Compact Oxford Dictionary, Thesaurus, and Wordpower Guide

Edited by
Sara Hawker

OXFORD
UNIVERSITY PRESS

OXFORD
UNIVERSITY PRESS

Great Clarendon Street, Oxford OX2 6DP

Oxford University Press is a department of the University of Oxford.
It furthers the University's objective of excellence in research, scholarship,
and education by publishing worldwide in

Oxford New York

Auckland Cape Town Dar es Salaam Hong Kong Karachi
Kuala Lumpur Madrid Melbourne Mexico City Nairobi
New Delhi Shanghai Taipei Toronto

With offices in

Argentina Austria Brazil Chile Czech Republic France Greece
Guatemala Hungary Italy Japan Poland Portugal Singapore
South Korea Switzerland Thailand Turkey Ukraine Vietnam

Oxford is a registered trade mark of Oxford University Press
in the UK and in certain other countries

© Oxford University Press 2002, 2006

Database right Oxford University Press (makers)

First published 2002
Second edition 2006
Dictionary text adapted from the *Colour Oxford English Dictionary*,
3rd edition, published 2006; thesaurus text first published 2006 as
the *Colour Oxford Thesaurus*, 3rd edition

British Library Cataloguing in Publication Data
Data available

Library of Congress Cataloging in Publication Data
Data available

ISBN 978-0-19-8614234

10 9 8 7 6 5 4 3 2

Typeset in Frutiger and Parable
by Interactive Sciences Ltd, Gloucester
Printed in Italy by
Legoprint S.p.A.

Contents

Introduction

The *Compact Oxford Dictionary, Thesaurus, and Wordpower Guide* is an invaluable three-in-one reference tool for anyone who wants to enrich their vocabulary and increase their command of the English language. This new edition has been fully revised and updated and now features an attractive two-colour design. It aims to provide a wide variety of information about language and the core vocabulary of current English in a conveniently sized volume and a readily accessible format. The dictionary and thesaurus components are combined in a way that enables quick and easy reference to both: the top section of each page contains the dictionary entries, while the lower section gives matching thesaurus entries for many of the words in the dictionary.

The dictionary section is adapted from the 3rd edition of the *Colour Oxford English Dictionary* and is based on our analysis of the hundreds of millions of words of real English, taken from books, newspapers, magazines, and the Internet, which are contained in the Oxford English Corpus. It focuses on clear explanations of meaning together with extra help on aspects of words which often cause difficulties in terms of spelling, pronunciation, grammar, or usage. Individual notes give clear guidance on confusable words (such as *accept* and *except*, or *flaunt* and *flout*), on points of good English (for example, whether to say 'different from' or 'different to'), and tricky spellings like *Mediterranean, skilful*, or *weird*. Information is presented in clear, concise language, avoiding the use of difficult or technical terms wherever possible. The pronunciations use a simple respelling system which makes them very easy to understand.

The thesaurus section is derived from the 3rd edition of the *Colour Oxford Thesaurus* and provides synonyms (words with the same or similar meanings) for around 7,000 entries in the dictionary section. The synonym lists are divided, where appropriate, into numbered senses relating to particular meanings of the word in question so that it is easy to select the sense that matches the context you are looking for. Synonyms are arranged in order of their closeness in meaning to the entry word, with the closest one given first and printed in blue. Words with opposite meanings (known as *antonyms*) are also provided for many entries.

The Wordpower Guide, located in the middle of the book, is made up of several sections designed to expand and enrich your vocabulary, to provide help with word games and puzzles, and to help you use English more confidently. It includes a section on foreign words and phrases that are often encountered in English; a list of words that are regularly spelled wrongly; a special 'word link' feature containing a wide selection of vocabulary linked to words from a range of subject areas; and a table of commonly confused words. There are also lists of useful factual information, such as countries of the world and their currencies, entertaining sections on topics such as collective names for animals and birds, and an article presenting a variety of interesting facts about the English language.

Guide to the dictionary and thesaurus

The dictionary and thesaurus is designed to be as easy to use and understand as possible. Here is an explanation of the main features that you will find in each half of the book.

1. Structure of dictionary entries

Part of speech (word class)

Headword

deny verb (**denies, denying, denied**) **1** state that something is not true. **2** refuse to admit something. **3** refuse to give someone a thing that they want. **4** (**deny yourself**) go without something you want.

Sense number

Typical pattern of use

desperate adjective **1** feeling, showing, or involving despair. **2** done when everything else has failed. **3** very serious: *a desperate shortage.* **4** needing or wanting something very much.
■ **desperately** adverb **desperation** noun.

Derivatives (words formed from the headword)

Example of use

Spelling note

☑ *desperate*, not *-parate*.

Plural form

donkey noun (plural **donkeys**) a domesticated animal of the horse family with long ears and a braying call.
□ **donkey jacket** Brit. a heavy jacket with a patch of waterproof material across the shoulders. **donkey's years** informal a very long time.

Phrases and compounds

Geographical label (showing where the term is used)

Adjective forms

classy adjective (**classier, classiest**) informal stylish and sophisticated.

Label showing the situation in which the word is used

flair noun **1** a natural ability or talent. **2** stylishness.

Usage note

! don't confuse **flair** with **flare**, which means 'burn' or 'gradually become wider'.

Homonym number, given for words that have the same spelling but for different meanings

Subject label

bail² noun Cricket either of the two small pieces of wood that rest on the stumps.

Alternative spelling of the headword

mackintosh or **macintosh** noun Brit. a full-length waterproof coat.

Cross reference to another dictionary entry

Pronunciation (for selected words)

discotheque /diss-kuh-tek/ = **DISCO**.

2. Structure of thesaurus entries

Headword

cheerful adjective **1** *he arrived looking cheerful:* happy, jolly, merry, bright, sunny, joyful, in good/high spirits, buoyant, cheery, animated, smiling, good-humoured; informal chipper, chirpy, full of beans. **2** *a cheerful room:* pleasant, attractive, bright, agreeable, sunny, friendly, welcoming.
OPPOSITES sad, gloomy.

Core synonym—
the closest synonym
to the headword

Example of use, to
help distinguish
different senses

Sense number

Words meaning the
opposite of the
headword; most other
entries of their own,
where a wider choice
will be found

everywhere adverb all over, all around, in every nook and cranny, far and wide, near and far, high and low, {here, there, and everywhere}, the world over, worldwide; informal all over the place; Brit. informal all over the shop; N. Amer. informal all over the map.
OPPOSITES nowhere.

Part of speech
(word class)

Brackets around a
phrase, to avoid
confusion

infant noun baby, newborn, young child, tiny tot, little one; Medicine neonate; Scottish & N. English bairn, wean; informal tiny, sprog.

Subject label,
indicating the field in
which the following
synonym is used

Label indicating the
region of the world in
which the following
synonym(s) are used

Label indicating the
level or style of English
in which the following
synonym(s) are used

root noun **1** *the root of the problem:* source, origin, cause, reason, basis, foundation, bottom, seat. **2** (roots) origins, beginnings, family, birth, heritage.
● verb *he rooted around in the cupboard:* rummage, hunt, search, rifle, delve, forage, dig, nose, poke.
□ **root something out eradicate,** eliminate, weed out, destroy, wipe out, stamp out, abolish, end, put a stop to.

Form of the
headword for which
synonyms are given

Phrase for which
synonyms are given

seldom adverb rarely, infrequently, hardly (ever), scarcely (ever); informal once in a blue moon.
OPPOSITES often.

Brackets to show
more than one
possibility: *hardly*
and *hardly ever*

Labels

Most of the words and senses in the dictionary and thesaurus are part of standard English. Some words, however, are only appropriate to certain situations (such as an informal conversation) or are found only in certain contexts (for example, in poetry or in official documents). Where this is the case a label (or a combination of labels) is used.

Register labels

Register labels refer to a particular level of use in language. They show that a term is informal or formal, old-fashioned, or technical, and so on.

- **formal:** normally used only in writing, especially in official documents (e.g. *dwelling* or *deceased*)
- **informal:** normally used only in speaking, or in informal writing or email (e.g. *gawp* or *barmy*)
- **dated:** no longer used by most people (e.g. *gramophone*)
- **old use:** not in ordinary use today, though sometimes used to give an old-fashioned effect and also found in the literature of the past (e.g. *farewell* or *maiden*)
- **historical:** only used today to refer to things that are no longer part of modern life (e.g. *blunderbuss* or *doublet*)
- **literary:** found only or mainly in poems, plays, and novels (e.g. *flaxen* or *serpent*)
- **technical:** normally used only in technical language (e.g. *node* or *fluvial*)
- **humorous:** used to sound amusing or playful (e.g. *underwhelmed*)
- **dialect:** used only in certain local regions of the UK (e.g. *aye* or *bide*)
- **disapproving:** meant to convey a low opinion or to insult someone (e.g. *pleb*)
- **offensive:** likely to cause offence, whether the person speaking means to or not

Geographical labels

English is spoken throughout the world, and while most of the words used in standard British English will be the same as those used in other varieties, there are some words which are only found in one type of English. For example, the normal American word for a lift is **elevator**. If a word or phrase has the geographical label Brit. in this book, this means that it is used in standard British English but not in American English, although it may be found in other varieties such as Australian English. The labels US and N. Amer., on the other hand, mean that the word or phrase is typically American and is not standard in British English, though it may be found elsewhere.

Subject labels

These are used to show that a word or sense is connected with a particular subject or specialist activity such as Music, Computing, or Rugby.

Cross references

Cross references are pointers to another entry. In the dictionary text they are indicated by an arrow (⇨) or an equals sign (=). The arrow means that the term is an alternative spelling of the one referred to (e.g. **caftan** ⇨ KAFTAN), while the equals sign shows that the term means the same as the one referred to (e.g. **groundnut** = PEANUT).

Pronunciations

Pronunciations are given for words which might cause difficulty, but not for everyday words which are assumed to be familiar to everyone (such as **table** or **happy**). The part of the pronunciation printed in **bold** is the syllable that is stressed when the word is spoken.

List of Symbols

Vowels	Examples	Vowels	Examples	Vowels	Examples
a	as in **cat**	ew	as in **few**	oy	as in **boy**
ah	as in **calm**	i	as in **pin**	u	as in **cup**
air	as in **hair**	I	as in **eye**	uh	as in **along**
ar	as in **bar**	o	as in **top**	uu	as in **book**
aw	as in **law**	oh	as in **most**	y	as in **cry**
ay	as in **say**	oi	as in **join**	yoo	as in **unit**
e	as in **bed**	oo	as in **soon**	yoor	as in **Europe**
ee	as in **meet**	oor	as in **poor**	yr	as in **fire**
eer	as in **beer**	or	as in **corn**		
er	as in **her**	ow	as in **cow**		

Consonants	Examples	Consonants	Examples	Consonants	Examples
b	as in **bat**	l	as in **leg**	t	as in **top**
ch	as in **chin**	m	as in **man**	th	as in **thin**
d	as in **day**	n	as in **not**	th	as in **this**
f	as in **fat**	ng	as in **sing, finger**	v	as in **van**
g	as in **get**	nk	as in **thank**	w	as in **will**
h	as in **hat**	p	as in **pen**	y	as in **yes**
j	as in **jam**	r	as in **red**	z	as in **zebra**
k	as in **king**	s	as in **sit**	zh	as in **vision**
kh	as in **loch**	sh	as in **shop**		

Note on trademarks and proprietary status

This dictionary includes some words which have, or are asserted to have, proprietary status as trademarks or otherwise. Their inclusion does not imply that they have acquired for legal purposes a non-proprietary or general significance, nor any other judgement concerning their legal status. In cases where the editorial staff have some evidence that a word has proprietary status this is indicated in the entry for that word by the label trademark, but no judgement concerning the legal status of such words is made or implied thereby.

Aa

A or **a** noun (plural **As** or **A's**) the first letter of the alphabet. • abbreviation **1** ampere(s). **2** (Å) angstroms.
□ **A level** (in the UK except Scotland) the higher of the two main levels of the GCE exam.

a determiner **1** used when mentioning someone or something for the first time; the indefinite article. **2** one single. **3** per.

AA abbreviation **1** Alcoholics Anonymous. **2** Automobile Association.

aardvark /ard-vark/ noun an African animal with a long snout, that eats ants and termites.

aback adverb (**be taken aback**) be shocked or surprised.

abacus /ab-uh-kuhss/ noun (plural **abacuses**) a frame with rows of wires along which you slide beads, used for counting.

abaft adverb & preposition at the back of or behind a ship.

abandon verb **1** leave a place or person permanently. **2** give up a practice completely. **3** (**abandon yourself to**) give in to a desire. • noun complete lack of self-consciousness or self-control.
■ **abandonment** noun.

abase verb (**abases**, **abasing**, **abased**) (**abase yourself**) behave in a very humble way.
■ **abasement** noun.

abashed adjective embarrassed or ashamed.

abate verb (**abates**, **abating**, **abated**) become less severe or widespread.
■ **abatement** noun.

abattoir /ab-uh-twar/ noun Brit. a slaughter-house.

abbess noun a woman who is the head of an abbey of nuns.

abbey noun (plural **abbeys**) a building occupied by a community of monks or nuns.

abbot noun a man who is the head of an abbey of monks.

abbreviate verb (**abbreviates**, **abbreviating**, **abbreviated**) shorten a word or phrase.

abbreviation noun a shortened form of a word or phrase.

ABC noun **1** the alphabet. **2** the basic facts of a subject.

abdicate verb (**abdicates**, **abdicating**, **abdicated**) **1** give up being king or queen. **2** fail to carry out a duty.
■ **abdication** noun.

abdomen /ab-duh-muhn/ noun **1** the part of the body that contains the organs used

---

THESAURUS

abandon verb **1** *he abandoned his wife:* desert, leave, turn your back on, cast aside, finish with, jilt, throw over; informal walk/run out on, dump, ditch; literary forsake. **2** *she had abandoned painting:* give up, stop, have done with; informal pack in, quit; Brit. informal jack in. **3** *they abandoned the car:* leave (behind), vacate, dump, quit, evacuate, discard, jettison. **4** *the party abandoned those policies:* renounce, relinquish, dispense with, discard, give up, drop; informal ditch, scrap, junk; formal forswear.
OPPOSITES keep, continue, retain.
• noun *with reckless abandon:* uninhibitedness, recklessness, lack of restraint, lack of inhibition.
OPPOSITES self-control.

abate verb *the storm had abated:* subside, die down/away/out, lessen, ease (off), let up, decrease, diminish, fade, weaken.
OPPOSITES intensify.

abatement noun **1** *the storm still rages with no sign of abatement:* subsiding, dying down/away/out, lessening, easing (off), let-up. **2** *noise abatement:* reduction, control.

abbreviate verb shorten, reduce, cut, contract, condense, compress, abridge.
OPPOSITES lengthen, expand.

abbreviation noun short form, contraction, acronym, initialism.

abdicate verb resign, retire, stand down, step down, renounce the throne.

abdomen noun stomach, belly, gut, middle; informal tummy, guts; Austral. informal bingy.

for digestion and reproduction. **2** the rear part of the body of an insect, spider, or crustacean.
■ **abdominal** adjective.

abduct verb take someone away, especially by force.
■ **abduction** noun **abductor** noun.

aberrant /uh-**berr**-uhnt/ adjective not normal or acceptable.

aberration /a-buh-**ray**-sh'n/ noun **1** an action or event which is not normal or acceptable. **2** an unexpected silly mistake.

abet verb (**abets, abetting, abetted**) encourage or help someone to do something wrong.

abeyance /uh-**bay**-uhnss/ noun (**in** or **into abeyance**) temporarily not occurring or in use.

abhor /uhb-**hor**/ verb (**abhors, abhorring, abhorred**) feel strong hatred for.

abhorrent adjective disgusting or hateful.
■ **abhorrence** noun.

abide verb (**abides, abiding, abided**)
1 (**abide by**) accept or obey a rule or decision. **2** (**cannot abide**) dislike very much. **3** (of a feeling or memory) last for a long time.

ability noun (plural **abilities**) **1** the power or capacity to do something. **2** skill or talent.

abject /**ab**-jekt/ adjective **1** very unpleasant and humiliating. **2** completely without pride or dignity.
■ **abjectly** adverb.

abjure /uhb-**joor**/ verb (**abjures, abjuring, abjured**) formal swear that you will give up a belief or claim.

ablaze adjective burning fiercely.

able adjective (**abler, ablest**) **1** having the power, skill, or means to do something. **2** skilful and capable.
□ **able-bodied** physically fit and healthy.
■ **ably** adverb.

ablutions /uh-**bloo**-shuhnz/ plural noun the act of washing yourself.

abnegation /ab-ni-**gay**-sh'n/ noun formal the giving up something wanted or valuable.
■ **abnegate** verb.

abnormal adjective different from what is usual or expected in a bad or worrying way.
■ **abnormality** noun **abnormally** adverb.

aboard adverb & preposition on or into a ship, train, or other vehicle.

abode noun a house or home.

abolish verb put an end to a custom or law.

abolition noun the abolishing of a custom or law.

THESAURUS

abdominal adjective **gastric,** intestinal, stomach, duodenal, visceral, coeliac, ventral.

abduct verb **kidnap,** carry off, seize, capture, run away/off with; informal snatch.

aberration noun **anomaly,** deviation, abnormality, irregularity, variation, freak, oddity, peculiarity, curiosity, mistake.

abhor verb **hate,** detest, loathe, despise, regard with disgust, shudder at; formal abominate.
OPPOSITES love, admire.

abhorrent adjective **hateful,** detestable, loathsome, abominable, repellent, repugnant, repulsive, revolting, disgusting, horrible, horrid, horrifying, awful, heinous.
OPPOSITES admirable.

abide verb **1** *I can't abide cigar smoke:* **stand,** bear; Brit. informal stick. **2** *one memory will abide:* **continue,** remain, survive, last, persist, live on.
□ **abide by comply with,** obey, observe, follow, keep to, adhere to, stick to, go along with, heed, accept.

abiding adjective **enduring,** lasting, everlasting, perpetual, eternal, unending, permanent.
OPPOSITES short-lived, ephemeral.

ability noun **1** *the ability to read:* **capacity,** capability, power, faculty, facility, wherewithal, means. **2** *leadership ability:*

talent, skill, aptitude, expertise, savoir faire, prowess, accomplishment, competence, proficiency, flair, gift, knack, genius; informal know-how.
OPPOSITES inability.

able adjective **1** *able to resume his duties:* **capable of,** competent to, up to, fit to, in a position to, allowed to, free to. **2** *an able student:* **intelligent,** clever, talented, skilful, skilled, accomplished, gifted, proficient, apt, adroit, adept, capable, competent.
OPPOSITES incompetent, incapable.

abnormal adjective **unusual,** uncommon, atypical, untypical, unrepresentative, irregular, anomalous, deviant, aberrant, freak, strange, odd, peculiar, bizarre, weird, unnatural, perverted, twisted, warped; informal funny, freaky, kinky.
OPPOSITES normal, typical, common.

abnormality noun **oddity,** strangeness, irregularity, anomaly, deviation, aberration, deformity, defect, malformation.
OPPOSITES normality.

abolish verb **put an end to,** get rid of, scrap, cancel, end, remove, dissolve, stop, ban; informal do away with, ditch.
OPPOSITES retain, create.

abolition noun **scrapping,** ending, cancellation, dissolution, removal.
OPPOSITES retention, creation.

abolitionist noun a person who supports the abolition of a custom or law.

abominable adjective **1** very unpleasant and causing disgust. **2** informal very bad.
□ Abominable Snowman = YETI.
■ abominably adverb.

abominate verb (**abominates, abominating, abominated**) feel strong hatred for.

abomination noun **1** something that you hate or find disgusting. **2** a feeling of hatred.

aboriginal adjective **1** existing in a country from the earliest times. **2** (**Aboriginal**) having to do with the Australian Aborigines. ● noun (**Aboriginal**) an Australian Aborigine.

Aborigine /ab-uh-**ri**-ji-nee/ noun a member of one of the original peoples of Australia.

abort verb **1** end a pregnancy early to stop the baby from developing and being born. **2** undergo a natural abortion. **3** end something early because of a problem or fault.

abortion noun **1** the deliberate ending of a human pregnancy. **2** the natural ending of a pregnancy before the fetus is able to survive on its own.

abortionist noun disapproving a person who carries out abortions.

abortive adjective failing to achieve the intended result; unsuccessful.

abound verb **1** exist in large numbers or amounts. **2** (**abound in** or **with**) have a large number or amount of something.

about preposition & adverb **1** on the subject of. **2** here and there within a particular area. **3** approximately.
□ about-turn Brit. **1** Military a turn made so as to face the opposite direction. **2** a complete change of opinion or policy.

above preposition & adverb **1** at a higher level than. **2** rather or more than. **3** (in printed writing) mentioned earlier.
□ above board lawful and honest.

abracadabra exclamation a word said by magicians when performing a trick.

abrade verb (**abrades, abrading, abraded**) scrape or wear away.

abrasion /uh-**bray**-zh'n/ noun **1** the process of scraping or wearing away. **2** an area of scraped skin.

abrasive /uh-**bray**-siv/ adjective **1** able to polish or clean a surface by rubbing or grinding. **2** harsh or unkind.
■ abrasively adverb.

abreast adverb **1** side by side and facing the same way. **2** (**abreast of**) up to date with.

abominable adjective loathsome, detestable, hateful, obnoxious, despicable, contemptible, disgusting, revolting, repellent, repulsive, repugnant, abhorrent, reprehensible, atrocious, foul, vile, wretched, horrible, awful, dreadful, appalling, nauseating; informal terrible, shocking, God-awful; Brit. informal beastly.
OPPOSITES good, admirable.

abort verb **1** miscarry, have a miscarriage, terminate. **2** *the crew aborted the take-off:* halt, stop, end, call off, abandon, discontinue, terminate, arrest; informal pull the plug on.

abortion noun termination, miscarriage.

abortive adjective unsuccessful, failed, vain, ineffective, ineffectual, unproductive.
OPPOSITES successful, fruitful.

abound verb **1** *cafes abound in the narrow streets:* be plentiful, be abundant, be numerous, be thick on the ground; informal grow on trees, be two/ten a penny. **2** *a stream which abounded with trout:* be full of, overflow with, teem with, be packed with, be crowded with; informal be stuffed with, be chock-a-block with.

about preposition *a book about Greece:* regarding, concerning, referring to, with regard to, with respect to, relating to, on, touching on, dealing with, on the subject of.
● adverb **1** *there were babies crawling about:*

around, here and there, to and fro, back and forth, in all directions. **2** *he was about somewhere:* near, nearby, around, hereabouts, in the vicinity, in the neighbourhood. **3** *about £15,000:* approximately, roughly, around, in the region of, circa, of the order of, or so, or thereabouts, more or less; Brit. getting on for; N. Amer. informal in the ballpark of.

above preposition **1** over, higher (up) than, on top of, on. **2** *those above the Colonel:* superior to, senior to, over, higher (up) than, more powerful than, in charge of, commanding.
OPPOSITES below.
● adverb overhead, on/at the top, high up, on high, up above, (up) in the sky.
□ above all **most importantly**, most of all, chiefly, primarily, first and foremost, essentially, in essence, at bottom; informal at the end of the day, when all is said and done.

abrasion noun **1** *he had abrasions to his forehead:* graze, cut, scrape, scratch, gash, laceration. **2** *the metal is resistant to abrasion:* erosion, wearing away/down.

abrasive adjective **1** *abrasive kitchen cleaners:* rough, coarse, harsh, scratchy. **2** *her abrasive manner:* curt, brusque, sharp, harsh, rough.
OPPOSITES gentle, friendly.

a

abridge verb (**abridges**, **abridging**, **abridged**) shorten a book or film.
■ **abridgement** noun.

abroad adverb **1** in or to a foreign country or countries. **2** felt or talked about by many people.

abrogate /ab-ruh-gayt/ verb (**abrogates**, **abrogating**, **abrogated**) formal cancel or do away with a law or agreement.
■ **abrogation** noun.

abrupt adjective **1** sudden and unexpected. **2** brief to the point of rudeness.
■ **abruptly** adverb **abruptness** noun.

abscess noun a swelling that contains pus.

> ☑ remember the *s* and *c*: ab**sc**ess.

abscond /uhb-**skond**/ verb leave quickly and secretly to escape from custody or avoid arrest.

abseil /ab-sayl/ verb Brit. climb down a rock face using a rope wrapped round the body and fixed at a higher point.

absence noun **1** the state of being away from a place or person. **2** (**absence of**) the lack of.

absent adjective /ab-s'nt/ **1** not present. **2** not paying attention. • verb /uhb-**sent**/ (**absent yourself**) go away.

□ **absent-minded** forgetful, or not paying attention.
■ **absently** adverb.

absentee noun a person who is absent.

absenteeism noun frequent absence from work or school without good reason.

absinthe /ab-sinth/ noun a green aniseed-flavoured liqueur.

absolute adjective **1** complete; total. **2** having unlimited power. **3** not related or compared to anything else.
□ **absolute zero** the lowest temperature theoretically possible (−273.15°C).
■ **absolutely** adverb.

absolution noun formal forgiveness of a person's sins.

absolutism noun the principle that the government or ruler should have unlimited power.
■ **absolutist** noun & adjective.

absolve /uhb-**zolv**/ verb (**absolves**, **absolving**, **absolved**) formally declare that someone is free from guilt, blame, or sin.

absorb verb **1** soak up liquid or another substance. **2** take in information. **3** take over something less powerful. **4** use up time or resources. **5** reduce the effect or strength of sound or an impact. **6** hold someone's attention.

THESAURUS

abridge verb **shorten**, cut (down), edit, abbreviate, condense, compress, truncate, prune, summarize, precis; (**abridged**) concise.
OPPOSITES extend.

abroad adverb **overseas**, out of the country, to/in foreign parts, to/in a foreign country/land.

abrupt adjective **1** *an abrupt halt:* **sudden**, rapid, quick, unexpected, unanticipated, unforeseen, precipitate. **2** *an abrupt manner:* **curt**, brusque, blunt, short, rude, sharp, terse, brisk, unceremonious.
OPPOSITES gradual, gentle.

absence noun **1** *his absence from the office:* **non-attendance**, absenteeism, truancy, leave, holiday, vacation, sabbatical. **2** *the absence of activity:* **lack**, want, non-existence, unavailability, scarcity, shortage, dearth.
OPPOSITES presence.

absent adjective **1** *she was absent from work:* **away**, off, out, elsewhere, off duty, on holiday, on leave; informal AWOL. **2** *symptoms were absent:* **non-existent**, lacking, missing. **3** *an absent look:* **distracted**, preoccupied, inattentive, vague, absorbed, dreamy, faraway, blank, empty, vacant.
OPPOSITES present, attentive, alert.
□ **absent yourself** **stay away**, be absent, go away, leave, withdraw.

absent-minded adjective **forgetful**, distracted, scatterbrained, preoccupied, inattentive; informal with a mind/memory like a sieve.

absolute adjective **1** *absolute silence | an absolute disgrace:* **complete**, total, utter, out-and-out, outright, perfect, pure, thorough, unqualified, unreserved, downright, unmitigated, sheer. **2** *absolute power:* **unlimited**, unrestricted, unrestrained, infinite, total, supreme, unconditional. **3** *an absolute ruler:* **autocratic**, dictatorial, all-powerful, omnipotent, supreme.
OPPOSITES partial, qualified, limited, democratic.

absolutely adverb **completely**, totally, utterly, perfectly, entirely, wholly, fully, quite, thoroughly, unreservedly, definitely, certainly, unquestionably, undoubtedly, without (a) doubt, without question, in every way/respect, one hundred per cent.
OPPOSITES partially.

absorb verb **1** *a material which absorbs water:* **soak up**, suck up, draw up/in, take up/in, mop up. **2** *she was absorbed in her book:* **engross**, captivate, occupy, preoccupy, engage, rivet, grip, hold, immerse, involve, enthral, spellbind, fascinate.

absorbent adjective able to soak up liquid easily.
■ **absorbency** noun.

absorption noun the process of absorbing, or of being absorbed.

abstain verb 1 (**abstain from**) stop yourself from doing something pleasant. 2 formally choose not to vote.

abstemious /uhb-**stee**-mi-uhss/ adjective not letting yourself have much food, alcohol, or enjoyment.

abstention /uhb-**sten**-sh'n/ noun 1 a deliberate decision not to vote. 2 abstinence.

abstinence /**ab**-sti-nuhnss/ noun the avoidance of something enjoyable, such as food or alcohol.
■ **abstinent** adjective.

abstract adjective /**ab**-strakt/ 1 having to do with ideas or qualities rather than physical or concrete things. 2 (of art) using colour and shapes to create an effect rather than attempting to represent real life accurately. • verb /uhb-**strakt**/ take out or remove. • noun /**ab**-strakt/ a summary of a book or article.
■ **abstractly** adverb.

abstracted adjective not paying attention to what is happening; preoccupied.
■ **abstractedly** adverb.

abstraction noun 1 the quality of being abstract. 2 something which exists only as an idea. 3 the state of being preoccupied.

abstruse /uhb-**strooss**/ adjective difficult to understand.

absurd adjective completely unreasonable or inappropriate.
■ **absurdity** noun **absurdly** adverb.

abundance noun a very large quantity or amount of something.

abundant adjective 1 existing in large quantities; plentiful. 2 (**abundant in**) having plenty of.
■ **abundantly** adverb.

abuse verb /uh-**byooz**/ (**abuses, abusing, abused**) 1 use something wrongly or badly. 2 treat someone cruelly or violently. 3 speak to someone in an insulting way. • noun /uh-**byooss**/ 1 the wrong or harmful use of something. 2 cruel and violent treatment. 3 insulting language.
■ **abuser** noun.

abusive adjective 1 very insulting.

absorbent adjective spongy, sponge-like, porous, permeable.

absorbing adjective fascinating, interesting, captivating, gripping, engrossing, compelling, compulsive, enthralling, riveting, spellbinding; informal unputdownable.
OPPOSITES boring.

absorption noun 1 the absorption of water: soaking up, sucking up. 2 her total absorption in the music: involvement, immersion, raptness, preoccupation, captivation, fascination, enthralment.

abstain verb 1 he abstained from wine: refrain, desist, forbear, give up, renounce, avoid, eschew, forgo, go/do without, refuse, decline; informal cut out. 2 one member abstained: not vote, decline to vote.

abstemious adjective moderate, restrained, temperate, self-disciplined, self-restrained, sober, austere, ascetic, puritanical, spartan.
OPPOSITES self-indulgent.

abstinence noun self-denial, self-restraint, teetotalism, temperance, sobriety, abstemiousness.

abstract adjective abstract concepts: theoretical, conceptual, intellectual, metaphysical, philosophical, academic.
OPPOSITES actual, concrete.
• noun an abstract of her speech: summary, synopsis, precis, résumé, outline; N. Amer. wrap-up.

abstruse adjective obscure, arcane, esoteric, rarefied, recondite, difficult, hard, cryptic, over/above your head, incomprehensible, unfathomable, impenetrable.

absurd adjective irrational, illogical, inappropriate, ridiculous, ludicrous, farcical, comical, stupid, foolish, silly, pointless, senseless, preposterous; informal crazy, cockeyed; Brit. informal barmy, daft.
OPPOSITES reasonable, sensible.

abundance noun plenty, plethora, profusion, riot, superabundance.
OPPOSITES lack, scarcity.

abundant adjective plentiful, copious, ample, profuse, large, huge, great, bumper, prolific, overflowing, teeming, superabundant; informal galore.
OPPOSITES scarce, sparse.

abuse verb 1 the judge abused his power: misuse, exploit, take advantage of. 2 he was accused of abusing women: mistreat, maltreat, ill-treat, molest, beat, sexually abuse, interfere with. 3 the referee was abused by players: insult, be rude to, swear at, shout at.
• noun 1 the abuse of power: misuse, exploitation. 2 the abuse of women: mistreatment, maltreatment, ill-treatment, molestation, beating, sexual abuse. 3 torrents of abuse: insults, expletives, swear words, swearing, name-calling, invective.

abusive adjective 1 abusive language: insulting, rude, offensive, derogatory,

2 involving cruelty and violence.
■ abusively adverb.

abut /uh-**but**/ verb (abuts, abutting, abutted) be next to or touching.

abysmal /uh-**biz**-m'l/ adjective very bad; terrible.
■ abysmally adverb.

abyss /uh-**biss**/ noun a very deep hole.

AC abbreviation alternating current.

acacia /uh-**kay**-shuh/ noun a tree or shrub with yellow or white flowers.

academia /a-kuh-**dee**-mi-uh/ noun the world of higher education.

academic adjective 1 having to do with education or study. 2 not related to a real situation; theoretical. • noun a teacher or scholar in a university or college.
■ academically adverb.

academy noun (plural academies) 1 a place where people study or are trained in a particular field. 2 a society of scholars, artists, or scientists.
□ Academy Award an Oscar.

acanthus /uh-**kan**-thuhss/ noun a plant or shrub with spiny leaves.

a cappella /a kuh-**pel**-luh/ adjective & adverb (of music) sung without instrumental accompaniment.

accede /uhk-**seed**/ verb (accedes, acceding, acceded) (usu. accede to) formal 1 agree to a demand or request. 2 take up a role or position: *accede to the throne.*

accelerate verb (accelerates, accelerating, accelerated) 1 begin to move more quickly. 2 begin to happen more quickly.
■ acceleration noun.

accelerator noun 1 a foot pedal which controls the speed of a vehicle. 2 Physics a machine that makes charged particles move at high speeds.

accent noun 1 a way of pronouncing a language. 2 an emphasis given to a syllable, word, or musical note. 3 a mark on a letter or word that shows how a sound is pronounced or stressed. 4 a particular emphasis. • verb /ak-**sent**/ 1 (accented) spoken with a particular accent. 2 stress or emphasize.

accentuate /uhk-**sen**-tyuu-ayt/ verb (accentuates, accentuating, accentuated) make a feature more noticeable.
■ accentuation noun.

accept verb 1 agree to receive or do something that is offered or suggested. 2 believe that something said is true or correct. 3 admit responsibility for something. 4 come to terms with something unwelcome.
■ acceptance noun.

❗ don't confuse **accept** with **except**, which means 'not including'.

acceptable adjective 1 able to be accepted.

THESAURUS

slanderous, libellous. 2 *an abusive husband:* violent, brutal, cruel, harsh, oppressive.
OPPOSITES polite, kind.

abysmal adjective terrible, dreadful, awful, frightful, atrocious, disgraceful, lamentable; informal rotten, appalling, pathetic, pitiful, woeful, useless, lousy, dire, poxy, the pits; Brit. informal chronic, shocking.

academic adjective 1 *an academic institution:* educational, scholastic. 2 *his academic turn of mind:* scholarly, learned, literary, intellectual, bookish, studious. 3 *only of academic interest:* theoretical, hypothetical, notional, speculative, conjectural, irrelevant, beside the point.
• noun *a group of academics:* scholar, intellectual, don, professor, man/woman of letters, thinker; informal egghead; Brit. informal boffin.

academy noun educational institution, school, college, university, institute.

accelerate verb 1 *the car accelerated:* speed up, go faster, gain momentum, increase speed, pick up speed, gather speed. 2 *sunlight accelerates growth:* hasten, quicken, speed up, further, advance, expedite; informal crank up.

OPPOSITES decelerate, delay.

acceleration noun speeding up, quickening, hastening.

accent noun 1 *a Scottish accent:* pronunciation, intonation, enunciation, articulation, inflection. 2 *the accent is on comfort:* emphasis, stress, priority, importance, prominence.

accept verb 1 *he accepted a pen as a present:* receive, take, get, obtain, acquire, pick up. 2 *just accept what you're told:* go along with, believe, respect, abide by, defer to, put up with, give in to, resign yourself to; informal buy, swallow.
OPPOSITES refuse, reject.

acceptable adjective satisfactory, adequate, reasonable, fair, good enough, sufficient, tolerable, passable.
OPPOSITES unacceptable.

acceptance noun 1 *the acceptance of an award:* receipt, receiving, taking. 2 *his acceptance of her ideas:* respect, acknowledgement, belief, toleration, consent, agreement, assent, compliance, acquiescence.

accepted adjective recognized, acknowledged, established, traditional, orthodox, agreed, approved, customary,

2 good enough; adequate.
■ **acceptability** noun **acceptably** adverb.

access noun **1** a way of approaching or entering a place. **2** the right or opportunity to use something or see someone. • verb **1** approach or enter a place. **2** obtain information stored in a computer.

accessible adjective **1** able to be reached or used. **2** friendly and easy to talk to. **3** easily understood or enjoyed.
■ **accessibility** noun **accessibly** adverb.

accession noun **1** the gaining of an important position or rank. **2** a new item added to a library or museum collection.

accessory noun (plural **accessories**) **1** a thing which can be added to or worn with something else to make it more useful or attractive. **2** Law a person who helps someone commit a crime without taking part in it.

accident noun **1** something harmful that happens unexpectedly or without being intended. **2** an incident that happens by chance or without apparent cause.

accidental adjective happening by chance.
■ **accidentally** adverb.

acclaim verb praise enthusiastically and publicly. • noun enthusiastic public praise.

acclamation noun enthusiastic approval or praise.

acclimatize or **acclimatise** verb (**acclimatizes, acclimatizing, acclimatized**) get used to a new climate or conditions.
■ **acclimatization** noun.

accolade /ak-kuh-layd/ noun something given as a special honour or as a reward for excellence.

accommodate verb (**accommodates, accommodating, accommodated**) **1** provide a room or rooms for someone, or space for something. **2** adapt to or fit in with.

☑ double c, double m: accommodate.

accommodating adjective willing to fit in with someone's wishes.

accommodation noun a room or building where someone may live or stay.

accompaniment noun **1** a musical part which accompanies an instrument, voice, or group. **2** something that adds to or improves something else.

accompany verb (**accompanies,**

normal, standard.
OPPOSITES unorthodox.

access noun **1** *the building has a side access:* entrance, entry, approach, path, drive, way in. **2** *they were denied access to the stadium:* admission, admittance, entry.

accessible adjective approachable, attainable, reachable, obtainable, available, understandable, comprehensible, intelligible; informal get-at-able.

accessory noun **1** *a car accessory:* extra, add-on, addition, supplement, attachment. **2** *an accessory to murder:* accomplice, abetter, collaborator, co-conspirator, henchman, associate.

accident noun **1** *an accident at work:* mishap, misadventure, disaster, tragedy, catastrophe, calamity. **2** *a road accident:* crash, collision, smash, bump, derailment; N. Amer. wreck; informal smash-up, pile-up; Brit. informal shunt. **3** *we met by accident:* chance, fate, fortune, luck, good luck, fluke, coincidence.

accidental adjective **1** *accidental death:* chance, coincidental, unexpected, incidental, fortuitous, serendipitous. **2** *accidental damage:* unintentional, unintended, unplanned, inadvertent, unwitting.
OPPOSITES predictable, intentional.

acclaim verb *the booklet has been acclaimed by teachers:* praise, applaud, cheer, commend, approve, welcome, hail.
OPPOSITES criticize.
• noun *she has won widespread acclaim:*

praise, applause, tributes, approval, admiration, congratulations, commendation.
OPPOSITES criticism.

acclimatize verb adjust, adapt, get used, familiarize yourself, find your feet, get your bearings; N. Amer. acclimate.

accommodate verb **1** *refugees were accommodated in army camps:* lodge, house, put up, billet, board. **2** *the cottages accommodate six people:* hold, take, have room for, sleep, seat. **3** *we tried to accommodate her:* help, assist, oblige, cater for, fit in with, satisfy.

accommodating adjective obliging, cooperative, helpful, amenable, hospitable, flexible.

accommodation noun housing, homes, lodging(s), (living) quarters, rooms, billet, shelter, a roof over your head; informal digs, pad; formal residence, dwelling, abode.

accompaniment noun **1** *a musical accompaniment:* backing, support, background, soundtrack. **2** *the wine makes a superb accompaniment to cheese:* complement, addition, adjunct, accessory, companion.

accompany verb **1** *the driver accompanied her to the door:* go with, travel with, keep someone company, partner, escort, show, see, usher, conduct. **2** *an illness accompanied by nausea:* go along with, occur with, go together with, attend, be linked with. **3** *he accompanied the choir on the piano:* back, play along with, support.

a

accompanying, accompanied) 1 go somewhere with someone. **2** be present or happen at the same time as. **3** play musical backing for an instrument or voice.
■ **accompanist** noun.

accomplice noun a person who helps another commit a crime.

accomplish verb achieve or complete something successfully.

accomplished adjective highly trained or skilled.

accomplishment noun **1** an activity that you can do well. **2** something that has been achieved successfully. **3** the successful achievement of a task.

accord verb **1** give power or recognition to. **2** (**accord with**) be consistent or in agreement with. ●noun **1** agreement in opinion or feeling. **2** an official agreement or treaty.
□ **of your own accord** willingly.

accordance noun (**in accordance with**) in a way that fits in with.

according adverb (**according to**) **1** as stated by. **2** in a way that corresponds to.

accordingly adverb **1** appropriately. **2** therefore.

accordion noun a musical instrument that you play by stretching and squeezing it with your hands and pressing buttons or keys.
■ **accordionist** noun.

accost verb approach someone and speak to them, often in a rude or aggressive way.

account noun **1** a description of an event. **2** a record of money that has been spent and received. **3** an arrangement by which you can keep money in a bank or buy things from a business on credit. **4** importance. ●verb consider in a particular way.
□ **account for 1** supply or make up an amount. **2** give an explanation of. **on account of** because of. **on no account** under no circumstances. **take account of** take into consideration.

accountable adjective expected to explain your actions or decisions.
■ **accountability** noun.

accountant noun a person who keeps or inspects financial accounts.
■ **accountancy** noun.

accoutrement /uh-koo-truh-muhnt/ (US spelling **accouterment**) noun an extra item of clothing or equipment.

accredit verb (**accredits, accrediting, accredited**) **1** (**accredit something to**) give someone the credit for something. **2** give official authorization to.
■ **accreditation** noun.

accretion noun **1** growth or increase by a gradual build-up. **2** something formed or added gradually.

accrue verb (**accrues, accruing, accrued**) **1** (of money) be received in regular or increasing amounts. **2** collect or receive payments or benefits.
■ **accrual** noun.

accumulate verb (**accumulates,**

THESAURUS

accomplice noun partner in crime, abetter, accessory, collaborator, co-conspirator, henchman, associate.

accomplish verb achieve, succeed in, realize, attain, manage, bring off, carry through, execute, effect, perform, complete.

accomplished adjective expert, skilled, skilful, masterly, virtuoso, master, consummate, talented, gifted, able, capable; informal mean, nifty, crack, ace.

accomplishment noun **1** *a remarkable accomplishment:* achievement, success, act, deed, exploit, effort, feat, coup. **2** *her many accomplishments:* talent, skill, gift, ability.

accord verb **1** *the national assembly accorded him more power:* give, grant, present, award, confer on, bestow on. **2** *his views accorded with mine:* correspond, agree, tally, match, concur, be in harmony, be in tune.
OPPOSITES withhold, disagree, differ.
●noun **1** *a peace accord:* pact, treaty, agreement, settlement, deal, entente, protocol. **2** *the two sides failed to reach*

accord: agreement, consensus, unanimity, harmony.
OPPOSITES disagreement.
□ **of your own accord voluntarily,** of your own free will, of your own volition, by choice, willingly, freely, readily.

account noun **1** *his account of the incident:* description, report, version, story, statement, explanation, tale, chronicle, history, record, log. **2** *the firm's accounts:* financial record, ledger, balance sheet, financial statement; (**accounts**) books. **3** *his background is of no account:* importance, import, significance, consequence, value.
□ **account for 1** *they must account for the delay:* explain, answer for, give reasons for, justify. **2** *excise duties account for over half the price:* constitute, make up, comprise, represent, be responsible for, produce.

accountability noun responsibility, liability, answerability.

accountable adjective responsible, liable, answerable, to blame.

accumulate verb gather, collect, amass, stockpile, pile up, build up, store (up),

a

accumulating, accumulated) **1** gather together a number or quantity of. **2** increase.
■ accumulation noun accumulative adjective.

> ☑ two cs, one m: accumulate.

accumulator noun Brit. **1** a large rechargeable electric battery. **2** a bet placed on a series of events, the winnings from each being placed on the next.

accurate adjective **1** correct in all details. **2** reaching an intended target.
■ accuracy noun accurately adverb.

accursed /uh-ker-sid, uh-kerst/ adjective literary under a curse.

accusation noun a claim that someone has done something illegal or wrong.

accusative noun Grammar (in some languages) the case used for the object of a verb.

accuse verb (accuses, accusing, accused) (often accuse someone of) claim that someone has done something wrong or illegal.
■ accusatory adjective accuser noun.

accustom verb **1** (accustom someone/thing to) make someone or something used to. **2** (be accustomed to) be used to.

accustomed adjective usual or habitual.

AC/DC adjective alternating current/direct current.

ace noun **1** a playing card with a single spot on it, the highest card in its suit in most games. **2** informal a person who is very good

at a particular activity. **3** Tennis a service that an opponent is unable to return.
● adjective informal very good.

acerbic /uh-ser-bik/ adjective sharp and direct.
■ acerbically adverb acerbity noun.

acetate /a-si-tayt/ noun **1** a kind of chemical compound made from acetic acid. **2** fibre or plastic made of cellulose acetate.

acetic acid /uh-see-tik/ noun the acid that gives vinegar its taste.

acetone /a-si-tohn/ noun a colourless liquid used as a solvent.

acetylene /uh-set-i-leen/ noun a gas which burns with a bright flame, used in welding.

ache noun a continuous or long-lasting dull pain. ● verb (aches, aching, ached) **1** suffer from an ache. **2** (ache for or to do) want very much to have or do something.
■ achy adjective.

achieve verb (achieves, achieving, achieved) manage to do something by effort, skill, or courage.
■ achievable adjective achiever noun.

> ☑ the usual rule is i before e except after c: achieve.

achievement noun **1** a thing that is achieved. **2** the process of achieving something.

Achilles heel /uh-kil-leez/ noun a weak point.

Achilles tendon noun the tendon connecting calf muscles to the heel.

acid noun **1** a substance that turns litmus

THESAURUS

hoard, lay in/up, increase, accrue, run up. OPPOSITES disperse.

accumulation noun mass, build-up, pile, collection, stock, store, stockpile, hoard.

accuracy noun correctness, precision, exactness, fidelity, truth, truthfulness, authenticity, realism.

accurate adjective **1** accurate information: correct, precise, exact, right, factual, literal, faithful, true, truthful, on the mark, authentic, realistic; Brit. informal spot on, bang on; N. Amer. informal on the money, on the button. **2** an accurate shot: well aimed, on target, unerring, deadly, true.

accusation noun allegation, charge, indictment, impeachment, claim, assertion, imputation.

accuse verb **1** four people were accused of assault: charge with, indict for, impeach for. **2** you accused the companies of causing job losses: blame for, hold responsible for, condemn for, criticize for, denounce for; informal point the finger at.
OPPOSITES absolve, exonerate.

accustom verb adapt, adjust, acclimatize, habituate, familiarize, become reconciled,

get used to, come to terms with, learn to live with; N. Amer. acclimate.

accustomed adjective customary, established, habitual, usual, normal, regular, routine.

ache noun pain, twinge, pang, soreness, tenderness, irritation, discomfort, burning, cramp.
● verb my legs were aching: hurt, be sore, be painful, be tender, burn, be in pain.

achieve verb attain, reach, realize, bring off, pull off, accomplish, carry through, fulfil, complete; informal wrap up, swing.

achievement noun **1** the achievement of high growth: attainment, realization, accomplishment, fulfilment, implementation, completion. **2** they were proud of their achievement: feat, exploit, triumph, coup, accomplishment, act, action, deed, effort, work, handiwork.

acid adjective **1** an acid flavour: sour, acidic, tart, sharp, vinegary. **2** acid remarks: sharp, sharp-tongued, sarcastic, scathing, cutting, biting, stinging, caustic; informal bitchy, catty.
OPPOSITES alkali, sweet, kind.

a

red, neutralizes alkalis, and dissolves some metals. **2** informal the drug LSD. •**adjective 1** sharp-tasting or sour. **2** (of a remark) bitter or cutting.

□ **acid rain** rainfall that has been made acidic by pollution. **acid test** a decisive test of something.

■ **acidic** adjective **acidity** noun **acidly** adverb.

acidify verb (**acidifies, acidifying, acidified**) make or become acid.

acknowledge verb (**acknowledges, acknowledging, acknowledged**) **1** accept that something exists or is true. **2** confirm that you have received something. **3** greet someone with words or gestures.

acknowledgement or **acknowledgment** noun **1** the action of acknowledging. **2** something done or given as thanks to someone. **3** a mention of someone in a book thanking them for work they have done.

acme /ak-mi/ noun the highest point of achievement or excellence.

acne noun a skin condition causing red pimples.

acolyte /ak-uh-lyt/ noun an assistant or follower.

acorn noun the fruit of the oak tree, a smooth oval nut in a cup-like base.

acoustic adjective **1** having to do with sound or hearing. **2** not electrically amplified. •**noun** (**acoustics**) **1** the aspects of a room or building that affect how well it transmits sound. **2** the branch of physics concerned with sound.

■ **acoustically** adverb.

acquaint verb **1** (**acquaint someone with**) make someone aware of or familiar with. **2** (**be acquainted with**) know someone personally.

☑ acquaint, acquiesce, acquire, acquit, and related words have a *c* before the *qu*: *acquaint*.

acquaintance noun **1** familiarity with someone or something. **2** a person you know slightly.

acquiesce /ak-wi-ess/ verb (**acquiesces, acquiescing, acquiesced**) accept something without protest.

acquiescent adjective ready to accept or do something without protest.

■ **acquiescence** noun.

acquire verb (**acquires, acquiring, acquired**) **1** buy or obtain an article. **2** learn or develop a skill or quality.

acquisition noun **1** something that you have recently obtained. **2** the action of obtaining or learning something.

acquisitive adjective too interested in gaining money or material things.

acquit verb (**acquits, acquitting, acquitted**) **1** formally state that someone is not guilty of a criminal charge. **2** (**acquit yourself**) behave or perform in a particular way.

■ **acquittal** noun.

acre noun a unit of land area equal to 4,840 square yards (0.405 hectare).

■ **acreage** noun.

acrid adjective unpleasantly bitter or sharp.

acrimonious adjective angry and bitter.

■ **acrimoniously** adverb.

acrimony noun feelings of anger and bitterness.

acrobat noun an entertainer who performs spectacular gymnastic feats.

acrobatic adjective involving or performing spectacular gymnastic feats. •**noun** (**acrobatics**) spectacular gymnastic feats.

■ **acrobatically** adverb.

acronym /ak-ruh-nim/ noun a word formed from the first letters of other words (e.g. *Aids*).

acropolis noun (in an ancient Greek city) a fortress built on high ground.

THESAURUS

acknowledge verb **1** *he acknowledges his unfitness for the role*: admit, accept, grant, allow, concede, confess, recognize. **2** *he did not acknowledge Colin*: greet, salute, address, nod to, wave to, say hello to. **3** *few people acknowledged my letters*: answer, reply to, respond to.
OPPOSITES reject, deny, ignore.

acquaint verb familiarize, make aware of, inform of, advise of; informal fill in on, clue in on.

acquaintance noun **1** *friends and business acquaintances*: contact, associate, colleague. **2** *I renewed my acquaintance with George*: association, relationship. **3** *she had some acquaintance with the language*: familiarity with, knowledge of, awareness of, experience of, understanding

of, grasp of.

acquire verb get, obtain, come by, receive, collect, gain, buy, earn, win, come into, secure, pick up; informal get your hands on, get hold of, land, bag, score.
OPPOSITES lose.

acquisition noun **1** *a new acquisition*: purchase, addition, investment, possession; informal buy. **2** *the acquisition of funds*: obtaining, collection, gaining, earning, winning, securing.

acquit verb **1** *the jury acquitted her*: clear, exonerate, find innocent, absolve, discharge, free, release; informal let off (the hook). **2** *the boys acquitted themselves well*: behave, conduct yourself, perform, act.
OPPOSITES convict.

across preposition & adverb from one side to the other of something.
□ **across the board** applying to all.

acrostic /uh-**kross**-tik/ noun a poem or puzzle in which certain letters in each line form a word or words.

acrylic adjective (of paint, fabric, etc.) made using **acrylic acid** (an organic acid).

act verb 1 do something. 2 have a particular effect. 3 behave in a particular way. 4 (**act as**) perform the function of. 5 (**acting**) temporarily doing the duties of another person. 6 perform a role in a play or film. • noun 1 a thing done. 2 a law passed formally by a parliament. 3 a pretence. 4 a main division of a play, ballet, or opera. 5 a set performance, or a performing group.
□ **act of God** an event caused by natural forces beyond human control.

actinium noun a rare radioactive metallic element.

action noun 1 the process of doing something to achieve an aim. 2 a thing done. 3 the effect of something such as a chemical. 4 a lawsuit. 5 fighting in a battle or war. 6 the way in which something works or moves. • verb deal with a particular matter.

actionable adjective giving someone grounds to take legal action.

activate verb (**activates, activating, activated**) make something start working.

■ **activation** noun.

active adjective 1 moving about often or energetically. 2 regularly taking part in something. 3 working; functioning. 4 (of a volcano) erupting or having erupted in the past. 5 Grammar (of a verb) having as its subject the person or thing doing the action (e.g. *she loved him* as opposed to the passive form *he was loved*).
□ **active service** military service in wartime.
■ **actively** adverb.

activist noun a person who campaigns for political or social change.
■ **activism** noun.

activity noun (plural **activities**) 1 a condition in which things are happening or being done. 2 busy or energetic action or movement. 3 an action, especially one done for interest or pleasure.

actor noun a person whose profession is acting.

actress noun a female actor.

actual adjective existing in fact or reality.

actuality noun (plural **actualities**) actual reality or fact.

actualize or **actualise** verb (**actualizes, actualizing, actualized**) make something real or actual.

actually adverb in truth; in reality.

actuary noun (plural **actuaries**) a person who calculates insurance risks.
■ **actuarial** adjective.

THESAURUS

act verb 1 *the Government must act:* take action, take steps, take measures, move. 2 *Alison began to act oddly:* behave, conduct yourself, react. 3 *I'll act as lookout:* function, work, serve, operate. 4 *he acted in a film:* perform, play, appear.
• noun 1 *acts of kindness:* deed, action, gesture, feat, exploit. 2 *the act will raise taxes:* law, decree, statute, bill, edict, ruling, order. 3 *a comedy act:* performance, turn, routine, number, sketch. 4 *it was all an act:* pretence, show, front, facade, masquerade, charade, pose; informal a put-on.

acting adjective temporary, interim, caretaker, pro tem, provisional, stopgap; N. Amer. informal pinch-hitting.
OPPOSITES permanent.

action noun 1 *their actions are inexcusable:* deed, act, undertaking, exploit, behaviour, conduct, activity. 2 *the need for local action:* measures, steps, activism, campaigning, pressure. 3 *the action of hormones:* operation, working, effect, influence, process, power. 4 *he died in action:* battle, combat, hostilities, fighting, active service. 5 *a civil action:* lawsuit, suit, case, prosecution, litigation, proceedings.

activate verb start (up), switch on, turn on, set going, trigger (off), set off, energize.
OPPOSITES switch off.

active adjective 1 *she kept active:* busy, mobile, lively, vigorous; informal on the go, full of beans. 2 *an active member of the union:* hard-working, industrious, tireless, energetic. 3 *the watermill was active until 1960:* working, operative, functioning, operational, in action, in operation, in force; informal (up and) running.
OPPOSITES listless, inactive.

activity noun 1 *there was a lot of activity:* action, bustle, movement, life; informal toing and froing, comings and goings. 2 *a leisure activity:* pursuit, occupation, hobby, pastime, recreation, diversion, venture, undertaking, enterprise, project, scheme.
OPPOSITES inactivity.

actor, actress noun performer, player, thespian, star, starlet; Brit. informal luvvy.

actual adjective real, true, genuine, authentic, confirmed, definite, hard, concrete; informal real live.
OPPOSITES imaginary.

actually adverb really, in (actual) fact, in point of fact, as a matter of fact, in reality, in truth, if truth be told, to tell the truth.

a

actuate verb **1** cause a machine to function. **2** motivate someone to act in a particular way.

acuity /uh-**kyoo**-i-ti/ noun sharpness of thought, vision, or hearing.

acumen /**ak**-yoo-muhn/ noun the ability to make good judgements and take quick decisions.

acupuncture noun a medical treatment in which very thin needles are inserted into the skin.
  ■ **acupuncturist** noun.

acute adjective **1** (of something bad) very serious. **2** intelligent and shrewd. **3** (of a physical sense or faculty) highly developed. **4** (of an angle) less than 90°.
  □ **acute accent** a mark (´) placed over certain letters in some languages to show pronunciation (e.g. in *fiancée*).
  ■ **acutely** adverb **acuteness** noun.

AD abbreviation used to indicate that a date comes a particular number of years after the traditional date of Jesus's birth.

> ❗ if a date is written in figures, AD should be placed **before** the numerals, e.g. *AD 375,* but when the date is spelled out, AD should be placed after it, as in *the third century AD.*

adage /**ad**-ij/ noun a popular saying expressing something that most people accept as true.

adagio /uh-**dah**-ji-oh/ noun (plural **adagios**) a piece of music to be played in slow time.

adamant adjective refusing to be persuaded or to change your mind.
  ■ **adamantly** adverb.

Adam's apple noun a projection at the front of the neck, more prominent in men than women.

adapt verb **1** make something suitable for a new use or purpose. **2** become adjusted to new conditions.

adaptable adjective able to adjust to, or be altered for, new conditions or uses.
  ■ **adaptability** noun **adaptably** adverb.

adaptation or **adaption** noun **1** the process of adapting. **2** a film or play adapted from a written work.

adaptor or **adapter** noun **1** a device for connecting pieces of equipment. **2** Brit. a device for connecting several electric plugs to one socket.

add verb **1** put something together with something else. **2** put together two or more numbers or amounts to find their total value. **3** (**add up**) increase in amount or number. **4** say as a further remark. **5** (**add up**) informal make sense.

addendum /uh-**den**-duhm/ noun (plural **addenda**) an extra item added at the end of a book or other publication.

adder noun a poisonous snake with a dark zigzag pattern on its back.

addict noun a person who is addicted to something.

addicted adjective (usu. **addicted to**) **1** physically dependent on a particular substance. **2** very keen on a particular interest or activity.

addiction noun the condition of being addicted to something.
  ■ **addictive** adjective.

addition noun **1** the action of adding. **2** a

THESAURUS

acute adjective **1** *acute food shortages:* severe, dire, terrible, grave, serious, desperate. **2** *acute pain:* excruciating, sharp, severe, stabbing, agonizing, racking, searing. **3** *his acute mind:* quick, astute, shrewd, sharp, keen, penetrating, razor-sharp, quick-witted, agile, nimble, intelligent, canny, discerning, perceptive. OPPOSITES mild, dull.

adamant adjective unshakeable, unwavering, unswerving, resolute, resolved, determined, firm, dead set.

adapt verb **1** *the policy can be adapted:* modify, alter, change, adjust, remodel, reorganize, customize, tailor; informal tweak. **2** *he adapts well to new surroundings:* adjust, conform, acclimatize, accommodate.

add verb **1** *the porch was added later:* attach, append, tack on, join on. **2** *they added the figures up:* total, count (up), reckon up, tally; Brit. tot up.
  OPPOSITES subtract.

□ **add to** increase, augment, magnify, amplify, enhance, intensify, heighten, deepen, exacerbate, aggravate, compound, reinforce. **add up to amount to,** come to, run to, make, total, equal, number.

addict noun **1** *a heroin addict:* abuser; informal junkie, druggy, -head, freak; N. Amer. informal hophead. **2** (informal) *skiing addicts:* enthusiast, fan, lover, devotee, aficionado; informal buff, freak, nut, fanatic.

addicted adjective dependent, obsessed, fixated, fanatical, passionate, a slave to; informal hooked.

addiction noun dependency, dependence, habit, obsession, infatuation, passion, love, mania, enslavement.

addictive adjective habit-forming, compulsive; Brit. informal moreish.

addition noun **1** *the addition of extra rooms:* adding, inclusion, incorporation, introduction. **2** *a useful addition:* add-on, person or thing that is added.

additional adjective added; extra.
■ **additionally** adverb.

additive noun a substance added to improve or preserve something.

addled adjective **1** humorous confused or puzzled. **2** (of an egg) rotten.

address noun **1** the details of where a building is or where someone lives. **2** a string of characters identifying a destination for email messages. **3** a formal speech. •verb **1** write a name and address on an envelope or parcel. **2** make a speech or remark to. **3** think about a task and begin to deal with it.

> ☑ two *d*s: address.

adduce verb (**adduces, adducing, adduced**) formal refer to something as evidence.

adenoids /ad-uh-noydz/ **plural noun** a mass of tissue between the back of the nose and the throat.

adept adjective /uh-**dept**, **ad**-ept/ very skilled or able. •noun /**ad**-ept/ an adept person.
■ **adeptly** adverb.

adequate adjective satisfactory or acceptable; good enough.
■ **adequacy** noun **adequately** adverb.

adhere verb (**adheres, adhering, adhered**) (**adhere to**) **1** stick firmly to. **2** follow or observe.
■ **adherence** noun.

adherent noun a person who supports a particular party, person, or set of ideas. •adjective sticking firmly to an object or surface.

adhesion noun the process of adhering.

adhesive noun a substance used to stick things together. •adjective sticky.

ad hoc adjective & adverb created or done for a particular purpose only.

adieu /uh-**dyoo**/ exclamation old use goodbye.

Adi Granth /ah-di **grunt**/ noun the main sacred scripture of Sikhism.

ad infinitum /ad in-fi-ny-tuhm/ adverb endlessly; forever.

adjacent /uh-**jay**-s'nt/ adjective near or next to something else.

adjective noun Grammar a word used to describe a noun or to make its meaning clearer, such as *sweet* or *red*.
■ **adjectival** adjective.

adjoin verb be next to and joined with.

adjourn /uh-**jern**/ verb **1** break off a meeting until later. **2** postpone a decision.
■ **adjournment** noun.

adjudge verb (**adjudges, adjudging, adjudged**) (of a law court or judge) formally decide.

adjudicate /uh-**joo**-di-kayt/ verb (**adjudicates, adjudicating, adjudicated**) **1** make a formal judgement. **2** judge a competition.
■ **adjudication** noun **adjudicator** noun.

adjunct noun an additional part or thing.

adjure verb (**adjures, adjuring, adjured**) formal urge someone to do something.

adjust verb **1** alter something slightly. **2** become used to a new situation. **3** decide the amount to be paid when settling an

THESAURUS

extra, adjunct, appendage, supplement, rider.
OPPOSITES subtraction, removal, essential.
□ **in addition**. See **ADDITIONALLY**.

additional adjective extra, added, supplementary, further, more, spare, other, new, fresh.

additionally adverb also, in addition, besides, too, as well, on top (of that), furthermore, moreover, into the bargain, to boot, to say nothing of.

address noun **1** *officers called at the address:* house, flat, apartment, home; formal residence, dwelling. **2** *his address to Parliament:* speech, lecture, talk, presentation, dissertation, sermon.
•verb *he addressed his audience:* speak to, talk to, give a talk to, make a speech to, hold forth to.

adept adjective expert, proficient, accomplished, skilful, practised, masterly, consummate.
OPPOSITES inept.

adequate adjective **1** *adequate financial resources:* sufficient, enough. **2** *an*

adequate service: satisfactory, acceptable, passable, reasonable, tolerable, fair, average, not bad, all right, middling; informal OK.
OPPOSITES insufficient, inadequate.

adhere verb stick, cling, bond, hold.
□ **adhere to abide by,** stick to, hold to, comply with, conform to, follow, obey, heed, observe, respect, uphold, fulfil.

adjacent adjective adjoining, neighbouring, next-door, abutting.
□ **adjacent to next to,** by the side of, bordering on, beside, alongside, touching.

adjoining adjective connecting, connected, interconnecting, bordering, abutting, attached, adjacent, neighbouring, next-door.

adjourn verb **1** *the hearing was adjourned:* suspend, break off, discontinue, interrupt, recess. **2** *sentencing was adjourned until June 9:* postpone, put off/back, defer, delay, hold over.

adjust verb **1** *he adjusted the brakes:* modify, alter, regulate, tune, fine-tune, balance, tailor, customize, rearrange,

insurance claim.
- **adjustable** adjective **adjustment** noun.

adjutant /a-juu-tuhnt/ noun a military officer who helps a senior officer with administrative work.

ad-lib verb (**ad-libs, ad-libbing, ad-libbed**) speak or perform in public without preparing first. • noun an unprepared remark or speech.

administer verb (**administers, administering, administered**) **1** organize or put into effect. **2** give out or apply a drug or remedy.

administrate verb (**administrates, administrating, administrated**) manage the affairs of a business or organization.
- **administrative** adjective **administrator** noun.

administration noun **1** the running of a business or system. **2** the action of giving out or applying something. **3** the government in power.

admirable /ad-mi-ruh-b'l/ adjective deserving respect and approval.
- **admirably** adverb.

admiral noun **1** the most senior commander of a fleet or navy. **2** a naval officer of the second most senior rank.

admire verb (**admires, admiring, admired**) **1** respect or approve of. **2** look at with pleasure.
- **admiration** noun **admirer** noun.

admissible adjective acceptable or valid.

admission noun **1** the process of being allowed in to a place. **2** a confession.

admit verb (**admits, admitting, admitted**) **1** confess that something is true or is the case. **2** allow someone to enter a place. **3** accept that something is valid.

admittance noun the process of entering, or of being allowed to enter.

admonish verb firmly tell someone off.
- **admonition** noun **admonitory** adjective.

ad nauseam /ad **naw**-zi-am/ adverb to an annoying or boring extent.

ado noun trouble; fuss.

adobe /uh-**doh**-bi/ noun a kind of clay used to make sun-dried bricks.

adolescent adjective in the process of developing from a child into an adult.

THESAURUS

change, reshape; informal tweak. **2** *Kate had adjusted to her new life:* adapt, become accustomed, get used, accommodate, acclimatize, habituate yourself, assimilate, come to terms with, blend in with, fit in with; N. Amer. acclimate.

adjustable adjective alterable, adaptable, modifiable, variable, multiway, versatile.

administer verb **1** *the union is administered by an executive:* manage, direct, control, operate, regulate, coordinate, conduct, handle, run, organize, govern, steer. **2** *the crew administered first aid:* dispense, issue, give out, provide, apply, offer, distribute, deliver, hand out, deal out, dole out.

administration noun **1** *the administration of the company:* management, direction, control, conduct, operation, running, coordination, governance, supervision, regulation. **2** *the Labour administration:* government, regime, executive, cabinet, authority, directorate, council, leadership, management, term of office, incumbency.

administrative adjective managerial, executive, operational, organizational, supervisory, directorial, governmental, regulatory.

administrator noun manager, director, executive, controller, official, coordinator, supervisor.

admirable adjective commendable, praiseworthy, laudable, creditable, exemplary, worthy, deserving, respectable, worthwhile, good, sterling, fine.
OPPOSITES deplorable.

admiration noun respect, approval, appreciation, (high) regard, esteem, recognition.
OPPOSITES scorn.

admire verb **1** *I admire your courage:* respect, think highly of, hold in high regard, rate highly, esteem, prize, approve of. **2** *Simon had admired her for a long time:* adore, love, worship, be taken with, be attracted to; informal carry a torch for, have a thing about.
OPPOSITES despise.

admirer noun fan, devotee, enthusiast, aficionado, supporter, adherent, follower, disciple.

admission noun **1** *an admission of liability:* confession, acknowledgement, acceptance, concession, disclosure, divulgence. **2** *free admission:* admittance, entry, entrance, access, entrée, acceptance, initiation.

admit verb **1** *Paul admitted that he was angry:* confess, acknowledge, concede, grant, accept, allow, reveal, disclose, divulge. **2** *he admitted the offence:* confess (to), plead guilty to, own up to. **3** *he was admitted to the college:* let in, accept, receive, initiate, take on.
OPPOSITES deny, exclude.

admittance noun entry, admission, entrance, access, entrée.
OPPOSITES exclusion.

adolescence noun teenage years, teens, youth, later childhood.

•**noun** an adolescent boy or girl.
■ **adolescence** noun.

Adonis /uh-**doh**-nis/ **noun** a very handsome young man.

adopt verb **1** legally take someone else's child and bring it up as your own. **2** choose an option or course of action.
■ **adoption** noun.

adoptive adjective (of a parent) having adopted a child.

adorable adjective very lovable or charming.
■ **adorably** adverb.

adore verb (**adores, adoring, adored**) love deeply.
■ **adoration** noun.

adorn verb make more attractive; decorate.
■ **adornment** noun.

adrenal /uh-**dree**-nuhl/ adjective having to do with the **adrenal glands**, a pair of glands above the kidneys.

adrenalin or **adrenaline** /uh-**dre**-nuh-lin/ noun a hormone produced by the adrenal glands in response to stress, that makes the body's natural processes work more quickly.

adrift adjective & adverb **1** (of a boat) drifting without control. **2** no longer fixed in position.

adroit adjective clever or skilful.
■ **adroitly** adverb.

adulation noun excessive admiration.
■ **adulatory** adjective.

adult noun a person who is fully grown and developed. •**adjective 1** fully grown and developed. **2** suitable for or typical of adults.
■ **adulthood** noun.

adulterate verb (**adulterates, adulterating, adulterated**) make something worse in quality by adding another substance.
■ **adulteration** noun.

adulterer noun (feminine **adulteress**) a person who has committed adultery.

adultery noun sex between a married person and a person who is not their husband or wife.
■ **adulterous** adjective.

adumbrate /ad-um-brayt/ verb (**adumbrates, adumbrating, adumbrated**) formal give a faint or general idea of.

advance verb (**advances, advancing, advanced**) **1** move forwards. **2** put forward a theory or suggestion. **3** hand over payment to someone as a loan or before it is due. •**noun 1** a forward movement. **2** a development or improvement. **3** an amount of money advanced. **4** an approach made with the aim of beginning a sexual or romantic relationship. •**adjective** done, sent, or supplied beforehand.

advanced adjective **1** far on in progress or life. **2** complex; not basic.
□ **advanced level** an A level.

advancement noun **1** the process of helping a cause or plan to develop or succeed. **2** the raising of a person to a

---

adolescent noun teenager, youth, juvenile; informal teen, teeny-bopper.
•**adjective** teenage, young, immature, childish, juvenile, infantile, puerile; informal teen.
OPPOSITES mature.

adopt verb take on, embrace, take up, espouse, assume, follow, choose, endorse, approve.
OPPOSITES abandon.

adore verb love, be devoted to, dote on, cherish, treasure, prize, think the world of, admire, look up to, revere, worship.
OPPOSITES hate.

adorn verb decorate, embellish, array, ornament, enhance.
OPPOSITES disfigure.

adrift adjective **1** adrift in a strange country: lost, off course, drifting, disorientated, confused, (all) at sea, rootless, unsettled. **2** (informal) the hook has come adrift: loose, free, detached, unsecured, unfastened.

adult adjective **1** an adult woman: mature, grown-up, fully grown, fully developed, of age. **2** an adult movie: (sexually) explicit, pornographic, obscene, dirty, erotic, sexy; informal porn, porno, naughty, blue, X-rated.

advance verb **1** the battalion advanced rapidly: move forward, press on, push on, attack, make progress, make headway, gain ground. **2** the move advanced his career: promote, further, forward, help, aid, assist, boost. **3** technology has advanced: progress, develop, evolve, make strides, move forward (in leaps and bounds), move on. **4** a relative advanced him some money: lend, loan, put up, come up with; Brit. informal sub.
OPPOSITES retreat, hinder, regress.
•**noun 1** the army's advance: progress, (forward) movement, attack. **2** a significant medical advance: breakthrough, development, step forward, (quantum) leap.
•**adjective** advance warning: early, prior.
□ in advance beforehand, before, ahead of time, earlier, previously, in readiness.

advanced adjective **1** advanced manufacturing techniques: state-of-the-art, modern, up to date, up to the minute, cutting-edge, new, the latest, pioneering, innovative, sophisticated. **2** an advanced course: higher-level, higher, tertiary.
OPPOSITES primitive, elementary.

a

higher rank or status. **3** a development or improvement.

advantage noun **1** something that puts you in a good position. **2** Tennis a score marking a point between deuce and winning the game.
□ **take advantage of 1** make unfair use of someone. **2** make good use of an opportunity.
■ **advantageous** adjective.

advent noun **1** the arrival of an important person or thing. **2** (**Advent**) (in Christian belief) the coming or second coming of Jesus. **3** (**Advent**) the time leading up to Christmas.

adventitious /ad-vuhn-ti-shuhss/ adjective formal happening by chance.

adventure noun **1** an unusual, exciting, and daring experience. **2** excitement resulting from danger or risk.

adventurer noun **1** a person willing to take risks or do dishonest things for personal gain. **2** a person who looks for adventure.

adventurous adjective **1** involving new or daring methods or experiences. **2** willing to take risks and try new things.
■ **adventurously** adverb.

adverb noun Grammar a word that gives more information about an adjective, verb, or other adverb (e.g. *gently*, *very*).
■ **adverbial** adjective.

adversarial /ad-ver-sair-i-uhl/ adjective having to do with conflict or opposition.

adversary /ad-ver-suh-ri/ noun (plural **adversaries**) an opponent or enemy.

adverse adjective harmful or unfavourable.
■ **adversely** adverb.

> ! don't confuse **adverse** with **averse**, which means 'strongly disliking or opposed to', as in *I am not averse to helping out.*

adversity noun (plural **adversities**) a difficult or unpleasant situation.

advert noun Brit. informal an advertisement.

advertise verb (**advertises**, **advertising**, **advertised**) **1** describe a product, service, or event in a publication or on television or radio in order to increase sales. **2** try to fill a job vacancy by publishing details of it. **3** make a fact known.
■ **advertiser** noun.

advertisement noun a notice or display advertising something.

advice noun guidance or recommendations about what someone should do in the future.

> ! don't confuse the noun **advice** and the verb **advise**.

advisable adjective sensible; to be recommended.
■ **advisability** noun.

advise verb (**advises**, **advising**, **advised**)

THESAURUS

advantage noun **1** *they have the advantage:* **upper hand**, edge, lead, sway, whip hand, superiority, dominance, supremacy. **2** *the advantage of belonging to a union:* benefit, value, good/strong point, asset, plus, bonus, boon, blessing, virtue, profit, good.
OPPOSITES disadvantage.

advantageous adjective **1** *an advantageous position:* superior, dominant, powerful, fortunate, lucky, favourable. **2** *the arrangement is advantageous to both sides:* beneficial, of benefit, helpful, of assistance, useful, of value, profitable, in someone's interests.
OPPOSITES disadvantageous.

adventure noun **1** *her adventures in Italy:* exploit, escapade, undertaking, experience, incident. **2** *in search of adventure:* excitement, thrills, action, stimulation, risk, danger.

adventurous adjective **1** *an adventurous traveller:* daring, intrepid, bold, fearless, brave; informal gutsy. **2** *adventurous activities:* risky, dangerous, perilous, hazardous, exciting.
OPPOSITES cautious, safe, predictable.

adversary noun opponent, rival, enemy, antagonist, challenger, contender,

competitor, opposition, competition; literary foe.
OPPOSITES ally, supporter.

adverse adjective **1** *adverse weather:* unfavourable, inclement, bad, poor, untoward. **2** *the drug's adverse side effects:* harmful, dangerous, injurious, detrimental. **3** *an adverse response:* hostile, unfavourable, antagonistic, unfriendly, negative.
OPPOSITES favourable, auspicious, beneficial.

advertise verb publicize, make public, announce, broadcast, proclaim, trumpet, promote; informal push, plug, hype; N. Amer. informal ballyhoo, flack.

advertisement noun announcement, commercial, promotion, blurb, write-up; informal ad, push, plug, puff; Brit. informal advert.

advice noun guidance, counselling, counsel, help, direction, recommendations, guidelines, suggestions, hints, tips, pointers.

advise verb **1** *her grandmother advised her about marriage:* counsel, give guidance, guide, give hints/tips/pointers, offer suggestions. **2** *he advised caution:* recommend, advocate, suggest, urge. **3** *you*

a

1 recommend that someone should do something. **2** tell someone about a fact or situation.
■ **adviser** (or **advisor**) noun.

advised adjective behaving as someone would recommend; sensible.
■ **advisedly** adverb.

advisory adjective having the power to make recommendations but not to make sure that they are carried out.

advocaat /ad-vuh-kah/ noun a liqueur made with eggs, sugar, and brandy.

advocate noun /ad-vuh-kuht/ **1** a person who publicly supports or recommends a cause or policy. **2** a person who argues a case on someone else's behalf. **3** Scottish a barrister. •verb /ad-vuh-kayt/ (**advocates**, **advocating**, **advocated**) publicly recommend or support.
■ **advocacy** noun.

adze /adz/ (US spelling **adz**) noun a tool like an axe, with an arched blade.

aegis /ee-jiss/ noun the protection, backing, or support of someone.

aeon /ee-on/ (US spelling **eon**) noun a very long period of time.

aerate verb bring air into something.
■ **aeration** noun.

aerial noun a wire, rod, etc. that sends out or receives radio or television signals.
•adjective **1** existing or taking place in the air. **2** involving the use of aircraft.

aerie US spelling of EYRIE.

aerobatics noun exciting and daring flying performed for display.
■ **aerobatic** adjective.

aerobic /air-oh-bik/ adjective (of exercise) intended to increase the amount of oxygen you breathe in and make it move around the body more quickly.
■ **aerobically** adverb.

aerobics noun exercises intended to strengthen the heart and lungs.

aerodrome noun Brit. an airfield.

aerodynamic adjective **1** relating to aerodynamics. **2** having a shape which moves through the air quickly. •noun (**aerodynamics**) the science concerned with the movement of objects through the air.
■ **aerodynamically** adverb.

aerofoil noun Brit. a curved structure, such as a wing, designed to give an aircraft lift.

aeronautics noun the study or practice of travel through the air.
■ **aeronautical** adjective.

aeroplane noun Brit. a powered flying vehicle with fixed wings.

aerosol noun a substance sealed in a container under pressure and released as a fine spray.

aerospace noun the technology and industry concerned with flight.

aesthete /eess-theet/ (US spelling **esthete**) noun a person who appreciates art and beauty.

aesthetic /ess-thet-ik/ (US spelling **esthetic**) adjective **1** concerned with beauty. **2** having a pleasant appearance. •noun a set of principles behind the work of an artist or artistic movement.
■ **aesthetically** adverb.

aesthetics (US spelling **esthetics**) noun **1** a set of principles concerned with beauty. **2** the branch of philosophy which deals with questions of beauty and artistic taste.

afar adverb at or to a distance.

affable adjective good-natured and friendly.
■ **affability** noun **affably** adverb.

affair noun **1** an event or series of events. **2** a matter that is a particular person's responsibility. **3** a love affair. **4** (**affairs**) matters of public interest and importance.

affect verb **1** make a difference to. **2** make someone feel sadness, pity, etc. **3** pretend to have a particular feeling. **4** wear something or behave in a particular way in

THESAURUS

will be advised of our decision: **inform**, notify, give notice, apprise, warn.

adviser noun **counsellor**, aide, mentor, guide, consultant, confidant, confidante, guru.

advocate noun **champion**, upholder, supporter, backer, promoter, proponent, campaigner, lobbyist; N. Amer. booster.
OPPOSITES critic.
•verb **recommend**, champion, uphold, support, back, promote, campaign for, urge, subscribe to, speak for, argue for, lobby for.
OPPOSITES oppose, advise against.

affair noun **1** *it was a strange affair*: **event**, incident, episode, case, matter, business. **2** *what you do is your affair*: **business**,

concern, matter, responsibility; Brit. informal lookout. **3** (**affairs**) *financial affairs*: **transactions**, activities, dealings, undertakings, ventures, business. **4** *his affair with Anthea was over*: **relationship**, romance, fling, dalliance, liaison, involvement, amour; informal hanky-panky; Brit. informal carry-on.

affect[1] verb **1** *this affected our decision*: **influence**, have an effect on, have an impact on, act on, change, alter, modify. **2** *he was visibly affected by the experience*: **move**, touch, hit (hard), make an impression on, upset, trouble, distress, disturb, shake (up).

affect[2] verb *he affected an air of boredom*: **put on**, assume, take on, adopt, feign.

an attempt to impress people.

> **!** don't confuse **affect** and **effect**. **Affect** chiefly means 'make a difference to', as in *the changes will affect everyone*. **Effect** is chiefly a noun meaning 'a result', as in *the effects of ageing*.

affectation noun behaviour that is designed to impress people.

affected adjective designed to impress people.
  ∎ **affectedly** adverb.

affection noun a feeling of fondness or liking.

affectionate adjective readily showing affection.
  ∎ **affectionately** adverb.

affidavit /af-fi-**day**-vit/ noun a written statement that a person swears is true and that can be used as evidence in a law court.

affiliate verb /uh-**fil**-i-ayt/ (**affiliates**, **affiliating**, **affiliated**) officially link a person or group to an organization. ∙ noun /uh-**fil**-i-uht/ an affiliated person or group.
  ∎ **affiliation** noun.

affinity noun (plural **affinities**) **1** a natural liking or understanding. **2** a close relationship between people or things with similar qualities.

affirm verb state firmly or publicly.
  ∎ **affirmation** noun.

affirmative adjective agreeing with a statement, or consenting to a request.
  ∎ **affirmatively** adverb.

affix verb /uh-**fiks**/ attach or fasten

something to something else. ∙ noun /**af**-fiks/ Grammar a prefix or suffix.

afflict verb cause pain or suffering to.
  ∎ **affliction** noun.

affluent adjective wealthy; rich.
  ∎ **affluence** noun.

afford verb **1** have enough money or time for. **2** provide an opportunity or facility.
  ∎ **affordable** adjective.

affray noun Law, dated a breach of the peace by fighting in a public place.

affront noun an action or remark that offends someone. ∙ verb offend someone.

Afghan /**af**-gan/ noun a person from Afghanistan. ∙ adjective relating to Afghanistan.

aficionado /uh-fi-shuh-**nah**-doh/ noun (plural **aficionados**) a person who knows a lot about an activity or subject and is very keen on it.

afield adverb to or at a distance.

aflame adjective in flames.

afloat adjective & adverb **1** floating in water. **2** out of debt or difficulty.

afoot adverb & adjective happening; in preparation or progress.

aforementioned adjective previously mentioned.

afraid adjective feeling fear.

afresh adverb in a new or different way.

African noun a person from Africa. ∙ adjective relating to Africa or Africans.

Afrikaans /af-ri-**kahns**/ noun a language of southern Africa that developed from Dutch.

THESAURUS

affectation noun pretension, pretentiousness, affectedness, artificiality, posturing, airs (and graces); Brit. informal side.

affection noun fondness, love, liking, tenderness, warmth, devotion, caring, attachment, friendship.

affectionate adjective fond, loving, adoring, devoted, caring, tender, warm, friendly, demonstrative; informal touchy-feely, lovey-dovey.
  OPPOSITES cold.

affiliate verb associate, unite, combine, join (up), join forces, link up, ally, align, amalgamate, merge.

affinity noun empathy, rapport, sympathy, accord, harmony, similarity, relationship, bond, closeness, understanding; informal chemistry.
  OPPOSITES aversion, dislike, dissimilarity.

affirm verb declare, state, assert, proclaim, pronounce, attest, swear.
  OPPOSITES deny.

affirmative adjective positive, assenting,

consenting, approving, favourable.
  OPPOSITES negative.

afflict verb trouble, burden, distress, beset, harass, worry, oppress, torment, plague.

affluent adjective wealthy, rich, prosperous, well off, well-to-do, of means; informal well heeled, rolling in it, made of money, loaded.
  OPPOSITES poor.

afford verb **1** *I can't afford a new car:* pay for, find the money for, run to, stretch to, stand, manage. **2** *can you afford the time?* spare, allow yourself. **3** *the terrace affords beautiful views:* give, offer, supply, provide, furnish, yield.

afraid adjective **1** *they ran away because they were afraid:* frightened, scared, terrified, fearful, nervous, petrified, intimidated, cowardly, faint-hearted; informal scared stiff; N. Amer. informal spooked. **2** *don't be afraid to ask awkward questions:* reluctant, hesitant, unwilling, slow, shy. **3** *I'm afraid I'm late:* sorry.
  OPPOSITES brave, confident, glad.

Afrikaner /af-ri-**kah**-ner/ noun an Afrikaans-speaking white person in South Africa.

aft adverb & adjective at or towards the rear of a ship or an aircraft.

after preposition 1 in the time following an event or another period of time. 2 next to and following in order or importance. 3 behind. 4 trying to find or get. 5 in reference to. • conjunction & adverb in the time following an event.
□ after-effect an effect that happens some time after its cause.

afterbirth noun the placenta and other material that passes out of the mother's womb after a birth.

afterlife noun life after death.

aftermath noun the situation that exists as a result of an unpleasant or disastrous event.

afternoon noun the time from noon or lunchtime to evening.

aftershave noun a scented liquid for men to apply to their skin after shaving.

afterthought noun something that is thought of or added later.

afterwards (US spelling **afterward**) adverb at a later or future time.

again adverb 1 once more. 2 returning to a previous position or condition. 3 in addition.

against preposition 1 in opposition to. 2 in resistance to. 3 in contrast to. 4 in or into contact with.

agape adjective (of a person's mouth) wide open.

agate /**ag**-uht/ noun an ornamental stone marked with bands of colour.

agave /uh-**gay**-vi, uh-**gah**-vi/ noun an American plant with narrow spiny leaves.

age noun 1 the length of time that a person or thing has existed. 2 a particular stage in someone's life. 3 old age. 4 a distinct period of history. • verb (**ages**, **ageing** or **aging**, **aged**) grow old or older.
□ age of consent the age at which a person can legally have sex. come of age be legally recognized as an adult.

aged adjective 1 /ayjd/ of a specified age. 2 /**ay**-jid/ old.

ageism noun prejudice or discrimination on the grounds of a person's age.
■ ageist adjective & noun.

ageless adjective not ageing or appearing to age.

agency noun 1 an organization providing a particular service. 2 action or intervention.

agenda noun 1 a list of items to be discussed at a meeting. 2 a list of matters to be dealt with.

agent noun 1 a person who provides a particular service. 2 a spy. 3 a person or thing that takes an active role or produces a particular effect.

agent provocateur /a-zhon pruh-vo-kuh-ter/ noun (plural **agents provocateurs** /a-zhon pruh-vo-kuh-**ter**/) a person who tempts suspected criminals to commit a crime and therefore be convicted.

agglomeration noun a mass or collection of things.

aggrandize or **aggrandise** verb (**aggrandizes**, **aggrandizing**, **aggrandized**) make more powerful, important, or impressive.
■ aggrandizement noun.

aggravate verb (**aggravates**, **aggravating**,

after preposition following, subsequent to, at the end of, in the wake of.

aftermath noun consequences, after-effects, results, repercussions, upshot.

afterwards adverb later, later on, subsequently, then, next, after this/that, in due course.

again adverb once more, another time, afresh, anew.

against preposition 1 *most delegates were against the motion:* opposed to, in opposition to, hostile to, antagonistic towards, unsympathetic to, at odds with, in disagreement with; informal anti, agin.
2 *swimming against the tide:* counter to, contrary to, in the opposite direction to, resisting. 3 *she leaned against the wall:* touching, in contact with, up against, abutting, on.
OPPOSITES in favour of, with.

age noun 1 *her hearing deteriorated with age:* old age, maturity, advancing years, elderliness, seniority. 2 *the Elizabethan age:* era, epoch, period, time.
• verb 1 *Cabernet Sauvignon ages well:* mature, mellow, ripen, soften, season, weather. 2 *the experience has aged her:* make old, wear out, weather. 3 *she has aged a lot:* grow old, decline, wither, fade.

agency noun business, organization, company, firm, office, bureau.

agenda noun programme, schedule, to-do list, timetable, plan.

agent noun 1 *the sale was arranged through an agent:* representative, intermediary, negotiator, go-between, proxy, broker, emissary, envoy, spokesperson; informal rep. 2 *a CIA agent:* spy, secret agent, operative, mole; N. Amer. informal spook, G-man.

aggravate verb 1 *the new law could aggravate the situation:* worsen, make worse, exacerbate, inflame, compound.

a

aggravated) 1 make worse. **2** informal annoy or exasperate.
■ **aggravation** noun.

aggregate noun /ag-gri-guht/ **1** a whole formed by combining several different elements. **2** the total score of a player or team in a fixture that is made up of more than one game or round. ● adjective /ag-gri-guht/ formed by combining many separate items. ● verb /ag-gri-gayt/ (**aggregates, aggregating, aggregated**) combine into a whole.

aggression noun hostile or violent behaviour or attitudes.

aggressive adjective **1** very angry or hostile. **2** too forceful.
■ **aggressively** adverb.

☑ double g, double s: aggressive.

aggressor noun a person or country that attacks another without being provoked.

aggrieved adjective resentful because you feel you have been treated unfairly.

aghast /uh-gahst/ adjective filled with horror or shock.

agile adjective **1** able to move quickly and easily. **2** able to think quickly and intelligently.
■ **agilely** adverb **agility** noun.

agitate verb (**agitates, agitating, agitated**) **1** make someone troubled or nervous. **2** try to arouse public concern about an issue. **3** stir or shake a liquid.

■ **agitation** noun.

agitator noun a person who urges other people to protest or rebel.

AGM abbreviation Brit. annual general meeting.

agnostic noun a person who believes it is impossible to know whether or not God exists.
■ **agnosticism** noun.

ago adverb before the present.

agog adjective very eager to hear or see something.

agonize or **agonise** verb (**agonizes, agonizing, agonized**) **1** worry about something very much. **2** (**agonizing**) very painful or worrying.

agony noun (plural **agonies**) extreme suffering.
□ **agony column** Brit. informal a column in a newspaper or magazine offering advice on readers' personal problems.

agoraphobia /ag-uh-ruh-foh-bi-uh/ noun abnormal fear of open or public places.
■ **agoraphobic** adjective & noun.

agrarian /uh-grair-i-uhn/ adjective having to do with agriculture.

agree verb (**agrees, agreeing, agreed**) **1** have the same opinion about something. **2** (**agree to**) say that you will do something that has been suggested by someone else. **3** (**agree with**) be consistent with. **4** (**agree with**) be good for.

agreeable adjective **1** pleasant. **2** willing to

THESAURUS

2 (informal) *you'll only aggravate him!* annoy, antagonize, irritate, exasperate, nettle, provoke, get on someone's nerves; Brit. rub up the wrong way; informal needle, hack off, get someone's goat, get up someone's nose; Brit. informal wind up; N. Amer. informal tick off.
OPPOSITES alleviate, improve, placate.

aggregate noun total, sum, grand total, combined score.

aggression noun **1** *an act of aggression:* hostility, belligerence, force, violence, attack. **2** *he played with unceasing aggression:* confidence, self-confidence, boldness, determination, forcefulness, vigour, energy, dynamism, commitment.

aggressive adjective **1** *aggressive behaviour:* violent, confrontational, antagonistic, pugnacious. **2** *aggressive foreign policy:* warmongering, warlike, warring, belligerent, bellicose, hawkish, militaristic, expansionist; informal gung-ho. **3** *an aggressive promotional drive:* assertive, forceful, vigorous, energetic, dynamic, audacious; informal in-your-face, feisty.
OPPOSITES peaceable, peaceful, laid-back.

agile adjective **1** *she was as agile as a monkey:* nimble, lithe, supple, acrobatic.

2 *an agile mind:* alert, sharp, acute, shrewd, astute, perceptive, quick.
OPPOSITES stiff, clumsy, dull.

agitate verb **1** *any mention of Clare agitates my grandmother:* upset, fluster, ruffle, disconcert, unnerve, disquiet, disturb, distress, unsettle; informal rattle, faze. **2** *agitate the solution:* shake, whisk, beat, stir.

agonizing adjective excruciating, painful, acute, harrowing, torturous.

agony noun suffering, torture, pain, torment, anguish.

agree verb **1** *I agree with you:* concur, see eye to eye, be in sympathy, be as one, be unanimous. **2** *they agreed to a ceasefire:* consent, assent, acquiesce; formal accede. **3** *the plan and the drawing do not agree:* match (up), correspond, conform, coincide, fit, tally, be consistent; informal square. **4** *they agreed a price:* settle, decide on, arrive at, negotiate, shake hands on.
OPPOSITES differ, reject, contradict.

agreeable adjective **1** *an agreeable atmosphere:* pleasant, pleasing, enjoyable, pleasurable, nice, appealing, relaxing, friendly, congenial. **2** *an agreeable man:*

agree to something. **3** acceptable.

■ **agreeably** adverb.

agreement noun **1** the state of sharing the same opinion or feeling. **2** an arrangement that has been made between people.

agriculture noun the science or practice of farming.

■ **agricultural** adjective **agriculturally** adverb.

agronomy noun the scientific study of the relationship between crop production and the environment.

■ **agronomist** noun.

aground adjective & adverb (of a ship) touching the bottom in shallow water.

ague /**ay**-gyoo/ noun old use malaria or some other illness involving fever and shivering.

ahead adverb **1** further forward. **2** in the lead.

ahoy exclamation a call used by people in ships or boats to attract attention.

aid noun **1** help or support. **2** food or money given to a country in need of help. •**verb** give help to.

aide /ayd/ noun an assistant to a political leader.

Aids noun a disease, caused by the HIV virus and transmitted in body fluids, which breaks down the sufferer's natural defences against infection.

aikido /I-**kee**-doh/ noun a Japanese martial art.

ail verb old use cause someone to suffer or have problems.

aileron /**ayl**-uh-ron/ noun a hinged part of an aircraft's wing, used to control the aircraft's balance.

ailing adjective in bad health.

ailment noun a minor illness.

aim verb **1** point a weapon, camera, etc. at a target. **2** try to achieve something. •**noun 1** a purpose or intention. **2** the aiming of a weapon or missile.

aimless adjective having no direction or purpose.

■ **aimlessly** adverb.

ain't short form informal **1** am not; are not; is not. **2** has not; have not.

> **!** do not use **ain't** when writing or speaking in a formal situation.

air noun **1** the invisible mixture of gases surrounding the earth. **2** the open space above the surface of the earth. **3** (**an air of**) an impression of. **4** (**airs**) a pretentious

likeable, amiable, affable, pleasant, nice, friendly, good-natured, sociable, genial. **3** *we should get together, if you're agreeable:* willing, amenable, in agreement.
OPPOSITES unpleasant.

agreement noun **1** *all heads nodded in agreement:* accord, concurrence, consensus, assent, acceptance, consent, acquiescence. **2** *an agreement on imports:* contract, treaty, pact, accord, settlement, understanding, bargain. **3** *there is some agreement between the two datasets:* correspondence, consistency, compatibility, accord, similarity, resemblance, likeness.
OPPOSITES discord, dissimilarity.

agricultural adjective farm, farming, agrarian, rural, rustic, countryside.
OPPOSITES urban.

agriculture noun farming, cultivation, husbandry, agribusiness, agronomy.

aid noun **1** *with the aid of his colleagues:* assistance, support, help, backing, cooperation. **2** *humanitarian aid:* relief, assistance, support, subsidy, funding, donations, grants; historical alms.
OPPOSITES hindrance.
•**verb** help, assist, support, encourage, further, boost, promote, facilitate.
OPPOSITES hinder.

aide noun assistant, helper, adviser, supporter, right-hand man/woman, adjutant, deputy, second (in command), lieutenant.

ailing adjective **1** *his ailing mother:* ill, sick, sickly, poorly, weak, in poor/bad health, infirm. **2** *the country's ailing economy:* failing, weak, poor, tottering, fragile, unstable.
OPPOSITES healthy.

ailment noun illness, disease, disorder, affliction, malady, complaint, infirmity; informal bug, virus.

aim verb **1** *he aimed the rifle:* point, direct, train, sight, line up. **2** *she aimed at the target:* take aim, fix on, zero in on, draw a bead on. **3** *this food is aimed at children:* target, intend, direct, design, tailor, market, pitch. **4** *we aim to give you good service:* intend, mean, hope, want, plan, propose.
•**noun** *our aim is to develop top gymnasts:* objective, object, goal, end, target, design, desire, intention, intent, plan, purpose, ambition, aspiration, wish, dream, hope.

aimless adjective purposeless, directionless, undirected, random.
OPPOSITES purposeful.

air noun **1** breeze, draught, wind, gust/puff of wind. **2** *an air of defiance:* look, appearance, impression, aspect, manner, tone, feel, atmosphere, mood.
•**verb 1** *a chance to air your views:* express, voice, make public, articulate, state, declare. **2** *the room needs airing:* ventilate,

or condescending way of behaving. **5** a tune. • **verb 1** express an opinion or complaint publicly. **2** broadcast a programme on radio or television. **3** expose something to fresh or warm air.
□ **air conditioning** a system that cools the air in a building or vehicle. **air force** the branch of the armed forces concerned with fighting in the air. **air gun** a gun which uses compressed air to fire pellets. **on the air** being broadcast on radio or television.
■ **airing** noun **airless** adjective.

airbase noun a base for military aircraft.

airborne adjective **1** carried or spread through the air. **2** (of an aircraft) in the air; flying.

airbrush noun a device for spraying paint by means of compressed air. • **verb** paint a picture or alter a photograph with an airbrush.

aircraft noun (plural **aircraft**) a plane, helicopter, or other machine that can fly.
■ **aircraft carrier** a large warship from which aircraft can take off and land.

Airedale noun a large black-and-tan breed of terrier with a rough coat.

airfield noun an area of ground where aircraft can take off and land.

airlift noun an act of transporting supplies by aircraft.

airline noun a company that provides regular flights for the public to use.

airliner noun a large passenger aircraft.

airlock noun **1** a bubble of air that stops the flow in a pump or pipe. **2** a compartment which allows people to move between areas that are at different pressures.

airmail noun a system of transporting mail overseas by air.

airman noun (plural **airmen**) a pilot or crew member in a military aircraft.

airplane noun N. Amer. a plane.

airport noun an area consisting of a set of runways and buildings where non-military aircraft can take off and land.

airship noun a large aircraft filled with gas

which is lighter than air.

airspace noun the part of the air above a particular country.

airstrip noun a strip of ground where aircraft can take off and land.

airtight adjective **1** not allowing air to escape or pass through. **2** unable to be proved false.

airwaves plural noun the radio frequencies used for broadcasting.

airway noun **1** the passage by which air reaches the lungs. **2** a recognized route followed by aircraft.

airworthy adjective (of an aircraft) safe to fly.

airy adjective (**airier**, **airiest**) **1** spacious and having plenty of fresh air. **2** showing that you feel something is not worth serious consideration.
■ **airily** adverb.

airy-fairy adjective informal vague and unrealistic or impractical.

aisle /rhymes with mile/ noun a passage between rows of seats in a public building, aircraft, or train or between shelves in a shop.

ajar adverb & adjective (of a door or window) slightly open.

aka abbreviation also known as.

akimbo /uh-**kim**-boh/ adverb with hands on the hips and elbows turned outwards.

akin adjective similar in nature or type.

alabaster /**al**-uh-bass-ter/ noun a white, semi-transparent mineral that is carved into ornaments.

à la carte /a la **kart**/ adjective & adverb (of a menu) offering dishes that are separately priced, rather than part of a set meal.

alacrity noun great eagerness or enthusiasm.

alarm noun **1** anxiety or fear caused by being aware of danger. **2** a warning of danger. **3** a sound or device that gives a warning of danger. • **verb 1** frighten or disturb. **2** (**be alarmed**) (of a car or

---

THESAURUS

freshen, refresh, cool.

airless adjective stuffy, close, stifling, suffocating, oppressive, unventilated.
OPPOSITES airy.

airy adjective spacious, uncluttered, light, bright, well ventilated, fresh.
OPPOSITES poky, stuffy.

aisle noun passage, passageway, lane, path, gangway, walkway.

akin adjective similar, related, close, near, comparable, equivalent, connected, alike, analogous.
OPPOSITES unlike.

alarm noun **1** the girl spun round in alarm:

fear, anxiety, apprehension, distress, agitation, consternation, fright, panic. **2** a fire alarm: warning, danger signal, siren, bell, detector, sensor.
OPPOSITES calmness, composure.
• verb the news alarmed her: frighten, scare, panic, unnerve, distress, agitate, upset, disconcert, shock, disturb; informal rattle, spook; Brit. informal put the wind up.
OPPOSITES reassure.

alarming adjective frightening, unnerving, shocking, worrying, upsetting, disconcerting, disturbing; informal scary.
OPPOSITES reassuring.

building) be fitted with an alarm.
◻ **alarm clock** a clock set to sound at a particular time to wake you up.

alarmist noun a person who exaggerates a danger and causes unnecessary alarm.

alas exclamation literary or humorous an expression of grief, pity, or concern.

albatross /al-buh-tross/ noun (plural **albatrosses**) a very large white seabird with long, narrow wings.

albeit /awl-**bee**-it/ conjunction though.

albino /al-**bee**-noh/ noun (plural **albinos**) a person or animal born with white skin and hair and pink eyes.

album noun 1 a blank book for displaying photographs, stamps, etc. 2 a collection of musical recordings issued as a single item.

albumen /al-byuu-muhn/ noun egg white.

alchemy /al-kuh-mi/ noun a medieval form of chemistry that was chiefly concerned with trying to convert ordinary metals into gold.
■ **alchemical** adjective **alchemist** noun.

alcohol noun 1 drinks containing a colourless liquid that can make people drunk, such as wine, beer, and spirits. 2 this liquid.

alcoholic adjective relating to alcohol. •noun a person suffering from alcoholism.

alcoholism noun addiction to alcoholic drink.

alcopop noun Brit. informal a ready-mixed fizzy drink containing alcohol.

alcove noun a recess in the wall of a room.

alder noun a tree of the birch family, which produces catkins.

alderman noun (plural **aldermen**) chiefly historical a member of a council below the rank of mayor.

ale noun chiefly Brit. beer, especially bitter.

alert adjective 1 quick to notice and respond to danger or change. 2 quick-thinking; intelligent. •noun 1 a watchful state. 2 a warning of danger. •verb warn someone of a danger or problem.
■ **alertly** adverb **alertness** noun.

alfalfa /al-**fal**-fuh/ noun a plant with bluish flowers, used as food for animals.

alfresco /al-**fress**-koh/ adverb & adjective in the open air.

algae /al-jee, al-gee/ plural noun simple plants that do not have true stems, roots, and leaves, such as seaweed.

algebra /al-ji-bruh/ noun the branch of mathematics in which letters and other symbols are used to represent numbers and quantities.
■ **algebraic** /al-ji-**bray**-ik/ adjective.

Algerian noun a person from Algeria. •adjective relating to Algeria.

algorithm /al-guh-ri-*th*'m/ noun a process or set of rules used in calculations.

alias /ay-li-uhss/ adverb also known as. •noun a false identity.

alibi /a-li-by/ noun (plural **alibis**) a piece of evidence that a person was somewhere else when a crime was committed.

alien adjective 1 belonging to a foreign country. 2 unfamiliar and unappealing. 3 from another world. •noun 1 a foreigner. 2 a being from another world.

alienate verb (**alienates**, **alienating**, **alienated**) 1 make someone feel isolated. 2 lose the support or sympathy of.
■ **alienation** noun.

alight¹ verb 1 get off a train or bus. 2 (of a bird) land on something.

alight² adverb & adjective 1 on fire. 2 shining brightly.

align verb 1 place something in a straight

alcoholic adjective **intoxicating**, strong, hard, stiff, fermented, brewed, distilled.
•noun **drunkard**, dipsomaniac, drunk, heavy drinker, problem drinker, alcohol-abuser; informal **boozer**, alky, dipso, soak, wino; Austral./NZ informal **hophead**.

alert adjective 1 *an alert sentry:* **vigilant**, watchful, attentive, observant, wide awake, on the lookout, on your guard/toes; informal keeping your eyes open/peeled. 2 *mentally alert:* **quick-witted**, sharp, bright, quick, perceptive, on your toes; informal on the ball, quick on the uptake, all there, with it.
OPPOSITES inattentive, dull.
•noun 1 *a state of alert:* **vigilance**, watchfulness, attentiveness, alertness. 2 *a flood alert:* **warning**, notification, notice, siren, alarm, signal.
•verb *police were alerted:* **warn**, notify, forewarn, put on your guard; informal tip off.

alien adjective **foreign**, unfamiliar, unknown, peculiar, exotic, strange.
OPPOSITES native, familiar.
•noun 1 *an illegal alien:* **foreigner**, non-native, immigrant, émigré, stranger. 2 *the alien's spaceship crashed:* **extraterrestrial**, ET; informal little green man.

alienate verb **isolate**, distance, estrange, cut off, turn away, drive apart, set at variance/odds, drive a wedge between.

alienation noun **isolation**, detachment, estrangement, separation.

alight adjective *the stable was alight:* **burning**, ablaze, on fire, in flames, blazing.

align verb 1 *the desks are aligned with the wall:* **line up**, straighten, even up, arrange, coordinate. 2 *he aligned himself with the workers:* **ally**, affiliate, associate, side, join forces, team up, band together, throw in your lot.

a

line or in the right position in relation to other things. **2** (**align yourself with**) be on the side of.
■ **alignment** noun.

alike adjective similar. • adverb in a similar way.

alimentary canal noun the passage along which food passes through the body.

alimony /a-li-muh-ni/ noun chiefly N. Amer. financial support for a husband or wife after separation or divorce.

alive adjective **1** living; not dead. **2** continuing in existence or use. **3** alert and active. **4** (**alive with**) full of. **5** (**alive to**) aware of and willing to respond to.

alkali /al-kuh-ly/ noun (plural **alkalis**) a substance whose chemical properties include turning litmus blue and neutralizing acids.
■ **alkaline** adjective.

all determiner **1** the whole quantity or extent of. **2** any whatever. **3** the greatest possible. • pronoun everything or everyone. • adverb **1** completely. **2** indicating an equal score: *one-all.*
□ **all and sundry** everyone. **the all clear** a signal that danger is over. **all in** informal exhausted. **all out** trying as hard as you can. **all-rounder** Brit. a person with a wide range of skills. **all told** in total. **on all fours** on hands and knees.

Allah /al-luh/ noun the Arabic name of God.

allay /uh-**lay**/ verb reduce or end fear, concern, or difficulty.

allegation noun a claim that someone has done something illegal or wrong.

allege verb (**alleges**, **alleging**, **alleged**) claim that someone has done something illegal or wrong.
■ **alleged** adjective **allegedly** adverb.

allegiance noun loyalty to a person, group, or cause.

allegory noun (plural **allegories**) a story, poem, or picture which contains a hidden meaning.
■ **allegorical** adjective.

allegro /uh-**lay**-groh/ noun (plural **allegros**) a piece of music that is to be played at a brisk speed.

alleluia ⇒ HALLELUJAH.

allergen noun a substance that causes an allergic reaction.

allergic adjective **1** caused by an allergy. **2** having an allergy.

allergy noun (plural **allergies**) a medical condition that makes you feel ill when you eat or come into contact with a particular substance.

alleviate verb (**alleviates**, **alleviating**, **alleviated**) make a pain or problem less severe.
■ **alleviation** noun.

alley noun (plural **alleys**) **1** (also **alleyway**) a narrow passageway between or behind buildings. **2** a path in a park or garden. **3** a long, narrow area in which skittles and bowling are played.

alliance noun **1** the state of being joined or associated. **2** an agreement made between countries or organizations to work together. **3** a relationship or connection.

allied adjective **1** joined by an alliance. **2** (**Allied**) relating to Britain and its allies

THESAURUS

alike adjective *all the doors looked alike:* similar, (much) the same, identical, indistinguishable, uniform, interchangeable; informal much of a muchness.
OPPOSITES different.
• adverb *great minds think alike:* similarly, the same, correspondingly, analogously, identically.
OPPOSITES differently.

alive adjective **1** *the synagogue has kept the Jewish faith alive:* active, in existence, functioning, in operation, operative, on the map. **2** *teachers need to be alive to their pupils' needs:* alert, awake, aware, conscious, mindful, heedful, sensitive, familiar.
OPPOSITES dead, unaware.

allay verb reduce, diminish, decrease, lessen, alleviate, ease, relieve, soothe, soften, calm.
OPPOSITES increase, intensify.

allegation noun claim, assertion, charge, accusation, contention.

allege verb claim, assert, charge, accuse, contend.

alleged adjective reported, supposed, so-called, claimed, professed, purported, ostensible, unproven.
OPPOSITES confirmed.

allegiance noun loyalty, faithfulness, fidelity, obedience, adherence, devotion.
OPPOSITES disloyalty, treachery.

alleviate verb ease, relieve, take the edge off, deaden, dull, lessen, reduce, moderate, allay, soothe, help, soften.
OPPOSITES aggravate.

alley noun passage, passageway, alleyway, backstreet, lane, path, pathway, walk.

alliance noun association, union, league, confederation, federation, coalition, marriage, cooperation.

allied adjective associated, united, related, connected, interconnected, linked, cooperating, in league, affiliated, combined, coupled, married.
OPPOSITES unrelated, independent.

in the First and Second World Wars.
3 (**allied to** or **with**) combined with.

alligator noun a large reptile similar to a crocodile.

alliteration noun the occurrence of the same letter or sound at the beginning of words that are next to or close to each other.
■ **alliterative** adjective.

allocate verb (**allocates, allocating, allocated**) assign or give to.
■ **allocation** noun.

allot verb (**allots, allotting, allotted**) give or share out something.

allotment noun **1** Brit. a small plot of rented land for growing vegetables or flowers.
2 the action of allotting something, or an amount of something allotted to someone.

allow verb **1** let someone do something.
2 (**allow for**) take into consideration.
3 provide or set aside. **4** admit that something is true.
■ **allowable** adjective.

> **!** don't confuse **allowed**, meaning 'permitted', with **aloud**, meaning 'out loud'.

allowance noun **1** the amount of something that is allowed. **2** a sum of money paid regularly to a person. **3** Brit. an amount of money that can be earned free of tax.
□ **make allowances for 1** take into consideration. **2** treat someone less harshly because they are in difficult circumstances.

alloy noun /**al**-loy/ **1** a mixture of two or more metals. **2** an inferior metal mixed with a precious one. ●verb /uh-**loy**/ mix metals to make an alloy.

all right adjective **1** satisfactory; acceptable. **2** allowed. ●adverb fairly well.

> ☑ use the spelling **all right** rather than alright.

allspice noun the dried fruit of a Caribbean tree, used as a spice in cookery.

allude verb (**alludes, alluding, alluded**) (**allude to**) **1** mention in passing. **2** hint at.

allure noun the quality of being very attractive or appealing.

alluring adjective very attractive or tempting.
■ **alluringly** adverb.

allusion noun an indirect reference to something.
■ **allusive** adjective.

alluvial adjective made of clay, silt, and sand that is left by flood water.

ally /**al**-ly/ noun (plural **allies**) **1** a person, organization, or country that cooperates with another. **2** (**the Allies**) the countries that fought with Britain in the First and Second World Wars. ●verb /uh-**ly**/ (**allies, allying, allied**)**1** (**ally something to** or **with**) combine one resource with another in a way that benefits both. **2** (**ally yourself with**) side with.

alma mater /al-muh **mah**-ter (or **may**-ter)/ noun the school, college, or university that a person once attended.

almanac or **almanack** /**al**-muh-nak/ noun **1** a calendar that gives important dates and

---

THESAURUS

allocate verb allot, assign, set aside, earmark, consign, distribute, apportion, share out, dole out, give out.

allocation noun **1** *the efficient allocation of resources:* allotment, assignment, distribution, sharing out, doling out, giving out. **2** *our annual allocation of funds:* allowance, allotment, consignment, quota, share, ration; informal cut; Brit. informal whack.

allow verb **1** *the police allowed him to go home:* permit, let, enable, authorize, give leave, license, entitle, consent to, assent to, acquiesce in, agree to, approve; informal give the go-ahead to, give the thumbs up to, OK, give the green light to; formal accede to. **2** *allow an hour or so for driving:* set aside, allocate, allot, earmark, designate, reserve.
OPPOSITES prevent, forbid.

allowance noun **1** *your baggage allowance:* allocation, allotment, quota, share, ration, grant, limit. **2** *her father gave her an allowance:* payment, pocket money, contribution, grant, handout, subsidy, maintenance.

all right adjective **1** *the tea was all right:* satisfactory, acceptable, adequate, passable, reasonable; informal so-so, OK. **2** *are you all right?* unhurt, uninjured, unharmed, in one piece, safe (and sound), alive and well; informal OK. **3** *it's all right for you to go:* permissible, permitted, allowed, acceptable, legal, lawful, authorized, approved, in order; informal OK, legit, cool.
OPPOSITES unsatisfactory, hurt, forbidden.
●adverb *the system works all right:* satisfactorily, adequately, fairly well, passably, acceptably, reasonably, well, fine; informal OK.
OPPOSITES unsatisfactorily.

ally noun *a political ally:* associate, colleague, friend, confederate, partner, supporter.
OPPOSITES enemy, opponent.
●verb *the Catholic powers allied with Philip II:* unite, combine, join (up), join forces, band together, team up, collaborate, side, align yourself.
OPPOSITES split.

a

also information about the sun, moon, tides, etc. **2** a book published yearly and containing useful information for that year.

almighty adjective **1** having unlimited or very great power. **2** informal enormous. • noun **(the Almighty)** God.

almond noun an oval nut with a woody shell, growing on a tree found in warm climates.

almost adverb very nearly.

alms /ahmz/ plural noun (in the past) money or goods given to the poor.

almshouse noun (in the past) a house built for poor people to live in.

aloe /a-loh/ noun a tropical plant with succulent leaves, whose bitter juice is used in medicine.

aloe vera /veer-uh/ noun a jelly-like substance obtained from a kind of aloe, used to soothe the skin.

aloft adjective & adverb up in or into the air.

alone adjective & adverb **1** on your own. **2** isolated and lonely. **3** only; exclusively.

along preposition & adverb **1** moving on a surface in a constant direction. **2** extending on a surface in a horizontal line. **3** in company with other people.

alongside preposition **1** close to the side of; next to. **2** at the same time as.

aloof adjective not friendly or showing an interest in other people. ▪ aloofness noun.

alopecia /a-luh-pee-shuh/ noun abnormal loss of hair.

aloud adverb not silently; out loud.

> **!** don't confuse **aloud**, meaning 'out loud', with **allowed**, meaning 'permitted'.

alp noun **1** a high mountain. **2** **(the Alps)** a high range of mountains in Switzerland and adjoining countries.

alpaca /al-pak-uh/ noun (plural **alpaca** or **alpacas**) a long-haired South American animal related to the llama.

alpha noun the first letter of the Greek alphabet (A, α). • adjective referring to the dominant animal or person in a group: *the alpha male.*

alphabet noun a set of letters or symbols used to represent the basic speech sounds of a language.

alphabetical adjective in the order of the letters of the alphabet. ▪ alphabetically adverb.

alpine adjective **1** relating to or found on high mountains. **2** **(Alpine)** relating to the Alps.

already adverb **1** before the time in question. **2** as surprisingly soon or early as this.

alright = ALL RIGHT.

Alsatian noun Brit. a German shepherd dog.

also adverb in addition. □ also-ran a loser in a race or contest.

altar noun **1** the table in a Christian church at which bread and wine are made sacred. **2** a table or block on which offerings are made to a god or goddess.

alter verb make or become different; change. ▪ alteration noun.

altercation noun a noisy argument or disagreement.

alter ego /awl-ter ee-goh/ noun **1** another side to a person's normal personality. **2** a close friend who is very like yourself.

alternate verb /awl-ter-nayt/ (**alternates, alternating, alternated**) **1** (of two things or people) repeatedly follow one another in turn. **2** keep changing between two states. • adjective /awl-ter-nuht/ **1** every other. **2** (of two things) each following and

THESAURUS

almost adverb nearly, (just) about, practically, virtually, all but, as good as, close to, not quite; informal pretty nearly/much/well; literary well nigh, nigh on.

alone adjective & adverb **1** *she was alone in the house:* by yourself, on your own, apart, solitary, single, solo; Brit. informal on your tod. **2** *she felt terribly alone:* lonely, isolated, deserted, abandoned, friendless.
OPPOSITES accompanied, loved.
• adverb *he travelled alone:* by yourself, on your own, solo, singly, independently, unaccompanied, without help.
OPPOSITES in company.

also adverb too, as well, besides, in addition, additionally, furthermore, further, moreover, into the bargain, on top (of that), what's more, to boot.

alter verb **1** *Eliot was persuaded to alter the passage:* change, adjust, adapt, amend, modify, revise, rework, redo, transform; informal tweak. **2** *the situation has altered:* change, become different, undergo a (sea) change, evolve, move on.
OPPOSITES preserve, stay the same.

alternate verb **1** *rows of trees alternate with dense shrub:* be interspersed, follow one another, take turns, take it in turns, oscillate, see-saw. **2** *we could alternate the two groups:* rotate, swap, exchange, interchange.
• adjective **1** *she attended on alternate days:* every other, every second, alternating. **2** (N. Amer.) *an alternate plan.* See ALTERNATIVE adjective sense 1.

succeeded by the other in a regular pattern.
□ **alternating current** an electric current that reverses its direction many times a second.
■ **alternately** adverb **alternation** noun.

alternative adjective **1** (of one or more things) available as another possibility. **2** different from what is usual or traditional: *alternative therapy*. • **noun** one of two or more available possibilities.
■ **alternatively** adverb.

alternator noun a dynamo that generates an alternating current.

although conjunction **1** in spite of the fact that. **2** but.

altimeter /al-ti-mee-ter/ noun an instrument which indicates the altitude that has been reached.

altitude noun the height of an object or point above sea level or ground level.

alto noun (plural **altos**) the highest adult male or lowest female singing voice.

altogether adverb **1** completely. **2** in total. **3** on the whole.

altruism /al-troo-iz'm/ noun unselfish concern for other people.
■ **altruist** noun **altruistic** adjective.

alum /al-uhm/ noun a compound of aluminium and potassium, used in dyeing and in making leather.

aluminium /al-yoo-**min**-i-uhm/ (US spelling **aluminum** /uh-**loo**-mi-nuhm/) noun a lightweight silvery-grey metal.

alumnus /uh-**lum**-nuhss/ noun (plural **alumni** /uh-**lum**-ny/) a former student of a particular school, college, or university.

alveolus /al-vee-oh-luhss/ noun (plural **alveoli** /al-vee-**oh**-lee/) any of the many tiny air sacs in the lungs.
■ **alveolar** adjective.

always adverb **1** at all times. **2** forever. **3** repeatedly. **4** failing all else.

Alzheimer's disease /alts-hy-merz/ noun a disease of the brain which can affect older people, causing memory loss and confusion.

AM abbreviation amplitude modulation.

am 1st person singular present of **be**.

a.m. abbreviation before noon.

amalgam noun **1** a mixture or blend of things. **2** an alloy of mercury with another metal.

amalgamate verb (**amalgamates**, **amalgamating**, **amalgamated**) combine two or more things to form one organization or structure.
■ **amalgamation** noun.

amanuensis /uh-man-yoo-en-siss/ noun (plural **amanuenses** /uh-man-yoo-en-seez/) a person who helps a writer with their work.

amass verb build up over time.

amateur noun **1** a person who takes part in a sport or other activity without being paid. **2** a person who is not skilled at an activity. • **adjective 1** non-professional. **2** not skilful.
■ **amateurism** noun.

☑ *-eur*, not *-uer*: amateur.

amateurish adjective not done or made very well; unskilful.

amatory /am-uh-tuh-ri/ adjective having to

THESAURUS

alternative adjective **1** *an alternative route:* different, other, second, substitute, replacement, standby, emergency, reserve, backup, auxiliary, fallback; N. Amer. alternate. **2** *an alternative lifestyle:* unorthodox, unconventional, nonconformist, radical, revolutionary, avant-garde; informal offbeat, way-out. • **noun** *we have no alternative:* (other) option, (other) choice, substitute, replacement.

altogether adverb **1** *he wasn't altogether happy:* completely, totally, entirely, absolutely, wholly, fully, thoroughly, utterly, perfectly, one hundred per cent, in all respects. **2** *we have five offices altogether:* in all, all told, in total.

always adverb **1** *he's always late:* every time, all the time, without fail, consistently, invariably, regularly, habitually, unfailingly. **2** *she's always complaining:* continually, continuously, constantly, forever, all the time, day and

night; informal 24-7. **3** *the place will always be dear to me:* forever, for good, for evermore, for ever and ever, until the end of time, eternally.
OPPOSITES never, seldom, sometimes.

amalgamate verb combine, merge, unite, join, fuse, blend, meld.
OPPOSITES separate.

amass verb gather, collect, assemble, accumulate, stockpile, hoard.
OPPOSITES disperse.

amateur noun **1** *the crew were all amateurs:* non-professional, non-specialist, layman, layperson, dilettante, dabbler. **2** *what a bunch of amateurs:* incompetent, bungler; Brit. informal bodger, cowboy, clown.
OPPOSITES professional, expert.
• adjective non-professional, unpaid, non-specialist, lay, dilettante.

amateurish adjective incompetent, inept, inexpert, amateur, clumsy, bumbling; Brit. informal bodged.

a

do with love or desire.

amaze verb (amazes, amazing, amazed) make someone feel very surprised.
■ **amazement** noun **amazing** adjective **amazingly** adverb.

Amazon noun **1** a member of a legendary race of female warriors. **2** a very tall, strong woman.
■ **Amazonian** adjective.

ambassador noun **1** a person sent by a state as its permanent representative in a foreign country. **2** a person who represents or promotes a particular activity.

amber noun **1** a hard, clear yellowish substance used in jewellery. **2** a yellowish colour.

ambergris /**am**-ber-greess/ noun a wax-like substance produced by sperm whales, used in making perfume.

ambidextrous /am-bi-**deks**-truhss/ adjective able to use the right and left hands equally well.

ambience or **ambiance** noun the character and atmosphere of a place.

ambient adjective **1** relating to the surroundings of something. **2** (of music) quiet and relaxing.

ambiguity noun (plural **ambiguities**) the quality of having more than one possible meaning.

ambiguous adjective **1** having more than one possible meaning. **2** not clear or decided.
■ **ambiguously** adverb.

ambit noun the scope or extent of something.

ambition noun **1** a strong desire to do or achieve something. **2** desire for success,

wealth, or fame.

ambitious adjective **1** having or showing determination to succeed. **2** intended to reach a high standard and therefore difficult to achieve.
■ **ambitiously** adverb.

ambivalent /am-**biv**-uh-luhnt/ adjective having mixed feelings about something or someone.
■ **ambivalence** noun **ambivalently** adverb.

amble verb (ambles, ambling, ambled) walk at a leisurely pace. • noun a leisurely walk.

ambrosia noun **1** Greek & Roman Mythology the food of the gods. **2** something very pleasing to taste or smell.

ambulance noun a vehicle for taking sick or injured people to and from hospital.

ambulatory adjective relating to walking, or able to walk or move.

ambush noun a surprise attack by people lying in wait in a hidden position. • verb make a surprise attack on someone from a hidden position.

ameba US spelling of **AMOEBA**.

ameliorate /uh-**mee**-li-uh-rayt/ verb (ameliorates, ameliorating, ameliorated) formal make something better.

amen /ah-**men**, ay-**men**/ exclamation a word said at the end of a prayer or hymn, meaning 'so be it'.

amenable /uh-**meen**-uh-b'l/ adjective **1** willing to be persuaded. **2** (**amenable to**) able to be affected by.

amend verb change or make minor improvements to.

amendment noun a minor change or improvement.

THESAURUS

amaze verb astonish, astound, surprise, stun, stagger, nonplus, shock, startle, stop someone in their tracks, leave open-mouthed, dumbfound; informal bowl over, flabbergast; Brit. informal knock for six; (**amazed**) thunderstruck, at a loss for words, speechless; Brit. informal gobsmacked.

amazement noun astonishment, surprise, shock, speechlessness, awe, wonder.

amazing adjective astonishing, astounding, surprising, stunning, staggering, breathtaking, awesome, awe-inspiring, sensational, remarkable, spectacular, stupendous, phenomenal, extraordinary, incredible, unbelievable; informal mind-blowing; literary wondrous.

ambassador noun envoy, emissary, representative, diplomat, minister, consul, attaché.

ambiguous adjective vague, unclear, ambivalent, equivocal, inconclusive, enigmatic, cryptic.

OPPOSITES clear.

ambition noun **1** *young people with ambition:* drive, determination, enterprise, initiative, eagerness, motivation, a sense of purpose; informal get-up-and-go. **2** *her ambition was to become a model:* aspiration, desire, dream, intention, goal, aim, objective, plan.

ambitious adjective **1** *an ambitious politician:* aspiring, determined, motivated, energetic, committed, purposeful, power-hungry; informal go-ahead, go-getting. **2** *an ambitious task:* challenging, exacting, demanding, formidable, difficult, hard, tough.
OPPOSITES laid-back, easy.

ambush verb surprise, waylay, trap, ensnare, attack, jump on, pounce on; N. Amer. bushwhack.

amend verb revise, alter, change, modify, adapt, adjust, edit, rewrite, redraft, rephrase, reword.

amends plural noun (**make amends**) make up for a wrongdoing.

amenity noun (plural **amenities**) a useful or desirable feature of a place.

American adjective relating to the United States or to the continents of America.
•noun a person from the United States or any of the countries of North, South, or Central America.
□ **American football** a kind of football played with an oval ball on a field marked with parallel lines. **American Indian** a member of one of the original peoples of America.

americium /am-uh-**riss**-i-uhm/ noun a radioactive metallic element.

amethyst /**am**-uh-thist/ noun a violet or purple precious stone.

amiable adjective friendly and pleasant.
■ **amiability** noun **amiably** adverb.

amicable adjective friendly and without disagreement.
■ **amicably** adverb.

amid or **amidst** preposition in the middle of.

amidships adverb & adjective in the middle of a ship.

amino acid /uh-**mee**-noh/ noun any of the natural substances which combine to form proteins.

amir ⇨ **EMIR**.

amiss adjective not quite right; inappropriate.
□ **take something amiss** be offended by something.

amity noun formal friendly relations between people or countries.

ammeter noun an instrument for measuring electric current.

ammo noun informal ammunition.

ammonia noun a colourless, strong-smelling gas which can be used to make a cleaning fluid.

ammonite noun an extinct sea creature with a spiral shell.

ammunition noun 1 a supply of bullets and shells. 2 points used to support your case in an argument.

amnesia /am-**nee**-zi-uh/ noun loss of memory.
■ **amnesiac** adjective.

amnesty noun (plural **amnesties**) 1 a pardon given to people who have committed an offence against the government. 2 a period during which people who admit to committing an offence are not punished.

amniocentesis /am-ni-oh-sen-**tee**-siss/ noun (plural **amniocenteses**/am-ni-oh-sen-tee-seez/) a medical procedure in which a sample of amniotic fluid is taken to check for possible abnormalities in the unborn baby.

amniotic fluid noun the fluid surrounding an unborn baby in the womb.

amoeba /uh-**mee**-buh/ (US spelling **ameba**) noun (plural **amoebas** or **amoebae** /uh-**mee**-bee/) a microscopic creature that is made up of a single cell and can change its shape.

amok /uh-**mok**/ or **amuck** /uh-**muk**/ adverb (**run amok**) behave in an uncontrolled way.

among or **amongst** preposition 1 surrounded by. 2 included or occurring in. 3 shared by; between.

amoral /ay-mo-ruhl/ adjective not concerned with doing what is right.
■ **amorality** noun.

amorous adjective showing or feeling sexual desire.
■ **amorously** adverb.

amorphous /uh-**mor**-fuhss/ adjective without a clear shape or form.

amortize or **amortise** verb (**amortizes, amortizing, amortized**) gradually pay off a debt.

amount noun 1 the total number, size, or value of something. 2 a quantity. •verb (**amount to**) 1 add up to. 2 be the same as.

ampere /**am**-pair/ noun a basic unit of electric current.

ampersand /**am**-per-sand/ noun the sign &, which means *and*.

amphetamine /am-**fet**-uh-meen/ noun a drug used as a stimulant.

amphibian noun an animal such as a frog or toad, which lives in the water when young and on the land as an adult.
■ **amphibious** adjective.

amphitheatre (US spelling **amphitheater**) noun a round building without a roof, in which tiers of seats surround a central

---

THESAURUS

amends plural noun
□ **make amends for make up for**, atone for, make good.
□ **make amends to compensate**, recompense, indemnify, make it up to.

amenity noun facility, service, resource, convenience, comfort.

amnesty noun pardon, reprieve, forgiveness, release, discharge; informal let-off.

amount noun quantity, number, total, aggregate, sum, quota, size, mass, weight, volume.
□ **amount to 1** *the bill amounted to £50:* **add up to**, come to, run to; Brit. tot up to. **2** *their actions amounted to conspiracy:*

space used for performing plays or for sports.

amphora /am-for-uh/ noun (plural **amphorae** /am-for-ee/ or **amphoras**) a tall ancient Greek or Roman jar with two handles and a narrow neck.

ample adjective **1** enough or more than enough; plentiful. **2** large.
■ **amply** adverb.

amplifier noun a device that makes sounds or radio signals louder.

amplify verb (**amplifies, amplifying, amplified**) **1** increase the strength of a sound or an electrical signal. **2** explain something in more detail.
■ **amplification** noun.

amplitude noun **1** the maximum amount by which a vibration such as an alternating current varies from its average level. **2** great size, range, or extent.

ampoule noun a small glass capsule containing liquid used in giving an injection.

amputate verb (**amputates, amputating, amputated**) cut off a limb in a surgical operation.
■ **amputation** noun.

amputee noun a person who has had a limb amputated.

amuck ⇨ AMOK.

amulet noun a small piece of jewellery worn as protection against evil.

amuse verb (**amuses, amusing, amused**) **1** make someone laugh or smile. **2** give someone something enjoyable to do.

amusement noun **1** the feeling that you have when something is funny. **2** a game or activity that provides entertainment and pleasure.

an determiner the form of the indefinite article 'a' used before words beginning with a vowel sound.

anabolic steroid /an-uh-**bol**-ik/ noun a synthetic hormone used to build up muscle.

anachronism /uh-**nak**-ruh-ni-z'm/ noun **1** something which seems to belong to another time. **2** something which is wrongly placed in a particular period.
■ **anachronistic** adjective.

anaconda /an-uh-**kon**-duh/ noun a very large snake of the boa family, found in South America.

anaemia /uh-**nee**-mi-uh/ (US spelling **anemia**) noun a shortage of red cells or haemoglobin in the blood, making a person pale and tired.
■ **anaemic** adjective.

anaesthetic /an-iss-**thet**-ik/ (US spelling **anesthetic**) noun a drug or gas that stops you feeling pain.

anaesthetize or **anaesthetise** /uh-**neess**-thuh-tyz/ (US spelling **anesthetize**) verb (**anaesthetizes, anaesthetizing, anaesthetized**) give an anaesthetic to.
■ **anaesthetist** noun.

anagram noun a word or phrase formed by rearranging the letters of another.

anal /**ay**-nuhl/ adjective having to do with the anus.

analgesic /an-uhl-**jee**-zik/ noun a pain-relieving drug.

analogous /uh-**nal**-uh-guhss/ adjective similar to and able to be compared with something else.

analogue /**an**-uh-log/ (US spelling **analog**) adjective using a variable physical effect, such as voltage or the position of a pointer, to represent information, rather than a digital display. • noun something that is similar to and can be compared with something else.

analogy /uh-**nal**-uh-ji/ noun (plural **analogies**) a way of explaining something

THESAURUS

constitute, comprise, be tantamount to.

ample adjective **1** *there is ample time for discussion:* enough, sufficient, adequate, plenty of, more than enough. **2** *an ample supply of wine:* plentiful, abundant, copious, profuse, lavish, liberal, generous; informal galore. **3** *his ample tunic:* spacious, full, capacious, roomy, voluminous, loose-fitting, baggy, sloppy.
OPPOSITES insufficient, meagre, tight.

amuse verb **1** *her annoyance simply amused him:* make someone laugh, entertain, delight, divert, cheer (up), please, charm, tickle; informal crack up; Brit. informal crease up. **2** *he amused himself by writing poetry:* occupy, engage, busy, absorb, engross, entertain.
OPPOSITES bore.

amusement noun **1** *the cause of much amusement:* mirth, merriment, hilarity, glee, delight. **2** *I read the book for amusement:* entertainment, pleasure, leisure, relaxation, fun, enjoyment, interest. **3** *a range of amusements:* activity, entertainment, diversion, pastime, recreation, game, sport.

amusing adjective funny, comical, humorous, light-hearted, jocular, witty, droll, entertaining, diverting; informal rib-tickling.
OPPOSITES solemn, boring.

analogy noun similarity, parallel, correspondence, likeness, resemblance, correlation, relation, comparison.
OPPOSITES dissimilarity.

by comparing it to something else.
■ **analogical** adjective.

analyse (US spelling **analyze**) verb
(**analyses, analysing, analysed**) **1** examine
something in detail to explain it or to find
out its structure or composition.
2 psychoanalyse someone.

analysis /uh-**nal**-i-siss/ noun (plural **analyses**
/uh-**nal**-i-seez/) **1** a detailed examination of
the elements or structure of something.
2 psychoanalysis.

analyst noun a person who carries out
analysis.

analytical or **analytic** adjective using
analysis.
■ **analytically** adverb.

anarchic /uh-**nar**-kik/ adjective not
controlled or governed by any rules or
principles.

anarchist noun a person who believes that
all government and laws should be
abolished.
■ **anarchism** noun **anarchistic** adjective.

anarchy noun **1** a situation in which no
rules or principles are being followed and
there is complete disorder. **2** a society with
no government.

anathema /uh-**na**-thuh-muh/ noun
something that you hate.

anatomy noun (plural **anatomies**) **1** the
scientific study of the structure of the
human body. **2** the structure of a person,
animal, or plant. **3** a detailed examination
or analysis.
■ **anatomical** adjective **anatomically** adverb
anatomist noun.

ancestor noun **1** a person from whom you
are descended. **2** something from which a
later species or version has developed.

ancestral /an-**sess**-truhl/ adjective inherited
from your ancestors.

ancestry noun (plural **ancestries**) your
ancestors or ethnic origins.

anchor noun a heavy object that is attached

to a boat by a rope or chain and is dropped
to the sea bed to stop the boat from
drifting. •verb **1** hold with an anchor.
2 secure or fix firmly in position.

anchorage noun a place where ships may
anchor safely.

anchorite /ang-kuh-ryt/ noun (in the past)
a person who lived alone for religious
reasons.

anchorman or **anchorwoman** noun
(plural **anchormen** or **anchorwomen**) a
person who presents a live television or
radio programme.

anchovy /an-chuh-vi/ noun (plural **anchovies**)
a small fish of the herring family, with a
strong flavour.

ancien régime /on-si-an ray-**zh**eem/ noun
(plural **anciens régimes** /on-si-an ray-**zh**eem/)
a political or social system that has been
replaced by a more modern one.

ancient adjective **1** belonging to the very
distant past. **2** very old. •noun (**the
ancients**) the people of ancient times.

ancillary adjective **1** providing support.
2 additional; extra.

and conjunction **1** used to connect words,
clauses, or sentences. **2** (connecting two
numbers) plus.

andante /an-**dan**-tay/ adverb & adjective Music
at a moderately slow pace.

androgynous /an-**dro**-ji-nuhss/ adjective
partly male and partly female.
■ **androgyny** noun.

android /**an**-droyd/ noun (in science fiction)
a robot with a human appearance.

anecdotal /an-ik-**doh**-t'l/ adjective (of a
story) not backed up by facts.

anecdote /**an**-ik-doht/ noun a short
entertaining story about a real incident or
person.

anemia US spelling of ANAEMIA.

anemometer noun an instrument for
measuring the speed of the wind.

THESAURUS

analyse verb examine, inspect, survey,
study, scrutinize, investigate, probe,
explore, evaluate.

analysis noun examination, inspection,
study, scrutiny, investigation, exploration,
evaluation.

analytical, analytic adjective systematic,
logical, scientific, methodical, precise,
meticulous, rigorous, investigative,
enquiring.
OPPOSITES unsystematic.

anarchy noun lawlessness, disorder, chaos,
pandemonium, riot, revolution.
OPPOSITES government, order.

anatomy noun structure, make-up,

composition, constitution, form, body,
physique.

ancestor noun forefather, forebear,
predecessor, antecedent, progenitor,
parent, grandparent.
OPPOSITES descendant.

ancient adjective **1** *ancient civilizations:*
early, prehistoric, primeval, primordial,
primitive. **2** *an ancient custom:* old, age-
old, archaic, antediluvian, time-honoured.
3 *I feel positively ancient:* antiquated,
decrepit, antediluvian, geriatric; informal out
of the ark; Brit. informal past its/your sell-
by date.
OPPOSITES recent, contemporary, young.

anecdote noun story, tale, urban myth,

anemone /uh-**nem**-uh-ni/ noun a plant with brightly coloured flowers.

anesthetic US spelling of ANAESTHETIC.

aneurysm or **aneurism** /an-yuu-ri-z'm/ noun a swelling of the wall of an artery.

anew adverb **1** in a new or different way. **2** once more; again.

angel noun **1** a messenger of God, pictured as being of human form but with wings. **2** a very beautiful or good person.
■ **angelic** adjective.

angelica /an-**jel**-li-kuh/ noun a plant whose stalks are preserved in sugar and used in cake decoration.

anger noun a strong feeling of extreme displeasure. ● verb (**angers, angering, angered**) make someone angry.

angina /an-**jy**-nuh/ or **angina pectoris** /**pek**-tuh-riss/ noun severe pain in the chest caused by an inadequate supply of blood to the heart.

angle[1] noun **1** the space between two lines or surfaces that meet. **2** a position from which something is viewed. **3** a way of thinking about something. ● verb (**angles, angling, angled**) **1** place something in a slanting position. **2** present information from a particular point of view.

angle[2] verb (**angles, angling, angled**) **1** fish with a rod and line. **2** try to get something without asking for it directly.
■ **angler** noun.

Anglican adjective relating to the Church of England. ● noun a member of the Church of England.
■ **Anglicanism** noun.

anglicize or **anglicise** verb (**anglicizes,**

anglicizing, anglicized) make something English.
■ **anglicization** noun.

Anglophile noun a person who admires England or Britain.

Anglo-Saxon noun **1** a person living in England between the 5th century and the Norman Conquest, whose ancestors came from north and west Europe. **2** the Old English language.

Angolan noun a person from Angola, a country in SW Africa. ● adjective relating to Angola.

angora /ang-**gor**-uh/ noun **1** a breed of cat, goat, or rabbit with long, soft hair. **2** fabric made from the hair of the angora goat or rabbit.

angostura /ang-guh-**styoor**-uh/ noun the bitter bark of a South American tree, used as a flavouring.

angry adjective (**angrier, angriest**) **1** feeling or showing anger. **2** (of a wound or sore) red and swollen.
■ **angrily** adverb.

angst noun a strong feeling of anxiety about life in general.

angstrom /ang-struhm/ noun a unit of length equal to one hundred-millionth of a centimetre.

anguish noun severe pain or suffering.
■ **anguished** adjective.

angular /ang-gyuu-ler/ adjective **1** having angles or sharp corners. **2** (of a person) lean and bony. **3** placed or directed at an angle.
■ **angularity** noun.

animal noun **1** a living being that can move about of its own accord and has specialized sense organs and nervous system. **2** a

THESAURUS

narrative, reminiscence; informal yarn.

angelic adjective **innocent**, pure, virtuous, saintly, cherubic, adorable.

anger noun **annoyance**, vexation, temper, indignation, rage, fury, wrath, outrage; literary ire.
OPPOSITES pleasure, good humour.
● verb **annoy**, irk, vex, enrage, incense, infuriate, rile, outrage.
OPPOSITES pacify, placate.

angle noun **1** *an angle of 33°:* **gradient**, slope, slant, inclination. **2** *right in the angle of the roof:* **corner**, point, fork, nook, crook, edge. **3** *consider the problem from a different angle:* **perspective**, point of view, viewpoint, standpoint, position, aspect, slant, direction, approach, tack.
● verb *Anna angled her camera upwards:* **tilt**, slant, twist, swivel, lean, tip, turn.

angry adjective **furious**, irate, vexed, irked, enraged, seething, infuriated, in a temper, fuming, outraged, cross; informal (hopping)

mad, up in arms, foaming at the mouth, steamed up, in a paddy; Brit. informal **shirty**; N. Amer. informal **sore**, teed off, ticked off; Austral./NZ informal **ropeable**, snaky.
OPPOSITES pleased, good-humoured.
□ **get angry lose your temper**, go berserk, flare up; informal go mad/crazy/wild, go bananas, hit the roof, go through the roof, go up the wall, see red, go off the deep end, fly off the handle, blow your top, blow a fuse/gasket, lose your rag, flip (your lid), have a fit, foam at the mouth, explode, go ballistic; Brit. informal go spare, do your nut; N. Amer. informal flip your wig, blow your lid/stack.

anguish noun **agony**, pain, torment, torture, suffering, distress, woe, misery, sorrow, heartache.
OPPOSITES happiness.

animal noun **1** **creature**, beast, (living) thing; (**animals**) wildlife, fauna. **2** *the man was an animal:* **beast**, brute, monster, devil, fiend; informal swine, bastard, pig.

a

mammal, as opposed to a bird, reptile, fish, or insect. • adjective **1** having to do with animals. **2** physical rather than spiritual or intellectual.
■ **animality** noun.

animate verb /**an**-i-mayt/ (animates, animating, animated) **1** bring life or energy to. **2** make drawings or models into an animated film. • adjective /**an**-i-muht/ living.
■ **animator** noun.

animated adjective **1** lively. **2** (of a film) made using animation.
■ **animatedly** adverb.

animation noun **1** liveliness. **2** the technique of filming a sequence of drawings or positions of models to give the appearance of movement. **3** the creation of moving images by means of a computer.

animism /**an**-i-mi-z'm/ noun the belief that all things in nature have a soul.
■ **animist** noun.

animosity noun (plural animosities) hatred or strong dislike.

animus noun hatred or dislike.

anion /**an**-I-uhn/ noun an ion with a negative charge.

aniseed noun the seed of the **anise plant**, used as a flavouring.

ankle noun the joint connecting the foot with the leg.

anklet noun a chain or band worn round the ankle.

annals plural noun a historical record of events made year by year.

anneal /uh-**neel**/ verb heat metal or glass

and allow it to cool slowly, so as to toughen it.

annex verb /an-**neks**/ **1** take possession of another country's land. **2** add something as an extra part. • noun (also **annexe**) /**an**-neks/ (plural annexes) **1** a building attached or near to a main building. **2** an addition to a document.
■ **annexation** noun.

annihilate /uh-**ny**-i-layt/ verb (annihilates, annihilating, annihilated) destroy completely.
■ **annihilation** noun.

anniversary noun (plural anniversaries) the date on which an event took place in a previous year.

annotate verb (annotates, annotating, annotated) add explanatory notes to.
■ **annotation** noun.

announce verb (announces, announcing, announced) **1** make a public statement about. **2** be a sign of.
■ **announcer** noun.

announcement noun a public statement.

annoy verb make someone slightly angry.
■ **annoyance** noun.

annual adjective **1** happening once a year. **2** calculated over or covering a year. **3** (of a plant) living for a year or less. • noun a book published once a year.
■ **annually** adverb.

annuity /uh-**nyoo**-i-ti/ noun (plural annuities) a fixed sum of money paid to someone each year.

THESAURUS

animate verb *the forces animating community life:* **enliven**, energize, invigorate, liven up, inspire, fire, rouse, excite, move.
OPPOSITES depress.
• adjective *an animate being:* **living**, alive, live, breathing, sentient.
OPPOSITES inanimate.

animated adjective **lively**, spirited, energetic, full of life, excited, enthusiastic, eager, alive, vigorous, vibrant, vivacious, exuberant, ebullient, bouncy, bubbly, perky; informal bright-eyed and bushy-tailed, full of beans, bright and breezy, chirpy, chipper.
OPPOSITES lethargic, lifeless.

animosity noun **hostility**, antipathy, antagonism, enmity, resentment, ill feeling/will, bad blood.
OPPOSITES goodwill, friendship.

annihilate verb **destroy**, obliterate, eradicate, wipe out, wipe off the face of the earth; informal rub out, snuff out.
OPPOSITES create.

announce verb **make public**, make known,

report, declare, state, give out, publicize, broadcast, publish, advertise, circulate, proclaim, release.

announcement noun **1** *an announcement by the Minister:* **statement**, declaration, proclamation, pronouncement, bulletin, communiqué; N. Amer. advisory. **2** *the announcement of the decision:* **declaration**, notification, reporting, publishing, broadcasting.

annoy verb **irritate**, bother, vex, make cross, exasperate, irk, anger, antagonize, nettle; Brit. rub up the wrong way; informal aggravate, peeve, miff, rile, needle, get (to), bug, hack off; Brit. informal wind up, nark, get on someone's wick; N. Amer. informal tee off, tick off, burn up, rankle, gravel.
OPPOSITES please, gratify.

annoyance noun **irritation**, exasperation, vexation, indignation, anger, displeasure, chagrin.

annual adjective **yearly**, once-a-year, year-long, twelve-month.

annually adverb **yearly**, once a year, each year, per annum.

a

annul /uh-**nul**/ verb (**annuls, annulling, annulled**) declare a law, marriage, or other legal contract to be no longer valid.
■ **annulment** noun.

annular /**an**-yuu-ler/ adjective technical ring-shaped.

Annunciation noun (**the Annunciation**) (in Christian belief) the announcement by the angel Gabriel to the Virgin Mary that she was to be the mother of Jesus.

anode /**an**-ohd/ noun an electrode with a positive charge.

anodized or **anodised** adjective (of metal) coated with a protective layer by the action of an electric current.

anodyne adjective not likely to cause offence or disagreement. ● noun a painkilling drug.

anoint verb dab or smear water or oil on someone as part of a religious ceremony.

anomalous adjective differing from what is standard or normal.

anomaly /uh-**nom**-uh-li/ noun (plural **anomalies**) something that is different from what is normal or expected.

anon adverb old use soon; shortly.

anonymous adjective 1 having a name that is not publicly known. 2 having no outstanding or individual features.
■ **anonymity** noun **anonymously** adverb.

anorak noun a waterproof jacket with a hood.

anorexia or **anorexia nervosa** noun a disorder in which a person refuses to eat because they are afraid of becoming fat.
■ **anorexic** adjective & noun.

another determiner & pronoun 1 one more. 2 different from the one already mentioned.

answer noun 1 something said or written in reaction to a question or statement. 2 the solution to a problem. ● verb (**answers, answering, answered**) 1 give an answer. 2 (**answer back**) give a cheeky reply. 3 (**answer to**) have to explain your actions

or decisions to someone. 4 (**answer for**) be responsible for the things you do. 5 meet a need.
□ **answering machine** a machine which gives a pre-recorded reply to a telephone call and can record a message from the caller.

answerable adjective 1 (**answerable to**) having to explain to someone why you have done the things you have done. 2 (**answerable for**) responsible for something.

ant noun a small insect that lives with many others in an organized group.

antacid /an-**tass**-id/ adjective (of a medicine) reducing excess acid in the stomach.

antagonism /an-**tag**-uh-ni-z'm/ noun the expression of hostile feelings.

antagonist noun an opponent or enemy.
■ **antagonistic** adjective.

antagonize or **antagonise** verb (**antagonizes, antagonizing, antagonized**) make someone feel hostile.

Antarctic adjective relating to the region surrounding the South Pole.

☑ remember the *c* after the *r*: Antarctic.

anteater noun an animal with a long snout and sticky tongue, that feeds on ants and termites.

antecedent noun 1 a thing that exists or comes before another. 2 (**antecedents**) a person's ancestors. ● adjective coming before in time or order.

antechamber noun an anteroom.

antedate verb (**antedates, antedating, antedated**) come or exist before something else.

antediluvian /an-ti-di-**loo**-vi-uhn/ adjective 1 belonging to the time before the biblical Flood. 2 very old-fashioned.

antelope noun a swift deer-like animal found in Africa and Asia.

antenatal adjective Brit. before birth; during pregnancy.

THESAURUS

annul verb declare invalid, declare null and void, nullify, invalidate, void, repeal, revoke.
OPPOSITES restore, enact.

anomaly noun oddity, peculiarity, abnormality, irregularity, inconsistency, aberration, quirk.

anonymous adjective 1 *an anonymous donor:* unnamed, nameless, unidentified, unknown, incognito. 2 *an anonymous letter:* unsigned, unattributed.
OPPOSITES known.

answer noun 1 *her answer was unequivocal:* reply, response, rejoinder, reaction, retort, riposte; informal comeback. 2 *the answer to*

this problem: solution, remedy, way out, explanation.
OPPOSITES question.
● verb *Steve was about to answer:* reply, respond, rejoin, retort, riposte.
□ **answer for** *he will answer for his crime:* pay for, be punished for, suffer for, make amends for.

antagonistic adjective hostile, opposed, antipathetic, ill-disposed, resistant, in disagreement; informal anti.
OPPOSITES pro.

antagonize verb provoke, intimidate, alienate, anger, annoy.
OPPOSITES pacify, disarm.

antenna /an-**ten**-nuh/ noun **1** (plural **antennae** /an-**ten**-nee/) each of a pair of long, thin feelers on the heads of some insects and shellfish. **2** (plural **antennae** or **antennas**) an aerial.

anterior adjective at or near the front.

anteroom noun a small room leading to a more important one.

anthem noun **1** a song chosen by a country to express patriotic feelings. **2** a musical setting of a religious work that is sung by a choir during a church service.

anther noun the part of a flower's stamen that contains the pollen.

anthill noun a mound of earth made by ants when they build a nest.

anthology noun (plural **anthologies**) a collection of poems or other pieces of writing or music.

anthracite noun hard coal that burns without producing much flame and smoke.

anthrax noun a serious disease of sheep and cattle, that can be passed to humans.

anthropoid adjective having to do with apes that resemble human beings in form, such as gorillas or chimpanzees.

anthropology noun the study of human origins, societies, and cultures.
■ **anthropological** adjective **anthropologist** noun.

anthropomorphic /an-thruh-puh-**mor**-fik/ adjective treating a god, animal, or object as if they were human.

antibiotic noun a medicine that kills bacteria.

antibody noun (plural **antibodies**) a protein produced in the blood to react against harmful substances.

Antichrist noun an enemy of Christ that some people believe will appear before the end of the world.

anticipate verb (**anticipates, anticipating, anticipated**) **1** be aware of and prepared for a future event. **2** look forward to. **3** do something earlier than someone else.
■ **anticipation** noun **anticipatory** adjective.

anticlimax noun a disappointing end to an exciting series of events.

■ **anticlimactic** adjective.

anticlockwise adverb & adjective Brit. in the opposite direction to the way in which a clock's hands move round.

antics plural noun silly or amusing behaviour.

anticyclone noun an area of high atmospheric pressure around which air slowly circulates, usually resulting in calm, fine weather.

antidote noun a medicine taken to undo the effect of a poison.

antifreeze noun a liquid added to water to prevent it from freezing, used in car radiators.

antigen /an-ti-jen/ noun a harmful substance which causes the body to produce antibodies.

anti-hero noun a central character in a story, film, or play who is either ordinary or unpleasant.

antihistamine noun a drug that is used in treating allergies.

antimacassar /an-ti-muh-**kass**-er/ noun a decorative piece of cloth put over the back of a chair to protect it from grease and dirt.

antimatter noun Physics matter consisting of particles with the same mass as those of normal matter but opposite electric or magnetic properties.

antimony /an-ti-muh-ni/ noun a brittle silvery-white metallic element.

antipasto /an-ti-**pas**-toh/ noun (plural **antipasti** /an-ti-**pas**-ti/) (in Italian cooking) a small savoury first course of a meal.

antipathy /an-ti-puh-thi/ noun (plural **antipathies**) a strong feeling of dislike.
■ **antipathetic** adjective.

antiperspirant noun a substance applied to the skin to prevent or reduce sweating.

antiphonal adjective sung or recited alternately by two groups.

Antipodes /an-ti-puh-deez/ plural noun (**the Antipodes**) Australia and New Zealand.
■ **Antipodean** adjective & noun.

antiquarian /an-ti-**kwair**-i-uhn/ adjective relating to the collection or study of

---

anthem noun hymn, song, chorale, chant, psalm, canticle.

anticipate verb **1** the police did not anticipate trouble: expect, foresee, predict, be prepared for, bargain on, reckon on; N. Amer. informal figure on. **2** we eagerly anticipated his arrival: look forward to, await, long for, can't wait for.

anticipation noun expectation, expectancy, prediction, hope, excitement, suspense.

anticlimax noun let-down, disappointment,

comedown, non-event, disillusionment; Brit. damp squib; informal washout.

antics plural noun capers, pranks, larks, high jinks, skylarking, horseplay, clowning; Brit. informal monkey tricks.

antidote noun remedy, cure, solution, countermeasure, corrective.

antipathy noun hostility, antagonism, animosity, aversion, animus, distaste, hatred, abhorrence, loathing.
OPPOSITES affinity, liking.

antiques or rare books.

antiquated adjective very old-fashioned or out of date.

antique noun an object or piece of furniture that is valuable because of its age. • adjective having value because of its age.

antiquity noun (plural **antiquities**) 1 the distant past. 2 an object from the distant past.

anti-Semitism noun hostility to or prejudice against Jews.
■ anti-Semite noun **anti-Semitic** adjective.

antiseptic adjective preventing the growth of germs that cause disease or infection. • noun an antiseptic substance.

antisocial adjective 1 behaving in a way that is unacceptable or annoying to other people. 2 not wanting to mix with other people.

antithesis /an-ti-thuh-siss/ noun (plural **antitheses** /an-ti-thuh-seez/) 1 a person or thing that is the direct opposite of another. 2 the putting together of contrasting ideas or words to produce an effect in writing or speaking.

antithetical /an-ti-thet-i-k'l/ adjective opposed to each other.

antler noun each of a pair of branched horns on the head of an adult male deer.

antonym /an-tuh-nim/ noun a word opposite in meaning to another.

anus /ay-nuhss/ noun the opening through which solid waste matter leaves the body.

anvil noun an iron block on which metal is hammered and shaped.

anxiety noun (plural **anxieties**) an anxious feeling or state.

anxious adjective 1 feeling worried or nervous. 2 very eager.
■ anxiously adverb.

any determiner & pronoun 1 one or some, no matter how much or how many. 2 whichever or whatever you choose. • adverb at all.

anybody pronoun anyone.

anyhow adverb 1 anyway. 2 in a careless or haphazard way.

anyone pronoun any person or people.

anything pronoun a thing of any kind.

anyway adverb 1 said to emphasize something just said or to change the subject. 2 nevertheless.

anywhere adverb in or to any place. • pronoun any place.

aorta /ay-or-tuh/ noun the main artery supplying blood from the heart to the rest of the body.

apace adverb literary quickly.

Apache /uh-pa-chi/ noun (plural **Apache** or **Apaches**) a member of an American Indian people living in New Mexico and Arizona.

apart adverb 1 separated by a distance. 2 into pieces.
□ apart from 1 except for. 2 as well as.

apartheid /uh-par-tayt/ noun the official system of racial segregation formerly in force in South Africa.

apartment noun 1 a flat. 2 (**apartments**) a private set of rooms in a large house.

☑ only one *p*: apartment.

apathetic adjective not interested or

THESAURUS

antiquated adjective outdated, outmoded, outworn, behind the times, old-fashioned, anachronistic; informal out of the ark; N. Amer. informal horse-and-buggy, clunky.
OPPOSITES modern, up to date.

antique noun collector's item, museum piece, period piece, bygone, antiquity. • adjective antique furniture: antiquarian, old, collectable, vintage, classic.
OPPOSITES modern.

antisocial adjective 1 antisocial behaviour: objectionable, offensive, unacceptable, disruptive, rowdy. 2 I'm feeling a bit antisocial: unsociable, unfriendly, uncommunicative, reclusive.
OPPOSITES acceptable, sociable.

anxiety noun worry, concern, apprehension, unease, fear, disquiet, doubts, nervousness, nerves; informal butterflies (in your stomach), the jitters, collywobbles.
OPPOSITES confidence.

anxious adjective 1 I'm anxious about her: worried, concerned, apprehensive, fearful, uneasy, disturbed, fretful, agitated,

nervous, on edge, worked up, jumpy; informal uptight, with butterflies in your stomach, jittery, twitchy; N. Amer. informal antsy, squirrelly, in a twit; Austral./NZ informal toey. 2 she was anxious for news: eager, keen, itching, impatient.
OPPOSITES confident, unconcerned.

apart adverb
□ apart from **except for,** but for, aside from, with the exception of, excepting, excluding, bar, barring, besides, other than; informal outside of.

apartment noun 1 a rented apartment: flat, suite, penthouse; Austral. home unit; N. Amer. informal crib. 2 the royal apartments: suite (of rooms), rooms, quarters, accommodation.

apathetic adjective uninterested, indifferent, unconcerned, unmoved, uninvolved, unemotional, lukewarm, lethargic; informal couldn't-care-less.
OPPOSITES interested, enthusiastic, involved.

enthusiastic.

apathy noun general lack of interest or enthusiasm.

apatosaurus /uh-pa-tuh-**sor**-uhss/ noun a huge plant-eating dinosaur with a long neck and tail; a brontosaurus.

ape noun an animal related to the monkeys but with no tail, such as a chimpanzee or gorilla. • verb (**apes, aping, aped**) imitate someone.

aperitif /uh-**pe**-ri-teef/ noun an alcoholic drink taken before a meal.

aperture noun 1 an opening, hole, or gap. 2 the variable opening by which light enters a camera.

apex /**ay**-peks/ noun (plural **apexes** or **apices** /**ay**-pi-seez/) the top or highest point of something.

aphid /**ay**-fid/ noun a small insect that feeds on the sap of plants.

aphorism noun a short clever phrase which makes a true point.

aphrodisiac /af-ruh-**diz**-i-ak/ noun a food, drink, or drug that makes people want to have sex.

apiary /**ay**-pee-uh-ri/ noun (plural **apiaries**) a place where bees are kept.

apiece adverb for or by each one.

aplenty adjective in large amounts.

aplomb /uh-**plom**/ noun calm self-confidence.

apocalypse noun a terrible event in which everything is destroyed.

apocalyptic/uh-po-kuh-**lip**-tik/ adjective having to do with or resembling the destruction of the world.

apocryphal adjective (of a story or piece of information) widely known but unlikely to be true.

apogee /**ap**-uh-jee/ noun 1 the highest point reached. 2 the point in the orbit of the moon or a satellite at which it is furthest from the earth.

apolitical adjective not interested or involved in politics.

apologetic adjective showing that you are sorry for making a mistake or doing something wrong.
■ **apologetically** adverb.

apologia /ap-uh-**loh**-ji-uh/ noun a formal defence of opinions or actions.

apologist noun a person who defends something controversial.

apologize or **apologise** verb (**apologizes, apologizing, apologized**) say that you are sorry for making a mistake or doing something wrong.

apology noun (plural **apologies**) 1 a statement in which someone apologizes for a mistake made or for harm done. 2 (**an apology for**) a very bad example of.

apoplectic /a-puh-**plek**-tik/ adjective 1 very angry. 2 old use relating to apoplexy (a stroke).

apoplexy /a-puh-**plek**-si/ noun (plural **apoplexies**) old use a stroke.

apostasy /uh-**poss**-tuh-si/ noun the abandoning of a belief or principle.

apostate /a-puh-stayt/ noun a person who abandons a belief or principle.

apostle noun 1 (**Apostle**) each of the twelve chief disciples of Jesus. 2 a person who strongly supports a policy, cause, etc.

apostrophe /uh-**poss**-truh-fi/ noun a punctuation mark (') used to show that something belongs to someone or to show that letters or numbers have been missed out.

apothecary /uh-**poth**-uh-kuh-ri/ noun (plural **apothecaries**) old use a person who prepared and sold medicines.

apotheosis /uh-po-thi-**oh**-siss/ noun (plural **apotheoses** /uh-po-thi-**oh**-seez/) the highest level in the development of something.

appal (US spelling **appall**) verb (**appals, appalling, appalled**) 1 make someone feel horror and dismay. 2 (**appalling**) informal very bad.
■ **appallingly** adverb.

apathy noun indifference, lack of interest, lack of enthusiasm, lack of concern, lack of involvement, unconcern, lethargy.
OPPOSITES enthusiasm, interest, concern.

aperture noun opening, hole, gap, slit, slot, vent, crevice, chink, crack; technical orifice.

apologetic adjective sorry, regretful, contrite, remorseful, penitent, repentant.
OPPOSITES unrepentant.

apologize verb say sorry, express regret, ask forgiveness, ask for pardon, eat humble pie.

apology noun regrets, expression of regret.
□ **apology for travesty of,** poor imitation

of, poor substitute for, pale shadow of; informal excuse for.

appal verb horrify, shock, dismay, distress, outrage, scandalize, disgust, revolt, sicken, nauseate, offend, make someone's blood run cold.

appalling adjective 1 *an appalling crime:* horrific, shocking, horrible, terrible, awful, dreadful, ghastly, hideous, horrendous, frightful, atrocious, abominable, outrageous. 2 (informal) *your schoolwork is appalling:* dreadful, terrible, atrocious, deplorable, hopeless, lamentable; informal rotten, crummy, woeful, useless, lousy,

apparatus noun (plural **apparatuses**) the equipment needed for a particular activity or task.

apparel /uh-**pa**-ruhl/ noun formal clothing.

apparent adjective 1 clearly seen or understood; obvious. 2 seeming real, but not necessarily so.
■ apparently adverb.

> ☑ -ent, not -ant: apparent.

apparition noun a remarkable thing making a sudden appearance, especially a ghost.

appeal verb 1 ask earnestly or formally for something. 2 be attractive or interesting. 3 ask a higher court of law to reverse the decision of a lower court. • noun 1 an act of appealing. 2 the quality of being attractive or interesting.

appealing adjective attractive or interesting.
■ appealingly adverb.

appear verb 1 come into view or start to exist. 2 seem. 3 present yourself as a performer or in a law court.

appearance noun 1 the way that someone or something looks or seems. 2 an act of appearing.

appease verb (**appeases, appeasing, appeased**) make someone calm or less hostile by agreeing to their demands.
■ appeasement noun.

appellation noun formal a name or title.

append verb add something to the end of a document.

appendage noun a thing that is attached to something larger or more important.

appendicitis noun inflammation of the appendix.

appendix noun (plural **appendices** or **appendixes**) 1 a small tube of tissue attached to the lower end of the large intestine. 2 a section of additional information at the end of a book.

appertain verb (**appertain to**) formal relate to.

appetite noun 1 a natural desire and physical need for food. 2 a liking or desire for something.

appetizer or **appetiser** noun a small dish of food or a drink taken before a meal to stimulate the appetite.

appetizing or **appetising** adjective stimulating the appetite.

applaud verb 1 show approval by clapping.

THESAURUS

abysmal, dire; Brit. informal chronic, shocking.

apparatus noun 1 *laboratory apparatus:* equipment, gear, tackle, mechanism, appliance, device. 2 *the apparatus of government:* system, machinery, framework, structure, organization.

apparent adjective 1 *their relief was all too apparent:* evident, plain, obvious, clear, manifest, visible, discernible, unmistakable. 2 *his apparent lack of concern:* seeming, ostensible, outward, superficial.
OPPOSITES unclear, real.

apparently adverb seemingly, evidently, ostensibly, outwardly.

appeal verb ask, request, call, plead, entreat, beg, implore.
□ appeal to **attract**, interest, fascinate, please, tempt, lure, draw; informal float someone's boat.
• noun 1 *an appeal for help:* plea, request, entreaty, cry, call. 2 *the cultural appeal of the island:* attraction, allure, charm, fascination, magnetism, pull.

appealing adjective attractive, engaging, alluring, enchanting, captivating, bewitching, fascinating, tempting, enticing, irresistible, charming; Brit. informal tasty.
OPPOSITES disagreeable, off-putting.

appear verb 1 become visible, come into view/sight, materialize. 2 *differences were beginning to appear:* be revealed, emerge, surface, manifest itself, become

apparent/evident, come to light, arrive, arise, crop up, show up. 3 *they appeared completely devoted:* seem, look, give the impression of being, come across as, strike someone as.
OPPOSITES vanish.

appearance noun 1 *her dishevelled appearance:* look, air, aspect, looks, mien, expression, behaviour. 2 *an appearance of respectability:* impression, air, (outward) show, semblance, illusion, facade, front, pretence. 3 *the appearance of these symptoms:* occurrence, manifestation, emergence, arrival, development, materialization.

appease verb placate, conciliate, pacify, mollify, reconcile, win over; informal sweeten.
OPPOSITES provoke, inflame.

appendix noun supplement, addendum, postscript, codicil, coda, epilogue, afterword, tailpiece.

appetite noun 1 hunger, taste, palate. 2 *my appetite for learning:* desire, liking, hunger, thirst, longing, yearning, passion, enthusiasm, keenness, eagerness; informal yen.

applaud verb 1 *the audience applauded:* clap, give a standing ovation, put your hands together; informal give someone a big hand. 2 *police have applauded the decision:* praise, commend, salute, welcome,

2 say that you approve of or admire something.

applause noun clapping.

apple noun a round fruit with green or red skin and crisp flesh.
□ **the apple of your eye** a person who you are very fond and proud of.

appliance noun an electrically operated machine for use in the home.

applicable adjective relevant to someone or something.
■ **applicability** noun.

applicant noun a person who applies for something.

application noun **1** a formal request to an authority. **2** the action of applying something. **3** practical use or relevance. **4** continued effort.

applicator noun a device for putting something into or on to something.

applied adjective (of a subject of study) used in a practical way.

appliqué /uh-**plee**-kay/ noun decorative needlework in which fabric shapes are fixed on to a background.

apply verb (**applies, applying, applied**)
1 make a formal request for something. **2** bring into operation or use. **3** be relevant. **4** put a substance on a surface. **5** (**apply yourself**) concentrate on what you are doing.

appoint verb **1** give someone a job or role. **2** decide on a time for something. **3** (**appointed**) equipped or furnished in a particular way.

appointment noun **1** an arrangement to meet. **2** the appointing of someone to a job. **3** (**appointments**) furniture or fittings.

apportion verb share out.
■ **apportionment** noun.

apposite adjective appropriate.

appraisal noun **1** an assessment of the quality or value of something. **2** a formal assessment of an employee's performance.

appraise verb (**appraises, appraising, appraised**) assess the quality or value of something.

appreciable adjective large or important enough to be noticed.
■ **appreciably** adverb.

appreciate verb (**appreciates, appreciating,**

THESAURUS

celebrate, approve of.
OPPOSITES boo, criticize.

applause noun clapping, (standing) ovation, cheering.

appliance noun device, machine, instrument, gadget, contraption, apparatus, mechanism, contrivance, labour-saving device; informal gizmo.

applicable adjective relevant, appropriate, pertinent, apposite, material, fitting, suitable, apt.
OPPOSITES inappropriate, irrelevant.

applicant noun candidate, interviewee, contender, entrant, claimant, petitioner, prospective student/employee, job-seeker.

application noun **1** *an application for an overdraft:* request, appeal, petition, approach, claim, demand. **2** *the application of anti-inflation policies:* implementation, use, exercise, employment, execution, enactment. **3** *the job requires a great deal of application:* hard work, diligence, industry, effort, commitment, dedication, devotion, perseverance, persistence, concentration.

apply verb **1** *300 people applied for the job:* bid, put in, try, audition, seek, solicit, claim, request, ask, petition. **2** *the Act did not apply to Scotland:* be relevant, pertain, relate, concern, affect, involve, cover, touch, deal with, have a bearing on.
3 *countries apply their own national rules:* implement, put into practice, introduce. **4** *she applied some ointment:* put on, rub in/on, work in, spread, smear on, slap on.

5 *steady pressure should be applied:* exert, administer, use, exercise, employ, utilize, bring to bear.
□ **apply yourself** work hard, exert yourself, make an effort, be industrious, show dedication, buckle down, persevere, persist, concentrate; informal put your back in it, knuckle down, get stuck in.

appoint verb nominate, name, designate, install, commission, engage, co-opt, select, choose, elect, vote in.
OPPOSITES reject.

appointed adjective **1** *at the appointed time:* scheduled, arranged, prearranged, specified, agreed, designated, allotted, set, fixed. **2** *a well appointed room:* furnished, decorated, fitted out, supplied.

appointment noun **1** *a six o'clock appointment:* meeting, engagement, interview, consultation, session. **2** *the appointment of directors:* nomination, naming, designation, installation, commissioning, engagement, co-option, selection, choosing, election. **3** *he held an appointment at the university:* job, post, position, situation, place, office.

appraisal noun assessment, evaluation, estimation, judgement, summing-up, consideration.

appreciate verb **1** *I'm not appreciated here:* value, admire, respect, think highly of, think much of, be grateful for, be glad of.
2 *we appreciate the problems:* recognize, realize, know, be aware of, be conscious of, be sensitive to, understand, sympathize

appreciated) 1 recognize the value of something. 2 understand a situation fully. 3 be grateful for. 4 rise in value or price.

appreciation noun 1 recognition of the value of something. 2 gratitude for something. 3 a piece of writing in which the qualities of a person or their work are discussed. 4 an increase in value.

appreciative adjective feeling or showing gratitude or pleasure.
■ **appreciatively** adverb.

apprehend verb 1 arrest someone for doing something wrong. 2 understand something.

apprehension noun 1 a feeling of worry or fear about what might happen. 2 understanding.

apprehensive adjective worried or afraid about what might happen.
■ **apprehensively** adverb.

apprentice noun a person learning a skilled trade from an employer. • verb (be

apprenticed) be employed as an apprentice.
■ **apprenticeship** noun.

apprise verb (**apprises, apprising, apprised**) (**apprise someone of**) make someone aware of.

approach verb 1 come near to. 2 go to someone with a proposal or request. 3 deal with something in a certain way. • noun 1 a way of dealing with something. 2 a proposal or request. 3 the action of approaching. 4 a way leading to a place.

approachable adjective 1 friendly and easy to talk to. 2 able to be reached from a particular direction.

approbation noun approval.

appropriate adjective /uh-**proh**-pri-uht/ suitable or right in the circumstances. • verb /uh-**proh**-pri-ayt/ (**appropriates, appropriating, appropriated**) 1 take something for your own use without permission. 2 set money aside for a special purpose.
■ **appropriately** adverb **appropriation** noun.

THESAURUS

with. 3 *a home will appreciate in value:* increase, gain, grow, rise, go up, soar.
OPPOSITES disparage, depreciate, decrease.

appreciation noun 1 *her appreciation of literature:* knowledge, awareness, enjoyment, love, feeling, discrimination, sensitivity. 2 *he showed his appreciation:* gratitude, thanks, gratefulness. 3 *an appreciation of the value of teamwork:* acknowledgement, recognition, realization, knowledge, awareness, consciousness, understanding. 4 *an appreciation of the professor's work:* review, critique, criticism, analysis, assessment, evaluation, judgement; Brit. informal crit. 5 *the appreciation of the euro against the pound:* increase, gain, growth, rise, inflation, escalation.
OPPOSITES ingratitude, unawareness, depreciation, decrease.

appreciative adjective 1 *we are appreciative of all your efforts:* grateful, thankful, obliged, indebted. 2 *an appreciative audience:* admiring, enthusiastic, approving, complimentary.
OPPOSITES ungrateful, disparaging.

apprehension noun 1 *he was filled with apprehension:* anxiety, worry, unease, nervousness, nerves, misgivings, disquiet, concern, trepidation. 2 *the apprehension of a criminal:* arrest, capture, seizure, detention.
OPPOSITES confidence.

apprehensive adjective anxious, worried, uneasy, nervous, concerned, agitated.
OPPOSITES confident.

apprentice noun trainee, learner, probationer, novice, beginner, starter,

pupil, student; N. Amer. tenderfoot; informal rookie; N. Amer. informal greenhorn.
OPPOSITES veteran, master, expert.

approach verb 1 *she approached the altar:* move towards, near, come near, close in on, close with, gain on. 2 *she approached him about a pay rise:* speak to, talk to, sound out, make a proposal to, proposition. 3 *he approached the problem in the best way:* tackle, address, manage, set about, go about, start work on.
OPPOSITES leave.
• noun 1 *the traditional British approach:* method, procedure, technique, modus operandi, style, way, strategy, tactic, system, means, line of action. 2 *he considered an approach to the High Court:* proposal, submission, application, appeal, plea, request. 3 *the dog barked at the approach of any intruder:* advance, arrival, appearance. 4 *the approach to the castle:* driveway, drive, road, path, entry, way.

approachable adjective 1 *students found the staff approachable:* friendly, welcoming, pleasant, agreeable, affable, sympathetic, congenial. 2 *the island is approachable by boat:* accessible, reachable, attainable; informal get-at-able.
OPPOSITES aloof, inaccessible.

appropriate adjective *this isn't the appropriate time:* suitable, proper, fitting, apt, right, convenient, opportune, relevant, apposite.
OPPOSITES inappropriate.
• verb *the barons appropriated church lands:* seize, commandeer, expropriate, usurp, take over, hijack, steal; informal swipe, rip off, nab; Brit. informal pinch, nick.

approval noun **1** a feeling that something is good or acceptable. **2** official permission or agreement.

approve verb (**approves, approving, approved**) **1** feel that something is good or acceptable. **2** officially accept something as satisfactory.

approximate adjective /uh-**prok**-si-muht/ almost but not completely accurate. • verb /uh-**prok**-si-mayt/ (**approximates, approximating, approximated**) come close or be similar to.
■ **approximately** adverb **approximation** noun.

appurtenances /uh-**per**-ti-nuhn-siz/ plural noun the things you need for a particular activity.

après-ski /ap-ray **skee**/ noun parties and entertainments which take place after a day's skiing.

apricot noun an orange-yellow fruit resembling a small peach.

April noun the fourth month of the year.

a priori /ay pry-**or**-I/ adjective & adverb using facts that are known to be true in order to decide what an unknown effect or result will be.

apron noun **1** a garment tied over the front of clothes to keep them clean. **2** an area on an airfield used for manoeuvring or parking aircraft. **3** a strip of stage extending in front of the curtain.

apropos /a-pruh-**poh**/ preposition (**apropos of**) with reference to.

apse noun a recess with a domed or arched roof at the end of a church.

apt adjective **1** suitable for the occasion; appropriate. **2** (**apt to**) tending to. **3** quick to learn.
■ **aptly** adverb.

aptitude noun a natural ability.

aqualung noun a piece of equipment worn by divers to enable them to breathe underwater.

aquamarine noun **1** a bluish-green precious stone. **2** a light bluish-green colour.

aquaplane verb (**aquaplanes, aquaplaning, aquaplaned**) (of a vehicle) slide uncontrollably on a wet surface.

aquarium noun (plural **aquaria** or **aquariums**) a water-filled glass tank in which fish and other water creatures are kept.

Aquarius /uh-**kwair**-i-uhss/ noun a sign of the zodiac (the Water Carrier), 21 January–20 February.

aquatic /uh-**kwat**-ik/ adjective **1** relating to water. **2** living in or near water.

aqueduct /**ak**-wuh-dukt/ noun a long channel or bridge-like structure for carrying water across country.

aqueous /**ay**-kwee-uhss/ adjective relating to or containing water.

aquiline /**ak**-wi-lyn/ adjective **1** (of a person's nose) curved like an eagle's beak. **2** like an eagle.

Arab noun a member of a people inhabiting much of the Middle East and North Africa.
■ **Arabian** noun & adjective.

arabesque noun **1** a ballet position in which one leg is extended horizontally backwards and the arms are outstretched. **2** an ornamental design of intertwined flowing lines.

Arabic noun the language of the Arabs, written from right to left. • adjective relating to the Arabs or Arabic.
□ **Arabic numeral** any of the numerals 0, 1, 2, 3, 4, 5, 6, 7, 8, and 9.

arable adjective (of land) able to be used for growing crops.

THESAURUS

approval noun **1** *their proposals went to the ministry for approval:* acceptance, agreement, consent, assent, permission, rubber stamp, sanction, blessing, endorsement, ratification, authorization; informal the go-ahead, the green light, the OK, the thumbs up. **2** *Lily looked at him with approval:* favour, liking, appreciation, admiration, regard, esteem, respect.
OPPOSITES refusal, disapproval.

approve verb agree to, accept, consent to, assent to, give your blessing to, bless, ratify, sanction, endorse, authorize, validate, pass; informal give the go-ahead to, give the green light to, give the OK to, give the thumbs-up to.
OPPOSITES refuse.
□ **approve of agree with,** hold with, endorse, support, be in favour of, favour, think well of, like, take kindly to, admire.

approximate adjective estimated, rough, imprecise, inexact, broad, loose; N. Amer. informal ballpark.
OPPOSITES precise.
□ **approximate to roughly equal,** come near/close to, approach, border on, verge on, resemble, be similar to.

approximately adverb roughly, about, around, circa, round about, more or less, nearly, almost, approaching; Brit. getting on for; informal pushing; N. Amer. informal in the ballpark of.
OPPOSITES precisely.

apt adjective **1** *a very apt description:* suitable, fitting, appropriate, relevant, apposite; Brit. informal spot on. **2** *they are apt to be a bit slipshod:* inclined, given, likely, liable, prone. **3** *an apt pupil:* bright, quick, clever, sharp, smart, able, gifted, talented.
OPPOSITES inappropriate, unlikely, slow.

arachnid /uh-**rak**-nid/ noun a creature of a class including spiders, scorpions, mites, and ticks.

arachnophobia /uh-rak-nuh-**foh**-bi-uh/ noun extreme fear of spiders.

Aran adjective (of knitted clothes) having a pattern involving thick raised stitches and large diamond designs.

arbiter /**ar**-bi-ter/ noun 1 a person who settles a dispute. 2 a person who has influence in a particular area.

arbitrary adjective 1 not seeming to be based on any plan or system. 2 (of power) used without restraint.
■ **arbitrarily** adverb.

arbitrate verb (**arbitrates, arbitrating, arbitrated**) act as an arbitrator to settle a dispute.
■ **arbitration** noun.

arbitrator noun a person or organization appointed to settle a dispute.

arboreal /ar-**bor**-i-uhl/ adjective 1 living in trees. 2 relating to trees.

arboretum /ar-buh-**ree**-tuhm/ noun (plural **arboretums** or **arboreta**) a garden in which trees are grown for study and display to the public.

arbour (US spelling **arbor**) noun a shady place in a garden, with a canopy of trees or climbing plants.

arc noun 1 a curve forming part of the circumference of a circle. 2 a curving movement through the air. 3 a glowing electrical discharge between two points.
•verb (**arcs, arcing, arced**) move in an arc.

arcade noun 1 a series of arches supporting a roof or wall. 2 a covered walk with shops along the sides.

Arcadian adjective literary having to do with a perfect country scene or way of life.

arcane adjective secret and mysterious.

arch¹ noun 1 a curved structure spanning an opening or supporting the weight of a bridge or roof. 2 the inner side of the foot.
•verb form an arch.

arch² adjective suggesting in a playful way that you know more than you are revealing.
■ **archly** adverb.

archaeology (US spelling **archeology**) noun the study of ancient history through the examination of objects, structures, and materials dug up from old sites.
■ **archaeological** adjective **archaeologist** noun.

archaic /ar-**kay**-ik/ adjective 1 very old or old-fashioned. 2 belonging to an earlier period.
■ **archaism** noun.

archangel /**ark**-ayn-j'l/ noun an angel of high rank.

archbishop noun a bishop of the highest rank.

archdeacon noun a senior Christian priest.

arch-enemy noun a chief enemy.

archer noun a person who shoots with a bow and arrows.
■ **archery** noun.

archetype /**ar**-ki-typ/ noun 1 a very typical example. 2 an original model which others follow.
■ **archetypal** adjective.

archipelago /ar-ki-**pel**-uh-goh/ noun (plural **archipelagos** or **archipelagoes**) a group of many islands and the sea surrounding them.

architect noun 1 a person who designs buildings. 2 the person responsible for something: *the architect of the reforms.*

architecture noun 1 the design and construction of buildings. 2 the complex structure of something.
■ **architectural** adjective.

architrave /**ar**-ki-trayv/ noun 1 (in classical architecture) a beam resting across the tops of columns. 2 the frame around a doorway or window.

archive /**ar**-kyv/ noun 1 a collection of historical documents or records. 2 a complete record of the data in a computer

THESAURUS

arbitrary adjective random, unpredictable, capricious, subjective, whimsical, wanton, motiveless, irrational, groundless, unjustified.
OPPOSITES reasoned, democratic.

arbitration noun adjudication, judgement, mediation, conciliation, intervention.

arbitrator noun adjudicator, arbiter, judge, referee, umpire, mediator, go-between.

arc noun curve, arch, bow, curl, crescent, semicircle, half-moon.

arch noun *a stone arch:* archway, vault, span.
•verb *she arched her eyebrows:* curve, arc, bend, bow, crook, hunch.

architect noun designer, planner,

originator, author, creator, founder, inventor.

architecture noun 1 *modern architecture:* building, planning, design, construction. 2 *computer architecture:* structure, construction, organization, layout, design, build, make-up; informal set-up.

archive noun 1 *the family archives:* records, papers, documents, files, annals, chronicles, history. 2 *the National Sound Archive:* record office, registry, repository, museum, library.
•verb *the videos are archived for future use:* file, log, catalogue, document, record, register, store.

system. • verb (**archives, archiving, archived**) put something in an archive.
■ **archival** adjective.

archivist /ar-ki-vist/ noun a person who is in charge of archives of historical material.

archway noun a curved structure forming a passage or entrance.

Arctic adjective relating to the regions around the North Pole.

> ☑ remember the first *c*: Arctic.

ardent adjective **1** feeling passionate about something. **2** old use burning; glowing.
■ **ardently** adverb.

ardour (US spelling **ardor**) noun passionate feelings.

arduous adjective difficult and tiring.
■ **arduously** adverb.

are 2nd person singular present and 1st, 2nd, and 3rd person plural present of **BE**.

> ❗ don't confuse **are** with **our**.

area noun **1** a part of a place, object, or surface. **2** the extent or measurement of a surface. **3** a subject or range of activity.

arena noun **1** a level area surrounded by seating, in which sports and other events are held. **2** an area of activity.

aren't short form **1** are not. **2** am not (only in questions).

areola /uh-**ree**-uh-luh/ noun (plural **areolae** /uh-**ree**-uh-lee/) the circular area of darker skin surrounding a human nipple.

Argentinian or **Argentine** noun a person from Argentina. • adjective relating to Argentina.

argon noun an inert gaseous element, present in small amounts in the air.

argot /**ar**-goh/ noun the jargon or slang of a particular group.

arguable adjective able to be argued or disagreed with.
■ **arguably** adverb.

argue verb (**argues, arguing, argued**)
1 discuss something in a serious or angry way with someone who disagrees with you.
2 make statements in support of an action or opinion.

argument noun **1** a serious or angry discussion between people who disagree with each other. **2** a set of reasons given in support of an action or opinion.

> ☑ no e in the middle: *argument*, not *argue-*

argumentative adjective tending to argue.

aria /**ah**-ri-uh/ noun a song for a solo voice in an opera.

arid adjective **1** very dry because having little or no rain. **2** dull and boring.
■ **aridity** noun.

Aries /**air**-eez/ noun a sign of the zodiac (the Ram), 20 March–20 April.

arise verb (**arises, arising, arose**; past participle **arisen**) **1** start to exist or be noticed.
2 (**arise from** or **out of**) happen as a result of. **3** formal stand up.

aristocracy noun (plural **aristocracies**) the highest social class, consisting of people whose families hold a title such as *Lord* or *Duke*.
■ **aristocrat** noun **aristocratic** adjective.

ardent adjective passionate, fervent, zealous, wholehearted, intense, enthusiastic, keen, eager, avid, committed, dedicated.
OPPOSITES apathetic.

arduous adjective tough, difficult, hard, heavy, laborious, onerous, taxing, strenuous, back-breaking, demanding, challenging, punishing, gruelling; informal killing; Brit. informal knackering.
OPPOSITES easy.

area noun **1** *an inner-city area:* district, zone, region, sector, quarter, locality, neighbourhood; informal neck of the woods; Brit. informal manor; N. Amer. informal turf. **2** *the dining area:* space, section, part, place, room. **3** *specific areas of knowledge:* field, sphere, realm, domain, sector, province, territory.

arena noun **1** *an ice-hockey arena:* stadium, amphitheatre, ground, field, ring, rink, pitch, court; N. Amer. bowl, park. **2** *the political arena:* scene, sphere, realm, province, domain, forum, territory, world.

argue verb **1** *they argued that the*

government was to blame: claim, maintain, insist, contend, assert, hold, reason, allege. **2** *the children are always arguing:* quarrel, disagree, dispute, row, squabble, bicker, have words, cross swords.

argument noun **1** *he had an argument with Tony:* quarrel, disagreement, squabble, dispute, altercation, row; informal slanging match; Brit. informal barney. **2** *an argument for the existence of God:* reasoning, justification, explanation, case, defence, vindication, evidence, reasons, grounds.

arise verb **1** *many problems arose:* come about, happen, occur, come into being, emerge, crop up, come to light, become apparent, appear, turn up, surface, spring up. **2** *injuries arising from defective products:* result, stem, originate, proceed, follow, ensue, be caused by.

aristocrat noun nobleman, noblewoman, lord, lady, peer (of the realm), patrician; informal aristo; Brit. informal toff, nob.
OPPOSITES commoner.

aristocratic adjective noble, titled, upper-class, blue-blooded, high-born; informal

arithmetic noun the use of numbers in counting and calculation.
■ **arithmetical** adjective **arithmetically** adverb.

ark noun **1** (in the Bible) the ship built by Noah to save two of every kind of animal from the Flood. **2** a chest or cupboard in a synagogue in which the holy scrolls are kept. **3** (**Ark of the Covenant**) the chest which contained the laws of the ancient Israelites.

arm¹ noun **1** each of the two upper limbs of the human body from the shoulder to the hand. **2** a side part of a chair supporting a sitter's arm. **3** a strip of water or land. **4** a branch or division of a company or organization.

arm² verb **1** supply with weapons. **2** provide with essential equipment or information. **3** make a bomb ready to explode.

armada noun a fleet of warships.

armadillo noun (plural **armadillos**) an insect-eating animal of Central and South America, with a body covered in bony plates.

Armageddon /ar-muh-ged-duhn/ noun **1** (in the Bible) the final battle between good and evil before the Last Judgement. **2** a terrible war with a catastrophic ending.

armament noun **1** (also **armaments**) military weapons and equipment. **2** the equipping of military forces.

armature noun **1** the rotating coil of a dynamo or electric motor. **2** a piece of iron placed across the poles of a magnet to preserve its power.

armchair noun a comfortable chair with padded sides on which to rest your arms.

armed adjective carrying a weapon.
□ **armed forces** a country's army, navy, and air force.

Armenian noun a person from Armenia.
● adjective relating to Armenia.

armistice /ar-miss-tiss/ noun an agreement to stop fighting.

armorial adjective relating to coats of arms.

armour (US spelling **armor**) noun **1** metal coverings worn in the past to protect the body in battle. **2** (also **armour plate**) the tough metal layer covering a military vehicle or ship.
■ **armoured** adjective.

armourer (US spelling **armorer**) noun a person who makes, supplies, or looks after weapons or armour.

armoury (US spelling **armory**) noun (plural **armouries**) a store of arms.

armpit noun a hollow under the arm at the shoulder.

arms plural noun **1** guns and other weapons. **2** the emblems on a coat of arms.
□ **up in arms** protesting strongly.

army noun (plural **armies**) **1** a military force that fights on land. **2** a large number of people or things.

aroma noun a pleasant smell.
■ **aromatic** adjective.

aromatherapy noun the use of aromatic oils for healing or to give pleasant feelings.
■ **aromatherapist** noun.

arose past of ARISE.

around adverb & preposition **1** on every side of something. **2** in or to many places throughout an area. ● adverb **1** so as to face in the opposite direction. **2** about; approximately. **3** available or present.

arouse verb (**arouses**, **arousing**, **aroused**) **1** bring about a feeling or response in someone. **2** excite someone sexually.

THESAURUS

upper crust, top drawer; Brit. informal posh.
OPPOSITES common.

arm verb equip, provide, supply, furnish, issue, fit out.

armaments plural noun arms, weapons, weaponry, firearms, guns, ordnance, artillery, munitions, materiel.

armoured adjective armour-plated, steel-plated, ironclad, bulletproof, bombproof, reinforced, toughened.

arms plural noun weapons, weaponry, firearms, guns, ordnance, artillery, armaments, munitions.

army noun **1** armed force, military force, land force(s), military, soldiery, infantry, militia, troops, soldiers. **2** *an army of tourists*: crowd, swarm, horde, mob, gang, throng, mass, flock, herd, pack.

aroma noun smell, odour, fragrance, scent, perfume, bouquet, nose.

aromatic adjective fragrant, scented, perfumed, fragranced.

around preposition **1** *the hills around the city*: surrounding, enclosing, on all sides of. **2** *around three miles*: approximately, about, round about, circa, roughly, more or less, nearly, almost, approaching; Brit. getting on for; N. Amer. informal in the ballpark of.
OPPOSITES precisely.

arouse verb **1** *they had aroused suspicion*: provoke, trigger, stir up, kindle, engender, cause. **2** *his ability to arouse the masses*: stir up, whip up, rouse, galvanize, electrify, stimulate, inspire, fire up, inflame, agitate, incite. **3** *she was aroused from sleep*: wake (up), awaken, bring to/round, rouse.
OPPOSITES allay, pacify.

3 awaken someone from sleep.
■ **arousal** noun.

arpeggio /ar-**pej**-ji-oh/ noun (plural **arpeggios**) the notes of a musical chord played in rapid succession.

arraign /uh-**rayn**/ verb call someone before a court to answer a criminal charge.
■ **arraignment** noun.

arrange verb (**arranges, arranging, arranged**) **1** put tidily or in a particular order. **2** organize or plan. **3** adapt a piece of music for performance.
■ **arranger** noun.

arrangement noun **1** a plan for a future event. **2** something made up of things arranged in a particular way. **3** an arranged piece of music.

arrant /**a**-ruhnt/ adjective complete; absolute: *arrant nonsense.*

array noun **1** an impressive display or range. **2** an ordered arrangement of troops. **3** literary elaborate clothing. • verb **1** (**be arrayed**) be displayed or arranged in a neat or impressive way. **2** (**be arrayed in**) be dressed in.

arrears plural noun money owed that should already have been paid.
□ **in arrears 1** behind with paying money that is owed. **2** (of wages or rent) paid at the end of each period of work or occupation.

arrest verb **1** seize someone and take them into custody. **2** stop the progress of something. **3** (**arresting**) attracting attention. • noun **1** the action of arresting someone. **2** a sudden stop.

arrival noun **1** the process of arriving somewhere. **2** a person or thing that has just arrived.

arrive verb (**arrives, arriving, arrived**) **1** reach a destination. **2** (of a particular moment) come about. **3** (**arrive at**) reach a conclusion or decision.

arrogant adjective behaving in an unpleasant way because you think that you are better than other people.
■ **arrogance** noun **arrogantly** adverb.

arrogate /a-ruh-**gayt**/ verb (**arrogates, arrogating, arrogated**) formal take or claim something that you have no right to.

arrow noun **1** a stick with a sharp point, shot from a bow. **2** a symbol resembling this, used to show direction or position.

arrowroot noun a starch obtained from a plant and used as a thickener in cookery.

arsenal noun a store of weapons and ammunition.

arsenic noun a brittle grey element from which a highly poisonous white powder is obtained.

arson noun the criminal act of deliberately setting fire to property.
■ **arsonist** noun.

THESAURUS

arrange verb **1** *she arranged the flowers in a vase:* set out, order, lay out, position, present, display, exhibit, group, sort, organize. **2** *they hoped to arrange a meeting:* organize, fix (up), plan, schedule, contrive, determine, agree. **3** *he arranged the piece for a full orchestra:* adapt, set, score, orchestrate.

arrangement noun **1** *the arrangement of the furniture:* positioning, presentation, grouping, organization, alignment. **2** *the arrangements for my trip:* preparation, plan, provision, planning. **3** *we had an arrangement:* agreement, deal, understanding, bargain, settlement, pact. **4** *an arrangement of Beethoven's symphonies:* adaptation, orchestration, scoring, interpretation.

array noun range, collection, selection, assortment, variety, arrangement, line-up, display, exhibition.
• verb arrange, assemble, group, order, range, place, position, set out, lay out, spread out, display, exhibit.

arrest verb **1** *police arrested him for murder:* detain, apprehend, seize, capture, take into custody; informal pick up, pull in, collar; Brit. informal nick. **2** *the spread of the disease can be arrested:* stop, halt, check, block, curb, prevent, obstruct.
OPPOSITES release, start.
• noun detention, apprehension, seizure, capture.

arresting adjective striking, eye-catching, conspicuous, impressive, imposing, spectacular, dramatic, breathtaking, stunning, awe-inspiring.
OPPOSITES inconspicuous.

arrival noun **1** *they awaited Ruth's arrival:* coming, appearance, entrance, entry, approach. **2** *the arrival of democracy:* emergence, appearance, advent, coming, dawn, onset.
OPPOSITES departure, end.

arrive verb **1** *more police arrived:* come, turn up, get here/there, make it, appear; informal show (up), roll in/up, blow in. **2** *virtual reality had arrived:* emerge, appear, surface, dawn, be born, come into being, arise.
OPPOSITES depart, leave.

arrogant adjective haughty, conceited, self-important, cocky, supercilious, full of yourself, condescending, overbearing, proud; informal high and mighty, too big for your boots.
OPPOSITES modest.

a

art noun 1 the expression of creative skill in a visual form such as painting or sculpture. 2 paintings, drawings, and sculpture as a whole. 3 (**the arts**) creative activities such as painting, music, and drama. 4 (**arts**) subjects of study concerned with human culture. 5 a skill.

artefact /**ar**-ti-fakt/ (US spelling **artifact**) noun a useful or decorative man-made object.

artery noun (plural **arteries**) 1 any of the tubes through which blood flows from the heart around the body. 2 an important transport route.
■ **arterial** adjective.

artesian well /ar-**tee**-zh'n/ noun a well in which water comes to the surface through natural pressure.

artful adjective clever in a cunning way.
■ **artfully** adverb.

arthritis /ar-**thry**-tiss/ noun painful inflammation and stiffness of the joints.
■ **arthritic** /ar-**thri**-tik/ adjective & noun.

arthropod /ar-**thruh**-pod/ noun an animal with a body that is divided into segments, such as an insect, spider, crab, etc.

artichoke noun a vegetable consisting of the unopened flower head of a thistle-like plant.

article noun 1 a particular object. 2 a piece of writing in a newspaper or magazine. 3 an item in a legal document. 4 (**articles**) a period of training in a company as a solicitor, accountant, etc. • verb (**be articled**) (of a solicitor, accountant, etc.) be employed as a trainee.

articulate adjective /ar-**tik**-yuu-luht/ 1 fluent and clear in speech. 2 having joints or jointed segments. • verb /ar-**tik**-yuu-layt/ (**articulates, articulating, articulated**) 1 pronounce words distinctly. 2 clearly express an idea or feeling. 3 (**articulated**) having sections connected by a flexible joint or joints.

■ **articulacy** noun **articulately** adverb **articulation** noun.

artifact US spelling of **ARTEFACT**.

artifice noun the clever use of tricks to deceive someone.

artificer noun a person skilled in making or planning things.

artificial adjective 1 made as a copy of something natural. 2 not sincere.
□ **artificial insemination** the injection of semen through a syringe into the vagina or womb. **artificial intelligence** the performance by computers of tasks that normally need human intelligence. **artificial respiration** the forcing of air into and out of a person's lungs to make them begin breathing again.
■ **artificiality** noun **artificially** adverb.

artillery noun 1 large guns used in warfare on land. 2 a branch of the armed forces that uses artillery.

artisan noun a skilled worker who makes things by hand.

artist noun 1 a person who paints or draws. 2 a person who practises or performs any of the creative arts.

artiste /ar-**teest**/ noun a professional singer or dancer.

artistic adjective 1 having creative skill. 2 having to do with art or artists.
■ **artistically** adverb.

artistry noun creative skill or ability.

artless adjective straightforward and sincere.
■ **artlessly** adverb.

artwork noun illustrations to be included in a publication.

arty (US spelling **artsy**) adjective informal displaying an obvious interest in the arts.
■ **artiness** noun.

arum lily /**air**-uhm/ noun a tall lily-like African plant.

Aryan /**air**-i-uhn/ noun 1 a member of an

THESAURUS

art noun 1 *he studied art:* fine art, design, artwork, aesthetics. 2 *the art of writing:* skill, craft, technique, knack, aptitude, talent, flair, mastery, expertise.

article noun 1 *household articles:* object, thing, item, piece, artefact, device, implement. 2 *an article in The Times:* report, account, story, essay, feature, item, piece (of writing), column, commentary. 3 *the crucial article of the treaty:* clause, section, paragraph, head, point, item.

articulate adjective *an articulate speaker:* eloquent, fluent, effective, persuasive, lucid, expressive, silver-tongued.
OPPOSITES unintelligible.
• verb *they were unable to articulate their*

emotions: express, voice, vocalize, put in words, communicate, state.

artificial adjective 1 *artificial flowers:* synthetic, fake, imitation, mock, ersatz, man-made, manufactured, plastic, faux; informal pretend. 2 *an artificial smile:* insincere, feigned, false, unnatural, contrived, put-on, forced, laboured, hollow; informal pretend, phoney.
OPPOSITES natural, genuine.

artistic adjective 1 *he's very artistic:* creative, imaginative, inventive, expressive, sensitive, perceptive, discerning. 2 *artistic dances:* aesthetic, beautiful, stylish, ornamental, graceful, ancient people of Europe and Asia. **2** (in Nazi thinking) a white person not of Jewish descent. • **adjective** relating to Aryans.

as adverb used in comparisons to refer to extent or amount. • **conjunction 1** while. **2** in the way that. **3** because. **4** even though. • **preposition 1** in the role of; being. **2** while; when.

asap abbreviation as soon as possible.

asbestos noun a fibrous grey-white mineral that does not burn.

asbestosis /az-bes-**toh**-sis/ noun a serious lung disease caused by breathing asbestos dust.

ASBO abbreviation Brit. antisocial behaviour order.

ascend verb go up; climb or rise.

ascendant adjective **1** rising in power or status. **2** (of a planet or sign of the zodiac) just above the eastern horizon.
■ **ascendancy** noun.

ascension noun **1** the action of reaching a higher position or status. **2** (**the Ascension**) the ascent of Jesus into heaven after the Resurrection.

ascent noun **1** the action of going up. **2** an upward slope.

ascertain /ass-er-**tayn**/ verb find something out for certain.
■ **ascertainable** adjective.

ascetic /uh-**set**-ik/ adjective choosing to live without pleasures and luxuries. • noun an ascetic person.
■ **asceticism** noun.

ascorbic acid /uh-**skor**-bik/ noun vitamin C.

ascribe verb (**ascribes, ascribing, ascribed**) (**ascribe something to**) say or believe that something is caused by.
■ **ascription** noun.

aseptic /ay-**sep**-tik/ adjective free from germs.

asexual adjective **1** without sex or sexual organs. **2** not having sexual feelings.

■ **asexually** adverb.

ash[1] noun **1** the powder remaining after something has been burned. **2** (**ashes**) the remains of a human body after cremation.

ash[2] noun a tree with winged fruits and hard pale wood.

ashamed adjective feeling embarrassed or guilty.

ashen adjective very pale from shock, fear, or illness.

ashlar noun large, thin slabs of stone used as the surface layer of a wall.

ashore adverb to or on the shore or land.

ashram /**ash**-ruhm/ noun a Hindu religious retreat or community.

ashtray noun a small container for tobacco ash and cigarette ends.

Asian noun a person from Asia, or whose family originally came from Asia. • adjective relating to Asia.

Asiatic adjective relating to Asia.

aside adverb **1** to one side; out of the way. **2** in reserve. • noun **1** an actor's remark spoken to the audience. **2** a remark not directly related to the subject being discussed.

asinine /**ass**-i-nyn/ adjective very foolish.

ask verb **1** say something so as to get an answer or some information. **2** say that you want someone to do, give, or allow something. **3** (**ask for**) say that you want to speak to. **4** expect something of someone. **5** invite someone to a social occasion.

askance /uh-**skanss**/ adverb with a suspicious or disapproving look.

askew /uh-**skyoo**/ adverb & adjective not straight or level.

aslant adverb & preposition at a slant or crossing something at a slant.

asleep adjective & adverb **1** in or into a state of sleep. **2** (of a limb) numb.

asp noun a small viper.

asparagus /uh-**spa**-ruh-guhss/ noun a vegetable consisting of the tender young

THESAURUS

subtle, expressive.
OPPOSITES unimaginative.

ascent noun **1** *the ascent of the Matterhorn:* climbing, scaling, conquest. **2** *the ascent grew steeper:* slope, incline, gradient.
OPPOSITES descent, drop.

ascertain verb find out, discover, get to know, work out, make out, fathom (out), learn, deduce, divine, establish, determine; informal figure out.

ashamed adjective **1** *she felt ashamed that she had hit him:* sorry, shamefaced, sheepish, guilty, contrite, remorseful, regretful, mortified, humiliated. **2** *he was ashamed to admit it:* reluctant, loath,

unwilling, afraid, embarrassed.
OPPOSITES proud, pleased.

ask verb **1** *he asked what time we opened:* enquire, want to know, question, interrogate, quiz. **2** *they'll ask a few questions:* put (forward), pose, raise, submit. **3** *do ask for advice:* request, demand, seek, solicit, apply, petition, call, appeal.
OPPOSITES answer.

asleep adjective sleeping, napping, dozing, drowsing; informal snoozing, dead to the world; humorous in the land of Nod.
OPPOSITES awake.

shoots of a tall plant.

aspartame /uh-**spah**-taym/ noun a low-calorie artificial sweetener.

aspect noun 1 a particular part or feature of something. 2 a particular appearance or quality. 3 the side of a building facing a particular direction.

aspen noun a poplar tree with small rounded leaves.

asperity /uh-**spe**-ri-ti/ noun harshness in the way you speak to or treat someone.

aspersion /uh-**sper**-sh'n/ noun (**cast aspersions on**) attack someone's character or reputation.

asphalt /**ass**-falt/ noun a tar-like substance used in surfacing roads or roofs.

asphyxia /uh-**sfik**-si-uh/ noun a condition in which someone cannot get enough oxygen and becomes unconscious or dies.

asphyxiate verb (**asphyxiates, asphyxiating, asphyxiated**) die or cause to die from lack of oxygen.
■ **asphyxiation** noun.

aspic noun a savoury jelly made with meat stock.

aspidistra /ass-pi-**diss**-truh/ noun a plant with broad tapering leaves.

aspirant noun a person with ambitions to do or be something.

aspiration noun a hope or ambition.
■ **aspirational** adjective.

aspire verb (**aspires, aspiring, aspired**) have a strong desire to achieve or become something.

aspirin noun (plural **aspirin** or **aspirins**) a medicine used to relieve pain and reduce fever and inflammation.

ass noun 1 a donkey or related small wild horse. 2 informal a stupid person.

assail verb 1 attack someone violently. 2 (of an unpleasant feeling) come over someone strongly.

assailant noun an attacker.

assassin noun a person who assassinates someone.

assassinate verb (**assassinates, assassinating, assassinated**) murder a political or religious leader.
■ **assassination** noun.

assault noun 1 a violent attack. 2 a determined attempt. • verb make an assault on.
□ **assault course** Brit. an obstacle course used for training soldiers.

assay noun the testing of a metal to see how pure it is. • verb test a metal.

assegai /**ass**-uh-gy/ noun (plural **assegais**) an iron-tipped spear used by southern African peoples.

assemblage noun 1 a collection or gathering of things or people. 2 something made of pieces fitted together.

assemble verb (**assembles, assembling, assembled**) 1 come or bring together. 2 construct something by fitting parts together.

assembly noun (plural **assemblies**) 1 a group of people gathered together. 2 a group of people with powers to make decisions and laws. 3 the action of fitting the parts of something together.
□ **assembly line** a series of workers and machines in a factory along which

THESAURUS

aspect noun 1 *every aspect of life:* feature, facet, side, characteristic, particular, detail. 2 *from every aspect:* point of view, position, standpoint, viewpoint, perspective, angle, slant. 3 *his face had a sinister aspect:* appearance, look, air, mien, demeanour, expression.

aspiration noun desire, hope, dream, wish, longing, yearning, aim, ambition, goal, target, expectation.

aspire verb *she aspired to be a writer:* desire, aim, hope, dream of, long, yearn, set your heart on, wish, want, seek, set your sights on.

aspiring adjective would-be, hopeful, budding, potential, prospective; informal wannabe.

assassin noun murderer, killer, gunman, executioner; informal hit man.

assassinate verb murder, kill, eliminate, liquidate, execute; N. Amer. terminate; informal hit.

assault verb *he assaulted a police officer:* attack, hit, strike, beat up, thump; informal wallop, belt, clobber, lay into, rough up; Austral. informal quilt.
• noun 1 *he was charged with assault:* violence, battery; Brit. grievous bodily harm, GBH, actual bodily harm, ABH. 2 *an assault on the city:* attack, strike, onslaught, offensive, charge, push, thrust, raid.

assemble verb 1 *a crowd had assembled:* gather, collect, get together, congregate, convene, meet, muster, rally. 2 *he assembled the suspects:* bring/call together, gather, collect, round up, marshal, muster. 3 *how to assemble the kite:* construct, build, erect, set up, put together, connect.
OPPOSITES disperse, dismantle.

assembly noun 1 *an assembly of dockers:* gathering, meeting, congregation, convention, council, rally, group, crowd; informal get-together. 2 *car assembly:* construction, manufacture, building, fabrication, erection.

identical products pass to be assembled in stages.

assent noun approval or agreement. • verb agree to a request or suggestion.

assert verb 1 confidently state that something is true. 2 (**assert yourself**) be confident and forceful.

assertion noun a confident and forceful statement.

assertive adjective speaking and doing things in a confident and forceful way. ■ assertively adverb assertiveness noun.

assess verb make a judgement about the value or quality of something. ■ assessment noun assessor noun.

asset noun 1 a useful or valuable thing or person. 2 (**assets**) property owned by a person or company.

assiduous /uh-**sid**-yoo-uhss/ adjective showing great care and thoroughness. ■ assiduity noun assiduously adverb.

assign verb give someone a task or duty.

assignation noun a secret meeting, especially between lovers.

assignment noun a piece of work that someone has been asked to do.

assimilate verb (**assimilates, assimilating, assimilated**) 1 take in and understand information. 2 absorb people or ideas into a society or culture. ■ assimilation noun.

assist verb help someone.

assistance noun help or support.

assistant noun a person employed to help someone more senior.

assize /uh-**syz**/ or **assizes** noun historical a court which sat at intervals in each county of England and Wales.

associate verb (**associates, associating, associated**) 1 (**associate something with**) mentally connect something with something else. 2 (**associate with**) frequently meet or have dealings with. 3 (**associate yourself with**) be involved with. • noun a work partner or colleague. • adjective 1 connected with an organization. 2 belonging to an association but not having full membership.

THESAURUS

assert verb 1 *she asserts that hysteria is universal:* declare, maintain, contend, argue, claim, insist. 2 *you should assert your rights:* insist on, stand up for, uphold, defend, press/push for.

assertion noun declaration, contention, statement, claim, opinion, protestation.

assertive adjective confident, self-confident, bold, decisive, forceful, insistent, determined, commanding, pushy; informal feisty. OPPOSITES timid.

assess verb 1 *the committee's power is hard to assess:* evaluate, judge, gauge, rate, estimate, appraise, weigh up; informal size up. 2 *the damage was assessed at £5 billion:* value, calculate, work out, determine, cost, price, estimate.

assessment noun 1 *a teacher's assessment of the pupil's abilities:* evaluation, judgement, rating, estimation, appraisal, opinion. 2 *some assessments valued the estate at £2 million:* valuation, calculation, costing, pricing, estimate.

asset noun 1 benefit, advantage, blessing, good/strong point, strength, forte, virtue, recommendation, attraction, resource. 2 (**assets**) property, resources, estate, holdings, funds, valuables, possessions, effects, belongings. OPPOSITES liability.

assign verb 1 *a young doctor was assigned the task:* allocate, allot, give, set, charge with, entrust. 2 *she was assigned to a new post:* appoint, promote, delegate, nominate, commission, post, co-opt; Military detail. 3 *we assign large sums of money to*

travel budgets: earmark, designate, set aside, reserve, appropriate, allot, allocate.

assignation noun rendezvous, date, appointment, meeting.

assignment noun task, job, duty, mission, errand, undertaking, exercise, project, homework.

assist verb 1 help, aid, lend a (helping) hand to, support, back (up), work with. OPPOSITES hinder. 2 *the aim was to assist cashflow:* facilitate, aid, ease, promote, boost, speed, benefit, encourage, further. OPPOSITES hinder.

assistance noun help, aid, a (helping) hand, support, backing, reinforcement. OPPOSITES hindrance.

assistant noun helper, aide, deputy, second (in command), number two, right-hand man/woman, PA, mate, auxiliary, attendant; informal sidekick, gofer; Brit. informal dogsbody, skivvy.

associate verb 1 *the colours that we associate with fire:* link, connect, relate, bracket, identify, equate. 2 *I was forced to associate with them:* mix, keep company, mingle, socialize, go around, have dealings; informal hobnob, hang out/around/round. OPPOSITES avoid. • noun *a business associate:* partner, colleague, co-worker, workmate, collaborator, comrade, ally; informal crony.

associated adjective related, connected, linked, similar, corresponding, attendant, accompanying, incidental. OPPOSITES unrelated.

association noun **1** a group of people organized for a joint purpose. **2** a connection or link.
□ Association Football soccer.

assonance /ass-uh-nuhnss/ noun a rhyming of vowel sounds.

assorted adjective made up of various sorts.

assortment noun a varied collection.

assuage /uh-swayj/ verb (**assuages, assuaging, assuaged**) **1** make an unpleasant feeling less strong. **2** relieve thirst or an appetite or desire.

assume verb (**assumes, assuming, assumed**) **1** think that something must be true but have no proof. **2** take responsibility or control. **3** begin to have. **4** pretend to have or feel.

assumption noun **1** a feeling that something must be true. **2** the taking on of responsibility or control.

assurance noun **1** something said to make someone feel confident about something. **2** self-confidence. **3** Brit. life insurance.

assure verb (**assures, assuring, assured**) **1** make someone feel confident about something. **2** make certain. **3** Brit. insure a person's life.

assured adjective **1** confident in yourself and your abilities. **2** certain; guaranteed.
■ **assuredly** adverb.

astatine /ass-tuh-teen/ noun a radioactive chemical element.

aster noun a plant of the daisy family, with pink or purple flowers.

asterisk noun a symbol (*) used as a pointer to a note.

☑ aster*isk*, not *-ix* (Astérix is a character in a cartoon strip).

astern adverb behind or towards the rear of a ship or aircraft.

asteroid /ass-tuh-royd/ noun a small rocky planet orbiting the sun.

asthma /ass-muh/ noun a medical condition that causes difficulty in breathing.
■ **asthmatic** adjective & noun.

astigmatism /uh-stig-muh-ti-z'm/ noun a fault in the shape of the eye which prevents clear vision.

astir adjective **1** in a state of excited movement. **2** awake and out of bed.

astonish verb surprise someone very much.
■ **astonishment** noun.

THESAURUS

association noun **1** *a trade association:* alliance, consortium, coalition, union, league, guild, syndicate, federation, confederation, cooperative, partnership. **2** *the association between man and environment:* relationship, relation, interrelation, connection, interconnection, link, bond, interdependence.

assorted adjective various, miscellaneous, mixed, varied, diverse, different, sundry.
OPPOSITES uniform.

assortment noun variety, mixture, array, mix, miscellany, selection, medley, ragbag, potpourri.

assume verb **1** *I assumed he wanted me to keep the book:* presume, suppose, take it (as given), take for granted, take as read, conclude, infer, think, fancy, believe, understand, gather; N. Amer. figure. **2** *he assumed a Southern accent:* affect, adopt, put on. **3** *they are to assume more responsibility:* accept, shoulder, bear, undertake, take on/up. **4** *he assumed control of their finances:* seize, take (over), appropriate, wrest, usurp.
OPPOSITES know, drop, give up.

assumed adjective false, fictitious, fake, bogus, invented, made-up; informal pretend, phoney.
OPPOSITES genuine.

assumption noun presumption, supposition, inference, conjecture, belief.
OPPOSITES knowledge.

assurance noun **1** *you have my assurance:* promise, word (of honour), pledge, vow, oath, undertaking, guarantee, commitment. **2** *her calm assurance:* confidence, self-confidence, self-assurance, self-possession, nerve, poise; informal cool. **3** *life assurance:* insurance, indemnity, protection, security, cover.
OPPOSITES self-doubt, nervousness.

assure verb **1** *we must assure him of our loyal support:* reassure, convince, satisfy, persuade. **2** *I assure you all is well:* promise, guarantee, swear, confirm, certify, vow. **3** *he wants to assure a favourable vote:* ensure, secure, guarantee, seal, clinch; informal sew up.
OPPOSITES avoid.

assured adjective **1** *an assured performance:* confident, self-confident, self-assured, self-possessed, poised, composed, unruffled, imperturbable; informal unflappable, together. **2** *an assured supply of weapons:* guaranteed, certain, sure, secure, reliable, dependable; informal sure-fire.
OPPOSITES nervous, uncertain.

astonish verb amaze, astound, stagger, startle, stun, confound, dumbfound, nonplus, take aback, leave open-mouthed; informal flabbergast, bowl over; Brit. informal knock for six.

astonishing adjective amazing, astounding, staggering, surprising, breathtaking, remarkable, extraordinary, incredible,

astound verb shock or surprise someone very much.

astrakhan /ass-truh-**kan**/ noun the dark curly fleece of young lambs from central Asia, used to make coats and hats.

astral adjective relating to the stars.

astray adverb away from the correct course.

astride preposition & adverb with a leg on each side of. • adverb (of a person's legs) apart.

astringent /uh-**strin**-juhnt/ adjective 1 causing body tissue to contract. 2 sharp or severe. • noun an astringent lotion.
■ astringency noun.

astrolabe /**ass**-truh-layb/ noun an instrument formerly used in navigation and for measuring the altitude of the stars.

astrology noun the study of the supposed influence of the stars and planets on human affairs.
■ astrologer noun **astrological** adjective.

astronaut noun a person trained to travel in a spacecraft.

astronomical adjective 1 relating to astronomy. 2 informal very large.
■ astronomic adjective **astronomically** adverb.

astronomy noun the scientific study of stars, planets, and the universe.
■ astronomer noun.

astrophysics noun the study of the physical nature of stars and planets.
■ astrophysicist noun.

astute /uh-**styoot**/ adjective good at making accurate judgements.
■ astutely adverb.

asunder adverb apart or into pieces.

asylum noun 1 protection from danger. 2 protection given to someone who has fled their country for political reasons. 3 dated an institution for people who are mentally ill.

asymmetrical adjective not symmetrical.
■ asymmetric adjective.

asymmetry noun (plural **asymmetries**) lack of symmetry.

at preposition used to express: 1 location, arrival, or time. 2 a value, rate, or point on a scale. 3 a state or condition. 4 direction towards. 5 the means by which something is done.

atavistic /at-uh-**viss**-tik/ adjective inherited from the earliest human beings.
■ atavism noun.

ate past of EAT.

atelier /uh-**tel**-i-ay/ noun a workshop or studio.

atheism /**ay**-thi-iz'm/ noun the belief that God does not exist.
■ atheist noun **atheistic** adjective.

athlete noun 1 a person who is good at sports. 2 a person who competes in track and field events.
□ athlete's foot a form of ringworm infection affecting the feet.

athletic adjective 1 fit and good at sport. 2 relating to athletics. • noun (**athletics**) Brit. the sport of competing in track and field events.
■ athletically adverb **athleticism** noun.

athwart preposition across from side to side.

Atlantic adjective having to do with the Atlantic Ocean.

atlas noun a book of maps or charts.

atmosphere noun 1 the gases surrounding the earth or another planet. 2 the quality of the air in a place. 3 an overall tone or mood. 4 a unit of pressure equal to the pressure of the atmosphere at sea level.

atmospheric adjective 1 relating to the atmosphere of a planet. 2 creating a distinctive mood. • noun (**atmospherics**) electrical disturbances in the atmosphere.

atoll noun a ring-shaped coral reef or chain of islands.

atom noun 1 the smallest particle of a chemical element that can exist. 2 a very small amount.
□ atom bomb (or **atomic bomb**) a bomb whose explosive power comes from the fission (splitting) of the nuclei of atoms.

THESAURUS

unbelievable, phenomenal; informal mind-boggling.
OPPOSITES unremarkable.

astound verb amaze, astonish, stagger, surprise, startle, stun, confound, dumbfound, take aback, leave open-mouthed; informal flabbergast, bowl over; Brit. informal knock for six.

astounding adjective amazing, astonishing, staggering, surprising, breathtaking, remarkable, extraordinary, incredible, unbelievable, phenomenal; informal mind-boggling.
OPPOSITES unremarkable.

astute adjective shrewd, sharp, acute, quick, clever, intelligent, bright, smart, canny, perceptive; informal quick on the uptake.
OPPOSITES stupid.

asylum noun political asylum: refuge, sanctuary, shelter, protection, immunity, a safe haven.

athletic adjective muscular, fit, strapping, well built, strong, sturdy, powerful, brawny, burly.
OPPOSITES puny.

atmosphere noun 1 air, sky; literary the heavens. 2 a relaxed atmosphere: spirit, ambience, air, mood, feel, feeling,

atomic adjective **1** relating to an atom or atoms. **2** relating to nuclear energy or weapons.

atomize or **atomise** verb (**atomizes, atomizing, atomized**) convert something into very fine particles or droplets.
■ **atomizer** noun.

atonal /ay-**toh**-n'l/ adjective not written in any musical key.

atone verb (**atones, atoning, atoned**) (**atone for**) do something to show you are sorry for something that happened in the past.
■ **atonement** noun.

atrium /**ay**-tri-uhm/ noun (plural **atria** /**ay**-tri-uh/ or **atriums**) **1** a central hall rising through several storeys. **2** an open central court in an ancient Roman house. **3** each of the two upper cavities of the heart.

atrocious adjective **1** horrifyingly wicked. **2** very bad or unpleasant.
■ **atrociously** adverb.

atrocity noun (plural **atrocities**) a very wicked or cruel act.

atrophy /a-truh-fi/ verb (**atrophies, atrophying, atrophied**) (of a part of the body) waste away. •noun the condition or process of atrophying.

attach verb **1** fasten; join. **2** believe that something has significance or importance.

3 (**be attached to**) be working with a group of people. **4** (**attached to**) very fond of.
■ **attachable** adjective.

☑ *-ach*, not *-atch*: att**ach**.

attaché /uh-**tash**-ay/ noun a person on an ambassador's staff.
□ **attaché case** a small, flat briefcase for carrying documents.

attachment noun **1** an extra part that is attached to something. **2** a computer file sent with an email.

attack verb **1** violently hurt or attempt to hurt. **2** have a harmful effect on. **3** fiercely criticize. **4** tackle something with determination. **5** (in sport) try to score goals or points. •noun **1** an instance of attacking. **2** a sudden period of illness.
■ **attacker** noun.

attain verb **1** succeed in doing. **2** reach.
■ **attainable** adjective.

attainment noun **1** the achieving of something. **2** an achievement.

attar /at-tar/ noun a sweet-smelling oil made from rose petals.

attempt verb make an effort to do something. •noun an effort to do something.

THESAURUS

character, tone, aura, quality; informal vibe.

atrocious adjective **1** *atrocious cruelties:* wicked, cruel, brutal, barbaric, vicious, monstrous, vile, inhuman, fiendish. **2** *the weather was atrocious:* appalling, dreadful, terrible, miserable; informal abysmal, dire, rotten, lousy; Brit. informal shocking.
OPPOSITES admirable, superb.

atrocity noun **1** *a number of atrocities:* outrage, horror, violation, abuse, massacre. **2** *scenes of hardship and atrocity:* wickedness, cruelty, brutality, barbarity, viciousness, savagery, inhumanity.
OPPOSITES humanity.

attach verb **1** *a weight is attached to the cord:* fasten, fix, join, secure, stick. **2** *they attach importance to research:* ascribe, assign, attribute, accredit, impute. **3** *the medical officer attached to HQ:* assign, appoint, allocate, second.
OPPOSITES detach.

attached adjective *she's very attached to him:* fond of, devoted to, keen on; informal mad about.

attachment noun **1** *a strong attachment to his mother:* bond, closeness, devotion, loyalty, fondness for, love for, affection for, feeling for, sympathy for. **2** *the shower had a massage attachment:* accessory, fitting, extension, add-on.

attack verb **1** *Chris was brutally attacked:*

assault, beat up, set upon, mug; N. Amer. beat up on; informal work over, rough up; Brit. informal duff up. **2** *the French attacked the fort:* strike at, assault, charge, pounce on, raid, storm. **3** *the clergy attacked government policies:* criticize, censure, condemn, disparage; informal knock, slam, lay into; Brit. informal slate, slag off, rubbish.
OPPOSITES defend, praise.
•noun **1** *an attack on their home:* assault, onslaught, offensive, strike, blitz, raid, charge, invasion. **2** *an attack on his leadership:* criticism, censure, condemnation, disparagement; Brit. informal slating. **3** *an asthmatic attack:* fit, seizure, spasm, convulsion, paroxysm, bout, episode.
OPPOSITES defence, praise.

attacker noun assailant, assaulter, mugger, aggressor, raider, invader.
OPPOSITES defender, victim.

attain verb achieve, accomplish, reach, obtain, gain, secure, get, win, earn, realize, fulfil; informal clinch, bag, wrap up.

attempt verb *I attempted to answer the question:* try, strive, aim, venture, endeavour, seek, have a go.
•noun *an attempt to reach the summit:* try, effort, endeavour, venture, bid, go; informal crack, shot, stab.

attend verb **1** be present at or go regularly to. **2** (**attend to**) deal with or pay attention to. **3** happen at the same time as or as a result of. **4** escort and help someone.

attendance noun **1** the action of attending. **2** the number of people present.

attendant noun **1** a person employed to help people in a public place. **2** an assistant to an important person. • adjective accompanying.

attention noun **1** special care, notice, or consideration. **2** (**attentions**) things done to help someone or to express sexual interest. **3** a straight standing position taken by soldiers.

attentive adjective **1** paying close attention. **2** considerate and helpful.
■ **attentively** adverb.

attenuate verb (**attenuates, attenuating, attenuated**) **1** make something weaker. **2** make something thin or thinner.
■ **attenuation** noun.

attest verb **1** provide or act as clear evidence of something. **2** declare something to be true.

■ **attestation** noun.

attic noun a space or room inside the roof of a building.

attire formal noun clothes of a particular kind. • verb (**be attired**) be wearing clothes of a particular kind.

attitude noun **1** a way of thinking. **2** a position of the body. **3** informal self-confident or aggressive behaviour.

attitudinize or **attitudinise** /at-ti-tyoo-di-nyz/ verb (**attitudinizes, attitudinizing, attitudinized**) adopt an attitude just for effect.

attorney /uh-ter-ni/ noun (plural **attorneys**) **1** a person who is appointed to act for someone else in legal matters. **2** chiefly US a lawyer.

attract verb **1** draw someone in by offering something interesting or appealing. **2** cause a particular reaction. **3** draw something closer by an unseen force.

attraction noun **1** the action or power of attracting. **2** something interesting or appealing.

attractive adjective **1** very pleasing to look

a

THESAURUS

attend verb **1** *they attended a carol service:* be present at, sit in on, take part in, appear at, turn up at, visit, go to; informal show up at. **2** *the children were not attending:* pay attention, listen, be attentive, concentrate.
OPPOSITES miss, take no notice.
□ **attend to something deal with**, see to, look after, manage, organize, sort out, handle, take care of, tackle. **attend to someone care for**, look after, minister to, see to, tend, treat, help.

attendance noun **1** *you requested the attendance of a doctor:* presence, appearance, attention. **2** *their gig attendances grew:* audience, turnout, house, gate, crowd; Austral. informal muster.
OPPOSITES absence.

attendant noun *a royal attendant:* assistant, aide, companion, steward, equerry, escort, servant, retainer, valet, maid.
• adjective *new discoveries and the attendant excitement:* accompanying, associated, related, connected, resulting, consequent.

attention noun **1** *the issue needs further attention:* consideration, contemplation, deliberation, thought, study, observation, mind, investigation, action. **2** *he tried to attract the attention of a policeman:* awareness, notice, scrutiny, eye, gaze. **3** *medical attention:* care, treatment, relief, aid, assistance.

attentive adjective **1** *an attentive pupil:* alert, perceptive, observant, acute, aware, heedful, focused, studious, diligent,

conscientious, earnest. **2** *the most attentive of husbands:* considerate, conscientious, thoughtful, kind, caring, solicitous, understanding, sympathetic.
OPPOSITES inattentive.

attic noun loft, roof space, garret.

attitude noun **1** *you seem ambivalent in your attitude:* view, viewpoint, outlook, perspective, stance, standpoint, position, approach, opinion. **2** *an attitude of prayer:* position, posture, pose, stance.

attract verb **1** *he was attracted by her smile:* entice, appeal to, tempt, lure, allure, charm, win, woo, captivate; informal turn on. **2** *electrical equipment attracts dust:* draw, pull, suck.
OPPOSITES repel, put off.

attraction noun **1** *she had lost her attraction:* appeal, attractiveness, pull, desirability, fascination, allure, charisma, charm. **2** *the town's attractions:* entertainment, activity, diversion, amenity, service. **3** *magnetic attraction:* pull, draw, force.
OPPOSITES repulsion.

attractive adjective **1** good-looking, beautiful, pretty, handsome, lovely, stunning, striking, arresting, gorgeous, prepossessing, fetching; Scottish & N. English bonny; informal drop-dead gorgeous; Brit. informal fit; N. Amer. informal cute; Austral./NZ informal spunky. **2** *an attractive career:* appealing, inviting, tempting, pleasing, interesting.
OPPOSITES unattractive, ugly, uninviting.

at. **2** arousing interest.
■ **attractively** adverb **attractiveness** noun.

attribute verb /uh-**trib**-yoot/ (**attributes, attributing, attributed**) (**attribute something to**) say or believe that something is the result of or belongs to. • noun /**at**-tri-byoot/ a quality or feature.
■ **attributable** adjective **attribution** noun.

attrition noun gradual wearing down through prolonged attack, pressure, or friction.

attune verb (**be attuned**) be receptive to and able to understand someone or something.

atypical adjective not typical.

aubergine /**oh**-ber-zheen/ noun a large vegetable with purple skin.

aubretia or **aubrietia** /aw-**bree**-shuh/ noun a plant with purple, pink, or white flowers.

auburn noun a reddish-brown colour.

auction noun a public sale in which each item is sold to the person who offers most for it. • verb sell something at an auction.

auctioneer noun a person who conducts auctions.

audacious adjective very confident and daring.
■ **audaciously** adverb **audacity** noun.

audible adjective able to be heard.
■ **audibility** noun **audibly** adverb.

audience noun **1** the people gathered to see or listen to a play, concert, film, etc. **2** a formal interview with a person in authority.

audio tape noun magnetic tape on which sound can be recorded.

audit noun an official inspection of an organization's accounts. • verb (**audits, auditing, audited**) inspect the accounts of.
■ **auditor** noun.

audition noun an interview for an actor, singer, etc. in which they give a practical demonstration of their skill. • verb assess or be assessed by an audition.

auditorium noun (plural **auditoriums** or **auditoria**) the part of a theatre or hall in which the audience sits.

auditory adjective relating to hearing.

au fait /oh **fay**/ adjective (**au fait with**) completely familiar with.

auger /**aw**-ger/ noun a tool for boring holes.

aught pronoun old use anything at all.

augment verb increase the amount or value of.
■ **augmentation** noun.

augur /**aw**-ger/ verb be a sign of a likely outcome.

augury /**aw**-gyoo-ri/ noun (plural **auguries**) a sign of what will happen in the future.

August noun the eighth month of the year.

august /aw-**gust**/ adjective inspiring respect and admiration.

auk noun a black and white seabird.

aunt noun the sister of your father or mother or the wife of your uncle.

au pair /oh **pair**/ noun a foreign girl employed to look after children and help with housework.

aura /**aw**-ruh/ noun (plural **auras**) the distinctive feeling that seems to surround a particular place or person.

aural /**aw**-ruhl/ adjective having to do with the ear or hearing.
■ **aurally** adverb.

aureole /**aw**-ri-ohl/ noun a circle of light around the sun or moon.

au revoir /aw ruh-**vwar**/ exclamation goodbye.

aurora borealis /aw-**raw**-ruh bo-ri-**ay**-liss/ noun streamers of light sometimes seen in the sky near the North Pole; the Northern Lights.

auspice /**awss**-piss/ noun (**under the auspices of**) with the support or protection of.

THESAURUS

attribute verb *they attributed their success to him:* ascribe, assign, accredit, credit, put down, chalk up, pin on.
• noun *the attributes of a top player:* quality, characteristic, trait, feature, element, aspect, property, sign, hallmark, mark.

audible adjective perceptible, discernible, detectable, clear, distinct.
OPPOSITES inaudible, faint.

audience noun **1** *the audience applauded:* spectators, listeners, viewers, onlookers, crowd, throng, gallery, congregation, turnout. **2** *an audience with the Pope:* meeting, interview, consultation, conference, hearing, reception.

augment verb increase, add to, supplement, enhance, build up, raise, up, hike up, enlarge, swell, expand, extend; informal jack up.
OPPOSITES decrease, reduce.

august adjective distinguished, respected, eminent, venerable, illustrious, prestigious, renowned, celebrated, honoured, acclaimed, esteemed.
OPPOSITES lowly, obscure, disreputable.

aura noun atmosphere, ambience, air, quality, character, mood, feeling; informal vibe.

auspicious /aw-**spi**-shuhss/ adjective suggesting that there is a good chance of success.
■ **auspiciously** adverb.

Aussie informal noun (plural **Aussies**) an Australian. • adjective Australian.

austere adjective **1** without luxuries or decoration; very simple and plain. **2** severe or strict in appearance or behaviour.
■ **austerely** adverb **austerity** noun.

Australasian adjective relating to Australasia, a region made up of Australia, New Zealand, and neighbouring islands.

Australian noun a person from Australia.
• adjective relating to Australia.

Austrian noun a person from Austria.
• adjective relating to Austria.

authentic adjective known to be real; genuine.
■ **authentically** adverb **authenticity** noun.

authenticate verb (**authenticates**,

authenticating, **authenticated**) prove or show that something is authentic.
■ **authentication** noun.

author noun **1** a writer of a book or article. **2** the inventor of something.
■ **authorship** noun.

authoritarian adjective demanding strict obedience of authority and rules. • noun an authoritarian person.

authoritative adjective **1** true or accurate and so able to be trusted. **2** commanding and self-confident. **3** official.
■ **authoritatively** adverb.

authority noun (plural **authorities**) **1** the power to give orders and make people obey you. **2** a person or organization that has official power. **3** recognized knowledge or expertise. **4** a person or book that is trusted as a source of knowledge.

authorize or **authorise** verb (**authorizes**, **authorizing**, **authorized**) give official

---

THESAURUS

auspicious adjective favourable, promising, encouraging, fortunate, opportune, timely, advantageous, good.
OPPOSITES inauspicious, unfavourable.

austere adjective **1** *an austere man:* severe, stern, strict, harsh, dour, grim, cold, frosty, unfriendly. **2** *an austere life:* spartan, frugal, ascetic, puritanical, abstemious, strict, simple, hard. **3** *an austere building:* plain, simple, basic, functional, unadorned, bleak, bare, clinical.
OPPOSITES easy-going, friendly, luxurious, extravagant, ornate.

authentic adjective **1** *an authentic document:* genuine, real, bona fide, true, legitimate; informal pukka, kosher; Austral./NZ informal dinkum. **2** *an authentic depiction of the situation:* accurate, factual, true, truthful, reliable, trustworthy, honest, faithful.
OPPOSITES fake, inaccurate, unreliable.

authenticate verb verify, validate, prove, substantiate, corroborate, confirm, support, back up.
OPPOSITES disprove.

author noun **1** *modern Canadian authors:* writer, novelist, poet, playwright, columnist, reporter, wordsmith; informal scribe, scribbler. **2** *the author of the peace plan:* creator, originator, founder, father, architect, designer, producer.

authoritarian adjective strict, autocratic, dictatorial, despotic, tyrannical, domineering, imperious, illiberal, undemocratic; informal bossy.
OPPOSITES democratic, liberal.
• noun disciplinarian, autocrat, dictator, despot, tyrant.
OPPOSITES democrat, liberal.

authoritative adjective **1** *authoritative information:* reliable, dependable, trustworthy, accurate, authentic, valid. **2** *the authoritative edition:* definitive, most reliable, best, authorized, approved. **3** *his authoritative manner:* commanding, masterful, assertive, self-assured, self-confident.
OPPOSITES unreliable, timid.

authority noun **1** *a rebellion against those in authority:* power, command, control, charge, dominance, jurisdiction, rule; informal clout. **2** *the authority to arrest drug traffickers:* right, authorization, power, mandate, prerogative, licence. **3** *the money was spent without parliamentary authority:* permission, authorization, consent, sanction, assent, agreement, approval, clearance; informal the go-ahead. **4** *the authorities:* officials, officialdom, government, administration, establishment, police; informal the powers that be. **5** *an authority on coins:* expert, specialist, professional, master, connoisseur, pundit, doyen/doyenne, guru.
OPPOSITES amateur, ignoramus.

authorize verb **1** *they authorized further action:* permit, sanction, allow, approve, consent to, assent to; informal give the go-ahead to, OK. **2** *the troops were authorized to fire:* empower, give authority, mandate, commission, entitle.
OPPOSITES forbid.

authorized adjective approved, sanctioned, accredited, recognized, licensed, certified, official, legal, legitimate.
OPPOSITES unauthorized, unofficial.

a

permission for.
■ **authorization** noun.

autism noun a mental condition in which a person has great difficulty in communicating with other people.
■ **autistic** adjective.

autobiography noun (plural **autobiographies**) an account of a person's life written by that person.
■ **autobiographical** adjective.

autocracy /aw-tok-ruh-si/ noun (plural **autocracies**) a system of government in which one person has total power.

autocrat noun 1 a ruler who has total power. 2 a person who expects obedience.
■ **autocratic** adjective.

autogiro or **autogyro** noun (plural **autogiros**) a type of aircraft that is powered by a propeller and has rotating horizontal blades like a helicopter.

autograph noun a celebrity's signature written for an admirer. ● verb write an autograph on something.

automate verb (**automates, automating, automated**) convert a process or machine so that it can operate automatically.
■ **automation** noun.

automatic adjective 1 operating by itself without human control. 2 (of a gun) able to fire continuously until the bullets run out. 3 done without conscious thought. 4 (of a punishment) applied without question because of a fixed rule.
□ **automatic pilot** a device for keeping an aircraft on course without the pilot having to control it.
■ **automatically** adverb.

automaton /aw-**tom**-uh-tuhn/ noun (plural **automata** /aw-**tom**-uh-tuh/ or **automatons**) a mechanical device that looks like a

human being.

automobile noun N. Amer. a car.

automotive adjective having to do with motor vehicles.

autonomous /aw-ton-uh-muhss/ adjective self-governing or independent.
■ **autonomously** adverb.

autonomy noun 1 self-government. 2 freedom of action.

autopsy /aw-top-si/ noun (plural **autopsies**) an examination of a dead body to discover the cause of death.

autumn noun chiefly Brit. the season after summer and before winter.
■ **autumnal** adjective.

auxiliary adjective providing extra help and support. ● noun (plural **auxiliaries**) an auxiliary person or thing.
□ **auxiliary verb** a verb such as be, do, and have, which is used to form tenses of other verbs.

avail verb (**avail yourself of**) formal use or take advantage of. ● noun use or benefit.

available adjective 1 able to be used or obtained. 2 not occupied.
■ **availability** noun.

avalanche /av-uh-lahnsh/ noun 1 a mass of snow and ice falling rapidly down a mountainside. 2 an overwhelming amount of something.

avant-garde /a-von gard/ adjective (in the arts) new and experimental.

avarice /av-uh-riss/ noun extreme greed for money or material things.

avaricious adjective very greedy for money or material things.

avatar /av-uh-tar/ noun (in Hinduism) a god or goddess appearing in physical form on earth.

avenge verb (**avenges, avenging, avenged**)

THESAURUS

automatic adjective 1 automatic garage doors: mechanized, powered, mechanical, automated, computerized, electronic, robotic. 2 an automatic reaction: instinctive, involuntary, unconscious, reflex, knee-jerk, subconscious, spontaneous, impulsive, unthinking, mechanical; informal gut. 3 the automatic choice: inevitable, unavoidable, inescapable, only possible.
OPPOSITES manual, conscious, deliberate.

autonomous adjective self-governing, independent, sovereign, free.
OPPOSITES dependent, repressed.

autonomy noun self-government, self-rule, home rule, self-determination, independence, sovereignty, freedom.
OPPOSITES dependence, repression.

auxiliary adjective additional, supplementary, extra, reserve, backup,

emergency, fallback, second.
OPPOSITES primary, regular.

available adjective 1 refreshments will be available: obtainable, accessible, to/at hand, to be had, on sale, untaken, unsold; informal up for grabs, on tap. 2 I'll see if he's available: free, unoccupied, on duty, contactable.
OPPOSITES unavailable, taken, busy.

avalanche noun an avalanche of enquiries: barrage, flood, deluge, torrent, wave.
OPPOSITES trickle.

avant-garde adjective experimental, modern, cutting-edge, progressive, unorthodox, unconventional; informal edgy, offbeat, way-out.
OPPOSITES conservative, established.

avarice noun greed, acquisitiveness, covetousness, materialism.
OPPOSITES generosity.

repay something bad that has been done to you by harming the person who did it. ■ **avenger** noun.

avenue noun **1** a broad road or path. **2** a way of making progress towards achieving something.

aver /uh-**ver**/ verb (**avers, averring, averred**) formal declare that something is the case.

average noun **1** the result obtained by adding several amounts together and then dividing the total by the number of amounts. **2** a usual amount or level. • adjective **1** being an average. **2** usual or ordinary. • verb (**averages, averaging, averaged**) **1** amount to a particular figure as an average. **2** calculate the average of several amounts.

averse adjective (**averse to**) strongly disliking or opposed to.

> ! don't confuse **averse** with **adverse**, which means 'harmful or unfavourable'.

aversion noun a strong dislike.

avert verb **1** turn away your eyes. **2** prevent something unpleasant happening.

avian /**ay**-vi-uhn/ adjective having to do with birds.

aviary noun (plural **aviaries**) a large enclosure for keeping birds in.

aviation noun the activity of operating and flying aircraft.

aviator noun dated a pilot.

avid adjective very interested or enthusiastic. ■ **avidly** adverb.

avionics plural noun electronics used in aviation.

avocado noun (plural **avocados**) a pear-shaped fruit with pale green flesh and a large stone.

avocet /**av**-uh-set/ noun a wading bird with long legs and an upturned bill.

avoid verb **1** keep away from, or stop yourself from doing. **2** prevent something from happening. **3** manage not to collide with. ■ **avoidable** adjective **avoidance** noun.

avoirdupois /av-war-dyoo-**pwah**/ noun the system of weights based on a pound of 16 ounces.

avow verb openly state or confess. ■ **avowed** adjective.

avuncular /uh-**vung**-kyuu-ler/ adjective kind and friendly towards a younger person.

await verb wait for.

awake verb (**awakes, awaking, awoke**; past participle **awoken**) **1** stop sleeping. **2** make or become active again. • adjective not asleep.

awaken verb **1** awake. **2** stir up a feeling.

THESAURUS

average noun the national average: mean, median, mode, norm, standard, rule, par. • adjective **1** the average temperature: mean, median, modal. **2** a woman of average height: ordinary, standard, normal, typical, regular. OPPOSITES abnormal, unusual. □ on average **normally,** usually, ordinarily, generally, typically, for the most part, as a rule, by and large, overall, on the whole.

averse adjective opposed, hostile, antagonistic, resistant, disinclined, reluctant, loath; informal anti. OPPOSITES keen.

aversion noun dislike, hatred, loathing, abhorrence, distaste, antipathy, hostility, reluctance, disinclination. OPPOSITES liking.

avert verb **1** she averted her gaze: turn aside, turn away, shift, redirect. **2** an attempt to avert political chaos: prevent, avoid, stave off, ward off, head off, forestall. OPPOSITES bring about, allow.

avid adjective keen, eager, enthusiastic, ardent, passionate, zealous, devoted. OPPOSITES apathetic.

avoid verb **1** I avoid situations that cause me stress: keep away from, steer clear of, give

a wide berth to. **2** he avoids responsibility: evade, dodge, sidestep, escape, run away from; informal duck, wriggle out of, get out of. **3** book early to avoid disappointment: prevent, preclude, stave off, forestall, head off, ward off. **4** he should avoid drinking alcohol: refrain from, abstain from, desist from, steer clear of. OPPOSITES confront, face up to, seek out, cause, allow, continue, insist on.

await verb **1** Peter was awaiting news: wait for, expect, look forward to, anticipate. **2** many dangers await them: be in store for, lie ahead of, lie in wait for, be waiting for, be round the corner.

awake verb she awoke early: wake up, wake, awaken, waken, stir, come to, come round, rouse, call. • adjective **1** she was still awake: sleepless, wide awake, restless, insomniac. **2** too few are awake to the dangers: aware of, conscious of, mindful of, alert to. OPPOSITES asleep, oblivious.

awaken verb **1** See **AWAKE** verb. **2** he had awakened strong emotions in her: arouse, bring out, trigger, stir up, stimulate, kindle, revive. OPPOSITES suppress.

award verb give an official prize or reward to. •noun **1** an official prize or reward. **2** the action of awarding.

aware adjective (usu. **aware of** or **that**) knowing about a situation or fact.
■ **awareness** noun.

awash adjective covered or flooded with water.

away adverb **1** to or at a distance. **2** into a place for storage. **3** out of existence. **4** constantly or continuously. •adjective (of a sports match) played at the opponents' ground.

awe noun a feeling of great respect mixed with fear. •verb (**awes**, **awing**, **awed**) fill someone with awe.

awesome adjective **1** inspiring awe. **2** informal excellent.
■ **awesomely** adverb.

awful adjective **1** very bad or unpleasant. **2** used to emphasize something: *an awful lot.*
■ **awfully** adverb.

awhile adverb for a short time.

awkward adjective **1** hard to do or deal with. **2** causing or feeling embarrassment. **3** inconvenient. **4** clumsy.
■ **awkwardly** adverb.

awl noun a small pointed tool used for making holes.

awning noun a sheet of canvas on a frame, used for shelter.

awoke past of AWAKE.

awoken past participle of AWAKE.

AWOL /ay-wol/ adjective (**go AWOL**) informal go missing.

awry /uh-ry/ adverb & adjective away from the expected course or position.

THESAURUS

award verb *the society awarded him a medal:* give, grant, accord, confer on, bestow on, present to, decorate with. •noun **1** *an award for long service:* prize, trophy, medal, decoration, reward; informal gong. **2** *an award of £1,500:* grant, scholarship, endowment; Brit. bursary.

aware adjective **1** *she is aware of the dangers:* conscious of, mindful of, informed about, acquainted with, familiar with, alive to, alert to; informal wise to, in the know about. **2** *environmentally aware:* sensitive, enlightened, knowledgeable, (well) informed; informal clued up; Brit. informal switched-on.
OPPOSITES unaware, ignorant.

awareness noun consciousness, recognition, realization, perception, understanding, grasp, appreciation, knowledge, familiarity.

away adverb *we'll be away for two weeks:* elsewhere, abroad, gone, off, out, absent, on holiday, on vacation.

awe noun wonder, wonderment, admiration, reverence, respect, fear, dread.

awesome adjective breathtaking, awe-inspiring, magnificent, amazing, stunning, staggering, imposing, formidable, intimidating; informal mind-boggling, mind-blowing, brilliant.
OPPOSITES unimpressive.

awful adjective **1** *the place smelled awful:* disgusting, terrible, dreadful, ghastly, horrible, vile, foul, revolting, repulsive, repugnant, sickening, nauseating; informal gross; Brit. informal beastly. **2** *an awful book:* dreadful, terrible, frightful, atrocious, lamentable; informal crummy, pathetic, rotten, woeful, lousy, appalling, abysmal, dismal, dire; Brit. informal rubbish. **3** *an awful accident:* serious, bad, terrible, dreadful,

shocking. **4** *I feel awful:* ill, unwell, sick, nauseous; Brit. off colour, poorly; Brit. informal grotty, ropy; Scottish informal wabbit, peely-wally; Austral./NZ informal crook.
OPPOSITES delightful, excellent, well.

awfully adverb **1** (informal) *an awfully nice man:* very, extremely, really, immensely, exceedingly, thoroughly, dreadfully, terrifically, terribly, exceptionally, remarkably, extraordinarily; N. English right; informal seriously, majorly; Brit. informal jolly, dead, well; N. Amer. informal real, mighty, awful; informal, dated frightfully. **2** *we played awfully:* terribly, dreadfully, atrociously, appallingly; informal abysmally, pitifully, diabolically.

awkward adjective **1** *the box was awkward to carry:* difficult, tricky, cumbersome, unwieldy; Brit. informal fiddly. **2** *you're being really awkward:* unreasonable, difficult, uncooperative, unhelpful, obstructive, contrary, stubborn, obstinate; Brit. informal bloody-minded, bolshie; N. Amer. informal balky. **3** *an awkward time:* inconvenient, inappropriate, inopportune, difficult. **4** *he put her in a very awkward position:* embarrassing, uncomfortable, unenviable, delicate, tricky, problematic, troublesome, humiliating, compromising; informal sticky. **5** *she felt awkward when alone with him:* uncomfortable, uneasy, tense, nervous, edgy, self-conscious, embarrassed. **6** *his awkward movements:* clumsy, ungainly, uncoordinated, graceless, inelegant, gauche, gawky, stiff, unskilful, inept, blundering; informal ham-fisted, cack-handed; Brit. informal all (fingers and) thumbs.
OPPOSITES easy, amenable, convenient, at ease, graceful, dexterous.

axe (US spelling **ax**) noun a tool with a heavy blade, used for chopping wood. • verb (**axes, axing, axed**) suddenly and ruthlessly cancel or dismiss.
□ **have an axe to grind** have a private reason for doing something.

axiom /ak-si-uhm/ noun a statement regarded as being obviously true.
■ **axiomatic** adjective.

axis /ak-sis/ noun (plural **axes** /ak-seez/) **1** an imaginary line around which an object or shape rotates. **2** a fixed line against which points on a graph are measured. **3** (**the Axis**) Germany and its allies in the Second World War.

axle noun a rod passing through the centre of a wheel or group of wheels.

ayatollah /I-uh-**tol**-luh/ noun a religious leader in Iran.

aye /rhymes with my/ exclamation old use or dialect yes.

azalea /uh-**zay**-li-uh/ noun a shrub with brightly coloured flowers.

Azerbaijani /a-zer-by-**jah**-ni/ noun (plural **Azerbaijanis**) a person from Azerbaijan. • adjective relating to Azerbaijan.

azimuth /**az**-i-muhth/ noun Astronomy the direction of a star measured horizontally as an angle from due north or south.

Aztec noun a member of an American Indian people that ruled Mexico before the Spanish conquest.

azure /**az**-yuur/ noun a bright blue colour like a cloudless sky.

axe noun hatchet, chopper, cleaver, adze; historical battleaxe.
• verb **1** the show was axed: cancel, withdraw, drop, scrap, cut, discontinue, end; informal ditch, dump, pull the plug on.

2 500 staff were axed: dismiss, make redundant, lay off, get rid of; informal sack, fire.
OPPOSITES start, launch, recruit.

axle noun shaft, spindle, rod.

Bb

B or **b** noun (plural **Bs** or **B's**) the second letter of the alphabet.

BA abbreviation Bachelor of Arts.

baa verb (**baas**, **baaing**, **baaed**) (of a sheep or lamb) bleat.

babble verb talk quickly in a silly or confused way. •noun silly or confused talk.

babe noun **1** literary a baby. **2** informal an attractive young woman.

babel /**bay**-b'l/ noun a confused noise made by many people speaking together.

baboon noun a large monkey with a long snout and a pink rump.

baby noun (plural **babies**) **1** a child or animal that has recently been born. **2** a timid or childish person. •adjective small or very young. •verb (**babies**, **babying**, **babied**) treat someone too protectively.
■ **babyhood** noun **babyish** adjective.

babysit verb (**babysits**, **babysitting**, **babysat**) look after a child or children while the parents are out.
■ **babysitter** noun.

baccalaureate /ba-kuh-**lor**-i-uht/ noun an exam taken in some countries to qualify for higher education.

baccarat /**bak**-kuh-rah/ noun a gambling card game.

bacchanalian /bak-kuh-**nay**-li-uhn/ adjective (of a party or celebration) drunken and wild.

bachelor noun **1** a man who has never been married. **2** a person who holds a first degree from a university.

bacillus /buh-**sil**-luhss/ noun (plural **bacilli** /buh-**sil**-lee/) a type of bacterium.

back noun **1** the rear surface of a person's body, or the upper part of an animal's body. **2** the side or part of something that is furthest from the front. **3** a defending

THESAURUS

babble verb prattle, rattle on, gabble, chatter, jabber, twitter, burble, blather; informal yatter, blabber, jaw, gas, shoot your mouth off; Brit. informal witter, rabbit, chunter, natter, waffle.

baby noun infant, newborn, child; Scottish & N. English bairn; technical neonate; informal sprog, tot; literary babe.
•adjective *baby carrots:* miniature, mini, little, toy, pocket, midget, dwarf; Scottish wee; N. Amer. vest-pocket; informal teeny, teensy, tiddly, bite-sized; Brit. informal titchy; N. Amer. informal little-bitty.
OPPOSITES large.

babyish adjective childish, infantile, juvenile, puerile, immature.
OPPOSITES mature.

back noun **1** spine, backbone, spinal column, vertebral column. **2** *the back of the house:* rear; Nautical stern. **3** *the back of the queue:* end, tail end, rear end; N. Amer. tag end. **4** *the back of a postcard:* reverse, other side, underside; informal flip side.
OPPOSITES front, bow, head, face.
•adverb **1** *he pushed his chair back:* backwards, behind you, to your rear,

rearwards, away. **2** *a few months back:* ago, earlier, previously, before.
OPPOSITES forward, ahead.
•verb **1** *companies backed the scheme generously:* sponsor, finance, fund, subsidize, underwrite; informal pick up the bill for. **2** *most people backed the idea:* support, endorse, sanction, approve of, give your blessing to, smile on, favour, advocate, promote, champion; informal throw your weight behind. **3** *he backed the horse at 33–1:* bet on, gamble on, stake money on. **4** *he backed away:* reverse, draw back, step back, pull back, retreat, withdraw.
OPPOSITES oppose, advance.
•adjective **1** *the back seats:* rear, rearmost, hind, hindmost, posterior. **2** *a back copy:* past, old, previous, earlier.
OPPOSITES front, future.
□ **back down give in**, concede defeat, surrender, yield, submit, climb down. **back out of renege on**, withdraw from, pull out of, fail to honour. **back something up substantiate**, corroborate, confirm, support, bear out, endorse, lend weight to. **back someone up support**, stand by, side with, take someone's part.

player in a team game. •adverb 1 in the opposite direction from the one in which you are facing or travelling. 2 so as to return to an earlier or normal position or state. 3 into the past. 4 in return. •adjective 1 at or towards the back. 2 in a remote or less important position. 3 relating to the past. •verb 1 give support to. 2 walk or drive backwards. 3 bet money on a person or animal to win a race or contest. 4 (back on to) (of a building) have its back facing or next to. 5 cover the back of an object. 6 provide musical backing for a singer or musician.

□ the back of beyond a very remote place. back down give in. back off stop opposing someone. back out withdraw from something you have promised to do. back-pedal go back on something previously said. back someone/thing up 1 support someone or something. 2 Computing make a spare copy of data or a disk. put someone's back up annoy someone.

■ backer noun.

backbencher noun an MP who does not hold a government or opposition post.

backbiting noun spiteful talk about a person who is not present.

backbone noun 1 the spine. 2 strength of character.

backchat noun Brit. informal rude or cheeky remarks.

backdate verb (backdates, backdating, backdated) Brit. make something valid from an earlier date.

backdrop noun 1 a painted cloth hung at the back of a theatre stage as part of the scenery. 2 the setting or background for a scene or event.

backfire verb (backfires, backfiring, backfired) 1 (of an engine) make a banging sound as a result of fuel igniting wrongly. 2 produce the opposite effect to what was intended.

backgammon noun a board game played with counters and a dice.

background noun 1 the part of a scene or picture behind the main figures. 2 information or circumstances that influence or explain something. 3 a person's education, experience, and early life.

backhand noun (in tennis and similar games) a stroke played with the back of the hand facing in the direction of the stroke.

backhanded adjective expressed in a way that is indirect or has more than one meaning: *a backhanded compliment.*

backhander noun 1 a backhand stroke or blow. 2 Brit. informal a bribe.

backing noun 1 support. 2 a layer of material that forms or strengthens the back of something. 3 music or singing accompanying a pop singer.

backlash noun an angry reaction by a large number of people.

backlog noun a build-up of things needing to be dealt with.

backpack noun a rucksack. •verb travel carrying your belongings in a rucksack.
■ backpacker noun.

backside noun informal a person's bottom.

backslapping noun the offering of hearty congratulations or praise.

backsliding noun a return to bad behaviour after an attempt to improve.

backstage adverb & adjective behind the stage in a theatre.

backstreet noun a less important street in a town or city.

backstroke noun a swimming stroke in which you lie on your back and lift your arms out of the water in a backward circular movement.

backtrack verb 1 retrace your steps. 2 change your opinion to the opposite of what it was.

backup noun 1 support. 2 a person or thing

THESAURUS

backer noun 1 *our financial backers:* sponsor, investor, underwriter, financier, patron, benefactor; informal angel. 2 *the backers of the proposition:* supporter, defender, advocate, promoter; N. Amer. booster.

backfire verb *Bernard's plan backfired on him:* rebound, boomerang, come back, fail; informal blow up in someone's face.

background noun 1 *a background of trees:* backdrop, backcloth, surrounding(s), setting, scene. 2 *students from different backgrounds:* social circumstances, family circumstances, environment, class, culture, tradition. 3 *her nursing background:*

experience, record, history, past, training, education.
OPPOSITES foreground.

backing noun 1 *he has the backing of his colleagues:* support, endorsement, approval, blessing. 2 *financial backing:* sponsorship, finance, funding, subsidy, patronage.

backlash noun adverse reaction, counterblast, repercussion, comeback, retaliation, reprisal.

backup noun *troops will provide backup:* help, support, assistance, aid, reserve, reinforcements.
•adjective *a backup supply:* reserve, spare,

b

kept ready to be used when needed.

backward adjective **1** directed towards the back. **2** having made less progress than is normal or expected. • adverb (also **backwards**) **1** towards the back, or back towards the starting point. **2** opposite to the usual direction or order.

backwash noun waves flowing outwards behind a ship.

backwater noun **1** a stretch of stagnant water on a river. **2** a place where change happens very slowly.

backwoods plural noun a remote area or region.

bacon noun salted or smoked meat from the back or sides of a pig.

bacteria plural noun (sing. **bacterium**) a group of microscopic organisms, many kinds of which can cause disease.
■ **bacterial** adjective.

> ! **bacteria** is actually a plural (the singular is **bacterium**), and should always be used with a plural verb, e.g. *the bacteria were multiplying.*

bad adjective (**worse**, **worst**) **1** low in quality; well below standard. **2** unpleasant. **3** severe; serious. **4** wicked or evil. **5** (**bad for**) harmful to. **6** injured, ill, or diseased. **7** (of food) decayed.
■ **badness** noun.

bade past of **BID²**.

badge noun a small flat object that a person pins to their clothing to show that they belong to an organization, have a particular rank, etc.

badger noun an animal with a black and white striped head which lives underground and is active at night. • verb (**badgers**, **badgering**, **badgered**) pester someone to do something.

badinage /bad-i-nah*zh*/ noun witty conversation.

badlands plural noun land where plants or crops will not grow.

badly adverb (**worse**, **worst**) **1** in a way that is not acceptable or satisfactory. **2** severely; seriously. **3** very much.
□ **badly off** poor.

badminton noun a game in which the players hit a shuttlecock across a high net with rackets.

THESAURUS

substitute, replacement, standby, fallback, emergency.

backward adjective **1** *a backward look:* rearward, towards the rear, behind you, reverse. **2** *the decision was a backward step:* retrograde, regressive, for the worse, in the wrong direction, downhill, negative. **3** *economically backward:* underdeveloped, undeveloped, primitive. **4** *he was not backward in displaying his talents:* hesitant, reticent, reluctant, shy, diffident, timid.
OPPOSITES forward, progressive, advanced, confident.

backwards adverb towards the rear, rearwards, behind you.
OPPOSITES forwards.

bad adjective **1** *bad workmanship:* unsatisfactory, substandard, poor, inferior, second-rate, second-class, inadequate, deficient, imperfect, defective, faulty, shoddy, negligent; informal crummy, rotten, pathetic, useless, woeful, lousy; Brit. informal duff, rubbish. **2** *the alcohol had a bad effect:* harmful, damaging, detrimental, injurious, hurtful, destructive. **3** *the bad guys:* wicked, evil, sinful, criminal, immoral, corrupt; informal crooked, bent. **4** *you bad girl!* naughty, badly behaved, disobedient, wayward, wilful, defiant, unruly, undisciplined. **5** *bad news:* unpleasant, disagreeable, unwelcome, unfavourable, unfortunate, grim, distressing, gloomy. **6** *a bad time to arrive:* unfavourable, inauspicious, inopportune,

unfortunate, disadvantageous, inappropriate, unsuitable. **7** *a bad accident:* serious, severe, grave, critical, acute. **8** *the meat's bad:* rotten, off, decayed, putrid, rancid, curdled, sour, mouldy. **9** *a bad knee:* injured, wounded, diseased; Brit. informal gammy, knackered; Austral./NZ informal crook.
OPPOSITES good, quality, beneficial, virtuous, well behaved, welcome, favourable, slight, fresh, healthy.

badge noun **1** brooch, pin, emblem, crest, insignia; N. Amer. button. **2** *a badge of success:* sign, symbol, indication, signal, mark, hallmark, trademark.

badger verb pester, harass, hound, harry, nag, bother, go on at; informal hassle, bug.

badly adverb **1** *the job had been badly done:* poorly, unsatisfactorily, inadequately, incorrectly, faultily, defectively, shoddily, amateurishly, carelessly, negligently, incompetently, inexpertly. **2** *try not to think badly of me:* unfavourably, ill, critically, disapprovingly. **3** *stop behaving badly:* naughtily, disobediently, wilfully, mischievously. **4** *he had been badly treated:* cruelly, wickedly, unkindly, harshly, shamefully, unfairly, unjustly, wrongly. **5** *it turned out badly:* unfavourably, unsuccessfully, adversely, unfortunately. **6** *some of the victims are badly hurt:* severely, seriously, gravely, acutely, critically.
OPPOSITES well, properly, humanely, fairly, favourably, slightly.

bad-tempered adjective irritable, irascible,

baffle verb (**baffles, baffling, baffled**) make someone feel puzzled. •noun a device for controlling the flow of sound, light, gas, or fluid.
■ **bafflement** noun.

bag noun **1** a flexible container with an opening at the top. **2** (**bags**) loose folds of skin under a person's eyes. **3** (**bags of**) Brit. informal plenty of. **4** informal an unpleasant or unattractive woman. •verb (**bags, bagging, bagged**) **1** put something in a bag. **2** manage to catch an animal. **3** informal manage to get.

bagatelle noun **1** a game in which you hit small balls into numbered holes on a board. **2** something unimportant or of little value.

bagel /**bay**-g'l/ noun a ring-shaped bread roll with a heavy texture.

baggage noun luggage packed with belongings for travelling.

baggy adjective (**baggier, baggiest**) loose and hanging in folds.

bagpipe or **bagpipes** noun a musical instrument with pipes that are sounded by wind squeezed from a bag.
■ **bagpiper** noun.

baguette /ba-**get**/ noun a long, narrow French loaf of bread.

bail[1] noun **1** the release of an accused person on condition that a sum of money is left with the court, which will be returned as long as the person attends their trial. **2** money paid to release an accused person. •verb release an accused person on payment of bail.

bail[2] noun Cricket either of the two small pieces of wood that rest on the stumps.

bail[3] or Brit. **bale** verb **1** scoop water out of

a ship or boat. **2** (**bail out**) make an emergency jump out of an aircraft, using a parachute. **3** (**bail someone out**) rescue someone who is in difficulties.

bailey noun (plural **baileys**) the outer wall of a castle.

bailiff noun a person who delivers writs and seizes the property of people who owe money for rent.

bailiwick noun **1** a district over which a bailiff has authority. **2** a person's area of activity or interest.

bairn noun Scottish & N. English a child.

bait noun food put on a hook or in a trap to attract fish or other animals. •verb **1** taunt or tease. **2** (**baiting**) the activity of setting dogs on an animal that is trapped or tied up. **3** put bait on a hook or in a trap.

baize noun a thick green material used for covering billiard tables.

bake verb (**bakes, baking, baked**) **1** cook food in an oven. **2** heat something to dry or harden it. **3** (**baking**) informal (of weather) very hot.
□ **baking soda** sodium bicarbonate.

baker noun a person whose job is making bread and cakes.
□ **baker's dozen** a group of thirteen.
■ **bakery** noun (plural **bakeries**).

baksheesh noun (in India and some other eastern countries) money given as charity, a tip, or a bribe.

balaclava /ba-luh-**klah**-vuh/ noun a close-fitting woollen hat covering the head and neck except for the face.

balalaika /ba-luh-**ly**-kuh/ noun a Russian musical instrument like a guitar, with a triangular body.

balance noun **1** a state in which weight is

tetchy, testy, grumpy, grouchy, crotchety, cross, in a (bad) mood, cantankerous, curmudgeonly, ill-tempered, ill-humoured, peevish, fractious, pettish, crabby; informal snappish, on a short fuse; Brit. informal shirty, stroppy, ratty; N. Amer. informal cranky, ornery; Austral./NZ informal snaky.
OPPOSITES good-humoured, affable.

baffle verb puzzle, perplex, bewilder, mystify, confuse; informal flummox, stump, beat, fox.
OPPOSITES enlighten.

bag noun suitcase, case, valise, holdall, grip. •verb **1** locals bagged the most fish: catch, land, capture, trap, net, snare. **2** he bagged seven medals: get, secure, obtain, acquire, pick up, win, achieve; informal land, net.

baggage noun luggage, suitcases, cases, bags.

baggy adjective loose, roomy, generously cut, sloppy, full, voluminous.

bail noun he was released on bail: surety, security, indemnity, bond, guarantee, pledge.
□ **bail out** the pilot bailed out: eject, parachute to safety. **bail someone/something out** rescue, save, relieve, finance, help (out), aid.

bait noun was she the bait to lure him into a trap? enticement, lure, decoy, snare, trap, inducement, siren, carrot, attraction; informal come-on.
•verb he was baited at school: taunt, tease, goad, pick on, torment, persecute; informal needle; Brit. informal wind up.

balance noun **1** I tripped and lost my balance: stability, equilibrium, steadiness, footing. **2** political balance in broadcasting: fairness, justice, impartiality, parity, equity, evenness, uniformity, comparability. **3** the balance of the rent:

b

evenly distributed, so that a person or object does not wobble or fall over. **2** a situation in which different parts are in the right proportions. **3** a piece of equipment for weighing. **4** an amount that is the difference between money received and money spent in an account. **5** an amount still owed when part of a debt has been paid. • verb (**balances, balancing, balanced**) **1** put your body, or an object, in a steady position. **2** compare the value of one thing with another. **3** give equal importance to two or more things. □ **balance of payments** the difference between payments into and out of a country over a period. **balance sheet** a written statement of what a business owns and what it owes.

balcony noun (plural **balconies**) **1** a platform with a railing or low wall, projecting from the outside of a building. **2** the highest level of seats in a theatre or cinema.

bald adjective **1** having no hair on the head. **2** (of a tyre) having the tread worn away. **3** plain or blunt. ■ **baldly** adverb **baldness** noun.

balderdash noun nonsense.

balding adjective going bald.

bale¹ noun a large bundle of paper, hay, or cloth. • verb (**bales, baling, baled**) make paper, hay, or cloth into bales.

bale² ⇒ **BAIL³**.

baleen /buh-leen/ noun whalebone.

baleful adjective threatening to cause harm. ■ **balefully** adverb.

balk US spelling of **BAULK**.

Balkan adjective relating to countries on the peninsula of SE Europe surrounded by the Adriatic, Ionian, Aegean, and the Black Seas.

ball¹ noun **1** a rounded object that is kicked, thrown, or hit in a game. **2** a single throw or kick of the ball in a game. **3** a rounded part or thing. • verb squeeze or form something into a ball. □ **ball bearing 1** a ring of small metal balls which separate moving parts to reduce rubbing. **2** one of these balls.

ball² noun a formal gathering for dancing

and meeting people.

ballad noun **1** a poem or song telling a story. **2** a slow, sentimental song.

ballast noun **1** a heavy substance carried by a ship or hot-air balloon to keep it stable. **2** stones used to form the base of a railway track or road.

ballcock noun a valve which automatically tops up a cistern when liquid is drawn from it.

ballerina noun a female ballet dancer.

ballet noun an artistic form of dancing performed to music, using set steps and gestures. ■ **balletic** adjective.

ballistic /buh-**liss**-tik/ adjective having to do with the flight of missiles, bullets, or similar objects. □ **ballistic missile** a missile which is fired into the air and falls on to its target.

balloon noun **1** a small rubber bag which is blown up and used as a toy or decoration. **2** (also **hot-air balloon**) a large bag filled with hot air or gas to make it rise in the air, with a basket for passengers attached to it. **3** a rounded outline in which the words of characters in a cartoon are written. • verb **1** swell outwards. **2** increase quickly. **3** (**ballooning**) travelling by hot-air balloon.

ballot noun **1** a way of voting on something secretly by putting paper slips in a box. **2** (**the ballot**) the total number of votes recorded. • verb (**ballots, balloting, balloted**) ask people to vote secretly about something.

ballpark noun N. Amer. a baseball ground. • adjective informal approximate: *a ballpark figure.*

ballpoint pen noun a pen with a tiny ball as its writing point.

ballroom noun a large room for formal dancing. □ **ballroom dancing** formal dancing for couples.

ballyhoo noun informal a lot of fuss.

balm noun **1** a sweet-smelling ointment

THESAURUS

remainder, outstanding amount, rest, residue, difference.
OPPOSITES instability, bias.
• verb **1** *she balanced the book on her head:* steady, stabilize, poise, level. **2** *he balanced his radical remarks with more familiar declarations:* counterbalance, balance out, offset, counteract, compensate for, make up for. **3** *their income and expenditure do not balance:* correspond, agree, tally, match up, coincide. **4** *you need to balance cost*

against benefit: weigh (up), compare, evaluate, consider, assess.

bald adjective **1** *a bald head:* hairless, smooth, shaven, depilated. **2** *a bald statement:* plain, simple, direct, blunt, unadorned, unvarnished; informal upfront.
OPPOSITES hairy, vague.

ball noun sphere, globe, orb, globule, spheroid.

ballot noun vote, poll, election, referendum, show of hands, plebiscite.

b

used to heal or soothe the skin.
2 something that soothes or heals.

balmy adjective (**balmier, balmiest**) (of the weather) pleasantly warm.

baloney noun informal nonsense.

balsa /bawl-suh/ noun very lightweight wood from a tropical American tree, used for making models.

balsam noun a scented substance obtained from some trees and shrubs, used in perfumes and medicines.

balti noun (plural **baltis**) a spicy Pakistani dish that is cooked in a small two-handled pan.

Baltic adjective relating to the Baltic Sea or the countries on its eastern shores.

baluster noun a short pillar forming part of a series supporting a rail.

balustrade noun a railing supported by balusters.

bamboo noun a giant tropical grass with hollow woody stems.

bamboozle verb (**bamboozles, bamboozling, bamboozled**) informal cheat or deceive.

ban verb (**bans, banning, banned**)
1 officially forbid something. **2** forbid someone to do something. •noun an official order forbidding something.

banal /buh-nahl/ adjective boring through being too ordinary and predictable.
■ **banality** noun (plural **banalities**) **banally** adverb.

banana noun a long curved fruit of a tropical tree, with yellow skin.

band¹ noun **1** a flat, thin strip or loop of material used for fastening, strengthening, or decoration. **2** a stripe or strip that is different from its surroundings.

■ **banded** adjective.

band² noun **1** a small group of musicians and singers who play pop, jazz, or rock music. **2** a group of musicians who play brass, wind, or percussion instruments. **3** a group of people with the same aim or a shared feature. •verb form a group with other people.

bandage noun a strip of material tied round a wound or an injury. •verb (**bandages, bandaging, bandaged**) tie a bandage round.

bandanna noun a square of cloth tied round the head or neck.

B. & B. abbreviation bed and breakfast.

bandit noun a member of a gang of armed robbers.
■ **banditry** noun.

bandolier /ban-duh-leer/ noun a belt with loops or pockets for carrying bullets, worn over the shoulder.

bandstand noun a covered outdoor platform for a band to play on.

bandwagon noun an activity or cause that has suddenly become fashionable or popular.

bandwidth noun **1** a range of frequencies used in telecommunications. **2** the ability of a computer network to transmit signals.

bandy¹ adjective (**bandier, bandiest**) (of a person's legs) curved outwards so that the knees are wide apart.

bandy² verb (**bandies, bandying, bandied**) use an idea or word frequently in casual talk.
□ **bandy words** exchange angry remarks.

bane noun a cause of great distress or annoyance.

bang noun **1** a sudden loud noise. **2** a

THESAURUS

ban verb **1** *smoking was banned:* **prohibit,** forbid, veto, proscribe, outlaw, make illegal, bar. **2** *Gary was banned from the playground:* **exclude,** bar, banish, expel, eject, evict, drive out, force out; informal kick out.
OPPOSITES permit, admit.
•noun **1** *a ban on smoking:* **prohibition,** veto, bar, proscription, moratorium, injunction. **2** *a ban from league football:* **exclusion,** bar, banishment, expulsion, ejection, eviction.
OPPOSITES permission, admission.

banal adjective **unoriginal,** unimaginative, trite, hackneyed, clichéd, commonplace, stereotyped, overused, stale, boring, obvious; informal corny.
OPPOSITES original.

band¹ noun *a band round his wrist:* **loop,** wristband, headband, ring, hoop, circlet, belt, sash, girdle, strap, strip, tape, circle.

band² noun **1** *a band of robbers:* **gang,** group, mob, pack, troop, troupe, company, set, party, crew, body, team; informal bunch.
2 *the band played on:* **group,** pop group, ensemble, orchestra; informal combo.

bandage noun **dressing,** covering, plaster, compress, gauze, lint.
•verb *she bandaged my knee:* **bind,** dress, cover, strap (up).

bandit noun **robber,** thief, raider, mugger, pirate, outlaw, hijacker, looter, gangster; literary brigand; historical rustler, highwayman.

bang noun **1** *the door slammed with a bang:* **thud,** thump, bump, crack, crash, smack, boom, blast, clap, report, explosion. **2** *a bang on the head:* **blow,** knock, thump, bump, hit, smack, crack; informal bash, whack.
•verb **1** *he banged the table with his fist:* **hit,** strike, beat, thump, hammer, knock, rap, pound, thud, punch, bump, smack, crack, slap, slam; informal bash, whack,

sudden painful blow. • verb **1** hit or put down forcefully and noisily. **2** make a bang. • adverb Brit. informal exactly: *bang on time.*

banger noun Brit. informal **1** a sausage. **2** an old car. **3** a loud explosive firework.

Bangladeshi noun (plural **Bangladeshis**) a person from Bangladesh. • adjective relating to Bangladesh.

bangle noun a bracelet of rigid material worn loosely on the wrist.

banish verb **1** make someone leave a place as a punishment. **2** get rid of; drive away.
■ **banishment** noun.

banister or **bannister** noun **1** the upright posts and handrail at the side of a staircase. **2** a single upright post at the side of a staircase.

banjo noun (plural **banjos** or **banjoes**) a musical instrument like a guitar, with a circular body.

bank¹ noun **1** the land alongside a river or lake. **2** a long, high slope, mound, or mass. **3** a set of similar things grouped together in rows. • verb **1** form into a bank. **2** (of an aircraft) tilt sideways in making a turn.

bank² noun **1** an organization that makes loans and keeps customers' money for them. **2** a stock or supply of something. **3** a site or container where you can leave something for recycling. • verb **1** put money in a bank. **2** have an account at a bank. **3** (**bank on**) rely on.
□ **bank holiday** Brit. a public holiday, when banks are officially closed. **break the bank** informal cost more than you can afford.
■ **banker** noun **banking** noun.

bankable adjective certain to bring profit and success.

banknote noun a piece of paper money.

bankroll verb informal give money to.

• **noun** N. Amer. a roll of banknotes.

bankrupt adjective officially declared not to have the money to pay your debts. • noun a bankrupt person. • verb make someone bankrupt.
■ **bankruptcy** noun (plural **bankruptcies**).

banner noun a long strip of cloth with a slogan or design, hung up or carried on poles.

bannister ⇨ BANISTER.

banns plural noun an announcement of an intended marriage read out in a church.

banquet noun an elaborate formal meal for many people. • verb (**banquets, banqueting, banqueted**) attend a banquet.

banshee noun (in Irish legend) a female spirit whose wailing warns of a death.

bantam noun a kind of small chicken.

banter noun friendly teasing. • verb (**banters, bantering, bantered**) make friendly teasing remarks.

banyan noun an Indian fig tree with spreading branches from which roots grow downwards to the ground and form new trunks.

baobab /bay-oh-bab/ noun a short African tree with a very thick trunk.

bap noun Brit. a soft, round, flattish bread roll.

baptism noun the Christian ceremony of sprinkling a person with water or dipping them in it to show that they have entered the Church.
□ **baptism of fire** a difficult new experience.
■ **baptismal** adjective.

Baptist noun a member of a Christian group believing that only adults, not babies, should be baptized.

THESAURUS

clobber, clout, wallop. **2** *fireworks banged in the air:* thud, thump, bump, crack, crash, boom, pound, explode, detonate, burst, blow up.

banish verb **1** *he was banished for his crime:* exile, expel, deport, eject, repatriate, transport, extradite, evict, throw out, exclude, shut out, ban. **2** *he tried to banish his fear:* dispel, dismiss, disperse, scatter, dissipate, drive away, chase away, shut out.
OPPOSITES admit, cause, induce.

bank¹ noun **1** *the banks of Lake Michigan:* edge, shore, side, embankment, levee, margin, verge, brink. **2** *a grassy bank:* slope, rise, incline, gradient, ramp, mound, pile, heap, ridge, hillock, knoll, bar, shoal, mass, drift. **3** *a bank of switches:* array, row, line, tier, group, series.
• verb **1** *they banked up the earth:* pile up, heap up, stack up, amass. **2** *the aircraft*

banked: tilt, lean, tip, slant, incline, angle, list, camber, pitch.
OPPOSITES level, spread out, level out.

bank² noun store, reserve, stock, stockpile, supply, pool, fund, cache, hoard, deposit.
• verb *I banked the money:* deposit, pay in, save.
OPPOSITES withdraw.

bankrupt adjective insolvent, ruined; Brit. in administration, in receivership; informal bust, broke, belly up, wiped out.
OPPOSITES solvent.

banner noun **1** *students waved banners:* placard, sign, poster, notice. **2** *banners fluttered above the troops:* flag, standard, ensign, colour(s), pennant, banderole.

banquet noun feast, dinner; informal spread, blowout; Brit. informal nosh-up, slap-up meal.
OPPOSITES snack.

b

baptize or **baptise** verb (**baptizes, baptizing, baptized**) **1** perform the baptism ceremony on someone. **2** give someone a name or nickname.

bar noun **1** a long rigid piece of wood, metal, etc. **2** a counter, room, or place where alcohol is served. **3** something that stops or delays progress. **4** any of the short units into which a piece of music is divided. **5** (**the bar**) the place in a courtroom where an accused person stands during a trial. **6** (**the Bar**) the profession of barrister. **7** Brit. a metal strip added to a medal as an additional honour. • verb (**bars, barring, barred**) **1** fasten with a bar or bars. **2** forbid or prevent. • preposition except for. □ **bar code** a row of printed stripes identifying a product and its price, able to be read by a computer.

barb noun **1** the backward-pointing part of a fish hook, the tip of an arrow, etc. **2** a spiteful remark.

barbarian noun **1** (in ancient times) a person who did not belong to the Greek, Roman, or Christian civilizations. **2** a very uncivilized or cruel person.

barbaric adjective **1** savagely cruel. **2** not cultured or civilized.

barbarism noun **1** great cruelty. **2** an uncivilized or primitive state. ■ **barbarity** noun (plural **barbarities**).

barbarous adjective **1** very cruel. **2** uncivilized or uncultured.

barbecue noun **1** an outdoor meal at which food is grilled over a charcoal fire. **2** a grill used at a barbecue. • verb (**barbecues, barbecuing, barbecued**) cook food on a barbecue.

barbed adjective **1** having a barb or barbs. **2** (of a remark) spiteful. ■ **barbed wire** wire with clusters of short, sharp spikes along it.

barbel noun **1** a long, thin growth hanging from the mouth or snout of some fish. **2** a freshwater fish with barbels.

barbell noun a long metal bar with discs of different weights attached at each end, used for weightlifting.

barber noun a person whose job is cutting men's hair and shaving or trimming their beards.

barbican noun a double tower above a gate or drawbridge of a castle.

barbiturate noun a kind of drug used as a sedative.

bard noun old use a poet.

bare adjective **1** not wearing clothes. **2** without the usual covering or contents. **3** without detail; basic. **4** only just enough. • verb (**bares, baring, bared**) uncover or reveal. ■ **barely** adverb **bareness** noun.

bareback adverb & adjective on a horse without a saddle.

barefaced adjective done openly and without shame.

barefoot or **barefooted** adjective wearing nothing on your feet.

THESAURUS

baptize verb **1** *he was baptized as a baby:* christen. **2** *they were baptized into the church:* admit, initiate, enrol, recruit. **3** *he was baptized Enoch:* name, call, dub.

bar noun **1** *an iron bar:* rod, stick, pole, batten, shaft, rail, spar, strut, crosspiece, beam. **2** *a bar of chocolate:* block, slab, cake, tablet, wedge, ingot. **3** *your drinks are on the bar:* counter, table, buffet. **4** *she had a drink in a bar:* inn, tavern, hostelry; Brit. pub, public house; Brit. informal local, boozer. **5** *a bar to promotion:* obstacle, impediment, hindrance, obstruction, block, hurdle, barrier.
OPPOSITES aid.
• verb **1** *they have barred the door:* bolt, lock, fasten, secure, block, barricade, obstruct. **2** *I was barred from entering:* prohibit, debar, preclude, forbid, ban, exclude, obstruct, prevent, hinder, block.
OPPOSITES open, admit, allow.

barbarian noun **1** *the city was besieged by barbarians:* savage, heathen. **2** *you arrogant barbarian!* brute, beast, philistine, boor, yahoo, oaf, lout; Brit. informal yob.

barbaric adjective **1** *barbaric crimes:* cruel, brutal, barbarous, brutish, savage, vicious, wicked, ruthless, vile, inhuman. **2** *barbaric cultures:* uncultured, uncivilized, barbarian, philistine, boorish, loutish; Brit. informal yobbish.
OPPOSITES civilized.

bare adjective **1** *he was bare to the waist:* naked, unclothed, undressed, uncovered, stripped, with nothing on, nude; informal without a stitch on, in the altogether; Brit. informal starkers; Scottish informal in the scud; N. Amer. informal buck naked. **2** *the room was bare:* empty, unfurnished, clear, undecorated, unadorned. **3** *the bare facts:* basic, essential, fundamental, plain, straightforward, simple, unembellished, pure, stark, bald, cold, hard.
OPPOSITES dressed, furnished, decorated, embellished.

barely adverb hardly, scarcely, only just, narrowly, by the skin of your teeth, by a hair's breadth; informal by a whisker; Brit. informal at a push.
OPPOSITES easily.

bargain noun **1** an agreement made between people to do something for each other. **2** a thing sold at a low price. • verb **1** discuss the terms of an agreement. **2** (**bargain for** or **on**) expect. □ into the bargain as well.

☑ remember the second *a*: bar*gain*.

barge noun a long flat-bottomed boat for carrying goods on canals and rivers. • verb (**barges, barging, barged**) **1** move forcefully or roughly. **2** (**barge in**) burst in on someone rudely.

baritone noun a man's singing voice between tenor and bass.

barium noun a chemical element that is a soft white metal.

bark¹ noun the sharp sudden cry of a dog, fox, or seal. • verb **1** give a bark. **2** say a command or question suddenly or fiercely. **3** (**barking**) Brit. informal completely mad.

bark² noun the tough outer covering of the trunk and branches of a tree. • verb scrape the skin off your shin by accidentally hitting it.

barley noun a type of cereal plant with a bristly head. □ barley sugar an orange sweet made of boiled sugar.

barmaid noun a woman who serves drinks in a bar or pub.

barman noun (plural **barmen**) a man who serves drinks in a bar or pub.

bar mitzvah /bar **mits**-vuh/ noun a religious ceremony in which a Jewish boy aged 13 takes on the responsibilities of an adult.

barmy adjective (**barmier, barmiest**) Brit. informal mad.

barn noun a large farm building used for storing hay or grain or keeping livestock. □ barn dance a party with country dancing.

barnacle noun a small shellfish which fixes itself to things.

barnstorming adjective done in a very showy, energetic way.

barnyard noun N. Amer. a farmyard.

barometer noun an instrument that measures the pressure of the atmosphere, used to forecast the weather.

baron noun **1** a man belonging to the lowest rank of the British nobility. **2** (in the Middle Ages) a man who held lands or property granted to him by the king or queen or a lord. **3** a powerful person in business or industry. ■ baronial adjective.

baroness noun **1** the wife or widow of a baron. **2** a woman holding the rank of baron.

baronet noun a man who holds a title below that of baron.

baroque /buh-**rok**/ adjective in a highly decorated style of European architecture, art, and music popular during the 17th and 18th centuries.

barque /bark/ noun **1** a sailing ship with three masts. **2** literary a boat.

barrack verb Brit. shout loud insulting comments at a performer or speaker.

barracks noun a building or set of buildings for soldiers to live in.

barracuda /ba-ruh-**koo**-duh/ noun (plural **barracuda** or **barracudas**) a large predatory fish found in tropical seas.

barrage noun **1** a continuous attack by heavy guns. **2** an overwhelming number of questions or complaints. **3** a barrier placed across a river to control the water level.

barrel noun **1** a large cylindrical container bulging out in the middle and with flat ends. **2** a tube forming part of a gun, pen, etc. □ barrel organ a small organ that plays a tune when you turn a handle.

THESAURUS

bargain noun **1** *I'll make a bargain with you*: agreement, arrangement, understanding, deal, contract, pact. **2** *this binder is a bargain at £1.98*: good value; informal good buy, cheap buy, snip, steal, giveaway.
OPPOSITES rip-off.
• verb haggle, negotiate, discuss terms, deal, barter.
□ bargain for/on expect, anticipate, be prepared for, allow for, plan for, reckon with, envisage, foresee, predict, count on, reckon on; N. Amer. informal figure on. into the bargain in addition, as well, also, besides, on top, to boot, for good measure.

bark¹ verb **1** *the dog barked*: woof, yap. **2** *'Okay, outside!' he barked*: shout, snap,

bawl, yell, roar, bellow, thunder; informal holler.
OPPOSITES whisper.

bark² noun *the bark of a tree*: rind, skin, peel, covering.

barracks plural noun garrison, camp, encampment, depot, billet, quarters, fort, cantonment.

barrage noun **1** *an artillery barrage*: bombardment, gunfire, shelling, salvo, volley, fusillade; historical broadside. **2** *a barrage of criticism*: deluge, stream, storm, torrent, onslaught, flood, spate, tide, avalanche, hail, blaze. **3** *a barrage across the river*: dam, barrier, weir, dyke, embankment, wall.

barrel noun cask, keg, butt, vat, tun, drum,

barren adjective **1** (of land) not good enough to produce plants or crops. **2** unable to produce children or young animals. **3** bleak.

barrette /ba-**ret**/ noun a hairslide.

barricade noun a makeshift barrier used to block a road or entrance. •verb (**barricades, barricading, barricaded**) block or defend with a barricade.

barrier noun something that stops people entering a place or making progress.

barring preposition except for; if not for.

barrister noun Brit. a lawyer qualified to argue a case in court.

barrow¹ noun Brit. a two-wheeled cart pushed by hand and used by street traders.

barrow² noun a mound of earth built over a grave in ancient times.

bartender noun a person serving drinks at a bar.

barter verb (**barters, bartering, bartered**) exchange goods or services for other goods or services. •noun trade by bartering.

basalt /ba-**sawlt**/ noun a dark volcanic rock.

base¹ noun **1** the lowest or supporting part of something. **2** the main place where a person works or stays. **3** a centre of operations: *a military base.* **4** a main element to which others are added. **5** Chemistry a substance able to react with an acid to form a salt and water. **6** Baseball each

of the four points that you must reach in turn to score a run. •verb (**bases, basing, based**) **1** (**base something on**) use something as the foundation for something else. **2** station someone or something at a particular base.

base² adjective **1** bad or immoral. **2** old use of low social class.
□ **base metal** a common non-precious metal.

baseball noun a game played with a bat and ball on a diamond-shaped circuit of four bases, which a batsman must run around to score.
□ **baseball cap** a cotton cap with a large peak.

baseless adjective not based on fact; untrue.

baseline noun **1** a starting point for comparisons. **2** (in tennis, volleyball, etc.) the line marking each end of a court.

basement noun a room or floor below ground level.

bases plural of **base**¹ and **basis**.

bash informal verb hit hard and violently. •noun **1** a heavy blow. **2** a party. **3** Brit. an attempt.

bashful adjective shy and easily embarrassed.
■ **bashfully** adverb.

basic adjective **1** forming an essential foundation; fundamental. **2** of the simplest or lowest kind or standard. •noun (**basics**)

THESAURUS

hogshead, firkin.

barren adjective unproductive, infertile, unfruitful, sterile, arid, desert.
OPPOSITES fertile.

barricade noun *a barricade across the street:* barrier, roadblock, blockade, obstacle, obstruction.
•verb *they barricaded the building:* seal up, close up, block off, shut off/up, defend, protect, fortify, occupy.

barrier noun **1** fence, railing, barricade, hurdle, bar, blockade, roadblock. **2** *a barrier to international trade:* obstacle, obstruction, hurdle, stumbling block, bar, impediment, hindrance, curb.

barter verb **1** *they bartered grain for salt:* trade, swap, exchange, sell. **2** *you can barter for souvenirs:* haggle, bargain, negotiate, deal.

base¹ noun **1** *the base of the tower:* foundation, bottom, foot, support, stand, pedestal, plinth. **2** *the system uses existing technology as its base:* basis, foundation, bedrock, starting point, source, origin, root(s), core, key component. **3** *the troops returned to their base:* headquarters, camp, site, station, settlement, post, centre.
OPPOSITES top.
•verb **1** *he based his idea on a movie:* found,

build, construct, form, ground; (**be based on**) derive from, spring from, stem from, depend on. **2** *the company was based in London:* locate, situate, position, install, station, site.

base² adjective *base motives:* sordid, ignoble, low, mean, immoral, unscrupulous, unprincipled, dishonest, dishonourable, shameful.
OPPOSITES noble.

bashful adjective shy, reserved, diffident, inhibited, retiring, reticent, reluctant, shrinking, timid, nervous.
OPPOSITES bold, confident.

basic adjective **1** *basic human rights:* fundamental, essential, vital, primary, principal, cardinal, elementary, intrinsic, central, pivotal, critical, key, focal. **2** *basic cooking facilities:* plain, simple, unsophisticated, straightforward, adequate, spartan, stark, severe, austere, limited, meagre, rudimentary, patchy, sketchy, minimal, crude, makeshift; informal bog-standard.
OPPOSITES secondary, unimportant, elaborate.

basically adverb fundamentally, essentially, first and foremost, primarily, at heart, at bottom, intrinsically, inherently,

b

essential facts or principles.
- **basically** adverb.

basil noun a herb used in cooking.

basilica /buh-**zil**-i-kuh/ noun a large church or hall with two rows of columns inside and a curved end with a dome.

basilisk /**baz**-i-lisk/ noun a mythical reptile that could kill people by looking at or breathing on them.

basin noun 1 a large bowl or open container for holding liquid. 2 a circular valley. 3 an area drained by a river. 4 an enclosed area of water for mooring boats.

basis noun (plural **bases** /**bay**-seez/) 1 the foundation of a theory or process. 2 the reasons why something is done.

bask verb 1 lie in the sun for pleasure. 2 (**bask in**) take great pleasure in.

basket noun 1 a container for carrying things, made from strips of cane or wire. 2 a net fixed on a hoop, used as the goal in basketball.

basketball noun a team game in which goals are scored by throwing a ball through a hoop.

basmati rice /baz-**mah**-ti/ noun a kind of long-grain Indian rice.

Basque /bask, bahsk/ noun 1 a member of a people living in the western Pyrenees in France and Spain. 2 the language of the Basques.

bass¹ /bayss/ noun 1 the lowest adult male singing voice. 2 a bass guitar or double bass. 3 the deep, low-frequency part of sound.
- **bassist** noun.

bass² /bass/ noun (plural **bass** or **basses**) a fish related to the perch, used for food.

basset hound noun a breed of hunting dog with a long body, short legs, and long, drooping ears.

bassoon noun a large low-pitched woodwind instrument.
- **bassoonist** noun.

bastard noun 1 old use a person whose parents were not married. 2 informal a nasty person.

bastardize or **bastardise** verb (**bastardizes, bastardizing, bastardized**) make something less good by adding new elements.

baste verb (**bastes, basting, basted**) pour fat or juices over meat while it cooks.

bastion noun 1 a part of a fortified building that sticks out. 2 something that protects or preserves particular principles or activities.

bat¹ noun a piece of wood with a handle and a solid surface, used in sports for hitting the ball. • verb (**bats, batting, batted**) 1 (in sport) take the role of hitting rather than throwing the ball. 2 hit with the flat of your hand.
□ **off your own bat** Brit. informal of your own accord.

bat² noun 1 a flying animal that is active at night. 2 (**old bat**) informal an unpleasant woman.

bat³ verb (**bats, batting, batted**) flutter your eyelashes.

batch noun a quantity of goods produced or dispatched at one time.

bated adjective (**with bated breath**) in great suspense.

☑ bated, not baited.

bath noun 1 a large tub that you fill with water and sit or lie in to wash your body. 2 an act of washing yourself in a bath. 3 (also **baths**) Brit. a building containing a public swimming pool or washing facilities. • verb Brit. wash in a bath.

bathe verb (**bathes, bathing, bathed**) 1 wash by putting your body in water. 2 Brit. have a swim. 3 soak or wipe gently with liquid. • noun Brit. a swim.
- **bather** noun.

bathos /**bay**-thoss/ noun (in literature) a

THESAURUS

principally, chiefly, above all, mostly, mainly, on the whole, by and large; informal at the end of the day.

basics plural noun fundamentals, essentials, first principles, foundations, preliminaries, groundwork, essence, basis, core; informal nitty-gritty, brass tacks, nuts and bolts, ABC.

basin noun bowl, dish, pan.

basis noun 1 the basis of his method: foundation, support, base, reasoning, rationale, defence, reason, grounds, justification. 2 the basis of discussion: starting point, base, point of departure, beginning, premise, fundamental point/principle, cornerstone, core, heart.

3 on a part-time basis: footing, condition, status, position, arrangement.

bask verb laze, lie, lounge, relax, sprawl, loll.

bass adjective low, deep, resonant, sonorous, rumbling, booming, resounding.
OPPOSITES high.

batch noun group, quantity, lot, bunch, cluster, raft, set, collection, bundle, pack, consignment, shipment.

bathe verb 1 I bathed in the pool: swim, take a dip. 2 they bathed his wounds: clean, wash, rinse, wet, soak. 3 the room was bathed in light: flood, cover, envelop, fill, wash, pervade, suffuse.

b

change from a serious mood to something trivial.

bathroom noun **1** a room containing a bath and usually also a washbasin and toilet. **2** N. Amer. a room containing a toilet.

batik /ba-**teek**/ noun a method of producing coloured designs on cloth using wax to cover the areas not to be dyed.

baton noun **1** a thin stick used to conduct an orchestra or choir. **2** a short stick passed from runner to runner in a relay race. **3** a police officer's truncheon.

batsman noun (plural **batsmen**) a player who bats in cricket.

battalion noun an army unit forming part of a brigade.

batten noun a long wooden or metal strip used for strengthening or securing something.
◻ **batten down the hatches** prepare for a crisis.

batter¹ verb (**batters**, **battering**, **battered**) hit repeatedly with hard blows.

batter² noun a mixture of flour, egg, and milk or water, used for making pancakes or coating food before frying.

battery noun (plural **batteries**) **1** a device containing one or more electrical cells, used as a source of power. **2** an extensive series: *a battery of tests.* **3** Brit. a series of small cages for keeping chickens in artificial conditions. **4** Law an unlawful physical attack on another person.

battle noun **1** a prolonged fight between organized armed forces. **2** a long and difficult struggle or conflict. •verb (**battles**, **battling**, **battled**) fight or struggle with determination.

battleaxe noun **1** a large axe used in ancient warfare. **2** informal an aggressive older woman.

battledress noun clothing worn by soldiers for fighting.

battlefield noun the piece of ground where a battle is fought.

battlement noun a wall at the top of a castle with gaps for firing through.

battleship noun a heavily armoured warship with large guns.

batty adjective (**battier, battiest**) informal mad.

bauble noun a small, showy trinket or decoration.

baulk /bawlk/ (US spelling **balk**) verb **1** (**baulk at**) hesitate to accept an idea. **2** prevent from getting or doing something.

bauxite noun a clay-like rock from which aluminium is obtained.

bawdy adjective (**bawdier, bawdiest**) referring to sex in an amusing way.

bawl verb **1** shout out noisily. **2** cry noisily. •noun a loud shout.

bay¹ noun an area of sea and coast forming a broad curve.

bay² noun a Mediterranean shrub whose leaves are used in cookery.

bay³ noun **1** a window area that sticks out from a wall. **2** an area for a particular purpose: *a loading bay.*
◻ **bay window** a window sticking out from a wall.

bay⁴ adjective (of a horse) mainly reddish-brown in colour.

bay⁵ verb (of a dog) bark or howl loudly.
◻ **at bay** trapped or cornered. **hold** (or **keep**) **someone/thing at bay** prevent someone or something from approaching or having an effect.

bayonet noun a long blade fixed to a rifle for hand-to-hand fighting. •verb (**bayonets, bayoneting, bayoneted**) stab someone with a bayonet.

THESAURUS

baton noun **1** *the conductor's baton:* stick, rod, staff, wand. **2** *police batons:* truncheon, club, cudgel, stick, mace, shillelagh; N. Amer. nightstick, blackjack; Brit. informal cosh.

batter verb beat up, hit repeatedly, pummel, pound, rain blows on, buffet, belabour, thrash; informal knock about/around, lay into, do over.

battle noun **1** *he was killed in the battle:* fight, engagement, armed conflict, clash, struggle, skirmish, fray, war, campaign, crusade, warfare, combat, action, hostilities; informal scrap, dogfight, shoot-out. **2** *a legal battle:* conflict, clash, struggle, disagreement, argument, dispute. OPPOSITES peace.
•verb fight, combat, contend with, resist,

withstand, stand up to, confront, war, feud, struggle, strive, work.

battlefield noun battleground, field of battle, field of operations, combat zone, lines, front, theatre of war.

bawl verb **1** *'Come on!' he bawled:* shout, yell, roar, bellow, screech, scream, shriek, bark, thunder; informal yammer, holler. **2** *the children continued to bawl:* cry, sob, weep, wail, whine, howl; Scottish informal greet. OPPOSITES whisper.

bay¹ noun *ships were anchored in the bay:* cove, inlet, gulf, sound, bight, basin, fjord.

bay² noun *there was a bay let into the wall:* alcove, recess, niche, nook, opening, inglenook.

b

bazaar noun **1** a market in a Middle Eastern country. **2** a sale of goods to raise funds.

bazooka noun a short-range rocket launcher used against tanks.

BBC abbreviation British Broadcasting Corporation.

BC abbreviation before Christ (used to show that a date is before the traditional date of Jesus's birth).

! write BC after the numerals, as in *72 BC*.

be verb (singular present **am**; **are**; **is**; plural present **are**; 1st and 3rd singular past **was**; 2nd singular past and plural past **were**; present participle **being**; past participle **been**) **1** exist; be present. **2** happen. **3** have the specified state, nature, or role. **4** come, go, or visit. • auxiliary verb **1** used with a present participle to form continuous tenses. **2** used with a past participle to form the passive voice. **3** used to show something that is due to, may, or should happen.

beach noun a shore of sand or pebbles at the edge of the sea. • verb bring something on to a beach from the water.

beachcomber noun a person who searches beaches for valuable things.

beacon noun **1** a fire lit on the top of a hill as a signal. **2** a light acting as a signal for ships or aircraft.

bead noun **1** a small piece of glass, stone, etc., threaded with others to make a necklace. **2** a drop of a liquid on a surface. ■ **beaded** adjective.

beadle noun Brit. **1** an official of a church, college, etc. **2** historical a parish officer who dealt with minor offenders.

beady adjective (of a person's eyes) small, round, and observant.

beagle noun a small short-legged breed of hound.

beak noun a bird's hard projecting jaws.

beaker noun Brit. **1** a tall plastic cup. **2** a cylindrical glass container used in laboratories.

beam noun **1** a long piece of timber or metal used as a support in building. **2** a narrow length of timber for balancing on in gymnastics. **3** a ray of light or particles. **4** a wide, happy smile. **5** the width of a ship. • verb **1** transmit a radio signal. **2** shine brightly. **3** smile broadly.

bean noun **1** an edible seed growing in long pods on certain plants. **2** the hard seed of a coffee or cocoa plant. □ **full of beans** informal in high spirits.

beanbag noun **1** a small bag filled with dried beans and used in children's games. **2** a large cushion filled with polystyrene beads, used as a seat.

bear¹ verb (**bears**, **bearing**, **bore**; past participle **borne**) **1** carry. **2** have a particular quality or visible mark. **3** support a weight.

THESAURUS

bazaar noun **1** *a Turkish bazaar:* market, marketplace, souk, mart. **2** *the church bazaar:* fete, fair, fund-raiser, charity event; Brit. jumble sale, bring-and-buy sale, car boot sale; N. Amer. tag sale.

beach noun sands, seaside, seashore, coast; literary strand.
• verb *they beached the boat:* land, ground, strand, run ashore.

beacon noun signal, light, fire, danger signal, bonfire, lighthouse.

bead noun **1** *a string of beads:* ball, pellet, pill, globule, sphere, spheroid, orb, round; (**beads**) necklace, rosary, chaplet. **2** *beads of sweat:* droplet, drop, drip, blob, pearl, dot.

beaker noun cup, tumbler, glass, mug, drinking vessel.

beam noun **1** *an oak beam:* plank, timber, joist, rafter, lintel, spar, girder, support. **2** *a beam of light:* ray, shaft, stream, streak, flash, gleam, glint. **3** *the beam on her face:* grin, smile.
OPPOSITES frown.
• verb **1** *the signal is beamed out:* broadcast, transmit, relay, disseminate, direct, send, aim. **2** *the sun beamed down:* shine, radiate, glare, gleam. **3** *he beamed broadly:* grin, smile, smirk.
OPPOSITES frown.

bear verb **1** *she was bearing a box:* carry, bring, transport, move, convey, take, fetch; informal tote. **2** *the bag bore my name:* display, be marked with, show, carry, exhibit. **3** *will it bear his weight?* support, withstand, sustain, stand, take, carry, hold up, cope with, handle. **4** *she bore no grudge:* harbour, foster, entertain, cherish, nurse. **5** *I can't bear sport:* endure, tolerate, put up with, stand, abide, countenance, stomach; informal hack, swallow; Brit. informal stick, wear, be doing with; formal brook. **6** *she bore a son:* give birth to, bring forth, deliver, have, produce, spawn. **7** *a shrub that bears berries:* produce, yield, give, provide, supply.
□ **bear fruit yield results,** succeed, be effective, be profitable, work; informal pay off, do the trick. **bear something out** confirm, corroborate, substantiate, endorse, vindicate, give credence to, support, justify, prove. **bear up remain cheerful,** cope, manage, get by, muddle through. **bear with be patient with,** make allowances for, tolerate, put up with, endure.

b

4 (**bear yourself**) behave in a particular way. **5** tolerate. **6** give birth to a child. **7** (of a tree or plant) produce fruit or flowers. **8** turn and go in a particular direction.
□ **bear down on** approach someone in a determined or threatening way. **bear something in mind** remember and take something into account. **bear something out** support or confirm something. **bear up** remain cheerful in difficult circumstances. **bear with** be patient with.
■ **bearable** adjective **bearably** adverb **bearer** noun.

bear² noun a large, heavy animal with thick fur.

beard noun a growth of hair on a man's chin and lower cheeks. •**verb** boldly confront or challenge an important or powerful person.
■ **bearded** adjective.

bearing noun **1** a person's way of standing, moving, or behaving. **2** relevance. **3** (**bearings**) a part of a machine that allows one part to rotate or move in contact with another. **4** direction or position in relation to a fixed point. **5** (**your bearings**) awareness of where you are.

bearskin noun a tall black fur cap worn on ceremonial occasions by some British troops.

beast noun **1** an animal, especially a large or dangerous mammal. **2** a very cruel or wicked person.
□ **beast of burden** an animal used for carrying loads.

beastly adjective Brit. informal very unpleasant.
■ **beastliness** noun.

beat verb (**beats, beating, beat**; past participle **beaten**) **1** hit someone repeatedly and violently. **2** hit something repeatedly to flatten it or make a noise. **3** defeat or be better than. **4** informal baffle someone. **5** (of the heart) throb. **6** (of a bird) move its wings up and down. **7** stir cooking ingredients vigorously. •**noun 1** an act of beating. **2** the main rhythm, or a unit of rhythm, in music or poetry. **3** a brief pause. **4** an area patrolled by a police officer.
•**adjective** informal completely exhausted.
□ **beat about the bush** discuss something without coming to the point. **beat it** informal leave. **beat someone up** hit or kick someone repeatedly. **off the beaten track** isolated.

beatific /bee-uh-**tif**-ik/ adjective feeling or expressing blissful happiness.
■ **beatifically** adverb.

beatify /bi-**at**-i-fy/ verb (**beatifies, beatifying, beatified**) state officially that a dead person is very holy (the first step towards making them a saint).

beatitude /bi-**at**-i-tyood/ noun very great happiness or blessedness.

beatnik noun a young person in the 1950s and early 1960s who rejected conventional society.

THESAURUS

bearer noun **1** *a lantern-bearer:* carrier, porter. **2** *the bearer of bad news:* bringer, messenger, agent, conveyor, emissary.

bearing noun **1** *a man of military bearing:* posture, stance, carriage, gait; Brit. deportment. **2** *a rather regal bearing:* demeanour, manner, air, aspect, attitude, style. **3** *this has no bearing on the matter:* relevance, pertinence, connection, import, significance. **4** *a bearing of 015°:* direction, orientation, course, trajectory, heading, tack, path. **5** (**bearings**) orientation, sense of direction, whereabouts, location, position.
OPPOSITES irrelevance.

beast noun **1** *the beasts of the forest:* animal, creature, brute; N. Amer. informal critter. **2** *he is a cruel beast:* monster, brute, savage, barbarian, animal, swine, ogre, fiend, sadist, demon, devil.

beat verb **1** hit, strike, batter, thump, bang, hammer, knock, thrash, pound, pummel, slap, rain blows on, assault; informal wallop, belt, bash, whack, clout, clobber. **2** *her heart was still beating:* throb, pulse, pulsate, pump, palpitate, pound, thump, thud, hammer, drum. **3** *the eagle beat its wings:* flap, flutter, thrash, wave, vibrate. **4** *beat the cream into the mixture:* whisk, mix, blend, whip. **5** *the team they need to beat:* defeat, conquer, vanquish, trounce, rout, overpower, overcome; informal lick, thrash, whip. **6** *he beat the record:* exceed, surpass, better, improve on, eclipse, transcend, top, trump, cap.
•**noun 1** *the song has a good beat:* rhythm, pulse, metre, time, measure, cadence, stress, accent. **2** *the beat of hooves:* pounding, banging, thumping, thudding, hammering, crashing. **3** *the beat of her heart:* pulse, pulsation, vibration, throb, palpitation, reverberation, pounding, thump, thud, hammering, drumming. **4** *a policeman on his beat:* circuit, round, route, path.
□ **beat someone/something off repel**, fight off, fend off, stave off, repulse, drive away/back, push back. **beat someone up** assault, attack, mug; informal knock about/around, do over, work over, rough up; Brit. informal duff someone up; N. Amer. informal beat up on.

beau /boh/ noun (plural **beaux** or **beaus** /bohz, boh/) dated a young woman's boyfriend.

Beaujolais /**boh**-zhuh-lay/ noun a light red wine from the Beaujolais district of France.

beauteous adjective literary beautiful.

beautician noun a person whose job is to give beauty treatments.

beautiful adjective 1 very pleasing to the senses. 2 of a very high standard; excellent. ■ **beautifully** adverb.

> ☑ remember the u before the t: bea*u*tiful.

beautify verb (**beautifies**, **beautifying**, **beautified**) make someone or something look more attractive.

beauty noun (plural **beauties**) 1 the quality of being very pleasing to the senses. 2 a beautiful woman. 3 an excellent example of something. 4 an attractive feature or advantage.

beaver noun (plural **beaver** or **beavers**) a large rodent that lives partly in water. • verb (**beavers**, **beavering**, **beavered**) (**beaver away**) informal work hard.

bebop /**bee**-bop/ noun a type of jazz with complex rhythms.

becalmed adjective (of a sailing ship) unable to move because there is no wind.

because conjunction for the reason that; since.

béchamel /**bay**-shuh-mel/ noun a rich white sauce flavoured with herbs and other seasonings.

beck noun (**at someone's beck and call**) always having to be ready to obey someone's orders.

beckon verb 1 make a movement encouraging someone to approach or follow. 2 seem appealing.

become verb (**becomes**, **becoming**, **became**; past participle **become**) 1 begin to be. 2 turn into. 3 (**become of**) happen to. 4 suit or be appropriate to.

becquerel /**bek**-kuh-rel/ noun a unit of radioactivity.

bed noun 1 a piece of furniture for sleeping on. 2 an area of ground where flowers and shrubs are grown. 3 a flat base. • verb (**beds**, **bedding**, **bedded**) 1 (**bed down**) sleep in a place where you do not usually sleep. 2 (**bed something in**) fix something firmly.

bedclothes plural noun coverings for a bed, such as sheets and blankets.

bedding noun 1 bedclothes. 2 straw for animals to sleep on.

bedevil verb (**bedevils**, **bedevilling**, **bedevilled**; US spelling **bedevils**, **bedeviling**, **bedeviled**) cause continual trouble to.

bedlam noun a scene of great confusion and noise.

Bedouin /**bed**-oo-in/ noun (plural **Bedouin**) an Arab living as a nomad in the desert.

bedpan noun a container used as a toilet by a bedridden patient.

bedraggled adjective untidy.

THESAURUS

beautiful adjective attractive, pretty, handsome, good-looking, fetching, lovely, charming, graceful, elegant, appealing, winsome, ravishing, gorgeous, stunning, glamorous; Scottish & N. English bonny; informal tasty, knockout, drop-dead gorgeous; Brit. informal smashing; N. Amer. informal cute, foxy; Austral./NZ informal beaut, spunky. OPPOSITES ugly.

beauty noun 1 attractiveness, prettiness, good looks, loveliness, appeal, winsomeness, charm, grace, elegance, exquisiteness, glamour; Scottish & N. English bonniness. 2 *she is a beauty:* belle, vision, goddess, picture, Venus; informal babe, looker, lovely, stunner, knockout, bombshell, bit of all right. OPPOSITES ugliness, hag, boot.

because conjunction since, as, seeing that, in view of the fact that, in that. □ **because of** on account of, as a result of, as a consequence of, owing to, due to, thanks to, by virtue of; formal by reason of.

beckon verb 1 *the guard beckoned to Benny:* gesture, signal, wave, gesticulate, motion. 2 *the countryside beckons you:* entice, invite, tempt, lure, charm, attract, draw, call.

become verb 1 *she became rich:* grow, get, turn, come to be, get to be. 2 *he became a tyrant:* turn into, change into, transform into, be converted into. 3 *he became Foreign Secretary:* be appointed, be assigned as, be nominated, be elected. 4 *the dress becomes her:* suit, flatter, look good on, set off; informal do something for. □ **become of** happen to, be the fate of, be the lot of, overtake.

becoming adjective flattering, fetching, attractive, pretty, elegant, handsome, well chosen, stylish, fashionable, tasteful.

bed noun 1 couch, berth, billet, cot; informal the sack. 2 *a flower bed:* patch, plot, border, strip. 3 *built on a bed of stones:* base, foundation, footing, support, basis. • verb *the tiles are bedded in mortar:* embed, set, fix, insert, inlay, implant, bury, plant. □ **go to bed** retire; informal hit the sack, hit the hay, turn in.

bedraggled adjective dishevelled, disordered, untidy, unkempt, tousled;

b

bedridden adjective unable to get out of bed because of illness or old age.

bedrock noun **1** a layer of solid rock under soil. **2** the central principles on which something is based.

bedroom noun a room for sleeping in.

bedsit or **bedsitter** noun Brit. a rented room consisting of a combined bedroom and living room, with cooking facilities.

bedsore noun a sore caused by lying in bed in one position for a long time.

bedspread noun a decorative cloth used to cover a bed.

bedstead noun the framework of a bed.

bee noun a winged insect which collects nectar and pollen from flowers and makes wax and honey.

beech noun a large tree with grey bark and pale wood.

beef noun the flesh of a cow, bull, or ox, used as food. • verb (**beef something up**) informal make something stronger or larger.

beefburger noun a fried or grilled cake of minced beef eaten in a bun.

beefy adjective (**beefier, beefiest**) informal muscular or strong.

beehive noun a structure in which bees are kept.

beeline noun (**make a beeline for**) hurry straight to.

Beelzebub /bi-el-zi-bub/ noun the Devil.

been past participle of **BE**.

beep noun a short, high-pitched sound made by electronic equipment or the horn of a vehicle. • verb produce a beep.

beer noun an alcoholic drink made from fermented malt flavoured with hops.

beeswax noun wax produced by bees to make honeycombs, used for wood polishes and candles.

beet noun a plant with a fleshy root, grown

as food and for making into sugar.

beetle noun an insect with hard, shiny covers over its wings.

beetroot noun Brit. the edible dark-red root of a kind of beet.

befall verb (**befalls, befalling, befell**; past participle **befallen**) literary (of something bad) happen to someone.

befit verb (**befits, befitting, befitted**) be appropriate for.
■ **befitting** adjective.

before preposition, conjunction, & adverb **1** during the time preceding. **2** in front of. **3** rather than.

beforehand adverb in advance.

befriend verb become a friend to.

befuddled adjective confused.

beg verb (**begs, begging, begged**) **1** humbly ask someone for something. **2** ask for food or money as charity.
□ **beg the question 1** (of a fact or action) invite a question or point that has not been dealt with. **2** assume that something is true without discussing it. **go begging** be available because other people do not want it.

beget /bi-get/ verb (**begets, begetting, begot** or **begat**; past participle **begotten**) old use **1** cause something. **2** become the father of a child.

beggar noun **1** a person who lives by begging for food or money. **2** informal a particular type of person: *lucky beggar!*
□ **beggar belief** be too extraordinary to be believed.
■ **beggarly** adjective.

begin verb (**begins, beginning, began**; past participle **begun**) **1** carry out or experience

---

N. Amer. informal mussed.
OPPOSITES neat.

before preposition **1** *he dressed up before going out:* prior to, previous to, earlier than, preparatory to, in advance of, ahead of, pre-.... **2** *he appeared before the judge:* in front of, in the presence of. **3** *death before dishonour:* in preference to, rather than, sooner than.
OPPOSITES after.
• adverb previously, before now/then, until now/then, up to now/then, earlier, in the past, formerly, hitherto.
OPPOSITES afterwards, later.

beforehand adverb in advance, in readiness, ahead of time, before, earlier (on), previously, already, sooner.
OPPOSITES afterwards.

beg verb **1** *he begged on the streets:* ask for money, seek charity; informal sponge, cadge, scrounge, bum. **2** *we begged for mercy:* plead for, request, ask for, appeal for, call for, sue for, solicit, seek. **3** *he begged her not to go:* implore, entreat, plead with, appeal to, pray to, call on, petition; literary beseech.

beggar noun tramp, vagrant, vagabond, mendicant; N. Amer. hobo; informal scrounger, sponger, cadger, freeloader; Brit. informal dosser; N. Amer. informal bum; Austral./NZ informal bagman.

begin verb **1** *we began work:* start, commence, set about, go about, embark on, launch into, get down to, take up, initiate, set in motion, get going, get off the ground, lead off, institute, inaugurate,

the first part of an action or activity.
2 come into being. **3** have a particular
starting point. **4** (**begin on**) set to work on.
■ **beginner** noun **beginning** noun.

begonia /bi-**goh**-ni-uh/ noun a plant with
brightly coloured flowers.

begrudge verb **1** feel envious that someone
possesses something. **2** give something
resentfully.

beguile verb charm or trick.

behalf noun (**on behalf of** or **on someone's
behalf**) **1** in the interests of a particular
person, group, or principle. **2** as a
representative of.

behave verb **1** act in a certain way. **2** (also
behave yourself) act in a polite or proper
way.

behaved adjective acting in a certain way: *a
well-behaved child.*

behaviour (US spelling **behavior**) noun the
way in which someone or something
behaves.
■ **behavioural** adjective.

behead verb execute someone by cutting
off their head.

behemoth /bi-**hee**-moth/ noun a huge
creature, or a very large organization.

behest /bi-**hest**/ noun (**at someone's behest**)
in response to someone's order.

behind preposition & adverb **1** at or to the
back or far side of. **2** further back than
other members of a group. **3** in support of.
4 responsible for an event or plan. **5** late in
doing something.

behold verb (**beholds, beholding, beheld**) old
use see or look at.

beholden adjective (**beholden to**) owing
something to someone because they have
done you a favour.

behove verb (**it behoves someone to do**)
formal it is right or appropriate for someone
to do.

beige noun a pale sandy colour.

being noun **1** existence. **2** the nature of a
person. **3** a living creature.

THESAURUS

open; informal get cracking on, kick off.
2 *when did the illness begin?* appear, arise,
become apparent, spring up, crop up, turn
up, come into existence, originate, start,
commence, develop.
OPPOSITES finish, end, disappear.

beginner noun novice, learner, starter,
(raw) recruit, newcomer, tyro, fresher,
probationer; N. Amer. tenderfoot; informal
rookie, new kid (on the block), newie;
N. Amer. informal greenhorn.
OPPOSITES expert, veteran.

beginning noun **1** *the beginning of
socialism:* start, commencement, creation,
birth, inception, conception, origination,
origin, genesis, emergence, rise, dawn,
launch, onset, outset, day one; informal kick-
off. **2** *the beginning of the article:* opening,
start, commencement, introduction, first
part, preamble.
OPPOSITES end, conclusion.

behalf noun
□ **on behalf of/on someone's behalf 1** *I am
writing on behalf of my client:* **as a
representative of,** as a spokesperson for,
for, in the name of, in place of, on the
authority of. **2** *a campaign on behalf of
cycling:* **in the interests of,** in support of,
for, for the benefit of, for the good of, for
the sake of.

behave verb **1** *she behaved badly:* act,
conduct yourself, acquit yourself. **2** *the
children behaved themselves:* act correctly,
be good, be well behaved, conduct yourself
well.
OPPOSITES misbehave.

behaviour noun **1** *his behaviour was
inexcusable:* conduct, actions, doings,

manners, ways, deportment, bearing,
etiquette. **2** *the behaviour of these
organisms:* functioning, action,
performance, operation, working, reaction,
response.

behind preposition **1** *he hid behind a tree:* at
the back/rear of, beyond, on the far/other
side of; N. Amer. in back of. **2** *a guard ran
behind him:* after, following, at the
back/rear of, hard on the heels of, in the
wake of. **3** *you are behind the rest of the
class:* less advanced than, slower than,
weaker than. **4** *he was behind the bombings:*
responsible for, at the bottom of, the
cause of, the perpetrator of, the organizer
of, to blame for, guilty of. **5** *they have the
nation behind them:* supporting, backing,
for, on the side of, in agreement with;
informal rooting for.
OPPOSITES in front of, ahead of, against.
• adverb **1** *a man followed behind:* after,
afterwards, at the back/end, in the rear. **2** *I
looked behind:* over your shoulder, towards
the back/rear, backwards. **3** *we're behind, so
don't stop:* running late, behind schedule,
behindhand, not on time. **4** *he was behind
with his subscription:* in arrears, overdue,
late, unpunctual, behindhand.
OPPOSITES in front, ahead, in advance.

being noun **1** *she is warmed by his very
being:* existence, living, life, reality,
lifeblood, vital force. **2** *God is alive in the
being of man:* soul, spirit, nature, essence,
psyche, heart, bosom, breast. **3** *an
enlightened being:* creature, life form,
organism, living thing, individual, person,
human.

b

bejewelled (US spelling **bejeweled**) **adjective** decorated with jewels.

belated adjective coming late or too late. ■ **belatedly** adverb.

belay /bi-**lay**/ verb fix a rope round a rock, pin, or other object to secure it.

belch verb **1** noisily expel wind from the stomach through the mouth. **2** give out smoke or flames with great force. •noun an act of belching.

beleaguered adjective **1** in difficulties. **2** under siege.

belfry noun (plural **belfries**) the place in a bell tower or steeple which contains the bells.

Belgian noun a person from Belgium. •adjective relating to Belgium.

belie verb (**belies, belying, belied**) **1** fail to give a true idea of. **2** show that something is not true.

belief noun **1** a feeling that something exists or is true. **2** a firmly held opinion. **3** (**belief in**) trust or confidence in. **4** religious faith.

believe verb (**believes, believing, believed**) **1** accept that something is true or someone is telling the truth. **2** (**believe in**) have faith that something is true or exists. **3** think or suppose. **4** have a religious faith. ■ **believable** adjective **believer** noun.

☑ *i* before e except after c: bel*ie*ve.

belittle verb (**belittles, belittling, belittled**) dismiss as unimportant.

Belizean or **Belizian** /be-**leez**-i-uhn/ noun a person from Belize, a country in Central America. •adjective relating to Belize.

bell noun **1** a deep metal cup held upside down, that sounds a clear musical note when struck. **2** a device that buzzes or rings to give a signal. □ ring a bell informal sound vaguely familiar.

belladonna noun **1** deadly nightshade. **2** a drug made from deadly nightshade.

belle noun a beautiful woman.

bellicose adjective aggressive and ready to fight.

belligerence noun aggressive or warlike behaviour.

belligerent adjective **1** hostile and aggressive. **2** taking part in a war or conflict. ■ **belligerently** adverb.

bellow verb **1** give a deep roar of pain or anger. **2** shout or sing very loudly. •noun a deep shout or noise.

bellows plural noun a device consisting of a bag with two handles, used for blowing air into a fire.

belly noun (plural **bellies**) **1** the front part of the body below the ribs, containing the stomach and bowels. **2** a person's stomach.

bellyache informal noun a stomach pain. •verb

belated adjective late, overdue, behindhand, delayed, tardy, unpunctual. OPPOSITES early, punctual.

beleaguered adjective **1** *the beleaguered garrison:* besieged, blockaded, surrounded, encircled, hemmed in, under attack. **2** *a beleaguered government:* troubled, hard-pressed, in difficulties, under pressure, in a tight corner; informal up against it.

belief noun **1** *it's my belief that age is irrelevant:* opinion, view, conviction, judgement, thinking, idea, theory. **2** *belief in God:* faith, trust, reliance, confidence, credence. **3** *traditional beliefs:* ideology, principle, ethic, tenet, doctrine, teaching, dogma, creed, credo. OPPOSITES disbelief, doubt.

believe verb **1** *I don't believe you:* trust, have confidence in, consider honest, consider truthful. **2** *do you believe that story?* accept, be convinced by, give credence to, credit, trust, put confidence in; informal swallow, buy, go for. **3** *I believe he worked for you:* think, be of the opinion that, have an idea that, imagine, assume, presume, take it, understand, gather; informal reckon, figure.
OPPOSITES doubt.

□ believe in **have faith in,** trust in, have every confidence in, cling to, set (great) store by, value, be convinced by, be persuaded by; informal swear by, rate.

believer noun disciple, follower, supporter, adherent, devotee, upholder, worshipper. OPPOSITES infidel, sceptic.

belittle verb disparage, denigrate, run down, deprecate, play down, trivialize, minimize; informal do down, pooh-pooh. OPPOSITES praise, magnify.

belligerent adjective **1** *a belligerent stare:* hostile, aggressive, threatening, antagonistic, pugnacious, bellicose, truculent, confrontational, contentious, militant, combative; informal spoiling for a fight; Brit. informal stroppy, bolshie; N. Amer. informal scrappy. **2** *the belligerent states:* warring, combatant, fighting, battling. OPPOSITES peaceable, neutral.

bellow verb roar, shout, bawl, thunder, boom, bark, yell, shriek, howl, scream; informal holler. OPPOSITES whisper.

belly noun stomach, abdomen, paunch, middle, midriff, girth; informal tummy, gut, insides.

b

complain noisily or often.

bellyflop noun informal a dive into water in which you land flat on your front.

belong verb **1** (**belong to**) be the property of. **2** (**belong to**) be a member of. **3** be rightly put into a particular position or class. **4** feel at ease in a particular place or situation.

belongings plural noun a person's movable possessions.

beloved adjective dearly loved.

below preposition & adverb **1** at a lower level than. **2** (in printed writing) mentioned further down.

belt noun **1** a strip of leather or fabric worn round the waist. **2** a continuous band in machinery that connects two wheels. **3** a strip or encircling area. • verb **1** fasten with a belt. **2** hit very hard. **3** (**belt something out**) informal sing or play something loudly. **4** (**belt up**) Brit. informal be quiet.
□ **below the belt** against the rules; unfair.

belying present participle of BELIE.

bemoan verb express sadness or regret about something.

bemused adjective confused or bewildered. ■ bemusement noun.

bench noun **1** a long seat for more than one person. **2** a long table for working at in a workshop or laboratory. **3** (**the bench**) the office of judge or magistrate. **4** (**the bench**) a seat at the side of a sports field for coaches and reserve players.

benchmark noun a standard against which things may be compared.

bend verb (**bends, bending, bent**) **1** change from being straight; make or become curved or angled. **2** lean or curve the body downwards. **3** change a rule to suit yourself. • noun **1** a place where something bends; a curve or turn. **2** (**the bends**) decompression sickness.
□ **round the bend** informal mad.

beneath preposition & adverb extending or directly underneath. • preposition of lower status or worth than.

THESAURUS

belong verb **1** *the house belongs to his mother:* be owned by, be the property of, be held by, be in the hands of. **2** *I belong to a union:* be a member of, be in, be affiliated to, be allied to, be associated with. **3** *the garden belongs to the flat:* be part of, be attached to, go with. **4** *she doesn't belong here:* fit in, be suited to; informal go, click.

belongings plural noun possessions, effects, worldly goods, chattels, property; informal gear, tackle, kit, things, stuff, bits and pieces; Brit. informal clobber.

beloved adjective *her beloved brother:* darling, dear, precious, adored, cherished, treasured, prized, valued, idolized.
OPPOSITES hated.
• noun *he watched his beloved:* sweetheart, love, darling, dearest, lover, girlfriend, boyfriend; informal steady, baby, angel, honey, pet.

below preposition **1** *the water rushed below them:* beneath, under, underneath, lower than. **2** *the sum is below average:* less than, lower than, under, not as much as, smaller than. **3** *a captain is below a major:* lower than, under, inferior to, subordinate to.
OPPOSITES above, over, more than.
• adverb **1** *I could see what was happening below:* further down, lower down, underneath, beneath. **2** *the statements below:* underneath, following, further on, at a later point.
OPPOSITES above.

belt noun **1** sash, girdle, band, strap, cummerbund. **2** *the commuter belt:* region, strip, stretch, zone, area, district, sector, territory.

bemused adjective bewildered, confused, puzzled, perplexed, baffled, mystified, nonplussed, dumbfounded, at sea, at a loss; informal flummoxed, bamboozled, fazed.

bench noun **1** *he sat on a bench:* seat, form, pew, stall, settle. **2** *a laboratory bench:* workbench, worktop, counter.

benchmark noun standard, point of reference, guide, guideline, norm, touchstone, yardstick, barometer, model, gauge, criterion, specification.

bend verb **1** *the frames can be bent to fit your face:* curve, crook, flex, angle, hook, bow, arch, buckle, warp, contort, distort, deform, twist. **2** *the highway bent to the left:* turn, curve, incline, swing, veer, fork, change course, curl, loop. **3** *he bent down to tie his shoe:* stoop, bow, crouch, hunch, lean down/over.
OPPOSITES straighten.
• noun *a bend in the road:* curve, turn, corner, kink, angle, arc, twist.
OPPOSITES straight.

beneath preposition **1** *we sat beneath the trees:* under, underneath, below, at the foot of, at the bottom of, lower than. **2** *the rank beneath theirs:* inferior to, below, lower than, subordinate to. **3** *such an attitude was beneath her:* unworthy of, unbecoming to, degrading to.
OPPOSITES above.
• adverb *sand with rock beneath:* underneath, below, further down, lower down.
OPPOSITES above.

benediction noun the speaking of a blessing.

benefactor noun a person who gives money or other help.

benefice /ben-i-fiss/ noun an arrangement by which a Christian priest is paid and given accommodation for being in charge of a parish.

beneficent /bi-nef-i-suhnt/ adjective doing or resulting in good.
■ **beneficence** noun.

beneficial adjective having a good effect.
■ **beneficially** adverb.

beneficiary noun (plural **beneficiaries**) a person who benefits from something, especially a trust or will.

benefit noun 1 advantage or profit. 2 payment made by the state to someone in need: *unemployment benefit*. 3 a public performance to raise money for a charity. • verb (**benefits**, **benefiting**, **benefited** or **benefitting**, **benefitted**) 1 get an advantage; profit. 2 bring advantage to.

☑ there is usually a single *t* in **benefited** and **benefiting**; the spelling with a double *t* is commoner in American English.

benevolent adjective 1 well meaning and kindly. 2 (of an organization) charitable rather than profit-making.

■ **benevolence** noun.

Bengali /ben-**gaw**-li/ noun (plural **Bengalis**) 1 a person from Bengal in the Indian subcontinent. 2 the language of Bangladesh and West Bengal. • adjective relating to Bengal.

benighted adjective ignorant or primitive.

benign /bi-**nyn**/ adjective 1 cheerful and kindly. 2 favourable; not harmful. 3 (of a tumour) not malignant.

Beninese /ben-i-**neez**/ noun a person from Benin, a country in West Africa. • adjective relating to Benin.

bent past and past participle of BEND. • adjective 1 Brit. informal dishonest or corrupt. 2 (**bent on**) determined to do. • noun a natural talent.

benzene noun a liquid present in coal tar and petroleum.

bequeath verb 1 leave property to someone by a will. 2 hand down or pass on.

bequest noun 1 something that is left to someone by a will. 2 the action of bequeathing.

berate verb (**berates**, **berating**, **berated**) angrily scold or criticize.

bereave verb (**be bereaved**) be deprived of a close relation or friend through their death.
■ **bereavement** noun.

benefactor noun patron, supporter, backer, sponsor, donor, contributor, subscriber; informal angel.

beneficial adjective advantageous, favourable, helpful, useful, of assistance, valuable, profitable, rewarding, gainful.
OPPOSITES disadvantageous.

beneficiary noun recipient, payee, heir, heiress, inheritor.

benefit noun 1 *for the benefit of others*: good, sake, welfare, well-being, advantage, comfort, ease, convenience, help, aid, assistance, service. 2 *the benefits of working for a large firm*: advantage, profit, plus point, boon, blessing, reward; informal perk. 3 *state benefit*: social security payment, welfare, charity; informal the dole; Scottish informal the broo.
OPPOSITES detriment, disadvantage.
• verb 1 *the deal benefited them both*: be advantageous to, be beneficial to, profit, do good to, be of service to, serve, be useful to, be helpful to, aid. 2 *they may benefit from drugs*: profit, gain, reap reward, make the most of, exploit, turn to your advantage, put to good use.
OPPOSITES disadvantage, harm, suffer.

benevolent adjective kind, kindly, kind-hearted, good-natured, compassionate, caring, altruistic, humanitarian,

philanthropic.
OPPOSITES unkind.

benign adjective 1 *a benign grandfatherly role*: kindly, kind, warm-hearted, good-natured, friendly, genial, tender-hearted, gentle, sympathetic, compassionate, caring, well disposed, benevolent. 2 *a benign climate*: mild, temperate, gentle, balmy, soft, pleasant, favourable, healthy. 3 (Medicine) *a benign tumour*: harmless, non-malignant, non-cancerous.
OPPOSITES unkind, unhealthy, hostile, malignant.

bent adjective 1 twisted, crooked, warped, contorted, deformed, misshapen, out of shape, bowed, arched, curved, angled, hooked, kinked; N. Amer. informal pretzeled. 2 *a mob bent on violence*: intent, determined, set, insistent, resolved.
OPPOSITES straight.
• noun *an artistic bent*: inclination, leaning, tendency, talent, gift, flair, aptitude, facility, skill.

bequeath verb leave, will, hand down, pass on, entrust, make over, grant, transfer, give, bestow on, confer on.

bequest noun legacy, estate, inheritance, endowment, settlement.

bereavement noun death in the family, loss, passing (away), demise.

b

bereft adjective **1** (**bereft of**) deprived of; without. **2** lonely and abandoned.

beret /be-ray/ noun a flat round cap of felt or cloth.

bergamot /ber-guh-mot/ noun an oily substance found in some oranges, used as a flavouring.

beriberi noun a disease caused by a lack of vitamin B₁.

berk noun Brit. informal a stupid person.

berkelium noun a radioactive metallic element.

berry noun (plural **berries**) a small, juicy round fruit without a stone.

berserk adjective out of control; wild and frenzied.

berth noun **1** a place in a harbour where a boat can stay. **2** a bunk on a ship or train. • verb moor a boat in a berth.
□ **give a wide berth to** stay well away from.

beryl noun a transparent pale green, blue, or yellow gemstone.

beryllium /buh-ril-li-uhm/ noun a hard, grey, lightweight metallic element.

beseech verb (**beseeches**, **beseeching**, **besought** or **beseeched**) ask in a pleading way.

beset verb (**besets**, **besetting**, **beset**) continually trouble or worry.

beside preposition **1** at the side of. **2** compared with. **3** (also **besides**) as well as. • adverb (**besides**) as well.
□ **beside yourself** frantic with worry.

besiege verb (**besieges**, **besieging**, **besieged**) **1** surround a place so that no one can come or go. **2** overwhelm someone with requests or complaints.

> ☑ remember, *i* before *e* except after *c*: bes*i*ege.

besmirch verb damage someone's reputation.

besom /bee-zuhm/ noun a broom made of twigs tied round a stick.

besotted adjective so much in love that you stop acting sensibly.

bespoke adjective Brit. made to a customer's requirements.

best adjective **1** of the highest quality. **2** most suitable or sensible. • adverb **1** to the highest degree; most. **2** most suitably or sensibly. • noun (**the best**) something which is of the highest quality.
□ **best man** a male friend or relative who helps a bridegroom at his wedding. **best-seller** a book or other product that sells in very large numbers. **make the best of** get what advantage you can from.

THESAURUS

berserk adjective mad, crazy, insane, out of your mind, hysterical, frenzied, crazed, demented, maniacal, manic, frantic, raving, wild, out of control, amok, on the rampage; informal off your head, off the deep end, ape, bananas, bonkers; Brit. informal spare; N. Amer. informal postal.

berth noun **1** *a 4-berth cabin:* bunk, bed, cot, couch, hammock. **2** *the vessel left its berth:* mooring, dock, pier, jetty, quay.
• verb *the ship berthed in London:* dock, moor, land, tie up, make fast.

beside preposition alongside, by/at the side of, next to, parallel to, abreast of, adjacent to, next door to, neighbouring.
□ **beside yourself** distraught, overcome, out of your mind, frantic, desperate, distracted, at your wits' end, frenzied, hysterical.

besides preposition *who did you ask besides Mary?* in addition to, as well as, over and above, on top of, apart from, other than, aside from, not counting, excluding, leaving aside; N. Amer. informal outside of.
• adverb **1** *there's a lot more besides:* in addition, as well, too, also, into the bargain, on top of that, to boot. **2** *besides, he's a man:* furthermore, moreover, further; informal what's more.

besiege verb **1** *the army besieged Leith:* lay siege to, beleaguer, blockade. **2** *he was*

besieged by fans: surround, mob, harass, pester, badger. **3** *we were besieged with requests:* overwhelm, bombard, inundate, deluge, flood, swamp, snow under.

best adjective **1** *the best hotel in Paris:* finest, premier, greatest, top, foremost, leading, pre-eminent, supreme, superlative, unrivalled, second to none, without equal, unsurpassed, unparalleled, unbeatable, optimum, ultimate, incomparable, record-breaking; informal star, number-one, a cut above the rest, top-drawer. **2** *do whatever you think best:* most advantageous, most useful, most suitable, most fitting, most appropriate, most advisable.
OPPOSITES worst.
• adverb **1** *the best-dressed man:* to the highest standard, in the best way. **2** *pizza was the food he liked best:* most, to the highest/greatest degree. **3** *this is best done at home:* most appropriately, most suitably, most fittingly, most usefully, most advantageously, most sensibly, most prudently, most wisely.
OPPOSITES worst, least.
• noun *only the best will do:* finest, choicest, top, cream, choice, prime, elite, crème de la crème, flower, jewel in the crown; informal tops, pick of the bunch.
OPPOSITES worst.

bestial adjective savagely cruel.

bestiality noun **1** savagely cruel behaviour. **2** sex between a person and an animal.

bestir verb (**bestirs, bestirring, bestirred**) (**bestir yourself**) make yourself start to do something

bestow verb give an honour, right, or gift.

bestride verb (**bestrides, bestriding, bestrode**; past participle **bestridden**) put a leg on either side of.

bet verb (**bets, betting, bet** or **betted**) **1** risk money against someone else's on the basis of the outcome of an unpredictable event such as a race. **2** informal feel sure. ● noun an act of betting or the money betted.

beta /bee-tuh/ noun the second letter of the Greek alphabet (**B, β**).
□ **beta blocker** a drug used to treat high blood pressure and angina.

bête noire /bet nwar/ noun (plural **bêtes noires** /bet nwar/) a person or thing that you greatly dislike.

betide verb (**betide, betiding, betided**) literary happen or happen to.

betimes adverb in good time; early.

betoken verb be a sign of.

betray verb **1** harm someone or something by giving information to an enemy. **2** be disloyal to someone. **3** reveal a secret without meaning to.
■ **betrayal** noun.

betrothed adjective engaged to be married.
■ **betrothal** noun.

better adjective **1** of a higher standard or quality. **2** partly or fully recovered from illness or injury. ● adverb **1** in a more satisfactory way. **2** to a greater degree; more. ● noun (**your betters**) people who have greater ability or are more important than you. ● verb **1** improve on something. **2** (**better yourself**) improve your social position.
□ **better off** having more money or being in a more desirable situation. **get the better of** defeat.

betterment noun improvement.

between preposition & adverb **1** at, into, or across the space separating two things. **2** in the period separating two points in time. **3** indicating a connection or relationship. **4** shared by two or more people or things.

betwixt preposition & adverb old use between.

bevel noun an edge cut at an angle in wood or glass. ● verb (**bevels, bevelling, bevelled**; US spelling **bevels, beveling, beveled**) cut the edge of wood or glass at an angle.

bestow verb confer on, grant, accord, afford, endow someone with, present, award, give, donate, entrust with, vouchsafe.

bet verb **1** *he bet £10 on the favourite:* wager, gamble, stake, risk, venture, hazard, chance; Brit. informal punt, have a flutter. **2** (informal) *I bet it was your idea:* be certain, be sure, be convinced, be confident, expect, predict, guess.
● noun **1** *a £20 bet:* wager, gamble, stake, ante; Brit. informal punt, flutter. **2** (informal) *your best bet is to go early:* option, choice, alternative, course of action, plan.

betray verb **1** *he betrayed his own brother:* be disloyal to, be unfaithful to, break faith with, play someone false, inform on/against, give away, denounce, sell out, stab in the back; informal split on, rat on, stitch up, do the dirty on, sell down the river; Brit. informal grass on, shop, sneak on; N. Amer. informal rat out, drop a/the dime on, finger; Austral./NZ informal dob in, point the bone at. **2** *he betrayed a secret:* reveal, disclose, divulge, tell, give away, leak, bring out into the open.
OPPOSITES be loyal to, keep.

betrayal noun disloyalty, treachery, bad faith, breach of faith, breach of trust, faithlessness, duplicity, deception, double-dealing, stab in the back, double-cross, sell-out.
OPPOSITES loyalty.

better adjective **1** *better facilities:* superior, finer, of higher quality, preferable; informal a cut above, streets ahead, head and shoulders above, ahead of the pack/field. **2** *there couldn't be a better time:* more advantageous, more suitable, more fitting, more appropriate, more useful, more valuable, more desirable. **3** *are you better?* healthier, fitter, stronger, well again, cured, healed, recovered, recovering, on the road to recovery, on the mend.
OPPOSITES worse, inferior.
● adverb **1** *I played better today:* to a higher standard, in a superior way, more effectively. **2** *this may suit you better:* more, to a greater degree/extent. **3** *the money could be better spent:* more wisely, more sensibly, more suitably, more fittingly, more advantageously, more usefully.
● verb **1** *he bettered the record:* surpass, improve on, beat, exceed, top, cap, trump, eclipse. **2** *refugees who want to better their lot:* improve, ameliorate, raise, advance, further, lift, upgrade, enhance.
OPPOSITES worsen.

between preposition **1** *Philip stood between his parents:* in the middle of, with one on either side, among; old use betwixt. **2** *the bond between her and her mother:* connecting, linking, joining, uniting, allying.

b

beverage noun a drink.

bevy noun (plural **bevies**) a large group.

bewail verb be very sorry or sad about.

beware verb be aware of danger.

bewilder verb (**bewilders, bewildering, bewildered**) puzzle or confuse.
∎ **bewilderment** noun.

bewitch verb **1** put a magic spell on. **2** attract and delight.

beyond preposition & adverb **1** at or to the further side of. **2** outside the range or limits of. **3** happening or continuing after. **4** except.

bhaji /**bah**-ji/ noun (plural **bhajis**) an Indian dish of vegetables fried in batter.

biannual adjective happening twice a year.
∎ **biannually** adverb.

bias noun **1** a feeling for or against a person or thing that is based on prejudice rather than reason. **2** a direction diagonal to the grain of a fabric.

biased adjective having a bias; prejudiced.

bib noun **1** a piece of cloth or plastic fastened under a baby's chin to protect its clothes when it is being fed. **2** the part of an apron or pair of dungarees that covers the chest.

Bible noun the book containing the writings of the Christian Church.
∎ **biblical** adjective.

bibliography noun (plural **bibliographies**) a list of books on a particular subject.
∎ **bibliographer** noun **bibliographic** adjective.

bibliophile /**bib**-li-oh-fyl/ noun a person who collects books.

bibulous adjective fond of drinking alcohol.

bicameral adjective (of a parliament) having two separate parts.

bicarbonate of soda noun a soluble white powder used in fizzy drinks and in baking.

bicentenary noun (plural **bicentenaries**) a two-hundredth anniversary.
∎ **bicentennial** noun & adjective.

biceps /**by**-seps/ noun (plural **biceps**) a large muscle in the upper arm which flexes the arm and forearm.

bicker verb (**bickers, bickering, bickered**) argue about unimportant things.

bicycle noun a two-wheeled vehicle that you ride by pushing the pedals with your feet.
• verb (**bicycles, bicycling, bicycled**) ride a bicycle.

bid[1] verb (**bids, bidding, bid**) **1** offer a price for something. **2** (**bid for**) offer to do work for a stated price. **3** (**bid for**) try to get.
• noun an act of bidding.

bid[2] verb (**bids, bidding, bid** or **bade**; past participle **bid**) **1** say a greeting. **2** old use command.

biddable adjective obedient.

biddy noun (plural **biddies**) informal an old woman.

bide verb (**bides, biding, bided**) old use or dialect stay in a place.
□ **bide your time** wait patiently for an opportunity to do something.

bidet /**bee**-day/ noun a low basin that you sit on to wash your bottom.

biennial adjective **1** taking place every other year. **2** (of a plant) living for two years.

bier /beer/ noun a platform on which a coffin or dead body is placed before burial.

bifocal adjective (of a lens) made in two sections, one for distant and one for close vision. • noun (**bifocals**) a pair of glasses with bifocal lenses.

THESAURUS

beware verb watch out, look out, mind out, be alert, keep your eyes open/peeled, keep an eye out, take care, be careful, be cautious, watch your step, guard against.

bewilder verb baffle, mystify, bemuse, perplex, puzzle, confuse; informal flummox, faze, stump, beat.
OPPOSITES enlighten.

beyond preposition **1** *beyond the trees:* on the far side of, on the other side of, further away than, behind, past, after. **2** *beyond six o'clock:* later than, past, after. **3** *inflation beyond 10 per cent:* greater than, more than, exceeding, in excess of, above, upwards of. **4** *little beyond food was provided:* apart from, except, other than, besides; informal outside of; formal save.

bias noun *he accused the media of bias:* prejudice, partiality, favouritism, unfairness, one-sidedness, discrimination, leaning, tendency, inclination.
OPPOSITES impartiality.
• verb *this may have biased the result:* prejudice, influence, colour, sway, predispose, distort, skew, slant.

biased adjective prejudiced, partial, partisan, one-sided, bigoted, discriminatory, distorted, warped, twisted, skewed.
OPPOSITES impartial.

bid verb *United bid £1 million for the striker:* offer, put up, tender, proffer, propose.
• noun **1** *a bid of £3,000:* offer, tender, proposal. **2** *a bid to cut crime:* attempt, effort, endeavour, try; informal crack, go, shot, stab.

bidding noun command, order, direction, instruction, decree, injunction, demand, beck and call.

big adjective (**bigger, biggest**) **1** large in size, amount, or extent. **2** very important or serious. **3** informal (of a brother or sister) older.
□ **Big Bang** the rapid expansion of dense matter which is thought to have started the formation of the universe. **big-headed** conceited. **big top** the main tent in a circus.

bigamy noun the crime of marrying someone when you are already married to someone else.
■ **bigamist** noun **bigamous** adjective.

bigot /**bi**-guht/ noun a prejudiced and intolerant person.
■ **bigoted** adjective **bigotry** noun.

bigwig noun informal an important person.

bijou /**bee**-zhoo/ adjective small and elegant.

bike informal noun a bicycle or motorcycle.
• verb (**bikes, biking, biked**) ride a bicycle or motorcycle.
■ **biker** noun.

bikini noun (plural **bikinis**) a woman's two-piece swimsuit.

bilateral adjective involving two countries or groups of people.

bilberry noun (plural **bilberries**) a small blue edible berry.

bile noun **1** a bitter fluid which is produced by the liver and helps digestion. **2** anger.

bilge noun the bottom of a ship's hull.

bilingual adjective **1** speaking two languages fluently. **2** expressed in two languages.

bilious adjective feeling sick.

bilk verb informal cheat someone.

bill[1] noun **1** a note saying how much a person owes for something. **2** a written proposal for a new law, presented to parliament for discussion. **3** a programme of entertainment at a theatre or cinema. **4** an advertising poster. **5** N. Amer. a banknote. • verb **1** send someone a bill saying what they owe. **2** list someone in a programme of entertainment. **3** (**bill someone/thing as**) describe someone or something as.
□ **fit the bill** be suitable.

bill[2] noun a bird's beak.

billabong noun Austral. a stretch of a river forming a backwater or stagnant pool.

billboard noun a large board for displaying advertising posters.

billet noun a private house where soldiers live temporarily. • verb (**be billeted**) (of a soldier) stay in a particular place.

billet-doux /**bil**-li-doo/ noun (plural **billets-doux** /**bil**-li-**dooz**/) a love letter.

billhook noun a tool with a curved blade, used for pruning.

billiards noun a game played on a table with pockets at the sides and corners, into which balls are struck with a cue.

billion cardinal number (plural **billions** or (with another word or number) **billion**) a thousand million; 1,000,000,000.
■ **billionth** ordinal number.

billionaire noun a person owning money and property worth at least a billion pounds or dollars.

billow verb **1** (of smoke, cloud, or steam) roll outward. **2** fill with air and swell out.
• noun **1** a large rolling mass of cloud,

THESAURUS

big adjective **1** *a big building:* large, sizeable, substantial, great, huge, immense, enormous, extensive, colossal, massive, vast, gigantic, giant, spacious; informal jumbo, whopping, thumping, bumper, mega; Brit. informal whacking, ginormous; formal commodious. **2** *a big man:* well built, sturdy, brawny, burly, broad-shouldered, muscular, bulky, hulking, strapping, hefty, tall, huge, fat, stout; informal hunky, beefy. **3** *my big brother:* grown-up, adult, mature, grown, elder, older. **4** *a big decision:* important, significant, major, momentous, weighty, far-reaching, key, vital, crucial. **5** *that was big of you:* generous, kind, kindly, caring, compassionate, loving.
OPPOSITES small, little, younger, minor, mean.

bigoted adjective prejudiced, biased, partial, one-sided, sectarian, discriminatory, opinionated, dogmatic, intolerant, narrow-minded, blinkered, illiberal.
OPPOSITES open-minded.

bill noun **1** *a bill for £6:* invoice, account, statement, list of charges; humorous the damage; N. Amer. check; N. Amer. informal tab. **2** *a parliamentary bill:* draft law, proposal, measure. **3** *she was top of the bill:* programme, line-up; N. Amer. playbill. **4** (N. Amer.) *a $10 bill:* banknote, note; US informal greenback. **5** *he had been posting bills:* poster, advertisement, notice, announcement, flyer, leaflet, handbill; informal ad; Brit. informal advert.
• verb **1** *please bill me for the work:* invoice, charge, debit. **2** *the concert went ahead as billed:* advertise, announce, schedule, programme, timetable; N. Amer. slate. **3** *he was billed as the new Sean Connery:* describe, call, style, label, dub, promote, talk up; informal hype.

billow noun *billows of smoke:* cloud, mass.
• verb **1** *her dress billowed around her:* puff up/out, balloon (out), swell, fill (out). **2** *smoke billowed from the chimney:* swirl, spiral, roll, undulate, eddy, pour, flow.

smoke, or steam. **2** literary a large sea wave.

billy or **billycan** noun (plural **billies**) Brit. a metal cooking pot with a lid and handle, used in camping.

billy goat noun a male goat.

bimbo noun (plural **bimbos**) informal an attractive but unintelligent young woman.

bin Brit. noun **1** a container for rubbish. **2** a large storage container. • verb (**bins, binning, binned**) throw away.

binary /by-nuh-ri/ adjective **1** composed of or involving two things. **2** relating to a system of numbers which has two as its base and uses only the digits 0 and 1.

bind verb (**binds, binding, bound**) **1** firmly tie, wrap, or fasten. **2** hold together in a united group or mass. **3** (**be bound by**) be hampered or restricted by. **4** require someone to do something by law or because of a contract. **5** (**bind someone over**) (of a court of law) require someone to do something. **6** enclose the pages of a book in a cover. **7** trim the edge of a piece of material with a fabric strip. • noun informal an annoying or difficult situation.

binder noun **1** a cover for holding loose papers together. **2** a machine that binds grain into sheaves. **3** a person who binds books.
■ **bindery** noun (plural **binderies**).

bindi noun (plural **bindis**) a decorative mark worn in the middle of the forehead by some Indian women.

binding noun **1** a strong covering holding the pages of a book together. **2** fabric in a strip, used for binding the edges of material. • adjective (of an agreement) legally compelling someone to do what is stated.

bindweed noun a plant that twines itself round things.

binge informal noun a short period of uncontrolled eating or drinking. • verb (**binges, bingeing, binged**) eat or drink in an uncontrolled way.

bingo noun a game in which players mark off on a card numbers called at random, the winner being the first to mark off all their numbers.

binocular adjective for or using both eyes. • noun (**binoculars**) an instrument with a separate lens for each eye, for viewing distant objects.

biochemistry noun the study of the chemical processes that take place within living things.
■ **biochemical** adjective **biochemist** noun.

biodegradable adjective able to be decomposed by bacteria or other living things.

biodiversity noun the variety of plant and animal life in the world or in a particular environment.

biography noun (plural **biographies**) an account of a person's life written by someone else.
■ **biographer** noun **biographical** adjective.

biological adjective **1** relating to biology or living things. **2** (of a parent or child) related by blood. **3** relating to the use of germs as a weapon in war. **4** (of a detergent) containing enzymes.
■ **biologically** adverb.

biology noun the scientific study of the life and structure of plants and animals.
■ **biologist** noun.

bionic adjective **1** (of an artificial body part) electronically powered. **2** informal having superhuman powers.

biopsy noun (plural **biopsies**) an examination of tissue taken from the body, to discover the presence or cause of a disease.

biorhythm noun a recurring cycle in the functioning of an animal or plant.

biosphere noun the parts of the earth in which plants and animals live.

bioterrorism noun the use of harmful organisms such as viruses or bacteria as weapons of terrorism.

bipartite adjective involving two separate groups or parties.

biped /by-ped/ noun an animal that walks on two feet.

biplane noun an early type of aircraft with two pairs of wings, one above the other.

bipolar adjective having two poles or outer limits.

birch noun **1** a slender tree with thin peeling bark. **2** (**the birch**) (in the past) the punishment of being beaten with a bundle of birch twigs.

bird noun **1** an animal with feathers, wings,

THESAURUS

bind verb **1** *they bound her hands:* tie up, fasten together, secure, make fast, attach, rope, lash, tether. **2** *Shelley bound up the wound:* bandage, dress, cover, wrap, strap up, tape up. **3** *the edges are bound in a contrasting colour:* trim, hem, edge, border, fringe. See also **BOUND**¹.
OPPOSITES untie.

binding adjective irrevocable, unalterable, inescapable, unbreakable, contractual, compulsory, obligatory, mandatory, incumbent.

binge noun (informal) bout, spell, fling, spree, orgy, drinking bout; informal bender, session, booze-up; Scottish informal skite; N. Amer. informal jag, toot.

and a beak, that lays eggs and is usually able to fly. **2** Brit. informal a young woman or girlfriend.

□ **bird of prey** (plural **birds of prey**) a bird that eats small animals or birds, such as an eagle or hawk. **bird's-eye view** a view of something from high above.

birdie noun (plural **birdies**) Golf a score of one stroke under par at a hole.

biro noun (plural **biros**) Brit. trademark a ballpoint pen.

birth noun **1** the process by which a baby or other young animal comes out of its mother's body. **2** the beginning of something. **3** a person's family origins.

□ **birth control** the use of contraceptives to prevent unwanted pregnancies. **give birth** produce a baby or young animal.

birthday noun the day in each year which is the same as the day on which a person was born.

birthmark noun an unusual mark on the body which is there from birth.

birthright noun **1** a right or privilege that a person inherits. **2** a basic right belonging to all human beings.

biscuit noun **1** Brit. a small, flat, crisp cake. **2** a light brown colour.

☑ don't forget the *u*: bisc*u*it.

bisect verb divide into two parts.

bisexual adjective **1** sexually attracted to both men and women. **2** Biology having both male and female organs. • noun a bisexual person.

■ **bisexuality** noun.

bishop noun (in the Christian Church) a senior minister who is in charge of a diocese (a district).

bismuth noun a brittle reddish-grey metallic element resembling lead.

bison noun (plural **bison**) a wild ox with a humped back and shaggy hair.

bistro /**bee**-stroh/ noun (plural **bistros**) a small, inexpensive restaurant.

bit[1] noun **1** a small piece or quantity. **2** (**a bit**) a short time or distance. **3** (**a bit**) rather; slightly.

□ **bit part** a small acting role in a play or a film.

bit[2] noun **1** a metal mouthpiece attached to a bridle, used to control a horse. **2** a tool or piece for boring or drilling.

bit[3] noun Computing the smallest unit of information, expressed as either a 0 or 1.

bitch noun **1** a female dog. **2** informal a spiteful or unpleasant woman. • verb informal say spiteful things about someone.

bitchy adjective (**bitchier**, **bitchiest**) informal spiteful.

■ **bitchiness** noun.

bite verb (**bites**, **biting**, **bit**; past participle **bitten**) **1** cut into something with your teeth. **2** (of a tool, tyre, etc.) grip a surface. **3** take effect in an unwelcome way. • noun **1** an act of biting or a piece bitten off. **2** informal a quick snack. **3** a feeling of cold in the air.

□ **bite the bullet** make yourself do something that is difficult or unpleasant.

biting adjective **1** (of a wind) painfully cold. **2** (of something said) cruel.

bitter adjective **1** having a sharp or sour

birth noun **1** childbirth, delivery, nativity. **2** *the birth of science*: beginning(s), emergence, genesis, dawn, dawning, rise, start. **3** *he is of noble birth*: ancestry, lineage, blood, descent, parentage, family, extraction, origin, stock.
OPPOSITES death, end.

□ **give birth to have,** bear, produce, be delivered of, bring into the world; N. Amer. birth; informal drop.

bit noun piece, portion, section, part, chunk, lump, hunk, fragment, scrap, shred, crumb, grain, speck, spot, drop, pinch, dash, morsel, mouthful, bite, sample, iota, jot, whit, atom, particle, trace, touch, suggestion, hint, tinge; informal smidgen, tad.
OPPOSITES lot.

bite verb **1** chew, sink your teeth into, munch, crunch, champ. **2** *my boots failed to bite*: grip, hold, get a purchase. **3** *the measures begin to bite*: take effect, work, act, have results.

• noun **1** *he took a bite at his sandwich*: chew, munch, nibble, gnaw, nip, snap. **2** *he ate it in two bites*: mouthful, piece, bit, morsel. **3** *the appetizer had a fiery bite*: piquancy, pungency, spiciness, tang, zest; informal kick, punch, zing.

biting adjective **1** *biting comments*: vicious, harsh, cruel, savage, cutting, sharp, bitter, scathing, caustic, acid, acerbic, acrimonious, spiteful, venomous. vitriolic; informal bitchy, catty. **2** *the biting wind*: freezing, icy, arctic, bitter, piercing, penetrating, raw.
OPPOSITES mild, pleasant, warm.

bitter adjective **1** *bitter coffee*: sharp, acid, acrid, tart, sour, vinegary. **2** *a bitter row*: acrimonious, hostile, angry, rancorous, spiteful, vicious, vitriolic, savage, ferocious, nasty. **3** *a bitter woman*: resentful, embittered, aggrieved, spiteful, jaundiced, sullen, sour. **4** *a bitter wind*: freezing, icy, arctic, biting, piercing, penetrating, raw.
OPPOSITES pleasant, sweet, amicable, magnanimous, content, mild, warm.

b

taste or smell; not sweet. **2** feeling or causing resentment or unhappiness. **3** (of a conflict) intense and full of hatred. **4** very cold. •**noun 1** Brit. bitter-tasting beer that is strongly flavoured with hops. **2** (**bitters**) bitter alcoholic spirits used in cocktails.
■ **bitterly** adverb **bitterness** noun.

bittern noun a wading bird with a very loud call.

bittersweet adjective **1** sweet with a bitter aftertaste. **2** bringing pleasure mixed with sadness.

bitty adjective (**bittier, bittiest**) Brit. informal made up of small unrelated parts.

bitumen noun a black sticky substance obtained from oil, used for covering roads and roofs.
■ **bituminous** adjective.

bivalve noun a creature that has a shell divided into two parts, such as an oyster or mussel.

bivouac noun a makeshift open-air camp without tents. •**verb** (**bivouacs, bivouacking, bivouacked**) stay overnight in such a camp.

bizarre adjective very strange or unusual.
■ **bizarrely** adverb.

| ✓ one *z*, two *r*s: bizarre. |

blab verb (**blabs, blabbing, blabbed**) informal give away a secret.

blabber verb (**blabbers, blabbering, blabbered**) informal talk in a silly or annoying way.

black adjective **1** of the very darkest colour. **2** relating to people who have dark-coloured skin. **3** (of coffee or tea) without milk. **4** indicating that bad or unwelcome things are likely to happen. **5** (of a joke) making something bad or unwelcome seem funny. **6** full of anger or hatred. •**noun 1** black colour. **2** a black person. •**verb 1** make something black. **2** (**black out**) faint. **3** (**black something out**) make a building dark by switching off lights and covering windows.
□ **black belt** a black belt awarded to an expert in judo, karate, and other martial arts. **black box** a machine that records what is happening to the controls in an aircraft during a flight. **black eye** an area of bruising around the eye. **black hole** an area in space where gravity is so strong that nothing, not even light, can escape. **black ice** a transparent coating of ice on a road. **black magic** magic in which evil spirits are called on. **black market** the illegal trade in goods that are officially controlled or hard to obtain. **black pudding** a pork sausage containing dried pig's blood. **black sheep** a person who is considered bad or embarrassing by the rest of their family. **black spot** a place that is dangerous or where problems arise. **black widow** a very poisonous American spider with a black body and red markings. **in the black** not owing any money.
■ **blackness** noun.

blackball verb prevent someone from joining a club.

blackberry noun (plural **blackberries**) a soft purple-black fruit that grows on a prickly bush.

blackbird noun a bird with black feathers and a yellow beak.

blackboard noun a board with a black surface for writing on with chalk.

blackcurrant noun a small round edible purple-black berry.

blacken verb **1** make or become black. **2** damage someone's reputation.

blackfly noun (plural **blackflies**) a small black fly which eats the young shoots of plants.

blackguard /**blag**-gerd/ noun dated a man who is dishonest or treats other people badly.

blackhead noun a lump of oily matter blocking a pore in the skin.

THESAURUS

bitterness noun **1** *the bitterness of the medicine:* sharpness, acidity, tartness, sourness. **2** *there was no bitterness between them:* acrimony, hostility, anger, antipathy, antagonism, enmity, animus, friction, rancour, vitriol, venom, nastiness, bad blood. **3** *his bitterness grew:* resentment, rancour, indignation, grudge, spite, sullenness, pique.
OPPOSITES sweetness, goodwill.

bizarre adjective strange, peculiar, odd, funny, fantastic, curious, outlandish, eccentric, unconventional, unorthodox; informal weird, wacky, oddball, way out, freaky; N. Amer. informal wacko.
OPPOSITES normal.

black adjective **1** *a black horse:* dark, pitch-black, jet-black, coal-black, ebony, inky, sable. **2** *the blackest day of the war:* tragic, dark, disastrous, calamitous, catastrophic, cataclysmic, fateful. **3** *Mary was in a black mood:* miserable, unhappy, sad, wretched, heartbroken, grief-stricken, sorrowful, anguished, desolate, despairing, disconsolate, downcast, dejected, gloomy; informal blue. **4** *black humour:* macabre, cynical, unhealthy, ghoulish, weird, morbid, gruesome; informal sick.
OPPOSITES white, bright, happy.
□ **black out** faint, lose consciousness, pass out, swoon.

blackleg noun Brit. disapproving a person who continues working when other workers are on strike.

blacklist noun a list of people who cannot be trusted or who are out of favour. • verb put someone on a blacklist.

blackmail noun 1 the demanding of money from someone in return for not giving away secret information about them. 2 the use of threats or other pressure to influence someone. • verb use blackmail on someone.

blackout noun 1 a period when all lights must be switched off or covered during an enemy air raid. 2 a sudden failure of electric lights. 3 a short loss of consciousness. 4 an official restriction on the publishing of news.

blacksmith noun a person who makes and repairs things made of iron.

blackthorn noun a thorny bush that has blue-black fruits (called sloes).

bladder noun a bag-like organ in the abdomen in which urine collects before it is passed from the body.

blade noun 1 the flat cutting edge of a knife or other tool or weapon. 2 the broad flat part of an oar, leaf, or other object. 3 a long, narrow leaf of grass.

blag verb (**blags, blagging, blagged**) Brit. informal get something by clever talk or lying.
■ **blagger** noun.

blame verb (**blames, blaming, blamed**) say that someone is responsible for something bad. • noun responsibility for something bad.

■ **blameworthy** adjective.

blameless adjective having done nothing bad; innocent.

blanch verb 1 become white or pale. 2 prepare vegetables by putting them briefly in boiling water.

blancmange /bluh-**monzh**/ noun Brit. a dessert like a milky jelly, made with cornflour and milk.

bland adjective 1 not having any interesting features or qualities. 2 showing no emotion or excitement.

blandishments plural noun nice things said to someone in order to persuade them to do something.

blank adjective 1 not marked or decorated. 2 not understanding or reacting. • noun 1 a space in a form left to be filled in. 2 a state in which you cannot understand or remember something. 3 a gun cartridge containing gunpowder but no bullet. • verb 1 (**blank something out**) hide or block out something. 2 Brit. informal deliberately ignore someone.
□ **blank verse** poetry that has a regular rhythm but does not rhyme.
■ **blankly** adverb **blankness** noun.

blanket noun 1 a large piece of woollen material used as a warm covering. 2 a thick mass or layer. • verb (**blankets, blanketing, blanketed**) cover with a thick layer.

blare verb (**blares, blaring, blared**) make a loud, harsh sound. • noun a loud, harsh sound.

blarney noun talk that is friendly and charming but may not be truthful.

THESAURUS

blacklist verb boycott, ostracize, avoid, embargo, ignore, refuse to employ.

blackmail noun *he was accused of blackmail:* extortion, demanding money with menaces, threats, intimidation.
• verb 1 *he was blackmailing the murderer:* extort money from, threaten, hold to ransom, intimidate. 2 *she blackmailed me into working for her:* coerce, pressure, force, dragoon; informal lean on, twist someone's arm.

blame verb 1 *he always blames others:* hold responsible, hold accountable, condemn, accuse, find/consider guilty. 2 *they blame youth crime on unemployment:* attribute to, ascribe to, impute to, lay at the door of, put down to; informal pin.
OPPOSITES absolve.
• noun *he was cleared of all blame:* responsibility, guilt, accountability, liability, culpability, fault.

blameless adjective innocent, guiltless, above reproach, unimpeachable, in the

clear, exemplary; informal squeaky clean.
OPPOSITES blameworthy.

bland adjective 1 *a bland film:* uninteresting, dull, boring, tedious, monotonous, ordinary, run-of-the-mill, drab, dreary, unexciting, lacklustre, flat, stale, trite. 2 *bland food:* tasteless, flavourless, plain, insipid, weak, watery, thin, wishy-washy.
OPPOSITES interesting, tangy.

blank adjective 1 *a blank sheet of paper:* empty, unmarked, unused, clear, free, bare, clean, plain. 2 *a blank face:* expressionless, deadpan, wooden, stony, impassive, glazed, fixed, lifeless, inscrutable.
OPPOSITES full, marked, expressive.
• noun *fill in the blanks:* space, gap.

blanket noun *a blanket of cloud:* covering, layer, coating, carpet, cloak, mantle, veil, pall, shroud.
• verb *snow blanketed the mountains:* cover, coat, carpet, cloak, shroud, swathe, envelop.

b

blasé /blah-zay/ adjective not impressed by something because you have experienced it often before.

blaspheme verb (**blasphemes, blaspheming, blasphemed**) speak rudely about God or use the name of God as a swear word.
■ blasphemous adjective blasphemy noun (plural **blasphemies**).

blast noun 1 an explosion, or the rush of compressed air spreading outwards from it. 2 a strong gust of wind. 3 a single loud note of a horn or whistle. •verb 1 blow something up with explosives. 2 (**blast off**) (of a rocket or spacecraft) take off. 3 produce loud music or noise.
□ blast furnace a furnace for extracting metal from ore, using blasts of hot compressed air.

blatant adjective done in an open and unashamed way.
■ blatancy noun blatantly adverb.

☑ -ant, not -ent: blatant.

blather verb (**blathers, blathering, blathered**) talk without making much sense. •noun rambling talk.

blaze noun 1 a very large or fierce fire. 2 a very bright light or display of colour. 3 a conspicuous display or outburst of something: *a blaze of publicity.* 4 a white stripe down the face of a horse. •verb (**blazes, blazing, blazed**) 1 burn or shine fiercely or brightly. 2 shoot repeatedly or wildly.
□ blaze a trail 1 mark out a path. 2 be the first to do something.

blazer noun 1 a jacket worn by schoolchildren or sports players as part of a uniform. 2 a man's smart jacket.

blazon /blay-zuhn/ verb display or proclaim something in a way that catches people's attention.

bleach verb lighten something by using a chemical or leaving it in sunlight. •noun a chemical used to remove stains and also to sterilize drains, sinks, etc.

bleak adjective 1 bare and exposed to the weather. 2 dreary and unwelcoming. 3 (of a situation) not hopeful.
■ bleakly adverb bleakness noun.

bleary adjective (**blearier, bleariest**) (of the eyes) tired and not focusing properly.
■ blearily adverb.

bleat verb 1 (of a sheep or goat) make a weak, wavering cry. 2 speak or complain in a weak or silly way. •noun a bleating sound.

bleed verb (**bleeds, bleeding, bled**) 1 lose blood from the body. 2 informal drain someone of money or resources. 3 (of dye or colour) seep into an adjoining colour or area. 4 allow fluid or gas to escape from a closed system through a valve. 5 (in the past) take blood from someone as a medical treatment. •noun an instance of bleeding.

bleep noun a short, high-pitched sound made by an electronic device. •verb make a bleep.
■ bleeper noun.

blemish noun a small mark or flaw. •verb spoil the appearance of.

blench verb flinch suddenly out of fear or pain.

blend verb 1 mix and combine one thing

THESAURUS

blast noun 1 *the blast from the bomb:* shock wave, pressure wave. 2 *Friday's blast killed two people:* explosion, detonation, discharge, burst. 3 *a blast of cold air:* gust, rush, gale, squall, flurry. 4 *the shrill blast of the trumpets:* blare, wail, roar, screech, shriek, hoot, honk, beep.
•verb 1 *bombers were blasting airfields:* blow up, bomb, blow (to pieces), dynamite, explode. 2 *guns were blasting away:* fire, shoot, blaze, let fly, discharge. 3 *he blasted his horn:* honk, beep, toot, sound. 4 *radios blasting out pop music:* blare, boom, roar, thunder, bellow, pump, shriek, screech.

blatant adjective flagrant, glaring, obvious, undisguised, open, shameless, barefaced, unashamed, brazen.
OPPOSITES inconspicuous, shamefaced.

blaze noun 1 fire, flames, conflagration, inferno, holocaust. 2 *a blaze of light:* glare, flash, burst, flare, streak, radiance, brilliance, beam, glitter.

•verb 1 *the fire blazed merrily:* burn, be alight, be on fire, be in flames. 2 *headlights blazed:* shine, flash, flare, glare, gleam, glitter, glisten. 3 *soldiers blazed away:* fire, shoot, blast, let fly.

bleach verb turn white, whiten, turn pale, blanch, lighten, fade.
OPPOSITES darken.

bleak adjective 1 *a bleak landscape:* bare, exposed, desolate, stark, desert, lunar, open, empty, windswept. 2 *the future is bleak:* unpromising, unfavourable, dim, gloomy, black, grim, discouraging, disheartening, depressing.
OPPOSITES lush, promising.

bleary adjective blurry, unfocused, fogged, clouded, misty, watery.
OPPOSITES clear.

blend verb 1 *blend the ingredients until smooth:* mix, mingle, combine, merge, amalgamate, stir, whisk, fold in. 2 *the new buildings blend with the older ones:* harmonize, go (well), fit (in), be in tune, with something else. **2** (**blend in**) become unnoticeable. • **noun** a mixture.

blender noun an electric device for liquidizing or chopping food.

bless verb **1** make something holy by saying a prayer over it. **2** ask God to protect a person or thing. **3** (**be blessed with**) have or be given something that is desired.

blessed /bless-id, blest/ adjective **1** holy and protected by God. **2** bringing welcome pleasure or relief.
■ **blessedly** adverb.

blessing noun **1** God's approval and protection, or a prayer asking for this. **2** something for which you are very grateful. **3** a person's approval or support.

blew past of BLOW¹.

blight noun **1** a plant disease caused by fungi. **2** a thing that spoils or damages something. • **verb** spoil or damage something.

blighter noun Brit. informal an annoying or unfortunate person.

blind adjective **1** not able to see. **2** done without being able to see or without certain information. **3** without awareness or judgement. **4** concealed, closed, or blocked off: *a blind alley.* • **verb 1** make someone blind. **2** stop someone thinking clearly or sensibly. **3** (**blind someone with**)

confuse someone by presenting them with something hard to understand. • **noun** a screen for a window.
□ **blind date** a meeting with a person you have not met before, arranged in the hope of starting a romantic relationship. **blind man's buff** a game in which a player tries to catch people while wearing a blindfold. **blind spot 1** an area where someone's view is obstructed. **2** an inability to understand something. **turn a blind eye** pretend not to notice.
■ **blindly** adverb **blindness** noun.

blindfold noun a piece of cloth covering someone's eyes, so that they cannot see. • **verb** cover someone's eyes with a blindfold.

blinding adjective **1** (of light) very bright. **2** (of pain) very severe.
■ **blindingly** adverb.

bling-bling or **bling** noun informal showy, expensive clothes and jewellery.

blink verb **1** shut and open the eyes quickly. **2** (of a light) flash on and off. • **noun** an act of blinking.
□ **on the blink** informal no longer working properly.

blinkered adjective having a limited point of view.

blinkers plural noun a pair of flaps used to

be compatible, coordinate, match, complement, suit.
• **noun** *a blend of bananas and ginger:* mixture, mix, combination, compound, amalgam, fusion, alloy.

bless verb **1** *the Cardinal blessed the memorial plaque:* consecrate, sanctify, dedicate to God, make holy; formal hallow. **2** *the gods blessed us with magical voices:* endow, bestow, furnish, give, favour, confer on. **3** *the government refused to bless the undertaking:* sanction, consent to, endorse, agree to, approve, back, support; informal give the green light to, OK.
OPPOSITES curse, trouble, oppose.

blessed adjective holy, sacred, hallowed, consecrated, sanctified, ordained, canonized, beatified.
OPPOSITES cursed.

blessing noun **1** *a blessing from the priest:* benediction, dedication, consecration, grace, invocation, intercession. **2** *Amanda gave the plan her blessing:* sanction, endorsement, approval, consent, assent, agreement, backing, support; informal the green light, OK. **3** *it was a blessing they didn't have far to go:* advantage, godsend, boon, benefit, help, bonus, plus, stroke of luck, windfall.
OPPOSITES condemnation, affliction.

blight noun **1** *potato blight:* disease, canker,

infestation, fungus, mildew, mould. **2** *the blight of aircraft noise:* curse, scourge, affliction, plague, menace, misfortune, bane, trouble, nuisance, pest.
OPPOSITES blessing.
• **verb** *scandal blighted his career:* ruin, wreck, spoil, mar, frustrate, disrupt, undo, scotch, destroy, shatter, devastate, demolish; informal mess up, foul up, put paid to, put the kibosh on, stymie; Brit. informal scupper.

blind adjective **1** sightless, unsighted, visually impaired, unseeing. **2** *blind acceptance of conventional opinion:* uncritical, unreasoned, unthinking, unquestioning, mindless, undiscerning, indiscriminate. **3** *she was blind to the realities of her position:* unaware of, oblivious to, ignorant of, unmindful of, heedless of, insensible to, indifferent to.
OPPOSITES sighted, discerning, mindful.
• **noun** *a window blind:* screen, shade, sunshade, curtain, awning, canopy, louvre, jalousie, shutter.

blindly adverb **1** *he ran blindly upstairs:* impetuously, impulsively, recklessly, heedlessly. **2** *they blindly followed US policy:* uncritically, unquestioningly, unthinkingly, mindlessly, indiscriminately.
OPPOSITES cautiously, critically, selectively.

prevent a horse from seeing sideways.

blip noun **1** a short, high-pitched sound made by an electronic device. **2** a small flashing point of light on a radar screen. **3** a temporary change in a situation or process that is generally steady. •verb (**blips, blipping, blipped**) make a blip.

bliss noun perfect happiness.

blissful adjective full of joy and happiness. ■ **blissfully** adverb.

blister noun **1** a small bubble on the skin filled with watery liquid. **2** a similar bubble on a surface. •verb (**blisters, blistering, blistered**) form blisters.

blistering adjective **1** (of heat) very strong. **2** very fierce or forceful.

blithe /bly*th*/ adjective **1** without thought or care. **2** very happy. ■ **blithely** adverb.

blithering adjective informal thoroughly stupid.

blitz noun **1** a sudden fierce military attack. **2** informal a sudden and concentrated effort. •verb make a sudden fierce attack on.

blizzard noun a snowstorm with high winds.

bloat verb cause something to swell with fluid or gas. ■ **bloated** adjective.

bloater noun a salted and smoked herring.

blob noun **1** a drop of a thick or sticky liquid. **2** a roundish mass or shape.

bloc noun a group of allied countries with similar political systems.

block noun **1** a large solid piece of material. **2** Brit. a large building divided into flats or offices. **3** a group of buildings with streets on all four sides. **4** an obstacle. •verb **1** prevent movement or flow in something. **2** prevent the progress of something. □ **block capitals** plain capital letters.

blockade noun a blocking of the way in or out of a place to prevent people or goods from entering or leaving it. •verb (**blockades, blockading, blockaded**) block the way in or out of a place.

blockage noun an obstruction.

blockbuster noun informal a film or book that is very successful.

blog noun a weblog. •verb (**blogs, blogging, blogged**) regularly update a weblog. ■ **blogger** noun.

bloke noun Brit. informal a man.

blonde adjective (also **blond**) **1** (of hair) pale yellow. **2** having pale yellow hair. •noun a woman with blonde hair.

blood noun **1** the red liquid that flows through the arteries and veins. **2** family background. •verb give someone their first experience of an activity. □ **blood-curdling** horrifying. **blood pressure** the pressure created by blood as it moves around the body. **blood poisoning** a serious illness that occurs when harmful bacteria have infected the blood. **blood sport** a sport involving the hunting or killing of animals. **blood vessel** a vein, artery, or capillary carrying blood through the body. **new** (or **fresh**) **blood** people who join a group and give it new ideas.

bloodbath noun an event in which many people are violently killed.

bloodhound noun a large hound used for following scents.

bloodless adjective **1** without violence or killing. **2** (of the skin) drained of colour. **3** lacking emotion or vitality.

bloodletting noun **1** violent conflict. **2** (in the past) the removal of some of a patient's blood, as a medical treatment.

THESAURUS

bliss noun joy, happiness, pleasure, delight, ecstasy, elation, rapture, euphoria. OPPOSITES misery.

blitz noun bombing, air raid, air strike, bombardment, barrage, attack, assault.

bloated adjective swollen, distended, bulging, inflated, dilated. OPPOSITES shrunken.

blob noun **1** *a blob of cold gravy*: drop, droplet, globule, bead, bubble. **2** *a blob of ink*: spot, dab, blotch, blot, dot, smudge; informal splodge.

bloc noun group, alliance, coalition, federation, confederation, league, union, axis, association.

block noun **1** *a block of cheese*: chunk, hunk, lump, wedge, cube, brick, slab, piece. **2** *an apartment block*: building, complex, structure, development. **3** *a block to development*: obstacle, bar, barrier,

impediment, hindrance, check, hurdle. OPPOSITES aid.
•verb **1** *weeds can block ditches*: clog, stop up, choke, plug, bung up, obstruct, gum up, dam up, congest, jam. **2** *picket lines blocked access to the factory*: hinder, hamper, obstruct, impede, inhibit, halt, stop, bar, check, prevent, fend off, hold off, repel. OPPOSITES clear, aid, allow.
□ **block something out keep out**, exclude, stop, conceal, blot out, obliterate.

blockage noun obstruction, stoppage, block, jam, congestion.

blonde, blond adjective fair, light, yellow, flaxen, golden. OPPOSITES dark.

blood noun **1** lifeblood, gore, vital fluid. **2** *a woman of noble blood*: ancestry, lineage, descent, parentage, family, birth, extraction, origin, stock.

b

bloodshed noun the killing or wounding of people.

bloodshot adjective (of the eyes) having tiny red blood vessels visible in the whites.

bloodstock noun thoroughbred horses.

bloodstream noun the blood circulating through the body.

bloodthirsty adjective (**bloodthirstier, bloodthirstiest**) taking pleasure in killing and violence.

bloody adjective (**bloodier, bloodiest**) **1** covered with or containing blood. **2** involving violence or cruelty. • verb (**bloodies, bloodying, bloodied**) cover or stain with blood.
□ **bloody-minded** Brit. informal deliberately unhelpful.

bloom verb **1** produce flowers; be in flower. **2** be healthy and happy. • noun **1** a flower. **2** a state or period of blooming. **3** a healthy glow in a person's complexion. **4** a powdery coating on the surface of some fruit.

bloomers plural noun **1** women's baggy knee-length knickers. **2** historical women's loose-fitting trousers.

blossom noun a flower or a mass of flowers on a tree. • verb **1** produce blossom. **2** become strong and healthy.

blot noun **1** a spot of ink. **2** a thing that spoils something good. • verb (**blots, blotting, blotted**) **1** dry something with an absorbent material. **2** mark or spoil. **3** (**blot something out**) hide something.
□ **blotting paper** absorbent paper used for drying ink when writing. **blot your copybook** Brit. spoil your good reputation.

blotch noun an irregular mark. • verb mark something with blotches.
■ **blotchy** adjective.

blotter noun a pad of blotting paper.

blouse noun a woman's top that is similar to a shirt.

blouson /bloo-zon/ noun a short loose-fitting jacket.

blow[1] verb (**blows, blowing, blew**; past participle **blown**) **1** (of the wind) move. **2** send out air through pursed lips. **3** force air into an instrument through the mouth. **4** sound a horn. **5** break something open with explosives. **6** burst through pressure or overheating. **7** informal spend money recklessly. **8** informal waste an opportunity. • noun an act of blowing.
□ **blow-dry** style the hair while drying it with a hand-held dryer. **blow hot and cold** keep changing your mind. **blow over** (of trouble) fade away. **blow up** explode. **blow something up 1** make something explode. **2** inflate something.

blow[2] noun **1** a powerful stroke with a hand

bloodshed noun slaughter, massacre, killing, wounding, carnage, butchery, bloodletting, bloodbath.

bloodthirsty adjective murderous, homicidal, violent, vicious, barbarous, barbaric, savage, brutal, cut-throat.

bloody adjective **1** his hands were all bloody: bloodstained, blood-soaked, gory, bleeding. **2** a bloody civil war: vicious, ferocious, savage, fierce, brutal, cruel, murderous, gory.
OPPOSITES clean, bloodless.

bloom verb **1** the geraniums bloomed: flower, blossom, open, mature. **2** the children bloomed in the Devonshire air: flourish, thrive, prosper, burgeon; informal be in the pink.
OPPOSITES wither, fade, decline.

blossom noun pink blossoms: flower, bloom, bud.
• verb **1** the snowdrops have blossomed: bloom, flower, open, mature. **2** the whole region had blossomed: develop, grow, mature, progress, evolve, burgeon, flourish, thrive, prosper, bloom.
OPPOSITES wither, fade, decline.

blot noun **1** an ink blot: patch, dab, smudge, blotch, mark, dot, spot; Brit. informal splodge. **2** the only blot on a clean campaign: blemish, taint, stain, blight, flaw, fault. **3** a

blot on the landscape: eyesore, monstrosity, carbuncle, mess; informal sight.
□ **blot something out 1** clouds were starting to blot out the stars: conceal, hide, obscure, exclude, obliterate, shadow, eclipse. **2** he urged her to blot out the memory: erase, blank out, wipe out, eradicate.

blow[1] verb **1** the icy wind blew around us: gust, puff, flurry, blast, roar, bluster, rush, storm. **2** his ship was blown on to the rocks: sweep, carry, toss, drive, push, force. **3** leaves blew across the road: drift, flutter, waft, float, glide, whirl, move. **4** he blew a smoke ring: exhale, puff. **5** he blew a trumpet: sound, blast, toot, play, pipe, trumpet.
□ **blow something out** extinguish, put out, snuff, douse, quench, smother. **blow up** a lorryload of shells blew up: explode, detonate, go off, ignite, erupt. **blow something up 1** they blew the plane up: explode, detonate, bomb, blast, destroy. **2** blow up the balloons: inflate, pump up, fill up, puff up, swell, expand.

blow[2] noun **1** a blow on the head: knock, bang, hit, punch, thump, smack, crack, rap; informal whack, bash, clout, wallop. **2** losing his wife must have been a blow: upset, disaster, setback, misfortune, disappointment, calamity, catastrophe, or weapon. **2** a sudden shock or disappointment.

blowfly noun (plural **blowflies**) a large fly which lays its eggs in meat.

blowhole noun the nostril of a whale or dolphin on the top of its head.

blowout noun the release of air or gas from a tyre, oil well, etc.

blowsy or **blowzy** /rhymes with drowsy/ adjective (of a woman) plump and untidy.

blowtorch or **blowlamp** noun a portable device producing a hot flame, used to burn off paint.

blowy adjective windy or windswept.

blub verb (**blubs**, **blubbing**, **blubbed**) informal cry noisily.

blubber[1] noun the fat of whales and seals.
■ **blubbery** adjective.

blubber[2] verb (**blubbers**, **blubbering**, **blubbered**) informal cry noisily.

bludgeon noun a thick, heavy stick used as a weapon. ●verb **1** hit someone with a thick, heavy stick. **2** bully someone into doing something.

blue adjective (**bluer**, **bluest**) **1** of the colour of the sky on a sunny day. **2** informal sad or depressed. **3** informal indecent or pornographic. ●noun a blue colour.
▢ **blue-blooded** from a royal or aristocratic family. **blue cheese** cheese having veins of mould in it. **blue-chip** (of an investment) safe and reliable. **blue-collar** relating to manual work. **out of the blue** unexpectedly.

bluebell noun a woodland plant with clusters of blue bell-shaped flowers.

blueberry noun (plural **blueberries**) a blue-black berry that grows on a North American bush.

bluebottle noun a large fly with a bluish body.

blueprint noun **1** a technical drawing or plan. **2** a model or prototype.

blues noun **1** slow, sad music of black American origin. **2** (**the blues**) informal feelings of sadness or depression.
■ **bluesy** adjective.

bluestocking noun a serious intellectual woman.

bluff[1] noun a pretence that you know or can do something when this is not true. ●verb pretend in this way.
▢ **call someone's bluff** challenge someone to do something, in the belief that they will not be able to.

bluff[2] adjective frank and direct in a good-natured way.

bluff[3] noun a steep cliff or bank.

bluish or **blueish** adjective having a blue tinge.

blunder noun a clumsy mistake. ●verb (**blunders**, **blundering**, **blundered**) **1** make a blunder. **2** move clumsily or as if unable to see.

blunderbuss noun historical a gun with a short, wide barrel.

blunt adjective **1** not having a sharp edge or point. **2** frank and direct. ●verb make or become blunt.
■ **bluntly** adverb.

THESAURUS

thunderbolt, bombshell, shock, surprise, jolt.

blue adjective sky-blue, azure, cobalt, sapphire, navy, ultramarine, aquamarine, cyan.

blueprint noun **1** *blueprints of the aircraft:* plan, design, diagram, drawing, sketch, layout. **2** *a blueprint for similar measures in other countries:* model, plan, template, pattern, example, guide, prototype, pilot.

bluff[1] noun *this offer was denounced as a bluff:* trick, deception, fraud, ruse, pretence, sham, fake, hoax, charade; informal put-on.
●verb **1** *they are bluffing to hide their guilt:* pretend, sham, fake, feign, lie, hoax, pose. **2** *I managed to bluff the board into believing me:* deceive, delude, mislead, trick, fool, hoodwink, dupe, hoax; informal con, kid, have on.

bluff[2] adjective *a bluff man:* plain-spoken, straightforward, blunt, direct, no-nonsense, frank, open, candid, forthright, unequivocal; informal upfront.

OPPOSITES guarded, secretive.

blunder noun *he shook his head at his blunder:* mistake, error, gaffe, slip, oversight, faux pas; informal slip-up, boo-boo; Brit. informal clanger, boob; N. Amer. informal blooper.
●verb **1** *the government admitted it had blundered:* make a mistake, err, miscalculate, bungle, trip up; informal slip up, screw up, blow it, goof; Brit. informal boob. **2** *she blundered down the steps:* stumble, lurch, stagger, flounder, grope.

blunt adjective **1** *a blunt knife:* dull, worn. **2** *the leaf is broad with a blunt tip:* rounded, flat, stubby. **3** *a blunt message:* straightforward, frank, plain-spoken, candid, direct, bluff, forthright, unequivocal, brusque, abrupt, curt, bald, brutal, harsh, stark; informal upfront.
OPPOSITES sharp, pointed, subtle.
●verb *age hasn't blunted my passion for life:* dull, deaden, dampen, numb, take the edge off, weaken, allay, diminish, lessen.
OPPOSITES intensify.

b

blur verb (**blurs, blurring, blurred**) make or become unclear or less distinct. • noun something that cannot be seen, heard, or remembered clearly.
■ **blurry** adjective.

blurb noun a short description written to promote a book, film, or other product.

blurt verb (**blurt something out**) say something suddenly and without thinking.

blush verb become red in the face from shyness or embarrassment. • noun a reddening of the face from shyness or embarrassment.

blusher noun a cosmetic used to give a reddish tinge to the cheeks.

bluster verb (**blusters, blustering, blustered**) 1 talk loudly or aggressively but without having any effect. 2 (of wind or rain) blow or beat fiercely and noisily. • noun loud and aggressive talk that does not have much effect.
■ **blustery** adjective.

boa noun 1 a large snake which winds itself round and crushes its prey. 2 a long, thin scarf of feathers or fur.

boar noun (plural **boar** or **boars**) 1 (also **wild boar**) a wild pig with tusks. 2 a male pig.

board noun 1 a long, narrow, flat piece of wood used in building. 2 a rectangular piece of stiff material used as a surface for a particular purpose. 3 the people who control and direct an organization. 4 regular meals provided in return for payment. • verb 1 get on a ship, aircraft, or other passenger vehicle. 2 (**board something up** or **over**) seal something in with pieces of wood. 3 have a bedroom and receive meals in return for payment. 4 (of a pupil) live in school during term time.
□ **board game** a game in which counters are moved around a board. **boarding house** a private house providing rooms and meals for paying guests. **boarding school** a school in which the pupils live during term time. **go by the board** (of a plan or principle) be rejected or abandoned. **on board** on or in a ship, aircraft, or other vehicle.

boarder noun a pupil who lives in school during term time.

boardroom noun a room in which a board of directors regularly meets.

boast verb 1 talk about yourself with too much pride. 2 (of a place or organization) have something as an impressive feature. • noun an act of boasting.
■ **boastful** adjective **boastfully** adverb.

boat noun a vehicle that travels on water and is smaller than a ship.
□ **be in the same boat** informal be in the same difficult situation as other people.

boater noun a flat-topped straw hat with a brim.

boathouse noun a shed at the edge of a river or lake in which boats are kept.

boatswain /boh-s'n/ noun an officer in charge of equipment and the crew on a ship.

---

blur verb 1 *she felt tears blur her vision:* cloud, fog, obscure, dim, make hazy, make fuzzy, soften, dull, numb, deaden, mute. 2 *the digits on the screen blurred:* become fuzzy, become dim, become hazy, become vague.
OPPOSITES sharpen, focus.
• noun *a blur on the horizon:* indistinct shape, smudge, haze, cloud, mist.

blurred adjective indistinct, fuzzy, hazy, misty, foggy, faint, unclear, vague, indefinite, unfocused.
OPPOSITES sharp, clear.

blurt verb *he blurted out the truth:* burst out with, exclaim, call out, divulge, disclose, reveal, betray, let slip, give away; informal blab, let on, spill the beans.

blush verb *Joan blushed at the compliment:* redden, go pink, go red, flush, colour, burn up.
• noun *the darkness hid her blush:* flush, rosiness, redness, pinkness, bloom, high colour, glow.

blustery adjective stormy, gusty, blowy, windy, squally, wild.
OPPOSITES calm.

board noun 1 *a wooden board:* plank, beam, panel, slat, batten, timber. 2 *the board of directors:* committee, council, panel, directorate, commission.
• verb 1 *he boarded the aircraft:* get on, go aboard, enter, mount, ascend, embark, catch. 2 *a number of students boarded with them:* lodge, live, reside, stay, be housed; N. Amer. room; informal put up.

boast verb 1 *his mother had been boasting about him:* brag, crow, swagger, swank, gloat, show off; informal talk big, lay it on thick; Austral./NZ informal skite. 2 *the hotel boasts a fine restaurant:* have, possess, own, enjoy, pride yourself/itself on, offer.
OPPOSITES hush up.
• noun 1 *the government's main boast seemed undone:* brag, exaggeration, overstatement; informal swank; Austral./NZ informal skite. 2 *the hall is the boast of the county:* pride, joy, pride and joy, apple of someone's eye, wonder, delight.

boastful adjective bragging, swaggering, bumptious, puffed up, full of yourself, cocky, conceited, arrogant; informal swanky, big-headed.
OPPOSITES modest.

b

bob¹ verb (**bobs, bobbing, bobbed**) **1** make a quick, short movement up and down. **2** curtsy briefly. ●noun a bobbing movement.

bob² noun a short hairstyle that hangs evenly all round. ●verb (**bobs, bobbing, bobbed**) cut hair in a bob.

bob³ noun (plural **bob**) Brit. informal, dated a shilling (five pence).

bobbin noun a reel for holding thread.

bobble noun a small ball made of strands of wool.

bobby noun (plural **bobbies**) Brit. informal, dated a police officer.

bobsleigh noun a sledge used for racing down an ice-covered run.

bode verb (**bodes, boding, boded**) (**bode well** or **ill**) be a sign of a good or bad outcome.

bodge verb (**bodges, bodging, bodged**) Brit. informal make or repair something badly or clumsily.

bodice noun **1** the part of a dress above the waist. **2** a woman's sleeveless undergarment.

bodily adjective relating to the body. ●adverb by taking hold of a person's body with force.

bodkin noun a thick needle with a blunt, rounded end.

body noun (plural **bodies**) **1** a person's or animal's physical structure. **2** the main part of the body, apart from the head and limbs. **3** the main or central part of something. **4** a mass or collection. **5** a group of people organized for a particular purpose. **6** Brit. a woman's stretchy garment for the upper body.
□ **body language** the showing of your feelings through the way in which you move or hold your body.

bodybuilder noun a person who enlarges

their muscles through exercise.

bodyguard noun a person paid to protect someone rich or famous.

bodywork noun the metal outer shell of a vehicle.

Boer /rhymes with more or mower/ noun a member of the Dutch people who settled in southern Africa.

boffin noun Brit. informal a scientist.

bog noun an area of soft, wet ground. ●verb (**be/get bogged down**) be prevented from making progress.
■ **boggy** adjective.

bogey or **bogy** noun (plural **bogeys**) **1** an evil spirit. **2** a cause of fear or alarm.

bogeyman or **bogyman** noun (plural **bogeymen**) an evil spirit.

boggle verb (**boggles, boggling, boggled**) informal **1** be astonished or baffled. **2** (**boggle at**) hesitate to do.

bogie /boh-gi/ noun (plural **bogies**) a supporting frame with wheels, fitted beneath the end of a railway vehicle.

bogus adjective not genuine or true.

Bohemian noun an artistic and unconventional person. ●adjective unconventional.

boil¹ verb **1** (of a liquid) reach a temperature where it bubbles and turns to vapour. **2** cook food in boiling water. **3** (**boil down to**) amount to. ●noun the process of boiling.

boil² noun an inflamed pus-filled swelling on the skin.

boiler noun a device for heating water.
□ **boiler suit** Brit. a pair of overalls worn for dirty work.

boiling adjective **1** (of a liquid) at or near the temperature at which it boils. **2** informal very hot.

THESAURUS

bob verb move up and down, bounce, toss, skip, dance, wobble, jiggle, joggle, jolt, jerk.

bodily adjective *bodily sensations:* physical, corporeal, corporal, mortal, material, tangible, concrete, real, actual.
OPPOSITES spiritual, mental.
●adverb *he hauled her bodily from the van:* forcefully, forcibly, violently, completely, entirely.

body noun **1** *the human body:* figure, frame, form, physique, anatomy, skeleton. **2** *he was hit by shrapnel in the head and body:* torso, trunk. **3** *the bodies were put in the fire:* corpse, carcass, skeleton, remains; informal stiff; Medicine cadaver. **4** *the body of the article:* main part, core, heart, hub. **5** *the representative body of the employers:*

association, organization, assembly, delegation, committee, executive, company, society, corporation, group.

bog noun marsh, swamp, mire, quagmire, morass, slough, fen, wetland.
□ **bog someone/something down** mire, stick, entangle, ensnare, embroil, hamper, hinder, impede, obstruct, swamp, overwhelm.

bogus adjective fake, spurious, false, fraudulent, sham, counterfeit, forged, feigned; informal phoney, pretend.
OPPOSITES genuine.

boil¹ verb *the soup is boiling:* simmer, bubble, stew, seethe, froth, foam.

boil² noun *a boil on her neck:* swelling, spot, pimple, blister, gathering, pustule, carbuncle, abscess.

boisterous adjective lively and high-spirited.
■ **boisterously** adverb.

bold adjective 1 brave and confident. 2 (of a colour or design) strong or vivid. 3 (of printed words or letters) in thick, dark type.
■ **boldly** adverb **boldness** noun.

bole noun a tree trunk.

bolero noun (plural **boleros**) 1 /buh-**lair**-oh/ a Spanish dance. 2 /**bol**-uh-roh/ a woman's short open jacket.

Bolivian noun a person from Bolivia.
• adjective relating to Bolivia.

boll noun the rounded seed capsule of plants such as cotton or flax.

bollard noun 1 Brit. a short post used to prevent traffic from entering an area. 2 a short post on a ship or quayside for securing a rope.

Bolshevik noun a member of the group which seized power in the Russian Revolution of 1917.
■ **Bolshevism** noun.

bolshie or **bolshy** adjective Brit. informal bad-tempered and uncooperative.

bolster noun a long, firm pillow. • verb (**bolsters**, **bolstering**, **bolstered**) support or strengthen.

bolt noun 1 a heavy metal pin with a head that screws into a nut, used to fasten things together. 2 a bar that slides into a socket to fasten a door or window. 3 a short, heavy arrow shot from a crossbow. 4 a flash of lightning. 5 a roll of fabric.
• verb 1 fasten with a bolt. 2 run away suddenly. 3 eat food quickly. 4 (of a plant)

grow quickly upwards and stop flowering as seeds develop.
□ **bolt-hole** a place to escape to and hide in. **bolt upright** with the back very straight. **make a bolt for** run suddenly towards.

bomb noun 1 a device designed to explode and cause damage. 2 (**the bomb**) nuclear weapons. 3 (**a bomb**) Brit. informal a large sum of money. • verb 1 attack with a bomb or bombs. 2 Brit. informal move very quickly. 3 informal fail badly.

bombard verb 1 attack continuously with bombs or other missiles. 2 direct a continuous flow of questions or information at.
■ **bombardment** noun.

bombardier /bom-buh-**deer**/ noun 1 a rank of non-commissioned officer in some artillery regiments. 2 a member of a bomber crew in the US air force who is responsible for releasing the bombs.

bombast noun language that sounds impressive but has little meaning.
■ **bombastic** adjective.

bomber noun 1 an aircraft designed for dropping bombs. 2 a person who plants bombs.

bombshell noun 1 a great surprise or shock. 2 informal a very attractive woman.

bona fide /boh-nuh **fy**-di/ adjective genuine; real.

bonanza noun 1 a situation creating wealth or success. 2 a large amount of something desirable.

bonbon noun a sweet.

bond noun 1 a thing used to tie or fasten

THESAURUS

boisterous adjective lively, animated, exuberant, spirited, noisy, loud, rowdy, unruly, wild, uproarious, unrestrained, uninhibited, uncontrolled, rough, disorderly, riotous; informal rumbustious.
OPPOSITES restrained.

bold adjective 1 bold adventurers: daring, intrepid, brave, courageous, valiant, fearless, dauntless, audacious, daredevil, adventurous, heroic, plucky; informal gutsy, spunky. 2 a bold pattern: striking, vivid, bright, strong, eye-catching, prominent, gaudy, lurid, garish.
OPPOSITES timid, pale, faint.

bolster verb strengthen, reinforce, boost, fortify, support, buoy up, shore up, maintain, help, augment, increase.
OPPOSITES undermine.

bolt noun 1 the bolt on the door: bar, lock, catch, latch, fastener. 2 nuts and bolts: pin, rivet, peg, screw.
• verb 1 he bolted the door: lock, bar, latch, fasten, secure. 2 the lid was bolted down: pin, rivet, peg, screw, fasten, fix. 3 Anna

bolted from the room: dash, dart, run, sprint, hurtle, rush, fly, shoot; informal tear, scoot, leg it. 4 he bolted his breakfast: gobble, gulp, wolf, guzzle, devour; informal demolish, polish off, shovel down; N. Amer. informal scarf, snarf.

bomb noun explosive, incendiary (device), missile, projectile.
• verb their headquarters were bombed: blow up, blast, shell, blitz, strafe, pound, bombard, attack, assault, destroy, demolish.

bombard verb 1 gun batteries bombarded the islands: shell, pound, blitz, strafe, bomb, batter, blast, pelt. 2 we were bombarded with information: swamp, inundate, flood, deluge, snow under, overwhelm.

bonanza noun windfall, godsend, blessing, bonus, stroke of luck; informal jackpot.

bond noun 1 the women forged a close bond: friendship, relationship, fellowship, partnership, association, affiliation, alliance, attachment. 2 I've broken my

b

things together. 2 (**bonds**) ropes or chains used to hold someone prisoner. 3 an instinct or feeling that draws people together. 4 a legally binding agreement. 5 a certificate issued by a government or public company promising to repay money lent to it at a fixed rate of interest and at a particular time. •verb 1 join or be joined securely to something else. 2 feel connected to someone.

bondage noun 1 the state of being a slave or of having no freedom. 2 sexual activity that involves the tying up of one partner.

bone noun 1 any of the pieces of hard material that make up the skeleton in vertebrates. 2 the hard material of which bones are made. •verb (**bones**, **boning**, **boned**) remove the bones from meat or fish before cooking.
□ bone china white porcelain that contains a mineral obtained from bone. bone dry completely dry. bone idle very lazy. bone of contention something argued about. close to the bone 1 (of a remark) accurate to the point of making you feel uncomfortable. 2 (of a joke or story) rather rude. have a bone to pick with informal have reason to quarrel with someone or to tell them off. make no bones about be direct in stating or dealing with.
■ boneless adjective.

bonemeal noun ground bones used as a fertilizer.

bonfire noun an open-air fire lit to burn rubbish or as a celebration.

bongo noun (plural **bongos**) each of a pair of small drums that are held between the knees.

bonhomie /**bon**-uh-mee/ noun good-natured friendliness.

bonkers adjective informal mad.

bonnet noun 1 a woman's or child's hat tied under the chin. 2 Brit. the hinged metal cover over the engine of a vehicle.

bonny or **bonnie** adjective (**bonnier**, **bonniest**) chiefly Scottish & N. English attractive and healthy-looking.

bonsai /**bon**-sy/ noun the art of growing miniature ornamental trees.

bonus noun 1 a sum of money added to a person's wages for good performance. 2 an unexpected extra benefit.

bon voyage /bon voy-**yahzh**/ exclamation have a good journey.

bony adjective (**bonier**, **boniest**) 1 containing or resembling bones. 2 so thin that the bones can be seen.

boo exclamation 1 said suddenly to surprise someone. 2 said to show disapproval or contempt. •verb (**boos**, **booing**, **booed**) say 'boo' to show disapproval or contempt.

boob Brit. informal noun an embarrassing mistake. •verb make an embarrassing mistake.

booby noun (plural **boobies**) informal a stupid person.
□ booby prize a prize given to someone who comes last in a contest. booby trap an object containing a hidden explosive device.

boogie verb (**boogies**, **boogieing**, **boogied**) informal dance to pop music.

book noun 1 a written or printed work consisting of pages fastened together along one side and bound in covers. 2 a main division of a literary work or of the Bible. 3 (**books**) a record of financial transactions. •verb 1 reserve accommodation or a ticket. 2 (**book in**) register your arrival at a hotel. 3 engage a performer or guest for an event. 4 (**be booked up**) have all places or dates reserved. 5 make an official note of the name of someone who has broken a law or rule.

bookcase noun a cabinet containing shelves on which books are kept.

bookend noun a support placed at the end of a row of books to keep them upright.

THESAURUS

bond: promise, pledge, vow, oath, word (of honour), guarantee, assurance, agreement, contract, pact, deal.
•verb *the extensions are bonded to your hair*: join, fasten, fix, affix, attach, secure, bind, stick, fuse.

bonus noun 1 *the extra work's a real bonus*: extra, plus, benefit, advantage, boon, blessing, godsend, stroke of luck, attraction. 2 *she's on a good salary and she gets a bonus*: gratuity, handout, gift, present, reward, prize, incentive; informal perk, sweetener.
OPPOSITES disadvantage.

bony adjective skinny, thin, lean, gaunt,

spare, skin and bone, skeletal, emaciated, underweight.
OPPOSITES plump.

book noun 1 *he published his first book in 1610*: volume, tome, publication, title, novel, treatise, manual. 2 *he scribbled in his book*: notepad, notebook, pad, exercise book, logbook, ledger, journal, diary; Brit. jotter, pocketbook; N. Amer. scratch pad.
•verb 1 *she booked a table at the restaurant*: reserve, prearrange, order; informal bag. 2 *we booked a number of events in the Festival*: arrange, programme, schedule, timetable, line up, lay on; N. Amer. slate.
□ book in **register**, check in, enrol.

b

bookie noun (plural **bookies**) informal a bookmaker.

bookish adjective very interested in reading and studying.

bookkeeping noun the keeping of records of financial transactions.

booklet noun a small, thin book with paper covers.

bookmaker noun a person who takes bets and pays out winnings.

bookmark noun **1** a strip of leather or card used to mark a place in a book. **2** a record of the address of a computer file, Internet page, etc., enabling a user to return to it quickly. ● **verb** record the address of a computer file, Internet page, etc.

bookworm noun informal a person who loves reading.

boom[1] noun **1** a deep, loud sound. **2** a period of fast economic growth. ● **verb 1** make a deep, loud sound. **2** experience fast economic growth.

boom[2] noun **1** a movable pole to which the bottom of a sail is attached. **2** a movable arm carrying a microphone or film camera. **3** a beam used to form a barrier across the mouth of a harbour.

boomerang noun a curved flat piece of wood that follows a circle through the air and returns to you when you throw it.

boon noun a very helpful thing.

boor noun a rough and bad-mannered person.
■ **boorish** adjective.

boost verb help or encourage. ● noun a source of help or encouragement.

booster noun **1** a dose of a vaccine that increases or renews the effect of an earlier

one. **2** the part of a rocket or spacecraft used to give acceleration after lift-off.

boot noun **1** an item of footwear covering the foot and the ankle or lower leg. **2** Brit. a space at the back of a car for carrying luggage. **3** informal a hard kick. **4** (**the boot**) informal dismissal from a job. ● **verb 1** informal kick someone hard. **2** (**boot someone out**) informal force someone to leave. **3** start a computer and make it ready to operate. □ **to boot** as well.

bootee or **bootie** noun **1** a baby's woollen shoe. **2** a woman's short boot.

booth noun **1** an enclosed compartment that gives you privacy when telephoning, voting, etc. **2** a small temporary structure used for selling goods or staging shows at a market or fair.

bootleg adjective made or distributed illegally.
■ **bootlegger** noun **bootlegging** noun.

booty noun valuable stolen goods.

booze informal noun alcoholic drink. ● **verb** (**boozes, boozing, boozed**) drink a lot of alcohol.
■ **boozer** noun **boozy** adjective.

bop informal noun a dance to pop music. ● **verb** (**bops, bopping, bopped**) dance to pop music.
■ **bopper** noun.

boracic adjective having to do with boric acid.

borage noun a plant with bright blue flowers and hairy leaves.

borax noun a white mineral used in making glass.

Bordeaux /bor-**doh**/ noun a wine from the Bordeaux region of France.

THESAURUS

booklet noun pamphlet, brochure, leaflet, tract; N. Amer. folder, mailer.

boom noun **1** *the boom of the waves on the rocks:* roar, rumble, thunder, crashing, drumming, pounding, echoing, resonance, reverberation. **2** *an unprecedented boom in sales:* increase, growth, advance, boost, escalation, improvement, upsurge, upturn. OPPOSITES slump.
● **verb 1** *thunder boomed overhead:* roar, rumble, thunder, crash, roll, clap, explode, bang, resound, blare, echo, resonate, reverberate. **2** *a voice boomed at her:* shout, yell, bellow, roar, thunder, bawl; informal holler. **3** *the market continued to boom:* flourish, thrive, prosper, burgeon, progress, improve, pick up, expand. OPPOSITES slump.

boorish adjective coarse, uncouth, rude, vulgar, uncivilized, unrefined, rough, thuggish, loutish, Neanderthal; Brit. informal yobbish; Austral. informal ocker.

OPPOSITES refined.

boost verb *they used advertising to boost sales:* increase, raise, escalate, improve, strengthen, inflate, push up, promote, advance, foster, stimulate, encourage, facilitate, help, assist, aid; informal hike, bump up.
OPPOSITES decrease.
● **noun 1** *a boost to your morale:* uplift, lift, spur, encouragement, help, inspiration, stimulus, fillip; informal shot in the arm. **2** *a boost in sales:* increase, expansion, upturn, upsurge, rise, escalation, improvement, advance, growth, boom; informal hike.
OPPOSITES decrease.

boot verb kick, punt, tap, propel, drive, knock.

booth noun **1** *booths for different traders:* stall, stand, kiosk. **2** *a phone booth:* cubicle, kiosk, box, enclosure, cabin.

booty noun loot, plunder, haul, spoils, ill-gotten gains, pickings; informal swag.

b

border noun **1** a boundary between two countries or areas. **2** a decorative band around the edge of something. **3** a strip of ground along the edge of a lawn where flowers or shrubs are planted. •verb (**borders, bordering, bordered**) **1** form a border around or along. **2** (of a country or area) be next to. **3** (**border on**) come near to.

borderline noun a boundary. •adjective on the boundary between two qualities or categories.

bore[1] verb (**bores, boring, bored**) make a hole in something with a drill or other tool. •noun the hollow part inside a gun barrel or other tube.

bore[2] noun a dull person or activity. •verb (**bores, boring, bored**) make someone feel tired and unenthusiastic by being dull. ■ **boring** adjective.

bore[3] past of BEAR[1].

bored adjective feeling tired and unenthusiastic because you have nothing interesting to do.

> ! use **bored by** or **bored with** rather than **bored of**.

boredom noun the state of feeling bored.

borehole noun a deep hole in the ground made to find water or oil.

boric acid noun a substance made from boron, used as an antiseptic.

born adjective **1** having come out of your mother's body; having started life.

2 having a particular natural ability: *a born engineer*. **3** (**born of**) existing as a result of a situation or feeling. □ **born-again** newly converted to Christianity or some other cause.

> ! don't confuse **born** with **borne**, which is the past participle of **bear** and means 'carried'.

borne past participle of BEAR[1].

Bornean /bor-ni-uhn/ noun a person from Borneo. •adjective relating to Borneo.

boron noun a chemical element used in making alloy steel and in nuclear reactors.

borough noun **1** Brit. a town with a corporation and privileges granted by a royal charter. **2** a part of London or New York City which has its own local council.

borrow verb take and use something belonging to someone else with the intention of returning it.

borscht or **borsch** /borsht, borsch/ noun a Russian or Polish soup made with beetroot.

borstal noun Brit. historical a type of prison for young offenders.

Bosnian /boz-ni-uhn/ noun a person from Bosnia. •adjective relating to Bosnia.

bosom noun **1** a woman's breast or chest. **2** loving care: *he went home to the bosom of his family*. •adjective (of a friend) very close.

boss[1] informal noun a person who is in charge

THESAURUS

border noun **1** *the border of a medieval manuscript:* edge, margin, perimeter, circumference, periphery, rim, fringe, verge, sides. **2** *the French border:* frontier, boundary, borderline, perimeter.
•verb **1** *the fields were bordered by hedges:* surround, enclose, encircle, edge, fringe, bound, flank. **2** *the straps are bordered with gold braid:* edge, fringe, hem, trim, pipe, finish. **3** *the forest bordered Broadmoor:* adjoin, abut, be next to, be adjacent to, touch.
□ **border on verge on,** approach, come close to, be comparable to, approximate to, be tantamount to.

bore[1] verb *bore a hole:* drill, pierce, perforate, puncture, punch, tunnel, burrow, mine, dig, gouge, sink.

bore[2] verb *the television news bored Philip:* weary, pall on, tire, fatigue, send to sleep, leave cold; informal turn off.
OPPOSITES interest.
•noun *you can be such a bore:* tedious person/thing, tiresome person/thing, bother, nuisance, pest, annoyance, trial, thorn in your flesh/side; informal drag, pain (in the neck), headache, hassle.

boredom noun tedium, ennui, apathy, weariness, dullness, monotony, repetitiveness, flatness, dreariness.
OPPOSITES interest, excitement.

boring adjective tedious, dull, dreary, monotonous, repetitive, uneventful, unimaginative, characterless, featureless, colourless, lifeless, uninteresting, unexciting, lacklustre, humdrum, mind-numbing, soul-destroying, wearisome, tiresome; informal deadly; Brit. informal samey; N. Amer. informal dullsville.
OPPOSITES interesting, exciting.

borrow verb **1** *we borrowed a lot of money:* loan, lease, hire; informal cadge, scrounge, bum, touch someone for; N. Amer. informal mooch; Austral./NZ informal bludge. **2** *adventurous chefs borrow foreign techniques:* adopt, take on, acquire, embrace.
OPPOSITES lend.

boss (informal) noun *the boss of a large company:* head, chief, principal, director, president, chief executive, chair, manager, supervisor, foreman, overseer, controller, employer, owner, proprietor; Brit. informal

b

of other people at work. • **verb** tell someone what to do in an arrogant or annoying way.

boss² noun a knob at the centre of a shield, propeller, or similar object.

bossa nova /bos-suh **noh**-vuh/ **noun** a dance like the samba, from Brazil.

boss-eyed adjective Brit. informal cross-eyed.

bossy adjective (**bossier, bossiest**) tending to tell people what to do in an arrogant or annoying way.
■ **bossiness** noun.

bosun or **bo'sun** /boh-suhn/ = BOATSWAIN.

botany noun the scientific study of plants.
■ **botanical** (or **botanic**) adjective **botanist** noun.

botch verb informal do something badly or carelessly.

both determiner & pronoun two people or things, considered together. • **adverb** applying to each of two alternatives.

bother verb (**bothers, bothering, bothered**)
1 take the trouble to do something.
2 annoy, worry, or upset someone.
3 (**bother with** or **about**) feel concern about or interest in. • **noun 1** trouble and fuss. **2** (**a bother**) a cause of trouble or fuss.

bothersome adjective troublesome.

Botswanan noun a person from Botswana, a country in southern Africa. • **adjective** relating to Botswana.

bottle noun **1** a container with a narrow neck, used for storing liquids. **2** Brit. informal courage. • **verb** (**bottles, bottling, bottled**)
1 place in bottles for storage. **2** (**bottle**

something **up**) hide your feelings.
□ **bottle green** dark green.

bottleneck noun a narrow section of road where the flow of traffic is restricted.

bottom noun **1** the lowest or furthest point or part of something. **2** the lowest position in a competition or ranking. **3** a person's buttocks. **4** (also **bottoms**) the lower half of a two-piece garment. • **adjective** in the lowest or furthest position. • **verb** (**bottom out**) (of a situation) reach the lowest point before becoming stable or improving.
□ **get to the bottom of** find an explanation for. **the bottom line** informal the most important factor.
■ **bottomless** adjective.

botulism /bot-yuu-li-z'm/ noun a dangerous form of food poisoning.

boudoir /boo-dwar/ noun a woman's bedroom or small private room.

bouffant /boo-fon/ adjective (of hair) styled so as to stand out from the head in a rounded shape.

bougainvillea /boo-guhn-**vil**-li-uh/ noun a tropical climbing plant with brightly coloured flower-like leaves (called bracts).

bough noun a large branch.

bought past and past participle of BUY.

> **!** don't confuse **bought** with **brought**, which is the past of **bring**.

boulder noun a large rock.

boulevard /boo-luh-vard/ noun a wide street.

bounce verb (**bounces, bouncing, bounced**)

---

gaffer, governor; N. Amer. informal head honcho.
• **verb** *you have no right to boss me about:* order about/around, dictate to, bully, push around/about, call the shots, lay down the law; informal bulldoze, walk all over, railroad.

bossy adjective (informal) domineering, pushy, overbearing, imperious, officious, authoritarian, dictatorial; informal high and mighty.
OPPOSITES submissive.

bother verb **1** *no one bothered her:* disturb, trouble, inconvenience, pester, badger, harass, molest, plague; informal hassle, bug; N. English informal mither; N. Amer. informal ride.
2 *the incident was too small to bother about:* mind, care, worry, concern yourself, trouble yourself. **3** *there was something bothering him:* worry, trouble, concern, perturb, disturb, disquiet; informal rattle.
• **noun 1** *I don't want to put you to any bother:* trouble, effort, exertion, inconvenience, fuss, pains; informal hassle.
2 *the food was such a bother to cook:* nuisance, pest, palaver, rigmarole, job,

trial, bind, bore, drag, inconvenience, trouble; informal hassle, headache, pain (in the neck). **3** *there was a spot of bother in the public bar:* disorder, fighting, trouble, disturbance, commotion, uproar; informal hoo-ha, aggro, argy-bargy, kerfuffle.

bottom noun **1** *the bottom of the stairs:* foot, lowest part, base, foundation. **2** *the bottom of the car:* underside, underneath, undersurface, underbelly. **3** *the bottom of Lake Ontario:* floor, bed, depths. **4** *the bottom of his garden:* farthest point, far end, extremity. **5** (Brit.) *I've got a tattoo on my bottom:* buttocks, rear (end), rump, seat; informal behind, backside; Brit. informal bum, botty, jacksie; N. Amer. informal butt, fanny; humorous posterior.
OPPOSITES top, surface.
• **adjective** *she sat on the bottom step:* lowest, last, bottommost.
OPPOSITES top.

bounce verb **1** *the ball bounced:* rebound, spring back, ricochet; N. Amer. carom.
2 *William bounced down the stairs:* bound, leap, jump, spring, bob, hop, skip, gambol,

b

1 move quickly up or away from a surface after hitting it. 2 move or jump up and down repeatedly. 3 informal (of a cheque) be returned by a bank when there is not enough money in an account for it to be paid. •noun 1 an act of bouncing. 2 lively confidence.

bouncer noun a person employed by a nightclub to control or keep out troublemakers.

bouncy adjective (**bouncier, bounciest**) 1 able to bounce, or making something bounce. 2 confident and lively.

bound¹ verb move with long, leaping strides. •noun a leaping movement.

bound² verb 1 form the boundary of. 2 restrict. •noun a boundary or restriction. □ out of bounds 1 (in sport) beyond the field of play. 2 beyond where you are allowed to go.

bound³ past and past participle of **BIND**. •adjective 1 restricted to or by a place or situation: *his job kept him city-bound.* 2 going towards somewhere: *a train bound for Edinburgh.* 3 (**bound to**) certain to be, do, or have.

boundary noun (plural **boundaries**) a line marking the limits of an area.

bounder noun Brit. informal, dated a man who is dishonest or treats other people badly.

boundless adjective unlimited.

bounteous adjective old use given or giving generously.

bountiful adjective 1 existing in large quantities. 2 giving generously.

bounty noun (plural **bounties**) 1 literary generosity, or something given in generous amounts. 2 a reward paid for killing or capturing someone.

bouquet /boo-**kay**, boh-**kay**/ noun 1 a bunch of flowers. 2 the pleasant smell of a particular wine or perfume.

bourbon /**ber**-buhn/ noun an American whisky made from maize and rye.

bourgeois /**boor**-zhwah/ adjective having to do with the middle class, especially in being concerned with wealth and social status.

bourgeoisie /boor-zhwah-**zee**/ noun the middle class.

bout noun 1 a short period of great activity, or of illness. 2 a wrestling or boxing match.

boutique /boo-**teek**/ noun a small shop selling fashionable clothes.

bovine /**boh**-vyn/ adjective 1 having to do with cattle. 2 rather slow and stupid.

bow¹ /rhymes with toe/ noun 1 a knot tied with two loops and two loose ends. 2 a weapon for shooting arrows, consisting of

THESAURUS

trip, prance.
•noun 1 *the pitch's uneven bounce:* springiness, resilience, elasticity, give. 2 *she had lost her bounce:* vitality, vigour, energy, vivacity, liveliness, animation, sparkle, verve, spirit; informal get-up-and-go, pep, zing.

bound¹ adjective 1 *he raised his bound ankles:* tied, restrained, fixed, fastened, secured. 2 *she seemed bound to win:* certain, sure, very likely, destined. 3 *bound by the Official Secrets Act:* constrained, obliged, compelled, required, obligated. 4 *religion and morality are bound up with one another:* connected, linked, tied, united, allied, interdependent.
OPPOSITES free, unlikely, independent.

bound² verb *Louis came bounding down the stairs:* leap, jump, spring, vault, bounce, hop, skip, dance, prance, gambol, gallop.

bound³ verb 1 *corporate freedom is bounded by law:* limit, restrict, confine, circumscribe, demarcate, delimit. 2 *the heath is bounded by a hedge:* enclose, surround, encircle, circle, border, close in/off, hem in. 3 *the garden was bounded by Mill Lane:* border, adjoin, abut, be next to, be adjacent to.

boundary noun 1 *the boundary between Israel and Jordan:* border, frontier, borderline, partition. 2 *the boundary*

between art and advertising: dividing line, division, borderline, cut-off point. 3 *the boundary of his estate:* limits, confines, bounds, margins, edges, fringes, border, periphery, perimeter.

bouquet noun 1 *her bridal bouquet:* posy, nosegay, spray, corsage, buttonhole, garland, wreath, arrangement. 2 *the Chardonnay has a fine bouquet:* aroma, nose, smell, fragrance, perfume, scent, odour.

bourgeois adjective middle-class, conservative, conformist, conventional, propertied, provincial, suburban, small-town.
OPPOSITES proletarian.

bout noun 1 *a bout of exercise:* spell, period, stretch, stint, session, burst, flurry, spurt. 2 *a coughing bout:* attack, fit, spasm. 3 *he is fighting only his fifth bout:* contest, fight, match, round, competition, meeting, encounter.

bow¹ verb 1 *the officers bowed:* nod, bend, stoop, bob, curtsy, kneel, genuflect. 2 *the mast quivered and bowed:* bend, buckle, curve, flex, deform. 3 *the government bowed to foreign pressure:* give in, submit, yield, surrender, succumb, capitulate.
•noun *a perfunctory bow:* nod, bob, obeisance, curtsy, genuflection.

a string held taut by a strip of bent wood.
3 a rod with horsehair stretched along its length, used for playing some stringed instruments.
□ **bow-legged** having legs that curve outwards at the knee. **bow tie** a man's tie that is tied in a bow.

bow² /rhymes with cow/ **verb 1** bend the head and upper body as a sign of respect. **2** bend with age or under a heavy weight. **3** give in to pressure. **4** (**bow out**) withdraw from an activity. • **noun** an act of bowing.
□ **bow and scrape** try too hard to please someone.

bow³ /rhymes with cow/ or **bows noun** the front end of a ship.

bowdlerize or **bowdlerise** /**bowd**-luh-ryz/ **verb** (**bowdlerizes, bowdlerizing, bowdlerized**) remove parts of a written work that might shock or offend people.

bowel noun 1 (also **bowels**) the intestine. **2** (**bowels**) the innermost parts of something.
□ **bowel movement** an act of emptying waste matter from the bowels.

bower noun a pleasant shady place under trees.

bowl¹ noun 1 a round, deep dish or basin. **2** a rounded, hollow part of an object.

bowl² verb 1 roll a round object along the ground. **2** Cricket (of a bowler) throw the ball towards the wicket. **3** Brit. move along rapidly and smoothly. • **noun** a heavy ball used in bowls or tenpin bowling.
□ **bowl someone over 1** knock someone down. **2** informal surprise or impress someone very much.

bowler¹ noun 1 Cricket a member of the fielding side who bowls. **2** a player at bowls or tenpin bowling.

bowler² noun a man's hard black felt hat

that is rounded at the top and has a rim.

bowling noun bowls, tenpin bowling, or skittles.

bowls noun a game played with wooden balls called bowls, in which you roll your bowl as close as possible to a small white ball (the jack).

box¹ noun 1 a square or rectangular container with a lid. **2** an enclosed area reserved for a group of people in a theatre or sports ground. **3** (**the box**) informal television. • **verb 1** put something in a box. **2** (**box someone in**) restrict or confine someone.
□ **box number** a number identifying an advertisement in a newspaper, used as an address for replies. **box office** the place at a theatre or cinema where tickets are sold. **box room** Brit. a small room used for storage.

box² verb take part in boxing. • **noun** a slap on the side of a person's head.
□ **box someone's ears** slap someone on both sides of the head.

box³ noun a shrub with small, round glossy leaves.

boxer noun 1 a person who boxes as a sport. **2** a breed of dog with a smooth brown coat and a flattened face.
□ **boxer shorts** men's underpants that look like shorts.

boxing noun a sport in which contestants fight each other wearing big padded gloves.

Boxing Day noun Brit. a public holiday on the day after Christmas Day.

boxy adjective 1 roughly square in shape. **2** (of a room or space) cramped.

boy noun a male child or youth.
■ **boyhood noun** **boyish adjective.**

boycott verb 1 refuse to have dealings with. **2** refuse to buy goods as a protest.

THESAURUS

bow² noun the bow of the tanker: prow, front, stem, nose, head.

bowels plural noun 1 a disorder of the bowels: intestines, entrails, viscera, innards, digestive system; Medicine gut; informal guts, insides. **2** the bowels of the ship: interior, inside, core, belly, depths, recesses; informal innards.

bowl¹ verb he bowled a hundred or so balls: throw, pitch, hurl, toss, lob, fling, roll, launch, propel; informal chuck, sling, bung.

bowl² noun dish, basin, pot, crock, vessel, receptacle.

box¹ noun 1 carton, pack, packet, case, crate, chest, coffer, casket. **2** a telephone box: booth, cubicle, compartment, kiosk, cabin, hut.

• **verb** Muriel boxed up his clothes: pack, package, parcel, encase, bundle, crate.

box² verb he began boxing professionally: fight, prizefight, spar, battle, brawl; informal scrap.

boxer noun fighter, pugilist, prizefighter; informal bruiser, scrapper.

boy noun lad, youth, young man, stripling; Scottish & N. English laddie; disapproving brat. See also **CHILD**.

boycott verb they boycotted the election: shun, snub, spurn, avoid, abstain from, reject, veto.
OPPOSITES support.
• **noun** a boycott on the use of tropical timbers: ban, veto, embargo, prohibition, sanction, restriction, avoidance, rejection.

b

•noun an act of boycotting someone or something.

boyfriend noun a person's regular male companion in a romantic or sexual relationship.

bra noun a woman's undergarment worn to support the breasts.

brace noun 1 a part that strengthens or supports something. 2 (**braces**) Brit. a pair of straps that pass over the shoulders and fasten to the top of trousers to hold them up. 3 a wire device used to straighten the teeth. 4 (plural **brace**) a pair. 5 (also **brace and bit**) a drilling tool with a crank handle and a socket to hold a bit. •verb (**braces, bracing, braced**) 1 make something stronger or firmer with a brace. 2 press your body firmly against something to stay balanced. 3 (**brace yourself**) prepare for something difficult or unpleasant.

bracelet noun an ornamental band or chain worn on the wrist or arm.

bracing adjective refreshing; making you feel full of energy.

bracken noun a tall fern.

bracket noun 1 each of a pair of marks ( ) [ ] { } < > used to enclose words or figures. 2 a category of similar people or things. 3 a right-angled support that sticks out from a wall. •verb (**brackets, bracketing, bracketed**) 1 enclose in brackets. 2 place in the same category.

brackish adjective (of water) slightly salty.

bract noun a leaf with a flower in the angle where it meets the stem.

brag verb (**brags, bragging, bragged**) speak boastfully. •noun a simplified form of the card game poker.

braggart /**brag**-gert/ noun a boastful person.

braid noun 1 threads woven into a decorative band. 2 a length of hair made up of strands plaited together. •verb 1 form hair into a braid. 2 trim something with braid.

Braille noun a written language for blind people, using raised dots.

brain noun 1 an organ contained in the skull that controls thought and feeling and is the centre of the nervous system. 2 intellectual ability. 3 (**the brains**) informal the main organizer within a group. •verb informal hit someone hard on the head.

brainchild noun informal an idea or invention thought up by a particular person.

brainless adjective very stupid.

brainstorm noun Brit. informal a moment in which you are suddenly unable to think clearly. •verb hold a group discussion to solve a problem or produce new ideas.

brainwash verb force someone to accept an idea or belief by putting pressure on them or repeating the same thing over and over again.

brainwave noun 1 an electrical impulse in the brain. 2 informal a sudden clever idea.

brainy adjective (**brainier, brainiest**) informal intelligent.

braise verb (**braises, braising, braised**) fry food lightly and then stew it slowly in a closed container.

brake noun a device for slowing or stopping a moving vehicle. •verb (**brakes, braking, braked**) slow or stop a vehicle with a brake.

> ❗ don't confuse **brake** with **break** which mainly means 'separate into pieces' or 'a pause or short rest'.

bramble noun 1 a blackberry bush or similar prickly shrub. 2 Brit. the fruit of the blackberry.

bran noun pieces of the outer husk left when grain is made into flour.

THESAURUS

boyfriend noun lover, sweetheart, beloved, darling, partner; informal fella, flame, fancy man; N. Amer. informal squeeze.

brace noun the aquarium is supported by wooden braces: prop, strut, stay, support, bracket.
•verb 1 the plane's wing is braced by rods: support, shore up, prop up, hold up, buttress, reinforce. 2 he braced his hand on the railing: steady, secure, stabilize, poise, fix. 3 brace yourself for disappointment: prepare, get ready, gear up, nerve, steel, fortify; informal psych yourself up.

bracing adjective invigorating, refreshing, stimulating, energizing, exhilarating, restorative, rejuvenating.

bracket noun 1 each speaker is fixed on a bracket: support, prop, stay, batten, rest, mounting, rack, frame. 2 a higher tax bracket: group, category, grade, classification, division.

brag verb boast, crow, swagger, swank, bluster, gloat, show off, blow your own trumpet, sing your own praises; informal talk big.

brain noun intelligence, intellect, brainpower, cleverness, wit(s), reasoning, wisdom, judgement, understanding, sense; informal nous, grey matter; N. Amer. informal smarts.

brake noun curb, check, restraint, control, limit, constraint.
OPPOSITES accelerator.
•verb slow (down), decelerate, reduce speed.
OPPOSITES accelerate.

b

branch noun **1** a part of a tree which grows out from the trunk. **2** a river, road, or railway extending out from a main one. **3** a division of a larger group. • verb **1** divide into one or more branches. **2** (**branch out**) start doing a different sort of activity.

brand noun **1** a type of product made by a company under a particular name. **2** (also **brand name**) a name given to a product by its maker. **3** a mark burned on farm animals with a piece of hot metal. **4** a piece of smouldering wood. • verb **1** mark with a piece of hot metal. **2** mark someone out as being bad in a particular way. **3** give a brand name to.
□ **brand new** completely new.

brandish verb wave something as a threat or in anger or excitement.

brandy noun (plural **brandies**) a strong alcoholic drink made from wine or fermented fruit juice.

brash adjective confident in a rather rude or aggressive way.
■ **brashly** adverb **brashness** noun.

brass noun **1** a yellowish metal made by mixing copper and zinc. **2** (also **horse brass**) Brit. a flat brass ornament for a horse's harness. **3** Brit. a brass plate fixed in a church in memory of someone. **4** brass wind instruments forming a section of an orchestra.
□ **brass band** a group of musicians playing brass instruments. **top brass** informal people in authority.

brasserie /brass-uh-ri/ noun (plural

brasseries) an inexpensive French or French-style restaurant.

brassica /brass-ik-uh/ noun a plant of a family that includes cabbages and swedes.

brassiere /braz-i-er/ noun a bra.

brassy adjective (**brassier, brassiest**) **1** resembling brass in colour. **2** unpleasantly bright or showy. **3** harsh or blaring like a brass instrument.

brat noun informal a badly behaved child.

bravado noun confidence or a show of confidence that is intended to impress.

brave adjective willing to do something that is dangerous or frightening; not afraid.
• noun dated an American Indian warrior.
• verb (**braves, braving, braved**) face or deal with something frightening or unpleasant.
■ **bravely** adverb **bravery** noun.

bravo exclamation shouted to express approval for a performer.

bravura /bruh-vyoor-uh/ noun **1** great skill; brilliance. **2** the display of great daring.

brawl noun a noisy fight or quarrel. • verb take part in a brawl.

brawn noun physical strength.
■ **brawny** adjective.

bray verb (of a donkey) make a loud, harsh cry. • noun the loud, harsh cry of a donkey.

brazen adjective not caring if other people think you are behaving badly; shameless.
• verb (**brazen it out**) endure an awkward situation without seeming ashamed or embarrassed.
■ **brazenly** adverb.

brazier /bray-zi-er/ noun a portable heater

THESAURUS

branch noun **1** the branches of a tree: bough, limb, arm, offshoot, twig. **2** the judicial branch of government: division, subdivision, section, subsection, department, unit, sector, wing. **3** the corporation's New York branch: office, bureau, agency, subsidiary.
• verb **1** the place where the road branches: fork, divide, split, bifurcate. **2** narrow paths branched off the road: diverge, deviate, split off, fan out, radiate.

brand noun **1** a new brand of margarine: make, line, label, marque, trade name, trademark, proprietary name. **2** her particular brand of humour: type, kind, sort, variety, class, category, genre, style, ilk; N. Amer. stripe.
• verb **1** the letter M was branded on each animal: mark, stamp, burn, sear. **2** the scene was branded on her brain: engrave, stamp, etch, imprint. **3** the media branded us as communists: stigmatize, mark out, denounce, discredit, vilify, label.

brandish verb flourish, wave, shake, wield, swing, swish.

brash adjective **1** a brash man: self-assertive, pushy, cocky, self-confident, arrogant, bold, audacious, brazen. **2** brash colours: garish, gaudy, loud, flamboyant, showy, tasteless; informal flashy, tacky.
OPPOSITES meek, subdued.

brave adjective courageous, intrepid, bold, plucky, heroic, fearless, daring, audacious, dauntless, valiant; informal game, gutsy.
OPPOSITES cowardly.
• verb fans braved freezing temperatures: endure, put up with, bear, withstand, weather, suffer, face, confront, defy.
OPPOSITES succumb to.

bravery noun courage, boldness, heroism, intrepidity, nerve, daring, fearlessness, audacity, pluck, valour; informal guts; Brit. informal bottle; N. Amer. informal moxie.

brawl noun fight, skirmish, scuffle, tussle, fray, melee, fracas, fisticuffs; informal scrap, set-to; Brit. informal punch-up.

brawny adjective strong, muscular, muscly, well built, powerful, strapping, burly, sturdy; informal beefy, hulking.
OPPOSITES puny, weak.

b

holding lighted coals.

Brazilian noun a person from Brazil.
• **adjective** relating to Brazil.

brazil nut noun the large three-sided nut of a South American forest tree.

breach verb 1 make a hole in; break through. 2 break a rule or agreement.
• **noun 1** a gap made in a wall or barrier. **2** an act that breaks a rule or agreement. **3** a quarrel or disagreement.
□ **step into the breach** replace someone who is suddenly unable to do a job.

bread noun 1 food made of flour, water, and yeast mixed together and baked. 2 informal money.
□ **bread and butter** a person's main source of income.

breadcrumb noun a very small fragment of bread.

breaded adjective (of food) coated with breadcrumbs and fried.

breadline noun (**on the breadline**) Brit. very poor.

breadth noun 1 the distance from side to side of something. 2 wide range.

breadwinner noun a person who supports their family with the money they earn.

break verb (**breaks**, **breaking**, **broke**; past participle **broken**) 1 separate into pieces as a result of a blow or strain. 2 stop working. 3 interrupt a sequence or course. 4 fail to obey a rule or agreement. 5 beat a record. 6 work out a code. 7 make a rush or dash. 8 soften a fall. 9 suddenly become public. 10 (of a person's voice) falter and change tone. 11 (of a teenage boy's voice) become deeper. 12 (of the weather) change suddenly. • noun 1 a pause or gap. 2 a short rest. 3 an instance of breaking, or the point where something is broken. 4 a sudden rush or dash. 5 informal a chance. 6 Tennis the winning of a game against an opponent's serve. 7 Snooker & Billiards a continuous series of successful shots. 8 a short solo in music.
□ **break away** escape. **break down 1** stop working. **2** lose control of your emotions when upset. **break in** force your way into a building. **break something in** make a horse used to being ridden. **break off** stop suddenly. **break out 1** (of something unwelcome) start suddenly. **2** escape. **break up 1** (of a gathering) end. **2** (of a couple)

THESAURUS

breach noun 1 *a breach of the regulations:* contravention, violation, infringement, infraction, transgression. **2** *a breach in the sea wall:* break, rupture, split, crack, fracture, opening, gap, hole, fissure. OPPOSITES observance.
• verb 1 *the river breached its banks:* break (through), burst, rupture. **2** *the changes breached union rules:* break, contravene, violate, infringe, defy, disobey, flout.

breadth noun 1 *a breadth of 100 metres:* width, broadness, thickness, span, diameter. **2** *the breadth of his knowledge:* range, extent, scope, depth, reach, compass, scale.

break verb 1 shatter, smash, crack, snap, fracture, fragment, splinter, split, burst; informal bust. **2** *the coffee machine has broken:* stop working, break down, give out, go wrong, malfunction, crash; informal go kaput, conk out; Brit. informal pack up. **3** *traders who break the law:* violate, contravene, infringe, breach, defy, flout, disobey. **4** *the film broke box-office records:* beat, surpass, exceed, better, cap, top, outdo, outstrip. **5** *he tried to break the news gently:* reveal, disclose, divulge, impart, tell, announce, release. OPPOSITES repair, obey.
• noun 1 *the magazine has been published without a break since 1950:* stop, interruption, gap, disruption, stoppage, cessation. **2** *let's have a break:* rest, respite, recess, pause, interval, intermission; informal breather, time out. **3** *a*

break in the wall: gap, opening, space, hole, breach, chink, crack, fracture, fissure, tear, split.
□ **break down 1** *his van broke down.* See **BREAK** verb sense 2. **2** *pay negotiations broke down:* **fail**, collapse, founder, fall through. **3** *Vicky broke down, sobbing loudly:* **burst into tears**, lose control, be overcome, go to pieces; informal crack up, lose it. **break something down 1** *police broke the door down:* **knock down**, kick down, smash in, pull down, tear down, demolish. **2** *the information can be broken down:* **analyse**, categorize, classify, sort, itemize, organize, divide, separate, split. **break something off 1** *I broke off a branch from the tree:* **snap off**, pull off, sever, detach. **2** *they threatened to break off diplomatic relations:* **end**, terminate, stop, cease, call a halt to, suspend, discontinue; informal pull the plug on. **break out 1** *he broke out of the detention centre:* **escape**, abscond, flee, get free. **2** *fighting broke out:* **flare up**, start suddenly, erupt, burst out. **break up 1** *the meeting broke up:* **end**, finish, stop, terminate, adjourn; N. Amer. recess. **2** *the crowd began to break up:* **disperse**, scatter, disband, part company. **3** *Danny and I broke up last year:* **split up**, separate, part (company), divorce. **break something up 1** *police tried to break up the crowd:* **disperse**, scatter, disband. **2** *I'm not going to let you break up my marriage:* **wreck**, ruin, destroy.

b

end a relationship. **3** end a school term.
break wind release gas from the anus.
■ **breakable** adjective.

breakage noun the action of breaking something.

breakaway noun **1** a major change from something established. **2** (in sport) a sudden attack or forward movement.

breakdown noun **1** a failure or collapse. **2** a careful analysis of costs or figures.

breaker noun **1** a heavy sea wave that breaks on the shore. **2** a person that breaks up old machinery.

breakfast noun the first meal of the day. • verb eat breakfast.

breakneck adjective dangerously fast.

breakthrough noun a sudden important development or success.

breakwater noun a barrier built out into the sea to protect a coast or harbour from waves.

bream noun (plural **bream**) a greenish-bronze freshwater fish.

breast noun **1** either of the two soft organs on a woman's chest which produce milk when she has had a baby. **2** a person's or animal's chest. • verb **1** reach the top of a hill. **2** move forwards while pushing against something.

breastbone noun a bone running down the centre of the chest and connecting the ribs.

breastfeed verb (**breastfeeds, breastfeeding, breastfed**) feed a baby with milk from the breast.

breastplate noun a piece of armour covering the chest.

breaststroke noun a swimming stroke in which you push your arms forwards and then sweep them back while kicking your legs out.

breath noun **1** air taken into or sent out of the lungs. **2** an instance of breathing in or out. **3** a slight movement of air. **4** a sign or hint.
■ **breathable** adjective.

breathalyser (US spelling **Breathalyzer** (trademark)) noun a device for measuring the amount of alcohol in a driver's breath.
■ **breathalyse** (US spelling **breathalyze**) verb.

breathe verb (**breathes, breathing, breathed**) **1** take air into the lungs and send it out again. **2** say quietly. **3** let air or moisture in or out.

breather noun informal a brief pause for rest.

breathless adjective **1** gasping for breath. **2** feeling or causing great excitement.
■ **breathlessly** adverb.

breathtaking adjective astonishing or awe-inspiring.
■ **breathtakingly** adverb.

breathy adjective (of speech or singing) having a noticeable sound of breathing.

breech noun the back part of a rifle or gun barrel.

breech birth noun a birth in which the baby's buttocks or feet are delivered first.

breeches plural noun short trousers fastened just below the knee.

breed verb (**breeds, breeding, bred**) **1** (of

breakdown noun **1** *the breakdown of the negotiations:* failure, collapse, disintegration, foundering. **2** *she suffered a breakdown:* nervous breakdown, collapse. **3** *a breakdown of the computer system:* malfunction, failure, crash. **4** *a breakdown of the figures:* analysis, itemization, classification, examination, investigation, explanation.

break-in noun burglary, robbery, theft, raid, breaking and entering; informal smash-and-grab.

breakthrough noun advance, development, step forward, success, improvement, discovery, innovation, revolution.
OPPOSITES setback.

breast noun **1** *the curve of her breasts:* bosom(s), bust; informal boobs, knockers. **2** *her heart was hammering in her breast:* chest, bosom, front.

breath noun inhalation, gulp of air, puff, gasp, exhalation; Medicine respiration.

breathe verb **1** *she breathed deeply:* inhale, exhale, respire, draw breath, puff, pant,

blow, gasp, wheeze; Medicine inspire, expire. **2** *'Together at last,' she breathed:* whisper, murmur, purr, sigh.

breathless adjective **1** *Will arrived breathless:* out of breath, panting, puffing, gasping, wheezing, winded; informal out of puff. **2** *the crowd were breathless with anticipation:* eager, agog, open-mouthed, excited, on the edge of your seat, on tenterhooks.

breathtaking adjective spectacular, magnificent, awe-inspiring, awesome, astonishing, amazing, stunning, thrilling; informal sensational, out of this world.
OPPOSITES run-of-the-mill.

breed verb **1** *elephants breed readily in captivity:* reproduce, produce offspring, procreate, multiply, mate. **2** *she was born and bred in the village:* bring up, rear, raise, nurture. **3** *the political system bred discontent:* cause, produce, bring about, give rise to, arouse, stir up, generate, foster.
OPPOSITES stifle.

• noun **1** *a breed of cow:* variety, stock,

b

animals) mate and then produce young.
2 keep animals for the young that they
produce. 3 produce or cause. •noun a
particular type of domestic or farm animal
that has been specially developed.
■ **breeder** noun.

breeding noun upper-class good manners.

breeze noun a gentle wind. •verb (**breezes,
breezing, breezed**) informal come or go
casually.

breeze block noun Brit. a lightweight
building brick made from sand, cement,
and pieces of partly burnt coal or wood.

breezy adjective (**breezier, breeziest**)
1 pleasantly windy. 2 relaxed and
cheerfully brisk.

brethren plural noun 1 old-fashioned plural
of **BROTHER**. 2 fellow Christians or members
of group.

Breton /bre-tuhn/ noun 1 a person from
Brittany. 2 the language of Brittany.

breve /rhymes with sleeve/ noun Music a note
twice as long as a semibreve.

brevity noun 1 economical and exact use of
words. 2 the fact of lasting a short time.

brew verb 1 make beer. 2 make tea or coffee
by mixing it with hot water. 3 begin to
develop. •noun something brewed.
■ **brewer** noun.

brewery noun (plural **breweries**) a place
where beer is made.

briar or **brier** noun a prickly shrub.

bribe verb (**bribes, bribing, bribed**) pay
someone to do something dishonest that
helps you. •noun an amount of money
offered in an attempt to bribe someone.
■ **bribery** noun.

bric-a-brac noun various objects of little
value.

brick noun a small rectangular block of fired
clay, used in building. •verb (**brick
something up**) block or enclose something
with a wall of bricks.

brickbat noun a critical remark.

bricklayer noun a person whose job is to
build structures with bricks.

bridal adjective relating to a bride or a
newly married couple.

bride noun a woman at the time of her
wedding.

bridegroom noun a man at the time of his
wedding.

bridesmaid noun a girl or woman who
accompanies a bride at her wedding.

bridge noun 1 a structure that allows
people or vehicles to cross a river, road,
etc. 2 the platform on a ship where the
captain and officers stand. 3 the upper
bony part of a person's nose. 4 the part on
a stringed instrument over which the
strings are stretched. 5 a card game played
by two teams of two players. •verb
(**bridges, bridging, bridged**) be or make a
bridge over.

bridgehead noun a strong position gained
by an army inside enemy territory.

bridle noun the harness used to control a
horse. •verb (**bridles, bridling, bridled**)
1 put a bridle on. 2 show resentment or
anger.

bridleway noun Brit. a path along which
horse riders have right of way.

brief adjective 1 lasting a short time. 2 using

THESAURUS

strain, race, species. 2 *a new breed of
journalist:* type, kind, sort, variety, class,
genre, generation.

breeding noun (good) manners, gentility,
refinement, cultivation, polish, urbanity;
informal class.

breeze noun gentle wind, puff of air, gust,
draught; literary zephyr.

breezy adjective 1 *a breezy day:* windy,
fresh, brisk, blowy, blustery, gusty. 2 *his
breezy manner:* jaunty, cheerful, cheery,
brisk, carefree, easy, casual, relaxed,
informal, light-hearted; informal upbeat.

brew verb 1 *this beer is brewed in Frankfurt:*
ferment, make. 2 *I'll brew some tea:*
prepare, infuse, make; Brit. informal mash.
3 *there's trouble brewing:* develop, loom, be
imminent, be on the horizon, be in the
offing, be just around the corner.
•noun 1 *home brew:* beer, ale. 2 *a hot
reviving brew:* drink, beverage. 3 *a rich
brew of myths and distortion:* mixture,
mix, blend, combination, amalgam,
cocktail.

bribe verb *they tried to bribe the police:* buy
off, pay off, suborn; informal grease
someone's palm, keep someone sweet,
square; Brit. informal nobble.
•noun *he accepted a bribe:* inducement;
informal backhander, pay-off, kickback,
sweetener.

bribery noun corruption; N. Amer. payola;
informal palm-greasing, graft, hush money.

brief adjective 1 *a brief account:* concise,
succinct, short, pithy, compact, thumbnail,
potted. 2 *a brief visit:* short, flying,
fleeting, hasty, hurried, quick, cursory,
perfunctory, temporary, short-lived.
OPPOSITES lengthy.
•noun 1 *my brief is to reorganize the
project:* instructions, directions, directive,
remit, mandate. 2 *a barrister's brief:* case,
summary, argument, contention, dossier.
•verb *employees were briefed about the
decision:* inform, tell, update, notify,
advise, prepare, prime, instruct; informal fill
in, put in the picture.

few words. **3** (of clothing) not covering much of the body. • noun Brit. **1** a set of instructions about a task. **2** a summary of the facts in a case given to a barrister to argue in court. **3** informal a solicitor or barrister. • verb give someone information to prepare them for a task.
■ **briefly** adverb.

briefcase noun a flat rectangular case for carrying documents.

briefing noun a meeting for giving information or instructions.

briefs plural noun short, close-fitting underpants.

brier ⇒ BRIAR.

brig noun a sailing ship with two masts.

brigade noun **1** a large army unit, forming part of a division. **2** disapproving a particular group of people: *the anti-smoking brigade.*

brigadier /bri-guh-**deer**/ noun a rank of officer in the British army, above colonel.

brigand /**brig**-uhnd/ noun a member of a gang of bandits.

bright adjective **1** giving out light, or filled with light. **2** (of colour) strong and eye-

catching. **3** intelligent and quick-witted. **4** (of sound) clear and high-pitched. **5** cheerfully lively. **6** (of prospects) good.
■ **brightly** adverb **brightness** noun.

brighten verb make or become brighter or more cheerful.

brilliant adjective **1** (of light or colour) very bright or vivid. **2** very clever or talented. **3** Brit. informal very good; marvellous.
■ **brilliance** noun **brilliantly** adverb.

brim noun **1** the projecting edge around the bottom of a hat. **2** the lip of a cup, bowl, etc. • verb (**brims**, **brimming**, **brimmed**) be full to the point of overflowing.

brimstone noun old use sulphur.

brindle or **brindled** adjective (of an animal) brownish with streaks of grey or black.

brine noun water which contains dissolved salt.

bring verb (**brings**, **bringing**, **brought**) **1** take someone or something to a place. **2** cause to be in a particular position or state. **3** cause someone to receive something.

THESAURUS

briefing noun **1** *a press briefing:* conference, meeting, interview. **2** *this briefing explains the systems:* information, rundown, guidance, instructions, directions, guidelines.

briefly adverb **1** *tell me as briefly as you can:* concisely, succinctly. **2** *Henry paused briefly:* momentarily, temporarily, fleetingly. **3** *briefly, the plot is as follows:* in short, in brief, in a word, in a nutshell, in essence.

briefs plural noun underpants, pants, knickers, bikini briefs; N. Amer. shorts; informal panties; Brit. informal kecks.

brigade noun squad, team, group, band, party, crew, force, outfit.

bright adjective **1** *the bright surface of the metal:* shining, brilliant, dazzling, glaring, sparkling, flashing, glittering, gleaming, glowing, luminous, shiny, glossy. **2** *a bright morning:* sunny, cloudless, clear, fair, fine. **3** *bright colours:* vivid, brilliant, intense, strong, vibrant, bold, gaudy, lurid, garish. **4** *a bright young graduate:* clever, intelligent, quick-witted, smart, canny, astute, perceptive, ingenious; informal brainy.
OPPOSITES dull, cloudy, dark, stupid.

brighten verb **1** *sunshine brightened the room:* illuminate, light up, lighten. **2** *the sky brightened:* become lighter, grow brighter, lighten. **3** *Sarah brightened up:* cheer up, perk up, rally, feel heartened; informal buck up.

brilliance noun **1** *the brilliance of the sunshine:* brightness, vividness, intensity, sparkle, glitter, blaze, luminosity, radiance.

2 *a philosopher of great brilliance:* genius, intelligence, talent, ability, prowess, skill, expertise, aptitude, flair, wisdom, intellect. **3** *the brilliance of Paris:* splendour, magnificence, grandeur, resplendence, glory.
OPPOSITES dullness, stupidity, simplicity, lowliness.

brilliant adjective **1** *a shaft of brilliant light:* bright, shining, blazing, dazzling, vivid, intense, glaring, luminous, radiant. **2** *a brilliant student:* clever, bright, intelligent, smart, able, talented, gifted, skilful, astute; informal brainy. **3** *his brilliant career:* superb, glorious, illustrious, successful, impressive, remarkable, exceptional.
OPPOSITES dim, stupid, undistinguished.

bring verb **1** *he brought over a tray:* fetch, carry, bear, take, convey, transport, shift. **2** *Philip brought his bride to his mansion:* escort, conduct, guide, lead. **3** *the wind brought rain:* cause, produce, create, generate, precipitate, occasion, provoke, lead to, give rise to, result in.
▫ **bring something about/on.** See BRING sense 3. **bring something in** introduce, launch, inaugurate, initiate, institute. **bring something off** achieve, accomplish, bring about, succeed in, pull off, carry off, manage. **bring something out** launch, establish, begin, start, found, set up, market, publish, issue. **bring someone up** rear, raise, nurture, look after. **bring something up** mention, raise, broach, introduce, air, suggest.

4 (**bring yourself to do**) force yourself to do something unpleasant. **5** begin legal action.
□ **bring something about** cause something to happen. **bring something off** achieve something successfully. **bring something on** cause something unpleasant to develop. **bring something out 1** produce and launch a new product. **2** emphasize a feature. **bring someone round 1** make someone conscious again. **2** persuade someone to agree to something. **bring someone/thing up 1** look after a child until it is an adult. **2** mention something in order to discuss it.
■ **bringer** noun.

brink noun **1** the edge of land before a steep slope or an area of water. **2** the stage just before a new situation.

brinkmanship noun the practice of continuing with a dangerous course of action to the limits of safety before stopping.

briny adjective salty. •noun (**the briny**) Brit. informal the sea.

brio /bree-oh/ noun energy or liveliness.

brioche /bree-osh/ noun a soft, sweet French roll.

brisk adjective **1** quick, active, or energetic. **2** (of a person's manner) practical and efficient.
■ **briskly** adverb.

brisket noun meat from the chest of a cow.

bristle noun a short, stiff hair. •verb (**bristles**, **bristling**, **bristled**) **1** (of hair or fur) stand upright away from the skin. **2** react angrily or defensively. **3** (**bristle with**) be covered with.
■ **bristly** adjective.

British adjective relating to Great Britain.

Briton noun a British person.

brittle adjective **1** hard but likely to break easily. **2** sharp or artificial: *a brittle laugh*.

broach verb **1** raise a subject for discussion. **2** pierce a container.

broad adjective **1** larger than usual from side to side; wide. **2** large in area or range. **3** without detail; general. **4** (of a hint) clear and unmistakable. **5** (of an accent) very strong. •noun N. Amer. informal a woman.
□ **broad bean** a large flat green bean. **broad-minded** not easily shocked; tolerant.
■ **broadly** adverb.

broadband noun a telecommunications technique which uses a wide range of frequencies, enabling messages to be sent at the same time.

broadcast verb (**broadcasts**, **broadcasting**, **broadcast**; past participle **broadcast** or **broadcasted**) **1** transmit on radio or television. **2** tell to a lot of people. •noun a radio or television programme.
■ **broadcaster** noun.

broaden verb make or become broader.

broadleaved or **broadleaf** adjective

THESAURUS

brink noun **1** *the brink of the crater:* edge, verge, margin, rim, lip, border, boundary. **2** *two countries on the brink of war:* verge, threshold, point, edge.

brisk adjective **1** *a brisk pace:* quick, rapid, fast, swift, speedy, hurried, energetic, lively; informal nippy. **2** *his tone became brisk:* no-nonsense, businesslike, decisive, brusque, abrupt, short, sharp, curt, blunt, terse; informal snappy.
OPPOSITES leisurely.

bristle noun **1** *the bristles on his chin:* hair, whisker; (**bristles**) stubble, five o'clock shadow. **2** *a hedgehog's bristles:* spine, prickle, quill, barb.
•verb **1** *the hair on the back of his neck bristled:* rise, stand up, stand on end. **2** *she bristled at his tone:* take offence, bridle, take umbrage, be offended. **3** *the roof bristled with antennae:* be crowded, be full, be packed, be jammed, be covered, overflow; informal be thick, be chock-full.

brittle adjective breakable, fragile, crisp, crumbly, delicate.
OPPOSITES flexible, solid.

broach verb bring up, raise, introduce, mention, touch on, air.

broad adjective **1** *a broad expanse of prairie:* wide, extensive, vast, immense, great, spacious, expansive, sizeable, sweeping. **2** *a broad range of opportunities:* comprehensive, inclusive, extensive, wide, all-embracing, unlimited. **3** *this report gives a broad outline:* general, non-specific, rough, approximate, basic, loose, vague.
OPPOSITES narrow, limited, detailed.

broadcast verb **1** *the show will be broadcast worldwide:* transmit, relay, air, beam, show, televise, screen. **2** *the result was broadcast far and wide:* report, announce, publicize, advertise, make public, proclaim, spread, circulate.
•noun *a live broadcast:* transmission, programme, show, telecast, production, screening.

broaden verb **1** *her smile broadened:* widen, expand, stretch (out), spread. **2** *the government tried to broaden its political base:* expand, enlarge, extend, widen, swell, increase, add to, develop.
OPPOSITES narrow, restrict.

broad-minded adjective liberal, tolerant, freethinking, indulgent, progressive, permissive, unshockable, unprejudiced, unbiased.
OPPOSITES intolerant.

having fairly wide flat leaves.

broadsheet noun a newspaper printed on large sheets of paper.

broadside noun 1 a fierce verbal or written criticism. 2 historical a firing of all the guns from one side of a warship.

broadsword noun a sword with a wide blade.

brocade noun a rich fabric woven with a raised pattern.

broccoli /brok-kuh-li/ noun a vegetable with heads of small green or purplish flower buds.

☑ two cs, one l: broccoli.

brochure /broh-sher/ noun a booklet or magazine containing information about a product or service.

brogue noun 1 a strong outdoor shoe with perforated patterns in the leather. 2 a strong regional accent.

broil verb N. Amer. cook meat or fish using direct heat.

broke past of BREAK. •adjective informal having no money.

broken past participle of BREAK. •adjective (of a language) spoken hesitantly and with many mistakes.
□ broken home a family in which the parents are divorced or separated.

broker noun a person who buys and sells things for other people. •verb arrange a deal or plan.

bromide noun a compound of bromine, used in medicine.

bromine noun a dark red liquid chemical element.

bronchial adjective relating to the tubes leading to the lungs.

bronchitis /brong-ky-tiss/ noun inflammation of the tubes that lead to the lungs.

bronco noun (plural **broncos**) a wild or half-tamed horse of the western US.

brontosaurus former term for APATOSAURUS.

bronze noun 1 a yellowish-brown metal made by mixing copper and tin. 2 a yellowish-brown colour. 3 (also **bronze medal**) a medal given for third place in a competition. •verb (**bronzes, bronzing, bronzed**) 1 give something a bronze surface. 2 make someone suntanned.
□ Bronze Age an ancient period when weapons and tools were made of bronze, following the Stone Age.

brooch noun an ornament fastened to clothing with a hinged pin.

brood noun a family of young animals born or hatched at one time. •verb 1 think deeply about an unpleasant subject. 2 (**brooding**) appearing mysterious or menacing. 3 (of a bird) sit on eggs to hatch them.

broody adjective (**broodier, broodiest**) 1 (of a hen) wanting to hatch eggs. 2 informal (of a woman) having a strong desire to have a baby. 3 thoughtful and unhappy.

brook[1] noun a small stream.

brook[2] verb formal tolerate.

broom noun 1 a long-handled brush used for sweeping. 2 a shrub with yellow flowers.

broomstick noun a brush with twigs at one end and a long handle, on which witches are said to fly.

Bros abbreviation brothers.

broth noun thin soup or stock, sometimes with chunks of meat or vegetables.

brothel noun a house where men visit prostitutes.

brother noun 1 a man or boy in relation to other children of his parents. 2 a male colleague or friend. 3 (plural **brothers** or **brethren**) a male fellow Christian or member of a religious order.
□ brother-in-law (plural **brothers-in-law**) 1 the brother of a person's wife or husband. 2 the husband of a person's sister

THESAURUS

brochure noun booklet, prospectus, catalogue, pamphlet, leaflet, circular, mailshot; N. Amer. folder.

broken adjective 1 smashed, shattered, fragmented, splintered, crushed, snapped, in bits, in pieces, cracked, split, fractured; informal in smithereens. 2 his video's broken: faulty, damaged, defective, not working, malfunctioning, out of order, broken down, down; informal kaput, bust, acting up; Brit. informal knackered. 3 a night of broken sleep: interrupted, disturbed, fitful, disrupted, discontinuous, intermittent. 4 she spoke in broken English: halting, hesitating, disjointed, faltering, imperfect.

OPPOSITES whole, working, uninterrupted, fluent, perfect.

broker noun dealer, agent, middleman, intermediary, mediator, factor, liaison, stockbroker.
•verb arrange, organize, orchestrate, work out, settle, clinch, negotiate, mediate.

brood noun she looked after her brood well: offspring, young, family, litter, clutch, progeny.
•verb he does brood a lot: think, ponder, contemplate, meditate, ruminate, muse, worry, fret, agonize.

brook noun stream, rill; N. English beck; Scottish & N. English burn; N. Amer. & Austral./NZ creek.

b

or sister-in-law.
■ **brotherly** adjective.

brotherhood noun 1 the relationship between brothers. 2 a feeling of friendliness and understanding between people. 3 a group of people linked by a shared interest.

brought past and past participle of **BRING**.

> ! don't confuse **brought** with **bought**, which is the past of **buy**.

brouhaha noun a noisy and overexcited reaction.

brow noun 1 a person's forehead. 2 an eyebrow. 3 the highest point of a hill.

browbeat verb (**browbeats, browbeating, browbeat**; past participle **browbeaten**) bully someone with aggressive or threatening words.

brown adjective 1 of a colour produced by mixing red, yellow, and blue. 2 dark-skinned or suntanned. • noun a brown colour. • verb 1 make or become brown by cooking. 2 (**be browned off**) Brit. informal be dissatisfied.

brownfield adjective Brit. (of a piece of land) having had buildings on it already.

Brownie noun (plural **Brownies**) 1 a member of the junior branch of the Guides Association. 2 (**brownie**) a small square of rich chocolate cake. 3 (**brownie**) a kind elf believed to do people's housework secretly.

browse verb (**browses, browsing, browsed**) 1 read or look at something in a leisurely way. 2 look at information on a computer. 3 (of an animal) feed on leaves, twigs, etc.

• noun an act of browsing.

browser noun 1 a person or animal that browses. 2 a computer program for navigating the World Wide Web.

bruise noun 1 an area of discoloured skin on the body, caused by a blow. 2 a damaged area on a fruit or vegetable. • verb (**bruises, bruising, bruised**) make a bruise appear on.

bruiser noun informal a tough, aggressive person.

brunch noun a late morning meal eaten instead of breakfast and lunch.

brunette noun a woman or girl with dark brown hair.

brunt noun the chief impact of something bad.

brush¹ noun 1 an object with a handle and a block of bristles, hair, or wire. 2 an act of brushing. 3 a slight, brief touch. 4 a brief encounter with something bad. 5 the bushy tail of a fox. • verb 1 clean, smooth, or apply with a brush. 2 touch lightly. 3 (**brush someone/thing off**) dismiss someone or something abruptly. 4 (**brush something up**) work to improve a skill you have not used for a long time.

brush² noun undergrowth, small trees, and shrubs.

brushwood noun undergrowth, twigs, and small branches.

brusque /bruusk/ adjective rather rude and abrupt.

■ **brusquely** adverb.

Brussels sprout noun a small green vegetable, the bud of a variety of cabbage.

THESAURUS

brotherly adjective fraternal, friendly, comradely, affectionate, amicable, kind, devoted, loyal.

brow noun 1 forehead, temple. 2 *the brow of the hill:* summit, peak, top, crest, crown, head, pinnacle, apex.

brown adjective 1 *brown eyes:* hazel, chocolate, coffee, brunette, sepia, fawn, mahogany, tan, café au lait, caramel, chestnut. 2 *his face was brown from the sun:* tanned, suntanned, bronzed.

• verb *the grill browns food evenly:* grill, toast, singe, sear, barbecue, sauté.

browse verb look round/over, scan, skim, glance, peruse, thumb, leaf, flick, dip into.

bruise noun *a bruise on her forehead:* contusion, bump, swelling, lump, mark, injury, welt.

• verb 1 *her face was badly bruised:* contuse, injure, mark, discolour, make black and blue. 2 *every one of the apples is bruised:* mark, discolour, blemish, damage, spoil.

brush¹ noun 1 *a dustpan and brush:* broom, sweeper, besom, whisk. 2 *he gave the seat a*

brush with his hand: clean, sweep, wipe, dust. 3 *a brush with the law:* encounter, clash, confrontation, conflict, altercation, incident; informal run-in, to-do; Brit. informal spot of bother.

• verb 1 *he spent his day brushing the floors:* sweep, clean, buff, polish, scrub. 2 *she brushed her hair:* groom, comb, neaten, tidy, smooth, arrange, curry. 3 *she felt his lips brush her cheek:* touch, stroke, caress, skim, sweep, graze, contact, kiss.

□ brush something aside **disregard**, ignore, dismiss, shrug off, wave aside, reject, spurn, laugh off, make light of; informal pooh-pooh. brush up (on) **revise**, read up, go over, improve, polish up, enhance, hone, perfect; informal bone up on; Brit. informal swot up (on).

brush² noun undergrowth, scrub, brushwood, shrubs, bushes; N. Amer. underbrush, chaparral.

brusque adjective curt, abrupt, blunt, short, sharp, brisk, peremptory, gruff.
OPPOSITES polite.

brutal adjective **1** savagely violent. **2** not attempting to hide something unpleasant: *brutal honesty*.
■ **brutality** noun **brutally** adverb.

brutalize or **brutalise** verb (**brutalizes, brutalizing, brutalized**) **1** make someone cruel or violent by frequently exposing them to violence. **2** treat someone in a violent way.

brute noun a violent or savage person, or a large and uncontrollable animal. ●adjective involving physical strength rather than reasoning: *brute force*.
■ **brutish** adjective.

BSE abbreviation bovine spongiform encephalopathy, a fatal brain disease in cattle.

BST abbreviation British Summer Time.

bubble noun **1** a thin ball of liquid enclosing a gas. **2** a ball filled with gas in a liquid or a material such as glass. **3** a transparent dome. ●verb (**bubbles, bubbling, bubbled**) **1** (of a liquid) contain rising bubbles of gas. **2** (**bubble with**) be filled with.

bubblegum noun chewing gum that can be blown into bubbles.

bubbly adjective (**bubblier, bubbliest**) **1** containing bubbles. **2** cheerful and high-spirited. ●noun informal champagne.

bubonic plague noun a form of plague passed on by rat fleas.

buccaneer noun **1** historical a pirate. **2** a recklessly adventurous person.
■ **buccaneering** adjective.

buck¹ noun **1** the male of some animals, e.g. deer and rabbits. **2** a vertical jump performed by a horse. **3** old use a fashionable young man. ●verb **1** (of a horse) perform a buck. **2** go against something: *don't try to buck the system.* **3** (**buck up** or **buck someone up**) informal

become or make someone more cheerful.
□ **buck teeth** teeth that stick out.

buck² noun N. Amer. & Austral./NZ informal a dollar.

buck³ noun an object placed in front of a poker player whose turn it is to deal.
□ **pass the buck** informal shift responsibility to someone else.

bucket noun **1** an open container with a handle, used to carry liquids. **2** (**buckets**) informal large quantities. ●verb (**buckets, bucketing, bucketed**) (**bucket down**) Brit. informal rain very heavily.

buckle noun a flat frame with a hinged pin, used as a fastener. ●verb (**buckles, buckling, buckled**) **1** fasten with a buckle. **2** bend and give way under pressure. **3** (**buckle down**) tackle a task with determination.

buckwheat noun a grain used for flour or animal feed.

bucolic /byoo-**kol**-ik/ adjective relating to country life.

bud noun a growth on a plant which develops into a leaf, flower, or shoot. ●verb (**buds, budding, budded**) form a bud or buds.

Buddhism /**buud**-di-z'm/ noun a religion based on the teachings of Buddha (real name Siddartha Gautama, *c*.563–*c*.460 BC).
■ **Buddhist** noun & adjective.

budding adjective beginning and showing signs of promise.

buddleia /**bud**-li-uh/ noun a shrub with clusters of lilac, white, or yellow flowers.

buddy noun (plural **buddies**) informal, chiefly N. Amer. a close friend.

budge verb (**budges, budging, budged**) **1** move very slightly. **2** change an opinion.

budgerigar noun a small Australian parakeet.

budget noun **1** an estimate of income and spending for a set period of time. **2** the

b

THESAURUS

brutal adjective **1** *a brutal attack:* savage, cruel, vicious, ferocious, barbaric, wicked, murderous, bloodthirsty, cold-blooded, callous, heartless, merciless, sadistic. **2** *brutal honesty:* harsh, unforgiving, pitiless, frank, blunt, tough, hard, bleak, disagreeable.
OPPOSITES gentle, kind.

bubbly adjective **1** *bubbly water:* fizzy, sparkling, effervescent, gassy, aerated, carbonated, frothy, foamy. **2** *she was bubbly and full of life:* vivacious, animated, ebullient, lively, high-spirited, bouncy, merry, happy, cheerful, sunny; informal chirpy.
OPPOSITES still, listless.

buckle noun *a belt buckle:* clasp, clip, catch, hasp, fastener.
●verb **1** *he buckled the belt round his waist:*

fasten, do up, hook, secure, clasp, clip. **2** *the front axle buckled:* bend, warp, twist, distort, contort, deform, crumple, collapse, give way.
OPPOSITES unbuckle, straighten.

budding adjective promising, up-and-coming, rising, in the making, aspiring, future, fledgling, developing.

budge verb **1** *the horses wouldn't budge:* move, shift, stir, go. **2** *I couldn't budge the door:* dislodge, shift, move, stir, reposition.

budget noun **1** *your budget for the week:* financial plan, forecast. **2** *the defence budget:* allowance, allocation, quota, funds, resources, capital.
●verb *we have to budget £7,000 for the work:* allocate, allot, allow, earmark, designate, set aside.

b

amount of money needed or available for a purpose. **3** (**Budget**) a regular estimate of national income and spending put forward by a finance minister. • verb (**budgets, budgeting, budgeted**) plan to spend a particular amount of money. • adjective inexpensive.

■ **budgetary** adjective.

budgie noun a budgerigar.

buff¹ noun a yellowish-beige colour. • verb polish something with a soft cloth.

□ **in the buff** informal naked.

buff² noun informal a person who knows a lot about a particular subject.

buffalo noun (plural **buffalo** or **buffaloes**) **1** a heavily built wild ox with backward-curving horns. **2** the North American bison.

buffer noun **1** (**buffers**) Brit. shock absorbers at the end of a railway track or on a railway vehicle. **2** a person or thing that lessens the impact of harmful effects.

buffet¹ /boo-fay, buf-fay/ noun **1** a meal made up of several dishes from which you serve yourself. **2** a counter at which snacks are sold.

buffet² /buf-fit/ verb (**buffets, buffeting, buffeted**) (especially of wind or waves) strike repeatedly.

buffoon noun a ridiculous but amusing person.

■ **buffoonery** noun.

bug noun **1** a small insect. **2** informal a germ, or an illness caused by one. **3** informal an enthusiasm for something: *the sailing bug.* **4** a microphone used for secret recording. **5** an error in a computer program or

system. • verb (**bugs, bugging, bugged**) **1** hide a microphone in a room or telephone. **2** informal annoy someone.

bugbear noun something that causes anxiety or irritation.

buggery noun anal sex.

buggy noun (plural **buggies**) **1** a kind of pushchair. **2** a small motor vehicle with an open top. **3** historical a light horse-drawn vehicle.

bugle noun a brass instrument like a small trumpet.

■ **bugler** noun.

build verb (**builds, building, built**) **1** make something by putting parts together. **2** (**build up**) increase over time. **3** (**build on**) use as a basis for further development. • noun the size or form of someone or something.

□ **build-up 1** a gradual increase. **2** a period of preparation before an event.

■ **builder** noun.

building noun **1** a structure with a roof and walls. **2** the process or trade of building houses and other structures.

□ **building society** Brit. a financial organization which pays interest on members' investments and lends money for mortgages.

built past and past participle of **BUILD**. • adjective of a particular physical build.

□ **built-in** included as part of a larger structure. **built-up** covered by many buildings.

bulb noun **1** the rounded base of the stem of some plants, from which the roots grow. **2** (also **light bulb**) a glass ball filled with

---

THESAURUS

buff¹ verb *he buffed the glass:* polish, burnish, shine, smooth, rub.

buff² noun (informal) *a film buff:* enthusiast, fan, devotee, lover, admirer, expert, aficionado, authority; informal freak, nut, addict.

buffer noun cushion, bulwark, shield, barrier, guard, safeguard.

buffet¹ noun **1** *a sumptuous buffet:* cold table, self-service meal, smorgasbord. **2** *a station buffet:* cafe, cafeteria, snack bar, canteen, restaurant.

buffet² verb *rough seas buffeted the coast:* batter, pound, lash, strike, hit.

bug noun **1** (informal) *a stomach bug:* illness, disease, sickness, disorder, upset, ailment, infection, virus; Brit. informal lurgy. **2** *bugs were crawling everywhere:* insect, minibeast; informal creepy-crawly, beastie. **3** *the bug planted on his phone:* listening device, hidden microphone, wire, wiretap, tap. **4** *the program developed a bug:* fault,

error, defect, flaw, virus; informal glitch, gremlin.

• verb *her conversations were bugged:* eavesdrop on, spy on, tap, monitor.

build verb construct, erect, put up, assemble, make, create, fashion, model, shape.

OPPOSITES demolish, dismantle.

• noun *a man of slim build:* physique, frame, body, figure, form, shape, stature, proportions; informal vital statistics.

□ **build up** increase, grow, mount up, intensify, strengthen. **build something up 1** *he built up his stamina:* boost, strengthen, increase, improve, augment, raise, enhance, swell. **2** *I have built up a collection of prints:* accumulate, amass, collect, gather.

building noun structure, construction, edifice, erection, property, premises, establishment.

build-up noun increase, growth, expansion, enlargement, escalation, accumulation, gas, which provides light when an electric current is passed through it.

bulbous adjective **1** round or bulging in shape. **2** (of a plant) growing from a bulb.

Bulgarian noun **1** a person from Bulgaria. **2** the language of Bulgaria. •adjective relating to Bulgaria.

bulge noun a rounded swelling on a flat surface. •verb (**bulges, bulging, bulged**) **1** swell or stick out unnaturally. **2** (**bulge with**) be full of.

bulimia /buu-lim-mi-uh/ noun a disorder marked by bouts of overeating, followed by fasting or vomiting.
■ **bulimic** adjective & noun.

bulk noun **1** the mass or size of something large. **2** the greater part of something. **3** a large mass or shape. •adjective large in quantity.
□ **in bulk** (of goods) in large quantities.

bulkhead noun an internal wall or barrier in a ship or aircraft.

bulky adjective (**bulkier, bulkiest**) large and unwieldy.

bull[1] noun **1** an adult male animal of the cattle group. **2** a large male animal, e.g. a whale or elephant.
□ **take the bull by the horns** deal decisively with a difficult situation.

bull[2] noun an order or announcement issued by the Pope.

bulldog noun a breed of dog with a flat wrinkled face and a broad chest.

bulldoze verb (**bulldozes, bulldozing, bulldozed**) clear or destroy with a bulldozer.

bulldozer noun a tractor with a broad curved blade at the front for clearing ground.

bullet noun a small piece of metal fired from a gun.

bulletin noun **1** a short official statement or summary of news. **2** a regular newsletter or report.
□ **bulletin board** a site on a computer system where any user can read or write messages.

bullfighting noun the sport of tormenting and killing bulls as a public entertainment.
■ **bullfight** noun **bullfighter** noun.

bullfinch noun a finch (songbird) with a reddish breast.

bullfrog noun a very large frog with a deep croak.

bullion noun gold or silver in bulk before being made into coins.

bullish adjective aggressively confident.

bullock noun a castrated bull.

bullring noun an arena where bullfights are held.

bullseye noun the centre of the target in sports such as archery and darts.

bully noun (plural **bullies**) a person who frightens or persecutes weaker people.
•verb (**bullies, bullying, bullied**) frighten or persecute a weaker person.

bulrush or **bullrush** noun a tall reed-like waterside plant.

bulwark /buul-werk/ noun **1** a defensive wall. **2** a person or thing that acts as a defence. **3** an extension of a ship's sides above deck level.

bum[1] noun Brit. informal a person's bottom.

bum[2] N. Amer. informal noun **1** a homeless person or beggar. **2** a lazy or worthless person. •verb (**bums, bumming, bummed**) **1** get something by asking or begging. **2** (**bum around**) laze around. •adjective bad.

bumble verb (**bumbles, bumbling, bumbled**) act or speak in an awkward or confused way.

bumblebee noun a large hairy bee with a loud hum.

THESAURUS

development.

bulbous adjective bulging, round, fat, rotund, swollen, distended, bloated.

bulge noun *a bulge under his jacket:* swelling, bump, lump, hump, protrusion.
•verb *the veins in his neck bulged:* swell, stick out, project, protrude, stand out, puff out, balloon (out), fill out, distend.

bulk noun **1** *the sheer bulk of the bags:* size, volume, dimensions, proportions, mass, scale. **2** *the bulk of entrants were British:* majority, mass, generality, main part, lion's share, preponderance.
OPPOSITES minority.

bulky adjective unwieldy, cumbersome, unmanageable, awkward, ponderous, outsize, oversized; informal hulking.
OPPOSITES manageable, handy.

bullet noun ball, shot, pellet; informal slug; (**bullets**) lead.

bulletin noun **1** *a news bulletin:* report, dispatch, story, flash, statement, announcement, message, communication, communiqué. **2** *the society's monthly bulletin:* newsletter, news-sheet, proceedings, newspaper, magazine, gazette, review.

bully noun *the school bully:* persecutor, oppressor, tyrant, tormentor, intimidator, bully boy, thug.
•verb **1** *the others bully him:* persecute, oppress, tyrannize, browbeat, intimidate, dominate; informal push around/about. **2** *she was bullied into helping:* coerce, pressure, press, push, prod, browbeat, dragoon, strong-arm; informal bulldoze, railroad, lean on.

b

bumf or **bumph** noun Brit. informal printed information.

bump noun 1 a light blow or collision. 2 a hump or projection on a level surface. • **verb** 1 knock or run into with a jolt. 2 move with a lot of jolting. 3 (**bump into**) meet by chance. 4 (**bump someone off**) informal murder someone. 5 (**bump something up**) informal increase something. ■ **bumpy** (**bumpier, bumpiest**) adjective.

bumper noun a bar fixed across the front or back of a vehicle to reduce damage in a collision. • **adjective** exceptionally large or successful.

bumpkin noun an unsophisticated person from the countryside.

bumptious adjective irritatingly confident and self-important.

bun noun 1 a small cake or bread roll. 2 a tight coil of hair at the back of the head.

bunch noun 1 a number of things grouped or held together. 2 informal a group of people. • **verb** collect or form into a bunch.

bundle noun a group of things tied or wrapped up together. • **verb** (**bundles, bundling, bundled**) 1 tie or roll up in a bundle. 2 (**be bundled up**) be dressed in a lot of warm clothes. 3 informal push or carry forcibly.

bunfight noun Brit. humorous a grand party or other large social event.

bung noun a stopper for a hole in a container. • **verb** 1 (**bung something up**) block something up. 2 Brit. informal put or throw something somewhere casually or carelessly.

bungalow noun a house with only one storey.

bungee jumping noun the sport of jumping from a high place to which you are attached with a long elastic cord tied to your ankles.

bungle verb (**bungles, bungling, bungled**) fail in performing a task. • **noun** a mistake or failure. ■ **bungler** noun.

bunion noun a painful swelling on the big toe.

bunk¹ noun a narrow shelf-like bed.

bunk² verb (**bunk off**) Brit. informal play truant from school. □ **do a bunk** leave hurriedly.

bunker noun 1 a large container for storing fuel. 2 an underground shelter for use in wartime. 3 a hollow filled with sand on a golf course.

bunkum noun informal, dated nonsense.

bunny noun (plural **bunnies**) informal a rabbit.

Bunsen burner noun a small gas burner used in laboratories.

bunting¹ noun a small bird with brown streaked feathers.

bunting² noun flags and streamers used as decorations.

buoy noun an anchored float used to mark an area of water. • **verb** (**be buoyed** or **buoyed up**) be cheered up and made more confident.

THESAURUS

bump noun 1 *I landed with a bump:* jolt, crash, smash, smack, crack, bang, thud, thump; informal whack, wallop. 2 *I was woken by a bump:* bang, crack, boom, clang, knock, thud, thump, clunk, crash, smash. 3 *a bump in the road:* hump, lump, ridge, bulge, knob. 4 *a bump on his head:* swelling, lump, bulge, injury, contusion. • **verb** 1 *cars bumped into each other:* hit, crash, smash, slam, bang, knock, run, plough, ram, collide with, strike; N. Amer. impact. 2 *a cart bumping along the road:* bounce, jolt, jerk, rattle, shake.

bumper adjective exceptional, large, abundant, rich, bountiful, good, plentiful, record, successful; informal whopping. OPPOSITES meagre.

bumpy adjective 1 *a bumpy road:* uneven, rough, rutted, pitted, potholed, lumpy, rocky. 2 *a bumpy ride:* bouncy, rough, uncomfortable, jolting, lurching, jerky, jarring, bone-shaking. OPPOSITES smooth.

bunch noun 1 *a bunch of flowers:* bouquet, posy, nosegay, spray, wreath, garland. 2 *a bunch of keys:* cluster, clump, knot, group.

• **verb** *the runners bunched up behind him:* cluster, huddle, gather, congregate, collect, amass, group, crowd. OPPOSITES scatter.

bundle noun *a bundle of clothes:* bunch, roll, clump, wad, parcel, sheaf, bale, pile, stack, heap, mass; informal load, wodge. • **verb** 1 *she bundled up her things:* tie, pack, parcel, wrap, swathe, roll, fold, bind. 2 (informal) *he was bundled into a van:* push, shove, thrust, throw, propel, jostle, manhandle.

bungle verb mishandle, mismanage, mess up, spoil, ruin; informal blow, botch, fluff, make a hash of, screw up; Brit. informal make a pig's ear of, cock up; N. Amer. informal goof up. OPPOSITES carry off.

bungling adjective incompetent, blundering, amateurish, inept, unskilful, clumsy, awkward, bumbling; informal ham-fisted, cack-handed. OPPOSITES competent.

buoy noun float, marker, beacon.

b

☑ the *u* comes before the *o* in b*u*oy and
b*u*oyant.

buoyant adjective 1 able to keep afloat.
2 cheerful and optimistic.
■ **buoyancy** noun.

burble verb (**burbles, burbling, burbled**)
1 make a continuous murmuring noise.
2 speak for a long time in a way that is
hard to understand. ●noun a continuous
murmuring noise.

burden noun 1 a heavy load. 2 something
that causes hardship, worry, or grief. 3 the
main responsibility for a task. ●verb 1 load
heavily. 2 cause someone worry, hardship,
or grief.

burdensome adjective causing worry or
difficulty.

burdock noun a plant with large leaves and
prickly flowers.

bureau /byoor-oh/ noun (plural **bureaux** or
bureaus) 1 Brit. a writing desk with a
sloping top. 2 N. Amer. a chest of drawers.
3 an office for carrying out particular
business. 4 a government department.

bureaucracy /byuu-**rok**-ruh-si/ noun (plural
bureaucracies) 1 administrative procedures
that are too complicated. 2 a system of
government in which most decisions are
taken by state officials.

bureaucrat noun a government official,
especially one who follows guidelines
rigidly.
■ **bureaucratic** adjective.

burgeon verb grow or increase rapidly.

burger noun a hamburger.

burgher /**ber**-guh/ noun old use a citizen of a
town or city.

burglar noun a person who burgles a
building.

burglary noun (plural **burglaries**) the action
of burgling a building.

burgle verb (**burgles, burgling, burgled**) go
into a building illegally to steal its
contents.

burgundy /**ber**-guhn-di/ noun (plural
burgundies) 1 a red wine from Burgundy
in France. 2 a deep red colour.

burial noun the burying of a dead body.

burlesque /ber-**lesk**/ noun 1 a comically
exaggerated imitation of something.
2 N. Amer. a variety show.

burly adjective (**burlier, burliest**) (of a man)
large and strong.

burn¹ verb (**burns, burning, burned** or chiefly
Brit. **burnt**) 1 (of a fire) produce flames and
heat while using up a fuel. 2 harm or
damage by fire. 3 (**be burning with**)
experience a very strong desire or emotion.
4 (**burn out**) become exhausted through
working too hard. 5 produce a CD by
copying from an original or master copy.
●noun an injury caused by burning.
▫ **burn your boats** (or **bridges**) do
something which makes turning back
impossible.

burn² noun Scottish a small stream.

burner noun a part of a cooker, lamp, etc.
that puts out a flame.
▫ **on the back burner** given a low priority.

THESAURUS

buoyant adjective 1 *a buoyant substance:*
floating, floatable. 2 *a buoyant mood:*
cheerful, cheery, happy, light-hearted,
carefree, joyful, bubbly, bouncy, sunny;
informal upbeat.
OPPOSITES gloomy.

burden noun *a financial burden:*
responsibility, onus, obligation, liability,
trouble, care, problem, worry, strain.
●verb *avoid burdening them with guilt:*
oppress, trouble, worry, weigh down,
harass, upset, distress, haunt, afflict.

bureau noun 1 *an oak bureau:* desk, writing
table, secretaire. 2 *the intelligence bureau:*
department, agency, office, division,
branch, section, station, unit.

bureaucracy noun 1 *the ranks of the
bureaucracy:* civil service, government,
administration, establishment, system,
powers that be, authorities. 2 *unnecessary
bureaucracy:* red tape, rules and
regulations, protocol, officialdom,
paperwork.

burgeon verb grow, increase, rocket,
mushroom, expand, escalate, swell, boom,

flourish, thrive, prosper.

burglar noun housebreaker, robber, thief,
raider, looter, cat burglar.

burglary noun 1 *a sentence for burglary:*
housebreaking, breaking and entering,
theft, stealing, robbery, larceny, looting,
pillaging. 2 *a series of burglaries:* break-in,
theft, robbery, raid; informal smash-and-grab;
N. Amer. informal heist.

burgle verb rob, loot, steal from, pillage.

burial noun funeral, interment, committal,
inhumation, entombment.
OPPOSITES exhumation.

burly adjective strapping, well built, strong,
muscular, muscly, hefty, sturdy, brawny;
informal hunky, beefy.
OPPOSITES puny.

burn verb 1 *the coal was burning:* be on fire,
be alight, blaze, go up (in smoke), be in
flames, smoulder, glow. 2 *he burned the
letters:* set fire to, set alight, set light to,
kindle, ignite, touch off, incinerate,
cremate; informal torch. 3 *I burned my dress
with the iron:* scorch, singe, sear, char,
blacken, brand.

burning adjective **1** very hot. **2** deeply felt. **3** important and urgent.

burnish verb polish something by rubbing it.

burnout noun physical or mental collapse.

burp informal verb belch. • noun a belch.

burr noun **1** a strong pronunciation of the letter *r*. **2** a prickly seed case or flower head that clings to clothing and animal fur.

burrow noun a hole or tunnel dug by a small animal to live in. • verb **1** make a burrow. **2** hide underneath or search inside something.

bursar noun a person who manages the financial affairs of a college or school.

bursary noun (plural **bursaries**) Brit. a grant for studying.

burst verb (**bursts**, **bursting**, **burst**) **1** break suddenly and violently apart. **2** (**be bursting**) be very full. **3** move or be opened suddenly and forcibly. **4** (**be bursting with**) feel full of an emotion. **5** (**burst out** or **into**) suddenly do something as a result of strong emotion. • noun **1** an instance of bursting. **2** a sudden brief outbreak. **3** a period of continuous effort.

bury verb (**buries**, **burying**, **buried**) **1** place or hide something underground. **2** make something disappear or be hidden. **3** (**bury yourself**) involve yourself deeply in something.

bus noun (plural **buses**; US also **busses**) a large motor vehicle that carries customers along a fixed route. • verb (**buses**, **busing**, **bused** or **busses**, **bussing**, **bussed**) transport or travel in a bus.
□ a busman's holiday leisure time spent doing the same thing that you do at work.

busby noun (plural **busbies**) a tall fur hat worn by certain military regiments.

bush noun **1** a shrub or clump of shrubs. **2** (**the bush**) (in Australia and Africa) wild or uncultivated country.

bushbaby noun (plural **bushbabies**) a small African animal with very large eyes.

bushel noun **1** Brit. a measure of capacity equal to 8 gallons (36.4 litres). **2** US a measure of capacity equal to 64 US pints (35.2 litres).

bushy adjective (**bushier**, **bushiest**) **1** growing thickly. **2** covered with bushes.

business noun **1** a person's regular occupation. **2** commercial activity. **3** a commercial organization. **4** work to be done or things to be attended to. **5** a person's concern: *it's none of your business*.

☑ remember the *i*: bus*i*ness.

businesslike adjective efficient and practical.

businessman or **businesswoman** noun (plural **businessmen** or **businesswomen**) a

---

THESAURUS

burning adjective **1** *burning coals:* on fire, blazing, flaming, fiery, glowing, red-hot, smouldering. **2** *a burning desire:* intense, passionate, deep-seated, profound, strong, ardent, fervent, urgent, fierce, consuming. **3** *burning issues:* important, crucial, critical, vital, essential, pivotal, urgent, pressing, compelling.

burrow noun *a rabbit's burrow:* warren, tunnel, hole, dugout, lair, set, den, earth. • verb *rabbits burrowed among the roots:* tunnel, dig, excavate, mine, bore, channel.

burst verb **1** *one balloon burst:* split (open), rupture, break, tear. **2** *a shell burst:* explode, blow up, detonate, go off. **3** *smoke burst through the hole:* gush, erupt, surge, rush, stream, flow, pour, spurt, jet. **4** *he burst into the room:* charge, plunge, barge, plough, hurtle, career, rush, dash, tear. • noun **1** *a burst in the tyre:* rupture, puncture, breach, split, blowout. **2** *mortar bursts:* explosion, detonation, blast, eruption, bang. **3** *a burst of gunfire:* volley, salvo, barrage, hail, rain. **4** *a burst of activity:* outbreak, eruption, flare-up, blaze, attack, fit, rush, storm, surge, spurt.

bury verb **1** *the dead were buried:* inter, lay to rest, entomb. **2** *she buried her face in her hands:* hide, conceal, cover, enfold, cup,

sink. **3** *the bullet buried itself in the wood:* embed, sink, implant, submerge, lodge.
OPPOSITES exhume.

bush noun **1** *a rose bush:* shrub, thicket; (**bushes**) undergrowth, shrubbery. **2** *the bush:* wilds, wilderness, backwoods; N. Amer. backcountry; Austral./NZ outback, backblocks; N. Amer. informal boondocks.

bushy adjective thick, shaggy, curly, fuzzy, bristly, fluffy, woolly.
OPPOSITES sleek, wispy.

business noun **1** *she has to smile in her business:* work, occupation, profession, career, employment, job, position. **2** *who do you do business with?* trade, commerce, dealing, traffic, dealings, transactions, negotiations. **3** *her own business:* firm, company, concern, enterprise, venture, organization, operation, undertaking; informal outfit. **4** *none of your business:* concern, affair, responsibility, duty. **5** *an odd business:* affair, matter, case, circumstance, situation, event, incident.

businessman, businesswoman noun executive, entrepreneur, industrialist, merchant, dealer, trader, manufacturer, tycoon, employer, broker, buyer, seller, tradesman, retailer, supplier.

person who works in business.

busk verb play music in the street in the hope of being given money by passers-by.
■ busker noun.

bust[1] noun 1 a woman's breasts. 2 a sculpture of a person's head, shoulders, and chest.

bust[2] informal verb (**busts, busting, busted** or **bust**) 1 break, split, or burst. 2 chiefly N. Amer. raid or search a building, or arrest someone. •noun 1 a period of economic difficulty. 2 a police raid. •adjective 1 Brit. damaged; broken. 2 bankrupt.
□ bust-up a serious quarrel or fight.

bustard noun a large fast-running bird with speckled feathers.

bustle[1] verb (**bustles, bustling, bustled**) 1 move energetically or noisily. 2 (of a place) be full of activity. •noun excited activity and movement.

bustle[2] noun a pad or frame formerly worn by women under a skirt to puff it out behind.

busy adjective (**busier, busiest**) 1 having a lot to do. 2 occupied with an activity. 3 crowded or full of activity. •verb (**busies, busying, busied**) (**busy yourself**) keep yourself occupied.
■ busily adverb.

busybody noun (plural **busybodies**) an interfering or nosy person.

but conjunction 1 nevertheless. 2 on the contrary. 3 other than; otherwise than.

4 old use without it being the case that. •preposition except; apart from. •adverb only.
□ but for 1 except for. 2 if it were not for.

butane /byoo-tayn/ noun a flammable gas present in petroleum and natural gas and used as a fuel.

butch adjective informal aggressively masculine.

butcher noun 1 a person who cuts up and sells meat as a trade. 2 a person who kills animals for food. 3 a person who kills brutally. •verb (**butchers, butchering, butchered**) 1 kill or cut up an animal for food. 2 kill someone brutally.
■ butchery noun.

butler noun the chief male servant of a house.

butt[1] verb 1 hit with the head or horns. 2 (**butt in**) interrupt a conversation. •noun a rough push with the head.

butt[2] noun 1 an object of criticism or ridicule. 2 a target in archery or shooting.

butt[3] noun 1 the thicker end of a tool or a weapon. 2 the stub of a cigar or a cigarette. 3 N. Amer. informal a person's bottom. •verb meet end to end.

butt[4] noun a cask used for wine, beer, or water.

butter noun a pale yellow fatty substance made by churning cream. •verb (**butters, buttering, buttered**) 1 spread with butter.

bust noun 1 *her large bust:* bosom, breasts, chest; informal boobs, knockers; N. Amer. informal bazooms. 2 *a bust of Caesar:* sculpture, carving, effigy, statue, head and shoulders.

bustle verb *people bustled about:* rush, dash, hurry, scurry, scuttle, scamper, scramble; informal scoot, beetle, buzz.
•noun *the bustle of the market:* activity, action, liveliness, excitement, tumult, commotion, hubbub, whirl; informal toing and froing.

bustling adjective busy, crowded, swarming, teeming, humming, buzzing, hectic, lively.
OPPOSITES leisurely, deserted.

busy adjective 1 *they are very busy at the moment:* hard at work, involved, rushed off your feet, hard-pressed, on the job; informal on the go, hard at it; Brit. informal on the hop. 2 *I'm sorry, Mr Harris is busy:* unavailable, engaged, occupied, absorbed, engrossed, immersed, preoccupied, working; informal tied up. 3 *a busy day:* hectic, active, lively, full, eventful, energetic, tiring.
OPPOSITES idle, free, quiet.
•verb *he busied himself with paperwork:* occupy, involve, engage, concern, absorb, engross, immerse, distract, divert.

but conjunction 1 *he stumbled but didn't fall:* however, nevertheless, nonetheless, even so, yet, still. 2 *I am clean but you aren't:* whereas, conversely.
•preposition *everyone but him:* except (for), apart from, other than, besides, aside from, with the exception of, bar.
□ but for *except for,* if it were not for, barring, notwithstanding.

butt[1] verb *she butted him:* ram, headbutt, bump, poke, prod, push, shove, thrust.
□ butt in **interrupt,** intrude, break in, cut in, interfere, put your oar in; informal poke your nose in; Brit. informal chip in.

butt[2] noun *the butt of a joke:* target, victim, object, dupe, laughing stock.

butt[3] noun 1 *the butt of a gun:* stock, end, handle, hilt, haft. 2 *a cigarette butt:* stub, end, stump; informal fag end, dog end.
•verb *the shop butts up against the house:* adjoin, abut, be next to, be adjacent to, border (on), neighbour.

buttocks plural noun bottom, rear (end), rump, seat; informal behind, backside; Brit. informal bum, botty, jacksie; N. Amer. informal butt, fanny; humorous posterior.

b

2 (**butter someone up**) informal flatter someone.
□ **butter bean** Brit. a large flat edible bean.

buttercream noun a mixture of butter and icing sugar used to ice cakes.

buttercup noun a plant with small bright yellow flowers.

butterfly noun (plural **butterflies**) **1** an insect with two pairs of large wings, which feeds on nectar. **2** (**butterflies**) informal a fluttering sensation in the stomach when you are nervous. **3** a stroke in swimming in which you raise both arms out of the water together.

buttermilk noun the slightly sour liquid left after butter has been churned.

butterscotch noun a sweet made with butter and brown sugar.

buttery adjective containing, resembling, or covered with butter. • noun (plural **butteries**) Brit. a room in a college where food is sold to students.

buttock noun either of the two round fleshy parts of the human body that form the bottom.

button noun **1** a small disc sewn on to a garment to fasten it by being pushed through a buttonhole. **2** a knob on a piece of equipment which is pressed to operate it. • verb fasten a garment with buttons.

buttonhole noun **1** a slit in a piece of clothing through which a button is pushed to fasten it. **2** Brit. a flower worn in a buttonhole of a lapel. • verb (**buttonholes, buttonholing, buttonholed**) informal stop someone and hold them in conversation.

buttress noun **1** a projecting support built against a wall. **2** a projecting part of a hill or mountain. • verb support or strengthen.

buxom adjective (of a woman) attractively plump and large-breasted.

buy verb (**buys, buying, bought**) **1** get something in return for payment. **2** informal accept that something is true. • noun informal something that has been bought.
□ **buy someone out** pay someone to give

up a share in something.
■ **buyer** noun.

buzz noun **1** a low continuous humming sound. **2** the sound of a buzzer or telephone. **3** an atmosphere of excitement and activity. **4** informal a thrill. • verb **1** make a humming sound. **2** call someone with a buzzer. **3** move quickly. **4** (**buzz off**) informal go away. **5** have an air of excitement or activity.

buzzard noun a large bird of prey.

buzzer noun an electrical device that makes a buzzing noise to attract attention.

buzzword noun informal a technical word or phrase that has become fashionable.

by preposition **1** through the action of. **2** indicating an amount or the size of a margin. **3** indicating the end of a time period. **4** beside. **5** past and beyond. **6** during. **7** according to. • adverb so as to go past.
□ **by and by** before long. **by the by** in passing. **by and large** on the whole.

bye[1] noun **1** the moving of a competitor straight to the next round of a competition because they have no opponent. **2** Cricket a run scored from a ball that passes the batsman without being hit.

bye[2] exclamation informal goodbye.

by-election noun Brit. an election held during a government's term of office to fill a vacant seat.

bygone adjective belonging to an earlier time.
□ **let bygones be bygones** decide to forget past disagreements.

by-law or **bye-law** noun **1** Brit. a rule made by a local authority. **2** a rule made by a company or society.

byline noun **1** a line in a newspaper naming the writer of an article. **2** (in soccer) the part of the goal line to either side of the goal.

bypass noun **1** a road passing round a town. **2** an operation to help the circulation of blood by directing it through a new

THESAURUS

buy verb *they bought a new house:* purchase, acquire, obtain, get, pick up, snap up, invest in; informal get hold of, score.
OPPOSITES sell.
• noun (informal) *a good buy:* purchase, deal, bargain, investment, acquisition.

buyer noun purchaser, customer, consumer, shopper; (**buyers**) clientele, market.

buzz noun **1** *the buzz of the bees:* hum, murmur, drone. **2** *an insistent buzz from her control panel:* tone, purr, ring, warble, note, beep, alarm, warning.

by preposition **1** *I broke it by forcing the lid:* through, as a result of, because of, by dint

of, by means of, with the help of, by virtue of. **2** *be there by midday:* no later than, in good time for, before. **3** *a house by the lake:* next to, beside, alongside, by/at the side of, adjacent to.
• adverb *people hurried by:* past, on, along.

bypass noun ring road, detour, diversion, alternative route; Brit. relief road.
• verb **1** *bypass the farm:* go round, go past, make a detour round, avoid. **2** *the system had been bypassed:* ignore, sidestep, avoid, evade, escape, elude, skirt, dodge, circumvent, get round, go over the head of, pass over; informal short-circuit, duck.

passage. •verb go past or round.

by-product noun **1** a product produced in the process of making something else. **2** an unintended but unavoidable secondary result.

byre noun Brit. a cowshed.

bystander noun a person who is present at an event but does not take part.

byte noun a unit of information stored in a computer, equal to eight bits.

byway noun a minor road or path.

byword noun **1** a notable example of something. **2** a saying.

Byzantine /bi-**zan**-tyn/ adjective **1** relating to Byzantium (now Istanbul) or the Eastern Orthodox Church. **2** very complicated and detailed.

THESAURUS

by-product noun spin-off, consequence, result, corollary, side effect, ramification, repercussion, fallout.

bystander noun onlooker, passer-by, observer, spectator, eyewitness, witness, looker-on.

Cc

C or **c** noun (plural **Cs** or **C's**) **1** the third letter of the alphabet. **2** the Roman numeral for 100. • **abbreviation 1** Celsius or centigrade. **2** (©) copyright. **3** (c) cents. **4** (c or ca.) circa. **5** (c.) century or centuries.

cab noun **1** a taxi. **2** the driver's compartment in a truck, bus, or train.

cabal /kuh-**bal**/ noun a secret political group.

cabaret /**kab**-uh-ray/ noun entertainment held in a nightclub or restaurant while the audience sit at tables.

cabbage noun a vegetable with thick green or purple leaves.

caber /**kay**-ber/ noun a tree trunk used in the Scottish Highland sport of tossing the caber.

cabin noun **1** a private compartment on a ship. **2** the passenger compartment in an aircraft. **3** a small wooden shelter or house.

cabinet noun **1** a cupboard with drawers or shelves for storing things. **2** a piece of furniture enclosing a radio, speaker, etc. **3** (**Cabinet**) a committee of senior government ministers.

cabinetmaker noun a person who makes fine wooden furniture as a job.

cable noun **1** a thick rope of wire or fibre. **2** a wire for transmitting electricity or telecommunication signals. □ **cable car** a small carriage that hangs from a moving cable and travels up and down the side of a mountain. **cable television** a system in which programmes are transmitted by cable.

caboodle noun (**the whole caboodle**) informal the whole number of people or things in question.

caboose /kuh-**booss**/ noun N. Amer. a guards' van on a goods train.

cabriolet /**kab**-ri-oh-lay/ noun **1** a car with a roof that folds down. **2** a horse-drawn carriage with a hood.

cacao /kuh-**kah**-oh/ noun the seeds of a tropical American tree, from which cocoa and chocolate are made.

cache /kash/ noun a hidden store of things.

cachet /ka-**shay**/ noun the state of being respected or admired; prestige.

cackle verb (**cackles, cackling, cackled**) **1** laugh noisily. **2** (of a hen) make a noisy clucking cry. • noun a noisy cry or laugh.

cacophony /kuh-**koff**-uh-ni/ noun (plural **cacophonies**) a mixture of loud and unpleasant sounds.
■ **cacophonous** adjective.

cactus /**kak**-tuhss/ noun (plural **cacti** /**kak**-ty/ or **cactuses**) a plant with a thick fleshy stem that has spines but no leaves.

cad noun dated or humorous a man who is dishonest or treats other people badly.
■ **caddish** adjective.

cadaver /kuh-**da**-ver/ noun Medicine a dead body.

cadaverous adjective very pale and thin.

caddie or **caddy** noun (plural **caddies**) a person who carries a golfer's clubs. • verb (**caddies, caddying, caddied**) work as a caddie.

caddy noun (plural **caddies**) a small storage container.

cadence /**kay**-duhnss/ noun **1** the rise and fall in pitch of the voice. **2** the close of a musical phrase.

cadenza /kuh-**den**-zuh/ noun a difficult solo passage in a piece of music.

cadet noun a young trainee in the armed services or police.

THESAURUS

cab noun taxi, taxi cab; Brit. minicab, hackney carriage; N. Amer. hack.

cabin noun **1** a ship's cabin: berth, stateroom, compartment. **2** a cabin by the lake: hut, log cabin, shanty, shack, chalet; Scottish bothy; N. Amer. cabana.

cabinet noun cupboard, bureau, chest of drawers.

cable noun **1** a thick cable moored the ship: rope, cord, line; Nautical hawser; N. Amer. choker. **2** electric cables: wire, lead, cord, power line; Brit. flex.

cache noun hoard, store, stockpile, stock, supply, reserve, arsenal; informal stash.

cadge verb (**cadges, cadging, cadged**) informal ask for or get something without paying or working for it.

cadmium /**kad**-mi-uhm/ noun a silvery-white metallic element.

cadre /**kah**-der/ noun a small group of people trained for a particular purpose or at the centre of a political organization.

Caesar /**see**-zer/ noun a title of Roman emperors.

✓ -ae-, not -ea-: Caesar.

Caesarean or **Caesarean section** /si-**zair**-i-uhn/ noun an operation for delivering a child by cutting through the wall of the mother's abdomen.

caesium /**see**-zi-uhm/ (US spelling **cesium**) noun a soft, silvery metallic element.

cafe /**ka**-fay/ noun a small restaurant selling light meals and drinks.

cafeteria /ka-fuh-**teer**-i-uh/ noun a self-service restaurant.

cafetière /ka-fuh-**tyair**/ noun a coffee pot containing a plunger to push the grounds to the bottom.

caffeine /**kaf**-feen/ noun a stimulating substance found in tea and coffee.

caftan ⇒ **KAFTAN**.

cage noun a structure of bars or wires used for confining animals. •verb (**cages, caging, caged**) confine an animal in a cage.

cagey adjective informal cautiously reluctant to speak.
■ **cagily** adverb.

cagoule /kuh-**gool**/ noun Brit. a lightweight hooded waterproof jacket.

cahoots /kuh-**hoots**/ plural noun (**in cahoots**) informal making secret plans together.

caiman /**kay**-muhn/ noun a tropical American reptile similar to an alligator.

cairn noun a mound of rough stones built as a memorial or landmark.

cajole /kuh-**johl**/ verb (**cajoles, cajoling, cajoled**) persuade someone to do something by flattering them.

cake noun **1** an item of soft sweet food made from baking a mixture of flour, fat, eggs, and sugar. **2** a flat round item of savoury food. •verb (**cakes, caking, caked**) (of a thick or sticky substance) cover and become encrusted on something.

calabrese /kal-uh-**breez**/ noun a bright green variety of broccoli.

calamine /**kal**-uh-myn/ noun a pink powder used to make a soothing lotion or ointment.

calamity noun (plural **calamities**) an event causing great and sudden damage or distress.
■ **calamitous** adjective.

calcified /**kal**-si-fyd/ adjective hardened by the addition of calcium salts.

calcium noun a soft grey metallic substance. □ **calcium carbonate** a white compound found as chalk, limestone, and marble.

calculate verb (**calculates, calculating, calculated**) **1** work out a number or amount using mathematics. **2** intend an action to have a particular effect.
■ **calculable** adjective.

calculated adjective done with awareness of the likely effect.

calculating adjective craftily planning things so as to benefit yourself.

calculation noun **1** a count or assessment done using mathematics. **2** an assessment of the risks or effects of a course of action.

calculator noun a small electronic device used for making mathematical calculations.

calculus /**kal**-kyuu-luhss/ noun the branch

C

THESAURUS

cafe noun snack bar, cafeteria, coffee bar/shop, tea room/shop, bistro, brasserie; N. Amer. diner, lunchroom.

cafeteria noun self-service restaurant, canteen, cafe, buffet, refectory, mess hall.

cage noun the lion's cage: enclosure, pen, pound, coop, hutch, birdcage, aviary.
•verb they were caged up like animals: confine, shut in/up, pen, coop up, enclose.

cagey adjective (informal) secretive, guarded, tight-lipped, reticent, evasive; informal playing your cards close to your chest.
OPPOSITES open.

cajole verb persuade, wheedle, coax, talk into, prevail on; informal sweet-talk, soft-soap.

cake noun **1** cream cakes: bun, pastry, gateau, slice. **2** a cake of soap: bar, tablet, block, slab, lump, wedge.

•verb boots caked with mud: coat, encrust, plaster, cover.

calculate verb **1** the interest is calculated daily: compute, work out, reckon, figure, add up/together, count up, tally, total; Brit. tot up. **2** his words were calculated to wound her: intend, mean, design.

calculated adjective deliberate, premeditated, planned, pre-planned, preconceived, intentional, intended.
OPPOSITES unintentional, rash.

calculating adjective cunning, crafty, wily, sly, scheming, devious, disingenuous.
OPPOSITES ingenuous, innocent.

calculation noun **1** the calculation of the overall cost: computation, reckoning, adding up, counting up, working out, figuring; Brit. totting up. **2** political calculations: assessment, judgement, forecast, projection, prediction.

of mathematics concerned with problems involving rates of change.

caldron US spelling of CAULDRON.

calendar noun 1 a chart showing the days, weeks, and months of a particular year. 2 a system by which the beginning and end of a year are fixed. 3 a list of special days or events.

calf[1] noun (plural **calves**) 1 a young cow or bull. 2 the young of some other large animals, e.g. elephants.

calf[2] noun (plural **calves**) the fleshy part at the back of a person's leg below the knee.

calibrate verb (**calibrates**, **calibrating**, **calibrated**) 1 mark a gauge or instrument with units of measurement. 2 compare the readings of an instrument with those of a standard.
■ **calibration** noun.

calibre (US spelling **caliber**) noun 1 the diameter of the inside of a gun barrel, or of a bullet or shell. 2 a person's quality or ability.

calico noun (plural **calicoes** or US **calicos**) 1 Brit. a type of plain white cotton cloth. 2 N. Amer. printed cotton fabric.

californium noun a radioactive metallic element that is produced artificially.

caliper or **calliper** noun 1 (also **calipers**) a measuring instrument with two hinged legs. 2 a metal support for a person's leg.

caliph /**kay**-lif/ noun (in the past) the chief Muslim ruler.

calk US spelling of CAULK.

call verb 1 shout to someone to attract their attention or ask them to come somewhere. 2 telephone someone. 3 (of a bird or animal) make its characteristic cry. 4 pay a brief visit. 5 name or describe someone or something. 6 predict the result of a vote or contest. ● noun 1 an act of calling someone. 2 an act of telephoning someone. 3 the cry of a bird or animal. 4 a brief visit. 5 (**call for**) demand or need for.
□ **call centre** an office in which large numbers of telephone calls are handled for an organization. **call for** require. **call something off** cancel something. **call on** turn to for help. **call the shots** (or **tune**) be in charge of how something should be done. **call someone up** summon someone to serve in the army or to play in a team.
■ **caller** noun.

calligraphy /kuh-**lig**-ruh-fi/ noun decorative handwriting.
■ **calligrapher** noun **calligraphic** adjective.

calling noun 1 a profession or occupation. 2 a strong feeling that you are suitable for a particular occupation; a vocation.

callisthenics /kal-liss-**then**-iks/ (US spelling **calisthenics**) plural noun gymnastic exercises.

callous adjective insensitive and cruel.
■ **callously** adverb.

THESAURUS

calendar noun *my social calendar:* schedule, programme, diary, timetable, agenda.

calibre noun 1 *a man of his calibre:* quality, merit, distinction, stature, excellence, ability, expertise, talent, capability. 2 *rugby of this calibre:* standard, level, quality. 3 *the calibre of a gun:* bore, diameter, gauge.

call verb 1 *'Wait for me!' she called:* cry out, shout, yell, sing out, chant, exclaim; informal holler. 2 *Mum called me in the morning:* wake (up), awaken, rouse; Brit. informal knock up. 3 *I'll call you tomorrow:* phone, telephone, give someone a call; Brit. ring (up), give someone a ring; informal call up; Brit. informal give someone a bell, get someone on the blower; N. Amer. informal get someone on the horn. 4 *Rose called a taxi:* summon, send for, order. 5 *he called at Ashgrove Cottage:* pay a visit to, visit, call/drop/look in on, drop/stop by, pop into, nip over to. 6 *the prime minister called a meeting:* convene, summon, assemble. 7 *they called their daughter Hannah:* name, christen, baptize, designate, style, term, dub. 8 *I would call him a friend:* describe as, regard as, look on as, think of as, consider to be.
● noun 1 *I heard calls from the auditorium:*

cry, shout, yell, chant, exclamation; informal holler. 2 *the call of the barn owl:* cry, song. 3 *I'll give you a call tomorrow:* phone call, telephone call; Brit. ring; informal buzz; Brit. informal bell. 4 *a call for party unity:* appeal, request, plea. 5 *there's no call for that kind of language:* need, necessity, reason, justification, excuse. 6 *there's no call for expensive wine here:* demand, desire, market. 7 *the call of the Cairngorms:* attraction, appeal, lure, allure, pull, draw.
□ **call for 1** *this calls for a celebration:* require, need, necessitate, make necessary, demand, be grounds for, justify, warrant. 2 *he called for an enquiry:* ask for, request, seek, apply for, appeal for, demand, insist on, order. **call something off** cancel, abandon, scrap, drop, axe; informal scrub; N. Amer. informal redline. **call someone up 1** (informal) *Roland called me up.* See CALL verb sense 3. 2 *they called up the reservists:* enlist, recruit, conscript; US draft.

calling noun profession, occupation, vocation, career.

callous adjective heartless, unfeeling, uncaring, cold, cold-hearted, hard, as hard as nails, hard-hearted, insensitive, unsympathetic.
OPPOSITES kind, compassionate.

callow adjective young and inexperienced.

callus or **callous** noun an area of thickened and hardened skin.

calm adjective **1** not nervous, angry, or excited. **2** peaceful and undisturbed. •noun a calm state or period. •verb (often **calm down** or **calm someone down**) become or make someone calm.
■ **calmly** adverb **calmness** noun.

calorie noun (plural **calories**) **1** a unit for measuring how much energy food will produce. **2** a unit of heat.

calorific adjective relating to the amount of energy contained in food or fuel.

calumny /ka-luhm-ni/ noun (plural **calumnies**) formal the making of false and damaging statements about someone.

calve verb (**calves**, **calving**, **calved**) give birth to a calf.

calves plural of CALF¹, CALF².

calypso noun (plural **calypsos**) a kind of West Indian song with improvised words on a topical theme.

calyx /kay-liks/ noun (plural **calyces** /kay-li-seez/ or **calyxes**) the ring of small leaves (sepals) which form a layer around the bud of a flower.

cam noun **1** a projecting part on a wheel or shaft, which comes into contact with another part while rotating and makes it move. **2** a camshaft.

camaraderie /kam-uh-**rah**-duh-ri/ noun trust and friendship between people.

camber noun a slightly curved shape of a horizontal surface such as a road.

Cambodian /kam-**boh**-di-uhn/ noun a person from Cambodia. •adjective relating to Cambodia.

cambric noun a lightweight white linen or cotton fabric.

camcorder noun a portable combined video camera and video recorder.

came past tense of COME.

camel noun a large long-necked animal with either one or two humps on its back.

camellia /kuh-**mee**-li-uh/ noun an evergreen shrub with bright flowers and shiny leaves.

cameo noun (plural **cameos**) **1** a piece of jewellery consisting of a carving of a head against a differently coloured background. **2** a short piece of writing giving a good description of a person or thing. **3** a small part played by a well-known actor.

camera noun a device for taking photographs or recording moving images. □ **in camera** Law in a judge's private rooms, without the press and public being present.

Cameroonian noun a person from Cameroon, a country in West Africa. •adjective relating to Cameroon.

camisole noun a woman's loose-fitting undergarment for the upper body.

camomile or **chamomile** /**kam**-uh-myl/ noun a plant with white and yellow flowers, used in herbal preparations.

camouflage /**kam**-uh-flah*z*h/ noun **1** the painting or covering of soldiers and military equipment to make them blend in with their surroundings. **2** clothing or materials used for this purpose. **3** the natural appearance of an animal which allows it to blend in with its surroundings. •verb (**camouflages**, **camouflaging**, **camouflaged**) disguise using camouflage.

camp¹ noun **1** a place where soldiers, refugees, etc. live temporarily in tents, huts, or cabins. **2** a complex of buildings for holidaymakers. **3** the supporters of a particular party or set of beliefs. •verb live in a tent while on holiday.
□ **camp bed** Brit. a folding portable bed.
camp follower a person who associates with a group without being a full member.
■ **camper** noun.

calm adjective **1** *she seemed very calm:* relaxed, serene, tranquil, unruffled, unperturbed, unflustered, untroubled, unexcitable, unemotional, phlegmatic, composed; informal unflappable, laid-back. **2** *the night was calm:* windless, still, quiet, tranquil, smooth.
OPPOSITES excited, nervous, stormy.
•noun **1** *his usual calm deserted him:* composure, coolness, calmness, self-possession, sangfroid, serenity, tranquillity; informal cool, unflappability. **2** *calm prevailed:* tranquillity, stillness, quiet, peace.
□ **calm down 1** *I tried to calm him down:* soothe, pacify, placate, mollify; Brit. quieten (down); Austral. square off. **2** *she forced*

herself to calm down: **compose yourself,** recover/regain your composure, control yourself, pull yourself together, simmer down, cool down/off, take it easy; Brit. quieten down; informal get a grip, keep your shirt on; N. Amer. informal decompress.

camouflage noun *the stripes act as camouflage:* disguise, mask, screen, cover, cloak, front, facade, blind, concealment, subterfuge.
•verb *I used cement to camouflage the hole:* disguise, hide, conceal, mask, screen, cover (up).

camp noun **1** *an army camp:* campsite, encampment, camping ground, bivouac, base, settlement. **2** *the liberal and conservative camps:* faction, wing, group,

C

camp[2] informal **adjective 1** (of a man) effeminate in an exaggerated way. **2** deliberately exaggerated and theatrical in style.
□ **camp it up** behave in a camp way.

campaign noun **1** a series of military operations in a particular area. **2** an organized course of action to achieve a goal. • verb work towards a goal.
■ **campaigner** noun.

campanile /kam-puh-**nee**-lay/ noun a bell tower.

campanology /kam-puh-**nol**-uh-ji/ noun the art of bell-ringing.

campanula noun a plant with blue, purple, or white bell-shaped flowers.

campfire noun an open-air fire in a camp.

camphor noun a strong-smelling white substance, used in medicine and in insect repellents.

campion noun a plant with pink or white flowers.

campus noun (plural **campuses**) the grounds and buildings of a university or college.

camshaft noun a shaft with one or more cams attached to it.

can[1] **modal verb** (3rd singular present **can**; past **could**) **1** be able to. **2** be allowed to.

> ! when you're asking to be allowed to do something, it is more polite to say **may** rather than **can** (*may we leave now?* rather than *can we leave now?*).

can[2] noun a cylindrical metal container. • verb (**cans, canning, canned**) preserve food in a can.
□ **a can of worms** a complicated matter that will prove difficult to manage.

Canadian noun a person from Canada. • adjective relating to Canada.

canal noun **1** a water-filled channel made for boats to travel on or to convey water to fields. **2** a passage in a plant or animal carrying food, liquid, or air.

canapé /**kan**-uh-pay/ noun a small piece of bread or pastry with a savoury topping.

canard /ka-**nard**/ noun a false rumour or story.

canary noun (plural **canaries**) a small bright yellow bird with a tuneful song.

canasta /kuh-**nass**-tuh/ noun a card game using two packs and usually played by two pairs of partners.

cancan noun a lively, high-kicking stage dance.

cancel verb (**cancels, cancelling, cancelled**; US spelling **cancels, canceling, canceled**) **1** decide that a planned event will not take place. **2** withdraw from or end an arrangement. **3** (**cancel something out**) (of one thing) have an equal but opposite effect on another thing. **4** mark a stamp, ticket, etc. to show that it has been used.
■ **cancellation** noun.

Cancer noun a sign of the zodiac (the Crab), 21 June–22 July.

cancer noun **1** a disease caused by an uncontrolled growth of abnormal cells in a part of the body. **2** a tumour. **3** something evil or destructive that is hard to contain or destroy.
■ **cancerous** adjective.

candela /kan-**dee**-luh/ noun the basic unit of luminous intensity.

candelabrum /kan-di-**lah**-bruhm/ noun (plural **candelabra** /kan-di-**lah**-bruh/) a large branched holder for several candles or lamps.

candid adjective truthful and straight-forward; frank.
■ **candidly** adverb.

candidate noun **1** a person who applies for a job or is nominated for election. **2** Brit. a person taking an exam.
■ **candidacy** noun.

candied adjective (of fruit) preserved in a sugar syrup.

candle noun a stick of wax with a central

THESAURUS

lobby, caucus, bloc.

campaign noun **1** *Napoleon's Russian campaign:* operation(s), manoeuvre(s), offensive, attack, war, battle, crusade. **2** *the campaign to reduce vehicle emissions:* effort, drive, push, struggle, movement, crusade, operation, strategy.
• verb *they are campaigning for political reform:* fight, battle, push, press, strive, struggle, lobby, agitate.

cancel verb **1** *the match was cancelled:* call off, abandon, scrap, drop, axe; informal scrub; N. Amer. informal redline. **2** *his visa has been cancelled:* annul, invalidate, declare null and void, void, revoke, rescind, retract,

withdraw.
□ **cancel out** neutralize, negate, nullify, wipe out, balance (out), make up for, compensate for, offset.
OPPOSITES arrange, confirm, reinstate, issue.

cancer noun (malignant) growth, tumour.

candid adjective frank, forthright, direct, blunt, open, honest, truthful, sincere; informal upfront; N. Amer. informal on the up and up.
OPPOSITES guarded.

candidate noun applicant, contender, competitor, entrant, claimant, nominee, interviewee, examinee, possible; Brit. informal runner.

wick which is lit to produce light as it burns.

candlestick noun a support or holder for a candle.

candlewick noun a thick, soft cotton fabric with a tufted pattern.

candour (US spelling **candor**) noun the quality of being open and honest.

candy noun (plural **candies**) N. Amer. sweets.

candyfloss noun Brit. a mass of pink or white fluffy spun sugar wrapped round a stick.

cane noun 1 the hollow stem of tall reeds, grasses, etc. 2 a length of cane used as a walking stick, for beating someone, etc. •verb (**canes, caning, caned**) beat someone with a cane as a punishment.

canine /**kay**-nyn/ adjective relating to or resembling a dog. •noun a pointed tooth next to the incisors.

canister noun a round or cylindrical container.

canker noun 1 a disease of trees and plants. 2 a condition in animals that causes open sores.

cannabis noun a drug made from the hemp plant.

canned adjective preserved in a sealed can.

cannelloni /kan-nuh-**loh**-ni/ plural noun rolls of pasta stuffed with a meat or vegetable mixture and cooked in a cheese sauce.

cannery noun (plural **canneries**) a factory where food is canned.

cannibal noun a person who eats the flesh of human beings.
■ cannibalism noun cannibalistic adjective.

cannibalize or **cannibalise** verb (**cannibalizes, cannibalizing, cannibalized**) use a machine as a source of spare parts for others.

cannon noun (plural **cannon** or **cannons**) 1 a large, heavy gun formerly used in warfare. 2 an automatic heavy gun that fires shells from an aircraft or tank. •verb (**cannons, cannoning, cannoned**) (**cannon into** or **off**) chiefly Brit. collide with.
□ cannon fodder soldiers seen merely as a resource to be used up in war.

cannonade /kan-nuh-**nayd**/ noun a period of continuous heavy gunfire.

cannonball noun a metal or stone ball fired from a cannon.

cannot short form can not.

canny adjective (**cannier, canniest**) shrewd, especially in financial matters.
■ cannily adverb.

canoe noun a narrow boat with pointed ends, propelled with a paddle. •verb (**canoes, canoeing, canoed**) travel in a canoe.
■ canoeist noun.

canon noun 1 a general rule or principle by which something is judged. 2 a Church decree or law. 3 the works of a particular author or artist that are recognized as genuine. 4 a list of literary works considered as being of the highest quality. 5 a member of the clergy on the staff of a cathedral. 6 a piece of music in which a theme is taken up by two or more parts that overlap.
□ canon law the laws of the Christian Church.

canonical /kuh-**non**-i-k'l/ adjective 1 accepted as authentic or as a standard. 2 according to the laws of the Christian Church.

canonize or **canonise** verb (**canonizes, canonizing, canonized**) officially declare a dead person to be a saint.
■ canonization noun.

canoodle verb (**canoodles, canoodling, canoodled**) informal kiss and cuddle lovingly.

canopy noun (plural **canopies**) 1 a cloth covering over a throne or bed. 2 a roof-like covering or shelter. 3 the expanding, umbrella-like part of a parachute.
■ canopied adjective.

cant[1] /rhymes with rant/ noun 1 insincere talk about moral or religious matters. 2 disapproving the language typical of a particular group.

cant[2] /rhymes with rant/ verb tilt or slope. •noun a slope or tilt.

can't short form cannot.

cantaloupe /**kan**-tuh-loop/ noun a small melon with orange flesh.

cantankerous adjective bad-tempered and uncooperative.

cantata /kan-**tah**-tuh/ noun a musical work with a solo voice and usually a chorus and orchestra.

canteen noun 1 a restaurant in a workplace, school, or college. 2 Brit. a case containing a set of cutlery. 3 a small water bottle used by soldiers or campers.

canter noun a pace of a horse between a trot and a gallop. •verb (**canters, cantering, cantered**) move at this pace.

canticle noun a hymn or chant forming part of a church service.

cantilever noun a long beam or girder fixed

THESAURUS

canny adjective shrewd, astute, smart, sharp, discerning, discriminating, perceptive.

canoe noun kayak, dugout, outrigger.
canopy noun awning, shade, sunshade, covering.

C

at only one end, used for supporting a bridge.

■ **cantilevered** adjective.

canto /**kan**-toh/ noun (plural **cantos**) a division of a long poem.

canton noun a political or administrative subdivision of a country, especially in Switzerland.

canvas noun (plural **canvases** or **canvasses**) 1 a strong, coarse cloth used to make sails, tents, etc. 2 an oil painting on canvas.

canvass verb 1 visit someone to ask for their vote in an election. 2 question someone to find out their opinion.

■ **canvasser** noun.

canyon noun a deep gorge.

cap noun 1 a soft flat hat with a peak. 2 Brit. a cap awarded to members of a national sports team. 3 a lid or cover. 4 an upper limit on spending or borrowing. 5 a small amount of explosive powder in a case that explodes when you hit it. 6 a contraceptive diaphragm. • verb (**caps, capping, capped**) 1 put a cap on. 2 be a fitting end to. 3 put a limit on. 4 (**be capped**) Brit. be chosen as a member of a national sports team. □ **cap in hand** humbly asking for a favour.

capability noun (plural **capabilities**) the power or ability to do something.

capable adjective 1 (**capable of**) having the ability to do something. 2 able to achieve what you need to do; competent.

■ **capably** adverb.

capacious adjective having a lot of space inside; roomy.

capacitance noun the ability to store electric charge.

capacitor noun a device used to store electric charge.

capacity noun (plural **capacities**) 1 the maximum amount that something can contain or produce. 2 the ability or power to do something. 3 a role or position.

cape[1] noun a short cloak.

cape[2] noun a piece of land that sticks out into the sea.

caper[1] verb (**capers, capering, capered**) skip or dance about in a lively or playful way. • noun informal a light-hearted or dishonest activity.

caper[2] noun the flower bud of a shrub, pickled and used in cooking.

capillarity noun capillary action.

capillary /kuh-**pil**-luh-ri/ noun (plural **capillaries**) 1 a very small blood vessel. 2 a tube with a very narrow diameter. □ **capillary action** the force which acts on a liquid in a narrow tube to push it up or down.

capital noun 1 the most important city or town of a country or region. 2 wealth that is owned or invested, lent, or borrowed. 3 a capital letter. 4 the top part of a pillar. • adjective informal, dated excellent. □ **capital letter** a large size of letter used to begin sentences and names. **capital offence** an offence that is punished by death. **capital punishment** the punishment of a crime by death. **make capital out of** use to your own advantage.

capitalism noun a system in which a country's trade and industry are controlled by private owners for profit.

■ **capitalist** noun & adjective.

capitalize or **capitalise** verb (**capitalizes, capitalizing, capitalized**) 1 (**capitalize on**) take advantage of. 2 convert into or

THESAURUS

canvass verb 1 *he's canvassing for the Green Party:* campaign, electioneer. 2 *they promised to canvass all members:* poll, question, survey, interview, consult.

canyon noun ravine, gorge, gully, chasm, abyss, gulf; N. Amer. gulch, coulee.

cap noun 1 *a white plastic cap:* lid, top, stopper, cork, bung; N. Amer. stopple. 2 *a cap on spending:* limit, ceiling, curb, check. • verb 1 *mountains capped with snow:* top, crown, cover, coat, tip. 2 *budgets will be capped:* limit, restrict, curb, control, peg.

capability noun ability, capacity, power, potential, competence, aptitude, faculty, skill, talent, flair; informal know-how.
OPPOSITES inability.

capable adjective able, competent, effective, proficient, accomplished, experienced, skilful, talented, gifted; informal useful.
OPPOSITES incompetent.

capacity noun 1 *the capacity of the freezer:* volume, size, dimensions, measurements, proportions. 2 *his capacity to inspire trust.* See CAPABILITY. 3 *in his capacity as Commander-in-Chief:* role, function, position, post, job, office.

cape[1] noun *a woollen cape:* cloak, mantle, poncho.

cape[2] noun *the ship rounded the cape:* headland, promontory, point, head, horn, mull, peninsula.

capital noun money, finance(s), funds, cash, wherewithal, means, assets, wealth, resources.

capitalism noun private enterprise, free enterprise, the free market, private ownership.
OPPOSITES communism.

capitalize verb *Wales failed to capitalize on their early lead:* take advantage of, profit from, make the most of, exploit, develop; informal cash in on.

provide with financial capital. **3** write in capital letters or with a capital first letter.
∎ **capitalization** noun.

capitation noun the payment of a fee or grant to a doctor, school, etc., the amount of which depends on the number of pupils, patients, etc. that are involved.

capitulate verb (**capitulates**, **capitulating**, **capitulated**) give in to an opponent.
∎ **capitulation** noun.

capon /**kay**-puhn/ noun a male chicken that has been fattened up for eating.

cappuccino /kap-puh-**chee**-noh/ noun (plural **cappuccinos**) coffee made with milk that has been frothed up with pressurized steam.

caprice /kuh-**preess**/ noun a sudden change of mood or behaviour.

capricious /kuh-**pri**-shuhss/ adjective having sudden changes of mood.
∎ **capriciously** adverb.

Capricorn noun a sign of the zodiac (the Goat), 21 December–20 January.

capsicum noun (plural **capsicums**) a sweet pepper or chilli pepper.

capsize verb (**capsizes**, **capsizing**, **capsized**) (of a boat) overturn in the water.

capstan noun a broad revolving cylinder for winding a heavy rope or cable.

capsule noun **1** a small gelatin container with a dose of medicine inside, swallowed whole. **2** a small case or compartment.

captain noun **1** the person in command of a ship or commercial aircraft. **2** the rank of naval officer above commander. **3** the rank of army officer above lieutenant. **4** the leader of a team. •verb be the captain of.
∎ **captaincy** noun.

caption noun **1** a title or explanation accompanying an illustration or cartoon. **2** a piece of writing appearing as part of a film or television broadcast. •verb provide a caption for.

captivate verb (**captivates**, **captivating**, **captivated**) attract and hold the interest of; charm.

captive noun a person who has been captured. •adjective unable to escape.
∎ **captivity** noun.

captor noun a person who captures another.

capture verb (**captures**, **capturing**, **captured**) **1** take prisoner, or forcibly get possession of. **2** record accurately in words or pictures. **3** cause data to be stored in a computer. •noun the action of capturing.

capybara /ka-pi-**bah**-ruh/ noun (plural **capybara** or **capybaras**) a large South American rodent.

car noun **1** a powered road vehicle designed to carry a small number of people. **2** a railway carriage or wagon.
□ **car park** Brit. an area or building where cars may be left temporarily.

carafe /kuh-**raf**/ noun a wide-necked glass bottle for serving wine.

caramel noun **1** sugar or syrup heated until it turns brown. **2** soft toffee made with sugar and butter.

carapace /**ka**-ruh-payss/ noun the hard upper shell of a tortoise, lobster, etc.

carat /**ka**-ruht/ noun **1** a unit of weight for precious stones and pearls. **2** a measure of the purity of gold.

caravan noun **1** a vehicle equipped for living in, designed to be towed by a car or a horse. **2** historical a group of people travelling together across a desert.

C

THESAURUS

capitulate verb surrender, give in, yield, concede defeat, give up (the struggle), submit, lay down your arms, throw in the towel/sponge.
OPPOSITES resist, hold out.

capricious adjective fickle, volatile, unpredictable, temperamental, erratic, wayward, whimsical, flighty, faddish.
OPPOSITES consistent.

capsule noun **1** *he swallowed a capsule:* pill, tablet, lozenge, pastille; informal tab. **2** *a space capsule:* module, craft, probe.

captain noun **1** *the ship's captain:* commander, master; informal skipper. **2** *the team captain:* leader, head, chief; informal boss, skipper.

caption noun title, heading, legend, description.

captivate verb enthral, charm, enchant, bewitch, fascinate, beguile, entrance, delight, attract, allure.

captive noun prisoner, convict, detainee, hostage, prisoner of war, internee.
•adjective confined, caged, incarcerated, locked up, jailed, imprisoned, interned, detained.
OPPOSITES free.

captivity noun imprisonment, incarceration, confinement, detention, internment.
OPPOSITES freedom.

capture verb **1** *Mark Dawes was captured in Moscow:* catch, apprehend, seize, arrest. **2** *guerrillas have captured several towns:* occupy, invade, conquer, seize, take (possession of).
OPPOSITES release, abandon, liberate.
•noun *he tried to avoid capture:* arrest, seizure.

car noun **1** *he drove up in his car:* motor, motor car, automobile; informal wheels; N. Amer. informal auto. **2** *the dining car:* carriage, coach; Brit. saloon.

caraway noun a plant whose seeds are used as a spice.

carbide noun a compound of carbon with a metal or other element.

carbine noun a light automatic rifle.

carbohydrate noun a substance (e.g. sugar and starch) containing carbon, hydrogen, and oxygen, found in food and used to give energy.

carbolic or **carbolic acid** noun a kind of disinfectant.

carbon noun a chemical element with two main pure forms (diamond and graphite), found in all organic compounds.
□ **carbon copy 1** a copy made with carbon paper. **2** a person or thing identical to another. **carbon dating** a method of finding out how old something is by measuring the amount of radioactive carbon-14 in it. **carbon dioxide** a gas produced by people and animals breathing out, and also by burning carbon, which is absorbed by plants in photosynthesis. **carbon monoxide** a poisonous gas formed when carbon is not completely burned. **carbon paper** thin paper coated with carbon, used for making a copy of a document.

carbonaceous adjective consisting of or containing carbon or its compounds.

carbonate noun a compound containing carbon and oxygen together with a metal.

carbonated adjective (of a drink) fizzy because it contains small bubbles of carbon dioxide.

carbonic acid noun a very weak acid formed from carbon dioxide and water.

carborundum noun a very hard black substance used for grinding and polishing.

carbuncle noun **1** a large abscess or boil in the skin. **2** a polished red gem.

carburettor (US spelling **carburetor**) noun a device in an engine that mixes the fuel with air.

carcass or **carcase** noun the dead body of an animal.

carcinogen /kar-sin-uh-juhn/ noun a substance that can cause cancer.
■ **carcinogenic** adjective.

carcinoma /kar-si-noh-muh/ noun (plural **carcinomas**) a cancer of the skin or of the internal organs.

card¹ noun **1** thick, stiff paper or thin cardboard. **2** a piece of card printed with information, greetings, etc. **3** a small rectangular piece of plastic used for obtaining money from a bank or paying for goods. **4** a playing card. **5** (**cards**) a game played with playing cards.
□ **card sharp** a person who cheats at cards. **on the cards** possible or likely.

card² verb disentangle the fibres of raw wool by combing it with a sharp-toothed instrument.

cardamom noun the seed and pods of a SE Asian plant, used as a spice.

cardboard noun thin board made from paper pulp.

cardiac adjective having to do with the heart.

cardigan noun a sweater with buttons down the front.

cardinal noun an important Roman Catholic priest, having the power to elect the Pope.
• adjective most important; chief.
□ **cardinal number** a number expressing quantity (one, two, three, etc.).

cardiograph noun an instrument for recording heart movements.

cardiology noun the branch of medicine concerned with the heart.

cardiovascular adjective having to do with the heart and blood vessels.

care noun **1** special attention or effort made to avoid damage, risk, or error. **2** the process of looking after and protecting someone or something. **3** a cause for anxiety, or a worried feeling. **4** the responsibility of a local authority to look after children, rather than their parents.
• verb (**cares**, **caring**, **cared**) **1** feel concern or interest. **2** feel affection or liking. **3** (**care for** or **to do**) like to have or be willing to do. **4** (**care for**) look after.
□ **care of** at the address of someone who will look after or pass on mail. **take care of** look after or deal with.

careen /kuh-**reen**/ verb (of a ship) tilt to one side.

THESAURUS

carcass noun corpse, dead body, remains; Medicine cadaver; informal stiff.

care noun **1** *the care of the child:* safe keeping, supervision, custody, charge, protection, responsibility, guardianship. **2** *she chose her words with care:* discretion, caution, sensitivity, thought, regard, consideration. **3** *the cares of the day:* worry, anxiety, trouble, concern, stress, pressure, strain.

OPPOSITES neglect, carelessness.
• verb *the teachers didn't care about our work:* be concerned, worry (yourself), trouble/concern yourself, bother, mind, be interested; informal give a damn/hoot.
□ **care for 1** *he cares for his children:* love, be fond of, be devoted to, treasure, adore, dote on, think the world of, worship. **2** *the hospice cares for the terminally ill:* look after, take care of, tend, attend to,

C

career noun an occupation which is undertaken for a long period of a person's life. •verb (**careers, careering, careered**) move very fast and in an uncontrolled way.

careerist noun a person whose only concern is to make progress in their career.
■ **careerism** noun.

carefree adjective free from anxiety or responsibility.

careful adjective **1** taking care to avoid harm; cautious. **2** showing a lot of thought and attention.
■ **carefully** adverb **carefulness** noun.

careless adjective not giving enough attention to avoiding harm or mistakes.
■ **carelessly** adverb **carelessness** noun.

carer noun someone who looks after a sick, elderly, or disabled person.

caress verb touch or stroke gently or lovingly. •noun a gentle or loving touch.

caretaker noun a person employed to look after a public building.

careworn adjective showing signs of prolonged worry.

cargo noun (plural **cargoes** or **cargos**) goods carried on a ship, aircraft, etc.

Caribbean /ka-rib-bee-uhn/ adjective relating to the Caribbean Sea and its islands.

☑ one *r* and two *b*s: Caribbean.

caribou /ka-ri-boo/ noun (plural **caribou**) N. Amer. a reindeer.

caricature /ka-ri-kuh-tyoor/ noun a picture in which a person's distinctive features are amusingly exaggerated. •verb (**caricatures, caricaturing, caricatured**) make a caricature of.

caries /kair-eez/ noun decay of a tooth or bone.

carjacking noun the action of stealing a car after attacking its driver or forcing them to abandon it.

carmine /kar-myn/ noun a vivid crimson colour.

carnage /kar-nij/ noun the killing of a large number of people.

carnal adjective relating to sexual needs and activities.
■ **carnality** noun.

carnation noun a plant with pink, white, or red flowers.

carnelian /kar-nee-li-uhn/ noun a dull red or pink semi-precious stone.

carnival noun a festival involving processions, music, and dancing.

carnivore /kar-ni-vor/ noun an animal that eats meat.

carnivorous /kar-niv-uh-ruhss/ adjective eating a diet of meat.

carob noun a substitute for chocolate made from the pod of an Arabian tree.

carol noun a religious song associated with Christmas. •verb (**carols, carolling, carolled**; US spelling **carols, caroling, caroled**) **1** sing carols in the streets. **2** sing or say happily.

carotene noun an orange or red substance found in carrots and other plants, important in the formation of vitamin A.

THESAURUS

career noun *a business career:* profession, occupation, vocation, calling, life's work, employment.
•verb *they careered down the hill:* hurtle, rush, shoot, race, speed, charge, hare, fly; informal belt, tear; Brit. informal bucket.

carefree adjective unworried, untroubled, blithe, nonchalant, happy-go-lucky, free and easy, easy-going, relaxed; informal laid-back.
OPPOSITES troubled.

careful adjective **1** *be careful when you go up the stairs:* cautious, alert, attentive, watchful, vigilant, wary, on your guard, circumspect. **2** *careful with money:* prudent, thrifty, economical, sparing, frugal. **3** *careful consideration of the facts:* attentive, conscientious, painstaking, meticulous, diligent, assiduous, scrupulous, methodical.
OPPOSITES careless, extravagant, casual.

careless adjective **1** *careless motorists:* inattentive, negligent, heedless, irresponsible, impetuous, reckless.
2 *careless work:* shoddy, slapdash, slipshod, scrappy, slovenly, sloppy, negligent, lax, slack, disorganized, hasty, hurried. **3** *a careless remark:* thoughtless, insensitive, indiscreet, unguarded, incautious, inadvertent.
OPPOSITES careful, attentive, meticulous, deliberate, calculated.

caress verb stroke, touch, fondle, brush, feel, skim.

caretaker noun janitor, attendant, porter, custodian, concierge; N. Amer. superintendent.
•adjective *the caretaker manager:* temporary, acting, provisional, substitute, interim, stand-in, fill-in, stopgap; N. Amer. informal pinch-hitting.
OPPOSITES permanent.

cargo noun freight, load, haul, consignment, delivery, shipment, goods, merchandise.

carnage noun slaughter, massacre, murder, butchery, bloodbath, bloodletting, holocaust.

carnival noun festival, fiesta, fete, fair, gala, Mardi Gras.

C

carotid artery /kuh-**rot**-id/ noun either of two main arteries carrying blood to the head.

carouse /kuh-**rowz**/ verb (**carouses, carousing, caroused**) drink alcohol and enjoy yourself with other people in a noisy, lively way.

carousel noun 1 a merry-go-round at a fair. 2 a rotating device for baggage collection at an airport.

carp[1] noun (plural **carp**) an edible freshwater fish.

carp[2] verb complain or find fault.

carpal adjective relating to the bones in the wrist.

carpel noun the female reproductive organ of a flower.

carpenter noun a person who makes objects and structures out of wood.
■ **carpentry** noun.

carpet noun 1 a floor covering made from thick woven fabric. 2 a thick or soft layer of something. • verb (**carpets, carpeting, carpeted**) 1 cover with a carpet. 2 informal tell someone off severely.
□ **carpet-bomb** bomb an area intensively.

carpetbagger noun informal, disapproving a politician who tries to get elected in an area where they have no local connections.

carport noun an open-sided shelter for a parked car.

carriage noun 1 a four-wheeled horse-drawn vehicle for passengers. 2 a passenger vehicle in a train. 3 the carrying of goods from one place to another. 4 a person's way of standing or moving. 5 a wheeled support for moving a gun.
□ **carriage clock** a portable clock with a handle on top.

carriageway noun 1 each of the two sides of a dual carriageway or motorway. 2 the part of a road intended for vehicles.

carrier noun 1 a person or thing that carries or holds something. 2 a company that transports goods or people for payment.
□ **carrier bag** a plastic or paper bag with

handles. **carrier pigeon** a homing pigeon trained to carry messages.

carrion noun the decaying flesh of dead animals.

carrot noun 1 a tapering orange root vegetable. 2 something tempting offered as a means of persuasion.

carry verb (**carries, carrying, carried**) 1 move or take from one place to another. 2 support the weight of. 3 take on or accept responsibility or blame. 4 have a particular feature or result. 5 approve a proposal by a majority of votes. 6 publish or broadcast something. 7 (of a sound or voice) travel a long way. 8 (**carry yourself**) stand and move in a particular way. 9 be pregnant with.
□ **be** (or **get**) **carried away** lose self-control. **carry the can** informal take responsibility for a mistake. **carry something off** succeed in doing something. **carry on** 1 continue with something. 2 informal have a love affair. **carry-on** informal 1 a fuss. 2 (also **carryings-on**) improper behaviour. **carry something out** perform a task. **carry something through** manage to complete something.

carrycot noun a baby's small portable cot.

cart noun 1 an open horse-drawn vehicle for carrying goods or people. 2 a shallow open container on wheels, pulled or pushed by hand. • verb 1 carry in a cart or similar vehicle. 2 informal carry a heavy object with difficulty.

carte blanche /kart **blahnsh**/ noun complete freedom to act as you wish.

cartel /kar-**tel**/ noun an association of manufacturers or suppliers formed to keep prices high.

carthorse noun a large, strong horse suitable for heavy work.

cartilage /**kar**-ti-lij/ noun firm, flexible tissue which covers the ends of joints and forms structures such as the external ear.
■ **cartilaginous** adjective.

cartography /kar-**tog**-ruh-fi/ noun the

THESAURUS

carp verb complain, find fault, quibble, grumble, grouse, whine; informal nit-pick, gripe, moan, bitch, whinge.
OPPOSITES praise.

carpenter noun woodworker, joiner, cabinetmaker; Brit. informal chippy.

carriage noun 1 a railway carriage: coach, car; Brit. saloon. 2 a horse and carriage: wagon, coach. 3 an erect carriage: posture, bearing, gait; Brit. deportment.

carry verb 1 she carried the box into the kitchen: convey, transfer, transport, move, take, bring, bear, fetch; informal cart, hump, lug. 2 satellites carry the signal over the

Atlantic: transmit, conduct, relay, communicate, convey, beam, send. 3 a resolution was carried: approve, pass, accept, endorse, ratify. 4 his voice carried across the quay: be audible, travel, reach, be heard.
OPPOSITES reject.
□ **carry on continue**, keep (on), go on, persist in; informal stick with/at. **carry something out** 1 they carried out an operation: conduct, perform, execute, implement. 2 I carried out my promise: keep, honour, fulfil, observe, abide by, comply with, adhere to, stick to.

C

science or practice of drawing maps.
■ **cartographer** noun **cartographic** adjective.

carton noun a light cardboard box or container.

cartoon noun 1 a humorous drawing in a newspaper or magazine. 2 (also **cartoon strip**) a sequence of cartoon drawings that tell a story. 3 a film made from a sequence of drawings, using animation techniques to give the appearance of movement. 4 a full-size drawing made as a preliminary design for a work of art.
■ **cartoonist** noun.

cartridge noun 1 a container holding film, ink, etc., designed to be inserted into a mechanism such as a camera or printer. 2 a casing containing explosives and a bullet or shot for a gun.
□ **cartridge paper** thick paper for drawing on.

cartwheel noun a sideways somersault performed with the arms and legs extended. •verb perform cartwheels.

carve verb (**carves**, **carving**, **carved**) 1 cut into a hard material to produce an object or design. 2 cut cooked meat into slices for eating. 3 (**carve something out**) develop a career, reputation, etc. through great effort. 4 (**carve something up**) divide something up ruthlessly.

carvery noun (plural **carveries**) a restaurant where cooked joints of meat are carved as required.

carving noun an object or design carved from wood or stone.

Casanova /ka-suh-**noh**-vuh/ noun a man known for seducing many women.

casbah ⇒ KASBAH.

cascade noun 1 a small waterfall. 2 a mass of something falling or hanging down.
•verb (**cascades**, **cascading**, **cascaded**) pour downwards in large quantities.

case[1] noun 1 an instance of something happening. 2 an incident being investigated by the police. 3 a legal action decided in a court of law. 4 a set of facts or arguments supporting one side of a debate or lawsuit. 5 a person or problem being given the attention of a doctor, social worker, etc. 6 Grammar a form of a noun, adjective, or pronoun expressing the relationship of the word to others in the sentence.
□ **in case** so as to allow for the possibility of something happening.

case[2] noun 1 a container or protective covering. 2 a suitcase. 3 a box containing twelve bottles of wine. •verb (**cases**, **casing**, **cased**) 1 enclose in a case. 2 informal examine a place before robbing it.

casein /**kay**-seen/ noun the main protein in milk and cheese.

casement noun a window hinged at the side so that it opens like a door.

cash noun 1 money in coins or notes. 2 money available for use. •verb 1 give or receive notes or coins for a cheque or money order. 2 (**cash something in**) convert an insurance policy, savings account, etc. into money. 3 (**cash in on**) informal take advantage of.
□ **cash crop** a crop produced for sale rather than for use by the grower. **cash flow** the total amount of money passing into and out of a business. **cash register** a machine used in shops for adding up and recording the amount of each sale and storing the

THESAURUS

carton noun box, package, cardboard box, case, container, pack, packet.

cartoon noun 1 *a cartoon of the Prime Minister:* caricature, parody, lampoon, satire; informal take-off, send-up. 2 *he was reading cartoons:* comic strip, comic, graphic novel. 3 *we watched Yogi Bear cartoons:* cartoon film, animated film, animation.

cartridge noun cassette, magazine, canister, case, container.

carve verb 1 *he carved horn handles:* sculpt, cut, hew, whittle, chisel, shape, fashion. 2 *I carved my initials on the tree:* engrave, incise, score, cut. 3 *he carved the roast chicken:* slice, cut up, chop.
□ **carve something up divide**, break up, partition, apportion, subdivide, split up, share out.

case[1] noun 1 *a classic case of overreaction:* instance, example, occurrence, occasion, demonstration, illustration. 2 *is that the*

case? situation, position, state of affairs, circumstances, conditions, facts; Brit. state of play; informal score. 3 *the officers on the case:* assignment, job, project, investigation, exercise. 4 *he lost his case:* lawsuit, legal action, trial, legal proceedings, litigation. 5 *the case against animal testing:* argument, defence, justification, vindication, exposition, thesis.

case[2] noun 1 *a cigarette case:* container, box, canister, holder. 2 *a seed case:* casing, cover, sheath, envelope, sleeve, jacket, shell. 3 (Brit.) *she threw some clothes into a case:* suitcase, travel bag, valise; (**cases**) luggage, baggage. 4 *a glass display case:* cabinet, cupboard.

cash noun 1 *a wallet stuffed with cash:* money, currency, bank notes, coins, change; N. Amer. bills; informal dough, loot; Brit. informal dosh, brass; N. Amer. informal dinero. 2 *a lack of cash:* finance, money, resources, funds, assets, means, wherewithal.

money received.

cashew noun an edible kidney-shaped nut.

cashier noun a person responsible for paying out and receiving money in a shop, bank, etc. • verb (**cashiers, cashiering, cashiered**) dismiss someone from the armed forces.

cashmere noun fine, soft wool from a breed of Himalayan goat.

casing noun a cover that protects or encloses something.

casino noun (plural **casinos**) a public building or room for gambling.

cask noun a large barrel for storing alcoholic drinks.

casket noun 1 a small ornamental box or chest for holding valuable objects. 2 chiefly N. Amer. a coffin.

cassava /kuh-**sah**-vuh/ noun the root of a tropical American tree, used as food.

casserole noun 1 a large dish with a lid, used for cooking food slowly in an oven. 2 a kind of stew cooked slowly in an oven. • verb (**casseroles, casseroling, casseroled**) cook food in a casserole.

cassette noun a sealed plastic case containing audio tape, videotape, film, etc., designed to be inserted into a player or camera.

cassock noun a long garment worn by Christian priests and members of church choirs.

cassowary /**kass**-uh-wuh-ri/ noun (plural **cassowaries**) a very large bird that cannot fly, found in New Guinea.

cast verb (**casts, casting, cast**) 1 throw forcefully. 2 make light or shadow appear on a surface. 3 direct your eyes or thoughts. 4 give a vote. 5 make a magic spell take effect. 6 throw a fishing line out into the water. 7 shed or discard. 8 shape metal by pouring it into a mould while molten. 9 give a part to an actor, or allocate parts in a play or film. • noun 1 the

actors taking part in a play or film. 2 (also **casting**) an object made by casting metal. 3 a bandage stiffened with plaster of Paris to support and protect a broken limb. 4 the appearance or character of a person or thing. 5 a slight squint.
□ **cast about** (or **around** or **round**) search far and wide. **casting vote** an extra vote used by a chairperson to decide an issue when votes on each side are equal. **cast iron** a hard alloy of iron and carbon which can be cast in a mould. **cast off** release a boat or ship from its moorings. **cast-off** abandoned or discarded.

castanets plural noun a pair of small curved pieces of wood, clicked together by the fingers to accompany Spanish dancing.

castaway noun a person who has been shipwrecked in an isolated place.

caste noun each of the classes of Hindu society.

castellated adjective having battlements.

castigate verb (**castigates, castigating, castigated**) tell someone off severely.
■ **castigation** noun.

castle noun 1 a large fortified building of the medieval period. 2 Chess a rook.
□ **castles in the air** dreams or plans that will never be achieved.

castor or **caster** noun 1 a small swivelling wheel fixed to the legs or base of a piece of furniture. 2 a small container with holes in the top, used for sprinkling salt, sugar, etc.
□ **castor oil** oil from the seeds of an African shrub, used as a laxative. **castor sugar** white sugar in fine granules.

castrate verb (**castrates, castrating, castrated**) 1 remove the testicles of. 2 make something less powerful or strong.
■ **castration** noun.

casual adjective 1 relaxed and unconcerned. 2 done without enough attention or proper

---

THESAURUS

cashier noun clerk, teller, banker, treasurer, bursar, purser.

cast verb 1 *he cast the stone into the stream:* throw, toss, fling, pitch, hurl, lob; informal chuck, sling, bung. 2 *she cast a fearful glance over her shoulder:* direct, shoot, throw, fling, send. 3 *each citizen cast a vote:* register, record, enter, file. 4 *the fire cast a soft light:* emit, give off, throw, send out, radiate. 5 *printing type was cast by hand:* mould, fashion, form, shape, forge. • noun 1 *a cast of his hand:* mould, die, matrix, shape, casting, model. 2 *the cast of 'Hamlet':* actors, performers, players, company, troupe, dramatis personae, characters.

caste noun class, rank, level, order, stratum, echelon, status.

castle noun fortress, fort, stronghold, fortification, keep, citadel, palace, chateau, tower.

casual adjective 1 *a casual attitude to life:* unconcerned, uncaring, indifferent, lackadaisical, nonchalant, offhand, flippant, easy-going, free and easy, blithe, carefree, devil-may-care; informal laid-back. 2 *a casual remark:* offhand, spontaneous, unthinking, unconsidered, impromptu, throwaway, unguarded; informal off-the-cuff. 3 *a casual glance:* cursory, perfunctory, superficial, passing, fleeting. 4 *a casual acquaintance:* slight, superficial. 5 *casual work:*

planning. **3** occasional or temporary: *casual work*. **4** happening by chance; accidental. **5** (of clothes) informal.
■ **casually** adverb.

casualty noun (plural **casualties**) **1** a person killed or injured in a war or accident. **2** a person or thing badly affected by an event or situation.

casuistry /**kazh**-oo-iss-tri/ noun the use of clever but false reasoning.

cat noun **1** a small furry animal kept as a pet. **2** a wild animal related to this, such as a lion or tiger.
▫ **cat burglar** a thief who enters a building by climbing to an upper storey. **cat's paw** a person used by another to carry out an unpleasant task. **the cat's whiskers** informal an excellent person or thing. **let the cat out of the bag** reveal a secret by mistake.

cataclysm /**kat**-uh-kli-z'm/ noun a violent upheaval or disaster.
■ **cataclysmic** adjective.

catacomb /**kat**-uh-koom/ noun an underground cemetery consisting of tunnels with recesses for tombs.

catafalque /**kat**-uh-falk/ noun a decorated wooden framework used to support a coffin.

catalepsy /**kat**-uh-lep-si/ noun a condition in which a person becomes unconscious and goes rigid.

catalogue (US spelling **catalog**) noun **1** a list of items arranged in order. **2** a publication containing details of items for sale. **3** a series of bad things: *a catalogue of failures*.
● verb (**catalogues, cataloguing, catalogued**; US spelling **catalogs, cataloging, cataloged**) list in a catalogue.

catalyse /**kat**-uh-lyz/ (US spelling **catalyze**) verb (**catalyses, catalysing, catalysed**) cause or speed up a reaction by acting as a catalyst.

catalysis /kuh-**tal**-i-siss/ noun the speeding up of a chemical reaction by a catalyst.
■ **catalytic** /kat-uh-**lit**-ik/ adjective.

catalyst /**kat**-uh-list/ noun **1** a substance that increases the rate of a chemical reaction while remaining unchanged itself. **2** a person or thing that causes something to happen.

catalytic converter noun a device in a motor vehicle which converts pollutant exhaust gases into less harmful ones.

catamaran /**kat**-uh-muh-ran/ noun a boat with twin parallel hulls.

catapult noun **1** a forked stick with elastic fastened to the two prongs, used for shooting small stones. **2** a device for launching a glider or aircraft. ● verb **1** throw forcefully. **2** move suddenly or very fast.

cataract noun **1** a large waterfall. **2** a condition in which the lens of the eye becomes cloudy, resulting in blurred vision.

catarrh /kuh-**tar**/ noun excessive mucus in the nose or throat.

catastrophe /kuh-**tass**-truh-fi/ noun a sudden event that causes great damage or suffering.
■ **catastrophic** adjective **catastrophically** adverb.

catatonia /kat-uh-**toh**-ni-uh/ noun a condition in which a person experiences both periods of near unconsciousness and periods of overactivity.
■ **catatonic** adjective.

catcall noun a shrill whistle or shout of mockery or disapproval. ● verb make a catcall.

catch verb (**catches, catching, caught**)

C

THESAURUS

temporary, freelance, irregular, occasional. **6** *a casual meeting changed his life*: chance, accidental, unplanned, unintended, unexpected, unforeseen. **7** *a casual shirt*: informal, leisure, everyday; informal sporty. **8** *the inn's casual atmosphere*: relaxed, friendly, informal, easy-going, free and easy; informal laid-back.
OPPOSITES serious, premeditated, careful, good, permanent, planned, formal.

casualty noun victim, sufferer, fatality, death, loss, wounded person, injured person.

cat noun feline, tomcat, tom, kitten; informal pussy (cat), puss, kitty; Brit. informal moggie, mog.

catalogue noun *a library catalogue*: directory, register, index, list, listing, record, schedule, archive, inventory.
● verb *the collection is fully catalogued*:

classify, categorize, index, list, archive, record, itemize.

catastrophe noun disaster, calamity, cataclysm, ruin, tragedy, fiasco, debacle.

catch verb **1** *he caught the ball*: seize, grab, snatch, grasp, grip, clutch, intercept, trap, receive, get. **2** *we've caught the thief*: capture, seize, apprehend, arrest, take prisoner, trap, snare, net; informal nab, collar; Brit. informal nick. **3** *her heel caught in a hole*: become trapped, become entangled, snag, jam, wedge, lodge, get stuck. **4** *they were caught siphoning petrol*: discover, find, come across, stumble on, chance on, surprise. **5** *he caught malaria*: contract, go/come down with, be taken ill with, develop, pick up.
OPPOSITES drop, miss, release.
● noun **1** *he inspected the catch*: haul, net, bag, yield. **2** *he slipped the catch*: latch,

c

1 seize and hold something moving.
2 capture a person or animal. 3 be in time to get on a vehicle or to see a person or event. 4 entangle or become entangled. 5 surprise someone in the act of doing something wrong or embarrassing. 6 (**be caught in**) unexpectedly find yourself in an unwelcome situation. 7 see, hear, or understand. 8 hit or strike. 9 become infected with an illness. 10 (**catching**) (of a disease) infectious. • **noun** 1 an act of catching. 2 a device for fastening a door, window, etc. 3 a hidden problem. 4 a break in a person's voice caused by emotion. 5 an amount of fish caught.
□ catch on informal 1 become popular. 2 understand. catch someone out discover that someone has done something wrong. catch-22 a difficult situation from which there is no escape because it involves conditions which conflict with each other. catch up do tasks which you should have done earlier. catch someone up succeed in reaching a person ahead of you.

catchment area **noun** 1 the area from which a hospital's patients or a school's pupils are drawn. 2 the area from which rainfall flows into a river, lake, or reservoir.

catchphrase **noun** a well-known sentence or phrase.

catchword **noun** a word or phrase frequently used to sum something up.

catchy **adjective** (**catchier**, **catchiest**) (of a tune or phrase) appealing and easy to remember.

catechism /**kat**-i-ki-z'm/ **noun** a summary of the principles of Christian religion in the form of questions and answers, used for teaching.

categorical **adjective** completely clear and direct.
■ categorically adverb.

categorize or **categorise** **verb**

(**categorizes**, **categorizing**, **categorized**) place in a category.
■ categorization noun.

category **noun** (plural **categories**) a class or group of people or things with shared characteristics.

cater **verb** 1 (**cater for**) Brit. provide food and drink at a social event. 2 (**cater for**) provide someone with what is needed. 3 (**cater to**) satisfy a need or demand.
■ caterer noun.

caterpillar **noun** a creature like a small worm with legs, which develops into a butterfly or moth.

caterwaul /**kat**-er-wawl/ **verb** make a shrill howling or wailing noise.

catfish **noun** (plural **catfish** or **catfishes**) a fish with whisker-like growths round its mouth.

catgut **noun** material used for the strings of musical instruments, made of the dried intestines of sheep or horses.

catharsis /kuh-**thar**-siss/ **noun** the process of releasing strong but pent-up emotions in such a way as to free yourself of them.
■ cathartic adjective.

cathedral **noun** the most important church of a diocese (district).

Catherine wheel **noun** Brit. a firework in the form of a spinning coil.

catheter /**kath**-i-ter/ **noun** a tube that is inserted into a body cavity to drain fluid.

cathode /**kath**-ohd/ **noun** an electrode with a negative charge.
□ cathode ray tube a tube in which beams of electrons produce a luminous image on a screen, as in a television.

catholic **adjective** 1 including a wide variety of things. 2 (**Catholic**) Roman Catholic.
• **noun** (**Catholic**) a Roman Catholic.
■ Catholicism noun.

cation /**kat**-I-uhn/ **noun** an ion with a positive charge.

catkin **noun** a spike of small, soft flowers

THESAURUS

lock, fastener, clasp, hasp. 3 *there must be a catch:* snag, disadvantage, drawback, stumbling block, hitch, complication, problem, trap, trick.
□ catch on (informal) 1 *radio soon caught on:* **become popular,** take off, boom, flourish, thrive. 2 *I caught on fast:* **understand,** comprehend, learn, see the light; informal cotton on, latch on.

catching adjective (informal) infectious, contagious, communicable; dated infective.
OPPOSITES non-infectious.

catchy adjective memorable, unforgettable, haunting, appealing, popular.
OPPOSITES forgettable.

categorical adjective unqualified,

unconditional, unequivocal, absolute, explicit, unambiguous, definite, direct, emphatic, positive, out-and-out.
OPPOSITES qualified, equivocal.

category noun class, classification, group, grouping, bracket, heading, set, type, sort, kind, grade, order, rank.

cater verb
□ cater for 1 *we cater for vegetarians:* **provide (food) for,** feed, serve, cook for. 2 *a resort catering for older holidaymakers:* serve, provide for, meet the needs/wants of, accommodate. 3 *he seemed to cater for all tastes:* **take into account/consideration,** allow for, consider, bear in mind, make provision for, have regard for.

hanging from trees such as willow and hazel.

catnap noun a short sleep during the day.

catseye noun Brit. trademark each of a series of reflective studs marking the lanes or edges of a road.

catsuit noun a woman's close-fitting one-piece garment with trouser legs.

cattery noun (plural **catteries**) a place where cats are kept while their owners are away.

cattle plural noun cows, bulls, and oxen.

catty adjective (**cattier, cattiest**) spiteful.

catwalk noun 1 a narrow platform along which models walk to display clothes. 2 a narrow raised walkway.

Caucasian adjective 1 relating to peoples from Europe, western Asia, and parts of India and North Africa. 2 white-skinned. • noun a Caucasian person.

caucus /kaw-kuhss/ noun (plural **caucuses**) 1 a meeting of a policymaking group of a political party. 2 a group of people within a larger organization who have similar interests.

caught past and past participle of CATCH.

caul /rhymes with ball/ noun a membrane that encloses an unborn baby in the womb.

cauldron (US spelling **caldron**) noun a large metal cooking pot.

cauliflower noun a vegetable with a large white edible flower head.

caulk (US spelling **calk**) noun a waterproof substance used to fill cracks and seal joins.

causal adjective relating to or being a cause. ■ **causally** adverb **causality** noun.

causation noun the process of causing an effect. ■ **causative** adjective.

cause noun 1 a person or thing that produces an effect. 2 a good reason for thinking or doing something. 3 a principle or movement. • verb (**causes, causing,**

caused) make something happen.

causeway noun a raised road or track across low or wet ground.

caustic adjective 1 able to burn through or wear away something by chemical action. 2 sarcastic in a hurtful way. □ **caustic soda** sodium hydroxide, used in industrial processes, such as soap-making. ■ **caustically** adverb.

cauterize or **cauterise** verb (**cauterizes, cauterizing, cauterized**) burn the area round a wound to stop bleeding or prevent infection.

caution noun 1 care taken to avoid danger or mistakes. 2 a warning to the public. 3 Brit. an official or legal warning given to someone who has committed a minor offence. • verb 1 warn or advise someone. 2 give someone a legal caution.

cautionary adjective acting as a warning.

cautious adjective taking care to avoid possible problems or dangers. ■ **cautiously** adverb.

cavalcade noun a procession of vehicles or people on horseback.

cavalier noun (**Cavalier**) a supporter of King Charles I in the English Civil War. • adjective showing a lack of proper concern.

cavalry noun (plural **cavalries**) (in the past) the part of the army that fought on horseback. ■ **cavalryman** noun.

cave noun a large natural hollow in the side of a hill or cliff, or underground. • verb (**caves, caving, caved**) 1 (**cave in**) give way or collapse. 2 (**cave in**) give in to demands. 3 (**caving**) the exploring of caves as a sport.

caveat /ka-vi-at/ noun a warning.

cavern noun a large cave.

cavernous /ka-ver-nuhss/ adjective huge, spacious, or gloomy.

caviar or **caviare** /ka-vi-ar/ noun the pickled roe of the sturgeon (a large fish).

THESAURUS

cattle plural noun cows, oxen, herd, livestock.

cause noun 1 *the cause of the fire:* source, root, origin, beginning(s), starting point, originator, author, creator, agent. 2 *there is no cause for alarm:* reason, grounds, justification, call, need, necessity, occasion, excuse. 3 *the cause of human rights | a good cause:* principle, ideal, belief, conviction, object, aim, objective, purpose, charity. • verb *this disease can cause blindness:* bring about, give rise to, lead to, result in, create, produce, generate, engender, spawn, bring on, precipitate, prompt, provoke, trigger, make happen, induce, inspire, promote, foster.

caution noun 1 *proceed with caution:* care,

attention, alertness, circumspection, discretion, prudence. 2 *a first offender may receive a caution:* warning, admonishment, injunction, reprimand, rebuke; informal telling-off, dressing-down; Brit. informal ticking-off. • verb 1 *advisers cautioned against tax increases:* advise, warn, counsel, urge. 2 *he was cautioned by the police:* warn, admonish, reprimand; informal tell off; Brit. informal tick off.

cautious adjective careful, attentive, alert, judicious, circumspect, prudent, tentative, guarded. OPPOSITES reckless.

cave noun cavern, grotto, pothole, chamber, gallery, hollow.

cavil /**ka**-vuhl/ verb (**cavils, cavilling, cavilled;** US spelling **cavils, caviling, caviled**) make unnecessary complaints. •noun an unnecessary complaint.

cavity noun (plural **cavities**) **1** a hollow space inside something solid. **2** a decayed part of a tooth.

cavort verb jump or dance around excitedly.

caw verb make a harsh cry.

cayenne /kay-**en**/ noun a hot-tasting red powder made from dried chillies.

CBE abbreviation Commander of the Order of the British Empire.

cc or **c.c.** abbreviation **1** carbon copy. **2** cubic centimetres.

CCTV abbreviation closed-circuit television.

CD abbreviation compact disc.

CD-ROM abbreviation a compact disc storing large amounts of information, used in a computer (*ROM* stands for 'read-only memory').

CDT abbreviation craft, design, and technology (as a school subject).

cease verb (**ceases, ceasing, ceased**) come or bring to an end; stop.

ceasefire noun a temporary period during a conflict when fighting stops.

ceaseless adjective not stopping.
■ **ceaselessly** adverb.

cedar noun a tall evergreen tree with sweet-smelling wood.

cede verb (**cedes, ceding, ceded**) give up power or territory.

cedilla /si-**dil**-luh/ noun a mark (¸) written under the letter *c* to show that it is pronounced like an *s* (e.g. *soupçon*).

ceilidh /**kay**-li/ noun a party with Scottish or Irish folk music and dancing.

ceiling noun **1** the top surface of a room. **2** a top limit set on prices, wages, or spending.

☑ *i* before *e* except after *c*: cei̯ling.

celandine noun a wild plant with small yellow flowers.

celebrate verb (**celebrates, celebrating, celebrated**) mark an important occasion by doing something special.
■ **celebration** noun **celebratory** adjective.

celebrity noun (plural **celebrities**) **1** a famous person. **2** the state of being famous.

celeriac /suh-**lair**-i-ak/ noun a vegetable with a large edible root.

celerity /si-**le**-ri-ti/ noun old use speed of movement.

celery noun a vegetable with crisp juicy stalks.

celestial adjective **1** relating to heaven. **2** relating to the sky or outer space.

celibate /**sel**-i-buht/ adjective not married or in a sexual relationship.
■ **celibacy** noun.

cell noun **1** a small room for a prisoner, monk, or nun. **2** the smallest unit of a living thing. **3** a small political group that is part of a larger organization. **4** a device for producing electricity by chemical action or light.

cellar noun **1** a room below ground level, used for storage. **2** a stock of wine.

cello /**chel**-loh/ noun (plural **cellos**) an instrument like a large violin, held upright on the floor between the legs of the seated player.
■ **cellist** noun.

THESAURUS

cavity noun space, chamber, hollow, hole, pocket, gap, crater, pit.

cease verb come/bring to an end, come/bring to a halt, end, halt, stop, conclude, terminate, finish, wind up, discontinue, suspend, break off.
OPPOSITES start, continue.

celebrate verb **1** *they were celebrating their wedding anniversary:* commemorate, observe, mark, keep, honour, remember. **2** *let's all celebrate!* enjoy yourself, make merry, have fun, have a good time, have a party; N. Amer. step out; informal party, whoop it up, have a ball. **3** *the priest celebrated mass:* perform, observe, officiate at, preside at.

celebrated adjective acclaimed, admired, highly rated, esteemed, exalted, vaunted, eminent, great, distinguished, prestigious, illustrious, notable.
OPPOSITES unsung.

celebration noun **1** *the celebration of his 50th birthday:* commemoration, observance, marking, keeping. **2** *a cause for celebration:* merrymaking, jollification, revelry, revels, festivities; informal partying. **3** *a birthday celebration:* party, function, gathering, festivities, festival, fete, carnival, jamboree; informal do, bash, rave; Brit. informal rave-up. **4** *the celebration of the Eucharist:* performance, observance, officiation, solemnization.

celebrity noun **1** *his celebrity grew:* fame, prominence, renown, stardom, popularity, distinction, prestige, stature, repute, reputation. **2** *a sporting celebrity:* famous person, VIP, personality, big name, household name, star, superstar; informal celeb, megastar.
OPPOSITES obscurity, nonentity.

cell noun **1** *a prison cell:* room, cubicle, chamber, dungeon, compartment, lock-up. **2** *terrorist cells:* unit, squad, detachment, group.

cellar noun basement, vault, crypt.

cellophane noun trademark a thin transparent wrapping material.

cellphone noun a mobile phone.

cellular adjective **1** relating to or made up of cells. **2** (of a mobile phone system) using a number of short-range radio stations to cover the area it serves.

cellulite noun fat that builds up under the skin, causing a dimpled effect.

celluloid noun a kind of transparent plastic formerly used for cinema film.

cellulose noun a substance found in all plant tissues, used in making paint, plastics, and fibres.

Celsius /**sel**-si-uhss/ noun a scale of temperature on which water freezes at 0° and boils at 100°.

Celt /kelt/ noun a member of a people who lived in Britain and elsewhere in Europe before the Romans arrived.

Celtic /**kel**-tik/ noun a group of languages including Irish, Scottish Gaelic, and Welsh. • adjective relating to Celtic languages or to the Celts.

cement noun a powdery substance made by heating lime and clay, used in making mortar and concrete. • verb **1** fix with cement. **2** make something stronger.

cemetery noun (plural **cemeteries**) a large burial ground.

> ☑ -tery, not -try or -tary: cemetery.

cenotaph noun a monument built to honour soldiers killed in a war.

censer noun a container in which incense is burnt.

censor noun an official who examines films, books, or documents and bans unacceptable parts. • verb ban unacceptable parts of a film, book, or document. ■ **censorship** noun.

censorious /sen-**sor**-i-uhss/ adjective very critical.

censure verb (**censures**, **censuring**, censured) criticize strongly. • noun strong disapproval or criticism.

census noun (plural **censuses**) an official count of a population.

cent noun a unit of money equal to one hundredth of a dollar, euro, or other decimal currency unit.

centaur noun (in Greek mythology) a creature with a man's head, arms, and upper body and a horse's lower body and legs.

centenarian /sen-ti-**nair**-i-uhn/ noun a person who has reached one hundred years of age.

centenary /sen-**tee**-nuh-ri/ noun (plural **centenaries**) Brit. the hundredth anniversary of an event.

centennial adjective relating to a hundredth anniversary. • noun a hundredth anniversary.

center US spelling of CENTRE.

centigrade adjective measured by the Celsius scale of temperature.

centilitre (US spelling **centiliter**) noun a metric unit equal to one hundredth of a litre.

centime /**son**-teem/ noun a unit of money equal to one hundredth of a franc.

centimetre (US spelling **centimeter**) noun a metric unit equal to one hundredth of a metre.

centipede noun an insect-like creature with a long, thin body and many legs.

central adjective **1** in or near the centre. **2** very important. □ **central heating** heating conducted from a boiler through pipes and radiators. **central nervous system** the system of nerve tissues in the brain and spinal cord in vertebrates. ■ **centrally** adverb.

centralize or **centralise** verb (**centralizes**, **centralizing**, **centralized**) bring under the control of a central authority. ■ **centralization** noun.

THESAURUS

cement noun adhesive, glue, fixative, gum, paste; N. Amer. mucilage; N. Amer. informal stickum.

cemetery noun graveyard, churchyard, burial ground, necropolis, garden of remembrance, mass grave; Scottish kirkyard.

censor verb letters home were censored: cut, edit, expurgate, sanitize, clean up, ban, delete.

censure verb he was censured for his conduct: condemn, criticize, attack, reprimand, rebuke, admonish, upbraid, reproach.
OPPOSITES defend, praise.
• noun a note of censure: condemnation, criticism, attack, reprimand, rebuke, admonishment, reproof, disapproval, reproach.
OPPOSITES approval, praise.

central adjective **1** occupying a central position: middle, centre, halfway, midway, mid. **2** central London: inner, innermost, middle, mid. **3** their central campaign issue: main, chief, principal, primary, foremost, key, crucial, vital, essential, basic, fundamental, core; informal number-one.
OPPOSITES side, extreme, outer, subordinate.

centralize verb concentrate, consolidate, amalgamate, condense, unify, focus.
OPPOSITES devolve.

centre (US spelling **center**) noun **1** a point in the middle of something. **2** a place where a particular activity takes place. **3** a point from which something spreads or to which something is directed. •verb (**centres, centring, centred**; US spelling **centers, centering, centered**) **1** place in the centre. **2** (**centre on** or **around**) have as a main concern or theme.
□ **centre back** (or **centre half**) (in soccer) a defender who plays in the middle of the field. **centre forward** (in soccer) an attacker who plays in the middle of the field. **centre of gravity** the central point in an object, around which its mass is evenly distributed.

centrefold noun the two middle pages of a magazine, usually containing a special feature.

centrepiece noun an item that is designed to have people's attention focused on it.

centrifugal force noun a force which appears to cause something travelling round a central point to fly outwards from its circular path.

centurion noun a commander of one hundred men in the army of ancient Rome.

century noun (plural **centuries**) **1** a period of one hundred years. **2** a batsman's score of a hundred runs in cricket. **3** a unit of a hundred men in the army of ancient Rome.

ceramic adjective made of fired clay. •noun (**ceramics**) the art of making ceramic articles.

cereal noun **1** a grass producing an edible grain, such as wheat, oats, maize, or rye. **2** a breakfast food made from the grain of cereals.

cerebellum /se-ri-**bel**-luhm/ noun (plural

cerebellums or cerebella) the part of the brain at the back of the skull.

cerebral /se-ri-**bruhl**, suh-**ree**-bruhl/ adjective **1** relating to the brain. **2** intellectual rather than emotional or physical.
□ **cerebral palsy** a condition in which a person has difficulty in controlling their muscles.

cerebrum /se-ri-**bruhm**/ noun (plural **cerebra**) the main part of the brain, in the front of the skull.

ceremonial adjective relating to or used in ceremonies.
■ **ceremonially** adverb.

ceremonious adjective done in a formal and grand way.
■ **ceremoniously** adverb.

ceremony noun (plural **ceremonies**) a formal occasion during which a set of special acts are performed.
□ **stand on ceremony** behave formally.

cerise /suh-**reess**/ noun a light pinkish-red colour.

cerium /**seer**-i-uhm/ noun a silvery-white metallic element.

certain adjective **1** able to be relied on to happen or be the case. **2** completely sure about something. **3** specific but not directly named or stated. •pronoun some but not all.

certainly adverb **1** without doubt; definitely. **2** yes.

certainty noun (plural **certainties**) **1** the state of being certain. **2** a fact that is true or an event that is definitely going to take place.

certifiable adjective able or needing to be officially declared insane.

certificate noun **1** an official document

THESAURUS

centre noun *the centre of the town:* middle, nucleus, heart, core, hub.
OPPOSITES edge.
•verb *the story centres on a doctor:* focus, concentrate, pivot, revolve, be based.

ceremonial adjective formal, official, state, public, ritual, ritualistic, stately, solemn.
OPPOSITES informal.

ceremony noun **1** *a wedding ceremony:* rite, ritual, observance, service, event, function, formality. **2** *the new Queen was proclaimed with due ceremony:* pomp, protocol, formalities, niceties, decorum, etiquette.

certain adjective **1** *I'm certain he's guilty:* sure, confident, positive, convinced, in no doubt, satisfied. **2** *it is certain that more changes are in the offing:* unquestionable, sure, definite, beyond question, indubitable, undeniable, indisputable. **3** *they are certain to win:* sure, bound, destined. **4** *certain defeat:* inevitable,

assured, unavoidable, inescapable, inexorable. **5** *there is no certain cure for this:* reliable, dependable, foolproof, guaranteed, sure, infallible; informal surefire.
OPPOSITES doubtful, unlikely, possible.

certainly adverb definitely, surely, assuredly, unquestionably, beyond/without question, undoubtedly, without doubt, indubitably, undeniably, irrefutably, indisputably.
OPPOSITES possibly.

certainty noun **1** *she knew with certainty that it was true:* confidence, sureness, conviction, assurance. **2** *he accepted defeat as a certainty:* inevitability, foregone conclusion; informal sure thing; Brit. informal (dead) cert.
OPPOSITES doubt, possibility.

certificate noun guarantee, document, authorization, authentication,

recording a particular fact, event, or achievement. **2** an official classification given to a cinema film, saying which age group it is suitable for.
■ **certification** noun.

certify verb (**certifies, certifying, certified**) **1** declare or confirm in a certificate or other official document. **2** officially declare someone insane.

certitude noun a feeling of complete certainty.

cervical /**ser**-vi-k'l, ser-**vy**-k'l/ adjective relating to the cervix.
□ **cervical smear** a specimen of cells taken from the neck of the womb and examined for signs of cancer.

cervix /**ser**-viks/ noun (plural **cervices** /**ser**-vi-seez/) the narrow neck-like passage between the lower end of the womb and the vagina.

Cesarean US spelling of **Caesarean**.

cesium US spelling of **caesium**.

cessation noun the stopping of something.

cession noun the giving up of rights or territory by a state.

cesspool or **cesspit** noun an underground tank or covered pit where sewage is collected.

cetacean /si-**tay**-sh'n/ noun the name in zoology for a whale or dolphin.

cf. abbreviation compare with.

CFC abbreviation chlorofluorocarbon, a gas used in fridges and aerosols that is harmful to the ozone layer.

CFE abbreviation College of Further Education.

Chablis /**shab**-lee/ noun a dry white French wine.

Chadian /**chad**-i-uhn/ noun a person from Chad, a country in central Africa. • adjective relating to Chad.

chador /**chah**-dor/ noun a piece of dark cloth worn by Muslim women around the head and upper body.

chafe verb (**chafes, chafing, chafed**) **1** make something sore or worn by rubbing against it. **2** rub a part of the body to warm it. **3** become impatient because of restrictions.

chaff[1] noun husks of grain that have been separated from the seed.

chaff[2] verb tease someone.

chaffinch noun a small finch (songbird) with a pink breast.

chagrin /**sha**-grin/ noun a feeling of disappointment or annoyance. • verb (**be chagrined**) feel disappointed or annoyed.

chain noun **1** a series of connected metal links. **2** a connected series, set, or sequence. • verb fasten or restrain with a chain.
□ **chain mail** armour made of small metal rings linked together. **chain reaction** a series of events, each caused by the previous one. **chain-smoke** smoke cigarettes one after the other. **chain store** each of a series of shops owned by one firm.

chainsaw noun a power-driven saw with teeth set on a moving chain.

chair noun **1** a seat for one person, with a back and four legs. **2** a person in charge of a meeting or an organization. **3** a post as professor. • verb be in charge of a meeting.

chairlift noun a lift for carrying skiers up and down a mountain, consisting of a series of chairs hung from a moving cable.

chairman or **chairwoman** noun (plural **chairmen** or **chairwomen**) a person in charge of a meeting or organization.

chairperson noun a person in charge of a meeting.

chaise longue /shayz **longg**/ noun (plural **chaises longues** /shayz **longg**/) a sofa with a backrest at only one end.

chalet /**sha**-lay/ noun **1** a wooden house with overhanging eaves, found in the Swiss Alps. **2** a wooden cabin used by holidaymakers.

chalice /**cha**-liss/ noun a large cup or glass for wine.

chalk noun **1** a soft white limestone. **2** a similar substance made into sticks and used for drawing or writing. • verb draw or write with chalk.
□ **by a long chalk** by far. **chalk something up** achieve something noteworthy.
■ **chalkiness** noun **chalky** adjective.

THESAURUS

accreditation, credentials, testimonial.

certify verb **1** *the aircraft was certified as airworthy:* verify, guarantee, attest, validate, confirm, endorse. **2** *a certified hospital:* accredit, recognize, license, authorize, approve.

cessation noun end, termination, halt, finish, stoppage, conclusion, winding up, pause, suspension.
OPPOSITES start, resumption.

chain noun **1** *he was held in chains:* fetters, shackles, irons, manacles, handcuffs; informal cuffs, bracelets. **2** *a chain of events:* series, succession, string, sequence, train, course.
• verb *she chained her bicycle to the railings:* secure, fasten, tie, tether, hitch, restrain, shackle, fetter, manacle, handcuff.

chairman, chairwoman noun chair, chairperson, president, chief executive, leader, master of ceremonies, MC.

C

challenge noun 1 an interesting but difficult task or situation. 2 an invitation to someone to take part in a contest or to prove something. •verb (**challenges, challenging, challenged**) 1 raise doubt as to whether something is true or genuine. 2 call on someone to fight or do something difficult. 3 (of a guard) call on someone to prove their identity.
■ **challenger** noun.

challenging adjective testing your abilities in an interesting way.

chamber noun 1 a large room used for formal or public events. 2 each of the houses of a parliament. 3 (**chambers**) rooms used by a barrister. 4 old use a bedroom. 5 a hollow space inside something. 6 the part of a gun bore that contains the explosive.
□ **chamber music** classical music played by a small group of musicians. **chamber pot** a bowl kept in a bedroom and used as a toilet.

chamberlain noun (in the past) a person who looked after the household of a king or queen, or a noble.

chambermaid noun a woman who cleans rooms in a hotel.

chameleon /kuh-**mee**-li-uhn/ noun a small lizard that is able to change colour to fit in with its surroundings.

chamfer /**cham**-fer/ verb (**chamfers, chamfering, chamfered**) (in carpentry) cut an angled edge on a piece of wood.

chamois /**sham**-wah/ noun (plural **chamois** /**sham**-wah, **sham**-wahz/) an antelope that lives in the mountains of southern Europe.
□ **chamois leather** /**sham**-mi/ very soft

leather made from the skin of sheep, goats, or deer.

chamomile ⇒ CAMOMILE.

champ verb munch noisily.
□ **champ at the bit** be very impatient.

champagne /sham-**payn**/ noun a white sparkling wine from the Champagne region of France.

champion noun 1 a person who has won a contest. 2 a person who argues or fights for a cause. •verb argue or fight in support of a cause. •adjective informal or dialect excellent.

championship noun a competition for the position of champion.

chance noun 1 (also **chances**) a possibility of something happening. 2 an opportunity. 3 the way that things happen without any obvious plan or cause: *they met by chance.* •verb (**chances, chancing, chanced**) 1 happen to do something. 2 informal do something even though it is risky.
□ **on the off chance** just in case.

chancel /**chahn**-s'l/ noun the part of a church near the altar, where the choir sits.

chancellor noun 1 a senior state or legal official. 2 (**Chancellor**) the head of the government in some European countries.
□ **Chancellor of the Exchequer** (in the UK) the government minister in charge of the country's finances.

chancer noun informal a person who makes the most of any opportunity.

chancy adjective (**chancier, chanciest**) informal uncertain and risky.

chandelier /shan-duh-**leer**/ noun an ornamental hanging light with holders for several candles or light bulbs.

THESAURUS

challenge noun 1 *he accepted the challenge:* dare, provocation, offer. 2 *a challenge to his leadership:* opposition, confrontation, stand, dispute, test. 3 *it was proving quite a challenge:* problem, difficult task, test, trial.
OPPOSITES cinch.
•verb 1 *we challenged their statistics:* question, dispute, take issue with, call into question. 2 *he challenged me to deny it:* dare, defy, invite, throw down the gauntlet to. 3 *changes that would challenge them:* test, tax, strain, make demands on, stretch.

challenging adjective demanding, testing, taxing, exacting.
OPPOSITES easy.

champion noun 1 *the world champion:* winner, title-holder, gold medallist, prizewinner; informal champ, number one. 2 *a champion of change:* advocate, proponent, promoter, supporter, defender, upholder, backer; N. Amer. booster.

•verb *championing the rights of tribal peoples:* advocate, promote, defend, uphold, support, espouse, stand up for, campaign for, lobby for, fight for.
OPPOSITES oppose.

chance noun 1 *there was a chance he might be released:* possibility, prospect, probability, likelihood, risk, threat, danger. 2 *I gave her a chance to answer:* opportunity, opening, occasion, window; N. Amer. & Austral./NZ show; Brit. informal look-in. 3 *Nigel took an awful chance:* risk, gamble, leap in the dark. 4 *pure chance:* accident, coincidence, fate, destiny, providence, happenstance, good fortune, luck, fluke.
OPPOSITES certainty.
•adjective *a chance discovery:* accidental, fortuitous, fluky, coincidental.
OPPOSITES planned.
□ **by chance** by accident, fortuitously, accidentally, coincidentally, unintentionally, inadvertently.

chandler noun a person who buys and sells supplies and equipment for ships and boats.
■ **chandlery** noun.

change verb (**changes**, **changing**, **changed**) **1** make or become different. **2** exchange one thing for something else. **3** (**change over**) move from one system or situation to another. **4** exchange a sum of money for the same sum in a different currency or different units. • noun **1** a process through which something becomes different. **2** money returned as the balance of the amount paid or given in exchange for the same amount in larger units. **3** coins as opposed to banknotes. **4** a clean set of clothes.
□ **change hands** pass to a different owner.

changeable adjective **1** likely to change in an unpredictable way. **2** able to be changed.

changeling noun a child believed to have been left by fairies in exchange for the parents' real child.

changeover noun a change from one system or situation to another.

channel noun **1** a band of frequencies used in radio and television broadcasting. **2** a means of communication. **3** a wide stretch of water joining two seas. **4** a passage along which liquid flows. **5** a passage that boats can pass through in a stretch of water. **6** an electric circuit which acts as a path for a signal. • verb (**channels**, **channelling**, **channelled**; US spelling **channels**, **channeling**, **channeled**) **1** direct something towards a particular purpose. **2** pass along or through a particular channel.

chant noun **1** a repeated rhythmic phrase that is called out or sung to music. **2** a tune to which the words of psalms are fitted by singing several syllables or words to the same note. • verb say, shout, or sing in a chant.

Chanukkah ⇒ **HANUKKAH**.

chaos /kay-oss/ noun complete confusion and disorder.

chaotic /kay-ot-ik/ adjective in a state of complete confusion and disorder.
■ **chaotically** adverb.

chap noun informal a man or boy.

chapatti /chuh-pah-ti/ noun (plural **chapattis**) (in Indian cookery) a flat round piece of unleavened bread.

chapel noun **1** a small building or room used for prayers. **2** a part of a large church with its own altar.

chaperone /shap-uh-rohn/ noun **1** a person who accompanies and looks after another person or group of people. **2** dated an older woman in charge of an unmarried girl at social occasions. • verb (**chaperones**, **chaperoning**, **chaperoned**) go with and look after.

chaplain noun a minister of the church attached to a chapel in an institution or military unit, or a private house.
■ **chaplaincy** noun.

chapped adjective (of the skin) cracked and sore through exposure to cold weather.

chapter noun **1** a main division of a book. **2** a particular period in history or in a person's life. **3** the group of people in charge of a cathedral or other religious community. **4** chiefly N. Amer. a local branch of a society.

THESAURUS

change verb **1** *this could change Britain | things have changed*: alter, make/become different, adjust, adapt, amend, modify, revise, vary, transform, metamorphose, evolve. **2** *he's changed his job*: exchange, substitute, swap, switch, replace, alternate.
OPPOSITES preserve, keep.
• noun **1** *a change of plan*: alteration, modification, variation, revision, amendment, adjustment, adaptation, metamorphosis, transformation, evolution. **2** *a change of government*: replacement, exchange, substitution, swap, switch.

channel noun **1** *the English Channel*: strait(s), sound, narrows, passage. **2** *the water ran down a channel*: duct, gutter, conduit, trough, sluice, drain. **3** *a channel of communication*: means, medium, instrument, mechanism, agency, vehicle, route, avenue.
• verb *many countries channel their aid through charities*: convey, transmit,

conduct, direct, relay, pass on, transfer.

chant noun shout, cry, call, slogan, chorus, refrain.
• verb shout, chorus, repeat, call.

chaos noun disorder, disorganization, confusion, mayhem, bedlam, pandemonium, havoc, turmoil, anarchy, lawlessness; Brit. a shambles; informal all hell broken loose.
OPPOSITES order.

chaotic adjective disorderly, disorganized, in confusion, in turmoil, topsy-turvy, anarchic, lawless; Brit. informal shambolic.

chap noun (informal) man, boy, fellow, individual, character; informal guy, geezer; Brit. informal bloke, lad; N. Amer. informal dude, hombre.

chapter noun **1** *the first chapter of the book*: section, part, division, topic, stage, episode. **2** *a new chapter in our history*: period, phase, page, stage, epoch, era.

char¹ verb (**chars, charring, charred**) partially burn something so as to blacken the surface.

char² noun informal a woman employed as a cleaner in a private house.

char³ noun informal tea.

character noun 1 the particular qualities that make a person or thing an individual and different from others. 2 strong personal qualities such as courage and determination. 3 a person's good reputation. 4 a person in a novel, play, or film. 5 informal an eccentric or amusing person. 6 a printed or written letter or symbol.
■ **characterful** adjective **characterless** adjective.

characteristic noun a quality typical of a person or thing. ● adjective typical of a particular person or thing.
■ **characteristically** adverb.

characterize or **characterise** verb (**characterizes, characterizing, characterized**) 1 describe the character of. 2 be typical of.
■ **characterization** noun.

charade /shuh-**rahd**/ noun 1 a pretence that something is true when it is clearly not. 2 (**charades**) a game of guessing a word or phrase from clues that are acted out.

charcoal noun 1 a form of carbon obtained when wood is burned slowly with little air.

2 a dark grey–black colour.

chard noun a vegetable with large leaves and thick leaf stalks.

Chardonnay noun a type of white wine.

charge verb (**charges, charging, charged**) 1 ask an amount as a price. 2 formally accuse someone of something. 3 rush forward in an attack. 4 (**charge someone with**) give someone a task or responsibility. 5 store electrical energy in a battery. 6 load or fill a container, gun, etc. 7 fill with an emotion or quality: *the air was charged with menace.* ● noun 1 a price asked. 2 a formal accusation. 3 responsibility for the care or control of a person or thing. 4 a person or thing handed over to someone's care. 5 a headlong rush forward. 6 the electricity naturally existing in a substance. 7 energy stored chemically in a battery. 8 a quantity of explosive needed to fire a gun.
□ **charge card** a kind of credit card issued by a large shop.
■ **chargeable** adjective.

chargé d'affaires /shar-zhay da-**fair**/ noun (plural **chargés d'affaires** /shar-zhay da-**fair**/) 1 an ambassador's deputy. 2 the diplomatic representative in a country to which an ambassador has not been sent.

charger noun 1 a device for charging a battery. 2 a strong horse formerly ridden by a knight or mounted soldier.

THESAURUS

character noun 1 *a forceful character | the character of a town:* personality, nature, quality, disposition, temperament, mentality, make-up, spirit, identity, tone, feel. 2 *a woman of character:* integrity, honour, moral strength/fibre, strength, backbone, resolve, grit, will power; informal guts; Brit. informal bottle. 3 *a stain on his character:* reputation, (good) name, standing, position, status. 4 (informal) *a bit of a character:* eccentric, oddity, crank, original, individualist, madcap, nonconformist; informal oddball. 5 *a boorish character:* person, man, woman, soul, creature, individual, customer; informal cookie; Brit. informal bod, guy. 6 *written in Cyrillic characters:* letter, figure, symbol, mark, device, sign, hieroglyph.

characteristic noun *the main characteristics of his poetry:* attribute, feature, quality, property, trait, aspect, idiosyncrasy, peculiarity, quirk.
● adjective *his characteristic eloquence:* typical, usual, normal, distinctive, representative, particular, special, peculiar, idiosyncratic.
OPPOSITES abnormal.

characterize verb 1 *the period was characterized by scientific advancement:* distinguish, mark, typify, set apart. 2 *the*

women are characterized as prophets of doom: portray, depict, present, represent, describe, categorize, class, brand.

charade noun pretence, act, masquerade, show, facade, pantomime, farce, travesty, mockery, parody.

charge verb 1 *he didn't charge much:* ask, demand, bill, invoice. 2 *two men were charged with murder:* accuse, indict, arraign, prosecute, try, put on trial; N. Amer. impeach. 3 *they charged him with reforming the system:* entrust, burden, encumber, saddle, tax. 4 *the cavalry charged the tanks:* attack, storm, assault, assail, descend on; informal lay into, tear into. 5 *we charged into the crowd:* rush, storm, stampede, push, plough, launch yourself, go headlong; informal steam; N. Amer. informal barrel. 6 *charge your glasses!* fill (up), top up, load (up), arm.
● noun 1 *all customers pay a charge:* fee, payment, price, rate, tariff, fare, levy. 2 *he pleaded guilty to the charge:* accusation, allegation, indictment, arraignment; N. Amer. impeachment. 3 *an infantry charge:* attack, assault, offensive, onslaught, drive, push. 4 *the child was in her charge:* care, protection, safe keeping, control, custody, hands.

chargrill verb grill food quickly at a very high heat.

chariot noun a two-wheeled horse-drawn vehicle, used in ancient warfare and racing.
∎ **charioteer** noun.

charisma /kuh-riz-muh/ noun attractiveness that inspires admiration or enthusiasm in other people.
∎ **charismatic** adjective.

charitable adjective 1 relating to help given to people in need. 2 showing kindness and understanding when judging other people.
∎ **charitably** adverb.

charity noun (plural **charities**) 1 an organization set up to help people in need. 2 the giving of money or other help to people in need. 3 kindness and understanding shown when judging other people.

charlatan /shar-luh-tuhn/ noun a person who claims to have skills or knowledge that they do not really have.

charleston noun a lively dance of the 1920s.

charm noun 1 the power or quality of delighting or fascinating other people. 2 a small ornament worn on a necklace or bracelet. 3 an object or saying believed to have magic power. ∎ verb 1 make someone feel great pleasure or delight. 2 use your charm in order to influence someone. 3 (**charmed**) unusually lucky as if protected by magic.
∎ **charmer** noun **charmless** adjective.

charming adjective 1 delightful; attractive. 2 very likeable.
∎ **charmingly** adverb.

charnel house noun a place formerly used for keeping dead bodies and bones in.

chart noun 1 a sheet of paper on which information is displayed in the form of a table, graph, or diagram. 2 a map used for navigation by sea or air. 3 (**the charts**) a weekly listing of the current best-selling pop records. ∎ verb 1 make a map of. 2 follow progress or record something on a chart.

charter noun 1 an official document stating that a ruler or government allows an institution to exist and setting out its rights. 2 a document listing and describing the functions of an organization. 3 the hiring of an aircraft, ship, or vehicle. ∎ verb 1 hire an aircraft, ship, or vehicle. 2 grant a charter to an institution.
▫ **charter flight** a flight by an aircraft that

charisma noun charm, presence, (force of) personality, strength of character, (animal) magnetism, appeal, allure.

charismatic adjective charming, magnetic, compelling, inspiring, captivating, mesmerizing, appealing, alluring, glamorous.

charitable adjective 1 *charitable activities:* philanthropic, humanitarian, altruistic, benevolent, public-spirited, non-profit-making. 2 *charitable people:* generous, open-handed, munificent. 3 *he was always charitable in his judgements:* magnanimous, generous, liberal, tolerant, sympathetic, understanding, lenient, indulgent, forgiving.
OPPOSITES commercial, mean, harsh.

charity noun 1 *an AIDS charity:* voluntary organization, charitable institution, fund, trust, foundation. 2 *we don't need charity:* aid, financial assistance, welfare, relief, donations, handouts, gifts, largesse; historical alms. 3 *his actions are motivated by charity:* philanthropy, humanitarianism, altruism, public-spiritedness, social conscience, benevolence. 4 *show a bit of charity:* goodwill, compassion, concern, consideration, kindness, sympathy, indulgence, tolerance, leniency.
OPPOSITES business, misanthropy, intolerance.

charm noun 1 *people were captivated by her charm:* appeal, attraction, fascination, beauty, loveliness, allure, seductiveness, magnetism, charisma; informal pulling power. 2 *magical charms:* spell, incantation, formula; N. Amer. mojo, hex. 3 *a lucky charm:* talisman, trinket, amulet, mascot, fetish.
∎ verb 1 *he charmed them with his singing:* delight, please, win (over), attract, captivate, lure, fascinate, enchant, beguile. 2 *he charmed his mother into agreeing:* coax, cajole, wheedle; informal sweet-talk, soft-soap.

charming adjective delightful, pleasing, endearing, lovely, adorable, appealing, attractive, good-looking, alluring, winning, fetching, captivating, enchanting, entrancing.
OPPOSITES repulsive.

chart noun *check your ideal weight on the chart:* graph, table, diagram, plan, map; Computing graphic.
∎ verb 1 *the changes were charted accurately:* plot, tabulate, graph, record, register, represent. 2 *the book charted his progress:* follow, trace, outline, describe, detail, record, document.

charter noun 1 *a Royal charter:* authority, authorization, sanction, dispensation, permit, licence, warrant. 2 *the UN Charter:* constitution, code, principles.
∎ verb *they chartered a bus:* hire, lease, rent, book.

C

has been hired for a specific journey.

chartered adjective (of an accountant, engineer, etc.) qualified as a member of a professional institution that has a royal charter.

chary /**chair**-i/ adjective (**charier, chariest**) cautious about doing something.

chase[1] verb (**chases, chasing, chased**) **1** go after someone in order to catch them. **2** rush or hurry. **3** try to make contact with or get hold of. •noun **1** an act of chasing. **2** (**the chase**) hunting as a sport.

chase[2] verb (**chases, chasing, chased**) engrave metal.

chaser noun informal a strong alcoholic drink taken after a weaker one.

chasm /**ka**-z'm/ noun **1** a deep crack in the earth. **2** a very big difference between two people or their opinions.

chassis /**sha**-si/ noun (plural **chassis** /**sha**-siz/) the framework forming the base of a vehicle.

chaste adjective **1** having sex only with your husband or wife, or not at all. **2** not expressing sexual interest; demure and modest.
■ **chastely** adverb.

chasten /**chay**-s'n/ verb make someone feel subdued and less confident about something.

chastise verb (**chastises, chastising, chastised**) tell someone off in a very strict way.

chastity noun the practice of having sex only with your husband or wife, or not at all.

chasuble /**chaz**-yuu-b'l/ noun a long sleeveless garment worn by a priest over other robes.

chat verb (**chats, chatting, chatted**) **1** talk informally. **2** (**chat someone up**) informal talk flirtatiously to someone. •noun an informal conversation.
□ **chat room** an area on the Internet where users can communicate.
■ **chatty** adjective.

chateau /**sha**-toh/ noun (plural **chateaux** or **chateaus** /**sha**-toh, **sha**-tohz/) a large French country house or castle.

chattel /**chat**-t'l/ noun a personal possession.

chatter verb (**chatters, chattering, chattered**) **1** talk informally about unimportant things. **2** (of a person's teeth) click together continuously from cold or fear. •noun informal or unimportant talk.

chatterbox noun informal a person who likes to chatter.

chauffeur noun a person who is employed to drive someone around in a car. •verb be a driver for someone.

chauvinism /**shoh**-vin-iz'm/ noun **1** a strong and unreasonable belief that your own country or group is better than others. **2** the belief held by some men that men are superior to women.
■ **chauvinist** adjective & noun **chauvinistic** adjective.

cheap adjective **1** low in price, or charging low prices. **2** low in price and of bad quality. **3** having no value because achieved in a bad way.
■ **cheaply** adverb **cheapness** noun.

cheapen verb lower the quality or value of something.

cheapskate noun informal a person who hates to spend money.

THESAURUS

chase verb **1** *the dogs chased the fox:* pursue, run after, follow, hunt, track, trail; informal tail. **2** *she chased away the donkeys:* drive, send, scare; informal send packing. **3** *she chased away all thoughts of him:* dispel, banish, dismiss, drive away, shut out, put out of your mind.
•noun *they gave up the chase:* pursuit, hunt, trail.

chat noun *I popped in for a chat:* talk, conversation, gossip; informal jaw, gas, confab; Brit. informal natter, chinwag.
•verb *they chatted with the guests:* talk, gossip; informal gas, jaw, chew the rag/fat; Brit. informal natter, have a chinwag; N. Amer. informal shoot the breeze/bull; Austral./NZ informal mag.

chatter verb *they chattered excitedly:* prattle, chat, gossip, jabber, babble; informal yatter; Brit. informal natter, chunter, rabbit on.
•noun *she tired him with her chatter:* prattle, chat, gossip, patter, jabber, babble;

informal chit-chat, yattering; Brit. informal nattering, chuntering, rabbiting on.

chatty adjective talkative, communicative, effusive, gossipy, loquacious, voluble; informal mouthy, gabby.
OPPOSITES taciturn.

cheap adjective **1** *cheap tickets:* inexpensive, low-priced, low-cost, economical, competitive, affordable, reasonable, budget, economy, bargain, cut-price, reduced, discounted; informal dirt cheap. **2** *plain without looking cheap:* poor-quality, second-rate, substandard, inferior, vulgar, shoddy, trashy, tawdry, cheap and nasty; informal rubbishy, cheapo, junky, tacky, kitsch; Brit. informal naff, duff, ropy, grotty; N. Amer. informal two-bit, dime-store. **3** *a cheap remark:* despicable, contemptible, immoral, unscrupulous, unprincipled, cynical.
OPPOSITES expensive, superior, kind.

cheat verb **1** act dishonestly or unfairly to gain an advantage. **2** deprive someone of something by tricking them. • **noun** a person who cheats.

check¹ verb **1** examine the accuracy, quality, or condition of. **2** make sure that something is the case. **3** stop or slow the progress of. • **noun 1** an act of checking accuracy, quality, or condition. **2** a control or restraint. **3** Chess a position in which a king is directly threatened. **4** N. Amer. the bill in a restaurant.
□ **check in** register at a hotel or airport. **check out** pay your hotel bill before leaving. **check something out** find out about something. **check-up** an examination by a doctor or dentist. **check up on** investigate. **in check** under control.

check² **noun** a pattern of small squares. • **adjective** (also **checked**) having a pattern of small squares.

check³ US spelling of CHEQUE.

checker US spelling of CHEQUER.

checklist noun a list of items to be considered or things to be done.

checkmate Chess **noun** a position of check from which a king cannot escape. • **verb** put a king into checkmate.

checkout noun a point at which goods are paid for in a supermarket or large shop.

checkpoint noun a barrier where security checks are carried out on travellers.

Cheddar noun a kind of firm, smooth cheese.

cheek noun 1 the area on either side of the face below the eye. **2** either of the buttocks. **3** rude or disrespectful behaviour. • **verb** informal speak to someone rudely or disrespectfully.
□ **cheek by jowl** close together. **turn the other cheek** stop yourself from fighting back.

cheekbone noun the rounded bone below the eye.

cheeky adjective (**cheekier, cheekiest**) showing a cheerful lack of respect.
■ **cheekily** adverb.

cheep noun a squeaky cry made by a young bird. • **verb** make a cheep.

cheer verb 1 shout for joy or in praise or encouragement. **2** praise or encourage a person or group. **3** (**cheer up** or **cheer someone up**) become or make someone less miserable. **4** give comfort to someone. • **noun 1** a shout of joy, encouragement, or praise. **2** (also **good cheer**) cheerfulness; optimism.

cheerful adjective 1 noticeably happy and

THESAURUS

cheat verb swindle, defraud, deceive, trick, dupe, hoodwink, double-cross, gull; informal diddle, rip off, con, pull a fast one on; N. Amer. informal sucker, goldbrick; Austral. informal rort.
• **noun** swindler, fraudster, confidence trickster, double-dealer, double-crosser, fraud, fake, charlatan; informal con artist; N. Amer. informal bunco artist, gold brick; Austral. informal shicer.

check verb 1 troops checked all vehicles: examine, inspect, look at/over, scrutinize, study, investigate, probe, look into, enquire into; informal check out, give something a/the once-over. **2** he checked that the gun was cocked: make sure, confirm, verify. **3** two defeats checked their progress: halt, stop, arrest, bar, obstruct, foil, thwart, curb, block.
• **noun 1** a check of the medical records: examination, inspection, scrutiny, perusal, study, investigation, test, check-up; informal once-over. **2** a check on the abuse of authority: control, restraint, constraint, curb, limitation.
□ **check in** register, book in, report. **check out** pay the bill, settle up, leave.

cheek noun impudence, impertinence, insolence, rudeness, disrespect; informal brass neck, lip, mouth, chutzpah; Brit. informal backchat; N. Amer. informal sass, nerviness, back talk.

cheeky adjective impudent, impertinent, insolent, rude, disrespectful; informal brass-necked, lippy, mouthy, fresh; N. Amer. informal sassy, nervy.
OPPOSITES respectful, polite.

cheer verb 1 they cheered their team: applaud, hail, salute, shout for, clap, put your hands together for, bring the house down; informal holler for, give someone a big hand; N. Amer. informal ballyhoo. **2** the bad weather did little to cheer me: raise/lift someone's spirits, brighten, buoy up, hearten, gladden, perk up, encourage; informal buck up.
OPPOSITES boo, depress.
• **noun** the cheers of the crowd: hurrah, hurray, whoop, bravo, shout; (**cheers**) acclaim, applause, ovation.
OPPOSITES boo.
□ **cheer up** perk up, brighten up, rally, revive, bounce back, take heart; informal buck up. **cheer someone up.** See CHEER verb sense 2.

cheerful adjective 1 he arrived looking cheerful: happy, jolly, merry, bright, sunny, joyful, in good/high spirits, buoyant, cheery, animated, smiling, good-humoured; informal chipper, chirpy, full of beans. **2** a cheerful room: pleasant, attractive, bright, agreeable, sunny, friendly, welcoming.
OPPOSITES sad, gloomy.

optimistic. **2** bright and pleasant.
■ **cheerfully** adverb **cheerfulness** noun.

cheerleader noun (in North America) a girl belonging to a group that performs organized chanting and dancing at sports events.

cheerless adjective gloomy; depressing.

cheers exclamation informal **1** said before having an alcoholic drink with other people. **2** said to express thanks or on parting.

cheery adjective (**cheerier, cheeriest**) happy and optimistic.
■ **cheerily** adverb.

cheese¹ noun a food made from the pressed curds of milk.
□ **cheese-paring** very careful about spending money; mean.

cheese² verb (**be cheesed off**) informal be irritated or bored.

cheeseburger noun a beefburger with a slice of cheese on it, served in a bread roll.

cheesecake noun a rich, sweet tart having a thick topping made with cream cheese.

cheesecloth noun thin, loosely woven cotton cloth.

cheesy adjective (**cheesier, cheesiest**) **1** like cheese. **2** informal sentimental or of bad quality.

cheetah noun a large spotted cat that can run very fast, found in Africa and parts of Asia.

chef noun a professional cook in a restaurant or hotel.

chef-d'œuvre /shay **derv**-ruh/ noun (plural **chefs-d'œuvre** /shay **derv**-ruh/) a masterpiece.

chemical adjective relating to chemistry or chemicals. ●**noun** a substance which has been artificially prepared or purified.
■ **chemically** adverb.

chemise /shuh-**meez**/ noun a woman's loose-fitting dress, nightdress, or petticoat.

chemist noun **1** a person who is authorized to give out or sell medicines. **2** a shop where medicines, toiletries, and cosmetics are sold. **3** a person who studies chemistry.

chemistry noun **1** the branch of science concerned with the nature of substances and how they react with each other. **2** attraction or interaction between two people.

chemotherapy noun the treatment of cancer with drugs.

chenille /shuh-**neel**/ noun a fabric with a thick velvety pile.

cheque (US spelling **check**) noun a written order to a bank to pay a stated sum from an account to a named person.
□ **cheque card** a card issued by a bank to guarantee payment of a customer's cheques.

chequer (US spelling **checker**) noun **1** (**chequers**) a pattern of alternately coloured squares. **2** (**checkers**) N. Amer. the game of draughts.

chequered adjective **1** divided into or marked with chequers. **2** having successful and unsuccessful periods: *a chequered career.*

cherish verb **1** protect and care for someone lovingly. **2** keep a thought or memory in your mind.

Cherokee noun (plural **Cherokee** or **Cherokees**) a member of an American Indian people formerly living in much of the southern US.

cheroot /shuh-**root**/ noun a cigar with both ends open.

cherry noun (plural **cherries**) **1** a small, round red fruit with a stone. **2** a bright red colour.

cherub noun **1** (plural **cherubim** or **cherubs**) a type of angel, shown in art as a plump child with wings. **2** (plural **cherubs**) a beautiful or innocent-looking child.
■ **cherubic** adjective /chuh-**roo**-bik/.

chervil noun a herb with an aniseed flavour.

chess noun a board game for two players, the object of which is to put the opponent's king under a direct attack, leading to checkmate.

chest noun **1** the front of a person's body between the neck and the stomach. **2** a large, strong box for storing or transporting things.
□ **chest of drawers** a piece of furniture fitted with a set of drawers.

chesterfield noun a sofa with a back of the same height as the arms.

chestnut noun **1** an edible nut with a glossy brown shell. **2** a deep reddish-brown colour. **3** (**old chestnut**) a joke, story, or

THESAURUS

chemist noun pharmacist, dispenser; N. Amer. druggist; old use apothecary.

cherish verb **1** *a woman he could cherish:* adore, love, dote on, be devoted to, revere, think the world of, care for, look after, protect, keep safe. **2** *I cherish her letters:* treasure, prize, hold dear. **3** they cherished *dreams of glory:* harbour, entertain, nurse, cling to, foster.
OPPOSITES hate, disdain.

chest noun **1** *a wound in the chest:* breast, upper body, torso, trunk, front. **2** *an oak chest:* box, case, casket, crate, trunk, coffer, strongbox.

subject that has become boring through being repeated too often.

chesty adjective informal having a lot of catarrh in the lungs.

chevron noun a V-shaped line or stripe, worn on the sleeve of a military uniform to show rank or length of service.

chew verb 1 grind food with the teeth to make it easier to swallow. 2 (**chew something over**) discuss or consider something at length. • noun a sweet meant for chewing.

▫ **chewing gum** flavoured gum for chewing.

chewy adjective needing a lot of chewing.

Chianti /ki-**an**-ti/ noun a red Italian wine produced in Tuscany.

chic /sheek/ adjective (**chicer, chicest**) smart and fashionable.

chicane /shi-**kayn**/ noun a sharp double bend in a motor-racing track.

chicanery noun the use of cunning tricks to get what you want.

chick noun 1 a newly hatched young bird. 2 informal a young woman.

chicken noun 1 a large domestic bird kept for its eggs or meat. 2 informal a coward. • adjective informal cowardly. • verb (**chicken out**) informal be too scared to do something.

chickenpox noun a disease causing itchy inflamed pimples.

chickpea noun a yellowish seed eaten as a vegetable.

chickweed noun a small white-flowered plant that grows as a garden weed.

chicory noun (plural **chicories**) a plant whose leaves are eaten and whose root can be used instead of coffee.

chide verb (**chides, chiding, chided**) tell someone off.

chief noun a leader or ruler. • adjective 1 having the highest rank or authority. 2 most important.

chiefly adverb mainly; mostly.

chieftain noun the leader of a people or clan.

chiffon noun a light, see-through fabric.

chignon /**sheen**-yon/ noun a knot or coil of hair arranged on the back of a woman's head.

chihuahua /chi-**wah**-wuh/ noun a very small breed of dog with smooth hair.

chilblain noun a painful, itchy swelling on a hand or foot caused by exposure to cold.

child noun (plural **children**) 1 a young human being below the age of full physical development. 2 a son or daughter of any age.

▪ **childhood** noun **childless** adjective.

childbirth noun the process of giving birth to a baby.

childish adjective 1 silly and immature. 2 like a child.

childlike adjective (of an adult) innocent and unsuspecting like a child.

childminder noun Brit. a person who is paid to look after other people's children.

Chilean /**chil**-i-uhn/ noun a person from Chile. • adjective relating to Chile.

chill noun 1 an unpleasant feeling of

THESAURUS

chew verb munch, champ, chomp, crunch, gnaw, bite, masticate.

chic adjective stylish, smart, elegant, sophisticated, fashionable; informal trendy; Brit. informal swish; N. Amer. informal kicky, tony. OPPOSITES unfashionable.

chief noun 1 *a Highland chief:* leader, chieftain, head, ruler, master, commander. 2 *the chief of the central bank:* head, chief executive, chief executive officer, CEO, president, chairman, chairwoman, principal, governor, director, manager; informal boss, (head) honcho; Brit. informal gaffer, guv'nor.
• adjective 1 *the chief rabbi:* head, leading, principal, premier, highest, supreme, arch. 2 *their chief aim:* main, principal, primary, prime, first, cardinal, central, key, crucial, essential; informal number-one.
OPPOSITES subordinate, minor.

chiefly adverb mainly, in the main, primarily, principally, predominantly, mostly, for the most part, usually, typically, commonly, generally, on the whole, largely.

child noun youngster, baby, infant, toddler, minor, juvenile, junior, descendant; Scottish & N. English bairn; informal kid, kiddie, nipper, tiny, tot; disapproving brat.

childbirth noun labour, delivery, birthing; old use confinement.

childhood noun youth, early years/life, infancy, babyhood, boyhood, girlhood, minority.
OPPOSITES adulthood.

childish adjective *childish behaviour:* immature, babyish, infantile, juvenile, puerile, silly.
OPPOSITES mature.

childlike adjective *childlike curiosity:* youthful, innocent, unsophisticated, naive, trusting, artless, unaffected, uninhibited, natural, spontaneous.
OPPOSITES adult.

chill noun 1 *a chill in the air:* coldness, chilliness, coolness, nip. 2 *he had a chill:* cold, dose of flu, fever. 3 *a chill ran down my spine:* shiver, frisson.
OPPOSITES warmth.
• verb *his quiet tone chilled Ruth:* scare, frighten, petrify, terrify, alarm, make

c

coldness. **2** a feverish cold. •**verb 1** make cold. **2** frighten or horrify. **3** (usu. **chill out**) informal relax. •**adjective** unpleasantly cold.

chilli (US spelling **chili**) noun (plural **chillies**) a small hot-tasting pepper, used in cookery and as a spice.
□ **chilli con carne** a stew of minced beef and beans flavoured with chilli.

chilly adjective (**chillier**, **chilliest**) **1** too cold to be comfortable. **2** unfriendly.

chime noun **1** a tuneful ringing sound. **2** a bell, bar, or tube used in a set to produce chimes when struck. •**verb** (**chimes**, **chiming**, **chimed**) **1** (of a bell or clock) make a tuneful ringing sound. **2** (**chime in**) interrupt a conversation with a remark.

chimera or **chimaera** /ky-**meer**-uh/ noun **1** (in Greek mythology) a female monster with a lion's head, a goat's body, and a snake's tail. **2** an unrealistic hope or dream.

chimerical /ky-**merr**-i-k'l/ adjective not real or possible.

chimney noun (plural **chimneys**) a pipe or channel which takes smoke and gases up from a fire or furnace.
□ **chimney breast** the part of an inside wall that surrounds a chimney.

chimpanzee noun an ape native to west and central Africa.

chin noun the part of the face below the mouth.

china noun **1** a delicate white ceramic material. **2** household objects made from china.

chinchilla /chin-**chil**-luh/ noun a small South American rodent with soft grey fur and a long bushy tail.

Chinese noun (plural **Chinese**) **1** the language of China. **2** a person from China. •**adjective** relating to China.

chink[1] noun **1** a narrow opening or crack. **2** a beam of light entering through a chink.

chink[2] verb make a high-pitched ringing sound. •**noun** a high-pitched ringing sound.

chinos /**chee**-nohz/ plural noun casual

trousers made from a smooth cotton fabric.

chintz noun patterned cotton fabric with a glazed finish, used for curtains and upholstery.

chintzy adjective **1** like chintz. **2** colourful but fussy and tasteless.

chip noun **1** a small piece cut or broken off from something hard. **2** Brit. a long, thin piece of deep-fried potato. **3** (also **potato chip**) chiefly N. Amer. a potato crisp. **4** a microchip. **5** a counter used in some gambling games to represent money. •**verb** (**chips**, **chipping**, **chipped**) **1** cut or break off a small piece from something hard. **2** (**chip away**) gradually make something smaller or weaker. **3** (**chip in**) add a contribution.
□ **a chip on your shoulder** informal a long-held feeling of resentment.

chipboard noun a building material made from chips of wood pressed and stuck together.

chipmunk noun a burrowing squirrel with light and dark stripes running down the body.

chipolata noun Brit. a small, thin sausage.

chipping noun a small fragment of stone, wood, or similar material.

chiropody /ki-**rop**-uh-di/ noun care and treatment of the feet.
■ **chiropodist** noun.

chiropractic /ky-roh-**prak**-tik/ noun a system of complementary medicine based on the manipulation of the joints, especially those of the spinal column.
■ **chiropractor** noun.

chirp verb (of a small bird) make a short, high-pitched sound. •**noun** a chirping sound.

chirpy adjective (**chirpier**, **chirpiest**) informal cheerful and lively.

chirrup verb (**chirrups**, **chirruping**, **chirruped**) chirp. •**noun** a chirping sound.

chisel noun a hand tool with a narrow blade,

THESAURUS

someone's blood run cold; informal scare the pants off; Brit. informal put the wind up.
OPPOSITES warm.
•**adjective** a chill wind: cold, chilly, cool, fresh, wintry, frosty, icy, arctic, bitter, freezing; informal nippy; Brit. informal parky.

chilly adjective **1** the weather had turned chilly: cold, cool, crisp, fresh, wintry, frosty, icy; informal nippy; Brit. informal parky. **2** a chilly reception: unfriendly, unwelcoming, cold, cool, frosty; informal stand-offish.
OPPOSITES warm.

china noun crockery, dishes, plates, cups and saucers, tableware, porcelain, dinnerware, dinner service, tea service.

chink noun a chink in the curtains: gap, crack, space, hole, aperture, fissure, cranny, cleft, split, slit.

chip noun **1** wood chips: fragment, sliver, splinter, shaving, shard, flake. **2** a chip in the glass: nick, crack, scratch. **3** gambling chips: counter, token; N. Amer. check.
•**verb 1** the teacup was chipped: nick, crack, scratch. **2** chip off the old plaster: cut, hack, chisel, carve, hew, whittle.

used with a hammer to cut or shape wood, stone, or metal. •verb (**chisels, chiselling, chiselled**; US spelling **chisels, chiseling, chiseled**) **1** cut or shape something with a chisel. **2** (**chiselled**) (of a man's facial features) clear and strong.

chit noun a short note recording a sum of money owed.

chivalrous adjective acting in a polite and charming way towards women.
■ **chivalrously** adverb.

chivalry noun **1** an honourable code of behaviour which knights in medieval times were expected to follow. **2** polite behaviour by a man towards women.

chives plural noun a plant with long, thin leaves that are used as a herb.

chivvy verb (**chivvies, chivvying, chivvied**) keep telling someone to do something.

chloride noun a compound of chlorine with another substance.

chlorinate verb (**chlorinates, chlorinating, chlorinated**) treat water with chlorine.
■ **chlorination** noun.

chlorine /klor-een/ noun a chemical element in the form of a green gas, sometimes added to water as a disinfectant.

chlorofluorocarbon ⇒ **CFC**.

chloroform noun a liquid used to dissolve things and formerly used as an anaesthetic.

chlorophyll /klo-ruh-fil/ noun a green pigment in plants which allows them to absorb sunlight and use it in photosynthesis.

chock noun a wedge or block placed against a wheel to prevent it from moving.
□ **chock-a-block** crammed full.

chocolate noun **1** a dark brown sweet food made from roasted cacao seeds. **2** a drink made by mixing milk or water with powdered chocolate.

choice noun **1** an act of choosing. **2** the right or ability to choose. **3** a range from which to choose. **4** something that has been chosen. •adjective of very good quality.

choir noun **1** an organized group of singers.

2 the part of a church between the altar and the nave, used by the choir.

choirboy noun a boy who sings in a church choir.

choke verb (**chokes, choking, choked**) **1** prevent someone from breathing by blocking their throat or depriving them of air. **2** have trouble breathing. **3** (**be choked with**) be blocked or filled with. •noun a valve used to reduce the amount of air in the fuel mixture of a petrol engine.

choker noun a close-fitting necklace.

cholera /kol-uh-ruh/ noun an infectious disease causing severe vomiting and diarrhoea.

choleric /ko-luh-rik/ adjective literary bad-tempered.

cholesterol /kuh-less-tuh-rol/ noun a substance in the body which is believed to cause disease of the arteries when there is too much of it in the blood.

chomp verb munch or chew food noisily.

choose verb (**chooses, choosing, chose**; past participle **chosen**) pick something out as being the closest to what you want or need.

choosy adjective (**choosier, choosiest**) informal very careful in making a choice.

chop verb (**chops, chopping, chopped**) **1** cut something into pieces with a knife or axe. **2** hit with a short downward stroke. •noun **1** a thick slice of meat cut from or including the rib bone. **2** a downward cutting movement. **3** (**the chop**) Brit. informal the cancellation or end of something.
□ **chop and change** Brit. informal keep changing your mind.

chopper noun **1** a short axe with a large blade. **2** informal a helicopter.

choppy adjective (of the sea) having many small waves.

chopstick noun each of a pair of thin sticks used by the Chinese and Japanese to eat with.

chop suey noun a Chinese-style dish of meat with bean sprouts, bamboo shoots,

---

THESAURUS

choice noun **1** *freedom of choice:* selection, choosing, picking, pick, preference, decision, say, vote. **2** *you have no other choice:* option, alternative, course of action. **3** *an extensive choice:* range, variety, selection, assortment.
•adjective *choice plums:* superior, first-class, first-rate, prime, premier, grade A, best, finest, select, quality, top, top-quality, high-grade, prize; informal A1, top-notch. OPPOSITES inferior.

choke verb **1** *Christopher started to choke:* gag, retch, cough, fight for breath. **2** *she*

had been choked to death: suffocate, asphyxiate, smother, stifle, strangle, throttle; informal strangulate. **3** *the guttering was choked with leaves:* clog (up), bung up, stop up, block, obstruct.

choose verb **1** *we chose a quiet country hotel:* select, pick (out), opt for, plump for, settle on, prefer, decide on, fix on, elect, adopt. **2** *I'll stay as long as I choose:* wish, want, desire, please, like.

chop verb cut (up), cube, dice, hew, split, fell; N. Amer. hash.

and onions.

choral adjective sung by a choir or chorus.

chorale noun a simple, stately hymn tune.

chord noun a group of three or more musical notes sounded together in harmony.

> **!** don't confuse **chord** with **cord**, which means 'thin string or rope'.

chore noun a boring or routine job or task.

choreograph /ko-ri-uh-grahf/ verb compose the sequence of steps for a ballet or dance routine.
■ choreographer noun choreography noun.

chorister noun a member of a church choir.

chortle verb (**chortles, chortling, chortled**) chuckle happily.

chorus noun (plural **choruses**) **1** a part of a song which is repeated after each verse. **2** a group of singers or dancers performing together in a supporting role in an opera, musical, etc. **3** something said at the same time by many people. • verb (**choruses, chorusing, chorused**) (of a group of people) say the same thing at the same time.

chose past of **CHOOSE**.

chosen past participle of **CHOOSE**.

choux pastry /shoo/ noun very light pastry made with egg.

chowder noun a rich soup containing fish, clams, or corn.

chow mein /chow **mayn**/ noun a Chinese-style dish of fried noodles served with shredded meat or seafood and vegetables.

Christ noun the title given to Jesus.

christen verb give a name to a baby while it is being baptized.

Christian adjective based on or believing in Christianity. • noun a person who believes in Christianity.
□ Christian name a person's first name.

Christianity noun the religion based on the life and teaching of Jesus.

Christmas noun (plural **Christmases**) the annual Christian festival celebrating the birth of Jesus, held on 25 December.
□ Christmas tree an evergreen tree

decorated with lights and ornaments at Christmas.

chromatic adjective **1** Music using notes that do not belong to the key in which the passage is written. **2** Music going up or down by semitones. **3** relating to or produced by colour.

chrome noun a hard, bright metal coating made from chromium.

chromium noun a hard white metallic element.

chromosome noun a thread-like structure found in the nuclei of most living cells, carrying genetic information in the form of genes.

chronic adjective **1** (of an illness or problem) lasting for a long time. **2** having a long-lasting illness or bad habit. **3** Brit. informal very bad.
■ chronically adverb.

chronicle noun a record of historical events made in the order in which they happened. • verb (**chronicles, chronicling, chronicled**) record a series of events in detail.
■ chronicler noun.

chronological adjective (of a record of events) starting with the earliest and following the order in which they happened.
■ chronologically adverb.

chronology /kruh-**nol**-uh-ji/ noun (plural **chronologies**) the arrangement of events or dates in the order in which they happened.

chronometer noun an instrument for measuring time.

chrysalis /**kriss**-uh-liss/ noun (plural **chrysalises**) a butterfly or moth when it is changing from a larva to the adult form, inside a hard case.

chrysanthemum /kri-**san**-thi-muhm/ noun (plural **chrysanthemums**) a garden plant with brightly coloured flowers.

chub noun a thick-bodied river fish.

chubby adjective (**chubbier, chubbiest**) plump and rounded.

chuck¹ verb informal throw something

THESAURUS

□ chop something off **cut off**, sever, lop, shear.

chore noun task, job, duty, errand, burden; informal hassle.

christen verb **1** she was christened Sara: baptize, name, give the name of, call. **2** a group who were christened 'The Magic Circle': call, name, dub, style, term, label, nickname.

chronicle noun a chronicle of the region's past: record, account, history, annals, archive(s), log, diary, journal.

• verb the events have been chronicled: record, write down, set down, document, report.

chubby adjective plump, tubby, flabby, rotund, portly, chunky; Brit. informal podgy; N. Amer. informal zaftig, corn-fed.
OPPOSITES skinny.

chuck verb (informal) **1** he chucked the letter on to the table: throw, toss, fling, hurl, pitch, cast, lob; informal sling, bung; Austral. informal hoy; NZ informal bish. **2** I chucked the rubbish: throw away/out, discard, dispose of, get carelessly or casually.

chuck² verb touch someone playfully under the chin.

chuckle verb (**chuckles, chuckling, chuckled**) laugh quietly. • noun a quiet laugh.

chuff verb (of a steam engine) move with a regular puffing sound.

chuffed adjective Brit. informal very pleased.

chug verb (**chugs, chugging, chugged**) (of a vehicle) move slowly with a loud, regular sound.

chum noun informal a close friend.
■ **chummy** adjective.

chump noun informal a silly person.

chunk noun a thick, solid piece.
■ **chunky** adjective.

church noun 1 a building where Christians go to worship. 2 (**Church**) a particular Christian organization. 3 (**the Church**) people within the Christian faith.

churchyard noun an enclosed area surrounding a church.

churlish adjective unfriendly and rude.
■ **churlishly** adverb.

churn noun 1 a machine for making butter by shaking milk or cream. 2 a large metal milk can. • verb 1 (of liquid) move about vigorously. 2 (**churn something out**) produce something in large quantities and without much thought. 3 shake milk or cream in a churn to produce butter.

chute noun 1 a sloping channel for moving things to a lower level. 2 a slide into a swimming pool.

chutney noun (plural **chutneys**) a spicy sauce made of fruits or vegetables with vinegar, spices, and sugar.

chutzpah /**khuuts**-puh/ noun informal extreme self-confidence.

CIA abbreviation (in the US) Central

Intelligence Agency.

ciabatta /chuh-**bah**-tuh/ noun a flat Italian bread made with olive oil.

cicada /si-**kah**-duh/ noun an insect which makes a shrill droning noise.

CID abbreviation Criminal Investigation Department.

cider noun an alcoholic drink made from apple juice.

cigar noun a cylinder of tobacco rolled in tobacco leaves for smoking.

cigarette noun a cylinder of finely cut tobacco rolled in paper for smoking.

cilium /**sil**-i-uhm/ noun (plural **cilia** /**sil**-i-uh/) a microscopic hair-like structure, found on the surface of certain cells.

cinch noun informal 1 a very easy task. 2 a certainty.

cinder noun a piece of partly burnt coal or wood.

cine adjective relating to or used for the making of films.

cinema noun Brit. 1 a place where films are shown. 2 the production of films as an art or industry.

cinematic adjective relating to the cinema, or like a film.

cinematography noun the skilled use of the camera in film-making.
■ **cinematographer** noun.

cinnamon noun a spice made from the bark of an Asian tree.

cipher or **cypher** noun 1 a code. 2 a key to a code. 3 an unimportant person or thing.

circa /**ser**-kuh/ preposition approximately.

circadian /ser-**kay**-di-uhn/ adjective relating to processes in the body that happen regularly every twenty-four hours.

circle noun 1 a round flat shape whose edge

THESAURUS

rid of, dump, bin, jettison; informal ditch, junk; N. Amer. informal trash. 3 *I've chucked my job*: give up, leave, resign from; informal quit, pack in; Brit. informal jack in. 4 *Mary chucked him for another guy*: leave, finish with, break off with, jilt; informal dump, ditch, give someone the elbow; Brit. informal give someone the push.

chuckle verb laugh, chortle, giggle, titter, snigger.

chum noun (informal) friend, companion, playmate, classmate, schoolmate, workmate; informal pal, crony; Brit. informal mate; N. Amer. informal buddy.
OPPOSITES enemy, stranger.

chunk noun lump, hunk, wedge, block, slab, square, nugget, brick, cube; informal wodge; N. Amer. informal gob.

churlish adjective rude, ill-mannered, discourteous, impolite, inconsiderate,

surly, sullen.
OPPOSITES polite.

churn verb disturb, stir up, agitate, beat.

cinema noun 1 *the local cinema*: the movies, the pictures; N. Amer. movie theatre/house; informal the flicks. 2 *British cinema*: films, film, movies, pictures, motion pictures.

circa preposition approximately, (round) about, around, in the region of, roughly, something like, or so, or thereabouts, more or less; informal as near as dammit; N. Amer. informal in the ballpark of.
OPPOSITES exactly.

circle noun 1 *a circle of gold stars*: ring, band, hoop, circlet, halo, disc. 2 *her circle of friends*: group, set, crowd, band, company, clique, coterie, club, society; informal gang, bunch.
• verb 1 *seagulls circled above*: wheel,

c

is at the same distance from the centre all the way round. **2** a group of people with shared interests, friends, etc. **3** Brit. a curved upper tier of seats in a theatre.
•verb (**circles, circling, circled**) **1** move or be placed all the way round. **2** draw a line round.

circuit noun **1** a roughly circular line, route, or movement. **2** Brit. a track used for motor racing. **3** a system of components forming a complete path for an electric current. **4** a series of sports events or entertainments.

circuitous /ser-**kyoo**-i-tuhss/ adjective (of a route) long and indirect.

circuitry noun (plural **circuitries**) a system of electric circuits.

circular adjective **1** having the form of a circle. **2** (of a letter or advertisement) for distribution to a large number of people.
•noun a circular letter or advertisement.

circulate verb (**circulates, circulating, circulated**) **1** move continuously through a system or area. **2** pass from place to place or person to person.

circulation noun **1** movement through a system or area. **2** the continuous movement of blood round the body. **3** the spreading or passing of something from one person or place to another. **4** the number of copies of a newspaper or magazine sold.

circumcise verb (**circumcises, circumcising, circumcised**) **1** cut off a boy's or man's foreskin. **2** cut off a girl's or woman's clitoris.
■ **circumcision** noun.

circumference noun **1** the boundary which encloses a circle. **2** the distance around something.

circumflex noun a mark (^) placed over a vowel in some languages to show a change in its sound.

circumlocution noun a way of saying something which uses more words than are necessary.

circumnavigate verb (**circumnavigates, circumnavigating, circumnavigated**) sail all the way around.
■ **circumnavigation** noun.

circumscribe verb (**circumscribes, circumscribing, circumscribed**) restrict the freedom or power of.

circumspect adjective not wanting to take risks; cautious.

circumstance noun **1** a fact or condition that is connected with an event or action. **2** things that happen that are beyond your control. **3** (**circumstances**) the practical things that affect a person's life.

circumstantial adjective (of evidence) consisting of facts that make something seem likely but do not prove it.
■ **circumstantially** adverb.

circumvent /ser-kuhm-**vent**/ verb find a way of avoiding a problem or obstacle.

circus noun (plural **circuses**) a travelling group of entertainers, including acrobats, clowns, and people who perform with trained animals.

cirrhosis /si-**roh**-siss/ noun a disease of the liver.

cirrus /**si**-ruhss/ noun (plural **cirri** /**si**-ry/) cloud forming wispy streaks high in the sky.

CIS abbreviation Commonwealth of Independent States.

cistern noun a tank connected to a toilet, in which the water used for flushing it is stored.

citadel noun a fortress protecting or overlooking a city.

citation noun **1** a quotation from a book or author. **2** an official mention of someone who has done something deserving praise.

cite verb (**cites, citing, cited**) quote a book or author as evidence for an argument.

citizen noun **1** a person who is legally recognized as being a member of a country. **2** an inhabitant of a town or city.
■ **citizenship** noun.

THESAURUS

revolve, rotate, whirl, spiral. **2** *satellites circling the earth:* go round, travel round, circumnavigate, orbit. **3** *the abbey was circled by a wall:* surround, encircle, ring, enclose.

circuit noun **1** *two circuits of the track:* lap, turn, round, circle. **2** (Brit.) *a racing circuit:* track, racetrack, course, route, stadium.

circular adjective *a circular room:* round, ring-shaped.
•noun leaflet, pamphlet, handbill, flyer, advertisement, notice.

circulate verb **1** *the news was widely circulated:* spread, communicate, disseminate, make known, make public,

broadcast, publicize, distribute. **2** *they circulated among the guests:* socialize, mingle, mix, wander, stroll.

circumstances plural noun situation, conditions, state of affairs, position, the lie of the land, (turn of) events, factors, facts, background, environment, context.

cite verb **1** *cite the passage in full:* quote, reproduce, excerpt. **2** *he cited the case of Leigh v. Gladstone:* refer to, allude to, instance, specify, mention, name.

citizen noun **1** *a British citizen:* subject, national, passport holder. **2** *the citizens of Edinburgh:* inhabitant, resident, native, townsman, townswoman, taxpayer, people;

citric acid noun a sharp-tasting acid present in the juice of lemons and other sour fruits.

citrus noun (plural **citruses**) a fruit of a group that includes the lemon, lime, orange, and grapefruit.

city noun (plural **cities**) 1 a large town, in particular (Brit.) a town that has been created a city by charter, usually containing a cathedral. 2 (**the City**) the part of London that is a centre of finance and business.
□ **city state** a city that forms an independent state.

civet /siv-it/ noun 1 a cat native to Africa and Asia. 2 a strong perfume obtained from the civet.

civic adjective having to do with a city or town.

civil adjective 1 relating to the lives of ordinary people rather than to military or church matters. 2 (of a court) dealing with personal legal matters rather than criminal offences. 3 polite.
□ **civil engineer** an engineer who designs roads, bridges, dams, etc. **civil liberties** a person's rights to freedom of action and speech (while staying within the law). **civil servant** a person who works in the civil service. **civil service** the departments that carry out the work of the government. **civil war** a war between groups of people within the same country.
■ **civilly** adverb.

civilian noun a person who is not a member of the armed services or the police force.
• adjective relating to a civilian.

civility noun (plural **civilities**) polite behaviour or speech.

civilization or **civilisation** noun 1 an advanced stage of human development in which people in a society behave well

towards each other and share a common culture. 2 the society, culture, and way of life of a particular area or period.

civilize or **civilise** verb (**civilizes, civilizing, civilized**) 1 bring a person or group to an advanced stage of social development. 2 (**civilized**) polite and good-mannered.

CJD abbreviation Creutzfeldt-Jakob disease, a fatal disease affecting the brain, possibly linked to BSE.

cl abbreviation centilitre.

clack verb make a sharp sound like that of one hard object hitting another. • noun a clacking sound.

clad adjective 1 clothed. 2 fitted with cladding.

cladding noun a protective or insulating covering or coating.

claim verb 1 say that something is true although you are not able to prove it. 2 request something that you believe you have a right to. 3 cause the loss of someone's life. 4 ask for money under the terms of an insurance policy. 5 call for someone's attention. • noun 1 a statement that something is true. 2 a statement requesting something that you believe you have a right to. 3 a request for compensation under the terms of an insurance policy.
■ **claimant** noun.

clairvoyant noun a person who claims that they are able to see into the future or communicate mentally with people who are dead or far away. • adjective able to see into the future.
■ **clairvoyance** noun.

clam noun a large shellfish with a hinged shell. • verb (**clams, clamming, clammed**) (**clam up**) informal suddenly stop talking about something.

THESAURUS

formal denizen.

city noun town, municipality, metropolis, conurbation, urban area; Scottish burgh; informal big smoke; N. Amer. informal burg.

civic adjective municipal, city, town, urban, metropolitan, public, community.

civil adjective 1 a civil marriage: secular, non-religious, lay. 2 civil aviation: non-military, civilian. 3 he behaved in a civil manner: polite, courteous, well mannered, gentlemanly, chivalrous, ladylike.
OPPOSITES religious, military, rude.

civilization noun 1 a higher stage of civilization: human development, advancement, progress, enlightenment, culture, refinement, sophistication. 2 ancient civilizations: culture, society, nation, people.

civilize verb enlighten, improve, educate, instruct, refine, cultivate, socialize.

civilized adjective 1 civilized society: advanced, developed, sophisticated, enlightened, educated, cultured, cultivated. 2 civilized behaviour: polite, courteous, well mannered, civil, refined, polished.
OPPOSITES unsophisticated, rude.

claim verb 1 he claimed that she was lying: assert, declare, profess, protest, maintain, insist, contend, allege. 2 you can claim compensation: request, ask for, apply for, demand.
• noun 1 her claim that she was robbed: assertion, declaration, profession, protestation, insistence, contention, allegation. 2 a claim for damages: application, request, demand.

c

clamber verb (**clambers, clambering, clambered**) climb or move using your hands and feet.

clammy adjective (**clammier, clammiest**) 1 unpleasantly damp and sticky. 2 (of air) cold and damp.

clamour (US spelling **clamor**) noun 1 a loud and confused noise. 2 a loud protest or demand. •verb shout or demand something loudly.
■ **clamorous** adjective.

clamp noun 1 a brace, band, or clasp for holding something tightly. 2 a device attached to the wheel of an illegally parked car to prevent it being driven away. •verb 1 fasten or hold with a clamp. 2 (**clamp down**) suppress or prevent something. 3 fit a wheel clamp to a car.

clan noun a group of families, especially in the Scottish Highlands.

clandestine /klan-dess-tin/ adjective done secretly.
■ **clandestinely** adverb.

clang noun a loud metallic sound. •verb make a clang.

clank noun a sharp sound like that of pieces of metal being struck together. •verb make a clank.

clannish adjective (of a group) tending to exclude people from outside the group.

clap verb (**claps, clapping, clapped**) 1 bring the palms of your hands together loudly and repeatedly to show that you approve of something. 2 slap someone encouragingly on the back. 3 suddenly place a hand over a part of your face as a gesture of dismay. •noun 1 an act of clapping. 2 a sudden loud sound of thunder.
□ **clapped-out** Brit. informal worn out from age or heavy use.

clapper noun the moving part inside a bell.

clapperboard noun a pair of hinged boards that are struck together at the beginning of filming so that the picture and sound can be matched.

claret /kla-ruht/ noun a red wine from Bordeaux in France.

clarify verb (**clarifies, clarifying, clarified**) 1 make something easier to understand. 2 melt butter to separate out the impurities.
■ **clarification** noun.

clarinet noun a woodwind instrument with holes that are stopped by keys.
■ **clarinettist** (US spelling **clarinetist**) noun.

clarion /kla-ri-uhn/ noun historical a war trumpet.
□ **clarion call** a loud, clear call for action.

clarity noun 1 the quality of being clear and easily understood. 2 transparency or purity.

clash verb 1 come into violent conflict. 2 disagree or be at odds. 3 (of colours) look unpleasant together. 4 (of events) happen inconveniently at the same time. 5 strike metal objects together, producing a loud harsh sound. •noun an act or sound of clashing.

clasp verb 1 grasp tightly with your hand. 2 place your arms tightly around. 3 fasten with a clasp. •noun 1 a device with interlocking parts used for fastening. 2 an

---

THESAURUS

clamour noun noise, din, racket, rumpus, uproar, shouting, commotion, hubbub; informal hullabaloo; Brit. informal row.

clamp verb fasten, secure, fix, attach, clench, grip, hold, press, clasp, screw, bolt.

clan noun family, house, dynasty, tribe.

clap verb the audience clapped: applaud, give someone a round of applause, put your hands together; informal give someone a (big) hand; N. Amer. informal give it up.
•noun 1 everybody gave him a clap: round of applause; informal hand. 2 a clap of thunder: crack, peal, crash, bang, boom.

clarify verb make clear, shed/throw light on, illuminate, elucidate, explain, interpret, spell out, clear up.
OPPOSITES confuse.

clarity noun 1 the clarity of his explanation: lucidity, precision, coherence, transparency, simplicity. 2 the clarity of the image: sharpness, clearness, crispness, definition. 3 the clarity of the water: transparency, clearness, limpidity, translucence.
OPPOSITES vagueness, blurriness, cloudiness.

clash noun 1 clashes between armed gangs: fight, battle, confrontation, skirmish, engagement, encounter, conflict. 2 clashes in parliament: argument, altercation, confrontation, quarrel, disagreement, dispute; informal run-in, slanging match. 3 the clash of cymbals: crash, clang, bang.
•verb 1 protesters clashed with police: fight, battle, confront, skirmish, contend, come to blows. 2 the prime minister clashed with union leaders: disagree, differ, wrangle, dispute, cross swords, lock horns, be at loggerheads. 3 the dates clash: conflict, coincide, overlap. 4 she clashed the cymbals together: bang, strike, clang, crash.

clasp verb Ruth clasped him to her: grasp, grip, clutch, hold, squeeze, seize, grab, embrace, hug.
•noun 1 a gold clasp: fastener, catch, clip, pin, buckle. 2 his tight clasp: grasp, grip, squeeze, embrace, hug.

act of clasping.

□ **clasp knife** a knife with a blade that folds into the handle.

class noun 1 a set or category of things that have something in common. 2 the division of people into different groups according to their social status. 3 a group of people of the same social status. 4 a group of students or pupils who are taught together. 5 a school or college lesson. 6 informal impressive stylishness. • verb place something in a particular category.

■ **classless** adjective.

classic adjective 1 judged over a period of time to be of the highest quality. 2 typical. • noun (**Classics**) the study of ancient Greek and Latin language and culture.

classical adjective 1 relating to the literature, art, or culture of ancient Greece and Rome. 2 representing the highest standard within a long-established form. 3 (of music) written in the tradition of formal European music.

■ **classically** adverb.

classicism noun the use of a simple and elegant style characteristic of the art, architecture, or literature of ancient Greece and Rome.

classicist noun a person who studies Classics.

classification noun 1 the arrangement of things in categories. 2 a category into which something is put.

classified adjective 1 (of newspaper or magazine advertisements) organized in

categories. 2 (of information or documents) officially secret.

classify verb (**classifies, classifying, classified**) 1 arrange things in groups according to features that they have in common. 2 put in a particular class or category.

classroom noun a room in which a class of pupils or students is taught.

classy adjective (**classier, classiest**) informal stylish and sophisticated.

clatter noun a loud rattling sound like that of hard objects hitting each other. • verb (**clatters, clattering, clattered**) make a clatter.

clause noun 1 a group of words that includes a subject and a verb and forms part of a sentence. 2 a part of a treaty, bill, or contract.

claustrophobia /kloss-truh-**foh**-bi-uh/ noun an extreme fear of being in a small or enclosed space.

■ **claustrophobic** adjective.

clavichord noun a small early keyboard instrument.

clavicle noun the collarbone.

claw noun 1 each of the horny nails on the feet of birds, lizards, and some mammals. 2 the pincer of a shellfish. • verb scratch or tear at something with the claws or fingernails.

clay noun sticky earth that can be moulded when wet and baked to make bricks and pottery.

clean adjective 1 free from dirt or harmful

C

THESAURUS

class noun 1 a new class of drug: kind, sort, type, variety, genre, category, grade, rating, classification. 2 mixing with people of her own class: group, grouping, rank, stratum, level, echelon, status, caste. • verb the 12-seater is classed as a commercial vehicle: classify, categorize, group, grade, order, rate, bracket, designate, label, rank.

classic adjective 1 the classic work on the subject: definitive, authoritative, outstanding, first-rate, first-class, best, finest, excellent, superior, masterly. 2 a classic example of Norman design: typical, archetypal, quintessential, model, representative, perfect, prime, textbook. 3 a classic look: timeless, traditional, simple, elegant, understated. OPPOSITES insignificant, second-rate, atypical, ephemeral. • noun a classic of the genre: definitive example, model, epitome, paradigm, exemplar, masterpiece.

classification noun categorization, classifying, grouping, grading, ranking, organization, sorting, codification.

classify verb categorize, group, grade, rank, order, organize, sort, type, codify, bracket.

classy adjective (informal) stylish, high-class, superior, exclusive, chic, elegant, smart, sophisticated; Brit. upmarket; N. Amer. high-toned; informal posh, ritzy, plush, swanky; Brit. informal swish.

clause noun section, paragraph, article, passage, subsection, chapter, condition, proviso, rider.

claw noun 1 a bird's claw: talon, nail. 2 a crab's claw: pincer, nipper. • verb her fingers clawed his shoulders: scratch, lacerate, tear, rip, scrape, dig into.

clean adjective 1 keep the wound clean: washed, scrubbed, cleansed, cleaned, laundered, spotless, unstained, unsullied, unblemished, immaculate, pristine, disinfected, sterilized, sterile, aseptic, decontaminated. 2 a clean sheet of paper: blank, empty, clear, plain, unused, new, pristine, fresh, unmarked. 3 clean air: pure, clear, fresh, uncontaminated, unpolluted. OPPOSITES dirty, polluted, used. • verb Dad cleaned the windows: wash,

substances. **2** not yet used or marked. **3** not obscene. **4** having no record of offences or crimes. **5** (of an action) smoothly and skilfully done. •**verb** make something free from dirt or harmful substances. •**noun** an act of cleaning.
□ **clean-cut** (of a person) clean and neat. **clean-shaven** (of a man) without a beard or moustache. **come clean** informal fully confess something.
■ **cleaner** noun **cleanly** adverb.

cleanliness /klen-li-nuhss/ noun the quality of being clean.

cleanse /klenz/ verb (**cleanses**, **cleansing**, **cleansed**) make something thoroughly clean or pure.
■ **cleanser** noun.

clear adjective **1** easy to see, hear, or understand. **2** leaving or feeling no doubt. **3** transparent. **4** free of obstructions or unwanted objects. **5** (of a period of time) free of commitments. **6** free from disease or guilt. **7** (**clear of**) not touching. •**verb 1** make or become clear. **2** get past or over something safely or without touching it. **3** show or state that someone is innocent. **4** give official approval to. **5** make people leave a place. **6** (of a cheque) be paid into someone's account.

□ **clear-cut** sharply defined; easy to see or understand. **clear off** informal go away. **clear up 1** (of an illness) become cured. **2** stop raining. **clear something up 1** tidy something. **2** solve or explain a mystery or misunderstanding. **in the clear** no longer in danger or under suspicion.
■ **clearly** adverb.

clearance noun **1** the action of clearing. **2** official permission for something to take place. **3** clear space allowed for a thing to move past or under another.

clearing noun an open space in a wood or forest.

clearway noun Brit. a main road other than a motorway on which vehicles are not allowed to stop.

cleat noun **1** a projection to which a rope may be attached. **2** a projecting wedge on a tool, the sole of a boot, etc., to prevent it slipping.

cleavage noun **1** the space between a woman's breasts. **2** a sharp difference or division between people.

cleave¹ verb (**cleaves**, **cleaving**, **clove** or **cleft** or **cleaved**; past participle **cloven** or **cleft** or **cleaved**) divide or split in two.

cleave² verb (**cleaves**, **cleaving**, **cleaved**) (**cleave to**) literary stick to something.

THESAURUS

cleanse, wipe, sponge, scrub, mop, rinse, scour, swab, shampoo, launder, dry-clean. OPPOSITES dirty.

cleanse verb **1** *the wound was cleansed:* clean (up), wash, bathe, rinse, disinfect. **2** *cleansing the environment of traces of lead:* rid, clear, free, purify, purge.

clear adjective **1** *clear instructions:* understandable, comprehensible, plain, intelligible, uncomplicated, explicit, lucid, coherent, simple, straightforward, unambiguous, clear-cut. **2** *a clear case of harassment:* obvious, evident, plain, sure, definite, unmistakable, manifest, indisputable, unambiguous, patent, incontrovertible, visible, conspicuous, overt, blatant, glaring. **3** *clear water:* transparent, limpid, translucent, crystal clear. **4** *a clear sky:* bright, cloudless, unclouded, visible, blue, sunny, starry. **5** *the road was clear:* unobstructed, passable, open, unrestricted, unhindered.
OPPOSITES vague, disputed, cloudy, obstructed.

•**verb 1** *the smoke had cleared:* disappear, go away, stop, die away, fade, wear off, lift, settle, evaporate, dissipate, decrease, lessen, shift. **2** *they cleared the table:* empty, unload, strip. **3** *clearing drains:* unblock, unstop. **4** *staff cleared the building:* evacuate, empty, leave. **5** *Karen cleared the dirty plates:* remove, take away,

carry away, tidy away/up. **6** *I cleared the bar at my first attempt:* go over, pass over, sail over, jump (over), vault (over), leap (over). **7** *he was cleared by the court:* acquit, declare innocent, find not guilty, absolve, exonerate; informal let off (the hook).

□ **clear something up 1** *clear up the garden:* tidy (up), put in order, straighten up, clean up, fix. **2** *we've cleared up the problem:* solve, resolve, straighten out, find an/the answer to, get to the bottom of, explain; informal crack, figure out, suss out.

clearance noun **1** *slum clearance:* removal, clearing, demolition. **2** *you must have Home Office clearance:* authorization, permission, consent, approval, leave, sanction, licence, dispensation; informal the go-ahead. **3** *there is plenty of clearance:* space, room (to spare), headroom, margin, leeway.

clear-cut adjective definite, distinct, precise, specific, explicit, unambiguous, unequivocal, black and white.
OPPOSITES vague.

clearly adverb **1** *write clearly:* intelligibly, plainly, distinctly, comprehensibly, legibly, audibly. **2** *clearly, substantial changes are needed:* obviously, evidently, patently, unquestionably, undoubtedly, without doubt, plainly, undeniably.

cleaver noun a tool with a broad, heavy blade, used for chopping meat.

clef noun Music a symbol placed next to the notes on a stave, to show their pitch.

cleft past and past participle of CLEAVE¹.
•adjective split or divided into two. •noun a split or indentation.
□ cleft lip an upper lip with an abnormal split in the centre. cleft palate a split in the roof of the mouth.

clematis /klem-uh-tiss/ noun an ornamental climbing plant.

clemency noun kind or merciful treatment.

clement adjective (of weather) mild.

clementine noun a small citrus fruit with bright orange-red skin.

clench verb 1 close your fist or hold your teeth or muscles together tightly in response to stress or anger. 2 grasp something tightly.

clerestory /kleer-stor-i/ noun (plural clerestories) a row of windows in the upper part of the wall of a church or other large building.

clergy /kler-ji/ noun (plural clergies) the priests and ministers in the Christian Church.

clergyman or **clergywoman** noun (plural clergymen or clergywomen) a Christian priest or minister.

cleric noun a priest or religious leader.

clerical adjective 1 relating to the normal work of an office clerk. 2 relating to the priests and ministers of the Christian Church.

clerk noun 1 a person employed in an office or bank to keep records or accounts and do other routine work. 2 a person in charge of the records of a local council or court.

clever adjective (**cleverer, cleverest**) 1 quick to understand and learn. 2 skilled at doing something.
■ cleverly adverb cleverness noun.

cliché /klee-shay/ noun a phrase or idea that has been used too much and is no longer fresh or interesting.
■ clichéd adjective.

click noun a short, sharp sound as of two hard objects coming into contact. •verb 1 make a click. 2 move or become secured with a click. 3 Computing press a mouse button. 4 informal become suddenly clear or understood.

client noun a person who uses the services of a professional person or organization.

clientele /klee-on-tel/ noun the clients or customers of a shop, restaurant, or professional service.

cliff noun a steep rock face at the edge of the sea.

cliffhanger noun a situation in a story which is exciting because you do not know what is going to happen next.

climacteric /kly-mak-tuh-rik/ noun the period in a person's life when their fertility has started to decline.

climactic /kly-mak-tik/ adjective forming an exciting climax.

climate noun 1 the general weather conditions in an area over a long period. 2 a general attitude or feeling among people.
■ climatic adjective.

climax noun 1 the most intense, exciting, or important point of something. 2 an orgasm. •verb reach a climax.

climb verb 1 go or come up to a higher position. 2 go up a hill, rock face, etc.

cleft noun split, crack, fissure, crevice.

clench verb grip, grasp, grab, clutch, clasp, clamp, hold tightly, seize, squeeze.

clergyman, clergywoman noun priest, cleric, minister, preacher, chaplain, padre, father, pastor, vicar, rector, parson, curate; Scottish kirkman.

clever adjective 1 intelligent, bright, smart, astute, quick-witted, shrewd, talented, gifted, capable, able, competent; informal brainy. 2 a clever scheme: ingenious, canny, cunning, crafty, artful, slick, neat. 3 she was clever with her hands: skilful, dexterous, adroit, adept, deft, nimble, handy, skilled, talented, gifted.
OPPOSITES stupid.

cliché noun platitude, hackneyed phrase, commonplace, banality, truism, stock phrase; informal old chestnut.

client noun customer, buyer, purchaser, shopper, patient, patron; Brit. informal punter.

cliff noun precipice, rock face, crag, bluff, ridge, escarpment, scar, scarp.

climate noun 1 a mild climate: (weather) conditions, weather. 2 the political climate: atmosphere, mood, spirit, ethos, feeling, ambience, environment.

climax noun the climax of his career: peak, pinnacle, height, high point, top, zenith, culmination.
OPPOSITES anticlimax, nadir.

climb verb 1 we climbed the hill: ascend, mount, scale, scramble up, clamber up, shin up, conquer. 2 the plane climbed: rise, ascend, go up, gain height, soar, rocket. 3 the road climbs steeply: slope (upwards), rise, go uphill, incline.
OPPOSITES descend.
□ climb down back down, retreat, give in, backtrack, eat your words, eat humble pie, do a U-turn; N. Amer. informal eat crow.

c

3 move somewhere, especially with effort or difficulty. 4 increase in value or amount. • noun 1 an act of climbing. 2 a route up a mountain or cliff. □ **climb down** admit that you are wrong about something. ■ **climber** noun.

clime noun literary a place considered in terms of its climate: *sunnier climes.*

clinch verb 1 settle a contract or contest. 2 settle something that has been uncertain or undecided. • noun 1 a tight hold in a fight or struggle. 2 informal a tight embrace.

cling verb (**clings, clinging, clung**) (**cling to** or **on to**) 1 hold on tightly to. 2 stick to. 3 be unwilling to give up a belief or hope. 4 be emotionally dependent on. □ **cling film** Brit. thin plastic film used to wrap or cover food. ■ **clingy** adjective.

clinic noun a place where medical treatment or advice is given.

clinical adjective 1 relating to the observation and treatment of patients. 2 (of a place) very clean and plain. 3 efficient and showing no emotion. ■ **clinically** adverb.

clink noun a sharp ringing sound. • verb make a clink.

clinker noun the stony remains from burnt coal or from a furnace.

clip¹ noun 1 a flexible or spring-loaded device for holding objects together or in place. 2 a piece of jewellery that is fastened to a garment with a clip. • verb (**clips, clipping, clipped**) fasten with a clip.

clip² verb (**clips, clipping, clipped**) 1 cut or trim with shears or scissors. 2 trim the hair or wool of an animal. 3 hit quickly or lightly. • noun 1 an act of clipping. 2 a short sequence taken from a film or broadcast. 3 informal a quick or light blow.

clipboard noun a board with a clip at the top, for holding papers and writing on.

clipped adjective (of speech) having short, sharp vowel sounds and clear pronunciation.

clipper noun 1 (**clippers**) an instrument for clipping. 2 (in the past) a type of fast sailing ship.

clipping noun 1 a small piece trimmed from something. 2 an article cut from a newspaper or magazine.

clique /rhymes with seek/ noun a small group of people who do not allow other people to join them. ■ **cliquey** adjective.

clitoris /kli-tuh-riss/ noun the small sensitive organ just in front of the vagina.

cloak noun an outer garment that hangs loosely from the shoulders to the knees or ankles. • verb cover or hide something. □ **cloak-and-dagger** involving secret activities.

cloakroom noun 1 a room where coats and bags may be left. 2 Brit. a room that contains a toilet.

clobber informal verb (**clobbers, clobbering, clobbered**) hit someone hard. • noun Brit. clothing and personal belongings.

cloche /klosh/ noun 1 a small cover for protecting young or tender plants. 2 a woman's close-fitting bell-shaped hat.

clock noun 1 an instrument that indicates the time. 2 informal a measuring device resembling a clock, such as a speedometer. • verb informal 1 reach a particular speed or distance. 2 (**clock in** or **out** or Brit. **on** or **off**) register the time you are arriving at or leaving work. 3 (**clock something up**) reach a total.

clockwise adverb & adjective in the direction

THESAURUS

clinch verb 1 *he clinched the deal:* secure, settle, conclude, close, confirm, seal, finalize; informal sew up. 2 *these findings clinched the matter:* settle, decide, determine, resolve. 3 *they clinched the title:* win, secure.
OPPOSITES lose.

cling verb *rice grains cling together:* stick, adhere, hold.
□ **cling (on) to** hold on, clutch, grip, grasp, clasp, hang on, embrace, hug.

clinical adjective 1 *he seemed so clinical:* detached, impersonal, dispassionate, indifferent, uninvolved, distant, remote, aloof, cold. 2 *the room was very clinical:* plain, stark, austere, spartan, bleak, bare, functional, basic, institutional.
OPPOSITES emotional, luxurious.

clip¹ noun *the clip on his briefcase:* fastener, clasp, hasp, catch, hook, buckle, lock. • verb *he clipped the pages together:* fasten, attach, fix, join, pin, staple, tack.

clip² verb 1 *I clipped the hedge:* trim, prune, cut, snip, crop, shear, lop. 2 *his lorry clipped a van:* hit, strike, graze, glance off, nudge, scrape. • noun 1 *a film clip:* extract, excerpt, snippet, fragment, trailer. 2 *I gave the dog a clip:* trim, cut, crop, haircut, shear.

cloak noun 1 *the cloak over his shoulders:* cape, robe, wrap, mantle. 2 *a cloak of secrecy:* cover, veil, mantle, shroud, screen, blanket. • verb *a peak cloaked in mist:* conceal, hide, cover, veil, shroud, mask, obscure, cloud, envelop, swathe, surround.

of the movement of the hands of a clock.

clockwork noun a mechanism which has a spring and a system of interlocking wheels, used to make a mechanical clock or other device work.
□ **like clockwork** very smoothly and easily.

clod noun **1** a lump of earth. **2** informal a stupid person.

clodhopper noun informal **1** a large, heavy shoe. **2** a clumsy person.

clog noun a shoe with a thick wooden sole. •verb (**clogs**, **clogging**, **clogged**) (often **clog something up**) block something up.

cloister noun a covered passage round an open courtyard in a convent, monastery, cathedral, etc.

cloistered adjective **1** having a cloister. **2** protected from the outside world.

clomp verb walk with a heavy tread. •noun the sound of a heavy tread.

clone noun an animal or plant created from the cells of another, to which it is genetically identical. •verb (**clones**, **cloning**, **cloned**) **1** create something as a clone. **2** make an identical copy of something.

close¹ /rhymes with dose/ adjective **1** only a short distance away or apart in space or time. **2** (of a connection or likeness) strong. **3** (of two people) very affectionate and friendly. **4** (of observation or examination) done in a careful and thorough way. •adverb so as to be very near; with very little space between. •noun Brit. a street of houses that is closed at one end.
□ **close-knit** (of a group of people) united by strong relationships. **at close quarters** (or **range**) from a position close to someone or something. **close shave** (or **close call**) informal a narrow escape from danger or disaster. **close-up** a photograph or sequence in a film that is taken from a

very short distance.
■ **closely** adverb.

close² /rhymes with nose/ verb (**closes**, **closing**, **closed**) **1** move something so as to cover an opening. **2** (also **close something up**) bring two parts of something together. **3** (**close on** or **in on**) gradually surround or get nearer to. **4** (**close around** or **over**) encircle and hold. **5** come or bring something to an end. **6** finish speaking or writing. **7** (often **close down**) stop trading or working. **8** bring a deal or arrangement to a conclusion. •noun the end of an event or of a period of time or activity.
□ **close season** (or **closed season**) a period in the year when fishing or hunting is officially forbidden, or when a sport is not played.

closed adjective **1** not open or allowing people to go in. **2** not communicating with or influenced by other people.
□ **closed-circuit television** a television system used to watch people within a building, shopping centre, etc. **closed shop** a place of work where all employees must belong to a particular trade union.

closet noun chiefly N. Amer. **1** a tall cupboard or wardrobe. **2** a small room. •verb (**closets**, **closeting**, **closeted**) shut yourself in a private room.
□ **in** (or **out of**) **the closet** not open (or open) about being homosexual.

closure noun **1** the closing of something. **2** a feeling that an upsetting experience has been resolved.

clot noun **1** a lump that is formed when a thick liquid substance dries or becomes thicker. **2** Brit. informal a stupid person. •verb (**clots**, **clotting**, **clotted**) form into clots.
□ **clotted cream** thick cream obtained by heating and cooling milk slowly.

cloth noun (plural **cloths**) **1** fabric made from a soft fibre such as wool or cotton. **2** a

---

THESAURUS

clog verb block, obstruct, congest, jam, choke, bung up, plug, stop up.

close¹ adjective **1** the town is close to Leeds: near, nearby, adjacent, neighbouring, adjoining, abutting, at hand. **2** a very close match: even, neck and neck. **3** close friends: intimate, dear, bosom, inseparable, close-knit, devoted, faithful, special, firm. **4** a close resemblance: noticeable, marked, distinct, pronounced, strong. **5** a close examination: careful, detailed, thorough, minute, searching, painstaking, meticulous, rigorous. **6** the weather was close: humid, muggy, stuffy, airless, heavy, sticky, sultry, stifling.
OPPOSITES far, distant, one-sided, slight, cursory, fresh.

close² verb **1** she closed the door: shut, pull

to, push to, slam. **2** close the hole: block, stop up, plug, seal, bung up, clog up, choke, obstruct. **3** he closed the meeting: end, conclude, finish, terminate, wind up. **4** the factory is to close: shut down, close down, cease production, cease trading, be wound up, go out of business; informal fold, go to the wall, go bust. **5** he closed a deal: clinch, settle, secure, seal, confirm, pull off, conclude, finalize; informal wrap up.
OPPOSITES open, start.
•noun the close of the talks: end, finish, conclusion.
OPPOSITES beginning.

cloth noun **1** a maker of cloth: fabric, material, textile(s). **2** a cloth to wipe the table: rag, wipe, duster, flannel; Austral. washer.

piece of cloth used for a particular purpose. **3** (**the cloth**) ministers of the Church.

clothe verb (**clothes**, **clothing**, **clothed**) **1** provide with clothes. **2** (**be clothed in**) be dressed in.

clothes plural noun things worn to cover the body.
□ **clothes horse** a frame on which washed clothes are hung to dry.

clothing noun clothes.

cloud noun **1** a mass of vapour floating in the atmosphere. **2** a mass of smoke, dust, etc. in the air. **3** a state or cause of gloom or anxiety. • verb **1** (**cloud over**) (of the sky) become full of clouds. **2** become less clear. **3** (of someone's face or eyes) show sadness, anxiety, or anger.
□ **cloud cuckoo land** a state of unrealistic fantasy. **on cloud nine** very happy. **under a cloud** out of favour or suspected of having done wrong.
■ **cloudless** adjective **cloudy** adjective.

cloudburst noun a sudden fall of very heavy rain.

clout informal noun **1** a heavy blow. **2** influence or power. • verb hit someone hard.

clove[1] noun the dried flower bud of a tropical tree, used as a spice.

clove[2] noun any of the segments making up a bulb of garlic.

clove[3] past of CLEAVE[1].
□ **clove hitch** a knot used to fasten a rope to a spar or another rope.

cloven past participle of CLEAVE[1].
□ **cloven hoof** the divided hoof of animals such as cattle, sheep, and deer.

clover noun a plant with white or pink flowers and a leaf with three lobes.
□ **in clover** in ease and luxury.

clown noun **1** an entertainer who does silly things to make people laugh. **2** a playful or silly person. • verb **1** perform as a clown. **2** behave in a funny or silly way.
■ **clownish** adjective.

cloying adjective **1** too sweet and making you feel slightly sick. **2** too sentimental.

club[1] noun **1** a group of people who meet regularly for a particular activity. **2** a place where members can relax, eat meals, or stay overnight. **3** a nightclub with dance music. • verb (**clubs**, **clubbing**, **clubbed**) **1** (**club together**) combine with other people to do something. **2** informal go out to nightclubs.
■ **clubber** noun.

club[2] noun **1** a heavy stick used as a weapon. **2** a heavy stick with a thick head, used to hit the ball in golf. **3** (**clubs**) one of the four suits in a pack of playing cards, represented by a design of three black clover leaves on a short stem. • verb (**clubs**, **clubbing**, **clubbed**) beat someone with a heavy stick.
□ **club foot** a deformed foot which is twisted so that the sole cannot be placed flat on the ground.

clubhouse noun a building having a bar and other facilities for club members.

cluck verb (of a hen) make a short, throaty sound. • noun the short, throaty sound made by a hen.

clue noun a fact or piece of evidence that helps to clear up a mystery or solve a problem.
□ **not have a clue** informal have no idea about something. **clued up** informal well informed.

THESAURUS

clothe verb dress, attire, robe, garb, costume, swathe, deck (out), turn out, fit out, rig (out); informal get up.

clothes plural noun clothing, garments, attire, garb, dress, wear, costume, wardrobe; informal gear, togs; Brit. informal clobber; N. Amer. informal threads.

clothing noun. See CLOTHES.

cloud noun a cloud of exhaust smoke: mass, billow, pall, mantle, blanket.
• verb anger clouded my judgement: confuse, muddle, obscure.

cloudy adjective **1** a cloudy sky: overcast, dark, grey, black, leaden, murky, gloomy, sunless, starless. **2** cloudy water: murky, muddy, milky, dirty, turbid.
OPPOSITES clear, sunny.

clown noun **1** the class clown: joker, comedian, comic, wag, wit, jester, buffoon. **2** bureaucratic clowns: fool, idiot, dolt, ass, ignoramus; informal moron, numbskull, halfwit, fathead; Brit. informal prat, berk, twit, twerp.
• verb Harvey clowned around: fool around/ about, play the fool, play about/around, monkey about/around, joke; informal mess about/around, lark (about/around); Brit. informal muck about/around.

club[1] noun **1** a canoeing club: society, association, group, circle, league, guild, union. **2** the city has great clubs: nightclub, bar; informal disco. **3** the top club in the league: team, squad, side.

club[2] noun a wooden club: stick, cudgel, truncheon, bludgeon, baton, mace, bat; N. Amer. blackjack, nightstick; Brit. informal cosh.
• verb he was clubbed with an iron bar: hit, beat, strike, cudgel, bludgeon, batter; informal clout, clobber; Brit. informal cosh.

clue noun hint, indication, sign, signal, pointer, lead, tip, evidence.

clueless adjective not able to understand or do something.

clump noun 1 a small group of trees or plants growing closely together. 2 a mass or lump of something. 3 the sound of a heavy tread. •verb 1 form into a clump or mass. 2 walk heavily.

clumpy adjective (of shoes or boots) thick and heavy.

clumsy adjective (**clumsier, clumsiest**) 1 awkward and badly coordinated. 2 tactless. ■ **clumsily** adverb **clumsiness** noun.

clung past and past participle of **CLING**.

clunk noun a dull, heavy sound. •verb make a clunk.

cluster noun a group of similar things placed or occurring closely together. •verb (**cluster, clustering, clustered**) form a cluster.

clutch[1] verb grasp something tightly. •noun 1 a tight grasp. 2 (**clutches**) power and control. 3 a mechanism in a vehicle that connects the engine with the axle and wheels.

clutch[2] noun 1 a group of eggs fertilized at the same time and laid in a single session. 2 a group of chicks hatched from the same clutch of eggs.

clutter verb (**clutters, cluttering, cluttered**) cover or fill with an untidy assortment of things. •noun things lying about untidily.

cm abbreviation centimetres.

Co. abbreviation 1 company. 2 county.

co- prefix joint; mutual; together with another or others: *coexist | co-star.*

c/o abbreviation care of.

coach[1] noun 1 Brit. a comfortable single-decker bus used for longer journeys. 2 a railway carriage. 3 a large horse-drawn carriage.

coach[2] noun 1 a person who trains someone in a sport. 2 a person who gives private lessons in a subject. •verb give private lessons or training to someone.

coagulate /koh-ag-yoo-layt/ verb (**coagulates, coagulating, coagulated**) (of a liquid) thicken or become solid. ■ **coagulant** noun **coagulation** noun.

coal noun a black rock used as fuel, consisting mainly of carbon formed from the remains of ancient plants. ☐ **coal tar** a thick black liquid produced when gas is made from coal.

coalesce /koh-uh-less/ verb (**coalesces, coalescing, coalesced**) come or bring together to form a single mass or whole.

coalface noun an exposed surface of coal in a mine.

coalfield noun a large area where there is a lot of coal underground.

coalition /koh-uh-li-sh'n/ noun a government made up of two political parties who have agreed to work together.

coarse adjective 1 having a rough texture. 2 consisting of large grains or particles. 3 rude or vulgar. ☐ **coarse fish** Brit. any freshwater fish other than salmon and trout. ■ **coarsely** adverb.

> ❗ don't confuse **coarse** with **course**, which means 'a direction', as in *the plane changed course.*

coarsen verb make or become coarse.

THESAURUS

clump noun 1 *a clump of trees:* cluster, thicket, group, bunch. 2 *a clump of earth:* lump, clod, mass, chunk.

clumsy adjective 1 *she was terribly clumsy:* awkward, uncoordinated, ungainly, graceless, lumbering, inelegant, inept, unskilful, accident-prone, all fingers and thumbs; informal cack-handed, ham-fisted, butterfingered, having two left feet; N. Amer. informal klutzy. 2 *a clumsy contraption:* unwieldy, cumbersome, bulky, awkward. OPPOSITES graceful, handy.

cluster noun *clusters of berries:* bunch, clump, mass, knot, group, clutch, huddle, crowd. •verb *they clustered around the television:* congregate, gather, collect, group, assemble, huddle, crowd.

clutch verb grip, grasp, clasp, cling to, hang on to, clench, hold, grab, snatch.

clutter noun disorder, chaos, disarray, untidiness, mess, confusion, litter, rubbish, junk. •verb litter, mess up, be strewn, be scattered, cover, bury.

coach[1] noun 1 *a journey by coach:* bus. 2 *a railway coach:* carriage, wagon; N. Amer. car.

coach[2] noun *a football coach:* instructor, trainer, teacher, tutor, mentor, guru. •verb *he coached Richard in maths:* instruct, teach, tutor, school, educate, drill, train.

coalition noun alliance, union, partnership, bloc, federation, league, association, confederation, consortium, syndicate, amalgamation, merger.

coarse adjective 1 *coarse blankets:* rough, scratchy, prickly, wiry, harsh. 2 *coarse manners:* uncouth, oafish, loutish, boorish, rude, impolite, ill-mannered, vulgar, common, rough. 3 *a coarse remark:* vulgar, crude, rude, off colour, lewd, smutty, indelicate. OPPOSITES soft, refined, polite.

c

coast noun a stretch of land next to or near the sea. • verb 1 move easily without using power. 2 do something without making much effort.

□ the coast is clear there is no danger of being seen or caught.

■ coastal adjective.

coaster noun 1 a small mat for a glass. 2 a ship that sails along the coast from port to port.

coastguard noun an organization or person that keeps watch over coastal waters.

coastline noun the shape or appearance of the land along a coast.

coat noun 1 a full-length outer garment with sleeves. 2 an animal's covering of fur or hair. 3 an outer layer or covering. 4 a single layer of paint. • verb form or provide with a layer or covering.

□ coat of arms a design used as a special symbol of a family, city, or organization.

coating noun a thin layer or covering.

coax verb 1 gently persuade someone to do something. 2 gently guide or move something.

coaxial /koh-**ak**-si-uhl/ adjective (of a cable) having two wires, one wrapped round the other but separated by insulation.

cob noun 1 Brit. a loaf of bread. 2 the central part of an ear of maize. 3 (also **cobnut**) a hazelnut or filbert. 4 a sturdily built horse.

cobalt noun a silvery-white metallic element.

cobber noun Austral./NZ informal a companion or friend.

cobble¹ or **cobblestone** noun a small round stone used to cover road surfaces.

■ cobbled adjective.

cobble² verb (**cobbles, cobbling, cobbled**) (**cobble something together**) make up something roughly from materials that happen to be available.

cobbler noun 1 a person whose job is mending shoes. 2 chiefly N. Amer. a fruit pie with a cake-like crust.

cobra noun a highly poisonous snake native to Africa and Asia.

cobweb noun a spider's web.

cocaine noun an addictive drug made from the leaves of a tropical plant.

coccyx /**kok**-siks/ noun (plural **coccyges** /**kok**-si-jeez/ or **coccyxes**) a small triangular bone at the base of the spine.

cochineal /koch-i-**neel**/ noun a bright red dye used for colouring food.

cochlea /**kok**-li-uh/ noun (plural **cochleae** /**kok**-li-ee/) the spiral cavity of the inner ear.

cock noun a male chicken or game bird. • verb 1 tilt or bend something in a particular direction. 2 raise the firing lever of a gun to make it ready to shoot. 3 (**cock something up**) Brit. informal spoil something by doing it badly.

□ cock-a-hoop very pleased. cock and bull story a very unlikely story.

cockade noun a rosette or knot of ribbons worn on a hat as part of a uniform.

cockatiel /kok-uh-**teel**/ noun a small Australian parrot with a crest.

cockatoo noun a kind of parrot with a crest.

cockcrow noun literary dawn.

cockerel noun a young cock.

cocker spaniel noun a small breed of spaniel with a silky coat.

cockeyed adjective informal 1 crooked. 2 stupid and impractical.

cockle noun an edible shellfish with a ribbed shell.

cockney noun (plural **cockneys**) 1 a person who was born in the East End of London. 2 the dialect or accent used in this area.

cockpit noun 1 a compartment for the pilot and crew in an aircraft or spacecraft. 2 the driver's compartment in a racing car.

cockroach noun a beetle-like insect with long antennae and legs.

cocksure adjective arrogantly confident.

cocktail noun 1 an alcoholic drink consisting of a spirit mixed with other ingredients. 2 a mixture.

cocky adjective (**cockier, cockiest**) too self-confident.

■ cockily adverb cockiness noun.

cocoa noun a drink made from powdered cacao seeds, mixed with hot milk.

coconut noun 1 the large brown seed of a kind of palm tree, consisting of a woody husk lined with edible white flesh. 2 the white flesh of a coconut.

□ coconut shy a sideshow at a fair, in which you throw balls at a coconut and

THESAURUS

coast noun the west coast: shore, coastline, seashore, seaboard, shoreline, seaside; literary strand, littoral.
  • verb the car coasted down a hill: freewheel, cruise, taxi, drift, glide, sail.

coat noun 1 a dog's coat: fur, hair, wool, fleece, hide, pelt, skin. 2 a coat of paint: layer, covering, coating, skin, film, deposit.
  • verb the tube was coated with wax: cover, surface, plate, spread, daub, smear, plaster, cake.

coax verb persuade, wheedle, cajole, get round, inveigle, manoeuvre; informal sweet-talk, soft-soap, twist someone's arm.

cocky adjective arrogant, conceited, overconfident, swollen-headed, self-important, egotistical, presumptuous, win it if you knock it off a stand.

☑ just -o-, not -oa-: coconut.

cocoon noun **1** a silky case spun by the larva of many insects, which protects it while it is turning into an adult. **2** something that envelops you in a protective or comforting way. ● verb wrap in a cocoon.

cod noun (plural **cod**) a large sea fish used for food.
▫ **cod liver oil** oil obtained from the liver of cod, rich in vitamins D and A.

coda /**koh**-duh/ noun an extra passage marking the end of a piece of music.

coddle verb (**coddles, coddling, coddled**) give someone too much care and attention.

code noun **1** a system of words, figures, or symbols used to represent others secretly or briefly. **2** (also **dialling code**) a sequence of numbers dialled to connect a telephone line with another exchange. **3** instructions for a computer program. **4** a set of laws or rules. ● verb (**codes, coding, coded**) **1** convert into a code. **2** (**coded**) expressed in an indirect way.

codeine /**koh**-deen/ noun a painkilling drug obtained from morphine.

codex nounj (plural **codices** /**koh**-di-seez/ or **codexes**) an ancient manuscript in the form of a book.

codger noun informal an elderly man.

codicil /**koh**-di-sil/ noun a part added to a will that explains or alters an earlier part.

codify /**koh**-di-fy/ verb (**codifies, codifying, codified**) arrange a set of rules as a formal code.
■ **codification** noun.

codpiece noun (in the past) a pouch worn by a man over his trousers, covering the groin.

codswallop noun Brit. informal nonsense.

co-education noun the teaching of boys and girls together in the same schools.
■ **co-educational** adjective.

coefficient noun **1** Maths a quantity which is placed before another which it multiplies (e.g. 4 in $4x^2$). **2** Physics a multiplier or factor that measures some property.

coerce /**koh**-erss/ verb (**coerces, coercing, coerced**) force someone to do something.
■ **coercion** noun **coercive** adjective.

coexist verb **1** exist at the same time or in the same place. **2** be together in harmony.
■ **coexistence** noun.

C. of E. abbreviation Church of England.

coffee noun a hot drink made from the seeds of a tropical shrub.
▫ **coffee table** a small low table for putting cups, books, etc. on.

coffer noun a small chest for holding money or valuable items.

coffin noun a long box in which a dead body is buried or cremated.

cog noun **1** (also **cogwheel**) a wheel or bar with projections on its edge, which transfers motion by engaging with projections on another wheel or bar. **2** a projection on a cog.

cogent /**koh**-juhnt/ adjective (of an argument) clear, logical, and convincing.
■ **cogency** noun **cogently** adverb.

cogitate /**koj**-i-tayt/ verb (**cogitates, cogitating, cogitated**) formal think carefully about something.
■ **cogitation** noun.

cognac /**kon**-yak/ noun brandy made in Cognac in western France.

cognition /kog-**ni**-sh'n/ noun the process of gaining knowledge through thought, experience, and the senses.
■ **cognitive** adjective.

cognizance or **cognisance** /**kog**-ni-zuhnss/ noun formal knowledge or awareness.
■ **cognizant** adjective.

cognoscenti /kog-nuh-**shen**-ti/ plural noun people who are well informed about a particular subject.

cohabit verb (**cohabits, cohabiting, cohabited**) live together and have a sexual relationship without being married.
■ **cohabitation** noun.

cohere verb (**coheres, cohering, cohered**) hold firmly together; form a whole.

coherent adjective **1** (of an argument or theory) logical and consistent. **2** able to speak clearly and logically.
■ **coherence** noun **coherently** adverb.

cohesion /koh-**hee**-zh'n/ noun the fact of

THESAURUS

boastful; informal too big for your boots.
OPPOSITES modest.

code noun **1** *a secret code:* cipher. **2** *a strict social code:* convention, etiquette, protocol, ethic. **3** *the penal code:* law(s), rules, regulations, constitution, system.

coerce verb pressure, press, push, constrain, force, compel, oblige, browbeat, bully, threaten, intimidate, dragoon, twist someone's arm; informal railroad, steamroller, lean on.

coherent adjective logical, reasoned, rational, sound, cogent, consistent, lucid, articulate, intelligible.
OPPOSITES muddled.

C

holding firmly together.

cohesive adjective holding or making something hold together.

cohort /koh-hort/ noun 1 a large group of people. 2 an ancient Roman military unit equal to one tenth of a legion.

coif noun /koyf/ a close-fitting cap worn by nuns under a veil. • verb /kwahf, kwof/ (**coifs**, **coiffing**, **coiffed**) arrange someone's hair.

coiffure /kwah-**fyoor**/ noun a person's hairstyle.
■ **coiffured** adjective.

coil noun 1 a length of something wound in loops. 2 a contraceptive in the form of a small coil, fitted into the womb. • verb arrange or form something into a coil.

coin noun a flat disc or piece of metal used as money. • verb 1 invent a new word or phrase. 2 make coins by stamping metal.

coinage noun 1 coins of a particular type. 2 a newly invented word or phrase.

coincide verb (**coincides**, **coinciding**, **coincided**) 1 happen at the same time or place. 2 be the same or similar; tally.

coincidence noun 1 a remarkable instance of things happening at the same time by chance. 2 the fact of things being the same or similar.
■ **coincidental** adjective **coincidentally** adverb.

coitus /**koh**-i-tuhss/ noun technical sexual intercourse.
■ **coital** adjective.

coke[1] noun a solid fuel made by heating coal in the absence of air.

coke[2] noun informal cocaine.

colander noun a bowl with holes in it, used to strain off liquid from food.

cold adjective 1 at a low temperature. 2 not feeling or showing emotion. 3 (of a colour) containing a lot of blue or grey and giving no impression of warmth. 4 (of a scent or trail) no longer fresh and easy to follow. 5 without preparation; unawares. • noun 1 cold weather. 2 an infection causing a streaming nose and sneezing.
□ **cold-blooded** 1 (of reptiles and fish) having a body that is the same temperature as the surrounding air. 2 heartless and cruel. **the cold shoulder** deliberately unfriendly behaviour. **cold sore** an inflamed blister near the mouth, caused by a virus. **cold snap** a brief period of cold weather. **cold turkey** unpleasant feelings experienced by someone who has suddenly stopped taking a drug to which they are addicted. **cold war** a state of hostility between the Soviet Union and its allies and the Western powers after the Second World War. **get cold feet** lose your nerve. **in cold blood** deliberately cruel.
■ **coldly** adverb **coldness** noun.

coleslaw noun a dish of shredded raw cabbage and carrots mixed with mayonnaise.

colic noun severe pain in the abdomen caused by wind or an obstruction in the intestines.
■ **colicky** adjective.

collaborate verb (**collaborates**, **collaborating**, **collaborated**) 1 work together on an activity. 2 cooperate with your country's enemy.
■ **collaboration** noun **collaborative** adjective **collaborator** noun.

collage /**kol**-lahzh/ noun a form of art in which various materials are arranged and stuck to a backing.

collagen noun a protein found in skin and bone.

collapse verb (**collapses**, **collapsing**,

THESAURUS

coil verb wind, loop, twist, curl, spiral, twine, wrap.

coin verb invent, create, make up, conceive, originate, think up, dream up.

coincide verb 1 *the events coincided:* occur simultaneously, happen together, co-occur, coexist. 2 *their interests do not always coincide:* tally, correspond, agree, accord, match up, be compatible, dovetail, mesh; informal square.
OPPOSITES differ.

coincidence noun accident, chance, providence, happenstance, fate, luck, fortune, fluke.

coincidental adjective accidental, chance, fluky, random, fortuitous.

cold adjective 1 *a cold day:* chilly, chill, cool, freezing, icy, wintry, frosty, bitter, raw; informal nippy; Brit. informal parky. 2 *a cold reception:* unfriendly, inhospitable,

unwelcoming, cool, frigid, frosty, distant, formal, stiff.
OPPOSITES hot, warm.

collaborate verb 1 *they collaborated on the project:* cooperate, join forces, work together, combine, pool resources, club together. 2 *they collaborated with the enemy:* fraternize, conspire, collude, cooperate, consort.

collaborator noun 1 *his collaborator on the book:* co-worker, partner, associate, colleague, confederate, assistant. 2 *a wartime collaborator:* sympathizer, traitor, quisling, fifth columnist.

collapse verb 1 *the roof collapsed:* cave in, fall in, subside, fall down, give (way), crumple, crumble, disintegrate. 2 *he collapsed last night:* faint, pass out, black out, lose consciousness. 3 *she collapsed in tears:* break down, go to pieces, be

C

collapsed) **1** suddenly fall down or give way. **2** fail and come to a sudden end. •noun **1** the falling down or giving way of a structure. **2** a sudden failure.

collapsible adjective able to be folded down.

collar noun **1** a band of material around the neck of a shirt or other garment. **2** a band put around the neck of a dog or cat. •verb informal seize someone.

collarbone noun either of the pair of bones joining the breastbone to the shoulder blades.

collate verb (**collates, collating, collated**) collect and combine documents or information.
■ collation noun.

collateral noun something that you promise to give to someone if you cannot repay a loan. •adjective additional but less important; secondary.

colleague noun a person that you work with.

collect verb **1** bring or gather things together. **2** come together and form a group. **3** go somewhere to fetch someone or something. **4** buy or find and keep items of a particular kind as a hobby.
■ collectable (or **collectible**) adjective collector noun.

collected adjective **1** calm. **2** brought together in one volume or edition.

collection noun **1** the action of collecting. **2** a group of things that have been collected. **3** a time when mail is picked up from a postbox, or when rubbish is taken away.

collective adjective **1** done by or belonging to all the members of a group. **2** taken as a whole. •noun a small business or project owned by all the people who work for it. ◻ collective noun a noun that refers to a group of people or things (e.g. *staff* or *herd*).
■ collectively adverb.

college noun **1** a place providing higher education or specialized training. **2** (in Britain) any of the independent institutions into which some universities are separated.

collegiate /kuh-**lee**-ji-uht/ adjective **1** having to do with a college or college students. **2** (of a university) composed of different colleges.

collide verb (**collides, colliding, collided**) move or bump into something.

collie noun (plural **collies**) a breed of sheepdog with long hair.

collier noun a coal miner.

colliery noun (plural **collieries**) a coal mine.

collision noun an instance when two or more things collide.

colloquial /kuh-**loh**-kwi-uhl/ adjective (of language) used in ordinary conversation.
■ colloquialism noun colloquially adverb.

colloquy /**kol**-luh-kwi/ noun (plural **colloquies**) formal a conference or conversation.

collude verb (**colludes, colluding, colluded**) make a secret plan with someone to do something illegal or dishonest.
■ collusion noun.

collywobbles plural noun informal anxiety or nervousness.

---

overcome; informal crack up. **4** *peace talks collapsed:* break down, fail, fall through, fold, founder; informal flop, fizzle out.
•noun **1** *the collapse of the roof:* cave-in, disintegration. **2** *the collapse of the talks:* breakdown, failure.

colleague noun co-worker, fellow worker, workmate, teammate, associate, partner, collaborator, ally, confederate.

collect verb **1** *he collected up the rubbish:* gather, accumulate, assemble, amass, stockpile, pile up, heap up, store (up), hoard, save. **2** *a crowd soon collected:* gather, assemble, meet, muster, congregate, convene, converge. **3** *I must collect the children:* fetch, pick up, go/come and get, call for, meet.
OPPOSITES distribute, disperse, deliver.

collected adjective calm, cool, self-possessed, self-controlled, composed, poised, serene, tranquil, relaxed; informal laid-back.
OPPOSITES excited, hysterical.

collection noun **1** *a collection of stolen items:* hoard, pile, heap, stock, store, stockpile, accumulation, reserve, supply, bank, pool, fund; informal stash. **2** *a collection of shoppers:* group, crowd, body, gathering, knot, cluster. **3** *a collection of short stories:* anthology, selection, compendium, compilation, miscellany. **4** *a collection for famine relief:* appeal; informal whip-round.

collective adjective common, shared, joint, combined, mutual, communal, pooled, united, allied, cooperative, collaborative.
OPPOSITES individual.

collide verb crash, hit, strike, run into, bump into.

collision noun crash, accident, smash; N. Amer. wreck; informal pile-up; Brit. informal shunt.

colloquial adjective informal, conversational, everyday, familiar, popular, casual, idiomatic, slangy, vernacular.
OPPOSITES formal.

cologne /kuh-**lohn**/ noun a type of light perfume.

Colombian noun a person from Colombia. ● adjective relating to Colombia.

colon[1] noun a punctuation mark (:) used before a list of items, a quotation, or an expansion or explanation.

colon[2] noun the main part of the large intestine, which leads to the rectum.
■ colonic adjective.

colonel /**ker**-nuhl/ noun a rank of officer in the army and in the US air force, above a lieutenant colonel.

colonial adjective having to do with a colony or with colonialism. ● noun a person who lives in a colony.

colonialism noun the practice of gaining control over other countries and occupying them with settlers.
■ colonialist noun & adjective.

colonist noun an inhabitant of a colony.

colonize or **colonise** verb (**colonizes, colonizing, colonized**) 1 make a colony in. 2 take over a place for your own use.
■ colonization noun.

colonnade noun a row of evenly spaced columns supporting a roof.

colony noun (plural **colonies**) 1 a country or area under the control of another country and occupied by settlers from that country. 2 a group of people of one nationality or race living in a foreign place. 3 a place where a group of people with a common interest live together. 4 a community of animals or plants living close together.

coloration or **colouration** noun the colours and markings of a plant or animal.

colossal adjective very large.
■ colossally adverb.

colossus /kuh-**loss**-uhss/ noun (plural **colossi** /kuh-**loss**-I/) a person or thing that is very important or large in size.

colostomy /kuh-**loss**-tuh-mi/ noun (plural **colostomies**) a surgical operation in which the colon is shortened and the cut end is moved to a new opening made in the wall of the abdomen.

colour (US spelling **color**) noun 1 an object's property of producing different sensations on the eye as a result of the way it reflects or gives out light. 2 one of the parts into which light can be separated. 3 the use of all colours in photography or television. 4 the natural colouring of the skin as an indication of someone's race. 5 redness of the complexion. 6 interest and excitement. ● verb 1 change the colour of something. 2 blush. 3 influence something.
▫ colour-blind not able to see certain colours.

coloured (US spelling **colored**) adjective 1 having a colour or colours. 2 offensive not having white skin. 3 (in South Africa) having parents who are of different races. ● noun 1 offensive a non-white person. 2 (in South Africa) a person with parents of different races.

colourful (US spelling **colorful**) adjective 1 having many or varied colours. 2 lively and exciting; vivid.
■ colourfully adverb.

colouring (US spelling **coloring**) noun 1 the process or art of applying colour. 2 visual appearance in terms of colour. 3 a substance used to colour something.

colourist (US spelling **colorist**) noun an artist or designer who uses colour in a special or skilful way.

colourless (US spelling **colorless**) adjective 1 without colour. 2 without character or interest; dull.

colt noun a young male horse.

coltish adjective energetic but awkward in movement or behaviour.

columbine noun a plant with purplish-blue flowers.

column noun 1 an upright pillar supporting a structure or standing alone as a

THESAURUS

colonize verb settle (in), people, populate, occupy, take over, invade.

colony noun territory, dependency, protectorate, satellite, settlement, outpost, province.

colossal adjective huge, massive, enormous, gigantic, giant, mammoth, vast, immense, monumental, mountainous; informal monster, whopping, humongous; Brit. informal ginormous.
OPPOSITES tiny.

colour noun 1 the lights changed colour: hue, shade, tint, tone, coloration. 2 oil colour: paint, pigment, colourant, dye, stain.

● verb 1 the wood was coloured blue: tint, dye, stain, tinge. 2 the experience coloured her outlook: influence, affect, taint, warp, skew, distort.

colourful adjective 1 a colourful picture: brightly coloured, vivid, vibrant, brilliant, radiant, gaudy, garish, multicoloured; informal jazzy. 2 a colourful account: vivid, graphic, lively, animated, dramatic, fascinating, interesting, stimulating, scintillating, evocative.
OPPOSITES drab, plain, boring.

column noun 1 arches supported by massive columns: pillar, post, support, upright, pier, pile. 2 a column in the paper: article, piece, monument. **2** a line of people or vehicles moving in the same direction. **3** a vertical division of a page or piece of writing. **4** a regular section of a newspaper or magazine on a particular subject or by a particular person.

columnist noun a journalist who writes a column in a newspaper or magazine.

coma noun a state of long-lasting deep unconsciousness.

Comanche /kuh-**man**-chi/ noun (plural **Comanche** or **Comanches**) a member of an American Indian people of the south-western US.

comatose adjective in a coma.

comb noun **1** an object with a row of narrow teeth, used for smoothing and neatening the hair. **2** a device for separating and smoothing the fibres of raw wool or cotton. **3** the red fleshy crest on the head of a chicken. •verb **1** neaten the hair with a comb. **2** search systematically through something. **3** prepare wool or cotton for manufacture with a comb.

combat noun fighting, especially between armed forces. •verb (**combats, combating, combated** or **combats, combatting, combatted**) take action to prevent something undesirable.

combatant noun a person or group that is fighting a battle or war.

combative adjective ready or eager to fight or argue.

combe /koom/ noun Brit. a short valley or hollow on a hillside or coastline.

combination noun **1** something that is made up of distinct parts. **2** the action of combining different things.
□ **combination lock** a lock that is opened using a sequence of letters or numbers.

combine verb /kuhm-**byn**/ (**combines, combining, combined**) **1** join or mix together. **2** join together to do something. •noun /**kom**-byn/ a group acting together for a commercial purpose.
□ **combine harvester** a farming machine that cuts a crop and separates out the grain in one process.

combust verb catch fire or burn.
■ **combustion** noun.

combustible adjective able to catch fire and burn easily.

come verb (**comes, coming, came**; past participle **come**) **1** move towards or into a place near to the speaker. **2** arrive. **3** happen; take place. **4** have or achieve a certain position. **5** be sold or available in a particular form. **6** (**coming**) likely to be successful in the future.
□ **come about** happen. **come across 1** give a particular impression. **2** meet or find by chance. **come by** manage to get. **come into** inherit. **come off** succeed. **come on 1** (of a state or condition) begin. **2** (also **come upon**) meet or find by chance. **come out 1** (of a fact) become known. **2** declare publicly that you are homosexual. **come round** Brit. **1** recover consciousness. **2** be converted to another person's opinion. **come to 1** recover consciousness. **2** (of an expense) amount to. **come up** happen.

comeback noun **1** a return to fame or

feature. **3** *we walked in a column:* line, file, queue, procession, convoy; informal crocodile.

comb verb **1** *she combed her hair:* groom, brush, untangle, smooth, straighten, neaten, tidy, arrange. **2** *police combed the area:* search, scour, explore, sweep.

combat noun *he was killed in combat:* battle, fighting, action, hostilities, conflict, war, warfare.
•verb *they tried to combat the disease:* fight, battle, tackle, attack, counter, resist.

combination noun mixture, mix, blend, fusion, amalgamation, amalgam, merger, marriage, synthesis.

combine verb **1** *he combines comedy with tragedy:* mix, blend, fuse, amalgamate, integrate, merge, marry. **2** *teachers combined to tackle the problem:* unite, collaborate, join forces, get together, team up.

come verb **1** *come and listen:* approach, advance, draw close/closer, draw near/nearer. **2** *they came last night:* arrive, get here/there, make it, appear, turn up,

materialize; informal show (up), roll up. **3** *they came to a stream:* reach, arrive at, get to, come across, run across, happen on, chance on, come upon, stumble on, end up at; informal wind up at. **4** *she comes from Belgium:* be from, be a native of, hail from, live in, reside in. **5** *attacks came without warning:* happen, occur, take place, come about, fall, crop up.
OPPOSITES go, leave.
□ **come about happen,** occur, take place, transpire, fall, arise. **come across meet,** run into, run across, come upon, chance on, stumble on, happen on, discover, encounter, find; informal bump into. **come on progress,** develop, shape up, take shape, come along, turn out, improve.

comeback noun return, recovery, resurgence, rally, upturn; Brit. fightback.

comedian noun **1** *a famous comedian:* comic, comedienne, funny man/woman, humorist, stand-up; N. Amer. tummler. **2** *Dad was such a comedian:* joker, wit, wag, comic, clown; informal laugh, hoot.

popularity. **2** informal a quick reply to a remark.

comedian noun (feminine **comedienne**) an entertainer whose act is intended to make people laugh.

comedown noun informal **1** a loss of status or importance. **2** a feeling of disappointment or depression.

comedy noun (plural **comedies**) **1** a film, play, or other entertainment intended to make people laugh. **2** a light-hearted play in which the characters find happiness after experiencing difficult situations.

comely /**kum**-li/ adjective old use pleasant to look at.

comestibles plural noun formal items of food.

comet noun a mass of ice and dust with a long tail, moving around the solar system.

comeuppance noun (**get your comeuppance**) informal get the punishment or fate that you deserve.

comfort noun **1** a pleasant state of ease and relaxation. **2** (**comforts**) things that contribute to comfort. **3** consolation for unhappiness or anxiety. • verb make someone less unhappy.
■ **comforter** noun.

comfortable adjective **1** giving or enjoying physical comfort. **2** free from financial worry. **3** (of a victory) easily achieved.
■ **comfortably** adverb.

comfrey /**kum**-fri/ noun (plural **comfreys**) a plant with clusters of purplish or white flowers.

comfy adjective (**comfier, comfiest**) informal comfortable.

comic adjective **1** making people laugh; amusing. **2** having to do with comedy.
• noun **1** a comedian. **2** a children's magazine that contains comic strips.
□ **comic strip** a sequence of drawings that tell an amusing story.

comical adjective causing laughter, especially through being ridiculous.
■ **comically** adverb.

comma noun a punctuation mark (,) showing a pause between parts of a sentence or separating items in a list.

command verb **1** give an order. **2** be in charge of a military unit. • noun **1** an order. **2** authority. **3** a group of officers in control of a particular group or operation. **4** the ability to use or control something. **5** an instruction which makes a computer carry out one of its basic functions.

commandant noun an officer in charge of a force or institution.

commandeer verb (**commandeers, commandeering, commandeered**) officially take possession of something for military purposes.

commander noun **1** a person in command.

THESAURUS

comedy noun the comedy in their work: humour, fun, hilarity, funny side, laughs, jokes.
OPPOSITES tragedy.

comfort noun **1** travel in comfort: ease, repose, luxury, prosperity. **2** words of comfort: consolation, condolence, sympathy, commiseration, support, reassurance, cheer.
OPPOSITES discomfort.
• verb a friend tried to comfort her: console, support, reassure, soothe, calm, cheer, hearten.
OPPOSITES distress, depress.

comfortable adjective **1** a comfortable lifestyle: pleasant, affluent, well-to-do, luxurious, opulent. **2** a comfortable room: cosy, snug, warm, pleasant, agreeable, homely; informal comfy. **3** comfortable clothes: loose, casual; informal comfy.
OPPOSITES hard, spartan, restricting.

comforting adjective soothing, reassuring, calming, heartening, cheering.
OPPOSITES upsetting.

comic adjective humorous, funny, amusing, hilarious, comical, zany, witty.
OPPOSITES serious.
• noun comedian, comedienne, funny man/woman, humorist, wit, joker.

comical adjective **1** he could be quite comical: funny, humorous, droll, witty, amusing, entertaining; informal wacky. **2** they look comical in those suits: silly, absurd, ridiculous, laughable, ludicrous, preposterous, foolish; informal crazy.
OPPOSITES serious, sensible.

coming adjective the coming election: forthcoming, imminent, impending, approaching.
• noun the coming of spring: approach, advance, advent, arrival, appearance, emergence.

command verb **1** he commanded his men to retreat: order, tell, direct, instruct, call on, require. **2** Jones commanded a tank squadron: be in charge of, be in command of, head, lead, control, direct, manage, supervise, oversee; informal head up.
• noun **1** officers shouted commands: order, instruction, direction. **2** he had 160 men under his command: authority, control, charge, power, direction, dominion, guidance, leadership, rule, government, management, supervision, jurisdiction. **3** a brilliant command of English: knowledge, mastery, grasp, comprehension, understanding.

commander noun leader, head, chief, overseer, director, controller; informal boss,

C

2 the rank of naval officer below captain. □ **commander-in-chief** (plural **commanders-in-chief**) an officer in charge of all of the armed forces of a country.

commanding adjective **1** having or showing authority. **2** having greater strength.

commandment noun a divine rule, especially one of the Ten Commandments.

commando noun (plural **commandos**) a soldier trained for carrying out raids.

commemorate verb (**commemorates, commemorating, commemorated**) honour the memory of.
■ **commemoration** noun **commemorative** adjective.

> ☑ the first *m* is double, but not the second: *commemorate*.

commence verb (**commences, commencing, commenced**) begin.

commencement noun the beginning of something.

commend verb **1** praise formally or officially. **2** recommend someone or something.
■ **commendation** noun.

commendable adjective deserving praise.
■ **commendably** adverb.

commensurable adjective formal able to be

measured by the same standard.

commensurate adjective (often **commensurate with**) matching something else in size, value, etc.

comment noun **1** a remark expressing an opinion or reaction. **2** discussion of an issue or event. •verb express an opinion or reaction.

commentary noun (plural **commentaries**) **1** a broadcast account of a sports match or other event as it happens. **2** the expression of opinions about an event or situation. **3** a set of explanatory notes on a written work.

commentate verb (**commentates, commentating, commentated**) give a commentary on an event.
■ **commentator** noun.

commerce noun the activity of buying and selling; trade.

commercial adjective **1** concerned with commerce. **2** making or intended to make a profit. •noun a television or radio advertisement.
■ **commercially** adverb.

commercialism noun emphasis on making as much profit as possible.

commercialize or **commercialise** verb (**commercializes, commercializing, commercialized**) manage something in a

skipper, head honcho; Brit. informal **gaffer**, guv'nor.

commanding adjective **dominant**, controlling, superior, powerful, advantageous, favourable.
OPPOSITES disadvantageous, weak.

commemorate verb **celebrate**, remember, recognize, acknowledge, observe, mark, pay tribute to, pay homage to, honour, salute.

commence verb **begin**, inaugurate, start, initiate, launch into, open, get the ball rolling, get going, get under way, get off the ground, set about, embark on; informal kick off.
OPPOSITES conclude.

commend verb **1** *we should commend him:* **praise**, compliment, congratulate, applaud, salute, honour, sing the praises of, pay tribute to. **2** *I commend her to you without reservation:* **recommend**, endorse, vouch for, speak for, support, back.
OPPOSITES criticize.

commendable adjective **admirable**, praiseworthy, creditable, laudable, meritorious, exemplary, honourable, respectable.
OPPOSITES reprehensible.

comment noun **1** *their comments on her appearance:* **remark**, observation,

statement, pronouncement, judgement, reflection, opinion, view. **2** *a great deal of comment:* **discussion**, debate, interest. **3** *a comment in the margin:* **note**, annotation, commentary, footnote, gloss, explanation.
•verb **1** *they commented on the food:* **remark on**, speak about, talk about, discuss, mention. **2** *'It will soon be night,' he commented:* **remark**, observe, say, state, note, point out; formal opine.

commentary noun **1** *the test match commentary:* **narration**, description, report, review, voice-over. **2** *textual commentary:* **explanation**, elucidation, interpretation, analysis, assessment, review, criticism, notes, comments.

commentator noun **1** *a sports commentator:* **reporter**, narrator, journalist, newscaster. **2** *a political commentator:* **analyst**, pundit, critic, columnist, leader-writer, opinion-former, monitor, observer.

commerce noun **trade**, trading, business, dealing, buying and selling, traffic, trafficking.

commercial adjective **1** *a vessel built for commercial purposes:* **trade**, trading, business, mercantile, sales. **2** *a commercial organization:* **profit-making**, materialistic, mercenary.
OPPOSITES non-profit-making.

way designed to make a profit.
■ commercialization noun.

commiserate verb (**commiserates, commiserating, commiserated**) express sympathy or pity; sympathize.
■ commiseration noun.

commissar noun an official of the Communist Party responsible for political education.

commission noun 1 an instruction, command, or duty. 2 a formal request for something to be produced. 3 a group of people given official authority to do something. 4 payment made to someone for selling goods or services. 5 the position of officer in the armed forces. • verb 1 order something to be made or produced. 2 bring something into working order. 3 (**commissioned**) having the rank of a military officer.
□ out of commission not in working order.

commissionaire noun Brit. a uniformed door attendant at a hotel, theatre, etc.

commissioner noun 1 a member of an official commission. 2 a representative of the highest authority in an area.

commit verb (**commits, committing, committed**) 1 do something wrong or bad. 2 set aside something for a particular use. 3 (**commit yourself**) say that you will definitely do something. 4 put something in a safe place. 5 send someone to prison or a psychiatric hospital.

commitment noun 1 the time, work, and loyalty that someone devotes to a cause, activity, or job. 2 a promise. 3 an engagement or duty that limits your freedom of action.

☑ there's a single *t* in the middle: commitment.

committal noun the sending of someone to prison or a psychiatric hospital, or for trial.

committed adjective devoting a lot of time and hard work to a cause, activity, or job.

committee noun a group of people appointed for a particular function by a larger group.

☑ double *m*, double *t*: committee.

commode noun a piece of furniture containing a concealed chamber pot.

commodious adjective formal roomy and comfortable.

commodity noun (plural **commodities**) 1 a raw material or agricultural product that can be bought and sold. 2 something useful or valuable.

commodore noun 1 the naval rank above captain. 2 the president of a yacht club.

common adjective (**commoner, commonest**) 1 happening, found, or done often; not rare. 2 without special qualities or position; ordinary. 3 of the most familiar type. 4 shared by two or more people or things. 5 belonging to or affecting the whole of a community. 6 Brit. not well mannered or tasteful, in a way supposedly typical of lower-class people. • noun 1 a piece of open land for the public to use. 2 (**the Commons**) the House of Commons.
□ common denominator 1 Maths a number that can be divided exactly by all the numbers below the line in a set of

THESAURUS

commission noun 1 *the dealer's commission:* percentage, share, premium, fee, bonus, royalty; informal cut, rake-off, slice; Brit. informal whack. 2 *a commission to design a monument:* contract, engagement, assignment, booking, job. 3 *an independent commission:* committee, board, council, panel, body.
• verb 1 *he was commissioned to paint a portrait:* engage, contract, book, employ, hire, recruit, take on, retain, appoint. 2 *they commissioned a sculpture:* order.

commit verb 1 *he committed a murder:* carry out, do, perpetrate, engage in, execute, accomplish, be responsible for; informal pull off. 2 *she was committed to their care:* entrust, consign, assign, deliver, hand over. 3 *the judge committed him to prison:* consign, send, confine.

commitment noun 1 *the pressure of his commitments:* responsibility, obligation, duty, liability, engagement, tie. 2 *her commitment to her students:* dedication, devotion, allegiance, loyalty. 3 *he made a*

commitment: promise, vow, pledge, undertaking.

committed adjective devoted, dedicated, staunch, loyal, faithful, devout, firm, steadfast, unwavering, passionate, ardent, sworn.
OPPOSITES apathetic.

common adjective 1 *a common occurrence:* frequent, regular, everyday, normal, usual, ordinary, familiar, standard, commonplace. 2 *a common belief:* widespread, general, universal, popular, mainstream, prevalent, rife, established, conventional, accepted. 3 *the common people:* ordinary, normal, average, unexceptional, typical, simple. 4 *the common good:* collective, communal, shared, community, public, popular, general. 5 *she's so common:* uncouth, vulgar, coarse, rough, uncivilized, unsophisticated, unrefined, inferior, plebeian; informal plebby.
OPPOSITES unusual, rare, individual, refined.

fractions. **2** a feature shared by all members of a group. **the common market** the European Union. **common** noun a noun referring to a class of things (e.g. *plant*, *sea*) as opposed to a particular person or thing. **common or garden** Brit. informal of the usual or ordinary type. **common room** a room in a school or college for students or staff to use outside teaching hours. **common sense** good sense and judgement in practical matters. **in common** shared.
■ **commonly** adverb.

commoner noun an ordinary person as opposed to an aristocrat.

commonplace adjective ordinary. • noun a remark that is not new or interesting.

commonsensical adjective having common sense.

commonwealth noun **1** (**the Commonwealth**) an association consisting of the UK together with countries that used to be part of the British Empire. **2** an independent state or community.

commotion noun a state of confused and noisy disturbance.

communal adjective shared or done by all members of a community.
■ **communally** adverb.

commune¹ /**kom**-myoon/ noun a group of people living together and sharing possessions.

commune² /kuh-**myoon**/ verb (**communes**, **communing**, **communed**) (**commune with**) share your intimate thoughts or feelings with.

communicable adjective (of a disease) able to be passed on to other people.

communicant noun a person who receives

Holy Communion.

communicate verb (**communicates**, **communicating**, **communicated**) **1** share or exchange information or ideas. **2** pass on or convey an emotion, disease, etc. **3** (**communicating**) (of two rooms) having a connecting door.

communication noun **1** the action of communicating. **2** a letter or message. **3** (**communications**) means of sending information or travelling.

communicative adjective willing or eager to talk or pass on information.

communion noun **1** the sharing of intimate thoughts and feelings. **2** (also **Holy Communion**) the service of Christian worship at which bread and wine are made holy and shared; the Eucharist.

communiqué /kuh-**myoo**-ni-kay/ noun an official announcement or statement.

communism noun **1** a political system in which all property is owned by the community. **2** a system of this kind based on Marxism.
■ **communist** noun & adjective.

community noun (plural **communities**) **1** a group of people living together in one place or having the same religion, race, etc. **2** (**the community**) the people of an area or country considered as a group. □ **community service** socially useful work that an offender is sentenced to do instead of going to prison.

commute verb (**commutes**, **commuting**, **commuted**) **1** regularly travel some distance between your home and place of work. **2** reduce a sentence given to an

THESAURUS

commonplace adjective. See **COMMON** sense 1.

common sense noun good sense, native wit, good judgement, level-headedness, prudence, wisdom; informal horse sense, nous; Brit. informal common; N. Amer. informal smarts.
OPPOSITES stupidity.

commotion noun disturbance, uproar, disorder, confusion, rumpus, fuss, furore, hue and cry, stir, storm, chaos, havoc, pandemonium.

communal adjective **1** *a communal kitchen:* shared, joint, common. **2** *they farm on a communal basis:* collective, cooperative, community.
OPPOSITES private, individual.

communicate verb **1** *they communicate daily:* liaise, be in touch, be in contact, have dealings, talk, speak. **2** *Jatinder communicated the news to his boss:* convey, tell, relay, transmit, impart, pass on, report,

recount, relate. **3** *the disease is communicated easily:* transmit, spread, transfer, pass on.

communication noun **1** *there was no communication between them:* contact, dealings, relations, connection, correspondence, dialogue, conversation. **2** *an official communication:* message, statement, announcement, report, dispatch, bulletin, disclosure, communiqué, letter, correspondence.

communicative adjective forthcoming, expansive, expressive, unreserved, vocal, outgoing, frank, open, candid, talkative, chatty.
OPPOSITES uncommunicative.

communist noun & adjective collectivist, Bolshevik, Marxist, Maoist, Soviet; informal, disapproving Commie, red.

community noun society, population, populace, people, public, residents, inhabitants, citizens.

c

offender to a less severe one.
■ **commuter** noun.

compact[1] adjective /kuhm-**pakt**/ **1** closely and neatly packed together; dense.
2 having all the necessary parts fitted into a small space. • verb /kuhm-**pakt**/ press something together into a small space.
• noun /**kom**-pakt/ a small case containing face powder, a mirror, and a powder puff.
□ **compact disc** a small disc on which music or other digital information is stored.

compact[2] /**kom**-pakt/ noun a formal agreement between two or more parties.

companion noun **1** a person that you spend time or travel with. **2** each of a pair of things intended to match each other, or that can be used together.
■ **companionship** noun.

companionable adjective friendly and sociable.
■ **companionably** adverb.

company noun (plural **companies**) **1** a commercial business. **2** the fact of being with other people. **3** a guest or guests. **4** a number of people gathered together. **5** a unit of soldiers. **6** a group of actors, singers, or dancers who perform together.

comparable adjective similar to someone or something else and able to be compared.
■ **comparably** adverb.

comparative adjective **1** measured or judged by comparing one thing with another. **2** involving comparison between two or more subjects. **3** (of an adjective or adverb) expressing a higher degree of a quality, but not the highest possible (e.g. *braver*).
■ **comparatively** adverb.

☑ compar*ative*, not *-itive*.

compare verb (**compares**, **comparing**, **compared**) **1** (often **compare something to** or **with**) estimate or measure the ways in which one person or thing is similar to or unlike another. **2** (**compare something to**) point out the ways in which one person or thing is similar to another. **3** (usu. **compare with**) be similar to another thing or person.

comparison noun **1** the action of comparing. **2** the quality of being similar.

compartment noun a separate section of a structure or container.

compartmentalize or **compartmentalise** verb (**compartmentalizes**, **compartmentalizing**, **compartmentalized**) divide into categories or sections.

compass noun **1** an instrument containing a pointer which shows the direction of magnetic north. **2** (also **compasses**) an instrument for drawing circles, consisting of two arms linked by a movable joint. **3** range or scope.

compassion noun sympathetic pity and

THESAURUS

compact[1] adjective **1** *extremely compact rugs:* dense, tightly packed, compressed, thick, tight, firm, solid. **2** *a very compact phone:* neat, small, handy, petite. **3** *her tale is compact and readable:* concise, succinct, condensed, brief, pithy, to the point, short and sweet; informal snappy.
OPPOSITES loose, bulky, lengthy.
• verb *the rubbish is then compacted:* compress, condense, pack down, tamp (down), flatten.

compact[2] noun *the warring states signed a compact:* treaty, pact, accord, agreement, contract, bargain, deal, settlement.

companion noun comrade, fellow ..., partner, associate, escort, compatriot, confederate, friend; informal pal, chum, crony; Brit. informal mate; N. Amer. informal buddy.

company noun **1** *an oil company:* firm, business, corporation, establishment, agency, office, house, institution, concern, enterprise, consortium, syndicate; informal outfit. **2** *I enjoy his company:* companionship, fellowship, society, presence. **3** *a company of infantry:* unit, section, detachment, corps, squad, platoon.

comparable adjective **1** *comparable incomes:* similar, close, near, approximate, equivalent, proportionate. **2** *nobody is comparable with him:* equal to, as good as, in the same league as, on a level with, a match for.
OPPOSITES incomparable.

compare verb **1** *we compared the two portraits:* contrast, balance, set against, weigh up. **2** *he was compared to Wagner:* liken, equate, class with, bracket with. **3** *the porcelain compares with Dresden china:* be as good as, be comparable to, bear comparison with, be the equal of, match up to, be on a par with, be in the same league as, come close to, rival.

comparison noun *there's no comparison between them:* resemblance, likeness, similarity, correspondence.

compartment noun bay, locker, recess, alcove, cell, cubicle, pod, pigeonhole, cubbyhole.

compass noun scope, range, extent, reach, span, breadth, ambit, limits, parameters, bounds.

compassion noun sympathy, empathy, understanding, fellow feeling, pity, care, concern, sensitivity, kindness.
OPPOSITES indifference, cruelty.

concern for the sufferings of other people.

compassionate adjective feeling or showing compassion.
■ **compassionately** adverb.

compatible adjective **1** able to exist or be used together. **2** (of two people) able to have a good relationship; well suited. **3** (usu. **compatible with**) consistent or in keeping.
■ **compatibility** noun.

☑ compat*ible*, not -*able*.

compatriot noun a person from the same country; a fellow citizen.

compel verb (**compels, compelling, compelled**) **1** force someone to do something. **2** make something happen.

compelling adjective powerfully gaining people's attention or admiration.
■ **compellingly** adverb.

compendium noun (plural **compendiums** or **compendia**) **1** a collection of information about a subject. **2** a collection of similar items.

compensate verb (**compensates, compensating, compensated**) **1** give someone something to reduce or balance

the bad effect of loss, suffering, or injury.
2 (**compensate for**) reduce or balance something bad by having an opposite force or effect.
■ **compensatory** adjective.

compensation noun **1** something given to compensate for loss, suffering, or injury. **2** something that compensates for something bad.

compère /**kom**-pair/ Brit. noun a person who introduces the different acts that are performing in one show. •verb (**compères, compèring, compèred**) act as a compère for.

compete verb (**competes, competing, competed**) try to gain or win something by defeating other people.

competent adjective **1** having the necessary skill or knowledge to do something successfully. **2** satisfactory, though not outstanding.
■ **competence** (or **competency**) noun **competently** adverb.

competition noun **1** the activity of competing against other people. **2** an event or contest in which people compete. **3** the person or people that you are competing against.

competitive adjective **1** involving

compassionate adjective sympathetic, understanding, pitying, caring, sensitive, warm, loving, kind.
OPPOSITES unsympathetic, uncaring.

compatible adjective well matched, (well) suited, like-minded, in tune, in harmony, in keeping, consistent, consonant; informal on the same wavelength.
OPPOSITES incompatible.

compel verb force, pressure, coerce, dragoon, press, push, oblige, require, make; informal lean on, railroad, put the screws on.

compelling adjective **1** *a compelling performance*: enthralling, captivating, gripping, riveting, spellbinding, mesmerizing, absorbing. **2** *a compelling argument*: convincing, persuasive, cogent, irresistible, powerful, strong.
OPPOSITES boring, weak.

compensate verb **1** *we agreed to compensate him for his loss*: recompense, repay, pay back, reimburse, remunerate, indemnify. **2** *his flair compensated for his faults*: balance (out), counterbalance, counteract, offset, make up for, cancel out.

compensation noun recompense, repayment, reimbursement, remuneration, redress, amends, damages; N. Amer. informal comp.

compete verb **1** *they competed in a tennis tournament*: take part, participate, be a contestant, play, enter, go in for. **2** *they had to compete with other firms*: contend, vie,

battle, jockey, go head to head, pit yourself against, challenge, take on.

competence noun **1** *my technical competence*: ability, capability, proficiency, accomplishment, expertise, skill, prowess; informal know-how. **2** *the competence of the system*: adequacy, suitability, fitness.
OPPOSITES incompetence.

competent adjective **1** *a competent carpenter*: able, capable, proficient, adept, accomplished, skilful, skilled, expert. **2** *the court was not competent to hear the case*: fit, suitable, suited, appropriate, qualified, empowered, authorized.
OPPOSITES incompetent, unfit.

competition noun **1** *Stephanie won the competition*: contest, tournament, championship. **2** *I'm not interested in competition*: rivalry, competitiveness, conflict; informal keeping up with the Joneses. **3** *we must stay ahead of the competition*: opposition, rivals, other side, field, enemy; informal other guy.

competitive adjective **1** *a competitive player*: ambitious, zealous, keen, combative, aggressive; informal go-ahead. **2** *a highly competitive industry*: ruthless, aggressive, fierce, cut-throat; informal dog-eat-dog. **3** *competitive prices*: reasonable, moderate, keen, low, cheap, budget, bargain, rock-bottom, bargain-basement.
OPPOSITES apathetic, exorbitant.

competition. **2** strongly wanting to be more successful than other people. **3** as good as or better than others of a similar nature.
■ **competitively** adverb.

competitor noun **1** a person who takes part in a sports contest. **2** an organization that competes with others in business.

compilation noun **1** a book, record, etc. compiled from different sources. **2** the process of compiling something.

compile verb (**compiles, compiling, compiled**) produce a book, record, etc. by bringing together material from different sources.
■ **compiler** noun.

complacent adjective smugly satisfied with yourself.
■ **complacency** noun **complacently** adverb.

complain verb **1** express dissatisfaction or annoyance. **2** (**complain of**) state that you are suffering from a particular symptom.

complainant noun Law a plaintiff.

complaint noun **1** an act of complaining. **2** a reason to be dissatisfied. **3** a minor illness or medical condition.

complaisant /kuhm-**play**-z'nt/ adjective willing to please other people or to accept their behaviour without protest.

complement noun /**kom**-pli-muhnt/ **1** a thing that contributes extra features to something else so as to improve it. **2** the number or quantity that makes something complete. **3** Grammar a word or words used with a verb to complete the meaning (e.g. *happy* in *we are happy*). • verb /**kom**-pli-ment/ add to something in a way that improves it.

> **!** don't confuse **complement** and **compliment**. **Complement** means 'add to something in a way that improves it', while **compliment** means 'politely congratulate or praise'.

complementary adjective combining so as to form a complete whole or to improve each other's qualities.
■ **complementary medicine** medical therapy that is not part of scientific medicine, e.g. acupuncture.

complete adjective **1** having all the necessary parts. **2** having run its course; finished. **3** to the greatest extent or degree; total. **4** skilled at every aspect of an activity. • verb (**completes, completing, completed**) **1** finish making or doing something. **2** make something complete. **3** write the required information on a form.
■ **completely** adverb **completion** noun.

complex adjective **1** consisting of many

THESAURUS

competitor noun **1** *the competitors in the race:* contestant, contender, challenger, participant, entrant, player. **2** *our European competitors:* rival, challenger, opponent, competition, opposition.
OPPOSITES partner, teammate, ally.

compile verb assemble, put together, make up, collate, compose, organize, arrange, gather, collect.

complacency noun smugness, self-satisfaction, self-congratulation, self-regard.

complacent adjective smug, self-satisfied, self-congratulatory, resting on your laurels.

complain verb protest, grumble, whine, bleat, carp, cavil, grouse, make a fuss, object, find fault; informal whinge, gripe, moan, bitch.

complaint noun **1** *they lodged a complaint:* protest, objection, grievance, grouse, grumble, criticism; informal gripe, whinge. **2** *a kidney complaint:* disorder, disease, illness, sickness, ailment, infection, condition, problem, upset, trouble.

complement noun **1** *the perfect complement to the food:* accompaniment, companion, addition, supplement, accessory, finishing touch. **2** *a full complement of lifeboats:* amount, contingent, capacity, allowance, quota.

OPPOSITES contrast.
• verb *this sauce complements the dessert:* accompany, go with, round off, set off, suit, harmonize with, enhance, complete.
OPPOSITES contrast with.

complementary adjective harmonious, compatible, corresponding, matching, reciprocal.
OPPOSITES incompatible.

complete adjective **1** *the complete text:* entire, whole, full, total, uncut, unabridged, unexpurgated. **2** *their research was complete:* finished, ended, concluded, completed; informal wrapped up, sewn up. **3** *a complete fool:* absolute, utter, out-and-out, total, downright, prize, perfect, unqualified, unmitigated, sheer; N. Amer. full-bore.
OPPOSITES partial, unfinished.
• verb **1** *he had to complete his training:* finish, end, conclude, finalize, wind up; informal wrap up. **2** *the outfit was completed with a veil:* finish off, round off, top off, crown, cap. **3** *complete the application form:* fill in/out, answer.

completely adverb totally, entirely, wholly, thoroughly, fully, utterly, absolutely, perfectly, downright.

complex adjective **1** *a complex structure:* compound, composite, multiplex. **2** *a*

C

different and connected parts. **2** not easy to understand; complicated. •**noun 1** a group of similar buildings or facilities on the same site. **2** a network of linked things. **3** a group of subconscious ideas or feelings that influence a person's mental state or behaviour.

■ **complexity** noun (plural **complexities**).

complexion noun **1** the natural condition of the skin of a person's face. **2** the general character of something.

compliance noun the action of complying.

compliant adjective **1** meeting rules or standards. **2** too ready to do what other people want.

complicate verb (**complicates, complicating, complicated**) make something less easy to understand or deal with.

complicated adjective **1** consisting of many connected elements; intricate. **2** involving many different and confusing aspects.

complication noun **1** a circumstance that complicates something; a difficulty. **2** an involved or confused state. **3** an extra disease or condition which makes an existing one worse.

complicit adjective involved with other people in an unlawful activity.

complicity noun involvement with other people in an unlawful activity.

compliment noun /kom-pli-muhnt/ **1** a remark that expresses praise or admiration. **2** (**compliments**) formal greetings. •**verb** /kom-pli-ment/ politely congratulate or praise.

> ! don't confuse **compliment** and **complement**: see the note at COMPLEMENT.

complimentary adjective **1** praising or approving. **2** given free of charge.

comply verb (**complies, complying, complied**) (**comply with**) **1** do what someone wants or tells you to do. **2** meet specified standards.

component noun a part of a larger whole.

comport verb (**comport yourself**) formal behave in a particular way.

compose verb (**composes, composing, composed**) **1** make up a whole. **2** create a work of art, especially music or poetry. **3** arrange in an orderly or artistic way. **4** (**composed**) calm and in control of your feelings.

■ **composer** noun.

complex situation: complicated, involved, intricate, convoluted, elaborate, difficult; Brit. informal fiddly.
OPPOSITES simple.
•**noun 1** *a complex of roads*: network, system, nexus, web. **2** (informal) *he had a complex about losing his hair*: obsession, fixation, preoccupation, neurosis; informal hang-up, thing.

complexion noun **1** *a pale complexion*: skin, skin colour/tone, colouring. **2** *governments of all complexions*: kind, nature, character, colour, persuasion, outlook.

complicate verb make (more) difficult, make complicated, mix up, confuse, muddle, compound.
OPPOSITES simplify.

complicated adjective **1** *a complicated stereo system*: compound, composite, multiplex. **2** *a long and complicated saga*: involved, intricate, complex, convoluted, elaborate, difficult; Brit. informal fiddly.
OPPOSITES simple, straightforward.

complication noun difficulty, problem, obstacle, hurdle, stumbling block, snag, catch, hitch; Brit. spanner in the works; informal headache.

compliment noun *an unexpected compliment*: tribute, accolade, pat on the back, commendation; (**compliments**) praise, acclaim, congratulations, admiration, flattery.

OPPOSITES criticism, insult.
•**verb** *they complimented him on his performance*: praise, pay tribute to, flatter, commend, acclaim, applaud, salute, congratulate.
OPPOSITES criticize.

complimentary adjective **1** *complimentary remarks*: flattering, appreciative, congratulatory, admiring, approving, favourable, glowing. **2** *complimentary tickets*: free (of charge), gratis, donated, courtesy; informal on the house.
OPPOSITES critical.

comply verb obey, observe, abide by, adhere to, conform to, follow, respect, go along with.
OPPOSITES disobey.

component noun part, piece, bit, element, constituent, ingredient, unit, module.

compose verb **1** *a poem composed by Shelley*: write, devise, make up, think up, produce, invent, pen, author. **2** *how to compose a photograph*: organize, arrange, construct, set out. **3** *the congress is composed of ten senators*: make up, constitute, form, comprise.
□ **compose yourself calm down**, control yourself, regain your composure, pull yourself together, steady yourself; informal get a grip.

composed adjective calm, collected, cool (as a cucumber), self-possessed, poised, serene, relaxed, at ease, unruffled,

C

composite /kom-puh-zit/ adjective made up of several parts. ● noun a thing made up of several parts.

composition noun 1 the way in which something is made up. 2 a work of music, literature, or art. 3 an essay written by a school pupil. 4 the action of composing.

compositor noun a person who arranges type or keys material for printing.

compos mentis /kom-poss **men**-tiss/ adjective having full control of your mind.

compost noun decayed organic material added to soil as a fertilizer.

composure noun the state of being calm and self-controlled.

compote /kom-poht/ noun fruit preserved or cooked in syrup.

compound¹ noun /kom-pownd/ 1 a thing made up of two or more separate elements. 2 a substance formed from two or more elements chemically united in fixed proportions. ● adjective /kom-pownd/ made up or consisting of several parts. ● verb /kuhm-**pownd**/ 1 make up a whole from several elements. 2 make something bad worse.
□ compound fracture an injury in which a broken bone pierces the skin.

compound² /kom-pownd/ noun a large open area enclosed by a fence.

comprehend verb understand something.

comprehensible adjective able to be understood.

comprehension noun 1 the action of understanding. 2 the ability to understand.

comprehensive adjective 1 including or dealing with all or nearly all aspects of something. 2 Brit. (of secondary education) in which children of all abilities are educated in one school. 3 (of a victory or defeat) by a large margin. ● noun Brit. a comprehensive school.
■ comprehensively adverb.

compress verb /kuhm-**press**/ 1 flatten by pressure; force into less space. 2 squeeze or press two things together. 3 alter the form of computer data so that it takes up less space on a disk or magnetic tape. ● noun /kom-press/ an absorbent pad pressed on to part of the body to relieve inflammation or stop bleeding.
■ compression noun.

compressor noun a machine used to supply air at increased pressure.

comprise verb (comprises, comprising, comprised) 1 be made up of; consist of. 2 (also be comprised of) make up a whole.

compromise noun 1 an agreement reached

THESAURUS

unperturbed; informal unflappable, together, laid-back.
OPPOSITES excited.

composition noun 1 the composition of the council: make-up, constitution, configuration, structure, formation, anatomy, organization. 2 a literary composition: work (of art), creation, opus, piece. 3 the composition of a poem: writing, creation, formulation, compilation. 4 a school composition: essay, paper, study, piece of writing; N. Amer. theme. 5 the composition of the painting: arrangement, layout, proportions, balance, symmetry.

compound noun a compound of two materials: amalgam, blend, mixture, mix, alloy.
● adjective the compound eye of a wasp: composite, complex, multiple.
OPPOSITES simple.
● verb 1 soap compounded with disinfectant: mix, combine, blend. 2 his illness compounds their problems: aggravate, exacerbate, worsen, add to, augment, intensify, heighten, increase.
OPPOSITES separate, alleviate.

comprehend verb understand, grasp, see, take in, follow, make sense of, fathom; informal work out, figure out, get.

comprehensible adjective intelligible, understandable, accessible, self-explanatory, clear, plain, straightforward.

comprehension noun understanding, grasp, mastery, conception, knowledge, awareness.
OPPOSITES ignorance.

comprehensive adjective inclusive, all-inclusive, complete, thorough, full, extensive, all-embracing, blanket, exhaustive, detailed, sweeping, wholesale, broad, wide-ranging.
OPPOSITES limited.

compress verb 1 it is coconut compressed into a slab: squeeze, press, squash, crush, compact. 2 the material has been compressed into 17 pages: shorten, abridge, condense, abbreviate, contract, telescope, summarize, precis.
OPPOSITES expand, pad out.

comprise verb 1 the country comprises twenty states: consist of, be made up of, be composed of, contain. 2 this breed comprises half the herd: make up, constitute, form, account for.

compromise noun they reached a compromise: agreement, understanding, settlement, terms, deal, trade-off, bargain, middle ground.
OPPOSITES intransigence.
● verb 1 we compromised: meet each other halfway, come to an understanding, make a deal, make concessions, find a happy medium, strike a balance. 2 his actions could compromise his reputation:

C

by each side giving way on some points. **2** something that is midway between different or conflicting elements: *a compromise between price and quality of output.* • verb (**compromises, compromising, compromised**) **1** give way on some points in order to settle a dispute. **2** accept something that is less good than you would like. **3** cause someone danger or embarrassment by behaving in an indiscreet or reckless way.

comptroller /kuhn-**troh**-ler, komp-**troh**-ler/ noun a person in charge of the financial affairs of an organization.

compulsion noun **1** pressure to do something. **2** an irresistible urge to do something.

compulsive adjective **1** done because of an irresistible urge. **2** unable to stop yourself doing something. **3** irresistibly exciting.
■ **compulsively** adverb.

compulsory adjective required by law or a rule; obligatory.

compunction noun a feeling of guilt about doing something wrong.

computation noun **1** mathematical calculation. **2** the use of computers.
■ **computational** adjective.

compute verb (**computes, computing, computed**) calculate a figure or amount.

computer noun an electronic device capable of storing and processing information according to a set of instructions.
■ **computing** noun.

computerize or **computerise** verb

(**computerizes, computerizing, computerized**) convert to a system controlled by or stored on computer.

comrade noun **1** (among men) a person who shares your activities or is a fellow member of an organization. **2** a fellow soldier.
■ **comradeship** noun.

con[1] informal verb (**cons, conning, conned**) deceive someone into doing or believing something. • noun a deception of this kind.
□ **con man** a man who cheats people after gaining their trust.

con[2] noun (usu. in **pros and cons**) a disadvantage of or argument against something.

concatenation noun a series of interconnected things.

concave adjective having an outline or surface that curves inwards.
■ **concavity** noun.

conceal verb **1** stop someone or something being seen. **2** keep something secret.
■ **concealment** noun.

concede verb (**concedes, conceding, conceded**) **1** finally admit that something is true. **2** give up a possession, advantage, or right. **3** admit defeat in a match or contest. **4** fail to prevent an opponent scoring a goal or point.

conceit noun **1** too much pride in yourself. **2** an artistic effect. **3** a complicated metaphor.

conceited adjective too proud of yourself.

conceivable adjective able to be imagined

THESAURUS

undermine, weaken, damage, harm, jeopardize, prejudice.
compulsion noun **1** *he is under no compulsion to go:* obligation, pressure, coercion. **2** *a compulsion to tell the truth:* urge, impulse, need, desire, drive, obsession, fixation, addiction.
compulsive adjective **1** *a compulsive desire:* irresistible, uncontrollable, compelling, overwhelming. **2** *compulsive eating:* obsessive, obsessional, addictive, uncontrollable. **3** *a compulsive liar:* inveterate, chronic, incorrigible, incurable, hopeless, persistent, habitual; informal pathological. **4** *it's compulsive viewing:* fascinating, compelling, gripping, riveting, engrossing, enthralling, captivating.
compulsory adjective obligatory, mandatory, required, requisite, necessary, binding, enforced, prescribed.
OPPOSITES optional.
compute verb calculate, work out, reckon, determine, evaluate, add up, total.
comrade noun companion, friend,

colleague, associate, partner, ally; Brit. informal mate; N. Amer. informal buddy.

conceal verb **1** *clouds concealed the sun:* hide, screen, cover, obscure, block out, blot out, mask. **2** *he concealed his true feelings:* keep secret, hide, disguise, mask, veil, bottle up; informal keep a/the lid on.
OPPOSITES reveal, confess.

concede verb **1** *I had to concede that I'd overreacted:* admit, acknowledge, accept, allow, grant, recognize, own, confess, agree. **2** *he eventually conceded the title:* surrender, yield, give up, relinquish, hand over.
OPPOSITES deny, retain.

conceit noun vanity, pride, arrogance, egotism, self-importance, narcissism, self-admiration.
OPPOSITES humility.

conceited adjective vain, proud, arrogant, egotistic, self-satisfied, self-important, narcissistic, full of yourself; informal big-headed, stuck-up.

C

or understood.
- **conceivably** adverb.

conceive verb (**conceives, conceiving, conceived**) **1** become pregnant with a child. **2** form an idea in your mind.

> ☑ *i* before *e* except after *c*: conce*i*ve.

concentrate verb (**concentrates, concentrating, concentrated**) **1** focus all your attention on something. **2** gather together in numbers or a mass at one point. **3** (**concentrated**) (of a solution) strong. • noun a concentrated substance or solution.

concentration noun **1** the action or power of concentrating. **2** a close gathering of people or things. **3** the amount of a particular substance in a solution or mixture.
- **concentration camp** a camp for holding political prisoners.

concentric adjective (of circles or arcs) sharing the same centre.

concept noun an abstract idea.

conception noun **1** the conceiving of a child. **2** the forming of a plan or idea. **3** an idea or concept. **4** ability to imagine or understand.

conceptual adjective having to do with concepts.
- **conceptually** adverb.

conceptualize or **conceptualise** verb (**conceptualizes, conceptualizing, conceptualized**) form an idea of something in your mind.

concern verb **1** relate to; be about. **2** affect or involve. **3** make someone worried. • noun **1** worry; anxiety. **2** a matter of interest or importance. **3** a business.

concerned adjective worried.

concerning preposition about.

concert noun a musical performance given in public.
- **in concert** acting together.

concerted adjective **1** jointly arranged or carried out. **2** done in a determined way.

concertina noun a small musical instrument which you play by stretching and squeezing it and pressing buttons. • verb (**concertinas, concertinaing, concertinaed**) compress in folds like those of a concertina.

concerto /kuhn-**cher**-toh/ noun (plural **concertos** or **concerti** /kuhn-**cher**-ti/) a musical work for an orchestra and one or more solo instruments.

THESAURUS

conceive verb **1** *the project was conceived in 1977:* think up, think of, dream up, devise, formulate, design, create, develop. **2** *I could hardly conceive what it must be like:* imagine, envisage, visualize, picture, grasp, appreciate.

concentrate verb **1** *the government concentrated its efforts on staying in power:* focus, direct, centre. **2** *she concentrated on the film:* focus on, pay attention to, keep your mind on, be absorbed in, be engrossed in, be immersed in. **3** *troops concentrated on the horizon:* collect, gather, congregate, converge, mass, rally.
OPPOSITES disperse.

concentrated adjective **1** *a concentrated effort:* strenuous, concerted, intensive, all-out, intense. **2** *a concentrated solution:* condensed, reduced, undiluted, strong.
OPPOSITES half-hearted, diluted.

concentration noun close attention, attentiveness, application, single-mindedness, absorption.
OPPOSITES inattention.

concept noun idea, notion, conception, abstraction, theory, hypothesis.

conception noun **1** *the fertility treatment resulted in conception:* pregnancy, fertilization, impregnation, insemination. **2** *the product's conception:* inception, genesis, origination, creation, invention, beginning, origin. **3** *his original conception:*
plan, idea, notion, scheme, project, proposal, intention, aim.

concern verb **1** *the report concerns the war:* be about, deal with, cover, relate to, pertain to. **2** *that doesn't concern you:* affect, involve, be relevant to, apply to, have a bearing on, impact on. **3** *one thing still concerns me:* worry, disturb, trouble, bother, perturb, unsettle. • noun **1** *a voice full of concern:* anxiety, worry, disquiet, apprehensiveness, unease, misgiving. **2** *his concern for others:* care, consideration, solicitude, sympathy. **3** *housing is the concern of the council:* responsibility, business, affair, duty, job; informal bailiwick; Brit. informal lookout. **4** *issues of concern to women:* interest, importance, relevance, significance. **5** *a publishing concern:* firm, business, company, enterprise, operation, corporation; informal outfit.
OPPOSITES indifference.

concerned adjective **1** *her mother looked concerned:* worried, anxious, upset, troubled, uneasy, bothered. **2** *all concerned parties:* interested, involved, affected, implicated.
OPPOSITES unconcerned.

concerning preposition about, regarding, relating to, with reference to, referring to, with regard to, as regards, touching, in connection with, re, apropos.

C

concession noun **1** something done or given up in order to settle a dispute. **2** a reduction allowed in the price of something. **3** the right to use land or other property for a particular purpose. **4** a stall, bar, or small shop selling things within a larger business or shop.
■ **concessionary** adjective.

conch noun (plural **conches**) a shellfish with a spiral shell.

concierge /kon-si-**airzh**/ noun (especially in France) a resident caretaker of a block of flats or small hotel.

conciliate verb (**conciliates, conciliating, conciliated**) **1** make someone calm and content. **2** try to bring the two sides in a dispute together.
■ **conciliation** noun **conciliatory** adjective.

concise adjective giving a lot of information clearly and in few words.
■ **concisely** adverb **concision** noun.

conclave noun a private meeting.

conclude verb (**concludes, concluding, concluded**) **1** bring or come to an end. **2** arrive at an opinion by reasoning. **3** formally settle or arrange a treaty or agreement.

conclusion noun **1** an end or finish. **2** the summing up of an argument or written work. **3** a decision reached by reasoning.

conclusive adjective decisive or convincing.
■ **conclusively** adverb.

concoct verb **1** make a dish by combining ingredients. **2** think up a story or plan.
■ **concoction** noun.

concomitant /kuhn-**kom**-i-tuhnt/ adjective formal naturally accompanying or connected with something else.

concord noun literary agreement; harmony.

concordance noun an alphabetical list of the important words in a written work.

concordat /kuhn-**kor**-dat/ noun an agreement or treaty.

concourse noun a large open area inside or in front of a public building.

concrete noun a building material made from gravel, sand, cement, and water.
• adjective **1** existing in a physical form; not abstract. **2** definite: *concrete proof.* • verb (**concretes, concreting, concreted**) cover with concrete.

concretion noun a hard solid mass.

concubine /**kong**-kyuu-byn/ noun (in some societies, especially in the past) a woman who lives with a man but has lower status than his wife or wives.

concur verb (**concurs, concurring, concurred**) (often **concur with**) agree.

concurrent adjective existing or happening at the same time.
■ **concurrently** adverb.

concussion noun temporary unconsciousness or confusion caused by a blow on the head.
■ **concussed** adjective.

condemn verb **1** express complete disapproval of someone or something. **2** (usu. **condemn someone to**) sentence someone to a punishment. **3** (**condemn someone to**) force someone to endure something unpleasant. **4** officially declare something to be unfit for use.
■ **condemnation** noun.

condensation noun **1** water from humid air collecting as droplets on a cold surface. **2** the conversion of a vapour or gas to a liquid.

concession noun **1** *the government made several concessions:* compromise, accommodation, trade-off, sop. **2** *tax concessions:* reduction, cut, discount, deduction, rebate; informal break. **3** *a logging concession:* right, privilege, licence, permit, franchise, warrant.

concise adjective succinct, pithy, brief, abridged, condensed, abbreviated, compact, potted.
OPPOSITES lengthy.

conclude verb **1** *the meeting concluded at ten:* finish, end, draw to a close, stop, cease. **2** *he concluded the press conference:* bring to an end, close, wind up, terminate; informal wrap up. **3** *an attempt to conclude a deal:* settle, clinch, finalize, tie up. **4** *I concluded that he was rather unpleasant:* deduce, infer, gather, judge, decide, surmise; N. Amer. figure.
OPPOSITES begin.

conclusion noun **1** *the conclusion of his speech:* end, ending, finish, close. **2** *the conclusion of a trade agreement:* settlement, clinching, completion, arrangement. **3** *his conclusions have been verified:* deduction, inference, interpretation, judgement, verdict.
OPPOSITES beginning.

concrete adjective **1** *concrete objects:* solid, material, real, physical, tangible. **2** *concrete proof:* definite, specific, firm, positive, conclusive, precise.
OPPOSITES abstract, imaginary.

condemn verb **1** *he condemned the suspended players:* censure, criticize, denounce; informal slam; Brit. informal slate, slag off. **2** *his illness condemned him to a lonely life:* doom, destine, damn, sentence.
OPPOSITES praise.

condemnation noun censure, criticism, denunciation; informal flak, a bad press.

condense verb (**condenses, condensing, condensed**) **1** change from a gas or vapour to a liquid. **2** make a liquid thicker or more concentrated. **3** express a piece of writing or a speech in fewer words.
□ **condensed milk** milk that has been thickened and sweetened.

condescend verb **1** behave as if you were better than someone else. **2** do something even though you think it is beneath your dignity. **3** (**condescending**) behaving as if you are better than other people.

condescension noun a patronizing attitude or way of behaving.

condiment noun something such as salt or mustard that is added to food to bring out its flavour.

condition noun **1** the state that someone or something is in as regards appearance, fitness, or working order. **2** (**conditions**) circumstances that affect the way something works or exists. **3** a situation that must exist before something else is possible. **4** an illness or medical problem. • verb **1** train or influence someone to behave in a certain way. **2** (**be conditioned by**) be influenced or determined by. **3** bring something into a good condition.

conditional adjective **1** depending on one or more conditions being fulfilled. **2** Grammar expressing something that must happen or be true before something else can happen or be true.
■ **conditionally** adverb.

conditioner noun a liquid added when washing hair or clothing, to make them softer.

condo = CONDOMINIUM.

condolence noun an expression of sympathy.

condom noun a rubber sheath that a man wears on his penis during sex to stop the woman getting pregnant or to protect against infection.

condominium /kon-duh-**min**-i-uhm/ noun (plural **condominiums**) N. Amer. a building containing a number of individually owned flats.

condone verb (**condones, condoning, condoned**) accept or forgive an offence or wrong.

condor noun a very large South American vulture.

conducive adjective (**conducive to**) contributing or helping towards.

conduct noun /**kon**-dukt/ **1** the way in which a person behaves. **2** management or direction. • verb /kuhn-**dukt**/ **1** organize and carry out. **2** direct the performance of a piece of music. **3** guide or lead someone to a place. **4** (**conduct yourself**) behave in a particular way. **5** transmit heat or electricity directly through a substance.
■ **conduction** noun.

conductance noun the degree to which a material conducts electricity.

conductive adjective conducting heat or electricity.
■ **conductivity** noun.

conductor noun **1** a person who conducts musicians. **2** a material or device that conducts heat or electricity. **3** a person who collects fares on a bus.

conduit /**kon**-dwit, **kon**-dyuu-it/ noun **1** a channel for moving water from one place to another. **2** a tube protecting electric wiring.

cone noun **1** an object which tapers from a circular base to a point. **2** the hard, dry fruit of a pine or fir tree.

coney noun (plural **coneys**) a rabbit.

THESAURUS

condense verb abridge, compress, summarize, shorten, cut, abbreviate, edit.
OPPOSITES expand.

condition noun **1** *check the condition of your wiring:* state, shape, order; Brit. informal nick. **2** *they had been living in appalling conditions:* circumstances, surroundings, environment, situation. **3** *she was in tip-top condition:* fitness, health, form, shape. **4** *a liver condition:* disorder, problem, complaint, illness, disease. **5** *a condition of employment:* stipulation, constraint, prerequisite, precondition, requirement, term, proviso.
• verb *our minds are conditioned by habit:* train, teach, educate, guide, accustom, adapt, habituate, mould.

conditional adjective qualified, dependent, contingent, with reservations, limited, provisional, provisory.

condone verb disregard, accept, allow, let pass, turn a blind eye to, overlook, forget, forgive, pardon, excuse.
OPPOSITES condemn.

conduct noun **1** *they complained about her conduct:* behaviour, actions, deeds, doings, exploits. **2** *the conduct of the elections:* management, running, direction, control, supervision, regulation, administration, organization, coordination, handling.
• verb **1** *the election was conducted lawfully:* manage, direct, run, administer, organize, coordinate, orchestrate, handle, carry out/on. **2** *he was conducted through the corridors:* escort, guide, lead, usher, steer. **3** *aluminium conducts heat:* transmit, convey, carry, channel.
□ **conduct yourself** behave, act, acquit yourself, bear yourself.

confection noun 1 an elaborate sweet dish. 2 something put together in an elaborate or complicated way.

confectionery noun (plural **confectioneries**) sweets and chocolates.

☑ the ending is -*ery*, not -*ary*: confection**ery**.

confederacy noun (plural **confederacies**) 1 an alliance of states or groups. 2 (**the Confederacy**) the Confederate states of the US.

confederate adjective /kuhn-**fed**-uh-ruht/ 1 joined by an agreement or treaty. 2 (**Confederate**) having to do with the southern states which separated from the US in 1860–1. • verb /kuhn-**fed**-uh-rayt/ (**confederates, confederating, confederated**) unite in an alliance.

confederation noun an alliance of states or groups.

confer verb (**confers, conferring, conferred**) 1 formally give a title, benefit, or right to someone. 2 have discussions. ■ **conferment** noun.

conference noun a formal meeting to discuss something.

confess verb 1 admit that you have done something criminal or wrong. 2 acknowledge something reluctantly. 3 formally declare your sins to a priest.

confession noun 1 an act of confessing. 2 formal declaration of your sins to a priest.

confessional noun 1 an enclosed box in a church, in which a priest sits to hear confessions. 2 a confession.

confessor noun a priest who hears confessions.

confetti noun small pieces of coloured paper traditionally thrown over a bride and groom after a marriage ceremony.

confidant noun (feminine **confidante**) a person you trust and confide in.

confide verb (**confides, confiding, confided**) (often **confide in**) tell someone about a secret or private matter.

confidence noun 1 faith in someone or something. 2 a positive feeling gained from a belief in your own ability to do things well. 3 a feeling of certainty about something. □ **confidence trick** an act of cheating someone after gaining their trust. **in confidence** as a secret.

confident adjective 1 feeling confidence in yourself. 2 feeling certain about something. ■ **confidently** adverb.

confidential adjective intended to be kept secret. ■ **confidentiality** noun **confidentially** adverb.

configuration noun a particular arrangement of parts.

configure verb (**configures, configuring, configured**) 1 arrange or set up in a particular way. 2 arrange a computer system so that it is able to do a particular task.

confine verb /kuhn-**fyn**/ (**confines, confining, confined**) 1 (**confine someone/thing to**) keep someone or something within certain limits. 2 (**be confined to**) be unable to leave a place due to illness or disability. • noun (**confines**) /**kon**-fynz/ limits, boundaries, or restrictions.

confined adjective (of a space) small and enclosed.

confinement noun 1 the state of being

confer verb 1 *she conferred a knighthood on him:* bestow on, present to, grant to, award to, decorate with. 2 *she went to confer with her colleagues:* consult, talk, speak, have a chat, converse, deliberate.

conference noun meeting, congress, convention, seminar, discussion, council, forum, summit.

confess verb 1 *he confessed that he had done it:* admit, acknowledge, reveal, disclose, divulge, own up; informal come clean. 2 *they could not make him confess:* own up, plead guilty, accept the blame; informal come clean. 3 *I confess I don't know:* acknowledge, admit, concede, grant, allow, own.
OPPOSITES deny.

confide verb reveal, disclose, divulge, impart, declare, vouchsafe, tell, confess.

confidence noun 1 *I have little confidence in these figures:* trust, belief, faith, credence. 2 *she's brimming with confidence:* self-assurance, self-confidence, self-possession, assertiveness, self-belief, conviction.
OPPOSITES distrust, doubt.

confident adjective 1 *we are confident that business will improve:* sure, certain, positive, convinced, in no doubt, satisfied. 2 *a confident girl:* self-assured, assured, self-confident, positive, assertive, self-possessed.

confidential adjective private, personal, intimate, quiet, secret, sensitive, classified, restricted; informal hush-hush.

confine verb 1 *they were confined in the house:* enclose, incarcerate, imprison, intern, hold captive, cage, lock up, coop up. 2 *he confined his remarks to the weather:* restrict, limit.

confined. **2** dated the time around which a woman gives birth to a baby.

confirm verb **1** state or establish that something is definitely true or correct. **2** make something definite or valid. **3** (**be confirmed**) go through the religious ceremony of confirmation.

confirmation noun **1** the action of confirming. **2** the ceremony at which a baptized person is admitted as a full member of the Christian Church.

confirmed adjective firmly established in a habit, belief, etc.

confiscate verb (**confiscates, confiscating, confiscated**) officially take or seize someone's property.

conflagration noun a large and destructive fire.

conflate verb (**conflates, conflating, conflated**) combine into one.
■ **conflation** noun.

conflict noun /kon-flikt/ **1** a serious disagreement. **2** a long-lasting armed struggle. **3** a difference of opinions, principles, etc. ●verb /kuhn-**flikt**/ (of

opinions, stories, etc.) disagree or be different.

confluence noun the junction of two rivers.

conform verb (often **conform to**) **1** obey a rule. **2** behave in an expected or conventional way. **3** be similar in form or type.
■ **conformity** noun.

conformist noun a person who behaves in an expected or conventional way.

confound verb **1** surprise or bewilder someone. **2** prove a person, theory, or expectation wrong. **3** (**confounded**) informal, dated used to express annoyance.

confront verb **1** meet an enemy or opponent face to face. **2** face up to and deal with a problem. **3** make someone face up to a problem.

confrontation noun a situation of angry disagreement or hostility.
■ **confrontational** adjective.

confuse verb (**confuses, confusing, confused**) **1** make someone bewildered or puzzled. **2** make something less easy to understand. **3** mistake one thing or person for another.

confused adjective **1** bewildered. **2** difficult

THESAURUS

confirm verb **1** *records confirm the latest evidence:* corroborate, verify, prove, substantiate, justify, vindicate, bear out. **2** *he confirmed that help was on the way:* affirm, reaffirm, assert, assure someone, repeat. **3** *his appointment was confirmed by the President:* ratify, approve, endorse, validate, sanction, authorize.
OPPOSITES contradict, deny.

confiscate verb impound, seize, commandeer, requisition, appropriate, expropriate, sequester.
OPPOSITES return.

conflict noun **1** *industrial conflicts:* dispute, quarrel, squabble, disagreement, clash, feud, discord, friction, strife, antagonism, hostility. **2** *the Vietnam conflict:* war, campaign, fighting, engagement, struggle, hostilities, warfare, combat. **3** *a conflict between work and home life:* clash, incompatibility, friction, mismatch, variance, contradiction.
OPPOSITES agreement, peace, harmony.
●verb *their interests sometimes conflict:* clash, be incompatible, be at odds, differ, diverge, disagree, collide.

conflicting adjective contradictory, incompatible, inconsistent, irreconcilable, contrary, opposite, opposing, clashing.

conform verb **1** *visitors have to conform to our rules:* comply with, abide by, obey, observe, follow, keep to, stick to, adhere to, uphold, heed, accept, go along with. **2** *they refuse to conform:* fit in, behave (yourself),

toe the line, obey the rules, informal play by the rules.
OPPOSITES flout, rebel.

confound verb baffle, bewilder, mystify, bemuse, perplex, puzzle, confuse, dumbfound, throw; informal flabbergast, flummox.

confront verb **1** *Martin confronted the burglar:* challenge, square up to, face (up to), come face to face with, meet, accost, stand up to, tackle. **2** *the problems that confront us:* face, plague, bother, trouble, beset, threaten. **3** *they must confront these issues:* tackle, address, face, get to grips with, grapple with. **4** *she confronted him with the evidence:* present, face.
OPPOSITES evade.

confrontation noun conflict, clash, fight, battle, encounter, head-to-head; informal set-to, run-in, dust-up, showdown.

confuse verb **1** *don't confuse students with too much detail:* bewilder, baffle, mystify, bemuse, perplex, puzzle, nonplus; informal flummox, faze. **2** *the authors have confused the issue:* complicate, muddle, blur, obscure, cloud. **3** *some confuse strokes with heart attacks:* mix up, muddle up, mistake for.
OPPOSITES enlighten, simplify.

confused adjective **1** *they are confused about what is going on:* puzzled, bemused, bewildered, perplexed, baffled, mystified; informal flummoxed. **2** *her confused elderly mother:* disorientated, bewildered, muddled, addled, befuddled, demented, to understand or distinguish.

confusion noun 1 uncertainty or bewilderment. 2 a situation of panic or disorder. 3 the mistaking of one person or thing for another.

confute verb (**confutes, confuting, confuted**) formal prove a person or argument to be wrong.

conga noun a Latin American dance performed by people in single file.

congeal /kuhn-jeel/ verb become semi-solid.

congenial /kuhn-jee-ni-uhl/ adjective suited or pleasing to your tastes.
■ congeniality noun.

congenital /kuhn-jen-i-t'l/ adjective 1 (of a disease or abnormality) present from birth. 2 having a particular characteristic as part of your character: *a congenital liar.*
■ congenitally adverb.

conger eel /kong-ger/ noun a large eel found in coastal waters.

congested adjective 1 so crowded that it is difficult to move freely. 2 abnormally full of blood. 3 blocked with mucus.
■ congestion noun.

conglomerate noun /kuhn-**glom**-muh-ruht/ 1 a large corporation formed by the merging of separate firms. 2 something consisting of a number of different and distinct things.
■ conglomeration noun.

Congolese /kong-guh-**leez**/ noun (plural **Congolese**) a person from the Congo or the Democratic Republic of Congo (formerly Zaire). • adjective relating to the Congo or the Democratic Republic of Congo.

congratulate verb (**congratulates, congratulating, congratulated**) 1 tell someone that you are pleased at their success or good fortune. 2 (**congratulate yourself**) think that you are fortunate or clever.
■ congratulatory adjective.

congratulation noun 1 (**congratulations**) good wishes given to someone who has had success or good fortune. 2 the action of congratulating someone.

congregate verb (**congregates, congregating, congregated**) gather into a crowd or mass.

congregation noun 1 a group of people assembled for religious worship. 2 a gathering or collection of people or things.

congress noun 1 a formal meeting or series of meetings between representatives of different groups. 2 (**Congress**) (in the US and some other countries) the group of people elected to pass laws.
■ congressional adjective.

congruent /kong-groo-uhnt/ adjective 1 in agreement or harmony. 2 Geometry (of figures) identical in form.
■ congruence noun.

conical adjective shaped like a cone.

conifer noun a tree that produces hard dry fruit (**cones**) and evergreen needle-like leaves.
■ coniferous adjective.

conjecture noun an opinion based on incomplete information; a guess. • verb (**conjectures, conjecturing, conjectured**) form a conjecture; guess.
■ conjectural adjective.

conjoin verb formal join; combine.

conjugal /kon-juu-g'l/ adjective having to do with marriage.

THESAURUS

senile. 3 *a confused recollection:* **vague,** unclear, indistinct, imprecise, blurred, hazy, dim. 4 *a confused mass of bones:* **disorderly,** disorganized, untidy, jumbled, mixed up, chaotic, topsy-turvy, tangled; informal higgledy-piggledy; Brit. informal shambolic.
OPPOSITES clear, lucid, precise, neat.

confusing adjective **puzzling,** baffling, perplexing, bewildering, mystifying, ambiguous, misleading, inconsistent, contradictory.

confusion noun 1 *there is confusion about the new system:* **uncertainty,** doubt, ignorance. 2 *she stared in confusion:* **bewilderment,** bafflement, perplexity, puzzlement, befuddlement. 3 *her life was in utter confusion:* **disorder,** disarray, chaos, mayhem, turmoil, muddle, mess; informal shambles.
OPPOSITES certainty, order.

congenial adjective 1 *very congenial people:* **sociable,** convivial, hospitable, genial, personable, agreeable, friendly, amiable. 2 *a congenial environment:* **pleasant,** agreeable, enjoyable, pleasurable, relaxing, welcoming, hospitable, favourable.
OPPOSITES unsociable, unpleasant.

congested adjective **blocked,** clogged, choked, jammed, obstructed, crowded, overcrowded, overflowing, packed; informal snarled up, gridlocked.
OPPOSITES clear.

congratulate verb **compliment,** wish someone happiness, pay tribute to, pat on the back, take your hat off to, praise, applaud, salute, honour.
OPPOSITES criticize.

congratulations plural noun **best wishes,** compliments, greetings, felicitations.

congregate verb **assemble,** gather, collect, come together, convene, rally, muster, meet, cluster, group.
OPPOSITES disperse.

C

conjugate /kon-juu-gayt/ verb (**conjugates, conjugating, conjugated**) Grammar give the different forms of a verb.
■ **conjugation** noun.

conjunction noun **1** a word used to connect words or clauses (e.g. *and*, *if*). **2** an instance of two or more things happening at the same time or being in the same place.

conjunctivitis /kuhn-jungk-ti-vy-tiss/ noun inflammation of the eye.

conjure verb (**conjures, conjuring, conjured**) (usu. **conjure something up**) **1** make something appear by magic, or as if by magic. **2** make something appear as an image in your mind.

conjuring noun entertainment in the form of seemingly magical tricks.
■ **conjuror** (or **conjurer**) noun.

conk informal verb (**conk out**) **1** (of a machine) break down. **2** faint or go to sleep. •noun a person's nose.

conker noun Brit. the dark brown nut of a horse chestnut tree.

connect verb **1** join or bring together; link. **2** (**be connected**) be related in some way.

connection or Brit. **connexion** noun **1** a link or relationship. **2** the action of linking one thing with another. **3** (**connections**) influential people that you know or are related to. **4** a train, bus, etc. that you can catch to continue a journey.

connective adjective connecting one thing to another. •noun a word or phrase that links parts of a sentence.

connive /kuh-nyv/ verb (**connives, conniving, connived**) **1** (**connive at** or **in**) secretly allow something wrong to be done. **2** (often **connive with**) conspire to do something wrong.
■ **connivance** noun.

connoisseur /kon-nuh-ser/ noun a person with great knowledge and appreciation of something.

connotation noun an idea or feeling that is suggested by a word in addition to its main meaning.

connote verb (**connotes, connoting, connoted**) (of a word) suggest something in addition to its main meaning.

connubial /kuh-nyoo-bi-uhl/ adjective having to do with marriage.

conquer verb (**conquers, conquering, conquered**) **1** take control of a country or its people by military force. **2** successfully overcome a problem.
■ **conqueror** noun.

conquest noun **1** the action of conquering. **2** a place that has been conquered. **3** a person whose affection you have won.

conscience noun a person's moral sense of right and wrong.

conscientious /kon-shi-en-shuhss/ adjective careful and thorough in carrying out your work or duty.
□ **conscientious objector** a person who refuses to serve in the armed forces for moral reasons.
■ **conscientiously** adverb.

conscious adjective **1** aware of and

THESAURUS

conjure verb **1** *he conjured a cigarette out of the air*: produce, magic, summon. **2** *the picture that his words conjured up*: bring to mind, call to mind, evoke, summon up, suggest.

connect verb **1** *electrodes were connected to the device*: attach, join, fasten, fix, link, hook (up), secure, hitch, stick. **2** *customs connected with Easter*: associate, link, couple, identify, relate to.
OPPOSITES detach.

connection noun **1** *the connection between commerce and art*: link, relationship, relation, interconnection, interdependence, association, bond, tie, tie-in, parallel, correspondence. **2** *he has the right connections*: contact, friend, acquaintance, ally, colleague, associate, relation.

conquer verb **1** *the Franks conquered the Visigoths*: defeat, beat, vanquish, triumph over, overcome, overwhelm, overpower, overthrow, subdue, subjugate. **2** *Peru was conquered by Spain*: seize, take (over), appropriate, capture, occupy, invade, annex, overrun. **3** *the first men to conquer*

Mount Everest: climb, ascend, scale. **4** *the way to conquer fear*: overcome, get the better of, control, master, deal with, cope with, rise above; informal lick.
OPPOSITES lose to, lose, give in to.

conquest noun **1** *the conquest of the Aztecs*: defeat, overthrow, subjugation. **2** *their conquest of the territory*: seizure, takeover, capture, occupation, invasion, annexation. **3** *the conquest of Everest*: ascent, climbing.

conscience noun sense of right and wrong, morals, standards, values, principles, ethics, beliefs, scruples, qualms.

conscientious adjective diligent, industrious, punctilious, painstaking, dedicated, careful, meticulous, thorough, attentive, hard-working, rigorous, scrupulous, religious.
OPPOSITES casual.

conscious adjective **1** *the patient was conscious*: aware, awake, responsive; informal with us. **2** *a conscious decision*: deliberate, purposeful, knowing, considered, wilful, calculated, premeditated.
OPPOSITES unaware, unconscious.

responding to your surroundings. **2** (usu. **conscious of**) aware. **3** deliberate; intentional.
■ **consciously** adverb **consciousness** noun.

conscript verb /kuhn-**skript**/ call someone up for compulsory military service. • noun /**kon**-skript/ a person who has been conscripted.
■ **conscription** noun.

consecrate verb (**consecrates, consecrating, consecrated**) **1** make or declare something holy. **2** officially make someone a bishop.
■ **consecration** noun.

consecutive adjective following one after another in unbroken sequence.
■ **consecutively** adverb.

consensual adjective relating to or involving consent or consensus.

consensus noun general agreement.

☑ consensus, not -cen-.

consent noun permission or agreement. • verb **1** give permission. **2** agree to do something.

consequence noun **1** a result or effect. **2** importance or relevance.

consequent adjective following as a consequence.
■ **consequently** adverb.

conservation noun **1** preservation or restoration of the natural environment. **2** preservation of historical sites and objects. **3** careful use of a resource.
■ **conservationist** noun.

conservative adjective **1** opposed to change and holding traditional values. **2** (in politics) favouring free enterprise and private ownership. **3** (**Conservative**) relating to the Conservative Party, a British right-wing political party favouring free enterprise and private ownership. **4** (of an estimate) deliberately low for the sake of caution. • noun **1** a conservative person. **2** (**Conservative**) a supporter or member of the Conservative Party.
■ **conservatism** noun **conservatively** adverb.

conservatory noun (plural **conservatories**) Brit. a room with a glass roof and walls, attached to a house.

conserve /kuhn-**serv**/ verb (**conserves, conserving, conserved**) protect something from being harmed or overused. • noun /kuhn-**serv**, kon-serv/ fruit jam.

consider verb (**considers, considering, considered**) **1** think carefully about. **2** believe or think. **3** take into account when making a judgement.

considerable adjective great in size,

consecutive adjective successive, succeeding, in succession, running, in a row, straight; informal on the trot.

consensus noun **1** *there was consensus among delegates:* agreement, unanimity, harmony, accord, unity, solidarity. **2** *the consensus was that they should act:* general opinion, common view.
OPPOSITES disagreement.

consent noun *the consent of all members:* agreement, assent, acceptance, approval, permission, authorization, sanction; informal go-ahead, green light, OK.
OPPOSITES dissent.
• verb *she consented to surgery:* agree, assent, submit, allow, sanction, approve, go along with.
OPPOSITES forbid, refuse.

consequence noun **1** *a consequence of inflation:* result, upshot, outcome, effect, repercussion, ramification, product, end result. **2** *the past is of no consequence:* importance, import, significance, account, value, concern.
OPPOSITES cause.

consequently adverb as a result, as a consequence, so, thus, therefore, accordingly, hence, for this/that reason, because of this/that.

conservation noun preservation, protection, safe keeping, husbandry,

upkeep, maintenance, repair, restoration.

conservative adjective **1** *the conservative wing of the party:* right-wing, reactionary, traditionalist. **2** *the conservative trade-union movement:* traditionalist, old-fashioned, dyed-in-the-wool, hidebound, unadventurous, reactionary, set in your ways; informal stick in the mud. **3** *a conservative suit:* conventional, sober, modest, sensible, restrained; informal square.
OPPOSITES socialist, radical, ostentatious.

conserve verb *fossil fuel should be conserved:* preserve, protect, save, safeguard, keep, look after, sustain, husband.
OPPOSITES squander.

consider verb **1** *Isabel considered her choices:* think about, contemplate, reflect on, mull over, ponder, deliberate on, chew over, meditate on, ruminate on, evaluate, weigh up, appraise, take account of, bear in mind; informal size up. **2** *I consider him irresponsible:* deem, think, believe, judge, rate, count, find, regard as, hold to be, reckon to be, view as, see as. **3** *he considered the painting:* look at, contemplate, observe, regard, survey, examine, inspect.

considerable adjective sizeable, substantial, appreciable, significant,

amount, or importance.
■ **considerably** adverb.

considerate adjective careful not to harm or inconvenience other people.
■ **considerately** adverb.

consideration noun **1** careful thought. **2** a fact taken into account when making a decision. **3** thoughtfulness towards other people.

considering preposition & conjunction taking something into account.

consign verb **1** deliver something to someone. **2** (**consign someone/thing to**) put someone or something in a place so as to be rid of them.

consignment noun a batch of goods that are delivered.

consist verb **1** (**consist of**) be composed or made up of. **2** (**consist in**) have as an essential feature.

consistency noun (plural **consistencies**) **1** the state of being consistent. **2** the thickness of a liquid or semi-liquid substance.

consistent adjective **1** always behaving in the same way; unchanging. **2** (usu. **consistent with**) in agreement.
■ **consistently** adverb.

consolation noun **1** comfort received after a loss or disappointment. **2** a source of such comfort.
□ **consolation prize** a prize given to a competitor who just fails to win.

console[1] /kuhn-**sohl**/ verb (**consoles**,

consoling, consoled) comfort someone who is unhappy or disappointed about something.

console[2] /**kon**-sohl/ noun **1** a panel or unit containing a set of controls. **2** a small machine for playing computerized video games.

consolidate verb (**consolidates, consolidating, consolidated**) **1** make stronger or more solid. **2** combine into a single unit.
■ **consolidation** noun.

consommé /kuhn-**som**-may/ noun a clear soup made with concentrated stock.

consonance noun formal agreement or compatibility.

consonant noun a letter of the alphabet representing a sound in which the breath is completely or partly obstructed.
•adjective (**consonant with**) formal in agreement or harmony with.

consort formal noun /**kon**-sort/ a wife, husband, or companion. •verb /kuhn-**sort**/ (**consort with**) habitually associate with.

consortium noun (plural **consortia** or **consortiums**) an association of several companies.

conspicuous /kuhn-**spik**-yoo-uhss/ adjective **1** clearly visible. **2** attracting notice.
■ **conspicuously** adverb.

conspiracy noun (plural **conspiracies**) a secret plan by a group to do something unlawful or harmful.

THESAURUS

plentiful, goodly; informal tidy.
OPPOSITES paltry.

considerably adverb greatly, (very) much, a great deal, a lot, lots, significantly, substantially, appreciably, markedly, noticeably; informal plenty.

considerate adjective attentive, thoughtful, solicitous, kind, unselfish, caring, polite, sensitive.

consideration noun **1** *your case needs careful consideration*: thought, deliberation, reflection, contemplation, examination, inspection, scrutiny, analysis, discussion, attention. **2** *his health is the prime consideration*: factor, issue, matter, concern, aspect, feature. **3** *firms should show more consideration*: attentiveness, concern, care, thoughtfulness, solicitude, understanding, respect, sensitivity.

considering preposition bearing in mind, taking into consideration, taking into account, in view of, in the light of.

consist verb *the crew consists of five men*: be composed of, be made up of, be formed of, comprise, include, contain.

consistent adjective **1** *consistent opinion-*

poll evidence: constant, regular, uniform, steady, stable, even, unchanging. **2** *her injuries were consistent with a knife attack*: compatible, in tune, in line, corresponding to, conforming to.
OPPOSITES irregular, incompatible.

consolation noun comfort, solace, sympathy, pity, commiseration, relief, encouragement, reassurance.

console verb comfort, sympathize with, commiserate with, show compassion for, help, support, cheer (up), hearten, encourage, reassure, soothe.
OPPOSITES upset.

consolidate verb **1** *we consolidated our position in the market*: strengthen, secure, stabilize, reinforce, fortify. **2** *consolidate the results into an action plan*: combine, unite, merge, integrate, amalgamate, fuse, synthesize.

conspicuous adjective obvious, evident, apparent, visible, noticeable, clear, plain, marked, patent, blatant.
OPPOSITES inconspicuous.

conspiracy noun plot, scheme, intrigue, plan, collusion, ploy.

conspire verb (**conspires, conspiring, conspired**) **1** jointly make secret plans to commit a wrongful act. **2** (of circumstances) seem to be working together to bring about something bad.
■ **conspirator** noun **conspiratorial** adjective.

constable noun Brit. a police officer of the lowest rank.

constabulary /kuhn-**stab**-yuu-luh-ri/ noun (plural **constabularies**) Brit. a police force.

constant adjective **1** occurring continuously. **2** remaining the same. **3** faithful and dependable. • noun **1** an unchanging situation. **2** Maths & Physics a number or quantity that does not change its value.
■ **constancy** noun **constantly** adverb.

constellation noun a group of stars forming a recognized pattern.

consternation noun anxiety or dismay.

constipated adjective suffering from constipation.

constipation noun difficulty in emptying the bowels.

constituency noun (plural **constituencies**) chiefly Brit. an area that elects a representative to a parliament.

constituent adjective being a part of a whole. • noun **1** a member of a constituency. **2** a part of a whole.

constitute verb (**constitutes, constituting, constituted**) **1** be a part of a whole. **2** be

equivalent to. **3** establish by law.

constitution noun **1** a set of principles according to which a state or organization is governed. **2** the composition or formation of something. **3** a person's physical or mental state.

constitutional adjective **1** relating or according to a constitution. **2** relating to a person's physical or mental state. • noun dated a walk taken regularly so as to stay healthy.
■ **constitutionally** adverb.

constrain verb **1** force someone to do something. **2** (**constrained**) appearing forced or unnatural. **3** severely restrict or limit.

constraint noun a limitation or restriction.

constrict verb **1** make or become narrower; tighten. **2** stop someone moving or acting freely.
■ **constriction** noun.

constrictor noun a snake that kills by squeezing and choking its prey.

construct verb /kuhn-**strukt**/ build or put together. • noun /**kon**-strukt/ an idea or theory containing various elements.

construction noun **1** the process of constructing something. **2** a building or other structure. **3** an interpretation of something.

constructive adjective having a useful and

THESAURUS

conspire verb **1** *they admitted conspiring to steal cars:* plot, scheme, intrigue, plan, manoeuvre. **2** *circumstances conspired against them:* combine, unite, join forces, work together.

constant adjective **1** *constant noise:* continuous, persistent, sustained, ceaseless, unceasing, perpetual, incessant, never-ending, eternal, endless, non-stop. **2** *a constant speed:* consistent, regular, steady, uniform, even, invariable, unvarying, unchanging. **3** *a constant friend:* faithful, loyal, devoted, true, fast, firm, unswerving.
OPPOSITES intermittent, variable, fickle.

constitute verb **1** *farmers constituted 10 per cent of the population:* comprise, make up, form, account for. **2** *this constitutes a breach of copyright:* amount to, be tantamount to, be equivalent to, represent. **3** *the courts were constituted in 1875:* establish, inaugurate, found, create, set up.

constitution noun **1** *the chemical constitution of the dye:* composition, make-up, structure, construction, arrangement, configuration, formation, anatomy. **2** *she has the constitution of an ox:* health,

condition, strength, stamina, build, physique.

constraint noun **1** *financial constraints:* restriction, limitation, curb, check, restraint, control. **2** *they were able to talk without constraint:* inhibition, uneasiness, embarrassment, self-consciousness, awkwardness.
OPPOSITES freedom, ease.

constrict verb narrow, tighten, compress, contract, squeeze, strangle.
OPPOSITES expand, dilate.

construct verb **1** *a bridge constructed by the army:* build, erect, put up, set up, assemble, fabricate. **2** *he constructed a faultless argument:* create, formulate, form, put together, devise, compose, work out, frame.
OPPOSITES demolish.

construction noun **1** *the station was a spectacular construction:* structure, building, edifice, work. **2** *you put such a sordid construction on it:* interpretation, explanation, analysis, reading, meaning; informal take.

constructive adjective useful, helpful, productive, positive, practical, valuable, profitable, worthwhile.
OPPOSITES unhelpful.

c

helpful effect.
■ **constructively** adverb.

construe verb (**construes, construing, construed**) interpret something in a particular way.

consul noun **1** an official who is based in a foreign city and protects their country's citizens and interests there. **2** (in ancient Rome) each of two elected officials who ruled the republic jointly for a year.
■ **consular** adjective.

consulate noun the place where a consul works.

consult verb **1** try to get advice or information from. **2** ask someone for permission or approval.
■ **consultation** noun **consultative** adjective.

consultancy noun (plural **consultancies**) a company that gives expert advice in a particular field.

consultant noun **1** a person who provides expert advice professionally. **2** Brit. a senior hospital doctor.

consume verb (**consumes, consuming, consumed**) **1** eat or drink. **2** use up. **3** (of a fire) completely destroy. **4** (of a feeling) absorb someone wholly.

consumer noun a person who buys a product or uses a service.

consumerism noun the preoccupation of society with buying goods.
■ **consumerist** adjective.

consummate verb /**kon**-syuu-mayt/ (**consummates, consummating,**

consummated) **1** make a marriage or relationship complete by having sex. **2** complete a transaction. •adjective /kuhn-sum-muht, **kon**-sum-muht/ showing great skill and flair.
■ **consummation** noun.

consumption noun **1** the process of consuming, or an amount consumed. **2** dated tuberculosis.
■ **consumptive** adjective (dated).

contact noun **1** physical touching. **2** communicating or meeting. **3** a person whom you can ask for information or help. **4** a connection for an electric current to pass from one thing to another. •verb get in touch with.
□ **contact lens** a plastic lens placed on the surface of the eye to help you see better.

contagion noun the passing of a disease from one person to another by close contact.

contagious adjective **1** (of a disease) spread by contact between people. **2** having a contagious disease.

contain verb **1** have or hold something inside. **2** control or restrain. **3** prevent a problem from becoming worse.

container noun **1** a box or similar object for holding something. **2** a large metal box for transporting goods.

containment noun the keeping of something harmful under control.

contaminate verb (**contaminates,**

THESAURUS

consult verb **1** *you need to consult a solicitor:* seek advice from, ask, call (on), turn to; informal pick someone's brains. **2** *the government must consult with interested parties:* confer, talk things over, communicate, deliberate, compare notes. **3** *she consulted her diary:* refer to, look at, check.

consultant noun adviser, expert, specialist, authority.

consultation noun **1** *the need for further consultation with industry:* discussion, dialogue, debate, negotiation, deliberation. **2** *a 30-minute consultation:* meeting, talk, discussion, interview, examination, audience, hearing.

consume verb **1** *vast amounts of food and drink were consumed:* eat, devour, swallow, gobble up, wolf down, guzzle, drink. **2** *natural resources are being consumed at an alarming rate:* use (up), expend, deplete, exhaust, spend. **3** *the fire consumed fifty houses:* destroy, demolish, lay waste, raze, devastate, gut, ruin, wreck. **4** *Carolyn was consumed with guilt:* eat up, devour, grip, overwhelm, absorb, obsess, preoccupy.

consumer noun buyer, purchaser, customer, shopper, user.

contact noun **1** *have you had any contact with him lately?* communication, correspondence, connection, relations, dealings, touch. **2** *he had many contacts in Germany:* connection, link, acquaintance, associate, friend.
•verb *he should contact the police:* get in touch with, communicate with, approach, notify, speak to, write to, come forward; informal get hold of.

contain verb **1** *the boat contained four people:* hold, carry, enclose, accommodate. **2** *the archive contains much unpublished material:* include, comprise, incorporate, involve, consist of, be made up of, be composed of. **3** *he must contain his anger:* restrain, control, curb, rein in, suppress, stifle, swallow, bottle up, keep in check.
OPPOSITES vent.

container noun receptacle, vessel, holder, repository.

contaminate verb pollute, taint, poison, stain, adulterate, defile, debase, corrupt.
OPPOSITES purify.

contaminating, contaminated) make something dirty or poisonous by allowing it to come into contact with harmful substances.
■ contamination noun.

contemplate verb (**contemplates, contemplating, contemplated**) **1** look at thoughtfully. **2** think about. **3** think deeply and at length.
■ contemplation noun contemplative adjective.

contemporaneous /kuhn-tem-puh-ray-ni-uhss/ adjective existing at or happening in the same period of time.

contemporary adjective **1** living or happening at the same time. **2** belonging to or happening in the present. **3** modern in style. • noun (plural **contemporaries**) a person living or working in the same period as another.

☑ contem*porary*, not -*pory*.

contempt noun **1** the feeling that someone or something is worthless. **2** (also **contempt of court**) the offence of disobeying or being disrespectful to a court of law.

contemptible adjective deserving contempt.
■ contemptibly adverb.

contemptuous adjective showing contempt.
■ contemptuously adverb.

contend verb **1** (**contend with** or **against**) struggle to deal with a difficulty. **2** (**contend for**) struggle to achieve. **3** put forward a view in an argument.
■ contender noun.

content[1] /kuhn-**tent**/ adjective peacefully happy or satisfied. • verb satisfy or please. • noun a state of happiness or satisfaction.
■ contentment noun.

content[2] /**kon**-tent/ noun **1** (**contents**) the things that are contained in something. **2** the amount of a particular thing occurring in a substance. **3** (**contents**) a list of chapters given at the front of a book or magazine. **4** the material in a piece of writing, as opposed to its form or style.

contented adjective happy or satisfied.
■ contentedly adverb.

contention noun **1** heated disagreement. **2** a point of view that is expressed.
□ in contention having a good chance of success in a contest.

contentious adjective causing disagreement or controversy; controversial.

contest noun /**kon**-test/ an event in which people compete to see who is the best.

contemplate verb **1** *she contemplated her image in the mirror:* look at, gaze at, stare at, view, regard, examine, inspect, observe, survey, study, eye. **2** *he contemplated his fate:* think about, ponder, reflect on, consider, mull over, muse on, dwell on, deliberate over, meditate on, ruminate on, chew over. **3** *he was contemplating legal action:* consider, think about, have in mind, intend, plan, propose.

contemporary adjective **1** *contemporary sources:* of the time, contemporaneous, concurrent, coexisting. **2** *contemporary society:* modern, present-day, present, current. **3** *a very contemporary design:* modern, up to date, up to the minute, fashionable, recent; informal trendy.
OPPOSITES older, newer, former, old-fashioned.

contempt noun scorn, disdain, derision, disgust, disrespect.
OPPOSITES respect.

contemptuous adjective scornful, disdainful, derisive, mocking, sneering, scoffing, condescending, dismissive.
OPPOSITES respectful.

contend verb **1** *three groups were contending for power:* compete, vie, battle, tussle, struggle, jostle, strive. **2** *he contends that the judge was wrong:* assert, maintain, hold, claim, argue, insist, allege.
□ contend with **cope with**, struggle with,

grapple with, deal with, take on, handle.

content[1] adjective *she seemed content with life:* satisfied, contented, pleased, fulfilled, happy, glad, at ease.
OPPOSITES dissatisfied.
• verb *her reply seemed to content him:* satisfy, comfort, gratify, gladden, please, soothe, placate, appease, mollify.

content[2] noun **1** *foods with a high fibre content:* amount, proportion, level. **2** (**contents**) *the contents of a vegetarian sausage:* constituents, ingredients, components. **3** *the content of the essay:* subject matter, theme, argument, thesis, message, substance, material, ideas.

contented adjective. See **CONTENT**[1] adjective.

contentious adjective **1** *a contentious issue:* controversial, debatable, disputed, open to debate, moot, vexed. **2** *contentious people:* quarrelsome, argumentative, confrontational; Brit. informal stroppy.

contest noun **1** *a boxing contest:* competition, match, tournament, game, bout. **2** *the contest for the party leadership:* fight, battle, tussle, struggle, competition, race.
• verb **1** *he intended to contest the seat:* compete for, contend for, vie for, fight for. **2** *a system where parties contest elections:* compete in, take part in, fight, enter. **3** *we contested the decision:* oppose, challenge, take issue with, question, call into

• **verb** /kuhn-**test**/ **1** take part in a competition or election. **2** challenge or dispute a decision or theory.

contestant noun a person who takes part in a contest.

context noun **1** the circumstances surrounding an event, statement, or idea. **2** the parts that come immediately before and after a word or passage and make its meaning clearer.
■ **contextual** adjective.

contiguous /kuhn-**tig**-yoo-uhss/ adjective sharing a border.

continent[1] noun **1** any of the world's main continuous expanses of land (Europe, Asia, Africa, North and South America, Australia, Antarctica). **2** (**the Continent**) the mainland of Europe as distinct from the British Isles.

continent[2] adjective **1** able to control movements of the bowels and bladder. **2** restrained; self-disciplined.
■ **continence** noun.

continental adjective **1** forming or belonging to a continent. **2** coming from or like mainland Europe. • noun a person from mainland Europe.
□ **continental breakfast** a light breakfast of coffee and bread rolls.

contingency noun (plural **contingencies**) a future event which may happen but cannot be predicted with certainty.

contingent noun a group of people with a common feature, forming part of a larger group. • adjective **1** (**contingent on**) dependent on. **2** depending on chance.

continual adjective happening constantly or often, with intervals in between: *he met with continual delays.*
■ **continually** adverb.

! note that **continual** and **continuous** don't mean exactly the same thing.

continuation noun **1** the action of continuing. **2** a part that is attached to something else and is an extension of it.

continue verb (**continues, continuing, continued**) **1** keep doing something; carry on with. **2** keep existing or happening. **3** carry on travelling in the same direction. **4** start doing something again.

continuity noun (plural **continuities**) **1** the fact of not stopping or changing. **2** an unbroken connection or line of development. **3** organization of a film or television programme so that the plot makes sense and clothing, scenery, etc. remain the same in different scenes.

continuous adjective forming an unbroken whole or sequence without interruptions or exceptions: *a day of continuous rain.*
■ **continuously** adverb.

continuum /kuhn-**tin**-yoo-uhm/ noun (plural **continua**) a continuous sequence in which the elements change gradually.

contort verb twist or bend something out of its normal shape.
■ **contortion** noun.

contortionist noun an entertainer who twists and bends their body into unnatural positions.

contour noun **1** an outline of the shape or form of something. **2** (also **contour line**) a line on a map joining points of equal height.
■ **contoured** adjective.

contraband noun goods that have been imported or exported illegally.

contraception noun the use of contraceptives.

contraceptive noun a device or drug used to prevent a woman becoming pregnant.

THESAURUS

question, object to.
OPPOSITES accept.

contestant noun competitor, participant, player, contender, candidate, entrant.

context noun circumstances, conditions, frame of reference, factors, state of affairs, situation, background, scene, setting.

contingency noun eventuality, possibility, chance event, incident, occurrence, accident, emergency.

continual adjective **1** *continual breakdowns:* frequent, repeated, constant, recurrent, recurring, regular. **2** *continual pain:* constant, continuous, unremitting, unrelenting, chronic, uninterrupted, unbroken.
OPPOSITES occasional, temporary.

continue verb **1** *he was unable to continue with his job:* carry on, proceed, pursue, go

on, keep on, persist, persevere, keep at; informal stick at. **2** *discussions continued throughout the year:* go on, carry on, last, extend, run on, drag on. **3** *we are keen to continue this relationship:* maintain, keep up, sustain, keep going, keep alive, preserve. **4** *his willingness to continue in office:* remain, stay, carry on, keep going. **5** *we continued our conversation after supper:* resume, pick up, take up, carry on with, return to, revisit.
OPPOSITES stop, break off, leave.

continuous adjective continual, persistent, sustained, ceaseless, unceasing, perpetual, incessant, never-ending, eternal, endless, non-stop.
OPPOSITES intermittent.

contort verb twist, bend out of shape, distort, misshape, warp, buckle, deform.

C

• **adjective** preventing a woman becoming pregnant.

contract noun /**kon**-trakt/ **1** an official, legally binding agreement. **2** informal an arrangement for someone to be murdered by a hired killer. • **verb** /kuhn-**trakt**/ **1** make or become smaller. **2** become shorter and tighter. **3** shorten a word or phrase. **4** make a formal and legally binding agreement to do something. **5** catch or develop a disease. ■ **contractual** adjective.

contraction noun **1** the process of contracting. **2** a shortening of the muscles of the womb happening at intervals during childbirth. **3** a shortened form of a word or words.

contractor noun a person or firm that undertakes to provide materials or labour for a job.

contradict verb deny the truth of a statement made by someone by saying the opposite.

contradiction noun **1** a combination of statements, ideas, or features which are opposed to one another. **2** saying the opposite to something already said.

contradictory adjective **1** inconsistent with or opposing each other. **2** containing inconsistent elements.

contradistinction noun distinction made by contrasting two things.

contraflow noun Brit. an arrangement by which the lanes of a dual carriageway normally carrying traffic in one direction become two-directional.

contralto /kuhn-**tral**-toh/ noun (plural **contraltos**) the lowest female singing voice.

contraption noun a machine or device that appears strange or unnecessarily complicated.

contrapuntal /kon-truh-**pun**-t'l/ adjective Music relating to or in counterpoint.

contrariwise adverb in the opposite way.

contrary /**kon**-truh-ri/ adjective **1** opposite in nature, direction, or meaning. **2** (of two or more statements, beliefs, etc.) opposed to one another. **3** /kuhn-**trair**-i/ deliberately inclined to do the opposite of what is expected or wanted. • noun (**the contrary**) the opposite. ■ **contrariness** noun.

contrast noun /**kon**-trahst/ **1** the state of being noticeably different from something else. **2** a thing or person noticeably different from another. **3** the amount of difference between tones in a television

THESAURUS

contract noun *a legally binding contract:* agreement, arrangement, commitment, settlement, understanding, compact, covenant, deal, bargain.
• verb **1** *the market began to contract:* shrink, diminish, reduce, decrease, dwindle, decline. **2** *her stomach muscles contracted:* tighten, tense, flex, constrict, draw in. **3** *the company was contracted to build the stadium:* engage, take on, hire, commission, employ. **4** *she contracted German measles:* catch, pick up, come/go down with, develop.
OPPOSITES expand, relax, lengthen.

contraction noun **1** *the contraction of the industry:* shrinking, shrinkage, decline, decrease, diminution, dwindling. **2** *the contraction of muscles:* tightening, tensing, flexing. **3** *'goodbye' is a contraction of 'God be with you':* abbreviation, short form, shortening.
OPPOSITES expansion, relaxation, lengthening.

contradict verb **1** *he contradicted the government's account:* deny, refute, rebut, dispute, challenge, counter. **2** *nobody dared contradict him:* argue with, go against, challenge, oppose.
OPPOSITES confirm, agree with.

contradiction noun **1** *the contradiction between his faith and his lifestyle:* conflict, clash, disagreement, inconsistency,

mismatch. **2** *a contradiction of his statement:* denial, refutation, rebuttal, countering.
OPPOSITES agreement, confirmation.

contradictory adjective inconsistent, incompatible, irreconcilable, opposed, opposite, contrary, conflicting, at variance.

contrary adjective **1** *contrary views:* opposite, opposing, contradictory, clashing, conflicting, antithetical, incompatible, irreconcilable. **2** *she was sulky and contrary:* perverse, awkward, difficult, uncooperative, obstinate, pig-headed, intractable; Brit. informal bloody-minded, stroppy; N. Amer. informal balky.
OPPOSITES compatible, accommodating.
• noun *in fact, the contrary is true:* opposite, reverse, converse, antithesis.

contrast noun **1** *the contrast between rural and urban trends:* difference, dissimilarity, disparity, divergence, variance, distinction, comparison. **2** *Jane was a complete contrast to Sarah:* opposite, antithesis, foil, complement.
OPPOSITES similarity.
• verb **1** *a view which contrasts with his earlier opinion:* differ, be at variance, be contrary, conflict, be at odds, disagree, clash. **2** *people contrasted her with her sister:* compare, juxtapose, measure, distinguish, differentiate.
OPPOSITES resemble, liken.

picture, photograph, etc. •verb /kuhn-**trahst**/ 1 be noticeably different.
2 compare two things to emphasize their differences.

contravene verb (**contravenes**, **contravening**, **contravened**) 1 do something that breaks a law, treaty, etc. 2 conflict with a right, principle, etc. ■ **contravention** noun.

contretemps /kon-truh-ton/ noun (plural **contretemps** /kon-truh-tonz/) a minor disagreement.

contribute verb (**contributes**, **contributing**, **contributed**) 1 give something in order to help an undertaking or effort.
2 (**contribute to**) help to cause or bring about. ■ **contribution** noun **contributor** noun.

contributory adjective 1 playing a part in bringing something about. 2 (of a pension or insurance scheme) operated by means of a fund into which people pay.

contrite adjective sorry for something that you have done. ■ **contritely** adverb **contrition** noun.

contrivance noun 1 a clever device or scheme. 2 the action of contriving something.

contrive verb (**contrives**, **contriving**, **contrived**) 1 plan or achieve something in a clever or skilful way. 2 manage to do something foolish.

contrived adjective deliberately created and seeming artificial; not natural or spontaneous.

control noun 1 the power to influence people's behaviour or the course of events. 2 the restriction of something: *crime control*. 3 a way of regulating or limiting

something: *controls on local spending*. 4 a person or thing used as a standard of comparison for checking the results of a survey or experiment. •verb (**controls**, **controlling**, **controlled**) 1 have control or command of. 2 limit or regulate. □ **control tower** a tall building at an airport from which the movements of aircraft are controlled. ■ **controllable** adjective **controller** noun.

controversial adjective causing or likely to cause controversy. ■ **controversially** adverb.

controversy /kon-truh-ver-si, kuhn-**trov**-er-si/ noun (plural **controversies**) debate or disagreement about a subject which arouses strong opinions.

contumely /kon-**tyoom**-li/ noun (plural **contumelies**) old use insulting language or treatment.

contusion noun a bruise.

conundrum /kuh-**nun**-druhm/ noun (plural **conundrums**) 1 a difficult problem or question. 2 a riddle.

conurbation /kon-er-**bay**-sh'n/ noun an area consisting of several towns merging together or with a city.

convalesce verb (**convalesces**, **convalescing**, **convalesced**) gradually get better after an illness or injury.

convalescent adjective recovering from an illness or injury. ■ **convalescence** noun.

convection noun the process by which heat moves through a gas or liquid as the warmer part rises and the cooler part sinks.

convector noun a heater that circulates

THESAURUS

contribute verb give, donate, put up, grant, provide, supply; informal chip in; Brit. informal stump up.
□ **contribute to play a part in**, be instrumental in, have a hand in, be conducive to, make for.

contribution noun gift, donation, offering, present, handout, grant, subsidy.

contributor noun donor, benefactor, supporter, backer, patron, sponsor.

contrive verb 1 *they contrived a plan*: create, engineer, manufacture, devise, concoct, construct, fabricate, hatch.
2 *Lomax contrived to bump into him*: manage, find a way, engineer a way, arrange, succeed in.
OPPOSITES fail.

contrived adjective forced, strained, laboured, overdone, unnatural, artificial, false, affected.
OPPOSITES natural.

control noun 1 *China retained control over the region*: power, authority, command, dominance, sway, management, direction, leadership, rule, government, sovereignty, supremacy. 2 *strict import controls*: limit, limitation, restriction, restraint, check, curb, regulation. 3 *her control deserted her*: self-control, self-restraint, composure, calm; informal cool.
•verb 1 *one family controlled the company*: run, manage, direct, preside over, supervise, command, rule, govern, lead, dominate. 2 *she struggled to control her temper*: restrain, keep in check, curb, hold back, suppress, repress. 3 *public spending was controlled*: limit, restrict, curb, cap.

controversial adjective disputed, contentious, moot, debatable, arguable, vexed.

controversy noun dispute, disagreement, argument, debate, contention, quarrel, war of words, storm; Brit. row.

warm air by convection.

convene verb (**convenes, convening, convened**) **1** call people together for a meeting. **2** come together for a meeting.
■ **convener** (or **convenor**) noun.

convenience noun **1** freedom from effort or difficulty. **2** a useful or helpful device or situation. **3** Brit. a public toilet.

convenient adjective **1** fitting in well with a person's needs, activities, and plans. **2** involving little trouble or effort.
■ **conveniently** adverb.

convent noun a building where nuns live together.

convention noun **1** a way in which something is usually done. **2** socially acceptable behaviour. **3** a large meeting or conference. **4** an agreement between countries.

conventional adjective **1** based on or following what is generally done. **2** not individual or adventurous. **3** (of weapons or power) non-nuclear.
■ **conventionally** adverb.

converge verb (**converges, converging, converged**) **1** come together from different directions. **2** (**converge on**) come from different directions and meet at.
■ **convergent** adjective.

conversant adjective (**conversant with**) familiar with or knowledgeable about.

conversation noun an informal talk between two or more people.
■ **conversational** adjective **conversationalist** noun.

converse[1] /kuhn-verss/ verb (**converses, conversing, conversed**) hold a conversation.

converse[2] /kon-verss/ noun something that is the opposite of another. ● adjective opposite.
■ **conversely** adverb.

conversion noun **1** the action of converting. **2** Brit. a building that has been converted to a new purpose. **3** Rugby a successful kick at goal after a try.

convert verb /kuhn-**vert**/ **1** change the form, character, or function of something. **2** change money or units into others of a different kind. **3** adapt a building for a new purpose. **4** change your religious faith.
● noun /kon-vert/ a person who has changed their religious faith.

convertible adjective **1** able to be converted. **2** (of a car) having a folding or detachable roof. ● noun a convertible car.

convex adjective having an outline or surface that curves outwards.

convene verb **1** *he convened a secret meeting:* summon, call, order. **2** *the committee convened for its final session:* assemble, gather, meet, come together; formal foregather.
OPPOSITES disperse.

convenience noun **1** *the convenience of the arrangement:* advantage, benefit, expedience, suitability. **2** *for convenience, the handset is wall-mounted:* ease of use, usefulness, utility, accessibility, availability.
OPPOSITES inconvenience.

convenient adjective **1** *a convenient time:* suitable, favourable, advantageous, appropriate, opportune, timely, expedient. **2** *a convenient shop:* nearby, handy, well situated, practical, useful, accessible.
OPPOSITES inconvenient.

convention noun **1** *social conventions:* custom, usage, practice, tradition, etiquette, protocol. **2** *a convention signed by 74 countries:* agreement, accord, protocol, pact, treaty. **3** *the party's biennial convention:* conference, meeting, congress, assembly, gathering.

conventional adjective **1** *conventional wisdom:* orthodox, traditional, established, accepted, received, prevailing. **2** *a conventional railway:* normal, standard, regular, ordinary, usual, traditional, typical.

3 *a very conventional woman:* conservative, traditional, conformist, old-fashioned; informal square, stick-in-the-mud. **4** *a conventional piece of work:* unoriginal, formulaic, predictable, unadventurous.
OPPOSITES unorthodox, unconventional, original.

converge verb *here the lines converge:* meet, intersect, cross, connect, link up, join, merge.
OPPOSITES diverge.
□ **converge on meet at,** arrive at, close in on, bear down on, descend on, approach, move towards.

conversation noun discussion, talk, chat, gossip, tête-à-tête, exchange, dialogue; Brit. informal chinwag, natter.

conversion noun **1** *the conversion of waste into energy:* change, transformation, metamorphosis. **2** *the conversion of the building:* adaptation, alteration, modification, redevelopment.

convert verb **1** *plants convert the sun's energy into chemical energy:* change, turn, transform, metamorphose. **2** *the factory was converted into flats:* adapt, turn, change, alter, modify, redevelop. **3** *they sought to convert sinners:* win over, claim, redeem, save, reform, re-educate, proselytize, evangelize.

C

convey verb 1 transport or carry to a place.
2 communicate an idea or feeling.

conveyance noun 1 the action of
conveying. 2 formal a means of transport.
3 the legal process of transferring property
from one owner to another.
∎ **conveyancing** noun.

conveyor belt noun a continuous moving
band used for transporting objects from
one place to another.

convict verb /kuhn-**vikt**/ officially declare
that someone is guilty of a criminal
offence. •noun /**kon**-vikt/ a person in prison
after being convicted of a criminal offence.

conviction noun 1 an instance of being
convicted of a criminal offence. 2 a firmly
held belief or opinion. 3 the quality of
showing that you believe strongly in what
you are saying or doing.

convince verb (**convinces, convincing,
convinced**) 1 cause someone to believe
firmly that something is true. 2 persuade
someone to do something.

convincing adjective 1 able to convince
someone. 2 (of a victory or a winner)
leaving no margin of doubt.
∎ **convincingly** adverb.

convivial adjective 1 (of an atmosphere or
event) friendly and lively. 2 (of a person)
cheerfully sociable.
∎ **conviviality** noun.

convoluted adjective 1 (of an argument or
account) very complex. 2 folded or twisted
in an elaborate way.

convolution noun 1 a coil or twist.

2 (**convolutions**) something complex and
difficult to follow.

convoy noun a group of ships or vehicles
travelling together under armed
protection.

convulse verb (**convulses, convulsing,
convulsed**) 1 suffer convulsions. 2 (**be
convulsed**) make sudden, uncontrollable
movements because of emotion, laughter,
etc.
∎ **convulsive** adjective.

convulsion noun 1 a sudden, irregular
movement of the body caused by muscles
contracting uncontrollably. 2 (**convulsions**)
uncontrollable laughter. 3 a violent
upheaval.

coo verb (**coos, cooing, cooed**) 1 (of a pigeon
or dove) make a soft murmuring sound.
2 speak in a soft, gentle voice. •noun a
cooing sound.

cook verb 1 prepare food or a meal by
heating the ingredients. 2 (of food) be
heated so as to become edible. 3 informal
alter accounts dishonestly. 4 (**cook
something up**) informal invent a story or
plan. •noun a person who cooks.

cooker noun Brit. an appliance for cooking
food.

cookery noun the practice or skill of
preparing and cooking food.

cookie noun (plural **cookies**) 1 N. Amer. a sweet
biscuit. 2 informal a person of a particular
kind: *she's a tough cookie.*

cool adjective 1 fairly cold. 2 stopping you

THESAURUS

convey verb 1 *taxis conveyed guests to the
station:* transport, carry, bring, take, fetch,
move. 2 *he conveyed the information to me:*
communicate, pass on, impart, relate,
relay, transmit, send. 3 *it's impossible to
convey how I felt:* express, communicate,
get across/over, put across/over, indicate.

convict verb find guilty, sentence.
OPPOSITES acquit.
•noun prisoner, inmate, criminal, offender,
felon; informal jailbird, con, (old) lag.

conviction noun 1 *his political convictions:*
beliefs, opinions, views, persuasion, ideals,
position, stance, values. 2 *she spoke with
conviction:* assurance, confidence,
certainty.
OPPOSITES diffidence.

convince verb 1 *he convinced me that I was
wrong:* assure, persuade, satisfy, prove to.
2 *I convinced her to marry me:* persuade,
induce, prevail on, talk into, talk round,
win over, coax, cajole, inveigle.

convincing adjective 1 *a convincing
argument:* persuasive, powerful, strong,
forceful, compelling, cogent, plausible,
irresistible, telling. 2 *a convincing 5–0 win:*

resounding, emphatic, decisive, conclusive.
OPPOSITES unconvincing, narrow.

cool adjective 1 *a cool breeze:* chilly, chill,
cold, bracing, brisk, crisp, fresh; informal
nippy; Brit. informal parky. 2 *a cool response to
the suggestion:* unenthusiastic, lukewarm,
tepid, indifferent, uninterested, apathetic.
3 *David seemed distinctly cool:* unfriendly,
distant, remote, aloof, cold, chilly, frosty,
unwelcoming; informal stand-offish. 4 *his
ability to keep cool in a crisis:* calm,
collected, composed, self-possessed, poised,
serene, relaxed, at ease, unruffled,
unperturbed; informal unflappable, together,
laid-back.
OPPOSITES warm, enthusiastic, friendly,
excited.
•noun 1 *the cool of the evening:* chill,
chilliness, coldness, coolness. 2 (informal) *Ken
lost his cool:* self-control, control,
composure, self-possession, calmness,
aplomb, poise.
OPPOSITES warmth.
•verb *cool the sauce in the fridge:* chill,
refrigerate, freeze.
OPPOSITES warm.

from becoming too hot. **3** unfriendly or unenthusiastic. **4** not anxious or excited. **5** informal fashionably attractive or impressive. **6** informal excellent. • **noun** the state of being calm and self-controlled. • **verb** (**cools, cooling, cooled**) make or become cool.
■ **cooler** noun **coolly** adverb **coolness** noun.

coolant noun a fluid used to cool an engine or other device.

coolie noun (plural **coolies**) dated an unskilled labourer in an Asian country.

coon noun N. Amer. a raccoon.

coop noun a cage or pen for poultry. • **verb** (**coop someone/thing up**) confine a person or animal in a small space.

cooper noun a person who makes or repairs casks and barrels.

cooperate or **co-operate** verb (**cooperates, cooperating, cooperated**) **1** work together towards the same end. **2** do what someone wants.
■ **cooperation** noun.

cooperative or **co-operative** adjective **1** involving cooperation. **2** willing to help. **3** (of a business) owned and run jointly by its members. • **noun** a cooperative organization.
■ **cooperatively** adverb.

co-opt verb **1** appoint someone as a member of a committee or other body. **2** adopt an idea or policy for your own use.

coordinate or **co-ordinate** verb /koh-or-di-nayt/ (**coordinates, coordinating, coordinated**) **1** bring the different elements of something together so that it works well. **2** (**coordinate with**) negotiate with other people to work together effectively. **3** (of different things) match or look attractive together. • **noun** /koh-or-di-nuht/ Maths each of a group of numbers used to indicate the position of a

point, line, or plane.
■ **coordinator** noun.

coordination or **co-ordination** noun **1** the process of coordinating. **2** the ability to move different parts of the body smoothly and at the same time.

coot noun a waterbird with black feathers and a white bill.

cop informal noun a police officer. • **verb** (**cops, copping, copped**) **1** arrest an offender. **2** receive or experience something unwelcome. **3** (**cop out**) avoid doing something that you ought to do.
□ **cop it** Brit. get into trouble. **not much cop** Brit. not very good.

cope[1] verb (**copes, coping, coped**) deal effectively with something difficult.

cope[2] noun a long cloak worn by a priest on ceremonial occasions.

copier noun a machine that makes exact copies of something.

co-pilot noun a second pilot in an aircraft.

coping noun the top line of bricks or stones in a wall.

copious adjective in large amounts; plentiful.
■ **copiously** adverb.

copper[1] noun **1** a reddish-brown metal. **2** (**coppers**) Brit. coins made of copper or bronze. **3** a reddish-brown colour.
□ **copper-bottomed** Brit. thoroughly reliable.

copper[2] noun Brit. informal a police officer.

copperplate noun an elaborate style of handwriting.

coppice noun an area of woodland in which the trees or shrubs are periodically cut back to ground level.

copse noun a small group of trees.

copulate verb (**copulates, copulating, copulated**) mate or have sex.
■ **copulation** noun.

copy noun (plural **copies**) **1** a thing made to

cooperate verb **1** *police and social services cooperated:* collaborate, work together, pull together, join forces, team up, unite, combine, pool resources. **2** *he was happy to cooperate:* assist, help, lend a hand, be of service, do your bit; informal play ball.

cooperation noun **1** *cooperation between management and workers:* collaboration, joint action, combined effort, teamwork, give and take, compromise. **2** *thank you for your cooperation:* assistance, help.

cooperative adjective **1** *a cooperative effort:* collaborative, collective, combined, joint, shared, united, concerted. **2** *pleasant and cooperative staff:* helpful, eager to help, obliging, accommodating, willing.

coordinate verb organize, arrange, order, synchronize, bring together, orchestrate.

cope verb **1** *she couldn't cope on her own:* manage, survive, look after yourself, fend for yourself, shift for yourself, get by/through, hold your own. **2** *his inability to cope with the situation:* deal with, handle, manage, address, face (up to), confront, tackle, get to grips with.

copy noun **1** *a copy of the report:* duplicate, facsimile, photocopy; trademark Xerox. **2** *a copy of a sketch by Leonardo da Vinci:* replica, reproduction, imitation, likeness, forgery, fake, counterfeit.

• **verb 1** *each form had to be copied:* duplicate, photocopy, xerox, photostat, reproduce. **2** *portraits copied from originals:* reproduce, replicate, forge, fake, counterfeit. **3** *their sound was copied by a lot of jazz players:* imitate, reproduce,

C

be similar or identical to another. **2** a single example of a particular book, record, etc. **3** material for a newspaper or magazine article. •verb (**copies, copying, copied**) **1** make a copy of. **2** imitate the behaviour or style of.
□ **copy-edit** check that written material is consistent and accurate.
■ **copyist** noun.

copyright noun the exclusive right to publish, perform, film, or record literary, artistic, or musical material.

copywriter noun a person who writes advertisements or publicity material.

coquette /ko-**ket**/ noun a flirtatious woman.
■ **coquetry** noun **coquettish** adjective.

coracle /ko-ruh-k'l/ noun a small round boat made of wickerwork covered with a watertight material.

coral noun **1** a hard substance found in warm seas which consists of the skeletons of small animals living together as a stationary group. **2** a pinkish-red colour.

cor anglais /kor ong-glay/ noun (plural **cors anglais** /kor ong-glay/) a woodwind instrument of the oboe family.

corbel noun a projection jutting out from a wall to support a structure above it.

cord noun **1** thin string or rope made from several twisted strands. **2** an electric flex. **3** corduroy. **4** (**cords**) trousers made of corduroy.
■ **cordless** adjective.

❗ don't confuse **cord** with **chord**, which means 'a group of musical notes'.

cordial adjective **1** warm and friendly. **2** sincere. •noun **1** Brit. a sweet fruit-flavoured drink, sold in concentrated form. **2** chiefly N. Amer. a liqueur.
■ **cordiality** noun **cordially** adverb.

cordite noun a kind of explosive.

cordon noun a line or circle of police, soldiers, or guards forming a barrier. •verb (**cordon something off**) close somewhere off by means of a cordon.

cordon bleu /kor-don **bler**/ adjective Cookery

of the highest class.

corduroy /kor-duh-roy/ noun a thick cotton fabric with velvety ridges.

core noun **1** the tough central part of a fruit. **2** the central or most important part of something. •verb (**cores, coring, cored**) remove the core from a fruit.

co-respondent noun a person named in a divorce case as having committed adultery with the respondent.

corgi noun (plural **corgis**) a breed of dog with short legs and a pointed face.

coriander /ko-ri-**an**-der/ noun a plant used as a herb in cookery.

cork noun **1** a light, soft brown substance obtained from the bark of a tree. **2** a bottle stopper made of cork. •verb **1** seal a bottle with a cork. **2** (**corked**) (of wine) spoilt by a faulty cork.

corker noun informal an excellent person or thing.
■ **corking** adjective.

corkscrew noun a device used for pulling corks from bottles. •verb move or twist in a spiral.

corm noun an underground part of certain plants.

cormorant /kor-muh-ruhnt/ noun a diving seabird with a long hooked bill and black feathers.

corn[1] noun **1** Brit. the chief cereal crop of a district (in England, wheat). **2** N. Amer. & Austral./NZ maize.
□ **corn on the cob** maize cooked and eaten straight from the cob.

corn[2] noun a painful area of thickened skin on the toes or foot.

cornea noun the transparent layer forming the front of the eye.

corned beef noun beef preserved with salt, often sold in tins.

corner noun **1** a place or angle where two or more sides or edges meet. **2** a place where two streets meet. **3** a secluded or remote area. **4** a difficult or awkward position. **5** Soccer a free kick taken by the attacking

THESAURUS

emulate, mimic; informal rip off.

cord noun string, thread, line, rope, cable, wire, twine, yarn.

cordon noun barrier, line, chain, ring, circle.
□ **cordon something off** close off, seal off, fence off, separate off, isolate, enclose, encircle, surround.

core noun **1** *the earth's core:* centre, interior, middle, nucleus. **2** *the core of the argument:* heart, nucleus, nub, kernel, meat, essence, crux, pith, substance; informal

nitty-gritty.
OPPOSITES edge, periphery.

corner noun **1** *the cart lurched round the corner:* bend, curve, turn, junction; Brit. hairpin bend. **2** *a charming corner of Italy:* district, region, area, quarter; informal neck of the woods.
•verb **1** *he was eventually cornered by police dogs:* surround, trap, hem in, pen in, cut off. **2** *crime syndicates have cornered the stolen car market:* gain control of, take over, dominate, monopolize, capture; informal sew up.

C

side from a corner of the field. • verb (**corners, cornering, cornered**) **1** force someone into a place or situation from which it is hard to escape. **2** go round a bend in a road. **3** control the trade in a particular type of goods.

cornerstone noun **1** a vital part. **2** a stone that forms the base of a corner of a building.

cornet noun **1** a brass instrument resembling a trumpet but shorter and wider. **2** Brit. a cone-shaped wafer for holding ice cream.

cornflour noun Brit. ground maize flour, used for thickening sauces.

cornflower noun a plant with deep blue flowers.

cornice /**kor**-niss/ noun a decorative border round the wall of a room just below the ceiling.

cornucopia /kor-nyuu-**koh**-pi-uh/ noun a plentiful supply of good things.

corny adjective (**cornier, corniest**) informal sentimental or unoriginal.

corolla /kuh-**rol**-luh/ noun the petals of a flower.

corollary /kuh-**rol**-luh-ri/ noun (plural **corollaries**) **1** a direct consequence or result. **2** a logical conclusion.

corona /kuh-**roh**-nuh/ noun (plural **coronae** /kuh-**roh**-nee/) **1** the gases surrounding the sun or a star. **2** a small circle of light around the sun or moon.

coronary /**ko**-ruh-nuh-ri/ adjective having to do with the heart, in particular with the arteries which supply it with blood. • noun (plural **coronaries**) (also **coronary thrombosis**) a blockage of the flow of blood to the heart.

coronation noun the ceremony of crowning a king or queen.

coroner noun an official who holds inquests into violent, sudden, or suspicious deaths.

coronet noun **1** a small or simple crown. **2** a decorative band put around the head.

corpora plural of **CORPUS**.

corporal[1] noun a rank of officer in the army, below sergeant.

corporal[2] adjective relating to the human body.
□ **corporal punishment** physical punishment, such as caning.

corporate adjective **1** relating to a business corporation. **2** relating to or shared by all members of a group.

corporation noun **1** a large company, or a group of companies acting as a single unit. **2** Brit. a group of people elected to govern a city, town, or borough.

corporeal /kor-**por**-i-uhl/ adjective relating to a person's body; physical rather than spiritual.

corps /kor/ noun (plural **corps** /korz/) **1** a large unit of an army. **2** a branch of an army with a particular kind of work. **3** a group of people involved in a particular activity.

corpse noun a dead body.

corpulent /**kor**-pyuu-luhnt/ adjective (of a person) fat.
■ **corpulence** noun.

corpus /**kor**-puhss/ noun (plural **corpora** /**kor**-puh-ruh/ or **corpuses**) a collection of written works.

corpuscle /**kor**-pus-s'l/ noun a red or white blood cell.

corral /kuh-**rahl**/ noun N. Amer. a pen for animals on a farm or ranch. • verb (**corrals, corralling, corralled**) **1** N. Amer. drive animals into a corral. **2** gather a group together.

correct adjective **1** free from mistakes; true or right. **2** following accepted social standards. • verb **1** put something right. **2** mark the mistakes in a piece of writing. **3** tell someone that they are wrong.
■ **correctly** adverb **correctness** noun.

correction noun **1** the process of correcting. **2** a change that corrects a mistake or inaccuracy.

corrective adjective designed to put something right.

correlate verb (**correlates, correlating, correlated**) place things together so that one thing depends on another and vice versa.

correlation noun **1** a situation in which one thing depends on another and vice versa.

THESAURUS

corporation noun company, firm, business, concern, operation, conglomerate, group, chain, multinational.

corpse noun dead body, carcass, remains; informal stiff; Medicine cadaver.

correct adjective **1** *the correct answer:* right, accurate, exact, true, perfect; informal spot on. **2** *correct behaviour:* proper, right, decent, seemly, respectable, decorous, suitable, appropriate, accepted.
OPPOSITES wrong, improper.

• verb *correct any mistakes:* rectify, right, put right, set right, amend, remedy, repair, reform, cure.

correction noun rectification, righting, amendment, repair, remedy, cure.

correctly adverb **1** *the questions were answered correctly:* accurately, right, perfectly, exactly, precisely. **2** *she behaved correctly at all times:* properly, decorously, with decorum, decently, fittingly,

C

2 the process of correlating two or more things.

correspond verb **1** match or agree almost exactly. **2** be similar or the same. **3** communicate by exchanging letters.

correspondence noun **1** letters sent or received. **2** a close connection or similarity. □ correspondence course a course of study in which student and tutors communicate by post.

> ☑ the ending is -ence, not -ance: correspondence.

correspondent noun **1** a journalist who reports on a particular subject. **2** a person who writes letters.

corridor noun **1** a passage in a building or train, with doors leading into rooms or compartments. **2** a strip of land linking two other areas.

> ☑ -dor, not -door: corridor.

corroborate verb (**corroborates, corroborating, corroborated**) confirm or give support to a statement or theory. ■ corroboration noun.

corrode verb (**corrodes, corroding, corroded**) **1** slowly wear away a hard material by the action of a chemical. **2** gradually weaken or destroy.

corrosion noun the process of corroding, or damage caused by it.

corrosive adjective tending to cause corrosion.

corrugated adjective shaped into alternate ridges and grooves. ■ corrugation noun.

corrupt adjective **1** willing to act dishonestly in return for money or other reward. **2** evil or immoral. **3** (of a written work or computer data) unreliable because of mistakes or alterations. ●verb make corrupt. ■ corruptly adverb.

corruption noun **1** dishonest or illegal behaviour. **2** the action of corrupting.

corsage /kor-**sahzh**/ noun a small bunch of flowers worn pinned to a woman's clothes.

corset noun a tight-fitting undergarment worn to shape a woman's figure or to support a person's back.

cortège /kor-**tezh**/ noun a funeral procession.

cortex /**kor**-teks/ noun (plural **cortices** /**kor**-ti-seez/) the outer layer of an organ or structure, especially the outer layer of the brain.

cortisone noun a hormone used to treat inflammation and allergies.

coruscating /**ko**-ruh-skay-ting/ adjective literary flashing or sparkling.

corvette /kor-**vet**/ noun a small warship designed for escorting convoys.

cos abbreviation cosine.

cosh noun a thick, heavy stick or bar used as a weapon. ●verb hit someone on the head with a cosh.

cosine /**koh**-syn/ noun Maths (in a right-angled triangle) the ratio of the side next to a particular acute angle to the longest side.

cosmetic adjective **1** (of treatment) intended to improve a person's appearance. **2** improving something only outwardly. ●noun (**cosmetics**) substances put on the

THESAURUS

appropriately, well.
OPPOSITES wrongly, improperly.

correspond verb **1** *the setting corresponds with the number on the dial:* be consistent, correlate, agree, accord, coincide, tally, tie in, match; informal square. **2** *a rank corresponding to a British sergeant:* be equivalent, be analogous, be comparable, equate. **3** *Debbie and I corresponded for years:* exchange letters, write, communicate.

correspondence noun **1** *there is some correspondence between the two variables:* parallel, correlation, agreement, consistency, conformity, similarity, resemblance, comparability. **2** *his private correspondence:* letters, messages, mail, post, communication.

correspondent noun reporter, journalist, columnist, writer, contributor, commentator.

corresponding adjective equivalent, related, parallel, matching, comparable, analogous.

corrupt adjective **1** *a corrupt official | corrupt practices:* dishonest, unscrupulous, criminal, fraudulent, illegal, unlawful; informal crooked; Brit. informal bent. **2** *he is utterly corrupt:* immoral, depraved, degenerate, debauched, vice-ridden, perverted, dissolute.
OPPOSITES honest, ethical, pure.
●verb deprave, pervert, lead astray, debauch, defile, pollute, sully.

corruption noun **1** *political corruption:* dishonesty, unscrupulousness, double-dealing, fraud, misconduct, bribery, venality; N. Amer. payola; informal graft, sleaze. **2** *his fall into corruption:* immorality, depravity, vice, degeneracy, perversion, debauchery, wickedness, evil, sin.
OPPOSITES honesty, morality, purity.

cosmetic adjective superficial, surface, skin-deep, outward, external.
OPPOSITES fundamental.

face and body to make them more attractive.

cosmic adjective relating to the universe.

cosmonaut noun a Russian astronaut.

cosmopolitan adjective **1** made up of people from many different countries and cultures. **2** familiar with many different countries.

cosmos noun the universe.

Cossack /koss-ak/ noun a member of a people of Russia and Ukraine famous for being good riders.

cosset verb (cossets, cosseting, cosseted) look after and protect someone in a way that is too indulgent.

cost verb (costs, costing, cost) **1** be able to be bought or done for a specific price. **2** involve the loss of. **3** (costs, costing, costed) estimate the cost of work that needs to be done. • noun **1** an amount given or required as payment. **2** the effort or loss necessary to achieve something. **3** (costs) legal expenses.
□ cost-effective effective or productive in relation to its cost.

co-star noun a performer appearing with another or others of equal importance.
• verb **1** appear in a film or play as a co-star. **2** (of a film or play) include someone as a co-star.

Costa Rican noun a person from Costa Rica. • adjective relating to Costa Rica.

costermonger noun dated a person who sells fruit and vegetables in the street.

costly adjective (costlier, costliest) **1** expensive. **2** causing suffering, loss, or disadvantage.
■ costliness noun.

costume noun **1** a set of clothes in a style typical of a particular country or historical period. **2** a set of clothes worn by an actor or performer for a role.

□ **costume jewellery** jewellery made with inexpensive materials or imitation gems.

costumier /koss-tyoo-mi-er/ noun a person who makes or supplies theatrical or fancy-dress costumes.

cosy (US spelling cozy) adjective (cosier, cosiest) **1** comfortable, warm, and secure. **2** not difficult or demanding. • noun (plural cosies) a cover to keep a teapot or a boiled egg hot.
■ cosily adverb cosiness noun.

cot noun a small bed with high barred sides for a baby or very young child.
□ cot death the unexplained death of a baby in its sleep.

coterie /koh-tuh-ri/ noun (plural coteries) a small, close-knit group of people.

cottage noun a small house in the country.
□ cottage cheese soft, lumpy white cheese.

cotter pin noun a metal pin used to fasten two parts of a mechanism together.

cotton noun **1** soft white fibres surrounding the seeds of a plant that grows in warm climates. **2** cloth or thread made from these fibres. • verb (cotton on) informal begin to understand.
□ cotton wool fluffy soft material used for cleaning the skin or a wound.

cotyledon /ko-ti-lee-duhn/ noun the first leaf that grows from a seed.

couch noun a long padded piece of furniture for sitting or lying on. • verb (couch something in) express something in language of a particular style.
□ couch potato informal a person who watches a lot of television.

couchette /koo-shet/ noun a bed or bunk on a train, converted from a seat or folded down from a wall.

cougar /koo-ger/ noun N. Amer. a puma.

THESAURUS

cosmopolitan adjective **1** *a cosmopolitan city:* multicultural, multiracial, international, worldwide, global. **2** *a very cosmopolitan chap:* sophisticated, cultivated, cultured, worldly, suave, urbane.

cost noun **1** *the cost of the equipment:* price, fee, tariff, fare, toll, levy, charge, payment, value, rate, outlay; humorous damage. **2** *the human cost of the conflict:* sacrifice, loss, toll, harm, damage, price. **3** (costs) *we need to cover our costs:* expenses, outgoings, overheads, expenditure, spend, outlay.
• verb **1** *the chair costs £186:* be priced at, sell for, be valued at, fetch, come to, amount to; informal set someone back, go for. **2** *the proposal has not yet been costed:* price, value, put a price/value/figure on.

costly adjective **1** *costly machinery:* expensive, dear, high-cost, overpriced; informal steep, pricey. **2** *a costly mistake:* catastrophic, disastrous, calamitous, ruinous, damaging, harmful, deleterious. OPPOSITES cheap.

costume noun clothes, garments, outfit, ensemble, dress, clothing, attire, garb, uniform, livery; formal apparel.

cosy adjective **1** *a cosy country cottage:* snug, comfortable, warm, homely, welcoming, safe, sheltered, secure; informal comfy. **2** *a cosy chat:* intimate, relaxed, informal, friendly.

cottage noun lodge, chalet, cabin, shack, shanty; (in Russia) dacha; Scottish bothy; Austral. informal weekender.

C

cough verb **1** send out air from the lungs with a sudden sharp sound. **2** (**cough something up**) informal reluctantly give money or information •noun **1** an act of coughing. **2** an illness of the throat or lungs causing coughing.

could modal verb past of CAN¹.

couldn't short form could not.

coulomb /koo-lom/ noun a unit of electric charge.

council noun **1** a group of people that meet regularly to discuss or organize something. **2** a group of people elected to manage the affairs of a city, county, or district. □ **council house** a house owned by a local council and rented to tenants. **council tax** (in the UK) a tax charged on households by local authorities.

councillor noun a member of a council.

! note the difference between **councillor** and **counsellor**.

counsel noun **1** advice. **2** (plural **counsel**) a barrister or other lawyer involved in a case. •verb (**counsels**, **counselling**, **counselled**; US spelling **counsels**, **counseling**, **counseled**) **1** advise or recommend. **2** give professional help and advice to someone with psychological or personal problems.

counsellor (US spelling **counselor**) noun a person trained to give advice on personal or psychological problems.

count¹ verb **1** find the total number of. **2** recite numbers in ascending order. **3** take into account. **4** regard as being: *people she counted as her friends.* **5** be important. **6** (**count on**) rely on. **7** (**count someone in** or **out**) include (or not include) someone in an activity. •noun **1** an act of counting.

2 a total found by counting. **3** a point to be discussed or considered. **4** Law each of the charges against an accused person. □ **out for the count 1** Boxing defeated by being knocked to the ground and unable to get up within ten seconds. **2** informal unconscious or asleep.

count² noun a foreign nobleman.

countdown noun an act of counting backwards to zero.

countenance noun a person's face or expression. •verb (**countenances**, **countenancing**, **countenanced**) tolerate or allow.

counter¹ noun **1** a long flat surface over which goods are sold or served or across which business is conducted with customers. **2** a small disc used in board games or to represent a coin. **3** a person or thing that counts something. □ **under the counter** bought or sold secretly and illegally.

counter² verb (**counters**, **countering**, **countered**) **1** argue against or reply to. **2** try to stop or prevent. •adverb (**counter to**) **1** in the opposite direction to. **2** in opposition to.

counteract verb do something to reduce or prevent the bad effects of.

counter-attack noun an attack made in response to an attack. •verb attack in response.

counterbalance noun **1** a weight that balances another. **2** something that has an equal but opposite effect to something else. •verb (**counterbalances**, **counterbalancing**, **counterbalanced**) have an equal but opposite effect on.

counter-espionage noun activities

THESAURUS

cough verb *he coughed loudly:* hack, hawk, bark, clear your throat.
•noun *a loud cough:* bark, hack; informal frog in your throat.

council noun **1** *the town council:* authority, government, administration, executive, chamber, assembly; Brit. corporation. **2** *the Schools Council:* committee, board, commission, assembly, panel, synod.

counsel noun **1** *his wise counsel:* advice, guidance, counselling, recommendations, suggestions, direction. **2** *the counsel for the defence:* barrister, lawyer; Scottish advocate; N. Amer. attorney, counselor(-at-law).
•verb *he counselled the team to withdraw:* advise, recommend, advocate, encourage, warn, caution, guide.

count verb **1** *she counted the money again:* add up, reckon up, total, tally, calculate, compute; Brit. tot up. **2** *250 employees, not counting overseas staff:* include, take into

account/consideration, take account of, allow for. **3** *I count it a privilege to be asked:* consider, think, feel, regard, look on as, view as, hold to be, judge, deem. **4** *it's your mother's feelings that count:* matter, be important, be of consequence, be significant, signify, carry weight, rate. □ **count on/upon rely on**, depend on, bank on, be sure of, have confidence in, believe in, put your faith in, take for granted, take as read.

counter verb **1** *workers countered accusations of dishonesty with claims of oppression:* respond to, parry, hit back at, answer. **2** *the second argument is more difficult to counter:* oppose, dispute, argue against/with, contradict, challenge, contest. OPPOSITES support. □ **counter to against,** in opposition to, contrary to, at variance with, in defiance of, in conflict with, at odds with.

designed to prevent spying by an enemy.

counterfeit /kown-ter-fit/ adjective made in exact imitation of something valuable so as to deceive or cheat people. • noun a forgery. • verb imitate something dishonestly.

counterfoil noun the part of a cheque, ticket, etc. that you keep when you give the other part up.

countermand verb cancel an order.

countermeasure noun something done to deal with a danger or threat.

counterpane noun dated a bedspread.

counterpart noun a person or thing that corresponds to another.

counterpoint noun 1 the playing of two or more tunes at the same time. 2 a tune played at the same time as another.

counterproductive adjective having the opposite effect to the one intended.

countersign verb sign a document that has already been signed by another person.

countersink verb (countersinks, countersinking, countersunk) insert a screw or bolt so that the head lies flat with the surface.

countertenor noun the highest male adult singing voice.

counterterrorism noun political or military activities designed to prevent terrorism.

countervailing adjective having an equal but opposite effect.

countess noun 1 the wife or widow of a count or earl. 2 a woman holding the rank of count or earl.

counting preposition taking account of; including.

countless adjective too many to be counted; very many.

countrified adjective characteristic of the country or country life.

country noun (plural countries) 1 a nation with its own government. 2 areas outside large towns and cities. 3 an area of land with particular physical features: *hilly country.*
□ country music (or country and western) a kind of popular music from country areas of the southern US.

countryside noun land and scenery outside towns and cities.

county noun (plural counties) each of the main areas into which some countries are divided for the purposes of local government.
□ county town the main town of a county, where its council is based.

coup /koo/ noun (plural coups /kooz/) 1 (also coup d'état /koo day-tah/) a sudden violent seizing of power from a government. 2 a successful move or action.

coupe /koo-pay, koop/ noun a sports car with a fixed roof and a sloping rear.

couple noun 1 two individuals of the same sort considered together. 2 two people who are married or in a romantic or sexual relationship. 3 informal an unspecified small number. • verb (couples, coupling, coupled) 1 connect or combine. 2 have sex.

couplet noun a pair of rhyming lines of poetry one after another.

coupling noun a device for connecting railway vehicles or parts of machinery together.

coupon noun 1 a voucher that gives you the right to claim a discount or buy something. 2 a form that can be sent off to ask for information or to enter a competition.

C

THESAURUS

counterpart noun equivalent, opposite number, peer, equal, parallel, complement, analogue, match, twin, mate, fellow.

countless adjective innumerable, numerous, untold, legion, numberless, limitless, incalculable; informal umpteen; N. Amer. informal gazillions of.
OPPOSITES few.

country noun 1 *foreign countries:* nation, state, kingdom, realm, land, territory, province. 2 *the country took to the streets:* people, public, population, populace, citizens, nation; Brit. informal Joe Public. 3 *thickly forested country:* terrain, land, territory, landscape, countryside, scenery, surroundings, environment. 4 *she hated living in the country:* countryside, provinces, rural areas, backwoods, hinterland; Austral./NZ outback, bush, back country; informal sticks.

countryside noun. See COUNTRY senses 3, 4.

county noun shire, province, territory, region, district, area.

coup noun 1 *a violent military coup:* takeover, coup d'état, overthrow, palace revolution, rebellion, uprising. 2 *a major publishing coup:* success, triumph, feat, masterstroke, accomplishment, achievement, scoop.

couple noun 1 *a couple of girls:* pair, duo, twosome, two, brace. 2 *a honeymoon couple:* husband and wife, twosome, partners, lovers; informal item.
• verb 1 *hope is coupled with a sense of loss:* combine, accompany, mix, incorporate, ally, add to. 2 *a cable is coupled to one of the wheels:* connect, attach, join, fasten, fix, link, secure, hook (up).
OPPOSITES detach.

coupon noun voucher, token, ticket, slip; N. Amer. informal rain check.

courage noun **1** the ability to do something frightening; bravery. **2** strength when faced with pain or grief.

courageous adjective having courage; brave.
■ **courageously** adverb.

courgette /koor-zhet/ noun Brit. a long, thin vegetable with green skin.

courier noun **1** a person employed to deliver goods or documents quickly. **2** a person employed to guide and help a group of tourists.

course noun **1** a direction that is taken or intended. **2** the way in which something progresses or develops. **3** (also **course of action**) a way of dealing with a situation. **4** a dish forming one of the stages of a meal. **5** a series of lectures or lessons in a particular subject. **6** a series of repeated treatments or doses of a drug. **7** an area prepared for racing, golf, or another sport. •verb (**courses**, **coursing**, **coursed**) **1** (of liquid) flow. **2** (**coursing**) the activity of hunting animals, especially hares, with greyhounds. □ **of course 1** as expected. **2** certainly; yes.

> ❗ don't confuse **course** with **coarse**, which means 'havng a rough texture'.

court noun **1** the judge, jury, and lawyers who sit and hear legal cases. **2** the place where a law court meets. **3** an area marked out for ball games such as tennis. **4** a courtyard. **5** the home, advisers, and staff of a king or queen. •verb **1** try to win someone's support. **2** behave in a way that might lead to something bad happening. **3** dated try to win the love of someone you want to marry. □ **court shoe** a woman's plain shoe with a low-cut upper and no fastening. **hold court** be the centre of attention.

courteous /ker-ti-uhss/ adjective polite and considerate.
■ **courteously** adverb.

courtesan /kor-ti-**zan**/ noun a prostitute with wealthy clients.

courtesy /ker-tuh-si/ noun (plural **courtesies**) **1** polite and considerate behaviour. **2** a polite speech or action. □ **courtesy of** given or allowed by.

courtier /**kor**-ti-er/ noun a companion or adviser of a king or queen.

courtly adjective (**courtlier**, **courtliest**) very dignified and polite.

court martial noun (plural **courts martial**) a court for trying people accused of breaking military law. •verb (**court-martial**) (**court-martials**, **court-martialling**, **court-martialled**) try someone in a court martial.

courtship noun **1** a period during which a couple develop a romantic relationship. **2** the process of trying to win someone's love or support.

courtyard noun an open area enclosed by walls or buildings.

couscous /**kuuss**-kuuss/ noun a North African dish of steamed or soaked semolina.

cousin noun (also **first cousin**) a child of

THESAURUS

courage noun bravery, pluck, valour, fearlessness, nerve, daring, audacity, boldness, grit, heroism, gallantry; informal guts; Brit. informal bottle.
OPPOSITES cowardice.

courageous adjective brave, plucky, fearless, intrepid, valiant, heroic, undaunted, dauntless; informal gutsy, have-a-go.
OPPOSITES cowardly.

course noun **1** the island was not far off our course: route, way, track, path, line, trail, trajectory, bearing, heading. **2** the best course to adopt: procedure, plan (of action), course of action, practice, approach, technique, policy, strategy, tactic. **3** a waterlogged course: racecourse, racetrack, track. **4** a French course: programme/course of study, curriculum, syllabus, classes, lectures, studies. **5** a course of antibiotics: programme, series, sequence, system, schedule, regime.
•verb tears coursed down her cheeks: flow, pour, stream, run, rush, gush, cascade, flood, roll.

□ **of course naturally**, as you would expect, needless to say, as a matter of course, obviously, it goes without saying.

court noun **1** the court found him guilty: court of law, law court, bench, bar, tribunal, assizes. **2** the King's court: household, retinue, entourage, train, courtiers, attendants.
•verb **1** he was courting a girl from the village: woo, go out with, date, go steady with. **2** an editor who was courted by politicians: cultivate, flatter, curry favour with, wine and dine; informal butter up. **3** he was courting public attention: seek, pursue, go after, strive for, solicit. **4** he's often courted controversy: risk, invite, attract, bring on yourself.

courteous adjective polite, well mannered, civil, respectful, well behaved, gracious, obliging, considerate.
OPPOSITES rude.

courtesy noun politeness, good manners, civility, respect, grace, consideration, thought.

your uncle or aunt.

□ **second cousin** a child of your mother's or father's first cousin.

couture /koo-**tyoor**/ noun the design and making of fashionable clothes, especially for a particular customer.

couturier /koo-**tyoo**-ri-ay/ noun a person who designs couture clothes.

cove noun a small sheltered bay.

coven /**kuv**-uhn/ noun a group of witches who meet regularly.

covenant /**kuv**-uh-nuhnt/ noun **1** a formal agreement. **2** an agreement to make regular payments to a charity.

cover verb (**covers**, **covering**, **covered**) **1** put something over or in front of a person or thing so as to protect or hide them. **2** spread or extend over an area. **3** deal with a subject. **4** travel a particular distance. **5** (of money) be enough to pay for something. **6** (of insurance) protect against a loss or accident. **7** (**cover something up**) try to hide or deny a mistake or crime. **8** (**cover for**) temporarily take over someone's job. **9** perform a cover version of a song. • noun **1** something that covers or protects. **2** a thick protective outer part or page of a book or magazine. **3** shelter. **4** a means of hiding an illegal or secret activity. **5** protection by insurance. **6** (also **cover version**) a performance of a song previously recorded by a different artist.

□ **break cover** suddenly leave shelter when being chased. **cover charge** a charge per person added to the bill in a restaurant. **covering letter** a letter sent with a document or parcel to explain what it is. **cover-up** an attempt to hide a mistake or crime.

coverage noun the extent to which something is covered.

coverlet noun a bedspread.

covert adjective /**kuv**-ert, **koh**-vert/ not done openly; secret. • noun /**kuv**-ert/ an area of bushes and undergrowth where game birds and animals can hide.

■ **covertly** adverb.

covet /**kuv**-it/ verb (**covets**, **coveting**, **coveted**) long to possess something belonging to someone else.

■ **covetous** adjective.

covey /**kuv**-i/ noun (plural **coveys**) a small flock of game birds.

cow[1] noun **1** a mature female animal of a domesticated breed of ox. **2** the female of certain other large animals. **3** informal a nasty woman.

cow[2] verb frighten someone so much that they do what you want.

coward noun a person who is too scared to do dangerous or unpleasant things.

■ **cowardliness** noun **cowardly** adjective.

cowardice noun lack of bravery.

cowboy noun **1** a man on horseback who herds cattle in the western US. **2** informal a dishonest or unqualified tradesman.

cower verb (**cowers**, **cowering**, **cowered**) crouch down or shrink back in fear.

cowl noun **1** a large, loose hood forming part of a monk's garment. **2** a hood-shaped covering for a chimney or ventilation shaft.

cowling noun a removable cover for a vehicle or aircraft engine.

cowrie noun (plural **cowries**) a shellfish whose glossy shell has a long, narrow opening.

cowslip noun a wild plant with clusters of yellow flowers.

cox noun the person who steers a rowing boat.

coxcomb noun old use a vain and conceited man.

coxswain /**kok**-suhn/ = **cox**.

C

THESAURUS

cove noun bay, inlet, fjord.

cover verb **1** *she covered her face with a towel:* protect, shield, shelter, hide, conceal, mask. **2** *his car was covered in mud:* cake, coat, encrust, plaster, smother. **3** *snow covered the fields:* blanket, carpet, coat, shroud, smother. **4** *a course covering all aspects of the business:* deal with, consider, take in, include, involve, incorporate, embrace.
OPPOSITES reveal.
• noun **1** *a protective cover:* covering, sleeve, wrapping, wrapper, envelope, sheath, housing, jacket, casing, cowling, canopy. **2** *a manhole cover:* lid, top, cap. **3** *a book cover:* binding, jacket, dust jacket, dust cover, wrapper. **4** *a thick cover of snow:*

coating, coat, covering, layer, carpet, blanket, film, sheet, veneer, crust, skin, cloak, mantle, veil, pall, shroud. **5** *panicking onlookers ran for cover:* shelter, protection, refuge, sanctuary.

coward noun mouse, baby; informal chicken, scaredy-cat, yellow-belly, sissy; Brit. informal big girl's blouse; N. Amer. informal pantywaist, pussy; Austral./NZ informal sook.
OPPOSITES hero.

cowardly adjective faint-hearted, lily-livered, spineless, craven, timid, timorous, fearful; informal yellow, chicken, gutless, yellow-bellied.
OPPOSITES brave.

cower verb cringe, shrink, flinch, crouch, blench.

coy adjective (**coyer, coyest**) **1** pretending to be shy or modest. **2** reluctant to give details about something.
■ **coyly** adverb.

coyote /koy-oh-ti/ noun (plural **coyote** or **coyotes**) a wolf-like wild dog found in North America.

coypu /koy-poo/ noun (plural **coypus**) a large South American rodent resembling a beaver.

cozy US spelling of **cosy**.

crab noun a sea creature with a broad shell and five pairs of legs.
□ **crab apple** a small, sour kind of apple.

crabbed adjective **1** (of writing) hard to read or understand. **2** bad-tempered.

crabby adjective (**crabbier, crabbiest**) informal bad-tempered.

crack noun **1** a narrow opening between two parts of something which has split or been broken. **2** a sudden sharp noise. **3** a sharp blow. **4** informal a joke. **5** informal an attempt to do something. **6** (also **crack cocaine**) a very strong form of cocaine. •verb **1** break without dividing into separate parts. **2** give way under pressure or strain. **3** make a sudden sharp sound. **4** hit hard. **5** (of a person's voice) suddenly change in pitch. **6** informal solve or decipher. •adjective very good or skilful: *a crack shot*.
□ **crack down on** informal deal severely with. **crack of dawn** daybreak. **crack a joke** tell a joke. **crack up** informal **1** suffer an emotional breakdown. **2** (**be cracked up to be**) be said to be.

crackdown noun a series of severe measures against undesirable or illegal behaviour.

cracker noun **1** a paper cylinder which makes a sharp noise and releases a small toy when it is pulled apart. **2** a firework that explodes with a crack. **3** a thin, dry biscuit. **4** informal a very good example of something.

crackers or **cracked** adjective informal mad.

cracking adjective informal **1** excellent. **2** fast: *a cracking pace*.

crackle verb (**crackles, crackling, crackled**) make a series of slight cracking noises. •noun a crackling sound.
■ **crackly** adjective.

crackling noun the crisp fatty skin of roast pork.

crackpot noun informal an eccentric or foolish person.

cradle noun **1** a baby's bed on rockers. **2** a place or period in which something originates or flourishes: *the cradle of civilization*. **3** a supporting framework. •verb (**cradles, cradling, cradled**) hold gently and protectively.

craft noun **1** an activity involving skill in making things by hand. **2** skill in carrying out work. **3** (**crafts**) things made by hand. **4** (plural **craft**) a boat, ship, or aircraft. **5** skill in deceiving people. •verb make something skilfully.

craftsman noun (plural **craftsmen**) a worker who is skilled in a particular craft.
■ **craftsmanship** noun.

crafty adjective (**craftier, craftiest**) clever at deceiving people; cunning.
■ **craftily** adverb.

crag noun a steep or rugged cliff or rock face.
■ **craggy** adjective.

THESAURUS

coy adjective demure, shy, modest, bashful, diffident, self-effacing, shrinking.
OPPOSITES brazen.

crack noun **1** *a crack in the glass*: split, break, chip, fracture, rupture. **2** *a crack between two rocks*: space, gap, crevice, fissure, cleft, cranny, chink. **3** *the crack of a rifle*: bang, report, explosion, detonation, clap, crash. **4** *a crack on the head*: blow, bang, hit, knock, rap, bump, smack, slap; informal bash, whack, clout.
•verb **1** *the glass cracked in the heat*: break, split, fracture, rupture, snap. **2** *he finally cracked*: break down, give way, cave in, go to pieces, give in, yield, succumb. **3** *she cracked him across the forehead*: hit, strike, smack, slap, beat, thump, knock, rap; informal bash, whack, clobber, clout, clip. **4** (informal) *the code proved hard to crack*: decipher, interpret, decode, break, solve.

cradle noun **1** *the baby's cradle*: crib, Moses basket, cot, carrycot. **2** *the cradle of democracy*: birthplace, fount, fountainhead, source, spring, origin.
•verb *she cradled his head in her arms*: hold, support, cushion, pillow, nurse, rest.

craft noun **1** *the historian's craft*: activity, occupation, trade, profession, work, line of work, job. **2** *she used craft and diplomacy*: cunning, craftiness, guile, wiliness, artfulness, deviousness, slyness, trickery, duplicity, dishonesty, deceit, deceitfulness, deception, intrigue, subterfuge, wiles, ploys, ruses, schemes, tricks. **3** *a sailing craft*: vessel, ship, boat, aircraft, spacecraft.

craftsman, craftswoman noun artisan, artist, skilled worker, technician, expert, master.

crafty adjective cunning, wily, sly, artful, devious, tricky, scheming, calculating, shrewd, canny, dishonest, deceitful.
OPPOSITES open, honest.

cram verb (**crams, cramming, crammed**)
1 force too many people or things into a space. 2 fill something to the point of overflowing. 3 study hard just before an exam.

crammer noun a college that prepares students for exams.

cramp noun 1 pain caused by a muscle or muscles tightening. 2 a tool for clamping two objects together. •verb restrict the development of.

cramped adjective 1 uncomfortably small or crowded. 2 (of handwriting) small and difficult to read.

crampon noun a spiked plate fixed to a boot for climbing on ice or rock.

cranberry noun (plural **cranberries**) a small sour-tasting red berry.

crane noun 1 a tall machine used for moving heavy objects by suspending them from a projecting arm. 2 a wading bird with long legs and a long neck. •verb (**cranes, craning, craned**) stretch out your neck to see something.
□ crane fly a flying insect with very long legs.

cranium /kray-ni-uhm/ noun (plural **craniums** or **crania** /kray-ni-uh/) the part of the skull that encloses the brain.
■ cranial adjective.

crank noun 1 a part of an axle or shaft that is bent at right angles, turned to produce motion. 2 an eccentric person. •verb 1 start an engine by turning a crankshaft. 2 (**crank something up**) informal make something more intense. 3 (**crank something out**) informal produce something regularly and routinely.

crankshaft noun a shaft driven by a crank.

cranky adjective (**crankier, crankiest**) informal 1 strange or eccentric. 2 bad-tempered.

cranny noun (plural **crannies**) a small, narrow space or opening.

crape noun black silk, formerly used for mourning clothes.

craps noun a North American gambling game played with two dice.

crash verb 1 (of a vehicle) collide violently with an obstacle or another vehicle. 2 (of an aircraft) fall from the sky and hit the land or sea. 3 move or fall with a sudden loud noise. 4 (of shares) fall suddenly in value. 5 Computing fail suddenly. 6 (also **crash out**) informal fall deeply asleep. 7 (**crashing**) informal complete; total: *a crashing bore.* •noun 1 an instance of crashing. 2 a sudden loud, deep noise. •adjective rapid and concentrated: *a crash course in Italian.*
□ crash helmet a helmet worn by a motorcyclist to protect the head. crash-land (of an aircraft) land roughly in an emergency.

crass adjective very thoughtless and stupid.
■ crassly adverb.

crate noun 1 a wooden case for transporting goods. 2 a square container divided into individual units for holding bottles.

crater noun a large hollow caused by an explosion or impact or forming the mouth of a volcano.

cravat /kruh-vat/ noun a strip of fabric worn by men round the neck and tucked inside a shirt.

C

THESAURUS

cram verb 1 *wardrobes crammed with clothes:* fill, stuff, pack, jam, fill to overflowing, overload, crowd, throng. 2 *they all crammed into the car:* crowd, pack, pile, squash. 3 *he crammed his clothes into a suitcase:* push, thrust, shove, force, ram, jam, stuff, pack, pile, squash, squeeze. 4 *the students are cramming for exams:* revise; informal swot, mug up, bone up.

cramp noun *stomach cramps:* spasm, pain, shooting pain, twinge, pang, convulsion. •verb *tighter rules will cramp economic growth:* hinder, impede, inhibit, hamper, constrain, hamstring, interfere with, restrict, limit, slow.

cramped adjective 1 *cramped accommodation:* poky, uncomfortable, confined, restricted, small, tiny, narrow, crowded, congested. 2 *cramped handwriting:* small, crabbed, illegible, unreadable, indecipherable.
OPPOSITES spacious, flamboyant.

crash verb 1 *the car crashed into a tree:* smash into, collide with, be in collision with, hit, strike, ram, cannon into, plough into, meet head-on; N. Amer. impact. 2 *he crashed his car:* smash, wreck; Brit. write off; Brit. informal prang; N. Amer. informal total. 3 *a tree crashed to the ground:* fall, drop, plummet, plunge, sink, dive, tumble. 4 (informal) *his company crashed:* collapse, fold, fail, go under, go bankrupt; informal go bust, go to the wall. •noun 1 *a crash on the motorway:* accident, collision, smash; N. Amer. wreck; informal pile-up; Brit. informal shunt. 2 *a loud crash:* bang, smash, smack, crack, bump, thud, explosion. 3 *the crash of her company:* collapse, failure, liquidation, bankruptcy.

crate noun packing case, chest, tea chest, box, container.

crater noun hollow, bowl, basin, hole, cavity, depression, dip; Geology caldera.

crave verb (**craves**, **craving**, **craved**) **1** feel a very strong desire for. **2** old use ask for.

craven adjective cowardly.

craving noun a very strong desire for something.

craw noun dated the part of a bird's throat where food is prepared for digestion.

crawl verb **1** move forward on the hands and knees or with the body close to the ground. **2** move very slowly along. **3** (**be crawling with**) be unpleasantly covered or crowded with. **4** feel an unpleasant sensation like that of something moving over the skin. **5** informal be too friendly or obedient in order to make someone like you. • noun **1** an act of crawling. **2** a very slow rate of movement. **3** a swimming stroke involving alternate overarm movements and rapid kicks of the legs.

crayfish noun (plural **crayfish** or **crayfishes**) a shellfish like a small lobster.

crayon noun a stick of coloured chalk or wax, used for drawing. • verb draw with a crayon or crayons.

craze noun a widespread but short-lived enthusiasm for something.

crazed adjective **1** behaving in a wild or mad way. **2** covered with fine cracks.

crazy adjective (**crazier**, **craziest**) **1** mad.

2 (usu. **crazy about**) informal very enthusiastic about or fond of. **3** foolish or ridiculous.
□ **crazy paving** paving made of irregular pieces of flat stone.
■ **crazily** adverb **craziness** noun.

creak verb make a harsh, high sound. • noun a creaking sound.
■ **creaky** adjective.

cream noun **1** the thick fatty liquid which rises to the top when milk is left to stand. **2** a food containing cream or having a creamy texture. **3** a thick liquid substance that is applied to the skin. **4** the very best of a group. **5** a very pale yellow or off-white colour. • verb **1** mash a cooked vegetable with milk or cream. **2** (**cream someone/thing off**) take away the best of a group.
□ **cream cheese** a soft, rich kind of cheese.
■ **creamy** adjective.

crease noun **1** a line or ridge produced on paper or cloth by folding or pressing it. **2** Cricket any of a number of lines marked on the pitch. • verb (**creases**, **creasing**, **creased**) make creases in.

create verb (**creates**, **creating**, **created**) **1** bring into existence. **2** cause something to happen. **3** informal make a fuss; complain.

creation noun **1** the action of creating. **2** a

THESAURUS

crave verb long for, yearn for, hanker after, desire, want, hunger for, thirst for, pine for; informal be dying for.

craving noun longing, yearning, desire, hankering, hunger, thirst, appetite.

crawl verb **1** *they crawled under the table:* creep, worm your way, go on all fours, wriggle, slither, squirm. **2** (informal) *I'm not crawling to him:* grovel, kowtow, pander, toady, bow and scrape, fawn; informal suck up, lick someone's boots.

craze noun fad, fashion, trend, vogue, enthusiasm, mania, passion, rage; informal thing.

crazy adjective (informal) **1** *a crazy old man:* mad, insane, out of your mind, deranged, demented, crazed, lunatic, unbalanced, unhinged; informal mental, off your head, round the bend; Brit. informal barmy, crackers, barking (mad), potty, round the twist. **2** *a crazy idea:* stupid, foolish, idiotic, silly, absurd, ridiculous, ludicrous, preposterous; informal cockeyed; Brit. informal barmy, daft. **3** *he's crazy about her:* passionate, very keen, enamoured, infatuated, smitten, enthusiastic, fanatical; informal wild, mad, nuts; Brit. informal potty.
OPPOSITES sane, sensible, apathetic.

cream noun **1** *skin cream:* lotion, ointment, moisturizer, cosmetic, salve, rub. **2** *the cream of the world's photographers:* best,

finest, pick, flower, crème de la crème, elite.
OPPOSITES dregs.
• adjective *a cream dress:* off-white, creamy, ivory.

creamy adjective smooth, thick, velvety, rich, buttery.
OPPOSITES lumpy.

crease noun **1** *trousers with creases:* fold, line, ridge, furrow, groove, corrugation. **2** *creases at the corners of her eyes:* wrinkle, line, crinkle, pucker, crow's foot. • verb *her skirt was creased:* crumple, wrinkle, crinkle, line, scrunch up, rumple.

create verb **1** *she has created a work of stunning originality:* produce, generate, bring into being, make, fashion, build, construct. **2** *regular socializing creates a good team spirit:* bring about, give rise to, lead to, result in, cause, breed, generate, engender, produce. **3** *the governments planned to create a free-trade zone:* establish, found, initiate, institute, constitute, inaugurate, launch, set up. **4** *she was created a life peer:* appoint, make.
OPPOSITES destroy, abolish.

creation noun **1** *the creation of a government:* establishment, formation, foundation, initiation, institution, inauguration, constitution, setting up. **2** *the whole of creation:* the world, the

thing which has been made or invented.
3 (Creation) literary the universe.

creative adjective involving the use of the imagination in order to create something.
■ **creatively** adverb **creativity** noun.

creator noun **1** a person or thing that creates. **2 (the Creator)** God.

creature noun a living being, in particular an animal rather than a person.
□ **creature comforts** things that make life comfortable.

crèche /kresh/ noun a place where babies and young children are looked after while their parents are at work.

credence /**kree**-duhnss/ noun belief that something is true.

credential /kri-**den**-sh'l/ noun **1** a qualification, achievement, or quality used to indicate how suitable a person is for something. **2 (credentials)** documents that prove a person's identity or qualifications.

credible adjective able to be believed; convincing.
■ **credibility** noun **credibly** adverb.

> **!** don't confuse **credible** with **creditable**: **credible** means 'believable or convincing', whereas **creditable** means 'deserving recognition and praise'.

credit noun **1** the system of doing business by trusting that a customer will pay at a later date for goods or services supplied. **2** public recognition or praise given for an achievement or quality. **3 (a credit to)** a source of pride to. **4 (credits)** a list of the

people who worked on a film or television programme, displayed at the end. **5** a unit of study counting towards a degree or diploma. **6** an entry in an account recording an amount received. •**verb** (**credits, crediting, credited**) **1 (credit someone with)** feel that someone is responsible for something good. **2** believe something surprising. **3** add an amount of money to an account.
□ **be in credit** (of an account) have money in it. **credit card** a plastic card that allows you to buy things and pay for them later.

creditable adjective deserving recognition and praise.
■ **creditably** adverb.

creditor noun a person or company to whom money is owed.

credo /**kree**-doh, **kray**-doh/ noun (plural **credos**) a statement of a person's beliefs or aims.

credulous adjective too ready to believe things.
■ **credulity** noun.

creed noun **1** a system of religious belief; a faith. **2** a set of beliefs or principles.

creek noun **1** a narrow stretch of water running inland from the coast. **2** N. Amer. & Austral./NZ a stream or small river.
□ **up the creek** informal in severe difficulty.

creel noun a large basket for carrying fish.

creep verb (**creeps, creeping, crept**) **1** move slowly and cautiously. **2** progress or develop gradually. •**noun** informal a person

---

universe, the cosmos, nature, the natural world. **3** *Dickens's literary creations:* work, work of art, production, opus, oeuvre, achievement, concoction, invention; informal brainchild.
OPPOSITES abolition, destruction.

creative adjective inventive, imaginative, innovative, experimental, original, artistic, inspired, visionary.
OPPOSITES unimaginative.

creativity noun inventiveness, imagination, innovation, originality, artistry, inspiration, vision.

creator noun maker, producer, author, designer, deviser, originator, inventor, architect.

creature noun animal, beast, brute, living thing, living being; N. Amer. informal critter.

credentials plural noun **1** *a biologist with impeccable credentials:* suitability, eligibility, attributes, qualifications, record, experience, background. **2** *examine the credentials of all callers:* documents, identity papers, ID, passport, testimonial, reference, certification.

credibility noun plausibility, believability, credence, trustworthiness, reliability, dependability, integrity.

credible adjective believable, plausible, conceivable, persuasive, convincing, tenable, probable, possible, feasible, reasonable.

credit noun *he got the credit for the work:* praise, commendation, acclaim, acknowledgement, recognition, kudos, glory, respect, appreciation.
•**verb** (Brit.) *you wouldn't credit it!* believe, accept, give credence to, trust, have faith in.
□ **credit someone with something ascribe something to someone,** attribute something to someone.

creed noun **1** *people of many creeds:* faith, religion, belief, religious persuasion. **2** *his political creed:* beliefs, principles, articles of faith, ideology, credo.

creek noun inlet, bay, estuary, fjord; Scottish firth.

creep verb tiptoe, steal, sneak, slink, edge, inch, skulk, prowl.

c

who is insincerely friendly or respectful.
□ **give you the creeps** make you feel disgust or fear.

creeper noun a plant that grows along the ground or another surface.

creepy adjective (**creepier**, **creepiest**) informal causing an unpleasant feeling of fear or unease.

cremate verb (**cremates**, **cremating**, **cremated**) dispose of a dead body by burning it.
■ **cremation** noun.

crematorium /kre-muh-**tor**-i-uhm/ noun (plural **crematoria** or **crematoriums**) a building where dead people are cremated.

crème de la crème /krem duh la **krem**/ noun the best person or thing of a particular kind.

crenellations plural noun battlements.
■ **crenellated** adjective.

Creole /**kree**-ohl/ noun **1** a person of mixed European and black descent. **2** a descendant of French settlers in the southern US. **3** a combination of a European language and an African language.

creosote /**kree**-uh-soht/ noun a dark brown oil painted on to wood to preserve it.

crêpe or **crepe** /krayp/ noun **1** a light, thin fabric with a wrinkled surface. **2** hard-wearing wrinkled rubber used for the soles of shoes. **3** /krayp, krep/ a thin pancake.
□ **crêpe paper** thin, crinkled paper.

crept past and past participle of **CREEP**.

crepuscular /kri-**puss**-kyuu-ler/ adjective literary resembling twilight; dim and shadowy.

crescendo /kri-**shen**-doh/ noun (plural **crescendos** or **crescendi** /kri-**shen**-di/) **1** a gradual increase in loudness in a piece of music. **2** a climax.

crescent noun a narrow curved shape tapering to a point at each end.

cress noun a plant with hot-tasting leaves.

crest noun **1** a tuft or growth of feathers,

fur, or skin on the head of a bird or animal. **2** a plume of feathers on a helmet. **3** the top of a ridge, wave, etc. **4** a distinctive design in heraldry representing a family or organization. • verb reach the top of.
■ **crested** adjective.

crestfallen adjective sad and disappointed.

cretin noun a stupid person.
■ **cretinous** adjective.

crevasse /kri-**vass**/ noun a deep open crack in a glacier.

crevice noun a narrow opening or crack in a rock or wall.

crew[1] noun **1** a group of people who work on a ship, aircraft, or train. **2** the members of a crew other than the officers. **3** a group of people who work together: *a film crew*.
• verb act as a member of a crew.
□ **crew cut** a very short haircut for men and boys. **crew neck** a close-fitting round neckline.

crew[2] past of **CROW**[2].

crib noun **1** chiefly N. Amer. a child's cot. **2** informal a list of answers or other information used, for example, by students to cheat in a test. **3** the card game cribbage. • verb (**cribs**, **cribbing**, **cribbed**) informal copy something dishonestly.

cribbage noun a card game for two players.

crick noun a painful stiff feeling in the neck or back. • verb twist or strain the neck or back.

cricket[1] noun a team game played with a bat, ball, and wickets.
■ **cricketer** noun.

cricket[2] noun an insect like a grasshopper, the male of which produces a shrill chirping sound.

cried past and past participle of **CRY**.

crime noun **1** an action that is against the law. **2** illegal actions as a whole. **3** something disgraceful or very unfair.

criminal noun a person who has committed

THESAURUS

creepy adjective (informal) frightening, eerie, disturbing, sinister, weird, menacing, threatening; informal spooky, scary.

crest noun **1** *the bird's crest:* tuft, comb, plume, crown. **2** *the crest of the hill:* summit, peak, top, ridge, pinnacle, brow, crown, apex. **3** *the Duke's crest:* insignia, emblem, coat of arms, arms, badge, device, regalia.

crevice noun crack, fissure, cleft, chink, cranny, slit, split.

crew noun **1** *the ship's crew:* company, complement, sailors, hands. **2** *a film crew:* team, squad, company, unit, party, gang.

crime noun **1** *kidnapping is a serious crime:* offence, unlawful act, illegal act, felony, violation, misdemeanour. **2** *the increase in crime:* lawbreaking, delinquency, wrongdoing, criminality, misconduct, illegality, villainy, vice.

criminal noun *a convicted criminal:* lawbreaker, offender, villain, delinquent, felon, culprit; informal crook; Austral./NZ informal crim.
• adjective **1** *criminal conduct:* unlawful, illegal, illicit, lawless, delinquent, corrupt; informal crooked; Brit. informal bent. **2** (informal) *a criminal waste of money:* deplorable, shameful, reprehensible, disgraceful,

a crime. •adjective **1** relating to crime or a crime. **2** informal disgraceful or very unfair.
■ **criminality** noun **criminally** adverb.

crimp verb press into small folds or ridges.

crimson noun a deep red colour.

cringe verb (**cringes, cringing, cringed**) **1** shrink back or cower in fear. **2** have a sudden feeling of embarrassment or disgust.

crinkle verb (**crinkle, crinkling, crinkled**) form small creases or wrinkles. •noun a small crease or wrinkle.
■ **crinkly** adjective.

crinoline /krin-uh-lin/ noun a petticoat stiffened with hoops, formerly worn to make a long skirt stand out.

cripple noun old use or offensive a person who is unable to walk or move properly because they are disabled or injured. •verb (**cripples, crippling, crippled**) **1** make someone unable to move or walk properly. **2** severely damage or weaken.

crisis noun (plural **crises**) **1** a time of severe difficulty or danger. **2** a time when a difficult decision must be made.

crisp adjective **1** firm, dry, and brittle. **2** (of the weather) cool and fresh. **3** brisk and decisive. •noun a thin, crisp slice of fried potato.

■ **crisply** adverb **crispy** adjective.

crispbread noun a thin, crisp biscuit made from rye or wheat.

criss-cross adjective with a pattern of crossing lines. •verb **1** form a criss-cross pattern on. **2** repeatedly go back and forth around a place.

criterion /kry-teer-i-uhn/ noun (plural **criteria** /kry-teer-i-uh/) a standard by which something may be judged.

> ❗ the singular form is **criterion** and the plural form is **criteria**. It's wrong to use **criteria** as a singular: say *further criteria need to be considered* not *a further criteria needs to be considered*.

critic noun **1** a person who finds fault with someone or something. **2** a person who assesses literary or artistic works.

critical adjective **1** expressing disapproving comments. **2** assessing a literary or artistic work. **3** very important in terms of the success or failure of something. **4** at a point of danger or crisis.
■ **critically** adverb.

criticism noun **1** expression of disapproval. **2** the assessment of literary or artistic works.

criticize or **criticise** verb (**criticizes,**

THESAURUS

inexcusable, outrageous, scandalous.
OPPOSITES lawful, reasonable.

cripple verb **1** *the accident crippled her:* disable, paralyse, immobilize, incapacitate, handicap. **2** *the company had been crippled by the recession:* damage, weaken, hamper, paralyse, ruin, destroy, wipe out, bring to a standstill, put out of action, put out of business.
OPPOSITES assist.

crippled adjective disabled, paralysed, incapacitated, (physically) handicapped, lame, immobilized, bedridden, confined to a wheelchair; euphemistic physically challenged.

crisis noun **1** *the current economic crisis:* emergency, disaster, catastrophe, calamity, meltdown, predicament, plight, dire straits. **2** *the situation had reached a crisis:* critical point, turning point, crossroads, head, moment of truth; informal crunch.

crisp adjective **1** *crisp bacon:* crunchy, crispy, brittle, breakable, dry. **2** *a crisp autumn day:* invigorating, cool, fresh, refreshing, exhilarating, brisk. **3** *crisp white bedlinen:* smooth, fresh, ironed, starched.
OPPOSITES soft, sultry, crumpled.

criterion noun standard, measure, gauge, test, benchmark, yardstick, touchstone, barometer.

critic noun **1** *a literary critic:* reviewer,

commentator, analyst, judge, pundit, expert. **2** *critics of the government:* detractor, attacker, fault-finder; informal knocker.

critical adjective **1** *a highly critical report:* disapproving, disparaging, scathing, fault-finding, judgemental, negative, unfavourable, censorious; informal nit-picking, picky. **2** *the situation is critical:* serious, grave, precarious, touch-and-go, in the balance, desperate, dire, acute, life-and-death. **3** *the choice of materials is critical:* crucial, vital, essential, all-important, paramount, fundamental, key, pivotal.
OPPOSITES complimentary, safe, unimportant.

criticism noun **1** *she was stung by his criticism:* fault-finding, censure, condemnation, disapproval, disparagement; informal flak, a bad press, panning; Brit. informal stick. **2** *literary criticism:* evaluation, assessment, appraisal, appreciation, analysis, critique, judgement, commentary.
OPPOSITES praise.

criticize verb find fault with, censure, condemn, attack, disparage, denigrate, run down; informal knock, pan, pull to pieces; Brit. informal slag off, slate, rubbish; N. Amer. informal pummel, trash; Austral./NZ informal bag.
OPPOSITES praise.

C

criticizing, criticized) **1** express disapproval of. **2** assess a literary or artistic work.

critique /kri-**teek**/ noun a critical assessment.

croak noun a deep, hoarse sound, like that made by a frog. • verb make a croak.
■ **croaky** adjective.

Croatian /kroh-**ay**-sh'n/ noun (also **Croat** /**kroh**-at/) **1** a person from Croatia. **2** the language of Croatia. • adjective relating to Croatia or Croatian.

crochet /**kroh**-shay/ noun a craft in which yarn is made into fabric with a hooked needle. • verb (**crochets, crocheting, crocheted**) make an article by means of crochet.

crock[1] noun informal a feeble and useless old person.

crock[2] noun an earthenware pot or jar.

crockery noun plates, dishes, cups, etc. made of earthenware or china.

crocodile noun **1** a large reptile with long jaws, a long tail, and a thick skin. **2** Brit. informal a line of schoolchildren walking in pairs.
☐ **crocodile tears** insincere tears or sorrow.

crocus noun (plural **crocuses**) a small plant with bright yellow, purple, or white flowers.

croft noun a small rented farm in Scotland or northern England.
■ **crofter** noun.

croissant /**krwass**-on/ noun a flaky crescent-shaped bread roll.

crone noun an ugly old woman.

crony noun (plural **cronies**) informal a close friend or companion.

crook noun **1** a shepherd's or bishop's hooked staff. **2** a bend at a person's elbow. **3** informal a criminal or dishonest person. • verb bend a finger or leg.

crooked adjective **1** bent or twisted out of shape or position. **2** informal dishonest or illegal.

croon verb hum, sing, or speak in a soft, low voice.
■ **crooner** noun.

crop noun **1** a plant grown in large quantities, especially as food. **2** an amount of a crop harvested at one time. **3** a very short hairstyle. **4** a pouch in a bird's throat where food is stored or prepared for digestion. **5** a short flexible whip used by horse riders. • verb (**crops, cropping, cropped**) **1** cut something very short. **2** (of an animal) bite off and eat the tops of plants. **3** (**crop up**) appear or happen unexpectedly.

cropper noun (**come a cropper**) informal fall or fail heavily.

croquet /**kroh**-kay/ noun a game in which wooden balls are hit through hoops with a mallet.

croquette /kroh-**ket**/ noun a small cake or roll of vegetables, meat, or fish, fried in breadcrumbs.

cross noun **1** a mark, object, or shape formed by two short intersecting lines or pieces (+ or ×). **2** a medal or monument shaped like a cross. **3** (**the Cross**) the wooden cross on which Jesus was crucified. **4** an animal

THESAURUS

crook noun (informal). See **CRIMINAL** noun.

crooked adjective **1** *narrow, crooked streets:* winding, twisting, zigzag, meandering, tortuous, serpentine. **2** *a crooked spine:* bent, twisted, misshapen, deformed, malformed, contorted, warped, bowed, distorted. **3** *the picture over the bed looked crooked:* lopsided, askew, awry, off-centre, out of true, at an angle, slanting, squint; Scottish agley; Brit. informal skew-whiff, wonky. **4** (informal) *a crooked deal:* dishonest, criminal, illegal, unlawful, nefarious, fraudulent, corrupt; informal shady; Brit. informal bent.
OPPOSITES straight, legal, honest.

crop noun *some farmers lost their entire crop:* harvest, yield, fruits, produce, vintage.
• verb **1** *she's had her hair cropped:* cut, clip, trim, shear, shave, lop off, chop off, hack off, dock. **2** *a flock of sheep were cropping the turf:* graze on, browse on, feed on, nibble, eat.
☐ **crop up** happen, occur, arise, turn up, pop up, emerge, materialize, surface,

appear, come to light.

cross noun **1** *we all have our crosses to bear:* burden, trouble, worry, trial, affliction, curse, misfortune, woe; informal hassle, headache. **2** *a cross between a yak and a cow:* mixture, blend, combination, amalgam, hybrid, cross-breed, mongrel.
• verb **1** *they crossed the hills on foot:* travel across, traverse, negotiate, navigate, cover. **2** *the two roads cross:* intersect, meet, join, connect. **3** *no one dared cross him:* oppose, resist, defy, obstruct, contradict, argue with, stand up to. **4** *the breed was crossed with Friesian:* hybridize, cross-breed, interbreed, cross-fertilize, cross-pollinate.
• adjective *Jane was getting cross:* angry, annoyed, irate, irritated, in a bad mood, put out; informal hot under the collar, peeved; Brit. informal shirty, ratty; N. Amer. informal sore, ticked off; Austral./NZ informal ropeable, snaky.
OPPOSITES pleased.
☐ **cross something out** delete, strike out, score out, cancel, obliterate.

or plant resulting from cross-breeding. **5** a mixture of two things. •verb **1** go or extend across or to the other side of. **2** pass in an opposite or different direction. **3** place crosswise. **4** draw a line or lines across. **5** Brit. mark a cheque with a pair of parallel lines to indicate that it must be paid into a named bank account. **6** Soccer pass the ball across the field towards the centre. **7** oppose or stand in the way of. **8** make an animal breed with another of a different species. •adjective annoyed.
□ **at cross purposes** misunderstanding or having different aims from one another. **cross-breed** produce an animal or plant by making two different species, breeds, or varieties breed. **cross-check** check figures or information by using a different source or method. **cross-country 1** across fields or countryside. **2** across a region or country. **cross-dressing** the wearing of clothes usually worn by the opposite sex. **cross-examine** question a witness called by the other party in a court of law. **cross-eyed** having one or both eyes turned inwards towards the nose. **cross-fertilize** fertilize a plant using pollen from another plant of the same species. **cross something off** remove an item from a list. **cross something out** remove a word or phrase by drawing a line through it. **cross-question** question in great detail. **cross reference** a reference to another written work, or part of one, given to provide further information. **cross section 1** a surface exposed by making a straight cut through a solid object at right angles to its length. **2** a sample of a larger group. **cross swords** have an argument or dispute.
■ **crossly** adverb.

crossbar noun **1** a horizontal bar between the two upright posts of a football goal. **2** a bar between the handlebars and saddle on a bicycle.

crossbow noun a bow with a mechanism for drawing and releasing the string.

crossfire noun gunfire from two or more directions passing through the same area.

cross-hatch verb shade an area with many intersecting parallel lines.

crossing noun **1** a place where roads or railway lines cross. **2** a place to cross a street or railway line.

crossroads noun a place where two or more roads cross each other.

crosswise or **crossways** adverb **1** in the form of a cross. **2** diagonally.

crossword noun a puzzle in which words crossing each other vertically and horizontally are written as answers to clues.

crotch noun the part of the human body between the legs.

crotchet noun a musical note that lasts half as long as a minim.

crotchety adjective irritable.

crouch verb bend the knees and bring the upper body forward and down. •noun a crouching position.

croup¹ /kroop/ noun an illness of children, with coughing and breathing difficulties.

croup² /kroop/ noun a horse's hindquarters.

croupier /kroo-pi-ay, kroo-pi-er/ noun the person in charge of a gambling table in a casino.

crouton /kroo-ton/ noun a small piece of fried or toasted bread served with soup.

crow¹ noun a large black bird with a harsh call.
□ **as the crow flies** in a straight line across country. **crow's feet** wrinkles at the outer corner of a person's eye. **crow's-nest** a platform at the top of a ship's mast to watch from.

crow² verb (**crows, crowing, crowed** or **crew**) **1** (of a cock) make its loud, shrill cry. **2** boastfully express pride or triumph. •noun the cry of a cock.

crowbar noun an iron bar with a flattened end, used as a lever.

crowd noun **1** a large number of people gathered together. **2** informal a group of

crouch verb squat, bend (down), hunker down, hunch over, stoop, duck, cower.

crow verb boast, brag, blow your own trumpet, swagger, swank, gloat.

crowd noun **1** *a crowd gathered:* throng, horde, mass, multitude, host, army, swarm, mob, rabble; informal gaggle. **2** *they're a nice crowd:* group, set, circle, clique; informal gang, bunch, crew, lot. **3** *the final attracted a capacity crowd:* audience, spectators, listeners, viewers, house, turnout, attendance, gate, congregation.
•verb **1** *reporters crowded round her:* cluster, flock, swarm, mill, throng, huddle,

gather, assemble, congregate, converge. **2** *the guests crowded into the dining room:* surge, throng, push, jostle, elbow your way, squeeze, pile, cram. **3** *the quayside was crowded:* throng, pack, jam, cram, fill.

crowded adjective packed, full, filled to capacity, full to bursting, congested, overflowing, teeming, swarming, thronged, populous, overpopulated, busy; informal jam-packed, stuffed, chock-a-block, chock-full, bursting at the seams, full to the gunwales, wall-to-wall, mobbed; Austral./NZ informal chocker.
OPPOSITES deserted.

people with a shared quality. • verb 1 fill a
space almost completely. 2 move or come
together as a crowd. 3 move or stand too
close to.

crown noun 1 a circular headdress worn by
a king or queen. 2 (**the Crown**) the
reigning king or queen. 3 a wreath of
leaves or flowers worn as an emblem of
victory. 4 an award gained by a victory.
5 the top or highest part of something.
6 an artificial replacement or covering for
the upper part of a tooth. 7 a former
British coin worth five shillings (25 pence).
• verb 1 place a crown on the head of
someone to declare them to be king or
queen. 2 rest on or form the top of.

crozier /kroh-zi-er/ noun a hooked staff
carried by a bishop.

crucial adjective very important, especially
in terms of the success or failure of
something.
■ **crucially** adverb.

crucible noun a container in which metals
or other substances may be melted or
heated.

crucifix noun a small cross with a figure of
Jesus on it.

crucifixion noun 1 the execution of a
person by crucifying them. 2 (**the
Crucifixion**) the crucifixion of Jesus.

cruciform adjective having the shape of a
cross.

crucify verb (**crucifies, crucifying, crucified**)

1 kill someone by nailing or tying them to
a cross. 2 informal criticize someone severely.

crude adjective 1 in a natural state; not yet
processed. 2 rough or simple. 3 coarse or
vulgar.
■ **crudely** adverb **crudity** noun.

cruel adjective (**crueller, cruellest** or **crueler,
cruelest**) 1 taking pleasure in the suffering
of other people. 2 causing suffering or
pain.
■ **cruelly** adverb.

cruelty noun (plural **cruelties**) cruel behaviour
or treatment.

cruet noun a small container or set of
containers for salt, pepper, oil, or vinegar.

cruise verb (**cruises, cruising, cruised**)
1 move slowly around without a definite
destination. 2 travel smoothly at a
moderate speed. • noun a voyage on a ship
taken as a holiday.

cruiser noun 1 a large, fast warship. 2 a
yacht or motorboat with passenger
accommodation.

crumb noun 1 a small fragment of bread,
cake, or biscuit. 2 a very small amount.

crumble verb (**crumbles, crumbling,
crumbled**) 1 break or fall apart into small
fragments. 2 gradually decline or fall apart.
• noun Brit. a baked pudding made with fruit
and a crumbly topping.
■ **crumbly** adjective.

crummy adjective (**crummier, crummiest**)
informal bad or unpleasant.

THESAURUS

crown noun 1 *the royal crown:* coronet,
diadem, tiara, circlet. 2 *loyal servants of
the Crown:* monarch, sovereign, king,
queen, emperor, empress, monarchy,
royalty. 3 *the crown of the hill:* top, crest,
summit, peak, pinnacle, tip, brow, apex.
• verb 1 *the building is crowned by a
balustrade:* top, cap, tip, head, surmount.
2 *a teaching post at Harvard crowned his
career:* round off, cap, be the climax of, be
the culmination of, top off, complete.

crucial adjective 1 *negotiations were at a
crucial stage:* pivotal, critical, key, decisive,
life-and-death. 2 *confidentiality is crucial:*
all-important, of the utmost importance,
of the essence, critical, paramount,
essential, vital.
OPPOSITES insignificant, unimportant.

crude adjective 1 *crude oil:* unrefined,
unpurified, unprocessed, untreated, coarse,
raw, natural. 2 *a crude barricade:*
primitive, simple, basic, homespun,
rudimentary, rough and ready, improvised.
3 *crude jokes:* vulgar, rude, dirty, naughty,
smutty, indecent, obscene, coarse; informal
blue.
OPPOSITES refined, sophisticated, clean.

cruel adjective 1 *a cruel man:* brutal, savage,
inhuman, barbaric, vicious, sadistic,
monstrous, callous, ruthless, merciless,
heartless, unkind, inhumane. 2 *her death
was a cruel blow:* harsh, severe, bitter,
heartbreaking, heart-rending, painful,
agonizing, traumatic.
OPPOSITES compassionate.

cruelty noun brutality, savagery,
inhumanity, barbarity, viciousness, sadism,
callousness, ruthlessness.

cruise noun *a cruise down the Nile:* (boat)
trip, voyage, sail.
• verb 1 *she cruised across the Atlantic:* sail,
voyage. 2 *a taxi cruised past:* drive slowly,
drift, sail; informal mosey, tootle; Brit. informal
pootle.

crumb noun fragment, bit, morsel, particle,
speck, scrap, shred, atom, trace, mite, jot,
ounce; informal smidgen, tad.

crumble verb 1 *the plaster was crumbling:*
disintegrate, fall apart, fall to pieces,
collapse, decompose, break up, decay,
become dilapidated. 2 *crumble the cheese
with your fingers:* break up, crush,
fragment. 3 *party unity began to crumble:*
collapse, deteriorate, degenerate, fail.

crumpet noun 1 a soft, flat cake with an open texture, eaten toasted and buttered. 2 Brit. informal sexually attractive women.

crumple verb (**crumples, crumpling, crumpled**) 1 crease something by crushing it. 2 collapse.

crunch verb 1 crush something hard or brittle with the teeth. 2 move with a noisy grinding sound. •noun 1 a crunching sound. 2 (**the crunch**) informal the crucial point of a situation.
■ **crunchy** adjective.

crusade noun 1 (**the Crusades**) a series of medieval military expeditions made by Europeans against Muslims in the Middle East. 2 an energetic organized campaign. •verb (**crusades, crusading, crusaded**) take part in a crusade.
■ **crusader** noun.

crush verb 1 squash, crease, or break up something by pressing it. 2 defeat completely. •noun 1 a crowd of people pressed closely together. 2 informal a strong, short-lived feeling of love for someone.

crust noun 1 the tough outer part of a loaf of bread. 2 a hardened layer, coating, or deposit. 3 the outermost layer of the earth. 4 a layer of pastry covering a pie. •verb form into a crust, or cover with a crust.

crustacean /kruss-**tay**-sh'n/ noun a hard-shelled creature such as a crab or lobster, usually living in water.

crusty adjective (**crustier, crustiest**) 1 having or consisting of a crust. 2 easily irritated.

crutch noun 1 a long stick with a bar at the top, used as a support by a lame person. 2 a person's crotch.

crux noun (**the crux**) the most important point that is being discussed.

cry verb (**cries, crying, cried**) 1 shed tears. 2 shout or scream loudly. 3 (of an animal) make a distinctive call. 4 (**cry out for**) demand or need. 5 (**cry off**) informal fail to keep to an arrangement. •noun (plural **cries**) 1 a period of shedding tears. 2 a loud shout or scream. 3 an animal's distinctive call.
□ a crying shame a very unfortunate situation.

cryogenics /kry-uh-**jen**-iks/ noun the branch of physics concerned with very low temperatures.
■ **cryogenic** adjective.

crypt noun an underground room beneath a church, used as a chapel or burial place.

cryptic adjective mysterious or obscure in meaning.
■ **cryptically** adverb.

crystal noun 1 a transparent mineral, especially quartz. 2 a piece of a solid substance that is formed naturally and has flat sides arranged symmetrically. 3 very clear glass.
□ crystal ball a globe of glass or crystal, used for predicting the future.

crystalline adjective 1 resembling a crystal. 2 literary very clear.

crystallize or **crystallise** verb (**crystallizes, crystallizing, crystallized**) 1 form crystals. 2 become definite and clear. 3 (**crystallized**) (of fruit) coated with and preserved in sugar.

cu. abbreviation cubic.

cub noun 1 the young of a fox, bear, lion, or other meat-eating mammal. 2 (also **Cub**

---

crumple verb 1 *she crumpled the note in her fist:* crush, scrunch up, screw up, squash, squeeze. 2 *his trousers were dirty and crumpled:* crease, wrinkle, crinkle, rumple. 3 *her resistance crumpled:* collapse, give way, cave in, go to pieces, break down, crumble.
OPPOSITES flatten out, iron, hold.

crunch verb munch, chomp, champ, bite into, crush, grind, break, smash.

crusade noun *a crusade against crime:* campaign, drive, push, movement, effort, struggle, battle, war, offensive.
•verb *he has crusaded for hopeless causes:* campaign, fight, battle, strive, struggle, agitate, lobby.

crush verb 1 *essential oils are released when the herbs are crushed:* squash, squeeze, press, pulp, mash, mangle, pulverize. 2 *your dress will get crushed:* crease, crumple, rumple, wrinkle, scrunch up. 3 *crush the biscuits with a rolling pin:* pulverize, pound, grind, break up, smash,

crumble. 4 *the new regime crushed all opposition:* suppress, put down, quell, stamp out, repress, subdue, extinguish. 5 *Alan was crushed by her words:* demoralize, deflate, flatten, squash, devastate, shatter, mortify, humiliate.
OPPOSITES allow, promote, encourage.
•noun *the crush of people:* crowd, throng, horde, swarm, press, mob.

crust noun covering, layer, coating, surface, topping, sheet, film, skin, shell, scab.

cry verb 1 *Mandy started to cry:* weep, shed tears, sob, wail, snivel, whimper; Scottish greet; informal blub, blubber; Brit. informal grizzle. 2 *'Wait!' he cried:* call, shout, exclaim, sing out, yell, bawl, bellow, roar; informal holler.
OPPOSITES laugh, whisper.
•noun call, shout, exclamation, yell, bawl, bellow, roar; informal holler.
□ cry off (informal) **back out,** pull out, cancel, withdraw, change your mind; informal get cold feet, cop out.

C

Scout) a member of the junior branch of the Scout Association.

Cuban noun a person from Cuba. • adjective relating to Cuba.

cubbyhole noun a small enclosed space or room.

cube noun 1 a three-dimensional shape with six equal square faces. 2 the result obtained when a number is multiplied by itself twice. • verb 1 cut food into small cubes. 2 find the cube of a number.
□ **cube root** the number which produces a given number when cubed.

cubic adjective 1 having the shape of a cube. 2 involving the cube of a quantity: *a cubic metre.*

cubicle noun a small area of a room that is separated off for privacy.

cubism noun a style of painting featuring regular lines and shapes.
■ **cubist** noun & adjective.

cubit noun an ancient measure of length, approximately equal to the length of a forearm.

cuckoo noun a bird known for laying its eggs in the nests of other birds. • adjective informal crazy.

cucumber noun a long green fruit with watery flesh, eaten in salads.

cud noun (usu. in **chew the cud**) partly digested food that cows and similar animals bring back from the first stomach to the mouth for further chewing.

cuddle verb (**cuddles, cuddling, cuddled**) 1 hold closely and lovingly in your arms. 2 (often **cuddle up to**) lie or sit close. • noun an affectionate hug.

cuddly adjective (**cuddlier, cuddliest**) pleasantly soft or plump.

cudgel noun a short, thick stick used as a weapon. • verb (**cudgels, cudgelling, cudgelled;** US spelling **cudgels, cudgeling, cudgeled**) beat with a cudgel.

cue¹ noun 1 a signal to an actor to enter or to begin their speech or performance. 2 a signal or prompt for action. • verb (**cues, cueing** or **cuing, cued**) 1 give a cue to. 2 set a piece of audio or video equipment to play a particular part of a recording.

cue² noun a long rod for hitting the ball in snooker, billiards, or pool.

cuff¹ noun 1 the end part of a sleeve, where the material of the sleeve is turned back or a separate band is sewn on. 2 chiefly N. Amer. a trouser turn-up.
□ **off the cuff** informal without preparation.

cuff² verb hit with an open hand. • noun a blow with an open hand.

cufflink noun a device for fastening together the sides of a shirt cuff.

cuisine /kwi-**zeen**/ noun a particular style of cooking.

cul-de-sac /**kul**-duh-sak/ noun (plural **cul-de-sacs**) a street or passage closed at one end.

culinary adjective having to do with cooking.

cull verb 1 kill a selected number of a certain kind of animal to reduce its population. 2 choose a few things from a wide range. • noun a selective killing of a certain kind of animal.

culminate verb (**culminates, culminating, culminated**) reach a climax or point of highest development.
■ **culmination** noun.

culottes /kyuu-**lots**/ plural noun women's wide-legged knee-length trousers.

culpable adjective deserving blame.
■ **culpability** noun.

culprit noun the person responsible for an offence.

cult noun 1 a system of religious worship directed towards a particular person or object. 2 a small, unconventional religious group. 3 something popular or fashionable among a particular group of people.

cultivate verb (**cultivates, cultivating,**

THESAURUS

cuddle verb 1 *she picked up the baby and cuddled her:* hug, embrace, clasp, hold in your arms. 2 *the pair were kissing and cuddling:* embrace, hug, caress, pet, fondle; informal canoodle, smooch. 3 *I cuddled up to him:* snuggle, nestle, curl, nuzzle.

cudgel noun club, truncheon, bludgeon, baton, shillelagh, mace; N. Amer. blackjack, nightstick; Brit. informal cosh.
• verb club, bludgeon, beat, batter, bash; Brit. informal cosh.

cue noun signal, sign, indication, prompt, reminder.

culminate verb come to a climax, come to a head, climax, end, finish, conclude, build up to, lead up to.

culpable adjective to blame, guilty, at fault, in the wrong, answerable, accountable, responsible.
OPPOSITES innocent.

culprit noun guilty party, offender, wrongdoer, miscreant, criminal, lawbreaker, felon, delinquent; informal baddy, crook.

cult noun 1 *a religious cult:* sect, group, movement. 2 *the cult of youth in Hollywood:* obsession, fixation, idolization, devotion, worship, veneration.

cultivate verb 1 *the peasants cultivated the land:* farm, work, till, plough, dig. 2 *they cultivated basic food crops:* grow, raise, rear, tend, plant, sow. 3 *Tessa tried to*

cultivated) **1** prepare and use land for crops or gardening. **2** grow plants or crops. **3** try to develop or gain a particular quality. **4** try to win the friendship or support of. **5** (**cultivated**) well educated and having good taste.
■ **cultivation** noun **cultivator** noun.

cultural adjective **1** relating to the culture of a society. **2** relating to the arts and intellectual achievements.
■ **culturally** adverb.

culture noun **1** the arts, customs, and institutions of a nation, people, or group. **2** the arts and intellectual achievements regarded as a whole. **3** a refined understanding or appreciation of culture. **4** a preparation of cells or bacteria grown for medical or scientific study.

cultured adjective **1** well educated and having good taste. **2** (of a pearl) formed round a foreign body inserted into an oyster.

culvert noun a tunnel carrying a stream or open drain under a road or railway.

cum preposition combined with.

cumbersome adjective **1** difficult to carry or use because of its size or weight. **2** complicated and time-consuming.

cumin /kyoo-min/ noun the seeds of a plant, used as a spice.

cummerbund noun a sash worn round the waist as part of a man's formal evening suit.

cumulative adjective increasing by successive additions.
■ **cumulatively** adverb.

cumulus /kyoo-myuu-luhss/ noun (plural

cumuli /kyoo-myuu-lee/) a type of cloud that forms rounded masses heaped on a flat base.

cuneiform /kyoo-ni-form/ adjective (of ancient writing systems) using wedge-shaped characters.

cunning adjective **1** skilled at deceiving people. **2** skilful or clever. •noun craftiness.
■ **cunningly** adverb.

cup noun **1** a small bowl-shaped drinking container with a handle. **2** a trophy in the shape of a cup on a stem, awarded as a prize in a sports contest. **3** a sports contest in which the winner is awarded a cup. **4** either of the two parts of a bra shaped to contain one breast. •verb (**cups**, **cupping**, **cupped**) **1** form your hand or hands into the curved shape of a cup. **2** place your curved hand or hands around.

cupboard noun a piece of furniture, or a recess in a wall with a door, used for storage.
□ **cupboard love** affection shown to someone in order to obtain something.

Cupid noun **1** the Roman god of love. **2** (also **cupid**) a picture or statue of a naked winged child carrying a bow.

cupidity noun greed for money or possessions.

cupola noun a rounded dome that forms or decorates a roof.

cur noun an aggressive mongrel dog.

curate noun an assistant to a parish priest.

curative adjective able to cure disease.

curator noun a keeper of a museum or other collection.

curb verb control or put a limit on. •noun **1** a

C

THESAURUS

cultivate her: woo, court, curry favour with, ingratiate yourself with; informal get in someone's good books. **4** he wants to cultivate his mind: improve, better, refine, educate, develop, enrich.

cultivated adjective. See **CULTURED**.

cultural adjective **1** cultural differences: social, lifestyle, sociological, societal, anthropological, racial, ethnic. **2** cultural achievements: aesthetic, artistic, intellectual, educational, civilizing.

culture noun **1** a lover of culture: the arts, high art. **2** a man of culture: education, cultivation, enlightenment, discernment, discrimination, taste, refinement, sophistication. **3** Afro-Caribbean culture: civilization, society, way of life, lifestyle, customs, traditions, heritage, values. **4** a corporate culture of greed and envy: philosophy, ethic, outlook, approach, rationale.

cultured adjective cultivated, artistic, enlightened, civilized, educated, well read,

learned, discerning, discriminating, refined, sophisticated; informal arty.
OPPOSITES ignorant.

cunning adjective **1** a cunning scheme: crafty, wily, artful, devious, sly, scheming, canny, dishonest, deceitful. **2** a cunning plan: clever, ingenious, imaginative, enterprising, inventive, creative, original, inspired, brilliant.
OPPOSITES open, honest, stupid.
•noun **1** his political cunning: guile, craftiness, deviousness, trickery, duplicity. **2** it took cunning just to survive: ingenuity, imagination, inventiveness, enterprise, creativity, brilliance.

curator noun custodian, keeper, conservator, guardian, caretaker.

curb noun a curb on imports: restraint, restriction, check, brake, rein, control, limit.
•verb a plan to curb consumer spending: restrain, hold back, keep in check, control, rein in, contain; informal keep a lid on.

C

control or limit on something. **2** a type of bit with a strap or chain which passes under a horse's lower jaw. **3** US spelling of **KERB**.

curd or **curds** noun a soft, white substance formed when milk coagulates.

curdle verb (**curdles, curdling, curdled**) form curds or lumps.

cure verb (**cures, curing, cured**) **1** make a person who is ill well again. **2** end a disease, condition, or problem by treatment or appropriate action. **3** preserve meat, fish, etc. by salting, drying, or smoking. • noun **1** something that cures; a remedy. **2** the healing of a person who is ill.
  ■ **curable** adjective.

curfew noun **1** a regulation requiring people to remain indoors between specific hours of the night. **2** the time at which a curfew begins.

curie noun (plural **curies**) a unit of radioactivity.

curio noun (plural **curios**) an object that is interesting because it is rare or unusual.

curiosity noun (plural **curiosities**) **1** a strong desire to know or learn something. **2** an unusual or interesting object or fact.

curious adjective **1** eager to know or learn something. **2** strange; unusual.
  ■ **curiously** adverb.

curium noun a radioactive metallic element that is produced artificially.

curl verb form a curved or spiral shape.

• noun something in the shape of a spiral or coil.
  ■ **curly** adjective.

curler noun a roller or clasp around which you wrap hair to curl it.

curlew /ker-lyoo/ noun (plural **curlew** or **curlews**) a large wading bird with a long curved bill.

curling noun a game played on ice, in which you slide large circular flat stones towards a mark.

curmudgeon noun a bad-tempered person.
  ■ **curmudgeonly** adjective.

currant noun a dried fruit made from a small seedless variety of grape.

currency noun (plural **currencies**) **1** a system of money used in a country. **2** the state or period of being current.

current adjective **1** happening or being used or done now. **2** in common or general use. • noun **1** a flow of water or air in a particular direction. **2** a flow of electrically charged particles.
  □ **current account** Brit. a bank or building society account from which you may withdraw money at any time.
  ■ **currently** adverb.

❗ don't confuse **current** with **currant**, which means 'a dried grape'.

curriculum noun (plural **curricula** or **curriculums**) the subjects that make up a course of study in a school or college.
  □ **curriculum vitae** /vee-ty/ a written

THESAURUS

cure verb **1** *he was cured of the disease:* heal, restore to health, make well/better. **2** *economic equality cannot cure all social ills:* rectify, remedy, put/set right, right, fix, mend, repair, solve, sort out, eliminate, end. **3** *some farmers cured their own bacon:* preserve, smoke, salt, dry, pickle.
• noun *a cure for cancer:* remedy, medicine, medication, antidote, treatment, therapy.

curiosity noun **1** *his evasiveness roused my curiosity:* interest, inquisitiveness, attention, prying; informal nosiness. **2** *the shop is full of curiosities:* oddity, curio, novelty, rarity.

curious adjective **1** *she was curious to know what had happened:* intrigued, interested, eager, inquisitive. **2** *her curious behaviour:* strange, odd, peculiar, funny, unusual, bizarre, weird, eccentric, extraordinary, abnormal, anomalous.
OPPOSITES uninterested, normal.

curl verb **1** *smoke curled up from his cigarette:* spiral, coil, wreathe, twirl, swirl, wind, curve, twist (and turn), snake, corkscrew. **2** *Ruth curled her arms around his neck:* wind, twine, entwine, wrap.

• noun **1** *the tangled curls of her hair:* ringlet, corkscrew, kink, lock. **2** *a curl of smoke:* spiral, coil, twirl, swirl, twist, corkscrew.

curly adjective wavy, curling, curled, frizzy, kinky, corkscrew.
OPPOSITES straight.

currency noun **1** *foreign currency:* money, legal tender, cash, banknotes, notes, coins; N. Amer. bills. **2** *a term which has gained new currency:* popularity, circulation, exposure, acceptance, prevalence.

current adjective **1** *current events:* contemporary, present-day, modern, topical, live, burning. **2** *the idea is still current:* prevalent, common, accepted, in circulation, popular, widespread. **3** *a current driving licence:* valid, usable, up to date. **4** *the current prime minister:* incumbent, present, in office, in power, reigning.
OPPOSITES past, out of date, former.
• noun **1** *a current of air:* flow, stream, draught, jet, tide. **2** *the current of human life:* course, progress, progression, flow, tide, movement.

account of a person's qualifications and previous jobs, sent with a job application. ■ **curricular** adjective.

curry[1] noun (plural **curries**) an Indian dish of meat, vegetables, or fish, cooked in a hot, spicy sauce.

curry[2] verb (**curry favour**) try to win someone's approval by flattering them and being very helpful.

curry comb noun a hand-held rubber device used for grooming horses.

curse noun **1** an appeal to a supernatural power to harm someone or something. **2** a cause of harm or misery. **3** an offensive word or phrase used to express anger or annoyance. •verb (**curses**, **cursing**, **cursed**) **1** use a curse against. **2** (**be cursed with**) continuously suffer from or be affected by. **3** say offensive words; swear.

cursor noun a mark on a computer screen identifying the point where typing or other input will take effect.

☑ -*or* at the end, not -*er*: cursor.

cursory adjective hasty and therefore not thorough. ■ **cursorily** adverb.

curt adjective (of a person's speech) rudely brief. ■ **curtly** adverb.

curtail verb cut short or restrict. ■ **curtailment** noun.

curtain noun a piece of material hung up to form a screen at a window or between the stage and the audience in a theatre. •verb provide or screen something with a curtain or curtains.

□ **curtain call** the appearance of a performer on stage after a performance to acknowledge applause. **curtain-raiser** an event happening just before a longer or more important one.

curtsy or **curtsey** noun (plural **curtsies** or **curtseys**) a woman's or girl's respectful greeting, made by bending the knees with one foot in front of the other. •verb (**curtsies**, **curtsying**, **curtsied** or **curtseys**, **curtseying**, **curtseyed**) perform a curtsy.

curvaceous adjective having an attractively curved shape.

curvature noun the fact of being curved; a curved shape.

curve noun a line which gradually turns from a straight course. •verb (**curves**, **curving**, **curved**) form a curve. ■ **curvy** adjective.

cushion noun **1** a bag of cloth stuffed with soft material, used to provide comfort when sitting. **2** something that gives protection against impact or something unpleasant. **3** the inner sides of a billiard table. •verb **1** soften the effect of an impact on. **2** lessen the bad effects of.

cushy adjective (**cushier**, **cushiest**) informal easy and undemanding.

cusp noun **1** a pointed end where two curves meet. **2** a point in between two different states.

custard noun **1** a sweet sauce made with milk and eggs, or milk and flavoured cornflour. **2** a baked dessert made from eggs and milk.

custodian noun a person responsible for looking after something.

custody noun **1** protective care.

THESAURUS

curse noun **1** *she'd put a curse on him:* jinx; N. Amer. hex. **2** *the curse of unemployment:* affliction, burden, misery, ordeal, evil, scourge. **3** *muffled curses:* swear word, expletive, oath, profanity, four-letter word, dirty word, obscenity; informal cuss word. •verb **1** *she was cursed with feelings of inadequacy:* afflict, trouble, plague, bedevil. **2** *he cursed loudly:* swear, take the Lord's name in vain; informal cuss, turn the air blue, eff and blind.

cursed adjective damned, doomed, ill-fated, ill-starred; informal jinxed.

cursory adjective brief, hasty, hurried, rapid, passing, perfunctory, desultory, casual. OPPOSITES thorough.

curt adjective terse, brusque, abrupt, clipped, blunt, short, sharp. OPPOSITES expansive.

curtail verb **1** *policies designed to curtail spending:* reduce, cut, cut down, decrease, trim, restrict, limit, curb, rein in/back; informal slash. **2** *his visit was curtailed:* shorten, cut short, truncate. OPPOSITES increase, extend.

curve noun *the curves of the river:* bend, turn, loop, arc, arch, bow, curvature. •verb *the road curved back on itself:* bend, turn, loop, wind, meander, snake, arc, arch.

curved adjective bent, arched, bowed, rounded, crescent. OPPOSITES straight.

cushion noun *a cushion against inflation:* protection, buffer, shield, defence, bulwark. •verb **1** *residents are cushioned from the outside world:* protect, shield, shelter, cocoon. **2** *to cushion the blow, pensions were increased:* soften, lessen, diminish, mitigate, alleviate, take the edge off, dull, deaden.

custody noun *custody of the child:* care, guardianship, charge, supervision, safe keeping, responsibility, protection. □ **in custody in prison**, in jail, imprisoned, incarcerated, under lock and key, on

2 imprisonment.
■ **custodial** adjective.

custom noun 1 a traditional way of behaving or doing something. 2 regular dealings with a shop or business by customers.
□ **custom-built** (or **custom-made**) made to a particular customer's order.

customary adjective usual or habitual.
■ **customarily** adverb.

customer noun 1 a person who buys goods or services from a shop or business. 2 a person or thing that you have to deal with: *a tough customer.*

customize or **customise** verb (**customizes, customizing, customized**) modify something to suit a person or task.

customs plural noun 1 charges made by a government on imported goods. 2 the official department that administers and collects customs charges.

cut verb (**cuts, cutting, cut**) 1 make an opening or wound with something sharp. 2 shorten, divide, or remove with something sharp. 3 make or design a garment in a particular way. 4 reduce the amount or quantity of. 5 go across or through an area. 6 stop filming or recording. 7 divide a pack of playing cards by lifting a portion from the top. • noun 1 a wound or opening resulting from cutting. 2 a reduction. 3 the style in which a garment or a person's hair is cut. 4 a piece of meat cut from a carcass. 5 informal a share of profits. 6 a version of a film after editing.
□ **cut and dried** already decided. **cut and**

thrust a competitive atmosphere or environment. **cut corners** do something badly to save time or money. **cut glass** glass with decorative patterns cut into it. **cut in** 1 interrupt. 2 pull in too closely in front of another vehicle. 3 (of a machine) begin operating automatically. **cut the mustard** informal reach the required standard. **cut no ice** informal have no influence or effect. **cut someone/thing off** 1 make it impossible to reach a place. 2 deprive someone of a supply. 3 break a telephone connection with someone. **cut out** (of an engine) suddenly stop operating. **cut someone out** exclude someone. **cut-throat** ruthless and fierce.

cutaneous /kyoo-**tay**-ni-uhss/ adjective having to do with the skin.

cutback noun a reduction.

cute adjective 1 charmingly pretty; sweet. 2 N. Amer. informal clever; shrewd.
■ **cutely** adverb.

cuticle /kyoo-ti-k'l/ noun the dead skin at the base of a fingernail or toenail.

cutlass noun a short sword with a slightly curved blade, formerly used by sailors.

cutlery noun knives, forks, and spoons used for eating or serving food.

cutlet noun 1 a lamb or veal chop from just behind the neck. 2 a flat cake of minced meat, nuts, etc., covered in breadcrumbs and fried.

cutter noun 1 a person or thing that cuts. 2 a light, fast patrol boat or sailing boat.

cutting noun 1 an article cut from a newspaper. 2 a piece cut from a plant to

THESAURUS

remand; informal behind bars, doing time, inside; Brit. informal banged up.

custom noun 1 *his unfamiliarity with local customs:* tradition, practice, usage, way, convention, formality, ritual, mores. 2 *it was his custom to sleep in a chair:* habit, practice, routine, way; formal wont.

customary adjective usual, traditional, normal, conventional, habitual, familiar, accepted, accustomed, routine, established, time-honoured, prevailing.
OPPOSITES unusual.

customer noun consumer, buyer, purchaser, patron, client, shopper; Brit. informal punter.

cut verb 1 *he cut his finger:* gash, slash, lacerate, slit, wound, scratch, graze, nick. 2 *cut the pepper into small pieces:* slice, chop, dice, cube, carve; N. Amer. hash. 3 *the name had been cut into the stone:* carve, engrave, incise, etch, score, chisel, whittle. 4 *the government will cut expenditure:* reduce, cut back/down on, decrease, lessen, mark down, discount, lower; informal

slash. 5 *the text has been substantially cut:* shorten, abridge, condense, abbreviate, truncate, edit, censor. 6 *you need to cut ten lines per page:* delete, remove, take out, excise.
• noun 1 *a cut on his jaw:* gash, slash, laceration, incision, wound, scratch, graze, nick. 2 *a cut of beef:* piece, joint, fillet, section. 3 (informal) *they want their cut:* share, portion, quota, percentage; informal slice (of the cake). 4 *a cut in interest rates:* reduction, cutback, decrease, lessening; N. Amer. rollback. 5 *the cut of his jacket:* style, design, line, fit.

cutback noun reduction, cut, decrease, economy, saving; N. Amer. rollback.
OPPOSITES increase.

cute adjective endearing, adorable, lovable, sweet, lovely, appealing, engaging, delightful, dear; informal twee; Brit. informal dinky.
OPPOSITES hateful, ugly.

cutting noun *a newspaper cutting:* clipping, article, piece, column, paragraph.

grow a new one. **3** a way dug through higher ground for a railway, road, etc. • **adjective** hurtful: *a cutting remark.* □ **the cutting edge** the most advanced or modern stage; the forefront.

cuttlefish noun (plural **cuttlefish** or **cuttlefishes**) a sea creature resembling a squid.

CV abbreviation curriculum vitae.

cwt abbreviation hundredweight.

cyan /sy-uhn/ noun a greenish-blue colour.

cyanide noun a highly poisonous compound containing a metal combined with carbon and nitrogen atoms.

cybercafe noun a cafe with computers on which customers can access the Internet, send emails, etc.

cybernetics noun the science of communications and control in machines (e.g. computers) and living things (e.g. by the nervous system). ■ **cybernetic** adjective.

cyberspace noun the hypothetical place in which communication over computer networks takes place.

cyclamen /sik-luh-muhn/ noun a plant having pink, red, or white flowers with backward-curving petals.

cycle noun **1** a series of events that are regularly repeated in the same order. **2** a complete sequence of changes associated with something recurring such as an alternating electric current. **3** a series of musical or literary works composed around a particular theme. **4** a bicycle. • **verb** (**cycles**, **cycling**, **cycled**) ride a bicycle. ■ **cyclist** noun.

cyclic /syk-lik, sik-lik/ or **cyclical** adjective happening in cycles.

cyclone noun **1** a system of winds rotating inwards to an area of low atmospheric pressure. **2** a violent tropical storm. ■ **cyclonic** adjective.

cygnet /sig-nit/ noun a young swan.

cylinder noun **1** a three-dimensional shape with straight parallel sides and circular or oval ends. **2** a chamber in which a piston moves in an engine. ■ **cylindrical** adjective.

cymbal noun a musical instrument consisting of a round brass plate which is either struck against another one or hit with a stick.

cynic noun **1** a person who believes that people always act from selfish motives. **2** a person who raises doubts about something. ■ **cynicism** noun.

cynical adjective **1** believing that people always act from selfish motives. **2** doubtful or sneering. **3** concerned only with your own interests. ■ **cynically** adverb.

cypher ⇒ **CIPHER.**

cypress noun an evergreen coniferous tree with small dark leaves.

Cypriot noun a person from Cyprus. • **adjective** relating to Cyprus.

Cyrillic /si-ril-lik/ noun the alphabet used for Russian and related languages.

cyst /sist/ noun an abnormal cavity in the body which contains fluid.

cystic adjective **1** having to do with cysts. **2** relating to the bladder or the gall bladder. □ **cystic fibrosis** an inherited disease which causes too much mucus to be produced and often leads to blockage of tubes in the body.

cystitis /si-sty-tiss/ noun inflammation of the bladder.

cytology /sy-tol-uh-ji/ noun the scientific study of plant and animal cells. ■ **cytological** adjective **cytologist** noun.

cytoplasm noun the material of a living cell, excluding the nucleus.

czar etc. ⇒ **TSAR** etc.

Czech /chek/ noun **1** a person from the Czech Republic or (formerly) Czechoslovakia. **2** the language spoken in the Czech Republic.

C

THESAURUS

• **adjective** *a cutting remark:* hurtful, wounding, barbed, scathing, caustic, sarcastic, snide, spiteful, malicious, cruel; informal bitchy; Brit. informal sarky; N. Amer. informal snarky.
OPPOSITES friendly, warm.

cycle noun **1** *the cycle of birth, death, and rebirth:* circle, round, pattern, rhythm, loop. **2** *a cycle of three plays:* series, set, sequence, succession, run.

cynic noun sceptic, doubter, doubting Thomas, pessimist, prophet of doom.
OPPOSITES idealist, optimist.

cynical adjective sceptical, doubtful, distrustful, suspicious, disbelieving, pessimistic, negative, world-weary, disillusioned, disenchanted, jaundiced.
OPPOSITES idealistic, optimistic.

Dd

D or **d** noun (plural **Ds** or **D's**) **1** the fourth letter of the alphabet. **2** the Roman numeral for 500. • **abbreviation** (**d**) (before decimal currency was brought in) penny or pence.

'd short form had or would.

DA abbreviation (in the US) district attorney.

dab verb (**dabs, dabbing, dabbed**) **1** press lightly with something absorbent. **2** apply with light, quick strokes. • noun a small amount of something applied lightly.
□ **dab hand** Brit. informal a person who is very good at something.

dabble verb (**dabbles, dabbling, dabbled**) **1** gently move your hands or feet around in water. **2** take part in an activity in a casual way.
■ **dabbler** noun.

dace noun (plural **dace**) a small freshwater fish related to the carp.

dachshund noun a breed of dog with a long body and very short legs.

dad or **daddy** noun (plural **dads** or **daddies**) informal your father.

daddy-long-legs noun Brit. informal a crane fly.

dado /day-doh/ noun (plural **dados**) the lower part of the wall of a room, when it is decorated differently from the upper part.

daffodil noun a plant that has bright yellow flowers with a long trumpet-shaped centre.

daft adjective informal silly; foolish.

dagger noun a short pointed knife, used as a weapon.

daguerreotype /duh-ger-ruh-typ/ noun an early kind of photograph produced using a silver-coated plate.

dahlia /day-li-uh/ noun a garden plant with brightly coloured flowers.

daily adjective & adverb every day or every weekday.

dainty adjective (**daintier, daintiest**) delicately small and pretty. • noun (plural **dainties**) a small, tasty item of food.
■ **daintily** adverb.

dairy noun (plural **dairies**) a building where milk and milk products are produced.
• adjective **1** made from milk. **2** involved in milk production.

dais /day-iss/ noun a low platform that supports a throne, or that people stand on to make a speech.

daisy noun (plural **daisies**) a small plant that has flowers with a yellow centre and white petals.

dale noun (in northern England) a valley.

dalliance noun a casual relationship.

dally verb (**dallies, dallying, dallied**) **1** do something in a leisurely way. **2** (**dally with**) have a casual relationship with.

Dalmatian /dal-may-sh'n/ noun a breed of large dog with short white hair and dark spots.

dam[1] noun a barrier constructed across a

THESAURUS

dab verb *she dabbed disinfectant on the cut:* pat, press, touch, swab, daub, wipe.
• noun *a dab of glue:* drop, spot, smear, splash, bit.

dabble verb toy with, dip into, flirt with, tinker with, play with.

daft adjective (Brit. informal) **1** *a daft idea:* absurd, preposterous, ridiculous, ludicrous, idiotic, stupid, foolish; informal crazy; Brit. informal barmy. **2** *he's really daft:* stupid, idiotic, empty-headed, unhinged, insane, mad; informal thick, dim, dopey; Brit. informal barmy, crackers. **3** *she's daft about him:* infatuated, smitten, besotted; informal crazy,

mad, nuts; Brit. informal potty.
OPPOSITES sensible, sane.

daily adjective *a daily event:* everyday, day-to-day; formal quotidian.
• adverb *the museum is open daily:* every day, once a day, day after day.

dainty adjective **1** *a dainty china cup:* delicate, fine, elegant, exquisite. **2** *a dainty eater:* fastidious, fussy, particular; informal choosy, picky; Brit. informal faddy.
OPPOSITES unwieldy, undiscriminating.

dam noun barrage, barrier, wall, embankment, barricade, obstruction.

river to hold back water. •verb (**dams, damming, dammed**) build a dam across.

dam² noun the female parent of an animal.

damage noun **1** physical harm that makes something less valuable or effective. **2** harmful effects. **3** (**damages**) money paid to compensate for a loss or injury. •verb (**damages, damaging, damaged**) cause harm to.

damask noun a rich, heavy fabric with a pattern woven into it.

dame noun **1** (**Dame**) (in the UK) the title of a woman awarded a knighthood, equivalent to *Sir*. **2** N. Amer. informal a woman. **3** Brit. a comic female character in pantomime, played by a man.

damn verb **1** (**be damned**) (in Christian belief) be condemned by God to eternal punishment in hell. **2** harshly condemn. **3** curse.

damnable /**dam**-nuh-b'l/ adjective very bad or unpleasant.

damnation noun the fate of being condemned to eternal punishment in hell.

damned adjective said to emphasize anger or frustration.

damp adjective slightly wet. •noun moisture in the air, on a surface, or in a solid substance. •verb **1** make something damp. **2** (**damp something down**) control a feeling or situation.
□ **damp course** a layer of waterproof material in a wall near the ground, to prevent rising damp. **damp squib** Brit. something that turns out to be a lot less impressive than expected.

dampen verb **1** make something damp. **2** make a feeling or reaction less strong or intense.

damper noun **1** a pad for silencing a piano string. **2** a movable metal plate for controlling the air flow in a chimney.
□ **put a damper on** informal make something less enjoyable or lively.

damsel noun old use a young unmarried woman.

damson noun a small purple-black fruit resembling a plum.

dance verb (**dances, dancing, danced**) **1** move rhythmically to music. **2** move in a quick and lively way. •noun **1** a series of steps and movements performed to music. **2** a social gathering at which people dance.
■ **dancer** noun.

dandelion noun a weed with large bright yellow flowers.

dander noun (**get your dander up**) informal lose your temper.

dandle verb (**dandles, dandling, dandled**) gently bounce a young child on your knees or in your arms.

dandruff noun flakes of dead skin on a person's scalp and in the hair.

dandy noun (plural **dandies**) a man who is too concerned with looking stylish and fashionable. •adjective (**dandier, dandiest**) N. Amer. informal excellent.
■ **dandified** adjective.

Dane noun a person from Denmark.

danger noun **1** the possibility of suffering harm or of experiencing something unpleasant. **2** a cause of harm.

d

THESAURUS

•verb block (up), obstruct, bung up, close, hold back.

damage noun **1** *did the thieves do any damage?* harm, destruction, vandalism, injury, ruin, devastation. **2** (**damages**) compensation, recompense, restitution, redress, reparation(s); N. Amer. informal comp. •verb *the parcel had been damaged:* harm, injure, deface, spoil, impair, vandalize, ruin, destroy, wreck; N. Amer. informal trash.
OPPOSITES repair.

damaging adjective harmful, detrimental, injurious, hurtful, destructive, ruinous, deleterious.
OPPOSITES beneficial.

damn verb condemn, censure, criticize, attack, denounce.
OPPOSITES bless, praise.

damning adjective incriminating, implicating, damaging, condemnatory, conclusive, irrefutable.

damp adjective *her hair was damp:* moist, humid, muggy, clammy, sweaty, dank, wet, rainy, drizzly, showery, misty, foggy, dewy.

OPPOSITES dry.
•noun *the damp in the air:* moisture, liquid, wet, wetness, dampness, humidity.
OPPOSITES dryness.

dampen verb **1** *the rain dampened her face:* moisten, damp, wet, soak. **2** *nothing could dampen her enthusiasm:* lessen, decrease, diminish, reduce, moderate, cool, suppress, stifle, inhibit.
OPPOSITES dry, heighten.

dance verb **1** *he danced with her:* trip, sway, twirl, whirl, pirouette, gyrate; informal bop, trip the light fantastic; N. Amer. informal get down. **2** *the girls danced round me:* caper, cavort, frolic, skip, prance, gambol, leap, hop, bounce.
•noun *the school dance:* ball; N. Amer. prom, hoedown; informal disco, rave, hop, bop.

danger noun **1** *an element of danger:* peril, hazard, risk, jeopardy. **2** *he is a danger to society:* menace, hazard, threat, risk. **3** *a serious danger of fire:* possibility, chance, risk, probability, likelihood.
OPPOSITES safety.

d

dangerous adjective likely to cause harm or injury.
  ∎ **dangerously** adverb.
dangle verb (**dangles, dangling, dangled**)
  1 hang or swing freely. **2** offer something to someone to persuade them to do something.
Danish adjective relating to Denmark or the Danes. ∙ noun the language of Denmark.
dank adjective damp and cold.
dapper adjective (of a man) neat in appearance; smart.
dapple verb (**dapples, dappling, dappled**) mark with patches of colour or of light and shadow.
  □ **dapple grey** (of a horse) grey with darker ring-shaped markings.
dare verb (**dares, daring, dared**) **1** have the courage to do something. **2** challenge someone to do something. ∙ noun a challenge to do something brave or risky.
daredevil noun a person who enjoys doing dangerous things.

daring adjective willing to do dangerous or risky things. ∙ noun the courage to do dangerous or risky things.
  ∎ **daringly** adverb.
dark adjective **1** with little or no light. **2** of a deep colour. **3** depressing or gloomy. **4** evil; wicked. **5** mysterious: *a dark secret.* ∙ noun **1** (**the dark**) the absence of light. **2** nightfall.
  □ **the Dark Ages** the period *c.*500–1100 in Europe, seen as lacking culture or learning. **dark horse** a person about whom little is known. **in the dark** knowing nothing about a situation or matter. **a shot in the dark** a wild guess.
  ∎ **darkly** adverb **darkness** noun.
darken verb **1** make or become darker. **2** become unhappy or angry.
darkroom noun a darkened room for developing photographs.
darling noun **1** an affectionate form of address. **2** a lovable person. ∙ adjective **1** much loved. **2** charming.

THESAURUS

dangerous adjective **1** *a dangerous animal:* menacing, threatening, treacherous. **2** *dangerous wiring:* hazardous, perilous, risky, unsafe, unpredictable, precarious, insecure; informal dicey, hairy; Brit. informal dodgy.
  OPPOSITES harmless, safe.
dangle verb **1** *a chain dangled from his belt:* hang, swing, droop, wave, trail, stream. **2** *he dangled the keys:* wave, swing, jiggle, brandish, flourish.
dank adjective damp, musty, chilly, clammy.
  OPPOSITES dry.
dapper adjective smart, spruce, trim, debonair, neat, well dressed, elegant; informal snappy, natty; N. Amer. informal spiffy, fly.
  OPPOSITES scruffy.
dare verb **1** *nobody dared to say a word:* be brave enough, have the courage, venture, have the nerve, risk, take the liberty of; N. Amer. take a flyer; informal stick your neck out. **2** *she dared him to go:* challenge, defy, invite, bid, provoke, goad.
  ∙ noun *she accepted the dare:* challenge, invitation, wager, bet.
daring adjective *a daring attack:* bold, audacious, intrepid, fearless, brave, heroic, dashing; informal gutsy.
  OPPOSITES cowardly, timid.
  ∙ noun *his sheer daring:* boldness, audacity, temerity, fearlessness, bravery, courage, pluck; informal nerve, guts; Brit. informal bottle; N. Amer. informal moxie.
  OPPOSITES cowardice.
dark adjective **1** *a dark night:* dingy, gloomy, shadowy, murky, poorly lit, grey, inky, black. **2** *dark hair:* brunette, dark brown,

sable, jet-black, ebony. **3** *dark skin:* swarthy, dusky, olive, black, ebony. **4** *dark thoughts:* gloomy, dismal, negative, downbeat, bleak, grim, fatalistic, black. **5** *a dark look:* angry, forbidding, threatening, ominous, moody, brooding, sullen, scowling, glowering. **6** *dark deeds:* evil, wicked, sinful, bad, iniquitous, ungodly, vile, foul, monstrous; informal dirty, crooked, shady.
  OPPOSITES bright, light, blonde, pale, white, happy, friendly, good.
  ∙ noun *walking in the dark:* night, night-time, darkness, nightfall, blackout.
  OPPOSITES light, day.
darken verb grow dark, make dark, blacken, grow dim, cloud over, lour.
  OPPOSITES lighten.
darkness noun **1** *lights shone in the darkness:* dark, blackness, gloom, dimness, murk, shadow, shade. **2** *darkness fell:* night, night-time, dark. **3** *the forces of darkness:* evil, wickedness, sin, ungodliness, the Devil.
darling noun **1** *good night, darling:* dear, dearest, love, sweetheart, beloved; informal honey, angel, pet, sweetie, baby, poppet. **2** *the darling of the media:* favourite, idol, hero, heroine; Brit. informal blue-eyed boy/girl.
  OPPOSITES bugbear, villain.
  ∙ adjective **1** *his darling wife:* dear, dearest, precious, beloved. **2** *a darling little hat:* adorable, charming, cute, sweet, dear, enchanting, delightful; Scottish & N. English bonny.
  OPPOSITES ugly.

darn[1] verb mend a hole in a knitted garment by weaving yarn across it.

darn[2] or **darned** adjective informal another way of saying **DAMNED**.

dart noun 1 a small pointed missile fired as a weapon or thrown in the game of darts. 2 (**darts**) an indoor game in which you throw darts at a circular board marked with numbers. 3 a sudden rapid movement. 4 a tapered tuck stitched into a garment to make it fit better. •verb move suddenly or rapidly.

dash verb 1 run or travel in a great hurry. 2 hit or throw with great force. 3 destroy: *his hopes were dashed.* 4 (**dash something off**) write something hurriedly. •noun 1 an act of dashing. 2 a small amount added to something. 3 a horizontal stroke in writing (—).

dashboard noun the panel of instruments and controls facing the driver of a vehicle.

dashing adjective (of a man) attractive, stylish, and confident.

dastardly /dass-terd-li/ adjective old use wicked and cruel.

data noun 1 facts, statistics, or other information. 2 information stored by a computer.

> ! **data** is the plural of the Latin word **datum**. Scientists use it as a plural noun, taking a plural verb (as in *the data were classified*). In everyday use, however, **data** is usually treated as a singular noun with a singular verb (as in *here is the data*).

database noun a set of data held in a computer.

date[1] noun 1 the day of the month or year as specified by a number. 2 a day or year when a particular event happened or will happen. 3 a social or romantic appointment. 4 a musical or theatrical performance. •verb (**dates, dating, dated**) 1 mark something with a date. 2 establish the date when something existed or was made. 3 (**date from** or **back to**) have existed since a particular time in the past. 4 informal go on a date or regular dates with. □ to date until now. ■ datable (or **dateable**) adjective.

date[2] noun the sweet, dark brown, oval fruit of a palm tree.

dated adjective old-fashioned.

dative noun Grammar (in Latin, Greek, German, etc.) the case of nouns and pronouns that indicates an indirect object or the person or thing affected by a verb.

datum noun (plural **data**) a piece of information.

daub verb smear something with a thick substance. •noun 1 plaster, clay, or a similar substance, used in building. 2 a smear of a thick substance.

daughter noun 1 a girl or woman in relation to her parents. 2 a female descendant. □ daughter-in-law (plural **daughters-in-law**) the wife of a person's son.

daunt verb make someone feel nervous or discouraged. ■ daunting adjective.

dart verb 1 *Karl darted across the road:* dash, rush, tear, shoot, sprint, bound, scurry, scamper; informal scoot, whip. 2 *he darted a glance at her:* direct, cast, throw, shoot, send, flash.

dash verb 1 *he dashed home:* rush, race, run, sprint, career, charge, shoot, hurtle, hare, fly, speed, zoom; informal tear, belt; Brit. informal bomb; N. Amer. informal barrel. 2 *he dashed the glass to the ground:* hurl, smash, fling, slam, throw, toss, cast; informal chuck, sling; N. Amer. informal peg. 3 *her hopes were dashed:* shatter, destroy, wreck, ruin, demolish, scotch, frustrate, thwart; informal put paid to; Brit. informal scupper.
OPPOSITES dawdle, raise.
•noun 1 *a dash for the door:* rush, race, run, sprint, bolt, dart, leap, charge, bound. 2 *a dash of salt:* pinch, touch, sprinkle, taste, spot, drop, dab, splash; informal smidgen, tad. 3 *he led off with such dash:* verve, style, flamboyance, gusto, zest, elan, flair, vigour, panache; informal pizzazz, oomph.

dashing adjective 1 *a dashing pilot:* debonair, devil-may-care, raffish, confident, flamboyant, swashbuckling. 2 *he looked very dashing:* stylish, smart, elegant, dapper, spruce, trim, debonair; informal natty; N. Amer. informal spiffy.

data noun facts, figures, statistics, details, particulars, information.

date noun 1 *at a later date:* day, occasion, time, year, age, period, era, epoch. 2 *a lunch date:* appointment, meeting, engagement, rendezvous, commitment. 3 (informal) *a date for tonight:* partner, escort, girlfriend, boyfriend.
•verb 1 *the best films don't date:* age, grow old, become dated, show its age, be of its time. 2 assign a date to, put a date on. 3 (informal) *he's dating Jill:* go out with, take out, go with, see; informal go steady with. □ date from be from, originate in, come from, belong to, go back to.

dated adjective old-fashioned, outdated, outmoded, unfashionable, passé, behind the times, archaic, obsolete, antiquated; informal old hat, out of the ark.
OPPOSITES modern.

daunting adjective intimidating,

dauntless adjective brave and determined.

dauphin /doh-fan/ noun (in the past) the eldest son of the King of France.

davit noun a small crane on a ship.

dawdle verb (dawdles, dawdling, dawdled) move slowly; take your time.

dawn noun **1** the first appearance of light in the sky in the morning. **2** the beginning of something new. • verb **1** (of a day) begin. **2** come into existence. **3** (**dawn on**) (of a fact) become clear to.
□ **dawn chorus** the early-morning singing of birds.

day noun **1** a period of twenty-four hours, reckoned from midnight to midnight. **2** the time between sunrise and sunset. **3** (usu. **days**) a particular period of the past. **4** (**the day**) the present time or the time in question.
□ **call it a day** decide to stop doing something.

daybreak noun dawn.

daydream noun a series of pleasant thoughts that distract your attention from the present. • verb have a daydream.

daylight noun **1** the natural light of the day. **2** dawn.
□ **daylight robbery** Brit. informal the fact of charging far too much for something.

daze noun a state of stunned confusion or bewilderment.
■ **dazed** adjective.

dazzle verb (dazzles, dazzling, dazzled) **1** (of a bright light) blind someone temporarily. **2** amaze someone by being very impressive. • noun blinding brightness.
■ **dazzling** adjective.

dB abbreviation decibels.

DC abbreviation **1** direct current. **2** District of Columbia.

DDT noun a compound used as an insecticide (now banned in many countries).

deacon /dee-kuhn/ noun **1** a Christian minister just below the rank of priest. **2** (in some Protestant Churches) a person who helps a minister but is not a member of the clergy.
■ **deaconess** noun.

deactivate verb (deactivates, deactivating, deactivated) stop equipment from working by disconnecting or destroying it.

dead adjective **1** no longer alive. **2** (of a part

THESAURUS

forbidding, challenging, formidable, unnerving, disconcerting, discouraging, disheartening, demoralizing, dismaying, scary, frightening, alarming.
OPPOSITES inviting, reassuring.

dawdle verb **1** *they dawdled over breakfast:* linger, take your time, be slow, waste time, dally; informal dilly-dally. **2** *Ruth dawdled home:* amble, stroll, trail, dally, move at a snail's pace; informal mosey, tootle; Brit. informal pootle.
OPPOSITES hurry.

dawn noun **1** *we got up at dawn:* daybreak, sunrise, first light, daylight, cockcrow; N. Amer. sunup. **2** *the dawn of civilization:* beginning, start, birth, inception, genesis, emergence, advent, appearance, arrival, rise, origin.
OPPOSITES dusk, end.
• verb **1** *Thursday dawned crisp and sunny:* begin, break, arrive, emerge. **2** *a bright new future has dawned:* begin, start, commence, be born, appear, arrive, emerge, arise, rise, unfold, develop. **3** *the reality dawned on him:* become evident, register, cross someone's mind, suggest itself, occur, come, strike, hit.
OPPOSITES end.

day noun **1** *I stayed for a day:* twenty-four hours. **2** *enjoy the beach during the day:* daytime, daylight, waking hours. **3** *the leading architect of the day:* period, time, date, age, era, generation.
OPPOSITES night.

daze verb *she was dazed by the revelations:* dumbfound, stupefy, stun, shock, stagger, bewilder, take aback, nonplus; informal flabbergast; Brit. informal knock for six.
• noun *she is in a daze:* stupor, trance, haze, spin, whirl, muddle, jumble.

dazzle verb **1** *she was dazzled by the headlights:* blind, confuse, disorient. **2** *I was dazzled by the exhibition:* overwhelm, overcome, impress, move, stir, touch, awe, overawe; informal bowl over, blow away, knock out.

dead adjective **1** *my parents are dead:* passed on/away, departed, late, lost, perished, fallen, killed, lifeless, extinct; informal six feet under, pushing up daisies; formal deceased. **2** *a dead issue/language:* obsolete, extinct, defunct, disused, abandoned, superseded, vanished, archaic, ancient. **3** *the phone was dead:* not working, out of order, inoperative, inactive, broken, defective; informal kaput, conked out, on the blink, bust; Brit. informal knackered. **4** *a dead town:* boring, uninteresting, unexciting, uninspiring, dull, flat, quiet, sleepy, slow, lifeless; informal one-horse; N. Amer. informal dullsville.
OPPOSITES alive, live, living, working, lively.
• adverb **1** *he was dead serious:* completely, absolutely, totally, utterly, deadly, perfectly, entirely, quite, thoroughly. **2** *flares were seen dead ahead:* directly, exactly, precisely, immediately, right, straight, due.

of the body) numb. **3** showing no emotion.
4 without activity or excitement.
5 complete: *dead silence.* •adverb
1 absolutely, exactly, or directly: *you're
dead right.* **2** Brit. informal very.
◻ **dead end** a road or passage that is closed
at one end. **dead heat** a result in a race in
which two or more competitors finish at
exactly the same time. **dead loss** a useless
person or thing. **dead reckoning** a way of
finding out your position by estimating the
direction and distance travelled. **dead
ringer** informal a person or thing very like
another.

deadbeat noun informal a lazy or aimless
person.

deaden verb **1** make a noise or sensation
less strong or intense. **2** make something
numb.

deadhead verb remove dead flower heads
from a plant.

deadline noun the time or date by which
you have to complete something.

deadlock noun **1** a situation in which no
one can make any progress. **2** Brit. a lock
operated by a key. •verb (**be deadlocked**)
be unable to make any progress.

deadly adjective (**deadlier, deadliest**)
1 causing or able to cause death. **2** (of a
voice, glance, etc.) filled with hate. **3** very
accurate or effective. **4** informal very boring.
•adverb very: *she was deadly serious.*
◻ **deadly nightshade** a plant with purple
flowers and poisonous black berries.

deadpan adjective not showing any

emotion; expressionless.

deadweight noun **1** the weight of a
motionless person or thing. **2** the total
weight which a ship can carry.

deaf adjective **1** unable to hear. **2** (**deaf
to**) unwilling to listen to.
◻ **deaf mute** offensive a person who is deaf
and unable to speak.
■ **deafness** noun.

deafen verb **1** make someone deaf.
2 (**deafening**) very loud.
■ **deafeningly** adverb.

deal[1] verb (**deals, dealing, dealt**) **1** (**deal
something out**) distribute something.
2 buy and sell a product commercially.
3 buy and sell illegal drugs. **4** give out
cards to players of a card game. •noun **1** an
agreement between two or more people or
groups. **2** a particular form of treatment
received.
◻ **deal with 1** do business with. **2** do
things to put a problem right. **3** cope with.
4 have something as a subject. **a good** (or
great) **deal** a lot.
■ **dealer** noun.

deal[2] noun fir or pine wood.

dealer noun **1** a person who buys and sells
goods. **2** a person who buys and sells
shares directly (rather than as a broker or
agent). **3** a player who deals cards in a card
game.

dean noun **1** the head of a cathedral's
governing body. **2** the head of a university
department or medical school.

dear adjective **1** much loved. **2** used in the

THESAURUS

deadline noun time limit, finishing date,
target date, cut-off point.

deadlock noun stalemate, impasse,
checkmate, stand-off, standstill, gridlock.

deadly adjective **1** *these drugs can be deadly:*
fatal, lethal, mortal, life-threatening,
noxious, toxic, poisonous. **2** *deadly enemies:*
mortal, irreconcilable, implacable, bitter,
sworn. **3** *his aim is deadly:* unerring,
unfailing, perfect, true, accurate; Brit. informal
spot on.
OPPOSITES harmless, inaccurate.

deafening adjective ear-splitting,
thunderous, crashing, almighty, booming.
OPPOSITES low, soft.

deal noun *completion of the deal:*
agreement, understanding, pact, bargain,
covenant, contract, treaty, arrangement,
compromise, settlement, terms.
•verb **1** *how to deal with difficult children:*
cope with, handle, manage, treat, take care
of, take charge of, take in hand, sort out,
tackle, take on, control. **2** *the article deals
with advances in biochemistry:* concern, be
about, have to do with, discuss, consider,

cover, tackle, explore, investigate, examine.
3 *the company deals in high-tech goods:*
trade in, buy and sell, purvey, supply,
market, traffic in. **4** *the cards were dealt:*
distribute, give out, share out, divide out,
hand out, pass out, pass round, dispense,
allocate.

dealer noun trader, merchant, salesman/
woman, seller, vendor, purveyor, pedlar,
distributor, supplier, shopkeeper, retailer,
wholesaler, tradesman, tradesperson;
Brit. stockist.

dear adjective **1** *a dear friend:* beloved,
precious, close, intimate, bosom. **2** *her
pictures were too dear to part with:*
precious, treasured, valued, prized,
cherished, special. **3** *such a dear man:*
endearing, adorable, lovable, appealing,
engaging, charming, captivating, lovely,
delightful, sweet, darling. **4** *rather dear
meals:* expensive, costly, high-priced,
overpriced, exorbitant, extortionate; Brit.
over the odds; informal pricey.
OPPOSITES disagreeable, cheap.
•noun *don't worry, my dear:* darling,
dearest, love, beloved, sweetheart,

polite introduction to a letter. **3** expensive. • **noun** a lovable person.

dearly adverb **1** very much. **2** at great cost.

dearth noun a lack of something.

death noun **1** an instance of a person or an animal dying. **2** the end of life; the state of being dead. **3** the end of something.
☐ **at death's door** so ill that you may die. **death knell** an event that signals the end of something. **death penalty** punishment by being executed. **death row** a block of cells for prisoners who have been sentenced to death. **death-watch beetle** a beetle that makes a ticking sound which people used to think was an omen of death.

deathly adjective suggesting death: *a deathly hush.*

debacle /day-**bah**-k'l/ noun an utter failure or disaster.

debar verb (**debars, debarring, debarred**) officially prevent someone from doing something.

debase verb (**debases, debasing, debased**) make something worse in quality, value, or character.
■ **debasement** noun.

debatable adjective open to discussion or argument.

debate noun **1** a formal discussion in which people present opposing arguments. **2** an argument. • verb (**debates, debating, debated**) **1** discuss or argue about. **2** consider a possible course of action.

debauched adjective indulging in a lot of pleasures in a way considered to be immoral.
■ **debauchery** noun.

debenture /di-**ben**-cher/ noun Brit. a certificate issued by a company confirming that it has borrowed money on which interest is being paid.

debilitate /di-**bil**-i-tayt/ verb (**debilitates, debilitating, debilitated**) severely weaken.

debility noun (plural **debilities**) physical weakness.

debit noun **1** an entry in an account recording a sum owed. **2** a payment that has been made or that is owed. • verb (**debits, debiting, debited**) (of a bank) remove money from a customer's account.
☐ **debit card** a card that lets you take money from your bank account electronically when buying something.

debonair adjective (of a man) confident, stylish, and charming.

debrief verb question someone in detail about a mission they have completed.

debris /**deb**-ree/ noun **1** scattered items or pieces of rubbish. **2** loose broken pieces of rock.

debt noun **1** a sum of money owed. **2** a situation where you owe someone money. **3** gratitude for a favour or service.

debtor noun a person who owes money.

debug verb (**debugs, debugging, debugged**) remove errors from computer hardware or software.

debunk verb show that something believed in by many people is false or exaggerated.

debut /**day**-byoo/ noun a person's first appearance in a role. • verb make a debut.

debutant /**deb**-yoo-ton(t)/ noun a person making a debut.

debutante /**deb**-yoo-tont/ noun a young upper-class woman making her first appearance in society.

decade noun a period of ten years.

decadent adjective **1** immoral and interested only in pleasure. **2** luxuriously self-indulgent.
■ **decadence** noun **decadently** adverb.

decaffeinated adjective (of tea or coffee) having had most or all of its caffeine removed.

decagon noun a figure with ten straight sides and angles.

THESAURUS

precious; informal sweetie, sugar, honey, baby, pet, poppet.

dearly adverb *I love him dearly:* very much, a great deal, greatly, deeply, profoundly.

dearth noun lack, scarcity, shortage, shortfall, deficiency, insufficiency, inadequacy, absence.
OPPOSITES surfeit.

death noun **1** *her father's death:* dying, demise, end, passing, loss of life; formal decease. **2** *the death of their dream:* end, finish, termination, extinction, extinguishing, collapse, destruction.
OPPOSITES life, birth, start.

deathly adjective deathlike, ghostly, ghastly, ashen, white, pale, pallid.

debacle noun fiasco, failure, catastrophe, disaster.

debate noun *a debate on the reforms:* discussion, argument, dispute, talks.
• verb **1** *MPs will debate our future:* discuss, talk over/through, talk about, thrash out, argue, dispute. **2** *he debated whether to call her:* consider, think over/about, chew over, mull over, weigh up, ponder, deliberate.

debris noun ruins, remains, rubble, wreckage, detritus, refuse, rubbish, waste, scrap, flotsam and jetsam.

debt noun **1** *he couldn't pay his debts:* bill, account, dues, arrears, charges. **2** *his debt to the author:* indebtedness, obligation, gratitude, appreciation.

d

decahedron /de-kuh-**hee**-druhn/ noun (plural **decahedra** or **decahedrons**) a solid figure with ten sides.

decamp verb depart suddenly or secretly.

decant /di-**kant**/ verb pour liquid from one container into another.

decanter noun a glass container with a stopper, for wine or spirits.

decapitate verb (**decapitates, decapitating, decapitated**) cut off the head of.
■ decapitation noun.

decathlon /di-**kath**-luhn/ noun an athletic event in which each competitor takes part in the same ten events.
■ decathlete noun.

decay verb **1** (of plant or animal material) rot. **2** become weaker or less good. •noun **1** the state or process of decaying. **2** rotten matter or tissue.

decease noun formal or Law death.

deceased formal or Law noun (**the deceased**) the recently dead person in question. •adjective recently dead.

deceit noun behaviour intended to make someone believe something that is not true.

deceitful adjective deliberately deceiving other people.
■ deceitfully adverb.

deceive verb (**deceives, deceiving, deceived**) **1** deliberately make someone believe something that is not true. **2** (of a thing) give a mistaken impression.
■ deceiver noun.

☑ *i* before *e* except after *c*: dece*i*ve.

decelerate verb (**decelerates, decelerating, decelerated**) slow down.
■ deceleration noun.

December noun the twelfth month of the year.

decency noun (plural **decencies**) **1** decent behaviour. **2** (**decencies**) standards of acceptable behaviour.

decennial /di-**sen**-i-uhl/ adjective happening every ten years.

decent adjective **1** having good moral standards. **2** of an acceptable quality. **3** Brit. informal kind or generous.
■ decently adverb.

decentralize or **decentralise** verb (**decentralizes, decentralizing, decentralized**) transfer authority from central to local government.
■ decentralization noun.

deception noun **1** the action of deceiving. **2** a thing that deceives.

deceptive adjective giving a false impression.
■ deceptively adverb.

decibel /**dess**-i-bel/ noun a unit for measuring the loudness of a sound or the power of an electrical signal.

THESAURUS

decay verb **1** *the corpses had decayed:* decompose, rot, putrefy, go bad, go off, spoil, fester, perish. **2** *the cities continue to decay:* deteriorate, degenerate, decline, go downhill, slump, slide, go to rack and ruin, go to seed; informal go to the dogs.
•noun **1** *signs of decay:* decomposition, putrefaction, rot. **2** *the decay of American values:* deterioration, degeneration, decline, weakening, crumbling, disintegration, collapse.

deceit noun deception, deceitfulness, duplicity, double-dealing, lies, fraud, cheating, trickery.
OPPOSITES honesty.

deceitful adjective dishonest, untruthful, insincere, false, untrustworthy, unscrupulous, unprincipled, two-faced, duplicitous, fraudulent, double-dealing; informal sneaky, tricky, crooked; Brit. informal bent.
OPPOSITES honest.

deceive verb trick, cheat, defraud, swindle, hoodwink, hoax, dupe, take in, mislead, delude, fool; informal con, pull the wool over someone's eyes; N. Amer. informal sucker, goldbrick; Austral. informal rort.

decency noun **1** *standards of taste and*

decency: propriety, decorum, good taste, respectability, morality, virtue, modesty. **2** *he didn't have the decency to tell me:* courtesy, politeness, good manners, civility, consideration, thoughtfulness.

decent adjective **1** *a decent burial:* proper, correct, right, appropriate, suitable, respectable, decorous, modest, seemly, accepted; informal pukka. **2** *a job with decent pay:* satisfactory, reasonable, fair, acceptable, adequate, sufficient, not bad, all right, tolerable, passable, suitable; informal OK. **3** (Brit. informal) *a very decent chap:* kind, generous, thoughtful, considerate, obliging, courteous, polite, well mannered, neighbourly, hospitable, pleasant, agreeable, amiable.
OPPOSITES indecent, unsatisfactory, unpleasant.

deception noun **1** *they obtained money by deception:* deceit, duplicity, double-dealing, fraud, cheating, trickery, guile, bluff, lying, pretence, treachery. **2** *it was all a deception:* trick, sham, fraud, pretence, hoax, ruse, scheme, dodge, cheat, swindle; informal con, set-up, scam.

deceptive adjective misleading, confusing, illusory, distorted, ambiguous.

decide verb (**decides, deciding, decided**)
1 think about something and make a judgement or decision. **2** settle an issue or contest.

decided adjective definite; clear.
■ **decidedly** adverb.

decider noun a contest that settles the winner of a series of contests.

deciduous adjective (of a tree or shrub) shedding its leaves annually.

decimal adjective having to do with a system of numbers based on the number ten. • noun a fractional number in the decimal system, written with figures either side of a full point.
□ **decimal place** the position of a digit to the right of a decimal point. **decimal point** a full point placed after the figure representing units in a decimal fraction.

decimate verb (**decimates, decimating, decimated**) **1** kill or destroy a large proportion of. **2** drastically reduce in strength.
■ **decimation** noun.

decipher verb (**deciphers, deciphering, deciphered**) **1** convert something from code into normal language. **2** succeed in understanding something that is hard to interpret.

decision noun **1** a choice or judgement made after considering something. **2** the ability to decide things quickly.

decisive adjective **1** having great importance for the outcome of a situation. **2** able to make decisions quickly.
■ **decisively** adverb **decisiveness** noun.

deck noun **1** a floor of a ship. **2** a floor or platform. **3** chiefly N. Amer. a pack of cards. **4** a player or recorder for discs or tapes. • verb decorate something.

deckchair noun a folding chair with a wooden frame and a canvas seat.

decking noun material used in making a deck.

declaim verb speak or recite in a dramatic or passionate way.

declamation noun the action of declaiming something.
■ **declamatory** adjective.

declaration noun **1** a formal statement or announcement. **2** the action of declaring.

declare verb (**declares, declaring, declared**) **1** announce something solemnly or officially. **2** (**declare yourself**) reveal your intentions or identity. **3** acknowledge that you have income or goods on which tax or duty should be paid. **4** Cricket voluntarily close an innings before all the players have batted.

declassify verb (**declassifies, declassifying, declassified**) officially declare information or documents to be no longer secret.

declension noun Grammar the changes in the form of a noun, pronoun, or adjective that identify its case, number, and gender.

decline verb (**declines, declining, declined**) **1** become smaller, weaker, or worse.

THESAURUS

decide verb **1** *she decided to become a writer:* resolve, determine, make up your mind, choose, opt, plan, aim, intend, have in mind, set your sights on. **2** *research to decide a variety of questions:* settle, resolve, determine, work out, answer; informal sort out. **3** *the court is to decide the case:* adjudicate, arbitrate, judge, pronounce on, give a verdict on, rule on.

decidedly adverb distinctly, clearly, markedly, obviously, noticeably, unmistakably, patently, manifestly, definitely, positively.

decision noun **1** *they came to a decision:* resolution, conclusion, settlement, choice, option, selection. **2** *the judge's decision:* verdict, finding, ruling, judgement, adjudication, sentence.

decisive adjective **1** *a decisive man:* resolute, firm, strong-minded, strong-willed, determined, purposeful. **2** *the decisive factor:* deciding, conclusive, determining, key, pivotal, critical, crucial.
OPPOSITES indecisive.

declaration noun **1** *they issued a declaration:* announcement, statement, communication, pronouncement, proclamation; N. Amer. advisory. **2** *a declaration of faith:* assertion, profession, affirmation, acknowledgement, revelation, disclosure, confirmation, testimony, avowal, protestation.

declare verb **1** *she declared her political principles:* announce, proclaim, state, reveal, air, voice, articulate, express, vent, set forth, publicize, broadcast. **2** *he declared that they were guilty:* assert, profess, affirm, maintain, state, contend, argue, insist.

decline verb **1** *she declined all invitations:* turn down, reject, brush aside, refuse, rebuff, spurn, repulse, dismiss, pass up, say no; informal give something a miss. **2** *the number of traders has declined:* decrease, reduce, lessen, diminish, dwindle, contract, shrink, fall off, tail off, drop, fall, go down. **3** *standards steadily declined:* deteriorate, degenerate, decay, crumble, collapse, slump, slip, slide, go downhill, worsen; informal go to the dogs.
OPPOSITES accept, increase, rise, improve.
• noun **1** *a decline in profits:* reduction, decrease, downturn, downswing, diminution, ebb, drop, slump, plunge.

2 politely refuse. **3** Grammar form a word according to its case, number, and gender. • **noun** a gradual loss of strength, numbers, or value.

declivity /di-**kliv**-i-ti/ **noun** (plural **declivities**) formal a downward slope.

decode **verb** (**decodes, decoding, decoded**) convert a coded message into understandable language.
■ **decoder** noun.

décolletage /day-kol-i-**tahz**h/ **noun** a low neckline on a woman's dress or top.

décolleté /day-**kol**-tay/ **adjective** having a low neckline.

decommission **verb** take a nuclear reactor or weapon out of use and make it safe.

decompose **verb** (**decomposes, decomposing, decomposed**) decay; rot.
■ **decomposition** noun.

decompress **verb** **1** reduce the pressure on. **2** expand compressed computer data to its normal size.

decompression **noun** **1** reduction in air pressure. **2** the decompressing of computer data.
□ **decompression sickness** a serious condition that results when a deep-sea diver surfaces too quickly.

decongestant **noun** a medicine used to relieve a blocked nose.

deconstruct **verb** reduce something to its basic elements in order to interpret it in a different way.
■ **deconstruction** noun.

decontaminate **verb** (**decontaminates, decontaminating, decontaminated**) remove dangerous substances from.
■ **decontamination** noun.

decor /**day**-kor/ **noun** the furnishing and decoration of a room.

decorate **verb** (**decorates, decorating, decorated**) **1** make something more attractive by adding extra items. **2** apply paint or wallpaper to the walls of a room or house. **3** give someone an award or medal.
■ **decorator** noun.

decoration **noun** **1** the process or art of decorating. **2** a decorative object or pattern. **3** the way in which something is decorated. **4** a medal or award given as an honour.

decorative **adjective** **1** making something look more attractive. **2** having to do with decoration.
■ **decoratively** adverb.

decorator **noun** a person who decorates, in particular (Brit.) a person whose job is to paint interior walls or hang wallpaper.

decorous **adjective** in good taste; polite and restrained.
■ **decorously** adverb.

decorum /di-**kor**-uhm/ **noun** polite and socially acceptable behaviour.

decoy **noun** **1** a real or imitation bird or animal, used by hunters to lure game. **2** a person or thing used to mislead or lure someone into a trap. • **verb** lure by means of a decoy.

decrease **verb** (**decreases, decreasing, decreased**) make or become smaller or fewer. • **noun** the process of decreasing, or the amount by which something decreases.

decree **noun** **1** an official order that has the force of law. **2** a judgement of certain law

THESAURUS

2 *habitat decline:* deterioration, degeneration, degradation, shrinkage, erosion.
OPPOSITES rise, improvement.

decor noun decoration, furnishing, colour scheme.

decorate verb **1** *the door was decorated with a wreath:* ornament, adorn, trim, embellish, garnish, furnish, enhance. **2** *he started to decorate his home:* paint, wallpaper, paper, refurbish, renovate, redecorate; informal do up, give something a facelift, give something a makeover. **3** *he was decorated for courage:* give a medal to, honour, cite, reward.

decoration noun **1** *a ceiling with rich decoration:* ornamentation, adornment, trimming, embellishment, beautification. **2** *a Christmas tree decoration:* ornament, bauble, trinket, knick-knack. **3** *a decoration won on the battlefield:* medal, award, prize; Brit. informal gong.

decorative adjective ornamental, fancy, ornate, attractive, pretty, showy.
OPPOSITES functional.

decrease verb **1** *pollution levels decreased:* lessen, reduce, drop, diminish, decline, dwindle, fall off, plummet, plunge.
2 *decrease the amount of fat in your body:* reduce, lessen, lower, cut, deplete, minimize; informal slash.
OPPOSITES increase.
• noun *a decrease in crime:* reduction, drop, decline, downturn, cut, cutback, diminution.
OPPOSITES increase.

decree noun **1** *a presidential decree:* order, command, commandment, edict, proclamation, law, statute, act. **2** *a court decree:* judgement, verdict, adjudication, finding, ruling, decision.
• verb *he decreed that a stadium should be built:* order, direct, command, rule, dictate, pronounce, proclaim, ordain.

courts. • verb (**decrees, decreeing, decreed**) order something officially.

decrepit adjective worn out or ruined because of age or neglect.
■ decrepitude noun.

decriminalize or **decriminalise** verb (**decriminalizes, decriminalizing, decriminalized**) change the law to make something no longer illegal.
■ decriminalization noun.

decry verb (**decries, decrying, decried**) publicly declare something to be wrong or bad.

decrypt verb convert a coded or unclear message into understandable language.

dedicate verb (**dedicates, dedicating, dedicated**) 1 give time or effort to a particular subject, task, or purpose. 2 address a book to someone as a sign of respect or affection.

dedicated adjective 1 devoting a lot of time and attention to a particular task or subject. 2 exclusively given over to a particular purpose.

dedication noun 1 devotion to a particular task or subject. 2 the action of dedicating. 3 the words with which a book is dedicated to someone.

deduce verb (**deduces, deducing, deduced**) reach a conclusion by thinking about the information or evidence that is available.

deduct verb take an amount away from a total.
■ deductible adjective.

deduction noun 1 the action of deducting something. 2 an amount that is or may be deducted. 3 the process of deducing something.
■ deductive adjective.

deed noun 1 something that is done deliberately. 2 (usu. **deeds**) a legal document.
□ deed poll Law a legal deed made by one party only.

deem verb formal consider in a particular way.

deep adjective 1 extending far down or in from the top or surface. 2 extending a specified distance from the top or surface. 3 (of sound) not shrill. 4 (of colour) dark. 5 very intense or extreme: *he was in deep trouble.* 6 difficult to understand. 7 (in ball games) far down or across the field. • noun (**the deep**) literary the sea.
□ deep freeze (or **deep freezer**) a freezer. deep-fry fry food in enough fat or oil to cover it completely.
■ deeply adverb.

deepen verb make or become deep or deeper.

deer noun (plural **deer**) a grazing animal with

THESAURUS

dedicate verb 1 *she dedicated her life to the sick:* devote, commit, pledge, give (up), sacrifice, set aside. 2 *the book is dedicated to his wife:* inscribe, address, offer. 3 *a chapel dedicated to St Jude:* devote, assign, bless, consecrate, sanctify.

dedicated adjective 1 *a dedicated supporter:* committed, devoted, staunch, firm, steadfast, loyal, faithful. 2 *a dedicated rail link:* specialized, custom-built, customized, purpose-built, exclusive.
OPPOSITES half-hearted, general-purpose.

dedication noun 1 *any sport requires dedication:* commitment, devotion, loyalty, allegiance, application, conscientiousness, resolve, perseverance. 2 *the book has a dedication to his wife:* inscription, message.
OPPOSITES apathy.

deduct verb subtract, take away, take off, debit, dock, stop; informal knock off.
OPPOSITES add.

deduction noun 1 *the deduction of tax:* subtraction, removal, debit. 2 *gross pay, before deductions:* stoppage, tax, expenses, rebate, discount, concession. 3 *she was right in her deduction:* conclusion, inference, supposition, hypothesis, assumption, presumption, suspicion.

deed noun 1 *heroic deeds:* act, action, feat, exploit, achievement, accomplishment, endeavour. 2 *mortgage deeds:* document, contract, instrument.

deep adjective 1 *a deep ravine:* cavernous, yawning, gaping, huge, extensive, bottomless, fathomless. 2 *deep affection:* intense, heartfelt, wholehearted, deep-seated, sincere, genuine, earnest, enthusiastic, great. 3 *a deep sleep:* sound, heavy. 4 *a deep thinker:* profound, serious, intelligent, intellectual, learned, wise, scholarly. 5 *he was deep in concentration:* rapt, absorbed, engrossed, preoccupied, intent, immersed, lost, gripped. 6 *a deep mystery:* obscure, complex, mysterious, unfathomable, opaque, abstruse, esoteric, enigmatic. 7 *his deep voice:* low-pitched, low, bass, rich, resonant, booming, sonorous. 8 *a deep red:* dark, intense, rich, strong, vivid.
OPPOSITES shallow, superficial, light, high, shrill.

deepen verb 1 *his love for her had deepened:* grow, increase, intensify, strengthen; informal step up. 2 *they deepened the hole:* dig out, dig deeper, excavate.

deeply adverb profoundly, greatly, enormously, extremely, strongly, intensely, keenly, acutely, thoroughly, completely, entirely, seriously, gravely; informal majorly.

hooves, the male of which usually has antlers.

deerstalker noun a soft cloth cap, with peaks in front and behind and ear flaps which can be tied together over the top.

deface verb (**defaces, defacing, defaced**) spoil the surface or appearance of.

de facto /day **fak**-toh/ adjective & adverb existing or happening in fact, whether it is supposed to or not.

defame verb (**defames, defaming, defamed**) damage the good reputation of.
■ **defamation** noun **defamatory** adjective.

default noun 1 failure to do something that is required by law. 2 an option adopted by a computer program or other mechanism when no alternative is specified. ● verb 1 fail to do something that is required by law. 2 (**default to**) go back automatically to a default option.
□ **by default** because there is no opposition or positive action.
■ **defaulter** noun.

defeat verb 1 win a victory against; beat. 2 prevent someone from achieving an aim. 3 reject or block a proposal or motion. ● noun an instance of defeating or of being defeated.

defeatist noun a person who gives in to difficulty or failure too easily.
■ **defeatism** noun.

defecate /**def**-uh-kayt/ verb expel waste matter from the bowels.
■ **defecation** noun.

defect¹ /**dee**-fekt/ noun a fault or

imperfection.

defect² /di-**fekt**/ verb abandon your country or cause in favour of an opposing one.
■ **defection** noun **defector** noun.

defective adjective not perfect; faulty.

defence (US spelling **defense**) noun 1 the action of defending something. 2 something that protects a building, country, etc. against attack. 3 an attempt to justify something. 4 the case presented by the person being accused or sued in a lawsuit. 5 (**the defence**) the lawyer or lawyers acting for the person being accused or sued in a lawsuit. 6 (in sport) the action of defending the goal or wicket, or the players who perform this role.

defenceless (US spelling **defenseless**) adjective completely vulnerable.

defend verb 1 protect from harm or danger. 2 argue in support of the person being accused or sued in a lawsuit. 3 attempt to justify. 4 compete to hold on to a title or seat in a contest or election. 5 (in sport) protect your goal or wicket rather than attempt to score against your opponents.
■ **defender** noun.

defendant noun a person sued or accused in a court of law.

defensible adjective 1 able to be justified by argument. 2 able to be protected.

defensive adjective 1 used or intended to defend or protect. 2 very anxious to defend yourself against criticism.
■ **defensively** adverb **defensiveness** noun.

defer¹ verb (**defers, deferring, deferred**) put

d

THESAURUS

defeat verb 1 *the army which defeated the Scots:* beat, conquer, win against, triumph over, get the better of, vanquish, rout, trounce, overcome, overpower; informal lick, thrash. 2 *this defeats the original point of the plan:* thwart, frustrate, foil, ruin, scotch, derail; informal put paid to, stymie; Brit. informal scupper.
● noun *a crippling defeat:* loss, conquest, rout; informal thrashing, hiding, drubbing, licking.
OPPOSITES victory.

defect noun *he spotted a defect in my work:* fault, flaw, imperfection, deficiency, deformity, blemish, mistake, error.

defective adjective faulty, flawed, imperfect, unsound, inoperative, malfunctioning, out of order, broken; informal on the blink; Brit. informal duff.
OPPOSITES perfect, working, intact.

defence noun 1 *the defence of the fortress:* protection, guarding, security, fortification, resistance. 2 *more spending on defence:* armaments, arms, weapons, weaponry, the military, the armed forces.

3 *the prisoner's defence:* justification, vindication, explanation, mitigation, excuse, alibi, denial, rebuttal, plea, pleading, argument, case.
OPPOSITES attack, prosecution.

defend verb 1 *a fort built to defend Ireland:* protect, guard, safeguard, secure, shield, fortify, watch over. 2 *he defended his policy:* justify, vindicate, explain, argue for, support, back, stand by, make a case for, stick up for.
OPPOSITES attack, criticize.

defender noun 1 *defenders of the environment:* protector, guardian, guard, custodian. 2 *a defender of colonialism:* supporter, upholder, backer, champion, advocate, apologist.

defensive adjective 1 *troops in defensive positions:* defending, protective, guarding. 2 *a defensive response:* self-justifying, oversensitive, prickly, paranoid, neurotic; informal twitchy.

defer verb postpone, put off, delay, hold over/off, put back, shelve, suspend; N. Amer.

something off to a later time.
■ **deferment** noun **deferral** noun.

defer² verb (**defers, deferring, deferred**)
(**defer to**) give in to or agree to accept.

deference noun polite respect.

deferential adjective polite and respectful.
■ **deferentially** adverb.

defiance noun open refusal to obey
someone or something.
■ **defiant** adjective **defiantly** adverb.

deficiency noun (plural **deficiencies**) **1** a lack
or shortage of something. **2** a failing or
shortcoming.

deficient adjective **1** not having enough of a
particular quality or ingredient.
2 inadequate in amount or quantity.

deficit noun **1** the amount by which a total
falls short of that required. **2** the amount
by which money spent is greater than
money earned in a particular period of
time.

defile¹ verb (**defiles, defiling, defiled**)
1 make dirty. **2** treat something sacred
with disrespect.
■ **defilement** noun.

defile² noun a narrow steep-sided gorge or
mountain pass.

define verb (**defines, defining, defined**)
1 describe the exact nature or scope of.
2 give the meaning of a word or phrase.
3 mark out the limits or outline of.
■ **definable** adjective.

definite adjective **1** clearly stated or
decided. **2** (of a person) certain about
something. **3** known to be true or real.
4 having exact and measurable physical
limits.

□ **the definite article** Grammar the word *the*.
■ **definitely** adverb.

☑ *-ite*, not *-ate*: defin*ite*.

definition noun **1** a statement of the exact
meaning of a word or the nature or scope
of something. **2** the degree of sharpness in
outline of an object or image.

definitive adjective **1** (of a conclusion or
agreement) final and not able to be
changed. **2** (of a written work) the most
accurate of its kind.
■ **definitively** adverb.

deflate verb (**deflates, deflating, deflated**)
1 let air or gas out of a tyre, balloon, etc.
2 make someone feel suddenly depressed.
3 reduce price levels in an economy.

deflation noun **1** the action of deflating
something. **2** reduction of the general level
of prices in an economy.
■ **deflationary** adjective.

deflect verb **1** turn something aside from a
straight course. **2** make someone change
their mind about doing something.
■ **deflection** noun.

deflower verb literary have sex with a woman
who is a virgin.

defoliate verb (**defoliates, defoliating,
defoliated**) remove the leaves from trees
or plants.
■ **defoliant** noun **defoliation** noun.

deforest verb clear an area of trees.
■ **deforestation** noun.

deform verb change or spoil the usual
shape of.
■ **deformed** adjective.

deformity noun (plural **deformities**) **1** a

THESAURUS

table; informal put on ice, put on the back
burner.

defiance noun resistance, opposition, non-
compliance, disobedience, insubordination,
rebellion, disregard, contempt, insolence.
OPPOSITES obedience.

defiant adjective disobedient, resistant,
obstinate, uncooperative, non-compliant,
recalcitrant, insubordinate; Brit. informal
stroppy, bolshie.
OPPOSITES cooperative.

deficiency noun **1** *a vitamin deficiency:*
lack, insufficiency, shortage, inadequacy,
deficit, shortfall, scarcity, dearth. **2** *the
team's big deficiency:* defect, fault, flaw,
failing, weakness, shortcoming, limitation.
OPPOSITES surplus, sufficiency, strength.

deficit noun shortfall, deficiency, shortage,
debt, arrears, loss.
OPPOSITES surplus.

definite adjective specific, explicit, express,
precise, exact, clear, clear-cut,
unambiguous, certain, sure, positive,

conclusive, decisive, firm, unequivocal,
unmistakable, proven, decided, marked,
distinct, identifiable.
OPPOSITES vague, ambiguous,
indeterminate.

definitely adverb certainly, surely, for sure,
unquestionably, without doubt,
undoubtedly, undeniably, clearly,
positively, absolutely, unmistakably.

definition noun **1** *the definition of
'intelligence':* meaning, sense,
interpretation, explanation, description.
2 *the definition of the picture:* clarity,
sharpness, focus, crispness, resolution.

definitive adjective **1** *a definitive decision:*
conclusive, final, unqualified, absolute,
categorical, positive, definite. **2** *the
definitive guide:* authoritative, best,
ultimate, classic, standard, recognized,
accepted, exhaustive.
OPPOSITES provisional, average.

deflect verb divert, turn away, draw away,
distract, fend off, parry, stave off.

deformed part. **2** the state of being deformed.

defraud verb illegally obtain money from someone by deception.

defray verb provide money to pay a cost.

defrock verb remove the official status of a Christian priest.

defrost verb **1** remove ice from something. **2** thaw frozen food.

deft adjective quick and neatly skilful. ■ **deftly** adverb **deftness** noun.

defunct adjective no longer existing or functioning.

defuse verb (**defuses, defusing, defused**) **1** make a situation less tense or difficult. **2** remove the fuse from an explosive device to prevent it from exploding.

> ! don't confuse **defuse** with **diffuse**, which means 'spread over a wide area'.

defy verb (**defies, defying, defied**) **1** openly resist or refuse to obey. **2** challenge someone to do or prove something.

degenerate verb /di-**jenn**-uh-rayt/ (**degenerates, degenerating, degenerated**) deteriorate physically or morally; get worse. • adjective /di-**jenn**-uh-ruht/ having very low moral standards. • noun /di-**jenn**-uh-ruht/ a person with very low moral standards.
■ **degeneracy** noun **degeneration** noun.

degenerative adjective (of a disease) becoming progressively worse.

degrade verb (**degrades, degrading, degraded**) **1** cause someone to lose dignity or self-respect. **2** make worse in character or quality. **3** make something break down or deteriorate chemically.
■ **degradable** adjective **degradation** noun.

degree noun **1** the amount, level, or extent to which something happens or is present. **2** a unit for measuring angles, equivalent to one ninetieth of a right angle. **3** a stage in a scale, e.g. of temperature or hardness. **4** a qualification awarded to someone who has successfully completed a course at a university.

dehumanize or **dehumanise** verb (**dehumanizes, dehumanizing, dehumanized**) remove the positive human qualities from.

dehumidify verb (**dehumidifies, dehumidifying, dehumidified**) remove moisture from the air or a gas.
■ **dehumidifier** noun.

dehydrate verb (**dehydrates, dehydrating, dehydrated**) **1** make someone lose a lot of water from their body. **2** remove water from food to preserve it.
■ **dehydration** noun.

de-ice verb (**de-ices, de-icing, de-iced**) remove ice from.
■ **de-icer** noun.

deify /**day**-i-fy/ verb (**deifies, deifying, deified**) treat or worship someone as a god.
■ **deification** noun.

deign verb (**deign to do**) do something that you think you are too important to do.

deity /**day**-i-ti/ noun (plural **deities**) a god or goddess.

déjà vu /**day**-zhah **voo**/ noun a feeling of having already experienced the present situation.

dejected adjective sad and in low spirits.
■ **dejection** noun.

dekko noun Brit. informal a quick look.

delay verb **1** make someone late or slow.

d

---

defraud verb swindle, cheat, rob, deceive, dupe, hoodwink, double-cross, trick; informal con, do, sting, diddle, rip off, shaft, pull a fast one on, put one over on, sell a pup to; N. Amer. informal sucker, snooker, stiff; Austral. informal pull a swifty on.

defy verb disobey, flout, disregard, ignore, break, violate, contravene, breach, challenge, confront.
OPPOSITES obey.

degenerate adjective *her degenerate brother:* corrupt, perverted, decadent, dissolute, dissipated, debauched, immoral, unprincipled, disreputable.
OPPOSITES upright, pure.
• verb *their quality of life had degenerated:* deteriorate, decline, slip, slide, worsen, go downhill; informal go to the dogs.
OPPOSITES improve.

degrade verb demean, debase, humiliate, humble, belittle, mortify, dehumanize,

brutalize.
OPPOSITES dignify.

degree noun level, standard, grade, stage, mark, amount, extent, measure, intensity, strength, proportion.

dejected adjective downcast, downhearted, despondent, disconsolate, dispirited, crestfallen, disheartened, depressed; informal down in the mouth, down in the dumps.
OPPOSITES cheerful.

delay verb **1** *we were delayed by the traffic:* detain, hold up, make late, slow up/down, bog down, hinder, hamper, impede, obstruct. **2** *don't delay:* linger, drag your feet, hold back, dawdle, waste time, stall, hesitate, dither, shilly-shally; informal dilly-dally. **3** *he may delay the cut in interest rates:* postpone, put off, defer, hold over, adjourn, reschedule.
OPPOSITES assist, hurry, advance.
• noun **1** *drivers will face lengthy delays:*

2 hesitate or be slow. **3** put off or postpone. •**noun** the period or length of time that someone or something is delayed.

delectable adjective lovely, delightful, or delicious.
■ **delectably** adverb.

delectation /dee-lek-**tay**-sh'n/ noun formal pleasure and delight.

delegate noun /**del**-i-guht/ **1** a person sent to represent other people. **2** a member of a committee. •**verb** /**del**-i-gayt/ (**delegates, delegating, delegated**) **1** give a task or responsibility to someone else, especially someone more junior. **2** authorize someone to act as a representative.

delegation noun **1** a group of delegates. **2** the process of delegating something.

delete verb (**deletes, deleting, deleted**) cross out or remove something written or printed or stored in a computer's memory.
■ **deletion** noun.

deleterious /de-li-**tee**-ri-uhss/ adjective formal causing harm or damage.

deli noun (plural **delis**) informal a delicatessen.

deliberate adjective /di-**lib**-uh-ruht/ **1** done on purpose; intentional. **2** careful and unhurried. •**verb** /di-**lib**-uh-rayt/ (**deliberates, deliberating, deliberated**) think about something carefully and for a long time.
■ **deliberately** adverb.

deliberation noun **1** long and careful consideration. **2** slow and careful movement or thought.

deliberative adjective having to do with consideration or discussion.

delicacy noun (plural **delicacies**) **1** intricate or fragile texture or structure. **2** discretion and tact. **3** a tasty, expensive food.

delicate adjective **1** attractively light and intricate in texture or structure. **2** easily broken or damaged. **3** tending to become ill easily. **4** needing or showing careful handling: *a delicate issue.* **5** (of colour or flavour) subtle and pleasant.
■ **delicately** adverb.

delicatessen noun a shop selling unusual or foreign prepared foods.

delicious adjective having a very pleasant taste or smell.
■ **deliciously** adverb.

THESAURUS

hold-up, wait, interruption, stoppage. **2** *the delay of his trial:* **postponement,** deferral, adjournment.

delegate noun *trade union delegates:* **representative,** envoy, emissary, agent, commissioner, deputy.
•**verb** *she must delegate routine tasks:* **assign,** entrust, pass on, hand on/over, turn over, devolve.

delegation noun **1** *the delegation from South Africa:* **deputation,** mission, commission, contingent, legation. **2** *the delegation of tasks to others:* **assignment,** entrusting, devolution.

delete verb **remove,** cut (out), take out, edit out, excise, cancel, cross out, strike out, obliterate, rub out, erase.
OPPOSITES add.

deliberate adjective **1** *a deliberate attempt to provoke him:* **intentional,** calculated, conscious, intended, planned, wilful, premeditated. **2** *small, deliberate steps:* **careful,** cautious, measured, regular, even, steady. **3** *a deliberate worker:* **methodical,** systematic, careful, painstaking, meticulous, thorough.
OPPOSITES accidental, hasty, careless.
•**verb** *she deliberated on his words:* **think about/over,** ponder, consider, contemplate, reflect on, muse on, meditate on, ruminate on, mull over; N. Amer. think on.

deliberately adverb **1** *he deliberately hurt me:* **intentionally,** on purpose, purposely, by design, knowingly, wittingly,

consciously, wilfully. **2** *he walked deliberately down the aisle:* **carefully,** cautiously, slowly, steadily, evenly.

deliberation noun **thought,** consideration, reflection, contemplation, discussion.

delicacy noun **1** *the delicacy of the fabric:* **fineness,** delicateness, fragility, thinness, lightness, flimsiness. **2** *the delicacy of the situation:* **difficulty,** trickiness, sensitivity, ticklishness, awkwardness. **3** *treat this matter with delicacy:* **care,** sensitivity, tact, discretion, diplomacy, subtlety. **4** *an Australian delicacy:* **treat,** luxury, titbit, speciality.

delicate adjective **1** *delicate embroidery:* **fine,** intricate, dainty. **2** *a delicate shade of blue:* **subtle,** soft, muted, pastel, pale, light. **3** *delicate china cups:* **fragile,** frail. **4** *his wife is very delicate:* **sickly,** unhealthy, frail, feeble, weak. **5** *a delicate issue:* **difficult,** tricky, sensitive, ticklish, awkward, touchy, embarrassing; informal sticky, dicey. **6** *the matter required delicate handling:* **careful,** sensitive, tactful, diplomatic, discreet, kid-glove, subtle. **7** *a delicate mechanism:* **sensitive,** light, precision.
OPPOSITES coarse, lurid, strong, robust, clumsy, crude.

delicious adjective **delectable,** mouth-watering, appetizing, tasty, flavoursome; informal scrumptious, moreish; N. Amer. informal finger-licking.
OPPOSITES unpalatable.

delight verb 1 please someone very much. 2 (**delight in**) take great pleasure in. • noun great pleasure, or something that causes it.

delighted adjective very pleased.
■ **delightedly** adverb.

delightful adjective causing delight; very pleasing.
■ **delightfully** adverb.

delineate /di-**lin**-i-ayt/ verb (**delineates, delineating, delineated**) describe or indicate something precisely.
■ **delineation** noun.

delinquency noun (plural **delinquencies**) minor crime.

delinquent adjective tending to commit crime. • noun a delinquent person.

deliquesce /de-li-**kwess**/ verb (**deliquesces, deliquescing, deliquesced**) (of a solid) become liquid by absorbing moisture.
■ **deliquescence** noun **deliquescent** adjective.

delirious adjective 1 suffering from delirium. 2 very excited or happy.
■ **deliriously** adverb.

☑ note there's an *i*, not an *e*, in the middle: del*i*rious.

delirium noun a disturbed state of mind in which a person becomes very restless, has illusions, and is unable to think clearly.

deliver verb 1 bring something and hand it over to the person who is supposed to receive it. 2 provide something promised or expected. 3 give a speech. 4 launch or aim a blow or attack. 5 save or set free. 6 assist in the birth of a baby. 7 give birth to a baby.

deliverance noun the process of being rescued or set free.

delivery noun (plural **deliveries**) 1 the action of delivering something. 2 the process of giving birth. 3 an act of throwing or bowling a ball.

dell noun literary a small valley.

delphinium /del-**fin**-i-uhm/ noun (plural **delphiniums**) a garden plant that has tall spikes of blue flowers.

delta noun 1 an area of land where the mouth of a river has split into several channels. 2 the fourth letter of the Greek alphabet (Δ, δ).

delude verb (**deludes, deluding, deluded**) persuade someone to believe something that is not true.

deluge noun 1 a severe flood or very heavy fall of rain. 2 a great quantity of something arriving at the same time: *a deluge of complaints*. • verb (**deluges, deluging, deluged**) 1 overwhelm someone with a great quantity of something. 2 flood a place.

delusion noun a mistaken belief or impression.
■ **delusional** adjective.

de luxe /di **luks**/ adjective of a higher quality than usual.

delve verb (**delves, delving, delved**) 1 reach inside a container and search for something. 2 research something very thoroughly.

demagnetize or **demagnetise** verb (**demagnetizes, demagnetizing, demagnetized**) stop something being magnetic.

demagogue /**dem**-uh-gog/ noun a political leader who appeals to people's desires and

d

THESAURUS

delight verb *her manners delighted him:* charm, enchant, captivate, entrance, thrill, entertain, amuse, divert; informal send, tickle pink, bowl over.
OPPOSITES dismay, disgust.
• noun *she squealed with delight:* pleasure, happiness, joy, glee, ecstasy, bliss, excitement, amusement.
OPPOSITES displeasure.
☐ **delight in** love, relish, savour, adore, lap up, take pleasure in, enjoy, revel in.

delighted adjective pleased, glad, happy, thrilled, overjoyed, ecstatic, elated, on cloud nine, walking on air, in seventh heaven, jumping for joy; enchanted, charmed; amused, diverted; gleeful, cock-a-hoop; informal over the moon, tickled pink, as pleased as Punch, on top of the world, as happy as Larry; Brit. informal chuffed; N. English informal made up; Austral. informal wrapped.

delightful adjective 1 *a delightful evening:* lovely, enjoyable, amusing, entertaining.

2 *a delightful girl:* charming, enchanting, captivating, bewitching, appealing, sweet, endearing, cute.

deliver verb 1 *the parcel was delivered to his house:* bring, take, convey, carry, transport, send, distribute, dispatch, ship. 2 *the court delivered its verdict:* state, utter, give, read, broadcast, pronounce, announce, declare, proclaim, hand down, return. 3 *she delivered a blow to his head:* administer, deal, inflict, give; informal land.

delivery noun 1 *the delivery of the goods:* conveyance, carriage, transportation, transport, distribution, dispatch, shipping. 2 *we get several deliveries a day:* consignment, load, shipment. 3 *her delivery was stilted:* speech, pronunciation, enunciation, articulation, elocution.

delusion noun misapprehension, misconception, false impression, misunderstanding, mistake, error, misconstruction, illusion, fantasy, fancy.

prejudices rather than using reasoned arguments.

demand noun **1** a very firm request for something. **2** (**demands**) tasks or requirements that are urgent or difficult. **3** the desire of consumers for a particular product or service. •verb **1** ask very firmly. **2** insist on having. **3** require; need. □ in demand wanted by many people.

demanding adjective needing a lot of skill or effort.

demarcate /dee-mar-kayt/ verb (**demarcates, demarcating, demarcated**) set the boundaries of.
■ demarcation noun.

dematerialize or **dematerialise** verb (**dematerializes, dematerializing, dematerialized**) stop being physically present.

demean verb make someone lose dignity or respect.

demeanour (US spelling **demeanor**) noun the way a person behaves or looks.

demented adjective **1** suffering from dementia. **2** informal wild and irrational.

dementia /di-men-shuh/ noun a disorder in which a person is unable to remember things or think clearly.

demerara sugar /dem-uh-rair-uh/ noun a type of light brown sugar.

demerit noun a fault or disadvantage.

demesne /di-mayn/ noun (in the past) land attached to a manor.

demigod noun a being that is partly a god and partly a human.

demilitarize or **demilitarise** verb (**demilitarizes, demilitarizing, demilitarized**) remove all military forces from an area.
■ demilitarization noun.

demi-monde /de-mi-mond/ noun a group of people on the fringes of respectable society.

demise /di-myz/ noun **1** a person's death. **2** the end or failure of something.

demo noun (plural **demos**) informal **1** a political demonstration. **2** a tape or disc containing a demonstration of a performer's music or a piece of software.

demob verb (**demobs, demobbing, demobbed**) Brit. informal demobilize.

demobilize or **demobilise** verb (**demobilizes, demobilizing, demobilized**) take troops out of active service.
■ demobilization noun.

democracy /di-mok-ruh-si/ noun (plural **democracies**) **1** a form of government in which the people can vote for representatives to govern the state on their behalf. **2** a state governed in this way.

democrat noun **1** a supporter of democracy. **2** (**Democrat**) (in the US) a member of the Democratic Party.

democratic adjective **1** relating to or supporting democracy. **2** based on the principle that everyone in society is equal. **3** (**Democratic**) (in the US) relating to or supporting the Democratic Party.
■ democratically adverb.

democratize or **democratise** verb (**democratizes, democratizing, democratized**) introduce a democratic system or democratic ideas to.
■ democratization noun.

demography noun the study of changes in human populations using records of the numbers of births, deaths, etc. in a particular area.
■ demographic adjective.

demolish /di-mol-ish/ verb **1** knock down a

THESAURUS

demand noun **1** *I gave in to her demands:* request, call, command, order, dictate. **2** *the demands of a young family:* requirement, need, claim, commitment, imposition. **3** *the big demand for such toys:* market, call, appetite, desire.
•verb **1** *workers demanded wage increases:* call for, ask for, request, push for, seek, claim. **2** *Harvey demanded that I tell him the truth:* order, command, enjoin, require, insist. **3** *'Where is she?' he demanded:* ask, enquire. **4** *an activity demanding detailed knowledge:* require, need, necessitate, call for, involve, entail. **5** *they demanded complete anonymity:* insist on, stipulate, expect, look for.

demanding adjective **1** *a demanding task:* difficult, challenging, taxing, exacting, tough, hard, onerous, formidable, arduous, gruelling, back-breaking, punishing. **2** *a demanding child:* nagging, trying, tiresome, hard to please, high-maintenance.
OPPOSITES easy.

demeaning adjective degrading, humiliating, shameful, undignified, menial; informal infra dig.

demise noun **1** *her tragic demise:* death, dying, passing, end. **2** *the demise of the Ottoman Empire:* end, break-up, disintegration, fall, downfall, collapse, overthrow.
OPPOSITES birth.

democratic adjective elected, representative, parliamentary, popular, egalitarian, self-governing.

demolish verb **1** *they demolished a block of flats:* knock down, pull down, tear down, destroy, flatten, raze to the ground, dismantle, level, bulldoze, blow up. **2** *he demolished her credibility:* destroy, ruin, wreck, overturn, explode, drive a coach and

building. **2** show that a theory is completely wrong. **3** *humorous* eat up food quickly.
■ **demolition** noun.

demon noun an evil spirit or devil. • **adjective** very forceful or skilful: *a demon cook.*

demoniac /di-**moh**-ni-ak/ or **demoniacal** /dee-muh-**ny**-u-k'l/ adjective demonic.

demonic /di-**mon**-ik/ adjective having to do with demons or evil spirits.
■ **demonically** adverb.

demonize or **demonise** verb (**demonizes, demonizing, demonized**) portray someone as wicked and threatening.

demonstrable adjective clearly apparent or able to be proved.
■ **demonstrably** adverb.

demonstrate verb (**demonstrates, demonstrating, demonstrated**) **1** clearly show that something exists or is true. **2** show and explain how something works. **3** express a feeling or quality by your actions. **4** take part in a public demonstration.
■ **demonstrator** noun.

demonstration noun **1** the action of demonstrating. **2** a public meeting or march expressing an opinion on an issue.

demonstrative /di-**mon**-struh-tiv/ adjective **1** tending to show your feelings openly. **2** demonstrating something.
■ **demonstratively** adverb.

demoralize or **demoralise** verb (**demoralizes, demoralizing, demoralized**) make someone lose confidence or hope.
■ **demoralization** noun.

demote verb (**demotes, demoting, demoted**) move someone to a less senior position.
■ **demotion** noun.

demotivate verb make someone less eager to work or make an effort.

demur /di-**mer**/ verb (**demurs, demurring, demurred**) show reluctance.
□ **without demur** without objecting or hesitating.
■ **demurral** noun.

demure adjective (of a woman) reserved, modest, and shy.
■ **demurely** adverb.

demystify verb (**demystifies, demystifying, demystified**) make a subject less difficult to understand.

den noun **1** a wild animal's lair or home. **2** *informal* a person's private room. **3** a place where people meet to do something immoral or forbidden: *an opium den.*

denationalize or **denationalise** verb (**denationalizes, denationalizing, denationalized**) transfer an industry or business from public to private ownership.

denial noun **1** a statement that something is not true. **2** the refusal to acknowledge or accept something unpleasant: *he's still in denial.*

denier /den-yer/ noun a unit for measuring the fineness of nylon or silk.

denigrate verb (**denigrates, denigrating, denigrated**) criticize someone unfairly.
■ **denigration** noun.

denim noun **1** a hard-wearing cotton fabric. **2** (**denims**) jeans or other clothes made of denim.

denizen /den-i-zuhn/ noun formal an inhabitant or occupant.

denominate verb (**denominates, denominating, denominated**) formal call; name.

denomination noun **1** a recognized branch

d

THESAURUS

horses through; *informal* shoot full of holes.
OPPOSITES build, strengthen.

demonstrate verb **1** *his findings demonstrate that boys commit more crimes:* show, indicate, establish, prove, confirm, verify. **2** *she demonstrated various drawing techniques:* show, display, present, illustrate, exemplify. **3** *his work demonstrated an analytical ability:* reveal, manifest, indicate, signify, signal, denote, show, display, exhibit. **4** *they demonstrated against the Government:* protest, march, parade, picket, strike.

demonstration noun **1** *a demonstration of carving:* exhibition, presentation, display. **2** *his paintings are a demonstration of his talent:* manifestation, indication, sign, mark, proof, testimony. **3** *an anti-racism demonstration:* protest, march, rally, mass lobby, sit-in, sit-down strike; *informal* demo.

demoralized adjective dispirited,

disheartened, downhearted, dejected, downcast, low, depressed, dismayed, daunted, discouraged.

demure adjective modest, reserved, shy, unassuming, decorous, decent, proper.
OPPOSITES brazen.

den noun **1** *the wolves' den:* lair, burrow, hole, shelter, hiding place, hideout. **2** *sulking in his den:* study, studio, workshop, retreat, sanctuary, hideaway; *informal* hidey-hole.

denial noun **1** *the reports met with a denial:* contradiction, rebuttal, repudiation, refutation, disclaimer. **2** *the denial of insurance to certain people:* refusal, withholding.

denomination noun **1** *a Christian denomination:* religious group, sect, cult, movement, persuasion, order, creed, school, church. **2** *banknotes in a number of*

d

of a Church or religion. **2** the face value of a banknote, coin, postage stamp, etc. **3** formal a name or designation.
■ denominational adjective.

denominator noun Maths the number below the line in a fraction, for example 4 in ¼.

denote verb (**denotes, denoting, denoted**) **1** be a sign of. **2** (of a word) have something as a main meaning.

denouement /day-noo-mon/ noun the final part of a play, film, or story, in which matters are explained or settled.

denounce verb (**denounces, denouncing, denounced**) publicly declare that someone is wrong or evil.

dense adjective **1** containing many people or things crowded closely together. **2** having a thick or closely packed texture. **3** informal stupid.
■ densely adverb.

density noun (plural **densities**) **1** the degree to which something is dense. **2** the quantity of people or things in a given area.

dent noun a slight hollow in a surface made by a blow or pressure. • verb **1** mark with a dent. **2** have a bad effect on.

dental adjective relating to the teeth or to dentistry.

dentine /den-teen/ noun the hard, bony tissue that teeth are made of.

dentist noun a person who is qualified to treat the diseases and conditions that affect the teeth and gums.
■ dentistry noun.

denture /den-cher/ noun a removable plate or frame fitted with one or more false teeth.

denude verb (**denudes, denuding, denuded**) make something bare or empty.

denunciation noun the action of denouncing.

deny verb (**denies, denying, denied**) **1** state that something is not true. **2** refuse to admit something. **3** refuse to give someone a thing that they want. **4** (**deny yourself**) go without something you want.

deodorant noun a substance which prevents unpleasant bodily odours.

deodorize or **deodorise** verb (**deodorizes, deodorizing, deodorized**) prevent an unpleasant smell in.

depart verb **1** leave; go away. **2** (**depart from**) do something different from the usual or accepted thing.

departed adjective deceased; dead.

department noun **1** a division of a business, government, or other large organization. **2** an administrative district in some countries, e.g. France. **3** informal a person's area of special knowledge or responsibility.
□ department store a large shop that stocks many types of goods in different departments.
■ departmental adjective departmentally adverb.

departure noun **1** the action of leaving. **2** a change from the usual way of doing something.

THESAURUS

denominations: value, unit, size.

denote verb indicate, be a mark of, signify, signal, designate, symbolize, represent.

denounce verb **1** the pope denounced his critics: condemn, attack, censure, decry, stigmatize, deprecate, disparage, revile, damn. **2** he was denounced as a traitor: expose, betray, inform on, incriminate, implicate, cite, accuse.
OPPOSITES praise.

dense adjective **1** a dense forest: thick, crowded, compact, solid, tight, overgrown, impenetrable, impassable. **2** dense smoke: thick, heavy, opaque, murky. **3** (informal) they were dense enough to believe me: stupid, brainless, foolish, slow, simple-minded, empty-headed, idiotic; informal thick, dim; Brit. informal daft.
OPPOSITES sparse, thin, clever.

dent noun a dent in his car: knock, indentation, dint, depression, hollow, crater, pit; N. Amer. informal ding.
• verb Jamie dented his car: knock, dint, mark; N. Amer. informal ding.

deny verb **1** the report was denied by witnesses: contradict, rebut, repudiate, refute, challenge, contest. **2** he denied the request: refuse, turn down, reject, rebuff, decline, veto, dismiss; informal give the thumbs down to.
OPPOSITES confirm, allow, accept.

depart verb **1** James departed after lunch: leave, go away, withdraw, absent yourself, quit, exit, decamp, retreat, retire, make off; informal make tracks, take off, split; Brit. informal sling your hook. **2** the budget departed from the norm: deviate, diverge, digress, stray, veer, differ, vary.
OPPOSITES arrive, stick to.

department noun division, section, sector, unit, branch, wing, office, bureau, agency, ministry.

departure noun **1** he tried to delay her departure: leaving, going, leave-taking, withdrawal, exit. **2** a departure from normality: deviation, divergence, digression, shift, variation. **3** an exciting departure for film-makers: change, innovation, novelty.

depend verb (**depend on**) **1** be determined by. **2** rely on.

dependable adjective trustworthy and reliable.
■ **dependability** noun **dependably** adverb.

dependant or **dependent** noun a person who relies on another for financial support.

> ☑ the noun can be spelled **dependant** or **dependent**. The adjective is always spelled **dependent**.

dependency noun (plural **dependencies**) **1** a country or province controlled by another. **2** the state of being dependent.

dependent adjective **1** (**dependent on**) determined by. **2** relying on someone or something for support. **3** (**dependent on**) unable to do without. • noun ⇒ **DEPENDANT**.
■ **dependence** noun **dependently** adverb.

depict verb **1** represent something by a drawing, painting, or other art form. **2** portray in words.
■ **depiction** noun.

depilate /dep-i-layt/ verb (**depilates**, **depilating**, **depilated**) remove the hair from.
■ **depilation** noun **depilatory** adjective.

deplete verb (**depletes**, **depleting**, **depleted**) reduce the number or quantity of.
■ **depletion** noun.

deplorable adjective shockingly bad.
■ **deplorably** adverb.

deplore verb (**deplores**, **deploring**, **deplored**) strongly disapprove of.

deploy verb **1** bring or move forces into position for military action. **2** use a resource or quality effectively.
■ **deployment** noun.

depopulate verb (**depopulates**, **depopulating**, **depopulated**) greatly reduce the population of a place.
■ **depopulation** noun.

deport verb expel a foreigner or immigrant from a country.
■ **deportation** noun **deportee** noun.

deportment noun **1** the way a person stands and walks. **2** N. Amer. a person's behaviour or manners.

depose verb (**deposes**, **deposing**, **deposed**) remove someone from office suddenly and forcefully.

deposit noun **1** a sum of money placed in an account. **2** a payment made as a first instalment in buying something. **3** a returnable sum paid when renting something, to cover possible loss or damage. **4** a layer of a substance that has built up. • verb (**deposits**, **depositing**, **deposited**) **1** put something down in a particular place. **2** store something

d

THESAURUS

depend verb **1** *her career depends on this reference:* be dependent on, hinge on, hang on, rest on, rely on. **2** *my family depends on me:* rely on, lean on, count on, bank on, trust (in), pin your hopes on.

dependent adjective **1** *she is dependent on drugs:* addicted, reliant; informal hooked. **2** *he is ill and dependent:* reliant, needy, helpless, infirm, invalid, incapable, debilitated, disabled.
OPPOSITES independent.
□ **dependent on 1** conditional on, contingent on, based on, subject to, determined by, influenced by. **2** reliant on, relying on, counting on, sustained by.

depict verb **1** *the painting depicts the Last Supper:* portray, show, represent, picture, illustrate, reproduce, render. **2** *the process depicted by Darwin's theory:* describe, detail, relate, present, set forth, set out, outline.

deplete verb reduce, decrease, diminish, exhaust, use up, consume, expend, drain, empty.
OPPOSITES augment.

deplore verb **1** *we deplore violence:* abhor, find unacceptable, frown on, disapprove of, take a dim view of, take exception to, condemn, denounce. **2** *he deplored their*

lack of flair: regret, lament, mourn, bemoan, bewail, complain about, grieve over, sigh over.
OPPOSITES applaud, rejoice at.

deploy verb **1** *forces were deployed at strategic points:* position, station, post, place, install, locate, base. **2** *she deployed all her skills:* use, utilize, employ, take advantage of, exploit, call on.

deport verb expel, banish, extradite, repatriate.
OPPOSITES admit.

depose verb overthrow, unseat, dethrone, topple, remove, supplant, displace, oust.

deposit noun **1** *a thick deposit of ash:* layer, covering, coating, blanket, accumulation, sediment. **2** *a copper deposit:* seam, vein, lode, layer, stratum, bed. **3** *they paid a deposit:* down payment, advance payment, prepayment, instalment, retainer, security.
• verb **1** *she deposited her books on the table:* put down, place, set down, unload, rest, drop; informal dump, park, plonk; N. Amer. informal plunk. **2** *the silt deposited by flood water:* leave (behind), precipitate, dump, wash up, cast up. **3** *the gold was deposited at the bank:* lodge, bank, house, store, stow.

d

somewhere for safekeeping. **3** pay a sum as a deposit. **4** lay down a layer of a substance.

deposition noun **1** the action of deposing someone from office. **2** Law a sworn statement to be used as evidence in a court of law. **3** the action of depositing.

depository noun (plural **depositories**) a place where things are stored.

depot /**dep**-oh/ noun **1** a place where large quantities of goods are stored. **2** a place where vehicles are kept and maintained. **3** N. Amer. /**dee**-poh/ a railway or bus station.

deprave verb (**depraves, depraving, depraved**) make someone morally bad; corrupt someone.

depravity /di-**prav**-i-ti/ noun immoral behaviour or character.

deprecate /**dep**-ri-kayt/ verb (**deprecates, deprecating, deprecated**) express disapproval of.
■ **deprecation** noun.

depreciate /di-**pree**-shi-ayt/ verb (**depreciates, depreciating, depreciated**) **1** decrease in value over a period of time. **2** dismiss something as being unimportant.
■ **depreciation** noun.

depredations plural noun acts that cause harm or damage.

depress verb **1** make someone feel very

unhappy. **2** make something less active. **3** push or pull down.

depressant noun a drug or other substance that slows down the natural processes of the body.

depressed adjective **1** feeling very unhappy and without hope. **2** suffering the damaging effects of an economic slump.

depression noun **1** a mental state in which a person has feelings of great unhappiness and hopelessness. **2** a long and severe slump in an economy or market. **3** the action of depressing. **4** a sunken or hollow place. **5** an area of low pressure which may bring rain.

depressive adjective tending to cause or feel depression.

deprivation /dep-ri-**vay**-sh'n/ noun **1** hardship resulting from not having enough of the things necessary for life. **2** the action of depriving someone of something.

deprive verb (**deprives, depriving, deprived**) prevent someone from having or using something.

deprived adjective not having enough of the things necessary for life.

Dept abbreviation Department.

depth noun **1** the distance from the top or surface down, or from front to back.

THESAURUS

depot noun **1** *the bus depot:* terminal, terminus, station, garage, headquarters, base. **2** *an arms depot:* storehouse, warehouse, store, repository, depository, cache, arsenal, armoury, dump.

depress verb **1** *the news depressed him:* sadden, dispirit, cast down, get down, dishearten, demoralize, crush, weigh down on. **2** *new economic policies depressed sales:* slow down, weaken, impair, inhibit, restrict. **3** *imports will depress farm prices:* reduce, lower, cut, cheapen, discount, deflate, diminish, depreciate, devalue. **4** *depress each key in turn:* press, push, hold down, tap.
OPPOSITES cheer, boost, raise, lift.

depressed adjective **1** *he felt lonely and depressed:* sad, unhappy, miserable, gloomy, dejected, downhearted, downcast, down, despondent, dispirited, low, morose, dismal, desolate; informal blue, down in the dumps, down in the mouth. **2** *a depressed economy:* weak, inactive, flat, slow, slack, sluggish, stagnant. **3** *a depressed area:* poverty-stricken, poor, disadvantaged, deprived, needy, distressed, run down.
OPPOSITES cheerful, strong, prosperous.

depressing adjective dismal, sad, unhappy, sombre, gloomy, grave, bleak, black, melancholy, dreary, grim, cheerless.

depression noun **1** *she ate to ease her depression:* unhappiness, sadness, melancholy, melancholia, misery, sorrow, gloom, despondency, low spirits. **2** *an economic depression:* recession, slump, decline, downturn. **3** *a depression in the ground:* hollow, indentation, dent, cavity, dip, pit, crater, basin, bowl.

deprivation noun **1** *unemployment and deprivation:* poverty, impoverishment, privation, hardship, destitution, need, want. **2** *deprivation of political rights:* dispossession, withholding, withdrawal, removal, seizure.
OPPOSITES prosperity, granting.

deprive verb dispossess, strip, divest, relieve, rob, cheat out of.

deprived adjective disadvantaged, underprivileged, poverty-stricken, impoverished, poor, destitute, needy.
OPPOSITES privileged.

depth noun **1** *the depth of the caves:* deepness, drop, height. **2** *the depth of his knowledge:* extent, range, scope, breadth, width. **3** *her lack of depth:* profundity, wisdom, understanding, intelligence, discernment, penetration, insight, awareness. **4** *depth of colour:* intensity, richness, vividness, strength, brilliance.
OPPOSITES triviality.

2 complex or meaningful thought. **3** extensive and detailed study. **4** strength of emotion. **5** (**the depths**) the deepest, lowest, or innermost part of something. □ **depth charge** a device designed to explode under water, used for attacking submarines.

deputation noun a group of people who are sent to do something on behalf of a larger group.

depute verb (**deputes, deputing, deputed**) instruct someone to do something that you are responsible for.

deputize or **deputise** verb (**deputizes, deputizing, deputized**) temporarily act on behalf of someone else.

deputy noun (plural **deputies**) a person appointed to do the work of a more senior person in that person's absence.

derail verb **1** make a train leave the tracks. **2** prevent a process from following its intended course.
■ **derailment** noun.

deranged adjective mad; insane.
■ **derangement** noun.

derby /**dar**-bi/ noun (plural **derbies**) a sports match between two rival teams from the same area.

deregulate verb (**deregulates, deregulating, deregulated**) remove regulations or restrictions from.
■ **deregulation** noun.

derelict /**de**-ri-likt/ adjective in a very bad condition as a result of disuse and neglect.
• noun a person without a home, job, or property.

dereliction noun **1** an abandoned and run-down state. **2** (usu. **dereliction of duty**) shameful failure to do something you are supposed to do.

deride verb (**derides, deriding, derided**) express contempt for; ridicule.

de rigueur /duh ri-**ger**/ adjective necessary if you want to be accepted socially.

derision noun scornful ridicule or mockery.

derisive /di-**ry**-siv/ adjective expressing contempt or ridicule.
■ **derisively** adverb.

derisory /di-**ry**-suh-ri/ adjective **1** ridiculously small or inadequate. **2** expressing contempt or ridicule; derisive.

derivation noun **1** the obtaining of something from a source. **2** the formation of a word from another word.

derivative adjective imitating the work of another artist, writer, etc.; not original.
• noun something which comes from or is based on another source.

derive verb (**derives, deriving, derived**) **1** (**derive something from**) obtain something from a source. **2** (**derive from**) originate or develop from.

dermatitis /der-muh-ty-tiss/ noun inflammation of the skin as a result of irritation or an allergic reaction.

dermatology noun the branch of medicine concerned with skin disorders.
■ **dermatological** adjective **dermatologist** noun.

derogatory /di-**rog**-uh-tri/ adjective critical or disrespectful.

derrick noun **1** a type of crane. **2** the framework over an oil well for holding the drilling machinery.

derring-do noun old use heroic actions.

dervish noun a member of a Muslim religious group, some orders of which are known for their wild rituals.

descant /**dess**-kant/ noun an independent melody sung or played above a basic melody.

descend verb **1** move down or downwards. **2** slope or lead downwards. **3** (**descend to**) do something very shameful. **4** (**descend on**) make a sudden attack on or unwelcome visit to. **5** (**be descended from**) have a particular person as an ancestor.

descendant noun a person that is

d

THESAURUS

deputy noun second in command, number two, assistant, aide, proxy, stand-in, replacement, substitute, representative, reserve.

derelict adjective *a derelict building:* dilapidated, ramshackle, run down, tumbledown, in ruins, falling down, disused, abandoned, deserted.
• noun *the derelicts who survive on the streets:* tramp, vagrant, down and out, homeless person, drifter, beggar, outcast; informal dosser, bag lady.

derision noun mockery, ridicule, jeers, sneers, taunts, disdain, disparagement, denigration, insults.

derogatory adjective disparaging,

disrespectful, demeaning, critical, pejorative, negative, unfavourable, uncomplimentary, unflattering, insulting, defamatory, slanderous, libellous.
OPPOSITES complimentary.

descend verb **1** *the plane started descending:* go down, come down, drop, fall, sink, dive, plummet, plunge, nosedive. **2** *she descended the stairs:* climb down, go down, come down, shin down, slide down. **3** *the road descends to a village:* slope, dip, slant, go down, fall away. **4** *she saw Leo descend from the bus:* alight, disembark, get down, get off, dismount.
OPPOSITES climb, board.
□ **descend on flock to,** besiege, surround,

descended from a particular ancestor.

> ☑ the correct spelling of the noun **descendant** is with -*ant*, not -*ent*, at the end.

descent noun **1** an act of descending. **2** a downward slope. **3** a person's origin or nationality.

describe verb (**describes, describing, described**) **1** give a detailed account of something in words. **2** mark out or draw a shape.

description noun **1** a spoken or written account. **2** the process of describing. **3** a sort, kind, or class: *people of any description.*

descriptive adjective describing something, especially in a vivid style.
■ **descriptively** adverb.

descry verb (**descries, descrying, descried**) literary catch sight of.

desecrate /dess-i-krayt/ verb (**desecrates, desecrating, desecrated**) damage something sacred or treat it with great disrespect.
■ **desecration** noun.

desegregate verb (**desegregates, desegregating, desegregated**) end a policy by which people of different races are kept separate.
■ **desegregation** noun.

deselect verb Brit. (of a local branch of a political party) reject an existing MP as a candidate in a forthcoming election.
■ **deselection** noun.

desensitize or **desensitise** verb (**desensitizes, desensitizing, desensitized**) make less sensitive.

desert¹ /di-zert/ verb **1** leave someone without help or support. **2** leave a place, making it seem empty. **3** illegally leave the armed forces.
□ **desert island** an uninhabited tropical island.
■ **deserter** noun **desertion** noun.

desert² /dez-ert/ noun an empty, waterless area of land with very few plants.

> ! don't confuse **desert** (a waterless area) with **dessert** (the sweet course)!

deserts /di-zerts/ plural noun (**get your just deserts**) get the reward or punishment that you deserve.

deserve verb (**deserves, deserving, deserved**) do something worthy of a particular reward or punishment.
■ **deservedly** adverb.

deserving adjective worthy of being treated well or helped.

déshabillé /day-za-bee-yay/ noun the state of being only partly clothed.

desiccate verb (**desiccates, desiccating, desiccated**) remove the moisture from.
■ **desiccation** noun.

design noun **1** a plan or drawing produced

THESAURUS

take over, invade, swoop on, occupy.

descent noun **1** *the plane began its descent:* dive, drop, fall, plunge, nosedive. **2** *a steep descent:* slope, incline, dip, drop, gradient. **3** *his descent into alcoholism:* decline, slide, fall, degeneration, deterioration. **4** *she is of Italian descent:* ancestry, parentage, ancestors, family, extraction, origin, derivation, birth, lineage, stock, blood, roots, origins.

describe verb **1** *he described his experiences:* report, recount, relate, narrate, tell of, set out, detail, give a rundown of. **2** *she described him as a pathetic figure:* portray, depict, paint, define, characterize, call, label, class, brand. **3** *the pen described a circle:* mark out, delineate, outline, trace, draw.

description noun **1** *a description of my travels:* account, report, relate, narrate, story, portrayal, portrait, sketch, details. **2** *the description of oil as 'black gold':* designation, labelling, naming, dubbing, characterization, definition, classification, branding. **3** *vehicles of every description:* sort, variety, kind, type.

desert¹ verb **1** *his wife deserted him:* abandon, leave, jilt, leave high and dry, leave in the lurch, leave behind, strand, maroon; informal walk/run out on, dump, ditch; literary forsake. **2** *soldiers deserted in droves:* abscond, defect, run away, decamp, flee, turn tail, take French leave; Military go AWOL.

desert² noun *an African desert:* wasteland, wastes, wilderness, dust bowl.

deserted adjective **1** *a deserted wife:* abandoned, jilted, cast aside, neglected, stranded, marooned, forlorn; literary forsaken. **2** *a deserted village:* empty, uninhabited, unoccupied, abandoned, evacuated, desolate, lonely, godforsaken.
OPPOSITES cherished, populous.

deserve verb merit, earn, warrant, rate, justify, be worthy of, be entitled to.

deserved adjective well earned, merited, warranted, justified, rightful, due, fitting, just, proper.

deserving adjective *a deserving cause:* worthy, commendable, praiseworthy, admirable, estimable, creditable.

design noun **1** *a design for the offices:* plan, blueprint, drawing, sketch, outline, map, plot, diagram, draft. **2** *a Celtic design:* pattern, motif, device, style, theme, layout.
•verb **1** *they designed a new engine:* invent,

before something is made. **2** the production of such plans or drawings. **3** purpose or deliberate planning. **4** a decorative pattern. • **verb 1** produce a design for. **2** (**be designed**) be intended for a purpose.

□ **have designs on** aim to obtain.

designate verb /**dez**-ig-nayt/ (**designates**, **designating**, **designated**) **1** officially give a particular status or name to. **2** appoint someone to a job or position. • adjective /**dez**-ig-nuht/ appointed to a position but not yet having taken it up: *the Director designate.*

designation noun **1** the action of designating. **2** an official title or description.

designer noun a person who designs things. • adjective made by a famous fashion designer: *designer jeans.*

desirable adjective **1** wished for as being attractive, useful, or necessary. **2** (of a person) sexually attractive.
■ **desirability** noun.

desire noun a strong feeling of wanting to have something or wishing for something to happen. • verb (**desires**, **desiring**, **desired**) **1** strongly wish for or want. **2** find someone attractive.

desirous adjective (**desirous of** or **to do**) wanting a particular thing.

desist verb stop doing something.

desk noun **1** a piece of furniture with a flat or sloping surface for writing on. **2** a counter in a hotel, bank, etc.

desktop noun **1** a computer suitable to be used at a desk. **2** the area of a computer screen that you can work in.

desolate adjective **1** (of a place) bleak and empty. **2** very unhappy. • verb (**be desolated**) be very unhappy.
■ **desolation** noun.

despair noun the complete loss or absence of hope. • verb lose hope, or be without hope.

☑ *des-*, not *dis-*: despair.

despatch ⇒ DISPATCH.

desperado /dess-puh-**rah**-doh/ noun (plural **desperadoes** or **desperados**) a reckless and dangerous criminal.

desperate adjective **1** feeling, showing, or involving despair. **2** done when everything else has failed. **3** very serious: *a desperate shortage.* **4** needing or wanting something very much.
■ **desperately** adverb **desperation** noun.

☑ desperate, not *-parate*.

despicable adjective deserving hatred and contempt.
■ **despicably** adverb.

d

THESAURUS

create, think up, come up with, devise, formulate, conceive; informal dream up. **2** *this paper is designed to provoke discussion:* intend, aim, mean.

designate verb **1** *some firms designate a press officer:* appoint, nominate, delegate, select, choose, pick, elect, name, identify, assign. **2** *the rivers are designated 'Sites of Special Scientific Interest':* classify, class, label, tag, name, call, term, dub.

desirable adjective **1** *a desirable location:* attractive, sought-after, in demand, popular, enviable; informal to die for, must-have. **2** *it is desirable that they should meet:* advantageous, advisable, wise, sensible, recommended, beneficial, preferable. **3** *a very desirable woman:* (sexually) attractive, beautiful, pretty, appealing, seductive, alluring, irresistible; informal sexy.
OPPOSITES unattractive, unwise, ugly.

desire noun **1** *a desire to see the world:* wish, want, aspiration, yearning, longing, craving, hankering, hunger; informal yen, itch. **2** *his eyes glittered with desire:* lust, passion, sensuality, sexuality, libido, lasciviousness, lechery.
• verb *they desired peace:* want, wish for, long for, yearn for, crave, hanker after, be desperate for, be bent on, covet, aspire to.

desolate adjective **1** *desolate moorlands:* bleak, stark, bare, dismal, grim, wild, inhospitable, deserted, uninhabited, godforsaken, abandoned, empty, isolated, remote. **2** *she is desolate:* miserable, despondent, depressed, disconsolate, devastated, despairing, inconsolable.
OPPOSITES populous, joyful.

despair noun desperation, anguish, unhappiness, despondency, depression, misery, wretchedness, hopelessness.
OPPOSITES hope, joy.
• verb lose hope, give up, lose heart, be discouraged, be despondent, be demoralized.

despatch verb & noun. See DISPATCH.

desperate adjective **1** *a desperate look:* despairing, hopeless, anguished, distressed, wretched, desolate, forlorn, distraught, at your wits' end, at the end of your tether. **2** *a desperate attempt to escape:* last-ditch, last-gasp, eleventh-hour, do-or-die, final, frantic, frenzied, wild. **3** *a desperate shortage of teachers:* grave, serious, critical, acute, urgent, pressing, drastic, extreme.

desperation noun hopelessness, despair, distress, anguish, agony, torment, misery.

d

despise verb (despise, despising, despised) hate or feel disgusted by.

despite preposition in spite of.

despoil verb literary steal valuable possessions from a place.

despondent adjective very sad and without much hope.
■ **despondency** noun **despondently** adverb.

despot /dess-pot/ noun a ruler with unlimited power.
■ **despotic** adjective **despotism** noun.

dessert /di-zert/ noun the sweet course eaten at the end of a meal.

> **!** don't confuse **dessert** (the sweet course) with **desert** (a waterless area)!

dessertspoon noun a spoon smaller than a tablespoon and larger than a teaspoon.

destabilize or **destabilise** verb (destabilizes, destabilizing, destabilized) make a country or government less stable.

destination noun the place to which someone or something is going or being sent.

destine verb 1 (**be destined for** or **to**) be intended for a particular purpose, or certain to do or be a particular thing. 2 (**be destined for**) be on the way to a particular place.

destiny noun (plural **destinies**) 1 the things that will happen to a person. 2 the hidden power believed to control what will happen in the future.

destitute adjective very poor and without a home or other things necessary for life.
■ **destitution** noun.

destroy verb 1 make something stop existing by damaging or attacking it. 2 kill a sick or unwanted animal using a humane method.

destroyer noun 1 a person or thing that destroys. 2 a small, fast warship.

destruction noun the destroying of something.

destructive adjective 1 causing destruction. 2 negative and unhelpful.
■ **destructively** adverb.

desultory /dez-uhl-tuh-ri/ adjective lacking enthusiasm or a definite plan.
■ **desultorily** adverb.

detach verb 1 remove something that is attached to something larger. 2 (**be detached**) Military be sent on a mission.
■ **detachable** adjective.

> ☑ -ach, not -atch: detach.

detached adjective 1 separate or disconnected. 2 not involved or interested; aloof.

detachment noun 1 a feeling of being

THESAURUS

despise verb detest, hate, loathe, abhor, deplore, scorn, disdain, deride, sneer at, revile, spurn, shun.
OPPOSITES adore, respect.

despite preposition in spite of, notwithstanding, regardless of, in the face of, in the teeth of, undeterred by, for all, even with.

destined adjective 1 *he is destined to lead a troubled life:* fated, ordained, predestined, doomed, meant, intended. 2 *computers destined for Pakistan:* heading, bound, en route, scheduled, headed.

destiny noun 1 *master of his own destiny:* future, fate, fortune, doom, lot. 2 *she was sent by destiny:* fate, providence, God, the stars, luck, fortune, chance, karma.

destroy verb 1 *their offices were destroyed by bombing:* demolish, knock down, level, raze to the ground, fell, blow up. 2 *traffic would destroy the conservation area:* spoil, ruin, wreck, blight, devastate, wreak havoc on. 3 *the horse had to be destroyed:* kill, put down, put to sleep, slaughter, cull. 4 *we had to destroy the enemy:* annihilate, wipe out, obliterate, eliminate, eradicate, liquidate, exterminate; informal take out; N. Amer. informal waste.
OPPOSITES build, preserve, spare.

destruction noun 1 *the destruction caused by allied bombers:* devastation, carnage, ruin, chaos, wreckage. 2 *the destruction of the countryside:* wrecking, ruining, annihilation, obliteration, elimination, eradication, devastation. 3 *the destruction of cattle:* killing, slaughter, putting down, extermination, culling.
OPPOSITES preservation.

destructive adjective devastating, ruinous, damaging, harmful, detrimental, injurious, hurtful, deleterious.

detach verb disconnect, separate, unfasten, disengage, uncouple, isolate, remove, loose, unhitch, unhook, free, pull off, cut off, break off, split off, sever.
OPPOSITES attach, join.

detached adjective 1 *a detached collar:* disconnected, separated, separate, unfastened, disengaged, uncoupled, isolated, loosened, unhitched, unhooked, free, severed, cut off. 2 *a detached observer:* dispassionate, disinterested, objective, outside, neutral, unbiased, impartial.

detachment noun 1 *she looked on with detachment:* objectivity, dispassion, disinterest, neutrality, impartiality. 2 *a detachment of soldiers:* unit, squad, detail, troop, contingent, task force, party, platoon.

uninvolved or aloof. **2** a group of troops, ships, etc. sent away on a mission.

detail noun **1** a small individual item or fact. **2** small items or facts as a group: *attention to detail.* **3** a small part of a picture reproduced separately. **4** a small group of troops or police officers given a special duty. • **verb 1** describe something item by item. **2** instruct someone to undertake a particular task.

detailed adjective having many details.

detain verb **1** keep someone back. **2** keep someone in custody.

detainee noun a person who is kept in custody.

detect verb **1** discover or notice that something is present. **2** discover or investigate a crime or criminal.
■ **detectable** adjective **detection** noun.

detective noun a person whose job is investigating crimes.

detector noun a device designed to detect that something, e.g. smoke or gas, is present.

détente /day-**tahnt**/ noun the easing of

hostility or strained relations between countries.

detention noun **1** the state of being kept in custody. **2** the punishment of being kept in school after hours.

deter verb (**deters, deterring, deterred**) **1** make someone decide not to do something because they are afraid of the consequences. **2** prevent something happening.

detergent noun a chemical substance used for removing dirt and grease.

deteriorate verb (**deteriorates, deteriorating, deteriorated**) become gradually worse.
■ **deterioration** noun.

determination noun **1** persistence in continuing to do something even when it is difficult. **2** the process of establishing something exactly.

determine verb **1** make something develop in a particular way or be of a particular type. **2** discover the facts about something by research or calculation. **3** firmly decide.

determined adjective persisting in doing

d

THESAURUS

detail noun **1** *the picture is correct in every detail:* particular, respect, feature, characteristic, specific, aspect, fact, point, element. **2** *that's just a detail:* triviality, technicality, nicety, fine point. **3** *a guard detail:* unit, detachment, squad, troop, contingent, outfit, task force, party, platoon.
• **verb** *the report details our objections:* describe, relate, catalogue, list, spell out, itemize, identify, specify.

detailed adjective comprehensive, full, complete, thorough, exhaustive, all-inclusive, elaborate, minute, precise, itemized, blow-by-blow.
OPPOSITES general.

detain verb **1** *they were detained for questioning:* hold, take into custody, confine, imprison, intern, seize, arrest, apprehend; informal pick up; Brit. informal nick. **2** *don't let me detain you:* delay, hold up, make late, keep, slow up/down, hinder.
OPPOSITES release.

detect verb **1** *I detected a note of urgency in her voice:* notice, perceive, discern, become aware of, note, make out, spot, recognize, identify, catch, sense. **2** *they are responsible for detecting fraud:* discover, uncover, turn up, unearth, dig up, root out, expose. **3** *the hackers were detected:* catch, hunt down, track down, find out, expose, reveal, unmask, smoke out.

detective noun investigator, police officer; informal private eye, sleuth; N. Amer. informal gumshoe.

detention noun custody, imprisonment, incarceration, internment, captivity, remand, arrest, quarantine.
OPPOSITES release.

deter verb **1** *the high cost deterred many:* discourage, dissuade, put off, scare off, dishearten, demoralize, daunt, intimidate. **2** *the presence of a caretaker deters crime:* prevent, stop, avert, stave off, ward off.
OPPOSITES encourage.

deteriorate verb worsen, decline, degenerate, fail, go downhill, wane.
OPPOSITES improve.

determination noun resolution, resolve, will power, strength of character, single-mindedness, dedication, perseverance, persistence, tenacity, staying power, doggedness; informal guts.

determine verb **1** *chromosomes determine the sex of the embryo:* control, decide, regulate, direct, dictate, govern. **2** *he determined to sell up:* resolve, decide, make up your mind, choose, elect, opt. **3** *the rent shall be determined by an accountant:* specify, set, fix, decide on, settle, establish, ordain, prescribe, decree. **4** *determine the composition of the fibres:* ascertain, find out, discover, learn, establish, calculate, work out; informal figure out.

determined adjective resolute, purposeful, adamant, single-minded, unswerving, unwavering, persevering, persistent, tenacious, dedicated, dogged.
OPPOSITES irresolute.

something even when it is difficult; resolute.

■ determinedly adverb.

determiner noun 1 a person or thing that determines. 2 Grammar a word that comes before a noun to show how the noun is being used, e.g. *a*, *the*, *every*.

deterrent noun a thing that deters or is intended to deter.

■ deterrence noun.

detest verb feel strong dislike for.

■ detestable adjective detestation noun.

dethrone verb (**dethrones, dethroning, dethroned**) remove a ruler from power.

detonate verb (**detonates, detonating, detonated**) explode, or make something explode.

■ detonation noun.

detonator noun a device used to detonate an explosive.

detour noun a long or roundabout route taken to avoid something or to visit something along the way.

detoxify verb (**detoxifies, detoxifying, detoxified**) remove poisonous substances from.

detract verb (**detract from**) make something seem less valuable or impressive.

detractor noun a person who is critical about someone or something.

detriment noun harm or damage.

■ detrimental adjective detrimentally adverb.

detritus /di-**try**-tuhss/ noun debris or waste material.

deuce /dyooss/ noun 1 Tennis the score of 40 all in a game, at which two consecutive points are needed to win the game. 2 (**the deuce**) informal said instead of 'devil' when making an exclamation.

Deutschmark /**doych**-mark/ noun the former basic unit of money in Germany.

devalue verb (**devalues, devaluing, devalued**) 1 make something seem less important than it is. 2 reduce the value of a currency in relation to other currencies.

■ devaluation noun.

devastate verb (**devastates, devastating, devastated**) 1 destroy or ruin. 2 (**be devastated**) be overwhelmed with shock or grief.

■ devastation noun.

devastating adjective 1 highly destructive. 2 very distressing. 3 informal very impressive or attractive.

■ devastatingly adverb.

develop verb (**develops, developing, developed**) 1 make or become larger or more advanced. 2 start to exist; come into being. 3 start to experience or possess something. 4 convert land to a new purpose. 5 treat a photographic film with chemicals to make a visible image.

■ developer noun.

> ☑ there is no *e* at the end: deve*lop*.

development noun 1 the action of developing. 2 a new product or idea. 3 a new stage in a changing situation. 4 an area of land with new buildings on it.

■ developmental adjective.

deviant adjective different from what is considered normal. • noun disapproving a deviant person.

■ deviance noun.

deviate verb (**deviates, deviating, deviated**) depart from an established course or from normal standards.

■ deviation noun.

device noun 1 a piece of equipment made

THESAURUS

deterrent noun disincentive, discouragement, damper, curb, check, restraint, inhibition.
OPPOSITES incentive.

detest verb hate, abhor, loathe, regard with disgust, be unable to bear, have an aversion to, find intolerable, disdain, despise.
OPPOSITES love.

devastate verb 1 *the city was devastated by an earthquake:* destroy, ruin, wreck, lay waste, ravage, demolish, raze to the ground, level, flatten. 2 *he was devastated by the news:* shatter, shock, stun, daze, dumbfound, traumatize, distress; informal knock sideways; Brit. informal knock for six.

devastation noun destruction, ruin, desolation, wreckage, ruins.

develop verb 1 *the industry developed rapidly:* grow, expand, spread, advance, progress, evolve, mature. 2 *a plan was*

developed: initiate, instigate, set in motion, originate, invent, form. 3 *children should develop their talents:* expand, augment, broaden, supplement, reinforce, enhance, refine, improve, polish, perfect. 4 *a row developed:* start, begin, emerge, erupt, break out, arise, break, unfold.
OPPOSITES shrink, regress.

development noun 1 *the development of the firm:* evolution, growth, expansion, enlargement, spread, progress. 2 *there have been a number of developments:* event, change, circumstance, incident, occurrence. 3 *a housing development:* estate, complex, site.

deviate verb diverge, digress, drift, stray, veer, swerve, get sidetracked, branch off, differ, vary.

device noun 1 *a device for measuring pressure:* implement, gadget, utensil, tool, appliance, apparatus, instrument, machine, for a particular purpose. **2** a plan or method with a particular aim. **3** an emblem or design.

☐ **leave someone to their own devices** leave someone to do as they wish.

devil noun **1** (**the Devil**) (in Christian and Jewish belief) the most powerful spirit of evil. **2** an evil spirit. **3** a very wicked or cruel person. **4** informal a person of a particular sort: *the poor devil.*

☐ **devil-may-care** cheerful and reckless. **devil's advocate** a person who expresses an opinion that they do not really hold in order to provoke discussion.

devilish adjective **1** like a devil in evil and cruelty. **2** mischievous. **3** very difficult to deal with.

■ **devilishly** adverb.

devilment noun mischievous behaviour.

devilry noun **1** wicked activity. **2** mischievous behaviour.

devious adjective **1** behaving in a cunning way to get what you want. **2** (of a route or journey) indirect.

■ **deviously** adverb **deviousness** noun.

devise verb (**devises**, **devising**, **devised**) plan or invent a complex procedure or device.

devoid adjective (**devoid of**) entirely without.

devolution noun the transfer of power by central government to local or regional governments.

devolve verb (**devolves**, **devolving**, **devolved**) **1** transfer power to a lower level. **2** (**devolve on** or **to**) (of duties or responsibility) pass to.

devote verb (**devotes**, **devoting**, **devoted**) (**devote something to**) give time or resources to.

devoted adjective very loving or loyal.

■ **devotedly** adverb.

devotee /dev-oh-**tee**/ noun **1** a person who is very enthusiastic about someone or something. **2** a follower of a particular religion or god.

devotion noun **1** great love or loyalty. **2** religious worship. **3** (**devotions**) prayers or other religious practices.

■ **devotional** adjective.

devour verb **1** eat something greedily. **2** (of a force) destroy something completely. **3** read something quickly and eagerly.

devout adjective **1** deeply religious. **2** earnestly sincere: *a devout hope.*

■ **devoutly** adverb.

dew noun tiny drops of moisture that form on cool surfaces at night, when water vapour in the air condenses.

■ **dewy** adjective.

dewlap noun a fold of loose skin hanging from the neck or throat of an animal or bird.

dexterity noun skill in performing tasks.

dexterous or **dextrous** adjective showing skill, especially with the hands.

■ **dexterously** adverb.

dextrose noun a form of glucose.

dhoti /**doh**-ti/ noun (plural **dhotis**) a long piece of cloth tied around the waist, worn by some Hindu men.

diabetes /dy-uh-**bee**-teez/ noun an illness in

d

THESAURUS

mechanism, contrivance, contraption; informal gizmo. **2** *an ingenious legal device:* ploy, tactic, move, stratagem, scheme, plot, trick, ruse, manoeuvre.

devil noun **1** *God and the Devil:* Satan, Beelzebub, Lucifer, the Prince of Darkness; informal Old Nick. **2** *they drove out the devils:* evil spirit, demon, fiend. **3** *he was a devil:* brute, beast, monster, fiend, villain, sadist, barbarian, ogre.

devious adjective **1** *the devious ways in which they bent the rules:* underhand, dishonest, crafty, cunning, conniving, scheming, sneaky, furtive; informal crooked, shady; Brit. informal dodgy. **2** *a devious route:* circuitous, roundabout, indirect, meandering, tortuous.
OPPOSITES open, honest, direct.

devise verb conceive, think up, dream up, work out, formulate, concoct, hatch, contrive, design, invent, coin; informal cook up.

devoid adjective *her voice was devoid of emotion:* empty of, free of, bereft of,

lacking, deficient in, without, wanting in; informal minus.

devote verb dedicate, allocate, assign, allot, commit, give (over), consign, pledge, set aside, earmark, reserve.

devoted adjective dedicated, committed, devout, loyal, faithful, true, staunch, steadfast, fond, loving.

devotee noun enthusiast, fan, lover, aficionado, admirer, supporter, disciple; informal buff, freak, nut, fanatic.

devotion noun **1** *wifely devotion:* loyalty, fidelity, commitment, allegiance, dedication, fondness, love, care. **2** *a life of devotion:* piety, spirituality, godliness, holiness, sanctity.

devour verb **1** *he devoured his meal:* gobble, guzzle, gulp down, bolt, wolf; informal polish off; Brit. informal scoff. **2** *flames devoured the house:* consume, engulf, envelop.

devout adjective dedicated, devoted, committed, loyal, sincere, fervent, pious, reverent, God-fearing, dutiful, churchgoing.

d

which the body cannot absorb sugar and starch properly because it does not have enough of the hormone insulin.

diabetic adjective having to do with diabetes. •noun a person with diabetes.

diabolical adjective **1** (also **diabolic**) relating to or like the Devil. **2** informal very bad.
■ **diabolically** adverb.

diadem noun a crown.

diagnose verb (**diagnoses, diagnosing, diagnosed**) identify which illness or problem a person is suffering from by examining the symptoms.
■ **diagnostic** adjective.

diagnosis noun (plural **diagnoses**) the identification of which illness or problem a person is suffering from by examining the symptoms.

diagonal adjective **1** (of a straight line) joining opposite corners of a rectangle, square, or other figure. **2** straight and at an angle; slanting. •noun a diagonal line.
■ **diagonally** adverb.

diagram noun a simplified drawing showing the appearance or structure of something.
■ **diagrammatic** adjective.

dial noun **1** a disc marked to show the time or to indicate a measurement. **2** a disc with numbered holes on a telephone, turned to make a call. **3** a disc turned to choose a setting on a radio, cooker, etc. •verb (**dials, dialling, dialled**; US spelling **dials, dialing, dialed**) call a telephone number by turning a dial or pressing numbered keys.

dialect noun a form of a language used in a particular region or by a particular social group.
■ **dialectal** adjective.

dialectic or **dialectics** noun a way of discovering whether ideas are true by discussion and logical argument.
■ **dialectical** adjective.

dialogue (US spelling **dialog**) noun **1** conversation between two or more people in a book, play, or film. **2** a discussion intended to explore a subject or solve a problem.

dialysis /dy-al-i-siss/ noun the use of a machine to purify the blood of a person whose kidneys do not work properly.

diamanté /dy-uh-**mon**-tay/ adjective decorated with glass that is cut to look like diamonds.

diameter noun a straight line passing from side to side through the centre of a circle or sphere.

diametrical adjective **1** complete: *the diametrical opposite*. **2** having to do with a diameter.
■ **diametrically** adverb.

diamond noun **1** a clear precious stone, the hardest naturally occurring substance. **2** a figure with four straight sides of equal length forming two opposite acute angles and two opposite obtuse angles.
◻ **diamond jubilee** the sixtieth anniversary of a notable event. **diamond wedding** Brit. the sixtieth anniversary of a wedding.

diaper /**dy**-uh-per/ noun N. Amer. a baby's nappy.

diaphanous /dy-**af**-uh-nuhss/ adjective light, delicate, and semi-transparent.

diaphragm /**dy**-uh-fram/ noun **1** a layer of muscle between the lungs and the stomach. **2** a piece of flexible material in mechanical or sound systems. **3** a thin rubber or plastic contraceptive device worn over the cervix.

diarist noun a person who writes a diary.

diarrhoea /dy-uh-**ree**-uh/ (US spelling **diarrhea**) noun a condition in which a person has frequent liquid bowel movements.

☑ two *rs*, and *-hoea* at the end: dia*rrhoea*.

diary noun (plural **diaries**) a book in which you keep a daily record of events and experiences, or note down future appointments.

diastole /dy-**ass**-tuh-li/ noun the stage of the heartbeat when the heart muscle

---

THESAURUS

diagnose verb identify, determine, distinguish, recognize, interpret, detect, pinpoint.

diagnosis noun **1** *the diagnosis of coeliac disease:* **identification**, detection, recognition, determination, discovery, pinpointing. **2** *the results confirmed his diagnosis:* **opinion**, judgement, verdict, conclusion.

diagonal adjective **crosswise**, crossways, slanting, slanted, oblique, angled, cornerways, cornerwise.

diagram noun **drawing**, representation, plan, outline, figure, chart, graph.

dialogue noun **conversation**, talk, discussion, chat, tête-à-tête, exchange, debate, conference, consultation; informal confab.

diary noun **1** *he put the date in his diary:* **appointment book**, engagement book, personal organizer; trademark Filofax. **2** *her World War II diaries:* **journal**, memoir, chronicle, log, logbook, history, annal, record, weblog, blog; N. Amer. daybook.

relaxes and the chambers fill with blood.
■ **diastolic** /dy-uh-**stol**-ik/ adjective.

diatonic /dy-uh-**ton**-ik/ adjective Music involving only the notes of the appropriate major or minor scale.

diatribe /**dy**-uh-tryb/ noun a speech or piece of writing forcefully attacking someone.

dice noun (plural **dice**) a small cube whose sides are marked with one to six spots, used in games of chance. • verb (**dices, dicing, diced**) **1** cut food into small cubes. **2** (**dice with**) take great risks with: *dicing with death.*

dicey adjective (**dicier, diciest**) informal difficult or risky.

dichotomy /dy-**kot**-uh-mi/ noun (plural **dichotomies**) a separation or contrast between two things.

dicky adjective Brit. informal not strong, healthy, or working properly.

dictate verb /dik-**tayt**/ (**dictates, dictating, dictated**) **1** give orders with great authority. **2** control or influence. **3** speak words for someone else to type or write down. • noun /**dik**-tayt/ an order or principle that must be obeyed.
■ **dictation** noun.

dictator noun a ruler who has total power over a country.
■ **dictatorial** adjective.

dictatorship noun **1** government by a dictator. **2** a country governed by a dictator.

diction noun **1** the choice and use of words in speech or writing. **2** a person's way of pronouncing words.

dictionary noun (plural **dictionaries**) a book that lists the words of a language and gives their meaning, or their equivalent in a different language.

dictum noun (plural **dicta** or **dictums**) **1** a

formal announcement made by someone in authority. **2** a short statement that expresses a general principle.

did past of DO.

didactic adjective intended to teach or give moral instruction.
■ **didactically** adverb.

diddle verb (**diddles, diddling, diddled**) informal cheat or swindle.

didgeridoo noun an Australian Aboriginal musical instrument in the form of a long wooden tube, which produces a deep sound when blown.

didn't short form did not.

die[1] verb (**dies, dying, died**) **1** stop living. **2** (**die out**) become extinct. **3** become less loud or strong. **4** (**be dying for** or **to do**) informal be very eager to have or do.

die[2] noun **1** a dice. **2** (plural **dies**) a device for cutting or moulding metal or for stamping a design on to coins or medals.
□ **die-cast** formed by pouring molten metal into a mould.

diehard noun a person who stubbornly continues to support something in spite of opposition or changing circumstances.

diesel /**dee**-zuhl/ noun **1** a type of engine in which heat produced by compressing air is used to ignite the fuel. **2** a form of petroleum used as fuel in diesel engines.

diet noun **1** the kinds of food that a person or animal usually eats. **2** a limited range or amount of food, eaten in order to lose weight or for medical reasons. • verb (**diets, dieting, dieted**) keep to a special diet in order to lose weight.

dietary /**dy**-uh-tri/ adjective **1** having to do with diets or dieting. **2** provided by the food you eat.

dietitian or **dietician** noun an expert on diet and nutrition.

THESAURUS

dictate verb **1** *his attempts to dictate policy:* prescribe, lay down, impose, set down, order, command, decree, ordain, direct. **2** *choice is often dictated by availability:* determine, control, govern, decide, influence, affect.
□ **dictate to give orders to,** order about/around, lord it over; informal boss about/around, push about/around.

dictator noun autocrat, despot, tyrant, absolute ruler.
OPPOSITES democrat.

dictatorial adjective domineering, autocratic, authoritarian, oppressive, imperious, overweening, overbearing, peremptory; informal bossy, high-handed.

dictionary noun lexicon, glossary, vocabulary.

die verb **1** *her father died last year:* pass

away, pass on, perish; informal give up the ghost, kick the bucket, croak; Brit. informal snuff it, peg out; N. Amer. informal buy the farm. **2** *the wind had died:* lessen, subside, drop, ease (off), let up, moderate, abate, fade, peter out, wane, ebb. **3** (informal) *the engine died:* fail, cut out, give out, break down, stop; informal conk out, go kaput; Brit. informal pack up.
OPPOSITES live, intensify.

diet noun **1** *a healthy diet:* food, nutrition, eating habits. **2** *she's on a diet:* dietary regime, regimen, restricted diet, fast, abstinence.
OPPOSITES binge.
• verb *I began dieting again:* be on a diet, slim, lose weight, watch your weight; N. Amer. reduce; N. Amer. informal slenderize.
OPPOSITES binge.

differ verb (**differs, differing, differed**) **1** be different. **2** disagree.

difference noun **1** a way in which people or things are unlike each other. **2** a disagreement or dispute. **3** what is left when one number or amount is subtracted from another.

different adjective **1** not the same as another or each other. **2** separate. **3** informal new and unusual.
■ **differently** adverb.

> ❗ say **different from**, not **different to** in British English; **different than** is American.

differential /dif-fuh-ren-sh'l/ adjective involving a difference. •noun **1** Brit. a difference in wages between industries or between categories of worker. **2** Maths a minute difference between successive values of a variable. **3** a gear that allows a vehicle's wheels to revolve at different speeds when going around corners.

differentiate /dif-fuh-ren-shi-ayt/ verb (**differentiates, differentiating, differentiated**) **1** recognize things as being different from each other; distinguish. **2** make things appear different from each other.

■ **differentiation** noun.

difficult adjective **1** needing a lot of effort or skill to do or understand; hard. **2** causing or involving problems. **3** not easy to please or satisfy; awkward.

difficulty noun (plural **difficulties**) **1** the state of being difficult. **2** a difficult or dangerous situation; a problem.

diffident adjective not having much self-confidence.
■ **diffidence** noun **diffidently** adverb.

diffract verb cause a beam of light to be spread out as a result of passing through a narrow opening or across an edge.
■ **diffraction** noun.

diffuse verb /dif-fyooz/ (**diffuses, diffusing, diffused**) **1** spread over a wide area. **2** (of a gas or liquid) become mingled with a substance. •adjective /dif-**fyooss**/ **1** spread out over a large area; not concentrated. **2** not clearly or concisely expressed.
■ **diffusely** adverb **diffusion** noun.

> ❗ don't confuse **diffuse** with **defuse**, which means 'make a situation less tense or difficult' or 'remove the fuse from'.

dig verb (**digs, digging, dug**) **1** cut into earth

THESAURUS

differ verb **1** *the second set of data differed from the first*: **contrast with**, be different to, vary from, deviate from, conflict with, run counter to, be at odds with, contradict. **2** *the two sides differed over this issue*: **disagree**, conflict, be at variance/odds, be in dispute, not see eye to eye.
OPPOSITES resemble, agree.

difference noun **1** *the difference between the two sets of data*: **dissimilarity**, contrast, distinction, differentiation, variance, variation, divergence, disparity, contradiction. **2** *we've had our differences*: **disagreement**, difference of opinion, dispute, argument, quarrel; Brit. row. **3** *I'll pay the difference*: **balance**, remainder, rest.
OPPOSITES similarity.

different adjective **1** *people with different lifestyles*: **dissimilar**, unlike, contrasting, differing, varying, disparate, poles apart, incompatible, mismatched; informal like chalk and cheese. **2** *suddenly everything in her life was different*: **changed**, altered, transformed, new, unfamiliar, unknown, strange. **3** *two different occasions*: **distinct**, separate, individual, independent. **4** (informal) *try something different*: **unusual**, out of the ordinary, unfamiliar, novel, new, fresh, original, unconventional, exotic.
OPPOSITES similar, normal, related, ordinary.

difficult adjective **1** *a very difficult job*: **laborious**, strenuous, arduous, hard, tough, demanding, punishing, gruelling, back-breaking, exhausting, tiring; informal hellish, killing, no picnic. **2** *a difficult problem*: **hard**, complicated, puzzling, baffling, problematic, thorny, ticklish. **3** *a difficult child*: **troublesome**, tiresome, trying, exasperating, awkward, demanding, contrary, uncooperative, fussy.
OPPOSITES easy, simple, cooperative, accommodating.

difficulty noun **1** *the difficulty of balancing motherhood with a career*: **strain**, trouble, problems, struggle, stress, laboriousness, arduousness; informal hassle. **2** *practical difficulties*: **problem**, complication, snag, hitch, obstacle, hurdle, stumbling block; Brit. spanner in the works; informal headache. **3** *Charles got into difficulties*: **trouble**, predicament, plight, hard times.
OPPOSITES ease.

dig verb **1** *she began to dig the soil*: **turn over**, work, break up. **2** *he dug a hole*: **excavate**, dig out, quarry, hollow out, scoop out, bore, burrow, mine. **3** *Winnie dug her elbow into his ribs*: **poke**, prod, jab, stab, shove, ram, push, thrust, drive, stick. **4** *he'd been digging into my past*: **delve**, probe, search, enquire, look, investigate, research.
•noun **1** *a dig in the ribs*: **poke**, prod, jab, stab, shove, push. **2** (informal) *they're always making digs at each other*: **snide remark**, cutting remark, jibe, taunt, sneer, insult;

in order to turn it over or move it. **2** remove or produce something by digging. **3** push or poke sharply. **4** (**dig into** or **through**) search or rummage in. **5** (**dig something out** or **up**) discover facts. **6** (**dig in**) start eating heartily. **7** informal, dated like. ▪ **noun 1** an act of digging. **2** an investigation of a site by archaeologists. **3** a sharp push or poke. **4** informal a critical remark. **5** (**digs**) informal temporary accommodation.
■ **digger** noun.

digest verb /dy-**jest**/ **1** break down food in the stomach and intestines so that it can be absorbed by the body. **2** reflect on and absorb information. ▪ noun /**dy**-jest/ a summary or collection of material or information.
■ **digestible** adjective.

digestion noun **1** the process of digesting food. **2** a person's ability to digest food.

digestive adjective relating to the digestion of food. ▪ noun Brit. a semi-sweet biscuit made with wholemeal flour.

digit noun **1** any of the numerals from 0 to 9. **2** a finger or thumb.

digital adjective **1** having to do with information represented as a series of binary digits, as in a computer. **2** having to do with computer technology. **3** (of a clock or watch) showing the time by displaying numbers electronically, rather than having a clock face. **4** having to do with a finger or fingers.
■ **digitally** adverb.

digitize or **digitise** verb (**digitizes, digitizing, digitized**) convert pictures or sound into a digital form.

dignified adjective having or showing dignity.

dignify verb (**dignifies, dignifying, dignified**) make something impressive or worthy of respect.

dignitary /**dig**-ni-tuh-ri/ noun (plural **dignitaries**) a very important or high-ranking person.

dignity noun (plural **dignities**) **1** the quality of being worthy of respect. **2** a calm or serious manner. **3** pride in yourself.

digress verb temporarily leave the main subject in speech or writing.
■ **digression** noun.

dike ⇒ DYKE.

diktat /**dik**-tat/ noun an order given by someone in power.

dilapidated adjective old and in bad condition.
■ **dilapidation** noun.

☑ *dil-*, not *del-*: *dil*apidated.

dilate verb (**dilates, dilating, dilated**) become wider, larger, or more open.
■ **dilation** noun.

dilatory /**di**-luh-tri/ adjective **1** slow to act. **2** intended to cause delay.

dilemma /di-**lem**-muh, dy-**lem**-muh/ noun a difficult situation in which you have to make a choice between alternatives.

dilettante /di-li-**tan**-ti/ noun (plural **dilettanti** or **dilettantes**) a person who does or studies something for enjoyment but does not take it very seriously.

diligent adjective showing care and effort in a task or duty.
■ **diligence** noun **diligently** adverb.

dill noun a herb used in cookery and medicine.

dilly-dally verb (**dilly-dallies, dilly-dallying, dilly-dallied**) informal be slow or indecisive.

dilute verb (**dilutes, diluting, diluted**) **1** make a liquid thinner or weaker by adding water or other liquid. **2** weaken something by modifying it or adding other

---

THESAURUS

informal **wisecrack, put-down.**
□ **dig something up exhume,** disinter, unearth.

digest verb *Liz digested this information:* **assimilate, absorb, take in, understand, comprehend, grasp.**
▪ noun *a digest of their findings:* **summary, synopsis, abstract, precis, résumé, summation.**

dignified adjective **stately, noble, majestic, distinguished, regal, imposing, impressive, grand, solemn, formal, ceremonious, decorous, sedate.**

dignity noun **1** *the dignity of the Crown:* **stateliness, nobility, majesty, grandeur, impressiveness, magnificence, ceremoniousness, formality, decorum,** propriety, respectability, worthiness, integrity, solemnity, gravitas. **2** *little regard for human dignity:* **self-respect,** pride, self-esteem, self-worth.
OPPOSITES informality.

dilemma noun **quandary,** predicament, catch-22, vicious circle, plight, conflict; informal **fix, tight spot/corner;** (**in a dilemma**) between the devil and the deep blue sea, between a rock and a hard place.

dilute verb **1** *strong bleach can be diluted with water:* **make weaker, water down, thin, doctor, adulterate;** informal **cut. 2** *the original plans have been diluted:* **weaken, moderate, tone down, water down, compromise.**
OPPOSITES **concentrate, beef up.**

elements. •adjective (of a liquid) diluted; weak.
■ dilution noun.

dim adjective (dimmer, dimmest) 1 not bright or well lit. 2 not clearly seen or remembered. 3 not able to see clearly. 4 informal stupid. •verb (dims, dimming, dimmed) make or become dim.
□ take a dim view of disapprove of.
■ dimly adverb dimness noun.

dime noun N. Amer. a ten-cent coin.

dimension noun 1 a measure of how long, broad, high, etc. something is. 2 an aspect or feature.
■ dimensional adjective.

diminish verb make or become smaller, weaker, or less.

diminution noun a reduction.

diminutive adjective very or unusually small. •noun a shortened form of a person's name.

dimmer noun a device for varying the brightness of an electric light.

dimple noun a small hollow formed in the cheeks when you smile.
■ dimpled adjective.

dimwit noun informal a stupid person.
■ dim-witted adjective.

din noun a prolonged loud and unpleasant noise. •verb (dins, dinning, dinned) (din something into) teach something to someone by constantly repeating it.

dine verb (dines, dining, dined) eat dinner.

diner noun 1 a person who dines. 2 a carriage providing meals on a train. 3 N. Amer. a small, cheap restaurant.

dinghy /ding-gi, ding-i/ noun (plural dinghies) 1 a small open boat with a mast and sails. 2 a small inflatable rubber boat.

dingo /ding-goh/ noun (plural dingoes or dingos) a wild or semi-domesticated Australian dog.

dingy /din-ji/ adjective (dingier, dingiest) gloomy and drab.
■ dinginess noun.

dinky adjective (dinkier, dinkiest) Brit. informal attractively small and neat.

dinner noun 1 the main meal of the day, eaten either around midday or in the evening. 2 a formal evening meal.
■ dinner jacket a black or white jacket worn by men for formal evening occasions.

dinosaur noun an extinct reptile that lived millions of years ago, some kinds of which were very large.

dint noun a dent.
□ by dint of by means of.

diocese /dy-uh-siss/ noun (plural dioceses /dy-uh-seez, dy-uh-seez-iz/) a district under the control of a bishop in the Christian Church.

diode noun an electrical device that has two terminals and allows current to flow in one direction only.

dioxide noun an oxide with two atoms of oxygen to one of a metal or other element.

dip verb (dips, dipping, dipped) 1 (dip

THESAURUS

dim adjective 1 the dim light: faint, weak, feeble, soft, pale, dull, subdued, muted. 2 long dim corridors: dark, badly lit, dingy, dismal, gloomy, murky. 3 a dim figure: indistinct, ill-defined, vague, shadowy, nebulous, blurred, fuzzy. 4 dim memories: vague, imprecise, imperfect, unclear, indistinct, sketchy, hazy. 5 (informal) I'm awfully dim. See STUPID.
OPPOSITES bright, distinct, clear.
•verb 1 the lights were dimmed: turn down, lower, soften, subdue. 2 memories have dimmed: fade, dwindle, dull.
OPPOSITES brighten.

dimension noun 1 the dimensions of the room: size, measurements, proportions, extent, length, width, breadth, depth. 2 the cultural dimensions of the problem: aspect, feature, element, angle, facet, side.

diminish verb 1 the pain will gradually diminish: decrease, lessen, decline, reduce, subside, dwindle, fade, slacken off, let up. 2 new legislation diminished the courts' authority: reduce, decrease, lessen, curtail, cut, limit, curb.
OPPOSITES increase.

din noun noise, racket, rumpus, cacophony, hubbub, uproar, commotion, clangour, clatter, clamour; informal hullabaloo; Brit. informal row.
OPPOSITES silence.

dine verb eat, have dinner, have lunch; dated sup.

dinner noun main meal, lunch, evening meal, supper, feast, banquet; Brit. tea.

dip verb 1 he dipped a rag in the water: immerse, submerge, plunge, dunk, bathe, sink. 2 the sun dipped below the horizon: sink, set, drop, fall, descend. 3 the president's popularity has dipped: decrease, fall, drop, fall off, decline, diminish, dwindle, slump, plummet, plunge. 4 the road dipped: slope down, descend, go down, drop (away), fall away.
OPPOSITES rise, increase.
•noun 1 a dip in the pool: swim, bathe, paddle. 2 the hedge at the bottom of the dip: slope, incline, decline, descent, hollow, depression, basin. 3 a sharp dip in sales: decrease, fall, drop, downturn, decline, falling-off, slump, reduction.
□ dip into 1 draw on, use, spend. 2 browse through, skim through, look through, flick through.

something in or into) put or lower something briefly in or into. **2** sink, drop, or slope downwards. **3** (of a level or amount) temporarily become lower or smaller. **4** lower something briefly. **5** (**dip into**) reach into a container to take something out. •**noun 1** an act of dipping. **2** a thick sauce in which you dip pieces of food before eating them. **3** a brief swim. **4** a brief downward slope followed by an upward one.

diphtheria /dip-**theer**-i-uh/ **noun** a serious illness that causes inflammation of the mucous membranes, especially in the throat.

diphthong /**dif**-thong, **dip**-thong/ **noun** a sound formed by the combination of two vowels in a single syllable (as in *coin*).

diploma **noun** a certificate awarded to someone who has successfully completed a course of study.

diplomacy **noun 1** the management of relations between countries. **2** skill and tact in dealing with people.

diplomat **noun** an official who represents a country abroad.

diplomatic **adjective 1** having to do with diplomacy. **2** tactful.
■ **diplomatically** adverb.

dipper **noun 1** a bird that dives into fast-flowing streams to feed. **2** a ladle.

dipsomania /dip-suh-**may**-ni-uh/ **noun** alcoholism.

■ **dipsomaniac** noun.

dipstick **noun** a rod for measuring the depth of a liquid.

dire **adjective 1** very serious or urgent. **2** informal of very bad quality.

direct **adjective 1** going from one place to another without changing direction or stopping. **2** with nothing or no one in between. **3** saying exactly what you mean; frank. **4** clear and explicit. •**adverb** in a direct way or by a direct route. •**verb 1** aim something towards. **2** tell or show someone the way. **3** control the operations of. **4** supervise the production of a film, play, etc. **5** give an order to.
□ **direct current** an electric current that flows in one direction only. **direct debit** Brit. an arrangement by which a bank transfers money from your account to pay a particular person or organization. **direct speech** the actual words of a speaker quoted in writing.

direction **noun 1** a course along which someone or something moves, or which leads to a destination. **2** a point to or from which someone or something moves or faces. **3** the directing or managing of people. **4** (**directions**) instructions on how to reach a destination or how to do something.
■ **directional** adjective.

directive **noun** an official instruction.

directly **adverb 1** in a direct way. **2** exactly

diplomacy noun **1** *diplomacy failed to win them independence:* statesmanship, statecraft, negotiation(s), discussion(s), talks. **2** *Jack's quiet diplomacy:* tact, tactfulness, sensitivity, discretion.

diplomat noun ambassador, attaché, consul, chargé d'affaires, envoy, emissary.

diplomatic adjective tactful, sensitive, subtle, delicate, polite, discreet, judicious, politic.
OPPOSITES tactless.

dire adjective terrible, dreadful, appalling, frightful, awful, grim, sore, alarming, acute, grave, serious, urgent, pressing, wretched, desperate, parlous.

direct adjective **1** *the most direct route:* straight, short, quick. **2** *a direct flight:* non-stop, through, unbroken, uninterrupted. **3** *he is very direct:* frank, candid, straightforward, open, blunt, plain-spoken, outspoken, forthright, no-nonsense, matter-of-fact; informal upfront. •verb **1** *an economic elite directed the nation's affairs:* manage, govern, run, administer, control, conduct, handle, be in charge of, preside over, lead, head, rule. **2** *was that remark directed at me?* aim, target, address to, intend for, mean for,

design for. **3** *a man in uniform directed them to the hall:* give directions, show the way, point someone in the direction of. **4** *the judge directed the jury to return a not guilty verdict:* instruct, tell, command, order, require.

direction noun **1** *a northerly direction:* way, route, course, line, bearing, orientation. **2** *his direction of the project:* running, management, administration, conduct, handling, supervision, superintendence, command, rule, leadership. **3** *explicit directions about nursing care:* instruction, order, command, rule, regulation, requirement.

directive noun instruction, direction, command, order, injunction, decree, dictum, edict.

directly adverb **1** *they flew directly to New York:* straight, as the crow flies. **2** *directly after breakfast:* immediately, right (away), straight (away), without delay, promptly. **3** *the houses directly opposite:* exactly, right, immediately, diametrically; informal bang. **4** *she spoke simply and directly:* frankly, candidly, openly, bluntly, forthrightly, without beating around the bush.

in a particular position: *the house directly opposite.* **3** immediately. ● conjunction Brit. as soon as.

director noun **1** a person who is in charge of an organization or activity. **2** a member of the board which manages a business. **3** a person responsible for directing a film, play, etc.
□ **director general** (plural **directors general**) the chief executive of a large organization.
■ **directorial** adjective.

directory noun (plural **directories**) a book that lists individuals or organizations and gives their addresses, telephone numbers, etc.

dirge noun **1** a piece of music expressing sadness for someone's death. **2** a slow, boring song or piece of music.

dirigible /di-rij-i-b'l/ noun an airship.

dirk noun a kind of short dagger formerly carried by Scottish Highlanders.

dirt noun **1** a substance that makes something dirty. **2** soil or earth. **3** informal scandalous or damaging information about someone.

dirty adjective (**dirtier, dirtiest**) **1** covered or marked with mud, dust, grease, etc.; not clean. **2** obscene. **3** unfair or dishonest.
● verb (**dirties, dirtying, dirtied**) make something dirty.
□ **dirty look** informal a look expressing disapproval, disgust, or anger.

disability noun (plural **disabilities**) **1** a physical or mental condition that restricts your movements, senses, or activities. **2** a disadvantage or handicap.

disable verb (**disables, disabling, disabled**) **1** cause someone to be disabled. **2** put something out of action.
■ **disablement** noun.

disabled adjective having a disability.

disabuse verb (**disabuses, disabusing, disabused**) (**disabuse someone of**) persuade someone that an idea or belief is mistaken.

disadvantage noun something that causes a problem or reduces the chances of success. ● verb (**disadvantages, disadvantaging, disadvantaged**) **1** put someone in an unfavourable position. **2** (**disadvantaged**) having less money and fewer opportunities than most people.
■ **disadvantageous** adjective.

disaffected adjective unhappy with the people in authority or with the organization you belong to, and no longer willing to support them.
■ **disaffection** noun.

disagree verb (**disagrees, disagreeing, disagreed**) **1** have a different opinion. **2** be inconsistent. **3** (**disagree with**) make someone slightly unwell.
■ **disagreement** noun.

THESAURUS

director noun manager, head, chief, principal, leader, governor, president, chair, chief executive; informal boss, gaffer.

dirt noun **1** *his face was streaked with dirt:* grime, filth, muck, dust, mud; Brit. informal gunge. **2** *a dirt road:* earth, soil, clay, ground.

dirty adjective **1** *a dirty sweatshirt / dirty water:* soiled, grimy, grubby, filthy, mucky, stained, unwashed, greasy, muddy, dusty, polluted, contaminated, foul, unhygienic; Brit. informal manky, grotty. **2** *a dirty joke:* obscene, indecent, rude, naughty, vulgar, smutty, coarse, crude, filthy, off colour, pornographic, explicit, X-rated; informal blue; euphemistic adult. **3** *a dirty look:* malevolent, hostile, black, angry, disapproving.
OPPOSITES clean, friendly.
● verb *the dog had dirtied her dress:* soil, stain, muddy, blacken, mess (up), mark, spatter, smudge, smear, splatter, sully, pollute, foul.
OPPOSITES clean.

disability noun handicap, incapacity, impairment, infirmity, defect, abnormality, condition, disorder, affliction.

disable verb **1** *an injury that could disable somebody for life:* incapacitate, put out of action, debilitate, handicap, cripple, lame, maim, immobilize, paralyse. **2** *the bomb squad disabled the device:* deactivate, defuse, disarm, make safe.

disabled adjective handicapped, incapacitated, infirm, crippled, lame, paralysed, immobilized, bedridden; euphemistic physically challenged, differently abled.
OPPOSITES able-bodied.

disadvantage noun **1** *that's the disadvantage of this scheme:* drawback, snag, downside, fly in the ointment, catch, nuisance, handicap, trouble, informal minus. **2** *she did nothing to his disadvantage:* detriment, prejudice, harm, loss, hurt.
OPPOSITES advantage.

disagree verb **1** *no one disagreed with him:* be of a different opinion, not see eye to eye, take issue, challenge, contradict, differ, dissent, be in dispute, clash. **2** *their accounts disagree:* differ, be dissimilar, be different, be at variance/odds, vary, contradict each other, conflict. **3** *the spicy food disagreed with her:* make ill, make unwell, nauseate, upset.
OPPOSITES agree.

disagreement noun dissent, difference of opinion, controversy, discord, division,

disagreeable adjective **1** unpleasant. **2** bad-tempered.

disallow verb declare to be invalid.

disappear verb **1** stop being visible. **2** cease to exist.
- **disappearance** noun.

> ☑ one *s*, two *ps*: disa*pp*ear.

disappoint verb **1** make someone sad or upset through failing to fulfil their hopes or expectations. **2** prevent hopes or expectations being fulfilled.
- **disappointed** adjective.

> ☑ one *s*, two *ps*: disa*pp*oint.

disappointment noun **1** sadness felt when hopes or expectations are not fulfilled. **2** a person or thing that causes disappointment.

disapprobation noun strong disapproval.

disapprove verb (**disapproves**, **disapproving**, **disapproved**) feel that someone or something is bad or immoral.
- **disapproval** noun.

disarm verb **1** take a weapon or weapons away from someone. **2** (of a country) reduce the size of its armed forces or give up its weapons. **3** win over a hostile or suspicious person, especially through being charming. **4** remove the fuse from a bomb.

disarmament noun the reduction or withdrawal of military forces and weapons.

disarrange verb (**disarranges**, **disarranging**, **disarranged**) make something untidy or disordered.

disarray noun disorder or confusion.

disassemble verb (**disassembles**, **disassembling**, **disassembled**) take to pieces.

disassociate = DISSOCIATE.

disaster noun **1** a sudden accident or natural event that causes great damage or loss of life. **2** a sudden misfortune.

disastrous adjective **1** causing great damage. **2** informal very unsuccessful.
- **disastrously** adverb.

> ☑ no *e*: disastrous, not -*erous*.

THESAURUS

dispute, quarrel.
OPPOSITES agreement.

disappear verb **1** *the mist had disappeared:* vanish, be lost to view/sight, recede, fade away, melt away, clear. **2** *this way of life has disappeared:* die out, cease to exist, end, go, pass away, pass into oblivion, perish, vanish.
OPPOSITES materialize, arise.

disappoint verb let down, fail, dissatisfy, upset, dismay, sadden, disenchant, disillusion, shatter someone's illusions.
OPPOSITES delight.

disappointed adjective upset, saddened, let down, displeased, dissatisfied, disheartened, downhearted, discouraged, crestfallen, disenchanted, disillusioned; informal choked, cut up; Brit. informal gutted, as sick as a parrot.
OPPOSITES delighted.

disappointment noun **1** *she tried to hide her disappointment:* sadness, sorrow, regret, dismay, displeasure, dissatisfaction, disenchantment, disillusionment. **2** *the trip was a disappointment:* let-down, non-event, anticlimax; Brit. damp squib; informal washout.
OPPOSITES delight, pleasant surprise.

disapproval noun disfavour, objection, dislike, dissatisfaction, distaste, displeasure, criticism, censure, condemnation, denunciation.
OPPOSITES approval.

disapprove verb *he strongly disapproved of smoking:* object to, take exception to, dislike, take a dim view of, look askance at,

frown on, be against, deplore, censure, condemn, denounce.

disarm verb **1** *the militia refused to disarm:* lay down your arms, demobilize, disband, demilitarize. **2** *police disarmed the bomb:* defuse, disable, deactivate, make safe. **3** *the warmth in his voice disarmed her:* win over, charm, persuade, soothe, mollify, appease, placate.
OPPOSITES arm, antagonize.

disarmament noun demilitarization, demobilization, disbandment, decommissioning, arms reduction, arms limitation.
OPPOSITES arming.

disarming adjective winning, charming, irresistible, persuasive, soothing, conciliatory, mollifying.
OPPOSITES infuriating.

disarray noun disorder, confusion, chaos, untidiness, disorganization, a mess, a muddle, a shambles.
OPPOSITES tidiness.

disaster noun **1** *a railway disaster:* catastrophe, calamity, cataclysm, tragedy, act of God, accident. **2** *a string of personal disasters:* misfortune, misadventure, mishap, setback, reversal, stroke of bad luck, blow. **3** (informal) *the film was a disaster:* failure, fiasco, catastrophe; informal flop, washout, dead loss.
OPPOSITES success.

disastrous adjective catastrophic, calamitous, cataclysmic, tragic, devastating, ruinous, terrible, awful.

d

disavow verb deny that you are responsible for or in favour of something.
■ **disavowal** noun.

disband verb (of an organized group) break up.

disbar verb (**disbars, disbarring, disbarred**) stop a barrister from working as a lawyer.

disbelief noun **1** inability or refusal to accept that something is true or real. **2** lack of faith.

disbelieve verb (**disbelieves, disbelieving, disbelieved**) be unable to believe.

disburse verb (**disburses, disbursing, disbursed**) pay out money from a fund.
■ **disbursement** noun.

disc (US spelling **disk**) noun **1** a flat, thin, round object. **2** (**disk**) a device on which computer data is stored. **3** a layer of cartilage that separates vertebrae in the spine. **4** a compact disc or record.
□ **disc jockey** a DJ.

discard verb /diss-**kard**/ get rid of something useless or unwanted. ● noun /**diss**-kard/ something that has been discarded.

discern /di-**sern**/ verb **1** recognize or be aware of. **2** see or hear something with difficulty.
■ **discernible** adjective.

discerning adjective having or showing good judgement.
■ **discernment** noun.

discharge verb (**discharges, discharging, discharged**) **1** dismiss or allow to leave. **2** send out a liquid, gas, or other substance. **3** fire a gun or missile. **4** fulfil a responsibility. ● noun **1** the action of discharging. **2** a substance that has been discharged.

disciple /di-**sy**-puhl/ noun **1** a person who followed Jesus during his life, especially one of the twelve Apostles. **2** a follower of a teacher, leader, or philosophy.

disciplinarian noun a person who enforces firm discipline.

disciplinary adjective having to do with discipline.

discipline noun **1** the training of people to obey rules or a code of behaviour. **2** controlled behaviour resulting from such training. **3** a branch of academic study.
● verb (**disciplines, disciplining, disciplined**) **1** train someone to be obedient or self-controlled. **2** formally punish someone for an offence. **3** (**disciplined**) behaving in a controlled way.

☑ there's a c in the middle: di*sc*ipline.

disclaim verb refuse to acknowledge that you are responsible for or interested in something.

disclaimer noun a statement disclaiming responsibility for something.

disclose verb (**discloses, disclosing,**

THESAURUS

disbelief noun incredulity, incredulousness, scepticism, doubt, cynicism, suspicion, distrust, mistrust.
OPPOSITES belief.

discard verb dispose of, throw away/out, get rid of, toss out, jettison, dispense with, scrap, reject, drop; informal ditch, bin, junk; Brit. informal get shot of; N. Amer. informal trash.
OPPOSITES keep.

discharge verb **1** *he was discharged from service:* dismiss, eject, expel, throw out, make redundant, release, let go; Military cashier; informal sack, fire. **2** *he was discharged from prison:* release, free, let out. **3** *oil is routinely discharged from ships:* release, eject, let out, pour out, give off, dump. **4** *he accidentally discharged a pistol:* fire, shoot, let off, set off, loose off, trigger, launch. **5** *the ferry was discharging passengers:* unload, offload, put off, remove. **6** *they discharged their duties efficiently:* carry out, perform, execute, conduct, fulfil, complete.
OPPOSITES recruit, imprison, take on.
● noun **1** *his discharge from the service:* dismissal, release, removal, ejection, expulsion; Military cashiering; informal the sack, the boot. **2** *her discharge from prison:*

release. **3** *a discharge of diesel oil into the river:* leak, leakage, emission, release, outflow. **4** *a watery discharge:* emission, secretion, excretion, suppuration, pus. **5** *the discharge of their duties:* carrying out, performance, execution, conduct, fulfilment, accomplishment, completion.

disciple noun follower, adherent, believer, admirer, devotee, acolyte, apostle, supporter, advocate.

discipline noun **1** *parental discipline:* control, regulation, direction, order, authority, strictness. **2** *he maintained discipline among his men:* good behaviour, order, control, obedience. **3** *sociology is a fairly new discipline:* field (of study), branch of knowledge, subject, area, speciality.
● verb **1** *she had disciplined herself to ignore the pain:* train, drill, teach, school, coach. **2** *he was disciplined by the management:* punish, penalize, bring to book, reprimand, rebuke; Brit. informal carpet.

disclose verb **1** *the information must not be disclosed:* reveal, make known, divulge, tell, impart, communicate, pass on, release, make public, broadcast, publish. **2** *surgery disclosed a growth:* uncover, reveal, show, disclosed) **1** make new or secret information known. **2** allow to be seen.

disclosure noun **1** the disclosing of information. **2** a secret that is disclosed.

disco noun (plural **discos**) a club or party at which people dance to pop music.

discolour (US spelling **discolor**) verb make something stained or unattractive in colour.
■ **discoloration** (or **discolouration**) noun.

discomfit /diss-**kum**-fit/ verb (**discomfits, discomfiting, discomfited**) make someone uneasy or embarrassed.
■ **discomfiture** noun.

discomfort noun **1** slight pain. **2** slight anxiety or embarrassment. ●verb cause someone discomfort.

discompose verb (**discomposes, discomposing, discomposed**) make someone feel worried or disturbed.

disconcert verb make someone feel worried, confused, or uneasy.

disconnect verb **1** break the connection between two things. **2** detach an electrical device from a power supply.
■ **disconnection** noun.

disconsolate adjective very unhappy and unable to be consoled.

discontent noun a feeling of unhappiness or dissatisfaction.
■ **discontented** adjective **discontentment** noun.

discontinue verb (**discontinues, discontinuing, discontinued**) stop doing, providing, or making.
■ **discontinuation** noun.

discontinuous adjective having intervals or gaps; not continuous.
■ **discontinuity** noun.

discord noun **1** lack of agreement or harmony. **2** lack of harmony between musical notes sounding together.

discordant adjective **1** not in harmony or agreement. **2** (of a sound or sounds) harsh and unpleasant.

discotheque /diss-kuh-tek/ = DISCO.

discount noun an amount by which the usual cost of something is reduced. ●verb **1** reduce the usual price of something. **2** decide not to believe something because you think it is unlikely.

discourage verb (**discourages, discouraging, discouraged**) **1** cause someone to lose confidence or enthusiasm. **2** try to persuade someone not to do something.
■ **discouragement** noun.

discourse noun **1** written or spoken communication or debate. **2** a formal discussion of a topic. ●verb (**discourses, discoursing, discoursed**) speak or write about something with authority.

discourteous adjective rude and without consideration for other people.

discourtesy noun (plural **discourtesies**) behaviour that is rude and inconsiderate.

discover verb (**discovers, discovering, discovered**) **1** find something unexpectedly or in the course of a search. **2** gain knowledge about, or become aware of. **3** be the first to find or observe something.

discovery noun (plural **discoveries**) **1** the

bring to light.
OPPOSITES keep secret, conceal.

discomfort noun **1** *discomfort caused by indigestion:* **pain,** aches and pains, soreness, aching, twinge, pang, throb, cramp. **2** *the discomforts of life at sea:* **inconvenience,** difficulty, problem, trial, tribulation, hardship. **3** *Thomas noticed her discomfort:* **embarrassment,** discomfiture, unease, awkwardness, discomposure, confusion, nervousness, distress, anxiety.

discontent noun **dissatisfaction,** disaffection, grievances, unhappiness, displeasure, resentment, envy, restlessness, unrest, unease.
OPPOSITES satisfaction.

discontented adjective **dissatisfied,** disgruntled, disaffected, unhappy, aggrieved, displeased, resentful, envious, restless, frustrated; informal fed up.
OPPOSITES satisfied.

discount noun *a 10 per cent discount:* **reduction,** deduction, markdown, price cut, concession, rebate.
●verb **1** *I discounted the rumours:*

disregard, pay no attention to, take no notice of, dismiss, ignore, overlook; informal pooh-pooh. **2** *the price is heavily discounted:* **reduce,** mark down, cut, lower; informal knock down.
OPPOSITES believe, increase.

discourage verb **1** *we want to discourage children from smoking:* **dissuade,** deter, put off, talk out of. **2** *she was discouraged by his hostile tone:* **dishearten,** dispirit, demoralize, disappoint, put off, unnerve, daunt, intimidate. **3** *he sought to discourage further speculation:* **prevent,** deter, stop, avert, inhibit, curb.
OPPOSITES encourage.

discover verb **1** *firemen discovered a body:* **find,** locate, come across/upon, stumble on, chance on, uncover, unearth, turn up. **2** *I discovered the truth:* **find out,** learn, realize, ascertain, work out, recognize; informal figure out; Brit. informal twig.

discovery noun **1** *the discovery of the body:* **finding,** location, uncovering, unearthing. **2** *the discovery that she was pregnant:* **realization,** recognition, revelation, action of discovering. **2** a person or thing discovered.

discredit verb (**discredits, discrediting, discredited**) **1** make someone seem less trustworthy or honourable. **2** make something seem false or unreliable. • **noun** damage to someone's reputation.

discreditable adjective causing damage to someone's reputation; shameful.

discreet adjective careful not to attract attention or give offence.
■ **discreetly** adverb.

! don't confuse **discreet** with **discrete**, which means 'separate'.

discrepancy noun (plural **discrepancies**) a difference between things that should be the same.

discrete adjective separate and distinct.

discretion noun **1** the quality of being discreet. **2** the freedom to decide what should be done in a particular situation.

discretionary adjective done or used according to the judgement of a particular person.

discriminate verb (**discriminates, discriminating, discriminated**) **1** recognize a difference between one thing and another. **2** treat people unfairly on the grounds of race, sex, or age.

discriminating adjective having or showing good taste or judgement.

discrimination noun **1** unfair treatment of people on the grounds of race, sex, or age. **2** recognition of the difference between one thing and another. **3** good judgement or taste.

discriminatory adjective showing discrimination or prejudice.

discursive adjective (of writing) moving from subject to subject.

discus noun (plural **discuses**) a heavy disc thrown in athletic contests.

discuss verb **1** talk about something in order to reach a decision. **2** talk or write about a topic in detail.

discussion noun **1** conversation or debate about something. **2** a detailed treatment of a topic in writing.

disdain noun the feeling that someone or

THESAURUS

disclosure. **3** *he failed to take out a patent on his discoveries:* find, finding, breakthrough, innovation.

discredit verb **1** *an attempt to discredit him:* bring into disrepute, disgrace, dishonour, blacken the name of, put/show in a bad light, compromise, smear, tarnish; N. Amer. slur. **2** *that theory has been discredited:* disprove, invalidate, explode, refute; informal debunk.
OPPOSITES honour, prove.
• **noun** *to his discredit:* dishonour, disgrace, shame, humiliation, ignominy.
OPPOSITES honour, glory.

discreet adjective tactful, circumspect, diplomatic, judicious, sensitive, careful, cautious, strategic.

discrepancy noun difference, disparity, variation, deviation, divergence, disagreement, inconsistency, mismatch, conflict.
OPPOSITES correspondence.

discretion noun **1** *you can rely on his discretion:* tact, diplomacy, delicacy, sensitivity, good sense, prudence, circumspection. **2** *at the discretion of the council:* choice, option, preference, disposition, pleasure, will, inclination.
OPPOSITES tactlessness.

discriminate verb **1** *he cannot discriminate between fact and opinion:* differentiate, distinguish, draw a distinction, tell the difference, tell apart, separate. **2** *policies that discriminate against women:* be biased, be prejudiced, treat differently, treat unfairly, put at a disadvantage,

victimize, pick on.

discriminating adjective discerning, perceptive, judicious, selective, tasteful, refined, sensitive, cultivated, cultured.
OPPOSITES indiscriminate.

discrimination noun **1** *racial discrimination:* prejudice, bias, bigotry, intolerance, favouritism, partisanship. **2** *a man with no discrimination:* discernment, judgement, perceptiveness, (good) taste, refinement, sensitivity, cultivation.
OPPOSITES impartiality.

discuss verb **1** *I discussed the matter with my wife:* talk over, talk about, talk through, debate, confer about. **2** *chapter three discusses this topic:* examine, explore, study, analyse, go into, deal with, consider, tackle.

discussion noun **1** *a long discussion with her husband:* conversation, talk, dialogue, conference, debate, exchange of views, consultation, deliberation; informal confab. **2** *see Chapter 7 for a detailed discussion:* examination, exploration, study, analysis, treatment, consideration.

disdain noun *she looked at him with disdain:* contempt, scorn, derision, disrespect, condescension, superciliousness, hauteur, haughtiness.
OPPOSITES respect.
• **verb** *she disdained exhibitionism:* scorn, deride, regard with contempt, sneer at, look down your nose at, look down on, despise.
OPPOSITES value.

something does not deserve respect. •verb treat with disdain.

■ **disdainful** adjective **disdainfully** adverb.

disease noun an illness in a human, animal, or plant.

■ **diseased** adjective.

disembark verb leave a ship, aircraft, or train.

■ **disembarkation** noun.

disembodied adjective **1** separated from the body, or existing without a body. **2** (of a sound) not having any obvious physical source.

disembowel verb (**disembowels, disembowelling, disembowelled**; US spelling **disembowels, disemboweling, disemboweled**) cut open and remove the internal organs of.

disempower verb (**disempowers, disempowering, disempowered**) make someone less powerful or confident.

disenchant verb make someone disillusioned.

■ **disenchantment** noun.

disenfranchise verb (**disenfranchises, disenfranchising, disenfranchised**) **1** deprive someone of the right to vote. **2** deprive someone of a right or privilege.

disengage verb (**disengages, disengaging, disengaged**) **1** release or detach. **2** remove troops from an area of conflict.

■ **disengagement** noun.

disentangle verb (**disentangles,**

disentangling, disentangled) stop something being tangled.

disestablish verb end the official status of a national Church.

disfavour (US spelling **disfavor**) noun disapproval or dislike.

disfigure verb (**disfigures, disfiguring, disfigured**) spoil the appearance of.

■ **disfigurement** noun.

disgorge verb (**disgorges, disgorging, disgorged**) **1** cause something to pour out. **2** bring up food from the stomach.

disgrace noun **1** the loss of other people's respect as the result of behaving badly. **2** a shamefully bad person or thing. •verb (**disgraces, disgracing, disgraced**) bring disgrace to.

disgraceful adjective shockingly unacceptable.

■ **disgracefully** adverb.

disgruntled adjective angry or dissatisfied.

■ **disgruntlement** noun.

disguise verb (**disguises, disguising, disguised**) **1** change the appearance of someone or something so they cannot be recognized. **2** hide a feeling or situation. •noun **1** a way of disguising yourself. **2** the state of being disguised.

disgust noun a strong feeling that something is unpleasant, offensive, or unacceptable. •verb give someone a feeling of disgust.

■ **disgusting** adjective.

THESAURUS

disease noun illness, sickness, ill health, infection, ailment, malady, disorder, condition, problem; informal bug, virus; Brit. informal lurgy.
OPPOSITES health.

diseased adjective unhealthy, ill, sick, unwell, ailing, infected, septic, rotten, bad.

disgrace noun **1** *he brought disgrace on the family:* dishonour, shame, discredit, ignominy, disrepute, infamy, scandal, stigma, humiliation, loss of face. **2** *the unemployment figures are a disgrace:* scandal, discredit, reproach, stain, blemish, blot, outrage, affront.
OPPOSITES honour, credit.
•verb *you have disgraced the family name:* shame, bring shame on, dishonour, discredit, stigmatize, taint, sully, tarnish, stain, blacken.
OPPOSITES honour.

disgraceful adjective shameful, scandalous, contemptible, dishonourable, discreditable, disreputable, reprehensible, blameworthy, unworthy, ignoble.
OPPOSITES admirable.

disgruntled adjective dissatisfied, fed up, discontented, aggrieved, resentful, put out, displeased, unhappy, disappointed,

annoyed; informal hacked off, browned off; Brit. informal cheesed off, narked; N. Amer. informal sore, ticked off.
OPPOSITES contented.

disguise verb camouflage, conceal, hide, cover up, mask, screen, veil, paper over.
OPPOSITES expose.

disgust noun **1** *the sight filled her with disgust:* revulsion, repugnance, aversion, distaste, abhorrence, loathing, hatred. **2** *the audience walked out in disgust:* disapproval, displeasure, indignation, annoyance, anger, fury, outrage, contempt, resentment.
OPPOSITES delight.
•verb **1** *they were disgusted by the violence:* revolt, repel, repulse, sicken, horrify, appal, turn someone's stomach; N. Amer. informal gross out. **2** *Toby's behaviour disgusted her:* displease, dissatisfy, arouse the disapproval of, annoy, anger, outrage, scandalize, offend, affront, dismay.
OPPOSITES delight.

disgusting adjective **1** *the food was disgusting:* revolting, repulsive, sickening, nauseating, stomach-turning, off-putting; N. Amer. vomitous; informal sick-making. **2** *I find racism disgusting:* outrageous,

d

dish noun **1** a shallow container for cooking or serving food. **2** (**the dishes**) all the crockery and utensils used for a meal. **3** a particular kind of food. **4** a shallow concave object. **5** informal an attractive person. • verb (**dish something out** or **up**) put food on to plates before a meal.

disharmony noun lack of harmony.

dishearten verb make someone lose determination or confidence.

dishevelled (US spelling **disheveled**) adjective untidy in appearance.

dishonest adjective not honest, trustworthy, or sincere.
  ■ **dishonestly** adverb **dishonesty** noun.

dishonour (US spelling **dishonor**) noun shame or disgrace. • verb **1** bring shame or disgrace to. **2** fail to keep an agreement.

dishonourable (US spelling **dishonorable**) adjective bringing shame or disgrace.

dishwasher noun a machine for washing dishes automatically.

dishy adjective (**dishier**, **dishiest**) informal good-looking.

disillusion verb make someone realize that a belief they hold is mistaken or unrealistic. • noun disappointment caused by discovering that your beliefs are mistaken or unrealistic.
  ■ **disillusionment** noun.

disincentive noun a factor that discourages someone from doing a particular thing.

disinclination noun a reluctance to do something.

disinclined adjective reluctant; unwilling.

disinfect verb clean with a disinfectant in order to destroy bacteria.
  ■ **disinfection** noun.

disinfectant noun a chemical liquid that destroys bacteria.

disinformation noun information which is intended to mislead people.

disingenuous adjective not sincere, especially in pretending ignorance about something.

disinherit verb (**disinherits**, **disinheriting**, **disinherited**) prevent a person from inheriting something.

disintegrate verb (**disintegrates**, **disintegrating**, **disintegrated**) break up into small parts as a result of impact or decay.
  ■ **disintegration** noun.

disinter /diss-in-**ter**/ verb (**disinters**, **disinterring**, **disinterred**) dig up something buried.

disinterest noun **1** impartiality. **2** lack of interest.

disinterested adjective not influenced by personal feelings; impartial.

> **!** don't confuse **disinterested** and **uninterested**. **Disinterested** means 'impartial', while **uninterested** means 'not interested'.

disjointed adjective not having a logical sequence or clear connection; disconnected.

disjunction noun a difference or lack of agreement between things that you might expect to be the same.

disk ⇨ DISC.
  □ **disk drive** a device which allows a computer to read from and write on to computer disks.

diskette noun a floppy disk.

dislike verb (**dislikes**, **disliking**, **disliked**) find someone or something unpleasant or offensive. • noun **1** a feeling that someone or something is unpleasant or offensive. **2** a person or thing that you dislike.

dislocate verb (**dislocates**, **dislocating**, **dislocated**) **1** put a bone out of its proper position in a joint. **2** stop something from working properly; disrupt.
  ■ **dislocation** noun.

dislodge verb (**dislodges**, **dislodging**,

THESAURUS

objectionable, abhorrent, repellent, loathsome, offensive, appalling, shocking, horrifying, scandalous, monstrous, detestable; informal gross, sick.
OPPOSITES delightful.

dish noun **1** *a china dish:* bowl, plate, platter, salver, pot. **2** *vegetarian dishes:* recipe, meal, course, fare.
□ **dish something out distribute,** dispense, issue, hand out/round, give out, pass round, deal out, dole out, allocate.

dishonest adjective fraudulent, cheating, underhand, devious, treacherous, unfair, dirty, criminal, illegal, unlawful, false, untruthful, deceitful, lying, corrupt, dishonourable, untrustworthy,

unscrupulous; informal crooked, shady, sharp; Brit. informal bent; Austral./NZ informal shonky.
OPPOSITES honest.

disintegrate verb break up, crumble, break apart, fall apart, fall to pieces, collapse, fragment, shatter, splinter.

disinterested adjective *disinterested advice:* unbiased, unprejudiced, impartial, neutral, detached, objective, dispassionate.

dislike verb *a man she had always disliked:* find distasteful, regard with distaste, be averse to, have an aversion to, hate, disapprove of, object to, take exception to.
OPPOSITES like.
• noun *she viewed the other woman with dislike:* distaste, aversion, disfavour,

dislodged) remove something from its position.

disloyal adjective not loyal or faithful.
■ disloyalty noun.

dismal adjective **1** causing or showing gloom or depression. **2** informal disgracefully bad.
■ dismally adverb.

dismantle verb (**dismantles, dismantling, dismantled**) take something to pieces.

dismay noun a feeling of unhappiness and discouragement. •verb cause someone to feel dismay.

dismember verb (**dismembers, dismembering, dismembered**) **1** tear or cut the limbs from. **2** divide up a territory or organization.
■ dismemberment noun.

dismiss verb **1** order or allow someone to leave. **2** order an employee to leave a job. **3** treat something as not being worthy of serious consideration. **4** refuse to allow a legal case to continue. **5** Cricket end the innings of a batsman or side.
■ dismissal noun.

dismissive adjective showing that you feel something is not worth serious consideration.
■ dismissively adverb.

dismount verb get off a horse or bicycle.

disobedient adjective failing or refusing to be obedient.
■ disobedience noun.

disobey verb fail or refuse to obey.

disorder noun **1** untidiness or disorganization. **2** the breakdown of peaceful and law-abiding behaviour. **3** an illness or disease.
■ disordered adjective.

disorderly adjective **1** involving a breakdown of peaceful behaviour. **2** untidy or disorganized.

disorganized or **disorganised** adjective **1** not well planned and controlled. **2** not able to plan your activities efficiently.
■ disorganization noun.

disorientate or **disorient** verb (**disorientates, disorientating, disorientated**) make someone lose their bearings or feel confused.
■ disorientation noun.

disown verb show or decide that you no longer want to have anything to do with someone.

disparage /diss-**pa**-rij/ verb (**disparages, disparaging, disparaged**) speak critically or negatively about.

disparate /diss-**puh**-ruht/ adjective **1** very different from one another. **2** containing elements that are very different from one another.

disparity noun (plural **disparities**) a great difference.

dispassionate adjective not influenced by

THESAURUS

antipathy, disgust, abhorrence, hatred.
OPPOSITES liking.

dismal adjective **1** *a dismal look:* gloomy, glum, melancholy, morose, doleful, woebegone, forlorn, dejected, downcast. **2** *dismal weather:* dim, dingy, dark, gloomy, dreary, drab, dull.
OPPOSITES cheerful, bright.

dismantle verb take apart, take to pieces/bits, pull to pieces, disassemble, break up, strip (down).
OPPOSITES build.

dismay noun *to his dismay:* alarm, distress, concern, surprise, consternation, disquiet.
OPPOSITES pleasure, relief.
•verb *he was dismayed by the answer:* concern, distress, disturb, worry, alarm, disconcert, take aback, unnerve, unsettle.
OPPOSITES encourage, please.

dismiss verb **1** *the president dismissed five ministers:* give someone their notice, discharge, lay off, make redundant; informal sack, fire. **2** *the guards were dismissed:* send away, let go, release. **3** *don't dismiss the idea so lightly:* reject, deny, repudiate, spurn. **4** *she dismissed the thought:* banish, set aside, put out of your mind.

OPPOSITES appoint, keep on, entertain, dwell on.

disobedient adjective naughty, insubordinate, defiant, unruly, wayward, badly behaved, delinquent, rebellious, mutinous, troublesome, wilful.
OPPOSITES obedient.

disobey verb defy, go against, flout, contravene, infringe, transgress, violate, disregard, ignore, pay no heed to.

disorder noun **1** *he hates disorder:* untidiness, mess, disarray, chaos, confusion, clutter, jumble, a muddle, a shambles. **2** *incidents of public disorder:* unrest, disturbance, turmoil, mayhem, violence, fighting, fracas, rioting, lawlessness, anarchy, breach of the peace. **3** *a blood disorder:* disease, infection, complaint, condition, affliction, malady, sickness, illness, ailment.
OPPOSITES order, tidiness, peace.

disorderly adjective **1** *a disorderly desk:* untidy, disorganized, messy, cluttered, in disarray; informal like a bomb's hit it, higgledy-piggledy; Brit. informal shambolic. **2** *disorderly behaviour:* unruly, riotous, disruptive, troublesome, lawless.
OPPOSITES tidy, peaceful.

strong feelings; impartial.

■ **dispassionately** adverb.

dispatch or **despatch** verb 1 send to a destination, especially for a particular purpose. 2 send a letter or parcel somewhere. 3 deal with a task or problem quickly and efficiently. 4 kill a person or animal. • noun 1 the action of dispatching. 2 a report on the latest situation in state or military affairs. 3 speed and efficiency.

dispel verb (**dispels, dispelling, dispelled**) make a doubt, feeling, or belief disappear.

dispensable adjective able to be replaced or done without.

dispensary noun (plural **dispensaries**) a room where medicines are prepared and provided.

dispensation noun 1 special permission not to obey a rule. 2 the religious system of a particular time. 3 the action of dispensing.

dispense verb (**dispenses, dispensing, dispensed**) 1 distribute something to a number of people. 2 (of a chemist) prepare and supply medicine according to a prescription. 3 (**dispense with**) get rid of or manage without.

■ **dispenser** noun.

disperse verb (**disperses, dispersing, dispersed**) 1 move apart and go in different directions. 2 (of gas, smoke, etc.) thin out and eventually disappear.

■ **dispersal** noun **dispersion** noun.

dispirited adjective discouraged or depressed.

■ **dispiriting** adjective.

displace verb (**displaces, displacing, displaced**) 1 move something from its proper or usual position. 2 take over the position or role of. 3 force someone to leave their home.

displacement noun 1 the action of displacing something, or the amount by which something is displaced. 2 the volume or weight of water displaced by a floating ship, used as a measure of the ship's size.

display verb 1 put something on show in a noticeable and attractive way. 2 show a quality or feeling. 3 show data or an image on a screen. • noun 1 a performance, show, or event for public entertainment. 2 the displaying of a quality or feeling. 3 a collection of objects being displayed. 4 the data or image shown on a screen.

displease verb (**displeases, displeasing, displeased**) annoy or upset.

displeasure noun annoyance or

THESAURUS

dispatch verb 1 *all the messages were dispatched:* send (off), post, mail, forward. 2 *the business was dispatched in the morning:* deal with, finish, conclude, settle, discharge, perform. 3 *the good guy dispatched a host of villains:* kill, put to death, massacre, wipe out, exterminate, eliminate, murder, assassinate, execute. • noun *the latest dispatch from the front:* message, report, communication, communiqué, bulletin, statement, letter, news, intelligence.

dispel verb banish, drive away/off, chase away, scatter, eliminate, dismiss, allay, ease, quell.
OPPOSITES form, give rise to.

dispense verb 1 *servants dispensed the drinks:* distribute, pass round, hand out, dole out, dish out, share out. 2 *the soldiers dispensed summary justice:* administer, deliver, issue, deal out, mete out.
3 *dispensing medicines:* prepare, make up, supply, provide.
□ **dispense with** 1 *let's dispense with the formalities:* waive, omit, drop, leave out, forgo, do away with; informal give something a miss. 2 *he dispensed with his crutches:* get rid of, throw away/out, dispose of, discard; informal ditch, scrap, dump, chuck out/away; Brit. informal get shot of.

disperse verb 1 *the crowd began to disperse / police dispersed the demonstrators:* break

up, split up, disband, scatter, leave, go their separate ways, drive away/off, chase away. 2 *the fog finally dispersed:* dissipate, dissolve, melt away, fade away, clear, lift. 3 *the seeds are dispersed by birds:* scatter, distribute, spread, disseminate.
OPPOSITES assemble, form, gather.

displace verb 1 *roof tiles were displaced by gales:* dislodge, dislocate, move out of place/position, shift. 2 *English displaced the local language:* replace, take the place of, supplant, supersede.
OPPOSITES replace.

display verb 1 *the Crown Jewels are displayed in London:* exhibit, show, arrange, array, present, lay out, set out. 2 *the play displays his many theatrical talents:* show off, parade, highlight, reveal, showcase. 3 *she displayed a vein of sharp humour:* manifest, show evidence of, reveal, demonstrate, show.
OPPOSITES conceal. • noun 1 *a display of dolls:* exhibition, exposition, array, arrangement, presentation, demonstration, spectacle, show, parade. 2 *his display of concern:* manifestation, expression, show, proof, demonstration, evidence.

displease verb annoy, irritate, anger, incense, irk, vex, nettle, put out, upset, exasperate.

dissatisfaction.

disport verb (**disport yourself**) old use enjoy yourself in an unrestrained way.

disposable adjective **1** intended to be used once and then thrown away. **2** (of money) available to be used.

disposal noun the action of disposing of something.
□ **at your disposal** available to be used whenever or however you wish.

dispose verb (**disposes, disposing, disposed**) **1** (**dispose of**) get rid of. **2** (**be disposed to**) be inclined to do or think something. **3** (**disposed**) having a particular attitude: *they were favourably disposed towards him.* **4** arrange something in a particular position.

disposition noun **1** the natural qualities of a person's character. **2** an inclination or tendency. **3** the way in which something is arranged.

dispossess verb deprive someone of a possession.
■ **dispossession** noun.

disproportionate adjective too large or too small in comparison with something else.
■ **disproportionately** adverb.

disprove verb (**disproves, disproving, disproved**) prove something to be false.

disputation noun debate or argument.

disputatious adjective fond of arguing.

dispute verb (**disputes, disputing, disputed**) **1** argue about. **2** question whether something is true or valid. **3** compete for.
•**noun** an argument or disagreement.
■ **disputable** adjective.

disqualify verb (**disqualifies, disqualifying, disqualified**) prevent someone performing an activity or taking an office because they have broken a rule or are not suitable.
■ **disqualification** noun.

disquiet noun a feeling of anxiety.
■ **disquieting** adjective.

disquisition noun a long or complex discussion of a topic.

disregard verb pay no attention to. •**noun** the action of disregarding something.

disrepair noun (**in disrepair**) in a bad condition as a result of being neglected.

disreputable adjective not respectable in appearance or character.

disrepute noun the state of having a bad reputation.

disrespect noun lack of respect or courtesy.
■ **disrespectful** adjective **disrespectfully** adverb.

disrobe verb (**disrobes, disrobing, disrobed**) take off your clothes.

disrupt verb interrupt or disturb an activity or process.
■ **disruption** noun.

disruptive adjective causing disruption.

dissatisfied adjective not content or happy.
■ **dissatisfaction** noun.

d

THESAURUS

dispose verb *a more sanitary way to dispose of waste:* **throw away/out,** get rid of, discard, jettison, scrap; informal **dump,** junk, ditch, chuck out/away; Brit. informal get shot of; N. Amer. informal trash.

disposition noun **1** *a nervous disposition:* **temperament,** nature, character, constitution, make-up, mentality. **2** *the disposition of the troops:* **arrangement,** positioning, placement, configuration, set-up, line-up, layout.

disprove verb **refute,** prove false, rebut, debunk, give the lie to, demolish; informal shoot full of holes, blow out of the water.

dispute noun **1** *a subject of dispute:* **debate,** discussion, argument, controversy, disagreement, dissent, conflict. **2** *they have settled their dispute:* **quarrel,** argument, altercation, squabble, falling-out, disagreement, difference of opinion, clash; Brit. row.
OPPOSITES agreement.
•**verb 1** *George disputed with him:* **debate,** discuss, exchange views, quarrel, argue, disagree, clash, fall out, wrangle, bicker, squabble. **2** *they disputed his proposals:* **challenge,** contest, question, call into question, quibble over, contradict, argue

about, disagree with, take issue with.
OPPOSITES accept.

disregard verb *Annie disregarded the remark:* **ignore,** take no notice of, pay no attention to, discount, overlook, turn a blind eye to, shut your eyes to, gloss over, brush off/aside, shrug off.
OPPOSITES heed.
•**noun** *blithe disregard for the rules:* **indifference,** non-observance, inattention, heedlessness, neglect, contempt.
OPPOSITES attention.

disrupt verb **interrupt,** disturb, interfere with, play havoc with, upset, unsettle, obstruct, impede, hold up, delay.

disruptive adjective **troublesome,** disturbing, upsetting, unsettling, unruly, badly behaved, rowdy, disorderly, undisciplined, unmanageable, uncontrollable, uncooperative.
OPPOSITES well behaved.

dissatisfaction noun **discontent,** disaffection, disquiet, unhappiness, disappointment, disgruntlement, displeasure, vexation, annoyance, irritation.

dissatisfied adjective **discontented,** disappointed, disaffected, displeased,

dissect verb 1 cut up the dead body of a person or animal to study its internal parts. 2 analyse in great detail.
■ **dissection** noun.

☑ **dissect** has a double *s*.

dissemble verb (**dissembles, dissembling, dissembled**) hide or disguise your motives or feelings.

disseminate verb (**disseminates, disseminating, disseminated**) spread information widely.
■ **dissemination** noun.

dissension noun disagreement that causes trouble within a group.

dissent verb 1 express disagreement with a widely held view. 2 disagree with the doctrine of an established Church. 3 (in sport) disagree with the referee's decision. • noun disagreement with a widely held view.
■ **dissenter** noun.

dissertation noun a long essay, especially one written for a university degree.

disservice noun a harmful action.

dissident noun a person who opposes official policy. • adjective opposing official policy.
■ **dissidence** noun.

dissimilar adjective not similar; different.
■ **dissimilarity** noun.

dissimulate verb (**dissimulates, dissimulating, dissimulated**) hide or disguise your thoughts or feelings.
■ **dissimulation** noun.

dissipate verb (**dissipates, dissipating, dissipated**) 1 disappear or disperse. 2 waste money, energy, or resources. 3 (**dissipated**)

indulging too much in alcohol and other physical pleasures.
■ **dissipation** noun.

dissociate verb (**dissociates, dissociating, dissociated**) 1 disconnect or separate. 2 (**dissociate yourself from**) say publicly that you are not connected with.
■ **dissociation** noun.

dissolute adjective indulging too much in physical pleasures.

dissolution noun 1 the formal closing down or ending of an official body or agreement. 2 the action of dissolving or decomposing.

dissolve verb (**dissolves, dissolving, dissolved**) 1 (of a solid) mix with a liquid and form a solution. 2 close down or end an assembly or agreement. 3 (**dissolve into** or **in**) give way to strong emotion.

dissonant adjective without harmony; discordant.
■ **dissonance** noun.

dissuade verb (**dissuades, dissuading, dissuaded**) persuade or advise someone not to do something.
■ **dissuasion** noun.

distaff /**diss**-tahf/ noun a stick or spindle on to which wool or flax is wound for spinning.
□ **distaff side** the female side of a family.

distance noun 1 the length of the space between two points. 2 the state of being distant. 3 a far-off point or place. 4 the full length or time of a race. • verb (**distances, distancing, distanced**) (**distance yourself**) become less friendly or supportive.

distant adjective 1 far away in space or

THESAURUS

disgruntled, aggrieved, unhappy.
OPPOSITES contented.

dissent verb disagree, differ, demur, be at variance/odds, take issue, protest, object.
OPPOSITES agree, conform.
• noun disagreement, difference of opinion, argument, dispute, resistance, objection, protest, opposition.
OPPOSITES agreement, conformity.

dissident noun dissenter, objector, protester, rebel, revolutionary, subversive, agitator, refusenik.
OPPOSITES conformist.
• adjective dissenting, opposing, objecting, protesting, rebellious, revolutionary, subversive, nonconformist.
OPPOSITES conformist.

dissociate verb separate, detach, disconnect, sever, cut off, divorce, isolate, alienate.
OPPOSITES relate.

dissolve verb 1 *sugar dissolves in water:*

break down, liquefy, melt, deliquesce, disintegrate. 2 *the crowd dissolved:* disperse, disband, break up, scatter. 3 *the assembly was dissolved:* disband, bring to an end, end, terminate, discontinue, close down, wind up/down, suspend, adjourn. 4 *their marriage was dissolved:* annul, nullify, void, invalidate, revoke.

dissuade verb discourage, deter, prevent, divert, stop, talk out of, persuade against, advise against, argue out of.
OPPOSITES encourage.

distance noun 1 they measured the distance: interval, space, span, gap, extent, length, range, reach. 2 *a mix of warmth and distance:* aloofness, remoteness, detachment, unfriendliness, reserve, reticence, formality; informal stand-offishness.
OPPOSITES proximity, friendliness.

distant adjective 1 *distant parts of the world:* faraway, far-off, far-flung, remote,

time. **2** at a specified distance. **3** far apart in terms of resemblance or relationship. **4** aloof or reserved.
■ **distantly** adverb.

distaste noun the feeling that something is unpleasant or offensive.

distasteful adjective unpleasant or disliked.
■ **distastefully** adverb.

distemper noun **1** a kind of paint used on walls. **2** a disease of dogs, causing fever and coughing.

distend verb swell because of internal pressure.
■ **distension** noun.

distil (US spelling **distill**) verb (**distils**, **distilling**, **distilled**) **1** purify a liquid by heating it until it vaporizes, then condensing the vapour and collecting the resulting liquid. **2** make alcoholic spirits such as whisky in this way. **3** extract the most important aspects of.
■ **distiller** noun **distillation** noun.

distillery noun (plural **distilleries**) a factory that makes alcoholic spirits.

distinct adjective **1** recognizably different.

2 able to be perceived clearly by the senses.
■ **distinctly** adverb.

distinction noun **1** a noticeable difference. **2** outstanding excellence. **3** a special honour or recognition.

distinctive adjective characteristic of a person or thing and distinguishing them from others.
■ **distinctively** adverb.

distinguish verb **1** recognize the difference between two people or things. **2** manage to see or hear. **3** be a characteristic that makes two people or things different. **4** (**distinguish yourself**) do something very well.
■ **distinguishable** adjective.

distinguished adjective **1** successful and greatly respected. **2** having a dignified appearance.

distort verb **1** pull or twist out of shape. **2** give a misleading account of.
■ **distortion** noun.

distract verb **1** prevent someone from giving their full attention to something. **2** take attention away from something.

distracted adjective unable to concentrate

---

out of the way, outlying. **2** *the distant past:* **remote**, bygone, ancient, prehistoric. **3** *a distant memory:* **vague**, faint, dim, hazy, indistinct, sketchy. **4** *my father was always very distant:* **aloof**, unapproachable, reserved, remote, detached, unfriendly; informal stand-offish. **5** *a distant look in his eyes:* **distracted**, absent, faraway, detached, vague.
OPPOSITES near, recent, clear, close, friendly, alert.

distinct adjective **1** *two distinct categories:* **discrete**, separate, different, unconnected, distinctive, contrasting. **2** *the tail has distinct black tips:* **clear**, well defined, unmistakable, easily distinguishable, recognizable, visible, obvious, pronounced, prominent, striking.
OPPOSITES overlapping, similar, indefinite.

distinction noun **1** *distinctions that we observed:* **difference**, contrast, variation, division, differentiation, discrepancy. **2** *a painter of distinction:* **merit**, worth, greatness, excellence, quality, repute, renown. **3** *he had served with distinction:* **honour**, credit, excellence, merit.
OPPOSITES similarity, mediocrity, dishonour.

distinctive adjective **distinguishing**, characteristic, typical, individual, particular, peculiar, unique, exclusive, special.
OPPOSITES common.

distinctly adverb **1** *there's something distinctly odd about him:* **decidedly**, markedly, definitely, unmistakably,

manifestly, patently. **2** *Laura spoke quite distinctly:* **clearly**, plainly, intelligibly, audibly.

distinguish verb **1** *he can distinguish reality from fantasy:* **differentiate**, tell apart, discriminate between, tell the difference between. **2** *he could distinguish shapes in the dark:* **discern**, see, perceive, make out, detect, recognize, identify. **3** *this is what distinguishes history from other disciplines:* **separate**, set apart, make distinctive, make different, single out, mark off.

distinguished adjective **eminent**, famous, renowned, prominent, well known, esteemed, respected, illustrious, acclaimed, celebrated.
OPPOSITES unknown, obscure.

distorted adjective **1** *a distorted face:* **twisted**, warped, contorted, buckled, deformed, malformed, misshapen, disfigured, crooked, out of shape. **2** *a distorted version:* **misrepresented**, perverted, twisted, falsified, misreported, misstated, garbled, inaccurate, biased, prejudiced.
OPPOSITES normal, straight, honest.

distract verb **divert**, sidetrack, draw away, lead astray, disturb, put off.

distracted adjective **preoccupied**, inattentive, vague, abstracted, absent-minded, faraway, in a world of your own, troubled, harassed, worried; informal miles away, not with it.
OPPOSITES attentive.

distraction noun **1** a thing that distracts someone's attention. **2** something that provides entertainment. **3** the state of being distracted.

distraught adjective very worried and upset.

distress noun **1** extreme unhappiness, pain, or suffering. **2** the state of a ship or aircraft when in danger or difficulty. • verb cause distress to.

distribute verb (**distributes, distributing, distributed**) **1** hand or share out to a number of people. **2** (**be distributed**) be spread over an area. **3** supply goods to retailers.

distribution noun **1** the action of distributing. **2** the way in which something is distributed.

distributor noun **1** a company that supplies goods to retailers. **2** a device in a petrol engine for passing electric current to each spark plug in turn.

district noun a particular area of a town or region.

distrust noun lack of trust. • verb have little trust in.
■ **distrustful** adjective.

disturb verb **1** interrupt the sleep, relaxation, or privacy of. **2** move something from its normal position. **3** make someone anxious. **4** (**disturbed**) having emotional or mental problems.

disturbance noun **1** the interruption of a normal or settled condition. **2** a riot or other breakdown of peaceful behaviour.

disunited adjective not united.
■ **disunity** noun.

disuse noun the state of not being used; neglect.
■ **disused** adjective.

THESAURUS

distraction noun **1** *a distraction from the real issues:* diversion, interruption, disturbance, interference. **2** *frivolous distractions:* amusement, entertainment, diversion, recreation, pastime, leisure pursuit.

distraught adjective distressed, frantic, fraught, overcome, overwrought, beside yourself, out of your mind, desperate, hysterical, worked up, at your wits' end; informal in a state.
OPPOSITES calm.

distress noun **1** *she concealed her distress:* anguish, suffering, pain, agony, torment, heartache, heartbreak, sorrow, sadness, unhappiness. **2** *a ship in distress:* danger, peril, difficulty, trouble, jeopardy, risk.
OPPOSITES happiness, safety.
• verb *he was distressed by the trial:* upset, pain, trouble, worry, perturb, disturb, disquiet, agitate, torment.
OPPOSITES comfort.

distribute verb **1** *the proceeds were distributed among his creditors:* give out, deal out, dole out, dish out, hand out/round, share out, divide out/up, parcel out. **2** *the newsletter is distributed free:* circulate, issue, deliver, disseminate, publish.
OPPOSITES gather in, pool.

distribution noun **1** *the distribution of aid:* giving out, dealing out, doling out, handing out/round, issuing, allocation, sharing out, dividing up/out, parcelling out. **2** *centres of food distribution:* supply, delivery, dispersal, transportation.
OPPOSITES gathering in, pooling, collection.

district noun area, region, quarter, sector, zone, territory, locality, neighbourhood, community.

distrust noun *distrust of Soviet intentions:* mistrust, suspicion, wariness, chariness, scepticism, doubt, cynicism, misgivings, qualms.
OPPOSITES trust.
• verb *the Army distrustsd the peace process:* mistrust, be suspicious of, be wary of, be chary of, regard with suspicion, suspect, be sceptical of, doubt, be unsure of/about, have misgivings about.
OPPOSITES trust.

disturb verb **1** *somewhere where we won't be disturbed:* interrupt, intrude on, butt in on, barge in on, distract, disrupt, bother, trouble, pester, harass. **2** *don't disturb his papers:* move, rearrange, mix up, interfere with, mess up, muddle. **3** *he wasn't disturbed by the allegations:* perturb, trouble, concern, worry, upset, fluster, disconcert, dismay, alarm, distress, unsettle.
OPPOSITES calm, reassure.

disturbance noun **1** *a disturbance to local residents:* disruption, distraction, interference, inconvenience, upset, annoyance, irritation, intrusion. **2** *disturbances in the town centre:* riot, fracas, brawl, street fight, free-for-all, commotion, disorder.
OPPOSITES order.

disturbed adjective **1** *disturbed sleep:* disrupted, interrupted, fitful, intermittent, broken. **2** *disturbed children:* troubled, distressed, upset, distraught, unbalanced, unstable, disordered, dysfunctional, maladjusted, neurotic, unhinged; informal screwed up.
OPPOSITES uninterrupted, well adjusted, sane.

ditch noun a narrow channel dug to hold or carry water. •verb **1** informal abandon or get rid of. **2** (of an aircraft) come down in a forced landing on the sea.

dither verb (**dithers**, **dithering**, **dithered**) be indecisive.

ditto noun **1** the same thing again (used in lists). **2** a symbol consisting of two apostrophes (״) placed under the item to be repeated.

ditty noun (plural **ditties**) a short, simple song.

diuretic /dy-uh-**ret**-ik/ adjective (of a drug) making you pass more urine.

diurnal /dy-**er**-n'l/ adjective **1** relating to or during the daytime. **2** daily.

diva /**dee**-vuh/ noun a famous female opera singer.

Divali ⇒ **DIWALI**.

divan noun **1** a bed consisting of a base and mattress but no headboard. **2** a long, low sofa without a back or arms.

dive verb (**dives**, **diving**, **dived**; US past and past participle also **dove** /dohv/) **1** plunge head first into water. **2** (of a submarine or swimmer) go under water. **3** plunge steeply downwards through the air. **4** move quickly or suddenly in a downward direction or under cover. •noun **1** an act of diving. **2** informal a disreputable nightclub or bar.

□ **dive-bomb** bomb a target while diving

steeply in an aircraft.

diver noun **1** a person who dives under water. **2** a large diving waterbird.

diverge verb (**diverges**, **diverging**, **diverged**) **1** (of a route or line) separate from another route and go in a different direction. **2** be different.

■ **divergence** noun **divergent** adjective.

diverse adjective widely varied.

diversify verb (**diversifies**, **diversifying**, **diversified**) **1** make or become more varied. **2** (of a company) expand its range of products or area of operation.

■ **diversification** noun.

diversion noun **1** the action of diverting something from its course. **2** Brit. an alternative route used when a road is closed. **3** something intended to distract attention. **4** a pastime or other pleasant activity.

■ **diversionary** adjective.

diversity noun (plural **diversities**) **1** the state of being varied. **2** a range of different things.

divert verb **1** change the direction or course of. **2** distract a person or their attention. **3** amuse or entertain.

divest verb **1** (**divest someone/thing of**) deprive someone or something of. **2** (**divest yourself of**) remove or get rid of.

divide verb (**divides**, **dividing**, **divided**)

ditch noun trench, trough, channel, dyke, drain, gutter, gully, watercourse.

dive verb **1** *they dived into the clear water* | *the plane was diving towards the ground:* plunge, nosedive, jump, plummet, fall, drop, pitch. **2** *they dived for cover:* leap, jump, lunge, throw/fling yourself, go headlong, duck.
•noun **1** *a dive into the pool:* plunge, nosedive, jump, fall, drop, swoop. **2** *a sideways dive:* lunge, spring, jump, leap.

diverge verb **1** *the two roads diverged:* separate, part, fork, divide, split, bifurcate, go in different directions. **2** *areas where our views diverge:* differ, be different, be dissimilar, disagree, be at variance/odds, conflict, clash.
OPPOSITES converge, agree.

diverse adjective various, sundry, varied, varying, miscellaneous, assorted, mixed, diversified, divergent, different, differing, distinct, unlike, dissimilar.
OPPOSITES similar.

diversion noun **1** *the diversion of the river:* re-routing, redirection, deflection, deviation, divergence. **2** *traffic diversions:* detour, deviation, alternative route. **3** *the noise created a diversion:* distraction,

disturbance, smokescreen; informal red herring. **4** *a city full of diversions:* entertainment, amusement, pastime, delight, fun, recreation, pleasure.

diversity noun variety, miscellany, assortment, mixture, mix, range, array, multiplicity, variation, diverseness, difference.
OPPOSITES uniformity.

divert verb **1** *a plan to divert Siberia's rivers:* re-route, redirect, change the course of, deflect, channel. **2** *he diverted her from her studies:* distract, sidetrack, disturb, draw away, put off. **3** *the story diverted them:* amuse, entertain, distract, delight, enchant, interest, fascinate, absorb, engross, rivet, grip.

divide verb **1** *he divided his kingdom into four:* split (up), cut up, carve up, dissect, bisect, halve, quarter. **2** *a curtain divided her cabin from the galley:* separate, segregate, partition, screen off, section off, split off. **3** *the stairs divide at the mezzanine:* diverge, separate, part, branch (off), fork, split (in two). **4** *Jack divided the cash:* share out, ration out, parcel out, deal out, dole out, dish out, distribute. **5** *he aimed to divide his opponents:* disunite,

d

1 separate into parts. **2** share out. **3** cause disagreement between people or groups. **4** form a boundary between. **5** find how many times one number contains another.
● **noun** a difference or disagreement between two groups.

dividend noun **1** a sum of money that is divided among a number of people, such as the part of a company's profits paid to its shareholders. **2** (**dividends**) benefits.

divider noun **1** a screen that divides a room into separate parts. **2** (**dividers**) a measuring compass.

divination noun the use of supernatural means to find out about the future or the unknown.

divine¹ adjective **1** having to do with God or a god. **2** informal excellent.
■ **divinely** adverb.

divine² verb (**divines, divining, divined**) **1** discover by guesswork or intuition. **2** have supernatural insight into the future.
■ **diviner** noun.

divinity noun (plural **divinities**) **1** the state of being divine. **2** a god or goddess. **3** the study of religion; theology.

divisible adjective **1** capable of being divided. **2** (of a number) containing another number a number of times without a remainder.

division noun **1** the action of dividing, or the state of being divided. **2** each of the parts into which something is divided. **3** a major section of an organization. **4** a

number of sports teams or competitors grouped to compete against each other. **5** a partition.
□ **division sign** the sign ÷, placed between two numbers showing that the first is to be divided by the second, as in $6 \div 3 = 2$.
■ **divisional** adjective.

divisive adjective causing disagreement or hostility between people.

divorce noun the legal ending of a marriage. ● **verb** (**divorces, divorcing, divorced**) **1** legally end your marriage with. **2** (**divorce something from**) separate something from.

divorcee noun a divorced person.

divot /di-vuht/ noun a piece of turf cut out of the ground.

divulge verb (**divulges, divulging, divulged**) reveal information.

Diwali or **Divali** /di-wah-li/ noun a Hindu festival at which lights, candles, etc. are lit, held in October and November.

DIY abbreviation Brit. do it yourself.

dizzy adjective (**dizzier, dizziest**) having a sensation of spinning around and losing your balance. ● **verb** (**dizzies, dizzying, dizzied**) make unsteady or confused.
■ **dizzily** adverb **dizziness** noun.

DJ noun a person who introduces and plays recorded pop music on radio or at a club.

DNA noun a substance carrying genetic information that is found in the cells of nearly all animals and plants.

do verb (**does, doing, did**; past participle **done**)

THESAURUS

drive apart, drive a wedge between, break up, split (up), separate, isolate, alienate.
OPPOSITES unify, converge, collect, unite.

divine¹ adjective **1** *a divine being:* godly, angelic, heavenly, celestial, holy. **2** *divine worship:* religious, holy, sacred, sanctified, consecrated, blessed, devotional.
OPPOSITES mortal, infernal.

divine² verb *Fergus divined how afraid she was:* guess, surmise, deduce, infer, discern, discover, perceive; informal figure (out); Brit. informal suss.

division noun **1** *the division of the island / cell division:* dividing (up), breaking up, break-up, carving up, splitting, dissection, partitioning, separation, segregation. **2** *the division of his estates:* sharing out, dividing up, parcelling out, dishing out, allocation, allotment, splitting up, carving up. **3** *the division between nomadic and urban cultures:* dividing line, divide, boundary, border, demarcation line, gap, gulf. **4** *each class is split into nine divisions:* section, subsection, subdivision, category, class, group, grouping, set. **5** *an independent division of the executive:*

department, branch, arm, wing. **6** *the causes of social division:* disunity, disunion, conflict, discord, disagreement, alienation, isolation.
OPPOSITES unification, unity.

divorce noun **1** *she wants a divorce:* dissolution, annulment, decree nisi, separation. **2** *a growing divorce between the church and people:* separation, division, split, disunity, alienation, schism, gulf.
OPPOSITES unity.
● **verb 1** *her parents have divorced:* split up, get a divorce, separate, end your marriage. **2** *religion cannot be divorced from morality:* separate, divide, detach, isolate, alienate, set apart, cut off.

divulge verb disclose, reveal, tell, communicate, pass on, publish, give away, let slip.
OPPOSITES conceal.

dizzy adjective giddy, light-headed, faint, unsteady, shaky, muzzy, wobbly; informal woozy.

do verb **1** *she does most of the work:* carry out, undertake, discharge, execute, perform, accomplish, achieve, bring about,

1 carry out or complete an action, duty, or task. **2** have a specified amount of success: *the team did well.* **3** make or provide something. **4** have a particular result or effect on. **5** work at for a living or take as a subject of study. **6** be suitable or acceptable. **7** informal swindle someone.
•**auxiliary verb 1** used before a verb in questions and negative statements. **2** used to refer back to a verb already mentioned. **3** used in commands, or to give emphasis to a verb. •**noun** (plural **dos** or **do's**) Brit. informal a party or other social event.
□ **do away with** informal put an end to or kill. **do something up 1** fasten or wrap something. **2** informal renovate or redecorate a room or building.

Dobermann or **Dobermann pinscher** /doh-ber-muhn **pin**-sher/ **noun** a large breed of dog with strong jaws.

docile **adjective** quiet and easy to control.
■ **docilely** adverb **docility** noun.

dock[1] **noun** an enclosed area of water in a port for loading, unloading, and repairing ships. •**verb 1** (of a ship) come into a dock. **2** (of a spacecraft) join with a space station or another spacecraft in space.

dock[2] **noun** the enclosure in a criminal court for a person on trial.

dock[3] **noun** a weed with broad leaves.

dock[4] **verb 1** take away money from a person's wages before they are paid. **2** cut short an animal's tail.

docker **noun** a person employed in a port to load and unload ships.

docket **noun** Brit. a document accompanying a batch of goods that lists its contents, shows that duty has been paid, etc.

dockyard **noun** an area with docks and equipment for repairing and building ships.

doctor **noun 1** a person who is qualified to practise medicine. **2** (**Doctor**) a person who holds the highest university degree. •**verb 1** change something in order to deceive people. **2** add a harmful or strong ingredient to food or drink. **3** Brit. remove the sexual organs of an animal.

doctoral **adjective** relating to a doctorate.

doctorate **noun** the highest degree awarded by a university.

doctrinaire **adjective** very strict in applying beliefs or principles.

doctrine /dok-trin/ **noun** a set of beliefs or principles held by a religious or political group.
■ **doctrinal** /dok-**try**-n'l/ adjective.

document **noun** a piece of written, printed, or electronic material that provides information or evidence. •**verb** record something in written or other form.

documentary **noun** (plural **documentaries**) a film or television or radio programme giving a factual report, using film, photographs, and sound recordings of real events. •**adjective** consisting of documents: *documentary evidence.*

documentation **noun** documents providing official information, evidence, or instructions.

dodder **verb** be slow and unsteady.
■ **doddery** adjective.

doddle **noun** Brit. informal a very easy task.

dodecagon /doh-**dek**-uh-guhn/ **noun** a figure with twelve straight sides and angles.

dodecahedron /doh-dek-uh-**hee**-druhn/ **noun** (plural **dodecahedra** or **dodecahedrons**)

d

THESAURUS

engineer; informal pull off. **2** *they can do as they please:* act, behave, conduct yourself. **3** *regular coffee will do:* suffice, be adequate, be satisfactory, fill/fit the bill, serve. **4** *a portrait I am doing:* make, create, produce, work on, design, manufacture.
□ **do away with** *they want to do away with the old customs:* **abolish,** get rid of, eliminate, discontinue, stop, end, terminate, drop, abandon, give up; informal scrap. **do without forgo,** dispense with, abstain from, refrain from, eschew, give up, cut out, renounce, manage without.

dock[1] **noun** *his boat was moored at the dock:* harbour, marina, port, wharf, quay, pier, jetty, landing stage.
•**verb** moor, berth, put in, tie up, anchor.

dock[2] **verb 1** *they docked the money from his salary:* deduct, subtract, remove, debit, take off/away; informal knock off. **2** *workers* *had their pay docked:* reduce, cut, decrease. **3** *the dog's tail was docked:* cut off, cut short, shorten, crop, lop.

doctor **noun** physician, medical practitioner, general practitioner, GP, clinician, consultant; informal doc, medic; Brit. informal quack.
•**verb 1** *he doctored Stephen's drink:* adulterate, tamper with, lace; informal spike. **2** *the reports have been doctored:* falsify, tamper with, interfere with, alter, change, forge, fake; Brit. informal fiddle.

doctrine **noun** creed, credo, dogma, belief, teaching, ideology, tenet, maxim, canon, principle.

document **noun** *a legal document:* paper, certificate, deed, form, contract, record, agreement, report.
•**verb** *its history is well documented:* record, register, report, log, chronicle, record, authenticate, verify.

d

a three-dimensional shape with twelve faces.

dodge verb (**dodges, dodging, dodged**) **1** avoid something by a sudden quick movement. **2** avoid something in a cunning or dishonest way. • noun an act of avoiding something.
■ **dodger** noun.

dodgem noun a small electric car driven at a funfair with the aim of bumping other such cars.

dodgy adjective Brit. informal **1** dishonest. **2** risky. **3** not good or reliable.

dodo noun (plural **dodos** or **dodoes**) a large extinct bird that could not fly, formerly found on Mauritius.

doe noun **1** a female deer or reindeer. **2** the female of some other animals, such as a rabbit or hare.

does 3rd person singular present of **DO**.

doesn't short form does not.

doff verb remove your hat when greeting someone.

dog noun **1** a four-legged meat-eating animal, kept as a pet or used for work or hunting. **2** any member of the dog family, such as the wolf or fox. **3** the male of an animal of the dog family. • verb (**dogs, dogging, dogged**) **1** follow someone closely and persistently. **2** cause continual trouble for.
□ **a dog in the manger** a person who stops other people having things that they do not need themselves. **dog collar** informal a white upright collar worn by Christian priests. **dog-eared** (of a book) having the corners of the pages curled or folded over from constant use. **dog-end** informal a cigarette end. **dog-leg** a sharp bend. **go to the dogs** informal get much worse.

doge /dohj/ noun (in the past) the chief magistrate of Venice or Genoa.

dogfight noun a close combat between military aircraft.

dogfish noun (plural **dogfish** or **dogfishes**) a

small shark with a long tail.

dogged /dog-gid/ adjective very persistent.
■ **doggedly** adverb.

doggerel noun badly written verse.

doggo adverb (**lie doggo**) informal hide by keeping still and quiet.

doggy-paddle noun a simple swimming stroke like that of a dog.

doghouse noun N. Amer. a dog's kennel.
□ **in the doghouse** informal in disgrace.

dogma noun a firm set of principles.

dogmatic adjective firmly putting forward your own opinions and not willing to accept those of other people.
■ **dogmatically** adverb.

dogsbody noun (plural **dogsbodies**) Brit. informal a person who is given boring tasks that no one else wants to do.

doily noun (plural **doilies**) a small decorative mat made of lace or paper.

doings plural noun a person's actions or activities.

doldrums plural noun (**the doldrums**) a state of being inactive or feeling depressed.

dole noun Brit. informal money paid by the state to unemployed people. • verb (**doles, doling, doled**) (**dole something out**) distribute something.

doleful adjective sad or depressing.
■ **dolefully** adverb.

doll noun a small model of a human figure, used as a child's toy. • verb (**be dolled up**) informal be dressed in smart or fancy clothes.

dollar noun the chief unit of money in the US, Canada, Australia, and some other countries.

dollop informal noun a shapeless mass or lump. • verb (**dollops, dolloping, dolloped**) casually add or serve out a mass of something.

dolmen noun a prehistoric tomb with a large flat stone laid on upright ones.

dolomite /dol-uh-myt/ noun a mineral or

THESAURUS

dodge verb **1** *he could easily dodge the two coppers:* elude, evade, avoid, escape, run away from, lose, shake (off); informal give someone the slip. **2** *the minister tried to dodge the debate:* avoid, evade, get out of, back out of, sidestep; informal duck, wriggle out of. **3** *she dodged into a telephone booth:* dart, bolt, dive, slip.
• noun *a clever dodge | a tax dodge:* ruse, ploy, scheme, tactic, stratagem, subterfuge, trick, hoax, cheat, deception, fraud; informal scam; Brit. informal wheeze; Austral. informal rort.

dog noun hound, canine, man's best friend, mongrel; informal pooch, mutt; Austral. informal bitzer.
• verb *the scheme was dogged by bad*

weather: plague, beset, bedevil, blight, trouble.

dogged adjective tenacious, determined, resolute, stubborn, obstinate, purposeful, persistent, persevering, single-minded, tireless.
OPPOSITES half-hearted, tentative.

dogmatic adjective opinionated, assertive, insistent, emphatic, adamant, doctrinaire, authoritarian, imperious, dictatorial, uncompromising.

dole verb *waitresses doled out plates of chicken:* distribute, share out, divide up, allocate, deal out, dispense, hand out, give out, dish out.

rock that consists of a carbonate of calcium and magnesium.

dolour /dol-er/ (US spelling **dolor**) noun literary great sorrow or distress.
■ **dolorous** adjective.

dolphin noun a small whale with a beak-like snout and a curved fin on the back.

dolphinarium noun (plural **dolphinariums** or **dolphinaria**) an aquarium in which dolphins are kept and trained for public entertainment.

dolt noun a stupid person.

domain noun **1** an area controlled by a ruler or government. **2** an area of activity or knowledge. **3** a set of websites whose addresses end with the same group of letters.

dome noun **1** a rounded roof with a circular base. **2** a stadium or other building with a rounded roof.
■ **domed** adjective.

domestic adjective **1** relating to a home or family. **2** for use in the home. **3** (of an animal) tame and kept by humans. **4** existing or occurring within a country; not foreign.
■ **domestically** adverb.

domesticate verb (**domesticates, domesticating, domesticated**) tame an animal and keep it as a pet or on a farm.
■ **domestication** noun.

domesticity noun home life.

domicile /dom-i-syl/ formal or Law noun **1** the country in which a person lives permanently. **2** a person's home. •verb (**be domiciled**) be living in a particular country or place.

dominant adjective **1** most important, powerful, or influential. **2** (of a gene) appearing in offspring even if a contrary gene is also inherited.
■ **dominance** noun **dominantly** adverb.

dominate verb (**dominates, dominating, dominated**) **1** have a very strong influence over. **2** be the most important or noticeable person or thing in.
■ **domination** noun.

domineering adjective arrogantly trying to control other people.

dominion noun **1** supreme power or control. **2** the territory of a ruler or government.

domino noun (plural **dominoes**) any of twenty-eight small oblong pieces marked with 0–6 pips in each half, used in the game of **dominoes**.

don[1] noun a university teacher.

don[2] verb (**dons, donning, donned**) put on an item of clothing.

donate verb (**donates, donating, donated**) give something to a charity or other good cause.

donation noun something given to a charity or other good cause.

done past participle of **DO**. •adjective **1** cooked thoroughly. **2** no longer happening or existing. **3** informal socially acceptable: *the done thing.*

doner kebab /doh-ner, don-er/ noun a Turkish dish of spiced lamb cooked on a spit and served in slices.

donkey noun (plural **donkeys**) a domesticated animal of the horse family with long ears and a braying call.
□ **donkey jacket** Brit. a heavy jacket with a patch of waterproof material across the shoulders. **donkey's years** informal a very long time.

domain noun **1** *they extended their domain:* realm, kingdom, empire, dominion, province, territory, land. **2** *the domain of art:* field, area, sphere, discipline, province, world.

domestic adjective **1** *domestic commitments:* family, home, household. **2** *she was not at all domestic:* domesticated, homely, home-loving. **3** *domestic animals:* tame, pet, domesticated, household. **4** *the domestic car industry:* national, state, home, internal.

dominant adjective **1** *the dominant classes:* ruling, governing, controlling, presiding, commanding. **2** *he has a dominant personality:* assertive, authoritative, forceful, domineering, commanding, controlling, pushy. **3** *the dominant issues in psychology:* main, principal, prime, chief, primary, central, key, crucial, core.
OPPOSITES subservient, subsidiary.

dominate verb **1** *the Russians dominated Iran in the nineteenth century:* control, influence, command, be in charge of, rule, govern, direct. **2** *the village is dominated by the viaduct:* overlook, command, tower above/over, loom over.

domination noun control, power, command, authority, dominion, rule, supremacy, superiority, ascendancy, sway, mastery.

don verb put on, get dressed in, dress (yourself) in, get into, slip into/on, change into.

donate verb give, contribute, gift, subscribe, grant, present, endow; informal chip in, stump up.

donation noun gift, contribution, subscription, present, handout, grant, offering.

d

donor noun a person who donates something.

don't short form do not.

donut US spelling of DOUGHNUT.

doodle verb (doodles, doodling, doodled) scribble absent-mindedly. • noun a drawing made absent-mindedly.

doom noun death, destruction, or another terrible fate. • verb (be doomed) be fated to fail or be destroyed.

doomsday noun 1 the last day of the world's existence. 2 (in religious belief) the day of the Last Judgement.

door noun a movable barrier at the entrance to a building, room, vehicle, etc.
□ out of doors in or into the open air.

doorman noun (plural doormen) a man who is on duty at the entrance to a large building.

doormat noun 1 a mat placed in a doorway for wiping your shoes. 2 informal a person who lets other people control them.

doorstep noun a step leading up to the outer door of a house.

doorstop noun an object that keeps a door open or in place.

doorway noun an entrance with a door.

dope noun 1 informal an illegal drug, especially cannabis. 2 a drug used to improve the performance of an athlete, racehorse, or greyhound. 3 informal a stupid person. • verb (dopes, doping, doped) give a drug to.

dopey or **dopy** adjective informal 1 in a semi-conscious state from sleepiness or a drug. 2 stupid.

doppelgänger /dop-puhl-gang-er/ noun a ghost or double of a living person.

Doppler effect noun an apparent change in the frequency of sound or light waves as the source and the observer move towards or away from each other.

dormant adjective 1 (of an animal) in a deep sleep. 2 (of a plant or bud) alive but not growing. 3 (of a volcano) temporarily inactive.
■ dormancy noun.

dormer window noun a window set vertically into a sloping roof.

dormitory noun (plural dormitories) a bedroom for a number of people in an institution. • adjective (of a town) from which people travel to work in a nearby city.

dormouse noun (plural dormice) a small mouse-like rodent with a bushy tail.

dorsal adjective relating to the upper side or back.

dose noun 1 a quantity of a medicine taken at one time. 2 an amount of radiation absorbed at one time. • verb (doses, dosing, dosed) give a dose of medicine to.
■ dosage noun.

dosh noun Brit. informal money.

doss verb Brit. informal 1 sleep in an uncomfortable place or without a proper bed. 2 spend time in a lazy or aimless way.
■ dosser noun.

dossier /doss-i-er, doss-i-ay/ noun a collection of documents about a person or subject.

dot noun a small round mark or spot. • verb (dots, dotting, dotted) 1 mark with a dot or dots. 2 cover an area with a scattering of something.
□ dot-com a company that carries out its business on the Internet. on the dot informal exactly on time.

dotage /doh-tij/ noun the period of life in which a person is old and weak.

dotard noun an old person who is weak or senile.

dote verb (dotes, doting, doted) (dote on) love someone very much, ignoring their faults.

dotty adjective Brit. informal slightly mad or eccentric.

THESAURUS

donor noun giver, contributor, benefactor, benefactress, subscriber, supporter, backer, patron, sponsor.
OPPOSITES beneficiary.

doom noun prepare to meet your doom: destruction, downfall, ruin, extinction, annihilation, death, nemesis.
• verb they were doomed to die: destine, fate, predestine, preordain, mean, condemn, sentence.

doomed adjective ill-fated, ill-starred, cursed, jinxed, damned.

dope verb 1 the horse was doped: drug, tamper with, interfere with, sedate; Brit. informal nobble. 2 they doped his drink: add drugs to, tamper with, adulterate, lace; informal spike, doctor.

dose noun a dose of medicine: measure, portion, draught, dosage.
• verb he dosed himself with vitamins: drug, fill (up), pump, prime, load, stuff, cram.

dot noun a pattern of dots: spot, speck, fleck, speckle, full stop, decimal point.
• verb 1 spots of rain dotted his shirt: spot, fleck, mark, spatter. 2 restaurants are dotted around the site: scatter, pepper, sprinkle, strew, spread.

dote verb his grandmother dotes on him: adore, love dearly, be devoted to, idolize, treasure, cherish, worship.

double adjective **1** consisting of two equal, identical, or similar parts or things. **2** having twice the usual size, quantity, or strength. **3** designed to be used by two people. **4** having two different roles or meanings. •adverb twice the amount or quantity. •noun **1** a thing which is twice as large as usual or is made up of two parts. **2** a person who looks exactly like another. **3** (**doubles**) a game involving sides made up of two players. •verb (**doubles**, **doubling**, **doubled**) **1** make or become double. **2** fold or bend over on itself. **3** (**double up**) curl up with pain or laughter. **4** (**double as**) be used in or play a different role.
□ **at the double** very fast. **double agent** an agent who pretends to act as a spy for one country while in fact acting for its enemy. **double back** go back in the direction you have come from. **double-barrelled** Brit. (of a surname) having two parts joined by a hyphen. **double bass** the largest and lowest-pitched instrument of the violin family. **double-breasted** (of a jacket or coat) having a large overlap at the front and two rows of buttons. **double chin** a roll of flesh below a person's chin. **double cream** Brit. thick cream with a high fat content. **double-cross** betray or deceive a person that you are supposed to be helping. **double-dealing** deceitful behaviour. **double-decker** a bus with two floors. **double Dutch** Brit. informal language that is hard to understand. **double glazing** windows having two layers of glass with a space between them. **double-jointed** (of a person) having unusually flexible joints. **double standard** a rule or principle applied unfairly in different ways to different people. **double take** a second reaction to something unexpected, immediately after your first one.
■ **doubly** adverb.

double entendre /doo-b'l on-**ton**-druh/ noun (plural **double entendres** /doo-b'l on-**ton**-druh/) a word or phrase with two meanings, one of which is usually rude.

doublet noun historical a man's short close-fitting padded jacket.

doubloon /dub-**loon**/ noun historical a Spanish gold coin.

doubt noun a feeling of uncertainty. •verb **1** feel uncertain about something. **2** disbelieve or mistrust someone. □ **no doubt** certainly; probably.

doubtful adjective **1** feeling uncertain. **2** causing uncertainty. **3** not likely or probable.
■ **doubtfully** adverb.

doubtless adverb very probably.

douche /doosh/ noun a jet of water applied to part of the body.

dough noun **1** a thick mixture of flour and liquid, for baking into bread or pastry. **2** informal money.
■ **doughy** adjective.

doughnut (US spelling **donut**) noun a small fried cake or ring of sweetened dough.

doughty /**dow**-ti/ adjective old use brave and

double adjective *a double garage:* **dual**, duplex, twin, binary, duplicate, coupled, matching, twofold, in pairs.
OPPOSITES single.
•noun *it must be her double:* **lookalike**, twin, clone, duplicate, exact likeness, replica, copy, facsimile, doppelgänger; informal spitting image, dead ringer.

doubt noun **1** *there was some doubt as to the caller's identity:* **uncertainty**, confusion, controversy. **2** *a weak leader racked by doubt:* **indecision**, hesitation, uncertainty, insecurity, hesitancy, vacillation. **3** *there is doubt about their motives:* **scepticism**, distrust, mistrust, suspicion, cynicism, wariness, reservations, misgivings, suspicions.
OPPOSITES certainty, conviction, trust.
•verb *they doubted my story:* **disbelieve**, distrust, mistrust, suspect, be suspicious of, have misgivings about.
OPPOSITES trust.
□ **in doubt 1** *the outcome is in doubt:* **doubtful**, uncertain, unconfirmed, unknown, undecided, unresolved, in the balance, up in the air; informal iffy. **2** *if you* are in doubt, ask for advice: **irresolute**, hesitant, doubtful, unsure, uncertain, in two minds, undecided, in a quandary/ dilemma. **no doubt doubtless**, undoubtedly, indubitably, without (a) doubt, unquestionably, undeniably, clearly, plainly, obviously, patently.

doubtful adjective **1** *I was doubtful about going:* **hesitant**, in doubt, unsure, uncertain, in two minds, in a quandary, in a dilemma. **2** *it is doubtful whether he will come:* **in doubt**, uncertain, open to question, unsure, debatable, up in the air. **3** *the whole trip is looking rather doubtful:* **unlikely**, improbable. **4** *they are doubtful of the methods used:* **distrustful**, mistrustful, suspicious, wary, chary, leery, sceptical. **5** *this decision is of doubtful validity:* **questionable**, arguable, debatable, controversial, contentious.
OPPOSITES confident, certain, probable, trusting.

doubtless adverb **undoubtedly**, no doubt, unquestionably, indisputably, undeniably, certainly, surely, of course.

determined.

dour /doo-er, dow-er/ adjective very severe, stern, or gloomy.

douse verb (**douses, dousing, doused**) **1** drench with liquid. **2** extinguish a fire.

dove[1] /duv/ noun **1** a bird with a cooing voice, very similar to a pigeon. **2** (in politics) a person who is in favour of a policy of peace and negotiation.

dove[2] US past and past participle of DIVE.

dovecote or **dovecot** /duv-kot/ noun a shelter with nest holes for domesticated pigeons.

dovetail verb fit together neatly. • noun a wedge-shaped joint formed by interlocking two pieces of wood.

dowager /dow-uh-jer/ noun **1** a widow who holds a title that belonged to her late husband. **2** a dignified elderly woman.

dowdy adjective unfashionable and dull in appearance.

dowel noun a peg used to hold together parts of a structure.

down[1] adverb **1** towards, in, or at a lower place, position, or level. **2** to a smaller amount or size. **3** in or into a weaker or worse position or condition. **4** away from a central place or the north. **5** from an earlier to a later point in time or order. **6** in or into writing. **7** (of a computer system) out of action. • preposition **1** from a higher to a lower point of. **2** at or to a point further along the course of. • adjective **1** directed or moving downwards. **2** unhappy or depressed. • verb informal drink something quickly.
□ **down and out** homeless and without money. **down at heel** shabby because of a lack of money. **down payment** an initial payment made when buying something on credit. **down-to-earth** practical and realistic. **down under** informal Australia and New Zealand.

down[2] noun fine, soft feathers or hairs.

downbeat adjective **1** gloomy. **2** relaxed and low-key.

downcast adjective **1** (of eyes) looking downwards. **2** unhappy; discouraged.

downer noun informal **1** a tranquillizing or depressant drug. **2** a depressing experience.

downfall noun a loss of power, wealth, or status.

downgrade verb (**downgrades, downgrading, downgraded**) bring someone down to a lower rank or level of importance.

downhearted adjective unhappy; discouraged.

downhill adverb & adjective **1** towards the bottom of a slope. **2** into a steadily worsening situation.

download verb copy data from one computer system to another. • noun data that has been downloaded.

downmarket adjective chiefly Brit. cheap and of low quality.

downplay verb make something appear less important than it really is.

downpour noun a heavy fall of rain.

downright adjective utter; complete. • adverb extremely.

downs noun gently rolling hills.

downshift verb change to a job or way of life that is simpler and less stressful.

downside noun the negative aspect of something.

Down's syndrome noun a medical condition in which a person is born with physical abnormalities and an intellectual ability that is lower than average.

downstairs adverb & adjective on or to a lower floor.

downstream or **downriver** adverb in the direction in which a stream or river flows.

downtown adjective & adverb chiefly N. Amer. in, to, or towards the central or main business area of a city.

downtrodden adjective treated badly by those in power.

downturn noun a decline in economic or other activity.

downward adjective & adverb towards a lower point or level.
■ **downwards** adverb.

downwind adverb in the direction in which the wind is blowing.

downy adjective covered with fine soft hair or feathers.

THESAURUS

douse verb **1** *a mob doused the thieves with petrol:* drench, soak, saturate, wet. **2** *a guard doused the flames:* extinguish, put out, quench, smother.

downfall noun ruin, ruination, undoing, defeat, overthrow, destruction, annihilation, end, collapse, fall, crash, failure.
OPPOSITES rise.

downgrade verb demote, reduce, relegate.
OPPOSITES promote.

downright adjective *downright lies:* complete, total, absolute, utter, thorough, out-and-out, outright, sheer, arrant, pure. • adverb *that's downright dangerous:* thoroughly, utterly, positively, profoundly, really, completely, totally, entirely.

dowry noun (plural **dowries**) property or money brought by a bride to her husband on their marriage.

dowse verb (**dowses, dowsing, dowsed**) search for underground water or minerals with a pointer which is supposedly moved by unseen influences.

doyen /doy-yen/ noun (feminine **doyenne** /doy-yen/) the most respected or prominent person in a field.

doze verb (**dozes, dozing, dozed**) sleep lightly. • noun a short, light sleep.
■ **dozy** adjective.

dozen noun 1 (plural **dozen**) a group or set of twelve. 2 (**dozens**) a lot.

DPhil abbreviation Doctor of Philosophy.

Dr abbreviation Doctor.

drab adjective (**drabber, drabbest**) dull and uninteresting.
■ **drabness** noun.

drachma /drak-muh/ noun (plural **drachmas** or **drachmae** /drak-mee/) the former basic unit of money in Greece.

draconian /druh-koh-ni-uhn/ adjective (of laws) very harsh and severe.

draft noun 1 a rough early version of a piece of writing. 2 a written order requesting a bank to pay a specific sum of money. 3 (**the draft**) US compulsory recruitment for military service. 4 US spelling of **DRAUGHT**.
• verb 1 prepare a rough version of a piece of writing. 2 select someone for a particular purpose. 3 (**be drafted**) US recruit someone for compulsory military service.

drafty US spelling of **DRAUGHTY**.

drag verb (**drags, dragging, dragged**) 1 pull along forcefully, roughly, or with difficulty. 2 trail along the ground. 3 (of time) pass slowly. 4 (**drag something out**) make something last longer than necessary. 5 move an image across a computer screen using a mouse. 6 search the bottom of an area of water with hooks or nets. • noun 1 informal a boring or annoying person or thing. 2 a person or thing that makes progress difficult. 3 informal an act of inhaling smoke from a cigarette. 4 the force exerted by air or water to slow down a moving object.
◻ **drag race** a short race between two cars from a standstill. **in drag** (of a man) wearing women's clothes.

dragnet noun a net drawn through water or across ground to trap fish or game.

dragon noun a mythical monster that can breathe out fire.

dragonfly noun (plural **dragonflies**) an insect with a long body and two pairs of large transparent wings.

dragoon noun a member of any of several British cavalry regiments. • verb force someone into doing something.

drain verb 1 make something empty or dry by removing the liquid from it. 2 (of liquid) run off or out. 3 make someone feel weak or tired. 4 use up a resource. 5 drink the entire contents of a glass or cup. • noun 1 a channel or pipe for carrying off rainwater or liquid waste. 2 a thing that uses up a resource or strength.
◻ **draining board** Brit. a surface next to a sink, on which crockery is left after it has been washed.
■ **drainage** noun.

drainpipe noun 1 a pipe for carrying off rainwater from a building. 2 (**drainpipes**) trousers with very narrow legs.

drake noun a male duck.

dram noun a small drink of spirits.

drama noun 1 a play. 2 plays as a literary

THESAURUS

drab adjective 1 *a drab interior:* colourless, grey, dull, washed out, dingy, dreary, dismal, cheerless, gloomy, sombre. 2 *a drab existence:* uninteresting, dull, boring, tedious, monotonous, dry, dreary.
OPPOSITES bright, cheerful, interesting.

draft noun 1 *the first draft of his speech:* version, sketch, attempt, effort, outline, plan. 2 *a banker's draft:* cheque, order, money order, bill of exchange.

drag verb *she dragged the chair backwards:* haul, pull, tug, heave, lug, draw, trail.
• noun 1 *the drag from the parachute:* pull, resistance, tug. 2 (informal) *work can be a drag:* bore, nuisance, bother, trouble, pest, annoyance, trial; informal pain (in the neck), bind, headache, hassle.

drain verb 1 *a valve for draining the tank:* empty (out), void, clear (out), evacuate, unload. 2 *drain off any surplus liquid:* draw off, extract, siphon off, pour out, pour off, bleed, tap, filter, discharge. 3 *the water drained away to the sea:* flow, pour, trickle, stream, run, rush, gush, flood, surge, leak, ooze, seep, dribble. 4 *more people would just drain our resources:* use up, exhaust, deplete, consume, expend, get through, sap, milk, bleed. 5 *he drained his drink:* drink (up/down), gulp (down), guzzle, quaff, swallow, finish off, toss off; informal sink, down, swig, swill (down), knock back.
OPPOSITES fill.
• noun 1 *the drain filled with water:* sewer, channel, ditch, culvert, duct, pipe, gutter. 2 *a drain on the battery:* strain, pressure, burden, load, demand.

drama noun 1 *a television drama:* play,

d

form. **3** an exciting series of events.

dramatic adjective **1** relating to drama. **2** sudden and striking. **3** exciting or impressive. • noun (**dramatics**) the practice of acting in and presenting plays.
■ **dramatically** adverb.

dramatist noun a person who writes plays.

dramatize or **dramatise** verb (**dramatizes, dramatizing, dramatized**) **1** present a novel or story as a play. **2** make something seem more exciting or serious than it really is.
■ **dramatization** noun.

drank past of **DRINK**.

drape verb (**drapes, draping, draped**) **1** arrange cloth or clothing loosely on or round something. **2** rest part of your body on something in a relaxed way. • noun (**drapes**) N. Amer. long curtains.

draper noun Brit. dated a person who sells fabrics.

drapery noun (plural **draperies**) curtains or fabric hanging in loose folds.

drastic adjective having a strong or far-reaching effect.

■ **drastically** adverb.

draught (US spelling **draft**) noun **1** a current of cool air indoors. **2** an act of drinking or breathing in. **3** old use a quantity of a medicinal liquid. **4** the depth of water needed to float a particular ship. **5** (**draughts**) Brit. a game played on a chequered board. • verb = **DRAFT**. • adjective **1** (of beer) served from a cask. **2** (of an animal) used for pulling heavy loads.

draughtsman noun (plural **draughtsmen**) **1** a person who makes detailed technical plans or drawings. **2** an artist skilled in drawing.

draughty (US spelling **drafty**) adjective uncomfortable because of draughts of cold air.

draw verb (**draws, drawing, drew**; past participle **drawn**) **1** produce a picture or diagram by making lines and marks on paper. **2** pull or drag a vehicle. **3** move in a particular direction. **4** pull curtains shut or open. **5** arrive at a point in time. **6** take from a container or source. **7** be the cause of a particular response. **8** attract people to

THESAURUS

show, piece, theatrical work, stage show, dramatization. **2** *he is studying drama:* acting, the theatre, the stage, dramatic art, stagecraft, dramaturgy. **3** *she liked to create a drama:* incident, scene, spectacle, crisis, disturbance, row, commotion, excitement, thrill, sensation, dramatics, theatrics, histrionics.

dramatic adjective **1** *dramatic art:* theatrical, thespian, stage, dramaturgical. **2** *a dramatic increase:* considerable, substantial, significant, remarkable, extraordinary, exceptional, phenomenal. **3** *there were dramatic scenes in the city:* exciting, stirring, action-packed, sensational, spectacular, startling, unexpected, tense, gripping, riveting, thrilling, hair-raising, lively. **4** *dramatic headlands:* striking, impressive, imposing, spectacular, breathtaking, dazzling, sensational, awesome, awe-inspiring, remarkable. **5** *a dramatic gesture:* exaggerated, theatrical, ostentatious, actressy, stagy, showy, melodramatic.
OPPOSITES insignificant, boring, unremarkable, unimposing, restrained.

dramatize verb **1** *the novel was dramatized for television:* turn into a play/film, adapt (for the stage/screen). **2** *the tabloids dramatized the event:* exaggerate, overdo, overstate, hyperbolize, magnify, amplify, inflate, sensationalize, embroider, colour, aggrandize, embellish, elaborate; informal blow up (out of all proportion).

drape verb wrap, cover, envelop, shroud, wind, swathe, festoon, hang.

drastic adjective extreme, serious, desperate, radical, far-reaching, momentous, substantial.
OPPOSITES moderate.

draught noun **1** *the draught made Robin shiver:* current of air, wind, breeze, gust, puff, waft. **2** *a draught of beer:* gulp, drink, swallow, mouthful; informal swig.

draw verb **1** *he drew the house:* sketch, outline, rough out, illustrate, render, represent, trace, portray, depict. **2** *she drew her chair in to the table:* pull, haul, drag, tug, heave, lug, tow; informal yank. **3** *the train drew into the station:* move, go, come, proceed, progress, pass, drive, inch, roll, glide, cruise, sweep. **4** *he drew his gun:* pull out, take out, produce, fish out, extract, withdraw, unsheathe. **5** *she drew huge audiences:* attract, win, capture, catch, engage, lure, entice, bring in.
• noun **1** *she won the Christmas draw:* raffle, lottery, sweepstake, sweep, tombola, ballot. **2** *the match ended in a draw:* tie, dead heat, stalemate. **3** *the draw of central London:* attraction, lure, allure, pull, appeal, temptation, charm, fascination.
□ **draw on call on,** have recourse to, turn to, look to, exploit, use, employ, utilize, bring into play. **draw something out** prolong, protract, drag out, spin out, string out, extend, lengthen. **draw something up** compose, formulate, frame, write down, draft, prepare, think up, devise, work out, create, invent, design.

a place or an event. **9** persuade someone to reveal something. **10** reach a conclusion. **11** finish a contest or game with an even score. **12** take in a breath. • **noun 1** a game or match that ends with the scores even. **2** an act of choosing names at random for prizes, sports fixtures, etc. **3** a person or thing that is very attractive or interesting. **4** an act of inhaling smoke from a cigarette.
□ **draw the line at** refuse to do or tolerate. **draw something out** make something last longer. **draw** (of a vehicle) come to a halt. **draw something up** prepare a plan or document.

> **!** don't confuse **draw** with **drawer**, which means 'a sliding storage compartment'.

drawback noun a disadvantage or problem.
drawbridge noun a bridge which is hinged at one end so that it can be raised.
drawer noun **1** a compartment for storage that slides horizontally in and out of a desk or chest. **2** (**drawers**) dated knickers or underpants. **3** a person who draws something.
drawing noun a picture or diagram made with a pencil, pen, or crayon.
□ **drawing pin** Brit. a short flat-headed pin for fastening paper to a surface. **drawing room** a sitting room.
drawl verb speak in a slow, lazy way with long vowel sounds. • **noun** a drawling accent.
drawn past participle of **DRAW**. • adjective

looking strained from illness or exhaustion.
drawstring noun a string in the seam of a garment or bag, which can be pulled to tighten or close it.
dray noun a low truck or cart for delivering barrels or other loads.
dread verb think about something with great fear or anxiety. • **noun** great fear or anxiety.
dreadful adjective **1** very bad or serious. **2** used for emphasis: *he's a dreadful flirt.*
■ **dreadfully** adverb.
dreadlocks plural noun a Rastafarian hairstyle in which the hair is twisted into tight braids or ringlets.
dream noun **1** a series of images and feelings that happen in your mind while you are asleep. **2** an ambition or wish. **3** informal a wonderful or perfect person or thing. • **verb** (**dreams, dreaming, dreamed** or **dreamt** /dremt/) **1** experience dreams during sleep. **2** have daydreams. **3** think of something as possible. **4** (**dream something up**) imagine or invent something.
■ **dreamer** noun.
dreamy adjective **1** tending to daydream. **2** having a magical or pleasantly unreal quality.
■ **dreamily** adverb.
dreary adjective (**drearier, dreariest**) dull, bleak, and depressing.
■ **drearily** adverb **dreariness** noun.
dredge verb (**dredges, dredging, dredged**)

---

drawback noun disadvantage, snag, downside, stumbling block, catch, hitch, pitfall, fly in the ointment, weak spot/point, weakness, imperfection; informal minus.
OPPOSITES benefit.
drawing noun sketch, picture, illustration, representation, portrayal, depiction, diagram, outline.
dread verb *I used to dread going to school:* fear, be afraid of, worry about, be anxious about, shudder at the thought of.
OPPOSITES look forward to.
• **noun** *she was filled with dread:* fear, apprehension, trepidation, anxiety, panic, alarm, terror, disquiet, unease.
OPPOSITES confidence.
dreadful adjective **1** *a dreadful accident:* terrible, frightful, horrible, grim, awful, horrifying, shocking, distressing, appalling, harrowing, ghastly, fearful, horrendous, tragic. **2** *a dreadful meal:* very bad, frightful, shocking, awful, abysmal, atrocious, disgraceful, deplorable; informal woeful, rotten, lousy, ropy; Brit. informal duff, rubbish. **3** *you're a dreadful flirt:*

outrageous, shocking, real, awful, terrible, inordinate, incorrigible, quite a.
OPPOSITES pleasant, wonderful, excellent.
dream noun **1** *she went around in a dream:* daydream, reverie, trance, daze, stupor. **2** *he realized his childhood dream:* ambition, aspiration, hope, goal, aim, objective, intention, desire, wish, daydream, fantasy. **3** *he's an absolute dream:* delight, joy, marvel, wonder, gem, treasure, beauty, vision.
OPPOSITES alertness, nightmare, horror.
• **verb 1** *I dreamed of making the Olympic team:* fantasize, daydream, wish, hope, long, yearn, hanker. **2** *she's always dreaming:* daydream, be in a trance, be lost in thought, be preoccupied, be abstracted, stare into space, be in cloud cuckoo land, be in a brown study.
□ **dream something up think up**, invent, concoct, devise, hatch, come up with.
dreary adjective dull, uninteresting, tedious, boring, unexciting, unstimulating, uninspiring, soul-destroying, monotonous, uneventful.
OPPOSITES exciting.

1 use a machine to scoop out mud and objects from the bed of a river, canal, etc. **2** (**dredge something up**) mention something unpleasant that people have forgotten.

■ **dredger** noun.

dregs plural noun **1** the last remaining amount of a liquid left in a cup, bottle, etc. together with any sediment. **2** the most worthless parts: *the dregs of society.*

drench verb wet thoroughly; soak.

dress verb **1** (also **get dressed**) put on your clothes. **2** put clothes on someone. **3** clean or apply a dressing to a wound. **4** prepare food for cooking or eating. **5** decorate or arrange in an artistic or attractive way.
• noun **1** a woman's garment that covers the body and extends down over the legs. **2** clothing of a particular kind.
□ **dress rehearsal** a final rehearsal in which costumes are worn and things are done as if it is a real performance. **dress up** dress in smart clothes or in a special costume.

dressage /dress-ahzh/ noun the training of a horse to perform a series of precise movements at the rider's command.

dresser noun a sideboard with shelves above it.

dressing noun **1** a sauce for salads, usually consisting of oil and vinegar with flavourings. **2** a piece of material placed on a wound to protect it.
□ **dressing-down** informal a severe telling-off or reprimand. **dressing gown** a long, loose garment worn after getting out of bed. **dressing room** a room in which performers change their clothes. **dressing table** a table with a mirror, used while dressing or putting on make-up.

dressmaker noun a person who makes women's clothes.
■ **dressmaking** noun.

dressy adjective (**dressier**, **dressiest**) (of clothes) smart or formal.

drew past of **DRAW**.

dribble verb (**dribbles**, **dribbling**, **dribbled**) **1** (of a liquid) fall slowly in drops or a thin stream. **2** let saliva run from the mouth. **3** (in sport) take the ball forward with slight touches. • noun a thin stream of liquid.

dribs and drabs plural noun (**in dribs and drabs**) informal in small amounts over a period of time.

dried past and past participle of **DRY**.

drier[1] ⇒ **DRYER**.

drier[2] comparative of **DRY**.

drift verb **1** be carried slowly by a current of air or water. **2** walk or move slowly or casually. **3** (of snow, leaves, etc.) be blown into heaps by the wind. • noun **1** a continuous slow movement from one place to another. **2** the general meaning of someone's remarks. **3** a large mass of snow, leaves, etc. piled up by the wind.

drifter noun a person who moves from place to place, with no fixed home or job.

driftwood noun pieces of wood floating on the sea or washed ashore.

drill noun **1** a tool or machine used for boring holes. **2** training in military exercises. **3** (**the drill**) informal the correct procedure. **4** a machine for sowing seed in rows. • verb **1** bore a hole with a drill. **2** give someone military training or other

---

THESAURUS

drench verb soak, saturate, wet through, douse, steep, flood, drown.

dress verb **1** *he dressed quickly:* put on clothes, clothe yourself, get dressed. **2** *she was dressed in a suit:* clothe, attire, deck out; informal get up. **3** *she enjoyed dressing the tree:* decorate, trim, adorn, arrange, prepare. **4** *they dressed his wounds:* bandage, cover, bind, wrap.
OPPOSITES undress.
• noun **1** *a long blue dress:* frock, gown, robe, shift. **2** *full evening dress:* clothes, clothing, garments, attire, costume, outfit; informal get-up; Brit. informal clobber.

dribble verb **1** *the baby started to dribble:* drool, slaver, slobber. **2** *rainwater dribbled down her face:* trickle, drip, roll, run, drizzle, ooze, seep, leak.

drift verb **1** *his raft drifted down the river:* be carried, be borne, float, bob, glide, coast, waft. **2** *the guests drifted away:* wander, meander, stray, stroll, dawdle,

float, roam. **3** *don't allow your attention to drift:* stray, digress, wander, deviate, be diverted. **4** *snow drifted over the path:* pile up, bank up, heap up, accumulate, gather, amass.
• noun **1** *a drift from the country to urban areas:* movement, shift, flow, transfer, gravitation. **2** *he caught the drift of her thoughts:* gist, meaning, sense, significance, thrust, import, tenor, intention, direction. **3** *a drift of deep snow:* pile, heap, bank, mound, mass, accumulation.

drill noun **1** *military drill:* training, instruction, coaching, teaching, (physical) exercises; informal square-bashing. **2** *Estelle knew the drill:* procedure, routine, practice, programme, schedule, method, system.
• verb **1** *drill the piece of wood:* bore, pierce, puncture, perforate. **2** *a sergeant drilling new recruits:* train, instruct, coach, teach, discipline, exercise.

strict instruction.

drily or **dryly** adverb in a matter-of-fact or ironically humorous way.

drink verb (**drinks, drinking, drank**; past participle **drunk**) **1** take a liquid into the mouth and swallow it. **2** drink alcohol. • noun **1** a liquid for drinking. **2** a quantity of liquid swallowed at one time. **3** alcohol, or an alcoholic drink. ▫ **drink-driving** Brit. the crime of driving a vehicle after drinking too much alcohol. ■ **drinkable** adjective **drinker** noun.

drip verb (**drips, dripping, dripped**) fall in small drops of liquid. • noun **1** a small drop of a liquid. **2** a device which slowly passes a liquid substance into a patient's body through a vein. **3** informal a weak person. ▫ **drip-feed** give a patient liquid nourishment through a drip. ■ **drippy** adjective.

dripping noun Brit. fat that has dripped from roasting meat. • adjective very wet.

drive verb (**drives, driving, drove**; past participle **driven**) **1** operate a motor vehicle. **2** take someone somewhere in a motor vehicle. **3** make someone or something move in a particular direction. **4** make someone behave in a particular way. **5** provide energy to make an engine or machine work. • noun **1** a journey in a car. **2** (also **driveway**) a short private road leading to a

house. **3** a natural urge. **4** an organized effort to achieve something. **5** determination and ambition. ■ **driver** noun.

drivel /driv-uhl/ noun nonsense.

drizzle noun light rain falling in fine drops. • verb (**it drizzles, it is drizzling, it drizzled**) rain lightly. ■ **drizzly** adjective.

droll /drohl/ adjective amusing in a strange or unusual way.

dromedary /drom-i-duh-ri/ noun (plural **dromedaries**) a kind of camel with one hump.

drone verb (**drones, droning, droned**) **1** make a low continuous humming sound. **2** talk for a long time in a boring way. • noun **1** a low continuous humming sound. **2** a male bee which does no work but can fertilize a queen.

drool verb (**drools, drooling, drooled**) **1** drop saliva uncontrollably from the mouth. **2** (often **drool over**) informal show great pleasure or desire.

droop verb bend, hang, or sag downwards limply or wearily. ■ **droopy** adjective.

droopy adjective (**droopier, droopiest**) **1** hanging down limply. **2** not having much strength or spirit.

drop verb (**drops, dropping, dropped**) **1** fall,

d

THESAURUS

drink verb **1** *she drank her coffee:* **swallow,** gulp (down), quaff, guzzle, imbibe, sip, drain; informal swig, down, knock back. **2** *he never drank:* **drink alcohol,** tipple, indulge, carouse; informal hit the bottle, booze; Brit. informal bevvy.
• noun **1** *cocoa is a nice drink:* **beverage,** liquid refreshment; Brit. informal bevvy. **2** *she turned to drink:* **alcohol,** intoxicating liquor, spirits; informal booze, the hard stuff, the bottle, grog. **3** *she took a drink of wine:* swallow, gulp, mouthful, draught, sip; informal swig, slug.

drip verb **1** *there was a tap dripping:* **dribble,** leak. **2** *sweat dripped from his chin:* drop, dribble, trickle, run, splash, sprinkle, leak.
• noun *a bucket caught the drips:* **drop,** dribble, spot, trickle, splash.

drive verb **1** *I can't drive a car:* **operate,** handle, manage, pilot, steer, work. **2** *he drove to the police station:* **go by car,** motor. **3** *I'll drive you to the airport:* **run,** chauffeur, give someone a lift, take, ferry, transport, convey. **4** *the engine drives the front wheels:* **power,** propel, move, push. **5** *he drove a nail into the boot:* **hammer,** screw, ram, sink, plunge, thrust, knock. **6** *she was driven to crime:* **force,** compel, prompt, precipitate, oblige, coerce,

pressure, spur, prod.
• noun **1** *an afternoon drive:* **excursion,** outing, trip, jaunt, tour, ride, run, journey; informal spin. **2** *she lacked the drive to succeed:* **motivation,** ambition, single-mindedness, will power, dedication, doggedness, tenacity, enthusiasm, zeal, commitment, energy, vigour; informal get-up-and-go. **3** *an anti-corruption drive:* **campaign,** crusade, movement, effort, push, initiative.

droop verb hang down, wilt, dangle, sag, flop, sink, slump, drop.

drop verb **1** *Eric dropped the box:* let fall, let go of, lose your grip on, release. **2** *a plane dropped out of the sky:* **fall,** descend, plunge, plummet, dive, sink, dip, tumble. **3** *the exchange rate dropped:* **decrease,** lessen, reduce, fall, decline, dwindle, sink, slump. **4** *let's drop this pretence:* **abandon,** give up, discontinue, finish with, renounce, reject, forgo, relinquish, dispense with, leave out; informal dump, pack in, quit. OPPOSITES rise, increase, keep.
• noun **1** *a drop of water:* **droplet,** blob, globule, bead. **2** *it needs a drop of oil:* **small amount,** little, bit, dash, spot, dribble, sprinkle, trickle, splash, mouthful; informal smidgen, tad. **3** *a small drop in profits:* **decrease,** reduction, decline, fall-off,

d

or let something fall. **2** make or become lower or less. **3** abandon a course of action. **4** (often **drop someone/thing off**) set down or unload a passenger or goods. **5** (in sport) lose a point or match. • noun **1** a small round or pear-shaped amount of liquid. **2** a small drink. **3** an abrupt fall or slope. **4** a type of sweet.
□ **drop kick** a kick made by dropping a ball and kicking it as it bounces. **drop off** fall asleep. **drop out 1** stop taking part in something. **2** start living an alternative lifestyle.

droplet noun a very small drop of a liquid.

dropout noun a person who has started living an alternative lifestyle, or abandoned a course of study.

droppings plural noun the excrement of animals.

dross noun rubbish.

drought /drowt/ noun a very long period of abnormally low rainfall.

drove¹ past of DRIVE.

drove² noun **1** a flock of animals being moved along. **2** a large number of people doing the same thing.

drown verb **1** die through taking water into the lungs, or kill someone in this way. **2** flood an area. **3** (usu. **drown something out**) make something impossible to hear by being much louder.

drowsy adjective (**drowsier, drowsiest**) sleepy.
■ **drowsily** adverb **drowsiness** noun.

drub verb (**drubs, drubbing, drubbed**) beat repeatedly.
■ **drubbing** noun.

drudge noun a person who is made to do hard or dull work.

drudgery noun hard or dull work.

drug noun **1** a substance used as a medicine. **2** an illegal substance taken for the effects it has on the body. • verb (**drugs, drugging, drugged**) make a person or animal unconscious or sleepy by giving them a drug.

drugstore noun N. Amer. a shop which sells medicines and also cosmetics and other articles.

Druid /droo-id/ noun a priest in the ancient Celtic religion.

drum noun **1** a percussion instrument which you play by hitting it with sticks or the hands. **2** a cylindrical object or part. • verb (**drums, drumming, drummed**) **1** play on a drum. **2** make a continuous rhythmic noise. **3** (**drum something into**) teach something to someone by constantly repeating it. **4** (**drum something up**) try hard to get support or business.
□ **drum and bass** a type of dance music consisting largely of electronic drums and bass.
■ **drummer** noun.

drumstick noun **1** a stick used for beating a drum. **2** the lower joint of the leg of a cooked chicken.

drunk past participle of DRINK. • adjective having drunk so much alcohol that you cannot think or speak clearly. • noun a person who is drunk or who often drinks too much.

drunkard noun a person who is often drunk.

drunken adjective **1** drunk. **2** caused by or showing the effects of drink.
■ **drunkenly** adverb **drunkenness** noun.

drupe noun Botany a fruit with a central stone, e.g. a plum or olive.

THESAURUS

downturn, slump. **4** *I walked to the edge of the drop:* cliff, precipice, slope, descent, incline.
OPPOSITES flood, increase.
□ **drop off fall asleep**, doze (off), nap, drowse; informal nod off, drift off, snooze, take forty winks. **drop out leave**, give up, withdraw, retire, pull out, abandon something, fall by the wayside; informal quit, pack something in, jack something in.

drug noun **1** *drugs prescribed by doctors:* medicine, medication, remedy, cure, antidote. **2** *she was under the influence of drugs:* narcotic, stimulant, hallucinogen; informal dope, gear.
• verb **1** *he was drugged:* anaesthetize, poison, knock out; informal dope. **2** *she drugged his coffee:* tamper with, lace, poison; informal dope, spike, doctor.

drum noun *a drum of radioactive waste:*

canister, barrel, cylinder, tank, bin, can.
• verb **1** *she drummed her fingers on the desk:* tap, beat, rap, thud, thump, tattoo, thrum. **2** *the rules were drummed into us at school:* instil, drive, din, hammer, drill, implant, ingrain, inculcate.
□ **drum something up round up**, gather, collect, summon, attract, canvass, solicit, petition.

drunk adjective intoxicated, inebriated, drunken, tipsy, under the influence; informal tight, merry, plastered, sloshed, pickled, tanked (up), ratted; Brit. informal legless, paralytic, Brahms and Liszt, trolleyed, tiddly; N. Amer. informal loaded, trashed, sauced.
OPPOSITES sober.
• noun drunkard, inebriate; informal boozer, soak, wino, alky.
OPPOSITES teetotaller.

dry adjective (**drier**, **driest**) **1** free from moisture. **2** dull and serious. **3** (of humour) subtle and expressed in a matter-of-fact way. **4** (of wine) not sweet. • verb (**dries**, **drying**, **dried**) **1** make or become dry. **2** preserve something by evaporating the moisture. **3** (**dry up**) (of a supply) decrease and stop.
□ dry-clean clean a garment with a chemical rather than by washing it. **dry rot** a fungus that causes wood to decay. **dry run** a rehearsal.
■ dryness noun.

dryer or **drier** noun a machine or device for drying something.

dryly ⇨ **DRILY**.

drystone adjective Brit. (of a stone wall) built without using mortar.

dual adjective consisting of two parts or aspects.
□ dual carriageway Brit. a road with two or more lanes in each direction.

dualism noun **1** division into two contrasted aspects, such as good and evil. **2** duality.
■ dualist noun & adjective.

duality noun (plural **dualities**) the state of having two parts or aspects.

dub¹ verb (**dubs**, **dubbing**, **dubbed**) **1** give an unofficial name to. **2** knight someone by touching their shoulder with a sword in a special ceremony.

dub² verb (**dubs**, **dubbing**, **dubbed**) **1** give a film a soundtrack in a different language from the original. **2** add sound effects or music to a film or recording.

dubbin noun Brit. a grease used for softening and waterproofing leather.

dubious adjective **1** hesitating or doubting. **2** probably not honest. **3** of uncertain quality or value.
■ dubiously adverb.

ducal /dyoo-k'l/ adjective relating to a duke or dukedom.

ducat /duk-uht/ noun a gold coin formerly used in Europe.

duchess noun **1** the wife or widow of a duke. **2** a woman holding a rank equivalent to duke.

duchy noun (plural **duchies**) the territory of a duke or duchess.

duck¹ noun (plural **duck** or **ducks**) **1** a waterbird with a broad blunt bill, short legs, and webbed feet. **2** a female duck.
□ duck-billed platypus ⇨ **PLATYPUS**.

duck² verb **1** lower yourself quickly to avoid being hit or seen. **2** push someone under water. **3** informal avoid an unwelcome duty.

duck³ noun Cricket a batsman's score of nought.

duckboards plural noun wooden slats joined together to form a path over muddy ground.

duckling noun a young duck.

duct noun **1** a tube or passageway for air, cables, etc. **2** a tube in the body through which fluid passes.

ductile adjective (of a metal) able to be drawn out into a thin wire.

dud informal noun a thing that fails to work properly. • adjective failing to work properly.

dude noun N. Amer. informal a man.

dudgeon noun deep resentment.

due adjective **1** expected at a certain time.

d

dry adjective **1** the dry desert: arid, parched, waterless, dehydrated, desiccated, withered, shrivelled, wizened. **2** a dry debate: dull, uninteresting, boring, unexciting, tedious, dreary, monotonous, unimaginative, sterile; informal deadly. **3** a dry sense of humour: wry, subtle, laconic, ironic, sardonic, sarcastic, cynical.
OPPOSITES wet, moist, interesting, lively, broad.
• verb **1** the sun dried the ground: parch, scorch, bake, sear, dehydrate, desiccate, wither, shrivel. **2** he dried the dishes: wipe, towel, rub dry, drain.
OPPOSITES wet, moisten.

dual adjective double, twofold, duplex, binary, twin, matching, paired, coupled.
OPPOSITES single.

dub verb name, call, nickname, label, christen, term, tag.

dubious adjective **1** I was rather dubious about the idea: doubtful, uncertain,

unsure, hesitant, sceptical, suspicious; informal iffy. **2** a dubious businessman: suspicious, suspect, untrustworthy, unreliable, questionable; informal shady; Brit. informal dodgy.
OPPOSITES certain, trustworthy.

duck verb **1** he ducked behind the wall: bob down, bend down, stoop, crouch, squat, hunch down, hunker down. **2** (informal) they cannot duck the issue forever: shirk, dodge, evade, avoid, elude, escape, sidestep.

duct noun tube, channel, canal, vessel, conduit, pipe, outlet, inlet, flue, shaft, vent.

due adjective **1** their fees were due: owing, owed, payable, outstanding, overdue, unpaid, unsettled. **2** the chancellor's statement is due today: expected, anticipated, scheduled for, awaited, required. **3** a little respect is due: deserved, merited, warranted, justified, owing, appropriate, fitting, right, rightful, proper.

d

2 owing; needing to be paid or given. **3** (of a person) owed or deserving something. **4** proper or adequate. •noun **1** (**someone's due** or **dues**) what someone deserves or is owed. **2** (**dues**) fees. •adverb directly: *head due south.*
□ **due to 1** caused by. **2** because of.

duel noun **1** historical a contest with deadly weapons between two people to settle a point of honour. **2** a contest between two parties. •verb (**duels, duelling, duelled;** US spelling **duels, dueling, dueled**) fight a duel.
■ **duellist** (US spelling **duelist**) noun.

duet noun **1** a performance by two singers or musicians. **2** a piece of music for two performers.

duff Brit. informal **adjective** of very bad quality; useless. •verb (**duff someone up**) beat someone up.

duffel bag or **duffle bag** noun a cylinder-shaped canvas bag closed by a drawstring.

duffel coat or **duffle coat** noun a hooded coat made of a rough woollen material.

duffer noun informal an incompetent or stupid person.

dug¹ past and past participle of DIG.

dug² noun the udder, teat, or nipple of a female animal.

dugout noun **1** a trench that is roofed over as a shelter for troops. **2** a low shelter at the side of a sports field for a team's coaches and substitutes. **3** a canoe made from a hollowed-out tree trunk.

duke noun **1** the highest rank of nobleman in Britain and certain other countries. **2** historical (in parts of Europe) a male ruler of a small independent state.
■ **dukedom** noun.

dulcet /dul-sit/ adjective (of a sound) sweet and soothing.

dulcimer /dul-si-mer/ noun a musical instrument which you play by hitting the strings with small hammers.

dull adjective **1** not very interesting. **2** not vivid or bright. **3** (of the weather) overcast. **4** slow to understand. •verb make or become dull.
■ **dullness** noun **dully** adverb.

dullard noun a slow or stupid person.

duly adverb in the proper or expected way.

dumb adjective **1** offensive unable to speak; not having the power of speech. **2** temporarily unable or unwilling to speak. **3** N. Amer. informal stupid. •verb (**dumb something down**) informal make something less intellectually challenging.
□ **dumb-bell** a short bar with a weight at each end, used for exercise. **dumb waiter** a small lift for carrying food and crockery between floors.

dumbfounded adjective greatly astonished.

dumbstruck adjective so shocked or surprised that you cannot speak.

dumdum bullet noun a kind of soft-nosed bullet that expands on impact.

THESAURUS

4 *he drove without due care:* **proper,** correct, suitable, appropriate, adequate, sufficient.
•noun *members have paid their dues:* **fee,** subscription, charge, payment, contribution, levy.
•adverb *due north:* **directly,** straight, exactly, precisely, dead.
□ **due to 1** *her death was due to an infection:* **attributable to,** caused by, because of, down to. **2** *the train was cancelled due to staff shortages:* **because of,** owing to, on account of, as a consequence of, as a result of, thanks to.

duel noun **1** *he was killed in a duel:* **single combat,** fight, confrontation, head-to-head; informal shoot-out. **2** *a snooker duel:* **contest,** match, game, meet, encounter, clash.

dull adjective **1** *a dull novel:* **uninteresting,** boring, tedious, monotonous, unimaginative, uneventful, characterless, featureless, colourless, lifeless, unexciting, uninspiring, flat, bland, stodgy, dreary; informal deadly; N. Amer. informal dullsville. **2** *a dull morning:* **overcast,** cloudy, gloomy, dark, dismal, dreary, sombre, grey, murky, sunless. **3** *dull colours:* **drab,** dreary, sombre, dark, subdued, muted. **4** *a dull sound:* **muffled,** muted, quiet, soft, faint, indistinct, stifled. **5** *the chisel became dull:* **blunt,** worn. **6** *a rather dull child:* **stupid,** unintelligent, slow, brainless, mindless, foolish, idiotic; informal dense, dim, half-witted, thick.
OPPOSITES interesting, bright, resonant, sharp, clever.
•verb *the pain was dulled by drugs:* **lessen,** decrease, diminish, reduce, dampen, blunt, deaden, allay, ease.
OPPOSITES intensify.

duly adverb **1** *the document was duly signed:* **properly,** correctly, appropriately, suitably, fittingly. **2** *he duly arrived to collect Alice:* **at the right time,** on time, punctually.

dumb adjective **1** *she stood dumb while he shouted:* **mute,** speechless, tongue-tied, silent, at a loss for words. **2** (informal) *he is not as dumb as you'd think:* **stupid,** unintelligent, ignorant, dense, brainless, foolish, slow, dull, simple; informal thick, dim; Brit. informal daft.
OPPOSITES talkative, clever.

dummy noun (plural **dummies**) **1** a model of a human being. **2** an object designed to resemble and take the place of the real one. **3** Brit. a rubber or plastic teat for a baby to suck on. **4** (in sport) a movement made to deceive an opponent into thinking that you are about to kick or pass the ball. **5** informal a stupid person.
□ dummy run a practice or trial.

dump noun **1** a place where rubbish or waste is left. **2** a temporary store of weapons or military provisions. **3** informal an unpleasant or boring place. • verb **1** get rid of something unwanted. **2** put down something carelessly. **3** informal abandon someone.

dumpling noun a small savoury ball of dough boiled in water or in a stew.

dumps plural noun (**down in the dumps**) informal depressed or unhappy.

dumpy adjective short and stout.

dun noun a dull greyish-brown colour.

dunce noun a person who is slow at learning.

dune noun a mound or ridge of sand formed by the wind.

dung noun manure.

dungarees /dung-guh-**reez**/ noun a garment consisting of trousers held up by straps over the shoulders.

dungeon noun a strong underground prison cell.

dunk verb **1** dip food into a drink or soup before eating it. **2** put something in water.

dunnock noun a small bird with a grey head and a reddish-brown back.

duo noun (plural **duos**) **1** a pair of people or things, especially in music or entertainment. **2** Music a duet.

duodenum /dyoo-uh-**dee**-nuhm/ noun (plural **duodenums**) the first part of the small intestine immediately beyond the stomach.

dupe verb (**dupes, duping, duped**) deceive; trick. • noun a person who is tricked or deceived.

duple /**dyoo**-p'l/ adjective Music (of rhythm) based on two main beats to the bar.

duplex /**dyoo**-pleks/ N. Amer. noun **1** a building divided into two flats. **2** a flat on two floors.

duplicate adjective /**dyoo**-pli-kuht/ **1** exactly like something else. **2** having two corresponding parts. • noun /**dyoo**-pli-kuht/ each of two or more identical things. • verb /**dyoo**-pli-kayt/ (**duplicates, duplicating, duplicated**) **1** make or be an exact copy of. **2** multiply by two. **3** do something again unnecessarily.
■ duplication noun duplicator noun.

duplicity /dyoo-**pli**-si-ti/ noun deceitful behaviour.
■ duplicitous adjective.

durable adjective **1** hard-wearing. **2** (of goods) not for immediate consumption and so able to be kept.
■ durability noun.

duration noun the time during which something continues.

duress noun threats or violence used to force a person to do something.

during preposition **1** throughout the course of. **2** at a particular point in the course of.

dusk noun the darker stage of twilight.

dusky adjective dark, or darkish in colour.

d

THESAURUS

dummy noun *a shop-window dummy:* mannequin, model, figure.
• adjective *a dummy attack:* simulated, practice, trial, mock, make-believe; informal pretend.
OPPOSITES real.

dump noun **1** *take the rubbish to the dump:* tip, rubbish dump, dumping ground, recycling centre. **2** (informal) *the house is a dump:* hovel, slum; informal hole, pigsty.
• verb **1** *he dumped his bag on the table:* put down, set down, deposit, place, shove, unload, drop, throw down; informal stick, park, plonk; Brit. informal bung. **2** *they will dump asbestos at the site:* dispose of, get rid of, throw away/out, discard, bin, jettison; informal ditch, junk.

dune noun bank, mound, hillock, hummock, knoll, ridge, heap, drift.

duplicate noun *a duplicate of the invoice:* copy, photocopy, facsimile, reprint, replica, reproduction, clone; trademark Xerox, photostat.
• adjective *duplicate keys:* matching, identical, twin, corresponding, equivalent.
• verb **1** *she will duplicate the newsletter:* copy, photocopy, photostat, xerox, reproduce, replicate, reprint, run off. **2** *a feat difficult to duplicate:* repeat, do again, redo, replicate.

durable adjective **1** *durable carpets:* hard-wearing, wear-resistant, heavy-duty, tough, long-lasting, strong, sturdy, robust. **2** *a durable peace:* lasting, long-lasting, long-term, enduring, persistent, abiding, permanent, undying, everlasting.
OPPOSITES delicate, short-lived.

duration noun length, time, period, term, span, extent, stretch.

dusk noun twilight, nightfall, sunset, sundown, evening, close of day, semi-darkness, gloom; literary gloaming.
OPPOSITES dawn.

d

dust noun fine, dry powder, especially tiny particles of earth, sand, etc. •verb **1** remove dust from the surface of. **2** cover lightly with a powdered substance.
□ dust-up informal a fight.
■ dusty adjective.

dustbin noun Brit. a large container for household rubbish.

dustcart noun Brit. a vehicle used for collecting household rubbish.

duster noun a cloth for dusting furniture.

dustman noun (plural **dustmen**) Brit. a man employed to remove rubbish from dustbins.

dustpan noun a hand-held container into which you sweep dust and waste.

Dutch adjective relating to the Netherlands or its language. •noun the language of the Netherlands.
□ Dutch courage confidence gained from drinking alcohol. go Dutch share the cost of a meal equally.

dutiable adjective on which duty needs to be paid.

dutiful adjective carrying out all your obligations; doing your duty.
■ dutifully adverb.

duty noun (plural **duties**) **1** a moral or legal obligation. **2** a person's regular work, or a task required as part of their job. **3** a charge made when some goods are

imported, exported, or sold.
□ duty-bound morally or legally obliged. duty-free not requiring duty to be paid.

duvet /dyoo-vay, doo-vay/ noun chiefly Brit. a thick quilt used instead of an upper sheet and blankets.

DVD abbreviation digital versatile disc.

dwarf noun (plural **dwarfs** or **dwarves**) **1** a member of a mythical race of short human-like creatures. **2** a person who is unusually small. •verb make something seem small in comparison.

dwell verb (**dwells**, **dwelling**, past and past participle **dwelt** or **dwelled**) **1** formal live in or at a place. **2** (**dwell on**) think about something at length.

dwelling noun formal a house or home.

dwindle verb (**dwindles**, **dwindling**, **dwindled**) gradually become smaller or weaker.

dye noun a substance used to colour something. •verb (**dyes**, **dyeing**, **dyed**) make something a particular colour with dye.
□ dyed in the wool having firm beliefs that never change.

dying present participle of **DIE¹**.

dyke or **dike** noun **1** a barrier built to prevent flooding from the sea. **2** a ditch or water-filled channel. **3** informal a lesbian.

dynamic adjective **1** full of energy,

THESAURUS

dust noun the desk was covered in dust: dirt, grime, grit, powder, particles.
•verb **1** she dusted her mantelpiece: wipe, clean, brush, sweep. **2** dust the cake with icing sugar: sprinkle, scatter, powder, dredge, sift, cover.

dusty adjective **1** the floor was dusty: dirty, grimy, grubby, mucky, unswept. **2** dusty sandstone: powdery, crumbly, chalky, granular, soft, gritty.
OPPOSITES clean, hard, smooth.

dutiful adjective conscientious, responsible, dedicated, devoted, attentive, obedient, respectful.
OPPOSITES remiss.

duty noun **1** a misguided sense of duty: responsibility, obligation, commitment, allegiance, loyalty. **2** it was his duty to attend the king: job, task, assignment, mission, function, role. **3** the duty was raised on alcohol: tax, levy, tariff, excise, toll, rate.

dwarf noun **1** small person, person of restricted growth, midget, pygmy. **2** the wizard captured the dwarf: gnome, goblin, hobgoblin, troll, imp, elf, brownie, leprechaun.
•adjective dwarf conifers: miniature, toy, pocket, baby, pygmy; informal mini.

OPPOSITES giant.
•verb **1** the buildings dwarf the trees: dominate, tower over, loom over, overshadow. **2** her progress was dwarfed by her sister's success: overshadow, outshine, surpass, exceed, outclass, outstrip, outdo, top.

dwell verb (formal) live, reside, be housed, lodge.
□ dwell on **brood about**, think about, linger on, be preoccupied by, obsess about, harp on about.

dwindle verb diminish, decrease, reduce, lessen, shrink, wane.
OPPOSITES increase.

dye noun a blue dye: colouring, dyestuff, pigment, tint, stain, wash.
•verb the gloves were dyed: colour, tint, pigment, stain, wash.

dying adjective **1** his dying aunt: terminally ill, at death's door, on your deathbed, fading fast, not long for this world, moribund, in extremis. **2** a dying art form: declining, vanishing, fading, waning; informal on the way out. **3** her dying words: final, last.
OPPOSITES thriving, first.

dynamic adjective energetic, spirited, active, lively, vigorous, forceful, high-

enthusiasm, and new ideas. **2** (of a process or system) constantly changing and developing. **3** Physics relating to forces that produce motion.
∎ **dynamically** adverb.

dynamics plural noun **1** the study of the forces involved in movement. **2** forces which stimulate change. **3** the varying levels of sound in a musical performance.

dynamism noun the quality of being full of energy, enthusiasm, and new ideas.

dynamite noun a kind of high explosive.
• verb (**dynamites, dynamiting, dynamited**) blow up something with dynamite.

dynamo noun (plural **dynamos**) a machine for converting mechanical energy into electrical energy.

dynasty /**di**-nuh-sti/ noun (plural **dynasties**) a series of rulers or powerful people who belong to the same family.

dysentery /**diss**-uhn-tri/ noun a disease of the intestines which results in severe diarrhoea.

dysfunctional adjective **1** not operating properly. **2** unable to deal with normal social relations.

dyslexia /diss-**lek**-si-uh/ noun a disorder involving difficulty in learning to read words and letters.
∎ **dyslexic** adjective & noun.

dyspepsia noun indigestion.

dyspeptic adjective **1** suffering from indigestion. **2** irritable.

d

THESAURUS

powered, aggressive, enterprising; informal go-getting, go-ahead.

dynasty noun family, house, line, lineage, regime, empire.

Ee

e

E or e noun 1 (plural Es or E's) the fifth letter of the alphabet. 2 (€) euro or euros.
• abbreviation 1 East or Eastern. 2 informal the drug Ecstasy.
□ E-number Brit. a code number starting with the letter E, given to food additives according to European Union instructions.

e- prefix referring to the use of electronic communication in order to send information, do business, etc., especially through the Internet: *e-commerce.*

each determiner & pronoun every one of two or more people or things, regarded separately. • adverb to, for, or by every one of a group.

eager adjective very much wanting to do or have something.
■ eagerly adverb.

eagle noun a large bird of prey with long, broad wings.
□ eagle-eyed very observant.

ear noun 1 the organ of hearing in humans and animals. 2 an ability to recognize and appreciate music or language. 3 the spike of seeds at the top of the stalk of a cereal plant.
□ within (or out of) earshot near enough (or too far away) to be heard.

earache noun pain inside the ear.

eardrum noun a membrane in the ear which vibrates in response to sound waves.

earl noun a British nobleman ranking above a viscount.
■ earldom noun.

early adjective (earlier, earliest) & adverb 1 before the expected time. 2 at the beginning of a particular time, period, or sequence.

earmark verb choose or set aside for a particular purpose.

earmuffs plural noun a pair of fabric coverings worn over the ears to protect them from cold or noise.

earn verb 1 be given money in return for work or services. 2 gain a reward for hard work or good qualities.
■ earner noun.

earnest adjective very serious.
□ in earnest sincere and serious about your intentions.
■ earnestly adverb.

earnings plural noun money or income earned.

THESAURUS

each adverb *they gave a tenner each:* apiece, per person, per head, per capita.

eager adjective 1 *small eager faces:* keen, enthusiastic, avid, ardent, highly motivated, committed, earnest. 2 *they were eager for news:* anxious, impatient, longing, yearning, wishing, hoping; informal itching, dying.
OPPOSITES apathetic.

early adjective 1 *early copies of the book:* advance, initial, preliminary, first. 2 *an early death:* untimely, premature, unseasonable. 3 *early man:* primitive, ancient, prehistoric, primeval. 4 *an early response:* prompt, timely, quick, speedy.
OPPOSITES late, timely, modern.
• adverb 1 *get your application in early:* in advance, in good time, ahead of schedule, with time to spare, before the last moment. 2 *she was widowed very early:*

prematurely, before the usual time, too soon, ahead of schedule.
OPPOSITES late.

earmark verb set aside, keep (back), reserve, designate, assign, allocate.

earn verb 1 *they earned £20,000:* be paid, take home, gross, receive, get, make, collect, bring in; informal pocket, bank. 2 *he has earned their trust:* deserve, merit, warrant, justify, be worthy of, gain, win, secure, obtain.
OPPOSITES lose.

earnest adjective 1 *he is dreadfully earnest:* serious, solemn, grave, humourless, staid, intense. 2 *earnest prayer:* devout, heartfelt, wholehearted, sincere, impassioned, fervent, intense.
OPPOSITES frivolous, half-hearted.

earnings plural noun income, pay, wages,

earphones plural noun devices worn on the ears to listen to radio, recorded sound, etc.

earpiece noun the part of a telephone or other device that is held to or put inside the ear during use.

earplug noun a piece of wax, cotton wool, etc., placed in the ear as protection against noise or water.

earring noun a piece of jewellery worn on the lobe or edge of the ear.

earth noun 1 (also **Earth**) the planet on which we live. 2 the ground. 3 soil. 4 Brit. a wire that connects an electrical circuit to the ground and makes it safe. 5 the underground lair of a badger or fox. • verb Brit. connect an electrical device to earth.

earthen adjective made of earth or baked clay.

earthenware noun pottery made of fired clay.

earthling noun (in science fiction) a person from the earth.

earthly adjective 1 having to do with the earth or human life. 2 remotely possible: *no earthly reason.*

earthquake noun a sudden violent shaking of the ground, caused by movements within the earth's crust.

earthwork noun a large man-made bank of soil.

earthworm noun a burrowing worm that lives in the soil.

earthy adjective (**earthier, earthiest**) 1 like soil. 2 direct and unembarrassed about sexual subjects or bodily functions.

earwig noun a small insect with a pair of pincers at its rear end.

ease noun 1 lack of difficulty or effort. 2 freedom from problems. • verb (**eases, easing, eased**) 1 make or become less serious or severe. 2 move carefully or gradually.

easel noun a wooden frame on legs used by artists for holding the picture they are working on.

east noun 1 the direction in which the sun rises. 2 the eastern part of a place. • adjective & adverb 1 towards or facing the east. 2 (of a wind) blowing from the east. ■ **eastward** adjective & adverb **eastwards** adverb.

Easter noun the Christian festival celebrating the resurrection of Jesus. □ **Easter egg** a chocolate egg given as a gift at Easter.

easterly adjective & adverb 1 facing or moving towards the east. 2 (of a wind) blowing from the east.

eastern adjective 1 situated in or facing the east. 2 (**Eastern**) having to do with the part of the world to the east of Europe.

easterner noun a person from the east of a region.

easy adjective (**easier, easiest**) 1 able to be done without great effort. 2 free from worry or problems. □ **easy chair** a comfortable armchair. **easy-going** having a relaxed and tolerant attitude. ■ **easily** adverb.

e

THESAURUS

salary, stipend, remuneration, fees, revenue, yield, profit, takings, proceeds.

earth noun 1 *the moon orbits the earth:* **world**, globe, planet. 2 *a trembling of the earth:* **land**, ground, terra firma, floor. 3 *he ploughed the earth:* **soil**, clay, dust, dirt, loam, ground, turf.

earthly adjective **worldly**, temporal, mortal, human, material, carnal, fleshly, bodily, physical, corporeal, sensual. OPPOSITES extraterrestrial, heavenly.

ease noun 1 *he defeated them all with ease:* **effortlessness**, no trouble, simplicity. 2 *his ease of manner:* **naturalness**, casualness, informality, composure, nonchalance, insouciance. 3 *a life of ease:* **affluence**, wealth, prosperity, luxury, plenty, comfort, enjoyment, well-being. OPPOSITES difficulty, formality, hardship. • verb 1 *the alcohol eased his pain:* **relieve**, alleviate, soothe, moderate, dull, deaden, numb. 2 *the rain eased off:* **let up**, abate, subside, die down, slacken off, diminish, lessen. 3 *work helped to ease her mind:* **calm**, quieten, pacify, soothe, comfort, console. 4 *he eased out the cork:* **slide**, slip,

squeeze, guide, manoeuvre, inch, edge. OPPOSITES aggravate, intensify, unsettle.

easily adverb **effortlessly**, comfortably, simply, without difficulty, readily, without a hitch.

easy adjective 1 *the task was very easy:* **uncomplicated**, undemanding, effortless, painless, trouble-free, simple, straightforward, elementary, plain sailing; informal a piece of cake, child's play, a cinch. 2 *an easy target:* **vulnerable**, susceptible, defenceless, naive, gullible, trusting. 3 *Vic's easy manner:* **natural**, casual, informal, unceremonious, unreserved, unaffected, easy-going, amiable, affable, genial, good-humoured, carefree, nonchalant, unconcerned; informal laid-back. 4 *an easy life:* **quiet**, tranquil, serene, peaceful, untroubled, contented, relaxed, comfortable, secure, safe; informal cushy. 5 *an easy pace:* **leisurely**, unhurried, comfortable, undemanding, easy-going, gentle, sedate, moderate, steady. OPPOSITES difficult, formal, hard, demanding.

eat verb (**eats, eating, ate**; past participle **eaten**)
1 put food into the mouth and chew and swallow it. **2** (**eat something away**) gradually wear away or destroy something. **3** (**eat something up**) use resources in very large quantities.
□ **eat your words** admit that what you previously said was wrong.
■ **eatable** adjective.

eatery noun (plural **eateries**) informal a cafe or restaurant.

eau de cologne /oh duh kuh-**lohn**/ = COLOGNE.

eaves plural noun the part of a roof that meets or overhangs the walls of a building.

eavesdrop verb (**eavesdrops, eavesdropping, eavesdropped**) secretly listen to a conversation.

ebb noun the movement of the tide out to sea. ● verb **1** (of the tide) move away from the land. **2** (**ebb away**) gradually become less or weaker.
□ **at a low ebb** in a weakened or depressed state.

ebony noun **1** heavy dark wood from a tree of tropical and warm regions. **2** a very dark brown or black colour.

ebullient /i-**bul**-yuhnt/ adjective cheerful and full of energy.
■ **ebullience** noun.

EC abbreviation European Community.

eccentric adjective unconventional and slightly strange. ● noun an eccentric person.
■ **eccentrically** adverb **eccentricity** noun.

ecclesiastical /i-klee-zi-**ass**-ti-k'l/ adjective relating to the Christian Church or its clergy.

echelon /**esh**-uh-lon/ noun a level or rank in an organization, profession, or society.

echo noun (plural **echoes**) **1** a sound caused by the reflection of sound waves from a surface back to the listener. **2** a reflected radio or radar beam. ● verb (**echoes, echoing, echoed**) **1** (of a sound) reverberate or be repeated after the original sound has stopped. **2** repeat someone's words or opinions.
■ **echoey** adjective.

eclair /i-**klair**, ay-**klair**/ noun a cake of light pastry filled with cream and topped with chocolate icing.

éclat /ay-**klah**/ noun a notably brilliant or successful effect.

eclectic adjective taking ideas from a wide range of sources.

eclipse noun **1** an occasion when one planet, the moon, etc. passes between another and the observer, or in front of a planet's source of light. **2** a sudden loss of significance or power. ● verb (**eclipses, eclipsing, eclipsed**) **1** (of a planet, the moon, etc.) obscure the light coming from or shining on another. **2** make less significant or powerful.

eco-friendly adjective not harmful to the environment.

ecology noun the study of how animals and plants relate to one another and to their surroundings.
■ **ecological** adjective **ecologically** adverb **ecologist** noun.

economic adjective **1** relating to economics or the economy of a country or region. **2** profitable, or concerned with profitability.

economical adjective **1** giving good value in

THESAURUS

eat verb **1** *we ate a hearty breakfast:* consume, devour, swallow, partake of, munch, chomp; informal tuck into, put away. **2** *we ate at a local restaurant:* have a meal, feed, snack, breakfast, lunch, dine; informal graze.

ebb verb **1** *the tide ebbed:* recede, go out, retreat. **2** *his courage began to ebb:* diminish, dwindle, wane, fade (away), peter out, decline, flag.
OPPOSITES flow, increase.

eccentric adjective *eccentric behaviour:* unconventional, abnormal, anomalous, odd, strange, peculiar, weird, bizarre, outlandish, idiosyncratic, quirky; informal oddball, kooky, cranky.
OPPOSITES conventional.
● noun *he was something of an eccentric:* oddity, free spirit, misfit; informal oddball, weirdo.

echo noun *a faint echo of my shout:* reverberation, reflection, ringing, repetition, repeat.
● verb **1** *his laughter echoed round the room:* reverberate, resonate, resound, reflect, ring, vibrate. **2** *Bill echoed Rex's words:* repeat, restate, reiterate, imitate, parrot, mimic, reproduce, recite.

eclipse verb outshine, overshadow, surpass, exceed, outclass, outstrip, outdo, transcend.

economic adjective **1** *economic reform:* financial, monetary, budgetary, fiscal, commercial. **2** *the firm cannot remain economic:* profitable, moneymaking, lucrative, remunerative, fruitful, productive.
OPPOSITES unprofitable.

economical adjective **1** *an economical car:* cheap, inexpensive, low-cost, budget, economy, cut-price, bargain. **2** *a very economical shopper:* thrifty, provident, prudent, sensible, frugal.
OPPOSITES expensive, spendthrift.

relation to the resources used or money spent. **2** careful in the use of resources or money.
■ **economically** adverb.

economics plural noun the study of the production, consumption, and transfer of wealth.

economist noun an expert in economics.

economize or **economise** verb (**economizes, economizing, economized**) spend less; be economical.

economy noun (plural **economies**) **1** the state of a country or region in terms of the production and consumption of goods and services and the supply of money. **2** careful management of resources. **3** a financial saving.

ecosystem noun all the plants and animals of a particular area considered in terms of how they interact with their environment.

ecstasy noun (plural **ecstasies**) **1** an overwhelming feeling of great happiness. **2** (**Ecstasy**) an illegal drug that produces feelings of excitement and happiness.

> ☑ no *x*: there is a -*cs*- at the beginning and an *s* at the end: ecstasy.

ecstatic adjective very happy or enthusiastic.
■ **ecstatically** adverb.

ectoplasm noun a substance that is thought by some people to come out of the body of a medium during a seance.

Ecuadorean or **Ecuadorian** /ek-wuh-**dor**-i-uhn/ noun a person from Ecuador.
• adjective relating to Ecuador.

ecumenical adjective **1** representing a number of different Christian Churches. **2** wishing for the world's Christian Churches to be united.

eczema /**eks**-muh/ noun a condition in which patches of skin become rough and inflamed.

eddy noun (plural **eddies**) a circular movement of water causing a small whirlpool. • verb (**eddies, eddying, eddied**) (of water, air, etc.) move in a circular way.

edelweiss /**ay**-duhl-vyss/ noun a mountain plant with small flowers.

edema US spelling of OEDEMA.

Eden noun **1** (also **Garden of Eden**) the place where Adam and Eve lived in the story of the Creation in the Bible. **2** a place of happiness or unspoilt beauty.

edge noun **1** the outside limit of an object, area, or surface. **2** the sharpened side of a blade. **3** the line along which two surfaces meet. **4** a slight advantage over close rivals.
• verb (**edges, edging, edged**) **1** provide with an edge. **2** move slowly and carefully.
□ **on edge** tense or irritable.

edgeways or **edgewise** adverb with the edge uppermost or towards the viewer.
□ **get a word in edgeways** manage to break into a conversation.

edgy adjective (**edgier, edgiest**) tense, nervous, or irritable.

edible adjective fit to be eaten.

edict /**ee**-dikt/ noun an official order or announcement.

edifice /**ed**-i-fiss/ noun formal a large, impressive building.

edify /**ed**-i-fy/ verb (**edifies, edifying, edified**) teach someone something that is educational or morally improving.
■ **edification** noun.

edit verb (**edits, editing, edited**) **1** prepare written material for publication by correcting or shortening it. **2** prepare material for a recording or broadcast. **3** be

economize verb save (money), cut costs, cut back, make cutbacks, retrench, scrimp.

economy noun **1** *the nation's economy:* wealth, financial resources, financial system, financial management. **2** *one can combine good living with economy:* thrift, thriftiness, prudence, careful budgeting, saving, restraint, frugality.
OPPOSITES extravagance.

ecstasy noun rapture, bliss, joy, elation, euphoria, rhapsodies.
OPPOSITES misery.

ecstatic adjective enraptured, elated, euphoric, rapturous, joyful, overjoyed, blissful; informal over the moon, on top of the world.

eddy noun *eddies at the river's edge:* swirl, whirlpool, vortex.
• verb *the snow eddied around her:* swirl, whirl, spiral, wind, twist.

edge noun **1** *the edge of the lake:* border, boundary, extremity, fringe, margin, side, lip, rim, brim, brink, verge, perimeter. **2** *she had an edge in her voice:* sharpness, severity, bite, sting, sarcasm, malice, spite, venom. **3** *they have an edge over their rivals:* advantage, lead, head start, the whip hand, the upper hand, dominance.
OPPOSITES middle, kindness, disadvantage.
• verb **1** *poplars edged the orchard:* border, fringe, skirt, surround, enclose, encircle, bound. **2** *a frock edged with lace:* trim, decorate, finish, border, fringe. **3** *he edged closer to the fire:* creep, inch, work your way, ease yourself, sidle, steal.
OPPOSITES stride.

edit verb correct, check, copy-edit, improve, polish, modify, adapt, revise, rewrite, reword, shorten, condense, cut, abridge.

editor of a newspaper or magazine.

edition noun 1 a particular form of a published written work. 2 the total number of copies of a book, newspaper, etc. that are issued. 3 a particular example of a regular programme or broadcast.

editor noun 1 a person who is in charge of a newspaper or magazine. 2 a person who prepares material for publication or broadcasting.

editorial adjective relating to the editing of material. •noun a newspaper article giving the editor's opinion.

educate verb (**educates, educating, educated**) train or instruct someone to improve their mind or character.

education noun 1 the process of teaching or learning. 2 the theory and practice of teaching. 3 training in a particular subject. ■ **educational** adjective **educationally** adverb.

Edwardian /ed-**wor**-di-uhn/ adjective relating to the reign of King Edward VII (1901–10).

EEC abbreviation European Economic Community.

eel noun a snake-like fish with a slender body.

eerie adjective (**eerier, eeriest**) strange and frightening.
■ **eerily** adverb.

efface verb (**effaces, effacing, effaced**) 1 rub off a mark from a surface. 2 make something disappear. 3 (**efface yourself**) make yourself appear unimportant.

effect noun 1 a change that something causes in something else; a result. 2 operation or effectiveness. 3 the extent to which something succeeds. 4 (**effects**) personal belongings. 5 (**effects**) the lighting, sound, or scenery used in a play or film. •verb make something happen. □ **in effect** in practice, even if not formally acknowledged.

> ! don't confuse **effect** and **affect**. Effect chiefly means 'a result', while **affect** is a verb whose main meaning is 'make a difference to'.

effective adjective 1 producing a desired or intended result; successful. 2 (of a law or policy) in operation. 3 existing in fact, though not formally acknowledged as such.
■ **effectively** adverb **effectiveness** noun.

effectual adjective producing the intended result; effective.

effeminate adjective disapproving (of a man) looking, behaving, or sounding like a woman.
■ **effeminacy** noun.

effervescent /ef-fuh-ve-suhnt/ adjective 1 (of a liquid) giving off bubbles; fizzy. 2 lively and enthusiastic.
■ **effervesce** verb **effervescence** noun.

effete /i-**feet**/ adjective 1 weak; feeble. 2 (of a man) effeminate.

THESAURUS

edition noun issue, number, volume, printing, impression, publication, programme, version.

educate verb teach, school, tutor, instruct, coach, train, inform, enlighten.

educated adjective informed, literate, schooled, tutored, well read, learned, knowledgeable, enlightened, intellectual, academic, erudite, scholarly, cultivated, cultured.
OPPOSITES uneducated.

education noun 1 *the education of young children:* teaching, schooling, tuition, tutoring, instruction, coaching, training, guidance, enlightenment. 2 *a woman of some education:* learning, knowledge, literacy, scholarship, enlightenment.

educational adjective 1 *an educational establishment:* academic, scholastic, learning, teaching, pedagogic. 2 *an educational experience:* instructive, instructional, educative, informative, illuminating; formal edifying.

eerie adjective uncanny, sinister, ghostly, unnatural, unearthly, supernatural, other-worldly, strange, abnormal, weird, freakish; informal creepy, scary, spooky.

effect noun 1 *the effect of these changes:* result, consequence, upshot, outcome, repercussions, end result, aftermath. 2 *the effect of the drug:* impact, action, effectiveness, power, potency, strength, success. 3 *the dead man's effects:* belongings, possessions, worldly goods, chattels, property; informal things, stuff; Brit. informal clobber.
OPPOSITES cause.
•verb *they effected many changes:* achieve, accomplish, carry out, manage, bring off, execute, conduct, engineer, perform, do, cause, bring about, produce.

effective adjective 1 *an effective treatment:* successful, effectual, potent, powerful, helpful, beneficial, advantageous, valuable, useful. 2 *an effective argument:* convincing, compelling, strong, forceful, persuasive, plausible, credible, logical, reasonable, cogent. 3 *the new law will be effective from next week:* operative, in force, in effect, valid, official, legal, binding. 4 *Korea was under effective Japanese control:* virtual, practical, essential, actual.
OPPOSITES ineffective, weak, invalid, theoretical.

efficacious /ef-fi-**kay**-shuhss/ **adjective** formal effective.

efficacy /**ef**-fi-kuh-si/ **noun** formal effectiveness.

efficient **adjective** working well with no waste of money or effort.
■ **efficiency** **noun** **efficiently** **adverb**.

effigy /**ef**-fi-ji/ **noun** (plural **effigies**) a sculpture or statue of a person.

effluent **noun** liquid waste or sewage that flows into a river or the sea.

effluvium /i-**floo**-vi-uhm/ **noun** (plural **effluvia** /i-**floo**-vi-uh/) an unpleasant or harmful smell.

effort **noun** 1 a determined attempt to do something. 2 the physical or mental energy needed to do something.

effortless **adjective** done or achieved without effort; natural and easy.
■ **effortlessly** **adverb**.

effrontery /i-**frun**-tuh-ri/ **noun** rude and disrespectful behaviour.

effusion **noun** an act of talking or writing in an unrestrained way.

effusive **adjective** expressing pleasure or approval in a warm and emotional way.
■ **effusively** **adverb**.

e.g. **abbreviation** for example.

egalitarian /i-gal-i-**tair**-i-uhn/ **adjective** believing that all people are equal and deserve equal rights and opportunities.
● **noun** an egalitarian person.
■ **egalitarianism** **noun**.

egg[1] **noun** 1 a small oval or round object laid by a female bird, reptile, fish, etc., and containing a cell which can develop into a new creature. 2 a female reproductive cell; an ovum.

egg[2] **verb** (**egg someone on**) urge someone to do something foolish.

egghead **noun** informal a very intelligent and hard-working person.

eggplant **noun** N. Amer. an aubergine.

ego /**ee**-goh/ **noun** (plural **egos**) 1 a person's sense of their own value and importance. 2 the part of the mind that is responsible for a person's sense of who they are.

egocentric **adjective** self-centred.

egomania **noun** an obsessive concern with yourself.

egotism or **egoism** **noun** the quality of being very conceited or self-absorbed.
■ **egotist** (or **egoist**) **noun** **egotistical** (or **egoistical**) **adjective**.

egregious /i-**gree**-juhss/ **adjective** formal very bad.

egress /**ee**-gress/ **noun** formal 1 the action of going out of a place. 2 a way out.

egret /**ee**-grit/ **noun** a kind of heron with white feathers.

Egyptian **noun** 1 a person from Egypt. 2 the language used in ancient Egypt. ● **adjective** relating to Egypt.

Egyptology **noun** the study of the language, history, and culture of ancient Egypt.
■ **Egyptologist** **noun**.

Eid or **Id** /eed/ **noun** 1 the Muslim festival marking the end of the fast of Ramadan. 2 the Muslim festival marking the end of the annual pilgrimage to Mecca.

eider /**I**-der/ **noun** (plural **eider** or **eiders**) a black and white duck that lives in northern countries.

eiderdown **noun** Brit. a quilt filled with down or another soft material.

eight **cardinal number** 1 one more than seven; 8. (Roman numeral: **viii** or **VIII**.) 2 a rowing boat with eight oars.

eighteen **cardinal number** one more than seventeen; 18. (Roman numeral: **xviii** or **XVIII**.)
■ **eighteenth** **ordinal number**.

eighth **ordinal number** 1 at number eight in a sequence; 8th. 2 (**an eighth** or **one eighth**) each of eight equal parts of something.

☑ there are two *h*s: eigh*th*.

eighty **cardinal number** (plural **eighties**) ten less than ninety; 80. (Roman numeral: **lxxx** or **LXXX**.)
■ **eightieth** **ordinal number**.

eisteddfod /**I**-steth-vod/ **noun** a Welsh festival with music and poetry competitions.

THESAURUS

efficiency **noun** 1 *we need reforms to bring efficiency:* economy, productivity, cost-effectiveness, organization, order, orderliness, regulation. 2 *I compliment you on your efficiency:* competence, capability, ability, proficiency, expertise, skill, effectiveness.
OPPOSITES inefficiency, incompetence.

efficient **adjective** 1 *efficient techniques:* economic, productive, effective, cost-effective, streamlined, organized, methodical, systematic, orderly. 2 *an*

efficient secretary: competent, capable, able, proficient, skilful, skilled, effective, productive, organized, businesslike.
OPPOSITES inefficient, incompetent.

effort **noun** 1 *an effort to work together:* attempt, try, endeavour; informal shot, stab, bash. 2 *a fine effort:* achievement, accomplishment, feat, undertaking, enterprise, work, result, outcome. 3 *the job requires little effort:* exertion, energy, work, application; informal elbow grease; Brit. informal graft.

e

either conjunction & adverb **1** used before the first of two alternatives specified. **2** used to indicate a similarity or link with a statement just made. **3** for that matter; moreover. •**determiner & pronoun 1** one or the other of two people or things. **2** each of two.

ejaculate verb (**ejaculates, ejaculating, ejaculated**) **1** (of a man or male animal) eject semen from the penis at the moment of orgasm. **2** dated say something suddenly. ■ **ejaculation** noun.

eject verb **1** force or throw out violently or suddenly. **2** force someone to leave a place. **3** (of a pilot) escape from an aircraft by means of an ejection seat.
□ **ejection seat** (or **ejector seat**) a seat that can throw the pilot out of the aircraft in an emergency.
■ **ejection** noun.

eke verb (**ekes, eking, eked**) (**eke something out**) **1** make a supply of something last a long time. **2** make a living with difficulty.

elaborate adjective /i-**lab**-uh-ruht/ involving many carefully arranged parts or details; complicated. •**verb** /i-**lab**-uh-rayt/ (**elaborates, elaborating, elaborated**) develop something in more detail.
■ **elaborately** adverb **elaboration** noun.

elan /ay-**lan**/ noun energy and stylishness.

elapse verb (**elapses, elapsing, elapsed**) (of time) pass.

elastic adjective **1** able to go back to its normal shape after being stretched or squeezed. **2** flexible. •**noun** cord or fabric which returns to its original length or shape after being stretched.
□ **elastic band** a rubber band.
■ **elasticity** noun.

elasticated adjective Brit. (of a garment or part of a garment) made elastic with rubber thread or tape.

elated adjective very happy and excited.

elation noun great happiness and excitement.

elbow noun the joint between the forearm and the upper arm. •**verb** push someone with your elbow.
□ **elbow grease** informal hard work in cleaning something.

elder[1] adjective older. •**noun 1** (**your elder**) a person who is older than you are. **2** a leader or senior figure in a tribe.

elder[2] noun a small tree or shrub with white flowers and bluish-black or red berries (**elderberries**).

elderly adjective old or ageing.

eldest adjective oldest.

elect verb **1** choose someone to hold a position by voting for them. **2** choose to do something. •**adjective** elected to a position but not yet in office: *the President-Elect.*

election noun **1** a procedure by which a person is elected. **2** the action of electing.

electioneering noun the action of campaigning to be elected.

elective adjective **1** using or chosen by election. **2** (of study, treatment, etc.) chosen; not compulsory.

elector noun a person who has the right to vote in an election.

electoral adjective relating to elections or electors.
□ **electoral roll** (or **electoral register**) an official list of the people in a district who are entitled to vote in an election.

electorate noun the people who are entitled to vote in an election.

electric adjective **1** of, worked by, or producing electricity. **2** very exciting. •**noun**

THESAURUS

eject verb **1** *the volcano ejected ash:* emit, spew out, discharge, give off, send out, belch, vent. **2** *the pilot had time to eject:* bail out, escape. **3** *they were ejected from the hall:* expel, throw out, remove, oust, evict, banish; informal kick out.
OPPOSITES admit.

elaborate adjective **1** *an elaborate plan:* complicated, complex, intricate, involved, detailed. **2** *an elaborate plasterwork ceiling:* ornate, decorated, embellished, adorned, ornamented, fancy, fussy, busy.
OPPOSITES simple, plain.
•**verb** *both sides refused to elaborate on their reasons:* expand on, enlarge on, add to, flesh out, develop, fill out, amplify.

elastic adjective **1** *elastic material:* stretchy, elasticated, springy, flexible, pliable, supple. **2** *an elastic concept of nationality:* adaptable, flexible, adjustable,

accommodating, variable, fluid, versatile.
OPPOSITES rigid.

elder adjective *his elder brother:* older, senior, big.
•**noun** *the church elders:* leader, patriarch, father.

elderly adjective aged, old, ageing, long in the tooth, grey-haired, in your dotage; informal getting on, over the hill.
OPPOSITES youthful.

elect verb **1** *a new president was elected:* vote in, vote for, return, cast your vote for, choose, pick, select. **2** *she elected to stay behind:* choose, decide, opt, prefer, vote.

election noun ballot, vote, poll; Brit. by-election; US primary.

electric adjective *the atmosphere was electric:* exciting, charged, electrifying, thrilling, dramatic, dynamic, stimulating, galvanizing.

(**electrics**) Brit. the system of electric wiring in a house or vehicle.
□ **electric chair** a chair in which convicted criminals are executed by electrocution. **electric shock** a sudden discharge of electricity through a part of the body.

electrical adjective concerned with, operating by, or producing electricity.
■ **electrically** adverb.

electrician noun a person who installs and maintains electrical equipment.

electricity noun 1 a form of energy resulting from charged particles. 2 the supply of electric current to a building for heating, lighting, etc.

electrify verb (**electrifies, electrifying, electrified**) 1 charge something with electricity. 2 convert something to use electrical power. 3 (**electrifying**) very exciting.

electroconvulsive adjective (of therapy for mental illness) using electric shocks applied to the brain.

electrocute verb (**electrocutes, electrocuting, electrocuted**) injure or kill by electric shock.
■ **electrocution** noun.

electrode noun a conductor through which electricity enters or leaves something.

electrolysis /i-lek-**trol**-i-siss/ noun 1 the separation of a liquid into its chemical parts by passing an electric current through it. 2 the removal of hair roots or small blemishes on the skin by means of an electric current.

electrolyte noun a liquid or gel that an electric current can pass through, e.g. in a battery.

electromagnet noun a metal core made into a magnet by passing electric current through a surrounding coil.

electromagnetic adjective relating to electric currents and magnetic fields.
■ **electromagnetism** noun.

electromotive adjective tending to produce an electric current.

electron noun Physics a subatomic particle with a negative charge, found in all atoms.
□ **electron microscope** a powerful microscope using electron beams instead of light.

electronic adjective 1 having parts such as microchips and transistors that control and direct electric currents. 2 relating to electrons or electronics. 3 carried out by means of a computer.
□ **electronic mail** email.
■ **electronically** adverb.

electronics plural noun 1 the use or study of electronic devices. 2 the study of the behaviour and movement of electrons. 3 circuits or devices using transistors, microchips, etc.

electroplate verb (**electroplates, electroplating, electroplated**) coat a metal object with another metal using electrolysis.

elegant adjective attractive, graceful, and stylish.
■ **elegance** noun **elegantly** adverb.

elegiac /el-i-**jy**-uhk/ adjective expressing sadness, especially about the past or a person who has died.

elegy /**el**-i-ji/ noun (plural **elegies**) a poem expressing sadness, especially for a person who has died.

element noun 1 a basic part of something. 2 each of more than one hundred substances that cannot be changed or broken down. 3 any of the four substances (earth, water, air, and fire) which were formerly believed to make up all matter. 4 a trace. 5 a distinct group within a larger group. 6 (**the elements**) weather conditions such as rain, wind, and cold. 7 a part in an electric device through which an electric current is passed to provide heat.

elemental adjective 1 fundamental. 2 having to do with or like the primitive forces of nature.

elementary adjective 1 relating to the most basic aspects of a subject.

THESAURUS

electrify verb excite, thrill, stimulate, arouse, rouse, inspire, stir (up), exhilarate, galvanize, fire (with enthusiasm), fire someone's imagination, invigorate, animate; N. Amer. light a fire under.

elegance noun 1 he was attracted by her elegance: style, grace, taste, sophistication, refinement, dignity, poise. 2 the elegance of the idea: neatness, simplicity.

elegant adjective 1 an elegant black outfit: stylish, graceful, tasteful, sophisticated, classic, chic, smart, poised, cultivated, polished, cultured. 2 an elegant solution: neat, simple.

element noun 1 an essential element of the local community: component, constituent, part, section, portion, piece, segment, aspect, factor, feature, facet, ingredient, strand, detail, member. 2 there is an element of truth in this stereotype: trace, touch, hint, smattering, soupçon.
3 (**elements**) I braved the elements: weather, climate, weather conditions.

elementary adjective 1 an elementary astronomy course: basic, rudimentary, preparatory, introductory. 2 a lot of the work is elementary: easy, simple, straightforward, uncomplicated,

2 straightforward and uncomplicated.

elephant noun (plural **elephant** or **elephants**) a very large animal with a trunk, long curved tusks, and large ears, found in Africa and Asia.

elephantine /el-i-fan-tyn/ adjective resembling an elephant.

elevate verb (**elevates, elevating, elevated**) **1** lift to a higher position. **2** raise to a higher level or status.

elevated adjective of a high intellectual or moral level.

elevation noun **1** the action of elevating. **2** height above a given level, especially sea level. **3** the angle of something with the horizontal.

elevator noun N. Amer. a lift in a building.

eleven cardinal number **1** one more than ten; 11. (Roman numeral: **xi** or **XI**.) **2** a sports team of eleven players.
□ **the eleventh hour** the latest possible moment.
■ **eleventh** ordinal number.

elevenses plural noun Brit. informal a mid-morning snack.

elf noun (plural **elves**) (in folk tales) a creature resembling a small human figure with pointed ears.

elfin adjective (of a person) small and delicate.

elicit /i-liss-it/ verb (**elicits, eliciting, elicited**) produce or draw out a response or reaction.

elide /i-lyd/ verb (**elides, eliding, elided**) **1** omit a sound or syllable when speaking. **2** join together.

eligible adjective **1** meeting the conditions to do or receive something. **2** desirable as a husband or wife.
■ **eligibility** noun.

eliminate verb (**eliminates, eliminating, eliminated**) **1** completely remove or get rid of. **2** exclude someone from a competition by beating them.
■ **elimination** noun.

elision /i-li-zh'n/ noun the omission of a sound or syllable in speech.

elite /i-leet/ noun a group of people regarded as the best in a particular society or organization.

elitism noun **1** the belief that a society should be run by an elite. **2** the superior attitude associated with an elite.
■ **elitist** adjective & noun.

elixir /i-lik-seer/ noun a drink believed to make people live for ever or have other magical effects.

Elizabethan adjective relating to the reign of Queen Elizabeth I (1558–1603).

elk noun (plural **elk** or **elks**) a kind of large deer.

ellipse noun a regular oval shape.

ellipsis /i-lip-siss/ noun (plural **ellipses** /i-lip-seez/) **1** the omission of words from speech or writing. **2** a set of dots indicating such an omission.

elliptical adjective **1** (of speech or writing) having a word or words deliberately left out. **2** (also **elliptic**) having the shape of an ellipse.

elm noun a tall tree with rough leaves.

elocution noun the skill of speaking clearly.

elongate verb (**elongates, elongating, elongated**) make or become longer.
■ **elongation** noun.

elope verb (**elopes, eloping, eloped**) run away secretly to get married.

eloquence noun fluent or persuasive speaking or writing.

eloquent adjective **1** fluent or persuasive in

THESAURUS

undemanding, painless, child's play, plain sailing; informal a piece of cake.
OPPOSITES advanced, difficult.

elevate verb **1** *we need a breeze to elevate the kite:* raise, lift (up), raise up/aloft, hoist, hike up, haul up. **2** *he was elevated to Secretary of State:* promote, upgrade, move up, raise; informal kick upstairs.
OPPOSITES lower, demote.

elevated adjective **1** *an elevated motorway:* raised, overhead, in the air, high up. **2** *elevated language:* lofty, grand, exalted, fine, sublime, inflated, pompous, bombastic. **3** *his elevated status:* high, high-ranking, lofty, exalted, grand, noble.
OPPOSITES sunken, everyday, lowly.

elicit verb obtain, draw out, extract, bring out, evoke, induce, prompt, generate, trigger, provoke.

eligible adjective **1** *those eligible to vote:* entitled, permitted, allowed, qualified, able. **2** *an eligible bachelor:* desirable, suitable, available, single, unmarried, unattached.

eliminate verb **1** *a policy that would eliminate inflation:* remove, get rid of, put an end to, do away with, end, stop, eradicate, destroy, stamp out. **2** *he was eliminated from the title race:* knock out, exclude, rule out, disqualify.

elite noun best, pick, cream, crème de la crème, flower, high society, beautiful people, aristocracy, ruling class.
OPPOSITES dregs.

eloquent adjective articulate, fluent, expressive, persuasive, well expressed, effective, lucid, vivid.
OPPOSITES inarticulate.

speech or writing. **2** clearly expressive.
■ **eloquently** adverb.

else adverb **1** in addition. **2** different; instead.
□ **or else** if not; otherwise.

elsewhere adverb in, at, or to some other place or other places.

elucidate verb (**elucidates, elucidating, elucidated**) make clear; explain.
■ **elucidation** noun.

elude verb (**eludes, eluding, eluded**) **1** cleverly escape from or avoid. **2** fail to be understood or achieved by.

elusive adjective difficult to find, catch, or achieve.

elver noun a young eel.

elves plural of **ELF**.

Elysian /i-**liz**-i-uhn/ adjective relating to or like paradise.

emaciated /i-**may**-si-ay-tid/ adjective abnormally thin and weak.
■ **emaciation** noun.

email or **e-mail** noun the sending of electronic messages from one computer user to another via a network, or a message sent in this way. • verb send someone a message using email.

emanate /**em**-uh-nayt/ verb (**emanates, emanating, emanated**) **1** (**emanate from**) come out from a place or source. **2** give out a feeling or quality.
■ **emanation** noun.

emancipate verb (**emancipates, emancipating, emancipated**) **1** set free from restrictions. **2** free from slavery.
■ **emancipation** noun.

emasculate verb (**emasculates, emasculating, emasculated**) **1** make weaker or less effective. **2** deprive a man of his

male role or identity.
■ **emasculation** noun.

embalm verb treat a dead body to preserve it from decay.

embankment noun **1** a wall or bank built to prevent flooding by a river. **2** a bank of earth or stone built to carry a road or railway over an area of low ground.

embargo /em-**bar**-goh/ noun (plural **embargoes**) an official ban, especially on trade with a particular country. • verb (**embargoes, embargoing, embargoed**) put an embargo on.

embark verb **1** go on board a ship or aircraft. **2** (**embark on**) begin a new project or course of action.
■ **embarkation** noun.

embarrass verb make someone feel awkward or ashamed.
■ **embarrassment** noun.

☑ double *r*, double *s*: emba*rrass*.

---

embassy noun (plural **embassies**) the official residence or offices of an ambassador.

embattled adjective **1** facing a lot of difficulties. **2** surrounded by enemy forces.

embed or **imbed** verb (**embeds, embedding, embedded**) fix something firmly in a surrounding mass.

embellish verb **1** make more attractive; decorate. **2** add extra details to a story.

ember noun a piece of burning wood or coal in a dying fire.

embezzle verb (**embezzles, embezzling, embezzled**) steal money that you have been given responsibility for.
■ **embezzlement** noun.

embittered adjective angry or resentful.

emblazon /im-**blay**-zuhn/ verb display a

e

THESAURUS

elusive adjective **1** *her elusive husband:* difficult to find, slippery. **2** *an elusive quality:* indefinable, intangible, impalpable, fugitive, fleeting, transitory, ambiguous.

embargo noun *an embargo on oil sales:* ban, bar, prohibition, stoppage, veto, moratorium, restriction, block, boycott. • verb *arms sales were embargoed:* ban, bar, prohibit, stop, outlaw, blacklist, restrict, block, boycott.
OPPOSITES allow.

embark verb board (ship), go on board, go aboard; informal hop on, jump on.
OPPOSITES disembark.
□ **embark on** begin, start, undertake, set out on, take up, turn your hand to, get down to, enter into, venture into, launch into, plunge into, engage in.

embarrass verb humiliate, shame, put someone to shame, abash, mortify, fluster,

discomfit; informal show up.

embarrassed adjective humiliated, mortified, red-faced, blushing, abashed, shamed, ashamed, shamefaced, self-conscious, uncomfortable, discomfited, disconcerted, flustered; informal with egg on your face.

embarrassing adjective humiliating, shameful, mortifying, ignominious, awkward, uncomfortable, compromising; discomfiting; informal cringeworthy, cringe-making, toe-curling.

embarrassment noun **1** *he was scarlet with embarrassment:* humiliation, mortification, shame, shamefacedness, awkwardness, self-consciousness, discomfort, discomfiture. **2** *his current financial embarrassment:* difficulty, predicament, plight, problem, mess; informal bind, pickle, fix.

design on something in a very noticeable way.

emblem noun a design or symbol as a badge of a nation, organization, or family.

emblematic adjective representing a particular quality or idea.

embody verb (**embodies, embodying, embodied**) **1** give a tangible or visible form to an idea or quality. **2** include or contain. ■ **embodiment** noun.

embolden verb make someone braver or more confident.

embolism /em-buh-li-z'm/ noun obstruction of an artery by a clot of blood or an air bubble.

emboss verb carve a raised design on.

embrace verb (**embraces, embracing, embraced**) **1** hold someone closely in your arms. **2** include or contain. **3** willingly accept or support a belief or change. •noun an act of embracing.

embrocation noun a liquid medication rubbed on the body to relieve pain from strains.

embroider verb (**embroiders, embroidering, embroidered**) **1** sew decorative needlework patterns on. **2** add false or exaggerated details to.

embroidery noun (plural **embroideries**) **1** the art of embroidering. **2** embroidered cloth.

embroil verb (**embroil someone in**) involve someone in a conflict or difficult situation.

embryo /em-bri-oh/ noun (plural **embryos**) an unborn or unhatched baby or animal in the early stages of development.

embryonic adjective **1** relating to an

embryo. **2** in a very early stage of development.

emend verb correct and revise a piece of writing.

emerald noun **1** a green precious stone. **2** a bright green colour.

emerge verb (**emerges, emerging, emerged**) **1** become gradually visible. **2** (of facts) become known. **3** recover from a difficult situation or experience. ■ **emergence** noun.

emergency noun (plural **emergencies**) a serious and unexpected situation requiring immediate action.

emergent adjective new and still developing.

emeritus /i-me-ri-tuhss/ adjective having retired but allowed to keep a title as an honour: *an emeritus professor.*

emery board noun a strip of thin wood or card coated with a rough material and used as a nail file.

emetic /i-met-ik/ adjective causing vomiting.

emigrant noun a person who emigrates.

emigrate verb (**emigrates, emigrating, emigrated**) leave your own country and settle permanently in another. ■ **emigration** noun.

émigré /em-i-gray/ noun a person who has emigrated.

eminence noun **1** the quality of being very famous and respected in a particular area of activity. **2** an important or distinguished person.

eminent adjective **1** very famous and

THESAURUS

emblem noun symbol, representation, token, image, figure, mark, sign, crest, badge, device, insignia, coat of arms, shield, logo, trademark.

embody verb **1** *Gradgrind embodies the spirit of industrial capitalism:* personify, manifest, symbolize, represent, express, epitomize, stand for, typify, exemplify. **2** *the changes embodied in the Act:* incorporate, include, contain.

embrace verb **1** *he embraced her warmly:* hug, take/hold in your arms, hold, cuddle, clasp to your bosom, squeeze, clutch, enfold. **2** *most western European countries have embraced the concept:* welcome, welcome with open arms, accept, take on board, take up, take to your heart, adopt, espouse. **3** *the faculty embraces a wide range of disciplines:* include, take in, comprise, contain, incorporate, encompass, cover, subsume. •noun *a fond embrace:* hug, cuddle, squeeze, clinch, caress.

emerge verb **1** *a policeman emerged from the alley:* come out, appear, come into

view, become visible, surface, materialize, issue, come forth. **2** *several unexpected facts emerged:* become known, become apparent, be revealed, come to light, come out, turn up, transpire, unfold, turn out, prove to be the case.

emergence noun appearance, arrival, coming, materialization, advent, inception, dawn, birth, origination, start, development.

emergency noun *a military emergency:* crisis, disaster, catastrophe, calamity, plight; informal panic stations. •adjective **1** *an emergency meeting:* urgent, crisis, extraordinary. **2** *emergency supplies:* reserve, standby, backup, fallback.

emigrate verb move abroad, move overseas, leave your country, migrate, relocate, resettle.
OPPOSITES immigrate.

eminent adjective illustrious, distinguished, renowned, esteemed, pre-eminent, notable, noted, noteworthy, great, prestigious, important, outstanding, celebrated,

respected; distinguished. **2** outstanding or obvious.
■ **eminently** adverb.

emir /e-**meer**/ or **amir** /uh-**meer**/ noun a title of some Muslim rulers.

emissary /**em**-i-suh-ri/ noun (plural **emissaries**) a person sent as a diplomatic representative on a mission.

emission noun **1** the action of emitting. **2** a substance which is emitted.

emit verb (**emits**, **emitting**, **emitted**) **1** give out light, heat, gas, etc. **2** make a sound.

emollient /i-**mol**-li-uhnt/ adjective **1** softening or soothing the skin. **2** attempting to avoid conflict; calming.
■ **emollience** noun.

emolument /i-**mol**-yuu-muhnt/ noun formal a salary or fee.

emotion noun **1** a strong feeling, such as joy or anger. **2** instinctive feeling as opposed to reasoning.

emotional adjective **1** relating to the emotions. **2** arousing or showing emotion.
■ **emotionally** adverb.

emotive adjective arousing strong feeling.

empathize or **empathise** verb (**empathizes**, **empathizing**, **empathized**) understand and share the feelings of someone else.

empathy noun the ability to understand and share the feelings of someone else.

emperor noun the ruler of an empire.

emphasis /**em**-fuh-siss/ noun (plural **emphases** /**em**-fuh-seez/) **1** special importance or value given to something. **2** stress put on a word or words in speaking.

emphasize or **emphasise** verb (**emphasizes**, **emphasizing**, **emphasized**) give special importance or prominence to.

emphatic adjective **1** showing or giving emphasis. **2** definite and clear.
■ **emphatically** adverb.

emphysema /em-fi-**see**-muh/ noun a condition that affects the lungs, causing breathlessness.

empire noun **1** a large group of countries under a single authority or ruler. **2** a large commercial organization under the control of one person or group.

empirical adjective based on observation or experience rather than theory or logic.
■ **empirically** adverb **empiricism** noun **empiricist** noun.

emplacement noun a structure or platform where a gun is placed for firing.

employ verb **1** give work to someone and

---

prominent, well known, acclaimed, exalted.
OPPOSITES unknown.

emission noun discharge, release, outpouring, outflow, outrush, leak.

emit verb **1** *hydrocarbons emitted from vehicle exhausts:* discharge, release, give out/off, pour out, radiate, leak, ooze, disgorge, eject, belch, spew out, exude. **2** *he emitted a loud cry:* utter, voice, let out, produce, give vent to, come out with.
OPPOSITES absorb, stifle.

emotion noun **1** *she was good at hiding her emotions:* feeling, sentiment, reaction, response, instinct, intuition, heart. **2** *overcome by emotion, she turned away:* passion, strength of feeling.

emotional adjective **1** *an emotional young man:* passionate, hot-blooded, ardent, fervent, excitable, temperamental, demonstrative. **2** *he paid an emotional tribute to his wife:* poignant, moving, touching, affecting, powerful, stirring, emotive, impassioned, dramatic; informal tear-jerking.
OPPOSITES cold, clinical.

emphasis noun **1** *the curriculum gave more emphasis to reading and writing:* prominence, importance, significance, value, stress, weight, accent, attention, priority. **2** *the emphasis is on the word 'little':* stress, accent, weight, beat.

emphasize verb stress, underline, highlight, focus attention on, point up, lay stress on, draw attention to, spotlight, foreground.
OPPOSITES understate.

emphatic adjective forceful, firm, vehement, wholehearted, energetic, vigorous, direct, insistent, certain, definite, out-and-out, decided, categorical, unqualified, unconditional, unequivocal, unambiguous, absolute, explicit, downright, outright, clear.
OPPOSITES hesitant.

empire noun **1** *the Ottoman Empire:* kingdom, realm, domain, territory, commonwealth, power. **2** *a worldwide shipping empire:* business, firm, company, corporation, multinational, conglomerate, group, consortium, operation.

employ verb **1** *she employed a chauffeur:* hire, engage, recruit, take on, sign up, appoint, retain. **2** *Sam was employed in carving a stone figure:* occupy, engage, involve, keep busy, tie up. **3** *the team employed subtle psychological tactics:* use, utilize, make use of, apply, exercise, put into practice, practise, exert, bring into play, bring to bear, draw on, resort to, turn to, have recourse to.
OPPOSITES dismiss.

employed adjective working, in work, in

pay them for it. **2** make use of. **3** keep someone occupied.

employee noun a person who is employed by a company or individual.

employer noun a company or individual that employs people.

employment noun **1** the state of having paid work. **2** a person's work or profession.

emporium /em-por-i-uhm/ noun (plural **emporia** or **emporiums**) a large store selling a wide variety of goods.

empower verb (**empowers**, **empowering**, **empowered**) **1** give authority or power to. **2** give strength and confidence to.
■ **empowerment** noun.

empress noun **1** a female emperor. **2** the wife or widow of an emperor.

empty adjective (**emptier**, **emptiest**) **1** containing nothing; not filled or occupied. **2** (of words or gestures) having no real meaning: *empty promises.* •verb (**empties**, **emptying**, **emptied**) **1** make or become empty. **2** (of a river) flow into the sea or a lake.
■ **emptiness** noun.

emu noun a large Australian bird which is unable to fly, similar to an ostrich.

emulate verb (**emulates**, **emulating**, **emulated**) try to do as well as or be better than.
■ **emulation** noun.

emulsify verb (**emulsifies**, **emulsifying**, **emulsified**) combine two liquids into a smooth mixture.
■ **emulsifier** noun.

emulsion noun **1** a mixture of two liquids in which particles of one are evenly

distributed in the other. **2** a type of paint for walls and ceilings. **3** a light-sensitive coating for photographic film.

enable verb (**enables**, **enabling**, **enabled**) **1** provide with the ability or means to do something. **2** make something possible.

enact verb **1** pass a law. **2** act out a role or play.
■ **enactment** noun.

enamel noun **1** a coloured glassy substance applied to metal, glass, or pottery for decoration or protection. **2** the hard substance that covers the crown of a tooth. **3** a paint that dries to give a hard coat. •verb (**enamels**, **enamelling**, **enamelled**; US spelling **enamels**, **enameling**, **enameled**) coat or decorate with enamel.

enamour (US spelling **enamor**) verb (**be enamoured of** or **with**) be filled with love or admiration for.

en bloc /on blok/ adverb all together, or all at once.

encamp verb settle in or set up a camp.

encampment noun a place where a camp is set up.

encapsulate verb (**encapsulates**, **encapsulating**, **encapsulated**) summarize clearly and in few words.

encase verb (**encases**, **encasing**, **encased**) enclose or cover in a case.

encephalitis /en-sef-uh-ly-tiss/ noun inflammation of the brain.

enchant verb **1** delight; charm. **2** put under a spell.
■ **enchanter** noun **enchantment** noun **enchantress** noun.

THESAURUS

employment, holding down a job, earning, salaried, waged.
OPPOSITES unemployed.

employee noun worker, member of staff, blue-collar worker, white-collar worker, workman, labourer, (hired) hand; (**employees**) personnel, staff, workforce.

employment noun work, labour, service, job, post, position, situation, occupation, profession, trade, business, line of work.

empower verb **1** *the act empowered Henry to punish heretics:* authorize, entitle, permit, allow, license, enable. **2** *movements to empower the poor:* emancipate, unshackle, set free, liberate, enfranchise.
OPPOSITES forbid.

empty adjective **1** *an empty house:* vacant, unoccupied, uninhabited, bare, clear, free. **2** *an empty threat:* meaningless, hollow, idle, vain, futile, worthless, useless, ineffectual. **3** *without her my life is empty:* futile, pointless, purposeless, worthless, meaningless, valueless, of no value,

aimless, senseless.
OPPOSITES full, occupied, serious, worthwhile.
•verb **1** *I emptied the dishwasher:* unload, unpack, clear, evacuate, drain. **2** *he emptied out the contents of the case:* remove, take out, extract, tip out, pour out.
OPPOSITES fill, replace.

emulate verb imitate, copy, mirror, echo, follow, model yourself on, take a leaf out of someone's book.

enable verb allow, permit, let, equip, empower, make able, fit, authorize, entitle, qualify.
OPPOSITES prevent.

enact verb **1** *the government enacted an environmental protection bill:* make law, pass, approve, ratify, validate, sanction, authorize. **2** *they are to enact a nativity play:* act out, perform, appear in, stage, mount, put on, present.
OPPOSITES repeal.

enchanting adjective delightfully charming or attractive.

enchilada /en-chi-lah-duh/ noun a tortilla filled with meat or cheese and served with chilli sauce.

encircle verb (encircles, encircling, encircled) form a circle around.

enclave /en-klayv/ noun a small area of one country's territory which is surrounded by another country.

enclose verb (encloses, enclosing, enclosed) 1 surround or close off on all sides. 2 put a document or object in an envelope along with a letter.

enclosure noun 1 an enclosed area. 2 a document or object put in an envelope along with a letter.

encode verb (encodes, encoding, encoded) convert into a coded form.

encompass verb 1 include a wide range of things. 2 surround or cover.

encore /ong-kor/ noun a short extra performance given at the end of a concert in response to calls by the audience.

encounter verb (encounters, encountering, encountered) unexpectedly meet or be faced with. • noun 1 an unexpected or casual meeting. 2 a confrontation.

encourage verb (encourages, encouraging, encouraged) 1 give support, confidence, or hope to. 2 help the development of.
■ **encouragement** noun **encouraging** adjective.

encroach verb 1 (encroach on) gradually intrude on a person's territory, rights, etc. 2 gradually advance beyond expected or acceptable limits.
■ **encroachment** noun.

encrust verb cover with a hard crust.

encrypt verb convert into code.
■ **encryption** noun.

encumber verb (encumbers, encumbering, encumbered) prevent someone from moving or acting freely.

encumbrance noun a thing that prevents someone from moving or acting freely.

encyclopedia or **encyclopaedia** noun a book or set of books giving information on many subjects.
■ **encyclopedic** adjective.

end noun 1 the final part of something. 2 the furthest or most extreme part. 3 the stopping of a state or situation. 4 a person's death or downfall. 5 a goal or desired result. • verb 1 come or bring to an

e

THESAURUS

enchanting adjective captivating, charming, delightful, adorable, lovely, attractive, appealing, engaging, fetching, irresistible, fascinating.

enclose verb 1 *tall trees enclosed the garden:* surround, circle, ring, encircle, bound, close in, wall in. 2 *please enclose a stamped addressed envelope:* include, insert, put in, send.

enclosure noun compound, pen, fold, stockade, ring, paddock, yard, run, coop; N. Amer. corral.

encompass verb include, cover, embrace, incorporate, take in, contain, comprise, involve, deal with.

encounter verb 1 *we encountered a slight problem:* experience, run into, meet, come up against, face, be faced with, confront, suffer. 2 *I encountered a girl I used to know:* meet, run into, come across/upon, stumble across/on, chance on, happen on; informal bump into.
• noun 1 *an unexpected encounter:* meeting, chance meeting. 2 *a violent encounter between police and demonstrators:* battle, fight, clash, scuffle, confrontation, struggle; informal run-in, scrap.

encourage verb 1 *the players were encouraged by the crowd:* hearten, cheer, buoy up, uplift, inspire, motivate, spur on, stir, fire up, stimulate, embolden; informal buck up. 2 *she encouraged him to go:* persuade, coax, urge, press, push, pressure, prod. 3 *the Government was keen to encourage local businesses:* support, back, promote, further, foster, nurture, cultivate, strengthen, stimulate.
OPPOSITES discourage, dissuade, hinder.

encouragement noun 1 *she needed a bit of encouragement:* support, cheering up, inspiration, motivation, stimulation, morale-boosting. 2 *they required no encouragement to get back to work:* persuasion, coaxing, urging, prodding, prompting, inducement, incentive, carrot. 3 *the encouragement of foreign investment:* support, backing, sponsorship, promotion, furtherance, fostering, nurture, cultivation, stimulation.

end noun 1 *the end of the novel:* conclusion, termination, ending, finish, close, resolution, climax, finale, culmination, denouement. 2 *the end of the road:* extremity, limit, edge, border, boundary, periphery, point, tip, head, top, bottom. 3 *wealth is not an end in itself:* aim, goal, purpose, objective, object, target, intention, aspiration, wish, desire, ambition.
OPPOSITES beginning, means.
• verb 1 *the show ended with a wedding scene:* finish, conclude, terminate, close, stop, cease, culminate, climax. 2 *she ended their relationship:* break off, call off, bring to an end, put an end to, stop, finish, terminate, discontinue, cancel.
OPPOSITES begin.

end. 2 (end in) have a particular result. **3 (end up)** eventually reach or come to a particular state or place.
□ **make ends meet** earn just enough money to live on.

endanger verb (**endangers, endangering, endangered**) put in danger.

endangered adjective in danger of extinction.

endear verb (**endear someone to**) make someone popular with or liked by.

endearing adjective inspiring affection; lovable.
■ **endearingly** adverb.

endearment noun **1** a word or phrase expressing affection. **2** love or affection.

endeavour (US spelling **endeavor**) verb try hard to achieve something. •noun **1** an attempt to achieve something. **2** concentrated hard work and effort.

endemic /en-**dem**-ik/ adjective **1** (of a disease or condition) regularly found among particular people or in a certain area. **2** (of a plant or animal) native to a certain area.

ending noun an end or final part.

endive /en-dyv, en-div/ noun a plant with bitter leaves, eaten in salads.

endless adjective having or seeming to have no end or limit.
■ **endlessly** adverb.

endocrine /en-duh-kryn/ adjective (of a gland) secreting hormones or other products directly into the blood.

endorphin /en-**dor**-fin/ noun a painkilling hormone within the brain and nervous system.

endorse verb (**endorses, endorsing, endorsed**) **1** publicly state that you approve of something. **2** sign a cheque on the back so that it can be paid into an account. **3** Brit. mark details of a driving offence on a driving licence.
■ **endorsement** noun.

endow verb **1** give someone your property, or leave it to them in your will. **2** donate a large sum of money to an institution, from which they will be able to receive a regular income. **3** (**be endowed with**) have as a natural quality or characteristic.

endowment noun **1** property or a regular income that has been given or left to a person or an institution. **2** a quality or ability that you are born with.
□ **endowment mortgage** Brit. a mortgage linked to an insurance policy, in which the sum received when the policy matures is used to pay back the money borrowed.

endpaper noun a sheet of paper at the beginning or end of a book, fixed to the inside of the cover.

endurance noun the ability to do or cope with something painful or difficult for a long time.

endure verb (**endures, enduring, endured**)

THESAURUS

endanger verb jeopardize, risk, put at risk, put in danger, be a danger to, threaten, compromise, imperil.
OPPOSITES safeguard.

endearing adjective charming, appealing, attractive, engaging, winning, captivating, enchanting, cute, sweet, delightful, lovely.

endeavour verb *the company endeavoured to expand:* try, attempt, seek, strive, struggle, labour, toil, work.
•noun **1** *an endeavour to build a more buoyant economy:* attempt, try, bid, effort. **2** *an extremely unwise endeavour:* undertaking, enterprise, venture, exercise, activity, exploit, deed, act, action, move.

ending noun end, finish, close, conclusion, resolution, summing-up, denouement, finale.
OPPOSITES beginning.

endless adjective **1** *a woman with endless energy:* unlimited, limitless, infinite, inexhaustible, boundless, unbounded, ceaseless, unending, everlasting, constant, continuous, interminable, unfailing, perpetual, eternal. **2** *we played endless games:* countless, innumerable, numerous, a multitude of; informal umpteen, no end of; literary myriad.

OPPOSITES limited, few.

endorse verb support, back, agree with, approve (of), favour, subscribe to, recommend, champion, uphold, sanction.
OPPOSITES oppose.

endorsement noun support, backing, approval, seal of approval, agreement, recommendation, patronage, sanction.

endow verb **1** *Henry II endowed the hospital:* finance, fund, pay for, subsidize, sponsor. **2** *he was endowed with great strength:* provide, supply, furnish, equip, favour, bless, grace.

endowment noun gift, present, grant, funding, award, donation, contribution, subsidy, sponsorship, bequest, legacy.

endurance noun **1** *she pushed him beyond endurance:* toleration, tolerance, forbearance, patience, acceptance, resignation, stoicism. **2** *an endurance test:* resistance, durability, permanence, longevity, strength, toughness, stamina, staying power, fortitude.

endure verb **1** *he endured much pain:* undergo, go through, live through, experience, cope with, deal with, face, suffer, tolerate, put up with, brave, bear, withstand. **2** *our love will endure:* last, live,

1 experience and be able to cope with prolonged pain or difficulty. 2 last for a long time.

enema /en-i-muh/ noun a process in which liquid is injected into the rectum to clean it out.

enemy noun (plural **enemies**) 1 a person who is hostile to you. 2 (**the enemy**) a country that your own is fighting in a war.

energetic adjective having a lot of energy.
■ **energetically** adverb.

energize or **energise** verb (**energizes, energizing, energized**) give energy and enthusiasm to.

energy noun (plural **energies**) 1 the strength and vitality that you need in order to be active. 2 (**energies**) a person's physical and mental powers. 3 power obtained from physical or chemical resources to provide light and heat or to work machines.

enervate /en-er-vayt/ verb (**enervates, enervating, enervated**) cause someone to feel drained of energy.

enfant terrible /on-fon te-ree-bluh/ noun (plural **enfants terribles** /on-fon te-**ree**-bluh/) a person who is known for behaving in an unconventional or controversial way.

enfeeble verb (**enfeebles, enfeebling, enfeebled**) make someone weak.

enfold verb envelop someone.

enforce verb (**enforces, enforcing, enforced**)

1 make sure a law or rule is obeyed. 2 force something to happen.
■ **enforceable** adjective **enforcement** noun **enforcer** noun.

enfranchise verb (**enfranchises, enfranchising, enfranchised**) 1 give a person or group the right to vote. 2 historical free a slave.
■ **enfranchisement** noun.

engage verb (**engages, engaging, engaged**) 1 attract or involve someone's interest or attention. 2 (**engage in** or **with**) become involved in. 3 employ or hire someone. 4 move a part of a machine or engine into position.

engaged adjective 1 occupied. 2 Brit. (of a telephone line) unavailable because already in use. 3 having formally agreed to get married.

engagement noun 1 a formal agreement to get married. 2 an appointment. 3 the state of being involved in something. 4 fighting between armed forces.

engaging adjective charming and attractive.
■ **engagingly** adverb.

engender verb (**engenders, engendering, engendered**) give rise to.

engine noun 1 a machine with moving parts that converts power into motion. 2 a railway locomotive.

e

THESAURUS

live on, go on, survive, abide, continue, persist, remain.
OPPOSITES fade.

enemy noun opponent, adversary, rival, antagonist, combatant, challenger, competitor, opposition, competition, the other side; literary foe.
OPPOSITES friend, ally.

energetic adjective 1 *an energetic woman:* active, lively, dynamic, spirited, animated, bouncy, bubbly, sprightly, tireless, indefatigable, enthusiastic; informal full of beans. 2 *energetic exercises:* vigorous, strenuous, brisk, hard, arduous, demanding, taxing, tough, rigorous. 3 *an energetic advertising campaign:* forceful, vigorous, aggressive, hard-hitting, high-powered, all-out, determined, bold, intensive; informal in-your-face.
OPPOSITES lethargic, gentle, half-hearted.

energy noun vitality, vigour, strength, stamina, animation, spirit, verve, enthusiasm, zest, exuberance, dynamism, drive; informal punch, bounce, oomph, go, get-up-and-go.

enforce verb 1 *the sheriff enforced the law:* impose, apply, administer, carry out, implement, bring to bear, put into effect. 2 *they cannot enforce cooperation:* force, compel, coerce, exact.

engage verb 1 *tasks which engage children's interest:* capture, catch, arrest, grab, draw, attract, gain, hold, grip, absorb, occupy. 2 *he engaged a secretary:* employ, hire, recruit, take on, enrol, appoint. 3 *the chance to engage in a wide range of pursuits:* participate in, join in, take part in, partake in/of, enter into, embark on. 4 *infantry units engaged the enemy:* attack, fall on, take on, clash with, encounter, meet, fight, do battle with.
OPPOSITES lose, dismiss.

engagement noun 1 *a business engagement:* appointment, meeting, arrangement, commitment, date, assignation, rendezvous. 2 *Britain's engagement in open trading:* participation, involvement. 3 *the first engagement of the war:* battle, fight, clash, confrontation, encounter, conflict, skirmish, action, hostilities.

engaging adjective charming, attractive, appealing, pleasing, pleasant, agreeable, likeable, lovable, sweet, winning, fetching; Scottish & N. English bonny.
OPPOSITES unappealing.

engine noun motor, generator, machine, turbine.

engineer noun **1** a person who is qualified in engineering. **2** a person who maintains or controls an engine or machine. • verb (**engineers, engineering, engineered**) **1** design and build. **2** arrange for something to happen.

engineering noun the study of the design, building, and use of engines, machines, and structures.

English noun the language of England, used in many varieties throughout the world. • adjective relating to England.

engorged adjective swollen.

engrained ⇒ INGRAINED.

engrave verb (**engraves, engraving, engraved**) **1** carve words or a design on a hard surface or object. **2** (**be engraved on** or **in**) be fixed in a person's mind.
■ **engraver** noun.

engraving noun **1** a print made from an engraved plate or block. **2** the process of engraving.

engross /in-**grohss**/ verb (often **be engrossed in**) absorb all of someone's attention.

engulf verb (of a natural force) sweep over someone or something and completely surround or cover them.

enhance verb (**enhances, enhancing, enhanced**) increase the quality, value, or extent of something.
■ **enhancement** noun.

enigma noun a mysterious or puzzling person or thing.
■ **enigmatic** adjective **enigmatically** adverb.

enjoin verb instruct or urge someone to do something.

enjoy verb **1** get pleasure from. **2** (**enjoy yourself**) have a good time. **3** have and benefit from.
■ **enjoyment** noun.

enjoyable adjective giving pleasure.
■ **enjoyably** adverb.

enlarge verb (**enlarges, enlarging, enlarged**) **1** make or become bigger. **2** (**enlarge on**) speak or write about something in greater detail.

enlargement noun **1** the state of being enlarged. **2** a photograph that is larger than the original negative or than an earlier print.

enlighten verb **1** give someone greater knowledge and understanding. **2** (**enlightened**) well informed and able to make good judgements.
■ **enlightenment** noun.

THESAURUS

engineer noun **1** *a structural engineer:* designer, planner, builder. **2** *a repair engineer:* mechanic, repairer, technician, maintenance man, operator, driver, controller.
• verb *he engineered a takeover deal:* bring about, arrange, pull off, bring off, contrive, manoeuvre, negotiate, organize, plan, mastermind.

engraving noun etching, print, plate, picture, illustration, inscription.

engulf verb swamp, inundate, flood, deluge, immerse, swallow up, submerge, bury, envelop, overwhelm.

enhance verb improve, add to, strengthen, boost, increase, intensify, heighten, magnify, amplify, inflate, build up, supplement, augment.
OPPOSITES diminish.

enjoy verb **1** *he enjoys playing the piano:* like, be fond of, take pleasure in, be keen on, delight in, relish, revel in, adore, lap up, savour, luxuriate in, bask in; informal get a thrill out of. **2** *she had always enjoyed good health:* benefit from, be blessed with, be favoured with, be endowed with, possess, own, boast.
OPPOSITES dislike, lack.
□ **enjoy yourself** have fun, have a good time, make merry, celebrate, revel; informal party, have a whale of a time, let your hair down.

enjoyable adjective entertaining, amusing,

delightful, pleasant, congenial, convivial, agreeable, pleasurable, satisfying.
OPPOSITES disagreeable.

enjoyment noun pleasure, fun, entertainment, amusement, recreation, relaxation, happiness, merriment, joy, satisfaction, liking.

enlarge verb **1** *they enlarged the scope of their research:* extend, expand, grow, add to, amplify, augment, magnify, build up, stretch, widen, broaden, lengthen, elongate, deepen, thicken. **2** *the lymph glands had enlarged:* swell, distend, bloat, bulge, dilate, blow up, puff up.
OPPOSITES reduce, shrink.
□ **enlarge on** elaborate on, expand on, add to, flesh out, add detail to, develop, fill out, embellish, embroider.

enlighten verb inform, tell, make aware, open someone's eyes, illuminate; informal put someone in the picture.

enlightened adjective informed, aware, sophisticated, liberal, open-minded, broad-minded, educated, knowledgeable, civilized, refined, cultured.
OPPOSITES benighted.

enlightenment noun insight, understanding, awareness, education, learning, knowledge, illumination, awakening, instruction, teaching, open-mindedness, broad-mindedness, culture, refinement, cultivation, civilization.

enlist verb **1** join the armed services. **2** ask for someone's help in doing something. ■ **enlistment** noun.

enliven verb **1** make something more interesting. **2** make someone more cheerful or animated.

en masse /on mass/ adverb all together.

enmesh verb (**be enmeshed in**) be involved in a complicated situation.

enmity noun (plural **enmities**) hostility.

ennoble verb (**ennobles, ennobling, ennobled**) give greater dignity to.

ennui /on-wee/ noun a feeling of listlessness, boredom, and dissatisfaction.

enormity noun (plural **enormities**) **1** (**the enormity of**) the extreme seriousness of something bad. **2** great size or scale. **3** a serious crime or sin.

enormous adjective very large. ■ **enormously** adverb.

enough determiner & pronoun as much or as many as is necessary or desirable. ●adverb **1** to the required degree. **2** to a moderate degree.

enquire verb (**enquires, enquiring, enquired**) **1** ask for information. **2** (**enquire after**) ask how someone is. **3** (**enquire into**) investigate.

enquiry noun (plural **enquiries**) **1** an act of asking for information. **2** an official investigation.

enrage verb (**enrages, enraging, enraged**) make someone very angry.

enrapture verb (**enraptures, enrapturing, enraptured**) make someone feel great pleasure or joy.

enrich verb **1** improve the quality or value of. **2** improve something by adding an extra item or ingredient. ■ **enrichment** noun.

enrol (US spelling **enroll**) verb (**enrols, enrolling, enrolled**) officially register or recruit someone as a member or student. ■ **enrolment** noun.

en route /on root/ adverb on the way.

ensconce verb (**ensconces, ensconcing, ensconced**) establish in a comfortable, safe, or secret place.

ensemble /on-som-buhl/ noun **1** a group of musicians, actors, or dancers who perform together. **2** a group of items viewed as a whole.

enshrine verb (**enshrines, enshrining, enshrined**) preserve a right, tradition, or

e

THESAURUS

enlist verb **1** *he enlisted in the Royal Engineers:* join up, enrol, sign up, volunteer, register. **2** *he was enlisted in the army:* recruit, call up, enrol, sign up, conscript, mobilize; US draft. **3** *he enlisted the help of a friend:* obtain, engage, secure, win, get.
OPPOSITES discharge, demobilize.

enormity noun **1** *the enormity of his crimes:* wickedness, vileness, heinousness, baseness, depravity, outrageousness. **2** *the enormity of the task:* immensity, hugeness, size, extent, magnitude.

enormous adjective huge, vast, immense, gigantic, giant, massive, colossal, mammoth, tremendous, extensive, mighty, monumental, mountainous; informal mega, monster, whopping; Brit. informal ginormous.
OPPOSITES tiny.

enough determiner *they had enough food:* sufficient, adequate, ample, abundant, the necessary; informal plenty of.
OPPOSITES insufficient.
●pronoun *there's enough for everyone:* sufficient, plenty, an adequate amount, as much as necessary, a sufficiency, an ample supply, one's fill.

enquire, inquire verb **1** *I enquired about training courses:* ask, make enquiries. **2** *the commission is to enquire into the payments:* investigate, probe, look into, research, examine, explore, delve into; informal check out.

enquiry, inquiry noun **1** *telephone enquiries:* question, query. **2** *an enquiry into alleged security leaks:* investigation, probe, examination, exploration, inquest, hearing.

enrage verb anger, infuriate, incense, madden, inflame, antagonize, provoke; informal drive mad/crazy, make someone see red, make someone's blood boil.
OPPOSITES placate.

enraged adjective furious, infuriated, irate, incensed, raging, incandescent, fuming, seething, beside yourself; informal mad, livid, foaming at the mouth.
OPPOSITES calm.

enrich verb enhance, improve, better, add to, augment, supplement, complement, refine.
OPPOSITES spoil.

enrol verb **1** *they both enrolled for the course:* register, sign on/up, put your name down, apply, volunteer, enter, join. **2** *280 new members were enrolled:* accept, admit, take on, sign on/up, recruit, engage.

ensemble noun **1** *a Bulgarian folk ensemble:* group, band, company, troupe, cast, chorus, corps; informal combo. **2** *the buildings present a charming provincial ensemble:* whole, unit, body, set, collection, combination, composite, package. **3** *a pink and black ensemble:* outfit, costume, suit; informal get-up.

idea in a form that ensures it will be respected.

enshroud verb completely envelop something and hide it from view.

ensign noun a flag.

enslave verb (**enslaves, enslaving, enslaved**) **1** make someone a slave. **2** make someone dependent on something.
■ **enslavement** noun.

ensnare verb (**ensnares, ensnaring, ensnared**) **1** catch an animal in a trap. **2** keep someone in a situation from which they cannot escape.

ensue verb (**ensues, ensuing, ensued**) happen afterwards or as a result.

en suite /on sweet/ adjective & adverb Brit. (of a bathroom) leading directly off a bedroom.

ensure verb (**ensures, ensuring, ensured**) **1** make certain that something will turn out in a particular way. **2** (**ensure against**) make sure that a problem does not happen.

entail verb involve something as an inevitable part or result.

entangle verb (**entangles, entangling, entangled**) **1** cause something to become tangled. **2** involve someone in complicated circumstances.
■ **entanglement** noun.

entente /on-tont/ or **entente cordiale** /on-tont kor-di-**ahl**/ noun a friendly understanding between people or countries.

enter verb (**enters, entering, entered**)

1 come or go into. **2** (often **enter into**) begin to be involved in or do. **3** join an institution or profession. **4** register as a participant in a competition or contest. **5** (**enter into**) undertake to be bound by an agreement. **6** record information in a book, computer, etc.

enterprise noun **1** a business or company. **2** a large project. **3** the ability to think of and set up new projects.

enterprising adjective having the ability to think of and set up new projects.

entertain verb **1** provide someone with interest or amusement. **2** receive someone as a guest and provide them with food and drink. **3** give consideration to.
■ **entertainer** noun.

entertaining adjective providing amusement or enjoyment.
■ **entertainingly** adverb.

entertainment noun **1** the action of entertaining. **2** an event or activity designed to entertain other people.

enthral (US spelling **enthrall**) verb (**enthrals, enthralling, enthralled**) fascinate someone and hold their attention.

> ☑ one *l* in **enthral** and **enthrals**, two in **enthralled** and **enthralling**.

enthrone verb (**enthrones, enthroning, enthroned**) mark the new reign of a king or queen by a ceremony in which they sit on a throne.
■ **enthronement** noun.

THESAURUS

ensue verb result, follow, develop, succeed, emerge, arise, proceed, stem.

ensure verb **1** *ensure that the surface is completely clean:* make sure, make certain, see to it, check, confirm, establish, verify. **2** *legislation to ensure equal opportunities for all:* secure, guarantee, assure, certify.

entail verb involve, necessitate, require, need, demand, call for, mean, imply, cause, give rise to, occasion.

enter verb **1** *police entered the house:* go into, come into, get into, set foot in, gain access to. **2** *a bullet entered his chest:* penetrate, pierce, puncture, perforate. **3** *they entered the Army at eighteen:* join, enrol in/for, enlist in, volunteer for, sign up for. **4** *she entered a cookery competition:* go in for, register for, enrol for, sign on/up for, compete in, take part in, participate in. **5** *the cashier entered the details in a ledger:* record, write, put down, take down, note, jot down, register, log. **6** *please enter your password:* key (in), type (in), tap in.
OPPOSITES leave.

enterprise noun **1** *a joint enterprise:* undertaking, endeavour, venture, exercise,

activity, operation, task, business, project, scheme. **2** *a woman with enterprise:* initiative, resourcefulness, imagination, ingenuity, inventiveness, originality, creativity. **3** *a profit-making enterprise:* business, company, firm, venture, organization, operation, concern, establishment; informal outfit.

enterprising adjective resourceful, entrepreneurial, imaginative, ingenious, inventive, creative, adventurous; informal go-ahead.
OPPOSITES unimaginative.

entertain verb **1** *he wrote stories to entertain them:* amuse, please, charm, cheer, interest, engage, occupy. **2** *he entertains foreign visitors:* receive, play host/hostess to, invite (round/over), throw a party for, wine and dine, feed. **3** *I would never entertain such an idea:* consider, contemplate, think of, hear of, countenance.
OPPOSITES bore, reject.

entertainment noun amusement, pleasure, leisure, recreation, relaxation, fun, enjoyment, interest.

enthuse verb (**enthuses, enthusing, enthused**) **1** express enthusiasm about something. **2** make someone enthusiastic.

enthusiasm noun excited interest in and enjoyment of something.

enthusiast noun a person who is very interested in a particular activity.

enthusiastic adjective feeling very interested in and happy about something.
 ■ **enthusiastically** adverb.

entice verb (**entices, enticing, enticed**) attract someone by offering them something desirable.
 ■ **enticingly** adverb.

entire adjective with no part left out; whole.

entirely adverb wholly; completely.

entirety noun (**the entirety**) the whole.
 ☐ **in its entirety** as a whole.

entitle verb (**entitles, entitling, entitled**) **1** give someone a right to do or have something. **2** give a title to a book, play, etc.
 ■ **entitlement** noun.

entity noun (plural **entities**) a thing which exists independently.

entomb verb **1** place someone in a tomb. **2** bury or completely cover.

entomology noun the study of insects.
 ■ **entomological** adjective **entomologist** noun.

entourage /on-toor-ahzh/ noun a group of people who accompany and assist an important person.

entrails plural noun a person's or animal's intestines or internal organs.

entrance[1] /en-truhnss/ noun **1** a door or passageway into a place. **2** an act of entering. **3** the right or opportunity to go into a place.

entrance[2] /in-trahnss/ verb (**entrances, entrancing, entranced**) **1** fill someone with wonder and delight. **2** cast a spell on.

entrant noun a person who joins or takes part in something.

entrap verb (**entraps, entrapping, entrapped**) **1** catch a person or animal in a trap. **2** trick someone into committing a crime in order to have them prosecuted.
 ■ **entrapment** noun.

entreat verb ask someone earnestly or anxiously to do something.

entreaty noun (plural **entreaties**) an earnest request.

entrée /on-tray/ noun **1** the main course of a meal. **2** Brit. a dish served between the first and main courses at a formal dinner. **3** the right to enter a place or social group.

entrecôte /on-truh-koht/ noun a steak cut off a sirloin of beef.

entrench verb **1** establish a military force in fortified positions. **2** (**be entrenched**) be so firmly established that change is difficult.
 ■ **entrenchment** noun.

entrepreneur /on-truh-pruh-**ner**/ noun a person who is successful in setting up businesses.
 ■ **entrepreneurial** /on-truh-pruh-**ner**-i-uhl/ adjective.

entropy noun Physics a quantity expressing how much of a system's thermal energy is not available for conversion into

---

THESAURUS

enthusiasm noun keenness, eagerness, passion, fervour, zeal, zest, gusto, energy, vigour, fire, spirit, interest, commitment, devotion; informal get-up-and-go.
 OPPOSITES apathy.

enthusiast noun fan, devotee, supporter, follower, aficionado, lover, admirer; informal buff.

enthusiastic adjective keen, eager, avid, ardent, fervent, passionate, zealous, excited, wholehearted, committed, devoted, fanatical, earnest.
 OPPOSITES apathetic.

entice verb tempt, lure, attract, appeal to, invite, persuade, beguile, coax, woo, lead on, seduce; informal sweet-talk.

entire adjective whole, complete, total, full.

entirely adverb **1** *that's entirely out of the question:* absolutely, completely, totally, wholly, utterly, quite, altogether, thoroughly. **2** *a gift entirely for charitable purposes:* solely, only, exclusively, purely, merely, just, alone.

entitle verb **1** *this pass entitles you to visit the museum:* qualify, make eligible, authorize, allow, permit, enable, empower. **2** *a chapter entitled 'Comedy and Tragedy':* name, title, call, label, designate, dub.

entity noun being, creature, individual, organism, life form, body, object, article, thing.

entrance[1] noun **1** *the main entrance:* entry, way in, access, approach, door, portal, gate, opening, mouth, foyer, lobby, porch; N. Amer. entryway. **2** *the entrance of Mrs Knight:* appearance, arrival, entry, coming. **3** *he was refused entrance:* admission, admittance, (right of) entry, entrée, access.
 OPPOSITES exit, departure.

entrance[2] verb *I was entranced by her beauty:* enchant, bewitch, beguile, captivate, mesmerize, hypnotize, spellbind, transfix, enthral, engross, absorb, fascinate, stun, electrify, charm, delight; informal bowl over, knock out.

entrant noun competitor, contestant, contender, participant, candidate, applicant.

mechanical work.

entrust verb make someone responsible for doing or looking after something.

entry noun (plural **entries**) **1** an act of entering. **2** a door or passageway into a place. **3** the right or opportunity to enter. **4** an item included in a list, reference book, etc.

entwine verb (**entwines, entwining, entwined**) wind or twist together.

enumerate verb (**enumerates, enumerating, enumerated**) mention a number of things one by one.
■ **enumeration** noun.

enunciate verb (**enunciates, enunciating, enunciated**) **1** say or pronounce clearly. **2** set something out clearly and precisely.
■ **enunciation** noun.

envelop /in-**vel**-uhp/ verb (**envelops, enveloping, enveloped**) wrap up, cover, or surround completely.

☑ unlike the noun *envelope*, the verb **envelop** has no e on the end.

envelope /en-vuh-lohp/ noun a flat paper container with a flap, used to enclose a letter or document.

enviable adjective offering something desirable.
■ **enviably** adverb.

envious adjective feeling discontented because you want something that someone else has.
■ **enviously** adverb.

environment noun **1** the surroundings in which a person, animal, or plant lives or operates. **2** (**the environment**) the natural world.
■ **environmental** adjective **environmentally** adverb.

☑ remember the *n*: environment.

environmentalist noun a person who is concerned with the protection of the environment.
■ **environmentalism** noun.

environs plural noun the surrounding area or district.

envisage /in-**viz**-ij/ verb (**envisages, envisaging, envisaged**) **1** see something as a possibility. **2** form a mental picture of.

envoy noun a messenger or representative.

envy noun (plural **envies**) **1** a feeling of wanting something that belongs to someone else. **2** (**the envy of**) a thing that is wanted by other people. • verb (**envies, envying, envied**) wish that you had the same possessions or opportunities as someone.

enzyme /en-zym/ noun a substance produced by an animal or plant which helps a chemical change happen without being changed itself.

eon US spelling of AEON.

epaulette /ep-uh-**let**/ (US spelling **epaulet**) noun a flap attached to the shoulder of a coat or jacket.

ephemera /i-**fem**-uh-ruh, i-**feem**-uh-ruh/ plural noun things that people use or are

THESAURUS

entrust verb **1** *he was entrusted with the task:* charge, give someone the responsibility for, present. **2** *the powers entrusted to the Home Secretary:* assign, confer on, bestow on, vest in, delegate, give, grant, vouchsafe.

entry noun **1** *my moment of entry:* appearance, arrival, entrance, coming. **2** *the entry to the flats:* entrance, way in, access, approach, door, portal, gate, entrance hall, foyer, lobby; N. Amer. entry-way. **3** *he was refused entry:* admission, admittance, entrance, access. **4** *entries in the cash book:* item, record, note, memo, memorandum. **5** *data entry:* recording, archiving, logging, documentation, capture. **6** *we must pick a winner from the entries:* submission, entry form, application.
OPPOSITES departure, exit.

envelop verb surround, cover, enfold, engulf, encircle, cocoon, sheathe, swathe, enclose, cloak, veil, shroud.

environment noun **1** *the hospital environment:* situation, setting, milieu, background, backdrop, context, conditions, ambience, atmosphere. **2** *the impact of pesticides on the environment:* the natural world, nature, the earth, the ecosystem, the biosphere, Mother Nature, wildlife, flora and fauna, the countryside.

environmentalist noun conservationist, ecologist, nature-lover, green; informal eco-warrior, tree-hugger.

envisage verb **1** *it was envisaged that the hospital would open soon:* foresee, predict, forecast, anticipate, expect, think likely. **2** *I cannot envisage what the future holds:* imagine, contemplate, picture, conceive of, think of.

envoy noun ambassador, emissary, diplomat, representative, delegate, spokesperson, agent, intermediary, mediator; informal go-between.

envy noun *feelings of envy:* jealousy, covetousness, resentment, bitterness.
• verb **1** *I admired and envied her:* be envious of, be jealous of, be resentful of. **2** *we envied her lifestyle:* covet, desire, aspire to, wish for, want, long for, yearn for, hanker after, crave.

interested in for only a short time.

ephemeral adjective lasting only for a short time.

epic noun **1** a long poem about the actions of great men or women or about a nation's history. **2** a long film or book dealing with a long period of time. • adjective **1** having to do with an epic. **2** great and impressive in scale or character.

epicene /e-pi-**seen**/ adjective having both male and female characteristics or no characteristics of either sex.

epicentre (US spelling **epicenter**) noun the point on the earth's surface where the effects of an earthquake are felt most strongly.

epicure noun a person who enjoys and is interested in good food and drink.
■ **epicurean** noun & adjective.

epidemic noun a situation in which a large number of people have caught the same infectious disease.

epidermis noun **1** the surface layer of an animal's skin, on top of the dermis. **2** the outer layer of tissue in a plant.
■ **epidermal** adjective.

epidural noun an anaesthetic injected into the space around the spinal cord, especially during childbirth.

epiglottis noun a flap of cartilage in the throat that descends during swallowing to cover the opening of the windpipe.

epigram noun **1** a concise and witty saying. **2** a short witty poem.
■ **epigrammatic** adjective.

epigraph noun **1** an inscription on a building, statue, or coin. **2** a short quotation introducing a book or chapter.

epilepsy noun a disorder of the nervous system that causes convulsions and loss of consciousness.
■ **epileptic** adjective & noun.

epilogue (US spelling **epilog**) noun a section at the end of a book or play which comments on what has happened.

epiphany noun (plural **epiphanies**) **1** (**Epiphany**) (in the Bible) the time when the Magi visited the baby Jesus in Bethlehem. **2** a sudden and inspiring revelation.

episcopacy /i-**piss**-kuh-puh-si/ noun (plural **episcopacies**) **1** government of a Church by bishops. **2** (**the episcopacy**) the bishops of a region or Church as a group.

episcopal /i-**piss**-kuh-puhl/ adjective having to do with a bishop or bishops.

episcopalian /i-**piss**-kuh-**pay**-li-uhn/ adjective having to do with the government of a Church by bishops. • noun a supporter of this type of Church government.

episode noun **1** an event or group of events happening as part of a sequence. **2** each of the separate parts into which a serialized story or programme is divided.

episodic adjective **1** made up of a series of separate events. **2** happening at irregular intervals.

epistemology /i-**piss**-ti-**mol**-uh-ji/ noun the branch of philosophy that deals with knowledge.

epistle /i-**piss**-uhl/ noun **1** formal a letter. **2** (**Epistle**) a book of the New Testament in the form of a letter from an Apostle.

epistolary adjective **1** relating to the writing of letters. **2** (of a literary work) in the form of letters.

epitaph noun words written in memory of a person who has died.

epithet noun a word or phrase describing someone or something's character or most important quality.

epitome /i-**pit**-uh-mi/ noun (**the epitome of**) a perfect example of something.

epitomize or **epitomise** verb (**epitomizes, epitomizing, epitomized**) be a perfect example of.

epoch /**ee**-pok/ noun a long and distinct period of time.

eponym /**ep**-uh-nim/ noun **1** a person after whom something is named. **2** a word or phrase based on someone's name.

eponymous /i-**pon**-i-muhss/ adjective **1** (of a person) giving their name to something. **2** (of a thing) named after a particular person.

equable /**ek**-wuh-b'l/ adjective **1** calm and even-tempered. **2** (of a climate) not changing very much.
■ **equably** adverb.

equal adjective **1** the same in quantity, size,

e

THESAURUS

epidemic noun **1** *an epidemic of typhoid:* outbreak, plague, pandemic. **2** *a joyriding epidemic:* spate, rash, wave, eruption, plague, outbreak, craze, upsurge.

episode noun **1** *the best episode of his career:* incident, event, occurrence, chapter, experience, occasion, interlude, adventure, exploit. **2** *the final episode of the series:* instalment, chapter, passage, part, portion, section, programme, show.

3 *an episode of illness:* period, spell, bout, attack, phase; informal dose.

equal adjective **1** *lines of equal length:* identical, uniform, alike, like, the same, matching, equivalent, corresponding. **2** *equal treatment before the law:* impartial, non-partisan, fair, just, equitable, unprejudiced, non-discriminatory. **3** *an equal contest:* evenly matched, even, balanced, level; informal level e

value, or status. **2** evenly balanced.
3 (**equal to**) able to face a challenge. • **noun** a person or thing that is equal to another.
• **verb** (**equals, equalling, equalled;** US spelling **equals, equaling, equaled**) **1** be equal to. **2** be as good as.
■ **equally** adverb.

equality noun the state of having the same rights, opportunities, or advantages as others.

equalize or **equalise** verb (**equalizes, equalizing, equalized**) **1** make things equal. **2** level the score in a match by scoring a goal.
■ **equalization** noun **equalizer** noun.

equanimity /ek-wuh-**nim**-i-ti/ noun calmness of temper.

equate verb (**equates, equating, equated**) consider one thing as equal to another.

equation noun **1** the process of equating one thing with another. **2** Maths a statement that the values of two mathematical expressions are equal (indicated by the sign =). **3** Chemistry a formula representing the changes which happen in a chemical reaction.

equator noun an imaginary line around the earth at an equal distance from the two poles, dividing the earth into northern and southern hemispheres.

equatorial adjective having to do with the equator.

equerry /ek-wuh-ri/ noun (plural **equerries**) a male officer of the British royal household who acts as an attendant to a member of the royal family.

equestrian /i-**kwess**-tri-uhn/ adjective relating to horse riding. • **noun** a person on horseback.

equestrianism noun the skill or sport of horse riding.

equidistant adjective at equal distances.

equilateral adjective having all its sides of the same length.

equilibrium noun (plural **equilibria**) **1** a state in which opposing forces are balanced. **2** the state of being physically balanced. **3** a calm state of mind.

equine adjective **1** relating to horses. **2** resembling a horse.

equinoctial adjective **1** having to do with the equinox. **2** at or near the equator.

equinox noun the time or date (twice each year, about 22 September and 20 March) when day and night are of equal length.

equip verb (**equips, equipping, equipped**) **1** supply someone with the things they need for a particular activity. **2** prepare someone for a situation or task.

equipment noun the items needed for a particular activity.

equitable adjective fair and impartial.
■ **equitably** adverb.

equity noun (plural **equities**) **1** the quality of being fair and impartial. **2** the value of the shares issued by a company. **3** the value of a mortgaged property after all charges and debts have been paid.

equivalent adjective (often **equivalent to**) **1** equal in value, amount, function, meaning, etc. **2** having the same effect.
• **noun** a person or thing that is equivalent to another.
■ **equivalence** noun.

equivocal /i-**kwiv**-uh-k'l/ adjective (of words or intentions) not clear because they can be interpreted in more than one way.
■ **equivocally** adverb.

equivocate /i-**kwiv**-uh-kayt/ verb (**equivocates, equivocating, equivocated**) use language that can be interpreted in more than one way in order to hide the

THESAURUS

pegging, neck and neck.
OPPOSITES different, discriminatory.
• **noun** *they did not treat him as their equal:* equivalent, peer, fellow, like, counterpart, match, parallel.
• **verb 1** *two plus two equals four:* be equal to, be equivalent to, be the same as, come to, amount to, make, total, add up to. **2** *he equalled the world record:* match, reach, parallel, be level with.

equality noun fairness, justice, equal rights, equal opportunities, impartiality, even-handedness.

equate verb **1** *he equates criticism with treachery:* identify, compare, bracket, class, associate, connect, link, relate. **2** *moves to equate supply and demand:* equalize, balance, even out/up, level, square, tally,

match.

equilibrium noun balance, stability, poise, symmetry, harmony.
OPPOSITES imbalance.

equip verb **1** *the boat was equipped with a flare gun:* provide, furnish, supply, issue, kit out, stock, provision, arm. **2** *the course will equip them for the workplace:* prepare, qualify, ready, suit, train.

equipment noun apparatus, paraphernalia, tools, utensils, implements, hardware, gadgetry, things; informal stuff, gear.

equivalent adjective *a degree or equivalent qualification:* comparable, corresponding, commensurate, similar, parallel, analogous.
• **noun** *Denmark's equivalent of the Daily Mirror:* counterpart, parallel, alternative, analogue, twin, opposite number.

truth or avoid committing yourself.
■ **equivocation** noun.

era noun a long and distinct period of history.

eradicate verb (**eradicates, eradicating, eradicated**) remove or destroy completely.
■ **eradication** noun.

erase verb (**erases, erasing, erased**) **1** rub out something written in pencil. **2** remove all traces of something.

eraser noun a piece of rubber or plastic used to rub out something written in pencil.

erbium noun a soft silvery-white metallic element.

ere /air/ **preposition & conjunction** old use before (in time).

erect adjective **1** rigidly upright. **2** (of the penis) enlarged and stiffened. •verb **1** put up a structure or object. **2** create or establish something.

erectile adjective able to become erect.

erection noun **1** the action of erecting a structure or object. **2** a building or other upright structure. **3** an erect state of the penis.

ergo /er-goh/ adverb therefore.

ergonomics /er-guh-**nom**-iks/ noun the study of people's efficiency in their working environment.
■ **ergonomic** adjective.

Eritrean /e-ri-**tray**-uhn/ noun a person from the independent state of Eritrea in NE Africa. •adjective relating to Eritrea.

ermine /**er**-min/ noun (plural **ermine** or **ermines**) **1** a stoat. **2** the white winter fur of the stoat.

erode verb (**erodes, eroding, eroded**)

1 gradually wear away. **2** gradually destroy.

erogenous /i-**roj**-i-nuhss/ adjective (of a part of the body) giving pleasure in a sexual way when it is touched.

erosion noun the process of eroding.

erotic adjective having to do with sexual desire or excitement.
■ **erotically** adverb.

erotica noun literature or art that is intended to make people feel sexually excited.

eroticism noun **1** the use of images that are intended to be sexually exciting. **2** sexual desire or excitement.

err verb **1** make a mistake. **2** do wrong.

errand noun a short journey made to deliver or collect something.

errant adjective **1** doing something wrong or unacceptable. **2** old use travelling in search of adventure.

erratic adjective happening, moving, or acting in an irregular or uneven way.
■ **erratically** adverb.

erratum /e-**rah**-tuhm/ noun (plural **errata**) a mistake in a book or printed document.

erroneous adjective incorrect.
■ **erroneously** adverb.

error noun **1** a mistake. **2** the state of being wrong.

ersatz adjective (of a product) artificial and not as good as the real thing.

erstwhile adjective former.

erudite adjective having or showing knowledge gained from reading and study.
■ **erudition** noun.

erupt verb **1** (of a volcano) become active and eject lava, ash, and gases. **2** break out suddenly. **3** show or express your feelings

e

THESAURUS

era noun age, epoch, period, time, date, day, generation.

eradicate verb eliminate, get rid of, remove, obliterate, extinguish, annihilate, exterminate, destroy, kill, wipe out.

erase verb **1** *they erased his name:* delete, rub out, wipe off, blank out, expunge, excise, remove, obliterate. **2** *the data had been erased:* wipe, kill, delete, record over, format.

erect adjective upright, straight, vertical, perpendicular, standing (on end), bristling, stiff.
OPPOSITES bent, flat.
•verb build, construct, put up, assemble, put together, fabricate, raise.
OPPOSITES demolish, dismantle, lower.

erode verb wear away/down, abrade, grind down, crumble, weather, undermine, weaken, deteriorate, destroy.

erosion noun wearing away, abrasion, attrition, weathering, dissolution, deterioration, disintegration, destruction.

erotic adjective sexually arousing, sexually stimulating, titillating, suggestive, pornographic, sexually explicit; informal blue, X-rated; euphemistic adult.

errand noun task, job, chore, assignment, mission.

erratic adjective unpredictable, inconsistent, changeable, variable, inconstant, irregular, fitful, unstable, varying, fluctuating, unreliable.
OPPOSITES consistent.

error noun mistake, inaccuracy, miscalculation, blunder, slip, oversight, misconception, delusion, misprint; Brit. informal boob.

erupt verb **1** *the volcano erupted:* give out lava, become active, explode. **2** *fighting erupted:* break out, flare up, start.

in a sudden and noisy way. **4** (of a spot, rash, etc.) suddenly appear on the skin.
■ **eruption** noun.

erythrocyte /i-**rith**-ruh-syt/ **noun** technical a red blood cell.

escalate verb (**escalates, escalating, escalated**) **1** increase rapidly. **2** become more serious.
■ **escalation** noun.

escalator noun a moving staircase consisting of a circulating belt of steps driven by a motor.

escalope /i-**ska**-luhp/ **noun** a thin slice of meat coated in breadcrumbs and fried.

escapade noun an adventure.

escape verb (**escapes, escaping, escaped**) **1** break free from captivity or control. **2** succeed in avoiding something bad. **3** fail to be noticed or remembered by. • **noun 1** an act of escaping. **2** a means of escaping.
■ **escapee** noun **escaper** noun.

escapism noun the habit of doing enjoyable things to stop you thinking about unpleasant realities.
■ **escapist** noun & adjective.

escapologist /ess-kuh-**pol**-uh-jist/ **noun** an entertainer whose act consists of breaking free from ropes and chains.
■ **escapology** noun.

escarpment noun a long, steep slope at the edge of an area of high land.

eschew /iss-**choo**/ **verb** deliberately avoid doing or having something.

escort noun **1** a person, vehicle, or group accompanying someone to protect or honour them. **2** a person who accompanies a member of the opposite sex to a social

event. • **verb** accompany someone as an escort.

escudo /ess-**kyoo**-doh/ **noun** (plural **escudos**) the former basic unit of money in Portugal.

escutcheon /i-**sku**-chuhn/ **noun** a shield on which a coat of arms is depicted.

Eskimo noun (plural **Eskimo** or **Eskimos**) a member of a people inhabiting northern Canada, Alaska, Greenland, and eastern Siberia.

> **!** many of the peoples traditionally called **Eskimos** now prefer to call themselves **Inuit**.

esophagus US spelling of **OESOPHAGUS**.

esoteric /e-suh-**te**-rik, ee-suh-**te**-rik/ **adjective** intended for or understood by only a small number of people with a specialized knowledge.

ESP abbreviation extrasensory perception.

espadrille /ess-puh-**dril**/ **noun** a light canvas shoe with a plaited fibre sole.

espalier /i-**spal**-yer/ **noun** a fruit tree or shrub whose branches are trained to grow flat against a wall.

especial adjective **1** special. **2** for or belonging chiefly to one person or thing.

especially adverb **1** in particular. **2** to a great extent.

espionage /ess-pi-uh-nah*zh*/ **noun** the practice of spying.

esplanade /ess-pluh-**nayd**/ **noun** a long, open, level area where people may walk for pleasure.

espouse /i-**spowz**/ **verb** (**espouses, espousing, espoused**) support or choose a

THESAURUS

eruption noun **1** *a volcanic eruption:* discharge, explosion, lava flow, pyroclastic flow. **2** *an eruption of violence:* outbreak, flare-up, upsurge, outburst, explosion, wave, spate.

escalate verb **1** *prices have escalated:* increase rapidly, soar, rocket, shoot up, spiral; informal go through the roof. **2** *the dispute escalated:* grow, develop, mushroom, increase, heighten, intensify, accelerate.
OPPOSITES plunge, subside.

escape verb **1** *he escaped from prison:* run away/off, get out, break out, break free, bolt, make your getaway, slip away; Brit. informal do a runner. **2** *he escaped his pursuers:* get away from, elude, avoid, dodge, shake off; informal give someone the slip. **3** *they escaped injury:* avoid, evade, elude, cheat, sidestep, circumvent, steer clear of, shirk. **4** *lethal gas escaped:* leak (out), spill (out), seep (out), discharge, flow (out), pour (out).

• **noun 1** *his escape from prison:* getaway, breakout, flight. **2** *a gas escape:* leak, spill, seepage, discharge, outflow, outpouring.

escort noun *a police escort:* guard, bodyguard, protector, minder, attendant, chaperone, entourage, retinue, protection, convoy.
• **verb 1** *he was escorted home by the police:* conduct, accompany, guide, usher, shepherd, take. **2** *he escorted her in to dinner:* accompany, partner, take, bring.

especially adverb **1** *work poured in, especially from Kent:* mainly, mostly, chiefly, particularly, principally, largely, primarily. **2** *a committee formed especially for the purpose:* expressly, specially, specifically, exclusively, just, particularly, explicitly. **3** *he is especially talented:* exceptionally, particularly, specially, unusually, extraordinarily, uncommonly, uniquely, remarkably, outstandingly; informal seriously, majorly.

particular belief or way of doing things.
■ **espousal** noun.

espresso /ess-**press**-oh/ noun (plural **espressos**) strong black coffee made by forcing steam through ground coffee beans.

> ☑ **espresso** is an Italian word (from *caffè espresso*, meaning 'pressed out coffee') and should be spelled the Italian way, with an *s*, not an *x*.

esprit de corps /e-spree duh **kor**/ noun a feeling of pride and loyalty that unites the members of a group.

espy verb (**espies**, **espying**, **espied**) literary catch sight of.

Esq. abbreviation Esquire.

Esquire /i-**skwy**-er/ noun Brit. a polite title placed after a man's name when no other title is used.

essay noun **1** a piece of writing on a particular subject. **2** formal an attempt. • verb formal attempt to do something.
■ **essayist** noun.

essence noun **1** the quality which is most important in making something what it is. **2** an extract obtained from a plant or other substance and used for flavouring or scent.

essential adjective **1** absolutely necessary. **2** relating to the most important part or basic nature of something. • noun (**essentials**) **1** things that are absolutely

necessary. **2** things that are part of the basic nature of something.
□ **essential oil** a natural oil extracted from a plant.
■ **essentially** adverb.

establish verb **1** set something up on a firm or permanent basis. **2** make someone or something accepted, recognized, or respected by other people. **3** show something to be true.

establishment noun **1** the action of establishing something. **2** a business, public institution, or household. **3** (**the Establishment**) the group in society who have control over policy and resist change.

estate noun **1** a property consisting of a large house with grounds. **2** Brit. a group of modern houses, or of buildings used by businesses. **3** a property where crops such as coffee or grapes are grown. **4** all the money and property owned by a person at the time of their death.
□ **estate agent** a person who sells or rents out houses or flats for clients. **estate car** Brit. a car with a large storage area behind the seats and an extra door at the rear.

esteem noun respect and admiration. • verb respect and admire someone.

ester noun Chemistry an organic compound formed by a reaction between an acid and an alcohol.

esthetic US spelling of **AESTHETIC**.

e

THESAURUS

essay noun article, composition, paper, dissertation, thesis, discourse, study, assignment, treatise, piece, feature; N. Amer. theme.

essence noun **1** *the very essence of economics*: nature, heart, core, substance, basis, principle, quintessence, soul, spirit, reality; informal nitty-gritty. **2** *essence of ginger*: extract, concentrate, elixir, juice, oil.

essential adjective **1** *it is essential to remove the paint*: crucial, key, vital, indispensable, all-important, critical, imperative. **2** *the essential simplicity of his style*: basic, inherent, fundamental, quintessential, intrinsic, underlying, characteristic, innate, primary.
OPPOSITES unimportant, incidental.
• noun **1** *an essential for broadcasters*: necessity, prerequisite; informal must. **2** *the essentials of the job*: fundamentals, basics, rudiments, first principles, foundations, essence, basis, core, kernel, crux; informal nitty-gritty, nuts and bolts.

establish verb **1** *they established an office in Moscow*: set up, start, initiate, institute, found, create, inaugurate. **2** *evidence to establish his guilt*: prove, demonstrate, show, indicate, determine, confirm.

establishment noun **1** *the establishment of a democracy*: foundation, institution, formation, inception, creation, installation, inauguration. **2** *a dressmaking establishment*: business, firm, company, concern, enterprise, venture, organization, operation; informal outfit. **3** *educational establishments*: institution, place, premises, institute. **4** *they dare to poke fun at the Establishment*: the authorities, the powers that be, the system, the ruling class.

estate noun **1** *the Balmoral estate*: property, grounds, garden(s), park, parkland, land(s), territory. **2** *a housing estate*: area, development, complex; Scottish scheme. **3** *a coffee estate*: plantation, farm, holding, forest, vineyard; N. Amer. ranch. **4** *he left an estate worth £610,000*: assets, capital, wealth, riches, holdings, fortune, property, effects, possessions, belongings.

esteem noun *she was held in high esteem*: respect, admiration, acclaim, appreciation, recognition, honour, reverence, estimation, regard.
• verb *such ceramics are highly esteemed*: respect, admire, value, regard, appreciate, like, prize, treasure, revere.

estimable adjective deserving respect and admiration.

estimate verb /ess-ti-mayt/ (**estimates, estimating, estimated**) roughly calculate the value, number, or amount of something. • noun /ess-ti-muht/ **1** a rough calculation. **2** a written statement giving the likely price that will be charged for work. **3** an opinion.
■ **estimation** noun.

Estonian noun a person from Estonia.
• adjective relating to Estonia.

estranged adjective **1** no longer friendly or in contact with someone. **2** (of someone's husband or wife) no longer living with them.
■ **estrangement** noun.

estrogen US spelling of **OESTROGEN**.

estuary noun (plural **estuaries**) the mouth of a large river where it becomes affected by tides.

et al. abbreviation and others.

etc. abbreviation et cetera.

et cetera or **etcetera** /et set-uh-ruh/ adverb and other similar things; and so on.

etch verb **1** engrave metal, glass, or stone by applying a coating, drawing on it with a needle, and then covering the surface with acid to attack the exposed parts. **2** cut words or a design on a surface. **3** (**be etched on** or **in**) be fixed permanently in someone's mind.

etching noun **1** the process of etching. **2** a print produced by etching.

eternal adjective lasting or existing forever.
■ **eternally** adverb.

eternity noun (plural **eternities**) **1** unending time. **2** (**an eternity**) informal an undesirably long period of time.

ethane noun a flammable gas present in petroleum and natural gas.

ether /ee-ther/ noun **1** a highly flammable liquid used as an anaesthetic and a solvent.

2 literary the upper regions of the air.

ethereal /i-theer-i-uhl/ adjective **1** very delicate and light. **2** heavenly or spiritual.

ethic noun **1** (also **ethics**) a set of principles concerning right and wrong and how people should behave. **2** (**ethics**) the branch of philosophy concerned with moral principles.

ethical adjective **1** having to do with principles about right and wrong. **2** morally correct.
■ **ethically** adverb.

Ethiopian noun a person from Ethiopia.
• adjective relating to Ethiopia.

ethnic adjective **1** having to do with people from the same national or cultural background. **2** referring to a person's origins rather than their present nationality. **3** belonging to a non-Western cultural tradition.
□ **ethnic cleansing** the removal or killing of members of one ethnic or religious group in an area by those of another. **ethnic minority** a group which has a different ethnic origin from the main population.
■ **ethnically** adverb **ethnicity** noun.

ethnology noun the study of different peoples and the differences and relationships between them.
■ **ethnological** adjective **ethnologist** noun.

ethos /ee-thoss/ noun the characteristic spirit of a culture, period, etc.

ethyl /eth-yl/ noun Chemistry a radical obtained from ethane, present in alcohol and ether.

etiolated /ee-ti-uh-lay-tid/ adjective (of a plant) pale and weak as a result of a lack of light.

etiquette noun the rules of polite or correct behaviour in a society.

etymology noun (plural **etymologies**) an account of the origins and the

THESAURUS

estimate verb **1** *estimate the cost:* **calculate roughly**, approximate, guess, evaluate, judge. **2** *we estimate it to be worth £50,000:* **consider**, believe, reckon, deem, judge, rate.
• noun *an estimate of the cost:* **rough calculation**, approximation, estimation, guess, costing, quotation, valuation, evaluation; informal guesstimate.

etch verb **engrave**, carve, inscribe, incise, score, mark, scratch, scrape.

etching noun **engraving**, print, plate.

eternal adjective **1** *eternal happiness:* **everlasting**, never-ending, endless, perpetual, undying, immortal, abiding, permanent, enduring. **2** *eternal vigilance:* **constant**, continual, continuous, perpetual,

sustained, uninterrupted, unbroken, non-stop, round-the-clock.
OPPOSITES transient, intermittent.

eternity noun **1** *the memory will remain for eternity:* **ever**, all time, perpetuity.
2 (informal) *I waited an eternity for you:* **a long time**, an age, ages, a lifetime, hours, years, forever.

ethical adjective **1** *an ethical dilemma:* **moral**. **2** *ethical investment:* **morally correct**, right-minded, principled, good, moral, just, honourable, fair.
OPPOSITES unethical.

ethics plural noun **morals**, morality, values, principles, ideals, standards (of behaviour).

ethnic adjective **racial**, race-related, national, cultural, folk, tribal, ethnological.

developments in meaning of a word.
■ **etymological** adjective.

EU abbreviation European Union.

eucalyptus /yoo-kuh-**lip**-tuhss/ noun (plural **eucalyptuses**) an evergreen Australasian tree whose leaves produce a strong-smelling oil.

Eucharist /**yoo**-kuh-rist/ noun **1** the Christian ceremony commemorating the Last Supper, in which consecrated bread and wine are consumed. **2** the consecrated bread and wine used in this ceremony.

eugenics /yoo-**jen**-iks/ noun the study of ways to increase the occurrence of desirable characteristics in a population by choosing which people become parents.

eulogize or **eulogise** /**yoo**-luh-jyz/ verb (**eulogizes, eulogizing, eulogized**) praise highly.

eulogy /**yoo**-luh-ji/ noun (plural **eulogies**) a speech or piece of writing that praises someone or something highly.

eunuch /**yoo**-nuhk/ noun a man who has had his testicles removed.

euphemism /**yoo**-fuh-mi-z'm/ noun a less direct word used instead of one that is blunt or offensive.
■ **euphemistic** adjective **euphemistically** adverb.

euphonious /yoo-**foh**-ni-uhss/ adjective sounding pleasant.
■ **euphoniously** adverb.

euphonium /yoo-**foh**-ni-uhm/ noun a brass musical instrument like a small tuba.

euphony /**yoo**-fuh-ni/ noun (plural **euphonies**) the quality of sounding pleasant.

euphoria /yoo-**for**-i-uh/ noun a feeling of great happiness.
■ **euphoric** adjective.

Eurasian adjective **1** of mixed European and Asian parentage. **2** relating to Eurasia (the land mass of Europe and Asia together).

eureka /yoo-**ree**-kuh/ exclamation a cry of joy or satisfaction when you discover something.

euro noun the basic unit of money in twelve states of the European Union.

European noun **1** a person from Europe. **2** a person who is of European parentage.

• adjective having to do with Europe or the European Union.
□ **European Union** an economic and political association of certain European countries.

europium noun a soft silvery-white metallic element.

Eustachian tube /yoo-**stay**-sh'n/ noun a narrow passage leading from the throat to the middle ear.

euthanasia /yoo-thuh-**nay**-zi-uh/ noun the painless killing of a patient suffering from an incurable disease.

evacuate verb (**evacuates, evacuating, evacuated**) **1** remove someone from a place of danger to a safer place. **2** leave a dangerous place. **3** empty the bowels.
■ **evacuation** noun.

evacuee noun a person who is evacuated from a place of danger.

evade verb (**evades, evading, evaded**) **1** escape or avoid. **2** avoid giving a direct answer to a question.

evaluate verb (**evaluates, evaluating, evaluated**) form an idea of the amount or value of.
■ **evaluation** noun.

evanescent /ev-uh-**ness**-uhnt/ adjective soon passing out of existence; fleeting.
■ **evanescence** noun.

evangelical adjective **1** having to do with a tradition within Protestant Christianity which emphasizes the authority of the Bible and salvation through personal faith in Jesus. **2** having to do with the teaching of the gospel or Christianity. **3** showing passionate support for something. • noun a member of the evangelical tradition in the Christian Church.
■ **evangelicalism** noun.

evangelist noun **1** a person who sets out to convert other people to Christianity. **2** the writer of one of the four Gospels. **3** a passionate supporter of something.
■ **evangelism** noun **evangelistic** adjective.

evangelize or **evangelise** verb (**evangelizes, evangelizing, evangelized**) **1** set out to convert people to Christianity. **2** preach the gospel.

THESAURUS

euphoria noun elation, happiness, joy, delight, glee, excitement, exhilaration, jubilation, exultation, ecstasy, bliss, rapture.
OPPOSITES misery.

evacuate verb **1** *local residents were evacuated*: remove, move out, take away. **2** *they evacuated the building*: leave, vacate, abandon, move out of, quit, withdraw from, retreat from, flee. **3** *police evacuated the area*: clear, empty.

evade verb **1** *they evaded the guards*: elude, avoid, dodge, escape (from), steer clear of, sidestep, lose, leave behind, shake off; informal give someone the slip. **2** *he evaded the question*: avoid, dodge, sidestep, bypass, skirt round; informal duck; Austral./NZ informal duck-shove.
OPPOSITES confront.

evaluate verb assess, judge, gauge, rate, estimate, appraise, weigh up; informal size up.

evaporate verb (**evaporates, evaporating, evaporated**) **1** turn from liquid into vapour. **2** cease to exist.
□ **evaporated milk** thick sweetened milk from which some of the liquid has been evaporated.
■ **evaporation** noun.

evasion noun the action of avoiding something.

evasive adjective **1** avoiding committing yourself or revealing things about yourself. **2** (of an action) intended to avoid or escape something.
■ **evasively** adverb.

eve noun **1** the day or period of time immediately before an event or occasion. **2** evening.

even¹ adjective **1** flat and smooth; level. **2** equal in number, amount, or value. **3** regular. **4** equally balanced. **5** placid; calm. **6** (of a number) able to be divided by two without a remainder. ● verb (**evens, evening, evened**) make or become even.
● adverb used for emphasis: *he knows even less than I do.*
□ **even-handed** fair and impartial.
■ **evenly** adverb **evenness** noun.

even² noun old use evening.

evening noun the period of time at the end of the day.

evensong noun a Christian service of evening prayers, psalms, and hymns.

event noun **1** a thing that happens or takes place. **2** a public or social occasion. **3** each of several contests making up a sports competition.

eventful adjective marked by interesting or exciting events.

eventual adjective occurring at the end of or resulting from a process or period of time.
■ **eventually** adverb.

eventuality noun (plural **eventualities**) a possible event or outcome.

ever adverb **1** at any time. **2** used for emphasis in comparisons and questions: *better than ever.* **3** always. **4** increasingly.

evergreen adjective (of a plant) having green leaves throughout the year.

everlasting adjective lasting forever or a very long time.
■ **everlastingly** adverb.

evermore adverb always; forever.

every determiner **1** used to refer to all the individual members of a set without exception. **2** used to indicate how often something happens: *every thirty minutes.* **3** all possible: *every effort was made.*

everybody pronoun every person.

everyday adjective **1** daily. **2** happening regularly.

THESAURUS

evaporate verb **1** *the water evaporated:* vaporize, dry up. **2** *the feeling has evaporated:* end, pass (away), fizzle out, peter out, wear off, vanish, fade, disappear, melt away.
OPPOSITES condense, materialize.

evasive adjective equivocal, prevaricating, elusive, ambiguous, non-committal, vague, unclear, oblique.

even adjective **1** *an even surface:* flat, smooth, uniform, level, plane. **2** *an even temperature:* uniform, constant, steady, stable, consistent, unvarying, unchanging, regular. **3** *the score was even:* level, drawn, tied, all square, neck and neck; Brit. level pegging; informal even-steven(s).
OPPOSITES bumpy, irregular, unequal.

evening noun dusk, twilight, nightfall, sunset, sundown, night.

event noun **1** *an annual event:* occurrence, happening, incident, affair, occasion, phenomenon, function, gathering; informal do. **2** *a team event:* competition, contest, tournament, match, fixture, race, game, sport, discipline.

eventful adjective busy, action-packed, full, lively, active, hectic.
OPPOSITES dull.

eventual adjective final, ultimate, resulting, ensuing, consequent, subsequent.

eventually adverb in the end, in due course, by and by, in time, after a time, finally, at last, ultimately, in the long run, at the end of the day, one day, some day, sometime, sooner or later.

ever adverb **1** *the best I've ever done:* at any time, at any point, on any occasion, under any circumstances, on any account, until now. **2** *he was ever the optimist:* always, forever, eternally. **3** *an ever increasing rate of crime:* continually, constantly, always, endlessly, perpetually, incessantly.

everlasting adjective eternal, endless, never-ending, perpetual, undying, abiding, enduring, infinite.
OPPOSITES transient, occasional.

every determiner **1** *he exercised every day:* each, each and every, every single. **2** *we make every effort to satisfy our clients:* all possible, the utmost.
OPPOSITES no.

everybody pronoun everyone, every person, each person, all, one and all, all and sundry, the whole world, the public.
OPPOSITES nobody.

everyday adjective **1** *the everyday demands of a baby:* daily, day-to-day, ongoing; formal quotidian. **2** *everyday drugs like aspirin:* commonplace, ordinary, common, usual, regular, familiar, conventional, routine,

everyone pronoun every person.

everything pronoun **1** all things, or all the things of a group. **2** the most important thing.

everywhere adverb **1** in or to all places. **2** in many places.

evict verb legally force someone to leave a property.
■ **eviction** noun.

evidence noun **1** information indicating whether something is true or valid. **2** information used to establish facts in a legal investigation. • verb (**evidences, evidencing, evidenced**) be or show evidence of.
◻ **in evidence** noticeable.

evident adjective easily seen or understood; obvious.
■ **evidently** adverb.

evil adjective **1** deeply immoral and wicked. **2** very unpleasant. • noun **1** extreme wickedness. **2** something harmful or undesirable.
■ **evilly** adverb.

evince verb (**evinces, evincing, evinced**) formal reveal the presence of.

eviscerate /i-viss-uh-rayt/ verb (**eviscerates, eviscerating, eviscerated**) formal remove the intestines of.
■ **evisceration** noun.

evocative adjective bringing strong images, memories, or feelings to mind.

evoke verb (**evokes, evoking, evoked**) **1** bring a feeling or memory into someone's mind. **2** obtain a response.
■ **evocation** noun.

evolution noun **1** the process by which different kinds of animals and plants develop from earlier forms. **2** gradual development.
■ **evolutionary** adjective.

evolve verb (**evolves, evolving, evolved**) **1** develop gradually. **2** (of an animal or plant) develop and change over many generations by evolution.

ewe noun a female sheep.

ewer /yoo-er/ noun a large jug with a wide mouth.

ex noun informal a former husband, wife, boyfriend, or girlfriend. • prefix (**ex-**) **1** out: *exclude.* **2** former: *ex-husband.*

exacerbate verb (**exacerbates, exacerbating, exacerbated**) make something that is already bad worse.
■ **exacerbation** noun.

exact adjective **1** precise. **2** accurate in all

run-of-the-mill, standard, stock, household, domestic; Brit. common or garden.
OPPOSITES unusual.

everyone pronoun. See EVERYBODY.

everything pronoun every single thing, each thing, the (whole) lot, all; informal the works.
OPPOSITES nothing.

everywhere adverb all over, all around, in every nook and cranny, far and wide, near and far, high and low, {here, there, and everywhere}, the world over, worldwide; informal all over the place; Brit. informal all over the shop; N. Amer. informal all over the map.
OPPOSITES nowhere.

evidence noun **1** *evidence of his infidelity:* proof, confirmation, verification, substantiation, corroboration. **2** *the court accepted her evidence:* testimony, witness statement, declaration, submission; Law deposition, affidavit. **3** *evidence of a struggle:* signs, indications, marks, traces, suggestions, hints.

evident adjective obvious, apparent, noticeable, conspicuous, visible, discernible, clear, plain, manifest, patent; informal as clear as day.

evidently adverb **1** *he was evidently upset:* obviously, clearly, plainly, unmistakably, manifestly, patently. **2** *evidently, she believed him:* seemingly, apparently, from all appearances, on the face of it, it seems, it appears.

evil adjective **1** *an evil deed:* wicked, bad, wrong, immoral, sinful, vile, iniquitous, villainous, vicious, malicious, malevolent, demonic, diabolical, fiendish, dark, monstrous. **2** *an evil spirit:* harmful, bad, malign. **3** *evil weather:* unpleasant, disagreeable, nasty, horrible, foul, filthy, vile.
OPPOSITES good, benign, pleasant.
• noun **1** *the evil in our midst:* wickedness, badness, wrongdoing, sin, sinfulness, immorality, vice, iniquity, corruption, villainy. **2** *nothing but evil will result:* harm, pain, misery, sorrow, suffering, trouble, disaster, misfortune, woe.
OPPOSITES good.

evoke verb bring to mind, put someone in mind of, conjure up, summon (up), invoke, elicit, induce, kindle, awaken, arouse.

evolution noun **1** *the evolution of Bolshevism:* development, progress, rise, expansion, growth. **2** *his interest in evolution:* natural selection, Darwinism, adaptation, development.

evolve verb develop, progress, advance, grow, expand, spread.

exact adjective **1** *an exact description:* precise, accurate, correct, faithful, close, true, literal, strict, perfect. **2** *an exact record keeper:* careful, meticulous, painstaking, punctilious, conscientious, details. • **verb 1** demand and obtain something from someone. **2** take revenge on someone.

■ **exactness** noun.

exacting adjective (of a task) making you concentrate or work very hard.

exactitude noun the quality of being exact.

exactly adverb **1** in an exact way. **2** used to agree with what has just been said.

exaggerate verb (**exaggerates, exaggerating, exaggerated**) make something seem larger, more important, etc. than it really is.

■ **exaggeration** noun.

☑ two *g*s: exa*gg*erate.

exalt verb **1** praise someone or something highly. **2** give someone or something a higher rank or status.

exaltation noun **1** extreme happiness. **2** the action of exalting.

exalted adjective **1** having high rank or status. **2** very grand or noble; high-flown.

exam noun an examination in a subject or skill.

examination noun **1** a detailed inspection. **2** a formal test of knowledge or ability in a subject or skill. **3** the action of examining.

examine verb (**examines, examining, examined**) **1** inspect something closely. **2** (of a doctor or dentist) look closely at a part of a person's body to detect any problems. **3** test someone's knowledge or ability.

■ **examinee** noun **examiner** noun.

example noun **1** a thing that is typical of or represents a particular group. **2** something that shows or supports a general rule. **3** a person or thing seen in terms of how suitable they are to be copied.

exasperate verb (**exasperates, exasperating, exasperated**) irritate someone very much.

■ **exasperation** noun.

excavate verb (**excavates, excavating, excavated**) **1** make a hole by digging. **2** carefully remove earth from an area in order to find buried remains. **3** dig material out of the ground.

■ **excavation** noun.

exceed verb **1** be greater in number or size than. **2** go beyond a set limit. **3** go beyond what is expected.

exceedingly adverb extremely.

excel verb (**excels, excelling, excelled**) **1** be very good at something. **2** (**excel yourself**) do something exceptionally well.

Excellency noun (plural **Excellencies**) (**His, Your,** etc. **Excellency**) a form of address for certain high officials of state or of the Roman Catholic Church.

excellent adjective very good; outstanding.

■ **excellence** noun **excellently** adverb.

THESAURUS

scrupulous.

OPPOSITES inaccurate, careless.

• verb **1** *he exacted certain promises:* demand, require, impose, extract, compel, force, wring. **2** *they exacted a terrible vengeance on him:* inflict, impose, administer, mete out, wreak.

exacting adjective demanding, stringent, testing, challenging, arduous, laborious, taxing, gruelling, punishing, hard, tough.

OPPOSITES easy, easy-going.

exactly adverb **1** *it's exactly as I expected:* precisely, entirely, absolutely, completely, totally, just, quite, in every respect. **2** *write it out exactly:* accurately, precisely, unerringly, faultlessly, perfectly, faithfully.

exaggerate verb overstate, overemphasize, overestimate, inflate, embellish, embroider, elaborate, overplay, dramatize; Brit. informal blow out of all proportion.

OPPOSITES understate.

examination noun **1** *artefacts spread out for examination:* scrutiny, inspection, perusal, study, investigation, consideration, analysis. **2** *a medical examination:* inspection, check-up, test, assessment, appraisal, scan. **3** *a school examination:* test, exam, assessment; N. Amer. quiz.

examine verb **1** *they examined the bank records:* inspect, scrutinize, investigate, look at, study, appraise, analyse, review, survey; informal check out. **2** *students were examined after a year:* test, quiz, question, assess, appraise.

example noun **1** *a fine example of Chinese porcelain:* specimen, sample, instance, case, illustration. **2** *we must follow their example:* precedent, lead, model, pattern, ideal, standard. **3** *he was hanged as an example to others:* warning, lesson, deterrent, disincentive.

excavate verb unearth, dig up, uncover, reveal, disinter, exhume, dig out, quarry, mine.

exceed verb be more than, be greater than, be over, go beyond, top, surpass.

excel verb shine, be excellent, be outstanding, be skilful, be talented, stand out, be second to none.

excellence noun distinction, quality, superiority, brilliance, greatness, calibre, eminence.

excellent adjective very good, superb, outstanding, exceptional, marvellous, wonderful, splendid; informal terrific, fantastic.

OPPOSITES inferior.

except preposition not including. •**conjunction** used before a statement that forms an exception to one just made. •**verb** exclude.

> ☑ don't forget the *c* in **except** and related words. Also, don't confuse **except** and **accept**, which means 'agree to receive or do something'.

excepting preposition except for.

exception noun a person or thing that is excluded or that does not follow a rule. □ **take exception to** object strongly to.

exceptionable adjective formal causing disapproval or offence.

exceptional adjective 1 unusual; not typical. 2 unusually good.
■ **exceptionally** adverb.

excerpt noun a short extract from a film or piece of music or writing.

excess noun 1 an amount that is too much. 2 (**excesses**) extreme or outrageous behaviour. 3 Brit. a part of an insurance claim to be paid by the person insured. •**adjective** going beyond an allowed or desirable amount.

excessive adjective more than is necessary, normal, or desirable.
■ **excessively** adverb.

exchange noun 1 an act of giving something and receiving something else in return. 2 a short conversation or argument.

3 the changing of money to its equivalent in another currency. 4 a building used for financial trading. 5 a set of equipment that connects telephone lines during a call.
•**verb** (**exchanges, exchanging, exchanged**) give something and receive something else in return.
□ **exchange rate** the value at which one currency may be exchanged for another.

exchequer noun 1 a royal or national treasury. 2 (**Exchequer**) Brit. the account at the Bank of England into which public money is paid.

excise[1] /ek-syz/ noun a tax charged on certain goods, such as alcohol.

excise[2] /ik-syz/ verb (**excises, excising, excised**) 1 cut something out. 2 remove a section from a written work or piece of music.
■ **excision** noun.

excitable adjective easily excited.
■ **excitability** noun **excitably** adverb.

excite verb (**excites, exciting, excited**) 1 make someone feel very enthusiastic and eager. 2 make someone feel sexually aroused. 3 give rise to. 4 increase the energy or activity in a physical or biological system.
■ **excitation** noun **exciting** adjective **excitingly** adverb.

> ☑ don't forget the *c*: excite.

---

except preposition excluding, not including, excepting, except for, omitting, not counting, but, besides, apart from, aside from, barring, bar, other than; informal outside of.
OPPOSITES including.

exception noun anomaly, irregularity, deviation, special case, peculiarity, abnormality, oddity.

exceptional adjective 1 *the drought was exceptional:* unusual, abnormal, atypical, out of the ordinary, rare, unprecedented, unexpected, surprising. 2 *her exceptional ability:* outstanding, extraordinary, remarkable, special, phenomenal, prodigious.
OPPOSITES normal, average.

excerpt noun extract, part, section, piece, portion, snippet, clip, citation, quotation, quote, line, passage, fragment.

excess noun 1 *an excess of calcium:* surplus, surfeit, over-abundance, superabundance, superfluity, glut. 2 *the excess is turned into fat:* extra, surplus, remainder, rest, residue. 3 *a life of excess:* overindulgence, intemperance, immoderation, profligacy, extravagance, self-indulgence.
OPPOSITES lack, restraint.
•**adjective** *excess oil:* surplus, superfluous,

redundant, unwanted, unneeded, excessive, extra.

excessive adjective 1 *excessive alcohol consumption:* immoderate, intemperate, overindulgent, unrestrained, uncontrolled, extravagant. 2 *the cost is excessive:* exorbitant, extortionate, unreasonable, outrageous, uncalled for, inordinate, unwarranted, disproportionate; informal over the top.

exchange noun 1 *the exchange of ideas:* interchange, trade, trading, swapping, traffic, trafficking. 2 *a brief exchange:* conversation, dialogue, chat, talk, discussion.
•**verb** *we exchanged shirts:* trade, swap, switch, change.

excite verb 1 *the prospect of a holiday excited me:* thrill, exhilarate, animate, enliven, rouse, stir, stimulate, galvanize. 2 *his clothes excited envy:* provoke, stir up, rouse, arouse, kindle, trigger, spark off, incite, cause.
OPPOSITES bore.

excitement noun 1 *the excitement of seeing a leopard in the wild:* thrill, pleasure, delight, joy; informal buzz. 2 *excitement in her eyes:* exhilaration, elation, animation, enthusiasm, eagerness, anticipation.

excitement noun 1 a feeling of great enthusiasm and eagerness. 2 something that arouses such a feeling. 3 sexual arousal.

exclaim verb cry out suddenly.

exclamation noun a sudden cry or remark. □ exclamation mark a punctuation mark (!) indicating an exclamation.
■ exclamatory adjective.

exclude verb (**excludes, excluding, excluded**) 1 choose not to include something in what you are counting or considering. 2 prevent someone from being a part of something.

exclusion noun the process of excluding, or the state of being excluded.

exclusive adjective 1 restricted to the person, group, or area concerned. 2 high-quality and expensive. 3 not including other things. 4 not published or broadcast elsewhere. • noun a story or film that has not been published or broadcast elsewhere.
■ exclusively adverb exclusivity noun.

excommunicate verb (**excommunicates, excommunicating, excommunicated**) officially bar someone from membership of the Christian Church.
■ excommunication noun.

excoriate verb (**excoriates, excoriating, excoriated**) 1 formal criticize someone severely. 2 Medicine damage or remove part of the surface of the skin.
■ excoriation noun.

excrement noun waste material passed from the body through the bowels.

excrescence noun an abnormal growth or lump on a part of the body or a plant.

excreta noun waste material that is passed out of the body.

excrete verb (**excretes, excreting, excreted**) pass waste material from the body.
■ excretion noun excretory adjective.

excruciating adjective 1 very painful. 2 very embarrassing, awkward, or boring.
■ excruciatingly adverb.

exculpate /eks-kul-payt/ verb (**exculpates, exculpating, exculpated**) formal say that someone is not guilty of doing something wrong.
■ exculpation noun.

excursion noun a short journey or trip taken for pleasure.

excuse verb /ik-skyooz/ (**excuses, excusing, excused**) 1 give reasons why something that someone has done wrong may be justified. 2 forgive someone for something they have done wrong. 3 allow someone to not do something that is usually required. 4 allow someone to leave a room or meeting. • noun /ik-skyooss/ 1 a reason put forward to justify a fault or wrongdoing. 2 something said to conceal the real reason for an action. 3 informal a very bad example of something.
■ excusable adjective.

ex-directory adjective Brit. not listed in a telephone directory at your own request.

execrable /ek-si-kruh-b'l/ adjective very bad or unpleasant.

execrate /ek-si-krayt/ verb (**execrates, execrating, execrated**) feel or express great hatred for.
■ execration noun.

execute verb (**executes, executing, executed**) 1 carry out a plan, order, etc.

THESAURUS

exciting adjective thrilling, exhilarating, stirring, rousing, stimulating, intoxicating, electrifying, invigorating, gripping, compelling, powerful, dramatic.

exclaim verb cry out, declare, proclaim, blurt out, call out, shout, yell.

exclude verb 1 *women were excluded from the club:* keep out, deny access to, shut out, bar, ban, prohibit. 2 *the clause excluded any judicial review:* rule out, preclude. 3 *the price excludes postage:* be exclusive of, not include.
OPPOSITES admit, include, allow for.

exclusive adjective 1 *an exclusive club:* select, chic, high-class, elite, fashionable, stylish, elegant, premier; Brit. upmarket; informal posh, classy; Brit. informal swish. 2 *a room for your exclusive use:* sole, unshared, unique, individual, personal, private. 3 *prices exclusive of VAT:* not including, excluding, leaving out, omitting, excepting.
OPPOSITES shared, inclusive.

excursion noun outing, trip, jaunt, expedition, journey, tour, day trip, day out, drive, run; informal spin.

excuse verb 1 *please excuse me:* forgive, pardon. 2 *such conduct cannot be excused:* justify, defend, condone, forgive, overlook, disregard, ignore, tolerate, explain, mitigate. 3 *she was excused from her duties:* let off, release, relieve, exempt, absolve, free.
OPPOSITES punish, blame, condemn.
• noun 1 *that's no excuse for stealing:* justification, defence, reason, explanation, mitigating circumstances, mitigation. 2 *an excuse to get away:* pretext, pretence; Brit. get-out; informal story, alibi.

execute verb 1 *he executed a series of financial deals:* carry out, accomplish, bring off/about, implement, achieve, complete, engineer; informal pull off. 2 *he was finally executed:* put to death, kill, hang, behead, electrocute, shoot.

2 carry out an activity or manoeuvre. **3** kill a condemned person as a legal punishment.

execution noun **1** the carrying out of something. **2** the killing of a person who has been condemned to death.

executioner noun an official who executes condemned criminals.

executive noun **1** a senior manager in a business. **2** a group of people who run an organization or business. **3** (**the executive**) the branch of a government responsible for putting plans, actions, or laws into effect. •adjective having the power to put plans, actions, or laws into effect.

executor /ig-**zek**-yuu-ter/ noun a person appointed by someone to carry out the terms of their will.

exegesis /ek-si-**jee**-siss/ noun (plural **exegeses** /ek-si-**jee**-seez/) an explanation or interpretation of a written work.

exemplar /ig-**zem**-pler/ noun a person or thing that is a good or typical example of something.

exemplary adjective **1** giving a good example to other people. **2** (of a punishment) acting as a warning.

exemplify verb (**exemplifies**, **exemplifying**, **exemplified**) be or give a typical example of.
■ **exemplification** noun.

exempt adjective not having to do or pay something that other people have to do or pay. •verb make someone exempt.
■ **exemption** noun.

exercise noun **1** physical activity done to stay healthy or become stronger. **2** a set of movements, activities, or questions that test your ability or help you practise a skill. **3** an activity carried out for a specific purpose. **4** the putting into practice of a power or right. •verb (**exercises**, **exercising**, **exercised**) **1** use or apply a power or right. **2** do physical exercise. **3** worry or puzzle someone.
□ **exercise book** Brit. a booklet with blank pages for students to write in.

exert verb **1** use a force, influence, or quality to make something happen. **2** (**exert yourself**) make a physical or mental effort.
■ **exertion** noun.

exeunt /**ek**-si-uhnt/ verb (in a play) a stage direction telling actors to leave the stage.

exfoliate verb (**exfoliates**, **exfoliating**, **exfoliated**) wash or rub the skin with a grainy substance to remove dead cells.
■ **exfoliation** noun.

exhale verb (**exhales**, **exhaling**, **exhaled**) **1** breathe out. **2** give off vapour or fumes.
■ **exhalation** noun.

exhaust verb **1** tire someone out. **2** use up all of something. **3** talk about a subject so

e

---

execution noun **1** *the execution of the plan:* **implementation**, carrying out, performance, accomplishment, bringing off/about, attainment, realization. **2** *public execution:* **killing**, capital punishment, the death penalty.

executive adjective *executive powers:* **administrative**, managerial, decision-making, law-making, governing, controlling.
•noun **1** *the company's chief executive:* **director**, manager, senior official, administrator; informal boss, exec, suit. **2** *the parliamentary executive:* **administration**, management, directorate, government, authority.

exemplary adjective **perfect**, ideal, model, faultless, flawless, impeccable, irreproachable.
OPPOSITES deplorable.

exemplify verb **typify**, epitomize, be an example of, be representative of, symbolize, illustrate, demonstrate.

exempt adjective **free**, not liable, not subject, immune, excepted, excused, absolved.
OPPOSITES subject to.
•verb **excuse**, free, release, exclude, grant immunity, spare, absolve; informal let off.

exemption noun **immunity**, exception, dispensation, indemnity, exclusion, freedom, release, relief, absolution.

exercise noun **1** *exercise improves your heart:* **physical activity**, a workout, working out, movement, training. **2** *translation exercises:* **task**, piece of work, problem, assignment, practice. **3** *a military exercise:* **manoeuvre**, operation, deployment.
•verb **1** *she exercised every day:* **work out**, do exercises, train. **2** *he must learn to exercise patience:* **use**, employ, make use of, utilize, practise, apply. **3** *the problem continued to exercise him:* **concern**, occupy, worry, trouble, bother, disturb, prey on someone's mind.

exert verb **bring to bear**, apply, use, utilize, deploy.
□ **exert yourself work hard**, labour, toil, make an effort, endeavour, slog away, push yourself.

exhaust verb **1** *the effort had exhausted him:* **tire out**, wear out, overtire, fatigue, weary, drain; informal take it out of you, shatter; Brit. informal knacker; N. Amer. informal poop, tucker out. **2** *the country has exhausted its reserves:* **use up**, get through, e

thoroughly that there is nothing left to say. • **noun 1** waste gases that are expelled from the engine of a car or other machine. **2** the system through which these gases are expelled.
■ **exhaustible** adjective.

exhaustion noun the state of being exhausted.

exhaustive adjective thoroughly covering all aspects of something.
■ **exhaustively** adverb.

exhibit verb **1** display an item in an art gallery or museum. **2** show a particular quality. • noun **1** an object or collection on display in an art gallery or museum. **2** an object produced in a court of law as evidence.
■ **exhibitor** noun.

exhibition noun **1** a public display of items in an art gallery or museum. **2** a display or demonstration of a skill or quality.

exhibitionism noun behaviour that is intended to make people notice you.
■ **exhibitionist** noun.

exhilarate verb (**exhilarates**, **exhilarating**, **exhilarated**) make someone feel very happy and full of energy.
■ **exhilaration** noun.

☑ the middle is -*lar*-, not -*ler*-: exhi*lar*ate.

exhort verb strongly urge someone to do something.
■ **exhortation** noun.

exhume verb (**exhumes**, **exhuming**, **exhumed**) dig out from the ground something that has been buried.

■ **exhumation** noun.

exigency /ek-si-juhn-si/ noun (plural **exigencies**) formal an urgent need.

exigent /ek-si-juhnt/ adjective formal needing urgent action; pressing.

exiguous /eg-**zig**-yoo-uhss/ adjective formal very small.

exile noun **1** the state of being forbidden to live or spend time in your own country. **2** a person who lives in exile. • verb (**exiles**, **exiling**, **exiled**) expel and bar someone from their own country.

exist verb **1** be present in a place or situation. **2** live.

existence noun **1** the fact or state of existing. **2** a way of living: *a rural existence.*

☑ -ence, not -ance: existence.

existential /eg-zi-**sten**-sh'l/ adjective **1** having to do with existence. **2** Philosophy concerned with existentialism.

existentialism noun a theory in philosophy which says that people are free individuals, responsible for their own actions.
■ **existentialist** noun & adjective.

exit noun **1** a way out of a place. **2** an act of leaving. • verb (**exits**, **exiting**, **exited**) go out of or leave a place.
□ **exit poll** an opinion poll in which people leaving a polling station are asked how they voted.

exocrine /ek-soh-kryn/ adjective (of a gland) secreting hormones or other

---

THESAURUS

consume, finish, deplete, spend, empty, drain; informal blow.
OPPOSITES invigorate, replenish.

exhaustion noun tiredness, overtiredness, fatigue, weariness.

exhibit verb **1** *the paintings were exhibited in Glasgow:* display, show, put on display, unveil, present. **2** *Luke exhibited signs of jealousy:* show, reveal, display, manifest, indicate, demonstrate, express.
• noun *an exhibit at the British Museum:* item, piece, artefact, display, collection.

exhibition noun **1** *a photography exhibition:* display, show, showing, presentation, exposition. **2** *a convincing exhibition of concern:* display, show, demonstration, manifestation, expression.

exhilarating adjective thrilling, exciting, invigorating, stimulating, intoxicating, electrifying.

exile noun **1** *his exile from his homeland:* banishment, expulsion, deportation, eviction, isolation. **2** *political exiles:* expatriate, émigré, deportee, displaced person, refugee.

exist verb **1** *animals that existed long ago:* live, be alive, be, be present. **2** *the liberal climate that now exists:* prevail, occur, be found, be in existence, be the case. **3** *she had to exist on a low income:* survive, subsist, live, support yourself, manage, make do, get by, scrape by, make ends meet.

existence noun **1** *the industry's continued existence:* survival, continuation. **2** *her suburban existence:* way of life, life, lifestyle, situation.
□ in existence **existing**, alive, surviving, remaining, extant, existent, in circulation, current.

exit noun **1** *a fire exit:* way out, door, escape route, egress. **2** *take the second exit:* turning, turn-off, junction. **3** *his sudden exit:* departure, leaving, withdrawal, going, retreat, flight, exodus, escape.
OPPOSITES entrance, arrival.
• verb *the doctor had just exited:* leave, go out, depart, withdraw, retreat.
OPPOSITES enter.

products through ducts rather than directly into the blood.

exodus noun a mass departure of people.

exonerate /ig-**zon**-uh-rayt/ verb (**exonerates, exonerating, exonerated**) officially state that someone has not done something wrong or illegal.
■ **exoneration** noun.

exorbitant adjective (of an amount charged) unreasonably high.
■ **exorbitantly** adverb.

☑ no h: exorbitant.

exorcize or **exorcise** verb (**exorcizes, exorcizing, exorcizes**) drive an evil spirit from a person or place.
■ **exorcism** noun **exorcist** noun.

exotic adjective 1 coming from or characteristic of a distant foreign country. 2 strikingly colourful or unusual.
■ **exotically** adverb **exoticism** noun.

expand verb 1 make or become larger or more extensive. 2 (**expand on**) give a fuller account of.
■ **expandable** adjective **expansion** noun.

expanse noun a wide continuous area of something.

expansive adjective 1 covering a wide area. 2 relaxed, friendly, and communicative.
■ **expansively** adverb.

expat = EXPATRIATE.

expatiate /ek-**spay**-shi-ayt/ verb (**expatiates, expatiating, expatiated**) (**expatiate on**) speak or write in detail about something.

expatriate noun /eks-**pat**-ri-uht/ a person who lives outside their own country.

expect verb 1 think something is likely to

happen. 2 think someone is likely to do or be something. 3 believe that someone will arrive soon. 4 assume or demand that someone will do something because it is their duty or responsibility. 5 (**be expecting**) informal be pregnant.

expectancy noun (plural **expectancies**) the belief or hope that something will happen.

expectant adjective 1 believing or hoping that something is about to happen. 2 (of a woman) pregnant.
■ **expectantly** adverb.

expectation noun 1 belief that something will happen or be the case. 2 a thing that is expected to happen.

expectorant noun a medicine which helps to bring up phlegm from the air passages, used to treat a cough.

expectorate verb (**expectorates, expectorating, expectorated**) cough or spit out phlegm from the throat or lungs.

expedient /ik-**spee**-di-uhnt/ adjective 1 useful or helpful for a particular purpose. 2 useful in achieving something, rather than morally correct. •noun a means of achieving something.
■ **expediency** (or **expedience**) noun.

expedite /**eks**-pi-dyt/ verb (**expedites, expediting, expedited**) make something happen more quickly.

expedition noun a journey with a particular purpose, made by a group of people.
■ **expeditionary** adjective.

expeditious /eks-pi-**di**-shuhss/ adjective quick and efficient.
■ **expeditiously** adverb.

expel verb (**expels, expelling, expelled**)

---

exotic adjective 1 *exotic birds:* foreign, non-native, alien, tropical. 2 *exotic places:* foreign, faraway, far-off, far-flung, distant. 3 *Linda's exotic appearance:* striking, colourful, eye-catching, unusual, unconventional, extravagant, outlandish.
OPPOSITES native, nearby, conventional.

expand verb 1 *metals expand when heated:* enlarge, increase in size, swell, lengthen, stretch, spread, thicken, fill out. 2 *the company is expanding:* grow, enlarge, increase in size, extend, augment, broaden, widen, develop, diversify, build up, branch out, spread.
OPPOSITES contract.
□ **expand on elaborate on,** enlarge on, go into detail about, flesh out, develop.

expansion noun 1 *expansion and contraction:* enlargement, swelling, lengthening, elongation, stretching, thickening. 2 *the expansion of the company:* growth, increase in size, enlargement,

extension, development, diversification, spread.
OPPOSITES contraction.

expect verb 1 *I expect she'll be late:* suppose, presume, imagine, assume, surmise; informal guess, reckon; N. Amer. informal figure. 2 *a 10 per cent rise was expected:* anticipate, envisage, await, look for, hope for, look forward to, contemplate, bargain for/on, predict, forecast. 3 *we expect total loyalty:* require, ask for, call for, want, insist on, demand.

expectation noun 1 *her expectations were unrealistic:* supposition, assumption, presumption, conjecture, calculation, prediction, hope. 2 *tense with expectation:* anticipation, expectancy, eagerness, excitement, suspense.

expedition noun journey, voyage, tour, safari, trek, mission, quest, hike, trip.

expel verb throw out, bar, ban, debar, drum

1 force someone to leave a school, organization, or place. **2** force something out.

expend verb spend or use up a resource.

expendable adjective able to be sacrificed in order to gain or achieve something.

expenditure noun **1** the action of spending money. **2** the amount of money spent.

expense noun **1** the amount something costs. **2** something on which money must be spent. **3** (**expenses**) money spent in doing a particular thing. **4** (**expenses**) money paid for meals, fares, etc. by an employee in the course of their work, which they can claim back from their employer.

expensive adjective costing a lot of money. ■ **expensively** adverb.

experience noun **1** the fact of being present at or taking part in something. **2** knowledge or skill gained over time. **3** an event which affects you in some way. • verb (**experiences, experiencing, experienced**) **1** be present at or be affected by something. **2** feel an emotion.

experienced adjective having gained a lot of knowledge or skill in a job or activity over time.

experiment noun **1** a scientific procedure carried out to make a discovery, test a theory, or demonstrate a fact. **2** a new course of action that you try out without being sure of the outcome. • verb **1** perform a scientific experiment. **2** try out new things. ■ **experimentation** noun.

experimental adjective **1** based on a new idea and not yet fully tested. **2** having to do with scientific experiments. **3** (of art, music, etc.) new and unconventional. ■ **experimentally** adverb.

expert noun a person who has great knowledge or skill in a particular field. • adjective having or involving great knowledge or skill. ■ **expertly** adverb.

expertise noun great skill or knowledge in a particular field.

expiate /ek-spi-ayt/ verb (**expiates, expiating, expiated**) do something to make up for having done something wrong. ■ **expiation** noun.

expire verb (**expires, expiring, expired**) **1** (of a document or agreement) cease to be valid. **2** (of a period of time) come to an end. **3** (of a person) die. **4** breathe out air from the lungs.

THESAURUS

out, banish, exile, deport, evict; informal chuck out.
OPPOSITES admit.

expense noun cost, expenditure, spending, outlay, outgoings, payment, price, charge, fees, overheads, tariff, bill.
OPPOSITES income, profit.

expensive adjective costly, dear, high-priced, overpriced, exorbitant, extortionate; informal steep, stiff, pricey.
OPPOSITES cheap.

experience noun **1** *qualifications and experience:* skill, practical knowledge, understanding, background, track record, history; informal know-how. **2** *an enjoyable experience:* incident, occurrence, event, happening, episode, adventure. **3** *his first experience of business:* involvement in, participation in, contact with, acquaintance with, exposure to.
• verb *they experience daily harassment:* undergo, go through, encounter, face, meet, come across, come up against.

experienced adjective knowledgeable, skilful, skilled, expert, proficient, trained, competent, capable, seasoned, practised, mature, veteran.
OPPOSITES inexperienced.

experiment noun *the calculations were confirmed by experiment:* test, investigation, trial, examination, observation, research, assessment,

evaluation, appraisal, analysis, study.
• verb *they experimented with new ideas:* carry out experiments, test, trial, try out, assess, appraise, evaluate.

experimental adjective **1** *the experimental stage:* exploratory, investigational, trial, test, pilot, speculative, tentative, preliminary. **2** *experimental music:* new, innovative, creative, radical, avant-garde, alternative, unorthodox, unconventional, cutting-edge; informal edgy.

expert noun specialist, authority, pundit, maestro, virtuoso, master, wizard, connoisseur, aficionado; informal ace, pro, hotshot; Brit. informal dab hand; N. Amer. informal maven.
OPPOSITES amateur.
• adjective skilful, skilled, adept, accomplished, experienced, practised, knowledgeable, talented, masterly, virtuoso; informal ace, crack, mean.
OPPOSITES incompetent.

expertise noun skill, prowess, proficiency, competence, knowledge, ability, aptitude, capability; informal know-how.

expire verb **1** *my contract has expired:* run out, become invalid, become void, lapse, end, finish, stop, terminate. **2** *the spot where he expired:* die, pass away, breathe your last; informal kick the bucket, croak; Brit. informal snuff it, peg out; N. Amer. informal buy the farm.

expiry noun the end of the period for which something is valid.

explain verb 1 describe something in a way that makes it easy to understand. 2 give a reason for something. 3 (**explain yourself**) say why you are doing something in order to justify or excuse it.
■ **explanation** noun.

explanatory adjective giving the reason for something, or making something clear.

expletive /ik-**splee**-tiv/ noun a swear word.

explicable adjective able to be explained.

explicit adjective 1 clear, detailed, and easy to understand. 2 showing or describing sexual activity openly and clearly.
■ **explicitly** adverb.

explode verb (**explodes, exploding, exploded**) 1 burst or shatter violently as a result of the release of internal energy. 2 show sudden violent emotion. 3 increase suddenly in number or extent. 4 show a belief to be false.

exploit verb /ik-**sployt**/ 1 make use of someone unfairly. 2 make good use of a resource. • noun /**ek**-sployt/ a daring act.
■ **exploitation** noun **exploitative** adjective.

explore verb (**explores, exploring, explored**) 1 travel through an unfamiliar area in order to learn about it. 2 examine or discuss something in detail. 3 investigate.
■ **exploration** noun **exploratory** adjective **explorer** noun.

explosion noun an instance of exploding.

explosive adjective 1 able or likely to explode. 2 likely to cause anger or controversy. 3 (of an increase) sudden and dramatic. • noun a substance which can be made to explode.
■ **explosively** adverb.

exponent /ik-**spoh**-nuhnt/ noun 1 a promoter of an idea or theory. 2 a person who does a particular thing skilfully. 3 Maths a raised figure beside a number indicating how many times that number is

e

explain verb 1 *he explained the procedure:* describe, make clear, spell out, put into words, define, elucidate, expound, clarify, throw light on. 2 *that could explain his behaviour:* account for, give a reason for, excuse.

explanation noun 1 *an explanation of his theory:* clarification, description, statement, interpretation, definition, commentary. 2 *I owe you an explanation:* account, reason, justification, answer, excuse, defence, vindication.

explicit adjective 1 *explicit instructions:* clear, plain, straightforward, crystal clear, precise, exact, specific, unequivocal, unambiguous, detailed. 2 *sexually explicit material:* graphic, candid, full-frontal, uncensored.
OPPOSITES vague, tasteful, decent.

explode verb 1 *a bomb has exploded:* blow up, detonate, go off, burst, erupt. 2 *exploding an atomic device:* detonate, set off, let off, discharge. 3 *he just exploded:* lose your temper, blow up; informal fly off the handle, hit the roof, blow your top; Brit. informal go spare; N. Amer. informal blow your lid/stack. 4 *the city's exploding population:* increase rapidly, mushroom, snowball, escalate, burgeon, rocket. 5 *exploding the myths about men:* disprove, refute, rebut, repudiate, debunk, give the lie to; informal shoot full of holes, blow out of the water.
OPPOSITES shrink.

exploit verb 1 *we should exploit this opportunity:* utilize, make use of, turn/put to good use, make the most of, capitalize on, benefit from; informal cash in on. 2 *exploiting the workers:* take advantage of, abuse, impose on, treat unfairly,

misuse, ill-treat; informal walk (all) over.
• noun *his exploits brought him notoriety:* feat, deed, act, adventure, stunt, escapade, achievement.

exploitation noun taking advantage, abuse, misuse, ill-treatment, unfair treatment, oppression.

exploration noun investigation, study, survey, research, inspection, examination, scrutiny, observation.

explore verb 1 *exploring Iceland:* travel through, tour, survey, scout, reconnoitre. 2 *they explored the possibilities:* investigate, look into, consider, examine, research, survey, scrutinize, study, review; informal check out.

explosion noun 1 *Ed heard the explosion:* detonation, eruption, bang, blast, boom. 2 *an explosion of anger:* outburst, flare-up, outbreak, eruption, storm, rush, surge, fit, paroxysm. 3 *a population explosion:* sudden increase, mushrooming, snowballing, escalation, multiplication, burgeoning, rocketing.

explosive adjective 1 *explosive gases:* volatile, inflammable, flammable, combustible, incendiary. 2 *Marco's explosive temper:* fiery, stormy, violent, volatile, passionate, tempestuous, turbulent, touchy, irascible. 3 *an explosive situation:* tense, highly charged, overwrought, dangerous, perilous, hazardous, sensitive, delicate, unstable, volatile.
OPPOSITES inert, cool, stable.
• noun *stocks of explosives:* bomb, charge, incendiary (device).

to be multiplied by itself (e.g. 3 in $2^3 = 2 \times 2 \times 2$).

exponential /eks-puh-**nen**-sh'l/ adjective 1 (of an increase) becoming more and more rapid. 2 Maths having to do with a mathematical exponent.
■ **exponentially** adverb.

export verb /ik-**sport**/ send goods or services to another country for sale. • noun /**ek**-sport/ 1 the exporting of goods or services. 2 an exported item.
■ **exportation** noun **exporter** noun.

expose verb (**exposes**, **exposing**, **exposed**) 1 uncover something and make it visible. 2 show the true nature of someone or something. 3 (**exposed**) not protected from the weather. 4 (**expose someone to**) make someone vulnerable to. 5 subject photographic film to light. 6 (**expose yourself**) show your sexual organs in public.

exposé /ik-**spoh**-zay/ noun a report in the news revealing shocking information about someone.

exposition noun 1 a careful setting out of the facts or ideas involved in something. 2 an exhibition. 3 Music the part of a movement in which the main themes are first presented.

expostulate verb (**expostulates**, **expostulating**, **expostulated**) express strong disapproval or disagreement.
■ **expostulation** noun.

exposure noun 1 the state of being exposed to something harmful. 2 a physical condition resulting from being exposed to severe weather conditions. 3 the revealing of the true facts about someone or something. 4 the fact of being discussed or mentioned on television, in newspapers, etc. 5 the quantity of light reaching a photographic film.

expound verb set out and explain the facts or ideas involved in something.

express[1] verb 1 show by words or actions what you are thinking or feeling. 2 squeeze out liquid or air.

express[2] adjective operating or delivered very quickly. • adverb by express train or delivery service. • noun 1 a train that travels quickly and stops at few stations. 2 a special delivery service.

express[3] adjective 1 stated very clearly. 2 excluding anything else.
■ **expressly** adverb.

expression noun 1 the action of expressing. 2 the look on someone's face. 3 a word or phrase expressing an idea. 4 Maths a collection of symbols expressing a quantity.
■ **expressionless** adjective.

expressionism noun a style in art, music, or drama in which the artist or writer shows the inner world of emotion rather than external reality.
■ **expressionist** noun & adjective.

expressive adjective clearly showing

THESAURUS

expose verb 1 *at low tide the rocks are exposed:* reveal, uncover, lay bare. 2 *he was exposed to radiation:* lay open, subject, put at risk of, put in jeopardy of, leave unprotected from. 3 *they were exposed to new ideas:* introduce to, bring into contact with, make aware of, familiarize with, acquaint with. 4 *he was exposed as a liar:* uncover, reveal, unveil, unmask, detect, find out, denounce, condemn; informal blow the whistle on.
OPPOSITES cover, protect from, insulate from, protect.

exposure noun 1 *suffering from exposure:* frostbite, cold, hypothermia. 2 *the exposure of a banking fraud:* uncovering, revelation, disclosure, unveiling, unmasking, discovery, detection. 3 *we're getting a lot of exposure:* publicity, advertising, public attention, media interest; informal hype.

express[1] verb communicate, convey, indicate, show, demonstrate, reveal, put across/over, get across/over, articulate, put into words, voice, give voice to, state, air, give vent to.
□ **express yourself** communicate your

thoughts/opinions/views, put thoughts into words, speak your mind, say what's on your mind.

express[2] adjective rapid, swift, fast, high-speed, non-stop, direct.
OPPOSITES slow.

express[3] adjective 1 *it was his express wish:* explicit, clear, direct, plain, distinct, unambiguous, categorical. 2 *his express purpose was to do work:* sole, specific, particular, special, specified.
OPPOSITES vague, implied.

expression noun 1 *the free expression of their views:* utterance, uttering, voicing, declaration, articulation. 2 *an expression of sympathy:* indication, demonstration, show, exhibition, token, communication, illustration. 3 *a sad expression:* look, appearance, air, manner, countenance. 4 *a well-known expression:* idiom, phrase, term, proverb, saying, adage, maxim. 5 *put more expression into it:* emotion, feeling, spirit, passion, intensity, style.

expressive adjective 1 *an expressive shrug:* eloquent, meaningful, demonstrative, suggestive. 2 *an expressive song:* emotional, passionate, poignant, moving,

thoughts or feelings.
■ **expressively** adverb **expressiveness** noun.

expropriate verb (**expropriates, expropriating, expropriated**) (of the state or an authority) take property from its owner.
■ **expropriation** noun.

expulsion noun the action of expelling.

expunge /ik-**spunj**/ verb (**expunges, expunging, expunged**) remove something completely.

expurgate /eks-per-gayt/ verb (**expurgates, expurgating, expurgated**) remove unsuitable material from a written work.
■ **expurgation** noun.

exquisite adjective **1** very beautiful and delicate. **2** showing great sensitivity or refinement. **3** strongly felt.
■ **exquisitely** adverb.

extant adjective still in existence.

extempore /ik-**stem**-puh-ri/ adjective & adverb spoken or done without preparation.

extemporize or **extemporise** verb (**extemporizes, extemporizing, extemporized**) make something up as you go along.

extend verb **1** make something larger in area. **2** make something last longer. **3** occupy a particular area or continue for a particular distance. **4** stretch out a part of your body. **5** offer something to someone.

□ **extended family** a family group consisting of parents and children and close relatives living nearby.
■ **extendable** (or **extendible**) adjective **extensible** adjective.

extension noun **1** the action of extending something. **2** a part added to a building to make it bigger. **3** an additional period of time. **4** an extra telephone on the same line as the main one.
□ **extension lead** a length of electric cable which can be plugged into a socket and has another socket on the end.

extensive adjective **1** covering a large area. **2** large in amount or scale.
■ **extensively** adverb.

extensor noun a muscle which makes a part of the body extend.

extent noun **1** the area covered by something. **2** size or scale. **3** the degree to which something is the case.

extenuating /ik-**sten**-yoo-ay-ting/ adjective serving to make an offence less serious by partially excusing it: *extenuating circumstances.*
■ **extenuation** noun.

exterior adjective having to do with the outside of something. • noun the outer surface or structure of something.

exterminate verb (**exterminates, exterminating, exterminated**) destroy

e

stirring, emotionally charged.
OPPOSITES undemonstrative, inexpressive.

expulsion noun **1** *expulsion from the party:* removal, debarment, dismissal, exclusion, ejection, banishment, eviction. **2** *the expulsion of waste:* discharge, ejection, excretion, voiding, evacuation, elimination, passing.
OPPOSITES admission.

exquisite adjective **1** *exquisite antiques:* beautiful, lovely, elegant, fine, delicate, fragile, dainty, subtle. **2** *exquisite taste:* discriminating, discerning, sensitive, fastidious, refined.

extend verb **1** *we've extended the kitchen:* expand, enlarge, increase, lengthen, widen, broaden. **2** *the garden extends to the road:* continue, carry on, stretch, reach. **3** *we have extended our range:* widen, expand, broaden, augment, supplement, increase, add to, enhance, develop. **4** *extending the life of parliament:* prolong, lengthen, increase, stretch out, protract, spin out, string out. **5** *he extended a hand:* hold out, reach out, hold forth, stretch out, offer, give, proffer. **6** *we wish to extend our thanks:* offer, proffer, give, accord.
OPPOSITES reduce, shorten, withdraw.
□ **extend to include**, take in, incorporate,

encompass.

extension noun **1** *they are planning an extension:* addition, add-on, adjunct, annex, wing. **2** *an extension of our knowledge:* expansion, increase, enlargement, widening, broadening, deepening, augmentation, enhancement, development, growth. **3** *an extension of opening hours:* prolongation, lengthening, increase.
OPPOSITES restriction, shortening.

extensive adjective **1** *extensive grounds:* large, sizeable, substantial, considerable, ample, great, vast. **2** *extensive knowledge:* comprehensive, thorough, exhaustive, broad, wide, wide-ranging, catholic.

extent noun **1** *two acres in extent:* area, size, expanse, length, proportions, dimensions. **2** *the full extent of her illness:* degree, scale, level, magnitude, scope, size, reach, range.

exterior adjective *the exterior surface:* outer, outside, outermost, outward, external.
OPPOSITES interior.
• noun *a beautiful exterior:* outside, external surface, outward appearance, facade.
OPPOSITES interior.

something completely.

■ **extermination** noun **exterminator** noun.

external adjective **1** having to do with the outside of something. **2** coming from outside an organization or situation. **3** having to do with another country or institution.

■ **externally** adverb.

externalize or **externalise** verb (**externalizes, externalizing, externalized**) express a thought or feeling in words or actions.

extinct adjective **1** no longer in existence. **2** (of a volcano) not having erupted in recorded history.

■ **extinction** noun.

extinguish verb **1** put out a fire or light. **2** put an end to.

■ **extinguisher** noun.

extirpate /ek-ster-payt/ verb (**extirpates, extirpating, extirpated**) search out and destroy something completely.

■ **extirpation** noun.

extol verb (**extols, extolling, extolled**) praise enthusiastically.

extort verb obtain something by force, threats, or other unfair means.

■ **extortion** noun.

extortionate adjective (of a price) much too high.

■ **extortionately** adverb.

extra adjective added to an existing or usual amount or number. ● adverb **1** to a greater extent than usual. **2** in addition. ● noun **1** an additional item, for which an extra charge

is made. **2** a person employed to take part in a crowd scene in a film or play. ● prefix (**extra-**) outside; beyond: *extramarital.*

extract verb /ik-**strakt**/ **1** remove something with care or effort. **2** obtain something from someone unwilling to give it. **3** separate out a substance by a special method. ● noun /ek-**strakt**/ **1** a short passage taken from a written work, film, or piece of music. **2** an extracted substance. □ **extractor fan** a device that removes steam and smells from a room.

extraction noun **1** the action of extracting. **2** the ethnic origin of someone's family.

extradite /ek-struh-dyt/ verb (**extradites, extraditing, extradited**) hand over a person accused or convicted of committing a crime in a foreign state to the legal authority of that state.

■ **extradition** noun.

extramarital adjective happening outside marriage.

extramural adjective Brit. (of a course of study) for people who are not full-time members of an educational establishment.

extraneous /ik-**stray**-ni-uhss/ adjective **1** unrelated to the subject being dealt with. **2** of external origin.

extraordinaire /ek-struh-or-di-**nair**/ adjective outstanding in a particular capacity: *she was a gardener extraordinaire.*

extraordinary adjective **1** very unusual or remarkable. **2** (of a meeting) held for a particular reason rather than being one of

THESAURUS

external adjective **1** *an external wall:* outer, outside, outermost, outward, exterior. **2** *an external examiner:* outside, independent, visiting.

OPPOSITES internal.

extinct adjective **1** *an extinct species:* vanished, lost, gone, died out, wiped out, destroyed. **2** *an extinct volcano:* inactive.

OPPOSITES living, dormant.

extinction noun dying out, disappearance, vanishing, extermination, destruction, elimination, eradication, annihilation.

extinguish verb douse, put out, quench, stamp out, smother, snuff out, stub out.

OPPOSITES light.

extort verb extract, exact, wring, wrest, screw, squeeze.

extortionate adjective exorbitant, excessive, outrageous, unreasonable, prohibitive, inflated; Brit. over the odds; informal over the top, daylight robbery.

extra adjective additional, more, added, supplementary, further, auxiliary, ancillary, subsidiary, secondary.

● adverb exceptionally, particularly, specially, especially, extremely.

● noun addition, supplement, bonus, adjunct, addendum, add-on.

extract verb **1** *he extracted the cassette:* take out, draw out, pull out, remove, withdraw, release, extricate. **2** *they extracted a confession:* wrest, exact, wring, screw, squeeze, obtain by force, extort. **3** *the roots are crushed to extract the juice:* squeeze out, press out, obtain.

OPPOSITES insert.

● noun **1** *an extract from his article:* excerpt, passage, citation, quotation. **2** *an extract of ginseng:* distillation, distillate, concentrate, essence, juice.

extraordinary adjective **1** *an extraordinary coincidence:* remarkable, exceptional, amazing, astonishing, astounding, sensational, stunning, incredible, unbelievable, phenomenal; informal fantastic. **2** *extraordinary speed:* very great, tremendous, enormous, immense, prodigious, stupendous, monumental.

OPPOSITES unremarkable, tiny.

a regular series.
■ **extraordinarily** adverb.

☑ the beginning is *extra-*, not just *extr-*: *extra*ordinary.

extrapolate /ik-**strap**-uh-layt/ **verb** (**extrapolates, extrapolating, extrapolated**) use a fact or conclusion that is valid for one situation and apply it to a larger or different one.
■ **extrapolation** noun.

extrasensory perception noun the supposed ability to perceive things by means other than the known senses, e.g. by telepathy.

extraterrestrial adjective having to do with things that come from beyond the earth or its atmosphere. • noun a fictional being from outer space.

extravagant adjective 1 spending or using more than is necessary or more than you can afford. 2 very expensive. 3 going beyond what is reasonable.
■ **extravagance** noun **extravagantly** adverb.

extravaganza noun an elaborate and spectacular entertainment.

extreme adjective 1 to the highest degree. 2 highly unusual. 3 very severe or serious. 4 not moderate. 5 furthest from the centre or a given point. • noun 1 either of two abstract things that are as different from each other as possible. 2 the most extreme degree.
■ **extremely** adverb.

extremist noun a person who holds extreme political or religious views.
■ **extremism** noun.

extremity noun (plural **extremities**) 1 the furthest point or limit. 2 (**extremities**) a

person's hands and feet. 3 extreme hardship.

extricate verb (**extricates, extricating, extricated**) 1 free someone from a difficult situation. 2 free something that is trapped.

extrinsic adjective coming from outside; not part of something's basic nature.

extrovert noun an outgoing, lively person. • adjective outgoing and lively.

☑ *extro-*, not *extra-*: *extro*vert.

extrude verb (**extrudes, extruding, extruded**) thrust or force something out.

exuberant adjective 1 lively and cheerful. 2 growing thickly.
■ **exuberance** noun **exuberantly** adverb.

exude verb (**exudes, exuding, exuded**) 1 send out or give off a liquid or smell slowly and steadily. 2 display an emotion or quality strongly and openly.

exult verb show or feel triumphant joy.
■ **exultant** adjective **exultantly** adverb **exultation** noun.

eye noun 1 the organ of sight in humans and animals. 2 the small hole in a needle through which the thread is passed. 3 a small metal loop into which a hook is fitted as a fastener on a garment. 4 a person's opinion or feelings. 5 the calm region at the centre of a storm. 6 a dark spot on a potato from which a new shoot grows. • verb (**eyes, eyeing** or **eying, eyed**) look at closely or with interest.
□ **see eye to eye** be in complete agreement.

eyeball noun the round part of the eye of a vertebrate, within the eyelids.

eyebrow noun the strip of hair growing on the ridge above a person's eye socket.

e

THESAURUS

extravagant adjective 1 *an extravagant lifestyle:* spendthrift, profligate, wasteful, prodigal, lavish. 2 *extravagant praise:* excessive, immoderate, exaggerated, gushing, unrestrained, effusive, fulsome. 3 *decorated in an extravagant style:* ornate, elaborate, fancy, over-elaborate, ostentatious, exaggerated; informal flashy.
OPPOSITES thrifty, moderate, plain.

extreme adjective 1 *extreme danger:* utmost, (very) great, greatest (possible), maximum, great, acute, enormous, severe, serious. 2 *extreme measures:* drastic, serious, desperate, dire, radical, far-reaching, draconian; Brit. swingeing. 3 *extreme views:* radical, extremist, immoderate, fanatical, revolutionary, subversive, militant. 4 *extreme sports:* dangerous, hazardous, risky, high-risk, adventurous; informal white-knuckle. 5 *the extreme north-west:*

furthest, farthest, utmost, remotest, ultra-.
OPPOSITES slight, moderate, safe, near.
• noun *the two extremes:* opposite, antithesis, side of the coin, (opposite) pole, limit, extremity, contrast.

extremely adverb very, exceptionally, especially, extraordinarily, tremendously, immensely, hugely, supremely, highly, mightily; informal awfully, terribly, seriously; Brit. informal jolly; N. Amer. informal mighty.
OPPOSITES slightly.

extremist noun fanatic, radical, zealot, fundamentalist, hardliner, militant, activist.
OPPOSITES moderate.

eye verb look at, observe, view, gaze at, stare at, regard, contemplate, survey, scrutinize, consider, glance at, watch; informal check out, size up; N. Amer. informal eyeball.

eyeglass noun a single lens for correcting eyesight.

eyelash noun each of the short hairs growing on the edges of the eyelids.

eyelet noun a small round hole with a metal ring around it, for threading a lace or cord through.

eyelid noun each of the upper and lower folds of skin which cover the eye when it is closed.

eyeliner noun a cosmetic applied as a line round the eyes.

eyeshadow noun a cosmetic applied to the skin around the eyes.

eyesight noun a person's ability to see.

eyesore noun a thing that is very ugly.

eyewitness noun a person who has seen something happen.

eyrie /eer-i, I-ri/ (US spelling **aerie**) noun a large nest of a bird of prey.

Ff

F or **f** noun (plural **Fs** or **F's**) the sixth letter of the alphabet. • **abbreviation** Fahrenheit.

FA abbreviation Football Association.

fable noun **1** a short story, often about animals, which teaches about right and wrong behaviour. **2** a story about mythical characters or events.

fabled adjective **1** famous. **2** described in myths and legends.

fabric noun **1** cloth. **2** the walls, floor, and roof of a building. **3** the basic structure of a system or organization.

fabricate verb (**fabricates, fabricating, fabricated**) **1** make up facts that are not true. **2** make an industrial product.
■ **fabrication** noun.

fabulous adjective **1** great; extraordinary. **2** informal wonderful. **3** existing in myths and legends.
■ **fabulously** adverb.

facade /fuh-**sahd**/ noun **1** the front of a building. **2** a misleading outward appearance.

face noun **1** the front part of the head from the forehead to the chin. **2** an expression on someone's face. **3** the surface of a thing. **4** a vertical or sloping side of a mountain or cliff. **5** an aspect of something. • **verb** (**faces, facing, faced**) **1** be positioned with the face or front towards something. **2** confront and deal with. **3** have a difficulty ahead of you. **4** cover the surface of something with a layer of material.
□ **face pack** Brit. a cream or gel spread over the face to improve the skin. **face the music** be confronted with the unpleasant results of your actions. **face value 1** the value stated on a coin or postage stamp. **2** the value that something seems to have before you look at it closely. **lose** (or **save**) **face** suffer (or avoid) humiliation.

facecloth noun a small towelling cloth for washing your face.

faceless adjective without character or individuality; impersonal.

facelift noun an operation to remove wrinkles in the face by tightening the skin.

facet noun **1** one of the sides of a cut gemstone. **2** an aspect of something.
■ **faceted** adjective.

facetious /fuh-**see**-shuhss/ **adjective** trying

THESAURUS

fable noun parable, allegory, myth, legend, story.

fabric noun **1** *the finest fabrics:* cloth, material, textile. **2** *the fabric of society:* structure, construction, make-up, organization, framework, essence.

fabulous adjective **1** *fabulous salaries:* stupendous, prodigious, phenomenal, exceptional, fantastic, breathtaking, staggering, unthinkable, unimaginable, incredible, undreamed of. **2** (informal) *we had a fabulous time.* See **EXCELLENT**.

facade noun **1** *a half-timbered facade:* front, frontage, face, elevation, exterior, outside. **2** *a facade of bonhomie:* show, front, appearance, pretence, simulation, affectation, act, charade, mask, veneer.

face noun **1** *a beautiful face:* countenance, physiognomy, features, profile. **2** *her face grew sad:* expression, look, appearance, countenance. **3** *he made a face:* grimace, scowl, wince, frown, pout. **4** *a cube has six faces:* side, aspect, surface, plane, facet, wall, elevation.
• **verb 1** *the hotel faces the sea:* look out on, front on to, look towards, look over/across, overlook, be opposite (to). **2** *you'll have to face the truth:* accept, get used to, adjust to, learn to live with, cope with, deal with, come to terms with, become resigned to. **3** *the problems facing our police force:* beset, worry, trouble, confront, torment, plague, bedevil. **4** *he faced the challenge:* brave, face up to, encounter, meet (head-on), confront. **5** *a wall faced with flint:* cover, clad, veneer, surface, dress, laminate, coat, line.

facelift noun renovation, redecoration, refurbishment, revamp, makeover.

facet noun aspect, feature, side, dimension, strand, component, element.

to be funny or clever about something that should be treated seriously.
■ **facetiously** adverb.

facia ⇨ FASCIA.

facial adjective having to do with the face.
•noun a beauty treatment for the face.
■ **facially** adverb.

facile /fa-syl/ adjective **1** produced without careful thought. **2** too simple, or too easily achieved.

facilitate verb (**facilitates, facilitating, facilitated**) make something possible or easier.
■ **facilitation** noun **facilitator** noun.

facility noun (plural **facilities**) **1** a building, service, or piece of equipment provided for a particular purpose. **2** a natural ability to do something well and easily.

facing noun **1** a strip of material sewn inside the neck, armhole, etc. of a piece of clothing to strengthen it. **2** an outer layer covering the surface of a wall.

facsimile /fak-**sim**-i-li/ noun an exact copy of written or printed material.

fact noun **1** a thing that is definitely the case. **2** (**facts**) information used as evidence or as part of a report.
◻ **the facts of life** information explaining things relating to sex.

faction noun a small group within a larger one.
■ **factional** adjective.

factious /fak-shuhss/ adjective having

opposing views.

factitious /fak-ti-shuhss/ adjective made up; not genuine.

factor noun **1** a circumstance, fact, or influence that helps to bring about a result. **2** Maths a number by which a larger number can be divided exactly. **3** the amount by which something increases or decreases. **4** any of a number of substances in the blood which are involved in clotting.
•verb (**factor something in** or **out**) consider (or ignore) something when making a decision.

factory noun (plural **factories**) a building where goods are made or assembled in large numbers.
◻ **factory farming** the rearing of poultry, pigs, or cattle indoors under strictly controlled conditions.

factotum /fak-**toh**-tuhm/ noun (plural **factotums**) an employee who does all kinds of jobs.

factual adjective based on or concerned with facts.
■ **factually** adverb.

faculty noun (plural **faculties**) **1** a basic mental or physical power. **2** a talent. **3** a department or group of related departments in a university.

fad noun **1** a craze. **2** a fussy like or dislike of something.
■ **faddish** adjective **faddy** adjective.

fade verb (**fades, fading, faded**) **1** gradually

THESAURUS

facilitate verb make easy/**easier**, ease, make possible, smooth the way for, enable, assist, help (along), aid, promote, hasten, speed up.
OPPOSITES impede.

facility noun **1** car-parking facilities: **provision**, space, means, equipment. **2** the camera has a zoom facility: **feature**, setting, mode, option. **3** a wealth of local facilities: **amenity**, resource, service. **4** a medical facility: **establishment**, centre, station, location, premises, site, post, base.

fact noun **1** a fact we cannot ignore: **reality**, actuality, certainty, truth, verity, gospel. **2** every fact was double-checked: **detail**, particular, finding, point, factor, feature, characteristic, aspect; (**facts**) information, data.
OPPOSITES lie, fiction.

faction noun **1** a faction of the Liberal Party: **clique**, coterie, caucus, bloc, camp, group, grouping, splinter group. **2** the council was split by faction: **infighting**, dissent, dispute, discord, strife, conflict, friction, argument, disagreement, disunity, schism.
OPPOSITES agreement, unity.

factor noun element, part, component,

ingredient, strand, constituent, feature, facet, aspect, characteristic, consideration, influence, circumstance.

factory noun works, plant, yard, mill, facility, workshop, shop.

factual adjective truthful, true, accurate, authentic, historical, genuine, true-to-life, correct, exact.
OPPOSITES fictitious.

faculty noun **1** the faculty of speech: **power**, capability, capacity, facility; (**faculties**) senses, wits, reason, intelligence. **2** the arts faculty: **department**, school.

fad noun craze, vogue, trend, fashion, mode, mania, rage.

fade verb **1** the paintwork has faded: **become pale**, become bleached, become washed out, lose colour, discolour. **2** sunlight had faded the picture: **bleach**, wash out, make pale, blanch. **3** the afternoon light began to fade: (**grow**) **dim**, grow faint, fail, dwindle, die away, wane, disappear, vanish, decline, melt away. **4** Communism was fading away: **decline**, die out, diminish, decay, crumble, collapse, fail.
OPPOSITES brighten, grow.

grow faint and disappear. **2** lose colour.
3 (**fade something in** or **out**) make a film
or video image or sound more or less clear
or loud.

faeces /fee-seez/ (US spelling **feces**) **plural
noun** waste matter passed out of the body
from the bowels.
■ **faecal** /fee-k'l/ adjective.

fag[1] **noun** Brit. informal a cigarette.

fag[2] Brit. informal **noun 1** a tiring or boring
task. **2** a junior schoolboy at a public
school who does minor chores for an older
one.

faggot noun 1 Brit. a ball of seasoned
chopped liver which is baked or fried. **2** a
bundle of sticks bound together as fuel.

Fahrenheit /fa-ruhn-hyt/ **noun** a scale of
temperature on which water freezes at 32°
and boils at 212°.

fail verb 1 not succeed in achieving
something. **2** be unable to meet the
standards set by a test. **3** not do something
that you should have done. **4** stop working
properly. **5** become weaker or less good.
6 let someone down. • **noun** a mark which is
not high enough to pass an exam.

□ **fail-safe 1** (of machinery) going back to a
safe condition if it is faulty. **2** unlikely or
unable to fail. **without fail** whatever
happens.

failing noun a weakness in a person's
character. • **preposition** if not.

failure noun 1 lack of success. **2** an
unsuccessful person or thing. **3** a situation
in which something stops working
properly. **4** an instance of not doing
something that is expected.

faint adjective 1 not clearly seen, heard, or
smelt. **2** slight: *a faint chance*. **3** close to
losing consciousness. • **verb** briefly lose
consciousness. • **noun** a sudden loss of
consciousness.
□ **faint-hearted** timid.
■ **faintly** adverb.

fair[1] **adjective 1** treating people equally.
2 reasonable or appropriate. **3** quite large
in size or amount. **4** quite good. **5** (of hair
or complexion) light; blonde. **6** (of
weather) fine and dry. **7** old use beautiful.
□ **fair game** a person or thing that people
feel they can criticize or exploit. **fair-
weather friend** a person who stops

fail verb 1 *the scheme had failed:* be
unsuccessful, fall through, fall flat,
collapse, founder, backfire, miscarry, come
unstuck; informal flop, bomb. **2** *he failed his
examination:* be unsuccessful in, not make
the grade; informal flunk. **3** *his friends had
failed him:* let down, disappoint, desert,
abandon, betray, be disloyal to. **4** *the
ventilation system has failed:* break
(down), stop working, cut out, crash,
malfunction, go wrong; informal conk out;
Brit. informal pack up. **5** *Ceri's health was
failing:* deteriorate, degenerate, decline,
fade. **6** *900 businesses are failing a week:*
collapse, crash, go under, go bankrupt,
cease trading, be wound up; informal fold, go
bust.
OPPOSITES succeed, pass, work, improve,
thrive.

failing noun fault, shortcoming, weakness,
imperfection, deficiency, defect, flaw,
frailty.
OPPOSITES strength.

failure noun 1 *the failure of the escape
attempt:* lack of success, defeat, collapse,
foundering. **2** *the scheme had been a
failure:* fiasco, debacle, catastrophe,
disaster; informal flop, washout, dead loss.
3 *she was a failure:* loser, underachiever,
ne'er-do-well, disappointment; informal no-
hoper. **4** *a failure on my part:* negligence,
dereliction, omission, oversight. **5** *the
failure of the heating system:* breaking
down, breakdown, malfunction, crash.
6 *company failures:* collapse, crash,

bankruptcy, insolvency, liquidation,
closure.
OPPOSITES success.

faint adjective 1 *a faint mark:* indistinct,
vague, unclear, indefinite, ill-defined,
imperceptible, pale, light, faded. **2** *a faint
cry:* quiet, muted, muffled, stifled, feeble,
weak, low, soft, gentle. **3** *a faint possibility:*
slight, slender, slim, small, tiny, remote,
vague. **4** *I suddenly felt faint:* dizzy, giddy,
light-headed, unsteady; informal woozy.
OPPOSITES clear, loud, strong.
• **verb** *he nearly fainted:* pass out, lose
consciousness, black out, keel over, swoon.
• **noun** *a dead faint:* blackout, fainting fit,
loss of consciousness, coma, swoon.

faintly adverb 1 *Maria called his name
faintly:* indistinctly, softly, gently, weakly,
in a whisper. **2** *he looked faintly
bewildered:* slightly, vaguely, somewhat,
quite, fairly, rather, a little, a bit, a touch, a
shade.
OPPOSITES loudly, extremely.

fair[1] **adjective 1** *the courts were generally
fair:* just, equitable, honest, impartial,
unbiased, unprejudiced, neutral, even-
handed. **2** *fair weather:* fine, dry, bright,
clear, sunny, cloudless. **3** *fair hair:*
blond(e), yellow, golden, flaxen, light.
4 *fair skin:* pale, light, pink, white, creamy.
5 *a fair achievement:* reasonable, passable,
tolerable, satisfactory, acceptable,
respectable, decent, all right, good enough,
pretty good.
OPPOSITES unfair, inclement, dark, poor.

being a friend when you have problems.

fair² noun **1** a gathering of sideshows and amusements for public entertainment. **2** an event held to promote or sell goods: *an antiques fair.*

fairground noun an outdoor area where a fair is held.

fairing noun a structure added to make a vehicle, boat, or aircraft more streamlined.

fairly adverb **1** in a fair way. **2** to some extent; quite.

fairway noun the part of a golf course between a tee and a green.

fairy noun (plural **fairies**) a small imaginary being that has magical powers.
□ **fairy godmother** a female character in fairy stories who brings good fortune to the hero or heroine. **fairy lights** small electric lights used to decorate a Christmas tree. **fairy tale** (or **fairy story**) **1** a children's story about magical beings and lands. **2** a lie.

fait accompli /fayt uh-**kom**-pli/ noun something that has been done and cannot be changed.

faith noun **1** complete trust or confidence.

2 belief in a religion. **3** a system of religious belief.
□ **faith healing** healing achieved by religious faith, rather than by medical treatment.

faithful adjective **1** remaining loyal and committed. **2** accurate; true to the facts.
• noun (**the faithful**) the people who believe in a particular religion.
■ **faithfully** adverb.

faithless adjective unable to be trusted; disloyal.

fake adjective not genuine. • noun a person or thing that is not genuine. • verb (**fakes, faking, faked**) **1** make a copy or imitation of something in order to deceive.
2 pretend to have an emotion or illness.

fakir /**fay**-keer/ noun a Muslim or Hindu holy man who lives by asking people for money or food.

falcon noun a fast-flying bird of prey with long pointed wings.

falconry noun the keeping and training of birds of prey.
■ **falconer** noun.

fall verb (**falls, falling, fell;** past participle **fallen**)

THESAURUS

fair² noun **1** *a country fair:* fete, gala, festival, carnival. **2** *an antiques fair:* market, bazaar, exchange, sale. **3** *an art fair:* exhibition, display, show, exposition.

fairly adverb **1** *we were treated fairly:* justly, equitably, impartially, without bias, without prejudice, even-handedly, equally. **2** *in fairly good condition:* reasonably, passably, tolerably, adequately, moderately, quite, relatively, comparatively; informal pretty. **3** *he fairly hauled her along the street:* positively, really, simply, actually, absolutely.
OPPOSITES unfairly.

fairy noun sprite, pixie, elf, imp, brownie, puck, leprechaun.

faith noun **1** *our faith in him:* trust, belief, confidence, conviction, reliance. **2** *she died for her faith:* religion, belief, creed, church, persuasion, ideology, doctrine.
OPPOSITES mistrust.

faithful adjective **1** *his faithful assistant:* loyal, constant, true, devoted, staunch, steadfast, dedicated, committed, trusty, dependable, reliable. **2** *a faithful copy:* accurate, precise, exact, true, strict, realistic, authentic.
OPPOSITES disloyal, inaccurate.

fake noun **1** *the sculpture was a fake:* forgery, counterfeit, copy, pirated copy, sham, fraud, hoax, imitation; informal phoney, rip-off. **2** *that doctor is a fake:* charlatan, quack, sham, fraud, impostor; informal phoney.
• adjective **1** *fake banknotes:* counterfeit,

forged, fraudulent, sham, pirated, false, bogus; informal phoney, dud. **2** *fake diamonds:* imitation, artificial, synthetic, simulated, reproduction, replica, ersatz, man-made, dummy, false, mock; informal pretend. **3** *a fake accent:* feigned, faked, put-on, assumed, invented, affected.
OPPOSITES genuine, real, authentic.
• verb **1** *the certificate was faked:* forge, counterfeit, falsify, copy, pirate. **2** *he faked a yawn:* feign, pretend, simulate, put on, affect.

fall verb **1** *bombs began to fall:* drop, descend, plummet, plunge, sink, dive, tumble, cascade. **2** *he tripped and fell:* topple over, tumble over, fall down/over, collapse. **3** *the water level began to fall:* subside, recede, drop, retreat, fall away, go down, sink. **4** *inflation will fall:* decrease, decline, diminish, fall off, drop off, lessen, dwindle, plummet, plunge, slump, sink. **5** *those who fell in the war:* die, perish, lose your life, be killed, be slain, be lost; informal bite the dust, buy it. **6** *the town fell to the barbarians:* surrender, yield, submit, give in, capitulate, succumb, be taken, be overwhelmed. **7** *Easter falls on 23rd April:* occur, take place, happen, come about.
OPPOSITES rise.
• noun **1** *an accidental fall:* tumble, trip, spill, topple. **2** *a fall in sales:* decline, fall-off, drop, decrease, cut, dip, reduction, slump; informal crash. **3** *the fall of the Roman Empire:* downfall, collapse, failure, decline, destruction, overthrow, demise. **4** *the fall*

1 move downwards quickly and without control. 2 collapse to the ground. 3 slope down. 4 become less or lower. 5 become. 6 happen; come about. 7 (of someone's face) show dismay. 8 be captured or defeated. • noun 1 an act of falling. 2 a thing which falls or has fallen. 3 (**falls**) a waterfall. 4 a drop in size or number. 5 a defeat or downfall. 6 N. Amer. autumn. □ fall back retreat. fall back on turn to something for help. fall for informal 1 fall in love with. 2 be tricked by. fall foul of come into conflict with. fall guy informal a person who is blamed for something that is not their fault. fall out have an argument. fall short fail to reach a required standard. fall through fail to happen or be completed.

fallacious /fuh-**lay**-shuhss/ adjective based on a mistaken belief.

fallacy /**fal**-luh-si/ noun (plural **fallacies**) 1 a mistaken belief. 2 a false or misleading argument.

fallback noun an alternative plan for use in an emergency.

fallible /**fal**-li-b'l/ adjective capable of making mistakes.
■ fallibility noun.

Fallopian tube /fuh-**loh**-pi-uhn/ noun either of a pair of tubes along which eggs travel from the ovaries to the uterus of a female mammal.

fallout noun 1 radioactive particles that are spread over a wide area after a nuclear explosion. 2 the bad effects of a situation.

fallow adjective (of farmland) ploughed but left for a period without being planted with crops.

fallow deer noun a small deer that has a white-spotted reddish-brown coat in summer.

false adjective 1 not correct or true; wrong. 2 fake; artificial. 3 based on something that is not true or correct: *a false sense of security.* 4 disloyal.
□ false alarm a warning given about something that does not happen. false pretences behaviour intended to deceive.
■ falsely adverb falsity noun.

falsehood noun 1 the state of being untrue. 2 a lie.

falsetto /fawl-**set**-toh/ noun (plural **falsettos**) a high-pitched voice used by male singers.

falsify verb (**falsifies, falsifying, falsified**) alter something in order to mislead people.
■ falsification noun.

falter verb (**falters, faltering, faltered**) 1 lose momentum. 2 move or speak hesitantly.

fame noun the state of being famous.

famed adjective famous; well known.

familial /fuh-**mil**-i-uhl/ adjective having to do with a family.

familiar adjective 1 well known. 2 frequently encountered; common. 3 (**familiar with**) having a good knowledge of. 4 friendly or informal. • noun a spirit believed to accompany a witch.
■ familiarity noun familiarly adverb.

☑ familiar is spelled with only one *l*.

f

of Berlin: surrender, capitulation, yielding, submission, defeat. **5** *a steep fall down to the ocean:* descent, slope, slant.
OPPOSITES rise.
□ fall back **retreat, withdraw,** back off, draw back, pull back, move away.fall back on **resort to,** turn to, look to, call on, have recourse to.fall for (informal) **1** *she fell for John:* **fall in love with,** take a fancy to, be smitten by, be attracted to. **2** *she won't fall for that trick:* **be deceived by,** be duped by, be fooled by, be taken in by; informal go for, buy, swallow. fall out **quarrel,** argue, row, fight, squabble, bicker. fall through **fail,** be unsuccessful, come to nothing, miscarry, go awry, collapse, founder, come to grief.

false adjective **1** *a false report:* incorrect, untrue, wrong, inaccurate, untruthful, fictitious, fabricated, invented, made up, trumped up, counterfeit, forged, fraudulent. **2** *a false friend:* disloyal, faithless, unfaithful, untrue, inconstant, treacherous, double-crossing, deceitful, dishonest, duplicitous. **3** *false pearls:* fake, artificial, imitation, synthetic, simulated, reproduction, replica, ersatz, man-made,

dummy, mock; informal pretend.
OPPOSITES correct, faithful, genuine.

falter verb hesitate, delay, drag your feet, stall, waver, vacillate, be indecisive, be irresolute; Brit. hum and haw; informal sit on the fence.

fame noun renown, celebrity, stardom, popularity, prominence, distinction, esteem, eminence, repute.
OPPOSITES obscurity.

familiar adjective **1** *a familiar task:* well known, recognized, accustomed, everyday, day-to-day, habitual, customary, routine. **2** *are you familiar with the subject?* acquainted, conversant, versed, knowledgeable, well informed, au fait; informal well up on. **3** *he is too familiar with the teachers:* overfamiliar, presumptuous, disrespectful, forward, bold, impudent, impertinent.
OPPOSITES unfamiliar, formal.

familiarity noun **1** *a familiarity with politics:* acquaintance with, awareness of, knowledge of, experience of, insight into, understanding of, comprehension of. **2** *she was affronted by his familiarity:* overfamiliarity, presumption, forwardness,

familiarize or **familiarise** verb
(**familiarizes, familiarizing, familiarized**)
(**familiarize someone with**) give someone
knowledge of something.
■ **familiarization** noun.

family noun (plural **families**) **1** a group of
parents and their children. **2** a group of
people related by marriage or through
having the same ancestors. **3** the children
of a person or couple. **4** a group of things
that are alike in some way. **5** a group of
related plants or animals. • **adjective**
designed to be suitable for children as well
as adults.
□ **family name** a surname. **family planning**
control of the number of children in a
family by using contraceptives. **family tree**
a diagram showing the relationship
between people in a family.

famine noun a period when there is a
severe shortage of food in a region.

famished adjective informal very hungry.

famous adjective **1** known about by many
people. **2** informal very good or impressive.
■ **famously** adverb.

fan¹ noun **1** a device which uses rotating
blades to create a current of air. **2** a
semicircular object that you wave to cool
yourself. • verb (**fans, fanning, fanned**)
1 make a current of air blow towards.
2 make a belief or emotion stronger. **3** (**fan
out**) spread out from a central point.
□ **fan belt** a belt driving the fan that cools
the radiator of a motor vehicle.

fan² noun a person who is very interested in
a sport, celebrity, etc.

fanatic noun a person who is too
enthusiastic about something.
■ **fanatical** adjective **fanatically** adverb
fanaticism noun.

fancier noun a person who keeps or breeds
a particular type of animal: *a pigeon
fancier.*

fanciful adjective **1** existing only in the
imagination. **2** very unusual or creative.
■ **fancifully** adverb.

fancy verb (**fancies, fancying, fancied**) **1** Brit.
informal want or want to do. **2** Brit. informal find
someone attractive. **3** imagine; think.
• **adjective** (**fancier, fanciest**) elaborate or
highly decorated. • noun (plural **fancies**) **1** a
brief feeling of attraction. **2** the ability to
imagine things. **3** a belief or idea that may
not be true.
□ **fancy dress** an unusual costume or
disguise worn at a party. **fancy-free** not in
a serious relationship. **take a fancy to**
become fond of.
■ **fanciness** noun.

fandango /fan-**dang**-goh/ noun (plural
fandangoes or **fandangos**) a lively Spanish
dance for two people.

fanfare noun a short tune played on brass
instruments to announce someone or
something.

fang noun **1** a long, pointed tooth of a dog
or wolf. **2** a tooth with which a snake
injects poison.

fanlight noun a small semicircular window
over a door or window.

fantasia /fan-**tay**-zi-uh/ noun a piece of
music that does not follow a conventional

THESAURUS

boldness, cheek, impudence, impertinence,
disrespect. **3** *our familiarity allows us to
tease each other:* closeness, intimacy,
friendliness, friendship.

family noun **1** *I met his family:* relatives,
relations, (next of) kin, clan, tribe; informal
folks. **2** *she is married with a family:*
children, little ones, youngsters; informal
kids. **3** *the cat family:* species, order, class,
genus, phylum.

famine noun **1** *a nation threatened by
famine:* food shortage, hunger, starvation,
malnutrition. **2** *the cotton famine:*
shortage, scarcity, lack, dearth, deficiency,
insufficiency, shortfall, drought.
OPPOSITES plenty.

famous adjective well known, prominent,
famed, popular, renowned, noted, eminent,
distinguished, celebrated.
OPPOSITES unknown.

fan noun enthusiast, devotee, admirer, lover,
supporter, follower, disciple, adherent;
informal buff.

fanatic noun extremist, militant, dogmatist,
bigot, zealot, radical, diehard; informal
maniac.

fancy verb **1** (Brit. informal) *I fancied a change
of scene:* wish for, want, desire, long for,
yearn for, crave, thirst for, hanker after,
dream of, covet. **2** (Brit. informal) *she fancied
him:* be attracted to, find attractive, be
infatuated with, be taken with; informal have
a crush on, carry a torch for. **3** *I fancied I
could see lights:* imagine, believe, think, be
under the impression; informal reckon.
• **adjective** *fancy clothes:* elaborate, ornate,
ornamental, decorative, embellished,
intricate, ostentatious, showy, flamboyant,
lavish, expensive; informal flashy, snazzy,
posh, classy, bling-bling; Brit. informal swish.
OPPOSITES plain.
• **noun 1** *a passing fancy:* whim, foible,
urge, whimsy, fascination, fad, craze,
enthusiasm, passion, caprice. **2** *a flight of
fancy:* fantasy, dreaming, imagination,
delusion, creativity.

form, or one based on several familiar tunes.

fantasize or **fantasise** verb (**fantasizes, fantasizing, fantasized**) daydream about something that you would like to do, or that you would like to happen.

fantastic adjective **1** hard to believe. **2** strange or exotic. **3** informal very good or large.
■ **fantastical** adjective **fantastically** adverb.

fantasy noun (plural **fantasies**) **1** the imagining of things that do not exist in reality. **2** an imagined situation or event that is desirable but unlikely to happen. **3** a type of fiction that involves magic and adventure.

fanzine noun a magazine for fans of a particular performer, team, etc.

FAQ abbreviation Computing frequently asked questions.

far adverb (**further, furthest** or **farther, farthest**) **1** at, to, or by a great distance in space or time. **2** by a great deal. ● adjective **1** distant in space or time. **2** extreme. □ **far-fetched** exaggerated or unlikely. **far-flung** spread out; scattered. **the Far East** China, Japan, and other countries of east Asia. **far-off** distant in space or time.

farad noun the basic unit of electrical capacitance.

faraway adjective **1** remote or distant. **2** lost in thought; dreamy.

farce noun **1** a comedy based on situations which are ridiculous and improbable. **2** an absurd event.

farcical adjective absurd or ridiculous.
■ **farcically** adverb.

fare noun **1** the money which a passenger pays to travel on public transport. **2** a range of food. ● verb (**fares, faring, fared**) get on in a particular situation: *the party fared badly in the elections.*

farewell exclamation old use goodbye. ● noun an act of leaving.

farinaceous /fa-ri-**nay**-shuhss/ adjective containing or like starch.

farm noun **1** an area of land and buildings used for growing crops and rearing animals. **2** a farmhouse. ● verb **1** make a living by growing crops or keeping animals. **2** (**farm something out**) give work to other people to do.

farmer noun a person who owns or manages a farm.

farmhouse noun a house attached to a farm.

farmstead noun a farm and its buildings.

farmyard noun a yard or enclosure surrounded by farm buildings

farrago /fuh-**rah**-goh/ noun (plural **farragos** or **farragoes**) a confused mixture.

farrier noun a person who shoes horses.

farrow noun a litter of pigs. ● verb (of a sow) give birth to piglets.

farther ⇨ FURTHER.

farthest ⇨ FURTHEST.

THESAURUS

fantastic adjective **1** *a fantastic notion:* fanciful, extravagant, extraordinary, irrational, wild, absurd, far-fetched, unthinkable, implausible, improbable, unlikely; informal crazy. **2** *fantastic shapes:* strange, weird, bizarre, outlandish, grotesque, surreal, exotic. **3** (informal) *a fantastic car:* marvellous, wonderful, sensational, outstanding, superb, excellent; informal terrific, fabulous; Brit. informal brilliant; Austral./NZ informal bonzer.
OPPOSITES rational, ordinary, indifferent.

fantasy noun **1** *a mix of fantasy and realism:* imagination, fancy, invention, make-believe, creativity, vision, daydreaming, reverie. **2** *his fantasy about being famous:* dream, daydream, pipe dream, fanciful notion, wish, fond hope, delusion; informal pie in the sky.
OPPOSITES realism.

far adverb **1** *far from the palace:* a long way, a great distance, a good way, afar. **2** *her charm far outweighs any flaws:* much, considerably, markedly, greatly, significantly, substantially, appreciably, by a long way, by a mile, easily.
OPPOSITES near, barely.

● adjective **1** *far places:* distant, faraway, far-off, remote, out of the way, far-flung, outlying. **2** *the far side:* further, opposite.
OPPOSITES near.

farce noun mockery, travesty, parody, sham, pretence, charade, joke; informal shambles.
OPPOSITES tragedy.

fare noun **1** *we paid the fare:* price, cost, charge, fee, toll, tariff. **2** *they eat simple fare:* food, meals, cooking, cuisine.
● verb *how are you faring?* get on, get along, cope, manage, do, survive; informal make out.

farewell exclamation *farewell, Patrick!* goodbye, so long, adieu, au revoir, ciao; informal bye, cheerio, see you (later); Brit. informal ta-ta, cheers.
● noun *an emotional farewell:* goodbye, adieu, leave-taking, parting, departure, send-off.

farming noun agriculture, cultivation, husbandry; Brit. crofting.

fascinating adjective interesting, captivating, engrossing, absorbing, enchanting, enthralling, spellbinding, riveting, engaging, compelling, compulsive, gripping, charming, attractive, intriguing, diverting, entertaining.

farthing noun a former UK coin, worth a quarter of an old penny.

fascia or Brit. **facia** /fay-shuh/ noun **1** a board covering the ends of rafters or other fittings. **2** Brit. a board above the entrance of a shop, displaying the shop's name. **3** the dashboard of a motor vehicle. **4** a detachable cover for the front of a mobile phone.

fascinate verb (**fascinates, fascinating, fascinated**) interest or charm someone greatly.
■ **fascination** noun.

> ☑ spell **fascinate** and **fascination** with an *s* before the *c*.

fascism /fash-i-z'm/ noun **1** a right-wing system of government with extreme nationalistic beliefs. **2** an attitude which is very intolerant or right-wing.
■ **fascist** noun & adjective.

fashion noun **1** a popular style of clothes, way of behaving, etc. **2** a way of doing something. •verb make or shape something.

fashionable adjective in a style that is currently popular.
■ **fashionably** adverb.

fast¹ adjective **1** moving or capable of moving very quickly. **2** taking place quickly. **3** (of a clock or watch) ahead of the correct time. **4** firmly fixed or attached. **5** (of a dye) not fading. •adverb **1** quickly. **2** firmly or securely.

fast² verb go without food or drink. •noun a period of fasting.

fasten verb **1** close or do up securely. **2** fix or hold in place. **3** (**fasten on**) pick out and concentrate on.
■ **fastener** noun **fastening** noun.

fastidious /fa-stid-i-uhss/ adjective **1** paying a lot of attention to detail. **2** very concerned about cleanliness.
■ **fastidiously** adverb.

fastness noun **1** a place that is secure and well protected. **2** the ability of a dye to keep its colour.

fat noun **1** an oily substance found in animals. **2** a substance used in cooking made from the fat of animals, or from plants. •adjective (**fatter, fattest**) **1** having too much fat. **2** informal large; substantial.
□ **fat cat** disapproving a wealthy and powerful businessman.
■ **fatness** noun.

fatal adjective **1** causing death. **2** leading to disaster.
■ **fatally** adverb.

THESAURUS

fascination noun interest, preoccupation, passion, obsession, compulsion, allure, lure, charm, attraction, appeal, pull, draw.

fashion noun **1** *the fashion for tight clothes:* vogue, trend, craze, rage, mania, fad, style, look, convention; informal thing. **2** *the world of fashion:* clothes, clothing design, couture; informal the rag trade. **3** *in a sensible fashion:* manner, way, method, style, approach.
• verb *fashioned from clay:* construct, build, make, manufacture, cast, shape, form, mould, sculpt, forge, hew, carve.

fashionable adjective in vogue, in fashion, popular, up to date, up to the minute, modern, all the rage, trendsetting, stylish, chic; informal trendy, classy, cool; N. Amer. informal tony.
OPPOSITES unfashionable.

fast¹ adjective **1** *a fast pace:* speedy, quick, swift, rapid, high-speed, accelerated, express, blistering, breakneck, hasty, hurried; informal nippy, scorching, supersonic; Brit. informal cracking. **2** *make the rope fast:* secure, fastened, tight, firm, closed, shut, immovable. **3** *fast friends:* loyal, devoted, faithful, firm, steadfast, staunch, true, boon, bosom, inseparable.
OPPOSITES slow, loose, temporary.
• adverb **1** *she drove fast:* quickly, rapidly, swiftly, speedily, briskly, at full tilt, hastily, hurriedly, in a hurry; informal double quick, nippily; N. Amer. informal lickety-split. **2** *his wheels were stuck fast:* securely, firmly, tight. **3** *he's fast asleep:* deeply, sound, completely.
OPPOSITES slowly, loosely, lightly.

fast² verb *we must fast and pray:* eat nothing, refrain from eating, go without food, go hungry, starve yourself, go on hunger strike.
OPPOSITES eat.
• noun *a five-day fast:* period of fasting, period of abstinence, hunger strike, diet.
OPPOSITES feast.

fasten verb **1** *he fastened the door:* bolt, lock, secure, make fast, chain, seal. **2** *they fastened splints to his leg:* attach, fix, affix, clip, pin, tack, stick, join. **3** *he fastened his horse to a tree:* tie (up), tether, hitch, truss, fetter, lash, anchor, strap, rope.
OPPOSITES unlock, remove, untie.

fat adjective **1** *a fat man:* obese, overweight, plump, stout, chubby, portly, flabby, paunchy, pot-bellied, corpulent; informal tubby; Brit. informal podgy. **2** *fat bacon:* fatty, greasy, oily. **3** *a fat book:* thick, big, chunky, substantial, long.
OPPOSITES thin, slim, lean.
• noun **1** *whale fat:* blubber, fatty tissue, adipose tissue, cellulite. **2** *eggs in sizzling fat:* oil, grease, lard, suet, butter, margarine.

fatal adjective **1** *a fatal disease:* deadly,

fatalism noun the belief that all events are decided in advance by a supernatural power.
■ **fatalist** noun **fatalistic** adjective.

fatality noun (plural **fatalities**) a death occurring in a war, or caused by an accident or disease.

fate noun 1 a supernatural power believed to control all events. 2 the things that will inevitably happen to someone or something. ● verb (**be fated**) be destined to happen in a particular way.

fateful adjective having important, often unpleasant, consequences.

father noun 1 a male parent. 2 an important figure in the early history of something. 3 literary a male ancestor. 4 a priest. 5 (**the Father**) God. ● verb (**fathers, fathering, fathered**) be the father of.
□ **father-in-law** (plural **fathers-in-law**) the father of a person's husband or wife.
■ **fatherhood** noun.

fatherland noun a person's native country.

fatherly adjective protective and affectionate.

fathom noun a measure of the depth of water, equal to six feet (1.8 metres). ● verb understand after a lot of thought.

fatigue noun 1 great tiredness. 2 weakness in metals caused by repeated stress. 3 (**fatigues**) loose-fitting clothing worn by soldiers. ● verb (**fatigues, fatiguing, fatigued**) make someone very tired.

fatten verb make or become fat or fatter.

fatty adjective (**fattier, fattiest**) containing a lot of fat.

fatuity /fuh-**tyoo**-i-ti/ noun 1 a silly remark. 2 foolishness.

fatuous adjective silly and pointless.
■ **fatuously** adverb.

fatwa /fat-wah/ noun a ruling on a point of Islamic law given by a recognized authority.

faucet /**faw**-sit/ noun N. Amer. a tap.

fault noun 1 a defect or mistake. 2 responsibility for an accident or unfortunate event. 3 (in tennis) a service that is against the rules. 4 a break in the layers of rock of the earth's crust. ● verb find a defect or mistake in someone or something.
■ **faultless** adjective.

faulty adjective (**faultier, faultiest**) having faults.

faun noun (in Roman mythology) a god of woods and fields, with a human body and a goat's horns, ears, legs, and tail.

fauna noun the animals of a particular region or period.

faux pas /foh pah/ noun (plural **faux pas**) a mistake which causes embarrassment in a social situation.

favour (US spelling **favor**) noun 1 approval

THESAURUS

lethal, mortal, death-dealing, terminal, incurable, untreatable, inoperable. 2 *a fatal mistake:* disastrous, devastating, ruinous, catastrophic, calamitous, dire.
OPPOSITES harmless, beneficial.

fate noun 1 *what has fate in store for me?* destiny, providence, the stars, chance, luck, serendipity, fortune, karma, kismet. 2 *my fate was in their hands:* future, destiny, outcome, end, lot. 3 *a similar fate would befall Harris:* death, demise, end, sentence. ● verb *she was fated to face the same problem:* predestine, preordain, destine, mean, doom.

father noun 1 informal dad, daddy, pop, pa, old man; informal, dated pater. 2 *the father of democracy:* originator, initiator, founder, inventor, creator, author, architect. ● verb sire, spawn, breed, give life to.

fatigue noun tiredness, weariness, exhaustion.
OPPOSITES energy.
● verb tire out, exhaust, wear out, drain, weary, overtire; informal knock out, take it out of; Brit. informal knacker.
OPPOSITES invigorate.

fatty adjective greasy, fat, oily, creamy, rich.
OPPOSITES lean.

fault noun 1 *he has his faults:* defect, failing, imperfection, flaw, blemish, shortcoming, weakness, vice. 2 *engineers have located the fault:* defect, flaw, imperfection, bug, error, mistake, inaccuracy; informal glitch. 3 *it was not my fault:* responsibility, liability, culpability, guilt.
OPPOSITES strength.
● verb *you can't fault their commitment:* find fault with, criticize, attack, condemn; informal knock; Brit. informal slag off.
□ **at fault** to blame, blameworthy, culpable, responsible, guilty, in the wrong.

faulty adjective 1 *a faulty electric blanket:* malfunctioning, broken, damaged, defective, not working, out of order; informal on the blink, acting up; Brit. informal playing up. 2 *her logic is faulty:* defective, flawed, unsound, inaccurate, incorrect, erroneous, wrong.
OPPOSITES working, sound.

favour noun 1 *will you do me a favour?* good turn, service, good deed, act of kindness, courtesy. 2 *she looked on him with favour:* approval, approbation, goodwill, kindness, benevolence.
OPPOSITES disservice, disapproval.
● verb 1 *the party favours electoral reform:* advocate, recommend, approve of, be in favour of, support, back, champion,

or liking. **2** a kind or helpful act. **3** special treatment of one person or group. •**verb 1** view or treat with favour. **2** work to the advantage of. **3** (**favour someone with**) give someone something they wish for. □ **in favour of 1** to be replaced by. **2** in support of.

favourable (US spelling **favorable**) adjective **1** expressing approval or consent. **2** advantageous or helpful.
■ **favourably** adverb.

favourite (US spelling **favorite**) adjective preferred to all other people or things of the same kind. •**noun 1** a favourite person or thing. **2** the competitor thought most likely to win.

favouritism (US spelling **favoritism**) noun the unfair favouring of one person or group.

fawn[1] noun **1** a young deer. **2** a light brown colour.

fawn[2] verb try to please someone by flattering them and being too attentive.

fax noun **1** a copy of a document which has been scanned and transmitted electronically. **2** a machine for transmitting and receiving faxes. •**verb** send a document by fax.

faze verb (**fazes, fazing, fazed**) informal shock or confuse.

FBI abbreviation (in the US) Federal Bureau of Investigation.

FC abbreviation Football Club.

fealty /fee-uhl-ti/ noun (in the feudal system) the loyalty sworn to a lord by a person who served him or worked for him.

fear noun **1** an unpleasant emotion caused by the threat of danger. **2** the likelihood of something unwelcome happening. •**verb 1** be afraid of. **2** (**fear for**) be anxious about.

fearful adjective **1** feeling afraid. **2** causing fear. **3** informal very great.
■ **fearfully** adverb.

fearless adjective having no fear; brave.
■ **fearlessly** adverb.

fearsome adjective very impressive and frightening.

feasible adjective **1** able to be done easily. **2** likely.
■ **feasibility** noun **feasibly** adverb.

> ! some people say **feasible** should not be used to mean 'likely', but this sense has been in the language for centuries and is generally considered to be acceptable.

THESAURUS

campaign for, press for, lobby for, promote; informal push for. **2** *Robyn favours loose clothes:* **prefer,** go for, choose, opt for, select, pick, plump for. **3** *Father always favoured George:* **prefer,** be biased towards, indulge, like more/better. **4** *the conditions favoured the other team:* **benefit,** be to the advantage of, help, assist, aid, be of service to.
OPPOSITES oppose, dislike, hinder.
□ **in favour of on the side of,** pro, for, giving support to, approving of, sympathetic to.

favourable adjective **1** *a favourable review:* **approving,** positive, complimentary, full of praise, flattering, glowing, enthusiastic, kind, good; informal rave. **2** *conditions are favourable:* **advantageous,** beneficial, in your favour, good, right, suitable, appropriate, auspicious, promising, encouraging. **3** *a favourable reply:* **positive,** affirmative, assenting, approving, encouraging, reassuring.
OPPOSITES critical, disadvantageous, negative.

favourite adjective favoured, preferred, chosen, choice, best-loved, dearest, pet. •**noun first choice,** pick, preference, pet, darling, the apple of your eye; informal golden boy, teacher's pet; Brit. informal blue-eyed boy/girl; N. Amer. informal fair-haired boy/girl.

fear noun **1** *she felt fear at entering the house:* **terror,** fright, fearfulness, horror, alarm, panic, trepidation, dread, anxiety, angst, apprehension, nervousness. **2** *a fear of heights:* **phobia,** aversion, antipathy, dread, nightmare, horror, terror; informal hang-up.
•**verb 1** *she feared her husband:* **be afraid of,** be fearful of, be scared of, be apprehensive of, dread, live in fear of, be terrified of. **2** *I fear you may be right:* **suspect,** be afraid, have a sneaking suspicion, be inclined to think, have a hunch.
□ **fear for worry about,** feel anxious about, feel concerned about, have anxieties about.

fearful adjective **1** *they are fearful of being overheard:* **afraid,** scared, frightened, scared stiff, scared to death, terrified, petrified, nervous, apprehensive, uneasy, anxious, timid; informal jittery. **2** *a fearful accident:* **terrible,** dreadful, awful, appalling, frightful, ghastly, horrific, horrible, shocking, gruesome.
OPPOSITES unafraid.

fearless adjective brave, courageous, bold, audacious, intrepid, valiant, plucky, heroic, daring, unafraid; informal gutsy.
OPPOSITES timid, cowardly.

feasible adjective practicable, practical, workable, achievable, attainable, realizable, viable, realistic, possible; informal doable.
OPPOSITES impracticable.

f

feast noun 1 a large meal marking a special occasion. 2 an annual religious celebration. • verb 1 have a feast. 2 (**feast on**) eat large quantities of.

feat noun an achievement requiring great courage, skill, or strength.

feather noun any of the structures growing from a bird's skin, consisting of a hollow shaft fringed with fine strands. • verb (**feathers, feathering, feathered**) turn an oar so that the blade passes through the air edgeways.
□ a feather in your cap an achievement to be proud of. feather your nest make money dishonestly.
■ feathery adjective.

feature noun 1 a distinctive element or aspect. 2 a part of the face. 3 a special article in a newspaper or magazine. 4 (also **feature film**) the main film showing at a cinema. • verb (**features, featuring, featured**) 1 have as a feature. 2 have an important part in something.
■ featureless adjective.

febrile /fee-bryl/ adjective 1 having the symptoms of a fever. 2 overactive and excitable.

February /feb-yuu-ri, feb-ruu-uh-ri/ noun (plural **Februaries**) the second month of the year.

☑ -ruary, not -uary: February.

feces US spelling of FAECES.

feckless adjective irresponsible and without strength of character.

fecund adjective very fertile.
■ fecundity noun.

fed past and past participle of FEED.
□ fed up informal annoyed or bored.

federal adjective 1 having a system of government in which several states unite under a central authority. 2 having to do with the central government of a federation. 3 (**Federal**) US historical having to do with the Northern States in the Civil War.
■ federalism noun federalist noun & adjective federally adverb.

federate verb (**federates, federating, federated**) join as a federation.

federation noun 1 a group of states united under a central authority in which individual states keep control of their internal affairs. 2 a group organized like a federation.

fedora /fi-dor-uh/ noun a soft felt hat with a curled brim.

fee noun 1 a payment given for professional advice or services. 2 a sum paid to be allowed to do something.

feeble adjective (**feebler, feeblest**) 1 weak. 2 not convincing or effective.
■ feebleness noun feebly adverb.

feed verb (**feeds, feeding, fed**) 1 give food to. 2 provide enough food for. 3 (of an

---

THESAURUS

feast noun a wedding feast: banquet, dinner, treat; informal spread; Brit. informal beanfeast, slap-up meal.
• verb they feasted on lobster: gorge, dine, binge; (**feast on**) devour, consume, partake of, eat your fill of; informal stuff your face with, pig out.

feat noun achievement, accomplishment, coup, triumph, undertaking, enterprise, venture, exploit, operation, exercise, endeavour, effort.

feather noun plume, quill; (**feathers**) plumage, down.

feature noun 1 a feature of Indian music: characteristic, attribute, quality, property, trait, hallmark, aspect, facet, factor, ingredient, component, element. 2 her delicate features: face, countenance, physiognomy; informal mug; Brit. informal mush, phizog. 3 she made a feature of her sculptures: centrepiece, special attraction, highlight, focal point, focus, conversation piece. 4 a series of short features: article, piece, item, report, story, column.
• verb 1 Radio 3 is featuring a week of live concerts: present, promote, make a feature of, spotlight, highlight, showcase, foreground. 2 she is to feature in a new movie: star, appear, participate.

federation noun confederation, confederacy, association, league, alliance, coalition, union, syndicate, guild, consortium.

fee noun payment, wage, salary, price, charge, bill, tariff, rate; (**fees**) remuneration, dues, earnings, pay; formal emolument.

feeble adjective 1 old and feeble: weak, weakened, debilitated, enfeebled, frail, decrepit, infirm, delicate, sickly, ailing, unwell, poorly. 2 a feeble argument: ineffective, unconvincing, implausible, unsatisfactory, poor, weak, flimsy, lame. 3 he's too feeble to stand up to her: cowardly, faint-hearted, spineless, timid, timorous, fearful, unassertive, weak, ineffectual; informal sissy, chicken; Brit. informal wet. 4 a feeble light: faint, dim, weak, pale, soft, subdued, muted.
OPPOSITES strong, well, brave.

feed verb 1 a large family to feed: cater for, provide for, cook for, dine, nourish. 2 cows feeding: eat, graze, browse, crop. 3 she fed secrets to the Russians: supply, provide, give, deliver, furnish, issue, leak.
• noun animal feed: fodder, food, provender.

f

f

animal or baby) eat. **4** supply with material or information. **5** pass something gradually through a confined space. •**noun 1** an act of feeding. **2** food for domestic animals.

feedback noun **1** comments made in response to something you have done. **2** the return of part of the output of an amplifier to its input, causing a whistling sound.

feeder noun **1** a thing that feeds or supplies something. **2** a minor route that links outlying areas with the main route.

feel verb (**feels**, **feeling**, **felt**) **1** be aware of, examine, or search by touch. **2** give a particular sensation when touched. **3** experience an emotion or sensation. **4** be affected by. **5** have a belief or opinion. •**noun 1** an act of feeling. **2** the sense of touch. **3** a sensation or impression. **4** (**a feel for**) a sensitive appreciation of.

feeler noun **1** an organ used by certain animals for testing things by touch. **2** a cautious proposal intended to find out someone's opinion.

feeling noun **1** an emotional state or reaction. **2** (**feelings**) the emotional side of a person's character. **3** strong emotion. **4** the ability to feel. **5** the sensation of touching or being touched. **6** a belief or opinion. **7** (**feeling for**) an understanding of.

feet plural of FOOT.

feign verb pretend to feel or have.

feint /faynt/ noun a movement made to deceive an opponent, especially in boxing or fencing. •**verb** make a feint.

feisty /fy-sti/ adjective (**feistier**, **feistiest**) lively and spirited.

feldspar or **felspar** noun a mineral that forms igneous rocks.

felicitations plural noun formal congratulations.

felicitous /fuh-li-si-tuhss/ adjective well chosen or appropriate.

felicity noun (plural **felicities**) **1** great happiness. **2** the ability to express yourself in an appropriate way. **3** a pleasing feature of an artistic work.

feline adjective having to do with a cat or cats. •**noun** a cat or other animal of the cat family.

fell[1] past of FALL.

fell[2] verb **1** cut down a tree. **2** knock someone down.

fell[3] noun a hill or stretch of high moorland in northern England.

fellow noun **1** a man or boy. **2** a person in the same situation as you. **3** a thing of the same kind as another. **4** a member of a learned society. **5** Brit. a senior member of certain universities or colleges. •**adjective** in the same situation: *a fellow sufferer*.

fellowship noun **1** friendship between

THESAURUS

feel verb **1** *she felt the fabric:* touch, stroke, caress, fondle, finger, paw, handle. **2** *she felt a breeze on her back:* perceive, sense, detect, discern, notice, be aware of, be conscious of. **3** *he will not feel any pain:* experience, undergo, go through, bear, endure, suffer. **4** *he felt his way towards the door:* grope, fumble, scrabble. **5** *he feels that he should go:* believe, think, consider it right, be of the opinion, hold, maintain, judge; informal reckon, figure.
•**noun 1** *the feel of the paper:* texture, finish, touch, consistency. **2** *the feel of the house:* atmosphere, ambience, aura, mood, feeling, air, impression, spirit; informal vibes. **3** *a feel for languages:* aptitude, knack, flair, bent, talent, gift, ability.

feeling noun **1** *a feeling of nausea:* sensation, sense. **2** *I had a feeling I would win:* (sneaking) suspicion, notion, inkling, hunch, intuition, funny feeling, fancy, idea. **3** *the strength of her feeling:* love, affection, fondness, tenderness, warmth, emotion, passion, desire. **4** *public feeling:* mood, (tide of) opinion, attitude, sentiment, emotion, belief, views, consensus. **5** *show some feeling:* compassion, sympathy, empathy, fellow feeling, concern, pity, sorrow,

commiseration. **6** *he had hurt her feelings:* sensibilities, sensitivities, self-esteem, pride. **7** *my feeling is that it is true:* opinion, belief, view, impression, intuition, instinct, hunch, estimation, guess. **8** *a feeling of peace:* atmosphere, ambience, aura, air, mood, impression, spirit; informal vibes. **9** *a remarkable feeling for language:* aptitude, knack, flair, bent, talent, feel, gift, ability.

fell verb **1** *the dead trees had to be felled:* cut down, chop down, hack down, saw down, clear. **2** *she felled him with one punch:* knock down, knock to the ground, floor, strike down, knock out; informal deck, flatten, lay out.

fellow noun **1** *he's a decent sort of fellow:* man, boy, person, individual, character; informal guy, lad; Brit. informal chap, bloke; N. Amer. informal dude. **2** *he exchanged glances with his fellows:* companion, friend, comrade, partner, associate, co-worker, colleague; informal pal, buddy; Brit. informal mate.

fellowship noun **1** *a community bound together in fellowship:* companionship, comradeship, camaraderie, friendship, sociability, solidarity. **2** *the church fellowship:* association, organization,

felon noun a person who has committed a felony.
■ **felonious** /fi-**loh**-ni-uhss/ adjective.

felony /**fe**-luh-ni/ noun (plural **felonies**) (in the US and formerly also in English Law) a serious crime.

felspar ⇨ FELDSPAR.

felt[1] noun cloth made from wool that has been rolled and pressed.
□ **felt-tip pen** a pen with a writing point made of felt or tightly packed fibres.

felt[2] past and past participle of FEEL.

female adjective 1 of the sex that can give birth to offspring or produce eggs. 2 having to do with women. 3 (of a plant or flower) having a pistil but no stamens. 4 (of a fitting) having a hollow so that a corresponding part can be inserted. ● noun a female person, animal, or plant.

feminine adjective 1 having qualities associated with women. 2 female. 3 Grammar (of nouns and adjectives in some languages) having a gender regarded as female.
■ **femininity** noun.

feminism noun a movement or theory that supports the rights of women.
■ **feminist** noun & adjective.

feminize or **feminise** verb (**feminizes**, **feminizing**, **feminized**) make more feminine or female.

femme fatale /fam fuh-**tahl**/ noun (plural **femmes fatales** /fam fuh-**tahl**/) an attractive and seductive woman.

femur /**fee**-mer/ noun (plural **femurs** or **femora** /**fem**-uh-ruh/) the bone of the thigh.
■ **femoral** adjective.

fen noun a low and marshy or frequently flooded area of land.

fence noun 1 a barrier made of wire or wood that encloses an area of land. 2 an obstacle for horses to jump over in a competition. 3 informal a person who buys and resells stolen goods. ● verb (**fences,**

fencing, fenced) 1 surround or protect with a fence. 2 take part in the sport of fencing.
□ **sit on the fence** avoid making a decision.
■ **fencer** noun.

fencing noun 1 the sport of fighting with blunted swords. 2 fences or material for making fences.

fend verb 1 (**fend for yourself**) look after yourself without help from other people. 2 (**fend someone/thing off**) defend yourself from an attack or attacker.

fender noun 1 a low frame around a fireplace to stop coals from falling out. 2 a soft object that is hung over the side of a ship to protect it from collisions. 3 N. Amer. the mudguard or area around the wheel of a vehicle.

feng shui /feng **shoo**-i, fung **shway**/ noun an ancient Chinese system of designing buildings and arranging objects in rooms to achieve a good flow of energy and so bring happiness or good luck.

fennel noun a plant whose leaves and seeds are used as a herb and whose bulb is eaten as a vegetable.

feral adjective 1 (of an animal) wild, especially after having been tame or kept as a pet. 2 savage or fierce.

ferment verb /fer-**ment**/ 1 undergo a chemical change by the action of yeast or bacteria. 2 stir up disorder. ● noun /**fer**-ment/ a state of widespread unrest or excitement.
■ **fermentation** noun.

fermium noun an unstable radioactive element that is produced artificially.

fern noun (plural **fern** or **ferns**) a plant which has feathery fronds and no flowers.

ferocious adjective very fierce or violent.
■ **ferociously** adverb.

ferocity noun the state of being ferocious.

ferret noun a small, fierce animal with a long thin body, used for catching rabbits. ● verb (**ferrets, ferreting, ferreted**) 1 search among a lot of things. 2 (**ferret something out**) discover something by searching thoroughly. 3 (**ferreting**) hunting with ferrets.

f

---

society, club, league, union, guild, alliance, fraternity, brotherhood.

feminine adjective womanly, ladylike, soft, gentle, tender, delicate, pretty.
OPPOSITES masculine.

fence noun barrier, paling, railing, enclosure, barricade, stockade.
● verb 1 *they fenced off the meadow:* enclose, surround, encircle. 2 *he fenced in his chickens:* confine, pen in, coop up, shut in/up, enclose, surround; N. Amer. corral.

fend verb *she tried to fend him off:* ward off,

head off, stave off, hold off, repel, repulse, resist, fight off.
□ **fend for yourself** take care of yourself, look after yourself, shift for yourself, cope, stand on your own two feet, provide for yourself.

ferocious adjective 1 *ferocious animals:* fierce, savage, wild, predatory, ravening, aggressive, dangerous. 2 *a ferocious attack:* brutal, vicious, violent, bloody, barbaric, savage, frenzied.
OPPOSITES gentle, mild.

Ferris wheel noun a fairground ride consisting of a large upright revolving wheel.

ferrous adjective (of a metal) containing iron.

ferrule noun a metal cap which protects the end of a stick or umbrella.

ferry noun (plural **ferries**) a boat or ship that transports passengers and goods as a regular service. • verb (**ferries, ferrying, ferried**) carry by ferry or other transport.

fertile adjective 1 (of soil or land) producing a lot of plants or crops. 2 (of a person, animal, or plant) able to produce offspring or seeds. 3 producing a lot of good results or ideas.
■ **fertility** noun.

fertilize or **fertilise** verb (**fertilizes, fertilizing, fertilized**) 1 introduce sperm or pollen into an egg or plant so that a new individual develops. 2 add fertilizer to soil.
■ **fertilization** noun.

fertilizer or **fertiliser** noun a chemical or natural substance added to soil to make it more fertile.

fervent adjective showing strong or passionate feeling.
■ **fervently** adverb.

fervid adjective fervent.

fervour (US spelling **fervor**) noun strong or passionate feeling.

festal adjective relating to a festival.

fester verb (**festers, festering, festered**) 1 (of a wound or sore) become septic. 2 become rotten. 3 become worse or more strongly felt.

festival noun 1 a time when people celebrate a special occasion. 2 an organized series of concerts, films, etc.

festive adjective relating to a period of celebration.

festivity noun (plural **festivities**) 1 joyful celebration. 2 (**festivities**) activities or events celebrating a special occasion.

festoon verb decorate with chains of flowers, ribbons, etc. • noun a decorative chain of flowers, ribbons, etc.

feta /fe-tuh/ noun a salty Greek cheese made from the milk of sheep or goats.

fetal or Brit. **foetal** adjective relating to a fetus.

fetch verb 1 go for something and bring it back. 2 be sold for a particular price. 3 (**fetching**) attractive.

fete or **fête** /fayt/ noun Brit. an outdoor event to raise funds for a special purpose. • verb (**fetes, feting, feted**) praise or entertain someone lavishly.

fetid or **foetid** adjective smelling very unpleasant.

fetish noun 1 a form of sexual desire in which pleasure is gained from a particular object or part of the body. 2 an object worshipped for its supposed magical powers.
■ **fetishism** noun **fetishist** noun.

fetlock noun a joint of a horse's leg between the knee and the hoof.

fetter verb (**fetters, fettering, fettered**) 1 limit the freedom of. 2 restrain with chains or shackles. • noun 1 (**fetters**) restraints or controls. 2 a chain placed around a prisoner's ankles.

fettle noun condition.

fettuccine /fet-tuh-**chee**-ni/ plural noun pasta made in long flat strips.

fetus or Brit. **foetus** noun (plural **fetuses**) an unborn baby of a mammal.

feud noun a long and bitter dispute. • verb take part in a feud.

feudal adjective having to do with feudalism.

feudalism noun the social system in medieval Europe, in which people worked and fought for a nobleman in return for land.

THESAURUS

ferry verb transport, convey, carry, run, ship, shuttle.

fertile adjective 1 *the soil is fertile:* productive, fruitful, fecund, rich, lush. 2 *a fertile imagination:* creative, inventive, innovative, visionary, original, ingenious, prolific.
OPPOSITES barren, uncreative.

fertilizer noun plant food, dressing, manure, muck, compost.

festival noun celebration, festivity, fete, fair, gala, carnival, fiesta, jamboree, feast day, holiday, holy day.

festive adjective jolly, merry, joyous, joyful, happy, jovial, light-hearted, cheerful, jubilant, celebratory, holiday, carnival.

fetch verb 1 *he went to fetch a doctor:* go and get, go for, call for, summon, pick up, collect, bring, carry, convey, transport. 2 *the land could fetch millions:* sell for, bring in, raise, realize, yield, make, command; informal go for.

fetching adjective attractive, appealing, sweet, pretty, lovely, delightful, charming, captivating, enchanting; Scottish & N. English bonny; Brit. informal fit.

feud noun *a long-standing feud:* vendetta, conflict, quarrel, row, rivalry, hostility, strife.
• verb *feuding families:* quarrel, fight, clash, argue, squabble, dispute.

fever noun **1** an abnormally high body temperature. **2** a state of nervous excitement.
■ **feverish** adjective.

fevered adjective **1** having a fever. **2** nervously excited.

few determiner, pronoun, & adjective **1** (**a few**) a small number of; some. **2** not many.
• noun (**the few**) a select minority.

> ❗ make sure you distinguish between **fewer** and **less**. Use **fewer** with plural nouns, as in *there were fewer tourists this year*; use **less** with nouns referring to things that can't be counted, as in *there is less blossom on this tree*. It's wrong to use **less** with a plural noun (as in *there were less tourists*).

fey adjective seeming vague or mysterious and unaware of the realities of life.

fez noun (plural **fezzes**) a conical red hat with a flat top, worn by men in some Muslim countries.

ff. abbreviation following pages.

fiancé /fi-on-say/ noun (feminine **fiancée** /fi-**on**-say/) a person to whom you are engaged to be married.

fiasco noun (plural **fiascos**) a ridiculous or humiliating failure.

fiat /fee-at/ noun an official order.

fib noun a trivial lie. • verb (**fibs, fibbing, fibbed**) tell a fib.
■ **fibber** noun.

fibre (US spelling **fiber**) noun **1** each of the thin threads which form plant or animal tissue, cloth, or minerals. **2** a material made from fibres. **3** the part of some foods

that is difficult to digest and which helps food to pass through the body. **4** strength of character.
□ **fibre optics** the use of glass fibres to send information in the form of light.
■ **fibrous** adjective.

fibreboard (US spelling **fiberboard**) noun a building material made of compressed wood fibres.

fibreglass (US spelling **fiberglass**) noun **1** a strong plastic material containing glass fibres. **2** a material made from woven glass fibres.

fibrillate verb (**fibrillates, fibrillating, fibrillated**) (of a muscle, especially in the heart) twitch irregularly.
■ **fibrillation** noun.

fibroid noun a lump consisting of mass of fibrous tissues, usually developing in a woman's womb.

fibula /fib-yuu-luh/ noun (plural **fibulae** /fib-yuu-lee/ or **fibulas**) the outer of the two bones between the knee and the ankle.

fickle adjective changeable in your loyalties.

fiction noun **1** literature describing imaginary events and people. **2** something that is invented and not true.
■ **fictional** adjective.

fictionalize or **fictionalise** verb (**fictionalizes, fictionalizing, fictionalized**) make into a fictional story.

fictitious /fik-**tish**-uhss/ adjective imaginary or invented; not real.

fiddle noun informal **1** a violin. **2** something done dishonestly in order to obtain money.
• verb (**fiddles, fiddling, fiddled**) **1** touch or

THESAURUS

fever noun **1** *he developed a fever:* feverishness, high temperature; Medicine pyrexia; informal temperature. **2** *World Cup fever:* excitement, mania, frenzy, agitation, passion.

few determiner *police are revealing few details:* not many, hardly any, scarcely any, a small number of, a handful of, a couple of, one or two.
OPPOSITES many.
• adjective *comforts here are few:* scarce, scant, meagre, sparse, in short supply, thin on the ground, few and far between.
OPPOSITES plentiful.

fiasco noun failure, disaster, catastrophe, debacle, farce, mess; informal flop, washout, shambles; Brit. informal cock-up; N. Amer. informal snafu; Austral./NZ informal fizzer.
OPPOSITES success.

fibre noun thread, strand, filament, wisp, yarn.

fickle adjective capricious, flighty, giddy, changeable, volatile, mercurial, erratic, unpredictable, unreliable, unsteady.
OPPOSITES constant.

fiction noun **1** *the traditions of British fiction:* novels, stories, literature, creative writing. **2** *this is an absolute fiction:* fabrication, invention, lie, fib, tall story, untruth, falsehood, fantasy, nonsense.
OPPOSITES non-fiction, fact.

fictitious adjective false, fake, fabricated, bogus, spurious, assumed, affected, adopted, invented, made up; informal pretend, phoney.
OPPOSITES genuine.

fiddle (informal) noun *a VAT fiddle:* fraud, swindle, confidence trick; informal racket, scam.
• verb **1** *he fiddled with a beer mat:* fidget, play, toy, finger, handle. **2** *he fiddled with the dials:* adjust, tinker, play about/around, fool about/around, meddle, interfere, tamper; informal tweak, mess about/around; Brit. informal muck about/around. **3** *fiddling the figures:* falsify, manipulate, massage, rig, distort, misrepresent, doctor, tamper with, interfere with; informal fix, cook (the books).

move something restlessly or nervously. **2** informal change the details of something dishonestly.

□ **play second fiddle** take a less important role.

■ **fiddler** noun.

fiddly adjective Brit. complicated and awkward to do or use.

fidelity noun **1** faithfulness to a person or belief. **2** the accuracy with which something is copied or reproduced.

fidget verb (**fidgets, fidgeting, fidgeted**) make small movements because you are nervous or impatient. • noun a person who fidgets.

■ **fidgety** adjective.

fief /feef/ noun historical a piece of land held under the feudal system.

■ **fiefdom** noun.

field noun **1** an enclosed area of land for growing crops or keeping animals. **2** a piece of land used for a sport or game. **3** a subject of study or area of activity. **4** an area within which a force has an effect: *a magnetic field*. **5** (**the field**) all the people taking part in a contest or sport. • verb **1** Cricket & Baseball attempt to catch or stop the ball after it has been hit. **2** try to deal with something. **3** choose someone to play in a game or to stand in an election.

□ **field day** a good opportunity to do something. **field events** athletic sports other than running. **field marshal** the highest rank of officer in the British army. **field sports** hunting, shooting, and fishing. **play the field** informal have a series of casual

sexual relationships.

■ **fielder** noun.

fiend noun **1** an evil spirit. **2** a very wicked or cruel person. **3** informal a person who is very enthusiastic about something: *an exercise fiend*.

fiendish adjective **1** very cruel or unpleasant. **2** informal very difficult.

■ **fiendishly** adverb.

fierce adjective **1** violent or aggressive. **2** strong or powerful.

■ **fiercely** adverb **fierceness** noun.

| ☑ *i* before e except after c: fierce. |

fiery adjective (**fierier, fieriest**) **1** consisting of or resembling fire. **2** quick-tempered or passionate.

fiesta noun (in Spanish-speaking countries) a religious festival.

fife noun a small, high-pitched flute used in military bands.

fifteen cardinal number one more than fourteen; 15. (Roman numeral: **xv** or **XV**.)

■ **fifteenth** ordinal number.

fifth ordinal number **1** being number five in a sequence; 5th. **2** (**a fifth** or **one fifth**) each of five equal parts of something.

□ **fifth column** a group within a country at war who are working for its enemies.

fifty cardinal number (plural **fifties**) ten less than sixty; 50. (Roman numeral: **l** or **L**.)

□ **fifty-fifty** with equal shares or chances.

■ **fiftieth** ordinal number.

fig noun a soft, sweet fruit with many small seeds.

fight verb (**fights, fighting, fought**) **1** take

THESAURUS

fidelity noun **1** *fidelity to her husband:* faithfulness, loyalty, constancy, allegiance, commitment, devotion. **2** *the fidelity of the reproduction:* accuracy, exactness, precision, correctness, strictness, closeness, authenticity.
OPPOSITES disloyalty, inaccuracy.

field noun **1** *a large ploughed field:* meadow, pasture, paddock, grassland. **2** *a football field:* pitch, ground; Brit. informal park. **3** *the field of biotechnology:* area, sphere, discipline, province, department, domain, territory, branch, subject. **4** *your field of vision:* scope, range, sweep, reach, extent. **5** *she is well ahead of the field:* competitors, entrants, competition, applicants, candidates, runners.
• verb **1** *she fielded the ball:* catch, stop, retrieve, return, throw back. **2** *fielding a great team:* send out, play, put up, assemble, offer. **3** *he fielded some awkward questions:* deal with, handle, cope with, answer, reply to, respond to.

fierce adjective **1** *a fierce black mastiff:* ferocious, savage, vicious, aggressive.

2 *fierce competition:* aggressive, cut-throat, keen, intense, strong, relentless. **3** *fierce jealousy:* intense, powerful, vehement, passionate, impassioned, fervent, ardent. **4** *a fierce wind:* powerful, strong, violent, forceful, stormy, howling, raging, tempestuous.
OPPOSITES gentle, mild.

fiery adjective **1** *a fiery blast:* burning, blazing, flaming, on fire, ablaze. **2** *a fiery red:* bright, brilliant, vivid, intense, rich. **3** *her fiery spirit:* passionate, impassioned, excitable, spirited, quick-tempered, volatile, explosive, impetuous.

fight verb **1** *two men were fighting:* brawl, exchange blows, scuffle, grapple, wrestle; informal scrap; Brit. informal have a punch-up; N. Amer. informal rough-house; Austral./NZ informal stoush. **2** *he fought in Vietnam:* do battle, serve your country, go to war, take up arms, engage, meet, clash, skirmish. **3** *a war fought for freedom:* wage, engage in, conduct, prosecute, undertake. **4** *they are always fighting:* quarrel, argue, row, bicker, squabble, fall out; informal scrap. **5** *fighting*

part in a violent struggle involving physical force. **2** (**fight someone off**) defend yourself against an attacker. **3** struggle to overcome or prevent. • noun a period of fighting.
◻ **fighting chance** a possibility of succeeding if you make an effort. **fighting fit** in very good health. **fight shy of** be unwilling to do or accept.

fighter noun **1** a person or animal that fights. **2** a fast military aircraft designed for attacking other aircraft.

figment noun a thing that exists only in the imagination.

figurative adjective **1** not using words in their literal sense; metaphorical. **2** (of art) representing things as they appear in real life.
■ **figuratively** adverb.

figure noun **1** a number or numerical symbol. **2** the shape of a person's body, especially that of a woman. **3** an important or distinctive person. **4** a shape defined by one or more lines. **5** a diagram or drawing. • verb (**figures, figuring, figured**) **1** play a significant part. **2** (**figure something out**) informal understand something. **3** N. Amer.

informal think; consider.
◻ **figure of speech** a word or phrase used in a way different from its usual sense. **figure skating** ice skating in set patterns.

figurehead noun **1** a leader without real power. **2** a wooden statue of a person at the front of a sailing ship.

figurine noun a small statue of a human form.

Fijian /fee-**jee**-uhn/ noun a person from Fiji. • adjective relating to Fiji.

filament noun **1** a long, thin thread-like piece of something. **2** a metal wire in a light bulb, which glows when an electric current is passed through it.

filbert noun a type of hazelnut.

filch verb informal steal something.

file[1] noun **1** a folder or box for keeping loose papers together. **2** a collection of computer data stored under a single name. **3** a line of people or things one behind another. • verb (**files, filing, filed**) **1** place in a file. **2** officially present a legal document, application, etc. so that it can be dealt with. **3** walk one behind the other.

file[2] noun a tool with a roughened surface,

THESAURUS

against injustice: campaign, strive, battle, struggle, contend, crusade, agitate, lobby, push, press. **6** *they will fight the decision:* oppose, contest, confront, challenge, appeal against, combat, dispute. **7** *Don fought the urge to cry:* repress, restrain, suppress, stifle, smother, hold back, fight back, keep in check, curb, choke back; informal keep the lid on, cork up.
• noun **1** *a fight outside a club:* brawl, scuffle, disturbance, fisticuffs, fracas, melee, skirmish, clash; informal scrap, dust-up; Brit. informal punch-up; N. Amer. informal rough house; Austral./NZ informal stoush. **2** *a heavyweight fight:* boxing match, bout, match, contest. **3** *the fight against terrorism:* battle, engagement, conflict, struggle, war, campaign, crusade, action, hostilities. **4** *a fight with my girlfriend:* argument, quarrel, squabble, row, wrangle, disagreement, falling-out, dispute; informal tiff, spat, scrap; Brit. informal barney, ding-dong. **5** *their fight for control of the company:* struggle, battle, campaign, push, effort. **6** *she had no fight left in her:* will, resistance, spirit, pluck, grit, strength, backbone, determination, resolution, resolve.

fighter noun **1** *a guerrilla fighter:* soldier, fighting man/woman, warrior, combatant, serviceman, servicewoman; (**fighters**) troops, personnel, militia. **2** *the fighter was knocked to the ground:* boxer, pugilist, prizefighter, wrestler.

figure noun **1** *the figure for April:* statistic,

number, quantity, amount, level, total, sum; (**figures**) data, statistics, information. **2** *the second figure was 9:* digit, numeral, character, symbol. **3** *he can't put a figure on it:* price, cost, amount, value, valuation. **4** *her petite figure:* shape, outline, form, silhouette, proportions, physique, build, frame. **5** *a figure of authority:* person, personage, individual, character, personality, celebrity. **6** *geometrical figures:* shape, pattern, design, motif. **7** *figure 1 shows an ignition circuit:* diagram, illustration, drawing, picture, plate.
• verb *he figures in many myths:* feature, appear, be featured, be mentioned, be referred to.
◻ **figure something out** (informal) **work out**, fathom, puzzle out, decipher, make sense of, think through, get to the bottom of, understand, comprehend, see, grasp, get the hang of; informal twig, crack; Brit. informal suss out.

file[1] noun **1** *he opened the file:* folder, portfolio, binder. **2** *we have files on all of you:* dossier, document, record, report, data, information, documentation, archives.
• verb **1** *file the documents correctly:* categorize, classify, organize, put in order, order, arrange, catalogue, store, archive. **2** *two women have filed a civil suit:* bring, press, lodge.

file[2] noun *a file of boys:* line, column, row, queue, string, chain, procession; Brit. informal crocodile.

used for smoothing or shaping. •verb (**files**, **filing**, **filed**) smooth or shape with a file.

filial adjective having to do with a son or daughter.

filibuster noun (in parliament) a very long speech made to prevent the passing of a new law.

filigree noun delicate ornamental work of thin wire.

filings plural noun small particles rubbed off by a file.

Filipino noun (plural **Filipinos**; feminine **Filipina**, plural **Filipinas**) **1** a person from the Philippines. **2** the national language of the Philippines. •adjective relating to the Philippines or to Filipinos.

fill verb **1** make or become full. **2** block up a hole or gap. **3** appoint a person to a vacant post. **4** hold a particular position or role. •noun (**your fill**) as much as you want or can bear. □ **fill in** act as a substitute. **fill something in** complete a form. **fill someone in** give someone information.

filler noun something used to fill a hole or gap, or to increase bulk.

fillet noun **1** a piece of meat without bones. **2** a piece of fish with the bones taken out. **3** a decorative band or ribbon worn round the head. •verb (**fillets**, **filleting**, **filleted**) take the bones out of a piece of fish.

filling noun a quantity or piece of material used to fill something. •adjective (of food) giving you a pleasantly full feeling.

fillip noun a stimulus or boost.

filly noun (plural **fillies**) **1** a young female horse. **2** humorous a lively girl or young woman.

film noun **1** a thin flexible strip coated with light-sensitive material, used in a camera to make photographs or motion pictures. **2** a story or event recorded by a camera and shown in a cinema or on television. **3** material in the form of a very thin flexible sheet. **4** a thin layer of something on a surface. •verb make a film of; record on film.

filmy adjective (**filmier**, **filmiest**) thin and almost transparent.

filter noun **1** a device or substance that lets liquid or gas pass through but holds back solid particles. **2** a screen, plate, or layer that absorbs some of the light passing through it. **3** Brit. (at a junction) a set of lights that lets vehicles turn but stops traffic waiting to go straight ahead. •verb (**filters**, **filtering**, **filtered**) **1** pass through a filter. **2** move gradually in or out of somewhere.

filth noun **1** disgusting dirt. **2** obscene and offensive language or material.

filthy adjective (**filthier**, **filthiest**) **1** disgustingly dirty. **2** obscene and offensive. **3** informal very unpleasant.

filtrate noun a liquid which has passed through a filter.

filtration noun the action of passing something through a filter.

fin noun **1** a flattened projection on the body of a fish or whale, used for swimming and balancing. **2** an underwater swimmer's flipper. **3** a projection on an aircraft,

THESAURUS

•verb *we filed out into the park:* **walk in a line,** queue, march, parade, troop.

file[3] verb *she filed her nails:* **smooth,** buff, rub down, polish, shape, scrape, abrade, rasp, manicure.

fill verb **1** *he filled a bowl:* **fill up,** top up, charge. **2** *guests filled the room:* **crowd into,** throng, pack (into), occupy, squeeze into, cram (into). **3** *he began filling his shelves:* **stock,** pack, load, supply, replenish. **4** *fill all the holes with putty:* **block up,** stop (up), plug, seal, caulk. **5** *the perfume filled the room:* **pervade,** permeate, suffuse, penetrate, infuse. **6** *the person who fills this vacancy:* **occupy,** hold, take up.
OPPOSITES empty, clear, leave.

filling noun *filling for cushions:* **stuffing,** padding, wadding, filler, contents.
•adjective *a filling meal:* **substantial,** hearty, ample, satisfying, square, heavy, stodgy.

film noun **1** *a film of sweat:* **layer,** coat, coating, covering, cover, skin, patina, tissue. **2** *Emma was watching a film:* **movie,** picture, feature film, motion

picture, video, DVD. **3** *she would like to work in film:* **cinema,** movies, the pictures, films, the silver screen, the big screen.
•verb **1** *he filmed the next scene:* **photograph,** record on film, shoot, capture on film, video. **2** *his eyes had filmed over:* **cloud,** mist, haze, blur.

filter noun *a carbon filter:* **strainer,** sifter, sieve, gauze, mesh, net.
•verb **1** *the farmers filter the water:* **sieve,** strain, sift, clarify, purify, refine, treat. **2** *the rain had filtered through her jacket:* **seep,** percolate, leak, trickle, ooze, leach.

filthy adjective **1** *the room was filthy:* **dirty,** mucky, grimy, foul, squalid, sordid, soiled, stained, polluted, contaminated, unwashed. **2** *filthy jokes:* **obscene,** rude, vulgar, dirty, smutty, improper, coarse, bawdy, lewd; informal blue. **3** *he was in a filthy mood:* **bad,** foul, irritable, grumpy, grouchy, cross; informal snappy; Brit. informal shirty, stroppy; N. Amer. informal cranky, ornery.
OPPOSITES clean, pleasant.

rocket, etc., for making it more stable.

final adjective **1** coming at the end; last. **2** allowing no further doubt or dispute. • noun **1** the last game in a tournament, which will decide the overall winner. **2** (**finals**) Brit. a series of exams at the end of a degree course. ■ **finally** adverb.

finale /fi-**nah**-li/ noun the last part of a piece of music or entertainment.

finalist noun a person or team competing in a final.

finality noun the fact or quality of being final.

finalize or **finalise** verb (**finalizes, finalizing, finalized**) complete or agree on the last part of a plan, agreement, etc.

finance noun **1** the management of large amounts of money by governments or large companies. **2** money to support an enterprise. **3** (**finances**) the money held by a state, organization, or person. • verb

(**finances, financing, financed**) provide funding for.

financial adjective relating to finance. ■ **financially** adverb.

financier noun a person who manages money for large organizations.

finch noun a small bird with a short, stubby bill.

find verb (**finds, finding, found**) **1** discover by chance or by searching. **2** discover that something is the case. **3** work out or confirm by research or calculation. **4** (of a law court) officially declare that a defendant is guilty or not guilty. • noun a valuable or interesting discovery. □ **find someone/thing out 1** discover information. **2** discover that someone has lied or been dishonest. ■ **finder** noun.

finding noun a conclusion reached as a result of an inquiry or trial.

fine[1] adjective **1** of very high quality.

THESAURUS

final adjective **1** *the final year of study:* last, closing, concluding, finishing, end, ultimate, eventual. **2** *their decisions are final:* irrevocable, unalterable, absolute, conclusive, irrefutable, incontrovertible, indisputable, unchallengeable, binding. OPPOSITES first, provisional.

finale noun climax, culmination, end, ending, finish, close, conclusion, termination, denouement. OPPOSITES opening.

finally adverb **1** *she finally got married:* eventually, ultimately, in the end, after a long time, at (long) last, in the long run, in the fullness of time. **2** *finally, attach the ribbon:* lastly, last, in conclusion. **3** *this should finally dispel that myth:* conclusively, irrevocably, decisively, definitively, for ever, for good, once and for all.

finance noun **1** *he knows about finance:* financial affairs, money matters, economics, commerce, business, investment. **2** *short-term finance:* funds, money, capital, cash, resources, assets, reserves, funding. • verb *a project financed by grants:* fund, pay for, back, capitalize, endow, subsidize, invest in, sponsor; N. Amer. informal bankroll.

financial adjective monetary, money, economic, pecuniary, fiscal, banking, commercial, business, investment.

find verb **1** *I found the book I wanted:* locate, spot, pinpoint, unearth, obtain, search out, track down, root out, come across/upon, run across/into, chance on, happen on, stumble on, encounter; informal bump into. **2** *they found a cure for rabies:* discover, invent, come up with, hit on.

3 *you'll find that it's a lively area:* discover, become aware, realize, observe, notice, note, learn. **4** *I find this strange:* consider, think, feel to be, look on as, view as, see as, judge, deem, regard as. **5** *he was found guilty:* judge, deem, rule, declare, pronounce. OPPOSITES lose. • noun **1** *an archaeological find:* discovery, acquisition. **2** *this table is a real find:* bargain, godsend, boon, catch, asset; informal good buy. □ **find something out** discover, become aware of, learn, detect, discern, observe, notice, note, get/come to know, realize, bring to light; informal figure out, cotton on, tumble; Brit. informal twig, suss.

fine[1] adjective **1** *fine wines:* good, choice, select, prime, quality, special, superior, of distinction, premium, classic, vintage. **2** *a fine piece of work:* excellent, first-class, first-rate, great, exceptional, outstanding, splendid, magnificent, exquisite, superb, wonderful, superlative; informal A1, top-notch. **3** *a fine fellow:* worthy, admirable, praiseworthy, laudable, upright, upstanding, respectable. **4** *that's fine, but it's not enough:* all right, acceptable, suitable, good (enough), passable, satisfactory, adequate, reasonable, tolerable; informal OK. **5** *I feel fine:* good, well, healthy, all right, (fighting) fit, blooming, in fine fettle, in good shape/condition; informal OK, great, in the pink. **6** *a fine day:* fair, dry, bright, clear, sunny, cloudless. **7** *fine clothes:* elegant, stylish, expensive, smart, chic, fashionable, fancy, sumptuous, lavish, opulent; informal flashy. **8** *a fine mind:* keen, quick, alert,

2 satisfactory. **3** in good health and feeling well. **4** (of the weather) bright and clear. **5** (of a thread, strand, or hair) thin. **6** consisting of small particles. **7** delicate or complex. **8** difficult to distinguish or describe accurately.

□ **fine art** art such as painting or sculpture. **fine-tune** make small adjustments to. **with a fine-tooth comb** (or **fine-toothed comb**) with a very thorough search or examination.

■ **finely** adverb **fineness** noun.

fine² noun a sum of money that has to be paid as a punishment. ●verb (**fines, fining, fined**) make a person, company, etc. pay a fine.

finery noun smart, colourful clothes or decoration.

finesse /fi-**ness**/ noun **1** elegant or delicate skill. **2** subtle skill in handling people or situations.

finger noun **1** each of the four long, thin parts attached to either hand (or five, if the thumb is included). **2** an object shaped like a finger. **3** an amount of alcohol in a glass equivalent to the width of a finger. ●verb (**fingers, fingering, fingered**) touch or feel with the fingers.

fingerboard noun a flat strip on the neck of a stringed instrument, against which you press the strings.

fingering noun a way of using the fingers to play a musical instrument.

fingernail noun the nail on the upper surface of the tip of each finger.

fingerprint noun a mark made on a surface by a person's fingertip, which can be used to identify the person. ●verb record the fingerprints of.

finial /**fin**-i-uhl/ noun a decorative part at the top of a roof, wall, or other structure.

finicky adjective fussy and hard to please.

finish verb **1** bring or come to an end. **2** (**finish with**) have nothing more to do with. **3** reach the end of a race or other competition. **4** (**finish someone off**) kill or completely defeat someone. **5** give an article an attractive surface appearance. ●noun **1** an end or final stage. **2** the place at which a race or competition ends. **3** the way in which a manufactured article is finished.

□ **finishing school** a college where girls are taught how to behave in fashionable society.

■ **finisher** noun.

finite /**fy**-nyt/ adjective limited in size or extent.

Finn noun a person from Finland.

Finnish noun the language of the Finns. ●adjective relating to Finland or the Finns.

fiord ⇒ **FJORD**.

fir noun an evergreen coniferous tree with needle-shaped leaves.

fire noun **1** the light, heat, and smoke

THESAURUS

sharp, bright, brilliant, astute, clever, intelligent. **9** *fine china*: delicate, dainty, thin, light, fragile. **10** *fine hair*: thin, light, delicate, wispy, flyaway. **11** *a fine point*: sharp, keen, acute, razor-sharp. **12** *fine material*: sheer, light, lightweight, thin, flimsy, diaphanous, filmy, see-through. **13** *fine sand*: fine-grained, powdery, dusty, ground, crushed. **14** *fine details*: intricate, delicate, detailed, elaborate, meticulous. **15** *a fine distinction*: subtle, ultra-fine, nice, hair-splitting.
OPPOSITES everyday, poor, contemptible, ill, dull, wet, coarse.

fine² noun *heavy fines*: financial penalty, forfeit, damages, sanction, fee, excess charge.

finger noun digit.
●verb *she fingered her brooch*: touch, feel, handle, stroke, rub, caress, fondle, toy with, play (about/around) with, fiddle with.

finish verb **1** *Pam finished her work*: complete, end, conclude, terminate, wind up, round off; informal wrap up, sew up, polish off. **2** *Hitch finished his dinner*: consume, eat, devour, drink, finish off, polish off, gulp (down), use (up), exhaust,

empty, drain, get through; informal down. **3** *the programme has finished*: end, come to an end, stop, conclude, come to a close, cease. **4** *finished in a black lacquer*: coat, surface, texture.
OPPOSITES start.
●noun **1** *the finish of filming*: end, ending, completion, conclusion, close, termination, finale, denouement. **2** *a shiny finish*: surface, texture, coating, covering, lacquer, glaze, veneer, gloss, patina, sheen, lustre.
OPPOSITES start.
□ **finish someone/something off 1** *the hunters finished them off*: kill, execute, terminate, exterminate, liquidate, get rid of; informal wipe out, bump off, dispose of; N. Amer. informal waste. **2** *financial difficulties finished us off*: overwhelm, overcome, defeat, get the better of, bring down; informal drive to the wall.

fire noun **1** *a fire broke out*: blaze, conflagration, inferno, flames, burning, combustion. **2** *he lacked fire*: dynamism, energy, vigour, animation, vitality, exuberance, zest, elan, passion, zeal, spirit, verve, vivacity, enthusiasm; informal go, get-up-and-go, oomph. **3** *machine-gun fire*: gunfire, firing, shooting, bombardment, produced when something burns. **2** an occasion in which a building is damaged or destroyed by a fire. **3** wood or coal that is burning for heating or cooking. **4** a heater for a room that uses electricity or gas as fuel. **5** passionate emotion or enthusiasm. **6** the firing of guns. •verb (**fires, firing, fired**) **1** send a bullet, shell, etc. from a gun or other weapon. **2** direct a rapid series of questions or statements towards someone. **3** informal dismiss an employee from a job. **4** supply a furnace or power station with fuel. **5** stimulate. **6** bake or dry pottery or bricks in a kiln. **7** old use set fire to. □ **fire brigade** Brit. a team of people employed to put out fires. **fire door** a strong door for preventing the spread of fire. **fire drill** a practice of the emergency procedures to be used in case of fire. **fire engine** a vehicle carrying firefighters and their equipment. **fire escape** a staircase or ladder for escaping from a burning building. **fire extinguisher** a device that sprays a jet of liquid, foam, or gas to put out a fire. **the firing line 1** the front line of troops in a battle. **2** a situation where you are likely to be criticized. **firing squad** a group of soldiers ordered to shoot a condemned person.

firearm noun a rifle, pistol, or other portable gun.

fireball noun a ball of flames.

firebomb noun a bomb intended to cause a fire.

firebrand noun a person who passionately supports a particular cause.

firebreak noun a strip of open space cleared in a forest to stop a fire from spreading.

firecracker noun a firework that makes a loud bang.

firefighter noun a person whose job is to put out fires.

firefly noun (plural **fireflies**) a kind of beetle which glows in the dark.

fireguard noun a protective screen or grid in front of an open fire.

fireman noun (plural **firemen**) a male firefighter.

fireplace noun a space at the base of a chimney for lighting a fire.

firepower noun the destructive capacity of guns, missiles, or forces.

fireproof adjective able to withstand fire or great heat.

firestorm noun a very fierce fire fanned by strong currents of air.

firewall noun a part of a computer system or network that prevents unauthorized access to the information stored in it.

firewood noun wood that is burnt as fuel.

firework noun **1** a device consisting of a small container of chemicals that produces spectacular effects and explosions when it is lit. **2** (**fireworks**) an outburst of anger or a display of skill.

firm¹ adjective **1** not giving way under pressure. **2** solidly in place and stable. **3** having steady power or strength. **4** showing determination and strength of character. **5** fixed or definite. •verb make firm.
■ **firmly** adverb **firmness** noun.

firm² noun a business organization.

firmament noun literary the heavens; the sky.

first ordinal number **1** coming before all

THESAURUS

shelling, volley, salvo, hail.
•verb **1** *howitzers firing shells:* launch, shoot, discharge, let fly with. **2** *someone fired a gun:* shoot, discharge, let off, set off. **3** (informal) *he was fired:* dismiss, discharge, give someone their notice, lay off, let go; informal sack. **4** *the story fired my imagination:* stimulate, stir up, excite, awaken, rouse, inflame, animate, inspire, motivate.
□ **catch fire ignite**, catch light, burst into flames, go up in flames. **set on fire ignite**, light, set fire to, set alight.

firm¹ adjective **1** *the ground is fairly firm:* hard, solid, unyielding, resistant, compacted, compressed, dense, stiff, rigid, set. **2** *firm foundations:* secure, stable, steady, strong, fixed, fast, tight, immovable, rooted, stationary, motionless. **3** *I was very firm | a firm supporter:* resolute, determined, decided, resolved, steadfast, adamant, emphatic, insistent,

single-minded, wholehearted, unfaltering, unwavering, unflinching, unswerving, unbending, committed. **4** *firm friends:* close, good, boon, intimate, inseparable, dear, special, constant, devoted, loving, faithful, long-standing, steady, steadfast. **5** *firm plans:* definite, fixed, settled, decided, cut-and-dried, established, confirmed, agreed.
OPPOSITES soft, unstable, irresolute, indefinite.

firm² noun *an accountancy firm:* business, company, concern, enterprise, organization, corporation, conglomerate, office, bureau, agency, consortium; informal outfit, operation.

first adjective **1** *the first chapter:* earliest, initial, opening, introductory. **2** *first principles:* fundamental, basic, rudimentary, primary, key, cardinal, central, chief, vital, essential. **3** *our first priority:* foremost, principal, highest,

others in time, order, or importance.
2 before doing something else. **3** Brit. a place in the top grade in an exam for a degree. **4** informal something that has never happened or been done before.

▫ **first aid** emergency medical help given to a sick or injured person. **first class 1** the best accommodation in a train, ship, etc. **2** very good. **first-degree** (of burns) causing only reddening of the skin. **first-hand** from the original source or personal experience; direct. **first lady** the wife of the President of the United States. **first name** a name given to someone when they are born or baptized. **first-rate** very good.

■ **firstly** adverb.

firstborn noun the first child to be born to someone.

firth noun a narrow channel of the sea that runs inland.

fiscal adjective relating to the income received by a government, especially from taxes.

■ **fiscally** adverb.

fish noun (plural **fish** or **fishes**) **1** a cold-blooded animal with a backbone, gills and fins, living in water. **2** the flesh of fish as food. • verb **1** try to catch fish. **2** (**fish something out**) take something out of water or a container. **3** (**fish for**) search or feel for something hidden. **4** (**fish for**) try to get something: *fishing for compliments.*

fisherman noun (plural **fishermen**) a person who catches fish for a living or as a sport.

fishery noun (plural **fisheries**) a place where fish are reared for food, or caught in large quantities.

fisheye lens noun a highly curved lens for a camera, covering a very wide angle of view.

fishmonger noun a person who sells fish for food.

fishnet noun an open mesh fabric resembling a fishing net.

fishwife noun (plural **fishwives**) a woman with a loud, coarse voice.

fishy adjective (**fishier**, **fishiest**) **1** resembling fish. **2** informal causing feelings of doubt or suspicion.

fissile adjective **1** able to undergo nuclear fission. **2** (of rock) easily split.

fission noun **1** the action of splitting into two or more parts. **2** a reaction in which an atomic nucleus splits in two, releasing a great deal of energy. **3** reproduction by means of a cell dividing into two or more new cells.

fissure noun a long, narrow crack.

fist noun a person's hand when the fingers are bent in towards the palm and held there tightly.

■ **fistful** noun.

fisticuffs plural noun fighting with the fists.

fit¹ adjective (**fitter**, **fittest**) **1** of a suitable quality, standard, or type. **2** in good health. • verb (**fits**, **fitting**, **fitted**) **1** be the right shape and size for. **2** be able to occupy a particular position or space. **3** fix into place. **4** provide with a part or attachment; equip. **5** be in harmony with; match. **6** (**fit in**) be well suited. • noun the way in which something fits.

■ **fitness** noun **fitter** noun.

THESAURUS

greatest, paramount, top, main, overriding, central, core; informal number-one. **4** *first prize:* top, best, prime, premier, winner's, winning.

OPPOSITES last.

• adverb **1** *the room they had first entered:* at first, to begin with, first of all, at the outset, initially. **2** *I'd like to eat first:* before anything else, now. **3** *she wouldn't go—she'd die first!* rather, sooner, in preference.

OPPOSITES last, later.

• noun *that's a first:* novelty, innovation, departure, break with tradition.

fish verb **1** *some people were fishing in the lake:* go fishing, angle, trawl. **2** *she fished for her purse:* search, delve, look, hunt, grope, fumble, ferret, rummage.

▫ **fish someone/something out pull out**, haul out, remove, extricate, extract, retrieve, rescue, save.

fit¹ adjective **1** *a fit subject for a book:* suitable, appropriate, suited, apposite, fitting, good enough, apt, -worthy. **2** *not fit*

to look after children: competent, able, capable, ready, prepared, equipped. **3** *tanned and fit:* healthy, well, in good health, in (good) shape, in trim, in good condition, fighting fit, athletic, muscular, strapping, strong, robust, hale and hearty.

OPPOSITES unsuitable, incapable, unfit.

• verb **1** *having carpets fitted:* lay, install, put in, position, place, fix, arrange. **2** *cameras fitted with autofocus:* equip, provide, supply, fit out, furnish. **3** *they fitted the slabs together:* join, connect, piece together, attach, unite, link. **4** *a sentence that fits his crime:* be appropriate to, suit, match, correspond to, tally with, go with, accord with. **5** *an MSc fits you for a scientific career:* qualify, prepare, make ready, train.

▫ **fit in conform**, be in harmony, blend in, be in line, be assimilated.

fit² noun **1** *an epileptic fit:* convulsion, spasm, paroxysm, seizure, attack. **2** *a fit of the giggles:* outbreak, outburst, attack, bout, spell. **3** *Mum would have a fit:*

fit² noun **1** a sudden attack when a person makes violent, uncontrolled movements. **2** a sudden attack of coughing, fainting, etc. **3** a sudden burst of strong feeling. •verb (**fits, fitting, fitted**) have a fit or convulsion.
▢ **in fits and starts** with irregular bursts of activity.

fitful adjective not steady or continuous.
■ **fitfully** adverb.

fitment noun Brit. a fixed item of furniture or piece of equipment.

fitted adjective made to fill a space or to cover something closely.

fitting noun **1** a small part attached to furniture or equipment. **2** (**fittings**) items which are fixed in a building but can be removed when the owner moves. **3** a time when someone tries on an item of clothing that is being made or altered. •adjective appropriate.
■ **fittingly** adverb.

five cardinal number one more than four; 5. (Roman numeral: **v** or **V.**) •noun (**fives**) a game in which a ball is hit with a gloved hand or a bat against a wall.

fiver noun Brit. informal a five-pound note.

fix verb **1** attach or position securely. **2** mend or repair. **3** decide or settle on. **4** make arrangements for. **5** make something unchanging or permanent. **6** informal dishonestly influence the outcome of. •noun informal **1** a difficult or awkward situation. **2** a dose of an addictive drug. **3** an act of fixing something.
■ **fixer** noun.

fixate verb (**fixates, fixating, fixated**) (**fixate on** or **be fixated on**) be obsessed with.

fixation noun an obsessive interest in someone or something.

fixative noun a substance used to fix or protect something.

fixity noun the state of being unchanging or permanent.

fixture noun **1** a piece of equipment or furniture which is fixed in position. **2** (**fixtures**) articles attached to a house that normally remain in place when the owner moves. **3** Brit. a sports event arranged to take place on a particular date.

fizz verb make a hissing sound, like gas escaping in bubbles from a liquid. •noun the sound of fizzing or the quality of being fizzy.

fizzle verb (**fizzles, fizzling, fizzled**) **1** make a weak hissing sound. **2** (**fizzle out**) end or fail in a weak or disappointing way.

fizzy adjective (**fizzier, fizziest**) (of a drink) containing bubbles of gas.

fjord or **fiord** /fyord, fee-ord/ noun a long, narrow inlet of the sea between high cliffs, especially in Norway.

fl. abbreviation fluid.

f

THESAURUS

tantrum, frenzy; informal paddy, heart attack; N. Amer. informal blowout.

fitness noun **1** *polo requires tremendous fitness:* good health, strength, robustness, vigour, athleticism, toughness, stamina. **2** *his fitness for active service:* suitability, capability, competence, ability, aptitude, readiness, preparedness.

fitting noun **1** *a light fitting:* attachment, part, piece, component, accessory, apparatus. **2** *bathroom fittings:* furnishings, furniture, fixtures, fitments, equipment.
•adjective *a fitting conclusion:* apt, appropriate, suitable, apposite, fit, proper, right, seemly, correct.
OPPOSITES unsuitable.

fix verb **1** *signs were fixed to lamp posts:* fasten, attach, affix, secure, connect, couple, link, install, stick, glue, pin, nail, screw, bolt, clamp, clip. **2** *his words are fixed in my memory:* stick, lodge, embed. **3** *his eyes were fixed on the ground:* focus, direct, level, point, train. **4** *he fixed my car:* repair, mend, put right, get working, restore. **5** *Jim fixed it for us to see the show:* arrange, organize, contrive, manage, engineer; informal swing, wangle. **6** (informal) *Laura was fixing her hair:* arrange, put in

order, adjust, style, groom, comb, brush; informal do. **7** (informal) *I'll fix supper:* prepare, cook, make, get; informal rustle up; Brit. informal knock up. **8** *let's fix a date:* decide on, select, choose, settle, set, arrange, establish, allot, designate, name, appoint, specify. **9** (informal) *the fight was fixed:* rig, tamper with, skew, influence; informal fiddle.
OPPOSITES remove.
•noun (informal) **1** *they are in a bit of a fix:* predicament, plight, difficulty, awkward situation, corner, tight spot, mess; informal pickle, jam, hole, scrape, bind. **2** *the result was a fix:* fraud, swindle, trick, charade, sham; informal set-up, fiddle.

fixed adjective predetermined, set, established, arranged, specified, decided, agreed, determined, confirmed, prescribed, definite, defined, explicit, precise.

fizz verb *the mixture fizzed like mad:* bubble, sparkle, effervesce, froth.
•noun **1** *the fizz in champagne:* bubbles, sparkle, fizziness, effervescence, gassiness, froth. **2** *the fizz of the static:* crackle, buzz, hiss, white noise.

fizzy adjective sparkling, effervescent, carbonated, gassy, bubbly, frothy.
OPPOSITES still, flat.

flab noun informal excess fat on a person's body.

flabbergasted adjective informal very surprised.

flabby adjective (**flabbier**, **flabbiest**) (of a part of a person's body) fat and floppy.
■ **flabbiness** noun.

flaccid /flass-id/ adjective soft and limp.
■ **flaccidity** noun.

flack ⇨ FLAK.

flag[1] noun a piece of cloth that is attached to a pole or rope and used as a symbol of a country or organization or as a signal.
● verb (**flags**, **flagging**, **flagged**) 1 mark something as needing attention. 2 (**flag someone down**) signal to a driver to stop.

flag[2] or **flagstone** noun a flat stone slab used for paving.

flag[3] verb (**flags**, **flagging**, **flagged**) become tired or less enthusiastic.

flagellate /fla-juh-layt/ verb whip someone as a form of religious punishment or for sexual pleasure.
■ **flagellation** noun.

flagon noun a large bottle or jug for wine, cider, or beer.

flagpole or **flagstaff** noun a pole used for flying a flag.

flagrant /flay-gruhnt/ adjective very obvious and unashamed.
■ **flagrantly** adverb.

flagship noun 1 the ship in a fleet which carries the admiral in command. 2 the best or most important thing owned or produced by an organization.

flail verb 1 swing something wildly. 2 (**flail around** or **about**) move around in an uncontrolled way. ● noun a tool or machine that is swung to separate grains of wheat from the husks.

flair noun 1 a natural ability or talent. 2 stylishness.

> ❗ don't confuse **flair** with **flare**, which means 'burn' or 'gradually become wider'.

flak or **flack** noun 1 anti-aircraft fire. 2 strong criticism.

flake noun a small, flat, very thin piece of something. ● verb (**flakes**, **flaking**, **flaked**) 1 come away from a surface in flakes. 2 separate into flakes. 3 (**flake out**) informal fall asleep or drop from exhaustion.
■ **flaky** adjective.

flambé /flom-bay/ verb (**flambés**, **flambéing**, **flambéed**) cover food with spirits and set it on fire briefly.

flamboyant adjective 1 very confident and lively. 2 brightly coloured or highly decorated.
■ **flamboyance** noun **flamboyantly** adverb.

flame noun 1 a glowing stream of burning gas produced by something on fire. 2 a brilliant orange-red colour. ● verb (**flames**, **flaming**, **flamed**) 1 give off flames. 2 set on fire. 3 (of a strong emotion) appear suddenly and fiercely. 4 informal send insulting email messages to.
□ **old flame** informal a former lover.

flamenco noun a lively style of Spanish guitar music accompanied by singing and dancing.

flamingo noun (plural **flamingos** or **flamingoes**) a wading bird with mainly pink or red feathers and a long neck and legs.

flammable adjective easily set on fire.

THESAURUS

flag[1] noun *the Irish flag:* banner, standard, ensign, pennant, streamer, colours; Brit. pendant.
● verb *flag the misspelled words:* indicate, identify, point out, mark, label, tag, highlight.
□ **flag someone/something down** hail, wave down, stop, halt.

flag[2] verb 1 *they were flagging towards the finish:* tire, grow tired, weaken, grow weak, wilt, droop. 2 *my energy flags in the afternoon:* fade, decline, wane, ebb, diminish, decrease, lessen, dwindle.
OPPOSITES revive.

flagrant adjective blatant, glaring, obvious, conspicuous, barefaced, shameless, brazen, undisguised.

flair noun 1 *a flair for publicity:* aptitude, talent, gift, instinct, ability, facility, knack, skill. 2 *she dressed with flair:* style, elegance, panache, dash, elan, poise, taste; informal class.

flake noun *a flake of paint:* sliver, wafer, shaving, paring, chip, fragment, scrap, shred.
● verb *the paint was flaking off:* peel (off), chip, blister, come off.

flamboyant adjective 1 *her flamboyant personality:* ostentatious, exuberant, confident, lively, animated, vibrant, vivacious. 2 *flamboyant clothes:* colourful, bright, vibrant, vivid, dazzling, bold, showy, gaudy, garish, loud; informal jazzy, flashy, bling-bling.
OPPOSITES restrained.

flame noun 1 *a sheet of flames:* fire, blaze, conflagration, inferno. 2 (informal) *an old flame:* sweetheart, boyfriend, girlfriend, lover, partner.
□ **in flames** on fire, burning, alight, flaming, blazing.

flan noun a baked dish consisting of an open pastry case with a savoury or sweet filling.

flange noun a projecting flat rim for strengthening an object or attaching it to something.
■ **flanged** adjective.

flank noun **1** the side of the body between the ribs and the hip. **2** the side of something such as a mountain. **3** the left or right side of a group of people. •verb be on the side of.

flannel noun **1** a kind of soft woollen or cotton fabric. **2** (**flannels**) men's trousers made of woollen flannel. **3** Brit. a small piece of towelling for washing yourself. **4** Brit. informal talk that does not have much meaning, used to avoid a difficult subject.

flannelette noun a soft cotton fabric resembling flannel.

flap verb (**flaps**, **flapping**, **flapped**) **1** move up and down or from side to side. **2** Brit. informal be very anxious; panic. •noun **1** a flat piece of paper, cloth, or metal that is attached to one side of something and covers an opening. **2** a movable section of an aircraft wing, used to control upward movement. **3** a flapping movement. **4** informal a panic.

flapjack noun **1** Brit. a soft biscuit made from oats and butter. **2** N. Amer. a pancake.

flapper noun informal a fashionable young woman of the 1920s.

flare noun **1** a sudden brief burst of flame or light. **2** a device that produces a very bright flame as a signal or marker. **3** (**flares**) trousers whose legs widen from the knees down. •verb (**flares**, **flaring**, **flared**) **1** burn or shine suddenly and strongly. **2** (usu. **flare up**) suddenly become intense or violent. **3** gradually become wider at one end.

! don't confuse **flare** with **flair**, which means 'a natural ability or talent'.

flash verb **1** shine with a bright but brief or irregular light. **2** move quickly. **3** display words or images briefly or repeatedly. **4** informal display something in an obvious way to impress people. **5** informal (of a man) show his genitals in public. •noun **1** a sudden brief burst of bright light. **2** a camera attachment that produces a flash of light, for taking photographs in bad light. **3** a sudden or brief occurrence. **4** Brit. a coloured patch on a uniform, used to identify a regiment, country, etc. •adjective informal stylish or expensive in a showy way. □ **flash flood** a sudden local flood resulting from very heavy rainfall. **flash in the pan** a sudden but brief success.
■ **flasher** noun.

flashback noun **1** a scene in a film or novel set in a time earlier than the main story. **2** a sudden vivid memory of a past event.

flashgun noun a device which gives a brief flash of intense light, used for taking photographs in bad light.

flashing noun a strip of metal used to seal the join of a roof with another surface.

flashlight noun **1** an electric torch with a strong beam. **2** a flashgun.

flashpoint noun a point or place at which anger or violence flares up.

flashy adjective (**flashier**, **flashiest**) attractive in a showy or cheap way.

flask noun **1** a bottle with a narrow neck. **2** Brit. a container that keeps a substance hot or cold by means of a double wall that encloses a vacuum.

THESAURUS

flank noun **1** *the horse's flanks:* **side**, haunch, quarter, thigh. **2** *the southern flank of the Eighth Army:* **side**, wing, sector, face, aspect.
•verb *the garden is flanked by two rivers:* **edge**, bound, line, border, fringe.

flap verb **1** *the mallards flapped their wings:* **beat**, flutter, agitate, vibrate, wag, thrash, flail. **2** *the flag flapped in the breeze:* **flutter**, wave, fly, blow, swing, ripple, stir. •noun **1** *a few flaps of its wing:* **beat**, stroke, flutter, movement. **2** (informal) *in a flap:* **panic**, fluster; informal state, stew, tizzy; N. Amer. informal twit.

flare noun **1** *the flare of the match:* **blaze**, flame, flash, burst, flicker. **2** *a flare set off by the crew:* **signal**, beacon, rocket, light, torch, maroon.
•verb **1** *the match flared:* **blaze**, flash, flare up, flame, burn, flicker. **2** *her nostrils flared:* **spread**, splay, broaden, widen, dilate.

flash verb **1** *a torch flashed:* **shine**, flare, blaze, gleam, glint, sparkle, burn, blink, wink, flicker, shimmer, twinkle, glimmer, glisten. **2** (informal) *flashing his money about:* **show off**, flaunt, flourish, display, parade. **3** *racing cars flashed past:* **zoom**, streak, tear, shoot, dash, dart, fly, whistle, hurtle, rush, bolt, race, speed, career; informal belt, zap; Brit. informal bomb, bucket; N. Amer. informal barrel.
•noun *a flash of light:* **flare**, blaze, burst, gleam, glint, sparkle, flicker, shimmer, twinkle, glimmer.

flashy adjective (informal) **ostentatious**, flamboyant, showy, conspicuous, extravagant, expensive, vulgar, tasteless, brash, garish, loud, gaudy; informal snazzy, fancy, swanky, flash, glitzy, bling-bling. OPPOSITES understated.

flat¹ adjective (**flatter, flattest**) **1** having a level and even surface. **2** not sloping; horizontal. **3** with a level surface and little height or depth. **4** not lively or interesting. **5** (of a sparkling drink) no longer fizzy. **6** (of something inflated) having lost its air. **7** Brit. (of a battery) having used up its charge. **8** (of a charge or price) fixed. **9** definite and firm. **10** (of a musical sound) below the proper pitch. **11** (of a note or key) lower by a semitone than a stated note or key. • **adverb** informal completely; absolutely. • **noun 1** the flat part of something. **2** (**flats**) low level ground near water. **3** informal a flat tyre. **4** (**the Flat**) Brit. flat racing. **5** a musical note that is a semitone lower than the named note, shown by the sign ♭.
□ **flat feet** feet with arches that are lower than usual. **flat out** as fast or as hard as possible. **flat race** a horse race over a course with no jumps.
■ **flatly** adverb **flatness** noun.

flat² noun Brit. a set of rooms on one floor forming an individual home within a larger building.

flatfish noun (plural **flatfish** or **flatfishes**) a sea fish, such as a plaice, that has both eyes on the upper side of its flattened body.

flatmate noun Brit. a person that you share a flat with.

flatten verb make or become flat or flatter.

flatter verb (**flatters, flattering, flattered**) **1** compliment someone too much or in an insincere way. **2** (**be flattered**) feel honoured and pleased. **3** make someone appear attractive.

flattery noun excessive or insincere praise.

flatulent adjective suffering from a build-up of gas in the intestines or stomach.
■ **flatulence** noun.

flatworm noun a type of worm with a simple flattened body.

flaunt verb display proudly or obviously.

> ! don't confuse **flaunt** with **flout**, which means 'ignore a rule'.

flautist noun a flute player.

flavour (US spelling **flavor**) noun **1** the

THESAURUS

flat¹ adjective **1** *a flat roof:* level, horizontal. **2** *the sea was flat:* calm, still, glassy, smooth, placid, like a millpond. **3** *plane the wood completely flat:* smooth, even, plane. **4** *a flat wooden box:* shallow, low, low-sided. **5** *his voice was flat:* monotonous, toneless, droning, boring, dull, tedious, uninteresting, unexciting. **6** *the market was flat:* slow, inactive, sluggish, slack, quiet, depressed. **7** (Brit.) *a flat battery:* run down, dead, used up, expired. **8** *a flat tyre:* deflated, punctured, burst, blown. **9** *a flat fee:* fixed, set, invariable, regular, constant. **10** *a flat denial:* outright, direct, absolute, definite, positive, straight, plain, explicit.
OPPOSITES sloping, vertical, rough, uneven, curved, tall, animated, lively, charged, new, inflated, variable, equivocal.
• adverb *she lay flat on the floor:* stretched out, outstretched, spreadeagled, sprawling, prone, prostrate.

flat² noun *a two-bedroom flat:* apartment, suite, penthouse, rooms.

flatten verb **1** *Tom flattened the crumpled paper:* make/become flat, even out, smooth out, level. **2** *the cows flattened the grass:* squash, compress, press down, crush, compact, trample. **3** *tornadoes can flatten buildings in seconds:* demolish, raze (to the ground), tear down, knock down, destroy, wreck, devastate.
OPPOSITES crumple, raise, build.

flatter verb **1** *it amused him to flatter her:* compliment, praise, express admiration for, fawn on, humour, wheedle, blarney; informal sweet-talk, soft-soap, butter up, play

up to. **2** *I was flattered to be asked:* honour, gratify, please, delight; informal tickle pink. **3** *a hairstyle that flattered her:* suit, become, look good on, go well with; informal do something for.
OPPOSITES insult, offend.

flattering adjective **1** *flattering remarks:* complimentary, praising, favourable, admiring, appreciative, fulsome, honeyed, obsequious, ingratiating, sycophantic. **2** *it was very flattering to be nominated:* pleasing, gratifying, an honour. **3** *her most flattering dress:* becoming, enhancing.
OPPOSITES unflattering.

flattery noun praise, adulation, compliments, blandishments, honeyed words, fawning, blarney; informal sweet talk, soft soap, buttering up, toadying.

flaunt verb show off, display, make a great show of, put on show/display, parade, draw attention to, brag about, crow about, vaunt; informal flash.

flavour noun **1** *the flavour of basil:* taste, savour, tang, smack. **2** *salami can give extra flavour:* flavouring, seasoning, taste, tang, relish, bite, piquancy, spice. **3** *a strong international flavour:* character, quality, feel, feeling, ambience, atmosphere, air, mood, tone, spirit. **4** *this excerpt will give you a flavour of the report:* impression, suggestion, hint, taste.
• verb *spices for flavouring food:* season, spice (up), add piquancy to, ginger up, enrich, infuse.

distinctive taste of a food or drink. **2** a particular quality. • **verb** give flavour to.
■ **flavouring** noun **flavourless** adjective.

flaw noun **1** a mark or fault that spoils something. **2** a weakness or mistake.
■ **flawed** adjective **flawless** adjective.

flax noun a blue-flowered plant that is grown for its seed (linseed) and for its stalks, from which thread is made.

flaxen adjective literary (of hair) pale yellow.

flay verb **1** strip the skin from a body. **2** whip or beat very harshly.

flea noun a small wingless jumping insect which feeds on the blood of mammals and birds.
□ **flea market** a street market selling second-hand goods.

fleapit noun Brit. informal a run-down cinema.

fleck noun **1** a very small patch of colour or light. **2** a very small piece of something. • **verb** mark or dot with flecks.

fledged /flejd/ adjective (of a young bird) having developed wing feathers that are large enough for it to fly.

fledgling or **fledgeling** noun a young bird that has just learned to fly.

flee verb (**flees**, **fleeing**, **fled**) run away.

fleece noun **1** the wool coat of a sheep. **2** a soft, warm fabric with a pile, or a jacket made from this. • **verb** (**fleeces**, **fleecing**, **fleeced**) informal swindle someone.
■ **fleecy** adjective.

fleet¹ noun **1** a group of ships travelling together. **2** a group of vehicles or aircraft with the same owner.

fleet² adjective literary fast in movement.

fleeting adjective lasting for a very short time.
■ **fleetingly** adverb.

Flemish noun **1** (**the Flemish**) the people of Flanders, a region divided between Belgium, France, and the Netherlands. **2** the form of the Dutch language spoken in Flanders. • **adjective** relating to Flanders or the Flemish.

flesh noun **1** the soft substance in the body consisting of muscle and fat. **2** the edible part of a fruit or vegetable. **3** (**the flesh**) the physical aspects and needs of the body. • **verb** (**flesh something out**) make something more detailed.
□ **in the flesh** in person.

fleshly adjective relating to the body and its needs.

fleshpots plural noun humorous places with a lot of nightlife and lively entertainment.

fleshy adjective (**fleshier**, **fleshiest**) **1** plump. **2** soft and thick.

fleur-de-lis or **fleur-de-lys** /fler-duh-lee/ noun (plural **fleurs-de-lis** /fler-duh-**lee**/) a design showing a lily made up of three petals bound together at the bottom.

flew past of **FLY**¹.

flex verb **1** bend a limb or joint. **2** tighten a muscle. • **noun** Brit. a cable for carrying electric current to an appliance.

flexible adjective **1** able to bend easily without breaking. **2** able to adapt to different circumstances.
■ **flexibility** noun **flexibly** adverb.

THESAURUS

flaw noun defect, blemish, fault, imperfection, deficiency, weakness, weak spot/point, failing; Computing bug; informal glitch.
OPPOSITES strength.

flawed adjective **1** *a flawed mirror:* faulty, defective, unsound, imperfect, blemished, broken, cracked, scratched; Brit. informal duff. **2** *the findings were flawed:* unsound, distorted, inaccurate, incorrect, erroneous, fallacious.
OPPOSITES flawless.

flee verb run (away/off), run for it, make off, take off, take to your heels, make a break for it, bolt, beat a (hasty) retreat, make a quick exit, escape; informal beat it, clear off/out, skedaddle, scram; Brit. informal scarper; N. Amer. informal light out.

fleet noun navy, naval force, (naval) task force, armada, flotilla, squadron, convoy.

fleeting adjective brief, short-lived, quick, momentary, cursory, transient, ephemeral, passing, transitory.
OPPOSITES lasting.

flesh noun **1** *his smooth, white flesh:* tissue, skin, body, muscle, fat. **2** *strip the flesh from the bone:* meat, muscle. **3** *a fruit with juicy flesh:* pulp, marrow, meat. **4** *the pleasures of the flesh:* the body, human nature, physicality, sensuality, sexuality.

flexibility noun **1** *the flexibility of wood:* pliability, suppleness, elasticity, stretchiness, springiness, spring, resilience, bounce; informal give. **2** *the flexibility of an endowment loan:* adaptability, adjustability, versatility, open-endedness, freedom, latitude. **3** *the flexibility shown by the local authority:* willingness to compromise, accommodation, give and take, amenability, cooperation, tolerance.
OPPOSITES rigidity, inflexibility, intransigence.

flexible adjective **1** *flexible tubing:* bendy, pliable, supple, pliant, plastic, elastic, stretchy, springy, resilient, bouncy. **2** *a flexible arrangement:* adaptable, adjustable, variable, versatile, open-ended, open. **3** *the need to be flexible towards*

flexitime noun a system that lets you vary your working hours.

flexor noun a muscle which makes a part of the body bend.

flick verb 1 hit or remove with a quick light movement. 2 make a sudden quick movement. 3 (**flick through**) look quickly through a book, magazine, etc. • noun 1 a sudden quick movement. 2 informal a cinema film.
□ **flick knife** Brit. a knife with a blade that springs out from the handle when you press a button.

flicker verb (**flickers, flickering, flickered**) 1 shine or burn unsteadily. 2 appear briefly. 3 make small, quick movements. • noun 1 a flickering movement or light. 2 a brief occurrence of a feeling.

flier ⇨ FLYER.

flight noun 1 the action of flying. 2 a journey made in an aircraft or in space. 3 the path of something through the air. 4 the action of running away. 5 a group of birds or aircraft flying together. 6 a series of steps between floors or levels. 7 the tail of an arrow or dart.
□ **flight deck** 1 the cockpit of a large aircraft. 2 the deck of an aircraft carrier. **flight of fancy** a very imaginative idea or story.
■ **flightless** adjective.

flighty adjective unreliable and uninterested in serious things.

flimsy adjective (**flimsier, flimsiest**) 1 weak and fragile. 2 (of clothing) light and thin. 3 unconvincing: *a flimsy excuse*.

flinch verb 1 make a quick, nervous movement as a reaction to fear or pain. 2 (**flinch from**) avoid something because you are scared or anxious.

fling verb (**flings, flinging, flung**) throw or move forcefully. • noun 1 a short period of enjoyment or wild behaviour. 2 a short sexual relationship.

flint noun 1 a hard grey rock. 2 a piece of flint or a metal alloy, used to produce a spark in a cigarette lighter.

flintlock noun an old-fashioned type of gun fired by a spark from a flint.

flip verb (**flips, flipping, flipped**) 1 turn over with a quick, smooth movement. 2 move or throw with a sudden sharp movement. 3 informal suddenly become very angry or lose your self-control. • noun a flipping action or movement. • adjective not serious or respectful; flippant.
□ **flip-flop** a light sandal with a thong that passes between the big and second toes. **flip side** informal the reverse and less welcome aspect of a situation.

flippant adjective not properly serious or respectful.
■ **flippancy** noun **flippantly** adverb.

flipper noun 1 a broad, flat limb used for swimming by sea creatures such as turtles.

THESAURUS

tenants: accommodating, amenable, willing to compromise, cooperative, tolerant.
OPPOSITES rigid, inflexible, intransigent.

flick noun *a flick of the wrist:* jerk, snap, flip, whisk.
• verb 1 *he flicked the switch:* click, snap, flip, jerk, throw. 2 *the horse flicked its tail:* swish, twitch, wave, wag, waggle, shake.
□ **flick through** thumb (through), leaf through, flip through, skim, scan, look through, browse through, dip into, glance at/through.

flicker verb 1 *the lights flickered:* glimmer, flare, dance, gutter, twinkle, sparkle, wink, flash. 2 *his eyelids flickered:* flutter, quiver, tremble, shiver, shudder, jerk, twitch.

flight noun 1 *the history of flight:* aviation, flying, air transport, aeronautics. 2 *a flight to Rome:* plane trip/journey, air trip/journey, service. 3 *the flight of the ball:* trajectory, path (through the air), track, orbit. 4 *a flight of birds:* flock, swarm, cloud, throng. 5 *his headlong flight from home:* escape, getaway, hasty departure, exit, exodus, breakout, bolt, disappearance; Brit. informal flit.

flimsy adjective 1 *a flimsy building:* insubstantial, fragile, frail, rickety, ramshackle, makeshift, jerry-built, shoddy. 2 *a flimsy dress:* thin, light, fine, filmy, floaty, diaphanous, sheer, delicate, gossamer, gauzy. 3 *flimsy evidence:* weak, feeble, poor, inadequate, insufficient, thin, unsubstantial, unconvincing, implausible.
OPPOSITES sturdy, thick, sound.

flinch verb 1 *he flinched at the noise:* wince, start, shudder, quiver, jerk. 2 *he never flinched from his duty:* shrink from, recoil from, shy away from, dodge, evade, avoid, duck, baulk at.

fling verb *he flung the axe into the river:* throw, hurl, toss, sling, launch, pitch, lob; informal chuck, heave.
• noun 1 *a birthday fling:* good time, party, spree, fun and games; informal binge, bash, night on the town. 2 *she had a brief fling with him:* affair, love affair, relationship, romance, liaison, entanglement, involvement.

flippant adjective frivolous, facetious, tongue-in-cheek, disrespectful, irreverent, cheeky; informal flip, saucy; N. Amer. informal sassy.
OPPOSITES serious, respectful.

2 a flat rubber attachment worn on each foot for swimming underwater.

flirt verb 1 behave as if you are trying to attract someone sexually, but without serious intentions. 2 (**flirt with**) show a casual interest in. 3 (**flirt with**) deliberately risk danger or death. •**noun** a person who likes to flirt.
■ **flirtation** noun **flirty** adjective.

flirtatious adjective liking to flirt.

flit verb (**flits, flitting, flitted**) move quickly and lightly.

flitter verb move quickly here and there.

float verb 1 rest on the surface of a liquid without sinking. 2 move or be held up in a liquid or the air. 3 put forward a suggestion. 4 (**floating**) not having fixed opinions or living in a fixed location. 5 put shares in a company on sale for the first time. •**noun** 1 a lightweight object designed to float on water. 2 a vehicle that carries a display in a procession. 3 Brit. a sum of money available for minor expenses.
■ **floaty** adjective.

floatation ⇨ **FLOTATION**.

flock[1] noun 1 a number of birds, sheep, or goats together. 2 (**a flock** or **flocks**) a large number or crowd. 3 a Christian congregation. •**verb** gather or move in a flock.

flock[2] noun 1 a soft material for stuffing

cushions and quilts. 2 powdered wool or cloth, used to give a raised pattern on wallpaper.

floe noun a sheet of floating ice.

flog verb (**flogs, flogging, flogged**) 1 beat with a whip or stick as a punishment. 2 Brit. informal sell.

flood noun 1 an overflow of a large amount of water over dry land. 2 an overwhelming quantity or amount. 3 the rising of the tide. •**verb** 1 cover with water in a flood. 2 (of a river) overflow its banks. 3 arrive in very large numbers.
□ **flood plain** an area of low ground next to a river that is regularly flooded. **flood tide** an incoming tide.

floodgate noun 1 a gate that can be opened or closed to control a flow of water. 2 (**floodgates**) controls that hold back something powerful.

floodlight noun a large, powerful lamp used to light up a sports ground. •**verb** (**floodlights, floodlighting, floodlit**) light up with floodlights.

floor noun 1 the lower surface of a room. 2 a storey of a building. 3 the bottom of the sea, a cave, etc. 4 (**the floor**) the part of a parliament or other law-making assembly in which members sit and from which they speak. •**verb** informal 1 knock someone to the

THESAURUS

flirt noun *Anna was quite a flirt:* tease, coquette, heartbreaker.
□ **flirt with** 1 *he liked to flirt with her:* **tease,** lead on, toy with. 2 *those who flirt with fascism:* **dabble in,** toy with, trifle with, play with, tinker with, dip into, scratch the surface of.

float verb 1 *oil floats on water:* stay afloat, stay on the surface, be buoyant, be buoyed up. 2 *the balloon floated in the air:* hover, levitate, be suspended, hang, defy gravity. 3 *a cloud floated across the moon:* drift, glide, sail, slip, slide, waft. 4 *the company was floated on the Stock Exchange:* launch, offer, sell, introduce.
OPPOSITES sink, drop, rush, take private.

floating adjective 1 *floating voters:* uncommitted, undecided, undeclared, wavering; informal sitting on the fence. 2 *a floating population:* unsettled, transient, temporary, migrant, wandering, nomadic, migratory, itinerant.
OPPOSITES committed, decided, settled.

flock noun 1 *a flock of sheep:* herd, drove. 2 *a flock of birds:* flight, swarm, cloud, gaggle, skein.
•**verb** 1 *people flocked around her:* gather, collect, congregate, assemble, converge, mass, crowd, throng, cluster, swarm.
2 *tourists flock to the place:* stream, go in

large numbers, swarm, crowd, troop.

flog verb whip, thrash, lash, scourge, birch, cane, beat.

flood noun 1 *a severe flood:* inundation, deluge, torrent, overflow, flash flood; Brit. spate. 2 *a flood of tears:* gush, outpouring, torrent, rush, stream, surge, cascade. 3 *a flood of complaints:* succession, series, string, barrage, volley, battery, avalanche, torrent, stream, storm.
OPPOSITES trickle.
•**verb** 1 *the town was flooded:* inundate, swamp, deluge, immerse, submerge, drown, engulf. 2 *the river could flood:* overflow, burst its banks, brim over, run over. 3 *cheap goods flooding the market:* glut, swamp, saturate. 4 *refugees flooded in:* pour, stream, flow, surge, swarm, pile, crowd.
OPPOSITES drain, starve, trickle.

floor noun 1 *he sat on the floor:* ground, flooring. 2 *the second floor:* storey, level, deck, tier, stage.
•**verb** 1 *he floored his attacker:* knock down, knock over, fell; informal deck, lay out. 2 (informal) *the question floored him:* baffle, defeat, confound, perplex, puzzle, disconcert; informal throw, beat, stump; N. Amer. informal buffalo.

ground. 2 surprise or confuse someone.
□ **floor show** an entertainment presented on the floor of a nightclub or restaurant. ■ **floored** adjective.

floorboard noun a long plank making up part of a wooden floor.

floozy or **floozie** noun (plural **floozies**) informal a girl or woman who has many sexual partners.

flop verb (**flops, flopping, flopped**) 1 hang or swing loosely. 2 sit or lie down heavily. 3 informal fail totally. ● noun 1 a heavy and clumsy fall. 2 informal a total failure.

floppy adjective not firm or rigid.
□ **floppy disk** a flexible disk used for storing computer data.

flora noun the plants of a particular area or period.

floral adjective having to do with flowers.

floret noun 1 each of the small flowers making up a flower head. 2 each of the flowering stems making up a head of cauliflower or broccoli.

florid adjective 1 having a red or flushed complexion. 2 too elaborate.

florin noun a former British coin worth two shillings (ten pence).

florist noun a person who sells cut flowers.

floss noun 1 (also **dental floss**) soft thread used to clean between the teeth. 2 silk thread used in embroidery. ● verb clean between the teeth with dental floss.

flotation or **floatation** noun 1 the action of floating. 2 the offering of a company's shares for sale for the first time.

flotilla noun a small fleet of ships or boats.

flotsam noun wreckage found floating on the sea.

flounce verb (**flounces, flouncing, flounced**) move in an angry or impatient way. ● noun 1 an exaggerated action expressing annoyance or impatience. 2 a wide strip of material sewn to a skirt or dress.

flounder[1] verb (**flounders, floundering, floundered**) 1 stagger clumsily in mud or water. 2 have trouble doing or understanding something.

flounder[2] noun a small flatfish.

flour noun a powder produced by grinding grain, used to make bread, cakes, and pastry. ■ **floury** adjective.

flourish verb 1 grow or develop well; thrive. 2 be successful. 3 wave something about in a noticeable way. ● noun 1 a dramatic or exaggerated movement or gesture. 2 a decorative flowing curve in handwriting. 3 a fanfare played by brass instruments.

flout verb openly fail to follow a rule, law, or custom.

❗ don't confuse **flout** with **flaunt**, which means 'display proudly or obviously'.

flow verb 1 move steadily and continuously in a current or stream. 2 hang loosely and elegantly. ● noun a steady, continuous stream.
□ **flow chart** a diagram that shows the

THESAURUS

flop verb 1 *he flopped into a chair:* collapse, slump, crumple, sink, drop. 2 *his hair flopped over his eyes:* hang (down), dangle, droop, sag, loll. 3 (informal) *the play flopped:* be unsuccessful, fail, fall flat, founder; informal bomb; N. Amer. informal tank.
OPPOSITES spring, succeed.
● noun (informal) *the play was a flop:* failure, disaster, fiasco, debacle, catastrophe; Brit. damp squib; informal washout, also-ran; N. Amer. informal clinker.
OPPOSITES success.

floppy adjective limp, flaccid, slack, flabby, relaxed, drooping, droopy, loose, flowing.
OPPOSITES erect, stiff.

flounder verb 1 *floundering in the water:* struggle, thrash, flail, twist and turn, splash, stagger, stumble, reel, lurch, blunder. 2 *she floundered, not knowing what to say:* struggle, be out of your depth, be confused; informal scratch your head, be flummoxed, be fazed, be floored.

flourish verb 1 *ferns flourish in the shade:* grow, thrive, prosper, do well, burgeon, increase, multiply, proliferate, run riot.
2 *the arts flourished:* thrive, prosper, bloom, be in good health, be vigorous, be in its heyday, make progress, advance, expand; informal go places. 3 *he flourished a sword:* brandish, wave, shake, wield, swing, display, show off.
OPPOSITES die, wither, decline.

flout verb defy, refuse to obey, disobey, break, violate, fail to comply with, fail to observe, contravene, infringe, breach, commit a breach of, transgress against, ignore, disregard; informal cock a snook at.
OPPOSITES observe.

flow verb 1 *the water flowed down the channel:* pour, run, course, circulate, stream, swirl, surge, sweep, gush, cascade, roll, rush, trickle, seep, ooze, dribble.
2 *many questions flow from today's announcement:* result, proceed, arise, follow, ensue, stem, originate, emanate, spring.
● noun *a good flow of water:* movement, motion, current, circulation, stream, swirl, surge, gush, rush, spate, tide, trickle, ooze.

sequence of stages making up a complex process.

flower noun **1** the part of a plant from which the seed or fruit develops, usually having brightly coloured petals. **2 (the flower of)** the best of a group. •**verb** (**flowers, flowering, flowered**) **1** produce flowers. **2** develop fully and well.

flowerpot noun a container for growing plants in.

flowery adjective **1** full of or decorated with flowers. **2** (of speech or writing) elaborate.

flown past participle of FLY¹.

flu noun influenza or any similar, milder infection.

fluctuate verb (**fluctuates, fluctuating, fluctuated**) rise and fall irregularly in number or amount.
■ **fluctuation** noun.

flue noun a pipe that takes smoke and gases away from a chimney, heater, etc.

fluent adjective **1** able to use a language in a clear and natural way. **2** smoothly graceful and easy.
■ **fluency** noun **fluently** adverb.

fluff noun **1** soft fibres gathered in small, light clumps. **2** the soft fur or feathers of a young animal or bird. •**verb 1** (**fluff something up**) make something fuller and softer by shaking or patting it. **2** informal fail to do something properly.

fluffy adjective (**fluffier, fluffiest**) **1** covered with fluff. **2** (of food) light in texture.

flugelhorn /floo-guhl-horn/ noun a brass musical instrument like a cornet but with a broader tone.

fluid noun a liquid or gas. •**adjective 1** able to flow easily. **2** not fixed or stable: *a fluid situation*. **3** graceful.
□ **fluid ounce** Brit. one twentieth of a pint (approximately 0.028 litre).
■ **fluidity** noun **fluidly** adverb.

fluke noun something lucky that happens by chance.

■ **fluky** adjective.

flume noun **1** an artificial channel for carrying water. **2** a water slide at a swimming pool or amusement park.

flummery noun (plural **flummeries**) empty talk or compliments.

flummox verb informal baffle someone completely.

flung past and past participle of FLING.

flunk verb informal, chiefly N. Amer. fail an exam.

flunkey or **flunky** noun (plural **flunkeys** or **flunkies**) **1** a uniformed male servant. **2** a person who does menial tasks for someone else.

fluoresce verb (**fluoresces, fluorescing, fluoresced**) shine or glow brightly.

fluorescent /fluu-uh-**ress**-uhnt/ adjective **1** giving off bright light when exposed to radiation such as ultraviolet light. **2** vividly colourful.
■ **fluorescence** noun.

☑ *fluor-*, not *flour-*: *fluorescent*.

fluoridate verb (**fluoridates, fluoridating, fluoridated**) add fluoride to a water supply.
■ **fluoridation** noun.

fluoride /**floo**-uh-ryd, **flor**-yd/ noun a compound of fluorine that is added to water supplies or toothpaste to reduce tooth decay.

fluorine /**floo**-uh-reen, **flor**-een/ noun a poisonous pale yellow gas.

fluorite /**floo**-uh-ryt, **flor**-yt/ noun a mineral found in the form of crystals.

fluorspar /**floo**-uh-spar, **flor**-spar/ = FLUORITE.

flurry noun (plural **flurries**) **1** a small swirling mass of snow, leaves, etc. moved by a gust of wind. **2** a sudden short period of activity or excitement. **3** a number of things arriving suddenly and at the same time.

flush¹ verb **1** (of a person's skin or face)

THESAURUS

flower noun & verb bloom, blossom.

fluctuate verb vary, change, shift, alter, waver, swing, oscillate, alternate, rise and fall.

fluent adjective articulate, eloquent, silver-tongued, communicative, natural, effortless.
OPPOSITES inarticulate.

fluid noun *the fluid seeps up the tube:* liquid, solution, liquor, gas, vapour.
OPPOSITES solid.
•adjective **1** *a fluid substance:* free-flowing, runny, liquid, liquefied, melted, molten, gaseous. **2** *he stood up in one fluid movement:* smooth, fluent, flowing, effortless, easy, continuous, graceful,

elegant.
OPPOSITES solid, jerky.

flurry noun **1** *a flurry of snow:* swirl, whirl, eddy, shower, gust. **2** *a flurry of activity:* burst, outbreak, spurt, fit, spell, bout, rash, eruption.
OPPOSITES dearth.

flush verb **1** *she flushed in embarrassment:* blush, redden, go pink, go red, go crimson, go scarlet, colour (up). **2** *flushing toxins from the body:* rinse, wash, sluice, swill, cleanse, clean; Brit. informal sloosh. **3** *they flushed out the snipers:* drive, chase, force, dislodge, expel.
OPPOSITES pale.
•noun *a flush crept over her face:* blush,

become red and hot. **2** (**be flushed with**) be very pleased by. **3** clean something by passing large quantities of water through it. **4** force a person or animal out into the open. • noun **1** a reddening of the face or skin. **2** a sudden rush of strong emotion. **3** a period of freshness and energy: *the first flush of youth.* **4** an act of flushing.

flush² adjective **1** completely level with another surface. **2** informal having plenty of money.

flush³ noun (in poker) a hand of cards all of the same suit.

fluster noun an agitated and confused state.

flustered adjective agitated and confused.

flute noun **1** a high-pitched wind instrument that you hold sideways and play by blowing across a hole at one end. **2** a tall, narrow wine glass.

fluted adjective decorated with a series of gently rounded grooves.

flutter verb (**flutters, fluttering, fluttered**) **1** fly unsteadily by flapping the wings quickly and lightly. **2** move or fall with a light trembling motion. **3** (of a pulse or heartbeat) beat feebly or irregularly. • noun **1** a state of nervous excitement. **2** Brit. informal a small bet.
■ **fluttery** adjective.

fluvial /floo-vi-uhl/ adjective technical having to do with a river.

flux noun **1** continuous change. **2** a flow.

fly¹ verb (**flies, flying, flew**; past participle **flown**) **1** (of a winged creature or aircraft) move through the air. **2** control the flight of an aircraft. **3** move quickly through the air. **4** go or move quickly. **5** (of a flag) be displayed on a flagpole. **6** (**fly at**) attack. **7** old use run away. • noun (plural **flies**) **1** (Brit. also **flies**) an opening at the crotch of a pair of trousers, closed with a zip or buttons. **2** a flap of material covering the opening of a tent. **3** (**the flies**) the space over the stage in a theatre.
□ **fly-by-night** unreliable or untrustworthy. **fly-post** Brit. put up advertising posters

without permission. **flying saucer** a disc-shaped flying spacecraft supposedly piloted by aliens. **flying squad** a division of a police force which is capable of reaching an incident quickly. **flying start** a good beginning that gives an advantage over competitors. **fly in the face of** do the opposite of what is usual or expected. **fly off the handle** informal lose your temper. **with flying colours** with distinction.

fly² noun (plural **flies**) **1** a flying insect with transparent wings. **2** an artificial fly used as a fishing bait.
□ **a fly in the ointment** a small irritation that spoils the enjoyment of something. **a fly on the wall** an unnoticed observer.

fly³ adjective (**flyer, flyest**) Brit. informal knowing and clever.

flyaway adjective (of hair) fine and difficult to control.

flyblown adjective contaminated by contact with flies.

flycatcher noun a small bird that catches flying insects.

flyer or **flier** noun **1** a person or thing that flies. **2** a small printed advertisement.

flyleaf noun (plural **flyleaves**) a blank page at the beginning or end of a book.

flyover noun Brit. a bridge carrying one road or railway line over another.

flysheet noun Brit. a cover over a tent for keeping the rain out.

flywheel noun a heavy revolving wheel in a machine that helps it to work smoothly.

FM abbreviation frequency modulation.

foal noun a young horse or related animal. • verb give birth to a foal.

foam noun **1** a mass of small bubbles formed on the surface of liquid. **2** a liquid substance containing many small bubbles. **3** a lightweight form of rubber or plastic that is full of small holes. • verb form or produce foam.
■ **foamy** adjective.

fob¹ noun **1** a chain attached to a watch for carrying in a pocket. **2** a tab on a key ring.

THESAURUS

colour, rosiness, pinkness, ruddiness, bloom.
OPPOSITES pallor.

flutter verb **1** *butterflies fluttered around:* flit, hover, dance. **2** *a tern was fluttering its wings:* flap, beat, quiver, agitate, vibrate. **3** *she fluttered her eyelashes:* flicker, bat. **4** *flags fluttered:* flap, wave, ripple, undulate, quiver, fly. **5** *her heart fluttered:* beat irregularly, palpitate, miss/skip a beat, quiver.

fly verb **1** *a bird flew overhead:* wing, glide, soar, wheel, take wing, take to the air. **2** *they flew to Paris:* travel by plane/air,

jet. **3** *we flew in supplies:* transport (by plane/air), airlift, lift, jet, drop, parachute. **4** *he can fly a plane:* pilot, operate, control, manoeuvre, steer. **5** *the ship was flying a French flag:* display, show, exhibit. **6** *flags flew in the town:* flutter, flap, wave. **7** *doesn't time fly?* go quickly, fly by/past, pass swiftly, rush past.

foam noun *the foam on the waves:* froth, spume, surf, spray, fizz, effervescence, bubbles, head, lather, suds.
• verb *the water foamed:* froth, fizz, effervesce, bubble, lather, ferment, boil, seethe.

fob² verb (**fobs, fobbing, fobbed**) **1** (**fob someone off**) try to deceive someone into accepting excuses or something inferior. **2** (**fob something off on**) give something inferior to.

focaccia /fuh-**kach**-uh/ noun a type of flat Italian bread made with olive oil.

focal adjective relating to a focus. □ **focal point 1** the point at which rays or waves of light, sound, etc. meet, or from which they seem to come. **2** the centre of interest or activity.

fo'c's'le ⇨ FORECASTLE.

focus /**foh**-kuhss/ noun (plural **focuses** or **foci** /**foh**-sy/) **1** the centre of interest or activity. **2** the state of having or producing a clear image: *his face is out of focus.* **3** the point at which an object must be situated for a lens or mirror to produce a clear image of it. **4** a focal point. • verb (**focuses, focusing** or **focussing, focused** or **focussed**) **1** adapt to the amount of light available and become able to see clearly. **2** (**focus on**) pay particular attention to. **3** adjust the focus of a telescope, camera, etc. **4** (of rays or waves) meet at a single point. □ **focus group** a group of people brought together to give their opinions of a new product, political campaign, etc.

fodder noun **1** food for cattle and other livestock. **2** a person or thing viewed only as material to satisfy a particular need.

foe noun an enemy or opponent.

foetid ⇨ FETID.

foetus ⇨ FETUS.

fog noun a thick cloud of water droplets which is difficult to see through. • verb (**fogs, fogging, fogged**) **1** become covered with steam. **2** confuse.

fogey noun (plural **fogeys** or **fogies**) a very old-fashioned or conservative person.

foggy adjective (**foggier, foggiest**) **1** full of fog. **2** confused or unclear.

foghorn noun a device that makes a loud, deep sound as a warning to ships in fog.

foible noun a slight peculiarity in a person's character or habits.

foil¹ verb **1** prevent something from happening. **2** stop someone from doing something.

foil² noun **1** metal in the form of a thin flexible sheet. **2** a person or thing that contrasts with and so emphasizes the qualities of another.

foil³ noun a light, blunt-edged fencing sword.

foist verb (**foist someone/thing on**) make someone accept an unwelcome person or thing.

fold¹ verb **1** bend something over on itself so that one part of it covers another. **2** be able to be folded into a flatter shape. **3** clasp someone in your arms. **4** informal (of a company) stop trading as a result of financial problems. **5** (**fold something in** or **into**) mix one ingredient gently with another. • noun **1** a folded part. **2** a line or crease produced by folding.

fold² noun **1** a pen or enclosure for livestock. **2** (**the fold**) a group or community.

folder noun a folding cover or wallet for storing loose papers.

foliage noun the leaves of plants.

folic acid noun a vitamin found especially in green vegetables, liver, and kidney.

folio /**foh**-li-oh/ noun (plural **folios**) **1** a sheet of paper folded once to form four pages of a book. **2** a large-sized book made up of such sheets.

folk plural noun **1** (also **folks**) informal people in general. **2** (**your folks**) informal, chiefly N. Amer. your family. **3** (also **folk music**) traditional music whose composer is unknown, passed on through

f

THESAURUS

focus noun **1** *a focus of community life:* **centre,** focal point, central point, centre of attention, hub, pivot, nucleus, heart, cornerstone, linchpin. **2** *the main focus of this chapter:* **subject,** theme, concern, subject matter, topic, point, essence, gist. • verb *he focused his binoculars on the tower:* **bring into focus,** aim, point, turn. □ **focus on concentrate,** centre, zero in, zoom in, address yourself to, pay attention to, pinpoint, revolve around.

fog noun **mist,** smog, murk, haze; informal pea-souper.

foil¹ verb *the escape attempt was foiled:* **thwart,** frustrate, stop, defeat, block, prevent, obstruct, hinder, snooker, scotch; informal put paid to; Brit. informal scupper.

OPPOSITES assist.

foil² noun *the wine was a perfect foil to pasta:* **contrast,** complement, antithesis.

fold verb **1** *I folded the cloth:* **double,** crease, turn, bend, tuck, pleat. **2** *the firm folded last year:* **fail,** collapse, founder, go bankrupt, cease trading, be wound up, be shut (down); informal crash, go bust, go under, go to the wall, go belly up. • noun *there was a fold in the paper:* **crease,** knife-edge, wrinkle, crinkle, pucker, furrow, pleat.

folk noun (informal) **1** *the local folk:* **people,** individuals, {men, women, and children}, (living) souls, citizenry, inhabitants, residents, populace, population. **2** *my folks live in Hull:* **relatives,** relations, family, performances.

□ **folk tale** a traditional story passed on by word of mouth.

folklore noun the traditional stories and customs of a community.

folksy adjective traditional and homely.

follicle noun one of the small holes in the skin that hair grows out of.

follow verb 1 go after or move along behind. 2 go along a route. 3 come after in time or order. 4 be a result or consequence. 5 act according to advice or an instruction. 6 understand or pay attention to. 7 (**follow something through**) continue an action or task to its end. 8 (**follow something up**) pursue something further.

□ **follow suit** do the same as someone else.

follower noun 1 a supporter, fan, or disciple. 2 a person who follows.

following preposition coming after or as a result of. • noun a group of supporters. • adjective 1 next in time or order. 2 about to be mentioned.

folly noun (plural **follies**) 1 foolishness. 2 a foolish act. 3 an ornamental building with no practical purpose.

foment /foh-**ment**/ verb stir up revolution or conflict.

fond adjective 1 (**fond of**) having a liking or

affection for. 2 affectionate. 3 hoped for but unlikely to be fulfilled.

■ **fondly** adverb **fondness** noun.

fondant noun a thick paste made of sugar and water, used in making sweets and icing cakes.

fondle verb (**fondles, fondling, fondled**) stroke or caress lovingly or in a sexual way.

fondue noun a dish in which you dip small pieces of food into melted cheese or a hot sauce.

font noun 1 a large stone bowl in a church for the water used in baptizing people. 2 (Brit. also **fount**) a set of printed letters of a particular size and design.

fontanelle (US spelling **fontanel**) noun a soft area between the bones of the skull in a baby or fetus.

food noun any substance that people or animals eat to stay alive.

□ **food chain** a series of creatures in which each depends on the next as a source of food. **food for thought** something that makes you think carefully about an issue. **food poisoning** illness caused by food contaminated by bacteria.

foodstuff noun a substance that can be eaten as food.

fool[1] noun 1 a person who behaves in a silly

THESAURUS

people; informal peeps.

follow verb 1 *we'll let the others follow:* come behind, come after, go behind, go after, walk behind. 2 *people who follow the band around:* accompany, go along with, go around with, travel with, escort, attend; informal tag along with. 3 *the police followed her everywhere:* shadow, trail, stalk, track; informal tail. 4 *follow the instructions:* obey, comply with, conform to, adhere to, stick to, keep to, act in accordance with, abide by, observe. 5 *I couldn't follow what he said:* understand, comprehend, take in, grasp, fathom, see; informal make head or tail of, figure out; Brit. informal suss out. 6 *he follows Manchester United:* be a fan of, be a supporter of, support, watch, keep up with.

OPPOSITES lead, flout, misunderstand.

follower noun 1 *a follower of Christ:* disciple, apostle, defender, champion, believer, worshipper. 2 *followers of Scottish football:* fan, enthusiast, admirer, devotee, lover, supporter, adherent.

OPPOSITES leader, opponent.

following noun *his devoted following:* admirers, supporters, backers, fans, adherents, devotees, public, audience.

OPPOSITES opposition.

• adjective 1 *the following day:* next, ensuing, succeeding, subsequent. 2 *the*

following questions: below, underneath, these.

OPPOSITES preceding, above.

folly noun foolishness, foolhardiness, stupidity, idiocy, lunacy, madness, rashness, recklessness, irresponsibility.

OPPOSITES wisdom.

fond adjective 1 *she was fond of dancing:* keen on, partial to, enthusiastic about, attached to, attracted to; informal into. 2 *his fond father:* adoring, devoted, doting, loving, caring, affectionate. 3 *a fond hope:* unrealistic, naive, foolish, over-optimistic, absurd, vain.

OPPOSITES indifferent, uncaring, realistic.

fondle verb caress, stroke, pat, pet, finger, tickle, play with.

food noun nourishment, sustenance, nutriment, fare, cooking, cuisine, foodstuffs, refreshments, meals, provisions, rations; informal eats, grub.

fool noun 1 *acting like a fool:* idiot, ass, halfwit, blockhead, dunce, simpleton; informal nincompoop, clod, dimwit, dummy, fathead, numbskull; Brit. informal nitwit, twit, clot, berk, prat, pillock, wally, dork, twerp, charlie; Scottish informal nyaff, balloon; N. Amer. informal schmuck, turkey; Austral./NZ informal drongo, nong, galah, boofhead. 2 *she made a fool of me:* laughing stock, dupe, gull;

or stupid way. **2** historical a jester or clown.
• **verb 1** trick or deceive. **2** (**fool about** or
around) act in a joking or silly way.
▫ **fool's gold** a yellowish mineral that can
be mistaken for gold. **fool's paradise** a
happy state that is based on ignoring
possible trouble.

fool² noun Brit. a cold dessert made of puréed
fruit and cream or custard.

foolhardy adjective recklessly daring.

foolish adjective silly or stupid.
■ **foolishly** adverb **foolishness** noun.

foolproof adjective incapable of going
wrong or being wrongly used.

foolscap noun Brit. a size of paper, about 330
× 200 (or 400) mm.

foot noun (plural **feet**) **1** the part of the leg
below the ankle, on which a person walks.
2 the bottom of something vertical. **3** the
end of a bed. **4** a unit of length equal to 12
inches (30.48 cm). **5** a group of syllables
making up a basic unit of rhythm in
poetry. • **verb** informal pay a bill.
▫ **foot-and-mouth disease** a disease of
cattle and sheep, causing ulcers on the
hoofs and around the mouth.

footage noun a length of film made for
cinema or television.

football noun **1** a team game involving
kicking a ball, in particular (in the UK)
soccer or (in the US) American football.
2 a large inflated ball used in football.
■ **footballer** noun.

footbridge noun a bridge for pedestrians.

footfall noun the sound of a footstep or
footsteps.

foothill noun a low hill at the base of a
mountain.

foothold noun **1** a place where you can put
a foot down securely while climbing. **2** a
secure position from which to make
further progress.

footing noun **1** a secure grip with the feet.
2 the basis on which something is
established or operates.

footlights plural noun a row of spotlights
along the front of a stage at the level of

the actors' feet.

footling adjective unimportant and
irritating.

footloose adjective free to do as you please.

footman noun (plural **footmen**) a servant
who lets in visitors and serves food at the
table.

footnote noun an additional piece of
information printed at the bottom of a
page.

footpad noun (in the past) a highwayman
who operated on foot.

footpath noun a path for people to walk
along.

footprint noun the mark left by a foot or
shoe on the ground.

footsore adjective having sore feet from
walking.

footstep noun a step taken in walking.

footstool noun a low stool for resting the
feet on when sitting.

fop noun a man who is too concerned with
his clothes and appearance.
■ **foppish** adjective.

for preposition **1** affecting or relating to. **2** in
favour of. **3** on behalf of. **4** because of. **5** so
as to get, have, or do. **6** in place of. **7** in
exchange for. **8** in the direction of. **9** over a
distance or during a period. **10** so as to
happen at. • **conjunction** literary because.

fora plural of **FORUM**.

forage verb (**forages, foraging, foraged**)
search for food. • **noun** food for horses and
cattle.

foray noun **1** a sudden attack or move into
enemy territory. **2** a brief but spirited
attempt to become involved in a new
activity.

forbear¹ /for-**bair**/ verb (**forbears,
forbearing, forbore**; past participle **forborne**)
stop yourself from doing something.

forbear² /for-**bair**/ ⇨ **FOREBEAR**.

forbearance noun patient self-control.

forbearing adjective patient and self-
controlled.

THESAURUS

informal **stooge, sucker, mug, fall guy**; N. Amer.
informal **sap**.
OPPOSITES **genius**.
• **verb 1** *he'd been fooled:* **deceive, trick,
hoax, dupe, take in, mislead, delude,
hoodwink, bluff, gull**; informal **bamboozle,
take for a ride, have on**; N. Amer. informal
sucker; Austral. informal **pull a swifty on. 2** *I'm
not fooling, I promise:* **pretend, make
believe, put on an act, act, sham, fake,
joke, jest**; informal **kid**; Brit. informal **have
someone on**.

foolish adjective **stupid, idiotic, mindless,**

**unintelligent, thoughtless, imprudent,
unwise, ill-advised, rash, reckless,
foolhardy**; informal **dumb, dim, dim-witted,
half-witted, thick, hare-brained**; Brit. informal
barmy, daft; Scottish & N. English informal **glaikit**;
N. Amer. informal **dumb-ass, chowderheaded.**
OPPOSITES **sensible, wise.**

footing noun **1** *a solid financial footing:*
basis, base, foundation. 2 *on an equal
footing:* **standing, status, position,
condition, arrangement, basis, relationship,
terms.**

forbid verb (**forbids, forbidding, forbade** or **forbad**; past participle **forbidden**) **1** refuse to allow something. **2** order someone not to do something.

forbidding adjective appearing unfriendly or threatening.
■ **forbiddingly** adverb.

force noun **1** physical strength or energy that makes something move. **2** violence used to obtain or achieve something. **3** effect or influence. **4** a person or thing that has influence. **5** an organized group of soldiers, police, or workers. **6** (**the forces**) Brit. the army, navy, and air force. ● verb (**forces, forcing, forced**) **1** make someone do something against their will. **2** use physical strength to move something. **3** achieve something by making an effort: *he forced a smile.* **4** (**force something on**) impose something on.
□ **force-feed** force someone to eat food. **in force 1** in great strength or numbers. **2** (of a law or rule) in effect.

forceful adjective powerful and confident.
■ **forcefully** adverb.

forcemeat noun chopped meat or vegetables used as a stuffing.

forceps /**for**-seps/ plural noun a pair of pincers used in surgery.

forcible adjective done by force.
■ **forcibly** adverb.

ford noun a shallow place in a river or stream where it can be crossed. ● verb cross a river or stream at a ford.

fore adjective found or placed in front. ● noun the front part of something. ● combining form (**fore-**) **1** in front. **2** in advance. **3** coming before: *forefather.* ● exclamation called out as a warning to people in the path of a golf ball.

forearm[1] noun the part of a person's arm from the elbow to the wrist or the fingertips.

forearm[2] verb (**be forearmed**) be prepared in advance for danger or attack.

forebear or **forbear** noun an ancestor.

foreboding noun a feeling that something bad will happen.

forecast verb (**forecasts, forecasting, forecast** or **forecasted**) predict what will happen in the future. ● noun a prediction.
■ **forecaster** noun.

forecastle or **fo'c's'le** /**fohk**-suhl/ noun the front part of a ship below the deck.

foreclose verb (**forecloses, foreclosing, foreclosed**) take possession of a property because the occupant has not kept up their mortgage payments.
■ **foreclosure** noun.

forecourt noun **1** an open area in front of a large building or petrol station. **2** Tennis the part of the court between the service line and the net.

forefather noun an ancestor.

forefinger noun the finger next to the thumb.

forefoot noun (plural **forefeet**) each of the two front feet of a four-legged animal.

THESAURUS

forbid verb prohibit, ban, outlaw, make illegal, veto, proscribe, embargo, bar, debar, rule out.
OPPOSITES permit.

forbidding adjective threatening, ominous, menacing, sinister, brooding, daunting.
OPPOSITES inviting.

force noun **1** *he pushed with all his force:* strength, power, energy, might, effort. **2** *they used force to achieve their aims:* coercion, compulsion, constraint, duress, pressure, oppression, harassment, intimidation, violence; informal arm-twisting. **3** *the force of the argument:* power, weight, effectiveness, validity, strength, significance, influence, authority; informal punch. **4** *a peacekeeping force:* body, group, outfit, party, team, detachment, unit, squad.
● verb **1** *he was forced to pay:* compel, coerce, make, constrain, oblige, impel, drive, pressure, press-gang, bully; informal lean on, twist someone's arm. **2** *the door had to be forced:* break open, knock/smash/break down, kick in. **3** *water was forced through a hole:* propel, push, thrust, shove, drive, press, pump.
□ **in force 1** *the law is now in force:* effective, in operation, operative, valid, current, binding. **2** *her fans were out in force:* **in great numbers**, in hordes/droves, in their hundreds/thousands.

forced adjective **1** *forced repatriation:* enforced, compulsory, obligatory, mandatory, involuntary, imposed, required. **2** *a forced smile:* strained, unnatural, artificial, false, feigned, simulated, contrived, laboured, affected, hollow; informal phoney, pretend, put on.
OPPOSITES voluntary, natural.

forceful adjective **1** *a forceful personality:* dynamic, energetic, assertive, authoritative, vigorous, powerful, strong, pushy; informal in-your-face, go-ahead, feisty. **2** *a forceful argument:* convincing, cogent, compelling, strong, powerful, persuasive, coherent.
OPPOSITES weak, submissive, unconvincing.

forecast verb *they forecast record profits:* predict, prophesy, foretell, foresee.
● noun *a gloomy forecast:* prediction, prophecy, prognostication, prognosis.

forefront noun the leading position.

forego[1] ⇒ FORGO.

forego[2] verb (**foregoes, foregoing, forewent**; past participle **foregone**) old use come before in place or time.
▫ **foregone conclusion** a result that can be easily predicted.

foregoing adjective previously mentioned.

foreground noun **1** the part of a view or image nearest to the observer. **2** the most important position.

forehand noun (in tennis and similar games) a stroke played with the palm of the hand facing in the direction of the stroke.

forehead noun the part of the face above the eyebrows.

foreign adjective **1** having to do with a country or language other than your own. **2** coming from outside. **3** (**foreign to**) not familiar to or typical of.
▫ **foreign body** a small piece of material that has entered the body from outside.

☑ -*eign*, not -*iegn*: for*eign*.

foreigner noun **1** a person from a foreign country. **2** informal a stranger.

foreknowledge noun awareness of something before it happens.

foreleg noun either of the front legs of a four-legged animal.

forelimb noun either of an animal's front limbs.

forelock noun a lock of hair growing just above the forehead.

foreman noun (plural **foremen**) **1** a worker who supervises other workers. **2** (in a law court) a person who is head of a jury.

foremast noun the mast of a ship nearest the bow.

foremost adjective highest in rank, importance, or position. • adverb in the first place.

forename noun a person's first name.

forensic /fuh-**ren**-sik/ adjective **1** having to do with the use of scientific methods in investigating crime. **2** having to do with courts of law.

foreplay noun activities such as kissing and touching that people may engage in before having sex.

forerunner noun a person or thing which exists before another comes or is developed.

foresee verb (**foresees, foreseeing, foresaw**; past participle **foreseen**) be aware of something before it happens; predict.
■ **foreseeable** adjective.

foreshadow verb be a warning or indication of a future event.

foreshore noun the part of a shore between the highest and lowest levels reached by the sea.

foreshorten verb **1** portray something as being closer or shallower than it really is. **2** end something before the usual or intended time.

foresight noun the ability to predict future events and needs.

foreskin noun the roll of skin covering the end of the penis.

forest noun **1** a large area covered thickly with trees and plants. **2** a large number of tangled or upright objects.
■ **forested** adjective.

forestall verb prevent or delay something by taking action in advance.

forestry noun the science or practice of planting and taking care of forests.
■ **forester** noun.

foretaste noun a sample of something that is to come.

foretell verb (**foretells, foretelling, foretold**) predict.

forethought noun careful consideration of what will be necessary or may happen in the future.

forever adverb **1** (also **for ever**) for all future time. **2** a very long time. **3** continually.

forewarn verb warn in advance.

THESAURUS

foreign adjective alien, overseas, non-native, imported, distant, external, far-off, exotic, strange.
OPPOSITES domestic, native.

foreigner noun alien, non-native, stranger, outsider, immigrant, settler, newcomer, incomer.
OPPOSITES native, national.

foremost adjective leading, principal, premier, prime, top, greatest, best, supreme, pre-eminent, outstanding, most important, most notable; N. Amer. ranking; informal number-one.
OPPOSITES minor.

foresee verb anticipate, expect, envisage, predict, forecast, foretell, prophesy.

foretell verb predict, forecast, prophesy, foresee, anticipate, envisage, warn of.

forever adverb **1** *their love would last forever:* for always, evermore, for ever and ever, for good, for all time, until the end of time, eternally; N. Amer. forevermore; informal until the cows come home. **2** *he was forever banging into things:* always, continually, constantly, perpetually, incessantly, endlessly, persistently, repeatedly, regularly; informal 24-7.
OPPOSITES never, occasionally.

forewent past of FOREGO¹, FOREGO².

foreword noun a short introduction to a book.

forfeit /for-fit/ verb (**forfeits, forfeiting, forfeited**) lose property or a right as a punishment for doing wrong. • noun a punishment for doing wrong.

forge¹ verb (**forges, forging, forged**) 1 shape a metal object by heating and hammering it. 2 create something through effort. 3 produce a copy of a banknote, signature, etc. to deceive people. • noun 1 a blacksmith's workshop. 2 a furnace for melting or refining metal.
■ **forger** noun **forgery** noun.

forge² verb (**forges, forging, forged**) 1 move forward gradually or steadily. 2 (**forge ahead**) make progress.

forget verb (**forgets, forgetting, forgot**; past participle **forgotten** or chiefly US **forgot**) 1 be unable to remember. 2 fail to remember to do something. 3 stop thinking of. 4 (**forget yourself**) behave in an inappropriate or unacceptable way.
□ **forget-me-not** a plant with light blue flowers.
■ **forgettable** adjective.

forgetful adjective tending to forget things.
■ **forgetfully** adverb.

forgive verb (**forgives, forgiving, forgave**; past participle **forgiven**) 1 stop feeling angry or resentful towards a person who has done something hurtful or wrong. 2 excuse an offence or mistake.
■ **forgivable** adjective.

forgiveness noun the action of forgiving, or the state of being forgiven.

forgo or **forego** verb (**forgoes, forgoing, forwent**; past participle **forgone**) go without something that you want.

fork noun 1 an object with two or more prongs used for lifting or holding food. 2 a similar-shaped farm or garden tool used for digging or lifting. 3 the point where a road, river, etc. divides into two parts. 4 either of two such parts. • verb 1 divide into two parts. 2 take one route or the other at a fork. 3 dig or lift with a fork. 4 (**fork something out**) informal pay money.

forked adjective 1 having a divided or fork-shaped end. 2 in the shape of a zigzag.

forklift truck noun a vehicle with a device on the front for lifting and carrying heavy loads.

forlorn /fer-**lorn**/ adjective 1 pitifully sad and lonely. 2 unlikely to succeed or be fulfilled: *a forlorn hope.*
■ **forlornly** adverb.

form noun 1 the shape or arrangement of

THESAURUS

forfeit verb lose, be deprived of, surrender, relinquish, sacrifice, give up, renounce, forgo.
OPPOSITES retain.
• noun penalty, sanction, punishment, penance, fine, confiscation, loss, forfeiture, surrender.

forge verb 1 *he forged a huge sword:* hammer out, beat out, fashion. 2 *they forged a partnership:* build, construct, form, create, establish, set up. 3 *he forged her signature:* fake, falsify, counterfeit, copy, imitate; informal pirate.

forged adjective fake, false, counterfeit, imitation, copied, pirate, bogus; informal phoney, dud.
OPPOSITES genuine.

forgery noun fake, counterfeit, fraud, imitation, replica, copy, pirate copy; informal phoney.

forget verb 1 *he forgot where he was:* fail to remember, be unable to remember. 2 *I never forget my briefcase:* leave behind, travel/leave home without. 3 *I forgot to close the door:* neglect, fail, omit.
OPPOSITES remember.

forgive verb 1 *she would not forgive him:* pardon, excuse, exonerate, absolve. 2 *you must forgive his rude conduct:* excuse, overlook, disregard, ignore, make

allowances for, turn a blind eye to, condone, indulge, tolerate.
OPPOSITES blame, resent.

forgiveness noun pardon, absolution, exoneration, indulgence, clemency, mercy, reprieve, amnesty; informal let-off.
OPPOSITES mercilessness, punishment.

fork verb split, branch, divide, separate, part, diverge, go in different directions, bifurcate.

form noun 1 *the form of the landscape:* shape, configuration, formation, structure, construction, arrangement, appearance, exterior, outline, format, layout, design. 2 *the human form:* body, shape, figure, frame, physique, anatomy; informal vital statistics. 3 *the infection takes different forms:* manifestation, appearance, embodiment, incarnation, semblance, shape, guise. 4 *sponsorship is a form of advertising:* kind, sort, type, class, category, variety, genre, brand, style. 5 *you have to fill in a form:* questionnaire, document, coupon, slip. 6 *what form is your daughter in?* class, year; N. Amer. grade. 7 *in good form:* condition, fettle, shape, health; Brit. informal nick.
• verb 1 *formed from mild steel:* make, construct, build, manufacture, fabricate, assemble, put together, create, fashion, shape. 2 *he formed a plan:* formulate,

something. **2** a particular way in which a thing exists. **3** a type. **4** a printed document with blank spaces for information to be filled in. **5** the current standard of play of a sports player or team. **6** a person's mood and state of health. **7** the way something is usually done. **8** Brit. a class or year in a school. •**verb 1** create something by shaping material or bringing together parts. **2** go to make up. **3** establish or develop.
■ **formless** adjective.

formal adjective **1** suitable for or referring to official or important occasions. **2** officially recognized. **3** arranged in a regular way, according to an exact plan.
■ **formally** adverb.

formaldehyde /for-mal-di-hyd/ noun a strong-smelling gas mixed with water and used as a preservative and disinfectant.

formalin /for-muh-lin/ noun a solution of formaldehyde in water.

formality noun (plural **formalities**) **1** a thing done to follow rules or usual customs. **2** correct and formal behaviour. **3** (**a formality**) a thing done or happening as a matter of course.

formalize or **formalise** verb (**formalizes, formalizing, formalized**) make an arrangement official.

format noun **1** the way in which something is arranged or presented. **2** the shape, size, and presentation of a book, document, etc. •**verb** (**formats, formatting, formatted**) give something a particular format.

formation noun **1** the action of forming. **2** something that has been formed. **3** a particular structure or arrangement.

formative adjective having a strong influence in the way something is formed.

former[1] adjective **1** having been previously: *her former boyfriend.* **2** in the past. **3** (**the former**) referring to the first of two things mentioned.

former[2] noun **1** a person or thing that forms something. **2** Brit. a person in a particular school year.

formerly adverb in the past.

Formica noun trademark a hard plastic material used for worktops, cupboard doors, etc.

formic acid noun an acid present in the fluid produced by some ants.

formidable adjective frightening or

devise, conceive, work out, think up, lay, draw up, put together, produce, fashion, concoct, forge, hatch; informal dream up. **3** *they formed a company:* set up, establish, found, launch, create, institute, start, inaugurate. **4** *a mist was forming:* materialize, come into being/existence, emerge, develop, take shape, gather, accumulate, collect, amass. **5** *his men formed themselves into a line:* arrange, draw up, line up, assemble, organize, sort, order. **6** *these parts form an integrated whole:* comprise, make, make up, constitute, compose, add up to.
OPPOSITES dissolve, disappear.

formal adjective **1** *a formal dinner:* ceremonial, ritualistic, ritual, official, conventional, traditional, stately, solemn, elaborate. **2** *a very formal manner:* aloof, reserved, remote, detached, stiff, unapproachable, stuffy, ceremonious, correct, proper; informal stand-offish. **3** *formal permission:* official, legal, authorized, approved, certified, endorsed, sanctioned, licensed, recognized.
OPPOSITES informal, friendly, casual, colloquial, unofficial.

formality noun **1** *the formality of the occasion:* ceremony, ritual, protocol, decorum, solemnity. **2** *his formality was off-putting:* aloofness, reserve, remoteness, detachment, unapproachability, stiffness, stuffiness, correctness; informal stand-offishness. **3** *we keep the formalities to a*

minimum: official procedure, bureaucracy, red tape, paperwork. **4** *the interview is just a formality:* routine, routine practice, normal procedure.
OPPOSITES informality, friendliness.

format noun design, style, appearance, look, form, shape, size, arrangement, plan, structure, scheme, composition, configuration.

formation noun **1** *the formation of the island:* emergence, genesis, development, evolution, shaping, origin. **2** *the formation of a new government:* establishment, setting up, institution, foundation, creation, inauguration. **3** *fighters flying in a V formation:* configuration, arrangement, grouping, pattern, array, alignment, order.
OPPOSITES destruction, dissolution.

former adjective **1** *the former bishop:* one-time, erstwhile, sometime, ex-, previous, preceding, earlier, prior, last; formal quondam. **2** *in former times:* earlier, old, past, bygone, olden, long ago, gone by, long past, of old. **3** *the former view:* first-mentioned, first.
OPPOSITES future, current, latter.

formerly adverb previously, earlier, before, until now/then, once, once upon a time, at one time, in the past.

formidable adjective **1** *a formidable beast:* intimidating, forbidding, alarming, frightening, awesome, fearsome, threatening. **2** *a formidable pianist:*

intimidating through being very large, powerful, or capable.
- **formidably** adverb.

formula noun (plural **formulae** /**for**-myuu-lee/ or **formulas**) **1** a mathematical relationship or rule expressed in symbols. **2** a set of chemical symbols showing what elements are present in a compound. **3** a method for achieving something. **4** a fixed form of words used in particular situations. **5** a list of ingredients with which something is made. **6** a powder-based milky drink for babies.

formulaic /for-myuu-**lay**-ik/ adjective **1** containing a set form of words. **2** made by closely following a rule or style.

formulate verb (**formulates, formulating, formulated**) **1** create or prepare something methodically. **2** express an idea clearly and briefly.
- **formulation** noun.

fornicate verb (**fornicates, fornicating, fornicated**) formal have sex with someone you are not married to.
- **fornication** noun **fornicator** noun.

forsake verb (**forsakes, forsaking, forsook**; past participle **forsaken**) literary **1** abandon. **2** give up.

forsooth adverb old use indeed.

forswear verb (**forswears, forswearing, forswore**; past participle **forsworn**) formal agree to give up or do without.

forsythia noun a shrub with bright yellow flowers.

fort noun a building constructed to defend a place against attack.
- ☐ **hold the fort** be responsible for something while a person is away.

forte /**for**-tay/ noun a thing for which someone has a particular talent.

forth adverb old use **1** forwards or into view. **2** onwards in time.

forthcoming adjective **1** about to happen or appear. **2** made available when required. **3** willing to reveal information.

forthright adjective direct and outspoken.

forthwith adverb without delay.

fortify verb (**fortifies, fortifying, fortified**) **1** strengthen a place to protect it against attack. **2** give strength or energy to. **3** add alcohol or vitamins to food or drink.
- **fortification** noun.

fortissimo /for-**tiss**-i-moh/ adverb & adjective Music very loud or loudly.

fortitude noun courage and strength when facing pain or trouble.

fortnight noun Brit. a period of two weeks.

fortnightly Brit. adjective & adverb happening or produced every two weeks.

fortress noun a building or town which has been strengthened against attack.

fortuitous /for-**tyoo**-i-tuhss/ adjective **1** happening by chance. **2** lucky.
- **fortuitously** adverb.

fortunate adjective **1** involving good luck. **2** advantageous or favourable.
- **fortunately** adverb.

THESAURUS

accomplished, masterly, virtuoso, expert, impressive, powerful, terrific, superb; informal tremendous, nifty, crack, ace, wizard, magic, mean, wicked, deadly. OPPOSITES pleasant-looking, comforting, poor.

formula noun **1** *a legal formula:* form of words, set expression, phrase, saying. **2** *a peace formula:* recipe, prescription, blueprint, plan, policy, method, procedure.

formulate verb **1** *the miners formulated a plan:* devise, conceive, work out, think up, lay, draw up, form, concoct, contrive, forge, hatch, prepare, develop. **2** *how Marx formulated his question:* express, phrase, word, define, specify, put into words, frame, couch, put, articulate, say.

fort noun fortress, castle, citadel, bunker, stronghold, fortification, bastion.

forte noun strength, strong point, speciality, strong suit, talent, skill, gift; informal thing. OPPOSITES weakness.

forthcoming adjective **1** *forthcoming events:* coming, upcoming, approaching, imminent, impending, future. **2** *no reply was forthcoming:* available, on offer, offered. **3** *he was not very forthcoming:*

communicative, talkative, chatty, expansive, expressive, frank, open, candid. OPPOSITES past, current, unavailable, uncommunicative.

fortify verb **1** *measures to fortify the building:* strengthen, secure, barricade, protect. **2** *I'll have a drink to fortify me:* invigorate, strengthen, energize, enliven, animate, vitalize; informal pep up, buck up. OPPOSITES weaken, sedate, subdue.

fortitude noun courage, bravery, endurance, resilience, mettle, strength of character, backbone, grit; informal guts; Brit. informal bottle. OPPOSITES faint-heartedness.

fortress noun fort, castle, citadel, bunker, stronghold, fortification.

fortunate adjective **1** *he was fortunate enough to survive:* lucky, favoured, blessed, blessed with good luck, in luck; Brit. informal jammy. **2** *we were in a fortunate position:* favourable, advantageous, happy. OPPOSITES unfortunate, unfavourable.

fortunately adverb luckily, by good luck, by good fortune, as luck would have it, happily, mercifully, thankfully.

fortune noun **1** chance or luck as it affects human affairs. **2** (**fortunes**) the success or failure of a person or undertaking. **3** a large amount of money or property.

forty cardinal number (plural **forties**) ten less than fifty; 40. (Roman numeral: **xl** or **XL**.) □ **forty winks** informal a short daytime sleep. ■ **fortieth** ordinal number.

> ☑ *for-*, not *four-*: *forty*.

forum noun (plural **forums**) **1** a meeting or opportunity for exchanging views. **2** (plural **fora**) (in ancient Roman cities) a square or marketplace used for public business.

forward adverb & adjective **1** in the direction that you are facing or travelling. **2** towards a successful end. **3** ahead in time. **4** in or near the front of a ship or aircraft. • adjective behaving in a way that is too confident or friendly. • noun an attacking player in sport. • verb send a letter, especially on to a further destination. ■ **forwards** adverb.

forwent past of FORGO.

fossil noun the remains of a prehistoric plant or animal that have become hardened into rock. □ **fossil fuel** a fuel such as coal or gas that is formed from the remains of animals and plants.

fossilize or **fossilise** verb (**fossilizes, fossilizing, fossilized**) preserve an animal or plant so that it becomes a fossil. ■ **fossilization** noun.

foster verb (**fosters, fostering, fostered**) **1** encourage the development of. **2** bring up a child that is not your own by birth.

fought past and past participle of FIGHT.

foul adjective **1** having a disgusting smell or taste. **2** very unpleasant. **3** wicked or obscene. **4** polluted. • noun (in sport) a piece of play that is not allowed by the rules. • verb **1** make foul or dirty. **2** (in sport) commit a foul against. **3** (**foul something up**) make a mistake with something. **4** make a cable or anchor become entangled or jammed. □ **foul-mouthed** using bad language. **foul play 1** unfair play in sport. **2** criminal or violent activity. ■ **foully** adverb.

found¹ past and past participle of FIND.

found² verb **1** establish an institution or organization. **2** (**be founded on**) be based on a particular concept.

found³ verb melt and mould metal to make an object.

foundation noun **1** the lowest part of a building, which supports the weight. **2** an

fortune noun **1** *fortune favoured him:* chance, accident, coincidence, serendipity, destiny, providence; N. Amer. happenstance. **2** *a change of fortune:* luck, fate, destiny, predestination, the stars, karma, kismet, lot. **3** *an upswing in Sheffield's fortunes:* circumstances, state of affairs, condition, position, situation. **4** *he made his fortune in steel:* wealth, money, riches, assets, resources, means, possessions, property, estate.

forum noun meeting, assembly, gathering, rally, conference, seminar, convention, symposium.

forward adverb **1** *the traffic moved forward:* ahead, forwards, onwards, onward, on, further. **2** *the winner stepped forward:* towards the front, out, forth, into view, up. **3** *from that day forward:* onward, onwards, on, forth, for ever. OPPOSITES backwards, back. • adjective **1** *a forward movement:* onward, advancing. **2** *the Red Army's forward bridgehead:* front, advance, foremost, leading. **3** *forward planning:* future, forward-looking, for the future, anticipatory. **4** *the girls were very forward:* bold, brazen, cheeky, shameless, familiar, overfamiliar, presumptuous; informal fresh. OPPOSITES backward, rear, shy. • verb **1** *my mother forwarded your letter:*

send on, post on, redirect, readdress, pass on. **2** *the goods were forwarded by sea:* send, dispatch, transmit, carry, convey, deliver, ship.

foster verb **1** *he fostered the arts:* encourage, promote, further, nurture, help, aid, assist, support, back. **2** *they fostered two children:* bring up, rear, raise, care for, take care of, look after, provide for. OPPOSITES suppress, neglect.

foul adjective **1** *a foul smell:* disgusting, revolting, repulsive, repugnant, abhorrent, loathsome, offensive, sickening, nauseating; informal ghastly, gruesome, gross. **2** *foul drinking water:* polluted, contaminated, infected, tainted, impure, filthy, dirty, unclean. **3** *foul language:* vulgar, crude, coarse, filthy, dirty, obscene, indecent, naughty, offensive; informal blue. OPPOSITES pleasant, clean. • verb **1** *the river had been fouled:* dirty, pollute, contaminate, poison, taint. **2** *the trawler had fouled its nets:* tangle up, entangle, snarl, catch, entwine. OPPOSITES clean up, disentangle.

found verb establish, set up, start, begin, get going, institute, inaugurate, launch. OPPOSITES dissolve.

foundation noun **1** *the foundations of the*

f

underlying basis or reason. **3** an institution or organization. **4** the action of founding something. **5** a cream or powder applied to the face as a base for other make-up.

founder[1] noun a person who founds an institution or settlement.

founder[2] verb (**founders, foundering, foundered**) **1** (of a plan or undertaking) fail; come to nothing. **2** (of a ship) fill with water and sink.

foundling noun a child that has been abandoned by its parents and is discovered and cared for by other people.

foundry noun (plural **foundries**) a workshop or factory for casting metal.

fount noun **1** a source of a desirable quality. **2** literary a spring or fountain. **3** ⇨ FONT.

fountain noun **1** a decorative structure in a pool or lake from which a jet of water is pumped into the air. **2** literary a natural spring of water.
□ **fountain pen** a pen with a container from which ink flows to the nib.

fountainhead noun an original source of something.

four cardinal number **1** one more than three; 4. (Roman numeral: **iv** or **IV**.) **2** Cricket a hit that reaches the boundary after first hitting the ground, scoring four runs.
□ **four-poster bed** a bed with a post at each corner holding up a canopy. **four-square** having a square shape and solid appearance.

foursome noun a group of four people.

fourteen cardinal number one more than thirteen; 14. (Roman numeral: **xiv** or **XIV**.)
■ **fourteenth** ordinal number.

fourth ordinal number **1** number four in a

sequence; 4th. **2** (**a fourth** or **one fourth**) a quarter.
■ **fourthly** adverb.

fowl noun (plural **fowl** or **fowls**) **1** a bird kept for its eggs or meat, such as a chicken or turkey. **2** birds as a group.

fox noun an animal with a pointed muzzle, bushy tail, and a reddish coat. • verb informal baffle or deceive.

foxglove noun a tall plant with spikes of flowers shaped like the fingers of gloves.

foxhole noun a hole in the ground used by troops as a shelter against the enemy or as a place to fire from.

foxhound noun a breed of dog trained to hunt foxes in packs.

foxtrot noun a ballroom dance which involves switching between slow and quick steps.

foxy adjective (**foxier, foxiest**) **1** like a fox. **2** crafty or sly.

foyer /foy-ay/ noun a large entrance hall in a hotel or theatre.

fracas /fra-kah/ noun (plural **fracas** /fra-kah or fra-kahz/) a noisy disturbance or quarrel.

fraction noun **1** a number that is not a whole number (e.g. ½, 0.5). **2** a very small part or amount.

fractional adjective **1** having to do with a fraction. **2** very small in amount.
■ **fractionally** adverb.

fractious adjective **1** bad-tempered. **2** difficult to control.

fracture noun **1** a crack or break. **2** the cracking or breaking of a hard object or material. • verb (**fractures, fracturing, fractured**) **1** break. **2** (of a group) break up.

fragile adjective **1** easily broken or damaged.

THESAURUS

wall: footing, foot, base, substructure, underpinning. **2** *there was no foundation for the claim:* justification, grounds, evidence, basis. **3** *an educational foundation:* endowed institution, charitable body, funding agency.

founder[1] noun *the founder of modern physics:* originator, creator, (founding) father, architect, developer, pioneer, author, inventor, mastermind.

founder[2] verb **1** *the ship foundered:* sink, go to the bottom, go down, be lost at sea. **2** *the scheme foundered:* fail, be unsuccessful, fall flat, fall through, collapse, backfire, meet with disaster; informal flop, bomb.
OPPOSITES be raised, succeed.

fountain noun **1** *a fountain of water:* jet, spray, spout, spurt, cascade, water feature. **2** *a fountain of knowledge:* source, fount, well, reservoir, fund, mine.

foyer noun entrance hall, hallway, entry, porch, reception area, atrium, concourse, lobby, anteroom; N. Amer. entryway.

fraction noun **1** *a fraction of the population:* tiny part, fragment, snippet, snatch. **2** *he moved a fraction closer:* tiny amount, little, bit, touch, soupçon, trifle, mite, shade, jot; informal smidgen, tad.
OPPOSITES whole.

fracture noun break, crack, split, rupture, fissure.
• verb break, crack, split, rupture, snap, shatter, fragment, splinter.

fragile adjective **1** *fragile vases:* breakable, delicate, brittle, flimsy, dainty, fine. **2** *the fragile ceasefire:* tenuous, shaky, insecure, vulnerable, flimsy. **3** *she is still very fragile:* weak, delicate, frail, debilitated, ill, unwell, poorly, sickly.
OPPOSITES sturdy, durable, robust.

2 (of a person) delicate and vulnerable.
■ **fragility** noun.

fragment noun /frag-muhnt/ a small part that has broken off or come from something larger. • verb /frag-**ment**/ break into fragments.
■ **fragmentary** adjective **fragmentation** noun.

fragrance noun **1** a pleasant, sweet smell. **2** a perfume or aftershave.

fragrant adjective having a pleasant, sweet smell.

frail adjective **1** weak and delicate. **2** easily damaged or broken.

frailty noun (plural **frailties**) the condition of being frail; weakness.

frame noun **1** a rigid structure surrounding a picture, door, etc. or giving support to a building or vehicle. **2** the structure of a person's body. **3** a single picture in a series forming a cinema or video film. **4** a single game of snooker. • verb (**frames, framing, framed**) **1** put a picture in a frame.
2 create or develop a plan or system.
3 informal produce false evidence against someone to make them appear guilty of a crime.
□ **frame of mind** a particular mood.

framework noun a supporting or

underlying structure.

franc noun the basic unit of money of Switzerland and some other countries, and formerly also of France, Belgium, and Luxembourg.

franchise noun **1** a licence allowing a person or company to use or sell certain products. **2** a business that has been given a franchise. **3** the right to vote in elections.

frank[1] adjective **1** honest and direct. **2** open or undisguised.
■ **frankly** adverb **frankness** noun.

frank[2] verb stamp a mark on a letter or parcel to indicate that postage has been paid or does not need to be paid.

frankfurter noun a seasoned smoked sausage made of beef and pork.

frankincense noun a kind of sweet-smelling gum that is burnt as incense.

frantic adjective **1** agitated because of fear, anxiety, etc. **2** done in a hurried and chaotic way.
■ **frantically** adverb.

fraternal adjective **1** brotherly. **2** having to do with a fraternity.

fraternity noun (plural **fraternities**) **1** a group

fragment noun **1** *meteorite fragments:* piece, bit, particle, speck, chip, shard, sliver, splinter, flake. **2** *a fragment of conversation:* snatch, snippet, scrap, bit.
• verb *explosions caused the chalk to fragment:* break up, crack open, shatter, splinter, fracture, disintegrate, fall to pieces, fall apart.

fragrance noun **1** *the fragrance of spring flowers:* sweet smell, scent, perfume, bouquet, aroma, nose. **2** *a daring new fragrance:* perfume, scent, eau de toilette.

fragrant adjective sweet-scented, sweet-smelling, scented, perfumed, aromatic.
OPPOSITES smelly.

frail adjective **1** *a frail old lady:* weak, delicate, feeble, infirm, ill, unwell, sickly, poorly. **2** *a frail structure:* fragile, easily damaged, delicate, flimsy, insubstantial, unsteady, unstable, rickety.
OPPOSITES strong, robust.

frame noun **1** *a tubular metal frame:* framework, structure, substructure, skeleton, casing, chassis, shell. **2** *his tall, slender frame:* body, figure, form, shape, physique, anatomy, build.
• verb **1** *he had the picture framed:* mount, set in a frame. **2** *those who frame the regulations:* formulate, draw up, draft, shape, compose, put together, form, devise.
□ **frame of mind** mood, state of mind, humour, temper, disposition.

framework noun **1** *a metal framework:*

frame, structure, skeleton, chassis, support, scaffolding. **2** *the framework of society:* structure, shape, fabric, order, scheme, system, organization, anatomy; informal make-up.

frank adjective **1** *he was quite frank with me:* candid, direct, forthright, plain, straight, to the point, matter-of-fact, open, honest; informal upfront. **2** *she looked at Sam with frank admiration:* open, undisguised, unconcealed, naked, unmistakable, clear, obvious, transparent, patent, evident.
OPPOSITES evasive, disguised.

frankly adverb **1** *frankly, I'm not interested:* to be frank, to be honest, to tell the truth, in all honesty. **2** *he stated the case quite frankly:* candidly, directly, plainly, straightforwardly, forthrightly, openly, honestly, without beating about the bush, bluntly.

frantic adjective panic-stricken, panicky, beside yourself, at your wits' end, distraught, overwrought, worked up, frenzied, frenetic, fraught, feverish, desperate; informal in a state, tearing your hair out; Brit. informal having kittens, in a flat spin.
OPPOSITES calm.

fraternity noun **1** *a spirit of fraternity:* brotherhood, fellowship, kinship, friendship, mutual support, solidarity, community. **2** *the teaching fraternity:* profession, community, trade, set, circle.

of people sharing a common profession or interests. **2** N. Amer. a male students' society in a university or college. **3** friendship and support within a group.

fraternize or **fraternise** verb (**fraternizes, fraternizing, fraternized**) be on friendly terms.
■ **fraternization** noun.

fratricide noun **1** the killing by someone of their brother or sister. **2** the accidental killing of your own forces in war.

fraud noun **1** the crime of deceiving someone in order to get money or goods. **2** a person who deceives other people by claiming to be something they are not.

fraudster noun a person who commits fraud.

fraudulent adjective **1** involving fraud. **2** deceitful or dishonest.
■ **fraudulently** adverb.

fraught adjective **1** (**fraught with**) filled with something undesirable. **2** causing or feeling anxiety or stress.

fray[1] verb **1** (of a fabric or rope) unravel or become worn at the edge. **2** (of a person's

nerves or temper) show the effects of strain.

fray[2] noun (**the fray**) **1** a battle or fight. **2** a very competitive situation.

frazzle noun (**a frazzle**) informal **1** an exhausted state. **2** a charred or burnt state.
■ **frazzled** adjective.

freak noun **1** informal a person who is obsessed with a particular interest: *a fitness freak.* **2** a very unusual and unexpected event. **3** a person, animal, or plant with a physical abnormality. ● verb (**freak out**) informal behave in a wild, excited, or shocked way.
■ **freakish** adjective **freaky** adjective.

freckle noun a small light brown spot on the skin.
■ **freckled** adjective **freckly** adjective.

free adjective (**freer, freest**) **1** not under the control of someone else. **2** not confined, obstructed, or fixed. **3** not being used. **4** (**free of** or **from**) not affected by. **5** given or available without charge. **6** (**free with**) giving something generously. ● adverb without cost or payment. ● verb (**frees,**

THESAURUS

3 (N. Amer.) *a college fraternity:* society, club, association, group.

fraud noun **1** *he was arrested for fraud:* deception, sharp practice, cheating, swindling, trickery, embezzlement, deceit, double-dealing, chicanery. **2** *social security frauds:* swindle, racket, deception, trick, cheat, hoax; informal scam, con, rip-off, sting, fiddle; N. Amer. informal hustle. **3** *they exposed him as a fraud:* impostor, fake, sham, charlatan, swindler, fraudster, confidence trickster; informal phoney.

fraudulent adjective dishonest, cheating, swindling, corrupt, criminal, deceitful, double-dealing, duplicitous; informal crooked, shady, dirty; Brit. informal bent, dodgy; Austral./NZ informal shonky.
OPPOSITES honest.

frayed adjective **1** *a frayed collar:* worn, threadbare, tattered, ragged, the worse for wear; informal tatty; N. Amer. informal raggedy. **2** *his frayed nerves:* strained, fraught, tense, edgy, stressed.

freak noun **1** *a genetically engineered freak:* aberration, abnormality, oddity, monster, monstrosity, mutant, chimera. **2** *the accident was a freak:* anomaly, aberration, rarity, oddity, one-off, fluke, twist of fate. **3** (informal) *a bunch of freaks:* oddity, eccentric, misfit, crank; informal oddball, weirdo, nut; Brit. informal nutter; N. Amer. informal wacko, kook. **4** (informal) *a fitness freak:* enthusiast, fan, devotee, lover,

aficionado; informal nut, fanatic, addict, maniac.
● adjective *a freak storm:* unusual, anomalous, aberrant, atypical, unrepresentative, irregular, exceptional, isolated.
OPPOSITES normal.

free adjective **1** *admission is free:* free of charge, without charge, for nothing, complimentary, gratis; informal for free, on the house. **2** *free of any pressures:* without, unencumbered by, unaffected by, clear of, rid of, exempt from, not liable to, safe from, immune to, excused. **3** *I'm free this afternoon:* unoccupied, not busy, available, off duty, off work, on holiday, on leave, at leisure, with time to spare. **4** *the bathroom's free:* vacant, empty, available, unoccupied, not in use. **5** *a free nation:* independent, self-governing, self-determining, sovereign, autonomous, democratic. **6** *the killer is still free:* on the loose, at liberty, at large, loose, unrestrained. **7** *you are free to leave:* able, in a position, allowed, permitted. **8** *the free flow of water:* unobstructed, unimpeded, unrestricted, unhampered, clear, open. **9** *she was free with her money:* generous, liberal, open-handed, unstinting.
OPPOSITES chargeable, busy, occupied, captive, confined, obstructed, mean.
● verb **1** *the hostages were freed:* release, set free, let go, liberate, set loose, untie. **2** *victims were freed by firefighters:* extricate, release, get out, cut free, pull

freeing, freed) make free.

□ **free enterprise** a system in which private businesses compete with each other. **free fall** unrestricted downward movement under the force of gravity. **free-for-all** a disorganized situation in which everyone may take part. **free-form** not in a regular or formal structure. **a free hand** freedom to do exactly what you want. **free house** Brit. a pub not controlled by a brewery. **free kick** (in soccer and rugby) an unopposed kick of the ball awarded when the opposition have broken the rules. **the free market** a system in which prices are determined by unrestricted competition between privately owned businesses. **free-range** referring to farming in which animals are kept in natural conditions where they can move around freely. **free-standing** not supported by another structure. **free trade** unrestricted international trade without taxes or regulations on imports and exports. **free will** the power to act according to your own wishes. **free verse** poetry that does not rhyme or have a regular rhythm.
■ **freely** adverb.

freebie noun informal a thing given free of charge.

freedom noun 1 the right to act or speak freely. 2 the state of not being a prisoner or slave. 3 (**freedom from**) not being affected by something undesirable. 4 unrestricted use of something. 5 Brit. a special honour given to someone by a city.

freehand adjective & adverb drawn by hand without a ruler or other aid.

freehold noun permanent ownership of land or property with the freedom to sell it whenever you want.
■ **freeholder** noun.

freelance adjective self-employed and working for different companies on particular assignments. • noun (also

freelancer) a freelance worker. • verb (**freelances, freelancing, freelanced**) work as a freelance.

freeloader noun informal a person who takes advantage of other people's generosity.

freeman noun (plural **freemen**) 1 Brit. a person who has been given the freedom of a city. 2 historical a person who was not a slave or serf.

Freemason noun a member of an organization whose members help each other and hold secret ceremonies.
■ **Freemasonry** noun.

freesia /free-zhuh/ noun a plant with sweet-smelling, colourful flowers.

freestyle adjective (of a contest or sport) having few restrictions on the technique that competitors use.

freethinker noun a person who questions or rejects accepted opinions.

freeway noun N. Amer. a dual-carriageway main road.

freewheel verb ride a bicycle without using the pedals.

freeze verb (**freezes, freezing, froze**; past participle **frozen**) 1 (of a liquid) turn into a solid as a result of extreme cold. 2 become blocked or rigid with ice. 3 be very cold. 4 preserve something by storing it at a very low temperature. 5 suddenly become motionless with fear, shock, etc. 6 (of a computer screen) suddenly become locked. 7 keep or hold at a fixed level. • noun 1 an act of freezing. 2 a period of very cold weather.

□ **freeze-dry** preserve something by rapidly freezing it and then drying it in a vacuum. **freeze-frame** the stopping of a film or videotape to obtain a single still image.

freezer noun a refrigerated cabinet or room for preserving food at very low temperatures.

freezing adjective 1 having a temperature

free, rescue.
OPPOSITES confine, trap.

freedom noun 1 *a desperate bid for freedom:* liberty, liberation, release, deliverance. 2 *the fight for freedom:* independence, self-government, self-determination, self-rule, home rule, sovereignty, autonomy, democracy. 3 *freedom from political accountability:* exemption, immunity, dispensation, impunity. 4 *patients have more freedom to choose who treats them:* right, entitlement, privilege, prerogative, discretion, latitude, elbow room, licence, free rein, a free hand, carte blanche.
OPPOSITES captivity, subjection, liability, obligation.

freely adverb 1 *may I speak freely?* openly, candidly, frankly, directly, without beating about the bush, without mincing your words. 2 *they gave their time and labour freely:* voluntarily, willingly, readily, of your own accord, of your own free will, without being told to.

freeze verb 1 *the stream had frozen:* ice over, ice up, solidify. 2 *she froze in horror:* stop dead in your tracks, stand (stock) still, go rigid, become motionless, become paralysed. 3 *the prices of basic foodstuffs were frozen:* fix, hold, peg, set, limit, restrict, cap.
OPPOSITES thaw.

freezing adjective 1 *a freezing wind:* icy, bitter, chill, frosty, glacial, arctic, wintry, below 0°C. **2** very cold.

freight noun goods transported by truck, train, ship, or aircraft. • verb transport goods by truck, train, etc.

freighter noun a large ship or aircraft designed to carry freight.

French adjective having to do with France or its language. • noun the language of France, also used in parts of Belgium, Switzerland, Canada, etc.
□ **French dressing** a salad dressing of vinegar, oil, and seasonings. **French fries** chiefly N. Amer. chips. **French horn** a brass instrument with a coiled tube and a wide opening at the end. **French kiss** a kiss with contact between tongues. **French polish** a kind of polish used on wood to give it a very glossy finish. **French windows** glazed doors in an outside wall.

frenetic adjective fast and energetic in a rather wild and uncontrolled way.
■ **frenetically** adverb.

frenzy noun (plural **frenzies**) a state of uncontrolled excitement or wild behaviour.
■ **frenzied** adjective **frenziedly** adverb.

frequency noun (plural **frequencies**) **1** the rate at which something happens. **2** the state of being frequent. **3** the number of cycles per second of a sound, light, or radio wave. **4** the particular waveband at which radio signals are transmitted.

frequent adjective /free-kwuhnt/ **1** happening or done many times at short intervals. **2** doing something often. • verb /fri-**kwent**/ visit a place often.
■ **frequently** adverb.

fresco noun (plural **frescoes** or **frescos**) a painting that is done on wet plaster on a wall or ceiling.

fresh adjective **1** new or different. **2** (of food) recently made or obtained. **3** recently created and not faded. **4** pleasantly clean and cool: *fresh air.* **5** (of the wind) cool and fairly strong. **6** (of water) not salty. **7** full of energy. **8** informal too familiar with someone.
■ **freshly** adverb **freshness** noun.

freshen verb **1** make or become fresh. **2** (**freshen up**) wash and tidy yourself.

fresher noun Brit. a first-year student at college or university.

freshman noun (plural **freshmen**) a first-year student at university or (N. Amer.) at high school.

fret[1] verb (**frets, fretting, fretted**) be anxious and restless.

fret[2] noun each of the ridges on the neck of guitars and similar instruments.

fretful adjective anxious and restless.
■ **fretfully** adverb.

fretwork noun decorative designs cut into in wood.

friable /fry-uh-b'l/ adjective easily crumbled.

friar noun a member of certain religious orders of men.

friary noun (plural **friaries**) a building or community occupied by friars.

fricassée /fri-kuh-say, fri-kuh-see/ noun a dish of stewed or fried pieces of meat served in a thick white sauce.

THESAURUS

sub-zero, raw, biting. **2** *you must be freezing:* frozen, numb with cold, chilled to the bone/marrow.
OPPOSITES balmy, hot.

freight noun goods, cargo, merchandise.

frenzied adjective frantic, wild, frenetic, hectic, feverish, fevered, mad, crazed, manic, furious, uncontrolled.
OPPOSITES calm.

frenzy noun hysteria, madness, mania, delirium, wild excitement, fever, lather, passion, panic, fury, rage.

frequent adjective *frequent complaints:* recurrent, recurring, repeated, periodic, continual, habitual, regular, successive, numerous, several.
OPPOSITES occasional.
• verb *he frequented chic clubs:* visit, patronize, spend time in, visit regularly, haunt; informal hang out at.

frequently adverb often, all the time, habitually, regularly, customarily, routinely, again and again, repeatedly, recurrently, continually; N. Amer. oftentimes.
OPPOSITES occasionally, rarely.

fresh adjective **1** *a fresh approach:* new, modern, original, novel, different, innovative. **2** *fresh food:* recently made, just picked, crisp, raw, natural, unprocessed. **3** *feeling fresh after a sleep:* refreshed, rested, restored, energetic, vigorous, invigorated, lively, sprightly, bright, alert, bouncing, perky; informal full of beans, bright-eyed and bushy-tailed. **4** *a fresh breeze:* strong, brisk, bracing, invigorating, chilly, cool; informal nippy; Brit. informal parky. **5** *the night air was fresh:* cool, crisp, refreshing, invigorating, pure, clean, clear. **6** (informal) *he's getting too fresh:* impudent, impertinent, insolent, presumptuous, forward, cheeky, disrespectful, rude; informal mouthy, saucy, lippy; N. Amer. informal sassy.
OPPOSITES stale, old, used, cooked, preserved, processed, tired, light, warm, sultry.

fret verb worry, be anxious, distress yourself, upset yourself, concern yourself, agonize, lose sleep.

friction noun **1** the resistance that one surface or object encounters when moving over another. **2** the action of one surface or object rubbing against another. **3** conflict or disagreement.

Friday noun the day of the week before Saturday and following Thursday.

fridge noun an appliance in which food and drink are stored at a low temperature.

fried past and past participle of **FRY**[1].

friend noun **1** a person that you know well and like. **2** a supporter of a cause or organization. **3** (**Friend**) a Quaker.
■ **friendless** adjective **friendship** noun.

☑ *-ie-*, not *-ei-*: friend.
---

friendly adjective (**friendlier, friendliest**)
1 treating someone as a friend; on good terms. **2** kind and pleasant. **3** not harmful to a particular thing: *environment-friendly*. • noun (plural **friendlies**) Brit. a game not forming part of a serious competition.
■ **friendliness** noun.

frieze noun a broad horizontal band of sculpted or painted decoration.

frigate noun a kind of fast warship.

fright noun **1** a sudden strong feeling of fear. **2** a shock.

frighten verb make someone afraid.
■ **frightening** adjective **frighteningly** adverb.

frightful adjective **1** very unpleasant, serious, or shocking. **2** informal terrible; awful.
■ **frightfully** adverb.

frigid /frij-id/ adjective **1** literary very cold. **2** disapproving (of a woman) not interested in sex.
■ **frigidity** noun.

frill noun **1** a decorative strip of gathered or pleated cloth attached to the edge of clothing or material. **2** (**frills**) unnecessary extra features.
■ **frilled** adjective **frilly** adjective.

fringe noun **1** a decorative border of threads or tassels attached to the edge of clothing or material. **2** Brit. a part of someone's hair that hangs over the forehead. **3** the outer part of an area, group, etc. • adjective not part of the mainstream: *fringe theatre*. • verb (**fringes, fringing, fringed**) add a fringe to something.
□ **fringe benefit** something extra given to someone as well as wages.

frippery noun (plural **fripperies**) showy or unnecessary decoration.

frisbee noun trademark a plastic disc that you skim through the air as an outdoor game.

frisk verb **1** pass your hands over someone in a search for hidden weapons or drugs. **2** skip or move playfully. • noun a playful skip or leap.

frisky adjective (**friskier, friskiest**) playful and full of energy.

---

friction noun **1** *lubrication reduces friction:* rubbing, chafing, grating, rasping, scraping, resistance, drag, abrasion. **2** *friction between father and son:* discord, disagreement, dissension, dispute, conflict, hostility, animosity, antipathy, antagonism, resentment, acrimony, bitterness, bad feeling.
OPPOSITES harmony.

friend noun companion, comrade, confidant, confidante, familiar, intimate, soul mate, playmate, playfellow, ally, associate; informal pal, chum; Brit. informal mate; N. Amer. informal buddy, amigo, compadre, homeboy.
OPPOSITES enemy.

friendly adjective **1** *a friendly woman:* amiable, companionable, sociable, gregarious, comradely, neighbourly, hospitable, easy to get on with, affable, genial, cordial, warm, affectionate, convivial; Scottish couthy; informal chummy, pally; Brit. informal matey; N. Amer. informal buddy-buddy. **2** *friendly conversation:* amicable, cordial, pleasant, easy, relaxed, casual, informal, unceremonious, close, intimate, familiar.
OPPOSITES unfriendly, hostile.

friendship noun **1** *lasting friendships:* relationship, attachment, association, bond, tie, link, union. **2** *ties of friendship:* friendliness, affection, camaraderie, comradeship, companionship, fellowship, closeness, affinity, unity, intimacy.
OPPOSITES hostility.

fright noun **1** *she was paralysed with fright:* fear, terror, horror, alarm, panic, dread, trepidation, dismay, nervousness. **2** *the experience gave everyone a fright:* scare, shock, surprise, turn, jolt, start.
OPPOSITES pleasant surprise.

frighten verb scare, startle, alarm, terrify, petrify, shock, chill, panic, unnerve, intimidate; informal spook; Brit. informal put the wind up.
OPPOSITES reassure.

frightful adjective horrible, horrific, ghastly, horrendous, awful, dreadful, terrible, nasty; informal horrid.

fringe noun **1** *the city's northern fringe:* edge, border, margin, extremity, perimeter, periphery, rim, limits, outskirts. **2** *blue curtains with a yellow fringe:* edging, border, trimming, frill, flounce, ruffle.
OPPOSITES middle.
• adjective *fringe theatre:* alternative, avant-garde, experimental, innovative, left-field, radical, off-Broadway.
OPPOSITES mainstream.

frisson /free-son/ noun a sudden shiver of excitement.

fritillary /fri-til-luh-ri/ noun (plural **fritillaries**) **1** a plant with hanging bell-like flowers. **2** a butterfly with orange-brown wings.

fritter[1] verb (**fritters, frittering, frittered**) (**fritter something away**) waste time or money on unimportant matters.

fritter[2] noun a piece of food that is coated in batter and deep-fried.

frivolous adjective **1** not having any serious purpose or value. **2** (of a person) not treating things seriously.
■ **frivolity** noun **frivolously** adverb.

frizz verb (of hair) form into a mass of tight curls. • noun a mass of tightly curled hair.
■ **frizzy** adjective.

frock noun **1** a dress. **2** a loose outer garment, worn by priests.
□ **frock coat** a man's long, double-breasted coat, worn on formal occasions.

frog noun an amphibian with a short body, very long hind legs for leaping, and no tail.
□ **have a frog in your throat** informal be hoarse.

frogman noun (plural **frogmen**) a diver equipped with a rubber suit, flippers, and breathing equipment.

frogmarch verb force someone to walk forward by holding their arms from behind.

frogspawn noun a mass of frogs' eggs surrounded by transparent jelly.

frolic verb (**frolics, frolicking, frolicked**) play or move about in a cheerful and lively way. • noun a playful action or movement.

frolicsome adjective lively and playful.

from preposition **1** indicating the point at which a journey, process, or action starts. **2** indicating the source of something. **3** indicating separation, removal, or prevention. **4** indicating a cause. **5** indicating a difference.

fromage frais /from-ahzh fray/ noun a type of smooth, soft cheese.

frond noun the leaf of a palm, fern, or similar plant.

front noun **1** the part of an object that faces forwards or that is normally seen first. **2** the position directly ahead. **3** the furthest position that an army has reached. **4** a particular situation or area of activity. **5** (in weather forecasting) the forward edge of an advancing mass of air. **6** a false appearance or way of behaving. **7** a person or organization that is a cover for secret or illegal activities. **8** a very confident manner. • adjective having to do with the front. • verb **1** have the front facing towards. **2** be at the front of. **3** (**be fronted with**) have the front covered with. **4** be the leader or presenter of.
□ **the front line** the part of an army that is closest to the enemy. **front runner** the leader in a competition.

frontage noun **1** the front of a building. **2** a strip of land next to a street or waterway.

frontal adjective having to do with the front.
■ **frontally** adverb.

frontier noun **1** a border separating two countries. **2** the furthest part of land that has been settled. **3** the limit of what is known about a subject or area of activity.

frontispiece noun an illustration facing the title page of a book.

frontman noun (plural **frontmen**) a person who represents an illegal organization to make it seem respectable.

frost noun **1** white ice crystals that form on surfaces when the temperature falls below freezing. **2** a period of cold weather when frost forms.

frostbite noun injury to parts of the body caused by exposure to extreme cold.
■ **frostbitten** adjective.

frosted adjective **1** covered with frost. **2** (of glass) having a semi-transparent textured surface. **3** N. Amer. (of a cake) covered with icing.

frosting noun N. Amer. icing.

frosty adjective (**frostier, frostiest**) **1** (of the

THESAURUS

frivolous adjective flippant, glib, facetious, joking, jokey, light-hearted, fatuous, inane; informal flip.
OPPOSITES serious.

front noun **1** the front of the boat: fore, foremost part, forepart, nose, head, bow, prow, foreground. **2** a shop front: frontage, face, facing, facade, window. **3** the front of the queue: head, beginning, start, top, lead. **4** a brave front: appearance, air, face, manner, exterior, veneer, (outward) show, act, pretence. **5** the shop was a front for his real business: cover, blind, disguise, facade,

mask, cloak, screen, smokescreen, camouflage.
OPPOSITES back.
• adjective leading, lead, first, foremost.
OPPOSITES back, last.
□ **in front ahead**, to/at the fore, at the head, up ahead, in the lead, leading, coming first, at the head of the queue; informal up front.

frontier noun border, boundary, borderline, dividing line, perimeter, limit, edge.

frosty adjective **1** a frosty morning: cold, freezing, frozen, icy, bitter, chill, wintry,

weather) very cold with frost forming on surfaces. **2** cold and unfriendly.
■ **frostily** adverb.

froth noun **1** a mass of small bubbles in liquid. **2** appealing but trivial ideas or activities. • verb produce or contain froth.
■ **frothy** adjective.

frown verb **1** make an angry or worried expression by bringing your eyebrows together so that lines appear on your forehead. **2** (**frown on**) disapprove of.
• noun a frowning expression.

frowsty adjective Brit. warm and stuffy.

frowzy or **frowsy** adjective scruffy and neglected in appearance.

froze past of FREEZE.

frozen past participle of FREEZE.

fructose /fruk-tohz/ noun a kind of sugar found in honey and fruit.

frugal /froo-g'l/ adjective **1** careful in the use of money or food. **2** (of a meal) plain and cheap.
■ **frugality** noun **frugally** adverb.

fruit noun **1** a fleshy part of a plant that contains seed and can be eaten as food. **2** Botany the part of a plant in which seeds develop, e.g. an acorn. **3** the result of work or activity. • verb produce fruit.
□ **fruit machine** Brit. a coin-operated gambling machine.

fruiterer noun a person who sells fruit.

fruitful adjective **1** producing a lot of fruit. **2** producing good results.
■ **fruitfully** adverb **fruitfulness** noun.

fruition /fruu-i-sh'n/ noun the fulfilment of a plan or project.

fruitless adjective failing to achieve the desired results.
■ **fruitlessly** adverb.

fruity adjective (**fruitier, fruitiest**) **1** having to do with fruit. **2** (of someone's voice) mellow, deep, and rich.

frump noun an unattractive woman who wears unfashionable clothes.
■ **frumpy** adjective.

frustrate verb (**frustrates, frustrating, frustrated**) **1** prevent a plan or action from succeeding. **2** prevent someone from doing or achieving something. **3** make someone feel dissatisfied or unfulfilled.
■ **frustrating** adjective **frustration** noun.

fry¹ verb (**fries, frying, fried**) cook in hot fat or oil. • noun (**fries**) French fries; chips.
□ **frying pan** a shallow pan used for frying food.
■ **fryer** (or **frier**) noun.

fry² plural noun young fish.

ft abbreviation foot or feet.

fuchsia /fyoo-shuh/ noun a shrub with drooping purplish-red flowers.

fuddled adjective not able to think clearly.

fuddy-duddy noun (plural **fuddy-duddies**) informal a person who is very old-fashioned and pompous.

fudge noun **1** a soft sweet made from sugar, butter, and milk or cream. **2** an attempt to present an issue in a vague way. • verb (**fudges, fudging, fudged**) present something in a vague or deceptive way.

fuel noun **1** material such as coal, gas, or oil that is burned to produce heat or power. **2** something that stirs up argument or strong emotion. • verb (**fuels, fuelling, fuelled**; US spelling **fuels, fueling, fueled**) **1** supply or power with fuel. **2** stir up strong feeling.
□ **fuel injection** the direct introduction of fuel into the cylinders of an engine.

fug noun Brit. informal a warm, stuffy

arctic; informal **nippy**; Brit. informal **parky**. **2** *a frosty reception*: **unfriendly**, cold, frigid, icy, glacial, inhospitable, unwelcoming, forbidding, hostile, stony.
OPPOSITES warm, friendly.

frown verb **scowl**, glower, glare, lour, make a face, look daggers, give someone a black look, knit your brows; informal give someone a dirty look.
OPPOSITES smile.
□ **frown on disapprove of,** take a dim view of, take exception to, object to, look askance at, not take kindly to.

fruitful adjective **productive,** constructive, useful, worthwhile, helpful, beneficial, valuable, rewarding, profitable, advantageous.
OPPOSITES barren, futile.

frustrate verb **1** *his plans were frustrated*: **thwart**, defeat, foil, block, stop, counter,

spoil, check, forestall, scotch, derail, snooker; informal **stymie**; Brit. informal **scupper**. **2** *the delays frustrated him*: **exasperate**, infuriate, discourage, dishearten, disappoint.
OPPOSITES further, satisfy.

frustration noun **1** *he clenched his fists in frustration*: **exasperation**, annoyance, anger, vexation, irritation, disappointment, dissatisfaction. **2** *the frustration of his plans*: **thwarting**, defeat, prevention, foiling, blocking, spoiling, forestalling, derailment, obstruction.

fudge verb **evade**, avoid, dodge, skirt, duck, gloss over, cloud, hedge, beat about the bush, equivocate.

fuel verb **1** *power stations fuelled by coal*: **power**, fire, drive, run. **2** *the rumours fuelled people's anxiety*: **fan**, feed, stoke up, inflame, intensify, stimulate, encourage, provoke, incite, sustain.

atmosphere.

fugitive /fyoo-ji-tiv/ **noun** a person who has escaped from captivity or is in hiding.

fugue /fyoog/ **noun** a piece of music in which a short melody is introduced and then successively taken up by other instruments or voices.

führer or **fuehrer** /fyoo-ruh/ **noun** the title that Hitler held as leader of Germany.

fulcrum /fuul-kruhm/ **noun** the point on which a lever turns or is supported.

fulfil (US spelling **fulfill**) **verb** (**fulfils, fulfilling, fulfilled**) **1** do or achieve something that was desired, promised, or predicted. **2** meet a requirement. **3** (**fulfil yourself**) fully develop your abilities.
■ **fulfilment** noun.

full **adjective 1** holding as much or as many as possible. **2** (**full of**) having a large number or quantity of. **3** (also **full up**) filled to capacity. **4** complete: *full details.* **5** plump or rounded. **6** (of flavour, sound, or colour) strong or rich. ●**adverb** straight; directly.
□ **full back** (in soccer and similar sports) a defender who plays at the side of the pitch. **full-blooded** wholehearted and enthusiastic. **full-blown** fully developed. **full board** Brit. accommodation at a hotel or guest house which includes all meals. **full-bodied** rich and satisfying in flavour or sound. **full-frontal** fully exposing the front of the body. **full house 1** a theatre that is filled to capacity. **2** a poker hand with three of a kind and a pair. **3** a winning card

at bingo. **full moon** the moon when its whole disc is illuminated. **full-scale 1** (of a model or plan) of the same size as the thing represented. **2** complete and thorough. **full stop** a punctuation mark (.) used at the end of a sentence or abbreviation. **full time** the end of a sports match. **full-time** working for the whole of the available time.
■ **fullness** (or **fulness**) noun.

fuller noun historical a person whose job was treating cloth to make it thicker.

fully **adverb 1** completely. **2** no less or fewer than.
□ **fully fledged** Brit. completely developed or established.

fulminate **verb** (**fulminates, fulminating, fulminated**) protest strongly.
■ **fulmination** noun.

fulsome **adjective 1** too flattering or complimentary. **2** of large size or quantity.
■ **fulsomely** adverb.

fumble **verb** (**fumbles, fumbling, fumbled**) **1** use the hands clumsily while doing something. **2** deal with something clumsily. **3** fail to catch a ball cleanly. ●**noun** an act of fumbling.

fume **noun** a gas or vapour that smells strongly or is dangerous to breathe in.
●**verb** (**fumes, fuming, fumed**) **1** send out fumes. **2** be very angry.

fumigate **verb** (**fumigates, fumigating, fumigated**) disinfect an area using chemical fumes.
■ **fumigation** noun.

fun **noun 1** light-hearted pleasure, or

THESAURUS

fugitive noun escapee, runaway, deserter, absconder, refugee.

fulfil verb **1** *he fulfilled a lifelong ambition:* **achieve**, attain, realize, make happen, succeed in, bring to completion, bring to fruition, satisfy. **2** *she failed to fulfil her duties:* **carry out**, perform, accomplish, execute, do, discharge, conduct. **3** *they fulfilled the criteria:* **meet**, satisfy, comply with, conform to, fill, answer.

fulfilled adjective **satisfied**, content, contented, happy, pleased, at peace.
OPPOSITES discontented.

full adjective **1** *her glass was full:* **filled**, brimming, brimful, packed, loaded, crammed, crowded, bursting, overflowing, congested; informal jam-packed, wall-to-wall, chock-a-block, chock-full, awash. **2** *I'm full:* **replete**, full up, satisfied, sated, satiated; informal stuffed. **3** *a full life:* **eventful**, interesting, exciting, lively, action-packed, busy, active. **4** *a full list of facilities:* **comprehensive**, thorough, exhaustive, all-inclusive, all-encompassing, all-embracing, in-depth, complete, entire, whole,

unabridged, uncut. **5** *at full speed:* **maximum**, top. **6** *a full figure:* **plump**, rounded, buxom, shapely, ample, curvaceous, voluptuous; informal busty, curvy, well endowed; N. Amer. informal zaftig. **7** *a full skirt:* **loose-fitting**, loose, baggy, voluminous, roomy, capacious, billowing.
OPPOSITES empty, hungry, uneventful, selective, low, thin, tight.

fully adverb **completely**, entirely, wholly, totally, perfectly, quite, altogether, thoroughly, in all respects, (up) to the hilt.
OPPOSITES partly, nearly.

fumble verb **grope**, fish, scrabble, feel.

fume noun *toxic fumes:* **smoke**, vapour, gas, exhaust, pollution.
●verb *Ella was fuming at his arrogance:* **be furious**, seethe, be livid, be incensed, boil, be beside yourself, spit; informal foam at the mouth, see red.

fumigate verb **disinfect**, purify, sterilize, sanitize, decontaminate, cleanse, clean out.
OPPOSITES soil.

fun noun **1** *I joined in with the fun:* **enjoyment**, entertainment, amusement,

something that provides it. **2** playfulness.
□ **make fun of** laugh at in a mocking way.

function noun **1** a purpose or natural activity of a person or thing. **2** a large social event. **3** a basic task of a computer. **4** Maths a quantity whose value depends on the varying values of others. • verb **1** work or operate. **2** (**function as**) fulfil the purpose of.

functional adjective **1** having to do with a function. **2** designed to be practical and useful. **3** working or operating.
■ **functionality** noun **functionally** adverb.

functionary noun (plural **functionaries**) an official.

fund noun **1** a sum of money saved or made available for a purpose. **2** (**funds**) financial resources. **3** a large stock. • verb provide money for.

fundamental adjective of basic importance. • noun a basic rule or principle.
■ **fundamentally** adverb.

fundamentalism noun strict following of the basic teachings of a religion.
■ **fundamentalist** noun & adjective.

funeral noun a ceremony in which a dead person is buried or cremated.
□ **funeral director** an undertaker.

funerary /fyoo-nuh-ruh-ri/ adjective having to do with a funeral or other rites in which dead people are remembered.

funereal /fyoo-**neer**-i-uhl/ adjective solemn, in a way appropriate to a funeral.

funfair noun Brit. a fair consisting of rides, sideshows, etc.

fungicide /**fun**-ji-syd, **fung**-gi-syd/ noun a chemical that destroys fungus.

fungus noun (plural **fungi** /**fung**-gy/) an organism, such as a mushroom, that has no leaves or flowers and grows on plants or decaying vegetable matter and reproduces by spores.
■ **fungal** adjective.

funicular railway /fyuu-**nik**-yuu-ler/ noun a railway on a steep slope which is operated by cable.

funk[1] noun a style of popular dance music with a strong rhythm.

funk[2] noun informal a state of panic or anxiety.

funky adjective (**funkier**, **funkiest**) informal **1** (of music) having a strong dance rhythm. **2** modern and stylish.

funnel noun **1** an object that is wide at the top and narrow at the bottom, used for guiding liquid or powder into a small opening. **2** a chimney on a ship or steam engine. • verb (**funnels**, **funnelling**, **funnelled**; US spelling **funnels**, **funneling**, **funneled**) guide through a funnel or narrow space.

THESAURUS

pleasure, jollification, merrymaking, recreation, leisure, relaxation, a good time; informal living it up, a ball. **2** *she's full of fun:* merriment, cheerfulness, jollity, joviality, high spirits, mirth, laughter, hilarity, light-heartedness, levity. **3** *he became a figure of fun:* ridicule, derision, mockery, scorn, contempt.
OPPOSITES boredom, misery, respect.
• adjective (informal) *a fun evening:* enjoyable, entertaining, amusing, pleasurable, pleasant, agreeable, convivial.
□ **make fun of** tease, poke fun at, ridicule, mock, laugh at, parody, caricature, satirize; informal take the mickey out of, send up; N. Amer. informal goof on.

function noun **1** *the main function of the machine:* purpose, task, use, role. **2** *my function is to train the recruits:* responsibility, duty, role, province, activity, assignment, task, job, mission. **3** *a function attended by local dignitaries:* social event, party, social occasion, affair, gathering, reception, soirée; N. Amer. levee; informal do, bash.
• verb **1** *the system had ceased to function:* work, go, run, be in working/running order, operate. **2** *the museum functions as an education centre:* act, serve, operate, perform, do duty.

functional adjective **1** *a small functional kitchen:* practical, useful, utilitarian, workaday, serviceable, no-frills. **2** *the machine is now fully functional:* working, in working order, functioning, in service, in use, going, running, operative; informal up and running.

fund noun **1** *an emergency fund:* collection, kitty, reserve, pool, purse, savings, coffers. **2** *short of funds:* money, cash, wealth, means, assets, resources, savings, capital, reserves, the wherewithal; informal dosh; Brit. informal lolly.
• verb *we were funded by the Treasury:* finance, pay for, back, capitalize, subsidize, endow, invest in, sponsor; N. Amer. informal bankroll.

fundamental adjective basic, underlying, core, rudimentary, root, primary, prime, cardinal, principal, chief, key, central, vital, essential.
OPPOSITES secondary, incidental.

fundamentally adverb essentially, in essence, basically, at heart, at bottom, deep down, profoundly, primarily, above all.

funeral noun burial, interment, entombment, committal, laying to rest, cremation.

funny adjective (**funnier, funniest**) **1** causing laughter or amusement. **2** strange; odd. **3** suspicious or illegal. **4** informal slightly unwell.
□ **funny bone** informal the part of the elbow over which a very sensitive nerve passes.
■ **funnily** adverb.

fur noun **1** the short, soft hair of certain animals. **2** the skin of an animal with fur on it, or a coat made from this. **3** Brit. a coating formed by hard water on the inside surface of a pipe, kettle, etc.
■ **furred** adjective.

furbelow noun **1** a strip of gathered or pleated material sewn on a skirt or petticoat. **2** (**furbelows**) showy decorations or ornaments.

furious adjective **1** very angry. **2** with great energy or speed.
■ **furiously** adverb.

furl verb roll or fold up neatly.

furlong noun an eighth of a mile, 220 yards.

furlough /fer-loh/ noun a time when you have permission to be away from your work or duties.

furnace noun **1** an enclosed space for heating material to very high temperatures. **2** a very hot place.

furnish verb **1** provide a room or building with furniture and fittings. **2** supply or provide.

furnishings noun furniture and fittings in a room or building.

furniture noun the movable articles that make a room or building suitable for living or working in.

furore /fyoo-**ror**-i/ (US spelling **furor** /fyoo-**ror**/) noun an outbreak of public anger or excitement.

furrier noun a person who deals in clothes made of fur.

furrow noun **1** a long, narrow trench made in the ground by a plough. **2** a deep wrinkle on a person's face. •verb make a furrow in.

furry adjective (**furrier, furriest**) covered with or like fur.

further adverb (also **farther**) **1** at, to, or by a greater distance. **2** at or to a more advanced stage. **3** in addition. •adjective **1** (also **farther**) more distant in space. **2** additional. •verb (**furthers, furthering, furthered**) help the progress of.
□ **further education** Brit. education below degree level for people older than school age.

furtherance noun the process of helping something to develop or succeed.

furthermore adverb in addition.

furthest or **farthest** adverb & adjective at or to the greatest distance.

furtive adjective secretively trying to avoid being noticed.
■ **furtively** adverb.

fury noun (plural **furies**) **1** extreme anger.

THESAURUS

funny adjective **1** *a very funny film:* amusing, humorous, witty, comic, comical, hilarious, hysterical, riotous, uproarious, farcical; informal rib-tickling, priceless. **2** *a funny coincidence:* strange, peculiar, odd, weird, bizarre, curious, freakish, quirky, unusual. **3** *there's something funny about him:* suspicious, suspect, dubious, untrustworthy, questionable; informal fishy; Brit. informal dodgy.
OPPOSITES unfunny, serious, unsurprising, trustworthy.

furious adjective **1** *he was furious when we told him:* very angry, enraged, infuriated, irate, incensed, fuming, ranting, raving, seething, beside yourself, outraged; informal hopping mad, wild, livid. **2** *a furious debate:* fierce, heated, passionate, fiery, tumultuous, turbulent, tempestuous, violent, stormy, acrimonious.
OPPOSITES pleased, calm.

furnish verb **1** *the bedrooms are elegantly furnished:* fit out, appoint, equip; Brit. informal do out. **2** *they furnished us with waterproofs:* supply, provide, equip, issue, kit out; informal fix up.

furore noun commotion, uproar, outcry, fuss, upset, brouhaha, stir; informal to-do,

hoo-ha, hullabaloo.

further adverb *further, it gave him an alibi.* See **FURTHERMORE**.
•adjective *further information:* additional, more, extra, supplementary, new, fresh.
OPPOSITES existing.
•verb *attempts to further his career:* promote, advance, forward, develop, facilitate, aid, assist, help, boost, encourage.
OPPOSITES impede.

furthermore adverb moreover, further, what's more, also, additionally, in addition, besides, as well, too, on top of that, into the bargain.

furthest adjective most distant, remotest, farthest, furthermost, farthermost, outer, outermost, extreme.
OPPOSITES nearest.

furtive adjective surreptitious, secretive, secret, clandestine, hidden, covert, conspiratorial, cloak-and-dagger, sneaky; informal shifty.
OPPOSITES open.

fury noun **1** *she exploded with fury:* rage, anger, wrath, outrage; literary ire. **2** *the fury of the storm:* ferocity, violence, turbulence, tempestuousness, savagery, severity,

2 extreme strength or violence. **3** (**the Furies**) Greek Mythology three goddesses who punished people for their crimes.

furze = GORSE.

fuse[1] verb (**fuses, fusing, fused**) **1** join or combine to form a whole. **2** melt something so it joins with something else. **3** Brit. (of an electrical appliance) stop working when a fuse melts. **4** fit a circuit or electrical appliance with a fuse. • noun **1** a safety device consisting of a strip of wire that melts and breaks an electric circuit if the current goes beyond a safe level. **2** a length of material which is lit to explode a bomb or firework. **3** a device in a bomb that controls the timing of the explosion.

fuselage /fyoo-zuh-lahzh/ noun the main body of an aircraft.

fusible adjective able to be melted easily.

Fusilier /fyoo-zi-leer/ noun a member of a British regiment formerly armed with muskets called **fusils**.

fusillade /fyoo-zi-layd, fyoo-zi-lahd/ noun a series of shots fired at the same time or quickly one after the other.

fusion noun **1** the joining of two or more things together to form a whole. **2** a reaction in which the nuclei of atoms fuse to form a heavier nucleus, releasing a great deal of energy.

fuss noun **1** unnecessary excitement or activity. **2** a protest or complaint. • verb (usu. **fuss over**) show unnecessary concern about something.

fussy adjective (**fussier, fussiest**) **1** hard to please. **2** full of unnecessary detail.
■ **fussily** adverb **fussiness** noun.

fusty adjective **1** smelling stale or damp. **2** old-fashioned.

futile adjective pointless.
■ **futilely** adverb **futility** noun.

futon /foo-ton/ noun a padded mattress that can be rolled up.

future noun **1** (**the future**) time that is still to come. **2** a prospect of success or happiness. • adjective **1** existing or happening in the future. **2** Grammar (of a verb) expressing an event yet to happen.

futuristic adjective **1** having very modern technology or design. **2** (of a film or book) set in the future.

futurity noun the future time.

fuzz noun **1** a frizzy mass of hair or fibre. **2** (**the fuzz**) informal the police.

fuzzy adjective (**fuzzier, fuzziest**) **1** having a frizzy texture or appearance. **2** blurred; not clear.

THESAURUS

intensity, vehemence, force.
OPPOSITES pleasure.

fuss noun **1** *what's all the fuss about?* commotion, excitement, stir, confusion, disturbance, brouhaha, uproar, furore, storm in a teacup; informal hoo-ha, to-do, song and dance, performance. **2** *he didn't put up too much of a fuss:* protest, complaint, objection, argument, row. **3** *they settled in with very little fuss:* trouble, bother, inconvenience, effort, exertion, labour; informal hassle.
• verb *he was still fussing about his clothes:* worry, fret, be agitated, be worked up, make a big thing out of, make a mountain out of a molehill; informal flap, be in a tizzy.

fussy adjective **1** *he's very fussy about what he eats:* particular, finicky, fastidious, hard to please, faddish; informal pernickety, choosy, picky; Brit. informal faddy; N. Amer. informal persnickety. **2** *a fussy bridal gown:* over-elaborate, ornate, fancy, busy, cluttered.

futile adjective fruitless, vain, pointless, useless, ineffectual, forlorn, hopeless.
OPPOSITES useful.

future noun **1** *plans for the future:* time to come, what lies ahead. **2** *her future lay in acting:* destiny, fate, fortune, prospects, chances.
OPPOSITES past.
• adjective **1** *a future date:* later, to come, following, ensuing, succeeding, subsequent, coming. **2** *his future wife:* to be, destined, intended, planned, prospective.
OPPOSITES previous, past.

fuzzy adjective **1** *her fuzzy hair:* frizzy, fluffy, woolly, downy. **2** *a fuzzy picture:* blurred, indistinct, unclear, out of focus, misty. **3** *a fuzzy concept:* unclear, imprecise, unfocused, nebulous, vague, hazy, loose, woolly.
OPPOSITES straight, smooth, sharp, clear.

Gg

G or **g** noun (plural **Gs** or **G's**) the seventh letter of the alphabet. • **abbreviation 1** grams. **2** gravity.
□ **G-string** a skimpy pair of knickers consisting of a narrow strip of cloth attached to a waistband.

gab verb (**gabs**, **gabbing**, **gabbed**) informal talk at length.
□ **the gift of the gab** the ability to speak in a fluent and persuasive way.

gabble verb (**gabbles**, **gabbling**, **gabbled**) talk very quickly and in a way that is difficult to understand. • **noun** talk that is fast and difficult to understand.

gaberdine or **gabardine** /ga-ber-**deen**/ noun a smooth, hard-wearing cloth used for making raincoats.

gable noun the triangular upper part of a wall at the end of a roof.

Gabonese /gab-uh-**neez**/ noun (plural **Gabonese**) a person from Gabon, a country in West Africa. • **adjective** relating to Gabon.

gad verb (**gads**, **gadding**, **gadded**) (**gad about**) informal enjoy yourself by visiting many different places.

gadfly noun (plural **gadflies**) **1** a fly that bites cattle. **2** an annoying person.

gadget noun a small mechanical device.
■ **gadgetry** noun.

gadolinium noun a soft silvery-white metallic element.

Gaelic /**gay**-lik, ga-lik/ noun a language

spoken in parts of Ireland and western Scotland.

gaff¹ noun a stick with a hook for landing large fish.

gaff² noun (**blow the gaff**) Brit. informal reveal a secret.

gaffe noun an embarrassing mistake made in a social situation.

gaffer noun informal **1** Brit. a person's boss. **2** an old man.

gag¹ noun a piece of cloth put over a person's mouth to stop them speaking. • **verb** (**gags**, **gagging**, **gagged**) **1** put a gag on. **2** choke or retch.

gag² noun a joke or funny story.

gaga /**gah**-gah/ adjective informal rambling in speech or thought, especially as a result of old age.

gage US spelling of **GAUGE**.

gaggle noun **1** a flock of geese. **2** informal a noisy group of people.

gaiety (US spelling **gayety**) noun (plural **gaieties**) light-hearted and cheerful mood or behaviour.

gaily adverb **1** in a light-hearted and cheerful way. **2** without thinking of the effect of your actions. **3** with a bright appearance.

gain verb **1** obtain or secure something. **2** reach a place. **3** (**gain on**) get closer to a person or thing that you are chasing. **4** increase in weight or speed. **5** (**gain in**)

THESAURUS

gadget noun device, appliance, apparatus, instrument, implement, tool, utensil, contrivance, contraption, machine, mechanism, invention; informal gizmo.

gag¹ verb **1** *the government tried to gag its critics*: silence, muzzle, suppress, stifle, censor, curb, restrain. **2** *the stench made her gag*: retch, heave.

gag² noun (informal) *he told a few gags*: joke, quip, jest, witticism; informal crack, wisecrack, one-liner.

gain verb **1** *he gained a scholarship*: obtain, get, secure, acquire, come by, procure,

attain, achieve, earn, win, capture; informal land. **2** *they stood to gain from the deal*: profit, make money, benefit, do well out of. **3** *she gained weight*: put on, increase in, build up. **4** *they were gaining on us*: catch up (with), catch, reduce someone's lead, narrow the gap.
OPPOSITES lose, fall behind.
• **noun 1** *his gain from the deal*: profit, earnings, income, yield, return, reward, advantage, benefit; informal take. **2** *weight gain*: increase, addition, rise, increment, advance.
OPPOSITES loss.

improve or progress in some respect. **6** (of a clock or watch) become fast. • noun **1** a thing that is gained. **2** an increase in wealth or resources.

gainful adjective (of employment) paid; profitable.
■ **gainfully** adverb.

gainsay verb (**gainsays, gainsaying, gainsaid**) formal deny or contradict.

gait noun a way of walking.

gaiter noun a covering of cloth or leather for the ankle and lower leg.

gala /gah-luh/ noun **1** a social occasion with special entertainments. **2** Brit. a special sports event, especially a swimming competition.

galactic adjective relating to a galaxy.

galaxy noun (plural **galaxies**) **1** a large system of stars. **2** (**the Galaxy**) the system of stars that includes the sun and the earth; the Milky Way.

gale noun **1** a very strong wind. **2** an outburst of laughter.

gall¹ noun disrespectful or rude behaviour. □ **gall bladder** a small organ beneath the liver, in which bile is stored.

gall² noun **1** annoyance; irritation. **2** a sore on the skin made by rubbing. • verb annoy; irritate.
■ **galling** adjective.

gallant adjective **1** /**gal**-luhnt/ brave or heroic. **2** /guh-**lant**/ (of a man) polite and charming to women. • noun /guh-**lant**/ a man who is polite and charming to women.
■ **gallantly** adverb.

gallantry noun (plural **gallantries**) **1** courageous behaviour. **2** polite attention given by men to women.

galleon noun historical a large sailing ship with three or more decks and masts.

gallery noun (plural **galleries**) **1** a room or building in which works of art are displayed or sold. **2** a balcony at the back of a large hall. **3** the highest part of a theatre.

galley noun (plural **galleys**) **1** historical a low, flat ship with one or more sails and up to three banks of oars. **2** a narrow kitchen in a ship or aircraft.

Gallic /**gal**-lik/ adjective having to do with

France or the French.

gallivant verb informal go from place to place enjoying yourself.

gallon noun **1** a unit of volume for measuring liquids, equal to eight pints (4.55 litres). **2** (**gallons**) informal large quantities.

gallop noun **1** the fastest speed a horse can run. **2** a ride on a horse at its fastest speed. • verb (**gallops, galloping, galloped**) **1** go at the speed of a gallop. **2** proceed very quickly.

gallows plural noun **1** a structure used for hanging a person. **2** (**the gallows**) execution by hanging.

gallstone noun a hard painful mass which can form in the gall bladder or bile ducts.

galore adjective in large numbers or amounts.

galoshes plural noun rubber shoes worn over normal shoes in wet weather.

galumph verb informal move in a clumsy or noisy way.

galvanic /gal-**van**-ik/ adjective relating to electric currents produced by chemical action.

galvanize or **galvanise** /gal-vuh-nyz/ verb (**galvanizes, galvanizing, galvanized**) **1** shock or excite someone into doing something. **2** (**galvanized**) (of iron or steel) coated with a protective layer of zinc.

galvanometer /gal-vuh-**nom**-i-ter/ noun an instrument for measuring small electric currents.

Gambian noun a person from Gambia. • adjective relating to Gambia.

gambit noun something that somebody says or does that is meant to give them an advantage.

gamble verb (**gambles, gambling, gambled**) **1** play games of chance for money. **2** bet a sum of money. **3** risk losing something in the hope that you will be successful. • noun a risky action.
■ **gambler** noun.

gambol verb (**gambols, gambolling, gambolled**; US spelling **gambols, gamboling, gamboled**) run or jump about playfully.

game¹ noun **1** an activity that you take part

g

THESAURUS

gala noun festival, fair, fete, carnival, pageant, jubilee, jamboree, celebration.

gale noun **1** *a howling gale:* high wind, blast, squall, storm, tempest, hurricane, tornado, cyclone, whirlwind, typhoon. **2** *gales of laughter:* peal, howl, hoot, shriek, scream, roar, fit, paroxysm.

gamble verb **1** *he started to gamble:* bet, place a bet, wager, hazard; Brit. informal punt,

have a flutter. **2** *investors are gambling that the pound will fall:* take a chance, take a risk; N. Amer. take a flyer; informal stick your neck out; Brit. informal chance your arm.
• noun *I took a gamble:* risk, chance, leap in the dark, speculation, lottery, pot luck.

game noun **1** *the children invented a new game:* pastime, diversion, entertainment, amusement, distraction, recreation, sport,

in for amusement. **2** a competitive activity or sport played according to rules. **3** a period of play, ending in a final result. **4** a section of a tennis match, forming a unit in scoring. **5** (**games**) a meeting for sporting competitions. **6** informal a type of activity or business regarded as a game. **7** wild animals or birds that people hunt for food or as a sport. •adjective eager and willing to do something that is new or challenging. •verb (**games, gaming, gamed**) play at games of chance for money.
■ **gamely** adverb.

game² adjective dated (of a person's leg) lame.

gamekeeper noun a person employed to breed and protect game for a large country estate.

gamesmanship noun the ability to win games by making your opponent feel less confident.

gamete /gam-eet/ noun Biology a cell which is able to unite with another of the opposite sex in sexual reproduction to form a zygote.

gamine /ga-meen/ adjective (of a girl) having a mischievous, boyish charm.

gamma /gam-muh/ noun the third letter of the Greek alphabet (Γ, γ).
□ **gamma rays** (or **gamma radiation**) electromagnetic radiation of shorter wavelength than X-rays.

gammon noun Brit. **1** ham which has been cured like bacon. **2** the part of a side of bacon that includes the hind leg.

gammy adjective Brit. informal (of a person's leg) injured or painful.

gamut /gam-uht/ noun the complete range or scope of something.
□ **run the gamut** experience or perform the complete range of something.

gander noun **1** a male goose. **2** informal a look.

gang noun **1** an organized group of criminals or rowdy young people. **2** informal

a group of people who regularly meet and do things together. **3** an organized group of people doing manual work. •verb **1** (**gang together**) form a group or gang. **2** (**gang up**) join together to oppose or intimidate someone.

gangling or **gangly** adjective (of a person) tall, thin, and awkward.

ganglion noun (plural **ganglia** or **ganglions**) **1** a mass of nerve cells. **2** a swelling in a tendon.

gangmaster noun Brit. a person who organizes and supervises the work of manual labourers employed on a casual basis.

gangplank noun a movable plank used as a bridge between a boat and the shore.

gangrene noun the decay of tissue in a part of the body, caused by an obstructed blood supply or by infection.
■ **gangrenous** adjective.

gangster noun a member of an organized gang of violent criminals.

gangway noun Brit. **1** a passage between rows of seats. **2** a bridge placed between a ship and the shore.

gannet noun **1** a large seabird. **2** Brit. informal a greedy person.

gantry noun (plural **gantries**) a bridge-like structure used as a support.

gaol ⇒ JAIL.

gap noun **1** a hole in an object or between two objects. **2** an empty space or period of time; a break in something.
■ **gappy** adjective.

gape verb (**gapes, gaping, gaped**) **1** stare with your mouth open wide in amazement. **2** be or become wide open.

garage /ga-rahj, ga-rij/ noun **1** a building in which a car or other vehicle is kept. **2** a business which sells fuel or which repairs and sells motor vehicles. **3** a type of music with elements of drum and bass, house, and soul. •verb (**garages, garaging,**

THESAURUS

activity. **2** *we lost the game:* match, contest, fixture, meeting, tie, clash.
•adjective *are you game?* willing, prepared, ready, disposed, interested, eager, keen, enthusiastic.

gang noun **1** *a gang of teenagers:* band, group, crowd, pack, horde, throng, mob, herd, swarm, troop; informal bunch, gaggle, load. **2** *a gang of workmen:* crew, team, group, squad, shift, detachment, unit.

gangster noun hoodlum, racketeer, thug, villain, criminal, Mafioso; informal mobster, crook, tough; N. Amer. informal hood.

gaol noun. See JAIL.

gap noun **1** *a gap in the shutters:* opening,

aperture, space, breach, chink, slit, crack, crevice, cleft, cavity, hole. **2** *a gap between meetings:* pause, intermission, interval, interlude, break, breathing space, breather, respite; N. Amer. recess. **3** *a gap in our records:* omission, blank. **4** *the gap between rich and poor:* chasm, gulf, separation, contrast, difference, disparity, divergence, imbalance.

gape verb **1** *she gaped at him in astonishment:* stare, stare open-mouthed, goggle, gaze, ogle; informal rubberneck; Brit. informal gawp. **2** *a jacket which gaped at every seam:* open, yawn, part, split.

gaping adjective wide, broad, vast, wide open, yawning, cavernous.

garaged) keep a vehicle in a garage.

garb noun unusual or distinctive clothes.
• verb (**be garbed in**) be dressed in distinctive clothes.

garbage noun chiefly N. Amer. **1** domestic rubbish or waste. **2** something worthless or meaningless.

garble verb (**garbles, garbling, garbled**) confuse or distort a message or transmission.

garden noun **1** a piece of ground next to or around a house. **2** (**gardens**) a public park.
• verb work in a garden.
■ **gardener** noun.

gardenia noun a tree or shrub with large white or yellow sweet-smelling flowers.

gargantuan adjective enormous.

gargle verb (**gargles, gargling, gargled**) hold liquid in your mouth and throat while slowly breathing out through it. • noun **1** an act of gargling. **2** a liquid used for gargling.

gargoyle noun a spout in the form of an ugly person or animal that carries water away from the roof of a building.

garish /gair-ish/ adjective unpleasantly bright and showy.
■ **garishly** adverb.

garland noun a wreath of flowers and leaves. • verb crown or decorate with a garland.

garlic noun a plant of the onion family with a strong taste and smell.

garment noun a piece of clothing.

garner verb (**garners, garnering, garnered**) gather or collect.

garnet noun a red semi-precious stone.

garnish verb decorate food. • noun a decoration for food.

garret noun a room in the roof of a house.

garrison noun a group of troops stationed in a fortress or town to defend it. • verb provide a place with a garrison.

garrotte /guh-rot/ (US spelling **garrote**) verb

(**garrottes, garrotting, garrotted**) strangle someone with a wire or cord. • noun a wire or cord used for garrotting.

garrulous adjective very talkative.
■ **garrulity** noun.

garter noun a band worn around the leg to keep up a stocking or sock.

gas noun (plural **gases** or chiefly US **gasses**) **1** an air-like substance which expands to fill any available space. **2** a type of gas used as a fuel. **3** a type of gas that stops you feeling pain, used during a medical operation. **4** N. Amer. gasoline. • verb (**gases, gassing, gassed**) **1** attack with, expose to, or kill with gas. **2** informal talk or chat at length.
□ **gas chamber** an airtight room that can be filled with poisonous gas to kill people or animals. **gas mask** a mask used as protection against poisonous gas.

☑ in British English, the spelling of the plural is *gases*: no double *s*.

gaseous /gass-i-uhss/ adjective relating to or like a gas.

gash noun a long deep cut or wound. • verb make a gash in.

gasket /gass-kit/ noun a rubber seal at the junction between two surfaces in an engine.

gaslight noun light from a gas lamp.
■ **gaslit** adjective.

gasoline noun N. Amer. petrol.

gasometer /ga-som-i-ter/ noun a large tank for the storage of gas.

gasp verb **1** take a quick breath with your mouth open, because you are surprised or in pain. **2** (**gasp for**) struggle for air. • noun a sudden quick breath.

gassy adjective (**gassier, gassiest**) full of gas.

gastric adjective having to do with the stomach.

gastritis /gas-try-tiss/ noun inflammation of the lining of the stomach.

gastro-enteritis noun inflammation of the

THESAURUS

garish adjective gaudy, lurid, loud, harsh, showy, glittering, brash, tasteless, vulgar; informal flashy.
OPPOSITES drab, subdued, tasteful.

garments plural noun clothes, clothing, dress, garb, wardrobe, costume; informal gear, togs, get-up; Brit. informal clobber; N. Amer. informal threads; formal attire.

garnish verb decorate, adorn, ornament, trim, dress, embellish.
• noun decoration, adornment, ornament, embellishment, enhancement, finishing touch.

garrison noun **1** *the English garrison had left:* troops, forces, militia, soldiers, force, detachment, unit. **2** *forces from three*

garrisons: base, camp, station, barracks, fort, command post.
• verb *troops were garrisoned in York:* station, post, deploy, base, site, place, billet.

gash noun cut, laceration, slash, slit, split, wound, injury.
• verb cut, lacerate, slash, slit, split, wound, injure.

gasp verb **1** *I gasped in surprise:* catch/draw in your breath, gulp. **2** *he fell on the ground, gasping:* pant, puff, puff and blow, wheeze, breathe hard/heavily, choke, fight for breath.
• noun *he could speak only between gasps:* gulp, pant, puff.

stomach and intestines.

gastronomy noun the practice or art of cooking and eating good food.
■ **gastronomic** adjective.

gastropod noun a mollusc such as a snail or slug.

gasworks plural noun a place where gas is processed.

gate noun **1** a hinged barrier used to close an opening in a wall, fence, or hedge. **2** an exit from an airport building to an aircraft. **3** a barrier that controls the flow of water on a river or canal. **4** the number of people who pay to attend a sports event.

gateau /gat-oh/ noun (plural **gateaus** or **gateaux** /gat-ohz/) Brit. a cake.

gatecrash verb go to a party without an invitation or ticket.
■ **gatecrasher** noun.

gatefold noun an oversized page in a book or magazine, intended to be opened out for reading.

gatehouse noun a house standing by the gateway to a country estate.

gatekeeper noun an attendant at a gate.

gatepost noun a post on which a gate is hinged or against which it shuts.

gateway noun **1** an opening that can be closed by a gate. **2** (**gateway to**) a means of entering somewhere or achieving something.

gather verb (**gathers, gathering, gathered**) **1** come or bring together. **2** increase in force, speed, etc. **3** understand something to be the case. **4** collect plants or fruits for food. **5** harvest a crop. **6** draw together or towards yourself. **7** pull fabric into folds by drawing thread through it. •**noun** (**gathers**) a part of a piece of clothing that is gathered.

gathering noun a group of people who have come together for a purpose.

gauche /gohsh/ adjective awkward in social situations.

gaucho /gow-choh/ noun (plural **gauchos**) a cowboy from the South American plains.

gaudy /gaw-di/ adjective (**gaudier, gaudiest**) tastelessly bright and showy.
■ **gaudily** adverb.

gauge /gayj/ (US spelling **gage**) noun **1** an instrument for measuring the amount or level of something. **2** the thickness or size of a wire, tube, bullet, etc. **3** the distance between the rails of a railway track. •**verb** (**gauges, gauging, gauged**) **1** judge a situation or mood. **2** estimate or measure something.

> ☑ spell **gauge** with -*au*- in the middle (the spelling **gage** is American).

gaunt adjective (of a person) looking thin and exhausted.

gauntlet noun **1** a strong glove with a long loose wrist. **2** a glove worn as part of medieval armour.
□ **run the gauntlet** have to face criticism or hostility from a large number of people. **throw down the gauntlet** set a challenge.

gauze noun **1** a thin transparent fabric. **2** a fine wire mesh.
■ **gauzy** adjective.

gave past of GIVE.

gavel noun a small hammer with which a judge or auctioneer hits a surface in order to get people's attention.

gavotte /guh-vot/ noun a French dance, popular in the 18th century.

gawk verb stare in a stupid or rude way.

gawky adjective awkward and clumsy.

gawp verb Brit. informal gawk.

gay adjective (**gayer, gayest**) **1** (especially of

THESAURUS

gate noun barrier, turnstile, gateway, doorway, entrance, exit, door, portal; N. Amer. entryway.

gather verb **1** *we gathered in the hotel lobby:* congregate, assemble, meet, collect, get together, convene, muster, rally, converge. **2** *he gathered his family:* summon, call together, bring together, assemble, convene, rally, round up, muster, marshal. **3** *they gathered the crops:* harvest, reap, crop, pick, pluck, collect. **4** *I gather he's a footballer:* understand, believe, be led to believe, conclude, infer, assume, take it, surmise, hear, learn, discover. **5** *her dress was gathered at the waist:* pleat, pucker, tuck, fold, ruffle.
OPPOSITES disperse.

gathering noun assembly, meeting, convention, rally, council, congress,

congregation, audience, crowd, group, throng, mass; informal get-together.

gaudy adjective garish, lurid, loud, glaring, harsh, showy, glittering, ostentatious, tasteless; informal flashy, tacky.
OPPOSITES drab, tasteful.

gauge noun *the temperature gauge:* meter, measure, indicator, dial, scale, display.
•verb **1** *astronomers can gauge the star's brightness:* measure, calculate, compute, work out, determine, ascertain, count, weigh, quantify, put a figure on. **2** *it is hard to gauge how effective the ban was:* assess, evaluate, determine, estimate, form an opinion of, appraise, weigh up, judge, guess; informal size up.

gaunt adjective haggard, drawn, thin, spare, bony, angular, pinched, scrawny, rawboned, cadaverous, skeletal, emaciated.

a man) homosexual. **2** relating to homosexuals. **3** dated light-hearted and carefree. **4** dated brightly coloured. • noun a homosexual person, especially a man.

gayety US spelling of GAIETY.

gaze verb (**gazes, gazing, gazed**) look steadily. • noun a steady look.

gazebo /guh-**zee**-boh/ noun (plural **gazebos**) a summer house with a pleasant view.

gazelle noun a small antelope.

gazette noun a journal or newspaper.

gazetteer /ga-zuh-**teer**/ noun a list of place names.

gazump /guh-**zump**/ verb Brit. informal offer or accept a higher price for a house after a lower offer has already been accepted.

GB abbreviation **1** Great Britain. **2** (also **Gb**) Computing gigabytes.

GBH abbreviation Brit. grievous bodily harm.

GC abbreviation George Cross.

GCE abbreviation General Certificate of Education.

GCSE abbreviation (in the UK except Scotland) General Certificate of Secondary Education (the lower of the two main levels of the GCE exam).

gear noun **1** (**gears**) a set of machinery that connects the engine to the wheels of a vehicle and controls its speed. **2** a particular position of gears in a vehicle: *fifth gear.* **3** informal equipment or clothing. • verb **1** adapt something for a particular purpose. **2** adjust the gears in a vehicle to a particular level. **3** (**gear up**) get prepared for something.
□ **gear lever** Brit. a lever used to change gear in a vehicle.

gearbox noun a set of gears with its casing.

gecko noun (plural **geckos** or **geckoes**) a lizard with adhesive pads on the feet, active at night.

gee exclamation **1** (**gee up**) a command to a horse to go faster. **2** (also **gee whiz**) N. Amer. informal a mild expression of surprise, enthusiasm, or sympathy.

geek noun informal **1** an awkward or unfashionable person. **2** a person who is obsessed with something: *a computer geek.*
■ **geeky** adjective.

geese plural of GOOSE.

geezer noun informal a man.

Geiger counter noun a device for measuring radioactivity.

geisha /**gay**-shuh/ noun (plural **geisha** or **geishas**) a Japanese woman who is paid to accompany and entertain men.

gel[1] noun a jelly-like substance used on the hair or skin. • verb (**gels, gelling, gelled**) smooth your hair with gel.

gel[2] (**gels, gelling, gelled**) **1** (of jelly or a similar substance) set or become firmer. **2** take definite form or begin to work well.

gelatin /**jel**-uh-tin/ or **gelatine** /**jel**-uh-teen/ noun a clear substance made from animal bones and used to make jelly, glue, and photographic film.
■ **gelatinous** /ji-**lat**-i-nuhss/ adjective.

geld verb castrate a male animal.

gelding noun a castrated male horse.

gelignite /**jel**-ig-nyt/ noun a powerful explosive made from nitroglycerine.

gem noun **1** a precious stone. **2** an outstanding person or thing.

Gemini noun a sign of the zodiac (the Twins), 21 May–20 June.

gemstone noun a gem used in a piece of jewellery.

gen Brit. informal noun information. • verb (**gens, genning, genned**) (**gen up on**) obtain information about something.

gendarme /**zhon**-darm/ noun a member of the French police force.

gender noun **1** Grammar each of the classes into which nouns and pronouns are divided in some languages, usually referred to as masculine, feminine, and neuter. **2** the state of being male or female (in terms of social or cultural differences rather than biological ones). **3** the members of one or other sex.

gene noun Biology a distinct sequence of DNA forming part of a chromosome, by which offspring inherit characteristics from a parent.

genealogy /jee-ni-**al**-uh-ji/ noun (plural **genealogies**) **1** a line of descent traced

g

---

gaze verb stare, gape, look fixedly, goggle, eye, scrutinize, ogle; informal rubberneck; Brit. informal gawp; N. Amer. informal eyeball.
• noun stare, gape, fixed look, regard, scrutiny.

gear noun **1** *fishing gear:* equipment, apparatus, paraphernalia, tools, utensils, implements, instruments, rig, tackle; Brit. informal clobber. **2** (informal) *I'll pick up my gear from my hotel:* belongings, possessions, effects, paraphernalia, bits and

pieces; informal things, stuff, kit; Brit. informal clobber, gubbins. **3** (informal) *the best designer gear:* clothes, clothing, garments, outfits, garb, wardrobe; informal togs; Brit. informal clobber, kit; N. Amer. informal threads; formal attire.

gem noun **1** *rubies and other gems:* jewel, precious stone, semi-precious stone; informal rock. **2** *a musical gem:* masterpiece, classic, treasure, prize, find; informal one in a million, the bee's knees.

from an ancestor. **2** the study of lines of descent.

■ **genealogical** adjective **genealogist** noun.

genera plural of GENUS.

general adjective **1** affecting or concerning all or most people or things. **2** involving only the main features of something; not detailed. **3** chief or principal: *the general manager.* •noun a commander of an army, or an army officer ranking above lieutenant general.

□ **general anaesthetic** an anaesthetic that affects the whole body and causes a loss of consciousness. **general election** the election of representatives to a parliament by all the people of a country. **general practitioner** a doctor who treats patients in a local community rather than at a hospital.

generality noun (plural **generalities**) **1** a general statement rather than one that is specific or detailed. **2** the quality or state of being general.

generalize or **generalise** verb (**generalizes, generalizing, generalized**) **1** make a general or broad statement. **2** make something more common or more widely applicable.

■ **generalization** noun.

generally adverb **1** in most cases. **2** without discussing the details of something. **3** widely.

generate verb (**generates, generating, generated**) create or produce something.

■ **generative** adjective.

generation noun **1** all the people born and living at about the same time. **2** the average period in which a person grows up and has children of their own. **3** a single

stage in the history of a family. **4** a stage in the development of a product. **5** the producing or creating of something.

generator noun a machine for producing electricity.

generic adjective **1** referring to a class or group of things. **2** (of goods) having no brand name.

■ **generically** adverb.

generous adjective **1** freely giving more than is necessary or expected. **2** kind towards other people. **3** larger or more plentiful than is usual.

■ **generosity** noun.

genesis /jen-i-siss/ noun the origin or development of something.

genetic adjective **1** relating to genes. **2** relating to genetics.

■ **genetically** adverb.

□ **genetically modified** (of an animal or plant) containing genetic material that has been altered in order to produce a desired characteristic. **genetic engineering** the changing of the characteristics of an animal or plant by altering its genetic material. **genetic fingerprinting** the analysis of genetic material in order to identify individual people.

genetics plural noun the study of the way characteristics are passed from one generation to another.

■ **geneticist** noun.

genial /jee-ni-uhl/ adjective friendly and cheerful.

■ **geniality** noun **genially** adverb.

genie /jee-ni/ noun (in Arabian folklore) a spirit.

genital adjective referring to the external

THESAURUS

general adjective **1** *suitable for general use:* widespread, common, extensive, universal, wide, popular, public, mainstream. **2** *a general pay increase:* comprehensive, overall, across the board, blanket, global, universal, mass, wholesale. **3** *the general practice:* usual, customary, habitual, traditional, normal, conventional, typical, standard, regular, accepted, prevailing, routine, established, everyday. **4** *a general description:* broad, rough, loose, approximate, unspecific, vague, imprecise, inexact.

OPPOSITES restricted, localized, exceptional, detailed.

generally adverb **1** *summers were generally hot:* normally, in general, as a rule, by and large, mainly, mostly, for the most part, predominantly, on the whole, usually. **2** *the idea was generally accepted:* widely, commonly, extensively, universally, popularly.

generate verb create, make, produce, engender, spawn, precipitate, prompt, provoke, trigger, spark off, stir up, induce.

generation noun **1** *people of the same generation:* age, age group, peer group. **2** *the next generation of computers:* crop, batch, wave, range.

generosity noun liberality, lavishness, magnanimity, bounty, munificence, open-handedness, largesse, unselfishness, altruism, charity.

OPPOSITES meanness, selfishness.

generous adjective **1** *she is generous with money:* liberal, lavish, magnanimous, giving, open-handed, bountiful, unselfish, ungrudging, free. **2** *a generous amount of fabric:* plentiful, copious, ample, liberal, large, abundant.

OPPOSITES mean, selfish, meagre.

genesis noun origin, source, root, beginning, start.

reproductive organs of a person or animal.
• noun (**genitals**) the external reproductive
organs.

genitalia /jen-i-**tay**-li-uh/ plural noun formal or
technical the genitals.

genitive /jen-i-tiv/ noun Grammar the form of
a noun, pronoun, or adjective used to show
possession.

genius noun (plural **geniuses**) **1** exceptional
natural ability. **2** an exceptionally
intelligent or able person.

genocide /jen-uh-syd/ noun the deliberate
killing of a very large number of people
from a particular ethnic group or nation.
■ **genocidal** adjective.

genre /**zhon**-ruh/ noun a type or style of art
or literature.

gent noun informal a gentleman.

genteel adjective polite and refined in an
affected or exaggerated way.
■ **gentility** noun.

gentian /jen-sh'n/ noun a small plant with
violet or blue flowers.

Gentile /jen-tyl/ adjective not Jewish. • noun
a person who is not Jewish.

gentle adjective (**gentler**, **gentlest**) **1** (of a
person) mild and kind. **2** moderate; not
harsh or severe.
■ **gentleness** noun **gently** adverb.

gentleman noun (plural **gentlemen**) **1** a
polite or honourable man. **2** a man of good
social position. **3** (in polite or formal use)
a man.

gentrify verb (**gentrifies**, **gentrifying**,
gentrified) renovate a house or district so
that it appeals to the tastes of middle-class
people.
■ **gentrification** noun.

gentry noun (**the gentry**) people of good
social position.

genuflect /jen-yuu-flekt/ verb lower your
body as a sign of respect by bending one
knee.
■ **genuflection** noun.

genuine adjective **1** truly what it is said to

be. **2** honest.
■ **genuinely** adverb.

genus /jee-nuhss/ noun (plural **genera**
/jen-uh-ruh/) a category in the
classification of animals and plants.

geodesic /jee-oh-**dess**-ik, jee-oh-**dee**-sik/
adjective relating to a method of
construction based on straight lines
between points on a curved surface.

geographical or **geographic** adjective
relating to geography.
■ **geographically** adverb.

geography noun **1** the study of the
physical features of the earth and how
people relate to them. **2** the way in which
places and physical features are arranged.
■ **geographer** noun.

geology noun **1** the scientific study of the
physical structure and substance of the
earth. **2** the geological features of a
particular area.
■ **geological** adjective **geologist** noun.

geometric adjective **1** relating to geometry.
2 (of a design) featuring regular lines and
shapes.
■ **geometrical** adjective **geometrically** adverb.

geometry noun (plural **geometries**) **1** the
branch of mathematics that deals with the
properties and relationships of lines,
angles, surfaces, and solids. **2** the shape
and relationship of the parts of something.

geopolitical adjective relating to political
relations between the countries of the
world.

Geordie noun Brit. informal a person from
Tyneside in NE England.

Georgian adjective relating to the reigns of
the British kings George I–IV (1714–1830).

geranium noun a plant with red, pink, or
white flowers.

gerbil noun a small rodent, often kept as a
pet.

geriatric adjective relating to old people.
• noun an old person, especially one
receiving special care.

g

genius noun **1** *the world knew of his genius:*
brilliance, intelligence, intellect,
cleverness, brains. **2** *he has a genius for
organization:* talent, gift, flair, aptitude,
facility, knack, ability, expertise, capacity,
faculty. **3** *he is a genius:* brilliant person,
gifted person, mastermind, Einstein,
intellectual, brain, prodigy; informal egghead,
bright spark; Brit. informal brainbox, clever
clogs; N. Amer. informal brainiac.
OPPOSITES stupidity, dunce.

genre noun category, class, classification,
group, set, type, sort, kind, variety.

gentle adjective **1** *his manner was gentle:*
kind, tender, sympathetic, considerate,

understanding, compassionate, humane,
mild, placid, serene. **2** *a gentle breeze |
gentle music:* light, soft, quiet, low, slow.
3 *a gentle slope:* gradual, slight, easy, slow,
imperceptible.
OPPOSITES brutal, strong, loud, steep.

genuine adjective **1** *a genuine Picasso:*
authentic, real, actual, original, bona fide,
true; informal pukka, the real McCoy, the
real thing, kosher; Austral./NZ informal dinkum.
2 *a very genuine person:* sincere, honest,
truthful, straightforward, direct, frank,
candid, open, natural; informal straight,
upfront.
OPPOSITES bogus, insincere.

g

germ noun 1 a microorganism, especially one which causes disease. 2 a part of an organism that is able to develop into a new one. 3 an initial stage from which something may develop.

German noun 1 a person from Germany. 2 the language of Germany, Austria, and parts of Switzerland. • adjective relating to Germany or German.
□ German measles = RUBELLA. German shepherd a large breed of dog often used as guard dogs; an Alsatian.

germane adjective (**germane to**) relevant or appropriate to.

Germanic adjective 1 of the language family that includes English, German, Dutch, and the Scandinavian languages. 2 characteristic of Germans or Germany.

germicide noun a substance which destroys germs.
■ germicidal adjective.

germinal adjective 1 relating to a gamete or embryo. 2 in the earliest stage of development.

germinate verb (**germinates, germinating, germinated**) (of a seed) begin to grow.
■ germination noun.

gerontology noun the scientific study of old age and old people.

gerrymander verb (**gerrymanders, gerrymandering, gerrymandered**) change the boundaries of a constituency so as to give an unfair advantage to one party in an election.

gerund /je-ruhnd/ noun Grammar a verb form which functions as a noun (e.g. *asking* in *do you mind my asking?*).

Gestapo /ge-stah-poh/ noun the German secret police under Nazi rule.

gestation noun 1 the growth of a baby inside its mother's body. 2 the development of a plan or idea over a period of time.

gesticulate verb (**gesticulates, gesticulating, gesticulated**) make gestures instead of speaking or in order to emphasize what you are saying.
■ gesticulation noun.

gesture noun 1 a movement of part of the body to express an idea or meaning. 2 an action performed to convey your feelings or intentions. • verb (**gestures, gesturing, gestured**) make a gesture.

get verb (**gets, getting, got**; past participle **got**, N. Amer. or old use **gotten**) 1 come to have or hold; receive. 2 succeed in achieving or experiencing. 3 experience or suffer. 4 fetch. 5 reach a particular state or condition: *it's getting late.* 6 move to or from a particular place. 7 travel by or catch a form of transport. 8 begin to be or do something.
□ get away with escape blame or punishment for. get by manage to live or do something with the things that you have. get off informal escape a punishment. get on 1 make progress with a task. 2 have a friendly relationship. 3 (**be getting on**) informal be old. get over recover from an illness or an unpleasant experience. get something over manage to communicate an idea. get your own back informal have your revenge. get-together an informal social gathering. get-up informal an unusual style of clothes.

getaway noun an escape.

geyser /gee-zer/ noun a hot spring that

THESAURUS

germ noun 1 *this detergent kills germs:* microbe, microorganism, bacillus, bacterium, virus; informal bug. 2 *the germ of an idea:* start, beginnings, seed, embryo, bud, root, origin, source.

gesture noun 1 *a gesture of surrender:* signal, sign, motion, indication, gesticulation. 2 *a symbolic gesture:* action, act, deed, move.
• verb *he gestured to her:* signal, motion, gesticulate, wave, indicate, give a sign.

get verb 1 *where did you get that hat?* obtain, acquire, come by, receive, gain, earn, win, be given; informal get hold of, score. 2 *your tea's getting cold:* become, grow, turn, go. 3 *get the children from school:* fetch, collect, go/come for, call for, pick up, bring, deliver, convey. 4 *did the police get him?* capture, catch, arrest, apprehend, seize; informal collar, grab, pick up; Brit. informal nick. 5 *she got flu:* contract, develop, go down with, catch, fall ill with.

6 *I didn't get what he said:* hear, catch, make out, follow, take in. 7 *I don't get the joke:* understand, comprehend, grasp, see, fathom, follow. 8 *we got there early:* arrive, reach, make it, turn up, appear, present yourself, come along; informal show up. 9 *we got her to agree:* persuade, induce, prevail on, influence, talk into. 10 *I'll get supper:* prepare, get ready, cook, make; informal fix, rustle up; Brit. informal knock up.
OPPOSITES give, shake off.
□ get something across **communicate**, get over, impart, convey, transmit, make clear, express. get along **be friendly**, be compatible, get on, agree, see eye to eye; informal hit it off. get away **escape**, run away/off, break free, bolt, flee, make off, take off, decamp; informal skedaddle, scarper; Brit. informal do a bunk, do a runner. get by **manage**, cope, survive, exist, subsist, muddle through/along, scrape by, make ends meet, make do; informal make out. get

sometimes sprays water and steam into the air.

Ghanaian /gah-**nay**-uhn/ noun a person from Ghana. • adjective relating to Ghana.

ghastly adjective (**ghastlier, ghastliest**) **1** causing great horror or fear. **2** informal very unpleasant. **3** looking very pale and ill.

■ **ghastliness** noun.

ghee /gee/ noun a kind of butter used in Indian cooking.

gherkin /**ger**-kin/ noun a small pickled cucumber.

ghetto /**get**-toh/ noun (plural **ghettos** or **ghettoes**) a part of a city lived in by people of a particular race, nationality, or ethnic group.

□ **ghetto blaster** informal a large portable radio and cassette or CD player.

ghost noun **1** a spirit of a dead person which is believed to appear to the living. **2** (**a** or **the ghost of**) a faint trace of.

□ **ghost town** a town in which no one lives any more. **ghost writer** a person who writes something for someone else who is named as the author.

ghostly adjective like a ghost; eerie.

ghoul /gool/ noun **1** an evil spirit or phantom. **2** a person who is too interested in death or disaster.

■ **ghoulish** adjective.

GI noun (plural **GIs**) a private soldier in the US army.

giant noun **1** (in stories) a person of superhuman size and strength. **2** an unusually large person, animal, or plant.

• adjective unusually large.

gibber /**jib**-ber/ verb speak quickly in a way that is difficult to understand.

■ **gibbering** adjective.

gibberish /**jib**-ber-ish/ noun speech or writing that is impossible to understand; nonsense.

gibbet /**jib**-bit/ noun (in the past) a post and beam used for hanging people, or for displaying the bodies of those who had been executed.

gibbon noun a small ape with long, powerful arms, native to SE Asia.

gibe ⇒ JIBE.

giblets /**jib**-lits/ plural noun the liver, heart, gizzard, and neck of a chicken or other bird.

giddy adjective (**giddier, giddiest**) **1** having the feeling that everything is moving and that you are going to fall. **2** excitable and silly.

■ **giddily** adverb **giddiness** noun.

gift noun **1** a thing that you give to someone; a present. **2** a natural ability or talent. • verb **1** give something as a gift. **2** (**gifted**) having exceptional talent or ability.

gig[1] noun (in the past) a light two-wheeled carriage pulled by one horse.

gig[2] noun informal a live performance by a musician.

gigabyte /**gig**-uh-byt, **jig**-uh-byt/ noun Computing a unit of information equal to one thousand million (10^9) bytes.

gigantic adjective of very great size or extent.

g

THESAURUS

out of evade, dodge, shirk, avoid, escape, sidestep; informal wriggle out of. **get round someone cajole,** persuade, wheedle, coax, prevail on, win over, bring round, sway, inveigle; informal sweet-talk, butter up. **get up get out of bed,** rise, stir, rouse yourself; informal surface.

ghastly adjective **1** *a ghastly murder:* terrible, frightful, horrible, grim, awful, horrifying, shocking, appalling, gruesome, horrendous, monstrous. **2** (informal) *a ghastly building:* unpleasant, objectionable, disagreeable, distasteful, awful, terrible, horrible, dreadful, frightful, detestable, vile; informal horrid.
OPPOSITES pleasant.

ghost noun spectre, phantom, wraith, spirit, presence, apparition; informal spook.

ghostly adjective supernatural, unearthly, spectral, phantom, unnatural, eerie, weird, uncanny; informal spooky.

giant noun colossus, mammoth, monster, leviathan, ogre.
OPPOSITES dwarf.

• adjective huge, colossal, massive, enormous, gigantic, mammoth, vast, immense, monumental, mountainous, titanic, towering, gargantuan; informal mega, monster, whopping; Brit. informal ginormous.
OPPOSITES miniature.

giddy adjective **1** *she felt giddy:* dizzy, light-headed, faint, unsteady, wobbly, reeling; informal woozy. **2** *she was young and giddy:* flighty, silly, frivolous, skittish, irresponsible, scatty; informal dizzy.
OPPOSITES steady, sensible.

gift noun **1** *he gave the staff a gift:* present, handout, donation, offering, bonus, award, endowment; informal prezzie. **2** *a gift for music:* talent, flair, aptitude, facility, knack, bent, ability, skill, capacity, faculty.

gifted adjective talented, skilled, accomplished, expert, able, proficient, intelligent, clever, bright, brilliant, precocious; informal crack, ace.
OPPOSITES inept.

gigantic adjective huge, enormous, vast, giant, massive, colossal, mammoth,

giggle verb (**giggles, giggling, giggled**) laugh lightly in a nervous or silly way. •noun **1** a laugh of this kind. **2** Brit. informal an amusing person or thing.
■ **giggly** adjective.

gigolo /jig-uh-loh/ noun (plural **gigolos**) a young man paid to be the companion or lover of an older woman.

gild verb **1** cover thinly with gold. **2** (**gilded**) wealthy and privileged.
■ **gilding** noun.

gilet /zhi-lay/ noun a light sleeveless padded jacket.

gill[1] /gil/ noun **1** the breathing organ in fish and some amphibians. **2** the plates on the underside of mushrooms and many toadstools.

gill[2] /jil/ noun a unit for measuring liquids, equal to a quarter of a pint.

gillie /gil-li/ noun (in Scotland) a man or boy who helps someone who is on a shooting or fishing trip.

gilt adjective covered thinly with gold. •noun a thin layer of gold on a surface.
□ **gilt-edged** (of investments) safe and reliable.

gimlet /gim-lit/ noun a T-shaped tool with a screw-tip for boring holes.

gimmick noun a trick or device intended to attract attention rather than fulfil a useful purpose.
■ **gimmicky** adjective.

gin[1] noun a strong, clear alcoholic drink flavoured with juniper berries.

gin[2] noun **1** a machine for separating cotton from its seeds. **2** a trap for catching small wild animals or birds.

ginger noun **1** a hot spice made from the stem of an Asian plant. **2** a light reddish-yellow colour.
□ **ginger ale** (or **ginger beer**) a fizzy drink flavoured with ginger.

gingerbread noun cake made with treacle

and flavoured with ginger.

gingerly adverb in a careful or cautious way.

gingham /ging-uhm/ noun lightweight cotton cloth, typically checked.

gingivitis /jin-ji-vy-tiss/ noun inflammation of the gums.

ginormous adjective Brit. informal very large.

ginseng /jin-seng/ noun the root of an east Asian and North American plant, used in some medicines.

Gipsy ⇨ **Gypsy**.

giraffe noun (plural **giraffe** or **giraffes**) a large African animal with a very long neck and forelegs.

gird verb (**girds, girding, girded**; past participle **girded** or **girt**) literary encircle with a belt or band.
□ **gird your loins** get ready to do something.

girder noun a large metal beam.

girdle noun **1** a belt or cord worn round the waist. **2** a corset encircling the body from waist to thigh. •verb (**girdles, girdling, girdled**) encircle with a girdle or belt.

girl noun **1** a female child. **2** a young woman.
■ **girlish** adjective.

girlfriend noun **1** a person's regular female romantic or sexual partner. **2** a woman's female friend.

giro noun (plural **giros**) **1** a system in which money is transferred electronically from one bank or post office account to another. **2** a cheque or payment by giro.

girt past participle of **GIRD**.

girth noun **1** the measurement around the middle of something. **2** a strap attached to a saddle and fastened round a horse's belly.

gist /jist/ noun the main or general meaning of a speech or piece of writing.

give verb (**gives, giving, gave**; past participle

THESAURUS

immense, monumental, mountainous, gargantuan; informal mega, monster, whopping, humongous; Brit. informal ginormous.
OPPOSITES tiny.

giggle verb & noun titter, snigger, chuckle, chortle, laugh.

girl noun young woman, young lady, miss; Scottish & N. English lass, lassie; Irish colleen; informal chick; Brit. informal bird; N. Amer. informal gal, broad, dame, babe; Austral./NZ informal sheila.

girlfriend noun sweetheart, lover, partner, significant other, girl, woman; informal steady; Brit. informal bird; N. Amer. informal squeeze.

give verb **1** he gave them £2,000: donate,

contribute, present with, award, grant, bestow, hand (over). **2** can I give him a message? convey, pass on, impart, communicate, transmit, send, deliver, relay. **3** he gave his life for them: sacrifice, give up, relinquish, devote, dedicate. **4** he gave a party: organize, arrange, lay on, throw, host, hold, have. **5** Dominic gave a bow: perform, execute, make, do. **6** she gave a shout: utter, let out, emit, produce, make.
OPPOSITES receive, take.
□ **give someone away** betray, inform on; informal split on, rat on; Brit. informal grass on, shop; N. Amer. informal finger; Austral./NZ informal dob in. **give in/up** capitulate, concede defeat, admit defeat, give up, surrender, yield, submit. **give something off** emit,

given) 1 make someone have, get, or experience something. 2 carry out an action or make a sound. 3 show: *he gave no sign of life.* 4 state information. 5 (**give something off** or **out**) send out a smell, heat, etc. 6 bend under pressure. • noun the ability of something to bend under pressure.
□ **give something away** reveal something secret. **give in** stop opposing something. **give out** stop operating. **give rise to** make happen. **give up** stop making an effort and accept that you have failed. **give something up** stop doing, eating, or drinking something regularly.

given past participle of GIVE. • adjective 1 already named or stated. 2 (**given to**) inclined to. • preposition taking into account.
□ **given name** a person's first name.

gizmo noun (plural **gizmos**) informal a gadget.

gizzard noun a muscular part of a bird's stomach for grinding food.

glacé /**gla**-say/ adjective (of fruit) preserved in sugar.

glacial /**glay**-sh'l, **glay**-si-uhl/ adjective 1 relating to ice and glaciers. 2 very cold.

glaciation noun the formation of glaciers.

glacier /**glass**-i-er, **glay**-si-er/ noun a slowly moving mass of ice formed by the accumulation of snow on mountains.

glad adjective (**gladder**, **gladdest**) 1 pleased; delighted. 2 (often **glad of**) grateful. 3 giving pleasure.
□ **glad rags** informal clothes for a party or special occasion.
■ **gladly** adverb.

gladden verb make glad.

glade noun an open space in a forest.

gladiator noun (in ancient Rome) a man trained to fight other men or animals in a public arena.
■ **gladiatorial** adjective.

gladiolus noun (plural **gladioli** /glad-i-**oh**-ly/) a plant with tall stems and brightly coloured flowers.

glamorize or **glamorise** verb (**glamorizes, glamorizing, glamorized**) often disapproving make something seem attractive or desirable.

glamorous adjective excitingly attractive.
■ **glamorously** adverb.

☑ **glamorous** drops the *u* of **glamour**: glam*o*rous.

glamour (US spelling **glamor**) noun an attractive and exciting quality.

glance verb (**glances, glancing, glanced**) 1 look briefly. 2 (**glance off**) hit something at an angle and bounce off. • noun a brief or hurried look.
■ **glancing** adjective.

gland noun an organ of the body which produces a particular chemical substance.

glandular adjective relating to a gland or glands.
□ **glandular fever** Brit. an infectious disease which causes swelling of the lymph glands and a persistent lack of energy.

glare verb (**glares, glaring, glared**) 1 stare in an angry way. 2 shine with a dazzling light. 3 (**glaring**) very obvious. • noun 1 a fierce or angry stare. 2 strong and dazzling light.

glasnost /**glaz**-nosst/ noun (in the former

g

THESAURUS

produce, send out, throw out, discharge, release. **give something up stop**, cease, discontinue, desist from, abstain from, cut out, renounce, forgo; informal quit; Brit. informal jack in.

glad adjective 1 *I'm really glad you're coming:* pleased, happy, delighted, thrilled; informal over the moon; Brit. informal chuffed; N. English informal made up. 2 *I'd be glad to help:* willing, eager, happy, pleased, delighted, ready, prepared.
OPPOSITES dismayed, reluctant.

gladly adverb with pleasure, happily, cheerfully, willingly, readily, eagerly, freely, ungrudgingly.

glamorous adjective 1 *a glamorous woman:* beautiful, elegant, chic, stylish, fashionable. 2 *a glamorous lifestyle:* exciting, glittering, glossy, colourful, exotic; informal glitzy, jet-setting.
OPPOSITES dowdy, dull.

glamour noun 1 *she had undeniable glamour:* beauty, allure, elegance, chic, style, charisma, charm, magnetism. 2 *the*

glamour of TV: allure, attraction, fascination, charm, magic, romance, excitement, thrill; informal glitz, glam.

glance verb 1 *Rachel glanced at him:* look briefly, look quickly, peek, peep. 2 *I glanced through the report:* read quickly, scan, skim, leaf, flick, flip, thumb, browse.
OPPOSITES study.
• noun *a glance at his watch:* peek, peep, brief look, quick look.

glare verb *she glared at him:* scowl, glower, look daggers, frown, lour; informal give someone a dirty look.
• noun 1 *a cold glare:* scowl, glower, angry stare, frown, black look; informal dirty look. 2 *the glare of the lights:* blaze, dazzle, shine, beam, brilliance.

glaring adjective 1 *glaring lights:* dazzling, blinding, blazing, strong, harsh. 2 *a glaring omission:* obvious, conspicuous, unmistakable, inescapable, unmissable, striking, flagrant, blatant.
OPPOSITES soft, inconspicuous.

Soviet Union) the policy of more open government.

glass noun **1** a hard transparent substance made by fusing sand with soda and lime. **2** a drinking container made of glass. **3** a mirror.
□ **glass-blowing** the craft of making glass objects by blowing semi-liquid glass through a long tube.
■ **glassy** adjective.

glasses plural noun a pair of lenses set in a frame that rests on the nose and ears, used to correct eyesight.

glasshouse noun Brit. a greenhouse.

glaucoma /glaw-**koh**-muh/ noun a condition of increased pressure within the eyeball, causing gradual loss of sight.

glaze verb (**glazes, glazing, glazed**) **1** fit panes of glass into a window frame or similar structure. **2** enclose or cover with glass. **3** cover with a glaze. **4** (**glaze over**) (of a person's eyes) lose brightness and liveliness. ●noun **1** a glass-like substance fused on to the surface of pottery to form a hard coating. **2** a liquid such as milk or beaten egg, used to form a shiny coating on food.

glazier /**glay**-zi-er/ noun a person who fits glass into windows and doors.

gleam verb shine brightly, especially with reflected light. ●noun **1** a faint or brief light. **2** a brief or faint show of a quality or emotion: *a gleam of hope.*

glean verb **1** collect information from various sources. **2** gather leftover grain after a harvest.

glee noun great delight.

gleeful adjective very happy, usually in a smug or gloating way.
■ **gleefully** adverb.

glen noun Scottish & Irish a narrow valley.

glib adjective using words easily but without much thought or sincerity.
■ **glibly** adverb.

glide verb (**glides, gliding, glided**) **1** move

with a smooth, quiet, continuous motion. **2** fly without power or in a glider. ●noun an instance of gliding.

glider noun a light aircraft that flies without an engine.

glimmer verb (**glimmers, glimmering, glimmered**) shine faintly with a wavering light. ●noun **1** a faint or wavering light. **2** a faint sign of a feeling or quality.

glimpse noun a brief look at something.
●verb (**glimpses, glimpsing, glimpsed**) see something briefly or partially.

glint verb give off small flashes of light.
●noun a sudden flash of light.

glisten verb (of something wet) shine or sparkle.

glitch noun informal a sudden problem or fault.

glitter verb **1** shine with a shimmering reflected light. **2** (**glittering**) impressively successful or glamorous. ●noun
1 shimmering reflected light. **2** tiny pieces of sparkling material used for decoration. **3** an attractive but superficial quality.
■ **glittery** adjective.

glitz noun superficial glamour.
■ **glitzy** adjective.

gloaming noun (**the gloaming**) literary twilight; dusk.

gloat verb be smug or pleased about your own success or another person's failure.

global adjective **1** relating to the whole world; worldwide. **2** relating to all the parts of something.
□ **global warming** a gradual increase in the temperature of the earth's atmosphere due to the increase of gases such as carbon dioxide.
■ **globally** adverb.

globalization or **globalisation** noun the process by which businesses start to operate on a global scale.
■ **globalize** verb.

globe noun **1** a spherical or rounded object.

THESAURUS

glaze verb *pastry glazed with caramel:* cover, coat, varnish, lacquer.
●noun *a cake with an apricot glaze:* coating, topping, varnish, lacquer, polish.

gleam verb *a light gleamed:* shine, glint, glitter, shimmer, glimmer, sparkle, twinkle, flicker, wink, glisten, flash.
●noun *a gleam of light:* flash, glimmer, glint, shimmer, twinkle, sparkle, flicker, beam, ray, shaft.

glide verb **1** *a gondola glided past:* slide, slip, sail, float, drift, flow. **2** *seagulls gliding over the waves:* soar, wheel, plane, fly.

glimpse noun *a glimpse of her face:* brief/quick look, glance, sight, sighting,

peek, peep.
●verb *he glimpsed a figure:* catch sight of, sight, spot, notice, discern, spy, pick out, make out.

glitter verb *crystal glittered in the candlelight:* sparkle, twinkle, glint, shimmer, glimmer, wink, flash, shine.
●noun *the glitter of light on the water:* sparkle, twinkle, glint, shimmer, glimmer, flicker, flash.

global adjective **1** *the global economy:* worldwide, international, world, intercontinental, universal. **2** *a global view of the problem:* comprehensive, overall, general, all-inclusive, all-encompassing,

2 (the globe) the earth. **3** a model of the earth with a map on its surface.

globetrotter noun informal a person who travels widely.

■ **globetrotting** noun & adjective.

globular adjective **1** shaped like a globe; spherical. **2** consisting of globules.

globule noun a small drop or ball of a substance.

globulin noun any of a group of simple proteins found in blood.

glockenspiel /glok-uhn-speel, glok-uhn-shpeel/ noun a musical instrument made of metal bars that you hit with small hammers.

gloom noun **1** darkness. **2** a feeling of sadness and hopelessness.

gloomy adjective (**gloomier, gloomiest**) **1** dark or badly lit. **2** sad or depressed.

■ **gloomily** adverb **gloominess** noun.

glorify verb (**glorifies, glorifying, glorified**) **1** represent something as admirable. **2** (**glorified**) made to appear more important than in reality. **3** praise and worship God.

glorious adjective **1** having or bringing glory. **2** very beautiful or impressive.

■ **gloriously** adverb.

glory noun (plural **glories**) **1** fame and honour. **2** magnificence; great beauty. **3** a very beautiful or impressive thing. **4** worship and praise of God. • verb (**glories, glorying, gloried**) (**glory in**) take great

pride or pleasure in.

gloss[1] noun **1** the shine on a smooth surface. **2** a type of paint which dries to a bright shiny surface. **3** an attractive appearance that hides something ordinary or less attractive. • verb **1** give a glossy appearance to. **2** (**gloss over**) give only brief or misleading details about something.

gloss[2] noun a translation or explanation of a word, phrase, or passage. • verb provide a gloss for.

glossary noun (plural **glossaries**) a list of words and their meanings.

glossy adjective (**glossier, glossiest**) **1** shiny and smooth. **2** appearing attractive and stylish.

glottal adjective having to do with the glottis.

□ **glottal stop** a speech sound made by opening and closing the glottis, sometimes used instead of a properly sounded *t*.

glottis noun the part of the larynx made up of the vocal cords and the narrow opening between them.

glove noun **1** a covering for the hand having separate parts for each finger. **2** a padded covering for the hand used in boxing and other sports.

□ **glove compartment** a small storage compartment in the dashboard of a car.

glow verb **1** give out a steady light. **2** have flushed skin, especially after exercising.

g

---

universal, broad.

gloom noun **1** *she peered into the gloom:* darkness, dark, murk, shadows, shade. **2** *his gloom deepened:* despondency, depression, dejection, melancholy, unhappiness, sadness, misery, woe, despair. OPPOSITES light, happiness.

gloomy adjective **1** *a gloomy room:* dark, shadowy, murky, sunless, dim, dingy. **2** *Joanna looked gloomy:* despondent, depressed, downcast, downhearted, dejected, dispirited, disheartened, demoralized, crestfallen, glum, melancholy; informal down in the mouth, down in the dumps. **3** *gloomy forecasts about the economy:* pessimistic, depressing, downbeat, disheartening, disappointing, unfavourable, bleak, black. OPPOSITES bright, cheerful, optimistic.

glorious adjective wonderful, marvellous, magnificent, superb, sublime, spectacular, lovely, fine, delightful; informal stunning, fantastic, terrific, tremendous, sensational, heavenly, divine, gorgeous, fabulous, awesome. OPPOSITES undistinguished.

glory noun **1** *a sport that won him glory:*

honour, distinction, prestige, fame, renown, kudos, eminence, acclaim, praise, celebrity, recognition. **2** *a house restored to its former glory:* magnificence, splendour, grandeur, majesty, greatness, nobility, opulence, beauty, elegance. OPPOSITES shame, obscurity, modesty. • verb *we gloried in our independence:* delight, triumph, revel, rejoice, exult, relish, savour, be proud of; informal get a kick out of.

gloss noun *the gloss of her hair:* shine, sheen, lustre, gleam, patina, polish, brilliance, shimmer. □ **gloss over conceal**, cover up, hide, disguise, mask, veil, play down, minimize, understate.

glossy adjective shiny, gleaming, lustrous, brilliant, glistening, glassy, polished, lacquered, glazed. OPPOSITES dull.

glow verb **1** *lights glowed in the windows:* shine, gleam, glimmer, flicker, flare. **2** *a fire glowed in the hearth:* smoulder, burn. • noun *the glow of the fire:* radiance, light, gleam, glimmer.

3 look very happy. •**noun** a steady light or heat.

▫ **glow-worm** a kind of beetle which gives out light.

glower /glow-er/ **verb** have an angry or sullen expression. •**noun** an angry or sullen look.

glowing adjective expressing great praise: *a glowing report.*

glucose /gloo-kohz/ **noun** a type of sugar that is easily changed into energy by the body.

glue noun a sticky substance used for joining things together. •**verb** (**glues, gluing** or **glueing, glued**) **1** join something with glue. **2** (**be glued to**) informal be paying very close attention to.

glum adjective sad or miserable.
■ **glumly** adverb.

glut noun more of something than is needed. •**verb** (**gluts, glutting, glutted**) supply or provide with too much of something.

gluten noun a substance containing protein, found in wheat and other cereal plants.

glutinous adjective like glue in texture; sticky.

glutton noun **1** a very greedy eater. **2** a person who is very eager for something difficult or challenging: *a glutton for punishment.*

gluttony noun the habit of eating too

much.

glycerine (US spelling **glycerin**) noun a liquid made from fats and oils, used in medicines and cosmetics.

GM abbreviation genetically modified.

gm abbreviation grams.

GMO abbreviation genetically modified organism.

GMT abbreviation Greenwich Mean Time.

gnarled /narld/ adjective knobbly or twisted.

gnash /nash/ verb grind your teeth together, especially as a sign of anger.

gnat /nat/ noun a small two-winged fly.

gnaw /naw/ verb **1** bite at or nibble something persistently. **2** cause persistent anxiety or pain.

gnome /nohm/ noun (in stories) a creature like a tiny man, who lives underground and guards treasure.

gnomic /noh-mik/ adjective clever but hard to understand.

Gnosticism /noss-ti-si-z'm/ noun a former religious movement teaching that the soul is saved through mystical knowledge.
■ **Gnostic** adjective.

GNP abbreviation gross national product.

gnu /noo/ noun a large African antelope with a long head and a mane.

GNVQ abbreviation General National Vocational Qualification.

go verb (**goes, going, went;** past participle **gone**)

THESAURUS

glowing adjective **1** *glowing coals:* bright, radiant, incandescent, luminous, smouldering. **2** *his glowing cheeks:* rosy, pink, red, ruddy, flushed, blushing, burning. **3** *glowing colours:* vivid, vibrant, bright, brilliant, rich, intense, radiant. **4** *a glowing report:* complimentary, favourable, enthusiastic, admiring, rapturous, fulsome; informal rave.
OPPOSITES dead, pale, drab, damning.

glue noun *a tube of glue:* adhesive, gum, paste, cement; N. Amer. mucilage; N. Amer. informal stickum.
•**verb** *the planks were glued together:* stick, gum, paste, fix, seal, cement.

glum adjective gloomy, downcast, dejected, despondent, effort, bid; informal shot, stab, crestfallen, disheartened, depressed, doleful, miserable, woebegone; informal fed up, down in the dumps.
OPPOSITES cheerful.

go verb **1** *he's gone into town:* travel, move, proceed, make your way, journey, advance, progress, pass. **2** *the road goes to London:* lead, stretch, reach, extend. **3** *it's time to go:* leave, depart, take yourself off, go away, withdraw, absent yourself, exit, set off, start out, get under way, be on your way; Brit. make a move; informal make tracks. **4** *all our money had gone:* be used up, be

spent, be exhausted, be consumed. **5** *his hair had gone grey:* become, get, turn, grow. **6** *everything went well:* turn out, work out, develop, progress, result, end (up); informal pan out. **7** *those colours don't go:* match, harmonize, blend, be complementary, coordinate, be compatible. **8** *my car won't go:* function, work, run, operate.
OPPOSITES arrive, come, return, clash, malfunction.
•**noun** (informal) **1** *here, have a go:* try, attempt, effort, bid; informal shot, stab, crack. **2** *whose go is it?:* turn, opportunity, chance, stint, spell, time.
▫ **go down 1** *the ship went down:* sink, founder. **2** *interest rates are going down:* decrease, get lower, fall, drop, decline, plummet, plunge, slump. **go in for take part in**, participate in, engage in, get involved in, join in, enter into, undertake, practise, pursue, espouse, adopt, embrace. **go into investigate**, examine, enquire into, look into, research, probe, explore, delve into, consider, review, analyse. **go off 1** *the bomb went off:* explode, detonate, blow up. **2** (Brit.) *the milk's gone off:* go bad, go stale, go sour, turn, spoil, go rancid. **go on 1** *the lecture went on for hours:* last, continue,

1 move to or from a place. **2** pass into or be in a particular state. **3** lie or extend in a certain direction. **4** come to an end. **5** disappear or be used up. **6** (of time) pass. **7** take part in a particular activity. **8** have a particular outcome. **9** (**be going to be** or **do**) used to express a future tense. **10** function or operate. **11** be harmonious or matching. **12** be acceptable or allowed. **13** fit into or be regularly kept in a particular place. **14** make a particular sound. •**noun** (plural **goes**) informal **1** an attempt. **2** a turn to do or use something. **3** spirit or energy.
□ **the go-ahead** informal permission to proceed. **go along with** agree to. **go back on** fail to keep a promise. **go-between** a person who acts as a messenger or negotiator. **go-cart** (or **go-kart**) a small racing car with a lightweight body. **go for 1** decide on. **2** try to gain. **3** attack. **go in for 1** enter a contest. **2** like or habitually take part in. **go into 1** investigate or enquire into. **2** (of a whole number) be capable of dividing another. **go off 1** (of a gun or bomb) explode or fire. **2** Brit. (of food) begin to decompose. **3** Brit. informal begin to dislike. **go on** continue. **go out 1** stop shining or burning. **2** have a regular romantic relationship with someone. **go over** examine or check the details of. **go through 1** undergo a difficult experience. **2** examine carefully. **go without** suffer lack or hardship. **have a go at** attack or criticize.
■ **goer** noun.

goad verb keep annoying or criticizing someone until they react. •noun **1** a thing that makes someone do something. **2** a spiked stick used for driving cattle.

goal noun **1** (in soccer, rugby, etc.) a wooden frame into or over which the ball has to be sent to score. **2** an instance of sending the ball into or over a goal. **3** an aim or desired result.
■ **goalless** adjective.

goalkeeper noun (in soccer, hockey, etc.) a player whose role is to stop the ball from

entering the goal.

goalpost noun either of the two upright posts of a goal.

goat noun an animal with horns and a hairy coat, often kept for milk.

goatee noun a small pointed beard like that of a goat.

goatherd noun a person who looks after goats.

gob noun Brit. informal a person's mouth.

gobbet noun a piece of flesh, food, or other matter.

gobble verb (**gobbles, gobbling, gobbled**) **1** eat hurriedly and noisily. **2** (of a turkey) make a swallowing sound in the throat.

gobbledegook or **gobbledygook** noun informal complicated language that is difficult to understand.

goblet noun a drinking glass with a foot and a stem.

goblin noun (in stories) a small, ugly, mischievous creature.

gobsmacked adjective Brit. informal utterly astonished.

gobstopper noun a hard round sweet.

goby /goh-bi/ noun (plural **gobies**) a small sea fish.

God noun **1** (in Christianity and some other religions) the creator and supreme ruler of the universe. **2** (**god**) a superhuman being or spirit.
□ **God-fearing** earnestly religious.

godchild noun (plural **godchildren**) a person in relation to a godparent.

god-daughter noun a female godchild.

goddess noun a female deity.

godfather noun **1** a male godparent. **2** the male leader of an illegal organization.

godforsaken adjective (of a place) remote, unattractive, or depressing.

godhead noun **1** (**the Godhead**) God. **2** divine nature.

godless adjective **1** not believing in God or a god. **2** wicked.

godly adjective very religious.

g

THESAURUS

carry on, run on, proceed, endure, persist, take. **2** *she went on about the sea:* **talk at length,** ramble, rattle on, chatter, prattle; Brit. informal witter, rabbit. **3** *I'm not sure what went on:* **happen,** take place, occur, transpire; N. Amer. informal go down. **go out 1** *the lights went out:* **be turned off,** be extinguished, stop burning. **2** *he's going out with Kate:* **see,** take out, be someone's boyfriend/girlfriend, be in a relationship with; informal date, go with. **go over.** See **GO THROUGH** 3. **go through 1** *the terrible things she has gone through:* **undergo,** experience,

face, suffer, live through, endure. **2** *he went through Susie's bag:* **search,** look, hunt, rummage, rifle. **3** *I went through the report:* **examine,** study, scrutinize, inspect, look over, scan, check.

goal noun objective, aim, end, target, intention, plan, purpose, ambition, aspiration.

gobble verb guzzle, bolt, gulp, devour, wolf; informal tuck into, put away, demolish; Brit. informal scoff; N. Amer. informal scarf (down/up).

god noun deity, goddess, divine being, divinity, immortal.

godmother noun a female godparent.

godparent noun a person who promises to be responsible for a child's religious education.

godsend noun something that is very helpful or welcome.

godson noun a male godchild.

goes 3rd person singular present of **GO**.

goggle verb (goggles, goggling, goggled) 1 look with wide open eyes. 2 (of the eyes) stick out or open wide. • noun (goggles) close-fitting protective glasses.

going noun 1 the condition of the ground in terms of its suitability for horse racing or walking. 2 conditions for an activity: *the going gets tough.* • adjective 1 existing or available. 2 (of a price) normal or current. □ going concern a thriving business. goings-on informal activities that are strange or dishonest.

goitre /**goy**-ter/ noun a swelling of the neck which is caused by enlargement of the thyroid gland.

gold noun 1 a yellow precious metal. 2 a deep yellow or yellow-brown colour. 3 things made of gold. □ gold leaf gold beaten into a very thin sheet. gold medal a medal awarded for first place in a race or competition. gold rush a rapid movement of people to a place where gold has been discovered.

goldcrest noun a very small bird with a yellow or orange crest.

golden adjective 1 made of or resembling gold. 2 (of a period) very happy and prosperous. 3 excellent. □ golden age the period when something is very successful. golden eagle a large eagle with yellow-tipped head feathers. golden handshake informal a payment given to someone who is made redundant or retires early. golden jubilee the fiftieth anniversary of an important event. golden rule a principle which should always be followed. golden wedding Brit. the fiftieth anniversary of a wedding.

goldfinch noun a brightly coloured finch with a yellow patch on each wing.

goldfish noun (plural **goldfish** or **goldfishes**) a small orange carp, often kept in ponds.

goldsmith noun a person who makes things out of gold.

golf noun a game played on an outdoor course, the aim of which is to hit a small ball into a series of small holes using a set of special clubs. ■ golfer noun.

golliwog noun a soft doll with a black face and fuzzy hair.

gonad /**goh**-nad/ noun an organ in the body that produces gametes; a testis or ovary.

gondola /**gon**-duh-luh/ noun a light flat-bottomed boat used on canals in Venice, worked by one oar at the stern.

gondolier /gon-duh-**leer**/ noun a person who propels a gondola.

gone past participle of **GO**. • adjective no longer present or in existence. • preposition Brit. 1 (of time) past. 2 (of age) older than.

goner /**gon**-er/ noun informal a person or thing that cannot be saved.

gong noun 1 a metal disc that makes a deep ringing sound when struck. 2 Brit. informal a medal or other award.

gonorrhoea /gon-uh-**ree**-uh/ (US spelling **gonorrhea**) noun a disease caused by bacteria that are passed on during sex.

goo noun informal a soft, sticky substance.

good adjective 1 having the right qualities;

THESAURUS

golden adjective blonde, yellow, fair, flaxen. OPPOSITES dark.

gone adjective 1 *I wasn't gone long:* away, absent, off, out, missing. 2 *those days are gone:* past, over (and done with), no more, done, finished, ended, forgotten. 3 *the milk's all gone:* used up, consumed, finished, spent, depleted. OPPOSITES present, here.

good adjective 1 *a good product:* fine, superior, excellent, superb, outstanding, magnificent, exceptional, marvellous, wonderful, first-rate, first-class, quality; informal great, ace, terrific, fantastic, fabulous, class, awesome, wicked; Brit. informal brilliant. 2 *a good person:* virtuous, righteous, upright, upstanding, moral, ethical, principled, law-abiding, blameless, honourable, decent, respectable, trustworthy; informal squeaky clean. 3 *the*

children are good at school: well behaved, obedient, dutiful, polite, courteous, respectful. 4 *a good driver:* capable, able, proficient, adept, adroit, accomplished, skilful, talented, masterly, expert; informal mean, wicked, nifty; N. Amer. informal crackerjack. 5 *a good friend:* close, intimate, dear, bosom, special, best, firm, loyal. 6 *we had a good time:* enjoyable, pleasant, agreeable, pleasurable, delightful, lovely, amusing. 7 *it was good of you to come:* kind, generous, charitable, gracious, noble, altruistic, unselfish. 8 *a good time to call:* convenient, suitable, appropriate, fitting, fit, opportune, timely, favourable. 9 *milk is good for you:* wholesome, healthy, nourishing, nutritious, beneficial. 10 *good food:* tasty, appetizing, flavoursome, palatable, succulent; informal scrumptious, scrummy, yummy; Brit. informal moreish; N. Amer. informal finger-licking. 11 *a good* of a high standard. **2** behaving in a way that is right, polite, or obedient. **3** enjoyable or satisfying. **4** suitable or appropriate. **5** (**good for**) having a useful or helpful effect on. **6** thorough. •**noun** (**goods**) **1** products or possessions. **2** Brit. freight.

□ **as good as** very nearly. **for good** forever. **good faith** honest or sincere intentions. **good-for-nothing** worthless. **Good Friday** the Friday before Easter Sunday, on which Christians commemorate the Crucifixion of Jesus. **good-looking** attractive. **good-natured** kind and unselfish. **make something good 1** compensate for loss or damage. **2** fulfil a promise or claim.
■ **goodness** noun.

goodbye exclamation used to express good wishes when parting or ending a conversation. •**noun** (plural **goodbyes**) a parting.

goodly adjective (**goodlier, goodliest**) quite large in size or quantity.

goodnight exclamation used to express good wishes when parting at night or before going to bed.

goodwill noun friendly or helpful feelings towards other people.

goody or **goodie** noun (plural **goodies**) informal **1** Brit. a good person, especially a hero in a story or film. **2** (**goodies**) tasty things to eat.

□ **goody-goody** informal a person who behaves well in order to impress other people.

gooey adjective informal soft and sticky.

goof informal, chiefly N. Amer. **verb 1** make a mistake. **2** fool around. •**noun** a mistake.

goofy adjective informal **1** chiefly N. Amer. silly. **2** having front teeth that stick out.

goon noun informal **1** a silly person. **2** N. Amer. a thug.

goose noun (plural **geese**) **1** a large waterbird with a long neck and webbed feet. **2** a female goose. **3** informal a silly person.

□ **goose pimples** little raised bumps on your skin, caused by feeling cold or frightened. **goose step** a way of marching in which the legs are kept straight.

gooseberry noun (plural **gooseberries**) **1** an edible yellowish-green berry with a hairy skin. **2** Brit. informal a third person in the company of two lovers.

gopher /goh-fer/ noun a burrowing rodent found in North America.

gore[1] noun blood that has been shed.

gore[2] verb (**gores, goring, gored**) (of an animal such as a bull) pierce with a horn or tusk.

gore[3] noun a triangular piece of material used in making a garment, sail, or umbrella.

gorge noun a narrow valley or ravine. •**verb** (**gorges, gorging, gorged**) eat a large amount greedily.

gorgeous adjective **1** beautiful. **2** informal

g

THESAURUS

reason: **valid,** genuine, authentic, legitimate, sound, bona fide, convincing, compelling. **12** *good weather:* fine, fair, dry, bright, clear, sunny, cloudless, calm, warm, mild.
OPPOSITES bad, wicked, naughty, mean, inconvenient.
•**noun 1** *issues of good and evil:* virtue, righteousness, goodness, morality, integrity, honesty, truth, honour. **2** *it's for your own good:* benefit, advantage, profit, gain, interest, welfare, well-being.
OPPOSITES wickedness, disadvantage.
□ **for good forever,** permanently, for always, (for) evermore, for ever and ever; N. Amer. forevermore; informal for keeps.

goodbye exclamation farewell, adieu, au revoir, ciao, adios; Austral./NZ hooray; informal bye, bye-bye, so long, see you (later); Brit. informal cheerio, cheers, ta-ta.

goodness noun **1** *he had some goodness in him:* virtue, good, righteousness, morality, integrity, rectitude, honesty, honour, decency, respectability, nobility, worth, merit. **2** *his goodness towards us:* kindness, humanity, benevolence, tenderness, warmth, affection, love, goodwill, sympathy, compassion, care, concern,

understanding, generosity, charity.

goods plural noun merchandise, wares, stock, commodities, produce, products, articles.

goodwill noun kindness, compassion, goodness, benevolence, consideration, charity, decency, neighbourliness.
OPPOSITES hostility.

gorge noun ravine, canyon, gully, defile, couloir, chasm, gulf; S. English chine; N. English gill; N. Amer. gulch, coulee.
□ **gorge yourself stuff yourself,** guzzle, overindulge; informal pig yourself, pig out, stuff your face.

gorgeous adjective **1** *a gorgeous girl:* good-looking, attractive, beautiful, pretty, handsome, lovely, stunning; Scottish & N. English bonny; informal fanciable, tasty, hot; Brit. informal fit; N. Amer. informal cute, foxy; old use comely. **2** *a gorgeous view:* spectacular, splendid, superb, wonderful, grand, impressive, awe-inspiring, awesome, stunning, breathtaking; informal sensational, fabulous, fantastic. **3** *gorgeous uniforms of scarlet and gold:* resplendent, magnificent, sumptuous, luxurious, elegant, dazzling, brilliant.
OPPOSITES ugly, dreary, drab.

very pleasant.

gorgon /gor-guhn/ noun Greek Mythology each of three sisters with snakes for hair, who had the power to turn anyone who looked at them to stone.

gorilla noun a powerfully built ape of central Africa.

gormless adjective Brit. informal stupid.

gorse noun a yellow-flowered shrub with spiny leaves.

gory adjective 1 involving violence and bloodshed. 2 covered in blood.

goshawk /goss-hawk/ noun a large hawk with short wings.

gosling noun a young goose.

gospel noun 1 the teachings of Jesus. 2 (the Gospel) the record of Jesus's life and teaching in the first four books of the New Testament. 3 (Gospel) each of these books. 4 (also gospel truth) something absolutely true. 5 (also gospel music) a style of black American religious singing.

gossamer noun a fine substance consisting of cobwebs spun by small spiders. • adjective very fine and flimsy.

gossip noun 1 casual conversation about other people. 2 disapproving a person who likes talking about other people. • verb (gossips, gossiping, gossiped) talk about other people.

got past and past participle of GET.

Gothic adjective 1 of the style of architecture common in western Europe in the 12th to 16th centuries. 2 very gloomy or horrifying.

gotten N. Amer. or old use past participle of GET.

gouache /goo-ash/ noun 1 a method of painting using watercolours thickened with glue. 2 paint used in this method.

gouge /gowj, gooj/ verb (gouges, gouging, gouged) 1 make a rough hole in a surface. 2 (gouge something out) cut something

out roughly. • noun 1 a chisel with a concave blade. 2 a hole or groove made by gouging.

goulash /goo-lash/ noun a rich Hungarian stew of meat and vegetables.

gourd /goord/ noun a fruit with a hard skin, usually used as a container rather than as food.

gourmand /goor-muhnd/ noun a person who enjoys eating.

gourmet /goor-may/ noun a person who knows a lot about good food. • adjective suitable for a gourmet.

gout noun a disease causing the joints to swell and become painful.

govern verb 1 control the laws and affairs of a state, organization, or community. 2 control or influence.

governance noun the action or style of governing.

governess noun a woman employed to teach the children of a family in their home.

government noun 1 the group of people who govern a state. 2 the system by which a state, organization, or community is governed.
■ governmental adjective.

> ☑ remember that **government** is spelled with an n before the m.

governor noun 1 an official appointed to govern a town or region. 2 the head of a public institution. 3 a member of a governing body.

gown noun 1 a long dress worn on formal occasions. 2 a protective garment worn in hospital by surgeons or patients. 3 a loose cloak showing your profession or status, worn by a lawyer, academic, or university student.

GP abbreviation general practitioner.

THESAURUS

gossip noun 1 *tell me all the gossip:* news, rumours, scandal, hearsay; informal dirt, buzz; Brit. informal goss; N. Amer. informal scuttlebutt. 2 *they went for a gossip:* chat, talk, conversation, chatter, heart-to-heart, tête-à-tête; informal jaw, gas; Brit. informal natter, chinwag; N. Amer. informal gabfest; Austral./NZ informal yarn. 3 *she's such a gossip:* gossip-monger, busybody, scandalmonger, rumour-monger, muckraker.
• verb 1 *she gossiped about his wife:* talk, whisper, tell tales; informal dish the dirt. 2 *people sat around gossiping:* chat, talk, converse, discuss things; informal gas, chew the fat, jaw; Brit. informal natter, chinwag; N. Amer. informal shoot the breeze.

gourmet noun gastronome, epicure, epicurean, connoisseur; informal foodie.

govern verb 1 *he governs the province:* rule, preside over, control, be in charge of, command, run, head, manage, oversee, supervise. 2 *the rules governing social behaviour:* determine, decide, control, constrain, regulate, direct, rule, dictate, shape, affect.

government noun administration, executive, regime, authority, council, powers that be, cabinet, ministry.

governor noun leader, ruler, chief, head, administrator, principal, director, chairman, chairwoman, chair, superintendent, commissioner, controller; informal boss.

gown noun dress, frock, robe, habit, costume.

gr. abbreviation **1** grains. **2** grams. **3** gross.

grab verb (**grabs, grabbing, grabbed**) **1** seize someone or something suddenly and roughly. **2** informal take the opportunity to get something. •noun a sudden attempt to seize someone or something.

grace noun **1** attractive smoothness of movement. **2** polite respect. **3** (**graces**) attractive qualities or behaviour. **4** (in Christian belief) the unearned favour of God. **5** the condition of being trusted and respected by someone. **6** a period officially allowed to do something: *three days' grace.* **7** a short prayer of thanks said at a meal. **8** (**His, Her,** or **Your Grace**) used as a way of addressing a duke, duchess, or archbishop. •verb (**graces, gracing, graced**) **1** bring honour to someone or something by your presence. **2** make something more attractive.
□ **grace note** Music an extra note which is not needed for the harmony or melody.

graceful adjective having or showing grace or elegance.
■ **gracefully** adverb.

graceless adjective without grace or charm.

gracious adjective **1** kind, pleasant, and polite. **2** showing the elegance associated with high social status or wealth. **3** (in Christian belief) showing divine grace.
■ **graciously** adverb.

gradation noun **1** a scale of gradual change from one thing to another. **2** a stage in such a scale.

grade noun **1** a level of rank or ability. **2** a mark indicating the quality of a student's work. **3** N. Amer. a class of school students grouped according to age or ability. •verb (**grades, grading, graded**) **1** arrange people or things in groups according to quality, ability, etc. **2** N. Amer. give a grade to a student or their work.
□ **make the grade** informal succeed.

gradient /gray-di-uhnt/ noun **1** a sloping part of a road or railway. **2** the degree to which something slopes.

gradual adjective **1** taking place in stages over a long period of time. **2** (of a slope) not steep.
■ **gradually** adverb.

graduate noun /grad-yuu-uht/ a person who has been awarded a university degree. •verb /grad-yoo-ayt/ (**graduates, graduating, graduated**) **1** successfully complete a degree or course. **2** (**graduate to**) move up to something more advanced. **3** change something gradually.
■ **graduation** noun.

graffiti /gruh-fee-ti/ noun writing or drawings on a wall in a public place.

☑ double *f*, single *t*: graffiti.

graft[1] noun **1** a shoot from one plant inserted into another to form a new growth. **2** a piece of body tissue that is transplanted from one part of the body to another part that has been damaged. •verb **1** insert or transplant as a graft. **2** add something to something else, especially in a way that seems inappropriate.

graft[2] Brit. informal noun hard work. •verb work hard.

THESAURUS

grab verb seize, grasp, snatch, take hold of, grip, clasp, clutch, catch.

grace noun **1** *the grace of a ballerina:* elegance, poise, finesse, polish, fluency, suppleness. **2** *he had the grace to apologize:* courtesy, decency, (good) manners, politeness, respect, tact. **3** *he fell from grace:* favour, approval, approbation, acceptance, esteem, regard, respect. OPPOSITES awkwardness, effrontery, disfavour.
•verb *a mosaic graced the floor:* adorn, embellish, decorate, ornament, enhance.

graceful adjective elegant, fluid, fluent, easy, polished, supple.

gracious adjective courteous, polite, civil, well mannered, tactful, diplomatic, kind, considerate, thoughtful, obliging, accommodating, hospitable. OPPOSITES ungracious.

grade noun **1** *hotels within the same grade:* category, class, classification, ranking, quality, grouping, group, bracket. **2** *his job is of the lowest grade:* rank, level, standing, position, class, status, order, echelon. **3** (N. Amer.) *the best grades in the school:* mark, score, assessment, evaluation, appraisal. **4** (N. Amer.) *the fifth grade:* year, form, class.
•verb *eggs are graded by size:* classify, class, categorize, bracket, sort, group, arrange, pigeonhole, rank, evaluate, rate, value.

gradient noun slope, incline, hill, rise, ramp, bank; N. Amer. grade.

gradual adjective **1** *a gradual transition:* slow, steady, measured, unhurried, cautious, piecemeal, step-by-step, bit-by-bit, progressive, continuous. **2** *a gradual slope:* gentle, moderate, slight, easy. OPPOSITES abrupt, steep.

gradually adverb slowly, steadily, slowly but surely, cautiously, gently, gingerly, piecemeal, bit by bit, by degrees, progressively, systematically. OPPOSITES abruptly.

graft noun *a skin graft:* transplant, implant.
•verb **1** *graft a bud on to the stem:* splice, join, insert, fix. **2** *tissue is grafted on to the cornea:* transplant, implant.

graft³ informal noun bribery and other illegal methods used to gain advantage in politics or business.

Grail noun (in medieval legend) the cup or dish used by Jesus at the Last Supper.

grain noun 1 wheat or another cereal plant grown for food. 2 a single seed or fruit of a cereal plant. 3 a small, hard particle of a substance such as sand. 4 the smallest unit of weight in the troy and avoirdupois systems. 5 the smallest possible amount. 6 the arrangement of fibres in wood, fabric, etc.
□ against the grain conflicting with your nature or instinct.
■ grainy adjective.

gram or Brit. **gramme** noun a metric unit of mass equal to one thousandth of a kilogram.

grammar noun 1 the whole system and structure of a language. 2 knowledge and use of the rules of grammar. 3 a book on grammar.
□ grammar school (in the UK, especially formerly) a state secondary school to which pupils are admitted on the basis of their ability.

> ☑ *-ar*, not *-er*: grammar.

grammatical adjective 1 having to do with grammar. 2 conforming to the rules of grammar.
■ grammatically adverb.

gramophone noun dated a record player.

grampus noun (plural **grampuses**) a killer whale or other animal of the dolphin family.

gran noun Brit. informal your grandmother.

granary noun (plural **granaries**) a storehouse for grain.

grand adjective 1 magnificent and impressive. 2 large or ambitious in scale. 3 of the highest importance or rank. 4 dignified, noble, or proud. 5 informal excellent. • noun (plural **grand**) informal a thousand dollars or pounds.
□ grand piano a large piano which has the strings arranged horizontally. grand slam the winning of each of a group of major sports championships or matches in the same year. grand total the final amount after everything is added up.
■ grandly adverb.

grandad or **granddad** noun informal your grandfather.

grandchild noun (plural **grandchildren**) the child of a person's son or daughter.

granddaughter noun the daughter of a person's son or daughter.

grandee noun a person of high status and social rank.

grandeur /gran-dyer/ noun 1 the quality of being grand and impressive. 2 high status and social rank.

grandfather noun the father of a person's father or mother.
□ grandfather clock a large clock in a tall wooden case.

grandiloquent adjective pompous in style and using long and fancy words.

grandiose adjective (of a plan or building) very large and ambitious and intended to impress.

grandma noun informal your grandmother.

grandmother noun the mother of a person's father or mother.

grandpa noun informal your grandfather.

grandparent noun a grandmother or grandfather.

Grand Prix /gron pree/ noun (plural **Grands Prix** /gron pree/) a race forming part of a motor-racing or motorcycling world championship.

grandson noun the son of a person's son or daughter.

grandstand noun the main stand at a racecourse or sports ground.

grange noun Brit. a country house with farm buildings attached.

granite noun a hard grey rock.

granny or **grannie** noun (plural **grannies**) informal your grandmother.
□ granny flat a small flat that is part of or

THESAURUS

grain noun 1 *fields of grain:* cereal. 2 *a grain of corn:* kernel, seed. 3 *grains of sand:* granule, particle, speck, bit, scrap, crumb, fragment, morsel. 4 *a grain of truth:* trace, hint, tinge, suggestion, shadow, soupçon, ounce, iota, jot, scrap, shred; informal smidgen. 5 *the grain in paper:* texture, weave, pattern.

grand adjective 1 *a grand hotel:* magnificent, imposing, impressive, awe-inspiring, splendid, resplendent, majestic, monumental, palatial, stately; Brit. upmarket; N. Amer. upscale; informal fancy, posh; Brit. informal swish. 2 *a grand scheme:* ambitious, bold, epic, big, extravagant. 3 *a grand old lady:* august, distinguished, illustrious, eminent, venerable, dignified, proud. 4 (informal) *you're doing a grand job:* excellent, marvellous, splendid, first-class, first-rate, wonderful, outstanding; informal superb, terrific, great, super; Brit. informal brilliant.
OPPOSITES humble, small-scale, poor.

grandeur noun splendour, magnificence, glory, resplendence, majesty, greatness, stateliness, pomp, ceremony.

attached to a house, in which an elderly relative can live. **granny knot** a reef knot with the ends crossed the wrong way and therefore liable to slip.

grant verb 1 agree to give something to someone or to allow them to do something. 2 give something formally or legally. 3 admit to someone that something is true. •noun a sum of money given by a government or public body for a particular purpose.

granted adverb admittedly; it is true.

granulated adjective in the form of granules.
■ granulation noun.

granule noun a small compact particle of a substance.
■ granular adjective.

grape noun a green or purple-black berry growing in clusters on a vine, eaten as fruit and used in making wine.

grapefruit noun (plural **grapefruit**) a large yellow citrus fruit with a slightly bitter taste.

grapeshot noun (in the past) ammunition consisting of a number of small iron balls fired together from a cannon.

grapevine noun 1 a vine which produces grapes. 2 (**the grapevine**) the spreading of information through talk or rumour.

graph noun a diagram showing how two or more sets of numbers relate to each other.
□ **graph paper** paper printed with small squares, used for graphs and diagrams.

graphic adjective 1 relating to visual art, especially involving drawing and the design of printed material. 2 giving vivid details. •noun 1 a pictorial image or symbol on a computer screen. 2 (**graphics**) the use

of designs or pictures to illustrate books, magazines, etc.
□ **graphic design** the design of books, posters, and other printed material.
■ graphically adverb.

graphite noun a grey form of carbon used as pencil lead and as a lubricant in machinery.

graphology noun the study of handwriting as a guide to personality.
■ graphologist noun.

grapnel /grap-nuhl/ or **grappling hook** noun a device with iron claws, used for dragging or grasping things.

grapple verb (**grapples, grappling, grappled**) 1 struggle or fight physically with someone. 2 (**grapple with**) struggle to deal with or understand.

grasp verb 1 seize and hold something firmly. 2 understand something. •noun 1 a firm grip. 2 a person's ability to achieve or understand something.

grasping adjective greedy.

grass noun 1 plants with long narrow leaves and stalks. 2 ground covered with grass. 3 informal cannabis. 4 Brit. informal a police informer. •verb 1 cover an area with grass. 2 Brit. informal inform the police about someone's criminal activity.
□ **grass roots** the ordinary people in an organization or society, rather than the leaders.
■ grassy adjective.

grasshopper noun an insect with long hind legs which it uses for jumping and for producing a chirping sound.

grate[1] verb (**grates, grating, grated**) 1 shred food by rubbing it on a grater. 2 make an

g

THESAURUS

grant verb 1 *he granted them leave of absence:* allow, permit, accord, afford. 2 *he granted them £20,000:* give, award, bestow on, confer on, present with, endow with. 3 *I grant that the difference is slight:* admit, accept, concede, allow, appreciate, recognize, acknowledge, confess.
OPPOSITES refuse, deny.
•noun *a grant from the council:* award, bursary, endowment, scholarship, allowance, subsidy, contribution, handout, donation, gift.

graphic adjective 1 *a graphic representation:* visual, pictorial, illustrative, diagrammatic. 2 *a graphic account:* vivid, explicit, detailed, realistic, descriptive, powerful, colourful, lurid, shocking.
OPPOSITES vague.

grapple verb 1 *the police grappled with him:* wrestle, struggle, tussle, scuffle, battle. 2 *grappling with addiction:* deal, cope, get to grips, tackle, confront, face.

grasp verb 1 *she grasped his hand:* grip, clutch, clasp, clench, squeeze, catch, seize, grab, snatch. 2 *he grasped the important points:* understand, comprehend, take in, see, apprehend, assimilate, absorb; informal get, take on board; Brit. informal twig.
OPPOSITES release, overlook.
•noun 1 *his grasp on her hand:* grip, hold, squeeze. 2 *a prize lay within their grasp:* reach, scope, power, range, sights. 3 *a grasp of history:* understanding, comprehension, awareness, grip, knowledge, mastery, command.

grasping adjective greedy, acquisitive, avaricious, rapacious, mercenary, materialistic; informal tight-fisted, tight, money-grubbing; N. Amer. informal grabby.

grate verb 1 *grate the cheese:* shred, pulverize, mince, grind, crush, crumble. 2 *her bones grated together:* grind, rub, rasp, scrape, jar, creak.

unpleasant rasping sound. **3** have an irritating effect.

grate² noun a metal frame or basket in a fireplace in which the coals or wood are placed.

grateful adjective feeling thankful and appreciative.
- **gratefully** adverb.

☑ *grateful*, not *greatful*.

grater noun a device having a surface covered with sharp-edged holes, used for grating food.

gratify verb (**gratifies, gratifying, gratified**) **1** give someone pleasure or satisfaction. **2** indulge or satisfy a desire.
- **gratification** noun.

grating¹ adjective **1** sounding harsh and unpleasant. **2** irritating.

grating² noun a grid of metal bars used as a barrier.

gratis /grat-iss, grah-tiss/ adverb & adjective free of charge.

gratitude noun the feeling of being grateful.

gratuitous /gruh-**tyoo**-i-tuhss/ adjective having no justifiable reason or purpose.
- **gratuitously** adverb.

gratuity noun (plural **gratuities**) formal a sum of money given to someone who has provided a service; a tip.

grave¹ noun a hole dug in the ground for a coffin or dead body.

grave² adjective **1** giving cause for alarm or concern. **2** solemn.
- **gravely** adverb.

grave accent /grahv/ noun a mark (`) placed over a vowel in some languages to indicate a change in its sound quality.

gravel noun a loose mixture of small stones

used for paths and roads.

gravelly adjective **1** resembling or containing gravel. **2** (of a voice) deep and rough.

graven image noun a carved figure.

gravestone noun a stone slab marking a grave.

graveyard noun a burial ground.

gravitas /gra-vi-tahss/ noun a serious and dignified manner.

gravitate verb (**gravitates, gravitating, gravitated**) (**gravitate to/towards**) be drawn towards.

gravitation noun movement towards a centre of gravity.
- **gravitational** adjective.

gravity noun **1** the force that attracts a body towards the centre of the earth, or towards any other physical body having mass. **2** extreme importance or seriousness. **3** a solemn manner.

gravy noun (plural **gravies**) a sauce made from the fat and juices that come out of meat during cooking.
□ **gravy boat** a long, narrow jug used for serving gravy.

gray US spelling of GREY.

graze¹ verb (**grazes, grazing, grazed**) (of cattle, sheep, etc.) eat grass.

graze² verb (**grazes, grazing, grazed**) **1** scrape the skin on a part of your body. **2** touch something lightly in passing. • noun an area where the skin has been scraped.

grazing noun grassland suitable for use as pasture.

grease noun **1** a thick oily substance used as a lubricant. **2** animal fat used or produced in cooking. • verb (**greases, greasing, greased**) smear or lubricate something with grease.
- **greasy** adjective.

THESAURUS

grateful adjective thankful, appreciative, indebted, obliged, in someone's debt, beholden.

gratitude noun thanks, gratefulness, thankfulness, appreciation, indebtedness, recognition, acknowledgement.

grave¹ noun *an unmarked grave:* tomb, burial place, last resting place, vault, mausoleum, sepulchre.

grave² adjective *a grave matter:* serious, important, weighty, profound, significant, momentous, critical, urgent, pressing, dire, terrible, dreadful. **2** *Jackie looked grave:* solemn, serious, sober, unsmiling, grim, sombre, dour.
OPPOSITES trivial, light-hearted.

graveyard noun cemetery, churchyard, burial ground, necropolis, garden of remembrance; Scottish kirkyard.

gravity noun **1** *the gravity of the situation:* seriousness, importance, significance, weight, consequence, magnitude, acuteness, urgency, dreadfulness. **2** *the gravity of his demeanour:* solemnity, seriousness, sobriety, severity, grimness, sombreness, dourness.
OPPOSITES triviality, light-heartedness.

graze¹ verb *the deer grazed:* feed, eat, crop, nibble, browse.

graze² verb **1** *he grazed his arm:* scrape, skin, scratch, chafe, scuff, rasp. **2** *his shot grazed the bar:* touch, brush, shave, skim, kiss, scrape, clip, glance off.
• noun *grazes on the skin:* scratch, scrape, abrasion.

grease noun oil, fat, lubricant.

greasy adjective oily, fatty, buttery,

greasepaint noun a waxy substance used as make-up by actors.

greaseproof adjective not allowing grease to pass through it.

great adjective 1 considerably above average in extent, amount, or strength. 2 considerably above average in ability or quality. 3 informal excellent. 4 used to emphasize something: *he's a great cricket fan.*
□ **great-aunt** (or **great-uncle**) an aunt (or uncle) of your mother or father.
■ **greatness** noun.

greatcoat noun a long heavy overcoat.

greatly adverb very much.

grebe noun a diving bird with a long neck.

Grecian /gree-sh'n/ adjective relating to ancient Greece.

greed noun 1 a strong and selfish desire for possessions, wealth, or power. 2 a desire to eat more food than you need.

greedy adjective (**greedier**, **greediest**) having or showing greed.
■ **greedily** adverb.

Greek noun 1 a person from Greece. 2 the ancient or modern language of Greece.
•**adjective** relating to Greece.

green adjective 1 of a colour between blue and yellow, like that of grass. 2 covered with grass or other plants. 3 (**Green**) concerned with or supporting protection of the environment. 4 inexperienced or naive.
•**noun** 1 a green colour. 2 a piece of grassy land for public use. 3 an area of smooth grass used for cricket or bowls, or surrounding a hole on a golf course. 4 (**greens**) cabbage or other green vegetables. 5 (**Green**) a supporter of a Green political party.
□ **green belt** an area of open land around a city, on which building is restricted. **green card** (in the US) a permit allowing a foreigner to live and work permanently in the US. **green fingers** Brit. natural ability in growing plants. **green light** permission to go ahead with a project. **green pepper** an unripe sweet pepper.
■ **greenness** noun.

greenery noun green leaves or plants.

greenfield adjective (of a site) previously undeveloped.

g

THESAURUS

oleaginous, slippery, slick, slimy, slithery; informal slippy.

great adjective 1 *they showed great interest:* considerable, substantial, significant, serious, exceptional, extraordinary. 2 *a great expanse of water:* large, big, extensive, expansive, broad, wide, vast, immense, huge, enormous, massive; informal humongous; Brit. informal whopping, ginormous. 3 *great writers:* prominent, eminent, distinguished, illustrious, celebrated, acclaimed, admired, esteemed, renowned, notable, famous, well known, leading, top, major. 4 *a great castle:* magnificent, imposing, impressive, awe-inspiring, grand, splendid, majestic. 5 *a great sportsman:* expert, skilful, skilled, adept, accomplished, talented, fine, masterly, master, brilliant, virtuoso, marvellous, outstanding, first-class, superb; informal crack, class. 6 *a great fan of rugby:* keen, eager, enthusiastic, devoted, ardent, fanatical, passionate, dedicated, committed. 7 *we had a great time:* enjoyable, delightful, lovely, excellent, marvellous, wonderful, fine, splendid; informal terrific, fantastic, fabulous, super, cool; Brit. informal brilliant.
OPPOSITES little, small, minor, modest, poor, apathetic, half-hearted, miserable.

greatly adverb very much, extremely, considerably, substantially, significantly, markedly, seriously, materially, enormously, vastly, immensely, tremendously, mightily; informal majorly.
OPPOSITES slightly.

greatness noun 1 *a woman destined for greatness:* eminence, distinction, celebrity, fame, prominence, renown, importance. 2 *his greatness as a writer:* brilliance, genius, prowess, talent, expertise, mastery, artistry, skill, proficiency, flair.

greed, greediness noun 1 *human greed:* avarice, acquisitiveness, covetousness, materialism, mercenariness; informal money-grubbing. 2 *her mouth watered with greed:* gluttony, hunger, voracity, self-indulgence; informal piggishness. 3 *their greed for power:* desire, appetite, hunger, thirst, craving, longing, yearning, hankering; informal itch.
OPPOSITES generosity, temperance, indifference.

greedy adjective 1 *a greedy eater:* gluttonous, ravenous, voracious; informal piggish, piggy. 2 *his greedy manager:* avaricious, acquisitive, covetous, grasping, materialistic, mercenary; informal money-grubbing; N. Amer. informal grabby.

green adjective 1 olive green, pea green, emerald green, lime green, avocado, pistachio, bottle green, Lincoln green, jade, sea green. 2 *a green island:* verdant, grassy, leafy. 3 *Green issues:* environmental, ecological, conservation, eco-. 4 *a green alternative to diesel:* environmentally friendly, eco-friendly. 5 *the new supervisor was very green:* inexperienced, callow, raw, unseasoned, untried, naive, innocent, unworldly; informal wet behind the ears.
OPPOSITES barren, experienced.

greenfinch noun a large finch with green and yellow feathers.

greenfly noun (plural **greenfly** or **greenflies**) a green aphid.

greengage noun a sweet greenish fruit like a small plum.

greengrocer noun Brit. a person who has a shop selling fruit and vegetables.

greenhouse noun a glass structure in which plants are kept to protect them from cold weather.
□ **greenhouse effect** the tendency of atmospheric temperature to rise because certain gases absorb infrared radiation from the earth. **greenhouse gas** a gas that contributes to the greenhouse effect by absorbing infrared radiation.

greet verb 1 give a word or sign of welcome when meeting someone. 2 acknowledge or react to someone or something in a particular way.

greeting noun 1 a word or sign of welcome when meeting someone. 2 (**greetings**) a formal expression of good wishes.

gregarious adjective 1 enjoying being with people; sociable. 2 (of animals) living in flocks or colonies.

Gregorian chant noun medieval church music for voices.

gremlin noun an imaginary mischievous creature regarded as responsible for unexplained mechanical or electrical faults.

grenade noun a small bomb that is thrown by hand.

grenadier /gre-nuh-**deer**/ noun 1 historical a soldier armed with grenades. 2 (**Grenadiers** or **Grenadier Guards**) a regiment of the royal household infantry.

grew past of GROW.

grey (US spelling **gray**) adjective 1 of a colour between black and white, like that of ashes or lead. 2 (of hair) turning grey or white with age. 3 (of the weather) cloudy and dull. • noun a grey colour. • verb (of hair) become grey with age.
□ **grey area** a subject or area of activity that does not easily fit into existing categories. **grey matter** informal the brain.

greyhound noun a swift, slender breed of dog used in racing.

grid noun 1 a set of bars lying parallel to or crossing each other. 2 a network of lines that cross each other to form a series of squares or rectangles. 3 a network of cables or pipes for distributing power.

griddle noun a heavy iron plate that is heated and used for cooking food.

gridiron /grid-I-uhn/ noun a frame of metal bars used for grilling food over an open fire.

gridlock noun a traffic jam affecting a whole network of intersecting streets.
■ **gridlocked** adjective.

grief noun 1 great sorrow and sadness, especially caused by someone's death. 2 informal trouble or annoyance.

grievance noun a cause for complaint.

grieve verb (**grieves, grieving, grieved**) 1 feel great sorrow and sadness. 2 cause someone distress.

grievous adjective formal (of something bad) very severe or serious.
□ **grievous bodily harm** Law, Brit. serious physical injury deliberately inflicted on someone.
■ **grievously** adverb.

griffin or **gryphon** noun a mythical creature with the head and wings of an eagle and the body of a lion.

griffon noun a small breed of dog.

grill noun Brit. 1 a device on a cooker that radiates heat downwards for cooking food. 2 a frame of metal bars used for cooking food on an open fire. 3 a dish of food cooked using a grill. 4 ⇒ GRILLE. • verb 1 cook food with a grill. 2 informal question someone in a relentless or aggressive way.

THESAURUS

greet verb 1 she greeted Hank cheerily: say hello to, address, salute, hail, welcome, meet, receive. 2 the decision was greeted with outrage: receive, respond to, react to, take.

greeting noun 1 he shouted a greeting: hello, salutation, welcome, reception. 2 birthday greetings: best wishes, good wishes, congratulations, compliments, regards, respects.
OPPOSITES farewell.

grey adjective 1 silvery, gunmetal, slate, charcoal, smoky. 2 a grey day: cloudy, overcast, dull, sunless, murky. 3 her face looked grey: pale, wan, ashen, pasty, pallid, colourless, waxen. 4 his grey existence: characterless, colourless, nondescript, flat, bland, dull, boring, tedious, monotonous. 5 a grey area: ambiguous, doubtful, unclear, uncertain, indefinite, debatable.
OPPOSITES sunny, ruddy, exciting, certain.

grief noun sorrow, misery, sadness, anguish, pain, distress, heartache, heartbreak, agony, woe, desolation.
OPPOSITES joy.

grievance noun complaint, objection, grumble, grouse, ill feeling, bad feeling, resentment; informal gripe.

grieve verb 1 she grieved for her father: mourn, sorrow, cry, sob, weep. 2 it grieved me to leave her: sadden, upset, distress, pain, hurt, wound, break someone's heart.
OPPOSITES rejoice, please.

grille or **grill** noun a framework of metal bars or wires.

grim adjective (**grimmer**, **grimmest**) **1** very serious and stern or forbidding. **2** horrifying or depressing.
■ **grimly** adverb.

grimace noun a twisted expression on a person's face, showing disgust, pain, or wry amusement. •verb (**grimaces**, **grimacing**, **grimaced**) make a grimace.

grime noun dirt ingrained on a surface.
■ **grimy** adjective.

grin verb (**grins**, **grinning**, **grinned**) smile broadly. •noun a broad smile.

grind verb (**grinds**, **grinding**, **ground**) **1** reduce something to small particles or powder by crushing it. **2** make something sharp or smooth by rubbing it against a hard or abrasive tool or surface. **3** rub together or move gratingly. **4** (**grind someone down**) wear someone down with continuous harsh treatment. **5** (**grind something out**) produce something slowly and with effort. **6** (**grinding**) (of an unpleasant situation) seemingly endless. •noun **1** an act or process of grinding. **2** hard dull work.

grindstone noun **1** a revolving disc of abrasive material used for sharpening or polishing metal objects. **2** a millstone.
□ **keep your nose to the grindstone** keep working hard.

grip verb (**grips**, **gripping**, **gripped**) **1** hold something tightly. **2** deeply affect someone. **3** hold someone's attention. •noun **1** a firm hold on something. **2** understanding of something. **3** a part or attachment by which something is held in the hand. **4** a travelling bag.

□ **come** (or **get**) **to grips with** begin to deal with or understand.

gripe verb (**gripes**, **griping**, **griped**) **1** informal grumble. **2** (**griping**) (of pain in the stomach or intestines) sudden and sharp. •noun **1** informal a trivial complaint. **2** pain in the stomach or intestines.

gripping adjective very interesting or exciting.

grisly /griz-li/ adjective (**grislier**, **grisliest**) causing horror or disgust.

> ! don't confuse **grisly** with **grizzly**, as in *grizzly bear*.

grist noun corn that is ground to make flour.
□ **grist to the mill** useful experience or knowledge.

gristle noun tough inedible cartilage in meat.
■ **gristly** adjective.

grit noun **1** small loose particles of stone or sand. **2** (also **gritstone**) a coarse sandstone. **3** courage and determination. •verb (**grits**, **gritting**, **gritted**) spread grit on an icy road.
□ **grit your teeth** resolve to do something difficult.

gritty adjective (**grittier**, **grittiest**) **1** containing or covered with grit. **2** brave and determined. **3** showing something unpleasant as it really is.
■ **grittily** adverb.

grizzle verb (**grizzles**, **grizzling**, **grizzled**) Brit. informal cry fretfully.

grizzled adjective having grey or grey-streaked hair.

grizzly bear noun a large brown bear, often with white-tipped fur.

groan verb make a deep sound of pain or

g

THESAURUS

grim adjective **1** *his grim expression:* stern, forbidding, uninviting, unsmiling, dour, formidable. **2** *grim secrets:* dreadful, ghastly, horrible, terrible, awful, appalling, frightful, shocking, grisly, gruesome, depressing, distressing, upsetting. **3** *a grim hovel:* bleak, dismal, dingy, wretched, miserable, depressing, cheerless, joyless, gloomy, uninviting.
OPPOSITES amiable, pleasant, cheerful.

grin verb & noun smile, beam, smirk.
OPPOSITES frown, scowl.

grind verb **1** *the ore is ground into powder:* crush, pound, pulverize, mill, crumble. **2** *one stone grinds against another:* rub, grate, scrape. **3** *the edge of the knife is then ground:* sharpen, whet, hone, put an edge on, mill, machine, polish, smooth. •noun *the daily grind:* drudgery, toil, labour, donkey work, exertion, chores, slog.

grip verb **1** *she gripped the edge of the table:* grasp, clutch, clasp, take hold of, clench,

cling to, grab, seize, squeeze. **2** *we were gripped by the drama:* engross, enthral, absorb, rivet, spellbind, fascinate, mesmerize.
OPPOSITES release.
•noun **1** *a tight grip:* grasp, hold. **2** *the wheels lost their grip on the road:* traction, purchase, friction, adhesion. **3** *in the grip of an obsession:* control, power, hold, stranglehold, clutches, influence.

gripping adjective engrossing, enthralling, absorbing, riveting, captivating, spellbinding, fascinating, compelling, thrilling, exciting, action-packed, dramatic.
OPPOSITES boring.

groan verb **1** *she groaned and rubbed her stomach:* moan, cry. **2** *they groan about everything:* complain, grumble, moan, mutter; informal grouse, bellyache, bitch, whinge. **3** *the tree groaned:* creak, grate, rasp.
•noun **1** *a groan of anguish:* moan, cry.

despair. • noun a groaning sound.

groat noun historical an English silver coin worth four old pence.

grocer noun a person who sells food and small household goods.

grocery noun (plural **groceries**) **1** a grocer's shop or business. **2** (**groceries**) items of food sold in a grocer's shop or supermarket.

grog noun spirits mixed with water.

groggy adjective (**groggier**, **groggiest**) dazed and unsteady.
■ **groggily** adverb.

groin noun **1** the area between the stomach and the thigh. **2** US spelling of **GROYNE**.

grommet noun **1** a protective metal ring or eyelet. **2** Brit. a tube fitted in the eardrum to drain fluid from the middle ear.

groom verb **1** brush and clean the coat of a horse or dog. **2** keep yourself neat and tidy in appearance. **3** train someone for a particular activity. • noun **1** a person employed to take care of horses. **2** a bridegroom.

groove noun **1** a long, narrow cut in a hard surface. **2** a spiral track cut in a music record. **3** a routine or habit. • verb (**grooves**, **grooving**, **grooved**) **1** make a groove or grooves in. **2** informal listen or dance to jazz or pop music.

groovy adjective (**groovier**, **grooviest**) informal, dated fashionable and exciting.

grope verb (**gropes**, **groping**, **groped**) **1** feel about with your hands. **2** ease your way forward using your hands to guide you. **3** informal feel someone's body for sexual pleasure.

gross adjective **1** unattractively large. **2** very obvious and unacceptable. **3** informal very unpleasant. **4** rude or vulgar. **5** (of income, profit, or interest) before tax has been deducted. **6** (of weight) including contents or other variable items. • adverb in total.
• verb earn a particular amount of money as gross profit or income. • noun **1** (plural **gross**) twelve dozen; 144. **2** (plural **grosses**) a gross profit or income.
■ **grossly** adverb.

grotesque /groh-**tesk**/ adjective **1** ugly or distorted in a way that is funny or frightening. **2** shocking. • noun a grotesque figure or image.
■ **grotesquely** adverb.

grotto noun (plural **grottoes** or **grottos**) a small cave, especially an artificial one.

grotty adjective (**grottier**, **grottiest**) Brit. informal **1** unpleasant and of bad quality. **2** unwell.

grouch noun informal **1** a grumpy person. **2** a complaint.
■ **grouchy** adjective.

ground[1] noun **1** the solid surface of the earth. **2** land or soil of a particular kind. **3** an area of land or sea with a particular use. **4** (**grounds**) an area of enclosed land

THESAURUS

2 she listens to all their moans and groans: complaint, grumble, grievance, moan, muttering; informal grouse, gripe, whinge.
3 the groan of the timbers: creaking, creak, grating, grinding.

groom verb **1** she groomed her pony: curry, brush, clean, rub down. **2** his hair was carefully groomed: brush, comb, arrange, do; informal fix. **3** groomed for stardom: prepare, prime, condition, coach, train, drill, teach, school.

groove noun furrow, channel, trench, trough, rut, gutter, canal, hollow, indentation.

grope verb fumble, scrabble, fish, ferret, rummage, feel, search, hunt.

gross adjective **1** (informal) the place smelled gross: disgusting, repulsive, revolting, foul, nasty, obnoxious, sickening, nauseating, stomach-churning. **2** a gross distortion of the truth: thorough, complete, utter, out and out, shameful, serious, unacceptable, flagrant, blatant, obvious, barefaced, shameless, brazen. **3** gross income: total, full, overall, combined, before deductions, before tax.
OPPOSITES pleasant, net.

• verb he grosses over a million a year: earn, make, bring in, take, get, receive; informal rake in.

grotesque adjective **1** a grotesque creature: misshapen, deformed, distorted, twisted, monstrous, hideous, freakish, unnatural, abnormal, strange; informal weird. **2** a grotesque exaggeration: outrageous, monstrous, shocking, appalling, preposterous, ridiculous, ludicrous, unbelievable, incredible.
OPPOSITES normal, sensible.

ground noun **1** she collapsed on the ground: floor, earth, terra firma; informal deck.
2 soggy ground: earth, soil, turf, land, terrain. **3** the team's home ground: stadium, pitch, field, arena, track; Brit. informal park.
4 the mansion's grounds: estate, gardens, park, land, property, surroundings, territory. **5** grounds for dismissal: reason, cause, basis, foundation, justification, rationale, argument, occasion, excuse, pretext.
• verb **1** the religious life must be grounded on the law: base, found, establish, root, build, form. **2** she was well grounded in the classics: teach, instruct, coach, tutor, educate, school, train, drill.

surrounding a large house. **5** (**grounds**) good reasons for doing or believing something. **6** (**grounds**) small pieces of solid matter in a liquid which settle at the bottom. •**verb 1** ban or prevent a pilot or aircraft from flying. **2** run a ship aground. **3** (**be grounded in** or **on**) have as a foundation or basis.
□ **ground control** the people who direct the flight and landing of aircraft or spacecraft. **ground floor** the floor of a building at ground level. **ground rent** Brit. rent paid by the owner of a building to the owner of the land on which it is built. **ground rules** basic rules controlling the way in which something is done.

ground² past and past participle of GRIND.

groundbreaking adjective involving completely new methods or discoveries.

grounding noun basic training or instruction in a subject.

groundless adjective not based on any good reason.

groundnut = PEANUT.

groundsel noun a plant with small yellow flowers.

groundsheet noun a waterproof sheet spread on the ground inside a tent.

groundsman noun (plural **groundsmen**) Brit. a person who maintains a sports ground or the grounds of a large building.

groundswell noun **1** a large swell in the sea. **2** a build-up of public opinion.

groundwork noun preliminary or basic work.

group noun **1** a number of people or things placed or classed together. **2** a band of pop musicians. •**verb** put into a group.

groupie noun informal a fan who follows a

pop group or celebrity around.

grouse¹ noun (plural **grouse**) a game bird with a plump body.

grouse² verb (**grouses**, **grousing**, **groused**) complain; grumble. •**noun** a grumble or complaint.

grout noun a substance used for filling the gaps between tiles. •**verb** fill between tiles with grout.

grove noun a small wood, orchard, or group of trees.

grovel verb (**grovels**, **grovelling**, **grovelled**; US spelling **grovels**, **groveling**, **groveled**) **1** crouch or crawl on the ground. **2** act very humbly towards someone to make them forgive you or treat you favourably.

grow verb (**grows**, **growing**, **grew**; past participle **grown**) **1** (of a living thing) develop and get bigger. **2** (**grow up**) become an adult. **3** become larger or greater over a period of time. **4** become gradually or increasingly: *we grew braver.* **5** (**grow on**) become gradually more appealing to.
□ **grown-up 1** adult. **2** informal an adult. ■ **grower** noun.

growl verb **1** (of a dog) make a low hostile sound in the throat. **2** say something in a low grating voice. **3** make a low or harsh rumbling sound. •**noun** a growling sound.

growth noun **1** the process of growing. **2** something that has grown or is growing. **3** a tumour.

groyne (US spelling **groin**) noun a low wall built out into the sea from a beach to prevent the beach from shifting or being eroded.

g

THESAURUS

group noun **1** *the exhibits are in three groups*: category, class, classification, grouping, cluster, set, batch, type, sort, kind, variety, family. **2** *a group of tourists*: crowd, party, body, band, company, gathering, congregation, assembly, collection, cluster, clump, knot, flock, pack, troop, gang; informal bunch. **3** *a folk group*: band, ensemble, act; informal line-up, combo, outfit.
•**verb 1** *patients were grouped according to age*: categorize, classify, class, catalogue, sort, bracket, pigeonhole. **2** *chairs were grouped in fours*: assemble, collect, organize, place, arrange, range, line up, lay out.

grow verb **1** enlarge, get bigger, get larger, get taller, expand, increase in size, extend, spread, swell, multiply, snowball, mushroom, balloon, build up, mount up, pile up. **2** *flowers grew among the rocks*: sprout, germinate, spring up, develop, bud,

bloom, flourish, thrive, run riot. **3** *he grew vegetables*: cultivate, produce, propagate, raise, rear, farm. **4** *Leonora grew bored*: become, get, turn, begin to be.
OPPOSITES shrink, decline.

grown-up adjective *she has two grown-up daughters*: adult, mature, of age, fully grown, independent.
OPPOSITES under age.
•**noun** *she wanted to be treated like a grown-up*: adult, woman, man, grown man/woman.
OPPOSITES child.

growth noun **1** *population growth*: enlargement, increase in size, expansion, extension, swelling, multiplication, mushrooming, snowballing, rise, escalation, build-up, development. **2** *a growth on his jaw*: tumour, malignancy, cancer, lump, swelling.
OPPOSITES shrinkage, decline.

grub noun **1** the larva of an insect. **2** informal food. • verb (**grubs, grubbing, grubbed**) **1** dig or poke about in soil. **2** (**grub something up**) dig something up.

grubby adjective (**grubbier, grubbiest**) **1** rather dirty. **2** dishonest or immoral.

grudge noun a persistent feeling of anger or dislike. • verb (**grudges, grudging, grudged**) **1** be unwilling to give or allow something. **2** feel resentful that someone has achieved something.

grudging adjective reluctantly given or allowed.
■ **grudgingly** adverb.

gruel noun a thin liquid food of oatmeal boiled in milk or water.

gruelling (US spelling **grueling**) adjective very tiring and demanding.

gruesome adjective causing disgust or horror.

gruff adjective **1** (of a voice) rough and low. **2** abrupt in manner.
■ **gruffly** adverb.

grumble verb (**grumbles, grumbling, grumbled**) **1** complain in a quiet but bad-tempered way. **2** make a low rumbling sound. • noun a complaint.

grumpy adjective (**grumpier, grumpiest**) bad-tempered and sulky.
■ **grumpily** adverb.

grunge noun a style of rock music with a raucous guitar sound.
■ **grungy** adjective.

grunt verb **1** (of an animal) make a short, low sound. **2** (of a person) make a low sound because of physical effort or to show agreement. • noun a grunting sound.

gryphon ⇒ GRIFFIN.

guano /gwah-noh/ noun the excrement of seabirds, used as fertilizer.

guarantee noun **1** a promise that certain things will be done. **2** a promise that a product will remain in working order for a particular length of time. **3** something that makes a particular outcome certain. **4** an undertaking to pay or do something on behalf of someone if they fail to do it.
• verb (**guarantees, guaranteeing, guaranteed**) **1** provide a guarantee for something. **2** promise something with certainty. **3** provide financial security for.

> ☑ gua-, not gau-: guarantee.

guarantor /ga-ruhn-**tor**/ noun a person or organization that gives a guarantee.

guard verb **1** watch over in order to protect or control. **2** (**guard against**) take precautions against. • noun **1** a person who guards or keeps watch. **2** a group of soldiers guarding a place or person. **3** a state of looking out for possible danger: *she was on guard.* **4** a device worn or fitted to prevent injury or damage. **5** Brit. an official in charge of a train. **6** N. Amer. a prison warder.

> ☑ gua-, not gau-: guard.

THESAURUS

grubby adjective dirty, grimy, filthy, mucky, unwashed, stained, soiled; informal cruddy, yucky; Brit. informal **manky**; Austral./NZ informal scungy.
OPPOSITES clean.

grudge noun grievance, resentment, bitterness, rancour, ill will, animosity, antipathy, antagonism; informal a chip on your shoulder.

gruelling adjective exhausting, tiring, taxing, draining, demanding, exacting, difficult, arduous, strenuous, back-breaking, punishing, crippling; informal murderous; Brit. informal knackering.

gruesome adjective grisly, ghastly, frightful, horrid, horrifying, hideous, horrible, grim, awful, dreadful, terrible, horrific; informal sick, sick-making, gross.
OPPOSITES pleasant.

grumble verb complain, grouse, whine, mutter, carp, make a fuss; informal moan, bellyache, bitch, whinge; N. English informal mither.
• noun complaint, grouse, grievance, protest; informal grouch, moan, whinge, beef, gripe.

grumpy adjective bad-tempered, crabby,

tetchy, touchy, irascible, cantankerous, curmudgeonly, surly, fractious; informal grouchy; Brit. informal ratty; N. Amer. informal cranky, ornery.
OPPOSITES good-humoured.

guarantee noun **1** *a one-year guarantee:* warranty. **2** *a guarantee that the hospital will stay open:* promise, assurance, word (of honour), pledge, vow, oath, commitment. **3** *a guarantee for loans:* collateral, security, surety, bond.
• verb **1** *I guarantee he will accept:* promise, swear, pledge, vow, give your word, give an assurance, give an undertaking. **2** *he agreed to guarantee the loan:* underwrite, stand surety.

guard verb *troops guarded the bridge:* protect, defend, shield, secure, cover, mind, stand guard over, watch, keep an eye on.
• noun **1** *border guards:* sentry, sentinel, nightwatchman, protector, defender, guardian, lookout, watch. **2** *a prison guard:* warder, warden, keeper, jailer; informal screw. **3** *a metal guard:* cover, shield, screen, fender, bumper, buffer.

guarded adjective cautious.

guardian noun 1 a person who defends and protects something. 2 a person who is legally responsible for someone who cannot take care of their own affairs. □ guardian angel a spirit who is believed to watch over and protect you. ■ guardianship noun.

Guatemalan /gwah-tuh-**mah**-luhn/ noun a person from Guatemala. • adjective relating to Guatemala.

guava /**gwah**-vuh/ noun a tropical fruit with pink juicy flesh.

gudgeon noun a small freshwater fish.

guerrilla or **guerilla** /guh-**ril**-luh/ noun a member of a small independent group fighting against the government or regular forces.

guess verb 1 estimate or suppose something without having the information you need to be sure. 2 correctly estimate or suppose. • noun an attempt to guess something.

guesswork noun the process or results of guessing.

guest noun 1 a person who is invited to someone's house or to a social occasion. 2 a person invited to take part in a broadcast or entertainment. 3 a person staying at a hotel. □ guest house a kind of small hotel.

guffaw noun a loud, deep laugh. • verb give a loud, deep laugh.

guidance noun advice and information given by an experienced or skilled person.

guide noun 1 a person who advises or shows the way to other people. 2 a thing that helps you to form an opinion or make a decision. 3 a book providing information on a subject. 4 a structure or marking which directs the movement or positioning of something. 5 (**Guide**) a member of the Guides Association, a girls' organization corresponding to the Scouts. • verb (**guides, guiding, guided**) 1 show someone the way. 2 direct the movement or positioning of something. 3 (**guided**) directed by remote control or internal equipment. □ guide dog a dog trained to lead a blind person.

guidebook noun a book containing information about a place for visitors.

guideline noun a general rule, principle, or piece of advice.

guild noun 1 a medieval association of craftsmen or merchants. 2 an association of people who do the same work or have the same interests.

guilder /gil-der/ noun (plural **guilder** or **guilders**) the former basic unit of money in the Netherlands.

guildhall noun 1 the meeting place of a guild or corporation. 2 Brit. a town hall.

guile noun clever but dishonest or deceitful behaviour.

guileless adjective innocent and honest.

guillemot /gil-li-mot/ noun a seabird with a narrow pointed bill.

guillotine /gil-luh-teen/ noun 1 a machine with a heavy blade, used for beheading people. 2 a piece of equipment with a

g

guarded adjective cautious, careful, circumspect, wary, chary, reluctant, non-committal; informal cagey.

guardian noun protector, defender, preserver, custodian, warden, guard, keeper, curator, caretaker, steward, trustee.

guerrilla noun rebel, irregular, partisan, freedom fighter, revolutionary, terrorist.

guess verb 1 he guessed that she was about 40: estimate, reckon, judge, speculate, conjecture, hypothesize, surmise. 2 (informal) I guess I owe you an apology: suppose, think, imagine, expect, suspect, dare say; informal reckon. • noun my guess was right: hypothesis, theory, conjecture, surmise, estimate, belief, opinion, supposition, speculation, suspicion, impression, feeling.

guest noun 1 we have guests: visitor, caller, company. 2 hotel guests: client, customer, resident, boarder, lodger, patron, diner, holidaymaker, tourist.
OPPOSITES host, staff.

guidance noun 1 she looked to him for guidance: advice, counsel, instruction, suggestions, tips, hints, pointers, guidelines. 2 under the guidance of an expert: direction, control, leadership, management, supervision.

guide noun 1 our guide took us back to the hotel: escort, attendant, courier, leader, usher. 2 the techniques given serve as a guide: outline, template, example, exemplar, model, pattern, guideline, yardstick, precedent. 3 a guide to Paris: guidebook, vade mecum, companion, handbook, manual, directory, A to Z, instructions, directions; informal bible. • verb 1 he guided her to her seat: lead, conduct, show, usher, shepherd, direct, steer, pilot, escort. 2 the chairman guides the meeting: direct, steer, manage, conduct, run, be in charge of, govern, preside over, supervise, oversee. 3 he was always there to guide me: advise, counsel, direct.

guild noun association, society, union, league, organization, company, fellowship, club, order, lodge.

descending or sliding blade used for cutting paper or sheet metal. • verb (**guillotines, guillotining, guillotined**) behead someone with a guillotine.

guilt noun 1 the fact of having committed an offence or crime. 2 a feeling of having done something wrong.
■ **guiltless** adjective.

guilty adjective (**guiltier, guiltiest**) 1 responsible for doing something wrong. 2 having or showing a feeling of guilt.
■ **guiltily** adverb.

guinea /gi-ni/ noun a former British gold coin worth 21 shillings (£1.05).

guineafowl noun (plural **guineafowl**) a large African bird with grey, white-spotted feathers.

Guinean /gin-i-uhn/ noun a person from Guinea, a country in West Africa. • adjective relating to Guinea.

guinea pig noun 1 a South American rodent without a tail. 2 a person or thing used as a subject for experiment.

guise /gyz/ noun an outward form, appearance, or manner.

guitar noun a stringed musical instrument which you play by plucking or strumming.
■ **guitarist** noun.

Gujarati /goo-juh-**rah**-ti/ noun (plural **Gujaratis**) 1 a person from the Indian state of Gujarat. 2 the language of the Gujaratis.

gulch noun N. Amer. a narrow ravine.

gulf noun 1 a deep inlet of the sea with a narrow mouth. 2 a deep ravine. 3 a large difference in opinion between two people or groups.

gull[1] noun a white seabird with long wings and a grey or black back.

gull[2] verb fool or deceive.

gullet noun the passage by which food passes from the mouth to the stomach.

gullible adjective easily believing what people tell you.
■ **gullibility** noun.

gully or **gulley** noun (plural **gullies** or **gulleys**) a ravine or channel formed by running water.

gulp verb 1 swallow food or drink quickly or in large mouthfuls. 2 swallow with difficulty because you are upset or nervous. • noun 1 an act of gulping. 2 a large mouthful of liquid hastily drunk.

gum[1] noun 1 a sticky substance produced by some trees. 2 glue used for sticking paper or other light materials together. 3 chewing gum.

gum[2] noun the firm area of flesh around the roots of the teeth.

gumboot noun Brit. dated a tall rubber boot; a wellington.

gumdrop noun a firm, jelly-like sweet.

gummy[1] adjective sticky.

gummy[2] adjective toothless.

gumption noun informal initiative and resourcefulness.

gun noun 1 a weapon with a metal tube from which bullets or shells are fired by means of a small explosion. 2 a device using pressure to send out a substance or object. • verb (**guns, gunning, gunned**) (**gun someone down**) shoot someone with a gun.
□ jump the gun act before the proper or right time. stick to your guns refuse to compromise.

gunboat noun a small ship armed with guns.

gunfire noun the repeated firing of a gun or guns.

gunge (N. Amer. also **gunk**) noun informal an unpleasantly sticky or messy substance.

gung-ho adjective too eager to take part in fighting or warfare.

THESAURUS

guilt noun 1 *the proof of his guilt:* culpability, blameworthiness, responsibility. 2 *a terrible feeling of guilt:* remorse, shame, regret, contrition, self-reproach, a guilty conscience.
OPPOSITES innocence, shamelessness.

guilty adjective 1 *the guilty party:* culpable, to blame, at fault, in the wrong. 2 *I still feel guilty about it:* ashamed, guilt-ridden, conscience-stricken, remorseful, sorry, contrite, repentant, penitent, regretful, rueful, shamefaced.
OPPOSITES innocent, unrepentant.

gulf noun 1 *our ship sailed into the gulf:* bay, inlet, cove, bight, fjord, estuary, sound; Scottish firth. 2 *a gulf between rich and poor:* gap, divide, separation, difference, contrast.

gulp verb 1 *she gulped her juice:* swallow, quaff, swill down; informal swig, down, knock back. 2 *he gulped down the rest of his meal:* gobble, guzzle, devour, bolt, wolf; informal shovel down; Brit. informal scoff. 3 *Jenny gulped back her tears:* choke back, fight/hold back, suppress, stifle, smother.
OPPOSITES sip, nibble, let out.
• noun *a gulp of cold beer:* mouthful, swallow, draught; informal swig.

gum noun *stuck down with gum:* glue, adhesive, paste, cement; N. Amer. mucilage; N. Amer. informal stickum.
• verb *the receipts were gummed in:* stick, glue, paste, cement, attach.

gun noun firearm, side arm, handgun, weapon; informal shooter; N. Amer. informal piece, shooting iron.

gunman noun (plural **gunmen**) a man who uses a gun to commit a crime.

gunmetal noun **1** a grey form of bronze containing zinc. **2** a dull bluish-grey colour.

gunnel ⇒ **GUNWALE**.

gunner noun **1** a person who operates a gun. **2** a British artillery soldier.

gunnery noun the design, manufacture, or firing of heavy guns.

gunpoint noun (**at gunpoint**) while threatening someone or being threatened with a gun.

gunpowder noun an explosive consisting of a powdered mixture of saltpetre, sulphur, and charcoal.

gunrunner noun a person involved in the illegal sale or importing of firearms.
■ **gunrunning** noun.

gunship noun a heavily armed helicopter.

gunwale or **gunnel** /gun-uhl/ noun the upper edge or planking of the side of a boat.

guppy noun (plural **guppies**) a small colourful fish.

gurdwara /goor-**dwah**-ruh/ noun a Sikh place of worship.

gurgle verb (**gurgles**, **gurgling**, **gurgled**) make a hollow bubbling sound. •noun a hollow bubbling sound.

Gurkha /ger-kuh/ noun a member of a Nepalese regiment in the British army.

gurn or **girn** verb Brit. pull a grotesque face.

gurnard /ger-nerd/ noun a small sea fish.

guru noun **1** a Hindu spiritual teacher. **2** a person who is an expert on a subject and has a lot of followers.

gush verb **1** flow in a strong, fast stream. **2** express approval very enthusiastically. •noun a strong, fast stream.

■ **gushing** adjective.

gusset noun a piece of material sewn into a garment to strengthen or enlarge a part of it.

gust noun **1** a brief, strong rush of wind. **2** a burst of sound or emotion. •verb blow in gusts.
■ **gusty** adjective.

gusto noun enthusiasm and energy.

gut noun **1** the stomach or intestine. **2** (**guts**) internal organs that have been removed or exposed. **3** (**guts**) the inner or most important part of something. **4** (**guts**) informal courage and determination. •verb (**guts**, **gutting**, **gutted**) **1** take out the internal organs of a fish before cooking. **2** remove or destroy the internal parts of something.

gutless adjective informal not showing courage or determination.

gutsy adjective (**gutsier**, **gutsiest**) informal brave and determined.

gutted adjective Brit. informal bitterly disappointed or upset.

gutter noun **1** a shallow trough beneath the edge of a roof, or a channel at the side of a street, for carrying off rainwater. **2** (**the gutter**) a very poor or unpleasant environment. •verb (**gutters**, **guttering**, **guttered**) (of a flame) flicker and burn unsteadily.

guttering noun the gutters of a building.

guttersnipe noun disapproving a scruffy, badly behaved child.

guttural adjective (of a speech sound) produced in the throat.

guy[1] noun **1** informal a man. **2** (**guys**) informal, chiefly N. Amer. people of either sex. **3** Brit. a stuffed figure that is traditionally burnt on a bonfire on 5 November. •verb make fun

g

---

gunman noun armed criminal, assassin, sniper, terrorist, gunfighter; informal hit man, gunslinger; N. Amer. informal shootist.

guru noun **1** *a Hindu guru and mystic:* spiritual teacher, tutor, sage, mentor, spiritual leader, master. **2** *a management guru:* expert, authority, pundit, leading light, master, specialist.
OPPOSITES disciple.

gush verb surge, stream, spout, spurt, jet, rush, pour, spill, cascade, flood; Brit. informal sloosh.
•noun surge, stream, spout, spurt, jet, rush, outpouring, spill, outflow, cascade, flood, torrent.

gushing, gushy adjective effusive, overenthusiastic, extravagant, fulsome, lavish; informal over the top.
OPPOSITES restrained.

gust noun flurry, blast, puff, blow, rush, squall.

gut noun **1** *an ache in his gut:* stomach, belly, abdomen, paunch, intestines; informal tummy, insides, innards. **2** (informal) *Nicola has a lot of guts:* courage, bravery, backbone, nerve, pluck, spirit, daring, grit, fearlessness, determination; Brit. informal bottle; N. Amer. informal moxie.
•adjective (informal) *a gut feeling:* instinctive, intuitive, deep-seated, involuntary, spontaneous, unthinking.
•verb **1** *gut the sardines:* clean (out), disembowel, draw. **2** *builders had gutted the old place:* strip, empty, devastate, lay waste, ravage, ruin, wreck.

gutter noun drain, trough, trench, ditch, sluice, sewer, channel, conduit, pipe.

guy noun (informal) man, fellow; informal lad; Brit.

of someone.

guy[2] noun a rope or line fixed to the ground to secure a tent.

Guyanese /gy-uh-neez/ noun (plural **Guyanese**) a person from Guyana, a country in South America. • adjective relating to Guyana.

guzzle verb (**guzzles**, **guzzling**, **guzzled**) eat or drink greedily.

gybe /jyb/ verb (**gybes**, **gybing**, **gybed**) Sailing change course by swinging the sail across a following wind.

gym noun 1 a gymnasium. 2 a private club with equipment for improving physical fitness. 3 gymnastics.

gymkhana /jim-kah-nuh/ noun a horse-riding event consisting of a series of competitions.

gymnasium noun (plural **gymnasiums** or **gymnasia**) a hall or building equipped for gymnastics and other sports.

gymnast noun a person trained in gymnastics.

gymnastics plural noun exercises involving physical agility and coordination.

■ **gymnastic** adjective.

gymslip noun Brit. a pinafore dress reaching from the shoulder to the knee, formerly worn by schoolgirls.

gynaecology /gy-ni-kol-uh-ji/ (US spelling **gynecology**) noun the branch of medicine concerned with conditions and diseases experienced by women.

■ **gynaecological** adjective **gynaecologist** noun.

gypsophila /jip-sof-fi-luh/ noun a garden plant with small pink or white flowers.

gypsum /jip-suhm/ noun a soft white or grey mineral used to make plaster of Paris and in the building industry.

Gypsy or **Gipsy** noun (plural **Gypsies**) a member of a travelling people.

gyrate /jy-rayt/ verb (**gyrates**, **gyrating**, **gyrated**) move in a circle or spiral.

■ **gyration** noun.

gyroscope noun a device, used to provide stability or maintain a fixed direction, consisting of a wheel or disc spinning rapidly about an axis which is itself free to alter in direction.

THESAURUS

informal chap, bloke; N. Amer. informal dude, hombre.

guzzle verb 1 *he guzzled his burger:* gobble, bolt, wolf, devour; informal tuck into, shovel down, hoover up; Brit. informal scoff; N. Amer. informal snarf, scarf. 2 *she guzzled down the orange juice:* gulp down, quaff, swill; informal knock back, swig, down, slug, neck.

gyrate verb rotate, revolve, wheel, turn, whirl, circle, pirouette, twirl, swirl, spin.

Hh

H or **h** noun (plural **Hs** or **H's**) the eighth letter of the alphabet. •**abbreviation** (**h**) hours. □ **H-bomb** a hydrogen bomb.

ha abbreviation hectares.

habeas corpus /hay-bi-uhss **kor**-puhss/ noun Law a written order saying that a person must come before a judge or court.

haberdashery noun Brit. materials used in dressmaking and sewing.

habit noun **1** a thing you do regularly and repeatedly. **2** informal an addiction to a drug. **3** a long, loose garment worn by a monk or nun.

habitable adjective suitable to live in.

habitat noun the natural home or environment of a plant or animal.

habitation noun **1** the fact of living somewhere. **2** formal a house or home.

habitual /huh-**bit**-yuu-uhl/ adjective **1** done constantly or as a habit. **2** regular; usual. ■ **habitually** adverb.

habituate verb (**habituates, habituating, habituated**) make or become accustomed to something.

habitué /huh-**bit**-yuu-ay/ noun a frequent visitor to a place.

hacienda /ha-si-**en**-duh/ noun (in Spanish-speaking countries) a large estate with a house.

hack¹ verb **1** cut or hit at something with rough or heavy blows. **2** use a computer to read or alter information in another computer system without permission. ■ **hacker** noun.

hack² noun **1** a journalist producing dull, unoriginal work. **2** a horse for ordinary riding.

hackles plural noun hairs along an animal's back which rise when it is angry or alarmed.

hackney noun (plural **hackneys**) (in the past) a horse-drawn vehicle kept for hire.

□ **hackney carriage** a taxi.

hackneyed adjective (especially of a phrase) not original or interesting.

hacksaw noun a saw with a narrow blade set in a frame.

had past and past participle of **HAVE**.

haddock noun (plural **haddock**) a silvery-grey sea fish used for food.

hadn't short form had not.

haematology /hee-muh-**tol**-uh-ji/ (US spelling **hematology**) noun the branch of medicine concerned with the blood.

haemoglobin /hee-muh-**gloh**-bin/ (US spelling **hemoglobin**) noun a red protein in the blood that carries oxygen.

haemophilia /hee-muh-**fi**-li-uh/ (US spelling **hemophilia**) noun a condition in which the ability of the blood to clot is reduced, causing severe bleeding from even a slight injury. ■ **haemophiliac** noun.

haemorrhage /**hem**-uh-rij/ (US spelling **hemorrhage**) noun an escape of blood from a burst blood vessel. •**verb** (**haemorrhages, haemorrhaging, haemorrhaged**) have a haemorrhage.

haemorrhoid /**hem**-uh-royd/ (US spelling **hemorrhoid**) noun a swollen vein in the region of the anus.

haft noun the handle of a knife, axe, or spear.

hafnium noun a hard silver-grey metal.

hag noun an ugly old woman.

haggard adjective looking exhausted and ill.

haggis noun (plural **haggis**) a Scottish dish consisting of the internal organs of a sheep or calf mixed with suet and oatmeal.

haggle verb (**haggles, haggling, haggled**) argue or negotiate with someone about the price of something. •**noun** a period of haggling.

hagiography /ha-gi-og-ruh-fi/ noun

---

habit noun **1** custom, practice, routine, way. **2** (informal) *his cocaine habit:* addiction, dependence, craving, fixation.

hack verb cut, chop, hew, lop, saw, slash.

haggle verb barter, bargain, negotiate, wrangle.

1 writing which is about the lives of saints. **2** a biography that presents its subject as better than in reality.

ha-ha noun a trench which forms a boundary to a park or garden without interrupting the view.

haiku /hy-koo/ noun (plural **haiku** or **haikus**) a Japanese poem of three lines and seventeen syllables.

hail¹ noun **1** pellets of frozen rain falling in showers. **2** a large number of things hurled forcefully through the air. • verb (**it hails, it is hailing, it hailed**) hail falls.

hail² verb **1** call out to someone to attract their attention. **2** (**hail someone/thing as**) enthusiastically describe someone or something as. **3** (**hail from**) have your home or origins in.

hailstone noun a pellet of hail.

hair noun **1** each of the thread-like strands growing from the skin of animals, or from plants. **2** strands of hair.
□ **hair-raising** very alarming or frightening. **hair shirt** (in the past) a shirt made of very rough cloth worn as a way of punishing yourself. **hair trigger** a firearm trigger set for release at the slightest pressure. **let your hair down** informal behave wildly or in a very relaxed way. **split hairs** make small and unnecessary distinctions.

hairband noun a band worn on the head to keep the hair off the face.

haircut noun **1** the style in which someone's hair is cut. **2** an act of cutting someone's hair.

hairdo noun (plural **hairdos**) informal the style of a person's hair.

hairdresser noun a person who cuts and styles hair.
■ **hairdressing** noun.

hairdryer or **hairdrier** noun an electrical device for drying the hair with warm air.

hairgrip noun Brit. a hairpin.

hairline noun the edge of a person's hair. • adjective very thin or fine.

hairnet noun a fine net for holding the hair in place.

hairpiece noun a piece of false hair worn with your own hair to make it look thicker.

hairpin noun a U-shaped pin for fastening the hair.
□ **hairpin bend** a sharp U-shaped bend in a road.

hairspray noun a solution sprayed on to hair to keep it in place.

hairstyle noun a way in which a person's hair is cut or arranged.
■ **hairstylist** noun.

hairy adjective (**hairier, hairiest**) **1** covered with or like hair. **2** informal dangerous or frightening.

Haitian /hay-shi-uhn, hay-shuhn/ noun a person from Haiti. • adjective relating to Haiti.

hajj or **haj** /haj/ noun the pilgrimage to Mecca which all Muslims are expected to make at least once if they can afford to.

hake noun a long-bodied sea fish used for food.

halal /huh-**lahl**/ adjective (of meat) prepared according to Muslim law.

halberd /**hal**-berd/ noun historical a combined spear and battleaxe.

halcyon /**hal**-si-uhn/ adjective (of a past time) very happy and peaceful.

hale adjective (of an old person) strong and healthy.

half noun (plural **halves**) **1** either of two equal parts into which something is or can be divided. **2** Brit. informal half a pint of beer. • pronoun an amount equal to a half. • adverb **1** to the extent of half. **2** partly.
□ **at half mast** (of a flag) flown halfway down its mast, as a mark of respect for a person who has died. **half-and-half** in equal parts. **half-baked** informal not well planned or considered. **half board** Brit. a type of accommodation at a hotel or guest house which includes breakfast and one main meal. **half-brother** (or **half-sister**) a brother (or sister) with whom you have one parent in common. **half-caste** offensive a person whose parents are of different races. **half-crown** (or **half a crown**) a former

---

THESAURUS

hail¹ noun *a hail of bullets:* barrage, volley, shower, stream, salvo.

hail² verb **1** *a friend hailed him:* call out to, shout to, address, greet, say hello to, salute. **2** *he hailed a cab:* flag down, wave down. **3** *critics hailed the film as a masterpiece:* acclaim, praise, applaud. **4** *Rick hails from Australia:* come, be, be a native of.

hair noun **1** head of hair, shock of hair, mane, mop, locks, tresses, curls. **2** hairstyle, haircut; informal hairdo. **3** fur,

wool, coat, fleece, mane.

hairdresser noun hairstylist, coiffeur, coiffeuse, barber.

hairy adjective **1** *animals with hairy coats:* shaggy, bushy, long-haired, woolly, furry, fleecy. **2** *his hairy face:* bearded, unshaven, stubbly, bristly; formal hirsute. **3** (informal) *a hairy situation:* risky, dangerous, perilous, hazardous, tricky; informal dicey; Brit. informal dodgy.

OPPOSITES short-haired, smooth-haired, shaven, safe.

British coin equal to two shillings and sixpence (12½p). **half-dozen** (or **half a dozen**) a group of six. **half-hearted** without enthusiasm or energy. **half-hour** (or **half an hour**) a period of thirty minutes. **half-life** the time taken for the radioactivity of a substance to fall to half its original value. **half measures** actions or policies that are not forceful or decisive enough. **half nelson** a hold in wrestling in which you pass one arm under your opponent's arm from behind while applying your other hand to their neck. **half-term** Brit. a short holiday halfway through a school term. **half-timbered** having walls with a timber frame and a brick or plaster filling. **half-time** (in sport) a short gap between two halves of a match. **not half 1** not nearly. **2** Brit. informal to an extreme degree.

halfback noun a player in a ball game whose position is between the forwards and fullbacks.

halfpenny or **ha'penny** /hayp-ni/ noun (plural **halfpennies** or **halfpence** /hay-p'nss/) a former British coin equal to half an old penny.

halfway adverb & adjective **1** at or to a point equal in distance between two others. **2** to some extent.

halfwit noun informal a stupid person.
■ **half-witted** adjective.

halibut noun (plural **halibut**) a large flat sea fish used for food.

halitosis /hali-toh-sis/ noun bad-smelling breath.

hall noun **1** (also **hallway**) a room or space inside a front door, or between a number of rooms. **2** a large room for meetings, concerts, etc. **3** (also **hall of residence**) Brit. a university building in which students live. **4** Brit. a large country house.

hallelujah /hal-li-**loo**-yuh/ or **alleluia** /al-li-**loo**-yuh/ exclamation God be praised.

hallmark noun **1** an official mark stamped on objects made of pure gold, silver, or platinum. **2** a distinctive feature. •verb stamp an object with a hallmark.

hallo ⇨ HELLO.

hallowed /hal-lohd/ adjective **1** made holy. **2** very honoured and respected.

Halloween or **Hallowe'en** noun the night of 31 October, the evening before All Saints' Day.

hallucinate verb (**hallucinates**, **hallucinating**, **hallucinated**) see something which is not actually there.
■ **hallucination** noun **hallucinatory** adjective.

hallucinogen /huh-**loo**-si-nuh-juhn/ noun a drug causing hallucinations.
■ **hallucinogenic** adjective.

halo /hay-loh/ noun (plural **haloes** or **halos**) **1** (in a painting) a circle of light surrounding the head of a holy person. **2** a circle of light round the sun or moon.

halogen /hal-uh-juhn/ noun any of a group of elements including fluorine, chlorine, bromine, and iodine.

halt[1] verb come or bring to a sudden stop.
•noun **1** a stopping of movement or activity. **2** Brit. a minor stopping place on a railway line.

halt[2] adjective old use lame.

halter noun a rope or strap placed around the head of an animal and used to lead it.
□ **halter neck** a style of woman's top that is fastened behind the neck, leaving the shoulders, upper back, and arms bare.

halting adjective slow and hesitant.

halve verb (**halves**, **halving**, **halved**) **1** divide into two halves. **2** reduce or be reduced by half.

halves plural of HALF.

halyard /hal-yerd/ noun a rope used for raising and lowering a sail, yard, or flag on a ship.

ham[1] noun **1** meat from the upper part of a pig's leg which is salted and dried or smoked. **2** (**hams**) the back of the thighs.
□ **ham-fisted** clumsy.

ham[2] noun **1** an actor who overacts. **2** (also **radio ham**) informal an amateur radio operator. •verb (**hams, hamming, hammed**) informal overact.
■ **hammy** adjective.

h

halfway adjective *the halfway point:* **midway**, middle, mid, central, centre, intermediate.
•adverb *halfway down the passage:* **midway**, in the middle, in the centre, part of the way.

hall noun **1** *entrance hall*, hallway, entry, entrance, lobby, foyer, vestibule, atrium. **2** *the village hall:* **assembly room**, meeting room, chamber, auditorium, theatre, house.

halo noun **aura**, nimbus, corona, aureole.

halt verb **1** *halt at the barrier:* **stop**, come to a halt, come to a stop, come to a standstill,

pull up, draw up. **2** *a strike has halted production:* **stop**, bring to a stop, put a stop to, suspend, arrest, check, curb, stem, staunch, block, stall.
OPPOSITES start, continue, restart.
•noun **1** *a bus screeched to a halt:* **stop**, standstill. **2** *a halt in production:* **stoppage**, break, pause, interval, interruption.
OPPOSITES start, resumption.

halting adjective **hesitant**, faltering, hesitating, stumbling, stammering, stuttering, broken, imperfect.
OPPOSITES fluent.

hamburger noun a small cake of minced beef, fried or grilled and typically served in a bread roll.

hamlet noun a small village.

hammer noun **1** a tool with a heavy metal head and a wooden handle, for driving in nails. **2** an auctioneer's mallet, tapped to indicate a sale. **3** a part of a mechanism that hits another. **4** a heavy metal ball attached to a wire for throwing in an athletic contest. • verb (**hammers, hammering, hammered**) **1** hit repeatedly with a hammer. **2** (**hammer away**) work hard and persistently. **3** (**hammer something in** or **into**) make something stick in someone's mind by constantly repeating it. **4** (**hammer something out**) work out the details of a plan or agreement.

hammerhead noun a shark with flattened extensions on either side of the head.

hammock noun a wide strip of canvas or rope mesh suspended at both ends, used as a bed.

hamper¹ noun a basket used for food and other items needed for a picnic.

hamper² verb (**hampers, hampering, hampered**) slow down or prevent the movement or progress of.

hamster noun a burrowing rodent with a short tail and large cheek pouches.

> ☑ no *p*: *hamster*, not *hamp*-.

hamstring noun any of five tendons at the back of a person's knee. • verb (**hamstrings, hamstringing**, past and past participle **hamstrung**) **1** cripple by cutting the hamstrings. **2** severely restrict.

hand noun **1** the end part of the arm beyond the wrist, with four fingers and a thumb. **2** a pointer on a clock or watch indicating the passing of time. **3** (**hands**) a person's power or control. **4** an active role. **5** help in doing something. **6** a person who does physical work. **7** a round of applause. **8** the set of cards dealt to a player in a card game. **9** a unit of measurement of a horse's height, equal to 4 inches (10.16 cm). • verb give or pass something to.
□ **at hand** (or **on** or **to hand**) near; easy to reach. **from hand to mouth** meeting only your immediate needs. **hand grenade** a grenade that is thrown by hand. **hand in glove** working very closely together. **hand-me-down** a piece of clothing that has been passed on from another person. **hand-pick** choose carefully. **hands-on** involving direct participation in something. **hand-to-hand** (of fighting) involving physical contact. **in hand** in progress. **out of hand 1** not under control. **2** without taking time to think.

handbag noun Brit. a small bag used by a woman to carry everyday personal items.

handball noun **1** a game in which the ball is hit with the hand in a walled court. **2** Soccer unlawful touching of the ball with the hand or arm.

handbill noun a small printed advertisement handed out in the street.

handbook noun a book giving basic information or instructions.

handbrake noun a brake operated by hand, used to hold an already stationary vehicle.

handcuff noun (**handcuffs**) a pair of lockable linked metal rings for securing a prisoner's wrists. • verb put handcuffs on.

handful noun **1** a quantity that fills the hand. **2** a small number or amount. **3** informal a person who is difficult to deal with or control.

handgun noun a gun designed for use with one hand.

handhold noun something for a hand to grip on.

handicap noun **1** a condition that limits a

THESAURUS

hammer verb **1** *hammered metal*: beat, forge, shape, form, mould, fashion. **2** *he hammered the nail in*: batter, bang, pummel, pound, knock, thump.

hamper verb hinder, obstruct, impede, inhibit, delay, slow down, hold up, interfere with, handicap, hamstring. OPPOSITES help.

hand noun **1** fist, palm; informal paw, mitt. **2** *written in his own hand*: handwriting, writing, script. **3** *a factory hand*: worker, employee, workman, labourer, operative, craftsman, roustabout. • verb *hand me a spanner*: pass, give, present, let someone have.

handbook noun manual, instructions, ABC, A to Z, companion, guide, guidebook, vade mecum.

handcuff verb *he was handcuffed*: manacle, shackle, clap/put someone in irons; informal cuff. • noun (**handcuffs**) manacles, shackles, irons; informal cuffs, bracelets.

handful noun few, small number, small amount, small quantity, sprinkling, smattering, one or two, some, not many. OPPOSITES lot.

handicap noun **1** disability, infirmity, defect, impairment, affliction. **2** *a handicap to industrial competitiveness*: impediment, hindrance, obstacle, barrier, constraint, disadvantage, stumbling block. OPPOSITES benefit, advantage. • verb *handicapped by lack of funding*: hamper, impede, hinder, impair, person's ability to function physically, mentally, or socially. **2** something that makes progress or success difficult. **3** a disadvantage given to a leading competitor in a sport in order to make the chances of winning more equal, such as the extra weight given to certain racehorses. **4** the number of strokes by which a golfer normally exceeds par for a course. • **verb** (**handicaps, handicapping, handicapped**) make it difficult for someone to do something.

handicapped adjective having a handicap or disability.

> ! when used to refer to people with physical and mental disabilities, the word **handicapped** sounds old-fashioned and may cause offence; it is better to use **disabled**, or, when referring to mental disability, **having learning difficulties**.

handicraft noun **1** the skilled making of decorative objects by hand. **2** an object made in this way.

handiwork noun **1** (**your handiwork**) something that you have made or done. **2** the making of things by hand.

handkerchief noun (plural **handkerchiefs** or **handkerchieves**) a square of material for wiping or blowing the nose on.

handle verb (**handles, handling, handled**) **1** feel or move something with the hands. **2** control an animal, vehicle, or tool. **3** deal with a situation. **4** control, manage, or deal in something commercially. **5** (**handle yourself**) behave. • noun **1** the part by which a thing is held, carried, or controlled. **2** a means of understanding or approaching a person or situation. ■ **handler** noun.

handlebar or **handlebars** noun the steering bar of a bicycle or motorbike.

handmade adjective made by hand rather than machine.

handmaid or **handmaiden** noun old use a female servant.

handout noun **1** a parcel of food, clothes, or money given to a person in need. **2** a piece of printed information provided free of charge.

handset noun **1** the part of a telephone that you speak into and listen to. **2** a hand-held control device for a piece of electronic equipment.

handshake noun an act of shaking a person's hand.

handsome adjective (**handsomer, handsomest**) **1** (of a man) good-looking. **2** (of a woman) striking and impressive rather than pretty. **3** (of a thing) impressive and of good quality. **4** (of an amount) large. ■ **handsomely** adverb.

handspring noun a jump through the air on to your hands followed by another on to your feet.

handstand noun an act of balancing on your hands with your legs in the air.

handwriting noun **1** writing with a pen or pencil rather than by typing or printing. **2** a person's particular style of writing. ■ **handwritten** adjective.

handy adjective (**handier, handiest**) **1** convenient to handle or use. **2** close by and ready for use. ■ **handily** adverb.

handyman noun (plural **handymen**) a person employed to do general building repairs.

hang verb (**hangs, hanging**, past and past

h

THESAURUS

hamstring, restrict, constrain. OPPOSITES help.

handle verb **1** *handle the vase carefully:* hold, pick up, grasp, grip, lift, finger. **2** *a car which is easy to handle:* control, drive, steer, operate, manoeuvre. **3** *she handled the job well:* deal with, manage, tackle, take care of, look after, take charge of, attend to, see to, sort out. **4** *the traders handled imported goods:* trade in, deal in, buy, sell, supply, peddle, traffic in. • noun *a knife handle:* grip, haft, hilt, stock, shaft.

handsome adjective **1** *a handsome man:* good-looking, attractive, striking; informal hunky, dishy, tasty, fanciable; Brit. informal fit; N. Amer. informal cute. **2** *a handsome woman:* striking, imposing, prepossessing, good-looking, attractive. **3** *a handsome profit:* substantial, considerable, sizeable, princely, generous, lavish, ample, bumper;

informal tidy, whopping; Brit. informal ginormous. OPPOSITES ugly, meagre.

handy adjective **1** *a handy gadget:* useful, convenient, practical, neat, easy to use, user-friendly, helpful. **2** *keep your credit card handy:* ready, to hand, within reach, accessible, readily available, nearby, at the ready. **3** *he's handy with a needle:* skilful, skilled, dexterous, deft, adept, proficient. OPPOSITES useless, unwieldy, inconvenient, inept.

hang verb **1** *lights hung from the trees:* be suspended, dangle, swing, sway, hover, float. **2** *hang the picture at eye level:* suspend, put up, pin up, display. **3** *the room was hung with streamers:* decorate, adorn, drape, festoon, deck out. **4** *he was hanged for murder:* send to the gallows, execute, lynch; informal string up.

participle **hung** except in sense 2) **1** suspend or be suspended from above with the lower part dangling freely. **2** (past and past participle **hanged**) kill someone by suspending them from a rope tied around the neck. **3** (of a piece of clothing) fall or drape in a particular way.

□ **get the hang of** informal learn how to do something. **hang-glider** a simple aircraft consisting of a framework from which a person is suspended while they glide through the air. **hang out** informal spend time relaxing or enjoying yourself. **hang-up** informal an emotional problem.

> ! **hang** has two past tense and past participle forms, **hanged** and **hung**: use **hung** in general situations, as in *they hung out the washing*, and **hanged** when talking about execution by hanging, as in *the prisoner was hanged*.

hangar /hang-er/ **noun** a large building in which aircraft are kept.

> ☑ *-ar*, not *-er*: hang**ar**.

hangdog adjective having a sad or guilty appearance.

hanger noun **1** a person who hangs something. **2** (also **coat hanger**) a curved frame with a hook at the top, for hanging clothes from a rail.
□ **hanger-on** (plural **hangers-on**) a person who tries to be friendly with someone of higher status.

hanging noun a decorative piece of fabric hung on the wall of a room or around a bed.

hangman noun (plural **hangmen**) an executioner who hangs condemned people.

hangnail noun a piece of torn skin at the root of a fingernail.

hangover noun **1** a headache or other after-effects caused by drinking too much alcohol. **2** a thing that has survived from the past.

hank noun a coil or length of wool, hair, or other material.

hanker verb (**hanker after** or **for** or **to do**) feel a desire for or to do.

hanky or **hankie** noun (plural **hankies**) informal a handkerchief.

hanky-panky noun informal naughty behaviour.

hansom /han-suhm/ or **hansom cab** noun (in the past) a horse-drawn carriage with two wheels and a hood, for two passengers.

Hanukkah or **Chanukkah** /han-uu-kuh/ noun a Jewish festival of lights held in December.

haphazard adjective having no particular order or plan.
■ **haphazardly** adverb.

hapless adjective unlucky.

happen verb **1** take place without being planned or as the result of something. **2** (**happen to do**) do by chance. **3** (**happen on**) come across by chance. **4** (**happen to**) be experienced by. **5** (**happen to**) become of.

happening noun an event or occurrence.
• adjective informal fashionable.

happy adjective (**happier**, **happiest**) **1** feeling or showing pleasure. **2** willing to do something. **3** fortunate and convenient.
□ **happy-go-lucky** cheerfully unconcerned about the future. **happy hour** a period of the day when drinks are sold at reduced prices in a bar.
■ **happily** adverb **happiness** noun.

hara-kiri /ha-ruh-ki-ri/ noun a Japanese method of ritual suicide in which a person cuts open their stomach with a sword.

harangue /huh-rang/ verb (**harangues**, **haranguing**, **harangued**) use loud and aggressive language in criticizing someone or trying to persuade them to do something. • noun an act of haranguing.

harass /ha-ruhss, huh-rass/ verb **1** torment

THESAURUS

hanker verb yearn, long, wish, hunger, thirst, lust, ache; informal itch.

happen verb **1** *remember what happened last time*: occur, take place, come about, develop, result, transpire; N. Amer. informal go down. **2** *they happened to be in London*: chance, have the good/bad luck.

happening noun occurrence, event, incident, episode, affair.

happily adverb **1** cheerfully, contentedly, cheerily, merrily, joyfully. **2** *I will happily do as you ask*: gladly, willingly, readily, freely. **3** *happily, we arrived just in time*: fortunately, luckily, thankfully, mercifully, as luck would have it.

happiness noun pleasure, contentment, satisfaction, cheerfulness, merriment, joy, delight, elation, jubilation.
OPPOSITES misery.

happy adjective **1** cheerful, cheery, merry, joyful, jovial, jolly, carefree, in good spirits, in a good mood, pleased, contented, content, satisfied, gratified, delighted, sunny, radiant, elated, jubilant; literary blithe. **2** *we will be happy to advise you*: glad, pleased, delighted, more than willing. **3** *a happy coincidence*: fortunate, lucky, timely, convenient.
OPPOSITES sad, unwilling, unfortunate.

harass verb persecute, intimidate, hound, pester, bother; informal hassle, bug; N. Amer.

someone by putting constant pressure on them or by being unpleasant. **2** (**harassed**) tired or tense as a result of having too many demands made on you. **3** make repeated small-scale attacks on an enemy in order to wear down resistance.
■ **harassment** noun.

☑ only one *r*: harass.

harbinger /**har**-bin-jer/ noun a person or thing that announces or signals the approach of something.

harbour (US spelling **harbor**) noun a sheltered area of coast, where ships can be moored. • verb **1** keep a thought or feeling secretly in your mind. **2** give a refuge or shelter to. **3** carry the germs of a disease.

hard adjective **1** solid, firm, and rigid. **2** needing a lot of endurance or effort; difficult. **3** (of a person) not showing any signs of weakness. **4** (of information) precise and definitely true. **5** harsh or unpleasant to the senses. **6** done with a lot of force or strength. **7** (of drink) strongly alcoholic. **8** (of a drug) very addictive.
• adverb **1** with a lot of effort or force. **2** so as to be solid or firm.
☐ **hard and fast** (of a rule) fixed and not able to be changed. **hard-boiled 1** (of an egg) boiled until the yolk is firm. **2** (of a person) tough and cynical. **hard cash** coins and banknotes as opposed to other forms of payment. **hard copy** a printed version of data held in a computer. **hard core 1** the most committed or uncompromising members of a group. **2** very explicit pornography. **3** pop music that is loud and aggressive in style. **hard disk** (or **hard drive**) (in a computer) a rigid magnetic disk on which a large amount of data can be stored. **hard done by** Brit. harshly or unfairly treated. **hard feelings** feelings of resentment. **hard-headed** tough and realistic. **hard-hearted** unsympathetic or uncaring. **hard line** a strict policy or attitude. **hard-nosed** realistic and tough-minded. **hard shoulder** Brit. a strip of road alongside a motorway for use in an emergency. **hard up** informal short of money.
■ **harden** verb **hardness** noun.

hardback noun a book bound in stiff covers.

hardbitten adjective tough and cynical.

hardboard noun stiff board made of compressed wood pulp.

hardly adverb **1** scarcely; barely. **2** only with great difficulty.

❗ don't use **hardly** in a negative sentence, such as *I can't hardly wait*; say *I can hardly wait* instead.

hardship noun severe suffering.

hardware noun **1** tools and other items

h

informal ride.

harassed adjective stressed, hard-pressed, careworn, worried, troubled; informal hassled.
OPPOSITES carefree.

harassment noun persecution, intimidation, victimization, trouble, bother; informal hassle.

harbour noun port, dock, haven, marina, mooring, wharf, anchorage, waterfront.
• verb **1** *he is harbouring a dangerous criminal*: shelter, conceal, hide, shield, protect, give asylum to. **2** *Rose harboured a grudge against him*: bear, hold, nurse, foster.

hard adjective **1** *hard ground*: firm, solid, rigid, stiff, unbreakable, unyielding, compacted, tough, strong. **2** *hard physical work*: arduous, strenuous, tiring, exhausting, back-breaking, gruelling, heavy, laborious, demanding; Brit. informal knackering. **3** *hard workers*: industrious, diligent, assiduous, conscientious, energetic, keen, enthusiastic, indefatigable. **4** *a hard problem*: difficult, puzzling, complicated, intricate, thorny, problematic. **5** *times are hard*: harsh, grim, austere, difficult, bad, bleak, tough. **6** *a hard blow*: forceful, heavy, strong, sharp, violent, powerful.
OPPOSITES soft, easy, lazy, gentle.
• adverb **1** *George pushed her hard*: forcefully, roughly, heavily, sharply, violently. **2** *they worked hard*: diligently, industriously, assiduously, conscientiously, energetically, doggedly; informal like mad, like crazy. **3** *she looked hard at me*: closely, intently, critically, carefully, searchingly.
OPPOSITES gently, lazily, casually.

harden verb **1** *this glue hardens in four hours*: solidify, set, stiffen, thicken. **2** *their suffering had hardened them*: toughen, desensitize, inure, season, train, numb.
OPPOSITES soften.

hardened adjective *a hardened criminal*: inveterate, seasoned, habitual, chronic, compulsive, confirmed, incorrigible.

hardly adverb scarcely, barely, only just, just.
OPPOSITES fully, easily.

hardship noun difficulty, privation, destitution, poverty, austerity, need, distress, suffering, adversity.
OPPOSITES prosperity, ease.

hardware noun equipment, apparatus, gear, paraphernalia, tackle, kit, machinery.

used in the home and in activities such as gardening. **2** the machines, wiring, and other parts of a computer. **3** heavy military equipment such as tanks and missiles.

hardwood noun the wood from a broadleaved tree as distinguished from that of conifers.

hardy adjective (**hardier, hardiest**) capable of surviving difficult conditions.
■ **hardiness** noun.

hare noun a fast-running animal like a large rabbit, with long hind legs. • verb (**hares, haring, hared**) run very fast.
□ **hare-brained** foolish and unlikely to succeed.

harebell noun a plant with pale blue bell-shaped flowers.

harelip noun offensive a cleft lip.

harem /**hah**-reem, hah-**reem**/ noun **1** the separate part of a Muslim household reserved for women. **2** the women living in a harem.

haricot /**ha**-ri-koh/ noun a round white bean.

hark verb **1** literary listen. **2** (**hark back to**) recall or remind you of something in the past.

harken ⇨ **HEARKEN**.

harlequin noun (**Harlequin**) (in traditional pantomime) a character who wears a mask and a diamond-patterned costume. • adjective in varied colours.

harlot noun old use a prostitute.

harm noun **1** hurt or injury to a person. **2** damage done to a thing. • verb **1** hurt or injure someone. **2** damage or have a bad effect on something.

harmful adjective causing or likely to cause harm.
■ **harmfully** adverb.

harmless adjective not able or likely to cause harm.
■ **harmlessly** adverb.

harmonic adjective relating to harmony.

harmonica noun a small rectangular wind instrument with a row of metal reeds that produce different notes.

harmonious adjective **1** tuneful. **2** arranged in a pleasing way so that each part goes well with the others. **3** free from conflict.
■ **harmoniously** adverb.

harmonium noun a keyboard instrument in which the notes are produced by air driven through metal reeds by foot-operated bellows.

harmonize or **harmonise** verb (**harmonizes, harmonizing, harmonized**) **1** add notes to a melody to produce harmony. **2** make or be harmonious.

harmony noun (plural **harmonies**) **1** the combination of musical notes sounded at the same time to produce chords with a pleasing effect. **2** a pleasing quality when things are arranged together well. **3** agreement.

harness noun **1** a set of straps by which a horse or other animal is fastened to a cart, plough, etc. **2** an arrangement of straps used for attaching a person's body to something. • verb **1** fit a person or animal with a harness. **2** control and make use of resources.

harp noun a musical instrument consisting of a frame supporting a series of strings of different lengths, played by plucking with the fingers. • verb (**harp on**) keep talking about something in a boring way.
■ **harpist** noun.

harpoon noun a barbed spear-like missile used for catching whales and other large sea creatures. • verb spear with a harpoon.

harpsichord noun a keyboard instrument with horizontal strings plucked by points operated by pressing the keys.

harpy noun (plural **harpies**) **1** Greek & Roman Mythology a cruel creature with a woman's head and body and a bird's wings and claws. **2** an unpleasant woman.

THESAURUS

hardy adjective robust, healthy, fit, strong, sturdy, tough, rugged.
OPPOSITES delicate.

harm noun it won't do you any harm: injury, damage, mischief.
OPPOSITES good.
• verb **1** he's never harmed anybody: hurt, injure, lay a finger on, mistreat, ill-treat. **2** this could harm his prospects: damage, spoil, affect, undermine, ruin.
OPPOSITES heal, help.

harmful adjective damaging, injurious, detrimental, dangerous, unhealthy, unwholesome, hurtful, destructive, hazardous.
OPPOSITES beneficial.

harmless adjective **1** a harmless substance: safe, innocuous, gentle, mild, non-toxic. **2** he seems harmless enough: inoffensive, innocuous, gentle.
OPPOSITES harmful, objectionable.

harmony noun **1** musical harmony: tunefulness, euphony, melodiousness, unison. **2** the villagers live together in harmony: accord, agreement, peace, friendship, fellowship, cooperation, understanding, rapport, unity.
OPPOSITES dissonance, disagreement.

harridan noun a bossy or aggressive old woman.

harrier noun 1 a hound used for hunting hares. 2 a bird of prey.

harrow noun a piece of equipment consisting of a heavy frame set with teeth which is dragged over ploughed land to break up or spread the soil. • verb draw a harrow over.

harrowing adjective very distressing.

harry verb (**harries, harrying, harried**) 1 carry out repeated attacks on an enemy. 2 pester continuously.

harsh adjective 1 unpleasantly rough or jarring to the senses. 2 cruel or severe. 3 (of climate or conditions) difficult to survive in; hostile.
■ **harshly** adverb **harshness** noun.

hart noun an adult male deer.

harum-scarum adjective reckless.

harvest noun 1 the process or period of gathering in crops. 2 the season's yield or crop. • verb gather in a crop.
■ **harvester** noun.

has 3rd person singular present of **HAVE**.
□ **has-been** informal a person who is no longer important.

hash¹ noun a dish of chopped cooked meat reheated with potatoes.
□ **make a hash of** informal make a mess of.

hash² = **HASHISH**.

hash³ noun Brit. the symbol #.

hashish /ha-sheesh/ noun cannabis.

hasn't short form has not.

hasp noun a hinged metal plate that is fitted over a metal loop and secured by a pin or padlock to fasten something.

hassle informal noun 1 annoying inconvenience. 2 a situation involving argument or disagreement. • verb (**hassles, hassling, hassled**) harass or pester someone.

hassock noun a cushion for kneeling on in church.

haste noun speed or urgency of action.

hasten verb 1 move or act quickly. 2 make something happen sooner than expected.

hasty adjective (**hastier, hastiest**) hurried; rushed.
■ **hastily** adverb.

hat noun a covering for the head.
□ **hat-trick** three successes of the same kind.

hatch¹ noun 1 a small opening in a floor, wall, or roof allowing access to an area. 2 a door in an aircraft, spacecraft, or submarine.

hatch² verb 1 (of a young bird, fish, or reptile) come out of its egg. 2 (of an egg) open and produce a young animal. 3 form a plot or plan.

hatch³ verb (in drawing) shade an area with closely drawn parallel lines.

hatchback noun a car with a door that opens upwards across the full width at the back end.

hatchet noun a small axe with a short handle.
□ **bury the hatchet** end a quarrel.

hatchling noun a newly hatched young animal.

hatchway noun an opening or hatch, especially in a ship's deck.

hate verb (**hates, hating, hated**) feel very

h

THESAURUS

harrowing adjective distressing, traumatic, upsetting, shocking, disturbing, painful, agonizing.

harry verb harass, hound, torment, pester, worry, badger, nag, plague; informal hassle, bug.

harsh adjective 1 *a harsh voice:* grating, rasping, strident, raucous, discordant. 2 *harsh colours:* glaring, loud, garish, gaudy, lurid. 3 *his harsh treatment of captives:* cruel, savage, barbarous, merciless, inhumane, ruthless. 4 *they took harsh measures to end the crisis:* severe, stringent, firm, stiff, stern, rigorous. 5 *harsh words:* rude, discourteous, unfriendly, sharp, bitter, unkind, critical, disparaging. 6 *harsh conditions:* austere, grim, spartan, hard, inhospitable. 7 *a harsh winter:* cold, freezing, icy, bitter, hard, severe, bleak.
OPPOSITES soft, subdued, kind, mild, friendly, comfortable.

harvest noun *a poor harvest:* crop, yield,

vintage, produce.
• verb *he harvested the wheat:* gather, bring in, reap, pick, collect.

hassle (informal) noun *parking is such a hassle:* inconvenience, bother, nuisance, trouble, annoyance, irritation, fuss; informal aggravation, headache, pain in the neck.
• verb *don't hassle me!* harass, pester, be on at, badger, hound, bother, nag, torment; informal bug; N. English informal mither.

hasten verb 1 *we hastened back:* hurry, rush, dash, race, fly, speed; informal hare, scoot, hotfoot it, zip; N. Amer. informal hightail. 2 *chemicals can hasten ageing:* speed up, bring on, precipitate, advance.
OPPOSITES dawdle, delay.

hasty adjective hurried, rash, impetuous, impulsive, reckless, precipitate, spur-of-the-moment.
OPPOSITES considered.

hate verb 1 *they hate each other:* loathe, detest, despise, dislike, abhor, shrink from, be unable to bear/stand. 2 *I hate to bother* strong dislike for. • noun 1 very strong dislike. 2 informal a disliked person or thing.

hateful adjective very unkind or unpleasant.

hatred noun very strong dislike; hate.

haughty adjective (**haughtier, haughtiest**) arrogant and superior towards other people.
■ **haughtily** adverb.

haul verb 1 pull or drag something with a lot of effort. 2 transport something in a lorry or cart. • noun 1 a quantity of something obtained, especially illegally. 2 a number of fish caught at one time.

haulage noun Brit. the commercial transport of goods.

haulier noun Brit. a person or company employed in the commercial transport of goods by road.

haulm /hawm/ noun a plant stalk.

haunch noun 1 a person's or animal's buttock and thigh. 2 the leg and loin of an animal, as food.

haunt verb 1 (of a ghost) appear regularly in a place. 2 (of a person) visit a place frequently. 3 keep coming into someone's mind in a disturbing way. • noun a place where a particular type of person frequently goes.

haunted adjective 1 visited by a ghost. 2 showing signs of mental suffering.

haunting adjective making someone feel sad or thoughtful.
■ **hauntingly** adverb.

haute couture /oht kuu-tyoor/ noun the designing and making of high-quality clothes by leading fashion houses.

haute cuisine /oht kwi-zeen/ noun high-quality cooking in the traditional French style.

have verb (**has, having, had**) 1 possess or own. 2 experience. 3 be able to make use of. 4 (**have to**) be obliged to; must. 5 perform an action. 6 show a personal characteristic. 7 suffer from an illness or disability. 8 cause something to be or be done. 9 place, hold, or keep something in a particular position. 10 eat or drink something. • auxiliary verb used with a past participle to form the perfect, pluperfect, and future perfect tenses, and the conditional mood.

> ! be careful not to write **of** when you mean **have** or **'ve**: I could've told you that not I could of told you that.

haven noun 1 a place of safety. 2 a harbour or small port.

haven't short form have not.

haver /hay-ver/ verb (**havers, havering, havered**) 1 Scottish talk foolishly. 2 Brit. be indecisive.

haversack noun a small, sturdy bag carried on the back or over the shoulder.

havoc noun great destruction, confusion, or disorder.
□ **play havoc with** completely disrupt.

Hawaiian /huh-wy-uhn/ noun a person from Hawaii. • adjective relating to Hawaii.

hawk¹ noun 1 a fast-flying bird of prey with a long tail. 2 a person in favour of aggressive policies in foreign affairs. • verb hunt with a trained hawk.
■ **hawkish** adjective.

hawk² verb offer goods for sale in the street.
■ **hawker** noun.

hawk³ verb clear the throat noisily.

hawser /haw-zer/ noun a thick rope for

THESAURUS

you: be sorry, be reluctant, be loath.
OPPOSITES love.
• noun feelings of hate: hatred, loathing, abhorrence, abomination, aversion, disgust.
OPPOSITES love.

hatred noun. See HATE noun.

haul verb she hauled the basket upstairs: drag, pull, heave, lug, hump.
• noun the thieves' haul: booty, loot, plunder, spoils, stolen goods; informal swag.

haunt verb the sight haunted me: torment, disturb, trouble, worry, plague, prey on.
• noun a favourite haunt of artists: meeting place, stamping ground, spot, venue; informal hang-out; N. Amer. stomping ground.

haunted adjective 1 the church is haunted: possessed, cursed, jinxed, eerie. 2 his haunted eyes: tormented, anguished, tortured, obsessed, troubled, worried.

haunting adjective evocative, affecting, stirring, powerful, poignant, memorable.

have verb 1 he had a new car: own, be in possession of, be blessed with, boast, enjoy. 2 the flat has five rooms: comprise, consist of, contain, include, incorporate, be composed of, be made up of. 3 they had tea: eat, drink, take. 4 let's have a party: organize, hold, give, throw, put on, lay on. 5 I have to get up at six: must, be obliged to, be required to, be compelled to, be forced to, be bound to.
□ **have someone on** (Brit. informal) play a trick on, play a joke on, pull someone's leg; Brit. informal wind someone up; N. Amer. informal put someone on. **have something on** be wearing, be dressed in, be clothed in, be decked out in, sport.

haven noun refuge, retreat, shelter, sanctuary, oasis.

havoc noun chaos, mayhem, bedlam, pandemonium, a shambles.

mooring or towing a ship.

hawthorn noun a thorny shrub or tree with small dark red fruits called **haws**.

hay noun grass that has been mown and dried for use as animal feed.
□ **hay fever** an allergy to pollen or dust, causing sneezing and watery eyes.

haystack or **hayrick** noun a large packed pile of hay.

haywire adjective informal out of control.

hazard noun 1 a danger. 2 an obstacle, such as a bunker, on a golf course. • verb 1 dare to say. 2 put at risk.

hazardous adjective dangerous.

haze noun 1 a thin mist caused by fine particles of dust, water, etc. 2 a state of mental confusion.

hazel noun 1 a shrub or small tree which produces round nuts called **hazelnuts**. 2 a rich reddish-brown colour.

hazy adjective (**hazier**, **haziest**) 1 covered by a haze. 2 vague or unclear.
■ **hazily** adverb.

he pronoun 1 used to refer to a man, boy, or male animal previously mentioned or easily identified. 2 used to refer to a person or animal whose sex is not specified.

> ! until recently, **he** was used to refer to any person, male or female (as in *every child needs to know that he is loved*), but many people now think that this is old-fashioned and sexist. One solution is to use **he or she**; another is to use **they**, as in *everyone needs to feel that they matter.*

head noun 1 the upper part of the body, containing the brain, mouth, and sense organs. 2 a person in charge. 3 the front, forward, or upper part of something. 4 a person considered as a unit: *fifty pounds per head*. 5 a particular number of cattle or sheep. 6 a compact mass of leaves or flowers at the top of a stem. 7 a part of a computer or a tape or video recorder which transfers information to and from a tape or disk. 8 the source of a river or stream. 9 the foam on top of a glass of beer. 10 (**heads**) the side of a coin showing the image of a head. 11 pressure of water or steam in an enclosed space. • adjective chief. • verb 1 be the head of. 2 move in a particular direction. 3 (**head someone/ thing off**) intercept someone or something and force them to change direction. 4 give a heading to. 5 Soccer hit the ball with the head.
□ **come to a head** reach a crisis. **head-on** 1 with the front of a vehicle. 2 involving direct confrontation. **head start** an advantage gained at the beginning of something.
■ **headless** adjective **headship** noun.

headache noun 1 a continuous pain in the head. 2 informal something that causes worry.

headband noun a band of fabric worn around the head.

headboard noun an upright panel at the head of a bed.

headbutt verb attack someone by hitting them with the head.

headdress noun a decorative covering for the head.

header noun 1 Soccer a shot or pass made with the head. 2 a line of writing at the top of each page of a book or document.

headhunt verb approach someone already employed elsewhere to fill a vacant post.

heading noun 1 a title at the head of a page or section of a book. 2 a direction or bearing.

headland noun a narrow piece of land that

THESAURUS

hazard noun danger, risk, peril, menace, jeopardy, threat.

hazardous adjective risky, dangerous, unsafe, perilous, fraught with danger, high-risk; informal dicey; Brit. informal dodgy. OPPOSITES safe, certain.

haze noun mist, fog, cloud, vapour.

head noun 1 *her head hit the wall:* skull, cranium; informal nut. 2 *he had to use his head:* brain(s), brainpower, intellect, intelligence, grey matter; Brit. informal loaf; N. Amer. informal smarts. 3 *she had a head for business:* aptitude, talent, gift, capacity. 4 *the head of the church:* leader, chief, controller, governor, superintendent, commander, captain, director, manager, principal, president; informal boss; Brit. informal gaffer, guv'nor. 5 *the head of the queue:* front, beginning, start, top.
• adjective *the head waiter:* chief, principal, leading, main, first, top, highest.
• verb *a team headed by a manager:* command, control, lead, manage, direct, supervise, superintend, oversee, preside over.
□ **head someone/something off 1** *he went to head off the visitors:* intercept, divert, redirect, re-route, turn away. 2 *they headed off an argument:* forestall, avert, stave off, nip in the bud, prevent, avoid, stop.

headache noun 1 *I've got a headache:* sore head, migraine. 2 (informal) *it was a real headache:* problem, worry, hassle, pain in the neck, bind.

heading noun title, caption, legend, rubric, headline.

sticks out into the sea.

headlight or **headlamp** noun a powerful light at the front of a motor vehicle.

headline noun 1 a heading at the top of a newspaper or magazine article. 2 (**the headlines**) a summary of the most important items of news. • verb (**headlines, headlining, headlined**) 1 give an article a headline. 2 appear as the star performer at a concert.

headlong adverb & adjective 1 with the head first. 2 in a rush.

headmaster or **headmistress** noun a teacher in charge of a school.

headphones plural noun a pair of earphones joined by a band placed over the head.

headquarters noun the place from which an organization or military operation is directed.

headset noun a set of headphones with a microphone attached.

headstone noun a stone slab set up at the head of a grave.

headstrong adjective very independent and determined to have your own way.

headway noun (**make headway**) make progress.

headwind noun a wind blowing from directly in front, towards someone or something.

headword noun a word which begins a separate entry in a dictionary or encyclopedia.

heady adjective (**headier, headiest**) 1 having a strong or exciting effect. 2 (of alcohol) strong.

heal verb 1 make or become healthy again. 2 put right.
■ **healer** noun.

health noun 1 the state of being free from illness or injury. 2 a person's mental or physical condition.
□ **health club** a private club where exercise facilities and beauty treatments are available. **health farm** a place where people stay in order to try to become healthier through dieting, exercise, and special treatments. **health food** natural food that is believed to be good for your health.

healthful adjective good for the health.

healthy adjective (**healthier, healthiest**) 1 in good health, or helping towards good health. 2 normal, sensible, or desirable. 3 of a very satisfactory size or amount.
■ **healthily** adverb.

heap noun 1 a pile of a substance or of a number of objects. 2 informal a large amount or number. 3 informal an old vehicle in bad condition. • verb 1 put in or form a heap. 2 (**heap something with**) load something heavily with. 3 (**heap something on**) give a lot of praise, criticism, etc. to.

hear verb (**hears, hearing, heard**) 1 be aware of a sound with the ears. 2 be told of. 3 (**have heard of**) be aware of the existence of. 4 (**hear from**) receive a letter, phone call, or email from. 5 listen to. 6 listen to and judge a case in a law court.
■ **hearer** noun.

hearing noun 1 the ability to hear sounds. 2 the range within which sounds can be heard. 3 an opportunity to state your case. 4 an act of listening to evidence.
□ **hearing aid** a small device worn by a partially deaf person to make them hear better.

hearken or **harken** /har-k'n/ verb (usu. **hearken to**) old use listen.

hearsay noun information received from other people which is possibly unreliable.

hearse /herss/ noun a vehicle for carrying

THESAURUS

heady adjective 1 *heady wine:* potent, intoxicating, strong. 2 *the heady days of my youth:* exhilarating, exciting, stimulating, thrilling, intoxicating.
OPPOSITES weak, boring.

heal verb 1 *he heals the sick:* cure, make better, restore to health, treat. 2 *his knee had healed:* get better, be cured, recover, mend. 3 *we tried to heal the rift:* put right, repair, resolve, settle; informal patch up.
OPPOSITES worsen, aggravate.

health noun 1 *he was restored to health:* well-being, fitness, good condition, strength, robustness, vigour. 2 *poor health:* condition, physical shape, constitution.
OPPOSITES illness.

healthy adjective 1 *a healthy baby:* well, fit, in good shape, in fine fettle, in tip-top condition, strong, fighting fit. 2 *a healthy diet:* wholesome, good for you, health-giving, nutritious, nourishing, invigorating, sanitary, hygienic.
OPPOSITES unhealthy.

heap noun *a heap of boxes:* pile, stack, mound, mountain.
• verb *she heaped logs on the fire:* pile (up), stack (up), make a mound of.

hear verb 1 *she could hear voices:* make out, catch, get, perceive, overhear. 2 *they heard that I had moved:* learn, find out, discover, gather, glean. 3 *a jury heard the case:* try, judge, adjudicate on.

hearing noun 1 *she moved out of hearing:* earshot, hearing distance. 2 *I had a fair hearing:* chance to speak, opportunity to be heard. 3 *he gave evidence at the hearing:*

the coffin to a funeral.

heart noun 1 the organ in the chest that pumps the blood around the body. 2 the central or innermost part of something. 3 a person's ability to feel love or compassion. 4 mood or feeling. 5 courage or enthusiasm.
□ **heart attack** a sudden failure of the heart to work properly. **heart-rending** very sad or upsetting. **heart-searching** thorough examination of your feelings and motives. **heart-throb** a very good-looking famous man. **heart-to-heart** (of a conversation) very intimate and personal. **heart-warming** arousing feelings of happiness or pleasure. **wear your heart on your sleeve** show your feelings openly.

heartache noun emotional suffering or grief.

heartbeat noun a pulsation of the heart.

heartbreak noun extreme distress.
■ **heartbreaking** adjective **heartbroken** adjective.

heartburn noun a form of indigestion felt as a burning sensation in the chest.

hearten verb make more cheerful or confident.
■ **heartening** adjective.

heartfelt adjective deeply and strongly felt.

hearth /harth/ noun the floor or surround of a fireplace.

hearthrug noun a rug laid in front of a fireplace.

heartily adverb 1 in a hearty way. 2 very.

heartless adjective feeling no pity for other people.

hearty adjective (**heartier, heartiest**) 1 enthusiastic and friendly. 2 strong and healthy. 3 heartfelt. 4 (of a meal) large and filling.

heat noun 1 the quality of being hot. 2 hot weather or high temperature. 3 strength of feeling. 4 (**the heat**) informal great pressure to do or achieve something. 5 one of a series of races or contests held to decide who will take part in the next stage of a competition. ● verb 1 make or become hot or warm. 2 (**heat up**) become more intense and exciting. 3 (**heated**) passionate.
□ **on heat** (of a female mammal) ready for mating.
■ **heatedly** adverb.

heater noun a device for heating something.

heath noun an area of open uncultivated land covered with heather, gorse, etc.

heathen /**hee**-*th*uhn/ noun old use a person who does not belong to a widely held religion.

heather noun a shrub with small purple flowers, found on moors and heaths.

heating noun equipment used to provide heat.

heatstroke noun a feverish condition caused by being exposed to very high temperatures.

h

THESAURUS

trial, court case, enquiry, inquest, tribunal.

heart noun 1 *he poured out his heart:* emotions, feelings, sentiments, soul, mind. 2 *he has no heart:* compassion, sympathy, humanity, feeling(s), empathy, understanding, soul, goodwill. 3 *they lost heart:* enthusiasm, spirit, determination, resolve, nerve; Brit. informal bottle. 4 *the heart of the city:* centre, middle, hub, core. 5 *the heart of the matter:* essence, crux, core, nub, root, meat, substance, kernel; informal nitty-gritty.
□ **at heart deep down,** basically, fundamentally, essentially, in essence, intrinsically. **by heart from memory,** off pat, word for word, verbatim, parrot-fashion, word-perfect. **take heart be encouraged,** be heartened, be comforted, be consoled.

heartily adverb 1 *we heartily welcome the changes:* wholeheartedly, warmly, profoundly, eagerly, enthusiastically. 2 *they were heartily sick of her:* thoroughly, completely, absolutely, exceedingly, downright; N. Amer. quite; informal seriously; Brit. informal jolly; N. Amer. informal real, mighty.

hearty adjective 1 *a hearty character:*

exuberant, jovial, ebullient, cheerful, lively, loud, animated, vivacious, energetic, spirited. 2 *hearty congratulations:* wholehearted, heartfelt, sincere, genuine, real. 3 *a hearty woman of sixty-five:* robust, healthy, hardy, fit, fit as a fiddle, vigorous, sturdy, strong. 4 *a hearty meal:* substantial, large, ample, satisfying, filling, generous, square.
OPPOSITES half-hearted, frail, light.

heat noun 1 *a plant sensitive to heat:* warmth, hotness, high temperature. 2 *he took the heat out of the dispute:* passion, intensity, vehemence, fervour, excitement, agitation, anger.
OPPOSITES cold, apathy.
● verb 1 *the food was heated:* warm (up), reheat, cook, keep warm. 2 *the pipes expand as they heat up:* get hot, get warm, warm up; Brit. informal hot up.
OPPOSITES cool.

heated adjective 1 *a heated argument:* vehement, passionate, impassioned, animated, lively, acrimonious, angry, bitter, furious, fierce. 2 *Robert grew heated as he spoke:* excited, animated, worked up, wound up, keyed up; informal het up.

heatwave noun a period of abnormally hot weather.

heave verb (heaves, heaving, heaved or chiefly Nautical **hove**) 1 lift or move with great effort. 2 produce a sigh noisily. 3 rise and fall. 4 try to vomit. 5 (**heave to**) Nautical come to a stop. 6 (**heaving**) Brit. informal very crowded.
□ **heave in sight** (or **into view**) Nautical come into view.

heaven noun 1 (in Christianity and some other religions) the place where God or the gods live and where good people go when they die. 2 (**the heavens**) literary the sky. 3 a place or state of great happiness.
□ **in seventh heaven** very happy.

heavenly adjective 1 having to do with heaven. 2 having to do with the sky. 3 informal wonderful.
□ **heavenly body** a planet, star, etc.

heavy adjective (heavier, heaviest) 1 of great weight. 2 thick or dense. 3 of more than the usual size, amount, or force. 4 hard or forceful. 5 needing a lot of physical effort. 6 informal very important or serious. • noun (plural **heavies**) informal 1 a large, strong man. 2 an important person.
□ **heavy-duty** designed to withstand a lot of use or wear. **heavy-handed** clumsy, insensitive, or too forceful. **heavy industry** large-scale production of large, heavy articles and materials. **heavy metal** very loud, forceful rock music.
■ **heavily** adverb **heaviness** noun.

heavyweight noun 1 the heaviest weight in boxing. 2 informal an influential person.

Hebrew /hee-broo/ noun an ancient language still spoken in Israel.

heckle verb (heckles, heckling, heckled) interrupt a public speaker with comments or abuse.
■ **heckler** noun.

hectare /hek-tair/ noun a unit of area equal to 10,000 square metres (2.471 acres).

hectic adjective full of frantic activity.
■ **hectically** adverb.

hector verb talk to someone in a bullying way.

he'd short form 1 he had. 2 he would.

hedge noun a fence formed by bushes growing closely together. • verb (hedges, hedging, hedged) 1 surround with a hedge. 2 avoid making a definite statement or decision.
□ **hedge your bets** avoid committing yourself.

hedgehog noun a small animal with a spiny coat, which can roll itself into a ball for defence.

hedgerow noun a hedge of wild shrubs and trees bordering a field.

hedonism noun behaviour based on the belief that pleasure is the most important thing in life.
■ **hedonist** noun **hedonistic** adjective.

heebie-jeebies plural noun (**the heebie-jeebies**) informal a state of nervous fear or anxiety.

heed verb pay attention to.
□ **pay** (or **take**) **heed** pay careful attention.

THESAURUS

heaven noun 1 *the good will have a place in heaven:* paradise, the hereafter, the next world, the afterworld, nirvana, Zion, Elysium. 2 *a good book is my idea of heaven:* bliss, ecstasy, rapture, contentment, happiness, delight, joy, paradise.
OPPOSITES hell, misery.

heavenly adjective 1 *heavenly choirs:* divine, holy, celestial, angelic. 2 *a heavenly body:* celestial, cosmic, stellar, sidereal. 3 (informal) *a heavenly morning:* delightful, wonderful, glorious, sublime, exquisite, beautiful, lovely, gorgeous, enchanting; informal divine, super, fantastic, fabulous.
OPPOSITES mortal, infernal, terrestrial, dreadful.

heavily adverb 1 *Dad walked heavily:* laboriously, slowly, ponderously, awkwardly, clumsily. 2 *we were heavily defeated:* decisively, conclusively, roundly, soundly, utterly, completely, thoroughly. 3 *he drank heavily:* excessively, immoderately, copiously, intemperately. 4 *the area is heavily planted with trees:* densely, closely, thickly. 5 *I became heavily involved:* deeply, extremely, greatly, exceedingly, tremendously, profoundly.
OPPOSITES easily, narrowly, moderately, thinly, slightly.

heavy adjective 1 *a heavy box:* weighty, hefty, substantial, ponderous, solid, dense. 2 *a heavy blow to the head:* forceful, hard, strong, violent, powerful, mighty, sharp, severe. 3 *heavy work:* strenuous, hard, physical, difficult, arduous, demanding, back-breaking, gruelling. 4 *heavy fighting:* intense, fierce, relentless, severe, serious. 5 *a heavy meal:* substantial, filling, stodgy, rich, big.
OPPOSITES light.

hectic adjective frantic, frenetic, frenzied, feverish, manic, busy, active, fast and furious.
OPPOSITES leisurely.

heed verb *heed the warnings:* pay attention to, take notice of, take note of, listen to, consider, take to heart, take into account, obey, adhere to, abide by, observe.
OPPOSITES disregard.
• noun *he paid no heed:* attention, notice,

heedless adjective showing a reckless lack of care or attention.

heel[1] noun 1 the back part of the foot below the ankle. 2 the part of a shoe or boot supporting the heel. • verb renew the heel on a shoe.

□ take to your heels run away.

heel[2] verb (of a ship) lean over to one side.

heft verb lift or carry something heavy.

hefty adjective (**heftier**, **heftiest**) 1 large, heavy, and powerful. 2 (of a number or amount) considerable.

hegemony /hi-**jem**-uh-ni, hi-**gem**-uh-ni/ noun formal leadership or dominance.

Hegira or **Hejira** /**hej**-i-ruh/ noun Muhammad's departure from Mecca to Medina in AD 622.

heifer /**hef**-er/ noun a young cow.

height noun 1 measurement from head to foot or from base to top. 2 distance above sea level or the ground. 3 the quality of being tall or high. 4 a high place. 5 the most intense or extreme part.

heighten verb 1 make or become more intense. 2 make higher.

heinous /**hay**-nuhss, **hee**-nuhss/ adjective very wicked.

heir /air/ noun 1 a person who will inherit the property or rank of another when that person dies. 2 a person who continues someone else's work.

□ heir apparent (plural **heirs apparent**) 1 an heir whose rights cannot be taken away by the birth of another heir. 2 someone who is most likely to take the job or role of another person.

heiress noun a female heir.

heirloom noun a valuable object that has belonged to a family for several generations.

heist /hyst/ noun informal a robbery.

held past and past participle of HOLD.

helical /**he**-li-k'l, **hee**-li-k'l/ adjective in the shape of a helix.

helicopter noun a type of aircraft which is powered and lifted by horizontally revolving blades.

heliotrope /**heel**-i-uh-trohp/ noun a plant with sweet-smelling purple or blue flowers.

heliport noun an airport or landing place for helicopters.

helium /**hee**-li-uhm/ noun a light colourless gas that does not burn.

helix /**hee**-liks/ noun (plural **helices** /**hee**-li-seez/) an object in the shape of a spiral.

hell noun 1 (in Christianity and some other religions) a place of evil and suffering where wicked people are sent after death. 2 a state or place of great suffering.

□ hell-bent determined to achieve something.

he'll short form 1 he shall. 2 he will.

hellebore /**hel**-i-bor/ noun a poisonous plant with large white, green, or purplish flowers.

Hellenic /he-**len**-ik/ adjective Greek.

hellhole noun a very unpleasant place.

hellish adjective informal very difficult or unpleasant.

■ hellishly adverb.

hello, hallo, or **hullo** exclamation 1 used as a greeting. 2 Brit. used to express surprise or to attract someone's attention.

hellraiser noun a person who causes trouble by drunken or outrageous behaviour.

helm noun 1 a wheel or tiller for steering a ship or boat. 2 (**the helm**) the position of leader.

helmet noun a hard or padded protective hat.

helmsman noun (plural **helmsmen**) a person who steers a boat.

help verb 1 make it easier for someone to

h

THESAURUS

note, regard, thought.

hefty adjective 1 *a hefty young man:* burly, sturdy, strapping, bulky, strong, muscular, big, solid, well built; informal hulking, beefy. 2 *a hefty kick:* powerful, violent, hard, forceful. 3 *a hefty fine:* substantial, sizeable, considerable, stiff, large, heavy; informal whopping.

OPPOSITES slight, feeble, light, small.

height noun 1 *the height of the wall:* tallness, stature, elevation, altitude. 2 *mountain heights:* summit, top, peak, crest, crown, tip, cap, pinnacle. 3 *the height of their fame:* highest point, peak, zenith, pinnacle, climax.

OPPOSITES width, depth, nadir.

heighten verb intensify, increase, enhance, add to, augment, boost, strengthen, deepen, magnify, reinforce.

OPPOSITES reduce.

heir, heiress noun successor, next in line, inheritor, beneficiary, legatee.

hell noun 1 the underworld, the netherworld, eternal damnation, perdition, hellfire, fire and brimstone, the Inferno, Hades. 2 *he made my life hell:* misery, torture, agony, purgatory, torment, a nightmare.

OPPOSITES heaven, bliss.

help verb 1 assist, aid, abet, lend a hand (to), give assistance to, come to the aid of, be of service to, do someone a favour, do someone a service, do someone a good turn, rally round, pitch in. 2 *this credit*

do something. **2** improve a situation or problem. **3** (**help yourself**) take something without asking for it first. **4** (**cannot help**) be unable to stop yourself doing. • noun a person or thing that helps someone.
■ helper noun.

helpful adjective **1** ready to give help. **2** useful.
■ helpfully adverb.

helping noun a portion of food served to one person at one time.

helpless adjective **1** unable to defend yourself or to act without help. **2** uncontrollable.
■ helplessly adverb.

helpline noun a telephone service providing help with problems.

helpmate or **helpmeet** noun a helpful companion.

helter-skelter adjective & adverb in a hasty and confused or disorganized way. • noun Brit. a tall slide winding around a tower at a fair.

hem noun the edge of a piece of cloth or clothing which has been turned under and sewn. • verb (**hems, hemming, hemmed**) **1** give something a hem. **2** (**hem someone/thing in**) surround someone or something and restrict their movement.

hematology etc. US spelling of HAEMATOLOGY etc.

hemisphere noun **1** a half of a sphere. **2** a half of the earth.
■ hemispherical adjective.

hemline noun the level of the lower edge of a skirt or coat.

hemlock noun a poison made from a plant with small white flowers.

hemp noun **1** the cannabis plant, the fibre of which is used to make rope, fabrics, etc. **2** the drug cannabis.

hen noun a female bird, especially of a domestic fowl.

□ **hen night** Brit. informal an all-female celebration for a woman who is about to get married.

hence adverb **1** for this reason. **2** from now.

henceforth or **henceforward** adverb from this time on.

henchman noun (plural **henchmen**) chiefly disapproving a faithful follower or assistant.

henna noun a reddish-brown dye made from the powdered leaves of a tropical shrub.
■ hennaed adjective.

henpecked adjective (of a man) continually nagged or criticized by his wife.

henry noun (plural **henries** or **henrys**) the basic unit for measuring inductance.

hepatitis /he-puh-ty-tiss/ noun a serious disease of the liver, mainly transmitted by viruses.

heptagon /hep-tuh-guhn/ noun a figure with seven straight sides and angles.
■ heptagonal adjective.

heptathlon noun an athletic contest for women that consists of seven separate events.
■ heptathlete noun.

her pronoun used as the object of a verb or preposition to refer to a female person or animal previously mentioned. • possessive determiner belonging to or associated with a female person or animal previously mentioned.

herald noun **1** (in the past) a person who carried official messages and supervised tournaments. **2** a sign that something is about to happen or arrive. • verb **1** be a sign that something is about to happen or arrive. **2** describe in enthusiastic terms.

heraldic /he-ral-dik/ adjective having to do with heraldry.

heraldry noun the system by which coats of arms are organized and controlled.

herb noun **1** a plant used for flavouring food

THESAURUS

card helps cancer research: support, contribute to, give money to, donate to, promote, boost, back. **3** *sore throats are helped by lozenges:* relieve, soothe, ease, alleviate, improve, lessen. **4** *he could not help laughing:* resist, avoid, refrain from, keep from, stop.
OPPOSITES hinder, impede, worsen.
• noun **1** *this could be of help:* assistance, aid, support, succour, benefit, use, advantage, service. **2** *help for his eczema:* relief, alleviation, improvement, healing.
OPPOSITES hindrance, aggravation.

helper noun assistant, aide, deputy, auxiliary, supporter, second, mate, right-hand man/woman, attendant.

helpful adjective **1** *the staff are very helpful:* obliging, of assistance, supportive, accommodating, cooperative, eager to please. **2** *we found your comments helpful:* useful, beneficial, valuable, constructive, informative, instructive. **3** *a helpful new tool:* handy, useful, convenient, practical, easy-to-use, serviceable; informal neat, nifty.
OPPOSITES unhelpful, useless.

helping noun portion, serving, piece, slice, share, plateful; informal dollop.

helpless adjective dependent, incapable, powerless, paralysed, defenceless, vulnerable, exposed, unprotected.
OPPOSITES independent.

hence adverb consequently, as a consequence, for this reason, therefore, so, accordingly, as a result, that being so.

or in medicine. **2** Botany a plant which dies down to the ground after flowering.
■ **herbal** adjective.

herbaceous /her-**bay**-shuhss/ **adjective** relating to herbs (in the botanical sense).
□ **herbaceous border** a garden border containing plants which flower every year.

herbalism noun the use of plants in medicine and cookery.
■ **herbalist** noun.

herbicide /**her**-bi-syd/ **noun** a substance used to kill unwanted plants.

herbivore /**her**-bi-vor/ **noun** an animal that feeds on plants.
■ **herbivorous** /her-**biv**-uh-ruhss/ adjective.

Herculean /her-kyuu-**lee**-uhn/ **adjective** needing great strength or effort: *a Herculean task.*

herd noun **1** a large group of animals that live or are kept together. **2** disapproving a large group of people. ● verb make animals or people move in a large group.

here adverb in, at, or to this place or position.

hereabouts or **hereabout** adverb near this place.

hereafter adverb formal from now on or at some time in the future. ● noun (**the hereafter**) life after death.

hereby adverb formal as a result of this.

hereditary adjective **1** passed on by parents to their children or young. **2** having to do with inheritance.

heredity /hi-**red**-i-ti/ **noun 1** the passing on of characteristics from one generation to another. **2** the inheriting of a title, office, etc.

herein adverb formal in this document, book, or matter.

heresy noun (plural **heresies**) **1** belief which goes against traditional religious teachings. **2** opinion which is very different from

what is generally accepted.

heretic noun a person who is guilty of heresy.
■ **heretical** adjective.

hereto adverb formal to this matter or document.

heretofore adverb formal before now.

herewith adverb formal with this.

heritable adjective able to be inherited.

heritage noun valued things such as historic buildings that have been passed down from previous generations.

hermaphrodite /her-**maf**-ruh-dyt/ **noun** a person, animal, or plant with both male and female sex organs or characteristics.

hermetic /her-**met**-ik/ **adjective** (of a seal or closure) complete and airtight.
■ **hermetically** adverb.

hermit noun a person who lives completely alone, especially for religious reasons.

hernia noun a condition in which part of an organ pushes through the wall of the cavity containing it.

hero noun (plural **heroes**) **1** a person who is admired for their courage or outstanding achievements. **2** the chief male character in a book, play, or film.
□ **hero worship** extreme admiration for someone.

heroic adjective **1** very brave. **2** very grand or ambitious in scale. ● noun (**heroics**) brave or dramatic behaviour or talk.
■ **heroically** adverb.

heroin noun a very addictive painkilling drug.

heroine noun **1** a woman admired for her courage or outstanding achievements. **2** the chief female character in a book, play, or film.

heroism noun great bravery.

heron noun a large fish-eating bird with

THESAURUS

herd noun drove, flock, pack, fold, swarm, mass, crowd, horde.

hereditary adjective **1** *a hereditary right:* inherited, bequeathed, handed down, passed down, family, ancestral. **2** *a hereditary disease:* genetic, inborn, inherited, inbred, innate, in the family, in the blood, in the genes.

heritage noun **1** *Europe's cultural heritage:* tradition, history, past, background, culture, customs. **2** *his Greek heritage:* ancestry, lineage, descent, extraction, parentage, roots, heredity.

hermit noun recluse, loner; historical anchorite, anchoress; old use eremite.

hero noun **1** *a sporting hero:* star, superstar, megastar, idol, celebrity, favourite, darling; informal celeb. **2** *the hero of the film:* main

character, starring role, male protagonist, (male) lead, leading man; informal good guy. OPPOSITES villain.

heroic adjective brave, courageous, valiant, intrepid, bold, fearless, daring; informal gutsy, spunky.
OPPOSITES cowardly.

heroine noun **1** *a sporting heroine:* star, superstar, megastar, idol, celebrity, favourite, darling; informal celeb. **2** *the film's heroine:* main character, female protagonist, lead, leading lady, prima donna, diva.

heroism noun bravery, courage, valour, daring, fearlessness, pluck; informal guts, spunk; Brit. informal bottle; N. Amer. informal moxie.
OPPOSITES cowardice.

long legs, a long neck, and a long pointed bill.

herpes /her-peez/ noun an infectious disease that causes blisters on the skin.

herring noun a silvery fish which is found in shoals and is used for food.

herringbone noun a zigzag pattern consisting of columns of short slanting parallel lines.

hers possessive pronoun used to refer to something belonging to or associated with a female person or animal previously mentioned.

☑ no apostrophe: **hers**.

herself pronoun 1 used as the object of a verb or preposition to refer to a female person or animal previously mentioned as the subject of the clause. 2 she or her personally.

hertz noun (plural **hertz**) the basic unit of frequency, equal to one cycle per second.

he's short form 1 he is. 2 he has.

hesitant adjective slow to act or speak through indecision or reluctance.
■ **hesitancy** noun **hesitantly** adverb.

hesitate verb (**hesitates, hesitating, hesitated**) 1 pause indecisively. 2 be reluctant to do something.
■ **hesitation** noun.

hessian noun a strong, coarse fabric.

heterodox adjective not following traditional standards or beliefs.
■ **heterodoxy** noun.

heterogeneous /het-uh-ruh-jee-ni-uhss/ adjective varied.
■ **heterogeneity** /het-uh-ruh-juh-nee-i-ti/ noun.

heterosexual adjective sexually attracted to people of the opposite sex. • noun a heterosexual person.
■ **heterosexuality** noun.

het up adjective informal angry and agitated.

hew verb (**hews, hewing, hewed**; past participle **hewn** or **hewed**) chop wood, coal, etc. with an axe or other tool.

hex N. Amer. verb cast a spell on. • noun a magic spell.

hexagon /hek-suh-guhn/ noun a figure with six straight sides and angles.
■ **hexagonal** adjective.

hexagram noun a six-pointed star formed by two intersecting triangles.

hexameter /hek-sam-i-ter/ noun a line of verse made up of six groups of syllables.

hey exclamation used to attract someone's attention or to express surprise, interest, etc.

heyday noun (**your heyday**) the period when you are most successful or active.

HGV abbreviation Brit. heavy goods vehicle.

hiatus /hy-ay-tuhss/ noun (plural **hiatuses**) a pause or gap in a series or sequence.

hibernate verb (**hibernates, hibernating, hibernated**) (of an animal) spend the winter in a state like deep sleep.
■ **hibernation** noun.

hibiscus /hi-biss-kuhss/ noun a plant with large brightly coloured flowers.

hiccup or **hiccough** /hik-up/ noun 1 a sudden gulping sound caused by an involuntary spasm of the diaphragm. 2 a minor setback. • verb (**hiccups, hiccuping, hiccuped**) make the sound of a hiccup.

hick noun informal, chiefly N. Amer. an unsophisticated country person.

hickory noun a tree with edible nuts.

hide¹ verb (**hides, hiding, hid**; past participle **hidden**) 1 put or keep something out of sight. 2 get into a place where you cannot be seen. 3 keep secret. • noun Brit. a concealed shelter used to watch wild animals or birds.
□ **hide-and-seek** a game in which one player hides and the others have to look for them.

THESAURUS

hesitant adjective 1 she is hesitant about buying: uncertain, undecided, unsure, doubtful, dubious, ambivalent, in two minds; Brit. havering, humming and hawing; informal iffy. 2 a hesitant child: timid, diffident, shy, bashful, insecure.
OPPOSITES certain, decisive, confident.

hesitate verb 1 she hesitated, unsure of what to say: pause, delay, wait, stall, be uncertain, be unsure, be doubtful, be indecisive, vacillate, waver; Brit. haver, hum and haw; informal dilly-dally. 2 don't hesitate to ask: be reluctant, be unwilling, be disinclined, scruple, have misgivings about, have qualms about, think twice about.
OPPOSITES plunge in.

hidden adjective 1 a hidden camera:

concealed, secret, invisible, unseen, camouflaged. 2 a hidden meaning: obscure, unclear, concealed, cryptic, mysterious, secret, covert, abstruse, deep.
OPPOSITES visible, obvious.

hide verb 1 he hid the money: conceal, secrete, put out of sight, cache; informal stash. 2 they hid in an air vent: conceal yourself, secrete yourself, take cover, lie low, go to ground; informal hole up. 3 clouds hid the moon: obscure, block out, blot out, obstruct, cloud, shroud, veil, eclipse. 4 he could not hide his dislike: conceal, keep secret, cover up, keep quiet about, bottle up, suppress, disguise, mask; informal keep a/the lid on.
OPPOSITES flaunt, reveal, emerge, betray.

hide² noun the skin of an animal.

hideaway noun a hiding place.

hidebound adjective unwilling to give up old-fashioned ideas in favour of new ways of thinking.

hideous adjective **1** very ugly. **2** very unpleasant.
■ **hideously** adverb.

hideout noun a hiding place.

hiding noun a physical beating.

hierarchy /**hy**-uh-rah-ki/ noun (plural **hierarchies**) **1** a system in which people are ranked one above the other according to status or authority. **2** a classification of things according to their relative importance.
■ **hierarchical** adjective.

> ☑ -ie-, not -ei-, and remember the second r: hierarchy.

hieroglyphics plural noun writing in which a picture represents a word, syllable, or sound, as used in ancient Egypt.

hi-fi noun (plural **hi-fis**) a set of equipment for reproducing high-fidelity sound. • adjective having to do with high-fidelity sound.

higgledy-piggledy adverb & adjective in confusion or disorder.

high adjective **1** extending far upwards. **2** of a particular height. **3** far above ground or sea level. **4** large in amount, size, or intensity. **5** (of a period or movement) at its peak. **6** great in status; important. **7** (of a sound or note) not deep or low. **8** informal under the influence of drugs or alcohol. **9** (of food) beginning to go bad. • noun **1** a high point, level, or figure. **2** an area of high atmospheric pressure. **3** informal a state of high spirits. • adverb (of a sound) at a

high pitch.

▢ **High Church** the section of the Church of England which gives an important place to ritual and the authority of bishops and priests. **high commission** an embassy of one Commonwealth country in another. **higher education** education to degree level or its equivalent, provided at universities and colleges. **high explosive** powerful chemical explosive used in shells and bombs. **high fidelity** the reproduction of sound with little distortion. **high-flown** grand-sounding. **high-flyer** (or **high-flier**) a very successful person. **high-handed** using authority without considering the feelings of other people. **high jinks** high-spirited fun. **high jump** an athletic event in which competitors try to jump over a bar. **high-rise** (of a building) having many storeys. **high school** a secondary school. **the high seas** the areas of the sea that are not under the control of any one country. **high-spirited** lively and cheerful. **high tea** Brit. a meal eaten in the late afternoon or early evening. **high-tech** (also **hi-tech**) using advanced technology. **high technology** advanced technology. **high tide** the time when the sea is closest to the land.

highbrow adjective very intellectual or refined in taste.

highfalutin /hy-fuh-**loo**-tin/ adjective informal grand or self-important in a pretentious way.

highland or **highlands** noun **1** an area of high or mountainous land. **2** (**the Highlands**) the mountainous northern part of Scotland.
■ **highlander** noun.

highlight noun **1** an outstanding part of an

h

THESAURUS

hideaway noun **retreat**, refuge, hiding place, hideout, safe house, den, bolt-hole; informal hidey-hole.

hideous adjective **1** *a hideous face:* **ugly**, repulsive, repellent, unsightly, revolting, grotesque. **2** *hideous cases of torture:* **horrific**, terrible, appalling, awful, dreadful, frightful, horrible, horrendous, horrifying, shocking, sickening, gruesome, ghastly.
OPPOSITES beautiful, pleasant.

hiding noun (informal) **beating**, thrashing, whipping, drubbing; informal licking, belting, pasting, walloping.

hierarchy noun **ranking**, order, pecking order, grading, ladder, scale.

high adjective **1** *a high mountain:* **tall**, lofty, towering, giant, big, multi-storey, high-rise, elevated. **2** *a high position in the government:* **high-ranking**, leading, top, prominent, senior, influential, powerful,

important, exalted; N. Amer. ranking. **3** *high prices:* **inflated**, excessive, unreasonable, expensive, exorbitant, extortionate, informal steep, stiff. **4** *a high voice:* **high-pitched**, shrill, piercing, squeaky, penetrating, soprano, treble, falsetto. **5** (informal) *high on drugs:* **intoxicated**, befuddled, delirious, hallucinating; informal high as a kite, stoned, wrecked, off your head.
OPPOSITES low, short, lowly, deep.
• adverb *a jet flew high overhead:* **at a great height**, high up, way up, at altitude, in the sky, aloft, overhead, to a great height.
OPPOSITES low.

highlight noun *the highlight of his career:* **high point**, climax, peak, pinnacle, height, zenith, summit, focus, feature.
OPPOSITES low point.
• verb *he has highlighted shortcomings in the plan:* **spotlight**, call attention to, focus on, underline, show up, bring out,

event or period of time. **2** a bright area in a picture. **3** (**highlights**) bright tints in hair, created by bleaching or dyeing. •**verb 1** draw attention to. **2** create highlights in hair.
■ **highlighter** noun.

highly adverb **1** to a high degree or level. **2** favourably.
□ **highly strung** Brit. very nervous and easily upset.

Highness noun (**His, Her, Your Highness**) a title given to a person of royal rank.

highway noun **1** chiefly N. Amer. a main road. **2** a public road.

highwayman noun (plural **highwaymen**) (in the past) a man who held up and robbed travellers.

hijack verb **1** illegally seize control of an aircraft while it is travelling somewhere. **2** take over something and use it for a different purpose. •**noun** an act of hijacking.
■ **hijacker** noun.

hike noun **1** a long walk or walking tour. **2** a sharp increase. •**verb** (**hikes, hiking, hiked**) **1** go on a hike. **2** pull or lift up clothing. **3** increase a price sharply.
■ **hiker** noun.

hilarious adjective very amusing.
■ **hilariously** adverb **hilarity** noun.

hill noun a naturally raised area of land, not as high as a mountain.
□ **over the hill** informal old and past your best.

hillbilly noun (plural **hillbillies**) N. Amer. informal an unsophisticated country person.

hillock noun a small hill or mound.

hilly adjective (**hillier, hilliest**) having many hills.

hilt noun the handle of a sword, dagger, or knife.
□ **to the hilt** completely.

him pronoun used as the object of a verb or preposition to refer to a male person or animal previously mentioned.

himself pronoun **1** used as the object of a verb or preposition to refer to a male person or animal previously mentioned as the subject of the clause. **2** he or him personally.

hind[1] adjective situated at the back.

hind[2] noun a female deer.

hinder verb (**hinders, hindering, hindered**) delay or obstruct.

Hindi noun a language of northern India.

hindmost adjective furthest back.

hindquarters plural noun the rear part and hind legs of a four-legged animal.

hindrance noun a thing that hinders someone or something.

☑ no e: hind**r**ance, not hind**er**ance.

hindsight noun understanding of a situation or event after it has happened.

Hindu noun (plural **Hindus**) a follower of Hinduism.

Hinduism noun a religion of the Indian subcontinent, with a large number of gods and goddesses.

hinge noun a movable joint or mechanism by which a door, gate, or lid opens and closes. •**verb** (**hinges, hingeing** or **hinging, hinged**) **1** attach or join with a hinge. **2** (**hinge on**) depend entirely on.

hint noun **1** a slight or indirect suggestion. **2** a very small trace of something. **3** a

THESAURUS

accentuate, accent, stress, emphasize.
OPPOSITES play down.

highly adverb very, extremely, immensely, thoroughly, decidedly, exceptionally, extraordinarily; N. English right; informal awfully, terribly, seriously; Brit. informal dead, jolly; N. Amer. informal real, mighty, awful.
OPPOSITES slightly.

hijack verb commandeer, seize, take over, appropriate, expropriate.

hike noun **1** a hike across country: walk, trek, tramp, trudge, slog, march, ramble. **2** a price hike: increase, advance, boom.
OPPOSITES reduction.
•**verb 1** they hiked across Europe: walk, trek, tramp, trudge, slog, march, ramble, backpack. **2** they hiked the price: increase, raise, up, put up, push up; informal jack up, bump up.
OPPOSITES reduce.

hilarious adjective very funny, hysterical,

uproarious, rib-tickling; informal side-splitting, priceless, a scream, a hoot.
OPPOSITES sad, serious.

hill noun high ground, hillock, hillside, rise, mound, knoll, hummock, fell, mountain; Scottish brae.

hinder verb hamper, impede, inhibit, thwart, foil, delay, interfere with, slow down, hold back, hold up, restrict, handicap, hamstring.
OPPOSITES facilitate.

hint noun **1** a hint that he would leave: clue, inkling, suggestion, indication, sign, signal, intimation. **2** handy hints about painting: tip, suggestion, pointer, guideline, recommendation. **3** a hint of garlic: trace, touch, suspicion, suggestion, dash, soupçon; informal smidgen, tad.
•**verb** what are you hinting? imply, insinuate, intimate, suggest, refer to, drive at, mean; informal get at.

small piece of practical information. • **verb** suggest indirectly.

hinterland noun **1** the areas of a country away from the coast. **2** the area around or beyond a major town.

hip¹ noun a projection formed by the pelvis and upper thigh bone on each side of the body.

hip² noun the fruit of a rose.

hip³ adjective (**hipper**, **hippest**) informal fashionable.
■ **hipness** noun.

hip hop noun a style of pop music featuring rap with an electronic backing.

hippo = HIPPOPOTAMUS.

hippopotamus noun (plural **hippopotamuses** or **hippopotami** /hip-puh-**pot**-uh-my/) a large African animal with massive jaws, living partly on land and partly in water.

hippy or **hippie** noun (plural **hippies**) a young person who rejects traditional social values and dresses in an unconventional way.

hipsters plural noun Brit. trousers cut to fit and fasten at the hips.

hire verb (**hires**, **hiring**, **hired**) **1** pay to be allowed to use something temporarily. **2** (**hire something out**) allow something to be used temporarily in return for payment. **3** pay someone to work for you. • **noun** the action of hiring.
□ **hire purchase** Brit. a system by which you pay for a thing in regular instalments while having the use of it.

hireling noun a person who is willing to do any kind of work as long as they are paid.

hirsute /her-syoot/ adjective hairy.

his possessive determiner & pronoun belonging to or associated with a male person or animal previously mentioned.

Hispanic adjective having to do with Spain or other Spanish-speaking countries.

hiss verb **1** make a sharp sound like that made when pronouncing the letter *s*. **2** whisper something in an urgent or angry way. • **noun** a hissing sound.

histamine /**hiss**-tuh-meen/ noun a substance which is released by cells in response to an injury or allergy.

histology noun the scientific study of the structure of living tissues.
■ **histologist** noun.

historian noun an expert in history.

historic adjective famous or important in history, or likely to be seen as such in the future.

historical adjective **1** having to do with history. **2** belonging to or set in the past.
■ **historically** adverb.

history noun (plural **histories**) **1** the study of past events. **2** the past considered as a whole. **3** the past events connected with someone or something. **4** a continuous record of past events or trends.

histrionic adjective too theatrical or dramatic. • **noun** (**histrionics**) exaggerated behaviour intended to attract attention.

hit verb (**hits**, **hitting**, **hit**) **1** bring your hand or a tool, weapon, bat, etc. against

h

THESAURUS

hire verb **1** *we hired a car:* rent, lease, charter. **2** *they hire workers locally:* employ, engage, recruit, appoint, take on, sign up.
OPPOSITES dismiss.

hiss verb **1** *the escaping gas hissed:* fizz, whistle, wheeze. **2** *the audience hissed:* jeer, catcall, whistle, hoot.
OPPOSITES cheer.
• **noun 1** *the hiss of steam:* fizz, whistle, wheeze. **2** *the speaker received hisses:* jeer, catcall, whistle, abuse, derision.
OPPOSITES cheer.

historic adjective significant, notable, important, momentous, memorable, groundbreaking; informal earth-shattering.
OPPOSITES insignificant.

historical adjective **1** *historical evidence:* documented, recorded, chronicled, authentic, factual, actual. **2** *historical figures:* past, bygone, ancient, old, former.
OPPOSITES anecdotal, contemporary.

history noun **1** *my interest in history:* the past, former times, the olden days, yesterday, antiquity. **2** *a history of the Civil*

War: chronicle, archive, record, report, narrative, account, study. **3** *she gave details of her history:* background, past, life story, experiences, record.

hit verb **1** strike, beat, punch, thump, thrash; informal whack, wallop, bash, clout, belt; Brit. informal stick one on; N. Amer. informal slug; Austral./NZ informal dong, quilt. **2** *a car hit the barrier:* crash into, run into, smash into, knock into, bump into, plough into, collide with, meet head-on. **3** *the tragedy hit her hard:* devastate, affect badly, upset, shatter, crush, traumatize; informal knock sideways; Brit. informal knock for six.
• **noun 1** blow, thump, punch, knock, bang; informal whack, wallop, bash, clout, belt; N. Amer. informal slug; Austral./NZ informal king-hit. **2** *he directed many big hits:* success, sell-out, winner, triumph, sensation, best-seller; informal smash hit, chart-topper, crowd-puller.
OPPOSITES failure.
□ **hit back** retaliate, respond, reply, react, counter. **hit it off** (informal) get on (well), get along, be compatible, be on the same

someone or something quickly and with force. **2** (of something moving) come into contact with someone or something quickly and forcefully. **3** reach a target. **4** cause harm or distress to. **5** be suddenly realized by. **6** (**hit out**) criticize or attack strongly. **7** informal reach. **8** (**hit on**) suddenly discover or think of. •**noun 1** an instance of hitting or being hit. **2** a successful film, pop record, etc. **3** an instance of a website being accessed or a word being found in an Internet search. **4** informal, chiefly N. Amer. a murder carried out by a criminal organization. **5** informal a dose of an addictive drug.
▫ **hit-and-miss** not done in a careful, planned way. **hit-and-run** (of a road accident) in which the driver responsible leaves rapidly without helping the other people involved. **hit it off** informal get on well with someone.

hitch verb **1** move into a different position with a jerk. **2** fasten with a rope. **3** travel by hitchhiking. •**noun** a temporary difficulty.
■ **hitcher** noun.

hitchhike verb travel by getting free lifts in passing vehicles.
■ **hitchhiker** noun.

hither adverb old use to or towards this place.

hitherto adverb until this time.

HIV abbreviation human immunodeficiency virus (the virus causing Aids).

hive noun **1** a beehive. **2** a place full of people working hard.
▫ **hive something off** transfer part of a business to new ownership.

hives plural noun a rash of red, itchy marks on the skin, caused by an allergy.

HM abbreviation Her (or His) Majesty or Majesty's.

HMS abbreviation Her or His Majesty's Ship.

HND abbreviation Higher National Diploma.

hoard noun a store of money, valued objects, or useful information. •**verb** build up a store of something.
■ **hoarder** noun.

❗ don't confuse **hoard** with **horde**: a **hoard** is a store of something valuable; a **horde** is a large group of people.

hoarding noun Brit. a large board used to display advertisements.

hoar frost noun a feathery greyish-white deposit of frost.

hoarse adjective (of a voice) rough and harsh.
■ **hoarsely** adverb.

hoary adjective (**hoarier**, **hoariest**) **1** greyish-white. **2** having grey hair. **3** old and unoriginal.

hoax noun a humorous or cruel trick. •**verb** deceive with a hoax.
■ **hoaxer** noun.

hob noun Brit. the flat top part of a cooker, with hotplates or burners.

hobble verb (**hobbles**, **hobbling**, **hobbled**) **1** walk awkwardly. **2** strap together the legs of a horse to stop it wandering away.

hobby noun (plural **hobbies**) an activity that you do regularly in your leisure time for pleasure.
▫ **hobby horse 1** a child's toy consisting of a stick with a model of a horse's head at one end. **2** something that a person talks about very often.

hobgoblin noun a mischievous imp.

hobnail noun a short nail used to strengthen the soles of boots.
■ **hobnailed** adjective.

hobnob verb (**hobnobs**, **hobnobbing**, **hobnobbed**) informal spend time with rich or important people.

hobo noun (plural **hoboes** or **hobos**) N. Amer. a homeless person.

Hobson's choice noun a choice of taking what is offered or nothing at all.

hock[1] noun the middle joint in an animal's back leg.

hock[2] noun Brit. a dry white wine from Germany.

hock[3] verb informal pawn an object.
▫ **in hock** in debt.

hockey noun a team game played using hooked sticks to drive a small, hard ball

THESAURUS

wavelength, see eye to eye, take to each other; informal click. **hit on/upon discover**, come up with, think of, conceive of, dream up, invent, devise.

hitch verb **1** she hitched the blanket around her: pull, lift, raise; informal yank. **2** Tom hitched the pony to his cart: harness, yoke, couple, fasten, connect, attach.
•**noun** it went without a hitch: problem, difficulty, snag, setback, obstacle, complication; informal glitch, hiccup.

hoard noun a secret hoard: cache, stockpile,

store, collection, supply, reserve; informal stash.
•**verb** they hoarded their rations: stockpile, store up, put aside, put by, lay by, set aside, cache, save, squirrel away; informal salt away.
OPPOSITES squander.

hoax noun practical joke, prank, trick, deception, fraud; informal con, spoof, wind-up, scam.

hobby noun pastime, leisure activity, sideline, diversion, relaxation, recreation, amusement.

towards a goal.

hocus-pocus noun **1** meaningless talk used to deceive people. **2** a form of words used by a magician.

hod noun **1** a builder's V-shaped open trough attached to a short pole, used for carrying bricks. **2** a metal container for storing coal.

hoe noun a long-handled gardening tool with a thin metal blade. •verb (**hoes, hoeing, hoed**) break up soil or dig up weeds with a hoe.

hoedown noun N. Amer. a lively folk dance.

hog noun a castrated male pig reared for its meat. •verb (**hogs, hogging, hogged**) informal take or hoard selfishly.
□ **go the whole hog** informal do something fully.

Hogmanay /hog-muh-nay/ noun (in Scotland) New Year's Eve.

hogshead noun a large cask.

hogwash noun informal nonsense.

hoick verb Brit. informal lift or pull with a jerk.

hoi polloi /hoy puh-**loy**/ plural noun disapproving the common people.

hoist verb **1** raise with ropes and pulleys. **2** haul or lift up. •noun a piece of equipment for hoisting something.

hoity-toity adjective informal snobbish.

hokey-cokey noun a group song and dance performed in a circle, involving the shaking of each limb in turn.

hokum /hoh-kuhm/ noun informal **1** nonsense. **2** unoriginal or sentimental material in a film, book, etc.

hold verb (**holds, holding, held**) **1** grasp, carry, or support. **2** contain or be able to contain. **3** have, own, or occupy. **4** keep or detain someone. **5** stay or keep at a certain level. **6** (**hold someone to**) make someone keep a promise. **7** (**hold someone/thing in**) have a particular attitude to someone or something. •noun **1** a grip. **2** a place to grip while climbing. **3** a degree of control. **4** a storage space in the lower part of a ship or aircraft.
□ **hold back** hesitate. **hold fast 1** remain tightly secured. **2** stick to a principle. **hold forth** talk at length. **hold someone/thing off** resist an attacker. **hold on 1** wait. **2** keep going in difficult circumstances. **hold out 1** resist difficult circumstances. **2** continue to be enough; last. **hold something over** postpone something. **hold someone/thing up 1** delay someone or something. **2** rob someone using the threat of violence. **hold-up 1** a cause of delay. **2** a robbery carried out with the threat of violence. **no holds barred** without restrictions. **on hold** waiting to be dealt with or connected by telephone.
■ **holder** noun.

holdall noun Brit. a large bag with handles and a shoulder strap.

holding noun **1** an area of land held by lease. **2** (**holdings**) stocks and property owned by a person or organization.

hole noun **1** a hollow space or opening in a solid object or surface. **2** (in golf) a hollow in the ground which you try to hit the ball into. **3** informal an awkward or unpleasant place or situation. •verb (**holes, holing, holed**) **1** make a hole or holes in. **2** (in golf) hit the ball into a hole. **3** (**hole up**) informal hide yourself.
■ **holey** adjective.

Holi /hoh-li/ noun a Hindu spring festival.

holiday noun **1** Brit. a time spent away from

hoist verb *we hoisted the mainsail:* raise, lift, haul up, heave up, winch up, pull up, elevate.
OPPOSITES lower.
•noun *a mechanical hoist:* crane, winch, pulley, windlass.

hold verb **1** *she held a suitcase:* clasp, clutch, grasp, grip, clench, cling to, hold on to, embrace, hug, squeeze. **2** *he was being held by police:* detain, imprison, lock up, keep behind bars, confine, intern, incarcerate. **3** *the tank held 250 gallons:* take, contain, accommodate, fit, have room for. **4** *the court held that there was no evidence:* maintain, consider, take the view, believe, think, feel, deem, be of the opinion, rule, decide; informal reckon. **5** *they held a meeting:* convene, call, summon, conduct, organize, run.
OPPOSITES release.
•noun **1** *she kept a hold on my hand:* grip, grasp, clasp, clutch. **2** *Tom had a hold over* *his father:* influence, power, control, dominance, authority, sway. **3** *the military tightened their hold on the capital:* control, grip, power, stranglehold.

holder noun **1** *the licence holder:* bearer, owner, possessor, keeper. **2** *a knife holder:* container, receptacle, case, cover, housing, sheath.

hold-up noun **1** *a hold-up in production:* delay, setback, hitch, snag, difficulty, problem, glitch, hiccup, traffic jam, tailback; informal snarl-up. **2** *a bank hold-up:* robbery, raid, armed robbery, mugging; informal stick-up; N. Amer. informal heist.

hole noun **1** *a hole in the roof:* opening, aperture, gap, space, vent, chink, breach, crack, rupture, puncture. **2** *a hole in the* *ground:* pit, crater, depression, hollow, cavern, cave, chamber. **3** *the badger's hole:* burrow, lair, den, earth, sett.

holiday noun vacation, break, rest, recess, time off, leave, day off, festival, feast day.

home for rest or enjoyment. **2** a day when most people do not have to work. •**verb** spend a holiday.

holidaymaker noun Brit. a tourist.

holiness noun **1** the state of being holy. **2** (**His** or **Your Holiness**) the title of the Pope and some other religious leaders.

holistic adjective treating the whole person rather than just the symptoms of a disease. ▪ **holism** noun.

hollandaise sauce /hol-uhn-**dayz**/ noun a creamy sauce made of butter, egg yolks, and vinegar.

holler informal verb (**hollers, hollering, hollered**) give a loud shout. •noun a loud shout.

hollow adjective **1** having empty space inside. **2** curving inwards. **3** (of a sound) echoing. **4** worthless or not sincere. •**noun 1** a hole. **2** a small valley. •verb (usu. **hollow something out**) form by making a hole.

holly noun an evergreen shrub with prickly dark green leaves and red berries.

hollyhock noun a tall plant with large showy flowers.

holocaust /hol-uh-kawst/ noun **1** destruction or killing on a very large scale. **2** (**the Holocaust**) the mass murder of Jews under the German Nazi regime in World War II.

hologram noun a picture that looks three-dimensional when it is lit up. ▪ **holographic** adjective.

holster noun a holder for carrying a handgun.

holy adjective (**holier, holiest**) **1** dedicated to God or a religious purpose. **2** morally and spiritually good.
□ **the holy of holies** a very sacred place. **Holy Spirit** (or **Holy Ghost**) (in Christianity) God as a spirit that is active in the world. **Holy Week** the week before Easter.

homage noun honour shown to someone in public.

homburg noun a man's felt hat with a narrow curled brim.

home noun **1** the place where you live. **2** a place where people who need special care live. **3** a place where something flourishes or where it started. •adjective **1** relating to your home. **2** relating to your own country. **3** (of a sports match) played at a team's own ground. •adverb **1** to or at your home. **2** to the intended position. •verb (**homes, homing, homed**) **1** (of an animal) return by instinct to its territory. **2** (**home in on**) move to or be aimed towards.
□ **home economics** the study of cookery and household management. **home page** the main page of an individual's or organization's Internet site. **home rule** the government of a place by its own citizens. **home run** Baseball a hit that allows the batter to make a run around all the bases. **home truth** an unpleasant fact about yourself that someone else tells you.
■ **homeless** adjective **homeward** adjective & adverb **homewards** adverb.

homeland noun a person's native land.

homely adjective (**homelier, homeliest**) **1** Brit. simple but comfortable. **2** Brit. unsophisticated. **3** N. Amer. (of a person) unattractive.

homeopathy or **homoeopathy**

THESAURUS

hollow adjective **1** *a hollow tube:* empty, hollowed out, void. **2** *hollow cheeks:* sunken, deep-set, concave, depressed, recessed. **3** *a hollow promise:* insincere, hypocritical, feigned.
OPPOSITES solid, chubby, convex, sincere.
•**noun 1** *a hollow under the tree:* hole, pit, cavity, crater, trough, depression, indentation, dip. **2** *the village lay in a hollow:* valley, vale, dale, dell.
OPPOSITES rise.
•**verb** *hollowed out of rock:* gouge, scoop, dig, cut, excavate, channel.

holy adjective **1** *holy men:* saintly, godly, pious, religious, devout, God-fearing, spiritual. **2** *a holy place:* sacred, consecrated, hallowed, sanctified, venerated, revered.
OPPOSITES sinful, irreligious, cursed.

homage noun respect, honour, reverence, worship, admiration, esteem, adulation, tribute.
OPPOSITES contempt.

home noun **1** *they fled their homes:* residence, house, accommodation, property, quarters, lodgings, address, place; informal pad; formal abode, dwelling. **2** *I am far from my home:* homeland, native land, home town, birthplace, roots, fatherland, mother country, motherland. **3** *a home for the elderly:* institution, hospice, shelter, refuge, retreat, asylum, hostel.
•**adjective** *the UK home market:* domestic, internal, local, national.
OPPOSITES foreign, international.

homeless adjective of no fixed abode, without a roof over your head, on the streets, vagrant, sleeping rough, destitute.

homely adjective **1** (Brit.) *a homely atmosphere:* cosy, comfortable, snug, welcoming, friendly; informal comfy. **2** (N. Amer.) *she's rather homely:* unattractive, plain, unprepossessing, ugly; Brit. informal no oil painting.
OPPOSITES uncomfortable, attractive.

/hoh-mi-**op**-uh-thi/ noun a system of treating diseases by tiny doses of substances that would normally produce symptoms of the disease.
■ **homeopath** noun **homeopathic** adjective.

homesick adjective feeling upset because you are missing your home.

homespun adjective simple and unsophisticated.

homestead noun a farmhouse with surrounding land and outbuildings.

homework noun **1** school work that you are expected to do at home. **2** preparation for an event.

homicide /hom-i-syd/ noun chiefly N. Amer. the killing of another person.
■ **homicidal** adjective.

homily /hom-i-li/ noun (plural **homilies**) **1** a talk on a religious subject. **2** a dull talk on a moral issue.

hominid noun a member of a family of primates which includes humans and the prehistoric creatures from which they developed.

homoeopathy ⇒ HOMEOPATHY.

homogeneous /hom-uh-**jee**-ni-uhss/ adjective **1** alike. **2** made up of parts which are all of the same kind.
■ **homogeneity** /hom-uh-ji-**nee**-i-ti/ noun.

> ☑ the ending is -eous, with an e, not -ous: homogeneous.

homogenize or **homogenise** verb (**homogenizes, homogenizing, homogenized**) **1** treat milk so that the cream is mixed in. **2** make different things more alike.

homograph noun a word that is spelled the same as another but has a different meaning (e.g. *bat* 'a flying animal' and *bat* 'a piece of wood for hitting a ball').

homonym /hom-uh-nim/ noun a word that is spelled or pronounced the same as another but has a different meaning.

homophobia noun extreme hatred or fear of homosexuality and homosexuals.
■ **homophobic** adjective.

homophone noun a word that is pronounced the same as another but has a different meaning or spelling (e.g. *new* and *knew*).

Homo sapiens /hoh-moh **sap**-i-enz/ noun the species to which modern humans belong.

homosexual adjective sexually attracted to people of your own sex. • noun a homosexual person.
■ **homosexuality** noun.

Hon. abbreviation Honorary or Honourable.

Honduran /hon-**dyoo**-ruhn/ noun a person from Honduras, a country in Central America. • adjective relating to Honduras.

hone verb (**hones, honing, honed**) **1** make better or more efficient. **2** sharpen a tool with a stone.

honest adjective **1** truthful and sincere. **2** fairly earned. **3** simple and straightforward.
■ **honestly** adverb.

honesty noun the quality of being honest.

honey noun (plural **honeys**) a sweet, sticky yellowish-brown fluid made by bees from flower nectar.

honeybee noun the common bee.

honeycomb noun a structure of six-sided wax compartments made by bees to store honey and eggs.

honeydew noun a sweet, sticky substance produced by small insects feeding on the sap of plants.
☐ **honeydew melon** a variety of melon with sweet green flesh.

honeyed adjective **1** containing or coated with honey. **2** (of words) soothing and soft.

honeymoon noun **1** a holiday taken by a newly married couple. **2** an initial period of enthusiasm or goodwill. • verb spend a honeymoon somewhere.

honeypot noun a place that many people are attracted to.

honeysuckle noun a climbing shrub with sweet-smelling flowers.

honk noun **1** the cry of a goose. **2** the sound

h

THESAURUS

homicide noun murder, manslaughter, killing, slaughter, butchery, assassination.

honest adjective **1** *an honest man:* upright, honourable, principled, virtuous, decent, law-abiding, trustworthy, scrupulous. **2** *I haven't been honest with you:* truthful, sincere, candid, frank, open, forthright, straight; informal upfront.
OPPOSITES dishonest.

honestly adverb **1** *he earned the money honestly:* fairly, lawfully, legally, legitimately, honourably, decently, ethically; informal on the level. **2** *we honestly*

believe this: sincerely, genuinely, truthfully, truly, wholeheartedly, to be honest, to be frank, in all honesty, in all sincerity.
OPPOSITES dishonestly.

honesty noun **1** *I can attest to his honesty:* integrity, uprightness, honour, righteousness, virtue, goodness, probity, trustworthiness. **2** *they spoke with honesty about their fears:* sincerity, candour, frankness, directness, truthfulness, truth, openness, straightforwardness.
OPPOSITES dishonesty, insincerity.

of a car horn. •verb make a honk.

honky-tonk noun informal **1** N. Amer. a bar. **2** ragtime piano music.

honorary adjective **1** (of a title or position) given as an honour. **2** Brit. unpaid.

> ☑ honor-, not honour-: honorary.

honorific adjective given as a mark of respect.

honour (US spelling **honor**) noun **1** great respect. **2** a privilege. **3** a clear sense of what is right. **4** a person or thing that brings credit. **5** an award or title given as a reward for achievement. **6** (**honours**) a university course of a higher level than an ordinary one. **7** (**His, Your**, etc. **Honour**) a title for a judge. •verb **1** regard or treat with great respect. **2** fulfil an obligation or keep an agreement.

honourable (US spelling **honorable**) adjective **1** deserving honour. **2** having high moral standards. **3** (**Honourable**) a title given to MPs, nobles, etc.
■ **honourably** adverb.

hooch noun informal alcoholic drink.

hood¹ noun **1** a covering for the head and neck with an opening for the face. **2** Brit. a folding waterproof cover of a vehicle. **3** N. Amer. the bonnet of a vehicle. **4** a protective canopy.
■ **hooded** adjective.

hood² noun N. Amer. informal a gangster or violent criminal.

hoodlum noun a gangster or violent criminal.

hoodoo noun **1** a run or cause of bad luck. **2** voodoo.

hoodwink verb deceive or trick.

hoody or **hoodie** noun (plural **hoodies**) a hooded sweatshirt or other top.

hoof noun (plural **hoofs** or **hooves**) the horny part of the foot of a horse, cow, etc. •verb informal **1** kick a ball powerfully. **2** (**hoof it**) go on foot.
■ **hoofed** adjective.

hook noun **1** a curved object for catching hold of things or hanging things on. **2** a punch made with the elbow bent and rigid. **3** a catchy passage in a song. •verb **1** catch or fasten with a hook. **2** (**hook someone/thing up**) link someone or something to electronic equipment. **3** (**be hooked**) informal be very interested or addicted. **4** (in sport) hit the ball in a curving path.
▢ **by hook or by crook** by any possible means. **hook, line, and sinker** completely.
■ **hooked** adjective.

hookah noun a kind of tobacco pipe in which the smoke is drawn through water to cool it.

hooker noun **1** informal a prostitute. **2** Rugby the player in the middle of the front row of the scrum.

hookworm noun a worm which can infest the intestines.

hooligan noun a violent young

THESAURUS

honorary adjective **1** *an honorary doctorate:* titular, nominal, in name only, unofficial, token. **2** (Brit.) *an honorary treasurer:* unpaid, unsalaried, voluntary, volunteer.
OPPOSITES paid.

honour noun **1** *a man of honour:* integrity, honesty, uprightness, morality, principles, high-mindedness, decency, probity, scrupulousness, fairness, justness. **2** *a mark of honour:* distinction, privilege, glory, kudos, cachet, prestige. **3** *our honour is at stake:* reputation, good name, character, repute, image, standing, status. **4** *the honour of meeting the Queen:* privilege, pleasure, compliment.
OPPOSITES unscrupulousness, shame.
•verb **1** *we should honour our parents:* respect, esteem, admire, look up to, value, cherish, revere, venerate. **2** *they were honoured at a special ceremony:* applaud, acclaim, praise, salute, recognize, celebrate, pay tribute to. **3** *he honoured the contract:* fulfil, observe, keep, obey, heed, follow, carry out, keep to, abide by, adhere to, comply with, conform to, be true to.
OPPOSITES scorn, disgrace, disobey, break.

honourable adjective **1** *an honourable man:*

honest, moral, principled, righteous, decent, respectable, virtuous, good, upstanding, upright, noble, fair, trustworthy, law-abiding. **2** *an honourable career:* illustrious, distinguished, eminent, great, glorious, prestigious.
OPPOSITES crooked, deplorable.

hook noun **1** *she hung her jacket on the hook:* peg, nail. **2** *the dress has six hooks:* fastener, clasp, hasp, clip.
•verb **1** *they hooked baskets onto the ladder:* attach, hitch, fasten, fix, secure, hang, clasp. **2** *he hooked a large pike:* catch, land, net, take, bag.

hooked adjective **1** *a hooked nose:* curved, hook-shaped, aquiline, angular, bent. **2** (informal) *hooked on cocaine:* addicted to, dependent on. **3** (informal) *he is hooked on crosswords:* keen on, enthusiastic about, addicted to, obsessed with, fanatical about; informal mad about.
OPPOSITES straight.

hooligan noun lout, thug, tearaway, vandal, ruffian, troublemaker; Austral. larrikin; informal tough, bruiser; Brit. informal yob, yobbo, lager lout; Scottish informal ned.

troublemaker.

■ **hooliganism** noun.

hoop noun **1** a rigid circular band. **2** a large ring used as a toy or for circus performers to jump through. **3** a metal arch through which you hit the balls in croquet. **4** a contrasting horizontal band on a sports shirt.

■ **hooped** adjective.

hoopla noun Brit. a game in which you try to throw rings over a prize.

hooray exclamation hurrah.

hoot noun **1** a low sound made by owls, or a similar sound made by a horn, siren, etc. **2** a shout of scorn or disapproval. **3** an outburst of laughter. **4** (**a hoot**) informal an amusing person or thing. • verb make a hoot.

■ **hooter** noun.

Hoover Brit. noun trademark a vacuum cleaner. • verb (**hoover**) (**hoovers, hoovering, hoovered**) clean with a vacuum cleaner.

hooves plural of HOOF.

hop verb (**hops, hopping, hopped**) **1** move by jumping on one foot. **2** (of a bird or animal) move by jumping. **3** (**hop it**) Brit. informal go away. • noun **1** a hopping movement. **2** an informal dance.

□ **on the hop** Brit. informal unprepared.

hope noun **1** a feeling that something you want may happen. **2** a cause for hope. **3** something that you wish for. • verb (**hopes, hoping, hoped**) **1** expect and want something to happen. **2** intend if possible to do something.

hopeful adjective feeling or inspiring hope. • noun a person likely or hoping to succeed.

hopefully adverb **1** in a hopeful way. **2** it is to be hoped that.

❗ although the meaning 'it is to be hoped that' (as in hopefully we'll see you tomorrow) is now the more common one, some people feel that it is wrong and so it is best avoided in formal writing.

hopeless adjective **1** feeling or causing despair. **2** not at all skilful.

■ **hopelessly** adverb.

hopper noun a container that tapers downwards and empties its contents at the bottom.

hops plural noun the dried flowers of a climbing plant, used to give beer a bitter flavour.

hopscotch noun a children's game in which you hop over squares marked on the ground.

horde noun chiefly disapproving a large group of people.

❗ don't confuse **horde** with **hoard**: a **horde** is a large group of people, whereas a **hoard** is a store of something valuable.

horizon noun **1** the line at which the earth's surface and the sky appear to meet. **2** (**horizons**) the limits of a person's understanding, experience, or interest.

horizontal adjective parallel to the horizon. • noun a horizontal line or surface.

■ **horizontally** adverb.

hormone noun a substance produced in the body that controls the action of particular cells or tissues.

■ **hormonal** adjective.

horn noun **1** a hard bony growth on the heads of cattle, sheep, and other animals. **2** the substance that horns are made of. **3** a

h

hoop noun ring, band, circle, wheel, circlet, loop.

hop verb & noun jump, bound, spring, bounce, skip, leap, prance, caper.

hope noun **1** I had high hopes: aspiration, desire, wish, expectation, ambition, aim, plan, dream. **2** a life filled with hope: optimism, expectation, confidence, faith, belief.

OPPOSITES pessimism.

• verb **1** he's hoping for a medal: expect, anticipate, look for, be hopeful of, dream of. **2** we're hoping to address this issue: aim, intend, be looking, have the intention, have in mind, plan.

hopeful adjective **1** he remained hopeful: optimistic, full of hope, confident, positive, buoyant, bullish. **2** hopeful signs: promising, encouraging, heartening, reassuring, favourable, optimistic.

OPPOSITES pessimistic, discouraging.

hopefully adverb **1** he rode on hopefully: optimistically, full of hope, confidently, buoyantly, expectantly. **2** hopefully it should finish soon: all being well, if all goes well, God willing, with luck, touch wood, fingers crossed.

hopeless adjective **1** a hopeless case: forlorn, beyond hope, lost, irreparable, irreversible, incurable, impossible, futile. **2** hopeless at maths: bad, poor, awful, terrible, dreadful, appalling, atrocious, incompetent; informal pathetic, useless, lousy, rotten; Brit. informal rubbish.

OPPOSITES competent.

hopelessly adverb utterly, completely, irretrievably, impossibly, extremely, totally.

horde noun crowd, mob, pack, gang, troop, army, swarm, mass, throng.

horizontal adjective level, flat, parallel.

OPPOSITES vertical.

wind instrument shaped like a cone or wound into a spiral. **4** an instrument sounding a signal.
- **horned** adjective.

hornbill noun a tropical bird with a very large curved beak.

hornblende /horn-blend/ noun a dark brown, black, or green mineral.

hornet noun a kind of large wasp.

hornpipe noun a lively solo dance traditionally performed by sailors.

horny adjective (**hornier, horniest**) **1** made of or resembling horn. **2** hard and rough.

horology /ho-rol-uh-ji/ noun **1** the study and measurement of time. **2** the art of making clocks and watches.

horoscope noun a forecast of a person's future based on the positions of the stars and planets at the time of their birth.

horrendous adjective very unpleasant or horrifying.
- **horrendously** adverb.

horrible adjective **1** causing horror. **2** very unpleasant.
- **horribly** adverb.

horrid adjective horrible.

horrific adjective causing horror.
- **horrifically** adverb.

horrify verb (**horrifies, horrifying, horrified**) fill with horror.

horror noun **1** a strong feeling of fear, shock, disgust, or dismay. **2** a thing causing such a feeling.

hors d'oeuvre /or derv/ noun (plural **hors d'oeuvre** or **hors d'oeuvres** /or **derv**, or **dervz/**) a small savoury first course of a meal.

horse noun **1** a large four-legged animal used for riding and for pulling loads. **2** cavalry. •verb (**horses, horsing, horsed**) (**horse around**) informal fool about.
□ **horse chestnut 1** a large tree that produces nuts (conkers) in a spiny case. **2** a conker. **horse sense** common sense.

- **horsey** (or **horsy**) adjective.

horseback noun (**on horseback**) mounted on a horse.

horsebox noun Brit. a vehicle or trailer for transporting horses.

horsefly noun (plural **horseflies**) a large fly that bites horses and other large animals.

horseman or **horsewoman** noun (plural **horsemen** or **horsewomen**) a rider on horseback.

horseplay noun rough, high-spirited play.

horsepower noun (plural **horsepower**) a unit measuring the power of an engine.

horseradish noun a plant with strong-tasting roots which are made into a sauce.

horseshoe noun a U-shaped iron band attached to the base of a horse's hoof.

horticulture noun the cultivation of gardens.
- **horticultural** adjective.

hosanna noun an exclamation of praise or joy used in the Bible.

hose noun **1** (Brit. also **hosepipe**) a flexible tube that conveys water. **2** historical men's breeches. •verb (**hoses, hosing, hosed**) spray with a hose.

hosiery /hoh-zi-uh-ri/ noun socks, tights, and stockings.

hospice noun a home for people who are very ill or dying.

hospitable adjective **1** friendly and welcoming to strangers or guests. **2** (of an environment) pleasant and favourable for living in.
- **hospitably** adverb.

hospital noun a place where sick or injured people are looked after.

hospitality noun the friendly and generous treatment of guests or strangers.

hospitalize or **hospitalise** verb (**hospitalizes, hospitalizing, hospitalized**)

THESAURUS

horrible adjective **1** *a horrible murder:* **dreadful**, awful, terrible, shocking, appalling, horrifying, horrific, horrendous, grisly, ghastly, gruesome, harrowing, unspeakable. **2** *a horrible little man:* **nasty**, horrid, disagreeable, obnoxious, hateful, odious, objectionable, insufferable.
OPPOSITES pleasant, agreeable.

horrific adjective **dreadful**, horrendous, horrible, terrible, atrocious, horrifying, shocking, appalling, harrowing, hideous, grisly, ghastly, sickening.

horrify verb **shock**, appal, outrage, scandalize, offend, disgust, revolt, nauseate, sicken.

horror noun **1** *children screamed in horror:* **terror**, fear, fright, alarm, panic. **2** *to her horror she found herself alone:* **dismay**, consternation, alarm, distress, disgust, shock.
OPPOSITES delight, satisfaction.

horse noun **mount**, charger, cob, nag, hack, colt, stallion, mare, filly; N. Amer. bronco; Austral./NZ moke, yarraman; informal gee-gee.

hospitable adjective **welcoming**, friendly, sociable, cordial, gracious, accommodating, warm.
OPPOSITES inhospitable.

hospitality noun **friendliness**, neighbourliness, sociability, welcome, warmth, kindness, cordiality, generosity.

admit someone to hospital.
■ **hospitalization** noun.

Host noun (**the Host**) the bread used in the Christian ceremony of Holy Communion.

host[1] noun **1** a person who receives or entertains guests. **2** the presenter of a television or radio programme. **3** the place that holds an event to which others are invited. **4** Biology an animal or plant on or in which a parasite lives. ● verb act as host at.

host[2] noun (**a host** or **hosts of**) a large number of.

hostage noun a person held prisoner in an attempt to make other people give in to a demand.

hostel noun a place which provides cheap food and accommodation for a particular group of people.

hostelry noun (plural **hostelries**) old use or humorous a pub.

hostess noun **1** a female host. **2** a woman employed to welcome customers at a nightclub or bar.

hostile adjective **1** aggressively unfriendly. **2** having to do with a military enemy.

hostility noun (plural **hostilities**) **1** hostile behaviour. **2** (**hostilities**) acts of warfare.

hot adjective (**hotter**, **hottest**) **1** having a high temperature. **2** feeling or producing an uncomfortable sensation of heat. **3** informal currently popular or interesting. **4** informal (of goods) stolen. **5** (**hot on**) informal knowing a lot about. **6** (**hot on**) informal strict about. ● verb (**hots**, **hotting**, **hotted**) (**hot up**) Brit. informal become more exciting.

□ **hot air** informal empty or boastful talk. **hot-blooded** passionate. **hot cross bun** a bun marked with a cross, eaten on Good Friday. **hot dog** a hot sausage served in a long, soft roll. **hot rod** a car specially adapted to be fast. **hot-water bottle** a container filled with hot water and used for warming a bed. **hot-wire** informal start a vehicle without using the ignition switch.
■ **hotly** adverb.

hotbed noun a place where a lot of a particular activity is happening.

hotchpotch noun a confused mixture.

hotel noun a place providing accommodation and meals for travellers.

hotelier noun a person who owns or manages a hotel.

hotfoot adverb quickly and eagerly.
□ **hotfoot it** hurry eagerly.

hothead noun an impetuous or quick-tempered person.

hothouse noun a heated greenhouse.

hotline noun a direct telephone line set up for a particular purpose.

hotplate noun a flat heated surface on an electric cooker.

hotpot noun Brit. a casserole of meat and vegetables with a covering layer of sliced potato.

hotshot noun informal an important or very skilled person.

houmous ⇨ HUMMUS.

hound noun a hunting dog. ● verb harass someone.

houndstooth noun a kind of large check pattern.

h

THESAURUS

host noun *the host of a TV series:* presenter, compère, anchor, anchorman, anchorwoman, announcer.
OPPOSITES guest.
● verb *the show is hosted by Angus:* present, introduce, compère, front, anchor.

hostage noun captive, prisoner, detainee, internee.

hostile adjective **1** *a hostile attitude:* unfriendly, unkind, unsympathetic, antagonistic, aggressive, confrontational, belligerent. **2** *hostile conditions:* unfavourable, adverse, bad, harsh, grim, inhospitable, forbidding. **3** *they are hostile to the idea:* opposed, averse, antagonistic, ill-disposed, unsympathetic, antipathetic, against; informal anti.
OPPOSITES friendly, favourable, in favour.

hostility noun **1** *he glared at her with hostility:* antagonism, unfriendliness, malevolence, venom, hatred, aggression, belligerence. **2** *their hostility to the present regime:* opposition, antagonism, animosity, antipathy. **3** *a cessation of hostilities:*

fighting, armed conflict, combat, warfare, war, bloodshed, violence.

hot adjective **1** *hot food:* heated, piping, sizzling, roasting, boiling, scorching, scalding, red-hot. **2** *a hot day:* very warm, balmy, summery, tropical, scorching, searing, blistering, sweltering; informal boiling, baking, roasting. **3** *a hot chilli:* spicy, peppery, fiery, strong, piquant, powerful. **4** *the competition was hot:* fierce, intense, keen, competitive, cut-throat, ruthless, aggressive, strong. **5** (informal) *she is hot on local history:* knowledgeable about, well informed about, au fait with, up on, well versed in; informal clued up about.
OPPOSITES cold, mild, weak.

hotel noun inn, motel, boarding house, guest house, bed and breakfast, B & B, hostel.

hotly adverb vehemently, vigorously, strenuously, fiercely, heatedly.
OPPOSITES calmly.

hound verb pursue, chase, stalk, harry, harass, pester, badger, torment.

hour noun **1** a twenty-fourth part of a day and night; 60 minutes. **2** (**hours**) a period set aside for a particular purpose. **3** a particular point in time. **4** (**hours**) informal a very long time.

hourglass noun an object consisting of two connected glass bulbs containing sand that takes an hour to fall from the upper to the lower bulb.

houri /hoo-ri/ noun (plural **houris**) (in Islam) one of the virgin companions of the faithful in paradise.

hourly adverb & adjective **1** every hour. **2** by the hour.

house noun /howss/ **1** a building for people to live in. **2** a firm or institution. **3** a group of pupils living in the same building at a boarding school. **4** a long-established and powerful family. **5** (also **house music**) a style of popular dance music. •verb /howz/ (**houses, housing, housed**) **1** provide with accommodation. **2** provide space for. **3** enclose something. □ **house arrest** the state of being kept as a prisoner in your own house. **House of Commons** the chamber of the UK Parliament whose members are elected. **House of Lords** the chamber of the UK Parliament whose members are peers and bishops. **house-proud** very concerned with the appearance of your home. **house-train** train a pet to urinate and defecate outside the house. **house-warming** a party held to celebrate moving into a new home. **on the house** at the management's expense.

houseboat noun a boat that people can live in.

housebound adjective unable to leave your house.

housebreaking noun the action of breaking into a building to commit a crime.

household noun a house and all the people living in it.
■ **householder** noun.

housekeeper noun a person employed to shop, cook, and clean the house.
■ **housekeeping** noun.

housemaid noun a female servant in a house.

housemaster or **housemistress** noun a teacher in charge of a house at a boarding school.

housemate noun a person with whom you share a house.

housewife noun (plural **housewives**) a woman whose main occupation is looking after her family and the home.

housework noun cleaning, cooking, etc. done in running a home.

housing noun **1** houses and flats as a whole. **2** a hard cover for a piece of equipment.

hove chiefly Nautical past tense of **HEAVE**.

hovel noun a small house that is dirty and run-down.

hover verb (**hovers, hovering, hovered**) **1** remain in one place in the air. **2** wait about uncertainly. **3** remain near a particular level or between two states.

hovercraft noun (plural **hovercraft**) a vehicle that travels over land or water on a cushion of air.

how adverb **1** in what way or by what means. **2** in what condition. **3** to what extent or degree. **4** the way in which.

howdah /how-duh/ noun a seat for riding on the back of an elephant.

however adverb **1** used to begin a statement that contrasts with something that has just been said. **2** in whatever way or to whatever extent.

howitzer /how-it-ser/ noun a short gun for firing shells at a high angle.

THESAURUS

house noun **1** residence, home; formal dwelling, habitation, domicile, abode. **2** the house of Stewart: family, clan, tribe, dynasty, line, bloodline, lineage. **3** a printing house: firm, business, company, corporation, enterprise, establishment, institution, concern, organization, operation; informal outfit. **4** the country's upper house: assembly, legislative body, chamber, council, parliament, congress, senate. •verb **1** we can house twelve adults: accommodate, give someone a roof over their head, lodge, quarter, board, billet, take in, sleep, put up. **2** this panel houses the main switch: contain, hold, store, cover, protect, enclose.

household noun the household was asleep: family, house, occupants, clan, tribe; informal brood. •adjective household goods: domestic, family, everyday, workaday.

housing noun **1** a housing development: houses, homes, residences, living quarters, accommodation; formal dwellings. **2** the housing for the equipment: casing, covering, case, cover, holder, fairing, sleeve.

hovel noun shack, slum, shanty, hut; informal dump, hole.

hover verb **1** helicopters hovered overhead: hang, be poised, be suspended, float, fly, drift. **2** a servant hovered nearby: wait, linger, loiter.

however adverb nevertheless, nonetheless, even so, but, for all that, despite that, in spite of that.

howl noun **1** a long wailing cry made by an animal. **2** a loud cry of pain, amusement, etc. •**verb** make a howl.

howler noun informal a stupid mistake.

h.p. or **HP** abbreviation **1** Brit. hire purchase. **2** horsepower.

HQ abbreviation headquarters.

HRH abbreviation Brit. Her (or His) Royal Highness.

HTML abbreviation Computing Hypertext Markup Language.

hub noun **1** the central part of a wheel. **2** the centre of an activity or region.

hubbub noun a loud confused noise caused by a crowd.

hubcap noun a cover for the hub of a motor vehicle's wheel.

hubris /hyoo-briss/ noun excessive pride or self-confidence.

huckster noun **1** a person who sells things forcefully. **2** a person who sells small items in the street.

huddle verb (**huddles, huddling, huddled**) **1** crowd together. **2** curl your body into a small space. •**noun** a number of people or things crowded together.

hue noun **1** a colour or shade. **2** a particular aspect of something.

hue and cry noun a strong public outcry.

huff verb (often **huff and puff**) breathe out noisily. •**noun** a bad mood.
∎ **huffy** adjective.

hug verb (**hugs, hugging, hugged**) **1** hold tightly in your arms. **2** keep close to. •**noun** an act of hugging.

huge adjective (**huger, hugest**) very large.
∎ **hugely** adverb **hugeness** noun.

hugger-mugger adjective confused or disorderly.

hula noun a dance performed by Hawaiian women, in which the dancers sway their hips.
□ **hula hoop** (also US trademark **Hula-Hoop**) a large hoop that you spin around your body by moving your hips.

hulk noun **1** an old ship stripped of fittings and no longer used. **2** a large or clumsy person or thing.

hulking adjective informal very large or clumsy.

hull[1] noun the main body of a ship.

hull[2] noun **1** the outer covering of a fruit or seed. **2** the cluster of leaves and stalk on a strawberry or raspberry. •**verb** remove the hulls from.

hullabaloo noun informal an uproar.

hullo ⇒ **HELLO.**

hum verb (**hums, humming, hummed**) **1** make a low continuous sound like that of a bee. **2** sing a tune with closed lips. **3** informal be in a state of great activity. •**noun** a low continuous sound.

human adjective **1** having to do with men,

howl noun **1** *the howl of a wolf:* baying, cry, bark, yelp. **2** *a howl of anguish:* wail, cry, yell, yelp, bellow, roar, shout, shriek, scream, screech.
•**verb 1** *dogs howled in the distance:* bay, cry, bark, yelp. **2** *a baby started to howl:* wail, cry, yell, bawl, bellow, shriek, scream, screech, caterwaul; informal holler.

hub noun centre, core, heart, focus, focal point, nucleus, kernel, nerve centre.
OPPOSITES periphery.

huddle verb **1** *they huddled together:* crowd, cluster, gather, bunch, throng, flock, collect, group, congregate. **2** *he huddled beneath the sheets:* curl up, snuggle, nestle, hunch up.
OPPOSITES disperse.
•**noun** *a huddle of passengers:* group, cluster, bunch, collection; informal gaggle.

hue noun colour, shade, tone, tint, tinge.

hug verb *they hugged each other:* embrace, cuddle, squeeze, clasp, clutch, hold tight.
•**noun** *there were hugs as we left:* embrace, cuddle, squeeze, bear hug.

huge adjective enormous, vast, immense, massive, colossal, prodigious, gigantic, gargantuan, mammoth, monumental, giant, towering, mountainous; informal mega,

monster, astronomical; Brit. informal ginormous.
OPPOSITES tiny.

hugely adverb extremely, very, tremendously, exceptionally, immensely, extraordinarily, vastly; informal terrifically, awfully, terribly, seriously; Brit. informal dead, jolly; N. Amer. informal real, mighty, awful.

hull noun *the ship's hull:* framework, body, shell, frame, skeleton, structure.

hum verb **1** *the engine was humming:* purr, drone, murmur, buzz, whirr, throb. **2** *the workshops are humming:* be busy, be active, be lively, buzz, bustle, be a hive of activity, throb.
•**noun** *a low hum of conversation:* murmur, drone, purr, buzz.

human adjective **1** *they're only human:* mortal, flesh and blood, fallible, weak, frail, imperfect, vulnerable, physical, bodily, fleshly. **2** *his human side:* compassionate, humane, kind, considerate, understanding, sympathetic.
OPPOSITES infallible, inhuman.
•**noun** *the link between humans and animals:* person, human being, Homo sapiens, man, woman, individual, mortal, (living) soul, earthling; (**humans**) the

women, or children. **2** showing the better qualities of people. **• noun** (also **human being**) a man, woman, or child.

□ **human rights** basic rights which belong to all people, such as freedom.

■ **humanly** adverb.

humane /hyuu-**mayn**/ adjective showing concern and kindness towards other people.

■ **humanely** adverb.

humanism noun a system of thought that sees people as able to live their lives without the need for religious beliefs.

■ **humanist** noun & adjective **humanistic** adjective.

humanitarian adjective concerned with the welfare of people. **• noun** a humanitarian person.

humanity noun **1** people as a whole. **2** the condition of being human. **3** sympathy and kindness towards other people.
4 (**humanities**) studies concerned with human culture, such as literature or history.

humanize or **humanise** verb (**humanizes, humanizing, humanized**) make more pleasant or suitable for people.

humankind noun people as a whole.

humanoid adjective like a human in appearance. **• noun** a humanoid being.

humble adjective (**humbler, humblest**)

1 having a modest or low opinion of your own importance. **2** of low rank. **3** not large or important. **• verb** (**humbles, humbling, humbled**) make someone seem less important.

□ **eat humble pie** make a humble apology.

■ **humbly** adverb.

humbug noun **1** false or misleading talk or behaviour. **2** a person who is not sincere or honest. **3** Brit. a boiled peppermint sweet.

humdrum adjective ordinary; dull.

humerus /**hyoo**-muh-ruhss/ noun (plural **humeri** /**hyoo**-muh-ry/) the bone of the upper arm, between the shoulder and the elbow.

humid adjective (of the air or weather) damp and warm.

■ **humidity** noun.

humiliate verb (**humiliates, humiliating, humiliated**) make someone feel ashamed or stupid.

■ **humiliation** noun.

humility noun the quality of being humble.

hummingbird noun a small bird able to hover by beating its wings very fast.

hummock noun a small hill or mound.

hummus or **houmous** /**huu**-muhss/ noun a Middle Eastern dip made from chickpeas, sesame seeds, etc.

humorist noun a writer or speaker who is

THESAURUS

human race, humanity, humankind, mankind, man, people.

humane adjective compassionate, kind, considerate, understanding, sympathetic, tolerant, forbearing, forgiving, merciful, humanitarian, charitable.
OPPOSITES cruel.

humanitarian adjective **1** *a humanitarian act:* compassionate, humane, unselfish, altruistic, generous. **2** *a humanitarian organization:* charitable, philanthropic, public-spirited, socially concerned, welfare, aid.
OPPOSITES selfish, commercial.
• noun philanthropist, altruist, benefactor, social reformer, good Samaritan, do-gooder.

humanity noun **1** *humanity evolved from the apes:* humankind, mankind, man, people, the human race, Homo sapiens.
2 *he praised them for their humanity:* compassion, brotherly love, fellow feeling, humaneness, kindness, consideration, understanding, sympathy, tolerance.

humble adjective **1** *she was very humble:* meek, deferential, respectful, submissive, self-effacing, unassertive, modest, unassuming, self-deprecating; Scottish mim.
2 *a humble background:* lowly, poor, undistinguished, mean, common, ordinary,

simple. **3** *my humble abode:* modest, plain, simple, ordinary, little.
OPPOSITES proud, illustrious, grand.
• verb *it humbled him to ask for help:* humiliate, demean, lower, degrade, debase, mortify, shame.

humid adjective muggy, close, sultry, sticky, steamy, clammy, heavy.
OPPOSITES dry, fresh.

humiliate verb embarrass, mortify, humble, shame, disgrace, chasten, deflate, crush, squash, demean, take down a peg or two; informal show up, put down, cut down to size; N. Amer. informal make someone eat crow.
OPPOSITES dignify.

humiliating adjective embarrassing, mortifying, humbling, ignominious, inglorious, shaming, undignified, chastening, demeaning, degrading, deflating.

humiliation noun embarrassment, mortification, shame, indignity, ignominy, disgrace, dishonour, degradation, discredit, loss of face, blow to your pride.
OPPOSITES honour.

humility noun modesty, humbleness, meekness, respect, deference, diffidence, unassertiveness.
OPPOSITES pride.

known for being amusing.

humorous adjective **1** causing amusement. **2** showing a sense of humour. ■ **humorously** adverb.

> ☑ -*or*- not -*our*-: humorous.

humour (US spelling **humor**) noun **1** the quality of being amusing. **2** a state of mind. •verb do as someone wishes in order to keep them happy. ■ **humourless** adjective.

hump noun **1** a rounded mass of earth or land. **2** a round part projecting from the back of a camel or other animal, or as an abnormal feature on a person's back. •verb informal lift or carry with difficulty. ■ **humped** adjective.

humus /hyoo-muhss/ noun a substance found in soil, made from dead leaves and plants.

hunch verb raise your shoulders and bend the top part of your body forward. •noun an idea based on a feeling rather than evidence.

hunchback noun offensive a person with an abnormal hump on their back.

hundred cardinal number **1** ten more than ninety; 100. (Roman numeral: **c** or **C**.) **2** (**hundreds**) informal a large number. ■ **hundredth** ordinal number.

hundredweight noun (plural **hundredweight** or **hundredweights**) **1** Brit. a unit of weight equal to 112 lb (about 50.8 kg). **2** US a unit of weight equal to 100 lb (about 45.4 kg).

hung past and past participle of **HANG**.

•adjective **1** having no political party with an overall majority. **2** (of a jury) unable to agree on a verdict. **3** (**hung up**) informal emotionally confused or disturbed.

Hungarian noun **1** a person from Hungary. **2** the language of Hungary. •adjective relating to Hungary.

hunger noun **1** a feeling of discomfort caused by a lack of food. **2** a strong desire. •verb (**hungers**, **hungering**, **hungered**) (**hunger after** or **for**) have a strong desire for.
□ **hunger strike** a refusal to eat for a long period, carried out as a protest about something.

hungover adjective suffering from a hangover.

hungry adjective (**hungrier**, **hungriest**) **1** feeling that you want to eat something. **2** having a strong desire for something. ■ **hungrily** adverb.

hunk noun **1** a large piece cut or broken from something larger. **2** informal a good-looking man. ■ **hunky** adjective.

hunky-dory adjective informal fine; satisfactory.

hunt verb **1** chase and kill a wild animal for food or as a sport. **2** search for something. **3** (**hunt someone down**) chase and capture someone. **4** (**hunted**) looking worried and as if you are being chased. •noun **1** an act of hunting. **2** a group of people who meet regularly to hunt animals as a sport. ■ **hunter** noun.

huntsman noun (plural **huntsmen**) a person

h

---

humorous adjective amusing, funny, comic, comical, entertaining, diverting, witty, jocular, light-hearted, hilarious.
OPPOSITES serious.

humour noun **1** *the humour of the situation*: comedy, funny side, hilarity, absurdity, ludicrousness, satire, irony. **2** *the stories are spiced up with humour*: jokes, jests, quips, witticisms, funny remarks, wit, comedy; informal gags, wisecracks. **3** *his good humour was infectious*: mood, temper, disposition, spirits.
OPPOSITES seriousness.
•verb *she was always humouring him*: indulge, accommodate, pander to, cater to, give in to, go along with, flatter, mollify, placate.
OPPOSITES stand up to.

hunch noun feeling, guess, suspicion, impression, inkling, idea, notion, fancy, intuition; informal gut feeling.

hunger noun **1** *she was faint with hunger*: lack of food, starvation, malnutrition,

undernourishment. **2** *a hunger for news*: desire, craving, longing, yearning, hankering, appetite, thirst; informal itch.
□ **hunger after/for** desire, crave, long for, yearn for, pine for, ache for, hanker after, thirst for, lust for; informal itch for, be dying for, be gagging for.

hungry adjective **1** *I was really hungry*: ravenous, starving, starved, famished, malnourished, undernourished, underfed; informal peckish. **2** *they are hungry for success*: eager, keen, avid, longing, yearning, aching, greedy, craving, desirous of, hankering after; informal itching, dying, gagging.
OPPOSITES full.

hunk noun chunk, wedge, block, slab, lump, square, gobbet; Brit. informal wodge.

hunt verb **1** *they hunted deer*: chase, stalk, pursue, course, track, trail. **2** *police are hunting for her*: search, seek, look high and low, scour the area.
•noun **1** *the thrill of the hunt*: chase, pursuit. **2** *a police hunt*: search, quest.

who hunts.

hurdle noun **1** each of a series of upright frames that an athlete jumps over in a race. **2** a frame used as a temporary fence. **3** an obstacle or difficulty. • verb (**hurdles, hurdling, hurdled**) jump over an obstacle while running.
■ **hurdler** noun.

hurdy-gurdy noun (plural **hurdy-gurdies**) a musical instrument played by turning a handle.

hurl verb **1** throw something with great force. **2** shout insults.

hurling or **hurley** noun an Irish game resembling hockey.

hurly-burly noun busy and noisy activity.

hurrah, hooray, or **hurray** exclamation used to express joy or approval.

hurricane noun a severe storm with a violent wind.

hurry verb (**hurries, hurrying, hurried**) **1** move or act quickly. **2** do something quickly or too quickly. • noun great haste.
■ **hurriedly** adverb.

hurt verb (**hurts, hurting, hurt**) **1** make someone feel physical pain. **2** feel pain. **3** upset someone. • noun injury, pain, or unhappiness.

hurtful adjective upsetting; unkind.
■ **hurtfully** adverb.

hurtle verb (**hurtles, hurtling, hurtled**) move very fast.

husband noun the man that a woman is married to. • verb use something carefully without wasting it.

husbandry noun **1** farming. **2** careful management of resources.

hush verb **1** make or become quiet. **2** (**hush something up**) stop something from becoming known. • noun a silence.

husk noun the dry outer covering of some fruits or seeds. • verb remove the husk from.

husky[1] adjective (**huskier, huskiest**) **1** (of a voice) deep and rough. **2** big and strong.
■ **huskily** adverb.

husky[2] noun (plural **huskies**) a powerful dog used for pulling sledges.

hussar /huu-zar/ noun historical a soldier in a light cavalry regiment.

hussy noun (plural **hussies**) a girl or woman who behaves in an immoral or cheeky way.

hustings noun the political meetings and speeches that take place before an election.

hustle verb (**hustles, hustling, hustled**) **1** push or move roughly. **2** informal, chiefly N. Amer. obtain something dishonestly. • noun busy movement and activity.
■ **hustler** noun.

THESAURUS

hurdle noun obstacle, difficulty, problem, barrier, bar, snag, stumbling block, impediment, obstruction, complication, hindrance.

hurl verb throw, toss, fling, launch, pitch, cast, lob; informal chuck, sling, bung.

hurricane noun cyclone, typhoon, tornado, storm, windstorm, whirlwind, gale, tempest; Austral. willy-willy; N. Amer. informal twister.

hurried adjective **1** *hurried glances:* quick, fast, swift, rapid, speedy, brisk, cursory, perfunctory, brief, short, fleeting. **2** *a hurried decision:* hasty, rushed, precipitate, spur-of-the-moment.
OPPOSITES slow, considered.

hurry verb **1** *hurry or you'll be late:* be quick, hurry up, hasten, speed up, run, dash, rush, race, scurry, scramble, scuttle, sprint; informal get a move on; Brit. informal get your skates on; N. Amer. informal get a wiggle on. **2** *she hurried him out:* hustle, hasten, push, urge, usher.
OPPOSITES dawdle, delay.
• noun *in all the hurry, we forgot:* rush, haste, speed, urgency, hustle and bustle.
OPPOSITES ease.

hurt verb **1** *my back hurts:* be painful, ache, be sore, be tender, smart, sting, burn, throb; informal be agony. **2** *Dad hurt his leg:* injure, wound, damage, disable, bruise, cut, gash, graze, scrape, scratch. **3** *his words hurt her:* distress, pain, wound, sting, upset, sadden, devastate, grieve, mortify.
OPPOSITES comfort.
• noun *all the hurt he had caused:* distress, pain, suffering, grief, misery, anguish, upset, sadness, sorrow.
OPPOSITES joy.
• adjective **1** *my hurt hand:* injured, wounded, bruised, grazed, cut, gashed, sore, painful, aching. **2** *Anne's hurt expression:* pained, aggrieved, offended, distressed, upset, sad, mortified; informal miffed.
OPPOSITES unhurt, pleased.

hurtful adjective upsetting, distressing, wounding, unkind, cruel, nasty, mean, malicious, spiteful.

hush verb *he tried to hush her:* silence, quieten (down), shush, gag, muzzle; informal shut up.
• noun *a hush descended:* silence, quiet, stillness, peace, calm, tranquillity.
OPPOSITES noise.
□ **hush something up** keep secret, conceal, hide, suppress, cover up, keep quiet about, sweep under the carpet.

hut noun a small, simple house or shelter.

hutch noun a box with a front made of wire, used for keeping rabbits.

hyacinth /hy-uh-sinth/ noun a plant with bell-shaped flowers.

hyaena ⇒ HYENA.

hybrid noun **1** the offspring of two plants or animals of different species or varieties. **2** something made by combining two different things.

hydra noun a minute freshwater creature with a tube-shaped body and tentacles around the mouth.

hydrangea /hy-drayn-juh/ noun a shrub with white, blue, or pink clusters of flowers.

hydrant noun a water pipe with a nozzle for attaching a fire hose.

hydrate verb (**hydrates, hydrating, hydrated**) make something absorb or combine with water.
■ **hydration** noun.

hydraulic adjective operated by a liquid moving through pipes under pressure.
•noun (**hydraulics**) the branch of science concerned with the use of liquids moving under pressure to provide mechanical force.
■ **hydraulically** adverb.

hydrocarbon noun any of the compounds of hydrogen and carbon.

hydrocephalus /hy-druh-sef-uh-luhss/ noun a condition in which fluid collects in the brain.

hydrochloric acid noun an acid containing hydrogen and chlorine.

hydroelectric adjective having to do with the use of flowing water to generate electricity.

hydrofoil noun a boat designed to rise above the water when it is travelling fast.

hydrogen noun a highly flammable gas which is the lightest of the chemical elements.
□ **hydrogen bomb** a very powerful nuclear bomb. **hydrogen sulphide** a poisonous gas with a smell of bad eggs.

hydrology noun the scientific study of the water on the earth's surface.

hydrophobia noun **1** extreme fear of water, especially as a symptom of rabies. **2** rabies.

■ **hydrophobic** adjective.

hydroplane noun a light, fast motorboat designed to skim over the surface of water.

hydrous adjective containing water.

hydroxide noun a compound containing oxygen and hydrogen together with a metallic element.

hyena or **hyaena** noun a doglike African animal.

hygiene noun the practice of keeping yourself and your surroundings clean in order to prevent illness and disease.

hygienic adjective clean and not likely to spread disease.
■ **hygienically** adverb.

☑ remember, *i* before *e* except after *c*: hyg*ie*nic.

hygienist noun a dental worker who specializes in oral hygiene.

hymen /hy-muhn/ noun a membrane which partially closes the opening of the vagina and is usually broken when a woman or girl first has sex.

hymn noun a religious song of praise, especially a Christian one. •verb praise or celebrate.

hymnal noun a book of hymns.

hype informal noun extravagant publicity given to a product. •verb (**hypes, hyping, hyped**) **1** publicize a product in an extravagant way. **2** (**be hyped up**) be very excited or tense.

hyper adjective informal having a lot of nervous energy.

hyperactive adjective very active; unable to keep still.

hyperbola /hy-per-buh-luh/ noun (plural **hyperbolas**) a symmetrical curve formed when a cone is cut by a plane nearly parallel to the cone's axis.

hyperbole /hy-per-buh-li/ noun a way of speaking or writing that exaggerates things and is not meant to be understood literally.

hyperbolic adjective **1** deliberately exaggerated. **2** relating to a hyperbola.

hyperlink noun Computing a link from a hypertext document to another location.

hypermarket noun Brit. a very large supermarket.

hypersensitive adjective too sensitive.

hypersonic adjective **1** relating to speeds of

h

THESAURUS

hut noun shack, shanty, cabin, shelter, shed, lean-to, hovel; Scottish bothy; N. Amer. cabana.

hybrid noun *a hybrid of a goose and a swan:* **cross**, cross-breed, mixture, blend, combination, composite, fusion, amalgam.
•adjective *hybrid roses:* **composite**, cross-bred, interbred, mixed, blended, compound.

hygiene noun **cleanliness**, sanitation, sterility, purity, disinfection.

hygienic adjective **sanitary**, clean, germ-free, disinfected, sterilized, sterile, antiseptic, aseptic.
OPPOSITES insanitary.

more than five times the speed of sound. **2** relating to sound frequencies above about a thousand million hertz.

hypertension noun abnormally high blood pressure.

hypertext noun Computing a system that lets you move quickly between documents or sections of data.

hyperventilate verb (**hyperventilates, hyperventilating, hyperventilated**) breathe at an abnormally rapid rate.
■ **hyperventilation** noun.

hyphen noun the sign (-) used to join words together or to divide a word into parts between one line and the next.

hyphenate verb (**hypenates hyphenating, hyphenated**) join or divide words with a hyphen.
■ **hyphenation** noun.

hypnosis noun the practice of causing a person to enter a state in which they respond very readily to suggestions or commands.

hypnotherapy noun the use of hypnosis to treat physical or mental problems.

hypnotic adjective **1** having to do with hypnosis. **2** making you feel very relaxed or sleepy.
■ **hypnotically** adverb.

hypnotism noun the study or practice of hypnosis.
■ **hypnotist** noun.

hypnotize or **hypnotise** verb (**hypnotizes, hypnotizing, hypnotized**) put someone into a state of hypnosis.

hypoallergenic adjective unlikely to cause an allergic reaction.

hypochondria /hy-puh-**kon**-dri-uh/ noun extreme anxiety about your health.

hypochondriac noun a person who is too anxious about their health.

hypocrisy /hi-**pok**-ruh-si/ noun behaviour in which a person pretends to have higher standards than they really have.

hypocrite noun a person who pretends to have higher standards than they really have.
■ **hypocritical** adjective.

hypodermic adjective (of a needle or syringe) used to inject a drug or other substance beneath the skin. • noun a hypodermic syringe or injection.

hypotension noun abnormally low blood pressure.

hypotenuse /hy-**pot**-uh-nyooz/ noun the longest side of a right-angled triangle, opposite the right angle.

hypothermia noun the condition of having an abnormally low body temperature.

hypothesis /hy-**po**-thi-siss/ noun (plural **hypotheses** /hy-**po**-thi-seez/) an idea that has not yet been proved to be true or correct.

hypothesize or **hypothesise** verb (**hypothesizes, hypothesizing, hypothesized**) put forward as a hypothesis.

hypothetical adjective based on a situation which is imagined rather than true.
■ **hypothetically** adverb.

hysterectomy noun (plural **hysterectomies**) a surgical operation to remove all or part of the womb.

hysteria noun **1** wild or uncontrollable emotion. **2** dated a medical condition in which a person loses control of their emotions.

hysterical adjective **1** affected by wild or uncontrolled emotion. **2** informal very funny.
■ **hysterically** adverb.

hysterics plural noun **1** wildly emotional behaviour. **2** informal uncontrollable laughter.

Hz abbreviation hertz.

THESAURUS

hypocritical adjective sanctimonious, pious, self-righteous, holier-than-thou, superior, insincere, two-faced.

hysteria noun frenzy, feverishness, hysterics, agitation, mania, panic, alarm, distress.
OPPOSITES calm.

hysterical adjective **1** *Janet became*

hysterical: overwrought, overemotional, out of control, frenzied, frantic, wild, beside yourself, manic, delirious; informal in a state. **2** *the film was hysterical:* (informal) very funny, hilarious, uproarious, rib-tickling; informal side-splitting, priceless, a scream, a hoot.
OPPOSITES calm, unfunny, serious.

I¹ or **i** noun (plural **Is** or **I's**) **1** the ninth letter of the alphabet. **2** the Roman numeral for one.

I² pronoun used by a speaker to refer to himself or herself.

iambic /I-**am**-bik/ adjective (of rhythm in poetry) having one unstressed syllable followed by one stressed syllable.

Iberian /I-**beer**-i-uhn/ adjective relating to Iberia (the peninsula that consists of modern Spain and Portugal).

ibex /I-beks/ noun (plural **ibexes**) a wild mountain goat with long horns.

ibid. adverb in the same book as the one that has just been mentioned.

ibis /I-biss/ noun (plural **ibises**) a large wading bird with a long curved bill.

ice noun **1** water that has frozen and become solid. **2** Brit. an ice cream. ●verb (**ices, icing, iced**) **1** decorate a cake with icing. **2** (**ice up** or **over**) become covered with ice.
□ **ice age** a period of time when ice covered much of the earth's surface. **ice cap** a large area that is permanently covered with ice, especially at the North and South Poles. **ice cream** a frozen dessert made with sweetened milk fat. **ice hockey** a form of hockey played on an ice rink. **ice pack** a bag filled with ice and held against part of the body to reduce swelling or lower temperature. **ice skate** a boot with a blade attached to the sole, used for skating on ice. **on thin ice** in a risky situation.

iceberg noun a large mass of ice floating in the sea.

icebox noun **1** a chilled container for keeping food cold. **2** Brit. a compartment in a fridge for making and storing ice.

iced adjective **1** cooled or mixed with ice. **2** decorated with icing.

Icelandic noun the language of Iceland. ●adjective relating to Iceland.

■ **Icelander** noun.

ichthyology /ik-thi-**ol**-uh-ji/ noun the branch of zoology concerned with fish.
■ **ichthyologist** noun.

icicle noun a hanging piece of ice formed when dripping water freezes.

icing noun Brit. a mixture of sugar and water or fat, used to cover cakes.
□ **icing sugar** finely powdered sugar used to make icing.

icon /I-kon/ noun **1** (also **ikon**) (in the Orthodox Church) a painting of a holy person that is also regarded as holy. **2** a person or thing that is seen as a symbol of something. **3** Computing a symbol on a computer screen that represents a program.
■ **iconic** adjective.

iconify /I-**kon**-i-fy/ verb (**iconifies, iconifying, iconified**) Computing reduce a window to an icon.

iconoclast /I-**kon**-uh-klast/ noun a person who attacks established customs and values.
■ **iconoclasm** noun **iconoclastic** adjective.

iconography /I-kuh-**nog**-ruh-fi/ noun **1** the use or study of pictures or symbols in visual arts. **2** the pictures or symbols associated with a person or movement.
■ **iconographic** adjective.

ICT abbreviation information and computing technology.

icy adjective (**icier, iciest**) **1** covered with ice. **2** very cold. **3** very unfriendly; hostile.
■ **icily** adverb.

ID abbreviation identification or identity.

Id ⇒ **EID**.

I'd short form **1** I had. **2** I should or I would.

id noun the part of the mind that consists of a person's unconscious instincts and feelings.

idea noun **1** a thought or suggestion about a

icy adjective **1** *icy roads:* iced (over), frozen, frosty, slippery, treacherous; literary rimy. **2** *an icy wind:* freezing, chill, biting, bitter, raw, arctic. **3** *an icy voice:* unfriendly, hostile, forbidding, cold, chilly, frosty, stern.

idea noun **1** *the idea of death:* concept, notion, conception, thought. **2** *our idea is* possible course of action. **2** a mental picture or impression. **3** a belief. **4** (**the idea**) the aim or purpose.

ideal adjective **1** most suitable; perfect. **2** existing only in the imagination. • noun **1** a person or thing regarded as perfect. **2** a principle or standard that is worth trying to achieve.
■ **ideally** adverb.

idealism noun **1** the belief that ideals can be achieved. **2** the representation of things as better than they really are.
■ **idealist** noun **idealistic** adjective.

idealize or **idealise** verb (**idealizes, idealizing, idealized**) represent someone or something as better than they really are.
■ **idealization** noun.

identical adjective **1** exactly alike. **2** the same. **3** (of twins) very similar in appearance.
■ **identically** adverb.

identification noun **1** the action of identifying. **2** an official document or other proof of your identity.

identify verb (**identifies, identifying, identified**) **1** prove or recognize that someone or something is a specified person or thing. **2** recognize as being worthy of attention. **3** (**identify with**) feel that you understand or share the feelings of. **4** (**identify someone/thing with**) associate someone or something closely with.
■ **identifiable** adjective.

identity noun (plural **identities**) **1** the fact of being who or what a person or thing is. **2** a close similarity or feeling of understanding.
☐ **identity parade** Brit. a group of people assembled so that an eyewitness may identify someone suspected of a crime from among them.

ideology /I-di-ol-uh-ji/ noun (plural **ideologies**) **1** a system of ideas that an economic or political theory is based on. **2** the set of beliefs held by a particular group.
■ **ideological** adjective **ideologically** adverb.

idiocy noun (plural **idiocies**) very stupid behaviour.

idiom noun **1** a group of words whose overall meaning is different from the meanings of the individual words (e.g. *over the moon*). **2** a form of language used by a particular group of people. **3** a style of music or art.

idiomatic adjective using expressions that are natural to a native speaker of a language.

idiosyncrasy /id-i-oh-**sing**-kruh-si/ noun (plural **idiosyncrasies**) a person's particular way of behaving or thinking.
■ **idiosyncratic** adjective.

☑ the ending is *-asy*, not *-acy*: idiosyncr*asy*.

idiot noun a stupid person.
■ **idiotic** adjective **idiotically** adverb.

idle adjective (**idler, idlest**) **1** avoiding work;

THESAURUS

to open a new shop: plan, scheme, design, proposal, proposition, suggestion, aim, intention, objective, goal. **3** *Liz had various ideas on the subject:* thought, theory, view, opinion, feeling, belief. **4** *I had an idea this might happen:* sense, feeling, suspicion, fancy, inkling, hunch, notion. **5** *an idea of the cost:* estimate, approximation, guess, conjecture; informal guesstimate.

ideal adjective *ideal flying weather:* perfect, faultless, exemplary, classic, model, ultimate, theoretical, utopian.
OPPOSITES bad, real.
• noun **1** *an ideal to aim at:* model, pattern, exemplar, example, perfection, epitome, last word. **2** *liberal ideals:* principle, standard, value, belief, conviction.

identical adjective (*exactly*) the same, indistinguishable, twin, duplicate, interchangeable, alike, matching.
OPPOSITES different.

identification noun **1** *the identification of the suspect:* recognition, singling out, pinpointing, naming. **2** *early identification of problems:* determination, establishment, ascertainment, discovery, diagnosis. **3** *may I see your identification?* ID, papers,

documents, credentials, card, pass, badge.

identify verb **1** *Gail identified her attacker:* recognize, pick out, spot, point out, pinpoint, put your finger on, name. **2** *I identified four problem areas:* determine, establish, ascertain, make out, discern, distinguish. **3** *we identify sport with glamour:* associate, link, connect, relate. **4** *Peter identifies with the team captain:* empathize, sympathize, understand, relate to, feel for.

identity noun individuality, self, personality, character, originality, distinctiveness, uniqueness.

idiot noun fool, ass, halfwit, blockhead, dunce, simpleton; informal nincompoop, clod, dimwit, dummy, fathead, numbskull; Brit. informal nitwit, twit, clot, berk, prat, pillock, wally, dork, twerp, charlie; Scottish informal nyaff, balloon; N. Amer. informal schmuck, turkey; Austral./NZ informal drongo, nong, galah, boofhead.
OPPOSITES genius.

idle adjective **1** *an idle fellow:* lazy, indolent, slothful, work-shy. **2** *I was bored with being idle:* unemployed, jobless, out of work, lazy. **2** not working or in use. **3** having no purpose or effect. •verb (**idles, idling, idled**) **1** spend time doing nothing. **2** (of an engine) run slowly while out of gear. ■ **idleness** noun **idler** noun **idly** adverb.

idol noun **1** a statue or picture of a god that is worshipped. **2** a person who is very much admired.

idolatry /I-**dol**-uh-tri/ noun worship of idols.

idolize or **idolise** verb (**idolizes, idolizing, idolized**) admire or love someone very much.

idyll /i-dil/ noun **1** a very happy or peaceful time or situation. **2** a short piece of writing describing a peaceful scene of country life.

idyllic adjective very happy, peaceful, or beautiful. ■ **idyllically** adverb.

i.e. abbreviation that is to say.

if conjunction **1** on the condition or in the event that. **2** despite the possibility that. **3** whether. **4** whenever.

igloo noun a dome-shaped Eskimo house built from blocks of solid snow.

igneous /ig-ni-uhss/ adjective (of rock) formed when molten rock has solidified.

ignite verb (**ignites, igniting, ignited**) **1** catch fire, or set on fire. **2** provoke or stir up.

ignition noun **1** the action of igniting. **2** the mechanism in a vehicle that ignites the fuel to start the engine.

ignoble adjective not good or honest; dishonourable.

ignominious /ig-nuh-**min**-i-uhss/ adjective deserving or causing disgrace or shame. ■ **ignominiously** adverb.

ignominy /ig-nuh-mi-ni/ noun public shame or disgrace.

ignoramus /ig-nuh-**ray**-muhss/ noun (plural **ignoramuses**) an ignorant or stupid person.

ignorance noun lack of knowledge or information.

ignorant adjective **1** lacking knowledge or information. **2** informal not polite; rude.

ignore verb (**ignores, ignoring, ignored**) **1** deliberately take no notice of. **2** fail to consider something important.

iguana /i-**gwah**-nuh/ noun a large tropical American lizard with a spiny crest along the back.

ikon ⇒ ICON.

ileum /il-i-uhm/ noun (plural **ilea** /il-i-uh/) the third part of the small intestine.

ilk noun a type.

I'll short form **1** I shall. **2** I will.

ill adjective **1** not in good health; unwell.

redundant, unoccupied; Brit. informal on the dole. **3** *their idle hours:* unoccupied, spare, empty, unfilled. **4** *idle remarks:* frivolous, trivial, trifling, minor, insignificant, unimportant, empty, meaningless, vain. OPPOSITES industrious, employed, busy, serious.

idol noun **1** *an idol in a shrine:* icon, effigy, statue, figurine, totem. **2** *the pop world's latest idol:* hero, heroine, star, superstar, icon, celebrity, darling; informal pin-up, heart throb.

if conjunction **1** *if the weather is fine, we can walk:* provided, providing, on condition that, presuming, supposing, assuming, as long as, in the event that. **2** *if I go out she gets nasty:* whenever, every time. **3** *I wonder if he noticed:* whether, whether or not. OPPOSITES unless.

ignite verb **1** *moments before the petrol ignited:* catch fire, burst into flames, explode. **2** *a cigarette ignited the fumes:* light, set fire to, set alight, kindle. OPPOSITES go out, extinguish.

ignorance noun **1** *their attitudes are based on ignorance:* lack of knowledge, lack of education, unenlightenment. **2** *his ignorance of economics:* unfamiliarity with, incomprehension, inexperience, innocence. OPPOSITES education, knowledge.

ignorant adjective **1** *an ignorant country girl:* uneducated, unschooled, illiterate, uninformed, unenlightened, inexperienced, unsophisticated. **2** *ignorant of working-class life:* unaware, unconscious, unfamiliar, unacquainted, uninformed; informal in the dark. OPPOSITES educated, knowledgeable.

ignore verb **1** *he ignored her:* take no notice of, pay no attention to, snub, look right through, cold-shoulder. **2** *doctors ignored her instructions:* disregard, take no account of, fail to observe, disobey, defy, overlook, brush aside. OPPOSITES acknowledge, obey.

ill adjective **1** *she was feeling rather ill:* unwell, sick, poorly, peaky, indisposed, nauseous, queasy; informal under the weather, rough; Brit. informal grotty; Austral./NZ informal crook. **2** *the ill effects of smoking:* harmful, damaging, detrimental, deleterious, adverse, injurious, destructive, dangerous. OPPOSITES well, beneficial. •noun *the ills of society:* problem, trouble, difficulty, misfortune, trial, tribulation; informal headache, hassle. •adverb **1** *he can ill afford the loss:* barely, scarcely, hardly, only just. **2** *we are ill prepared:* inadequately, insufficiently, poorly, badly. OPPOSITES easily, well.

2 bad or harmful. ● adverb 1 badly or wrongly. 2 only with difficulty. ● noun 1 a problem or misfortune. 2 evil or harm. □ ill-advised not sensible or well thought out. ill at ease uncomfortable or embarrassed. ill-fated destined to fail or be unlucky. ill-favoured unattractive. ill-gotten obtained by illegal or unfair means. ill-starred unlucky. ill-treat treat in a cruel or unkind way. ill will hostility.

illegal adjective against the law.
■ **illegality** noun **illegally** adverb.

illegible adjective not clear enough to be read.
■ **illegibility** noun.

illegitimate adjective 1 not allowed by law or rules. 2 (of a child) born to parents who are not married to each other.
■ **illegitimacy** noun.

illiberal adjective not allowing freedom of thought or behaviour.

illicit adjective forbidden by law, rules, or standards.
■ **illicitly** adverb.

illiterate adjective 1 unable to read or write. 2 not knowing very much about a particular subject.
■ **illiteracy** noun.

illness noun a disease, or a period of being ill.

illogical adjective not sensible or based on sound reasoning.
■ **illogicality** noun **illogically** adverb.

illuminate verb (illuminates, illuminating,

illuminated) 1 light something up. 2 help to explain something. 3 decorate a manuscript with coloured designs.

illumination noun 1 lighting or light. 2 (**illuminations**) lights used in decorating a building for a special occasion. 3 understanding.

illumine verb literary light up; illuminate.

illusion noun 1 a false idea or belief. 2 a thing that seems to be something that it is not.

illusionist noun a magician or conjuror.

illusory or **illusive** adjective not real, although seeming to be.

illustrate verb (illustrates, illustrating, illustrated) 1 provide a book or magazine with pictures. 2 make something clear by using examples, charts, etc. 3 act as an example of.
■ **illustrative** adjective **illustrator** noun.

illustration noun 1 a picture illustrating a book or magazine. 2 the action of illustrating. 3 an example that helps to explain something.

illustrious adjective famous and admired for what you have achieved.

I'm short form I am.

image noun 1 a picture or statue of someone or something. 2 a picture seen on a television or computer screen, through a lens, or reflected in a mirror. 3 a picture in the mind. 4 the impression that a person or group gives to the public. 5 (**the image of**) a person or thing that looks very

THESAURUS

illegal adjective unlawful, criminal, illicit, illegitimate, fraudulent, corrupt, dishonest, outlawed, banned, forbidden, prohibited, proscribed, unlicensed, unauthorized; informal crooked, shady; Brit. informal bent, dodgy.
OPPOSITES legal.

illegible adjective unreadable, indecipherable, unintelligible.

illicit adjective illegal, unlawful, criminal, outlawed, banned, forbidden, prohibited, proscribed, unlicensed, unauthorized, improper, disapproved of.
OPPOSITES legal, approved.

illness noun sickness, poor health, disease, ailment, disorder, complaint, malady, affliction, infection, indisposition; informal bug, virus.
OPPOSITES health.

illuminating adjective informative, enlightening, revealing, explanatory, instructive, helpful, educational.
OPPOSITES confusing.

illumination noun light, lighting, radiance, gleam, glow, glare.

illusion noun 1 I had no illusions: delusion,

misapprehension, misconception, false impression, mistaken impression, fantasy, dream, fancy. 2 the illusion of depth: appearance, impression, semblance. 3 it's just an illusion: mirage, hallucination, apparition, figment of the imagination, trick of the light.

illustrate verb 1 the photographs that illustrate the text: decorate, ornament, accompany, support, explain, elucidate, clarify; informal get across/over. 2 this can be illustrated through a brief example: demonstrate, show, exemplify, bring home.

illustration noun 1 the illustrations in children's books: picture, drawing, sketch, figure, plate, image, print. 2 an illustration of such a dilemma: example, sample, case, instance, exemplification, demonstration.

image noun 1 images of the Queen: likeness, depiction, portrayal, representation, painting, picture, portrait, drawing, photograph. 2 the image of this country as a democracy: conception, impression, idea, perception, notion. 3 his public image: persona, profile, face.

similar to another. **6** a word or phrase
describing something in an imaginative
way; a simile or metaphor. •verb (**images,
imaging, imaged**) make or form an image
of.

imagery noun **1** language that produces
images in the mind. **2** pictures as a whole.

imaginary adjective existing only in the
imagination.

> ☑ the ending is -*ary* not -*ery*: imagin*ary*.

imagination noun **1** the part of the mind
that imagines things. **2** the ability to be
creative or solve problems.

imaginative adjective using the
imagination in a creative or inventive way.
■ **imaginatively** adverb.

imagine verb (**imagines, imagining,
imagined**) **1** form a mental picture of.
2 think that something is probable.
3 believe that something unreal exists.
■ **imaginable** adjective.

imago /i-**may**-goh/ noun (plural **imagos** or
imagines /i-**may**-ji-neez/) the final and
fully developed adult stage of an insect.

imam /i-**mahm**/ noun the person who leads
prayers in a mosque.

imbalance noun a lack of proportion or
balance.

imbecile /**im**-bi-seel/ noun informal a stupid
person.
■ **imbecilic** adjective **imbecility** noun.

imbed ⇒ EMBED.

imbibe verb (**imbibes, imbibing, imbibed**)
1 formal drink alcohol. **2** absorb ideas or
knowledge.

imbroglio /im-**broh**-li-oh/ noun (plural
imbroglios) a very confused or complicated
situation.

imbue verb (**imbues, imbuing, imbued**) fill
with a feeling or quality.

imitate verb (**imitates, imitating, imitated**)
1 follow as a model; copy. **2** copy the way
that a person speaks or behaves in order to
amuse people.
■ **imitator** noun.

imitation noun **1** a copy. **2** the action of
imitating.

imitative /**im**-i-tuh-tiv/ adjective imitating
or copying something.

immaculate adjective **1** completely clean or
tidy. **2** free from mistakes; perfect.
■ **immaculately** adverb.

immanent adjective present within or
throughout something.
■ **immanence** noun.

immaterial adjective **1** unimportant under
the circumstances. **2** spiritual rather than
physical.

immature adjective **1** not fully developed.
2 behaving in a way that is typical of
someone younger.
■ **immaturity** noun.

immeasurable adjective too large or
extreme to measure.
■ **immeasurably** adverb.

immediate adjective **1** happening or done
at once. **2** nearest in time, space, or

i

THESAURUS

imaginary adjective unreal, non-existent,
fictional, pretend, make-believe, invented,
made-up, illusory.
OPPOSITES real.

imagination noun **1** *in your imagination:*
mind's eye, fancy. **2** *a lack of imagination:*
creativity, vision, inventiveness, ingenuity,
originality.

imaginative adjective creative, visionary,
inventive, resourceful, ingenious, original,
innovative.

imagine verb **1** *you can imagine the scene:*
visualize, envisage, picture, see in the
mind's eye, dream up, think up/of,
conceive. **2** *I imagine he was at home:*
assume, presume, expect, take it (as read),
suppose.

imitate verb **1** *other artists have imitated
his style:* copy, emulate, follow, echo, ape,
parrot; informal rip off. **2** *he could imitate
Winston Churchill:* mimic, do an
impression of, impersonate; informal take
someone off.

imitation noun **1** *an imitation of a sailor's
hat:* copy, simulation, reproduction,

replica, forgery. **2** *learning by imitation:*
emulation, copying. **3** *a perfect imitation
of Francis:* impersonation, impression,
caricature; informal take-off, spoof.
•adjective *imitation ivory:* artificial,
synthetic, mock, fake, simulated, man-
made, manufactured, ersatz, substitute.
OPPOSITES real.

immaculate adjective **1** *an immaculate
white shirt:* clean, spotless, shining, shiny,
gleaming. **2** *immaculate condition:* perfect,
pristine, mint, flawless, faultless,
unblemished; informal tip-top, A1. **3** *his
immaculate record:* unblemished, spotless,
impeccable, unsullied, untarnished; informal
squeaky clean.
OPPOSITES dirty, damaged, sullied.

immediate adjective **1** *the UN called for
immediate action:* instant, instantaneous,
prompt, swift, speedy, rapid, quick. **2** *their
immediate concerns:* current, present,
urgent, pressing. **3** *our immediate
neighbours:* nearest, close, next-door,
adjacent, adjoining.
OPPOSITES delayed.

relationship. **3** most urgent; current.
4 without anything coming between;
direct.
■ **immediacy** noun.

immediately adverb **1** at once. **2** very close
in time, space, or relationship. • **conjunction**
chiefly Brit. as soon as.

☑ -*tely*, not -*tly*: immedia*tely*.

immemorial adjective existing for longer
than people can remember.

immense adjective very large or great.
■ **immensely** adverb **immensity** noun.

immerse verb (**immerses**, **immersing**,
immersed) **1** dip or cover completely in a
liquid. **2** (**immerse yourself in**) involve
yourself deeply in an activity.

immersion noun **1** the action of immersing.
2 deep involvement in an activity.
□ **immersion heater** an electric device in a
water tank which heats water for a house.

immigrant noun a person who comes to
live permanently in a foreign country.

immigration noun the action of coming to
live permanently in a foreign country.
■ **immigrate** verb.

imminent adjective about to happen.
■ **imminence** noun **imminently** adverb.

immiscible /i-**miss**-i-b'l/ adjective (of
liquids) not able to be mixed together.

immobile adjective not moving or able to
move.
■ **immobility** noun.

immobilize or **immobilise** verb
(**immobilizes**, **immobilizing**, **immobilized**)

prevent from moving or operating
normally.
■ **immobilization** noun.

immoderate adjective not sensible or
controlled; excessive.

immodest adjective **1** conceited or boastful.
2 showing too much of the body.

immolate verb kill or sacrifice by burning.
■ **immolation** noun.

immoral adjective not following accepted
standards of morality.
■ **immorality** noun.

immortal adjective **1** living forever.
2 deserving to be remembered forever.
• **noun 1** an immortal god. **2** a person who
will be famous for a very long time.
■ **immortality** noun.

immortalize or **immortalise** verb
(**immortalizes**, **immortalizing**, **immortalized**)
prevent someone or something from being
forgotten for a very long time.

immovable adjective **1** not able to be
moved. **2** unable to be changed or
persuaded.

immune adjective **1** having a natural ability
to resist a particular infection. **2** not
affected by something. **3** exempt or
protected from something.

immunity noun (plural **immunities**) **1** the
body's ability to resist a particular
infection. **2** freedom from a duty or
punishment.

immunize or **immunise** verb (**immunizes**,
immunizing, **immunized**) make immune to
infection.
■ **immunization** noun.

THESAURUS

immediately adverb **1** *you must decide
immediately:* straight away, at once, right
away, instantly, now, directly, forthwith,
there and then. **2** *I sat immediately behind
him:* directly, right, exactly, precisely,
squarely, just, dead; informal slap bang;
N. Amer. informal smack dab.
OPPOSITES sometime, later, somewhere.

immense adjective huge, vast, massive,
enormous, gigantic, colossal, monumental,
towering, giant, mammoth; informal monster,
whopping (great); Brit. informal ginormous.
OPPOSITES tiny.

immerse verb **1** *the metal was immersed in
acid:* dip, submerge, dunk, duck, sink.
2 *Elliot was immersed in his work:* absorb,
engross, occupy, engage, involve, bury,
preoccupy; informal lose.

immigrant noun newcomer, settler,
incomer, migrant, non-native, foreigner,
alien.
OPPOSITES native.

imminent adjective near, close (at hand),
impending, approaching, coming,

forthcoming, on the way, expected,
looming.
OPPOSITES distant.

immoral adjective wicked, bad, wrong,
unethical, unprincipled, unscrupulous,
dishonest, corrupt, sinful, impure.
OPPOSITES ethical, pure.

immortal adjective **1** *our immortal souls:*
undying, deathless, eternal, everlasting,
imperishable, indestructible. **2** *an immortal
children's story:* timeless, perennial, classic,
time-honoured, enduring, evergreen.
OPPOSITES mortal, ephemeral.

immune adjective resistant, not subject, not
liable, not vulnerable, protected from, safe
from, secure against.
OPPOSITES susceptible, liable.

immunity noun **1** *immunity to malaria:*
resistance, protection, defence.
2 *immunity from prosecution:* exemption,
exception, freedom. **3** *diplomatic
immunity:* indemnity, privilege,
prerogative, licence, exemption, impunity,
protection.
OPPOSITES susceptibility, liability.

immunology noun the branch of medicine and biology concerned with immunity to infection.
■ **immunological** adjective **immunologist** noun.

immure verb (**immures, immuring, immured**) literary shut someone up in a place.

immutable /im-**myoo**-tuh-b'l/ adjective not changing or able to be changed.

imp noun **1** (in stories) a small, mischievous devil. **2** a mischievous child.

impact noun /im-pakt/ **1** an instance of one object hitting another. **2** a noticeable effect or influence. • verb /im-pakt/ **1** hit another object with force. **2** (**impact on**) have a strong effect on. **3** (**impacted**) (of a tooth) wedged between another tooth and the jaw.

impair verb weaken or damage.
■ **impairment** noun.

impala /im-**pah**-luh/ noun (plural **impala**) an African antelope with curved horns.

impale verb (**impales, impaling, impaled**) pierce with a sharp instrument.

impalpable adjective **1** unable to be felt by touch. **2** not easily understood.

impart verb **1** communicate information. **2** give a particular quality to.

impartial adjective not favouring one person or thing more than another.
■ **impartiality** noun **impartially** adverb.

impassable adjective impossible to travel along or over.

impasse /am-pahss/ noun a situation in which no progress is possible.

impassioned adjective filled with or showing great emotion.

impassive adjective not feeling or showing emotion.
■ **impassively** adverb.

impasto /im-**pass**-toh/ noun the technique of laying on paint thickly so that it stands out from the surface of a painting.

impatient adjective **1** not having much patience or tolerance. **2** restlessly eager.
■ **impatience** noun **impatiently** adverb.

impeach verb chiefly US charge a person who holds an important public office with a serious crime.
■ **impeachment** noun.

impeccable adjective without faults or mistakes.
■ **impeccably** adverb.

impecunious /im-pi-**kyoo**-ni-uhss/ adjective having little or no money.

impedance noun the total resistance of an electric circuit to the flow of alternating current.

impede verb (**impedes, impeding, impeded**) delay or block the progress of.

impediment noun **1** something that delays or blocks progress. **2** (also **speech impediment**) a defect in a person's speech, such as a stammer.

impel verb (**impels, impelling, impelled**) force to do something.

impending adjective be about to happen.

impenetrable adjective **1** impossible to get through or into. **2** impossible to understand.

impenitent adjective not feeling shame or regret.

imperative adjective **1** of vital importance. **2** giving a command. **3** Grammar (of a verb) expressing a command, as in *come here!* • noun an essential or urgent thing.

THESAURUS

impact noun **1** *the force of the impact:* **collision**, crash, smash, bump, knock. **2** *the job losses will have a major impact:* **effect**, influence, consequences, repercussions, ramifications.
• verb **1** *an asteroid impacted the earth:* **crash into**, smash into, collide with, hit, strike, smack into, bang into. **2** *interest rates have impacted on spending:* **affect**, influence, hit, have an effect, make an impression.

impair verb **weaken**, damage, harm, have a negative effect on, undermine, diminish, reduce, lessen, decrease.
OPPOSITES improve, enhance.

impart verb **communicate**, pass on, convey, transmit, relay, relate, tell, make known, report, announce.

impartial adjective **unbiased**, unprejudiced, neutral, non-partisan, disinterested, detached, dispassionate, objective.
OPPOSITES biased, partisan.

impasse noun **deadlock**, dead end, stalemate, stand-off, standstill.

impatient adjective **1** *Melissa grew impatient:* **restless**, agitated, nervous, anxious. **2** *they are impatient to get back home:* **anxious**, eager, keen; informal itching, dying. **3** *an impatient gesture:* **irritated**, annoyed, angry, tetchy, snappy, cross, curt, brusque.
OPPOSITES patient, reluctant, calm.

impeccable adjective **flawless**, faultless, unblemished, spotless, stainless, perfect, exemplary, irreproachable; informal squeaky clean.
OPPOSITES imperfect.

impede verb **hinder**, obstruct, hamper, hold back/up, delay, interfere with, disrupt, retard, slow (down).
OPPOSITES facilitate.

imperative adjective **vital**, crucial, critical, essential, pressing, urgent.
OPPOSITES unimportant.

imperceptible adjective too slight or gradual to be seen or felt.
- **imperceptibly** adverb.

imperfect adjective **1** faulty or incomplete. **2** Grammar (of a verb) referring to a past action that is not yet completed.
- **imperfection** noun **imperfectly** adverb.

imperial adjective **1** relating to an empire or an emperor. **2** (of weights and measures) in a non-metric system formerly used in the UK.

imperialism noun a system in which one country extends its power and influence by defeating other countries in war, forming colonies, etc.
- **imperialist** noun & adjective.

imperil verb (**imperils, imperilling, imperilled**; US spelling **imperils, imperiling, imperiled**) put into danger.

imperious /im-peer-i-uhss/ adjective expecting to be obeyed.
- **imperiously** adverb.

impermanent adjective not permanent.
- **impermanence** noun.

impermeable adjective not allowing a liquid or gas to pass through.

impersonal adjective **1** not influenced by or involving personal feelings. **2** lacking human feelings or atmosphere. **3** Grammar (of a verb) used only with *it* as a subject (as in *it is snowing*).
- **impersonality** noun **impersonally** adverb.

impersonate verb (**impersonates, impersonating, impersonated**) pretend to be another person in order to entertain or deceive people.
- **impersonation** noun **impersonator** noun.

impertinent adjective not showing proper respect.
- **impertinence** noun.

imperturbable adjective not easily upset or excited.

impervious adjective **1** not allowing a liquid or a gas to pass through. **2** (**impervious to**) unable to be affected by.

impetuous adjective acting quickly and without thinking or being careful.
- **impetuously** adverb.

impetus noun **1** the force or energy with which something moves. **2** the force that makes something happen.

impinge verb (**impinges, impinging, impinged**) (**impinge on**) have an effect or impact on.

impious /im-pi-uhss/ adjective not showing respect or reverence.

implacable adjective **1** unwilling to stop being hostile towards someone or something. **2** (of strong negative feelings) unable to be changed.
- **implacably** adverb.

implant verb /im-**plahnt**/ **1** put tissue or an artificial object into someone's body, by means of a surgical operation. **2** fix an idea firmly in someone's mind. • noun /im-plahnt/ a thing that is implanted.
- **implantation** noun.

implausible adjective not seeming reasonable or probable.
- **implausibility** noun **implausibly** adverb.

implement noun /im-pli-muhnt/ a tool that is used for a particular purpose. • verb /im-pli-ment/ put something into effect.
- **implementation** noun.

implicate verb (**implicates, implicating, implicated**) **1** show that someone is involved in a crime. **2** (**be implicated in**) be partly responsible for.

implication noun **1** a conclusion that can

THESAURUS

imperfect adjective faulty, flawed, defective, inferior, second-rate, shoddy, substandard, damaged, blemished, torn, broken, cracked, scratched; Brit. informal duff.
OPPOSITES perfect.

impertinent adjective rude, insolent, impolite, ill-mannered, disrespectful, impudent, cheeky, presumptuous, forward; informal brass-necked.
OPPOSITES polite, respectful.

impetuous adjective impulsive, rash, hasty, reckless, foolhardy, imprudent, ill-considered, spontaneous, impromptu, spur-of-the-moment.
OPPOSITES considered, cautious.

implant verb **1** *the collagen is implanted under the skin:* insert, embed, bury, inject, transplant, graft. **2** *he implanted the idea in my mind:* instil, inculcate, introduce, plant, sow.

implement noun *garden implements:* tool, utensil, instrument, device, apparatus, gadget, contraption, appliance; informal gizmo.
• verb *the cost of implementing the new law:* execute, apply, put into effect/action, put into practice, carry out/through, perform, enact, fulfil.
OPPOSITES abolish, cancel.

implicate verb **1** *he had been implicated in a financial scandal:* incriminate, involve, connect, embroil, enmesh. **2** *viruses are implicated in the development of cancer:* involve in, concern with, associate with, connect with.

implication noun **1** *he was smarting at their implication:* suggestion, inference, insinuation, innuendo, intimation, imputation. **2** *important political implications:* consequence, result, ramification, repercussion, reverberation, be drawn from something. **2** a possible effect. **3** involvement in something.

implicit adjective **1** suggested without being directly expressed. **2** (**implicit in**) forming part of something. **3** not doubted or questioned.
■ **implicitly** adverb.

implode verb (**implodes, imploding, imploded**) collapse violently inwards.
■ **implosion** noun.

implore verb (**implores, imploring, implored**) beg earnestly or desperately.

imply verb (**implies, implying, implied**)
1 suggest rather than state directly.
2 suggest as a possible effect.

> **!** don't confuse the words **imply** and **infer**. They can describe the same situation, but from different points of view. If you **imply** something, it means that you are suggesting something though not saying it directly. If you **infer** something from what has been said, you come to the conclusion that this is what the speaker really means, although they are not saying it directly.

impolite adjective not having good manners.

impolitic adjective unwise.

imponderable noun something that is difficult or impossible to assess. • adjective difficult or impossible to assess.

import verb /im-**port**/ **1** bring goods into a country from abroad. **2** transfer computer data into a file. • noun /**im**-port/ **1** an imported article. **2** the action of importing. **3** the implied meaning of something. **4** importance.
■ **importation** noun **importer** noun.

important adjective **1** having a great effect or value. **2** (of a person) having great authority or influence.
■ **importance** noun **importantly** adverb.

importunate /im-**por**-tyuu-nuht/ adjective very persistent.

importune verb (**importunes, importuning, importuned**) ask someone persistently for something.

impose verb (**imposes, imposing, imposed**)
1 force something to be accepted. **2** (often **impose on**) take unfair advantage of someone.

imposing adjective grand and impressive.

imposition noun **1** the action of imposing

i

THESAURUS

effect. **3** *his implication in the murder:* incrimination, involvement, connection, entanglement, association.
OPPOSITES exoneration.

implore verb plead with, beg, entreat, appeal to, ask, request, call on, exhort, urge.

imply verb **1** *are you implying he is mad?* insinuate, suggest, infer, hint, intimate, give someone to understand, make out. **2** *the forecast traffic increase implies more roads:* involve, entail, mean, point to, signify, indicate, presuppose.

impolite adjective rude, bad-mannered, ill-mannered, discourteous, disrespectful, uncivil, insolent, impudent, impertinent, cheeky; informal lippy.
OPPOSITES polite.

import verb *the UK imports iron ore:* bring in, buy in, ship in.
OPPOSITES export.
• noun **1** *a matter of great import:* importance, significance, consequence, momentousness, magnitude, substance, weight, note, gravity, seriousness. **2** *the full import of her words:* meaning, sense, essence, gist, drift, message, thrust, substance, implication.
OPPOSITES insignificance.

importance noun **1** *an event of immense importance:* significance, momentousness, moment, import, consequence, note, weight, seriousness, gravity. **2** *she had an exaggerated sense of her own importance:*

status, eminence, prestige, worth, influence, power, authority.
OPPOSITES insignificance.

important adjective **1** *an important meeting:* significant, consequential, momentous, of great import, major, valuable, necessary, crucial, vital, essential, pivotal, decisive, far-reaching, historic. **2** *he was an important man:* powerful, influential, well connected, high-ranking, prominent, eminent, notable, distinguished, esteemed, respected, prestigious.
OPPOSITES unimportant, insignificant.

impose verb **1** *he imposed his ideas on everyone:* foist, force, inflict, press, saddle someone with. **2** *new taxes will be imposed:* levy, charge, apply, enforce, set, establish, institute, introduce, bring into effect.
OPPOSITES abolish.
□ **impose on** take advantage of, exploit, take liberties with, bother, trouble, disturb, inconvenience, put out, put to trouble.

imposing adjective impressive, striking, dramatic, spectacular, commanding, arresting, awesome, formidable, splendid, grand, majestic.
OPPOSITES modest.

imposition noun **1** *the imposition of an alien culture:* imposing, foisting, forcing, inflicting. **2** *the imposition of VAT:* levying, charging, application, enforcement, enforcing, setting, establishment, something. **2** an unreasonable thing that you are asked or expected to do or accept.

impossible adjective **1** not able to exist or be done. **2** very difficult to deal with.
■ impossibility noun impossibly adverb.

impostor or **imposter** noun a person who pretends to be someone else in order to deceive other people.

imposture noun an act of pretending to be someone else in order to deceive.

impotent /im-puh-tuhnt/ adjective **1** helpless or powerless. **2** (of a man) unable to achieve an erection.
■ impotence noun.

impound verb **1** officially seize something. **2** shut up domestic animals in an enclosure.

impoverish verb **1** make someone poor. **2** make something worse in quality.
■ impoverishment noun.

impracticable adjective not able to be done.

impractical adjective not sensible or realistic.

imprecation noun formal a spoken curse.

imprecise adjective not exact.
■ imprecision noun.

impregnable adjective **1** (of a building) unable to be captured or broken into. **2** unable to be defeated.

impregnate verb (**impregnates**, **impregnating**, **impregnated**) **1** soak with a substance. **2** fill with a feeling or quality.

3 make pregnant.
■ impregnation noun.

impresario /im-pri-**sah**-ri-oh/ noun (plural **impresarios**) a person who organizes plays, concerts, or operas.

impress verb **1** make someone feel admiration and respect. **2** (**impress something on**) make someone aware of something important. **3** make a mark or design using a stamp or seal.

impression noun **1** an idea, feeling, or opinion. **2** the effect that something has on someone. **3** an imitation of the way that a person speaks or behaves done in order to entertain people. **4** a mark made by pressing on a surface.

impressionable adjective easily influenced.

Impressionism noun a style of painting concerned with showing the visual impression of a particular moment.
■ Impressionist noun & adjective.

impressionist noun an entertainer who impersonates famous people.

impressionistic adjective based on personal ideas or feelings.

impressive adjective arousing admiration through size, quality, or skill.
■ impressively adverb.

imprimatur /im-pri-**mah**-ter/ noun the authority or approval of someone.

imprint verb /im-**print**/ make a mark on an object by pressing something on to it.

THESAURUS

introduction. **3** *it would be no imposition:* burden, encumbrance, liberty, bother, worry; informal hassle.
OPPOSITES abolition.

impossible adjective **1** *the winds made fishing impossible:* out of the question, impracticable, non-viable, unworkable. **2** *an impossible dream:* unattainable, unachievable, unobtainable, hopeless, impracticable, unworkable. **3** *food shortages made life impossible:* unbearable, intolerable, unendurable. **4** (informal) *an impossible woman:* unreasonable, difficult, awkward, intolerable, unbearable, exasperating, maddening, infuriating.
OPPOSITES possible, attainable, bearable, reasonable.

impound verb confiscate, appropriate, take possession of, seize, commandeer, expropriate, requisition, take over.
OPPOSITES release.

impress verb *Hazel had impressed him mightily:* make an impression on, have an impact on, influence, affect, move, stir, rouse, excite, inspire, dazzle, awe.
OPPOSITES disappoint.
□ impress something on someone

emphasize to, stress to, bring home to, instil in, inculcate into, drum into.

impression noun **1** *he got the impression she was hiding something:* feeling, sense, fancy, (sneaking) suspicion, inkling, intuition, hunch, notion, idea. **2** *a favourable impression:* opinion, view, image, picture, perception, reaction, judgement, verdict, estimation. **3** *school made a profound impression on me:* impact, effect, influence. **4** *the lid had left a circular impression:* indentation, dent, mark, outline, imprint. **5** *he did a good impression of their science teacher:* impersonation, imitation, caricature; informal take-off.

impressive adjective magnificent, majestic, imposing, splendid, spectacular, grand, awe-inspiring, stunning, breathtaking.
OPPOSITES unimpressive.

imprint verb *patterns can be imprinted in the clay:* stamp, print, impress, mark, emboss.
● noun *her feet left imprints on the floor:* impression, print, mark, stamp, indentation.

• **noun** /**im**-print/ **1** a mark made by pressing something on to an object. **2** a publisher's name and other details printed in a book.

imprison verb put or keep in prison.
■ **imprisonment** noun.

improbable adjective not likely to be true or to happen.
■ **improbability** noun **improbably** adverb.

impromptu /im-**promp**-tyoo/ adjective & adverb done without being planned or rehearsed.

improper adjective **1** not fitting in with accepted standards of behaviour. **2** not modest or decent.

impropriety /im-pruh-**pry**-uh-ti/ noun (plural **improprieties**) improper behaviour.

improve verb (**improves, improving, improved**) **1** make or become better. **2** (**improve on**) produce something better than.
■ **improvement** noun.

improvident adjective not thinking about or preparing for the future.

improvise verb (**improvises, improvising, improvised**) **1** invent and perform music or drama without planning it in advance. **2** make something from whatever is available.
■ **improvisation** noun.

imprudent adjective not sensible or careful.

impudent adjective not showing respect for another person.
■ **impudence** noun **impudently** adverb.

impugn /im-**pyoon**/ verb formal express doubts about whether something is true or honest.

impulse noun **1** a sudden urge to do something. **2** a force that makes something happen.

impulsive adjective acting without thinking ahead.
■ **impulsively** adverb.

impunity /im-**pyoo**-ni-ti/ noun freedom from being punished or hurt.

impure adjective **1** mixed with unwanted substances. **2** morally wrong.

impurity noun (plural **impurities**) **1** the state of being impure. **2** a thing which makes something less pure.

impute /im-**pyoot**/ verb (**imputes, imputing, imputed**) (**impute something to**) believe that something has been done or caused by.
■ **imputation** noun.

in preposition **1** expressing the position of something that is enclosed or surrounded. **2** expressing movement which results in something being enclosed or surrounded. **3** expressing a period of time before or during which something happens. **4** expressing a state or quality. **5** indicating that something is included or involved.

i

THESAURUS

imprison verb incarcerate, send to prison, jail, lock up, put away, intern, detain, hold prisoner, hold captive; informal send down; Brit. informal bang up.
OPPOSITES release.

improbable adjective **1** *it seemed improbable that the hot weather would continue*: unlikely, doubtful, dubious, debatable, questionable, uncertain. **2** *an improbable exaggeration*: unconvincing, unbelievable, implausible, unlikely.
OPPOSITES probable, believable.

improper adjective **1** *it is improper for police to accept gifts*: unacceptable, unprofessional, irregular, unethical, dishonest. **2** *it was improper for young ladies to drive a young man home*: unseemly, unfitting, unbecoming, unladylike, ungentlemanly, inappropriate, indelicate, indecent, immodest, indecorous, immoral. **3** *an extremely improper poem*: indecent, risqué, suggestive, naughty, dirty, filthy, vulgar, crude, rude, obscene, lewd; informal blue, raunchy, steamy.
OPPOSITES acceptable, decent, clean.

improve verb **1** *ways to improve the service*: make better, ameliorate, upgrade, refine, enhance, boost, build on, raise. **2** *communications improved*: get better,

advance, progress, develop, make headway, make progress, pick up, look up, move forward. **3** *the patient is improving*: recover, get better, recuperate, rally, revive, be on the mend.
OPPOSITES worsen, deteriorate.

improvement noun advance, development, upgrade, refinement, enhancement, betterment, amelioration, boost, augmentation, rally, recovery, upswing.

improvise verb **1** *she was improvising in front of the cameras*: extemporize, ad-lib; informal speak off the cuff, play it by ear, busk it, wing it. **2** *she improvised a sandpit*: contrive, devise, throw together, cobble together, rig up; informal whip up, rustle up; Brit. informal knock up.

impulse noun **1** *she had an impulse to hide*: urge, instinct, drive, compulsion, itch, whim, desire, fancy, notion. **2** *a man of impulse*: spontaneity, impetuosity, recklessness, rashness.
OPPOSITES forethought.

impulsive adjective **1** *he had an impulsive nature*: impetuous, spontaneous, hasty, passionate, emotional. **2** *an impulsive decision*: impromptu, snap, spontaneous, unpremeditated, spur-of-the-moment.
OPPOSITES cautious, premeditated.

6 indicating the language or material used by someone. 7 used to express a value as a proportion of a whole. ● adverb 1 expressing the state of being enclosed or surrounded. 2 expressing movement which results in being enclosed or surrounded. 3 present at your home or office. 4 having arrived at a destination. 5 (of the tide) rising or at its highest level. ● adjective informal fashionable. □ in-depth thorough and detailed. in-house within an organization. in-joke a joke shared only by a small group. the ins and outs informal all the details.

in. abbreviation inches.

inability noun the state of being unable to do something.

in absentia /in ab-sen-ti-uh/ adverb while not present.

inaccessible adjective 1 unable to be reached or used. 2 difficult to understand.

inaccurate adjective not accurate.
■ **inaccuracy** noun (plural **inaccuracies**) **inaccurately** adverb.

inactive adjective not active or working.
■ **inaction** noun **inactivity** noun.

inadequate adjective 1 not enough or not good enough. 2 unable to deal with a situation.
■ **inadequacy** noun (plural **inadequacies**) **inadequately** adverb.

inadmissible adjective (of evidence in court) not accepted as valid.

inadvertent adjective not deliberate or intentional.
■ **inadvertently** adverb.

☑ -ent, not -ant: inadvertent.

inadvisable adjective likely to have unfortunate results.

inalienable adjective unable to be taken away or given away.

inane adjective silly or stupid.
■ **inanely** adverb **inanity** noun.

inanimate adjective not alive.

inapplicable adjective not relevant or appropriate.

inappropriate adjective not suitable or appropriate.
■ **inappropriately** adverb.

inarticulate adjective 1 unable to express your ideas clearly. 2 not expressed in words.

inasmuch adverb (**inasmuch as**) 1 to the extent that. 2 considering that; since.

inattentive adjective not paying attention.
■ **inattention** noun.

inaudible adjective unable to be heard.
■ **inaudibly** adverb.

inaugural adjective marking the start of something important.

inaugurate verb (**inaugurates, inaugurating, inaugurated**) 1 begin or introduce a system or project. 2 mark the beginning of an organization or the opening of a building with a ceremony.
■ **inauguration** noun.

inauspicious adjective not likely to lead to success.

inauthentic noun not genuine or sincere.

inborn adjective existing from birth.

inbred adjective 1 produced by breeding from closely related people or animals. 2 existing from birth; inborn.

inbreeding noun breeding from closely related people or animals.

inbuilt adjective existing as an original or important part.

Inc. abbreviation N. Amer. Incorporated.

Inca noun a member of a South American Indian people living in the Andes before the Spanish conquest.

incalculable adjective too great to be calculated or estimated.

incandescent adjective glowing as a result

THESAURUS

inaccurate adjective inexact, imprecise, incorrect, wrong, erroneous, faulty, imperfect, defective, unreliable, false, mistaken, untrue; Brit. informal adrift.
OPPOSITES accurate.

inactivity noun inaction, inertia, idleness, non-intervention, negligence, apathy, indolence, laziness, slothfulness.
OPPOSITES action.

inadequate adjective 1 *inadequate water supplies:* insufficient, deficient, poor, scant, scarce, sparse, in short supply, paltry, meagre. 2 *he's a bit inadequate:* incapable, incompetent, immature; informal not up to scratch.
OPPOSITES adequate.

inadvertently adverb accidentally, by accident, unintentionally, by mistake,

mistakenly, unwittingly.
OPPOSITES intentionally.

inappropriate adjective unsuitable, unfitting, unseemly, unbecoming, out of place/keeping, improper, inapposite; informal out of order.
OPPOSITES appropriate.

inaudible adjective unclear, indistinct, faint, muted, soft, low, muffled, whispered, muttered, murmured, mumbled.

inaugurate verb 1 *he inaugurated a new policy:* initiate, begin, start, institute, launch, get going, get under way, establish, bring in, usher in; informal kick off. 2 *the new President will be inaugurated:* install, instate, swear in, invest, ordain, crown.
OPPOSITES terminate, abolish, dismiss.

of being heated.
■ **incandescence** noun.

incantation noun a magic spell or charm.
■ **incantatory** adjective.

incapable adjective 1 (**incapable of**) not able to do something. 2 not able to look after yourself.

incapacitate verb (**incapacitates, incapacitating, incapacitated**) prevent from working in a normal way.
■ **incapacitation** noun.

incapacity noun (plural **incapacities**) inability to do something.

incarcerate verb (**incarcerates, incarcerating, incarcerated**) imprison.
■ **incarceration** noun.

incarnate adjective in human form.

incarnation noun 1 a god, spirit, or quality in human form. 2 (**the Incarnation**) (in Christian belief) God taking human form as Jesus.

incautious adjective not concerned about possible problems.

incendiary adjective 1 (of a bomb) designed to cause fires. 2 tending to cause strong feelings. • noun (plural **incendiaries**) an incendiary bomb.

incense¹ /in-senss/ noun a substance that produces a sweet smell when you burn it.

incense² /in-senss/ verb (**incenses, incensing, incensed**) make very angry.

incentive noun something that influences or encourages you to do something.

inception noun the beginning of an organization or activity.

incessant adjective never stopping.
■ **incessantly** adverb.

incest noun sex between people who are very closely related in a family.

incestuous adjective 1 involving incest. 2 involving a group of people who are very close and do not want to include others.

inch noun 1 a unit of length equal to one twelfth of a foot (2.54 cm). 2 a very small amount or distance. • verb move along slowly and carefully.

inchoate /in-koh-uht/ adjective just beginning and so not fully formed or developed.

incidence noun 1 the extent to which something happens. 2 Physics the meeting of a line or ray with a surface.

incident noun 1 something that happens. 2 a violent event.

incidental adjective 1 occurring in connection with something else. 2 relatively unimportant.
□ **incidental music** background music in a film or play.
■ **incidentally** adverb.

incinerate verb (**incinerates, incinerating, incinerated**) destroy by burning.
■ **incineration** noun.

incinerator noun a device for burning rubbish.

incipient adjective beginning to happen or develop.

incise verb (**incises, incising, incised**) mark a surface by cutting into it.

incision noun 1 a cut made as part of a surgical operation. 2 the action of cutting into something.

incisive adjective 1 showing clear thought and good understanding. 2 quick and direct.

i

---

incapable adjective incompetent, inept, inadequate, ineffective, ineffectual, unfit, unqualified, unequal to the task; informal not up to it.
OPPOSITES competent.

incense verb enrage, infuriate, anger, madden, outrage, exasperate, antagonize, provoke; informal make someone see red; N. Amer. informal burn someone up.
OPPOSITES placate, please.

incensed adjective enraged, furious, infuriated, irate, raging, incandescent, fuming, seething, beside yourself, outraged; informal mad, hopping mad, wild, livid.
OPPOSITES pleased.

incentive noun inducement, motivation, motive, reason, stimulus, spur, impetus, encouragement, carrot; informal sweetener.
OPPOSITES deterrent.

incident noun 1 *incidents in his youth:* event, occurrence, episode, happening, affair, business, adventure, exploit, escapade. 2 *police are investigating another incident:* disturbance, commotion, clash, confrontation, accident, shooting, explosion, scene, situation. 3 *the journey was not without incident:* excitement, adventure, drama, crisis, danger.

incidental adjective 1 *incidental details:* secondary, subsidiary, minor, peripheral, background, by-the-by, unimportant, insignificant, tangential. 2 *an incidental discovery:* chance, accidental, random, fluky, fortuitous, serendipitous, unlooked-for, coincidental.
OPPOSITES essential.

incidentally adverb 1 *incidentally, I haven't had a reply yet:* by the way, by the by, in passing, speaking of which; informal as it happens. 2 *the infection was discovered incidentally:* by chance, by accident, accidentally, fortuitously, by a fluke, by happenstance.

incisor noun a narrow-edged tooth at the front of the mouth.

incite verb (**incites, inciting, incited**) encourage someone to do something violent or unlawful.
■ **incitement** noun.

incivility noun rude speech or behaviour.

inclement /in-**klem**-uhnt/ adjective (of the weather) unpleasantly cold or wet.
■ **inclemency** noun.

inclination noun 1 a tendency to do things in a particular way. 2 (**inclination for** or **to do**) an interest in or liking for. 3 a slope or slant.

incline verb /in-**klyn**/ (**inclines, inclining, inclined**) 1 (**incline to** or **be inclined to**) tend to do or think in a particular way. 2 lean or bend. • noun /in-**klyn**/ a slope.

include verb (**includes, including, included**) 1 have something as part of a whole. 2 make part of a whole.

including preposition having as part of a whole.

inclusion noun 1 the act of including. 2 a person or thing that is included.

inclusive adjective 1 including everything expected or required. 2 between the limits stated.

incognito /in-kog-**nee**-toh/ adjective & adverb having your true identity concealed.

incoherent adjective 1 hard to understand; not clear. 2 not logical or well organized.
■ **incoherence** noun **incoherently** adverb.

incombustible adjective (of a material) that does not burn.

income noun money received for work or from investments.
□ **income tax** tax that must be paid on personal income.

incomer noun Brit. a person who has come to live in an area in which they have not grown up.

incoming adjective 1 coming in or arriving. 2 (of a public official) having just been chosen to replace someone.

incommensurable /in-kuh-**men**-shuh-ruh-b'l/ adjective not able to be compared.

incommode verb (**incommodes, incommoding, incommoded**) formal cause someone difficulties or problems.

incommunicado /in-kuh-myoo-ni-**kah**-doh/ adjective & adverb not able to communicate with other people.

incomparable /in-**kom**-puh-ruh-b'l/ adjective so good that nothing can be compared to it.
■ **incomparably** adverb.

incompatible adjective 1 (of two things) not able to exist or be used together. 2 (of two people) unable to live or work together without disagreeing.
■ **incompatibility** noun.

THESAURUS

incite verb 1 *he was arrested for inciting racial hatred:* stir up, whip up, encourage, stoke up, fuel, kindle, inflame, instigate, provoke, excite, trigger, spark off. 2 *she incited him to commit murder:* provoke, encourage, urge, goad, spur on, egg on, drive, prod, prompt; informal put up to.
OPPOSITES discourage, deter.

inclination noun tendency, propensity, leaning, predisposition, predilection, impulse, bent, liking, taste, penchant, preference.
OPPOSITES aversion.

incline verb 1 *his prejudice inclines him to overlook obvious facts:* predispose, lead, make, dispose, prejudice, prompt, induce. 2 *I incline to the opposite view:* tend, lean, swing, veer, gravitate, be drawn, prefer, favour, go for. 3 *he inclined his head:* bend, bow, nod, bob, lower, dip.
• noun *a steep incline:* slope, gradient, pitch, ramp, bank, ascent, rise, hill, dip, descent; N. Amer. grade.

inclined adjective 1 *I'm inclined to believe her:* disposed, minded, of a mind. 2 *she's inclined to gossip:* prone, given, in the habit of, liable, apt.

include verb 1 *activities include drama and music:* incorporate, comprise, encompass, cover, embrace, take in, number, contain. 2 *include the cost of repairs:* allow for, count, take into account, take into consideration. 3 *include your address:* add, insert, put in, append, enter.
OPPOSITES exclude, leave out.

inclusive adjective all-in, comprehensive, overall, full, all-round, umbrella, catch-all, all-encompassing.
OPPOSITES exclusive, limited.

income noun earnings, salary, wages, pay, remuneration, revenue, receipts, takings, profits, proceeds, yield, dividend; N. Amer. take.
OPPOSITES expenditure, outgoings.

incoming adjective 1 *incoming flights:* arriving, approaching, inbound, inward, returning, homeward. 2 *the incoming president:* new, next, future, ... elect, ... designate.
OPPOSITES outward, outgoing.

incompatible adjective mismatched, unsuited, poles apart, irreconcilable, inconsistent, conflicting, opposed, opposite, contradictory, at odds, at variance.
OPPOSITES well matched, harmonious, consistent.

incompetent adjective not having the skill to do something well.
■ **incompetence** noun **incompetently** adverb.

incomplete adjective not complete.
■ **incompletely** adverb.

incomprehensible adjective not able to be understood.
■ **incomprehension** noun.

inconceivable adjective not able to be imagined or believed.
■ **inconceivably** adverb.

inconclusive adjective not leading to a firm conclusion.
■ **inconclusively** adverb.

incongruous /in-kong-groo-uhss/ adjective out of place.
■ **incongruity** noun **incongruously** adverb.

inconsequential adjective not important.
■ **inconsequentially** adverb.

inconsiderable adjective small in size or amount.

inconsiderate adjective not thinking about other people's feelings.

inconsistent adjective **1** having parts that contradict each other. **2** (**inconsistent with**) not in keeping with.
■ **inconsistency** noun (plural **inconsistencies**).

inconsolable adjective not able to be comforted.

inconspicuous adjective not noticeable.
■ **inconspicuously** adverb.

inconstant adjective **1** formal not faithful or dependable. **2** frequently changing.

incontestable adjective not able to be disputed.

incontinent adjective **1** unable to control your bladder or bowels. **2** lacking self-control.
■ **incontinence** noun.

incontrovertible adjective not able to be denied or disputed.
■ **incontrovertibly** adverb.

inconvenience noun slight trouble or difficulty. • verb (**inconveniences, inconveniencing, inconvenienced**) cause someone inconvenience.
■ **inconvenient** adjective **inconveniently** adverb.

incorporate verb (**incorporates, incorporating, incorporated**) include something as part of a whole.
■ **incorporation** noun.

incorporated adjective (of a company) formed into a legal corporation.

incorporeal /in-kor-por-i-uhl/ adjective without a body or form.

incorrect adjective not true or accurate.
■ **incorrectly** adverb.

incorrigible adjective having bad habits that cannot be changed.

incorruptible adjective too honest to be corrupted by taking bribes.

increase verb /in-**kreess**/ (**increases,**

i

incompetent adjective inept, unskilled, inexpert, amateurish, unprofessional, bungling, blundering, clumsy; informal useless, not up to it.
OPPOSITES competent.

incomplete adjective **1** the manuscript is still incomplete: unfinished, uncompleted, partial, half-finished. **2** incomplete information: deficient, insufficient, partial, sketchy, fragmentary, scrappy, bitty.
OPPOSITES completed, full.

incomprehensible adjective unintelligible, impenetrable, unclear, indecipherable, unfathomable, abstruse, difficult, involved; Brit. informal double Dutch.
OPPOSITES intelligible, clear.

inconsistent adjective **1** inconsistent behaviour: erratic, changeable, unpredictable, variable, unstable, fickle, unreliable, volatile; informal up and down.
2 he had done nothing inconsistent with his morality: incompatible, conflicting, at odds, at variance, irreconcilable, out of keeping, contrary to.
OPPOSITES consistent.

inconvenience noun **1** we apologize for any inconvenience caused: trouble, bother, problems, disruption, difficulty, disturbance; informal aggravation, hassle.

2 his early arrival was clearly an inconvenience: nuisance, trouble, bother, problem; informal headache, pain, pain in the neck, hassle.
• verb I don't want to inconvenience you: trouble, bother, put out, put to any trouble, disturb, impose on.

inconvenient adjective awkward, difficult, inopportune, badly timed, unsuitable, inappropriate, unfortunate.
OPPOSITES convenient.

incorporate verb **1** the region was incorporated into Moldavian territory: absorb, include, subsume, assimilate, integrate, swallow up. **2** the model incorporates advanced features: include, contain, embrace, build in, offer, boast. **3** incorporate the salt and the butter: blend, mix, combine, fold in, stir in.
OPPOSITES partition, separate.

incorrect adjective **1** an incorrect answer: wrong, erroneous, mistaken, untrue, false. **2** incorrect behaviour: inappropriate, unsuitable, unacceptable, improper, unseemly; informal out of order.
OPPOSITES correct.

increase verb **1** demand is likely to increase: grow, get bigger, get larger, enlarge, expand, swell, rise, climb, mount, intensify,

increasing, increased) make or become greater in size, amount, or strength. • noun /**in**-kreess/ a rise in amount, size, or strength.

increasingly adverb more and more.

incredible adjective 1 impossible or hard to believe. 2 informal very good.
■ **incredibly** adverb.

incredulity /in-kre-**dyoo**-li-ti/ noun unwillingness or inability to believe something.

incredulous adjective unwilling or unable to believe something.
■ **incredulously** adverb.

increment /**ing**-kri-muhnt/ noun an increase in a number or amount.
■ **incremental** adjective.

incriminate verb (**incriminates, incriminating, incriminated**) make it look as though someone has done something wrong or illegal.
■ **incrimination** noun.

incubate verb (**incubates, incubating, incubated**) 1 (of a bird) sit on eggs to keep them warm so that they hatch. 2 keep bacteria and cells at a suitable temperature so that they develop. 3 (of an infectious disease) develop slowly without obvious signs.
■ **incubation** noun **incubator** noun.

incubus /**ing**-kyuu-buhss/ noun (plural **incubi** /**ing**-kyuu-by/) (in folkore) a male demon believed to have sex with sleeping women.

inculcate /**in**-kul-kayt/ verb (**inculcates, inculcating, inculcated**) fix ideas in someone's mind by repeating them.
■ **inculcation** noun.

incumbency noun (plural **incumbencies**) the period during which an official position is held.

incumbent adjective 1 (**incumbent on**) necessary for someone as a duty. 2 currently holding an official position. • noun the holder of an official position.

incur verb (**incurs, incurring, incurred**) make something unwelcome happen.

incurable adjective not able to be cured.
■ **incurably** adverb.

incurious adjective not curious.

incursion noun a sudden invasion or attack.

indebted adjective 1 feeling grateful to someone. 2 owing money.

indecent adjective 1 causing offence by showing too much of the body or involving sex. 2 not appropriate.
■ **indecency** noun **indecently** adverb.

indecipherable adjective not able to be read or understood.

indecisive adjective 1 not able to make decisions quickly. 2 not settling an issue.
■ **indecision** noun **indecisively** adverb **indecisiveness** noun.

indeed adverb 1 used to emphasize a statement. 2 used to introduce a further and stronger point.

indefatigable adjective never tiring.

indefensible adjective not able to be justified or defended.

indefinable adjective not able to be defined or described exactly.

indefinite adjective 1 not clearly stated, seen, or heard; vague. 2 lasting for an unknown length of time.
□ **indefinite article** Grammar the word *a* or *an*.
■ **indefinitely** adverb.

indelible adjective 1 (of ink or a mark) unable to be removed. 2 unable to be forgotten.
■ **indelibly** adverb.

indelicate adjective likely to be thought rude or embarrassing.

indemnify verb (**indemnifies, indemnifying, indemnified**) 1 pay money to someone to compensate for harm or loss. 2 insure someone against legal responsibility for their actions.

indemnity noun (plural **indemnities**) 1 insurance against legal responsibility for

---

THESAURUS

strengthen, extend, spread, widen. 2 *higher expectations will increase user demand:* add to, make larger, make bigger, augment, supplement, top up, build up, extend, raise, swell, inflate, intensify, heighten; informal up, bump up.
OPPOSITES decrease, reduce.
• noun *the increase in size | an increase in demand:* growth, rise, enlargement, expansion, extension, increment, gain, addition, augmentation, surge; informal hike.
OPPOSITES decrease.

incredible adjective 1 *I find his story incredible:* unbelievable, unconvincing, far-fetched, implausible, improbable,

inconceivable, unimaginable. 2 *an incredible feat of engineering:* wonderful, marvellous, spectacular, remarkable, phenomenal, prodigious, breathtaking; informal fantastic, terrific.
OPPOSITES believable, unremarkable.

incur verb bring on yourself, expose yourself to, lay yourself open to, run up, earn, sustain, experience.

indecent adjective 1 *indecent photographs:* obscene, dirty, filthy, rude, naughty, vulgar, smutty, pornographic; informal blue; euphemistic adult. 2 *indecent haste:* unseemly, improper, unbecoming, inappropriate.

your actions. **2** a sum of money paid to compensate for damage or loss.

indent verb /in-**dent**/ **1** form hollows or notches in. **2** begin a line of writing further from the margin than the other lines. • noun /**in**-dent/ Brit. an official order for goods.
■ **indentation** noun.

indenture noun a formal agreement or contract.

independent adjective **1** free from the control or influence of others. **2** (of a country) self-governing. **3** having or earning enough money to support yourself. **4** not connected with another; separate.
• noun an independent person or body.
■ **independence** noun **independently** adverb.

> ☑ -ent, not -ant: independent.

indescribable adjective too extreme or unusual to be described.
■ **indescribably** adverb.

indestructible adjective not able to be destroyed.

indeterminate adjective not certain; vague.

index noun (plural **indexes** or **indices** /**in**-di-seez/) **1** a list of names or subjects referred to in a book, arranged in alphabetical order. **2** an alphabetical list or catalogue of books or documents. **3** a sign or measure of something. • verb record in or provide with an index.

□ **index finger** the forefinger.

Indian noun **1** a person from India. **2** an American Indian. • adjective **1** relating to India. **2** relating to American Indians. □ **Indian ink** deep black ink used in drawing. **Indian summer** a period of dry, warm weather in late autumn.

indicate verb (**indicates, indicating, indicated**) **1** point something out. **2** be a sign of. **3** mention briefly. **4** (**be indicated**) formal be necessary or recommended.
■ **indication** noun.

indicative /in-**dik**-uh-tiv/ adjective **1** acting as a sign. **2** Grammar (of a verb) expressing a simple statement of fact (e.g. *she left*).

indicator noun **1** a thing that shows the state or level of something. **2** a light on a vehicle that flashes to show that it is about to turn left or right.

indict /in-**dyt**/ verb formally accuse someone of a serious crime.
■ **indictable** adjective.

indictment /in-**dyt**-muhnt/ noun **1** a formal accusation that someone has committed a serious crime. **2** an indication that something is bad and deserves to be condemned.

indifferent adjective **1** not interested in or caring about something. **2** not very good; mediocre.
■ **indifference** noun **indifferently** adverb.

independence noun **1** *the struggle for American independence:* self-government, self-rule, home rule, self-determination, sovereignty, autonomy. **2** *the adviser's independence:* impartiality, neutrality, disinterestedness, detachment, objectivity.
OPPOSITES dependence, partiality.

independent adjective **1** *an independent country:* self-governing, self-ruling, self-determining, sovereign, autonomous, non-aligned, free. **2** *two independent groups verified the results:* separate, different, unconnected, unrelated, discrete. **3** *an independent school:* private, non-state-run, private-sector, fee-paying, privatized, deregulated, denationalized. **4** *independent advice:* impartial, unbiased, unprejudiced, neutral, disinterested, uninvolved, detached, dispassionate, objective, non-partisan, with no axe to grind.
OPPOSITES dependent, related, state, public, biased.

independently adverb alone, on your own, separately, individually, unaccompanied, solo, unaided, unassisted, without help, by your own efforts, under your own steam, single-handedly.

index noun list, listing, inventory, catalogue, register, directory, database.

indicate verb **1** *sales indicate a growing market:* point to, be a sign of, be evidence of, demonstrate, show, testify to, be symptomatic of, denote, mark, signal, reflect, signify, suggest, imply. **2** *the president indicated his willingness to use force:* state, declare, make known, communicate, announce, put on record. **3** *please indicate your choice of prize on the form:* specify, designate, stipulate, show.

indication noun sign, signal, indicator, symptom, mark, demonstration, pointer, guide, hint, clue, omen, warning.

indicator noun measure, gauge, meter, barometer, guide, index, mark, sign, signal.

indictment noun charge, accusation, arraignment, prosecution, citation, summons; N. Amer. impeachment.

indifference noun detachment, lack of concern, disinterest, lack of interest, nonchalance, boredom, unresponsiveness, impassivity, coolness.
OPPOSITES concern.

indifferent adjective **1** *an indifferent shrug:* detached, unconcerned, uninterested, uncaring, casual, nonchalant, offhand, unenthusiastic, unimpressed, unmoved, impassive, cool. **2** *an indifferent performance:* mediocre, ordinary, average,

indigenous /in-**dij**-i-nuhss/ adjective belonging to a place; native.

indigent /**in**-di-juhnt/ adjective poor; needy.

indigestible adjective difficult or impossible to digest.

indigestion noun pain or discomfort caused by difficulty in digesting food.

indignant adjective feeling or showing indignation.
∎ **indignantly** adverb.

indignation noun anger caused by something that you consider to be unfair.

indignity noun (plural **indignities**) a thing that causes you to feel ashamed or embarrassed.

indigo /**in**-di-goh/ noun a dark blue colour or dye.

indirect adjective **1** not going in a straight line. **2** not saying something in a straightforward way. **3** happening as a secondary effect or consequence.
□ **indirect speech** reported speech.
∎ **indirectly** adverb.

indiscipline noun lack of discipline.

indiscreet adjective too ready to reveal things that should remain secret or private.
∎ **indiscreetly** adverb.

indiscretion noun **1** indiscreet behaviour. **2** an indiscreet act or remark.

indiscriminate adjective done or acting without careful judgement.
∎ **indiscriminately** adverb.

indispensable adjective absolutely necessary.

> ☑ -able, not -ible: indispens**able**.

indisposed adjective **1** slightly unwell. **2** unwilling.

indisposition noun a slight illness.

indisputable adjective unable to be challenged or denied.

∎ **indisputably** adverb.

indissoluble adjective unable to be destroyed; lasting.

indistinct adjective not clear or sharply defined.
∎ **indistinctly** adverb.

indistinguishable adjective not able to be distinguished.
∎ **indistinguishably** adverb.

indium noun a soft silvery-white metallic element.

individual adjective **1** considered separately; single. **2** having to do with one particular person. **3** striking or unusual; original. ● noun **1** a single person or item as distinct from a group. **2** a distinctive or original person.
∎ **individually** adverb.

individualism noun **1** the quality of doing things in your own way; independence. **2** the belief that individual people should have freedom of action.
∎ **individualist** noun & adjective **individualistic** adjective.

individuality noun the quality or character of a person or thing that makes them different from other people or things.

individualize or **individualise** verb (**individualizes**, **individualizing**, **individualized**) give something an individual character.

indivisible adjective unable to be divided or separated.

indoctrinate verb (**indoctrinates**, **indoctrinating**, **indoctrinated**) force someone to accept a set of beliefs.
∎ **indoctrination** noun.

Indo-European noun the family of languages spoken over most of Europe and Asia as far as northern India. ● adjective relating to Indo-European.

THESAURUS

middle-of-the-road, undistinguished, uninspired, unexceptional, pedestrian, forgettable, amateurish; informal no great shakes, not up to much.
OPPOSITES enthusiastic, brilliant.

indignant adjective aggrieved, affronted, displeased, resentful, angry, annoyed, offended, exasperated; informal peeved, irked, put out; Brit. informal narked; N. Amer. informal sore.

indirect adjective **1** *an indirect effect:* incidental, secondary, subordinate, ancillary, collateral, concomitant, contingent. **2** *an indirect route:* roundabout, circuitous, meandering, winding, tortuous. **3** *an indirect attack:* oblique, implicit, implied.
OPPOSITES direct.

individual adjective **1** *exhibitions devoted to individual artists:* single, separate, discrete, independent, lone. **2** *he had his own individual style of music:* unique, characteristic, distinctive, distinct, particular, idiosyncratic, peculiar, personal, special. **3** *a highly individual apartment:* original, exclusive, different, striking, unusual, novel, unorthodox, out of the ordinary.
OPPOSITES multiple, shared, ordinary.
● noun *a rather stuffy individual:* person, human being, soul, creature, character; informal type, sort, customer.

individually adverb separately, singly, one by one, one at a time, independently.
OPPOSITES together.

indolent /in-duh-luhnt/ adjective lazy.
■ indolence noun.

indomitable /in-dom-i-tuh-b'l/ adjective impossible to defeat or subdue.

Indonesian noun **1** a person from Indonesia. **2** the group of languages spoken in Indonesia. ● adjective relating to Indonesia.

indoor adjective situated, done, or used inside a building. ● adverb (**indoors**) into or inside a building.

indubitable /in-dyoo-bi-tuh-b'l/ adjective impossible to doubt; certain.
■ indubitably adverb.

induce verb (**induces, inducing, induced**) **1** persuade or influence someone to do something. **2** bring about or cause. **3** make a woman begin to give birth to her baby by means of special drugs.

inducement noun a thing that persuades someone to do something.

induct verb formally admit someone to an organization or establish them in a position of authority.

inductance noun a process by which a change in the current of an electric circuit produces an electromotive force.

induction noun **1** introduction to a post or organization. **2** the action of inducing. **3** a method of reasoning in which a general rule or conclusion is drawn from particular facts or examples. **4** the passing of electricity or magnetism from one object to another without them touching.
■ inductive adjective.

indulge verb (**indulges, indulging, indulged**) **1** (**indulge in**) allow yourself to do something that you enjoy. **2** satisfy a desire or interest. **3** allow someone to do or have whatever they wish.

indulgence noun **1** the action of indulging in something. **2** a thing that is indulged in; a luxury. **3** willingness to tolerate someone's faults.

indulgent adjective allowing someone to do or have whatever they want or overlooking their faults.
■ indulgently adverb.

industrial adjective having to do with industry.
□ **industrial action** Brit. a strike or other action taken by workers as a protest. **industrial estate** Brit. an area of land developed as a site for factories.
■ industrially adverb.

industrialist noun a person who owns or controls a large factory or manufacturing business.

industrialize or **industrialise** verb (**industrializes, industrializing, industrialized**) develop industries in a country or region on a wide scale.
■ industrialization noun.

industrious adjective hard-working.
■ industriously adverb.

industry noun (plural **industries**) **1** the manufacture of goods in factories. **2** a branch of economic or commercial activity. **3** hard work.

THESAURUS

induce verb **1** *the pickets induced many workers to stay away:* persuade, convince, prevail on, get, make, prompt, encourage, cajole into, talk into. **2** *these activities induce a feeling of togetherness:* bring about, cause, produce, create, give rise to, generate, engender.
OPPOSITES dissuade, prevent.

indulge verb **1** *Sally indulged her passion for chocolate:* satisfy, gratify, fulfil, feed, yield to, give in to. **2** *she did not like her children to be indulged:* pamper, spoil, overindulge, coddle, mollycoddle, cosset, pander to, wait on hand and foot.
□ **indulge in carry out,** become involved in, participate in, commit, yield to. **indulge yourself treat yourself,** splash out; informal go to town, splurge.

indulgence noun **1** *the indulgence of all his desires:* satisfaction, gratification, fulfilment. **2** *indulgence contributed to his ill-health:* self-gratification, self-indulgence, overindulgence, intemperance, excess, lack of restraint, extravagance, hedonism. **3** *they viewed holidays as an*

indulgence: extravagance, luxury, treat, non-essential, extra, frill. **4** *her indulgence left him spoilt:* pampering, coddling, mollycoddling, cosseting. **5** *his parents view his lapses with indulgence:* tolerance, forbearance, understanding, compassion, sympathy, leniency.
OPPOSITES asceticism, intolerance.

indulgent adjective generous, permissive, easy-going, liberal, tolerant, forgiving, forbearing, lenient, kind, kindly, soft-hearted.
OPPOSITES strict.

industrialist noun manufacturer, factory owner, captain of industry, magnate, tycoon.

industry noun **1** *British industry:* manufacturing, production, construction, trade, commerce. **2** *the publishing industry:* business, trade, field, line of business, profession. **3** *the kitchen was a hive of industry:* activity, energy, effort, endeavour, hard work, industriousness, diligence, application.

inebriated /i-**nee**-bri-ay-tid/ adjective
drunk.
■ inebriation noun.

inedible adjective not fit for eating.

ineffable adjective too great or extreme to
be expressed in words.

ineffective adjective not having any effect
or achieving what you want.
■ ineffectively adverb.

ineffectual adjective **1** ineffective. **2** not
forceful enough to do something well.
■ ineffectually adverb.

inefficient adjective failing to make the
best use of time or resources.
■ inefficiency noun inefficiently adverb.

inelegant adjective not elegant or graceful.

ineligible adjective not qualified to have or
do something.

ineluctable adjective rare unable to be
resisted or avoided.

inept adjective lacking skill.
■ ineptitude noun ineptly adverb.

inequality noun (plural **inequalities**) lack of
equality.

inequitable adjective unfair; unjust.

inequity noun (plural **inequities**) lack of
fairness or justice.

ineradicable adjective unable to be rooted
out or destroyed.

inert adjective **1** lacking the ability or
strength to move or act. **2** without active
chemical properties.

inertia /i-**ner**-shuh/ noun **1** a tendency to do
nothing or to remain unchanged. **2** Physics a
property by which matter remains still or
continues moving unless acted on by an
external force.

inescapable adjective unable to be avoided
or denied.

inessential adjective not absolutely
necessary.

inestimable adjective too great to be
measured.

inevitable adjective certain to happen;
unavoidable.
■ inevitability noun inevitably adverb.

inexact adjective not quite accurate.

inexcusable adjective too bad to be
justified or tolerated.

inexhaustible adjective (of a supply) never
ending because available in unlimited
quantities.

inexorable /in-ek-suh-ruh-b'l/ adjective
1 impossible to stop or prevent. **2** unable
to be persuaded.
■ inexorably adverb.

inexpensive adjective not costing a lot of
money.

inexperience noun lack of experience.
■ inexperienced adjective.

inexpert adjective lacking skill or
knowledge in a particular field.

inexplicable adjective unable to be
explained.
■ inexplicably adverb.

inexpressive adjective showing no feelings.

in extremis /in ek-**stree**-miss/ adverb **1** in a
very difficult situation. **2** at the point of
death.

inextricable adjective impossible to
untangle or separate.
■ inextricably adverb.

infallible adjective incapable of making
mistakes or being wrong.
■ infallibility noun infallibly adverb.

infamous /in-fuh-muhss/ adjective well
known for some bad quality or act.
■ infamously adverb infamy noun.

THESAURUS

ineffective adjective **1** *an ineffective
scheme:* unsuccessful, unproductive,
unprofitable, ineffectual. **2** *an ineffective
president:* ineffectual, inefficient,
inadequate, incompetent, incapable, unfit,
inept; informal useless, hopeless.
OPPOSITES effective.

inefficient adjective **1** *an inefficient worker:*
ineffective, ineffectual, incompetent,
inept, disorganized, unprepared.
2 *inefficient processes:* uneconomical,
wasteful, unproductive, time-wasting, slow,
unsystematic.
OPPOSITES efficient.

inequality noun imbalance, inequity,
inconsistency, disparity, discrepancy,
dissimilarity, difference, bias, prejudice,
discrimination, unfairness.
OPPOSITES equality.

inevitable adjective unavoidable,

inescapable, inexorable, assured, certain,
sure.
OPPOSITES avoidable.

inevitably adverb unavoidably, necessarily,
automatically, naturally, as a matter of
course, of necessity, inescapably, certainly,
surely; informal like it or not.

inexpensive adjective cheap, affordable,
low-cost, economical, competitive,
reasonable, budget, economy, bargain, cut-
price, reduced.
OPPOSITES expensive.

inexperienced adjective inexpert,
untrained, unqualified, unskilled,
unseasoned, naive, new, callow, immature;
informal wet behind the ears, wide-eyed.
OPPOSITES experienced.

infamous adjective notorious, disreputable,
scandalous.
OPPOSITES reputable.

infancy noun **1** the state or period of early childhood or babyhood. **2** an early stage of development.

infant noun **1** a very young child or baby. **2** Brit. a schoolchild between the ages of about four and seven.

infanticide /in-**fan**-ti-syd/ noun the killing of a child.

infantile adjective **1** relating to infants. **2** disapproving childish.

infantry noun soldiers who fight on foot.

infatuate verb (**be infatuated with**) have a strong but short-lived feeling of love for.
■ **infatuation** noun.

infect verb **1** pass a germ that causes disease to a person, animal, or plant. **2** contaminate with something harmful.

infection noun **1** the process of infecting. **2** an infectious disease.

infectious adjective **1** (of a disease or germ) able to be passed on through the environment. **2** liable to spread infection. **3** likely to spread to or influence other people.
■ **infectiously** adverb.

infer verb (**infers, inferring, inferred**) work something out from the information you have available.

> ❗ on the difference between the words **imply** and **infer**, see the note at IMPLY.

inference noun **1** a conclusion drawn from the information available to you. **2** the process of inferring.

inferior adjective lower in quality or status.
● noun a person who is lower in status or less good at doing something.
■ **inferiority** noun.

infernal adjective **1** having to do with hell or the underworld. **2** informal very annoying.

inferno noun (plural **infernos**) a large uncontrollable fire.

infertile adjective **1** unable to have babies or other young. **2** (of land) unable to produce crops or plants.
■ **infertility** noun.

infest verb (especially of insects or rats) be present in large numbers so as to cause damage or disease.
■ **infestation** noun.

infidel /in-fi-duhl/ noun old use a person who has no religion or whose religion is not that of the majority.

infidelity noun (plural **infidelities**) the action or state of not being faithful to your sexual partner.

infighting noun conflict within a group or organization.

infiltrate verb enter or gain access to an organization or place secretly and gradually.
■ **infiltration** noun **infiltrator** noun.

infinite adjective **1** having no limits and impossible to measure. **2** very great in amount or degree.
■ **infinitely** adverb.

infinitesimal /in-fi-ni-tess-i-muhl/ adjective very small.
■ **infinitesimally** adverb.

i

---

infancy noun beginnings, early days, early stages, emergence, dawn, outset, birth, inception.
OPPOSITES end.

infant noun baby, newborn, young child, tiny tot, little one; Medicine neonate; Scottish & N. English bairn, wean; informal tiny, sprog.

infect verb **1** they can infect their children: pass infection to, contaminate. **2** nitrates were infecting rivers: contaminate, pollute, taint, foul, poison.

infection noun **1** a kidney infection: disease, virus, illness, ailment, disorder, sickness; informal bug. **2** the infection in his wounds: contamination, poison, bacteria, germs; Medicine sepsis.

infectious adjective **1** infectious diseases: communicable, contagious, transmittable, transmissible, transferable; informal catching. **2** her laughter is infectious: irresistible, compelling, contagious; informal catching.

inferior adjective **1** she regards him as inferior: second-class, lower-ranking, subordinate, junior, minor, lowly, humble, menial, beneath someone. **2** inferior accommodation: second-rate, substandard, low-grade, unsatisfactory, shoddy, poor; informal crummy, lousy.
OPPOSITES superior, luxury.
● noun how dare she treat him as an inferior? subordinate, junior, underling, minion.
OPPOSITES superior.

infertility noun barrenness, sterility, childlessness.
OPPOSITES fertility.

infested adjective overrun, swarming, teeming, crawling, alive, plagued.

infiltrate verb penetrate, insinuate yourself into, worm your way into, sneak into, slip into, creep into, invade.

infiltrator noun spy, secret agent, plant, intruder, interloper, subversive, informer, mole, fifth columnist; N. Amer. informal spook.

infinite adjective **1** the universe is infinite: boundless, unbounded, unlimited, limitless, never-ending, incalculable, untold. **2** in infinite combinations: countless, uncountable, innumerable, numberless, immeasurable.
OPPOSITES finite, limited.

infinitive /in-fin-i-tiv/ noun the basic form of a verb, normally occurring in English with the word *to* (as in *to see, to ask*).

infinity noun (plural **infinities**) **1** the state or quality of being infinite. **2** a very great number or amount.

infirm adjective physically weak.

infirmary noun (plural **infirmaries**) a place where sick people are cared for.

infirmity noun (plural **infirmities**) physical or mental weakness.

inflame verb (**inflames, inflaming, inflamed**) **1** make someone feel something passionately. **2** make a difficult situation worse. **3** (**inflamed**) (of a part of the body) red, swollen, and hot as a result of infection or injury.

inflammable adjective easily set on fire.

> ❗ **inflammable** and **flammable** both mean 'easily set on fire'. It's safer to use **flammable**, however, because **inflammable** is sometimes taken to mean 'non-flammable'.

inflammation noun a condition in which an area of the skin is red, swollen, and hot.

inflammatory adjective **1** making people feel angry. **2** relating to or causing inflammation.

inflatable adjective capable of being inflated. • noun an inflatable plastic or rubber boat.

inflate verb (**inflates, inflating, inflated**) **1** expand something by filling it with air or gas. **2** increase the cost or price of something by a large amount. **3** (**inflated**) exaggerated.

inflation noun **1** the action of inflating. **2** a general increase in prices and fall in the value of money.
■ **inflationary** adjective.

inflect verb **1** Grammar (of a word) be changed by inflection. **2** vary the tone or pitch of your voice.

inflection noun **1** Grammar a change in the form of a word to show its grammatical function, number, or gender. **2** a variation in the tone or pitch of a voice.

inflexible adjective **1** not able to be altered or adapted. **2** unwilling to change or compromise. **3** not able to be bent.
■ **inflexibility** noun.

inflict verb (**inflict something on**) make someone experience something unpleasant or painful.
■ **infliction** noun.

inflorescence /in-fluh-ress-uhnss/ noun Botany a cluster of flowers on a single stem.

influence noun **1** the power or ability to affect someone's beliefs or actions. **2** a person or thing with such ability or power. **3** the power arising out of status, contacts, or wealth. • verb (**influences, influencing, influenced**) have an influence on.

influential adjective having great influence.

influenza noun a disease spread by a virus and causing fever, aching, and catarrh.

influx noun the arrival or entry of large numbers of people or things.

inform verb **1** give facts or information to.

THESAURUS

inflame verb **1** *his opinions inflamed his rival:* enrage, incense, anger, madden, infuriate, exasperate, provoke, antagonize; informal make someone see red. **2** *he inflamed a sensitive situation:* aggravate, exacerbate, intensify, worsen, compound. OPPOSITES placate, calm.

inflamed adjective swollen, red, hot, burning, itchy, sore, painful, tender, infected.

inflate verb **1** *inflate the balloon:* blow up, pump up, fill, puff up/out, dilate, distend, swell, bloat. **2** *the demand inflated prices:* increase, raise, boost, escalate, put up; informal hike up, jack up. OPPOSITES deflate, lower.

inflated adjective **1** *inflated prices:* high, sky-high, excessive, unreasonable, outrageous, exorbitant, extortionate; Brit. over the odds; informal steep. **2** *an inflated opinion of himself:* exaggerated, immoderate, overblown, overstated. OPPOSITES low, modest.

inflict verb **1** *he inflicted an injury on Frank:* give, administer, deal out, mete out, cause

someone something, exact, wreak. **2** *I won't inflict my views on my children:* impose, force, thrust, foist. OPPOSITES spare.

influence noun **1** *the influence of parents on their children:* effect, impact, control, spell, hold, magic. **2** *a bad influence on young girls:* example to, role model for, inspiration to. **3** *political influence:* power, authority, sway, leverage, weight, pull; informal clout.
• verb **1** *bosses can influence our careers:* affect, have an impact on, determine, guide, control, shape, govern, decide, change, alter. **2** *an attempt to influence the jury:* sway, bias, prejudice, suborn, pressurize, coerce, intimidate; informal lean on; Brit. informal nobble.

influential adjective powerful, controlling, important, authoritative, leading, significant, instrumental, guiding.

inform verb **1** *she informed him that she was ill:* tell, notify, apprise, advise, impart to, communicate to, let someone know, brief, enlighten, send word to. **2** *he*

2 (**inform on**) give information about someone's involvement in a crime to the police.

informal adjective **1** relaxed and friendly, and not following strict rules of behaviour. **2** (of clothes) suitable for wearing when relaxing. **3** (of language) used in everyday speech and writing, rather than official contexts.
∎ **informality** noun **informally** adverb.

informant noun a person who gives information to another.

information noun facts or details supplied to or learned by someone.
▫ **information technology** the use of computers and telecommunications for storing, retrieving, and sending information.

informative adjective providing useful information.

informed adjective **1** having or showing knowledge. **2** (of a judgement) based on a sound understanding of the facts.

informer noun a person who informs on another person to the police.

infraction noun a breaking of a law or agreement.

infra dig /in-fruh dig/ adjective informal beneath your dignity.

infrared adjective (of electromagnetic radiation) having a wavelength just greater than that of red light.

infrastructure noun the basic things (e.g. buildings, roads, power supplies) needed for the operation of a society or enterprise.

infrequent adjective not happening often.
∎ **infrequency** noun **infrequently** adverb.

infringe verb **1** break a law or agreement. **2** restrict a right or privilege.
∎ **infringement** noun.

infuriate verb (**infuriates, infuriating, infuriated**) make someone angry.

∎ **infuriating** adjective.

infuse verb (**infuses, infusing, infused**) **1** spread throughout something. **2** soak tea or herbs to extract the flavour or healing properties.

infusion noun **1** a drink prepared by soaking tea or herbs. **2** the action of infusing.

ingenious adjective clever, original, and inventive.
∎ **ingeniously** adverb.

ingénue /an-zhuh-nyoo/ noun a naive young woman.

ingenuity noun the quality of being ingenious.

ingenuous /in-jen-yoo-uhss/ adjective innocent and unsuspecting.

ingest verb take food or drink into the body by swallowing it.
∎ **ingestion** noun.

inglenook noun a space on either side of a large fireplace.

inglorious adjective not making you feel proud; rather shameful.

ingoing adjective going towards or into.

ingot noun a rectangular block of steel, gold, or other metal.

ingrained or **engrained** adjective **1** (of a habit or belief) firmly established. **2** (of dirt) deeply embedded.

ingratiate /in-gray-shi-ayt/ verb (**ingratiates, ingratiating, ingratiated**) (**ingratiate yourself**) do things in order to make someone like you.

ingratitude noun a lack of appropriate gratitude.

ingredient noun **1** any of the substances that are combined to make a particular dish. **2** a component part or element.

ingress noun **1** the action of entering or coming in. **2** a place or means of access.

i

THESAURUS

informed on two colleagues: betray, give away, denounce, incriminate, report; informal rat, squeal, split, tell, blow the whistle, snitch; Brit. informal grass, shop; N. Amer. informal finger; Austral./NZ informal dob in.

informal adjective **1** *an informal discussion:* unofficial, casual, relaxed, easy-going, low-key. **2** *informal language:* colloquial, vernacular, idiomatic, popular, familiar, everyday; informal slangy, chatty. **3** *informal clothes:* casual, relaxed, comfortable, everyday, sloppy, leisure; informal comfy.
OPPOSITES formal, official, literary, smart.

information noun facts, particulars, details, figures, statistics, data, knowledge, intelligence; informal info, gen.

informative adjective instructive, illuminating, enlightening, revealing,

explanatory, factual, educational, edifying.

informed adjective knowledgeable, enlightened, educated, briefed, up to date, up to speed, in the picture, in the know, au fait; informal clued up.
OPPOSITES ignorant.

infuriate verb enrage, incense, provoke, anger, madden, exasperate; informal make someone see red; Brit. informal wind up.
OPPOSITES please.

ingenious adjective inventive, creative, imaginative, original, innovative, pioneering, resourceful, enterprising, inspired, clever.
OPPOSITES unimaginative.

ingredient noun constituent, component, element, item, part, strand, unit, feature, aspect, attribute.

ingrown or **ingrowing** adjective (of a toenail) having grown into the flesh.

inhabit verb (**inhabits, inhabiting, inhabited**) live in or occupy.
■ **inhabitable** adjective.

inhabitant noun a person or animal that lives in or occupies a place.

inhale verb (**inhales, inhaling, inhaled**) breathe in air, smoke, etc.
■ **inhalation** noun.

inhaler noun a portable device used for inhaling a drug.

inherent adjective existing in something as a permanent or essential quality.
■ **inherently** adverb.

inherit verb (**inherits, inheriting, inherited**) **1** receive money or property from someone when they die. **2** have a quality or characteristic passed on to you from your parents or ancestors. **3** be left with something previously belonging to someone else.

inheritance noun **1** a thing that is inherited. **2** the action of inheriting.

inhibit verb (**inhibits, inhibiting, inhibited**) **1** prevent or slow down a process. **2** make someone unable to act in a relaxed and natural way.

inhibition noun a feeling that makes you unable to act in a relaxed and natural way.

inhospitable adjective (of an environment) harsh and difficult to live in.

inhuman adjective **1** lacking positive human qualities; cruel and barbaric. **2** not human in nature or character.

inhumane adjective without pity; cruel.

inhumanity noun (plural **inhumanities**) cruel and brutal behaviour.

inimical adjective having a harmful effect on something; not helpful.

inimitable adjective impossible to imitate; unique.
■ **inimitably** adverb.

iniquity noun (plural **iniquities**) great injustice or unfairness.
■ **iniquitous** adjective.

initial adjective existing or occurring at the beginning. •noun the first letter of a name or word. •verb (**initials, initialling, initialled**; N. Amer. **initials, initialing, initialed**) mark something with your initials as a sign of approval or agreement.
■ **initially** adverb.

initiate verb (**initiates, initiating, initiated**) **1** make a process or action start. **2** admit someone into a society or group with a formal ceremony. **3** introduce someone to a new activity.
■ **initiation** noun.

initiative noun **1** the ability to act independently and with a fresh approach. **2** the power or opportunity to act before other people do. **3** a new development or approach to a problem.

inject verb **1** put a drug or other substance

THESAURUS

inhabit verb live in, occupy, settle, people, populate, colonize.

inhabitant noun resident, occupant, occupier, settler, local, native; (**inhabitants**) population, populace, people, public, community, citizenry, townsfolk, townspeople.

inhale verb breathe in, draw in, suck in, sniff in, drink in, gasp.
OPPOSITES exhale.

inherit verb **1** *she inherited the farm:* be left, be bequeathed, be willed, come into. **2** *Richard inherited the title:* succeed to, assume, take over.
OPPOSITES leave.

inheritance noun legacy, bequest, endowment, birthright, heritage, patrimony.

inhibit verb impede, hinder, hamper, hold back, discourage, interfere with, obstruct, slow down, retard.
OPPOSITES assist, allow.

inhibited adjective reserved, reticent, guarded, self-conscious, insecure, withdrawn, repressed, undemonstrative, shy, diffident, bashful; informal uptight.
OPPOSITES uninhibited.

initial adjective beginning, opening, commencing, starting, first, earliest, primary, preliminary, preparatory, introductory, inaugural.
OPPOSITES final.

initially adverb at first, at the start, at the outset, in/at the beginning, to begin with, to start with, originally.

initiate verb **1** *the government initiated the scheme:* begin, start (off), commence, institute, inaugurate, launch, instigate, establish, set up. **2** *he was initiated into a religious cult:* introduce, admit, induct, install, swear in, ordain, invest.
OPPOSITES finish, expel.

initiative noun **1** *employers are looking for initiative:* enterprise, resourcefulness, inventiveness, imagination, ingenuity, originality, creativity. **2** *he has lost the initiative:* advantage, upper hand, edge, lead, start. **3** *a recent initiative on recycling:* scheme, plan, strategy, measure, proposal, step, action.
OPPOSITES apathy.

inject verb **1** *he injected the codeine:* administer, take; informal shoot (up), mainline, fix. **2** *troops were injected with the vaccine:* inoculate, vaccinate. **3** *a pump*

into the body with a syringe. **2** add a new or different quality.
■ **injection** noun.

injudicious adjective unwise.

injunction noun **1** Law an order saying that someone must or must not carry out a certain action. **2** a strong warning.

injure verb (**injures, injuring, injured**) **1** do physical harm to; wound. **2** have a bad effect on; damage.

injurious /in-**joor**-i-uhss/ adjective causing or likely to cause injury.

injury noun (plural **injuries**) **1** harm done to the body. **2** hurt feelings.

injustice noun **1** lack of justice. **2** an unjust act.

ink noun **1** a coloured fluid used for writing, drawing, or printing. **2** a black liquid produced by a cuttlefish, octopus, or squid.
■ **inky** adjective.

inkling noun a slight suspicion; a hint.

inland adjective & adverb in or into the interior of a country.
□ **inland revenue** Brit. the government department responsible for collecting income tax.

in-law noun a relative by marriage.

inlay verb (**inlays, inlaying, inlaid**) fix pieces of a different material into a surface as a

form of decoration. ● noun decoration of this type.

inlet noun **1** a small arm of the sea, a lake, or a river. **2** a place or means of entry.

in loco parentis /in loh-koh puh-**ren**-tiss/ adverb having the same responsibility for a child or young person as a parent has.

inmate noun a person living in an institution such as a prison or hospital.

inn noun a pub, especially in the country.
■ **innkeeper** noun (old use).

innards plural noun informal **1** internal organs. **2** the internal workings of a machine.

innate adjective natural or inborn.
■ **innately** adverb.

inner adjective **1** situated inside or close to the centre. **2** private; not expressed. **3** mental or spiritual.
□ **inner city** an area in or near the centre of a large city. **inner tube** a separate inflatable tube inside a tyre.

innermost adjective **1** furthest in; closest to the centre. **2** (of thoughts) most private.

innings noun (plural **innings**) Cricket each of the divisions of a game during which one side has a turn at batting.

innocent adjective **1** not guilty of a crime or offence. **2** having little experience of life. **3** not intended to cause offence. ● noun an

---

injects air into the valve: insert, introduce, feed, push, force, shoot. **4** *he injected new life into the team:* introduce, instil, infuse, imbue, breathe.

injection noun **1** *injections against diphtheria:* inoculation, vaccination, immunization, booster; informal jab, shot. **2** *a cash injection:* addition, introduction, investment, dose, infusion, insertion.

injunction noun order, ruling, direction, directive, command, instruction, mandate.

injure verb **1** *he injured his foot:* hurt, wound, damage, harm, disable, break; Medicine traumatize; Brit. informal knacker. **2** *a libel injured her reputation:* damage, mar, spoil, ruin, blight, blemish, tarnish, blacken.
OPPOSITES boost.

injured adjective **1** *his injured arm:* hurt, wounded, damaged, sore, bruised, broken, fractured; Medicine traumatized; Brit. informal gammy. **2** *an injured tone:* upset, hurt, wounded, offended, reproachful, pained, aggrieved.
OPPOSITES healthy.

injury noun **1** *minor injuries:* wound, bruise, cut, gash, scratch, graze; Medicine trauma, lesion. **2** *they escaped without injury:* harm, hurt, damage, pain, suffering. **3** *injury to his feelings:* offence, abuse, injustice, disservice, affront, insult.

injustice noun **1** *the injustice of the world:* unfairness, one-sidedness, inequity, bias, prejudice, discrimination, intolerance, exploitation, corruption. **2** *his sacking was an injustice:* wrong, offence, crime, sin, outrage, scandal, disgrace, affront.
OPPOSITES justice, just deserts.

inland adjective interior, inshore, internal, upcountry.
OPPOSITES coastal.

inlet noun **1** *a rocky inlet:* cove, bay, bight, creek, estuary, fjord, sound; Scottish firth. **2** *an air inlet:* vent, flue, shaft, duct, channel, pipe.

inmate noun **1** *the inmates of the hospital:* patient, inpatient, resident, occupant. **2** *prison inmates:* prisoner, convict, captive, detainee, internee.

inner adjective **1** *inner London:* central, downtown, innermost. **2** *the inner gates:* internal, interior, inside, innermost. **3** *the inner meaning:* hidden, secret, deep, underlying, veiled, esoteric.
OPPOSITES outer, apparent.

innocence noun **1** *he protested his innocence:* guiltlessness, blamelessness. **2** *she took advantage of his innocence:* naivety, credulity, inexperience, gullibility, ingenuousness.

innocent person.

■ **innocence** noun **innocently** adverb.

innocuous /in-**nok**-yoo-uhss/ adjective not harmful or offensive.

innovate verb (**innovates, innovating, innovated**) introduce new ideas or products.

■ **innovative** adjective **innovator** noun.

innovation noun **1** the introduction of new ideas or products. **2** a new idea or product.

innuendo /in-yuu-**en**-doh/ noun (plural **innuendoes** or **innuendos**) a remark which makes a vague and indirect reference to something.

innumerable adjective too many to be counted.

innumerate adjective without a basic knowledge of mathematics and arithmetic.

inoculate verb treat someone with a vaccine to stop them getting a disease.

■ **inoculation** noun.

☑ one *n*, one *c*: i*noc*ulate.

inoffensive adjective causing no offence or harm.

inoperable adjective **1** (of an illness) not able to be cured by an operation. **2** not able to be used or operated.

inoperative adjective not working or taking effect.

inopportune adjective happening at an inconvenient time.

inordinate adjective much greater than is usual or expected; excessive.

■ **inordinately** adverb.

inorganic adjective **1** not consisting of or coming from living matter. **2** (of a chemical compound) not containing carbon.

inpatient noun a patient who is staying day and night in a hospital.

input noun **1** what is put or taken into a system or process. **2** the putting or feeding in of something. **3** a person's contribution.

•verb (**inputs, inputting, input** or **inputted**) put data into a computer.

inquest noun **1** a legal inquiry to gather the facts relating to an incident. **2** Brit. an inquiry by a coroner's court into the cause of a death.

inquire = ENQUIRE.

inquiry = ENQUIRY.

inquisition noun a long period of questioning or investigation.

inquisitive adjective **1** eager to find things out. **2** prying.

■ **inquisitively** adverb.

inquisitor noun a person conducting an inquisition.

inroad noun a gradual entry into or effect on a place or situation.

inrush noun a sudden inward rush or flow.

insalubrious /in-suh-**loo**-bri-uhss/ adjective unpleasant because not clean or well kept.

insane adjective **1** seriously mentally ill. **2** very foolish.

■ **insanely** adverb **insanity** noun.

insanitary adjective so dirty as to be a danger to health.

insatiable /in-**say**-shuh-b'l/ adjective always wanting more and not able to be satisfied.

■ **insatiably** adverb.

inscribe verb (**inscribes, inscribing, inscribed**) **1** write or carve something on a surface. **2** write a dedication to someone in a book.

inscription noun words or symbols written or carved on a surface or in a book.

inscrutable adjective impossible to understand or interpret.

■ **inscrutably** adverb.

insect noun a small animal with six legs and no backbone.

insecticide noun a substance used for

THESAURUS

innocent adjective **1** *he was entirely innocent:* guiltless, blameless, clean, irreproachable, honest, upright, law-abiding. **2** *innocent fun:* harmless, innocuous, safe, inoffensive. **3** *innocent foreign students:* naive, ingenuous, trusting, credulous, impressionable, easily led, inexperienced, unsophisticated, artless. OPPOSITES guilty, dangerous, worldly.

innovation noun change, alteration, upheaval, reorganization, restructuring, novelty, departure.

innovative adjective original, new, novel, fresh, unusual, experimental, inventive, ingenious, pioneering, groundbreaking, revolutionary, radical.

inquest noun enquiry, investigation, probe, examination, review, hearing.

inquire, inquiring, inquiry see ENQUIRE etc.

insane adjective **1** *she was declared insane:* mad, of unsound mind, certifiable, psychotic, schizophrenic, unhinged; informal crazy, (stark) raving mad, bonkers, loony, round the bend; Brit. informal crackers, off your trolley; N. Amer. informal nutso, out of your tree; Austral./NZ informal bushed. **2** *an insane suggestion:* stupid, idiotic, nonsensical, absurd, ridiculous, ludicrous, preposterous; informal crazy, mad; Brit. informal daft, barmy.

OPPOSITES sane, sensible.

insect noun bug; informal creepy-crawly; Brit. informal minibeast.

killing insects.

insectivore noun an animal that eats insects.
- insectivorous adjective.

insecure adjective **1** not confident or assured. **2** not firm or firmly fixed.
- insecurity noun (plural **insecurities**).

inseminate verb (**inseminates, inseminating, inseminated**) introduce semen into a woman or a female animal.
- insemination noun.

insensate adjective lacking physical sensation.

insensible adjective **1** unconscious. **2** numb; without feeling.

insensitive adjective **1** showing or feeling no concern for the feelings of other people. **2** not sensitive to physical sensation. **3** not aware of or able to respond to something.
- insensitively adverb insensitivity noun.

inseparable adjective unable to be separated or treated separately.
- inseparably adverb.

insert verb /in-**sert**/ place, fit, or incorporate something into something else. • noun /**in**-sert/ a loose page or section in a magazine.
- insertion noun.

inset noun /**in**-set/ a thing inserted. • verb /**in**-set/ (**insets, insetting, inset** or **insetted**) insert.

inshore adjective & adverb **1** at sea but close to the shore. **2** towards the shore.

inside noun **1** the inner side or surface of a thing. **2** the inner part; the interior. **3** (**insides**) informal a person's stomach and bowels. • adjective situated on or in the inside. • preposition & adverb **1** situated or moving within. **2** informal in prison. **3** within a particular time.
- inside out with the inner surface turned outwards.

insider noun a person working within an organization.

insidious adjective proceeding in a gradual and harmful way.
- insidiously adverb.

insight noun **1** the ability to understand the truth about people and situations. **2** understanding of this kind.
- insightful adjective.

insignia /in-**sig**-ni-uh/ noun (plural **insignia**) a badge or symbol showing someone's rank, position, or membership of an organization.

insignificant adjective having very little importance or value.
- insignificance noun insignificantly adverb.

insincere adjective saying or doing things that you do not mean.
- insincerely adverb insincerity noun.

insinuate verb (**insinuates, insinuating, insinuated**) **1** suggest or hint at something bad in an indirect way. **2** (**insinuate yourself into**) move yourself gradually into a favourable position.

insinuation noun an unpleasant hint or suggestion.

insipid adjective **1** having almost no flavour.

THESAURUS

insecure adjective **1** *an insecure young man:* unconfident, uncertain, unsure, doubtful, diffident, hesitant, self-conscious, anxious, fearful. **2** *insecure windows:* unprotected, unguarded, vulnerable, unsecured. **3** *an insecure footbridge:* unstable, rickety, wobbly, shaky, unsteady, precarious.
OPPOSITES confident, secure, stable.

insecurity noun lack of confidence, uncertainty, self-doubt, diffidence, hesitancy, nervousness, self-consciousness, anxiety, worry, unease.

insert verb put, place, push, thrust, slide, slip, load, fit, slot, install; informal pop, stick, bung.
OPPOSITES extract, remove.

inside noun **1** *the inside of the volcano:* interior, centre, core, middle, heart, bowels. **2** (informal) *my insides are out of order:* stomach, gut, bowels, intestines; informal tummy, belly, guts.
OPPOSITES outside.
• adjective **1** *his inside pocket:* inner, interior, internal, innermost. **2** *inside information:* confidential, classified,

restricted, privileged, private, secret, exclusive; informal hush-hush.
OPPOSITES outside, public.
• adverb *she ushered me inside:* indoors, within, in.
OPPOSITES outside.

insight noun **1** *your insight has been invaluable:* intuition, perception, understanding, comprehension, appreciation, judgement, vision, imagination; informal nous, savvy. **2** *an insight into the government:* understanding of, appreciation of, introduction to; informal eye-opener.
OPPOSITES stupidity.

insignificant adjective unimportant, trivial, trifling, negligible, inconsequential, of no account, paltry, petty, insubstantial; informal piddling.
OPPOSITES significant.

insincere adjective false, fake, hollow, artificial, feigned, pretended, put-on, disingenuous, hypocritical, cynical; informal phoney, pretend.
OPPOSITES sincere.

2 not interesting or lively.

insist verb 1 demand forcefully that something is done. 2 firmly state that something is the case, without letting anyone disagree. 3 (**insist on**) persist in doing something.

insistent adjective 1 insisting that someone does something or that something is the case. 2 continuing for a long time and demanding attention.
■ **insistence** noun **insistently** adverb.

☑ -ent, not -ant: insist*ent*.

in situ /in **sit**-yoo/ adverb & adjective in the natural or original place.

insole noun the inner sole of a boot or shoe.

insolent adjective rude and disrespectful.
■ **insolence** noun **insolently** adverb.

insoluble adjective 1 impossible to solve. 2 (of a substance) incapable of being dissolved.

insolvent adjective not having enough money to pay your debts.
■ **insolvency** noun.

insomnia noun inability to sleep.
■ **insomniac** noun & adjective.

insouciant /in-**soo**-si-uhnt/ adjective carefree and unconcerned.
■ **insouciance** noun.

inspect verb 1 look at something closely. 2 make an official visit to a school, factory, etc. to check on standards.
■ **inspection** noun.

inspector noun 1 an official who makes sure that regulations are obeyed. 2 a police officer ranking below a chief inspector.

inspiration noun 1 the process of being inspired. 2 a person or thing that inspires. 3 a sudden clever idea.
■ **inspirational** adjective.

inspire verb (**inspires, inspiring, inspired**) 1 fill someone with the urge or ability to do something. 2 create a feeling in a person. 3 give rise to.

inspired adjective showing great creativity or imagination.

instability noun (plural **instabilities**) lack of stability.

install verb (**installs, installing, installed**) 1 place or fix equipment in position ready for use. 2 establish someone in a new place or role.

THESAURUS

insist verb 1 *be prepared to insist:* stand firm, stand your ground, be resolute, be determined, hold out, persist, be emphatic, lay down the law, not take no for an answer; informal stick to your guns, put your foot down. 2 *she insisted that they pay up:* demand, command, order, require. 3 *he insisted that he knew nothing:* maintain, assert, protest, swear, declare, repeat.

insistent adjective 1 *Tony's insistent questioning:* persistent, determined, tenacious, unyielding, dogged, unrelenting, inexorable. 2 *an insistent buzzing:* incessant, constant, unremitting.

inspect verb examine, check, scrutinize, investigate, vet, test, monitor, survey, study, look over; informal check out, give something a/the once-over.

inspection noun examination, check-up, survey, scrutiny, exploration, investigation; informal once-over, going-over.

inspector noun examiner, scrutineer, investigator, surveyor, assessor, supervisor, monitor, watchdog, ombudsman, auditor.

inspiration noun 1 *she's an inspiration to others:* stimulus, motivation, spur, fillip, encouragement, influence; informal a shot in the arm. 2 *his work lacks inspiration:* creativity, invention, innovation, ingenuity, imagination, originality, insight, vision. 3 *she had a sudden inspiration:* bright idea, revelation; informal brainwave; N. Amer. informal brainstorm.

inspire verb 1 *the landscape inspired him to write:* stimulate, motivate, encourage,

influence, move, spur, energize, galvanize. 2 *the film inspired a musical:* give rise to, lead to, bring about, prompt, spawn, engender. 3 *Charles inspired awe in her:* arouse, awaken, prompt, induce, ignite, trigger, kindle, produce, bring out.

inspired adjective outstanding, wonderful, marvellous, excellent, magnificent, exceptional, first-class, virtuoso, superlative; informal tremendous, superb, awesome, out of this world; Brit. informal brilliant.
OPPOSITES uninspired.

inspiring adjective inspirational, encouraging, heartening, uplifting, stirring, rousing, electrifying, moving.
OPPOSITES uninspiring.

instability noun 1 *the instability of political life:* unreliability, uncertainty, unpredictability, insecurity, volatility, capriciousness, changeability, mutability. 2 *emotional instability:* volatility, unpredictability, variability, inconsistency.
OPPOSITES steadiness.

install verb 1 *a photocopier was installed in the office:* put, place, station, site, insert. 2 *they installed a new president:* swear in, induct, inaugurate, invest, appoint, ordain, consecrate, anoint, enthrone, crown. 3 *she installed herself behind the table:* ensconce, position, settle, seat, plant, sit (down); informal plonk, park.
OPPOSITES remove.

installation noun 1 the installing of something. 2 a large piece of equipment installed for use. 3 a military or industrial establishment. 4 a large piece of art constructed within a gallery.

instalment (US spelling **installment**) noun 1 each of several payments made over a period of time. 2 each of several parts of something published or broadcast at intervals.

> ☑ **instalment** is spelled with only one *l* in British English, while **install** is spelled with two.

instance noun a particular example or occurrence of something. • verb (**instances, instancing, instanced**) mention something as an example.
□ **for instance** as an example.

instant adjective 1 happening immediately. 2 (of food) processed so that it can be prepared very quickly. • noun 1 a precise moment of time. 2 a very short time.
■ **instantly** adverb.

instantaneous adjective happening or done immediately or at the same time.
■ **instantaneously** adverb.

instead adverb 1 as an alternative. 2 (**instead of**) in place of.

instep noun the part of a person's foot between the ball and the ankle.

instigate verb (**instigates, instigating, instigated**) make something happen or come about.
■ **instigation** noun **instigator** noun.

instil or **instill** verb (**instils, instilling, instilled**) gradually but firmly establish an idea or attitude in someone's mind.

instinct noun 1 an inborn tendency to behave in a certain way. 2 a natural ability or skill.
■ **instinctual** adjective.

instinctive adjective based on instinct rather than thought or training.
■ **instinctively** adverb.

institute noun an organization for the promotion of science, education, or a profession. • verb (**institutes, instituting, instituted**) set up or establish.

institution noun 1 an important organization or public body. 2 an organization providing residential care for people who have special needs. 3 an established law or custom.
■ **institutional** adjective.

institutionalize or **institutionalise** verb (**institutionalizes, institutionalizing,**

i

---

instalment noun 1 *they paid by monthly instalments:* payment, tranche, repayment, part payment, planned payment, regular payment. 2 *the book was published in instalments:* part, episode, chapter, issue, programme, section, volume.

instance noun example, occasion, occurrence, case, illustration, sample.

instant adjective 1 *instant access to your money:* immediate, instantaneous, on-the-spot, prompt, swift, speedy, rapid, quick; informal snappy. 2 *instant meals:* prepared, pre-cooked, microwaveable, convenience. OPPOSITES delayed.
• noun 1 *come here this instant!* moment, minute, second. 2 *it all happened in an instant:* flash, trice, moment, minute, (split) second, twinkling of an eye, no time (at all); informal jiffy.

instantly adverb immediately, at once, straight away, right away, instantaneously, forthwith, there and then, here and now, this/that minute, this/that second.

instead adverb as an alternative, in lieu, alternatively, rather, on second thoughts; N. Amer. alternately.
OPPOSITES as well.
□ **instead of as an alternative to,** as a substitute for, as a replacement for, in place of, in lieu of, in preference to, rather than.

instinct noun 1 *some instinct told me to be careful:* inclination, urge, drive, compulsion, intuition, feeling, sixth sense, nose. 2 *a good instinct for acting:* talent, gift, ability, aptitude, skill, flair, feel, knack.

instinctive adjective intuitive, natural, instinctual, innate, inborn, inherent, unconscious, subconscious, automatic, reflex, knee-jerk; informal gut.
OPPOSITES learned.

institute noun organization, establishment, institution, foundation, centre, academy, school, college, university, society, association, federation, body.
• verb set up, inaugurate, found, establish, organize, initiate, set in motion, get under way, get off the ground, start, launch.
OPPOSITES abolish, end.

institution noun 1 *an academic institution:* establishment, organization, institute, foundation, centre, academy, school, college, university, society, association, body. 2 *they spent their lives in institutions:* (residential) home, hospital, asylum, prison. 3 *the institution of marriage:* practice, custom, convention, tradition.

institutional adjective organized, established, bureaucratic, conventional, procedural, formal, formalized, systematic, systematized, structured, regulated.
OPPOSITES free and easy.

institutionalized) **1** establish something as a feature of an organization or culture. **2** place someone in a residential institution. **3** (**become institutionalized**) lose your individuality as a result of staying for a long time in a residential institution.

instruct verb **1** tell or order someone to do something. **2** teach. **3** inform someone of a fact or situation.

instruction noun **1** an order. **2** a piece of information about how something should be done. **3** teaching or education.
■ **instructional** adjective.

instructive adjective useful and informative.

instructor noun a teacher.

instrument noun **1** a tool or piece of equipment used for delicate or scientific work. **2** a measuring device. **3** (also **musical instrument**) a device for producing musical sounds.

instrumental adjective **1** important in making something happen. **2** (of music) performed on instruments. ● noun a piece of music performed by instruments, with no vocals.

instrumentalist noun a player of a musical instrument.

instrumentation noun **1** the instruments used in a piece of music. **2** the arrangement of a piece of music for particular instruments.

insubordinate adjective disobedient.
■ **insubordination** noun.

insubstantial adjective not strong or solid.

insufferable adjective unbearable.
■ **insufferably** adverb.

insufficient adjective not enough.
■ **insufficiency** noun **insufficiently** adverb.

insular adjective **1** narrow-minded through being isolated from outside influences. **2** relating to an island.
■ **insularity** noun.

insulate verb (**insulates, insulating, insulated**) **1** place material between one thing and another to prevent loss of heat or intrusion of sound. **2** cover something with non-conducting material to prevent the passage of electricity. **3** protect from something unpleasant.
■ **insulation** noun **insulator** noun.

insulin noun a hormone which regulates glucose levels in the blood.

insult verb /in-sult/ say or do hurtful or disrespectful things to someone. ● noun /in-sult/ an insulting remark or action.

insuperable adjective impossible to overcome.

insupportable adjective **1** unable to be justified. **2** unbearable.

insurance noun **1** an arrangement by which you make regular payments to a company who pay an agreed amount if something is lost or damaged or someone is hurt or killed. **2** money paid by or to an insurance company. **3** a thing that provides protection in case anything bad happens.

THESAURUS

instruct verb **1** *the union instructed them to strike:* order, direct, command, tell, mandate. **2** *nobody instructed him in how to operate it:* teach, coach, train, educate, tutor, guide, school, show.

instruction noun **1** *obey my instructions:* order, command, directive, direction, decree, injunction, mandate, commandment. **2** *read the instructions:* directions, handbook, manual, guide, advice, guidance. **3** *he gave instruction in self defence:* tuition, teaching, coaching, schooling, lessons, classes, lectures, training, drill, guidance.

instructor noun trainer, coach, teacher, tutor, adviser, counsellor, guide.

instrument noun **1** *a wound made with a sharp instrument:* implement, tool, utensil, device, apparatus, gadget. **2** *cockpit instruments:* gauge, meter, indicator, dial, display. **3** *an instrument of learning:* agent, agency, cause, channel, medium, means, vehicle.

instrumental adjective
□ **be instrumental in** play a part in, contribute to, be a factor in, have a hand

in, promote, advance, further.

insufficient adjective inadequate, deficient, poor, scant, scanty, not enough, too little, too few.

insulate verb **1** *pipes must be insulated:* wrap, sheathe, cover, encase, enclose, lag, soundproof. **2** *they were insulated from the impact of the war:* protect, save, shield, shelter, screen, cushion, cocoon.

insult verb abuse, be rude to, call someone names, slight, disparage, discredit, malign, defame, denigrate, offend, hurt, humiliate; informal bad-mouth, dis; Brit. informal slag off.
OPPOSITES compliment.
● noun jibe, affront, slight, slur, barb, indignity, abuse, aspersions; informal dig, put-down.

insulting adjective abusive, rude, offensive, disparaging, belittling, derogatory, deprecating, disrespectful, uncomplimentary; informal bitchy, catty.

insurance noun indemnity, assurance, protection, security, cover, safeguard, warranty.

insure verb (insures, insuring, insured) **1** pay money in order to receive financial compensation if something is lost or damaged or someone is hurt or killed. **2** (insure against) provide protection in case anything bad happens. **3** = ENSURE.

insurgent noun a rebel or revolutionary. • adjective fighting against a system or authority.
■ insurgency noun.

insurmountable adjective too great to be overcome.

insurrection noun a violent uprising against authority.

intact adjective not damaged.

intaglio /in-ta-li-oh/ noun (plural intaglios) an engraved design.

intake noun **1** an amount or quantity of something that is taken in. **2** a set of people entering a school or college at a particular time.

intangible adjective **1** not solid or real. **2** vague and abstract. • noun an intangible thing.
■ intangibly adverb.

integer /in-ti-jer/ noun a whole number.

integral /in-ti-gruhl, in-teg-ruhl/ adjective **1** necessary to make a whole complete; fundamental. **2** included as part of a whole.

integrate verb (integrates, integrating, integrated) **1** combine with something to form a whole. **2** make someone accepted within a social group.
■ integration noun.

integrity noun **1** the quality of being honest, fair, and good. **2** the state of being whole or unified.

intellect noun the power of using your mind to think logically and understand things.

intellectual adjective **1** relating or appealing to the intellect. **2** having a highly developed intellect. • noun a person with a highly developed intellect.
■ intellectually adverb.

intellectualize or **intellectualise** verb (intellectualizes, intellectualizing, intellectualized) talk or write in an intellectual way.

intelligence noun **1** the ability to gain and apply knowledge and skills. **2** the secret gathering of information about an enemy or opponent. **3** information of this sort.

intelligent adjective good at learning, understanding, and thinking.
■ intelligently adverb.

intelligentsia /in-tel-li-jent-si-uh/ noun intellectuals or highly educated people.

intelligible adjective able to be understood.
■ intelligibly adverb.

THESAURUS

insure verb provide insurance for, indemnify, cover, assure, protect, underwrite, warrant.

intact adjective whole, entire, complete, unbroken, undamaged, unscathed, unblemished, unmarked, in one piece.
OPPOSITES damaged.

integral adjective **1** *an integral part of human behaviour:* essential, fundamental, component, basic, intrinsic, inherent, vital, necessary. **2** *the dryer has an integral heat sensor:* built-in, inbuilt, integrated, inboard, fitted. **3** *an integral approach to learning:* unified, integrated, comprehensive, holistic, joined-up, all-embracing.
OPPOSITES peripheral, supplementary, fragmented.

integrate verb combine, amalgamate, merge, unite, fuse, blend, consolidate, meld, mix, incorporate, assimilate, homogenize, desegregate.
OPPOSITES separate.

integrity noun **1** *I never doubted his integrity:* honesty, probity, rectitude, honour, sincerity, truthfulness, trustworthiness. **2** *the integrity of the federation:* unity, coherence, cohesion, solidity. **3** *the structural integrity of the aircraft:* soundness, strength, sturdiness, solidity, durability, stability, rigidity.
OPPOSITES dishonesty, division, fragility.

intellect noun mind, brain(s), intelligence, reason, judgement, grey matter, brain cells.

intellectual adjective **1** *his intellectual capacity:* mental, rational, conceptual, theoretical, analytical, logical. **2** *an intellectual man:* learned, cerebral, academic, erudite, bookish, highbrow, scholarly.
OPPOSITES physical, stupid.

intelligence noun **1** *a man of great intelligence:* cleverness, intellect, brainpower, judgement, reasoning, acumen, wit, insight, perception. **2** *intelligence from our agents:* information, facts, details, particulars, data, knowledge; informal info.

intelligent adjective **1** *an intelligent woman:* clever, bright, quick-witted, smart, astute, insightful, perceptive; informal brainy. **2** *intelligent machines:* self-regulating, capable of learning, smart.
OPPOSITES unintelligent, dumb.

intelligible adjective comprehensible, understandable, accessible, digestible, user-friendly, clear, coherent, plain, unambiguous.

intemperate adjective lacking self-control.
■ **intemperance** noun.

intend verb **1** have something as your aim or plan. **2** plan that something should be, do, or mean something. **3** (**intend something for** or **to do**) design or plan something for a particular purpose.

intense adjective (**intenser, intensest**) **1** of great force or strength. **2** very earnest or serious.
■ **intensely** adverb **intensity** noun (plural **intensities**).

intensify verb (**intensifies, intensifying, intensified**) make or become more intense.

intensive adjective **1** involving a lot of effort over a short time. **2** (of agriculture) aiming to produce the highest possible yields.
□ **intensive care** special medical treatment given to a dangerously ill patient.
■ **intensively** adverb.

intent noun intention or purpose. • adjective **1** (**intent on**) determined to do. **2** (**intent on**) giving all your attention to. **3** showing great interest and attention.
□ **to all intents and purposes** in all important respects.
■ **intently** adverb.

intention noun **1** an aim or plan. **2** the fact of intending something. **3** (**intentions**) a man's plans about getting married.

intentional adjective deliberate.
■ **intentionally** adverb.

inter /in-ter/ verb (**inters, interring, interred**) place a dead body in a grave or tomb.

interact verb (of two people or things) do things which have an effect on each other.

■ **interaction** noun.

interactive adjective **1** influencing each other. **2** (of a computer or other electronic device) allowing a two-way flow of information between it and a user.

interbreed verb (**interbreeds, interbreeding, interbred**) breed with an animal of a different species.

intercede verb intervene on behalf of someone else.

intercept verb stop someone or something and prevent them from continuing to a destination.
■ **interceptor** noun **interception** noun.

intercession noun **1** the action of interceding. **2** the saying of a prayer on behalf of another person.

interchange verb /in-ter-chaynj/ (**interchanges, interchanging, interchanged**) **1** (of two people) exchange things with each other. **2** put each of two things in the place of the other. • noun /in-ter-chaynj/ **1** the action of interchanging things. **2** an exchange of words. **3** a road junction built on several levels.
■ **interchangeable** adjective **interchangeably** adverb.

intercity adjective existing or travelling between cities.

intercom noun a system of communication by telephone or radio inside a building or group of buildings.

interconnect verb (of two things) connect with each other.

intercontinental adjective relating to or travelling between continents.

THESAURUS

intend verb plan, mean, have in mind, aim, propose, hope, expect, envisage.

intense adjective **1** *intense heat:* extreme, great, acute, fierce, severe, high, exceptional, extraordinary, harsh, strong, powerful; informal serious. **2** *a very intense young man:* passionate, impassioned, zealous, vehement, earnest, eager, committed.
OPPOSITES mild, apathetic.

intensify verb escalate, increase, step up, raise, strengthen, reinforce, pick up, build up, heighten, deepen, extend, expand, amplify, magnify, aggravate, exacerbate, worsen, inflame, compound.
OPPOSITES abate.

intensity noun **1** *the intensity of the sun:* strength, power, force, severity, ferocity, fierceness, harshness. **2** *his eyes had a glowing intensity:* passion, ardour, fervour, vehemence, fire, emotion, eagerness.

intensive adjective thorough, thoroughgoing, in-depth, rigorous, exhaustive, vigorous, detailed, minute, meticulous, painstaking, methodical, extensive.
OPPOSITES cursory.

intent noun *he tried to divine his father's intent:* aim, intention, purpose, objective, goal.
• adjective **1** *he was intent on proving his point:* bent, set, determined, insistent, resolved, hell-bent, keen, committed to, determined to. **2** *an intent expression:* attentive, absorbed, engrossed, fascinated, enthralled, rapt, focused, preoccupied.
OPPOSITES distracted.

intention noun aim, purpose, intent, objective, goal.

intentional adjective deliberate, done on purpose, wilful, calculated, conscious, intended, planned, meant, knowing.

inter verb bury, lay to rest, consign to the grave, entomb.
OPPOSITES exhume.

intercept verb stop, head off, cut off, catch, seize, block, interrupt.

intercourse noun 1 communication or dealings between people. 2 sexual intercourse.

intercut verb (**intercuts, intercutting, intercut**) alternate scenes with contrasting scenes in a film.

interdependent adjective (of two or more people or things) dependent on each other.

interdisciplinary adjective relating to more than one branch of knowledge.

interest noun 1 the state of wanting to know about something or someone. 2 the quality of making someone curious or holding their attention. 3 a subject about which you are concerned or enthusiastic. 4 money that is paid for the use of money lent. 5 a person's advantage or benefit. 6 a share, right, or stake in property or a financial undertaking. • verb 1 make someone curious or attentive.
2 (**interested**) not impartial.
■ **interesting** adjective **interestingly** adverb.

interface noun 1 a point where two things meet and interact. 2 a device or program enabling a user to communicate with a computer, or for connecting two items of hardware or software. • verb (**interfaces, interfacing, interfaced**) (**interface with**)

connect with another computer by an interface.

interfere verb (**interferes, interfering, interfered**) 1 (**interfere with**) prevent something from continuing or being carried out properly. 2 (**interfere with**) handle or adjust something without permission. 3 become involved in something without being asked.
4 (**interfere with**) Brit. sexually molest someone.

interference noun 1 the action of interfering. 2 disturbance to radio signals caused by unwanted signals from other sources.

interferon /in-ter-**feer**-on/ noun a protein released by animal cells which prevents a virus from reproducing itself.

intergalactic adjective relating to or situated between galaxies.

interim noun (**the interim**) the time between two events. • adjective lasting for a short time, until a replacement is found.

interior adjective 1 situated within or inside; inner. 2 remote from the coast or frontier; inland. • noun 1 the interior part. 2 the internal affairs of a country.

interject verb say something suddenly as an interruption.

i

---

intercourse noun 1 *social intercourse:* dealings, relations, relationships, contact, interchange, communication. 2 *she did not consent to intercourse:* sexual intercourse, sex, sexual relations, mating, copulation; technical coitus; formal fornication.

interdict noun prohibition, ban, bar, veto, embargo, moratorium, injunction.
OPPOSITES permission.

interest noun 1 *we listened with interest:* attentiveness, attention, regard, notice, curiosity, enjoyment, delight. 2 *this will be of interest:* concern, consequence, importance, import, significance, note, relevance, value. 3 *her interests include reading:* hobby, pastime, leisure pursuit, amusement, recreation, diversion, passion. 4 *a financial interest in the firm:* stake, share, claim, investment, involvement, concern.
OPPOSITES boredom.
• verb *a topic that interests you:* appeal to, be of interest to, attract, intrigue, amuse, divert, entertain, arouse someone's curiosity, whet someone's appetite; informal tickle someone's fancy.
OPPOSITES put off.

interested adjective 1 *an interested crowd:* attentive, fascinated, riveted, gripped, captivated, agog, intrigued, curious, keen, eager. 2 *the government consulted with interested bodies:* concerned, involved, affected.

interesting adjective absorbing, engrossing, fascinating, riveting, gripping, compelling, captivating, engaging, enthralling, appealing, amusing, entertaining, stimulating, diverting, intriguing.

interfere verb *she tried not to interfere:* butt in, barge in, intrude, meddle, tamper, encroach; informal poke your nose in, stick your oar in.
□ **interfere with impede**, obstruct, stand in the way of, hinder, inhibit, restrict, constrain, hamper, handicap, disturb, disrupt, influence, affect, confuse.

interference noun 1 *they resent state interference:* intrusion, intervention, involvement, meddling, prying. 2 *radio interference:* disruption, disturbance, static, noise.

interior adjective 1 *the house has interior panelling:* inside, inner, internal. 2 *the interior deserts of the US:* inland, upcountry, inner, central. 3 *the country's interior affairs:* internal, home, domestic, national, state, civil, local. 4 *an interior monologue:* inner, mental, spiritual, psychological, private, personal, secret.
OPPOSITES exterior, border, coastal, foreign.
• noun 1 *the interior of the castle:* inside, depths, recesses, bowels, belly, heart. 2 *the country's interior:* centre, heartland.
OPPOSITES exterior, borders, coast.

interjection noun an exclamation (e.g. *ah!*).

interlace verb (**interlaces, interlacing, interlaced**) weave together.

interleave verb **1** insert between the pages of a book. **2** place between the layers of something else.

interlock verb (of two parts, fibres, etc.) engage with each other by overlapping or fitting together.

interlocutor /in-ter-**lok**-yuu-ter/ noun formal a person who takes part in a conversation.

interloper noun a person who is in a place or situation where they are not wanted or do not belong.

interlude noun **1** a period of time that contrasts with what goes before and after. **2** a pause between the acts of a play. **3** a piece of music played between other pieces.

intermarry verb (**intermarries, intermarrying, intermarried**) (of people of different races or religions) marry each other.
■ intermarriage noun.

intermediary noun (plural **intermediaries**) a person who tries to settle a dispute between other people.

intermediate adjective **1** coming between two things in time, place, character, etc. **2** having more than basic knowledge or skills but not yet advanced. •noun an intermediate person or thing.

interment /in-**ter**-muhnt/ noun the burial of a dead body.

intermezzo /in-ter-**met**-soh/ noun (plural **intermezzi** /in-ter-**met**-si/ or **intermezzos**) a short piece of music connecting parts of an opera or other work.

interminable adjective lasting a very long time and therefore boring.
■ interminably adverb.

intermingle verb (**intermingles, intermingling, intermingled**) mix or mingle together.

intermission noun **1** a pause or break. **2** an interval between parts of a play or film.

intermittent adjective stopping and starting at irregular intervals.
■ intermittently adverb.

intern verb /in-**tern**/ confine someone as a prisoner. •noun /**in**-tern/ N. Amer. **1** a recent medical graduate receiving supervised training in a hospital. **2** a student or trainee doing a job to gain work experience.
■ internment noun.

internal adjective **1** relating to or situated on the inside. **2** inside the body. **3** relating to affairs and activities within a country. **4** existing or used within an organization. **5** within the mind.
□ internal-combustion engine an engine in which power is generated by the expansion of hot gases from the burning of fuel with air inside the engine.
■ internally adverb.

internalize or **internalise** verb (**internalizes, internalizing, internalized**) make a feeling or belief part of the way you think.

international adjective **1** existing or happening between nations. **2** agreed on or used by all or many nations. •noun Brit. a game or contest between teams representing different countries.
■ internationally adverb.

internationalism noun belief in the value of cooperation between nations.

internationalize or **internationalise** verb (**internationalizes, internationalizing, internationalized**) make something international.

internecine /in-ter-**nee**-syn/ adjective (of fighting) taking place between members of the same country or group.

Internet noun a very large international computer network.

interpersonal adjective having to do with relationships or communication between people.

interplanetary adjective situated or travelling between planets.

interplay noun the way in which things interact.

interpolate /in-ter-**puh**-layt/ verb (**interpolates, interpolating, interpolated**) **1** add a remark to a conversation. **2** add something to a piece of writing.
■ interpolation noun.

interpose verb (**interposes, interposing,**

THESAURUS

intermediary noun mediator, go-between, negotiator, arbitrator, peacemaker, middleman, broker.

intermediate adjective halfway, midway, in-between, middle, mid, intervening, transitional.

intermittent adjective sporadic, irregular, fitful, spasmodic, discontinuous, isolated, random, patchy, scattered, occasional, periodic.

OPPOSITES continuous.

internal adjective **1** *an internal courtyard:* inner, interior, inside, central. **2** *the state's internal affairs:* domestic, home, interior, civil, local, national, state.
OPPOSITES external, foreign.

international adjective global, worldwide, world, intercontinental, universal, cosmopolitan, multiracial, multinational.
OPPOSITES national, local.

interposed) **1** place something between two other things. **2** say something as an interruption.

interpret verb (**interprets, interpreting, interpreted**) **1** explain the meaning of. **2** translate aloud the words of a person speaking a different language. **3** understand something as having a particular meaning.
■ **interpretation** noun **interpreter** noun.

interracial adjective existing between or involving different races.

interregnum /in-ter-**reg**-nuhm/ noun (plural **interregnums**) a period between regimes when normal government is suspended.

interrelate verb (**interrelates, interrelating, interrelated**) (of two people or things) relate or connect to one other.
■ **interrelation** noun.

interrogate verb (**interrogates, interrogating, interrogated**) ask someone a lot of questions, often in an aggressive way.
■ **interrogation** noun **interrogator** noun.

interrogative /in-ter-**rog**-uh-tiv/ adjective in the form of or used in a question. • noun a word used in questions, e.g. *how* or *what*.

interrupt verb **1** stop the continuous progress of. **2** stop a person who is speaking by saying or doing something. **3** break the continuity of a line, surface, or view.
■ **interruption** noun.

☑ double *r* in the middle: inte*rr*upt.

intersect verb **1** divide something by passing or lying across it. **2** (of lines, roads, etc.) cross or cut each other.

intersection noun **1** a point or line where lines or surfaces intersect. **2** a point where roads intersect.

intersperse verb (**intersperses, interspersing, interspersed**) place or scatter among or between other things.

interstate adjective existing or carried on between states.

interstellar adjective occurring or situated between stars.

interstice /in-ter-**stiss**/ noun a small crack or space in something.

intertwine verb (**intertwines, intertwining, intertwined**) twist or twine together.

interval noun **1** a period of time between two events. **2** a pause or break. **3** Brit. a pause between parts of a play, concert, etc. **4** the difference in pitch between two sounds.

intervene verb (**intervenes, intervening, intervened**) **1** become involved in a situation in order to improve or control it. **2** happen in the time or space between other things.
■ **intervention** noun.

interview noun **1** a meeting at which a journalist asks someone questions about their work or their opinions. **2** a formal meeting at which someone is asked questions to judge whether they are suitable for a job, college place, etc. • verb ask someone questions in an interview.
■ **interviewee** noun **interviewer** noun.

interweave verb (**interweaves, interweaving, interwove**; past participle **interwoven**) weave two or more fibres or strands together.

i

interpret verb **1** *the rabbis interpret the Jewish law:* explain, elucidate, expound, clarify. **2** *the remark was interpreted as an invitation:* understand, construe, take (to mean), see, regard. **3** *the symbols are difficult to interpret:* decipher, decode, translate, understand.

interpretation noun **1** *the interpretation of the Bible's teachings:* explanation, elucidation, exposition, clarification, analysis. **2** *she did not care what interpretation he put on her haste:* meaning, understanding, explanation, inference. **3** *his interpretation of Mozart:* rendition, execution, presentation, performance, reading, playing, singing.

interrupt verb **1** *she opened her mouth to interrupt:* cut in (on), break in (on), barge in (on), intrude, intervene; informal butt in (on), chime in (on); Brit. informal chip in (on). **2** *the band had to interrupt their tour:* suspend, adjourn, break off, stop, halt; informal put on ice.

interruption noun **1** *he was not pleased at her interruption:* cutting in, barging in, interference, intervention, intrusion; informal butting in. **2** *an interruption of the power supply:* suspension, breaking off, cutting.

interval noun intermission, interlude, break, recess, time out.

intervene verb intercede, involve yourself, get involved, step in, interfere, intrude.

interview noun *all applicants will be called for an interview:* meeting, discussion, interrogation, cross-examination, debriefing, audience, talk, chat; informal grilling.
• verb *we interviewed seventy subjects for the survey:* talk to, question, quiz, interrogate, cross-examine, debrief, poll, canvass, sound out; informal grill, pump.

interviewer noun questioner, interrogator, examiner, assessor, journalist, reporter, inquisitor.

i

intestate /in-tess-tayt/ adjective (of someone who has died) not having made a will.

intestine or **intestines** noun the long tube leading from the stomach to the anus.
■ **intestinal** adjective.

intimacy noun (plural **intimacies**) 1 close familiarity or friendship. 2 an intimate act or remark.

intimate[1] /in-ti-muht/ adjective 1 familiar. 2 private and personal. 3 (of two people) having a sexual relationship. 4 involving very close connection. 5 (of knowledge) detailed. 6 having a friendly, informal atmosphere. ● noun a very close friend.
■ **intimately** adverb.

intimate[2] /in-ti-mayt/ verb (**intimates**, **intimating**, **intimated**) say or suggest that something is the case.
■ **intimation** noun.

intimidate verb (**intimidates**, **intimidating**, **intimidated**) frighten or threaten someone, especially to force them to do something.
■ **intimidation** noun.

into preposition 1 expressing motion or direction to a point on or within. 2 expressing a change of state or the result of an action. 3 indicating the direction towards which something is turned. 4 indicating an object of interest. 5 expressing division.

intolerable adjective unable to be endured.
■ **intolerably** adverb.

intolerant adjective not willing to accept ideas or ways of behaving that are different from your own.
■ **intolerance** noun.

intonation noun the rise and fall of the voice in speaking.

intone verb (**intones**, **intoning**, **intoned**) say or recite something with your voice hardly rising or falling.

intoxicate verb (**intoxicates**, **intoxicating**, **intoxicated**) 1 (of alcoholic drink or a drug) make someone lose control of themselves. 2 (**be intoxicated**) be excited or exhilarated by something.
■ **intoxication** noun.

intractable adjective 1 hard to solve or deal with. 2 stubborn.

intranet noun a computer network for use within an organization.

intransigent /in-tran-si-juhnt/ adjective refusing to change your views or behaviour.
■ **intransigence** noun.

intransitive adjective (of a verb) not taking a direct object, e.g. *look* in *look at the sky*.

intrauterine /in-truh-yoo-tuh-ryn/ adjective within the womb.

intravenous /in-truh-vee-nuhss/ adjective within or into a vein.

intrepid adjective not afraid of danger or difficulties.
■ **intrepidly** adverb.

intricacy noun (plural **intricacies**) 1 the quality of being intricate. 2 (**intricacies**) details.

intricate adjective very complicated or detailed.
■ **intricately** adverb.

intrigue verb /in-treeg/ (**intrigues**, **intriguing**, **intrigued**) 1 arouse great curiosity in someone. 2 plot something illegal or harmful. ● noun /in-treeg/ 1 the plotting of something illegal or harmful. 2 a secret plan or relationship.
■ **intriguing** adjective **intriguingly** adverb.

intrinsic adjective part of the real and fundamental nature of something.
■ **intrinsically** adverb.

introduce verb (**introduces**, **introducing**,

THESAURUS

intimacy noun closeness, togetherness, rapport, attachment, familiarity, friendliness, affection, warmth.
OPPOSITES formality.

intimate[1] adjective 1 *an intimate friend:* close, bosom, dear, cherished, fast, firm. 2 *an intimate atmosphere:* friendly, warm, welcoming, hospitable, relaxed, informal, cosy, comfortable. 3 *intimate thoughts:* personal, private, confidential, secret, inward. 4 *an intimate knowledge:* detailed, thorough, exhaustive, deep, in-depth, profound.
OPPOSITES distant, formal, cold, public, sketchy.

intimate[2] verb 1 *he intimated his decision:* announce, state, proclaim, make known, make public, disclose, reveal, divulge. 2 *her feelings were subtly intimated:* imply,

suggest, hint at, indicate.

intimidate verb frighten, menace, scare, terrorize, threaten, browbeat, bully, harass, hound; informal lean on.

intricate adjective complex, complicated, convoluted, tangled, elaborate, ornate, detailed.
OPPOSITES simple.

intrigue verb *her answer intrigued him:* interest, fascinate, arouse someone's curiosity, attract, engage.
● noun *the cabinet was a nest of intrigue:* plotting, conniving, scheming, machination, double-dealing, subterfuge.

intriguing adjective interesting, fascinating, absorbing, engaging.

introduce verb 1 *he has introduced a new system:* institute, initiate, launch, inaugurate, establish, found, bring in, set

introduced) **1** bring something into use or operation for the first time. **2** present someone by name. **3** (**introduce something to**) bring a subject to someone's attention for the first time. **4** insert or bring something into. **5** happen at the start of. **6** provide an opening announcement for.

introduction noun **1** the action of introducing or being introduced. **2** a thing which introduces another, such as a section at the beginning of a book. **3** a thing newly brought in. **4** a book or course intended to introduce a newcomer to a subject of study. **5** a person's first experience of a subject or activity.

introductory adjective forming an introduction; basic.

introspection noun concentration on your own thoughts or feelings.
  ■ **introspective** adjective.

introvert noun a shy, quiet person who is focused on their own thoughts and feelings. • adjective (also **introverted**) characteristic of an introvert.

intrude verb (**intrudes, intruding, intruded**) come into a place or situation where you are unwelcome or uninvited.

intruder noun **1** a person who intrudes. **2** a person who goes into a building or an area illegally.

intrusion noun **1** the action of intruding. **2** a thing that has intruded.

intrusive adjective having a disturbing and unwelcome effect.

intuit /in-**tyoo**-it/ verb understand or work something out by intuition.

intuition noun the ability to understand or know something without conscious reasoning.

intuitive adjective able to understand or know something without conscious reasoning.
  ■ **intuitively** adverb.

Inuit /**in**-yuu-it, **in**-uu-it/ noun (plural **Inuit** or **Inuits**) a member of a people of northern Canada and parts of Greenland and Alaska; an Eskimo.

> **!** **Inuit** is the official term in Canada, and many of the peoples traditionally called **Eskimos** prefer it.

inundate verb (**inundates, inundating, inundated**) **1** give or send someone so many things that they cannot deal with them all. **2** flood a place.
  ■ **inundation** noun.

inure /i-**nyoor**/ verb (**be inured to**) make someone used to something unpleasant.

invade verb (**invades, invading, invaded**) **1** enter a country so as to conquer or occupy it. **2** enter a place in large numbers. **3** intrude on. **4** (of a parasite or disease) spread into.
  ■ **invader** noun.

invalid[1] /in-**vuh**-lid/ noun a person suffering from an illness or injury. • verb (**be invalided**) be removed from active military service because of injury or illness.

THESAURUS

in motion, start, begin, get going. **2** *she introduced Lindsey to the young man:* present, make known, acquaint with. **3** *introducing nitrogen into canned beer:* insert, inject, put, force, shoot, feed. **4** *she introduced a note of seriousness:* instil, infuse, inject, add.
OPPOSITES end, remove.

introduction noun **1** *the introduction of democratic reforms:* institution, establishment, initiation, launch, inauguration, foundation. **2** *an introduction to the king:* presentation, meeting, audience. **3** *the introduction to the book:* foreword, preface, preamble, prologue, prelude; informal intro.
OPPOSITES ending, epilogue.

introductory adjective **1** *the introductory chapter:* opening, initial, starting, first, preliminary. **2** *an introductory course:* elementary, basic, rudimentary, entry-level.
OPPOSITES final, advanced.

intrude verb encroach, impinge, trespass, infringe, invade, violate, disturb, disrupt.

intruder noun trespasser, interloper,

invader, infiltrator, burglar, housebreaker; informal gatecrasher.

intuition noun **1** *he works by intuition:* instinct, feeling, insight, sixth sense. **2** *this confirms an intuition I had:* hunch, feeling in your bones, inkling, sneaking suspicion, premonition; informal gut feeling.

intuitive adjective instinctive, innate, inborn, inherent, natural, unconscious, subconscious; informal gut.

invade verb **1** *the island was invaded:* occupy, conquer, capture, seize, take (over), annex, overrun, storm. **2** *someone had invaded our privacy:* intrude on, violate, encroach on, infringe on, trespass on, disturb, disrupt.
OPPOSITES leave, liberate.

invader noun attacker, raider, marauder, occupier, conqueror, intruder, trespasser.

invalid[1] adjective *her invalid husband:* ill, sick, ailing, infirm, incapacitated, bedridden, frail, sickly, poorly.
OPPOSITES healthy.
• verb *an officer invalided by a chest wound:* disable, incapacitate, hospitalize, put out of action, lay up.

invalid² /in-**val**-id/ adjective **1** not legally or officially recognized. **2** not correct because based on a mistake.

invalidate verb (**invalidates, invalidating, invalidated**) make something invalid.

invalidity noun **1** Brit. the condition of being an invalid. **2** the fact of not being valid.

invaluable adjective very useful.

invariable adjective **1** never changing. **2** Maths (of a quantity) constant.

invariably adverb always.

invasion noun **1** an act of invading a country. **2** the arrival of a large number of unwelcome people or things.

invasive adjective **1** tending to invade or intrude. **2** (of medical procedures) involving the introduction of instruments or other objects into the body.

invective noun strongly abusive or critical language.

inveigh /in-**vay**/ verb (**inveigh against**) speak or write about someone or something with great hostility.

inveigle /in-**vay**-g'l, in-**vee**-g'l/ verb (**inveigles, inveigling, inveigled**) (**inveigle someone into**) cleverly persuade someone to do something.

invent verb **1** create or design a new device or process. **2** make up a false story, name, etc.
■ **inventor** noun.

invention noun **1** the action of inventing.

2 a thing that has been invented. **3** a false story. **4** creative ability.

inventive adjective having or showing creativity or original thought.
■ **inventively** adverb.

inventory /in-vuhn-tuh-ri/ noun (plural **inventories**) **1** a complete list of items. **2** a quantity of goods in stock.

inverse adjective opposite in position, direction, order, or effect. • noun **1** a thing that is the opposite or reverse of another. **2** Maths a reciprocal quantity.
■ **inversion** noun.

invert verb put something upside down or in the opposite position, order, or arrangement.
□ **inverted comma** a quotation mark.

invertebrate /in-ver-ti-bruht/ noun an animal that has no backbone.

invest verb **1** put money into financial schemes, shares, or property in the hope of making a profit. **2** put time or energy into something in the hope of worthwhile results. **3** (**invest in**) buy something expensive. **4** (**invest something with**) give something a particular quality. **5** give someone a rank, honour, official title, etc. in a special ceremony.
■ **investor** noun.

investigate verb **1** carry out a systematic inquiry so as to establish the truth of

THESAURUS

invalid² adjective **1** *the law was invalid:* void, null and void, not binding, illegitimate, inapplicable. **2** *the whole theory is invalid:* false, fallacious, spurious, unsound, wrong, untenable.
OPPOSITES binding, in force, true.

invaluable adjective indispensable, irreplaceable, all-important, crucial, vital, worth its weight in gold.
OPPOSITES dispensable.

invariably adverb always, at all times, without fail, without exception, consistently, habitually, unfailingly.
OPPOSITES sometimes, never.

invasion noun **1** *the invasion of the islands:* occupation, conquering, capture, seizure, annexation, takeover. **2** *an invasion of my privacy:* violation, infringement, interruption, encroachment, disturbance, disruption, breach.
OPPOSITES withdrawal, liberation.

invent verb **1** *he invented television:* originate, create, design, devise, contrive, develop. **2** *they invented the story:* make up, fabricate, concoct, hatch, dream up; informal cook up.

invention noun **1** *the invention of the telescope:* origination, creation, development, design, discovery. **2** *medieval*

inventions: innovation, creation, contraption, contrivance, device, gadget. **3** *a journalistic invention:* fabrication, concoction, (piece of) fiction, story, tale, lie, untruth, falsehood, fib.

inventive adjective **1** *the most inventive composer of his time:* creative, original, innovative, imaginative, resourceful. **2** *a fresh, inventive comedy:* original, innovative, unusual, fresh, novel, new, groundbreaking, unorthodox, unconventional.
OPPOSITES unimaginative, hackneyed.

inventor noun originator, creator, designer, deviser, developer, author, architect, father.

inventory noun list, listing, catalogue, record, register, checklist, log, archive.

invest verb *they invested £18 million:* put in, plough in, put up, advance, expend, spend; informal lay out.
□ **invest in** put money into, sink money into, plough money into, fund, back, finance, underwrite.

investigate verb enquire into, look into, go into, probe, explore, scrutinize, analyse, study, examine; informal check out, suss out.

something. **2** carry out research into a subject.

■ **investigation** noun **investigative** adjective **investigator** noun.

investiture noun **1** the action of formally giving a person a rank, honour, or special title. **2** a ceremony at which this takes place.

investment noun **1** the process of investing in something. **2** a thing worth buying because it may be profitable or useful in the future.

inveterate adjective **1** having done a particular thing so often that you are now unlikely to stop doing it. **2** (of a feeling or habit) firmly established.

invidious adjective unfair and likely to arouse resentment or anger in other people.

invigilate verb (**invigilates, invigilating, invigilated**) Brit. supervise candidates. during an exam.

■ **invigilation** noun **invigilator** noun.

invigorate verb (**invigorates, invigorating, invigorated**) give strength or energy to.

invincible adjective too powerful to be defeated or overcome.

inviolable adjective that must be respected; never to be broken or attacked.

inviolate adjective free from injury or violation.

invisible adjective not able to be seen.

■ **invisibility** noun **invisibly** adverb.

invitation noun **1** a request that someone should join you in going somewhere or doing something. **2** the action of inviting.

3 a situation or action that is likely to provoke a particular outcome or response.

invite verb (**invites, inviting, invited**) **1** ask someone to join you in going somewhere or doing something. **2** ask formally or politely for a response to something. **3** tend to provoke a particular outcome or response. ● noun informal an invitation.

inviting adjective tempting or attractive.

■ **invitingly** adverb.

in vitro /in vee-troh/ adjective & adverb taking place in a test tube, culture dish, or elsewhere outside a living animal or plant.

invocation noun **1** the action of invoking. **2** an appeal to a god or supernatural being.

invoice noun a list of goods or services provided, with a statement of the payment that is due. ● verb (**invoices, invoicing, invoiced**) send an invoice to someone.

invoke verb (**invokes, invoking, invoked**) **1** appeal to someone or something as an authority or in support of an argument. **2** call on a god or supernatural being. **3** call earnestly on.

involuntary adjective **1** done without conscious control. **2** (especially of muscles or nerves) unable to be consciously controlled. **3** done against someone's will.

■ **involuntarily** adverb.

involve verb (**involves, involving, involved**) **1** (of a situation or event) include something as a necessary part or result. **2** make someone experience or take part in something.

■ **involvement** noun.

involved adjective **1** connected with

THESAURUS

investigation noun examination, enquiry, study, inspection, exploration, analysis, research, scrutiny, probe, review.

investigator noun researcher, examiner, analyst, inspector, scrutineer, detective.

investment noun **1** *investment in industry:* investing, speculation, outlay, funding, backing, financing, underwriting, buying shares. **2** *an investment of £305,000:* stake, payment, outlay, venture, proposition.

invisible adjective unseen, imperceptible, undetectable, inconspicuous, unnoticed, unobserved, hidden, out of sight.
OPPOSITES visible.

invitation noun request, call, summons; informal invite.

invite verb **1** *they invited us to lunch:* ask, summon, have someone over/round. **2** *applications are invited for the post:* ask for, request, call for, appeal for, solicit, seek. **3** *airing such views invites trouble:* cause, induce, provoke, ask for, encourage, lead to, bring on yourself, arouse.

inviting adjective tempting, enticing,

alluring, attractive, appealing, appetizing, mouth-watering, intriguing, seductive.
OPPOSITES repellent.

involve verb **1** *the inspection involved a lot of work:* entail, require, necessitate, demand, call for. **2** *I try to involve everyone in key decisions:* include, bring in, consult.
OPPOSITES preclude, exclude.

involved adjective **1** *social workers involved in the case:* associated, connected, concerned. **2** *he had been involved in burglaries:* implicated, caught up, mixed up. **3** *a long and involved story:* complicated, intricate, complex, convoluted. **4** *they were totally involved in their work:* engrossed, absorbed, immersed, caught up, preoccupied, intent.
OPPOSITES unconnected, straightforward.

involvement noun **1** *his involvement in the plot:* participation, collaboration, collusion, complicity, association, connection, entanglement. **2** *emotional involvement:* attachment, friendship, intimacy, commitment.

someone or something on an emotional or personal level. **2** complicated.

invulnerable adjective impossible to harm or damage.

inwards or **inward** adverb **1** towards the inside. **2** towards the mind, spirit, or soul.
■ **inwardly** adverb.

iodine /I-uh-deen, I-uh-dyn/ noun **1** a black, non-metallic chemical element. **2** a solution of iodine in alcohol used as an antiseptic.

ion noun an atom or molecule with a net electric charge through loss or gain of electrons.
■ **ionic** adjective.

ionize or **ionise** verb convert an atom, molecule, or substance into an ion or ions.
■ **ionization** noun.

ionizer noun a device which produces ions, used to improve the air quality in a room.

ionosphere /I-on-uh-sfeer/ noun the layer of the atmosphere above the mesosphere.

iota /I-oh-tuh/ noun a very small amount.

IOU noun a signed document acknowledging a debt.

ipso facto /ip-soh fak-toh/ adverb by that very fact or act.

IQ abbreviation intelligence quotient, a number representing a person's ability to reason, calculated from the results of special tests.

IRA abbreviation Irish Republican Army.

Iranian noun a person from Iran. •adjective relating to Iran.

Iraqi noun (plural **Iraqis**) a person from Iraq. •adjective relating to Iraq.

irascible /i-rass-i-b'l/ adjective irritable; hot-tempered.

irate adjective very angry.

ire /rhymes with fire/ noun literary anger.

iridescent adjective showing bright colours that seem to change when seen from different angles.
■ **iridescence** noun.

☑ just one *r*: iridescent.

iridium noun a hard silvery-white metallic element.

iris noun **1** the round coloured part of the eye, with the pupil in the centre. **2** a plant with sword-shaped leaves and purple, yellow, or white flowers.

Irish noun (also **Irish Gaelic**) the language of Ireland. •adjective relating to Ireland or Irish.
□ **Irish coffee** coffee mixed with a dash of Irish whisky.

irk verb irritate; annoy.

irksome adjective irritating; annoying.

iron noun **1** a strong magnetic silvery-grey metal. **2** a tool made of iron. **3** a hand-held piece of equipment with a heated steel base, used to smooth clothes. **4** a golf club used for hitting the ball at a high angle. **5** (**irons**) handcuffs or chains used as a restraint. •verb **1** smooth clothes with an iron. **2** (**iron something out**) settle a difficulty or problem.
□ **Iron Age** an ancient period when weapons and tools were made of iron. **Iron Curtain** an imaginary barrier separating the communist countries of the former Soviet bloc and western Europe.

ironic /I-ron-ik/ adjective **1** using irony. **2** happening in the opposite way to what is expected.
■ **ironically** adverb.

ironmonger noun Brit. a person who sells tools and other hardware.
■ **ironmongery** noun.

ironworks noun a place where iron is smelted or iron goods are made.

irony noun (plural **ironies**) **1** the use of words that say the opposite of what you really mean in order to be funny or to make a point. **2** aspects of a situation that are opposite to what are expected.

irradiate verb (**irradiates**, **irradiating**, **irradiated**) **1** expose to radiation. **2** shine light on.
■ **irradiation** noun.

irrational adjective not logical or

THESAURUS

inwards adverb inside, towards the inside, into the interior, inward, within.

iron adjective **1** *an iron bar:* ferric, ferrous. **2** *an iron will:* uncompromising, unrelenting, unyielding, unbending, rigid, steely.
OPPOSITES flexible.
□ **iron something out 1** *John had ironed out all the minor snags:* resolve, straighten out, sort out, clear up, put right, solve, rectify; informal fix. **2** *ironing out differences in national systems:* eliminate, eradicate, reconcile, resolve.

ironic adjective **1** *Edward's tone was ironic:* sarcastic, sardonic, dry, caustic, scathing, acerbic, bitter, trenchant, mocking, derisive, scornful; Brit. informal sarky. **2** *it's ironic that I've ended up writing:* paradoxical, funny, strange; informal typical.
OPPOSITES sincere.

irony noun **1** *that note of irony in her voice:* sarcasm, bitterness, mockery, ridicule, derision, scorn; Brit. informal sarkiness. **2** *the irony of the situation:* paradox.
OPPOSITES sincerity.

irrational adjective unreasonable, illogical,

reasonable.
- irrationality noun **irrationally** adverb.

irreconcilable adjective **1** incompatible.
2 (of differences) not able to be settled.

irrecoverable adjective not able to be recovered.

irredeemable adjective not able to be saved, improved, or corrected.

irreducible adjective not able to be reduced or simplified.

irrefutable adjective impossible to deny or disprove.

irregular adjective **1** not regular in shape, arrangement, or occurrence. **2** against a rule, standard, or convention. **3** not belonging to regular army units. **4** Grammar (of a word) having inflections that do not conform to the usual rules.
- irregularity noun (plural **irregularities**).

irrelevant adjective not relevant.
- irrelevance noun **irrelevantly** adverb.

☑ *-ant*, not *-ent*: irrelev*ant*.

irreligious adjective indifferent or hostile to religion.

irremediable /ir-ri-**mee**-di-uh-b'l/ adjective impossible to cure or put right.

irreparable /ir-**rep**-uh-ruh-b'l/ adjective impossible to put right or repair.
- irreparably adverb.

irreplaceable adjective impossible to replace if lost or damaged.

irrepressible adjective not able to be restrained.

irreproachable adjective very good and unable to be criticized.

irresistible adjective too tempting or powerful to be resisted.
- irresistibly adverb.

☑ *-ible*, not *-able*: irresist*ible*.

irresolute adjective uncertain.

irrespective adjective (**irrespective of**) regardless of.

irresponsible adjective not showing a proper sense of responsibility.
- irresponsibility noun **irresponsibly** adverb.

irretrievable adjective not able to be brought back or made right.
- irretrievably adverb.

irreverent adjective disrespectful.
- irreverence noun **irreverently** adverb.

irreversible adjective impossible to be reversed or altered.
- irreversibly adverb.

irrevocable /ir-**rev**-uh-kuh-b'l/ adjective not able to be changed or reversed.
- irrevocably adverb.

irrigate verb (**irrigates, irrigating, irrigated**) supply water to land or crops through channels.
- irrigation noun.

irritable adjective **1** easily annoyed or angered. **2** Medicine unusually sensitive.
- irritability noun **irritably** adverb.

irritant noun **1** a substance that irritates the skin or a part of the body. **2** a source of continual annoyance.

irritate verb (**irritates, irritating, irritated**)
1 make someone annoyed or angry. **2** cause

THESAURUS

groundless, baseless, unfounded, unjustifiable.
OPPOSITES logical.

irregular adjective **1** *an irregular coastline:* uneven, crooked, misshapen, lopsided, asymmetrical, twisted. **2** *irregular surfaces:* rough, bumpy, uneven, pitted, rutted, lumpy, knobbly, gnarled. **3** *an irregular heartbeat:* inconsistent, unsteady, uneven, fitful, patchy, variable, varying, changeable, inconstant, erratic, unstable, spasmodic, intermittent. **4** *irregular financial dealings:* improper, illegitimate, unethical, unprofessional; informal shady, dodgy. **5** *an irregular army:* guerrilla, underground, paramilitary, partisan, mercenary, terrorist.
OPPOSITES regular, above board.
• noun *gun-toting irregulars:* guerrilla, paramilitary, resistance fighter, partisan, mercenary, terrorist.
OPPOSITES regular.

irrelevant adjective beside the point, immaterial, unconnected, unrelated, peripheral, extraneous.

irresistible adjective **1** *her irresistible smile:* captivating, enticing, alluring, enchanting. **2** *an irresistible impulse:* uncontrollable, overwhelming, overpowering, ungovernable.

irresponsible adjective reckless, rash, careless, unwise, imprudent, ill-advised, injudicious, hasty, impetuous, foolhardy, foolish, unreliable, undependable, untrustworthy.
OPPOSITES responsible.

irritable adjective bad-tempered, short-tempered, irascible, tetchy, testy, grumpy, grouchy, crotchety, cantankerous, fractious, curmudgeonly.
OPPOSITES good-humoured.

irritate verb **1** *his tone irritated her:* annoy, bother, vex, make cross, exasperate, infuriate, anger, madden; Brit. rub up the wrong way; informal aggravate, peeve, rile, needle, get (to), bug, hack off; Brit. informal nark, get on someone's wick; N. Amer. informal tee off, tick off, burn up. **2** *some sand irritated my eyes:* inflame, hurt, chafe, scratch, scrape, rub.
OPPOSITES delight, soothe.

soreness, itching, or inflammation.
■ **irritation** noun.

is 3rd person singular present of **BE**.

ISA abbreviation individual savings account.

Islam noun **1** the religion of the Muslims, revealed through Muhammad as the Prophet of Allah. **2** the Muslim world.
■ **Islamic** adjective.

island noun **1** a piece of land surrounded by water. **2** a thing that is isolated, detached, or surrounded.
■ **islander** noun.

isle noun literary an island.

islet /I-lit/ noun a small island.

isn't short form is not.

isobar /I-soh-bar/ noun a line on a map connecting points having the same atmospheric pressure.

isolate verb (**isolates**, **isolating**, **isolated**) **1** place something or someone apart from others and on their own. **2** extract a substance in a pure form.
■ **isolation** noun.

isolated adjective **1** (of a place) remote. **2** (of a person) cut off from other people; lonely. **3** single; exceptional.

isolationism noun a policy of remaining apart from the political affairs of other countries.

isomer /I-suh-mer/ noun Chemistry each of two or more compounds with the same formula but a different arrangement of atoms.

isometric adjective having equal dimensions.

isosceles /I-soss-i-leez/ adjective (of a

triangle) having two sides of equal length.

isotherm /I-soh-therm/ noun a line on a map or diagram connecting points having the same temperature.

isotope /I-suh-tohp/ noun each of two or more forms of the same element that contain equal numbers of protons but different numbers of neutrons in their nuclei.

ISP abbreviation Internet service provider.

Israeli /iz-ray-li/ noun (plural **Israelis**) a person from Israel. ●adjective relating to the modern country of Israel.

Israelite /iz-ruh-lyt/ noun a member of the people of ancient Israel.

issue noun **1** an important topic to be discussed or settled. **2** a problem or difficulty. **3** each of a regular series of publications. **4** the action of supplying something. ●verb (**issues**, **issuing**, **issued**) **1** supply or give out. **2** formally send out or make known. **3** (**issue from**) come, go, or flow out from.
□ **take issue with** challenge someone.

isthmus /isth-muhss, iss-muhss/ noun (plural **isthmuses**) a narrow strip of land with sea on either side, linking two larger areas of land.

IT abbreviation information technology.

it pronoun **1** used to refer to a thing previously mentioned or easily identified. **2** referring to an animal or child whose sex is not specified. **3** used in the normal subject position in statements about time, distance, or weather. **4** the situation or circumstances.

Italian noun **1** a person from Italy. **2** the

THESAURUS

irritation noun annoyance, exasperation, vexation, indignation, anger, displeasure, chagrin.
OPPOSITES delight.

island noun isle, islet, atoll; Brit. holm; (**islands**) archipelago.

isolate verb separate, segregate, detach, cut off, shut away, alienate, distance, cloister, seclude, cordon off, seal off, close off, fence off.
OPPOSITES integrate.

isolated adjective **1** *isolated communities:* remote, out of the way, outlying, off the beaten track, in the back of beyond, godforsaken, inaccessible, cut-off; informal in the middle of nowhere, in the sticks; N. Amer. informal jerkwater, in the tall timbers; Austral./NZ informal beyond the black stump. **2** *he lived a very isolated existence:* solitary, lonely, secluded, reclusive, hermit-like; N. Amer. lonesome. **3** *an isolated incident:* unique, lone, solitary, unusual,

exceptional, untypical, freak; informal one-off.
OPPOSITES accessible, sociable, common.

isolation noun **1** *their feeling of isolation:* solitariness, loneliness, friendlessness. **2** *the isolation of some mental hospitals:* remoteness, inaccessibility.
OPPOSITES contact.

issue noun **1** *the committee discussed the issue:* matter, question, point at issue, affair, case, subject, topic, problem, situation. **2** *the latest issue of our magazine:* edition, number, instalment, copy. **3** *the issue of a special stamp:* issuing, release, publication.
●verb **1** *the minister issued a statement:* release, put out, deliver, publish, broadcast, circulate, distribute. **2** *the captain issued the crew with guns:* supply, provide, furnish, arm, equip, fit out, rig out, kit out; informal fix up.
OPPOSITES withdraw, collect in.
□ **take issue with someone/something** disagree with, challenge, dispute, (call

language of Italy. •**adjective** relating to Italy or Italian.

italic adjective (of a typeface) sloping to the right, used especially for emphasis and for foreign words. •**noun** (also **italics**) an italic typeface or letter.
■ **italicize** (or **italicise**) **verb**.

itch noun 1 an uncomfortable sensation that makes you want to scratch your skin. **2** informal an impatient desire. •**verb 1** experience an itch. **2** informal feel an impatient desire to do something.
■ **itchy** adjective.

it'd short form 1 it had. **2** it would.

item noun an individual article or unit.

itemize or **itemise verb** (**itemizes, itemizing, itemized**) present a quantity as a list of individual items or parts.

itinerant /I-**tin**-uh-ruhnt/ **adjective** travelling from place to place. •**noun** an itinerant person.

itinerary /I-**tin**-uh-ruh-ri/ **noun** (plural **itineraries**) a planned route or journey.

☑ itinerary, not -ery.

it'll short form 1 it shall. **2** it will.

its possessive determiner 1 belonging to or associated with a thing previously

mentioned or easily identified. **2** belonging to or associated with a child or animal whose sex is not specified.

❗ don't confuse the possessive **its** (as in turn the camera on its side) with the form **it's** (short for either **it is** or **it has**, as in it's my fault or it's been a hot day).

it's short form 1 it is. **2** it has.

itself pronoun 1 used to refer to something previously mentioned as the subject of the clause. **2** used to emphasize a particular thing mentioned.

ITV abbreviation Independent Television.

IUD abbreviation intrauterine device.

I've short form I have.

IVF abbreviation in vitro fertilization.

Ivorian /I-**vor**-i-uhn/ **noun** a person from the Ivory Coast, a country in West Africa. •**adjective** relating to the Ivory Coast.

ivory noun (plural **ivories**) **1** the hard creamy-white substance which elephants' tusks are made of. **2** the creamy-white colour of ivory.
▫ **ivory tower** a situation in which someone leads a privileged life and does not have to face normal difficulties.

ivy noun an evergreen climbing plant.

i

THESAURUS

into) question.

itch noun 1 I have an itch on my back: tingling, irritation, itchiness, prickle. **2** (informal) the itch to travel: longing, yearning, craving, ache, hunger, thirst, urge, hankering; informal yen.
•**verb 1** my chilblains really itch: tingle, be irritated, be itchy, sting, hurt, be sore. **2** (informal) he itched to do something to help: long, yearn, ache, burn, crave, hanker for/after, hunger, thirst, be eager, be

desperate; informal be dying, be gagging.

item noun 1 an item of farm equipment: thing, article, object, piece, element, constituent, component, ingredient. **2** the meeting discussed the item: issue, matter, affair, case, subject, topic, question, point. **3** a news item: report, story, article, piece, write-up, bulletin, feature, review.

itinerary noun route, plan, schedule, timetable, programme.

J or **j** noun (plural **Js** or **J's**) the tenth letter of the alphabet. • abbreviation joules.

jab verb (**jabs, jabbing, jabbed**) poke someone with something sharp or pointed. • noun **1** a quick, sharp poke or blow. **2** Brit. informal a vaccination.

jabber verb (**jabbers, jabbering, jabbered**) talk quickly and excitedly but without making much sense.

jack noun **1** a device for lifting a vehicle off the ground so that a wheel can be changed or the underside examined. **2** a playing card ranking next below a queen. **3** a connection between two pieces of electrical equipment. **4** (in bowls) a small white ball at which players aim the bowls. • verb (**jack something up**) **1** raise something with a jack. **2** informal increase something by a large amount.
□ **jack-in-the-box** a toy consisting of a box containing a figure on a spring, which pops up when the lid is opened.

jackal noun a wild dog that often hunts or scavenges in packs.

jackass noun **1** a stupid person. **2** a male ass or donkey.

jackdaw noun a small crow with a grey head.

jacket noun **1** an outer garment reaching to the waist or hips, with sleeves. **2** a covering placed around something for protection or insulation. **3** Brit. the skin of a potato.
□ **jacket potato** Brit. a potato that is baked and served with the skin on.

jackknife noun (plural **jackknives**) a large knife with a folding blade. • verb (**jackknifes, jackknifing, jackknifed**) (of an articulated lorry or truck) bend into a V-shape in an uncontrolled skidding movement.

jackpot noun a large cash prize in a game or lottery.
□ **hit the jackpot** have great or unexpected success.

Jack Russell noun a small breed of terrier with short legs.

Jacobean /jak-uh-bee-uhn/ adjective having to do with the reign of James I of England (1603–1625). • noun a person who lived in the Jacobean period.

Jacobite /jak-uh-byt/ noun a supporter of the deposed James II and his descendants in their claim to the British throne.

jacquard /ja-kard/ noun a fabric with a woven pattern.

jacuzzi /juh-koo-zi/ noun (plural **jacuzzis**) trademark a large, wide bath with jets of water to massage the body.

jade noun a hard bluish-green precious stone.

jaded adjective tired out or lacking enthusiasm after having had too much of something.

jagged /jag-gid/ adjective with rough, sharp points or edges sticking out.

jaguar /jag-yuu-er/ noun a large cat with a spotted coat, found in Central and South America.

jail or Brit. **gaol** noun a place for holding people who are accused or convicted of a

THESAURUS

jab verb & noun poke, prod, dig, nudge, thrust, stab, push.

jacket noun wrapping, wrapper, sleeve, coat, cover, covering, sheath.

jagged adjective spiky, barbed, ragged, rough, uneven, irregular, serrated.
OPPOSITES smooth.

jail noun *he was thrown into jail:* prison, lock-up, detention centre; N. Amer.

penitentiary, jailhouse, correctional facility; informal clink, cooler, the slammer, inside; Brit. informal nick; N. Amer. informal can, pen, slam, pokey.
• verb *she was jailed for killing her husband:* send to prison/jail, put in prison/jail, imprison, incarcerate, lock up, put away, detain; informal send down, put behind bars, put inside; Brit. informal bang up.
OPPOSITES acquit, release.

crime. •verb put someone in jail.
■ **jailer** (or Brit. **gaoler**) noun.

jalopy /juh-**lop**-i/ noun (plural **jalopies**) informal an old car.

jam¹ verb (**jams**, **jamming**, **jammed**)
1 squeeze or pack tightly into a space.
2 push something roughly and forcibly into a position. **3** block something through crowding. **4** make or become unable to function because a part is stuck. **5** (**jam something on**) apply a brake suddenly and with force. **6** interrupt a radio transmission by causing interference. **7** informal improvise with other musicians. •noun **1** an instance of something being jammed. **2** informal a difficult situation. **3** informal an improvised performance by a group of musicians.

jam² noun chiefly Brit. a spread made from fruit and sugar.

Jamaican noun a person from Jamaica.
•adjective relating to Jamaica.

jamb /jam/ noun a side post of a doorway, window, or fireplace.

jamboree noun a large celebration or party.

jammy adjective (**jammier**, **jammiest**)
1 covered or filled with jam. **2** Brit. informal lucky.

jangle verb (**jangles**, **jangling**, **jangled**)
1 make a ringing metallic sound. **2** (of your nerves) be set on edge. •noun a ringing metallic sound.
■ **jangly** adjective.

janitor noun a caretaker of a building.

January noun (plural **Januaries**) the first month of the year.

Japanese noun (plural **Japanese**) **1** a person from Japan. **2** the language of Japan.
•adjective relating to Japan.

jape noun a practical joke.

jar¹ noun a cylindrical container made of glass or pottery.

jar² verb (**jars**, **jarring**, **jarred**) **1** send a painful shock through a part of the body.

2 hit something with an unpleasant vibration or jolt. **3** have an unpleasant or strange effect. •noun an instance of jarring.

jardinière /zhar-din-**yair**/ noun an ornamental pot or stand for displaying plants.

jargon noun words or phrases used by a particular group that are difficult for other people to understand.

jasmine noun a shrub or climbing plant with sweet-smelling flowers.

jasper noun a reddish-brown variety of quartz.

jaundice /**jawn**-diss/ noun **1** a condition in which the skin takes on a yellow colour.
2 bitterness or resentment.
■ **jaundiced** adjective.

jaunt noun a short trip or journey taken for pleasure.

jaunty adjective (**jauntier**, **jauntiest**) lively and self-confident.
■ **jauntily** adverb.

javelin noun a long spear thrown in a competitive sport or as a weapon.

jaw noun each of the upper and lower bony structures forming the framework of the mouth and containing the teeth. •verb informal talk at length.

jawbone noun the lower jaw, or the lower part of the face.

jay noun a noisy bird of the crow family with brightly coloured feathers.

jaywalk verb chiefly N. Amer. walk in or across a road without paying proper attention to the traffic.
■ **jaywalker** noun.

jazz noun a type of music that is mainly instrumental, in which the players often improvise. •verb (**jazz something up**) make something more lively.

jazzy adjective (**jazzier**, **jazziest**) **1** in the style of jazz. **2** bright, colourful, and showy.

jealous adjective **1** envious of someone

j

THESAURUS

jam verb **1** *he jammed a finger in each ear:* stuff, shove, force, ram, thrust, press, push, stick, cram. **2** *hundreds of people jammed into the hall:* crowd, pack, pile, press, squeeze, cram, throng, mob, fill, block, clog, congest. **3** *the rudder had jammed:* stick, become stuck, catch, seize (up).
4 *dust can jam the mechanism:* immobilize, paralyse, disable, clog, block; informal bung up.
•noun *a traffic jam:* tailback, hold-up, queue, congestion, bottleneck; N. Amer. gridlock; informal snarl-up.

jar¹ noun *a jar of honey:* pot, container, crock.

jar² verb **1** *each step jarred my whole body:*

jolt, jerk, shake, vibrate. **2** *her shrill voice jarred on him:* grate, set someone's teeth on edge, irritate, annoy, get on someone's nerves. **3** *the verse jars with the words that follow:* clash, conflict, contrast, be at odds, be incompatible, be at variance, be inconsistent.

jargon noun slang, idiom, cant, argot, patter, gobbledegook; informal lingo, -speak, -ese.

jaws plural noun mouth, maw, muzzle; informal chops.

jealous adjective **1** *jealous of his brother:* envious, covetous, resentful, grudging, green with envy. **2** *a jealous lover:* suspicious, distrustful, possessive,

else's achievements or advantages.
2 resentful of someone who you think is a sexual rival. **3** very protective of your rights or possessions.
■ **jealously** adverb **jealousy** noun.

jeans noun casual trousers made of denim.

jeep noun trademark a sturdy motor vehicle with four-wheel drive.

jeer verb (**jeers, jeering, jeered**) shout rude and mocking remarks at someone. ● noun a rude and mocking remark.

Jehovah /ji-**hoh**-vuh/ noun a form of the Hebrew name of God used in some translations of the Bible.

jejune /ji-**joon**/ adjective **1** naive and simplistic. **2** not interesting.

jejunum /ji-**joo**-nuhm/ noun the part of the small intestine between the duodenum and ileum.

jell verb ⇨ **GEL**².

jelly noun (plural **jellies**) **1** Brit. a dessert consisting of a fruit-flavoured liquid set with gelatin to form a semi-solid mass. **2** a substance with a similar semi-solid consistency.
■ **jellied** adjective.

jellyfish noun (plural **jellyfish** or **jellyfishes**) a sea creature with a soft jelly-like body that has stinging tentacles around the edge.

jemmy noun (plural **jemmies**) a short crowbar.

je ne sais quoi /zhuh nuh say **kwah**/ noun a quality that cannot be easily identified.

jenny noun (plural **jennies**) a female donkey or ass.

jeopardize or **jeopardise** verb (**jeopardizes, jeopardizing, jeopardized**) risk harming or destroying something.

jeopardy noun danger of loss, harm, or failure.

jerboa /jer-**boh**-uh/ noun a desert rodent with very long hind legs.

jerk noun **1** a quick, sharp, sudden movement. **2** informal a stupid person. ● verb move or raise with a jerk.

jerkin noun a sleeveless jacket.

jerky adjective (**jerkier, jerkiest**) moving in sudden stops and starts.
■ **jerkily** adverb.

jerry-built adjective badly or quickly built, using cheap materials.

jerrycan or **jerrican** noun a large flat-sided metal container for liquids.

jersey noun (plural **jerseys**) **1** a knitted garment with long sleeves. **2** a distinctive shirt worn by people who play certain sports. **3** a soft knitted fabric. **4** (**Jersey**) a breed of light brown dairy cattle.

Jerusalem artichoke noun a knobbly root vegetable with white flesh.

jest noun a joke. ● verb speak or behave in a joking way.

jester noun a man who entertained people in a medieval court.

Jesuit /**jez**-yuu-it/ noun a member of the Society of Jesus, a Roman Catholic order.

Jesus or **Jesus Christ** noun the central figure of the Christian religion, considered by Christians to be the son of God.

jet¹ noun **1** a rapid stream of liquid or gas forced out of a small opening. **2** an aircraft powered by jet engines. ● verb (**jets, jetting, jetted**) **1** spurt out in a jet. **2** travel by jet aircraft.
□ **jet engine** an aircraft engine which gives propulsion by sending out a high-speed jet of gas obtained by burning fuel. **jet lag** extreme tiredness felt after a long flight across different time zones. **the jet set** informal wealthy people who frequently travel abroad for pleasure. **jet ski** trademark a small vehicle which skims across the surface of water.

jet² noun **1** a hard black semi-precious mineral. **2** (also **jet black**) a glossy black colour.

THESAURUS

proprietorial, overprotective. **3** *jealous of their rights:* protective, vigilant, watchful, mindful, careful.
OPPOSITES proud, trusting, careless.

jealousy noun envy, resentment, bitterness, the green-eyed monster.

jeer verb *the demonstrators jeered the police:* taunt, mock, scoff at, ridicule, sneer at, deride, insult, abuse, heckle, catcall (at), boo (at), whistle at; Brit. barrack.
OPPOSITES applaud, cheer.
● noun *the jeers of the crowd:* taunt, sneer, insult, shout, jibe, boo, catcall, derision, teasing, scoffing, abuse, scorn, heckling, catcalling; Brit. barracking.
OPPOSITES applause, cheer.

jeopardize verb threaten, endanger, imperil, risk, put in danger/jeopardy, compromise, prejudice.
OPPOSITES safeguard.

jeopardy noun danger, peril, risk.

jerk noun **1** *she gave the reins a jerk:* yank, tug, pull, wrench. **2** *he let the clutch in with a jerk:* jolt, lurch, bump, judder, jump, bounce, shake.
● verb **1** *she jerked her arm free:* yank, tug, pull, wrench, wrest, drag, snatch. **2** *the car jerked along:* jolt, lurch, bump, judder, bounce.

jet noun **1** *a jet of water:* stream, spurt, spray, spout, gush, surge, burst.
2 *carburettor jets:* nozzle, head, spout.

jetsam noun unwanted material thrown overboard from a ship and washed ashore.

jettison verb 1 throw or drop something from an aircraft or ship. 2 abandon or get rid of something.

jetty noun (plural **jetties**) a landing stage or small pier where boats can be moored.

Jew noun a member of the people whose religion is Judaism and who trace their origins to the Hebrew people of ancient Israel.
◻ **Jew's harp** a small musical instrument like a U-shaped harp, held between the teeth and struck with a finger.

jewel noun 1 a precious stone. 2 (**jewels**) pieces of jewellery. 3 a highly valued person or thing.
■ **jewelled** (US spelling **jeweled**) adjective.

jeweller (US spelling **jeweler**) noun a person who makes or sells jewellery.

jewellery (US spelling **jewelry**) noun objects such as necklaces, rings, or bracelets worn on the body for decoration.

Jewish adjective having to do with Jews or Judaism.
■ **Jewishness** noun.

Jewry noun Jews as a group.

Jezebel noun an immoral woman.

jib¹ noun 1 Sailing a triangular sail in front of the mast. 2 the projecting arm of a crane.

jib² verb (**jibs**, **jibbing**, **jibbed**) 1 (**jib at**) be unwilling to do or accept something. 2 (of a horse) stop and refuse to go on.

jibe or **gibe** noun an insulting remark. • verb (**jibes**, **jibing**, **jibed**) make insulting remarks.

jiffy or **jiff** noun informal a moment.

jig noun 1 a lively dance. 2 a device that holds something in position and guides the tools working on it. • verb (**jigs**, **jigging**, **jigged**) move up and down with a quick,

jerky motion.

jiggery-pokery noun informal suspicious behaviour.

jiggle verb (**jiggles**, **jiggling**, **jiggled**) move lightly and quickly from side to side or up and down. • noun a quick, light shake.
■ **jiggly** adjective.

jigsaw noun 1 a picture printed on cardboard or wood and cut into many interlocking shapes that have to be fitted together. 2 a machine saw with a fine blade allowing it to cut curved lines in a sheet of wood, metal, etc.

jihad /ji-**hahd**/ noun (in Islam) a war or struggle against non-Muslims.

jilt verb abruptly break off a relationship with a lover.

jingle noun 1 a light ringing sound. 2 a short easily remembered slogan, verse, or tune. • verb (**jingles**, **jingling**, **jingled**) make a jingle.
■ **jingly** adjective.

jingoism noun too much pride in your country.
■ **jingoistic** adjective.

jinx noun a person or thing that brings bad luck. • verb bring bad luck to.

jitterbug noun a fast dance performed to swing music, popular in the 1940s.

jitters noun informal a feeling of being very nervous.
■ **jittery** adjective.

jive noun a style of lively dance popular in the 1940s and 1950s, performed to swing music or rock and roll. • verb (**jives**, **jiving**, **jived**) dance the jive.

job noun 1 a paid position of regular employment. 2 a task. 3 informal a crime. 4 informal a procedure to improve the appearance of something. • verb (**jobs**,

j

THESAURUS

jettison verb dump, drop, ditch, throw out, get rid of, discard, dispose of, scrap.
OPPOSITES retain.

jewel noun 1 priceless jewels: gem, gemstone, (precious) stone; informal sparkler, rock. 2 the jewel of his collection: showpiece, pride (and joy), cream, crème de la crème, jewel in the crown, prize, pick.

jewellery noun jewels, gems, gemstones, precious stones, regalia, finery, ornaments, trinkets.

jibe noun cruel jibes: snide remark, taunt, sneer, jeer, insult, barb; informal dig, put-down.

jilt verb leave, walk out on, throw over, finish with, break up with, stand up, leave standing at the altar; informal chuck, ditch, dump, drop, run out on, give someone the

push/elbow, give someone the big E.

jingle noun & verb clink, chink, tinkle, jangle, ring.

jinx noun the jinx struck six days later: curse, spell, the evil eye, black magic, voodoo, bad luck; N. Amer. hex.
• verb the family is jinxed: curse, cast a spell on, put the evil eye on; Austral. point the bone at; N. Amer. hex.

job noun 1 my job involves a lot of travelling: position, post, situation, appointment, occupation, profession, trade, career, work, vocation, calling. 2 this job will take three months: task, piece of work, assignment, project, chore, undertaking, venture, operation. 3 it's your job to protect her: responsibility, duty, charge, task, role, function, mission; informal department.

jobbing, jobbed) do casual or occasional work.
□ **job lot** a batch of articles sold or bought at one time. **job-share** (of two part-time employees) share a single full-time job.
■ **jobless** adjective.

jobcentre noun (in the UK) a government office which gives out information about available jobs to unemployed people.

jockey noun (plural **jockeys**) a professional rider in horse races. • verb (**jockeys, jockeying, jockeyed**) struggle to gain or achieve something.

jockstrap noun a support or protection for the male genitals.

jocose /juh-**kohss**/ adjective formal playful or humorous.

jocular /**jok**-yuu-ler/ adjective humorous.
■ **jocularity** noun **jocularly** adverb.

jocund /**jok**-uhnd/ adjective formal cheerful and light-hearted.

jodhpurs /**jod**-perz/ plural noun trousers worn for horse riding that are close-fitting below the knee.

jog verb (**jogs, jogging, jogged**) **1** run at a steady, gentle pace. **2** (**jog along** or **on**) continue in a steady, uneventful way. **3** knock or nudge slightly. • noun **1** a period of jogging. **2** a gentle running pace. **3** a slight knock or nudge.
□ **jog someone's memory** make someone remember something.
■ **jogger** noun.

joggle verb (**joggles, joggling, joggled**) move with repeated small jerks.

joie de vivre /zhwah duh **vee**-vruh/ noun lively and cheerful enjoyment of life.

join verb **1** connect things together, or become connected. **2** come together to form a whole. **3** become a member or employee of. **4** (also **join in**) take part in an activity. **5** (**join up**) become a member of the armed forces. **6** do something or go somewhere with someone else. • noun a place where two or more things are joined.

joiner noun a person who puts together the wooden parts of a building.

joinery noun **1** the wooden parts of a building. **2** the work of a joiner.

joint noun **1** a point at which parts are joined. **2** a structure in a body which joins two bones. **3** the part of a plant stem from which a leaf or branch grows. **4** Brit. a large piece of meat. **5** informal a particular kind of place: *a burger joint.* **6** informal a cannabis cigarette. • adjective **1** shared, held, or made by two or more people. **2** sharing in an achievement or activity. • verb cut the body of an animal into joints.
■ **jointed** adjective **jointly** adverb.

joist noun a length of timber or steel supporting the floor or ceiling of a building.

jojoba /huh-**hoh**-buh/ noun an oil extracted from the seeds of a North American shrub.

joke noun **1** a thing that someone says to cause amusement or laughter. **2** a trick played for fun. **3** informal a person or thing that is ridiculously inadequate. • verb (**jokes, joking, joked**) make jokes.
■ **jokey** (or **joky**) adjective.

joker noun **1** a person who likes making or playing jokes. **2** a playing card with the figure of a jester, used as a wild card.

jollification noun time spent having fun.

THESAURUS

jobless adjective unemployed, out of work, out of a job, unwaged, redundant, laid off; Brit. informal on the dole, resting; Austral./NZ informal on the wallaby track.
OPPOSITES employed.

jog verb **1** *he jogged along the road:* run, trot, lope. **2** *a hand jogged his elbow:* nudge, prod, poke, push, bump, jar.
• noun *he set off at a jog:* run, trot, lope.

join verb **1** *the two parts of the mould are joined with clay:* connect, unite, couple, fix, affix, attach, fasten, stick, glue, fuse, weld, amalgamate, bond, link, merge, secure, make fast, tie, bind. **2** *here the path joins a major road:* meet, touch, reach. **3** *I'm off to join the search party:* help in, participate in, get involved in, contribute to, enlist in, join up, sign up, band together, get together, team up.
OPPOSITES separate, leave.

joint noun *a leaky joint:* join, junction, intersection, link, connection, weld, seam.
• adjective *a joint effort:* common, shared,

communal, collective, mutual, cooperative, collaborative, concerted, combined, united.
OPPOSITES separate.

jointly adverb together, in partnership, in cooperation, cooperatively, in conjunction, in combination, mutually.
OPPOSITES separately.

joke noun **1** *telling jokes:* funny story, jest, witticism, quip, pun; informal gag, wisecrack, crack, funny, one-liner; N. Amer. informal boffola. **2** *playing stupid jokes:* trick, prank, stunt, hoax, jape; informal leg-pull, spoof, wind-up. **3** (informal) *he soon became a joke:* laughing stock, figure of fun, object of ridicule. **4** (informal) *the present system is a joke:* farce, travesty, waste of time; informal shambles; N. Amer. informal shuck.
• verb *she joked with the guests:* tell jokes, jest, banter, quip; informal wisecrack, josh.

joker noun comedian, comedienne, comic, humorist, wit, jester, prankster, practical joker, clown.

jollity noun 1 lively and cheerful activity. 2 the quality of being cheerful.

jolly adjective (jollier, jolliest) 1 happy and cheerful. 2 lively and entertaining. • verb (jollies, jollying, jollied) (jolly someone along) informal encourage someone in a friendly way. • adverb Brit. informal very.

jolt verb 1 push or shake abruptly and roughly. 2 shock someone into taking action. • noun 1 an act of jolting. 2 a shock.

Jordanian noun a person from Jordan. • adjective relating to Jordan.

josh verb informal tease playfully.

joss stick noun a thin stick covered with a substance that produces a sweet smell when you burn it.

jostle verb (jostles, jostling, jostled) 1 push or bump against someone roughly. 2 (jostle for) struggle for.

jot verb (jots, jotting, jotted) write something quickly. • noun a very small amount.

jotter noun Brit. a small notebook.

joule /jool/ noun a unit of work or energy.

journal noun 1 a newspaper or magazine dealing with a particular subject. 2 a diary or daily record.

journalese noun informal a bad writing style thought to be typical of that used in newspapers.

journalism noun the activity or profession of being a journalist.

journalist noun a person who writes for newspapers or magazines or prepares news to be broadcast.
■ journalistic adjective.

journey noun (plural journeys) an act of travelling from one place to another. • verb (journeys, journeying, journeyed) travel.

journeyman noun (plural journeymen) a worker who is reliable but not outstanding.

joust verb (of medieval knights) fight each other with lances while on horseback. • noun a jousting contest.

jovial adjective cheerful and friendly.
■ joviality noun jovially adverb.

jowl noun the lower part of a person's or animal's cheek.
■ jowly adjective.

joy noun 1 great pleasure and happiness. 2 something that brings joy. 3 Brit. informal success or satisfaction.
■ joyless adjective.

joyful adjective feeling or causing joy.
■ joyfully adverb.

joyous adjective full of happiness and joy.
■ joyously adverb.

joyriding noun informal the crime of stealing a vehicle and driving it in a fast and dangerous way.
■ joyride noun joyrider noun.

j

THESAURUS

jolly adjective cheerful, happy, cheery, good-humoured, jovial, merry, sunny, joyful, light-hearted, in high spirits, bubbly, genial; informal chipper, chirpy, perky, bright-eyed and bushy-tailed.
OPPOSITES miserable.

jolt verb 1 the train jolted the passengers to one side: push, thrust, jar, bump, knock, bang, shake, jog. 2 the car jolted along: bump, bounce, jerk, rattle, lurch, shudder, judder. 3 she was jolted out of her reverie: startle, surprise, shock, stun, shake; informal rock, knock sideways.
• noun 1 a series of sickening jolts: bump, bounce, shake, jerk, lurch. 2 he woke up with a jolt: start, jerk, jump. 3 the sight of the dagger gave him a jolt: fright, shock, scare, surprise; informal turn.

jostle verb 1 she was jostled by noisy students: push, shove, elbow, barge. 2 people jostled for the best position: struggle, vie, jockey, scramble, fight.

journal noun 1 a medical journal: periodical, magazine, gazette, review, newsletter, news-sheet, bulletin, newspaper, paper, daily, weekly, monthly, quarterly. 2 he keeps a journal: diary, log, weblog, blog, logbook, chronicle, history, yearbook; N. Amer. daybook.

journalist noun reporter, correspondent, newspaperman, newspaperwoman, newsman, newswoman, columnist; informal news hound, hack, hackette, stringer, journo; N. Amer. informal newsie.

journey noun his journey round the world: trip, expedition, tour, trek, voyage, cruise, ride, drive, crossing, passage, flight, odyssey, pilgrimage.
• verb they journeyed south: travel, go, voyage, sail, cruise, fly, hike, trek, ride, drive, make your way.

jovial adjective cheerful, jolly, happy, cheery, good-humoured, convivial, genial, good-natured, affable, outgoing, smiling, merry, sunny.
OPPOSITES miserable.

joy noun delight, pleasure, jubilation, triumph, exultation, rejoicing, happiness, gladness, elation, euphoria, bliss, ecstasy, rapture.
OPPOSITES misery.

joyful adjective 1 his joyful mood: cheerful, happy, jolly, merry, sunny, joyous, cheery, smiling, mirthful, jubilant, gleeful, jovial. 2 joyful news: pleasing, happy, good, cheering, gladdening, welcome, heart-warming.
OPPOSITES sad.

joystick noun informal **1** the rod used for controlling an aircraft. **2** a lever for controlling the movement of an image on a computer screen.

JP abbreviation Justice of the Peace.

JPEG noun Computing a format for reducing the size of images.

jubilant adjective happy and triumphant.
■ **jubilantly** adverb.

jubilation noun a feeling of great happiness and triumph.

jubilee noun a special anniversary.

Judaism /joo-day-i-z'm/ noun the religion of the Jews, based on the Old Testament and the Talmud.
■ **Judaic** adjective.

Judas noun a person who betrays a friend.

judder verb (**judders, juddering, juddered**) shake rapidly and violently.
■ **juddery** adjective.

judge noun **1** a public official who has the authority to decide cases in a law court. **2** a person who decides the results of a competition. **3** a person who is qualified to give an opinion. ● verb (**judges, judging, judged**) **1** form an opinion about something. **2** give a verdict on a case or person in a law court. **3** decide the results of a competition.

judgement or **judgment** noun **1** the ability to make good decisions or form sensible opinions. **2** an opinion or conclusion. **3** a decision of a law court or judge.
□ Judgement Day the time of the Last Judgement.

judgemental or **judgmental** adjective **1** having to do with the use of judgement.

2 too critical of other people.

judicature noun the organization and putting into practice of justice.

judicial adjective having to do with a law court or judge.
■ **judicially** adverb.

judiciary noun (**the judiciary**) judges as a group.

judicious /joo-di-shuhss/ adjective having or done with good judgement.
■ **judiciously** adverb.

judo noun a kind of unarmed combat performed as a sport.

jug noun a cylindrical container with a handle and a lip, for holding and pouring liquids.
□ jugged hare a dish made with hare that has been cooked slowly in a covered container.

juggernaut noun Brit. a large, heavy lorry.

juggle verb (**juggles, juggling, juggled**) **1** continuously toss and catch a number of objects so as to keep at least one in the air at any time. **2** do several things at the same time. **3** present facts or figures in a way that makes them seem good.
■ **juggler** noun.

jugular or **jugular vein** noun any of several large veins in the neck, carrying blood from the head.

juice noun **1** the liquid present in fruit and vegetables. **2** a drink made from this liquid. **3** (**juices**) fluid produced by the stomach. **4** (**juices**) liquid coming from food during cooking. ● verb (**juices, juicing, juiced**) extract the juice from.

juicy adjective (**juicier, juiciest**) **1** full of juice.

THESAURUS

jubilant adjective overjoyed, exultant, triumphant, joyful, cock-a-hoop, elated, thrilled, gleeful, euphoric, ecstatic; informal over the moon.
OPPOSITES despondent.

jubilee noun anniversary, commemoration, celebration, festival.

judge noun **1** the judge sentenced him to five years: justice, magistrate, recorder, sheriff, His/Her/Your Honour; N. Amer. jurist; Brit. informal beak. **2** a panel of judges will select the winner: adjudicator, referee, umpire, arbiter, assessor, examiner, moderator, scrutineer.
● verb **1** I judged that she was exhausted: conclude, decide, consider, believe, think, deduce, infer, gauge, estimate, guess, surmise, conjecture, regard as, rate as, class as; informal reckon, figure. **2** she was judged innocent: pronounce, decree, rule, find. **3** the competition will be judged by Alan Amey: adjudicate, arbitrate, moderate, referee, umpire. **4** entries were judged by a

panel of experts: assess, appraise, evaluate, examine, review.

judgement noun **1** an error of judgement: sense, discernment, perception, discrimination, understanding, powers of reasoning, reason, logic. **2** his beliefs affect his judgement of Milton: opinion, view, estimate, appraisal, conclusion, diagnosis, assessment, impression, conviction, perception, thinking. **3** a court judgement: verdict, decision, adjudication, ruling, pronouncement, decree, finding, sentence.

judicious adjective wise, sensible, prudent, shrewd, astute, canny, discerning.
OPPOSITES ill-advised.

jug noun pitcher, ewer, crock, jar, urn, carafe, flask, flagon, decanter; N. Amer. creamer.

juice noun liquid, fluid, sap, milk, gum, extract, concentrate, essence.

juicy adjective succulent, tender, moist, ripe.
OPPOSITES dry.

2 informal (of gossip) very interesting.

ju-jitsu /joo jit-soo/ noun a Japanese system of unarmed combat.

jukebox noun a machine that plays a selected musical recording when a coin is inserted.

julep /joo-lep/ noun a sweet drink made from sugar syrup.

July noun (plural **Julys**) the seventh month of the year.

jumble noun **1** an untidy collection of things. **2** Brit. articles collected for a jumble sale. •verb (**jumbles, jumbling, jumbled**) mix things up in a confused way. □ jumble sale Brit. a sale of second-hand items.

jumbo informal noun (plural **jumbos**) **1** a very large person or thing. **2** (also **jumbo jet**) a very large airliner. •adjective very large.

jump verb **1** push yourself off the ground using the muscles in your legs and feet. **2** move over something by jumping. **3** make a sudden involuntary movement in surprise. **4** (**jump at** or **on**) accept something eagerly. **5** (often **jump on**) informal attack someone suddenly. **6** pass abruptly from one subject or state to another. •noun **1** an act of jumping. **2** a large or sudden increase. **3** an obstacle to be jumped by a horse. □ jumped-up informal considering yourself to be more important than you really are. jump jet a jet aircraft that can take off and land without a runway. jump leads Brit. a pair of cables used to recharge a battery in a vehicle by connecting it to the battery of a vehicle whose engine is running. jump the queue move ahead of your proper place in a queue. jump ship (of a sailor) leave a ship without permission. jump-start start a car with jump leads or by a sudden release of the clutch while it is being pushed.

jumper noun **1** Brit. a pullover or sweater.

2 N. Amer. a pinafore dress. **3** a person or animal that jumps.

jumpsuit noun a one-piece garment incorporating trousers and a sleeved top.

jumpy adjective (**jumpier, jumpiest**) informal anxious and uneasy.

junction noun **1** a point where things meet or are joined. **2** a place where roads or railway lines meet.

juncture noun **1** a particular point in time. **2** a place where things join.

June noun the sixth month of the year.

jungle noun **1** an area of land with thick forest and tangled vegetation. **2** a very bewildering or competitive situation.

junior adjective **1** having to do with young or younger people. **2** Brit. having to do with schoolchildren aged 7–11. **3** (after a name) referring to the younger of two with the same name in a family. **4** low or lower in status. •noun **1** a person who is a stated number of years younger than someone else: *he's five years her junior.* **2** Brit. a child at a junior school. **3** a person with low status.

juniper noun an evergreen shrub with sweet-smelling berries.

junk[1] noun informal useless or worthless articles. □ junk food unhealthy food. junk mail unwanted advertising material sent to you in the post.

junk[2] noun a flat-bottomed sailing boat used in China and the East Indies.

junket noun **1** informal a trip or excursion made by government officials and paid for using public funds. **2** a dish of sweetened curds of milk.

junkie or **junky** noun informal a drug addict.

junta noun a group ruling a country after taking power by force.

Jupiter noun the largest planet in the solar system.

j

THESAURUS

jumble noun *the books were in a jumble:* heap, muddle, mess, tangle, confusion, disarray, chaos, hotchpotch; N. Amer. hodgepodge; informal shambles.
•verb *the photographs are all jumbled up:* mix up, muddle up, disorganize, disorder, tangle.

jump verb **1** *the cat jumped off his lap:* leap, spring, bound, hop, skip, caper, dance, prance, frolic, cavort. **2** *he jumped the fence:* vault (over), leap over, clear, sail over, hop over. **3** *pre-tax profits jumped:* rise, go up, shoot up, soar, surge, climb, increase; informal skyrocket. **4** *the noise made her jump:* start, jolt, flinch, recoil, shudder.
•noun **1** *the short jump across the gully:* leap, spring, bound, hop, skip. **2** *a jump in*

profits: rise, leap, increase, upsurge, upswing; informal hike. **3** *I woke up with a jump:* start, jerk, spasm, shudder.

jumper noun (Brit.) sweater, pullover, jersey; informal woolly.

junction noun crossroads, intersection, interchange, T-junction, turn, turn-off, exit; Brit. roundabout; N. Amer. turnout, cloverleaf.

junior adjective **1** *the junior members of the family:* younger, youngest. **2** *a junior minister:* minor, subordinate, lower, lesser, low-ranking, secondary.
OPPOSITES senior, older.

junk noun (informal) rubbish, clutter, odds and ends, bits and pieces, bric-a-brac, refuse, litter, scrap, waste, debris; N. Amer. trash; Austral./NZ mullock.

jurisdiction noun **1** the official power to make legal decisions. **2** the area over which the legal authority of a court or other institution extends.

jurisprudence noun the study of law.

jurist noun an expert in law.

juror noun a member of a jury.

jury noun (plural **juries**) **1** a group of people who are required to attend a legal case and come to a verdict based on the evidence given in court. **2** a group of people judging a competition.

just adjective **1** right and fair. **2** deserved. **3** (of an opinion) based on good evidence or reasons. • adverb **1** exactly. **2** exactly or nearly at that moment. **3** very recently. **4** barely. **5** only.
■ **justly** adverb.

justice noun **1** just behaviour or treatment. **2** the quality of being fair and reasonable. **3** a judge or magistrate.
□ **Justice of the Peace** (in the UK) a non-professional magistrate appointed to hear minor cases.

justifiable adjective able to be shown to be right or reasonable.
■ **justifiably** adverb.

justify verb (**justifies, justifying, justified**) **1** prove something to be right or reasonable. **2** be a good reason for. **3** adjust lines of type so that they form straight edges at both sides.
■ **justification** noun.

jut verb (**juts, jutting, jutted**) extend out beyond the main body or line of something.

jute noun rough fibre made from the stems of a tropical plant, used for making rope or woven into sacking.

juvenile adjective **1** having to do with young people, birds, or animals. **2** childish. • noun **1** a young person, bird, or animal. **2** Law a person below the age at which they have adult status in law (18 in most countries).
□ **juvenile delinquent** a young person who regularly commits crimes.

juxtapose verb (**juxtaposes, juxtaposing, juxtaposed**) place two things close together.
■ **juxtaposition** noun.

THESAURUS

just adjective **1** *a just society:* fair, fair-minded, equitable, even-handed, impartial, unbiased, objective, neutral, disinterested, unprejudiced, honourable, upright, decent, principled. **2** *a just reward:* deserved, well deserved, well earned, merited, rightful, due, proper, fitting, appropriate.
OPPOSITES unfair, undeserved.
• adverb **1** *I just saw him:* a moment ago, a short time ago, very recently, not long ago. **2** *she's just right for him:* exactly, precisely, absolutely, completely, totally, entirely, perfectly, utterly, thoroughly; informal dead. **3** *we just made it:* narrowly, only just, by a hair's breadth, by the skin of your teeth, barely, scarcely, hardly; informal by a whisker. **4** *she's just a child:* only, merely, simply, (nothing) but, no more than.
OPPOSITES hardly, easily.

justice noun **1** *I appealed to his sense of justice:* fairness, justness, fair play, fair-mindedness, equity, right, even-handedness, honesty, morality. **2** *the justice of his case:* validity, justification, soundness, well-foundedness, legitimacy.

3 judge, magistrate, recorder, sheriff; N. Amer. jurist.

justifiable adjective valid, legitimate, warranted, well founded, justified, just, reasonable, defensible.
OPPOSITES unjustifiable.

justification noun grounds, reason, basis, rationale, premise, vindication, explanation, defence, argument, case.

justify verb **1** *directors must justify the expenditure:* give grounds for, give reasons for, explain, account for, defend, vindicate, excuse, exonerate. **2** *the situation justified further investigation:* warrant, be good reason for, be a justification for.

juvenile adjective **1** *juvenile offenders:* young, teenage, adolescent, junior, pubescent. **2** *juvenile behaviour:* childish, immature, puerile, infantile, babyish.
OPPOSITES adult, mature.
• noun *many victims are juveniles:* young person, youngster, child, teenager, adolescent, minor, junior; informal kid.
OPPOSITES adult.

Kk

K or **k** noun (plural **Ks** or **K's**) the eleventh letter of the alphabet. •**abbreviation** informal a thousand.

kaftan or **caftan** noun **1** a woman's long, loose dress or top. **2** a man's long tunic, worn in the East.

kaiser /ky-zer/ noun historical the German or Austrian Emperor.

kale noun a type of cabbage with large curly leaves.

kaleidoscope /kuh-ly-duh-skohp/ noun **1** a tube containing mirrors and pieces of coloured glass or paper, whose reflections produce changing patterns when the tube is turned. **2** a constantly changing pattern. ■ **kaleidoscopic** adjective.

kameez /kuh-meez/ noun (plural **kameez** or **kameezes**) a long tunic worn by people from the Indian subcontinent.

kamikaze /ka-mi-kah-zi/ noun (in the Second World War) a Japanese aircraft loaded with explosives and deliberately crashed on to an enemy target in a suicide mission. •**adjective** potentially causing death or harm to yourself.

kangaroo noun a large Australian animal with a long powerful tail and strong hind legs that enable it to travel by leaping. □ **kangaroo court** a court set up unofficially with the aim of finding someone guilty.

kaolin /kay-uh-lin/ noun a fine soft white clay, used for making china and in medicine.

kapok /kay-pok/ noun a substance resembling cotton wool which grows around the seeds of a tropical tree, used as padding.

kaput /kuh-puut/ adjective informal broken and useless.

karaoke /ka-ri-oh-ki/ noun a form of entertainment in which people sing popular songs over pre-recorded backing tracks.

karate /kuh-rah-ti/ noun a Japanese system of fighting using the hands and feet rather than weapons.

karma noun (in Hinduism and Buddhism) a person's actions in this and previous lives, seen as affecting their future fate.

karst noun a limestone region with underground streams and many cavities in the rock.

kart noun a small racing car with no suspension and having the engine at the back.

kasbah or **casbah** noun a fortress in the old part of a North African city, and the narrow streets that surround it.

kayak /ky-ak/ noun a canoe made of a light frame with a watertight covering. •**verb** (**kayaks, kayaking, kayaked**) travel in a kayak.

kazoo noun a simple musical instrument consisting of a pipe that produces a buzzing sound when you hum into it.

kebab noun a dish of pieces of meat, fish, or vegetables roasted or grilled on a skewer or spit.

kedgeree /kej-uh-ree/ noun a dish of smoked fish, rice, and hard-boiled eggs.

keel noun a structure running along the length of the base of a ship. •**verb** (**keel over**) **1** (of a boat or ship) turn over on its side. **2** fall over.

keelhaul verb (in the past) punish someone by dragging them through the water from one side of a boat to the other.

keen¹ adjective **1** eager and enthusiastic.

k

THESAURUS

keen adjective **1** *his publishers were keen to capitalize on his success:* eager, anxious, intent, impatient, determined; informal raring, itching, dying. **2** *a keen birdwatcher:* enthusiastic, avid, eager, ardent, fervent, conscientious, committed, dedicated. **3** *a girl he was keen on:* attracted to, passionate about, interested in, fond of, taken with, smitten with, enamoured of, infatuated with; informal struck on, gone on, mad about. **4** *a keen cutting edge:* sharp, well honed, razor-sharp. **5** *a keen mind:* acute, penetrating, astute, incisive, sharp, perceptive, piercing,

2 (of a blade) sharp. **3** quick to understand. **4** (of a sense) highly developed. **5** Brit. (of prices) very low.
■ **keenly** adverb **keenness** noun.

keen² verb **1** wail in grief for a person who has died. **2** make an eerie wailing sound.

keep verb (**keeps, keeping, kept**) **1** continue to have something. **2** save something for use in the future. **3** store something in a regular place. **4** continue in a particular condition, position, or activity: *she kept quiet.* **5** do something that you have promised or agreed to do. **6** (of food) remain in good condition. **7** make a note about something, or write a diary. **8** provide accommodation and food for someone. **9** (**kept**) dated supported financially in return for sex. ● noun **1** food, clothes, and other essentials for living. **2** the strongest or central tower of a castle.
□ **keep-fit** regular exercises done to improve fitness. **keep up** move at the same rate as someone or something else. **keep something up** continue a course of action.

keeper noun **1** a person who manages or looks after something or someone. **2** a goalkeeper or wicketkeeper.

keeping noun (**in** (or **out of**) **keeping with**) in (or not in) harmony or agreement with.

keepsake noun a small item kept in memory of the person who gave it or originally owned it.

keg noun a small barrel.

kelim ⇒ KILIM.

kelp noun a very large brown seaweed.

kelvin noun a unit of temperature, equal to one degree Celsius.

ken noun (**your ken**) the range of your

knowledge and experience. ● verb (**kens, kenning, kenned** or **kent**) Scottish & N. English know or recognize.

kendo noun a Japanese form of fencing with two-handed bamboo swords.

kennel noun **1** a small shelter for a dog. **2** (**kennels**) a place where dogs are looked after or bred.

Kenyan /ken-yuhn/ noun a person from Kenya. ● adjective relating to Kenya.

kept past and past participle of KEEP.

keratin /ke-ruh-tin/ noun a protein forming the basis of hair, feathers, hoofs, claws, and horns.

kerb (US spelling **curb**) noun a stone edging to a pavement.
□ **kerb-crawling** Brit. driving slowly along the edge of the road in search of a prostitute.

kerbstone noun a long, narrow stone or concrete block, laid end to end with others to form a kerb.

kerchief /ker-chif/ noun **1** a piece of fabric used to cover the head. **2** dated a handkerchief.

kerfuffle noun Brit. informal a fuss or commotion.

kernel noun **1** the softer part inside the shell of a nut, seed, or fruit stone. **2** the seed and hard husk of a cereal. **3** the central part of something.

☑ *-el,* not *-al:* kern*el.*

kerosene noun N. Amer. paraffin.

kestrel noun a small falcon that hovers in the air with rapidly beating wings.

ketch noun a small sailing boat with two masts.

THESAURUS

razor-sharp, shrewd, discerning, clever, intelligent, brilliant, bright, smart, wise, insightful. **6** *a keen sense of duty:* intense, acute, fierce, passionate, burning, fervent, ardent, strong, powerful.
OPPOSITES reluctant, unenthusiastic, dull.

keep verb **1** *you should keep all the old forms:* retain (possession of), hold on to, not part with, save, store, put by/aside, set aside; N. Amer. set by; informal hang on to. **2** *I tried to keep calm:* remain, stay, carry on being. **3** *he keeps going on about the murder:* persist in, keep on, carry on, continue, insist on. **4** *I shan't keep you long:* detain, keep waiting, delay, hold up, slow down. **5** *most people kept the rules:* comply with, obey, observe, conform to, abide by, adhere to, stick to, heed, follow, carry out, act on, make good, honour, keep to, stand by. **6** *keeping the old traditions:* preserve, keep alive/up, keep going, carry on, perpetuate, maintain, uphold. **7** *where is her umbrella kept?* store, house, stow,

put (away), place, deposit. **8** *he stole to keep his family:* provide for, support, feed, maintain, sustain, take care of, look after. **9** *she keeps rabbits:* breed, rear, raise, farm, own. **10** *his parents kept a shop:* manage, run, own, operate.
OPPOSITES throw away, break, abandon.
● noun *money to pay for his keep:* maintenance, upkeep, sustenance, board (and lodging), food, livelihood.
□ **keep off avoid,** steer clear of, stay away from, not go near.

keeper noun curator, custodian, guardian, administrator, overseer, steward, caretaker, attendant, concierge.

keeping noun care, custody, charge, guardianship, possession, trust, protection.
□ **in keeping with consistent with,** in harmony with, in accord with, in agreement with, in line with, in character with, compatible with, appropriate to, befitting, suitable for.

k

ketchup noun a spicy sauce made from tomatoes and vinegar.

kettle noun a container with a spout and handle, used for boiling water.

kettledrum noun a large drum shaped like a bowl.

key noun (plural **keys**) **1** a small piece of shaped metal which is inserted into a lock and turned to open or close it. **2** a lever pressed down by the finger in playing an instrument such as the organ, piano, or flute. **3** each of several buttons on a panel for operating a computer or typewriter. **4** a list explaining the symbols used in a map or table. **5** a word or system for solving a code. **6** Music a group of notes making up a scale. • **adjective** of great importance. • **verb** (**keys, keying, keyed**) **1** enter data using a computer keyboard. **2** (**be keyed up**) be nervous, tense, or excited.

keyboard noun **1** a panel of keys for use with a computer or typewriter. **2** a set of keys on a musical instrument. **3** an electronic musical instrument with keys arranged as on a piano. • **verb** enter data by means of a keyboard.
■ **keyboarder** noun.

keyhole noun a hole in a lock into which the key is inserted.
□ **keyhole surgery** surgery carried out through a very small cut in the patient's body.

keynote noun **1** a central theme of a book, speech, etc. **2** Music the note on which a key is based. • **adjective** (of a speech) setting out the theme of a conference.

keypad noun a small keyboard or set of buttons for operating a portable electronic device or telephone.

keystone noun **1** the most important part of a policy or system. **2** a central stone at the top of an arch.

keystroke noun a single act of pressing a key on a keyboard.

keyword noun **1** a significant word mentioned in an index. **2** a word used in a computer system to indicate the content of a document.

kg abbreviation kilograms.

khaki /kah-ki/ noun (plural **khakis**) **1** a dull greenish- or yellowish-brown colour. **2** a cotton or wool fabric of this colour.

khan noun a title given to rulers and officials in central Asia, Afghanistan, and certain other Muslim countries.

kHz abbreviation kilohertz.

kibbutz /kib-**buuts**/ noun a farming settlement in Israel in which work is shared between all of its members.

kibosh /ky-bosh/ noun (**put the kibosh on**) informal firmly put an end to.

kick verb **1** hit or propel something forcibly with the foot. **2** hit out with the foot or feet. **3** informal succeed in giving up a habit. **4** (**kick off**) (of a football match) start or restart with a kick of the ball from the centre. **5** (**kick someone out**) informal force someone to leave. **6** (of a gun) spring back when fired. • **noun 1** an instance of kicking. **2** informal a thrill of excitement. **3** informal the strong effect of alcohol or a drug.
□ **kick-boxing** a form of martial art which combines boxing with kicking with bare feet. **kick-off** the start of a football match. **kick-start 1** start a motorcycle engine with a downward thrust of a lever. **2** take action to make something start or develop more quickly. **kick the bucket** informal die.
■ **kicker** noun.

kickback noun **1** informal an underhand payment to someone who has helped in a business deal. **2** an instance of a gun springing back when fired.

kid[1] noun **1** informal a child or young person. **2** a young goat.

kid[2] verb (**kids, kidding, kidded**) informal fool someone into believing something.

kidnap verb (**kidnaps, kidnapping, kidnapped**; US spelling **kidnaps, kidnaping,**

k

---

key noun **1** *the key to the mystery:* **answer**, clue, solution, explanation, basis, foundation. **2** *the key to success:* **means**, way, route, path, passport, secret, formula. • **adjective** *a key figure:* **crucial**, central, essential, indispensable, pivotal, critical, dominant, vital, principal, prime, major, leading, main, important.
OPPOSITES peripheral.

kick verb *kick the ball:* **boot**, punt.
• **noun** (informal) *I get a kick out of driving:* **thrill**, excitement, stimulation, tingle, frisson; informal buzz, high; N. Amer. informal charge.
□ **kick off** (informal) **start**, commence, begin,

get going, get off the ground, get under way, open, start off, set in motion, launch, initiate, introduce, inaugurate. **kick someone out** (informal) **expel**, eject, throw out, oust, evict, get rid of, dismiss, discharge; informal chuck out, send packing, boot out, sack, fire.

kid noun (informal) **child**, youngster, little one, baby, toddler, tot, infant, boy, girl, young person, minor, juvenile, adolescent, teenager, youth, stripling; Scottish bairn; informal kiddie, nipper, kiddiewink; Brit. informal sprog; N. Amer. informal rug rat; Austral./NZ ankle-biter; disapproving brat.

kidnap verb **abduct**, carry off, capture,

kidnaped) take someone by force and hold them captive. • noun an instance of kidnapping someone.
■ **kidnapper** noun.

kidney noun (plural **kidneys**) **1** each of a pair of organs that remove waste products from the blood and produce urine. **2** the kidney of a sheep, ox, or pig as food.
□ **kidney bean** an edible dark red bean shaped like a kidney. **kidney machine** a device that performs the functions of a kidney, used if a person has a damaged kidney. **kidney stone** a hard mass formed in the kidneys.

kilim or **kelim** /ki-**leem**/ noun a carpet or rug of a kind made in Turkey and neighbouring areas.

kill verb **1** cause the death of. **2** put an end to. **3** informal cause someone pain. **4** pass time. • noun **1** an act of killing. **2** an animal or animals killed by a hunter or another animal.

killer noun **1** a person or thing that kills. **2** informal something that is very difficult or very impressive.
□ **killer whale** = ORCA.

killing noun an act of causing death. • adjective informal exhausting.
□ **make a killing** make a lot of money out of something.

killjoy noun a person who spoils the enjoyment of other people.

kiln noun a furnace for baking or drying things.

kilo noun (plural **kilos**) a kilogram.

kilobyte noun Computing a unit of memory or data equal to 1,024 bytes.

kilocalorie noun a unit of energy of one thousand calories.

kilogram or **kilogramme** noun a unit of mass, equal to 1,000 grams (approximately 2.205 lb).

kilohertz noun a measure of frequency equal to 1,000 hertz.

kilometre /**kil**-uh-mee-ter, ki-**lom**-i-ter/ (US spelling **kilometer**) noun a metric unit of measurement equal to 1,000 metres (0.62 miles).

kiloton or **kilotonne** noun a unit of explosive power equivalent to 1,000 tons of TNT.

kilovolt noun 1,000 volts.

kilowatt noun 1,000 watts.
□ **kilowatt-hour** a measure of electrical energy equivalent to one kilowatt operating for one hour.

kilt noun a skirt of pleated tartan cloth, traditionally worn by men as part of Scottish Highland dress.

kilter noun (**out of kilter**) out of balance.

kimono /ki-**moh**-noh/ noun (plural **kimonos**) a long, loose Japanese robe with wide sleeves, tied with a sash.

kin plural noun your family and relations.

kind¹ noun a class or type of similar people or things.
□ **in kind 1** in the same way. **2** (of payment) in goods or services instead of money.

> ! use **this kind of** to refer to a singular noun (e.g. *this kind of behaviour is not acceptable*), and **these kinds of** to refer to a plural noun (e.g. *these kinds of questions are not relevant*).

kind² adjective considerate and generous.

kindergarten noun a nursery school.

kindle verb (**kindles, kindling, kindled**) **1** light a flame; make a fire start burning. **2** arouse an emotion.

kindling noun small sticks used for lighting fires.

kindly adverb **1** in a kind way. **2** please

THESAURUS

seize, snatch, take hostage.

kill verb **1** murder, take the life of, assassinate, eliminate, terminate, dispatch, finish off, put to death, execute, slaughter, exterminate; informal bump off, do away with, do in, top, take out, blow away; N. Amer. informal rub out, waste; literary slay. **2** (informal) *Congress killed the bill:* veto, defeat, vote down, rule against, reject, throw out, overturn, put a stop to.

killer noun murderer, assassin, butcher, serial killer, gunman, terminator, executioner; informal hit man.

killing noun murder, assassination, homicide, manslaughter, execution, slaughter, massacre, butchery, bloodshed, extermination, carnage, genocide.

kind¹ noun *all kinds of gifts:* sort, type, variety, style, form, class, category, genre.

kind² adjective *a kind and caring person:* kindly, good-natured, kind-hearted, warm-hearted, caring, affectionate, loving, warm, considerate, obliging, compassionate, sympathetic, understanding, benevolent, benign, unselfish, selfless, altruistic, public-spirited; Brit. informal decent.
OPPOSITES unkind.

kindly adjective *a kindly old lady:* benevolent, kind, kind-hearted, warm-hearted, generous, good-natured, gentle, warm, compassionate, caring, loving, benign, well meaning, considerate.
OPPOSITES unkind, cruel.
• adverb *he looked at her kindly:* nicely, warmly, affectionately, tenderly, lovingly, compassionately, considerately, obligingly, generously.
OPPOSITES unkindly, harshly.

(used in a polite request). • adjective (**kindlier**, **kindliest**) kind.
□ **not take kindly to** not be pleased by.
■ **kindliness** noun.

kindness noun **1** the quality of being kind. **2** a kind act.

kindred plural noun your family and relations. • adjective having similar qualities.
□ **kindred spirit** a person whose interests or attitudes are similar to your own.

kinetic adjective relating to or resulting from motion.
■ **kinetically** adverb.

king noun **1** the male ruler of an independent state. **2** the best or most important person or thing of their kind. **3** a playing card ranking next below an ace. **4** the most important chess piece, which the opponent has to checkmate in order to win.
□ **king-sized** (or **king-size**) of a larger than normal size.
■ **kingly** adjective **kingship** noun.

kingdom noun **1** a country, state, or territory ruled by a king or queen. **2** each of the three divisions (animal, vegetable, and mineral) in which natural objects are classified.

kingfisher noun a colourful bird with a long sharp beak which dives to catch fish in streams and ponds.

kingpin noun **1** a person or thing that is essential to the success of an organization or operation. **2** a large bolt in a central position.

kink noun **1** a sharp twist in something long and narrow. **2** a flaw or difficulty. **3** a peculiar habit or characteristic. • verb form a kink.

kinky adjective (**kinkier**, **kinkiest**) **1** informal having to do with unusual sexual behaviour. **2** having kinks or twists.

kinsfolk or **kinfolk** plural noun your family and relations.

kinship noun **1** the relationship between members of the same family. **2** a state of having similar characteristics or origins.

kinsman or **kinswoman** noun (plural **kinsmen** or **kinswomen**) one of your relations.

kiosk noun **1** a small open-fronted hut from which newspapers, refreshments, or tickets are sold. **2** Brit. a public telephone booth.

kip Brit. informal noun a sleep. • verb (**kips**, **kipping**, **kipped**) sleep.

kipper noun a herring that has been split open, salted, and dried or smoked.
□ **kipper tie** a very wide tie.

kirk noun Scottish & N. English a church.

kismet /kiz-mit/ noun fate.

kiss verb touch someone or something with the lips as a sign of love, affection, or greeting. • noun an act of kissing.
□ **kiss curl** a small curl of hair on the forehead or in front of the ear. **the kiss of life** mouth-to-mouth resuscitation.

kit noun **1** a set of equipment or clothes for a specific purpose. **2** a set of drums, cymbals, and other percussion instruments. • verb (**kits**, **kitting**, **kitted**) (**kit someone out**) provide someone with the clothes or equipment needed for a particular activity.

kitbag noun a long canvas bag for carrying a soldier's possessions.

kitchen noun **1** a room where food is prepared and cooked. **2** a set of fittings and units installed in a kitchen.
□ **kitchen garden** a part of a garden where vegetables, fruit, and herbs are grown.

kitchenette noun a small kitchen or cooking area.

kite noun **1** a toy consisting of a light frame with thin material stretched over it, flown in the wind at the end of a long string. **2** a long-winged bird of prey with a forked tail. **3** Geometry a four-sided figure having two pairs of equal sides next to each other.

k

THESAURUS

kindness noun kindliness, affection, warmth, gentleness, concern, care, consideration, altruism, compassion, sympathy, benevolence, generosity.
OPPOSITES unkindness.

king noun ruler, sovereign, monarch, Crown, His Majesty, emperor, prince, potentate.

kingdom noun realm, domain, dominion, country, empire, land, territory, nation, (sovereign) state, province.

kiss verb **1** *he kissed her:* informal peck, smooch, canoodle, neck, pet; Brit. informal snog; N. Amer. informal buss; formal osculate.
2 *the ball just kissed the crossbar:* brush (against), caress, touch, stroke, skim.

• noun informal peck, smack, smacker, smooch; Brit. informal snog; N. Amer. informal buss.

kit noun **1** *the dental kit for the hospital:* equipment, tools, implements, instruments, gadgets, utensils, appliances, gear, tackle, hardware, paraphernalia; informal things, stuff; Military accoutrements. **2** (Brit. informal) *their football kit:* clothes, clothing, garments, outfit, dress, costume, attire, garb; informal gear, get-up, rig-out. **3** *a tool kit:* set, selection, collection, pack.
□ **kit someone/something out** equip, fit (out/up), furnish, supply, provide, issue, dress, clothe, attire, rig out, deck out; informal fix up.

kith noun (**kith and kin**) your family and relations.

kitsch /kich/ noun art, objects, or design that are thought to be unpleasantly bright and showy or too sentimental.
■ **kitschy** adjective.

kitten noun a young cat.

kittenish adjective playful, lively, or flirtatious.

kittiwake noun a small gull that nests on sea cliffs.

kitty¹ noun (plural **kitties**) 1 a fund of money for use by a number of people. 2 a pool of money in some card games.

kitty² noun (plural **kitties**) informal a cat.

kiwi noun (plural **kiwis**) 1 a bird from New Zealand that cannot fly. 2 (**Kiwi**) informal a person from New Zealand.
□ **kiwi fruit** the fruit of an Asian plant, with green flesh and black seeds.

klaxon /klak-suhn/ noun trademark a vehicle horn or warning hooter.

kleptomania noun a compulsive urge to steal.
■ **kleptomaniac** noun & adjective.

km abbreviation kilometres.

knack noun 1 a skill at performing a task. 2 a habit of doing something.

knacker verb (**knackers, knackering, knackered**) Brit. informal 1 damage or injure something. 2 (**knackered**) very tired.

knacker's yard noun Brit. informal a place where old or injured animals are taken to be killed.

knapsack noun a bag with shoulder straps, carried on the back.

knave noun 1 old use a dishonest man. 2 (in cards) a jack.
■ **knavish** adjective.

knead verb 1 work dough or clay with the hands. 2 massage something as if kneading it.

knee noun 1 the joint between the thigh and the lower leg. 2 the upper surface of your thigh when you are in a sitting position.
● verb (**knees, kneeing, kneed**) hit someone with your knee.
□ **knee-jerk** done automatically and without thinking. **knees-up** Brit. informal a

lively party.

kneecap noun the bone in front of the knee joint. ● verb (**kneecaps, kneecapping, kneecapped**) shoot someone in the knee.

kneel verb (**kneels, kneeling, knelt** or **kneeled**) be in a position in which you rest your weight on your knees.

knell noun literary the sound of a bell ringing to mark a person's death.

knew past of KNOW.

knickerbockers plural noun loose-fitting trousers or knickers gathered at the knee or calf.

knickers plural noun Brit. women's or girls' underpants.

knick-knack noun a small worthless object.

knife noun (plural **knives**) a cutting tool consisting of a blade fixed into a handle.
● verb (**knifes, knifing, knifed**) 1 stab someone with a knife. 2 cut through or into something like a knife.
□ **at knifepoint** under threat of injury from a knife. **knife-edge** a very tense or dangerous situation.

knight noun 1 (in the Middle Ages) a man of noble rank with a duty to fight for his king. 2 (in the UK) a man awarded a title by the king or queen and entitled to use 'Sir' in front of his name. 3 a chess piece that moves by jumping to the opposite corner of a rectangle two squares by three.
● verb give a man the title of knight.
■ **knighthood** noun.

knit verb (**knits, knitting, knitted** or **knit**) 1 make a garment by looping yarn together with knitting needles or on a machine. 2 make a plain stitch in knitting. 3 join together. 4 tighten your eyebrows in a frown.

knitwear noun knitted clothes.

knob noun 1 a rounded lump at the end or on the surface of something. 2 a ball-shaped handle. 3 a round button on a machine. 4 a small lump of something.

knobble noun Brit. a small lump on something.
■ **knobbly** adjective.

THESAURUS

knack noun 1 *a knack for making money:* gift, talent, flair, genius, instinct, ability, capability, capacity, aptitude, bent, facility, trick; informal the hang of something. 2 *he has a knack of getting injured:* tendency, habit, liability, propensity.

knickers plural noun (Brit.) underpants, briefs; Brit. pants; informal panties, undies; Brit. informal knicks, smalls; dated drawers; historical bloomers.

knife noun blade, cutter.

● verb *he was knifed in the back:* stab, hack, gash, slash, lacerate, cut, bayonet.

knit verb 1 *disparate regions began to knit together:* unite, unify, come together, bond, fuse, coalesce, merge, meld, blend. 2 *we expect broken bones to knit:* heal, mend, join, fuse. 3 *Marcus knitted his brows:* furrow, contract, gather, wrinkle.

knob noun lump, bump, protrusion, bulge, swelling, knot, boss.

knock verb **1** hit a surface noisily to attract attention. **2** collide with. **3** hit someone or something so that they move or fall. **4** make a hole, dent, etc. in something by hitting it. **5** informal criticize. **6** (of a motor) make a thumping or rattling noise. •noun **1** a sound of knocking. **2** a blow or collision. **3** a setback.
□ **knock-kneed** having legs that curve inward at the knee. **knock off** informal stop work. **knock something off** informal produce a piece of work quickly and easily. **knock-on effect** an effect or result that causes a series of other things to happen. **knock someone out 1** make someone unconscious. **2** eliminate a person or team from a knockout competition.

knockabout adjective (of comedy) lively and involving deliberately clumsy or rough actions.

knocker noun a hinged object fixed to a door and rapped by visitors to attract attention.

knockout noun **1** an act of knocking someone out. **2** Brit. a competition in which the loser in each round is eliminated. **3** informal a very impressive person or thing.

knoll noun a small hill or mound.

knot noun **1** a fastening made by looping a piece of string or rope and tightening it. **2** a tangled mass in hair, wool, etc. **3** a hard mass in wood at the point where the trunk and a branch join. **4** a hard lump of muscle tissue. **5** a small group of people. **6** a unit of speed of a ship, aircraft, or the wind, equivalent to one nautical mile per hour. •verb (**knots, knotting, knotted**) **1** fasten with a knot. **2** tangle. **3** make a muscle tense and hard.
□ **tie the knot** informal get married.

knotty adjective (**knottier, knottiest**) **1** full of knots. **2** very complex.

know verb (**knows, knowing, knew**; past participle **known**) **1** be aware of something as a result of observing, asking, or being told. **2** be absolutely sure of something. **3** be familiar with. **4** have a good grasp of a subject or language. **5** have personal experience of. **6** (**be known as**) be thought of as having a particular quality or title.
□ **be in the know** informal be aware of something known only to a few people. **know-all** informal a person who behaves as if they know everything. **know-how** practical knowledge or skill. **know the ropes** have experience of the right way of doing something.
■ **knowable** adjective.

knowing adjective suggesting that you know something that is meant to be secret.
■ **knowingly** adverb.

knowledge noun **1** information and awareness gained through experience or education. **2** the state of knowing about something.

☑ remember the *d*: knowle*d*ge.

k

---

knock verb **1** *he knocked on the door:* bang, tap, rap, thump, pound, hammer, beat, strike, hit. **2** *she knocked her knee on the table:* bump, bang, hit, strike, crack, injure, hurt, bruise; informal bash, whack. **3** *he knocked into an elderly man:* collide with, bump into, bang into, run into, crash into, smash into, plough into; N. Amer. impact; informal bash into.
•noun **1** *a knock at the door:* tap, rap, rat-tat, knocking, bang, banging, pounding, hammering, thump, thud. **2** *the casing can withstand knocks:* bump, blow, bang, jolt, jar, shock, collision, crash, smash, impact.
□ **knock someone down** fell, floor, flatten, bring down, knock to the ground, knock over, run over/down. **knock something down** demolish, pull down, tear down, destroy, raze (to the ground), level, flatten, bulldoze. **knock someone out** knock unconscious, knock senseless, floor, prostrate; informal lay out, KO, fell.

knot noun *a knot of people:* cluster, group, band, huddle, bunch, circle, ring.
•verb *a scarf knotted round her throat:* tie, fasten, secure, bind, do up.

knotted adjective tangled, matted, snarled, unkempt, tousled; informal mussed up.

know verb **1** *she doesn't know I'm here:* be aware, realize, be conscious. **2** *do you know the rules:* be familiar with, be conversant with, be acquainted with, be versed in, have a grasp of, understand, comprehend; informal be clued up on. **3** *I don't know many people here:* be acquainted with, have met, be familiar with; Scottish ken.

know-how noun (informal) expertise, skill, proficiency, knowledge, understanding, mastery, technique; informal savvy.

knowing adjective significant, meaningful, expressive, suggestive, superior.

knowledge noun **1** *his knowledge of history:* understanding, comprehension, grasp, command, mastery; informal know-how. **2** *people anxious to display their knowledge:* learning, erudition, education, scholarship, schooling, wisdom. **3** *he slipped away without my knowledge:* awareness, consciousness, realization, cognition, apprehension, perception, appreciation. **4** *a knowledge of the countryside:* familiarity, acquaintance, conversance, intimacy.
OPPOSITES ignorance.

knowledgeable or **knowledgable** adjective intelligent and well informed. ■ **knowledgeably** adverb.

known past participle of **KNOW**. • adjective 1 identified as being: *a known criminal.* 2 Maths (of a quantity or variable) having a value that can be stated.

knuckle noun 1 each of the joints of a finger. 2 a knee joint of a four-legged animal, or the part joining the leg to the foot. • verb (**knuckles, knuckling, knuckled**) 1 (**knuckle down**) apply yourself seriously to a task. 2 (**knuckle under**) accept someone's authority.

knuckleduster noun a metal fitting worn over the knuckles in fighting to increase the effect of blows.

koala /koh-**ah**-luh/ noun a bear-like Australian animal that lives in trees.

kohl noun a black powder used as eye make-up.

kohlrabi noun a variety of cabbage with an edible thick, round stem.

kookaburra /**kuu**-kuh-bur-ruh/ noun a very large, noisy kingfisher found in Australia and New Zealand.

Koran /ko-**rahn**/ noun the sacred book of Islam, believed to be the word of God as told to Muhammad and written down in Arabic.

Korean noun 1 a person from Korea. 2 the language of Korea. • adjective relating to Korea.

kosher /**koh**-sher/ adjective 1 (of food) prepared according to the requirements of Jewish law. 2 informal genuine and legitimate.

kowtow /kow-**tow**/ verb 1 be too meek and obedient towards someone. 2 (in the past, as part of Chinese custom) kneel and touch the ground with the forehead, in worship or as a sign of respect.

kraal /krahl/ noun S. African 1 a traditional African village of huts. 2 an enclosure for sheep and cattle.

krill plural noun small shrimp-like crustaceans which are the main food of baleen whales.

krona noun 1 (plural **kronor**) the basic unit of money of Sweden. 2 (plural **kronur**) the unit of money of Iceland.

krone /**kroh**-nuh/ noun (plural **kroner**) the basic unit of money of Denmark and Norway.

krypton /**krip**-ton/ noun a gaseous chemical element used in some kinds of electric light.

kudos noun praise and honour.

> ! **kudos** is a singular word and it is wrong to use it as if it were a plural; for example, you should say *he received much kudos for his work*, not *he received many kudos for his work*.

kumquat /**kum**-kwot/ noun a very small orange-like fruit.

kung fu /kung **foo**/ noun a Chinese martial art resembling karate.

Kurd noun a member of a mainly Islamic people living in Kurdistan, a region in the Middle East.

Kuwaiti /kuu-**way**-ti/ noun a person from Kuwait. • adjective relating to Kuwait.

kV abbreviation kilovolts.

kW abbreviation kilowatts.

THESAURUS

knowledgeable adjective 1 *a knowledgeable old man:* well informed, learned, well read, (well) educated, erudite, scholarly, cultured, cultivated, enlightened. 2 *he is knowledgeable about modern art:* conversant with, familiar with, well acquainted with, au fait with, up on, up to date with, abreast of; informal clued up on.
OPPOSITES ignorant.

known adjective *a known criminal:* recognized, well known, widely known, noted, celebrated, notable, notorious, acknowledged.

LI

L or **I** noun (plural **Ls** or **L's**) **1** the twelfth letter of the alphabet. **2** the Roman numeral for 50. • **abbreviation 1** Brit. learner driver: *L-plates*. **2** (**l**) litres. **3** (**l.**) old use pounds.

£ abbreviation pounds.

lab noun informal a laboratory.

label noun **1** a small piece of paper, fabric, etc. attached to an object and giving information about it. **2** the name or trademark of a fashion company. **3** a company that produces recorded music. **4** a classifying name given to a person or thing. • verb (**labels, labelling, labelled**; US spelling **labels, labeling, labeled**) **1** attach a label to. **2** put someone or something in a category.

☑ *-el*, not *-le*: label.

labia /lay-bi-uh/ plural noun (singular **labium**) the inner and outer folds of a woman's genitals. ■ **labial** adjective.

labor etc. US spelling of LABOUR etc.

laboratory noun (plural **laboratories**) a room or building for scientific research or teaching, or for the making of drugs or chemicals.

laborious adjective **1** needing a lot of time and effort. **2** showing obvious signs of effort. ■ **laboriously** adverb.

labour (US spelling **labor**) noun **1** work. **2** workers as a group. **3** (**Labour** or the **Labour Party**) a left-wing political party formed to represent ordinary working people. **4** the process of giving birth. • verb **1** do hard physical work. **2** have difficulty doing something in spite of working hard. **3** move with difficulty and effort. **4** (**labour under**) believe something that is not true. □ **labour camp** a prison camp where prisoners have to do hard physical work. **labour force** the members of a population who are able to work. **labour-intensive** needing a lot of work. **labour the point** repeat something that has already been said and understood.

laboured (US spelling **labored**) adjective

THESAURUS

label noun **1** *the price is clearly stated on the label*: tag, ticket, tab, sticker, marker, docket. **2** *a designer label*: brand (name), (trade) name, trademark, make, logo. **3** *the label the media came up with for me*: designation, description, tag, name, epithet, nickname, title.
• verb **1** *label each jar with the date*: tag, ticket, mark, stamp. **2** *tests labelled him an underachiever*: categorize, classify, class, describe, designate, identify, mark, stamp, brand, call, name, term, dub.

laborious adjective **1** *a laborious job*: arduous, hard, heavy, difficult, strenuous, gruelling, punishing, exacting, tough, onerous, burdensome, back-breaking, trying, challenging. **2** *Doug's laborious style*: laboured, strained, forced, stiff, stilted, unnatural, artificial, overwrought, heavy, ponderous.
OPPOSITES easy, effortless.

labour noun **1** *manual labour*: work, toil, exertion, industry, drudgery, effort; informal slog, grind. **2** *the conflict between capital and labour*: workers, employees, working people, labourers, workforce, staff, labour force. **3** *a difficult labour*: childbirth, birth, delivery.
OPPOSITES rest, management.
• verb **1** *a project on which he had laboured for many years*: work (hard), toil, slave (away), grind away, struggle, strive, exert yourself; informal slog away, plug away. **2** *Newcastle laboured to break down their defence*: strive, struggle, endeavour, work, try hard, make every effort, do your best, do your utmost, do all you can, give your all, go all out, fight, exert yourself; informal bend/lean over backwards, pull out all the stops.

laboured adjective **1** *laboured breathing*: strained, difficult, forced, laborious. **2** *a rather laboured joke*: contrived, strained, forced, unconvincing, unnatural, artificial, overdone, ponderous, over-elaborate.
OPPOSITES natural, easy.

1 done with great difficulty. **2** not spontaneous or natural.

labourer (US spelling **laborer**) noun a person who does hard physical work that does not need any special skill or training.

Labrador noun a breed of dog with a black or yellow coat, used as a retriever and as a guide dog.

laburnum noun a small tree with hanging clusters of yellow flowers.

labyrinth noun a complicated network of passages.
■ **labyrinthine** /lab-uh-**rin**-thyn/ adjective.

lace noun **1** a delicate open fabric made by looping, twisting, or knitting thread in patterns. **2** a cord used to fasten a shoe or garment. • verb (**laces, lacing, laced**) **1** fasten something with a lace or laces. **2** add an ingredient to a drink or dish to make it stronger or improve the flavour.

lacerate verb (**lacerates, lacerating, lacerated**) tear or deeply cut the flesh or skin.
■ **laceration** noun.

lachrymal or **lacrimal** /**lak**-ri-muhl/ adjective connected with weeping or tears.

lachrymose /**lak**-ri-mohss/ adjective literary tearful.

lack noun the state of being without or not having enough of something. • verb (also **lack for**) be without or without enough of.

lackadaisical adjective not showing enthusiasm or thoroughness.

lackey noun (plural **lackeys**) **1** a servant. **2** a person who is too willing to serve or obey other people.

lacklustre (US spelling **lackluster**) adjective **1** not exciting or interesting. **2** (of the hair or eyes) not shining.

laconic /luh-**kon**-ik/ adjective using very few words.
■ **laconically** adverb.

lacquer /**lak**-ker/ noun **1** a liquid applied to wood or metal to give it a hard, glossy surface. **2** decorative wooden goods coated with lacquer. **3** hairspray.
■ **lacquered** adjective.

lacrimal ➪ **LACHRYMAL**.

lacrosse /luh-**kross**/ noun a team game in which a ball is thrown, caught, and carried with a long-handled stick which has a net at one end.

lactate /lak-**tayt**/ verb (**lactates, lactating, lactated**) (of a woman or female animal) produce milk in the breasts or mammary glands, for feeding babies or young.
■ **lactation** noun.

lactic adjective relating to or obtained from milk.
☐ **lactic acid** an acid present in sour milk, and produced in the muscles during strenuous exercise.

lactose noun a sugar present in milk.

lacuna /luh-**kyoo**-nuh/ noun (plural **lacunae** /luh-**kyoo**-nee/ or **lacunas**) a gap or missing part.

lacy adjective (**lacier, laciest**) made of, resembling, or trimmed with lace.

lad noun informal a boy or young man.

ladder noun **1** a structure consisting of a series of bars or steps between two uprights, used for climbing up or down. **2** a series of stages by which progress can be made: *the career ladder*. **3** Brit. a hole in tights or stockings where the threads have come undone. • verb (**ladders, laddering, laddered**) Brit. cause a ladder to develop in a pair of tights or a stocking.

laddish adjective behaving in a way thought to be typical of young men, especially in being rowdy or drinking too much.

laden adjective heavily loaded or weighed down.

la-di-da or **lah-di-dah** adjective informal affected or snobbish.

ladle noun a large spoon with a cup-shaped bowl and a long handle, for serving soup, stew, etc. • verb (**ladles, ladling, ladled**)

THESAURUS

labourer noun workman, worker, working man, manual worker, unskilled worker, blue-collar worker, (hired) hand, roustabout, drudge, menial; Austral./NZ rouseabout.

lace verb **1** *he laced up his running shoes:* fasten, do up, tie up, secure, knot. **2** *tea laced with rum:* flavour, mix, blend, fortify, strengthen, season, spice (up), liven up, doctor, adulterate; informal spike.
OPPOSITES untie.

lack noun *a lack of cash:* absence, want, need, deficiency, dearth, shortage, shortfall, scarcity, paucity, scarceness.
OPPOSITES abundance.

• verb *she lacks judgement:* be without, be in need of, be short of, be deficient in, be low on, be pressed for; informal be strapped for.
OPPOSITES have, possess.

lad noun (informal) **1** *a young lad:* boy, schoolboy, youth, youngster, juvenile, stripling; informal kid, nipper; Scottish informal laddie; disapproving brat. **2** *a hard-working lad:* (young) man, fellow; informal guy, geezer; Brit. informal chap, bloke; N. Amer. informal dude, hombre.

laden adjective loaded, burdened, weighed down, overloaded, piled high, full, packed, stuffed, crammed; informal chock-full, serve or transfer soup, stew, etc. with a ladle.

lady noun (plural **ladies**) **1** (in polite or formal use) a woman. **2** a well-mannered woman, or a woman of high social position. **3** (**Lady**) a title used by peeresses, female relatives of peers, and the wives and widows of knights.
□ **lady-in-waiting** (plural **ladies-in-waiting**) a woman who accompanies and looks after a queen or princess.

ladybird noun a small beetle that has a red back with black spots.

ladykiller noun informal a man who is successful in seducing women.

ladylike adjective typical of a well-mannered woman or girl.

Ladyship noun (**Her/Your Ladyship**) a respectful way of referring to or addressing a Lady.

lag[1] verb (**lags, lagging, lagged**) fall behind. • noun (also **time lag**) a period of time between two events.

lag[2] verb (**lags, lagging, lagged**) cover a water tank or pipes with material designed to prevent heat loss.

lager noun a light fizzy beer.

laggard noun a person who falls behind other people.

lagging noun material wrapped round a water tank and pipes to prevent heat loss.

lagoon noun a stretch of salt water separated from the sea by a low sandbank or coral reef.

lah-di-dah ⇒ **LA-DI-DA**.

laid past and past participle of LAY[1].
□ **laid-back** informal relaxed and easy-going.

lain past participle of LIE[1].

lair noun **1** a wild animal's resting place. **2** a person's secret den.

laird noun (in Scotland) a person who owns a large estate.

laissez-faire /less-ay-**fair**/ noun a policy of leaving things to take their own course, without interfering.

laity /**lay**-i-ti/ noun (**the laity**) people who

are not priests or ministers of the Church; ordinary people.

lake noun a large area of water surrounded by land.

lama /**lah**-muh/ noun **1** a title given to a spiritual leader in Tibetan Buddhism. **2** a Tibetan or Mongolian Buddhist monk.

lamb noun **1** a young sheep. **2** a gentle or innocent person. • verb (of a female sheep) give birth to lambs.
■ **lambing** noun.

lambada /lam-**bah**-duh/ noun a fast Brazilian dance.

lambaste /lam-**bayst**/ or **lambast** /lam-**bast**/ verb (**lambastes** or **lambasts, lambasting, lambasted**) criticize someone harshly.

lambent /**lam**-buhnt/ adjective literary lit up or flickering with a soft glow.

lame adjective **1** walking with difficulty because of an injury or illness affecting the leg or foot. **2** (of an explanation or excuse) unconvincing and feeble. **3** (of something meant to be entertaining) dull. • verb (**lames, laming, lamed**) make a person or animal lame.
□ **lame duck** an unsuccessful person or thing.
■ **lamely** adverb **lameness** noun.

lamé /**lah**-may/ noun fabric with interwoven gold or silver threads.

lament /luh-**ment**/ noun **1** a passionate expression of grief. **2** a song or poem expressing grief or regret. • verb **1** mourn a person's death. **2** express regret or disappointment about.
■ **lamentation** noun.

lamentable /**la**-muhn-tuh-b'l/ adjective very bad or disappointing.
■ **lamentably** adverb.

laminate verb /**lam**-i-nayt/ (**laminates, laminating, laminated**) **1** cover a flat surface with a layer of protective material. **2** make something by sticking layers of material together. **3** split into layers or leaves. **4** beat or roll metal into thin plates.

THESAURUS

chock-a-block.

lady noun **1** *several ladies were present:* **woman**, female, girl; Scottish & N. English lass, lassie; N. Amer. informal dame. **2** *lords and ladies:* **noblewoman**, duchess, countess, peeress, viscountess, baroness.

laid-back adjective (informal) **relaxed**, easy-going, free and easy, casual, nonchalant, unexcitable, blasé, cool, calm, unconcerned, leisurely, unhurried; informal unflappable.
OPPOSITES uptight.

lake noun **pool**, pond, tarn, reservoir, lagoon, waterhole, inland sea; Scottish loch; Anglo-Irish

lough; N. Amer. bayou.

lame adjective **1** *the mare was lame:* **limping**, hobbling, crippled, disabled, incapacitated; informal gammy. **2** *a lame excuse:* **feeble**, weak, thin, flimsy, poor, unconvincing, implausible, unlikely.
OPPOSITES sound, convincing.

lament verb **1** *he was lamenting the death of his daughter:* **mourn**, grieve, sorrow, weep, cry. **2** *entrepreneurs lamented the red tape:* **complain about**, bewail, bemoan, deplore, be disappointed at.
OPPOSITES celebrate, welcome.

• noun /**lam**-i-nuht/ a laminated product or material.

■ **lamination** noun.

lamp noun a device using electricity, oil, or gas to give light.

lampoon verb mock or ridicule. • noun a mocking attack.

lamprey /**lam**-pri/ noun (plural **lampreys**) a fish like an eel, having a round sucking mouth with horny teeth.

lance noun (in the past) a weapon with a long shaft and a pointed steel head, used by people on horseback. • verb (**lances, lancing, lanced**) Medicine prick or cut open a boil or wound with a sharp instrument.
□ **lance corporal** a rank of non-commissioned officer in the army, below corporal.

lancer noun (in the past) a soldier armed with a lance.

lancet /**lahn**-sit/ noun a small two-edged knife with a sharp point, used in surgery.

land noun 1 the part of the earth's surface that is not covered by water. 2 an area of ground. 3 (**the land**) ground or soil used for farming. 4 a country or state. • verb 1 put or go ashore. 2 come or bring something down to the ground. 3 bring a fish out of the water with a net or rod. 4 informal succeed in obtaining or achieving something. 5 (**land up**) reach a particular place or destination. 6 (**land someone in**) informal put someone in a difficult situation. 7 (**land someone with**) inflict something unwelcome on someone. 8 informal inflict a blow on someone.

landau /**lan**-dor/ noun an enclosed horse-drawn carriage.

landed adjective owning a lot of land.

landfall noun arrival on land after a sea journey.

landfill noun 1 the disposal of rubbish by burying it. 2 buried rubbish.

landing noun 1 a level area at the top of a staircase. 2 a place where people and goods can be landed from a boat.
□ **landing gear** the undercarriage of an aircraft.

landless adjective owning no land.

landlocked adjective (of a place) surrounded by land.

landlord or **landlady** noun 1 a person who rents out property or land. 2 Brit. a person who runs a pub.

landlubber noun informal a person who is not familiar with the sea or sailing.

landmark noun 1 an object or feature that is easily seen from a distance. 2 an important stage or turning point.

landmine noun an explosive mine laid on or just under the surface of the ground.

landscape noun 1 all the visible features of an area of land. 2 a picture of an area of countryside. • verb (**landscapes, landscaping, landscaped**) improve the appearance of land by changing its contours, planting trees and shrubs, etc.

landslide noun 1 (Brit. also **landslip**) a mass of earth or rock that slides down a mountain or cliff. 2 an overwhelming majority of votes for one party in an election.

lane noun 1 a narrow road. 2 a division of a road for a single line of traffic. 3 a strip of track or water for each of the competitors in a race. 4 a course followed by ships or aircraft.

THESAURUS

land noun 1 *the lookout sighted land:* dry land, terra firma, coast, coastline, shore. 2 *Lyme Park has 1323 acres of land:* grounds, fields, open space, property, territory, acres, acreage, estate, lands, real estate. 3 *many people are leaving the land:* the countryside, the country, rural areas. 4 *Tunisia is a land of variety:* country, nation, state, realm, kingdom, province, region, area, domain. • verb 1 *Allied troops landed in France:* disembark, go ashore, debark, alight, get off. 2 *the ship landed at Le Havre:* berth, dock, moor, (drop) anchor, tie up, put in. 3 *their plane landed at Chicago:* touch down, make a landing, come in to land, come down. 4 (informal) *Nick landed the job of editor:* get, obtain, acquire, secure, gain, net, win, achieve, attain, bag, carry off; informal swing.
OPPOSITES embark, take off.
landlady, landlord noun 1 *the landlady*

had objected to the noise: owner, proprietor, lessor, householder, landowner. 2 *the landlord of the pub:* licensee, innkeeper, owner, hotelier, restaurateur; Brit. publican.
OPPOSITES tenant.

landmark noun 1 *one of London's most famous landmarks:* feature, sight, monument, building. 2 *the ruling was hailed as a landmark:* turning point, milestone, watershed, critical point.

landscape noun scenery, country, countryside, topography, terrain, view, panorama.

landslide noun 1 *floods and landslides:* landslip, rockfall, mudslide, avalanche. 2 *the Labour landslide:* decisive victory, runaway triumph, overwhelming majority; informal whitewash.

lane noun country road, track, course, trail, street, alley, alleyway, passage.

language noun **1** human communication through the use of spoken or written words. **2** a particular system or style of spoken or written communication. **3** a system of symbols and rules for writing computer programs.

> ☑ *-guage*, not *-gauge*: lan*guage*.

languid /lang-gwid/ adjective relaxed and not inclined to be physically active.
■ **languidly** adverb.

languish verb **1** become weak or faint. **2** be kept in an unpleasant place or situation.

languor /lang-ger/ noun a pleasant feeling of being tired or without energy.
■ **languorous** adjective.

lank adjective (of hair) long, limp, and straight.

lanky adjective (**lankier**, **lankiest**) tall, thin, and moving in an awkward or ungraceful way.

lanolin noun a fatty substance from sheep's wool, used in skin cream.

lantern noun a lamp enclosed in a metal frame with glass panels.

lanthanum /lan-thuh-nuhm/ noun a silvery-white metallic element.

lanyard /lan-yerd/ noun **1** a rope used on a ship. **2** a cord around the neck or shoulder for holding a whistle or similar object.

lap¹ noun the flat area between the waist and knees of a seated person.

lap² noun **1** one circuit of a track or racetrack. **2** an overlapping part. • verb (**laps**, **lapping**, **lapped**) overtake a competitor in a race to become a lap ahead.

lap³ verb (**laps**, **lapping**, **lapped**) **1** (of an animal) take up liquid with the tongue. **2** (**lap something up**) accept something with obvious pleasure. **3** (of water) wash against something with a gentle rippling sound.

lapdog noun **1** a small pampered pet dog. **2** a person who is completely under the influence of someone else.

lapel noun the part which is folded back at the front opening of a jacket or coat.

lapidary /la-pi-duh-ri/ adjective **1** relating to the engraving, cutting, or polishing of stone or gems. **2** (of language) elegant and concise.

lapis lazuli /lap-iss laz-yuu-ly/ noun a bright blue stone used in jewellery.

Lapp noun a member of a people of the extreme north of Scandinavia.

> ❗ the people themselves prefer to be called **Sami**.

lapse noun **1** a brief failure of concentration, memory, or judgement. **2** a decline from previously high standards. **3** an interval of time. • verb (**lapses**, **lapsing**, **lapsed**) **1** (of a right, agreement, etc.) become invalid because it is not used or renewed. **2** stop following a religion or doctrine. **3** (**lapse into**) pass gradually into a different state.

laptop noun a portable computer.

lapwing noun a black and white bird with a crest on the head.

larboard = PORT³.

larceny /lar-suh-ni/ noun (plural **larcenies**) theft of personal property.

larch noun a coniferous tree with needles

THESAURUS

language noun **1** *the structure of language:* speech, speaking, conversation, talking, talk, discourse, communication, words, writing, vocabulary, text. **2** *the English language:* tongue, mother tongue, native tongue, dialect; informal lingo. **3** *the booklet is written in simple, everyday language:* wording, phrasing, phraseology, style, vocabulary, terminology, expressions, turn of phrase, parlance; informal lingo.

languish verb **1** *the plants languished and died:* weaken, deteriorate, decline, go downhill, wither, droop, wilt, fade, waste away. **2** *the general is languishing in prison:* waste away, rot, be abandoned, be neglected, be forgotten, suffer, lie.
OPPOSITES thrive.

lap¹ verb **1** *waves lapped against the sea wall:* splash, wash, swish, slosh, break. **2** *the dog lapped water out of a puddle:* drink, lick up, sup, swallow, slurp, gulp.
◻ **lap something up relish**, revel in, savour, delight in, wallow in, glory in, enjoy.

lap² noun *a race of eight laps:* circuit, leg, circle, revolution, round.
• verb *she lapped the other runners:* overtake, outstrip, leave behind, pass, go past, catch up with.

lapse noun **1** *a lapse of concentration:* failure, slip, error, mistake, blunder, fault, omission; informal slip-up. **2** *his lapse into petty crime:* decline, fall, falling, slipping, deterioration, degeneration, backsliding, regression. **3** *a lapse of time:* interval, gap, pause, interlude, lull, hiatus, break.
• verb **1** *the planning permission has lapsed:* expire, become void, become invalid, run out. **2** *do not let friendships lapse:* (come to an) end, cease, stop, terminate, pass, fade, wither, die. **3** *she lapsed into silence:* revert, relapse, drift, slide, slip, sink.

lapsed adjective **1** *a lapsed Catholic:* non-practising, backsliding, apostate. **2** *a lapsed season ticket:* expired, void, invalid, out of date.
OPPOSITES practising, valid.

that fall in winter.

lard noun fat from a pig, used in cooking. • verb **1** insert strips of fat or bacon in meat before cooking. **2** add technical or obscure expressions to talk or writing.

larder noun a room or large cupboard for storing food.

large adjective **1** of relatively great size, extent, or capacity. **2** of wide range or scope.
□ **at large 1** escaped or not yet captured. **2** as a whole.

largely adverb on the whole; mostly.

largesse /lar-**zhess**/ noun **1** generosity. **2** money or gifts given generously.

largo /**lar**-goh/ adverb & adjective Music in a slow tempo and dignified style.

lariat /**la**-ri-uht/ noun a rope used as a lasso or for tying an animal to a post.

lark[1] noun a brown bird that sings while flying.

lark[2] informal noun **1** something done for fun or as a joke. **2** Brit. an activity viewed as foolish or a waste of time. • verb (**lark about** or **around**) behave in a playful and mischievous way.

larkspur noun a plant resembling a delphinium, with tall spikes of blue, pink, or white flowers.

larva noun (plural **larvae** /**lar**-vee/) an immature form of an insect that looks very different from the adult creature, e.g. a caterpillar.

laryngitis /la-rin-**jy**-tiss/ noun inflammation of the larynx.

larynx /**la**-ringks/ noun (plural **larynxes** or **larynges** /luh-**rin**-jeez/) the area at the top of the throat forming an air passage to the lungs and containing the vocal cords.

lasagne /luh-**zan**-yuh/ noun pasta in the form of sheets, baked in layers with meat or vegetables and a cheese sauce.

lascivious /luh-**siv**-i-uhss/ adjective showing strong or inappropriate sexual desire. ■ **lasciviously** adverb **lasciviousness** noun.

laser noun a device that produces an intense narrow beam of light.

laserdisc noun a disc resembling a large compact disc, used for high-quality video and multimedia.

lash verb **1** beat with a whip or stick. **2** beat strongly against. **3** (**lash out**) attack someone verbally or physically. **4** (of an animal) move its tail quickly and violently. **5** fasten securely with a cord or rope. • noun **1** an eyelash. **2** a sharp blow with a whip or stick. **3** the flexible part of a whip.

lashings plural noun Brit. informal a large amount of something.

lass or **lassie** noun Scottish & N. English a girl or young woman.

lassitude noun lack of energy.

lasso /luh-**soo**/ noun (plural **lassos** or **lassoes**) a rope with a noose at one end, used for catching cattle. • verb (**lassoes**, **lassoing**, **lassoed**) catch with a lasso.

last[1] adjective **1** coming after all others in time or order. **2** most recent in time. **3** lowest in importance or rank. **4** (**the last**) the least likely or suitable. **5** only remaining. • adverb on the last occasion before the present. • noun (plural **last**) **1** the last person or thing. **2** (**the last of**) the only remaining part of.
□ **Last Judgement** (in some religions) judgement of humankind expected to take place at the end of the world. **last rites** a Christian religious ceremony performed

THESAURUS

large adjective big, great, substantial, sizeable, considerable, extensive, voluminous, vast, huge, immense, enormous, colossal, massive, heavy, mammoth, gigantic, giant, fat, stout, bulky. OPPOSITES small.

largely adverb mostly, mainly, to a large/ great extent, chiefly, predominantly, primarily, principally, for the most part, in the main, typically, commonly.

lash verb **1** *rain lashed the window panes:* beat against, dash against, pound, batter, strike, drum. **2** *the tiger lashed his tail:* swish, flick, twitch, whip. **3** *two boats were lashed together:* fasten, bind, tie (up), tether, hitch, knot, rope.
• noun *he brought the lash down upon the prisoner's back:* whip, scourge, flail, birch, cane; historical cat-o'-nine-tails, cat.
□ **lash out 1** *the president lashed out at the opposition:* criticize, attack, disparage,

condemn, run down; informal lay into, dis; Brit. informal slag off, have a go at. **2** *Norman lashed out with a knife:* hit out at, strike, let fly at, take a swing at, set upon/about, turn on, round on, attack; informal lay into, pitch into.

last[1] adjective **1** *Rembrandt's last years:* final, closing, concluding, end, terminal, later, latter. **2** *the last woman in the queue:* rearmost, hindmost, endmost, furthest (back), ultimate. **3** *last year:* previous, preceding, prior, former. **4** *the last edition:* latest, most recent. OPPOSITES first, next.
• adverb *the candidate coming last is eliminated:* at the end, at/in the rear, bringing up the rear, at the back. OPPOSITES first.
□ **at last** finally, in the end, eventually, ultimately, at long last, after a long time, in time, in (the fullness of) time.

for a person who is about to die.
■ **lastly** adverb.

last² verb **1** continue for a particular period of time. **2** remain operating for a considerable or particular length of time. **3** be enough for someone to use for a particular length of time.

last³ noun a block used by a shoemaker for shaping or repairing shoes.

latch noun **1** a bar with a catch and lever used for fastening a door or gate. **2** a type of door lock which can be opened from the outside only with a key. • verb **1** fasten a door or gate with a latch. **2** (**latch on to**) associate yourself enthusiastically with.

latchkey noun (plural **latchkeys**) a key to an outer door of a house.

late adjective **1** acting, arriving, or happening after the proper or usual time. **2** far on in a period. **3** far on in the day or night. **4** (**the late**) (of a person) recently dead. **5** (**latest**) of most recent date or origin. • adverb **1** after the proper or usual time. **2** towards the end of a period. **3** far on in the day or night. **4** (**later**) afterwards or in the near future. □ **of late** recently. ■ **lateness** noun.

lately adverb recently; not long ago.

latent adjective existing but not yet developed, showing, or active. ■ **latency** noun.

lateral adjective of, at, towards, or from the side or sides. □ **lateral thinking** chiefly Brit. the solving of a

problem by thinking of new ways to approach it. ■ **laterally** adverb.

latex noun **1** a milky fluid in some plants which thickens when exposed to the air. **2** a synthetic product resembling this, used to make paints, coatings, etc.

lath /lahth, lath/ noun (plural **laths**) a thin, flat strip of wood.

lathe noun a machine that shapes pieces of wood or metal by turning them against a cutting tool.

lather noun **1** a frothy mass of bubbles produced by soap when mixed with water. **2** heavy sweat visible on a horse's coat as a white foam. • verb (**lathers, lathering, lathered**) **1** cover with or form a lather. **2** cover or spread generously with a substance.

Latin noun the language of ancient Rome and its empire. • adjective relating to the Latin language. □ **Latin America** the parts of the American continent where Spanish or Portuguese is spoken.

Latino /luh-tee-noh/ noun (plural **Latinos**) N. Amer. a Latin American inhabitant of the United States.

latitude noun **1** the distance of a place north or south of the equator. **2** (**latitudes**) regions at a particular distance from the equator. **3** scope for freedom of action or thought.

latrine noun a communal toilet, especially a temporary one in a camp.

latter adjective **1** nearer to the end than to

THESAURUS

last² verb **1** *the hearing lasted for six days:* continue, go on, carry on, keep on/going, take. **2** *how long will he last as manager?* survive, endure, hold on/out, keep going, persevere, persist, stay, remain; informal stick it out, hang on, go the distance. **3** *the car is built to last:* endure, wear well, stand up, bear up; informal go the distance.
OPPOSITES end, wear out.

lasting adjective enduring, long-lasting, long-lived, abiding, continuing, long-term, permanent, durable, stable, secure, long-standing, eternal, undying, everlasting, unending, never-ending.
OPPOSITES ephemeral.

late adjective **1** *the train was late:* behind schedule, tardy, overdue, delayed. **2** *her late husband:* dead, departed, lamented, passed on/away; formal deceased. **3** *some late news:* recent, fresh, new, up to date, latter-day, current.
OPPOSITES punctual, early, living, old.
• adverb *she had arrived late:* behind schedule, belatedly, tardily, at the last minute.

lately adverb recently, not long ago, of late, latterly, in recent times.

later adjective *a later chapter:* subsequent, following, succeeding, future, upcoming, to come, ensuing, next.
OPPOSITES earlier, preceding.
• adverb *later, the film rights were sold:* subsequently, eventually, then, next, later on, after this/that, afterwards, at a later date, in the future, in due course, by and by, in a while, in time; formal thereafter.

latest adjective most recent, newest, just out, up to the minute, state-of-the-art, current; informal in, with it, trendy, hip, hot, happening, cool.
OPPOSITES old.

latitude noun freedom, scope, leeway, (breathing) space, flexibility, liberty, independence, free rein, licence, slack.
OPPOSITES restriction.

latter adjective **1** *the latter half of the season:* later, closing, end, concluding, final. **2** *the latter option:* last-mentioned, second, last, final.
OPPOSITES earlier, former.

the beginning. **2** recent. **3** (**the latter**) referring to the second-mentioned of two people or things.
▫ **latter-day** modern or contemporary.
■ **latterly** adverb.

lattice noun a structure or pattern of strips crossing each other with square or diamond-shaped spaces left between.

Latvian noun a person from Latvia.
● adjective relating to Latvia.

laud /lawd/ verb formal praise highly.

laudable adjective deserving praise.

laudanum /law-duh-nuhm/ noun a liquid containing opium, formerly used as a sedative.

laudatory /law-duh-tuh-ri/ adjective formal expressing praise.

laugh verb **1** make sounds and movements that express amusement. **2** (**laugh at**) make fun of. **3** (**laugh something off**) dismiss something by treating it light-heartedly.
● noun **1** an act of laughing. **2** (**a laugh**) informal someone or something that makes people laugh.
▫ **laughing gas** nitrous oxide, used as an anaesthetic. **laughing stock** a person who is made fun of.

laughable adjective ridiculous or absurd; deserving to be laughed at.
■ **laughably** adverb.

laughter noun the action or sound of laughing.

launch[1] verb **1** move a boat or ship from land into the water. **2** send a rocket or missile on its course. **3** begin an enterprise or introduce a new product. **4** (**launch into**)

begin something energetically and enthusiastically. ● noun an act of launching something.
■ **launcher** noun.

launch[2] noun a large motorboat.

launder verb (**launders, laundering, laundered**) **1** wash and iron clothes, sheets, etc. **2** informal pass illegally obtained money through a bank or business to conceal its origins.

launderette or **laundrette** noun Brit. a place with coin-operated washing machines and dryers for public use.

laundry noun (plural **laundries**) **1** clothes, sheets, etc. that need to be washed or that have been newly washed. **2** a room or building where clothes, sheets, etc. are washed.

laurel noun **1** an evergreen shrub or small tree with dark green glossy leaves. **2** (**laurels**) a crown of bay leaves awarded as a mark of honour in classical times. **3** (**laurels**) honour or praise.
▫ **rest on your laurels** be so satisfied with what you have achieved that you make no more effort.

lava noun hot molten rock that erupts from a volcano, or solid rock formed when this cools.

lavatorial adjective (of humour) referring to bodily functions in a rude way.

lavatory noun (plural **lavatories**) a toilet.

lavender noun **1** a strong-smelling shrub with bluish-purple flowers. **2** a pale bluish-purple colour.

lavish adjective **1** very rich, elaborate, or

THESAURUS

laugh verb *he started to laugh:* chuckle, chortle, guffaw, giggle, titter, snigger, roar, hoot with laughter, split your sides; informal be in stitches, be rolling in the aisles, crease up, fall about, crack up; Brit. informal kill yourself.
● noun **1** *he gave a short laugh:* chuckle, chortle, guffaw, giggle, titter, snigger, roar, hoot, shriek. **2** (informal) *I entered the contest for a laugh:* joke, prank, bit of fun, jest; informal lark, hoot, scream.
▫ **laugh at ridicule**, mock, deride, scoff at, jeer at, sneer at, jibe at, make fun of, poke fun at; informal take the mickey out of; Austral./NZ informal poke mullock at. **laugh something off dismiss**, make a joke of, make light of, shrug off, brush aside, scoff at; informal pooh-pooh.

laughter noun **1** *the laughter subsided:* laughing, chuckling, chortling, guffawing, giggling, tittering, sniggering. **2** *a source of laughter:* amusement, entertainment, humour, mirth, merriment, gaiety, hilarity, jollity, fun.

launch verb **1** *a chair was launched at him:* propel, throw, hurl, fling, pitch, lob, let fly, fire, shoot; informal chuck, heave, sling. **2** *the government launched a new campaign:* start, begin, initiate, put in place, set up, inaugurate, introduce; informal kick off.

lavatory noun toilet, WC, convenience, privy, latrine; Brit. cloakroom; N. Amer. washroom, bathroom, rest room, men's/ladies' room, comfort station; informal little girls'/boys' room, smallest room; Brit. informal loo, bog, the Ladies, the Gents, khazi; N. Amer. informal can, john; Austral./NZ informal dunny.

lavish adjective **1** *a lavish apartment:* sumptuous, luxurious, gorgeous, costly, expensive, opulent, grand, splendid, rich, fancy; informal posh. **2** *he was lavish with his hospitality:* generous, liberal, bountiful, unstinting, unsparing, free, munificent, extravagant, prodigal. **3** *lavish praise:* extravagant, excessive, wasteful, prodigal, fulsome, effusive. **4** *lavish amounts of champagne:* abundant, copious, plentiful,

luxurious. **2** giving or given in large amounts. • **verb** give something in large or generous quantities.
■ **lavishly** adverb.

law noun **1** a rule or system of rules that regulates the actions of the people in a country or community. **2** a rule laying down the correct procedure or behaviour in a sport. **3** a statement of fact to the effect that a particular phenomenon always occurs if certain conditions are present.

lawful adjective allowed by or obeying law or rules.
■ **lawfully** adverb.

lawless adjective not governed by or obeying laws.
■ **lawlessness** noun.

lawn noun **1** an area of mown grass in a garden or park. **2** a fine linen or cotton fabric.

lawnmower noun a machine for cutting the grass on a lawn.

lawrencium noun a radioactive metallic element that is produced artificially.

lawsuit noun a claim brought to a law court to be decided.

lawyer noun a person who practises or studies law.

lax adjective **1** not strict, severe, or careful enough. **2** (of limbs or muscles) relaxed.
■ **laxity** noun.

laxative adjective tending to make someone empty their bowels. • **noun** a laxative drug or medicine.

lay[1] verb (**lays**, **laying**, past and past participle **laid**) **1** put something down gently or carefully. **2** put something down in position for use. **3** assign or place. **4** (of a female bird, reptile, etc.) produce an egg from inside the body. **5** stake an amount of money in a bet.
□ **lay-by** (plural **lay-bys**) Brit. an area at the side of a road where vehicles may stop. **lay off** informal stop doing something. **lay someone off** dismiss a worker because of a shortage of work. **lay something on** Brit. provide food or entertainment. **lay something out** construct or arrange something according to a plan.

> **!** don't confuse **lay** and **lie**. You *lay* something, as in *they are going to lay the carpet*, but you *lie* down on a bed or other flat surface. The past tense and past participle of **lay** is **laid**, as in *they laid the groundwork*; the past tense of **lie** is **lay** (*he lay on the floor*) and the past participle is **lain** (*she had lain on the bed for hours*).

lay[2] adjective **1** not having an official position in the Church. **2** not having professional qualifications or expert knowledge.

lay[3] noun a short poem intended to be sung.

lay[4] past of LIE[1].

---

liberal, prolific, generous; literary plenteous.
OPPOSITES meagre, mean, frugal.
• **verb** *she lavished money on her children:* shower, heap, pour, deluge, throw at, squander, dissipate.
OPPOSITES begrudge, stint.

law noun **1** *the law:* legislation, constitution, rules, regulations, legal code. **2** *a new law:* regulation, statute, act, bill, decree, edict, rule, ruling, dictum, command, order, directive, dictate, diktat, fiat, by-law; N. Amer. formal ordinance. **3** *the laws of the game:* rule, regulation, principle, convention, instruction, guideline. **4** *a moral law:* principle, rule, precept, commandment, belief, creed, credo, maxim, tenet, doctrine, canon.

lawyer noun legal adviser, solicitor, barrister, advocate, counsel, Queen's Counsel, QC; N. Amer. attorney, counselor(-at-law); informal brief, legal eagle.

lay[1] verb **1** *Curtis laid the newspaper on the table:* put (down), place, set (down), deposit, rest, position, shove; informal stick, dump, park, plonk; Brit. informal bung. **2** *I'd lay money on it:* bet, wager, gamble, stake. **3** *we laid plans for the next voyage:* devise,

arrange, prepare, work out, hatch, design, plan, scheme, plot, conceive, put together, draw up, produce, develop, formulate; informal cook up.
□ **lay something down 1** *they laid down their weapons:* **relinquish,** surrender, give up, abandon. **2** *the ground rules have been laid down:* **formulate,** set down, draw up, frame, prescribe, ordain, dictate, decree, enact, pass, decide, determine. **lay something in stock up with/on,** stockpile, store (up), amass, hoard, stow (away), put aside/away/by, garner, squirrel away; informal salt away, stash away. **lay off** (informal) **give up,** stop, refrain from, abstain from, desist from, cut out; informal pack in, leave off, quit. **lay someone off make redundant,** dismiss, let go, discharge, give notice to; informal sack, fire. **lay something on provide,** supply, furnish, line up, organize, prepare, produce, make available; informal fix up. **lay someone out** (informal) **knock out/down,** knock unconscious, fell, floor, flatten; informal KO, kayo; Brit. informal knock for six.

lay[2] adjective **1** *a lay preacher:* non-ordained, non-clerical. **2** *a lay audience:* non-expert, non-professional, non-specialist, non-technical, amateur, unqualified, untrained.

layabout noun disapproving a person who does little or no work.

layer noun a sheet or thickness of material covering a surface. ● verb arrange or cut in a layer or layers.

layette noun a set of clothing and bedclothes for a newborn baby.

layman or **laywoman** noun (plural **laymen** or **laywomen**) 1 a member of a Church who is not a priest or minister. 2 a person without professional or specialized knowledge.

layout noun the way in which something is laid out.

laze verb (**lazes, lazing, lazed**) spend time relaxing or doing very little.

lazy adjective (**lazier, laziest**) 1 unwilling to work or use energy. 2 showing a lack of effort or care.
■ **lazily** adverb **laziness** noun.

lazybones noun informal a lazy person.

lb abbreviation pounds (in weight).

lbw abbreviation Cricket leg before wicket.

lea noun literary an area of grassy land.

leach verb (of chemicals or minerals) be removed from soil by water passing through it.

lead¹ verb (**leads, leading, led**) 1 cause a person or animal to go with you. 2 be a route or means of access. 3 (**lead to**) result in. 4 cause someone to do or believe something. 5 be in charge of. 6 have the advantage in a race or game. 7 have a particular way of life. 8 (**lead up to**) come before or result in. 9 (**lead someone on**) deceive someone into believing that you are attracted to them. ● noun 1 an example for other people to copy. 2 a position of advantage in a contest. 3 the chief part in a play or film. 4 a clue to follow when trying to solve a problem. 5 Brit. a strap or cord for controlling and guiding a dog. 6 a wire conveying electric current.

lead² noun 1 a heavy bluish-grey metal. 2 the part of a pencil that makes a mark.

leaded adjective 1 framed or covered with lead. 2 (of petrol) containing lead.

leaden adjective 1 dull, heavy, or slow. 2 dull grey in colour.

leader noun 1 a person or thing that leads. 2 the most successful or advanced person or thing in a particular area. 3 the main player in a music group. 4 a newspaper article giving the editor's opinion.
■ **leadership** noun.

THESAURUS

layer noun sheet, stratum, level, tier, seam, coat, coating, film, covering, blanket, skin.

layout noun arrangement, design, plan, formation, format, configuration, composition, organization, geography, structure.

laze verb idle, relax, unwind, do nothing, loaf around/about, lounge around/about, loll around/about, lie around/about, take it easy; informal hang around, chill out, veg out.

lazy adjective 1 *a lazy worker:* idle, indolent, slothful, bone idle, work-shy, shiftless. 2 *a lazy stream:* slow, slow-moving, languid, leisurely, lethargic, sluggish.
OPPOSITES industrious, fast.

lead verb 1 *Michelle led them into the house:* guide, conduct, show (the way), usher, escort, steer, shepherd, accompany, see, take. 2 *he led us to believe they were lying:* cause, induce, prompt, move, persuade, drive, make. 3 *she led a coalition of radicals:* control, preside over, head, command, govern, run, manage, rule, be in charge of; informal head up. 4 *Rangers were leading at half-time:* be ahead, be winning, be (out) in front, be in the lead, be first. 5 *the champion was leading the field:* be ahead of, head, outrun, outstrip, outpace, leave behind, outdo, outclass, beat. 6 *I just want to lead a normal life:* live, have, spend, follow, pass, enjoy.
OPPOSITES follow.

● noun 1 *I was in the lead early on:* first place, winning position, vanguard. 2 *Newcastle built up a 3-0 lead:* margin, advantage, gap, edge, interval. 3 *sixth-formers should give a lead to younger pupils:* example, model, pattern, standard, guidance, direction, role model. 4 *playing the lead:* leading role, star/starring role, title role, principal role. 5 *a dog on a lead:* leash, tether, rope, chain. 6 *detectives were following up a new lead:* clue, pointer, hint, tip, tip-off, suggestion, indication, sign.
● adjective *the lead position:* leading, first, top, foremost, front, pole, head, chief, principal, premier.
□ **lead to** result in, cause, bring on/about, give rise to, create, produce, occasion, effect, generate, contribute to, promote, provoke, stir up, spark off.

leader noun chief, head, principal, commander, captain, controller, superior, chairman, chair, director, manager, superintendent, supervisor, overseer, master, mistress, prime minister, president, premier, governor, ruler, monarch, sovereign; informal boss, skipper, gaffer, guv'nor, number one.
OPPOSITES follower, supporter.

leadership noun 1 *the leadership of the Party:* control, rule, command, dominion, headship, directorship, premiership, chairmanship, governorship, captaincy. 2 *firm leadership:* guidance, direction,

leading adjective most important, or in first place.
□ **leading light** a prominent or influential person. **leading question** a question that encourages someone to give the answer that you want.

leaf noun (plural **leaves**) **1** a flat green part of a plant that is attached to a stem. **2** a single sheet of paper in a book. **3** gold or silver in the form of a very thin sheet. **4** a hinged or detachable part of a table. • verb (**leaf through**) turn over pages or papers, reading them quickly or casually.
□ **turn over a new leaf** start to behave in a better way.
■ **leafy** adjective.

leaflet noun **1** a printed sheet of paper containing information or advertising. **2** a small leaf. • verb (**leaflets, leafleting, leafleted**) distribute leaflets to.

league¹ noun **1** a collection of people, countries, or groups that combine to help or protect each other. **2** a group of sports clubs that play each other over a period for a championship. **3** a class of quality or excellence.
□ **in league** (of two or more people) making secret plans.

league² noun a former measure of distance, of about three miles.

leak verb **1** accidentally allow contents to escape or enter through a hole or crack. **2** (of liquid, gas, etc.) escape or enter accidentally through a hole or crack. **3** deliberately give out secret information. • noun **1** a hole or crack through which contents leak. **2** an instance of leaking.
■ **leakage** noun **leaky** adjective.

lean¹ verb (**leans, leaning,** past and past participle **leaned** or Brit. **leant**) **1** be in a sloping position. **2** (**lean against** or **on**) rest against. **3** (**lean on**) rely on for support. **4** (**lean to** or **towards**) favour a particular point of view.
□ **lean-to** (plural **lean-tos**) a small building sharing a wall with a larger building.

lean² adjective **1** (of a person) having little fat; thin. **2** (of meat) containing little fat. **3** (of a period of time) unproductive.

leaning noun a tendency or preference.

leap verb (**leaps, leaping,** past and past participle **leaped** or **leapt**) **1** jump high or a long way. **2** move quickly and suddenly. **3** (**leap at**) accept something eagerly. **4** increase dramatically. • noun an act of leaping.
□ **leap year** a year with 366 days, occurring every four years.

leapfrog noun a game in which players in turn jump over others who are bending down. • verb (**leapfrogs, leapfrogging, leapfrogged**) **1** jump over someone in leapfrog. **2** overtake others to move into a leading position.

---

authority, management, supervision, government.

leading adjective main, chief, top, front, major, prime, principal, foremost, key, central, dominant, most powerful, most important, greatest, pre-eminent, star. OPPOSITES subordinate, minor.

leaf noun *a folder of loose leaves:* page, sheet, folio.
• verb *he leafed through the documents:* flick, flip, thumb, skim, browse, glance, riffle, scan, run your eye over, peruse.

leaflet noun pamphlet, booklet, brochure, handbill, circular, flyer, handout; N. Amer. folder, dodger.

league noun **1** *a league of nations:* alliance, confederation, confederacy, federation, union, association, coalition, consortium, affiliation, cooperative, partnership, fellowship, syndicate. **2** *the store is not in the same league:* class, group, category, level, standard.
□ **in league** collaborating, cooperating, in alliance, allied, conspiring, hand in glove; informal in cahoots.

leak verb **1** *oil was leaking from the tanker:* seep, escape, ooze, drip, dribble, drain, run. **2** *civil servants leaking information:* disclose, divulge, reveal, make public, tell, expose, release, bring into the open.
• noun **1** *check that there are no leaks in the bag:* hole, opening, puncture, perforation, gash, slit, break, crack, fissure, rupture, tear. **2** *a gas leak:* escape, leakage, discharge, seepage. **3** *leaks to the media:* disclosure, revelation, exposé.

lean¹ verb **1** *Polly leaned against the door:* rest, recline. **2** *trees leaning in the wind:* slant, incline, bend, tilt, slope, tip, list. **3** *he leans towards existentialist philosophy:* tend, incline, gravitate, have a preference for, have an affinity with. **4** *someone to lean on:* depend, rely, count, bank, trust in.

lean² adjective **1** *a tall, lean man:* slim, thin, slender, spare, spindly, wiry, lanky. **2** *a lean harvest:* meagre, sparse, poor, mean, inadequate, insufficient, paltry. OPPOSITES fat, abundant.

leaning noun inclination, tendency, bent, propensity, penchant, preference, predisposition, predilection.

leap verb **1** *he leapt over the gate:* jump, vault, spring, bound, hop, clear. **2** *profits leapt by 55%:* rise, jump, soar, rocket, skyrocket, shoot up.
• noun *a leap of 33%:* rise, surge, upsurge, upswing, upturn.

learn verb (**learns**, **learning**, past and past participle **learned** or **learnt**) **1** gain knowledge or skill through study or experience. **2** become aware of something through observing or hearing about it. **3** memorize. ■ **learner** noun.

learned /ler-nid/ adjective having gained a lot of knowledge by studying.

learning noun knowledge or skills gained by studying.

lease noun an agreement by which one person uses land, property, etc. which belongs to another person for a stated time in return for payment. •verb (**leases**, **leasing**, **leased**) let out or rent land, property, etc. by a lease.

leasehold noun the holding of property by a lease.

leash noun a dog's lead.

least determiner & pronoun (usu. **the least**) smallest in amount, extent, or significance. •adverb to the smallest extent or degree. □ **at least 1** not less than. **2** if nothing else. **3** anyway.

leather noun a material made from the skin of an animal by tanning or a similar process.

leathery adjective tough and hard like leather.

leave[1] verb (**leaves**, **leaving**, **left**) **1** go away from. **2** stop attending or working for. **3** go away without taking someone or something. **4** (**be left**) remain to be used or dealt with. **5** let someone do something without interfering. **6** put something somewhere to be collected or dealt with. **7** give something to someone in a will. **8** (**leave someone/thing out**) fail to include someone or something. ■ **leaver** noun.

leave[2] noun **1** (also **leave of absence**) time when you have permission to be absent from work or duty. **2** formal permission. □ **take your leave** formal say goodbye.

leaven /lev-uhn/ noun a substance added to dough to make it ferment and rise. •verb make something less serious or dull by adding something.

leaves plural of **LEAF**.

Lebanese /le-buh-**neez**/ noun (plural **Lebanese**) a person from Lebanon. •adjective relating to Lebanon.

lecher noun a lecherous man. ■ **lechery** noun.

lecherous adjective (of a man) showing sexual desire in an offensive way.

lectern noun a tall stand with a sloping top

THESAURUS

learn verb **1** *learn a foreign language:* acquire, grasp, master, take in, absorb, assimilate, digest, familiarize yourself with, be taught; informal get the hang of. **2** *she learnt the poem:* memorize, learn by heart, commit to memory, learn parrot-fashion, get off/down pat. **3** *he learned that the school would be closing:* discover, find out, become aware, be informed, hear, understand, gather; informal get wind of the fact.

learned adjective scholarly, erudite, knowledgeable, widely read, cultured, intellectual, academic, literary, bookish, highbrow; informal brainy.
OPPOSITES ignorant.

learner noun beginner, novice, starter, trainee, apprentice, pupil, student, fledgling.
OPPOSITES expert, veteran.

learning noun study, knowledge, education, schooling, tuition, teaching, scholarship, erudition, research, understanding, wisdom.
OPPOSITES ignorance.

lease verb **1** *the film crew leased a large hangar:* rent, hire, charter. **2** *they leased the mill to a reputable family:* rent (out), let (out), hire (out), charter (out), loan (out).

leave[1] verb **1** *I left the hotel:* go away from, depart from, withdraw from, retire from, take yourself off from, take your leave of, pull out of, quit, escape from, flee, abandon, desert, vacate; informal push off, shove off, clear out/off, split, make tracks. **2** *the next morning we left for Leicester:* set off, head, make, set sail, get going. **3** *he's left his wife:* abandon, desert, jilt, leave in the lurch, leave high and dry, throw over; informal dump, ditch, walk/run out on. **4** *he left his job in November:* resign from, retire from, step down from, withdraw from, pull out of, give up; informal quit, jack in. **5** *she left her handbag on a bus:* leave behind, forget, lose, mislay. **6** *I thought I'd leave it to the experts:* entrust, hand over, pass on, refer, delegate. **7** *he left her £100,000:* bequeath, will, endow, hand down.
OPPOSITES arrive.
□ **leave someone/something out 1** *Adam left out the address:* miss out, omit, overlook, forget, skip, miss. **2** *he was left out of the England squad:* exclude, omit, drop, pass over.

leave[2] noun **1** *the judge granted leave to appeal:* permission, consent, authorization, sanction, dispensation, approval, clearance, blessing, agreement, assent; informal the go-ahead, the green light. **2** *he was on leave:* holiday, vacation, break, furlough, sabbatical, leave of absence; informal vac.

from which a speaker can read while standing up.

lecture noun **1** an educational talk to an audience. **2** a long telling-off or critical talk. • verb (**lectures, lecturing, lectured**) **1** give a lecture, or a series of lectures. **2** give someone a long telling-off. ■ **lecturer** noun.

led past and past participle of **LEAD**[1].

ledge noun a narrow horizontal surface sticking out from a wall, cliff, etc.

ledger noun a book in which financial accounts are kept.

lee noun the side of something that provides shelter from wind or weather.

leech noun **1** a worm that sucks the blood of animals or people. **2** a person who lives off other people.

leek noun a plant with a long cylindrical bulb which is eaten as a vegetable.

leer verb look or smile at someone in a lustful or unpleasant way. • noun a lustful or unpleasant look or smile.

leery adjective informal wary.

lees /leez/ plural noun the sediment left in the bottom of a bottle or barrel of wine.

leeward adjective & adverb on or towards the side that is sheltered from the wind.

leeway noun the amount of freedom to move or act that is available.

left[1] adjective **1** on or towards the side of a person or thing which is to the west when the person or thing is facing north. **2** left-wing. • adverb on or to the left side. • noun **1** (**the left**) the left-hand part, side, or direction. **2** a left turn. **3** (often **the Left**) a left-wing group or party.

▢ **left-field** unconventional or experimental. **left wing** socialist, or supporting political or social change.

left[2] past and past participle of **LEAVE**[1].

leftovers plural noun food remaining after the rest has been eaten. • adjective (**leftover**) remaining after the rest of something has been used.

leg noun **1** each of the limbs on which a person or animal moves and stands. **2** each of the parts of a table, chair, etc. that rest on the floor and support its weight. **3** a section of a journey, race, etc. **4** (in sport) each of two or more games making up a round of a competition. • verb (**legs, legging, legged**) (**leg it**) informal run away.

legacy noun (plural **legacies**) **1** an amount of money or property left to someone in a will. **2** something handed down by a predecessor.

legal adjective **1** having to do with the law. **2** permitted by law.
▢ **legal aid** money given to people who cannot afford to pay for a lawyer. **legal tender** accepted methods of payment such as coins or banknotes.
■ **legality** noun **legally** adverb.

legalize or **legalise** verb (**legalizes, legalizing, legalized**) make something legal. ■ **legalization** noun.

legate /le-guht/ noun a representative of the Pope.

legation /li-gay-sh'n/ noun **1** a diplomat below the rank of ambassador, and their staff. **2** the official residence of a diplomat.

legato /li-gah-toh/ adverb & adjective Music in a smooth, flowing way.

legend noun **1** a traditional story from long

lecture noun **1** *a lecture on children's literature:* speech, talk, address, discourse, presentation, oration. **2** *Dave got a severe lecture:* reprimand, scolding, rebuke, reproach; informal dressing-down, telling-off, talking-to, tongue-lashing.
• verb **1** *he lectures on drugs:* talk, speak, discourse, hold forth, teach; informal spout, sound off. **2** *he was lectured by the headmaster:* reprimand, scold, rebuke, reproach, take to task, upbraid, castigate; informal tell off, bawl out; Brit. informal tick off, carpet.
OPPOSITES praise.

leeway noun freedom, scope, latitude, space, room, liberty, flexibility, licence, free hand, free rein.

left adjective left-hand, sinistral; Nautical port. OPPOSITES right, starboard.

left-wing adjective socialist, communist, leftist, Labour; informal Commie, lefty, red, pinko.
OPPOSITES right-wing, conservative.

leg noun *the first leg of a European tour:* part, stage, section, phase, stretch, lap.

legacy noun **1** *a legacy from a great aunt:* bequest, inheritance, endowment, gift, birthright, estate, heirloom. **2** *the legacy of the war:* consequence, effect, repercussion, aftermath, by-product, result.

legal adjective **1** *a legal tax-avoidance scheme:* lawful, legitimate, within the law, legalized, valid, permissible, permitted, allowable, allowed, above board, acceptable, constitutional; informal legit. **2** *the legal profession:* judicial, juridical, forensic.
OPPOSITES illegal.

legend noun **1** *the Arthurian legends:* myth, saga, epic, folk tale, folk story, fable, lore, folklore, mythology, folk tradition. **2** *pop legends:* celebrity, star, superstar, icon, phenomenon, luminary, giant, hero; informal celeb, megastar. **3** *the wording of the legend:* caption, inscription, dedication, slogan, heading, title.

ago which is not definitely true. **2** a very famous person. **3** an inscription, caption, or list explaining the symbols used in a map or table.

legendary adjective **1** described in legends. **2** remarkable enough to be famous.

legerdemain /lej-er-di-**mayn**/ noun **1** skilful use of your hands when performing magic tricks. **2** trickery.

leggings plural noun **1** women's tight-fitting stretchy trousers. **2** strong protective coverings for the legs, worn over trousers.

leggy adjective (**leggier, leggiest**) long-legged.

legible adjective (of handwriting or print) clear enough to read.
■ **legibility** noun **legibly** adverb.

legion noun **1** a division of 3,000 to 6,000 men in the army of ancient Rome. **2** (**a legion** or **legions of**) a vast number of.
●**adjective** literary great in number.

legionary noun (plural **legionaries**) a soldier in an ancient Roman legion.

legionnaire /lee-juh-**nair**/ noun a member of a legion.
□ **legionnaires' disease** a form of pneumonia.

legislate verb (**legislates, legislating, legislated**) **1** make laws. **2** (**legislate for** or **against**) prepare for or try to prevent a situation.
■ **legislator** noun.

legislation noun laws.

legislative adjective **1** having the power to make laws. **2** relating to laws.

legislature noun the group of people who make a country's laws.

legitimate adjective /li-**jit**-i-muht/ **1** allowed by the law or rules. **2** able to be defended; reasonable. **3** (of a child) born to parents

who are married to each other. ●verb /li-jit-i-mayt/ (**legitimates, legitimating, legitimated**) make something legitimate.
■ **legitimacy** noun **legitimately** adverb.

☑ leg-, not lig-: legitimate.

legitimize or **legitimise** verb (**legitimizes, legitimizing, legitimized**) make something legitimate.

legume /**leg**-yoom/ noun a plant with seeds in pods, such as the pea.
■ **leguminous** adjective.

leisure noun time for relaxation or enjoyment.
□ **at leisure 1** not occupied; free. **2** in an unhurried way.

leisurely adjective relaxed and unhurried.
●adverb without hurry.

lemming noun a small Arctic rodent, some kinds of which periodically migrate in large numbers (they are popularly believed to run headlong into the sea and drown).

lemon noun **1** a pale yellow citrus fruit with thick skin and acidic juice. **2** a pale yellow colour.
□ **lemon curd** a sweet spread made with lemons.

lemonade noun a sweet drink made with lemon juice or flavouring.

lemur /**lee**-mer/ noun an animal resembling a monkey, found only in Madagascar.

lend verb (**lends, lending, lent**) **1** allow someone to use something on the understanding that they will return it. **2** give someone money on condition that they will pay it back later. **3** add or contribute a particular quality. **4** (**lend itself to**) be suitable for.
■ **lender** noun.

length noun **1** the measurement or extent

THESAURUS

legendary adjective **1** legendary kings: fabled, heroic, traditional, fairy-tale, storybook, mythical, mythological. **2** a legendary figure in the trade-union movement: famous, celebrated, famed, renowned, acclaimed, illustrious, esteemed, honoured, exalted, venerable, distinguished, great, eminent.
OPPOSITES historical, insignificant.

legion noun horde, throng, multitude, crowd, mass, mob, gang, swarm, flock, herd, army.

legislation noun law, rules, rulings, regulations, acts, bills, statutes; N. Amer. formal ordinances.

legitimate adjective **1** legitimate gambling: legal, lawful, authorized, permitted, sanctioned, approved, licensed; informal legit. **2** the legitimate heir: rightful, lawful, genuine, authentic, real, true, proper.

3 legitimate grounds for unease: valid, sound, admissible, acceptable, well founded, justifiable, reasonable, sensible, just, fair, bona fide.
OPPOSITES illegal, invalid.

leisure noun free time, spare time, time off, rest, recreation, relaxation.
OPPOSITES work.

leisurely adjective unhurried, relaxed, easy, gentle, sedate, comfortable, restful, undemanding, slow.
OPPOSITES hurried.

lend verb **1** I'll lend you my towel: loan, let someone use, advance; Brit. informal sub. **2** these examples lend weight to his assertions: add, impart, give, bestow, confer, provide, supply, furnish, contribute.
OPPOSITES borrow.

length noun **1** the whole length of the valley: extent, distance, span, reach, area, expanse, of something from end to end. **2** the amount of time that something lasts. **3** the quality of being long. **4** a stretch or piece of something. **5** the extent to which someone does something: *going to great lengths.*

lengthen verb make or become longer.

lengthways or **lengthwise** adverb in a direction parallel with a thing's length.

lengthy adjective (**lengthier, lengthiest**) lasting a long time.
■ lengthily adverb.

lenient /**lee**-ni-uhnt/ adjective not strict; merciful or tolerant.
■ leniency noun leniently adverb.

lens noun **1** a piece of transparent curved material that concentrates or spreads out light rays, used in cameras, glasses, etc. **2** the transparent part of the eye that focuses light on to the retina.

Lent noun (in the Christian Church) the period immediately before Easter.

lent past and past participle of **LEND**.

lentil noun an edible seed with one flat and one curved side.

lento adverb & adjective Music slow or slowly.

Leo noun a sign of the zodiac (the Lion), 23 July–22 August.

leonine /**lee**-uh-nyn/ adjective relating to or like a lion or lions.

leopard noun (feminine **leopardess**) a large cat with a spotted coat, found in Africa and southern Asia.

leotard /**lee**-uh-tard/ noun a close-fitting, stretchy one-piece garment covering the body to the top of the thighs, worn for dance, exercise, etc.

leper noun **1** a person who has leprosy. **2** someone who is rejected or avoided by other people.

lepidopterist noun a person who studies or collects butterflies or moths.

leprechaun /**lep**-ruh-kawn/ noun (in Irish folklore) a mischievous elf.

leprosy noun a contagious disease that affects the skin and can cause deformities.
■ leprous adjective.

lesbian noun a woman who is sexually attracted to other women. ● adjective relating to lesbians.
■ lesbianism noun.

lesion /**lee**-zhuhn/ noun an area of skin or part of the body which has been damaged.

less determiner & pronoun **1** a smaller amount of; not as much. **2** fewer in number. ● adverb to a smaller extent; not so much. ● preposition minus.

> **!** make sure you distinguish between **less** and **fewer**. Use **fewer** with plural nouns, as in *there are fewer tourists this year;* use **less** with nouns referring to things that cannot be counted, as in *there is less blossom on this tree.* Using **less** with a plural noun (*less tourists*) is wrong.

lessee noun a person who holds the lease of a property.

lessen verb make or become less.

lesser adjective not so great, large, or important as the other or the rest.

lesson noun **1** a period of learning or teaching. **2** a thing that has been learned. **3** a thing that acts as a warning or encouragement. **4** a passage from the Bible read aloud during a church service.

THESAURUS

stretch, range, scope. **2** *a considerable length of time:* period, duration, stretch, span. **3** *a length of blue silk:* piece, strip.
□ at length **1** *he spoke at length:* **for a long time**, for ages, for hours, interminably, endlessly, ceaselessly, unendingly. **2** *his search led him, at length, to Seattle:* **eventually**, in time, finally, at (long) last, in the end, ultimately.

lengthen verb **1** *he lengthened his stride:* elongate, make longer, extend, expand, widen, broaden, enlarge. **2** *you'll need to lengthen the cooking time:* prolong, make longer, increase, extend, expand, protract, stretch out.
OPPOSITES shorten.

lengthy adjective (very) long, long-lasting, protracted, extended, long-drawn-out, prolonged, interminable, time-consuming, long-winded.
OPPOSITES short.

lenient adjective merciful, forgiving,

forbearing, tolerant, charitable, humane, indulgent, magnanimous.
OPPOSITES severe.

lessen verb **1** *exercise lessens the risk of heart disease:* reduce, make less/smaller, minimize, decrease, attenuate, narrow, moderate. **2** *the pain began to lessen:* grow less, grow smaller, decrease, diminish, decline, subside, slacken, abate, fade, die down, let up, ease off, tail off, drop (off/away), dwindle, ebb, wane, recede.
OPPOSITES increase.

lesser adjective **1** *a lesser offence:* less important, minor, secondary, subsidiary, peripheral. **2** *you look down at us lesser mortals:* subordinate, minor, inferior, second-class, subservient, lowly, humble.
OPPOSITES greater, superior.

lesson noun **1** *a maths lesson:* class, session, seminar, tutorial, lecture, period. **2** *Stuart's accident should be a lesson to all parents:* warning, deterrent, caution, example,

lessor noun a person who lets a property to someone else.

lest conjunction formal **1** with the intention of preventing; to avoid the risk of. **2** because of the possibility of.

let verb (**lets, letting, let**) **1** allow. **2** used to express an intention, suggestion, or order: *let's have a drink.* **3** allow someone to use a room or property in return for payment. ▪ noun **1** Brit. a period during which a room or property is rented. **2** (in racket sports) a situation in which a point is not counted and is played for again. □ **let alone** not to mention. **let someone down** fail to support or help someone. **let someone go** allow someone to go free. **let yourself go 1** act in a relaxed way. **2** become careless in your habits or appearance. **let someone off 1** choose not to punish someone. **2** excuse someone from a task. **let something off** cause a gun, firework, etc. to fire or explode. **let up** informal become less strong or severe.

lethal adjective **1** able to cause death. **2** very harmful or destructive.
▪ **lethally** adverb.

lethargic adjective lacking energy or enthusiasm.
▪ **lethargically** adverb.

lethargy /leth-er-ji/ noun a lack of energy and enthusiasm.

let's short form let us.

letter noun **1** any of the symbols of an alphabet. **2** a written communication, usually sent by post. **3** (**letters**) old use knowledge of literature. ▪ verb (**letters, lettering, lettered**) **1** write something with letters. **2** (**lettered**) old use able to read and write.
□ **letter bomb** an explosive device hidden in a small package, which explodes when the package is opened. **letter box** a slot in a door through which letters are delivered. **the letter of the law** the precise terms of a law or rule.

letterhead noun a printed heading on stationery.

lettuce noun a plant whose leaves are eaten in salads.

leucocyte or **leukocyte** /loo-koh-syt/ noun technical a white blood cell.

leukaemia /loo-kee-mi-uh/ (US spelling **leukemia**) noun a serious disease in which too many white blood cells are produced.

levee /lev-i/ noun an embankment built to stop a river overflowing.

level noun **1** a position on a scale. **2** the

THESAURUS

message, moral.

let verb **1** *let him sleep for now:* allow, permit, give permission to, give leave to, authorize, license, empower, enable, entitle. **2** *they've let their flat:* rent (out), let out, lease, hire (out).
OPPOSITES prevent, prohibit.
□ **let someone down** fail, disappoint, disillusion, abandon, desert, leave in the lurch. **let go** release (your hold on), loose your hold on, relinquish. **let something off** detonate, discharge, explode, set off, fire (off), launch. **let someone off 1** (informal) *I'll let you off this time:* pardon, forgive, acquit, absolve, exonerate, clear, vindicate; informal let someone off the hook. **2** *he let me off work:* excuse from, exempt from, spare from. **let something out 1** *I let out a cry of triumph:* utter, emit, give (vent to), produce, issue, express, voice, release. **2** *she let out that he'd given her a lift home:* reveal, make known, tell, disclose, mention, divulge, let slip, give away, let it be known, blurt out. **let someone out** release, liberate, (set) free, let go, discharge, set/turn loose. **let up** (informal) **1** *the rain has let up.* See **LESSEN** sense 2. **2** *you never let up, do you?* relax, ease up/off, slow down, pause, break (off), take a break, rest, stop.

lethal adjective fatal, deadly, mortal, terminal, life-threatening, murderous,

poisonous, toxic, noxious, venomous, dangerous.
OPPOSITES harmless, safe.

letter noun **1** *capital letters:* character, sign, symbol, figure. **2** *she received a letter:* message, note, line, missive, dispatch, communication, correspondence, post, mail; formal epistle.

level adjective **1** *a smooth and level surface:* flat, smooth, even, uniform, plane, flush, horizontal. **2** *he kept his voice level:* steady, even, uniform, regular, constant. **3** *the scores were level:* equal, even, drawn, tied, all square, neck and neck, level pegging, on a par, evenly matched; informal even-stevens. **4** *his eyes were level with hers:* at the same height, on a level, in line.
OPPOSITES uneven, unsteady, unequal.
▪ noun **1** *the post is at a senior level:* rank, position, degree, grade, stage, standard, class, group, set, classification. **2** *a high level of employment:* quantity, amount, extent, measure, degree, volume.
▪ verb **1** *tilt the tin to level the mixture:* even off/out, flatten, smooth (out).
2 *bulldozers levelled the building:* raze (to the ground), demolish, flatten, bulldoze, destroy. **3** *Carl levelled the score:* equalize, equal, even (up), make level. **4** *he levelled his pistol at me:* aim, point, direct, train, focus, turn.
□ **on the level** (informal) genuine, straight,

amount of something that is present. **3** a horizontal line or surface. **4** height in relation to the ground. **5** a particular floor in a building. ● adjective **1** having a flat horizontal surface. **2** having the same relative height or position as someone or something else. ● verb (**levels, levelling, levelled**; US spelling **levels, leveling, leveled**) **1** make or become level. **2** aim or direct a weapon, criticism, or accusation. **3** (**level with**) informal be honest with. □ **level crossing** Brit. a place where a road crosses a railway at the same level. **level-headed** calm and sensible. ■ **levelly** adverb.

lever noun **1** a bar used to move a load with one end when pressure is applied to the other. **2** an arm or handle that is moved to operate a mechanism. ● verb (**levers, levering, levered**) lift or move with a lever.

leverage noun **1** the application of force with a lever. **2** the power to influence other people.

leveret noun a young hare.

leviathan /li-vy-uh-thuhn/ noun **1** (in the Bible) a sea monster. **2** a very large or powerful thing.

levitate verb (**levitates, levitating, levitated**) rise and hover in the air. ■ **levitation** noun.

levity noun the treatment of a serious matter with humour or lack of respect.

levy verb (**levies, levying, levied**) make a person, organization, etc. pay a tax or fine. ● noun (plural **levies**) **1** a sum of money paid as a tax. **2** old use a group of enlisted troops.

lewd adjective referring to sex in a crude

and offensive way.

lexical adjective relating to the words of a language.

lexicography noun the writing of dictionaries. ■ **lexicographer** noun.

lexicon noun **1** the vocabulary of a person, language, or branch of knowledge. **2** a dictionary.

ley line noun a line of energy believed by some people to connect some ancient sites.

liability noun (plural **liabilities**) **1** the state of being liable. **2** an amount of money that a person or company owes. **3** a person or thing likely to cause you embarrassment or trouble.

liable adjective **1** responsible by law. **2** (**liable to**) able to be punished by law for something. **3** (**liable to do**) likely to do or to be affected by.

liaise /li-ayz/ verb (**liaises, liaising, liaised**) **1** (of two or more people or groups) cooperate with each other and share information. **2** (**liaise between**) act as a link between two or more people or groups.

> ☑ remember the second *i* in **liaise** and **liaison**.

liaison noun **1** communication or cooperation between people or organizations. **2** a sexual relationship.

liana noun a tropical climbing plant that hangs from trees.

liar noun a person who tells lies.

libation noun (in the past) a drink poured

THESAURUS

honest, above board, fair, true, sincere, straightforward; informal upfront; N. Amer. informal on the up and up.

lever noun *the lid can be removed with a lever:* handle, arm, switch, crowbar, bar, jemmy. ● verb *he levered the door open:* prise, force, wrench; N. Amer. pry; informal jemmy.

leverage noun **1** *the long handles provide increased leverage:* force, purchase, grip, hold, anchorage. **2** *they have significant leverage in negotiations:* influence, power, authority, weight, sway, pull, control, say, advantage, pressure; informal clout, muscle, teeth.

levy verb impose, charge, exact, raise, collect. ● noun tax, tariff, toll, excise, duty.

liability noun **1** *they have big liabilities:* obligations, debts, arrears, dues, commitments. **2** *he's become a bit of a liability:* hindrance, encumbrance, burden, handicap, nuisance, inconvenience,

embarrassment, impediment, disadvantage, millstone. OPPOSITES asset.

liable adjective **1** *they are liable for negligence:* responsible, accountable, answerable, chargeable, blameworthy, at fault, culpable, guilty. **2** *my income is liable to fluctuate wildly:* likely, inclined, tending, apt, prone, given. **3** *areas liable to flooding:* exposed, prone, subject, susceptible, vulnerable, in danger of, at risk of.

liaise verb cooperate, collaborate, communicate, network, interface, link up.

liaison noun **1** *the branches work in close liaison:* cooperation, contact, association, connection, collaboration, communication, alliance, partnership. **2** *Dave was my White House liaison:* intermediary, mediator, middleman, contact, link, go-between. **3** *a secret liaison:* love affair, relationship, romance, attachment, fling.

liar noun fibber, deceiver, perjurer, dissembler, faker, hoaxer, impostor.

as an offering to a god.

libel noun the crime of publishing something false that is damaging to a person's reputation. •**verb** (**libels, libelling, libelled**; US spelling **libels, libeling, libeled**) publish something false about.
■ **libellous** (US spelling **libelous**) adjective.

liberal adjective **1** willing to respect and accept behaviour or opinions different from your own. **2** (in politics) supporting the freedom of individuals and in favour of moderate political reform. **3** (**Liberal**) relating to the Liberal or Liberal Democrat Party. **4** generous in applying or adding something. •**noun 1** a person with liberal views. **2** (**Liberal**) a supporter of the Liberal or Liberal Democrat Party.
■ **liberalism** noun **liberality** noun **liberally** adverb.

liberalize or **liberalise** verb (**liberalizes, liberalizing, liberalized**) remove or loosen restrictions on.
■ **liberalization** noun.

liberate verb (**liberates, liberating, liberated**) **1** set free. **2** (**liberated**) free from traditional ideas about social behaviour.
■ **liberation** noun **liberator** noun.

libertarian noun a person who believes that people should have the freedom to act and think as they wish.

libertine noun a man who is immoral and indulges too much in sexual pleasure.

liberty noun (plural **liberties**) **1** the state of being free. **2** a right or privilege. **3** the ability to act as you please. **4** informal a rude remark or disrespectful act.
□ **take liberties** behave in a disrespectful or overfamiliar way.

libidinous /li-**bid**-i-nuhss/ adjective having a strong sexual drive.

libido /li-**bee**-doh/ noun (plural **libidos**) sexual desire.

Libra /**lee**-bruh/ noun a sign of the zodiac (the Scales or Balance), 23 September–22 October.

librarian noun a person who works in a library.

library noun (plural **libraries**) **1** a building or room containing a collection of books which people can read or borrow. **2** a private collection of books.

libretto noun (plural **libretti** /li-**bret**-ti/ or **librettos**) the words of an opera or musical.
■ **librettist** noun.

Libyan noun a person from Libya. •**adjective** relating to Libya.

lice plural of **LOUSE**.

licence (US spelling **license**) noun **1** an official permit to own, use, or do something. **2** the freedom to do or say what you want.
□ **license plate** N. Amer. a number plate.

> ☑ **licence** is the spelling for the noun, and **license** for the verb; in American English the *-ense* spelling is used for both.

THESAURUS

libel noun *she sued two newspapers for libel:* defamation (of character), character assassination, calumny, misrepresentation, scandalmongering, aspersions, malicious gossip, slur, smear; informal mud-slinging.
•**verb** *she claimed the magazine had libelled her:* defame, malign, blacken someone's name, smear, cast aspersions on, drag someone's name through the mud/mire, denigrate; N. Amer. slur.

liberal adjective **1** *the values of a liberal society:* tolerant, unprejudiced, broad-minded, open-minded, enlightened, permissive, free (and easy), easy-going, libertarian, indulgent, lenient. **2** *a liberal social agenda:* progressive, advanced, modern, forward-looking, forward-thinking, enlightened, reformist, radical; informal go-ahead. **3** *a liberal interpretation of divorce laws:* flexible, broad, loose, rough, free, non-literal. **4** *liberal coatings of paint:* abundant, copious, ample, plentiful, generous, lavish. **5** *they were liberal with their cash:* generous, open-handed, unsparing, unstinting, lavish, free, munificent.
OPPOSITES reactionary, strict, miserly.

liberate verb (set) free, release, let out, let go, set loose, save, rescue, emancipate, enfranchise.
OPPOSITES imprison, enslave.

liberty noun freedom, independence, immunity, self-determination, autonomy, emancipation, sovereignty, self-government, self-rule, self determination, civil liberties, human rights.
OPPOSITES constraint, slavery.
□ **at liberty 1** *he was at liberty for three months:* free, loose, on the loose, at large, on the run, out. **2** *I am not at liberty to say:* free, able, entitled, permitted.

licence noun **1** *a driving licence:* permit, certificate, document, documentation, authorization, warrant, credentials, pass, papers. **2** *they manufacture footwear under licence:* franchise, consent, sanction, warrant, charter, concession. **3** *the army have too much licence:* freedom, liberty, free rein, latitude, independence, scope, carte blanche; informal a blank cheque.
4 *poetic licence:* disregard, inventiveness, invention, creativity, imagination, fancy, freedom.

license verb (licenses, licensing, licensed) 1 grant a licence to. 2 authorize or permit.

licensee noun a person who holds a licence to sell alcoholic drinks.

licentious /ly-sen-shuhss/ adjective behaving in a sexually immoral way.

lichen /ly-kuhn, li-chuhn/ noun a plant resembling moss which grows on rocks, walls, and trees.

lick verb 1 pass the tongue over something. 2 move lightly and quickly. • noun 1 an act of licking. 2 informal a small amount or quick application of something.

licorice US spelling of LIQUORICE.

lid noun 1 a removable or hinged cover for the top of a container. 2 an eyelid.

lido /lee-doh/ noun (plural lidos) a public open-air swimming pool.

lie[1] verb (lies, lying, lay; past participle lain) 1 be in a horizontal position on a supporting surface. 2 be in a particular state. 3 be situated or found.
□ the lie of the land 1 the features or characteristics of an area. 2 the current situation.

! don't confuse lay and lie: see the note at LAY[1].

lie[2] noun a false statement made deliberately by someone who knows it is not true. • verb (lies, lying, lied) tell a lie or lies.

liege /leej/ noun historical 1 (also liege lord) a lord under the feudal system. 2 a person who served a feudal lord.

lieu /lyoo/ noun (in lieu of) instead of.

lieutenant /lef-ten-uhnt/ noun 1 a deputy or substitute acting for a superior. 2 a rank of officer in the army and navy.

life noun (plural lives) 1 the condition of being alive. 2 the existence of an individual human being or animal. 3 a particular type or aspect of existence: college life. 4 living things and their activity. 5 vitality or energy. 6 informal a sentence of imprisonment for life.
□ life insurance (or life assurance) insurance that pays out money either when the insured person dies or after a set period. life jacket a jacket for keeping a person afloat in water. life peer (in the UK) a peer whose title cannot be inherited. life raft an inflatable raft used in an emergency at sea.

lifebelt noun a ring used to help a person who has fallen into water to stay afloat.

lifeblood noun a vital factor or force.

lifeboat noun a boat which is launched from land to rescue people at sea, or which is kept on a ship for use in an emergency.

lifeguard noun a person employed to rescue people who get into difficulty at a beach or swimming pool.

lifeless adjective 1 dead or apparently dead. 2 not containing living things. 3 lacking energy or excitement.

lifelike adjective accurate in its representation of a living person or thing.

lifeline noun 1 a thing on which someone or something depends. 2 a rope thrown to rescue someone in difficulties in water.

lifelong adjective lasting or remaining throughout a person's life.

lifespan noun the length of time that a person or animal is likely to live.

lifestyle noun the way in which a person lives.

THESAURUS

license verb permit, allow, authorize, grant/give authority to, grant/give permission to, certify, empower, entitle, enable, sanction.
OPPOSITES ban.

lid noun cover, top, cap, covering.

lie[1] noun it was a lie: untruth, falsehood, fib, fabrication, deception, invention, (piece of) fiction, falsification, white lie; informal tall story, whopper; humorous terminological inexactitude.
OPPOSITES truth.
• verb he had lied to the police: tell a lie, fib, dissemble, tell a white lie, perjure yourself.

lie[2] verb 1 he was lying on the bed: recline, lie down/back, be recumbent, be prostrate, be supine, be prone, be stretched out, sprawl, rest, repose, lounge, loll. 2 her handbag lay on the chair: be, be situated, be positioned, be located, be placed, be found, be sited, be arranged, rest.
OPPOSITES stand.

life noun 1 the joy of giving life to a child: existence, being, living, animation, sentience, creation, viability. 2 life on Earth: living beings/creatures, human/animal/plant life, fauna, flora, the ecosystem, the biosphere, the ecosphere. 3 an easy life: way of life, lifestyle, situation, fate, lot. 4 the last nine months of his life: lifetime, lifespan, days, time (on earth), existence. 5 the life of a Parliament: duration, lifetime, existence. 6 he is full of life: vitality, animation, liveliness, vivacity, verve, high spirits, exuberance, zest, enthusiasm, energy, vigour, dynamism, elan, gusto, bounce, spirit, fire. 7 a life of Chopin: biography, autobiography, life story/history, chronicle, account, memoirs, diary.
OPPOSITES death.

lifestyle noun way of life, life, situation, conduct, behaviour, ways, habits, mores.

lifetime noun the length of time that a person lives or a thing functions.

lift verb **1** raise to a higher position. **2** pick up and move to a different position. **3** formally end a restriction. **4** (**lift off**) (of an aircraft, spacecraft, etc.) take off. •noun **1** Brit. a device for moving people or things between different levels of a building. **2** a free ride in another person's vehicle. **3** a device for carrying people up or down a mountain. **4** a feeling of increased cheerfulness. **5** upward force exerted by the air on an aircraft wing or similar structure.

ligament /lig-uh-muhnt/ noun a band of tissue which connects two bones or holds together a joint.

ligature /lig-uh-cher/ noun a thing used for tying something tightly, especially a cord used to stop the flow of blood from a bleeding artery.

light¹ noun **1** the natural energy that makes things visible. **2** a device that uses electricity, oil, or gas to give light. **3** a match or cigarette lighter. **4** understanding or enlightenment. •verb (**lights, lighting, lit;** past participle **lit** or **lighted**) **1** provide an area or object with light. **2** make something start burning. **3** (**light up**) become lively or happy. **4** (**light on**) discover by chance. •adjective **1** having a lot of light. **2** pale in colour.
□ **in the light of** taking something into consideration. **light-fingered** informal tending to steal things. **light-headed** dizzy and slightly faint. **light-hearted 1** amusing and entertaining. **2** cheerful and carefree. **light year** the distance that light travels in one year, nearly 6 million million miles.

light² adjective **1** of little weight; not heavy. **2** not heavy enough. **3** not strongly or heavily built. **4** relatively low in density, amount, or strength. **5** gentle or delicate. **6** not profound or serious.
■ **lightly** adverb **lightness** noun.

lighten verb **1** make or become lighter in weight. **2** make or become brighter.

lighter¹ noun a device producing a small flame, used to light cigarettes.

lighter² noun a barge used to transfer goods to and from ships in harbour.

lighthouse noun a tower containing a powerful light to guide ships at sea.

THESAURUS

lifetime noun lifespan, life, days, time (on earth), existence, career.

lift verb **1** lift the pack on to your back: raise, hoist, heave, haul up, heft, raise up/aloft, elevate, hold high, pick up, grab, take up, winch up, jack up; informal hump. **2** the fog had lifted: clear, rise, disperse, dissipate, disappear, vanish, dissolve. **3** the ban has been lifted: cancel, remove, withdraw, revoke, rescind, end, stop, terminate. OPPOSITES drop, put down.
•noun **1** give me a lift up: push, hand, heave, thrust, shove. **2** he gave me a lift to the airport: ride, run, drive. **3** that goal will give his confidence a real lift: boost, fillip, impetus, encouragement, spur, push; informal shot in the arm.
□ **lift off** take off, become airborne, be launched, take to the air, blast off.

light¹ noun **1** the light of the candles: illumination, brightness, shining, gleam, brilliance, radiance, glow, blaze, glare. **2** there was a light on in the hall: lamp, lantern, torch, beacon, candle, bulb. **3** we'll be driving in the light: daylight, daytime, day, natural light, sunlight. OPPOSITES darkness.
•adjective **1** a light bedroom: bright, well lit, sunny. **2** light blue: pale, pastel, delicate, subtle, insipid, faint. OPPOSITES dark.

light² adjective **1** it's light and compact: lightweight, portable, underweight. **2** a light cotton dress: flimsy, lightweight, thin, floaty, gauzy, diaphanous. **3** she is light on her feet: nimble, agile, lithe, graceful, quick, sprightly. **4** a light dinner: small, modest, simple, insubstantial, quick. **5** light duties: easy, simple, undemanding, untaxing; informal cushy. **6** light reading: entertaining, lightweight, diverting, undemanding, middle-of-the-road, lowbrow, mainstream, frivolous, trivial, superficial. **7** a light touch: gentle, delicate, dainty, soft, faint, careful, sensitive, subtle. OPPOSITES heavy.

lighten¹ verb **1** the sky was beginning to lighten: become/grow/get lighter, brighten. **2** the first touch of dawn lightened the sky: brighten, make brighter, light up, illuminate. **3** he used lemon juice to lighten his hair: make lighter, whiten, bleach, blanch. OPPOSITES darken.

lighten² verb **1** lightening the burden of taxation: reduce, lessen, decrease, diminish, ease, alleviate, relieve. **2** an attempt to lighten her mood: cheer (up), brighten, gladden, lift, boost, buoy (up), revive, restore, revitalize. OPPOSITES increase, depress.

lightly adverb **1** Maisie kissed him lightly on the cheek: softly, gently, faintly, delicately. **2** season very lightly: sparingly, sparsely, moderately, delicately, subtly. **3** her views are not to be dismissed lightly: carelessly, airily, readily, heedlessly, uncaringly, unthinkingly, thoughtlessly, flippantly. OPPOSITES hard, heavily, seriously.

lighting noun 1 equipment for producing light. 2 the arrangement or effect of lights.

lightning noun a flow of high-voltage electricity between a cloud and the ground or within a cloud, accompanied by a bright flash. • adjective very quick.
□ **lightning conductor** (or N. Amer. **lightning rod**) a rod or wire fixed to a high place to divert lightning into the ground.

☑ the spelling is **lightning**, not -*tening*.

lights plural noun the lungs of sheep, pigs, or bullocks as food.

lightweight noun 1 a weight in boxing between featherweight and welterweight. 2 informal a person who is not very important: *a political lightweight.*

ligneous /lig-ni-uhss/ adjective consisting of, or resembling, wood.

lignite noun soft brownish coal.

like[1] preposition 1 similar to. 2 in a similar way to. 3 in a way appropriate to. 4 such as. • conjunction informal 1 in the same way that. 2 as though. • noun (**the like**) things of the same kind. • adjective having similar characteristics to someone or something else.

❗ don't use **like** to mean 'as if', as in *he's behaving like he owns the place.* Use **as if** or **as though** instead.

like[2] verb (**likes, liking, liked**) 1 find pleasant or satisfactory. 2 wish for; want. • noun (**likes**) the things that you like.

likeable or **likable** adjective pleasant; easy to like.

likelihood noun the state of being likely; probability.

likely adjective (**likelier, likeliest**) 1 probable. 2 promising. • adverb probably.

liken verb (**liken someone/thing to**) point out the resemblance of someone or something to.

likeness noun 1 resemblance. 2 outward appearance. 3 a portrait or representation.

likewise adverb 1 also; moreover. 2 similarly.

liking noun 1 a fondness for someone or something. 2 (**your liking**) your taste: *the coffee was just to her liking.*

lilac noun 1 a shrub or small tree with sweet-smelling violet, pink, or white blossom. 2 a pale pinkish-violet colour.

lilo noun (plural **lilos**) an inflatable mattress used for floating on water.

lilt noun 1 a rising and falling of the voice

lightweight adjective 1 *a lightweight jacket:* thin, light, flimsy, insubstantial, summery. 2 *lightweight entertainment:* trivial, insubstantial, superficial, shallow, undemanding, frivolous.
OPPOSITES heavy, serious.

like[1] verb 1 *I like him:* be fond of, have a soft spot for, think well/highly of, admire, respect, be attracted to, fancy, find attractive, be keen on, be taken with; informal rate. 2 *she likes gardening:* enjoy, have a taste for, have a liking for, be partial to, find/take pleasure in, be keen on, appreciate, love, adore, relish; informal have a thing about, be into, be mad about/for, be hooked on. 3 *feel free to say what you like:* choose, please, wish, want, see/think fit, care to, will.
OPPOSITES hate.

like[2] preposition 1 *you're just like a teacher:* similar to, the same as, identical to, akin to, resembling. 2 *the figure landed like a cat:* in the manner of, in the same way/manner as, in a similar way to. 3 *big cities, like Birmingham:* such as, for example, for instance, in particular, namely, viz. 4 *Richard sounded mean, which isn't like him:* characteristic of, typical of, in character with.
OPPOSITES unlike.

likelihood noun probability, chance,

prospect, possibility, odds, risk, threat, danger, hope, promise.

likely adjective 1 *it seemed likely that a scandal would break:* probable, (distinctly) possible, odds-on, plausible, imaginable; informal on the cards. 2 *a likely explanation:* plausible, reasonable, feasible, acceptable, believable, credible, tenable.
OPPOSITES improbable, unbelievable.

liken verb compare, equate, set beside.
OPPOSITES contrast.

likeness noun 1 *her likeness to Anne is quite uncanny:* resemblance, similarity, correspondence. 2 *a likeness of the president:* representation, image, depiction, portrayal, picture, drawing, sketch, painting, portrait, photograph, study.
OPPOSITES dissimilarity.

likewise adverb 1 *an ambush was out of the question, likewise poison:* also, equally, in addition, too, as well, to boot, besides, moreover, furthermore. 2 *encourage your family and friends to do likewise:* the same, similarly, correspondingly.
OPPOSITES differently.

liking noun fondness, love, affection, penchant, attachment, taste, passion, preference, partiality, predilection.
OPPOSITES dislike.

when speaking. **2** a gentle rhythm in a tune.

■ **lilting** adjective.

lily noun (plural **lilies**) a plant with large trumpet-shaped flowers on a tall, slender stem.

□ **lily-livered** cowardly. **lily of the valley** a plant with broad leaves and white bell-shaped flowers.

limb noun **1** an arm, leg, or wing. **2** a large branch of a tree.

□ **out on a limb** not supported by other people.

limber verb (**limbers, limbering, limbered**) (**limber up**) warm up in preparation for exercise or activity. ●**adjective** supple; flexible.

limbo¹ noun an uncertain period of waiting.

limbo² noun (plural **limbos**) a West Indian dance in which you bend backwards to pass under a horizontal bar.

lime¹ noun a white alkaline substance used as a building material or fertilizer.

lime² noun **1** a green citrus fruit similar to a lemon. **2** a bright light green colour.

lime³ noun a deciduous tree with heart-shaped leaves and yellowish blossom.

limelight noun (**the limelight**) the focus of public attention.

limerick noun a humorous five-line poem with a rhyme scheme *aabba*.

limestone noun a hard rock composed mainly of calcium carbonate.

limit noun **1** a point beyond which

something does not or may not pass. **2** a restriction on the size or amount of something. ●**verb** (**limits, limiting, limited**) put a limit on.

□ **off limits** out of bounds.

■ **limitless** adjective.

limitation noun **1** a restriction. **2** a fault or failing.

limited adjective restricted in size, amount, extent, or ability.

□ **limited company** Brit. a company whose owners have only a limited responsibility for its debts.

limo noun (plural **limos**) informal a limousine.

limousine noun a large, luxurious car.

limp¹ verb **1** walk with difficulty because of an injured leg or foot. **2** (of a damaged ship or aircraft) proceed with difficulty. ●**noun** a limping walk.

limp² adjective **1** not stiff or firm. **2** without energy or strength.

■ **limply** adverb.

limpet noun a shellfish with a muscular foot for clinging tightly to rocks.

limpid adjective (of a liquid or the eyes) clear.

linchpin or **lynchpin** noun **1** a very important person or thing. **2** a pin through the end of an axle keeping a wheel in position.

linctus noun Brit. thick liquid medicine, especially cough mixture.

line¹ noun **1** a long, narrow mark or band.

THESAURUS

limb noun arm, leg, wing, appendage; old use member.

limelight noun attention, interest, scrutiny, the public eye/gaze, the glare of publicity, prominence, the spotlight, fame, celebrity.
OPPOSITES obscurity.

limit noun **1** *the city limits:* boundary (line), border, frontier, edge, perimeter, margin. **2** *a limit of 4,500 supporters:* maximum, ceiling, upper limit.
●verb *the pressure to limit costs:* restrict, curb, cap, (hold in) check, restrain, limit, regulate, control, govern.

limitation noun **1** *a limitation on the number of newcomers:* restriction, curb, restraint, control, check. **2** *he is aware of his own limitations:* imperfection, flaw, defect, failing, shortcoming, weak point, deficiency, frailty, weakness.
OPPOSITES strength.

limited adjective restricted, finite, small, tight, slight, in short supply, short, meagre, scanty, sparse, inadequate, insufficient, paltry, poor, minimal.
OPPOSITES limitless, ample.

limp¹ verb *she limped out of the house:*

hobble, hop, lurch, stagger, shuffle, shamble.

limp² adjective *a limp handshake:* soft, flaccid, loose, slack, lax, floppy, drooping, droopy, sagging.
OPPOSITES firm.

line noun **1** *he drew a line through the name:* stroke, dash, score, underline, underscore, slash, stripe, strip, band, belt; Brit. oblique. **2** *there were lines round her eyes:* wrinkle, furrow, crease, crinkle, crow's foot. **3** *the classic lines of the Bentley:* contour, outline, configuration, shape, design, profile. **4** *the county line:* boundary, limit, border, frontier, touchline, margin, perimeter. **5** *the clothes line:* cord, rope, cable, wire, thread, string. **6** *a line of soldiers:* file, rank, column, string, train, procession, row, queue; Brit. informal crocodile. **7** *their line of flight:* course, route, track, path, trajectory.
●verb **1** *her face was lined with age:* furrow, wrinkle, crease. **2** *the driveway was lined by poplars:* border, edge, fringe, bound.
□ **in line 1** *standing in line for food:* **in a queue**, in a row, in a file. **2** *the adverts are in line with the editorial style:* **in**

2 a length of cord, wire, etc. 3 a row or series of people or things. 4 a row of written or printed words. 5 a direction, course, or channel. 6 a telephone connection. 7 a railway track or route. 8 a series of military defences facing an enemy force. 9 a wrinkle in the skin. 10 a range of commercial products. 11 an area of activity: *their line of work*. 12 (**lines**) a way of doing or thinking about something. 13 (**lines**) the words of an actor's part. 14 (**lines**) Brit. a school punishment in which you have to write out the same sentence a stated number of times. •verb (**lines, lining, lined**) 1 be positioned at intervals along a route. 2 (**line someone/ thing up**) arrange people or things in a row. 3 (**line something up**) have something prepared. 4 (**lined**) marked or covered with lines.
▢ in line under control. in line for likely to receive. line dancing country and western dancing in which a line of dancers follow a set pattern of steps. line-up 1 a group of people or things assembled for a particular purpose. 2 an identity parade. on the line at serious risk. out of line informal behaving badly or wrongly.

line² verb (**lines, lining, lined**) cover the inner surface of something with different material.

lineage /lin-i-ij/ noun ancestry or pedigree.

lineal /lin-i-uhl/ adjective in a direct line of descent or ancestry.

lineament /lin-i-uh-muhnt/ noun literary a distinctive feature, especially of the face.

linear /lin-i-er/ adjective 1 arranged in or extending along a straight line. 2 consisting of lines or outlines. 3 involving one dimension only. 4 progressing from one stage to another in

a series of steps.
■ linearity noun.

linen noun 1 cloth woven from flax. 2 articles such as sheets, pillowcases, and duvet covers.

liner¹ noun 1 a large passenger ship. 2 a cosmetic for outlining or emphasizing a facial feature.

liner² noun a lining of a garment, container, etc.

linesman noun (plural **linesmen**) (in sport) an official who helps the referee or umpire to decide whether the ball is out of play.

ling¹ noun a long-bodied sea fish.

ling² noun heather.

linger verb 1 be slow or reluctant to leave. 2 (**linger over**) spend a long time over. 3 be slow to fade, disappear, or die.

lingerie /lan-zhuh-ri/ noun women's underwear and nightclothes.

lingo noun (plural **lingos** or **lingoes**) informal 1 a foreign language. 2 the jargon of a particular subject or group.

lingua franca /ling-gwuh **frang**-kuh/ noun (plural **lingua francas**) a language used as a common language between speakers whose native languages are different.

linguine /ling-gwee-ni/ plural noun small ribbons of pasta.

linguist noun 1 a person who is good at foreign languages. 2 a person who studies linguistics.

linguistic adjective relating to language or linguistics.

linguistics plural noun the scientific study of language.

liniment noun an ointment rubbed on the body to relieve pain or bruising.

lining noun a layer of material covering or attached to the inside of something.

link noun 1 a relationship or connection

THESAURUS

agreement, in accord, in accordance, in harmony, in step, in compliance. 3 *in line with the goal:* aligned, level, alongside, abreast, side by side. in line for a candidate for, in the running for, due for; informal up for. line up form a queue/line, queue up, fall in. line someone/something up assemble, get together, organize, prepare, arrange, fix up, lay on, book, schedule, timetable.

lined¹ adjective 1 *lined paper:* ruled, feint, striped, banded. 2 *his lined face:* wrinkled, wrinkly, furrowed, wizened.
OPPOSITES plain, smooth.

lined² adjective *lined curtains:* covered, backed, padded, insulated, sealed.

line-up noun 1 *a star-studded line-up:* cast, bill, programme. 2 *United's line-up:* team, squad, side, configuration.

linger verb 1 *the crowd lingered:* wait (around), stand (around), remain, loiter; informal stick around, hang around/round. 2 *the infection can linger for years:* persist, continue, remain, stay, endure, carry on, last.
OPPOSITES vanish.

lining noun backing, facing, padding, insulation.

link noun 1 *the links between transport and the environment:* connection, relationship, association, linkage, tie-up. 2 *their links with the labour movement:* bond, tie, attachment, connection, association, affiliation.
•verb 1 *four boxes were linked together:* join, connect, fasten, attach, bind, secure, fix, tie, couple, yoke. 2 *the evidence linking him with the body:* associate, connect,

between people or things. **2** something that lets people communicate. **3** a means of contact or transport between two places. **4** a code or instruction that connects one part of a computer program, website, etc. to another. **5** a loop in a chain. ▪ verb connect or join.

linkage noun **1** the action of linking or the state of being linked. **2** a system of links.

links plural noun a golf course, especially one near the sea.

linnet noun a type of finch (songbird).

lino noun Brit. informal linoleum.

linoleum /li-noh-li-uhm/ noun a floor covering made from a mixture of linseed oil and powdered cork.

linseed noun the seeds of the flax plant, which are crushed to make an oil used in paint, varnish, etc.

lint noun **1** short, fine fibres which separate from cloth when it is being made. **2** a fabric used for dressing wounds.

lintel noun a horizontal support across the top of a door or window.

lion noun (feminine **lioness**) a large cat of Africa and NW India, the male of which has a shaggy mane.
□ **the lion's share** the largest part of something.

lionize or **lionise** verb (**lionizes, lionizing, lionized**) treat as a celebrity.

lip noun **1** either of the two fleshy parts forming the edges of the mouth opening. **2** the edge of a hollow container or an opening. **3** informal cheeky talk.
□ **lip-read** understand speech from watching a speaker's lip movements.

liposuction noun a technique in cosmetic surgery for sucking out excess fat from under the skin.

lippy adjective informal cheeky.

lipstick noun coloured cosmetic applied to the lips from a small solid stick.

liquefy /lik-wi-fy/ verb (**liquefies, liquefying, liquefied**) make or become liquid.

■ **liquefaction** noun.

☑ lique**fy**, not -*ify*.

liqueur /li-**kyoor**/ noun a strong, sweet alcoholic drink.

liquid noun a substance such as water or oil that flows freely. ▪ adjective **1** in the form of a liquid. **2** clear, like water. **3** (of assets) held in cash, or easily converted into cash.

liquidate verb (**liquidates, liquidating, liquidated**) **1** close a business and sell what it owns so as to pay its debts. **2** convert assets into cash. **3** pay off a debt. **4** informal kill.
■ **liquidation** noun.

liquidity /li-**kwid**-i-ti/ noun the state of owning assets that are held in or easily converted to cash.

liquidize or **liquidise** verb (**liquidizes, liquidizing, liquidized**) Brit. convert solid food into a liquid or purée.
■ **liquidizer** noun.

liquor /**lik**-er/ noun **1** alcoholic drink, especially spirits. **2** liquid that has been produced in cooking.

liquorice /**lik**-uh-riss, **lik**-uh-rish/ (US spelling **licorice**) noun a black substance made from the juice of a root and used as a sweet and in medicine.

lira /**leer**-uh/ noun (plural **lire** /**leer**-uh/) the basic unit of money of Turkey and formerly also of Italy.

lisp noun a speech defect in which the sound *s* is pronounced like *th*. ▪ verb speak with a lisp.

lissom or **lissome** adjective slim, supple, and graceful.

list¹ noun a number of connected items or names written one after the other. ▪ verb **1** make a list of. **2** include in a list.

list² verb (of a ship) lean over to one side.

listed adjective (of a building in the UK) officially protected because of its historical

THESAURUS

relate, bracket.
OPPOSITES separate.

lip noun *the lip of the crater:* edge, rim, brim, border, verge, brink.

liquid noun *a vat of liquid:* fluid, moisture, liquor, solution, juice, sap.
OPPOSITES solid.
▪ adjective *liquid fuels:* fluid, liquefied, melted, molten, thawed, dissolved.
OPPOSITES solid.

liquor noun **1** *alcoholic liquor:* alcohol, spirits, (alcoholic) drink; informal booze, the hard stuff, hooch, moonshine. **2** *strain the*

liquor into the sauce: stock, broth, bouillon, juice, liquid.

list¹ noun *a list of the world's wealthiest people:* catalogue, inventory, record, register, roll, file, index, directory, checklist.
▪ verb *the accounts are listed below:* record, register, enter, itemize, enumerate, catalogue, log, minute, categorize, inventory, classify, group, sort, rank, index.

list² verb *the boat listed to one side:* lean (over), tilt, tip, heel (over), pitch, incline, slant, slope, bank.

importance.

listen verb **1** give your attention to a sound. **2** make an effort to hear something. **3** pay attention to advice or a request. •noun an act of listening.
■ **listener** noun.

listeria noun a type of bacterium which infects humans and animals through contaminated food.

listing noun **1** a list or catalogue. **2** an entry in a list.

listless adjective lacking energy or enthusiasm.
■ **listlessly** adverb.

lit past and past participle of LIGHT[1].

litany noun (plural **litanies**) **1** a series of prayers to God used in church services. **2** a long, boring list of complaints, reasons, etc.

liter US spelling of LITRE.

literacy noun the ability to read and write.

literal adjective **1** using or interpreting words in their usual or most basic sense. **2** (of a translation) representing the exact words of the original piece of writing. **3** not exaggerated or distorted.

literally adverb **1** in a literal way. **2** informal used to emphasize what you are saying: *we were literally killing ourselves laughing.*

literary adjective **1** having to do with literature. **2** (of language) characteristic of literature or formal writing.

literate adjective **1** able to read and write. **2** knowledgeable in a particular field: *computer-literate.*

literati /li-tuh-**rah**-ti/ plural noun educated people who are interested in literature.

literature noun **1** written works that are regarded as having artistic merit. **2** books and printed information on a particular subject.

lithe /lyth/ adjective slim, supple, and graceful.

lithium /**li**-thi-uhm/ noun a silver-white metallic element.

lithograph /**li**-thuh-grahf/ noun a print made by lithography.

lithography /li-**thog**-ruh-fi/ noun printing from a flat metal surface which has been prepared so that ink sticks only where it is required.

Lithuanian noun a person from Lithuania. •adjective relating to Lithuania.

litigant noun a person who is involved in a dispute or claim being heard in a law court.

litigation noun the process of taking a dispute to a law court.

litigious /li-**ti**-juhss/ adjective frequently choosing to go to a law court to settle a dispute.

litmus noun a dye that is red under acid conditions and blue under alkaline conditions.
□ **litmus paper** paper stained with litmus, used as a test for acids or alkalis. **litmus test** a reliable test of the quality or truth of something.

litre (US spelling **liter**) noun a metric unit of capacity equal to 1,000 cubic centimetres (about 1.75 pints).

litter noun **1** rubbish left in an open or public place. **2** an untidy collection of things. **3** a number of young born to an animal at one time. **4** (also **cat litter**) absorbent material that is put into a tray for a cat to use as a toilet indoors. **5** straw or other material used as bedding for animals. **6** (also **leaf litter**) decomposing leaves forming a layer on top of soil. **7** (in the past) an enclosed chair or bed carried by men or animals. •verb (**litters**, **littering**, **littered**) make a place untidy by dropping litter.

THESAURUS

listen verb **1** *are you listening?* pay attention, be attentive, attend, concentrate, keep your ears open, prick up your ears; informal be all ears. **2** *policymakers should listen to popular opinion:* heed, take heed of, take notice/note of, bear in mind, take into consideration/account.

literal adjective strict, technical, concrete, original, true.
OPPOSITES figurative.

literary adjective **1** *literary works:* artistic, poetic, dramatic. **2** *her literary friends:* scholarly, intellectual, academic, bookish, erudite.

literate adjective (well) educated, well read, widely read, scholarly, learned, knowledgeable, cultured, cultivated.
OPPOSITES ignorant.

literature noun **1** *English literature:* writing, poetry, drama, prose. **2** *the literature on prototype theory:* publications, reports, studies, material. **3** *election literature:* documentation, material, publicity, blurb, propaganda, advertising; informal bumf.

litigation noun legal/judicial proceedings, legal action, lawsuit, legal dispute, legal case, prosecution, indictment.

litter noun **1** *never drop litter:* rubbish, refuse, junk, waste, debris; N. Amer. trash, garbage. **2** *the litter of glasses around her:* clutter, jumble, muddle, mess, heap; informal shambles.
•verb *clothes littered the floor:* cover, be strewn around, clutter up, pepper.

little adjective **1** small in size, amount, or degree. **2** (of a person) young or younger. **3** (of distance or time) short. • **determiner & pronoun** not much. • **adverb** hardly, or not at all.
□ a little **1** a small amount of. **2** a short time or distance. **3** to a limited extent.

littoral adjective relating to the shore of the sea or a lake.

liturgy /li-ter-ji/ noun (plural **liturgies**) a set form of public worship used in the Christian Church.
■ **liturgical** adjective.

live¹ /liv/ verb (**lives, living, lived**) **1** remain alive. **2** be alive at a particular time. **3** spend your life in a particular way. **4** have your home in a particular place. **5** obtain the things necessary for staying alive.
□ live something down manage to make other people forget something embarrassing. live rough live outdoors with no home.
■ **liveable** (or **livable**) adjective.

live² /lyv/ adjective **1** living. **2** (of music) played in front of an audience; not recorded. **3** (of a broadcast) transmitted at the time it happens, rather than recorded. **4** (of a wire or device) connected to a source of electric current. **5** containing explosive that can be detonated. • **adverb** as a live performance.
□ live wire informal an energetic and lively person.

livelihood noun a way of earning enough money to live on.

lively adjective (**livelier, liveliest**) **1** full of life and energy. **2** (of a place) full of activity.
■ **liveliness** noun.

liven verb (**liven someone/thing up** or **liven up**) make or become more lively or interesting.

liver noun **1** a large organ in the abdomen that produces bile. **2** the liver of some animals used as food.

livery noun (plural **liveries**) **1** a special uniform worn by a servant or official. **2** a

---

THESAURUS

little adjective **1** *a little writing desk:* small, compact, miniature, tiny, toy, baby, undersized, dwarf, midget; Scottish wee; informal teeny-weeny; Brit. informal titchy, dinky; N. Amer. informal vest-pocket. **2** *a little man:* short, small, slight, petite, elfin, diminutive, tiny; Scottish wee; informal teeny-weeny, pint-sized. **3** *my little sister:* young, younger, baby. **4** *a little while:* brief, short, quick, hasty, cursory. **5** *a few little problems:* minor, unimportant, trivial, insignificant, trifling, petty, paltry, inconsequential.
OPPOSITES big, large, elder, major.
• determiner *they have little political influence:* hardly any, not much, scant, limited, restricted, modest, little or no, minimal, negligible.
OPPOSITES considerable.
• adverb **1** *he is little known as a teacher:* hardly, barely, scarcely, not much, only slightly. **2** *this disease is little seen nowadays:* rarely, seldom, infrequently, hardly (ever), scarcely ever, not much.
OPPOSITES well, often.
□ a little **1** *add a little water:* some, a bit of, a touch of, a dash of, a taste of, a spot of, a hint of, a dribble of, a splash of, a pinch of, a sprinkling of, a speck of; informal a smidgen of, a tad of. **2** *after a little, Oliver came in:* a short time, a while, a bit, an interval, a short period, a minute, a moment, a second, an instant; informal a sec, a mo, a jiffy. **3** *this reminds me a little of the Adriatic:* slightly, somewhat, a little bit, quite, to some degree.

live¹ verb **1** *the greatest mathematician who ever lived:* exist, be alive, be, have life,
breathe, draw breath, walk the earth. **2** *I live in London:* reside, have your home, lodge, inhabit, occupy, populate; Scottish stay. **3** *she had lived a difficult life:* experience, spend, pass, lead, have, go through, undergo. **4** *Freddy lived by scavenging:* survive, make a living, eke out a living, subsist, support yourself, sustain yourself, make ends meet, keep body and soul together.
OPPOSITES die, be dead.

live² adjective **1** *live bait:* living, alive, conscious. **2** *a live rail:* electrified, charged, powered up, active, switched on. **3** *a live grenade:* unexploded, explosive, active, primed. **4** *a live issue:* topical, current, controversial, burning, pressing, important, relevant.
OPPOSITES dead, inanimate.

livelihood noun (source of) income, means of support, living, subsistence, bread and butter, job, work, employment, occupation.

lively adjective **1** *a lively young woman:* energetic, active, animated, dynamic, full of life, outgoing, spirited, high-spirited, vivacious, enthusiastic, vibrant, buoyant, exuberant, effervescent, cheerful; informal full of beans. **2** *a lively bar:* busy, crowded, bustling, buzzing, vibrant, boisterous, jolly. **3** *a lively debate:* heated, vigorous, animated, spirited, enthusiastic, forceful. **4** *a lively portrait of the local community:* vivid, colourful, striking, graphic. **5** *he bowled at a lively pace:* brisk, quick, fast, rapid, swift, speedy, smart.
OPPOSITES quiet, dull, slow.

distinctive design and colour scheme used on the vehicles or products of a company. □ **livery stable** a stable where people can pay to keep their horses, or hire a horse to ride. ■ **liveried** adjective.

lives plural of LIFE.

livestock noun farm animals.

livid adjective **1** furiously angry. **2** dark bluish grey in colour.

living noun **1** being alive. **2** an income which is enough to live on. ●adjective alive. □ **living room** a room in a house used for relaxing in.

lizard noun a small four-legged reptile with a long body and tail.

llama /lah-muh/ noun a South American animal related to the camel.

lo exclamation old use used to draw attention to something.

loach noun a small freshwater fish.

load noun **1** a heavy or bulky thing that is being carried. **2** a weight or source of pressure. **3** the total number or amount carried in a vehicle or container. **4** (**a load** or **loads of**) informal a lot of. ●verb **1** put a load on or in. **2** put ammunition into a gun. **3** put something into a device so that it will operate.

loaded adjective **1** carrying or supporting a load. **2** biased towards a particular outcome. **3** having an underlying meaning: *a loaded question.* **4** informal wealthy.

loaf¹ noun (plural **loaves**) a quantity of bread that is shaped and baked in one piece.

loaf² verb spend your time in a lazy or aimless way.

loafer noun **1** a person who spends their time in a lazy or aimless way. **2** a casual leather shoe with a flat heel.

loam noun a fertile soil of clay and sand containing hummus.

loan noun **1** a sum of money that is lent to someone. **2** the action of lending something. ●verb give something as a loan. □ **loan shark** informal a moneylender who charges very high rates of interest.

loath or **loth** adjective (**loath to do**) reluctant or unwilling to do.

! don't confuse **loath** with **loathe**, which means 'feel hatred for'.

loathe verb (**loathes**, **loathing**, **loathed**) feel hatred or disgust for.

loathsome adjective causing hatred or disgust.

loaves plural of LOAF¹.

lob verb (**lobs**, **lobbing**, **lobbed**) throw or hit something in a high arc. ●noun (in soccer

THESAURUS

livid adjective (informal) **very angry**, enraged, furious, infuriated, irate, incensed, fuming, ranting, raving, seething, beside yourself, outraged; informal hopping mad, wild.

living noun **1** *she cleaned floors for a living:* **livelihood**, (source of) income, means of support, subsistence, keep, daily bread, bread and butter, job, work, employment, occupation. **2** *healthy living:* **way of life**, lifestyle, life, conduct, behaviour, activities, habits. ●adjective **1** *living organisms:* **alive**, live, animate, sentient, breathing, existing. **2** *a living language:* **current**, contemporary, active. OPPOSITES dead, extinct.

load noun **1** *MacDowell's got a load to deliver:* **cargo**, freight, consignment, delivery, shipment, goods, pack, bundle, parcel. **2** *a heavy teaching load:* **commitment**, responsibility, duty, obligation, burden. ●verb **1** *we quickly loaded the van:* **fill** (up), pack, charge, stock, stack; old use lade. **2** *Larry loaded boxes into the jeep:* **pack**, stow, store, stack, bundle, place, deposit, put away. **3** *loading the committee with responsibilities:* **burden**, weigh down, saddle, charge, overburden, overwhelm, encumber, tax, strain, trouble, worry. **4** *he loaded a gun:* **prime**, charge, set up,

prepare. **5** *load the cassette into the camcorder:* **insert**, put, place, slot, slide.

loaded adjective **1** *a loaded freight train:* **full**, filled, laden, packed, stuffed, crammed, brimming, stacked; informal chock-full, chock-a-block. **2** *a politically loaded word:* **charged**, emotive, sensitive, delicate.

loaf verb **laze**, lounge, loll, idle; informal hang around/round; Brit. informal hang about, mooch about/around; N. Amer. informal bum around.

loan noun **credit**, advance, mortgage, overdraft, Brit. informal sub.

loath adjective **reluctant**, unwilling, disinclined, averse, opposed, resistant. OPPOSITES willing.

loathe verb **hate**, detest, abhor, not be able to bear/stand. OPPOSITES love.

loathing noun **hatred**, hate, abhorrence, antipathy, dislike, hostility, animosity, malice, enmity, repugnance.

loathsome adjective **hateful**, detestable, abhorrent, repulsive, odious, repugnant, repellent, disgusting, revolting, sickening, abominable, despicable, contemptible, reprehensible, vile, horrible, nasty, obnoxious, gross, foul; informal horrid; literary noisome.

or tennis) a ball lobbed over an opponent.

lobby noun (plural **lobbies**) **1** an open area inside the entrance of a public building. **2** any of several large halls in the Houses of Parliament in which MPs meet members of the public. **3** each of two corridors in the Houses of Parliament where MPs vote. **4** a group of people who try to influence politicians on a particular issue. • verb (**lobbies, lobbying, lobbied**) try to influence a politician on an issue. ■ **lobbyist** noun.

lobe noun **1** a roundish and flattish part that projects from or divides something. **2** the rounded fleshy part at the lower edge of the ear. **3** each of the sections of the main part of the brain.

lobelia /luh-**bee**-li-uh/ noun a garden plant with blue or red flowers.

lobotomy /luh-**bot**-uh-mi/ noun (plural **lobotomies**) an operation that involves cutting into part of the brain, formerly used to treat mental illness.

lobster noun a large edible shellfish with large pincers.
□ **lobster pot** a basket-like trap in which lobsters are caught.

local adjective having to do with a particular area, or with the place where you live. • noun **1** a person who lives in a particular place. **2** Brit. informal a pub near where you live.
□ **local anaesthetic** an anaesthetic that causes a loss of feeling in a particular part of the body. ■ **locally** adverb.

locale /loh-**kahl**/ noun a place where something happens.

locality noun (plural **localities**) **1** an area or neighbourhood. **2** the position or site of something.

localize or **localise** verb (**localizes, localizing, localized**) restrict to a particular place.
■ **localization** noun.

locate verb (**locates, locating, located**) **1** discover the exact place or position of. **2** (**be located**) be situated in a particular place.

location noun **1** a place where something is located. **2** the action of locating someone or something. **3** an actual place in which a film or broadcast is made, as distinct from a studio.

loch /lok, lokh/ noun Scottish a lake, or a narrow strip of sea that is almost surrounded by land.

loci plural of **LOCUS**.

lock¹ noun **1** a mechanism for keeping a door or container fastened, operated by a key. **2** a similar device used to prevent a vehicle or other machine from operating. **3** a short section of a canal or river with gates at each end which can be opened or closed to change the water level, used for raising and lowering boats. **4** a hold in wrestling that prevents an opponent from moving a limb. **5** the maximum extent that the front wheels of a vehicle can be turned. • verb **1** fasten with a lock. **2** shut in or imprison by locking a door. **3** become

THESAURUS

lobby noun **1** *the hotel lobby:* entrance (hall), hallway, hall, vestibule, foyer, reception area. **2** *the anti-hunt lobby:* pressure group, interest group, movement, campaign, crusade, faction, camp.
• verb **1** *readers are urged to lobby their MPs:* approach, contact, importune, sway, petition, solicit, appeal to, pressurize. **2** *a group lobbying for better rail services:* campaign, crusade, press, push, ask, call, demand, promote, advocate, champion.

local adjective **1** *the local council:* community, district, neighbourhood, regional, town, municipal, provincial, village, parish. **2** *a local restaurant:* neighbourhood, nearby, near, at hand, close by, handy, convenient. **3** *a local infection:* confined, restricted, contained, localized.
OPPOSITES national, widespread.
• noun *complaints from the locals:* local person, native, inhabitant, resident, parishioner.
OPPOSITES outsider.

locate verb **1** *spotter planes located the*

submarines: find, pinpoint, track down, unearth, sniff out, smoke out, search out, uncover. **2** *a company located near Pittsburgh:* situate, site, position, place, base, put, build, establish, station.

location noun position, place, situation, site, locality, locale, spot, whereabouts, scene, setting, area, environment, venue, address.

lock¹ noun *the lock on the door:* bolt, catch, fastener, clasp, hasp, latch.
• verb **1** *he locked the door:* bolt, fasten, secure, padlock, latch, chain. **2** *the police locked arms:* join, interlock, link, engage, combine, connect, couple. **3** *the wheels locked:* become stuck, stick, jam, seize. **4** *he locked her in an embrace:* clasp, clench, grasp, embrace, hug, squeeze.
OPPOSITES unlock, open, separate, divide.
□ **lock someone up** imprison, jail, incarcerate, intern, send to prison, put behind bars, put under lock and key, cage, pen, coop up; informal send down, put away, put inside.

fixed in one position.
□ **lock, stock, and barrel** including everything. **lock-up 1** a place used as a temporary jail. **2** Brit. a small shop or rented garage that is separate from other premises.
■ **lockable** adjective.

lock² noun **1** a coil or hanging piece of a person's hair. **2** (**locks**) literary a person's hair.

locker noun a small cupboard or compartment that can be locked.

locket noun a piece of jewellery in the form of a small case on a chain, worn round a person's neck and used to hold a tiny photograph, a lock of hair, etc.

lockjaw noun a form of the disease tetanus in which the jaws become stiff and tightly closed.

lockout noun a situation in which an employer refuses to allow employees to enter their place of work until they agree to certain conditions.

locksmith noun a person who makes and repairs locks.

locomotion noun movement from one place to another.

locomotive noun a powered railway vehicle used for pulling trains. • **adjective** relating to locomotion.

locum /loh-kuhm/ noun a doctor or priest standing in for another who is temporarily away.

locus /loh-kuhss/ noun (plural **loci** /loh-sy/) technical a particular position, point, or place.

locust noun a large tropical grasshopper which migrates in vast swarms.

locution noun **1** a word or phrase. **2** a person's particular way of speaking.

lode noun a vein of metal ore in the earth.

lodestone noun a piece of magnetic iron ore used as a magnet.

lodge noun **1** a small house at the gates of a large house with grounds. **2** a room for a porter at the entrance of a large building. **3** a small country house where people stay while hunting and shooting. **4** a branch of an organization such as the Freemasons. **5** a beaver's den. • **verb** (**lodges, lodging, lodged**) **1** formally present a complaint, appeal, etc. **2** firmly fix something in a place. **3** rent accommodation in another person's house. **4** leave something valuable in a safe place or with someone reliable.

lodger noun a person who pays rent to live in a house or flat with the owner.

lodging noun **1** temporary accommodation. **2** (usu. **lodgings**) a rented room or rooms, usually in the same house as the owner.

loft noun **1** a room or storage space directly under the roof of a house. **2** a large, open flat in a converted warehouse or factory. **3** a gallery in a church or hall. • **verb** kick, hit, or throw a ball high into the air.

lofty adjective (**loftier, loftiest**) **1** tall and impressive. **2** morally good; noble. **3** proud and superior.
■ **loftily** adverb.

log¹ noun **1** a part of the trunk or a large branch of a tree that has fallen or been cut off. **2** an official record of the voyage of a ship or aircraft. • **verb** (**logs, logging, logged**) **1** record facts in a log. **2** achieve a certain distance, speed, or time. **3** (**log in/on** or **out/off**) begin or finish using a computer system. **4** cut down an area of forest to use the wood commercially.
■ **logger** noun.

log² noun a logarithm.

I

---

lock² noun *a lock of hair:* tuft, tress, curl, ringlet, hank, strand, wisp, coil.

locker noun cupboard, cabinet, chest, safe, box, case, coffer, storeroom.

lodge noun **1** *the porter's lodge:* gatehouse, cottage. **2** *a hunting lodge:* house, cottage, cabin, chalet. **3** *a Masonic lodge:* section, branch, wing, hall, clubhouse, meeting room; N. Amer. chapter.
• **verb 1** *William lodged at our house:* reside, board, stay, live, stop; N. Amer. room. **2** *the government lodged a protest:* submit, register, enter, put forward, advance, lay, present, tender, proffer, put on record, record, table, file. **3** *the money was lodged in a bank:* deposit, put, bank, stash, store, stow, put away. **4** *the bullet lodged in his back:* become embedded, get/become stuck, stick, catch, become caught, wedge.

lodging noun accommodation, rooms, chambers, living quarters, a roof over your head, housing, shelter; informal digs; formal residence, dwelling.

lofty adjective **1** *a lofty tower:* tall, high. **2** *lofty ideals:* noble, exalted, high, high-minded, worthy, grand, fine, elevated. **3** *lofty disdain:* haughty, arrogant, disdainful, supercilious, condescending, scornful, contemptuous, self-important, conceited, snobbish; informal stuck-up, snooty; Brit. informal toffee-nosed.
OPPOSITES low, short, base, lowly, modest.

log noun *a log of phone calls:* record, register, logbook, journal, diary, minutes, chronicle, record book, ledger, account, tally.
• **verb 1** *all complaints are logged:* register, record, note, write down, put in writing, enter, file. **2** *the pilot had logged 95 hours:* attain, achieve, chalk up, make, do, go, cover, clock up.

loganberry noun (plural **loganberries**) an edible red soft fruit, similar to a raspberry.

logarithm noun each of a series of numbers which allow you to do calculations by adding and subtracting rather than multiplying and dividing.
■ logarithmic adjective.

logbook noun **1** a log of a ship or aircraft. **2** Brit. a document recording details about a vehicle and its owner.

loggerheads plural noun (**at loggerheads**) in strong disagreement.

loggia /loh-juh/ noun a long room with one or more open sides.

logic noun **1** the science of reasoning. **2** clear, sound reasoning. **3** a set of principles used in preparing a computer or electronic device to perform a task.
■ logician noun.

logical adjective **1** following the rules of logic. **2** using clear, sound reasoning. **3** expected or reasonable under the circumstances.
■ logically adverb.

logistics noun the detailed organization of a large and complex project or event.
● adjective relating to logistics.
■ logistic adjective logistical adjective.

logjam noun a situation in which progress is difficult or impossible.

logo /loh-goh/ noun (plural **logos**) a design or symbol used by an organization to identify its products.

loin noun **1** the part of the body between the ribs and the hip bones. **2** a joint of meat from this part of an animal. **3** (**loins**) literary a person's sexual organs.

loincloth noun a piece of cloth wrapped round the hips, worn by men in some hot countries.

loiter verb (**loiters, loitering, loitered**) stand around without any obvious purpose.

loll verb **1** sit, lie, or stand in a lazy, relaxed way. **2** hang loosely.

lollipop noun a large, flat, rounded boiled sweet on the end of a stick.

lollop verb (**lollops, lolloping, lolloped**) move in a series of clumsy bounding steps.

lolly noun (plural **lollies**) Brit. informal **1** a lollipop. **2** (also **ice lolly**) a piece of flavoured ice or ice cream on a stick. **3** money.

lone adjective **1** having no companions. **2** not having the support of other people.
□ lone wolf a person who prefers to be alone.

lonely adjective (**lonelier, loneliest**) **1** sad because of having no friends or company. **2** (of time) spent alone. **3** (of a place) remote.
■ loneliness noun.

loner noun a person who prefers to be alone.

lonesome adjective N. Amer. lonely.

long[1] adjective (**longer, longest**) **1** of great length in space or time. **2** having or lasting a particular length, distance, or time. **3** (of odds in betting) reflecting a low level of probability. ● adverb (**longer, longest**) **1** for a long time. **2** at a distant time. **3** throughout a stated period of time.
□ long-haul involving transport over a long distance. long in the tooth rather old. long johns informal underpants with close-fitting legs extending to the ankles. long jump an athletic event in which competitors jump as far as possible. long-lived living or lasting a long time. long shot a scheme or guess that has only the slightest chance of succeeding. long-sighted unable to see things clearly if they are close to the eyes. long-suffering

THESAURUS

logic noun **1** *this case appears to defy all logic:* reason, judgement, rationality, wisdom, sense, good sense, common sense, sanity. **2** *the logic of their argument:* reasoning, line, rationale, argument.

logical adjective **1** *information displayed in a logical fashion:* reasoned, rational, sound, cogent, valid, coherent, clear, systematic, orderly, methodical, analytical, consistent. **2** *the logical outcome:* natural, reasonable, sensible, understandable, predictable, unsurprising, likely.
OPPOSITES illogical, unlikely.

lone adjective **1** *a lone police officer:* solitary, single, solo, unaccompanied, sole, isolated. **2** *a lone parent:* single, unmarried, separated, divorced, widowed.

loneliness noun **1** *his loneliness was unbearable:* isolation, friendlessness, abandonment, rejection; N. Amer. lonesomeness. **2** *the enforced loneliness of a prison cell:* solitariness, solitude, aloneness, separation, seclusion.
OPPOSITES popularity, company.

lonely adjective **1** *I felt very lonely:* isolated, alone, friendless, with no one to turn to, abandoned, rejected, unloved, unwanted; N. Amer. lonesome. **2** *a lonely road:* deserted, uninhabited, desolate, solitary, isolated, remote, out of the way, secluded, in the back of beyond, godforsaken; informal in the middle of nowhere.
OPPOSITES popular, crowded.

long[1] adjective *a long silence:* lengthy, extended, prolonged, protracted, long-lasting, drawn-out, endless, lingering, interminable.
OPPOSITES short, brief.

patiently putting up with problems or annoying behaviour. **long-winded** long and boring.

long[2] verb (**long for** or **to do**) have a strong wish to do or have something.

longboat noun **1** historical the largest boat carried by a sailing ship. **2** = LONGSHIP.

longbow noun a large bow formerly used for shooting arrows.

longevity /lon-jev-i-ti/ noun long life.

longhand noun ordinary handwriting (as opposed to shorthand, typing, or printing).

longing noun a strong wish to do or have something. •adjective strongly wishing for something.
■ **longingly** adverb.

longitude /long-i-tyood/ noun the distance of a place east or west of the Greenwich meridian, measured in degrees.

longitudinal /long-i-**tyoo**-di-n'l/ adjective **1** extending lengthwise. **2** relating to longitude.
■ **longitudinally** adverb.

longship noun a long, narrow warship with oars and a sail, used by the Vikings.

longways adverb lengthways.

loo noun Brit. informal a toilet.

loofah /**loo**-fuh/ noun a long, rough object used to wash yourself with in the bath, consisting of the dried inner parts of a tropical fruit.

look verb **1** direct your eyes in a particular direction. **2** have the appearance of being; seem. **3** face in a particular direction. •noun **1** an act of looking. **2** appearance. **3** (**looks**) a person's facial appearance. **4** a style or fashion.
□ **look after** take care of. **look down on** think that you are better than. **look for** try to find. **looking glass** a mirror. **look into** investigate. **look on** watch without getting involved. **look out** be alert for possible trouble. **look up** improve. **look someone/thing up 1** search for information in a reference book. **2** informal visit or contact a friend. **look up to** have a lot of respect for.

lookalike noun a person who looks very similar to another.

lookout noun **1** a place from which you can

long[2] verb *I longed for the holidays:* yearn, pine, ache, hanker for/after, hunger, thirst, itch, be eager, be desperate, crave, dream of; informal be dying.

longing noun yearning, craving, ache, burning, hunger, thirst, hankering; informal yen, itch.

long-standing adjective well established, long-established, time-honoured, traditional, abiding, enduring.
OPPOSITES new, recent.

look verb **1** *Mrs Wright looked at him:* glance, gaze, stare, gape, peer, peep, peek, watch, observe, view, regard, examine, inspect, eye, scan, scrutinize, survey, study, contemplate, take in, ogle; informal take a gander, rubberneck, get a load of; Brit. informal gawp; N. Amer. informal eyeball. **2** *they looked shocked:* seem (to be), appear (to be), come across/over as.
OPPOSITES ignore.
•noun **1** *have a look at this report:* glance, examination, study, inspection, scrutiny, peep, peek, glimpse; informal eyeful, once-over, squint. **2** *the look on her face:* expression, mien. **3** *that rustic look:* appearance, air, aspect, manner, mien, demeanour, impression, effect, ambience. **4** *this season's look:* fashion, style; informal thing.
□ **look after** take care of, care for, attend to, minister to, tend, mind, keep an eye on, keep safe, be responsible for, protect, nurse, babysit, childmind. **look down on** disdain, scorn, look down your nose at, sneer at, despise. **look for** search for, hunt,

try to find, seek, cast about/around/round for, try to track down, forage for. **look forward to** await with pleasure, eagerly anticipate, lick your lips over, be unable to wait for, count the days until. **look into** investigate, enquire into, go into, probe, explore, follow up, research, study, examine; informal check out; N. Amer. informal scope out. **look like** resemble, bear a resemblance to, look similar to, take after, remind you of, make you think of; informal be the (spitting) image of, be a dead ringer for. **look out** beware, watch out, mind out, be on your guard, be alert, be wary, be vigilant, be careful, take care, be cautious, pay attention, keep your eyes open/peeled, keep an eye out, watch your step. **look something over** inspect, examine, scrutinize, cast an eye over, take stock of, vet, view, peruse, read through; informal give something a/the once-over; N. Amer. check out; N. Amer. informal eyeball. **look up** improve, get better, pick up, come along/on, progress, make progress, make headway, perk up, rally, take a turn for the better. **look someone up** (informal) **visit,** pay a visit to, call on, go to see, look in on; N. Amer. visit with, go see; informal drop in on. **look up to** admire, have a high opinion of, think highly of, hold in high regard, regard highly, respect, esteem, venerate, idolize.

lookout noun **1** *the lookout sighted sails:* watchman, watch, guard, sentry, sentinel, observer. **2** (Brit. informal) *that's your lookout:* problem, concern, business, affair, keep watch or view landscape. **2** a person who keeps watch for danger or trouble.

loom[1] noun a machine for weaving cloth.

loom[2] verb **1** appear as a vague and threatening shape. **2** (of something bad) seem about to happen.

loony informal noun (plural **loonies**) a mad or silly person. • adjective mad or silly.

loop noun **1** a shape produced by a curve that bends round and crosses itself. **2** a strip of tape or film with the ends joined, which allows sounds or images to be continuously repeated. **3** a complete circuit for an electric current. • verb form into or have the shape of a loop.
□ **loop the loop** (of an aircraft) fly in a vertical circle.

loophole noun a mistake or piece of vague wording that lets someone avoid obeying a law or keeping to a contract.

loopy adjective informal mad or silly.

loose adjective **1** not firmly or tightly fixed in place. **2** not fastened or packaged together. **3** not tied up or shut in. **4** (of a garment) not fitting tightly. **5** not exact: *a loose translation.* **6** careless and indiscreet. **7** dated immoral. • verb (**looses, loosing, loosed**) **1** unfasten or set free. **2** (**loose something off**) fire a shot, bullet, etc.
□ **be at a loose end** have nothing definite to do. **loose cannon** a person who behaves in an unpredictable and potentially

harmful way. **loose-leaf** (of a folder) having sheets of paper that can be added or removed.
■ **loosely** adverb **looseness** noun.

> **!** don't confuse **loose** with **lose**, which means 'no longer have' or 'become unable to find'.

loosen verb **1** make or become loose. **2** (**loosen up**) warm up in preparation for an activity.

loot verb steal goods from empty buildings during a war, riot, etc. • noun **1** goods stolen from empty buildings during a war, riot, etc. **2** goods stolen by a thief. **3** informal money.
■ **looter** noun.

lop verb (**lops, lopping, lopped**) cut off a branch or limb from a tree or body.
□ **lop-eared** (of an animal) having drooping ears.

lope verb (**lopes, loping, loped**) run with long, relaxed strides.

lopsided adjective with one side lower or smaller than the other.

loquacious /luh-**kway**-shuhss/ adjective formal talkative.
■ **loquacity** noun.

lord noun **1** a nobleman. **2** (**Lord**) a title given to certain British peers or high officials. **3** (**the Lords**) the House of Lords. **4** a master or ruler. **5** (**Lord**) a name for

---

THESAURUS

responsibility, worry; informal pigeon.
□ **be on the lookout keep watch,** keep an eye out, keep your eyes peeled, be alert.

loom verb **1** *ghostly shapes loomed out of the fog:* emerge, appear, materialize, reveal itself. **2** *the church loomed above him:* soar, tower, rise, rear up, hang, overshadow. **3** *without reforms, disaster looms:* be imminent, be on the horizon, impend, threaten, brew, be just around the corner.

loop noun *a loop of rope:* coil, ring, circle, noose, spiral, curl, bend, curve, arc, twirl, whorl, twist, helix.
• verb **1** *Dave looped rope around their hands:* coil, wind, twist, snake, spiral, curve, bend, turn. **2** *he looped the cables together:* fasten, tie, join, connect, knot, bind.

loophole noun flaw, discrepancy, inconsistency, ambiguity, omission, excuse; Brit. get-out.

loose adjective **1** *a loose floorboard:* not secure, unsecured, unattached, detached, wobbly, unsteady, dangling, free. **2** *she wore her hair loose:* untied, free, down. **3** *there's a wolf loose:* free, at large, at liberty, on the loose, escaped. **4** *a loose interpretation:* vague, imprecise,

approximate, broad, general, rough, liberal. **5** *a loose jacket:* baggy, generously cut, slack, roomy, oversized, shapeless, sloppy.
OPPOSITES secure, literal, narrow, tight.
• verb **1** *the hounds have been loosed:* free, let loose, release, untie, unchain, unfasten, unleash. **2** *the fingers loosed their hold:* relax, slacken, loosen.
OPPOSITES confine, tighten.

loosen verb **1** *you simply loosen two screws:* undo, slacken, unfasten, detach, release, disconnect. **2** *her fingers loosened:* slacken, become loose, let go, ease. **3** *Philip loosened his grip:* weaken, relax, slacken, loose.
OPPOSITES tighten.

loot noun *a bag full of loot:* booty, spoils, plunder, stolen goods, contraband, informal swag.
• verb *troops looted the cathedral:* plunder, pillage, ransack, sack, rifle, rob, strip, gut.

lord noun **1** *lords and ladies:* noble, nobleman, peer, aristocrat. **2** *it is my duty to obey my lord's wishes:* master, ruler, leader, chief, superior, monarch, sovereign, king, emperor, prince, governor, commander.
OPPOSITES commoner, servant, inferior.

God or Jesus.
□ **lord it over** act in an arrogant and bullying way towards someone. **Lord Mayor** the title of the mayor in London and some other large cities.

lordly adjective proud or superior.

Lordship noun (**His/Your Lordship**) a form of address to a judge, bishop, or nobleman.

lore noun all the traditions and knowledge relating to a particular subject.

lorgnette or **lorgnettes** /lor-nyet/ noun a pair of glasses held by a long handle at one side.

lorry noun (plural **lorries**) Brit. a large motor vehicle for transporting goods.

lose verb (**loses, losing, lost**) 1 have something or someone taken away from you; no longer have. 2 become unable to find. 3 fail to win a game or contest. 4 earn less money than you are spending. 5 waste an opportunity. 6 (**be lost**) be destroyed or killed. 7 escape from. 8 (**lose yourself in** or **be lost in**) be or become deeply involved in. 9 (of a clock or watch) become slow.
□ **lose out** not get a fair chance or share.

> ! don't confuse **lose** with **loose**, which means 'not fixed in place or tied up'.

loser noun 1 the person who loses a contest. 2 informal a person who is generally unsuccessful in life.

loss noun 1 the losing of something or someone. 2 a person or thing that is lost. 3 the feeling of sadness after losing a valued person or thing.
□ **at a loss** 1 uncertain or puzzled. 2 losing more money than is being made. **loss-leader** a product sold at a very low price to attract customers.

lost past and past participle of **LOSE**.
□ **be lost for words** be so surprised or upset that you cannot think what to say. **be lost on** not be noticed or understood by. **lost cause** something that has no chance of success.

lot pronoun & adverb (**a lot** or informal **lots**) a large number or amount. •noun 1 an item or set of items for sale at an auction. 2 informal a particular group of people. 3 (**the lot**) informal the whole number or quantity. 4 a method of deciding something by chance in which one piece is chosen from a number of marked pieces of paper. 5 a person's luck or situation in life. 6 chiefly N. Amer. a plot of land.

> ☑ **a lot** is a two-word phrase; don't spell it as one word.

loth ⇨ **LOATH**.

Lothario /luh-thah-ri-oh/ noun (plural **Lotharios**) a man who has many casual sexual relationships with women.

THESAURUS

lose verb 1 *I've lost my watch:* mislay, misplace, be unable to find, lose track of. 2 *he lost his pursuers:* escape from, evade, elude, dodge, avoid, give someone the slip, shake off, throw off, leave behind, outdistance, outrun. 3 *you've lost your opportunity:* waste, squander, let pass, miss; informal pass up, blow. 4 *they always lose at football:* be defeated, be/get beaten; informal come a cropper, go down.
OPPOSITES find, seize, win.

loser noun (informal) failure, underachiever, dead loss, write-off, has-been, informal also-ran, non-starter, no-hoper.
OPPOSITES success.

loss noun 1 *the loss of the papers:* mislaying, misplacement, destruction, theft. 2 *loss of earnings:* forfeiture, diminution, erosion, reduction, depletion. 3 *the loss of her husband:* death, demise, passing away, end. 4 *British losses in the war:* casualty, fatality, victim, dead. 5 *a loss of £15,000:* deficit, debit, debt.
OPPOSITES recovery, profit.
□ **at a loss** baffled, nonplussed, mystified, puzzled, perplexed, bewildered, confused, stumped, stuck; informal flummoxed, beaten.

lost adjective 1 *her lost keys:* missing, mislaid, misplaced, stolen. 2 *I think we're lost:* off course, going round in circles,
adrift, at sea. 3 *a lost opportunity:* missed, wasted, squandered, gone by the board; informal down the drain. 4 *lost traditions:* bygone, past, former, old, vanished, forgotten, dead. 5 *lost species and habitats:* extinct, died out, defunct, vanished, gone, destroyed, wiped out, exterminated. 6 *lost in thought:* engrossed, absorbed, rapt, immersed, deep, intent, engaged, wrapped up.
OPPOSITES current, living, saved.

lot pronoun *a lot of money | lots of friends:* a large amount, a good/great deal, an abundance, a wealth, a profusion, plenty, many, a great many, a large number, a considerable number; informal hundreds, loads, masses, heaps, piles, stacks, tons, oodles; Brit. informal a shedload, lashings.
OPPOSITES a little, a few.
•adverb *I work in pastels a lot:* a great deal, a good deal, much, often, frequently, regularly.
OPPOSITES a little.
•noun 1 (informal) *what do your lot think?* group, crowd, circle, crew; informal bunch, gang, mob. 2 *an auction lot:* item, article, batch, group, bundle, parcel. 3 *his lot in life:* fate, destiny, fortune, situation, circumstances, plight, predicament.

lotion noun a creamy liquid put on the skin as a medicine or cosmetic.

lottery noun (plural **lotteries**) **1** a way of raising money by selling numbered tickets and giving prizes to the holders of numbers drawn at random. **2** something whose success is controlled by luck.

lotus noun a kind of large water lily.
□ **lotus position** a cross-legged position with the feet resting on the thighs, used in meditation.

louche /loosh/ adjective having a bad reputation but still attractive.

loud adjective **1** producing a lot of noise. **2** expressed forcefully. **3** very brightly coloured and in bad taste.
■ **loudly** adverb **loudness** noun.

loudhailer noun an electronic device for making the voice louder.

loudspeaker noun a device that converts electrical impulses into sound.

lough /lok, lokh/ noun Irish a loch.

lounge verb (**lounges, lounging, lounged**) lie, sit, or stand in a relaxed way. ● noun **1** Brit. a sitting room. **2** a room in a hotel, airport, etc. in which people can relax or wait.
□ **lounge bar** Brit. a bar in a pub or hotel that is more comfortable than the public bar. **lounge suit** Brit. a man's ordinary suit.

lounger noun an outdoor chair that you can lie back in.

lour or **lower** /rhymes with flour/ verb **1** (of the sky) look dark and threatening. **2** scowl.

louse noun **1** (plural **lice**) a small insect which lives as a parasite on animals or plants. **2** (plural **louses**) informal an unpleasant person.

lousy adjective (**lousier, lousiest**) informal very bad.

lout noun a rude or aggressive man or boy.
■ **loutish** adjective.

louvre /loo-ver/ (US spelling **louver**) noun each of a set of slanting slats fixed at intervals in a door, shutter, etc. to allow air or light through.

lovable or **loveable** adjective easy to love or feel affection for.

lovage noun a herb used in cookery.

love noun **1** a very strong feeling of affection. **2** a strong feeling of affection linked with sexual attraction. **3** a great interest and pleasure in something. **4** a person or thing that you love. **5** (in tennis, squash, etc.) a score of zero. ● verb (**loves, loving, loved**) **1** feel love for. **2** like very much.
□ **love affair** a romantic or sexual relationship between two people who are not married to each other. **love child** a child born to parents who are not married to each other. **make love** have sex.
■ **loveless** adjective **lover** noun.

lovelorn adjective unhappy because you

THESAURUS

lotion noun ointment, cream, balm, rub, moisturizer, lubricant, embrocation.

lottery noun raffle, (prize) draw, sweepstake, sweep, tombola, lotto, pools.

loud adjective **1** *loud music:* noisy, blaring, booming, deafening, roaring, thunderous, ear-splitting, powerful, stentorian; Music forte, fortissimo. **2** *loud complaints:* vociferous, clamorous, insistent, vehement, emphatic. **3** *a loud T-shirt:* garish, gaudy, lurid, showy, ostentatious, vulgar, tasteless; informal flashy.
OPPOSITES quiet, gentle, sober, tasteful.

loudly adverb at high volume, at the top of your voice, noisily, stridently, vociferously, shrilly.
OPPOSITES quietly.

lounge verb *lounging around:* laze, lie, loll, recline, relax, rest, take it easy, sprawl, slump, slouch, loaf, idle, do nothing. ● noun *sitting in the lounge:* living room, sitting room, front room, drawing room.

lout noun hooligan, ruffian, thug, boor, oaf, rowdy; informal tough, bruiser; Brit. informal yob, yobbo.
OPPOSITES gentleman.

love noun **1** *a friendship that blossomed into love:* infatuation, adoration, attachment, devotion, fondness, tenderness, warmth, intimacy, passion, desire, lust, yearning, besottedness. **2** *her love of fashion:* liking, taste, passion, zeal, zest, enthusiasm, keenness, fondness, weakness, partiality, predilection, penchant. **3** *their love for their fellow human beings:* compassion, care, regard, concern, altruism, unselfishness, philanthropy, benevolence, humanity. **4** *he was her one true love:* beloved, loved one, dearest, darling, sweetheart, sweet, angel, honey.
OPPOSITES hatred.
● verb **1** *she loves him dearly:* be in love with, be infatuated with, be smitten with, be besotted with, adore, idolize, worship, think the world of, be devoted to, dote on, care for, hold dear; informal be mad/crazy about, carry a torch for. **2** *Laura loved painting:* like, delight in, enjoy, have a passion for, take pleasure in, have a weakness for, be partial to, be taken with; informal have a thing about, be mad/crazy about, be hooked on.
OPPOSITES hate.

love affair noun relationship, affair, romance, liaison, fling, entanglement, involvement, intrigue, amour; Brit. informal carry-on.

love someone who does not feel the same way about you.

lovely adjective (**lovelier, loveliest**) **1** very beautiful. **2** very pleasant.
■ **loveliness** noun.

lovemaking noun sex and other sexual activity.

lover noun **1** a person having a sexual or romantic relationship with someone. **2** a person who enjoys a particular thing.

lovesick adjective unable to think clearly or act normally as a result of being in love.

low¹ adjective **1** not high or tall or far above the ground. **2** below average in amount, extent, or strength. **3** not good or important. **4** (of a sound) deep or quiet. **5** depressed or without energy. **6** not honest or moral. • noun **1** a low point or level. **2** an area of low atmospheric pressure. • adverb (of a sound) at a low pitch.
□ **Low Church** the section of the Church of England that places little emphasis on ritual and the authority of bishops and priests. **the low-down** informal the important facts about something. **lowest common denominator** the lowest number that the bottom number of a group of fractions can be divided into exactly. **low-key** not

elaborate or showy. **low life** dishonest or immoral people or activities. **low tide** the time when the sea is furthest out.

low² verb (of a cow) moo.

lowbrow adjective not intellectual or interested in culture.

lower¹ adjective **1** less high. **2** (in place names) situated to the south. • verb (**lowers, lowering, lowered**) **1** make or become lower. **2** move downwards. **3** (**lower yourself**) behave in a way that makes other people lose respect for you.
□ **lower case** small letters as opposed to capitals.

lower² ⇨ **LOUR**.

lowland or **lowlands** noun **1** low-lying country. **2** (**the Lowlands**) the part of Scotland lying south and east of the Highlands.
■ **lowlander** noun.

lowly adjective (**lowlier, lowliest**) low in status or importance.
■ **lowliness** noun.

loyal adjective firm and faithful in your support for a person, organization, etc.
■ **loyally** adverb.

loyalist noun **1** a person who remains loyal to the established ruler or government.

lovely adjective **1** *a lovely young woman:* **beautiful**, pretty, attractive, good-looking, handsome, adorable, enchanting, gorgeous, alluring, ravishing, glamorous; Scottish & N. English bonny; informal tasty, stunning, drop-dead gorgeous; Brit. informal fit; N. Amer. informal cute, foxy. **2** *a lovely view:* **scenic**, picturesque, pleasing, magnificent, stunning, splendid. **3** (informal) *we had a lovely day:* **delightful**, very pleasant, very nice, marvellous, wonderful, sublime, superb; informal terrific, fabulous, heavenly, divine, amazing, glorious.
OPPOSITES ugly, horrible.

lover noun **1** *she had a secret lover:* **boyfriend**, girlfriend, beloved, sweetheart, mistress, partner; informal bit on the side, fancy man, fancy woman; dated beau; old use swain, paramour. **2** *a dog lover:* **devotee**, admirer, fan, enthusiast, aficionado; informal buff, nut, ...head.

loving adjective **affectionate**, fond, devoted, adoring, doting, caring, tender, warm, close, amorous, passionate.
OPPOSITES cold, cruel.

low adjective **1** *a low fence:* **short**, small, little, squat, stubby, stunted. **2** *low prices:* **cheap**, economical, moderate, reasonable, affordable, modest, bargain, bargain-basement, rock-bottom. **3** *supplies were low:* **scarce**, scant, meagre, sparse, few, little, reduced, depleted, diminished. **4** *low

quality:* **inferior**, substandard, poor, low-grade, unsatisfactory. **5** *a low voice:* **quiet**, soft, faint, gentle, muted, subdued, muffled, hushed. **6** *a low note:* **bass**, low-pitched, deep, rumbling, booming, sonorous. **7** *she was feeling low:* **depressed**, dejected, despondent, downhearted, downcast, down, miserable, dispirited, flat; informal fed up, down in the dumps, blue.
OPPOSITES high, expensive, plentiful, loud.

lower¹ adjective **1** *the lower house of parliament:* **subordinate**, inferior, lesser, junior, minor, secondary, subsidiary, subservient. **2** *her lower lip:* **bottom**, bottommost, nether, under. **3** *a lower price:* **cheaper**, reduced, cut.
OPPOSITES upper, higher, increased.

lower² verb **1** *she lowered the mask:* **let down**, take down, drop, let fall. **2** *lower your voice:* **soften**, modulate, quieten, hush, tone down, muffle, turn down. **3** *they are lowering their prices:* **reduce**, decrease, lessen, bring down, cut, slash.
OPPOSITES raise, increase.

lowly adjective **humble**, low, low-ranking, common, ordinary, plain, modest, simple, obscure.
OPPOSITES aristocratic, exalted.

loyal adjective **faithful**, true, devoted, constant, steadfast, staunch, dependable, reliable, trustworthy, trusty, patriotic.
OPPOSITES disloyal.

2 (**Loyalist**) a person who believes that Northern Ireland should remain part of Great Britain.
■ **loyalism** noun.

loyalty noun (plural **loyalties**) 1 the state of being loyal. 2 a strong feeling of support.

lozenge noun 1 a tablet of medicine that is sucked to soothe a sore throat. 2 a diamond-shaped figure.

LP abbreviation long-playing (record).

LSD noun lysergic acid diethylamide, a drug that causes hallucinations.

Ltd abbreviation Brit. Limited.

lubricant noun a substance, e.g. oil, for lubricating part of a machine.

lubricate /**loo**-bri-kayt/ verb (**lubricates, lubricating, lubricated**) apply oil or grease to machinery so that it moves easily.
■ **lubrication** noun.

lubricious /loo-**bri**-shuhss/ adjective formal referring to sexual matters in a rude or offensive way.

lucid /**loo**-sid/ adjective 1 easy to understand; clear. 2 able to think clearly.
■ **lucidity** noun **lucidly** adverb.

Lucifer /**loo**-si-fer/ noun the Devil.

luck noun 1 good things that happen by chance. 2 chance considered as a force that causes good or bad things to happen.

luckily adverb it is fortunate that.

luckless adjective unlucky.

lucky adjective (**luckier, luckiest**) having, bringing, or resulting from good luck.

□ **lucky dip** Brit. a game in which prizes are hidden in a container for people to pick out at random.

lucrative adjective making a large profit.

lucre /**loo**-ker/ noun money.

Luddite /**lud**-dyt/ noun a person who is opposed to new technology.

ludicrous /**loo**-di-kruhss/ adjective absurd; ridiculous.
■ **ludicrously** adverb.

ludo noun Brit. a board game in which players move counters according to throws of a dice.

lug[1] verb (**lugs, lugging, lugged**) carry or drag with great effort.

lug[2] noun 1 informal an ear. 2 a projection on an object for carrying it or fixing it in place.

luggage noun suitcases or other bags for a traveller's belongings.

lugubrious /luu-**goo**-bri-uhss/ adjective sad and gloomy.

lukewarm adjective 1 only slightly warm. 2 unenthusiastic.

lull verb 1 make someone relaxed or calm. 2 make someone feel safe or confident, even if they are at risk of something bad.
● noun a quiet period between times of activity.

lullaby noun (plural **lullabies**) a soothing song sung to send a child to sleep.

lumbago /lum-**bay**-goh/ noun pain in the lower back.

THESAURUS

loyalty noun allegiance, faithfulness, obedience, adherence, devotion, steadfastness, staunchness, dedication, commitment, patriotism.
OPPOSITES disloyalty.

lucid adjective rational, sane, in possession of your faculties, compos mentis, clear-headed, sober; informal all there.
OPPOSITES confused.

luck noun 1 *with luck you'll make it:* good fortune, good luck, stroke of luck; informal lucky break. 2 *I wish you luck:* success, prosperity, good fortune, good luck. 3 *it is a matter of luck whether it hits or misses:* fortune, fate, serendipity, chance, accident, a twist of fate.
OPPOSITES bad luck, misfortune.

luckily adverb fortunately, happily, providentially, by good fortune, as luck would have it, mercifully, thankfully.

lucky adjective 1 *the lucky winner:* fortunate, in luck, favoured, charmed, successful; Brit. informal jammy. 2 *a lucky escape:* providential, fortunate, timely, opportune, serendipitous, chance, fortuitous, accidental.
OPPOSITES unlucky.

lucrative adjective profitable, gainful, remunerative, moneymaking, well paid, rewarding, worthwhile.
OPPOSITES unprofitable.

ludicrous adjective absurd, ridiculous, farcical, laughable, risible, preposterous, mad, insane, idiotic, stupid, asinine, nonsensical; informal crazy.
OPPOSITES sensible.

luggage noun baggage, bags, suitcases, cases.

lukewarm adjective 1 *lukewarm coffee:* tepid, warmish, at room temperature. 2 *a lukewarm response:* indifferent, cool, half-hearted, apathetic, unenthusiastic, tepid, offhand.
OPPOSITES hot, cold, warm.

lull verb *the sound of the bells lulled us to sleep:* soothe, calm, hush, rock to sleep.
OPPOSITES waken, arouse.
● noun 1 *a lull in the fighting:* pause, respite, interval, break, suspension, breathing space; informal let-up, breather. 2 *the lull before the storm:* calm, stillness, quiet, tranquillity, peace, silence, hush.
OPPOSITES agitation, activity.

lumbar adjective relating to the lower back.

lumber noun 1 Brit. disused furniture. 2 chiefly N. Amer. timber sawn into rough planks. • verb (**lumbers, lumbering, lumbered**) 1 Brit. informal give someone an unwanted responsibility. 2 move in a heavy, awkward way.

lumberjack noun a person who cuts down trees and saws them into logs.

luminary /loo-mi-nuh-ri/ noun (plural **luminaries**) an important or influential person.

luminescence noun light given off by a substance that has not been heated, e.g. fluorescent light.
■ **luminescent** adjective.

luminous adjective bright or shining, especially in the dark.
■ **luminosity** noun **luminously** adverb.

lump noun 1 an irregularly shaped piece of something hard or solid. 2 a swelling under the skin. • verb (**lump together**) casually group different people or things together.
□ **lump it** informal put up with something whether you like it or not. **lump sum** a single payment as opposed to a number of smaller payments.
■ **lumpy** adjective.

lumpen adjective 1 lumpy and misshapen. 2 stupid or loutish.

lunacy noun 1 insanity; mental illness. 2 great stupidity.

lunar adjective having to do with the moon.
□ **lunar eclipse** an eclipse in which the moon is hidden by the earth's shadow.

lunatic noun 1 a person who is mentally ill. 2 a very foolish person.

lunch noun a meal eaten in the middle of the day. • verb eat lunch.

luncheon noun formal lunch.

lung noun each of a pair of organs in the chest into which humans and animals draw air when breathing.

lunge noun a sudden forward movement of the body. • verb (**lunges, lunging** or **lungeing, lunged**) make a sudden forward movement.

lupin noun a plant with spikes of tall flowers.

lupine /loo-pyn/ adjective resembling a wolf.

lurch verb make a sudden, unsteady movement. • noun a sudden, unsteady movement.
□ **leave someone in the lurch** leave someone in a difficult situation without help or support.

lurcher noun Brit. a dog that is a cross between a greyhound and a retriever, collie, or sheepdog.

lure verb (**lures, luring, lured**) tempt someone to do something by offering a reward. • noun 1 the attractive and tempting qualities of something. 2 a type of bait used in fishing or hunting.

lurex noun trademark yarn or fabric containing a glittering metallic thread.

lurid adjective 1 unpleasantly bright in colour. 2 (of a description) deliberately containing many shocking details.
■ **luridly** adverb.

lurk verb wait in hiding to attack someone.

luscious adjective 1 having a pleasantly rich, sweet taste. 2 (of a woman) very attractive.

THESAURUS

lumber[1] verb elephants lumbered past: trundle, stumble, lurch, shamble, shuffle, trudge, clump.

lumber[2] verb (Brit. informal) she was lumbered with debt: burden, saddle, encumber, land.
OPPOSITES free.

lumbering adjective clumsy, awkward, slow, blundering, bumbling, ponderous; informal clodhopping.
OPPOSITES nimble, agile.

lump noun 1 a lump of coal: chunk, hunk, piece, block, wedge, slab, ball, knob, clod. 2 a lump on his head: swelling, bump, bulge, protuberance, protrusion, growth, tumour, nodule.
• verb it is convenient to lump them together: combine, put, group, bunch, throw.

lunatic noun he drives like a lunatic: maniac, madman, madwoman, fool, idiot; informal loony, nutcase; Brit. informal nutter; N. Amer. informal screwball.

• adjective a lunatic idea: stupid, foolish, idiotic, absurd, ludicrous, preposterous; informal crazy, mad; Brit. informal barmy, daft.
OPPOSITES sensible.

lunge noun Darren made a lunge at his attacker: thrust, dive, rush, charge, grab.
• verb he lunged at Finn with a knife: thrust, dive, spring, launch yourself, rush.

lurch verb 1 he lurched into the kitchen: stagger, stumble, sway, reel, roll, totter. 2 the car lurched to the left: swing, list, roll, pitch, veer, swerve.

lure verb consumers are frequently lured into debt: tempt, entice, attract, induce, coax, persuade, inveigle, seduce.
OPPOSITES deter, put off.
• noun the lure of the stage: temptation, attraction, pull, draw, appeal, inducement, allure, fascination, interest, glamour.

lurk verb skulk, loiter, lie in wait, hide.

lush adjective **1** (of plants) growing thickly and strongly. **2** rich or luxurious. • noun N. Amer. informal a drunkard.
■ **lushly** adverb **lushness** noun.

lust noun **1** strong sexual desire. **2** a passionate desire for something. • verb feel lust.
■ **lustful** adjective.

lustre (US spelling **luster**) noun **1** a soft glow or shine. **2** prestige or honour.
■ **lustrous** adjective.

lusty adjective (**lustier, lustiest**) healthy and strong.
■ **lustily** adverb.

lute noun a stringed instrument with a long neck and a rounded body, which you play by plucking.

lutetium /loo-tee-shi-uhm/ noun a rare silvery-white metallic element.

luxuriant /lug-zhoor-i-uhnt/ adjective growing thickly and strongly.
■ **luxuriance** noun **luxuriantly** adverb.

luxuriate /lug-zhoor-i-ayt/ verb (**luxuriates, luxuriating, luxuriated**) (**luxuriate in**) relax and enjoy something very pleasant.

luxurious adjective very comfortable or elegant and expensive.
■ **luxuriously** adverb.

luxury noun (plural **luxuries**) **1** comfortable and expensive living or surroundings. **2** something that is expensive and enjoyable but not essential.

lychee /ly-chee/ noun a small, sweet fruit with thin, rough skin.

lychgate noun a roofed gateway to a churchyard.

Lycra noun trademark an elastic fabric used for close-fitting clothing.

lye noun an alkaline solution used for washing or cleaning.

lying present participle of LIE¹, LIE².

lymph noun a colourless fluid in the body that contains white blood cells.
□ **lymph node** (or **lymph gland**) each of a number of small swellings where lymph is filtered.
■ **lymphatic** adjective.

lymphocyte /lim-fuh-syt/ noun a type of white blood cell.

lynch verb (of a group) kill someone believed to be guilty of a crime without a legal trial.

lynchpin ⇨ LINCHPIN.

lynx noun a wild cat with a short tail and tufted ears.

lyre noun a stringed instrument like a small harp, used in ancient Greece.

lyric noun **1** (also **lyrics**) the words of a song. **2** a poem that expresses the writer's thoughts and emotions. • adjective (of poetry) expressing the writer's thoughts and emotions.

lyrical adjective **1** (of writing or music) expressing the writer's emotions in an imaginative and beautiful way. **2** relating to the words of a popular song.

THESAURUS

lush adjective **1** *lush vegetation:* profuse, rich, abundant, luxuriant, riotous, vigorous, dense, thick, rampant. **2** *a lush apartment:* luxurious, sumptuous, palatial, opulent, lavish, elaborate, extravagant, fancy; informal plush, posh, swanky; Brit. informal swish; N. Amer. informal swank.
OPPOSITES sparse, shrivelled, austere.

lust noun **1** *his lust for her:* desire, longing, passion, libido, sex drive, sexuality, lechery, lasciviousness; informal horniness; Brit. informal randiness. **2** *a lust for power:* greed, desire, craving, eagerness, longing, yearning, hunger, thirst, appetite, hankering.
OPPOSITES dread, aversion.
□ **lust after someone** *he lusted after his employer's wife:* desire, be consumed with desire for; informal fancy, have a thing about/for, drool over. **lust for/after something** *she lusted after adventure:* crave, desire, want, long for, yearn for, dream of, hanker for/after, hunger for, thirst for, ache for.

luxurious adjective opulent, sumptuous, grand, palatial, magnificent, extravagant, fancy; Brit. upmarket; informal plush, posh, classy, swanky, bling-bling; Brit. informal swish; N. Amer. informal swank.
OPPOSITES plain, basic.

luxury noun **1** *we'll live in luxury:* opulence, sumptuousness, grandeur, magnificence, splendour, affluence. **2** *a TV is his only luxury:* indulgence, extravagance, treat, extra, frill.
OPPOSITES simplicity, necessity.

lying noun *she was no good at lying:* dishonesty, fabrication, fibbing, perjury, untruthfulness, mendacity, misrepresentation, deceit, duplicity.
OPPOSITES honesty.
• adjective *he was a lying womanizer:* dishonest, false, untruthful, mendacious, deceitful, duplicitous, double-dealing, two-faced.
OPPOSITES honest.

lyrical adjective **1** *a subtle, lyrical film:* expressive, emotional, deeply felt, personal, passionate. **2** *she was lyrical about her success:* enthusiastic, effusive, rapturous, ecstatic, euphoric.
OPPOSITES unenthusiastic.

◻ **wax lyrical** talk about something in a very enthusiastic way.

▪ **lyrically** adverb.

lyricism noun expression of emotion in writing or music in an imaginative and beautiful way.

lyricist noun a person who writes the words to popular songs.

l

Wordpower Guide

The Wordpower Guide contains twelve separate sections providing a wealth of information on a variety of topics, ranging from extra help with spelling and usage to a handy quick-reference list of countries and currencies. Several sections should be useful for crosswords or word games, while others reveal fascinating facts about English and an entertaining selection of unusual vocabulary. Which is the longest word, for example, and which word has the most synonyms? What's the term for a fear of the number thirteen, or for a person who collects teddy bears? Find the answers in the sections *FAQ and facts about English*, *Phobias and fears*, and *Collectors and enthusiasts*.

Contents

Word links

In this section you will find a useful selection of vocabulary linked to words from a range of subject areas. The main entry **earthquake**, for example, includes the term for the scientific study of earthquakes (seismology), the name of the system for measuring the strength of an earthquake (Richter scale), and the word for a tidal wave caused by an earthquake (tsunami). The section is designed to guide you to a word or expression that is on the tip of your tongue but which you cannot quite bring to mind. It will be a great help with word games, and might also enrich your vocabulary!

abdomen coeliac, ventral (*relating to the abdomen*); colic (*severe pain in the abdomen caused by wind or blockage*), laparotomy (*surgical incision of the abdomen*).

acid alkali, base (*substances reacting with acid*), litmus test (*test for acid or alkali*), neutral (*neither acid nor alkali*), pH (*scale of acidity or alkalinity*).

actor histrionic, thespian (*relating to actors or drama*); audition (*interview for an actor*), cast (*list of actors in a play or film*), greasepaint (*actors' make-up*), green room (*backstage room for actors to relax in*), ham (*bad actor*), trouper (*experienced actor*).

aircraft aerofoil, aileron, bulkhead, cockpit, fairing, fin, flaps, fuselage, hold, joystick, rudder, spoiler, stabilizer, tailplane, undercarriage (*parts of aircraft*); jet, piston engine, ramjet, turbofan, turbojet (*kinds of aircraft engine*); aerodynamics, aeronautics (*science of aircraft flight*), aviation (*business of operating aircraft*), avionics (*aircraft electronics*).

alcohol alcoholism, dipsomania (*addiction to alcohol*), cirrhosis (*liver disease caused by drinking alcohol*), Dutch courage (*confidence gained from drinking alcohol*), teetotalism, temperance (*refusal to drink alcohol*).

alloy some common alloys: amalgam (*mercury with other metals*), brass (*copper and zinc*), bronze (*copper and tin*), ormolu (*copper, zinc, and tin*), pewter (*tin with copper and antimony*), solder (*lead and tin*), steel (*iron with carbon and other metals*).

angle acute (*less than 90°*), obtuse (*more than 90° and less than 180°*), reflex (*more than 180°*), right angle (*exactly 90°*); trigonometry (*branch of mathematics concerned with angles*), protractor, set square (*instruments for measuring or drawing angles*).

animal carnivore (*meat-eating animal*), fauna (*animals of a particular region*), herbivore (*plant-eating animal*), invertebrates (*animals without backbones*), ruminants (*animals that chew the cud*) vertebrates (*animals with backbones*),

zoology (*scientific study of animals*).

archery fletcher (*maker of arrows*), toxophilite (*lover of archery*).

Arab Bedouin (*Arab nomad living in the desert*), burnous, djellaba (*types of Arab cloak*), emir (*title of various Arab rulers*), sheikh (*leader of an Arab tribe, family, or village*), souk (*Arab market*).

architecture some architectural styles: art nouveau, baroque, classical, Georgian, Gothic, neoclassical, Palladian, quattrocento, Regency, rococo, Romanesque.

art some art schools and styles: art deco, art nouveau, baroque, classicism, cubism, Dada, expressionism, Fauvism, Futurism, Impressionism, Mannerism, post-Impressionism, Pre-Raphaelitism, Renaissance, surrealism, Vorticism.

astrology cusp (*initial point of an astrological sign*), horoscope (*astrological forecast of a person's future*), zodiac (*area of the sky divided by astrologers into twelve equal signs*).

atmosphere layers of the earth's atmosphere, from lowest to highest: troposphere, stratosphere, mesosphere, thermosphere, ionosphere; barometer (*instrument measuring atmospheric pressure*), meteorology (*study of the atmosphere*).

back dorsal (*on the back or upper side*), lumbar (*relating to the lower back*), posterior (*further back in position*), supine (*lying on your back*); lumbago (*back pain*); disc (*layer of cartilage separating the vertebrae*), vertebrae (*the small bones forming the spine*).

bacteria some kinds of bacteria: E. coli, legionella, listeria, meningococcus, pneumococcus, salmonella, staphylococcus, streptococcus; bacillus (*rod-shaped bacterium*), coccus (*rounded bacterium*), sepsis, septicaemia, toxaemia (*presence of bacteria in tissues or blood*).

bagpipes chanter (*pipe on which the melody is played*), drone (*pipe sounding a continuous low note*), pibroch (*elaborate Scottish music for bagpipes*), skirl (*shrill* sound of bagpipes), uillean pipes (*Irish bagpipes*).

ballet arabesque, entrechat, jeté, pirouette, plié (*ballet steps and movements*); balletomane (*person who loves ballet*), barre (*bar used during exercises*), choreography (*design of dance movements*), pas de deux (*dance for two*), pointe (*tips of the toes*), tutu (*ballet dancer's dress*).

bankrupt insolvent (*relating to bankruptcy*), receiver (*official managing bankrupt business*), sequestrate (*take possession of property of bankrupt person*).

barrel cooper (*maker of barrels*), hogshead, keg, tun (*kinds of barrel*), hoop (*metal band around a barrel*), spigot (*plug for a barrel vent*), stave (*plank from which barrels are made*).

bee apiary (*place where bees are kept*), apiculture (*keeping of bees*), drone (*male bee*), honeycomb (*wax structure built by bees*), royal jelly (*food for queen bee larvae*), swarm (*large group of bees*).

beetle some common beetles: Colorado beetle, death-watch beetle, ladybird, scarab, weevil; coleopterist (*person who collects beetles*).

bell belfry (*place in a bell tower where bells are kept*), campanile (*a bell tower*), campanology (*art of bell-ringing*), clapper (*moving part inside a bell*), knell (*sound of a bell, especially at a funeral*), peal (*ringing of bells, or set of bells*), tocsin (*alarm bell*).

biology cytology (*biology of cells*), ecology (*study of interrelations between animals, plants, and their surroundings*), morphology (*study of forms of living things*), physiology (*study of normal functions of living things*), taxonomy (*classification of living things*).

bird avian (*relating to birds*); aviary (*place where birds are kept*), ornithology (*study of birds*).

birth antenatal (*before birth*), Caesarean section (*operation to deliver child*), congenital (*present from birth*), natal (*relating to the place and time of birth*), neonate (*newborn child*), obstetrics (*branch of medicine concerned with childbirth*), perinatal (*near to the time of birth*), postpartum (*following birth*).

blood components of blood: corpuscle, erythrocyte, haemoglobin, leucocyte, plasma, platelet, rhesus factor, serum; haematology (*branch of medicine concerned with blood*).

blue shades of blue: aquamarine, azure, cerulean, cobalt, cornflower, cyan, duck-egg blue, indigo, lapis lazuli, lavender, midnight blue, navy, periwinkle, royal blue, sapphire, saxe blue, sky blue, teal, turquoise, ultramarine.

body corporal, corporeal, somatic (*relating to the body*); anatomy (*study of the structure of the body*), circadian (*relating to body processes that happen every twenty-four hours*), metabolism (*the body's chemical processes*), posture (*a body position*).

bone marrow (*soft substance in the hollow of bones*), orthopaedics (*branch of medicine concerned with bones*), osteoporosis (*brittleness of the bones*), osteoarthritis (*pain and stiffness in the joints*), sinew, tendon (*cord of tissue connecting a muscle to a bone*).

book appendix (*information at the end of a book*), bibliography (*list of books*), bibliophile (*person who loves or collects books*); recto (*right-hand page of an open book*), verso (*left-hand page of an open book*).

brass brass musical instruments: bugle, cornet, euphonium, flugelhorn, French horn, horn, trombone, trumpet, tuba.

bridge aqueduct (*bridge carrying water*), drawbridge (*bridge that can be raised*), humpback bridge (*small road bridge with a steep curve*), span (*part of a bridge between supports*), suspension bridge (*bridge suspended from cables*); pontoon (*floating object used to support a bridge*).

brother fraternal (*relating to or like a brother*); confraternity (*a brotherhood*), fratricide (*murder of your own brother or sister*), sibling (*brother or sister*).

brown shades of brown: auburn, beige, bronze, buff, camel, chestnut, chocolate, coffee, copper, dun, fawn, hazel, sepia, tan, taupe, tawny, terracotta, umber.

butterfly caterpillar (*butterfly larva*), chrysalis (*butterfly pupa*), lepidopterist (*person who collects butterflies and moths*), metamorphosis (*transformation of butterfly larva to adult*).

camp billy (*cooking pot used when camping*), bivouac (*temporary camp without tents*), canteen (*small water bottle used when camping*), latrine (*communal toilet in a camp*).

cancer types of cancer: carcinoma, lymphoma, melanoma, sarcoma; treatments for cancer: chemotherapy, radiotherapy; carcinogen (*substance causing cancer*); oncology (*branch of medicine concerned with cancer*).

candle candelabrum (*branched candlestick*), chandelier (*hanging light with branches for several candles*), menorah (*Jewish branched candlestick*), sconce (*ornamental candle holder on wall*); tallow (*substance used in making candles*).

castle parts of a castle: bailey, barbican, battlement, drawbridge, dungeon, keep, moat, portcullis, rampart, turret.

cat feline (*relating to or like cats*); wild cats: bobcat, cheetah, cougar, jaguar, leopard, lion, lynx, ocelot, panther, puma, tiger, wildcat.

cave grotto (*small picturesque cave*), potholer, speleologist (*person who explores caves*), speleology (*study or exploration of *caves*), stalactite, stalagmite (*rock formations within cave*), troglodyte (*cave-dweller*).

cell erythrocyte (*red blood cell*), gamete (*sex cell*), leucocyte (*white blood cell*), neuron (*nerve cell*), zygote (*cell formed by fusion of gametes*); meiosis, mitosis (*division of cells*).

child crèche (*a nursery*), infanticide (*murder of a child*), foundling (*child abandoned by its parents*), orphan (*child whose parents are dead*), paediatrics (*branch of medicine concerned with childhood diseases*).

Chinese Chinese life and culture: Cantonese (*form of the Chinese language*), feng shui (*ancient system of designing and arranging buildings and objects*), kung fu (*martial art*), Mandarin (*official form of the Chinese language*), mah-jong (*game played with small rectangular tiles*), qigong, t'ai chi (*exercise systems*), sinology (*study of Chinese language and culture*), Taoism (*philosophical system*) triad (*secret society involved in organized crime*), yuan (*basic unit of money in China*).

Christianity dates in the Christian calendar: Advent, Ascension, Ash Wednesday, Candlemas, Christmas, Easter, Epiphany, Lent, Palm Sunday, Pentecost, Whit Sunday.

church parts of a church: aisle, apse, chancel, choir, clerestory, crypt, font, nave, pew, pulpit, sacristy, sanctuary, spire, steeple, transept, vestry

circle parts of a circle: arc, circumference, diameter, radius, segment.

city civic, metropolitan, urban (*relating to a city*); citadel (*fortress protecting a city*), conurbation (*area consisting of several towns merging with a city*), mayor (*elected head of a city*), metropolis (*main city of a region*), suburb (*district of private housing on the outskirts of a city*).

coal anthracite, lignite (*kinds of coal*); Carboniferous (*geological period when many coal deposits were laid down*), clinker (*stony remains from burnt coal*), coke (*fuel made by heating coal in the absence of air*), colliery (*coal mine*).

coast littoral (*relating to the coast or shore*); bight (*long inward curve in a coastline*), corniche (*road running along a coast*), riviera (*coastal region with subtropical climate*).

code cipher (*simple kind of code*), cryptogram (*a text written in code*), cryptography (*art of writing or solving codes*), decipher, decrypt (*convert code into normal language*), encipher, encrypt (*convert normal language into code*).

coffin bier, catafalque (*platform or framework supporting a coffin*), hearse (*vehicle carrying a coffin*), pall (*cloth spread over a coffin*), pall-bearer (*person carrying a coffin*), sarcophagus (*stone coffin*).

coin numismatics (*study or collection of coins*), obverse (*side of coin with the head or main design*), reverse (*secondary side of coin*), mint (*place where money is made*).

comedy kinds of comedy: burlesque, farce, satire, slapstick, stand-up, vaudeville.

computer kinds of computer: desktop, laptop, mainframe, microcomputer, notebook, notepad, palmtop, workstation; parts of a computer: disk drive, hard disk, hardware, keyboard, monitor, motherboard, mouse, software, VDU, viewscreen; cyber- (*relating to computers*), modem (*device connecting a computer to a telephone line*).

country bucolic, pastoral, rural, rustic (*relating to the country or the countryside*).

cross types of cross: crucifix, St George's cross, saltire, swastika; cruciform (*cross-shaped*).

curve concave (*curving inwards*), convex (*curving outwards*), arc (*curve forming part of circumference of a circle*).

dance some dances: beguine, bolero, bossa nova, cancan, cha-cha, charleston, conga, eightsome reel, fandango, flamenco, foxtrot, galliard, gavotte, Highland fling, hornpipe, jitterbug, jive, lambada, limbo, mambo, mazurka, merengue, minuet, paso doble, polka, polonaise, quickstep, rumba, salsa, samba, tango, tarantella, twist, two-step, waltz; choreography (*sequence of steps for a dance routine*); terpsichorean (*relating to dancing*).

death autopsy, post-mortem (*examination of a dead body to discover cause of death*), euthanasia (*painless killing of someone suffering from an incurable disease*), inquest (*inquiry into the cause of a death*), memento mori (*object kept as a reminder of death*), moribund (*at the point of death*), necromancy (*attempted communication with dead people so as to predict the future*), necropolis (*a cemetery*), posthumous (*happening after someone has died*), rigor mortis (*stiffening of joints and muscles after death*), thanatology (*scientific study of death*).

devil diabolical (*relating to or like the Devil*); names for the Devil: Beelzebub, the Lord of the Flies, Lucifer, Old Nick, Satan.

dictionary gazetteer (*geographical dictionary*), lexicographer (*person who compiles dictionaries*), thesaurus (*dictionary of synonyms*).

disease aetiology (*study of the causes of disease*), communicable, infectious (*referring to a disease which can be passed to other people*), contagious (*referring to a disease spread by contact*), epidemic (*widespread occurrence of a disease*), epidemiology (*study of the spread of disease*), pathogen (*microorganism that can cause disease*), pathology (*branch of medicine concerned with diseases*).

doctor doctors and their specialties: cardiologist

(*heart disorders*), dermatologist (*skin disorders*), gynaecologist (*female reproductive system*), neurologist (*nervous system*), obstetrician (*childbirth*), oncologist (*cancer*), ophthalmologist (*eye disorders*), paediatrician (*childhood disorders*), pathologist (*causes and effects of diseases*).

document archive (*collection of historical documents*), manuscript (*handwritten document*), pro forma (*standard document*), recto (*front of a loose document*), rubric (*heading on a document*), verso (*back of a loose document*).

dog canine (*relating to or like dogs*); **members of the dog family:** coyote, dingo, fox, jackal, wolf.

ear auditory (*relating to hearing*), aural (*relating to the ear*); **some parts of the ear:** auricle *or* pinna, cochlea, eardrum *or* tympanum, labyrinth; grommet (*drainage tube in the eardrum*), tinnitus (*ringing in the ears*).

earth terrestrial (*relating to the earth*); circumnavigate (*travel around the earth*), geography (*study of physical features of the earth*), geology (*science of physical structure and substance of the earth*), mantle (*inner part of the earth*), tectonic (*relating to the earth's crust*).

earthquake seismic (*relating to earthquakes*); aftershock (*smaller earthquake following larger one*), epicentre (*point on surface directly above focus*), focus (*point of origin of earthquake*), Richter scale (*measuring earthquake intensity*), seismograph (*instrument for measuring earthquakes*), seismology (*scientific study of earthquakes*), tremor (*slight earthquake*), tsunami (*sea wave caused by earthquake*).

egg albumen (*egg white*), clutch (*set of eggs laid together*), incubate (*keep eggs warm for hatching*), ovate, oviform, ovoid (*egg-shaped*), oviparous (*egg-laying*), roe (*fish eggs*), spawn (*fish or amphibian eggs*).

eight octagon (*figure with eight straight sides and eight angles*), octahedron (*three-dimensional shape with eight faces*), octave (*series of eight musical notes between [and including] two notes*), octet (*group of eight musicians*).

election candidate (*person put forward for election*), canvass (*visit someone to seek their vote in an election*), hustings (*public political meetings before an election*), psephology (*study of elections and voting patterns*); franchise, suffrage (*the right to vote in political elections*).

element allotrope (*different form of a chemical element*), atom (*smallest particle of an element*), compound (*substance formed from two or more elements*), isotope (*form of the same element having different atomic mass*), periodic table (*table of the chemical elements*), valency (*combining power of an element*).

environment conservationist (*person dedicated to protecting the environment*), ecology (*study of animals' and plants' relationships with each other and with the environment*), habitat (*natural environment of an animal or plant*).

eye ocular, optic (*relating to the eye*); ophthalmologist (*specialist in eye diseases*), ophthalmoscope (*instrument for inspecting eyes*), optician (*person qualified to prescribe glasses and contact lenses*); **parts of the eye:** conjunctiva, cornea, iris, pupil, retina; **eye conditions or diseases:** astigmatism, cataract, conjunctivitis, glaucoma, myopia (= *short-sightedness*), nystagmus.

feather down (*soft, fine feathers*), pinnate (*shaped like a feather*), plumage (*bird's feathers*), plume (*long, soft feather or group of feathers*), preen (*of a bird: clean its feathers with its beak*); quill (*bird's main wing or tail feather*).

female distaff side (*female side of a family*), gynaecology (*branch of medicine concerned with women's conditions and diseases*), matrilineal (*descent through the female line*), yin (*in Chinese philosophy, the female presence in the universe*).

fetus amniotic fluid (*fluid surrounding a fetus*), caul (*membrane enclosing a fetus*), placenta (*organ that supplies nourishment to the fetus*), umbilical cord (*cord attaching the fetus to the placenta*).

figure **plane figures:** triangle (*three sides*), quadrilateral (*four sides*), pentagon (*five sides*), hexagon (*six sides*), heptagon (*seven sides*), octagon (*eight sides*), nonagon (*nine sides*), decagon (*ten sides*).

fire arson (*act of deliberately setting fire to property*); combustible, flammable, inflammable (*able to catch fire easily*); douse (*extinguish a fire*), ember (*piece of burning wood or coal in a dying fire*), incendiary (*bomb designed to cause fires*), ignite (*catch fire or set on fire*); pyromania (*strong urge to set fire to things*).

fish piscatorial (*relating to fishing*), piscine (*relating to fish*); fry (*young fish*), ichthyology (*study of fish*), milt (*fish sperm*), pisciculture (*breeding and rearing of fish*), roe, spawn (*fish eggs*).

five pentagon (*figure with five straight sides and five angles*), pentathlon (*athletic event made up of five different events*), quintet (*group of five musicians*), quintuplet (*each of five children born at one birth*).

flower **parts of a flower:** anther, bract, calyx, carpel, corolla, pistil, sepal, stamen.

foot chiropody, podiatry (*medical treatment of the feet*); athlete's foot (*ringworm infection of the feet*), bunion (*painful swelling on big toe*), corn (*painful area of thickened skin*), verruca (*wart on the sole of* *the foot*); metatarsus (*bones of the foot*), pedicure (*cosmetic treatment of the feet*), pedometer (*instrument measuring distance travelled on foot*).

four quadrilateral (*four-sided figure*), quadruped (*animal with four feet*), quadruplet (*each of four children born at one birth*), quartet (*group or set of four; group of four musicians*), quatrain (*poem or verse of four lines*), tetralogy (*group of four related books, plays, operas, etc.*).

fraction decimal fraction (*fraction with numbers either side of a decimal point*), denominator (*number below the line in a vulgar fraction*), numerator (*number above the line in a vulgar fraction*), vulgar fraction (*fraction shown by numbers above and below a line, not decimally*).

funeral bier, catafalque (*platform or framework supporting a coffin*), cortège (*funeral procession*), cremate (*burn a dead body*), hearse (*vehicle for carrying the coffin*), inter (*place a dead body in a grave or tomb*), obsequies (*funeral ceremonies*), pall (*cloth spread over a coffin, hearse, or tomb*), undertaker (*person who organizes funerals*), wake (*party held after a funeral*).

gene chromosome (*thread-like structure in a cell carrying genetic information*), clone (*genetically identical individual*), dominant (*gene appearing in offspring when inherited from only one parent*), GMO (*genetically modified organism*), recessive (*gene appearing in offspring only when inherited from both parents*).

God atheism (*belief that God does not exist*), agnosticism (*belief that it is not possible to know whether or not God exists*), blasphemy (*disrespectful talk about God*), divine (*relating to God or a god*), monotheism (*belief that there is only one god*), pantheon (*all the gods of a people or religion*), polytheism (*belief in more than one god*), theology (*the study of God and religious belief*).

gold alchemy (*medieval form of chemistry that tried to turn ordinary metal into gold*), bullion (*gold or silver in bulk before being made into coins*), carat (*measure of purity for gold*), gild (*cover with gold*), Midas touch (*power of turning everything into gold*), nugget (*small lump of gold in the earth*).

green shades of green: apple green, aquamarine, avocado, bottle green, eau de nil, emerald, jade, khaki, lime, olive, sage green; chlorophyll (*green pigment in leaves*), patina, verdigris (*green sheen or film formed on copper or brass*), verdant (*green with grass or other lush vegetation*) verdure (*lush green vegetation*).

gun parts of a gun: barrel, bore, breech, butt, chamber, magazine, muzzle, rifling, stock, trigger; ballistics (*science of firearms and missiles*), calibre (*diameter of a gun barrel*);

barrage, cannonade (*period of heavy gunfire*), fusillade, salvo, volley (*rapid gunfire*).

hair alopecia (*abnormal hair loss*), coiffure (*hairstyle*), depilate (*remove hair*), follicle (*sheath surrounding the root of a hair*), hirsute (*hairy*), toupee (*small wig worn to cover a bald spot*), tonsorial (*relating to hairdressing*), trichology (*branch of medicine concerned with the hair and scalp*).

hand ambidextrous (*able to use right or left hands equally well*), dexterity (*skill with the hands*), manicure (*cosmetic treatment of the hands*), manual (*involving the hands*), metacarpus (*bones of the hand*).

health convalesce (*gradually recover your health after illness*), hypochondriac, valetudinarian (*person abnormally anxious about their health*), salubrious (*health-giving or healthy*), sanitary (*relating to conditions affecting health*).

heart cardiac (*relating to the heart*); cardiology (*branch of medicine concerned with the heart*), coronary (*relating to the arteries that supply the heart*), pacemaker (*artificial device for regulating the heart muscle*); parts of the heart: aorta, atrium, mitral valve, pericardium, vena cava, ventricle

heartbeat arrhythmia (*irregular heartbeat*), bradycardia (*abnormally slow heartbeat*), diastole (*phase when the heart muscle relaxes*), palpitation (*rapid, strong, or irregular heartbeat*), systole (*phase when the heart muscle contracts*), tachycardia (*abnormally rapid heart rate*).

Hinduism ashram (*Hindu religious retreat*), avatar (*Hindu god or goddess appearing in bodily form on earth*), caste (*each of the hereditary classes of Hindu society*), Diwali (*Hindu festival of lights*), guru (*Hindu spiritual teacher*), Holi (*Hindu spring festival*) Maharishi, Mahatma (*wise or holy Hindu teacher or leader*), swami (*male Hindu religious teacher*), Veda (*ancient Hindu scriptures*).

horse equestrian (*relating to horse-riding*), equine (*relating to or like a horse or horses*); colt (*young uncastrated male horse*), foal (*young horse*), farrier (*person who shoes horses*), filly (*young female horse*), gelding (*castrated male horse*), mare (*female horse*), stallion (*uncastrated adult male horse*), stud (*establishment where horses are kept for breeding*).

idea abstract (*relating to ideas rather than objects*), ideology (*system of ideas*), plagiarism (*stealing someone else's idea*), sacred cow (*idea believed by many to be above criticism*), stereotype (*widely held fixed idea of something*).

illusion hallucination (*illusion experienced as real*), mirage (*optical illusion caused by atmospheric conditions*), trompe l'œil (*method of painting which creates an illusion*).

image definition, resolution (*degree of sharpness of an image*), graphic (*image on a computer screen*), hologram (*three-dimensional image*), iconography (*use or study of images*), pixel (*each of the tiny areas of light on a computer screen which make up an image*).

imitation burlesque (*comically exaggerated imitation*), ersatz (*referring to an inferior imitation of something*), parody (*mocking imitation*), pastiche (*imitation of an artistic style*).

Indian Indian languages: Sanskrit (*ancient language of India*), Bengali, Gujarati, Hindi, Hindustani, Marathi, Punjabi, Tamil, Urdu.

inherit heirloom (*valuable inherited article*), hereditary (*gained by inheritance*), legacy (*inherited amount of money or property*), patrimony (*property inherited from a person's father or male ancestor*), primogeniture (*eldest son's right of inheritance*).

injection inoculate, vaccinate (*give someone an injection*); ampoule (*glass capsule of liquid for injecting*), hypodermic (*referring to injection beneath the skin*), intravenous (*referring to injection into a vein*), syringe (*instrument for giving injections*).

insect grub, larva (*immature form of an insect*), chrysalis, pupa (*insect in the form between larva and adult*), imago (*final, fully developed adult stage of an insect*); metamorphosis (*transformation of insect from immature to adult form*); entomology (*study of insects*).

Irish Irish life and culture: ceilidh (*social event with folk music, singing, and traditional dancing*); Dáil (*lower House of Parliament in the Irish Republic*), Hibernian (*relating to Ireland*), hurling (*game resembling hockey*), shamrock (*national emblem of Ireland*), Taoiseach (*Prime Minister of the Irish Republic*).

Islam ayatollah (*Shiite religious leader*), hajj (*pilgrimage to Mecca*), imam (*leader of prayers in a mosque*), jihad (*war or struggle against unbelievers*), Koran (*sacred book of Islam*), mosque (*Muslim place of worship*), minaret (*slender tower of a mosque*), muezzin (*man who calls Muslims to prayer*), mullah (*expert in Islamic theology and sacred law*), Ramadan (*month of fasting*), sharia (*Islamic law*), Shia, Sunni (*two main branches of Islam*).

island insular (*relating to an island*); archipelago (*large group of islands*), atoll (*ring-shaped chain of islands*), key (*low-lying island*).

Japanese Japanese life and culture: aikido, ju-jitsu, karate (*martial arts*), bonsai (*art of growing miniature trees*), futon (*padded mattress*), geisha (*hostess*), haiku (*poem of 17 syllables*), hara-kiri (*method of ritual suicide*), kabuki (*drama performed by men*), kendo (*form of fencing*), kimono (*loose robe*), manga (*fantasy cartoons and animation*), Noh (*traditional theatre with dance and song*), origami (*art of folding paper into decorative shapes*), sake (*alcoholic drink made from rice*), samurai (*in the past, a member of powerful military class*) Shinto (*religion of spirit worship*), shogun (*in the past, a hereditary leader of the army*), sumo (*form of wrestling*), sushi (*dish of cold rice with raw seafood*), yen (*basic unit of money in Japan*).

joint arthritis (*inflammation and stiffness of a joint of the body*), articulation (*the state of being jointed*), chiropractic (*manipulative treatment of joints*), dislocation (*injury in which a joint is disturbed*).

Judaism bar mitzvah (*ceremony in which a Jewish boy comes of age*), cantor (*person who leads prayers in a synagogue*), Hanukkah (*Jewish festival of lights*), kosher (*referring to food prepared in accordance with Jewish law*), menorah (*large candlestick*), Passover (*festival commemorating the Israelites' liberation from slavery*), Pentecost (*festival 50 days after Passover*), rabbi (*Jewish scholar, teacher, or religious leader*), Rosh Hashana (*New Year festival*), synagogue (*building used for Jewish worship*), Talmud (*ancient writings on Jewish law and legend*), Torah (*law of God as revealed to Moses*), yarmulke (*skullcap worn by Jewish men*), Yom Kippur (*day of prayer, fasting, and penitence*).

kill euthanasia (*painless killing of a patient with an incurable disease*), genocide (*killing of a whole people*), homicide (*killing of another person*), manslaughter (*unintentional killing*), suicide (*killing of yourself*).

knight charger (*horse ridden by a knight*), chivalry (*medieval knights' code of behaviour*), dub (*make someone a knight by touching their shoulder with a sword*), joust, tilt, tourney (*knights' mock combat*), quest (*a knight's expedition*).

knowledge erudite (*knowing a great deal*), omniscient (*knowing everything*), philosophy (*study of the nature of knowledge*), polymath (*person who has wide knowledge of many subjects*), prescient (*knowing something in advance*).

language bilingual (*speaking or expressed in two languages*), dialect (*regional form of a language*), linguist (*person who studies language or languages*), monolingual (*speaking or expressed in only one language*), multilingual (*in or using several languages*), polyglot (*person who knows several languages*), vernacular (*language spoken by ordinary people*).

leaf deciduous (*referring to trees that shed*

leaves annually), evergreen (*referring to trees that have green leaves throughout the year*), foliage (*leaves in general*), frond (*leaf of a palm or fern*), vein (*thin rib running through a leaf*).

light chiaroscuro (*treatment of light and shade in drawing and painting*); opaque (*not allowing light through*), translucent (*allowing light to pass through partially*), transparent (*allowing light to pass through so that objects behind can be clearly seen*).

lung pulmonary (*relating to the lungs*); asbestosis (*disease caused by breathing asbestos dust*), alveoli (*tiny air sacs in the lungs*), bronchi (*air passages of the lungs*), emphysema (*condition causing breathlessness*), pleura (*membranes enclosing the lungs*), pleurisy (*inflammation of the membranes enclosing the lungs*), pneumonia (*lung infection in which pus collects in the lungs*).

magic amulet, fetish, talisman (*objects thought to have magical powers*); elixir (*magic potion*), incantation (*words said as a magic spell or charm*), necromancy (*black magic*), numerology (*magical power of numbers*), occult (*world of magic and the supernatural*), pentagram (*five-pointed star used as magical symbol*).

-mania dipsomania (*alcoholism*), kleptomania (*uncontrollable need to steal*), megalomania (*obsession with power*), monomania (*obsession with one thing*), nymphomania (*uncontrollable sexual desire in a woman*), pyromania (*obsession with setting things on fire*).

map cartography (*science of map-making*), isobar (*line on a map connecting points with the same atmospheric pressure*), Ordnance Survey (*official UK map-making organization*), projection (*way of representing the earth's surface on a map*), relief map (*map showing contours by shading*), topography (*representation of an area's physical features on a map*).

marriage bridal, conjugal, connubial, marital, matrimonial, nuptial (*relating to marriage*); banns (*announcement in church of intended marriage*), dowry (*money or property brought by bride on her marriage*), elope (*run away secretly to get married*), maiden name (*surname of woman before her marriage*), spouse (*husband or wife*), trousseau (*clothes etc. collected by a bride for her marriage*); monogamy (*practice of having only one spouse at a time*), bigamy (*crime of having more than one spouse at one time*), polygamy (*custom of having several spouses at one time*).

mathematics branches of mathematics: algebra, arithmetic, calculus, geometry, statistics, trigonometry.

meaning antonym (*word which is opposite in meaning*), nuance (*slight difference in meaning*), synonym (*word which is the same in meaning*), semantics (*study of meaning*).

memory amnesia (*loss of memory*), keepsake, memento (*small item kept in memory of someone or as a reminder of something*), mnemonic (*aid to memory*).

missile ballistic missile (*missile which is fired into the air and falls on to its target*), cruise missile (*flying bomb guided by an on-board computer*), heat-seeking missile (*able to home in on heat emitted by target*), payload, warhead (*explosive head of a missile*), silo (*underground launcher for missile*), torpedo (*underwater missile*).

moisture dehydrated, desiccated (*lacking moisture*), humidity (*amount of moisture in the air*), saturated (*full of moisture*).

monastery abbot (*head of a monastery*), chapter (*monastery's governing body*), cloister (*covered passage round an open courtyard*), refectory (*dining hall*).

money pecuniary (*relating to money*); avarice, cupidity (*greed for money*), economics (*study of the getting and spending of money*), mercenary (*interested only in money*), numismatist (*collector of notes and coins*), specie (*money in the form of coins*).

monk cowl (*monk's hood*), habit (*monk's robe*), novice, postulant (*monk who has recently entered a religious order*), scapular (*monk's short cloak*), tonsure (*shaven part of monk's head*).

motion kinetic (*relating to or resulting from motion*); inertia (*tendency to remain in motion or motionless*), impetus, momentum (*energy associated with motion*).

mountain alpine (*relating to high mountains*); arête (*sharp mountain ridge*), col (*high mountain pass*), massif (*compact group of mountains*), peak (*pointed top of a mountain*), sierra (*long mountain chain*), summit (*highest point of a mountain*), tarn (*mountain lake*).

mouth oral, buccal (*relating to the mouth*); epiglottis (*flap of cartilage at the back of the mouth*), palate (*roof of the mouth*), tonsil (*mass of tissue at the back of the mouth*).

music some musical forms: concerto, fantasia, fugue, madrigal, march, motet, nocturne, opera, operetta, oratorio, prelude, rhapsody, requiem, sonata, song, symphony, toccata.

musician ensemble (*group of musicians performing together*), maestro, virtuoso (*distinguished musician*), minstrel (*medieval musician*).

name alias (*false name or identity*), anonymous (*not identified by name*), diminutive (*shortened form of a name*), eponymous (*referring to a person after whom something is named*), misnomer (*name that is wrong or inaccurate*), nom de plume (*pen name*), nomenclature (*system of names*), onomastics (*study of proper names*), pen name (*name used by a writer*), pseudonym (*fictitious name*), toponym (*place name*).

number cardinal number (*number expressing quantity, e.g. five*), ordinal number (*number defining position in a series, e.g. fifth*), prime number (*number divisible only by itself and 1*), root (*number that when multiplied by itself gives a specified number*), square (*product of a number multiplied by itself*).

nun coif (*nun's close-fitting cap*), convent, nunnery (*community of nuns*), novice (*nun who has recently entered a religious order*), wimple (*nun's headdress*).

oath affidavit (*statement made under oath*), deposition (*evidence given under oath*), Hippocratic oath (*oath formerly taken by trainee doctors*), perjury (*offence of lying in court under oath*).

old antiquarian (*person who collects or studies old things*); dotage (*period of life when a person is old and weak*), geriatric (*relating to old people*), gerontology (*study of old age*), senile (*mentally weakened through old age*).

opera aria (*song for a soloist in an opera*), diva (*famous female opera singer*), libretto (*words of an opera*), prima donna (*chief female singer in an opera*), surtitle (*running translation of an opera displayed above the stage*).

operation some operations: angioplasty (*repair of a blood vessel*), amputation (*cutting off of a limb*), appendectomy (*removal of the appendix*), bypass (*creation of a new passage for blood to flow through*), Caesarean section (*delivery of a child by cutting through the mother's abdomen*), colostomy (*removal of part of the colon*), hysterectomy (*removal of all or part of the womb*), lobotomy (*cutting into part of the brain*), mastectomy (*removal of a breast*), tonsillectomy (*removal of the tonsils*).

page centrefold (*two middle pages of a magazine*), flyleaf (*blank page at the start or end of a book*), footnote (*extra information printed at the bottom of a page*), gatefold (*oversized page opened out for reading*), paginate (*to number the pages of a book*), recto (*right-hand page of open book*), verso (*left-hand page of open book*).

pain anaesthetic (*drug that stops you feeling pain*), analgesic (*medicine relieving pain*), embrocation (*liquid painkiller rubbed on the body*), masochist (*person who enjoys experiencing pain*), neuralgia (*intense pain along a nerve*), sadist (*person who enjoys inflicting pain*).

painting chiaroscuro (*treatment of light and shade*), diptych (*painting on two hinged panels*), fresco (*painting on wet plaster*), gouache (*method of painting using thickened watercolours*), impasto (*technique of applying paint in thick layers*), mural

(*painting on a wall*), triptych (*painting on three hinged panels*), trompe l'œil (*method of painting which creates an illusion*).

parliament act (*law passed by parliament*), backbencher (*MP who does not hold a government or opposition post*), bicameral (*referring to a parliament with two chambers*), bill (*draft of a proposed law presented to parliament*), filibuster (*very long speech made to prevent a new law from being passed*), Hansard (*record of UK parliamentary debates*), hung parliament (*with no party having a majority*), prorogue (*discontinue a session of parliament*), recess (*break between parliamentary sessions*).

people demotic, plebeian (*relating to ordinary people*), hoi polloi (*a derogatory term for common people*), proletariat (*working-class people*), vernacular (*language spoken by ordinary people*).

percussion percussion instruments: bells, castanets, cymbals, drum, glockenspiel, gong, Jew's harp, maracas, piano, tambourine, vibraphone, xylophone.

photograph daguerreotype (*early kind of photograph*), darkroom (*room for developing photographs*), microfiche (*piece of film containing very small-sized photographs*), paparazzi (*photographers who try to photograph celebrities*).

plant botany (*study of plants*), chlorophyll (*green pigment of plants*), flora (*plants of a region*), herbivorous (*feeding on plants*), photosynthesis (*process by which plants use sunlight to form nutrients*), succulent (*plant that stores water in its leaves or stem*), transpiration (*loss of water vapour from the leaves of a plant*), annual (*plant living one year*), biennial (*two years*), perennial (*three or more years*).

play types of play: comedy, farce, melodrama, pantomime, tragedy; denouement (*final part of a play in which all is resolved*), dialogue (*conversation between people in a play*), dramatize (*turn something into a play*), epilogue (*address to the audience at the end of a play*), prologue (*address to the audience at the start of a play*), soliloquy (*speech in which a character speaks their thoughts aloud*).

poem forms of poem: acrostic, ballad, elegy, epic, haiku, lay, limerick, lyric, ode, sonnet; anthology (*collection of poems*), blank verse (*unrhymed poetry*), metre (*rhythmic pattern of a poem*), prosody (*study of forms and rhythms of poetry*), stanza (*group of lines forming basic unit of a poem*).

poison antidote (*medicine which works against a poison*), toxin (*poison produced by a microorganism*), toxicology (*study of poisons*), venom (*snake poison*).

pope papal, pontifical (*relating to popes or the Pope*); bull (*order or announcement issued by the Pope*), encyclical (*letter from the Pope to all Catholic bishops), legate (*papal representative*), nuncio (*papal ambassador*), papacy, pontificate (*the position or role of the Pope*), pontiff (*another term for 'pope'*), Vatican (*official residence of the Pope*).

population census (*official survey of a population*), demography (*study of human populations*), eugenics (*improving a population's characteristics by choosing which people become parents*).

power carte blanche (*complete freedom to act as you wish*), megalomaniac (*person obsessed with exercising power*), omnipotence (*unlimited power*), usurp (*seize power unlawfully*).

praise encomium, eulogy, panegyric (*speeches or pieces of writing praising someone*); laudatory (*expressing praise*).

pregnancy abortion (*deliberate bringing to an end of a pregnancy*), conceive (*become pregnant*), ectopic (*involving growth of the fetus outside the womb*), gestation (*process of growing inside the womb*), in vitro (*referring to conception achieved outside the body*), miscarriage (*birth of a fetus before it can survive outside the womb*), progesterone (*hormone stimulating the uterus to prepare for pregnancy*).

pressure barometer (*device to measure pressure*), isobar (*line of equal pressure on a weather map*), pneumatic (*operated by air or gas under pressure*).

priest clerical, sacerdotal (*relating to priests*); neophyte (*newly ordained priest*), ordain (*make someone a priest*), presbytery (*house of a Roman Catholic parish priest*), seminary (*college for priests*), theocracy (*system of government by priests*).

prison custodial (*relating to prisons and imprisonment*); incarcerate (*lock someone up in prison*), parole (*release of a prisoner on promise of good behaviour*), remission (*reduction of a prison sentence*).

protein albumin (*blood protein*), amino acids (*compounds which are building blocks of proteins*), casein (*milk protein*), gluten (*cereal protein*).

punishment penal (*relating to punishment*), punitive (*intended as punishment*); impunity (*freedom from being punished*), nemesis (*unavoidable punishment*), reprieve (*cancellation or postponement of punishment*).

rabbit buck (*male rabbit*), doe (*female rabbit*), kitten (*young rabbit*), myxomatosis (*disease of rabbits*), scut (*rabbit's short tail*), warren (*network of rabbit burrows*).

railway metro, subway, Tube (*underground railways*); funicular (*railway on a steep slope, operated by a cable*); couchette, wagon lit (*railway carriage with sleeping berths*); siderodromophobia (*fear of rail travel*).

read dyslexia (*reading disorder*), illegible

(*not clear enough to be read*), illiterate (*unable to read or write*), literacy (*ability to read and write*), phonics (*method of teaching people to read based on sounds that letters represent*).

red shades of red: burgundy, carmine, cerise, cherry, claret, crimson, magenta, maroon, puce, ruby, scarlet, vermilion.

religion denomination (*recognized branch of a Church or religion*), divinity, theology (*study of religion*), fundamentalism (*strict following of the doctrines of a religion*), heresy (*belief which goes against traditional teachings*), scripture (*sacred writings of a religion*); proselytize (*convert someone from one religion to another*); major religions: Baha'i, Buddhism, Christianity, Hinduism, Islam, Jainism, Judaism, Shinto, Sikhism, Zoroastrianism.

rifle bayonet (*blade fixed to the muzzle of a rifle*), breech (*back part of a rifle barrel*), carbine (*light automatic rifle*).

river fluvial (*relating to rivers*); backwater (*stretch of stagnant water on a river*), billabong (*Australian backwater*), confluence (*junction of two rivers*), delta (*triangular area where mouth of a river splits into several channels*), embankment (*wall or bank built to prevent a river flooding*), estuary (*mouth of a large river*), oxbow (*loop formed by a bend in a river*), tributary (*river or stream flowing into a larger river*).

rock crevice (*narrow crack in rock*), lava (*hot molten rock*), moraine (*rocks and stones deposited by a glacier*), pinnacle (*high pointed piece of rock*), precipice (*tall, steep rock face*), scree (*loose pieces of rock on a mountain slope*); types of rock: igneous, metamorphic, sedimentary.

Russian Russian life and culture: Cyrillic (*alphabet used for Russian language*), dacha (*holiday home in the country*), Duma (*lower chamber of parliament*), glasnost (*policy of more open government*), Kremlin (*building housing Russian government*), perestroika (*reforms introduced in the former Soviet Union in the 1980s*), rouble (*basic unit of money in Russia*), samovar (*decorated tea urn*), steppe (*large area of flat grassland*), troika (*vehicle pulled by three horses*), tsar, czar (*emperor of Russia before 1917*).

sacred blaspheme (*speak rudely about sacred things*), consecrate (*make or declare sacred*), desecrate (*treat something holy with great disrespect*), sacrilege (*the treating of something sacred with great disrespect*), sanctum (*sacred place*).

saddle parts of a saddle: cantle, crupper, girth, pommel, stirrup.

saint beatification (*first step towards making someone a saint*), canonize (*officially declare someone a saint*), hagiography (*writing about the lives of saints*).

salt brackish (*referring to water that is slightly salty*), brine (*very salty water*), desalinate (*remove salt from seawater*), saline (*containing salt*).

school scholastic (*relating to schools and education*); alma mater (*the school that a person attended*), alumnus (*former student of a school*), catchment (*area from which a school's pupils are drawn*).

Scottish Scottish life and culture: Caledonian (*relating to Scotland*), clan (*group of related families*), claymore (*large sword*), curling (*game played on ice*), dirk (*short dagger*), haggis (*dish consisting of offal and suet or oatmeal*), Highland fling (*vigorous solo dance*), Hogmanay (*New Year's Eve*), sporran (*pouch worn round the waist as part of Highland dress*), tossing the caber (*Highland sport*).

sea marine (*relating to the sea*), maritime (*relating to shipping or the sea*); oceanography (*scientific study of the sea*), submarine (*existing or happening under the surface of the sea*).

seed seminal (*relating to seeds*); dicotyledon (*plant whose seeds have two seed leaves*), germinate (*of a seed: begin to grow*), monocotyledon (*plant whose seeds have a single seed leaf*).

sense aural (*relating to the sense of hearing*), olfactory (*relating to the sense of smell*), sensory (*relating to the senses*), tactile (*relating to the sense of touch*), visual (*relating to the sense of sight*).

seven heptagon (*figure with seven straight sides and seven angles*), heptathlon (*athletic contest consisting of seven separate events*), septet (*group of seven musicians*), septuple (*made up of seven parts or elements*).

sew embroidery (*art of decorative sewing*), haberdashery (*materials used in sewing and dressmaking*), needlewoman, seamstress (*woman skilled at sewing*); baste, tack (*sew loosely with long stitches*).

sex aphrodisiac (*food, drink, etc. that arouses sexual desire*), celibate, chaste (*abstaining from sexual relationships*), libido (*sexual desire*), Platonic (*referring to non-sexual love*), post-coital (*after sexual intercourse*).

sheep fleece (*wool coat of a sheep*), ovine (*relating to or like sheep*); ewe (*female sheep*), mutton (*flesh of a mature sheep used as food*), ram, tup (*male sheep*).

shell bivalve (*mollusc with a shell divided in two parts*), carapace (*the hard upper shell of a tortoise*), crustacean (*animal with a hard shell, such as a crab*).

ship maritime (*relating to shipping or the sea*); bow (*front end of a ship*), port (*side of a ship on the left when you are facing forward*), starboard (*side of a ship on the right when you are facing forward*), stern (*rear end of a ship*); load line, Plimsoll line (*line on ship's side showing legal limit of

submersion*); chandler (*dealer in ship supplies and equipment*).

side lateral (*relating to or at the side*); equilateral (*having equal sides*), juxtapose (*place side by side*), polygon (*figure with many sides*).

sin absolve (*declare someone free from sin*), mortal (*referring to serious sin believed to result in damnation*), penance (*punishment given by a priest after someone has confessed their sins*), purgatory (*in RC belief, the place where the souls of sinners make up for their sins*), redeem (*save someone from sin*), venial (*referring to sin that will not result in damnation*).

sister sororal (*like a sister*); sibling (*brother or sister*), sorority (*sisterhood*).

six hexagon (*figure with six straight sides and six angles*), hexagram (*six-pointed star*), sextet (*group of six musicians*), sextuple (*made up of six parts or elements*), sextuplet (*each of six children born at one birth*).

ski après-ski (*social activities following a day's skiing*), langlauf (*cross-country skiing*), nursery slopes (*gentle ski slopes for beginners*), piste (*ski slope with compacted snow*), salopettes (*padded trousers worn for skiing*), slalom (*ski race down a winding course*).

skin cutaneous (*relating to the skin*); dermatology (*branch of medicine concerned with the skin*), dermis, epidermis (*layers of the skin*); dermatitis, eczema, psoriasis (*inflammation of the skin*), melanoma (*type of skin cancer*).

skull cranial (*relating to the skull*); cranium (*part of skull containing the brain*), fontanelle (*soft area of a baby's skull*), phrenology (*study of skull shape as supposed indicator of character*), trepan (*saw used by surgeons to make holes in the skull*).

slave servile (*like a slave*); bondage, servitude (*state of being a slave*); emancipate, enfranchise (*release someone from slavery*).

sleep dormant (*in or as if in a deep sleep*), hibernation (*deep sleep lasting throughout the winter*), insomnia (*inability to sleep*), narcolepsy (*abnormal tendency to fall asleep in relaxing surroundings*), sedative, soporific (*causing sleep*), somnambulism (*sleepwalking*).

song kinds of song: anthem, aria, ballad, calypso, carol, ditty, hymn, lullaby, madrigal, psalm, shanty, spiritual.

speech elocution (*skill of speaking clearly*), oral (*spoken rather than written*), oratory (*public speaking*), phonetic, phonic (*relating to speech sounds*), phonetics (*study and classification of speech sounds*).

speed Mach number (*indicating ratio of speed to the speed of sound*), supersonic (*faster than the speed of sound*), tachometer (*instrument measuring the working speed of an engine), tempo (*speed at which a piece of music is played*).

star astral, stellar (*relating to a star or stars*); constellation (*group of stars forming a pattern*), galaxy (*large system of stars*), interstellar (*occurring or situated between stars*), magnitude (*degree of brightness of a star*), nova (*star that suddenly becomes very bright*), supernova (*exploding star*).

story allegory (*story with a hidden symbolic meaning*), fable, parable (*story illustrating moral lesson*), saga (*long traditional story*); folklore, legend, mythology (*traditional stories in a culture*); narrator (*storyteller*), raconteur (*skilled storyteller*).

string stringed instruments: banjo, cello, double bass, guitar, harp, lute, lyre, mandolin, sitar, viola, violin.

sugar dextrose, fructose, glucose (*types of sugar*); insulin (*hormone regulating glucose levels in the blood*), diabetes (*disease in which the body cannot absorb sugar properly*); saccharin (*artificial sugar substitute*).

sun solar (*relating to the sun*); heliocentric (*having the sun at the centre*), solstice (*times of the year when sun reaches its highest or lowest point in the sky at noon*), zenith (*sun's highest point in the sky*).

surgery amputation (*surgical removal of a body part*), ligature (*cord used in surgery to tie an artery*), prosthetics (*surgical fitting of artificial body parts*), scalpel, lancet (*sharp knives used by a surgeon*).

swimming aqualung, scuba (*swimmer's underwater breathing apparatus*), flume (*water slide at a swimming pool*), lido (*public open-air swimming pool*), natation (*technical word for swimming*), snorkel (*tube for a swimmer to breathe through*).

sword fencing (*sport of fighting with blunted swords*), hilt (*sword handle*), pommel (*knob on sword's handle*), scabbard (*sheath for sword*).

tax fiscal (*relating to taxes*); black economy (*part of country's economy not taxed by government*), excise (*tax payable on alcohol etc.*), tariff (*tax to be paid on particular class of imports and exports*), tithe (*one tenth of income formerly paid as tax to support the Church*).

temperature Celsius, centigrade (*referring to temperature scale on which water freezes at 0°*), Fahrenheit (*referring to temperature scale on which water freezes at 32°*); cryogenics (*branch of physics concerned with very low temperatures*), hypothermia (*abnormally low body temperature*), isotherm (*line on a map connecting points with the same temperature*), thermostat (*device that regulates temperature*).

ten decade (*period of ten years*), decagon (*figure with ten straight sides and ten angles*), decahedron (*solid figure with ten sides*), Decalogue (*the Ten Commandments*),

decathlon (*athletic event in which each competitor takes part in the same ten events*), decimal (*referring to a number system based on the number ten*).

theatre thespian (*relating to the theatre*); dramaturgy (*theory and practice of writing plays*), impresario (*person who finances theatrical productions*), repertory (*performance of a theatre company's repertoire at regular intervals*); seats in a theatre, lowest to highest: stalls, dress circle, circle, gallery (*or balcony*).

theology divinity (*study of religion*), eschatology (*part of theology concerned with death, judgement, and destiny*), scholasticism (*medieval system of theology and philosophy*).

three hat-trick (*three successes of the same kind*), triathlon (*athletic contest consisting of three different events*), triplet (*each of three children born at one birth*), triennial (*lasting for or recurring every three years*), trio (*group or set of three*), triad (*group of three*), trilogy (*group of three related novels, plays, etc.*), triplicate (*existing in three copies*), triptych (*painting on three panels*), trireme (*ancient ship with three banks of oars*), triumvirate (*group of three powerful people*).

tide ebb (*movement of the tide out to sea*), flood (*rising of the tide*), neap tide (*tide when there is least difference between high and low water*), spring tide (*tide when there is the greatest difference between high and low water*).

time temporal (*relating to time*); anachronism (*something which seems to belong to another time period*), chronological (*relating to dates and time sequences*), horology (*study and measurement of time*), synchronous (*existing or occurring at the same time*).

toe bunion (*painful swelling on the big toe*), corn (*painful area of thickened skin on the toes or foot*), hammer toe (*toe that is bent downwards*), pedicure (*cosmetic treatment of the feet and toenails*).

tomb catacomb (*underground cemetery*), cromlech, dolmen (*prehistoric or ancient tombs*), inter (*place someone in a tomb*), mausoleum (*building containing a tomb or tombs*), monumental mason (*person who makes tombstones*), sepulchre (*stone tomb*).

tooth dental (*relating to teeth*); caries (*tooth decay*), dentine (*hard bony tissue that teeth are made of*), dentition (*arrangement or condition of the teeth*), denture (*frame fitted with false teeth*), enamel (*hard substance covering the crown of a tooth*), orthodontics (*treatment of irregularities of the teeth*), plaque, tartar (*deposits which form on the teeth*); human teeth: bicuspids, canines, incisors, molars, premolars, tricuspids, wisdom teeth.

touch palpable (*able to be touched or felt*), tactile (*relating to the sense of touch*), tangible (*perceptible by touch*).

tower types of tower: belfry, campanile, donjon, keep, minaret, steeple, turret, watchtower, ziggurat.

tree arboreal (*relating to trees*); arboretum (*garden where trees are grown for study etc.*), deciduous (*referring to trees that shed their leaves annually*), evergreen (*referring to trees that have green leaves throughout the year*), lumberjack (*person who cuts down trees*), silviculture (*growing and cultivation of trees*), topiary (*art of clipping shrubs or trees into attractive shapes*).

triangle types of triangle: equilateral (*having sides of equal length*), isosceles (*having two sides equal*), scalene (*having all sides unequal*); hypotenuse (*longest side of a right-angled triangle*).

twelve dodecagon (*figure with twelve straight sides and twelve angles*), dodecahedron (*three-dimensional shape with twelve faces*), duodecimal (*relating to a counting system based on twelve*), gross (*twelve dozen, 144*).

twin fraternal, dizygotic (*referring to twins developing from separate ova*); identical, monozygotic (*referring to twins developing from a single ovum*); conjoined, Siamese (*referring to twins whose bodies are joined at birth*).

two biannual (*taking place twice a year*), biennial (*taking place every two years*), bilateral (*involving two groups*), bilingual (*in or able to speak two languages*), binary (*composed of or involving two things*), bisect (*divide into two parts*), dichotomy (*separation or contrast between two things*), diptych (*painting on two panels*), dual (*consisting of two parts or aspects*), duet (*performance by two singers or musicians*).

unconscious catalepsy (*condition in which person becomes unconscious and goes rigid*), coma (*state of deep unconsciousness*), comatose (*deeply unconscious*), concussion (*temporary unconsciousness produced by a blow to the head*), narcosis (*unconsciousness produced by drugs*), resuscitate (*revive someone from unconsciousness*).

universe cosmic (*relating to the universe*); astronomy (*science of stars, planets, and the universe*), Big Bang (*expansion of matter thought to have started the formation of the universe*) cosmology, cosmogony (*science of the origin and development of the universe*).

university alumnus (*former student of a particular university*), campus (*university site and buildings*), dissertation, thesis (*long university essay*), don (*university teacher*), faculty (*university department*), fresher (*newly arrived first-year student*), graduation (*the receiving of a degree*), matriculation (*enrolment in a university*).

valley kinds of valley: basin, canyon, combe, dale, dell, dene, dingle, glen, gorge, ravine, rift valley, strath (*in Scotland*), wadi (*in Arabic-speaking countries*).

verse blank verse (*verse without rhyme*), couplet (*pair of successive lines of rhyming verse*), doggerel (*badly written verse*), meter, prosody (*patterns of rhythm and sound in verse*), scansion (*rhythm of a line of verse*).

vitamin diseases caused by lack of a vitamin: beriberi (*vitamin B_1*), pernicious anaemia (*vitamin B_{12}*), rickets (*vitamin D*), scurvy (*vitamin C*).

voice vocal (*relating to the voice*); cadence (*rise and fall in the pitch of the voice*), intonation (*rise and fall of the voice in speaking*), register (*particular part of the range of a person's voice*), timbre (*quality of the voice as distinct from its pitch and strength*).

volcano states of a volcano: active (*erupting or having erupted in the past*), dormant (*not currently erupting*), extinct (*not having erupted in recorded history*); caldera (*large volcanic crater*), crater (*mouth of volcano*), fumarole (*opening through which hot gases emerge*), lava (*molten rock that erupts from a volcano*), volcanology, vulcanology (*study of volcanoes*).

vote abstain (*formally choose not to vote*), disenfranchise (*deprive someone of the right to vote*), electoral roll (*official list of people in a district entitled to vote*), electorate (*people in a district entitled to vote*), enfranchise (*give someone the right to vote*), floating voter (*person who does not vote for the same party all the time*), franchise, suffrage (*the right to vote*), poll (*process of voting or number of votes cast*), psephology (*study of voting patterns*), referendum, plebiscite (*general vote by the electorate on a single political question*).

walk ambulatory (*relating to walking*); circumambulate (*walk all the way round*), pedestrian (*person walking on a road*), perambulate (*walk from place to place*), promenade (*place for public walking*).

war martial (*relating to war*); Armageddon (*terrible war with catastrophic ending*), belligerent (*taking part in a war*), ceasefire (*temporary period in a war when fighting stops*), cenotaph (*monument honouring soldiers killed in a war*), neutral (*not supporting either side in a war*), pacifism (*belief that disputes should be settled through peaceful means rather than war*), shell shock (*mental condition resulting from battle experiences*).

watch analogue (*referring to a watch with hands*), digital (*referring to a watch with a numerical display*), fob (*chain attached to a watch*), horology (*art of making clocks and watches*), synchronize (*set one watch to the* *same time as another*).

water aquatic (*living in water*), aqueduct (*bridge carrying water*), aqueous, hydrous (*containing water*), dehydrate (*remove water from something*), dowse (*search for underground water with a special pointer*), hydraulic (*operated by water*), hydrolysis (*chemical breakdown of substances in water*), irrigate (*supply water to land or crops*).

wave crest (*the top of the ridge of a wave*), spindrift (*spray blown from waves*), spume (*froth on waves*), tsunami (*tidal wave produced by an earthquake*), undulate (*move with a wave-like motion*).

wealth magnate, tycoon (*very wealthy businessman*); arriviste, nouveau riche, parvenu (*person who has recently become wealthy*); avarice (*excessive greed for wealth*), Mammon (*wealth seen as an evil influence*), plutocracy (*rule by rich people*).

Welsh Welsh life and culture: coracle (*small round wickerwork boat*), cromlech (*ancient stone tomb*), Cymru (*Welsh word for Wales*), eisteddfod (*competitive festival of music and poetry*), hwyl (*stirring emotional feeling associated with the Welsh*).

whale ambergris (*substance produced by sperm whales, used in making perfume*), blubber (*the fat of whales and other sea mammals*), baleen whales (*whales having plates of whalebone in the mouth for feeding on plankton*), cetacean (*a whale or related mammal, e.g. a dolphin or porpoise*), harpoon (*missile used for catching whales*), krill (*shrimp-like crustaceans eaten by whales*), pod (*group of whales*).

wheel hub, nave (*centre of a wheel*), linchpin (*pin through the end of an axle keeping a wheel in position*), sprocket (*projecting tooth on a wheel*).

will codicil (*supplement to a will*), executor (*person appointed to carry out the terms of a will*), intestate (*having left no will*), legacy (*something left to someone in a will*), probate (*official process of proving that a will is valid*), testate (*having made a valid will*), testator (*a person making a will*).

wind anemometer (*instrument for measuring wind speed), Beaufort Scale (scale of wind speeds*), leeward (*on or towards the side sheltered from the wind*), windward (*on or towards the side facing the wind*); bora (*cold wind blowing in the Adriatic*), mistral (*cold wind blowing through southern France*), meltemi (*summer wind blowing in eastern Mediterranean*), monsoon (*seasonal wind in India and SE Asia*), sirocco (*hot wind blowing from North Africa to Europe*).

window types of window: bay, casement, clerestory, dormer, fanlight, oriel, porthole, sash window, skylight.

wine vinous (*relating to or like wine*); bouquet, nose (*scent of a wine*), carafe (*flask for serving wine*), chambré (*referring to red wine at room temperature*), lees (*sediment in wine*), oenology (*study of wines*), vintage (*year or place in which wine was produced*), vintner (*wine merchant*); brut (*referring to very dry sparkling wine*), demi-sec (*medium dry*), mousseux, pétillant (*slightly sparkling*), sec (*dry*).

witch coven (*group of witches*), familiar (*spirit accompanying a witch*), warlock (*man who practises witchcraft*), Wicca (*religious cult of modern witchcraft*).

wood creosote (*wood preservative*), joinery (*wooden parts of a building*), ligneous (*made or consisting of wood*), marquetry (*furniture decoration of inlaid wood*), parquet (*flooring of wooden blocks*), veneer (*thin decorative covering of wood*), wainscot (*area of wooden panelling in a room*).

woodwind woodwind instruments: bassoon, clarinet, cor anglais, flute, oboe, piccolo, recorder.

word verbal (*relating to or in words*), lexical (*relating to the vocabulary of a language*); acronym (*word formed from initial letters*), anagram (*word formed from the letters of another*), antonym (*word having opposite meaning*), etymology (*account of a word's origins*), malapropism (*the use of a similar-sounding but wrong word*), neologism, coinage (*newly invented word*), nonce word (*word invented for a particular occasion*), onomatopoeic (*referring to a word that sounds like the thing it refers to*), palindrome (*word or phrase spelled the same backwards as forwards*), synonym (*word having same meaning*), verbatim (*in exactly the same words*).

writing calligraphy (*decorative handwriting*), copperplate (*elaborate handwriting style*), cursive (*referring to joined-up writing*), epistolary (*relating to the writing of letters*), graphology (*study of handwriting*), hieroglyphs (*ancient Egyptian picture writing*) palaeography (*study of ancient writing systems*).

X-ray barium meal (*mixture swallowed to allow X-rays to be made of the stomach or intestines*), mammography (*the use of X-rays to diagnose tumours of the breasts*), radiography (*the production of images by X-rays*), radiology (*the science of X-rays*), radiotherapy (*the treatment of disease using X-rays*).

year annals (*history of events year by year*), annual (*occurring once a year; covering a year*), annuity (*sum of money paid to someone each year*), biannual (*occurring twice a year*), biennial (*occurring every other year*), perennial (*lasting through a year or several years*).

yellow shades of yellow: amber, canary, daffodil, flaxen, gold, lemon, mustard, primrose, saffron.

Commonly confused words

There are many words in English which look or sound alike but have quite different meanings. These words are very easy to confuse and most spellcheckers will not be able to help in those situations in which a word is spelled correctly but used in the wrong context. This section provides a quick-reference guide to the differences between those pairs of words that commonly cause problems.

Word 1	Meaning	Word 2	Meaning
accept	to agree to receive or do	except	not including; apart from
access	the means to enter somewhere or opportunity to use something	excess	an amount that is too much
adverse	unfavourable or harmful	averse	strongly disliking or opposed
advice	recommendations about what to do	advise	to recommend something
affect	to change or make a difference to	effect	a result; to bring about a result
aisle	a passage between rows of seats	isle	an island
all together	all in one place or all at once	altogether	in total; completely; on the whole
allusion	an indirect reference	illusion	a false idea or belief
aloud	out loud	allowed	permitted
altar	a sacred table in a church	alter	to change
amoral	not concerned with right or wrong	immoral	not following accepted moral standards
ante-	before (e.g. *antedate*)	anti-	against (e.g. *antidepressant*)
appraise	to assess	apprise	to inform someone
assent	approval or agreement	ascent	an act of going up something
augur	to be a sign of a good or bad outcome	auger	a tool for boring holes
aural	relating to the ears or hearing	oral	relating to the mouth; spoken
balmy	pleasantly warm	barmy	crazy
bare	naked; to uncover	bear	to carry; to tolerate
base	the lowest or supporting part; a centre of operations	bass	the lowest male singing voice; the deep low-frequency part of sound
bated	with **bated** breath (i.e. in great suspense)	baited	taunted
bazaar	a Middle Eastern market	bizarre	very strange
berth	a bunk in a ship, train, etc.	birth	the process of being born
blanch	make or become white or pale	blench	flinch through fear or pain
born	having started life	borne	carried
brake	a device for stopping a vehicle; to stop a vehicle	break	to separate into pieces; a pause
breach	a gap in a barrier; an act that breaks a rule or agreement	breech	the back part of a rifle or gun barrel
broach	to raise a subject for discussion	brooch	a piece of jewellery
canvas	a type of strong cloth	canvass	to ask for people's votes
cannon	a large heavy gun	canon	a rule or law; a list of books; a clergyman
censure	to criticize severely	censor	to ban parts of a book or film; an official who does this

Word 1	Meaning	Word 2	Meaning
chord	a group of musical notes	cord	a length of string; a cord-like body part
climactic	forming a climax	climatic	relating to climate
coarse	rough	course	a direction; one of the stages of a meal; a series of lectures or lessons
complacent	smugly self-satisfied	complaisant	willing to please
complement	to add to so as to improve; an addition that improves something	compliment	to politely congratulate or praise; a polite expression of praise
complementary	combining to form a whole or to improve something	complimentary	praising; given free of charge
council	a group of people who manage or advise	counsel	advice; to advise
councillor	a member of a council	counsellor	a person giving guidance on personal problems
credible	believable; convincing	credulous	too ready to believe things
cue	a signal for action; a wooden rod	queue	a line of people or vehicles
curb	to control or put a limit on; a control or limit	kerb	(in British English) the stone edge of a pavement
currant	a dried grape	current	happening now; a flow of water, air, or electricity
defuse	to make a situation less tense	diffuse	to spread over a wide area
dependant	a person who relies on another for support	dependent	determined; relying on
desert	a waterless, empty area	dessert	the sweet course of a meal
discreet	careful not to attract attention or give offence	discrete	separate and distinct
disinterested	impartial	uninterested	not interested
draught	a current of air	draft	a first version of a piece of writing; to write such a version
draw	to produce a picture; to pull; an even score at the end of a game	drawer	a sliding storage compartment
dual	having two parts	duel	a fight or contest between two people
elicit	to draw out a response or reaction	illicit	forbidden by law or rules
emigrant	a person who leaves their country to settle permanently in another	immigrant	a person who has come to live permanently in a foreign country
emotional	showing strong feeling	emotive	arousing strong feeling
empathy	the ability to understand another person's feelings	sympathy	the feeling of being sorry for someone
ensure	to make certain that something will happen	insure	to pay money in order to receive financial compensation if a person dies or property is damaged
envelop	to cover or surround	envelope	a paper container for a letter
exceptional	unusual or unusually good	exceptionable	causing disapproval or offence
exercise	physical activity; to do physical activity	exorcize	to drive out an evil spirit

Word 1	Meaning	Word 2	Meaning
faint	to lose consciousness; not clearly seen, heard, or smelled	feint	a pretended attacking movement; to make such a movement
fawn	a young deer; light brown	faun	a mythical being, part man, part goat
flair	a natural ability or talent	flare	a brief burst of flame or light; to gradually become wider
flaunt	to display in a way intended to attract attention	flout	to openly fail to follow a rule
flounder	to have trouble doing something	founder	to fail
forbear	to stop yourself from doing something	forebear	an ancestor
foreword	an introduction to a book	forward	onwards; ahead
freeze	to turn to ice	frieze	a decoration along a wall
Gallic	French	Gaelic	Celtic
grisly	causing horror or disgust	grizzly	a type of bear
hanger	a person who hangs something, or a frame to hang clothes on	hangar	a building in which aircraft are kept
historic	famous or important in history	historical	relating to history
hoard	a store of money or valuable objects	horde	a large crowd of people
hummus or houmous	a chickpea dip	humus	a substance found in soil
imply	to suggest indirectly	infer	to draw a conclusion about something not directly stated
incredible	impossible to believe	incredulous	unwilling or unable to believe something
internment	imprisonment	interment	burial
its	belonging to it	it's	short for *it is* or *it has*
judicial	relating to a law court or judge	judicious	sensible
lama	a Buddhist monk	llama	an animal related to the camel
licence	a permit to own or do something	license	to grant a licence or authorize something
lightening	getting lighter	lightning	a high-voltage electrical discharge; very quick
loath	reluctant or unwilling	loathe	to hate
loose	to unfasten or set free; not fixed in place	lose	to have something taken away; to be unable to find
meter	a measuring device	metre	a unit of measurement; rhythm in poetry
militate	to make it very difficult for something to happen or exist	mitigate	to make something less severe
muscle	tissue that moves a body part	mussel	a shellfish
omit	to leave out	emit	to give out light, heat, gas, etc.
pain	an unpleasant feeling	pane	a sheet of glass
palate	the roof of the mouth	palette	a board for mixing colours
pedal	a foot-operated lever; to work the pedals of a bicycle	peddle	to sell goods or spread an idea
peninsula	a piece of land jutting out into the sea	peninsular	relating to a peninsula
perpetrate	to carry out a bad or illegal act	perpetuate	to make something continue for a long time
pole	a long, thin piece of wood; each of the two opposite points of a magnet	poll	the process of voting in an election
pore	a tiny opening; to study or read something closely	pour	to flow in a steady stream

Word 1	Meaning	Word 2	Meaning
practice	the use of an idea or method; the work or business of a doctor, dentist, etc.	practise	to do something repeatedly to improve your skill; to carry something out regularly
prescribe	to authorize the use of a medicine; to order authoritatively	proscribe	to officially forbid something
principal	most important; the most important person in an organization	principle	a law or theory on which something is based; a belief
prophecy	a prediction of a future event	prophesy	to predict a future event
quiet	making little or no noise	quite	moderately; completely
reign	the period that a monarch rules; to rule as a monarch	rein	a strap used to control a horse; also used in the phrase **a free rein**
role	a part played by an actor	roll	to move by turning over and over; a rolling movement
sceptic	a person who tends to question accepted opinions	septic	infected with bacteria
shear	to cut the wool off a sheep	sheer	nothing but; to change course quickly
sight	the ability to see	site	a location
silicon	an element used in electronics	silicone	a substance used in cosmetic implants
stationary	not moving	stationery	paper and writing materials
storey	a level of a building	story	a tale or account
straight	without a curve or bend	strait	a narrow passage of water; (**straits**) trouble or difficulty
summary	a brief statement of the main points	summery	typical of summer
swat	to hit or crush	swot	to study hard
tail	the rear or end part	tale	a story
team	a group of people playing or working together	teem	to be full of something; to pour down
their	belonging to them	there	in, at, or to that place
titillate	to interest or excite, especially sexually	titivate	to make more attractive
to	in the direction of	too	excessively; in addition
toe	part of the foot; also in **toe the line**	tow	to pull something along behind a vehicle or boat
tortuous	full of twists and turns; complicated	torturous	full of pain or suffering
vain	having too high an opinion of yourself	vein	a tube that carries blood around the body
venal	open to bribery	venial	(of a sin) slight and able to be forgiven
waive	to choose not to insist on a right	wave	to move to and fro; a ridge of water
who's	short for *who is* or *who has*	whose	belonging to which person
wreath	an arrangement of flowers	wreathe	to surround or encircle
your	belonging to you	you're	short for *you are*

Common spelling errors

For historical reasons, English is full of irregularities of spelling and a lot of words can cause problems. The same sounds can be written in many different ways (e.g. the -oo- sound in *moon, threw, through,* and *lute*), while the same group of letters can represent completely different sounds in different words (e.g. -ough in *bough, though, through, enough,* and *cough*). Different spellings of the same word are sometimes permitted (e.g. *banister* and *bannister* or *judgement* and *judgment*) and sometimes disallowed (for example, *accomodation* is not a permitted variant of *accommodation,* nor *millenium* of *millennium,* though these forms are often seen in writing).

This section, which is based on evidence of real mistakes, contains a checklist of the words in the language which people most often spell wrongly, together with pointers to help you spell them right.

word	comment
abscess	-*scess,* not -*sess*
abseil	-*seil,* not -*sail*
accommodation	double *c,* double *m*
accumulate	double *c,* single *m*
achieve	*i* before *e*
acquaint	remember the *c*
acquire	remember the *c*
address	two *d*s
aggressive	double *g,* double *s*
aggrieved	*i* before *e*
amateur	-*eur,* not -*uer*
anaesthetic	remember the -*ae-*
anoint	only one *n* in the middle
Antarctic	remember the *c* after the *r*
apartment	only one *p*
appal	double *p,* single *l*
appalling	double *p,* double *l*
apparent	-*ent,* not -*ant*
applaud, applause	double *p*
aqueduct	*aque-,* not *aqua-*
archaeology	remember the -*ae-*
Arctic	remember the first *c*
argument	no *e* in the middle
assess	double *s,* double *s*
attach	not -*atch*
bargain	remember the second *a*
beautiful	remember the *u* before the *t*
believe	*i* before *e*
besiege	*i* before *e*
bizarre	single *z,* double *r*
blatant	-*ant,* not -*ent*
broccoli	double *c,* single *l*
buoy, buoyant	*u* before *o*

word	comment
business	remember the *i* in the middle
cappuccino	double *p,* double *c*
Caribbean	single *r,* double *b*
ceiling	*i* before *e*
cemetery	-*tery,* not -*try* or -*tary*
civilian	single *l*
coconut	just -*o-,* not -*oa-*
commemorate	double *m* followed by single *m*
commitment	single *t* in the middle
committee	double *m,* double *t*
comparative	-*ative,* not -*itive*
compatible	-*ible,* not -*able*
competent	-*ent,* not -*ant*
conceive	*i* before *e*
confectionery	-*ery,* not -*ary*
consensus	not -*census*
contemporary	-*porary,* not -*pory*
correspondence	-*ence,* not -*ance*
corridor	-*dor,* not -*door*
counterfeit	-*eit* at the end
cursor	-*or,* not -*er*
deceive	*i* before *e*
definite	-*ite,* not -*ate*
delirious	*delir-,* not *deler-*
despair	*des-,* not *dis-*
desperate	-*perate,* not -*parate*
detach	-*ach,* not -*atch*
develop	no *e* at the end
dilapidated	*dil-,* not *del-*
disappear	single *s,* double *p*
disappoint	single *s,* double *p*
disastrous	no *e* in the middle
discipline	remember the *c* in the middle

word	comment
dissect	double *s*
ecstasy	no *x*: -*cs*- at the beginning and -*s*- at the end
eighth	remember that there are two *hs*
embarrass	double *r*, double *s*
environment	remember the *n* in the middle
espresso	*es*-, not *ex*-
exaggerate	double *g*
except	remember the *c*
exercise	*exe*-, not *exce*-
exhilarate	-*lar*-, not -*ler*-
existence	-*ence*, not -*ance*
exorbitant	there is no *h* after the *x*
extraordinary	*extraor*-, not *extror*-
extrovert	*extro*-, not *extra*-
familiar	only one *l*
fascinate	-*sc*- in the middle
February	-*ruary*, not -*uary*
fierce	*i* before *e*
fluorescent	*fluor*-, not *flour*-
foreign	-*eign*, not -*iegn*
forty	no *u* in the middle
friend	-*ie*-, not -*ei*-
fulfil, fulfilment	no double *l* in British English
gauge	-*au*- in the middle
glamorous	drops the *u* of glamour
government	remember the *n* in the middle
graffiti	double *f*, single *t*
grammar	-*ar*, not -*er*
grateful	*grate*-, not *great*-
grief, grieve	*i* before *e*
guarantee	*gua*-, not *gau*-
guard, guardian	*gua*-, not *gau*-
hamster	no *p* in the middle
handkerchief	remember the *d*
harass, harassment	single *r*, double *s*
height	remember the *e* before the *i*
hierarchy	the beginning is *hier*-
hindrance	no *e* in the middle
homogeneous	-*eous* at the end, not -*ous*
honorary	*honor*-, not *honour*-
humorous	*humor*-, not *humour*-
hygienic	*i* before *e*
idiosyncrasy	-*asy*, not -*acy*
imaginary	-*ary*, not -*ery*
immediately	remember the *e* after the *t*
inadvertent	-*ent*, not -*ant*
independent	-*ent*, not -*ant*
indispensable	-*able*, not -*ible*
inoculate	single *n*, single *c*

word	comment
install	double *l*
instalment	single *l* in British English
interrupt	double *r*
introvert	*intro*-, not *intra*-
irrelevant	-*ent*, not -*ant*
irresistible	-*ible*, not -*able*
itinerary	-*erary*, not -*ary*
jubilee	single *l*
kernel	-*el*, not -*al*
knowledge	remember the *d*
label	-*el*, not -*le*
language	-*guage*, not -*gage*
legitimate	*leg*-, and the ending is -*ate*
liaison, liaise	remember the second *i*
lightning	no *e* in the middle
liquefy	-*efy*, not -*ify*
maintenance	-*ten*-, not -*tan*-
manoeuvre	-*oeu*- in the middle
medicine	remember the first *i*
Mediterranean	single *d*, single *t*, double *r*
millennium	double *l*, double *n*
millionaire	double *l*, single *n*
miniature	-*ia*- in the middle
minuscule	-*uscule*, not -*iscule*
mischievous	-*vous*, not -*vious*
moreover	remember the *e* in the middle
necessary	single *c*, double *s*
negotiate	-*tiate*, not -*ciate*
neither	-*ei*-, not -*ie*-
niece	*i* before *e*
noticeable	remember the first *e*
occasion	double *c*, single *s*
occurrence	double *c*, double *r*
omit, omission	only one *m*
omelette	remember the first *e*; the ending is -*ette*
opportunity	double *p*
oppress	double *p*, double *s*
parallel	double *l* in the middle
parliament	-*liament*, not -*lament*
particularly	-*cularly*, not -*culy*
peculiar	-*ar*, not -*er*
perceive	*i* before *e*
permanent	-*ent*, not -*ant*
persistent	-*ent*, not -*ant*
pharaoh	the ending is -*aoh*
piece	*i* before *e*
pigeon	no *d* before the *g*
pollute, pollution	double *l*
Portuguese	-*guese*, not -*gese*
possess	double *s*, double *s*
potato	no -*e* in the singular
prejudice	*prej*-, not *predj*-
presumptuous	-*tuous*, not -*tious*

word	comment	word	comment
privilege	*-ege*, not *-edge*	success, successful	double *c*, double *s*
professional	only one *f*	supersede	*-sede*, not *-cede*
pronunciation	no *o* in the middle	suppress	double *p*, double *s*
propaganda	*propa-*, not *propo-*	surprise	remember the first *r*
protein	*-ein*, not *-ien*	tariff	single *r*, double *f*
protuberance	no *r* after the t	temperature	*-era-* in the middle
publicly	*-cly*, not *-cally*	tendency	*-ency*, not *-ancy*
purify	*-ify*, not *-efy*	thief	*i* before *e*
pursue	*pur-*, not *per-*	threshold	single *h* in the middle
questionnaire	double *n*	tomato	no *e* in the singular
rarefied	*-ref-*, not *-rif-*	tomorrow	single *m*, double *r*
receive	*i* before *e*	traitor	the ending is *-or*
recommend	single *c*, double *m*	truly	there is no *e*
reference	single *r* in the middle	twelfth	remember the *f* after the *l*
refrigerator	no *d* in the middle	underrate	double *r*
relevant	*-ant*, not *-ent*	unforeseen	remember the first *e*
relieve	*i* before *e*	unnecessary	double *n*, single *c*, double *s*
religious	*-gious*, not *-gous*	until	just one *l*
responsible	*-ible*, not *-able*	unwieldy	*i* before *e*
restaurateur	no *n* in the middle	usually	double *l*
resuscitate	*-susc-*, not *-suss-*	vaccine, vaccination	double *c*
rhyme, rhythm	remember the first *h*	vegetable	*vege-*, not *vega-*
risotto	single *s*, double *t*	veterinary	*-er-* before *-in-*
sacrilege	*-rilege*, not *-relige*	vicious	no *s* in the middle
secretary	*-ary*, not *-ery*	vigorous	drops the *u* of vigour
seize	*-ei-*, not *-ie-*	vulnerable	remember the first *l*
sentence	*-ence*, not *-ance*	Wednesday	remember the first *d*
separate	*-parate*, not *-perate*	weird	*-ei-*, not *-ie-*
sherbet	*-bet*, not *-bert*	wholly	two *l*s, no *e*
siege	*i* before *e*	wield	*i* before *e*
sieve	*i* before *e*	wilful	single *l* in the middle in British English
simultaneous	*-eous*, not *-ious*		
skilful	single *l* in the middle in British English	wintry	*-try*, not *-tery*
sponsor	*-or*, not *-er*	withhold	double *h*
stiletto	single *l*, double *t*	yield	*i* before *e*
strength	remember the *g*		
subtle	remember the *b*		

Foreign words and phrases

Over the centuries, English has absorbed thousands of words from other languages, most of which are now so established that we never think of them as foreign imports. In fact, it's been estimated that about half of all English words come from languages other than Old English. Old French, for example, has given us everyday terms such **coat**, **message**, or **marriage**, as well as familiar items from the breakfast or dinner table like **toast**, **bacon**, **soup**, **salad**, and **cream**. Indian languages have contributed **shampoo**, **shawl**, and **bungalow**, while we owe **anorak** to Greenland Eskimo and **chocolate** to Nahuatl, a language of Central America. But other words and phrases, though they are frequently encountered in British English, still have a foreign flavour and you may often see them printed in italics in books, magazines, or newspapers.

ab initio from the beginning. [Latin]

a cappella sung without instrumental accompaniment: *an a cappella performance of a medieval mass*. [Italian, 'in chapel style']

à deux for or involving two people: *dinner à deux*. [French]

ad hoc made or done for a particular purpose: *an ad hoc meeting of ministers and civil servants*. [Latin, 'to this']

ad infinitum endlessly; forever. [Latin, 'to infinity']

ad interim for the meantime. [Latin]

ad nauseam to an annoying or boring extent: *a phrase repeated ad nauseam in the media*. [Latin, 'to sickness']

affaire de (or **du**) **coeur** a love affair. [French]

a fortiori more conclusively. [Latin, 'from stronger']

agent provocateur a person who tempts a suspected criminal to commit a crime and so be caught and convicted. [Latin, 'provocative agent']

à huis clos in private. [French, literally 'with closed doors']

aide-de-campe a military officer who acts as a personal assistant to a senior officer. [French, 'camp adjutant']

à la carte (of a menu) offering dishes that are separately priced, rather than part of a set meal. [French, 'according to the menu']

al dente (of food) cooked so as to be still firm when bitten. [Italian, 'to the tooth']

alfresco in the open air: *lunch was served alfresco*. [Italian]

amour fou uncontrollable or obsessive passion. [French, 'mad love']

amour propre self-respect. [French, 'love of yourself']

ancien régime a political or social system that has been replaced by another. [French, 'old rule']

annus horribilis a year of disaster or bad luck: *1992 had been an annus horribilis for the royal family*. [Latin]

annus mirabilis a remarkable or very good year. [Latin]

antipasti Italian hors-d'oeuvres. [Italian, 'before food']

a posteriori based on reasoning from known facts or past events rather than on assumptions or predictions. [Latin, 'from what comes after']

appellation contrôlée a guarantee of the origin of a French wine. [French]

a priori based on deduction rather than experience: *a priori assumptions about human nature*. [Latin, 'from what is before']

au courant well informed; up to date: *they're not au courant with the Japanese literary scene*. [French, 'in the (regular) course']

au fait having a good or detailed knowledge: *he's evidently au fait with the technology*. [French, 'to the point']

au fond basically; in essence: *au fond, she's quite a reasonable woman*. [French, 'at the bottom']

au naturel in the most simple or natural way. [French]

avant-garde (in the arts) new and experimental: *an avant-garde Japanese designer*. [French, 'vanguard']

beau geste a noble and generous act. [French, 'splendid gesture']

beau idéal the highest standard of excellence. [French, 'ideal beauty']

beau monde fashionable society. [French, 'fine world']

beaux arts the fine arts. [French]

belles-lettres literary works written and read for their elegant style. [French, 'fine letters']

bête noire a person or thing that you

particularly dislike. [French, 'black beast']

bêtise a foolish remark or action [French, 'stupidity']

bien pensant having a conventional attitude: *it's always the quiet, bien pensant girls who seem to end up with a boyfriend.* [French, 'well thinking']

Bildungsroman a novel about a person's formative years or spiritual education. [German, 'education novel']

billet-doux a love letter. [French, 'sweet note']

blitzkrieg an intense, violent military campaign intended to bring about a rapid victory. [German, 'lightning war']

bona fide genuine; real: *a bona fide money-back guarantee.* [Latin, 'with good faith']

bona fides evidence proving that a person is what they claim to be. [Latin, 'good faith']

bon mot a clever or witty remark. [French, 'good word']

bonne bouche a delicious thing to eat. [French, 'a good taste in the mouth']

bon vivant a person with a sociable and luxurious lifestyle. [French, 'person living well']

brasserie an informal or inexpensive restaurant. [French, 'brewery']

carpe diem make the most of the present time. [Latin, 'seize the day!']

carte blanche complete freedom to act as you wish: *he was given carte blanche to make whatever changes he saw fit.* [French, 'blank paper']

casus belli an act or situation that provokes or justifies a war. [Latin, 'cause of war']

cause célèbre a controversial issue attracting a lot of public attention. [French, 'famous case']

caveat emptor the buyer is responsible for checking the quality of goods before buying them. [Latin, 'let the buyer beware']

c'est la vie used to express resigned acceptance of a difficult or unpleasant situation: *she couldn't get the time off work—c'est la vie.* [French, 'that's life'. Another French expression with the same meaning is **c'est la guerre**, literally 'that's war']

chacun à son gout everyone to their own taste. [French]

chambré (of red wine) at room temperature. [French]

chef-d'œuvre a masterpiece. [French, 'chief work']

cherchez la femme there is certain to be a woman at the bottom of a problem or mystery. [French, 'look for the woman']

cognoscenti people who are well informed about something: *a man regarded by the cognoscenti as the greatest pianist in Europe.* [Italian, 'people who know']

comme ci, comme ça used to express the view that something is neither very bad, nor very good. [French, 'like this, like that']

comme il faut correct in behaviour or etiquette. [French, 'as is necessary']

compos mentis having full control of your mind: *are you sure he was totally compos mentis?* [Latin]

cordon bleu of the highest standard of skill in cooking: *a cordon-bleu chef.* [French, 'blue ribbon' (a blue ribbon once indicated the highest order of French chivalry)]

cordon sanitaire a guarded line placed around an area infected by disease to prevent anyone from leaving. [French, 'sanitary line']

Cosa Nostra a US criminal organization related to the Mafia. [Italian, 'our thing']

coup de foudre love at first sight. [French 'stroke of lightning']

coup de grâce a blow by which a mortally wounded person or thing is mercifully killed. [French, 'stroke of grace']

coup de main a sudden surprise attack. [French, 'stroke of hand']

coup d'état a sudden violent seizure of power. [French, 'blow of state']

coup de théâtre a dramatically sudden development or change in a situation. [French, 'blow of the theatre]

crème de la crème the best person or thing of a particular kind: *the crème de la crème of London café society.* [French, 'cream of the cream']

cri de cœur a passionate appeal or protest. [French, 'cry from the heart']

cui bono? who stands to gain? (implying that this person may have been responsible for a crime). [Latin, 'to whom (is it) a benefit?']

cum laude with distinction: *he graduated cum laude in 1922.* [Latin, 'with praise']

de facto in fact, whether by right or not: *the de facto president of the republic.* [Latin]

de haut en bas in a condescending or superior way: *he never addressed his students de haut en bas.* [French, 'from above to below']

Dei gratia by the grace of God. [Latin]

déjà vu the sense of having experienced the present situation before. [French, 'already seen']

de jure rightful; by right: *a de jure claim to the territory.* [Latin, 'of law']

de nos jours contemporary: *a kind of Oscar Wilde de nos jours.* [French, 'of our days']

Deo gratias thanks be to God. [Latin]

Deo volente God willing. [Latin]

de profundis expressing your deepest feelings. [Latin, 'from the depths']

de rigueur necessary if you want to be accepted socially: *black tie was de rigueur on* *such occasions.* [French, 'in strictness']

dernier cri the very latest fashion: *a dark suit in the cut that was the dernier cri of that time.* [French, 'the last cry']

de trop not wanted; unwelcome: *she hovered uncertainly in the doorway, feeling rather de trop.* [French, 'excessive']

deus ex machina an unexpected event that saves an apparently hopeless situation. [Latin, 'god from the machinery']

dolce far niente a state of pleasant inactivity or idleness. [Italian, 'sweet doing nothing']

dolce vita a life of pleasure and luxury. [Italian, 'sweet life']

doppelgänger an apparition or double of a living person. [German, 'double-goer']

double entendre a word or phrase with two possible interpretations. [from former French, 'double understanding']

dramatis personae the characters in a play. [Latin, 'persons of the drama']

du jour currently popular: *black comedy is the genre du jour.* [French, 'of the day']

embarras de richesse more options or resources than you know what to do with. [French, 'embarrassment of riches']

éminence grise a person who has power or influence without holding an official position. [French, 'grey eminence']

en bloc all together, or all at the same time: *they rejected the government's proposals en bloc.* [French]

en déshabille only partly dressed. [French]

en famille with your family; in an informal way: *we ate en famille at the kitchen table.* [French, 'in family']

enfant gâté a person who is flattered or indulged. [French, 'spoilt child']

enfant terrible a person whose behaviour is unconventional or controversial: *for years, he was the enfant terrible of contemporary British art.* [French, 'terrible child']

en fête holding or prepared for a party or celebration. [French, 'in festival']

en masse all together: *the cabinet resigned en masse.* [French, 'in a mass']

en passant by the way: *what is interesting, en passant, is that it is a pre-war model.* [French, 'in passing']

en route during the course of a journey. [French]

entente or **entente cordiale** a friendly understanding between people or countries [French]

entre nous between ourselves: *entre nous, I'll be glad when he retires.* [French]

e pluribus unum one out of many (the motto of the US). [Latin]

esprit de corps a feeling of pride and loyalty uniting the members of a group. [French, 'spirit of the body']

eureka a cry of joy or satisfaction when you discover something. [Greek, 'I have found it!]

ex gratia (of payment) given as a favour rather than because of any legal obligation. [Latin, 'from favour']

ex officio by virtue of your position or status: *an ex officio member of the committee.* [French, 'out of duty']

fait accompli a thing that has been done or decided and cannot now be altered. [French, 'accomplished fact']

faute de mieux for want of a better alternative. [French]

faux pas an embarrassing mistake: *wearing knitwear after dark is no longer a fashion faux pas.* [French, 'false step']

femme fatale a seductive woman. [French, 'disastrous woman']

fête champêtre an outdoor entertainment such as a garden party. [French, 'rural festival']

fin de siècle relating to the end of a century. [French]

folie à deux delusion or mental illness shared by two people. [French, 'shared madness']

folie de grandeur delusions of grandeur. [French]

force majeure superior strength. [French]

froideur coolness or reserve between people: *they are now back on speaking terms after a period of palpable froideur.* [French]

gemütlich pleasant and cheerful. [German]

gîte a small furnished holiday house in France. [French]

gran turismo a high-performance car. [Italian, 'great touring']

grande dame a woman who is influential within a particular sphere: *the grande dame of British sculpture.* [French, 'grand lady']

haute couture the designing and making of clothes by leading fashion houses. [French, 'high dressmaking']

haute cuisine high-quality cooking. [French, 'high cookery']

haut monde fashionable society. [French, 'high world']

hoi polloi the common people: *a dance club and cocktail lounge whose dress code and hefty cover charges deter the hoi polloi.* [Greek, 'the many']

hors de combat out of action due to injury or damage: *the juke box is currently hors de combat.* [French, 'out of the fight']

hor-d'oeuvre a small savoury first course of a meal. [French, 'outside the work']

idée fixe an obsession. [French, 'fixed idea']

in absentia while not present: *he was sentenced to death in absentia.* [Latin, 'in absence']

in camera in private: *the meeting will be*

held in camera. [Latin, 'in the chamber']

in extremis in an extremely difficult situation; at the point of death. [Latin, 'in the most extreme or furthest']

in loco parentis in the place of a parent: *the head teacher was acting in loco parentis.* [Latin]

in medias res in or into the middle of a sequence of events: *he began his story in medias res.* [Latin, 'in the middle of things']

in memoriam in memory of someone. [Latin]

in propria persona in his or her own person. [Latin]

in situ in the original or appropriate position. [Latin, 'in place']

inter alia among other things: *charges of, inter alia, insider dealing and stock manipulation.* [Latin, 'among others']

in toto as a whole: *he rejected the proposals in toto.* [Latin]

in vino veritas under the influence of alcohol, a person tells the truth. [Latin, 'truth in wine']

in vitro taking place in a test tube or elsewhere outside a living animal or plant: *in vitro fertilization.* [Latin, 'in glass']

ipso facto by that very fact or act: *the enemy of one's enemy may be ipso facto a friend.* [Latin, 'by the fact itself']

je ne sais quoi a quality that is hard to describe: *an actor possessed of that certain je ne sais quoi that makes someone a star.* [French, 'I do not know what']

jeu d'esprit a light-hearted display of wit. [French, 'game of the mind']

jeunesse dorée wealthy, fashionable young people. [French, 'gilded youth']

joie de vivre exuberant enjoyment of life. [French, 'joy of living']

jolie laide a woman who is attractive despite having ugly features. [French]

laissez-faire a policy of leaving things to take their own course without interfering. [French, 'allow to do']

locum tenens a temporary deputy or stand-in. [Latin, 'person holding a place']

locus classicus the best-known or most authoritative piece of writing on a subject; a classic case or example of something: *the Left Bank has always been the locus classicus of intellectual life.* [Latin, 'classical place']

magna cum laude with great distinction: *he graduated magna cum laude in mathematics.* [Latin, 'with great praise']

magnum opus the most important work of an artist, writer, etc. [Latin, 'great work']

manqué having failed to become what you might have been: *he fancied himself as an architect manqué.* [French, from *manquer*, 'to lack']

mal de mer sea-sickness. [French]

mea culpa an acknowledgement that something is your own fault. [Latin, 'by my fault']

memento mori something kept as a reminder that death is inevitable. [Latin, 'remember (that you have) to die']

ménage à trois an arrangement in which a married couple and the lover of one of them live together. [French, 'household of three']

mise en scène the setting or surroundings of an event. [French, 'putting on stage']

modus operandi a way of doing something: *we believe the crimes are linked, because the same modus operandi was used in each case.* [Latin, 'way of operating']

modus vivendi a way of living or existing together peacefully. [Latin, 'way of living']

mot juste the most exact or appropriate word or expression. [French]

mutatis mutandis making necessary alterations while not affecting the main point at issue. [Latin, 'things being changed that have to be changed']

nem. con. unanimously: *the motions were carried nem. con.* [short for Latin *nemine contradicente* 'with nobody disagreeing']

ne plus ultra the best example of something: *the ne plus ultra of Parisian tea rooms.* [Latin, 'not further beyond']

nil desperandum do not despair. [Latin, 'no need to despair']

noblesse oblige noble or wealthy people should help those who are less fortunate. [French, 'nobility obligates']

nolens volens whether you want or like something or not. [Latin, from *nolens* 'not willing' + *volens* 'willing']

nom de guerre a false name, especially one used by a person taking part in some military activity. [French, 'war name']

non sequitur a statement that does not follow on logically from what has just been said. [Latin, 'it does not follow']

nouveau riche people who have recently become rich and who display their wealth in an obvious or tasteless way. [French, 'new rich']

nuit blanche a sleepless night. [French, 'white night']

objet d'art a small decorative or artistic object. [French]

on dit a piece of gossip. [French, 'they say']

par excellence better or more than all others of the same kind: *a singer-songwriter par excellence.* [French, 'by excellence']

parti pris a preconceived view; a bias. [French, 'side taken']

per annum for each year. [Latin]

per capita for each person. [Latin, 'by heads']

per se by or in itself or themselves: *he's not*

against reform per se, just certain kinds of reform. [Latin]

persona non grata a person who is not welcome somewhere. [Latin]

pièce de résistance the most important or impressive item: *the pièce de résistance was chocolate cake laced with kirsch.* [French, 'piece (i.e. means) of resistance']

pied-à-terre a small flat or house kept for occasional use. [French, 'foot to earth']

pis aller a last resort. [French, from *pis* 'worse' + *aller* 'to go']

plat du jour a special dish prepared by a restaurant on a particular day. [French, 'dish of the day']

plus ça change used to express resigned acknowledgement of the fact that certain things never change. [French, from *plus ça change, plus c'est la même chose* 'the more it changes, the more it stays the same']

prima facie accepted as so until proved otherwise: *a prima facie case of professional misconduct.* [Latin, from *primus* 'first' + *facies* 'face']

primus inter pares the senior or representative member of a group: *Wordsworth emerged primus inter pares among the other Romantic poets.* [Latin, 'first among equals']

pro rata proportional; proportionally: *salary from £25,000 (pro rata for the part-time posts).* [Latin, 'according to the rate']

proxime accessit the person who comes second in an exam or is runner-up for an award. [Latin, 'came very near']

que sera sera used to express resigned acceptance that future events are out of your control. [Spanish, 'what will be, will be']

quid pro quo a favour given in return for something: *the pardon was a quid pro quo for their help in releasing hostages.* [Latin, 'something for something']

quod erat demonstrandum used to say that something proves the truth of a theory or claim. [Latin, 'which was to be demonstrated'; usually abbreviated to QED]

raison d'être the most important reason for someone or something's existence: *football appeared to be his sole raison d'être.* [French, 'reason for being']

reductio ad absurdam a method of disproving a premise by showing that its logical conclusion is absurd. [Latin, 'reduction to the absurd']

roman-à-clef a novel in which real people or events appear with invented names. [French, 'novel with a key']

sangfroid the ability to stay calm in difficult circumstances: *the region's inhabitants continue to exhibit remarkable sangfroid in the face of imminent catastrophe.* [French, 'cold blood']

savoir faire the ability to act appropriately in social situations. [French, 'know how to do']

Schadenfreude pleasure that someone gains from another person's misfortune. [German, from *Schaden* 'harm' and *Freude* 'joy']

sine die (of proceedings) adjourned indefinitely. [Latin, 'without a day']

sine qua non a thing that is absolutely essential: *tennis courts are a sine qua non for any summer camp.* [Latin, 'without which not']

soi-disant self-styled; so-called: *a soi-disant novelist.* [French, from *soi* 'oneself' + *disant* 'saying']

sotto voce in a quiet voice. [Italian, from *sotto* 'under' + *voce* 'voice']

sub judice being considered by a court of law and therefore not to be publicly discussed elsewhere. [Latin, 'under a judge']

sub rosa happening or done in secret: *the inspection must be sub rosa.* [Latin, 'under the rose' (the rose being an emblem of secrecy)]

succès de scandale a success which is due to a person or thing's notoriety. [French, 'success of scandal']

sui generis unique: *each of his novels is sui generis.* [Latin, 'of its own kind']

tableau vivant a silent motionless group of people arranged to represent a scene or incident. [French, 'living picture']

table d'hôte a restaurant meal offered at a fixed price, with few if any choices. [French, 'host's table']

tabula rasa 1 a situation in which there are no preconceived ideas about how something should be done. **2** the human mind as it is at birth, empty of ideas or thoughts. [Latin, 'scraped writing tablet']

tant mieux so much the better. [French]

tant pis so much the worse; too bad: *oh well, if you're on a diet, tant pis.* [French]

terra firma dry land; the ground. [Latin, 'firm land']

terra incognita unknown territory: *for centuries the interior of the country was terra incognita to the Western world.* [Latin]

tête-à-tête a private conversation. [French, 'head-to-head']

tour de force a thing accomplished with great skill: *the aria is a musical tour de force.* [French, 'feat of strength']

tour d'horizon a broad general survey of something: *a tour d'horizon of Brazilian literature.* [French, 'tour of the horizon']

tout court with no addition or qualification; in short: *he saw religion as an illusion, tout court.* [French, 'very short']

tout de suite at once. [French, 'quite in sequence']

trompe l'oeil a painting that creates the illusion of a real three-dimensional object or space. [French, 'deceives the eye']

verboten forbidden: *smoking in the studio is strictly verboten.* [German]

vernissage a private view of paintings before they are shown to the general public. [French, 'varnishing' (referring originally to the day before an exhibition when artists were allowed to retouch and varnish their work)]

via media a compromise. [Latin, 'middle way']

victor ludorum the overall champion in a sports competition. [Latin, 'victor of the games']

vis-à-vis in relation to; as compared with: *the value of the dollar vis-à-vis other currencies.* [French, 'face-to-face']

voila there it is, or there you are: *add a dash of mustard and a few drops of olive oil: voila!* [French]

volte-face an abrupt and complete change of attitude or policy: *the government's volte-face on tuition fees raises a serious question.* [French]

vox populi public opinion. [Latin, 'the people's voice']

Weltangschaung a particular philosophy or view of life. [German, from *Welt* 'world' and *Anschauung* 'perception']

Weltschmerz a feeling of melancholy and world-weariness. [German, from *Welt* 'world' and *Schmerz* 'pain']

zeitgeist the characteristic spirit or mood of a particular historical period: *the subtext of the film tapped right into the zeitgeist of the '90s.* [German, from *Zeit* 'time' + *Geist* 'spirit']

Useful words for games and puzzles

In many word games, it's handy to know some very short words or words with unusual spellings, especially those which are not in everyday use. Two-letter words, short words containing an *x* or a *z*, words containing a *q* not followed by a *u*, and words beginning with *x* can be particularly useful and a wide selection is included here, with brief explanations of their meaning. Proper names and abbreviations which are not pronounced as they are spelled (such as *Dr* or *Mr*) are not included, as most word games don't allow them.

Two-letter words

aa rough cindery lava

ab an abdominal muscle

ad an advertisement

ag S. African expressing various emotions, e.g. irritation, grief, or pleasure

ah expressing surprise, sympathy, pleasure, etc.

ai the three-toed sloth

am the present tense of **be**

an a form of the indefinite article

as used to convey relative extent or degree

at expressing location or time

aw expressing mild protest, entreaty, etc.

ax dialect form of **ask**

ay variant spelling of **aye**

ba (in Egyptian mythology) the soul

be to exist

bi bisexual

bo a kind of fig tree

by beside

da a person's father

DJ a disc jockey

do to perform an action

dy a type of sediment

ee dialect form of **oh**

eh seeking explanation or agreement

El an elevated railway or section of railway

em a measuring unit in printing

en a measuring unit in printing

er expressing doubt or hesitation

ex a former spouse or partner

fa a musical note

Ga a member of a people living in Ghana

GI a soldier in the US army

go to move or travel

ha expressing surprise, triumph, etc.

he a male person or animal previously mentioned

hi used as a greeting

ho expressing surprise, triumph, etc.

id a part of the mind

if introducing a conditional clause

in within

io a North American moth

is the present tense of **be**

it a thing previously mentioned

ja (S. African) yes

jo (Scottish, old use): a sweetheart

Ju a kind of Chinese pottery

ka (in Egyptian mythology) the spirit

ki a plant of the lily family

KO a knockout in boxing match

la a musical note

li a Chinese unit of distance

lo (old use) used to draw attention to something

ma a person's mother

MD (Brit.) a managing director

me the objective case of **I**

mi a musical note

mo a moment

MP a Member of Parliament

mu the 12th letter of the Greek alphabet

my belonging to me

no not any

nu the 13th letter of the Greek alphabet

ob a type of gene

od a power once thought to pervade the natural world

of belonging to

og (Australian, old use) a shilling

oh expressing surprise, anger, disappointment, etc.

oi used to attract attention

OJ orange juice

OK used to express assent, agreement, etc.

om a mystic syllable which constitutes a sacred mantra

on supported by or covering

op an operation

or used to link alternatives

os a bone

ou a Hawaiian bird

ow expressing pain

ox a cow or bull

oy = oi

Oz Australia

pa a person's father

pi the 16th letter of the Greek alphabet

po a chamber pot

qi (in Chinese philosophy) the life force

ra (in Norway and Sweden) a moraine

re a musical note

ri a Japanese unit of length

se a Chinese musical instrument

si = te
so therefore
ta thank you
te a musical note
ti = te
TV television
uh expressing hesitation
um expressing hesitation

up towards a higher position
us the objective case of **we**
Wa a member of a people living on the borders of China and Burma
we oneself and other people
Wu a dialect of Chinese
xi the 14th letter of Greek alphabet

xu a Vietnamese unit of money
ye (old use) the plural form of **thou**
Yi a people living in parts of China
yo used as a greeting
yu an ancient Chinese wine container

Three-letter words containing x or z

axe a tool for chopping wood etc.
biz business
box a container
coz (old use) a cousin
cox the person who steers a rowing boat
dux (Scottish) the top pupil in a school or class
dzo a crossbreed of a cow and a yak
fax an electronic copy of a document
fez a type of hat
fix to attach something
fox an animal with a bushy tail
hex (N. Amer.) to cast a spell on someone
lax not strict or careful enough

lox (N. Amer.) smoked salmon
lux a unit for measuring illumination
max maximum
Mex Mexican
mix to blend or combine
nix nothing
pax a call for a truce
pix pictures
pox a disease
pyx the container which holds the consecrated bread used in Holy Communion
Rex the reigning king
sax a saxophone
saz a musical instrument
sex being male or female
six one more than five
tax money paid to the government

tux a tuxedo
Uzi a type of sub-machine gun
vex to annoy
vox vocals; voice
wax substance used to make candles etc.
wiz = whizz
zag a sharp change of direction
zap to destroy
zed the letter Z
zee (N. Amer.) the letter Z
Zen a type of Buddhism
zig a sharp change of direction
zip a fastener
zit a spot
zol (S. African) a hand-rolled cigarette
zoo a place where wild animals are kept

Words with a q not followed by a u

burqa = burka, a garment worn by Muslim women
fiqh the theory or philosophy of Islamic law
Iraqi a person from Iraq; relating to Iraq
niqab a Muslim woman's veil
qadi a Muslim judge
qanat an irrigation tunnel
qasida an Arabic or Persian poem

qawwal a qawwali singer
qawwali Muslim devotional music
qi (in Chinese philosophy) the life force
qibla the direction towards Mecca
qigong a Chinese system of physical exercises
qin a Chinese musical instrument

qintar a monetary unit of Albania
qiviut wool from the musk ox
qwerty the standard layout of typewriters and keyboards
tariqa the Sufi method of spiritual learning

Words beginning with x

xanthan a polysaccharide
xanthate a chemical compound
xanthene a chemical compound
xanthic yellowish
xanthin a yellow colouring matter

xanthine a biochemical compound
xanthoma a yellow patch on the skin
xebec a sailing ship
xeme a fork-tailed gull
xenia gifts to a guest or guests

xenial relating to hospitality
xenon a gaseous chemical element
xeric very dry
xeroma abnormal dryness of a body part
xerophyte a plant needing very little water

xerox to photocopy

Xhosa a South African people or their language

xi the 14th letter of the Greek alphabet

Xiang a dialect of Chinese

xiphoid sword-shaped

Xmas Christmas

xoanon a wooden image of a god

xography a photographic process

xu a Vietnamese unit of money

xylan a compound found in wood

xylary of or relating to xylem

xylem plant tissue

xylene a liquid hydrocarbon

xylite a volatile liquid

xylitol a chemical substance

xylol = xylene

xylose a plant sugar

xyrid a sedge-like herb

xyster a surgical instrument

xyston an ancient Greek spear

xystus an ancient Greek portico

FAQs and facts about English

English is spoken by or used by an estimated one third of the world's population. It has always been an adaptable, flexible, and ever-changing language and modern technology has ensured that its reach now spreads even into the smallest settlements in the remotest corners of the world.

The English Dictionaries Department at Oxford University Press receives hundreds of letters and emails every year from around the world which reflect the global nature of the language and people's fascination with it. Here is a selection of frequently asked questions and facts about English, based on the kinds of enquiries that we receive.

What is English?

English belongs to the West Germanic group of Indo-European languages and comes from the language spoken by the Germanic invaders of Britain (Angles, Saxons, and Jutes), though its vocabulary has been much influenced by Latin, Greek, and Norman French and, more recently, by many other languages including Dutch, Spanish, Portuguese, Arabic, and Hindi. Old English (formerly called *Anglo-Saxon*) is the English language of the period ending soon after the Norman Conquest (up until around 1150); Middle English is used to describe the language from then to about 1500; Modern English extends from around 1500 to the present day.

How many people speak English?

Today, English is spoken in Britain, Ireland, Australia, New Zealand, the US, Canada, South Africa, and many other countries. It is the first language of an estimated 400 million people, and the second language of more than 1.5 billion. This makes it the world's second most widely spoken first language, after Chinese, but the world's most commonly learned second language.

How many words are there in English?

The full *Oxford English Dictionary* aims to record the history of all the words used in English, past and present. This means that it contains words that are now very rare or that have not been used for a long time (such as **spurrier** 'a person who makes spurs' and **frore** 'frosty') as well as recently coined words such as **bling** and **podcasting**. The second edition of the *OED*, published in 1989 and consisting of twenty volumes, contains more than 615,000 entries, and the third, available online, is expanding all the time, with batches of 1,800 new and revised items being added in regular quarterly updates.

But even the *OED* does not include every specialized technical term or obscure dialect expression. Furthermore, what exactly is a word? We are on safe ground with words such as **cat** and **dog**, **climb** and **walk**, or **quickly** and **happiness**. But what about compounds such as **walking stick**, which are made up of two pre-existing words? Does **walking stick** itself count as a word? There is an almost unlimited number of such two-word compounds, which cannot all be included in a dictionary. Then there is the question of proper names, such as **London**, **Nelson**, or

Everest: are they words? Finally, **climb** and **mountain** are single words, but what about the verb tenses **climbs**, **climbing**, and **climbed**, and the plural form **mountains**? As you can see, the question is not straightforward and is almost impossible to answer.

Where do new words come from?

New words enter English in a number of different ways:

- **completely new terms:** perhaps surprisingly, these account for less than 1 per cent of new vocabulary. Many of them are or were originally trademarks (often named after their inventor, such as **Hoover** and **biro**), some are technical coinages, and others are invented by writers such as Lewis Carroll (**chortle**) and J. R. R. Tolkien (**hobbit**).

- **from other languages:** it has been estimated that about half of all English words come from languages other than Old English, notably classical Latin and Greek. Norman French was very influential after the Norman Conquest in 1066, and, more recently, English has absorbed vocabulary from over 120 of the world's languages, from Italian (**casino**) and German (**sketch**) to Japanese (**futon**) and Turkish (**yogurt**).

- **from combinations of existing words:** an enormous amount of new words are formed from words, or parts of words, that already exist, for example **broadband**, **health club**, **ringtone**, **alcopop**, **bioterrorism**, **carjacking**.

- **from new senses of existing words:** the new meaning may take its place alongside existing senses of the word (for example, **attachment** now has the additional meaning 'a computer file sent with an email'), or may eventually replace the original meaning of the word altogether (**hoodwink** originally meant 'to blindfold someone').

- **by conversion:** this is the process by which a word begins as one part of speech, for example a noun, and then becomes another part of speech, such as a verb. For example, the noun **text** (in the sense 'a text message') quickly developed as a verb (I *texted* her).

What's the longest English word?

The longest words without hyphens in most larger dictionaries are **deinstitutionalization** at 22 letters (meaning 'the release of long-term inmates from institutions such as psychiatric hospitals or prisons') and **antidisestablishmentarianism** at 28 letters (meaning 'belief that the Church of England should not be disestablished' or deprived of its official status). The latter word is very occasionally found in genuine use, but it is most often quoted just as an example of a very long word.

Other extremely long words are **floccinaucinihilipilification**, 'the action or habit of estimating something as worthless', and **pneumonoultramicroscopicsilico-volcanoconiosis** (the longest word in the *Oxford English Dictionary*), which is said to mean a lung disease caused by inhaling very fine ash and sand dust, but has never been a real medical term.

The longest word encountered in Britain is the Welsh place name **Llanfairpwllgwyngyllgogerychwyrndrobwllllantysiliogogogoch**, which is usually abbreviated to **Llanfair PG**. Created in the mid-nineteenth century so as to be able to claim the record for the longest railway station name in the UK, this name translates as 'the church of St Mary in the hollow of white hazel trees near the rapid whirlpool by St Tysilio's of the red cave'.

What's the longest word containing no letter more than once?

There are two 15-letter words in standard use that we know of: **uncopyrightable** and **dermatoglyphics** (the study of skin markings on fingers, hands, and feet).

What's the longest one-syllable word?

There are several candidates for this in general use, all of which are nine letters long:

screeched   scrounged   stretched   strengths   scratched   scrunched   straights

Which word has the most meanings?

The three words with the most meanings listed in the *Oxford English Dictionary* are all verbs to do with movement and position:

- **set** has 156 main senses
- **stand** has 104 main senses
- **fall** has 101.

Which word has the most synonyms?

Given our tendency to criticize rather than praise, it's perhaps not surprising that there seem to be more synonyms for words with negative or unpleasant connotations than for words on the other side of the spectrum! The following list is drawn from the *Oxford Thesaurus of English*, 2nd edition:

Term	Number of synonyms	Term	Number of synonyms
1. stupid or foolish person	135	11. very	78
2. drunk	112	12. penis	77
3. wicked or morally bad	90	13. reprimand someone	75
4. annoy someone	89	14. servant	75
5. angry	88	15. kind or good natured	74
6. very good; excellent	87	16. worried	73
7. very unpleasant	87	17. happy	72
8. boring	86	18. go away	72
9. mad	85	19. speak	72
10. hurry	79	20. criticize strongly	72

Which words contain all five vowels?

Abstemious and **facetious** are the only words in this dictionary that contain all five vowels (a, e, i, o, u) in alphabetical order, used once only.

If you would like to explore further, you can find out more information about the English language by visiting our websites:

www.oup.com
www.AskOxford.com
www.oed.com

Collective names for animals and birds

Many of these names are humorous terms which were probably rarely if ever used: they were taken up by a writer called Joseph Strutt in 'Sports & Pastimes of England' (1801) and then by other antiquarian writers. The list is arranged in the alphabetical order of the birds and animals themselves.

a shrewdness of apes
a herd or pace of asses
a troop of baboons
a cete of badgers
a sloth of bears
a swarm, drift, or hive of bees
a flock, flight, or pod of birds
a herd, gang, or obstinacy of buffalo
a bellowing of bullfinches
a drove of bullocks
a clowder or glaring of cats
an army of caterpillars
a herd or drove of cattle
a brood, clutch, or peep of chickens
a chattering of choughs
a rag or rake of colts
a covert of coots
a herd of cranes
a bask of crocodiles
a murder of crows
a litter of cubs
a herd of curlew
a herd or mob of deer
a pack or kennel of dogs
a school of dolphins
a trip of dotterel (type of plover)
a flight, dole, or piteousness of doves
a paddling of ducks (on water)
a safe of ducks (on land)
a fling of dunlin
a herd or parade of elephants
a herd or gang of elk
a busyness of ferrets
a charm of finches
a shoal or run of fish
a swarm or cloud of flies
a skulk of foxes
a gaggle of geese (on land)
a skein, team, or wedge of geese (in flight)

a herd of giraffe
a cloud of gnats
a flock, herd, or trip of goats
a band of gorillas
a pack or covey of grouse
a down, mute, or husk of hares
a cast of hawks
a siege of herons
a bloat of hippopotami
a drove, string, stud, or team of horses
a pack, cry, or kennel of hounds
a flight or swarm of insects
a fluther or smack of jellyfish
a mob or troop of kangaroos
a litter or kindle of kittens
a desert of lapwings
a bevy or exaltation of larks
a leap of leopards
a pride or sawt of lions
a tiding of magpies
a sord or suit of mallard
a stud of mares
a richesse of martens
a labour of moles
a troop of monkeys
a span or barren of mules
a watch of nightingales
a parliament or stare of owls
a yoke of oxen
a pandemonium of parrots
a covey of partridges
a muster of peacocks
a muster, parcel, or rookery of penguins
a bevy or head of pheasants
a litter or herd of pigs
a kit of pigeons (in flight)
a congregation, stand, or wing of plovers
a rush or flight of pochards
a pod, school, herd, or turmoil of porpoises

a covey of ptarmigan
a litter of pups
a bevy or drift of quail
a bury of rabbits
a string of racehorses
an unkindness of ravens
a crash of rhinoceros
a bevy of roe deer
a parliament, building, or rookery of rooks
a hill of ruffs (type of fish)
a pod, herd, or rookery of seals
a flock, herd, trip, or mob of sheep
a dopping of sheldrake (type of duck)
a wisp or walk of snipe
a host of sparrows
a murmuration of starlings
a flight of swallows
a game or herd of swans (on land)
a wedge of swans (in flight)
a drift, herd, or sounder of swine
a spring of teal
a knot of toads
a hover of trout
a rafter of turkeys
a bale or turn of turtles
a bunch or knob of waterfowl
a school, herd, pod, or gam of whales
a company or trip of wigeon
a sounder of wild boar
a team of wild ducks (in flight)
a bunch, trip, plump, or knob of wildfowl
a pack or rout of wolves
a fall of woodcock
a descent of woodpeckers
a herd of wrens
a zeal of zebras

Phobias and fears

The word **phobia** comes from the Greek *phobos*, meaning 'fear'. It forms part of many English terms describing an extreme or irrational fear of a particular object, event, or situation. Some of the words and conditions listed below will be familiar, like **claustrophobia**, the fear of enclosed spaces, or its opposite **agoraphobia**, the fear of open spaces. Others, if not so familiar, seem entirely understandable, such as the fear of death (**thanatophobia**), fire (**pyrophobia**), or being buried alive (**taphephobia**). Certain objects of fear, however, seem rather more surprising or unexpected: that of beards, for example, (**pogonophobia**), snow (**chionophobia**), or even the essential bodily function of swallowing (**phagophobia**).

Object of Fear	Phobia	Object of Fear	Phobia
animals	zoophobia	fear	phobophobia
beards	pogonophobia	feathers	pteronophobia
beating	mastigophobia	fire	pyrophobia
bed	clinophobia	fish	ichthyophobia
bees	apiphobia	flesh	selaphobia
being buried alive	taphephobia	floods	antlophobia
being looked at	scopophobia	flowers	anthophobia
birds	ornithophobia	fog	homichlophobia
blood	haemophobia	food	sitophobia/cibophobia
blushing	erythrophobia	foreigners	xenophobia
body odour	bromidrosiphobia	fur	doraphobia
bridges	gephyrobia	ghosts	phasmophobia
bullets	ballistophobia	giving birth to monsters	teratophobia
cats	ailurophobia		
childbirth	tocophobia	glass	nelaphobia
church	ecclesiophobia	hair	trichophobia
clouds	nephephobia	heat	thermophobia
cold	cheimaphobia	heaven	uranophobia
colour	chromophobia	hell	stygiophobia
computers/technology	cyberphobia	high places	acrophobia/hypsophobia
		home	oikophobia
constipation	coprostasophobia	horses	hippophobia
corpses	necrophobia	ice	cryophobia
correspondence	epistolophobia	idleness	thassophobia
clowns	coulrophobia	illness	nosophobia
crowds	ochlophobia	injury	traumatophobia
dampness	hygrophobia	insanity	lyssophobia
darkness	scotophobia	insects	entomophobia
death	thanatophobia	insect stings	cnidophobia
dirt	mysophobia	itching	acarophobia
disease/illness	nosophobia	lakes	limnophobia
dogs	cynophobia	lice	pediculophobia
dreams	oneirophobia	light	photophobia
drink	potophobia	lightning	astrapophobia
dust	koniophobia	loneliness	autophobia
enclosed spaces	claustrophobia	magic	rhabdophobia
everything	panophobia/pantophobia	marriage	gametophobia
eyes	ommetophobia	men	androphobia
faeces	coprophobia	mice	musophobia

Object of Fear	Phobia	Object of Fear	Phobia
mirrors	eisoptrophobia	slime	blennophobia
mobs	ochlophobia	snakes	ophidiophobia
money	chrematophobia	snow	chionophobia
names	onomatophobia	solitude	eremophobia
needles	belonephobia	speed	tachophobia
new things	neophobia	spiders	arachnophobia
night	nyctophobia	stars	siderophobia
nudity	gymnophobia	stealing	kleptophobia
open spaces	agoraphobia	string	linonophobia
pain	algophobia	stuttering	laliophobia
people	anthropophobia	sun	heliophobia
pins	enetophobia	swallowing	phagophobia
pleasure	hedenophobia	teeth	odontophobia
precipices	cremnophobia	thirteen	triskaidekaphobia
priests	hierophobia	thunder	brontophobia
rabies	hydrophobophobia	touch	haptophobia
rail travel	siderodromophobia	travel	hodophobia
reptiles	batrachophobia	tuberculosis	phthisiophobia
rivers	potomaphobia	water	hydrophobia
robbers	harpaxophobia	waves	cymophobia
saints	hagiophobia	wind	anemophobia
sea	thalassophobia	women	gynophobia
sex	erotophobia	words	logophobia
shadows	sciophobia	work	ergophobia
sin	hamartophobia	worms	helminthophobia
sleep	hypnophobia	writing	graphophobia

Collectors and enthusiasts

Many of the English terms for people with particular hobbies or enthusiasms contain the elements *-phile* or *-philist*, which come from the Greek word *philos* meaning 'loving', or *-mane* (from *mania*). More recently there has been a trend for terms employing the endings *-head*, as in *petrolhead*, meaning 'a car fanatic', and *-ista* (from Spanish), as in *fashionista* 'a devoted follower of fashion'.

Hobby/object of enthusiasm	Enthusiast	Hobby/object of enthusiasm	Enthusiast
amateur radio	ham	heavy metal music	headbanger
animals/ conservation	bunny-hugger	hi-fi	audiophile
		horses	hippophile
arts	culture-vulture	horse racing	turfman
ballet	balletomane	jazz	jazzbo
bees	apiarist	making money	breadhead
boating	boatie	malt beer/whisky	malt worm
books	bibliophile	metal detection	detectorist
cars/motorbikes	petrolhead (*or* motorhead)	mushrooms	mycophile
		music	melomane
cats	ailurophile	oysters	ostreophage
caves	speleologist	parks	parkomane
chocolate	chocoholic	pigeons	columbarian
climbing buildings	stegophilist	photography	shutterbug
computers	propeller-head/ Nethead	railway/trains	gricer
		rockets	rocketeer
crosswords	cruciverbalist	sport	jock
dogs	canophilist	stamps	philatelist
fashion	fashionista	Star Trek	Trekkie
films/cinema	cineaste/cinephile	television	televisionary
folk music	folkie	trees	dendrophile
gold	chyrosophilist	tulips	tulipomaniac
good food and drink	epicurean	wine	oenophile
Greece/Greek culture	philhellene	words	logophile

Thing collected	Collector	Thing collected	Collector
anything	completist	flies	dipterist
autographs	autographizer	gramophone records	discophile
banknotes	notaphilist	matchboxes or their labels	phillumenist
beer mats	tegestologist		
beetles	coleopterist	mineral specimens	rockhound
birds' eggs	oologist (*or* egger)	money boxes	argyrothecologist
book plates	ex-librist	old bond and share certificates	scripophilist
early books	incunabulist		
butterflies	lepidopterist	postcards	deltiologist
cigarette cards/ postcards	cartophilist	shells	conchologist
		sightings of rare birds	twitcher
coins	numismatist		
dolls houses	miniaturist	teddy bears	arctophile

Ways of foretelling the future

The urge to find out what is going to happen in the future seems to be a fundamental and enduring part of human nature. Over the centuries people have used a variety of supernatural methods with this aim in view, making use of objects and phenomena ranging from the everyday or prosaic (flour, playing cards, keys) to the seemingly bizarre (for example, the cracks on a burnt shoulder blade). The technical term for these practices is **divination**.

Method	Thing used	Method	Thing used
aeromancy	air	lampadomancy	candles and lamps
alectryomancy	a cock and grains of corn	leconomancy	inspecting water in a basin
aleuromancy	flour	lithomancy	stones
ambulomancy	walking	metopomancy	lines or wrinkles on the forehead
arithmancy	numbers		
astragalomancy	dice	molybdomancy	observing the behaviour of molten lead
astrology	the stars		
augury	the flight of birds	myomancy	mice
austromancy	observation of the winds	necromancy	communication with the dead
axinomancy	an axe head		
belomancy	arrows	oenomancy	wine
bibliomancy	books, especially the Bible	omphalomancy	the navel
capnomancy	smoke	oneiromancy	dreams
cartomancy	playing cards	onomancy	people's names
catoptromancy	mirrors	onychomancy	fingernails
cephalomancy	an ass's head	ooscopy	birds' eggs
ceromancy	figures produced by dropping melted wax into water	ophiomancy	snakes
		ornithomancy	the flight and song of birds
		osteomancy	bones
chiromancy	the lines on the palms of the hands	palmistry	lines on the palms of the hands
cleidomancy	a key	pedomancy	the soles of the feet
cleromancy	drawing lots	pegomancy	springs and fountains
cosinomancy	the turning of a sieve	pessomancy	pebbles
crithomancy	meal or grain strewed over sacrificed animals	pyromancy	fire
		rhabdomancy	rods or wands
dactyliomancy	rings	scapulimancy	the cracks in a burnt shoulder blade
gastromancy	the belly		
hydromancy	water	scatomancy	faeces
geomancy	earth	sciomancy	communication with the dead
graptomancy	handwriting		
gyromancy	walking in a circle until dizzy	scyphomancy	a cup
		sideromancy	the stars (or burning straws on red-hot iron)
halomancy	salt		
hieromancy	observing objects offered as religious sacrifices	sortilege	drawing cards at random
		spodomancy	ashes
haruspicy	the entrails of animals	sycomancy	figs or fig leaves
hydromancy	water and tides	tephromancy	ashes
geloscopy	a person's laughter	tyromancy	cheese
ichthyomancy	the heads or entrails of fish	zoomancy	animals

Countries of the world

Country	Capital	Currency unit
Afghanistan	Kabul	afghani = 100 puls
Albania	Tirana	lek = 100 quintars
Algeria	Algiers	dinar = 100 centimes
Andorra	Andorra la Vella	euro = 100 cents
Angola	Luanda	kwanza = 100 lwei
Antigua and Barbuda	St John's	dollar = 100 cents
Argentina	Buenos Aires	peso = 100 centavos
Armenia	Yerevan	dram = 100 luma
Australia	Canberra	dollar = 100 cents
Austria	Vienna	euro = 100 cents
Azerbaijan	Baku	manat = 100 gopik
Bahamas	Nassau	dollar = 100 cents
Bahrain	Manama	dinar = 1,000 fils
Bangladesh	Dhaka	taka = 100 poisha
Barbados	Bridgetown	dollar = 100 cents
Belarus	Minsk	Belarusian rouble
Belgium	Brussels	euro = 100 cents
Belize	Belmopan	dollar = 100 cents
Benin	Porto Novo	franc = 100 centimes
Bhutan	Thimphu	ngultrum = 100 chetrum, Indian rupee
Bolivia	La Paz	boliviano = 100 centavos
Bosnia-Herzegovina	Sarajevo	dinar = 100 paras
Botswana	Gaborone	pula = 100 thebe
Brazil	Brasilia	real = 100 centavos
Brunei	Bandar Seri Begawan	dollar = 100 sen
Bulgaria	Sofia	lev = 100 stotinki
Burkina Faso	Ouagadougou	franc = 100 centimes
Burma (Myanmar)	Pyinmana	kyat = 100 pyas
Burundi	Bujumbura	franc = 100 centimes
Cambodia	Phnom Penh	riel = 100 sen
Cameroon	Yaoundé	franc = 100 centimes
Canada	Ottawa	dollar = 100 cents
Cape Verde Islands	Praia	escudo = 100 centavos
Central African Republic	Bangui	franc = 100 centimes
Chad	N'Djamena	franc = 100 centimes
Chile	Santiago	peso = 100 centavos
China	Beijing	yuan = 10 jiao or 100 fen
Colombia	Bogotá	peso = 100 centavos
Comoros	Moroni	franc = 100 centimes
Congo	Brazzaville	franc = 100 centimes
Congo, Democratic Republic of (Zaire)	Kinshasa	franc = 100 centimes
Costa Rica	San José	colón = 100 centimos
Croatia	Zagreb	kuna = 100 lipa
Cuba	Havana	peso = 100 centavos
Cyprus	Nicosia	pound = 100 cents
Czech Republic	Prague	koruna = 100 halers
Denmark	Copenhagen	krone = 100 øre
Djibouti	Djibouti	franc = 100 centimes

Country	Capital	Currency unit
Dominica	Roseau	dollar = 100 cents
Dominican Republic	Santo Domingo	peso = 100 centavos
Ecuador	Quito	sucre = 100 centavos
Egypt	Cairo	pound = 100 piastres or 1,000 milliemes
El Salvador	San Salvador	colón = 100 centavos
Equatorial Guinea	Malabo	franc = 100 centimes
Eritrea	Asmara	nakfa; Ethiopian birr
Estonia	Tallinn	kroon = 100 sents
Ethiopia	Addis Ababa	birr = 100 cents
Fiji	Suva	dollar = 100 cents
Finland	Helsinki	euro = 100 cents
France	Paris	euro = 100 cents
Gabon	Libreville	franc = 100 centimes
Gambia	Banjul	dalasi = 100 butut
Georgia	Tbilisi	lari = 100 tetri
Germany	Berlin	euro = 100 cents
Ghana	Accra	cedi = 100 pesewas
Greece	Athens	euro = 100 cents
Grenada	St George's	dollar = 100 cents
Guatemala	Guatemala City	quetzal = 100 centavos
Guinea	Conakry	franc = 100 centimes
Guinea-Bissau	Bissau	peso = 100 centavos
Guyana	Georgetown	dollar = 100 cents
Haiti	Port-au-Prince	gourde = 100 centimes
Holland (*see* **Netherlands**)		
Honduras	Tegucigalpa	lempira = 100 centavos
Hungary	Budapest	forint = 100 filler
Iceland	Reykjavik	krona = 100 aurar
India	New Delhi	rupee = 100 paisa
Indonesia	Djakarta	rupiah = 100 sen
Iran	Tehran	rial = 100 dinars
Iraq	Baghdad	dinar = 1,000 fils
Ireland, Republic of	Dublin	euro = 100 cents
Israel	Jerusalem	shekel = 100 agora
Italy	Rome	euro = 100 cents
Ivory Coast	Yamoussoukro	franc = 100 centimes
Jamaica	Kingston	dollar = 100 cents
Japan	Tokyo	yen = 100 sen
Jordan	Amman	dinar = 1,000 fils
Kazakhstan	Astana	tenge = 100 teins
Kenya	Nairobi	shilling = 100 cents
Kiribati	Bairiki	Australian dollar
Kuwait	Kuwait City	dinar = 1,000 fils
Kyrgyzstan	Bishkek	som = 100 tiyin
Laos	Vientiane	kip = 100 ats
Latvia	Riga	lat = 100 santims
Lebanon	Beirut	pound = 100 piastres
Lesotho	Maseru	loti = 100 lisente
Liberia	Monrovia	dollar = 100 cents
Libya	Tripoli	dinar = 1,000 dirhams
Liechtenstein	Vaduz	franc = 100 centimes
Lithuania	Vilnius	litas = 100 centas
Luxembourg	Luxembourg	euro = 100 cents
Macedonia	Skopje	denar = 100 deni

Country	Capital	Currency unit
Madagascar	Antananarivo	franc = 100 centimes
Malawi	Lilongwe	kwacha = 100 tambala
Malaysia	Kuala Lumpur	ringgit = 100 sen
Maldives	Male	rufiyaa = 100 laris
Mali	Bamako	franc = 100 centimes
Malta	Valletta	lira = 100 cents
Marshall Islands	Majuro	US dollar
Mauritania	Nouakchott	ouguiya = 5 khoums
Mauritius	Port Louis	rupee = 100 cents
Mexico	Mexico City	peso = 100 centavos
Micronesia	Kolonia	US dollar
Moldova	Chisinau	leu = 100 bani
Monaco	–	euro = 100 cents
Mongolia	Ulan Bator	tugrik = 100 mongos
Montenegro (see **Union of Serbia and Montenegro**)		
Morocco	Rabat	dirham = 100 centimes
Mozambique	Maputo	metical = 100 centavos
Myanmar (see **Burma**)		
Namibia	Windhoek	dollar = 100 cents
Nauru	–	Australian dollar
Nepal	Kathmandu	rupee = 100 paisa
Netherlands	Amsterdam	euro = 100 cents
New Zealand	Wellington	dollar = 100 cents
Nicaragua	Managua	cordoba = 100 centavos
Niger	Niamey	franc = 100 centimes
Nigeria	Abuja	naira = 100 kobo
North Korea	Pyongyang	won = 100 jun
Norway	Oslo	krone = 100 øre
Oman	Muscat	rial = 1,000 baiza
Pakistan	Islamabad	rupee = 100 paisa
Panama	Panama City	balboa = 100 centésimos
Papua New Guinea	Port Moresby	kina = 100 toea
Paraguay	Asunción	guarani = 100 centimos
Peru	Lima	sol = 100 cents
Philippines	Manila	peso = 100 centavos
Poland	Warsaw	zloty = 100 groszy
Portugal	Lisbon	euro = 100 cents
Qatar	Doha	riyal = 100 dirhams
Romania	Bucharest	leu = 100 bani
Russia	Moscow	rouble = 100 copecks
Rwanda	Kigali	franc = 100 centimes
St Kitts and Nevis	Basseterre	dollar = 100 cents
St Lucia	Castries	dollar = 100 cents
St Vincent and the Grenadines	Kingstown	dollar = 100 cents
Samoa	Apia	tala = 100 sene
San Marino	San Marino	euro = 100 cents
São Tomé and Principe	São Tomé	dobra = 100 centavos
Saudi Arabia	Riyadh	riyal = 20 qursh or 100 halalas
Senegal	Dakar	franc = 100 centimes
Serbia (see **Union of Serbia and Montenegro**)		
Seychelles	Victoria	rupee = 100 cents
Sierra Leone	Freetown	leone = 100 cents
Singapore	Singapore City	dollar = 100 cents
Slovakia	Bratislava	koruna = 100 haliers

Country	Capital	Currency unit
Slovenia	Ljubljana	tolar = 100 stotins
Solomon Islands	Honiara	dollar = 100 cents
Somalia	Mogadishu	shilling = 100 cents
South Africa	Pretoria	rand = 100 cents
South Korea	Seoul	won = 100 jeon
Spain	Madrid	euro = 100 cents
Sri Lanka	Colombo	rupee = 100 cents
Sudan	Khartoum	dinar = 10 pounds
Suriname	Paramaribo	guilder = 100 cents
Swaziland	Mbabane	lilangeni = 100 cents
Sweden	Stockholm	krona = 100 öre
Switzerland	Berne	franc = 100 centimes
Syria	Damascus	pound = 100 piastres
Taiwan	Taipei	New Taiwan dollar = 100 cents
Tajikistan	Dushanbe	somoni = 100 dirams
Tanzania	Dodoma	shilling = 100 cents
Thailand	Bangkok	baht = 100 satangs
Togo	Lomé	franc = 100 centimes
Tonga	Nuku'alofa	pa'anga = 100 seniti
Trinidad and Tobago	Port-of-Spain	dollar = 100 cents
Tunisia	Tunis	dinar = 1,000 milliemes
Turkey	Ankara	lira = 100 kurus
Turkmenistan	Ashgabat	manat = 100 tenesi
Tuvalu	Funafuti	dollar = 100 cents
Uganda	Kampala	shilling = 100 cents
Ukraine	Kiev	hryvna = 100 kopiykas
Union of Serbia and Montenegro	Belgrade	dinar = 100 paras
United Arab Emirates	Abu Dhabi	dirham = 100 fils
United Kingdom	London	pound = 100 pence
United States	Washington DC	dollar = 100 cents
Uruguay	Montevideo	peso = 100 centésimos
Uzbekistan	Tashkent	som = 100 tiyin
Vanuatu	Vila	vatu = 100 centimes
Vatican City	–	euro = 100 cents
Venezuela	Caracas	bolivar = 100 centimos
Vietnam	Hanoi	dong = 100 xu
Yemen	Sana'a	riyal = 100 fils
Zambia	Lusaka	kwacha = 100 ngwee
Zimbabwe	Harare	dollar = 100 cents

Chemical elements and symbols

actinium	Ac	gold	Au	praseodymium	Pr
aluminium	Al	hafnium	Hf	promethium	Pm
americium	Am	hassium	Hs	protactinium	Pa
antimony	Sb	helium	He	radium	Ra
argon	Ar	holmium	Ho	radon	Rn
arsenic	As	hydrogen	H	rhenium	Re
astatine	At	indium	In	rhodium	Rh
barium	Ba	iodine	I	roentgenium	Rg
berkelium	Bk	iridium	Ir	rubidium	Rb
beryllium	Be	iron	Fe	ruthenium	Ru
bismuth	Bi	krypton	Kr	rutherfordium	Rf
bohrium	Bh	lanthanum	La	samarium	Sm
boron	B	lawrencium	Lr	scandium	Sc
bromine	Br	lead	Pb	seaborgium	Sg
cadmium	Cd	lithium	Li	selenium	Se
caesium	Cs	lutetium	Lu	silicon	Si
calcium	Ca	magnesium	Mg	silver	Ag
californium	Cf	manganese	Mn	sodium	Na
carbon	C	meitnerium	Mt	strontium	Sr
cerium	Ce	mendelevium	Md	sulphur	S
chlorine	Cl	mercury	Hg	tantalum	Ta
chromium	Cr	molybdenum	Mo	technetium	Tc
cobalt	Co	neodymium	Nd	tellurium	Te
copper	Cu	neon	Ne	terbium	Tb
curium	Cm	neptunium	Np	thallium	Tl
darmstadtium	Ds	nickel	Ni	thorium	Th
dubnium	Db	niobium	Nb	thulium	Tm
dysprosium	Dy	nitrogen	N	tin	Sn
einsteinium	Es	nobelium	Nb	titanium	Ti
erbium	Er	osmium	Os	tungsten	W
europium	Eu	oxygen	O	uranium	U
fermium	Fm	palladium	Pd	vanadium	V
fluorine	F	phosphorus	P	xenon	Xe
francium	Fr	platinum	Pt	ytterbium	Yb
gadolinium	Gd	plutonium	Pu	yttrium	Y
gallium	Ga	polonium	Po	zinc	Zn
germanium	Ge	potassium	K	zirconium	Zr

Mm

M or **m** noun (plural **Ms** or **M's**) **1** the thirteenth letter of the alphabet. **2** the Roman numeral for 1,000. •**abbreviation 1** Monsieur. **2** motorway. **3** (m) metres. **4** (m) miles. **5** (m) millions.

MA abbreviation Master of Arts.

ma'am noun madam.

mac noun Brit. informal a mackintosh.

macabre /muh-**kah**-bruh/ adjective disturbing and horrifying because concerned with death and injury.

macadam noun broken stone used for surfacing roads and paths.

macadamia noun the round edible nut of an Australian tree.

macaque /muh-**kak**/ noun a monkey with a long face and cheek pouches for holding food.

macaroni noun pasta in the form of narrow tubes.

macaroon noun a light biscuit made with ground almonds or coconut.

macaw /muh-**kaw**/ noun a brightly coloured parrot found in Central and South America.

mace¹ noun **1** a decorated stick carried by an official such as a mayor. **2** (in the past) a heavy club with a spiked metal head.

mace² noun a spice made from the dried outer covering of nutmeg.

Macedonian /mass-i-**doh**-ni-uhn/ noun a person from the republic of Macedonia (formerly part of Yugoslavia), ancient Macedonia, or the modern Greek region of Macedonia. •adjective relating to Macedonia.

macerate /**mass**-uh-rayt/ verb (**macerates, macerating, macerated**) soften food by soaking it in a liquid.
■ maceration noun.

Mach /mak/ noun (**Mach 1, Mach 2,** etc.) the speed of sound, twice the speed of sound, etc.

machete /muh-**shet**-i/ noun a broad, heavy knife used as a tool or weapon.

Machiavellian /ma-ki-uh-**vel**-li-uhn/ adjective using cunning and underhand methods to get what you want.

machinations /ma-shi-**nay**-shuhnz/ plural noun plots and scheming.

machine noun **1** a mechanical device for performing a particular task. **2** an efficient group of influential people. •verb (**machines, machining, machined**) make or work on something with a machine.
□ machine gun a gun that fires many bullets in rapid succession. machine-readable in a form that a computer can process.

machinery noun **1** machines as a whole, or the parts of a machine. **2** an organized system or structure.

machinist noun a person who operates a machine or makes machinery.

machismo /muh-**kiz**-moh/ noun strong or aggressive male pride.

macho /**mach**-oh/ adjective showing aggressive pride in being male.

mackerel noun an edible sea fish.

mackintosh or **macintosh** noun Brit. a full-length waterproof coat.

macramé /muh-**krah**-mi/ noun the craft of knotting cord to make decorative articles.

macrobiotic adjective (of diet) consisting of foods grown or produced without the use of chemicals.

macrocosm noun the whole of a complex structure, contrasted with a small or representative part of it (a microcosm).

m

THESAURUS

machine noun **1** device, appliance, apparatus, engine, gadget, mechanism. **2** *an efficient publicity machine:* organization, system, structure, machinery; informal set-up.

machinery noun **1** equipment, apparatus, plant, hardware, gear, gadgetry, technology.

2 *the machinery of local government:* workings, organization, system, structure, institution; informal set-up.

macho adjective manly, male, masculine, virile, red-blooded; informal butch, laddish. OPPOSITES wimpish.

mad adjective (**madder, maddest**) **1** seriously mentally ill. **2** very foolish. **3** done without thought or control. **4** informal very enthusiastic about something. **5** informal very angry.
□ **mad cow disease** BSE.
■ **madly** adverb **madness** noun.

Madagascan noun a person from Madagascar. • adjective relating to Madagascar.

madam noun **1** a polite form of address for a woman. **2** Brit. informal a bossy or cheeky girl. **3** a woman who runs a brothel.

Madame /muh-**dam**/ noun (plural **Mesdames** /may-**dam**/) a form of address for a French woman.

madcap adjective acting without thought; reckless.

madden verb make someone mad or very annoyed.

madder noun a red dye obtained from the roots of a plant.

made past and past participle of **MAKE**.

Madeira noun a strong sweet white wine from the island of Madeira.
□ **Madeira cake** Brit. a rich kind of sponge cake.

Mademoiselle /ma-duh-mwah-**zel**/ noun (plural **Mesdemoiselles** /may-duh-mwa-**zel**/)

a form of address for an unmarried French woman.

Madonna noun (**the Madonna**) the Virgin Mary.

madrigal noun a 16th- or 17th-century song for several voices without instrumental accompaniment.

maelstrom /**mayl**-struhm/ noun **1** a situation of confusion or upheaval. **2** a powerful whirlpool.

maestro /**my**-stroh/ noun (plural **maestros**) a famous and talented man, especially a classical musician.

Mafia noun **1** (**the Mafia**) an international criminal organization originating in Sicily. **2** (**mafia**) a powerful group who secretly influence matters.

Mafioso /ma-fi-**oh**-soh/ noun (plural **Mafiosi** /ma-fi-**oh**-si/) a member of the Mafia.

magazine noun **1** a weekly or monthly publication that contains articles and pictures. **2** the part of a gun that holds bullets before they are fired. **3** a store for weapons, ammunition, and explosives.

magenta noun a light crimson.

maggot noun the soft-bodied larva of a fly or other insect.

Magi /**may**-jy/ plural noun the three wise men from the East who brought gifts to the infant Jesus.

magic noun **1** the use of mysterious or

THESAURUS

mad adjective **1** *he was killed by his mad brother:* insane, out of your mind, deranged, demented, crazed, lunatic, unbalanced, unhinged; informal crazy, mental, off your head, round the bend; Brit. informal barmy, crackers, barking (mad), potty, round the twist. **2** (informal) *I'm still mad at him:* angry, furious, infuriated, enraged, fuming, incensed, beside yourself; informal livid, spare; N. Amer. informal sore. **3** *some mad scheme:* foolish, insane, stupid, lunatic, idiotic, absurd, silly, asinine, wild; informal crazy, crackpot; Brit. informal daft. **4** (informal) *he's mad about jazz:* passionate, fanatical, ardent, fervent, devoted to, infatuated with, in love with; informal crazy, dotty, nuts, wild, hooked on; Brit. informal potty; N. Amer. informal nutso. **5** *it was a mad dash to get ready:* frenzied, frantic, frenetic, feverish, hysterical, wild, hectic, manic.
OPPOSITES sane, pleased, sensible, indifferent, calm.

madden verb infuriate, exasperate, irritate, incense, anger, enrage, provoke, make someone see red; informal aggravate, make someone's blood boil; Brit. informal nark; N. Amer. informal tee off, tick off.
OPPOSITES calm.

madly adverb **1** *she was smiling madly:* insanely, wildly; informal crazily. **2** *it was*

fun, hurtling madly downhill: furiously, hurriedly, speedily, energetically; informal like mad, like crazy. **3** (informal) *he loved her madly:* intensely, fervently, wildly, to distraction. **4** (informal) *his job isn't madly exciting:* very, tremendously, wildly, all that, hugely; informal awfully, terribly.
OPPOSITES sanely, slowly, slightly.

madman, madwoman noun lunatic, maniac, psychotic, psychopath; informal loony, nut, nutcase, head case; Brit. informal nutter; N. Amer. informal screwball.

madness noun **1** *today madness is called mental illness:* insanity, mental illness, dementia, derangement, lunacy, mania, psychosis. **2** *it would be madness to do otherwise:* folly, foolishness, idiocy, stupidity, insanity, lunacy. **3** *it's absolute madness in here:* bedlam, mayhem, chaos, pandemonium, uproar, turmoil, all hell broken loose; N. Amer. three-ring circus.
OPPOSITES sanity, sense.

magazine noun journal, periodical, supplement, colour supplement; informal glossy, mag, 'zine.

magic noun **1** *do you believe in magic?* sorcery, witchcraft, wizardry, necromancy, enchantment, the supernatural, occultism, the occult, black magic, the black arts, voodoo. **2** *he does magic at children's parties:* conjuring (tricks), illusion, sleight

supernatural forces to influence events.
2 conjuring tricks performed to entertain
people. **3** a mysterious or wonderful
quality. •adjective **1** having supernatural
powers. **2** informal wonderful. •verb (**magics,
magicking, magicked**) use magic to make
something happen.

magical adjective **1** relating to or using
magic. **2** wonderful; very enjoyable.
■ **magically** adverb.

magician noun **1** a person with magic
powers. **2** a conjuror.

magisterial /ma-ji-**steer**-i-uhl/ adjective
1 having or showing great authority.
2 relating to a magistrate.

magistrate noun an official who judges
minor cases and holds preliminary
hearings.
■ **magistracy** noun (plural **magistracies**).

magma /**mag**-muh/ noun very hot fluid or
semi-fluid rock under the earth's crust.

magnanimous adjective generous or
forgiving towards a rival or enemy.
■ **magnanimity** noun.

magnate noun a wealthy and influential
person, especially in business.

magnesium /mag-**nee**-zi-uhm/ noun a
silvery-white substance which burns with a
brilliant white flame.

magnet noun **1** a piece of iron that attracts
objects containing iron and that points
north and south when suspended. **2** (in the
Indian subcontinent and SE Asia) a person,
place, etc. that someone or something is
strongly attracted to.

magnetic adjective **1** having the property of
magnetism. **2** very attractive.
□ **magnetic pole** each of the points near
the geographical North and South Poles,
which the needle of a compass points to.
magnetic tape tape used in recording

sound, pictures, or computer data.
■ **magnetically** adverb.

magnetism noun **1** the property displayed
by magnets of attracting or pushing away
metal objects. **2** the ability to attract and
charm people.

magnetize or **magnetise** verb
(**magnetizes, magnetizing, magnetized**)
make magnetic.

magneto /mag-**nee**-toh/ noun (plural
magnetos) a small generator that uses a
magnet to produce pulses of electricity.

magnification noun **1** the action of
magnifying something. **2** the degree to
which something is magnified.

magnificent adjective **1** very attractive and
impressive; splendid. **2** very good.
■ **magnificence** noun **magnificently** adverb.

magnify verb (**magnifies, magnifying,
magnified**) **1** make something appear
larger than it is with a lens or microscope.
2 make larger or stronger. **3** old use praise.
□ **magnifying glass** a lens used to help you
see something very small by magnifying it.

magnitude noun **1** great size or
importance. **2** size.

magnolia noun a tree or shrub with large
white or pale pink flowers.

magnum noun (plural **magnums**) a wine
bottle of twice the standard size, normally
1½ litres.

magnum opus noun a work of art, music,
or literature which is the most important
that a person has produced.

magpie noun **1** a black and white bird with
a long tail. **2** a person who collects things
of little use or value.

Magyar /**mag**-yar/ noun **1** a member of the
predominant people in Hungary. **2** the
Hungarian language.

m

THESAURUS

of hand; formal prestidigitation. **3** *the magic
of the stage:* allure, excitement,
fascination, charm, glamour. **4** *the old
Liverpool magic:* brilliance, skill,
accomplishment, expertise, art, finesse,
talent.

magical adjective **1** *magical powers:*
supernatural, magic, mystical, other-
worldly. **2** *the news had a magical effect:*
extraordinary, remarkable, incredible,
amazing, astonishing, astounding,
staggering, miraculous. **3** *this magical
island:* enchanting, entrancing,
spellbinding, bewitching, fascinating,
captivating, alluring, enthralling,
charming, lovely, delightful, beautiful;
informal heavenly, gorgeous.
OPPOSITES predictable, boring.

magician noun **1** sorcerer, sorceress, witch,
wizard, warlock, enchanter, enchantress,

necromancer. **2** conjuror, illusionist; formal
prestidigitator.

magnetic adjective attractive, irresistible,
seductive, charismatic, hypnotic, alluring,
fascinating, captivating.
OPPOSITES repellent.

magnificent adjective **1** *a magnificent view:*
splendid, spectacular, impressive, striking,
glorious, superb, majestic, awe-inspiring,
breathtaking. **2** *a magnificent apartment:*
sumptuous, grand, impressive, imposing,
monumental, palatial, opulent, luxurious,
lavish, rich, dazzling, beautiful; informal
posh, classy; Brit. informal swish.
OPPOSITES uninspiring, modest, tawdry.

magnify verb enlarge, increase, augment,
extend, expand, boost, enhance, maximize,
amplify, intensify; informal blow up.
OPPOSITES reduce, minimize, understate.

maharaja or **maharajah** noun (in the past) an Indian prince.

mah-jong or **mah-jongg** /mah-jong/ noun a Chinese game played with small rectangular tiles.

mahogany noun 1 hard reddish-brown wood from a tropical tree. 2 a rich reddish-brown colour.

mahout /muh-howt/ noun (in the Indian subcontinent and SE Asia) a person who works with elephants.

maid noun 1 a female servant. 2 old use a girl or young unmarried woman.

maiden noun 1 old use a girl or young unmarried woman. 2 (also **maiden over**) Cricket an over in which no runs are scored. • adjective first of its kind: *a maiden voyage*. □ **maiden name** the surname of a married woman before her marriage.

maidenhair fern noun a fern with long, thin stems and delicate leaves.

maidenhead noun old use a girl's or woman's virginity.

mail¹ noun 1 letters and parcels sent by post. 2 the postal system. 3 email. • verb 1 send by post. 2 send post or email to. □ **mail order** the buying or selling of goods by post.

mail² noun (in the past) armour made of metal rings or plates.

mailshot noun Brit. a piece of advertising material posted to a large number of people.

maim verb inflict a permanent injury on.

main adjective greatest or most important. • noun 1 a chief water or gas pipe or electricity cable. 2 (**the mains**) Brit. the network of pipes and cables supplying water, gas, and electricity. □ **in the main** on the whole.

mainframe noun a large high-speed computer supporting a network of workstations.

mainland noun the main area of land of a country, not including islands and separate territories.

mainly adverb for the most part; chiefly.

mainspring noun the most important or influential part of something.

mainstay noun a thing on which something depends or is based.

mainstream noun the ideas, attitudes, or activities that are shared by most people.

maintain verb 1 keep something in the same state or at the same level. 2 regularly check and repair a building, machine, etc. 3 provide someone with financial support. 4 strongly state that something is the case.

maintenance noun 1 the action of maintaining something. 2 Brit. financial support that someone gives to their former husband or wife after divorce.

☑ -ten-, not -tain-: maintenance.

maisonette noun a flat on two storeys of a larger building.

maize noun Brit. a cereal plant whose large yellow grains are eaten as a vegetable.

majestic adjective impressively grand or beautiful. ■ **majestically** adverb.

majesty noun (plural **majesties**) 1 impressive

THESAURUS

mail noun 1 *the mail arrived:* post, letters, correspondence, email. 2 *we sent it by mail:* post, postal system, postal service, post office; informal snail mail; N. Amer. the mails. • verb *we mailed the parcels:* send, post, dispatch, forward, ship, email.

maim verb injure, wound, cripple, disable, incapacitate, mutilate, disfigure, mangle.

main adjective principal, chief, leading, foremost, most important, major, dominant, central, focal, key, prime, primary, first, fundamental, predominant, pre-eminent.
OPPOSITES subsidiary, minor.

mainly adverb mostly, for the most part, in the main, on the whole, largely, by and large, to a large extent, predominantly, chiefly, principally, primarily.

maintain verb 1 *they wanted to maintain peace:* preserve, conserve, keep, retain, keep going, prolong, perpetuate, sustain, carry on, continue. 2 *the council maintains the roads:* look after, service, care for, take care of. 3 *the costs of maintaining a family:* support, provide for, keep, sustain. 4 *he maintains that he is innocent:* insist, declare, assert, protest, affirm, profess, claim, contend, argue.
OPPOSITES break, discontinue, neglect, deny.

maintenance noun 1 *the maintenance of peace:* preservation, conservation, keeping, carrying on, prolongation, continuation. 2 *car maintenance:* servicing, service, repair(s), running repairs, care. 3 *the maintenance of his children:* support, keeping, upkeep, sustenance, nurture. 4 *absent fathers are forced to pay maintenance:* financial support, child support, alimony, upkeep.
OPPOSITES breakdown, discontinuation, neglect.

majestic adjective stately, dignified, distinguished, solemn, magnificent, grand, splendid, glorious, impressive, noble, awe-inspiring, monumental, palatial, imposing.
OPPOSITES modest, wretched.

majesty noun stateliness, dignity, solemnity, magnificence, pomp, grandeur, beauty or grandeur. **2** (**His, Your,** etc. **Majesty**) a title given to a king or queen or their wife or widow.

major adjective **1** important or serious. **2** greater or more important; main. **3** Music (of a scale) having intervals of a semitone between the third and fourth, and seventh and eighth notes. •noun **1** the rank of army officer above captain. **2** N. Amer. a student specializing in a particular subject. •verb (**major in**) N. Amer. & Austral./NZ specialize in a particular subject at college or university. □ **major general** the rank of army officer above brigadier.

major-domo noun (plural **major-domos**) a person employed to manage a large household.

majority noun (plural **majorities**) **1** the greater number. **2** Brit. the number of votes by which one party or candidate in an election defeats the opposition. **3** the age when a person is legally an adult, usually 18 or 21.

make verb (**makes, making, made**) **1** form something by putting parts together or mixing substances. **2** cause something to happen or come into existence. **3** force someone to do something. **4** add up to. **5** be suitable as. **6** estimate as or decide on. **7** earn money or profit. **8** arrive at or achieve. **9** prepare to go in a particular direction or to do something. •noun the manufacturer or trade name of a product. □ **make-believe** fantasy or pretence. **make do** manage with something that is not satisfactory. **make for** move towards. **make it** become successful. **make off** leave hurriedly. **make off with** steal. **make out** claim or pretend to be. **make something out** manage with difficulty to see, hear, or understand something. **make up** be friendly again after a quarrel. **make someone up** apply cosmetics to someone. **make something up 1** put something together from parts or ingredients. **2** invent a story. **make-up** cosmetics applied to the face. **make up for** compensate for. **make up your mind** make a decision. **on the make** informal trying to

THESAURUS

grandness, splendour, glory, nobility, impressiveness.
OPPOSITES modesty, wretchedness.

major adjective **1** *the major English poets:* greatest, best, finest, most important, chief, main, prime, principal, leading, foremost, outstanding, pre-eminent. **2** *a major factor:* crucial, vital, important, big, significant, considerable, weighty, serious, key, utmost, great, paramount, prime.
OPPOSITES minor, trivial.

majority noun **1** *the majority of cases:* most, bulk, mass, larger part/number, best/better part, more than half, lion's share, (main) body, preponderance, predominance. **2** *a majority in the election:* (winning) margin, landslide, whitewash.
OPPOSITES minority.

make verb **1** *he makes models:* construct, build, assemble, put together, manufacture, produce, fabricate, create, form, fashion, model, improvise. **2** *she made me drink it:* force, compel, coerce, press, drive, pressurize, oblige, require; informal railroad, steamroller. **3** *don't make such a noise:* cause, create, produce, generate, effect. **4** *she made a little bow:* perform, execute, give, do, accomplish, achieve, bring off, carry out. **5** *they made him chairman:* appoint, designate, name, nominate, select, elect, vote in. **6** *he's made a lot of money:* acquire, obtain, gain, get, secure, win, earn. **7** *he made tea:* prepare, get ready, put together, concoct, cook, dish up, throw together, whip up, brew; informal fix.
OPPOSITES destroy, lose.

•noun brand, marque, label.
□ **make for contribute to,** be conducive to, produce, promote, facilitate, foster. **make it 1** *he never made it as a singer:* succeed, be a success, make good; informal make the grade, arrive. **2** *she's very ill—is she going to make it?* survive, pull through, get better, recover. **make off run away/off,** take to your heels, flee, take off, take flight, bolt; informal clear off/out, beat it, split, scram; Brit. informal scarper, do a runner; N. Amer. informal take a powder; Austral./NZ informal shoot through. **make something out 1** *I could just make out a figure in the distance:* see, discern, distinguish, detect, observe, recognize. **2** *he couldn't make out what she was saying:* understand, grasp, follow, work out, make sense of, interpret, decipher, make head or tail of, catch. **3** *she made out that he was violent:* allege, claim, suggest, imply, hint, insinuate, indicate, intimate. **make up 1** *let's kiss and make up:* be friends again, bury the hatchet, make peace, forgive and forget, shake hands, settle your differences. **2** *she tried to make up for what she'd said:* atone, make amends, compensate. **make something up 1** *exports make up 42% of earnings:* comprise, form, compose, constitute, account for. **2** *he made up an excuse:* invent, fabricate, concoct, think up; informal cook up. **make up for** *job satisfaction can make up for low pay:* offset, counterbalance, counteract, compensate for, cancel out.

maker noun creator, manufacturer,

m

make money or gain an advantage.
■ **maker** noun.

makeover noun a transformation of someone's appearance with cosmetics, hairstyling, and clothes.

makeshift adjective temporary and improvised.

makeweight noun an unimportant person or thing that is only added or included to make up the correct number, amount, etc.

malachite /**ma**-luh-kyt/ noun a bright green mineral.

maladjusted adjective not able to cope well with normal life.

maladroit /mal-uh-**droyt**/ adjective clumsy.

malady noun (plural **maladies**) literary a disease or illness.

malaise /ma-**layz**/ noun **1** a general feeling of illness or low spirits. **2** a long-standing problem that is difficult to identify.

malapropism /**mal**-uh-prop-i-z'm/ noun the mistaken use of a word in place of a similar-sounding one.

malaria noun a disease that causes fever and is transmitted by the bite of some mosquitoes.
■ **malarial** adjective.

malarkey noun informal nonsense.

Malawian /muh-**lah**-wi-uhn/ noun a person from Malawi, a country in Africa. • adjective relating to Malawi.

Malay noun **1** a member of a people inhabiting Malaysia and Indonesia. **2** the language of the Malays.

Malayan noun = MALAY. • adjective relating to Malays or Malaya (which is now part of Malaysia).

Malaysian noun a person from Malaysia. • adjective relating to Malaysia.

malcontent noun a person who is dissatisfied and rebellious.

Maldivian /mawl-**div**-i-uhn/ noun a person from the Maldives. • adjective relating to the Maldives.

male adjective **1** of the sex that can fertilize or inseminate the female. **2** having to do

with men. **3** (of a plant or flower) having stamens but not a pistil. **4** (of a fitting) made to fit inside a corresponding part. • noun a male person, animal, or plant.

malediction /mal-i-**dik**-sh'n/ noun formal a curse.

malefactor /**mal**-i-fak-ter/ noun formal a criminal or wrongdoer.

malevolent /muh-**lev**-uh-luhnt/ adjective wishing to harm other people.
■ **malevolence** noun.

malformation noun the state of being abnormally shaped or formed.
■ **malformed** adjective.

malfunction verb (of equipment or machinery) fail to function normally. • noun a failure to function normally.

Malian /**mah**-li-uhn/ noun a person from Mali, a country in West Africa. • adjective relating to Mali.

malice noun the desire to harm someone.

malicious adjective meaning to harm other people.
■ **maliciously** adverb.

malign /muh-**lyn**/ adjective harmful or evil. • verb say unpleasant things about.
■ **malignity** /muh-**lig**-ni-ti/ noun.

malignancy noun (plural **malignancies**) **1** a cancerous growth. **2** the quality of being harmful or evil.

malignant adjective **1** (of a tumour) cancerous. **2** having or showing a desire to harm other people.

malinger verb (**malingers, malingering, malingered**) pretend to be ill in order to avoid work.
■ **malingerer** noun.

mall /mawl/ noun **1** a large enclosed shopping area. **2** a sheltered walk.

mallard noun a kind of duck, the male of which has a dark green head.

malleable /**mal**-li-uh-b'l/ adjective **1** able to be hammered or pressed into shape. **2** easily influenced.

mallet noun **1** a hammer with a large wooden head. **2** a wooden stick with a

THESAURUS

constructor, builder, producer.

makeshift adjective **temporary**, provisional, stopgap, standby, rough and ready, improvised, ad hoc.
OPPOSITES permanent.

make-up noun **1** *she used too much make-up:* **cosmetics**; informal warpaint, slap. **2** *the cellular make-up of plants:* **composition**, constitution, structure, configuration, arrangement. **3** *jealousy isn't part of his make-up:* **character**, nature, temperament, personality, mentality, persona.

makings plural noun qualities,

characteristics, ingredients, potential, capacity, capability, stuff.

male adjective **masculine**, manly, virile, macho.
OPPOSITES female.

malfunction verb *the computer has malfunctioned:* **crash**, go wrong, break down, fail, stop working; informal conk out, go kaput; Brit. informal play up, pack up.

malicious adjective **spiteful**, malevolent, vindictive, vengeful, resentful, malign, nasty, hurtful, cruel.
OPPOSITES benevolent.

head like a hammer, for hitting a croquet or polo ball.

mallow noun a plant with pink or purple flowers.

malnourished adjective suffering from malnutrition.

malnutrition noun bad health caused by not having enough food, or not enough of the right food.

malodorous adjective smelling very unpleasant.

malpractice noun illegal, corrupt, or careless behaviour by a professional person.

malt noun barley or other grain that has been soaked in water and then dried.
■ **malted** adjective.

maltreat verb treat badly or cruelly.
■ **maltreatment** noun.

mama or **mamma** noun dated or N. Amer. your mother.

mamba noun a large, highly poisonous African snake.

mammal noun a warm-blooded animal that has hair or fur, produces milk, and gives birth to live young.
■ **mammalian** adjective.

mammary adjective relating to the breasts or the milk-producing organs of other mammals.

Mammon noun money thought of as being worshipped like a god.

mammoth noun a large extinct form of elephant with a hairy coat and long curved tusks. •adjective huge.

man noun (plural **men**) **1** an adult human male. **2** a person. **3** human beings in general. **4** a figure or token used in a board game. •verb (**mans, manning, manned**) provide a place or machine with people to operate or defend it.
□ **man-made** made or caused by human beings. **man-of-war** historical an armed sailing ship.
■ **manhood** noun.

manacle noun a metal band fastened round a person's hands or ankles to restrict their movement. •verb (**manacles, manacling, manacled**) restrict someone with manacles.

manage verb (**manages, managing, managed**) **1** be in charge of people or an organization. **2** succeed in doing. **3** be able to cope despite difficulties. **4** control the use of money or other resources.
■ **manageable** adjective.

management noun **1** the action of managing. **2** the managers of an organization.

manager noun **1** a person who manages staff, an organization, or a sports team. **2** a person in charge of the business affairs of a performer, group of musicians, etc.
■ **managerial** adjective.

manageress noun a woman who manages a business.

manatee /man-uh-tee/ noun a large plant-eating animal that lives in tropical seas.

mandarin noun **1** (**Mandarin**) the official form of the Chinese language. **2** (in the past) a high-ranking Chinese official. **3** a powerful official. **4** a small citrus fruit with a loose yellow-orange skin.

m

THESAURUS

maltreat verb ill-treat, mistreat, abuse, ill-use, mishandle, persecute, molest.

man noun **1** *a handsome man:* male, adult male, gentleman, fellow, youth; informal guy, gent; Brit. informal bloke, chap, lad; N. Amer. informal dude, hombre. **2** *all men are mortal:* human being, human, person, mortal, individual, soul. **3** *the evolution of man:* the human race, the human species, Homo sapiens, humankind, humanity, human beings, humans, people, mankind.
•verb **1** *the office is manned from 9 to 5:* staff, crew, occupy, people. **2** *firemen manned the pumps:* operate, work, use.

manage verb **1** *she manages a staff of 80:* be in charge of, run, head, direct, control, preside over, lead, govern, rule, command, supervise, oversee, administer; informal head up. **2** *how much work can you manage this week?* accomplish, achieve, carry out, perform, undertake, deal with, cope with, get through. **3** *will you be able to manage without him?* cope, get along/on, make do, do all right, carry on, survive, get by,

muddle through/along, make ends meet; informal make out, hack it.

management noun **1** *he's responsible for the management of the firm:* administration, running, managing, organization, direction, leadership, control, governance, rule, command, supervision, guidance, operation. **2** *workers are in dispute with the management:* managers, employers, directors, board, directorate, executive, administration; informal bosses. OPPOSITES employees, workforce.

manager noun executive, head, supervisor, principal, director, superintendent, foreman, forewoman, overseer, organizer, administrator; informal boss, chief, governor; Brit. informal gaffer, guv'nor.

mandate noun **1** *he sought a mandate for his policies:* authority, approval, ratification, endorsement, sanction, authorization. **2** *a mandate from the UN:* instruction, directive, decree, command, order, injunction.

mandate noun /**man**-dayt/ **1** an official order or permission to do something. **2** the authority to carry out a policy that is given by voters to the winner of an election. • verb /man-**dayt**/ (**mandates, mandating, mandated**) give someone authority to do something.

mandatory /**man**-duh-tuh-ri/ adjective required by law or rules; compulsory.

mandible noun **1** the lower jawbone in mammals or fish. **2** either of the upper and lower parts of a bird's beak. **3** either of the parts of an insect's mouth that crush its food.

mandolin noun a musical instrument with a rounded back and metal strings.

mandrake noun a plant whose root is used in herbal medicine and magic.

mandrill noun a large baboon with a red and blue face.

mane noun **1** a growth of long hair on the neck of a horse, lion, etc. **2** a person's long hair.

maneuver US spelling of MANOEUVRE.

manful adjective brave and determined. ■ **manfully** adverb.

manganese noun a hard grey metallic element.

mange noun a skin disease of some animals that causes itching and hair loss.

mangel-wurzel noun a variety of beet grown as feed for farm animals.

manger noun a long trough from which horses or cattle eat.

mangetout /monz*h*-too/ noun (plural **mangetout** or **mangetouts** /monz*h*-too/) chiefly Brit. a variety of pea with an edible pod.

mangle verb (**mangles, mangling, mangled**) destroy or severely damage by crushing or twisting. • noun a machine with rollers for squeezing wet laundry to remove the water.

mango noun (plural **mangoes** or **mangos**) a tropical fruit with yellow flesh.

mangrove noun a tropical tree or shrub found in coastal swamps.

mangy /**mayn**-ji/ adjective **1** (of an animal) having mange. **2** in bad condition; shabby.

manhandle verb (**manhandles, manhandling, manhandled**) **1** move a heavy object with effort. **2** push or drag someone roughly.

manhole noun a covered opening giving access to a sewer or other underground structure.

mania /**may**-ni-uh/ noun **1** mental illness in which a person imagines things and has periods of wild excitement. **2** an extreme enthusiasm.

maniac /**may**-ni-ak/ noun **1** a person who behaves in a very wild or violent way. **2** informal a person who is very enthusiastic about something. ■ **maniacal** /muh-**ny**-uh-k'l/ adjective.

manic adjective **1** having to do with mania. **2** showing wild excitement and energy. □ **manic depression** a mental disorder with alternating periods of excitement and depression. ■ **manically** adverb.

manicure noun treatment to improve the appearance of the hands and nails. ■ **manicured** adjective **manicurist** noun.

manifest adjective clear and obvious. • verb **1** show or display. **2** appear; become apparent. • noun a document listing the cargo, crew, and passengers of a ship or aircraft. ■ **manifestly** adverb.

manifestation noun **1** a sign or evidence of something. **2** an appearance of a ghost or spirit.

manifesto noun (plural **manifestos**) a public declaration of the policy and aims of a political party.

manifold adjective of many kinds. • noun a

m

THESAURUS

mandatory adjective obligatory, compulsory, binding, required, requisite, necessary.
OPPOSITES optional.

mania noun obsession, compulsion, fixation, fetish, fascination, preoccupation, passion, enthusiasm, desire, urge, craving, craze, fad, rage; informal thing.

maniac noun lunatic, madman, madwoman, psychopath; informal loony, nutcase, nut, head case, headbanger, sicko; Brit. informal nutter; N. Amer. informal screwball.

manifest verb display, show, exhibit, demonstrate, betray, present, reveal.
OPPOSITES hide.
• adjective obvious, clear, plain, apparent,

evident, patent, distinct, definite, blatant, overt, transparent, conspicuous, undisguised.
OPPOSITES secret.

manifestation noun **1** *the manifestation of anxiety:* display, demonstration, show, exhibition, presentation. **2** *manifestations of global warming:* sign, indication, evidence, symptom, testimony, proof, mark, reflection, example, instance.

manipulate verb **1** *he manipulated some levers:* operate, work, turn, pull, push, twist, slide. **2** *the government tried to manipulate the situation:* control, influence, use to your advantage, exploit, twist.

pipe with several openings, especially in a car engine.

manikin noun a very small person.

Manila or **Manilla** noun strong brown paper, used especially for envelopes.

manioc /man-i-ok/ = CASSAVA.

manipulate verb (**manipulates, manipulating, manipulated**) 1 handle skilfully. 2 control or influence in a clever or underhand way.
∎ **manipulation** noun **manipulator** noun.

manipulative adjective manipulating other people in a clever or underhand way.

mankind noun human beings as a whole.

manky adjective Brit. informal dirty or of bad quality.

manly adjective (**manlier, manliest**) 1 having good qualities associated with men, such as courage and strength. 2 suitable for a man.
∎ **manliness** noun.

manna noun 1 (in the Bible) the substance supplied by God as food to the Israelites in the wilderness. 2 something unexpected and beneficial.

mannequin /man-ni-kin/ noun a dummy used to display clothes in a shop window.

manner noun 1 a way in which something is done or happens. 2 a person's outward behaviour. 3 (**manners**) polite social behaviour. 4 literary a kind or sort.

mannered adjective 1 behaving in a particular way: *a well-mannered girl.* 2 artificial and exaggerated.

mannerism noun a distinctive gesture or way of speaking.

mannerly adjective well mannered; polite.

mannish adjective (of a woman) like a man in appearance or behaviour.

manoeuvre /muh-**noo**-ver/ (US spelling **maneuver**) noun 1 a movement or series of moves needing skill and care. 2 a carefully planned scheme. 3 (**manoeuvres**) a large-scale military exercise. •verb (**manoeuvres, manoeuvring, manoeuvred**) 1 make a movement or series of moves skilfully and carefully. 2 cleverly influence someone or something in order to achieve an aim.
∎ **manoeuvrable** adjective.

☑ the British spelling has -*oeu*- in the middle and -*re* at the end: man*oeu*vre.

manometer noun an instrument for measuring the pressure of fluids.

manor noun a large country house with lands.
∎ **manorial** adjective.

manpower noun the number of people working or available for work.

manse noun the house provided for a minister of certain Christian Churches.

mansion noun a large, impressive house.

manslaughter noun the crime of killing a person without meaning to do so.

mantel noun a mantelpiece or mantelshelf.

mantelpiece noun 1 a structure surrounding a fireplace. 2 (also **mantelshelf**) a shelf forming the top of a mantelpiece.

mantilla /man-**til**-luh/ noun a lace or silk scarf worn by Spanish women over the hair and shoulders.

m

THESAURUS

mankind noun the human race, humankind, humanity, human beings, humans, Homo sapiens, people, man, men and women.

manly adjective virile, masculine, strong, all-male, red-blooded, muscular, muscly, strapping, well built, rugged, tough, powerful, brawny; informal hunky.
OPPOSITES effeminate.

man-made adjective artificial, synthetic, manufactured, imitation, ersatz, simulated, mock, fake.
OPPOSITES natural, real.

manner noun 1 *it was dealt with in a very efficient manner:* way, fashion, mode, means, method, system, style, approach, technique, procedure, process. 2 *her rather unfriendly manner:* behaviour, attitude, demeanour, air, aspect, bearing, conduct. 3 *the life and manners of Victorian society:* customs, habits, ways, practices, mores, conventions, usages. 4 *you ought to teach him some manners:* etiquette, social graces,

protocol, politeness, decorum, propriety, civility, Ps and Qs.

mannerism noun idiosyncrasy, quirk, oddity, foible, trait, peculiarity, habit, characteristic.

manoeuvre verb 1 *I manoeuvred the car into the space:* steer, guide, drive, negotiate, navigate, pilot, direct, manipulate, move, work. 2 *he manoeuvred things to suit himself:* manipulate, contrive, manage, engineer, fix, organize, arrange, orchestrate, choreograph, stage-manage; informal wangle.
•noun 1 *a tricky parking manoeuvre:* operation, exercise, move, movement, action. 2 *diplomatic manoeuvres:* stratagem, tactic, gambit, ploy, trick, dodge, ruse, scheme, device, plot, machination, artifice, subterfuge, intrigue.

mansion noun country house, stately home, hall, manor house; informal palace, pile.
OPPOSITES hovel.

mantis or **praying mantis** noun (plural mantis or mantises) a large insect that waits for its prey with its forelegs folded like hands in prayer.

mantle noun 1 a woman's loose sleeveless cloak. 2 a close covering, e.g. of snow. 3 a cover around a gas jet that produces a glowing light when heated. 4 a role or responsibility that passes from one person to another. 5 the region of very hot, dense rock between the earth's crust and its core.

mantra noun a word or sound repeated to aid concentration when meditating.

manual adjective 1 having to do with the hands. 2 operated by or using the hands. • noun a book giving instructions or information. ■ **manually** adverb.

manufacture verb (manufactures, manufacturing, manufactured) 1 make something on a large scale using machinery. 2 invent evidence or a story. • noun the manufacturing of things. ■ **manufacturer** noun.

manure noun animal dung used for fertilizing land.

manuscript noun 1 a handwritten book, document, etc. 2 an author's handwritten or typed work, before printing and publication.

Manx adjective relating to the Isle of Man. □ Manx cat a breed of cat that has no tail.

many determiner, pronoun, & adjective a large number of. • noun (the many) the majority of people.

Maori /mow-ri/ noun (plural Maori or Maoris)

a member of the aboriginal people of New Zealand.

map noun a flat diagram of an area showing physical features, cities, roads, etc. • verb (maps, mapping, mapped) 1 show something on a map. 2 (map something out) plan something in detail.

maple noun a tree with five-pointed leaves.

mar verb (mars, marring, marred) spoil the appearance or quality of.

maraca /muh-**rak**-uh/ noun a container filled with small beans or stones, shaken as a musical instrument.

marathon noun 1 a long-distance running race, strictly one of 26 miles 385 yards (42.195 km). 2 a long-lasting and difficult task.

maraud verb go about a place in search of things to steal or people to attack. ■ **marauder** noun.

marble noun 1 a hard stone, usually white with coloured streaks, which can be polished and used in sculpture and building. 2 a small ball of coloured glass used as a toy.

marbled adjective patterned with coloured streaks.

marcasite /**mar**-kuh-syt, **mar**-kuh-zeet/ noun a semi-precious stone used in jewellery.

March noun the third month of the year.

march verb 1 walk in time and with regular paces, like a soldier. 2 walk quickly and with determination. 3 force someone to walk quickly. 4 take part in an organized procession to make a protest. • noun 1 an act of marching. 2 a procession organized

m

THESAURUS

manual adjective 1 manual work: physical, labouring, blue-collar. 2 a manual typewriter: hand-operated, hand. • noun a training manual: handbook, instructions, guide, companion, ABC, guidebook; informal bible.

manufacture verb 1 the company manufactures laser printers: make, produce, mass-produce, build, construct, assemble, put together, turn out. 2 a story manufactured by the press: make up, invent, fabricate, concoct, hatch, dream up, think up, contrive; informal cook up. • noun the manufacture of aircraft engines: production, making, manufacturing, mass production, construction, building, assembly.

manufacturer noun maker, producer, builder, constructor, industrialist.

many determiner & adjective numerous, a lot of, plenty of, countless, innumerable, scores of, untold, copious, abundant; informal lots of, umpteen, loads of, masses of, stacks of, heaps of, oodles of, a slew of; Brit. informal

a shedload of; Austral./NZ informal a swag of; literary myriad.
OPPOSITES few.

map noun plan, chart, A to Z, atlas. • verb the region was mapped from the air: chart, plot, draw, record.

mar verb 1 an ugly bruise marred his features: spoil, impair, disfigure, blemish, scar. 2 the celebrations were marred by violence: spoil, ruin, damage, wreck, taint, tarnish.
OPPOSITES enhance.

march verb 1 the men marched past: stride, walk, troop, step, pace, tread, slog, tramp, hike, trudge, parade, file. 2 she marched in without even knocking: stride, stalk, strut, flounce, storm, stomp, sweep. • noun 1 a 20-mile march: walk, trek, slog, route march, hike. 2 police sought to ban the march: parade, procession, cortège, demonstration; informal demo. 3 the march of technology: progress, advance, development, evolution, passage.

as a protest. **3** (**Marches**) land on the border between two territories.
■ **marcher** noun.

marchioness /mar-shuh-**ness**/ noun **1** the wife or widow of a marquess. **2** a woman who holds the rank of marquess.

Mardi Gras /mar-di **grah**/ noun a carnival held in some countries on Shrove Tuesday.

mare noun the female of a horse or related animal.

margarine noun a butter substitute made from vegetable oils or animal fats.

margin noun **1** an edge or border. **2** the blank border on each side of the print on a page. **3** an amount by which something is won.
□ **margin of** (or **for**) **error** a small amount allowed for or included so as to be sure of success or safety.

marginal adjective **1** in a margin. **2** slight, or of minor importance. **3** Brit. (of a parliamentary seat) held by only a small majority.
■ **marginality** noun **marginally** adverb.

marginalize or **marginalise** verb (**marginalizes, marginalizing, marginalized**) reduce the power or importance of.
■ **marginalization** noun.

marigold noun a plant of the daisy family with yellow or orange flowers.

marijuana /ma-ri-**hwah**-nuh/ noun cannabis.

marina noun a purpose-built harbour with moorings for yachts and small boats.

marinade noun /ma-ri-**nayd**/ a mixture of ingredients in which food is soaked before cooking to flavour or soften it. • verb /**ma**-ri-nayd/ (**marinades, marinading, marinaded**) = **MARINATE**.

marinate verb (**marinates, marinating, marinated**) soak food in a marinade.

marine adjective **1** relating to the sea. **2** relating to shipping or matters concerning a navy. • noun a soldier trained to serve on land or sea.

mariner noun literary a sailor.

marionette noun a puppet worked by strings.

marital adjective having to do with marriage.

maritime adjective **1** relating to shipping or other activity taking place at sea. **2** living or found in or near the sea. **3** (of a climate) moist and having a mild temperature due to the influence of the sea.

marjoram noun **1** a sweet-smelling plant of the mint family, used as a herb in cooking.
2 = **OREGANO**.

mark[1] noun **1** a small area on a surface having a different colour from its surroundings. **2** something that indicates position or acts as a pointer. **3** a line, figure, or symbol made to identify or record something. **4** a sign of a quality or feeling. **5** a characteristic feature of something. **6** a point awarded for a correct answer or for a piece of work. **7** a

m

THESAURUS

margin noun **1** *the margin of the lake:* edge, side, verge, border, perimeter, brink, brim, rim, fringe, boundary, periphery, extremity. **2** *there's no margin for error:* leeway, latitude, scope, room, space, allowance. **3** *they won by a narrow margin:* gap, majority, amount.

marginal adjective **1** *the difference is marginal:* slight, small, tiny, minute, insignificant, minimal, negligible. **2** *a very marginal case:* borderline, disputable, questionable, doubtful.
OPPOSITES considerable, clear-cut.

marine adjective **1** *marine plants:* seawater, sea, saltwater, aquatic. **2** *a marine insurance company:* maritime, nautical, naval, seafaring, seagoing, ocean-going.

mariner noun sailor, seaman, seafarer; informal tar, matelot.

marital adjective matrimonial, married, wedded, conjugal, nuptial.

maritime adjective naval, marine, nautical, seafaring, seagoing, sea, ocean-going.

mark noun **1** *a dirty mark:* blemish, streak, spot, fleck, blot, stain, smear, speck, smudge; informal splodge. **2** *a punctuation*

mark: symbol, sign, character, accent, diacritic. **3** *the mark of a well-known bookseller:* logo, seal, stamp, symbol, emblem, device, insignia, badge, brand, trademark, monogram, hallmark. **4** *a mark of respect:* sign, token, symbol, indication, symptom, proof. **5** *the mark of a civilized society:* characteristic, feature, trait, attribute, quality, hallmark, indicator. **6** *he got a good mark for maths:* grade, grading, rating, score, percentage.
• verb **1** *be careful not to mark the paintwork:* discolour, stain, smear, smudge, streak, dirty; informal splodge. **2** *her possessions were clearly marked:* label, identify, flag, initial, name. **3** *I've marked the relevant passages:* indicate, label, tick, identify, highlight. **4** *a festival to mark the town's 200th anniversary:* celebrate, observe, recognize, acknowledge, keep, honour, commemorate, remember. **5** *these incidents marked a new phase:* represent, signify, indicate, herald. **6** *his style is marked by simplicity:* characterize, distinguish, identify, typify. **7** *I have a pile of essays to mark:* assess, evaluate, appraise, correct; N. Amer. grade.

particular model of a vehicle or machine.
•verb 1 make a mark on. 2 write a word or symbol on an object in order to identify it. 3 indicate the position of. 4 (mark someone/thing out) show someone or something to be different or special. 5 do something to celebrate or remember a significant event. 6 (mark something up or down) increase or reduce the price of an item. 7 assess and give a mark to a piece of work. 8 pay careful attention to. 9 Brit. (in team games) stay close to an opponent in order to prevent them getting or passing the ball.
□ mark time 1 fill in time with routine activities. 2 (of troops) march on the spot without moving forward. on your marks be ready to start (used to instruct competitors in a race). up to the mark up to the required standard.

mark² noun the former basic unit of money in Germany.

marked adjective 1 having an identifying mark. 2 clearly noticeable. 3 singled out as a target for attack.
■ markedly adverb.

marker noun 1 an object used to indicate a position, place, or route. 2 a felt-tip pen with a broad tip. 3 (in team games) a player who marks an opponent.

market noun 1 a regular gathering for the buying and selling of food, livestock, or other goods. 2 an outdoor space or large hall where traders offer their goods for sale. 3 a particular area of trade or competitive activity. 4 demand for a particular product or service. •verb (markets, marketing, marketed) advertise or promote a product.
□ market garden a place where vegetables and fruit are grown to be sold. market research the gathering of information about what people choose to buy. market town a medium-sized town where a regular market is held. market value the amount for which something can be sold. on the market available for sale.
■ marketable adjective.

marketing noun the promoting and selling of products or services.

marketplace noun 1 an open space where a market is held. 2 the world of trade and commerce.

marking noun 1 an identification mark. 2 (also markings) a pattern of marks on an animal's fur, feathers, or skin.

marksman noun (plural marksmen) a person skilled in shooting.
■ marksmanship noun.

markup noun the difference between the basic cost of producing something and the amount it is sold for.

marl¹ noun a rock or soil consisting of clay and lime.

marl² noun a type of yarn or fabric with differently coloured threads.

marlin noun a large edible fish with a pointed snout.

marmalade noun a thick spread made from oranges.

marmoreal /mar-mor-i-uhl/ adjective literary made of or resembling marble.

marmoset noun a small tropical American monkey with a long tail.

marmot noun a heavily built burrowing rodent.

maroon¹ noun a dark brownish-red colour.

maroon² verb (be marooned) be abandoned or isolated in a place which cannot be reached.

marque noun a make of car, as distinct from a specific model.

marquee noun 1 chiefly Brit. a large tent used for special events. 2 N. Amer. a roof-like canopy over the entrance to a building.

marquess noun a British nobleman ranking above an earl and below a duke.

marquetry /mar-ki-tri/ noun patterns or pictures made from small pieces of coloured wood inlaid into a surface, used to decorate furniture.

marquis /mar-kwiss/ noun (in some European countries) a nobleman ranking above a count and below a duke.

marquise /mar-keez/ noun the wife or widow of a marquis, or a woman holding the rank of marquis in her own right.

marriage noun 1 the formal union of a man and woman, by which they become husband and wife. 2 the relationship between a husband and wife.
■ marriageable adjective.

m

THESAURUS

marked adjective noticeable, pronounced, decided, distinct, striking, clear, unmistakable, obvious, conspicuous, notable.
OPPOSITES imperceptible.

market noun shopping centre, marketplace, mart, bazaar, souk, fair.
•verb the product was marketed worldwide: sell, retail, merchandise, trade, advertise, promote.

marriage noun 1 a proposal of marriage: matrimony, wedlock. 2 the marriage took place at St Margaret's: wedding, wedding ceremony, nuptials, union, match. 3 a marriage of jazz, pop, and gospel: union, fusion, mixture, mix, blend, amalgamation, combination, hybrid.
OPPOSITES divorce, separation.

marrow noun **1** Brit. a long vegetable with a green skin and white flesh. **2** (also **bone marrow**) a soft fatty substance inside bones, in which blood cells are produced.

marrowbone noun a bone containing edible bone marrow.

marry verb (**marries, marrying, married**) **1** become the husband or wife of. **2** join two people in marriage. **3** join two things together.

Mars noun the fourth planet from the sun in the solar system and the nearest to the earth.

marsh noun an area of low-lying land which usually remains waterlogged.
■ **marshy** adjective.

marshal noun **1** an officer of the highest rank in the armed forces of some countries. **2** (in the US) a type of law enforcement officer. **3** an official responsible for supervising public events. • verb (**marshals, marshalling, marshalled**; US spelling **marshals, marshaling, marshaled**) **1** assemble a group of people in order. **2** bring facts together in an organized way.

marshmallow noun a spongy sweet made from sugar, egg white, and gelatin.

marsupial /mar-soo-pi-uhl/ noun a mammal whose young are carried and suckled in a pouch on the mother's belly.

mart noun **1** N. Amer. a shop. **2** a trade centre or market.

marten noun a forest animal resembling a weasel.

martial adjective having to do with war. □ **martial arts** sports which started as forms of self-defence or attack, such as judo and karate. **martial law** government by the military forces of a country.

Martian noun a supposed inhabitant of the planet Mars. • adjective relating to Mars.

martin noun a small short-tailed swallow.

martinet noun a person who is very strict and insists on being obeyed.

martingale noun a strap running from the noseband or reins to the girth of a horse's saddle, which prevents the horse from raising its head too high.

martyr noun **1** a person who is killed because of their beliefs. **2** a person who exaggerates their difficulties in order to obtain sympathy or admiration. • verb make a martyr of.
■ **martyrdom** noun.

marvel verb (**marvels, marvelling, marvelled**; US spelling **marvels, marveling, marveled**) be filled with wonder. • noun a person or thing that causes a feeling of wonder.

marvellous (US spelling **marvelous**) adjective wonderful; very good.
■ **marvellously** adverb.

Marxism noun the political and economic theories of Karl Marx and Friedrich Engels, which formed the basis for communism.
■ **Marxist** noun & adjective.

marzipan noun a sweet paste of ground almonds, sugar, and egg whites.

mascara noun a cosmetic for darkening the eyelashes.

mascot noun a person, animal, or object that is supposed to bring good luck.

masculine adjective **1** relating to men. **2** having the qualities or appearance traditionally associated with men. **3** Grammar referring to a gender of nouns and adjectives seen as male.
■ **masculinity** noun.

mash verb crush or beat something into a

m

THESAURUS

marry verb **1** *the couple married last year:* get/be married, wed, be wed, become man and wife; informal tie the knot, walk down the aisle, get spliced, get hitched, say 'I do'. **2** *John wanted to marry her:* wed; informal make an honest woman of. **3** *the show marries poetry with art:* join, unite, combine, fuse, mix, blend, merge, amalgamate.
OPPOSITES divorce, separate.

marsh noun swamp, marshland, bog, swampland, morass, mire, quagmire, slough, fen.

marshal verb assemble, gather (together), collect, muster, call together, draw up, line up, array, organize, group, arrange, deploy, position, summon, round up.

martial adjective military, soldierly, army, warlike, fighting, militaristic; informal gung-ho.

marvel verb *she marvelled at their courage:* be amazed, be astonished, be in awe, wonder; informal be gobsmacked.
• noun *a marvel of technology:* wonder, miracle, sensation, spectacle, phenomenon.

marvellous adjective excellent, splendid, wonderful, magnificent, superb, glorious, sublime, lovely, delightful; informal super, great, amazing, fantastic, terrific, tremendous; Brit. informal smashing, brilliant.
OPPOSITES commonplace, awful.

masculine adjective **1** *a masculine trait:* male, man's, men's, male-oriented. **2** *a powerfully masculine man:* virile, macho, manly, all-male, muscular, muscly, strong, strapping, well built, rugged, robust, brawny, powerful, red-blooded, vigorous; informal hunky. **3** *a rather masculine woman:* mannish, unfeminine, unladylike; informal butch.
OPPOSITES feminine, effeminate.

soft mass. •noun 1 a soft mass made by crushing a substance. 2 Brit. informal boiled and mashed potatoes.

mask noun 1 a covering for all or part of the face, worn for protection, as a disguise, or for theatrical effect. 2 a likeness of a person's face moulded in clay or wax. •verb 1 (**masked**) wearing a mask. 2 conceal or disguise.

masochism /mass-uh-ki-z'm/ noun enjoyment felt in being hurt or humiliated by someone. ■ **masochist** noun **masochistic** adjective.

mason noun 1 a person who works with stone. 2 (**Mason**) a Freemason.

Masonic adjective relating to Freemasons.

masonry noun the parts of a building that are made of stone.

masque /mahsk/ noun (in the past) a form of entertainment consisting of dancing and acting performed by masked players.

masquerade /mass-kuh-**rayd**/ noun 1 a pretence. 2 a ball at which people wear masks. •verb (**masquerades, masquerading, masqueraded**) pretend to be someone or something else.

Mass noun 1 the Christian service of the Eucharist or Holy Communion. 2 a musical setting of parts of this service.

mass noun 1 an amount of matter with no definite shape. 2 a large number of people or objects gathered together. 3 (**the masses**) the ordinary people. 4 (**a mass of**) a large amount of. 5 Physics the quantity of

matter which something contains. •verb gather together in a mass.

□ **mass-market** (of goods) produced in large quantities and appealing to a large number of people. **mass-produce** produce goods in large quantities in a factory.

massacre noun a brutal killing of a large number of people. •verb (**massacres, massacring, massacred**) brutally kill a large number of people.

massage noun the rubbing and kneading of parts of the body with the hands to relieve tension or pain. •verb (**massages, massaging, massaged**) 1 give a massage to. 2 alter facts or figures to make them seem better than they really are. □ **massage parlour** 1 a place where massage is provided. 2 a brothel.

masseur /ma-**ser**/ noun (feminine **masseuse** /ma-**serz**/) a person who gives massages professionally.

massif /ma-**seef**/ noun a compact group of mountains.

massive adjective 1 large and heavy or solid. 2 very large, powerful, or severe. ■ **massively** adverb.

mast[1] noun 1 a tall upright post on a boat carrying a sail or sails. 2 any tall upright post or structure.

mast[2] noun nuts and other fruit that has fallen from trees.

mastectomy noun (plural **mastectomies**) an operation to remove a breast.

master noun 1 a man in a position of

THESAURUS

mask noun *a mask of respectability:* pretence, semblance, veil, screen, front, facade, veneer, disguise, cover, cloak, camouflage.
•verb *poplar trees masked the factory:* hide, conceal, disguise, cover up, obscure, screen, cloak, camouflage.

mass noun 1 *a soggy mass of fallen leaves:* pile, heap, accumulation, mess, mat, tangle. 2 *a mass of cyclists:* crowd, horde, throng, host, troop, army, herd, flock, swarm, mob, pack, flood, multitude. 3 *the mass of the population:* majority, greater part/number, best/better part, major part, bulk, main body.
•adjective *mass hysteria:* widespread, general, extensive, large-scale, wholesale, universal, indiscriminate.
•verb *they began massing troops in the region:* assemble, gather together, collect, rally.

massacre noun *a cold-blooded massacre:* slaughter, mass killing, mass murder, mass execution, ethnic cleansing, genocide, holocaust, annihilation, liquidation, extermination, carnage, butchery,

bloodbath, bloodletting.
•verb *thousands were massacred:* slaughter, butcher, murder, kill, annihilate, exterminate, execute, liquidate, eliminate, mow down, cut to pieces.

massage noun rub, rub-down, kneading.
•verb 1 *he massaged her tired muscles:* rub, knead, manipulate, pummel, work. 2 *the statistics have been massaged:* alter, tamper with, manipulate, doctor, falsify, juggle, fiddle with, tinker with, distort, rig; informal cook, fiddle.

massive adjective huge, enormous, vast, immense, mighty, great, colossal, tremendous, gigantic, giant, mammoth, monumental, mountainous; informal monster, whopping, astronomical; Brit. informal whacking, ginormous.
OPPOSITES tiny.

master noun 1 (historical) *he acceded to his master's wishes:* lord, ruler, sovereign, monarch. 2 *a chess master:* expert, genius, maestro, virtuoso, authority; informal ace, wizard, whizz, hotshot; Brit. informal dab hand; N. Amer. informal maven, crackerjack. 3 *the geography master:* teacher,

m

authority, control, or ownership. **2** a person skilled in a particular art or activity. **3** the head of a college or school. **4** chiefly Brit. a male schoolteacher. **5** a person who holds a second or further degree. **6** an original film, recording, or document from which copies can be made. • verb (**masters, mastering, mastered**) **1** gain great knowledge of or skill in. **2** gain control of. ▫ **master key** a key that opens several locks, each of which has its own key. **master of ceremonies** a person in charge of proceedings at a special event.

masterclass noun a class given to students by a leading musician.

masterful adjective **1** powerful and able to control other people. **2** performed or performing very skilfully. ▪ **masterfully** adverb.

masterly adjective performed or performing very skilfully.

mastermind noun a person who plans and directs a complex scheme or project. • verb plan and direct a complex scheme or project.

masterpiece noun a work of outstanding skill.

mastery noun **1** complete knowledge or command of a subject or skill. **2** control or superiority.

masthead noun **1** the highest part of a ship's mast. **2** the name of a newspaper or

magazine printed at the top of the first page.

mastic noun **1** a gum from the bark of a Mediterranean tree, used in making varnish and chewing gum. **2** a waterproof substance like putty, used in building.

masticate verb (**masticates, masticating, masticated**) chew food. ▪ **mastication** noun.

mastiff noun a dog of a large, strong breed with drooping ears and lips.

mastitis /ma-sty-tiss/ noun painful inflammation of glands in the breast or udder.

mastodon noun a large extinct elephant-like mammal.

mastoid noun a part of the bone behind the ear, which has air spaces linked to the middle ear.

masturbate verb (**masturbates, masturbating, masturbated**) stimulate your genitals with your hand for sexual pleasure. ▪ **masturbation** noun.

mat noun **1** a thick piece of material placed on the floor, used for decoration or to protect the floor. **2** a piece of springy material for landing on in gymnastics or similar sports. **3** a small piece of material placed on a surface to protect it. **4** a thick layer of hairy or woolly material.

matador noun a bullfighter.

match[1] noun **1** an event at which two

m

schoolteacher, schoolmaster, tutor, instructor. **4** *their spiritual master:* guru, teacher, leader, guide, mentor.
OPPOSITES servant, amateur, pupil.
• verb **1** *I managed to master my fears:* overcome, conquer, beat, quell, suppress, control, triumph over, subdue, vanquish, subjugate, curb, check, defeat, get the better of; informal lick. **2** *it took ages to master the technique:* learn, become proficient in, pick up, grasp, understand; informal get the hang of.
OPPOSITES succumb to.
• adjective *a master craftsman:* expert, adept, proficient, skilled, skilful, deft, dexterous, adroit, practised, experienced, masterly, accomplished; informal crack, ace; N. Amer. informal crackerjack.
OPPOSITES amateur.

masterful adjective commanding, powerful, imposing, authoritative.
OPPOSITES weak.

masterly adjective expert, adept, skilful, skilled, adroit, proficient, deft, dexterous, accomplished, polished, consummate.
OPPOSITES inept.

mastermind noun *the mastermind behind*

the project: genius, intellect, informal brain, brains.
• verb *he masterminded the whole campaign:* plan, control, direct, be in charge of, run, conduct, organize, arrange, preside over, orchestrate, stage-manage, engineer, manage, coordinate.

masterpiece noun magnum opus, chef-d'œuvre, masterwork, pièce de résistance, tour de force, classic.

mastery noun **1** *her mastery of the language:* proficiency, ability, capability, knowledge, understanding, comprehension, command, grasp. **2** *man's mastery over nature:* control, domination, command, supremacy, superiority, power, authority, jurisdiction, dominion, sovereignty.

mat noun **1** *the hall mat:* rug, carpet, doormat, runner. **2** *a thick mat of hair:* mass, tangle, mop, thatch, shock, mane.

match noun **1** *a football match:* contest, competition, game, tournament, tie, fixture, meet, friendly, (local) derby, bout, fight. **2** *the vase was an exact match of hers:* lookalike, double, twin, duplicate, mate, companion, counterpart, pair, replica, copy; informal spitting image, dead ringer.

people or teams compete against each other. **2** a person or thing that can compete with another as an equal in quality or strength. **3** an exact equivalent. **4** a pair of things which correspond or are very similar. •**verb 1** correspond or fit with something. **2** be equal to. **3** place a person or team in competition with another. □ **match point** (in sports) a point which if won by one of the players will also win them the match.

match² noun a short, thin stick tipped with a substance that ignites when rubbed against a rough surface.

matchbox noun a small box in which matches are sold.

matchless adjective so good that nothing is an equal.

matchmaker noun a person who tries to bring about marriages or relationships between other people.

matchstick noun the stem of a match.

mate noun **1** Brit. informal a friend. **2** the sexual partner of an animal. **3** an assistant to a skilled worker. •**verb** (**mates, mating, mated**) (of animals or birds) come together for breeding.

matelot /mat-loh/ noun Brit. informal a sailor.

material noun **1** the matter from which something is or can be made. **2** items needed for doing or creating something. **3** cloth. •**adjective 1** having to do with physical things rather than the mind or spirit. **2** essential or relevant. ■ **materially** adverb.

materialism noun a strong interest in possessions and physical comfort rather than spiritual values.

■ **materialist** adjective & noun **materialistic** adjective.

materialize or **materialise** verb (**materialize, materializing, materialized**) **1** happen. **2** appear suddenly.

maternal adjective **1** having to do with a mother. **2** related through the mother's side of the family. ■ **maternally** adverb.

maternity noun motherhood.

matey adjective (**matier, matiest**) Brit. informal very friendly.

mathematics noun the branch of science concerned with numbers, quantities, and space. ■ **mathematical** adjective **mathematically** adverb **mathematician** noun.

maths or N. Amer. **math** noun mathematics.

matinee /ma-ti-nay/ noun an afternoon performance in a theatre or cinema.

matins noun a Christian service of morning prayer.

matriarch /may-tri-ark/ noun a woman who is the head of a family or tribe.

matriarchy noun a society led or controlled by women. ■ **matriarchal** adjective.

matricide /ma-tri-syd/ noun **1** the killing by someone of their own mother. **2** a person who kills their mother.

matriculate verb (**matriculates, matriculating, matriculated**) enrol or be enrolled at a college or university. ■ **matriculation** noun.

matrimony noun the state of being married. ■ **matrimonial** adjective.

THESAURUS

•**verb 1** *the curtains matched the duvet cover:* go with, coordinate with, complement, suit, set off. **2** *did their statements match?* correspond, tally, agree, match up, coincide, square. **3** *no one can match him at chess:* equal, compare with, be in the same league as, touch, rival, compete with; informal hold a candle to.

matching adjective corresponding, equivalent, parallel, complementary, paired, twin, identical, alike.
OPPOSITES different, clashing.

mate noun **1** (Brit. informal) *he's gone out with his mates:* friend, companion, schoolmate, classmate, workmate; informal pal, chum; N. Amer. informal buddy, amigo, compadre. **2** *she's finally found her ideal mate:* partner, husband, wife, spouse, consort, lover; informal better half; Brit. informal other half. **3** *a plumber's mate:* assistant, helper, apprentice.
•**verb** *pandas rarely mate in captivity:* breed, couple, pair.

material noun **1** *organic material:* matter, substance, stuff. **2** *the materials for a new building:* constituent, raw material, component, supplies. **3** *cleaning materials:* things, items, articles, stuff, supplies; Brit. informal gubbins. **4** *curtain material:* fabric, cloth, textiles. **5** *material for a magazine article:* information, data, facts, facts and figures, statistics, evidence, details, particulars, background, notes; informal info.
•**adjective 1** *the material world:* physical, corporeal, tangible, mundane, worldly, earthly, secular, temporal, concrete, real. **2** *she was too fond of material pleasures:* sensual, physical, carnal, corporal, fleshly, bodily. **3** *information that could be material to the enquiry:* relevant, pertinent, applicable, germane, vital, essential, key.
OPPOSITES spiritual, aesthetic, irrelevant.

maternal adjective motherly, protective, caring, nurturing, maternalistic.

matrix /**may**-triks/ noun (plural **matrices** /**may**-tri-seez/ or **matrixes**) **1** an environment or material in which something develops. **2** a mould in which something is cast or shaped. **3** a grid-like arrangement of elements.

matron noun **1** a woman in charge of medical and living arrangements at a boarding school. **2** Brit. dated a woman in charge of nursing in a hospital. **3** an older married woman.
□ matron of honour a married woman attending the bride at a wedding.
■ **matronly** adjective.

matt or **matte** adjective not shiny.

matted adjective (of hair or fur) tangled into a thick mass.

matter noun **1** physical substance or material. **2** a subject or situation to be considered or dealt with. **3** (**the matter**) the reason for a problem. •verb (**matters, mattering, mattered**) be important.
□ matter-of-fact unemotional and practical.

mattock noun a farming tool similar to a pickaxe.

mattress noun a fabric case filled with soft or firm material and sometimes incorporating springs, used for sleeping on.

mature adjective **1** fully grown. **2** like a sensible adult. **3** (of certain foods or drinks) developed over a long period in order to achieve a full flavour. •verb (**matures, maturing, matured**) **1** become mature. **2** (of an insurance policy) reach the end of its term and so become payable.
■ **maturation** noun **maturely** adverb.

maturity noun **1** the state or period of being mature. **2** the time when an insurance policy matures.

maudlin /**mawd**-lin/ adjective sentimental in a self-pitying way.

maul verb **1** wound by scratching and tearing. **2** treat roughly.

maunder verb (**maunders, maundering, maundered**) move, talk, or act in a rambling way.

Mauritanian noun a person from Mauritania, a country in West Africa.
•adjective relating to Mauritania.

mausoleum /maw-suh-**lee**-uhm/ noun (plural **mausolea** /maw-suh-**lee**-uh/ or **mausoleums**) a building containing a tomb or tombs.

mauve noun a pale or reddish-purple colour.

maverick noun an unconventional and independent-minded person.

maw noun the jaws or throat.

mawkish adjective foolishly sentimental.

max abbreviation maximum.

maxim noun a short statement expressing a general truth or rule of behaviour.

maximize or **maximise** verb (**maximizes, maximizing, maximized**) **1** make something as large or great as possible. **2** make the best use of.

maximum noun (plural **maxima** or **maximums**) the greatest amount, size, or strength that is possible or that has been gained. •adjective greatest in amount, size, or strength.
■ **maximal** adjective.

m

matted adjective tangled, knotted, tousled, dishevelled, uncombed, unkempt, ratty.

matter noun **1** *vegetable matter:* material, stuff, substance. **2** *a serious matter:* affair, business, situation, concern, incident, episode, subject, topic, issue, question, point at issue, case.
•verb *it doesn't matter what you wear:* be important, make any difference, be of consequence, be relevant, count.

matter-of-fact adjective unemotional, practical, down-to-earth, sensible, realistic, unsentimental, pragmatic, businesslike, commonsensical, level-headed, hard-headed, no-nonsense, straightforward.

mature adjective **1** *a mature woman:* adult, grown, fully grown, in your prime. **2** *he's very mature for his age:* grown-up, sensible, responsible, adult, level-headed. **3** *mature cheese:* ripe, mellow, rich, strong, flavoursome, full-bodied.
OPPOSITES immature.
•verb **1** *kittens mature when they are about a year old:* become fully grown, come of age, reach adulthood, reach maturity. **2** *he's*

matured since he left home: grow up, blossom. **3** *leave the cheese to mature:* ripen, mellow, age. **4** *their friendship didn't have time to mature:* develop, grow, evolve, bloom, blossom, flourish, thrive.

maturity noun **1** *her progress from childhood to maturity:* adulthood, coming of age, manhood, womanhood. **2** *he displayed a maturity beyond his years:* responsibility, sense, level-headedness.

maul verb savage, attack, claw, scratch, lacerate, mangle, tear.

maverick noun individualist, nonconformist, free spirit, original, eccentric, rebel, dissenter, dissident.
OPPOSITES conformist.

maximum adjective *the maximum amount:* greatest, highest, biggest, largest, top, most, utmost.
OPPOSITES minimum.
•noun *production levels are near their maximum:* upper limit, limit, utmost, greatest, most, peak, height, ceiling, top.
OPPOSITES minimum.

May noun **1** the fifth month of the year. **2** (**may**) the hawthorn or its blossom.

may modal verb (3rd singular present **may**; past **might**) **1** expressing possibility. **2** expressing permission. **3** expressing a wish or hope.

maybe adverb perhaps.

Mayday noun an international distress signal used by ships and aircraft.

mayfly noun (plural **mayflies**) an insect which lives as an adult for only a very short time.

mayhem noun violent disorder.

mayn't short form may not.

mayonnaise /may-uh-**nayz**/ noun a creamy dressing made from egg yolks, oil, and vinegar.

mayor noun the elected head of a city or borough council.
■ **mayoral** adjective.

mayoralty /**mair**-uhl-ti/ noun (plural **mayoralties**) the period of office of a mayor.

mayoress noun **1** the wife of a mayor. **2** a woman elected as mayor.

maypole noun a decorated pole with long ribbons attached to the top, traditionally used for dancing round on the first day of May.

maze noun a complicated network of paths and walls or hedges designed as a challenge to find a way through.

mazurka noun a lively Polish dance.

MBA abbreviation Master of Business Administration.

MBE abbreviation Member of the Order of the British Empire.

MC abbreviation **1** master of ceremonies. **2** Military Cross.

MD abbreviation **1** Doctor of Medicine. **2** Brit. Managing Director.

ME abbreviation myalgic encephalomyelitis, a medical condition causing aching and prolonged tiredness.

me pronoun used as the object of a verb or preposition or after 'than', 'as', or the verb 'to be', to refer to the speaker himself or herself.

> **!** it is wrong to use *me* as the subject of a verb, as in *John and me went to the shops*; in this case use *I* instead.

mead noun an alcoholic drink made from fermented honey and water.

meadow noun an area of grassland.

meadowsweet noun a tall plant with creamy-white sweet-smelling flowers.

meagre (US spelling **meager**) adjective small in quantity and of bad quality.
■ **meagreness** noun.

meal[1] noun **1** any of the regular daily occasions when food is eaten. **2** the food eaten on such an occasion.

meal[2] noun the edible part of any grain or pulse ground to powder.
■ **mealy** adjective.

mealy-mouthed adjective not wanting to speak honestly or frankly.

mean[1] verb (**means**, **meaning**, **meant**) **1** intend to say or show something. **2** (of a word) have as its explanation in the same language or its equivalent in another language. **3** intend something to happen or be the case. **4** have something as a result. **5** intend something for a particular purpose. **6** have a particular level of importance: *animals mean more to him than people.*

mean[2] adjective **1** unwilling to give or share things. **2** unkind or unfair. **3** N. Amer. vicious or aggressive. **4** (of a place) poor and dirty in appearance.
■ **meanly** adverb **meanness** noun.

mean[3] noun **1** the average value of a set of quantities. **2** something in the middle of two extremes. • adjective **1** calculated as a mean. **2** equally far from two extremes.

meander /mi-**an**-der/ verb (**meanders**, **meandering**, **meandered**) **1** follow a winding course. **2** wander in a leisurely way. • noun a winding bend of a river or road.

THESAURUS

maybe adverb perhaps, possibly, for all you know; N. English happen; literary perchance.

mayhem noun chaos, havoc, bedlam, pandemonium, uproar, turmoil, a riot, anarchy; informal a madhouse.

maze noun labyrinth, network, warren, web, tangle, confusion, jungle.

meadow noun field, paddock, pasture; literary lea.

mean[1] verb **1** *flashing lights mean the road is blocked:* signify, denote, indicate, show, express, spell out, stand for, represent, symbolize, imply, suggest, intimate. **2** *she didn't mean to break it:* intend, aim, plan,

have in mind, set out, want. **3** *this will mean war:* entail, involve, necessitate, lead to, result in, give rise to, bring about, cause, engender, produce.

mean[2] adjective **1** *he's too mean to leave a tip:* miserly, niggardly, parsimonious, penny-pinching, cheese-paring; informal tight-fisted, stingy, tight; N. Amer. informal cheap. **2** *a mean trick:* unkind, nasty, unpleasant, spiteful, malicious, unfair, shabby, despicable, contemptible, horrible, obnoxious, vile, loathsome, base, low; informal rotten.
OPPOSITES generous, kind.

meaning noun **1** the thing or idea that a word, signal, or action represents. **2** a sense of purpose.

meaningful adjective **1** having meaning. **2** worthwhile. **3** expressive.
■ **meaningfully** adverb.

meaningless adjective having no meaning or significance.
■ **meaninglessly** adverb.

means noun **1** a thing or method used to achieve a result. **2** money or wealth.
□ **by all means** of course. **by no means** certainly not. **means test** an official investigation into how much money or income a person has, to find out whether they qualify for welfare benefits.

meant past and past participle of MEAN¹.

meantime adverb (**in the meantime**) meanwhile.

meanwhile adverb **1** in the period of time between two events. **2** at the same time.

measles noun an infectious disease causing fever and a red rash.

measly adjective informal ridiculously small or few.

measure verb (**measures, measuring, measured**) **1** find out what the size, amount, or degree of something is in standard units. **2** be of a particular size, amount, or degree. **3** (**measure something out**) take an exact quantity of. **4** (**measure**

up) reach the required standard. ● noun **1** a course of action taken to achieve a purpose. **2** a proposal for a new law. **3** a standard unit used to express size, amount, or degree. **4** a measuring device marked with such units. **5** (**a measure of**) an indication of the extent or quality of.
□ **for good measure** as an amount or item that is additional to what is strictly necessary. **have the measure of** understand the character of.
■ **measurable** adjective **measurably** adverb.

measured adjective **1** slow and regular in rhythm. **2** carefully considered.

measurement noun **1** the action of measuring. **2** an amount, size, or extent found by measuring.

meat noun the flesh of an animal used as food.

meatball noun a ball of minced or chopped meat.

meaty adjective (**meatier, meatiest**) **1** full of meat. **2** fleshy or muscular. **3** substantial or challenging.

Mecca noun **1** the holiest city for Muslims, in Saudi Arabia. **2** a place which attracts many people.

mechanic noun a skilled worker who repairs and maintains machinery.

mechanical adjective **1** relating to or

m

meaning noun **1** *the meaning of his remark:* significance, sense, signification, import, gist, thrust, drift, implication, message. **2** *the word has several different meanings:* definition, sense, explanation, interpretation.

meaningful adjective **1** *a meaningful remark:* significant, relevant, important, telling. **2** *a meaningful relationship:* sincere, deep, serious, earnest, significant, important. **3** *a meaningful glance:* expressive, eloquent, pointed, pregnant, revealing, suggestive.
OPPOSITES inconsequential, insincere.

meaningless adjective unintelligible, incomprehensible, incoherent.

means plural noun **1** *the best means to achieve your goal:* method, way, manner, course, procedure. **2** *she doesn't have the means to support herself:* money, resources, capital, income, finance, funds, cash, the wherewithal, assets, wealth, riches, affluence, fortune.

meanwhile, meantime adverb
1 *meanwhile, I'll stay here:* for now, for the moment, for the present, for the time being, in the meanwhile, in the meantime, in the interim. **2** *cook for a further half hour; meanwhile, make the stuffing:* at the same time, simultaneously, concurrently.

measure verb quantify, gauge, size, count, weigh, evaluate, assess, determine, calculate, compute.
● noun **1** *cost-cutting measures:* action, act, course of action, deed, procedure, step, expedient, initiative, programme. **2** *the Senate passed the measure:* statute, act, bill, law. **3** *use a measure to check the size:* ruler, tape measure, gauge, meter, scale, level. **4** *sales are the measure of the company's success:* yardstick, test, standard, barometer, touchstone, benchmark.

measured adjective **1** *his measured tread:* regular, steady, even, rhythmic, unfaltering, slow, dignified, stately, sedate, leisurely, unhurried. **2** *his measured tones:* thoughtful, careful, considered, deliberate, restrained.

measurement noun **1** *measurement of the effect is difficult:* quantification, evaluation, assessment, calculation, computation, mensuration. **2** *all measurements are in metric units:* size, dimension, proportions, value, amount, quantity.

mechanical adjective **1** *a mechanical device:* mechanized, machine-driven, automated, automatic. **2** *a mechanical response:* automatic, knee-jerk, unthinking,

operated by a machine or machinery.
2 done without thought. **3** relating to physical forces or movement.
■ **mechanically** adverb.

mechanics noun **1** the branch of study concerned with the forces producing movement. **2** machinery or working parts. **3** the practical aspects of something.

mechanism noun **1** a piece of machinery. **2** the way in which something works or is made to happen.

mechanize or **mechanise** verb (**mechanizes, mechanizing, mechanized**) equip with machines or automatic devices.
■ **mechanization** noun.

medal noun a metal disc with an inscription or design on it, awarded to someone for a special achievement.

medallion noun **1** a piece of jewellery in the shape of a medal, worn as a pendant. **2** a decorative oval or circular painting, panel, or design.

medallist (US spelling **medalist**) noun a person who has been awarded a medal.

meddle verb (**meddles, meddling, meddled**) interfere in something that is not your concern.
■ **meddler** noun.

meddlesome adjective fond of interfering in other people's affairs.

media noun **1** television, radio, and newspapers as providers of information. **2** plural of MEDIUM.

! the word **media** comes from the Latin plural of **medium**. In its normal sense, 'television, radio, and newspapers', it can be used with either a singular or a plural verb.

mediaeval ⇨ MEDIEVAL.

medial /mee-di-uhl/ adjective situated in the middle.

median adjective technical situated in the middle. •noun **1** a median value. **2** Geometry a straight line drawn from one of the angles of a triangle to the middle of the opposite side.

mediate verb (**mediates, mediating, mediated**) try to settle a dispute between other people or groups.
■ **mediation** noun **mediator** noun.

medic noun informal a doctor or medical student.

medical adjective relating to the science or practice of medicine. •noun an examination to see how healthy someone is.
■ **medically** adverb.

medicament noun a medicine.

medicate verb (**medicates, medicating, medicated**) **1** give medicine or a drug to. **2** (**medicated**) containing a substance that has healing properties.

medication noun **1** a medicine or drug. **2** treatment with medicines.

medicinal adjective **1** having healing properties. **2** relating to medicines.
■ **medicinally** adverb.

medicine noun **1** the science or practice of the treatment and prevention of disease. **2** a substance taken by mouth in order to treat or prevent disease.
□ **medicine man** a person believed to have supernatural healing powers.

medieval or **mediaeval** /me-di-ee-v'l/ adjective relating to the Middle Ages, the period between about 1000 and 1450.

medievalist or **mediaevalist** noun a person who studies medieval history or literature.

mediocre /mee-di-oh-ker/ adjective of only

THESAURUS

instinctive, habitual, routine, unemotional, unfeeling.
OPPOSITES manual, thoughtful.

mechanism noun **1** electrical mechanisms: apparatus, machine, appliance, device, instrument, contraption, gadget; informal gizmo. **2** the train's safety mechanism: machinery, gear, system, equipment. **3** a complaints mechanism: procedure, process, system, method, means, medium, channel.

mediate verb **1** Austria tried to mediate between the two sides: arbitrate, conciliate, moderate, make peace, intervene, intercede, act as an intermediary, liaise. **2** a tribunal was set up to mediate disputes: resolve, settle, arbitrate in, umpire, reconcile, referee, mend, clear up; informal patch up.

mediation noun arbitration, conciliation, reconciliation, intervention, intercession, negotiation, shuttle diplomacy.

mediator noun arbitrator, arbiter, negotiator, conciliator, peacemaker, go-between, middleman, intermediary, moderator, honest broker, liaison officer, umpire, referee, adjudicator, judge.

medicine noun medication, drug, prescription, treatment, remedy, cure, nostrum, panacea, cure-all.

mediocre adjective average, ordinary, undistinguished, uninspired, indifferent, unexceptional, unexciting, unremarkable, run-of-the-mill, pedestrian, prosaic, lacklustre, forgettable, amateurish; informal so-so.
OPPOSITES excellent.

average or fairly low quality.
■ **mediocrity** noun.

meditate verb (**meditates, meditating, meditated**) **1** focus your mind and free it of uncontrolled thoughts, as a spiritual exercise or for relaxation. **2** (**meditate on** or **about**) think carefully about.
■ **meditation** noun **meditative** adjective **meditatively** adverb.

Mediterranean adjective relating to the Mediterranean Sea or the countries around it.

☑ one *d*, one *t*, double *r*: Medi*terr*anean.

medium noun (plural **media** or **mediums**) **1** a means by which something is communicated or achieved. **2** a substance that something lives or exists in, or through which it travels. **3** the type of material used by an artist. **4** (plural **mediums**) a person who claims to be able to communicate with the spirits of dead people. **5** the middle state between two extremes. • **adjective** between two extremes.

medlar noun a fruit resembling a small brown apple.

medley noun (plural **medleys**) a varied mixture.

meek adjective quiet, gentle, and obedient.
■ **meekly** adverb.

meerkat noun a small southern African mongoose.

meet verb (**meets, meeting, met**) **1** come together with someone at the same place and time. **2** be introduced to or come across someone for the first time. **3** touch or join. **4** come across a situation. **5** (**meet with**) receive a particular reaction. **6** fulfil

or satisfy a requirement. • **noun** a gathering or meeting.

meeting noun **1** an occasion when people meet to discuss or decide something. **2** a situation in which people come together.

mega adjective informal **1** very large. **2** excellent.

megabyte noun Computing a unit of information equal to one million bytes.

megalith noun a large stone that forms a prehistoric monument or part of one.
■ **megalithic** adjective.

megalomania noun **1** the false belief that you are very powerful and important. **2** a strong desire for power.
■ **megalomaniac** noun & adjective.

megaphone noun a cone-shaped device for making the voice sound louder.

megapixel noun a unit for measuring the resolution of a digital image, equal to one million pixels.

megaton noun a unit for measuring the power of an explosive, equivalent to one million tons of TNT.

megawatt noun a unit of power equal to one million watts.

melamine /mel-uh-meen/ noun a hard plastic used to coat the surfaces of tables or worktops.

melancholia /me-luhn-**koh**-li-uh/ noun great sadness or depression.

melancholy noun deep and long-lasting sadness. • **adjective** sad or depressed.
■ **melancholic** adjective.

melanin noun a dark pigment in the hair and skin, responsible for the tanning of skin exposed to sunlight.

melanoma noun a form of skin cancer.

m

THESAURUS

meditate verb contemplate, think, consider, ponder, muse, reflect, deliberate, ruminate, brood, mull over.

medium noun *a medium of expression:* means, method, avenue, channel, vehicle, organ, instrument, mechanism.
• **adjective** *he is of medium build:* average, middling, medium-sized, middle-sized, moderate, normal, standard.

meet verb **1** *I met an old friend on the train:* encounter, come face to face with, run into, run across, come across/upon, chance on, happen on, stumble across; informal bump into. **2** *she first met Paul at a party:* get to know, be introduced to, make the acquaintance of. **3** *the committee met on Saturday:* assemble, gather, come together, get together, congregate, convene. **4** *the place where three roads meet:* converge, connect, touch, link up, intersect, cross, join.

meeting noun **1** *he stood up to address the*

meeting: gathering, assembly, conference, congregation, convention, summit, rally; informal get-together. **2** *she demanded a meeting with the minister:* consultation, audience, interview. **3** *he intrigued her on their first meeting:* encounter, contact, appointment, assignation, rendezvous. **4** *the meeting of land and sea:* convergence, coming together, confluence, conjunction, union, intersection, crossing. **5** *an athletics meeting:* event, tournament, meet, rally, competition, match, game, contest.

melancholy adjective *a melancholy mood:* sad, sorrowful, unhappy, gloomy, despondent, glum, miserable, morose; informal down in the dumps, blue.
OPPOSITES cheerful.
• **noun** *a feeling of melancholy:* sadness, sorrow, unhappiness, depression, despondency, dejection, gloom, misery; informal the blues.
OPPOSITES happiness.

meld verb blend.

melee /mel-ay/ noun **1** a confused fight or scuffle. **2** a disorderly crowd of people.

mellifluous adjective pleasingly smooth and musical to hear.

mellow adjective **1** pleasantly smooth or soft in sound, taste, or colour. **2** relaxed and good-humoured. •verb make or become mellow.

melodic adjective **1** relating to melody. **2** sounding pleasant.
■ melodically adverb.

melodious adjective tuneful.

melodrama noun **1** a play full of exciting events, in which the characters seem too exaggerated to be realistic. **2** behaviour or events that are very dramatic.

melodramatic adjective too dramatic and exaggerated.
■ melodramatically adverb.

melody noun (plural **melodies**) **1** a piece of music with a clear or simple tune. **2** the main tune in a piece of music.

melon noun a large round fruit with sweet pulpy flesh.

melt verb **1** make or become liquid by heating. **2** (**melt away**) gradually disappear. **3** become more tender or loving. □ melting pot a place where different peoples, ideas, or styles are mixed together.

meltdown noun an accident in a nuclear reactor in which the fuel overheats and melts the reactor core.

member noun **1** a person or organization belonging to a group or society. **2** old use a part of the body.
■ membership noun.

membrane noun **1** a skin-like tissue that connects, covers, or lines cells or parts of the body. **2** a layer of thin, skin-like material.
■ membranous adjective.

memento noun (plural **mementos** or **mementoes**) an object kept as a reminder.

memo noun (plural **memos**) a written note sent from one person to another within an organization.

memoir /mem-war/ noun **1** a historical account or biography written from personal knowledge. **2** (**memoirs**) an account written by a public figure of their life and experiences.

memorabilia plural noun objects kept or collected because of their associations with people or events.

memorable adjective worth remembering or easily remembered.
■ memorably adverb.

memorandum noun (plural **memoranda** or **memorandums**) **1** formal a memo. **2** a note recording something for future use.

memorial noun a column or other structure made or built in memory of a person or event. •adjective created or done in memory of someone.

memorize or **memorise** verb (**memorizes, memorizing, memorized**) learn and remember exactly.

memory noun (plural **memories**) **1** the power that the mind has to store and remember information. **2** a thing remembered. **3** the length of time over which you can remember things. **4** a computer's equipment or capacity for storing data.

men plural of **MAN.**

THESAURUS

mellow adjective **1** *she loved the mellow tone of his voice:* **sweet-sounding**, dulcet, soft, smooth, warm, full, rich. **2** *a mellow wine:* **full-bodied**, mature, full-flavoured, rich, smooth. **3** *a mellow mood:* **genial**, affable, amiable, good-humoured, good-natured, pleasant, relaxed, easy-going.
OPPOSITES harsh, rough, irritable.

melody noun tune, air, strain, theme, song, refrain.

melt verb **1** *the snow was beginning to melt:* **liquefy**, thaw, defrost, soften, dissolve. **2** *his anger melted away:* **vanish**, disappear, fade, dissolve, evaporate.
OPPOSITES freeze, grow.

member noun subscriber, associate, supporter, fellow, representative.

memoir noun **1** *a touching memoir of her childhood:* **account**, history, record, chronicle, narrative, story, portrayal, depiction, portrait, profile. **2** *he published his memoirs in 1955:* **autobiography**, life

story, journal, diary.

memorable adjective unforgettable, indelible, catchy, haunting, momentous, significant, historic, notable, noteworthy, outstanding, arresting.

memorial noun **1** *the war memorial:* **monument**, cenotaph, mausoleum, statue, plaque, cairn, shrine. **2** *the festival is a memorial to his life's work:* **tribute**, testimonial, remembrance, memento. •adjective *a memorial service:* **commemorative**, remembrance.

memorize verb commit to memory, remember, learn (by heart), become word-perfect in, get off pat.

memory noun **1** *happy memories of her childhood:* **recollection**, remembrance, reminiscence. **2** *the town built a statue in memory of him:* **commemoration**, remembrance, honour, tribute, recognition, respect.

m

menace noun **1** a dangerous or troublesome person or thing. **2** a threatening quality. • verb (**menaces, menacing, menaced**) threaten.

ménage à trois /may-nahzh ah trwah/ noun an arrangement in which a married couple and the lover of one of them live together.

menagerie /muh-**naj**-uh-ri/ noun a small zoo.

mend verb **1** restore something so that it is no longer broken, torn, or out of action. **2** improve an unpleasant situation. • noun a repair.

mendacious /men-**day**-shuss/ adjective untruthful; lying.
■ **mendacity** noun.

mendicant /**men**-di-kuhnt/ adjective **1** living by begging. **2** (of a religious order) originally dependent on charitable donations. • noun **1** a beggar. **2** a member of a mendicant religious order.

menhir /**men**-heer/ noun a tall upright prehistoric stone erected as a monument.

menial /**mee**-ni-uhl/ adjective (of work) needing little skill and lacking status. • noun a person with a menial job.

meningitis /men-in-**jy**-tiss/ noun an infectious disease in which the membranes enclosing the brain and spinal cord become inflamed.

meniscus /mi-**niss**-kuhss/ noun (plural **menisci** /mi-**niss**-l/) **1** the curved upper surface of a liquid in a tube. **2** a thin lens curving outwards on one side and inwards on the other.

menopause noun the time when a woman gradually stops having menstrual periods, on average around the age of 50.

■ **menopausal** adjective.

menorah /mi-**nor**-uh/ noun a large candlestick with several branches, used in Jewish worship.

menstrual adjective having to do with menstruation.

menstruate verb (**menstruates, menstruating, menstruated**) (of a woman) have a flow of blood from the lining of the womb each month.
■ **menstruation** noun.

mental adjective **1** having to do with the mind. **2** relating to disorders of the mind. **3** informal mad.
■ **mentally** adverb.

mentality noun (plural **mentalities**) a characteristic way of thinking.

menthol noun a substance found in peppermint oil, used in medicines and as a flavouring.
■ **mentholated** adjective.

mention verb refer to something or someone briefly. • noun **1** a brief reference to someone or something. **2** a formal acknowledgement that someone has done something well.

mentor noun an experienced person who advises you over a period of time.

menu noun **1** a list of dishes available in a restaurant. **2** the food to be served in a restaurant or at a meal. **3** Computing a list of commands or facilities displayed on screen.

meow ⇒ MIAOW.

MEP abbreviation Member of the European Parliament.

mercantile /**mer**-kuhn-tyl/ adjective relating to trade or commerce.

mercenary adjective wanting to do only things that make you money. • noun (plural

m

menace noun **1** *an atmosphere full of menace:* threat, intimidation, malevolence, oppression. **2** *a menace to society:* danger, peril, risk, hazard, threat. **3** *that child is a menace:* nuisance, pest, troublemaker, mischief-maker; informal bad news.
• verb **1** *the elephants are still menaced by poaching:* threaten, endanger, put at risk, jeopardize, imperil. **2** *a gang of skinheads menaced local residents:* intimidate, threaten, terrorize, frighten, scare, terrify.

menacing adjective threatening, ominous, intimidating, frightening, forbidding, hostile, sinister, baleful.
OPPOSITES friendly.

mend verb repair, fix, restore, sew (up), stitch, darn, patch, renew, renovate, fill in; informal patch up.
OPPOSITES break.

mental adjective **1** *mental faculties:* intellectual, cerebral, rational, cognitive.

2 *a mental disorder:* psychiatric, psychological, behavioural.
OPPOSITES physical.

mentality noun way of thinking, mind set, mind, psychology, attitude, outlook, make-up.

mentally adverb psychologically, intellectually, in your mind, in your head, inwardly, internally.

mention verb **1** *don't mention the war:* allude to, refer to, touch on/upon, bring up, raise, broach. **2** *Jim mentioned that he'd met them before:* state, say, indicate, let someone know, disclose, divulge, reveal.
• noun reference, allusion, comment, citation; informal namecheck, plug.

mentor noun adviser, counsellor, guide, guru, consultant, confidant(e), trainer, teacher, tutor, instructor.

menu noun bill of fare, tariff, carte du jour, set menu, table d'hôte.

mercenaries) a professional soldier who is hired to serve in a foreign army.

merchandise noun goods for sale.

merchant noun a trader who sells goods in large quantities. •adjective (of ships, sailors, or shipping activity) involved with commerce.
□ **merchant bank** a bank whose customers are large businesses. **merchant navy** a country's commercial shipping.

merchantable adjective suitable for sale.

merciful adjective **1** showing mercy. **2** giving relief from suffering.
■ **mercifully** adverb.

merciless adjective showing no mercy.
■ **mercilessly** adverb.

mercurial /mer-**kyoor**-i-uhl/ adjective **1** tending to change mood suddenly. **2** having to do with the element mercury.

mercury noun **1** a heavy silvery-white liquid metallic element used in some thermometers and barometers. **2** (**Mercury**) the planet closest to the sun in the solar system.

mercy noun (plural **mercies**) **1** kindness or forgiveness shown towards someone who is in your power. **2** something to be grateful for.
□ **at the mercy of** in the power of.

mere adjective **1** being no more than what is stated or described. **2** (**the merest**) the smallest or slightest.

merely adverb only.

meretricious /me-ri-**tri**-shuhss/ adjective superficially attractive but having no real value.

merge verb (**merges**, **merging**, **merged**) **1** combine or be combined into a whole.

2 blend gradually into something else.

merger noun a merging of two organizations into one.

meridian noun a circle passing at the same longitude through a given place on the earth's surface and the two poles.

meringue /muh-**rang**/ noun beaten egg whites and sugar baked until crisp.

merino noun (plural **merinos**) a soft wool obtained from a breed of sheep with a long fleece.

merit noun **1** the quality of being good and deserving praise. **2** a good point or feature.
•verb (**merits**, **meriting**, **merited**) deserve.

meritocracy noun (plural **meritocracies**) a society in which power is held by those people who have the greatest ability.
■ **meritocratic** adjective.

meritorious adjective deserving reward or praise.

merlin noun a small falcon.

Merlot /**mer**-loh/ noun a type of red wine.

mermaid noun a mythical sea creature with a woman's head and body and a fish's tail instead of legs.

merriment noun fun.

merry adjective (**merrier**, **merriest**) **1** cheerful and lively. **2** informal slightly drunk.
□ **merry-go-round** a revolving platform fitted with model horses or cars, on which people ride for fun.
■ **merrily** adverb.

merrymaking noun lively celebration and fun.

Mesdames plural of **MADAME**.

Mesdemoiselles plural of **MADEMOISELLE**.

THESAURUS

merchandise noun goods, wares, stock, commodities, produce, products.

merchant noun trader, tradesman, dealer, wholesaler, broker, agent, seller, retailer, supplier, buyer, vendor, distributor.

mercy noun pity, compassion, leniency, clemency, charity, forgiveness, forbearance, kindness, sympathy, indulgence, tolerance, generosity, magnanimity.
OPPOSITES ruthlessness, cruelty.

merely adverb only, purely, solely, simply, just, but.

merge verb **1** *the company merged with a European firm:* join (together), join forces, amalgamate, unite, affiliate, team up. **2** *the organizations were merged:* amalgamate, bring together, join, consolidate, conflate, unite, unify, combine, incorporate, integrate. **3** *the two colours merged:* blend, mingle, fuse, mix, intermix, intermingle, coalesce.
OPPOSITES separate.

merger noun amalgamation, combination, union, fusion, coalition, affiliation, unification, incorporation, consolidation, link-up, alliance.
OPPOSITES split.

merit noun **1** *composers of outstanding merit:* excellence, quality, calibre, worth, value, distinction, eminence. **2** *the merits of the scheme:* good point, strong point, advantage, benefit, value, asset, plus.
OPPOSITES inferiority, fault, disadvantage.
•verb *the accusation did not merit a response:* deserve, warrant, justify, earn, rate, be worthy of, be entitled to, have a right to, have a claim to/on.

merry adjective cheerful, cheery, in high spirits, sunny, smiling, light-hearted, lively, carefree, joyful, joyous, jolly, convivial, festive, gleeful, happy, laughing; informal chirpy.
OPPOSITES miserable.

mesh noun **1** material made of a network of wire or thread. **2** the spacing of the strands of a net. •verb **1** fit together or be in harmony. **2** (of a gearwheel) lock together with another.

mesmeric adjective hypnotic.

mesmerism noun hypnotism.

mesmerize or **mesmerise** verb (mesmerizes, mesmerizing, mesmerized) capture someone's attention so that they are completely enthralled.

Mesolithic adjective relating to the middle part of the Stone Age.

mess noun **1** a dirty or untidy state. **2** a state of confusion or difficulty. **3** a portion of semi-solid food. **4** a dog or cat's excrement. **5** a place where members of the armed forces eat and relax. •verb **1** make something untidy or dirty. **2** (**mess about** or **around**) behave in a silly or playful way. **3** (**mess with**) informal meddle with.

message noun **1** a spoken, written, or electronic communication. **2** a significant point or central theme. •verb (**messages, messaging, messaged**) send a message to.

messenger noun a person who carries a message.

messiah noun **1** (**the Messiah**) (in Judaism) the person who will be sent by God as the saviour of the Jewish people. **2** (**the Messiah**) (in Christianity) Jesus, regarded as this saviour. **3** a great leader seen as the saviour of a country, group, etc.

messianic /mess-i-**an**-ik/ adjective relating to a messiah.

Messieurs plural of **Monsieur**.

Messrs plural of **Mr**.

messy adjective (**messier, messiest**) **1** untidy or dirty. **2** confused and difficult to deal with.
■ **messily** adverb **messiness** noun.

met past and past participle of **meet**.

metabolism /mi-**tab**-uh-li-z'm/ noun the process by which food is used for the growth of tissue or the production of energy.
■ **metabolic** adjective.

metabolize or **metabolise** verb (**metabolizes, metabolizing, metabolized**) process by metabolism.

metal noun **1** a hard, solid, shiny material which conducts electricity and heat. **2** (also **road metal**) broken stone used in making road surfaces.

metalled adjective Brit. (of a road) having a hard surface.

metallic adjective **1** having to do with metal. **2** (of sound) sharp and ringing.

metallurgy /mi-**tal**-ler-ji, **met**-uh-ler-ji/ noun the scientific study of metals.
■ **metallurgical** adjective **metallurgist** noun.

metamorphic adjective (of rock) having been changed by heat and pressure.

metamorphosis /met-uh-**mor**-fuh-siss/ noun (plural **metamorphoses** /met-uh-**mor**-fuh-seez/) **1** the transformation of an insect or amphibian from an immature form or larva to an adult form. **2** a change in form or nature.
■ **metamorphose** verb.

metaphor /**met**-uh-fer/ noun a word or

m

mesh noun *wire mesh*: netting, net, grille, screen, lattice, gauze.
•verb **1** *one gear meshes with the input gear*: engage, connect, lock, interlock. **2** *our ideas just do not mesh*: harmonize, fit together, match, dovetail, connect, interconnect.

mess noun **1** *please clear up the mess*: untidiness, disorder, disarray, clutter, muddle, chaos; informal shambles; Brit. informal tip. **2** *I've got to get out of this mess*: plight, predicament, tight spot, tight corner, difficulty, trouble, quandary, dilemma, problem, muddle, mix-up; informal jam, fix, pickle, hole.
□ **mess about/around** **potter about**, fiddle about/around, footle about/around, play about/around, fool about/around, fidget, toy, trifle, tamper, tinker, interfere, meddle, monkey (about/around); Brit. informal muck about/around. **mess something up dirty**, clutter up, jumble, dishevel, rumple; N. Amer. informal muss up.

message noun **1** *are there any messages for me?* communication, news, note, memo, email, letter, missive, report, bulletin, communiqué, dispatch. **2** *the message of his teaching*: meaning, sense, import, idea, point, thrust, moral, gist, essence, implication.

messenger noun courier, postman, runner, dispatch rider, envoy, emissary, agent, go-between.

messy adjective **1** *messy clothes*: dirty, filthy, grubby, soiled, grimy, mucky, muddy, stained, smeared, smudged, dishevelled, scruffy, unkempt, rumpled, matted, tousled; informal yucky. **2** *a messy kitchen*: untidy, disordered, in a muddle, chaotic, confused, disorganized, in disarray, cluttered, in a jumble; informal like a bomb's hit it; Brit. informal shambolic. **3** *a messy legal battle*: complex, tangled, confused, convoluted, unpleasant, nasty, bitter, acrimonious.
OPPOSITES clean, tidy.

metaphor noun figure of speech, image, trope, analogy, comparison, symbol.

phrase used in an imaginative way to represent or stand for something else (e.g. *the long arm of the law*).

metaphorical /met-uh-fo-ri-k'l/ or **metaphoric** adjective having to do with metaphor.
■ **metaphorically** adverb.

metaphysical adjective 1 relating to metaphysics. 2 beyond physical matter.
■ **metaphysically** adverb.

metaphysics noun the branch of philosophy dealing with the nature of existence, truth, and knowledge.

mete verb (**metes, meting, meted**) (**mete something out**) give someone a punishment, or subject them to harsh treatment.

meteor noun a small body of matter from space that glows as a result of friction with the earth's atmosphere, and appears as a shooting star.

meteoric adjective 1 relating to meteors or meteorites. 2 rapid in achieving success or promotion.

meteorite noun a piece of rock or metal that has fallen to the earth from space.

meteorology noun the study of conditions in the atmosphere, especially for weather forecasting.
■ **meteorological** adjective **meteorologist** noun.

meter¹ noun a device that measures and records the quantity, degree, or rate of something. ● verb (**meters, metering, metered**) measure something with a meter.

meter² US spelling of METRE¹, METRE².

methadone noun a powerful painkiller, used as a substitute for morphine and heroin in treating people addicted to these drugs.

methane noun a flammable gas which is the main constituent of natural gas.

methanol noun a poisonous flammable alcohol, used to make methylated spirit.

methinks verb (past **methought**) old use it seems to me.

method noun 1 a way of doing something. 2 the quality of being well planned and organized.

methodical or **methodic** adjective done or doing something in a well-organized and systematic way.

■ **methodically** adverb.

Methodist noun a member of a Christian Protestant group which separated from the Church of England in the 18th century.
● adjective relating to Methodists or their beliefs.
■ **Methodism** noun.

methodology noun (plural **methodologies**) a particular system of methods.
■ **methodological** adjective.

meths noun Brit. informal methylated spirit.

methylated spirit or **methylated spirits** noun alcohol for use as a solvent or fuel, made unfit for drinking by the addition of methanol and a violet dye.

meticulous adjective very careful and precise.
■ **meticulously** adverb.

métier /**may**-ti-ay/ noun a person's trade, profession, or special ability.

metre¹ (US spelling **meter**) noun the basic unit of length in the metric system, equal to 100 centimetres (approximately 39.37 inches).

metre² (US spelling **meter**) noun the rhythm of a piece of poetry.

metric adjective relating to or using the metric system.
□ **metric system** the decimal measuring system based on the metre, litre, and gram. **metric ton** (or **metric tonne**) a unit of weight equal to 1,000 kilograms (2,205 lb).

metrical adjective having to do with poetic metre.
■ **metrically** adverb.

metricate verb (**metricates, metricating, metricated**) convert a system of measurement to the metric system.
■ **metrication** noun.

metro noun (plural **metros**) an underground railway system in a city.

metronome noun a device that marks time at a selected rate by giving a regular tick, used by musicians.
■ **metronomic** adjective.

metropolis noun the main city of a country or region.

metropolitan adjective relating to the

THESAURUS

method noun 1 *they use very old-fashioned methods:* procedure, technique, system, practice, routine, modus operandi, process, strategy, tactic, approach. 2 *there's no method in his approach:* order, structure, organization, form, system, logic, planning, design, consistency.
OPPOSITES disorder.

methodical adjective orderly, well ordered,

well organized, (well) planned, efficient, businesslike, systematic, structured, logical, disciplined, consistent, scientific.

meticulous adjective careful, conscientious, diligent, scrupulous, punctilious, painstaking, thorough, studious, rigorous, detailed, perfectionist, fastidious.
OPPOSITES careless.

m

main city of a country or region.

mettle noun spirit and strength of character.

mew verb (of a cat or gull) make a soft, high-pitched sound like a cry.

mewl verb 1 cry feebly. 2 mew.

mews noun (plural **mews**) Brit. a row of houses or flats converted from stables in a small street or square.

Mexican noun a person from Mexico. • adjective relating to Mexico.

mezzanine /mets-uh-neen/ noun a floor extending over only part of the full area of a building, built between two full floors.

mezzo /met-soh/ or **mezzo-soprano** noun (plural **mezzos**) a female singer with a voice pitched between soprano and contralto.

mg abbreviation milligrams.

MHz abbreviation megahertz.

miaow or **meow** noun the cry of a cat. • verb make a miaow.

miasma /mi-az-muh/ noun an unpleasant or unhealthy atmosphere.

mica /my-kuh/ noun a mineral found as tiny shiny scales in rocks.

mice plural of MOUSE.

mickey noun (**take the mickey**) Brit. informal tease or mock someone.

microbe noun a bacterium; a germ. ▪ microbial adjective.

microbiology noun the scientific study of living creatures that are so tiny that they can only be seen using a microscope.

microchip noun a miniature electronic circuit made from a tiny wafer of silicon.

microclimate noun the climate of a very small or restricted area.

microcosm noun a thing that has the features and qualities of something much larger.

microfiche /my-kroh-feesh/ or **microfilm** noun a piece of film containing very small-sized photographs of the pages of a newspaper, book, etc.

microlight noun Brit. a very small, light, one- or two-seater aircraft.

micrometer /my-krom-i-ter/ noun an instrument which measures small distances or thicknesses.

microorganism noun an organism that is so small that it can only be seen using a microscope.

microphone noun an instrument for changing sound waves into electrical energy which is then amplified and transmitted or recorded.

microprocessor noun an integrated circuit which can function as the main part of a computer.

microscope noun an instrument for magnifying very small objects.

microscopic adjective so small as to be visible only with a microscope. ▪ microscopically adverb.

microscopy /my-kross-kuh-pi/ noun the use of a microscope.

microsurgery noun surgery performed using very small instruments and a microscope.

microwave noun 1 an electromagnetic wave with a wavelength in the range 0.001–0.3 m. 2 (also **microwave oven**) an oven that uses microwaves to cook or heat food. • verb (**microwaves, microwaving, microwaved**) cook food in a microwave oven.

mid adjective having to do with the middle position of a range. • preposition literary amid; in the middle of.

Midas touch noun the ability to make a lot of money out of anything you do.

midday noun twelve o'clock in the day; noon.

midden noun a heap of dung.

middle adjective 1 positioned at an equal distance from the edges or ends of something. 2 medium in rank, quality, or ability. • noun 1 a middle point or position. 2 informal a person's waist and stomach. □ middle age the period when a person is between about 45 and 60 in age. Middle Ages the period of European history between about 1000 and 1450. middle class the social group between the aristocracy and the working class. middle ear the air-filled central cavity of the ear, behind the eardrum. Middle East an area of SW Asia and northern Africa, stretching from the Mediterranean to Pakistan. middle-of-the-road 1 (of views) not extreme. 2 (of music) generally popular but rather unadventurous.

middleman noun (plural **middlemen**) 1 a person who buys goods from the company who makes them and sells them on to shops or consumers. 2 a person who arranges business or political deals

m

microbe noun microorganism, bacterium, bacillus, germ; informal bug.

midday noun noon, twelve noon, high noon, noonday.
OPPOSITES midnight.

middle noun 1 centre, midpoint, halfway point, dead centre, hub, eye, heart, core, kernel. 2 *he had a towel round his middle:* midriff, waist, belly, stomach; informal tummy.
OPPOSITES edge.
• adjective *the middle point:* central, mid,

middling adjective average in size, amount, or rank.

midfield noun the central part of a sports field.
■ **midfielder** noun.

midge noun a small fly that breeds near water.

midget noun a very small person. •adjective very small.

midland noun **1** the middle part of a country. **2 (the Midlands)** the inland counties of central England.

midnight noun twelve o'clock at night.

midriff noun the front of the body between the chest and the waist.

midship noun the middle part of a ship or boat.

midshipman noun (plural **midshipmen**) a low-ranking officer in the Royal Navy.

midships = **AMIDSHIPS**.

midst old use preposition in the middle of.
•noun the middle point or part.

midstream noun the middle of a stream or river.

midsummer noun **1** the middle part of summer. **2** the summer solstice.
□ **Midsummer Day** (or **Midsummer's Day**) 24 June.

midterm noun the middle of a period of office, an academic term, or a pregnancy.

midway adverb & adjective in or towards the middle.

midweek noun the middle of the week.
•adjective & adverb in the middle of the week.

midwife noun (plural **midwives**) a nurse trained to help women during childbirth.
■ **midwifery** /mid-**wif**-uh-ri/ noun.

midwinter noun **1** the middle part of winter. **2** the winter solstice.

mien /meen/ noun a person's look or manner.

miffed adjective informal slightly angry or upset.

might¹ modal verb (3rd singular present **might**)

past of **MAY**. **1** used to express possibility or make a suggestion. **2** used politely in questions and requests.

might² noun great power or strength.

mightn't short form might not.

mighty adjective (**mightier**, **mightiest**) very strong or powerful. •adverb informal very.
■ **mightily** adverb.

migraine /**mee**-grayn, **my**-grayn/ noun a severe headache which is accompanied by symptoms such as nausea and disturbed vision.

migrant noun **1** a worker who moves from one place to another to find work. **2** an animal that migrates. •adjective tending to migrate or having migrated.

migrate verb (**migrates**, **migrating**, **migrated**) **1** (of an animal) move to warmer regions in the winter and back to colder regions in the summer. **2** move to settle in a new area in order to find work.
■ **migration** noun **migratory** adjective.

mike noun informal a microphone.

milch adjective (of an animal) giving or kept for milk.

mild adjective **1** not severe or harsh. **2** (of weather) fairly warm. **3** not sharp or strong in flavour. **4** (of a person or their behaviour) calm and gentle. •noun Brit. a kind of dark beer not strongly flavoured with hops.
■ **mildly** adverb **mildness** noun.

mildew noun a coating of tiny fungi on plants or damp material such as paper or leather.
■ **mildewed** adjective.

mile noun **1** a unit of length equal to 1,760 yards (approximately 1.609 kilometres). **2 (miles)** informal a very long way.

mileage noun **1** a number of miles covered. **2** informal advantage.

mileometer ⇨ **MILOMETER**.

milestone noun **1** a stone set up beside a road, marking the distance in miles to a place further along the road. **2** an event marking a significant new development or stage.

THESAURUS

mean, medium, median, midway, halfway.

might noun strength, force, power, vigour, energy, brawn.

mighty adjective powerful, forceful, hard, heavy, violent, vigorous, hefty.
OPPOSITES feeble.

migrant noun *economic migrants:* immigrant, emigrant, nomad, itinerant, traveller, transient, wanderer, drifter.
•adjective *migrant workers:* travelling, mobile, wandering, drifting, nomadic, itinerant, transient.

migrate verb **1** *rural populations migrated to towns:* relocate, resettle, move (house), emigrate, go abroad. **2** *wildebeest migrate across the Serengeti:* roam, wander, drift, rove, travel.

mild adjective **1** *a mild tone of voice:* gentle, tender, soft, sympathetic, peaceable, quiet, reasonable. **2** *a mild punishment:* lenient, light. **3** *he was eyeing her with mild interest:* slight, faint, vague. **4** *mild weather:* warm, balmy, temperate, clement. **5** *a mild curry:* bland, light, insipid.
OPPOSITES harsh, strong, cold, severe, hot.

m

milieu /mee-lyer/ noun (plural **milieux** /mee-lyer/ or **milieus** /mee-lyerz/) the social environment that you live or work in.

militant adjective supporting a cause in a forceful and aggressive way. • noun a militant person.
■ **militancy** noun **militantly** adverb.

militarism noun a belief in the value of military strength.
■ **militarist** noun & adjective **militaristic** adjective.

militarized or **militarised** adjective supplied with soldiers and military equipment.

military adjective having to do with soldiers or armed forces. • noun (**the military**) the armed forces of a country.
■ **militarily** adverb.

militate verb (**militates**, **militating**, **militated**) (**militate against**) make it very difficult for something to happen or exist.

> ! don't confuse **militate** with **mitigate**, which means 'make something bad less severe'.

militia /mi-li-shuh/ noun 1 a group of people who are not professional soldiers but who act as an army. 2 a rebel force opposing a regular army.

milk noun 1 a white fluid produced by female mammals to feed their young. 2 the milk of cows as a food and drink for humans. 3 the milk-like juice of certain plants. • verb 1 draw milk from an animal. 2 take money from someone dishonestly and over a period of time. 3 take full advantage of a situation.
□ **milk chocolate** solid chocolate made with milk. **milk float** Brit. an electrically powered van with open sides, used for delivering milk to houses. **milk tooth** a temporary tooth in a child or young mammal.

milkmaid noun old use a girl or woman who worked in a dairy.

milkman noun (plural **milkmen**) a man who delivers milk to houses.

milkshake noun a cold drink made from milk whisked with ice cream or a flavouring.

milksop noun a timid person.

milky adjective 1 containing milk. 2 having a soft white colour or clouded appearance.
□ **Milky Way** the galaxy of which our solar system is a part, visible at night as a faint band of light crossing the sky.
■ **milkily** adverb **milkiness** noun.

mill noun 1 a building equipped with machinery for grinding grain into flour. 2 a device for grinding coffee beans, peppercorns, etc. 3 a building fitted with machinery for a manufacturing process. • verb 1 grind something in a mill. 2 cut or shape metal with a rotating tool. 3 (**milled**) (of a coin) having ribbed markings on the edge. 4 (**mill about** or **around**) move around in a confused mass.
□ **mill wheel** a wheel used to drive a watermill.

millennium /mi-len-i-uhm/ noun (plural **millennia** or **millenniums**) 1 a period of a thousand years. 2 (**the millennium**) the point at which one period of a thousand years ends and another begins. 3 an anniversary of a thousand years.
■ **millennial** adjective.

> ☑ double *l*, double *n*: mil*lennium*.

miller noun a person who owns or works in a grain mill.

millet noun a cereal plant used to make flour or alcoholic drinks.

millibar noun a unit for measuring the pressure of the atmosphere.

milligram or **milligramme** noun one thousandth of a gram.

millilitre (US spelling **milliliter**) noun one thousandth of a litre.

millimetre (US spelling **millimeter**) noun one thousandth of a metre.

milliner noun a person who makes or sells women's hats.
■ **millinery** noun.

million cardinal number (plural **millions** or (with another word or number) **million**) 1 a thousand times a thousand; 1,000,000.

m

THESAURUS

militant adjective *militant workers:* hard-line, extreme, active, extremist, committed, zealous, fanatical, radical.
• noun *a confrontation with militants:* activist, extremist, radical, zealot.

military adjective fighting, service, army, armed, defence, martial.
OPPOSITES civilian.
• noun *the military took power:* (armed) forces, services, militia, army, navy, air force, marines.

militate verb *laws that militate against personal freedom:* work against, hinder, discourage, be prejudicial to, be detrimental to.

milk verb *milking rich clients:* exploit, take advantage of, suck dry; informal bleed, squeeze, fleece.

mill noun *a steel mill:* factory, plant, works, workshop, shop, foundry.
• verb *the wheat is milled into flour:* grind, pulverize, powder, granulate, pound, crush, press.
□ **mill around/about wander**, drift, swarm,

2 (also **millions**) informal a very large number or amount.
■ **millionth** ordinal number.

millionaire noun a person whose money and property are worth one million pounds or dollars or more.

☑ just one *n*: millionaire.

millipede noun an insect-like creature with a long body and a lot of legs.

millisecond noun one thousandth of a second.

millpond noun **1** a pool created to provide the water that turns the wheel of a watermill. **2** a very still and calm stretch of water.

millstone noun **1** each of a pair of circular stones used for grinding grain. **2** a heavy responsibility that you cannot escape from.

milometer or **mileometer** /my-lom-i-ter/ noun Brit. an instrument on a vehicle for recording the number of miles travelled.

mime noun the use of silent gestures and facial expressions to tell a story or show feelings. •**verb** (**mimes, miming, mimed**) **1** use mime to tell a story or show feelings. **2** pretend to sing or play an instrument as a recording is being played.

mimic verb (**mimics, mimicking, mimicked**) **1** imitate the voice or actions of someone else. **2** (of an animal or plant) take on the appearance of another in order to hide or for protection. •**noun** a person skilled in mimicking others.
■ **mimicry** noun.

mimosa noun an acacia tree with delicate leaves and yellow flowers.

minaret /min-uh-**ret**/ noun a slender tower of a mosque, with a balcony from which Muslims are called to prayer.

minatory /min-uh-tuh-ri/ adjective formal threatening.

mince verb **1** cut or grind meat into very small pieces. **2** walk with short, quick steps and swinging hips. •**noun** Brit. minced meat. ❑ **mince pie** a small tart containing mincemeat, eaten at Christmas. **not mince your words** speak plainly.

mincemeat noun a mixture of dried fruit, candied peel, sugar, spices, and suet.

mind noun **1** the faculty of consciousness and thought. **2** a person's intellect or memory. **3** a person's attention or will. •**verb** **1** be upset or annoyed by. **2** remember or take care to do. **3** watch out for. **4** temporarily take care of. **5** (**be minded**) be inclined to do. ❑ **out of your mind** not thinking sensibly; crazy.

minded adjective inclined to think in a particular way.

minder noun a person whose job is to take care of or protect someone or something.

mindful adjective (**mindful of** or **that**) aware of or recognizing that.

mindless adjective **1** acting or done without good reason and with no concern for the consequences. **2** (of an activity) simple and repetitive.
■ **mindlessly** adverb.

mindset noun a person's particular way of thinking and set of beliefs.

mine¹ possessive pronoun referring to a thing or things belonging to or associated with the person speaking. •**possessive determiner** old use my.

mine² noun **1** a hole or channel dug in the earth for extracting coal or other minerals. **2** an abundant source. **3** a type of bomb placed on or in the ground or water, which explodes on contact. •**verb** (**mines, mining, mined**) **1** obtain coal or other minerals from a mine. **2** lay explosive mines on or in.

THESAURUS

crowd, pack, fill.

mimic verb imitate, copy, impersonate, do an impression of, ape, caricature, parody; informal send up, take off.
•**noun** impersonator, impressionist; informal copycat.

mince verb grind, chop up, cut up, dice, crumble; N. Amer. hash.

mind noun **1** *a good teacher must stretch pupils' minds*: brain, intelligence, intellect, brains, brainpower, wits, understanding, reasoning, judgement, sense, head; informal grey matter; N. Amer. informal smarts. **2** *he kept his mind on the job*: attention, thoughts, concentration. **3** *the tragedy affected her mind*: sanity, mental faculties, senses, wits, reason, reasoning, judgement. **4** *a great*

mind: intellect, thinker, brain, scholar.
•**verb** **1** *do you mind if I smoke?* object, care, be bothered, be annoyed, be upset, take offence, disapprove, look askance; informal give/care a damn. **2** *mind the step!* be careful of, watch out for, look out for, beware of. **3** *mind you wipe your feet*: make sure, see, remember to, don't forget to. **4** *her husband was minding the baby*: look after, take care of, keep an eye on, attend to, care for.

mine noun **1** *a coal mine*: pit, colliery, excavation, quarry. **2** *a mine of information*: store, storehouse, reservoir, repository, gold mine, treasure house, treasury.
•**verb** *the iron ore was mined from shallow pits*: quarry, excavate, dig, extract.

minefield noun **1** an area planted with explosive mines. **2** a subject or situation presenting unseen dangers.

miner noun a person who works in a mine.

mineral noun **1** a solid substance occurring naturally, such as copper and silicon. **2** an inorganic substance needed by the human body for good health, such as calcium and iron.
□ **mineral water** water from a natural spring, containing dissolved mineral salts.

mineralogy noun the scientific study of minerals.
■ **mineralogical** adjective **mineralogist** noun.

mineshaft noun a deep, narrow shaft that gives access to a mine.

minestrone /mi-ni-stroh-ni/ noun an Italian soup containing vegetables and pasta.

minesweeper noun a warship equipped for detecting and removing or destroying explosive mines.

mingle verb (**mingles, mingling, mingled**) mix together.

mingy /min-ji/ adjective informal not generous.

mini adjective very small of its kind. • noun (plural **minis**) a very short skirt.

miniature adjective of a much smaller size than normal. • noun **1** a thing that is much smaller than normal. **2** a tiny, detailed portrait or picture.

> ☑ -ia- in the middle: min*ia*ture.

miniaturist noun an artist who paints miniatures.

miniaturize or **miniaturise** verb (**miniaturizes, miniaturizing, miniaturized**) make a smaller version of.

minibar noun a small fridge in a hotel room

containing a selection of drinks.

minibus noun a small bus for about ten to fifteen passengers.

minicab noun Brit. a taxi that you order by telephone but cannot hail in the street.

minidisc noun a disc similar to a small CD but able to record sound or data as well as play it back.

minim noun a musical note that lasts as long as two crotchets.

minimal adjective of a minimum amount, quantity, or degree.
■ **minimally** adverb.

minimalist adjective **1** (of art) using simple forms and structures. **2** deliberately simple or basic in design. • noun an artist who uses simple forms and structures.
■ **minimalism** noun.

minimize or **minimise** verb (**minimizes, minimizing, minimized**) **1** make something as small as possible. **2** represent something as less important or significant than it really is.

minimum noun (plural **minima** or **minimums**) the smallest amount, extent, or strength possible. • adjective smallest in amount, extent, or strength.

minion noun a worker or assistant who has a low or unimportant status.

miniskirt noun a very short skirt.

minister noun **1** a head of a government department. **2** a person who represents their government in a foreign country. **3** a person who carries out religious duties in the Christian Church. • verb (**ministers, ministering, ministered**) (**minister to**) attend to the needs of.
■ **ministerial** adjective.

ministrations plural noun the providing of

THESAURUS

mingle verb **1** *fact and fiction are mingled:* mix, blend, intermingle, intermix, interweave, interlace, combine, merge, fuse, unite, join, amalgamate. **2** *guests mingled in the marquee:* socialize, circulate, associate, fraternize, get together; informal hobnob.
OPPOSITES separate.

miniature adjective small, mini, little, small-scale, baby, toy, pocket, diminutive; Scottish wee; N. Amer. vest-pocket.
OPPOSITES giant.

minimal adjective very little/small, minimum, the least (possible), nominal, token, negligible.
OPPOSITES maximum.

minimize verb **1** *the aim is to minimize costs:* keep down, keep to a minimum, reduce, decrease, cut (down), lessen, curtail, prune; informal slash. **2** *we should not minimize his contribution:* belittle, make

light of, play down, underrate, downplay, undervalue.
OPPOSITES maximize, exaggerate.

minimum noun *costs will be kept to the minimum:* lowest level, lower limit, rock bottom, least, lowest, slightest.
OPPOSITES maximum.
• adjective *with the minimum effort:* minimal, least, smallest, least possible, slightest, lowest, minutest.
OPPOSITES maximum.

minister noun **1** *a government minister:* member of the government, member of the cabinet, secretary of state. **2** *a minister of religion:* clergyman, clergywoman, cleric, pastor, vicar, rector, priest, parson, curate; informal reverend, padre.
• verb *doctors were ministering to the injured:* tend, care for, take care of, look after, nurse, treat, attend to, see to, help.

m

ministry noun (plural **ministries**) **1** a government department headed by a minister. **2** a period of government under one Prime Minister. **3** the work of a minister in the Christian Church.

mink noun a small stoat-like animal that is farmed for its fur.

minnow noun a small freshwater fish.

minor adjective **1** not important or serious. **2** Music (of a scale) having intervals of a semitone between the second and third, fifth and sixth, and seventh and eighth notes. •noun a person under the age of full legal responsibility.

minority noun (plural **minorities**) **1** the smaller number or part. **2** a relatively small group of people differing from the majority in race, religion, etc.

minster noun Brit. a large or important church.

minstrel noun a medieval singer or musician.

mint¹ noun **1** a sweet-smelling plant, used as a herb in cookery. **2** the flavour of mint. **3** a peppermint sweet. ■ **minty** adjective.

mint² noun **1** a place where money is made. **2** (**a mint**) informal a large sum of money. •verb make a coin by stamping metal. □ in mint condition new, or as good as new.

minuet noun a ballroom dance popular in the 18th century.

minus preposition **1** with the subtraction of. **2** (of temperature) falling below zero by. **3** informal lacking. •adjective **1** (before a number) below zero. **2** (after a grade) slightly below. **3** having a negative electric charge. •noun **1** (also **minus sign**) the symbol –, indicating subtraction or a

negative value. **2** informal a disadvantage.

minuscule /min-uhss-kyool/ adjective very tiny.

☑ -u-, not -i-, in the middle: min**u**scule.

minute¹ /mi-nit/ noun **1** a period of time equal to sixty seconds or a sixtieth of an hour. **2** (**a minute**) informal a very short time. **3** a measurement of an angle equal to one sixtieth of a degree.

minute² /my-nyoot/ adjective (**minutest**) **1** very small. **2** precise and careful. ■ **minutely** adverb.

minute³ /mi-nit/ noun **1** (**minutes**) a written summary of the points discussed at a meeting. **2** an official written message. •verb (**minutes, minuting, minuted**) record the points discussed at a meeting.

minutiae /mi-**nyoo**-shi-ee/ plural noun small or precise details.

minx noun a cheeky, cunning, or flirtatious girl or young woman.

miracle noun **1** a welcome event that is so extraordinary that it is thought to be the work of God or a saint. **2** an outstanding example or achievement. □ miracle play a medieval play based on stories from the Bible.

miraculous adjective like a miracle; very surprising and amazing. ■ **miraculously** adverb.

mirage /mi-**rahzh**/ noun **1** an effect caused by hot air, in which a sheet of water seems to appear in a desert or on a hot road. **2** something that appears real or possible but is not in fact so.

mire noun **1** a stretch of swampy or boggy ground. **2** a difficult situation from which it is hard to escape. •verb (**be mired**)

THESAURUS

ministry noun **1** *the ministry for foreign affairs:* department, bureau, agency, office. **2** *he's training for the ministry:* the priesthood, holy orders, the cloth, the church.

minor adjective **1** *a minor problem:* slight, small, unimportant, insignificant, inconsequential, negligible, trivial, trifling, paltry, petty; N. Amer. nickel-and-dime; informal piffling. **2** *a minor Elizabethan poet:* little known, unknown, lesser, unimportant, insignificant, obscure; N. Amer. minor-league; informal small-time; N. Amer. informal two-bit. OPPOSITES major, important.
•noun *the accused was a minor:* child, infant, youth, adolescent, teenager, boy, girl; informal kid. OPPOSITES adult.

mint verb coin, stamp, strike, cast, manufacture.

minute¹ noun **1** *it'll only take a minute:*

moment, short time, little while, second, instant; informal sec, jiffy; Brit. informal tick, mo, two ticks. **2** *at that minute, Tony walked in:* point (in time), moment, instant, second, juncture. **3** *their objection was noted in the minutes:* record(s), proceedings, log, notes, transcript, summary.

minute² adjective **1** *minute particles:* tiny, minuscule, microscopic, miniature; Scottish wee; informal teeny, teeny-weeny; Brit. informal titchy, tiddly. **2** *a minute chance of success:* negligible, slight, infinitesimal, minimal. **3** *in minute detail:* exhaustive, painstaking, meticulous, rigorous, thorough. OPPOSITES huge.

miracle noun wonder, marvel, sensation, phenomenon.

miraculous adjective amazing, astounding, remarkable, extraordinary, incredible, unbelievable, sensational, phenomenal.

1 become stuck in mud. **2** be in a difficult situation.

mirror noun **1** a surface which reflects a clear image. **2** something that accurately represents something else. •verb reflect.
□ **mirror image** an image which is identical in form to another but is reversed, as if seen in a mirror.

mirth noun laughter.
■ mirthful adjective.

misadventure noun **1** (also **death by misadventure**) Law death caused accidentally and not involving crime. **2** a mishap.

misalliance noun an unsuitable or unhappy relationship or marriage.

misanthrope /mi-zuhn-throhp/ noun a person who dislikes and avoids other people.
■ misanthropic adjective misanthropy noun.

misapprehension noun a mistaken belief.

misappropriate verb (**misappropriates, misappropriating, misappropriated**) dishonestly take something for your own use.
■ misappropriation noun.

misbegotten adjective badly thought out or planned.

misbehave verb (**misbehaves, misbehaving, misbehaved**) behave badly.
■ misbehaviour noun.

miscalculate verb (**miscalculates, miscalculating, miscalculated**) calculate or assess wrongly.
■ miscalculation noun.

miscarriage noun the birth of a baby or fetus before it is able to survive outside the mother's womb.
□ **miscarriage of justice** a situation in which a court of law fails to achieve justice.

miscarry verb (**miscarries, miscarrying, miscarried**) **1** (of a pregnant woman) have a miscarriage. **2** (of a plan) fail.

miscast verb (**be miscast**) (of an actor) be given an unsuitable role.

miscellaneous /mi-suh-**lay**-ni-uhss/ adjective consisting of many different kinds.

miscellany /mi-**sel**-luh-ni/ noun (plural **miscellanies**) a collection of different things.

mischance noun bad luck.

mischief noun **1** playful bad behaviour that does not cause serious damage or harm. **2** harm caused by someone or something.

mischievous /miss-chi-vuhss/ adjective **1** causing mischief. **2** intended to cause trouble.
■ mischievously adverb.

☑ the ending is -ous, not -ious: mischievous.

miscible /miss-i-b'l/ adjective (of liquids) able to be mixed together.

misconceived adjective badly judged or planned.

misconception noun a failure to understand something correctly.

misconduct noun /miss-kon-dukt/ bad behaviour.

misconstruction noun a failure to interpret something correctly.

misconstrue verb (**misconstrues, misconstruing, misconstrued**) interpret something wrongly.

miscreant /miss-kri-uhnt/ noun a person who behaves badly or unlawfully.

misdeed noun a bad or evil act.

misdemeanour (US spelling **misdemeanor**) noun an action that is bad or unacceptable, but does not amount to a serious crime.

misdiagnose verb (**misdiagnoses, misdiagnosing, misdiagnosed**) diagnose something incorrectly.
■ misdiagnosis noun.

misdirect verb direct or instruct wrongly.
■ misdirection noun.

miser noun a person who hoards wealth and spends as little as possible.

miserable adjective **1** very unhappy or depressed. **2** causing unhappiness or discomfort. **3** (of a person) gloomy and humourless. **4** very small or inadequate.
■ miserably adverb.

m

THESAURUS

mirror noun **1** *a quick look in the mirror:* looking glass; Brit. glass. **2** *the Frenchman's life was a mirror of his own:* reflection, replica, copy, match, parallel.
•verb *pop music mirrored the mood of desperation:* reflect, match, reproduce, imitate, copy, mimic, echo, parallel.

misbehave verb behave badly, be naughty, be disobedient, get up to mischief, get up to no good, be rude, informal carry on, act up.

miscellaneous adjective various, varied, different, assorted, mixed, sundry, diverse, disparate.

mischief noun **1** *the boys are always getting up to mischief:* naughtiness, bad behaviour, misbehaviour, misconduct, disobedience. **2** *the mischief in her eyes:* impishness, roguishness, glint, twinkle.

miser noun penny-pincher, Scrooge; informal skinflint, cheapskate; N. Amer. informal tightwad.
OPPOSITES spendthrift.

miserable adjective **1** *I'm too miserable to*

misericord /mi-zerr-i-kord/ noun a ledge projecting from the underside of a hinged seat in the choir of a church, giving support to someone standing when the seat is folded up.

miserly adjective 1 not willing to spend money. 2 (of a quantity) too small.
■ miserliness noun.

misery noun (plural miseries) 1 great unhappiness. 2 a cause of this. 3 Brit. informal a person who is constantly miserable.

misfire verb (misfires, misfiring, misfired) 1 (of a gun) fail to fire properly. 2 (of an internal-combustion engine) fail to ignite the fuel correctly. 3 fail to produce the intended result.

misfit noun a person whose attitudes and actions set them apart from other people.

misfortune noun 1 bad luck. 2 an unfortunate event.

misgivings plural noun feelings of doubt or worry.

misguided adjective badly judged.

mishandle verb (mishandles, mishandling, mishandled) handle a situation badly or wrongly.

mishap noun an unlucky accident.

mishear verb (mishears, mishearing, misheard) hear incorrectly.

mishit verb (mishits, mishitting, mishit) hit or kick a ball badly.

mishmash noun a confused mixture.

misinform verb give someone false or inaccurate information.
■ misinformation noun.

misinterpret verb (misinterprets, misinterpreting, misinterpreted) interpret something wrongly.
■ misinterpretation noun.

misjudge verb (misjudges, misjudging, misjudged) 1 form a wrong opinion about.
2 estimate wrongly.
■ misjudgement (or misjudgment) noun.

mislay verb (mislays, mislaying, mislaid) lose something because you have forgotten where you put it.

mislead verb (misleads, misleading, misled) give someone a wrong impression or wrong information.

mismanage verb (mismanages, mismanaging, mismanaged) manage something badly or wrongly.
■ mismanagement noun.

mismatch noun a combination of things or people that do not go together well. •verb match people or things unsuitably or incorrectly.

misnomer /miss-noh-mer/ noun 1 a name or term that is wrong or inaccurate. 2 the wrong use of a name or term.

misogynist /mi-soj-uh-nist/ noun a man who hates women.
■ misogynistic adjective misogyny noun.

misplace verb (misplaces, misplacing, misplaced) put in the wrong place.

misplaced adjective 1 wrongly placed. 2 unwise or inappropriate.

misprint noun a mistake in printed material.

mispronounce verb (mispronounces, mispronouncing, mispronounced) pronounce wrongly.
■ mispronunciation noun.

misquote verb (misquotes, misquoting, misquoted) quote inaccurately.

misread verb (misreads, misreading, misread) read or interpret wrongly.

misrepresent verb give a false or misleading account of.
■ misrepresentation noun.

misrule noun 1 bad government. 2 disorder.

miss[1] verb 1 fail to hit, reach, or come into

THESAURUS

eat: unhappy, sad, sorrowful, dejected, depressed, down, despondent, disconsolate, wretched, glum, forlorn, woebegone; informal blue, down in the dumps. 2 *their miserable surroundings:* dreary, dismal, gloomy, drab, wretched, depressing, grim, cheerless, bleak, desolate.
OPPOSITES cheerful, lovely.

misery noun unhappiness, distress, wretchedness, suffering, anguish, anxiety, angst, torment, pain, grief, heartache, heartbreak, despair, despondency, dejection, depression, gloom, sorrow; informal the blues.
OPPOSITES contentment, pleasure.

misfortune noun problem, difficulty, setback, trouble, adversity, (stroke of) bad luck, misadventure, mishap, blow, failure, accident, disaster.

misguided adjective unwise, ill-advised, ill-judged, ill-considered, injudicious, imprudent, unsound, mistaken, misplaced.
OPPOSITES wise.

mislay verb lose, misplace, be unable to find.
OPPOSITES find.

mislead verb deceive, delude, take in, lie to, fool, hoodwink, misinform; informal lead up the garden path; N. Amer. informal give someone a bum steer.

misleading adjective deceptive, confusing, deceiving, equivocal, false.
OPPOSITES clear, honest, straightforward.

miss verb 1 *the shot missed her by inches:* go wide of, fall short of, pass, overshoot. 2 *I left early to miss the traffic:* avoid, beat, evade, escape, dodge, sidestep, elude, circumvent, bypass. 3 *she missed him when* contact with. **2** be too late for. **3** fail to notice, hear, or understand. **4** fail to be present at. **5** avoid something unpleasant. **6** (**miss someone/thing out**) fail to include someone or something. **7** feel sad because of the absence of. •**noun** a failure to hit, catch, or reach something.

miss² noun **1** (**Miss**) a title coming before the name of an unmarried woman or girl. **2** (**Miss**) used as a form of address to a teacher. **3** a girl or young woman.

missal noun a book containing the prayers and responses used in the Catholic Mass.

misshapen adjective not having the normal or natural shape.

missile noun an object or weapon that is thrown or fired at a target.

missing adjective **1** absent and unable to be found. **2** not present when expected to be.

mission noun **1** an important assignment, typically involving travel abroad. **2** an organization involved in a long-term assignment abroad. **3** a military or scientific expedition. **4** the work of teaching people about Christianity. **5** a strongly felt aim or calling.

missionary noun (plural **missionaries**) a person sent on a religious mission. •**adjective** having to do with a religious mission.

missive noun formal a letter.

misspell verb (**misspells, misspelling**, past and past participle **misspelled** or chiefly Brit. **misspelt**) spell wrongly.

misspend verb (**misspends, misspending**, **misspent**) spend time or money foolishly.

mist noun a thin cloud of tiny water droplets that makes it difficult to see. •**verb** cover or become covered with mist.

mistake noun **1** a thing that is incorrect. **2** an error of judgement. •**verb** (**mistakes, mistaking, mistook**; past participle **mistaken**) **1** be wrong about. **2** (**mistake someone/thing for**) confuse someone or something with.

mistaken adjective **1** wrong in your opinion or judgement. **2** based on or resulting from a misunderstanding.
■ **mistakenly** adverb.

mister noun **1** (**Mister**) = **Mr**. **2** informal a form of address to a man.

mistime verb (**mistimes, mistiming, mistimed**) choose an inappropriate moment to do or say something.

mistletoe noun a plant which grows as a parasite on trees, producing white berries in winter.

mistral /miss-truhl, mis-trahl/ noun a strong north-westerly wind that blows through southern France.

mistreat verb treat badly or unfairly.
■ **mistreatment** noun.

mistress noun **1** a woman in a position of authority. **2** a woman who is very skilled in something. **3** a woman having a sexual relationship with a man who is married to someone else. **4** Brit. a female schoolteacher. **5** (**Mistress**) old use Mrs.

mistrial noun a trial that is not considered valid because of a mistake in proceedings.

m

THESAURUS

he was away: pine for, yearn for, ache for, long for. **4** she never missed a meeting: fail to attend, be absent from, play truant from, cut, skip, omit; Brit. informal skive off.
OPPOSITES hit, catch, attend.
•noun one hit and three misses: failure, omission, slip, error, mistake.
□ miss someone/something out **leave out**, exclude, miss (off), fail to mention, pass over, skip, omit, ignore.

missing adjective **1** his wallet is missing: lost, mislaid, misplaced, absent, gone (astray), unaccounted for. **2** passion was missing from her life: absent, lacking, gone, wanting.
OPPOSITES present.

mission noun **1** a mercy mission to Romania: assignment, commission, expedition, journey, trip, undertaking, operation, project. **2** her mission in life: vocation, calling, goal, aim, quest, purpose, function, task, job, labour, work, duty.

missionary noun evangelist, apostle, proselytizer, preacher.

mist noun haze, fog, smog, murk, cloud,

vapour, steam, spray, condensation.

mistake noun it was all a mistake: error, fault, inaccuracy, omission, slip, blunder, miscalculation, misunderstanding, oversight, misinterpretation, gaffe, faux pas; informal slip-up, boo-boo, howler; Brit. informal boob, clanger; N. Amer. informal goof.
•verb **1** men are apt to mistake their own feelings: misunderstand, misinterpret, get wrong, misconstrue, misread. **2** children often mistake pills for sweets: confuse with, mix up with, take for.
□ make a mistake **make an error etc.**, go wrong, err, blunder, miscalculate.

mistaken adjective **1** such a mistaken view: inaccurate, wrong, erroneous, incorrect, off beam, false, fallacious, unfounded, misguided. **2** you are mistaken there: misinformed, wrong, in error, under a misapprehension, barking up the wrong tree.
OPPOSITES correct.

mistimed adjective ill-timed, badly timed, inopportune, inappropriate, untimely.
OPPOSITES opportune.

mistrust verb have no trust in. •noun lack of trust.

misty adjective (mistier, mistiest) 1 covered with mist. 2 having an outline that is not clear.

misunderstand verb (misunderstands, misunderstanding, misunderstood) fail to understand correctly.
■ misunderstanding noun.

misuse verb (misuses, misusing, misused) 1 use wrongly. 2 treat badly or unfairly. •noun the action of misusing.

mite noun 1 a tiny insect-like creature. 2 a small child or animal. 3 a very small amount.

mitigate verb (mitigates, mitigating, mitigated) make something bad less severe or serious.
■ mitigation noun.

> **!** don't confuse **mitigate** with **militate**: **militate against** means 'make it very difficult for something to happen or exist'.

mitre (US spelling **miter**) noun 1 a tall headdress that tapers to a point at the front and back, worn by bishops. 2 a joint made between two pieces of wood cut at an angle in order to form a corner of 90°.

mitt noun 1 a mitten. 2 informal a person's hand.

mitten noun a glove having a single section for all four fingers, with a separate section for the thumb.

mix verb 1 combine or be combined to form a whole. 2 make by mixing ingredients. 3 combine different recordings to form one piece of music. 4 (**mix something up**) spoil the arrangement of something. 5 (**mix someone/thing up**) confuse one person or thing with another. 6 meet different people socially. •noun 1 a mixture. 2 the proportion of different people or things making up a mixture. 3 a version of a piece of music mixed in a different way from the original.
□ **mix-up** informal a misunderstanding or mistake.

mixed adjective 1 made up of different qualities or things. 2 having to do with males and females.
□ **mixed bag** an assortment of people or things of very different types.

mixer noun 1 a machine or device for mixing things. 2 a soft drink that can be mixed with alcohol.

mixture noun 1 a substance made by mixing other substances together. 2 (**a mixture of**) a combination of different things in which each thing is distinct.

mizzen or **mizzenmast** noun the mast behind a ship's mainmast.

ml abbreviation 1 miles. 2 millilitres.

mm abbreviation millimetres.

MMR abbreviation measles, mumps, and rubella (a vaccination given to children).

mnemonic /ni-mon-ik/ noun a pattern of letters or words used to help remember

THESAURUS

mistrust verb be suspicious of, be sceptical of, be wary of, be chary of, distrust, have doubts about, have misgivings about, have reservations about, suspect.

misunderstand verb misapprehend, misinterpret, misconstrue, misconceive, mistake, misread, be mistaken, get the wrong idea; informal get (hold of) the wrong end of the stick.

misunderstanding noun 1 *a misunderstanding of juvenile crime:* misinterpretation, misreading, the wrong idea, misapprehension, misconception, false impression. 2 *we have had some misunderstandings:* disagreement, difference (of opinion), dispute, falling-out, quarrel, argument, clash.

misuse verb *misusing public funds:* embezzle, misappropriate, abuse, waste, squander.
•noun *a misuse of company assets:* embezzlement, fraud, squandering, waste.

mix verb 1 *mix all the ingredients together:* blend, mingle, combine, jumble, fuse, unite, join, amalgamate, incorporate, meld, homogenize; technical admix; literary commingle. 2 *she mixes with all sorts:* associate, socialize, keep company, consort, mingle, circulate; Brit. rub shoulders; N. Amer. rub elbows; informal hang out/around, hobnob.
OPPOSITES separate.
•noun *a mix of ancient and modern:* mixture, blend, combination, compound, fusion, union, amalgamation, medley, selection, assortment, variety.

mixed adjective 1 *a mixed collection:* assorted, varied, variegated, miscellaneous, disparate, diverse, diversified, motley, sundry, jumbled, heterogeneous. 2 *mixed reactions:* ambivalent, equivocal, contradictory, conflicting, confused, muddled.
OPPOSITES homogeneous.

mixture noun 1 *the pudding mixture:* blend, mix, brew, combination, concoction, composition, compound, alloy, amalgam. 2 *a strange mixture of people:* assortment, miscellany, medley, blend, variety, mixed bag, mix, diversity, collection, selection, hotchpotch, ragbag; N. Amer. hodgepodge.

mix-up noun confusion, muddle, misunderstanding, mistake, error.

something. •**adjective** designed to help remember something.

moan noun **1** a low mournful sound, usually expressing suffering. **2** informal a complaint. •**verb 1** make a moan. **2** complain; grumble.

moat noun a wide defensive ditch surrounding a castle or town.

mob noun **1** a disorderly crowd of people. **2** Brit. informal a group of people. **3** (**the Mob**) N. Amer. the Mafia. **4** (**the mob**) disapproving the ordinary people. •**verb** (**mobs, mobbing, mobbed**) (of a large group of people) crowd round someone.

mobile adjective **1** able to move or be moved freely or easily. **2** (of a shop, library, etc.) set up inside a vehicle and able to travel around. **3** able to change your occupation, social class, or where you live. **4** (of a person's face) easily changing expression. •**noun 1** a decoration that is hung so as to turn freely in the air. **2** (also **mobile phone**) a portable telephone.

mobility noun the quality of being mobile.

mobilize or **mobilise** verb (**mobilizes, mobilizing, mobilized**) **1** organize troops for active service. **2** organize people or resources for a particular task. ■ **mobilization** noun.

mobster noun informal a gangster.

moccasin noun a soft leather shoe with the sole turned up and sewn to the upper,

originally worn by North American Indians.

mocha /mok-uh/ noun **1** a type of fine-quality coffee. **2** a drink made with coffee and chocolate.

mock verb tease or imitate someone in an unkind way. •**adjective 1** not genuine or real. **2** (of an exam, battle, etc.) arranged for training or practice. •**noun** (**mocks**) Brit. informal exams taken in school as a practice for public exams. ▫ **mock-up** a model of a machine or structure that is used for teaching or testing.

mockery noun (plural **mockeries**) **1** unkind teasing; ridicule. **2** (**a mockery of**) an absurd or worthless version of something. ▫ **make a mockery of** make something seem ridiculous or useless.

mockingbird noun a long-tailed American songbird, noted for copying the calls of other birds.

modal verb noun Grammar an auxiliary verb expressing necessity or possibility, e.g. *must, shall, will.*

mode noun **1** a way in which something occurs or is done. **2** a style in clothes, art, etc.

model noun **1** a three-dimensional representation of something. **2** something used as an example. **3** a person or thing seen as an excellent example of a quality: *he was a model of self-control.* **4** a person

m

moan verb **1** *he moaned in agony:* groan, wail, whimper, sob, cry. **2** (informal) *you're always moaning about the weather:* complain, grouse, grumble, whine, carp; informal gripe, grouch, bellyache, bitch, beef, whinge.

mob noun *troops dispersed the mob:* crowd, horde, multitude, rabble, mass, throng, gathering, assembly. •**verb** *the Chancellor was mobbed:* surround, crowd round, besiege, jostle.

mobile adjective **1** *both patients are mobile:* able to move, able to walk, walking; informal up and about. **2** *a mobile library:* travelling, transportable, portable, movable, itinerant, peripatetic. OPPOSITES immobilized, fixed.

mobilize verb **1** *the government mobilized the troops:* marshal, deploy, muster, rally, call up, assemble, mass, organize, prepare. **2** *mobilizing support for the party:* generate, arouse, awaken, excite, stir up, stimulate, encourage, inspire, whip up.

mock verb *the local children mocked the old people:* ridicule, jeer at, sneer at, deride, make fun of, laugh at, scoff at, tease, taunt; informal take the mickey out of; N. Amer. informal goof on, rag on; Austral./NZ informal

chiack, sling off at. •**adjective** *mock leather:* imitation, artificial, man-made, simulated, synthetic, ersatz, fake, reproduction, false, counterfeit; informal pretend. OPPOSITES genuine.

mocking adjective sneering, derisive, contemptuous, scornful, sardonic, ironic, sarcastic.

mode noun **1** *an informal mode of policing:* manner, way, means, method, system, style, approach. **2** *the camera is in manual mode:* function, position, operation, setting, option.

model noun **1** *a working model:* replica, copy, representation, mock-up, dummy, imitation, duplicate, reproduction, facsimile. **2** *the American model of airline deregulation:* prototype, archetype, type, version, mould, template, framework, pattern, design, blueprint. **3** *a top model:* fashion model, supermodel, mannequin; informal clothes horse. •**adjective 1** *model trains:* replica, toy, miniature, dummy, imitation, duplicate, reproduction, facsimile. **2** *a model teacher:* ideal, perfect, exemplary, classic, flawless, faultless.

whose job is to display clothes by wearing them. **5** a person who poses for an artist or photographer. **6** a particular design or version of a product. **7** a simplified mathematical description of a system or process. • verb (**models, modelling, modelled**; US spelling **models, modeling, modeled**) **1** make a figure in clay, wax, etc. **2** (**model something on**) design or plan something using another thing as an example. **3** work as a fashion model. **4** devise a mathematical model of.

modem /moh-dem/ noun a device that connects a computer to a telephone line.

moderate adjective **1** average in amount, strength, or degree. **2** (of a political position) not extreme. • noun a person with moderate views. • verb (**moderates, moderating, moderated**) **1** make or become less extreme or strong. **2** check exam papers to ensure that they have been marked consistently.
■ **moderately** adverb.

moderation noun **1** the avoidance of extremes in your actions or opinions. **2** the process of moderating.

moderator noun **1** a person who helps others to solve a dispute. **2** a chairman of a debate. **3** a person who moderates exam papers.

modern adjective **1** relating to the present or to recent times. **2** using the most up-to-date techniques or equipment. **3** (of art, architecture, music, etc.) new and intended to be different from traditional styles.
■ **modernity** noun.

modernism noun **1** modern ideas, methods, or styles. **2** a movement in the arts or religion that aims to break with traditional forms or ideas.
■ **modernist** noun & adjective.

modernize or **modernise** verb (**modernizes, modernizing, modernized**) bring up to date with modern equipment, techniques, etc.
■ **modernization** noun.

modest adjective **1** not boasting about your abilities or achievements. **2** relatively moderate, limited, or small. **3** not showing off the body; decent.
■ **modestly** adverb **modesty** noun.

modicum /mod-i-kuhm/ noun a small quantity of something.

modification noun **1** the action of modifying something. **2** a change made.

modifier noun **1** a person or thing that modifies. **2** Grammar a word that qualifies the sense of a noun (e.g. *family* in *a family house*).

modify verb (**modifies, modifying, modified**) make partial changes to.

modish adjective fashionable.

modular adjective made up of separate units.

modulate verb (**modulates, modulating, modulated**) **1** adjust, change, or control

THESAURUS

moderate adjective **1** *moderate success:* **average,** modest, medium, middling, tolerable, passable, adequate, fair; informal OK, so-so, bog-standard, fair-to-middling. **2** *moderate prices:* **reasonable,** acceptable, affordable, inexpensive, fair, modest. **3** *moderate views:* **middle-of-the-road,** non-extremist, liberal, pragmatic.
OPPOSITES great, unreasonable, extreme.
• verb **1** *the wind has moderated:* **die down,** abate, let up, calm down, lessen, decrease, diminish, recede, weaken, subside. **2** *you can help her moderate her temper:* **curb,** control, check, temper, restrain, subdue, tame, lessen, decrease, lower, reduce, diminish, alleviate, allay, appease, ease, soothe, calm, tone down.
OPPOSITES increase.

moderately adverb **somewhat,** quite, fairly, reasonably, comparatively, relatively, to some extent, tolerably, adequately; informal pretty.

modern adjective **1** *modern times:* **present-day,** contemporary, present, current, twenty-first-century, latter-day, recent. **2** *her clothes are very modern:* **fashionable,** up to date, trendsetting, stylish, chic, à la mode, the latest, new, newest, newfangled, advanced; informal trendy, cool, funky.
OPPOSITES past, old-fashioned.

modest adjective **1** *she was modest about her poetry:* **humble,** self-deprecating, self-effacing, unassuming, shy, diffident, reserved, coy. **2** *modest success:* **moderate,** fair, limited, tolerable, passable, adequate, satisfactory, acceptable, unexceptional. **3** *a modest house:* **small,** ordinary, simple, plain, humble, inexpensive, unostentatious, unpretentious. **4** *her modest dress:* **demure,** decent, seemly, decorous, proper.
OPPOSITES conceited, great, grand, indecent.

modesty noun **humility,** self-effacement, shyness, bashfulness, self-consciousness, reserve.

modification noun **change,** adjustment, alteration, adaptation, refinement, revision, amendment; informal tweak.

modify verb **1** *their economic policy has been modified:* **change,** alter, adjust, adapt, amend, revise, refine; informal tweak. **2** *he modified his more extreme views:* **moderate,** temper, soften, tone down, qualify.

something. **2** vary the strength, tone, or pitch of your voice. **3** Music change from one key to another.
■ **modulation** noun.

module noun **1** each of a set of parts or units that can be used to create a more complex structure. **2** a unit forming part of a course. **3** an independent unit of a spacecraft.

moggie or **moggy** noun (plural **moggies**) Brit. informal a cat.

mogul /moh-guhl/ noun informal an important or powerful person.

mohair noun a yarn or fabric made from the hair of the angora goat.

Mohican /moh-hee-kuhn/ noun a hair style in which the sides of the head are shaved and a central strip of hair is made to stand up.

moiety /moy-i-ti/ noun (plural **moieties**) formal a half.

moist adjective slightly wet; damp.
■ **moisten** verb.

moisture noun tiny droplets of water making something damp.

moisturize or **moisturise** verb (**moisturizes, moisturizing, moisturized**) make something, especially the skin, less dry.
■ **moisturizer** noun.

molar noun a grinding tooth at the back of the mouth.

molasses /muh-lass-iz/ noun a thick brown liquid obtained from raw sugar.

mold US spelling of **MOULD¹, MOULD²**.

Moldovan /mol-doh-vuhn/ noun a person from Moldova, a country in SE Europe.
•**adjective** relating to Moldova.

mole¹ noun **1** a small burrowing mammal with dark fur, a long muzzle, and very small eyes. **2** someone within an organization who secretly passes confidential information to another organization or country.

mole² noun a dark brown mark on the skin.

mole³ noun **1** a pier, breakwater, or causeway. **2** a harbour formed by a mole.

mole⁴ noun Chemistry the amount of a particular substance which contains as many atoms or molecules as there are atoms in a standard amount of carbon.

molecule /mol-i-kyool/ noun a group of atoms forming the smallest unit into which a substance can be divided.
■ **molecular** adjective.

molehill noun a small mound of earth thrown up by a burrowing mole.

moleskin noun **1** the skin of a mole used as fur. **2** a thick cotton fabric with a soft surface.

molest verb **1** sexually assault someone. **2** dated pester someone in a hostile way.
■ **molestation** noun **molester** noun.

moll noun informal a gangster's girlfriend.

mollify verb (**mollifies, mollifying, mollified**) make someone feel less angry.

mollusc (US spelling **mollusk**) noun an animal of a group with a soft unsegmented body and often an external shell, such as slugs and snails.

mollycoddle verb (**mollycoddles, mollycoddling, mollycoddled**) treat someone too indulgently or protectively.

molt US spelling of **MOULT**.

molten adjective (especially of metal and glass) made liquid by heat.

molto /mol-toh/ adverb Music very.

molybdenum /muh-lib-duh-nuhm/ noun a brittle silver-grey metallic element.

mom N. Amer. = **MUM¹**.

moment noun **1** a brief period of time. **2** an exact point in time. **3** formal importance.

momentarily adverb **1** for a very short time. **2** N. Amer. very soon.

momentary adjective very brief or short-lived.

momentous adjective of great importance or significance.

momentum noun (plural **momenta**) **1** the force gained by a moving object. **2** the force caused by the development of something.

m

moist adjective **1** the air was moist: damp, steamy, humid, muggy, clammy, dank, wet, soggy, sweaty, sticky. **2** a moist fruitcake: succulent, juicy, soft, tender.
OPPOSITES dry.

moisten verb dampen, wet, damp, water, humidify.

moisture noun wetness, wet, water, liquid, condensation, steam, vapour, dampness, damp, humidity.

moment noun **1** he thought for a moment: little while, short time, bit, minute, instant, (split) second; informal sec, jiffy; Brit.

informal tick, mo, two ticks. **2** just at that moment: point (in time), stage, juncture, instant, time, hour, second, minute, day.

momentary adjective brief, short, short-lived, fleeting, passing.
OPPOSITES lengthy.

momentous adjective important, significant, historic, critical, crucial, decisive, pivotal, consequential, far-reaching; informal earth-shattering.
OPPOSITES insignificant.

momentum noun impetus, energy, force, power, strength, thrust, speed, velocity.

mommy N. Amer. = MUMMY[1].

monarch noun a king, queen, or emperor.
■ **monarchical** adjective.

monarchist noun someone who believes a country should be ruled by a king or queen.
■ **monarchism** noun.

monarchy noun (plural **monarchies**)
1 government by a monarch. 2 a state with a monarch.

monastery noun (plural **monasteries**) a community of monks living under religious vows.

monastic adjective 1 relating to monks or nuns. 2 resembling monks or their way of life.

Monday noun the day of the week before Tuesday and following Sunday.

monetarism noun the theory that inflation is best controlled by limiting the supply of money.
■ **monetarist** noun & adjective.

monetary adjective having to do with money.

money noun 1 a means of paying for things in the form of coins and banknotes.
2 wealth. 3 payment or financial gain.
4 (**moneys** or **monies**) formal sums of money.
□ **money order** a postal order. **money spider** a very small black spider.

moneyed or **monied** adjective having a lot of money.

Mongol noun 1 a person from Mongolia.
2 (**mongol**) offensive a person with Down's syndrome.
■ **Mongolian** noun & adjective.

mongoose noun (plural **mongooses**) a small meat-eating animal with a long body and tail, native to Africa and Asia.

mongrel noun a dog of no definite breed.

moniker noun informal a name.

monitor noun 1 a person or device that monitors something. 2 a television used to view a picture from a particular camera or a display from a computer. 3 a school pupil with special duties. 4 (also **monitor lizard**) a large tropical lizard. • verb keep under observation.

monk noun a man belonging to a religious community typically living under vows of poverty, chastity, and obedience.

monkey noun (plural **monkeys**) a primate typically having a long tail and living in trees in tropical countries. • verb (**monkeys, monkeying, monkeyed**) 1 (**monkey about** or **around**) behave in a silly or playful way.
2 (**monkey with**) tamper with.
□ **monkey nut** Brit. a peanut. **monkey puzzle** a coniferous tree with branches covered in spirals of tough spiny leaves. **monkey wrench** a spanner with large adjustable jaws.

mono noun sound reproduction which uses only one transmission channel.

monochrome adjective (of a photograph or picture) produced in black and white or in varying tones of one colour.
■ **monochromatic** adjective.

monocle noun a single lens worn at one eye.

monogamy /muh-**nog**-uh-mi/ noun the practice of having only one wife or husband at any one time.
■ **monogamous** adjective.

monogram noun a motif of two or more interwoven letters, typically a person's initials.
■ **monogrammed** adjective.

monograph noun a book or academic paper written on a single subject.

monolingual adjective speaking or expressed in only one language.

monolith noun a large single upright block of stone.

monolithic adjective 1 formed of a single large block of stone. 2 very large and impersonal.

monologue noun 1 a long speech by one actor in a play or film. 2 a long, boring speech by one person.

monomania noun an obsession with one thing.
■ **monomaniac** noun.

monomer /**mon**-uh-mer/ noun Chemistry a molecule that can be linked to other identical molecules to form a polymer.

monophonic adjective (of sound

THESAURUS

monarch noun sovereign, ruler, Crown, crowned head, potentate, king, queen, emperor, empress, prince, princess.

monastery noun monastic community, friary, abbey, priory, cloister.

monetary adjective financial, fiscal, pecuniary, money, cash, capital, economic, budgetary.

money noun cash, hard cash, means, wherewithal, funds, capital, finances, notes, coins, change, currency; informal

dough, bread, loot; Brit. informal dosh, brass, lolly; N. Amer. informal dinero, mazuma.

monitor noun 1 *monitors covered all entrances*: detector, scanner, recorder, sensor, security camera, CCTV. 2 *UN monitors*: observer, watchdog, overseer, supervisor, scrutineer. 3 *a computer monitor*: screen, display, VDU.
• verb *his movements were closely monitored*: observe, watch, track, keep an eye on, keep under surveillance, record,

reproduction) using only one channel.

monoplane noun an aircraft with one pair of wings.

monopolize or **monopolise** verb (monopolizes, monopolizing, monopolized) dominate or take control of.

monopoly noun (plural **monopolies**) the complete control of the supply of a product or service by one person or organization.

monorail noun a railway in which the track consists of a single rail.

monosodium glutamate noun a compound used to add flavour to food.

monosyllabic adjective **1** (of a word) having one syllable. **2** (of a person) saying very little.

monosyllable noun a word of one syllable.

monotheism /mon-oh-thee-i-z'm/ noun the belief that there is only one god.
■ **monotheistic** adjective.

monotone noun a continuing sound that does not change pitch.

monotonous adjective boring and unchanging.
■ **monotonously** adverb **monotony** noun.

monoxide noun Chemistry an oxide containing one atom of oxygen.

Monsieur /muh-**syer**/ noun (plural **Messieurs** /mess-**yer**/) a title for a French man, corresponding to *Mr* or *sir*.

Monsignor /mon-**seen**-yer/ noun (plural **Monsignori** /mon-seen-**yor**-i/) the title of a senior Roman Catholic priest.

monsoon noun **1** a seasonal wind in the Indian subcontinent and SE Asia. **2** the rainy season accompanying the monsoon.

monster noun **1** a frightening imaginary creature. **2** a cruel or wicked person.

3 something that is very large: *a monster of a book.*

monstrosity noun (plural **monstrosities**) something that is very large and ugly.

monstrous adjective **1** very large, ugly, or frightening. **2** shocking and morally wrong.
■ **monstrously** adverb.

montage /mon-**tahzh**/ noun a picture or film made by putting together pieces from other pictures or films.

month noun **1** each of the twelve periods of time into which a year is divided. **2** a period of time between a date in one month and the same date in the next month. **3** a period of 28 days or four weeks.

monthly adjective & adverb happening or produced once a month.

monty noun (**the full monty**) Brit. informal the full amount or extent.

monument noun **1** a statue or structure built in memory of a person or event. **2** a site of historical importance. **3** a lasting example of something: *a monument to good taste.*

monumental adjective **1** very large or impressive. **2** forming a monument.
■ **monumentally** adverb.

moo verb (**moos**, **mooing**, **mooed**) (of a cow) make a long, deep sound.

mooch verb Brit. informal stand or walk around in a bored way.

mood noun **1** the way you feel at a particular time. **2** a period of being bad-tempered. **3** the atmosphere of a work of art. **4** Grammar a form of a verb expressing fact, command, question, wish, or a condition.

moody adjective (**moodier**, **moodiest**)

m

THESAURUS

note, oversee; informal keep tabs on.

monster noun **1** *legendary sea monsters:* giant, mammoth, demon, dragon, colossus, leviathan, creature. **2** *her husband is a monster:* fiend, animal, beast, devil, demon, barbarian, savage, brute; informal swine.

monstrous adjective **1** *a monstrous creature:* grotesque, hideous, ugly, ghastly, gruesome, horrible, horrific, horrifying, grisly, disgusting, repulsive, dreadful, frightening, terrible, terrifying. **2** *monstrous acts of violence:* appalling, wicked, abominable, terrible, horrible, dreadful, vile, outrageous, unspeakable, despicable, vicious, savage, barbaric, inhuman.
OPPOSITES lovely, kind.

monument noun memorial, statue, pillar, cairn, column, obelisk, cross, cenotaph, tomb, mausoleum, shrine.

monumental adjective **1** *a monumental task:* huge, enormous, gigantic, massive, colossal, mammoth, immense, tremendous, mighty, stupendous. **2** *his monumental career:* significant, important, majestic, memorable, noteworthy, momentous, defining, grand, awe-inspiring, heroic, epic.
OPPOSITES tiny, insignificant.

mood noun **1** *she's in a good mood:* frame of mind, state of mind, humour, temper. **2** *he's obviously in a mood:* bad mood, temper, bad temper, sulk, low spirits, the doldrums, the blues; Brit. informal paddy. **3** *the mood of the film:* atmosphere, feeling, spirit, ambience, aura, character, flavour, feel, tone.

moody adjective temperamental, emotional, volatile, capricious, sullen, sulky, morose, glum, depressed, dejected, despondent, doleful.
OPPOSITES cheerful.

1 having moods that change quickly.
2 gloomy or bad-tempered.

moon noun 1 (also **Moon**) the natural satellite of the earth. 2 a natural satellite of any planet. 3 literary a month. • verb 1 (**moon about** or **around**) behave or walk about in a dreamy way. 2 informal expose your buttocks to someone as an insult or joke.
□ **over the moon** informal delighted.

moonlight noun the light of the moon. • verb (**moonlights, moonlighting, moonlighted**) informal do a second job without declaring it for tax purposes.
■ **moonlit** adjective.

moonscape noun a landscape that is rocky and barren like the moon.

moonshine noun informal 1 foolish talk or ideas. 2 N. Amer. alcohol that is made and sold illegally.

moonstone noun a white semi-precious mineral.

moony adjective dreamy as a result of being in love.

Moor noun a member of a NW African Muslim people.
■ **Moorish** adjective.

moor[1] noun a high open area of land that is not cultivated.

moor[2] verb fasten a boat to the shore or to an anchor.

moorhen noun a waterbird with black feathers.

mooring or **moorings** noun a place where a boat is moored, or the ropes used to moor it.

moose = ELK.

moot adjective uncertain or undecided: *a moot point.* • verb put forward a topic for discussion.

mop noun 1 a bundle of thick strings or a sponge attached to a handle, used for wiping floors. 2 a thick mass of hair. • verb (**mops, mopping, mopped**) 1 clean or soak up by wiping. 2 (**mop something up**) complete something by dealing with the things that remain.

mope verb (**mopes, moping, moped**) be listless and gloomy.

moped /**mow**-ped/ noun a motorcycle with a small engine.

moraine noun rocks and stones deposited by a glacier.

moral adjective 1 concerned with the principles of right and wrong behaviour. 2 conforming to accepted standards of behaviour. • noun 1 a lesson about right or wrong that you learn from a story or experience. 2 (**morals**) standards of good behaviour.
■ **morally** adverb.

morale noun a feeling of confidence and satisfaction.

moralist noun a person with strict views about morals.
■ **moralistic** adjective.

morality noun (plural **moralities**) 1 principles concerning the difference between right and wrong or good and bad behaviour. 2 moral behaviour. 3 the extent to which an action is right or wrong.

moralize or **moralise** verb (**moralizes, moralizing, moralized**) comment on moral issues, usually in a disapproving way.

morass /muh-**rass**/ noun 1 an area of muddy or boggy ground. 2 a complicated or confused situation.

moratorium noun (plural **moratoriums** or **moratoria**) a temporary ban on an activity.

moray or **moray eel** noun an eel-like fish.

morbid adjective 1 having a strong interest

m

THESAURUS

moon verb 1 *stop mooning about:* waste time, loaf, idle, mope; Brit. informal mooch; N. Amer. informal lollygag. 2 *he's mooning over her photograph:* mope, pine, brood, daydream.

moor[1] verb *a boat was moored to the quay:* tie (up), secure, make fast, berth, dock.

moor[2] noun *a walk on the moor:* upland, heath, moorland; Brit. fell, wold.

mop noun *her tousled mop of hair:* shock, mane, tangle, mass.
• verb *a man was mopping the floor:* wash, clean, wipe, sponge.

moral adjective 1 *moral issues:* ethical. 2 *a very moral man:* good, virtuous, righteous, upright, upstanding, high-minded, principled, honourable, honest, just, noble. 3 *moral support:* psychological, emotional, mental.

OPPOSITES dishonourable, practical.
• noun 1 *the moral of the story:* lesson, message, meaning, significance, import, point, teaching. 2 (**morals**) moral code, code of ethics, values, principles, standards, (sense of) morality, scruples.

morale noun confidence, self-confidence, self-esteem, spirit(s), team spirit, motivation.

morality noun 1 *the morality of nuclear weapons:* ethics, rights and wrongs, whys and wherefores. 2 *a sharp decline in morality:* virtue, good behaviour, righteousness, uprightness, morals, principles, honesty, integrity, propriety, honour, decency. 3 *Christian morality:* morals, standards, ethics, principles, mores.

morbid adjective ghoulish, macabre,

in unpleasant subjects, especially death and disease. **2** Medicine having to do with disease.
■ **morbidity** noun **morbidly** adverb.

mordant adjective (of humour) sharply sarcastic.

more determiner & pronoun a greater or additional amount or degree. • adverb **1** forming the comparative of adjectives and adverbs. **2** to a greater extent. **3** again. **4** (**more than**) very.

morel /muh-**rel**/ noun an edible fungus with a brown cap.

morello noun (plural **morellos**) a kind of sour dark cherry.

moreover adverb in addition to what has been said already.

mores /**mor**-ayz/ plural noun the customs of a community.

morgue noun a mortuary.

moribund adjective **1** at the point of death. **2** about to come to an end.

Mormon noun a member of the Church of Jesus Christ of Latter-Day Saints.
■ **Mormonism** noun.

morn noun literary morning.

morning noun **1** the period of time between midnight and noon, especially from sunrise to noon. **2** sunrise.
□ **morning sickness** nausea felt by a woman when she is pregnant.

Moroccan noun a person from Morocco. • adjective relating to Morocco.

moron noun informal a stupid person.
■ **moronic** adjective.

morose adjective unhappy and bad-tempered.
■ **morosely** adverb.

morph verb (in computer animation) change smoothly and gradually from one image to another.

morphine noun a drug made from opium and used to relieve pain.

morphology noun the scientific study of the form and structure of animals and plants, or of the forms of words.
■ **morphological** adjective.

morris dancing noun traditional English folk dancing.

morrow noun (**the morrow**) old use the next day.

Morse or **Morse code** noun a code in which letters are represented by combinations of long and short sounds or flashes of light.

morsel noun a small piece of food.

mortal adjective **1** having to die at some time. **2** causing death. **3** (of a battle or enemy) lasting until death. • noun a human being.
□ **mortal sin** (in Christian belief) a sin so serious as to result in damnation.
■ **mortally** adverb.

mortality noun **1** the state of being mortal. **2** death. **3** (also **mortality rate**) the number of deaths in a particular area or period of time.

mortar noun **1** a mixture of lime with cement, sand, and water, used to stick bricks or stones together. **2** a cup-shaped container in which substances are crushed with a pestle. **3** a short cannon for firing shells at high angles.
□ **mortar board** an academic cap with a flat square top and a tassel.

mortgage noun **1** a legal agreement by which a bank or building society lends you money, using your house as security. **2** an amount of money borrowed or lent under such an agreement. • verb (**mortgages, mortgaging, mortgaged**) give a bank or building society the right to hold your house as security for the money they agree to lend you.

mortician noun N. Amer. an undertaker.

mortify verb (**mortifies, mortifying, mortified**) make someone feel embarrassed or ashamed.
■ **mortification** noun.

mortise or **mortice** noun a slot cut in a piece of wood in order to hold the end of another piece of wood.
□ **mortise lock** a lock fitted into a hole in a door.

m

---

unhealthy, gruesome, unwholesome; informal sick.
OPPOSITES wholesome.

more determiner *some more clothes:* extra, further, added, additional, supplementary, increased, new.
OPPOSITES less, fewer.

moreover adverb besides, furthermore, what's more, in addition, also, as well, too, to boot, additionally, on top of that, into the bargain.

morning noun **1** *I've got a meeting this*

morning: before lunch(time), a.m.; literary morn; Nautical & N. Amer. forenoon. **2** *morning is on its way:* dawn, daybreak, sunrise, first light; N. Amer. sunup.

mortal adjective **1** *all men are mortal:* perishable, physical, bodily, corporeal, human, fleshly, earthly, impermanent, transient, ephemeral. **2** *a mortal blow:* deadly, fatal, lethal, death-dealing, murderous, terminal.
OPPOSITES eternal.
• noun *we are mere mortals:* human

mortuary noun (plural **mortuaries**) a room or building in which dead bodies are kept until they are buried or cremated.

mosaic noun a picture or pattern made by fitting together small coloured pieces of stone, tile, or glass.

mosey verb (**moseys, moseying, moseyed**) informal walk in a leisurely way.

Moslem ⇨ MUSLIM.

mosque noun a Muslim place of worship.

mosquito noun (plural **mosquitoes**) a small long-legged fly, some kinds of which transmit diseases through their bite.

moss noun a very small green spreading plant which grows in damp places.
■ **mossy** adjective.

most determiner & pronoun 1 greatest in amount or degree. 2 the majority of.
•adverb 1 to the greatest extent. 2 forming the superlative of adjectives and adverbs. 3 very.

mostly adverb 1 on the whole; mainly. 2 usually.

mote noun a speck.

motel noun a roadside hotel designed for motorists.

motet /moh-**tet**/ noun a short piece of choral music.

moth noun an insect like a butterfly, which is active at night.
□ **moth-eaten** 1 eaten by the larvae of moths. 2 shabby and worn.

mothball noun a small ball of camphor, placed among stored clothes to deter moths.

mother noun 1 a female parent. 2 (**Mother**) (especially as a title or form of address) the head of a convent. •verb look after somebody protectively.
□ **mother-in-law** (plural **mothers-in-law**) the mother of a person's husband or wife.
mother-of-pearl a smooth pearly substance lining the shells of oysters. **mother tongue** a person's native language.
■ **motherhood** noun **motherly** adjective.

motherland noun your native country.

motif /moh-**teef**/ noun 1 a pattern or design. 2 a theme that is repeated in a work of literature or piece of music.

motion noun 1 the action of moving. 2 a movement or gesture. 3 a formal proposal that is discussed at a meeting. 4 Brit. an emptying of the bowels. •verb direct someone with a gesture.
□ **motion picture** N. Amer. a cinema film.
■ **motionless** adjective.

motivate verb (**motivates, motivating, motivated**) 1 provide someone with a motive for doing something. 2 make someone want to do something.
■ **motivator** noun.

motivation noun 1 the reason for your actions or behaviour. 2 enthusiasm.
■ **motivational** adjective.

motive noun something that makes someone act in a particular way. •adjective causing motion.

motley adjective made up of a variety of different things.

motocross noun cross-country racing on motorcycles.

motor noun 1 a device that produces power and movement for a vehicle or machine.

m

THESAURUS

(being), person, man, woman, earthling.

mortuary noun morgue, funeral parlour; Brit. chapel of rest.

mostly adverb 1 *the other passengers were mostly businessmen:* mainly, for the most part, on the whole, in the main, largely, chiefly, predominantly, principally, primarily. 2 *I mostly wear jeans:* usually, generally, in general, as a rule, ordinarily, normally, customarily, typically, most of the time, almost always.

mother noun informal ma; Brit. informal mum, mummy; N. Amer. informal mom, mommy; Brit. informal, dated mater.
•verb *her colleagues mothered her:* look after, care for, take care of, nurse, protect, tend, raise, rear, pamper, coddle, cosset, fuss over.
OPPOSITES neglect.

motherly adjective maternal, maternalistic, protective, caring, loving, affectionate, nurturing.

motif noun 1 *a colourful tulip motif:* design, pattern, decoration, figure, shape, device,

emblem. 2 *a recurring motif in Pinter's work:* theme, idea, concept, subject, topic, leitmotif.

motion noun 1 *a planet's motion around the sun:* movement, locomotion, progress, passage, transit, course, travel, orbit. 2 *a motion of the hand:* gesture, movement, signal, sign, indication, wave, nod, gesticulation. 3 *the motion was passed:* proposal, proposition, recommendation.
•verb *he motioned her to sit down:* gesture, signal, direct, indicate, wave, beckon, nod.

motivate verb 1 *motivated by greed:* prompt, drive, move, inspire, stimulate, influence, activate, impel, propel, spur (on). 2 *the teacher must motivate the child:* inspire, stimulate, encourage, spur (on), excite, incentivize, fire (with enthusiasm).

motivation noun motive, motivating force, incentive, stimulus, stimulation, inspiration, inducement, incitement, spur.

motive noun reason, motivation, motivating force, rationale, grounds, cause, basis.

2 Brit. informal a car. •**adjective** giving or producing motion. •**verb** travel in a car.
□ **motor vehicle** a road vehicle powered by an engine.
■ **motorized** adjective.

motorbike noun a motorcycle.

motorboat noun a boat powered by a motor.

motorcade noun a procession of motor vehicles.

motorcycle noun a two-wheeled vehicle powered by a motor.
■ **motorcycling** noun **motorcyclist** noun.

motorist noun the driver of a car.

motorway noun Brit. a road designed for fast traffic, typically with three lanes in each direction.

mottled adjective marked with patches of a different colour.

motto noun (plural **mottoes** or **mottos**) a short sentence or phrase that expresses a belief or aim.

mould¹ (US spelling **mold**) noun **1** a container into which you pour hot liquid in order to produce a solid object of a desired shape when it cools. **2** a distinctive style or character. •**verb 1** form an object of a particular shape out of a soft substance. **2** influence the development of something.

mould² (US spelling **mold**) noun a furry growth of tiny fungi that occurs in moist warm conditions.
■ **mouldy** adjective.

moulder (US spelling **molder**) verb (**moulders, mouldering, mouldered**) slowly decay.

moulding (US spelling **molding**) noun a carved or moulded strip of wood, stone, or plaster as a decorative feature on a building.

moult (US spelling **molt**) verb shed old feathers, hair, or skin. •**noun** a period of moulting.

mound noun **1** a raised mass of earth or other material. **2** a small hill. **3** a heap or pile. •**verb** heap up into a mound.

mount¹ verb **1** climb up or on to. **2** get up on an animal or bicycle to ride it. **3** increase in size, number, or strength. **4** organize a campaign, bid, etc. **5** put or fix something in place or on a support. •**noun 1** (also **mounting**) something on which an object is mounted for support or display. **2** a horse used for riding.

mount² noun old use a mountain or hill.

mountain noun **1** a very high and steep hill. **2** a large pile or quantity.

mountaineering noun the sport or activity of climbing mountains.
■ **mountaineer** noun.

mountainous adjective **1** having many mountains. **2** huge.

mountebank noun a person who tricks people in order to get money from them.

mourn verb feel deep sorrow following the death or loss of.

mourner noun a person who attends a funeral.

mournful adjective very sad or depressing.
■ **mournfully** adverb.

mourning noun **1** the expression of deep sorrow for someone who has died. **2** black clothes worn in a period of mourning.

mouse noun (plural **mice**) **1** a small rodent

m

THESAURUS

motto noun slogan, maxim, saying, proverb, aphorism, adage, saw, axiom, formula, catchphrase.

mould noun **1** *a clay mould:* cast, die, form, matrix, shape, template, pattern, frame. **2** *an actress in the traditional Hollywood mould:* pattern, form, type, style, tradition, school.
•**verb 1** *a figure moulded from clay:* shape, form, fashion, model, work, construct, make, create, sculpt, cast. **2** *the ideas that mould US policy:* determine, direct, control, guide, influence, shape, form, fashion, make.

mound noun **1** *a mound of books:* heap, pile, stack, mountain. **2** *high on the mound:* hillock, hill, knoll, rise, hummock, hump; Scottish brae.

mount verb **1** *he mounted the stairs:* go up, ascend, climb (up), scale. **2** *they mounted their horses:* get on to, bestride, climb on to, leap on to, hop on to. **3** *the museum is mounting an exhibition:* put on, present, install, organize, stage, set up, prepare, launch, set in motion. **4** *their losses mounted rapidly:* increase, grow, rise, escalate, soar, spiral, shoot up, rocket, climb, accumulate, build up, multiply. OPPOSITES descend, dismount, fall.
•**noun** *a picture mount:* setting, backing, support, mounting, frame, stand.

mountain noun **1** *climb a mountain:* peak, summit; (**mountains**) range, massif, sierra; Scottish ben. **2** *a mountain of work:* lot; informal heap, pile, stack, slew, lots, loads, tons, masses.

mourn verb **1** *Isobel mourned her husband:* grieve for, sorrow over, lament for, weep for. **2** *he mourned the loss of the beautiful buildings:* deplore, bewail, bemoan, rue, regret.

mourning noun grief, grieving, sorrowing, lamentation.

with a pointed snout and a long thin tail. **2** a timid and quiet person. **3** (plural also **mouses**) Computing a small hand-held device which controls the cursor on a computer screen.

moussaka /moo-sah-kuh/ noun a Greek dish of minced lamb layered with aubergines and tomatoes and topped with a cheese sauce.

mousse noun **1** a dish made from whipped cream and egg whites. **2** a light substance used to style hair.

moustache (US spelling **mustache**) noun a strip of hair above a man's upper lip.

mousy or **mousey** adjective **1** (of hair) of a light brown colour. **2** timid and shy.

mouth noun **1** the opening in the body through which food is taken and sounds are made. **2** an opening or entrance to something. **3** the place where a river enters the sea. •verb **1** move your lips as if you were saying something. **2** say something in a pompous way. ▢ **mouth organ** a harmonica. **mouth-watering** smelling or looking delicious.

mouthful noun **1** an amount of food or drink that fills your mouth. **2** a long or complicated word or phrase.

mouthpiece noun a part of a musical instrument, telephone, etc. that is put in or against the mouth.

mouthwash noun an antiseptic liquid for rinsing the mouth or gargling.

mouthy adjective informal inclined to talk a lot.

move verb (**moves, moving, moved**) **1** go or make something go in a particular direction or way. **2** change or make something change position. **3** change the place where you live. **4** change from one state or activity to another. **5** take action. **6** make progress. **7** provoke a strong feeling in someone. •noun **1** an instance of moving. **2** an action taken towards achieving a purpose. **3** a player's turn during a board game. ■ **movable** (or **moveable**) adjective.

movement noun **1** an act of moving. **2** the process of moving. **3** a group of people who share the same aims. **4** a trend or development. **5** (**movements**) a person's activities during a particular period of time. **6** a main division of a piece of music.

movie noun N. Amer. a cinema film.

moving adjective **1** in motion. **2** arousing strong emotion. ■ **movingly** adverb.

mow verb (**mows, mowing, mowed**; past participle **mowed** or **mown**) **1** cut down or trim grass, hay, etc. **2** (**mow someone down**) kill someone with a gun or by knocking them down with a vehicle. ■ **mower** noun.

Mozambican noun a person from Mozambique, a country in southern Africa. •adjective relating to Mozambique.

mozzarella /mot-suh-rel-luh/ noun a firm

THESAURUS

mouth noun **1** lips, jaws, muzzle; informal trap, chops, kisser; Brit. informal gob; N. Amer. informal puss, bazoo. **2** the mouth of the cave: entrance, opening. **3** the mouth of the river: estuary, delta, firth, outlet, outfall.

move verb **1** she moved to the door | don't move! go, walk, step, proceed, progress, advance, budge, stir, shift, change position. **2** he moved the chair closer to the fire: carry, transfer, shift, push, pull, lift, slide. **3** things were moving too fast: go, progress, advance, develop, evolve, change, happen. **4** he urged the council to move quickly: act, take steps, do something, take measures; informal get moving. **5** she's moved to Cambridge: relocate, move house, move away/out, change address, go (away), decamp. **6** I was deeply moved by the story: affect, touch, impress, shake, upset, disturb. **7** she was moved to find out more about it: inspire, prompt, stimulate, motivate, provoke, influence, rouse, induce, incite. **8** I move that we adjourn: propose, submit, suggest, advocate, recommend, urge. •noun **1** his eyes followed her every move: movement, motion, action, gesture. **2** his

recent move to London: relocation, change of house/address, transfer, posting. **3** the latest move in the war against drugs: initiative, step, action, measure, manoeuvre, tactic, stratagem. **4** it's your move: turn, go; Scottish shot.

movement noun **1** Rachel made a sudden movement: motion, move, gesture, sign, signal, action. **2** the movement of supplies: transportation, shifting, conveyance, moving, transfer. **3** a political movement: group, party, faction, wing, lobby, camp. **4** a movement to declare war on poverty: campaign, crusade, drive, push, initiative.

movie noun film, picture, feature film; informal flick.

moving adjective **1** in motion, operating, operational, working, on the move, active, movable, mobile. **2** a moving book: affecting, touching, poignant, heart-warming, heart-rending, emotional, life-affirming, inspiring, inspirational, stimulating, stirring. OPPOSITES stationary, fixed.

mow verb cut, trim, crop, clip, shear.

white Italian cheese made from buffalo's or cow's milk.

MP abbreviation Member of Parliament.

MP3 noun a method of compressing a sound sequence into a very small file, used as a way of downloading sound files from the Internet.

Mr noun a title used before a man's surname or full name.

Mrs noun a title used before a married woman's surname or full name.

MS abbreviation 1 manuscript. 2 multiple sclerosis.

Ms noun a title used before a married or unmarried woman's surname or full name.

MSc abbreviation Master of Science.

Mt abbreviation Mount.

much determiner & pronoun a large amount. •adverb 1 to a great extent. 2 often.

muck noun 1 dirt or rubbish. 2 manure. •verb chiefly Brit. 1 (muck something up) informal spoil something. 2 (muck about or around) informal behave in a silly way. 3 (muck about with or around with) informal interfere with. 4 (muck in) informal share a task. 5 (muck something out) remove manure and dirt from a stable.
■ mucky adjective (muckier, muckiest).

mucous /myoo-kuhss/ adjective having to do with mucus.
□ mucous membrane a tissue that produces mucus, lining the nose, mouth, and other organs.

mucus /myoo-kuhss/ noun a slimy substance produced by the mucous membranes.

mud noun soft, wet, sticky earth.

muddle verb (muddles, muddling, muddled) 1 put things in the wrong order or mix them up. 2 confuse someone. 3 (muddle

something up) confuse two or more things with each other. 4 (muddle along or through) manage to cope in spite of a lack of skill, knowledge, etc. •noun a muddled state.

muddy adjective (muddier, muddiest) 1 covered in mud. 2 not bright or clear. •verb (muddies, muddying, muddied) make something muddy.

mudflap noun a flap hung behind the wheel of a vehicle to protect against mud and stones thrown up from the road.

mudflat noun a stretch of muddy land left uncovered at low tide.

mudguard noun a curved strip fitted over a wheel of a bicycle or motorcycle to protect against water and dirt thrown up from the road.

muesli /myooz-li/ noun (plural mueslis) a mixture of oats, dried fruit, and nuts, eaten with milk.

muezzin /moo-ez-zin/ noun a man who calls Muslims to prayer.

muff¹ noun a short tube made of fur or other warm material into which you place your hands for warmth.

muff² verb informal handle something clumsily or badly.

muffin noun 1 a type of flat bread roll, usually eaten toasted with butter. 2 a type of small cake.

muffle verb (muffles, muffling, muffled) 1 wrap or cover for warmth. 2 make a sound quieter.

muffler noun a scarf.

mufti /muf-ti/ noun (plural muftis) 1 a Muslim legal expert allowed to give rulings on religious matters. 2 civilian

m

THESAURUS

much determiner *is there much food?* a lot of, a great/good deal of, a great/large amount of, plenty of, ample, abundant, plentiful; informal lots of, loads of, heaps of, masses of, tons of, stacks of.
OPPOSITES little.
•adverb 1 *it didn't hurt much:* greatly, a great deal, a lot, considerably, appreciably. 2 *does he come here much?* often, frequently, many times, regularly, habitually, routinely, usually, normally, commonly; informal a lot.
•pronoun *he did much for our team:* a lot, a great/good deal, plenty; informal lots, loads, heaps, masses, tons.

muck noun 1 *I'll just clean off the muck:* dirt, grime, filth, mud, mess; Brit. informal gunge; N. Amer. informal guck. 2 *spreading muck on the fields:* dung, manure, excrement, droppings.

mud noun dirt, sludge, ooze, silt, clay, mire, soil.

muddle verb 1 *the papers have got muddled up:* confuse, mix up, jumble (up), disarrange, disorganize, disorder, mess up. 2 *it would only muddle you:* bewilder, confuse, bemuse, perplex, puzzle, baffle, nonplus, mystify.
•noun mess, confusion, jumble, tangle, chaos, disorder, disarray, disorganization.

muddy adjective 1 *muddy ground:* marshy, boggy, swampy, waterlogged, squelchy, squishy, mucky, slimy, wet, soft. 2 *muddy boots:* dirty, filthy, mucky, grimy, soiled. 3 *muddy water:* murky, cloudy, turbid.
OPPOSITES clean, clear.

muffle verb 1 *everyone was muffled up in coats:* wrap (up), swathe, enfold, envelop, cloak. 2 *the sound of their footsteps was muffled:* deaden, dull, dampen, mute, soften, quieten, mask, stifle, smother.

clothes when worn by military or police staff.

mug¹ noun **1** a large cylindrical cup with a handle. **2** informal a person's face. **3** Brit. informal a stupid or gullible person. • verb **(mugs, mugging, mugged)** attack and rob someone in a public place.

mug² verb **(mugs, mugging, mugged)** **(mug something up)** Brit. informal learn as much as you can about a subject in a short time.

mugger noun a person who attacks and robs someone in a public place.

muggins noun **(plural muggins or mugginses)** Brit. informal a foolish person.

muggy adjective (of the weather) unpleasantly warm and humid.

mugshot noun informal a photograph of a person's face made for an official purpose.

mulatto noun **(plural mulattoes or mulattos)** offensive a person with one white and one black parent.

mulberry noun **(plural mulberries)** **1** a dark red or white fruit resembling the loganberry. **2** a dark red or purple colour.

mulch noun a mass of leaves or compost, used to protect the base of a plant or to enrich the soil. • verb cover with mulch.

mule noun the offspring of a male donkey and a female horse.

mulish adjective stubborn.

mull¹ verb **(mull something over)** think about something at length.

mull² verb warm wine or beer and add sugar and spices to it.

mullah /muul-luh/ noun a Muslim who is an expert in Islamic theology and sacred law.

mullet noun a sea fish that is caught for food.

mulligatawny noun a spicy meat soup originally made in India.

mullion noun a vertical bar between the panes of glass in a window.
■ **mullioned** adjective.

multicoloured or **multicolour** (US spelling **multicolored** or **multicolor**) adjective having many colours.

multicultural adjective relating to or made up of several cultural or ethnic groups.
■ **multiculturalism** noun.

multifaceted adjective having many sides or aspects.

multifarious adjective having great variety.

multilateral adjective involving three or more participants.

multilingual adjective in or using several languages.

multimedia noun the use of sound and pictures as well as text on a computer screen.

multinational adjective involving several countries. • noun a company operating in several countries.

multiple adjective **1** having or involving several parts or elements. **2** (of a disease or injury) affecting several parts of the body. • noun a number that may be divided by another number without a remainder. □ **multiple-choice** (of a question in an exam) giving several possible answers, from which you must choose one. **multiple sclerosis** ⇒ **SCLEROSIS**.

multiplex noun a cinema with several separate screens.

multiplication noun the process of multiplying.
□ **multiplication sign** the symbol ×, indicating that one number is to be multiplied by another.

multiplicity noun **(plural multiplicities)** a large number or variety of something.

multiply verb **(multiplies, multiplying, multiplied)** **1** add a number to itself a stated number of times. **2** increase in number or quantity. **3** increase in number by reproducing.
■ **multiplier** noun.

multiracial adjective having to do with people of many races.

multi-storey adjective (of a building) having several storeys. • noun Brit. a multi-storey car park.

THESAURUS

mug noun *a china mug:* beaker, cup, tankard, glass, stein.
• verb (informal) *he was mugged by youths:* assault, attack, set upon, beat up, rob; informal jump.

muggy adjective humid, close, sultry, sticky, oppressive, airless, stifling, suffocating, stuffy, heavy.
OPPOSITES fresh.

mull verb *she began to mull over the possibilities:* ponder, consider, think over/about, reflect on, contemplate, chew over; formal cogitate on.

multicoloured adjective kaleidoscopic, psychedelic, colourful, rainbow, jazzy, variegated.
OPPOSITES monochrome.

multiple adjective numerous, many, various, different, diverse, several, manifold.
OPPOSITES single.

multiply verb increase, grow, accumulate, proliferate, mount up, mushroom, snowball.
OPPOSITES decrease.

multitask verb 1 Computing operate more than one program at the same time. 2 do several things at the same time.

multitude noun 1 a large number of people or things. 2 (**the multitude**) the mass of ordinary people.

multitudinous adjective very numerous.

mum[1] noun Brit. informal your mother.

mum[2] adjective (**keep mum**) informal stay silent so as not to reveal a secret. □ mum's the word it's a secret.

mumble verb (**mumbles, mumbling, mumbled**) say something in a quiet voice that is difficult to hear or understand. •noun quiet speech that is difficult to hear or understand.

mumbo-jumbo noun informal language that sounds mysterious but has no real meaning.

mummify verb (**mummifies, mummifying, mummified**) preserve a body as a mummy. ■ mummification noun.

mummy[1] noun (plural **mummies**) Brit. informal your mother.

mummy[2] noun (plural **mummies**) (especially in ancient Egypt) a body that has been embalmed and wrapped in bandages in order to preserve it.

mumps plural noun a disease causing swelling of the glands at the sides of the face.

munch verb eat something steadily and often noisily.

mundane adjective lacking interest or excitement.

municipal adjective relating to a municipality.

municipality noun (plural **municipalities**) a town or district with its own local government.

munificent adjective very generous. ■ munificence noun.

munitions plural noun military weapons, ammunition, and equipment.

mural noun a painting done directly on a wall.

murder noun the unlawful planned killing of one person by another. •verb (**murders, murdering, murdered**) kill someone unlawfully, having planned to in advance. ■ murderer noun murderess noun.

murderous adjective capable of murdering someone or being very violent.

murk noun darkness or fog.

murky adjective (**murkier, murkiest**) 1 dark and gloomy. 2 (of water) dirty or cloudy. 3 suspicious and kept hidden.

murmur verb 1 say something quietly. 2 make a low continuous sound. •noun 1 the sound made by a person speaking quietly. 2 a low continuous background noise.

muscle noun 1 a band of body tissue that can be tightened or relaxed in order to move a part of the body. 2 power or strength. •verb (**muscle in**) informal involve yourself in something that does not concern you. ■ muscly adjective.

m

THESAURUS

mumble verb mutter, murmur, talk under your breath.

mundane adjective humdrum, dull, boring, tedious, monotonous, tiresome, unexciting, uninteresting, uneventful, unremarkable, routine, ordinary.
OPPOSITES extraordinary.

municipal adjective civic, civil, metropolitan, urban, city, town, borough, council.
OPPOSITES private, rural.

murder noun a brutal murder: killing, homicide, assassination, extermination, execution, slaughter, butchery, massacre, manslaughter; literary slaying.
•verb someone tried to murder him: kill, put/do to death, assassinate, execute, butcher, slaughter, massacre, wipe out; informal bump off; N. Amer. informal ice, waste; literary slay.

murderer, murderess noun killer, assassin, serial killer, butcher; informal hit man, hired gun.

murderous adjective homicidal, brutal, violent, savage, ferocious, fierce, vicious, bloodthirsty, barbarous, barbaric, fatal, lethal, deadly.

murky adjective 1 a murky winter afternoon: dark, gloomy, grey, leaden, dull, dim, overcast, cloudy, clouded, sunless, dismal, dreary, bleak. 2 murky water: dirty, muddy, cloudy, turbid.
OPPOSITES bright, clear.

murmur noun 1 his voice was a murmur: whisper, mutter, mumble. 2 the murmur of bees: hum, buzz, drone.
•verb he heard them murmuring in the hall: mutter, mumble, whisper, talk under your breath.

muscle noun 1 he had muscle but no brains: strength, power, brawn; informal beef, beefiness. 2 financial muscle: influence, power, strength, might, force, forcefulness, weight; informal clout.
□ muscle in (informal) interfere, force your way in, impose yourself, encroach; informal horn in.

muscular adjective **1** having to do with the muscles. **2** having well-developed muscles. □ **muscular dystrophy** an inherited condition in which the muscles gradually become weaker.

musculature noun the arrangement of muscles in a body.

muse¹ noun **1** (**Muse**) (in Greek and Roman mythology) each of nine goddesses representing or associated with a particular art or science. **2** a woman who is the inspiration for a creative artist.

muse² verb (**muses, musing, mused**) **1** be absorbed in thought. **2** say something to yourself in a thoughtful way.

museum noun a building in which objects of interest are kept and shown to the public.

mush noun **1** a soft, wet, pulpy mass. **2** something that is too sentimental. ■ **mushy** adjective.

mushroom noun a fungus in the form of a domed cap on a short stalk, many kinds of which are edible. • verb increase or develop quickly.
■ **mushroom cloud** a mushroom-shaped cloud of dust formed after a nuclear explosion.

music noun **1** the sounds of voices or instruments arranged in a pleasing way. **2** the art of writing or playing music. **3** the written or printed signs representing a piece of music. □ **music hall 1** (in the past) a popular form of entertainment involving singing, dancing, and comedy. **2** a theatre where such entertainment took place.

musical adjective **1** relating to or accompanied by music. **2** fond of or skilled in music. **3** having a pleasant sound. • noun a play or film which involves singing or dancing. ■ **musically** adverb.

musician noun a person who plays a musical instrument or writes music. ■ **musicianship** noun.

musicology noun the study of the history and theory of music.

musk noun a strong-smelling substance produced by the male of a small breed of deer, used as an ingredient in perfume. ■ **musky** adjective.

musket noun (in the past) a light gun with a long barrel.

musketeer noun (in the past) a soldier armed with a musket.

muskrat noun a large North American rodent with a musky smell.

Muslim or **Moslem** noun a follower of Islam. • adjective relating to Muslims or Islam.

muslin noun lightweight cotton cloth in a plain weave.

musquash noun Brit. the fur of the muskrat.

mussel noun a small shellfish with a dark brown or purplish-black shell.

must¹ modal verb (past **had to** or in reported speech **must**) **1** be obliged to; should. **2** used to insist on something. **3** used to say that something is very likely: *you must be tired.* • noun informal something that should not be missed.

must² noun grape juice before it is fermented.

mustache US spelling of MOUSTACHE.

mustang noun a small wild horse of the south-western US.

mustard noun **1** a hot-tasting yellow or brown paste made from the crushed seeds of a plant. **2** a brownish-yellow colour. ■ **mustard gas** a liquid whose vapour causes severe irritation and blistering of the skin, used in chemical weapons.

muster verb (**musters, mustering, mustered**) **1** summon up a feeling or attitude. **2** bring troops together in preparation for battle. **3** (of people) gather together. • noun an instance of mustering troops. □ **pass muster** be accepted as satisfactory.

mustn't short form must not.

musty adjective having a stale or mouldy smell. ■ **mustiness** noun.

mutable adjective able or tending to change. ■ **mutability** noun.

mutant adjective resulting from or showing

THESAURUS

muscular adjective strong, brawny, muscly, well built, burly, strapping, sturdy, sinewy, powerful, athletic; informal hunky, beefy; N. Amer. informal buff.

muse verb ponder, consider, think over/about, mull over, reflect on, contemplate, turn over in your mind, chew over.

musical adjective tuneful, melodic, melodious, harmonious, sweet-sounding. OPPOSITES discordant.

must verb ought to, should, have (got) to, need to, be obliged to, be required to, be compelled to.

muster verb **1** *they mustered 50,000 troops:* assemble, mobilize, rally, raise, summon, gather, mass, call up, call to arms, recruit, conscript; US draft. **2** *reporters mustered outside her house:* congregate, assemble, gather (together), come together, collect, convene, mass, rally. **3** *she mustered her courage:* summon (up), screw up, call up, rally.

the effect of mutation. •noun a mutant form.

mutate verb (**mutates, mutating, mutated**) undergo mutation.

mutation noun **1** the process of changing. **2** a change in genetic structure which may be passed on to subsequent generations. **3** a distinct form resulting from such a change.

mute adjective **1** not speaking. **2** unable to speak. **3** (of a letter) not pronounced. •noun **1** dated a person who is unable to speak. **2** a device used to make the sound of a musical instrument quieter or softer. •verb (**mutes, muting, muted**) **1** make the sound of something quieter or softer. **2** reduce the strength or intensity of. ■ **mutely** adverb.

mutilate verb (**mutilates, mutilating, mutilated**) severely injure or damage. ■ **mutilation** noun.

mutineer noun a person who takes part in a mutiny.

mutinous adjective rebellious.

mutiny noun (plural **mutinies**) an open rebellion against authority, especially by soldiers or sailors against their officers. •verb (**mutinies, mutinying, mutinied**) take part in a mutiny; rebel.

mutt noun informal a mongrel dog.

mutter verb (**mutters, muttering, muttered**) **1** say something in a voice which can barely be heard. **2** talk or grumble in private. •noun speech that can barely be heard.

mutton noun the flesh of a fully grown sheep used as food.

mutual adjective **1** experienced by two or

more people equally. **2** shared by two or more people: *a mutual friend.* ■ **mutuality** noun **mutually** adverb.

muzzle noun **1** the nose and mouth of an animal. **2** a guard fitted over an animal's muzzle to stop it biting. **3** the open end of the barrel of a gun. •verb (**muzzles, muzzling, muzzled**) **1** put a muzzle on an animal. **2** prevent someone speaking freely.

muzzy adjective **1** dazed or confused. **2** blurred or indistinct.

my possessive determiner belonging to or associated with the speaker.

myalgia /my-al-juh/ noun pain in a muscle.

mycology noun the scientific study of fungi.

mynah bird noun an Asian or Australasian bird, some kinds of which can mimic human speech.

myopia /my-oh-pi-uh/ noun short-sightedness. ■ **myopic** adjective.

myriad /mi-ri-uhd/ noun (also **myriads**) a countless or very great number. •adjective countless.

myrrh /mer/ noun a sweet-smelling substance obtained from certain trees, used in perfumes and incense.

myrtle noun an evergreen shrub with white flowers and purple-black berries.

myself pronoun **1** used by a speaker to refer to himself or herself as the object of a verb or preposition when he or she is the subject of the clause. **2** I or me personally.

mysterious adjective difficult or impossible

m

THESAURUS

mutation noun **1** alteration, change, transformation, metamorphosis, transmutation. **2** *a genetic mutation:* mutant, freak (of nature), deviant, monstrosity, monster.

mute adjective **1** *Yasmin remained mute:* silent, speechless, dumb, unspeaking, tight-lipped, taciturn; informal mum. **2** *a mute appeal:* wordless, silent, dumb, unspoken. OPPOSITES voluble, spoken.

muted adjective **1** *the muted hum of traffic:* muffled, faint, indistinct, quiet, soft, low, distant, faraway. **2** *muted tones:* subdued, pastel, delicate, subtle, understated, restrained.

mutilate verb **1** *the bodies had been mutilated:* mangle, maim, disfigure, dismember, slash, hack. **2** *the carved screen had been mutilated:* vandalize, damage, slash, hack, deface, violate, desecrate.

mutiny noun *a naval mutiny:* insurrection, rebellion, revolt, riot, uprising, insurgence, insubordination. •verb *the crew mutinied:* rise up, rebel, revolt, riot, strike.

mutter verb **1** *a group of men stood muttering:* talk under your breath, murmur, mumble, whisper. **2** *residents muttered about the charge:* grumble, complain, grouse, carp, whine; informal moan, whinge.

mutual adjective reciprocal, reciprocated, requited, returned, common, joint, shared.

mysterious adjective **1** *mysterious circumstances:* puzzling, strange, peculiar, curious, funny, odd, weird, bizarre, mystifying, inexplicable, baffling, perplexing. **2** *he was being very mysterious:* secretive, inscrutable, enigmatic, reticent, evasive, furtive, surreptitious. OPPOSITES straightforward.

to understand or explain.
■ **mysteriously** adverb.

mystery noun (plural **mysteries**) **1** something
that is difficult or impossible to
understand or explain. **2** secrecy. **3** a novel,
film, etc. dealing with a puzzling crime.
□ **mystery play** a medieval play based on
biblical stories or the lives of the saints.

mystic noun a person who seeks to know
God through prayer and contemplation.
• adjective mystical.

mystical adjective **1** relating to mystics or
mysticism. **2** having a spiritual significance
that goes beyond human understanding.
3 inspiring a sense of spiritual mystery and
awe.

mysticism noun **1** the belief that
knowledge of God can be found through
prayer and contemplation. **2** vague or ill-
defined religious or spiritual belief.

mystify verb (**mystifies, mystifying,**
mystified) **1** completely bewilder someone.
2 make something uncertain or
mysterious.
■ **mystification** noun.

mystique noun a quality of mystery,
glamour, or power that makes someone or
something seem impressive or attractive.

myth noun **1** a traditional story that
describes the early history of a people or
explains a natural event. **2** a widely held
but false belief. **3** an imaginary person or
thing.

mythical adjective **1** found in or
characteristic of myths or folk tales.
2 imaginary or not real.

mythology noun (plural **mythologies**) **1** a
collection of myths. **2** a set of widely held
but exaggerated or false beliefs.
■ **mythological** adjective.

myxomatosis /mik-suh-muh-**toh**-siss/ noun
a highly infectious and usually fatal
disease of rabbits.

THESAURUS

mystery noun **1** *his death remains a
mystery:* puzzle, enigma, conundrum,
riddle, secret, paradox. **2** *her past is
shrouded in mystery:* secrecy, obscurity,
uncertainty, mystique.

mystic, mystical adjective spiritual,
religious, transcendental, paranormal,
other-worldly, supernatural, occult,
metaphysical.

mystify verb bewilder, puzzle, perplex,
baffle, confuse, confound, bemuse, throw;
informal flummox, stump, bamboozle.

myth noun **1** *ancient Greek myths:* folk tale,
folk story, legend, fable, saga, lore,
folklore. **2** *the myths surrounding
childbirth:* misconception, fallacy, old
wives' tale, fairy story, fiction; informal cock
and bull story.

m

Nn

N or **n** noun (plural **Ns** or **N's**) the fourteenth letter of the alphabet. •**abbreviation** North or Northern.

n/a abbreviation not applicable.

naan ⇨ NAN².

nab verb (**nabs, nabbing, nabbed**) informal catch a wrongdoer.

nacho /na-choh/ noun (plural **nachos**) a small piece of tortilla topped with melted cheese, peppers, etc.

nadir /nay-deer/ noun **1** the lowest or most unsuccessful point. **2** the point in space directly opposite the zenith and below an observer.

naevus /nee-vuhss/ (US spelling **nevus**) noun (plural **naevi** /nee-vy/) a birthmark or a mole on the skin.

naff adjective Brit. informal lacking taste or style.

nag¹ verb (**nags, nagging, nagged**) **1** constantly tell someone they should be doing something. **2** be constantly worrying or painful. •**noun 1** a person who nags. **2** a persistent feeling of anxiety.

nag² noun informal an old horse.

naiad /ny-ad/ noun (in classical mythology) a water nymph.

nail noun **1** a small metal spike with a flat head, used for joining pieces of wood together. **2** a thin hard layer covering the upper part of the tip of the finger and toe. •**verb 1** fasten with a nail or nails. **2** informal catch a criminal.

▫ **nail-biting** making you feel great anxiety or tension.

naive or **naïve** /ny-eev/ adjective lacking experience or judgement.

■ **naively** adverb.

naivety /ny-eev-ti/ or **naiveté** /ny-eev-tay/ noun lack of experience, wisdom, or judgement.

naked adjective **1** without clothes. **2** (of an object) without the usual covering or protection. **3** (of feelings) not hidden; open. **4** vulnerable.

▫ **the naked eye** the normal power of the eyes, without using a telescope, microscope, etc.

■ **nakedly** adverb **nakedness** noun.

namby-pamby adjective lacking strength or courage; feeble.

name noun **1** a word or words by which someone or something is known. **2** a famous person. **3** a reputation: *he made a name for himself.* •**verb (names, naming, named) 1** give a name to. **2** identify or mention by name. **3** specify a sum of money, time, or place.

▫ **name-dropping** mentioning the names of

n

THESAURUS

nag verb **1** *she's constantly nagging me:* harass, keep on at, go on at, badger, chivvy, hound, criticize, find fault with, moan at, grumble at, henpeck; informal hassle; N. Amer. informal ride. **2** *this has been nagging me for weeks:* trouble, worry, bother, plague, torment, niggle, prey on your mind; informal bug.

nail noun tack, pin, brad, clout, spike, staple. •**verb fasten,** attach, fix, affix, secure, tack, hammer, pin.

naive adjective **innocent,** unsophisticated, artless, inexperienced, unworldly, trusting, gullible, credulous, immature, callow, raw, green; informal wet behind the ears.
OPPOSITES worldly.

naked adjective **nude,** bare, in the nude, stark naked, having nothing on, stripped, unclothed, undressed; informal without a stitch on, in your birthday suit, in the raw/buff, in the altogether; Brit. informal starkers; N. Amer. informal buck naked.
OPPOSITES clothed.

name noun *her name's Gemma:* title, honorific, designation, tag, epithet, label; informal moniker, handle; formal appellation, denomination.
•**verb 1** *they named the child Pamela:* call, dub, label, style, term, title, baptize, christen. **2** *he has named his successor:* nominate, designate, select, pick, decide on, choose.

famous people as if you know them, in order to impress other people.

nameless adjective **1** having no name. **2** having a name that is kept secret.

namely adverb that is to say.

namesake noun a person or thing with the same name as another.

Namibian /nuh-**mib**-i-uhn/ noun a person from Namibia, a country in southern Africa. • adjective relating to Namibia.

nan[1] noun Brit. informal your grandmother.

nan[2] or **naan** /nahn/ noun a type of soft flat Indian bread.

nanny noun (plural **nannies**) **1** a woman employed to look after a child in its own home. **2** (also **nanny goat**) a female goat.

nanosecond noun one thousand millionth of a second.

nap[1] noun a short sleep. • verb (**naps, napping, napped**) have a nap.

nap[2] noun short raised fibres on the surface of certain fabrics.

napalm /**nay**-pahm/ noun a highly flammable form of petrol, used in firebombs.

nape noun the back of the neck.

naphtha /**naf**-thuh/ noun a flammable oil extracted from coal and petroleum.

napkin noun a piece of cloth or paper used at a meal to wipe the fingers or lips and to protect clothes.

nappy noun (plural **nappies**) Brit. a piece of material wrapped round a baby's bottom and between its legs to absorb urine and faeces.

narcissism /**nar**-si-si-z'm/ noun too much interest in yourself and your appearance. ■ **narcissist** noun **narcissistic** adjective.

narcissus /nar-si-**suhss**/ noun (plural **narcissi** /nar-si-sy/ or **narcissuses**) a daffodil with a flower that has pale outer petals and an orange or yellow centre.

narcotic noun **1** an addictive drug which affects mood or behaviour. **2** a drug which causes drowsiness or unconsciousness, or relieves pain. • adjective relating to narcotics.

nark Brit. informal noun a police informer. • verb annoy.

narrate verb (**narrates, narrating, narrated**) **1** give an account of something. **2** provide a commentary for a film, television programme, etc. ■ **narration** noun **narrator** noun.

narrative noun an account of connected events; a story. • adjective having to do with stories or the telling of stories.

narrow adjective (**narrower, narrowest**) **1** of small width in comparison to length. **2** limited in extent, amount, or scope. **3** only just achieved: *a narrow escape.* • verb **1** become or make narrower. **2** (**narrow something down**) reduce the number of possibilities of something. • noun (**narrows**) a narrow channel connecting two larger areas of water. □ **narrow-minded** unwilling to listen to or accept the views of other people. ■ **narrowly** adverb **narrowness** noun.

narrowboat noun Brit. a canal boat less than 7 ft (2.1 metres) wide.

NASA abbreviation (in the US) National Aeronautics and Space Administration.

nasal adjective relating to the nose. ■ **nasally** adverb.

nascent /**na**-suhnt, **nay**-suhnt/ adjective just

THESAURUS

namely adverb that is (to say), to be specific, specifically, viz., to wit, in other words.

nap noun sleep, catnap, siesta, doze, lie-down, rest; informal snooze, forty winks, shut-eye; Brit. informal kip.

narcotic noun *illegal narcotics:* drug, sedative, opiate, painkiller, analgesic, palliative. • adjective *a narcotic effect:* soporific, sedative, calming, sleep-inducing, opiate, painkilling, pain-relieving, analgesic, anodyne.

narrate verb tell, relate, recount, describe, chronicle, report, present.

narrative noun account, chronicle, history, description, record, report, story, tale.

narrator noun storyteller, relater, chronicler, commentator, presenter, author. OPPOSITES listener, audience.

narrow adjective **1** *her narrow waist:*

slender, slim, small, slight, spare, attenuated, tapering, thin, tiny. **2** *a narrow space:* confined, cramped, tight, restricted, limited, constricted, small, tiny. **3** *a narrow range of products:* limited, restricted, small, inadequate, insufficient, deficient. OPPOSITES wide, broad.
• verb *narrowing the gap between rich and poor:* become/make narrower, become/make smaller, taper, diminish, decrease, reduce, contract, shrink, constrict. OPPOSITES widen.

narrowly adverb (only) just, barely, scarcely, hardly, by a hair's breadth; informal by a whisker.

narrow-minded adjective intolerant, illiberal, reactionary, conservative, parochial, provincial, insular, small-minded, petty, blinkered, inward-looking, narrow, hidebound, prejudiced, bigoted. OPPOSITES tolerant.

coming into existence and beginning to develop.

nasturtium /nuh-ster-shuhm/ noun a garden plant with bright orange, yellow, or red flowers.

nasty adjective (**nastier, nastiest**) **1** unpleasant or disgusting. **2** spiteful, violent, or bad-tempered. **3** painful or harmful: *a nasty bang on the head.*
■ **nastily** adverb **nastiness** noun.

natal /nay-t'l/ adjective relating to the place or time of your birth.

nation noun a large group of people sharing the same language, culture, or history and inhabiting a particular territory.

national adjective **1** having to do with a nation. **2** owned, controlled, or financially supported by the state. •**noun** a citizen of a particular country.
▫ **national curriculum** a programme of study that must be taught in state schools. **national debt** the total amount of money which a country's government has borrowed. **national grid** Brit. **1** the network of power lines between major power stations. **2** the system of geographical coordinates used in maps of the British Isles. **National Insurance** (in the UK) a system of payments made by employees and employers to provide help for people who are ill, unemployed, or retired. **national park** an area of countryside that is protected by the state. **national service** a period of compulsory service in the armed forces during peacetime.
■ **nationally** adverb.

nationalism noun **1** very strong feelings of support for and pride in your own country. **2** belief in independence for a particular country.

■ **nationalist** noun & adjective **nationalistic** adjective.

nationality noun (plural **nationalities**) **1** the status of belonging to a particular nation. **2** an ethnic group.

nationalize or **nationalise** verb (**nationalizes, nationalizing, nationalized**) put an industry or business under the control of the government.
■ **nationalization** noun.

nationwide adjective & adverb throughout the whole nation.

native noun **1** a person born in a particular place. **2** a local inhabitant. **3** an animal or plant that lives or grows naturally in a particular area. **4** dated, offensive a non-white person living in a country before the arrival of white colonists or settlers.
•**adjective 1** associated with the place where you were born. **2** (of a plant or animal) living or growing naturally in a place. **3** having to do with the original inhabitants of a place. **4** in a person's character: *his native wit.*
▫ **native speaker** a person who has spoken a particular language from earliest childhood. **Native American** a member of any of the original peoples of North and South America.

nativity noun (plural **nativities**) **1** (**the Nativity**) the birth of Jesus. **2** formal a person's birth.

NATO or **Nato** abbreviation North Atlantic Treaty Organization.

natter informal verb (**natters, nattering, nattered**) chat for a long time. •**noun** a long chat.

natty adjective (**nattier, nattiest**) informal smart and fashionable.
■ **nattily** adverb.

natural adjective **1** existing in or obtained

n

THESAURUS

nasty adjective **1** *a nasty smell:* unpleasant, disagreeable, disgusting, vile, foul, abominable, revolting, repulsive, repellent, obnoxious, unsavoury, noxious, foul-smelling, smelly, stinking, rank; informal ghastly, horrid, yucky; N. Amer. informal lousy. **2** *she can be really nasty:* unkind, unpleasant, unfriendly, disagreeable, rude, spiteful, malicious, mean, vicious, malevolent, hurtful. **3** *a nasty accident:* serious, dangerous, bad, awful, dreadful, terrible, severe, painful, ugly.
OPPOSITES nice, slight.

nation noun country, state, land, realm, people, race, tribe, clan.

national adjective **1** *national politics:* state, public, federal, governmental. **2** *a national strike:* nationwide, countrywide, state, general, widespread.
OPPOSITES local, international.

•**noun** *a French national:* citizen, subject, native, resident, inhabitant, voter, passport holder.

nationalism noun patriotism, allegiance, xenophobia, chauvinism, jingoism.

nationwide adjective national, countrywide, state, general, widespread, extensive.
OPPOSITES local.

native noun *a native of Sweden:* inhabitant, resident, local, citizen, national, countryman.
OPPOSITES foreigner.

•**adjective 1** *the native population:* indigenous, original. **2** *native produce:* domestic, home-grown, home-made, local, indigenous. **3** *her native tongue:* mother, home, local, vernacular.
OPPOSITES immigrant, imported.

natural adjective **1** *a natural occurrence:*

from nature; not made or caused by people. **2** as you would expect; normal. **3** born with a particular skill or quality: *a natural leader.* **4** having a relaxed, easy manner. **5** (of a parent or child) related by blood. **6** Music (of a note) not sharp or flat. • noun **1** a person with a particular gift or talent. **2** Music a natural note or a sign (♮) denoting one. □ **natural gas** gas found underground and used as fuel. **natural history** the scientific study of animals or plants. **natural selection** the evolutionary process by which creatures better adapted to their environment tend to survive and produce more offspring. ■ **naturally** adverb.

naturalism noun a style in art or literature that shows things how they are in everyday life.

naturalist noun a person who studies animals or plants.

naturalistic adjective **1** having to do with real life or nature. **2** based on the theory of naturalism.

naturalize or **naturalise** verb (**naturalizes, naturalizing, naturalized**) **1** make a foreigner a citizen of a country. **2** introduce a plant or animal into a region where it is not native.

nature noun **1** the physical world, including plants, animals, and all things that are not made by people. **2** the typical qualities or character of a person, animal, or thing. **3** a type or kind of something.

naturism noun nudism. ■ **naturist** noun & adjective.

naught pronoun old use nothing.

naughty adjective (**naughtier, naughtiest**) **1** (of a child) disobedient; badly behaved. **2** informal mildly rude or indecent. ■ **naughtily** adverb **naughtiness** noun.

nausea /naw-zi-uh/ noun a feeling of sickness and wanting to vomit.

nauseate verb (**nauseates, nauseating, nauseated**) make someone feel sick or disgusted.

nauseous adjective **1** suffering from nausea. **2** causing nausea.

nautical adjective having to do with sailors or navigation. □ **nautical mile** a unit used to measure distances at sea, equal to 1,852 metres (approximately 2,025 yards).

nautilus noun (plural **nautiluses**) a swimming mollusc with a spiral shell and short tentacles round the mouth.

naval adjective having to do with a navy or navies.

nave noun the central part of a church.

navel noun the small hollow in the centre of a person's belly where the umbilical cord was cut at birth.

navigable adjective able to be used by boats and ships.

navigate verb (**navigates, navigating,**

THESAURUS

normal, ordinary, everyday, usual, regular, common, commonplace, typical, routine, standard. **2** *natural products:* unprocessed, organic, pure, unrefined, additive-free, green, GM-free. **3** *Alex is a natural leader:* born, instinctive, congenital, pathological. **4** *his natural instincts:* innate, inborn, inherent, native, hereditary, inherited, inbred. **5** *she seemed very natural:* unaffected, spontaneous, uninhibited, relaxed, unselfconscious, genuine, open, artless, guileless, unpretentious. **6** *it was quite natural to think she admired him:* reasonable, logical, understandable, (only) to be expected, predictable.
OPPOSITES abnormal, artificial, affected.

naturally adverb **1** *he's naturally shy:* by nature, by character, inherently, innately, congenitally, pathologically. **2** *try to act naturally:* normally, in a natural manner, spontaneously, genuinely, unpretentiously; informal natural. **3** *naturally, they wanted everything kept quiet:* of course, as might be expected, needless to say, obviously, clearly, it goes without saying.
OPPOSITES self-consciously.

nature noun **1** *the beauty of nature:* the natural world, the environment, the

universe, the cosmos, wildlife, the countryside, the land, the landscape. **2** *the very nature of such crimes:* essence, inherent features, character, complexion. **3** *nastiness was not in her nature:* character, personality, disposition, temperament, make-up, psyche. **4** *experiments of a similar nature:* kind, sort, type, variety, category, genre, order; N. Amer. stripe.

naughty adjective **1** *a naughty boy:* badly behaved, disobedient, bad, wayward, defiant, unruly, insubordinate, wilful, delinquent, undisciplined, disruptive, mischievous, impish. **2** *naughty jokes:* indecent, risqué, rude, racy, vulgar, dirty, filthy, smutty, crude, coarse.
OPPOSITES well behaved, clean.

nausea noun sickness, biliousness, queasiness, vomiting, retching.

nautical adjective maritime, marine, naval, seafaring, boating, sailing.

navigate verb **1** *he navigated the yacht across the Atlantic:* steer, pilot, guide, direct, captain; informal skipper. **2** *I'll drive— you can navigate:* map-read, give directions.

navigated) 1 plan and direct the route of a ship, aircraft, etc. **2** guide a boat or vehicle over a particular route.
■ **navigator** noun.

navigation noun **1** the activity of navigating. **2** the movement of ships.
■ **navigational** adjective.

navvy noun (plural **navvies**) Brit. dated a labourer employed in building a road, railway, or canal.

navy noun (plural **navies**) **1** the branch of a country's armed forces which fights at sea. **2** (also **navy blue**) a dark blue colour.

nay adverb old use or dialect no.

Nazi /naht-si/ noun (plural **Nazis**) historical a member of the far-right National Socialist German Workers' Party.
■ **Nazism** noun.

NB abbreviation note well.

NE abbreviation north-east or north-eastern.

Neanderthal /ni-an-der-tahl/ noun an extinct human living in Europe between about 120,000 and 35,000 years ago.

neap tide noun the tide when there is least difference between high and low water.

near adverb **1** at or to a short distance in space or time. **2** almost. •**preposition** (also **near to**) **1** at or to a short distance in space or time from. **2** close to. •**adjective 1** at a short distance away. **2** close to being. •**verb** approach.
□ **Near East** the countries of SW Asia between the Mediterranean and India

(including the Middle East).
■ **nearness** noun.

nearby adjective & adverb not far away.

nearly adverb very close to; almost.

nearside noun the side of a vehicle nearest the kerb.

nearsighted adjective chiefly N. Amer. short-sighted.

neat adjective **1** tidy or carefully arranged. **2** clever but simple. **3** (of a drink of spirits) not diluted. **4** N. Amer. informal excellent.
■ **neatly** adverb.

neaten verb make something neat.

nebula /neb-yuu-luh/ noun (plural **nebulae** /neb-yuu-lee/ or **nebulas**) a cloud of gas or dust in outer space.

nebulous adjective not clearly defined; vague.

necessarily adverb as a necessary result; unable to be avoided.

necessary adjective **1** needing to be present, or to be done or achieved. **2** unavoidable.

☑ one c, double s: necessary.

necessitate verb (**necessitates**, **necessitating**, **necessitated**) make something necessary.

necessity noun (plural **necessities**) **1** the fact of being necessary. **2** a thing that it is essential to have.

neck noun **1** the part connecting the head to the rest of the body. **2** the part of a bottle

n

navy noun fleet, flotilla, armada, squadron, task force.

near adjective **1** *the house is quite near:* close, nearby, (close/near) at hand, a stone's throw away, within reach, accessible, handy, convenient; informal within spitting distance. **2** *the final judgement is near:* imminent, in the offing, (close/near) at hand, (just) around the corner, on its way, coming, impending, looming.
OPPOSITES far, distant.

nearby adjective not far away/off, close at hand, close by, near, within reach, neighbouring, local, accessible, handy, convenient.
OPPOSITES faraway.

nearly adverb almost, just about, more or less, practically, virtually, all but, as good as, not far off, to all intents and purposes, not quite; informal pretty well.

neat adjective **1** *the bedroom was neat and clean:* tidy, orderly, well ordered, in (good) order, spick and span, uncluttered, straight, trim. **2** *he's very neat:* smart, spruce, dapper, trim, well groomed, well turned out; informal natty. **3** *her neat*

handwriting: clear, regular, precise, elegant; informal easy to read. **4** *this neat little gadget:* compact, well designed, handy; Brit. informal dinky, nifty. **5** *his neat footwork:* skilful, deft, dexterous, adroit, adept, expert; informal nifty. **6** *a neat solution:* clever, ingenious, inventive, imaginative. **7** *neat gin:* undiluted, straight, unmixed; N. Amer. informal straight up.
OPPOSITES untidy.

necessarily adverb as a consequence, as a result, automatically, as a matter of course, certainly, incontrovertibly, inevitably, unavoidably, inescapably, of necessity.

necessary adjective **1** *planning permission is necessary:* obligatory, requisite, required, compulsory, mandatory, imperative, needed. **2** *a necessary consequence:* inevitable, unavoidable, inescapable, inexorable.

necessity noun **1** *the VCR is now regarded as a necessity:* essential, requisite, prerequisite, necessary, basic; informal must-have. **2** *political necessity forced him to resign:* force of circumstance, obligation, need, call, exigency.

near the mouth. **3** the part of a violin, guitar, etc. to which the fingerboard is fixed. • **verb** informal kiss and caress. □ **neck and neck** level in a race or other competition.

neckerchief noun a square of cloth worn round the neck.

necklace noun a piece of jewellery consisting of a chain, string of beads, etc., worn round the neck.

necklet noun a close-fitting ornament worn round the neck.

neckline noun the edge of a dress or top at or below the neck.

necromancy /nek-ruh-man-si/ noun **1** attempted communication with dead people in order to predict the future. **2** witchcraft or black magic. ■ **necromancer** noun.

necrophilia /nek-ruh-fil-i-uh/ noun sexual activity with or interest in dead bodies. ■ **necrophiliac** noun.

necropolis /ne-krop-uh-liss/ noun a cemetery.

necrosis /ne-kroh-siss/ noun the death of cells in an organ or tissue.

nectar noun **1** a fluid produced by flowers and made into honey by bees. **2** (in Greek and Roman mythology) the drink of the gods.

nectarine noun a variety of peach with smooth skin.

née /nay/ adjective born (used in giving a married woman's maiden name).

need verb **1** require something because it is essential or very important. **2** used to express what should or must be done. • **noun 1** a situation in which something is necessary or must be done. **2** a thing that is needed. **3** the state of being very poor.

needful adjective formal necessary.

needle noun **1** a very thin pointed piece of metal with a hole or eye for thread at the blunter end, used in sewing. **2** a long, thin rod used in knitting. **3** the pointed hollow end of a hypodermic syringe. **4** a stylus used to play records. **5** a thin pointer on a dial, compass, etc. **6** the thin, stiff leaf of a fir or pine tree. • **verb** (**needles, needling, needled**) informal deliberately annoy someone.

needlecord noun Brit. a lightweight corduroy fabric with narrow ridges.

needlepoint noun closely stitched embroidery done on canvas.

needless adjective unnecessary; avoidable. ■ **needlessly** adverb.

needlework noun sewing or embroidery.

needn't short form need not.

needy adjective (**needier, neediest**) very poor.

ne'er /nair/ short form old use or dialect never. □ **ne'er-do-well** a useless or lazy person.

nefarious /ni-fair-i-uhss/ adjective bad or illegal.

negate verb (**negates, negating, negated**) **1** stop or undo the effect of. **2** say that something does not exist. ■ **negation** noun.

negative adjective **1** showing the absence rather than the presence of something. **2** expressing denial, disagreement, or refusal. **3** not hopeful or favourable. **4** (of a quantity) less than zero. **5** having to do with the kind of electric charge carried by electrons. **6** (of a photograph) showing light and shade or colours reversed from those of the original. • **noun 1** a negative word or statement. **2** a negative photograph, from which positive prints may be made. ■ **negatively** adverb **negativity** noun.

THESAURUS

need verb **1** *do you need money?* require, be in/have need of, want, be crying out for, be desperate for, demand, call for, necessitate, entail, involve, lack, be without, be short of. **2** *do I need to come?* have to, be meant to, be supposed to, be expected to. • **noun 1** *there's no need to apologize:* necessity, requirement, call, demand. **2** *basic human needs:* requirement, necessity, want, requisite, prerequisite. **3** *my hour of need:* difficulty, trouble, distress, crisis, emergency, urgency, extremity.

needed adjective necessary, required, called for, wanted, desired, lacking. OPPOSITES optional.

needless adjective unnecessary, unneeded, uncalled for, gratuitous, pointless, superfluous, redundant, excessive.

OPPOSITES necessary.

needy adjective poor, deprived, disadvantaged, underprivileged, in need, needful, hard up, poverty-stricken, impoverished, destitute, penniless; informal broke, strapped (for cash); Brit. informal skint. OPPOSITES wealthy.

negative adjective **1** *a negative reply:* opposing, opposed, contrary, anti-, dissenting, in the negative. **2** *stop being so negative:* pessimistic, defeatist, gloomy, Eeyorish, cynical, fatalistic, dismissive, unenthusiastic, apathetic, unresponsive. **3** *a negative effect on the economy:* harmful, bad, adverse, damaging, detrimental, unfavourable, disadvantageous. OPPOSITES positive, optimistic, favourable.

neglect verb **1** fail to give enough care or attention to. **2** fail to do. • noun the action of neglecting.

neglectful adjective failing to give enough care or attention.

negligee /neg-li-zhay/ noun a woman's dressing gown made of a very light, thin fabric.

negligence noun a failure to give someone or something enough care or attention. ▪ negligent adjective.

negligible adjective so small or unimportant as to be not worth considering.

negotiate verb (**negotiates**, **negotiating**, **negotiated**) **1** reach an agreement by discussion. **2** bring something about by discussion. **3** find a way through a difficult path or route. ▪ negotiable adjective **negotiation** noun **negotiator** noun.

☑ -tiate, not -ciate: negotiate.

Negro noun (plural **Negroes**) a black person.

❗ the term **Negro** is now regarded as old-fashioned or even offensive.

neigh noun a high-pitched cry made by a horse. • verb make this cry.

neighbour (US spelling **neighbor**) noun a person who lives next door to you, or very close by. ▪ neighbourly adjective.

neighbourhood (US spelling **neighborhood**) noun **1** a district within a town or city. **2** the area surrounding a place, person, or object.

neighbouring adjective situated next to or very near something.

neither determiner & pronoun not either. • adverb used to show that a negative statement is true of two things, or also true of something else.

☑ remember that **neither** is spelled with the e before the i.

nematode /nem-uh-tohd/ noun a type of worm with a thin tube-shaped body.

nemesis noun (plural **nemeses** /nem-i-seez/) something that brings about someone's deserved and unavoidable downfall.

neoclassical adjective relating to the revival of a classical style in the arts. ▪ neoclassicism noun.

neodymium noun a silvery-white metallic element.

THESAURUS

neglect verb **1** she neglected the children: fail to look after, leave alone, abandon. **2** he's neglecting his work: pay no attention to, let slide, not attend to, be remiss about, be lax about, leave undone. **3** I neglected to inform her: fail, omit, forget.
OPPOSITES cherish, heed, remember.
• noun **1** the place had an air of neglect: disrepair, dilapidation, shabbiness, disuse, abandonment. **2** her doctor was guilty of neglect: negligence, dereliction (of duty), carelessness, irresponsibility, laxity, slackness.
OPPOSITES care.

neglected adjective **1** neglected animals: uncared for, abandoned, mistreated, maltreated. **2** a neglected cottage: derelict, dilapidated, tumbledown, ramshackle, untended. **3** a neglected masterpiece: disregarded, forgotten, overlooked, ignored, unrecognized, unnoticed, unsung, underrated.

negligent adjective neglectful, remiss, careless, lax, irresponsible, inattentive, thoughtless, unmindful, forgetful, slack, sloppy; N. Amer. derelict.
OPPOSITES dutiful.

negligible adjective trivial, trifling, insignificant, unimportant, minor, inconsequential, minimal, small, slight, infinitesimal, minuscule.
OPPOSITES significant.

negotiate verb **1** she refused to negotiate: discuss (terms), talk, consult, confer, debate, compromise, bargain, haggle. **2** he negotiated a new contract: arrange, broker, work out, thrash out, agree on. **3** I negotiated the obstacles: get round, get past, get over, clear, cross, surmount, overcome, deal with, cope with.

negotiation noun **1** the negotiations resume next week: discussion(s), talks, conference, debate, dialogue, consultation. **2** the negotiation of a deal: arrangement, brokering, settlement, conclusion, completion.

negotiator noun mediator, arbitrator, go-between, middleman, intermediary, representative, spokesperson, broker.

neighbourhood noun **1** a quiet neighbourhood: district, area, locality, locale, quarter, community; N. Amer. informal hood, nabe. **2** in the neighbourhood of Canterbury: vicinity, environs.

neighbouring adjective adjacent, adjoining, bordering, connecting, next-door, nearby.
OPPOSITES remote.

neighbourly adjective obliging, helpful, friendly, kind, considerate, amicable, sociable, hospitable, companionable, civil, cordial.
OPPOSITES unfriendly.

n

Neolithic adjective relating to the later part of the Stone Age.

neologism /ni-ol-uh-ji-z'm/ noun a new word or expression.

neon noun a gas that glows when electricity is passed through it, used in fluorescent lighting.

neonatal adjective relating to birth and newborn children.

neophyte /nee-oh-fyt/ noun **1** a person who is new to a subject, skill, or belief. **2** a novice in a religious order, or a newly ordained priest.

Nepali /ni-paw-li/ noun (plural **Nepali** or **Nepalis**) a person from Nepal.
■ **Nepalese** noun & adjective.

nephew noun a son of your brother or sister.

nephritis /ni-fry-tiss/ noun inflammation of the kidneys.

nepotism /nep-uh-ti-z'm/ noun favouritism shown to relatives or friends.

Neptune noun the eighth planet from the sun in the solar system.

neptunium noun a rare radioactive metallic element.

nerd noun informal an unfashionable person who is obsessed with a particular subject or interest.

nerve noun **1** a fibre or bundle of fibres in the body along which impulses of sensation pass. **2** steadiness and courage in a difficult or demanding situation. **3** (**nerves**) nervousness. **4** informal cheekily disrespectful or inappropriate behaviour.
•verb (**nerves, nerving, nerved**) (**nerve yourself**) brace yourself for a difficult situation.
□ **get on someone's nerves** informal irritate someone. **nerve cell** a neuron. **nerve gas** a poisonous gas which affects the nervous

system. **nerve-racking** (or **nerve-wracking**) causing nervousness or fear.

nerveless adjective **1** lacking strength or feeling. **2** confident.

nervous adjective **1** easily frightened or worried. **2** anxious. **3** having to do with the nerves.
□ **nervous breakdown** a period of mental illness resulting from severe depression or stress. **nervous system** the network of nerves which transmits nerve impulses between parts of the body.
■ **nervously** adverb **nervousness** noun.

nervy adjective (**nervier, nerviest**) Brit. nervous or tense.

nest noun **1** a structure made by a bird in which it lays eggs and shelters its young. **2** a place where an animal or insect breeds or shelters. **3** a set of similar objects that are designed to fit inside each other. •verb **1** use or build a nest. **2** fit an object inside a larger one.
□ **nest egg** a sum of money saved for the future.

nestle verb (**nestles, nestling, nestled**) **1** settle comfortably within or against something. **2** (of a place) lie in a sheltered position.

nestling noun a bird that is too young to leave the nest.

net¹ noun **1** a material made of strands of cord or string that are knotted together to form small open squares. **2** a piece or structure of net for catching fish or insects, surrounding a goal, etc. **3** a thin fabric with a very open weave. **4** (**the Net**) the Internet. •verb (**nets, netting, netted**) **1** catch something in a net. **2** earn or obtain something.

net² or Brit. **nett** adjective **1** (of a sum of money) remaining after tax or expenses have been deducted. **2** (of a weight) not

---

THESAURUS

nerve noun **1** *the match will be a test of nerve:* confidence, assurance, courage, bravery, determination, will power, spirit, grit; informal guts; Brit. informal bottle; N. Amer. informal moxie. **2** *he had the nerve to chat her up:* audacity, cheek, effrontery, gall, temerity, presumption, impudence, impertinence, arrogance; informal face, front, brass neck, chutzpah. **3** (**nerves**) anxiety, tension, nervousness, stress, worry, cold feet, apprehension; informal butterflies (in your stomach), collywobbles, jitters.

nervous adjective **1** *a nervous woman:* highly strung, anxious, edgy, nervy, tense, excitable, jumpy, neurotic. **2** *he was so nervous he couldn't eat:* anxious, worried, apprehensive, on edge, edgy, tense, stressed, agitated, uneasy, restless, worked up, keyed up, overwrought; informal jittery,

twitchy, in a state, uptight, wired, in a flap; Brit. informal having kittens; N. Amer. informal squirrelly.
OPPOSITES relaxed, calm.

nestle verb snuggle, cuddle, huddle, nuzzle, settle, burrow.

net¹ noun *a dress of green net:* netting, mesh, tulle, fishnet, lace.
•verb *they netted some big criminals:* catch, capture, trap, snare; informal nab, bag, collar, bust; Brit. informal nick.

net² adjective **1** *net earnings:* after tax, after deductions, take-home, clear, final; informal bottom line. **2** *the net result:* final, end, ultimate, closing, overall, actual, effective.
OPPOSITES gross.
•verb *she netted £50,000:* earn, make, clear, take home, bring in, pocket, realize, be paid.

including the packaging. **3** (of an effect or result) overall. • verb (**nets, netting, netted**) gain a sum of money as clear profit.

netball noun a team game in which goals are scored by throwing a ball through a net hanging from a hoop.

nether adjective lower in position.

nettle noun a plant with leaves that are covered with stinging hairs. • verb (**nettles, nettling, nettled**) annoy.

network noun **1** an arrangement of intersecting horizontal and vertical lines. **2** a complex system of railways, roads, etc., that cross or connect with each other. **3** a group of radio or television stations that connect to broadcast a programme at the same time. **4** a number of interconnected computers, operations, etc. **5** a group of people who keep in contact with each other to exchange information. • verb keep in contact with other people to exchange information.
■ **networker** noun.

neural /nyoor-uhl/ adjective relating to a nerve or the nervous system.

neuralgia /nyoo-ral-juh/ noun severe pain along a nerve in the head or face.
■ **neuralgic** adjective.

neurology noun the branch of medicine concerned with the nervous system.
■ **neurological** adjective **neurologist** noun.

neuron or **neurone** noun a cell that transmits nerve impulses.

neurosis /nyoo-roh-siss/ noun (plural **neuroses** /nyoo-roh-seez/) a mild mental illness in which a person feels depressed or anxious, or behaves in an obsessive way.

neurosurgery noun surgery performed on the nervous system.
■ **neurosurgeon** noun.

neurotic adjective **1** having to do with

neurosis. **2** informal obsessive, or too sensitive or anxious.

neuter adjective **1** (of a noun) neither masculine nor feminine. **2** having no sexual or reproductive organs. • verb (**neuters, neutering, neutered**) operate on an animal so that it cannot produce young.

neutral adjective **1** not supporting either side in a dispute or war. **2** lacking noticeable or strong qualities. **3** Chemistry neither acid nor alkaline; having a pH of about 7. • noun a position of a gear mechanism in which the engine is disconnected from the driven parts.
■ **neutrality** noun **neutrally** adverb.

neutralize or **neutralise** verb (**neutralizes, neutralizing, neutralized**) **1** stop something from having an effect. **2** make neutral.
■ **neutralization** noun.

neutrino /nyoo-tree-noh/ noun (plural **neutrinos**) a subatomic particle with a mass close to zero and no electric charge.

neutron noun a subatomic particle of about the same mass as a proton but without an electric charge.

never adverb **1** not ever. **2** not at all.
□ the never-never Brit. informal hire purchase.

nevermore adverb never again.

nevertheless adverb in spite of that.

nevus US spelling of NAEVUS.

new adjective **1** made, introduced, discovered, or experienced recently. **2** not previously used or owned. **3** (**new to**) not experienced in. **4** different from a recent previous one. **5** better than before; renewed or reformed. • adverb newly.
□ New Age an alternative movement concerned with spirituality, care for the environment, etc. new moon the phase of the moon when it first appears as a thin crescent. New Testament the second part

n

THESAURUS

network noun **1** *a network of arteries:* web, lattice, net, matrix, mesh, criss-cross, grid. **2** *a network of lanes:* maze, labyrinth, warren, tangle.

neurotic adjective overanxious, highly strung, oversensitive, nervous, tense, paranoid, obsessive, fixated, hysterical, overwrought, irrational.
OPPOSITES stable, calm.

neutral adjective **1** *she's neutral on this issue:* impartial, unbiased, unprejudiced, objective, open-minded, non-partisan, even-handed, disinterested, dispassionate, detached. **2** *Switzerland remained neutral:* unaligned, non-aligned, unaffiliated, uninvolved, non-combatant. **3** *a neutral topic of conversation:* inoffensive, bland, unobjectionable, unexceptionable, anodyne, uncontroversial, safe, harmless,

innocuous. **4** *a neutral background:* pale, light, colourless, indeterminate, drab, insipid, nondescript, dull.
OPPOSITES biased, partisan, provocative, colourful.

new adjective **1** *new technology:* recent, up to date, the latest, current, state-of-the-art, contemporary, advanced, cutting-edge, modern; informal edgy. **2** *is your boat new?* unused, brand new, pristine, fresh. **3** *new neighbours moved in:* different, another, alternative, unfamiliar, unknown, strange. **4** *they had a new classroom built:* additional, extra, supplementary, further, another, fresh. **5** *I came back a new woman:* reinvigorated, restored, revived, improved, refreshed, regenerated.
OPPOSITES old, hackneyed, second-hand, present.

of the Christian Bible, recording the life and teachings of Jesus. **New World** North and South America. **new year** the calendar year that has just begun or is about to begin, following 31 December.

newborn adjective recently born.

newcomer noun **1** a person who has recently arrived. **2** a person who is new to an activity or situation.

newel /nyoo-uhl/ noun the post at the top or bottom of a stair rail.

newfangled adjective disapproving newly developed and unfamiliar.

newly adverb recently.
□ **newly-wed** a person who has recently married.

news noun **1** new information about recent events. **2** (**the news**) a broadcast or published news report.

newsagent noun Brit. a shopkeeper who sells newspapers and magazines.

newscast noun N. Amer. a broadcast news report.
■ **newscaster** noun.

newsflash noun a brief item of important news, interrupting other radio or television programmes.

newsgroup noun a group of Internet users who exchange information about a particular subject online.

newsletter noun a bulletin issued on a regular basis to the members of a society or organization.

newspaper noun a daily or weekly publication containing news and articles on current affairs.

newsprint noun cheap, low-quality paper used for newspapers.

newsreader noun Brit. a person who reads

the news on radio or television.

newsreel noun a short cinema film showing news and current affairs.

newsroom noun the area in a newspaper or broadcasting office where news is processed.

newsworthy adjective important enough to be mentioned as news.

newt noun a small animal with a slender body and a long tail, that can live in water or on land.

newton noun Physics a unit of force.

next adjective **1** coming immediately after the present one in time, space, or order. **2** (of a day of the week) nearest (or the nearest but one) after the present. ● adverb immediately afterwards.
□ **next door** in or to the next house or room. **next of kin** a person's closest living relative or relatives.

nexus noun (plural **nexus** or **nexuses**) a connection or series of connections.

NHS abbreviation National Health Service.

nib noun the pointed end part of a pen.

nibble verb (**nibbles**, **nibbling**, **nibbled**) **1** take small bites out of. **2** bite gently. ● noun **1** a small piece of food bitten off. **2** (**nibbles**) informal small savoury snacks.

Nicaraguan /ni-kuh-rag-yuu-uhn/ noun a person from Nicaragua. ● adjective relating to Nicaragua.

nice adjective **1** enjoyable or attractive; pleasant. **2** good-natured; kind. **3** involving a very small detail or difference.
■ **nicely** adverb **niceness** noun.

nicety noun (plural **niceties**) **1** a very small detail or difference. **2** accuracy.

niche /neesh, nich/ noun **1** a small hollow in

THESAURUS

newcomer noun **1** *a newcomer to the village*: new arrival, immigrant, incomer, settler, stranger, outsider, foreigner, alien; informal new kid on the block; Austral. informal blow-in. **2** *photography tips for the newcomer*: beginner, novice, learner, trainee, apprentice, probationer; N. Amer. tenderfoot; informal rookie, newbie.

newly adverb recently, only just, lately, freshly, not long ago, a short time ago.

news noun report, story, account, announcement, press release, communication, communiqué, bulletin, intelligence, disclosure, revelation, gossip; informal scoop; literary tidings.

next adjective **1** *the next chapter*: following, succeeding, upcoming, to come. **2** *the next house in the street*: neighbouring, adjacent, adjoining, next-door, bordering, connected, closest, nearest.
OPPOSITES previous.

● adverb *where shall we go next?* then, after, afterwards, later, subsequently; formal thereafter.
OPPOSITES before.

nice adjective **1** *have a nice time*: enjoyable, pleasant, agreeable, good, satisfying, entertaining, amusing; informal lovely, great; N. Amer. informal neat. **2** *nice people*: pleasant, likeable, agreeable, personable, congenial, amiable, affable, genial, friendly, charming, delightful, engaging, sympathetic. **3** *nice manners*: polite, courteous, civil, refined, polished, genteel, elegant. **4** *that's a rather nice distinction*: subtle, fine, delicate, precise, strict, close, careful, meticulous, scrupulous. **5** *it's a nice day*: fine, pleasant, agreeable, dry, sunny, warm, mild.
OPPOSITES unpleasant, nasty, rough.

niche noun **1** *a niche in the wall*: recess, alcove, nook, cranny, hollow, bay, cavity, cubbyhole, pigeonhole. **2** *he found his* a wall. **2** (**your niche**) a role or job that suits you.

nick noun **1** a small cut. **2** (**the nick**) Brit. informal prison or a police station. **3** Brit. informal condition. • verb **1** make a nick or nicks in. **2** Brit. informal steal. **3** Brit. informal arrest.

□ **in the nick of time** only just in time.

nickel noun **1** a silvery-white metallic element. **2** N. Amer. a five-cent coin.

nickname noun another name by which someone is known. • verb (**nicknames, nicknaming, nicknamed**) give a nickname to.

nicotine noun a poisonous oily liquid found in tobacco.

niece noun a daughter of your brother or sister.

☑ *i* before *e* except after *c*: n*i*ece.

nifty adjective (**niftier, niftiest**) informal very skilful, effective, or useful.

Nigerian noun a person from Nigeria. • adjective relating to Nigeria.

niggardly adjective not generous; mean.

nigger noun offensive a black person.

niggle verb (**niggles, niggling, niggled**) slightly worry or annoy. • noun a minor worry or criticism.

nigh adverb, preposition, & adjective old use near.

night noun **1** the time from sunset to sunrise. **2** an evening.

nightcap noun **1** a hot or alcoholic drink taken at bedtime. **2** (in the past) a soft hat worn in bed.

nightclub noun a club that is open at night, with a bar and music.

nightdress or **nightgown** noun a light, loose garment worn by a woman or girl in bed.

nightfall noun dusk.

nightie noun informal a nightdress.

nightingale noun a small bird with a

tuneful song, often heard at night.

nightjar noun a bird with grey-brown feathers and a distinctive call, active at night.

nightlife noun social activities or entertainment available at night.

nightly adjective & adverb happening or done every night.

nightmare noun **1** a frightening or unpleasant dream. **2** a very unpleasant experience.
■ **nightmarish** adjective.

nightshirt noun a long shirt worn in bed.

nightspot noun informal a nightclub.

nihilism /ny-hi-li-z'm/ noun the belief that nothing has any value.
■ **nihilist** noun **nihilistic** adjective.

nil noun nothing; zero.

nimble adjective (**nimbler, nimblest**) **1** quick and light in movement. **2** able to think and understand quickly.
■ **nimbly** adverb.

nimbus noun (plural **nimbi** /nim-by/ or **nimbuses**) a large grey rain cloud.

nincompoop noun a stupid person.

nine cardinal number one less than ten; 9. (Roman numeral: **ix** or **IX**.)

nineteen cardinal number one more than eighteen; 19. (Roman numeral: **xix** or **XIX**.)
■ **nineteenth** ordinal number.

ninety cardinal number (plural **nineties**) ten less than one hundred; 90. (Roman numeral: **xc** or **XC**.)
■ **ninetieth** ordinal number.

ninny noun (plural **ninnies**) informal a silly person.

ninth ordinal number **1** at number nine in a sequence; 9th. **2** (**a ninth** or **one ninth**) each of nine equal parts into which something is divided.

niobium noun a silver-grey metallic element.

niche in life: (**ideal**) position, slot, place, function, vocation, calling, métier, station, job, level.

nick noun *a slight nick in the blade*: cut, scratch, incision, notch, chip, dent, indentation.
• verb *I nicked the edge of the table*: cut, scratch, graze, chip, dent.

nickname noun pet name, diminutive, endearment, tag, label, sobriquet, epithet; informal moniker.

night noun night-time, (hours of) darkness, dark.
opposites day.

nightly adjective **1** *nightly raids*: every night, night after night. **2** *his nightly wanderings*: nocturnal, night-time.

• adverb *a band plays there nightly*: every night, each night, night after night.

nightmare noun ordeal, trial, hell, misery, agony, torture, murder, purgatory, disaster; informal the pits.

nil noun nothing, none, nought, zero; Tennis love; Cricket a duck.

nimble adjective **1** *he was nimble on his feet*: agile, sprightly, light, spry, quick, lithe, skilful, deft, dexterous, adroit; informal nippy. **2** *a nimble mind*: quick, alert, lively, astute, perceptive, penetrating, discerning, shrewd, sharp, intelligent, bright, smart, clever, brilliant; informal quick on the uptake.
opposites clumsy, dull.

nip[1] verb (**nips, nipping, nipped**) **1** pinch, squeeze, or bite sharply. **2** Brit. informal go quickly. •noun **1** a sharp bite or pinch. **2** a sharp feeling of coldness.

nip[2] noun a small quantity or sip of spirits.

nipper noun informal a child.

nipple noun a small projection in the centre of each breast, from which (in a woman who has recently had a baby) a baby is able to suck milk.

nippy adjective (**nippier, nippiest**) informal **1** able to move quickly. **2** chilly.

nirvana /neer-**vah**-nuh/ noun (in Buddhism) a state of perfect happiness.

nit noun informal **1** the egg of a human head louse. **2** Brit. a stupid person.
□ **nit-picking** criticism of small or unimportant details.

nitrate noun a salt or ester of nitric acid.

nitric acid noun a very corrosive acid.

nitrite noun a salt or ester of nitrous acid.

nitrogen noun a gas forming about 78 per cent of the earth's atmosphere.

nitroglycerine (US spelling **nitroglycerin**) noun an explosive liquid used in dynamite.

nitrous oxide noun a colourless gas used as an anaesthetic.

nitty-gritty noun informal the most important details.

nitwit noun informal a stupid person.

no determiner not any. •exclamation used to refuse or disagree with something. •adverb not at all. •noun (plural **noes**) a decision or vote against something.
□ **no-claims bonus** Brit. a reduction in an insurance premium when no claim has been made over an agreed period. **no-ball** a ball in cricket that is unlawfully bowled, counting as an extra run to the batting side.

no. abbreviation number.

nob noun Brit. informal an upper-class person.

nobble verb (**nobbles, nobbling, nobbled**) Brit. informal **1** try to influence someone using unfair or illegal methods. **2** stop someone and talk to them.

nobelium noun a radioactive chemical element that is produced artificially.

nobility noun **1** the quality of being noble. **2** the aristocracy.

noble adjective (**nobler, noblest**) **1** belonging to the aristocracy. **2** having personal qualities that people admire, such as courage and honesty. **3** magnificent; impressive. •noun a nobleman or noblewoman.
■ **nobly** adverb.

nobleman or **noblewoman** noun (plural **noblemen** or **noblewomen**) a member of the aristocracy.

nobody pronoun no person. •noun (plural **nobodies**) a person who is not considered important.

nocturnal adjective done or active at night.
■ **nocturnally** adverb.

nocturne noun a short piece of music in a dreamy, romantic style.

nod verb (**nods, nodding, nodded**) **1** lower and raise your head briefly to show agreement or as a greeting or signal. **2** let your head fall forward when you are drowsy or asleep. **3** (**nod off**) informal fall asleep. •noun an act of nodding.

node noun technical **1** a point in a network at which lines cross or branch. **2** the part of a plant stem from which one or more leaves grow. **3** a small mass of tissue in the body.

nodule noun a small swelling or lump.
■ **nodular** adjective.

Noel noun Christmas.

noggin noun a small quantity of alcoholic drink.

Noh noun a type of traditional Japanese theatre with dance and song.

noise noun **1** a sound or series of sounds, especially an unpleasant one. **2** disturbances that accompany and

THESAURUS

nip verb & noun bite, nibble, peck, pinch, tweak.

no adverb absolutely not, definitely not, of course not, under no circumstances, not at all, negative, never; informal nope, no way, not a chance; Brit. informal no fear; old use nay.
OPPOSITES yes.

noble adjective **1** a noble family: aristocratic, blue-blooded, high-born, titled, patrician. **2** a noble cause: worthy, righteous, virtuous, good, honourable, worthwhile. **3** a noble pine forest: magnificent, splendid, grand, stately, imposing, dignified, proud, striking, majestic.

OPPOSITES humble, base, unimpressive.
•noun Scottish nobles: aristocrat, nobleman, noblewoman, lord, lady, peer (of the realm), peeress, patrician; informal aristo.
OPPOSITES commoner.

nod verb **1** she nodded her head: incline, bob, bow, dip. **2** he nodded to me to start: signal, gesture, gesticulate, motion, sign, indicate.
•noun **1** a nod of his head: inclination, bob, bow, dip. **2** she gave a nod to the manager: signal, indication, sign, cue, gesture.

noise noun sound, din, hubbub, clamour, racket, uproar, tumult, commotion; informal hullabaloo; Brit. informal row.
OPPOSITES silence.

interfere with an electrical signal.
■ **noiseless** adjective.

noisome /**noy**-suhm/ adjective literary having a very unpleasant smell.

noisy adjective (**noisier, noisiest**) full of or making a lot of noise.
■ **noisily** adverb.

nomad noun a member of a people that travels from place to place to find fresh pasture for its animals.

nomadic adjective having the life of a nomad; wandering.

nom de plume /nom duh **ploom**/ noun (plural **noms de plume** /nom duh **ploom**/) a name used by a writer instead of their real name; a pen name.

nomenclature /noh-**men**-kluh-cher/ noun a system of names used in a particular subject.

nominal adjective **1** in name but not in reality. **2** (of a sum of money) very small.
■ **nominally** adverb.

nominate verb (**nominates, nominating, nominated**) **1** put someone forward as a candidate for a job or award. **2** arrange a time, date, or place.
■ **nomination** noun **nominee** noun.

nominative noun Grammar the case used for the subject of a verb.

non- prefix not: *non-existent.*

nonagenarian /noh-nuh-juh-**nair**-i-uhn/ noun a person between 90 and 99 years old.

nonchalant /**non**-shuh-luhnt/ adjective relaxed and unconcerned.
■ **nonchalance** noun **nonchalantly** adverb.

non-commissioned adjective (of a military officer) appointed from the lower ranks.

non-committal adjective not showing what you think or which side you are on.
■ **non-committally** adverb.

non compos mentis /non kom-poss **men**-tiss/ adjective not in your right mind; distracted or mad.

nonconformist noun **1** a person who does not follow accepted ideas or behaviour. **2** (**Nonconformist**) a member of a Protestant Church which does not follow the beliefs of the established Church of England.
■ **nonconformity** noun.

nondescript adjective having no interesting or special features.

none pronoun **1** not any. **2** no one. • adverb (**none the**) not at all.

nonentity noun (plural **nonentities**) an unimportant person or thing.

nonetheless or **none the less** adverb in spite of that; nevertheless.

non-event noun a very disappointing or uninteresting event.

non-existent adjective not real or present.

no-nonsense adjective simple and straightforward; sensible.

nonpareil /non-puh-**rayl**/ noun a person or thing that is better than all others of the same kind.

nonplussed adjective surprised and confused.

non-proliferation noun the prevention of an increase in the number of nuclear weapons that are produced.

nonsense noun **1** words or statements that make no sense. **2** silly behaviour.

nonsensical adjective making no sense; ridiculous.

non sequitur /non sek-wi-ter/ noun a statement that does not follow on logically from what has just been said.

non-starter noun informal something that has no chance of succeeding.

non-stick adjective (of a pan) covered with

n

THESAURUS

noisy adjective **1** *a noisy crowd:* rowdy, raucous, clamorous, boisterous, chattering, talkative, vociferous, shouting, screaming. **2** *noisy music:* loud, blaring, booming, deafening, thunderous, ear-splitting, piercing, strident, cacophonous.
OPPOSITES quiet, soft.

nominal adjective **1** *the nominal head of the campaign:* in name only, titular, formal, official, theoretical, supposed, ostensible, so-called. **2** *a nominal rent:* token, symbolic, minimal; Brit. peppercorn.
OPPOSITES real, considerable.

nominate verb **1** *any member may nominate a candidate:* propose, put forward, put up, submit, present, recommend, suggest. **2** *the President nominated her to the Supreme Court:* appoint, designate, assign, select, choose,

decide on, promote.

non-existent adjective imaginary, imagined, unreal, fictional, fictitious, made up, invented, fanciful, mythical, illusory.
OPPOSITES real.

nonsense noun **1** *he was talking nonsense:* rubbish, gibberish, claptrap, garbage; informal baloney, tripe, drivel, gobbledegook, twaddle; Brit. informal cobblers, codswallop, double Dutch; Scottish & N. English informal havers; N. Amer. informal flapdoodle, bushwa, applesauce. **2** *she stands no nonsense:* mischief, messing about, misbehaviour, funny business; informal tomfoolery, monkey business, shenanigans; Brit. informal monkey tricks, jiggery-pokery. **3** *the whole thing is a nonsense:* joke, farce, travesty, insanity, madness.
OPPOSITES sense, wisdom.

a substance that prevents food sticking to it during cooking.

non-stop adjective & adverb **1** continuing without stopping. **2** having no stops on the way to a destination.

noodles plural noun thin, long strips of pasta.

nook noun a place that is sheltered or hidden.

noon noun twelve o'clock in the day; midday.

noonday adjective taking place or appearing in the middle of the day.

no one pronoun no person.

noose noun a loop with a knot which tightens as the rope or wire is pulled, used to hang people or trap animals.

nor conjunction & adverb and not; and not either.

Nordic adjective relating to Scandinavia, Finland, and Iceland.

norm noun **1** (**the norm**) the usual or standard thing. **2** a standard that is required or acceptable.

normal adjective usual and typical; what you would expect. • noun the normal state or condition.
■ normality noun normally adverb.

normalize or **normalise** verb (**normalizes, normalizing, normalized**) make or become normal.
■ normalization noun.

Norman noun a member of a people from Normandy in northern France who conquered England in 1066. • adjective relating to the Normans or Normandy.

normative adjective relating to or setting a standard or norm.

Norse noun ancient or medieval Norwegian

or another Scandinavian language.
• adjective relating to ancient or medieval Norway or Scandinavia.

north noun **1** the direction which is on your left-hand side when you are facing east. **2** the northern part of a place. • adjective **1** lying towards or facing the north. **2** (of a wind) blowing from the north. • adverb to or towards the north.
■ northward adjective & adverb northwards adverb.

north-east noun the direction or region halfway between north and east. • adjective & adverb **1** towards or facing the north-east. **2** (of a wind) blowing from the north-east.
■ north-eastern adjective.

north-easterly adjective & adverb **1** facing or moving towards the north-east. **2** (of a wind) blowing from the north-east.

northerly adjective & adverb **1** facing or moving towards the north. **2** (of a wind) blowing from the north.

northern adjective **1** situated in or facing the north. **2** coming from or characteristic of the north.
□ Northern Lights the aurora borealis.

northerner noun a person from the north of a region.

north-west noun the direction or region halfway between north and west. • adjective & adverb **1** towards or facing the north-west. **2** (of a wind) blowing from the north-west.
■ north-western adjective.

north-westerly adjective & adverb **1** facing or moving towards the north-west. **2** (of a wind) blowing from the north-west.

Norwegian noun **1** a person from Norway. **2** the language spoken in Norway. • adjective

THESAURUS

non-stop adjective *non-stop entertainment:* continuous, constant, continual, incessant, ceaseless, uninterrupted, perpetual, round-the-clock, unremitting, relentless, persistent.
OPPOSITES intermittent, occasional.
• adverb *we worked non-stop:* continuously, continually, incessantly, ceaselessly, all the time, constantly, perpetually, round the clock, steadily, relentlessly, persistently; informal 24-7.
OPPOSITES intermittently, occasionally.

noon noun midday, twelve o'clock, twelve hundred hours, twelve noon, high noon, noonday.

norm noun **1** *norms of behaviour:* standard, convention, criterion, yardstick, benchmark, touchstone, rule, formula, pattern. **2** *such teams are now the norm:* normal, usual, the rule, standard, typical, average, par for the course, expected.

normal adjective **1** *they issue books in the normal way:* usual, standard, ordinary, customary, conventional, habitual, accustomed, typical, common, regular, routine, traditional. **2** *a normal couple:* ordinary, average, typical, run-of-the-mill, middle-of-the-road, common, conventional, mainstream; N. Amer. garden-variety; Brit. informal common or garden, bog-standard. **3** *the man was not normal:* sane, in your right mind, right in the head, of sound mind, compos mentis; informal all there.
OPPOSITES unusual, insane.

normally adverb **1** *she wanted to be able to walk normally:* naturally, conventionally, properly, like everyone else. **2** *normally we'd keep quiet about this:* usually, ordinarily, as a rule, generally, in general, mostly, for the most part, by and large, mainly, most of the time, on the whole, typically, traditionally.

relating to Norway.

nose noun **1** the part of the face containing the nostrils and used in breathing and smelling. **2** the front end of an aircraft, car, or other vehicle. **3** a talent for finding something. **4** the characteristic smell of a wine. • verb (**noses, nosing, nosed**) **1** make your way slowly forward. **2** look around or pry into something. **3** (of an animal) push its nose against or into.

nosebag noun a bag containing fodder, hung from a horse's head.

nosebleed noun an instance of bleeding from the nose.

nosedive noun **1** a sudden dramatic decline. **2** a steep downward plunge by an aircraft. • verb (**nosedives, nosediving, nosedived**) **1** fall or decline suddenly. **2** (of an aircraft) make a nosedive.

nosegay noun a small bunch of flowers.

nosh informal noun food. • verb eat enthusiastically.

nostalgia noun longing for a happier or better time in the past.
  ■ **nostalgic** adjective **nostalgically** adverb.

nostril noun either of the two openings of the nose through which air passes to the lungs.

nostrum noun **1** a favourite method for

improving something. **2** an ineffective medicine.

nosy or **nosey** adjective (**nosier, nosiest**) informal too inquisitive about other people's affairs.

not adverb **1** used to express a negative. **2** less than.

notable adjective deserving to be noticed or given attention. • noun a famous or important person.
  ■ **notably** adverb.

notary noun (plural **notaries**) a lawyer who is authorized to be a witness when people sign documents.

notation noun a system of symbols used in music, mathematics, etc.

notch noun **1** a V-shaped cut on an edge or surface. **2** a point or level on a scale. • verb **1** make notches in. **2** (**notch something up**) score or achieve something.

note noun **1** a brief written record of something. **2** a short written message. **3** Brit. a banknote. **4** a single sound of a particular pitch and length made by a musical instrument or voice, or a symbol representing this. • verb (**notes, noting, noted**) **1** pay attention to. **2** record something in writing.
  □ **of note** important. **take note** pay attention.

notebook noun **1** a small book for writing

---

nose noun **1** snout, muzzle, proboscis, trunk; informal beak, conk, schnozz, schnozzle, hooter. **2** *a nose for scandal:* instinct, feeling, sixth sense, intuition, insight, feel. • verb **1** *she's nosing into my business:* pry, enquire, poke about/around, interfere (in), meddle (in), be a busybody, stick/poke your nose in; informal be nosy (about), snoop; Austral./NZ informal stickybeak. **2** *he nosed the car into the traffic:* ease, inch, edge, move, manoeuvre, steer, guide.

nostalgia noun reminiscence, remembrance, recollection, wistfulness, regret, sentimentality.

nostalgic adjective wistful, romantic, sentimental, emotional, homesick, regretful, dewy-eyed, maudlin.

notable adjective **1** *notable examples of workmanship:* noteworthy, remarkable, outstanding, important, significant, memorable, marked, striking, impressive. **2** *a notable author:* prominent, important, well known, famous, famed, noted.
  OPPOSITES unremarkable, unknown.
  • noun *movie stars and other notables:* celebrity, public figure, VIP, dignitary, luminary, star, superstar, big name; informal celeb, bigwig, megastar.
  OPPOSITES nonentity.

notably adverb **1** *other countries, notably the USA:* in particular, particularly,

especially, primarily, principally. **2** *these are notably short-lived birds:* remarkably, especially, exceptionally, singularly, particularly, peculiarly, distinctly, significantly, unusually, uncommonly, conspicuously.

notch noun nick, cut, incision, score, scratch, slit, snick, slot, groove.

note noun **1** *a note in her diary:* record, entry, reminder; informal memo. **2** *notes of the meeting:* minutes, record, details, report, account, transcript, summary. **3** *notes in the margins:* annotation, footnote, comment. **4** *he wrote me a note:* message, letter, line. **5** (Brit.) *a £20 note:* banknote; N. Amer. bill; US informal greenback. **6** *a note of hopelessness in her voice:* tone, hint, indication, sign, element, suggestion, sense.
  • verb **1** *we will note your suggestion:* bear in mind, be mindful of, consider, take notice of, register, record, enter. **2** *the letter noted the ministers' concern:* mention, refer to, touch on, indicate, point out, make known, state. **3** *note the date in your diary:* write down, put down, jot down, take down, enter, mark, record, register, pencil.

notebook noun notepad, exercise book, register, logbook, log, diary, journal, record; Brit. jotter, pocketbook.

notes in. **2** a portable computer smaller than a laptop.

noted adjective well known.

notepaper noun paper for writing letters on.

noteworthy adjective interesting or important.

nothing pronoun **1** not anything. **2** something that is not important or interesting. **3** nought. •adverb not at all.

nothingness noun a state of not existing, or in which nothing exists.

notice noun **1** the fact of being aware of or paying attention to something. **2** warning that something is going to happen. **3** a formal statement that you are going to leave a job or end an agreement. **4** a sheet of paper displaying information. **5** a small published announcement or advertisement in a newspaper. **6** a short published review of a new film, play, or book. •verb (**notices, noticing, noticed**) become aware of.

noticeable adjective easily seen or noticed.
■ **noticeably** adverb.

> ☑ remember the e in the middle: noticeable.

notifiable adjective (of an infectious disease) that must be reported to the health authorities.

notify verb (**notifies, notifying, notified**) formally tell someone about something.
■ **notification** noun.

notion noun **1** an idea or belief. **2** an understanding.

notional adjective based on an idea rather than reality.
■ **notionally** adverb.

notoriety /noh-tuh-**ry**-i-ti/ noun the state of being notorious.

notorious adjective famous for something bad.
■ **notoriously** adverb.

notwithstanding preposition in spite of.
•adverb nevertheless.

nougat /**noo**-gah, **nug**-uht/ noun a sweet made from sugar or honey, nuts, and egg white.

nought noun the figure 0. •pronoun nothing.

noun noun a word (other than a pronoun) that refers to a person, place, or thing.

nourish verb **1** give a person, animal, or plant the food and other substances they need in order to grow and be healthy. **2** keep a feeling or belief in your mind for a long time.

nourishment noun the food and other substances necessary for life, growth, and good health.

nous /nowss/ noun Brit. informal common sense.

nouveau riche /noo-voh **reesh**/ noun people who have recently become rich and who display their wealth in an obvious or tasteless way.

nova noun (plural **novae** /**noh**-vee/ or **novas**) a

n

THESAURUS

noted adjective famous, famed, well known, renowned, prominent, notable, important, eminent, acclaimed, celebrated.
OPPOSITES unknown.

nothing noun **1** *there's nothing I can do:* not a thing, zero; N. English nowt; informal zilch, sweet FA, not a dicky bird; Brit. informal damn all, not a sausage; N. Amer. informal zip, nada, diddly-squat. **2** *the price fell to nothing:* zero, nought, nil, 0; Tennis love; Cricket a duck.
OPPOSITES something.

notice noun **1** *nothing escaped his notice:* attention, observation, awareness, consciousness, perception, regard, consideration, scrutiny. **2** *a notice on the wall:* sign, announcement, advertisement, poster, flyer, handbill, bill, bulletin. **3** *we will give you notice of any changes:* notification, (advance) warning, news, word. •verb *I noticed that the door was open:* observe, note, see, discern, detect, spot; Brit. informal clock.
OPPOSITES overlook.

noticeable adjective obvious, evident, apparent, manifest, plain, clear, conspicuous, perceptible, discernible, detectable, observable, visible, appreciable.

notify verb inform, tell, advise, give (advance) warning, let someone know, alert, warn.

notion noun **1** *he had a notion that something was wrong:* idea, impression, (funny) feeling, (sneaking) suspicion, intuition, hunch, belief, opinion. **2** *Claire had no notion of what he meant:* understanding, idea, clue, inkling.

notorious adjective infamous, scandalous, disreputable.

nought noun nil, zero, nothing; Tennis love; Cricket a duck; informal zilch; Brit. informal not a sausage; N. Amer. informal zip, nada.

nourish verb **1** *patients must be well nourished:* feed, sustain, provide for, maintain. **2** *we nourish the talents of children:* encourage, promote, foster, nurture, cultivate, boost, strengthen, enrich.

nourishing adjective nutritious, wholesome, good for you, full of goodness, healthy, health-giving, beneficial.
OPPOSITES unhealthy.

star that suddenly becomes very bright for a short period.

novel¹ noun a story of book length about imaginary people and events.

novel² adjective new in an interesting or unusual way.

novelist noun a person who writes novels.

novella /nuh-**vel**-luh/ noun a short novel or long short story.

novelty noun (plural **novelties**) **1** the quality of being new and unusual. **2** a new or unfamiliar thing. **3** a small toy or ornament.

November noun the eleventh month of the year.

novice noun **1** a person who is new to and lacks experience in a job or situation. **2** a person who has entered a religious community but has not yet taken their vows.

novitiate or **noviciate** noun a period of being a novice in a religious community.

now adverb **1** at the present time. **2** immediately. • conjunction as a result of the fact.

nowadays adverb at the present time, in contrast with the past.

nowhere adverb not anywhere. • pronoun no place.

noxious adjective harmful or very unpleasant.

nozzle noun a spout used to control a stream of liquid or gas.

nuance /**nyoo**-ahnss/ noun a very slight difference in meaning, expression, sound, etc.

nub noun **1** (**the nub**) the central point of a

matter. **2** a small lump.

nubile adjective (of a girl or young woman) sexually attractive.

nubuck /**nyoo**-buk/ noun a type of leather which has been rubbed on one side to make it feel like suede.

nuclear adjective **1** relating to the nucleus of an atom or cell. **2** using energy released in the fission (splitting) or fusion of atomic nuclei. **3** possessing or involving nuclear weapons.
□ **nuclear family** a couple and their children. **nuclear physics** the science of atomic nuclei and the way they interact.

nucleic acid /nyoo-**klay**-ik/ noun either of two substances, DNA and RNA, that are present in all living cells.

nucleus /**nyoo**-kli-uhss/ noun (plural **nuclei** /**nyoo**-kli-I/) **1** the central and most important part of an object or group. **2** Physics the positively charged central core of an atom. **3** Biology a structure present in most cells, containing the genetic material.

nude adjective wearing no clothes. • noun a painting or sculpture of a naked human figure.
■ **nudity** noun.

nudge verb (**nudges, nudging, nudged**) **1** prod someone with your elbow to attract their attention. **2** touch or push something gently. • noun a light prod or push.

nudist noun a person who prefers to wear no clothes.
■ **nudism** noun.

nugatory /**noo**-guh-tuh-ri/ adjective formal having no purpose or value.

nugget noun a small lump of precious metal found in the earth.

THESAURUS

novel¹ noun a good novel: story, tale, narrative, romance.

novel² adjective a novel way of making money: new, original, unusual, unconventional, unorthodox, different, fresh, imaginative, innovative.
OPPOSITES traditional.

novelty noun **1** the novelty of our approach: originality, newness, freshness, unconventionality, creativity, innovation, unfamiliarity. **2** we sell seasonal novelties: knick-knack, trinket, bauble, toy, trifle, ornament; N. Amer. kickshaw.

novice noun beginner, learner, newcomer, fledgling, trainee, probationer, student, pupil, apprentice, tyro, neophyte; N. Amer. tenderfoot; informal rookie, newie; N. Amer. informal greenhorn.
OPPOSITES expert, veteran.

now adverb **1** I'm busy now: at the moment, at present, at this moment in time, at this time, currently; N. Amer. presently.

2 television is now the main source of news: nowadays, these days, today, in this day and age. **3** you must leave now: at once, straight away, right away, this minute, this instant, immediately, instantly, directly; informal pronto, asap.

nucleus noun core, centre, heart, hub, middle, focal point, pivot, crux.

nude adjective naked, stark naked, bare, unclothed, undressed, stripped, with nothing on; informal without a stitch on, in your birthday suit, in the raw/buff, in the altogether; Brit. informal starkers; N. Amer. informal buck naked.
OPPOSITES dressed.

nudge verb **1** he nudged Ben: prod, elbow, dig, poke, jab. **2** the canoe nudged the bank: touch, bump (against), push (against), run into. **3** we nudged them towards a decision: prompt, encourage, persuade, prod.
• noun Maggie gave him a nudge: prod, dig (in the ribs), poke, jab, push.

n

nuisance noun a person or thing that causes annoyance or difficulty.

nuke informal noun a nuclear weapon. •verb (**nukes, nuking, nuked**) attack with nuclear weapons.

null adjective (**null and void**) having no legal force; invalid.

nullify verb (**nullifies, nullifying, nullified**) **1** make something legally invalid. **2** cancel out the effect of.
■ nullification noun.

nullity noun the state of being legally invalid.

numb adjective **1** (of a part of the body) having no sensation. **2** lacking the power to feel, think, or react. •verb make something numb.
■ numbly adverb **numbness** noun.

number noun **1** a quantity or value expressed by a word or symbol. **2** a quantity or amount: *huge numbers of visitors.* **3** (**a number of**) several. **4** a single issue of a magazine. **5** a song, dance, or piece of music. **6** a grammatical classification of words depending on whether one or more people or things are being referred to. •verb (**numbers, numbering, numbered**) **1** amount to. **2** give a number to each thing in a series. **3** count. **4** include as a member of a group.
□ **number plate** Brit. a sign on the front and rear of a vehicle showing its registration number.

numberless adjective too many to be counted.

numbskull or **numskull** noun informal a stupid person.

numeral noun a symbol or word representing a number.

numerate /nyoo-muh-ruht/ adjective having a good basic knowledge of arithmetic.

■ numeracy noun.

numeration noun the action of numbering or calculating.

numerator noun Maths the number above the line in a fraction.

numerical adjective having to do with numbers.
■ numerically adverb.

numerology noun the study of the supposed magical power of numbers.
■ numerologist noun.

numerous adjective **1** many. **2** consisting of many members.

numinous adjective having a strong religious or spiritual quality.

numismatic adjective having to do with coins or medals. •noun (**numismatics**) the study or collection of coins, banknotes, and medals.
■ numismatist noun.

numskull ⇨ NUMBSKULL.

nun noun a member of a female religious community who has taken vows of chastity and obedience.

nuncio /nun-si-oh/ noun (plural **nuncios**) a person who represents the Pope in a foreign country.

nunnery noun (plural **nunneries**) a convent.

nuptial /nup-sh'l/ adjective having to do with marriage or weddings. •noun (**nuptials**) a wedding.

nurse noun **1** a person who is trained to care for sick or injured people. **2** dated a person employed to look after young children. •verb (**nurses, nursing, nursed**) **1** look after a sick person. **2** treat or hold carefully or protectively. **3** feed a baby from the breast. **4** hold on to a belief or feeling for a long time.
□ **nursing home** a place providing

THESAURUS

nuisance noun annoyance, inconvenience, bore, bother, irritation, trial, burden, pest; informal pain (in the neck), hassle, bind, drag, headache.
OPPOSITES blessing.

numb adjective **1** *my fingers are numb:* dead, without sensation, without feeling, numbed, desensitized, insensible, frozen, anaesthetized. **2** *the news left me numb:* dazed, stunned, unfeeling, stupefied, paralysed, immobilized.
OPPOSITES sensitive.
•verb **1** *the cold weather numbed his fingers:* deaden, desensitize, anaesthetize, immobilize, freeze. **2** *the news updates numb us:* daze, stun, dull, stupefy, paralyse, immobilize.
OPPOSITES sensitize.

number noun **1** *a whole number:* numeral,

integer, figure, digit, character. **2** *a large number of complaints:* quantity, total, aggregate, tally, quota. **3** *the wedding of one of their number:* group, crowd, circle, party, band, crew, set, company; informal gang. **4** *the band performed another number:* song, piece, tune, track, dance.
•verb **1** *visitors numbered more than two million:* add up to, amount to, total, come to. **2** *he numbers her among his friends:* include, count, reckon, deem.

numerous adjective many, a number of, a lot of, several, plenty of, copious, an abundance of, frequent; informal umpteen.
OPPOSITES few.

nurse verb **1** *they nursed smallpox patients:* care for, take care of, look after, tend, minister to. **2** *they nursed old grievances:* harbour, foster, bear, have, hold (on to), retain.

accommodation and health care for old people.

nursemaid noun dated a woman or girl employed to look after a young child.

nursery noun (plural **nurseries**) **1** a room in a house where young children sleep or play. **2** a nursery school. **3** a place where young plants and trees are grown for sale or for planting elsewhere.
□ **nursery rhyme** a simple traditional song or poem for children. **nursery school** a school for young children between the ages of three and five.

nurture verb (**nurtures**, **nurturing**, **nurtured**) **1** care for and protect a child or young plant while they are growing and developing. **2** have a feeling or belief for a long time. •**noun** the state of being nurtured.

nut noun **1** a fruit consisting of a hard shell around an edible kernel. **2** the kernel of such a fruit. **3** a small flat piece of metal with a hole through the centre, for screwing on to a bolt. **4** (also **nutcase**) informal a crazy person. **5** (**nuts**) informal mad. **6** informal a person's head.
□ **in a nutshell** in the fewest possible words. **nuts and bolts** informal basic facts or practical details.
■ **nutty** adjective.

nutcrackers plural noun a device for cracking nuts.

nutmeg noun a spice made from the seed of a tropical tree.

nutrient noun a substance that provides nourishment.

nutriment noun nourishment.

nutrition noun the process of eating or taking nourishment.
■ **nutritional** adjective **nutritionist** noun.

nutritious adjective full of nourishing things; good for you.

nutritive adjective **1** having to do with nutrition. **2** nutritious.

nutter noun Brit. informal a mad person.

nuzzle verb (**nuzzles**, **nuzzling**, **nuzzled**) gently rub or push against someone or something with the nose.

NVQ abbreviation National Vocational Qualification.

NW abbreviation north-west or north-western.

nylon noun **1** a strong, lightweight synthetic material. **2** (**nylons**) nylon stockings or tights.

nymph noun **1** (in Greek and Roman mythology) a spirit in the form of a beautiful young woman. **2** an immature form of an insect such as a dragonfly.

nymphet noun an attractive and sexually mature young girl.

nymphomania noun uncontrollable or abnormally strong sexual desire in a woman.
■ **nymphomaniac** noun.

n

THESAURUS

nurture verb **1** *she nurtured her children into adulthood:* **bring up**, care for, take care of, look after, tend, rear, support. **2** *we nurtured these plants:* **cultivate**, grow, keep, tend, raise. **3** *he nurtured my love of art:* **encourage**, promote, stimulate, develop, foster, cultivate, boost, strengthen, fuel.
OPPOSITES neglect, hinder.

nut noun **1** (informal) *some nut arrived at the office:* **maniac**, lunatic, madman, madwoman; informal loony, nutcase, head case; Brit. informal nutter; N. Amer. informal screwball. **2** (informal) *a movie nut:* **enthusiast**, fan, devotee, aficionado; informal freak, fanatic, addict, buff.

nutritious adjective **nourishing**, nutritive, wholesome, good for you, full of goodness, healthy, health-giving, beneficial, healthful.

Oo

O or **o** noun (plural **Os** or **O's**) **1** the fifteenth letter of the alphabet. **2** zero.
▫ **O level** (in the past) the lower of the two main levels of the GCE exam.

oaf noun a stupid, rude, or clumsy man.
■ **oafish** adjective.

oak noun a large tree which produces acorns and a hard wood used in building and for furniture.

oaken adjective literary made of oak.

OAP abbreviation Brit. old-age pensioner.

oar noun a pole with a flat blade, used for rowing a boat.

oarsman or **oarswoman** noun (plural **oarsmen** or **oarswomen**) a rower.

oasis noun (plural **oases**) a fertile place in a desert where water rises to ground level.

oast house noun a building containing a kiln for drying hops.

oat noun **1** a cereal plant grown in cool climates. **2** (**oats**) the grain of this plant.

oatcake noun an oatmeal biscuit.

oath noun (plural **oaths**) **1** a solemn promise to do something or that something is true. **2** a swear word.

oatmeal noun ground oats, used in making porridge and oatcakes.

obdurate /ob-dyuu-ruht/ adjective refusing to change your mind; stubborn.
■ **obduracy** noun.

OBE abbreviation Officer of the Order of the British Empire.

obedient adjective willingly doing what you are told.
■ **obedience** noun **obediently** adverb.

obeisance /oh-**bay**-suhnss/ noun **1** respect for someone and willingness to obey them. **2** a gesture expressing this, such as a bow.

obelisk noun a stone pillar that tapers to a point, set up as a monument.

obese adjective very fat.
■ **obesity** noun.

obey verb do what a person or a rule tells you to do.

obfuscate /ob-**fuss**-kayt/ verb (**obfuscates**, **obfuscating**, **obfuscated**) make something unclear or hard to understand.
■ **obfuscation** noun.

obituary /oh-**bi**-tyuu-ri/ noun (plural **obituaries**) a short piece of writing about a person and their life which is published in a newspaper when they die.

object noun /ob-jikt/ **1** a thing that you can see and touch. **2** a person or thing to which an action or feeling is directed. **3** a purpose. **4** Grammar a noun acted on by a transitive verb or by a preposition. •**verb** /uhb-**jekt**/ say that you disagree with or disapprove of something.
■ **objector** noun.

objectify verb (**objectifies**, **objectifying**,

THESAURUS

oath noun **1** *an oath of allegiance:* vow, pledge, promise, affirmation, word (of honour), guarantee. **2** *a stream of oaths:* swear word, profanity, expletive, four-letter word, dirty word, obscenity, curse.

obedient adjective compliant, biddable, acquiescent, good, law-abiding, deferential, governable, docile, submissive.
OPPOSITES rebellious.

obey verb **1** *I obeyed him:* do what someone says, submit to, defer to, do as you are told. **2** *he refused to obey the order:* carry out, perform, act on, execute, discharge, implement. **3** *the rules have to be obeyed:* comply with, adhere to, observe, abide by, act in accordance with, conform to, respect,

follow, keep to, stick to.
OPPOSITES defy, ignore.

object noun **1** *wooden objects:* thing, article, item, entity. **2** *the object of criticism:* target, butt, focus, recipient, victim. **3** *his object was to resolve the crisis:* objective, aim, goal, target, purpose, end, plan, point, ambition, intention, idea.
•**verb** *teachers objected to the scheme:* protest about, oppose, take exception to, take issue with, take a stand against, argue against, quarrel with, condemn, draw the line at, demur at, mind, complain about; informal kick up a fuss/stink about.
OPPOSITES approve of, accept.

objectified) 1 refer to something abstract as if it has a physical form. **2** treat someone as an object rather than a person. ■ **objectification** noun.

objection noun a statement expressing disagreement or disapproval.

objectionable adjective unpleasant or offensive.

objective adjective **1** considering the facts about something without being influenced by personal feelings or opinions. **2** having actual existence outside the mind. •**noun** a goal or aim.
■ **objectively** adverb **objectivity** noun.

objet d'art /ob-zhay **dar**/ noun (plural **objets d'art** /ob-zhay **dar**/) a small decorative object or piece of art.

oblation noun a thing presented or offered to a god.

obligate verb (**be obligated**) having a moral or legal duty to do something.

obligation noun **1** something you must do in order to keep to an agreement or fulfil a duty. **2** the state of having to do something of this kind.

obligatory adjective required by a law, rule, or custom; compulsory.

oblige verb (**obliges**, **obliging**, **obliged**) **1** make someone do something because it is a law, a necessity, or their duty. **2** do something to help someone. **3** (**be obliged**) be grateful.

obliging adjective willing to help.

■ **obligingly** adverb.

oblique /uh-**bleek**/ adjective **1** at an angle; slanting. **2** not done in a direct way.
■ **obliquely** adverb.

obliterate /uh-**bli**-tuh-rayt/ verb (**obliterates**, **obliterating**, **obliterated**) destroy or remove all signs of something.
■ **obliteration** noun.

oblivion noun **1** the state of being unaware of what is happening around you. **2** the state of being forgotten or destroyed.

oblivious adjective not aware of what is happening around you.

oblong adjective rectangular in shape. •**noun** an oblong shape.

obloquy /ob-luh-kwi/ noun **1** strong public criticism. **2** disgrace.

obnoxious /uhb-**nok**-shuhss/ adjective very unpleasant and offensive.

oboe noun a woodwind instrument of treble pitch, that you play by blowing through a reed.
■ **oboist** noun.

obscene adjective **1** dealing with sex in an offensive way. **2** (of a payment, pay rise, etc.) unacceptably large.
■ **obscenely** adverb.

obscenity noun (plural **obscenities**) obscene language or behaviour, or an obscene action or word.

obscure adjective **1** not discovered or known

---

objection noun protest, protestation, complaint, opposition, demurral, counter-argument, disagreement, disapproval, dissent.

objective adjective **1** *try to be objective:* impartial, unbiased, unprejudiced, non-partisan, disinterested, neutral, even-handed, fair, dispassionate, detached. **2** *objective knowledge:* factual, actual, real, empirical, verifiable.
OPPOSITES subjective, emotional.
•noun *our objective is to make a profit:* aim, intention, purpose, target, goal, object, idea, plan.

objectively adverb impartially, without bias/prejudice, even-handedly, fairly, dispassionately, with an open mind, without fear or favour.

obligation noun **1** *professional obligations:* commitment, duty, responsibility, function, task, job, charge, onus, liability, requirement, debt. **2** *a sense of obligation:* duty, compulsion, indebtedness, necessity, pressure, constraint.

obligatory adjective compulsory, mandatory, prescribed, required, statutory,

enforced, binding, requisite, necessary, imperative.
OPPOSITES optional.

oblige verb **1** *we are obliged to accept the decision:* compel, force, require, bind, constrain. **2** *I'll be happy to oblige you:* do someone a favour, accommodate, help, assist, indulge, humour.

obliged adjective thankful, grateful, appreciative, beholden, indebted, in someone's debt.

obliging adjective helpful, accommodating, cooperative, agreeable, amenable, generous, kind; Brit. informal decent.
OPPOSITES unhelpful.

obscene adjective **1** *obscene literature:* pornographic, indecent, smutty, dirty, filthy, X-rated, explicit, lewd, rude, vulgar, coarse, scatological; informal blue, porn; euphemistic adult. **2** *an obscene amount:* scandalous, shocking, outrageous, immoral.
OPPOSITES clean, family.

obscure adjective **1** *his origins remain obscure:* unclear, uncertain, unknown, mysterious, hazy, vague, indeterminate. **2** *obscure references to Proust:* abstruse, oblique, opaque, cryptic, enigmatic,

about. 2 hard to understand or see. • verb
(**obscures, obscuring, obscured**) make
something difficult to see, hear, or
understand.
■ **obscurely** adverb.

obscurity noun (plural **obscurities**) 1 the
state of being unknown or forgotten. 2 the
quality of being hard to understand.

obsequies /ob-si-kwiz/ plural noun funeral
ceremonies.

obsequious /uhb-**see**-kwi-uhss/ adjective
too attentive and respectful towards
someone.
■ **obsequiously** adverb **obsequiousness** noun.

observance noun 1 the obeying of a rule or
following of a custom. 2 (**observances**) acts
performed for religious or ceremonial
reasons.

observant adjective quick to notice things.

observation noun 1 the close watching of
someone or something. 2 the ability to
notice important details. 3 a comment.
■ **observational** adjective.

observatory noun (plural **observatories**) a
building containing a telescope for looking
at the stars and planets.

observe verb (**observes, observing,
observed**) 1 notice. 2 watch something

carefully. 3 make a remark. 4 obey a rule.
5 celebrate or take part in a particular
festival.
■ **observable** adjective **observer** noun.

obsess verb preoccupy someone to a
disturbing extent.

obsession noun 1 the state of being
obsessed. 2 something that you cannot
stop thinking about.
■ **obsessional** adjective.

obsessive adjective unable to stop thinking
about someone or something.
■ **obsessively** adverb **obsessiveness** noun.

obsidian /uhb-**sid**-i-uhn/ noun a dark glass-
like volcanic rock.

obsolescent /ob-suh-**less**-uhnt/ adjective
becoming obsolete.
■ **obsolescence** noun.

obsolete adjective no longer produced or
used; out of date.

obstacle noun a thing that blocks the way
or makes it difficult to do something.

obstetrician /ob-stuh-**tri**-sh'n/ noun a
doctor who is trained in obstetrics.

obstetrics noun the branch of medicine
concerned with childbirth.
■ **obstetric** adjective.

obstinate adjective 1 refusing to change

THESAURUS

puzzling, perplexing, baffling, elliptical.
3 *an obscure Peruvian painter:* little
known, unknown, unheard of, unsung,
unrecognized, forgotten.
OPPOSITES clear, plain, famous.
• verb 1 *clouds obscured the sun:* hide,
conceal, cover, veil, shroud, screen, mask,
cloak, block, obliterate, eclipse. 2 *recent
events have obscured the issue:* confuse,
complicate, obfuscate, cloud, blur, muddy.
OPPOSITES reveal, clarify.

observation noun 1 *detailed observation of
their behaviour:* monitoring, watching,
scrutiny, survey, surveillance, attention,
study. 2 *his observations were correct:*
remark, comment, opinion, impression,
thought, reflection.

observe verb 1 *she observed that he was
drunk:* notice, see, note, perceive, discern,
spot. 2 *he had been observing her:* watch,
look at, contemplate, view, survey, regard,
keep an eye on, scrutinize, keep under
surveillance, keep watch on, monitor;
informal keep tabs on, keep a beady eye on.
3 *'You look tired,' she observed:* remark,
comment, say, mention, declare, announce,
state; formal opine. 4 *they agreed to observe
the ceasefire:* comply with, abide by, keep,
obey, adhere to, heed, honour, fulfil,
respect, follow, consent to, accept.

observer noun 1 *the casual observer:*
spectator, onlooker, watcher, fly on the

wall, viewer, witness. 2 *industry observers
are worried:* commentator, reporter,
monitor.

obsessed adjective fixated, possessed,
consumed, infatuated, besotted; informal
smitten, hung up; N. Amer. informal hipped.

obsession noun fixation, passion, mania,
compulsion, preoccupation, infatuation,
hobby horse, phobia, complex, neurosis;
informal bee in your bonnet, hang-up, thing.

obsessive adjective consuming, all-
consuming, compulsive, controlling,
fanatical, neurotic, excessive; informal
pathological.

obsolete adjective out of date, outdated,
outmoded, old-fashioned, passé,
antiquated, antediluvian, anachronistic,
archaic, ancient, fossilized, extinct,
defunct; informal out of the ark; Brit. informal
past its sell-by date.
OPPOSITES current, modern.

obstacle noun barrier, hurdle, stumbling
block, obstruction, bar, block, impediment,
hindrance, snag, catch, drawback, hitch, fly
in the ointment, handicap, difficulty,
problem, disadvantage; Brit. spanner in the
works.
OPPOSITES advantage, aid.

obstinate adjective stubborn, pig-headed,
unyielding, inflexible, unbending,
intransigent, intractable, self-willed.
OPPOSITES compliant.

your mind or stop what you are doing.
2 hard to deal with.
■ **obstinacy** noun **obstinately** adverb.

obstreperous adjective noisy and difficult to control.

obstruct verb be in the way or stop the progress of.

obstruction noun **1** a thing that is in the way; an obstacle or blockage. **2** the obstructing of someone or something.

obstructive adjective deliberately causing a delay or difficulty.

obtain verb **1** get possession of. **2** formal be established or usual.
■ **obtainable** adjective.

obtrude verb (**obtrudes, obtruding, obtruded**) become noticeable in an unpleasant or unwelcome way.

obtrusive adjective noticeable in an unwelcome way.

obtuse /uhb-**tyooss**/ adjective **1** annoyingly slow to understand. **2** (of an angle) more than 90° and less than 180°. **3** not sharp or pointed; blunt.

obverse noun **1** the side of a coin or medal showing the head or main design. **2** the opposite of something.

obviate /**ob**-vi-ayt/ verb (**obviates, obviating, obviated**) remove or prevent a need or difficulty.

obvious adjective easily seen or understood; clear.
■ **obviously** adverb.

ocarina /o-kuh-**ree**-nuh/ noun a small egg-shaped wind instrument with holes for the fingers.

occasion noun **1** a particular event, or the time at which it happens. **2** a special event or celebration. **3** a suitable time for something. **4** formal reason or cause. • verb formal cause.

☑ two cs and one s: occasion.

occasional adjective happening or done from time to time.
■ **occasionally** adverb.

occidental /ok-si-**den**-tuhl/ adjective relating to the countries of the West.

occlude verb (**occludes, occluding, occluded**) technical close up; block.

occult /o-**kult**, **o**-kult/ noun (**the occult**) the world of magic and supernatural beliefs and practices. • adjective relating to the occult.
■ **occultism** noun **occultist** noun.

occupancy noun **1** the action of occupying a place. **2** the proportion of accommodation that is occupied.

occupant noun a person who occupies a place.

THESAURUS

obstruct verb **1** *ensure that vents are not obstructed:* block (up), clog (up), occlude, cut off, bung up, choke, dam up. **2** *he was obstructing the traffic:* hold up, bring to a standstill, stop, halt, block. **3** *they may obstruct aid distribution:* impede, hinder, interfere with, hamper, block, interrupt, hold up, stand in the way of, frustrate, slow down, delay.
OPPOSITES clear, facilitate.

obstruction noun obstacle, barrier, stumbling block, impediment, hindrance, difficulty, check, restriction, blockage, stoppage, congestion, bottleneck, hold-up.

obtain verb get, acquire, come by, secure, procure, pick up, be given, gain, earn, achieve, attain; informal get hold of, lay your hands on, land.
OPPOSITES lose.

obtainable adjective available, to be had, in circulation, on the market, on offer, in season, at your disposal, accessible; informal up for grabs, on tap.

obvious adjective clear, plain, evident, apparent, manifest, conspicuous, pronounced, prominent, distinct, palpable, noticeable, perceptible, visible; informal sticking out a mile.
OPPOSITES imperceptible.

obviously adverb clearly, plainly, evidently,

patently, visibly, discernibly, manifestly, noticeably, of course, naturally, needless to say, it goes without saying.
OPPOSITES perhaps.

occasion noun **1** *a previous occasion:* time, instance, juncture, point, moment, experience, case. **2** *a special occasion:* event, affair, function, celebration, party, get-together, gathering; informal do, bash.

occasional adjective infrequent, intermittent, irregular, periodic, sporadic, odd; N. Amer. sometime.
OPPOSITES regular, frequent.

occasionally adverb sometimes, from time to time, (every) now and then, (every) now and again, at times, every so often, (every) once in a while, on occasion, periodically.
OPPOSITES often.

occult adjective supernatural, magic, magical, satanic, mystical, unearthly, esoteric, psychic.
□ **the occult** the supernatural, magic, black magic, witchcraft, necromancy, the black arts, occultism.

occupant noun resident, inhabitant, owner, householder, tenant, leaseholder, lessee; Brit. occupier, owner-occupier.

o

occupation noun **1** a job or profession. **2** a way of spending time. **3** the occupying of a place.

occupational adjective having to do with a job or profession.
□ occupational therapy the use of certain activities and crafts to help someone recover from an illness.

occupy verb (occupies, occupying, occupied) **1** live or work in a building. **2** fill or take up a space, time, or position. **3** keep someone busy. **4** enter and take control of a place.
■ occupier noun.

occur verb (occurs, occurring, occurred) **1** happen. **2** be found or present. **3** (occur to) come into someone's mind.

☑ double **c**, and there is a double **r** in occurred, occurring, and occurrence.

occurrence /uh-kur-ruhnss/ noun **1** a thing that happens or exists. **2** the fact of something happening or existing.

ocean noun a very large area of sea.

oceanic /oh-si-an-ik/ adjective relating to the ocean.

oceanography noun the study of the sea.
■ oceanographer noun.

ocelot /oss-i-lot/ noun a medium-sized striped and spotted wild cat, found in South and Central America.

ochre /oh-ker/ (US spelling ocher) noun a type of light yellow or reddish earth, used as a pigment.

o'clock adverb used to say which hour it is when telling the time.

octagon noun a figure with eight straight sides and eight angles.
■ octagonal adjective.

octahedron /ok-tuh-hee-druhn/ noun (plural octahedra or octahedrons) a three-dimensional shape with eight flat faces.

octane noun a liquid hydrocarbon present in petroleum.

octave noun **1** a series of eight musical notes occupying the interval between (and including) two notes. **2** the interval between two such notes.

octavo /ok-tah-voh/ noun (plural octavos) a size of book page that results from folding each printed sheet into eight leaves (sixteen pages).

octet noun **1** a group of eight musicians. **2** a piece of music for an octet.

October noun the tenth month of the year.

octogenarian /ok-tuh-ji-nair-i-uhn/ noun a person who is between 80 and 89 years old.

octopus noun (plural octopuses) a sea creature with a soft body and eight long tentacles.

ocular adjective having to do with the eyes.

OD verb (OD's, OD'ing, OD'd) informal take an overdose of a drug.

odd adjective **1** unusual or unexpected;

THESAURUS

occupation noun **1** his father's occupation: job, profession, work, line of work, trade, employment, business, career, métier, calling. **2** among her leisure occupations is birdwatching: pastime, activity, leisure activity, hobby, pursuit, interest, entertainment, recreation. **3** the Roman occupation of Britain: conquest, capture, invasion, seizure, annexation, colonization, subjugation.

occupied adjective **1** tasks which kept her occupied: busy, working, at work, active; informal tied up, hard at it, on the go. **2** the table was occupied: in use, full, engaged, taken. **3** only two flats are occupied: inhabited, lived in.
OPPOSITES free, vacant.

occupy verb **1** Carol occupied the basement flat: live in, inhabit, lodge in, move into, people, populate, settle. **2** he occupies a post at the Treasury: hold, fill, have; informal hold down. **3** something to occupy my mind: engage, busy, distract, absorb, engross, hold, interest, involve, entertain. **4** the region was occupied by Japan: capture, seize, conquer, invade, colonize, annex, subjugate.

occur verb **1** an accident occurred at 3.30: happen, take place, come about; N. Amer. informal go down. **2** the disease occurs in the tropics: be found, be present, exist, appear, develop.
□ occur to enter someone's head/mind, cross someone's mind, come/spring to mind, strike someone, come to someone, dawn on someone, suggest itself.

occurrence noun **1** a rare occurrence: event, incident, happening, phenomenon, circumstance. **2** the occurrence of cancer: existence, instance, appearance, frequency, incidence, rate, prevalence; Statistics distribution.

odd adjective **1** an odd man: strange, peculiar, queer, funny, bizarre, eccentric, unusual, weird, quirky, zany; informal wacky, off the wall. **2** some odd things had happened: unusual, strange, peculiar, funny, curious, weird, bizarre, queer, abnormal, puzzling, mystifying, baffling, unaccountable. **3** he does odd jobs: occasional, casual, irregular, isolated, sporadic, periodic, miscellaneous, various, varied, sundry. **4** an odd shoe: mismatched, unmatched, unpaired, single, lone, solitary, strange. **2** (of whole numbers such as 3 and 5) having one left over as a remainder when divided by two. **3** occasional. **4** spare; available. **5** separated from a pair or set. **6** in the region of.

■ **oddly** adverb **oddness** noun.

oddball noun informal a strange or eccentric person.

oddity noun (plural **oddities**) **1** the quality of being strange. **2** a strange person or thing.

oddment noun an item or piece left over from a larger piece or set.

odds plural noun **1** the ratio between the amount placed as a bet and the money which would be received if the bet was won. **2** (**the odds**) the chances of something happening. **3** (**the odds**) the advantage thought to be possessed by one person or side compared to another.

□ **at odds** in conflict or disagreement. **odds-on 1** (of a horse) with betting odds in favour of winning. **2** very likely to happen or succeed.

ode noun a poem addressed to a person or thing or celebrating an event.

odious adjective very unpleasant.

odium noun widespread hatred or disgust.

odoriferous adjective smelly.

odour (US spelling **odor**) noun a smell.

■ **odorous** adjective **odourless** adjective.

odyssey /od-i-si/ noun (plural **odysseys**) a long, eventful journey.

oedema /i-dee-muh/ (US spelling **edema**) noun a build-up of watery fluid in the tissues of the body.

oesophagus /i-so-fuh-guhss/ (US spelling **esophagus**) noun (plural **oesophagi** /i-so-fuh-jy/) the muscular tube which connects the throat to the stomach.

oestrogen /ee-struh-juhn/ (US spelling **estrogen**) noun a hormone which produces female physical and sexual characteristics.

oeuvre /er-vruh/ noun all the works of a particular artist, composer, or author.

of preposition **1** expressing the relationship between a part and a whole. **2** belonging to; coming from. **3** used in expressions of measurement, value, or age. **4** made from. **5** used to show position. **6** used to show that something belongs to a category.

! it is wrong to write **of** instead of **have** in sentences such as I could have told you (don't write I could of told you).

off adverb **1** away from a place. **2** so as to be removed or separated. **3** starting a journey or race. **4** so as to finish or be discontinued. **5** (of an electrical appliance or power supply) not working or connected. **6** having a particular level of wealth. • preposition **1** away from. **2** situated or leading in a direction away from. **3** so as to be removed or separated from. **4** having a temporary dislike of. • adjective (of food) no longer fresh. • noun Brit. informal the start of a race or journey.

□ **off-colour** Brit. slightly unwell. **off-licence** Brit. a shop selling alcoholic drink to be drunk elsewhere. **off-peak** at a time when demand is less. **off-putting** unpleasant or unsettling. **off white** a white colour with a grey or yellowish tinge.

! use **off**, not **off of**, in a sentence like the cup fell off the table.

offal noun the internal organs of an animal used as food.

offbeat adjective unconventional; unusual.

offcut noun a piece of wood, fabric, etc. left behind after a larger piece has been cut off.

offence (US spelling **offense**) noun **1** an act that breaks a law or rule. **2** a feeling of hurt or annoyance.

offend verb **1** make someone feel upset, insulted, or annoyed. **2** seem unpleasant

THESAURUS

extra, leftover, spare.

OPPOSITES normal, ordinary, regular.

odds plural noun likelihood, probability, chances.

□ **odds and ends** bits and pieces, bits and bobs, stuff, paraphernalia, things, sundries, bric-a-brac, knick-knacks, oddments; informal junk; Brit. informal odds and sods, clobber, gubbins.

odour noun smell, stench, stink, reek, aroma, bouquet, scent, perfume, fragrance; Brit. informal pong, whiff; N. Amer. informal funk.

odyssey noun journey, voyage, trip, trek, travels, quest, crusade, pilgrimage.

off adjective **1** Kate's off today: away, absent, not at work, off duty, on holiday, on leave,

free; N. Amer. on vacation. **2** the game's off: cancelled, postponed, called off. **3** the fish was off: rotten, bad, stale, mouldy, sour, rancid, turned, spoiled.

OPPOSITES in, on, good.

offence noun **1** he has committed an offence: crime, illegal act, misdemeanour, breach of the law, felony, infringement, violation, wrongdoing, sin. **2** I do not want to cause offence: annoyance, resentment, indignation, displeasure, bad feeling, animosity.

offend verb **1** I'm sorry if I offended him: upset, give offence to, affront, hurt someone's feelings, insult, hurt, wound, slight. **2** criminals who offend repeatedly: break the law, commit a crime, do wrong.

to. **3** do something illegal.
■ **offender** noun.

offensive adjective **1** causing someone to feel upset, insulted, or annoyed. **2** used in attack. •noun a campaign to attack or achieve something.
■ **offensively** adverb.

offer verb (**offers, offering, offered**)
1 present something for a person to accept or reject as they wish. **2** say you are willing to do something for someone. **3** provide.
•noun **1** an expression of readiness to do or give something. **2** an amount of money that someone is willing to pay for something. **3** a specially reduced price.
□ **on offer 1** available. **2** for sale at a reduced price.

offering noun something that is offered; a gift or contribution.

offertory /off-er-tuh-ri/ noun (plural **offertories**) **1** the offering of the bread and wine at the Christian service of Holy Communion. **2** a collection of money made at a Christian church service.

offhand adjective rudely casual or cool in manner. •adverb without previous thought.

office noun **1** a room, set of rooms, or building where people work at desks. **2** a position of authority. **3** (**offices**) formal things done for other people.

officer noun **1** a person holding a position of authority, especially in the armed forces. **2** a policeman or policewoman.

official adjective **1** relating to an authority or public organization. **2** agreed or done by a person or group in a position of authority. •noun a person holding public office or having official duties.
■ **officialdom** noun **officially** adverb.

officiate /uh-fi-shi-ayt/ verb (**officiates, officiating, officiated**) **1** act as an official in charge of something. **2** perform a religious service or ceremony.

officious adjective using your authority or interfering in a bossy way.

offing noun (**in the offing**) likely to happen or appear soon.

offline adjective not connected to a computer.

offload verb **1** unload a cargo. **2** get rid of.

offset verb (**offsets, offsetting, offset**) cancel out something with an equal and opposite force or effect.

offshoot noun a thing that develops from something else.

offshore adjective & adverb **1** at sea some distance from the shore. **2** (of the wind) blowing towards the sea from the land. **3** situated or registered abroad.

THESAURUS

offender noun wrongdoer, criminal, lawbreaker, crook, villain, miscreant, felon, delinquent, culprit, guilty party.

offensive adjective **1** *offensive remarks:* insulting, rude, derogatory, disrespectful, personal, hurtful, upsetting, wounding, abusive. **2** *an offensive smell:* unpleasant, disagreeable, nasty, distasteful, horrible, objectionable, off-putting, dreadful, frightful, obnoxious, abominable, disgusting, repulsive, repellent, vile, foul, sickening, nauseating; informal ghastly, horrid, gross; Brit. informal beastly. **3** *offensive operations:* hostile, attacking, aggressive, invading, incursive, combative, threatening, martial, warlike, belligerent, bellicose.
OPPOSITES complimentary, pleasant, defensive.
•noun *a military offensive:* attack, assault, onslaught, invasion, push, thrust, charge, raid, incursion, blitz, campaign.

offer verb **1** *Frank offered a suggestion:* put forward, proffer, give, present, come up with, suggest, propose, advance, submit, tender. **2** *she offered to help:* volunteer, step/come forward, show willing. **3** *he offered $200:* bid, tender, put in a bid/offer of.
OPPOSITES withdraw, refuse.
•noun **1** *an offer of help:* proposal,

proposition, suggestion, submission, approach, overture. **2** *the highest offer:* bid, tender, bidding price.

offering noun contribution, donation, gift, present, sacrifice, tribute.

office noun **1** *we met at her office:* place of work, place of business, workplace, workroom. **2** *the company's Paris office:* branch, division, section, bureau, department. **3** *the office of President:* post, position, appointment, job, occupation, role, situation, function.

officer noun official, office-holder, committee member, board member, functionary, executive.

official adjective **1** *an official enquiry:* authorized, approved, validated, authenticated, certified, accredited, endorsed, sanctioned, licensed, recognized, legitimate, legal, lawful, valid, bona fide, proper; informal kosher. **2** *an official function:* ceremonial, formal, solemn, bureaucratic.
OPPOSITES unauthorized, informal.
•noun *a union official:* officer, office-holder, executive, functionary, administrator, bureaucrat, mandarin, representative, agent; disapproving apparatchik.

offset verb counteract, balance (out), even out/up, counterbalance, compensate for, make up for, neutralize, cancel (out).

offside adjective & adverb (in games such as football) occupying a position on the field where playing the ball is not allowed.

offspring noun (plural **offspring**) a person's child or children.

offstage adjective & adverb (in a theatre) not on the stage.

often adverb **1** frequently. **2** in many instances.

ogle verb (**ogles**, **ogling**, **ogled**) stare at someone in a lecherous way.

ogre /oh-guh/ noun **1** (in stories) a man-eating giant. **2** a cruel or terrifying person.

ohm noun the basic unit of electrical resistance.

oik noun informal a rude person.

oil noun **1** a thick, sticky liquid obtained from petroleum. **2** a thick liquid which cannot be dissolved in water and is obtained from plants. **3** (also **oils**) oil paint. •verb treat or coat with oil.
□ **oil paint** artist's paint made from powder mixed with linseed or other oil.

oilcloth noun cotton fabric treated with oil to make it waterproof.

oilfield noun an area where oil is found beneath the ground or seabed.

oilskin noun **1** heavy cotton cloth waterproofed with oil. **2** (**oilskins**) a set of clothes made of oilskin.

oily adjective (**oilier**, **oiliest**) **1** containing, covered with, or like oil. **2** (of a person) insincerely polite and flattering.
■ **oiliness** noun.

oink noun the grunting sound made by a pig. •verb make such a sound.

ointment noun a smooth substance that is rubbed on the skin to heal a wound or sore place.

OK or **okay** informal **exclamation** said to express agreement or acceptance. •**adjective 1** satisfactory, but not especially good. **2** allowed. •**adverb** in a satisfactory way. •**noun** permission to do something. •**verb** (**OK's**, **OK'ing**, **OK'd**) approve or authorize.

okapi /oh-kah-pi/ noun (plural **okapi** or **okapis**) a large plant-eating African animal with stripes on the hindquarters and upper legs.

okra /ok-ruh/ noun the long seed pods of a tropical plant, eaten as a vegetable.

old adjective (**older**, **oldest**) **1** having lived for a long time. **2** made, built, or originating long ago. **3** owned or used for a long time. **4** former. **5** of a stated age.
□ **old age** the later part of normal life. **Old English** the language spoken in England until about 1150. **old-fashioned** no longer current or modern. **the old guard** the long-standing members of a group, who are often unwilling to accept change. **old hand** a very experienced person. **old hat** informal boringly familiar or out of date. **old maid** disapproving a single woman thought of as too old for marriage. **old master** a great painter of former times. **Old Nick** the Devil. **Old Testament** the first part of the Christian Bible. **old wives' tale** a widely held traditional belief that is incorrect. **Old World** Europe, Asia, and Africa.

olden adjective of a former age.

oleaginous /oh-li-aj-i-nuhss/ adjective **1** oily. **2** insincerely flattering.

oleander /oh-li-an-der/ noun an evergreen shrub with white, pink, or red flowers.

olfactory /ol-fak-tuh-ri/ adjective relating to the sense of smell.

oligarch /ol-i-gark/ noun a ruler in an oligarchy.

oligarchy noun (plural **oligarchies**) **1** a small group of people having control of a state. **2** a state governed by a small group of people.
■ **oligarchic** adjective.

THESAURUS

offspring noun **children**, sons and daughters, progeny, youngsters, babies, infants, brood, descendants, heirs, successors; informal kids; Brit. informal sprogs, brats.

often adverb **frequently**, many times, on many/numerous occasions, a lot, repeatedly, again and again, regularly, commonly, generally, ordinarily; N. Amer. oftentimes.
OPPOSITES seldom.

oily adjective **greasy**, fatty, buttery, rich, oleaginous.

ointment noun **lotion**, cream, salve, liniment, embrocation, rub, gel, balm, emollient, unguent.

old adjective **1** old people: **elderly**, aged, older, senior, venerable, in your dotage, long in the tooth, ancient, decrepit, doddery, senescent, senile; informal getting on, past it, over the hill. **2** old clothes: **worn**, worn out, shabby, threadbare, frayed, patched, tattered, moth-eaten, ragged; informal tatty. **3** old cars: **antique**, veteran, vintage, classic. **4** an old girlfriend: **former**, previous, earlier, past, ex-, one-time, sometime, erstwhile.
OPPOSITES young, new, modern current.

old-fashioned adjective **out of date**, outdated, dated, out of fashion, outmoded, unfashionable, passé, outworn, behind the times, archaic, obsolescent, obsolete; informal out of the ark; N. Amer. informal horse-and-buggy.
OPPOSITES modern.

olive noun **1** a small oval fruit with a hard stone and bitter flesh. **2** (also **olive green**) a greyish-green colour like that of an unripe olive. •adjective (of a person's complexion) yellowish brown.
□ **olive branch** an offer to restore friendly relations. **olive oil** oil obtained from olives, used in cookery and salad dressing.

Olympiad noun a staging of the Olympic Games.

Olympian adjective **1** relating to the Olympic Games. **2** having to do with Mount Olympus, traditional home of the Greek gods. •noun **1** a competitor in the Olympic Games. **2** any of the twelve main Greek gods.

Olympic adjective relating to the Olympic Games. •noun (**the Olympics** or **the Olympic Games**) a sports competition held every four years, or the ancient Greek festival of sport and arts that it was based on.

ombudsman /om-buudz-muhn/ noun (plural **ombudsmen**) an official who investigates people's complaints against companies or the government.

omega /oh-mi-guh/ noun the last letter of the Greek alphabet (Ω, ω).

omelette (US spelling **omelet**) noun a dish of beaten eggs cooked in a frying pan, usually with a savoury filling.

omen noun an event seen as a sign of future good or bad luck.

ominous adjective giving the impression that something bad is going to happen.
■ **ominously** adverb.

omission noun **1** the action of leaving something out. **2** a failure to do something. **3** something that has been left out or not done.

omit verb (**omits**, **omitting**, **omitted**) **1** leave out or exclude. **2** fail to do.

☑ just one *m*: omit.

omni- combining form **1** of all things: *omniscient*. **2** in all ways or places: *omnipresent*.

omnibus noun **1** a volume containing several works previously published separately. **2** a single edition of two or more programmes previously broadcast separately. **3** dated a bus.

omnipotent /om-ni-puh-tuhnt/ adjective having unlimited or very great power.
■ **omnipotence** noun.

omnipresent adjective **1** (of God) present everywhere at the same time. **2** widespread.
■ **omnipresence** noun.

omniscient /om-ni-si-uhnt/ adjective knowing everything.
■ **omniscience** noun.

omnivore /om-ni-vor/ noun an animal that eats both plants and meat.

omnivorous /om-ni-vuh-ruhss/ adjective eating both plants and meat.

on preposition & adverb in contact with and supported by a surface. •preposition **1** (also **on to**) into contact with a surface, or aboard a vehicle. **2** about; concerning. **3** as a member of. **4** stored in or broadcast by. **5** in the course of. **6** indicating a day or date when something takes place. **7** engaged in. **8** regularly taking a drug or medicine. **9** informal paid for by. •adverb **1** with continued movement or action. **2** (of clothing) being worn. **3** taking place or being presented. **4** (of an electrical appliance or power supply) functioning.

once adverb **1** on one occasion or for one time only. **2** formerly. **3** multiplied by one. •conjunction as soon as.
□ **at once 1** immediately. **2** at the same time. **once-over** informal a quick inspection, or act of cleaning something.

THESAURUS

ominous adjective threatening, menacing, baleful, forbidding, foreboding, fateful, sinister, black, dark, gloomy.
OPPOSITES promising.

omission noun **1** *the omission of certain news items*: exclusion, leaving out, deletion, elimination. **2** *I regret any omission on my part*: negligence, neglect, dereliction, oversight, lapse, failure.

omit verb **1** *they omitted his name from the list*: leave out, exclude, leave off, miss out, miss, cut, drop, skip. **2** *I omitted to mention this*: forget, neglect, fail.
OPPOSITES add, include, remember.

once adverb **1** *I only met him once*: on one occasion, one time. **2** *he didn't help once*: ever, at any time, on any occasion, at all. **3** *they were friends once*: formerly, previously, in the past, at one time, at one point, once upon a time, in days/times gone by, in the (good) old days, long ago.
OPPOSITES often, now.

•conjunction *once she's gone*: as soon as, the moment, when, after.
□ **at once 1** *leave at once*: immediately, right away, right now, this moment/instant/second/minute, straight away, instantly, directly, forthwith, without delay/hesitation, without further ado. **2** *they all arrived at once*: at the same time, (all) together, simultaneously, as a group, in unison.

one-sided adjective **1** *a one-sided account*: biased, prejudiced, partisan, partial, slanted, distorted, unfair. **2** *a one-sided game*: unequal, uneven, unbalanced.
OPPOSITES impartial, equal.

o

oncology /ong-**kol**-uh-ji/ noun the study and treatment of tumours.
 ■ **oncologist** noun.

oncoming adjective moving towards you.

one cardinal number **1** the lowest cardinal number; 1. (Roman numeral: **i** or **I**.) **2** single, or a single person or thing. **3** (before a person's name) a certain. **4** the same. •pronoun **1** used to refer to a person or thing previously mentioned or easily identified. **2** used to refer to the speaker, or to represent people in general.
 □ **one-armed bandit** informal a fruit machine operated by pulling a long handle at the side. **one-liner** informal a short joke or witty remark. **one-off** Brit. informal done, made, or happening only once. **one-upmanship** informal the technique of gaining an advantage over someone else.

oneness noun the state of being whole or in agreement.

onerous /**oh**-nuh-ruhss/ adjective involving a lot of effort and difficulty.

oneself pronoun **1** used as the object of a verb or preposition when this is the same as the subject of the clause and the subject is 'one'. **2** used to emphasize that one is doing something individually or without help. **3** in one's normal state of body or mind.

ongoing adjective still in progress.

onion noun a vegetable consisting of a round bulb with a strong taste and smell.

online adjective & adverb **1** controlled by or connected to a computer. **2** available on or carried out via the Internet.

onlooker noun a spectator.

only adverb **1** and no one or nothing more besides. **2** no longer ago than. **3** not until. **4** with the negative result that. •adjective **1** single or solitary. **2** alone deserving consideration. •conjunction informal except that.

onomatopoeia /on-uh-mat-uh-**pee**-uh/ noun the use of words that sound like the thing they refer to (e.g. *sizzle*).
 ■ **onomatopoeic** adjective.

onrush noun a surging rush forward.
 ■ **onrushing** adjective.

onset noun the beginning of something.

onshore adjective & adverb **1** situated on land. **2** (of the wind) blowing from the sea towards the land.

onside adjective & adverb (in sport) not offside.

onslaught noun **1** a fierce or destructive attack. **2** an overwhelmingly large quantity of people or things.

onstage adjective & adverb (in a theatre) on the stage.

onto ⇒ on to (see **on**).

ontology noun philosophy concerned with the nature of being.
 ■ **ontological** adjective.

onus noun a duty or responsibility.

onward adjective & adverb in a forward direction.
 ■ **onwards** adverb.

onyx /**on**-iks/ noun a semi-precious stone with layers of different colours.

oodles plural noun informal a very great number or amount.

oomph noun informal excitement or energy.

ooze verb (**oozes, oozing, oozed**) slowly seep out. •noun the very slow flow of a liquid.
 ■ **oozy** adjective.

opacity /oh-**pa**-si-ti/ noun the condition of being opaque.

opal noun a semi-transparent gemstone in which small points of shifting colour can be seen.

opalescent adjective having small points of shifting colour.

opaque /oh-**payk**/ adjective **1** not able to be seen through. **2** difficult or impossible to understand.

op. cit. adverb in the work already cited.

open adjective **1** not closed, fastened, or

THESAURUS

ongoing adjective in progress, under way, going on, continuing, proceeding.

onlooker noun eyewitness, witness, observer, spectator, bystander; informal rubberneck.

only adverb **1** *only enough for two:* at most, at best, just, no more than, hardly, barely, scarcely. **2** *for your eyes only:* exclusively, solely, purely. **3** *you're only saying that:* merely, simply, just.
 •adjective *their only son:* sole, single, one (and only), solitary, lone, unique, exclusive.

onset noun start, beginning, inception, commencement, arrival, appearance, day one, outbreak.
 OPPOSITES end.

onslaught noun attack, assault, offensive, advance, charge, blitz, bombardment, barrage.

ooze verb **1** *blood oozed from the wound:* seep, discharge, flow, exude, trickle, drip, dribble, drain, leak. **2** *positively oozing charm:* exude, gush, drip, emanate, radiate.

open adjective **1** *the door's open:* unlatched, unlocked, off the latch, ajar, gaping, yawning. **2** *a silk shirt, open at the neck:* unfastened, undone, unbuttoned,

restricted. **2** not covered or protected. **3** (**open to**) likely to suffer from or be affected by. **4** spread out, expanded, or unfolded. **5** accessible or available. **6** not hiding thoughts and feelings. **7** not disguised or hidden. **8** not finally settled. •**verb 1** make or become open. **2** formally begin or establish. **3** (**open on to** or **into**) give access to. **4** (**open out** or **up**) begin to talk freely. •**noun** (**the open**) fresh air or open countryside.
□ **the open air** an unenclosed space outdoors. **open-and-shut** straightforward. **open-heart surgery** surgery in which the heart is exposed. **open house** a place or situation in which all visitors are welcome. **open letter** a letter addressed to a particular person but intended to be published. **open market** a situation in which companies can trade without restrictions. **open-minded** willing to consider new ideas. **open-plan** having large rooms with few or no dividing walls. **open verdict** Law a verdict that a person's death is suspicious but that the cause is

not known.
■ **opener** noun **openly** adverb **openness** noun.

opencast adjective Brit. (of mining) in which coal or ore is extracted from a level near the earth's surface, rather than from shafts.

opening noun **1** a gap. **2** the beginning of something. **3** a ceremony at which a building, show, etc. is declared to be open. **4** an opportunity to achieve something. **5** an available job or position. •**adjective** coming at the beginning.

opera[1] noun a dramatic work that is set to music for singers and musicians.
□ **opera glasses** small binoculars used at the opera or theatre.

opera[2] plural of OPUS.

operable adjective **1** able to be used. **2** able to be treated by a surgical operation.

operate verb (**operates, operating, operated**) **1** function or work. **2** use or control a machine. **3** (of an organization or armed force) carry out activities. **4** be in effect. **5** carry out a surgical operation.

THESAURUS

unzipped. **3** *an open packet:* opened, undone, unsealed, uncorked, unstoppered. **4** *open countryside | open spaces:* unenclosed, rolling, sweeping, wide open, exposed, spacious, uncluttered. **5** *a map was open beside him:* spread out, unfolded, unfurled, unrolled, stretched out. **6** *the bank wasn't open:* open for business, open to the public, working, accessible. **7** *the position is still open:* available, vacant, free, unfilled; informal up for grabs. **8** *open to abuse:* vulnerable, subject, susceptible, liable, exposed. **9** *she was very open about her feelings:* frank, candid, honest, forthcoming, communicative, forthright, direct, unreserved, plain-spoken, outspoken; informal upfront. **10** *open hostility:* overt, manifest, conspicuous, plain, undisguised, unconcealed, clear, naked, blatant, flagrant, barefaced, brazen. **11** *I'm always open to suggestions:* receptive, amenable, willing to listen, responsive. **12** *what other options are open to us?* available, accessible, on hand, on offer. **13** *an open meeting:* public, general, unrestricted.
OPPOSITES shut, fastened, enclosed, closed, reticent, suppressed, private.
•**verb 1** *she opened the front door:* unfasten, unlock, throw wide. **2** *Katherine opened the parcel:* unwrap, undo, untie. **3** *shall I open another bottle?* uncork, crack open. **4** *Adam opened the map:* spread out, unfold, unfurl, unroll, straighten out. **5** *we'll be opening next week:* start trading, set up shop. **6** *Bryan opened the meeting:* begin, start, commence, initiate, set in motion, get going, get under way, get off

the ground; informal kick off. **7** *the lounge opens on to a patio:* give access, lead.
OPPOSITES close, shut, end.

open-air adjective outdoor, out-of-doors, outside, alfresco.
OPPOSITES indoor.

opening noun **1** *an opening in the roof:* hole, gap, aperture, orifice, vent, crack, slit, chink. **2** *the opening of the session:* beginning, start, commencement, outset; informal kick-off. **3** *a gallery opening:* launch, inauguration, opening/first night, premiere.
•**adjective** *her opening remarks:* first, initial, introductory, preliminary, maiden, inaugural.
OPPOSITES final, closing.

openly adverb **1** *drugs were openly on sale:* publicly, blatantly, flagrantly, overtly. **2** *he spoke openly of his problems:* frankly, candidly, explicitly, honestly, sincerely, forthrightly, freely.
OPPOSITES secretly, privately.

open-minded adjective unbiased, unprejudiced, neutral, objective, disinterested, tolerant, liberal, permissive, broad-minded.
OPPOSITES prejudiced, narrow-minded.

operate verb **1** *he can operate the crane:* work, run, use, handle, control, manage, drive, steer, manoeuvre. **2** *the machine ceased to operate:* function, work, go, run. **3** *the way the law operates:* take effect, act, apply, work, function. **4** *we operated the mines until 1979:* direct, control, manage, run, be in control/charge of.

operatic adjective having to do with opera.

operation noun 1 the action of operating. 2 an act of cutting into a patient's body to remove or repair a damaged part. 3 an organized action involving a number of people. 4 a business organization.

operational adjective 1 ready for use, or being used. 2 relating to the functioning of an organization.
■ **operationally** adverb.

operative adjective 1 working or functioning. 2 (of a word) having the most significance in a phrase. 3 relating to surgery. •**noun** a worker.

operator noun 1 a person who operates equipment or a machine. 2 a person who works at the switchboard of a telephone exchange. 3 a person or company that runs a business or enterprise. 4 informal a person who acts in a particular way: *a smooth operator*.

operetta noun a short opera on a light or humorous theme.

ophthalmic adjective relating to the eye and its diseases.

ophthalmology /off-thal-**mol**-uh-ji, op-thal-**mol**-uh-ji/ noun the study and treatment of disorders and diseases of the eye.
■ **ophthalmologist** noun.

opiate /**oh**-pi-uht/ noun a drug containing opium.

opine verb (**opines, opining, opined**) formal say something as your opinion.

opinion noun 1 a personal view not necessarily based on fact or knowledge. 2 the views of people in general. 3 a formal statement of advice by an expert. □ **opinion poll** the questioning of a small number of people in order to assess the views of people in general.

opinionated adjective having strong opinions that you are not willing to change.

opium noun an addictive drug made from the juice of a poppy.

opossum /uh-**poss**-uhm/ noun 1 an American animal with a tail which it can use for grasping. 2 Austral./NZ a possum.

opponent noun 1 a person who competes with another in a contest or argument. 2 a person who disagrees with a proposal or practice.

opportune /**op**-per-tyoon/ adjective happening at a good or convenient time.

opportunist noun a person who takes advantage of opportunities without worrying about whether or not they are right to do so. •**adjective** (also **opportunistic**) taking advantage of opportunities when they come up.
■ **opportunism** noun.

opportunity noun (plural **opportunities**) 1 a good time or set of circumstances for doing something. 2 a chance for employment or promotion.

☑ two *ps*: opportunity.

oppose verb (**opposes, opposing, opposed**) 1 (also **be opposed to**) disapprove of and try to prevent or resist. 2 compete with or

O

THESAURUS

operation noun 1 *the sliders ensure smooth operation:* functioning, working, running, performance, action. 2 *the operation of the factory:* management, running, administration, supervision. 3 *a military operation:* action, exercise, undertaking, enterprise, manoeuvre, campaign. 4 *their mining operation:* business, enterprise, company, firm.

operational adjective running, up and running, working, functioning, operative, in operation, in use, in action, ready for use, in working order, serviceable, functional.

operative adjective 1 *the steam railway is operative:* running, up and running, working, functioning, operational, in operation, in use, in action, in effect. 2 *the operative word:* key, significant, relevant, crucial, critical.
OPPOSITES inoperative, invalid.
•noun 1 *the operatives clean the machines:* machinist, operator, mechanic, engineer, worker, workman, (factory) hand. 2 *a CIA operative:* agent, secret/undercover agent,

spy, mole, plant; N. Amer. informal spook.

operator noun 1 *a machine operator:* operative, mechanic, handler, driver, worker, engineer, machinist. 2 *a tour operator:* contractor, entrepreneur, promoter.

opinion noun belief, thought(s), idea, way of thinking, feeling, mind, view, point of view, assessment, estimation, judgement.

opponent noun 1 *his Republican opponent:* rival, adversary, competitor, enemy, antagonist, combatant, contender, challenger. 2 *an opponent of the reforms:* critic, objector, dissenter.
OPPOSITES ally, supporter.

opportunity noun chance, time, occasion, moment, opening, option, window, possibility, scope, freedom; informal shot, break, look-in.

oppose verb be against, object to, be hostile to, disagree with, disapprove of, resist, take a stand against, put up a fight against, fight, counter, challenge; informal be anti.
OPPOSITES support.

fight. **3** (**opposed**) (of two or more things) contrasting or conflicting. **4** (**opposing**) opposite.

opposite adjective **1** facing. **2** completely different. **3** being the other of a contrasted pair: *the opposite sex.* • **noun** an opposite person or thing. • **adverb** in an opposite position. • **preposition** in a position opposite to.

opposition noun **1** resistance or disagreement. **2** a group of opponents. **3** (**the Opposition**) Brit. the main party in parliament that is opposed to the one in government. **4** a contrast or direct opposite.
■ **oppositional** adjective.

oppress verb **1** treat in a harsh and unfair way. **2** make someone feel distressed or anxious.
■ **oppression** noun **oppressor** noun.

☑ double *p*, double *s*: *oppress.*

oppressive adjective **1** harsh and unfair. **2** causing depression or anxiety. **3** (of weather) hot and airless.
■ **oppressively** adverb.

opprobrious /uh-**proh**-bri-uhss/ adjective formal very critical or scornful.

opprobrium /uh-**proh**-bri-uhm/ noun formal **1** harsh criticism or scorn. **2** public disgrace as a result of bad behaviour.

opt verb make a choice.
□ **opt out** choose not to take part.

optic adjective relating to the eye or vision. • **noun** Brit. trademark a device fastened to the neck of an upside-down bottle for measuring out spirits.

optical adjective relating to vision, light, or optics.
□ **optical fibre** a thin glass fibre through which light can be transmitted. **optical illusion** something that deceives the eye by appearing to be different from what it really is.
■ **optically** adverb.

optician noun a person qualified to examine people's eyes and to prescribe glasses and contact lenses.

optics noun the study of vision and the behaviour of light.

optimal adjective best or most favourable.
■ **optimally** adverb.

optimism noun hopefulness and confidence about the future or success of something.
■ **optimist** noun.

optimistic adjective hopeful and confident about the future.
■ **optimistically** adverb.

optimize or **optimise** verb (**optimizes, optimizing, optimized**) make the best use of.

optimum adjective most likely to lead to a

THESAURUS

opposed adjective *he was opposed to discrimination:* against, dead set against, averse to, hostile to, antagonistic to, antipathetic to; informal anti.

opposing adjective **1** *opposing points of view:* conflicting, contrasting, opposite, incompatible, irreconcilable, contradictory, clashing, at variance, at odds, opposed. **2** *opposing sides:* rival, opposite, enemy, competing.
OPPOSITES similar, allied.

opposite adjective **1** *they sat opposite each other:* facing, face to face with, across from. **2** *the opposite page:* facing, opposing. **3** *opposite views:* conflicting, contrasting, incompatible, irreconcilable, contradictory, at variance, at odds, differing. **4** *opposite sides:* rival, opposing, competing, enemy.
OPPOSITES same, similar, allied.
• **noun** *the opposite was true:* reverse, converse, antithesis, contrary.
OPPOSITES same.

opposition noun **1** *the proposal met with opposition:* resistance, hostility, antagonism, antipathy, objection, dissent, disapproval. **2** *they beat the opposition:* opponent(s), opposing side, other side/team, competition, rival(s), adversary,

adversaries.
OPPOSITES agreement, goodwill.

oppress verb persecute, tyrannize, crush, repress, subjugate, subdue, keep down.

oppression noun persecution, abuse, ill-treatment, tyranny, repression, suppression, subjection, subjugation, cruelty, brutality, injustice.
OPPOSITES freedom.

oppressive adjective **1** *an oppressive dictatorship:* harsh, cruel, brutal, repressive, tyrannical, despotic, ruthless, merciless, pitiless. **2** *it was overcast and oppressive:* muggy, close, heavy, hot, humid, sticky, airless, stuffy, stifling, sultry.
OPPOSITES kindly, fresh.

opt verb choose, select, pick, decide, elect.
□ **opt for choose**, select, pick (out), decide on, go for, settle on, plump for.

optimistic adjective **1** *she felt optimistic about the future:* positive, confident, hopeful, sanguine, bullish, buoyant; informal upbeat. **2** *an optimistic forecast:* encouraging, promising, hopeful, reassuring, favourable.
OPPOSITES pessimistic, depressing.

optimum adjective best, most favourable,

favourable outcome. •noun (plural **optima** or **optimums**) the most favourable conditions for growth or success.

option noun **1** a thing that you may choose. **2** the freedom or right to choose. **3** a right to buy or sell something at a stated price within a set time.

optional adjective available to be chosen, but not compulsory.
■ **optionally** adverb.

optometry noun the occupation of measuring people's eyesight, prescribing lenses, and detecting eye disease.
■ **optometrist** noun.

opulent adjective expensive and luxurious.
■ **opulence** noun **opulently** adverb.

opus /oh-puhss/ noun (plural **opuses** or **opera**) **1** a musical work or set of works. **2** a literary work.

or conjunction **1** used to link alternatives. **2** introducing a word that means the same as a preceding word or phrase, or that explains it. **3** otherwise.

oracle noun (in ancient Greece or Rome) a priest or priestess through whom the gods were believed to give prophecies about the future.

oracular /o-rak-yuu-ler/ adjective having to do with an oracle.

oral adjective **1** spoken rather than written. **2** relating to the mouth. **3** done or taken by the mouth. •noun a spoken exam.
■ **orally** adverb.

orange noun **1** a large round citrus fruit with a tough reddish-yellow rind. **2** a bright reddish-yellow colour.

orangeade noun Brit. a fizzy soft drink flavoured with orange.

orangery noun (plural **orangeries**) a type of large conservatory where orange trees are grown.

orang-utan or **orang-utang** noun a large ape with long reddish hair.

oration noun a formal speech.

orator /o-ruh-ter/ noun a person who is good at public speaking.

oratorio noun (plural **oratorios**) a large-scale musical work on a religious theme for orchestra and voices.

oratory[1] noun (plural **oratories**) a small chapel.

oratory[2] noun **1** formal public speaking. **2** exciting and inspiring speech.
■ **oratorical** adjective.

orb noun **1** an object shaped like a ball. **2** a golden globe with a cross on top, carried by a king or queen.

orbit noun **1** the regularly repeated course of a moon, spacecraft, etc. around a star or planet. **2** a particular area of activity or influence. •verb (**orbits, orbiting, orbited**) move in orbit round a star or planet.

orbital adjective **1** relating to an orbit or orbits. **2** Brit. (of a road) passing round the outside of a town.

orca noun a large whale with teeth and black and white markings.

orchard noun a piece of enclosed land planted with fruit trees.

orchestra noun **1** a large group of musicians with string, woodwind, brass, and percussion sections. **2** (also **orchestra pit**) the part of a theatre where the orchestra plays.
■ **orchestral** adjective.

orchestrate verb (**orchestrates, orchestrating, orchestrated**) **1** arrange music to be performed by an orchestra. **2** organize a situation to produce a particular effect.
■ **orchestration** noun.

orchid noun a plant with bright, unusually shaped flowers.

ordain verb **1** make someone a priest or minister. **2** order officially.

THESAURUS

most advantageous, ideal, perfect, prime, optimal.

option noun choice, preference, alternative, selection, possibility.
OPPOSITES impossibility.

optional adjective voluntary, non-compulsory, elective, discretionary.
OPPOSITES compulsory.

opulent adjective luxurious, sumptuous, palatial, lavishly appointed, rich, splendid, magnificent, grand, fancy; informal plush; Brit. informal swish; N. Amer. informal swank.
OPPOSITES spartan.

oral adjective spoken, verbal, unwritten, vocal, uttered.
OPPOSITES written.

orbit noun circuit, course, path, track,

trajectory, rotation, revolution.
•verb circle, go round, revolve round, travel round, circumnavigate.

orchestra noun ensemble, group; informal band, combo.

orchestrate verb **1** *the piece was orchestrated by Mozart:* arrange, adapt, score, set. **2** *orchestrating a protest campaign:* organize, arrange, plan, set up, mobilize, mount, stage, mastermind, coordinate, direct.

ordain verb **1** *the decision to ordain women:* confer holy orders on, admit to the priesthood, priest, appoint, anoint, consecrate. **2** *the path ordained by God:* determine, predestine, preordain, predetermine, prescribe, designate.

ordeal noun a prolonged painful or horrific experience.

order noun **1** the arrangement of people or things according to a particular sequence or method. **2** a situation in which everything is in its correct or appropriate place. **3** a situation in which the law is being obeyed and no one is behaving badly. **4** a statement telling someone to do something. **5** a request for something to be made, supplied, or served. **6** the procedure followed in a meeting, court, or religious service. **7** quality or class. **8** a social class or system. **9** a classifying category of plants and animals. **10** (**orders** or **holy orders**) the rank of an ordained Christian minister. **11** a group of people living in a religious community. **12** an institution founded by a ruler to honour people: *the Order of the Garter.* • verb (**orders, ordering, ordered**) **1** tell someone to do something. **2** request that something be made, supplied, or served. **3** organize or arrange. □ **of** (or **in**) **the order of** approximately. **out of order 1** not functioning. **2** Brit. informal unacceptable.

orderly adjective **1** arranged in a neat, organized way. **2** well behaved. • noun (plural **orderlies**) **1** a hospital attendant who is responsible for various non-medical tasks. **2** a soldier who carries orders or performs minor tasks.

■ **orderliness** noun.

ordinal adjective relating to order in a series. □ **ordinal number** a number defining a thing's position in a series, such as 'first' or 'second'.

ordinance noun formal **1** an official order. **2** a religious rite.

ordinary adjective **1** normal or usual. **2** not interesting or exceptional. □ **out of the ordinary** unusual. ■ **ordinarily** adverb **ordinariness** noun.

ordination noun the ordaining of someone as a priest or minister.

ordnance noun **1** mounted guns. **2** US military equipment and stores.

ordure noun formal dung; excrement.

ore noun a naturally occurring material from which a metal or mineral can be extracted.

oregano /o-ri-**gah**-noh/ noun a sweet-smelling plant used in cooking.

organ noun **1** a part of the body that has a particular function, e.g. the heart or kidneys. **2** a musical keyboard instrument with rows of pipes supplied with air from bellows, or one that produces similar sounds electronically. **3** a newspaper which puts forward particular views. ■ **organist** noun.

organdie noun a thin, slightly stiff cotton fabric.

THESAURUS

O

ordeal noun **unpleasant experience**, trial, hardship, suffering, nightmare, trauma, hell, torture, torment, agony.

order noun **1** *alphabetical order:* **sequence**, arrangement, organization, system, series, succession. **2** *some semblance of order:* **tidiness**, neatness, orderliness. **3** *the police managed to keep order:* **peace**, control, law and order, calm. **4** *his sense of order:* **orderliness**, organization, method, symmetry, uniformity, regularity, routine. **5** *in good order:* **condition**, state, repair, shape; Brit. informal nick. **6** *I had to obey his orders:* **command**, instruction, directive, direction, decree, edict, injunction. **7** *the company has won the order:* **commission**, request, requisition. **8** *the lower orders of society:* **class**, level, rank, grade, caste. **9** *a religious order:* **community**, brotherhood, sisterhood. **10** *the Orange Order:* **society**, organization, association, fellowship, fraternity, lodge, guild, league, union, club. OPPOSITES chaos. • verb **1** *he ordered me to return:* **instruct**, tell, command, direct, charge, require, enjoin. **2** *he ordered that their assets be confiscated:* **rule**, ordain, decree, direct. **3** *order your tickets by phone:* **request**, apply for, book, reserve. **4** *the messages are ordered chronologically:* **organize**, arrange, sort out, lay out, group, classify, categorize, catalogue. OPPOSITES forbid.

orderly adjective **1** *an orderly desk:* **neat**, tidy, well ordered, in order, shipshape, trim, in apple-pie order. **2** *the orderly presentation of information:* **organized**, efficient, methodical, systematic, coherent, structured, logical. **3** *the crowd was orderly:* **well behaved**, law-abiding, disciplined, peaceful, peaceable, non-violent. OPPOSITES untidy, disorganized, unruly.

ordinary adjective **1** *the ordinary course of events:* **usual**, normal, standard, typical, common, customary, habitual, everyday, regular, routine, day-to-day. **2** *my life seemed very ordinary:* **average**, normal, run-of-the-mill, standard, typical, middle-of-the-road, conventional, unremarkable, unexceptional; informal bog-standard; Brit. informal common or garden; N. Amer. informal garden-variety. OPPOSITES unusual.

organ noun **newspaper**, paper, journal, periodical, magazine, voice, mouthpiece.

organic adjective **1** having to do with living matter. **2** produced without the aid of artificial chemicals such as fertilizers. **3** (of chemical compounds) containing carbon. **4** having to do with an organ of the body. **5** (of development or change) continuous or natural.
■ **organically** adverb.

organism noun **1** an individual animal, plant, or life form. **2** a whole made up of parts which are dependent on each other.

organization or **organisation** noun **1** an organized group of people, e.g. a business. **2** the action of organizing. **3** a systematic arrangement or approach.
■ **organizational** adjective.

organize or **organise** verb (**organizes, organizing, organized**) **1** arrange in a particular order or structure. **2** make arrangements for an event or activity.
■ **organizer** noun.

orgasm noun an intensely pleasurable sensation that is felt as the climax of sexual activity. •**verb** have an orgasm.
■ **orgasmic** adjective.

orgiastic /or-ji-**ass**-tik/ adjective like an orgy.

orgy noun (plural **orgies**) **1** a wild party with a lot of drinking and sexual activity. **2** an excessive amount of a particular activity.

oriel noun a projecting part of an upper storey with a window.

orient noun (**the Orient**) literary the countries of the East. •**verb** (also **orientate**) **1** position something in relation to the points of a compass or other points. **2** (**orient yourself**) find your position in relation to your surroundings. **3** adapt something to meet particular needs.

oriental adjective having to do with the Far East. •**noun** dated or offensive a person of Far Eastern descent.

orientation noun **1** the action of orienting. **2** a position in relation to something else. **3** a person's attitude or natural tendency.

orienteering noun the sport of finding your way across country using a map and compass.

orifice noun an opening.

origami /o-ri-**gah**-mi/ noun the Japanese art of folding paper into decorative shapes.

origin noun **1** the point where something begins. **2** a person's background or ancestry.

original adjective **1** existing from the beginning. **2** not a copy. **3** new in an interesting or unusual way. •**noun** the

---

THESAURUS

organic adjective **1** *organic matter:* living, live, animate, biological. **2** *organic vegetables:* additive-free, chemical-free, pesticide-free, bio-, natural. **3** *a society is an organic whole:* structured, organized, coherent, integrated, coordinated, ordered, harmonious.

organism noun **1** *fish and other organisms:* living thing, being, creature, animal, plant, life form. **2** *a complex political organism:* structure, system, organization, entity.

organization noun **1** *the organization of conferences:* planning, arrangement, coordination, organizing, running, management. **2** *the overall organization of the book:* structure, arrangement, plan, pattern, order, form, format, framework, composition. **3** *his lack of organization:* efficiency, order, orderliness, planning. **4** *a large organization:* institution, body, group, company, firm, business, corporation, agency, association, society; informal outfit.

organize verb **1** *organize the information:* order, arrange, sort, assemble, marshal, put straight, group, classify, collate, categorize, catalogue. **2** *they organized a search party:* arrange, coordinate, sort out, put together, fix up, set up, lay on, orchestrate, see to, mobilize.
OPPOSITES muddle.

orient, orientate verb **1** *she found it hard* to orient herself: acclimatize, familiarize, adjust, accustom, find your feet, get/find your bearings. **2** *oriented to the business community:* aim, direct, pitch, design, intend. **3** *the stones are oriented from north to south:* align, place, position, arrange.

orientation noun **1** *the orientation of the radar station:* positioning, location, position, situation, placement, alignment. **2** *broadly Marxist in orientation:* attitude, inclination. **3** *orientation courses:* induction, training, initiation, briefing.

origin noun **1** *the origins of life:* beginning, start, genesis, birth, dawning, dawn, emergence, creation, source, basis, cause, root(s). **2** *the origin of the word:* source, derivation, root(s), provenance, etymology; N. Amer. provenience. **3** *his Scottish origins:* descent, ancestry, parentage, pedigree, lineage, line (of descent), heritage, birth, extraction, family, roots.

original adjective **1** *the original inhabitants:* indigenous, native, first, earliest, early. **2** *an original Rembrandt:* authentic, genuine, actual, true, bona fide. **3** *a highly original film:* innovative, creative, imaginative, inventive, new, novel, fresh, unusual, unconventional, unorthodox, groundbreaking, pioneering, unique, distinctive.
•**noun** *a copy of the original:* prototype, source, master.

earliest form of something, from which copies can be made.

□ **original sin** (in Christian belief) the tendency to be sinful that is thought to be present in all people.

■ **originality** noun **originally** adverb.

originate verb (**originates**, **originating**, **originated**) 1 begin in a particular place or situation. 2 create.

■ **origination** noun **originator** noun.

oriole /**or**-i-ohl/ noun a brightly coloured songbird.

ormolu noun a gold-coloured alloy of copper, zinc, and tin.

ornament noun 1 an object used as a decoration. 2 decorative items considered together.

■ **ornamental** adjective **ornamentation** noun.

ornate adjective elaborately decorated.

■ **ornately** adverb.

ornithology noun the scientific study of birds.

■ **ornithological** adjective **ornithologist** noun.

orphan noun a child whose parents are dead. • verb (**be orphaned**) (of a child) be made an orphan.

orphanage noun a place where orphans are looked after.

orthodontist /or-thuh-**don**-tist/ noun a dentist who treats irregularities in the position of the teeth and jaws.

■ **orthodontic** adjective **orthodontics** noun.

orthodox adjective 1 in keeping with generally accepted beliefs. 2 normal. 3 (**Orthodox**) relating to the Orthodox Church.

□ **Orthodox Church** a branch of the Christian Church in Greece and eastern Europe.

orthodoxy noun (plural **orthodoxies**) 1 the traditional beliefs or practices of a religion. 2 a generally accepted idea.

orthography noun (plural **orthographies**) the spelling system of a language.

■ **orthographic** adjective.

orthopaedics /or-thuh-**pee**-diks/ (US spelling **orthopedics**) noun the branch of medicine concerned with bones and muscles.

■ **orthopaedic** adjective.

Oscar noun a gold statuette given annually for achievement in various categories of film-making; an Academy award.

oscillate /**oss**-i-layt/ verb (**oscillates**, **oscillating**, **oscillated**) 1 move back and forth in a regular rhythm. 2 waver in your opinions or emotions.

■ **oscillation** noun **oscillator** noun.

osier /**oh**-zi-er/ noun a type of willow tree with long, flexible shoots that are used for making baskets.

osmium noun a hard, dense silvery-white metallic element.

osmosis /oz-**moh**-siss/ noun 1 a process by which molecules pass through a membrane from a less concentrated solution into a more concentrated one. 2 the gradual absorbing of ideas.

■ **osmotic** adjective.

osprey noun (plural **ospreys**) a large fish-eating bird of prey.

osseous /**oss**-i-uhss/ adjective consisting of bone.

ossify /**oss**-i-fy/ verb (**ossifies**, **ossifying**, **ossified**) 1 turn into bone or bony tissue. 2 stop developing or progressing.

■ **ossification** noun.

ostensible adjective apparently true, but not necessarily so.

■ **ostensibly** adverb.

ostentation noun a showy display of wealth, knowledge, etc. which is intended to impress.

ostentatious adjective expensive or showy in a way that is designed to impress.

■ **ostentatiously** adverb.

osteoarthritis noun a disease that causes pain and stiffness in the joints of the body.

osteopathy /oss-ti-**op**-uh-thi/ noun a system of complementary medicine

---

THESAURUS

originally adverb at first, in the beginning, to begin with, initially, in the first place, at the outset.

originate verb 1 *the disease originates from Africa:* arise, have its origin, begin, start, stem, spring, emerge, emanate. 2 *Bill originated the idea:* invent, create, devise, think up, dream up, conceive, formulate, form, develop, produce, mastermind, pioneer.

ornament noun 1 *cheap ornaments:* knick-knack, trinket, bauble; N. Amer. informal tchotchke, kickshaw. 2 *a dress with no ornament at all:* decoration, adornment, embellishment, ornamentation, trimming,

accessories, frills.

ornamental adjective decorative, fancy, ornate, ornamented, for show.

ornate adjective elaborate, decorated, embellished, adorned, ornamented, fancy, fussy, ostentatious, showy; informal flashy. OPPOSITES plain.

orthodox adjective 1 *orthodox views:* conventional, mainstream, conformist, established, traditional, traditionalist, prevalent, popular, conservative, received. 2 *an orthodox Hindu:* conservative, traditional, observant, devout, strict. OPPOSITES unconventional, liberal.

involving manipulation of the bones and muscles.
■ **osteopath** noun.

osteoporosis /oss-ti-oh-puh-**roh**-siss/ noun a medical condition in which the bones become brittle.

ostinato /oss-ti-**nah**-toh/ noun (plural **ostinatos** or **ostinati** /oss-ti-**nah**-ti/) a continually repeated musical phrase or rhythm.

ostler /**oss**-ler/ noun (in the past) a man employed at an inn to look after customers' horses.

ostracize or **ostracise** verb (**ostracizes**, **ostracizing**, **ostracized**) exclude someone from a society or group.
■ **ostracism** noun.

ostrich noun a large African bird with a long neck and long legs which is unable to fly.

other adjective & pronoun **1** used to refer to a person or thing that is different from one already mentioned or known. **2** additional. **3** the alternative of two. **4** those not already mentioned.
□ **other-worldly 1** relating to an imaginary or spiritual world. **2** not aware of the realities of life.

otherness noun the quality of being different or unusual.

otherwise adverb **1** in different circumstances. **2** in other respects. **3** in a different way. **4** alternatively.

otiose /**oh**-ti-ohss/ adjective serving no practical purpose.

otter noun a fish-eating animal with a long body, living partly in water and partly on land.

ottoman noun (plural **ottomans**) a low padded seat without a back or arms.

oubliette /oo-bli-**et**/ noun a secret dungeon with access only through a trapdoor in its ceiling.

ought modal verb (3rd singular present and past **ought**) **1** used to indicate duty or correctness. **2** used to indicate something that is probable. **3** used to indicate a desirable or expected state. **4** used to give or ask advice.

> **!** when using **ought** in a negative sentence, say, for example, *he ought not to have gone* rather than *he didn't/hadn't ought to have gone.*

oughtn't short form ought not.

Ouija board /**wee**-juh/ noun trademark a board marked with letters, used at a seance supposedly to receive messages from dead people.

ounce noun **1** a unit of weight of one sixteenth of a pound (approximately 28 grams). **2** a very small amount.

our possessive determiner **1** belonging to or associated with the speaker and one or more other people. **2** belonging to or associated with people in general.

ours possessive pronoun used to refer to something belonging to or associated with the speaker and one or more other people.

> ☑ no apostrophe: **ours**.

ourselves pronoun **1** used as the object of a verb or preposition when this is the same as the subject of the clause and the subject is the speaker and one or more other people. **2** we or us personally.

oust verb force someone out from a job or position.

out adverb **1** away from a place. **2** away from your home or office. **3** outdoors. **4** so as to be revealed, heard, or known. **5** to an end. **6** not possible or worth considering. **7** (of the tide) falling or at its lowest level. **8** (of the ball in tennis, squash, etc.) not in the playing area. **9** (in cricket, baseball, etc.) no longer batting. •**verb** informal reveal that

O

THESAURUS

other adjective **1** *these homes use other fuels:* alternative, different, distinct, separate, various. **2** *are there any other questions?* more, further, additional, extra, fresh, new, added, supplementary.

otherwise adverb **1** *hurry up, otherwise we'll be late:* or (else), if not. **2** *she's exhausted, but otherwise she's fine:* in other respects, apart from that. **3** *he could not have acted otherwise:* in any other way, differently.

oust verb expel, drive out, force out, remove from office/power, eject, get rid of, depose, topple, unseat, overthrow, bring down, overturn, dismiss, dislodge.

out adjective & adverb **1** *she's out at the moment:* not here, not at home, not in,

away, gone away, elsewhere. **2** *the secret was out:* revealed, (out) in the open, common/public knowledge. **3** *the roses are out:* in flower, flowering, in (full) bloom, blooming, in blossom, blossoming. **4** *the book should be out soon:* available, obtainable, to be had, in the shops, published, in print. **5** (informal) *grunge is out:* unfashionable, out of fashion, dated, outdated, passé; informal old hat. **6** *smoking is out:* forbidden, not permitted, not allowed, unacceptable; informal not on. **7** *he was slightly out in his calculations:* mistaken, inaccurate, incorrect, wrong, in error.
OPPOSITES in.
•**verb** (informal) *it was not our intention to out him:* expose, unmask.

someone is homosexual.
☐ out of **1** from. **2** not having a supply of something. out of date **1** old-fashioned. **2** no longer valid.

> **!** you should say **out of** rather than just **out** in sentences such as *he threw it out of the window.*

outback noun (**the outback**) the part of Australia that is remote and has few inhabitants.

outbid verb (**outbids, outbidding, outbid**) bid more than.

outboard adjective & adverb on, towards, or near the outside of a ship or aircraft.
☐ **outboard motor** a motor attached to the outside of a boat.

outbreak noun a sudden occurrence of war, disease, etc.

outbuilding noun a smaller building in the grounds of a main building.

outburst noun **1** a sudden release of strong emotion. **2** a sudden or violent occurrence of something.

outcast noun a person who is rejected by their social group.

outclass verb be far better than.

outcome noun a result or effect.

outcrop noun a part of a rock formation that is visible on the surface.

outcry noun (plural **outcries**) a strong expression of public disapproval.

outdated adjective no longer used or fashionable.

outdistance verb (**outdistances, outdistancing, outdistanced**) leave a competitor or pursuer far behind.

outdo verb (**outdoes, outdoing, outdid**; past participle **outdone**) do better than someone else.

outdoor adjective done, situated, or used outdoors.

outdoors adverb in or into the open air.
• noun any area outside buildings or shelter.

outer adjective **1** outside. **2** further from the centre or the inside.
☐ **outer space** the universe beyond the earth's atmosphere.

outermost adjective furthest from the centre.

outface verb (**outfaces, outfacing, outfaced**) unsettle or defeat someone by confronting them in a brave or confident way.

outfall noun the place where a river or drain empties into the sea, a river, or a lake.

outfit noun **1** a set of clothes worn together. **2** informal a group of people working together as a business, team, etc. • verb (**outfits, outfitting, outfitted**) provide someone with an outfit of clothes.
■ **outfitter** noun.

outflank verb **1** surround in order to attack. **2** defeat.

outgoing adjective **1** friendly and confident. **2** leaving an office or position. **3** going out or away from a place. • noun (**outgoings**) Brit. money that you spend regularly.

outgrow verb (**outgrows, outgrowing, outgrew**; past participle **outgrown**) **1** grow too big for. **2** stop doing something as you grow older.

THESAURUS

outbreak noun **1** *outbreaks of violence:* eruption, flare-up, upsurge, rash, wave, spate, burst, flurry. **2** *the outbreak of war:* start, beginning, commencement, onset.

outburst noun eruption, explosion, flare-up, storm, outpouring, surge, fit.

outcome noun result, end result, net result, consequence, upshot, conclusion, end product; informal pay-off.

outcry noun protest, protestation, complaints, objections, furore, fuss, uproar, opposition, dissent; informal hullabaloo, ructions, stink.

outdated adjective old-fashioned, out of date, outmoded, out of fashion, dated, unfashionable, passé, old, behind the times; informal out, old hat, square; N. Amer. informal horse-and-buggy.
OPPOSITES modern.

outdoor adjective open-air, out-of-doors, outside, al fresco.
OPPOSITES indoor.

outer adjective **1** *the outer layer:* outside, outermost, outward, exterior, external, surface. **2** *the outer islands:* outlying, distant, remote, faraway, far-flung, furthest.
OPPOSITES inner.

outfit noun **1** *a new outfit:* costume, suit, uniform, ensemble, clothes, clothing, dress, garb; informal get-up, gear; Brit. informal kit. **2** (informal) *a local manufacturing outfit:* organization, enterprise, company, firm, business, group, body, team; informal set-up.

outgoing adjective **1** *he's very outgoing:* extrovert, uninhibited, unreserved, demonstrative, affectionate, warm, sociable, convivial, lively, gregarious. **2** *the outgoing president:* departing, retiring, leaving.
OPPOSITES introverted, incoming.

outgoings plural noun expenses, expenditure, spending, outlay, payments, costs, overheads.

outing noun trip, excursion, jaunt, expedition, day out, tour, drive, ride, run; informal spin, junket.

outhouse noun a smaller building attached or close to a house.

outing noun a short trip made for pleasure.

outlandish adjective bizarre or unfamiliar.

outlast verb last longer than.

outlaw noun a person who has broken the law and remains at large. •verb make something illegal.

outlay noun an amount of money spent.

outlet noun 1 a pipe or hole through which water or gas may escape. 2 a point from which goods are sold or distributed. 3 a way of expressing your talents, energy, or emotions.

outline noun 1 a sketch or diagram showing the shape of an object. 2 the outer edges of an object. 3 a general description of something, with no detail. •verb (**outlines, outlining, outlined**) 1 draw the outer edge or shape of. 2 give a summary of.

outlive verb live or last longer than.

outlook noun 1 a person's attitude to life. 2 a view. 3 what is likely to happen in the future.

outlying adjective situated far from a centre.

outmanoeuvre verb (**outmanoeuvres, outmanoeuvring, outmanoeuvred**) gain an advantage over an opponent by using skill and cunning.

outmoded adjective old-fashioned.

outnumber verb (**outnumbers, outnumbering, outnumbered**) be more numerous than.

outpace verb (**outpaces, outpacing, outpaced**) go faster than.

outpatient noun a patient attending a hospital for treatment without staying overnight.

outperform verb perform better than.

outplay verb play better than.

outpost noun 1 a small military camp at a distance from the main army. 2 a remote part of a country or empire.

outpouring noun 1 something that streams out rapidly. 2 an outburst of strong emotion.

output noun 1 the amount of something produced. 2 the process of producing something. 3 the power, energy, etc. supplied by a device or system. 4 a place where power, information, etc. leaves a system.

outrage noun 1 a very strong reaction of anger or annoyance. 2 a very immoral or shocking act. •verb (**outrages, outraging, outraged**) make someone feel outrage.

outrageous adjective 1 shockingly bad or unacceptable. 2 very unusual and slightly shocking.
■ **outrageously** adverb.

outran past of OUTRUN.

outrank verb have a higher rank than.

outré /oo-tray/ adjective unusual and rather shocking.

THESAURUS   **o**

outlaw noun *a band of outlaws:* fugitive, wanted criminal, bandit, robber.
•verb *fox-hunting has been outlawed:* ban, bar, prohibit, forbid, make illegal, proscribe.
OPPOSITES permit.

outlet noun 1 *a central-heating outlet:* vent, way out, outfall, opening, channel, conduit, duct. 2 *an outlet for farm produce:* market, retail outlet, shop, store. 3 *an outlet for their energies:* means of expression, means of release, vent, avenue, channel.

outline noun 1 *the outline of the building:* silhouette, profile, shape, contours, form, lines. 2 *an outline of our proposal:* rough idea, thumbnail sketch, rundown, summary, synopsis, résumé, precis, main points, gist, bare bones.
•verb *she outlined the plan briefly:* rough out, sketch out, draft, give a rough idea of, summarize, precis.

outlook noun 1 *a positive outlook:* point of view, viewpoint, way of thinking, perspective, attitude, standpoint, stance, frame of mind. 2 *a lovely open outlook:* view, vista, prospect, panorama. 3 *the outlook for the economy:* prospects, future, expectations, prognosis.

out of date adjective 1 *the design is out of date:* old-fashioned, outmoded, outdated, dated, old, passé, behind the times, obsolete, antiquated, anachronistic; informal old hat; N. Amer. informal horse-and-buggy, clunky. 2 *your ticket is out of date:* expired, lapsed, invalid, void. 3 *your information is out of date:* obsolete, incorrect, inaccurate.
OPPOSITES fashionable, valid, current.

output noun production, yield, product, productivity, work, result, processed data.

outrage noun 1 *public outrage:* indignation, fury, anger, rage, wrath; literary ire. 2 *it is an outrage:* scandal, offence, insult, affront, disgrace, atrocity.
•verb *his remarks outraged everyone:* enrage, infuriate, incense, anger, scandalize, offend, affront, shock.

outrageous adjective 1 *outrageous behaviour:* shocking, disgraceful, scandalous, atrocious, appalling, dreadful. 2 *an outrageous claim:* exaggerated, improbable, preposterous, ridiculous, unwarranted. 3 *outrageous clothes:* eye-catching, flamboyant, showy, gaudy, ostentatious; informal flashy.

outreach noun an organization's involvement with the community.

outrider noun a person in a vehicle or on horseback who escorts another vehicle.

outrigger noun a structure fixed to a boat's side to help keep it stable.

outright adverb **1** altogether. **2** openly. **3** immediately. • adjective **1** open and direct. **2** complete.

outrun verb (**outruns, outrunning, outran**; past participle **outrun**) run or travel faster or further than.

outsell verb (**outsells, outselling, outsold**) be sold in greater quantities than.

outset noun the beginning.

outshine verb (**outshines, outshining, outshone**) **1** shine more brightly than. **2** be much better than.

outside noun **1** the external side or surface of something. **2** the external appearance of someone or something. **3** the side of a curve where the edge is longer. • adjective **1** situated on or near the outside. **2** not belonging to a particular group. • preposition & adverb **1** situated or moving beyond the boundaries of. **2** beyond the limits of. **3** not being a member of.

outsider noun **1** a person who does not belong to a particular group. **2** a competitor thought to have little chance of success.

outsize or **outsized** adjective very large.

outskirts plural noun the outer parts of a town or city.

outsmart verb defeat someone by being cleverer than them.

outsold past and past participle of **outsell**.

outspoken adjective stating your opinions in an open and direct way.

outstanding adjective **1** exceptionally good. **2** clearly noticeable. **3** not yet dealt with or paid.
■ **outstandingly** adverb.

outstay verb stay for longer than the expected or allowed time.

outstrip verb (**outstrips, outstripping, outstripped**) **1** move faster than. **2** surpass.

outvote verb (**outvotes, outvoting, outvoted**) defeat by gaining more votes.

outward adjective & adverb **1** on or from the outside. **2** out or away from a place.
■ **outwardly** adverb **outwards** adverb.

outweigh verb be more significant than.

outwit verb (**outwits, outwitting, outwitted**) deceive someone through being cleverer than them.

ouzo /oo-zoh/ noun an aniseed-flavoured Greek spirit.

ova plural of **ovum**.

oval adjective having a rounded and slightly elongated outline. • noun an oval object or design.

ovary noun (plural **ovaries**) **1** a female reproductive organ in which eggs are

THESAURUS

outright adverb **1** *he rejected the proposal outright:* completely, entirely, wholly, totally, categorically, absolutely, utterly, flatly, unreservedly, out of hand. **2** *I told her outright:* explicitly, directly, frankly, candidly, bluntly, plainly, to someone's face; Brit. informal straight up. **3** *they were killed outright:* instantly, instantaneously, immediately, at once, straight away, then and there, on the spot.
• adjective **1** *an outright lie:* complete, absolute, out-and-out, downright, utter, sheer, categorical. **2** *the outright winner:* definite, unequivocal, clear, unmistakable, overall.

outset noun start, starting point, beginning, inception; informal the word go.

outside noun *the outside of the building:* exterior, outer/external surface, case, skin, shell, covering, facade.
• adjective **1** *outside lights:* exterior, external, outer, outdoor, out-of-doors. **2** *outside contractors:* independent, freelance, consultant, external.
• adverb *shall we eat outside?* outdoors, out of doors, alfresco.
OPPOSITES inside.

outsider noun stranger, visitor, non-member, foreigner, alien, interloper, immigrant, incomer, newcomer.

outskirts plural noun edges, fringes, suburbs, suburbia, periphery.

outspoken adjective forthright, direct, candid, frank, straightforward, open, straight from the shoulder, plain-spoken, blunt.

outstanding adjective **1** *an outstanding painter:* excellent, marvellous, magnificent, superb, fine, wonderful, superlative, exceptional; informal great, terrific, tremendous, super; Brit. informal brilliant; N. Amer. informal neat. **2** *how much work is still outstanding?* to be done, undone, unfinished, incomplete, remaining, pending. **3** *outstanding debts:* unpaid, unsettled, owing, owed, to be paid, payable, due, overdue; N. Amer. delinquent.

outward adjective external, surface, superficial, seeming, apparent, ostensible.
OPPOSITES inward.

outweigh verb be greater than, exceed, be superior to, prevail over, override, supersede, offset, cancel out, more than make up for, outbalance, compensate for.

produced. **2** the base of the reproductive organ of a flower.

■ **ovarian** adjective.

ovation noun a long, enthusiastic round of applause.

oven noun **1** an enclosed compartment in which food is cooked or heated. **2** a small furnace or kiln.

ovenproof adjective suitable for use in an oven.

over preposition & adverb **1** expressing movement across an area. **2** beyond and falling or hanging from a point. •preposition **1** extending upwards from or above. **2** above so as to cover or protect. **3** expressing length of time. **4** higher or more than. **5** expressing authority or control. •adverb **1** in or to the place indicated. **2** expressing action and result. **3** finished. **4** expressing repetition of a process. •noun Cricket a sequence of six balls bowled by a bowler from one end of the pitch.

overact verb act a role in an exaggerated way.

overactive adjective more active than is normal or desirable.

overall adjective & adverb including everything; taken as a whole. •noun (also **overalls**) Brit. a loose-fitting garment worn over ordinary clothes to protect them.

overarching adjective covering or dealing with everything.

overarm adjective & adverb done with the hand brought forward and down from above shoulder level.

overawe verb (**overawes, overawing, overawed**) impress someone so much that they are nervous or silent.

overbalance verb (**overbalances, overbalancing, overbalanced**) fall due to loss of balance.

overbearing adjective trying to control other people; domineering.

overblown adjective made to seem more important or impressive than it really is.

overboard adverb from a ship into the water.

□ **go overboard** be very enthusiastic.

overcast adjective cloudy.

overcharge verb (**overcharges, overcharging, overcharged**) charge too high a price.

overcoat noun **1** a long, warm coat. **2** a top layer of paint or varnish.

overcome verb (**overcomes, overcoming, overcame;** past participle **overcome**) **1** succeed in dealing with a problem. **2** defeat; overpower.

overcompensate verb (**overcompensates, overcompensating, overcompensated**) do too much when trying to correct a problem.

overcrowded adjective filled beyond what is usual or comfortable.

overdo verb (**overdoes, overdoing, overdid;** past participle **overdone**) **1** do something excessively or in an exaggerated way. **2** (**overdone**) cooked too much.

overdose noun an excessive and dangerous dose of a drug. •verb (**overdoses, overdosing, overdosed**) take an overdose.

overdraft noun an arrangement with a bank that lets you take out more money than your account holds.

overdrawn adjective having taken out more money than there is in your bank account.

overdressed adjective dressed too elaborately or formally.

overdrive noun **1** a mechanism in a motor vehicle providing an extra gear above the usual top gear. **2** a state of high activity.

O

THESAURUS

ovation noun applause, round of applause, cheers, bravos, acclaim, standing ovation; informal (big) hand.

over preposition **1** *there was cloud over the hills:* above, on top of, higher (up) than, atop, covering. **2** *he walked over the grass:* across, on. **3** *he has three people over him:* superior to, above, higher up than, in charge of, responsible for. **4** *over 2,000 people:* more than, above, in excess of, upwards of. **5** *an argument over money:* about, on the subject of, concerning, with reference to, regarding, relating to, in connection with.
OPPOSITES under.

•adverb **1** *a plane flew over:* overhead, past, by. **2** *the relationship is over:* at an end, finished, ended, no more, a thing of the past.

overall adjective *the overall cost:* total, all-inclusive, gross, final, inclusive, complete, entire.

•adverb *overall, things are better:* generally (speaking), in general, altogether, all in all, on balance, on average, for the most part, in the main, on the whole, by and large.

overcome verb *he overcame his pain:* conquer, defeat, beat, prevail over, control, get/bring under control, master, get the better of; informal lick, best.

•adjective *she was overcome with excitement:* overwhelmed, moved, affected, speechless.

overdue adjective not having arrived, happened, or been done at the expected or required time.

overestimate verb (overestimates, overestimating, overestimated) estimate that something is larger or better than it really is. • noun an estimate which is too high.

overexpose verb (overexposes, overexposing, overexposed) 1 subject photographic film to too much light. 2 (overexposed) seen too much on television, in the newspapers, etc.

overflow verb 1 flow over the edge of a container. 2 be too full or crowded. 3 (overflow with) be very full of an emotion. • noun 1 the number of people or things that do not fit into a particular space. 2 an outlet for excess water.

overground adverb & adjective on or above the ground.

overgrown adjective 1 covered with plants that have grown wild. 2 having grown too large.

overhang verb (overhangs, overhanging, overhung) project outwards over. • noun an overhanging part.

overhaul verb 1 examine and repair or improve something. 2 Brit. overtake. • noun an act of overhauling something.

overhead adverb & adjective above your head. • noun (overheads) regular expenses involved in running a business or organization.

overhear verb (overhears, overhearing, overheard) hear something accidentally.

overheat verb make or become too hot.

overindulge verb (overindulges, overindulging, overindulged) 1 have too much of something enjoyable. 2 give in to the wishes of someone too easily. ▪ overindulgence noun.

overjoyed adjective very happy.

overkill noun too much of something.

overland adjective & adverb by land.

overlap verb (overlaps, overlapping, overlapped) 1 extend over something so as to cover it partially. 2 (of two events) happen at the same time for part of their duration. • noun an overlapping part or amount.

overlay verb (overlays, overlaying, overlaid) 1 coat the surface of. 2 add a quality, feeling, etc. to. • noun a covering.

overleaf adverb on the other side of the page.

overload verb 1 load too heavily. 2 put too great a demand on. • noun too much of something.

overlook verb 1 fail to notice. 2 ignore or disregard. 3 have a view of something from above.

overlord noun a ruler.

overly adverb excessively.

overmuch adverb & pronoun too much.

overnight adverb & adjective 1 during or for a night. 2 happening suddenly or very quickly.

overpass noun a bridge by which a road or railway line passes over another.

overplay verb give too much importance to.

overpower verb (overpowers,

THESAURUS

overdue adjective 1 *the ship is overdue:* late, behind schedule, behind time, delayed. 2 *overdue payments:* unpaid, unsettled, owing, owed, payable, due, outstanding, undischarged; N. Amer. delinquent.
OPPOSITES early, punctual.

overflow verb *chemicals overflowed from the tank:* spill over, flow over, brim over, well over, flood.
• noun *offices to accommodate the overflow:* surplus, excess, additional people/things, extra, remainder, overspill.

overhaul verb service, maintain, repair, mend, fix up, rebuild, renovate, recondition, refit, refurbish.

overhead adverb *the sky overhead:* above, high up, in the sky, on high, above your head.
OPPOSITES below.
• adjective *overhead lines:* aerial, elevated, raised, suspended, overhanging.
OPPOSITES surface, underground.

overheads plural noun running costs, operating costs, fixed costs, expenses.

overlook verb 1 *he overlooked the mistake:* fail to notice, fail to spot, miss. 2 *his work has been overlooked:* disregard, neglect, ignore, pass over, forget. 3 *she was willing to overlook his faults:* ignore, disregard, take no notice of, make allowances for, turn a blind eye to, excuse, pardon, forgive. 4 *the lounge overlooks the garden:* have a view of, look over/across, look on to, look out on/over.

overpower verb overwhelm, get the better of, overthrow, subdue, suppress, subjugate, repress, bring someone to their knees.

overpowering adjective 1 *overpowering grief:* overwhelming, oppressive, unbearable, unendurable, intolerable, shattering. 2 *an overpowering smell:* stifling, suffocating, strong, pungent, powerful, nauseating, offensive, acrid, fetid.

overrate verb overestimate, overvalue, think too much of.
OPPOSITES underestimate.

overpowering, overpowered) 1 defeat through having greater strength. **2** overwhelm.

overpriced adjective too expensive.

overqualified adjective too highly qualified.

overrated adjective rated more highly than is deserved.

overreach verb (**overreach yourself**) fail through being too ambitious or trying too hard.

overreact verb react more strongly than is justified.
 ■ **overreaction** noun.

override verb (**overrides, overriding, overrode**; past participle **overridden**) **1** use your authority to reject someone else's decision or order. **2** be more important than. **3** interrupt the action of an automatic device. •noun a device on a machine for overriding an automatic process.

overrule verb (**overrules, overruling, overruled**) use your authority to reject someone else's decision or order.

overrun verb (**overruns, overrunning, overran**; past participle **overrun**) **1** occupy a place in large numbers. **2** use more time or money than expected.

overseas adverb & adjective in or to a foreign country.

oversee verb (**oversees, overseeing, oversaw**; past participle **overseen**) supervise.
 ■ **overseer** noun.

oversexed adjective having unusually strong sexual desires.

overshadow verb **1** appear more important or successful than. **2** make something sad or less enjoyable. **3** tower above and cast a shadow over.

overshoot verb (**overshoots, overshooting,**

overshot) go past the place you intended to stop at.

oversight noun an unintentional failure to notice or do something.

oversimplify verb (**oversimplifies, oversimplifying, oversimplified**) simplify something so much that an inaccurate impression of it is given.

oversized or **oversize** adjective bigger than the usual size.

oversleep verb (**oversleeps, oversleeping, overslept**) sleep later than you intended to.

overspend verb (**overspends, overspending, overspent**) spend too much.

overspill noun Brit. people who move from an overcrowded area to live elsewhere.

overstate verb (**overstates, overstating, overstated**) state too strongly; exaggerate.
 ■ **overstatement** noun.

overstay verb stay longer than is allowed by.

overstep verb (**oversteps, overstepping, overstepped**) go beyond a limit.

overstretch verb make too many demands on a resource.

oversubscribed adjective offering too few places to satisfy demand.

overt adjective done or shown openly.
 ■ **overtly** adverb.

overtake verb (**overtakes, overtaking, overtook**; past participle **overtaken**) **1** pass while travelling in the same direction. **2** suddenly affect.

overthrow verb (**overthrows, overthrowing, overthrew**; past participle **overthrown**) remove from power by force. •noun a removal from power.

overtime noun time worked in addition to normal working hours.

overtone noun a subtle or secondary quality or implication.

O

THESAURUS

override verb **1** *the court overrode the decision:* disallow, overrule, countermand, veto, quash, overturn, overthrow, cancel, reverse, rescind, revoke, repeal. **2** *our interests should override all others:* outweigh, supersede, take precedence over, take priority over, be more important than, cancel out, outbalance.

overrule verb countermand, cancel, reverse, rescind, repeal, revoke, disallow, override, veto, quash, overturn, overthrow.

overrun verb invade, storm, occupy, swarm into, surge into, inundate, overwhelm.

overshadow verb outshine, eclipse, surpass, exceed, outclass, outstrip, outdo, upstage; informal be head and shoulders above.

overt adjective undisguised, unconcealed,

plain (to see), clear, conspicuous, obvious, noticeable, manifest, patent, open, blatant. OPPOSITES covert.

overtake verb **1** *a green car overtook us:* pass, go past, pull ahead of. **2** *Goa overtook Ibiza as the favourite destination:* outstrip, surpass, overshadow, eclipse, outshine, outclass, exceed, top, cap. **3** *the calamity which overtook us:* befall, happen to, come upon, hit, strike, overwhelm, overcome.

overthrow verb *the regime was overthrown:* oust, remove, bring down, topple, depose, displace, unseat, defeat, conquer.
 •noun *the overthrow of capitalism:* ousting, removal, downfall, toppling, supplanting, displacement, unseating, defeat, fall, collapse, demise.

overture noun **1** an orchestral piece at the beginning of a musical work. **2** an orchestral composition in one movement. **3** (**overtures**) approaches made with the aim of opening negotiations or establishing a relationship.

overturn verb **1** turn over and come to rest upside down. **2** abolish or reverse a decision, system, etc.

overuse verb (**overuses, overusing, overused**) use too much. • noun excessive use.

overview noun a general review or summary.

overweening adjective showing too much confidence or pride.

overweight adjective heavier or fatter than is usual or desirable.

overwhelm verb **1** have a strong emotional effect on. **2** overpower. **3** bury or drown beneath a huge mass.

overwork verb **1** work too hard. **2** use a word or idea too much. • noun too much work.

overwrite verb (**overwrites, overwriting, overwrote**; past participle **overwritten**) destroy computer data by entering new data in its place.

overwrought adjective **1** in a state of nervous excitement or anxiety. **2** too elaborate or complicated.

ovoid /oh-voyd/ adjective **1** egg-shaped. **2** oval.

ovulate /ov-yuu-layt/ verb (**ovulates, ovulating, ovulated**) (of a woman or female animal) release ova (reproductive cells) from the ovary.
■ ovulation noun.

ovule /ov-yool/ noun the part of the ovary of plants that after fertilization becomes the seed.

ovum /oh-vuhm/ noun (plural **ova**) a female reproductive cell, which can develop into an embryo if fertilized by a male cell.

owe verb (**owes, owing, owed**) **1** be required to give money or goods to someone in return for something received. **2** be obliged to show someone gratitude, respect, etc. **3** (**owe something to**) have something because of.

owing adjective yet to be paid or supplied.
□ owing to because of.

owl noun a bird of prey with large eyes, which is active at night.

owlish adjective resembling an owl.

own adjective & pronoun belonging to or done by the person specified. • verb **1** have something as your property. **2** formal admit that something is the case. **3** (**own up**) admit that you have done something wrong or embarrassing.
□ come into your own become fully effective. hold your own remain in a strong position.

owner noun a person who owns something.
■ ownership noun.

THESAURUS

overture noun **1** the overture to a long debate: preliminary, prelude, introduction, lead-in, precursor, start, beginning. **2** peace overtures: opening move, approach, advances, feeler, signal.

overturn verb **1** the boat overturned: capsize, turn turtle, keel over, tip over, topple over. **2** I overturned the stool: upset, tip over, topple over, turn over, knock over, upend. **3** the Senate may overturn this ruling: cancel, reverse, rescind, repeal, revoke, countermand, disallow, override, overrule, veto, quash, overthrow.

overweight adjective fat, obese, stout, plump, portly, chubby, pot-bellied, flabby; informal tubby; Brit. informal podgy.
OPPOSITES underweight.

overwhelm verb **1** Spain overwhelmed Russia in the hockey: defeat heavily, trounce, rout, beat hollow, conquer, be victorious over, crush; informal thrash, lick, wipe the floor with. **2** Elizabeth was overwhelmed by a sense of tragedy: overcome, move, stir, affect, touch, strike, dumbfound, shake, leave speechless; informal bowl over, knock sideways, floor; Brit. informal knock/hit for six.

overwhelming adjective **1** an overwhelming number of people: very large, enormous, immense, inordinate, massive, huge. **2** an overwhelming desire to laugh: very strong, powerful, uncontrollable, irrepressible, irresistible, overpowering, compelling.

owe verb be in debt (to), be indebted (to), be in arrears (to), be under an obligation (to).

owing adjective the rent was owing: unpaid, to be paid, payable, due, overdue, undischarged, owed, outstanding, in arrears; N. Amer. delinquent.
OPPOSITES paid.
□ owing to **because of**, as a result of, on account of, due to, as a consequence of, thanks to, in view of.

own adjective he has his own reasons: personal, individual, particular, private, personalized, unique.
• verb I own this house: possess, keep, hold, be the owner of, have to your name.

owner noun possessor, holder, proprietor, homeowner, freeholder, landlord, landlady.

ownership noun possession, freehold, proprietorship, proprietary rights, title.

ox noun (plural **oxen**) **1** a cow or bull. **2** a castrated bull.

Oxbridge noun Oxford and Cambridge universities classed together.

oxidation noun the process of oxidizing, or the result of being oxidized.

oxide noun a compound of oxygen with another substance.

oxidize or **oxidise** verb (**oxidizes, oxidizing, oxidized**) cause to combine with oxygen.

■ **oxidization** noun.

oxtail noun the tail of an ox, used in making soup.

oxygen noun a colourless, odourless gas that forms about 20 per cent of the earth's atmosphere.

oxygenate verb (**oxygenates, oxygenating, oxygenated**) supply or treat with oxygen.

oxymoron /ok-si-**mor**-on/ noun a figure of speech in which apparently contradictory terms appear together (e.g. *bittersweet*).

oyster noun **1** a shellfish with two hinged shells, some kinds of which are edible. **2** a shade of greyish white.

oystercatcher noun a wading bird with black or black-and-white feathers.

oz abbreviation ounces.

ozone noun **1** a strong-smelling, poisonous form of oxygen. **2** informal fresh air blowing from the sea.

□ **ozone layer** a layer in the stratosphere containing a lot of ozone, which protects the earth from the sun's ultraviolet radiation.

O

Pp

P or **p** noun (plural **Ps** or **P's**) the sixteenth letter of the alphabet. • abbreviation 1 page. 2 Brit. penny or pence.

PA abbreviation 1 Brit. personal assistant. 2 public address.

p.a. abbreviation per year.

pace noun 1 a single step taken when walking or running. 2 the rate at which something happens or develops. • verb (**paces, pacing, paced**) 1 walk to and fro in a small area. 2 measure a distance by counting the number of steps taken to cover it. 3 (**pace yourself**) do something at a controlled and steady rate.
□ keep pace with progress at the same speed as. put someone through their paces make someone demonstrate their abilities.

pacemaker noun a device for stimulating and regulating the heart muscle.

pachyderm /pak-i-derm/ noun an elephant or other very large mammal with thick skin.

pacific adjective 1 formal peaceful. 2 (**Pacific**) having to do with the Pacific Ocean.

pacifism noun the belief that disputes should be settled by peaceful means and that violence should never be used.
■ pacifist noun & adjective.

pacify verb (**pacifies, pacifying, pacified**) 1 make someone less angry or upset. 2 make a country peaceful.
■ pacification noun.

pack noun 1 a cardboard or paper container and the items inside it. 2 Brit. a set of playing cards. 3 a group of animals that live and hunt together. 4 chiefly disapproving a group of similar things or people. 5 (**the pack**) the main group of competitors following the leader in a race. 6 Rugby a team's forwards. 7 (**Pack**) an organized group of Cub Scouts or Brownies. 8 a rucksack. 9 an absorbent pad used for treating an injury. • verb 1 fill a bag with items needed for travel. 2 put something in a container for transport or storage. 3 cram a large number of things into. 4 (**packed**) crowded. 5 cover, surround, or fill.
□ pack ice a mass of ice floating in the sea. pack something in informal give up an activity or job. pack someone off informal send someone somewhere without much notice. pack up Brit. informal (of a machine) break down. send someone packing informal dismiss someone abruptly.

package noun 1 an object or group of objects wrapped in paper or packed in a box. 2 N. Amer. a packet. 3 a set of proposals or terms as a whole. • verb (**packages, packaging, packaged**) 1 put into a box or wrapping. 2 present in an attractive way.

packet noun 1 a paper or cardboard container or parcel. 2 (**a packet**) informal a lot of money.

packhorse noun a horse that is used to

THESAURUS

pace noun 1 *ten paces*: step. 2 *a slow, steady pace*: gait, stride, walk, march. 3 *a furious pace*: speed, rate, velocity, tempo.
• verb *she paced up and down*: walk, stride, march, pound.

pack noun 1 *a pack of cigarettes*: packet, container, package, box, carton, parcel. 2 *a pack of wolves*: group, herd, troop. 3 *a pack of hooligans*: crowd, mob, group, band, party, set, gang, rabble, horde, throng, huddle, mass, assembly, gathering, host; informal crew, bunch.
• verb 1 *she helped pack the car*: fill (up), put things in, load. 2 *they packed their*

belongings: stow, put away, store, box up. 3 *the glasses were packed in straw*: wrap (up), package, parcel, swathe, swaddle, encase, envelop, bundle. 4 *shoppers packed the store*: throng, crowd, fill, cram, jam, squash into, squeeze into.

package noun 1 *the delivery of a package*: parcel, packet, box. 2 *a package of services*: collection, bundle, combination, range, complement, raft, platform.
• verb *goods packaged in recyclable materials*: wrap, gift-wrap, pack, box, seal.

packet noun pack, carton, container, case, package.

carry loads.

pact noun a formal agreement between two or more people, groups, or countries.

pacy adjective fast-moving.

pad noun 1 a thick piece of soft or absorbent material. 2 a number of sheets of blank paper fastened together at one edge. 3 the fleshy underpart of an animal's foot or of a human finger. 4 a protective guard worn by a sports player. 5 a structure or area used for helicopter take-off and landing or for launching rockets. 6 informal a person's home. •verb (**pads, padding, padded**) 1 fill or cover with padding. 2 (**pad something out**) add unnecessary material to a speech, article, or book to make it longer. 3 walk with quiet, steady steps.

padding noun 1 soft material used to pad or stuff something. 2 unnecessary material added to make a speech, article, or book longer

paddle noun 1 a short pole with a broad end, used to propel a small boat. 2 a paddle-shaped tool for stirring or mixing. 3 a short-handled bat used e.g. in table tennis. •verb (**paddles, paddling, paddled**) 1 walk with bare feet in shallow water. 2 propel a boat with a paddle or paddles. □ **paddle steamer** a boat powered by steam and propelled by large wheels which move the water as they turn.

paddock noun 1 a small field or enclosure for horses. 2 an enclosure where horses or cars are displayed before a race.

paddy[1] noun (plural **paddies**) a field where rice is grown.

paddy[2] noun Brit. informal a fit of temper.

padlock noun a detachable lock which is attached by a hinged hook. •verb secure with a padlock.

padre /**pah**-dray/ noun informal a chaplain in the armed services.

paean /pee-uhn/ noun formal a song of praise or triumph.

paediatrics /pee-di-at-riks/ (US spelling **pediatrics**) noun the branch of medicine concerned with children and their diseases. ▪ **paediatric** adjective **paediatrician** noun.

paedophile /pee-duh-fyl/ (US spelling **pedophile**) noun a person who is sexually attracted to children. ▪ **paedophilia** noun.

paella /py-el-luh/ noun a Spanish dish of rice, chicken, seafood, etc.

pagan noun a person who holds religious beliefs other than those of the main world religions. •adjective relating to pagans or their beliefs. ▪ **paganism** noun.

page[1] noun 1 one side of a sheet of paper in a book, magazine, etc. 2 both sides of such a sheet of paper considered as a single unit. 3 a section of data displayed on a computer screen. •verb (**pages, paging, paged**) (**page through**) turn the pages of a book, magazine, etc.

page[2] noun 1 a boy or young man employed in a hotel to run errands, open doors, etc. 2 a young boy who attends a bride at a wedding. 3 historical a boy in training for knighthood. •verb (**pages, paging, paged**) summon someone over a public address system or with a pager.

pageant /pa-juhnt/ noun an entertainment performed by people in elaborate or historical costumes.

pageantry noun elaborate display or ceremonial events.

pageboy noun a page in a hotel or attending a bride at a wedding.

pager noun a small device which bleeps or vibrates to inform you that it has received a message.

p

THESAURUS

pact noun agreement, treaty, entente, protocol, deal, settlement, armistice, truce.

pad[1] noun 1 *a pad over the eye:* dressing, pack, wad. 2 *making notes on a pad:* notebook, notepad, writing pad, jotter; N. Amer. scratch pad.

pad[2] verb *he padded along the landing:* creep, sneak, steal, tiptoe, pussyfoot.

padded adjective cushioned, insulated, lined, quilted, stuffed, lagged.

padding noun 1 *padding around the ankle:* wadding, cushioning, stuffing, packing, filling, lining. 2 *a concise style with no padding:* verbiage, wordiness; Brit. informal waffle.

paddle[1] noun *use the paddles to row ashore:* oar, scull.
•verb *we paddled around the bay:* row, pull, scull.

paddle[2] verb *children were paddling in the water:* splash (about), dabble, wade.

pagan noun & adjective heathen, infidel, non-Christian.

page[1] noun folio, sheet, side, leaf.

page[2] noun 1 *a page in a hotel:* errand boy, messenger boy; N. Amer. bellboy, bellhop. 2 *a page at a wedding:* attendant, pageboy, train-bearer.
•verb *could you please page Mr Johnson?* call (for), summon, send for.

pageant noun parade, procession, cavalcade, tableau, spectacle, extravaganza, show.

pageantry noun spectacle, display, ceremony, magnificence, pomp, splendour, grandeur, show; informal razzle-dazzle, razzmatazz.

paginate verb (**paginates, paginating, paginated**) give numbers to the pages of a book, magazine, etc.
■ **pagination** noun.

pagoda noun a Hindu or Buddhist temple or other sacred building.

paid past and past participle of **PAY**.
□ **put paid to** informal stop something abruptly.

pail noun a bucket.

pain noun 1 a strongly unpleasant physical sensation caused by illness or injury. 2 mental suffering. 3 (**pains**) great care or trouble. 4 informal an annoying or boring person or thing. • verb 1 cause pain to. 2 (**pained**) showing that you are annoyed or upset.
□ **on** (or **under**) **pain of** with the threat of being punished by.

painful adjective suffering or causing pain.
■ **painfully** adverb.

painkiller noun a medicine for relieving pain.

painless adjective 1 not causing pain. 2 involving little effort or stress.
■ **painlessly** adverb.

painstaking adjective very careful and thorough.
■ **painstakingly** adverb.

paint noun a coloured substance which is spread over a surface to give a thin decorative or protective coating. • verb 1 put paint on something. 2 produce a picture with paint. 3 give a description of.

painter[1] noun 1 an artist who paints pictures. 2 a person who paints buildings.

painter[2] noun a rope attached to the bow of a boat for tying it to a quay.

painting noun 1 the action of painting. 2 a painted picture.

paintwork noun painted surfaces in a building or on a vehicle.

pair noun 1 a set of two things used together or seen as a unit. 2 an article consisting of two joined or corresponding parts. 3 two people or animals related in some way or considered together. • verb 1 join or connect to form a pair. 2 (**pair off** or **up**) form a couple.

paisley noun an intricate pattern of curved feather-shaped figures.

pajamas US spelling of **PYJAMAS**.

Pakistani noun a person from Pakistan.
• adjective relating to Pakistan.

pal informal noun a friend. • verb (**pals, palling, palled**) (**pal up**) form a friendship.

palace noun a large building where a king, queen, president, etc. lives.

palaeography /pa-li-og-ruh-fi/ (US spelling **paleography**) noun the study of ancient writing systems and manuscripts.

Palaeolithic /pa-li-uh-**li**-thik/ (US spelling **Paleolithic**) adjective relating to the early part of the Stone Age.

palaeontology /pa-li-on-**tol**-uh-ji/ (US spelling **paleontology**) noun the study of fossil animals and plants.
■ **palaeontologist** noun.

palatable adjective 1 pleasant to taste. 2 acceptable.

palate noun 1 the roof of the mouth. 2 a person's ability to distinguish between different flavours.

THESAURUS

pain noun 1 *she endured great pain:* suffering, agony, torture, torment. 2 *a pain in the stomach:* ache, aching, soreness, throbbing, sting, twinge, stab, pang, discomfort, irritation. 3 *the pain of losing a loved one:* sorrow, grief, heartache, heartbreak, sadness, unhappiness, distress, misery, despair, agony, torment, torture. 4 *he took great pains to hide his feelings:* care, effort, bother, trouble.
• verb *it pained him to watch:* sadden, grieve, distress, trouble, perturb, oppress, cause anguish to.

painful adjective 1 *a painful arm:* sore, hurting, tender, aching, throbbing. 2 *a painful experience:* disagreeable, unpleasant, nasty, distressing, upsetting, traumatic, miserable, sad, heartbreaking, agonizing, harrowing.

painfully adverb distressingly, disturbingly, uncomfortably, unpleasantly, dreadfully.

painstaking adjective careful, meticulous, thorough, assiduous, attentive, conscientious, punctilious, scrupulous, rigorous.
OPPOSITES slapdash.

paint noun colouring, colour, tint, dye, stain, pigment.
• verb 1 *I painted the ceiling:* colour, decorate, whitewash, emulsion, gloss, spray-paint, airbrush. 2 *painting slogans on a wall:* daub, smear, spray-paint, airbrush. 3 *Rembrandt painted his mother:* portray, picture, paint a picture/portrait of, depict, represent.

painting noun picture, illustration, portrayal, depiction, representation, image, artwork, canvas, oil, watercolour.

pair noun *a matching pair:* set, brace, couple, duo, two.
• verb *a cardigan paired with a matching skirt:* match, put together, couple, combine.

palace noun castle, château, mansion, stately home, schloss.

palatial /puh-**lay**-sh'l/ adjective large and impressive, like a palace.

palaver /puh-**lah**-ver/ noun informal a lot of fuss about something.

pale[1] adjective 1 of a light shade or colour. 2 (of a person's face) having little colour, especially as a result of illness or shock. •verb (**pales, paling, paled**) 1 become pale in your face. 2 seem or become less important.

pale[2] noun 1 a wooden stake used with others to form a fence. 2 a boundary. ☐ **beyond the pale** (of behaviour) considered by most people to be unacceptable.

Palestinian adjective relating to Palestine. •noun a member of the native Arab population of Palestine.

palette /**pa**-lit/ noun 1 a thin board on which an artist lays and mixes paints. 2 the range of colours used by an artist. ☐ **palette knife** a blunt knife with a flexible blade, for applying or removing paint.

palimpsest noun an ancient sheet of parchment from which the original writing has been removed to make room for new writing.

palindrome noun a word or phrase that reads the same backwards as forwards, e.g. *madam*.

paling noun 1 a fence made from stakes. 2 a stake used in such a fence.

palisade noun a fence of stakes or iron railings.

pall[1] /pawl/ noun 1 a cloth spread over a coffin, hearse, or tomb. 2 a dark cloud of smoke or dust. 3 a general atmosphere of gloom or fear. ☐ **pall-bearer** a person helping to carry a coffin at a funeral.

pall[2] /pawl/ verb become less appealing through being too familiar.

palladium noun a rare silvery-white metallic element.

pallet noun 1 a portable platform on which goods can be moved, stacked, and stored. 2 a straw mattress.

palliate verb (**palliates, palliating, palliated**) 1 reduce the pain or bad effects of a disease, though not curing it. 2 make something bad easier to cope with. ■ **palliative** adjective.

pallid adjective 1 pale, especially because of bad health. 2 (of colours or light) not strong or bright.

pallor noun an unhealthy pale appearance.

pally adjective informal having a close, friendly relationship.

palm[1] noun an evergreen tree of warm regions, with a crown of large feathered or fan-shaped leaves.

palm[2] noun the inner surface of the hand between the wrist and fingers. •verb informal 1 (**palm something off**) sell or dispose of something in a way that is dishonest or unfair. 2 (**palm someone off with**) persuade someone to accept something that is unwanted or has no value.

palmistry noun the activity of interpreting a person's character or predicting their future by examining the palm of their hand. ■ **palmist** noun.

palmtop noun a computer small and light enough to be held in one hand.

palmy adjective comfortable and prosperous.

palomino /pa-luh-**mee**-noh/ noun (plural **palominos**) a tan-coloured horse with a white mane and tail.

palpable adjective 1 able to be touched or felt. 2 (of a feeling or quality) very strong or obvious. ■ **palpably** adverb.

palpate verb (**palpates, palpating, palpated**) (of a doctor or nurse) examine a part of the body by touching it.

palpitate verb (**palpitates, palpitating, palpitated**) 1 (of the heart) beat fast or irregularly. 2 shake; tremble.

palpitations plural noun a noticeably fast, strong, or irregular heartbeat.

palsy /**pawl**-zi/ noun (plural **palsies**) dated paralysis. ■ **palsied** adjective.

paltry adjective (**paltrier, paltriest**) (of an amount) very small.

pampas noun large treeless plains in South America.

pamper verb (**pampers, pampering, pampered**) give someone a great deal of care and attention.

pamphlet noun a small booklet or leaflet.

p

THESAURUS

pale adjective 1 *she looked pale:* white, pallid, pasty, wan, colourless, anaemic, washed out, peaky, ashen, sickly; informal like death warmed up. 2 *pale colours:* light, pastel, muted, subtle, soft, faded, bleached, washed out. 3 *the pale light of morning:* dim, faint, weak, feeble. OPPOSITES rosy-cheeked, dark.

•verb *he paled at the news:* go/turn white, grow/turn pale, blanch, lose colour.

pamper verb spoil, indulge, overindulge, cosset, mollycoddle, coddle, baby, wait on someone hand and foot.

pamphlet noun brochure, leaflet, booklet, circular; N. Amer. mailer, folder.

pan¹ noun **1** a metal container for cooking food in. **2** a bowl fitted at either end of a pair of scales. **3** Brit. the bowl of a toilet. **4** a hollow in the ground in which water collects. • verb (**pans, panning, panned**) **1** informal criticize harshly. **2** (**pan out**) informal end up or conclude. **3** wash gravel in a pan to separate out gold.

pan² verb (**pans, panning, panned**) swing a video or film camera to give a wide view or follow a subject.

pan- combining form including everything or everyone: *pan-African*.

panacea /pan-uh-see-uh/ noun something that will cure all diseases or solve all difficulties.

panache /puh-**nash**/ noun impressive skill and confidence.

panama noun a man's wide-brimmed hat made of straw-like material.

Panamanian /pan-uh-**may**-ni-uhn/ noun a person from Panama. • adjective relating to Panama.

panatella noun a long, thin cigar.

pancake noun a thin, flat cake of batter, cooked in a frying pan.

pancreas /**pang**-kri-uhss/ noun (plural **pancreases**) a large gland behind the stomach which produces insulin and a liquid used in digestion.
■ **pancreatic** adjective.

panda noun **1** (also **giant panda**) a large black and white bear-like animal native to bamboo forests in China. **2** (also **red panda**) a Himalayan animal like a raccoon, with thick reddish-brown fur and a bushy tail.

pandemic /pan-**dem**-ik/ adjective (of a disease) widespread over a whole country or large part of the world. • noun an outbreak of such a disease.

pandemonium noun a state of uproar and confusion.

pander verb (**panders, pandering, pandered**) (**pander to**) indulge someone in an unreasonable desire or bad habit.

pane noun a single sheet of glass in a window or door.

panegyric /pa-ni-**ji**-rik/ noun a speech or piece of writing praising someone or something.

panel noun **1** a section in a door, vehicle, garment, etc. **2** a flat board on which instruments or controls are fixed. **3** a small group of people brought together to investigate a matter, or to take part in a broadcast quiz or game.
■ **panelled** (US spelling **paneled**) adjective **panellist** (US spelling **panelist**) noun.

pang noun a sudden sharp pain or painful emotion.

panic noun **1** sudden uncontrollable fear or anxiety. **2** frenzied hurry to do something. • verb (**panics, panicking, panicked**) feel sudden uncontrollable fear or anxiety.
■ **panicky** adjective.

pannier noun each of a pair of bags, boxes, or baskets fitted on either side of a bicycle or motorcycle, or carried by a horse or donkey.

panoply /**pan**-uh-pli/ noun a large and impressive collection or number of things.

panorama noun **1** a broad view of a surrounding region. **2** a complete survey of a subject or sequence of events.
■ **panoramic** adjective.

pan pipes plural noun a musical instrument made from a row of short pipes fixed together.

pansy noun **1** a garden plant with brightly coloured flowers. **2** informal a homosexual man.

pant verb breathe with short, quick breaths. • noun a short, quick breath.

pantaloons plural noun **1** women's baggy trousers gathered at the ankles. **2** (in the past) men's close-fitting trousers fastened below the calf or at the foot.

pantechnicon noun Brit. dated a large van for transporting furniture.

pantheism /**pan**-thee-i-z'm/ noun the belief

p

THESAURUS

pan¹ noun *a pan of water:* saucepan, pot, bowl, frying pan, skillet.

pan² verb *the camera panned to the building:* swing (round), sweep, move, turn.

panel noun **1** *a control panel:* console, instrument panel, dashboard, instruments, controls, dials, array. **2** *a panel of judges:* group, team, body, committee, board.

panic noun *a wave of panic:* alarm, anxiety, fear, fright, trepidation, dread, terror, hysteria, apprehension; informal flap, fluster, cold sweat; N. Amer. informal swivet.
OPPOSITES calm.
• verb **1** *there's no need to panic:* be

alarmed, be scared, be afraid, take fright, be hysterical, lose your nerve, get overwrought, get worked up; informal get in a flap, run around like a headless chicken; Brit. informal get the wind up, go into a flat spin, have kittens. **2** *talk of love panicked her:* frighten, alarm, scare, unnerve; Brit. informal put the wind up.
OPPOSITES stay calm, calm down.

panorama noun view, vista, prospect, scenery, landscape, seascape, cityscape, skyline.

pant verb breathe heavily, breathe hard, puff and blow, huff and puff, gasp, that God is all around us and is present in all things.

■ **pantheist** noun **pantheistic** adjective.

pantheon /pan-thi-uhn/ noun **1** all the gods of a people or religion. **2** an ancient temple dedicated to all the gods. **3** a group of particularly famous or important people.

panther noun **1** a black leopard. **2** N. Amer. a puma or a jaguar.

panties plural noun knickers.

pantile /pan-tyl/ noun a curved roof tile, fitted to overlap its neighbour.

panto noun (plural **pantos**) Brit. informal a pantomime.

pantomime noun Brit. an entertainment in the theatre involving music and slapstick comedy.

pantry noun (plural **pantries**) a small room or cupboard for storing food.

pants plural noun **1** Brit. underpants or knickers. **2** chiefly N. Amer. trousers.

pantyhose plural noun N. Amer. women's thin nylon tights.

pap noun **1** bland soft or semi-liquid food suitable for babies or invalids. **2** trivial books, television programmes, etc.

papa noun N. Amer. or dated your father.

papacy noun (plural **papacies**) the position or role of the Pope.

papal adjective relating to the Pope or the papacy.

paparazzo /pa-puh-**rat**-soh/ noun (plural **paparazzi** /pa-puh-**rat**-si/) a photographer who follows celebrities to get photographs of them.

papaya /puh-**py**-uh/ noun a tropical fruit like a long melon, with orange flesh and small black seeds.

paper noun **1** material manufactured in thin sheets from the pulp of wood, used for writing or printing on or as wrapping material. **2** (**papers**) sheets of paper covered with writing or printing. **3** a newspaper. **4** a government report or policy document. **5** an academic article read at a conference or published in a journal. **6** a set of exam questions. •verb (**papers**, **papering**, **papered**) **1** cover a wall with wallpaper. **2** (**paper something over**)

conceal or disguise an awkward problem instead of resolving it.

□ **on paper 1** in writing. **2** in theory rather than in reality. **paper clip** a piece of bent wire or plastic used for holding sheets of paper together. **paper tiger** a person or thing that appears threatening but is actually weak.

■ **papery** adjective.

paperback noun a book bound in stiff paper or thin cardboard.

paperknife noun a blunt knife used for opening envelopes.

paperweight noun a small, heavy object for keeping loose papers in place.

paperwork noun routine work involving written documents.

papier mâché /pa-pi-ay **mash**-ay/ noun a mixture of paper and glue that becomes hard when dry.

papist /**pay**-pist/ noun disapproving a Roman Catholic.

paprika /**pap**-ri-kuh, puh-**pree**-kuh/ noun a powdered spice made from sweet red peppers.

papyrus /puh-**py**-ruhss/ noun (plural **papyri** /puh-**py**-ry/ or **papyruses**) a material made in ancient Egypt from the stem of a water plant, used for writing or painting on.

par noun Golf the number of strokes a first-class player normally requires for a particular hole or course.

□ **above** (or **below** or **under**) **par** above (or below) the usual or expected level or amount. **on a par with** equal to.

parable noun a simple story that teaches a moral or spiritual lesson.

parabola /puh-**rab**-uh-luh/ noun (plural **parabolas** or **parabolae** /puh-**rab**-uh-lee/) a curve of the kind formed by the intersection of a cone with a plane parallel to its side.

■ **parabolic** adjective.

paracetamol noun (plural **paracetamol** or **paracetamols**) Brit. a drug used to relieve pain and reduce fever.

parachute noun a cloth canopy which allows a person or heavy object attached to it to descend slowly when dropped from a

p

THESAURUS

heave, wheeze.

pants plural noun **1** (Brit.) underpants, briefs, boxer shorts, boxers, knickers; N. Amer. shorts, undershorts; informal panties; dated drawers, bloomers. **2** (N. Amer.) trousers, slacks; Brit. informal trews, strides, kecks; Austral. informal daks.

paper noun **1** newspaper, journal, gazette, periodical, tabloid, broadsheet, daily, weekly; informal rag; N. Amer. informal tab. **2** *a three-hour paper*: exam, examination, test.

3 *he has written a paper on global warming*: essay, article, monograph, thesis, work, dissertation, treatise, study, report, analysis; N. Amer. theme. **4** *personal papers*: document, certificate, letter, file, deed, record, archive; (**papers**) paperwork, documentation. **5** *they asked us for our papers*: identification, identity card, ID, credentials.

parable noun allegory, moral tale, fable.

high position. • verb (**parachutes, parachuting, parachuted**) drop by parachute.
■ **parachutist** noun.

parade noun 1 a public procession. 2 a formal occasion when soldiers march or stand in line in order to be inspected or for display. 3 a series or succession. 4 Brit. a row of shops. • verb (**parades, parading, paraded**) 1 walk, march, or display in a parade. 2 display something publicly in order to impress people or attract attention.

paradigm /pa-ruh-dym/ noun a typical example, pattern, or model of something.
■ **paradigmatic** adjective.

paradise noun 1 (in some religions) heaven. 2 the Garden of Eden. 3 an ideal place or state.

paradox noun 1 a statement that sounds absurd or seems to contradict itself, but is in fact true. 2 a person or thing that combines two contradictory features or qualities.
■ **paradoxical** adjective **paradoxically** adverb.

paraffin noun 1 Brit. an oily liquid obtained from petroleum, used as a fuel. 2 a waxy substance obtained from petroleum, used for sealing and waterproofing and in candles.

paragliding noun a sport in which a person glides through the air attached to a wide parachute after jumping from a high place.

paragon noun a model of excellence or of a particular quality.

paragraph noun a distinct section of a piece of writing, beginning on a new line.

Paraguayan /pa-ruh-gwy-uhn/ noun a person from Paraguay. • adjective relating to Paraguay.

parakeet or **parrakeet** noun a small parrot with green feathers and a long tail.

parallax noun the apparent difference in the position of an object when viewed from different positions.

parallel adjective 1 (of lines or surfaces) side by side and having the same distance continuously between them. 2 happening or existing at the same time or in a similar way; corresponding. • noun 1 a person or thing that is similar to or can be compared to another. 2 a similarity or comparison. 3 each of the imaginary parallel circles of latitude on the earth's surface. • verb (**parallels, paralleling, paralleled**) correspond to or happen at the same time as.

☑ double *l* in the middle: para*ll*el.

parallelogram noun a figure with four straight sides and opposite sides parallel.

paralyse (US spelling **paralyze**) verb (**paralyses, paralysing, paralysed**) 1 make someone unable to move a part of their body. 2 prevent something from functioning normally.

paralysis /puh-**ral**-i-siss/ noun (plural **paralyses** /puh-**ral**-i-seez/) 1 the loss of the ability to move part of the body. 2 inability to do things or function normally.

paralytic adjective 1 relating to paralysis.

---

p # THESAURUS

parade noun 1 *a victory parade:* procession, march, cavalcade, motorcade, spectacle, display, pageant, review, tattoo; Brit. march past. 2 *she walked along the parade:* promenade, walkway, esplanade, mall; N. Amer. boardwalk; Brit. informal prom.
• verb 1 *the teams paraded through the city:* march, process, file, troop. 2 *she paraded up and down:* strut, swagger, stride. 3 *he was keen to parade his knowledge:* display, exhibit, make a show of, flaunt, show (off), demonstrate.

paradise noun 1 heaven, the promised land, the Elysian Fields. 2 *a tropical paradise:* Utopia, Shangri-La, Eden, heaven, idyll. 3 *this is sheer paradise!* bliss, heaven, ecstasy, delight, joy, happiness, heaven on earth.
OPPOSITES hell.

paradox noun contradiction, self-contradiction, inconsistency, incongruity, conflict, enigma, puzzle, conundrum.

paragraph noun section, division, part, portion, segment, passage, clause.

parallel adjective 1 *parallel lines:* aligned,

side by side, equidistant. 2 *parallel careers:* similar, analogous, comparable, corresponding, like, equivalent, matching.
OPPOSITES divergent, different.
• noun 1 *an exact parallel:* counterpart, analogue, equivalent, match, twin, duplicate, mirror. 2 *there is an interesting parallel between these figures:* similarity, likeness, resemblance, analogy, correspondence, comparison, equivalence, symmetry.
OPPOSITES divergence, difference.

paralyse verb 1 *both of his legs were paralysed:* disable, cripple, immobilize, incapacitate; (**paralysed**) Medicine paraplegic, quadriplegic. 2 *the capital was paralysed by a strike:* bring to a standstill, immobilize, bring to a halt, freeze, cripple, disable.

paralysis noun 1 *the disease can cause paralysis:* immobility, powerlessness, incapacity; Medicine paraplegia, quadriplegia. 2 *complete paralysis of the ports:* shutdown, immobilization, stoppage, gridlock, standstill, blockage.

2 informal very drunk.

paramedic noun a person who is trained to do medical work but is not a fully qualified doctor.

parameter /puh-**ram**-i-ter/ noun a thing which decides or limits the way in which something can be done.

paramilitary adjective organized on similar lines to a military force. •noun (plural **paramilitaries**) a member of a paramilitary organization.

paramount adjective **1** more important than anything else. **2** having the highest position or the greatest power.

paramour noun old use a person's lover.

paranoia noun a mental condition in which someone wrongly believes that other people want to harm them, or that they are very important.

paranoid adjective **1** wrongly believing that other people want to harm you. **2** having to do with paranoia.

paranormal adjective beyond the scope of scientific knowledge.

parapet noun a low wall along the edge of a roof, bridge, or balcony.

paraphernalia noun the objects needed for a particular activity.

paraphrase verb (**paraphrases, paraphrasing, paraphrased**) express the meaning of something using different words. •noun a rewording of something written or spoken.

paraplegia /pa-ruh-**plee**-juh/ noun paralysis of the legs and lower body.
■ **paraplegic** adjective & noun.

paraquat noun a powerful weedkiller.

parasite noun **1** an animal or plant which lives on or inside another, and gets its food from it. **2** a person who relies on or benefits from someone else but gives nothing in return.
■ **parasitic** adjective **parasitism** noun.

parasol noun a light umbrella used to give shade from the sun.

paratroops plural noun troops trained to be

dropped by parachute from aircraft.
■ **paratrooper** noun.

parboil verb boil something until it is partly cooked.

parcel noun an object or collection of objects wrapped in paper in order to be carried or sent by post. •verb (**parcels, parcelling, parcelled**; US spelling **parcels, parceling, parceled**) **1** (**parcel something up**) make something into a parcel. **2** (**parcel something out**) divide something between several people.

parch verb **1** make something dry through strong heat. **2** (**parched**) informal very thirsty.

parchment noun **1** (in the past) a stiff material made from the skin of a sheep or goat and used for writing on. **2** thick paper resembling parchment.

pardon noun **1** forgiveness for a mistake, sin, or crime. **2** a cancellation of the punishment for a crime. •verb **1** forgive or excuse a person, mistake, sin, or crime. **2** give an offender a pardon. •exclamation used to ask a speaker to repeat something because you did not hear or understand it.
■ **pardonable** adjective.

pare verb (**pares, paring, pared**) **1** trim something by cutting away the outer edges. **2** (**pare something away** or **down**) gradually reduce the amount of something.

parent noun **1** a father or mother. **2** an animal or plant from which young or new ones are produced. **3** an organization or company which owns or controls a number of smaller organizations or companies. •verb be or act as a parent to.
■ **parental** adjective **parenthood** noun.

parentage noun the identity and origins of your parents.

parenthesis /puh-**ren**-thi-siss/ noun (plural **parentheses** /puh-**ren**-thi-seez/) **1** a word or phrase added as an explanation or afterthought, indicated in writing by a pair of brackets, dashes, or commas. **2** (**parentheses**) a pair of round brackets ()

p

THESAURUS

paramount adjective most important, supreme, chief, overriding, predominant, foremost, prime, primary, principal, main, key, central; informal number-one.

paranoid adjective suspicious, mistrustful, anxious, fearful, insecure, obsessive.

paraphrase verb reword, rephrase, express differently, rewrite, gloss.

parasite noun hanger-on, cadger, leech, passenger; informal sponger, scrounger, freeloader; N. Amer. informal mooch; Austral./NZ informal bludger.

parcel noun *a parcel of clothes*: package,

packet, pack, bundle, box, case, bale.
•verb *she parcelled up the papers*: pack (up), package, wrap (up), gift-wrap, tie up, bundle up.

pardon noun **1** *pardon for your sins*: forgiveness, absolution. **2** *he offered them a full pardon*: reprieve, amnesty, exoneration, release, acquittal, discharge.
•verb **1** *I know she will pardon me*: forgive, absolve. **2** *they were subsequently pardoned*: exonerate, acquit, reprieve; informal let off.
OPPOSITES blame, punish.

surrounding a word or phrase.
■ **parenthetic** (or **parenthetical**) adjective.

par excellence /par ek-suh-**lonss**/ adjective better or more than all others of the same kind: *a designer par excellence.*

pariah /puh-**ry**-uh/ noun a person who is rejected by other people; an outcast.

parings plural noun thin strips pared off from something.

parish noun 1 (in the Christian Church) a district with its own church and church ministers. 2 Brit. the smallest unit of local government in country areas.

parishioner noun a person who lives in a particular Church parish.

parity noun the quality of being equal with or equivalent to something.

park noun 1 a large public garden in a town. 2 a large area of land attached to a country house. 3 an area used for a particular purpose. ● **verb** leave a vehicle somewhere for a time.

parka noun a windproof hooded jacket.

Parkinson's disease noun a disease of the brain and nervous system marked by trembling, stiffness in the muscles, and slowness of movement.

parky adjective Brit. informal chilly.

parlance noun a way of speaking.

parley noun (plural **parleys**) a meeting between enemies to discuss terms for a truce. ● **verb** (**parleys**, **parleying**, **parleyed**) hold a parley.

parliament noun 1 (**Parliament**) (in the UK) the assembly that makes laws, consisting of the king or queen, the House of Lords, and the House of Commons. 2 a similar assembly in other countries.
■ **parliamentary** adjective.

☑ -lia- in the middle, not -la-: parl*ia*ment.

parliamentarian noun a member of a parliament.

parlour (US spelling **parlor**) noun 1 dated a

sitting room. 2 a shop providing particular goods or services.

parlous /**par**-luhss/ adjective old use dangerously uncertain; precarious.

Parmesan /**par**-mi-zan/ noun a hard, dry Italian cheese.

parochial /puh-**roh**-ki-uhl/ adjective 1 relating to a parish. 2 having a narrow outlook.
■ **parochialism** noun.

parody noun (plural **parodies**) a piece of writing, art, or music that deliberately copies the style of someone or something, in order to be funny. ● **verb** (**parodies**, **parodying**, **parodied**) produce a parody of.

parole noun the temporary or permanent release of a prisoner before the end of their sentence, on the condition that they behave well. ● **verb** (**paroles**, **paroling**, **paroled**) release a prisoner on parole.

paroxysm /pa-**ruhk**-si-z'm/ noun a sudden attack of pain, coughing, etc., or a sudden feeling of overwhelming emotion.

parquet /**par**-kay/ noun flooring consisting of wooden blocks arranged in a geometric pattern.

parrakeet ⇨ **PARAKEET**.

parricide noun the killing by someone of their own parent or other close relative.

parrot noun a tropical bird with brightly coloured feathers and a hooked bill, some kinds of which can copy human speech.
● **verb** (**parrots**, **parroting**, **parroted**) repeat something mechanically, without thought or understanding.
□ **parrot-fashion** repeated without thought or understanding.

parry verb (**parries**, **parrying**, **parried**) 1 ward off a weapon or attack. 2 say something in order to avoid answering a question directly.

parse /parz/ verb analyse a sentence in terms of grammar.

parsimony /**par**-si-muh-ni/ noun the fact of

THESAURUS

parish noun 1 *the parish of Upton:* district, community. 2 *the vicar scandalized the parish:* parishioners, churchgoers, congregation, fold, flock, community.

park noun 1 public garden, recreation ground, playground, play area. 2 parkland, grassland, woodland, garden(s), lawns, grounds, estate.
● **verb** 1 *he parked his car:* leave, position, stop, pull up. 2 (informal) *park your bag by the door:* put (down), place, deposit, leave, stick, shove, dump; informal plonk; Brit. informal bung.

parliament noun legislature, assembly, chamber, house, congress, senate, diet.

parliamentary adjective legislative, law-

making, governmental, congressional, democratic, elected.

parochial adjective narrow-minded, small-minded, provincial, small-town, conservative; N. Amer. informal jerkwater.
OPPOSITES broad-minded.

parody noun 1 *a parody of the news:* satire, burlesque, lampoon, pastiche, caricature, imitation; informal spoof, take-off, send-up. 2 *a parody of the truth:* distortion, travesty, caricature, misrepresentation, perversion, corruption.

parry verb 1 *Sharpe parried the blow:* ward off, fend off, deflect, block. 2 *I parried her questions:* evade, sidestep, avoid, dodge, field.

p

being very unwilling to spend money.
■ **parsimonious** adjective.

parsley noun a herb with crinkly or flat leaves, used in cooking.

parsnip noun a long tapering cream-coloured root vegetable.

parson noun (in the Church of England) a parish priest.

parsonage noun a house provided by the Church for a parson.

part noun 1 a piece or section which is combined with others to make up a whole. 2 some but not all of something. 3 a role played by an actor or actress. 4 a person's contribution to an action or situation. 5 (**parts**) informal a region. • verb 1 move apart or divide to leave a central space. 2 (of two or more people) leave each other. 3 (**part with**) give up possession of; hand over. • adverb partly.
□ **part company** go in different directions. **part of speech** a category in which a word is placed according to its function in grammar, e.g. noun, adjective, and verb. **part song** a song with three or more voice parts and no musical accompaniment. **part-time** for only part of the usual working day

or week. **take part** join in or be involved in an activity. **take someone's part** support someone in an argument.

partake verb (**partakes, partaking, partook;** past participle **partaken**) formal 1 (**partake of**) eat or drink. 2 (**partake in**) participate in.

partial adjective 1 not complete or whole. 2 favouring one side in a dispute. 3 (**partial to**) liking something.
■ **partiality** noun **partially** adverb.

participate verb (**participates, participating, participated**) join in something; take part.
■ **participant** noun **participation** noun **participatory** adjective.

participle noun Grammar a word such as *going* or *burnt* that is formed from a verb and used as an adjective or noun (as in *burnt toast* or *the going was good*), or to make compound verb forms (as in *was going*).

particle noun 1 a tiny portion of matter. 2 a minute piece of matter smaller than an atom, e.g. an electron.

particular adjective 1 relating to an individual member of a group or class. 2 more than is usual. 3 very careful or concerned about something. • noun a detail.
□ **in particular** especially.

THESAURUS

parson noun priest, minister, clergyman, vicar, rector, cleric, chaplain, pastor, curate; informal reverend, padre; Austral. informal josser.

part noun 1 *a large part of their life:* piece, amount, portion, proportion, percentage, fraction; informal slice, chunk. 2 *car parts:* component, bit, constituent, element, module. 3 *body parts:* organ, limb, member. 4 *the third part of the book:* section, division, volume, chapter, act, scene, instalment. 5 *another part of the country:* district, neighbourhood, quarter, section, area, region. 6 *the part of Juliet:* role, character. 7 *he was jailed for his part in the affair:* involvement, role, function, hand, responsibility, capacity, participation, contribution; informal bit.
OPPOSITES whole.
• verb 1 *the curtains parted:* separate, divide, split, move apart. 2 *we parted on bad terms:* part company, say goodbye/farewell, go your separate ways, take your leave.
OPPOSITES join, meet.
□ **part with** give away, give up, relinquish, forgo, surrender, hand over. **take part** participate, join in, get involved, enter, play a part, play a role, be a participant, contribute, have a hand; informal get in on the act.

partial adjective 1 *a partial recovery:* incomplete, limited, qualified, imperfect, fragmentary, unfinished. 2 *a very partial*

view of the situation: biased, prejudiced, partisan, one-sided, slanted, skewed, coloured, unbalanced.
OPPOSITES complete, unbiased.
□ **be partial to** like, love, enjoy, be fond of, be keen on, have a soft spot for, have a taste for, have a penchant for.

partially adverb somewhat, to a limited extent, to a certain extent, partly, in part, up to a point, slightly.
OPPOSITES wholly.

participant noun participator, contributor, party, member, entrant, competitor, player, contestant, candidate.

participate verb take part, join, engage, get involved, share, play a part, play a role, contribute, partake, have a hand in.

particle noun (tiny) bit, (tiny) piece, speck, spot, fragment, sliver, splinter.

particular adjective 1 *a particular group of companies:* specific, certain, distinct, separate, definite, precise. 2 *an issue of particular importance:* special, exceptional, unusual, uncommon, notable, noteworthy, remarkable, unique. 3 *he was particular about what he ate:* fussy, fastidious, finicky, discriminating, selective; informal pernickety, choosy, picky; Brit. informal faddy.
OPPOSITES general, indiscriminate.
• noun *the same in every particular:* detail, item, point, element, fact, circumstance, feature.

p

particularly adverb **1** more than is usual. **2** in particular; especially.

☑ particu*larly*, not -*culy*.

parting noun **1** an act of leaving someone and going away. **2** Brit. a line of scalp which is visible when the hair is combed in different directions.

partisan /par-ti-zan/ noun **1** a committed supporter of a cause, group, or person. **2** a member of an armed group fighting secretly against an occupying force. •adjective prejudiced.

partition noun **1** a structure that divides a space into separate areas. **2** division into parts. •verb **1** divide into parts. **2** divide a room with a partition.

partly adverb not completely but to some extent.

partner noun **1** each of two people doing something as a pair. **2** the person you are having a sexual relationship with. **3** each of two or more people who are involved in a project or undertaking or who own a business. •verb (**partners, partnering, partnered**) be the partner of.

■ **partnership** noun.

partook past of PARTAKE.

partridge noun (plural **partridge** or **partridges**) a game bird with brown feathers and a short tail.

parturition noun formal or technical the action of giving birth.

party noun (plural **parties**) **1** a social event with food and drink and sometimes dancing. **2** an organized political group that puts forward candidates for election to government. **3** a group of people taking part in an activity or trip. **4** a person or group forming one side in an agreement or dispute. •verb (**parties, partying, partied**) informal enjoy yourself at a party.
□ **be party to** be involved in. **party line** a policy officially adopted by a political party. **party wall** a wall between two adjoining houses or rooms.

parvenu /par-vuh-nyoo/ noun disapproving a person from a poor background who has recently joined a group of wealthy or famous people.

pascal noun a unit of pressure.

pass[1] verb **1** move or go onward, past,

THESAURUS

particularly adverb **1** *the acoustics are particularly good*: especially, specially, exceptionally, unusually, remarkably, outstandingly, uncommonly, uniquely. **2** *he particularly asked that I should help you*: specifically, explicitly, expressly, in particular, especially, specially.

parting noun *an emotional parting*: farewell, leave-taking, goodbye, adieu, departure.

partisan noun guerrilla, freedom fighter, resistance fighter, underground fighter, irregular.
•adjective biased, prejudiced, one-sided, discriminatory, partial, sectarian, factional. OPPOSITES unbiased.

partition noun **1** *the partition of Palestine*: division, partitioning, separation, dividing up, splitting up, breaking up, break-up. **2** *room partitions*: screen, room divider, dividing wall, barrier, panel.
•verb **1** *moves to partition Poland*: divide, separate, split up, break up. **2** *the hall was partitioned*: subdivide, divide (up), separate, section off, screen off.

partly adverb in part, partially, somewhat, a little, up to a point, in some measure, slightly, to some extent. OPPOSITES wholly.

partner noun **1** *business partners*: colleague, associate, co-worker, fellow worker, collaborator, comrade, teammate; Austral./NZ informal offsider. **2** *his partner in crime*: accomplice, confederate, accessory, collaborator, fellow conspirator, helper;

informal sidekick. **3** *your relationship with your partner*: spouse, husband, wife, lover, girlfriend, boyfriend, fiancé, fiancée, significant other, live-in lover, mate; Brit. informal other half.

partnership noun **1** *close partnership*: cooperation, association, collaboration, coalition, alliance, union, affiliation, connection. **2** *thriving partnerships*: company, association, consortium, syndicate, firm, business, organization.

party noun **1** *150 people attended the party*: social gathering, function, get-together, celebration, reunion, festivity, reception, soirée, social; informal bash, do; Austral./NZ informal shivoo. **2** *a party of visitors*: group, company, body, gang, band, crowd, pack, contingent; informal bunch, crew, load. **3** *a left-wing party*: faction, group, bloc, camp, caucus, alliance.

pass verb **1** *the traffic passing through the village*: go, proceed, move, progress, make your way, travel. **2** *a car passed him*: overtake, go past/by, pull ahead of, leave behind. **3** *time passed*: elapse, go by/past, advance, wear on, roll by, tick by. **4** *he passed the time reading*: occupy, spend, fill, use (up), employ, while away. **5** *pass the salt*: hand, let someone have, give, reach. **6** *her estate passed to her grandson*: be transferred, go, be left, be bequeathed, be handed down/on, be passed on; Law devolve. **7** *his death passed unnoticed*: happen, occur, take place. **8** *the storm passed*: come to an end, fade (away), blow

through, or across. **2** change from one state or condition to another. **3** transfer something to someone. **4** kick, hit, or throw the ball to a teammate. **5** (of time) go by. **6** spend time. **7** be done or said. **8** come to an end. **9** be successful in an exam or test. **10** declare something to be satisfactory. **11** approve a proposal or law by voting. **12** express an opinion or judgement. • **noun 1** an act of passing. **2** a success in an exam. **3** an official document which allows you to go somewhere or use something. **4** informal a sexual advance. **5** a particular situation.
□ **pass away** die. **pass off** happen in a particular way. **pass something off as** pretend that something is something else. **pass out** become unconscious. **pass something up** choose not to take up an opportunity.

pass² noun a route over or through mountains.

passable adjective **1** acceptable, but not outstanding. **2** able to be travelled along or on.
■ **passably** adverb.

passage noun **1** the passing of someone or something. **2** a way through or across something. **3** a journey by sea or air. **4** the right to pass through a place. **5** a short section from a book, document, or musical work.

passageway noun a corridor or other

narrow passage between buildings or rooms.

passé /pass-ay/ adjective no longer fashionable.

passenger noun a person travelling in a car, bus, train, ship, or aircraft, other than the driver, pilot, or crew.

passer-by noun (plural **passers-by**) a person who happens to be walking past something or someone.

passerine /pass-uh-ryn, pass-uh-reen/ adjective referring to birds whose feet are adapted for perching (including all songbirds).

passim adverb used to show that a reference appears at various places throughout a document.

passing adjective **1** done quickly and casually. **2** (of a similarity) slight. • **noun 1** the ending of something. **2** a person's death.

passion noun **1** very strong emotion. **2** strong sexual love. **3** a strong enthusiasm for something. **4** (**the Passion**) Jesus's suffering and death on the Cross.
□ **passion flower** a climbing plant with distinctive flowers. **passion fruit** the edible fruit of some species of passion flower. **passion play** a play about Jesus's crucifixion.

passionate adjective showing or caused by passion.
■ **passionately** adverb.

p

over, run its course, die out/down, finish, end, cease. **9** *he passed the exam:* be successful in, succeed in, gain a pass in, get through; informal sail through, scrape through. **10** *the Senate passed the bill:* approve, vote for, accept, ratify, adopt, agree to, authorize, endorse, legalize, enact; informal OK.
• **noun** *you must show your pass:* permit, warrant, authorization, licence.
□ **pass as/for** be mistaken for, be taken for, be accepted as. **pass out** faint, lose consciousness, black out. **pass something up** turn down, reject, refuse, decline, give up, forgo, let pass, miss (out on); informal give something a miss.

passage noun **1** *their passage through the country:* progress, transit, advance, journey, trip, voyage. **2** *the passage of time:* passing, advance, course, march. **3** *clearing a passage to the front door:* way, route, path. **4** *the passage to the kitchen:* corridor, hall, hallway. **5** *a passage between the buildings:* alley, alleyway, passageway, lane, path, footpath, track, thoroughfare; N. Amer. areaway. **6** *a passage from 'Macbeth':* extract, excerpt, quotation, quote.

passenger noun traveller, commuter, fare-payer, rider, fare.

passing adjective **1** *of passing interest:* fleeting, transient, transitory, ephemeral, brief, short-lived, temporary, momentary. **2** *a passing glance:* hasty, rapid, hurried, brief, quick, cursory, superficial, casual, perfunctory.
• **noun 1** *the passing of time:* passage, course, progress, advance. **2** *Jack's passing:* death, demise, passing away, end, loss.

passion noun **1** *the passion of activists:* enthusiasm, ardour, fervour, eagerness, zeal, vigour, fire, energy, spirit, fanaticism. **2** *he worked himself up into a passion:* rage, fit of anger, temper, tantrum, fury, frenzy; Brit. informal paddy. **3** *hot with passion:* love, desire, lust, ardour, lasciviousness, lustfulness. **4** *his passion for football:* enthusiasm, love, mania, fascination, obsession, preoccupation, fanaticism, fixation, compulsion, appetite, addiction; informal thing.
OPPOSITES apathy, calm.

passionate adjective **1** *a passionate entreaty:* intense, impassioned, ardent, fervent, vehement, fiery, heated, emotional, heartfelt, excited. **2** *McGregor is*

passive adjective **1** accepting what happens without resisting or trying to change anything. **2** Grammar (of a verb) having the form used when the subject is affected by the action of the verb (e.g. *they were killed* as opposed to the active form *he killed them*).
□ **passive smoking** the inhaling of smoke from other people's cigarettes.
■ **passively** adverb **passivity** noun.

Passover noun the major Jewish spring festival, commemorating the liberation of the Israelites from slavery in Egypt.

passport noun an official document that identifies you as a citizen of a particular country and is required in order to enter and leave other countries.

password noun a secret word or phrase used to enter a place or use a computer.

past adjective **1** gone by in time and no longer existing. **2** (of time) that has gone by. **3** Grammar (of a tense of a verb) expressing a past action or state. •noun **1** a past period or the events in it. **2** a person's or thing's history or earlier life. •preposition **1** beyond in time or space. **2** in front of or from one side to the other of. **3** beyond the scope or power of. •adverb **1** so as to pass from one side to the other. **2** used to indicate the passage of time.
□ **past master** a person who is an expert in a particular activity. **past participle** Grammar the form of a verb which is used in perfect tenses (e.g. *have you looked?*), to form passive sentences (e.g. *it was broken*), and sometimes as an adjective (e.g. *lost property*).

pasta noun a type of food made from flour and water, formed into various shapes and cooked in boiling water.

paste noun **1** a soft, moist substance. **2** a glue made from water and starch. **3** a hard substance used in making imitation gems. •verb (**pastes, pasting, pasted**) **1** coat or stick with paste. **2** (in computing) insert a section of text into a document.

pasteboard noun thin board made by pasting together sheets of paper.

pastel noun **1** a soft coloured chalk or crayon used for drawing. **2** a pale shade of a colour. •adjective (of a colour) pale.

pasteurize or **pasteurise** verb (**pasteurizes, pasteurizing, pasteurized**) destroy the germs in milk by a process of heating and cooling.
■ **pasteurization** noun.

pastiche /pa-steesh/ noun a piece of writing or work of art produced in a style which imitates that of another work, artist, or period.

pastille /pass-tuhl/ noun a small sweet or throat lozenge.

pastime noun an activity done regularly for enjoyment.

pastor noun a minister in charge of a Christian church or group.

pastoral adjective **1** relating to or portraying country life. **2** relating to the farming or grazing of sheep or cattle. **3** relating to the work of a Christian minister in giving personal and spiritual guidance. **4** relating to a teacher's responsibility for the well-being of

p

THESAURUS

passionate about sport: very keen, very enthusiastic, addicted; informal mad, crazy, hooked; Austral./NZ informal shook. **3** *a passionate kiss:* amorous, ardent, hot-blooded, loving, sexy, sensual, erotic, lustful; informal steamy, hot, turned on.
OPPOSITES apathetic, cool.

passive adjective **1** *a passive role:* inactive, non-active, non-participative, uninvolved. **2** *passive victims:* submissive, acquiescent, unresisting, compliant, docile.
OPPOSITES active, resistant.

past adjective **1** *times past:* gone by, bygone, former, previous, old, of old, olden, long-ago. **2** *the past few months:* last, recent, preceding. **3** *a past chairman:* previous, former, foregoing, erstwhile, one-time, sometime, ex-.
OPPOSITES present, future.
•noun *Michael's colourful past:* history, background, past life, life story.
•preposition **1** *I drove past the cafe:* in front of, by. **2** *it's past 9 o'clock:* beyond, after, later than.

•adverb *they hurried past:* along, by, on.

paste noun **1** *blend the ingredients to a paste:* purée, pulp, mush, spread, pâté. **2** *wallpaper paste:* adhesive, glue, gum; N. Amer. mucilage.
•verb *a notice was pasted on the door:* stick, glue, gum, fix, affix.

pastel adjective pale, soft, light, delicate, muted.
OPPOSITES dark, bright.

pastime noun hobby, leisure activity, leisure pursuit, recreation, game, amusement, diversion, entertainment, interest.

pastor noun priest, minister, parson, clergyman, cleric, chaplain, vicar, rector, curate; informal reverend, padre; Austral. informal josser.

pastoral adjective **1** *a pastoral scene:* rural, country, rustic, agricultural, bucolic; literary Arcadian. **2** *his pastoral duties:* priestly, clerical, ecclesiastical, ministerial.
OPPOSITES urban, lay.

students. • **noun** a pastoral poem, picture, or piece of music.

pastrami /pass-**trah**-mi/ **noun** highly seasoned smoked beef.

pastry **noun** (plural **pastries**) 1 dough made from flour, fat, and water, used in baked dishes such as pies. 2 a cake consisting of sweet pastry with a filling.

pasture **noun** land covered with grass, suitable for grazing cattle or sheep. • **verb** (**pastures, pasturing, pastured**) put animals to graze in a pasture.
■ **pasturage** noun.

pasty[1] or **pastie** /**pass**-ti/ **noun** (plural **pasties**) Brit. a folded pastry case filled with seasoned meat and vegetables.

pasty[2] /**pay**-sti/ **adjective** (**pastier, pastiest**) (of a person's skin) unhealthily pale.

pat[1] **verb** (**pats, patting, patted**) tap quickly and gently with the flat of your hand.
• **noun** 1 an act of patting. 2 a compact mass of a soft substance.

pat[2] **adjective** (of something said) too quick or easy; not convincing.
□ **have something off pat** know facts or words perfectly so that you can repeat them without hesitation.

patch **noun** 1 a small area differing in colour or texture from its surroundings. 2 a piece of material used to mend a hole or strengthen a weak point. 3 a cover worn over an injured eye. 4 a small plot of land. 5 Brit. informal a period of time. 6 Brit. informal an area for which someone is responsible or in which they operate. • **verb** 1 mend, strengthen, or protect with a patch. 2 (**patch something up**) treat injuries or repair damage quickly or temporarily.
□ **not a patch on** Brit. informal much less good than.

patchwork **noun** needlework in which small pieces of cloth of different colours are sewn edge to edge.

patchy **adjective** (**patchier, patchiest**) 1 existing or happening in small, isolated areas. 2 uneven in quality; inconsistent.

pate /*rhymes with* gate/ **noun** old use a person's head.

pâté /**pa**-tay/ **noun** a rich savoury paste made from meat, fish, etc.

patella /puh-**tel**-luh/ **noun** (plural **patellae** /puh-**tel**-lee/) the kneecap.

patent /**pay**-t'nt, **pa**-t'nt/ **noun** a government licence giving someone the sole right to make, use, or sell their invention for a set period. • **verb** obtain a patent for. • **adjective** 1 /**pay**-t'nt/ easily recognizable; obvious. 2 made and marketed under a patent.
□ **patent leather** shiny varnished leather.
■ **patently** adverb.

paterfamilias /pay-ter-fuh-**mi**-li-ass/ **noun** the man who is the head of a family or household.

paternal **adjective** 1 having to do with or like a father. 2 related through the father.
■ **paternally** adverb.

paternalism **noun** the policy of protecting the people you have control over but also of restricting their freedom.
■ **paternalist** noun & adjective **paternalistic** adjective.

paternity **noun** 1 the state of being a father. 2 descent from a father.

paternoster **noun** (in the Roman Catholic Church) the Lord's Prayer.

path **noun** 1 a way or track laid down for walking or made by repeated treading. 2 the direction in which a person or thing moves. 3 a course of action.

pathetic **adjective** 1 arousing pity or sadness. 2 informal weak or inadequate.
■ **pathetically** adverb.

pathogen /pa-**thuh**-juhn/ **noun** a microscopic organism that can cause disease.
■ **pathogenic** adjective.

pathological **adjective** 1 relating to or caused by a disease. 2 informal unable to stop yourself doing something; compulsive.
■ **pathologically** adverb.

pathology **noun** 1 the study of the causes

p

pasture noun grassland, grass, grazing, meadow, field; literary lea.

pat verb & noun tap, clap, touch, stroke.

patch noun 1 *a reddish patch on her wrist*: blotch, mark, spot, smudge, smear, stain, streak, blemish; informal splodge. 2 *a patch of ground*: plot, area, piece, strip, tract, parcel, bed; Brit. allotment; N. Amer. lot. 3 (Brit. informal) *she's going through a difficult patch*: period, time, spell, phase, stretch.
• verb *her jeans were neatly patched*: mend, repair, sew up, stitch up, cover, reinforce.

patent adjective 1 *patent nonsense*: obvious, clear, plain, evident, manifest, conspicuous, blatant, barefaced, flagrant. 2 *patent*

medicines: proprietary, patented, licensed, branded.

path noun 1 *the path to the beach*: footpath, pathway, track, trail, bridle path, lane, cycle track; N. Amer. bikeway. 2 *journalists blocked his path*: route, way, course, direction, orbit, trajectory. 3 *the best path to follow*: course of action, route, road, avenue, line, approach, tack.

pathetic adjective 1 *a pathetic sight*: pitiful, moving, touching, poignant, plaintive, wretched. 2 (informal) *a pathetic excuse*: feeble, woeful, sorry, poor, weak, pitiful, lamentable, deplorable, contemptible.

and effects of diseases. **2** the typical behaviour of a disease.
■ **pathologist** noun.

pathos /**pay**-thoss/ noun a quality that arouses pity or sadness.

pathway noun a path or route.

patience noun **1** the ability to accept delay, trouble, or suffering without becoming angry or upset. **2** Brit. a card game for one player.

patient adjective having or showing patience. •noun a person receiving or registered to receive medical treatment.
■ **patiently** adverb.

patina /**pa**-ti-nuh/ noun **1** a green or brown film on the surface of old bronze. **2** a soft glow on wooden furniture produced by age and polishing.

patio noun (plural **patios**) a paved area outside a house.

patisserie /puh-**tiss**-uh-ri/ noun a shop where pastries and cakes are sold.

patois /**pat**-wah/ noun (plural **patois** /**pat**-wahz/) the dialect of a region.

patriarch /**pay**-tri-ark/ noun **1** a man who is the head of a family or tribe. **2** a biblical figure regarded as a father of the human race. **3** a respected older man.

patriarchy noun (plural **patriarchies**) a society led or controlled by men.
■ **patriarchal** adjective.

patrician /puh-**tri**-sh'n/ noun an aristocrat. •adjective relating to or characteristic of aristocrats.

patricide noun **1** the killing by someone of

their own father. **2** a person who kills their father.

patrimony /**pa**-tri-muh-ni/ noun (plural **patrimonies**) property inherited from your father or male ancestor.

patriot noun a person who strongly supports their country and is prepared to defend it.
■ **patriotic** adjective **patriotism** noun.

patrol noun **1** a person or group sent to keep watch over an area. **2** the action of patrolling an area. •verb (**patrols, patrolling, patrolled**) keep watch over an area by regularly walking or travelling around it.

patron noun **1** a person who gives financial support to a person or organization. **2** a regular customer of a restaurant, hotel, etc.
□ **patron saint** a saint who is believed to protect a particular place or group of people.

patronage noun **1** support given by a patron. **2** custom attracted by a restaurant, hotel, etc.

patronize or **patronise** verb (**patronizes, patronizing, patronized**) **1** treat someone as if they lack experience or are not very intelligent. **2** go regularly to a restaurant, hotel, etc.

patter[1] verb (**patters, pattering, pattered**) make a repeated light tapping sound. •noun a repeated light tapping sound.

patter[2] noun fast continuous talk.

pattern noun **1** a repeated decorative

THESAURUS

patience noun **1** *she tried everyone's patience:* forbearance, tolerance, restraint, equanimity, understanding, indulgence. **2** *a task requiring patience:* perseverance, persistence, endurance, tenacity, application, staying power, doggedness.

patient adjective **1** *I must ask you to be patient:* forbearing, uncomplaining, tolerant, long-suffering, accommodating, understanding, indulgent. **2** *patient research:* persevering, persistent, dogged, tenacious, determined.
•noun *a doctor's patient:* sick person, case, sufferer.

patriotic adjective nationalistic, loyalist, loyal, chauvinistic, jingoistic, flag-waving.
OPPOSITES traitorous.

patrol noun **1** *ships on patrol in the straits:* guard, watch, vigil. **2** *the patrol stopped a woman:* squad, detachment, party, force.
•verb *a guard was patrolling the estate:* guard, keep watch on, police, make the rounds of, stand guard (over), defend, safeguard.

patron noun **1** *a patron of the arts:* sponsor, backer, benefactor, contributor, subscriber, donor, philanthropist, promoter, friend, supporter. **2** *club patrons:* customer, client, consumer, user, visitor, guest; informal regular.

patronage noun **1** *arts patronage:* sponsorship, backing, funding, financing, assistance, support. **2** *thank you for your patronage:* custom, trade, business.

patronize verb **1** *don't patronize me!* talk down to, treat like a child. **2** *they patronized local tradesmen:* use, buy from, shop at, be a customer/client of, deal with, frequent, support.

patronizing adjective condescending, supercilious, superior, imperious, scornful; informal uppity, high and mighty.

pattern noun **1** *the pattern on the wallpaper:* design, decoration, motif, device, marking. **2** *working patterns:* system, order, arrangement, form, method, structure, scheme, plan, format. **3** *this set the pattern for a generation:* model, design. **2** a regular form or order in which a series of things happen. **3** a model, design, or set of instructions for making something. **4** an example for other people to follow.

patterned adjective decorated with a pattern.

patty noun (plural **patties**) a small pie or pasty.

paucity /paw-si-ti/ noun a very small or inadequate amount of something.

paunch noun an abdomen or stomach that is large and sticks out.
■ **paunchy** adjective.

pauper noun a very poor person.

pause verb (**pauses, pausing, paused**) stop talking or doing something for a short time before continuing again. • noun a temporary stop.

pave verb (**paves, paving, paved**) cover a piece of ground with flat stones.
■ **paving** noun.

pavement noun Brit. a raised path for pedestrians at the side of a road.

pavilion noun **1** Brit. a building at a sports ground used for changing and taking refreshments. **2** a summer house in a park or large garden. **3** a temporary display stand at a trade exhibition.

pavlova noun a dessert consisting of a meringue base covered with whipped cream and fruit.

paw noun an animal's foot that has claws and pads. • verb **1** feel or scrape something with a paw or hoof. **2** informal touch someone in a way that is clumsy or unwanted.

pawn[1] noun **1** a chess piece of the smallest size and value. **2** a person used by more powerful people for their own purposes.

pawn[2] verb leave an object with a pawnbroker in exchange for money.

pawnbroker noun a person who is licensed to lend money in exchange for an object that is left with them, and which they can sell if the borrower fails to pay the money back.

pawnshop noun a pawnbroker's shop.

pawpaw noun Brit. a papaya.

pay verb (**pays, paying, paid**) **1** give someone money for work or goods. **2** give a sum of money that is owed. **3** be profitable, or result in an advantage. **4** suffer something as a result of an action. **5** give someone attention, respect, or a compliment. **6** make a visit or a call to. • noun money that you get for work that you have done. □ **pay someone back** take revenge on someone. **pay-off** informal a payment made to someone as a bribe or so that they will not cause trouble.
■ **payable** adjective.

PAYE abbreviation pay as you earn, a system by which employers pay their employees' income tax directly to the government.

payee noun a person to whom money is paid.

payload noun **1** passengers and cargo as the part of a vehicle's load for which money is paid. **2** an explosive warhead carried by an aircraft or missile.

paymaster noun an official who pays troops or workers.

payment noun **1** the process of paying

p

THESAURUS

example, criterion, standard, norm, yardstick, touchstone, benchmark, blueprint.

pause noun *five minutes' pause:* break, interruption, lull, respite, breathing space, gap, interlude, adjournment, rest, wait, hesitation; informal let-up, breather.
• verb *let's pause here:* stop, break off, take a break, adjourn, rest, wait, hesitate; informal take a breather.

pave verb surface, floor, cover, tile, flag.

pavement noun footpath, walkway; N. Amer. sidewalk.

pay verb **1** *I must pay him for his work:* reward, reimburse, recompense, remunerate. **2** *I paid £7 for a ticket:* spend, pay out; informal lay out, shell out, fork out, cough up; N. Amer. informal ante up, pony up. **3** *he paid his debts:* discharge, settle, pay off, clear. **4** *he made the buses pay:* be profitable, make money, make a profit. **5** *it may pay you to be early:* be advantageous to, benefit, be of advantage to, be

beneficial to. **6** *he will pay for his mistakes:* suffer (the consequences), be punished, atone, pay the penalty/price.
• noun *equal pay:* salary, wages, payment, earnings, remuneration, fee, reimbursement, income, revenue.
□ **pay someone back** get your revenge on, get back at, get even with, settle the score. **pay something back** repay, pay off, give back, return, reimburse, refund. **pay something off** pay (in full), settle, discharge, clear, liquidate. **pay off** (informal) **meet with success**, be successful, be effective, get results, work.

payable adjective due, owed, owing, outstanding, unpaid, overdue; N. Amer. delinquent.

payment noun **1** *discounts for early payment:* remittance, settlement, discharge, clearance. **2** *monthly payments:* instalment, premium. **3** *extra payment for good performance:* salary, wages, pay, earnings, fees, remuneration, someone or of being paid. **2** an amount that is paid.

payola /pay-**oh**-luh/ noun N. Amer. the illegal payment of money to someone in return for their promoting a product in the media.

payroll noun a list of a company's employees and the amount of money they are to be paid.

PC abbreviation **1** personal computer. **2** police constable. **3** politically correct, or political correctness.

PDF noun Computing a kind of electronic file which can be sent by any system and displayed on any computer.

PE abbreviation physical education.

pea noun an edible round green seed growing in pods on a climbing plant.

peace noun **1** freedom from disturbance, noise, or anxiety. **2** freedom from war, or the ending of war.

peaceable adjective **1** wanting to avoid war. **2** free from conflict; peaceful.
■ **peaceably** adverb.

peaceful adjective **1** free from disturbance or noise. **2** not involving war or violence. **3** wanting to avoid conflict.
■ **peacefully** adverb.

peach noun **1** a round fruit with yellow and red skin and juicy yellow flesh, with a rough stone inside. **2** a pinkish-orange colour.

peacock noun a large, colourful bird with very long tail feathers that can be fanned out in display.

peahen noun the female of the peacock.

peak noun **1** the pointed top of a mountain, or a mountain with a pointed top. **2** a stiff brim at the front of a cap. **3** the point of highest strength, activity, or achievement. •**verb** reach a maximum or the highest point. •**adjective 1** greatest; maximum. **2** involving the greatest number of people; busiest.

peaked¹ adjective (of a cap) having a peak.

peaked² or **peaky** adjective pale from illness or tiredness.

peal noun **1** the loud ringing sound of a bell or bells. **2** a loud sound of thunder or laughter. **3** a set of bells. •**verb** ring or sound loudly.

peanut noun **1** an oval edible seed that develops in a pod underground. **2** (**peanuts**) informal a very small sum of money.
□ **peanut butter** a spread made from ground roasted peanuts.

pear noun a green edible fruit which has a narrow top and rounded base.

pearl noun **1** a small hard, shiny white ball that sometimes forms inside the shell of an oyster and has great value as a gem. **2** a thing that is highly valued.
□ **pearl barley** barley that is reduced to small round grains by grinding.
■ **pearly** adjective.

pearlescent adjective seeming to shine with many soft colours, like mother-of-pearl.

peasant noun (in the past, or in poor countries) an agricultural worker.
■ **peasantry** noun.

peat noun a soft brown or black substance formed in damp areas from decayed plants.
■ **peaty** adjective.

pebble noun a small, smooth round stone.
□ **pebble-dash** mortar mixed with small pebbles, used to coat the outside of houses.
■ **pebbly** adjective.

pecan /pee-k'n/ noun the smooth edible nut of a hickory tree of the southern US.

peccadillo /pek-kuh-**dil**-loh/ noun (plural **peccadilloes** or **peccadillos**) a small sin or fault.

peck¹ verb **1** (of a bird) hit or bite something with its beak. **2** kiss someone lightly or casually. •**noun 1** an act of pecking. **2** a light or casual kiss.
□ **pecking order** the order of importance that people or animals give each other within a group.

peck² noun a measure of dry goods, equal to

p

THESAURUS

reimbursement, income.

peace noun **1** *peace at last!* quiet, silence, peace and quiet, hush, stillness, still. **2** *peace of mind:* serenity, peacefulness, tranquillity, calm, calmness, composure, ease, contentment. **3** *we pray for peace:* order, harmony, agreement. **4** *a lasting peace:* treaty, truce, ceasefire, armistice.
OPPOSITES noise, agitation, war.

peaceful adjective **1** *peaceful surroundings:* tranquil, calm, restful, quiet, still, relaxing. **2** *his peaceful mood:* serene, calm, tranquil, composed, placid, at ease, untroubled,

unworried, content. **3** *peaceful relations:* harmonious, on good terms, amicable, friendly, cordial, non-violent.
OPPOSITES noisy, agitated, hostile.

peak noun **1** *the peaks of the mountains:* summit, top, crest, pinnacle, cap. **2** *the highest peak:* mountain, hill, height. **3** *the peak of his career:* height, high point, pinnacle, summit, top, climax, culmination, apex, zenith, acme.
•**verb** *Labour support has peaked:* reach its height, climax, culminate.
•**adjective** *at peak times:* maximum,

a quarter of a bushel.

pecker noun (**keep your pecker up**) Brit. informal remain cheerful.

peckish adjective informal hungry.

pectin noun a substance present in ripe fruits, used as a setting agent in jams and jellies.

pectoral adjective relating to the breast or chest. • noun each of four large paired muscles which cover the front of the ribcage.

peculiar adjective **1** strange or odd. **2** (**peculiar to**) belonging only to.
■ **peculiarly** adverb.

> ☑ -ar, not -er: peculiar.

peculiarity noun (plural **peculiarities**) **1** a feature or habit that is strange or unusual, or that belongs only to a particular person, thing, or place. **2** the state of being peculiar.

pecuniary /pi-**kyoo**-ni-uh-ri/ adjective formal relating to money.

pedagogue /**ped**-uh-gog/ noun formal a teacher.
■ **pedagogy** noun.

pedal noun **1** each of a pair of levers that you press with your foot to make a bicycle move along. **2** a lever that you press with your foot to operate an accelerator, brake, or clutch in a motor vehicle. **3** a similar lever on a piano or organ used to sustain or soften the tone. • verb (**pedals, pedalling, pedalled**; US spelling **pedals, pedaling, pedaled**) work the pedals of a bicycle to move along.

> ! don't confuse **pedal** with **peddle**, which means 'sell goods'.

pedalo /**ped**-uh-loh/ noun (plural **pedalos** or **pedaloes**) Brit. a small pedal-operated pleasure boat.

pedant noun a person who cares too much about small details or rules.
■ **pedantic** adjective **pedantry** noun.

peddle verb (**peddles, peddling, peddled**)
1 sell goods by going from house to house.
2 sell an illegal drug or stolen item.
3 disapproving spread an idea or view widely or persistently.

> ! don't confuse **peddle** with **pedal**.

peddler ⇨ PEDLAR.

pederast /**ped**-uh-rasst/ noun a man who has sexual intercourse with a boy.
■ **pederasty** noun.

pedestal noun **1** the base or support on which a statue or column is mounted.
2 the supporting column of a washbasin or toilet.

pedestrian noun a person who is walking rather than travelling in a vehicle.
• adjective dull.

pediatrics US spelling of PAEDIATRICS.

pedicure noun treatment to improve the appearance of the feet and toenails.

pedigree noun **1** the record of an animal's origins, showing that all the animals from which it is descended are of the same breed. **2** a person's family history and background.

pediment noun the triangular upper part of the front of a classical building, above the columns.

pedlar or **peddler** noun **1** a trader who sells goods by going from house to house.
2 a person who sells illegal drugs or stolen goods.

pedometer /pi-**dom**-i-ter/ noun an instrument for estimating how far you are walking by recording the number of steps you take.

peek verb **1** look quickly or secretly. **2** be just visible. • noun a quick look.

peel verb **1** remove the skin or rind from a

p

THESAURUS

greatest, busiest, highest.

peculiar adjective **1** *something peculiar happened:* strange, unusual, odd, funny, curious, bizarre, weird, eccentric, queer, abnormal, unconventional, outlandish, anomalous, out of the ordinary, unexpected; informal wacky. **2** *customs peculiar to this area:* distinctive, exclusive, unique, characteristic, distinct, individual, typical, special, personal.
OPPOSITES ordinary.

pedantic adjective finicky, fussy, fastidious, dogmatic, purist, hair-splitting, quibbling; informal nit-picking, pernickety.

peddle verb sell, hawk, tout, trade, deal in, traffic in.

pedestrian adjective dull, boring, tedious, monotonous, unremarkable, uninspired, unimaginative, unexciting, routine, commonplace, ordinary, everyday, run-of-the-mill, mundane, humdrum; informal bog-standard.
OPPOSITES exciting.

pedigree noun *a fine pedigree:* ancestry, lineage, line, descent, genealogy, extraction, parentage, bloodline, family tree.
• adjective *a pedigree cat:* pure-bred, full-blooded, thoroughbred.

peel verb **1** *peel and core the fruit:* pare, skin, hull, shell. **2** *the wallpaper was peeling:* flake (off), come off, fall off.
• noun *orange peel:* rind, skin, covering, zest.

fruit or vegetable. **2** remove a thin covering or layer from. **3** (of a surface) come off in small pieces. •noun the outer covering or rind of a fruit or vegetable.

peep[1] verb **1** look quickly and secretly. **2** (**peep out**) be just visible. •noun **1** a quick or secret look. **2** a momentary or partial view of something.
□ **peeping Tom** a person who likes to spy on people undressing or having sex. **peep show** a series of pictures in a box which you look at through a small opening.

peep[2] noun a short, high-pitched sound. •verb make a short, high-pitched sound.

peephole noun a small hole in a door or wall which you can look through.

peer[1] verb (**peers, peering, peered**) **1** look at something with difficulty or concentration. **2** be just visible.

peer[2] noun **1** a member of the nobility in Britain or Ireland. **2** a person who is the same age or has the same social status as you.
□ **peer group** a group of people of approximately the same age, status, and interests.

peerage noun **1** the title and rank of peer or peeress. **2** (**the peerage**) all the peers in Britain or Ireland.

peeress noun **1** a woman holding the rank of a peer in her own right. **2** the wife or widow of a peer.

peerless adjective better than all others.

peeved adjective informal annoyed; irritated.

peevish adjective irritable.

peewit noun Brit. a lapwing.

peg noun **1** a pin or bolt used for hanging things on, securing something in place, or marking a position. **2** a clip for holding things together or hanging up clothes. •verb (**pegs, pegging, pegged**) **1** fix, attach, or mark something with a peg or pegs. **2** fix a price, rate, etc. at a particular level.
□ **off the peg** (of clothes) not made to order; ready-made.

peignoir /**pay**-nwar/ noun a woman's light dressing gown or negligee.

pejorative /pi-**jorr**-uh-tiv/ adjective expressing contempt or disapproval.
■ **pejoratively** adverb.

Pekinese noun (plural **Pekinese**) a small dog with long hair and a snub nose.

pelican noun a large waterbird with a bag of skin hanging from a long bill.
□ **pelican crossing** (in the UK) a pedestrian crossing with traffic lights that are operated by the pedestrians.

pellagra /pel-**lag**-ruh/ noun a disease caused by an inadequate diet, whose symptoms include inflamed skin and diarrhoea.

pellet noun **1** a small compressed mass of a substance. **2** a lightweight bullet or piece of small shot.

pell-mell adjective & adverb in a confused or rushed way.

pellucid /pel-**loo**-sid/ adjective translucent or transparent; clear.

pelmet noun a structure or strip of fabric fitted across the top of a window to conceal the curtain fittings.

pelt[1] verb **1** hurl missiles at. **2** (**pelt down**) fall very heavily.
□ (**at**) **full pelt** as fast as possible.

pelt[2] noun the skin of an animal with the fur, wool, or hair still on it.

pelvis noun the large bony frame at the base of the spine to which the legs are attached.
■ **pelvic** adjective.

pen[1] noun an instrument for writing or drawing with ink. •verb (**pens, penning, penned**) write or compose.
□ **pen name** a name used by a writer that is not their real name.

pen[2] noun a small enclosure for farm animals. •verb (**pens, penning, penned**) **1** put or keep animals in a pen. **2** (**pen someone/thing up** or **in**) shut a person or animal up in a small space.

penal adjective **1** relating to the use of punishment as part of the legal system. **2** very severe.

penalize or **penalise** verb (**penalizes,**

THESAURUS

peep verb *I peeped through the keyhole:* peek, look, sneak a look, glance; informal squint.
•noun *I'll just take a peep:* peek, look, glance; informal squint, dekko.

peer[1] verb *he peered at the manuscript:* look closely, squint, gaze.

peer[2] noun **1** *hereditary peers:* aristocrat, lord, lady, noble, nobleman, noblewoman. **2** *his academic peers:* equal, fellow, contemporary.

peg noun *a tent peg:* pin, nail, dowel.
•verb **1** *the flysheet is pegged to the ground:*

fix, pin, attach, fasten, secure. **2** *we decided to peg our prices:* set, hold, fix, freeze, keep down, hold down.

pen[1] verb *he penned a number of articles:* write, compose, draft, dash off, scribble.

pen[2] noun *a sheep pen:* enclosure, fold, pound, compound, stockade, sty, coop; N. Amer. corral.
•verb *the hostages were penned up in a basement:* confine, coop, cage, shut, box, lock, trap, imprison, incarcerate.

penalize verb **1** *if you break the rules you will be penalized:* punish, discipline. **2** *a* penalizing, penalized) **1** give someone a penalty or punishment. **2** put in an unfavourable position.

penalty noun (plural **penalties**) **1** a punishment given to someone for breaking a law, rule, or contract. **2** something unpleasant suffered as a result of an action or circumstance. **3** (also **penalty kick**) Soccer a free shot at the goal awarded to the attacking team after a foul within the area around the goal (the **penalty area**).

penance noun **1** something that you yourself do or that a priest gives you to do as punishment for having done wrong. **2** a religious act in which someone confesses their sins to a priest and is given penance or formal forgiveness.

pence plural of PENNY.

> **!** it is wrong to use **pence** in the singular to mean 'penny'; say one penny not one pence.

penchant /pon-shon/ noun a strong liking for something.

pencil noun an instrument for writing or drawing, consisting of a thin stick of graphite enclosed in a wooden case. • verb (**pencils, pencilling, pencilled**; US spelling **pencils, penciling, penciled**) **1** write or draw something with a pencil. **2** (**pencil something in**) enter a time or date in your diary on the understanding that it might have to be changed later.

pendant noun **1** a piece of jewellery worn hanging from a chain around the neck. **2** a light designed to hang from the ceiling. • adjective (also **pendent**) hanging downwards.

pending adjective **1** waiting to be decided or settled. **2** about to happen. • preposition awaiting the outcome of.

pendulous adjective hanging down; drooping.

pendulum noun a weight hung from a

fixed point so that it can swing freely, used in regulating the mechanism of a clock.

penetrate verb (**penetrates, penetrating, penetrated**) **1** force a way into or through. **2** gain access to an enemy organization or a competitor's market. **3** understand something. **4** (**penetrating**) (of a sound) clearly heard through or above other sounds. **5** (of a man) insert the penis into the vagina or anus of a sexual partner.
■ **penetration** noun **penetrative** adjective.

penfriend noun a person with whom you form a friendship through exchanging letters.

penguin noun a black and white seabird living in the Antarctic and unable to fly.

penicillin noun a type of antibiotic.

peninsula noun a long, narrow piece of land projecting into the sea.
■ **peninsular** adjective.

penis noun the male organ used for urinating and having sex.

penitent adjective feeling sorrow and regret for having done wrong. • noun a person who is doing penance.
■ **penitence** noun **penitential** adjective.

penitentiary /pen-i-ten-shuh-ri/ noun (plural **penitentiaries**) N. Amer. a prison for people convicted of serious crimes.

penknife noun a small knife with a blade which folds into the handle.

pennant noun a long, narrow pointed flag.

penne /pen-nay/ plural noun pasta in the form of short wide tubes.

penniless adjective having no money.

pennon = PENNANT.

penny noun (plural **pennies** (for separate coins); **pence** (for a sum of money)) **1** a British bronze coin worth one hundredth of a pound. **2** (in the past) a British coin worth one twelfth of a shilling and 240th of a pound.
□ **penny-farthing** an early type of bicycle

p

new tax would penalize the poor: handicap, disadvantage, discriminate against.
OPPOSITES reward, benefit.

penalty noun punishment, sanction, fine, forfeit, sentence.
OPPOSITES reward.

pending adjective **1** nine cases were still pending: unresolved, undecided, unsettled, up in the air, ongoing, outstanding; informal on the back burner. **2** with a general election pending: imminent, impending, about to happen, forthcoming, on the way, coming, approaching, looming, near, on the horizon, in the offing.
• preposition they were released on bail pending an appeal: awaiting, until.

penetrate verb **1** the knife penetrated his lungs: pierce, puncture, enter, perforate, stab, gore. **2** they penetrated enemy lines: infiltrate, slip through, enter. **3** his words finally penetrated: register, sink in, become clear, fall into place; informal click.

penetrating adjective **1** a penetrating wind: cold, cutting, biting, keen, sharp, harsh, raw, freezing, chill, bitter. **2** a penetrating voice: shrill, strident, piercing, ear-splitting. **3** her penetrating gaze: intent, searching, piercing, probing, sharp, keen. **4** a penetrating analysis: perceptive, insightful, keen, sharp, intelligent, clever, smart, incisive, trenchant, astute.
OPPOSITES mild, soft.

with a very large front wheel and a small rear wheel. **penny-pinching** unwilling to spend money.

pension[1] /pen-sh'n/ noun a regular payment made to retired people, widows, etc., either by the state or from an investment fund. •verb (**pension someone off**) dismiss someone from employment and pay them a pension.
■ **pensionable** adjective **pensioner** noun.

pension[2] /pon-syon/ noun a small hotel in France and other European countries.

pensive adjective thinking deeply about something.
■ **pensively** adverb.

pentacle noun a pentagram.

pentagon noun **1** a figure with five straight sides and five angles. **2** (**the Pentagon**) the headquarters of the US Department of Defense.

pentagram noun a five-pointed star used as a magical symbol.

pentameter /pen-tam-i-ter/ noun a line of poetry with five stressed syllables.

Pentateuch /pen-tuh-tyook/ noun the first five books of the Old Testament and Hebrew Scriptures.

pentathlon noun an athletic event consisting of five different activities.
■ **pentathlete** noun.

Pentecost noun **1** the Christian festival celebrating the coming of the Holy Spirit to the disciples of Jesus after his Ascension. **2** a Jewish festival that takes place fifty days after the second day of Passover.

Pentecostal adjective having to do with a Christian movement which emphasizes the gifts of the Holy Spirit, e.g. the healing of the sick.

penthouse noun a flat on the top floor of a tall building.

pent-up adjective not expressed or released.

penultimate adjective last but one.

penumbra /pi-num-bruh/ noun the partially shaded outer part of a shadow.

penurious /pi-nyoor-i-uhss/ adjective formal very poor.

penury /pen-yuu-ri/ noun extreme poverty.

peony /pee-uh-ni/ noun a plant with large red, pink, or white flowers.

people plural noun **1** human beings in general. **2** (**the people**) all those living in a country or society. **3** (plural **peoples**) the members of a particular nation, community, or ethnic group. •verb (**peoples, peopling, peopled**) live in a place or fill it with people.

pep informal verb (**peps, pepping, pepped**) (**pep someone/thing up**) make someone or something more lively. •noun liveliness.
□ **pep talk** a talk given to someone to make them feel braver or more enthusiastic.

pepper noun **1** a hot-tasting powder made from peppercorns, used to flavour food. **2** the fruit of a tropical American plant, of which sweet peppers and chilli peppers are varieties. •verb (**peppers, peppering, peppered**) **1** season food with pepper. **2** (**pepper something with**) scatter large amounts of something over an area. **3** hit a place repeatedly with small missiles or gunshot.
■ **pepperiness** noun **peppery** adjective.

peppercorn noun the dried berry of a climbing vine, used whole as a spice or crushed to make pepper.
□ **peppercorn rent** a very low rent.

peppermint noun **1** a plant of the mint family whose leaves and oil are used as a flavouring in food. **2** a sweet flavoured with peppermint oil.

pepperoni /pep-puh-roh-ni/ noun a dried sausage made from beef and pork and seasoned with pepper.

peptic adjective relating to digestion.
□ **peptic ulcer** an ulcer in the lining of the stomach or small intestine.

THESAURUS

pension noun old-age pension, retirement pension, superannuation, allowance, benefit, support, welfare.

pensioner noun retired person, old-age pensioner, OAP, senior citizen; N. Amer. senior, retiree, golden ager.

people plural noun **1** *crowds of people:* human beings, persons, individuals, humans, mortals, living souls, personages, {men, women, and children}; informal folk. **2** *the British people:* citizens, subjects, electors, voters, taxpayers, residents, inhabitants, public, citizenry, nation, population, populace. **3** *a man of the people:* the common people, the

proletariat, the masses, the populace, the rank and file; disapproving the hoi polloi; informal, disapproving the proles, the plebs. **4** *her people don't live far away:* family, parents, relatives, relations, folk, kinsfolk, flesh and blood, nearest and dearest; informal folks. **5** (singular) *a proud people:* race, ethnic group, tribe, clan, nation.
•verb *an ancient region peopled by warring clans:* populate, settle (in), colonize, inhabit, live in, occupy.

pepper verb **1** *stars peppered the desert skies:* sprinkle, fleck, dot, spot, stipple. **2** *gunfire peppered the area:* bombard, pelt, shower, rain down on, strafe, rake, blitz.

p

per preposition **1** for each. **2** by means of. **3** (as per) according to.

perambulate verb (perambulates, perambulating, perambulated) formal walk or travel from place to place.
■ **perambulation** noun.

perambulator noun dated a pram.

per annum adverb for each year.

per capita adverb & adjective for each person.

perceive verb (perceives, perceiving, perceived) **1** become aware of something through starting to see, smell, or hear it. **2** (perceive something as) understand or interpret something in a particular way.
■ **perceivable** adjective.

☑ remember, *i* before *e* except after *c*: perce*i*ve.

per cent or US **percent** adverb by a stated amount in or for every hundred. ● noun one part in every hundred.

percentage noun **1** a rate, number, or amount in each hundred. **2** a proportion or share of a whole.

percentile /per-sen-tyl/ noun Statistics each of 100 equal groups into which a population can be divided.

perceptible adjective able to be noticed or felt.
■ **perceptibly** adverb.

perception noun **1** the ability to see, hear, or become aware of something. **2** a particular understanding of something. **3** the process of perceiving.

perceptive adjective having a good understanding of people and situations.
■ **perceptively** adverb.

perceptual adjective relating to the ability to perceive.

perch¹ noun **1** a branch, bar, or ledge on which a bird rests or roosts. **2** a high or narrow seat or resting place. ● verb **1** sit or

rest somewhere. **2** place or balance something somewhere.

perch² noun (plural **perch** or **perches**) a freshwater fish with a spiny fin on its back.

perchance adverb old use perhaps.

percipient adjective having good insight or understanding.

percolate verb (percolates, percolating, percolated) **1** filter through a porous surface or substance. **2** (of information or ideas) spread gradually through a group of people. **3** prepare coffee in a percolator.
■ **percolation** noun.

percolator noun a machine for making coffee, consisting of a pot in which boiling water is circulated through a small chamber that holds the ground beans.

percussion noun musical instruments that you play by hitting or shaking them.
■ **percussionist** noun.

perdition noun (in Christian thinking) a state of eternal damnation into which people who have sinned and not repented pass when they die.

peregrinations plural noun old use journeys or wanderings from place to place.

peregrine noun a powerful falcon with a bluish-grey back and wings.

peremptory adjective insisting on immediate attention or obedience.
■ **peremptorily** adverb.

perennial adjective **1** lasting or doing something for a very long time. **2** (of a plant) living for several years. ● noun a perennial plant.
■ **perennially** adverb.

perestroika /pe-ri-stroy-kuh/ noun (in the former Soviet Union) the economic and political reforms introduced during the 1980s.

perfect adjective /per-fikt/ **1** having all the

P

THESAURUS

perceive verb **1** *he perceived a tear in her eye:* see, discern, detect, catch sight of, spot, observe, notice. **2** *he was perceived as too negative:* regard, look on, view, think of, consider, judge, deem.

perception noun **1** *popular perceptions about old age:* impression, idea, conception, notion, thought, belief. **2** *he talks with great perception:* insight, perceptiveness, understanding, intelligence, intuition, incisiveness.

perceptive adjective insightful, discerning, sensitive, intuitive, observant, penetrating, intelligent, clever, canny, keen, sharp, astute, shrewd, quick, smart, acute; informal on the ball; N. Amer. informal heads-up.
OPPOSITES obtuse.

perch verb **1** *a swallow perched on the telegraph wire:* sit, rest, alight, settle, land, roost. **2** *she perched her glasses on her nose:* put, place, set, rest, balance.

perennial adjective lasting, enduring, abiding, long-lasting, long-lived, perpetual, continuing, continual, recurring.
OPPOSITES ephemeral.

perfect adjective **1** *a perfect wife:* ideal, model, faultless, flawless, consummate, exemplary, best, ultimate, copybook. **2** *in perfect condition:* flawless, mint, as good as new, pristine, immaculate, optimum, prime, peak; informal tip-top, A1. **3** *a perfect copy:* exact, precise, accurate, faithful, true; Brit. informal spot on; N. Amer. informal on the money. **4** *the perfect Christmas present:*

parts and qualities that are needed or wanted, and no flaws or weaknesses. **2** total; complete: *it made perfect sense.* **3** Grammar (of a verb) referring to a completed action or to a state in the past. •verb /per-**fekt**/ make something perfect. ■ **perfectly** adverb.

perfection noun the process of perfecting, or the state of being perfect.

perfectionism noun the refusal to be satisfied with something unless it is done perfectly. ■ **perfectionist** noun & adjective.

perfidious /per-**fid**-i-uhss/ adjective deceitful and disloyal.

perfidy /per-fi-di/ noun literary deceit; disloyalty.

perforate verb (**perforates, perforating, perforated**) pierce and make a hole or holes in. ■ **perforation** noun.

perforce adverb formal necessarily; inevitably.

perform verb **1** carry out an action, task, or function. **2** work, function, or do something to a particular standard. **3** entertain an audience by playing a piece of music, acting in a play, etc. ■ **performer** noun.

performance noun **1** an act of performing a play, piece of music, etc. **2** the process of performing. **3** informal a fuss. **4** the capabilities of a machine or product. □ **performance art** an art form that combines visual art with drama.

perfume /per-fyoom/ noun **1** a sweet-smelling liquid put on the body. **2** a pleasant smell. •verb /per-**fyoom**/ (**perfumes, perfuming, perfumed**) **1** give a pleasant smell to. **2** put perfume on or in. ■ **perfumery** noun.

perfunctory adjective carried out without much care or effort. ■ **perfunctorily** adverb.

pergola /per-guh-luh/ noun an arched structure forming a framework for climbing plants.

perhaps adverb possibly; maybe.

peril noun a situation of serious and immediate danger.

perilous adjective full of danger or risk. ■ **perilously** adverb.

perimeter noun the boundary or outside edge of something.

perinatal /per-i-**nay**-t'l/ adjective at the time immediately before and after a birth.

perineum /pe-ri-**nee**-uhm/ noun (plural **perinea**) the area between the anus and the genitals.

THESAURUS

ideal, just right, appropriate, fitting, suitable, tailor-made, very; Brit. informal spot on, just the job. **5** *she felt a perfect idiot:* **absolute,** complete, total, real, out-and-out, thorough, downright, utter; Brit. informal right; Austral./NZ informal fair.
•verb *he's perfecting his style:* **improve,** polish (up), hone, refine, brush up, fine-tune.

perfection noun the ideal, a paragon, the last word, the ultimate; informal the tops, the bee's knees.

perfectly adverb **1** *a perfectly cooked meal:* **superbly,** superlatively, excellently, flawlessly, faultlessly, to perfection, immaculately, exquisitely, consummately; N. Amer. to a fare-thee-well; informal like a dream, to a T. **2** *we understand each other perfectly:* **absolutely,** completely, totally, altogether, entirely, wholly, fully, in every respect.
OPPOSITES badly, partly.

perform verb **1** *duties to perform:* **carry out,** do, execute, discharge, conduct, implement; informal pull off. **2** *the car performs well:* **function,** work, operate, run, go, respond, behave, act. **3** *the play was performed in Britain:* **stage,** put on, present, mount, act, produce. **4** *the band performed live:* **play,** sing, appear.
OPPOSITES neglect.

performance noun **1** *the evening performance:* **show,** production, showing, presentation, staging, concert, recital; informal gig. **2** *their performance was excellent:* **rendition,** interpretation, playing, acting. **3** *the performance of his duty:* **carrying out,** execution, discharge, completion, fulfilment. **4** *the performance of the processor:* **functioning,** working, operation, running, behaviour, response, economy.

performer noun actor, actress, artiste, artist, entertainer, trouper, player, musician, singer, dancer, comic, comedian, comedienne.

perfume noun **1** *a bottle of perfume:* **scent,** fragrance, eau de toilette, toilet water. **2** *the heady perfume of lilacs:* **smell,** scent, fragrance, aroma, bouquet.

perhaps adverb maybe, for all you know, it could be, it may be, it's possible, possibly, conceivably; N. English happen.

peril noun danger, jeopardy, risk, hazard, menace, threat.
OPPOSITES safety.

perimeter noun boundary, border, limits, bounds, edge, margin, fringe(s), periphery.
OPPOSITES centre.

p

period noun **1** a length or portion of time. **2** a lesson in a school. **3** (also **menstrual period**) a flow of blood each month from the lining of a woman's womb. **4** N. Amer. a full stop. • adjective belonging to or characteristic of a past historical time. □ period piece an object made or a book or play set in an earlier period.

periodic adjective appearing or happening at intervals. □ periodic table a table of all the chemical elements.

periodical adjective **1** happening or appearing at intervals. **2** (of a magazine or newspaper) published at regular intervals. • noun a periodical magazine or newspaper. ■ periodically adverb.

peripatetic /pe-ri-puh-**tet**-ik/ adjective travelling from place to place.

peripheral /puh-**rif**-uh-ruhl/ adjective **1** relating to or situated on an edge or boundary. **2** outside the most important part of something; marginal. ■ peripherally adverb.

periphery /puh-**rif**-uh-ri/ noun (plural **peripheries**) **1** the outside edge or boundary of something. **2** an area of activity that is outside the most important part of something.

periscope noun a device consisting of a tube attached to a set of mirrors, through which you can see things that are above or behind something else.

perish verb **1** die. **2** be completely ruined or destroyed. **3** (of rubber or a similar material) rot or decay. **4** (**be perished**) Brit. informal feel very cold. **5** (**perishing**) Brit. informal very cold.

perishable adjective (of food) not able to be kept beyond a certain time because it will rot or decay.

peristalsis noun the contraction and relaxation of muscles in the digestive

system and intestines, creating wave-like movements which push food through the body.

peritoneum /pe-ri-tuh-**nee**-uhm/ noun (plural **peritoneums** or **peritonea** /pe-ri-tuh-**nee**-uh/) a membrane lining the inside of the abdomen. ■ peritoneal adjective.

peritonitis noun inflammation of the peritoneum.

periwinkle noun **1** a plant with purple flowers and glossy leaves. **2** = WINKLE.

perjure verb (**perjures**, **perjuring**, **perjured**) (**perjure yourself**) tell a lie in court after swearing to tell the truth.

perjury /**per**-juh-ri/ noun the offence of deliberately telling a lie in court after swearing to tell the truth.

perk¹ verb (**perk up**) become more cheerful or lively.

perk² noun informal an extra benefit given to an employee in addition to their wages.

perky adjective (**perkier**, **perkiest**) cheerful and lively.

perm noun (also **permanent wave**) a method of setting the hair in waves or curls and treating it with chemicals so that the style lasts for several months. • verb treat hair in such a way.

permafrost noun a layer of soil beneath the surface that remains below freezing point throughout the year.

permanent adjective lasting for a long time or forever. ■ permanence noun permanently adverb.

☑ permanent, not -ant.

permeable adjective allowing liquids or gases to pass through.

permeate verb (**permeates**, **permeating**, **permeated**) spread throughout.

permissible adjective permitted.

p

THESAURUS

period noun **1** *a six-week period:* time, spell, interval, stretch, term, span, phase, bout; Brit. informal patch. **2** *the post-war period:* era, age, epoch, time, days, years.

periodic adjective regular, at fixed intervals, recurrent, recurring, repeated, cyclical, seasonal, occasional, intermittent, sporadic, odd.

periodical noun journal, magazine, newspaper, paper, review, digest, gazette, newsletter, organ; informal mag, glossy.

peripheral adjective secondary, subsidiary, incidental, tangential, marginal, minor, unimportant, ancillary.
OPPOSITES central.

perish verb **1** *millions of soldiers perished:* die, lose your life, be killed, fall, be lost;

informal buy it. **2** *the rubber had perished:* go bad, spoil, rot, decay, decompose.

perk noun fringe benefit, advantage, bonus, extra, plus; informal freebie.

permanent adjective **1** *permanent brain damage:* lasting, enduring, indefinite, continuing, constant, irreparable, irreversible, lifelong, indelible, standing. **2** *a permanent job:* long-term, stable, secure.
OPPOSITES temporary.

permanently adverb **1** *the attack left her permanently disabled:* forever, for all time, for good, irreversibly, incurably, irreparably, indelibly; informal for keeps. **2** *I was permanently hungry:* continually, constantly, perpetually, always.

permission noun the act of allowing someone to do something.

permissive adjective allowing someone a lot of freedom of behaviour.
■ **permissiveness** noun.

permit verb /per-**mit**/ (**permits, permitting, permitted**) **1** say that someone is allowed to do something. **2** make something possible. •**noun** /**per**-mit/ an official document saying that someone is allowed to do something or go somewhere.

permutation noun each of several possible ways in which a number of things can be ordered or arranged.

pernicious adjective having a harmful effect.

pernickety adjective fussy.

peroration noun the concluding part of a speech.

peroxide noun (also **hydrogen peroxide**) a chemical that is used as a bleach or disinfectant.

perpendicular adjective at an angle of 90° to the ground, or to another line or surface. •**noun** a perpendicular line.

perpetrate verb (**perpetrates, perpetrating, perpetrated**) carry out a bad or illegal action.
■ **perpetration** noun **perpetrator** noun.

perpetual adjective **1** never ending or changing. **2** so frequent as to seem continual.
■ **perpetually** adverb.

perpetuate verb (**perpetuates, perpetuating, perpetuated**) cause something to continue indefinitely.

■ **perpetuation** noun.

perpetuity noun (plural **perpetuities**) the state of lasting forever.

perplex verb puzzle someone very much.

perplexity noun (plural **perplexities**) **1** the state of being puzzled. **2** a puzzling situation or thing.

perquisite /**per**-kwi-zit/ noun formal a special right or privilege.

perry noun (plural **perries**) an alcoholic drink made from pear juice.

per se /per **say**/ adverb in itself.

persecute verb (**persecutes, persecuting, persecuted**) **1** treat badly over a long period. **2** harass.
■ **persecution** noun **persecutor** noun.

persevere verb continue doing something in spite of difficulty or lack of success.
■ **perseverance** noun.

Persian noun **1** a person from Persia (now Iran). **2** the language of ancient Persia or modern Iran. **3** a breed of cat with long hair. •**adjective** relating to Persia or Iran.

persiflage /**per**-si-flah*zh*/ noun formal light teasing or joking.

persimmon /per-**sim**-muhn/ noun a fruit that looks like a large tomato but is very sweet.

persist verb **1** continue doing something in spite of difficulty or opposition. **2** continue to exist.

persistent adjective **1** continuing to do something in spite of difficulty or opposition. **2** continuing or recurring over

p

THESAURUS

permission noun authorization, consent, leave, authority, sanction, licence, dispensation, assent, agreement, approval, blessing, clearance; informal the go-ahead, the green light, say-so.
OPPOSITES ban.

permit verb *other synthetic drugs would be permitted:* allow, let, authorize, sanction, grant, license, consent to, assent to; informal give the go-ahead to, give the green light to.
OPPOSITES ban.
•**noun** *a work permit:* authorization, licence, pass, ticket, warrant, passport, visa.

perpetual adjective **1** *a perpetual state of fear:* constant, permanent, uninterrupted, continuous, unremitting, unending, everlasting, eternal, unceasing, without end, persistent, lasting, abiding.
2 *perpetual nagging:* interminable, incessant, ceaseless, endless, relentless, unrelenting, persistent, continual, continuous, non-stop, never-ending, repeated, unremitting, round-the-clock,

unabating; informal eternal.
OPPOSITES temporary, intermittent.

perplexing adjective puzzling, baffling, mystifying, mysterious, bewildering, confusing, disconcerting, worrying.

persecute verb **1** *they were persecuted for their beliefs:* oppress, abuse, victimize, ill-treat, mistreat, maltreat, torment, torture. **2** *she was persecuted by the press:* harass, hound, plague, badger, harry, intimidate, pick on, pester; informal hassle.

persist verb **1** *Corbett persisted with his questioning:* persevere, continue, carry on, go on, keep on, keep going, hammer away, keep at it; informal soldier on, plug away. **2** *if dry weather persists, water the lawn thoroughly:* continue, hold, carry on, last, keep on, remain, linger, stay, endure.
OPPOSITES give up, stop.

persistence noun perseverance, tenacity, determination, staying power, endurance, doggedness, stamina; informal stickability; N. Amer. informal stick-to-it-iveness; formal pertinacity.

a long period.
■ **persistence** noun **persistently** adverb.

> ☑ persist**ent**, not -*ant*.

person noun (plural **people** or **persons**) **1** an individual human being. **2** a person's body. **3** Grammar a category used in classifying pronouns and verb forms according to whether they indicate the speaker (**first person**), the person spoken to (**second person**), or a third party (**third person**).
□ **in person** physically present.

persona /per-soh-nuh/ noun (plural **personas** or **personae** /per-soh-nee/) the part of a person's character that is revealed to other people.

personable adjective having a pleasant appearance and manner.

personage noun a person of importance or high status.

personal adjective **1** having to do with or belonging to a particular person. **2** done by a particular person themselves, rather than someone acting for them. **3** concerning a person's private rather than professional or public life. **4** referring to someone's character or appearance in a way that is offensive. **5** relating to a person's body.
□ **personal pronoun** Grammar each of the pronouns that show person, gender, number, and case (such as *I, you, he, she,* etc.). **personal stereo** a small portable cassette or compact disc player, used with headphones.
■ **personally** adverb.

personality noun (plural **personalities**) **1** the qualities that form a person's character.

2 qualities that make someone interesting or popular. **3** a celebrity.

personalize or **personalise** verb (**personalizes, personalizing, personalized**) **1** design or produce something to meet someone's individual requirements. **2** cause an issue or argument to become concerned with personalities or feelings.

persona non grata /per-soh-nuh nohn grah-tuh/ noun a person who is not welcome in a place.

personify verb (**personifies, personifying, personified**) **1** give human characteristics to something that is not human. **2** be an example of a quality or characteristic.
■ **personification** noun.

personnel plural noun people employed in an organization.

perspective noun **1** the art of representing things in a picture so that they seem to have height, width, depth, and relative distance. **2** a way of seeing something. **3** understanding of how important things are in relation to others.

perspex noun trademark a tough transparent plastic.

perspicacious adjective quickly gaining insight into things.
■ **perspicacity** noun.

perspicuous adjective **1** clearly expressed and easily understood. **2** (of a person) expressing things clearly.

perspiration noun **1** sweat. **2** the process of sweating.

perspire verb (**perspires, perspiring, perspired**) produce sweat through the pores of your skin.

p

persistent adjective **1** *a very persistent man:* tenacious, determined, resolute, dogged, tireless, indefatigable, insistent, unrelenting; formal pertinacious. **2** *persistent rain:* constant, continuous, continuing, continual, non-stop, never-ending, steady, uninterrupted, unbroken, interminable, incessant, endless, unending, unrelenting. **3** *a persistent cough:* chronic, nagging, frequent, repeated, habitual.
OPPOSITES irresolute, intermittent.

person noun human being, individual, man, woman, human, being, living soul, mortal, creature; informal type, sort, beggar, cookie.
□ **in person physically,** in the flesh, personally, yourself.

personal adjective **1** *a highly personal style:* distinctive, characteristic, unique, individual, idiosyncratic. **2** *a personal appearance:* in person, in the flesh, actual, live, physical. **3** *his personal life:* private, intimate. **4** *personal remarks:* derogatory, disparaging, belittling, insulting, rude,

disrespectful, offensive, pejorative.
OPPOSITES common, public, complimentary.

personality noun **1** *her cheerful personality:* character, nature, disposition, temperament, make-up, psyche. **2** *she had loads of personality:* charisma, magnetism, character, charm, presence. **3** *a famous personality:* celebrity, VIP, star, superstar, big name, somebody, leading light, luminary, notable; informal celeb.
OPPOSITES nobody.

personally adverb **1** *I'd like to thank him personally:* in person, yourself. **2** *every pupil is known personally:* individually, specially. **3** *personally, I like it:* for my part, for myself, as far as I am concerned, subjectively.

personnel noun staff, employees, workforce, workers, labour force, manpower, human resources.

perspective noun outlook, view, viewpoint, point of view, standpoint, position, stand, stance, angle, slant, attitude.

persuade verb (**persuades, persuading, persuaded**) use reasoning or argument to make someone do or believe something.

persuasion noun **1** the process of persuading or of being persuaded. **2** a belief or set of beliefs.

persuasive adjective **1** good at persuading someone to do or believe something. **2** providing evidence or reasoning that makes you believe something.
■ **persuasively** adverb.

pert adjective **1** attractively lively or cheeky. **2** (of a bodily feature) attractively small and firm.

pertain verb (**pertain to**) be appropriate, related, or relevant to.

pertinacious adjective formal persistent.
■ **pertinacity** noun.

pertinent adjective relevant or appropriate.
■ **pertinence** noun **pertinently** adverb.

perturb verb make someone worried or anxious.
■ **perturbation** noun.

peruse verb (**peruses, perusing, perused**) formal read or examine thoroughly or carefully.
■ **perusal** noun.

Peruvian /puh-**roo**-vi-uhn/ noun a person from Peru. •adjective relating to Peru.

pervade verb (**pervades, pervading, pervaded**) spread or be present throughout.

pervasive adjective spreading widely through something.
■ **pervasively** adverb **pervasiveness** noun.

perverse adjective **1** deliberately choosing to behave in a way that other people find unacceptable. **2** contrary to what is accepted or expected.
■ **perversely** adverb **perversity** noun.

perversion noun **1** the action of perverting. **2** abnormal or unacceptable sexual behaviour.

pervert verb **1** change the form or meaning of something in a way that distorts it. **2** make someone perverted. •noun a person whose sexual behaviour is abnormal and unacceptable.

perverted adjective sexually abnormal or unacceptable.

pervious /per-vi-uhss/ adjective allowing water to pass through.

peseta /puh-**say**-tuh/ noun the former basic unit of money in Spain.

pesky adjective informal annoying.

peso /**pay**-soh/ noun (plural **pesos**) the basic unit of money of several Latin American countries.

pessary noun (plural **pessaries**) a solid medical preparation designed to dissolve after being inserted into the vagina, used to treat infection or as a contraceptive.

pessimism noun a tendency to expect the worst to happen.
■ **pessimist** noun **pessimistic** adjective **pessimistically** adverb.

pest noun **1** a destructive insect or other animal that attacks plants, crops, or livestock. **2** informal an annoying person or thing.

p THESAURUS

persuade verb **1** *he persuaded her to go with him:* prevail on, talk into, coax, convince, get, induce, win over, bring round, influence, sway; informal sweet-talk. **2** *lack of money persuaded them to abandon the scheme:* cause, lead, move, dispose, incline.
OPPOSITES dissuade, deter.

persuasion noun **1** *Monica needed a lot of persuasion:* coaxing, urging, inducement, convincing, encouragement, enticement; informal sweet-talking. **2** *various religious persuasions:* group, grouping, sect, denomination, party, camp, side, faction, school of thought, belief, creed, faith.

persuasive adjective convincing, compelling, effective, telling, forceful, powerful, eloquent, impressive, sound, cogent, valid, strong, plausible, credible.
OPPOSITES unconvincing.

pertinent adjective relevant, to the point, apposite, appropriate, suitable, applicable, material, germane.
OPPOSITES irrelevant.

perverse adjective **1** *he is being deliberately*

perverse: awkward, contrary, difficult, unreasonable, uncooperative, unhelpful, obstructive, stubborn, obstinate; Brit. informal bloody-minded, bolshie. **2** *a verdict that is manifestly perverse:* illogical, irrational, wrong-headed.
OPPOSITES accommodating, reasonable.

pervert verb *perverting the course of justice:* distort, warp, corrupt, subvert, twist, bend, abuse, divert.
•noun *a nasty pervert:* deviant, degenerate; informal perv, dirty old man, sicko.

perverted adjective unnatural, deviant, warped, twisted, abnormal, unhealthy, depraved, perverse, aberrant, debased, degenerate; informal sick, kinky.

pessimistic adjective gloomy, negative, defeatist, downbeat, cynical, bleak, fatalistic, depressed.
OPPOSITES optimistic.

pest noun nuisance, annoyance, irritant, thorn in your flesh/side, trial, menace, trouble, problem, worry, bother; informal pain in the neck, headache.

pester verb (pesters, pestering, pestered) annoy someone with repeated questions or requests.

pesticide noun a substance for destroying insects or other pests.

pestilence noun old use a disease that spreads widely and causes many deaths.
■ **pestilent** adjective.

pestilential adjective **1** old use relating to or causing a pestilence. **2** informal annoying.

pestle /pess-uhl/ noun a small, heavy tool with a rounded end, used for grinding substances in a mortar.

pesto noun a sauce of crushed basil leaves, pine nuts, garlic, Parmesan cheese, and olive oil, served with pasta.

pet noun **1** an animal or bird that you keep for pleasure. **2** a person treated with special favour. • adjective favourite. • verb (pets, petting, petted) **1** stroke or pat an animal. **2** caress someone sexually.
□ **pet name** a name used to express fondness or familiarity.

petal noun each of the segments forming the outer part of a flower.

petard /pi-tard/ noun (be hoist with your own petard) have problems when your schemes against other people backfire on you.

peter verb (peters, petering, petered) (peter out) gradually come to an end.

petite adjective (of a woman) small and dainty.

petit four /puh-ti for/ noun (plural petits fours /puh-ti forz/) a very small fancy cake, biscuit, or sweet.

petition noun **1** an appeal or request, especially a written one signed by a large number of people and presented formally to someone in authority. **2** Law an application to a court for a writ, legal action, etc. • verb make or present a petition to.

petrel noun a seabird that flies far from land.

Petri dish noun a shallow transparent dish with a flat lid, used in laboratories.

petrify verb (petrifies, petrifying, petrified) **1** make someone so frightened that they cannot move. **2** change organic matter into stone.

petrochemical adjective relating to petroleum and natural gas. • noun a chemical obtained from petroleum and natural gas.

petrol noun Brit. a liquid obtained by refining petroleum, used as fuel in motor vehicles.
□ **petrol bomb** a simple firebomb consisting of a bottle containing petrol and a cloth wick.

petroleum noun an oil that is refined to produce fuels including petrol, paraffin, and diesel oil.

petticoat noun a woman's light undergarment in the form of a skirt or dress.

pettifogging adjective petty; trivial.

pettish adjective childishly sulky.
■ **pettishly** adverb.

petty adjective (pettier, pettiest) **1** of little importance. **2** too concerned with unimportant things. **3** minor.
□ **petty cash** a store of money that is available for spending on small items.
petty officer a rank of naval officer.
■ **pettiness** noun.

petulant adjective childishly sulky or bad-tempered.
■ **petulance** noun **petulantly** adverb.

petunia noun a plant with white, purple, or red funnel-shaped flowers.

pew noun **1** a long wooden bench with a back, arranged with others in rows to provide seating in a church. **2** Brit. informal a seat.

pewter noun a metal made by mixing tin with copper and antimony.

pfennig /pfen-nig/ noun a former unit of money in Germany, equal to one hundredth of a mark.

PG abbreviation Brit. (in film classification) parental guidance.

pH noun a figure expressing how acid or alkaline a substance is.

p

---

pester verb badger, hound, harass, plague, annoy, bother, harry; informal hassle, bug.

pet adjective **1** *a pet lamb:* tame, domesticated, companion; Brit. house-trained; N. Amer. housebroken. **2** *his pet theory:* favourite, favoured, cherished, particular, special, personal.
• verb **1** *the cats came to be petted:* stroke, caress, fondle, pat, tickle. **2** *couples petting in their cars:* cuddle, embrace, caress, kiss; informal canoodle, neck, smooch; Brit. informal snog; N. Amer. informal make out.

petition noun *2,500 people have signed a*

petition: appeal, round robin, letter, request, entreaty, application, plea.
• verb *the islanders petitioned the government to help them:* appeal to, request, ask, call on, entreat, beg, implore, plead with, apply to, press, urge.

petty adjective **1** *petty regulations:* trivial, trifling, minor, insignificant, paltry, negligible, unimportant, inconsequential, footling; informal piffling. **2** *a petty form of revenge:* small-minded, mean, shabby, spiteful.
OPPOSITES important, magnanimous.

phalanx noun (plural **phalanxes**) a group of people standing or moving forward closely together.

phallic adjective relating to or resembling a penis.

phallus noun (plural **phalli** /**fal**-lee/ or **phalluses**) a penis.

phantasm noun literary a thing that exists only in the imagination.

phantasmagoria noun a sequence of real or imaginary images like that seen in a dream.

phantom noun **1** a ghost. **2** a thing that exists only in the imagination. •**adjective** not really existing.

pharaoh /**fair**-oh/ noun a ruler in ancient Egypt.

☑ remember, -*aoh*, not -*oah*: phar*aoh*.

Pharisee noun a member of an ancient Jewish sect who followed religious laws very strictly.

pharmaceutical adjective relating to medicinal drugs. •**noun** a medicinal drug.

pharmacist noun a person who is qualified to prepare and dispense medicinal drugs.

pharmacology noun the branch of medicine concerned with drugs.
■ **pharmacological** adjective **pharmacologist** noun.

pharmacy noun (plural **pharmacies**) **1** a place where medicinal drugs are prepared or sold. **2** the science or practice of preparing and dispensing medicinal drugs.

pharynx noun (plural **pharynges** /fa-**rin**-jeez/) the cavity connecting the nose and mouth to the throat.

phase noun a distinct period or stage in a process of change or development. •**verb** (**phases, phasing, phased**) **1** carry something out in gradual stages. **2** (**phase something in** or **out**) gradually introduce or withdraw something.

PhD abbreviation Doctor of Philosophy.

pheasant noun a large long-tailed game bird.

phenomenal adjective remarkable or outstanding.
■ **phenomenally** adverb.

phenomenon noun (plural **phenomena**) **1** a fact or situation that is known to exist or happen. **2** a remarkable person or thing.

❗ the word **phenomenon** comes from Greek, and its plural form is **phenomena**. Don't use **phenomena** as a singular form: say *this is a strange phenomenon*, not *this is a strange phenomena*.

pheromone /**ferr**-uh-mohn/ noun a chemical substance released by an animal and causing a response in others of its species.

phial /**fy**-uhl/ noun a small cylindrical glass bottle.

philander verb (**philanders, philandering, philandered**) (of a man) have many casual sexual relationships with women.
■ **philanderer** noun.

philanthropy noun the practice of helping people in need.
■ **philanthropic** adjective **philanthropist** noun.

philately /fi-**lat**-uh-li/ noun the hobby of collecting postage stamps.
■ **philatelist** noun.

philharmonic adjective devoted to music (used in the names of orchestras).

philippic noun a verbal attack.

Philistine noun **1** a member of a people of ancient Palestine who fought with the Israelites. **2** (**philistine**) a person who is not interested in culture and the arts.
■ **philistinism** noun.

philology noun the study of the structure and development of language and the relationships between languages.
■ **philological** adjective **philologist** noun.

philosopher noun **1** a person who is engaged in philosophy. **2** a person who thinks deeply about things.

philosophical adjective **1** relating to the

THESAURUS

phantom noun ghost, apparition, spirit, spectre, wraith; informal spook.

phase noun **1** *the final phase of the campaign:* stage, period, chapter, episode, part, step. **2** *he's going through a difficult phase:* period, stage, time, spell; Brit. informal patch.
□ **phase something in** introduce gradually, ease in. **phase something out** withdraw gradually, discontinue, stop using, run down, wind down.

phenomenal adjective remarkable, exceptional, extraordinary, marvellous, miraculous, wonderful, outstanding,

unprecedented; informal fantastic, terrific, tremendous, stupendous.
OPPOSITES ordinary.

phenomenon noun **1** *a rare phenomenon:* occurrence, event, happening, fact, situation, circumstance, experience, case, incident, episode. **2** *a pop phenomenon:* marvel, sensation, wonder, prodigy.

philosopher noun thinker, theorist, theoretician, scholar, intellectual, sage.

philosophical adjective **1** *a philosophical question:* theoretical, metaphysical. **2** *a philosophical mood:* thoughtful, reflective, pensive, meditative, contemplative,

p

study of philosophy. **2** having a calm attitude when things are difficult.
■ **philosophically** adverb.

philosophize or **philosophise** verb (**philosophizes, philosophizing, philosophized**) talk about serious issues, especially in a boring way.

philosophy noun (plural **philosophies**) **1** the study of the fundamental nature of knowledge, reality, and existence. **2** a set or system of beliefs.

phlegm /flem/ noun mucus in the nose and throat.

phlegmatic /fleg-**mat**-ik/ adjective calm and reasonable, and tending not to get upset.

phlox /floks/ noun a garden plant with colourful sweet-scented flowers.

phobia noun a strong irrational fear of something.
■ **phobic** adjective.

phoenix /**fee**-niks/ noun (in classical mythology) a bird that lived for hundreds of years before burning itself to death and being born again from its ashes.

☑ -oe-, not -eo-: phoenix.

phone noun a telephone. • verb (**phones, phoning, phoned**) make a telephone call to someone.
□ **phone-in** a radio or television programme in which listeners or viewers participate over the telephone.

phonecard noun a card which you can use instead of cash to make calls on a public telephone.

phonetic adjective **1** having to do with speech sounds. **2** (of a system of writing) using symbols that represent sounds. • noun (**phonetics**) the study of speech sounds.
■ **phonetically** adverb.

phoney or **phony** informal adjective (**phonier, phoniest**) not genuine. • noun (plural **phoneys** or **phonies**) a person or thing that

is not genuine.

phonic adjective relating to speech sounds.
• noun (**phonics**) a way of teaching people to read based on the sounds that letters represent.

phonograph noun **1** Brit. an early form of record player that could record as well as reproduce sound. **2** N. Amer. a record player.

phonology noun the relationships between the speech sounds of a language.

phosphate noun a salt or ester of phosphoric acid.

phosphorescence noun a faint light that is given out by a substance with little or no heat.
■ **phosphorescent** adjective.

phosphorus noun a yellowish waxy solid which can ignite spontaneously and which glows in the dark.
■ **phosphorous** adjective.

photo noun (plural **photos**) a photograph.
□ **photo finish** a close finish of a race in which the winner can be identified only from a photograph of competitors crossing the line.

photocall noun Brit. a prearranged occasion on which famous people pose for photographers.

photocopy noun (plural **photocopies**) a photographic copy of something produced by a process involving the action of light on a specially prepared surface. • verb (**photocopies, photocopying, photocopied**) make a photocopy of.
■ **photocopier** noun.

photoelectric adjective involving the production of electrons as a result of the action of light on a surface.

photofit noun Brit. a picture of a person made up from photographs of parts of other people's faces.

photogenic adjective looking attractive in photographs.

THESAURUS

introspective. **3** *he was very philosophical about it*: stoical, self-possessed, serene, dispassionate, phlegmatic, long-suffering, resigned.

philosophy noun **1** *the philosophy of Aristotle*: thinking, thought, reasoning, logic. **2** *her political philosophy*: beliefs, credo, ideology, ideas, thinking, theories, doctrine, principles, views, outlook.

phobia noun fear, dread, horror, terror, aversion, antipathy, revulsion; informal hang-up.

phone noun *she spent hours on the phone*: telephone, mobile; Brit. informal blower.
• verb *I'll phone you later*: call, telephone; Brit. ring, ring up, give someone a ring; informal call up, give someone a buzz; Brit.

informal give someone a bell, give someone a tinkle, get on the blower to; N. Amer. informal get someone on the horn.

phoney (informal) adjective *a phoney address*: bogus, false, fake, fraudulent, counterfeit, forged, imitation, affected, insincere; informal pretend; Brit. informal cod.
OPPOSITES authentic.
• noun **1** *he's a phoney*: impostor, sham, fake, fraud, charlatan; informal con artist. **2** *the diamond's a phoney*: fake, imitation, counterfeit, forgery.

photocopy noun *a photocopy of the letter*: copy, duplicate, reproduction, facsimile; trademark Xerox, photostat.
• verb *I photocopied the form*: copy, duplicate, xerox, photostat, reproduce.

photograph noun a picture made with a camera. •verb take a photograph of.
■ **photographer** noun **photographic** adjective.

photography noun the taking and processing of photographs.

photometer /foh-**tom**-i-ter/ noun an instrument measuring the strength of light.

photon /**foh**-ton/ noun a particle representing a quantum of light or other electromagnetic radiation.

photosensitive adjective responding to light.

photostat noun trademark **1** a type of machine for making photocopies on special paper. **2** a copy made by a photostat. •verb (**photostats, photostatting, photostatted**) copy something with a photostat.

photosynthesis noun the process by which green plants use sunlight to form nutrients from carbon dioxide and water.

phrase noun **1** a group of words forming a unit within a sentence. **2** Music a group of notes forming a unit within a longer passage. •verb (**phrases, phrasing, phrased**) put an idea into a particular form of words.
□ **phrase book** a book listing and translating useful phrases in a foreign language.
■ **phrasal** adjective.

phraseology /fray-zi-**ol**-uh-ji/ noun (plural **phraseologies**) a form of words used to express an idea.

phrenology noun (mainly in the past) the study of the shape and size of the skull in the belief that this can indicate someone's character.

phylum /**fy**-luhm/ noun (plural **phyla** /**fy**-luh/) a category used in the classification of animals.

physical adjective **1** relating to the body rather than the mind. **2** relating to things that you can see, hear, or feel. **3** involving bodily contact or activity. **4** relating to physics and natural forces such as heat, light, sound, etc. •noun a medical examination to find out the state of someone's health.
□ **physical education** instruction in physical exercise, sports, and games.
■ **physicality** noun **physically** adverb.

physician noun a person qualified to practise medicine.

physics noun the branch of science concerned with the nature and properties of matter and energy.
■ **physicist** noun.

physiognomy /fi-zi-**on**-uh-mi/ noun (plural **physiognomies**) a person's face or facial expression.

physiology noun the scientific study of the way in which living things function.
■ **physiological** adjective **physiologist** noun.

physiotherapy noun Brit. the treatment of disease and injury by massage and exercise.
■ **physiotherapist** noun.

physique noun the shape and size of a person's body.

pi /py/ noun the numerical value of the ratio of the circumference of a circle to its diameter (approximately 3.14159).

pianissimo /pi-uh-**niss**-i-moh/ adverb & adjective Music very soft or softly.

piano[1] /pi-**an**-oh/ noun (plural **pianos**) a musical instrument which you play by pressing black or white keys on a large keyboard, the sound being produced by small hammers hitting metal strings.
■ **pianist** noun.

piano[2] /pi-**ah**-noh/ adverb & adjective Music soft or softly.

pianoforte /pi-an-oh-**for**-tay/ formal a piano.

piazza /pi-**at**-suh/ noun a public square or marketplace.

picador noun (in bullfighting) a person on horseback who goads the bull with a lance.

picaresque adjective (of fiction) dealing with the adventures of a dishonest but appealing hero.

piccalilli noun a pickle of chopped

p

THESAURUS

photograph noun *a colour photograph:* picture, photo, snap, snapshot, shot, print, still.
•verb *he was photographed in Paris:* take a picture/photo of, take someone's picture, snap, shoot, film.

photographic adjective **1** *a photographic record:* pictorial, graphic, in photographs. **2** *a photographic memory:* detailed, exact, precise, accurate, vivid.

phrase noun *an elegant phrase:* expression, construction, term, turn of phrase, idiom, saying.
•verb *how did you phrase the question?* express, put into words, put, word, formulate, couch, frame.

physical adjective **1** *physical pleasure:* bodily, corporeal, corporal, carnal, fleshly, non-spiritual. **2** *physical work:* manual, labouring, blue-collar. **3** *the physical universe:* material, concrete, tangible, palpable, solid, substantial, real, actual, visible.
OPPOSITES mental, spiritual.

physician noun doctor, medical practitioner, general practitioner, GP, clinician, specialist, consultant; informal doc, medic, quack.

vegetables, mustard, and hot spices.

piccaninny noun (plural **piccaninnies**) offensive a small black child.

piccolo noun (plural **piccolos**) a small flute sounding an octave higher than the ordinary flute.

pick¹ verb 1 choose from a number of alternatives. 2 (often **pick something up**) take hold of something and lift or move it. 3 remove a flower or fruit from where it is growing. •noun 1 an act of choosing something. 2 (**the pick of**) the best person or thing in a particular group. ▫ pick at 1 repeatedly pull at something with your fingers. 2 eat food in small amounts. pick a fight provoke an argument or fight. pick holes in criticize. pick a lock open a lock with something other than the proper key. pick on single someone out for unfair treatment. pick someone's pockets steal something from a person's pocket. pick up improve or increase. pick someone/thing up 1 go to collect someone. 2 informal flirtatiously start talking to a stranger with the aim of having a sexual relationship with them. 3 detect or receive a signal or sound. 4 obtain or learn something. ▪ picker noun.

pick² noun 1 (also **pickaxe**) a tool consisting of a curved iron bar with pointed ends and a wooden handle, used for breaking up hard ground or rock. 2 a plectrum.

picket noun 1 a group of people standing outside a workplace and trying to persuade others not to work during a strike. 2 a pointed wooden stake driven into the ground. •verb (**pickets**, **picketing**, **picketed**) act as a picket outside a workplace.

pickings plural noun 1 profits or gains. 2 scraps or leftovers.

pickle noun 1 Brit. a thick, spicy, cold sauce made from chopped vegetables and fruit. 2 a preserve of vegetables or fruit in vinegar or salt water. 3 (**a pickle**) informal a difficult situation. •verb (**pickles**, **pickling**, **pickled**) preserve food in vinegar or salt water.

pickpocket noun a person who steals from people's pockets.

pickup noun 1 a small truck with low sides. 2 the part of a record player that holds the stylus. 3 a device on an electric guitar which converts sound vibration into electrical signals for amplification.

picky adjective informal fussy.

picnic noun a meal that is eaten outdoors and away from home. •verb (**picnics**, **picnicking**, **picnicked**) have a picnic. ▪ picnicker noun.

Pict noun a member of an ancient people inhabiting northern Scotland in Roman times.

pictograph or **pictogram** noun a small image or picture representing a word or phrase.

pictorial adjective having to do with or

THESAURUS

pick verb 1 *picking apples:* harvest, gather (in), collect, pluck. 2 *pick a time that suits you:* choose, select, single out, opt for, plump for, elect, decide on, settle on, fix on, name, nominate, identify. 3 *he tried to pick a fight:* provoke, start, cause, incite, instigate, prompt. OPPOSITES reject, avoid. •noun *the pick of the crop:* best, finest, choice, choicest, cream, flower, crème de la crème, elite. ▫ pick on **bully**, victimize, torment, persecute, taunt, tease; informal get at, needle. pick someone/something out **see**, make out, distinguish, discern, spot, perceive, detect, notice, recognize, identify, catch sight of, glimpse. pick up **improve**, recover, rally, bounce back, perk up, look up, take a turn for the better, turn the corner, be on the mend, make headway, make progress. pick someone/something up 1 *he picked up the baby:* **lift**, take up, raise, hoist, scoop up, gather up, snatch up. 2 *I'll pick up the parcel on my way:* **fetch**, collect, call for. pick someone up (informal) 1 *he was picked up by the police:* **arrest**, apprehend, detain, take into custody, seize;

informal nab, run in; Brit. informal nick. 2 *he picked her up in a club:* **meet**; informal get off with, pull, cop off with. pick something up 1 *we picked it up at a flea market:* **find**, discover, come across, stumble across, happen on, chance on, acquire, obtain, come by, get, buy, purchase; informal get hold of, get your hands on. 2 *he picked up the story in the 1950s:* **resume**, take up, start again, recommence, continue, carry/go on with. 3 *she picked up a virus:* **catch**, contract, get, go/come down with. 4 *all the gossip he'd picked up:* **hear**, hear tell, get wind of, be told, learn, glean. 5 *we're picking up a distress signal:* **receive**, detect, get, hear.

picket noun 1 *forty pickets were arrested:* demonstrator, striker, protester. 2 *they organized a picket:* demonstration, picket line, blockade, boycott, strike. •verb *workers picketed the factory:* demonstrate at, blockade, boycott.

pickup noun improvement, recovery, revival, upturn, upswing, rally, resurgence, renewal, turnaround. OPPOSITES slump.

expressed in pictures.

picture noun 1 a painting, drawing, or photograph. 2 an image on a television screen. 3 a cinema film. 4 (**the pictures**) the cinema. 5 an image formed in the mind. •verb (**pictures, picturing, pictured**) 1 represent in a picture. 2 form an image of something in your mind.
□ picture window a large window consisting of a single pane of glass.

picturesque adjective (of a place) very pleasant to look at.

pidgin noun a simple form of a language with elements taken from local languages.

pie noun a baked dish of meat, vegetables, fruit, etc. inside a pastry case.
□ pie chart a diagram in which a circle is divided into segments to show the size of particular amounts in relation to the whole.

piebald adjective (of a horse) having irregular patches of two colours.

piece noun 1 a portion that is separated or seen separately from the whole. 2 an item used in building something or forming part of a set. 3 a musical or written work. 4 a token used to make moves in a board game. 5 a coin of a particular value. •verb (**pieces, piecing, pieced**) (**piece something together**) assemble something from individual parts.

pièce de résistance /pyess duh ray-ziss-tonss/ noun the most important or impressive part of something.

piecemeal adjective & adverb done in stages over a period of time.

piecework noun work that is paid for by the amount done and not the hours worked.

pied /rhymes with ride/ adjective having two or more different colours.

pied-à-terre /pyay-dah-**tair**/ noun (plural **pieds-à-terre** /pyay-dah-**tair**/) a small flat or house kept for occasional use.

pier noun 1 a structure leading out to sea or into a lake, used as a landing stage for boats. 2 a pillar supporting an arch or bridge.

pierce verb (**pierces, piercing, pierced**) 1 make a hole in something with a sharp object. 2 force or cut a way through. 3 (**piercing**) very sharp, cold, or high-pitched.

piety /**py**-uh-ti/ noun (plural **pieties**) the quality of being religious in a respectful and serious way.

piffle noun informal nonsense.

pig noun 1 an animal with a short, curly tail and a flat snout. 2 informal a greedy, dirty, or unpleasant person. •verb (**pigs, pigging, pigged**) informal eat too much food.
□ pig-headed stupidly stubborn. pig iron iron when it is first taken out of a smelting furnace.
■ piggish adjective piglet noun.

pigeon noun a plump grey and white bird with a cooing voice.
□ pigeon-toed having the toes and feet turned inwards.

☑ note that there is no *d*: pi*geon*.

pigeonhole noun 1 a small hole in a wall leading into a place where pigeons nest. 2 each of a set of small compartments in a workplace, college, etc. where letters or messages may be left for individuals. 3 a

p

THESAURUS

picture noun 1 *pictures in an art gallery:* painting, drawing, sketch, watercolour, print, canvas, portrait, illustration, depiction, likeness, representation, image. 2 *we were told not to take pictures:* photograph, photo, snap, snapshot, shot, frame, exposure, still, print. 3 *my picture of the ideal woman:* concept, idea, impression, (mental) image, vision, visualization, notion. 4 *the picture of health:* personification, embodiment, epitome, essence, quintessence, soul, model.
•verb 1 *they were pictured playing in the snow:* depict, portray, show, represent, draw, sketch, photograph, paint. 2 *Anne still pictured Richard as he had been:* visualize, see (in your mind's eye), imagine, remember.

picturesque adjective attractive, pretty, beautiful, lovely, scenic, charming, quaint, pleasing, delightful.
OPPOSITES ugly.

piece noun 1 *a piece of cheese:* bit, slice, chunk, segment, section, lump, hunk, wedge, slab, block, cake, bar, stick, length. 2 *the pieces of a clock:* component, part, bit, constituent, element, section, unit, module. 3 *a piece of furniture:* item, article, specimen. 4 *a piece of the profit:* share, portion, slice, quota, part, percentage, amount, quantity, ration, fraction; Brit. informal whack. 5 *pieces from his collection:* work (of art), artwork, artefact, composition, opus. 6 *the reporter who wrote the piece:* article, item, story, report, essay, feature, review, column.

pier noun jetty, quay, wharf, dock, landing stage.

pierce verb penetrate, puncture, perforate, prick, spike, stab, drill, bore.

piercing adjective 1 *a piercing shriek:* shrill, ear-splitting, high-pitched, penetrating, strident. 2 *his piercing gaze:* searching, probing, penetrating, sharp, keen.

category in which someone or something is put. •verb (**pigeonholes, pigeonholing, pigeonholed**) put into a particular category.

piggery noun (plural **piggeries**) a place where pigs are kept.

piggy noun (plural **piggies**) a child's word for a pig or piglet. •adjective like a pig.
□ **piggy bank** a money box shaped like a pig.

piggyback noun a ride on someone's back and shoulders. •adverb on the back and shoulders of another person.

pigment noun **1** the substance that gives natural colouring to animal or plant tissue. **2** a coloured powder mixed with a liquid to make paints, crayons, etc.
■ **pigmentation** noun **pigmented** adjective.

pigmy ⇨ PYGMY.

pigskin noun leather made from the hide of a pig.

pigsty noun (plural **pigsties**) **1** an enclosure for a pig or pigs. **2** a very dirty or untidy place.

pigswill noun kitchen refuse and scraps fed to pigs.

pigtail noun a length of hair worn in a plait at the back or on each side of the head.

pike¹ noun (plural **pike**) a freshwater fish with a long body and sharp teeth.

pike² noun (in the past) a weapon with a pointed metal head on a long wooden shaft.

pikestaff noun (**as plain as a pikestaff**) very obvious.

pilaster /pi-**lass**-ter/ noun a column that projects from a wall.

pilchard noun a small fish of the herring family.

pile¹ noun **1** a heap of things lying one on top of another. **2** informal a large amount. **3** a large and impressive building. •verb (**piles,**

piling, piled) **1** place things one on top of the other. **2** (**pile up**) form a pile or very large quantity. **3** (**pile into** or **out of**) get into or out of a vehicle in a disorganized way.
□ **pile-up** a crash involving a lot of vehicles.

pile² noun the soft surface of a carpet or a fabric, consisting of the cut ends of many small threads.

pile³ noun a heavy post driven into the ground to support foundations.

piledriver noun a machine for driving piles into the ground.

piles plural noun haemorrhoids.

pilfer verb (**pilfers, pilfering, pilfered**) steal small items of little value.

pilgrim noun a person who travels to a sacred place for religious reasons.

pilgrimage noun a pilgrim's journey.

pill noun **1** a small round mass of solid medicine for swallowing whole. **2** (**the Pill**) a contraceptive pill.

pillage verb (**pillages, pillaging, pillaged**) steal from a place in a rough and violent way. •noun the action of pillaging.

pillar noun **1** a tall upright structure used as a support for a building. **2** a source of help and support.
□ **from pillar to post** from one place to another without achieving anything. **pillar box** (in the UK) a red cylindrical public postbox.

pillbox noun **1** a small round hat with a flat top and no brim. **2** a small concrete fort.

pillion noun a seat for a passenger behind a motorcyclist.

pillory noun (plural **pillories**) (in the past) a wooden framework with holes for the head and hands, in which people were locked and left on display as a punishment. •verb (**pillories, pillorying, pilloried**) criticize or ridicule someone publicly.

p

THESAURUS

pigment noun colouring, colour, tint, dye, stain.

pile¹ noun **1** *a pile of stones:* heap, stack, mound, pyramid, mass, collection, accumulation, assemblage, stockpile, hoard. **2** (informal) *I've a pile of work to do:* lot, mountain, reams, abundance; informal load, heap, mass, slew, stack, ton, oodles; Brit. informal shedload; Austral./NZ informal swag.
•verb **1** *he piled up the plates:* heap, stack. **2** *he piled his plate with salad:* load, heap, fill (up), stack, charge. **3** *we piled into the car:* crowd, clamber, pack, squeeze, scramble, struggle.
□ **pile up accumulate,** grow, mount up, build up, multiply, escalate, soar, spiral, rocket, increase.

pile² noun *a carpet with a short pile:* nap,

fibres, threads.

pile-up noun crash, collision, smash, accident; Brit. RTA; N. Amer. wreck; Brit. informal shunt.

pilgrim noun traveller, wayfarer, worshipper, devotee, believer; Islam haji; old use palmer.

pilgrimage noun journey, expedition, mission, hajj, visit, trek, trip, odyssey.

pill noun tablet, capsule, pellet, lozenge, pastille.

pillar noun **1** *stone pillars:* column, post, support, upright, pier, pile, prop, stanchion, obelisk. **2** *a pillar of the community:* stalwart, mainstay, bastion, leading light, worthy, backbone, supporter, upholder, champion.

pillow noun a soft pad used to support the head when you lie down in bed.
◻ pillow talk intimate conversation between a couple in bed.

pillowcase noun a removable cloth cover for a pillow.

pilot noun 1 a person who flies an aircraft. 2 a person qualified to take charge of a ship entering or leaving a harbour. 3 something done or produced as a test before being introduced more widely. •verb (pilots, piloting, piloted) 1 act as a pilot of an aircraft or ship. 2 test a scheme, project, etc. before introducing it more widely.
◻ pilot light a small gas burner that is kept alight permanently, used to fire a boiler.

pimento or **pimiento** noun (plural pimentos) a sweet red pepper.

pimp noun a man who controls prostitutes and takes part of their earnings. •verb act as a pimp.

pimple noun a small inflamed lump on the skin.
■ pimply adjective.

PIN or **PIN number** abbreviation personal identification number.

pin noun 1 a very thin pointed piece of metal with a round head, used to hold pieces of fabric together or as a fastener. 2 a metal projection from an electric plug. 3 a small brooch. 4 a steel rod used to join the ends of broken bones while they heal. 5 a metal peg in a hand grenade that prevents it exploding. 6 a skittle in bowling. 7 (pins) informal legs. •verb (pins, pinning, pinned) 1 attach or fasten with a pin or pins. 2 hold someone firmly so they are unable to move. 3 (pin someone down) force someone to be specific about their plans. 4 (pin someone down) trap an enemy by firing at them. 5 (pin something

on) fix blame or responsibility on.
◻ pin money a small sum of money for spending on everyday items. pins and needles a tingling sensation in a part of the body that is recovering from numbness. pin-up a poster of an attractive person.

pinafore noun a collarless, sleeveless dress worn over a blouse or jumper.

pinball noun a game in which balls are shot across a sloping board and score points by hitting targets.

pince-nez /panss-nay/ noun a pair of glasses kept in place with a nose clip instead of parts that rest on the ears.

pincer noun 1 (pincers) a metal tool with blunt inward-curving jaws for gripping and pulling things. 2 a front claw of a lobster or similar shellfish.

pinch verb 1 grip flesh tightly between your finger and thumb. 2 (of a shoe) hurt a foot by being too tight. 3 informal steal. •noun 1 an act of pinching. 2 an amount of an ingredient that can be held between your fingers and thumb.
◻ feel the pinch experience financial hardship.

pinched adjective (of a person's face) tight with cold or suffering.

pincushion noun a small pad into which you stick pins to store them.

pine¹ noun an evergreen tree that produces cones and has clusters of long needle-shaped leaves.
◻ pine nut the edible seed of various pines. pine marten an animal resembling a weasel that lives in trees.

pine² verb (pines, pining, pined) 1 become very sad or weak because you miss someone so much. 2 (pine for) miss or long for.

THESAURUS

pilot noun 1 *a fighter pilot:* airman, flyer, captain; informal skipper; N. Amer. informal jock; dated aviator. 2 *a harbour pilot:* navigator, helmsman, steersman, coxswain. 3 *a pilot for a TV series:* trial, sample, experiment.
•adjective *a pilot project:* experimental, exploratory, trial, test, sample, preliminary.
•verb *he piloted the jet to safety:* navigate, guide, manoeuvre, steer, control, direct, captain, fly, drive, sail; informal skipper.

pin noun 1 *fasten the hem with a pin:* tack, safety pin, nail, staple, fastener. 2 *a broken pin in the machine:* bolt, peg, rod, rivet, dowel. 3 *they wore name pins:* badge, brooch.
•verb 1 *she pinned the brooch to her dress:* attach, fasten, affix, fix, join, secure, clip, nail. 2 *they pinned him to the ground:* hold, press, pinion.

◻ pin someone/something down confine, trap, hem in, corner, close in, shut in, pen in. pin something on someone blame for, hold responsible for, attribute to, ascribe to, lay something at someone's door; informal stick on.

pinch verb 1 *he pinched my arm:* nip, tweak, squeeze, grasp. 2 *my new shoes pinch my toes:* hurt, squeeze, crush, cramp.
•noun 1 *he gave her arm a pinch:* nip, tweak, squeeze. 2 *a pinch of salt:* bit, touch, dash, spot, trace, soupçon, speck, taste; informal smidgen, tad.

pine verb *she thinks I am pining away from love:* fade, waste away, weaken, decline, languish, wilt, sicken.
◻ pine for long for, yearn for, ache for, sigh for, hunger for, thirst for, itch for, carry a torch for, miss, mourn.

pineapple noun a large juicy tropical fruit consisting of yellow flesh surrounded by a tough skin.

ping noun a short high-pitched ringing sound. •verb make such a sound.
□ ping-pong (also US trademark **Ping-Pong**) informal table tennis.

pinion¹ verb tie or hold someone's arms or legs so that they cannot move. •noun the outer part of a bird's wing.

pinion² noun a small cogwheel or spindle that engages with a large cogwheel.

pink¹ adjective of a colour midway between red and white. •noun a pink colour.
□ in the pink informal in the best condition.

pink² noun a plant with sweet-smelling pink or white flowers.

pinking shears plural noun scissors with a thick serrated blade, used for cutting a zigzag edge on fabric to prevent it fraying.

pinky or **pinkie** noun informal the little finger.

pinnace /pin-nis/ noun a small boat forming part of the equipment of a larger one.

pinnacle noun 1 the most successful point. 2 a high pointed piece of rock. 3 a small pointed turret on a roof.

pinpoint verb locate or identify something precisely. •adjective absolutely precise. •noun a tiny dot.

pinprick noun a very small dot or amount.

pinstripe noun a very narrow white stripe woven into dark material.
■ pinstriped adjective.

pint noun 1 a unit of liquid or dry capacity equal to one eighth of a gallon, in Britain equal to 0.568 litre. 2 Brit. a pint of beer.
□ pint-sized informal very small.

pinwheel noun chiefly N. Amer. a Catherine wheel firework.

pioneer noun 1 a person who explores or settles in a new region. 2 a developer of new ideas or techniques. •verb (**pioneers, pioneering, pioneered**) be a pioneer of a new idea or technique.

pious adjective 1 religious in a very respectful and serious way. 2 pretending to be moral and good in order to impress other people. 3 (of a hope) very much wanted, but unlikely to be achieved.
■ piously adverb.

pip noun 1 a small hard seed in a fruit. 2 Brit. a short, high-pitched sound used as a signal on the radio or in a telephone.
□ pip someone at (or to) the post Brit. informal defeat someone by a small margin or at the last moment.

pipe noun 1 a tube through which water, gas, oil, etc. can flow. 2 a device for smoking tobacco, consisting of a narrow tube that opens into a small bowl in which the tobacco is burned. 3 a wind instrument consisting of a single tube with holes along its length that you cover with your fingers to produce different notes. 4 each of the tubes by which notes are produced in an organ. 5 (**pipes**) bagpipes. •verb (**pipes, piping, piped**) 1 send a liquid through a pipe. 2 transmit music, a programme, a signal, etc. by wire or cable. 3 play a tune on a pipe. 4 sing or say something in a high voice. 5 decorate something with piping.
□ piped music pre-recorded background music played through loudspeakers. pipe dream a hope or plan that is impossible to achieve. pipe down informal be less noisy. pipe up informal say something suddenly.

pipeline noun a long pipe for carrying oil, gas, etc. over a distance.
□ in the pipeline in the process of being developed.

piper noun a person who plays a pipe or bagpipes.

pipette noun a thin tube used in a

p

---

pink adjective rose, rosy, rosé, pale red, salmon, coral, flushed, blushing.

pinnacle noun 1 the pinnacle of his career: height, peak, high point, top, apex, zenith, acme. 2 pinnacles of rock: peak, needle, crag, tor.
OPPOSITES nadir.

pinpoint adjective pinpoint accuracy: precise, exact, strict, absolute, complete, scientific.
•verb the technology can pinpoint a cellphone's position: identify, determine, distinguish, discover, find, locate, detect, track down, spot, diagnose, recognize, pin down, home in on.

pioneer noun 1 the pioneers of the Wild West: settler, colonist, colonizer, frontiersman, explorer. 2 a pioneer of motoring: developer, innovator, trailblazer, groundbreaker, founding father, architect, creator.
•verb he pioneered the sale of insurance: introduce, develop, launch, instigate, initiate, spearhead, institute, establish, found.

pious adjective religious, devout, God-fearing, churchgoing, holy, godly, saintly, reverent, righteous.
OPPOSITES irreligious.

pipe noun a central-heating pipe: tube, conduit, hose, main, duct, line, channel, pipeline, drain.
•verb 1 the beer is piped into barrels: feed, siphon, channel, run, convey.
2 programmes piped in from London: relay, feed, patch, transmit.

laboratory for transferring small quantities of liquid.

piping noun **1** lengths of pipe. **2** lines of icing or cream used to decorate cakes and desserts. **3** thin cord covered in fabric and used for decorating a garment or piece of furniture.
□ **piping hot** (of food or water) very hot.

pipistrelle noun a small insect-eating bat.

pipit noun a bird that lives on the ground in open country.

pippin noun a sweet red and yellow apple.

pipsqueak noun informal an unimportant person.

piquant /pee-kuhnt/ adjective having a pleasantly strong and sharp taste.
■ **piquancy** noun **piquantly** adverb.

pique /peek/ noun a feeling of irritation mixed with hurt pride. • verb (**piques, piquing, piqued**) **1** (**be piqued**) feel both irritated and hurt. **2** stimulate someone's interest.

piracy noun **1** the attacking and robbing of ships at sea. **2** the reproduction of a film or recording without permission and so as to make a profit.

piranha /pi-rah-nuh/ noun a freshwater fish with very sharp teeth.

pirate noun a person who attacks and robs ships at sea. • adjective **1** (of a film or recording) having been reproduced and used for profit without permission. **2** (of an organization) broadcasting without permission. • verb (**pirates, pirating, pirated**) reproduce a film or recording for profit without permission.

pirouette noun a movement in ballet involving spinning on one foot. • verb (**pirouettes, pirouetting, pirouetted**) perform a pirouette.

piscatorial /piss-kuh-tor-i-uhl/ adjective having to do with fish.

Pisces /py-seez/ noun a sign of the zodiac (the Fish or Fishes), 21 February–19 March.

pistachio /pi-stah-shi-oh/ noun (plural **pistachios**) a small pale green nut.

piste /peest/ noun a course or run for skiing.

pistil noun Botany the female organs of a flower (the stigma, style, and ovary).

pistol noun a small gun designed to be held in one hand.

piston noun a sliding disc or cylinder fitting closely inside a tube in which it moves up and down as part of an engine or pump.

pit¹ noun **1** a large hole in the ground. **2** a mine for coal, chalk, etc. **3** a hollow in a surface. **4** a sunken area in a workshop floor where people can work on the underside of vehicles. **5** an area at the side of a track where racing cars are serviced and refuelled. **6** a part of a theatre where the orchestra plays. **7** (**the pits**) informal a very bad place or situation. • verb (**pits, pitting, pitted**) **1** (**pit someone/thing against**) test someone or something in a contest with. **2** make a hollow in the surface of something.
□ **pit bull terrier** a fierce breed of bull terrier. **the pit of the stomach** an area low down in the stomach.

pit² noun chiefly N. Amer. the stone of a fruit. • verb (**pits, pitting, pitted**) remove the stone from a fruit.

pitch¹ noun **1** Brit. an area of ground used for outdoor team games. **2** the degree of highness or lowness in a sound or tone. **3** a particular level of intensity. **4** a form of words used when trying to sell something: *a sales pitch.* **5** Brit. a place on a street where someone performing or selling something has settled. **6** the steepness of a roof. • verb **1** throw heavily or roughly. **2** set your voice, a sound, or a piece of music at a particular pitch. **3** aim something at a particular level, target, or audience. **4** set up a tent or camp. **5** (**pitch in**) informal join in enthusiastically with an activity. **6** (**pitch up**) informal arrive. **7** (of a moving ship, aircraft, or vehicle) rock up and down. **8** (**pitched**) (of a roof) sloping.
□ **pitched battle** a battle in which the time and place are decided beforehand.

pitch² noun a sticky black substance made

THESAURUS

pirate noun *pirates boarded the ship:* **raider**, hijacker, marauder, freebooter; historical privateer, buccaneer; old use corsair.
• verb *designers may pirate good ideas:* **steal**, copy, plagiarize, poach, appropriate, bootleg; informal crib, lift, rip off.

pit noun **1** *we dug a pit:* **hole**, trough, hollow, excavation, cavity, crater, pothole. **2** *pit closures:* **coal mine**, colliery, quarry, shaft.
• verb *his skin had been pitted by acne:* **mark**, pockmark, pock, scar, dent, indent.

pitch noun **1** *a football pitch:* **playing field**, ground, sports field, stadium; Brit. park.

2 *her voice rose in pitch:* **tone**, key, modulation, frequency. **3** *the pitch of the roof:* **gradient**, slope, slant, angle, tilt, incline. **4** *at fever pitch:* **level**, intensity, point, degree, height, extent. **5** *his sales pitch:* **patter**, talk; informal spiel, line.
• verb **1** *a kid pitched a snowball:* **throw**, toss, fling, hurl, cast, lob, flip; informal chuck, sling, heave, bung. **2** *he pitched overboard:* **fall**, tumble, topple, plunge, plummet. **3** *they pitched their tents:* **put up**, set up, erect, raise. **4** *the boat pitched:* **lurch**, toss, plunge, roll, reel, sway, rock, list.

p

from tar or turpentine and used for waterproofing.
□ **pitch-black** (or **pitch-dark**) completely dark.

pitcher noun a large jug.

pitchfork noun a farm tool with a long handle and two sharp metal prongs, used for lifting hay.

piteous adjective deserving or arousing pity.
■ **piteously** adverb.

pitfall noun a hidden danger or difficulty.

pith noun **1** spongy white tissue lining the rind of citrus fruits. **2** spongy tissue in the stems and branches of many plants. **3** the most important part of something.
□ **pith helmet** a lightweight hat made from the dried pith of a plant, used for protection from the sun.

pithead noun the top of a mineshaft and the area around it.

pithy adjective (**pithier, pithiest**) (of language) concise and clear.

pitiable adjective **1** deserving or arousing pity. **2** deserving contempt.

pitiful adjective **1** deserving or arousing pity. **2** very small or inadequate.
■ **pitifully** adverb.

pitiless adjective showing no pity.

piton noun (in rock climbing) a peg or spike driven into a crack to support a climber or hold a rope.

pitta noun a type of flat bread which can be split open to hold a filling.

pittance noun a very small or inadequate amount of money.

pitter-patter noun the sound of quick light

steps or taps.

pituitary gland /pi-tyoo-i-tuh-ri/ noun a gland at the base of the brain which controls growth and development.

pity noun (plural **pities**) **1** a feeling of sympathy and sadness caused by the suffering of other people. **2** a cause for regret or disappointment. •verb (**pities, pitying, pitied**) feel pity for.

pivot noun the central point, pin, or shaft on which a mechanism turns or is balanced. •verb (**pivots, pivoting, pivoted**) **1** turn on or as if on a pivot. **2** (**pivot on**) depend on.

pivotal adjective of central importance.

pixel noun any of the tiny areas of light on a computer screen which make up an image.

pixie or **pixy** noun (plural **pixies**) an imaginary being portrayed as a tiny man with pointed ears.

pizza noun a flat, round base of dough baked with a topping of tomatoes, cheese, and other ingredients.

pizzeria /peet-suh-**ree**-uh/ noun a pizza restaurant.

pizzicato /pit-si-**kah**-toh/ adverb & adjective plucking the strings of a stringed instrument such as a violin with your finger.

placard noun a large written sign fixed to a wall or carried during a demonstration.

placate verb (**placates, placating, placated**) make someone less angry or upset.
■ **placatory** adjective.

place noun **1** a particular position or

pitfall noun hazard, danger, risk, peril, difficulty, catch, snag, stumbling block, drawback.

pity noun **1** *a voice full of pity:* compassion, commiseration, condolence, sympathy, fellow feeling, understanding. **2** *it's a pity he never had children:* shame, misfortune, too bad; informal bummer.
OPPOSITES indifference, cruelty.
•verb *they pitied me:* feel sorry for, feel for, sympathize with, empathize with, commiserate with, take pity on, be moved by, bleed for.

place noun **1** *an ideal place for dinner:* location, site, spot, setting, position, situation, area, region, locale, venue. **2** *foreign places:* country, state, area, region, town, city. **3** *a place of her own:* home, house, flat, apartment, pied-à-terre, accommodation, property, rooms, quarters; informal pad; Brit. informal gaff; formal residence, abode, dwelling. **4** *in your place, I'd agree:* situation, position, circumstances; informal shoes. **5** *a place was reserved for her:* seat,

chair, space. **6** *I offered him a place in the company:* job, position, post, appointment, situation, employment. **7** *I know my place:* status, position, standing, rank, niche; dated estate. **8** *it was not her place to sort it out:* responsibility, duty, job, task, role, function, concern, affair, charge.
•verb **1** *books were placed on the table:* put (down), set (down), lay, deposit, position, plant, rest, stand, station, situate, leave; informal stick, dump, bung, park, plonk, pop; N. Amer. informal plunk. **2** *the trust you placed in me:* put, lay, set, invest. **3** *a survey placed the company sixth:* rank, order, grade, class, classify, put. **4** *Joe couldn't quite place her:* identify, recognize, remember, put a name to, pin down, locate, pinpoint. **5** *we were placed with foster parents:* accommodate, house, home, allocate, assign.
□ **in place of** instead of, rather than, as a substitute for, as a replacement for, in exchange for, in lieu of, in someone's stead. **out of place 1** *he said something out of place:* inappropriate, unsuitable,

location. **2** an opportunity to study on a course or be a member of a team. **3** a position in a sequence. **4** (in place names) a square or short street. • verb (**places, placing, placed**) **1** put something in a particular position or situation. **2** find an appropriate place or role for. **3** remember where you have seen someone before. **4** make a reservation or order. □ **take place** happen.

placebo /pluh-see-boh/ noun (plural **placebos**) a medicine given to a patient to make them feel happier or more confident rather than for any physical effect.

placement noun **1** the action of placing. **2** a temporary job undertaken to gain work experience.

placenta /pluh-sen-tuh/ noun (plural **placentae** /pluh-sen-tee/ or **placentas**) an organ that is formed in the womb during pregnancy and which supplies blood and nourishment to the fetus through the umbilical cord.

placid adjective not easily upset or excited.
■ **placidity** noun **placidly** adverb.

placket noun an opening in a garment, covering fastenings or giving access to a pocket.

plagiarize or **plagiarise** /play-juh-ryz/ verb (**plagiarizes, plagiarizing, plagiarized**) copy another person's words or ideas and pretend that they are your own.
■ **plagiarism** noun **plagiarist** noun.

plague noun **1** an infectious disease causing fever and delirium. **2** an unusually and unpleasantly large number of insects or animals. • verb (**plagues, plaguing, plagued**) **1** cause continual trouble to. **2** pester someone.

plaice noun (plural **plaice**) a flat brown fish with orange spots, used for food.

plaid /plad/ noun fabric woven in a chequered or tartan design.

plain adjective **1** simple or ordinary. **2** without a pattern. **3** unmarked. **4** easy to understand; clear. **5** (of a woman or girl) not attractive. • noun a large area of flat land with few trees.
□ **plain chocolate** Brit. dark, slightly bitter chocolate made without added milk. **plain clothes** ordinary clothes rather than uniform. **plain sailing** smooth and easy progress.
■ **plainly** adverb **plainness** noun.

plainsong or **plainchant** noun a kind of medieval church music that was sung by a number of voices without any accompanying instruments.

plaintiff noun a person who brings a case against someone in a court of law.

plaintive adjective sounding sad and mournful.
■ **plaintively** adverb.

plait noun Brit. a length of hair or rope made up of strands woven together. • verb form into a plait or plaits.

plan noun **1** a detailed proposal for doing or

THESAURUS

unseemly, improper, untoward, out of keeping, unbecoming. **2** *she seemed out of place in a launderette:* **incongruous**, out of your element, like a fish out of water, uncomfortable, uneasy. **take place happen**, occur, come about, go on, transpire; N. Amer. informal go down. **take the place of replace**, stand in for, substitute for, act for, fill in for, cover for, relieve.

plague noun **1** *they died in a plague:* **pandemic**, epidemic, disease, sickness; dated contagion; old use pestilence. **2** *a plague of fleas:* **infestation**, invasion, swarm, epidemic.
• verb **1** *he was plagued by poor health:* **afflict**, trouble, torment, beset, dog, curse, bedevil. **2** *he plagued her with questions:* **pester**, harass, badger, bother, torment, harry, hound, trouble, nag, molest; informal hassle, bug; N. English informal mither; N. Amer. informal devil.

plain adjective **1** *it was plain that something was wrong:* **obvious**, clear, evident, apparent, manifest, unmistakable. **2** *plain English:* **intelligible**, comprehensible, understandable, clear, lucid, simple, straightforward, user-friendly. **3** *plain*

speaking: **candid**, frank, outspoken, forthright, direct, honest, truthful, blunt, bald, unequivocal; informal upfront. **4** *a plain dress:* **simple**, ordinary, unadorned, homely, basic, modest, unsophisticated, restrained. **5** *a plain girl:* **unattractive**, unprepossessing, ugly, ordinary; N. Amer. homely; Brit. informal no oil painting. **6** *it was plain bad luck:* **sheer**, pure, downright, out-and-out.
OPPOSITES obscure, fancy, attractive, pretentious.
• noun *the plains of North America:* **grassland**, flatland, prairie, savannah, steppe, tundra, pampas, veld, plateau.

plan noun **1** *a plan for raising money:* **scheme**, idea, proposal, proposition, project, programme, system, method, strategy, stratagem, formula, recipe. **2** *her plan was to break even:* **intention**, aim, idea, objective, object, goal, target, ambition. **3** *a plan of the new office:* **map**, diagram, chart, blueprint, drawing, sketch, impression; N. Amer. plat.
• verb **1** *plan your route in advance:* **organize**, arrange, work out, outline, map out, prepare, formulate, frame, develop, devise. **2** *he plans to buy a house:* **intend**,

achieving something. **2** an intention. **3** a map or diagram. **4** a scheme for making regular payments towards a pension, insurance policy, etc. •**verb** (**plans, planning, planned**) **1** decide on and arrange something in advance. **2** intend to do something. **3** (**plan for**) make preparations for. **4** make a plan of a building, town, garden, etc.
■ **planner** noun.

plane[1] **noun 1** a completely flat surface. **2** a level of existence or thought. •**adjective 1** completely flat. **2** relating to two-dimensional surfaces or sizes. •**verb** (**planes, planing, planed**) **1** (of a bird) soar without moving its wings. **2** skim over the surface of water.

plane[2] **noun** an aeroplane.

plane[3] or **planer noun** a tool used to smooth a wooden surface by cutting thin shavings from it. •**verb** (**planes, planing, planed**) smooth a surface with a plane.

plane[4] **noun** a tall tree with broad leaves and peeling bark.

planet noun a large round mass in space that orbits a star.
■ **planetary** adjective.

planetarium noun (plural **planetariums** or **planetaria** /plan-i-**tair**-i-uh/) a building in which images of stars, planets, and constellations are projected on to a domed ceiling.

plangent /plan-juhnt/ **adjective** (of a sound) loud and melancholy.

plank noun a long, flat piece of timber.

plankton noun tiny creatures living in the sea or fresh water.

plant noun 1 a living thing that absorbs substances through its roots and makes nutrients in its leaves by photosynthesis. **2** a place where a manufacturing process takes place. **3** machinery used in a

manufacturing process. **4** a person placed in a group as a spy. •**verb 1** place a seed, bulb, or plant in the ground so that it can grow. **2** place in a particular position. **3** secretly place a bomb. **4** hide something among someone's belongings to make them appear guilty of something. **5** send someone to join a group to act as a spy. **6** fix an idea in someone's mind.
■ **planter** noun.

Plantagenet /plan-**taj**-uh-nuht/ **noun** a member of the English royal house which ruled 1154–1485.

plantain noun 1 a type of banana eaten as a vegetable. **2** a wild plant with small green flowers and broad leaves that spread out near the ground.

plantation noun 1 a large estate on which crops such as coffee, sugar, and tobacco are grown. **2** an area in which trees have been planted.

plaque noun 1 an ornamental tablet fixed to a wall in memory of a person or event. **2** a sticky deposit that forms on teeth and in which bacteria grow quickly.

plasma /**plaz**-muh/ **noun 1** the clear fluid part of blood in which blood cells are suspended. **2** a gas of positive ions and free electrons with little or no overall electric charge.

plaster noun 1 a soft mixture of lime with sand or cement and water for spreading on walls and ceilings to form a smooth, hard surface when dried. **2** (also **plaster of Paris**) a hard white substance made by adding water to powdered gypsum, used for setting broken bones and making sculptures and casts. **3** a sticky strip of material for covering cuts and wounds. •**verb** (**plasters, plastering, plastered**) **1** apply plaster to. **2** coat something thickly. **3** make hair lie flat by applying

p

THESAURUS

aim, propose, mean, hope. **3** *I'm planning a new garden:* design, draw up a plan for, sketch out, map out; N. Amer. plat.

plane[1] **noun** *a higher plane of achievement:* level, degree, standard, stratum, dimension.
•**verb** *boats planed across the water:* skim, glide.

plane[2] **noun** *the plane took off:* aircraft, airliner, jet, flying machine; Brit. aeroplane; N. Amer. airplane, ship.

plant noun 1 *garden plants:* flower, shrub, vegetable, herb, bush, weed; (**plants**) vegetation, greenery, flora. **2** *a CIA plant:* spy, informant, informer, secret agent, mole, infiltrator, operative; N. Amer. informal spook. **3** *a chemical plant:* factory, works, facility, refinery, mill. **4** *investment in new*

plant: machinery, machines, equipment, apparatus, appliances, gear.
•**verb 1** *plant the seeds:* sow, scatter. **2** *he planted his feet on the ground:* place, put, set, position, situate, settle; informal plonk. **3** *she planted the idea in his mind:* instil, implant, put, place, introduce, fix, establish, lodge.

plaster noun 1 *the plaster covering the bricks:* plasterwork, stucco. **2** *a statuette made of plaster:* plaster of Paris, gypsum. **3** *waterproof plasters:* sticking plaster, adhesive dressing; trademark Elastoplast, Band-Aid.
•**verb 1** *bread plastered with butter:* spread, smother, smear, cake, coat. **2** *his hair was plastered down with sweat:* flatten (down), smooth down, slick down.

liquid to it. **4 (plastered)** informal drunk.
■ **plasterer** noun.

plasterboard noun board made of plaster
set between two sheets of paper, used to
line interior walls and ceilings.

plastic noun a chemically produced material
that can be moulded into shape while soft
and then set into a hard or slightly flexible
form. • **adjective 1** made of plastic. **2** easily
shaped.
□ **plastic surgery** surgery performed to
repair or reconstruct parts of the body.
■ **plasticity** noun **plasticky** adjective.

plasticine noun trademark a soft modelling
material.

plate noun **1** a flat dish for holding food.
2 bowls, cups, and other utensils made of
gold or silver. **3** a thin, flat piece of metal,
plastic, etc. **4** a small, flat piece of metal
with writing on it, fixed to a wall or door.
5 a printed photograph or illustration in a
book. **6** each of the several rigid pieces
which together make up the earth's
surface. • **verb** (**plates, plating, plated**)
cover a metal object with a thin coating of
a different metal.
□ **plate glass** thick glass used for shop
windows and doors.

plateau /plat-oh/ noun (plural **plateaux**
/plat-ohz/ or **plateaus**) **1** an area of fairly
level high ground. **2** a state of little or no
change after a period of activity or
progress. • **verb** (**plateaus, plateauing,
plateaued**) reach a plateau.

platelet noun a disc-shaped cell fragment
found in large numbers in blood and
involved in clotting.

platen /plat-uhn/ noun a cylindrical roller in
a typewriter against which the paper is
held.

platform noun **1** a raised level surface on
which people or things can stand. **2** a
raised structure along the side of a railway
track where passengers get on and off
trains. **3** a raised structure standing in the
sea from which oil or gas wells can be
drilled. **4** the stated policy of a political
party or group. **5** an opportunity for the
expression or exchange of views. **6** a very
thick sole on a shoe.

platinum noun a precious silvery-white
metallic element.

platitude noun a remark that has been used
too often to be interesting.
■ **platitudinous** adjective.

platonic /pluh-ton-ik/ adjective **1** (of love or
friendship) intimate and affectionate but
not sexual. **2** (**Platonic**) having to do with
the ideas of Plato, a philosopher of ancient
Greece.

platoon noun a subdivision of a company of
soldiers.

platter noun a large flat serving dish.

platypus or **duck-billed platypus** noun
(plural **platypuses**) an animal with a duck-
like bill and webbed feet, which lays eggs.

plaudits plural noun praise.

plausible adjective **1** seeming reasonable or
probable. **2** skilled at making people
believe something.
■ **plausibility** noun **plausibly** adverb.

play verb **1** take part in games for

p

THESAURUS

plastic adjective **1** *at high temperatures the
rocks become plastic:* soft, pliable, pliant,
flexible, malleable, workable, mouldable;
informal bendy. **2** *a plastic smile:* artificial,
false, fake, bogus, insincere; informal phoney,
pretend.
OPPOSITES rigid, genuine.

plate noun **1** *a dinner plate:* dish, platter,
salver; historical trencher; old use charger. **2** *a
plate of spaghetti:* plateful, helping,
portion, serving. **3** *steel plates:* panel,
sheet, slab. **4** *a brass plate on the door:*
plaque, sign, tablet. **5** *the book has colour
plates:* picture, print, illustration,
photograph, photo.
• **verb** *the roof was plated with steel:* cover,
coat, overlay, laminate, veneer, armour,
gild, chrome.

plateau noun upland, mesa, highland,
tableland.

platform noun **1** *he made a speech from the
platform:* stage, dais, rostrum, podium,
stand. **2** *the Democratic Party's platform:*

programme, manifesto, policies, principles,
party line.

plausible adjective credible, believable,
reasonable, likely, possible, conceivable,
imaginable, convincing, persuasive.
OPPOSITES unlikely.

play verb **1** *the children played with toys:*
amuse yourself, entertain yourself, enjoy
yourself, have fun, relax, occupy yourself,
frolic, romp; informal mess about/around. **2** *I
used to play football:* take part in,
participate in, be involved in, compete in,
do. **3** *Liverpool play Oxford on Sunday:*
compete against, take on, meet. **4** *he was
to play Macbeth:* act the part of, take the
role of, appear as, portray, perform.
• **noun 1** *work and play:* amusement,
relaxation, recreation, diversion, leisure,
enjoyment, pleasure, fun. **2** *a Shakespeare
play:* drama, theatrical work, piece,
comedy, tragedy, production, performance.
3 *there was no play in the rope:* movement,
slack, give.
□ **play something down make light of,**

enjoyment. **2** take part in a sport or contest. **3** compete against another player or team. **4** act the role of a character in a play or film. **5** perform on a musical instrument. **6** perform a piece of music. **7** make a CD, tape, or record produce sounds. **8** move a piece or display a playing card when it is your turn in a game. **9** move or flicker over a surface. •noun **1** a piece of writing performed by actors. **2** games that people take part in for enjoyment. **3** the performing of a sports match. **4** a move in a sport or game. **5** freedom of movement. **6** constantly changing movement. □ make a play for informal attempt to attract or gain. play along pretend to cooperate with someone. play something by ear **1** perform music without having seen a score. **2** (**play it by ear**) informal proceed without having formed a plan. play something down disguise the importance of something. playing card each of a set of rectangular pieces of card with numbers and symbols on one side, used in various games. play-off an extra match played to decide the outcome of a contest. play on take advantage of someone's weak point. play up Brit. informal cause problems.

playboy noun a wealthy man who spends his time enjoying himself.

player noun **1** a person taking part in a sport or game. **2** a person who plays a musical instrument. **3** a device for playing CDs, cassettes, etc. **4** a person who has influence in a particular area. **5** an actor.

playful adjective **1** fond of games and amusement. **2** light-hearted.
■ playfully adverb.

playground noun an outdoor area provided for children to play in.

playgroup or **playschool** noun Brit. a regular supervised play session for preschool children.

playhouse noun **1** a theatre. **2** a toy house for children to play in.

playmate noun a friend with whom a child plays.

playpen noun a small portable enclosure in which a baby or small child can play safely.

plaything noun **1** a person who is treated as amusing but unimportant. **2** a toy.

playwright noun a person who writes plays.

plaza noun **1** an open public space in a built-up area. **2** N. Amer. a shopping centre.

plc or **PLC** abbreviation Brit. public limited company.

plea noun **1** a request made in an urgent and emotional way. **2** a formal statement made by or on behalf of a person charged with an offence in a law court.

plead verb (**pleads**, **pleading**, **pleaded** or US & dialect **pled**) **1** make an emotional appeal. **2** argue in support of something. **3** state formally in court whether you are guilty or not guilty of the offence with which you are charged. **4** present something as an excuse for doing or not doing something.
■ pleadingly adverb.

pleasant adjective **1** satisfactory and enjoyable. **2** friendly and likeable.
■ pleasantly adverb.

pleasantry noun (plural **pleasantries**) **1** an unimportant remark made as part of a polite conversation. **2** a mildly amusing joke.

please verb (**pleases**, **pleasing**, **pleased**)

p

THESAURUS

make little of, gloss over, downplay, understate, soft-pedal, diminish, trivialize.
play up (Brit. informal) **1** *the boys really did play up:* **misbehave**, be bad, be naughty. **2** *the boiler's playing up:* **malfunction**, not work, be defective, be faulty; informal be on the blink, act up. **3** *his leg was playing up:* **be painful**, hurt, ache, be sore; informal kill someone, give someone gyp.

player noun **1** *a tournament for young players:* participant, contestant, competitor, contender, sportsman, sportswoman. **2** *the players in the orchestra:* musician, performer, artist, virtuoso, instrumentalist. **3** *the players of the Royal Shakespeare Company:* actor, actress, performer, thespian, entertainer, artiste, trouper.

playful adjective **1** *a playful mood:* frisky, lively, full of fun, frolicsome, high-spirited, exuberant, mischievous, impish; informal full of beans. **2** *a playful remark:* light-hearted,

jokey, teasing, humorous, jocular, facetious, frivolous, flippant.
OPPOSITES serious.

plea noun appeal, entreaty, supplication, petition, request, call.

plead verb *she pleaded ignorance:* claim, use as an excuse, assert, allege, argue.
□ plead with **beg**, implore, entreat, appeal to, ask.

pleasant adjective **1** *a pleasant evening:* enjoyable, pleasurable, nice, agreeable, entertaining, amusing, delightful, charming; informal lovely, great. **2** *the staff are pleasant:* friendly, charming, agreeable, amiable, nice, delightful, sweet, genial, cordial, good-natured, personable, hospitable, polite.
OPPOSITES unpleasant.

please verb **1** *he'd do anything to please her:* make happy, give pleasure to, make someone feel good, delight, charm, amuse,

1 make someone feel happy and satisfied. **2** wish or choose to do something. **3** (**please yourself**) consider only your own wishes. •adverb used in polite requests or questions, or to accept an offer.

pleased adjective feeling or showing pleasure and satisfaction.

pleasurable adjective enjoyable.
■ **pleasurably** adverb.

pleasure noun **1** a feeling of happy satisfaction and enjoyment. **2** an event or activity which you enjoy. •verb (**pleasures**, **pleasuring**, **pleasured**) give pleasure to.

pleat noun a fold in fabric, held by stitching at the top or side. •verb fold or form into pleats.

pleb noun informal, disapproving a member of the lower social classes.

plebeian /pli-bee-uhn/ adjective ordinary or unsophisticated. •noun a member of the ordinary people or the lower classes.

plebiscite /pleb-i-syt/ noun a vote made by everyone entitled to do so on an important public question.

plectrum noun (plural **plectrums** or **plectra**) a thin flat piece of plastic used to pluck the strings of a guitar.

pled US or dialect past participle of PLEAD.

pledge noun **1** a solemn promise or undertaking. **2** something valuable promised as a guarantee that a debt will be paid or a promise kept. **3** a thing given as a token of love or loyalty. •verb (**pledges**, **pledging**, **pledged**) **1** solemnly undertake to do or give something. **2** promise something as a pledge.

plenary /plee-nuh-ri/ adjective **1** (of a meeting at a conference or assembly) to be attended by all participants. **2** full; complete.

plenipotentiary /plen-i-puh-ten-shuh-ri/ noun (plural **plenipotentiaries**) a person given full power by a government to act on its behalf. •adjective having full power to take independent action.

plenitude noun formal a large amount of something.

plenteous adjective literary plentiful.

plentiful adjective existing in or producing great quantities.
■ **plentifully** adverb.

plenty pronoun as much as is wanted or needed; quite enough. •noun a situation in which food and other necessities are available in large enough quantities.

plenum /plee-nuhm/ noun an assembly of all the members of a group or committee.

plethora /pleth-uh-ruh/ noun an excessive amount or number of something.

pleurisy /ploor-i-si/ noun inflammation of the membranes around the lungs, causing pain during breathing.

plexus noun (plural **plexus** or **plexuses**) a complex network or web-like structure.

pliable /ply-uh-b'l/ adjective **1** easily bent. **2** easily influenced or persuaded.
■ **pliability** noun.

pliant adjective pliable.

pliers plural noun pincers having jaws with flat surfaces, used for gripping small

p

THESAURUS

satisfy, gratify, humour, oblige. **2** *do as you please:* like, want, wish, desire, see fit, think fit, choose, will, prefer.
OPPOSITES annoy.

pleased adjective happy, glad, delighted, gratified, grateful, thankful, content, contented, satisfied, thrilled; informal over the moon, on cloud nine; Brit. informal chuffed; N. English informal made up; Austral. informal wrapped.
OPPOSITES unhappy.

pleasing adjective **1** *a pleasing result:* good, agreeable, pleasant, pleasurable, satisfying, gratifying, great. **2** *her pleasing manner:* friendly, amiable, pleasant, agreeable, affable, nice, genial, likeable, charming, engaging, delightful; informal lovely.
OPPOSITES poor, unfriendly.

pleasure noun **1** *she smiled with pleasure:* happiness, delight, joy, gladness, glee, satisfaction, gratification, contentment, enjoyment, amusement. **2** *his greatest pleasure in life:* joy, amusement, diversion, recreation, pastime, treat, thrill. **3** *don't*

mix business and pleasure: enjoyment, fun, entertainment, recreation, leisure, relaxation.
OPPOSITES unhappiness.

pledge noun *his election pledge:* promise, vow, undertaking, word, commitment, assurance, oath, guarantee.
•verb *he pledged to root out corruption:* promise, vow, undertake, swear, commit yourself, declare, affirm.

plentiful adjective abundant, copious, ample, profuse, rich, lavish, generous, bountiful, bumper, prolific; informal galore.
OPPOSITES scarce.

plenty pronoun *there are plenty of books:* a lot of, many, a great deal of, a plethora of, enough and to spare, no lack of, a wealth of; informal loads of, heaps of, stacks of, masses of, oodles of.
•noun *times of plenty:* prosperity, wealth, affluence, opulence, comfort, luxury, abundance.

objects and bending or cutting wire.

plight[1] noun a dangerous or difficult situation.

plight[2] verb (**plight your troth**) old use promise to marry.

plimsoll noun Brit. a light rubber-soled canvas sports shoe.

plinth noun a heavy block or slab supporting a statue or forming the base of a column.

PLO abbreviation Palestine Liberation Organization.

plod verb (**plods, plodding, plodded**) 1 walk slowly with heavy steps. 2 work slowly and steadily at a dull task. •noun a slow, heavy walk.

plonk[1] verb informal put something down heavily or carelessly.

plonk[2] noun Brit. informal cheap wine.

plop noun a sound like that of a small, solid object dropping into water without a splash. •verb (**plops, plopping, plopped**) fall or drop with a plop.

plot noun 1 a secret plan to do something illegal or harmful. 2 the main sequence of events in a play, novel, or film. 3 a small piece of ground marked out for building, gardening, etc. •verb (**plots, plotting, plotted**) 1 secretly make plans to carry out something illegal or harmful. 2 mark a route or position on a chart or graph.
■ **plotter** noun.

plough (US spelling **plow**) noun 1 a piece of farming equipment with one or more blades fixed in a frame, used to turn over soil. 2 (**the Plough**) a formation of seven stars shaped like a simple plough, in the constellation Ursa Major (the Great Bear). •verb 1 turn earth with a plough. 2 move forward with difficulty or force. 3 (of a ship or boat) travel through an area of water. 4 (**plough something in**) invest money in a business.

ploughman's lunch noun Brit. a meal of bread, cheese, and pickle.

ploughshare noun the main cutting blade of a plough.

plover /rhymes with lover/ noun a wading bird with a short bill.

ploy noun a cunning act performed to gain an advantage.

pluck verb 1 take hold of something and quickly remove it from its place. 2 pull out a hair or feather. 3 pull the feathers from a bird's carcass to prepare it for cooking. 4 pull at. 5 sound a stringed instrument with your fingers or a plectrum. •noun courage.
□ **pluck up courage** summon up enough courage to do something frightening.

plucky adjective (**pluckier, pluckiest**) having a lot of courage and determination.
■ **pluckily** adverb.

plug noun 1 a piece of solid material that tightly blocks a hole. 2 a device with metal pins that fit into holes in a socket to make an electrical connection. 3 an electrical socket. 4 informal a piece of publicity promoting a product or event. •verb (**plugs, plugging, plugged**) 1 block a hole. 2 (**plug something in**) connect an appliance to an electric circuit. 3 informal promote a product or event by mentioning it publicly. 4 (**plug away**) informal proceed steadily with a task.

p

THESAURUS

plight noun predicament, difficult situation, dire straits, trouble, difficulty, bind; informal tight corner, tight spot, hole, pickle, jam, fix.

plod verb trudge, walk heavily, clump, stomp, tramp, lumber, slog.
OPPOSITES stride, skip.

plot noun 1 a plot to overthrow him: conspiracy, intrigue, stratagem, plan. 2 the plot of her novel: storyline, story, scenario, action, thread, narrative. 3 a three-acre plot: piece of ground, patch, area, tract, acreage; Brit. allotment; N. Amer. lot, plat; N. Amer. & Austral./NZ homesite.
•verb 1 he plotted their downfall: plan, scheme, arrange, organize, contrive. 2 his brother was plotting against him: conspire, scheme, intrigue, connive. 3 the points were plotted on a graph: mark, chart, map.

plough verb 1 the fields were ploughed: till, furrow, harrow, cultivate, work. 2 the car ploughed into a wall: crash, smash, career, plunge, bulldoze, hurtle, cannon.

ploy noun ruse, tactic, move, device, stratagem, scheme, trick, gambit, plan, manoeuvre, dodge, subterfuge; Brit. informal wheeze.

pluck verb 1 he plucked a thread from his lapel: remove, pick, pull, extract. 2 she plucked at his T-shirt: pull, tug, clutch, snatch, grab, catch, tweak, jerk; informal yank. 3 she plucked the guitar strings: strum, pick, thrum, twang.
•noun it took a lot of pluck: courage, bravery, nerve, daring, spirit, grit; informal guts; Brit. informal bottle; N. Amer. informal moxie.

plug noun 1 she pulled out the plug: stopper, bung, cork, connector; N. Amer. stopple. 2 (informal) a plug for his new book: advertisement, promotion, commercial, recommendation, mention, good word; informal hype, push, puff.
•verb 1 plug the holes: stop, seal, close, block, fill. 2 (informal) she plugged her new film: publicize, promote, advertise, mention, bang the drum for, draw attention to; informal hype, push.

plughole noun Brit. a hole at the bottom or end of a sink or bath, through which the water drains away.

plum noun 1 an oval fruit which is purple, reddish, or yellow when ripe. 2 a reddish-purple colour. • adjective informal highly desirable: *a plum job.*

plumage noun a bird's feathers.

plumb¹ verb 1 explore or experience something fully. 2 measure the depth of water. 3 test an upright surface to find out if it is vertical. • noun a heavy object attached to a plumb line. • adverb informal exactly. • adjective vertical.
□ **plumb line** a line with a heavy object attached to it, used for measuring the depth of water or checking that a wall, post, etc. is vertical.

plumb² verb (**plumb something in**) install a bath, washing machine, etc. and connect it to water and drainage pipes.

plumber noun a person who fits and repairs the pipes and fittings used in the supply of water and heating in a building.

plumbing noun the system of pipes and fittings required for the water supply and heating in a building.

plume noun 1 a long, soft feather or group of feathers. 2 a long spreading cloud of smoke or vapour.
■ **plumed** adjective.

plummet verb (**plummets, plummeting, plummeted**) 1 fall straight down very quickly. 2 decrease rapidly in value or amount. • noun a steep and rapid fall or drop.

plummy adjective (**plummier, plummiest**) Brit. informal (of a person's voice) typical of the English upper classes.

plump¹ adjective 1 rather fat. 2 full and rounded in shape. • verb (**plump something up**) make something more full and rounded.

plump² verb 1 set or sit down heavily. 2 (**plump for**) decide in favour of one of two or more possibilities.

plunder verb (**plunders, plundering, plundered**) force your way into a place and steal everything of value. • noun 1 goods obtained by plundering. 2 the action of plundering.

plunge verb (**plunges, plunging, plunged**) 1 fall or move suddenly and uncontrollably. 2 jump or dive quickly. 3 push or thrust something quickly. 4 (**plunge in**) begin a course of action without thought or care. 5 (**be plunged into**) be suddenly brought into a particular state. • noun an act of plunging.
□ **take the plunge** informal finally decide to do something difficult or challenging.

plunger noun 1 a part of a device that works with a plunging or thrusting movement. 2 a rubber cup on a long handle, used to clear blocked pipes by means of suction.

pluperfect adjective Grammar (of a tense) referring to an action completed earlier than some past point of time, formed by *had* and the past participle (as in *he had gone by then*).

plural adjective 1 more than one in number. 2 Grammar (of a word or form) referring to more than one. • noun Grammar a plural word or form.

pluralism noun 1 a system in which power is shared among a number of political

p

THESAURUS

plumb verb *an attempt to plumb her psyche:* explore, probe, delve into, search, examine, investigate, fathom, penetrate, understand.
• adverb (informal) *it went plumb through the screen:* right, exactly, precisely, directly, dead, straight; informal (slap) bang.

plummet verb 1 *the plane plummeted to the ground:* plunge, dive, drop, fall, hurtle. 2 *share prices plummeted:* fall steeply, plunge, tumble, drop rapidly, slump; informal crash, nosedive.
OPPOSITES soar.

plump adjective fat, chubby, rotund, ample, round, stout, portly, overweight; informal tubby, roly-poly, pudgy; Brit. informal podgy; N. Amer. informal zaftig, corn-fed.
OPPOSITES thin.

plunder verb 1 *enemy soldiers plundered the countryside:* pillage, loot, ransack, rob, raid, rifle, strip, sack. 2 *money plundered from pension funds:* steal, seize, thieve, pilfer, embezzle.

• noun *huge quantities of plunder:* booty, loot, stolen goods, spoils, ill-gotten gains; informal swag.

plunge verb 1 *Joy plunged into the sea:* dive, jump, throw yourself. 2 *the aircraft plunged to the ground:* plummet, nosedive, drop, fall, tumble, descend. 3 *the car plunged down an alley:* charge, hurtle, career, plough, tear; N. Amer. informal barrel. 4 *oil prices plunged:* fall sharply, plummet, drop, tumble, slump; informal crash, nosedive. 5 *he plunged the dagger into her back:* thrust, stab, sink, stick, ram, drive, push, shove, force. 6 *plunge the pears into water:* immerse, submerge, dip, dunk. 7 *the room was plunged into darkness:* throw, cast.
OPPOSITES rise.
• noun 1 *a plunge in the pool:* dive, jump, dip. 2 *a plunge in profits:* fall, drop, slump; informal nosedive, crash.
OPPOSITES rise.

parties. **2** the acceptance within a society of a number of groups with different beliefs or ethnic backgrounds.
■ **pluralist** noun & adjective.

plurality noun (plural **pluralities**) **1** the fact or state of being plural. **2** a large number of people or things.

plus preposition **1** with the addition of. **2** together with; as well as. •**adjective 1** (after a number or amount) at least. **2** (after a grade) rather better than. **3** (before a number) above zero. **4** having a positive electric charge. •**noun 1** (also **plus sign**) the symbol +, indicating addition or a positive value. **2** informal an advantage. •**conjunction** informal also.
□ **plus fours** men's trousers that are cut wide over the thigh and are gathered in at mid-calf length.

plush noun a fabric with a thick, velvety surface. •**adjective** informal luxurious.

Pluto noun the furthest planet from the sun in the solar system.

plutocracy /ploo-**tok**-ruh-si/ noun (plural **plutocracies**) **1** government by the richest people in a country. **2** a society governed by the richest people in it.

plutocrat noun a person who is powerful because of their wealth.

plutonium /ploo-**toh**-ni-uhm/ noun a radioactive metallic element used as a fuel in nuclear reactors and as an explosive in atomic weapons.

ply[1] noun (plural **plies**) a thickness or layer of a material.

ply[2] verb (**plies, plying, plied**) **1** (**ply someone with**) keep presenting someone with food or drink, or asking them questions. **2** (of a ship or vehicle) travel regularly over a route. **3** work steadily with a tool.
□ **ply your trade** do your job or business.

plywood noun board consisting of layers of wood glued together.

PM abbreviation Prime Minister.

p.m. abbreviation after noon.

pneumatic /nyoo-**mat**-ik/ adjective containing or operated by air or gas under pressure.

pneumonia /nyoo-**moh**-ni-uh/ noun an infection causing inflammation in the lungs.

poach[1] verb cook something by simmering it in a small amount of liquid.

poach[2] verb **1** hunt game or catch fish illegally from private or protected areas. **2** unfairly entice customers, workers, etc. away from someone else.
■ **poacher** noun.

pocked adjective having pockmarks.

pocket noun **1** a small bag sewn into or on clothing, used for carrying small articles. **2** a small area or group that is different from its surroundings. **3** informal the money that you have available: *gifts to suit every pocket.* **4** an opening at the corner or on the side of a billiard table into which balls are struck. •**verb** (**pockets, pocketing, pocketed**) **1** put something into your pocket. **2** take something that is not yours.
□ **pocket money 1** a small amount of money given to children regularly by their parents. **2** a small amount of money for minor expenses.

pockmark noun **1** a hollow scar or mark on the skin left by a spot. **2** a mark or hollow area on a surface.
■ **pockmarked** adjective.

p

---

plus preposition *four novels plus various poems:* as well as, together with, along with, in addition to, and, added to, not to mention.
OPPOSITES minus.
•**noun** (informal) *one of the pluses of the job:* advantage, good point, asset, pro, benefit, bonus, attraction; informal perk.
OPPOSITES disadvantage.

plush adjective (informal) luxurious, luxury, de luxe, sumptuous, opulent, magnificent, rich, expensive, fancy; Brit. upmarket; informal posh, classy; Brit. informal swish; N. Amer. informal swank.
OPPOSITES austere.

ply verb **1** *he plied a profitable trade:* engage in, carry on, pursue, conduct, practise. **2** *ferries ply between all lake resorts:* travel, shuttle, go back and forth. **3** *she plied me with scones:* provide, supply, shower. **4** *he plied her with questions:*

bombard, assail, pester, plague, harass; informal hassle.

poach verb **1** *he's been poaching salmon:* hunt illegally, catch illegally, steal. **2** *workers were poached by other firms:* steal, appropriate, headhunt; informal nab, swipe; Brit. informal nick, pinch.

pocket noun **1** *a bag with two pockets:* pouch, compartment. **2** *pockets of resistance:* area, patch, region, cluster.
•**adjective** *a pocket dictionary:* small, little, miniature, mini, compact, concise, abridged, portable, travel; N. Amer. vest-pocket.
•**verb 1** *he pocketed $4m for a few months' work:* acquire, obtain, gain, get, secure, win, make, earn. **2** *they were pocketing money supposed to be used for repairs:* steal, appropriate, purloin, misappropriate, embezzle.

pod[1] noun a long seed case of a pea, bean, etc. • verb (**pods, podding, podded**) remove peas or beans from their pods before cooking.

pod[2] noun a small herd of whales or similar sea mammals.

podcast noun a digital recording of a radio broadcast which is made available on the Internet for downloading to a personal computer or MP3 player.
■ **podcasting** noun.

podgy adjective (**podgier, podgiest**) Brit. informal rather fat.

podium noun (plural **podiums** or **podia**) a small platform on which a person stands to conduct an orchestra or give a speech.

poem noun a piece of imaginative writing in verse.

poesy /poh-i-zi/ noun old use poetry.

poet noun a person who writes poems.
□ **Poet Laureate** (plural **Poets Laureate**) a poet appointed by the British king or queen, formerly responsible for writing poems for important occasions.

poetic or **poetical** adjective 1 having to do with poetry. 2 expressed in a sensitive and imaginative way.
□ **poetic justice** a situation in which something bad happens to someone who has done something wrong. **poetic licence** freedom to change facts or the normal rules of language to achieve a special effect in writing.
■ **poetically** adverb.

poetry noun 1 poems as a whole or as a form of literature. 2 a quality of beauty and sensitivity.

po-faced adjective Brit. informal serious and disapproving.

pogo stick noun a toy for bouncing around

on, consisting of a pole on a spring, with a bar to stand on and a handle at the top.

pogrom noun an organized massacre of an ethnic group, originally that of Jews in Russia or eastern Europe.

poignant /poy-nyuhnt/ adjective making you feel sadness or regret.
■ **poignancy** noun **poignantly** adverb.

poinsettia noun a shrub with large red leaves which resemble petals.

point noun 1 the tapered, sharp end of a tool, weapon, or other object. 2 a particular place or moment. 3 an item, detail, or idea. 4 (**the point**) the most important part of what is being discussed. 5 the advantage or purpose of something. 6 a unit of scoring, value, or measurement. 7 a small dot used as punctuation or in decimal numbers. 8 each of thirty-two directions marked at equal distances round a compass. 9 a narrow piece of land jutting out into the sea. 10 (**points**) Brit. a junction of two railway lines. 11 (also **power point**) Brit. an electrical socket. 12 (**points**) a set of electrical contacts in the distributor of a motor vehicle. • verb 1 direct someone's attention by extending your finger. 2 aim, indicate, or face in a particular direction. 3 (**point something out**) make someone aware of something. 4 (**point to**) indicate that something is likely to happen. 5 fill in the joints of brickwork or tiling with mortar or cement.
□ **point-blank** 1 (of a shot or missile) fired from very close to its target. 2 in a blunt and very direct way. **point of view** a particular attitude or opinion. **point-to-point** (plural **point-to-points**) Brit. a cross-country race for horses used in hunting.

pointed adjective 1 having a sharpened or

THESAURUS

pod noun shell, husk, hull, case; N. Amer. shuck.

podium noun platform, stage, dais, rostrum, stand.

poem noun verse, rhyme, lyric, piece of poetry.

poetic adjective expressive, figurative, symbolic, flowery, artistic, imaginative, creative.

poetry noun poems, verse, versification, rhyme.

poignant adjective touching, moving, sad, affecting, pitiful, pathetic, plaintive.

point noun 1 *the point of a needle:* tip, (sharp) end, extremity, prong, spike, tine, nib, barb. 2 *points of light:* pinpoint, dot, spot, speck. 3 *a meeting point:* place, position, location, site, spot. 4 *this point in her life:* time, stage, juncture, period,

phase. 5 *the tension had reached such a high point:* level, degree, stage, pitch, extent. 6 *an important point:* detail, item, fact, thing, argument, consideration, factor, element, subject, issue, topic, question, matter. 7 *get to the point:* heart of the matter, essence, nub, core, crux; informal nitty-gritty. 8 *what's the point of this?* purpose, aim, object, objective, goal, intention, use, sense, value, advantage. 9 *he had his good points:* attribute, characteristic, feature, trait, quality, property, aspect, side.
• verb *she pointed the gun at him:* aim, direct, level, train.
□ **point something out identify,** show, draw attention to, indicate, specify, detail, mention. **point to something indicate,** suggest, evidence, signal, signify, denote.

pointed adjective 1 *a pointed stick:* sharp,

tapered tip or end. **2** (of a remark or look) directed towards a particular person and expressing a clear message.

pointer noun **1** a long, thin piece of metal on a scale or dial which moves to give a reading. **2** a hint or tip. **3** a breed of dog that, when it scents game, stands rigid and looks towards it.

pointless adjective having little or no sense or purpose.
■ **pointlessly** adverb.

poise noun **1** a graceful way of holding your body. **2** a calm and confident manner. •verb **1** cause something to be balanced or suspended. **2** (**poised**) calm and confident. **3** (**be poised to do**) be ready to do.

poison noun **1** a substance that causes death or injury to a person or animal that swallows or absorbs it. **2** a harmful influence. •verb **1** harm or kill a person or animal with poison. **2** put poison on or in. **3** have a harmful effect on.
■ **poisoner** noun **poisonous** adjective.

poke verb (**pokes, poking, poked**) **1** prod with a finger or a sharp object. **2** (**poke about** or **around**) look or search around. **3** push or stick out in a particular direction. •noun an act of poking.

poker¹ noun a metal rod used for prodding an open fire.

poker² noun a card game in which the players bet on the value of the hands dealt to them.
□ **poker face** a blank expression that hides your true feelings.

poky or **pokey** adjective (**pokier, pokiest**) (of a room or building) uncomfortably small and cramped.

polar adjective **1** relating to the North or South Poles or the regions around them. **2** having an electrical or magnetic field. **3** completely opposite.
□ **polar bear** a large white bear from the Arctic.

polarity noun (plural **polarities**) **1** the state of having poles or opposites. **2** the direction of a magnetic or electric field.

polarize or **polarise** verb (**polarizes, polarizing, polarized**) **1** divide people into two sharply contrasting groups with different opinions. **2** Physics restrict the vibrations of a wave of light to one direction. **3** give magnetic or electric polarity to.
■ **polarization** noun.

Polaroid noun trademark **1** a material that polarizes the light passing through it, used in sunglasses. **2** a camera that produces a finished print rapidly after each exposure.

polder noun (in the Netherlands) a piece of land reclaimed from the sea or a river.

Pole noun a person from Poland.

pole¹ noun a long, thin rounded piece of wood or metal, used as a support.
□ **pole position** the most favourable position at the start of a motor race. **pole vault** an athletic event in which competitors vault over a high bar with the aid of a long pole.

spiky, spiked, tapering, barbed; informal pointy. **2** *a pointed remark:* cutting, biting, incisive, trenchant, acerbic, caustic, scathing, venomous, sarcastic; informal sarky; N. Amer. informal snarky.

pointer noun **1** *the pointer moved to 100rpm:* indicator, needle, arrow, hand. **2** *a pointer to the outcome of the election:* indication, indicator, clue, hint, sign, signal, evidence. **3** *I can give you a few pointers:* tip, hint, suggestion, guideline, recommendation.

pointless adjective senseless, futile, hopeless, unavailing, aimless, idle, worthless, valueless.
OPPOSITES valuable.

poise noun **1** *poise and good deportment:* grace, gracefulness, elegance, balance, control. **2** *in spite of the setback she retained her poise:* composure, equanimity, self-possession, aplomb, self-assurance, self-control, sangfroid, dignity, presence of mind; informal cool.

poised adjective **1** *she was poised on one foot:* balanced, suspended, motionless, hanging, hovering. **2** *he was poised for*

action: prepared, ready, braced, geared up, all set, standing by.

poison noun toxin, venom.
•verb **1** *the Amazon is being poisoned:* pollute, contaminate, taint, spoil. **2** *they poisoned his mind:* twist, warp, corrupt.

poisonous adjective **1** *a poisonous snake:* venomous, deadly. **2** *a poisonous chemical:* toxic, noxious, deadly, fatal, lethal, mortal. **3** *a poisonous glance:* malicious, malevolent, hostile, spiteful, bitter, venomous, malign.
OPPOSITES harmless.

poke verb **1** *she poked him in the ribs:* prod, jab, dig, elbow, nudge, shove, jolt, stab, stick. **2** *leave the cable poking out:* stick out, jut out, protrude, project, extend. •noun *Carrie gave him a poke:* prod, jab, dig, elbow, nudge.

poky adjective small, little, tiny, cramped, confined, restricted, boxy.
OPPOSITES spacious.

pole noun post, pillar, stanchion, stake, support, prop, stick, paling, staff.

pole² noun 1 either of the two points (**North Pole** or **South Pole**) at opposite ends of the earth's axis. 2 each of the two opposite points of a magnet at which magnetic forces are strongest. 3 the positive or negative terminal of an electric cell or battery.
□ be poles apart have nothing in common.

poleaxe (US spelling **poleax**) verb (**poleaxes, poleaxing, poleaxed**) 1 kill or knock down with a heavy blow. 2 shock someone very much.

polecat noun 1 a dark brown weasel-like animal with an unpleasant smell. 2 N. Amer. a skunk.

polemic /puh-lem-ik/ noun 1 a speech or piece of writing that argues strongly for or against something. 2 (also **polemics**) the practice of using fierce argument or discussion. • adjective (also **polemical**) having to do with fierce argument or discussion.
■ **polemicist** noun.

police noun an official body of people employed by a state to prevent and solve crime and keep public order. • verb (**polices, policing, policed**) 1 keep law and order in an area. 2 make sure that a particular set of rules is obeyed.
□ **police state** a state in which the government requires the police to watch people secretly and control their activities.

policeman or **policewoman** noun (plural **policemen** or **policewomen**) a member of a police force.

policy noun (plural **policies**) 1 a plan of action adopted by an organization or person. 2 a contract of insurance.

polio or **poliomyelitis** /poh-li-oh-my-uh-ly-tiss/ noun a disease that can cause temporary or permanent paralysis.

Polish noun the language of Poland.
• adjective relating to Poland.

polish verb 1 make something smooth and shiny by rubbing. 2 (**polish something up**) improve a skill. 3 (**polish something off**) finish eating or doing something quickly. • noun 1 a substance used to polish something. 2 an act of polishing. 3 a shiny appearance produced by polishing. 4 refinement or elegance.
■ **polisher** noun.

polite adjective (**politer, politest**) 1 respectful and considerate towards other people; courteous. 2 civilized or refined.
■ **politely** adverb **politeness** noun.

politic adjective (of an action) sensible and wise in the circumstances.

political adjective 1 relating to the government or public affairs of a country. 2 related to or interested in politics.
□ **political correctness** the avoidance of language or behaviour that could offend certain groups of people. **political prisoner** a person who is imprisoned for their beliefs rather than because they have committed a crime.
■ **politically** adverb.

politician noun a person who holds an

THESAURUS

police noun police force, police service, police officers, policemen, policewomen; Brit. constabulary; informal the cops, the fuzz, the law, the boys in blue; Brit. informal the (Old) Bill; N. Amer. informal the heat.
• verb 1 we must police the area: guard, watch over, protect, defend, patrol. 2 the regulations will be policed by the ministry: enforce, regulate, oversee, supervise, monitor, observe, check.

police officer noun policeman, policewoman; Brit. constable; N. Amer. patrolman, trooper, roundsman; informal cop; Brit. informal rozzer; N. Amer. informal uniform.

policy noun plans, approach, code, system, guidelines, theory, line, position, stance.

polish verb 1 I polished his shoes: shine, wax, buff, rub up/down, gloss, burnish. 2 polish up your essay: perfect, refine, improve, hone, enhance, brush up, revise, edit, correct, rewrite, go over, touch up.
• noun his poetry has clarity and polish: sophistication, refinement, urbanity, suaveness, elegance, style, grace, finesse; informal class.

polished adjective 1 a polished table: shiny, glossy, gleaming, lustrous, glassy, waxed, buffed, burnished. 2 a polished performance: expert, accomplished, masterly, skilful, adept, adroit, dexterous, consummate, superb, superlative.
OPPOSITES dull, inexpert.

polite adjective 1 a very polite girl: well mannered, civil, courteous, respectful, well behaved, well bred, gentlemanly, ladylike, genteel, gracious, tactful, diplomatic. 2 polite society: civilized, refined, cultured, sophisticated.
OPPOSITES rude, uncivilized.

politic adjective wise, prudent, sensible, shrewd, astute, judicious, expedient, advantageous, beneficial, profitable.
OPPOSITES unwise.

political adjective governmental, government, constitutional, ministerial, parliamentary, diplomatic, legislative, administrative.

politician noun legislator, Member of Parliament, MP, representative, minister, statesman, stateswoman, senator, congressman, congresswoman; informal politico.

elected position within the government.

politicize or **politicise** verb (**politicizes, politicizing, politicized**) **1** make someone interested in politics. **2** make something a political issue.
■ **politicization** noun.

politics noun **1** the activities concerned with governing a country or area. **2** a particular set of political beliefs. **3** activities concerned with gaining or using power within an organization or group: *office politics*.

polity noun (plural **polities**) **1** a form of government. **2** a society as a politically organized state.

polka noun a lively dance for couples.
□ **polka dot** each of a number of dots that are evenly spaced to form a pattern.

poll /*rhymes with* pole *or* doll/ noun **1** the process of voting in an election. **2** a record of the number of votes cast. • verb **1** record the opinion or vote of. **2** (of a candidate in an election) receive a particular number of votes.
□ **poll tax** a tax paid at the same rate by every adult.

pollard verb cut off the top and side branches of a tree to encourage new growth.

pollen noun a powder produced by the male part of a flower, which is carried by bees, the wind, etc. and can fertilize other flowers.
□ **pollen count** a measure of the amount of pollen in the air.

pollinate verb (**pollinates, pollinating, pollinated**) carry pollen to and fertilize a flower or plant.
■ **pollination** noun.

pollster noun a person who carries out opinion polls.

pollutant noun a substance that causes pollution.

pollute verb (**pollutes, polluting, polluted**) make something dirty or poisonous with unwanted or harmful substances.
■ **polluter** noun.

pollution noun the presence in the air, soil, or water of a substance with unpleasant or harmful effects.

polo noun a game similar to hockey, played on horseback with a long-handled mallet.
□ **polo neck** Brit. a high, tight, turned-over collar on a sweater. **polo shirt** a casual short-sleeved shirt with a collar and two or three buttons at the neck.

polonium noun a rare radioactive metallic element.

poltergeist /**pol**-ter-gyst/ noun a kind of ghost that is said to make loud noises and throw objects around.

polychrome adjective consisting of several colours.
■ **polychromatic** adjective.

polyester noun a synthetic fibre used to make fabric for clothes.

polygamy /puh-**lig**-uh-mi/ noun the practice of having more than one wife or husband at the same time.
■ **polygamist** noun **polygamous** adjective.

polyglot adjective knowing or using several languages.

polygon noun a figure with three or more straight sides and angles.

polygraph noun a lie detector.

polyhedron /po-li-**hee**-druhn/ noun (plural **polyhedra** or **polyhedrons**) a solid figure with many sides.

polymath noun a person with a wide knowledge of many subjects.

polymer noun a substance with a molecular structure formed from many identical small molecules bonded together.

polymorphic or **polymorphous** adjective having several different forms.

Polynesian noun a person from Polynesia, a large group of Pacific islands including New Zealand and Hawaii. • adjective relating to Polynesia.

polyp noun **1** a simple sea creature which remains fixed in the same place, such as coral. **2** Medicine a small lump sticking out from a mucous membrane.

polyphony /puh-**li**-fuh-ni/ noun the combination of a number of musical parts, each forming an individual melody and harmonizing with each other.
■ **polyphonic** adjective.

p

THESAURUS

politics noun **1** *a career in politics:* government, affairs of state, public affairs, diplomacy. **2** *he studies politics:* political science, civics. **3** *what are his politics?* political views, political leanings. **4** *office politics:* power struggles, machinations, manoeuvring, realpolitik.

poll noun **1** *the poll to elect a new leader:* vote, ballot, show of hands, referendum, plebiscite, election. **2** *a poll to investigate*

holiday choices: survey, opinion poll, market research, census.
• verb **1** *most of those polled supported him:* canvass, survey, ask, question, interview, ballot. **2** *she polled 119 votes:* get, gain, register, record, return.

pollute verb contaminate, taint, poison, foul, dirty, soil, infect.
OPPOSITES purify.

pollution noun contamination, impurity,

polystyrene noun a light synthetic material.

polysyllabic adjective having more than one syllable.

polytechnic noun (in the past in the UK) a college offering courses at degree level (now called a university).

polytheism /po-li-thee-i-z'm/ noun the worship of more than one god.
■ **polytheistic** adjective.

polythene noun Brit. a tough, light, flexible plastic.

polyunsaturated adjective (of a fat) having a chemical structure that is thought not to lead to the formation of cholesterol in the blood.

polyurethane noun a synthetic material used in paints and varnishes.

Pom noun Austral./NZ informal a British person.
■ **Pommy** adjective & noun.

pomade noun a scented oil or cream for making the hair glossy and smooth.

pomander noun a ball or container of sweet-smelling substances used to perfume a room or cupboard.

pomegranate noun a round tropical fruit with a tough orange outer skin and red flesh containing many seeds.

pommel noun 1 the curving or projecting front part of a saddle. 2 a rounded knob on the handle of a sword.

pomp noun the special clothes, music, and customs that are part of a grand public ceremony.

pompom noun a small woollen ball attached to a garment for decoration.

pompous adjective showing in a rather solemn or arrogant way that you have a high opinion of yourself and your own views.
■ **pomposity** noun **pompously** adverb.

ponce Brit. informal noun 1 a man who lives off a prostitute's earnings. 2 disapproving an effeminate man. • verb (**ponces, poncing, ponced**) (**ponce about** or **around**) behave in a way that wastes time or looks silly.
■ **poncey** (or **poncy**) adjective.

poncho noun (plural **ponchos**) a garment made of a thick piece of cloth with a slit in the middle for the head.

pond noun a small area of still water.

ponder verb (**ponders, pondering, pondered**) consider something carefully.

ponderous adjective 1 moving slowly and heavily. 2 boringly solemn or long-winded.
■ **ponderously** adverb.

pondweed noun a plant that grows in still or running water.

pong Brit. informal noun a strong, unpleasant smell. • verb smell strongly and unpleasantly.
■ **pongy** adjective.

pontiff noun the Pope.

pontifical adjective having to do with a pope; papal.

pontificate verb /pon-ti-fi-kayt/ (**pontificates, pontificating, pontificated**) express your opinions in a pompous and overbearing way. • noun (**the Pontificate**) /pon-ti-fi-kuht/ the official position of a pope or bishop.

pontoon[1] noun Brit. a card game in which players try to obtain cards with a value totalling twenty-one.

pontoon[2] noun 1 a flat-bottomed boat or hollow cylinder used with others to support a temporary bridge or floating landing stage. 2 a bridge or landing stage supported by pontoons.

pony noun (plural **ponies**) a small breed of horse, especially one below 15 hands.
□ **pony-trekking** Brit. the riding of ponies across country as a leisure activity.

ponytail noun a hairstyle in which the hair is drawn back and tied at the back of the head.

pooch noun informal a dog.

poodle noun a breed of dog with a curly coat that is usually clipped.

poof or **pouf** noun Brit. informal a homosexual man.

pooh-pooh verb informal dismiss an idea as being silly or impractical.

pool[1] noun 1 a small area of still water. 2 (also **swimming pool**) an artificial pool for swimming in. 3 a small, shallow patch of liquid on a surface.

pool[2] noun 1 a supply of vehicles, goods,

THESAURUS

dirt, filth, infection.

pompous adjective self-important, overbearing, sententious, grandiose, affected, pretentious, puffed up, haughty, proud, conceited, supercilious, condescending, patronizing.
OPPOSITES modest.

ponder verb think about, contemplate, consider, review, reflect on, mull over, meditate on, muse on, dwell on.

pool[1] noun 1 *pools of water:* puddle, pond, lake. 2 *the hotel has a pool:* swimming pool, baths; Brit. swimming baths; N. Amer. natatorium.

pool[2] noun 1 *a pool of skilled labour:* supply, reserve(s), reservoir, fund, store, bank, stock, cache. 2 *a pool of money for emergencies:* fund, reserve, kitty, pot, bank, purse.
• verb *they pooled their skills:* combine,

money, etc. that is shared between a number of people and available for use when needed. **2 (the pools** or **football pools)** a form of gambling on the results of football matches. **3** a game played on a billiard table using sixteen balls. •**verb** put something into a common fund to be used by a number of people.

poop or **poop deck** noun a raised deck at the back of a ship.

poor adjective **1** having very little money. **2** of a low standard or quality. **3 (poor in)** not having enough of something. **4** deserving pity or sympathy.

poorhouse noun Brit. a workhouse.

poorly adverb badly. •**adjective** chiefly Brit. unwell.

pootle verb **(pootles, pootling, pootled)** Brit. informal move or travel in a leisurely way.

pop¹ verb **(pops, popping, popped) 1** make a sudden short explosive sound. **2** go or come quickly or unexpectedly. **3** put something somewhere quickly or for a short time. **4** (of a person's eyes) open wide and appear to bulge. •**noun 1** a sudden short explosive sound. **2** informal, dated a sweet fizzy drink.

pop² noun **(also pop music)** modern popular music, usually with a strong melody and beat. •**adjective 1** relating to pop music. **2** often disapproving made easy for the general public to understand; popularized: *pop psychology.*
□ **pop art** a style of art that uses images taken from popular culture, such as advertisements or films.

pop³ noun informal, chiefly US father.

popcorn noun a snack consisting of maize kernels which are heated until they burst open.

pope noun the Bishop of Rome as head of the Roman Catholic Church.

popery noun disapproving Roman Catholicism. ■ **popish** adjective.

popinjay noun old use a person who is vain and dresses in a showy way.

poplar noun a tall, slender tree with soft wood.

poplin noun a cotton fabric with a finely ribbed surface.

poppadom noun (in Indian cookery) a thin circular piece of spiced bread that is fried until crisp.

popper noun Brit. informal a press stud.

poppet noun Brit. informal a pretty or charming child.

poppy noun a plant with bright flowers and small black seeds.

poppycock noun informal nonsense.

populace noun the general public.

popular adjective **1** liked or admired by many people. **2** suited to the tastes of the general public. **3** connected with or carried out by ordinary people. ■ **popularly** adverb.

popularity noun the state of being liked or supported by many people.

popularize or **popularise** verb **(popularizes, popularizing, popularized) 1** make something popular. **2** make something understandable or interesting to the general public. ■ **popularization** noun.

populate verb **(populates, populating,**

p

group, join, unite, merge, share.

poor adjective **1** *a poor family:* poverty-stricken, penniless, impoverished, impecunious, needy, destitute; Brit. on the breadline; informal hard up, strapped, on your uppers; formal penurious. **2** *poor workmanship:* substandard, bad, deficient, defective, faulty, imperfect, inferior, unsatisfactory, shoddy, crude, inadequate, unacceptable; informal crummy, rubbishy, rotten; Brit. informal ropy, duff, rubbish, dodgy. **3** *a poor crop:* meagre, scanty, scant, paltry, reduced, modest, sparse, spare, deficient, insubstantial, skimpy, lean; informal measly, stingy. **4** *the poor thing:* unfortunate, unlucky, unhappy, hapless, wretched.
OPPOSITES rich, superior, abundant, lucky.

poorly adverb *the text is poorly written:* badly, imperfectly, incompetently, crudely, shoddily, inadequately.
•**adjective** *she felt poorly:* ill, unwell, not very well, ailing, indisposed, out of sorts,

under par, peaky; Brit. off colour; informal under the weather, rough; Brit. informal ropy, grotty; Scottish informal wabbit; Austral./NZ informal crook.

pop verb **1** *champagne corks popped:* go bang, go off, crack, snap, burst, explode. **2** *I'm just popping home:* go; informal tootle, whip; Brit. informal nip. **3** *pop a bag over the pot:* put, place, slip, throw, slide, stick, set, lay, position.
•**noun** *the balloons burst with a pop:* bang, crack, snap, explosion, report.

popular adjective **1** *the restaurant is very popular:* well liked, sought-after, in demand, commercial, marketable, fashionable, in vogue, all the rage, hot; informal in, cool, big. **2** *popular science books:* non-specialist, non-technical, amateur, lay person's, general, middle-of-the-road, accessible, simplified, understandable, mass-market. **3** *popular opinion:* widespread, general, common, current, prevailing, standard, ordinary, populated) **1** live in an area and form its population. **2** cause people to settle in an area.

population noun **1** all the people living in an area. **2** the number of people living in an area.

populist adjective aiming to appeal to ordinary people, especially in politics.
• noun a populist politician.
■ **populism** noun.

populous adjective having a large population.

porcelain /por-suh-lin/ noun a type of delicate china.

porch noun a covered shelter at the entrance to a building.

porcine /por-syn/ adjective relating to pigs, or like a pig.

porcupine noun an animal with long protective spines on the body and tail.

pore¹ noun each of many tiny openings in the skin or another surface.

pore² verb (**pores, poring, pored**) (**pore over** or **through**) study or read something with close attention.

> ! don't confuse **pore** and **pour**: you **pore over** a book, not **pour over** it.

pork noun the flesh of a pig used as food.

porker noun a young pig raised and fattened for food.

porn noun informal pornography.

pornography noun pictures, writing, or films that are intended to arouse sexual excitement.
■ **pornographic** adjective.

porous adjective having tiny spaces through which liquid or air can pass.
■ **porosity** noun.

porpoise noun a type of small whale with a rounded snout.

porridge noun a dish consisting of oats or oatmeal boiled with water or milk.

port¹ noun **1** a town or city with a harbour. **2** a harbour.
□ **port of call** a place where a ship or person stops on a journey.

port² noun a strong, sweet dark red wine from Portugal.

port³ noun the side of a ship or aircraft that is on the left when you are facing forward.

port⁴ noun **1** an opening in the side of a ship for boarding or loading. **2** an opening in an aircraft or vehicle through which a gun can be fired. **3** a socket in a computer network into which a device can be plugged.

portable adjective able to be carried or moved easily.
■ **portability** noun.

portal noun a large and impressive doorway or gate.

portcullis noun a strong, heavy grating that can be lowered to block a gateway to a castle.

portend verb be a sign or warning that something important or unpleasant is likely to happen.

portent noun a sign or warning that something important or unpleasant is likely to happen.

portentous adjective **1** warning or showing that something important is likely to happen. **2** very serious or solemn.
■ **portentously** adverb.

porter noun **1** a person employed to carry luggage and other loads. **2** a hospital employee who moves equipment or patients. **3** Brit. an employee in charge of the entrance of a large building. **4** dark brown bitter beer.

portfolio noun (plural **portfolios**) **1** a thin, flat case for carrying drawings, maps, etc. **2** a set of pieces of creative work collected together to show someone's ability. **3** a range of investments held by a person or organization. **4** the position and duties of a government minister.

porthole noun a small window in the side of a ship or aircraft.

portico noun (plural **porticoes** or **porticos**) a roof supported by columns, built over the entrance to a building.

portion noun **1** a part or share of something. **2** an amount of food for one

---

THESAURUS

conventional.
OPPOSITES unpopular, specialist, restricted.

population noun **inhabitants,** residents, people, citizens, public, community, populace, society, natives, occupants.

pornographic adjective **obscene,** indecent, dirty, smutty, filthy, erotic, titillating, sexy, risqué, X-rated, adult.

port noun **harbour,** docks, marina, haven, seaport.

portable adjective **transportable,** movable, mobile, battery, wireless, lightweight,

compact, handy, convenient.

porter¹ noun *a porter helped with the bags:* **carrier,** bearer; N. Amer. redcap, skycap.

porter² noun (Brit.) *the college porter:* **doorman,** doorkeeper, commissionaire, gatekeeper, concierge, security officer.

portion noun **1** *the upper portion of the chimney:* **part,** piece, bit, section, segment. **2** *her portion of the allowance:* **share,** slice, quota, ration, allocation, tranche; Brit. informal whack. **3** *a portion of cake:* **helping,** serving, plateful, slice, piece.

p

person. •**verb** share something out in portions.

portly adjective rather fat.

portmanteau /port-**man**-toh/ noun (plural **portmanteaus** or **portmanteaux** /port-**man**-tohz/) a large travelling bag that opens into two parts.

portrait noun **1** a painting, drawing, or photograph of a particular person. **2** a piece of writing or film about a particular person.

portraiture noun the art of making portraits.

portray verb **1** show or describe in a work of art or literature. **2** describe in a particular way.
■ **portrayal** noun.

Portuguese noun (plural **Portuguese**) **1** a person from Portugal. **2** the language of Portugal and Brazil. •**adjective** relating to Portugal.

☑ -*guese*, not -*gese*: Portuguese.

pose verb (**poses, posing, posed**) **1** present a problem, question, etc. **2** sit or stand in a particular position in order to be photographed, painted, or drawn. **3** (**pose as**) pretend to be. **4** behave in a way that is intended to impress people. •**noun 1** a position adopted in order to be painted, drawn, or photographed. **2** a way of behaving that is intended to impress people.

poser noun **1** a person who behaves in a way intended to impress other people. **2** a puzzling question or problem.

poseur /poh-**zer**/ noun a person who poses in order to impress; a poser.

posh adjective informal **1** very elegant or luxurious. **2** chiefly Brit. upper-class.

posit verb (**posits, positing, posited**) present something as a fact or as a basis for argument.

position noun **1** a place where something is situated. **2** a way in which someone or something is placed or arranged. **3** a situation or set of circumstances. **4** a job. **5** a person's place or importance in relation to others. **6** a point of view. •**verb** put or arrange in a particular position.
■ **positional** adjective.

positive adjective **1** indicating agreement

---

portrait noun **1** *a portrait of the King:* picture, likeness, painting, drawing, photograph, image. **2** *a vivid portrait of Italy:* description, portrayal, depiction, representation, impression, account, profile.

portray verb **1** *he always portrays Windermere in sunny weather:* paint, draw, sketch, picture, depict, represent, illustrate, render, show. **2** *the man portrayed by Waugh:* describe, depict, characterize, represent, present. **3** *the actor portrays a spy:* play, act the part of, take the role of, represent, appear as.

portrayal noun **1** *her portrayal of adolescence:* description, representation, characterization, depiction, evocation. **2** *Brando's portrayal of Corleone:* performance as, representation, interpretation, rendering.

pose verb **1** *pollution poses a threat to health:* constitute, present, offer. **2** *the question posed earlier:* raise, ask, put, submit, advance, propose. **3** *the guys posing at the bar:* posture, attitudinize, put on airs; informal show off, ponce about. •**noun 1** *a formal pose:* posture, position, stance, attitude. **2** *her pose of aggrieved innocence:* act, affectation, show, display, posture, expression.
□ **pose as pretend to be,** impersonate, pass yourself off as, masquerade as; formal personate.

posh adjective **1** (informal) *a posh hotel:* smart, stylish, fancy, high-class, fashionable, chic, luxurious, luxury, exclusive; Brit. upmarket; informal classy, plush, flash; Brit. informal swish; N. Amer. informal swank, tony. **2** (Brit. informal) *a posh accent:* upper-class, aristocratic.

position noun **1** *the aircraft's position:* location, place, situation, spot, site, locality, setting, area, whereabouts, bearings. **2** *a standing position:* posture, stance, attitude, pose. **3** *our financial position:* situation, state, condition, circumstances, predicament, plight. **4** *their position in society:* status, place, level, rank, standing, stature, prestige, reputation. **5** *a secretarial position:* job, post, situation, appointment, opening, vacancy, placement. **6** *the government's position on the matter:* viewpoint, opinion, outlook, attitude, stand, standpoint, stance, perspective, thinking, policy, feelings. •**verb** *he positioned a chair between them:* put, place, locate, situate, set, site, stand, station, plant, stick; informal plonk, park.

positive adjective **1** *a positive response:* affirmative, favourable, good, enthusiastic, supportive, encouraging. **2** *say something positive:* constructive, useful, productive, helpful, worthwhile, beneficial. **3** *she seems a lot more positive:* optimistic, hopeful, confident, cheerful, sanguine, buoyant; informal upbeat. **4** *positive economic signs:* favourable, good, promising, encouraging, heartening, propitious, auspicious. **5** *positive proof:* definite, certain, reliable, concrete, tangible, clear-cut, explicit, firm,

p

with or support for something. **2** hopeful, favourable, or confident. **3** with no possibility of doubt; certain. **4** (of the results of a test or experiment) showing the presence of something. **5** (of a quantity) greater than zero. **6** having to do with the kind of electric charge opposite to that carried by electrons. **7** (of an adjective or adverb) expressing the basic degree of a quality (e.g. *brave*). • noun a positive quality.

□ **positive discrimination** Brit. the policy of giving jobs or other opportunities to people who belong to groups which suffer discrimination.

■ **positively** adverb **positivity** noun.

positivism noun a system of philosophy that recognizes only things that can be scientifically or logically proved.

■ **positivist** noun & adjective.

positron noun a subatomic particle with the same mass as an electron and an equal but positive charge.

posse /poss-i/ **noun 1** N. Amer. (in the past) a group of men summoned by a sheriff to enforce the law. **2** informal a group of people.

possess verb **1** have or own something. **2** (also **be possessed of**) have a particular ability or quality. **3** dominate or have complete power over someone.

■ **possessor** noun.

☑ double *s* in the middle as well as at the end: possess.

---

possession noun **1** the state of having or owning something. **2** a thing owned.

possessive adjective **1** demanding someone's total attention and love. **2** unwilling to share your possessions. **3** Grammar (of a pronoun or determiner) showing that someone owns something. ■ **possessively** adverb.

possibility noun (plural **possibilities**) **1** a thing that is possible. **2** the state of being possible. **3** (**possibilities**) qualities suggesting that something might be good or could be improved.

possible adjective **1** capable of existing, happening, or being done. **2** that may be so. • noun a person or thing that may be chosen.

possibly adverb **1** perhaps. **2** in accordance with what is possible.

possum noun **1** a marsupial that lives in trees. **2** N. Amer. informal an opossum.

post¹ noun **1** a strong, upright piece of timber or metal used as a support or a marker. **2** (**the post**) a post marking the start or finish of a race. • verb **1** display a notice in a public place. **2** send a message to an Internet bulletin board or newsgroup.

post² chiefly Brit. **noun 1** the official service or

THESAURUS

decisive, real, actual. **6** *I'm positive he's coming back:* certain, sure, convinced, confident, satisfied.
OPPOSITES negative, pessimistic, doubtful, unsure.

positively adverb **1** *I could not positively identify the voice:* confidently, definitely, firmly, categorically, with certainty, conclusively. **2** *he was positively livid:* absolutely, utterly, downright, simply, virtually; informal plain.

possess verb **1** *the only hat she possessed:* own, have (to your name), be in possession of. **2** *he did not possess a sense of humour:* have, be blessed with, be endowed with, enjoy, boast. **3** *an evil force possessed him:* take control of, take over, bewitch, enchant, enslave.

possession noun **1** *the estate came into their possession:* ownership, control, hands, keeping, care, custody, charge. **2** *she packed her possessions:* belongings, things, property, worldly goods, personal effects, stuff, bits and pieces; informal gear, junk; Brit. informal clobber.

possibility noun **1** *a possibility that he might be alive:* chance, likelihood, probability, potentiality, hope, risk, hazard, danger, fear. **2** *buying a smaller house is*

one possibility: option, alternative, choice, course of action, solution. **3** *the idea has distinct possibilities:* potential, promise, prospects.

possible adjective **1** *it's not possible to check the figures:* feasible, practicable, viable, attainable, achievable, workable; informal on, doable. **2** *a possible reason for his disappearance:* likely, plausible, imaginable, believable, potential, probable, credible. **3** *a possible future leader:* potential, prospective, likely, probable. OPPOSITES unlikely.

possibly adverb **1** *possibly he took her with him:* perhaps, maybe, it is possible. **2** *you can't possibly refuse:* conceivably, under any circumstances, by any means. **3** *could you possibly help me?* please, kindly, be so good as to.

post¹ noun *wooden posts:* pole, stake, upright, shaft, prop, support, picket, strut, pillar.
• verb **1** *the notice posted on the wall:* affix, attach, fasten, display, pin up, put up, stick up. **2** *the group posted a net profit:* announce, report, make known, publish.

post² noun (Brit.) **1** *the winners will be notified by post:* mail; informal snail mail. **2** *did we get any post?* letters, mail, system that delivers letters and parcels. **2** letters and parcels delivered. **3** a single collection or delivery of post. •**verb** send something via the postal system.

□ **keep someone posted** keep someone up to date with the latest news about something. **post office 1** the organization responsible for postal services. **2** a building where postal business is carried out.

post³ noun 1 a place where someone is on duty or where an activity is carried out. **2** a job. •**verb 1** put a soldier, police officer, etc. in a particular place. **2** send someone to a place to take up a job.

post- prefix after: *postgraduate.*

postage noun 1 the sending of letters and parcels by post. **2** the charge for sending something by post.

postal adjective relating to or carried out by post.

□ **postal order** Brit. a document that can be bought from a post office and sent to someone who exchanges it for money.

postbox noun a large public box into which letters are posted for collection by the post office.

postcard noun a card for sending a message by post without an envelope.

postcode noun Brit. a group of letters and numbers added to a postal address to help in the sorting of mail.

post-date verb 1 put a date later than the actual one on a cheque or document. **2** happen, exist, or be found later than.

poster noun a large picture or notice used for decoration or advertisement.

poste restante /pohst **ress**-tuhnt/ **noun** Brit. a department in a post office that keeps people's letters until they are collected.

posterior adjective at or near the rear. •**noun** humorous a person's bottom.

posterity noun all future generations of people.

postgraduate adjective relating to study done after completing a first degree. •**noun**

a person taking a course of postgraduate study.

post-haste adverb very fast.

posthumous /**poss**-tyuu-muhss/ **adjective** happening or appearing after the person involved has died.

■ **posthumously** adverb.

posting¹ noun chiefly Brit. an appointment to a job abroad.

posting² noun a message sent to an Internet bulletin board or newsgroup.

postman noun (plural **postmen**) Brit. a man employed to deliver or collect post.

postmark noun an official mark stamped on a letter or parcel, giving the date of posting and cancelling the postage stamp. •**verb** stamp a letter or parcel with a postmark.

postmaster or **postmistress noun** a person in charge of a post office.

postmodernism noun a movement in the arts that features a deliberate mixing of different styles.

■ **postmodern** adjective **postmodernist** noun & adjective.

post-mortem noun an examination of a dead body to find out the cause of death.

post-natal adjective having to do with the period after childbirth.

postpone verb (**postpones, postponing, postponed**) arrange for something to take place at a time later than that first planned.

■ **postponement** noun.

postscript noun a remark added at the end of a letter.

postulant noun a person who has recently entered a religious order.

postulate verb (**postulates, postulating, postulated**) assume that something is true, as a basis for a theory or discussion.

■ **postulation** noun.

posture noun 1 a particular position of the body. **2** the usual way in which a person holds their body. **3** an approach or attitude

p

correspondence.

•**verb** (Brit.) *post the order form today:* send (off), mail, put in the post/mail.

□ **keep someone posted keep informed,** keep up to date, keep in the picture.

post³ noun 1 *there were seventy candidates for the post:* job, position, appointment, situation, place, vacancy, opening. **2** *back to your posts:* assigned position, station, place, base.

•**verb 1** *he'd been posted to Berlin:* send, assign, dispatch. **2** *armed guards were posted:* put on duty, mount, station.

poster noun notice, placard, bill, sign,

advertisement, playbill.

postpone verb put off, put back, delay, defer, hold over, reschedule, adjourn, shelve; informal put on ice, put on the back burner.

OPPOSITES bring forward.

posture noun 1 *a kneeling posture:* position, pose, attitude, stance. **2** *good posture:* bearing, carriage, stance, comportment; Brit. deportment. **3** *trade unions adopted a militant posture:* attitude, stance, standpoint, point of view, opinion, position.

•**verb** *Keith postured, flexing his biceps:*

towards something. • verb (**postures, posturing, postured**) behave in a way that is meant to impress or mislead other people.

■ **postural** adjective.

posy noun (plural **posies**) a small bunch of flowers.

pot¹ noun a rounded container used for storage or cooking. • verb (**pots, potting, potted**) 1 plant a young plant in a flowerpot. 2 preserve food in a sealed pot or jar. 3 Billiards & Snooker hit a ball into a pocket. 4 informal hit or kill by shooting. □ **go to pot** informal be ruined through neglect. **pot belly** a large stomach that sticks out. **pot luck** a situation in which you take a chance that whatever is available will be acceptable. **potting shed** a shed used for potting plants and storing garden tools.

pot² noun informal cannabis.

potable /**poh**-tuh-b'l/ adjective formal (of water) safe to drink.

potash noun a substance obtained from potassium, used in making soap and fertilizers.

potassium noun a soft silvery-white metallic element.

potato noun (plural **potatoes**) an oval vegetable with starchy white or yellow flesh and a brown skin, that grows underground as a tuber.

☑ the singular has no e on the end: potato.

potent adjective 1 very powerful. 2 (of a man) able to achieve an erection.
■ **potency** noun.

potentate noun a monarch or ruler.

potential adjective capable of becoming or developing into something. • noun 1 qualities or abilities that may be developed and lead to future success. 2 the possibility of something happening.
■ **potentiality** noun **potentially** adverb.

pothole noun 1 a deep underground cave. 2 a hole in the surface of a road.

■ **potholed** adjective.

potholing noun exploring potholes as a pastime.

potion noun a drink with healing, magical, or poisonous powers.

potpourri /poh-puh-**ree**/ noun (plural **potpourris**) a mixture of dried petals and spices used to perfume a room.

potshot noun a shot aimed unexpectedly or at random.

pottage noun old use soup or stew.

potted adjective 1 preserved in a sealed pot. 2 put into a short, easily understandable form.

potter¹ verb (**potters, pottering, pottered**) 1 spend your time doing small tasks in a relaxed way. 2 move in an unhurried way.

potter² noun a person who makes pottery.

pottery noun (plural **potteries**) 1 articles made of fired clay. 2 the craft of making such articles. 3 a place where pottery is made.

potty¹ adjective (**pottier, pottiest**) Brit. informal 1 mad; crazy. 2 very enthusiastic about someone or something.

potty² noun (plural **potties**) a bowl for a child to sit on and use as a toilet.

pouch noun 1 a small flexible bag. 2 a pocket of skin in an animal's body, especially that in which animals such as kangaroos carry their young.

pouf ⇨ POOF or POUFFE.

pouffe or **pouf** /poof/ noun a large, firm cushion used as a seat or for resting your feet on.

poulterer noun Brit. a person who sells poultry.

poultice /**pohl**-tiss/ noun a soft, moist mass of flour or plant material that is put on the skin to reduce inflammation.

poultry noun chickens, turkeys, ducks, and geese.

pounce verb (**pounces, pouncing, pounced**) 1 suddenly spring to seize or attack something. 2 (**pounce on**) quickly notice and criticize something that someone has

THESAURUS

pose, strike an attitude, strut.

pot noun 1 *a pot of soup:* pan, saucepan, casserole. 2 *Neolithic pots:* vessel, bowl, earthenware, pottery.

potent adjective 1 *a potent political force:* powerful, strong, mighty, formidable, influential, dominant. 2 *a potent argument:* forceful, convincing, cogent, compelling, persuasive, powerful, strong. 3 *a potent drug:* strong, powerful, effective; formal efficacious.
OPPOSITES weak.

potential adjective *a potential source of*

conflict: possible, likely, prospective, future, probable.
• noun *he has great potential:* possibilities, potentiality, prospects, promise, capability, capacity.

potter verb amble, wander, meander, stroll, saunter; informal mosey, tootle, toddle; N. Amer. informal putter.

pottery noun ceramics, crockery, earthenware, terracotta, stoneware, china, porcelain.

pounce verb jump, spring, leap, dive, lunge, swoop, attack.

said or done. • noun an act of pouncing.

pound[1] noun 1 a unit of weight equal to 16 oz avoirdupois (0.4536 kg), or 12 oz troy (0.3732 kg). 2 (also **pound sterling**) the basic unit of money of the UK, equal to 100 pence.

pound[2] verb 1 hit something heavily again and again. 2 walk or run with heavy steps. 3 beat or throb with a strong regular rhythm. 4 crush or grind something into a powder or paste.

pound[3] noun a place where stray dogs or illegally parked vehicles are officially taken and kept until claimed.

pour verb 1 flow or cause to flow in a steady stream. 2 (of rain) fall heavily. 3 prepare and serve a drink. 4 come or go in large numbers. 5 (**pour something out**) express your feelings freely.

❗ don't confuse **pour** and **pore**: you **pore over** a book, not **pour over** it.

---

pout verb push your lips forward as a sign of sulking or to make yourself look sexually attractive. • noun a pouting expression.
■ **pouty** adjective.

poverty noun 1 the state of being very poor. 2 the state of lacking in a particular quality.

powder noun 1 a mass of fine dry particles.

2 a cosmetic in this form applied to a person's face. • verb (**powders, powdering, powdered**) 1 sprinkle powder over. 2 make something into a powder.
□ **powder room** a women's toilet in a public building.
■ **powdery** adjective.

power noun 1 the ability to do something. 2 the ability to influence people or events. 3 the right or authority to do something. 4 political authority or control. 5 a country seen as having international influence and military strength. 6 strength, force, or energy. 7 capacity or performance of an engine or other device. 8 energy that is produced by mechanical, electrical, or other means. 9 Physics the rate of doing work, measured in watts or horse power. 10 Maths the product obtained when a number is multiplied by itself a certain number of times. • verb (**powers, powering, powered**) 1 supply with power. 2 move with speed or force.
□ **power cut** a temporary interruption in an electricity supply. **power station** a building where electrical power is generated. **power steering** steering aided by power from a vehicle's engine.

powerboat noun a fast motorboat.

powerful adjective having power.
■ **powerfully** adverb.

---

p

pound[1] verb 1 *the two men pounded him with their fists:* beat, strike, hit, batter, thump, pummel, punch, rain blows on, belabour, hammer; informal bash, clobber, wallop. 2 *waves pounded the seafront:* beat against, crash against, batter, dash against, lash, buffet. 3 *gunships pounded the capital:* bombard, bomb, shell. 4 *pound the garlic to a paste:* crush, grind, pulverize, mash, pulp. 5 *I heard him pounding along the gangway:* stomp, stamp, clomp, clump, tramp, lumber. 6 *her heart was pounding:* throb, thump, thud, hammer, pulse, race.

pound[2] noun *a dog pound:* enclosure, compound, pen, yard, corral.

pour verb 1 *blood was pouring from his nose:* stream, flow, run, gush, course, jet, spurt, surge, spill. 2 *Amy poured wine into his glass:* tip, splash, spill, decant; informal slosh, slop. 3 *it was pouring:* rain heavily/hard, teem down, pelt down, tip down, rain cats and dogs; informal be chucking it down; Brit. informal bucket down; N. Amer. informal rain pitchforks. 4 *people poured off the train:* crowd, throng, swarm, stream, flood.

poverty noun 1 *abject poverty:* pennilessness, destitution, penury, impoverishment, neediness, hardship, impecuniousness. 2 *the poverty of choice:* scarcity, deficiency, dearth, shortage,

paucity, absence, lack. 3 *the poverty of her imagination:* inferiority, mediocrity, sterility.
OPPOSITES wealth, abundance, fertility.

powdery adjective fine, dry, fine-grained, powder-like, dusty, chalky, floury, sandy, crumbly, friable.

power noun 1 *the power of speech:* ability, capacity, capability, potential, faculty. 2 *the union has enormous power:* control, authority, influence, dominance, sway, leverage; informal clout, teeth; N. Amer. informal drag. 3 *the power to stop and search:* authority, right, authorization. 4 *a major European power:* state, country, nation. 5 *he hit the ball with as much power as he could:* strength, might, force, vigour, energy; Brit. informal welly. 6 *the power of his arguments:* forcefulness, powerfulness, strength, force, cogency, persuasiveness. 7 *the new engine has more power:* driving force, horsepower, acceleration, torque; informal oomph, poke. 8 *generating power from waste:* energy, electricity.
OPPOSITES inability, weakness.

powerful adjective 1 *powerful shoulders:* strong, muscular, muscly, sturdy, strapping, robust, brawny, burly, athletic, manly, well built, solid; informal beefy. 2 *a powerful drink:* intoxicating, hard, strong,

powerhouse noun a person or thing having great energy or power.

powerless adjective without the power to take action.

powwow noun **1** informal a meeting for discussion. **2** a North American Indian ceremony involving feasting and dancing.

pox noun **1** any disease that produces a rash of pus-filled pimples that leave pockmarks on healing. **2** (**the pox**) informal syphilis.

poxy adjective Brit. informal of bad quality.

pp or **p.p.** abbreviation used when signing a letter on someone else's behalf.

PR abbreviation **1** proportional representation. **2** public relations.

practicable adjective able to be done successfully.
■ **practicability** noun.

practical adjective **1** relating to the actual doing or use of something rather than theory. **2** likely to be successful or useful. **3** skilled at making or doing things. •noun Brit. an exam or lesson in which students have to do or make things.
□ **practical joke** a trick played on someone to make them look silly.

practicality noun (plural **practicalities**) **1** the state of being practical. **2** (**practicalities**) the real facts or aspects of a situation.

practically adverb **1** almost; virtually. **2** in a practical way.

practice noun **1** the actual doing of something rather than the theories about it. **2** the usual way of doing something. **3** the work, business, or place of work of a doctor, dentist, or lawyer. **4** the doing of something repeatedly to improve your skill. •verb US spelling of **PRACTISE**.

> ! do you mean **practice** or **practise**?
> **Practice** is the spelling for the noun, and in America for the verb as well; **practise** is the British spelling of the verb.

practise (US spelling **practice**) verb (**practises**, **practising**, **practised**) **1** do something repeatedly to improve your skill. **2** do something regularly as part of your normal behaviour. **3** be working in a particular profession. **4** (**practised**) skilful as a result of experience. **5** follow the teaching and rules of a religion.

practitioner noun a person who practises a profession or activity.

pragmatic adjective dealing with things in

THESAURUS

stiff. **3** *a powerful blow:* violent, forceful, hard, mighty. **4** *he felt a powerful urge to kiss her:* intense, keen, fierce, strong, irresistible, overpowering, overwhelming. **5** *a powerful nation:* influential, strong, important, dominant, commanding, formidable. **6** *a powerful critique:* cogent, compelling, convincing, persuasive, forceful.
OPPOSITES weak, gentle.

powerless adjective impotent, helpless, ineffectual, ineffective, useless, defenceless, vulnerable.

practicable adjective realistic, feasible, possible, viable, reasonable, sensible, workable, achievable; informal doable.

practical adjective **1** *practical experience:* empirical, hands-on, actual. **2** *there are no practical alternatives:* feasible, practicable, realistic, viable, workable, possible, reasonable, sensible; informal doable. **3** *practical clothes:* functional, sensible, utilitarian. **4** *try to be more practical:* realistic, sensible, down-to-earth, businesslike, commonsensical, hard-headed, no-nonsense; informal hard-nosed. **5** *a practical certainty:* virtual, effective, near.
OPPOSITES theoretical, impractical.

practically adverb **1** *the cinema was practically empty:* almost, very nearly, virtually, just about, all but, more or less, as good as, to all intents and purposes;

informal pretty nearly, pretty well. **2** *'You can't afford it,' he pointed out practically:* realistically, sensibly, reasonably, rationally, matter-of-factly.

practice noun **1** *the practice of radiotherapy:* application, exercise, use, operation, implementation, execution. **2** *it is common practice:* custom, procedure, policy, convention, tradition. **3** *the team's final practice:* training, rehearsal, repetition, preparation, dummy run, run-through; informal dry run. **4** *the practice of medicine:* profession, career, business, work. **5** *a small legal practice:* business, firm, office, company; informal outfit.

practise verb **1** *he practised the songs every day:* rehearse, run through, go over/through, work on/at, polish, perfect. **2** *the performers were practising:* train, rehearse, prepare, go through your paces. **3** *we still practise these rituals today:* carry out, perform, observe. **4** *she practises medicine:* work at/in, pursue a career in.

practised adjective expert, experienced, seasoned, skilled, skilful, accomplished, proficient, talented, able, adept.

pragmatic adjective practical, matter of fact, sensible, down-to-earth, hard-headed, commonsensical, businesslike, no-nonsense; informal hard-nosed.
OPPOSITES impractical.

p

a sensible and realistic way.
■ **pragmatically** adverb.

pragmatism noun a realistic and sensible attitude or approach to something.
■ **pragmatist** noun.

prairie noun (in North America) a large open area of grassland.

praise verb (**praises, praising, praised**)
1 show approval of or admiration for.
2 express thanks to or respect for God.
• noun words that show approval or admiration.

praiseworthy adjective deserving praise.

praline /prah-leen, pray-leen/ noun a sweet substance made from nuts boiled in sugar.

pram noun Brit. a four-wheeled vehicle for a baby, pushed by a person on foot.

prance verb (**prances, prancing, pranced**) walk with exaggerated steps.

prang verb Brit. informal crash a motor vehicle or aircraft.

prank noun a practical joke or mischievous act.

prankster noun a person who is fond of playing pranks.

prat noun Brit. informal a stupid person.

prate verb (**prates, prating, prated**) talk too much in a silly or boring way.

prattle verb (**prattles, prattling, prattled**) talk too much in a silly or trivial way.
• noun foolish or silly talk.

prawn noun an edible shellfish like a large shrimp.

pray verb **1** say a prayer. **2** hope strongly for something. • adverb formal or old use please.
□ **praying mantis** ⇒ **MANTIS.**

prayer noun **1** a request for help or expression of thanks made to God or a god.
2 (**prayers**) a religious service at which people gather to pray together. **3** an

earnest hope or wish.

pre- prefix before: *prearrange.*

preach verb **1** give a religious talk to a group of people. **2** recommend a particular way of thinking or behaving. **3** (**preach at**) tell someone how they should think or behave in a way that is boring or annoying.
■ **preacher** noun.

preamble /pree-am-b'l/ noun an opening statement; an introduction.

prearrange verb (**prearranges, prearranging, prearranged**) arrange something in advance.

prebendary noun (plural **prebendaries**) (in the Church of England) a person holding an administrative or honorary position at certain cathedrals.

precarious adjective **1** likely to tip over or fall. **2** (of a situation) not safe or certain.
■ **precariously** adverb.

precaution noun something done to avoid problems or danger.
■ **precautionary** adjective.

precede verb (**precedes, preceding, preceded**) **1** happen before something in time or order. **2** go somewhere in front of someone.

precedence noun the state of coming before others in order or importance.

precedent noun an earlier event, action, or legal case that is taken as an example to be followed in similar situations.

precept noun a general rule about how to behave.

precinct noun **1** Brit. an area in a town that is closed to traffic. **2** an enclosed area around a place or building. **3** N. Amer. each of the districts into which a city or town is divided for elections or policing.

precious adjective **1** rare and worth a lot of

p

THESAURUS

praise verb commend, applaud, pay tribute to, speak highly of, compliment, congratulate, sing the praises of, rave about.
OPPOSITES criticize.
• noun approval, acclaim, admiration, approbation, plaudits, congratulations, commendation, accolade, compliment, a pat on the back, eulogy.
OPPOSITES criticism.

preach verb **1** *he preached to a large congregation:* give a sermon, sermonize, address, speak. **2** *preaching the gospel:* proclaim, teach, spread, propagate, expound. **3** *they preach toleration:* advocate, recommend, advise, urge, teach, counsel.

precarious adjective insecure, uncertain, unpredictable, risky, parlous, hazardous, dangerous, unsafe, unstable, unsteady,

shaky; informal dicey, iffy; Brit. informal dodgy.
OPPOSITES safe.

precaution noun safeguard, preventive measure, safety measure, insurance; informal backstop.

precede verb **1** *adverts preceded the film:* go/come before, lead up to, pave the way for, herald, introduce, usher in.
2 *Catherine preceded him into the studio:* go ahead of, go in front of, lead the way.
OPPOSITES follow.

precedent noun model, exemplar, example, pattern, paradigm, criterion, yardstick, standard.

precinct noun district, zone, sector, quarter, area.

precious adjective **1** *precious works of art:* valuable, costly, expensive, invaluable, priceless. **2** *her most precious possession:* valued, cherished, treasured, prized,

money. **2** greatly loved or valued.
3 sophisticated in a way that is artificial and exaggerated.
□ **precious little** (or **few**) informal very little (or few). **precious metal** a valuable metal such as gold, silver, or platinum. **precious stone** an attractive and valuable piece of mineral, used in jewellery.

precipice noun a tall and very steep rock face or cliff.

precipitate verb /pri-**sip**-i-tayt/ (**precipitates, precipitating, precipitated**) **1** make something bad happen suddenly or sooner than it should. **2** make something move or happen suddenly and with force. **3** Chemistry cause a substance to be deposited in solid form from a solution. **4** cause moisture in the air to condense and fall as rain, snow, etc. •adjective /pri-**sip**-i-tuht/ done or happening suddenly or without careful thought. •noun /pri-**sip**-i-tayt/ Chemistry a substance precipitated from a solution.

precipitation noun **1** rain, snow, sleet, or hail. **2** Chemistry the action of precipitating a substance from a solution.

precipitous adjective dangerously high or steep.

precis /**pray**-si/ (also **précis**) noun (plural **precis** /**pray**-si, **pray**-seez/) a short summary. •verb (**precises** /**pray**-seez/, **precising** /**pray**-see-ing/, **precised** /**pray**-seed/) make a precis of.

precise adjective **1** presented in a detailed and accurate way. **2** taking care to be exact and accurate. **3** particular.
■ **precisely** adverb.

precision noun the quality of being exact, accurate, and careful.

preclude verb (**precludes, precluding, precluded**) prevent something from happening.

precocious adjective having developed certain abilities or tendencies at an earlier age than usual.
■ **precocity** noun.

precognition noun knowledge of an event before it happens.

preconceived adjective (of an idea or opinion) formed before full knowledge or evidence is available.

preconception noun a preconceived idea or opinion.

precondition noun something that must exist or happen before other things can happen or be done.

precursor noun a person or thing that comes before another of the same kind.

pre-date verb happen, exist, or be found earlier than.

predation /pri-**day**-sh'n/ noun the preying of one animal on others.

predator noun an animal that hunts and kills others for food.

predatory adjective **1** (of an animal) killing other animals for food. **2** taking advantage of weaker people.

predecease verb (**predeceases, predeceasing, predeceased**) formal die before another person.

predecessor noun **1** a person who held a job or office before the current holder. **2** a thing that has been followed or replaced by another.

predestination noun the belief that everything that happens has been decided in advance by God or fate.

p

THESAURUS

favourite, dear, beloved, special. **3** *his precious manners:* affected, pretentious; informal la-di-da; Brit. informal poncey.

precipitate verb **1** *the incident precipitated a crisis:* bring about/on, cause, lead to, give rise to, instigate, trigger, spark off, touch off, provoke. **2** *they were precipitated down the mountain:* hurl, catapult, throw, plunge, launch, fling, propel.
•adjective *their actions were precipitate:* hasty, overhasty, rash, hurried, rushed, impetuous, impulsive, precipitous, incautious, imprudent, injudicious, ill-advised, reckless.

precipitous adjective **1** *a precipitous drop:* steep, sheer, perpendicular, abrupt, sharp, vertical. **2** *his precipitous fall from power:* sudden, rapid, swift, abrupt, headlong, speedy, quick, fast.

precise adjective **1** *precise measurements:* exact, accurate, correct, specific, detailed, explicit, careful, meticulous, strict,

rigorous. **2** *at that precise moment:* exact, particular, very, specific.
OPPOSITES inaccurate.

precisely adverb **1** *at 2 o'clock precisely:* exactly, sharp, on the dot, promptly, on the stroke of ...; informal bang (on); Brit. informal spot on; N. Amer. informal on the button.
2 *precisely the man I am looking for:* exactly, just, in all respects; informal to a T.
3 *fertilization can be timed precisely:* accurately, exactly. **4** *'So you knew?' 'Precisely.':* yes, exactly, absolutely, (that's) right, quite so.

precision noun exactness, accuracy, exactitude, correctness, care, meticulousness, scrupulousness, punctiliousness, rigour.

predecessor noun **1** *the Prime Minister's predecessor:* forerunner, precursor, antecedent. **2** *our Victorian predecessors:* ancestor, forefather, forebear, antecedent.
OPPOSITES successor, descendant.

predestined adjective already decided by God or fate.

predetermine verb (**predetermines, predetermining, predetermined**) establish or decide in advance.

predicament noun a difficult situation.

predicate noun /pred-i-kuht/ Grammar the part of a sentence or clause containing a verb and stating something about the subject (e.g. *went home* in *she went home*). • verb /pred-i-kayt/ (**predicates, predicating, predicated**) (**predicate something on**) base something on.

predicative /pri-dik-uh-tiv/ adjective Grammar (of an adjective) coming after a verb, as *old* in *the dog is old*.

predict verb state that an event will happen in the future.
■ **predictive** adjective **predictor** noun.

predictable adjective 1 able to be predicted. 2 always behaving or happening in the way that you would expect.
■ **predictability** noun **predictably** adverb.

prediction noun 1 a statement saying that something will happen; a forecast. 2 the action of predicting.

predilection /pree-di-lek-sh'n/ noun a preference or special liking for something.

predispose verb (**predisposes, predisposing, predisposed**) make someone likely to be, do, or think something.
■ **predisposition** noun.

predominant adjective 1 present as the main part of something. 2 having the greatest power.
■ **predominance** noun **predominantly** adverb.

predominate verb (**predominates, predominating, predominated**) 1 be the main part of something. 2 have control or power.

pre-eminent adjective better than all others.
■ **pre-eminence** noun.

pre-empt verb 1 take action so as to prevent something happening. 2 stop

someone from saying something by speaking first.
■ **pre-emption** noun **pre-emptive** adjective.

preen verb 1 (of a bird) tidy and clean its feathers with its beak. 2 attend to and admire your appearance. 3 (**preen yourself**) feel very pleased with yourself.

pre-existing adjective existing from an earlier time.

prefab noun informal a prefabricated building.

prefabricated adjective (of a building) made in previously constructed sections that can be easily put together on site.

preface /pref-uhss/ noun an introduction to a book. • verb (**prefaces, prefacing, prefaced**) (**preface something with** or **by**) say or do something to introduce a book, speech, or event.

prefect noun 1 Brit. a senior pupil in a school who has some authority over younger pupils. 2 a chief officer or regional governor in certain countries.

prefecture noun (in certain countries) a district administered by a prefect.

prefer verb (**prefers, preferring, preferred**) like one person or thing better than another.

☑ double the *r* when forming the past tense: preferred.

preferable adjective more desirable or suitable.
■ **preferably** adverb.

preference noun 1 a greater liking for one person or thing than another. 2 a thing preferred. 3 favour shown to one person over another.

preferential adjective favouring a particular person or group.
■ **preferentially** adverb.

preferment noun formal promotion to a job or position.

prefigure verb (**prefigures, prefiguring, prefigured**) be an early sign or version of.

prefix noun 1 a letter or group of letters

p

THESAURUS

predicament noun difficulty, mess, plight, quandary, muddle, dilemma; informal hole, fix, jam, pickle.

predict verb forecast, foretell, prophesy, foresee; old use augur.

predictable adjective foreseeable, to be expected, anticipated, likely, foreseen, unsurprising, reliable, inevitable.

prediction noun forecast, prophecy, prognosis, prognostication.

predominantly adverb mainly, mostly, for the most part, chiefly, principally, primarily, in the main, on the whole, largely, by and large, typically, generally, usually.

prefer verb like better, would rather (have), would sooner (have), favour, be more partial to, choose, select, pick, opt for, go for, plump for.

preferable adjective better, best, more desirable, more suitable, advantageous, superior, preferred, recommended.

preferably adverb ideally, if possible, for preference, from choice.

preference noun 1 *her preference for gin*: liking, partiality, fondness, taste, inclination, leaning, bent, penchant, predisposition. 2 *preference was given to female applicants*: priority, favour, precedence, preferential treatment.

placed at the beginning of a word to alter its meaning (e.g. *non-*). **2** a word, letter, or number placed before another. •**verb** add a prefix to.

pregnancy noun (plural **pregnancies**) the state or period of being pregnant.

pregnant adjective **1** (of a woman) having a baby developing inside her womb. **2** full of meaning.

prehensile /pri-**hen**-syl/ adjective (of an animal's limb or tail) capable of grasping things.

prehistoric adjective relating to the period before written records of events were made.

prehistory noun **1** the period of time before written records were made. **2** the early stages in the development of something.

pre-industrial adjective before the development of industries.

prejudge verb (**prejudges**, **prejudging**, **prejudged**) make a judgement before you have all the necessary information.

prejudice noun **1** an opinion that is not based on reason or experience. **2** unfair reactions or behaviour based on such opinions. •**verb** (**prejudices**, **prejudicing**, **prejudiced**) **1** influence someone so that they form an opinion that is not based on reason or experience. **2** cause harm to.

prejudicial adjective harmful to someone or something.

prelate /**prel**-uht/ noun a bishop or other high-ranking minister in the Christian Church.

preliminary adjective taking place before a main action or event. •**noun** (plural **preliminaries**) a preliminary action or event.

prelude noun **1** an action or event acting as an introduction to something more important. **2** a piece of music introducing a longer piece.

premarital adjective happening before marriage.

premature adjective **1** happening or done before the proper time. **2** (of a baby) born before the normal length of pregnancy is completed.
■ **prematurely** adverb.

premeditated adjective (of a crime or other bad action) planned in advance.
■ **premeditation** noun.

premenstrual adjective happening or experienced in the days of the month before menstruation.

premier adjective first in importance, order, or position. •**noun** a Prime Minister or other head of government.
■ **premiership** noun.

premiere /**prem**-i-air/ noun the first performance or showing of a play, film, ballet, etc.

premise or Brit. **premiss** /**prem**-iss/ noun a statement or idea that forms the basis for a theory or argument.

THESAURUS

p

pregnant adjective **1** *she is pregnant:* expecting, expectant, carrying a child; informal in the family way, preggers. **2** *a pregnant pause:* meaningful, significant, suggestive, expressive, charged.

prejudice noun **1** *male prejudices about women:* preconceived idea, preconception. **2** *they are motivated by prejudice:* bigotry, bias, partiality, intolerance, discrimination, unfairness, inequality.
•**verb 1** *the article could prejudice the jury:* bias, influence, sway, predispose, make partial, colour. **2** *this could prejudice his chances:* damage, be detrimental to, be prejudicial to, injure, harm, hurt, spoil, impair, undermine, compromise.

prejudiced adjective biased, bigoted, discriminatory, partisan, intolerant, narrow-minded, unfair, unjust, inequitable, coloured.
OPPOSITES impartial.

preliminary adjective *at a preliminary stage:* preparatory, introductory, initial, opening, early, exploratory.
OPPOSITES final.
•**noun** *he began without any preliminaries:*

introduction, preamble, preface, opening remarks, formalities.

prelude noun preliminary, overture, opening, preparation, introduction, lead-in, precursor.

premature adjective **1** *his premature death:* untimely, too early, before time, unseasonable. **2** *such a step would be premature:* rash, overhasty, hasty, precipitate, impulsive, impetuous; informal previous.
OPPOSITES overdue.

premier adjective *Germany's premier rock band:* leading, foremost, chief, principal, head, top-ranking, top, prime, primary, first, highest, pre-eminent, senior, outstanding; N. Amer. ranking.
•**noun** *the British premier:* head of government, prime minister, PM, president, chancellor.

premiere noun first performance, first night, opening night, debut.

premise noun proposition, assumption, hypothesis, thesis, presupposition, supposition, presumption, assertion.

premises plural noun the building and land occupied by a business.

premium noun (plural **premiums**) 1 an amount paid for an insurance policy. 2 an extra sum added to a basic price. • adjective of high quality and more expensive.
□ **at a premium** 1 scarce and in demand. 2 above the usual price.

premonition noun a strong feeling that something is going to happen.
■ premonitory adjective.

prenatal adjective N. Amer. before birth.

preoccupation noun 1 the state of being preoccupied. 2 a matter that preoccupies someone.

preoccupy verb (**preoccupies, preoccupying, preoccupied**) completely fill someone's mind.

preordained adjective decided or determined beforehand.

prep noun Brit. informal school work done outside lessons.
□ **prep school** a preparatory school.

prepaid adjective paid for in advance.

preparation noun 1 the process of getting ready for something. 2 something that is done to get ready for something. 3 a substance prepared for use as a medicine, cosmetic, etc.

preparatory adjective done in order to prepare for something.
□ **preparatory school** Brit. a private school for pupils aged seven to thirteen.

prepare verb (**prepares, preparing, prepared**) 1 make something ready for use. 2 get ready to do or deal with something. 3 (**be prepared to do**) be willing to do.

preparedness noun readiness.

preponderance noun a greater number or incidence of something.

preponderant adjective greater in number or happening more often.

preposition /prep-uh-zi-sh'n/ noun Grammar a word used with a noun or pronoun to show place, time, or method.
■ prepositional adjective.

prepossessing adjective attractive or appealing in appearance.

preposterous adjective completely ridiculous or outrageous.
■ preposterously adverb.

prepubescent adjective having to do with the period before puberty.

prerequisite /pree-**rek**-wi-zit/ noun a thing that must exist or happen before something else can exist or happen.

prerogative /pri-**rog**-uh-tiv/ noun a right or privilege belonging to a particular person or group.

presage /**press**-ij/ verb /also pri-**sayj**/ (**presages, presaging, presaged**) be a sign or warning of. • noun an omen.

Presbyterian /prez-bi-**teer**-i-uhn/ adjective relating to a Protestant Church governed by elders who are all of equal rank. • noun a member of a Presbyterian Church.
■ Presbyterianism noun.

presbytery /**prez**-bi-tuh-ri/ noun (plural **presbyteries**) 1 an administrative body in a Presbyterian Church. 2 the house of a Roman Catholic parish priest. 3 the eastern part of a church near the altar.

prescient /**press**-i-uhnt/ adjective knowing about things before they happen.
■ prescience noun.

THESAURUS

premises plural noun building(s), property, site, office, establishment.

premium noun 1 *monthly premiums of £30:* (regular) payment, instalment. 2 *you must pay a premium for organic fruit:* surcharge, additional payment, extra.
□ **at a premium scarce**, in great demand, hard to come by, in short supply, thin on the ground, like gold dust.

preoccupation noun obsession, fixation, concern, passion, enthusiasm, hobby horse; informal bee in your bonnet.

preoccupied adjective 1 *he's preoccupied with work:* obsessed, fixated, concerned, absorbed, engrossed, involved, wrapped up. 2 *she looked preoccupied:* lost in thought, deep in thought, oblivious, pensive, distracted.

preparation noun 1 *the preparation of a plan:* devising, putting together, drawing up, construction, composition, production, getting ready, development. 2 *preparations for the party:* arrangements, planning, plans, groundwork, provisions. 3 *a preparation to kill mites:* mixture, compound, concoction, solution, medicine, potion.

prepare verb 1 *I will prepare a report:* make/get ready, put together, draw up, produce, arrange, assemble, construct, compose, formulate. 2 *the meal is easy to prepare:* cook, make, get, put together, concoct; informal fix, rustle up; Brit. informal knock up. 3 *preparing for war:* get ready, make preparations, arrange things, make provision. 4 *athletes preparing for the Olympics:* train, get into shape, practise, get ready, warm up, limber up. 5 *prepare yourself for a shock:* brace, ready, tense, steel, steady.

prepared adjective 1 *prepared for action:* ready, (all) set, equipped, primed, waiting, poised. 2 *I'm prepared to negotiate:* willing, ready, disposed, (favourably) inclined, of a mind, minded.

prescribe verb (prescribes, prescribing, prescribed) 1 (of a doctor) state officially that someone should take a particular medicine or have a particular treatment. 2 state officially that something should be done.

prescription noun 1 a piece of paper on which a doctor states that a patient may be supplied with a medicine or treatment. 2 the action of prescribing a medicine or treatment.

prescriptive adjective stating what should be done.

presence noun 1 the state of being in a particular place. 2 a person's impressive manner or appearance. 3 a person or thing that seems to be present but is not seen. □ presence of mind the ability to remain calm and act sensibly in a difficult situation.

present¹ /pre-z'nt/ adjective 1 being or existing in a particular place. 2 existing or happening now. 3 Grammar (of a tense of a verb) expressing an action or state happening or existing now. • noun the period of time happening now. □ present participle Grammar the form of a verb, ending in -ing, which is used in forming tenses describing continuous action (e.g. I'm thinking), as a noun (e.g.

good thinking), and as an adjective (e.g. running water).

present² verb /pri-zent/ 1 formally give someone something. 2 offer something for consideration or payment. 3 formally introduce someone to someone else. 4 produce a show, broadcast, etc. for the public. 5 introduce and take part in a television or radio show. 6 be the cause of a problem. 7 give a particular impression to other people: we must present a united front. 8 (present yourself) appear at or attend a formal or official occasion. • noun /pre-z'nt/ a thing given to someone as a gift.
  ■ presenter noun.

presentable adjective looking smart enough to be seen in public.

presentation noun the action of presenting something, or the way in which it is presented.
  ■ presentational adjective.

presentiment /pri-zen-ti-muhnt/ noun a feeling that something unpleasant is going to happen.

presently adverb 1 soon. 2 now.

preservative noun a substance used to prevent food or wood from decaying.

preserve verb (preserves, preserving, preserved) 1 keep something in its original

---

THESAURUS

prescribe verb 1 a doctor may prescribe antibiotics: advise, recommend, advocate, suggest. 2 rules prescribing your duty: stipulate, lay down, dictate, order, direct, specify, determine.

presence noun 1 the presence of an intruder: existence. 2 I requested the presence of a lawyer: attendance, appearance. 3 a woman of great presence: aura, charisma, personality.
OPPOSITES absence.
□ presence of mind composure, self-possession, level-headedness, self-assurance, calmness, alertness, quick-wittedness; informal cool, unflappability.

present¹ adjective 1 a doctor must be present: in attendance, here, there, near, nearby, at hand, available. 2 organic compounds are present: in existence, detectable, occurring, here, there. 3 the present economic climate: current, present-day, existing, extant.
OPPOSITES absent.
• noun think about the present: now, today, the present time, the here and now, modern times.
OPPOSITES past, future.
□ at present at the moment, just now, right now, at the present time, currently, at this moment in time.

present² verb 1 Eddy presented a cheque to

the winner: hand over, give (out), confer, bestow, award, grant, accord. 2 the committee presented its report: submit, set forth, put forward, offer, tender, table. 3 may I present my wife? introduce, make known, acquaint someone with. 4 she presents a TV show: host, introduce, compère; N. Amer. informal emcee. 5 they present him as a criminal: represent, describe, portray, depict.

present³ noun a birthday present: gift, donation, offering, contribution, gratuity, tip, hand-out; informal prezzie.

presentation noun 1 the presentation of his certificate: awarding, presenting, giving, handing over, bestowal, granting. 2 the presentation of food: appearance, arrangement, packaging, layout. 3 a sales presentation: demonstration, talk, lecture, address, speech, show, exhibition, display, introduction, launch, launching, unveiling.

presently adverb 1 I shall see you presently: soon, shortly, quite soon, in a short time, in a little while, at any moment/minute/second, before long; N. Amer. momentarily; Brit. informal in a mo. 2 he is presently abroad: at present, currently, at the/this moment.

preservation noun 1 wood preservation: conservation, protection, care. 2 the preservation of the status quo:

state or in good condition. **2** keep someone safe from harm. **3** treat food to prevent it from decaying. • **noun 1** a food preserved in sugar, salt, vinegar, or alcohol, such as jam or pickle. **2** something reserved for a particular person or group. **3** a place where game is protected and kept for private hunting.

■ **preservation** noun **preserver** noun.

preset verb (**presets**, **presetting**, **preset**) set the controls of an electrical device before it is used.

preside verb (**presides**, **presiding**, **presided**) lead or be in charge of a meeting or event.

presidency noun (plural **presidencies**) the job of president, or the period of time it is held.

president noun **1** the elected head of a republic. **2** the head of an organization.

■ **presidential** adjective.

presidium /pri-si-di-uhm/ noun a permanent decision-making committee within a political organization, especially a communist one.

press¹ verb **1** (**press against** or **to**) move into contact with something by using steady force. **2** push something that operates a device. **3** apply pressure to something to flatten or shape it. **4** move by pushing. **5** (**press on** or **ahead**) continue in what you are doing. **6** express or repeat an opinion or claim in a forceful way. **7** make strong efforts to persuade someone to do something. **8** (**be pressed for**) have too little of. **9** (**be pressed to do**) have difficulty doing. • **noun 1** a device for crushing, flattening, or shaping something. **2** a printing press. **3** (**the press**) newspapers or journalists as a whole.

□ **press conference** a meeting with journalists in order to make an announcement or answer questions. **press release** a statement or piece of publicity issued to journalists. **press stud** Brit. a small fastener with two parts that fit together when pressed. **press-up** Brit. an exercise in which you lie face down on the floor and push your body up by pressing down with your hands and arms.

press² verb (in the past) force someone to serve in the army or navy.

□ **press gang** (in the past) a group of men employed to force men to serve in the army or navy. **press-gang** force someone into doing something. **press someone/thing into service** use someone or something for a particular purpose as a temporary or emergency measure.

pressing adjective **1** needing urgent action. **2** strongly expressed and difficult to refuse or ignore. • **noun** an object made by pressing.

pressure noun **1** steady force applied to an

continuation, conservation, maintenance, upholding, sustaining, perpetuation.

preserve verb **1** *oil preserves the wood:* conserve, protect, maintain, care for, look after. **2** *the wish to preserve the status quo:* continue (with), conserve, keep going, maintain, uphold, sustain, perpetuate, prolong. **3** *preserving him from harm:* guard, protect, keep, defend, safeguard, shelter, shield.

OPPOSITES attack, abandon.

• **noun 1** *the preserve of the rich:* domain, area, field, sphere, orbit, realm, province, territory; informal turf, bailiwick. **2** *a game preserve:* sanctuary, (game) reserve, reservation.

preside verb *the President continued to preside over cabinet meetings:* be in charge of, be responsible for, head, manage, administer, control, direct, chair, conduct, officiate at, lead, govern, rule, command, supervise, oversee; informal head up.

press verb **1** *press the paper down firmly:* push (down), press down, depress, hold down, force, thrust, squeeze, compress. **2** *his shirt was pressed:* iron. **3** *she pressed the child to her bosom:* clasp, hold close, hug, cuddle, squeeze, clutch, grasp, embrace. **4** *the crowd pressed round:* cluster, gather, converge, congregate, flock,

swarm, crowd. **5** *the government pressed its claim:* plead, urge, advance, present, submit, put forward. **6** *they pressed him to agree:* urge, put pressure on, pressurize, force, push, coerce, dragoon, steamroller, browbeat; informal lean on, put the screws on, twist someone's arm, railroad, bulldoze. **7** *they pressed for a ban:* call, ask, clamour, push, campaign, demand.

• **noun 1** *the freedom of the press:* the media, the newspapers, journalism, reporters, the fourth estate; Brit. dated Fleet Street. **2** *the company had some bad press:* (press) reports, press coverage, press articles, press reviews.

pressing adjective **1** *a pressing problem:* urgent, critical, crucial, acute, desperate, serious, grave, life-and-death. **2** *a pressing engagement:* important, high-priority, critical, crucial, unavoidable.

pressure noun **1** *atmospheric pressure:* force, load, stress, thrust, compression, weight. **2** *there was pressure to conform:* persuasion, intimidation, coercion, compulsion, duress, harassment, nagging, badgering. **3** *she had a lot of pressure at work:* strain, stress, tension, trouble, difficulty, burden; informal hassle.

• **verb** *they pressured him into resigning:* coerce, push, persuade, force, bulldoze,

p

object by something that is in contact with it. **2** the use of persuasion or threats to make someone do something. **3** a feeling of stress caused by the need to do something. **4** the force per unit area applied by a fluid against a surface. •**verb** (**pressures, pressuring, pressured**) persuade or force someone into doing something. □ **pressure cooker** a large airtight saucepan in which food is cooked quickly in steam held under pressure. **pressure group** a group that tries to influence the government or public opinion in order to help a cause.

pressurize or **pressurise verb** (**pressurizes, pressurizing, pressurized**) **1** persuade or force someone into doing something. **2** keep the air pressure in an aircraft cabin the same as it is at ground level.

prestige noun respect and admiration resulting from achievements or high quality.

prestigious /press-ti-juhss/ **adjective** having or bringing prestige.

presto adverb & adjective Music in a quick tempo.

prestressed adjective (of concrete) strengthened by means of rods inserted under tension before setting.

presumably adverb as may be supposed.

presume verb (**presumes, presuming, presumed**) **1** suppose that something is probably true. **2** show a lack of respect by doing something that you do not have authority or permission to do. **3** (**presume on**) take advantage of someone's kindness, friendship, etc.

presumption noun 1 something that is

thought to be true or probable. **2** an act of presuming. **3** behaviour that is too confident.

presumptuous adjective behaving too confidently.
■ **presumptuously adverb.**

☑ *-uous*, not *-ious*: presumpt*uous*.

presuppose verb (**presupposes, presupposing, presupposed**) **1** need something to have happened in order to exist or be true. **2** assume, without knowing for sure, that something exists or is true and act on that basis.
■ **presupposition noun.**

pretence (US spelling **pretense**) **noun 1** an act of pretending. **2** a claim to have or be something.

pretend verb 1 make it seem that something is the case when in fact it is not. **2** give the appearance of feeling or having an emotion or quality. **3** (**pretend to**) claim to have a skill, quality, or title.

pretender noun a person who claims a right to a title or position.

pretension noun 1 the act of trying to appear more important or better than you actually are. **2** (also **pretensions**) a claim to have or be something.

pretentious adjective trying to appear more important or better than you actually are so as to impress other people.
■ **pretentiousness noun.**

preternatural adjective beyond what is normal or natural.
■ **preternaturally adverb.**

pretext noun a false reason used to justify an action.

THESAURUS

hound, nag, badger, browbeat, bully, intimidate, dragoon, twist someone's arm; informal **railroad**, lean on; N. Amer. informal hustle.

pressurize verb *he pressurized us into selling:* **coerce**, pressure, push, persuade, force, bulldoze, hound, nag, badger, browbeat, bully, bludgeon, intimidate, dragoon, twist someone's arm; informal railroad, lean on; N. Amer. informal hustle.

prestige noun status, standing, kudos, cachet, stature, reputation, repute, renown, honour, esteem, importance, prominence.

prestigious adjective reputable, distinguished, respected, high-status, esteemed, eminent, highly regarded, renowned, influential.
OPPOSITES disreputable, obscure.

presumably adverb I presume, I expect, I assume, I take it, I imagine, I dare say, doubtless, no doubt, apparently, probably.

presume verb 1 *I presume it was once an*

attic: assume, suppose, surmise, imagine, take it, expect. **2** *I wouldn't presume to advise you:* dare, venture, have the effrontery, be so bold as, go so far as, take the liberty of.

pretence noun 1 *cease this pretence:* make-believe, acting, faking, play-acting, posturing, deception, trickery. **2** *he made a pretence of being concerned:* (false) show, semblance, affectation, (false) appearance, outward appearance, impression, guise, facade.
OPPOSITES honesty.

pretend verb 1 *they pretend to listen:* make as if, act like, affect, go through the motions, fake it. **2** *I'll pretend to be the dragon:* make believe, play at, act, impersonate.
•**adjective** (informal) mock, fake, sham, simulated, artificial, false, pseudo; informal phoney, faux.

p

prettify verb (**prettifies, prettifying, prettified**) try to make something look pretty.

pretty adjective (**prettier, prettiest**) **1** (of a woman or girl) having an attractive face. **2** pleasant to look at. • adverb informal to a certain extent; fairly.
■ **prettily** adverb **prettiness** noun.

pretzel noun a crisp salty biscuit in the shape of a knot or stick.

prevail verb **1** be widespread or current. **2** (**prevail against** or **over**) be more powerful than. **3** (**prevail on**) persuade someone to do something.

prevalent adjective widespread; common.
■ **prevalence** noun.

prevaricate verb (**prevaricates, prevaricating, prevaricated**) avoid giving a direct answer to a question.
■ **prevarication** noun.

prevent verb **1** keep something from happening. **2** stop someone from doing something.
■ **preventable** adjective **prevention** noun.

preventive or **preventative** adjective designed to prevent something from happening.

preview noun **1** a viewing or showing of something before it becomes generally available. **2** a review of a forthcoming film, book, or performance.

previous adjective **1** coming before something else in time or order.

2 (**previous to**) before.
■ **previously** adverb.

prey noun **1** an animal that is hunted and killed by another for food. **2** a person who is harmed or deceived by someone or something. • verb (**prey on**) **1** hunt and kill another animal for food. **2** take advantage of or cause distress to someone.

price noun **1** the amount of money for which something is bought or sold. **2** something unwelcome that must be done in order to achieve something. **3** the odds in betting. • verb (**prices, pricing, priced**) decide the price of.

priceless adjective **1** very valuable. **2** informal very amusing.

pricey adjective (**pricier, priciest**) informal expensive.

prick verb **1** make a small hole in something with a sharp point. **2** cause someone to feel a small, sharp pain. • noun a mark, hole, or pain caused by pricking.
□ **prick up your ears 1** (of a horse or dog) raise the ears when alert. **2** suddenly begin to pay attention.

prickle noun **1** a small thorn on a plant or a pointed spine on an animal. **2** a tingling feeling on the skin. • verb (**prickles, prickling, prickled**) have a tingling feeling on the skin.

prickly adjective **1** having prickles. **2** causing a prickling feeling. **3** easily offended or annoyed.
□ **prickly pear** a cactus which produces

THESAURUS

pretty adjective *a pretty girl:* attractive, good-looking, nice-looking, personable, fetching, prepossessing, appealing, charming, delightful, cute; Scottish & N. English bonny; old use fair, comely.
OPPOSITES plain, ugly.
• adverb (informal) *it's pretty cold:* quite, rather, somewhat, fairly.

prevail verb **1** *common sense will prevail:* win (out/through), triumph, be victorious, carry the day, come out on top, succeed, rule, reign. **2** *the conditions that prevailed in the 1950s:* exist, be present, be the case, occur, be prevalent, be in force.

prevailing adjective current, existing, prevalent, usual, common, general, widespread.

prevalent adjective widespread, frequent, usual, common, current, popular, general.
OPPOSITES rare.

prevent verb stop, avert, nip in the bud, foil, inhibit, thwart, prohibit, forbid.
OPPOSITES allow.

previous adjective **1** *the previous five years:* preceding, foregoing, prior, past, last. **2** *her previous boyfriend:* former, preceding, old, earlier, ex-, past, last, sometime, one-time,

erstwhile; formal quondam. **3** (informal) *I was a bit previous:* overhasty, hasty, premature; informal ahead of yourself.
OPPOSITES next.

previously adverb formerly, earlier (on), before, hitherto, at one time, in the past.

prey noun **1** *the lions' prey:* quarry, kill. **2** *con men choose their prey carefully:* victim, target, dupe; informal sucker; Brit. informal mug.
OPPOSITES predator.

price noun **1** *the purchase price:* cost, charge, fee, fare, amount, sum; informal damage. **2** *the price of success:* consequence, result, cost, penalty, toll, sacrifice, downside, drawback, disadvantage, minus.

priceless adjective invaluable, beyond price, irreplaceable, expensive, costly.
OPPOSITES worthless, cheap.

prick verb *prick the potatoes:* pierce, puncture, stab, perforate, spike, penetrate, jab.
• noun *a prick in the leg:* jab, sting, pinprick, stab, pinhole, wound.

prickly adjective spiky, spiked, thorny, barbed, spiny, bristly.

prickly, pear-shaped fruits.

pride noun **1** deep pleasure or satisfaction felt if you or people close to you have done something well. **2** a source of pride: *the team is the pride of the town.* **3** self-respect. **4** the feeling that you are better than other people. **5** a group of lions. •verb (**prides, priding, prided**) (**pride yourself on**) be especially proud of a quality or skill.
□ **pride of place** the most noticeable or important position.

priest noun **1** a person who is qualified to perform religious ceremonies in the Christian Church. **2** (also **priestess**) a person who performs ceremonies in a non-Christian religion.
■ **priesthood** noun **priestly** adjective.

prig noun a person who behaves as if they are morally superior to other people.
■ **priggish** adjective.

prim adjective very formal and correct and disapproving of anything rude.
■ **primly** adverb.

prima ballerina /pree-muh bal-luh-ree-nuh/ noun the chief female dancer in a ballet company.

primacy noun the fact of being most important.

prima donna /pree-muh **don**-uh/ noun **1** the chief female singer in an opera. **2** a very temperamental and self-important person.

primaeval ⇨ PRIMEVAL.

prima facie /pry-muh **fay**-shi-ee/ adjective & adverb Law accepted as correct until proved otherwise.

primal adjective having to do with early human life; primeval.

primarily adverb for the most part; mainly.

primary adjective **1** of chief importance. **2** earliest in time or order. **3** (of education) for children between the ages of about five and eleven. •noun (plural **primaries**) (in the US) a preliminary election to appoint delegates to a party conference or to choose candidates for an election.
□ **primary colour** each of the colours blue, red, and yellow, from which all other colours can be obtained by mixing.

primate noun **1** an animal belonging to the group that includes monkeys, apes, and humans. **2** (in the Christian Church) an archbishop.

prime¹ adjective **1** of chief importance. **2** of the highest quality; excellent. **3** (of a number) that can be divided only by itself and one (e.g. 2, 3, 5). •noun the time in a person's life when they are the strongest and most successful.
□ **prime minister** the head of a government. **prime time** the time at which a radio or television audience is greatest.

prime² verb (**primes, priming, primed**) **1** prepare someone for a situation by giving them information. **2** make something ready for use or action. **3** cover a surface with primer.

primer noun **1** a substance painted on a surface as a base coat. **2** a book for teaching children to read or giving a basic introduction to a subject.

primeval or **primaeval** /pry-**mee**-v'l/ adjective relating to the earliest times in history.

primitive adjective **1** relating to the earliest times in history or stages in development.

p

THESAURUS

pride noun **1** *a source of pride:* self-esteem, dignity, honour, self-respect. **2** *pride in a job well done:* pleasure, joy, delight, gratification, fulfilment, satisfaction, sense of achievement. **3** *he refused out of pride:* arrogance, vanity, self-importance, hubris, conceitedness, egotism, snobbery.
OPPOSITES shame, humility.

priest noun clergyman, clergywoman, minister, cleric, pastor, vicar, rector, parson, churchman, churchwoman, father, curate; Scottish kirkman; N. Amer. dominie; informal reverend, padre.

primarily adverb **1** *he was primarily a singer:* first and foremost, firstly, essentially, in essence, fundamentally, principally, predominantly. **2** *work is done primarily for large institutions:* mostly, for the most part, chiefly, mainly, in the main, on the whole, largely, principally, predominantly.

primary adjective main, chief, key, prime, central, principal, foremost, first, most important, predominant, paramount; informal number-one.
OPPOSITES secondary.

prime¹ adjective **1** *his prime reason for leaving:* main, chief, key, primary, central, principal, foremost, first, most important, paramount, major; informal number-one. **2** *prime agricultural land:* top-quality, top, best, first-class, superior, choice, select, finest; informal tip-top, A1.
OPPOSITES secondary, inferior.
•noun *he is in his prime:* heyday, peak, pinnacle, high point/spot, zenith, flower, bloom, flush.

prime² verb *Lucy had primed him carefully:* brief, fill in, prepare, advise, instruct, coach, drill, train.

primitive adjective **1** *primitive times:* ancient, earliest, first, prehistoric, primordial, primeval. **2** *primitive tools:* crude, simple, rough (and ready), basic,

2 offering a very basic level of comfort.
3 (of behaviour or emotion) not based on reason; instinctive.
■ **primitively** adverb.

primogeniture noun **1** the state of being the first child born in a family. **2** the system by which the eldest son inherits all his parents' property.

primordial /pry-**mor**-di-uhl/ adjective existing at the beginning of time.

primp verb make small adjustments to your appearance.

primrose noun a plant of woods and hedges with pale yellow flowers.

primula noun a plant of a group that includes primroses and cowslips.

prince noun a son or other close male relative of a king or queen.
□ **prince consort** the husband of a reigning queen who is himself a prince. **Prince of Wales** the title given to the eldest son of a British king or queen.

princeling noun **1** the ruler of a small country. **2** a young prince.

princely adjective **1** relating to or suitable for a prince. **2** (of a sum of money) generous.

princess noun **1** a daughter or other close female relative of a king or queen. **2** the wife or widow of a prince.
□ **Princess Royal** a title given to the eldest daughter of a British king or queen.

principal adjective most important; main.
● noun **1** the most important person in an organization or group. **2** the head of a school or college. **3** a sum of money lent or invested, on which interest is paid.
□ **principal boy** Brit. a woman who takes the leading male role in a pantomime.

■ **principally** adverb.

> **!** don't confuse the words **principal** and **principle**. **Principal** is usually an adjective meaning 'main or most important', whereas **principle** is a noun meaning 'a law, rule, or theory on which something is based'.

principality noun (plural **principalities**) **1** a state ruled by a prince. **2** (**the Principality**) Brit. Wales.

principle noun **1** a law, rule, or theory on which something is based. **2** (**principles**) rules or beliefs that govern the way you behave. **3** a scientific theorem or natural law that explains why something happens or how it works.
□ **in principle** in theory. **on principle** because of your moral principles.

principled adjective acting according to strong moral principles.

print verb **1** produce a book, newspaper, etc. by a process involving the transfer of words or pictures to paper. **2** produce a photographic print from a negative. **3** write words clearly without joining the letters. **4** mark fabric with a coloured design. ● noun **1** printed words in a book, newspaper, etc. **2** a mark where something has pressed or touched a surface. **3** a printed picture or design.
□ **in** (or **out of**) **print** (of a book) available (or no longer available) from the publisher.
■ **printer** noun.

printing noun **1** the transfer of words or pictures to paper in the production of books, newspapers, etc. **2** handwriting in which the letters are written separately.
□ **printing press** a machine for printing

p

THESAURUS

rudimentary, makeshift.
OPPOSITES modern, sophisticated.

prince noun ruler, sovereign, monarch, crowned head.

principal adjective main, chief, primary, leading, foremost, first, most important, predominant, dominant, pre-eminent, highest, top; informal number-one.
OPPOSITES minor.
● noun head teacher, headmaster, headmistress, head, dean, rector, master, mistress, chancellor, vice-chancellor, president, provost, warden; N. Amer. informal prexy.

principally adverb mainly, mostly, chiefly, for the most part, in the main, on the whole, largely, predominantly, primarily.

principle noun **1** *a basic principle of science:* truth, concept, idea, theory, fundamental, essential, precept, rule, law. **2** *the principle of laissez-faire:* doctrine, belief, creed,

credo, code, ethic. **3** *a woman of principle:* morals, morality, ethics, ideals, standards, integrity, virtue, probity, honour, decency, conscience, scruples.
□ **in principle 1** *there is no reason, in principle, why not:* in theory, theoretically, on paper, ideally. **2** *he accepted the idea in principle:* in general, in essence, on the whole, in the main.

print verb **1** *when was the book printed?* publish, issue, release, circulate, run off, copy, reproduce. **2** *patterns were printed on the cloth:* imprint, impress, stamp, mark.
● noun **1** *large print:* type, printing, letters, lettering, characters, typeface, font. **2** *a print of his left hand:* impression, handprint, fingerprint, footprint. **3** *sporting prints:* picture, engraving, etching, lithograph, woodcut. **4** *prints and negatives:* photograph, photo, snap, snapshot, picture, still, enlargement, copy,

books, newspapers, etc. by pressing an ink-covered surface on to paper.

printout noun a page of printed material from a computer's printer.

prion /pree-on/ noun a protein particle believed to be the cause of brain diseases such as BSE and CJD.

prior[1] adjective **1** coming before in time, order, or importance. **2 (prior to)** before.

prior[2] noun (feminine **prioress**) **1** (in an abbey) the person next in rank below an abbot or abbess. **2** the head of a house of friars or nuns.

prioritize or **prioritise** verb (**prioritizes, prioritizing, prioritized**) **1** decide the order of importance of a number of tasks. **2** treat something as being more important than other things.

priority noun (plural **priorities**) **1** the condition of being more important than other things. **2** a thing seen as more important than others. **3** Brit. the right to go before other traffic.

priory noun (plural **priories**) a monastery or nunnery governed by a prior or prioress.

prise (US spelling **prize**) verb (**prises, prising, prised**) force something open or apart.

prism noun **1** a piece of glass or other transparent material with facets, used to separate white light into a spectrum of colours. **2** a solid geometric figure whose two ends are parallel and of the same size and shape, and whose sides are parallelograms.

■ **prismatic** adjective.

prison noun a building where criminals are kept as a punishment.

prisoner noun **1** a person who has been found guilty of a crime and sent to prison. **2** a person who has been captured by someone and kept confined.
□ **prisoner of war** a person captured and imprisoned by the enemy in war.

prissy adjective too concerned with behaving in a correct and respectable way.

pristine adjective **1** in its original condition. **2** clean and fresh as if new.

privacy noun a state in which you are not watched or disturbed by other people.

private adjective **1** intended for or involving a particular person or group. **2** (of thoughts, feelings, etc.) that you do not tell other people about. **3** not sharing thoughts and feelings with other people. **4** where you will not be disturbed; secluded. **5** (of a service or industry) provided by an individual or commercial company rather than the state. **6** not connected with a person's work or official role. •noun (also **private soldier**) a soldier of the lowest rank in the army.
□ **private company** Brit. a company whose shares may not be offered to the public for sale. **private detective** a detective who is not a police officer and who carries out investigations for clients. **private enterprise** business or industry managed by independent companies rather than the state. **private eye** informal a private detective. **private member** a member of

---

THESAURUS

reproduction.

prior adjective earlier, previous, preceding, advance, pre-existing.
OPPOSITES subsequent.
□ **prior to before**, until, up to, previous to, preceding, earlier than, in advance of.

priority noun **1** *safety is our priority:* prime concern, main consideration. **2** *giving priority to education:* precedence, preference, pre-eminence, predominance, primacy. **3** *oncoming traffic has priority:* right of way, precedence, supremacy, seniority.

prison noun jail, penal institution; N. Amer. jailhouse, penitentiary, correctional facility; informal clink, slammer; Brit. informal nick; N. Amer. informal can, pen.
□ **in prison behind bars**; informal inside, doing time; Brit. informal doing porridge.

prisoner noun **1** *a prisoner serving a life sentence:* convict, detainee, inmate; informal jailbird, con; Brit. informal lag; N. Amer. informal yardbird. **2** *the army took many prisoners:* prisoner of war, POW, internee, captive, hostage.

pristine adjective immaculate, perfect, in mint condition, as new, spotless, unspoilt.
OPPOSITES dirty, spoilt.

privacy noun seclusion, solitude, isolation.

private adjective **1** *his private plane:* personal, own, special, exclusive. **2** *private talks:* confidential, secret, classified. **3** *private thoughts:* intimate, personal, secret, innermost, undisclosed, unspoken, unvoiced. **4** *a very private man:* reserved, introverted, self-contained, reticent, retiring, unsociable, withdrawn, solitary, reclusive. **5** *somewhere private to talk:* secluded, undisturbed, remote, isolated. **6** *in a private capacity:* unofficial, personal. **7** *private industry:* independent, non-state, privatized, commercial, private-enterprise.
OPPOSITES public, open, official, state, nationalized.
•noun *a private in the army:* private soldier, trooper; Brit. sapper, gunner; US GI; Brit. informal Tommy, squaddie.
□ **in private in secret**, secretly, privately, behind closed doors, in camera.

parliament who does not hold a government office. **private parts** a person's genitals. **private practice** the work of a doctor, lawyer, etc. who is self-employed. **private school** Brit. an independent school financed mainly by the fees paid by pupils. **private secretary 1** a secretary who deals with the personal matters of their employer. **2** a civil servant acting as an assistant to a senior government official. **private sector** the part of the national economy not under direct state control. ■ **privately** adverb.

privateer noun (in the past) an armed but privately owned ship, authorized by a government for use in war.

privation noun a state in which you do not have the basic things you need, such as food and warmth.

privatize or **privatise** verb (**privatizes**, **privatizing**, **privatized**) transfer a business or industry from ownership by the state to private ownership. ■ **privatization** noun.

privet noun a shrub with small white flowers.

privilege noun **1** a special right or advantage for a particular person or group. **2** an opportunity to do something regarded as a special honour. **3** the advantages available to people who are rich and powerful.

> ☑ -il-, not -el-, and no d: pri*vil*ege.

privileged adjective **1** having a privilege or privileges. **2** (of information) protected from being made public.

privy adjective (**privy to**) sharing in the knowledge of something secret. ● **noun** (plural **privies**) a toilet in a small shed outside a house.
□ **Privy Council** a group of politicians appointed to advise a king or queen.

prize[1] noun **1** a thing given to someone who wins a competition or race or to mark an outstanding achievement. **2** something that is worth struggling to achieve. ● **adjective 1** having been awarded a prize. **2** outstanding. ● **verb** (**prizes**, **prizing**, **prized**) value highly.

prize[2] US spelling of PRISE.

pro[1] informal **noun** (plural **pros**) a professional, especially in sport. ● **adjective** professional.

pro[2] noun (plural **pros**) (usu. **in pros and cons**) an advantage of or argument in favour of something.

proactive adjective creating or controlling a situation rather than just responding to it. ■ **proactively** adverb.

probability noun (plural **probabilities**) **1** the extent to which something is probable. **2** an event that is likely to happen.

probable adjective likely to happen or be the case.

probably adverb almost certainly.

probate noun the official process of proving that a will is valid.

probation noun **1** a system in which a person who has committed a crime does not have to go to prison if they behave well and report regularly to an official. **2** a period of training and testing when you start a new job. ■ **probationary** adjective **probationer** noun.

probe noun **1** an investigation. **2** a surgical

p

THESAURUS

privilege noun **1** *senior pupils have certain privileges:* advantage, benefit, prerogative, entitlement, right, concession, freedom, liberty. **2** *it was a privilege to meet her:* honour, pleasure.

privileged adjective **1** *a privileged background:* wealthy, rich, affluent, prosperous, born with a silver spoon in your mouth. **2** *I feel very lucky and privileged:* honoured, advantaged, favoured, valued, appreciated. **3** *privileged information:* confidential, private, secret, restricted, classified, not for publication, off the record, inside; informal hush-hush.
OPPOSITES underprivileged, disadvantaged, public.

prize noun *an art prize:* award, reward, trophy, medal, cup, winnings, purse, honour.
● **adjective 1** *a prize bull:* champion, award-winning, top, best. **2** *a prize idiot:* utter, complete, total, absolute, real, perfect; Brit. informal right.

probability noun **1** *the probability of winning:* likelihood, prospect, expectation, chance(s), odds. **2** *relegation is a distinct probability:* prospect, possibility.

probable adjective likely, odds-on, expected, anticipated, predictable; informal on the cards, a safe bet.
OPPOSITES improbable, unlikely.

probably adverb in all likelihood, in all probability, as likely as not, ten to one, the chances are, doubtless.

probation noun trial, trial period, test period, apprenticeship, training.

probe noun *a probe into city hall corruption:* investigation, enquiry, examination, inquest, study.
● **verb 1** *their long beaks are suited to probing the ground:* prod, poke, dig into, delve into, explore, feel around in, examine. **2** *an enquiry probed the cause of the disaster:* investigate, enquire into, look into, go into, study, examine, explore.

instrument used to examine the body. **3** a small device for measuring or testing something. **4** (also **space probe**) an unmanned spacecraft used for exploration. •**verb** (**probes**, **probing**, **probed**) **1** physically explore or examine something. **2** investigate something closely.
■ **probing** adjective.

probiotic noun a substance which stimulates the growth of beneficial microorganisms in the body.

probity noun formal the quality of being honest and having high moral standards.

problem noun a thing that is difficult to deal with or understand.

problematic or **problematical** adjective difficult to deal with or understand.

proboscis /pruh-**boss**-iss/ noun (plural **probosces** /pruh-**boss**-eez/ or **proboscises**) **1** a mammal's long, flexible snout, e.g. an elephant's trunk. **2** the long, thin mouth of some insects.

procedure noun **1** an established or official way of doing something. **2** a series of actions done in a certain way.
■ **procedural** adjective.

proceed verb **1** begin a course of action. **2** go on to do something. **3** carry on or continue.

proceedings plural noun **1** an event or a series of actions. **2** action taken in a law court to settle a dispute.

proceeds plural noun money obtained from an event or activity.

process[1] /proh-sess/ noun **1** a series of actions that are done to achieve a particular end. **2** a natural series of changes: *the ageing process.* •**verb** **1** perform a series of actions on something to change or preserve it. **2** deal with someone or something using an established procedure.
■ **processor** noun.

process[2] /pruh-**sess**/ verb walk in procession.

procession noun **1** a number of people or vehicles moving forward in an orderly way. **2** a large number of people or things that come one after another.

proclaim verb **1** announce officially or publicly. **2** show something clearly.
■ **proclamation** noun.

proclivity noun (plural **proclivities**) a tendency to do something regularly.

procrastinate verb (**procrastinates**, **procrastinating**, **procrastinated**) delay or postpone action.
■ **procrastination** noun.

procreate verb (**procreates**, **procreating**, **procreated**) produce a baby or young animal.
■ **procreation** noun.

proctor noun Brit. an officer in charge of discipline at some universities.

procurator fiscal noun (plural **procurators fiscal** or **procurator fiscals**) (in Scotland) a local coroner and public prosecutor.

procure verb (**procures**, **procuring**,

THESAURUS

p

problem noun **1** *there's a problem:* difficulty, worry, complication, snag, hitch, drawback, stumbling block, obstacle, hiccup, setback, catch; informal dilemma, headache, fly in the ointment. **2** *I don't want to be a problem:* nuisance, bother; informal drag, pain. **3** *arithmetical problems:* puzzle, question, poser, riddle, conundrum; informal brain-teaser.

problematic adjective difficult, tricky, troublesome, awkward, controversial, ticklish, complicated, complex, knotty. OPPOSITES easy, straightforward.

procedure noun course of action, method, system, strategy, way, approach, formula, mechanism, technique, routine, drill, practice.

proceed verb **1** *she was uncertain how to proceed:* begin, make a start, get going, move. **2** *he proceeded down the road:* go, make your way, advance, move, progress, carry on, press on, push on. **3** *we should proceed with the talks:* go ahead, carry on, go on, continue, keep on, get on. OPPOSITES stop.

proceedings plural noun **1** *the evening's*

proceedings: events, activities, happenings, goings-on. **2** *the proceedings of the meeting:* report, transactions, minutes, account, story, record(s). **3** *legal proceedings:* legal action, litigation, lawsuit, case, prosecution.

proceeds plural noun profits, earnings, receipts, returns, takings, income, revenue, profit, yield; Sport gate (money); N. Amer. take.

process noun **1** *investigation is a long process:* procedure, operation, action, activity, exercise, affair, business, job, task, undertaking. **2** *a new canning process:* method, system, technique, means, practice, way, approach.
•**verb** *applications are processed rapidly:* deal with, attend to, see to, sort out, handle, take care of.

procession noun parade, march, march past, cavalcade, motorcade, cortège, column, file; Brit. informal crocodile.

proclaim verb declare, announce, pronounce, state, make known, give out, advertise, publish, broadcast, trumpet.

procured) obtain.
■ **procurement** noun.

prod verb (**prods, prodding, prodded**) **1** push someone or something with a finger or pointed object. **2** prompt or remind someone to do something. • noun **1** an act of prodding. **2** a prompt or reminder. **3** a pointed object like a stick.

prodigal adjective **1** using time, money, etc. in a wasteful way. **2** lavish. • noun (also **prodigal son**) a person who leaves home and leads a wasteful life but is later sorry for their actions and returns.
■ **prodigality** noun.

prodigious adjective impressively large.
■ **prodigiously** adverb.

prodigy noun (plural **prodigies**) a young person with exceptional abilities.

produce verb /pruh-**dyooss**/ (**produces, producing, produced**) **1** make, manufacture, or create. **2** make something happen or exist. **3** show or provide something for consideration. **4** be in charge of the financial aspects of a film or the staging of a play. **5** supervise the making of a musical recording. • noun /**prod**-yooss/ things that have been produced or grown.

■ **producer** noun.

product noun **1** an article or substance manufactured for sale. **2** a result of an action or process. **3** a substance produced during a natural, chemical, or manufacturing process. **4** Maths a quantity obtained by multiplying one number by another.

production noun **1** the action of producing something. **2** the amount of something produced.
□ **production line** an assembly line.

productive adjective **1** producing large amounts of goods or crops. **2** doing or achieving a lot.
■ **productively** adverb.

productivity noun **1** the quality of being productive. **2** the efficiency with which things are produced.

profane adjective **1** not religious; secular. **2** not having respect for God or holy things. • verb (**profanes, profaning, profaned**) treat something holy with a lack of respect.

profanity noun (plural **profanities**) **1** language or behaviour that shows a lack of respect for God or holy things. **2** a swear word.

THESAURUS

prod verb **1** *Cassie prodded him in the chest:* poke, jab, stab, dig, nudge, elbow. **2** *the Department was prodded into action:* spur, stimulate, prompt, push, galvanize, persuade, urge, chivvy, remind.
• noun **1** *a sharp prod in the ribs:* poke, jab, stab, dig, nudge, elbow. **2** *he might need a prod to get him to come:* urging, stimulus, push, prompt, reminder, chivvying.

prodigal adjective wasteful, extravagant, spendthrift.
OPPOSITES thrifty.

prodigy noun genius, mastermind, virtuoso, wunderkind; informal whizz-kid, whizz.
OPPOSITES dunce.

produce verb **1** *the company produces furniture:* manufacture, make, construct, build, fabricate, put together, assemble, turn out, create, mass-produce. **2** *the vineyards produce excellent wines:* yield, grow, give, supply, provide, furnish, bear. **3** *she produced ten puppies:* give birth to, bear, deliver, bring forth, bring into the world. **4** *he produced five novels:* create, fashion, turn out, compose, write, pen, paint. **5** *she produced an ID card:* pull out, extract, fish out, present, offer, proffer, show. **6** *that will produce a reaction:* cause, bring about, give rise to, occasion, generate, lead to, result in, provoke, precipitate, spark off, trigger. **7** *James produced the play:* stage, put on, mount, present, exhibit.

• noun *local produce:* food, foodstuff(s), products, crops, fruit and vegetables.

producer noun **1** *a car producer:* manufacturer, maker, builder, constructor. **2** *coffee producers:* grower, farmer. **3** *the producer of the show:* impresario, manager, administrator, promoter, director.

product noun **1** *household products:* artefact, commodity; (**products**) goods, ware(s), merchandise, produce. **2** *a product of experience:* result, consequence, outcome, effect, upshot.

production noun **1** *the production of cars:* manufacture, making, construction, building, fabrication, assembly, creation, mass production. **2** *the production of literary works:* creation, origination, fashioning, composition, writing. **3** *agricultural production:* output, yield, productivity. **4** *a theatre production:* performance, staging, presentation, show, piece, play.

productive adjective **1** *a productive artist:* prolific, inventive, creative. **2** *productive talks:* useful, constructive, profitable, fruitful, valuable, effective, worthwhile, helpful. **3** *productive land:* fertile, fruitful, rich, fecund.
OPPOSITES unproductive.

productivity noun efficiency, work rate, output, yield, production.

p

profess verb **1** claim that something is true. **2** declare your faith in a religion.

profession noun **1** a job that needs special training and a formal qualification. **2** all the people working in a particular profession. **3** a claim. **4** a declaration of belief in a religion.

professional adjective **1** relating to or belonging to a profession. **2** doing something as a job rather than as a hobby. **3** having the skills or qualities of a professional person. •noun **1** a professional person. **2** a person who is very skilled in a particular activity. ■ **professionally** adverb.

☑ only one *f*: professional.

professionalism noun the ability or skill that you expect from a professional person.

professor noun **1** a university teacher or scholar of the highest rank. **2** N. Amer. a university teacher. ■ **professorial** adjective **professorship** noun.

proffer verb (**proffers, proffering, proffered**) offer something for someone to accept.

proficient adjective competent; skilled. ■ **proficiency** noun.

profile noun **1** an outline of someone's face, seen from the side. **2** a short article that describes someone or something. **3** the extent to which someone attracts attention: *her high profile.* •verb (**profiles, profiling, profiled**) describe in a short article.
□ **keep a low profile** try not to attract attention.

profit noun **1** a financial gain. **2** advantage or benefit. •verb (**profits, profiting, profited**) benefit someone.
□ **profit margin** the difference between the cost of producing something and the price at which it is sold.

☑ note that the forms **profited** and **profiting** have a single rather than a double *t*.

profitable adjective **1** (of a business or activity) making a profit. **2** useful. ■ **profitability** noun **profitably** adverb.

profiteering noun the making of a large profit in an unfair way. ■ **profiteer** noun.

profiterole noun a small ball of choux pastry filled with cream and covered with chocolate.

profligate adjective **1** using time, money, in a wasteful or extravagant way. **2** indulging too much in physical pleasures. •noun a profligate person. ■ **profligacy** noun.

THESAURUS

profess verb **1** *he professed his love:* declare, announce, proclaim, assert, state, affirm, maintain, protest. **2** *she professed to loathe publicity:* claim, pretend, purport, affect, make out.

professed adjective **1** *their professed independence:* claimed, supposed, ostensible, self-styled, apparent, pretended, purported. **2** *a professed Christian:* declared, self-acknowledged, self-confessed, confessed, sworn, confirmed.

profession noun career, occupation, calling, vocation, métier, line of work, job, business, trade, craft.

professional adjective **1** *professional occupations:* white-collar, non-manual, graduate, qualified, chartered. **2** *a professional cricketer:* paid, salaried. **3** *a very professional job:* expert, accomplished, skilful, masterly, fine, polished, skilled, proficient, competent, able, businesslike, deft. **4** *not a professional way to behave:* appropriate, fitting, proper, honourable, ethical. OPPOSITES manual, amateur, amateurish, unethical.
•noun *she was a real professional:* expert, virtuoso, old hand, master, maestro, past master; informal pro, ace. OPPOSITES amateur.

profile noun **1** *his handsome profile:* outline, silhouette, side view, contour, shape, form, lines. **2** *a profile of the organization:* description, account, study, portrait, rundown, sketch, outline.

profit noun **1** *the firm made a profit:* financial gain, return(s), yield, proceeds, earnings, winnings, surplus; informal pay dirt, bottom line. **2** *there was little profit in going on:* advantage, benefit, value, use, good; informal mileage. OPPOSITES loss, disadvantage.
•verb **1** *we will not profit from the deal:* make money, earn; informal rake it in, clean up, make a killing; N. Amer. informal make a fast buck. **2** *how will that profit us?* benefit, be advantageous to, be of use to, do someone good, help, be of service to, serve. OPPOSITES lose, disadvantage.

profitable adjective **1** *a profitable company:* moneymaking, profit-making, paying, lucrative, commercial, successful, money-spinning, gainful. **2** *profitable study:* beneficial, useful, advantageous, valuable, productive, worthwhile, rewarding, fruitful, illuminating, informative, well spent. OPPOSITES unprofitable, loss-making, fruitless, useless.

p

profound adjective (**profounder, profoundest**) **1** very great. **2** showing great knowledge or understanding. **3** needing a lot of study or thought.
■ **profoundly** adverb **profundity** noun.

profuse adjective produced or appearing in large quantities.
■ **profusely** adverb.

profusion noun a very large quantity of something.

progenitor /proh-**jen**-i-ter/ noun **1** an ancestor or parent. **2** the person who started an artistic, political, or intellectual movement.

progeny /**proj**-uh-ni/ noun offspring.

progesterone /pruh-**jess**-tuh-rohn/ noun a hormone that stimulates the uterus to prepare for pregnancy.

prognosis /prog-**noh**-siss/ noun (plural **prognoses** /prog-**noh**-seez/) **1** an opinion about how an illness is likely to develop. **2** the likely course of a situation.
■ **prognostic** adjective.

programmatic adjective having to do with or following a programme.

programme (US spelling **program**) noun **1** a plan of future events or things to be done.

2 a radio or television broadcast. **3** a sheet or booklet giving details about a play, concert, etc. **4** (**program**) a series of software instructions to control the operation of a computer. • verb (**programmes**, **programming**, **programmed**) **1** (**program**) provide a computer with a program. **2** make something behave in a particular way. **3** arrange something according to a plan.
■ **programmable** adjective **programmer** noun.

progress noun **1** forward movement towards a place. **2** the process of improving or developing. • verb **1** move forwards. **2** improve or develop.

progression noun **1** a gradual movement from one place or state to another. **2** a number of things coming one after another.

progressive adjective **1** proceeding gradually or in stages. **2** favouring new ideas or social reform. • noun a person who is in favour of social reform.
■ **progressively** adverb.

prohibit verb (**prohibits**, **prohibiting**, **prohibited**) **1** formally forbid something by law. **2** prevent something from happening.

prohibition noun **1** the action of

THESAURUS

profound adjective **1** *profound relief:* heartfelt, intense, keen, extreme, acute, severe, sincere, earnest, deep, deep-seated, overpowering, overwhelming. **2** *a profound change:* far-reaching, radical, extensive, sweeping, exhaustive, thoroughgoing. **3** *a profound analysis:* wise, learned, intelligent, scholarly, discerning, penetrating, perceptive, astute, thoughtful, insightful.
OPPOSITES superficial, mild, slight.

programme noun **1** *our programme for the day:* schedule, agenda, calendar, timetable, order, line-up. **2** *the government's reform programme:* scheme, plan, package, strategy, initiative, proposal. **3** *a television programme:* broadcast, production, show, presentation, transmission, performance; informal prog. **4** *a programme of study:* course, syllabus, curriculum.
• verb *they programmed the day well:* arrange, organize, schedule, plan, map out, timetable, line up; N. Amer. slate.

progress noun **1** *snow made progress difficult:* (forward) movement, advance, going, headway, passage. **2** *scientific progress:* development, advance, advancement, headway, step forward, improvement, growth.
OPPOSITES regression.
• verb **1** *they progressed slowly down the road:* go, make your way, move, proceed, advance, go on, continue, make headway, work your way. **2** *the school has progressed*

rapidly: develop, make progress, advance, make headway, take steps forward, move on, get on, gain ground, improve, get better, come on, come along, make strides; informal be getting there.
OPPOSITES regress, lapse.
□ **in progress under way,** going on, ongoing, happening, occurring, taking place, proceeding, continuing.

progression noun **1** *progression to the next stage:* progress, advancement, movement, passage, development, evolution, growth. **2** *a progression of peaks on the graph:* succession, series, sequence, string, stream, chain, train, row, cycle.

progressive adjective **1** *progressive deterioration:* continuing, continuous, ongoing, gradual, step-by-step, cumulative. **2** *progressive views:* modern, liberal, advanced, forward-thinking, enlightened, pioneering, reforming, reformist, radical; informal go-ahead.
OPPOSITES sporadic, conservative, reactionary.

prohibit verb **1** *state law prohibits gambling:* forbid, ban, bar, proscribe, make illegal, outlaw, disallow. **2** *a cash shortage prohibited the visit:* prevent, stop, rule out, preclude, make impossible.
OPPOSITES allow.

prohibition noun ban, bar, veto, embargo, boycott, injunction, moratorium.

p

prohibiting. **2** an order that forbids something.

prohibitive adjective **1** forbidding or restricting something. **2** (of a price) too high.
■ **prohibitively** adverb.

project noun /**pro**-jekt/ **1** a piece of work that is carefully planned to achieve a particular aim. **2** a piece of work by a school or college student in which they carry out their own research. •verb /pruh-**jekt**/ **1** estimate or predict something based on what is happening now. **2** (**be projected**) be planned. **3** stick out beyond something else. **4** make light or an image fall on a surface or screen. **5** present yourself to other people in a particular way.

projectile noun an object that is fired or thrown at a target.

projection noun **1** a prediction about something based on what is happening now. **2** the projecting of an image, sound, etc. **3** a thing that sticks out from something else.
■ **projectionist** noun.

projector noun a device for projecting slides or film on to a screen.

prolapse noun a condition in which an organ of the body has slipped forward or down from its normal position.

proletarian /proh-li-**tair**-i-uhn/ adjective relating to the proletariat. •noun a member of the proletariat.

proletariat noun workers or working-class people.

proliferate verb (**proliferates, proliferating, proliferated**) reproduce rapidly; increase rapidly in number.
■ **proliferation** noun.

prolific adjective **1** (of a plant or animal) producing a lot of fruit, leaves, or young. **2** (of an artist, author, etc.) producing many works.
■ **prolifically** adverb.

prolix /proh-liks/ adjective (of speech or writing) long and boring.
■ **prolixity** noun.

prologue noun **1** a separate introductory part of a play, book, or piece of music. **2** an event that leads to another.

prolong verb make something last longer.
■ **prolongation** noun.

prolonged adjective continuing for a long time.

prom noun informal **1** Brit. a promenade by the sea. **2** Brit. a promenade concert. **3** N. Amer. a formal dance at a high school or college.

promenade noun **1** a paved walkway along a seafront. **2** a leisurely walk. •verb (**promenades, promenading, promenaded**) go for a leisurely walk.
□ **promenade concert** Brit. a concert of classical music at which part of the audience stands.

promethium noun a radioactive metallic element.

prominence noun the state of being prominent.

prominent adjective **1** important; famous.

THESAURUS

project noun **1** *an engineering project:* scheme, plan, programme, enterprise, undertaking, venture, proposal, idea, concept. **2** *a history project:* assignment, piece of work, piece of research, task. •verb **1** *profits are projected to rise:* forecast, predict, expect, estimate, calculate, reckon. **2** *his projected book:* intend, plan, propose. **3** *balconies projected over the lake:* stick out, jut (out), protrude, extend, stand out, bulge out. **4** *the sun projected his shadow on the wall:* cast, throw, send, shed, shine.

projection noun **1** *a sales projection:* forecast, prediction, prognosis, expectation, estimate. **2** *tiny projections on the cliff face:* outcrop, outgrowth, overhang, ledge, shelf, prominence, protrusion, protuberance.

proliferate verb increase, grow, multiply, rocket, mushroom, snowball, burgeon, spread, expand, run riot.
OPPOSITES decrease, dwindle.

prolific adjective **1** *a prolific crop of* tomatoes: plentiful, abundant, bountiful, profuse, copious, luxuriant, rich, lush, fruitful. **2** *a prolific composer:* productive, fertile, creative, inventive.
OPPOSITES meagre, unproductive.

prolong verb lengthen, extend, drag out, draw out, protract, spin out, carry on, continue, keep up, perpetuate.
OPPOSITES shorten.

prominence noun **1** *his rise to prominence:* fame, celebrity, eminence, importance, distinction, greatness, prestige, stature, standing. **2** *the press gave prominence to the reports:* wide coverage, importance, precedence, weight, a high profile, top billing.

prominent adjective **1** *a prominent surgeon:* important, well known, leading, eminent, distinguished, notable, noteworthy, noted, illustrious, celebrated, famous, renowned; N. Amer. major-league. **2** *prominent cheekbones:* jutting (out), protruding, projecting, protuberant, standing out, sticking out, proud, bulging. **3** *a prominent feature of the landscape:* conspicuous,

2 sticking out. **3** particularly noticeable.
■ **prominently** adverb.

promiscuous /pruh-**miss**-kyuu-uhss/
adjective having a lot of sexual
relationships.
■ **promiscuity** noun.

promise noun **1** an assurance that you will
do something or that something will
happen. **2** qualities or abilities that may
lead to future success. • verb (**promises,
promising, promised**) **1** make a promise.
2 give good grounds for expecting
something.

promising adjective showing signs of
future success.
■ **promisingly** adverb.

promissory note noun a signed document
containing a written promise to pay a
stated amount of money.

promo noun (plural **promos**) informal a
promotional film, video, etc.

promontory /**prom**-uhn-tuh-ri/ noun (plural
promontories) a point of high land jutting

out into the sea.

promote verb (**promotes, promoting,
promoted**) **1** help something to happen.
2 give publicity to a product, event, etc. in
order to increase sales or make people
aware of it. **3** raise someone to a higher
position or rank.
■ **promoter** noun.

promotion noun **1** activity that supports or
encourages a cause or aim. **2** the action of
promoting a product, event, etc.
3 movement to a higher position or rank.
■ **promotional** adjective.

prompt verb **1** make something happen.
2 (**prompt someone to**) make someone
take a course of action. **3** encourage
someone to speak. **4** tell an actor a word
that they have forgotten. • noun **1** a word or
phrase used to prompt an actor. **2** a symbol
on a computer screen to show that more
input is needed. • adjective done without
delay. • adverb Brit. exactly or punctually.
■ **prompter** noun **promptly** adverb.

THESAURUS

noticeable, obvious, unmistakable, eye-
catching, pronounced, salient, striking,
dominant, obtrusive.
OPPOSITES unimportant, unknown, flat,
inconspicuous.

promise noun **1** *you broke your promise:*
word (of honour), assurance, pledge, vow,
guarantee, oath, bond, undertaking,
agreement, commitment, contract. **2** *he
shows promise:* potential, ability, talent,
aptitude, possibility.
• verb **1** *she promised to go:* give your word,
swear, pledge, vow, undertake, guarantee,
warrant, contract, give an assurance,
commit yourself. **2** *the skies promised
sunshine:* indicate, lead one to expect,
point to, be a sign of, give hope of, augur,
herald, portend.

promising adjective **1** *a promising start:*
good, encouraging, favourable, hopeful,
auspicious, propitious, bright, rosy,
heartening. **2** *a promising actor:* with
potential, gifted, talented, budding, up-
and-coming, rising, coming, in the making.
OPPOSITES unfavourable, hopeless.

promote verb **1** *she's been promoted:*
upgrade, give promotion to, elevate,
advance, move up. **2** *an organization
promoting justice:* encourage, further,
advance, foster, develop, boost, stimulate,
work for. **3** *she is promoting her new film:*
advertise, publicize, give publicity to,
beat/bang the drum for, market,
merchandise; informal push, plug, hype.

promotion noun **1** *her promotion at work:*
upgrading, preferment, elevation,

advancement, step up (the ladder). **2** *the
promotion of justice:* encouragement,
furtherance, furthering, advancement,
contribution to, fostering, boosting,
stimulation; N. Amer. boosterism. **3** *the
promotion for her new film:* advertising,
marketing, publicity, campaign,
propaganda; informal hard sell, plug, hype,
puff.

prompt verb **1** *curiosity prompted him to
look:* induce, make, move, motivate, lead,
dispose, persuade, incline, encourage,
stimulate, prod, impel, spur on, inspire.
2 *the statement prompted a hostile reaction:*
give rise to, bring about, cause, occasion,
result in, lead to, elicit, produce,
precipitate, trigger, spark off, provoke.
3 *the actors needed prompting:* remind,
cue, feed, help out, jog someone's memory.
OPPOSITES deter, avoid.
• adjective *a prompt reply:* quick, swift,
rapid, speedy, fast, direct, immediate,
instant, early, punctual, in good time, on
time.
OPPOSITES slow, late.
• adverb *at 3.30 prompt:* exactly, precisely,
sharp, on the dot, dead, punctually; informal
bang on; N. Amer. informal on the button, on
the nose.

promptly adverb **1** *William arrived
promptly at 7.30:* punctually, on time;
informal on the dot, bang on; Brit. informal spot
on; N. Amer. informal on the button, on the
nose. **2** *I expect the matter to be dealt with
promptly:* without delay, straight/right
away, at once, immediately, now, as soon as
possible, quickly, swiftly, rapidly, speedily,

p

promulgate verb (**promulgates, promulgating, promulgated**) **1** make an idea widely known. **2** announce the official beginning of a new law.
■ **promulgation** noun.

prone adjective **1** (**prone to** or **to do**) likely to suffer from, do, or experience something unfortunate. **2** lying flat, especially face downwards.

prong noun **1** each of two or more long pointed parts on a fork. **2** each of the separate parts of an attack.
■ **pronged** adjective.

pronoun noun a word used instead of a noun to indicate someone or something already mentioned or known, e.g. *I, this*.

pronounce verb (**pronounces, pronouncing, pronounced**) **1** make the sound of a word or part of a word. **2** declare or announce. **3** (**pronounce on**) pass judgement or make a decision on.
■ **pronouncement** noun.

pronounced adjective very noticeable.

pronto adverb informal promptly.

pronunciation noun the way in which a word is pronounced.

☑ **pronunciation** has no o in the middle.

proof noun **1** evidence that shows that something is true. **2** the process of finding out whether something is true. **3** a series of stages in the solving of a mathematical problem. **4** a copy of printed material used for making corrections before final printing. **5** a standard used to measure the strength of alcohol. •**adjective** resistant to: *damp-proof.*

proofread verb read written or printed material and mark any mistakes.
■ **proofreader** noun.

prop[1] noun **1** a pole or beam used as a temporary support. **2** a source of support or assistance. **3** (also **prop forward**) Rugby a forward at either end of the front row of a scrum. •verb (**props, propping, propped**) **1** support with a prop. **2** lean something against something else. **3** (**prop something up**) help something that is in difficulty.

prop[2] noun a portable object used by actors during a play or film.

propaganda noun false or exaggerated information, used to win support for a political cause or point of view.
■ **propagandist** noun.

☑ *propa-*, not *propo-*: *propa*ganda.

propagate verb (**propagates, propagating, propagated**) **1** grow a new plant from a parent plant. **2** spread an idea or information widely.
■ **propagation** noun.

propane noun a flammable gas present in natural gas and used as fuel.

propel verb (**propels, propelling, propelled**) drive or push forwards.

propellant noun a gas which forces out the contents of an aerosol.

propeller or **propellor** noun a device which uses two or more angled blades to propel a ship or aircraft.

propensity noun (plural **propensities**) a tendency to behave in a particular way.

proper adjective **1** truly what it is said to be;

p

THESAURUS

fast; informal pronto, asap.
OPPOSITES late, slowly.

prone adjective **1** *softwood is prone to rotting:* susceptible, vulnerable, subject, open, liable, given, predisposed, likely, disposed, inclined, apt. **2** *his prone body:* lying face down, on your stomach/front, lying flat, lying down, horizontal, prostrate.
OPPOSITES resistant, immune, upright.

pronounce verb **1** *his name is difficult to pronounce:* say, enunciate, utter, voice, sound, vocalize, get your tongue round. **2** *the doctor pronounced her fit for work:* declare, proclaim, judge, rule, decree.

pronounced adjective noticeable, marked, strong, conspicuous, striking, distinct, prominent, unmistakable, obvious.
OPPOSITES slight.

proof noun evidence, verification, corroboration, demonstration, authentication, confirmation, certification, documentation.
•adjective resistant, immune, unaffected,

impervious.

prop noun **1** *the roof is held up by props:* pole, post, support, upright, brace, buttress, stay, strut. **2** *a prop for the economy:* mainstay, pillar, anchor, support, cornerstone.
•verb *he propped his bike against the wall:* lean, rest, stand, balance.
□ prop something up **1** *this post is propping the wall up:* hold up, shore up, buttress, support, brace, underpin. **2** *they prop up loss-making industries:* subsidize, underwrite, fund, finance.

propaganda noun information, promotion, advertising, publicity, disinformation; informal hype.

propel verb **1** *a boat propelled by oars:* move, power, push, drive. **2** *the impact propelled him into the street:* throw, thrust, toss, fling, hurl, pitch, send, shoot.

proper adjective **1** *he's not a proper scientist:* real, genuine, actual, true, bona fide; informal kosher. **2** *the proper channels:* right, correct, accepted, conventional,

real. **2** in its true form: *the World Cup proper.* **3** appropriate or correct. **4** (**proper to**) belonging exclusively to.
□ **proper fraction** a fraction that is less than one. **proper noun** (or **proper name**) a name of a person, place, or organization, written with a capital letter.
■ **properly** adverb.

property noun (plural **properties**) **1** a thing or things belonging to someone. **2** a building and the land belonging to it. **3** a characteristic or quality.

prophecy /prof-i-si/ noun (plural **prophecies**) **1** a prediction about what will happen in the future. **2** the ability to predict the future.

prophesy /prof-i-sy/ verb (**prophesies**, **prophesying**, **prophesied**) predict that a particular thing will happen in the future.

prophet noun **1** a person regarded as being sent by God to teach people. **2** a person who predicts the future.

prophetic adjective **1** accurately predicting the future. **2** having to do with a prophet or prophecy.

prophylactic /prof-i-**lak**-tik/ adjective intended to prevent disease. •noun a medicine intended to prevent disease.

propinquity /pruh-**ping**-kwi-ti/ noun nearness in time or space.

propitiate verb (**propitiates**, **propitiating**, **propitiated**) win or regain the favour of.
■ **propitiation** noun **propitiatory** adjective.

propitious adjective indicating a good

chance of success; favourable.

proponent noun a person who proposes a theory or plan.

proportion noun **1** a part or share of a whole. **2** the relationship of one thing to another in terms of quantity or size. **3** the correct relationship between one thing and another. **4** (**proportions**) the size and shape of something.

proportional or **proportionate** adjective corresponding in size or amount to something else.
□ **proportional representation** an electoral system in which parties gain seats in proportion to the number of votes cast for them.
■ **proportionally** adverb.

proposal noun **1** a plan or suggestion. **2** the action of proposing something. **3** an offer of marriage.

propose verb (**proposes, proposing, proposed**) **1** put forward an idea or plan for consideration by other people. **2** nominate someone for an official position. **3** plan or intend to do something. **4** make an offer of marriage to someone.

proposition noun **1** a statement that expresses an opinion. **2** a plan of action. **3** a problem to be dealt with. •verb informal offer to have sex with someone.

propound verb put forward an idea or theory for consideration.

p

established, official, regular, acceptable, appropriate. **3** *they were terribly proper:* formal, conventional, correct, orthodox, polite, punctilious, respectable.
OPPOSITES fake, inappropriate, wrong, unconventional.

property noun **1** *lost property:* possessions, belongings, things, effects, stuff, goods; informal gear. **2** *private property:* building(s), premises, house(s), land; N. Amer. real estate. **3** *healing properties:* quality, attribute, characteristic, feature, power, trait, hallmark.

prophecy noun prediction, forecast, prognostication, prognosis, divination.

prophesy verb predict, foretell, forecast, foresee, prognosticate.

prophet, prophetess noun forecaster, seer, soothsayer, fortune teller, clairvoyant, oracle.

proportion noun **1** *a proportion of the land:* part, portion, amount, quantity, bit, piece, percentage, fraction, section, segment, share. **2** *the proportion of water to alcohol:* ratio, distribution, relative amount/ number, relationship. **3** *a sense of proportion:* balance, symmetry, harmony,

correspondence, correlation, agreement. **4** *men of huge proportions:* size, dimensions, magnitude, measurements, mass, volume, bulk, expanse, extent.

proportional, proportionate adjective corresponding, comparable, in proportion, pro rata, commensurate, equivalent, consistent.
OPPOSITES disproportionate.

proposal noun scheme, plan, idea, project, programme, motion, proposition, suggestion, submission.

propose verb **1** *he proposed a solution:* put forward, suggest, submit, advance, offer, present, move, come up with. **2** *do you propose to go?* intend, mean, plan, have in mind, aim. **3** *he proposed to her!* ask someone to marry you, ask for someone's hand in marriage; informal pop the question.
OPPOSITES withdraw.

proposition noun **1** *a business proposition:* proposal, scheme, plan, project, idea, programme. **2** *doing it for real is a very different proposition:* task, job, undertaking, venture, activity, affair.

proprietary adjective **1** having to do with an owner or ownership. **2** (of a product) marketed under a registered trademark. □ **proprietary name** a name of a product or service registered as a trademark.

proprietor noun the owner of a business.

proprietorial adjective behaving as if you owned something; possessive.

propriety noun (plural **proprieties**) **1** correctness of behaviour or morals. **2** the condition of being right or appropriate.

propulsion noun the action of propelling or driving something forward.
▪ **propulsive** adjective.

pro rata /proh **rah**-tuh/ adjective proportional. • adverb proportionally.

prosaic /proh-**zay**-ik/ adjective ordinary or unimaginative; dull.
▪ **prosaically** adverb.

proscenium /pruh-**see**-ni-uhm/ noun (plural **prosceniums** or **proscenia** /pruh-**see**-ni-uh/) **1** the part of a stage in front of the curtain. **2** (also **proscenium arch**) an arch framing the opening between the stage and the part of the theatre in which the audience sits.

proscribe verb (**proscribes**, **proscribing**, **proscribed**) **1** forbid. **2** criticize or condemn.

prose noun ordinary written or spoken language.

prosecute verb (**prosecutes**, **prosecuting**, **prosecuted**) **1** take legal proceedings against someone. **2** continue doing or taking part in something.
▪ **prosecutor** noun.

prosecution noun **1** the action of prosecuting. **2** (**the prosecution**) the party prosecuting someone in a lawsuit.

proselyte /**pross**-i-lyt/ noun a person who has converted from one religion or belief to another.

proselytize or **proselytise** /**pross**-i-li-tyz/ verb (**proselytizes**, **proselytizing**, **proselytized**) convert someone from one religion or belief to another.

prosody /**pross**-uh-di/ noun **1** the patterns of rhythm and sound used in poetry. **2** the study of these patterns.

prospect noun **1** a possibility of something happening. **2** an idea about what will happen in the future. **3** (**prospects**) chances of being successful. **4** a person who is likely to be successful. • verb search for mineral deposits.
▪ **prospector** noun.

prospective adjective expected or likely to happen or be something in the future.
▪ **prospectively** adverb.

prospectus noun (plural **prospectuses**) a printed booklet advertising a school, university, or business.

prosper verb (**prospers**, **prospering**, **prospered**) be successful, especially in making money.

prosperous adjective rich and successful.
▪ **prosperity** noun.

prostate noun a gland in men and male mammals that produces the fluid part of semen.

prostitute noun a person who has sex for

p

THESAURUS

proprietor, proprietress noun owner, possessor, holder, householder, master, mistress, landowner, landlord, landlady, shopkeeper.

prosecute verb charge, take to court, take legal action against, sue, try, bring to trial, put on trial, put in the dock, indict; N. Amer. impeach.
OPPOSITES defend, let off.

prospect noun **1** *there is little prospect of success:* likelihood, hope, expectation, chance, odds, probability, possibility, promise, lookout, fear, danger. **2** *her job prospects:* possibilities, potential, expectations, outlook. **3** *a daunting prospect:* vision, thought, idea, task, undertaking.
• verb *prospecting for oil:* search, look, explore, survey, scout, hunt, dowse.

prospective adjective potential, possible, probable, likely, future, eventual, -to-be, soon-to-be, in the making, intending, aspiring, would-be.

prospectus noun brochure, syllabus,

curriculum, catalogue, programme, list, schedule.

prosper verb flourish, thrive, do well, bloom, blossom, burgeon, progress, do all right for yourself, get ahead, get on (in the world), be successful; informal go places.
OPPOSITES fail, flounder.

prosperity noun success, affluence, wealth, ease, plenty.
OPPOSITES hardship, failure.

prosperous adjective thriving, flourishing, successful, strong, vigorous, profitable, lucrative, expanding, booming, burgeoning, affluent, wealthy, rich, moneyed, well off, well-to-do; informal in the money.
OPPOSITES ailing, poor.

prostitute noun whore, sex worker, call girl, courtesan; informal working girl; N. Amer. informal hooker, hustler.
• verb *they prostituted their art:* betray, sacrifice, sell, sell out, debase, degrade, demean, devalue, cheapen, lower, shame, misuse.

money. •verb (**prostitutes, prostituting, prostituted**) (**prostitute yourself**) **1** work as a prostitute. **2** put your talents to an unworthy use in order to earn money.
■ **prostitution** noun.

prostrate adjective /**pross**-trayt/ **1** lying stretched out on the ground with the face downwards. **2** completely overcome or helpless. •verb /pross-**trayt**/ (**prostrates, prostrating, prostrated**) **1** (**prostrate yourself**) throw yourself flat on the ground. **2** (**be prostrated**) be completely overcome with stress or exhaustion.
■ **prostration** noun.

protactinium noun a rare radioactive metallic element.

protagonist noun **1** the leading character in a drama, film, or novel. **2** an important person in a real event.

protean /proh-**tee**-uhn/ adjective tending or able to change or adapt.

protect verb keep someone or something safe from harm or injury.
■ **protector** noun.

protection noun **1** the action of protecting. **2** a person or thing that protects. **3** the payment of money to criminals so that they will not attack your property.

protectionism noun the practice of protecting a country's industries from foreign competition by taxing imported goods.
■ **protectionist** noun & adjective.

protective adjective **1** protecting someone or something. **2** having a strong wish to protect someone.
■ **protectively** adverb.

protectorate noun a state that is controlled and protected by another.

protégé /**prot**-i-zhay/ noun (feminine **protégée**) a person who is guided and supported by an older and more experienced person.

protein noun a substance which forms part of body tissues and is an important part of the human diet.

> ☑ **protein** is an exception to the usual rule of *i* before *e* except after *c*.

protest noun /**proh**-test/ a statement or action expressing disapproval or objection to something. •verb /pruh-**test**/ **1** express an objection to what someone has said or done. **2** take part in a public protest. **3** state something strongly in response to an accusation: *she protested her innocence.*
■ **protester** (or **protestor**) noun.

Protestant /pro-**tiss**-tuhnt/ noun a member or follower of any of the Western Christian Churches that are separate from the Roman Catholic Church. •adjective relating to or belonging to any of the Protestant Churches.
■ **Protestantism** noun.

protestation noun **1** a firm declaration that something is or is not the case. **2** an objection or protest.

proto- combining form original, primitive, or first: *prototype* | *protozoan.*

protocol noun **1** the system of rules governing formal occasions. **2** the accepted way to behave in a particular situation.

proton noun a subatomic particle with a positive electric charge.

p

THESAURUS

protect verb keep safe, keep from harm, guard, defend, shield, save, safeguard, preserve, cushion, insulate, shelter, screen, keep, look after.
OPPOSITES expose, neglect, attack, harm.

protection noun **1** *protection against frost:* defence, security, safeguard, safety, sanctuary, shelter, refuge, immunity, indemnity. **2** *the protection of the Church:* safe keeping, care, charge, umbrella, guardianship, support, aegis, patronage. **3** *a good protection against noise:* barrier, buffer, shield, screen, cushion, bulwark, armour, insulation.

protective adjective **1** *protective clothing:* special, safety, thick, heavy, insulated, ...-proof, ...-resistant. **2** *he felt protective towards her:* solicitous, caring, defensive, paternal, maternal, overprotective, possessive, jealous.

protector noun **1** *a protector of the environment:* defender, preserver, guardian, champion, patron, custodian.

2 *ear protectors:* guard, shield, buffer, cushion, pad, screen.

protest noun **1** *a storm of protest:* objection, complaint, challenge, dissent, demurral, remonstration, fuss, outcry. **2** *the women staged a protest:* demonstration, rally, vigil, sit-in, occupation, work-to-rule, stoppage, strike, walkout, mutiny, picket, boycott; informal demo.
OPPOSITES support, approval.
•verb **1** *residents protested at the plans:* object, express opposition, dissent, take issue, take a stand, put up a fight, take exception, complain, express disapproval, disagree, make a fuss, speak out; informal kick up a fuss. **2** *he protested his innocence:* insist on, maintain, assert, affirm, announce, proclaim, declare, profess.
OPPOSITES acquiesce, support, deny.

protocol noun etiquette, convention, formalities, custom, the rules, procedure, ritual, decorum, the done thing.

prototype noun a first form of something from which other forms are copied or developed.

protozoan /proh-tuh-zoh-uhn/ noun a microscopic animal that is made up of a single cell.

protracted adjective lasting for a long time.

protractor noun an instrument for measuring angles, in the form of a flat semicircle marked with degrees.

protrude verb (protrudes, protruding, protruded) stick out from a surface.
■ protrusion noun.

protuberance noun a thing that sticks out from a surface.
■ protuberant adjective.

☑ there is no *r* immediately after the *t*: pro*tuberance*.

proud adjective 1 feeling pleased or satisfied by your own or another's achievements. 2 having too high an opinion of yourself. 3 having respect for yourself. 4 slightly sticking out from a surface.
■ proudly adverb.

prove verb (proves, proving, proved; past participle **proved** or **proven** /proo-v'n or proh-v'n/) 1 use evidence to show that something is true or exists. 2 be found to be. 3 (**prove yourself**) show your abilities or courage. 4 (**proven**) found through experience to be effective or true.
■ provable adjective.

provenance noun the place where something originally comes from.

provender noun old use food or animal fodder.

proverb noun a short saying that gives advice or states something that is generally true.

proverbial adjective 1 referred to in a proverb. 2 well known.
■ proverbially adverb.

provide verb (provides, providing, provided) 1 make something available for someone to use. 2 (**provide for**) make enough preparation for a possible event.

provided or **providing** conjunction on the condition that.

providence noun 1 the protective care of God or of nature. 2 careful preparation for the future.

provident adjective careful in preparing for the future.

providential adjective happening at a favourable time.

province noun 1 a main administrative division of a country or empire. 2 (**the provinces**) the whole of a country outside the capital city.

THESAURUS

prototype noun original, master, template, pattern, sample.

protracted adjective prolonged, extended, long-drawn-out, lengthy, long.
OPPOSITES short.

proud adjective 1 *the proud parents:* pleased, glad, happy, delighted, thrilled, satisfied, gratified. 2 *a proud day:* pleasing, gratifying, satisfying, cheering, heart-warming, happy, glorious. 3 *he is too proud to admit to being in the wrong:* arrogant, conceited, vain, self-important, full of yourself, overbearing, bumptious, presumptuous, overweening, haughty, high and mighty; informal big-headed, too big for your boots, stuck-up.
OPPOSITES ashamed, shameful, humble, modest.

prove verb 1 *that proves I'm right:* show (to be true), demonstrate (the truth of), provide proof, substantiate, verify, validate, authenticate. 2 *the rumour proved to be correct:* turn out, be found.
OPPOSITES disprove.

proverb noun saying, adage, saw, maxim, axiom, motto, aphorism, epigram.

provide verb 1 *we will provide funds:* supply, give, furnish, come up with, dispense, produce, yield, deliver, donate, contribute; informal fork out, lay out. 2 *he was provided with tools:* equip, furnish, issue, supply, fit out, rig out, kit out, arm, provision; informal fix up. 3 *the test may provide the answer:* offer, present, afford, give, add, bring, yield, impart, reveal.
OPPOSITES refuse, withhold, deprive, neglect.
□ provide for feed, nurture, nourish, support, maintain, keep, sustain.

provided, providing conjunction if, on condition that, provided that, presuming (that), assuming (that), as long as, with/on the understanding that.

provider noun supplier, donor, giver, contributor, source.

province noun 1 *a province of the Roman Empire:* territory, region, state, department, canton, area, district, sector, zone, division. 2 (**the provinces**) the regions, the rest of the country, rural areas/districts, the countryside; informal the sticks, the middle of nowhere; N. Amer. informal the boondocks. 3 *that's outside my province, I'm afraid:* domain, area, department, responsibility, sphere, world, realm, field, discipline, territory; informal bailiwick.

provincial adjective **1** relating to a province or the provinces. **2** unsophisticated or narrow-minded. •noun a person who lives in a province.
■ **provincialism** noun.

provision noun **1** the action of providing. **2** something supplied or provided. **3** (**provision for** or **against**) arrangements for possible future events or needs. **4** (**provisions**) supplies of food, drink, or equipment. **5** a condition or requirement in a legal document. •verb supply with provisions.

provisional adjective arranged for the present time only, possibly to be changed later.
■ **provisionally** adverb.

proviso /pruh-vy-zoh/ noun (plural **provisos**) a condition attached to an agreement.

provocation noun action or speech that makes someone angry or causes a strong reaction.

provocative adjective **1** intended to make someone annoyed or angry. **2** intended to make someone sexually interested.
■ **provocatively** adverb.

provoke verb (provokes, provoking, provoked) **1** cause a strong reaction. **2** deliberately make someone feel angry. **3** stir someone up to do something.

provost noun **1** Brit. the head of certain university colleges and public schools. **2** N. Amer. a senior administrative officer in certain universities. **3** Scottish a mayor.

prow noun the pointed front part of a ship.

prowess noun skill or expertise.

prowl verb move about stealthily or restlessly.
□ **on the prowl** moving about in a stealthy way.
■ **prowler** noun.

proximity noun nearness or closeness.
■ **proximate** adjective.

proxy noun (plural **proxies**) **1** the authority to represent someone else. **2** a person authorized to act on behalf of another.

prude noun a person who is easily shocked by matters relating to sex.
■ **prudish** adjective.

prudent adjective acting in a cautious and sensible way.
■ **prudence** noun **prudently** adverb.

prudential adjective prudent.

prune[1] noun a dried plum.

THESAURUS

provincial adjective **1** *the provincial government:* **regional**, state, territorial, district, local, county. **2** *provincial areas:* **rural**, country, rustic, small-town, outlying, backwoods, backwater; informal one-horse. **3** *they're so dull and provincial:* **unsophisticated**, narrow-minded, parochial, small-town, suburban, insular, inward-looking; N. Amer. informal corn-fed.
OPPOSITES national, metropolitan, cosmopolitan, sophisticated, broad-minded.

provision noun **1** *the provision of weapons to guerrillas:* **supply**, giving, donation, equipping, furnishing, distribution. **2** *limited provision for young children:* **facilities**, services, amenities, resource(s), arrangements, means, funds, assistance. **3** (**provisions**) *provisions for the trip:* **supplies**, food and drink, stores, groceries, foodstuff(s), rations. **4** *the provisions of the Act:* **term**, requirement, specification, stipulation.

provisional adjective **interim**, temporary, transitional, changeover, stopgap, short-term, fill-in, acting, working.
OPPOSITES permanent, definite.

provocation noun **goading**, prodding, incitement, pressure, harassment, teasing, taunting, torment; informal hassle, aggravation.

provocative adjective **annoying**, irritating, maddening, galling, insulting, offensive, inflammatory, incendiary, like a red rag to a bull; informal aggravating.

provoke verb **1** *the plan has provoked outrage:* **arouse**, produce, evoke, cause, give rise to, excite, spark off, touch off, kindle, generate, engender, instigate, result in, lead to, bring on, precipitate, prompt, trigger. **2** *he was provoked into replying:* **goad**, spur, prick, sting, prod, incite, rouse, stimulate. **3** *he's dangerous if provoked:* **annoy**, anger, enrage, irritate, madden, nettle; Brit. rub up the wrong way; informal aggravate, rile, needle, get/put someone's back up; Brit. informal wind up.
OPPOSITES allay, deter, pacify, appease.

prowess noun **skill**, expertise, mastery, ability, capability, capacity, talent, aptitude, dexterity, proficiency, finesse; informal know-how.
OPPOSITES inability, ineptitude.

prowl verb **steal**, slink, skulk, sneak, stalk, creep; informal snoop.

proxy noun **deputy**, representative, substitute, delegate, agent, surrogate, stand-in, go-between.

prudent adjective **1** *it is prudent to obtain consent:* **wise**, sensible, politic, judicious, shrewd, advisable. **2** *a prudent approach to borrowing:* **cautious**, careful, provident, far-sighted, judicious, shrewd, circumspect, thrifty, economical.
OPPOSITES unwise, reckless, extravagant.

prune verb **1** *I pruned the roses:* **cut back**, trim, clip, shear, shorten, thin, shape. **2** *staff numbers have been pruned:* **reduce**,

p

prune² verb (**prunes, pruning, pruned**) **1** trim a tree or bush by cutting away dead or overgrown branches. **2** remove unwanted parts from. • noun an instance of pruning.

prurient adjective having too much interest in sexual matters.
■ **prurience** noun.

pry¹ verb (**pries, prying, pried**) ask someone unwelcome questions about their private life.

pry² = PRISE.

PS abbreviation postscript.

psalm /sahm/ noun a song or poem that praises God.

psalter /sawl-ter/ noun a copy of the Book of Psalms in the Bible.

pseudo adjective informal not genuine; false.

pseudonym noun a false name, especially one used by an author.

PSHE abbreviation personal, social, and health education (as a school subject).

psoriasis /suh-ry-uh-siss/ noun a condition in which patches of skin become red and itchy.

psych /syk/ verb **1** (**psych yourself up**) informal prepare yourself mentally for a difficult task. **2** (**psych someone out**) intimidate an opponent by appearing very confident or aggressive.

psyche /sy-ki/ noun the human soul, mind, or spirit.

psychedelia /sy-kuh-dee-li-uh/ noun music or art based on the experiences produced by taking psychedelic drugs.

psychedelic /sy-kuh-del-ik/ adjective **1** (of drugs) producing hallucinations. **2** having a strong, vivid colour or a swirling abstract pattern.

psychiatry noun the branch of medicine concerned with mental illness.
■ **psychiatric** adjective **psychiatrist** noun.

psychic adjective **1** relating to or possessing abilities that cannot be explained by science, e.g. telepathy or clairvoyance. **2** relating to the mind. • noun a person considered or claiming to have psychic

powers.
■ **psychically** adverb.

psycho noun (plural **psychos**) informal a psychopath.

psychoanalyse (US spelling **psychoanalyze**) verb (**psychoanalyses, psychoanalysing, psychoanalysed**) treat someone using psychoanalysis.

psychoanalysis noun a method of treating mental disorders by investigating the unconscious elements of the mind.
■ **psychoanalyst** noun **psychoanalytic** adjective.

psychological adjective **1** having to do with the mind. **2** relating to psychology.
■ **psychologically** adverb.

psychology noun **1** the scientific study of the human mind. **2** the way in which someone thinks or behaves.
■ **psychologist** noun.

psychopath noun a person suffering from a serious mental illness which makes them behave violently.
■ **psychopathic** adjective.

psychosis /sy-koh-siss/ noun (plural **psychoses** /sy-koh-seez/) a serious mental illness in which a person loses contact with external reality.

psychosomatic adjective (of a physical illness) caused or made worse by a mental factor such as stress.

psychotherapy noun the treatment of mental disorders by psychological rather than medical means.
■ **psychotherapist** noun.

psychotic /sy-kot-ik/ adjective relating to or suffering from a psychosis.

PT abbreviation physical training.

Pt abbreviation **1** Part. **2** (**pt**) pint. **3** (in scoring) point.

PTA abbreviation parent–teacher association.

ptarmigan /tar-mi-guhn/ noun a grouse with grey and black feathers which change to white in winter.

Pte abbreviation Private (in the army).

pterodactyl /te-ruh-dak-til/ noun a fossil

p

THESAURUS

cut (back/down), pare (down), slim down, trim, downsize, axe, shrink; informal slash.
OPPOSITES increase.

psychiatrist noun psychotherapist, psychoanalyst, analyst; informal shrink.

psychic adjective **1** *psychic powers:* **supernatural,** paranormal, other-worldly, metaphysical, extrasensory, magic(al), mystic(al), occult. **2** *I'm not psychic:* **clairvoyant,** telepathic.
OPPOSITES normal.
• noun *she is a psychic:* **clairvoyant,** fortune teller, medium, spiritualist, telepath, mind-

reader.

psychological adjective **1** *his psychological state:* **mental,** emotional, inner, cognitive. **2** *her pain was psychological:* **(all) in the mind,** psychosomatic, emotional, subjective, subconscious, unconscious.
OPPOSITES physical.

psychology noun *the psychology of the road user:* **mind,** mindset, thought processes, way of thinking, mentality, psyche, attitude(s), make-up, character, temperament; informal what makes someone tick.

flying reptile with a long, slender head and neck.

PTO abbreviation please turn over.

pub noun Brit. a building in which beer and other drinks are served.

puberty noun the period during which adolescents reach sexual maturity.

pubes /pyoo-beez/ noun the lower front part of the abdomen.

pubescence noun the time when puberty begins.

■ **pubescent** adjective & noun.

pubic adjective relating to the pubes or pubis.

pubis /pyoo-biss/ noun (plural **pubes** /pyoo-beez/) either of a pair of bones forming the two sides of the pelvis.

public adjective **1** having to do with the people as a whole. **2** involved in the affairs of the community: *a public figure.* **3** intended to be seen or heard by people in general. **4** provided by the government rather than an independent company. •noun **1** (**the public**) ordinary people in general. **2** a group of people with a particular interest: *the reading public.* □ **in public** when other people are present. **public address system** a system of microphones and loudspeakers used to amplify speech or music. **public company** (or **public limited company**) a company whose shares are traded freely on a stock exchange. **public house** a pub. **public relations** the business of creating a good public image for an organization or famous person. **public school** (in the UK) a private

fee-paying secondary school. **public sector** the part of an economy that is controlled by the state. **public transport** buses, trains, and other forms of transport that are available to the public and run on fixed routes.

■ **publicly** adverb.

publican noun Brit. a person who owns or manages a pub.

publication noun **1** the action of publishing something. **2** a book or journal that is published.

publicist noun a person responsible for publicizing a product or celebrity.

publicity noun **1** attention given to someone or something by television, newspapers, etc. **2** information used for advertising or promoting a product, person, event, etc.

publicize or **publicise** verb (**publicizes, publicizing, publicized**) **1** make something widely known. **2** give out information about a product, person, event, etc. in order to advertise or promote them.

publish verb **1** produce a book, newspaper, etc., for public sale. **2** print something in a book or newspaper.

■ **publisher** noun.

puce /pyooss/ noun a dark red or purple-brown colour.

puck noun a black disc made of hard rubber, used in ice hockey.

pucker verb (**puckers, puckering, puckered**) tightly gather into wrinkles or small folds. •noun a wrinkle or small fold.

pudding noun chiefly Brit. **1** a cooked sweet

THESAURUS p

pub noun (Brit.) **bar**, inn, tavern, hostelry; Brit. public house; Austral./NZ hotel; informal watering hole; Brit. informal local, boozer; N. Amer. historical saloon.

public adjective **1** *public affairs:* **state**, national, government, constitutional, civic, civil, official, social, municipal, community, nationalized. **2** *by public demand:* **popular**, general, common, communal, collective, shared, joint, universal, widespread. **3** *a public figure:* **prominent**, well known, important, leading, eminent, distinguished, celebrated, household, famous; N. Amer. major-league. **4** *public places:* **open (to the public)**, communal, available, free, unrestricted, community. **5** *the news became public:* **known**, published, publicized, open, obvious.
OPPOSITES private, obscure, unknown, restricted, secret.
•noun **1** *the British public:* **people**, citizens, subjects, electors, electorate, voters, taxpayers, residents, inhabitants, citizenry, population, populace, community, society, country, nation, everyone. **2** *his adoring*

public: **audience**, spectators, followers, following, fans, devotees, admirers.

publication noun **1** *the author of this publication:* **book**, volume, title, opus, tome, newspaper, paper, magazine, periodical, newsletter, bulletin, journal, report. **2** *the publication of her new book:* **issuing**, publishing, printing, distribution, spreading, appearance.

publicity noun **1** *the blaze of publicity:* **public attention/interest**, media attention/interest, exposure, glare, limelight. **2** *publicity should boost sales:* **promotion**, advertising, propaganda, boost, push; informal hype, ballyhoo, puff, build-up, plug.

publish verb **1** *we publish novels:* **issue**, bring out, produce, print. **2** *he ought to publish his views:* **make known**, make public, publicize, announce, broadcast, issue, put out, distribute, spread, promulgate, disseminate, circulate, air.

pudding noun **dessert**, sweet, last course; Brit. informal afters, pud.

dish eaten at the end of a meal. **2** the dessert course of a meal. **3** a savoury dish made with suet and flour.

puddle noun a small pool of liquid, especially of rain on the ground.

pudgy adjective (**pudgier, pudgiest**) informal rather fat.

puerile /**pyoor**-yl/ adjective childishly silly.

Puerto Rican /pwair-toh **ree**-kuhn/ noun a person from Puerto Rico. • adjective relating to Puerto Rico.

puff noun **1** a small amount of air or smoke that is blown out from somewhere. **2** an act of breathing in smoke from a pipe, cigarette, or cigar. **3** a hollow piece of light pastry that is filled with cream or jam. **4** informal breath: *out of puff.* • verb **1** breathe in repeated short gasps. **2** move with short, noisy puffs of air or steam. **3** smoke a pipe, cigarette, or cigar. **4** (**be puffed** or **puffed out**) informal be out of breath. **5** (**puff out** or **up**) swell.
□ **puff pastry** light flaky pastry.

puffball noun a fungus with a round head that bursts to release its seeds.

puffin noun a seabird with a large brightly coloured triangular bill.

puffy adjective (**puffier, puffiest**) **1** (of a part of the body) swollen and soft. **2** softly rounded: *puffy clouds.*

pug noun a very small breed of dog with a broad flat nose and a wrinkled face.

pugilist /**pyoo**-ji-list/ noun chiefly humorous a boxer.
■ **pugilistic** adjective.

pugnacious adjective eager or quick to argue or fight.
■ **pugnaciously** adverb **pugnacity** noun.

puke informal verb (**pukes, puking, puked**) vomit. • noun vomit.

pukka informal adjective **1** genuine. **2** socially acceptable. **3** excellent.

pulchritude /**pul**-kri-tyood/ noun literary beauty.

pull verb **1** apply force to something so as to move it towards yourself. **2** remove from a place by pulling. **3** move steadily: *the bus pulled away.* **4** strain a muscle. **5** attract someone as a customer. **6** Brit. informal attract a potential sexual partner. **7** informal bring out a weapon for use. • noun **1** an act of pulling. **2** a force, influence, or attraction. **3** a deep drink of something or a deep breath of smoke from a cigarette, pipe, etc.
□ **pull back** retreat. **pull someone's leg** deceive someone for a joke. **pull something off** informal succeed in doing something difficult. **pull out** withdraw. **pull strings** use your influence to gain an advantage. **pull yourself together** regain your self-control. **pull your weight** do your fair share of work.

pullet noun a young hen.

pulley noun (plural **pulleys**) a wheel around which a rope or chain passes, used to raise heavy objects.

pullover noun a knitted garment for the upper body.

pulmonary /**pul**-muh-nuh-ri/ adjective relating to the lungs.

pulp noun **1** a soft, wet mass of crushed material. **2** the soft fleshy part of a fruit. • verb crush into a pulp. • adjective (of writing) popular and badly written: *pulp fiction.*
■ **pulpy** adjective.

pulpit noun a raised platform in a church from which the preacher gives a sermon.

pulsar noun a star that gives off regular rapid pulses of radio waves.

pulsate verb (**pulsates, pulsating, pulsated**) **1** expand and contract with strong regular movements. **2** produce a regular throbbing sensation or sound.
■ **pulsation** noun.

THESAURUS

puff noun **1** *a puff of wind:* gust, blast, flurry, rush, draught, waft, breeze, breath. **2** *he took a puff at his cigar:* pull; informal drag, toke.
• verb **1** *he walked fast, puffing a little:* breathe heavily, pant, blow, gasp. **2** *she puffed at her cigarette:* smoke, draw on, drag on, suck at/on, inhale; informal toke on.

pull verb **1** *he pulled the box towards him:* tug, haul, drag, draw, tow, heave, jerk, wrench; informal yank. **2** *she pulled a muscle:* strain, sprain, wrench, tear. **3** *race day pulled big crowds:* attract, draw, bring in, pull in, lure, seduce, entice, tempt.
OPPOSITES push, repel.
• noun **1** *give the chain a pull:* tug, jerk, heave; informal yank. **2** *she took a pull at her beer:* gulp, draught, drink, swallow,

mouthful, slug; informal swig. **3** *a pull on a cigarette:* puff; informal drag, toke. **4** *the pull of the theatre:* attraction, draw, lure, magnetism, fascination, appeal, allure.
□ **pull something off achieve**, fulfil, succeed in, accomplish, bring off, carry off, clinch, fix. **pull out withdraw**, resign, leave, retire, step down, bow out, back out, give up; informal quit. **pull through get better**, get well again, improve, recover, rally, come through, recuperate.

pulp noun **1** *he ground it into a pulp:* mush, mash, paste, purée, slop, slush, mulch. **2** *the sweet pulp on cocoa seeds:* flesh, marrow, meat.
• verb *pulp the gooseberries:* mash, purée, cream, crush, press, liquidize.

pulse[1] noun 1 the regular beat of the blood as it is pumped around the body. 2 a single vibration or short burst of sound, electric current, light, etc. 3 a regular musical rhythm. •verb (**pulses, pulsing, pulsed**) pulsate.

pulse[2] noun the edible seeds of various plants, such as lentils or beans.

pulverize or **pulverise** verb (**pulverizes, pulverizing, pulverized**) 1 crush into fine particles. 2 informal completely defeat.

puma noun a large American wild cat with a yellowish-brown or grey coat.

pumice /pum-iss/ noun a very light rock formed from lava.

pummel verb (**pummels, pummelling, pummelled**; US spelling **pummels, pummeling, pummeled**) hit repeatedly with the fists.

pump[1] noun a device used to move liquids and gases or to force air into inflatable objects. •verb 1 move with a pump, or with something that works like a pump. 2 fill something with liquid, gas, etc. 3 move something up and down energetically. 4 informal try to get information from someone.
□ **pump iron** informal exercise with weights.

pump[2] noun 1 chiefly N. English a plimsoll. 2 a light shoe for dancing.

pumpkin noun 1 a large round fruit with a thick orange skin and edible flesh. 2 Brit. = **SQUASH**[2].

pun noun a joke that uses a word or words with more than one meaning. •verb (**puns, punning, punned**) make a pun.

punch[1] verb 1 hit with the fist. 2 press a button or key on a machine. •noun 1 a blow with the fist. 2 informal the power to impress someone.
□ **punch-drunk** 1 dazed by a series of punches. 2 very confused or shocked.
punch-up informal a fight.

punch[2] noun a device for cutting holes in paper, metal, leather, etc. •verb pierce a hole in something.

punch[3] noun a drink made from wine or spirits mixed with water, fruit juices, and spices.

punchbag noun Brit. a heavy bag hung on a rope, used for punching as exercise or training.

punchline noun the final part of a joke that makes it funny.

punchy adjective (**punchier, punchiest**) effective; forceful.

punctilious adjective showing great attention to detail or correct behaviour.

punctual adjective happening or doing something at the agreed or proper time.
■ **punctuality** noun **punctually** adverb.

punctuate verb (**punctuates, punctuating, punctuated**) 1 interrupt something at intervals. 2 add punctuation marks to a piece of writing.

punctuation noun the marks, such as full stop, comma, and brackets, used in writing to separate sentences and make meaning clear.

puncture noun a small hole caused by a sharp object. •verb (**punctures, puncturing, punctured**) make a puncture in.

pundit noun a person who frequently gives opinions about a subject in public.

pungent adjective 1 having a sharply strong taste or smell. 2 (of remarks or humour) having a strong effect.
■ **pungency** noun.

p

pulse noun 1 *the pulse in her neck:* heartbeat, heart rate. 2 *the pulse of the engine:* rhythm, beat, tempo, pounding, throbbing, thudding, drumming. 3 *pulses of ultrasound:* burst, blast, surge.
•verb *music pulsed through the building:* throb, pulsate, vibrate, beat, pound, thud, thump, drum, reverberate, echo.

pump verb 1 *they pumped air down the tube:* force, drive, push, inject, suck, draw. 2 *she pumped up the tyre:* inflate, blow up, fill up, swell, enlarge, distend, expand, dilate, puff up. 3 *blood was pumping from his leg:* spurt, spout, squirt, jet, surge, spew, gush, stream, flow, pour, spill, well, cascade.

punch[1] verb *Jim punched him in the face:* hit, strike, thump, jab, smash; informal sock, slug, biff, bop; Brit. informal stick one on, slosh; N. Amer. informal boff, bust; Austral./NZ informal quilt.
•noun *a punch on the nose:* blow, hit, knock, thump, box, jab, clip; informal sock, slug, biff, bop; N. Amer. informal boff, bust.

punch[2] verb *he punched her ticket:* perforate, puncture, pierce, prick, hole, spike, skewer.

punctual adjective on time, prompt, on schedule, in (good) time; informal on the dot.
OPPOSITES late.

punctuate verb break up, interrupt, intersperse, pepper, sprinkle, scatter.

puncture noun 1 *the tyre developed a puncture:* hole, perforation, rupture, cut, gash, slit, leak. 2 *my car has a puncture:* flat tyre; informal flat.
•verb *he punctured the balloon:* prick, pierce, stab, rupture, perforate, cut, slit, deflate.

punish verb **1** make someone experience something unpleasant because they have done something criminal or wrong. **2** treat harshly or unfairly.
■ **punishable** adjective.

punishment noun **1** an unpleasant experience imposed on someone because they have done something criminal or wrong. **2** the action of punishing. **3** harsh or rough treatment.

punitive /pyoo-ni-tiv/ adjective intended as punishment.

Punjabi noun (plural **Punjabis**) **1** a person from Punjab, a region of NW India and Pakistan. **2** the language of Punjab.

punk noun **1** (also **punk rock**) a loud and aggressive form of rock music. **2** (also **punk rocker**) a person who likes or plays punk music. **3** N. Amer. informal a worthless person.

punnet noun Brit. a small container for fruit or vegetables.

punt[1] noun a long, narrow boat with a flat bottom, moved forward with a long pole. • verb travel in a punt.

punt[2] verb kick a ball after it has dropped from the hands and before it reaches the ground. • noun a kick of this kind.

punt[3] noun Brit. informal a bet.

punt[4] /puunt/ noun the former basic unit of money in the Republic of Ireland.

punter noun Brit. informal **1** a person who gambles. **2** a customer or client.

puny adjective (**punier**, **puniest**) **1** small and weak. **2** not very impressive.

pup noun **1** a young dog. **2** a young wolf, seal, rat, or other animal.

pupa /pyoo-puh/ noun (plural **pupae** /pyoo-pee/) an insect in the form between larva and adult.
■ **pupal** adjective.

pupate verb (**pupates**, **pupating**, **pupated**) become a pupa.

pupil[1] noun a person who is being taught.

pupil[2] noun the dark circular opening in the centre of the iris of the eye.

puppet noun **1** a model of a person or animal which can be moved either by strings or by a hand inside it. **2** a person under the control of someone else.
■ **puppeteer** noun **puppetry** noun.

puppy noun (plural **puppies**) a young dog. □ **puppy fat** fat on a child's body that disappears as they grow up. **puppy love** strong but short-lived love.

purblind adjective literary **1** partially sighted. **2** lacking awareness or understanding.

purchase verb (**purchases**, **purchasing**, **purchased**) buy. • noun **1** the action of buying. **2** a thing bought. **3** firm contact or grip.
■ **purchaser** noun.

purdah noun the practice in certain Muslim and Hindu societies of screening women from men or strangers.

pure adjective **1** not mixed with any other

THESAURUS

p

punish verb **1** *they punished their children:* discipline, penalize, correct, sentence, teach someone a lesson; informal come down on (like a ton of bricks), have someone's guts for garters; dated chastise. **2** *higher charges would punish the poor:* disadvantage, handicap, hurt, penalize.

punishing adjective arduous, demanding, taxing, strenuous, rigorous, stressful, trying, heavy, difficult, tough, exhausting, tiring, gruelling.
OPPOSITES easy.

punishment noun penalty, sanction, penance, discipline, forfeit, sentence.

punitive adjective penal, disciplinary, corrective, retributive, retaliatory.

puny adjective **1** *a puny boy:* small, weak, feeble, slight, undersized, stunted; informal weedy. **2** *their puny efforts:* pitiful, pitiable, miserable, sorry, meagre, paltry; informal pathetic, measly.
OPPOSITES sturdy, substantial.

pupil noun **1** *former pupils of the school:* student, scholar, schoolchild, schoolboy, schoolgirl. **2** *the guru's pupils:* disciple, follower, student, protégé, apprentice, trainee, novice.

puppet noun **1** *a show with puppets:* marionette, glove puppet, finger puppet. **2** *a puppet of the government:* pawn, tool, instrument, cat's paw, poodle, mouthpiece, stooge.

purchase verb *we purchased new software:* buy, acquire, obtain, pick up, procure, pay for, invest in; informal get hold of, score.
OPPOSITES sell.
• noun **1** *he's happy with his purchase:* acquisition, buy, investment, order, bargain, shopping, goods. **2** *he could get no purchase on the wall:* grip, grasp, hold, foothold, toehold, anchorage, support, traction, leverage.
OPPOSITES sale.

pure adjective **1** *pure gold:* unadulterated, undiluted, sterling, solid, 100%. **2** *the air is so pure:* clean, clear, fresh, sparkling, unpolluted, uncontaminated, untainted. **3** *pure in body and mind:* virtuous, moral, good, righteous, honourable, reputable, wholesome, clean, honest, upright, upstanding, exemplary, chaste, decent, worthy, noble; informal squeaky clean. **4** *three hours of pure magic:* sheer, utter,

substance or material: *pure wool*. **2** not containing any harmful or polluting substances. **3** innocent or morally good. **4** sheer; nothing but: *a shout of pure anger.* **5** theoretical rather than practical: *pure mathematics.* **6** (of a sound) perfectly in tune and with a clear tone.
■ **purely** adverb.

purée /pyoor-ay/ noun a mass of crushed fruit or vegetables. •verb (**purées, puréeing, puréed**) make a purée of.

purgative adjective having a strong laxative effect. •noun a laxative.

purgatory noun (plural **purgatories**) (in Roman Catholic belief) a place inhabited by the souls of sinners who are making up for their sins before going to heaven.
■ **purgatorial** adjective.

purge verb (**purges, purging, purged**) rid someone or something of undesirable or harmful people or things. •noun an act of purging.

purify verb (**purifies, purifying, purified**) make something pure.
■ **purification** noun.

☑ *i* not *e*: pur*i*fy.

purist noun a person who insists on following traditional rules, especially in language or style.
■ **purism** noun.

puritan noun **1** (**Puritan**) a member of a group of English Protestants in the 16th and 17th centuries who tried to simplify forms of worship. **2** a person with strong

moral beliefs who is critical of the behaviour of other people.
■ **puritanical** adjective.

purity noun the state of being pure.

purl adjective (of a knitting stitch) made by putting the needle through the front of the stitch from right to left. •verb knit with a purl stitch.

purlieus /per-lyooz/ plural noun literary the area around or near a place.

purloin verb formal steal.

purple adjective of a colour between red and blue. •noun a purple colour.
☐ **purple patch** informal a run of success or good luck. **purple prose** prose that is too elaborate.

purport verb /per-**port**/ appear or claim to be or do. •noun /**per**-port/ the meaning or purpose of something.

purpose noun **1** the reason for which something is done or for which something exists. **2** strong determination.
☐ **on purpose** intentionally.

purposeful adjective **1** having or showing determination. **2** having a purpose.
■ **purposefully** adverb.

purposely adverb on purpose.

purposive adjective having or done with a purpose.

purr verb **1** (of a cat) make a low continuous sound expressing contentment. **2** (of an engine) run smoothly while making a similar sound. •noun a purring sound.

purse noun **1** chiefly Brit. a small pouch for

THESAURUS

absolute, out-and-out, complete, total, perfect.
OPPOSITES adulterated, polluted, immoral, practical.

purely adverb entirely, wholly, exclusively, solely, only, just, merely.

purge verb **1** *this purges the system of impurities:* cleanse, clear, purify, rid, empty, strip, scour. **2** *the founders were purged from the firm:* remove, get rid of, eliminate, clear out, sweep out, expel, eject, evict, dismiss, sack, oust, axe, depose, root out, weed out.
•noun removal, elimination, expulsion, ejection, exclusion, eviction, dismissal, sacking, ousting.

purify verb clean, cleanse, refine, decontaminate, filter, clear, freshen, deodorize, sanitize, disinfect, sterilize.

purity noun **1** *the purity of our tap water:* cleanness, freshness, cleanliness, wholesomeness. **2** *they sought purity in a foul world:* virtue, morality, goodness, righteousness, piety, honour, honesty, integrity, decency, innocence.

purpose noun **1** *the purpose of his visit:*

motive, motivation, grounds, occasion, reason, point, basis, justification. **2** *their purpose was to subvert the economy:* intention, aim, object, objective, goal, plan, ambition, aspiration. **3** *the original purpose of the porch:* function, role, use. **4** *they started with some purpose:* determination, resolution, resolve, enthusiasm, ambition, motivation, commitment, conviction, dedication; informal get-up-and-go.
☐ **on purpose** deliberately, intentionally, purposely, wilfully, knowingly, consciously.

purposeful adjective determined, resolute, steadfast, single-minded, committed.
OPPOSITES aimless.

purposely adverb deliberately, intentionally, on purpose, wilfully, knowingly, consciously.

purse noun **1** *the money fell out of her purse:* wallet, money bag; N. Amer. change purse, billfold. **2** (N. Amer.) *a woman's purse:* handbag, shoulder bag, clutch bag; N. Amer. pocketbook. **3** *the fight will net him a $75,000 purse:* prize, reward, winnings, stake(s).
•verb *he pursed his lips:* press together,

p

carrying money. **2** N. Amer. a handbag.
3 money for spending. **4** a sum of money
given as a prize. • verb (**purses, pursing,
pursed**) form the lips into a tight round
shape.

purser noun a ship's officer who keeps the
accounts.

pursuance noun formal the carrying out of a
plan or action.

pursuant adverb (**pursuant to**) formal in
accordance with.

pursue verb (**pursues, pursuing, pursued**)
1 follow someone or something in order to
catch or attack them. **2** try to achieve a
goal. **3** follow a course of action.
4 continue to investigate or discuss a topic.
■ **pursuer** noun.

> ✓ *pur-*, not *per-*: *pursue*.

pursuit noun **1** the action of pursuing
someone or something. **2** a leisure or
sporting activity.

purulent /pyoor-uh-luhnt/ adjective made
up of or giving out pus.

purvey verb formal provide or supply food or
drink as a business.
■ **purveyor** noun.

purview noun formal the range of
something's influence or concerns.

pus noun a thick yellowish or greenish
liquid produced in infected body tissue.

push verb **1** apply force to something so as
to move it away from yourself. **2** move part
of your body into a particular position.
3 move by using force. **4** encourage
someone to work hard. **5** (**push for**)
repeatedly demand something. **6** informal
promote the use, sale, or acceptance of.
7 informal sell an illegal drug. • noun **1** an act
of pushing. **2** a great effort: *one last push*.
■ **pusher** noun.

pushbike noun Brit. informal a bicycle.

pushchair noun Brit. a folding chair on
wheels, in which a young child can be
pushed along.

pushover noun informal **1** a person who is
easy to influence or defeat. **2** a thing that
is easily done.

pushy adjective (**pushier, pushiest**) too
assertive or ambitious.

pusillanimous adjective weak or cowardly.
■ **pusillanimity** noun.

pussy or **puss** noun (plural **pussies** or **pusses**)
(also **pussycat**) informal a cat.
□ **pussy willow** a willow with soft, fluffy
catkins that appear before the leaves.

pussyfoot verb (**pussyfoots, pussyfooting,
pussyfooted**) act very cautiously.

pustule noun a small blister on the skin
containing pus.
■ **pustular** adjective.

put verb (**puts, putting, put**) **1** move
something into a particular position.

THESAURUS

compress, tighten, pucker, pout.

pursue verb **1** *I pursued him down the
garden:* follow, run after, chase, hunt,
stalk, track, trail, hound. **2** *pursue the goal
of political union:* strive for, work towards,
seek, search for, aim at/for, aspire to. **3** *she
pursued a political career:* engage in, be
occupied in, practise, follow, conduct, ply,
take up, undertake, carry on, continue,
take further, stick with/at.
OPPOSITES avoid, shun.

pursuit noun **1** *the pursuit of profit:* striving
for, quest after/for, search for. **2** *a range of
leisure pursuits:* activity, hobby, pastime,
diversion, recreation, amusement,
occupation.

push verb **1** *she tried to push him away:*
shove, thrust, propel, send, drive, force,
prod, poke, nudge, elbow, shoulder, sweep,
ram. **2** *she pushed her way into the flat:*
force, shove, thrust, squeeze, jostle, elbow,
shoulder, bundle, hustle, work, inch. **3** *he
pushed the panic button:* press, depress,
hold down, squeeze, operate, activate.
4 *don't push her to join in:* urge, press,
pressure, pressurize, force, coerce, nag;
informal lean on, twist someone's arm.
OPPOSITES pull.

• noun **1** *I felt a push in the back:* shove,
thrust, nudge, bump, jolt, prod, poke. **2** *the
army's eastward push:* advance, drive,
thrust, charge, attack, assault, onrush,
offensive.

put verb **1** *she put the parcel on a chair:*
place, set, lay, deposit, position, leave,
plant; informal stick, dump, park, plonk, pop;
N. Amer. informal plunk. **2** *she put it bluntly:*
express, word, phrase, frame, formulate,
render, convey, state.
□ **put something across/over** communicate,
convey, get across/over, explain, make
clear, spell out. **put someone off** deter,
discourage, dissuade, daunt, unnerve,
intimidate, scare off; informal turn off. **put
something off** postpone, defer, delay, put
back, adjourn, hold over, reschedule,
shelve; N. Amer. informal table; informal put on ice, put
on the back burner. **put someone out**
1 *Maria was put out by the slur:* annoy,
anger, irritate, offend, displease, irk, gall,
upset; informal rile, miff. **2** *I don't want to
put you out:* inconvenience, trouble,
bother, impose on. **put something out**
1 *firemen put out the blaze:* extinguish,
quench, douse, smother, blow out, snuff
out. **2** *he put out a press release:* issue,
publish, release, bring out, circulate,
publicize, post. **put someone up 1** *we can*

2 bring into a particular state or condition: *she tried to put me at ease.* **3** (**put something on** or **on to**) make a person or thing subject to something. **4** give a value, figure, or limit to. **5** express something in a particular way. **6** (of a ship) go in a particular direction: *the boat put out to sea.* **7** throw a shot or weight as a sport. □ **put someone/thing down 1** end a riot by using force. **2** kill a sick, old, or injured animal. **3** pay a sum as a deposit. **4** informal criticize someone in public. **put someone/thing off 1** postpone something. **2** make someone feel dislike or lose enthusiasm. **3** distract someone. **put something on 1** organize an event. **2** gain weight. **3** adopt an expression, accent, etc. **put someone out** cause someone trouble or inconvenience. **put someone/thing up 1** present, provide, or offer something. **2** give someone a place to stay. **put someone up to** informal encourage someone to do something wrong. **put up with** tolerate.

putative /pyoo-tuh-tiv/ adjective formal generally considered to be.

putrefy verb (**putrefies, putrefying, putrefied**) decay or rot and produce a very unpleasant smell.
■ **putrefaction** noun.

putrid adjective **1** decaying or rotting and producing a very unpleasant smell. **2** informal very unpleasant.

putsch /puuch/ noun a violent attempt to overthrow a government.

putt verb (**putts, putting, putted**) hit a golf ball gently so that it rolls into or near a hole. •noun a stroke of this kind.
□ **putting green** a smooth area of short grass surrounding a hole on a golf course.

putter[1] noun a golf club designed for putting.

putter[2] noun the rapid irregular sound of a small petrol engine. •verb (**putters, puttering, puttered**) move with this sound.

putty noun a soft paste that hardens as it sets, used for sealing glass in window frames.

puzzle verb (**puzzles, puzzling, puzzled**) **1** make someone feel confused because they cannot understand something. **2** think hard about something difficult to understand. •noun **1** a game, toy, or problem designed to test mental skills or knowledge. **2** a person or thing that is difficult to understand.
■ **puzzlement** noun **puzzler** noun.

PVC abbreviation polyvinyl chloride, a sort of plastic.

pygmy or **pigmy** noun (plural **pygmies**) **1** (**Pygmy**) a member of a race of very short people living in parts of Africa. **2** a very small person or thing. •adjective very small.

pyjamas (US spelling **pajamas**) plural noun a loose jacket and trousers for sleeping in.

pylon noun a tall tower-like structure for carrying electricity cables.

pyramid noun a very large stone structure with a square or triangular base and sloping sides that meet in a point at the top.
■ **pyramidal** adjective.

pyre noun a large pile of wood for the ritual burning of a dead body.

pyrites /py-ry-teez/ or **pyrite** noun a shiny yellow mineral that is a compound of iron and sulphur.

pyromania noun a strong urge to set fire to things.
■ **pyromaniac** noun.

pyrotechnics plural noun **1** a firework display. **2** the art of making fireworks or staging firework displays.
■ **pyrotechnic** adjective.

pyrrhic /pir-rik/ adjective (of a victory) won at too great a cost to have been worthwhile.

python noun a large snake which crushes its prey.

p

THESAURUS

put him up for a few days: **accommodate**, house, take in, give someone a roof over their head. **2** *they put up a candidate:* **nominate**, propose, put forward, recommend. **put something up 1** *the building was put up 100 years ago:* **build**, construct, erect, raise. **2** *she put up a poster:* **display**, pin up, stick up, hang up, post. **3** *he put up most of the funding:* **provide**, supply, furnish, give, contribute, donate, pledge, pay; informal cough up, shell out; N. Amer. informal ante up, pony up. **put up with tolerate**, take, stand (for), accept,

stomach, swallow, endure, bear, abide; informal lump it; Brit. informal stick, be doing with; formal brook.

puzzle verb *her decision puzzled me:* **baffle**, perplex, bewilder, confuse, bemuse, mystify, nonplus; informal flummox, stump, beat.
•noun *the poem has always been a puzzle:* **enigma**, mystery, paradox, conundrum, poser, riddle, problem.

puzzling adjective **baffling**, perplexing, bewildering, confusing, complicated, unclear, mysterious, enigmatic.

Qq

Q or **q** noun (plural **Qs** or **Q's**) the seventeenth letter of the alphabet. • abbreviation question.

Qatari /ka-**tah**-ri/ noun a person from Qatar, a country in the Persian Gulf. • adjective relating to Qatar.

QC abbreviation Law Queen's Counsel.

QED abbreviation used to say that something proves the truth of your claim.

qt abbreviation quarts.

qua /kway, kwah/ conjunction formal in the role or capacity of.

quack¹ noun the harsh sound made by a duck. • verb make this sound.

quack² noun **1** an unqualified person who claims to have medical knowledge. **2** Brit. informal a doctor.

quad noun **1** a quadrangle. **2** a quadruplet. □ **quad bike** a motorcycle with four large tyres, for off-road use.

quadrangle noun **1** a square or rectangular courtyard enclosed by buildings. **2** a four-sided geometrical figure.
■ **quadrangular** adjective.

quadrant noun **1** a quarter of a circle or of a circle's circumference. **2** historical an instrument for measuring angles in astronomy and navigation.

quadraphonic or **quadrophonic** /kwod-ruh-**fon**-ik/ adjective (of sound reproduction) using four channels.

quadratic /kwod-**rat**-ik/ adjective Maths involving the second and no higher power of an unknown quantity.

quadriceps /**kwod**-ri-seps/ noun (plural **quadriceps**) a large muscle at the front of the thigh.

quadrilateral noun a four-sided figure. • adjective having four straight sides.

quadrille /kwod-**ril**/ noun a square dance performed by four couples.

quadriplegia /kwod-ri-**plee**-juh/ noun paralysis of all four limbs.
■ **quadriplegic** adjective & noun.

quadruped /**kwod**-ruu-ped/ noun an animal which has four feet.

quadruple adjective **1** consisting of four parts. **2** four times as much or as many. • verb (**quadruples**, **quadrupling**, **quadrupled**) multiply by four.

quadruplet noun each of four children born at one birth.

quaff /kwoff/ verb drink a large amount of something quickly.

quagmire /**kwog**-my-er/ noun a soft, wet area of land.

quail¹ noun (plural **quail** or **quails**) a small short-tailed game bird.

quail² verb feel or show fear.

quaint adjective attractively unusual or old-fashioned.
■ **quaintly** adverb.

quake verb (**quakes**, **quaking**, **quaked**) **1** (especially of the earth) shake or tremble. **2** shudder with fear. • noun informal an earthquake.

Quaker noun a member of the Religious Society of Friends, a Christian movement devoted to peaceful principles and rejecting set forms of worship.
■ **Quakerism** noun.

qualification noun **1** the action of

THESAURUS

quaint adjective **1** *a quaint town:* picturesque, charming, sweet, attractive, old-fashioned, old-world; Brit. twee. **2** *quaint customs:* unusual, curious, eccentric, quirky, bizarre, whimsical, unconventional; informal offbeat.
OPPOSITES ugly.

quake verb shake, tremble, quiver, shudder, sway, rock, wobble, move, heave, convulse.

qualification noun **1** *a teaching qualification:* certificate, diploma, degree, licence, document, warrant. **2** *I can't accept it without qualification:* modification, limitation, reservation, stipulation, alteration, amendment, revision, moderation, mitigation, condition, proviso, caveat.

qualified adjective **1** *a qualified engineer:*

qualifying. **2** a pass of an exam or an official completion of a course. **3** a quality that makes someone suitable for a job or activity. **4** a statement that limits the meaning of another statement.

qualify verb (**qualifies, qualifying, qualified**) **1** meet the necessary standard or conditions to be able to do or receive something. **2** become officially recognized as able to do a particular job. **3** add something to a statement to limit its meaning. **4** Grammar (of a word or phrase) give a quality to another word.
■ **qualifier** noun.

qualitative /kwol-i-tuh-tiv/ adjective relating to or measured by quality.
■ **qualitatively** adverb.

quality noun (plural **qualities**) **1** the standard of something as measured against other similar things; how good or bad something is. **2** general excellence. **3** a distinctive characteristic.

qualm /kwahm/ noun a feeling of doubt about what you are doing.

quandary /kwon-duh-ri/ noun (plural **quandaries**) a state of uncertainty.

quango /kwang-goh/ noun (plural **quangos**) disapproving an organization that works independently but with support from the government.

quantify verb (**quantifies, quantifying, quantified**) express or measure the quantity of.
■ **quantifiable** adjective.

quantitative /kwon-ti-tuh-tiv/ adjective relating to or measured by quantity.
■ **quantitatively** adverb.

quantity noun (plural **quantities**) **1** a certain amount or number. **2** the property of something that can be measured in number, amount, size, or weight. **3** a large number or amount.
□ **quantity surveyor** Brit. a person who calculates the amount and cost of materials needed for building work.

quantum /kwon-tuhm/ noun (plural **quanta**) Physics a distinct quantity of energy corresponding to that involved in the absorption or emission of energy by an atom.
□ **quantum leap** a sudden large increase or advance. **quantum mechanics** the branch of physics concerned with describing the behaviour of subatomic particles in terms of quanta.

quarantine noun a period of time when an animal or person that may have a disease is kept in isolation. •verb (**quarantines, quarantining, quarantined**) put in quarantine.

quark /kwark/ noun any of a group of subatomic particles which carry a very small electric charge and are believed to form protons, neutrons, and other particles.

quarrel noun **1** an angry argument or disagreement. **2** a reason for disagreement. •verb (**quarrels, quarrelling, quarrelled**; US spelling **quarrels, quarreling, quarreled**) **1** have a quarrel. **2** (**quarrel with**) disagree with.

quarrelsome adjective tending to quarrel with people.

quarry¹ noun (plural **quarries**) a place where stone or other materials are dug out of the earth. •verb (**quarries, quarrying, quarried**)

certified, certificated, chartered, licensed, professional. **2** *qualified approval:* limited, conditional, restricted, contingent, circumscribed, guarded, equivocal, modified, adapted, amended, adjusted, moderated, reduced.
OPPOSITES unqualified, wholehearted.

qualify verb **1** *I qualify for free travel:* be eligible, meet the requirements, be entitled to, be permitted. **2** *they qualify as refugees:* count, be considered, be designated, be eligible. **3** *she qualified as a solicitor:* be certified, be licensed, pass, graduate, succeed. **4** *the course qualified them to teach:* authorize, empower, allow, permit, license. **5** *they qualified their findings:* modify, limit, restrict, make conditional, moderate, temper, modulate, mitigate.

quality noun **1** *a poor quality of signal:* standard, grade, class, calibre, condition, character, nature, form, rank, value, level. **2** *work of such quality:* excellence, superiority, merit, worth, value, virtue, calibre, distinction. **3** *her good qualities:* feature, trait, attribute, characteristic, point, aspect, facet, side, property.

quantity noun amount, total, aggregate, sum, quota, mass, weight, volume, bulk.

quarrel noun *they had a quarrel:* argument, disagreement, squabble, fight, dispute, wrangle, clash, altercation, feud; Brit. row; informal tiff, slanging match, run-in; Brit. informal bust-up.
OPPOSITES agreement, harmony.
•verb *don't quarrel over it:* argue, fight, disagree, fall out, differ, be at odds, bicker, squabble, cross swords; Brit. row.
OPPOSITES agree, get on.
□ **quarrel with** *you can't quarrel with the verdict:* fault, criticize, object to, oppose, take exception to, attack, take issue with, impugn, contradict, dispute, controvert; informal knock; formal gainsay.

quarry noun prey, victim, object, goal, target, kill, game, prize.

dig out stone or other materials from a quarry.

quarry² noun (plural **quarries**) an animal or person that is being hunted or chased.

quart noun a unit of liquid capacity equal to a quarter of a gallon or two pints, in Britain equal to 1.13 litres and in the US to 0.94 litre.

quarter noun 1 each of four equal parts of something. 2 a period of three months. 3 a quarter of an hour; fifteen minutes. 4 one fourth of a pound weight, equal to 4 oz avoirdupois. 5 a part of a town. 6 a US or Canadian coin worth 25 cents. 7 one fourth of a hundredweight, in Britain equal to 28 lb and in the US equal to 25 lb. 8 (**quarters**) rooms to live in. 9 a person or area seen as the source of something: *help from an unexpected quarter.* 10 mercy shown to an opponent. • verb (**quarters, quartering, quartered**) 1 divide into quarters. 2 (**be quartered**) be provided with rooms to live in. 3 historical cut the body of an executed person into four parts. □ **quarter-final** a match of a competition coming before the semi-final.

quarterdeck noun the part of a ship's upper deck near the stern.

quarterly adjective & adverb produced or happening once every quarter of a year. • noun (plural **quarterlies**) a publication produced four times a year.

quartermaster noun an army officer in charge of accommodation and supplies.

quartet noun 1 a group of four people playing music or singing together. 2 a piece of music for a quartet. 3 a set of four.

quarto /kwor-toh/ noun (plural **quartos**) a size of page for a book, resulting from folding a sheet into four leaves.

quartz noun a hard mineral consisting of silica.

quasar /kway-zar/ noun (in astronomy) a kind of galaxy which gives off enormous amounts of energy.

quash verb 1 officially declare that a legal decision is no longer valid. 2 put an end to.

quasi- /kway-zy/ combining form seemingly; as if: *quasi-scientific.*

quatrain /kwot-rayn/ noun a poem or verse of four lines.

quaver verb (**quavers, quavering, quavered**) (of a voice) tremble. • noun 1 a tremble in a voice. 2 chiefly Brit. a musical note that lasts as long as half a crotchet.
■ **quavery** adjective.

quay /kee/ noun a platform in a harbour for loading and unloading ships.

quayside noun a quay and the area around it.

queasy adjective (**queasier, queasiest**) feeling sick.
■ **queasiness** noun.

queen noun 1 the female ruler of an independent state. 2 (also **queen consort**) a king's wife. 3 the best or most important woman or thing in a particular group. 4 a playing card ranking next below a king. 5 the most powerful chess piece, able to move in any direction. 6 a female that lays eggs for a colony of ants, bees, wasps, or termites. 7 informal a homosexual man who behaves like a woman. □ **queen mother** the widow of a king who is also mother of the current king or queen.
■ **queenly** adjective.

Queensberry Rules plural noun the standard rules of boxing.

queer adjective 1 strange; odd. 2 disapproving (of a man) homosexual. • noun disapproving a homosexual man.

quell verb 1 put an end to a rebellion by force. 2 suppress a feeling.

quench verb 1 satisfy thirst by drinking. 2 put out a fire.

querulous /kwe-ruu-luhss/ adjective complaining in an irritable way.
■ **querulously** adverb.

query noun (plural **queries**) a question, especially one expressing a doubt about something. • verb (**queries, querying, queried**) ask a question expressing doubt about something.

THESAURUS

quash verb 1 *he may quash the sentence:* cancel, reverse, rescind, repeal, revoke, retract, countermand, withdraw, overturn, overrule. 2 *we want to quash these rumours:* stop, put an end to, stamp out, crush, put down, check, curb, nip in the bud, squash, suppress, stifle.
OPPOSITES validate, encourage, perpetuate.

queen noun monarch, sovereign, ruler, head of state, Crown, Her Majesty.

queer adjective odd, strange, unusual, funny, peculiar, curious, bizarre, weird, uncanny, freakish, eerie, unnatural, abnormal,

anomalous; informal spooky.
OPPOSITES normal.

query noun 1 *we can answer any queries:* question, enquiry. 2 *there was a query as to who owned the hotel:* doubt, uncertainty, question (mark), reservation.
• verb 1 *'Why do that?' queried Isobel:* ask, enquire, question; Brit. informal quiz. 2 *folk may query his credentials:* challenge, question, dispute, doubt, have suspicions about, distrust.
OPPOSITES accept, trust.

q

quest noun a long or difficult search. •verb search for something.

question noun 1 a sentence worded so as to obtain information. 2 doubt, or the raising of a doubt about something. 3 a problem needing to be solved. 4 a matter depending on stated conditions: *it's only a question of time.* •verb 1 ask someone questions. 2 express doubt about something. □ out of the question not possible. question mark a punctuation mark (?) indicating a question. ■ questioner noun.

questionable adjective likely to be wrong.

questionnaire noun a set of questions written for a survey.

☑ there are two *ns*: questio*nn*aire.

queue noun a line of people or vehicles waiting their turn for something. •verb (**queues, queuing** or **queueing, queued**) wait in a queue. □ queue-jump Brit. move forward out of turn in a queue.

quibble noun a minor objection. •verb (**quibbles, quibbling, quibbled**) raise a minor objection.

quiche /keesh/ noun a baked flan with a savoury filling thickened with eggs.

quick adjective 1 moving fast. 2 lasting or taking a short time. 3 with little or no delay. 4 intelligent. 5 (of temper) easily roused. •noun (**the quick**) the tender flesh below the growing part of a fingernail or toenail. □ cut someone to the quick upset someone very much. quick-tempered easily angered. quick-witted able to think or respond quickly. ■ quickly adverb.

quicken verb 1 make or become quicker. 2 make or become active or alive.

quicklime noun a white alkaline substance consisting of calcium oxide, obtained by heating limestone.

quicksand or **quicksands** noun loose wet sand that sucks in anything resting on it.

quicksilver noun mercury. •adjective moving or changing rapidly.

quickstep noun a fast foxtrot.

quid noun (plural **quid**) Brit. informal one pound sterling.

quid pro quo /kwid proh **kwoh**/ noun (plural **quid pro quos**) a favour given in return for something.

quest noun 1 *their quest for her killer:* search, hunt, pursuance of. 2 *Sir Galahad's quest:* expedition, journey, voyage, trek, travels, odyssey, adventure, exploration, search, crusade, mission, pilgrimage.

question noun 1 *please answer my question:* enquiry, query, interrogation. 2 *there is no question that he is ill:* doubt, dispute, argument, debate, uncertainty, reservation. 3 *the political questions of the day:* issue, matter, topic, business, problem, concern, debate, argument, dispute, controversy. OPPOSITES answer, certainty.
•verb 1 *the magistrate questions the suspect:* interrogate, cross-examine, cross-question, quiz, interview, debrief, examine; informal grill, pump. 2 *she questioned his motives:* query, challenge, dispute, cast aspersions on, doubt, suspect. □ out of the question impossible, impracticable, unfeasible, unworkable, inconceivable, unimaginable, unrealizable, unsuitable; informal not on.

questionable adjective suspicious, suspect, dubious, irregular, odd, strange, murky, dark, unsavoury, disreputable; informal funny, fishy, shady, iffy; Brit. informal dodgy.

questionnaire noun question sheet, survey form, opinion poll, test, quiz.

queue noun row, column, file, chain, string, procession, waiting list; N. Amer. line, wait list.

quick adjective 1 *a quick worker:* fast, swift, rapid, speedy, brisk, smart, lightning, whirlwind, whistle-stop, breakneck; informal nippy, zippy. 2 *a quick look:* hasty, hurried, cursory, perfunctory, desultory, superficial, brief. 3 *a quick end to the recession:* sudden, instantaneous, instant, immediate, abrupt, precipitate. 4 *she isn't as quick as the others:* intelligent, bright, clever, gifted, able, astute, sharp-witted, smart, alert, sharp, perceptive; informal brainy, on the ball. OPPOSITES slow, long.

quicken verb 1 *she quickened her pace:* speed up, accelerate, step up, hasten, hurry (up). 2 *the film quickened his interest in nature:* stimulate, excite, arouse, rouse, stir up, activate, whet, inspire, kindle.

quickly adverb 1 *he walked quickly:* fast, swiftly, briskly, rapidly, speedily, at full tilt, at a gallop, at the double, post-haste, hotfoot; informal like (greased) lightning, hell for leather, like blazes, like the wind; Brit. informal like the clappers, like billy-o; N. Amer. informal lickety-split. 2 *you'd better leave quickly:* immediately, directly, at once, straight away, right away, instantly, forthwith; N. Amer. momentarily; informal like a shot, asap, p.d.q., pronto. 3 *he quickly inspected it:* briefly, fleetingly, briskly, hastily, hurriedly, cursorily, perfunctorily, superficially, desultorily.

q

quiescent /kwi-ess-uhnt/ **adjective** not active.
■ **quiescence** noun.

quiet adjective (**quieter**, **quietest**) **1** making little or no noise. **2** free from activity or excitement. **3** without being disturbed: *a quiet drink*. **4** discreet: *a quiet word*. **5** (of a person) shy and not tending to talk very much. ● **noun** absence of noise or disturbance. ● **verb** N. Amer. make or become quiet.
■ **quietly** adverb.

quieten verb Brit. make or become quiet and calm.

quietude noun a state of calmness and quiet.

quiff noun Brit. a piece of hair brushed upwards and backwards from the forehead.

quill noun **1** a main wing or tail feather of a bird. **2** the hollow shaft of a feather. **3** a pen made from a quill. **4** a spine of a porcupine or hedgehog.

quilt noun a warm bed covering made of padding enclosed between layers of fabric.
■ **quilting** noun.

quilted adjective made of two layers of cloth filled with padding.

quin noun Brit. informal a quintuplet.

quince noun a hard yellow pear-shaped fruit.

quinine /kwi-neen/ noun a bitter drug made from the bark of a South American tree.

quintessence noun **1** a perfect example of something. **2** the central and most important part or quality of something.

quintessential adjective representing the most perfect example.

■ **quintessentially** adverb.

quintet noun **1** a group of five people playing music or singing together. **2** a piece of music for a quintet. **3** a set of five.

quintuple adjective **1** consisting of five parts or elements. **2** five times as much or as many.

quintuplet noun each of five children born at one birth.

quip noun a witty remark. ● **verb** (**quips**, **quipping**, **quipped**) make a witty remark.

quire noun **1** four sheets of paper folded to form eight leaves. **2** 25 sheets of paper.

quirk noun **1** a peculiar habit. **2** a strange thing that happens by chance.

quirky adjective (**quirkier**, **quirkiest**) having peculiar or unexpected habits or qualities.

quisling noun a traitor who collaborates with an enemy force that has occupied their country.

quit verb (**quits**, **quitting**, **quitted** or **quit**) **1** leave a place. **2** resign from a job. **3** informal, chiefly N. Amer. stop doing something.
■ **quitter** noun.

quite adverb **1** to a certain extent; fairly. **2** to the greatest degree; completely. ● **exclamation** expressing agreement.

quits adjective on equal terms because a debt or score has been settled.

quiver[1] verb (**quivers**, **quivering**, **quivered**) shake or vibrate slightly. ● **noun** a quivering movement.

quiver[2] noun a case for carrying arrows.

quixotic /kwik-sot-ik/ adjective idealistic but impractical.

quiz noun (plural **quizzes**) a competition in

THESAURUS

q

quiet adjective **1** *the whole pub went quiet:* silent, still, hushed, noiseless, soundless, mute, dumb, speechless. **2** *a quiet voice:* soft, low, muted, muffled, faint, hushed, whispered, suppressed. **3** *a quiet village:* peaceful, sleepy, tranquil, calm, still, restful.
OPPOSITES loud, busy.
● noun *the quiet of the countryside:* silence, still, hush, restfulness, calm, tranquillity, serenity, peace.

quietly adverb **1** *she read quietly:* silently, noiselessly, soundlessly, inaudibly. **2** *he spoke quietly:* softly, faintly, in a low voice, in a whisper, in a murmur, under your breath, in an undertone.
OPPOSITES out loud, loudly.

quilt noun duvet, cover(s); Brit. eiderdown; N. Amer. comforter; Austral. trademark Doona.

quirk noun **1** *they all know his quirks:* idiosyncrasy, peculiarity, oddity, eccentricity, foible, whim, vagary, habit, characteristic, trait, fad. **2** *a quirk of fate:* chance, fluke, freak, anomaly, twist.

quirky adjective eccentric, idiosyncratic, unconventional, unorthodox, unusual, strange, bizarre, peculiar, zany; informal wacky, way-out, offbeat.
OPPOSITES conventional.

quit verb **1** *he quit the office at 12.30:* leave, vacate, exit, depart from. **2** (informal) *he quit his job:* resign from, leave, give up, hand in your notice; informal chuck, pack in.
3 (informal) *quit living in the past:* give up, stop, discontinue, drop, abandon, abstain from; informal pack in, leave off.
OPPOSITES arrive at, continue, start.

quite adverb **1** *two quite different types:* completely, entirely, totally, wholly, absolutely, utterly, thoroughly, altogether.
2 *red hair was quite common:* fairly, rather, somewhat, relatively, comparatively, moderately, reasonably; informal pretty.
OPPOSITES slightly, not at all.

quiz noun competition, test of knowledge.
● verb *a man was quizzed by police:* question, interrogate, cross-examine, cross-

which people answer questions that test their knowledge. • verb (**quizzes, quizzing, quizzed**) question someone.

quizzical adjective showing mild or amused puzzlement.
■ **quizzically** adverb.

quoin /koyn, kwoyn/ noun **1** an external angle of a wall or building. **2** a cornerstone.

quoit /koyt, kwoyt/ noun a ring that you throw over an upright peg in the game of **quoits**.

quorate /kwor-uht/ adjective Brit. (of a meeting) having a quorum.

quorum noun (plural **quorums**) the minimum number of people that must be present at a meeting to make its business valid.

quota noun **1** a limited quantity of people or things that is officially allowed. **2** a share of something that you have to contribute.

quotation noun **1** a passage or remark repeated by someone other than the person who originally said or wrote it. **2** a formal statement of the estimated cost of a job or service.
▫ **quotation marks** a pair of punctuation marks, (' ') or (" "), used to mark the beginning and end of a quotation or passage of speech.

quote verb (**quotes, quoting, quoted**) **1** repeat a passage or remark by another person. **2** (**quote something as**) mention something as an example to support a point. **3** give someone an estimated price. **4** give a company a listing on a stock exchange. • noun **1** a quotation. **2** (**quotes**) quotation marks.
■ **quotable** adjective.

quoth /rhymes with oath/ verb old use said.

quotidian /kwuh-**tid**-i-uhn/ adjective formal **1** daily. **2** ordinary or everyday.

quotient /kwoh-shuhnt/ noun Maths a result obtained by dividing one quantity by another.

q.v. abbreviation used to direct a reader to another part of a book for further information.

---

question, interview; informal grill, pump.

quota noun share, allocation, allowance, ration, portion, slice, percentage; Brit. informal whack.

quotation noun **1** *a quotation from Dryden:* extract, quote, citation, excerpt, passage; N. Amer. cite. **2** *a quotation for the work:*
estimate, quote, price, tender, bid, costing.

quote verb **1** *he quoted from the book:* recite, repeat, reproduce, retell, echo. **2** *she quoted one case in which a girl died:* mention, cite, refer to, name, instance, allude to, point out.
• noun. See **QUOTATION** senses 1, 2.

q

Rr

R or **r** noun (plural **Rs** or **R's**) the eighteenth letter of the alphabet. • **abbreviation 1** Regina or Rex. **2** (**R.**) River.

rabbi /rab-by/ noun (plural **rabbis**) a Jewish religious leader or teacher of Jewish law.
■ **rabbinic** (or **rabbinical**) adjective.

rabbit noun a burrowing animal with long ears and a short tail. • verb (**rabbits, rabbiting, rabbited**) Brit. informal chatter.

rabble noun **1** a disorderly crowd of people. **2** (**the rabble**) disapproving ordinary people.
□ **rabble-rouser** a person who makes speeches intended to make people angry or excited, usually for political reasons.

rabid /rab-id, ray-bid/ adjective **1** having extreme opinions; fanatical. **2** having rabies.
■ **rabidly** adverb.

rabies /ray-beez/ noun a dangerous disease of dogs and other animals, that can be transmitted through saliva to humans.

raccoon or **racoon** noun a greyish-brown American animal with a black face and striped tail.

race[1] noun **1** a competition to see who or which is fastest over a set course. **2** a strong current flowing through a narrow channel. • verb (**races, racing, raced**) **1** compete against someone or something in a race. **2** move or progress rapidly. **3** (of an engine) operate at too high a speed.
■ **racer** noun.

race[2] noun **1** each of the major divisions of humankind. **2** a group of people or things with a common feature. **3** a subdivision of a species.
□ **race relations** relations between members of different races within a country.

racecourse noun a ground or track for horse or dog racing.

racehorse noun a horse bred and trained for racing.

raceme /ra-seem/ noun a flower cluster with separate flowers along a central stem.

racetrack noun **1** a racecourse. **2** a track for motor racing.

racial adjective **1** having to do with race. **2** relating to relations or differences between races.
■ **racially** adverb.

racialism noun racism.
■ **racialist** noun & adjective.

racism noun **1** the belief that certain races are better than others. **2** discrimination against, or hostility towards, other races.
■ **racist** noun & adjective.

rack noun **1** a framework for holding or storing things. **2** (**the rack**) (in the past) a frame on which people were tortured by being stretched. **3** a joint of meat that includes the front ribs. • verb **1** (also **wrack**) cause great pain to. **2** (**rack something up**) achieve a score or amount.
□ **go to rack and ruin** fall into a bad condition. **rack** (or **wrack**) **your brains** think very hard.

racket[1] or **racquet** noun **1** a bat with a

THESAURUS

race[1] noun **1** *Dave won the race:* contest, competition, event, fixture, heat, trial(s). **2** *the race for naval domination:* competition, rivalry, contention, quest. • verb **1** *he will race in the final:* compete, contend, run. **2** *Claire raced after him:* hurry, dash, rush, run, sprint, bolt, charge, shoot, hurtle, hare, fly, speed; informal tear, belt.

race[2] noun **1** *pupils of different races:* ethnic group, racial type, origin, stock, blood, tribe. **2** *a bloodthirsty race:* people, nation.

racial adjective ethnic, ethnological, race-related, cultural, national, tribal, genetic.

rack noun *the boots live on that rack:* frame, framework, stand, holder, trestle, support, shelf.
• verb *he was racked with guilt:* torment, afflict, torture, agonize, harrow, plague, persecute, trouble, worry.

racket noun **1** noise, din, hubbub, clamour, uproar, tumult, commotion, rumpus; informal hullabaloo; Brit. informal row. **2** (informal) *a gold-smuggling racket:* fraud, swindle, sharp round or oval frame, used in tennis, badminton, and squash. **2** (**rackets**) a ball game played with rackets in a four-walled court.

racket² noun **1** a loud, unpleasant noise. **2** informal a dishonest scheme for making money.
■ **rackety** adjective.

racketeer noun a person who makes money through dishonest activities.
■ **racketeering** noun.

raconteur /ra-kon-ter/ noun a person who tells stories in an interesting and amusing way.

racoon ⇨ **RACCOON**.

racy adjective lively and exciting.

radar noun a system for detecting aircraft, ships, etc., by sending out radio waves which are reflected back off the object.

raddled adjective showing signs of age and tiredness.

radial adjective **1** arranged in lines coming out from a central point to the edge of a circle. **2** (of a tyre) in which the layers of fabric run at right angles to the circumference of the tyre.
■ **radially** adverb.

radian /ray-di-uhn/ noun an angle of 57.3 degrees, equal to the angle at the centre of a circle formed by an arc equal in length to the radius.

radiant adjective **1** shining or glowing brightly. **2** glowing with joy, love, or health. **3** transmitted by radiation.
■ **radiance** noun **radiantly** adverb.

radiate verb (**radiates, radiating, radiated**) **1** (of light, heat, or other energy) be sent out in rays or waves. **2** show a strong feeling or quality. **3** spread out from a central point.

radiation noun energy sent out as electromagnetic waves or subatomic particles.

radiator noun **1** a metal device for heating a room, usually filled with hot water pumped in through pipes. **2** a cooling device in a vehicle or aircraft engine.

radical adjective **1** having to do with the basic nature of something; fundamental. **2** supporting complete political or social reform. **3** departing from tradition; new.

4 Maths relating to the root of a number or quantity. •noun **1** a supporter of radical reform. **2** Chemistry a group of atoms behaving as a unit in a compound.
■ **radicalism** noun **radically** adverb.

radii plural of **RADIUS**.

radio noun (plural **radios**) **1** the sending and receiving of electromagnetic waves carrying sound messages. **2** the activity or medium of broadcasting in sound. **3** a device for receiving radio programmes, or for sending and receiving radio messages. •verb (**radioes, radioing, radioed**) send a message to someone by radio.

radioactive adjective giving out harmful radiation or particles.

radioactivity noun harmful radiation or particles sent out when atomic nuclei break up.

radiocarbon noun a radioactive isotope of carbon used in carbon dating.

radiogram noun Brit. dated a combined radio and record player.

radiography noun the production of images by X-rays or other radiation.
■ **radiographer** noun.

radioisotope noun a radioactive isotope.

radiology noun the science of X-rays and similar radiation, especially as used in medicine.
■ **radiologist** noun.

radiotherapy noun the treatment of disease using X-rays or similar radiation.

radish noun a crisp, hot-tasting root vegetable, eaten raw in salads.

radium noun a radioactive metallic element.

radius noun (plural **radii** /ray-di-I/ or **radiuses**) **1** a straight line from the centre to the edge of a circle or sphere. **2** a stated distance from a centre in all directions. **3** the thicker and shorter of the two bones in the human forearm.

radon noun a rare radioactive gas.

RAF abbreviation Royal Air Force.

raffia noun fibre from the leaves of a tropical palm tree.

raffish adjective slightly disreputable, but in an attractive way.

raffle noun a lottery with goods as prizes. •verb (**raffles, raffling, raffled**) offer

r

THESAURUS

practice; informal game, scam, rip-off.

radiate verb **1** stars radiate energy: emit, give off, discharge, diffuse, scatter, shed, cast. **2** light radiated from the hall: shine, beam, emanate, pour. **3** four spokes radiate from the hub: fan out, spread out, branch out/off, extend, issue.

radical adjective **1** radical reform: thorough, complete, total, comprehensive, exhaustive,

sweeping, far-reaching, wide-ranging, extensive, profound, major. **2** radical differences between the two theories: fundamental, basic, essential, quintessential, structural, deep-seated. **3** a radical political movement: revolutionary, progressive, reformist, revisionist, progressivist, extreme, fanatical, militant. OPPOSITES superficial, minor, conservative.

something as a prize in a raffle.

raft noun **1** a flat structure used as a boat or floating platform. **2** a small inflatable boat. **3** a large amount.

rafter noun a beam forming part of the internal framework of a roof.

rag noun **1** a piece of old cloth. **2** (**rags**) old or tattered clothes. **3** informal a low-quality newspaper. **4** Brit. a programme of entertainments organized by students to raise money for charity. **5** a piece of ragtime music.
□ **the rag trade** informal the clothing or fashion industry.

ragamuffin noun a person in ragged, dirty clothes.

ragbag noun a collection of widely different things.

rage noun violent, uncontrollable anger.
• verb (**rages, raging, raged**) **1** feel or express rage. **2** continue with great force.
□ **all the rage** temporarily very popular or fashionable.

ragged adjective **1** (of cloth or clothes) old and torn. **2** rough or irregular. **3** not smooth or steady.
■ **raggedly** adverb.

ragout /ra-goo/ noun a spicy stew of meat and vegetables.

ragtag adjective disorganized and made up of a mixture of different types of people.

ragtime noun an early form of jazz played especially on the piano.

ragwort noun a plant with yellow flowers and ragged leaves.

raid noun **1** a sudden attack on an enemy, or on a building to commit a crime. **2** a surprise visit by police to arrest suspects or seize illegal goods. • verb make a raid on.
■ **raider** noun.

rail[1] noun **1** a fixed bar forming part of a fence or barrier or used to hang things on. **2** each of the two metal bars laid on the ground to form a railway track. **3** railways as a means of transport. • verb **1** enclose with a rail or rails. **2** (**rail against** or **at**) complain strongly about.
□ **go off the rails** informal behave in an uncontrolled way.

rail[2] noun a waterside bird with grey and brown feathers.

railing noun a fence or barrier made of rails.

raillery noun good-humoured teasing.

railroad noun N. Amer. a railway. • verb informal rush or force someone into doing something.

railway noun Brit. **1** a track made of rails along which trains run. **2** a system of tracks and trains.

raiment /ray-muhnt/ noun old use or literary clothing.

rain noun **1** condensed moisture from the atmosphere falling in separate drops. **2** (**rains**) falls of rain. **3** a large quantity of things falling together. • verb **1** (**it rains, it is raining, it rained**) rain falls. **2** (**be rained off**) (of an event) be prevented by rain from continuing or taking place. **3** fall in large quantities.

rainbow noun an arch of colours in the sky, caused by the sun shining through water droplets in the atmosphere.

raincoat noun a coat made from water-resistant fabric.

rainfall noun the amount of rain falling.

rainforest noun a dense forest found in tropical areas with consistently heavy rainfall.

rainy adjective (**rainier, rainiest**) having a lot of rain.
□ **a rainy day** a time in the future when

THESAURUS

r

rage noun **1** *his rage is due to frustration:* fury, anger, wrath, outrage, indignation, temper, spleen, resentment, pique, annoyance, vexation, displeasure; formal ire. **2** *the current rage for DIY:* craze, passion, fashion, taste, trend, vogue, fad, mania; informal thing.
• verb *she raged silently:* be angry, be furious, be enraged, be incensed, seethe, be beside yourself, rave, storm, fume, spit; informal be livid, be wild, be steamed up.

ragged adjective **1** *ragged jeans:* tattered, torn, ripped, frayed, worn (out), threadbare, scruffy, shabby; informal tatty. **2** *a ragged coastline:* jagged, craggy, rugged, uneven, rough, irregular, indented. OPPOSITES new, smart, sound, smooth.

raid noun **1** *the raid on Dieppe:* attack, assault, descent, blitz, incursion, sortie, onslaught, storming. **2** *a raid on a shop:* robbery, burglary, hold-up, break-in, ram raid; informal smash-and-grab, stick-up; N. Amer. informal heist. **3** *a police raid:* swoop, search; N. Amer. informal bust, takedown.
• verb **1** *they raided shipping in the harbour:* attack, assault, set upon, descend on, swoop on, storm. **2** *armed men raided the store:* rob, hold up, break into, plunder, steal from, pillage, loot, ransack; informal stick up. **3** *homes were raided by police:* search, swoop on; N. Amer. informal bust.

raider noun robber, burglar, thief, housebreaker, plunderer, pillager, looter, marauder, attacker, assailant, invader.

railing noun fence, fencing, rail(s), palisade, balustrade, banister.

rainy adjective wet, showery, drizzly, damp, inclement.
OPPOSITES dry, fine.

money may be needed.

raise verb (**raises, raising, raised**) **1** lift or move upwards or into an upright position. **2** increase the amount, level, or strength of. **3** express doubts, objections, etc. **4** collect money. **5** bring up a child. **6** breed or grow animals or plants. **7** (**raise something to**) Maths multiply a quantity to a particular power. •noun N. Amer. an increase in salary.
◻ **raise the roof** cheer very loudly.

raisin noun a partially dried grape.

raison d'être /ray-zon det-ruh/ noun (plural **raisons d'être** /ray-zon det-ruh/) the most important reason for someone or something's existence.

Raj /rahj/ noun (**the Raj**) the period of British rule in India.

raja or **rajah** /rah-juh/ noun historical an Indian king or prince.

rake[1] noun a pole with metal prongs at the end, used for drawing together leaves, smoothing soil, etc. •verb (**rakes, raking, raked**) **1** draw together or smooth with a rake. **2** scratch or sweep with a long broad movement. **3** search through.
◻ **rake it in** informal make a lot of money. **rake something up** bring up something that is best forgotten.

rake[2] noun a fashionable, rich, but immoral man.

rake[3] verb (**rakes, raking, raked**) set something at a sloping angle. •noun the angle at which something slopes.

rakish adjective having a dashing, jaunty, or slightly disreputable appearance.

rally noun (plural **rallies**) **1** a mass meeting held as a protest or in support of a cause. **2** a long-distance competition for motor vehicles over roads or rough ground. **3** a quick or strong recovery. **4** (in tennis and similar games) a long exchange of strokes between players. •verb (**rallies, rallying, rallied**) **1** (of troops) come together again to continue fighting. **2** come together to support a person or cause. **3** recover health or strength. **4** (of shares or currency) increase in value after a fall. **5** (**rallying**) the sport of taking part in a motor rally.

ram noun **1** an adult male sheep. **2** a long, heavy object swung against a door to break it down. **3** a striking or plunging device in a machine. •verb (**rams, ramming, rammed**) **1** hit with force. **2** roughly force into place.
◻ **ram raid** a robbery in which people ram a shop window with a vehicle to steal goods.

Ramadan /ram-uh-dan/ noun the ninth month of the Muslim year, during which Muslims do not eat from dawn to sunset.

ramble verb (**rambles, rambling, rambled**) **1** walk for pleasure in the countryside. **2** talk or write in a confused way. •noun a country walk taken for pleasure.
∎ **rambler** noun.

ramekin /ra-mi-kin/ noun a small dish for baking and serving an individual portion of food.

ramifications plural noun complex results of an action or event.

ramp noun **1** a sloping surface joining two

r

raise verb **1** *he raised a hand:* lift (up), hold aloft, elevate, uplift, hoist, haul up, hitch up; Brit. informal hoick up. **2** *they raised prices:* increase, put up, push up, mark up, inflate; informal hike (up), jack up, bump up. **3** *he raised his voice:* amplify, louden, magnify, intensify, boost, lift, increase. **4** *how will you raise the money?* get, obtain, acquire, accumulate, amass, collect, fetch, net, make. **5** *he raised several objections:* bring up, air, present, table, propose, submit, advance, suggest, put forward. **6** *the disaster raised doubts about safety:* give rise to, occasion, cause, produce, engender, elicit, create, result in, lead to, prompt. **7** *most parents raise their children well:* bring up, rear, nurture. **8** *he raised cattle:* breed, rear, nurture, keep, tend, farm, produce.
OPPOSITES lower, reduce, demolish.

rake verb **1** *he raked the leaves into a pile:* scrape, collect, gather. **2** *she raked the gravel:* smooth (out), level, even out, flatten, comb. **3** *I raked through my pockets:* rummage, search, hunt, sift, rifle.

rally verb **1** *the troops rallied and held their ground:* regroup, reassemble, re-form, reunite. **2** *share prices rallied:* recover, improve, get better, pick up, revive, bounce back, perk up, look up, turn a corner.
OPPOSITES disperse, slump.
•noun **1** *a rally in support of the strike:* (mass) meeting, gathering, assembly, demonstration, (protest) march; informal demo. **2** *a rally in oil prices:* recovery, upturn, improvement, comeback, resurgence.
OPPOSITES slump.

ram verb **1** *he rammed his sword into its sheath:* force, thrust, plunge, stab, push, sink, dig, stick, cram, jam, stuff. **2** *a van rammed the car:* hit, strike, crash into, collide with, impact, smash into, butt.

ramble verb **1** *we rambled around the lanes:* walk, hike, tramp, trek, backpack. **2** *she does ramble on:* chatter, babble, prattle, blather, gabble, jabber, twitter, rattle; Brit. informal witter, chunter, rabbit.

ramp noun slope, bank, incline, gradient, rise, drop.

rampage verb /ram-payj/ (**rampages, rampaging, rampaged**) rush around in a wild and violent way. • noun /ram-payj/ a period of wild and violent behaviour.

rampant adjective **1** flourishing or spreading in an uncontrolled way. **2** Heraldry (of an animal) shown standing on its left hind foot with its forefeet in the air.

rampart noun a wall defending a castle or town, having a broad top with a walkway.

ramrod noun a rod formerly used to ram down the charge of a firearm.

ramshackle adjective in a very bad condition.

ran past of RUN.

ranch noun a large farm in America where cattle or other animals are bred.
■ **rancher** noun.

rancid adjective (of fatty or oily food) stale and smelling or tasting unpleasant.

rancour (US spelling **rancor**) noun bitter feeling or resentment.
■ **rancorous** adjective.

rand noun the basic unit of money of South Africa.

R & B abbreviation **1** rhythm and blues. **2** a kind of pop music with soulful vocals.

random adjective done or happening without any plan, purpose, or regular pattern.
◻ **at random** without thinking or planning in advance.
■ **randomly** adverb **randomness** noun.

randy adjective (**randier, randiest**) Brit. informal sexually excited.

rang past of RING².

range noun **1** the limits between which something varies. **2** a set of different things of the same general type. **3** the distance over which a sound, missile, etc. can travel. **4** a line of mountains or hills. **5** a large area of open land for grazing or hunting. **6** an area for testing military equipment or practising shooting. **7** a large stove with several burners or hotplates.
• verb (**ranges, ranging, ranged**) **1** vary between particular limits. **2** arrange things in a particular way. **3** (**be ranged against**) be in opposition to. **4** travel over a wide area.

ranger noun a keeper of a park, forest, or area of countryside.

rangy /rayn-ji/ adjective (of a person) tall and slim with long limbs.

rank¹ noun **1** a position within the armed forces or an organization. **2** a row of people or things. **3** high social position. **4** (**the ranks**) (in the armed forces) those who are not commissioned officers. • verb **1** give a rank to. **2** hold a particular rank. **3** arrange in a row or rows.
◻ **close ranks** unite to defend shared interests. **pull rank** use your higher rank to take advantage of someone. **rank and file** the ordinary members of an organization.

rank² adjective **1** having a very unpleasant smell. **2** complete: *a rank amateur*. **3** (of plants) growing too thickly.

THESAURUS

rampage verb riot, run amok, go berserk, storm, charge, tear.
◻ **go on the rampage** riot, go berserk, get out of control, run amok; N. Amer. informal go postal.

rampant adjective uncontrolled, unchecked, unrestrained, unbridled, out of control, out of hand, widespread, rife, spreading.
OPPOSITES controlled.

random adjective unsystematic, arbitrary, unmethodical, unplanned, chance, casual, indiscriminate, non-specific, haphazard, stray, erratic.
OPPOSITES systematic, deliberate.
◻ **at random** unsystematically, arbitrarily, randomly, unmethodically, haphazardly.

range noun **1** *his range of vision:* extent, limit, reach, span, scope, compass, sweep, area, field, orbit, ambit, horizon, latitude. **2** *a range of mountains:* row, chain, sierra, ridge, massif. **3** *a range of foods:* assortment, variety, diversity, mixture, collection, array, selection, choice.
• verb **1** *charges range from 1% to 5%:* vary,

fluctuate, differ, extend, stretch, reach, go, run, cover. **2** *they ranged over the steppes:* roam, wander, travel, journey, rove, traverse, walk, hike, trek.

rank¹ noun **1** *he was elevated to ministerial rank:* position, level, grade, echelon, class, status, standing. **2** *a family of rank:* high standing, blue blood, high birth, nobility, aristocracy. **3** *a rank of riflemen:* row, line, file, column, string, train, procession.
• verb **1** *the plant is ranked as endangered:* classify, class, categorize, rate, grade, bracket, group, designate, list. **2** *tulips were ranked like guardsmen:* line up, align, order, arrange, dispose, set out, array, range.

rank² adjective **1** *rank vegetation:* abundant, lush, luxuriant, dense, profuse, vigorous, overgrown; informal jungly. **2** *a rank smell:* offensive, nasty, revolting, sickening, obnoxious, foul, fetid, high, rancid, putrid; Brit. informal pongy, humming. **3** *rank stupidity:* downright, utter, out-and-out, absolute, complete, sheer, blatant, arrant, thorough, unqualified.
OPPOSITES sparse, pleasant.

r

rankle verb (**rankles, rankling, rankled**) cause continuing annoyance or resentment.

ransack verb go hurriedly through a place stealing or searching for things.

ransom noun a sum of money demanded for the release of someone who is held captive. •verb cause someone to be released by paying a ransom.
▫ **hold someone to ransom 1** hold someone captive and demand payment for their release. **2** force someone to do something by threatening them.

rant verb speak in a loud, angry, and forceful way.

rap verb (**raps, rapping, rapped**) **1** hit a hard surface several times. **2** hit sharply. **3** informal criticize sharply. **4** say sharply or suddenly. •noun **1** a quick, sharp knock or blow. **2** a type of popular music in which words are spoken rhythmically over an instrumental backing.
▫ **take the rap** informal be punished or blamed for something.
■ **rapper** noun.

rapacious adjective very greedy.

rapacity /ruh-**pa**-si-ti/ noun greed.

rape[1] verb (**rapes, raping, raped**) **1** (of a man) force someone to have sex with him against their will. **2** spoil or destroy a place. •noun an act of raping.

rape[2] noun a plant with bright yellow flowers, grown for its oil-rich seed.

rapid adjective very fast. •noun (**rapids**) a part of a river where the water flows very fast.
■ **rapidity** noun **rapidly** adverb.

rapier noun a thin, light sword.

rapist noun a man who commits rape.

rapport /rap-**por**/ noun a close relationship in which people understand each other and communicate well.

rapprochement /ra-**prosh**-mon/ noun a renewal of friendly relations between two countries or groups.

rapscallion noun old use a rascal.

rapt adjective completely fascinated or absorbed.

raptor noun a bird of prey.

rapture noun **1** great pleasure or joy. **2** (**raptures**) the expression of great pleasure or enthusiasm.

rapturous adjective very pleased or enthusiastic.
■ **rapturously** adverb.

rare adjective (**rarer, rarest**) **1** not happening or found very often. **2** unusually good. **3** (of red meat) lightly cooked, so that the inside is still red.
■ **rarely** adverb.

rarebit = Welsh rarebit.

rarefied adjective **1** (of air) of lower pressure than usual; thin. **2** understood by only a limited group of people.

☑ -ref-, not -rif-: rarefied.

raring adjective (**raring to do**) informal very eager to do something.

rarity noun (plural **rarities**) **1** the state of being rare. **2** a rare thing.

rascal noun **1** a mischievous or cheeky person. **2** a dishonest man.
■ **rascally** adjective.

rash[1] adjective acting or done without careful consideration of the possible results.
■ **rashly** adverb.

rash[2] noun **1** an area of red spots or patches

---

r

ransom noun pay-off, payment, sum, price.

rant verb shout, sound off, hold forth, go on, fulminate, spout, bluster; informal mouth off.

rap verb hit, knock, strike, smack, bang; informal whack, thwack, bash, wallop.

rapid adjective quick, fast, swift, speedy, express, brisk, lightning, meteoric, whirlwind, sudden, instantaneous, instant, immediate.
OPPOSITES slow.

rare adjective **1** rare moments of privacy: infrequent, scarce, sparse, few and far between, occasional, limited, odd, isolated, unaccustomed. **2** rare stamps: unusual, recherché, uncommon, thin on the ground, like gold dust, unfamiliar, atypical. **3** a man of rare talent: exceptional, beyond compare, outstanding, unparalleled, peerless, matchless, unique, unrivalled.
OPPOSITES common, commonplace.

rarely adverb seldom, infrequently, hardly (ever), scarcely.
OPPOSITES often.

raring adjective eager, keen, enthusiastic, impatient, longing, desperate; informal dying, itching, gagging.

rarity noun **1** the rarity of earthquakes in the UK: infrequency, scarcity. **2** this book is a rarity: curiosity, oddity, collector's item, rare bird, wonder, nonpareil, one of a kind; Brit. informal one-off.

rash[1] noun **1** he broke out in a rash: spots, eruption, nettlerash, hives. **2** a rash of articles in the press: series, succession, spate, wave, flood, deluge, torrent, outbreak, epidemic, flurry.

rash[2] adjective reckless, impulsive, impetuous, hasty, foolhardy, incautious, precipitate, careless, heedless, thoughtless, imprudent, foolish.
OPPOSITES prudent.

on a person's skin. **2** a series of unpleasant things happening within a short time.

rasher noun a thin slice of bacon.

rasp noun **1** a harsh, grating noise. **2** a tool with a rough edge, used for smoothing surfaces. • verb **1** make a harsh, grating noise. **2** scrape roughly. **3** file with a rasp.

raspberry noun (plural **raspberries**) **1** a reddish-pink soft fruit. **2** informal a rude sound made with the tongue and lips.

Rasta noun informal a Rastafarian.

Rastafarian /rass-tuh-**fair**-i-uhn/ noun a member of a Jamaican religious movement which worships Haile Selassie, the former Emperor of Ethiopia.
■ **Rastafarianism** noun.

rat noun **1** a rodent resembling a large mouse. **2** informal an unpleasant person.
• verb (**rats, ratting, ratted**) (**rat on**) informal **1** inform on someone. **2** break an agreement or promise.
□ **the rat race** informal a way of life which is a fiercely competitive struggle for money or power.

ratatouille /ra-tuh-**too**-i/ noun a vegetable dish of stewed onions, courgettes, tomatoes, etc.

ratchet noun a device with a set of angled teeth in which a cog, tooth, or bar fits, allowing movement in one direction only.

rate¹ noun **1** a measure, quantity, or frequency measured against another. **2** the speed of something. **3** a fixed price paid or charged for something. **4** (**rates**) (in the UK) a tax on land and buildings paid to a local authority by a business. • verb (**rates, rating, rated**) **1** give something a standard or value according to a particular scale. **2** consider to be of a certain quality or

standard. **3** be worthy of; deserve. **4** informal have a high opinion of.
■ **rateable** (or **ratable**) adjective.

rate² verb old use scold angrily.

rather adverb **1** (**would rather**) would prefer. **2** to some extent; fairly. **3** used to correct something you have said or to be more precise. **4** instead of.

ratify verb (**ratifies, ratifying, ratified**) make a treaty, contract, etc. valid by signing or agreeing to it.
■ **ratification** noun.

rating noun **1** a classification based on quality, standard, or performance.
2 (**ratings**) the estimated audience size of a television or radio programme. **3** Brit. a sailor in the navy who does not hold a commission.

ratio noun (plural **ratios**) an indication of the relationship between two amounts, showing the number of times one contains the other.

ratiocination /ra-ti-oss-i-**nay**-sh'n/ noun formal the process of thinking in a logical way; reasoning.

ration noun **1** a fixed amount of food, fuel, etc., officially allowed to each person.
2 (**rations**) a regular allowance of food supplied to members of the armed forces.
• verb limit the supply of food, fuel, etc.

rational adjective **1** based on reason or logic. **2** able to think sensibly or logically.
■ **rationality** noun **rationally** adverb.

rationale /ra-shuh-**nahl**/ noun the reasons for doing or believing something.

rationalism noun the belief that opinions and actions should be based on reason rather than on religious belief or emotions.
■ **rationalist** noun.

THESAURUS

rate noun **1** *a fixed rate of interest:* percentage, ratio, proportion, scale, standard. **2** *an hourly rate of £30:* charge, price, cost, tariff, fare, fee, remuneration, payment. **3** *the rate of change:* speed, pace, tempo, velocity.
• verb **1** *they rated their ability at driving:* assess, evaluate, appraise, judge, weigh up, estimate, gauge. **2** *he rated only a brief mention:* merit, deserve, warrant, be worthy of.
□ **at any rate** in any case, anyhow, anyway, in any event, come what may.

rather adverb **1** *I'd rather you went:* sooner, by preference, by choice. **2** *the situation is rather complicated:* quite, a bit, a little, fairly, slightly, somewhat, relatively, comparatively; informal pretty. **3** *she seemed sad rather than angry:* more, as opposed to, instead of.

ratify verb confirm, approve, sanction,

endorse, agree to, accept, uphold, authorize, formalize, sign.
OPPOSITES reject.

rating noun grade, classification, ranking, position, category, assessment, evaluation, mark, score.

ratio noun proportion, relationship, rate, percentage, fraction, correlation.

ration noun **1** *a daily ration of chocolate:* allowance, allocation, quota, share, portion, helping. **2** *the garrison ran out of rations:* supplies, provisions, food, stores.
• verb *fuel supplies were rationed:* control, limit, restrict, conserve.

rational adjective logical, reasoned, sensible, reasonable, realistic, cogent, intelligent, shrewd, common-sense, sane, sound.
OPPOSITES irrational.

rationale noun reason(s), thinking, logic, grounds, sense.

rationalize or **rationalise** verb (rationalizes, rationalizing, rationalized) **1** try to find a logical reason for an action or attitude. **2** reorganize a business, system, etc. to make it more efficient. ■ rationalization noun.

rattan /ruh-**tan**/ noun the thin stems of a tropical palm, used to make furniture.

rattle verb (rattles, rattling, rattled) **1** make a rapid series of short, sharp sounds. **2** informal make someone nervous or irritated. **3** (**rattle something off**) say or do something quickly and easily. • noun **1** a rattling sound. **2** a toy that makes a rattling sound.

rattlesnake noun an American viper with horny rings on the tail that produce a rattling sound.

ratty adjective Brit. informal irritable.

raucous adjective sounding loud and harsh. ■ raucously adverb.

raunchy adjective (raunchier, raunchiest) informal sexually exciting or explicit.

ravage verb (ravages, ravaging, ravaged) cause great damage to. • noun (**ravages**) the destruction caused by something.

rave verb (raves, raving, raved) **1** talk angrily or without making sense. **2** speak or write about someone or something with great enthusiasm. • noun a large event with dancing to loud, fast electronic music.

raven noun a large black crow. • adjective (of hair) of a glossy black colour.

ravening adjective literary very fierce and hungry.

ravenous adjective very hungry. ■ ravenously adverb.

raver noun informal a person who has an exciting or wild social life.

ravine noun a deep, narrow gorge.

raving noun (ravings) wild talk that makes no sense. • adjective & adverb informal used for emphasis: raving mad.

ravioli /rav-i-**oh**-li/ plural noun small pasta cases containing minced meat, cheese, or vegetables.

ravish verb **1** dated rape. **2** (**ravishing**) very beautiful.

raw adjective **1** (of food) not cooked. **2** (of a material) in its natural state. **3** (of the skin) red and painful from being rubbed or scraped. **4** (of an emotion or quality) strong and undisguised. **5** (of the weather) cold and damp. **6** new to an activity and lacking experience. □ a raw deal unfair treatment. ■ rawness noun.

ray[1] noun **1** a narrow line or beam of light or radiation. **2** a trace of something good: a ray of hope.

ray[2] noun a broad flat fish with a long, thin tail.

rayon noun a synthetic fabric made from viscose.

raze verb (razes, razing, razed) completely destroy a building, town, etc.

razor noun an instrument used to shave hair.

razzle noun (**on the razzle**) Brit. informal out celebrating or enjoying yourself.

razzmatazz or **razzamatazz** noun informal noisy and exciting activity designed to attract attention.

RC abbreviation Roman Catholic.

re /ree, ray/ preposition with reference to.

reach verb **1** stretch out an arm to touch or

rattle verb **1** hailstones rattled against the window: clatter, patter, clink, clunk. **2** he rattled some coins: jingle, jangle, clink, tinkle. **3** the government was rattled by the strike: unnerve, disconcert, disturb, fluster, shake, perturb, throw; informal faze.

ravage verb lay waste, devastate, ruin, destroy, wreak havoc on.

rave verb **1** I raved and swore at them: rant, rage, lose your temper, storm, fume, shout; informal fly off the handle, hit the roof; Brit. informal go spare; N. Amer. informal flip your wig. **2** he raved about her talent: enthuse, go into raptures, wax lyrical, rhapsodize, sing the praises of, acclaim, eulogize, extol; N. Amer. informal ballyhoo.
OPPOSITES criticize.

raw adjective **1** raw carrot: uncooked, fresh, natural. **2** raw materials: unprocessed, untreated, unrefined, crude, natural. **3** raw recruits: inexperienced, new, untrained, untried, untested, callow, green. **4** his skin is raw: sore, red, painful, tender, chafed.
OPPOSITES cooked, processed, experienced, sound.

ray noun beam, shaft, stream, streak, flash, glimmer, flicker, spark.

reach verb **1** Travis reached out a hand: extend, stretch, outstretch, thrust, stick, hold. **2** she reached Helen's house before lunch: arrive at, get to, come to, end up at. **3** the temperature reached 94 degrees: attain, get to, rise to, fall to, sink to, drop to; informal hit. **4** the leaders reached an agreement: achieve, work out, draw up, put together, negotiate, thrash out, hammer out. **5** I have been trying to reach you all day: contact, get in touch with, get through to, get, speak to; informal get hold of.
• noun **1** Bobby moved out of her reach: grasp, range, stretch. **2** small goals within your reach: capabilities, capacity. **3** beyond the reach of the law: jurisdiction,

grasp something. **2** be able to touch something with an outstretched arm or leg. **3** arrive at; get as far as. **4** come to a particular level or point. **5** make contact with. •noun **1** the distance to which someone can stretch out their arm or arms to touch something. **2** a continuous stretch of river between two bends.

react verb **1** respond to something in a particular way. **2** interact and undergo a chemical or physical change.
■ **reactive** adjective.

reaction noun **1** something done or experienced as a result of an event. **2 (reactions)** a person's ability to respond to an event. **3** a bad response by the body to a drug or substance. **4** a process in which substances interact causing chemical or physical change. **5** a force exerted in opposition to an applied force.

reactionary adjective opposing political or social progress or reform. •noun (plural **reactionaries**) a person holding reactionary views.

reactivate verb (**reactivates, reactivating, reactivated**) bring something back into action.
■ **reactivation** noun.

reactor noun an apparatus in which material is made to undergo a controlled nuclear reaction that releases energy.

read verb (**reads, reading, read**)
1 understand the meaning of written or printed words or symbols. **2** speak written or printed words aloud. **3** have a particular wording. **4** understand the nature or meaning of. **5** (**read something into**) think that something has a meaning that it may not possess. **6** Brit. study a subject at a university. **7** (of an instrument) show a measurement or figure. •noun informal a book that is interesting to read.
□ **take something as read** assume something.
■ **readable** adjective **reader** noun.

readership noun the readers of a publication regarded as a group.

readily adverb **1** willingly. **2** easily.

reading noun **1** the action of reading. **2** something that is read. **3** a figure recorded on a measuring instrument.

readjust verb **1** adjust again. **2** adapt to a changed situation.
■ **readjustment** noun.

ready adjective (**readier, readiest**) **1** prepared for an activity or situation. **2** made available for immediate use. **3** easily available or obtained. **4** (**ready to do**) willing or eager to do. **5** immediate or quick. •noun (**readies** or **the ready**) Brit. informal available money. •verb (**readies, readying, readied**) prepare.
■ **readiness** noun.

THESAURUS

authority, influence, power, scope, range, compass, ambit.

react verb respond, act in response, reply, answer, behave.

reaction noun **1** *his reaction bewildered her:* response, answer, reply, rejoinder, retort, riposte; informal comeback. **2** *a reaction against modernism:* backlash, counteraction.

reactionary adjective *a reactionary policy:* right-wing, conservative, traditionalist, conventional.
OPPOSITES radical, progressive.
•noun *an extreme reactionary:* right-winger, conservative, traditionalist.
OPPOSITES radical.

read verb **1** *he was reading the newspaper:* peruse, study, scrutinize, look through, pore over, run your eye over, cast an eye over, leaf through, scan. **2** *he read the letter to me:* read out/aloud, recite, declaim. **3** *I can't read my writing:* understand, make out, make sense of, interpret, decipher.

readily adverb **1** *Durkin readily offered to drive:* willingly, unhesitatingly, gladly, happily, eagerly. **2** *the island is readily accessible:* easily, without difficulty.
OPPOSITES reluctantly, with difficulty.

readiness noun **1** *their readiness to accept change:* willingness, eagerness, keenness, enthusiasm. **2** *a state of readiness:* preparedness.
□ **in readiness (at the) ready,** available, on hand, accessible, handy.

reading noun **1** *a cursory reading of the page:* perusal, study, scanning, browse, look, glance, leaf. **2** *a man of wide reading:* learning, scholarship, education, erudition. **3** *a poetry reading:* recital, recitation, performance. **4** *a Bible reading:* lesson, passage, excerpt. **5** *my reading of the situation:* interpretation, understanding, explanation, analysis, construction.

ready adjective **1** *are you ready?* prepared, all set, organized, primed; informal fit, psyched up, geared up. **2** *everything is ready:* completed, finished, prepared, organized, done, arranged, fixed. **3** *he's always ready to help:* willing, prepared, pleased, inclined, disposed, eager, keen, happy, glad; informal game. **4** *a ready supply of food:* (easily) available, accessible, handy, close/near at hand, to/on hand, convenient, within reach, near, at your fingertips. **5** *a ready answer:* prompt, quick, swift, speedy, fast, immediate, unhesitating, clever, sharp, astute, shrewd, keen, perceptive, discerning.

reagent /ri-ay-juhnt/ noun a substance that produces a chemical reaction, used to detect the presence of another substance.

real adjective **1** actually existing or happening. **2** not artificial; genuine. **3** worthy of the description; proper. • adverb N. Amer. informal really; very. ▫ **real estate** N. Amer. land or housing. **real tennis** the original form of tennis, played with a solid ball on an enclosed court.

realign verb change something to a different position or state. ■ **realignment** noun.

realism noun **1** the acceptance of a situation as it is. **2** the presentation of things in a way that is accurate and true to life. ■ **realist** noun.

realistic adjective **1** having a sensible and practical idea of what can be achieved. **2** showing things in a way that is accurate and true to life. ■ **realistically** adverb.

reality noun (plural **realities**) **1** the state of things as they actually exist. **2** a thing that is real. **3** the state of being real.

▫ **reality TV** television programmes based on real people or situations, presented as entertainment.

realize or **realise** verb (**realizes, realizing, realized**) **1** become fully aware of a fact. **2** achieve or fulfil a wish or plan. **3** be sold for a particular amount. **4** convert property, shares, etc. into money by selling them. ■ **realization** noun.

really adverb **1** in actual fact. **2** very; thoroughly. • exclamation expressing interest, surprise, doubt, etc.

realm noun **1** chiefly literary a kingdom. **2** an area of activity or interest.

ream noun **1** 500 sheets of paper. **2** (**reams**) a large quantity.

reap verb **1** gather in a crop or harvest. **2** receive a reward or benefit as a result of your actions.

reaper noun a person or machine that harvests a crop. ▫ **the Grim Reaper** death, shown as a cloaked skeleton holding a scythe.

rear[1] noun the back part of something.

THESAURUS

• verb prepare, organize, gear up; informal psych up.

real adjective **1** *based on real events:* actual, true, non-fictional, factual, historical, material, physical, tangible, concrete. **2** *real gold:* genuine, authentic, bona fide; informal pukka, kosher. **3** *tears of real grief:* sincere, genuine, true, unfeigned, heartfelt. **4** *a real man:* proper, true; informal regular. **5** *you're a real idiot:* complete, utter, thorough, absolute, total, prize, perfect; Brit. informal right, proper.
OPPOSITES imaginary, imitation.

realism noun **1** *optimism tinged with realism:* pragmatism, practicality, common sense, level-headedness. **2** *a degree of realism:* authenticity, accuracy, fidelity, verisimilitude, truthfulness.
OPPOSITES fancy, inauthenticity.

realistic adjective **1** *you've got to be realistic:* practical, pragmatic, matter-of-fact, down-to-earth, sensible, commonsensical, rational, level-headed; informal no-nonsense. **2** *a realistic aim:* achievable, attainable, feasible, practicable, reasonable, sensible, workable; informal doable. **3** *a realistic portrayal of war:* authentic, accurate, true to life, lifelike, truthful, faithful, natural, naturalistic.
OPPOSITES idealistic, impracticable, inauthentic.

reality noun **1** *distinguishing fantasy from reality:* the real world, real life, actuality, truth. **2** *the harsh realities of life:* fact, actuality, truth. **3** *the reality of the detail:* authenticity, verisimilitude, fidelity,

truthfulness, accuracy.
OPPOSITES fantasy, inaccuracy.

realization noun **1** *a growing realization of the danger:* awareness, understanding, comprehension, consciousness, appreciation, recognition, discernment. **2** *the realization of our dreams:* fulfilment, achievement, accomplishment, attainment.

realize verb **1** *he suddenly realized what she meant:* register, perceive, understand, grasp, comprehend, see, recognize; informal tumble to; Brit. informal twig. **2** *they realized their dream:* fulfil, achieve, accomplish, make happen, bring to fruition, bring about/off. **3** *the company realized significant profits:* make, clear, gain, earn, return, produce. **4** *the goods realized £30:* be sold for, fetch, go for, make, net.

really adverb **1** *he is really very wealthy:* in (actual) fact, actually, in reality, in truth. **2** *he really likes her:* genuinely, truly, certainly, honestly, undoubtedly, unquestionably.

realm noun **1** *peace in the realm:* kingdom, country, land, dominion, nation. **2** *the realm of academia:* domain, sphere, area, field, world, province, territory.

reap verb **1** *the corn was reaped:* harvest, cut, pick, gather, garner. **2** *reaping the benefits:* receive, obtain, get, derive, acquire, secure, realize.

rear[1] noun **1** *the rear of the building:* back (part), hind part; Nautical stern. **2** *the rear of the queue:* end, tail (end), back (end).
OPPOSITES front, bow, head.
• adjective *the rear bumper:* back, end,

r

•**adjective** at the back.
□ **rear admiral** the naval rank above commodore.
■ **rearmost** adjective **rearward** adjective & adverb **rearwards** adverb.

rear² verb **1** bring up offspring. **2** breed animals. **3** (of an animal) raise itself upright on its hind legs. **4** extend to a great height.

rearguard noun a group of soldiers protecting the rear of the main force.

rearm verb provide with or obtain a new supply of weapons.
■ **rearmament** noun.

rearrange verb (**rearranges, rearranging, rearranged**) arrange again in a different way.
■ **rearrangement** noun.

reason noun **1** a cause or explanation. **2** good or obvious cause to do something. **3** the power to think and draw conclusions logically. **4** (**your reason**) your sanity. **5** what is right, practical, or possible. •**verb 1** think and draw conclusions logically.

2 (**reason with**) persuade someone by using logical arguments.
□ **stand to reason** be logical.

reasonable adjective **1** fair and sensible. **2** appropriate in a particular situation. **3** fairly good. **4** not too expensive.
■ **reasonably** adverb.

reassure verb (**reassures, reassuring, reassured**) make someone feel less worried or afraid.
■ **reassurance** noun.

rebarbative adjective unpleasant.

rebate /ree-bayt/ noun **1** a partial refund to someone who has paid too much for tax, rent, etc. **2** a discount on a sum that is due.

rebel verb /ri-bel/ (**rebels, rebelling, rebelled**) **1** refuse to obey the government or ruler. **2** oppose authority, or refuse to behave conventionally. •**noun** /reb-uhl/ a person who rebels.

rebellion noun **1** an act of rebelling. **2** opposition to authority or control.

rebellious adjective choosing to rebel.
■ **rebelliously** adverb.

rebirth noun a return to life or activity.

THESAURUS

rearmost, hind, last.
OPPOSITES front.

rear² verb **1** *I was reared in Newcastle:* **bring up**, care for, look after, nurture; N. Amer. raise. **2** *he reared cattle:* **breed**, raise, keep. **3** *laboratory-reared plants:* **grow**, cultivate. **4** *houses reared up on either side:* **rise**, tower, soar, loom.

reason noun **1** *the main reason for his decision:* **cause**, ground(s), basis, rationale, motive, explanation, justification, defence, vindication, excuse. **2** *postmodern voices railing against reason:* **rationality**, logic, cognition. **3** *he was losing his reason:* **sanity**, mind, mental faculties, senses, wits; informal marbles.
•**verb** *Scott reasoned that Annabel might be ill:* **calculate**, conclude, reckon, think, judge, deduce, infer, surmise; informal figure.
□ **reason something out** **work out**, think through, make sense of, get to the bottom of, puzzle out; informal figure out. **reason with** **talk round**, bring round, persuade, prevail on, convince.

reasonable adjective **1** *a reasonable explanation:* **sensible**, rational, logical, fair, just, equitable, intelligent, wise, level-headed, practical, realistic, sound, valid, commonsensical, tenable, plausible, credible, believable. **2** *take all reasonable precautions:* **practicable**, sensible, within reason, appropriate, suitable. **3** *the car was in reasonable condition:* **fairly good**, acceptable, satisfactory, average, adequate, fair, tolerable, passable; informal OK. **4** *a reasonable price:* **inexpensive**, affordable, moderate, low, cheap, bargain.

reassure verb put someone's mind at rest, encourage, hearten, buoy up, cheer up, comfort, soothe.
OPPOSITES alarm.

rebate noun partial refund, partial repayment, discount, deduction, reduction.

rebel noun **1** *the rebels took control of the capital:* **revolutionary**, insurgent, insurrectionist, mutineer, guerrilla, terrorist, freedom fighter. **2** *the concept of the artist as a rebel:* **nonconformist**, dissenter, dissident, maverick.
OPPOSITES loyalist, conformist.
•**verb** *the citizens rebelled:* **revolt**, mutiny, riot, rise up, take up arms.
OPPOSITES comply.
•**adjective 1** *rebel troops:* **rebellious**, insurgent, revolutionary, mutinous. **2** *rebel MPs:* **defiant**, disobedient, insubordinate, subversive, rebellious, nonconformist, maverick.
OPPOSITES loyal, compliant.
□ **rebel against** **defy**, disobey, kick against, challenge, oppose, resist.

rebellion noun **1** *troops suppressed the rebellion:* **revolt**, uprising, insurrection, mutiny, revolution, insurgence. **2** *an act of rebellion:* **defiance**, disobedience, insubordination, subversion, resistance.
OPPOSITES compliance.

rebellious adjective **1** *rebellious troops:* **rebel**, insurgent, mutinous, revolutionary. **2** *a rebellious adolescent:* **defiant**, disobedient, insubordinate, unruly, mutinous, obstreperous, recalcitrant,

r

reborn adjective brought back to life or activity.

rebound verb /ri-**bownd**/ **1** bounce back after hitting a hard surface. **2** increase again. **3** (**rebound on**) have an unexpected and unpleasant effect on. • noun /**ree**-bownd/ a ball or shot that rebounds. □ **on the rebound** while still upset after the ending of a romantic relationship.

rebuff verb reject in an abrupt or unkind way. • noun an abrupt or unkind rejection.

rebuke verb (**rebukes, rebuking, rebuked**) sharply criticize or tell off. • noun a sharp criticism.

rebus noun (plural **rebuses**) a puzzle in which words are represented by combinations of pictures and letters.

rebut verb (**rebuts, rebutting, rebutted**) claim or prove that something is false. ■ **rebuttal** noun.

recalcitrant /ri-**kal**-si-truhnt/ adjective unwilling to cooperate; disobedient. ■ **recalcitrance** noun.

recall verb **1** remember. **2** make someone think of; bring to mind. **3** officially order someone to return. **4** (of a manufacturer) ask for faulty products to be returned. • noun **1** the action of remembering. **2** an official order for someone to return.

recant verb withdraw a former opinion or belief.

recap verb (**recaps, recapping, recapped**) recapitulate.

recapitulate verb (**recapitulates, recapitulating, recapitulated**) give a summary of. ■ **recapitulation** noun.

recapture verb (**recaptures, recapturing, recaptured**) **1** capture a person or animal that has escaped. **2** recover something taken or lost. **3** bring back or experience again a past time or feeling. • noun an act of recapturing.

recast verb (**recasts, recasting, recast**) present something in a different form.

recce /**rek**-ki/ noun Brit. informal a reconnaissance.

recede verb (**recedes, receding, receded**) **1** move back or further away. **2** gradually become weaker or smaller. **3** (**receding**) (of part of the face) sloping backwards.

receipt noun **1** a written statement confirming that something has been paid for or received. **2** the action of receiving something. **3** (**receipts**) the amount of money received over a period by a business.

receive verb (**receives, receiving, received**) **1** be given or paid. **2** accept something sent or offered. **3** experience or meet with. **4** form an idea or impression from an experience. **5** entertain someone as a guest. **6** detect or pick up broadcast signals. **7** (**received**) widely accepted as true. □ **received pronunciation** the standard form

intractable; Brit. informal bolshie.
OPPOSITES loyal, compliant.

rebound verb **1** *the ball rebounded:* bounce (back), spring back, ricochet, boomerang. **2** *Thomas's tactics rebounded on him:* backfire, boomerang.

rebuff verb *his offer was rebuffed:* reject, turn down, spurn, refuse, decline, snub, slight, dismiss, brush off.
OPPOSITES accept.
• noun *her fear of a rebuff:* rejection, snub, slight, refusal, spurning; informal brush-off, kick in the teeth, slap in the face.

rebuke verb *she never rebuked him:* reprimand, reproach, scold, admonish, reprove, chastise, upbraid, berate, take to task; informal tell off; Brit. informal tick off; N. Amer. informal chew out.
OPPOSITES praise.
• noun *a severe rebuke:* reprimand, reproach, scolding, admonition; informal telling-off; Brit. informal ticking-off.
OPPOSITES praise.

recall verb **1** *he recalled his student days:* remember, recollect, call to mind, think back on/to, reminisce about. **2** *their exploits recall the days of chivalry:* remind someone of, bring to mind, call up, conjure up, evoke. **3** *the ambassador was recalled:* call back, order home, withdraw.
OPPOSITES forget.
• noun **1** *their recall of dreams:* recollection, remembrance, memory. **2** *the recall of the ambassador:* calling back, ordering home, withdrawal.

recede verb **1** *the waters receded:* retreat, go back/down/away, withdraw, ebb, subside, abate, return, retire. **2** *fears of violence have receded:* diminish, lessen, dwindle, fade, abate, subside.
OPPOSITES advance, grow.

receipt noun **1** *the receipt of a letter:* receiving, getting, obtaining, gaining. **2** *make sure you get a receipt:* proof of purchase, sales ticket, till receipt, acknowledgement.

receive verb **1** *Tony received an award:* be given, be presented with, be awarded, be sent, be told, hear, collect, get, obtain, gain, acquire, be paid. **2** *he received her suggestion with a lack of interest:* hear, listen to, respond to, react to. **3** *she received an injury:* experience, sustain, undergo, meet with, suffer, bear.
OPPOSITES give, send, inflict.

r

of British English pronunciation, based on educated speech in southern England.

☑ remember, the rule is *i* before *e* except after *c*: rece*i*ve.

receiver noun **1** a radio or television apparatus that converts broadcast signals into sound or images. **2** the part of a telephone that converts electrical signals into sounds. **3** (also **official receiver**) a person appointed to manage the financial affairs of a bankrupt business.
■ **receivership** noun.

recent adjective having happened or been done shortly before the present.
■ **recently** adverb.

receptacle noun an object used to contain something.

reception noun **1** the action of receiving. **2** the way in which people react to something. **3** a formal social occasion held to welcome someone or celebrate an event. **4** the area in a hotel, office, etc. where visitors are greeted. **5** the quality with which broadcast signals are received.

receptionist noun a person who greets and deals with visitors to an office, hotel, etc.

receptive adjective **1** able or willing to receive something. **2** willing to consider new ideas.
■ **receptivity** noun.

receptor noun a nerve ending in the body that responds to a stimulus such as light.

recess noun **1** a small space set back in a wall or in a surface. **2** a break between sessions of a parliament, law court, etc. **3** (**recesses**) remote or hidden places. •verb fit something so that it is set back into a surface.

recession noun a period during which trade and industrial activity in a country are reduced.

recessive adjective (of a gene) appearing in offspring only if a contrary gene is not also inherited.

recharge verb (**recharges, recharging, recharged**) charge a battery or device again.
■ **rechargeable** adjective **recharger** noun.

recherché /ruh-**shair**-shay/ adjective unusual and not easily understood.

recidivist /ri-**sid**-i-vist/ noun a person who constantly commits crimes.
■ **recidivism** noun.

recipe noun **1** a list of ingredients and instructions for preparing a dish. **2** something likely to lead to a particular outcome: *a recipe for disaster.*

recipient noun a person who receives something.

reciprocal /ri-**sip**-ruh-k'l/ adjective **1** given or done in return. **2** affecting two parties equally.
■ **reciprocally** adverb.

reciprocate verb (**reciprocates, reciprocating, reciprocated**) respond to an action or emotion with a similar one.

reciprocity /re-si-**pross**-i-ti/ noun a situation in which two parties provide the same help to each other.

recital noun **1** the performance of a programme of music by a soloist or small group. **2** a long account of a series of facts or events.

recite verb (**recites, reciting, recited**) **1** repeat a passage aloud from memory. **2** state facts, events, etc. in order.
■ **recitation** noun.

reckless adjective without thought or care for the results of an action.
■ **recklessly** adverb **recklessness** noun.

r

THESAURUS

recent adjective **new**, the latest, current, fresh, modern, late, contemporary, up to date, up to the minute.
OPPOSITES old.

recently adverb **not long ago**, a little while back, just now, newly, freshly, of late, lately, latterly.

reception noun **1** *a chilly reception:* **response**, reaction, treatment, welcome. **2** *a wedding reception:* **party**, function, social occasion, celebration, get-together, gathering, soirée; N. Amer. levee; informal do.

recess noun **1** *two recesses fitted with bookshelves:* **alcove**, bay, niche, nook, corner. **2** *the Christmas recess:* **break**, adjournment, interlude, interval, rest, holiday, vacation.

recession noun **downturn**, depression,

slump, slowdown.
OPPOSITES boom.

recipe noun *a recipe for success:* **formula**, prescription, blueprint.

recital noun **1** *a piano recital:* **performance**, concert, rendering, recitation, reading. **2** *her recital of Adam's failures:* **report**, account, listing, catalogue, litany.

recite verb **1** *he began to recite the Koran:* **quote**, say, speak, read aloud, declaim, deliver, render. **2** *Sir John recited the facts:* **recount**, list, detail, reel off, relate, enumerate.

reckless adjective **rash**, careless, devil-may-care, thoughtless, heedless, precipitate, impetuous, impulsive, irresponsible, foolhardy.
OPPOSITES cautious.

reckon verb **1** have an opinion about something; think. **2** (**reckon on**) rely on or expect. **3** calculate. **4** (**reckon with** or **without**) take (or fail to take) something into account.
□ **to be reckoned with** to be treated as important.

reckoning noun **1** the action of calculating or estimating something. **2** punishment for past actions.

reclaim verb **1** get possession of something again. **2** make land usable.
■ **reclamation** noun.

recline verb (**reclines, reclining, reclined**) lie back in a relaxed position.

recluse /ri-klooss/ noun a person who avoids other people and lives alone.
■ **reclusive** adjective.

recognition noun **1** the action of recognizing. **2** appreciation or acknowledgement.

recognize or **recognise** verb (**recognizes, recognizing, recognized**) **1** know someone or something from having come across them before. **2** accept something as genuine, legal, or valid. **3** show official appreciation of.
■ **recognizable** adjective.

recoil verb **1** suddenly move back in fear, horror, or disgust. **2** (of a gun) suddenly move backwards as a reaction on being fired. **3** (**recoil on**) have an unpleasant effect on. • noun the action of recoiling.

recollect verb remember.
■ **recollection** noun.

recommend verb **1** say that someone or something is suitable for a particular purpose or role. **2** make something seem appealing or desirable.
■ **recommendation** noun.

☑ one *c* and two *m*s: recommend.

recompense /rek-uhm-penss/ verb (**recompenses, recompensing, recompensed**) **1** compensate someone for loss or harm suffered. **2** pay or reward someone for effort or work. • noun compensation or reward.

reconcile verb (**reconciles, reconciling, reconciled**) **1** make two people or groups friendly again. **2** find a satisfactory way of dealing with opposing facts, ideas, etc. **3** (**reconcile someone to**) make someone accept something unwelcome.

reconciliation noun **1** the end of a disagreement and the return to friendly relations. **2** the action of reconciling opposing ideas, facts, etc.

recondite /rek-uhn-dyt/ adjective not known about or understood by many people.

reckon verb **1** *the cost was reckoned at £60:* calculate, compute, work out, figure, count (up), add up, total; Brit. tot up. **2** *Anselm reckoned Hugh among his friends:* include, count, regard as, look on as. **3** *it was reckoned a failure:* regard as, consider, judge, think of as, deem, rate, gauge, count.
□ **reckon on/with** **take into account,** take into consideration, bargain for/on, anticipate, foresee, be prepared for, consider.

reckoning noun calculation, estimation, computation, working out, addition, count.

reclaim verb **1** *expenses can be reclaimed:* get back, claim back, recover, retrieve, recoup. **2** *Henrietta had reclaimed him from a life of vice:* save, rescue, redeem, salvage.

recline verb lie (down/back), lean back, relax, loll, lounge, sprawl, stretch out.

recognition noun **1** *there was no sign of recognition on his face:* identification, recollection, remembrance. **2** *his recognition of his lack of experience:* acknowledgement, acceptance, admission, confession. **3** *you deserve recognition for your work:* appreciation, gratitude, thanks, congratulations, credit, commendation, acclaim, acknowledgement.

recognize verb **1** *Hannah recognized him at once:* identify, place, know, put a name to, remember, recall, recollect; Scottish & N. English ken. **2** *they recognized Alan's ability:* acknowledge, accept, admit, concede, confess, realize. **3** *the Trust recognized their hard work:* pay tribute to, appreciate, be grateful for, acclaim, commend.

recollect verb remember, recall, call to mind, think of, think back to, reminisce about.
OPPOSITES forget.

recollection noun memory, recall, remembrance, impression, reminiscence.

recommend verb **1** *his former employer recommended him:* advocate, endorse, commend, suggest, put forward, propose, nominate, put up, speak favourably of, put in a good word for, vouch for; informal plug. **2** *the committee recommended a cautious approach:* advise, counsel, urge, exhort, enjoin, prescribe, argue for, back, support.
OPPOSITES advise against.

recommendation noun **1** *the adviser's recommendations:* advice, counsel, guidance, suggestion, proposal. **2** *a personal recommendation:* commendation, endorsement, good word, testimonial, tip; informal plug.

r

recondition verb Brit. bring back to a good condition; renovate.

reconnaissance /ri-**kon**-ni-suhnss/ **noun** military observation of an area to gain information.

reconnoitre /rek-uh-**noy**-ter/ (US spelling **reconnoiter**) verb (**reconnoitres, reconnoitring, reconnoitred**) make a military observation of an area.

reconsider verb (**reconsiders, reconsidering, reconsidered**) consider again, with the possibility of changing a decision.
■ **reconsideration** noun.

reconstitute verb (**reconstitutes, reconstituting, reconstituted**) 1 change the form of an organization. 2 restore dried food to its original state by adding water.
■ **reconstitution** noun.

reconstruct verb 1 construct again. 2 show how a past event happened by using the evidence that has been gathered.
■ **reconstruction** noun.

record noun /**rek**-ord/ 1 a permanent account of something, kept for evidence or information. 2 the previous behaviour or performance of a person or thing. 3 (also **criminal record**) a list of a person's previous criminal convictions. 4 the best performance of its kind that has been officially recognized. 5 a thin plastic disc carrying recorded sound in grooves on each surface. •verb /ri-**kord**/ 1 make a record of. 2 convert sound or vision into a permanent form so that it can be reproduced later.

□ **off the record** not made as an official statement. **record player** a device for playing records.
■ **recording** noun.

recorder noun 1 a device for recording sound, pictures, etc. 2 a person who keeps records. 3 a musical instrument which you play by blowing through a mouthpiece and putting your fingers over holes.

recount[1] verb describe something to someone.

recount[2] verb count again. •noun an act of counting something again.

recoup verb recover an amount of money that has been lost or spent.

recourse noun 1 a source of help in a difficult situation. 2 (**recourse to**) the use of a particular source of help.

recover verb (**recovers, recovering, recovered**) 1 return to a normal state of health or strength. 2 regain possession or control of. 3 regain an amount of money that has been spent or lent.
■ **recoverable** adjective.

recovery noun (plural **recoveries**) the action or an act of recovering.

recreate verb (**recreates, recreating, recreated**) make or do again.

recreation[1] /rek-ri-**ay**-sh'n/ **noun** enjoyable leisure activity.
■ **recreational** adjective.

recreation[2] /ree-kri-**ay**-sh'n/ **noun** the action of recreating something.

recrimination noun an accusation made in

THESAURUS

reconsider verb rethink, review, revise, re-evaluate, reassess, have second thoughts, change your mind.

reconstruct verb 1 *the building had to be reconstructed:* rebuild, recreate, remake, restore, reassemble. 2 *reconstructing events:* recreate, piece together, re-enact.

record noun 1 *written records:* account, document, data, file, dossier, evidence, report, annals, archive, chronicle, minutes, transactions, proceedings, transcript, certificate, deed, register, log. 2 *listening to records:* album, vinyl, LP, single. 3 *a good attendance record:* previous conduct, previous performance, history, reputation. 4 *a new British record:* best performance, highest achievement, best time, fastest time.
•verb 1 *the doctor recorded her blood pressure:* write down, take down, note, jot down, put down on paper, document, enter, minute, register, log. 2 *the thermometer recorded a high temperature:* indicate, register, show, display. 3 *the recital was recorded live:* capture on film/tape/disk, film, photograph, tape,

tape-record, video-record, videotape.

recount verb tell, relate, narrate, describe, report, relay, convey, communicate, impart.

recover verb 1 *he's recovering from a heart attack:* get better, improve, recuperate, convalesce, be on the mend, respond to treatment, heal, bounce back. 2 *later, shares recovered:* rally, improve, pick up, rebound, bounce back. 3 *the stolen material has been recovered:* retrieve, regain, get back, recoup, reclaim, repossess. 4 *gold coins recovered from a wreck:* salvage, save, rescue, retrieve.
OPPOSITES deteriorate, lose.

recovery noun 1 *her recovery may be slow:* improvement, recuperation, convalescence. 2 *the recovery of stolen goods:* retrieval, repossession, reclamation.
OPPOSITES relapse, loss.

recreation noun 1 *she cycles for recreation:* pleasure, leisure, relaxation, fun, enjoyment, entertainment, amusement. 2 *his favourite recreations:* pastime, hobby, leisure activity.
OPPOSITES work.

r

response to one from someone else.

recrudescence /ree-kroo-dess-'nss/ **noun** formal a recurrence.

recruit verb take on someone to serve in the armed forces or work for an organization. • noun a newly recruited person. ■ **recruitment** noun.

rectal adjective relating to or affecting the rectum.

rectangle noun a flat shape with four right angles and four straight sides, two of which are longer than the others. ■ **rectangular** adjective.

rectify verb (**rectifies, rectifying, rectified**) **1** put right; correct. **2** convert alternating current to direct current. ■ **rectification** noun **rectifier** noun.

rectilinear adjective having or moving in a straight line or lines.

rectitude noun morally correct behaviour.

recto noun (plural **rectos**) a right-hand page of an open book, or the front of a loose document.

rector noun **1** a Christian priest in charge of a parish. **2** the head of certain universities, colleges, and schools.

rectory noun (plural **rectories**) the house of a rector.

rectum noun the final section of the large intestine, ending at the anus.

recumbent adjective lying down.

recuperate verb (**recuperates, recuperating, recuperated**) **1** recover from illness or tiredness. **2** get back something that has been lost or spent. ■ **recuperation** noun.

recur verb (**recurs, recurring, recurred**) happen again or repeatedly. ■ **recurrence** noun.

recurrent adjective happening often or repeatedly.

recycle verb (**recycles, recycling, recycled**) **1** convert waste into a form in which it can be reused. **2** use something again. ■ **recyclable** adjective.

red adjective (**redder, reddest**) **1** of the colour of blood or fire. **2** (of hair or fur) of a reddish-brown colour. • noun **1** red colour. **2** informal, chiefly disapproving a communist or socialist. ◻ in the red having spent more than is in your bank account. **red blood cell** a blood cell which contains haemoglobin and carries oxygen to the tissues. **red-blooded** (of a man) energetic and healthy. **red-brick** (of a British university) founded in the late 19th or early 20th century. **red card** (in soccer) a red card shown by the referee to a player being sent off the field. **red-handed** in the act of doing something wrong. **red herring** a thing that takes people's attention away from something important. **red-hot 1** so hot that it glows red. **2** very exciting. **Red Indian** dated, often offensive an American Indian. **red-letter day** an important or memorable day. **red-light district** an area with many brothels, strip clubs, etc. **red pepper** a ripe sweet pepper. **red tape** complicated official rules which cause irritation because they take up your time. **see red** informal suddenly become very angry. ■ **reddish** adjective.

redcurrant noun a small edible red berry.

redden verb make or become red.

redeem verb **1** make up for the faults of. **2** save someone from sin or evil. **3** fulfil a promise. **4** pay a debt. **5** exchange a coupon for goods or money. **6** regain possession of something in exchange for payment.

Redeemer noun (**the Redeemer**) Jesus.

redemption noun the action of redeeming.

THESAURUS

recruit verb **1** *more soldiers were recruited:* enlist, call up, conscript; US draft. **2** *the king recruited an army:* muster, form, raise, mobilize. **3** *the company is recruiting staff:* hire, employ, take on, enrol, sign up, engage.
OPPOSITES demobilize, disband, dismiss.
• noun **1** *new recruits were enlisted:* conscript; US draftee; N. Amer. informal yardbird. **2** *top-quality recruits:* new member, newcomer, initiate, joiner, beginner, novice.

recur verb happen again, reoccur, repeat (itself), come back, return, reappear.

recycle verb reuse, reprocess, reclaim, recover, salvage.

red adjective **1** *a red dress:* scarlet, vermilion, ruby, cherry, cerise, cardinal, carmine, crimson, maroon, magenta, burgundy, claret. **2** *he was red in the face:* flushed, blushing, pink, rosy, florid, ruddy. **3** *red hair:* auburn, Titian, chestnut, carroty, ginger.

redeem verb **1** *redeeming sinners:* save, deliver from sin, absolve. **2** *Billy redeemed his drums from the pawnbrokers:* retrieve, regain, recover, get back, reclaim, repossess, buy back. **3** *this voucher can be redeemed at any branch:* exchange, convert, trade in, cash in.
OPPOSITES damn, pawn, buy.

redemption noun **1** *God's redemption of his people:* saving, freeing from sin, absolution. **2** *the redemption of their possessions:* retrieval, recovery, reclamation, repossession, return. **3** *the redemption of vouchers:* exchange, conversion, trade-in, cashing in.

r

redeploy verb move troops, resources, etc. to a new place or task.
∎ **redeployment** noun.

redhead noun a person with red hair.

redneck noun US informal a conservative working-class white person.

redolent /red-uh-luhnt/ adjective (**redolent of** or **with**) **1** making you think of a particular thing. **2** literary smelling of.
∎ **redolence** noun.

redouble verb (**redoubles, redoubling, redoubled**) make or become greater or stronger.

redoubt noun a small or temporary structure from which soldiers can defend a place under attack.

redoubtable adjective worthy of respect or fear; formidable.

redound verb (**redound to**) formal be to someone's credit.

redress /ri-dress/ verb put right something that is unfair or wrong. •**noun** payment or action to make amends for a wrong.

redskin noun dated or offensive an American Indian.

reduce verb (**reduces, reducing, reduced**) **1** make or become less. **2** (**reduce something to**) change something to a simpler form. **3** (**reduce someone to**) bring someone to a particular state or condition. **4** boil a liquid so that it becomes thicker.
□ **reduced circumstances** a state in which you have become poorer than you were before.
∎ **reducible** adjective.

reduction noun **1** the action of reducing. **2** the amount by which something is reduced.

reductive adjective presenting something in an oversimplified form.

redundant adjective **1** Brit. unemployed because your job is no longer needed. **2** no longer needed or useful.
∎ **redundancy** noun (plural **redundancies**).

redwood noun a giant coniferous tree with reddish wood.

reed noun **1** a tall, slender plant that grows in water or on marshy ground. **2** a piece of thin cane or metal in musical instruments such as the clarinet, which vibrates when air is blown over it and produces sound.

reedy adjective **1** (of a sound or voice) high and thin in tone. **2** full of reeds.

reef noun **1** a ridge of jagged rock or coral just above or below the surface of the sea. **2** each of several strips across a sail that can be taken in when the wind is strong.
•**verb** make a sail smaller by taking in a reef.
□ **reef knot** a type of secure knot.

reefer noun informal a cannabis cigarette.

reefer jacket noun a thick close-fitting double-breasted jacket.

reek verb have a very unpleasant smell.
•**noun** a very unpleasant smell.

reel noun **1** a cylinder on which film, thread, etc. can be wound. **2** a lively Scottish or Irish folk dance. •**verb 1** (**reel something in**) bring something towards you by turning a reel. **2** (**reel something off**) recite something quickly and with ease. **3** stagger. **4** feel giddy, shocked, or bewildered.

re-entry noun (plural **re-entries**) **1** the action of entering again. **2** the return of a spacecraft or missile into the earth's atmosphere.

refectory noun (plural **refectories**) a room used for meals in an educational or religious institution.

refer verb (**refers, referring, referred**) (**refer**

THESAURUS

redress verb **1** *we redressed the problem:* rectify, correct, right, compensate for, amend, remedy, make good. **2** *we aim to redress the balance:* even up, regulate, equalize.
•**noun** *your best hope of redress:* compensation, reparation, restitution, recompense, repayment, amends.

reduce verb **1** *the aim to reduce pollution:* lessen, make smaller, lower, bring down, decrease, diminish, minimize, shrink, narrow, contract, shorten; informal chop. **2** *he reduced her to tears:* bring to, drive to. OPPOSITES increase.

reduction noun **1** *a reduction in pollution:* lessening, lowering, decrease, diminution. **2** *a reduction in staff:* cut, cutback, axing, downsizing.

redundancy noun dismissal, sacking, lay-off, discharge, unemployment.

redundant adjective *redundant churches:* unnecessary, not required, unneeded, surplus (to requirements), superfluous.
□ **make someone redundant** dismiss, lay off, give someone their notice, discharge; informal sack, fire.

reel verb **1** *he reeled as the ship began to roll:* stagger, lurch, sway, rock, stumble, totter, wobble. **2** *the room reeled:* go round (and round), whirl, spin, revolve, swirl, twirl, turn, swim.

refer verb *the matter has been referred to my insurers:* pass, direct, hand on/over, send on, transfer, entrust, assign.
□ **refer to 1** *he referred to errors in the article:* mention, allude to, touch on, speak of/about, talk of/about, write about,

to) **1** write or say something about; mention. **2** (of a word or phrase) describe. **3** turn to a person, book, etc. for information. **4** (**refer someone/thing to**) pass a person or matter on to someone else for help or a decision.

referee noun **1** an official who supervises a game to ensure that players keep to the rules. **2** Brit. a person who is willing to provide a reference for a person applying for a job. **3** a person who reads academic work before it is published. • verb (**referees, refereeing, refereed**) be a referee of.

reference noun **1** the action of referring to something. **2** a mention of a source of information in a book or article. **3** a letter giving information about how suitable someone is for a new job.

☑ one *r* in the middle, not two: reference.

referendum noun (plural **referendums** or **referenda**) a vote by the people of a country on a single political issue.

referral noun the action of referring someone or something to a specialist or higher authority.

refine verb (**refines, refining, refined**) **1** make something pure by removing unwanted substances. **2** improve something by making minor changes. **3** (**refined**) well educated, elegant, and having good taste.

refinement noun **1** the process of refining. **2** an improvement. **3** the quality of being well educated, elegant, and having good taste.

refinery noun (plural **refineries**) a factory where a substance such as oil is refined.

refit verb (**refits, refitting, refitted**) replace or repair equipment and fittings in a ship, building, etc. • noun an act of refitting.

reflect verb **1** throw back heat, light, or sound from a surface. **2** (of a mirror) show an image of. **3** show in a realistic or appropriate way. **4** (**reflect well** or **badly on**) give a good or bad impression of. **5** (**reflect on**) think seriously about.

reflection noun **1** the process of reflecting. **2** a reflected image. **3** a sign of something's true nature. **4** something that brings discredit. **5** serious thought.

reflective adjective **1** providing a reflection. **2** thoughtful. ■ **reflectively** adverb.

reflector noun a piece of glass or plastic on the back of a vehicle for reflecting light.

reflex noun an action done without conscious thought as a response to something. • adjective **1** done as a reflex. **2** (of an angle) more than 180°.

reflexive adjective Grammar referring back to the subject of a clause or verb, e.g. *myself* in *I hurt myself.*

reflexology noun a system of massage used to relieve tension and treat illness. ■ **reflexologist** noun.

refocus verb (**refocuses, refocusing** or **refocussing, refocused** or **refocussed**) **1** adjust the focus of a lens or your eyes. **2** focus attention on something new or different.

THESAURUS

comment on, point out, call attention to. **2** *these figures refer only to 2001:* **apply to,** relate to, pertain to, be relevant to, concern, be connected with. **3** *the constable referred to his notes:* **consult,** turn to, look at, have recourse to.

referee noun **1** *the referee blew his whistle:* **umpire,** judge, adjudicator; informal ref. **2** *include the names of two referees:* **supporter,** character witness, advocate. • verb *he refereed the game:* **umpire,** judge, adjudicate; informal ref.

reference noun **1** *a reference to his book:* **mention,** allusion, quotation, comment, remark. **2** *references are given in the bibliography:* **source,** citation, authority, credit. **3** *a glowing reference:* **testimonial,** recommendation, character reference, credentials.

referendum noun (popular) **vote,** ballot, poll, plebiscite.

refine verb **1** *refining our cereal foods:* **purify,** filter, distil, process, treat. **2** *helping students to refine their skills:* **improve,** perfect, polish (up), hone, fine-tune.

refined adjective **1** *refined sugar:* **purified,** processed, treated. **2** *a refined lady:* **cultivated,** cultured, polished, elegant, sophisticated, urbane, polite, gracious, well bred. **3** *a person of refined taste:* **discriminating,** discerning, fastidious, exquisite, impeccable, fine. OPPOSITES crude, coarse.

reflect verb **1** *the snow reflects light:* **mirror,** send back, throw back, echo. **2** *their expressions reflected their feelings:* **indicate,** show, display, demonstrate, be evidence of, reveal, betray. **3** *he reflected on his task:* **think,** consider, review, mull, contemplate, cogitate, meditate, muse, brood.

reflection noun **1** *her reflection in the mirror:* **image,** likeness. **2** *your hands are a reflection of your well-being:* **indication,** display, demonstration, manifestation, expression, evidence. **3** *after some reflection, he turned it down:* **thought,** consideration, contemplation, deliberation, pondering, meditation, musing.

r

reform verb **1** change something to improve it. **2** make someone improve their behaviour. •noun an act of reforming.
■ **reformer** noun.

reformation noun **1** the action of reforming. **2** (**the Reformation**) a 16th-century movement for reforming the Roman Catholic Church, leading to the establishment of the Protestant Churches.

reformist adjective supporting political or social reform. •noun a supporter of such reform.
■ **reformism** noun.

refract verb (of water, air, or glass) make a ray of light change direction when it enters at an angle.
■ **refraction** noun **refractive** adjective.

refractory adjective **1** stubborn or difficult to control. **2** (of an illness) not responding to treatment.

refrain[1] verb (**refrain from**) stop yourself from doing something.

refrain[2] noun a part of a song that is repeated at the end of each verse.

refresh verb make someone feel less tired or hot.

refresher noun a course intended to improve or update your skills or knowledge.

refreshing adjective **1** making you feel less tired or hot. **2** pleasingly new or different.

■ **refreshingly** adverb.

refreshment noun **1** a snack or drink. **2** the giving of fresh energy.

refrigerate verb (**refrigerates, refrigerating, refrigerated**) make food or drink cold to keep it fresh.
■ **refrigeration** noun.

refrigerator noun a fridge.

> ☑ no *d* in the middle: re*frig*erator, not -*ridg*-.

refuel verb (**refuels, refuelling, refuelled;** US spelling **refuels, refueling, refueled**) supply with more fuel.

refuge noun **1** shelter from danger or trouble. **2** a safe place.

refugee noun a person who has been forced to leave their country because of a war or because they are being persecuted.

refulgent /ri-ful-juhnt/ adjective literary shining very brightly.

refund verb pay back money to. •noun a repayment of a sum of money.

refurbish verb redecorate and improve a building or room.
■ **refurbishment** noun.

refuse[1] /ri-fyooz/ verb (**refuses, refusing, refused**) say that you are unwilling to do or accept something.
■ **refusal** noun.

THESAURUS

reform verb **1** *a plan to reform the system:* improve, better, ameliorate, correct, rectify, restore, revise, refine, adapt, revamp, redesign, reconstruct, reorganize. **2** *after his marriage he reformed:* mend your ways, change for the better, turn over a new leaf.
•noun *the reform of the prison system:* improvement, amelioration, refinement, rectification, restoration, adaptation, revision, redesign, revamp, reconstruction, reorganization.

refrain verb abstain, desist, hold back, stop yourself, forbear, avoid; informal swear off.

refresh verb **1** *the cool air will refresh me:* reinvigorate, revitalize, revive, freshen, perk up, brace, freshen, wake up; informal buck up. **2** *let me refresh your memory:* jog, stimulate, prompt, prod.
OPPOSITES weary.

refreshing adjective **1** *a refreshing drink:* invigorating, revitalizing, reviving, bracing, fortifying, enlivening, stimulating. **2** *a refreshing change of direction:* welcome, stimulating, fresh, new, imaginative, innovative.
OPPOSITES wearying.

refreshment noun food and drink, snacks, titbits; informal nibbles.

refuge noun **1** *homeless people seeking refuge:* shelter, protection, safety, security, asylum, sanctuary. **2** *a refuge for mountain gorillas:* sanctuary, shelter, haven, sanctum, retreat, bolt-hole, hiding place.

refugee noun asylum seeker, fugitive, displaced person, exile, émigré.

refund verb **1** *we will refund your money:* repay, give back, return, pay back. **2** *they refunded the subscribers:* reimburse, compensate, recompense.
•noun *a full refund:* repayment, reimbursement, compensation, rebate.

refurbish verb renovate, recondition, rehabilitate, revamp, overhaul, restore, redecorate, upgrade, refit; informal do up.

refusal noun **1** *we had one refusal to our invitation:* non-acceptance, no, rejection, rebuff, turndown; informal knock-back. **2** *the refusal of planning permission:* withholding, denial.
OPPOSITES acceptance, granting.

refuse[1] verb **1** *he refused the invitation:* decline, turn down, say no to, reject, spurn, rebuff; informal pass up. **2** *the Council refused planning permission:* withhold, deny.
OPPOSITES accept, grant.

r

refuse² /ref-yooss/ noun things thrown away; rubbish.

refute verb (refutes, refuting, refuted) prove a statement or person to be wrong.
■ **refutation** noun.

regain verb 1 get something back after losing possession of it. 2 get back to a place.

regal adjective having to do with a king or queen, especially in being magnificent or dignified.
■ **regally** adverb.

regale verb (regales, regaling, regaled) 1 entertain someone with anecdotes or stories. 2 supply someone generously with food or drink.

regalia /ri-gay-li-uh/ noun 1 objects such as the crown and sceptre used at coronations or other state occasions. 2 the distinctive clothes and items worn or carried on official occasions by important people.

regard verb 1 think of in a particular way. 2 look steadily at. • noun 1 concern or care. 2 high opinion; respect. 3 (regards) best wishes.
□ **as regards** (or **with regard to**) concerning.

regarding preposition about; concerning.

regardless adverb 1 (regardless of) without concern for. 2 despite what is happening.

regatta noun a sports event consisting of a series of boat or yacht races.

regency /ree-juhn-si/ noun (plural regencies) 1 a period of government by a regent.

2 (**the Regency**) the period when George, Prince of Wales, acted as regent in Britain (1811–20).

regenerate verb (regenerates, regenerating, regenerated) 1 bring new life or strength to. 2 grow new tissue.
■ **regeneration** noun.

regent noun a person appointed to rule a state because the king or queen is too young or ill to rule, or is absent.

reggae /reg-gay/ noun a style of popular music originating in Jamaica.

regicide noun 1 the killing of a king. 2 a person who kills a king.

regime /ray-zheem/ noun 1 a government, especially one that strictly controls a state. 2 an ordered way of doing something; a system.

regimen /rej-i-muhn/ noun a course of medical treatment, diet, or exercise.

regiment noun 1 a permanent unit of an army. 2 a large number of people.
■ **regimental** adjective.

regimented adjective organized according to a strict system.

Regina noun the reigning queen (used in referring to lawsuits).

region noun 1 an area of a country or the world. 2 an administrative district of a city or country. 3 (**the regions**) the parts of a country outside the capital. 4 a part of the body.
□ **in the region of** approximately.
■ **regional** adjective **regionally** adverb.

---

refuse² noun *piles of refuse:* **rubbish,** waste, litter; N. Amer. garbage, trash; informal dreck, junk.

regain verb 1 *government troops regained the capital:* **recover,** get back, win back, recoup, retrieve, repossess, take back, retake, recapture, reconquer. 2 *they regained dry land:* **return to,** get back to, reach again, rejoin.

regal adjective 1 *a regal feast.* See **SPLENDID** sense 1. 2 *his regal forebears:* **royal,** kingly, queenly, princely, majestic.

regard verb 1 *we regard the results as encouraging:* **consider,** look on, view, see, think of, judge, deem, estimate, assess, reckon, rate. 2 *he regarded her coldly:* **look at,** contemplate, eye, gaze at, stare at, observe, view, study, scrutinize.
• noun 1 *he has no regard for life:* **consideration,** care, concern, thought, notice, heed, attention. 2 *doctors are held in high regard:* **esteem,** respect, admiration, approval, honour, estimation. 3 *his steady regard:* **(fixed) look,** gaze, stare, observation, contemplation, study, scrutiny. 4 (**regards**) best wishes,

greetings, respects, compliments, best, love.

regarding preposition concerning, as regards, with/in regard to, with respect to, with reference to, relating to, respecting, re, about, apropos, on the subject of, in connection with, vis-à-vis.

regardless adverb anyway, anyhow, in any case, nevertheless, nonetheless, despite everything, even so, all the same, in any event, come what may.
□ **regardless of** irrespective of, without reference to, without consideration of, discounting, ignoring, notwithstanding, no matter.

regime noun 1 *regime change:* **government,** administration, leadership, authority, control, rule, command. 2 *a health regime:* **system,** arrangement, scheme, policy, method, course, plan, programme.

region noun **district,** province, territory, division, area, section, sector, zone, belt, quarter.

regional adjective 1 *regional variation:* **geographical,** territorial. 2 *a regional parliament:* **local,** provincial, district,

r

register noun **1** an official list or record. **2** a particular part of the range of a musical instrument or voice. **3** the level and style of a piece of writing or speech (e.g. informal, formal). •verb (**registers, registering, registered**) **1** enter in a register. **2** put your name on a register. **3** express an opinion or emotion. **4** become aware of. **5** (of a measuring instrument) show a reading.
□ **register office** (in the UK) a government building where marriages are performed and births, marriages, and deaths are recorded.

registrar noun **1** an official responsible for keeping official records. **2** Brit. a hospital doctor who is training to be a specialist.

registration noun **1** the action of registering. **2** (also **registration number**) Brit. the series of letters and figures shown on a vehicle's number plate.

registry noun (plural **registries**) a place where registers are kept.
□ **registry office** a register office.

regress /ri-**gress**/ verb return to an earlier or less advanced state.
■ **regression** noun.

regressive adjective **1** returning to a less advanced state. **2** (of a tax) taking a proportionally greater amount from those on lower incomes.

regret verb (**regrets, regretting, regretted**) feel sorry or disappointed about something you have done or should have done. •noun a feeling of regretting something.

regretful adjective feeling or showing regret.
■ **regretfully** adverb.

regrettable adjective causing regret.
■ **regrettably** adverb.

regular adjective **1** following or arranged in an evenly spaced pattern or sequence. **2** done or happening frequently. **3** doing the same thing often. **4** following an accepted standard. **5** usual. **6** Grammar (of a word) following the normal pattern of inflection. **7** belonging to the permanent professional armed forces of a country. **8** (of a geometrical figure) having all sides and angles equal. •noun a regular customer, member of a team, etc.
■ **regularity** noun **regularly** adverb.

regularize or **regularise** verb (**regularizes, regularizing, regularized**) **1** make regular. **2** make a temporary situation legal or official.

regulate verb (**regulates, regulating, regulated**) **1** control the rate or speed of a machine or process. **2** control or supervise by means of rules.
■ **regulator** noun **regulatory** adjective.

regulation noun **1** a rule made by an authority. **2** the action of regulating.

regurgitate /ri-**ger**-ji-tayt/ verb (**regurgitates, regurgitating, regurgitated**) **1** bring swallowed food up again to the mouth. **2** repeat information without understanding it.
■ **regurgitation** noun.

THESAURUS

parochial, zonal.
OPPOSITES national.

register noun **1** *the register of electors:* list, roll, roster, index, directory, catalogue, inventory. **2** *the parish register:* record, chronicle, log, ledger, archive, annals, files. •verb **1** *I wish to register a complaint:* record, enter, file, lodge, write down, submit, report, note, minute, log. **2** *I'd like to register for the course:* enrol, put your name down, enlist, sign on/up, apply. **3** *the dial registered 100mph:* indicate, read, record, show. **4** *her face registered anger:* display, show, express, exhibit, betray, reveal.

regret verb **1** *they came to regret their decision:* be sorry about, feel contrite about, feel remorse for, rue. **2** *regretting the passing of youth:* mourn, grieve for/over, weep over, sigh over, lament, sorrow for.
OPPOSITES welcome.
•noun **1** *both players expressed regret:* remorse, contrition, repentance, compunction. **2** *they left with genuine regret:* sadness, sorrow, disappointment,

unhappiness, grief.
OPPOSITES satisfaction.

regular adjective **1** *plant them at regular intervals:* uniform, even, consistent, constant, unchanging, unvarying, fixed. **2** *the subject of regular protests:* frequent, repeated, continual, recurrent, periodic, constant, perpetual, numerous. **3** *his regular route to work:* usual, normal, customary, habitual, routine, typical, accustomed, established.
OPPOSITES erratic, occasional, unusual.

regulate verb **1** *the flow has been regulated:* control, adjust, manage, govern. **2** *a new act regulating businesses:* police, supervise, monitor, check (up on), be responsible for, control, manage, direct, govern.

regulation noun **1** *EC regulations:* rule, order, directive, act, law, by-law, statute, dictate, decree. **2** *the regulation of blood sugar:* adjustment, control, management, balancing. **3** *the regulation of financial services:* policing, supervision, superintendence, monitoring, control, governance, management, responsibility for.

r

rehabilitate verb (**rehabilitates, rehabilitating, rehabilitated**) **1** help someone who has been ill or in prison to return to normal life. **2** restore the reputation of someone previously out of favour.
■ **rehabilitation** noun.

rehash verb reuse old ideas or material.
• noun a reuse of old ideas or material.

rehearsal noun a trial performance of a play or other work for later public performance.

rehearse verb (**rehearses, rehearsing, rehearsed**) **1** practise a play, piece of music, etc. for later public performance. **2** state points that have been made many times before.

rehydrate verb (**rehydrates, rehydrating, rehydrated**) add moisture to something dehydrated.
■ **rehydration** noun.

Reich /ryk, rykh/ noun the former German state, in particular the **Third Reich** (the Nazi regime, 1933–45).

reign verb **1** rule as king or queen. **2** be the main quality or aspect: *confusion reigned.* **3** (**reigning**) currently holding a particular title in sport. • noun the period of rule of a king or queen.

reimburse verb (**reimburses, reimbursing, reimbursed**) repay money to.
■ **reimbursement** noun.

rein noun (**reins**) **1** long, narrow straps

attached to a horse's bit, used to control the horse. **2** the power to direct and control something. • verb **1** control a horse by pulling on its reins. **2** (**rein someone/thing in** or **back**) restrain someone or something.
□ **free rein** freedom of action.

reincarnate verb (**be reincarnated**) be born again in another body.
■ **reincarnation** noun.

reindeer noun (plural **reindeer** or **reindeers**) a deer with large antlers, found in cold northern regions.

reinforce verb (**reinforces, reinforcing, reinforced**) **1** make something stronger. **2** strengthen a military force with additional personnel.

reinforcement noun **1** the action of reinforcing. **2** (**reinforcements**) extra personnel sent to strengthen a military force.

reinstate verb (**reinstates, reinstating, reinstated**) restore to a former position.
■ **reinstatement** noun.

reiterate verb (**reiterates, reiterating, reiterated**) say something again or repeatedly.
■ **reiteration** noun.

reject verb /ri-jekt/ **1** refuse to accept or agree to. **2** fail to show proper affection or concern for. **3** (of the body) react against a transplanted organ or tissue. • noun

THESAURUS

rehearsal noun practice, trial performance, read-through, run-through, drill, training, coaching; informal dry run.

rehearse verb **1** *I rehearsed the role:* prepare, practise, read through, run through/over, go over. **2** *he rehearsed the Vienna Philharmonic:* train, drill, prepare, coach. **3** *the document rehearsed all the arguments:* list, enumerate, itemize, detail, spell out, catalogue, recite, repeat, go over, run through; informal recap.

reign verb **1** *Robert II reigned for nineteen years:* be king/queen, sit on the throne, wear the crown, be supreme, rule. **2** *chaos reigned:* prevail, exist, be present, be the case, occur, be rife, be rampant, be the order of the day.
• noun *Henry VII's reign:* rule, sovereignty, monarchy, dominion.

rein verb *they reined back costs:* restrain, check, curb, constrain, hold back/in, keep under control, regulate, restrict, control, curtail, limit.
□ **free rein** freedom, a free hand, leeway, latitude, flexibility, liberty, independence, licence, room to manoeuvre, carte blanche.
keep a tight rein on regulate, discipline, regiment, keep in line.

reinforce verb **1** *contractors reinforced the dam:* strengthen, fortify, bolster up, shore up, buttress, prop up, underpin, brace, support. **2** *reinforcing links between colleges and companies:* strengthen, fortify, cement, boost, deepen, enrich, enhance, intensify, improve. **3** *the need to reinforce NATO troops:* augment, increase, add to, supplement, boost, top up.

reinforcement noun **1** *the reinforcement of our defences:* strengthening, fortification, bolstering, shoring up, buttressing, bracing. **2** (**reinforcements**) additional troops, auxiliaries, reserves, support, backup, help.

reinstate verb restore, put back, bring back, reinstitute, reinstall, re-establish.

reject verb **1** *the miners rejected the offer:* turn down, refuse, decline, say no to, spurn. **2** *Jamie rejected her:* rebuff, spurn, shun, snub, cast off/aside, discard, abandon, desert, turn your back on.
OPPOSITES accept, welcome.
• noun **1** *what a reject!* failure, loser, incompetent. **2** *it is only a reject:* second, discard, misshape, faulty item, cast-off.

r

/**ree**-jekt/ a rejected person or thing.
■ rejection noun.

rejig verb (**rejigs, rejigging, rejigged**) Brit. rearrange.

rejoice verb (**rejoices, rejoicing, rejoiced**) feel or show great joy.

rejoin[1] verb join again.

rejoin[2] verb formal say in reply; retort.

rejoinder noun a quick reply.

rejuvenate verb (**rejuvenates, rejuvenating, rejuvenated**) make more lively or youthful.
■ rejuvenation noun.

rekindle verb (**rekindles, rekindling, rekindled**) 1 revive a past feeling, relationship, etc. 2 relight a fire.

relapse /ri-**laps**/ verb (**relapses, relapsing, relapsed**) 1 become ill again after a period of improvement. 2 (**relapse into**) return to a worse state. •noun /**ree**-laps/ a return to bad health after a temporary improvement.

relate verb (**relates, relating, related**) 1 make or show a connection between. 2 (**be related**) be connected by blood or marriage. 3 (**relate to**) have to do with; concern. 4 (**relate to**) feel sympathy with. 5 give a spoken or written account of.

relation noun 1 the way in which people or things are connected or related. 2 (**relations**) the way in which people or groups behave towards each other. 3 a relative.

relationship noun 1 the way in which people or things are connected or related. 2 the way in which people or groups behave towards each other. 3 an emotional and sexual association between two people.

relative adjective 1 considered in relation or in proportion to something else. 2 existing or possessing a quality only in comparison to something else. 3 Grammar referring to an earlier noun, sentence, or clause. •noun a person connected to another by blood or marriage.

relatively adverb 1 in comparison or proportion to something else. 2 quite.

relativism noun the idea that truth, morality, etc. exist only in relation to other things and are not absolute.
■ relativist noun.

relativity noun 1 the state of being relative; ability to be judged only in comparison with something else. 2 Physics a description of matter, energy, space, and time according to Albert Einstein's theories.

relax verb 1 become less tense, anxious, or

THESAURUS

rejection noun 1 *a rejection of the offer:* refusal, declining, turning down, dismissal, spurning. 2 *Madeleine's rejection of him:* repudiation, rebuff, spurning, abandonment, desertion; informal brush-off.
OPPOSITES agreement, acceptance, welcome.

rejoice verb be happy, be glad, be delighted, celebrate, make merry; informal be over the moon.
OPPOSITES mourn.
□ rejoice in **delight in,** enjoy, revel in, glory in, relish, savour.

rejoin verb return to, be reunited with, join again, reach again, regain.

relate verb *he related stories:* tell, recount, narrate, report, recite.
□ relate to 1 *mortality is related to unemployment levels:* **connect with,** associate with, link with, ally with, couple with. 2 *the charges relate to other offences:* **apply to,** concern, pertain to, have a bearing on, involve. 3 *she cannot relate to her father:* **have a rapport with,** get on (well) with, feel sympathy with, identify with, empathize with, understand; informal hit it off with.

related adjective connected, interconnected, associated, linked, allied, corresponding, analogous, parallel, comparable, equivalent.
OPPOSITES unrelated.

relation noun 1 *the relation between church and state:* connection, relationship, association, link, correlation, correspondence, parallel. 2 *are you a relation of his?* relative, member of the family, kinsman, kinswoman; (**relations**) family, kin, kith and kin, kindred. 3 (**relations**) *improving relations with India:* dealings, communication, relationship, connections, contact, interaction.

relationship noun 1 *the relationship between diet and diabetes:* connection, relation, association, link, correlation, correspondence, parallel. 2 *their relationship to a common ancestor:* family ties/connections, blood relationship, kinship, affinity, common ancestry/lineage. 3 *the end of their relationship:* romance, affair, love affair, liaison, amour, fling.

relative adjective 1 *the relative importance of each factor:* comparative, respective, comparable. 2 *food required is relative to body weight:* proportionate, in proportion, commensurate, corresponding.
OPPOSITES disproportionate.
•noun *he's a relative of mine:* relation, member of the family, kinsman, kinswoman; (**relatives**) family, kin, kith and kin, kindred.

relax verb 1 *relax after work:* rest, loosen up, ease up/off, slow down, de-stress, unbend, unwind, put your feet up, take it easy; informal chill out; N. Amer. informal hang loose. 2 *a walk will relax you:* calm, unwind, rest, loosen up, make less tense,

rigid. **2** rest from work; do something recreational. **3** make a rule or restriction less strict.
■ **relaxation** noun.

relay noun **1** a group of people or animals carrying out a task for a time and then replaced by a similar group. **2** a race between teams of runners, each team member in turn covering part of the total distance. **3** an electrical device which opens or closes a circuit in response to a current in another circuit. **4** a device which receives, strengthens, and transmits a signal again. • verb **1** receive and pass on information. **2** broadcast something by means of a relay.

release verb (**releases, releasing, released**) **1** set someone free from a place where they have been kept or trapped. **2** free someone from a duty, responsibility, etc. **3** allow to move freely. **4** allow information to be made available. **5** make a film or recording available to the public. • noun **1** the action of releasing. **2** a film or recording made available to the public.

relegate verb (**relegates, relegating, relegated**) **1** place in a lower rank or position. **2** Brit. transfer a sports team to a lower division of a league.
■ **relegation** noun.

relent verb **1** finally agree to something after first refusing it. **2** become less severe or intense.

relentless adjective **1** never stopping or ending. **2** harsh or inflexible.
■ **relentlessly** adverb.

relevant adjective closely connected or appropriate to the current subject.
■ **relevance** noun.

☑ -ant, not -ent: relevant.

reliable adjective able to be depended on or trusted.
■ **reliability** noun **reliably** adverb.

reliance noun dependence on or trust in someone or something.
■ **reliant** adjective.

relic noun **1** an object or custom that survives from an earlier time. **2** a part of a holy person's body or belongings kept after their death.

relief noun **1** a feeling of reassurance and relaxation after anxiety or stress. **2** a cause of relief. **3** the action of relieving. **4** (also

THESAURUS

make less uptight, soothe. **3** *he relaxed his grip:* loosen, slacken, unclench, weaken, lessen. **4** *they relaxed the restrictions:* moderate, temper, ease, loosen, lighten, dilute, weaken, reduce, decrease; informal let up on.
OPPOSITES tense, tighten.

relaxation noun recreation, enjoyment, amusement, entertainment, fun, pleasure, leisure.
OPPOSITES activity, work.

relay noun *a live relay of the performance:* broadcast, transmission, showing, feed.
• verb *I'd relayed the messages:* pass on, hand on, transfer, repeat, communicate, send, transmit, circulate.

release verb **1** *all prisoners were released:* free, set free, let go/out, liberate, discharge. **2** *Burke released the animal:* untie, undo, loose, let go, unleash. **3** *police released the news yesterday:* make public, make known, issue, put out, publish, broadcast, circulate, launch.
OPPOSITES imprison, tie up, embargo.
• noun **1** *the release of political prisoners:* freeing, liberation, deliverance, freedom, liberty. **2** *the release of the news:* issuing, announcement, publication, broadcasting, circulation, launch.
OPPOSITES imprisonment, embargo.

relegate verb downgrade, demote, lower, put down, move down.
OPPOSITES upgrade, promote.

relentless adjective **1** *their relentless pursuit of quality:* persistent, unfaltering, unremitting, unflagging, untiring, unwavering, dogged, single-minded, tireless, indefatigable. **2** *a relentless taskmaster:* harsh, cruel, remorseless, merciless, pitiless, implacable, ruthless.

relevant adjective pertinent, applicable, apposite, material, apropos, to the point, germane.
OPPOSITES irrelevant.

reliable adjective dependable, trustworthy, good, safe, authentic, faithful, genuine, sound, true, loyal, unfailing; humorous trusty.
OPPOSITES unreliable.

reliance noun **1** *reliance on the state:* dependence. **2** *reliance on his judgement:* trust, confidence, faith, belief, conviction.

relic noun artefact, historical object, antiquity, remnant, vestige, remains.

relief noun **1** *a bit of relief from work:* freedom, release, liberation, deliverance, comfort, respite, diversion. **2** *pain relief:* alleviation, relieving, palliation, soothing, easing, lessening. **3** *a little light relief:* respite, amusement, diversion, entertainment, jollity, recreation. **4** *bringing relief to the starving:* help, aid, assistance, charity. **5** *his relief arrived to take over:* replacement, substitute, deputy, reserve, cover, stand-in, supply, locum, understudy.

r

light relief) a temporary break in a tense or boring situation. **5** help given to people in need or difficulty. **6** a person or group replacing others who have been on duty. **7** a way of carving in which the design stands out from the surface.
□ **relief map** a map that indicates hills and valleys by shading.

relieve verb (**relieves, relieving, relieved**) **1** lessen or remove pain, difficulty, etc. **2** (**be relieved**) stop feeling anxious or stressed. **3** replace someone who is on duty. **4** (**relieve someone of**) take a responsibility from someone. **5** bring military support for a place which is surrounded by the enemy. **6** make something less boring. **7** (**relieve yourself**) go to the toilet.

> ☑ *i* before *e* except after *c*: rel*ie*ve.

religion noun **1** belief in and worship of a God or gods. **2** a particular system of faith and worship.

religious adjective **1** concerned with or believing in a religion. **2** very careful and regular.
■ **religiously** adverb.

> ☑ rel*igi*ous, not -*gous*.

relinquish verb give up something,

especially unwillingly.

reliquary /rel-i-kwuh-ri/ noun (plural **reliquaries**) a container for holy relics.

relish noun **1** great enjoyment or anticipation. **2** a strongly flavoured sauce or pickle. •verb enjoy or look forward to.

relive verb (**relives, reliving, relived**) live through an experience or feeling again in your mind.

reload verb load something, especially a gun, again.

relocate verb (**relocates, relocating, relocated**) move your home or business to a new place.
■ **relocation** noun.

reluctant adjective unwilling and hesitant.
■ **reluctance** noun **reluctantly** adverb.

rely verb (**relies, relying, relied**) (**rely on**) **1** need or be dependent on. **2** have faith in; trust.

remain verb **1** still be in the same place or condition. **2** continue to be: *he remained alert.* **3** be left over.

remainder noun **1** a part, number, or amount that is left over. **2** a part that is still to come. **3** the number left over when one quantity does not exactly divide another.

THESAURUS

relieve verb **1** *this helps relieve pain:* alleviate, mitigate, ease, counteract, dull, reduce. **2** *the helpers relieved us:* replace, take over from, stand in for, fill in for, substitute for, deputize for, cover for. **3** *this relieves the teacher of a heavy load:* free, release, exempt, excuse, absolve, let off.
OPPOSITES aggravate.

religion noun faith, belief, worship, creed, church, sect, denomination, cult.

religious adjective **1** *a religious person:* devout, pious, reverent, godly, God-fearing, churchgoing. **2** *religious beliefs:* spiritual, theological, scriptural, doctrinal, ecclesiastical, church, holy, divine, sacred. **3** *religious attention to detail:* scrupulous, conscientious, meticulous, punctilious, strict, rigorous.
OPPOSITES atheistic, secular.

relinquish verb **1** *he relinquished control of the company:* renounce, give up/away, hand over, let go of. **2** *he relinquished his post:* leave, resign from, stand down from, bow out of, give up; informal quit, chuck.
OPPOSITES retain, continue.

relish noun **1** *he dug into his food with relish:* enjoyment, gusto, delight, pleasure, glee, appreciation, enthusiasm. **2** *a hot relish:* condiment, sauce, dressing.
OPPOSITES distaste.

•verb **1** *he was relishing his moment of glory:* enjoy, delight in, love, adore, take pleasure in, rejoice in, appreciate, savour, revel in, luxuriate in, glory in. **2** *I don't relish the drive:* look forward to, fancy.
OPPOSITES dislike.

reluctance noun unwillingness, disinclination, hesitation, wavering, vacillation, doubts, second thoughts, misgivings.

reluctant adjective unwilling, disinclined, unenthusiastic, resistant, opposed, hesitant, loath.
OPPOSITES willing, eager.

rely verb *I knew I could rely on him:* depend on, count on, bank on, be confident of, be sure of, have faith in, trust in; informal swear by; N. Amer. informal figure on.

remain verb **1** *the problem will remain:* continue, endure, last, abide, carry on, persist, stay around, survive, live on. **2** *he remained in hospital:* stay, stay behind, stay put, wait behind, be left, hang on; informal hang around/round. **3** *union leaders remain sceptical:* continue to be, stay, keep.

remainder noun rest, balance, residue, others, remnant(s), leftovers, surplus, extra, excess.

r

remains plural noun **1** things that remain or are left. **2** historical or archaeological relics. **3** a person's body after death.

remand verb send a defendant to wait for their trial, either on bail or in jail.
□ **on remand** in jail before being tried.

remark verb **1** say as a comment. **2** notice.
• noun a comment.

remarkable adjective extraordinary or striking.
■ **remarkably** adverb.

rematch noun a second match between two teams or players.

remedial adjective **1** intended as a remedy. **2** provided for children with learning difficulties.

remedy noun (plural **remedies**) **1** a medicine or treatment for a disease or injury. **2** a means of dealing with something undesirable. • verb (**remedies, remedying, remedied**) put right an undesirable situation.

remember verb (**remembers, remembering, remembered**) **1** have in your mind someone or something from the past. **2** not forget to do something necessary or important. **3** (**remember someone to**) pass on greetings from one person to another.

remembrance noun **1** the action of remembering. **2** a memory. **3** a thing acting as a reminder of someone.

remind verb **1** help someone to remember something. **2** (**remind someone of**) make someone think of someone or something because of a resemblance.

reminder noun a thing that makes someone remember something.

reminisce /re-mi-**niss**/ verb (**reminisces, reminiscing, reminisced**) think or talk about the past.

reminiscence noun **1** an account of something that you remember. **2** the enjoyable remembering of past events.

reminiscent adjective **1** (**reminiscent of**) tending to remind you of something. **2** absorbed in memories.

remiss /ri-**miss**/ adjective not giving something proper attention or care.

remission noun **1** a temporary period during which a serious illness becomes less severe. **2** Brit. the reduction of a prison sentence as a reward for good behaviour. **3** the cancellation of a debt, penalty, etc.

remit noun /**ree**-mit/ the task or area of activity officially given to a person or organization. • verb /ri-**mit**/ (**remits, remitting, remitted**) **1** send money in payment. **2** cancel a debt or punishment. **3** refer a matter to an authority for a decision.

remittance noun **1** a sum of money sent as payment. **2** the action of remitting money.

remix verb produce a different version of a musical recording by altering the balance of the separate parts. • noun a remixed recording.

remnant noun a small remaining quantity of something.

remonstrate /**rem**-uhn-strayt/ verb (**remonstrates, remonstrating,**

---

remains plural noun **1** *the remains of her drink:* remainder, residue, rest, remnant(s), leftovers. **2** *Roman remains:* antiquities, relics, artefacts. **3** *the saint's remains:* corpse, body, carcass, bones.

remark verb *'You're quiet,' he remarked:* comment, say, observe, mention, reflect; formal opine.
• noun *he made a few remarks:* comment, statement, utterance, observation, reflection.

remarkable adjective extraordinary, exceptional, outstanding, notable, striking, memorable, unusual, conspicuous, momentous.
OPPOSITES ordinary.

remedy noun **1** *herbal remedies:* treatment, cure, medicine, medication, medicament, drug. **2** *a remedy for all kinds of problems:* solution, answer, cure, fix, antidote.
• verb *remedying the situation:* put right, set right, rectify, solve, sort out, straighten out, resolve, correct, repair, mend, fix.

remember verb **1** *remembering happy times:* recall, call to mind, recollect, think

of, reminisce about, look back on. **2** *can you remember all that?* memorize, retain, learn off by heart. **3** *you must remember she's only five:* bear in mind, be mindful of, take into account. **4** *remember to feed the cat:* be sure, be certain, mind that you, make sure that you. **5** *the nation remembered those who gave their lives:* commemorate, pay tribute to, honour, salute, pay homage to.
OPPOSITES forget.

remembrance noun **1** *an expression of remembrance:* recollection, reminiscence, recall. **2** *we sold poppies in remembrance:* commemoration, memory, recognition.

remind verb jog someone's memory, prompt.
□ **remind someone of** make someone think of, cause someone to remember, put someone in mind of, call to mind, evoke.

reminiscent adjective similar to, comparable with, evocative of, suggestive of, redolent of.

remnant noun remains, remainder, leftovers, offcut, residue, rest.

r

remonstrated) complain or protest strongly.
- ■ **remonstrance** noun **remonstration** noun.

remorse noun deep regret or guilt for something wrong that you have done.
- ■ **remorseful** adjective.

remorseless adjective **1** (of something unpleasant) never ending or improving. **2** without remorse.
- ■ **remorselessly** adverb.

remote adjective (**remoter, remotest**) **1** far away in space or time. **2** situated far from the main centres of population. **3** having very little connection. **4** (of a chance or possibility) unlikely to happen. **5** unfriendly and distant in manner. **6** operating or operated by means of radio or infrared signals.
- □ **remote control 1** control of a machine from a distance by means of signals transmitted from a radio or electronic device. **2** a device that controls a machine in this way.
- ■ **remotely** adverb **remoteness** noun.

removal noun **1** the action of removing. **2** Brit. the transfer of furniture and other items when moving house.

remove verb (**removes, removing, removed**) **1** take something away from the position it occupies. **2** abolish or get rid of. **3** dismiss from a post. **4** (**be removed**) be very different from. **5** (**removed**) separated by a particular number of steps of descent: *a second cousin once removed.* •noun the amount by which things are separated.
- ■ **removable** adjective.

remunerate /ri-myoo-nuh-rayt/ verb (**remunerates, remunerating, remunerated**)

formal pay someone for work they have done.
- ■ **remuneration** noun.

remunerative adjective formal paying a lot of money.

Renaissance /ri-nay-sonss/ noun **1** the revival of classical styles in art and literature in the 14th–16th centuries. **2** (**renaissance**) a period of renewed interest in something.

renal /ree-n'l/ adjective technical having to do with the kidneys.

rename verb (**renames, renaming, renamed**) give a new name to.

renascence /ri-nass-uhnss/ noun formal a revival or rebirth.
- ■ **renascent** adjective.

rend verb (**rends, rending, rent**) literary tear something to pieces.

render verb (**renders, rendering, rendered**) **1** provide or give a service, help, etc. **2** hand over for inspection, consideration, or payment. **3** cause to be or become: *he was rendered speechless.* **4** perform a piece of music or drama. **5** melt down fat to separate out its impurities. **6** cover a wall with a coat of plaster.

rendezvous /ron-day-voo/ noun (plural **rendezvous** /ron-day-voo/ or /ron-day-vooz/) **1** a meeting at an agreed time and place. **2** a meeting place. •verb (**rendezvouses** /ron-day-vooz/, **rendezvousing** /ron-day-voo-ing/, **rendezvoused** /ron-day-vood/) meet at an agreed time and place.

rendition noun a performance or version of a piece of music or drama.

THESAURUS

remorse noun regret, guilt, contrition, repentance, shame.

remote adjective **1** *a remote village:* isolated, faraway, distant, out of the way, off the beaten track, secluded, lonely; N. Amer. in the backwoods; informal in the middle of nowhere. **2** *a remote possibility:* unlikely, improbable, doubtful, dubious, faint, slight, slim, small, slender. **3** *she seems very remote:* aloof, distant, detached, withdrawn, unforthcoming, unfriendly, unapproachable, unresponsive, unsociable, introspective, introverted; informal stand-offish.
OPPOSITES close, distinct, friendly.

removal noun **1** *the removal of church treasures:* taking away, moving, carrying away, transporting. **2** *his removal from office:* dismissal, ejection, expulsion, ousting; N. Amer. ouster; informal sacking, firing. **3** *the removal of customs barriers:* withdrawal, elimination, abolition, taking away. **4** *her removal to France:* move,

transfer, relocation.
OPPOSITES installation, appointment, imposition.

remove verb **1** *she removed the lid:* take off, take away, take out, pull out, withdraw, detach, undo, unfasten, disconnect. **2** *he was removed from his post:* dismiss, discharge, get rid of, expel, oust, depose; informal sack, fire, kick out. **3** *tax relief was removed:* abolish, withdraw, eliminate, get rid of, do away with, stop, cut, axe.
OPPOSITES attach, insert, replace, appoint, impose.

renaissance noun revival, renewal, resurrection, reawakening, re-emergence, rebirth, reappearance, resurgence.

render verb **1** *her fury rendered her speechless:* make, cause to be/become, leave, turn. **2** *rendering assistance:* give, provide, supply, furnish, contribute. **3** *the characters are vividly rendered:* act, perform, play, depict, portray, interpret, represent, draw, paint, execute.

renegade /ren-i-gayd/ noun a person who deserts and betrays an organization, country, or set of principles.

renege /ri-nayg, ri-neeg/ verb (**reneges, reneging, reneged**) go back on an agreement or promise.

renew verb **1** start doing something again after an interruption. **2** give fresh life or strength to. **3** make a licence, subscription, etc. valid for a further period. **4** replace something broken or worn out.
■ **renewable** adjective **renewal** noun.

rennet noun a substance used to curdle milk in order to make cheese.

renounce verb (**renounces, renouncing, renounced**) **1** formally give up a title or possession. **2** state that you no longer have a particular belief or allegiance. **3** abandon a cause, habit, etc.

renovate verb (**renovates, renovating, renovated**) restore something old to a good state; repair.
■ **renovation** noun.

renown noun the state of being famous.
■ **renowned** adjective.

rent¹ noun a regular payment made for the use of property or land. •verb **1** regularly pay money to someone for the use of property or land. **2** let someone use property or land in return for payment.

rent² past and past participle of **REND**. •noun a large tear in a piece of fabric.

rental noun **1** an amount paid as rent. **2** the action of renting.

renunciation noun the action of renouncing or giving up something.

reorganize or **reorganise** verb (**reorganizes, reorganizing, reorganized**) change the organization of.
■ **reorganization** noun.

rep noun informal **1** a representative. **2** repertory.

repaid past and past participle of **REPAY**.

repair¹ verb restore something damaged or worn to a good condition. •noun **1** an act of repairing something. **2** the condition of an object: *in good repair.*
■ **repairer** noun.

repair² verb (**repair to**) go to a place.

reparable adjective able to be repaired.

reparation noun **1** something done to make up for a wrong. **2** (**reparations**) compensation for war damage paid by a defeated country.

repartee /rep-ar-tee/ noun quick, witty comments or conversation.

repast /ri-pahst/ noun formal a meal.

repatriate /ree-pat-ri-ayt/ verb (**repatriates, repatriating, repatriated**) send someone back to their own country.
■ **repatriation** noun.

repay verb (**repays, repaying, repaid**) **1** pay back money owed to someone. **2** do something as a reward for a favour or kindness. **3** be worthy of investigation,

renew verb **1** *I renewed my search:* resume, return to, take up again, come back to, begin again, restart, recommence, continue (with), carry on (with). **2** *they renewed their vows:* reaffirm, repeat, reiterate, restate. **3** *something to renew her interest in life:* revive, regenerate, revitalize, reinvigorate, restore, resuscitate. **4** *the hotel was completely renewed:* renovate, restore, refurbish, revamp, remodel, modernize; informal do up; N. Amer. informal rehab.

renounce verb **1** *Edward renounced his claim to the throne:* give up, relinquish, abandon, surrender, waive, forego, desist from, keep off; informal say goodbye to. **2** *she renounced her family:* reject, repudiate, deny, abandon, wash your hands of, turn your back on, disown, spurn, shun.

renovate verb modernize, restore, refurbish, revamp, recondition, update, rehabilitate, upgrade, refit; informal do up; N. Amer. informal rehab.

renowned adjective famous, well known, celebrated, famed, eminent, distinguished, acclaimed, illustrious, prominent, great, esteemed.
OPPOSITES unknown.

rent noun *I can't afford to pay the rent:* hire, charge, rental.
•verb **1** *she rented a car:* hire, lease, charter. **2** *why don't you rent it out?* let (out), lease (out), hire (out), charter (out).

repair verb **1** *the car was repaired:* mend, fix (up), put/set right, restore (to working order), darn; informal patch up. **2** *repairing relations with other countries:* put/set right, mend, fix, straighten out, improve; informal patch up. **3** *she sought to repair the wrong she had done:* rectify, make good, (put) right, correct, make up for, make amends for.
•noun **1** *in need of repair:* restoration, fixing (up), mending, renovation. **2** *an invisible repair:* mend, darn, patch. **3** *in good repair:* condition, working order, state, shape, fettle; Brit. informal nick.

repay verb **1** *repaying customers who have been cheated:* reimburse, refund, pay back, recompense, compensate. **2** *the grants have to be repaid:* pay back, return, refund, reimburse. **3** *I'd like to repay her generosity:* reciprocate, return, requite, reward.

r

attention, etc.
■ **repayment** noun.

repeal verb make a law no longer valid.
•noun the action of repealing.

repeat verb 1 say or do again. 2 (repeat yourself) say the same thing again.
3 (repeat itself) happen again in the same way or form. •noun 1 something that happens or is done again. 2 a repeated broadcast of a television or radio programme.
■ **repeatedly** adverb.

repel verb (repels, repelling, repelled)
1 drive back or away. 2 make someone feel disgust. 3 force away something with a similar magnetic charge.

repellent adjective 1 causing disgust or distaste. 2 able to keep a particular substance out: *water-repellent nylon.* •noun
1 a substance that keeps insects away. 2 a substance used to treat something so that water cannot pass through it.

repent verb feel sorry for something bad that you have done.
■ **repentance** noun **repentant** adjective.

repercussions plural noun the consequences of an event or action.

repertoire /rep-er-twar/ noun the material known or regularly performed by a performer or company.

repertory /rep-er-tuh-ri/ noun (plural repertories) 1 the performance by a company of various plays, operas, etc. at regular intervals. 2 a repertoire.

repetition noun 1 the action of repeating. 2 a repeat of something.

repetitious adjective having too much repetition; repetitive.

repetitive adjective involving repetition; repeated many or too many times.
■ **repetitively** adverb.

rephrase verb (rephrases, rephrasing, rephrased) express something in an alternative way.

repine verb (repines, repining, repined) literary be unhappy or anxious.

replace verb (replaces, replacing, replaced)
1 take the place of. 2 provide a substitute for. 3 put something back in its previous position.
■ **replaceable** adjective.

replacement noun 1 the action of replacing. 2 a person or thing that takes the place of another.

replay noun 1 a match that is played again because the previous game was a draw.
2 an act of playing a recording again. •verb
1 play back a recording. 2 play a match again.

THESAURUS

repeal verb *the Act was repealed:* cancel, abolish, reverse, rescind, revoke, annul, quash.
OPPOSITES enact.
•noun *the repeal of the law:* cancellation, abolition, reversal, rescinding, annulment.

repeat verb 1 *she repeated her story:* say again, restate, reiterate, go/run through again, recapitulate; informal recap. 2 *children can repeat chunks of text:* recite, quote, parrot, regurgitate, echo; informal trot out.
3 *Steele was invited to repeat his work:* do again, redo, replicate, duplicate. 4 *the episodes were repeated:* rebroadcast, rerun, reshow.
•noun 1 *a repeat of the previous year's final:* repetition, replication, duplicate. 2 *repeats of his TV show:* rerun, reshowing, replay.

repeatedly adverb frequently, often, again and again, over and over (again), time and (time) again, many times, persistently, recurrently, constantly, continually, regularly; N. Amer. oftentimes.

repel verb 1 *the US repelled an Iraqi attack:* fight off, repulse, drive back, force back, beat back, hold off; Brit. see off. 2 *the sight of the food repelled me:* revolt, disgust, repulse, sicken, nauseate, turn someone's stomach; informal turn off; N. Amer. informal gross out.
OPPOSITES attract, delight.

repertoire noun collection, range, repertory, list, store, stock, repository, supply.

repetition noun 1 *the statistics bear repetition:* reiteration, restatement, retelling. 2 *a repetition of the scene in the kitchen:* recurrence, rerun, repeat. 3 *there is some repetition:* repetitiousness, repetitiveness, redundancy, tautology.

repetitive, repetitious adjective recurring, recurrent, repeated, unvaried, unchanging, routine, mechanical, automatic, monotonous, boring.
OPPOSITES unique, varied.

replace verb 1 *Adam replaced the receiver:* put back, return, restore. 2 *a new chairman came in to replace him:* take the place of, succeed, take over from, supersede, stand in for, substitute for, deputize for; informal step into someone's shoes/boots. 3 *she replaced the spoon with a fork:* substitute, exchange, change, swap.
OPPOSITES remove.

replacement noun 1 *we have to find a replacement:* substitute, stand-in, locum, understudy, relief, cover, successor. 2 *the wiring was in need of replacement:* renewal.

r

replenish verb fill up a supply again after using some of it.
■ **replenishment** noun.

replete adjective 1 (**replete with**) filled or well supplied with. 2 very full with food.
■ **repletion** noun.

replica noun an exact copy or model of something.

replicate verb (**replicates, replicating, replicated**) make an exact copy of.
■ **replication** noun.

reply verb (**replies, replying, replied**) 1 say or write a response to something said or written. 2 respond with a similar action. • noun (plural **replies**) a spoken or written response.

report verb 1 give a spoken or written account of something. 2 (**be reported**) be said or rumoured. 3 make a formal complaint about. 4 tell someone in authority that you have arrived or are ready to do something. 5 (**report to**) be responsible to a manager. • noun 1 a spoken or written account of something. 2 Brit. a teacher's written assessment of a pupil's progress. 3 the sound of an explosion or a gun being fired.

reportage /rep-or-**tahzh**/ noun the reporting of news by the press and the broadcasting media.

reporter noun a person who reports news for a newspaper or broadcasting company.

repose noun a state of restfulness, peace, or calm. • verb (**reposes, reposing, reposed**) lie or be kept in a particular place.

repository noun (plural **repositories**) 1 a place or container for storage. 2 a place where a lot of something is found.

repossess verb take possession of something when a buyer fails to make the required payments.
■ **repossession** noun.

reprehensible adjective deserving condemnation; bad.

represent verb 1 act and speak on behalf of. 2 amount to. 3 be a specimen or example of. 4 show or describe in a particular way. 5 depict in a work of art. 6 signify or symbolize.

representation noun 1 the action of representing. 2 an image, model, etc. of something. 3 (**representations**) statements made to an authority.

representational adjective 1 relating to representation. 2 (of art) not abstract.

representative adjective 1 typical of a class or group. 2 consisting of people

replica noun 1 *is it real or a replica?* copy, model, duplicate, reproduction, dummy, imitation, facsimile. 2 *a replica of her mother:* perfect likeness, double, lookalike, living image, twin, clone; informal spitting image, dead ringer.

reply verb *Rachel didn't reply:* respond, answer, write back, rejoin, retort, riposte, counter, come back. • noun *he waited for a reply:* answer, response, rejoinder, retort, riposte; informal comeback.

report verb 1 *the press reported the story:* communicate, announce, divulge, disclose, reveal, make public, publish, broadcast, proclaim, publicize. 2 *I reported him to the police:* inform on; informal shop, tell on, squeal on, rat on; Brit. informal grass on. 3 *Juliet reported for duty:* present yourself, arrive, turn up; informal show up. • noun 1 *a full report on the meeting:* account, record, minutes, proceedings, transcript. 2 *reports of drug dealing:* news, information, word, intelligence. 3 *newspaper reports:* story, account, article, piece, item, column, feature, bulletin, dispatch. 4 (Brit.) *a school report:* assessment, evaluation, appraisal. 5 *reports of his imminent resignation:* rumour, whisper; informal buzz. 6 *the report of a gun:* bang, crack, explosion, boom.

reporter noun journalist, correspondent, newsman, newswoman, columnist; Brit. pressman; informal hack, stringer, journo; N. Amer. informal newsie.

represent verb 1 *a character representing a single quality:* stand for, symbolize, personify, epitomize, typify, embody, illustrate. 2 *Hathor is represented as a woman with cow's horns:* depict, portray, render, picture, delineate, show, illustrate. 3 *his solicitor represented him in court:* appear for, act for, speak on behalf of. 4 *the Queen was represented by Lord Lewin:* deputize for, substitute for, stand in for.

representation noun 1 *Rossetti's representation of women:* portrayal, depiction, presentation, rendition. 2 *representations of the human form:* likeness, painting, drawing, picture, illustration, sketch, image, model, figure, statue.

representative adjective 1 *a representative sample:* typical, characteristic, illustrative. 2 *a female figure representative of Britain:* symbolic, emblematic.
OPPOSITES atypical.
• noun 1 *a representative of the Royal Society:* spokesperson, spokesman, spokeswoman, agent, official, mouthpiece. 2 *a sales representative:* salesman, saleswoman, commercial traveller, agent, negotiator; informal rep; N. Amer. informal drummer. 3 *he acted as his father's*

r

chosen to act and speak on behalf of a wider group. **3** portraying or symbolizing something. •noun **1** a person chosen to act and speak for another or others. **2** a person who travels around trying to sell their company's products. **3** an example of a class or group.

repress verb **1** bring under control by force. **2** try not to have or show a thought or feeling. **3** (**repressed**) tending to keep your feelings or desires hidden.
■ repression noun.

repressive adjective restricting personal freedom.

reprieve noun **1** the cancellation or postponement of a punishment, especially the death penalty. **2** a brief delay before something undesirable happens. •verb (**reprieves, reprieving, reprieved**) give someone a reprieve.

reprimand verb speak severely to someone because they have done something wrong. •noun an act of reprimanding someone.

reprint verb print again. •noun **1** an act of reprinting. **2** a copy of a book that has been reprinted.

reprisal noun an act of retaliation.

reprise /ri-**preez**/ noun **1** a repeated passage in music. **2** a further performance of something. •verb (**reprises, reprising, reprised**) repeat a piece of music or a performance.

reproach verb express disapproval of or disappointment with. •noun an expression of disapproval or disappointment.
■ reproachful adjective **reproachfully** adverb.

reprobate /**rep**-ruh-bayt/ noun a person

who behaves in an immoral way.

reproduce verb (**reproduces, reproducing, reproduced**) **1** produce a copy or representation of. **2** recreate in a different medium or context. **3** produce young or offspring.

reproduction noun **1** the process of reproducing. **2** a copy of a work of art.
■ reproductive adjective.

reproof noun a reprimand.

reprove verb (**reproves, reproving, reproved**) reprimand; tell off.

reptile noun a cold-blooded animal of a class that includes snakes, lizards, crocodiles, and tortoises.
■ reptilian adjective.

republic noun a state in which power is held by the people and their elected representatives, and which has a president rather than a king or queen.

republican adjective **1** belonging to or characteristic of a republic. **2** in favour of republican government. **3** (**Republican**) (in the US) relating to or supporting the Republican Party. •noun **1** a person in favour of republican government. **2** (**Republican**) (in the US) a member or supporter of the Republican Party. **3** (**Republican**) a person who wants Ireland to be one country.
■ republicanism noun.

repudiate verb (**repudiates, repudiating, repudiated**) **1** refuse to accept or support. **2** deny that something is true or valid.
■ repudiation noun.

repugnance noun great disgust.

THESAURUS

representative: deputy, substitute, stand-in, proxy, delegate, ambassador, emissary.

repress verb **1** the rebellion was repressed: suppress, quell, quash, subdue, put down, crush, extinguish, stamp out, defeat, contain. **2** the peasants were repressed: oppress, subjugate, keep down, tyrannize. **3** these emotions may well be repressed: restrain, hold back/in, suppress, keep in check, control, curb, stifle, bottle up; informal button up, keep the lid on.
OPPOSITES express.

repression noun **1** the repression of the protests: suppression, quashing, subduing, crushing, stamping out. **2** political repression: oppression, subjugation, suppression, tyranny, authoritarianism. **3** the repression of sexual urges: restraint, suppression, control, curbing, stifling, bottling up.

reprieve verb she was reprieved: pardon, spare, amnesty; informal let off (the hook). •noun she was given a reprieve: pardon, stay of execution, amnesty.

reprimand verb he was publicly reprimanded: rebuke, reproach, scold, admonish, reprove, chastise, upbraid, berate, take to task, castigate; informal tell off; Brit. informal tick off; N. Amer. informal chew out. •noun a severe reprimand: rebuke, reproach, scolding, admonition; informal telling-off; Brit. informal ticking-off.

reproduce verb **1** each artwork is reproduced in colour: copy, duplicate, replicate, photocopy, xerox, photostat, print. **2** this work has not been reproduced in other laboratories: repeat, replicate, recreate, redo, simulate, imitate, emulate, mimic. **3** some animals reproduce prolifically: breed, procreate, propagate, multiply.

reproduction noun **1** a reproduction of the original: print, copy, reprint, duplicate, facsimile, photocopy; trademark Xerox. **2** the process of reproduction: breeding, procreation, multiplying, propagation.

repugnant adjective very unpleasant.

repulse verb (**repulses, repulsing, repulsed**) **1** drive back by force. **2** reject or refuse to accept. **3** give someone a feeling of strong disgust. •**noun** the action of repulsing.

repulsion noun **1** a feeling of strong disgust. **2** a force by which objects tend to push each other away.

repulsive adjective arousing a feeling of strong disgust.

reputable /rep-yuu-tuh-b'l/ adjective having a good reputation.

reputation noun the beliefs or opinions that people generally hold about someone or something.

repute noun **1** the opinion that people have of someone or something. **2** good reputation. •**verb 1** (**be reputed**) have a particular reputation. **2** (**reputed**) believed to exist.
■ **reputedly** adverb.

request noun **1** an act of asking politely or formally for something. **2** something that is asked for in this way. •**verb** politely or formally ask for something, or ask someone to do something.

requiem /rek-wi-em/ noun **1** a Christian Mass for the souls of dead people. **2** a musical work based on such a Mass.

require verb (**requires, requiring, required**) **1** need or want something for a purpose. **2** instruct or expect someone to do something. **3** regard a particular thing as necessary or compulsory.

requirement noun **1** something that you need or want. **2** something that is compulsory.

requisite /rek-wi-zit/ adjective necessary because of circumstances or regulations. •**noun** a thing that is needed for a particular purpose.

requisition noun **1** an official order allowing property or materials to be taken or used. **2** the taking of goods for military or public use. •**verb** officially take possession of something, especially during a war.

reredos /reer-doss/ noun (plural **reredos**) an ornamental screen at the back of an altar in a church.

rerun verb (**reruns, rerunning, reran**; past participle **rerun**) show, stage, or perform again. •**noun** a rerun event, competition, or programme.

resat past and past participle of RESIT.

reschedule verb (**reschedules, rescheduling, rescheduled**) change the timing of.

rescind /ri-sind/ verb cancel or repeal a law, order, etc.

rescue verb (**rescues, rescuing, rescued**) save from danger or distress. •**noun** an act of rescuing or being rescued.
■ **rescuer** noun.

research noun the study of materials and sources in order to establish facts and reach new conclusions. •**verb** carry out research into a subject, or for a book, programme, etc.
■ **researcher** noun.

resemblance noun **1** the state of resembling. **2** a way in which things

---

THESAURUS

repulsive adjective disgusting, revolting, foul, nasty, obnoxious, sickening, nauseating, stomach-churning.
OPPOSITES attractive.

reputation noun name, good name, character, repute, standing, stature, position, renown, esteem, prestige.

request noun **1** requests for assistance: appeal, entreaty, plea, petition, application, demand, call. **2** Charlotte spoke, at Ursula's request: bidding, entreaty, demand, insistence. **3** indicate your requests on the form: requirement, wish, desire, choice.
•**verb 1** the government requested aid: ask for, appeal for, call for, seek, solicit, plead for, apply for, demand. **2** I requested him to help: ask, call on, beg, entreat, implore; literary beseech.

require verb **1** the child required hospital treatment: need. **2** a situation requiring patience: necessitate, demand, call for, involve, entail. **3** unquestioning obedience is required: demand, insist on, call for, ask for, expect. **4** she was required to pay costs: order, instruct, command, enjoin, oblige,

compel, force. **5** do you require anything else? want, desire, lack, be short of.

requirement noun need, necessity, prerequisite, stipulation, demand, want, essential.

rescue verb **1** an attempt to rescue the hostages: save, free, set free, release, liberate, deliver. **2** Boyd rescued his papers: retrieve, recover, salvage.
•**noun** the rescue of ten crewmen: saving, rescuing, release, freeing, liberation, deliverance.

research noun medical research: investigation, experimentation, testing, analysis, fact-finding, examination, scrutiny.
•**verb** the phenomenon has been widely researched: investigate, study, enquire into, look into, probe, explore, analyse, examine, scrutinize.

resemblance noun similarity, likeness, similitude, correspondence, congruence, conformity, comparability, parallel.
OPPOSITES dissimilarity.

r

resemble each other.

resemble verb (resembles, resembling, resembled) look or be like.

resent verb feel bitter towards.

resentful adjective bitter about something you think is unfair.
■ **resentfully** adverb.

resentment noun a feeling of bitterness about something unfair.

reservation noun **1** the action of reserving. **2** an arrangement for something to be reserved. **3** an area of land set aside for a native people. **4** an expression of doubt about a statement.

reserve verb (reserves, reserving, reserved) **1** keep something to be used in the future. **2** arrange for a seat, ticket, etc. to be kept for a particular person. **3** have or keep a right or power. ● noun **1** a supply of something available for use if required. **2** money kept available by a bank, company, etc. **3** a military force kept to reinforce others or for use in an emergency. **4** an extra player in a team, who can be called on to play if necessary. **5** (**the reserves**) the second-choice team. **6** an area of land set aside for wildlife or

for a native people. **7** a lack of warmth or openness.

reserved adjective slow to reveal emotion or opinions.

reservist noun a member of a military reserve force.

reservoir noun **1** a large lake used as a source of water supply. **2** a place where fluid collects. **3** a supply or source of something.

reshuffle verb (reshuffles, reshuffling, reshuffled) **1** change the roles or positions of government ministers. **2** rearrange.
● noun an act of reshuffling.

reside verb (resides, residing, resided) formal **1** live in a particular place. **2** (**reside in** or **with**) (of a right or power) belong to a person or group. **3** (**reside in**) (of a quality) be naturally present in.

residence noun **1** the fact of living somewhere. **2** the place where a person lives.

residency noun (plural **residencies**) the fact of living in a place.

resident noun **1** a person who lives somewhere on a long-term basis. **2** Brit. a guest in a hotel. ● adjective living somewhere on a long-term basis.

THESAURUS

resemble verb look like, be similar to, remind you of, take after, approximate to, smack of, correspond to, echo, mirror, parallel.
OPPOSITES differ from.

resent verb begrudge, feel aggrieved at/about, feel bitter about, grudge, be resentful of, take exception to, object to, take amiss, take offence at.
OPPOSITES welcome.

resentment noun bitterness, indignation, irritation, pique, dissatisfaction, disgruntlement, discontentment, acrimony, rancour.

reservation noun **1** grave reservations: doubt, qualm, scruple; (**reservations**) misgivings, scepticism, unease, hesitation, objection. **2** an Indian reservation: reserve, enclave, sanctuary, territory, homeland.

reserve verb **1** ask your newsagent to reserve you a copy: put aside, set aside, keep (back), save, hold back, keep in reserve, earmark. **2** he reserved a table: book, order, arrange for, secure. **3** all rights reserved: retain, keep, hold. **4** reserve your judgement until you know him better: defer, postpone, put off, delay, withhold.
● noun **1** reserves of petrol and oil: stock, store, supply, stockpile, pool, hoard, cache. **2** the army are calling up reserves: reinforcements, extras, auxiliaries. **3** a nature reserve: national park, sanctuary,

preserve, conservation area. **4** his natural reserve: shyness, diffidence, timidity, taciturnity, inhibition, reticence, detachment, distance, remoteness. **5** she trusted him without reserve: reservation, qualification, condition, limitation, hesitation, doubt.
● adjective a reserve goalkeeper: substitute, stand-in, relief, replacement, fallback, spare, extra.

reserved adjective **1** Sewell is rather reserved: uncommunicative, reticent, unforthcoming, quiet, silent, taciturn, withdrawn, secretive, shy, retiring, diffident, timid, introverted; informal standoffish. **2** that table is reserved: booked, taken, spoken for, prearranged.
OPPOSITES outgoing.

reservoir noun **1** sailing on the reservoir: lake, pool, pond, basin. **2** an ink reservoir: receptacle, container, holder, tank. **3** the reservoir of managerial talent: stock, store, stockpile, reserve(s), supply, bank, pool.

residence noun (informal) home, house, address, quarters, lodgings; informal pad; formal dwelling, domicile, abode.

resident noun the residents of New York City: inhabitant, local, citizen, native, householder, homeowner, occupier, tenant; humorous denizen.
● adjective **1** resident in the UK: living, residing; formal dwelling. **2** a resident nanny: live-in.

r

residential adjective **1** involving residence. **2** providing accommodation. **3** occupied by private houses.

residual adjective remaining after the greater part has gone or been taken away.

residue noun a small amount of something that remains after the main part has gone or been taken.

resign verb **1** voluntarily leave a job or position of office. **2** (**be resigned**) accept that something bad cannot be avoided.

resignation noun **1** an act of resigning. **2** a document stating that you intend to resign. **3** acceptance of something bad but inevitable.

resilient adjective **1** able to spring back into shape after bending, stretching, or being compressed. **2** able to withstand or recover quickly from difficult conditions.
■ **resilience** noun.

resin noun **1** a sticky substance produced by some trees. **2** a synthetic substance used as the basis of plastics, adhesives, etc.

resist verb **1** withstand the action or effect of. **2** try to prevent or fight against. **3** stop yourself having or doing something tempting.

resistance noun **1** the action of resisting. **2** a secret organization that fights against an occupying enemy. **3** the ability not to be affected by something. **4** the degree to which a material or device resists the passage of an electric current.
■ **resistant** adjective.

resistor noun a device that resists the passage of an electric current.

resit verb (**resits, resitting, resat**) Brit. take an exam again after failing.

resolute /rez-uh-loot/ adjective determined.
■ **resolutely** adverb.

resolution noun **1** a firm decision. **2** a formal statement of opinion by a parliament. **3** determination. **4** the resolving of a problem or dispute. **5** the degree to which detail is visible in a photograph or an image on a computer or television screen.

resolve verb (**resolves, resolving, resolved**) **1** find a solution to. **2** decide firmly on a course of action. **3** take a decision by a formal vote. **4** (**resolve into**) separate into different parts. •noun determination.

resonant adjective **1** (of sound) deep, clear, and ringing. **2** having the power to bring images, memories, or feelings into your mind.
■ **resonance** noun.

THESAURUS

residue noun remainder, rest, remnant(s), surplus, extra, excess, remains, leftovers.

resign verb **1** *the manager resigned:* leave, give notice, stand down, step down; informal quit. **2** *19 MPs resigned their seats:* give up, leave, vacate, stand down from; informal quit, pack in.
□ **resign yourself to reconcile yourself to**, come to terms with.

resignation noun **1** *his resignation from his post:* departure, leaving, standing down, stepping down; informal quitting. **2** *he accepted his fate with resignation:* patience, forbearance, stoicism, fortitude, fatalism, acceptance.

resigned adjective patient, long-suffering, uncomplaining, forbearing, stoical, philosophical, fatalistic.

resist verb **1** *built to resist cold winters:* withstand, be proof against, combat, weather, endure, be resistant to, keep out. **2** *they resisted his attempts to change things:* oppose, fight against, object to, defy, kick against; informal be anti. **3** *I resisted the urge to retort:* refrain from, abstain from, forbear from, desist from, not give in to, restrain yourself from.
OPPOSITES welcome, submit to.

resistance noun **1** *resistance to change:* opposition, hostility. **2** *a spirited resistance:* struggle, fight, battle, stand, opposition, defiance. **3** *the body's resistance to disease:* immunity from, defences against. **4** *the French resistance:* freedom fighters, underground, partisans.

resistant adjective **1** *resistant to water:* impervious, immune, invulnerable, proof, unaffected. **2** *resistant to change:* opposed, averse, hostile, inimical, against; informal anti.
OPPOSITES vulnerable, favourable.

resolution noun **1** *her resolution not to smoke:* intention, resolve, decision, intent, aim, plan, commitment, pledge, promise. **2** *the committee passed the resolution:* motion, proposal, proposition; N. Amer. resolve. **3** *she handled the work with resolution:* determination, purpose, resolve, single-mindedness; informal guts. **4** *a satisfactory resolution of the problem:* solution, answer, end, settlement, conclusion.

resolve verb **1** *this matter cannot be resolved overnight:* settle, sort out, solve, fix, straighten out, deal with, put right, rectify; informal hammer out, thrash out. **2** *David resolved to wait:* determine, decide, make up your mind. **3** *the committee resolved that the project should proceed:* vote, rule, decide formally, agree. •noun *he reaffirmed his resolve:* determination, purpose, resolution, single-mindedness; informal guts.

r

resonate verb (**resonates, resonating, resonated**) make a deep, clear, ringing sound.

resort noun **1** a place visited for holidays. **2** a strategy or course of action. • verb (**resort to**) turn to a strategy or course of action so as to resolve a difficult situation.

resound verb **1** make a ringing, booming, or echoing sound. **2** (**resounding**) definite; unmistakable.

resource noun **1** (**resources**) a stock or supply of materials or assets. **2** something that can be used to help achieve an aim. **3** (**resources**) personal qualities that help you to cope with difficult circumstances. • verb (**be resourced**) be provided with resources.

resourceful adjective able to find quick and clever ways to overcome difficulties. ■ **resourcefully** adverb **resourcefulness** noun.

respect noun **1** a feeling of admiration for someone because of their qualities or achievements. **2** consideration for the feelings or rights of other people. **3** (**respects**) polite greetings. **4** a particular aspect, point, or detail. • verb **1** have respect for. **2** avoid harming or interfering

with. **3** agree to observe a law, principle, etc.

respectable adjective **1** regarded by society as being correct or proper. **2** adequate or acceptable. ■ **respectability** noun **respectably** adverb.

respectful adjective feeling or showing respect. ■ **respectfully** adverb.

respecting preposition with reference to.

respective adjective belonging or relating separately to each of two or more people or things.

respectively adverb individually and in the order already mentioned.

respiration noun the action of breathing.

respirator noun **1** a device worn over the face to prevent you breathing in dust, smoke, etc. **2** a device that enables someone to breathe when they cannot do so naturally.

respiratory /ri-spi-ruh-tuh-ri/ adjective relating to breathing.

respire verb (**respires, respiring, respired**) technical breathe.

respite /ress-pyt/ noun a short period of rest or relief from something difficult or unpleasant.

THESAURUS

resort noun *strike action is our last resort:* **option**, alternative, choice, possibility, hope, measure, step, recourse, expedient. □ **resort to fall back on**, have recourse to, turn to, make use of, use, avail yourself of.

resound verb **echo**, reverberate, ring, boom, thunder, rumble, resonate.

resounding adjective **1** *a resounding voice:* **reverberating**, resonating, echoing, ringing, sonorous, deep, rich. **2** *a resounding success:* **enormous**, huge, very great, tremendous, terrific, colossal, emphatic, outstanding, remarkable, phenomenal.

resource noun **1** *your tutor is there as a resource:* **facility**, amenity, aid, help, support. **2** *a person of resource:* **initiative**, resourcefulness, enterprise, ingenuity, inventiveness. **3** (**resources**) *use your resources efficiently:* **assets**, funds, wealth, money, capital, supplies, materials, stores, stocks, reserves.

resourceful adjective **ingenious**, enterprising, inventive, creative, clever, talented, able, capable.

respect noun **1** *the respect due to a great artist:* **esteem**, regard, high opinion, admiration, reverence, deference, honour. **2** *he spoke to her with respect:* **due regard**, politeness, courtesy, civility, deference. **3** (**respects**) *paying your respects:* **regards**, compliments, greetings, best/good wishes. **4** *the report was accurate in every respect:*

aspect, regard, feature, way, sense, particular, point, detail. OPPOSITES contempt. • verb **1** *he is highly respected for his industry:* **esteem**, admire, think highly of, have a high opinion of, look up to, revere, honour. **2** *they respected our privacy:* **show consideration for**, have regard for, observe, be mindful of, be heedful of. **3** *father respected her wishes:* **abide by**, comply with, follow, adhere to, conform to, act in accordance with, obey, observe, keep (to). OPPOSITES despise, disregard, disobey.

respectable adjective **1** *a respectable middle-class background:* **reputable**, upright, honest, honourable, trustworthy, decent, good, well bred, clean-living. **2** *a respectable salary:* **fairly good**, decent, fair-sized, reasonable, moderately good, large, sizeable, considerable. OPPOSITES disreputable, paltry.

respectful adjective **deferential**, reverent, dutiful, polite, well mannered, civil, courteous, gracious. OPPOSITES rude.

respective adjective **separate**, personal, own, particular, individual, specific, special.

respite noun **rest**, break, breathing space, interval, lull, pause, time out, relief; informal breather, let-up.

r

resplendent adjective attractive and impressive.

respond verb say or do something in reply or as a reaction.

respondent noun 1 Law a person against whom a petition is filed, especially one in a divorce case. 2 a person who responds to a questionnaire or advertisement.

response noun an answer or reaction.

responsibility noun (plural **responsibilities**) 1 the state of being responsible. 2 the opportunity to act independently. 3 a thing which you are required to do as part of a job, role, or obligation.

responsible adjective 1 obliged to do something or look after someone. 2 being the cause of something and so able to be blamed or credited for it. 3 able to be trusted. 4 (of a job) involving important duties or decisions. 5 (**responsible to**) having to report to a senior person. ■ **responsibly** adverb.

☑ responsi*ble*, not -*able*.

responsive adjective responding readily and positively.

rest¹ verb 1 stop working or moving in order to relax or recover your strength. 2 place something so that it stays in a particular position. 3 remain or be left in a particular condition: *rest assured*. 4 (**rest on**) depend or be based on. 5 (**rest with**) (of power, responsibility, etc.) belong to. •noun 1 a period of resting. 2 a motionless state. 3 an object that is used to hold or support something. 4 a brief interval of silence in a piece of music.

rest² noun the remaining part, people, or things.

restaurant /ress-tuh-ront/ noun a place where people pay to sit and eat meals that are cooked on the premises.

restaurateur /ress-tuh-ruh-ter/ noun a person who owns and manages a restaurant.

☑ note that there is no *n*: restau*rateur*.

restful adjective having a quiet and soothing quality.

restitution noun 1 the restoration of something lost or stolen to its proper owner. 2 payment for injury or loss that has been suffered.

restive adjective unable to keep still or silent; restless.

THESAURUS

respond verb 1 *they do not respond to questions:* answer, reply, write back, come back, rejoin, retort, riposte, counter. 2 *they were slow to respond:* react, reciprocate, retaliate.

response noun 1 *his response to the question:* answer, reply, rejoinder, retort, riposte; informal comeback. 2 *an angry response:* reaction, reply, retaliation; informal comeback.
OPPOSITES question.

responsibility noun 1 *it was his responsibility to find witnesses:* duty, task, function, job, role, business; Brit. informal pigeon. 2 *they denied responsibility for the attack:* blame, fault, guilt, culpability, liability. 3 *a sense of responsibility:* trustworthiness, (common) sense, maturity, reliability, dependability. 4 *managerial responsibility:* authority, control, power, leadership.
OPPOSITES irresponsibility.

responsible adjective 1 *who is responsible for prisons?* in charge of, in control of, at the helm of, accountable for, liable for. 2 *I am responsible for the error:* accountable, answerable, to blame, guilty, culpable, blameworthy, at fault, in the wrong. 3 *a responsible job:* important, powerful, executive. 4 *a responsible tenant:* trustworthy, sensible, mature, reliable, dependable.
OPPOSITES irresponsible.

responsive adjective reactive, receptive, open to suggestions, amenable, flexible, forthcoming.
OPPOSITES unresponsive.

rest¹ verb 1 *he needed to rest:* relax, ease up/off, let up, slow down, have/take a break, unbend, unwind, take it easy, put your feet up; informal take five, have/take a breather, chill out. 2 *his hands rested on the rail:* lie, be laid, repose, be placed, be positioned, be supported by. 3 *she rested her basket on the ground:* support, prop (up), lean, lay, set, stand, position, place, put.
•noun 1 *get some rest:* relaxation, repose, leisure, respite, time off, breathing space; informal lie-down. 2 *a short rest from work:* holiday, vacation, break, breathing space, interval, interlude, intermission, time off/out; informal breather. 3 *she took the poker from its rest:* stand, base, holder, support, rack, frame, shelf. 4 *we came to rest 100 metres lower:* a standstill, a halt, a stop.

rest² noun *the rest of the board are appointees:* remainder, residue, balance, others, those left, remnant(s), surplus, excess.

restful adjective relaxing, quiet, calm, tranquil, soothing, peaceful, leisurely, undisturbed, untroubled.
OPPOSITES exciting.

r

restless adjective unable to rest or relax.
■ **restlessly** adverb.

restorative adjective able to restore health or strength.

restore verb (**restores, restoring, restored**) 1 bring back a previous practice, situation, etc. 2 return someone or something to a previous condition, place, position, etc. 3 repair or renovate a building, work of art, etc.
■ **restoration** noun **restorer** noun.

restrain verb 1 keep under control or within limits. 2 stop someone moving or acting freely.

restrained adjective 1 reserved or unemotional. 2 not richly decorated or brightly coloured; subtle.

restraint noun 1 the action of keeping someone or something under control. 2 a

device which limits or prevents freedom of movement. 3 self-controlled behaviour.

restrict verb 1 put a limit on. 2 stop someone moving or acting freely.

restricted adjective 1 limited in extent, number, or scope. 2 not open to the public; secret.

restriction noun 1 a rule, law, etc. that prevents free movement or action. 2 the action of restricting.

restrictive adjective preventing freedom of action or movement.

restroom noun N. Amer. a toilet in a public building.

restructure verb (**restructures, restructuring, restructured**) 1 organize differently. 2 convert a debt into another debt that can be repaid at a later time.

result noun 1 a thing that is caused or

THESAURUS

restless adjective 1 *Maria was restless:* uneasy, ill at ease, fidgety, edgy, tense, worked up, nervous, nervy, agitated, anxious; informal jumpy, jittery, twitchy, uptight. 2 *a restless night:* sleepless, wakeful, fitful, broken, disturbed, troubled, unsettled.

restoration noun 1 *the restoration of democracy:* reinstatement, reinstitution, re-establishment, reimposition, return. 2 *the restoration of derelict housing:* repair, renovation, mending, refurbishment, reconditioning, rehabilitation, rebuilding, reconstruction; N. Amer. informal rehab.

restore verb 1 *the aim to restore democracy:* reinstate, bring back, reinstitute, reimpose, reinstall, re-establish. 2 *he restored it to its rightful owner:* return, give back, hand back. 3 *the building has been restored:* repair, fix, mend, refurbish, recondition, rehabilitate, renovate; informal do up; N. Amer. informal rehab. 4 *a good sleep can restore you:* reinvigorate, revitalize, revive, refresh, energize, freshen.
OPPOSITES abolish, tire.

restrain verb 1 *Charles restrained his anger:* control, check, curb, suppress, contain, rein back/in; informal keep the lid on. 2 *she could barely restrain herself from swearing:* prevent, stop, keep, hold back.

restrained adjective 1 *Julie was quite restrained:* self-controlled, not given to excesses, sober, steady, unemotional, undemonstrative. 2 *restrained elegance:* muted, soft, discreet, subtle, quiet, unobtrusive, unostentatious, understated, tasteful.
OPPOSITES impetuous.

restraint noun 1 *a restraint on their impulsiveness:* constraint, check, control, restriction, limitation, curtailment, rein,

brake. 2 *the customary restraint of the police:* self-control, self-discipline, control, moderation, judiciousness. 3 *the room has been decorated with restraint:* subtlety, understatedness, taste, discretion, discrimination.
OPPOSITES impetuousness.

restrict verb 1 *a busy job restricted his leisure activities:* limit, keep within bounds, regulate, control, moderate, cut down. 2 *the belt rather restricts movement:* hinder, interfere with, impede, hamper, obstruct, block, check, curb.

restricted adjective 1 *restricted space:* cramped, confined, constricted, small, narrow, tight. 2 *a restricted calorie intake:* limited, controlled, regulated, reduced. 3 *a restricted zone:* out of bounds, off limits, private, exclusive. 4 *restricted information:* secret, classified; informal hush-hush.
OPPOSITES generous, unlimited, public, open.

restriction noun 1 *there is no restriction on the number of places:* limitation, constraint, control, check, curb. 2 *the restriction of personal freedom:* reduction, limitation, diminution, curtailment. 3 *restriction of movement:* hindrance, impediment, slowing, reduction, limitation.

result noun *stress is the result of overwork:* consequence, outcome, upshot, sequel, effect, reaction, repercussion.
OPPOSITES cause.
● verb *anger may result from an argument:* follow, ensue, develop, stem, spring, arise, derive, proceed; (**result from**) be caused by, be brought about by, be produced by, originate in.
□ **result in end in**, culminate in, lead to, trigger, cause, bring about, occasion, effect, give rise to, produce.

r

produced by something else. **2** a piece of information obtained by experiment or calculation. **3** a final score or mark in an exam or sports event. **4** a satisfactory or favourable outcome. •**verb 1** happen because of something else. **2** (**result in**) have a particular outcome.

resultant adjective happening or produced as a result.

resume verb (**resumes, resuming, resumed**) begin again or continue after a pause.
■ **resumption** noun.

résumé /rez-yuu-may/ noun **1** a summary. **2** N. Amer. a curriculum vitae.

resurgent adjective becoming stronger or more popular again.
■ **resurgence** noun.

resurrect verb **1** restore to life. **2** start using or doing again.

resurrection noun **1** the action of resurrecting. **2** (**the Resurrection**) (in Christian belief) the time when Jesus rose from the dead.

resuscitate /ri-suss-i-tayt/ verb (**resuscitates, resuscitating, resuscitated**) make someone conscious again.
■ **resuscitation** noun.

☑ note that it is -susc-, not -suss-: resuscitate.

retail noun the sale of goods to the public. •**verb 1** sell goods to the public. **2** (**retail at** or **for**) be sold for a particular price.
■ **retailer** noun.

retain verb **1** continue to have; keep possession of. **2** absorb and continue to hold a substance. **3** (**retaining**) keeping something in place.

retainer noun **1** a fee paid in advance to a barrister to secure their services. **2** a servant who has worked for a family for a long time.

retake verb (**retakes, retaking, retook**; past participle **retaken**) **1** take a test or exam again. **2** regain possession of. •**noun** a test or exam that is retaken.

retaliate verb (**retaliates, retaliating, retaliated**) make an attack in return for a similar attack.
■ **retaliation** noun **retaliatory** adjective.

retard verb stop from developing or progressing.
■ **retardation** noun.

retarded adjective offensive less developed mentally than is usual at a particular age.

retch verb make the sound and movements of vomiting.

retention noun the action of retaining, or the state of being retained.

retentive adjective (of a person's memory) effective in retaining facts and impressions.

rethink verb (**rethinks, rethinking, rethought**) consider a policy or course of action again. •**noun** an instance of rethinking.

reticent /ret-i-suhnt/ adjective not revealing your thoughts or feelings readily.
■ **reticence** noun.

retina noun (plural **retinas** or **retinae** /ret-i-nee/) a layer at the back of the eyeball that is sensitive to light and sends impulses to the brain.

retinue noun a group of assistants accompanying an important person.

retire verb (**retires, retiring, retired**) **1** leave

THESAURUS

resume verb restart, recommence, begin again, start again, reopen, renew, return to, continue with, carry on with.
OPPOSITES suspend, abandon.

résumé noun summary, precis, synopsis, abstract, outline, abridgement, overview.

resumption noun restart, continuation, recommencement, reopening, renewal, return, revival.

resurgence noun renewal, revival, renaissance, recovery, comeback, reawakening, resurrection, reappearance, re-emergence, resumption, continuation.

resurrect verb revive, restore, regenerate, revitalize, breathe new life into, reinvigorate, resuscitate, rejuvenate, re-establish, relaunch.

retain verb **1** the government retained a share in the industries: keep (possession of), keep hold of, hang on to. **2** existing footpaths are to be retained: maintain, keep, preserve, conserve.

OPPOSITES give up, abolish.

retaliate verb fight back, hit back, respond, react, reply, reciprocate, counter-attack, get back at someone, pay someone back; informal get your own back.

retaliation noun revenge, vengeance, reprisal, retribution, repayment, response, reaction, reply, counter-attack.

retard verb delay, slow down/up, hold back/up, postpone, detain, decelerate, hinder, impede, check.
OPPOSITES accelerate, bring forward.

reticent adjective uncommunicative, unforthcoming, unresponsive, tight-lipped, quiet, taciturn, silent, reserved.
OPPOSITES expansive.

retire verb **1** he has retired: give up work, stop work. **2** Gillian retired to her office: withdraw, go away, take yourself off, shut yourself away. **3** everyone retired early: go to bed, call it a day; informal turn in, hit

your job and stop working, especially because you have reached a particular age. **2** withdraw from a race or match because of accident or injury. **3** formal leave a place. **4** (of a jury) leave the courtroom to decide the verdict of a trial. **5** go to bed.
■ **retired** adjective.

retirement noun **1** the action of retiring. **2** the period of life after retiring from work.

retiring adjective tending to avoid company; shy.

retook past of RETAKE.

retort[1] verb say something sharp or witty in answer to a remark or accusation. • noun a sharp or witty reply.

retort[2] noun a glass container with a long neck, used for distilling liquids and heating chemicals.

retouch verb make slight improvements to a painting, photograph, etc.

retrace verb (**retraces**, **retracing**, **retraced**) **1** go back over the route that you have just taken. **2** follow a route taken by someone else. **3** trace something back to its source.

retract verb **1** draw something back. **2** withdraw a statement or accusation. **3** go back on an undertaking.
■ **retractable** adjective **retraction** noun.

retreat verb **1** (of an army) withdraw from confrontation with enemy forces. **2** move back from a difficult situation. **3** withdraw to a quiet or secluded place. • noun **1** an act of retreating. **2** a quiet or secluded place. **3** a quiet place where people go for a time to pray and meditate.

retrench verb reduce costs or spending in

times of economic difficulty.
■ **retrenchment** noun.

retrial noun a second or further trial.

retribution noun severe punishment inflicted as revenge.

retrieve verb (**retrieves**, **retrieving**, **retrieved**) **1** get or bring back. **2** find or extract information stored in a computer. **3** improve a bad situation.
■ **retrieval** noun.

retriever noun a breed of dog used for finding and bringing back game that has been shot.

retrograde adjective directed or moving backwards or to a worse state.

retrogressive adjective going back to an earlier and inferior state.
■ **retrogression** noun.

retrorocket noun a small rocket on a spacecraft or missile, fired in the direction of travel to slow it down.

retrospect noun (**in retrospect**) when looking back on a past event.

retrospective adjective **1** looking back on or dealing with past events or situations. **2** taking effect from a date in the past. • noun an exhibition showing the development of an artist's work over a period of time.
■ **retrospectively** adverb.

retroussé /ruh-**troo**-say/ adjective (of a person's nose) turned up at the tip.

retsina /ret-**see**-nuh/ noun a Greek white wine flavoured with resin.

return verb **1** come or go back to a place. **2** (**return to**) go back to a particular state or activity. **3** give, send, or put back. **4** feel,

THESAURUS

the hay/sack.
OPPOSITES emerge, get up.

retiring adjective shy, diffident, self-effacing, unassuming, reserved, reticent, quiet, timid.

retort verb '*Oh, sure,*' *she retorted:* answer, reply, respond, return, counter, riposte, retaliate.
• noun *a sarcastic retort:* answer, reply, response, counter, rejoinder, riposte, retaliation; informal comeback.

retract verb take back, withdraw, recant, disavow, go back on, backtrack on.

retreat verb *the army retreated:* withdraw, retire, draw back, pull back/out, fall back, give way, give ground.
OPPOSITES advance.
• noun **1** *the retreat of the army:* withdrawal, retirement, pullback, flight. **2** *her rural retreat:* refuge, haven, sanctuary, hideaway, hideout, hiding place; informal hidey-hole.

retrieve verb **1** *I retrieved our ball from*

their garden: get back, bring back, recover, recapture, regain, recoup. **2** *they tried to retrieve the situation:* put/set right, rectify, remedy, restore, sort out, straighten out, resolve.

return verb **1** *he returned to London:* go back, come back, arrive back, come home. **2** *the symptoms returned:* recur, reoccur, repeat (itself), reappear. **3** *he returned the money:* give back, hand back, pay back, repay. **4** *Peter returned the book to the shelf:* restore, put back, replace, reinstall. **5** *the jury returned a verdict:* deliver, bring in, hand down.
OPPOSITES keep.
• noun **1** *the return of hard times:* recurrence, reoccurrence, repeat, repetition, reappearance. **2** *I requested the return of my books:* giving back, handing back, replacement, restoration, restitution, reinstatement. **3** *a quick return on investments:* yield, profit, gain, revenue, interest, dividend.

say, or do the same thing in response. **5** (in tennis) hit the ball back to an opponent. **6** (of a judge or jury) give a verdict. **7** produce a profit. **8** elect someone to a political office. •**noun 1** an act of returning. **2** a profit from an investment. **3** Brit. a ticket that lets you travel to a place and back again.

reunify verb (**reunifies, reunifying, reunified**) make a place a united country again.
■ **reunification** noun.

reunion noun **1** the process of reuniting. **2** a gathering of people who have not seen each other for some time.

reunite verb (**reunites, reuniting, reunited**) bring two or more people or things together again.

reuse verb (**reuses, reusing, reused**) use something again.
■ **reusable** adjective.

Rev. or **Revd** abbreviation Reverend.

rev informal noun (**revs**) the number of revolutions of an engine per minute. •**verb** (**revs, revving, revved**) make an engine run quickly by pressing the accelerator.

revamp verb alter something so as to improve it. •**noun** a new and improved version of something.

reveal verb **1** make previously unknown or secret information known. **2** allow something hidden to be seen.

revealing adjective **1** giving out interesting or significant information. **2** (of a piece of clothing) allowing a lot of your body to be seen.

reveille /ri-**val**-li/ noun a signal sounded on

a bugle, drum, etc. to wake up soldiers in the morning.

revel verb (**revels, revelling, revelled**; US spelling **revels, reveling, reveled**) **1** spend time enjoying yourself in a lively, noisy way. **2** (**revel in**) get great pleasure from. •**noun** (**revels**) lively, noisy celebrations.
■ **reveller** noun **revelry** noun (plural **revelries**).

revelation noun **1** the revealing of something previously unknown. **2** a surprising or remarkable thing.

revelatory adjective revealing something previously unknown.

revenge noun something harmful done to someone in return for something bad that they did to you. •**verb** (**revenges, revenging, revenged**) (**revenge yourself** or **be revenged**) harm someone in return for something bad that they did to you.

revenue noun the income received by an organization, or by a government from taxes.

reverberate verb (**reverberates, reverberating, reverberated**) **1** (of a loud noise) be repeated as an echo. **2** have continuing serious effects.
■ **reverberation** noun.

revere verb (**reveres, revering, revered**) respect or admire deeply.

reverence noun deep respect.

reverend adjective a title given to Christian ministers.

reverent adjective showing reverence; deeply respectful.
■ **reverential** adjective **reverently** adverb.

reverie /**rev**-uh-ri/ noun a daydream.

reversal noun **1** a change to an opposite

THESAURUS

revamp verb renovate, redecorate, refurbish, refashion, redesign, restyle; informal do up, give something a facelift, give something a makeover, vamp up; Brit. informal tart up.

reveal verb **1** *the police can't reveal his whereabouts:* disclose, make known, make public, broadcast, publicize, circulate, divulge, tell, let slip/drop, give away/out, blurt out, release, leak; informal let on. **2** *he revealed his new car:* show, display, exhibit, unveil, uncover.
OPPOSITES keep secret, hide.

revel verb *they revelled all night:* celebrate, make merry; informal party, live it up, whoop it up, paint the town red.
•**noun** *late-night revels:* celebration, festivity, jollification, merrymaking, party; informal rave, shindig, bash; Brit. informal rave-up; N. Amer. informal wingding, blast.
□ **revel in** enjoy, delight in, love, like, adore, take pleasure in, relish, lap up, savour; informal get a kick out of.

revelation noun **1** *revelations about his personal life:* disclosure, announcement, report, admission, confession. **2** *the revelation of a secret:* disclosure, divulging, letting slip/drop, giving away/out, leak, betrayal, publicizing.

revenge noun *she is seeking revenge:* retaliation, retribution, vengeance, reprisal, recrimination, an eye for an eye (and a tooth for a tooth), redress.
OPPOSITES forgiveness.
•**verb** *he revenged his brother's murder:* avenge, exact retribution for, take reprisals for, get redress for, make someone pay for; informal get your own back for.
OPPOSITES forgive.

revenue noun income, takings, receipts, proceeds, earnings, profit(s), gain, yield.
OPPOSITES expenditure.

revere verb respect, admire, think highly of, esteem, venerate, look up to, be in awe of.
OPPOSITES despise.

r

direction, position, or course of action. **2** a harmful change of fortune.

reverse verb (**reverses, reversing, reversed**) **1** move backwards. **2** make something the opposite of what it was. **3** turn something the other way round. **4** cancel a judgement by a lower court. • **adjective 1** going in or turned towards the opposite direction. **2** opposite to the usual way. • **noun 1** a complete change of direction or action. **2** (**the reverse**) the opposite or contrary. **3** a setback or defeat. **4** the opposite side of something to the observer.
■ **reversible** adjective.

reversion noun a return to a previous state, practice, etc.

revert verb (**revert to**) return to a previous state, practice, etc.

review noun **1** an examination of something to decide whether changes are necessary. **2** a critical assessment of a book, play, etc. **3** a report of an event that has already happened. **4** a ceremonial display of military forces. • **verb 1** examine or consider something again. **2** write a review of.
■ **reviewer** noun.

revile verb (**reviles, reviling, reviled**) criticize in a rude or scornful way.

revise verb (**revises, revising, revised**) **1** examine and alter a piece of writing. **2** reconsider and change an opinion. **3** Brit. reread work in order to prepare for an exam.
■ **revision** noun.

revisionism noun disapproving the changing of accepted theories or principles.
■ **revisionist** noun & adjective.

revitalize or **revitalise** verb (**revitalizes, revitalizing, revitalized**) give new life and vitality to.
■ **revitalization** noun.

revival noun **1** an improvement in the condition, strength, or popularity of something. **2** a new production of an old play.

revivalism noun **1** the process of trying to reawaken interest in a particular religious faith. **2** the practice of returning to former customs, fashions, etc.
■ **revivalist** noun & adjective.

revive verb (**revives, reviving, revived**) **1** make conscious, healthy, or strong again.

THESAURUS

reverse verb **1** *the car reversed:* back, move back/backwards. **2** *reverse the bottle in the ice bucket:* turn upside down, turn over, upend, invert, turn back to front. **3** *reverse your roles:* swap (round), change (round), exchange, switch (round), transpose. **4** *the umpire reversed the decision:* alter, change, overturn, overthrow, disallow, override, overrule, veto, revoke.
• **adjective** *in reverse order:* backward(s), inverted, transposed, opposite.
• **noun 1** *the reverse is the case:* opposite, contrary, converse, inverse, antithesis. **2** *successes and reverses:* setback, reversal, upset, failure, misfortune, mishap, disaster, blow, disappointment, adversity, hardship, affliction, vicissitude, defeat. **3** *the reverse of the page:* other side, back, underside, wrong side.
OPPOSITES success, front.

revert verb return, go back, change back, default, relapse.

review noun **1** *the Council undertook a review:* analysis, evaluation, assessment, appraisal, examination, investigation, enquiry, probe, inspection, study. **2** *the rent is due for review:* reconsideration, reassessment, re-evaluation, reappraisal. **3** *book reviews:* criticism, critique, assessment, evaluation, commentary.
• **verb 1** *I reviewed the evidence:* survey, study, research, consider, analyse, examine, scrutinize, explore, look into, probe, investigate, inspect, assess, appraise; informal size up. **2** *the referee reviewed his decision:*

reconsider, re-examine, reassess, re-evaluate, reappraise, rethink. **3** *she reviewed the play:* comment on, evaluate, assess, appraise, judge, criticize.

reviewer noun critic, commentator, judge.

revise verb **1** *she revised her opinion:* reconsider, review, re-examine, reassess, re-evaluate, reappraise, rethink, change, alter, modify. **2** *the editor revised the text:* amend, correct, alter, change, edit, rewrite, redraft, rephrase, rework. **3** (Brit.) *revise your lecture notes:* go over, reread, memorize, cram; informal bone up on; Brit. informal swot up (on), mug up (on).

revision noun **1** *a revision of the Prayer Book:* alteration, adaptation, editing, rewriting, redrafting, correction, updating. **2** *a major revision of the system:* reconsideration, review, re-examination, reassessment, re-evaluation, reappraisal, rethink, change, alteration, modification. **3** (Brit.) *he was doing some revision:* rereading, memorizing, cramming; Brit. informal swotting.

revival noun **1** *a revival in the economy:* improvement, rallying, picking up, turn for the better, upturn, upswing, resurgence. **2** *the revival of traditional crafts:* comeback, re-establishment, reintroduction, restoration, reappearance, resurrection.
OPPOSITES downturn, disappearance.

revive verb **1** *attempts to revive her failed:* resuscitate, bring round, bring back to

2 start doing, using, or performing something again.

revivify /ri-viv-i-fy/ verb (**revivifies, revivifying, revivified**) formal revive.

revoke verb (**revokes, revoking, revoked**) make a decree, law, etc. no longer valid. ■ **revocation** noun.

revolt noun an act of rebellion or defiance. •verb **1** rebel against an authority. **2** make someone feel disgust.

revolting adjective very unpleasant; disgusting.

revolution noun **1** the overthrow of a government by force, in favour of a new system. **2** a dramatic and far-reaching change. **3** a single circular movement around a central point.

revolutionary adjective **1** involving or causing dramatic change. **2** taking part in, or relating to, political revolution. •noun (plural **revolutionaries**) a person who starts or supports a political revolution.

revolutionize or **revolutionise** verb (**revolutionizes, revolutionizing, revolutionized**) change something completely or fundamentally.

revolve verb (**revolves, revolving, revolved**) **1** move in a circle around a central point. **2** (**revolve around**) treat as the most important element.

revolver noun a pistol with revolving chambers that allow several shots to be fired without reloading.

revue noun a theatrical show with short sketches, songs, and dances.

revulsion noun a sense of disgust and loathing.

reward noun something given in recognition of service, effort, or achievement. •verb **1** give a reward to. **2** show appreciation of an action or quality by giving a reward.

rewarding adjective providing satisfaction.

rewind verb (**rewinds, rewinding, rewound**) wind a film or tape back to the beginning.

rewire verb (**rewires, rewiring, rewired**) provide with new wiring.

rework verb alter something in order to improve or update it.

rhapsodize or **rhapsodise** verb (**rhapsodizes, rhapsodizing, rhapsodized**) express great enthusiasm about someone or something.

rhapsody noun (plural **rhapsodies**) **1** an expression of great enthusiasm. **2** a piece of music in one extended movement. ■ **rhapsodic** adjective.

rhenium /ree-ni-uhm/ noun a rare silvery-white metallic element.

rheostat /ree-uh-stat/ noun a device for varying the amount of resistance in an electrical circuit.

rhesus factor /ree-suhss/ noun a substance found in the red blood cells of many humans.

THESAURUS

consciousness. **2** *the man soon revived:* regain consciousness, come round, wake up. **3** *a cup of tea revived her:* reinvigorate, revitalize, refresh, energize, reanimate. **4** *reviving old traditions:* reintroduce, re-establish, restore, resurrect, bring back.

revolt verb **1** *the people revolted:* rebel, rise up, take to the streets, riot, mutiny. **2** *the smell revolted him:* disgust, sicken, nauseate, turn someone's stomach, put off, offend; informal turn off; N. Amer. informal gross out. •noun *an armed revolt:* rebellion, revolution, insurrection, mutiny, uprising, riot, insurgence, coup (d'état).

revolting adjective disgusting, sickening, nauseating, stomach-turning, repulsive, repugnant, hideous, nasty, foul, offensive; N. Amer. vomitous; informal ghastly, horrid, gross. OPPOSITES attractive, pleasant.

revolution noun **1** *the French Revolution:* rebellion, revolt, insurrection, mutiny, rising, uprising, riot, insurgence, coup (d'état). **2** *a revolution in printing techniques:* dramatic change, sea change, metamorphosis, transformation, innovation, reorganization, restructuring;

informal shake-up; N. Amer. informal shakedown. **3** *one revolution of a wheel:* (single) turn, rotation, circle, spin, orbit, circuit, lap.

revolutionary adjective **1** *revolutionary troops:* rebellious, rebel, insurgent, rioting, mutinous, renegade. **2** *a revolutionary kind of wheelchair:* new, novel, original, unusual, unconventional, unorthodox, newfangled, innovatory, modern, state-of-the-art, futuristic, pioneering. •noun *political revolutionaries:* rebel, insurgent, mutineer, insurrectionist, agitator.

revolve verb **1** *a fan revolved slowly:* go round, turn round, rotate, spin. **2** *the moon revolves around the earth:* circle, travel, orbit.

reward noun *a reward for long service:* award, honour, decoration, bonus, premium, bounty, present, gift, payment, recompense, prize; informal pay-off. •verb *they were well rewarded for their efforts:* recompense, pay, remunerate. OPPOSITES punish.

rewarding adjective satisfying, gratifying, pleasing, fulfilling, enriching, illuminating, worthwhile, productive, fruitful.

r

rhesus monkey noun a small monkey found in southern Asia.

rhetoric /ret-uh-rik/ noun **1** effective or persuasive public speaking. **2** persuasive but insincere language.

rhetorical /ri-torr-i-k'l/ adjective **1** relating to rhetoric. **2** intended to persuade or impress. **3** (of a question) asked for effect or to make a statement rather than to obtain an answer.
■ **rhetorically** adverb.

rheumatic adjective relating to, or suffering from, rheumatism.

rheumatism /roo-muh-ti-z'm/ noun a disease with inflammation and pain in the joints and muscles.

rheumy /roo-mi/ adjective (of a person's eyes) watery.

rhinestone noun an imitation diamond.

rhino noun (plural **rhino** or **rhinos**) informal a rhinoceros.

rhinoceros /ry-noss-uh-ruhss/ noun (plural **rhinoceros** or **rhinoceroses**) a large plant-eating animal with one or two horns on the nose and thick skin, found in Africa and Asia.

rhizome /ry-zohm/ noun a horizontal underground plant stem producing both roots and shoots.

rhodium /roh-di-uhm/ noun a hard silvery-white metallic element.

rhododendron noun a shrub with large clusters of bright flowers.

rhombus noun (plural **rhombuses** or **rhombi** /rom-by/) a flat shape with four straight sides of equal length.

rhubarb noun the thick leaf stalks of a plant, cooked and eaten as fruit.

rhumba ⇒ RUMBA.

rhyme noun **1** a word that has the same sound or ends with the same sound as another. **2** similarity of sound between words or the endings of words. **3** a short poem with rhyming lines. • verb (**rhymes**, **rhyming**, **rhymed**) have or end with the same sound as another word or line.
□ **rhyming slang** slang in which you use words that rhyme with the word you mean (e.g. *butcher's*, short for *butcher's hook*, meaning 'look').

> ☑ remember the first *h*, following the *r*, in rhyme and rhythm.

rhythm noun **1** a strong, regular repeated pattern of sound and movement. **2** a regularly recurring sequence of events or actions.
□ **rhythm and blues** a type of music that is a combination of blues and jazz.

rhythmic adjective **1** having or relating to rhythm. **2** happening regularly.
■ **rhythmically** adverb.

rib noun **1** each of a series of bones that are attached to the spine and curve around the chest. **2** a curved structure supporting an arched roof or forming part of a boat's framework. • verb (**ribs**, **ribbing**, **ribbed**) informal tease someone good-naturedly.

ribald adjective referring to sex in a rude but humorous way.
■ **ribaldry** noun.

riband noun old use a ribbon.

ribbed adjective having a pattern of raised bands.

ribbon noun **1** a long, narrow strip of fabric, used for tying something or for decoration. **2** a long, narrow strip. **3** a narrow band of inked material used to produce the characters in some typewriters.

ribcage noun the bony frame formed by the ribs.

riboflavin /ry-boh-flay-vin/ noun vitamin B₂.

rice noun grains of a cereal plant which is grown for food on wet land in warm countries.

ricepaper noun thin edible paper made from a type of plant, used in oriental painting and in baking biscuits and cakes.

rich adjective **1** having a lot of money, assets,

THESAURUS

rhetoric noun **1** *a form of rhetoric:* oratory, eloquence, command of language, way with words. **2** *empty rhetoric:* wordiness, verbosity, grandiloquence, bombast, pomposity, extravagant language, purple prose, turgidity; informal hot air.

rhetorical adjective **1** *rhetorical devices:* stylistic, oratorical, linguistic, verbal. **2** *rhetorical exchanges in parliament:* extravagant, grandiloquent, high-flown, bombastic, grandiose, pompous, pretentious, overblown, oratorical, turgid, flowery; informal highfalutin.

rhyme noun poem, verse, ode; (**rhymes**) poetry, doggerel.

rhythm noun **1** *the rhythm of the music:* beat, cadence, tempo, time, pulse, throb, swing. **2** *poetic features such as rhythm:* metre, measure, stress, accent, cadence. **3** *the rhythm of daily life:* pattern, flow, tempo.

rich adjective **1** *rich people:* wealthy, affluent, moneyed, well off, well-to-do, prosperous; informal loaded, well heeled, made of money. **2** *rich furnishings:* sumptuous, opulent, luxurious, lavish, gorgeous, splendid, magnificent, costly, expensive, fancy; informal plush; Brit. informal swish; N. Amer. informal swank. **3** *a garden rich in flowers:* well stocked, well provided, abounding,

r

or resources. **2** made of expensive materials. **3** plentiful. **4** having or producing something in large amounts. **5** (of food) containing a lot of fat, sugar, etc. **6** (of a colour, sound, or smell) pleasantly deep and strong. **7** (of soil or land) fertile.
■ **richness** noun.

riches plural noun **1** large amounts of money or valuable possessions. **2** valuable natural resources.

richly adverb **1** in a rich way. **2** fully; thoroughly.

Richter scale /rik-ter/ noun a scale for measuring the severity of an earthquake.

rick¹ noun a stack of hay, corn, or straw.

rick² Brit. verb strain part of your body slightly. •noun a slight sprain or strain.

rickets /ri-kits/ noun a disease of children in which the bones are softened and distorted.

rickety adjective badly made and likely to collapse.

rickshaw noun a light two-wheeled vehicle pulled by a person walking or riding a bicycle.

ricochet /ri-kuh-shay/ verb (**ricochets, ricocheting, ricocheted**) (of a bullet or other fast-moving object) rebound off a surface. •noun a shot or hit that ricochets.

rictus noun a fixed grimace or grin.

rid verb (**rids, ridding, rid**) **1** (**rid someone/thing of**) free a person or place of something unwanted. **2** (**be** or **get rid of**) be or make yourself free of.

riddance noun (**good riddance**) said when expressing relief at getting rid of someone or something.

ridden past participle of RIDE. •adjective full of a particular unpleasant thing; *disease-ridden.*

riddle¹ noun **1** a cleverly worded question that is asked as a game. **2** a puzzling person or thing.

riddle² verb (usu. **be riddled with**) **1** make a lot of holes in. **2** fill with something bad or unpleasant. •noun a type of large sieve.

ride verb (**rides, riding, rode**; past participle **ridden**) **1** sit on and control the movement of a horse, bicycle, or motorcycle. **2** travel in a vehicle. **3** be carried or supported by. **4** (**ride up**) (of clothing) gradually move upwards out of its proper position. **5** (**ride on**) depend on. •noun **1** an act of riding. **2** a roller coaster, roundabout, etc. ridden at a fair or amusement park. **3** a path for horse riding.
□ **take someone for a ride** informal deceive someone.

rider noun **1** a person who rides a horse, bicycle, etc. **2** an added condition on an official document.

ridge noun **1** a long, narrow hilltop or mountain range. **2** a narrow raised band on a surface. **3** the edge formed where the two sloping sides of a roof meet at the top.
■ **ridged** adjective.

ridicule noun making fun of someone in an unkind way; mockery. •verb (**ridicules, ridiculing, ridiculed**) make fun of.

ridiculous adjective very silly or

---

crammed, packed, teeming, bursting. **4** *a rich supply of restaurants:* plentiful, abundant, copious, ample, profuse, lavish, liberal, generous. **5** *rich soil:* fertile, productive, fruitful. **6** *a rich sauce:* creamy, fatty, heavy, full-flavoured. **7** *rich colours:* strong, deep, full, intense, vivid, brilliant. OPPOSITES poor, cheap, light.

riches plural noun money, wealth, funds, cash, means, assets, capital, resources; informal bread, loot; Brit. informal dosh, brass, lolly, spondulicks; N. Amer. informal bucks; US informal greenbacks.

richly adverb **1** *a richly furnished room:* sumptuously, opulently, luxuriously, lavishly, gorgeously, splendidly, magnificently. **2** *the joy she richly deserves:* fully, amply, well, thoroughly, completely, wholly, totally, entirely, absolutely, utterly. OPPOSITES meanly.

rid verb *the aim was to rid the town of malaria:* clear, free, purge, empty, strip.
□ **get rid of** dispose of, throw away/out, clear out, discard, scrap, dump, bin, jettison, expel, eliminate; informal chuck

(away), ditch, junk; Brit. informal get shot of; N. Amer. informal trash.

riddle noun puzzle, conundrum, brain-teaser, problem, question, poser, enigma, mystery.

ride verb **1** *she can ride a horse:* sit on, mount, control, manage, handle. **2** *riding round the town:* travel, move, proceed, drive, cycle, trot, canter, gallop.
•noun *he took us for a ride:* trip, journey, drive, run, excursion, outing, jaunt, lift; informal spin.

ridicule noun *he was subjected to ridicule:* mockery, derision, laughter, scorn, scoffing, jeering.
OPPOSITES respect.
•verb *his theory was ridiculed:* mock, deride, laugh at, heap scorn on, jeer at, make fun of, scoff at, satirize, caricature, parody.
OPPOSITES respect.

ridiculous adjective **1** *that looks ridiculous:* laughable, absurd, comical, funny, hilarious, risible, droll, amusing, farcical. **2** *a ridiculous suggestion:* foolish, silly,

r

unreasonable; absurd.
- **ridiculously** adverb.

riding noun each of three former administrative divisions of Yorkshire.

Riesling /reez-ling/ noun a type of dry white wine.

rife adjective **1** (of something bad or unpleasant) widespread. **2** (**rife with**) full of something bad or unpleasant.

riff noun a short repeated phrase in pop music or jazz.

riffle verb (**riffles, riffling, riffled**) (**riffle through**) turn over the pages of a book quickly and casually.

riff-raff noun people who are considered socially undesirable.

rifle noun a gun with a long barrel. • verb (**rifles, rifling, rifled**) **1** search through something hurriedly to find or steal something. **2** hit or kick a ball hard and straight.

rift noun **1** a crack, split, or break. **2** a serious break in friendly relations.

rig verb (**rigs, rigging, rigged**) **1** secretly arrange something in order to gain an advantage. **2** fit sails and rigging on a boat. **3** (often **rig something up**) set up a device or structure. **4** (**rig someone out**) provide with clothes of a particular type. • noun **1** a piece of equipment for a particular purpose: *a lighting rig.* **2** a large piece of equipment for extracting oil or gas from the ground.

rigging noun the system of ropes or chains supporting a ship's masts.

right adjective **1** on or towards the side of a person or thing which is to the east when the person or thing is facing north. **2** justified or morally good. **3** factually correct. **4** most appropriate. **5** satisfactory, sound, or normal. **6** right-wing. • adverb **1** on or to the right side. **2** completely;

THESAURUS

senseless, foolhardy, stupid, idiotic. **3** *a ridiculous exaggeration*: absurd, ludicrous, preposterous, laughable, risible, nonsensical, outrageous.
OPPOSITES sensible.

rife adjective widespread, general, common, universal, extensive, ubiquitous, endemic, inescapable.

rifle verb **1** *she rifled through her wardrobe*: rummage, search, hunt, forage. **2** *a thief rifled her home*: burgle, rob, steal from, loot, raid, plunder, ransack.

rift noun **1** *a deep rift in the ice*: crack, split, breach, fissure, fracture, cleft, crevice, opening. **2** *the rift between them*: breach, division, split, quarrel, disagreement, falling-out, row, conflict, feud; Brit. informal bust-up.

rig[1] verb **1** *the boats were rigged with a single sail*: equip, kit out, fit out, supply, furnish, provide, arm. **2** *I rigged myself out in black*: dress, clothe, attire, robe, garb, get up; informal doll up. **3** *he will rig up a shelter*: set up, erect, assemble, put together, whip up, improvise, contrive; Brit. informal knock up.

rig[2] verb *the results of the election were rigged*: manipulate, engineer, distort, misrepresent, pervert, tamper with, falsify, fake; informal fix; Brit. informal fiddle.

right adjective **1** *it wouldn't be right to do that*: just, fair, proper, good, upright, righteous, virtuous, moral, ethical, honourable, honest, lawful, legal. **2** *the right answer*: correct, accurate, exact, precise, proper, valid, conventional, established, official, formal; Brit. informal spot on. **3** *the right person for the job*: suitable, appropriate, fitting, correct, proper,

desirable, preferable, ideal. **4** *you've come at the right time*: opportune, advantageous, favourable, good, lucky, fortunate. **5** *on my right side*: right-hand; Nautical starboard.
OPPOSITES wrong, bad, left, port.
• adverb **1** *she was right at the limit of her patience*: completely, fully, totally, absolutely, utterly, thoroughly, quite. **2** *right in the middle of the village*: exactly, precisely, directly, immediately, just, squarely, dead; informal (slap) bang, smack, plumb. **3** *I think I heard right*: correctly, accurately, properly, precisely, perfectly. **4** *make sure you're treated right*: well, properly, justly, fairly, equitably, impartially, honourably, lawfully, legally. **5** *things will turn out right*: well, for the best, favourably, happily, advantageously, profitably, luckily, conveniently.
OPPOSITES wrong, badly.
• noun **1** *the difference between right and wrong*: goodness, righteousness, virtue, integrity, propriety, morality, truth, honesty, honour, justice, fairness, equity. **2** *you have the right to say no*: entitlement, prerogative, privilege, liberty, authority, power, licence, permission, dispensation, leave, due.
OPPOSITES wrong.
• verb *we must right the situation*: remedy, rectify, retrieve, fix, resolve, sort out, settle, square, straighten out, correct, repair, mend, redress.
□ **right away** at once, straight away, (right) now, this (very) minute, this instant, immediately, instantly, directly, forthwith, without further ado, promptly, quickly, without delay, asap, as soon as possible; N. Amer. in short order; informal straight off, pronto.

r

totally. **3** exactly; directly. **4** correctly or satisfactorily. •noun **1** what is morally right. **2** an entitlement to have or do something. **3** (**rights**) the authority to perform, publish, or film a work or event. **4** (**the right**) the right-hand part, side, or direction. **5** a right turn. **6** (often **the Right**) a right-wing group or party. •verb **1** put something back in a normal or upright position. **2** correct or make up for a wrong.

□ **by rights** if things were fair or correct. **in your own right** as a result of your own qualifications or efforts. **right angle** an angle of 90°, as in a corner of a square. **right of way 1** the legal right to go through someone's property along a specific route. **2** a public path through someone's property. **3** the right to proceed before another vehicle. **right wing** conservative or opposed to political or social change.

■ **rightly** adverb.

righteous /ry-chuhss/ adjective morally right.

■ **righteously** adverb.

rightful adjective **1** having a clear right to something. **2** proper; fitting.

■ **rightfully** adverb.

rigid adjective **1** unable to bend or be put out of shape. **2** (of a person) stiff and unmoving. **3** not able to be changed or adapted.

■ **rigidity** noun **rigidly** adverb.

rigmarole /**rig**-muh-rohl/ noun a lengthy and complicated procedure.

rigor mortis /ri-ger **mor**-tiss/ noun stiffening of the joints and muscles that

happens a few hours after death.

rigorous adjective **1** very thorough or accurate. **2** (of a rule, system, etc.) strictly applied or followed. **3** harsh or severe.

■ **rigorously** adverb.

rigour (US spelling **rigor**) noun **1** the quality of being rigorous. **2** (**rigours**) difficult or extreme conditions.

rile verb (**riles, riling, riled**) informal annoy or irritate.

rill noun literary a small stream.

rim noun **1** the upper or outer edge of something circular. **2** a limit or boundary. •verb (**rims, rimming, rimmed**) provide with a rim.

rime noun literary hoar frost.

rind noun a tough outer layer or covering of fruit, cheese, bacon, etc.

ring[1] noun **1** a small circular metal band worn on a finger. **2** a circular band, object, or mark. **3** an enclosed space in which a sport, performance, or show takes place. **4** each of the flat plates on a cooker that are used for cooking on. **5** a group of people with a shared interest or goal. •verb **1** surround. **2** draw a circle round.

□ **ring binder** a binder with ring-shaped clasps. **ring pull** Brit. a ring on a can that you pull to open it. **ring road** Brit. a road encircling a town.

ring[2] verb (**rings, ringing, rang**; past participle **rung**) **1** make a clear and repeated or long-lasting sound. **2** (**ring with**) echo with such a sound. **3** Brit. telephone someone. **4** (**ring off**) Brit. end a telephone call by replacing the receiver. **5** call for attention by sounding a bell. **6** (of the ears) be filled

---

righteous adjective good, virtuous, upright, upstanding, decent, ethical, principled, moral, honest, honourable, blameless. OPPOSITES wicked.

right-wing adjective conservative, rightist, reactionary, traditionalist, conventional. OPPOSITES left-wing.

rigid adjective **1** *a rigid container:* stiff, hard, firm, inflexible, unbending, unyielding. **2** *a rigid routine:* fixed, set, firm, inflexible, invariable, hard and fast, cast-iron. **3** *a rigid approach to funding:* strict, stringent, rigorous, inflexible, uncompromising, intransigent. OPPOSITES flexible, lenient.

rigorous adjective **1** *rigorous attention to detail:* meticulous, conscientious, punctilious, careful, scrupulous, painstaking, exact, precise, accurate, particular, strict. **2** *the rigorous enforcement of rules:* strict, stringent, rigid, inflexible, draconian, intransigent, uncompromising. **3** *rigorous conditions:*

harsh, severe, bleak, extreme, demanding. OPPOSITES slapdash, lax, mild.

rim noun edge, brim, lip, border, side, margin, brink, boundary, perimeter, circumference, limits, periphery.

ring[1] noun **1** *a ring round the moon:* circle, band, halo, disc. **2** *the horses entered the ring:* arena, enclosure, amphitheatre, bowl. **3** *a spy ring:* gang, syndicate, cartel, mob, band, circle, organization, association, society, alliance, league.

•verb *police ringed the building:* surround, circle, encircle, enclose, hem in, confine, seal off.

ring[2] verb **1** *church bells rang:* chime, sound, peal, toll, clang, bong; literary knell. **2** *the room rang with laughter:* resound, reverberate, resonate, echo. **3** *I'll ring you tomorrow:* telephone, phone (up), call (up); informal give someone a buzz; Brit. informal give someone a bell, give someone a tinkle, get on the blower to.

r

with a buzzing or humming sound. **7** (**ring something up**) record an amount on a cash register. • **noun 1** an act of ringing. **2** a loud, clear sound or tone. **3** a quality or feeling conveyed by words: *a ring of truth.*
□ **give someone a ring** Brit. informal telephone someone.
■ **ringer** noun.

ringing adjective **1** having a clear, resonant sound. **2** forceful and clear.

ringleader noun a person who leads others in committing a crime or causing trouble.

ringlet noun a corkscrew-shaped curl of hair.

ringmaster noun the person who directs a circus performance.

ringside noun the area beside a boxing ring or circus ring.

ringtone noun a sound made by a mobile phone when an incoming call is received.

ringworm noun a skin disease that causes small, itchy circular patches.

rink noun **1** (also **ice rink**) an enclosed area of ice for skating, ice hockey, or curling. **2** the strip of a bowling green used for a match.

rinse verb (**rinses, rinsing, rinsed**) **1** wash with clean water to remove soap or dirt. **2** remove soap or dirt by rinsing. • **noun 1** an act of rinsing. **2** an antiseptic solution for cleaning the mouth. **3** a liquid for conditioning or colouring the hair.

Rioja /ri-o-kuh/ noun a red or white Spanish wine.

riot noun **1** a violent disturbance caused by an angry crowd. **2** a confused combination or display. **3** (**a riot**) informal a very entertaining person or thing. • **verb** take part in a riot.
□ **run riot** behave in an uncontrolled way.

■ **rioter** noun.

riotous adjective **1** wild and uncontrolled. **2** involving public disorder.

RIP abbreviation rest in peace.

rip verb (**rips, ripping, ripped**) **1** suddenly tear or become torn. **2** pull forcibly away. • **noun** a long tear.
□ **let rip** informal move or act without restraint. **rip someone/thing off** informal **1** cheat someone. **2** steal something. **rip-roaring** very energetic and exciting. **rip tide** a stretch of fast-flowing rough water caused by currents meeting.

riparian /ri-**pair**-i-uhn/ adjective technical relating to or on the banks of a river.

ripcord noun a cord that you pull to open a parachute.

ripe adjective **1** ready for harvesting and eating. **2** (of a cheese or wine) fully matured. **3** (**ripe for**) having reached the right time for. **4** (of a person's age) advanced.
■ **ripely** adverb **ripeness** noun.

ripen verb become or make ripe.

riposte /ri-**posst**/ noun a quick reply.

ripple noun **1** a small wave or series of waves. **2** a feeling, effect, or sound that spreads through someone or something. **3** ice cream with wavy lines of syrup running through it. • **verb** (**ripples, rippling, rippled**) **1** form ripples. **2** (of a sound, feeling, etc.) spread through a person or place.

rise verb (**rises, rising, rose**; past participle **risen**) **1** come or go up. **2** get up after lying, sitting, or kneeling. **3** increase in number, size, strength, etc. **4** (of land) slope upwards. **5** (of the sun, moon, or stars) appear above the horizon. **6** (**rise above**) manage not to be restricted by. **7** (**rise to**)

THESAURUS

rinse verb wash (out), clean, cleanse, bathe, dip, drench, splash, swill, sluice.

riot noun **1** *a riot in the capital:* disorder, disturbance, lawlesssness, upheaval, uproar, commotion. **2** *a riot of colour:* mass, sea, splash, show, profusion.
• **verb** *the miners rioted:* (go on the) rampage, run wild, run amok, run riot, go berserk; informal raise hell.
□ **run riot grow profusely**, spread uncontrolled, burgeon, multiply, rocket.

rip verb **1** *he ripped the posters down:* tug, wrench, pull, snatch, tear, heave, drag, peel, pluck; informal yank. **2** *she ripped Leo's note into pieces:* tear, claw, hack, slit.

ripe adjective **1** *a ripe tomato:* mature, full grown. **2** *ripe for development:* ready, fit, suitable, right. **3** *the time is ripe for his return:* opportune, advantageous, favourable, auspicious, good, right.

rise verb **1** *the sun rose:* climb, come up, arise, ascend, mount, soar. **2** *the mountains rising above us:* loom, tower, soar. **3** *prices rose:* go up, increase, soar, shoot up, surge, leap, jump, rocket, escalate, spiral. **4** *living standards have risen:* improve, get better, advance. **5** *his voice rose:* get higher, grow, increase, become louder, swell, intensify. **6** *he rose from his chair:* stand up, get to your feet, get up, jump up, leap up. **7** *he rises at dawn:* get up, stir, bestir yourself, be up and about; informal surface.
OPPOSITES fall, sit down, go to bed.
• **noun 1** *a price rise:* increase, hike, leap, upsurge, upswing, climb. **2** *he got a rise of 4%:* raise, increase, hike, increment. **3** *a rise in standards:* improvement, advance. **4** *his rise to power:* progress, climb, promotion, elevation. **5** *we walked up the rise:* slope, incline, hill.
OPPOSITES fall, drop.

respond well to a difficult situation. **8** (**rise up**) rebel. **9** (of a river) have its source. •noun **1** an act of rising. **2** an upward slope or hill. **3** Brit. a pay increase.

riser noun **1** a person who gets up at a particular time. **2** a vertical section between the treads of a staircase.

risible /ri-zi-b'l/ **adjective** causing laughter. ■ **risibly** adverb.

rising noun a rebellion or revolt. •**adjective** approaching a particular age. □ **rising damp** Brit. moisture absorbed from the ground into a wall.

risk noun **1** a situation that involves being exposed to danger. **2** the possibility that something bad will happen. **3** a person or thing that causes a risk. •**verb 1** expose to danger or loss. **2** act in such a way that there is a chance of something bad happening.

risky adjective (**riskier**, **riskiest**) involving the possibility of danger or a bad outcome. ■ **riskily** adverb **riskiness** noun.

risotto noun (plural **risottos**) a dish of rice with meat, seafood, etc.

> ☑ only one *s*: risotto.

risqué /riss-kay/ **adjective** slightly indecent or rude.

rissole noun Brit. a small flat mass of chopped meat that is coated in breadcrumbs and fried.

rite noun a religious ceremony, or other solemn procedure. □ **rite of passage** a ceremony or event that marks an important stage in someone's life.

ritual noun **1** a ceremony that involves a series of actions performed in a set order. **2** something that is habitually done in the same way. •**adjective** done as a ritual. ■ **ritually** adverb.

ritzy adjective (**ritzier**, **ritziest**) informal expensively stylish.

rival noun **1** a person or thing competing with another for the same thing. **2** a person or thing equal to another in quality. •**verb** (**rivals**, **rivalling**, **rivalled**; US spelling **rivals**, **rivaling**, **rivaled**) be comparable to. ■ **rivalry** noun (plural **rivalries**).

riven /ri-vuhn/ **adjective** literary torn apart; split.

river noun **1** a large natural flow of water moving in a channel to the sea or another river. **2** a large quantity of a flowing substance.

rivet noun a short metal pin or bolt for holding together two metal plates. •**verb** (**rivets**, **riveting**, **riveted**) **1** fasten with a rivet or rivets. **2** (**be riveted**) be completely fascinated by something.

riviera /ri-vi-air-uh/ noun a coastal area of a warm country, especially in southern France and northern Italy.

rivulet noun a small stream.

RN abbreviation Royal Navy.

RNA noun a substance in living cells which carries instructions from DNA.

roach[1] noun (plural **roach**) a common freshwater fish of the carp family.

roach[2] noun N. Amer. informal a cockroach.

risk noun **1** *there is a certain amount of risk:* chance, uncertainty, unpredictability, instability, insecurity. **2** *the risk of fire:* possibility, chance, probability, likelihood, danger, peril, threat, menace, prospect. OPPOSITES certainty, safety, impossibility. •**verb** *he risked his life to save them:* endanger, imperil, jeopardize, hazard, gamble (with), chance, put on the line.

risky adjective dangerous, hazardous, perilous, unsafe, insecure, precarious, touch-and-go, treacherous, uncertain, unpredictable; informal dicey; N. Amer. informal gnarly.

rite noun ceremony, ritual, ceremonial, custom, service, observance, liturgy, worship, office.

ritual noun *an elaborate civic ritual:* ceremony, rite, act, practice, custom, tradition, convention, formality, protocol. •**adjective** *a ritual burial:* ceremonial, prescribed, set, formal, traditional, conventional.

rival noun **1** *his rival for the nomination:* opponent, challenger, competitor, contender, adversary, antagonist, enemy. **2** *the tool has no rival:* equal, match, peer, equivalent. OPPOSITES ally. •**verb** *few countries can rival it for scenery:* match, compare with, compete with, vie with, equal, measure up to, touch; informal hold a candle to. •**adjective** *rival candidates:* competing, opposing.

rivalry noun competition, contention, opposition, conflict, feuding; informal keeping up with the Joneses.

river noun **1** stream, brook, watercourse, rivulet, tributary; Scottish & N. English burn; N. English beck; S. English bourn; N. Amer. & Austral./NZ creek. **2** *a river of molten lava:* stream, torrent, flood, deluge, cascade.

riveting adjective fascinating, gripping, engrossing, intriguing, absorbing, captivating, enthralling, compelling, spellbinding, mesmerizing; informal unputdownable. OPPOSITES boring.

r

road noun **1** a wide track with a hard surface for vehicles to travel on. **2** a way to achieving a particular outcome.
□ **road rage** informal violent anger caused by conflict with the driver of another vehicle. **road test** a test of the performance of a vehicle or of other equipment.

roadblock noun a barrier put across a road by the police or army to stop and examine traffic.

roadholding noun the ability of a moving vehicle to remain stable.

roadie noun informal a person who sets up equipment for a rock group.

roadshow noun **1** a show broadcast from a different place each day. **2** a touring political or promotional campaign.

roadster noun an open-top sports car.

roadway noun **1** a road. **2** the part of a road intended for vehicles.

roadworks plural noun Brit. repairs to roads or to pipes under roads.

roadworthy adjective (of a vehicle) fit to be used on the road.

roam verb travel aimlessly over a wide area.

roaming noun the use of a mobile phone on another operator's network, typically while abroad.

roan adjective (of a horse) having a bay, chestnut, or black coat mixed with hairs of another colour.

roar noun a loud, deep sound made by a lion, engine, etc., or by a person who is angry, amused, or in pain. • verb **1** make a roar. **2** laugh loudly. **3** move very fast.
□ **a roaring trade** informal very good business.

roast verb **1** cook food in an oven or over a fire. **2** make or become very warm.
• adjective (of food) having been roasted.
• noun a joint of meat that has been roasted.

roasting informal adjective very hot and dry.
• noun a severe telling-off.

rob verb (**robs**, **robbing**, **robbed**) **1** steal property from a person or place by using force or threatening violence. **2** deprive someone of something.
■ **robber** noun.

robbery noun (plural **robberies**) the action of robbing a person or place.

robe noun **1** a loose garment reaching to the ankles, worn on formal or ceremonial occasions. **2** a dressing gown. • verb (**robes**, **robing**, **robed**) clothe someone in a robe.

robin noun a small bird with a red breast and brown back and wings.

robot noun a machine capable of carrying out a complex series of actions automatically.

robotic adjective **1** relating to robots. **2** mechanical, stiff, or unemotional.

robotics plural noun the science of constructing and using robots.

robust adjective **1** sturdy or able to withstand difficult conditions. **2** strong and healthy. **3** determined and forceful.
■ **robustly** adverb.

rock[1] noun **1** the hard material that makes up the earth's crust. **2** a projecting mass of rock. **3** a boulder. **4** Brit. a hard sweet in the form of a cylindrical stick. **5** informal a diamond or other precious stone.
□ **on the rocks** informal **1** in difficulties and

THESAURUS

r

road noun **1** street, thoroughfare, roadway, highway, lane; Brit. motorway. **2** on the road to recovery: way, path, route, course.

roam verb wander, rove, ramble, drift, walk, traipse, range, travel, tramp, trek; Scottish & Irish stravaig; informal cruise, mosey.

roar noun **1** the roars of the crowd: shout, bellow, yell, cry, howl, clamour; informal holler. **2** the roar of the sea: boom, crash, rumble, roll, thunder.
• verb **1** 'Get out!' roared Angus: bellow, yell, shout, bawl, howl; informal holler. **2** thunder roared: boom, rumble, crash, roll, thunder.

roaring adjective a roaring fire: blazing, burning, flaming.

rob verb **1** the gang robbed a bank: burgle, steal from, hold up, break into, raid, loot, plunder, pillage; N. Amer. burglarize. **2** he robbed an old woman: steal from, hold up; informal mug. **3** he was robbed of his savings: cheat, swindle, defraud; informal do out of, con out of. **4** defeat robbed him of his title: deprive, strip, deny.

robber noun burglar, thief, housebreaker, mugger, shoplifter, raider, looter.

robbery noun they were arrested for the robbery: burglary, theft, stealing, housebreaking, shoplifting, embezzlement, fraud, hold-up, raid; informal mugging, smash-and-grab, stick-up; N. Amer. informal heist.

robe noun **1** the women wore black robes: cloak, kaftan, djellaba, wrap, mantle, cape; N. Amer. wrapper. **2** ceremonial robes: garb, regalia, costume, finery, vestments.

robot noun machine, automaton, android, golem; informal bot, droid.

robust adjective **1** a robust man: strong, vigorous, sturdy, tough, powerful, solid, rugged, hardy, strapping, healthy, (fighting) fit, hale and hearty. **2** these knives are robust: durable, resilient, tough, hard-wearing, long-lasting, sturdy, strong.
OPPOSITES frail, fragile.

rock[1] noun boulder, stone, pebble.

likely to fail. **2** (of a drink) served undiluted and with ice cubes. **rock bottom** the lowest possible level. **rock salt** salt occurring naturally as a mineral.

rock² verb **1** move gently to and fro or from side to side. **2** shake violently. **3** shock or distress very much. •noun **1** (also **rock music**) a type of loud popular music with a heavy beat. **2** a rocking movement.
□ **rock and roll** a type of popular music with simple melodies, originating in the 1950s. **rocking chair** a chair mounted on curved bars. **rocking horse** a model horse mounted on curved bars for a child to ride on.

rockabilly noun music that combines rock and roll and country music.

rocker noun **1** a curved piece of wood on the bottom of a rocking chair. **2** a person who performs or likes rock music.
□ **off your rocker** informal mad.

rockery noun (plural **rockeries**) an arrangement of rocks in a garden with plants growing between them.

rocket noun **1** a tube-shaped missile or spacecraft propelled by a stream of burning gases. **2** a firework that shoots high in the air and explodes. **3** Brit. informal a severe telling-off. **4** a plant similar to lettuce, eaten in salads. •verb (**rockets, rocketing, rocketed**) move or increase very quickly and suddenly.

rocky adjective (**rockier, rockiest**)
1 consisting or formed of rock. **2** full of rocks. **3** unsteady or unstable.

rococo /ruh-**koh**-koh/ adjective (of furniture or architecture) in a highly decorated style popular in the 18th century.

rod noun **1** a thin straight bar of wood, metal, etc. **2** (also **fishing rod**) a long stick

with a line and hook attached, for catching fish.

rode past of **RIDE**.

rodent noun a mammal of a large group including rats, mice, and squirrels, with large front teeth.

rodeo /**roh**-di-oh/ noun (plural **rodeos**) a contest or entertainment in which cowboys show their horse-riding and lassoing skills.

roe noun the eggs or sperm of a fish, used as food.

roebuck noun a male roe deer.

roe deer noun a small deer with a coat that is reddish in summer.

roentgen /**runt**-yuhn/ noun a unit of radiation.

rogue noun **1** a dishonest or immoral man. **2** a mischievous but likeable person. **3** an elephant that is living apart from the herd.

roguish adjective mischievous.

roister verb (**roisters, roistering, roistered**) old use enjoy yourself in a lively, noisy way.

role noun **1** an actor's part in a play, film, etc. **2** a person's or thing's function in a particular situation.
□ **role model** a person that others look up to as an example to be imitated. **role play** the acting out of a role or situation.

> ! don't confuse **role** with **roll**, which mainly means 'move by turning over and over' or 'a rolling movement'.

roll verb **1** move by turning over and over. **2** move forward on wheels or with a smooth motion. **3** (of a moving ship, aircraft, etc.) sway from side to side. **4** (of a machine or device) begin operating. **5** (often **roll something up**) turn something flexible over and over on itself. **6** (**roll up**) curl up tightly. **7** (**roll something out**) officially launch a new product. **8** flatten

---

rock² verb **1** *the ship rocked on the water:* move to and fro, sway, see-saw, roll, pitch, plunge, toss, lurch. **2** *Wall Street was rocked by the news:* stun, shock, stagger, astonish, startle, surprise, shake, take aback, throw, unnerve, disconcert.

rocky¹ adjective *a rocky path:* stony, pebbly, shingly, rough, bumpy, craggy, mountainous.

rocky² adjective unsteady, shaky, unstable, wobbly, tottery, rickety.
OPPOSITES steady, stable.

rod noun bar, stick, pole, baton, staff, shaft, strut, rail, spoke.

rogue noun **1** *a rogue without ethics:* scoundrel, rascal, good-for-nothing, wretch, villain, criminal, lawbreaker; informal crook. **2** *your boy's a little rogue:* rascal,

imp, devil, monkey; informal scamp, scallywag.

role noun **1** *a small role in the film:* part, character. **2** *his role as President:* capacity, position, function, job, post, office, duty, responsibility.

roll verb **1** *the bottle rolled down the table:* bowl, turn over and over, spin, rotate, wheel, trundle. **2** *tears rolled down her cheeks:* flow, run, course, stream, pour, trickle. **3** *he rolled his handkerchief into a ball:* wind, coil, fold, curl, twist. **4** *the ship began to roll:* rock, sway, reel, list, pitch, plunge, lurch, toss.
•noun **1** *a roll of paper:* cylinder, tube, scroll, reel, spool. **2** *a roll of the dice:* throw, toss, turn, spin. **3** *the electoral roll:* list, register, directory, record, file, index, catalogue, inventory. **4** *a roll of thunder:*

with a roller. **9** (of a loud, deep sound) reverberate. **10** (**roll up**) informal arrive.
• noun **1** a cylinder formed by rolling flexible material. **2** a rolling movement. **3** a long, deep, reverberating sound. **4** a very small loaf of bread. **5** an official list or register of names.
□ **roll call** an occasion when a list of names is read out to discover who is present. **rolling pin** a cylinder for rolling out dough. **rolling stock** locomotives, carriages, and other vehicles used on a railway. **roll neck** a high turned-over collar. **roll-on** applied by means of a rotating ball.

! don't confuse **roll** with **role**, which means 'an actor's part in a play or film'.

roller noun **1** a rotating cylinder used to move, flatten, or spread something. **2** a small cylinder on which you roll your hair to make it curly. **3** a long wave moving towards the shore.
□ **roller coaster** a fairground attraction in which you ride in an open carriage on a steep, twisting track. **roller skate** a boot with wheels on which you can glide across a hard surface.

Rollerblade noun trademark a roller skate with wheels in a single line along the sole.
■ **rollerblading** noun.

rollicking adjective cheerfully lively and amusing. • noun Brit. informal a severe telling-off.

rollmop noun a rolled pickled herring fillet.

roly-poly adjective informal round and plump.
• noun Brit. a hot pudding made of suet pastry covered with jam and rolled up.

Roman adjective **1** relating to Rome or its ancient empire. **2** referring to the alphabet used for writing Latin, English, and most European languages. **3** (**roman**) (of a typeface) plain and upright, used in ordinary print. • noun **1** an inhabitant of Rome. **2** (**roman**) roman type.
□ **Roman Catholic 1** of the Christian Church which has the Pope as its head. **2** a member of the Roman Catholic Church.

Roman numeral each of the letters, I, V, X, L, C, D, and M, used in ancient Rome to represent numbers.

romance /roh-**manss**/ noun **1** a pleasurable feeling of excitement associated with love. **2** a love affair. **3** a book or film that deals with love in a sentimental or idealized way. **4** a feeling of mystery, excitement, and remoteness from everyday life. **5** (**Romance**) French, Spanish, Italian, and other languages descended from Latin.
• verb (**romances, romancing, romanced**) try to win the love of someone.

Romanesque /roh-muh-**nesk**/ adjective relating to a style of architecture common in Europe c.900–1200.

Romanian or **Rumanian** noun **1** a person from Romania. **2** the language of Romania.
• adjective relating to Romania.

romantic adjective **1** having to do with love or romance. **2** thinking about or showing life in an idealized rather than realistic way. **3** (**Romantic**) relating to the artistic and literary movement of Romanticism.
• noun **1** a person with romantic beliefs or attitudes. **2** (**Romantic**) an artist or writer of the Romantic movement.
■ **romantically** adverb.

Romanticism noun a literary and artistic movement which emphasized creative inspiration and individual feeling.

romanticize or **romanticise** verb (**romanticizes, romanticizing, romanticized**) make something seem more attractive and inspiring than it really is.

Romany /roh-muh-ni/ noun (plural **Romanies**) **1** the language of the Gypsies. **2** a Gypsy.

Romeo noun (plural **Romeos**) an attractive, passionate male lover.

romp verb **1** play about roughly and energetically. **2** (**romp ahead** or **home**) easily lead or win a race. **3** (**romp through**) informal do or achieve something easily.

rompers or **romper suit** plural noun a young child's one-piece garment.

rondo noun (plural **rondos**) a piece of music

THESAURUS

rumble, reverberation, echo, boom, clap, crack, roar.

romance noun **1** *he's had many romances:* **love affair,** relationship, liaison, courtship, attachment, amour. **2** *an author of romances:* **story,** tale, legend, fairy tale. **3** *the romance of the Far East:* **mystery,** glamour, excitement, exoticism, mystique, appeal, allure, charm.

romantic adjective **1** *he's so romantic:* **loving,** amorous, passionate, tender, affectionate; informal lovey-dovey.
2 *romantic songs:* **sentimental,** hearts-and-flowers, mawkish, sickly, saccharine,

syrupy; informal slushy, mushy, sloppy, schmaltzy; Brit. informal soppy. **3** *a romantic setting:* **idyllic,** picturesque, fairy-tale, beautiful, lovely, charming, pretty.
4 *romantic notions of rural communities:* **idealistic,** unrealistic, fanciful, impractical, head-in-the-clouds, starry-eyed, utopian, fairy-tale.
OPPOSITES unsentimental, realistic.
• noun *an incurable romantic:* **idealist,** sentimentalist, dreamer, fantasist.
OPPOSITES realist.

romp verb **play,** frolic, frisk, gambol, skip, prance, caper, cavort.

with a recurring leading theme.

röntgen = ROENTGEN.

rood screen noun a screen of wood or stone separating the nave from the chancel of a church.

roof noun (plural **roofs**) **1** the upper covering of a building or vehicle. **2** the top inner surface of a covered space. •verb put a roof over.
□ **roof rack** a framework for carrying luggage on the roof of a vehicle.

roofer noun a person who builds or repairs roofs.

rook[1] noun a crow that nests in colonies in treetops.

rook[2] noun a chess piece that can move in any direction.

rookery noun (plural **rookeries**) **1** a collection of rooks' nests high in a clump of trees. **2** a breeding place of seabirds.

rookie noun informal a new recruit.

room noun **1** a part of a building enclosed by walls, a floor, and a ceiling. **2** (**rooms**) a set of rooms rented out to a lodger. **3** empty space in which you can do or put things. •verb N. Amer. share a rented room or flat.

roomy adjective (**roomier**, **roomiest**) having plenty of space.

roost noun a place where birds regularly settle to rest. •verb (of a bird or birds) settle or gather for rest.

rooster noun N. Amer. a male chicken.

root[1] noun **1** the part of a plant that is normally below ground, which acts as a support and collects water and nourishment. **2** the part of a hair, tooth, nail, etc. that is fixed in the body tissue. **3** the basic cause or origin of something. **4** (**roots**) your family or origins. **5** Maths a number that when multiplied by itself one or more times gives a particular number. •verb **1** (of a plant or cutting) grow roots. **2** (**be rooted**) be firmly established. **3** (**root something out**) find and get rid of something.
□ **root vegetable** a vegetable which grows as the root of a plant.

root[2] verb **1** (of an animal) turn up the ground with its snout in search of food. **2** rummage. **3** (**root for**) informal support someone enthusiastically.

rootless adjective having nowhere where you feel settled and at home.

rootstock noun **1** a rhizome. **2** a plant on to which another variety is grafted.

rope noun **1** a length of thick cord made by twisting together thinner strands of fibre. **2** a number of objects strung together. **3** (**the ropes**) the ropes enclosing a boxing or wrestling ring. **4** (**the ropes**) informal the established way of doing something. •verb (**ropes, roping, roped**) **1** secure something with rope. **2** (**rope someone in** or **into**) informal persuade someone to take part in something.

ropy or **ropey** adjective Brit. informal of bad quality, or in bad health.

rosary noun (plural **rosaries**) a string of beads used by some Roman Catholics for keeping count of how many prayers they have said.

rose[1] noun **1** a sweet-smelling flower that grows on a prickly bush. **2** a cap with holes in it attached to a spout, hose, shower, etc. to produce a spray. **3** a soft pink colour.
□ **rose hip** the fruit of a rose.

rose[2] past of RISE.

rosé /roh-zay/ noun light pink wine made from red grapes, coloured by only brief contact with the skins.

rosemary noun an evergreen shrub with sweet-smelling leaves which are used as a herb in cooking.

rosette noun **1** a rose-shaped decoration made of ribbon, worn by supporters of a sports team or political party or awarded as a prize. **2** a piece of decoration in the shape of a rose.

rosewood noun the wood of a tropical tree, used for making furniture and musical instruments.

Rosh Hashana or **Rosh Hashanah** /rosh huh-**shah**-nuh/ noun the Jewish New Year festival.

rosin /ro-zin/ noun a kind of resin that is rubbed on the bows of stringed instruments.

roster noun **1** a list of people's names and the jobs they have to do at a particular time. **2** a list of sports players available for team selection. •verb (**rosters, rostering, rostered**) put a person's name on a roster.

rostrum noun (plural **rostra** or **rostrums**) a platform on which a person stands to make

r

THESAURUS

room noun **1** *there isn't much room:* space, headroom, legroom, area, expanse, extent. **2** *room for improvement:* scope, capacity, leeway, latitude, freedom.

root noun **1** *the root of the problem:* source, origin, cause, reason, basis, foundation, bottom, seat. **2** (**roots**) origins, beginnings, family, birth, heritage.

•verb *he rooted around in the cupboard:* rummage, hunt, search, rifle, delve, forage, dig, nose, poke.
□ **root something out eradicate**, eliminate, weed out, destroy, wipe out, stamp out, abolish, end, put a stop to.

rope noun cord, cable, line, hawser, string.

a speech, receive a prize, or conduct an orchestra.

rosy adjective (**rosier, rosiest**) **1** of a soft pink colour. **2** promising: *a rosy future.*

rot verb (**rots, rotting, rotted**) gradually decay. • noun **1** the process of decaying. **2** informal rubbish.

rota noun Brit. a list showing when each of a number of people has to do a particular job.

rotary adjective **1** revolving around a centre or axis. **2** having a rotating part or parts.

rotate verb (**rotates, rotating, rotated**) **1** move in a circle round an axis. **2** (of a job) pass on a regular basis to each member of a group in turn. **3** grow different crops one after the other on a piece of land.
■ **rotation** noun **rotator** noun **rotatory** adjective.

rote noun regular repetition of something to be learned.

rotisserie /roh-tiss-uh-ri/ noun a rotating spit for roasting meat.

rotor noun **1** the rotating part of a turbine, electric motor, or other device. **2** a hub with a number of blades spreading out from it that is rotated to provide the lift

for a helicopter.

rotten adjective **1** decayed. **2** corrupt. **3** informal very bad.

rotter noun informal, dated an unkind or unpleasant person.

Rottweiler /rot-vy-ler/ noun a large, powerful breed of dog.

rotund adjective rounded and plump.

rotunda noun a round building or room.

rouble or **ruble** /roo-b'l/ noun the basic unit of money in Russia.

roué /roo-ay/ noun a man who leads an immoral life.

rouge /roozh/ noun a red powder or cream used for colouring the cheeks.

rough adjective **1** not smooth or level. **2** not gentle. **3** (of weather or the sea) wild and stormy. **4** plain and basic. **5** not worked out in every detail. **6** harsh in sound or taste. **7** unsophisticated. **8** informal difficult and unpleasant. • noun **1** a basic draft of a design, piece of writing, etc. **2** (on a golf course) the area of longer grass around the fairway and the green. • verb **1** (**rough something out**) make a draft or first version of something. **2** (**rough it**) informal

THESAURUS

rosy adjective **1** *a rosy complexion:* pink, roseate, reddish, glowing, healthy, fresh, radiant, blooming, blushing, flushed, ruddy. **2** *his future looks rosy:* promising, optimistic, auspicious, hopeful, encouraging, favourable, bright, golden.
OPPOSITES pale, bleak.

rot verb **1** *the floorboards rotted:* decay, decompose, disintegrate, crumble, perish. **2** *the meat began to rot:* go bad, go off, spoil, moulder, putrefy, fester. **3** *poor neighbourhoods have been left to rot:* deteriorate, degenerate, decline, decay, go to seed, go downhill; informal go to pot, go to the dogs.
• noun *the leaves turned black with rot:* decay, decomposition, mould, mildew, blight, canker.

rotate verb **1** *the wheels rotate continually:* revolve, go round, turn (round), spin, gyrate, whirl, twirl, swivel, circle, pivot. **2** *many nurses rotate jobs:* alternate, take turns, change, switch, interchange, exchange, swap.

rotation noun **1** *the rotation of the wheels:* revolving, turning, spinning, gyration, circling. **2** *a rotation of the Earth:* turn, revolution, orbit, spin. **3** *each member is chair for six months in rotation:* sequence, succession, alternation, cycle.

rotten adjective **1** *rotten meat:* decaying, bad, off, decomposing, putrid, perished, rancid, festering, fetid. **2** *he's rotten to the*

core: corrupt, unprincipled, dishonest, dishonourable, unscrupulous, untrustworthy, immoral; informal crooked; Brit. informal bent.
OPPOSITES fresh, honourable.

rough adjective **1** *rough ground:* uneven, irregular, bumpy, stony, rocky, rugged, rutted, pitted. **2** *the terrier's rough coat:* coarse, bristly, scratchy, prickly, shaggy, hairy, bushy. **3** *rough skin:* dry, leathery, weather-beaten, chapped, calloused, scaly. **4** *his voice was rough:* gruff, hoarse, harsh, rasping, husky, gravelly. **5** *he gets rough when he's drunk:* violent, brutal, vicious, aggressive, belligerent, pugnacious, boisterous, rowdy, disorderly, unruly, riotous. **6** *a machine that can take rough handling:* careless, clumsy, inept, unskilful. **7** *rough manners:* boorish, loutish, oafish, brutish, coarse, crude, uncouth, vulgar, unrefined, unladylike, ungentlemanly, uncultured. **8** *rough seas:* turbulent, stormy, tempestuous, violent, heavy, choppy. **9** *a rough draft:* preliminary, hasty, quick, sketchy, cursory, basic, crude, rudimentary, raw, unpolished, incomplete, unfinished. **10** *a rough estimate:* approximate, inexact, imprecise, vague, estimated; N. Amer. informal ballpark.
OPPOSITES smooth, sleek, soft, dulcet, gentle, careful, refined, calm, exact.
• noun *the artist's initial roughs:* sketch, draft, outline, mock-up.

r

live with only very basic necessities.
3 (rough someone up) informal beat someone up.

□ **rough diamond** Brit. a person who lacks good manners and education but has a good character. **rough justice** treatment that is not fair or in accordance with the law. **sleep rough** Brit. sleep outside or without a bed.

■ **roughness** noun.

roughage noun material in cereals, fruit, and vegetables that cannot be digested.

roughen verb make or become rough.

roughly adverb **1** in a rough way. **2** approximately.

roughneck noun informal **1** a rough, rude person. **2** a person who works on an oil rig.

roughshod adjective **(ride roughshod over)** fail to consider someone's needs or wishes.

roulette noun a gambling game in which a ball is dropped on to a revolving wheel.

round adjective **1** shaped like a circle, sphere, or cylinder. **2** having a curved surface with no sharp projections. **3** (of a person's shoulders) bent forward. **4** (of a sound) rich and smooth. **5** (of a number) expressed in convenient units rather than exactly. •noun **1** a circular shape or piece. **2** a route by which you visit a number of people or places in turn. **3** a sequence of things that you do regularly. **4** each of a sequence of stages in a process. **5** a single division of a boxing or wrestling match. **6** a song for three or more voices or parts, each singing the same theme but starting one after another. **7** the amount of ammunition needed to fire one shot. **8** a set of drinks bought for all the members of a group. **9** Brit. the quantity of sandwiches made from two slices of bread. •adverb Brit. **1** so as to rotate or cause rotation. **2** so as to cover the whole area surrounding a particular centre. **3** so as to turn and face in the opposite direction. **4** used in describing the position of something: *the wrong way round.* **5** so as to surround someone or something. **6** so as to reach a new place or position. •preposition chiefly Brit. **1** on every side of. **2** so as to encircle. **3** from or on the other side of. **4** so as to cover the whole area of. •verb **1** pass and go round. **2 (round something up** or **down)** make a figure less exact but easier to use in calculations. **3** make or become round in shape.

□ **round something off** complete in a suitable or satisfying way. **round on** make a sudden attack on. **round robin 1** a tournament in which every player or team plays against every other player or team. **2** a petition. **round trip** a journey to a place and back again. **round someone/thing up** collect a number of people or animals together.

roundabout noun Brit. **1** a road junction at which traffic moves in one direction round a central island to reach one of the roads leading off it. **2** a large revolving device in a playground, for children to ride on. **3** a merry-go-round. •adjective not following a direct route.

rounded adjective **1** round or curved. **2** complete and balanced.

roundel noun a small disc or circular design.

rounders noun a ball game in which players run round a circuit after hitting the ball with a cylindrical wooden bat.

Roundhead noun a supporter of the Parliamentary party in the English Civil War.

roundly adverb in a firm or thorough way.

roundworm noun a parasitic worm found in the intestines of animals.

rouse verb **(rouses, rousing, roused) 1** wake

THESAURUS

round adjective *a round window:* circular, spherical, globular, cylindrical.
•noun **1** *mould the dough into rounds:* ball, sphere, globe, orb, circle, disc, ring, hoop. **2** *a policeman on his rounds:* circuit, beat, route, tour. **3** *the first round of the contest:* stage, level, heat, game, bout, contest. **4** *an endless round of parties:* succession, series, sequence, cycle.
•preposition **1** *the alleys round the station:* around, about, encircling, near, orbiting. **2** *casinos dotted round France:* throughout, all over.
•verb *the ship rounded the point:* go round, travel round, skirt, circumnavigate, orbit.
□ **round something off** complete, finish off, crown, cap, top, conclude, close, end. **round someone/something up gather together,**
herd together, muster, marshal, rally, assemble, collect, group; N. Amer. corral.

roundabout adjective **1** *a roundabout route:* circuitous, indirect, meandering, serpentine, tortuous. **2** *I asked in a roundabout sort of way:* indirect, oblique, circuitous, circumlocutory.
OPPOSITES direct.

rouse verb **1** *he roused Ralph at dawn:* wake (up), awaken, arouse; Brit. informal knock up. **2** *she roused and looked around:* wake up, awake, come to, get up, rise, bestir yourself. **3** *he roused the crowd:* stir up, excite, galvanize, electrify, stimulate, inspire, inspirit, move, inflame, agitate, goad, provoke, prompt. **4** *he's got a temper when he's roused:* provoke, annoy, anger, infuriate, madden, incense, vex, irk;

someone up. 2 make someone move or take an interest in something.

rousing adjective stirring.

rout /rowt/ noun 1 a disorderly retreat of defeated troops. 2 a decisive defeat. • verb defeat troops decisively and force them to retreat.

route /root/ noun a way taken in getting from a starting point to a destination.
• verb (**routes**, **routeing** or **routing**, **routed**) send along a particular route.

routine noun 1 the order and way in which you regularly do things. 2 a set sequence in a stage performance. • adjective 1 performed as part of a regular procedure. 2 without variety.
■ **routinely** adverb.

roux /roo/ noun (plural **roux**) a mixture of butter and flour used in making sauces.

rove verb (**roves**, **roving**, **roved**) 1 travel from place to place without a fixed destination. 2 (of eyes) look around in all directions.
■ **rover** noun.

row¹ /roh/ noun a number of people or things in a more or less straight line.

row² /roh/ verb move a boat through water with oars.

row³ /row/ Brit. noun 1 an angry quarrel. 2 a loud noise. • verb have an angry quarrel.

rowan /roh-uhn/ noun a small tree with white flowers and red berries.

rowdy adjective (**rowdier**, **rowdiest**) noisy and disorderly. • noun (plural **rowdies**) a rowdy person.
■ **rowdily** adverb **rowdiness** noun.

rowlock /rol-luhk/ noun a fitting on the side of a boat for holding an oar.

royal adjective 1 having the status of a king or queen or a member of their family. 2 having to do with a king or queen. 3 of a quality or size suitable for a king or queen.
• noun informal a member of a royal family.
□ **royal blue** a deep, vivid blue. **royal jelly** a substance produced by worker bees and fed by them to larvae raised to be queen bees.
■ **royally** adverb.

royalist noun a person who supports the principle of having a king or queen.

royalty noun (plural **royalties**) 1 the members of a royal family. 2 the status or power of a king or queen. 3 a sum of money paid for the use of a patent, to an author for each copy of a book sold, or to a composer for each performance of a work.

RSPCA abbreviation Royal Society for the Prevention of Cruelty to Animals.

RSVP abbreviation please reply.

Rt Hon. abbreviation Brit. Right Honourable.

rub verb (**rubs**, **rubbing**, **rubbed**) 1 move your hand, a cloth, etc. over the surface while pressing down firmly. 2 apply a

---

THESAURUS

informal aggravate.
OPPOSITES calm, pacify, allay.

rousing adjective stirring, inspiring, exciting, stimulating, moving, electrifying, invigorating, energizing, exhilarating.

rout noun *the army's ignominious rout:* defeat, beating, retreat, flight; informal licking, hammering, thrashing, pasting, drubbing.
OPPOSITES victory.
• verb *his army was routed:* defeat, beat, conquer, vanquish, crush, put to flight, drive off, scatter; informal lick, hammer, clobber, thrash; Brit. informal stuff.

route noun way, course, road, path, direction.

routine noun 1 *his morning routine:* procedure, practice, pattern, drill, regime, programme, schedule, plan. 2 *a stand-up routine:* act, performance, number, turn, piece; informal spiel, patter.
• adjective 1 *a routine health check:* standard, regular, customary, normal, usual, ordinary, typical, everyday. 2 *a routine action movie:* boring, tedious, monotonous, humdrum, run-of-the-mill, pedestrian, predictable, hackneyed, unimaginative, unoriginal, banal, trite.
OPPOSITES unusual.

row¹ noun 1 *rows of children:* line, column, file, queue, procession, chain, string, succession; informal crocodile. 2 *the middle row of seats:* tier, line, rank, bank.
□ **in a row** consecutively, in succession, running, straight; informal on the trot.

row² (Brit.) noun 1 *have you two had a row?* argument, quarrel, squabble, fight, dispute; informal tiff, run-in, slanging match, spat; Brit. informal bust-up. 2 *I couldn't hear for the row:* din, noise, racket, uproar, hubbub, rumpus; informal hullabaloo.
• verb *they rowed about money:* argue, quarrel, squabble, bicker, fight, fall out, disagree, have words; informal scrap.

royal adjective regal, kingly, queenly, princely, sovereign.

rub verb 1 *Polly rubbed her arm:* massage, knead, stroke, pat. 2 *he rubbed sun lotion on her back:* apply, smear, spread, work in. 3 *my shoes rub painfully:* chafe, scrape, pinch.
• noun 1 *she gave his back a rub:* massage, rub-down. 2 *I gave my shoes a rub:* polish, wipe, clean.
□ **rub something down** clean, sponge, wash. **rub something out** erase, delete, remove, obliterate, expunge.

r

substance with a rubbing action. **3 (rub off)** come off a surface through being rubbed. **4 (rub something out)** erase pencil marks with a rubber. **5 (rub something down)** dry, smooth, or clean something by rubbing. **6 (rub it in)** informal keep reminding someone of an embarrassing fact they would rather forget. • noun **1** an act of rubbing. **2** a substance for rubbing on the skin.

rubber[1] noun **1** a tough stretchy waterproof substance obtained from a tropical plant or from chemicals. **2** Brit. a piece of this or a similar substance used for erasing pencil marks. **3** N. Amer. informal a condom.
□ **rubber band** a stretchy loop of rubber for holding things together. **rubber plant** an evergreen plant with large shiny leaves. **rubber-stamp** approve something automatically without proper consideration.
■ **rubbery** adjective.

rubber[2] noun a unit of play in the card game bridge.

rubberneck verb informal turn to look at something as you pass it.

rubbing noun **1** the action of rubbing. **2** an impression of a design on brass or stone, made by placing paper over it and rubbing it with chalk or pencil.

rubbish Brit. noun **1** waste material and discarded items. **2** something that has no value or makes no sense. • verb informal say that something is bad.
■ **rubbishy** adjective.

rubble noun rough fragments of stone, brick, or concrete.

rubella /roo-**bel**-luh/ noun a disease with symptoms like mild measles.

rubicund /roo-bi-kuhnd/ adjective having a red complexion.

ruble ⇒ ROUBLE.

rubric /roo-brik/ noun **1** a heading on a document. **2** a set of instructions.

ruby noun (plural **rubies**) **1** a deep red precious stone. **2** a deep red colour.
□ **ruby wedding** Brit. the fortieth anniversary of a wedding.

ruche /roosh/ noun a frill or pleat of fabric.
■ **ruched** adjective.

ruck[1] noun **1** Rugby a loose scrum formed around a player with the ball on the ground. **2** a crowd of people.

ruck[2] verb (often **ruck up**) form creases or folds. • noun a crease.

rucksack noun a bag with two shoulder straps, that you carry on your back.

ruckus noun a row or commotion.

ructions plural noun Brit. informal angry reactions or protests.

rudder noun a flat piece hinged in an upright position at the back of a boat, used for steering.

ruddy adjective (**ruddier, ruddiest**) **1** (of a person's face) having a healthy red colour. **2** reddish.

rude adjective **1** saying impolite things that offend and hurt someone. **2** referring to sex or the body in a way that people find offensive or embarrassing. **3** very abrupt. **4** Brit. hearty: *rude health.*
■ **rudely** adverb **rudeness** noun.

rudimentary /roo-di-**men**-tuh-ri/ adjective **1** involving only basic matters or facts. **2** undeveloped.

rudiments /roo-di-muhnts/ plural noun **1** the essential matters or facts relating to a subject. **2** a basic form of something.

rue verb (**rues, rueing** or **ruing, rued**) bitterly regret a past event or action.

rueful adjective expressing regret.
■ **ruefully** adverb.

ruff noun **1** a frill worn round the neck. **2** a ring of feathers or hair round the neck of a bird or mammal.

ruffian noun a rough person.

ruffle verb (**ruffles, ruffling, ruffled**) **1** disturb the smooth surface of. **2** upset or worry. **3** (**ruffled**) gathered into a frill. • noun a gathered frill on a garment.

rug noun **1** a small carpet. **2** Brit. a thick woollen blanket.

rugby or **rugby football** noun a team game played with an oval ball that may be kicked, carried, and passed by hand.

r

THESAURUS

rubbish noun **1** *throw away that rubbish:* refuse, waste, litter, scrap, dross; N. Amer. garbage, trash; informal dreck, junk. **2** *she's talking rubbish:* nonsense, gibberish, claptrap, garbage; informal baloney, tripe, drivel, bilge, bunk, piffle, poppycock, twaddle, gobbledegook; Brit. informal codswallop, cobblers, tosh.

rude adjective **1** *a rude man:* ill-mannered, bad-mannered, impolite, discourteous, uncivil, impertinent, insolent, impudent, disparaging, abusive. **2** *rude jokes:* vulgar,

coarse, smutty, dirty, filthy, crude, lewd, obscene, risqué; informal blue; Brit. informal near the knuckle. **3** *a rude awakening:* abrupt, sudden, sharp.
OPPOSITES polite, clean, gentle.

ruffle verb **1** *he ruffled her hair:* disarrange, tousle, dishevel, rumple, mess up; N. Amer. informal muss up. **2** *don't let him ruffle you:* disconcert, unnerve, fluster, agitate, upset, disturb, discomfit, put off, perturb, unsettle; informal faze, throw, get to.
OPPOSITES smooth, calm.

rugged /rug-gid/ adjective **1** having a rocky surface. **2** tough and determined. **3** (of a man) having attractively masculine features.
■ **ruggedly** adverb **ruggedness** noun.

rugger noun Brit. informal rugby.

ruin verb **1** completely spoil or destroy something. **2** make someone bankrupt or very poor. •noun **1** the destruction or collapse of something. **2** (also **ruins**) a building that has been badly damaged. **3** the complete loss of a person's money and property.

ruination noun the process of ruining something.

ruinous adjective **1** disastrous or destructive. **2** in ruins.

rule noun **1** a statement saying what you must or must not do. **2** authority and control over a people or country. **3** (**the rule**) the normal state of things. **4** a ruler (for measuring or drawing). •verb (**rules, ruling, ruled**) **1** have authority and control over a people or country. **2** control or influence. **3** state with legal authority that

something is the case. **4** (**rule something out**) say that something is not possible. **5** (**ruled**) (of paper) marked with thin horizontal lines.
□ **rule of thumb** a rough guide.

ruler noun **1** a person who has authority and control over a people or country. **2** a strip of rigid material marked with centimetres or inches, used to measure short distances or draw straight lines.

ruling noun a decision or statement made by an authority.

rum[1] noun a strong alcoholic drink made from sugar cane.

rum[2] adjective (**rummer, rummest**) Brit. informal, dated peculiar.

Rumanian ⇨ **ROMANIAN**.

rumba or **rhumba** noun a rhythmic dance with Spanish and African elements.

rumble verb (**rumbles, rumbling, rumbled**) **1** make a continuous deep sound, like distant thunder. **2** (**rumble on**) (of a dispute) continue in a low-key way. **3** Brit. informal discover that someone is doing something wrong. •noun a continuous deep

THESAURUS

rugged adjective **1** *the rugged path:* rough, uneven, bumpy, rocky, stony, pitted. **2** *a rugged vehicle:* robust, durable, sturdy, strong, tough, resilient. **3** *rugged manly types:* well built, burly, strong, muscular, muscly, brawny, strapping, tough, hardy, robust, sturdy, solid; informal hunky. **4** *his rugged features:* strong, craggy, rough-hewn, manly, masculine.
OPPOSITES smooth, flimsy, weedy, delicate.

ruin noun **1** *the buildings were saved from ruin:* disintegration, decay, disrepair, dilapidation, destruction, demolition. **2** *the ruins of a church:* remains, remnants, fragments, rubble, debris, wreckage. **3** *electoral ruin for Labour:* downfall, collapse, defeat, undoing, failure. **4** *shopkeepers are facing ruin:* bankruptcy, insolvency, penury, poverty, destitution.
OPPOSITES preservation, triumph, wealth.
•verb **1** *don't ruin my plans:* spoil, wreck, blight, shatter, dash, torpedo, scotch, mess up, sabotage; informal screw up; Brit. informal scupper. **2** *the bank's collapse ruined them:* bankrupt, make insolvent, impoverish, pauperize, wipe out, break, cripple, bring someone to their knees. **3** *a country ruined by civil war:* destroy, devastate, lay waste, ravage, raze, demolish, wreck, wipe out, flatten.
OPPOSITES save, rebuild.

rule noun **1** *health and safety rules:* regulation, directive, order, law, statute. **2** *church attendance on Sunday was the general rule:* procedure, practice, protocol, convention, norm, routine, custom, habit.

3 *moderation is the golden rule:* principle, precept, standard, axiom, truth, maxim. **4** *under British rule:* government, jurisdiction, command, power, dominion, control, administration, sovereignty, leadership.
•verb **1** *El Salvador was ruled by Spain:* govern, preside over, control, lead, dominate, run, head, administer. **2** *Mary ruled for six years:* reign, be on the throne, be in power, govern. **3** *the judge ruled that they be set free:* decree, order, pronounce, judge, adjudge, ordain, decide, find. **4** *subversion ruled:* prevail, predominate, be the order of the day, reign supreme.
□ **as a rule** usually, in general, normally, ordinarily, customarily, for the most part, on the whole, by and large, in the main, mostly, commonly, typically. **rule something out** exclude, eliminate, disregard, preclude, prohibit, prevent, disallow.

ruler noun leader, sovereign, monarch, potentate, king, queen, emperor, empress, prince, princess, crowned head, head of state, president, premier, governor.
OPPOSITES subject.

ruling noun *the judge's ruling:* judgement, decision, adjudication, finding, verdict, pronouncement, resolution, decree, injunction.
•adjective **1** *Japan's ruling party:* governing, controlling, commanding, supreme. **2** *football was their ruling passion:* main, chief, principal, major, dominating, consuming; informal number-one.

sound like that of distant thunder.

rumbustious /rum-**buss**-chuhss/ adjective Brit. informal high-spirited or difficult to control.

ruminant noun an animal that chews the cud, such as a cow or sheep.

ruminate verb (**ruminates, ruminating, ruminated**) 1 think deeply about something. 2 (of an animal) chew the cud.

rummage verb (**rummages, rummaging, rummaged**) search for something by turning things over or moving them about in an untidy way. • noun an act of rummaging.

rummy noun a card game in which the players try to form sets and sequences of cards.

rumour (US spelling **rumor**) noun a piece of information spread among a number of people which is not confirmed and may be false. • verb (**be rumoured**) be spread as a rumour.

rump noun 1 the hind part of the body of a mammal. 2 a piece left over from something larger.

rumple verb (**rumples, rumpling, rumpled**) make something less smooth and neat.

rumpus noun (plural **rumpuses**) a noisy disturbance.

run verb (**runs, running, ran**; past participle **run**)

1 move at a speed faster than a walk, never having both feet on the ground at the same time. 2 be in charge of people or an organization. 3 continue, operate, or proceed. 4 function or cause to function. 5 pass into or reach a particular state or level. 6 (of a liquid) flow. 7 (**run in**) (of a quality) be common or lasting in. 8 (of dye or colour) dissolve and spread when wet. 9 stand as a candidate in an election. 10 compete in a race. 11 (of a bus or train) make a regular journey on a particular route. 12 take someone somewhere in a car. 13 publish a story in a newspaper. 14 smuggle goods. • noun 1 an act or period of running. 2 a journey or route. 3 a course that is regularly used: *a ski run.* 4 a continuous period or sequence. 5 an enclosed area in which chickens or animals can run around. 6 (**the run of**) unrestricted use of or access to a place. 7 a point scored in cricket or baseball. 8 a ladder in stockings or tights.

□ **run across** meet or find by chance. **run down** gradually lose power. **run someone down** 1 knock someone down with a vehicle. 2 criticize someone unfairly or unkindly. **run-down** 1 in a bad or neglected state. 2 tired and rather unwell. **run-of-the-mill** ordinary. **run into** 1 collide with. 2 meet someone by chance. **run out** 1 be used up. 2 be no longer valid. **run someone**

rumour noun gossip, hearsay, talk, tittle-tattle, speculation, word, report, story, whisper; informal the grapevine, the word on the street, the buzz.

run verb 1 *she ran across the road:* sprint, race, dart, rush, dash, hasten, hurry, scurry, scamper, gallop, jog, trot; informal leg it. 2 *the robbers turned and ran:* flee, take flight, make off, take off, take to your heels, bolt, make your getaway, escape; informal beat it, clear off/out, scram; Brit. informal scarper. 3 *the road runs the length of the valley:* extend, stretch, reach, continue. 4 *water ran from the eaves:* flow, pour, stream, gush, flood, cascade, roll, course, spill, trickle, drip, dribble, leak. 5 *a bus runs to Sorrento:* travel, shuttle, go. 6 *he runs a transport company:* be in charge of, manage, direct, control, head, govern, supervise, superintend, oversee. 7 *it's expensive to run a car:* maintain, keep, own, possess, have, use, operate. 8 *he left the engine running:* operate, function, work, go. 9 *the lease runs for twenty years:* last, continue, survive.
• noun 1 *his morning run:* jog, sprint, dash, gallop, trot. 2 *she did the school run:* route, journey, circuit, round, beat. 3 *a run in the car:* drive, ride, turn, trip, excursion, outing, jaunt; informal spin, tootle. 4 *an unbeaten run of victories:* series,

succession, sequence, string, streak, spate. 5 *a chicken run:* enclosure, pen, coop. 6 *a ski run:* slope, track, piste; N. Amer. trail.
□ **run someone down** 1 *he was run down by joyriders:* run over, knock down/over, hit. 2 *she ran him down in front of other people:* criticize, denigrate, belittle, disparage, deprecate, find fault with; informal put down, knock, bad-mouth; Brit. informal rubbish, slag off. **run into** 1 *a car ran into his van:* collide with, hit, strike, crash into, smash into, plough into, ram. 2 *I ran into Hugo the other day:* meet (by chance), run across, chance on, stumble on, happen on; informal bump into. 3 *we ran into a problem:* experience, encounter, meet with, be faced with, be confronted with. **run out** 1 *supplies ran out:* be used up, dry up, be exhausted, be finished, peter out. 2 *her contract ran out:* expire, end, terminate, finish, lapse. **run over** 1 *the bathwater ran over:* overflow, spill over, brim over. 2 *the project ran over budget:* exceed, go over, overshoot, overreach. 3 *he quickly ran over the story:* review, repeat, run through, go over, reiterate, recapitulate, look over, read through; informal recap on. **run someone over.** See RUN SOMEONE DOWN sense 1.

rundown noun summary, synopsis, precis, run-through, review, overview, briefing, sketch, outline; informal low-down, recap.

r

out Cricket dismiss a batsman by hitting the bails with the ball while the batsman is still running. **run someone over** knock someone down with a vehicle. **run through** (or **over**) go over something as a quick rehearsal or reminder. **run something up** 1 allow a bill to build up. 2 make something quickly. **run-up** the period before an important event.

runaway noun a person who has run away from their home or an institution. •adjective 1 (of an animal or vehicle) running out of control. 2 happening or done quickly or uncontrollably.

rundown noun a brief summary.

rune noun 1 a letter of an ancient Germanic alphabet. 2 a symbol with mysterious or magical significance.
■ **runic** adjective.

rung¹ noun 1 a horizontal support on a ladder for the foot. 2 a level or rank.

rung² past participle of RING².

runnel noun 1 a gutter. 2 a stream.

runner noun 1 a person who runs in a race or for exercise. 2 a messenger. 3 a rod, groove, or blade on which something slides. 4 a shoot which grows along the ground and can take root at points along its length. 5 a long, narrow rug.
□ **runner bean** a climbing bean plant with long edible pods. **runner-up** (plural **runners-up**) a competitor who comes second.

running noun 1 the activity or movement of a runner. 2 the action of managing or operating something. •adjective 1 (of water) flowing naturally or supplied through pipes and taps. 2 producing liquid or pus. 3 continuous or recurring. 4 done while running. 5 in succession: *the third week running.*
□ **in** (or **out of**) **the running** in (or no longer in) with a chance of success. **running board** a board acting as a step which extends along the side of a vehicle. **running commentary** a description of events given as they happen.

runny adjective (**runnier**, **runniest**) 1 more liquid than is usual. 2 (of a person's nose) producing mucus.

runt noun the smallest animal in a litter.

runway noun a strip of hard ground where aircraft take off and land.

rupee /roo-pee/ noun the basic unit of money of India and Pakistan.

rupture verb (**ruptures, rupturing, ruptured**) 1 break or burst suddenly. 2 (**be ruptured** or **rupture yourself**) develop a hernia in the abdomen. •noun 1 an instance of rupturing. 2 a hernia in the abdomen.

rural adjective having to do with the countryside.
■ **rurally** adverb.

ruse noun something done to deceive or trick someone.

rush¹ verb 1 move or act very quickly, often

THESAURUS

run down adjective 1 *a run-down area of London:* dilapidated, tumbledown, ramshackle, derelict, crumbling, neglected, uncared-for, slummy. 2 *she was feeling rather run down:* unwell, ill, poorly, unhealthy, peaky, tired, drained, exhausted, worn out, below par, washed out; Brit. off colour; informal under the weather; Brit. informal off; Austral./NZ informal crook.

runner noun 1 athlete, sprinter, hurdler, racer, jogger. 2 *the bookmaker employed runners:* messenger, courier, errand boy; informal gofer.

running noun 1 *the day-to-day running of the school:* administration, management, organization, coordination, orchestration, handling, direction, control, supervision. 2 *the smooth running of her department:* operation, working, function, performance. •adjective 1 *running water:* flowing, gushing, rushing, moving. 2 *a running argument:* ongoing, continuous, incessant, ceaseless, constant, perpetual. 3 *she was late two days running:* in succession, in a row, in sequence, consecutively, straight, together; informal on the trot.

runny adjective liquid, liquefied, fluid, melted, molten, watery, thin.
OPPOSITES solid, thick.

rupture noun & verb break, fracture, crack, burst, split, fissure, breach.

rural adjective country, rustic, bucolic, pastoral, agricultural, agrarian.
OPPOSITES urban.

ruse noun ploy, stratagem, tactic, scheme, trick, gambit, dodge, subterfuge, machination, wile; Brit. informal wheeze.

rush verb 1 *she rushed home:* hurry, dash, run, race, sprint, bolt, dart, gallop, career, charge, shoot, hurtle, hare, fly, speed, zoom, scurry, scuttle, scamper, hasten; informal tear, belt, pelt, scoot, zip, whip; Brit. informal bomb. 2 *water rushed along gutters:* gush, pour, surge, stream, course, cascade. 3 *the tax was rushed through parliament:* push, hurry, hasten, speed, hustle, press, force. 4 *they rushed the cordon of troops:* attack, charge, storm. •noun 1 *Tim made a rush for the exit:* dash, run, sprint, dart, bolt, charge, scramble. 2 *the lunchtime rush:* hustle and bustle, commotion, hubbub, hurly-burly, stir. 3 *a rush for tickets:* demand, clamour, call,

r

too quickly. **2** produce, deal with, or transport very quickly. **3** (of air or a liquid) flow strongly. **4** dash towards a person or place as a form of attack. • noun **1** a sudden quick movement towards something. **2** a sudden period of hasty activity. **3** a sudden strong demand for a product. **4** a sudden strong feeling. **5** informal a sudden thrill experienced after taking certain drugs. **6** (**rushes**) the first prints made of a film after a period of shooting.
▫ **rush hour** a time at the start and end of the working day when traffic is at its heaviest.

rush² noun a water plant used in making mats, baskets, etc.

rusk noun a dry biscuit or piece of baked bread.

russet adjective reddish brown. • noun a kind of apple with a greenish-brown skin.

Russian noun **1** a person from Russia. **2** the language of Russia. • adjective relating to Russia.
▫ **Russian roulette** a dangerous game of chance in which a person loads one bullet into a revolver, spins the cylinder, and then pulls the trigger while pointing the gun at their own head.

rust noun a brown flaky coating which forms on iron or steel when it is wet. • verb be affected by rust.

rustic adjective **1** having to do with life in the country. **2** simple and charming in a way seen as typical of the countryside. • noun an unsophisticated country person.
■ **rusticity** noun.

rustle verb **1** make a soft crackling sound. **2** round up and steal cattle, horses, or sheep. **3** (**rustle something up**) informal produce food or a drink quickly. • noun a rustling sound.
■ **rustler** noun.

rusty adjective **1** affected by rust. **2** of the colour of rust; reddish-brown. **3** (of knowledge or a skill) less good than it used to be because of a lack of recent practice.

rut¹ noun **1** a long deep track made by the wheels of vehicles. **2** a way of living or working that has become routine and dull but is hard to change.

rut² noun an annual period of sexual activity in deer and some other animals, during which the males fight each other for access to the females. • verb (**ruts, rutting, rutted**) be in such a period of activity.

ruthenium noun a hard silvery-white metallic element.

ruthless adjective hard, determined, and showing no sympathy.
■ **ruthlessly** adverb **ruthlessness** noun.

Rwandan /ruu-an-duhn/ noun a person from Rwanda, a country in central Africa. • adjective relating to Rwanda.

rye noun **1** a type of cereal plant. **2** whisky made from rye.

ryegrass noun a grass used for lawns and as food for farm animals.

THESAURUS

request, run on. **4** *he was in no rush to leave:* hurry, haste, urgency. **5** *I made a sudden rush at him:* charge, onslaught, attack, assault.
• adjective *a rush job:* urgent, high-priority, emergency, hurried, hasty, fast, quick, swift.

rust verb corrode, oxidize, tarnish.

rustic adjective **1** *a rustic setting:* rural, country, pastoral, bucolic, agricultural, agrarian; literary Arcadian. **2** *rustic wooden tables:* plain, simple, homely, unsophisticated, rough, crude.
OPPOSITES urban, ornate, sophisticated.
• noun peasant, countryman, country-woman, bumpkin, yokel, country cousin; N. Amer. informal hillbilly, hayseed, hick; Austral./NZ informal bushy.

ruthless adjective merciless, pitiless, cruel, heartless, hard-hearted, cold-hearted, cold-blooded, harsh, callous.
OPPOSITES merciful.

r

Ss

S or **s** noun (plural **Ss** or **S's**) the nineteenth letter of the alphabet. •**abbreviation** South or Southern.

sabbath noun (often **the Sabbath**) a day for rest and religious worship.

sabbatical noun a period of paid leave for study or travel.

sable noun a marten native to Japan and Siberia, hunted for its dark brown fur.

sabotage /sab-uh-tahzh/ verb (**sabotages, sabotaging, sabotaged**) deliberately damage or destroy. •**noun** the action of sabotaging.

saboteur /sab-uh-**ter**/ noun a person who sabotages something.

sabre /**say**-ber/ (US spelling **saber**) noun **1** a heavy sword with a curved blade. **2** a light fencing sword with a thin blade.

sabretooth tiger or **sabre-toothed tiger** noun a large extinct member of the cat family with massive curved upper canine teeth.

sac noun a hollow, flexible structure resembling a bag or pouch.

saccharin /**sak**-kuh-rin/ noun a sweet-tasting substance used as a low-calorie substitute for sugar.

saccharine /**sak**-kuh-rin/ adjective too sweet or sentimental.

sacerdotal /sak-er-**doh**-t'l/ adjective relating to priests.

sachet /**sa**-shay/ noun Brit. a small sealed bag or packet.

sack[1] noun **1** a large bag made of rough material or thick paper, used for storing and carrying goods. **2** (**the sack**) informal dismissal from employment. **3** (**the sack**) informal bed. •**verb** informal dismiss someone from employment.
■ **sackable** adjective.

sack[2] verb violently attack, steal from, and destroy a town or city (used when talking about the past). •**noun** the sacking of a town or city.

sackcloth noun a rough fabric woven from flax or hemp.

sacra plural of **sacrum**.

sacrament /**sak**-ruh-muhnt/ noun **1** (in the Christian Church) an important religious ceremony in which the people taking part are believed to receive the grace of God. **2** (also **the Blessed Sacrament** or **the Holy Sacrament**) (in Catholic use) the bread and wine used in the Mass.
■ **sacramental** adjective.

sacred /**say**-krid/ adjective **1** connected with God or a god or goddess, and treated as holy. **2** (of a piece of writing) containing the teachings of a religion. **3** religious.
□ **sacred cow** a thing that people believe must not be criticized.

sacrifice noun **1** the killing of an animal or person or giving up of a possession as an

THESAURUS

sabotage noun vandalism, wrecking, destruction, damage, obstruction, disruption.
•**verb** vandalize, wreck, damage, destroy, incapacitate, obstruct, disrupt, spoil, ruin, undermine; Brit. informal throw a spanner in the works.

sack noun bag, pouch, pocket, pack.
•**verb** (informal) dismiss, discharge, lay off, make redundant, let go, throw out; informal fire, give someone the sack; Brit. informal give someone their cards.
□ **the sack** (informal) dismissal, discharge, redundancy; informal the boot, the axe, the

heave-ho, the push.

sacred adjective **1** *a sacred place:* holy, hallowed, blessed, consecrated, sanctified. **2** *sacred music:* religious, spiritual, devotional, church, ecclesiastical.
OPPOSITES secular, profane.

sacrifice noun **1** *the sacrifice of animals:* (ritual) slaughter, (votive) offering. **2** *the sacrifice of privileges:* surrender, giving up, abandonment, renunciation.
•**verb 1** *two goats were sacrificed:* offer up, slaughter. **2** *he sacrificed his principles:* give up, abandon, renounce, relinquish, betray. **3** *he sacrificed his life:* give (up),

S

offering to a god or goddess. **2** an animal, person, or object offered in this way. **3** an act of giving up something you value for the sake of something that is more important. • verb (**sacrifices, sacrificing, sacrificed**) offer as a sacrifice.
■ sacrificial adjective.

sacrilege /sak-ri-lij/ noun an act of treating a sacred or highly valued thing without respect.
■ sacrilegious adjective.

☑ sacrilege, not -relige or -rilige.

sacristan noun a person in charge of a sacristy.

sacristy noun (plural **sacristies**) a room in a church where a priest prepares for a service.

sacrosanct adjective too important or valuable to be changed.

sacrum /say-kruhm/ noun (plural **sacra** or **sacrums**) a triangular bone in the lower back between the two hip bones.

sad adjective (**sadder, saddest**) **1** unhappy. **2** causing sorrow. **3** informal very inadequate or unfashionable.
■ sadly adverb sadness noun.

sadden verb make someone unhappy.

saddle noun **1** a seat with a raised ridge at the front and back, fastened on the back of a horse for riding. **2** a seat on a bicycle or motorcycle. **3** a piece of meat from the back of an animal. • verb (**saddles, saddling, saddled**) **1** put a saddle on a horse. **2** (**saddle someone with**) give someone an unpleasant responsibility or task.

saddlebag noun a bag attached to a saddle.

saddler noun a person who makes, sells, and repairs saddles and other equipment for horses.
■ saddlery (plural **saddleries**).

sadism /say-di-z'm/ noun enjoyment felt in hurting or humiliating other people.
■ sadist noun sadistic adjective.

sadomasochism /say-doh-mass-uh-ki-z'm/ noun enjoyment felt in hurting or being hurt by someone else, especially during sex.
■ sadomasochist noun sadomasochistic adjective.

safari noun (plural **safaris**) an expedition to observe or hunt animals in their natural environment.
□ safari park an area of parkland where wild animals are kept in the open and may be observed by visitors.

safe adjective **1** protected from danger or risk. **2** not leading to harm or injury; not risky. **3** (of a place) giving security or protection. **4** based on good reasons and not likely to be proved wrong. • noun a strong fireproof cabinet with a complex lock, used for storing valuable items.
□ safe house a house in a secret location, used by people in hiding.
■ safely adverb.

safeguard noun a thing done in order to protect or prevent something. • verb protect with a safeguard.

safekeeping noun the keeping of something in a safe place.

safety noun (plural **safeties**) the condition of

THESAURUS

lay down, surrender, forfeit.

sad adjective **1** *we felt sad:* unhappy, sorrowful, depressed, downcast, miserable, down, despondent, wretched, glum, gloomy, doleful, melancholy, mournful, woebegone, forlorn, heartbroken; informal blue, down in the mouth, down in the dumps. **2** *a sad story:* tragic, unhappy, miserable, wretched, sorry, pitiful, pathetic, heartbreaking, heart-rending. **3** *a sad state of affairs:* unfortunate, regrettable, sorry, deplorable, lamentable, pitiful, shameful, disgraceful.
OPPOSITES happy, cheerful, fortunate.

sadden verb depress, dispirit, deject, dishearten, grieve, discourage, upset, get down.

saddle verb burden, encumber, lumber, land, impose something on.

sadness noun unhappiness, sorrow, dejection, depression, misery, despondency, wretchedness, gloom, gloominess, melancholy.

safe adjective **1** *the jewels are safe in the*

bank: secure, protected, out of harm's way. **2** *the children are all safe:* unharmed, unhurt, uninjured, unscathed, all right, fine, well, in one piece, out of danger. **3** *a safe place:* secure, sound, impregnable, invulnerable, secret. **4** *a safe driver:* cautious, circumspect, prudent, careful, unadventurous, conservative. **5** *the drug is safe:* harmless, innocuous, benign, non-toxic, non-poisonous.
OPPOSITES insecure, dangerous, reckless, harmful.

safeguard noun protection, defence, buffer, provision, security, cover, insurance.
• verb protect, preserve, conserve, save, secure, shield, guard, keep safe.
OPPOSITES jeopardize.

safety noun **1** *the safety of the residents:* welfare, well-being, protection, security. **2** *the safety of ferries:* security, soundness, dependability, reliability. **3** *the safety of the shore:* shelter, sanctuary, refuge.

S

being safe.

□ **safety belt** a belt that secures a person to their seat in a vehicle or aircraft. **safety net 1** a net placed to catch an acrobat should they fall. **2** something arranged as a safeguard. **safety pin** a pin with a point that is bent back to the head and held in a guard when closed.

saffron noun a yellow spice made from the dried stigmas of a crocus.

sag verb (**sags, sagging, sagged**) **1** sink downwards gradually under weight or pressure or through weakness. **2** hang down loosely or unevenly. • noun an instance of sagging.
  ■ **saggy** adjective.

saga noun **1** a long traditional story describing brave acts. **2** a story which covers a long period of time. **3** a long and complicated series of incidents.

sagacious adjective having good judgement; wise.
  ■ **sagacity** noun.

sage[1] noun a sweet-smelling Mediterranean plant with greyish-green leaves, used as a herb in cookery.

sage[2] noun a very wise man. • adjective wise.
  ■ **sagely** adverb.

Sagittarius /saj-i-**tair**-i-uhss/ noun a sign of the zodiac (the Archer), 22 November–20 December.

sago noun a pudding made with starchy granules obtained from a palm tree, cooked with milk.

sahib /sahb/ noun Indian a polite form of address for a man.

said past and past participle of **SAY**.
  • adjective referring to someone or something already mentioned.

sail noun **1** a piece of material spread on a mast to catch the wind and propel a boat or ship. **2** a trip in a sailing boat or ship. **3** a flat board attached to the arm of a windmill. • verb **1** travel in a sailing boat as a sport or pastime. **2** travel in a ship or boat using sails or engine power. **3** begin a voyage. **4** direct or control a boat or ship. **5** move smoothly or confidently. **6** (**sail through**) informal succeed easily at.

□ **sail close to the wind** take risks. **sailing boat** (N. Amer. **sailboat**) a boat propelled by sails.

sailboard noun a board with a mast and a sail, used in windsurfing.

sailcloth noun strong fabric used for making sails.

sailor noun **1** a member of the crew of a ship or boat. **2** a person who sails as a sport or pastime. **3** (**a good** or **bad sailor**) a person who rarely (or often) becomes seasick.

saint noun **1** a good person who Christians believe will go to heaven when they die. **2** a person of great goodness who after their death is formally declared by the Church to be a saint, and to whom people offer prayers. **3** informal a very good or kind person.

□ **saint's day** (in the Christian Church) a day each year when a particular saint is honoured.
  ■ **sainthood** noun.

sainted adjective dated very good or kind, like a saint.

St George's cross noun a red cross on a white background.

saintly adjective very holy or good.
  ■ **saintliness** noun.

sake[1] noun **1** (**for the sake of**) in the interest of. **2** (**for the sake of**) out of consideration for. **3** (**for old times' sake**) in memory of former times.

sake[2] /**sah**-ki/ noun a Japanese alcoholic drink made from rice.

salaam /suh-**lahm**/ noun a low bow with the hand touching the forehead, used by Muslims as a gesture of respect. • verb make a salaam.

salacious /suh-**lay**-shuhss/ adjective containing too much sexual detail.

salad noun a cold dish of raw vegetables.
  □ **your salad days** the time when you are young and inexperienced.

salamander noun **1** an animal like a newt that can live in water or on land. **2** a mythical creature resembling a lizard, said to be able to stay alive in fire.

salami noun (plural **salami** or **salamis**) a type

S

THESAURUS

sag verb **1** *he sagged back in his chair:* sink, slump, loll, flop, crumple. **2** *the floors all sag:* dip, droop, bulge, bag.

saga noun **1** *Icelandic sagas:* epic, legend, (folk) tale, romance, narrative, myth. **2** *the saga of how they met:* story, tale, yarn.

sage noun wise man/woman, philosopher, scholar, guru, prophet, mystic.

sail verb **1** *we sailed across the Atlantic:* voyage, travel, navigate, cruise. **2** *we sail tonight:* set sail, put to sea, leave, weigh

anchor. **3** *who is sailing the ship?* steer, pilot, captain; informal skipper. **4** *clouds were sailing past:* glide, drift, float, flow, sweep, skim, coast, flit, scud.

sailor noun seaman, seafarer, mariner, yachtsman, yachtswoman, hand, merchant seaman; informal old salt, matelot, tar.

sake noun **1** *for the sake of clarity:* purpose(s), reason(s). **2** *for her son's sake:* benefit, advantage, good, well-being, welfare.

of spicy preserved sausage.

salary noun (plural **salaries**) a fixed payment made every month to an employee.
■ **salaried** adjective.

sale noun 1 the exchange of something for money. 2 (**sales**) the activity or profession of selling. 3 a period in which goods in a shop are sold at reduced prices. 4 a public event at which goods are sold or auctioned.
■ **saleable** (or **salable**) adjective.

saleroom or **salesroom** noun a room in which auctions are held or cars are sold.

salesman or **saleswoman** noun (plural **salesmen** or **saleswomen**) a person whose job involves selling goods.
■ **salesmanship** noun.

salient /**say**-li-uhnt/ adjective most noticeable or important.
■ **salience** noun.

saline /**say**-lyn/ adjective containing salt.
■ **salinity** noun.

saliva noun a watery liquid in the mouth produced by glands, that helps chewing, swallowing, and digestion.
■ **salivary** adjective.

salivate verb (**salivates, salivating, salivated**) have a lot of saliva in the mouth.
■ **salivation** noun.

sallow adjective (of a person's skin) yellowish or pale brown in colour.

sally noun (plural **sallies**) 1 a sudden charge out of a place surrounded by an enemy. 2 a witty or lively reply. • verb (**sallies, sallying, sallied**) (**sally forth**) set out.

salmon /rhymes with gammon/ noun (plural **salmon** or **salmons**) a large fish with pink flesh, that matures in the sea and moves to freshwater streams to release eggs.

salmonella /sal-muh-**nel**-luh/ noun a germ that can cause food poisoning.

salon noun 1 a place where a hairdresser, beautician, or clothes designer works. 2 a reception room in a large house. 3 (in the past) a regular gathering of writers and artists held in someone's house.

saloon noun 1 Brit. a car with a separate boot. 2 Brit. a lounge bar in a pub. 3 a large room for use as a public lounge on a ship. 4 N. Amer. old use a bar.

salopettes /sal-uh-**pets**/ plural noun padded trousers with a high waist and shoulder straps, worn for skiing.

salsa noun 1 a Latin American dance performed to music that combines jazz and rock. 2 a spicy sauce.

salt noun 1 sodium chloride, a white substance in the form of crystals, used for flavouring or preserving food. 2 Chemistry any compound formed by the reaction of an acid with a base. • verb 1 season or preserve food with salt. 2 sprinkle a road or path with salt in order to melt snow or ice.
□ **salt cellar** a container for salt. **the salt of the earth** a person who is very kind, reliable, or honest. **take something with a pinch** (or **grain**) **of salt** recognize that something may be exaggerated or untrue.

saltings noun Brit. an area of coastal land regularly covered by the tide.

saltpetre /sawlt-**pee**-ter/ (US spelling **saltpeter**) noun a white powder (potassium nitrate) used to make gunpowder and preserve meat.

salty adjective (**saltier, saltiest**) 1 containing or tasting of salt. 2 (of language or humour) rather rude.
■ **saltiness** noun.

salubrious adjective 1 good for your health. 2 (of a place) well maintained and pleasant to be in.

salutary /**sal**-yuu-tuh-ri/ adjective (with reference to something unpleasant) producing a good effect because it teaches you something.

salutation noun a greeting.

salute noun 1 a raising of a hand to the head, made as a formal gesture of respect by a member of a military force. 2 a gesture of admiration or respect. 3 the shooting of a gun or guns as a formal sign of respect or celebration. • verb (**salutes, saluting, saluted**) 1 make a formal salute to. 2 greet. 3 express admiration and respect for.

Salvadorean /sal-vuh-**dor**-i-uhn/ noun a person from El Salvador, a country in Central America. • adjective relating to El Salvador.

salvage verb (**salvages, salvaging, salvaged**) 1 rescue something that is in danger of being lost or destroyed. 2 rescue a ship or its contents from being lost at sea. • noun 1 the action of salvaging. 2 contents

S

THESAURUS

salary noun pay, wages, earnings, payment, remuneration, fee(s), stipend, income.

sale noun 1 the sale of firearms: selling, dealing, trading. 2 they make a sale every minute: deal, transaction, bargain.
OPPOSITES purchase.

salty adjective salt, salted, saline, briny, brackish.

salute noun tribute, testimonial, homage, honour, celebration (of), acknowledgement (of).
• verb pay tribute to, pay homage to, honour, celebrate, acknowledge, take your hat off to.

salvage verb rescue, save, recover, retrieve, reclaim.

rescued from a wrecked ship.
□ **salvage yard** a place where disused machinery and vehicles are broken up so that the metal or parts can be used again.

salvation noun **1** the saving of a person from sin and its consequences, believed by Christians to be brought about by faith in Jesus. **2** the protecting or saving of someone or something from harm or loss.

salve noun **1** an ointment that soothes the skin. **2** something that makes you feel less guilty. •verb (**salves, salving, salved**) reduce feelings of guilt.

salver noun a tray.

salvia noun a plant with bright red flowers.

salvo noun (plural **salvos** or **salvoes**) **1** a shooting of a number of guns at the same time. **2** a sudden series of aggressive statements or acts.

salwar /sul-**wah**/ (also **shalwar**) noun light, loose trousers that fit tightly around the ankles, worn by women from the Indian subcontinent.

Samaritan noun **1** (**good Samaritan**) a helpful person. **2** a member of a people living in Samaria, an ancient city and region of Palestine.

samba /**sam**-buh/ noun a Brazilian dance of African origin.

same adjective **1** (**the same**) exactly alike. **2** (**this** or **that same**) referring to a person or thing just mentioned. •pronoun **1** (**the same**) the same thing as previously mentioned. **2** (**the same**) identical people or things. •adverb in the same way.
■ **sameness** noun.

samey adjective Brit. informal lacking in variety.

Samoan noun a person from Samoa.
•adjective relating to Samoa.

samovar /sam-uh-var/ noun a highly decorated Russian tea urn.

sampan noun (in SE Asia) a small flat-bottomed boat propelled with an oar.

samphire noun a plant which grows on rocks near the sea.

sample noun **1** a small part or quantity of something intended to show what the whole is like. **2** a specimen taken for scientific testing. •verb (**samples, sampling, sampled**) **1** take a sample of. **2** try out. **3** take a short extract from one musical recording and reuse it as part of another recording.

sampler noun **1** a piece of fabric decorated with a number of different embroidery stitches. **2** a device for sampling music.

samurai /**sam**-yuu-ry/ noun (plural **samurai**) (in the past) a member of a powerful Japanese military class.

sanatorium noun (plural **sanatoriums** or **sanatoria**) **1** a place like a hospital where people who have a long-term illness or who are recovering from an illness are treated. **2** Brit. a place in a boarding school for children who are ill.

sanctify verb (**sanctifies, sanctifying, sanctified**) **1** make something holy. **2** make something legal or right.
■ **sanctification** noun.

sanctimonious adjective disapproving making a show of being morally superior to other people.

sanction noun **1** (**sanctions**) measures taken by a state to try to force another state to behave well. **2** a penalty for disobeying a law or rule. **3** official permission or approval. •verb give official permission for.

sanctity noun (plural **sanctities**) **1** the state of being holy. **2** the state of being very important.

THESAURUS

S

salvation noun **1** *praying for salvation:* redemption, deliverance. **2** *that man was her salvation:* lifeline, means of escape, saviour.
OPPOSITES damnation, ruin.

same adjective **1** *we stayed at the same hotel:* identical, selfsame, very same. **2** *they had the same symptoms:* matching, identical, alike, carbon-copy, twin, indistinguishable, interchangeable, corresponding, equivalent, parallel, like, comparable, similar.
OPPOSITES another, different, dissimilar, varying.
□ **the same** unchanging, unvarying, unvaried, consistent, uniform.

sample noun **1** *a sample of the fabric:* specimen, example, snippet, swatch, taste, taster. **2** *a representative sample:* cross section, selection.

•verb *we sampled the food:* try (out), taste, test, put to the test, appraise, evaluate; informal check out.
•adjective *a sample copy:* specimen, test, trial, pilot, dummy.

sanction noun **1** *trade sanctions:* penalty, punishment, deterrent, restriction, embargo, ban, prohibition, boycott. **2** *the scheme has the sanction of the court:* authorization, consent, leave, permission, authority, dispensation, assent, acquiescence, agreement, approval, endorsement, blessing; informal the thumbs up, the OK.
OPPOSITES reward, prohibition.
•verb *the rally was sanctioned by the government:* authorize, permit, allow, endorse, approve, accept, back, support; informal OK.
OPPOSITES prohibit.

sanctuary noun (plural **sanctuaries**) **1** a place of safety. **2** a nature reserve. **3** a place where injured or unwanted animals are cared for. **4** a holy place. **5** the part of the chancel of a church containing the high altar.

sanctum noun **1** a sacred place. **2** a private place.

sand noun **1** a substance consisting of very fine particles resulting from the wearing down of rocks, found in beaches and deserts and on the seabed. **2** (**sands**) a wide area of sand. • verb smooth a surface with sandpaper or a sander.

sandal noun a shoe with a partly open upper part or straps attaching the sole to the foot.

sandalwood noun the sweet-smelling wood of an Asian tree.

sandbag noun a bag of sand, used to protect or strengthen a structure or as a weight.

sandbank noun a deposit of sand forming a shallow area in the sea or a river.

sandbar noun a long, narrow sandbank.

sandblast verb roughen or clean a surface with a jet of sand.

sandcastle noun a model of a castle built out of sand.

sander noun a power tool used for smoothing a surface.

sandpaper noun paper coated with sand or another rough substance, used for smoothing surfaces. • verb smooth with sandpaper.

sandpiper noun a wading bird with a long bill and long legs.

sandpit noun Brit. a shallow box or hollow containing sand, for children to play in.

sandstone noun rock formed from compressed sand.

sandstorm noun a strong wind in a desert carrying clouds of sand.

sandwich noun two pieces of bread with a filling between them. • verb (**sandwich someone/thing between**) squeeze someone or something between two people or things.
□ **sandwich board** a pair of boards hung in front of and behind a person's body as they walk around, used especially to advertise something. **sandwich course** Brit. a course of study which includes periods working in business or industry.

sandy adjective (**sandier**, **sandiest**) **1** covered in or consisting of sand. **2** light yellowish brown.

sane adjective **1** not mad. **2** sensible.

sang past of SING.

sangfroid /song-frwah/ noun the ability to stay calm in difficult circumstances.

sangria noun a Spanish drink of red wine and lemonade with fruit and spices.

sanguinary /sang-gwi-nuh-ri/ adjective old use involving a lot of bloodshed.

sanguine /sang-gwin/ adjective cheerful and confident about things that are going to happen.

sanitarium US = SANATORIUM.

sanitary adjective **1** relating to sanitation. **2** hygienic.
□ **sanitary towel** a pad worn by women to absorb blood during a menstrual period.

sanitation noun arrangements to protect public health, such as the provision of clean drinking water and the disposal of sewage.

sanitize or **sanitise** verb (**sanitizes**, **sanitizing**, **sanitized**) **1** make something hygienic. **2** make something unpleasant seem more acceptable.

sanity noun **1** the condition of being sane. **2** reasonable behaviour.

sank past of SINK.

Sanskrit /san-skrit/ noun an ancient language of India.

Santa Claus noun Father Christmas.

sap noun the liquid that circulates in plants, carrying food to all parts. • verb (**saps**, **sapping**, **sapped**) gradually weaken a person's strength.

sapient /say-pi-uhnt/ adjective formal wise or intelligent.

sapling noun a young tree.

sapper noun a military engineer who lays or finds and defuses mines or (Brit.) a soldier in the Royal Engineers.

sapphic /saf-fik/ adjective literary relating to lesbians.

sapphire /saf-fy-er/ noun **1** a transparent blue precious stone. **2** a bright blue colour.

S

THESAURUS

sanctuary noun **1** *the garden is our sanctuary:* refuge, haven, oasis, shelter, retreat, bolt-hole, hideaway. **2** *he was given sanctuary in the embassy:* safety, shelter, protection, immunity, asylum. **3** *a bird sanctuary:* reserve, park.

sane adjective **1** *he is presumed to be sane:* of sound mind, in your right mind, compos mentis, lucid, rational, balanced, normal; informal all there. **2** *a sane suggestion:* sensible, practical, realistic, prudent, reasonable, rational, level-headed, commonsensical.
OPPOSITES mad, foolish.

sap noun juice, secretion, fluid, liquid.
• verb *illness sapped his energy:* erode, wear away/down, deplete, reduce, lessen, undermine, drain, bleed.

saprophyte /sap-ruh-fyt/ noun a plant or fungus that lives on decaying matter.
■ **saprophytic** adjective.

Saracen noun an Arab or Muslim at the time of the Crusades.

sarcasm noun the use of words which say the opposite of what you mean, as a way of hurting or mocking someone.

sarcastic adjective using sarcasm.
■ **sarcastically** adverb.

sarcoma /sar-**koh**-muh/ noun (plural **sarcomas**) a cancer that grows in parts of the body such as muscle or bone.

sarcophagus /sar-**kof**-fuh-guhss/ noun (plural **sarcophagi** /sar-**kof**-fuh-gy/) a stone coffin.

sardine noun a small edible sea fish.

sardonic adjective mocking.
■ **sardonically** adverb.

sari or **saree** noun (plural **saris** or **sarees**) a length of fabric draped around the body, worn by women from the Indian subcontinent.

sarky adjective Brit. informal sarcastic.
■ **sarkily** adverb.

sarnie noun Brit. informal a sandwich.

sarong noun a long piece of cloth wrapped round the body and tucked at the waist or under the armpits.

sartorial adjective having to do with the way a person dresses.
■ **sartorially** adverb.

sash[1] noun a strip of fabric worn over one shoulder or round the waist.

sash[2] noun a frame holding the glass in a window.
□ **sash window** a window with two sashes which can be slid up and down to open it.

sashay verb informal swing the hips from side to side when walking.

Sassenach /sass-uh-nak/ Scottish & Irish disapproving noun an English person. •adjective English.

sassy adjective (**sassier**, **sassiest**) informal confident, spirited, and cheeky.

SAT abbreviation standard assessment task.

sat past and past participle of SIT.

Satan noun the Devil.

satanic adjective having to do with Satan or the worship of Satan.

satanism noun the worship of Satan.
■ **satanist** noun & adjective.

satay or **saté** /sat-ay/ noun an Indonesian and Malaysian dish consisting of small pieces of meat grilled on a skewer, usually served with a peanut sauce.

satchel noun a bag with a long strap worn over one shoulder.

sated adjective having had as much or more of something than you want.

satellite noun 1 a man-made device placed in orbit round the earth or another planet in order to collect information or for communication. 2 a celestial body that moves in orbit round a planet. 3 a thing that is separate from but controlled by something else.
□ **satellite television** television in which the signals are broadcast via satellite.

satiate /say-shi-ayt/ verb give someone as much or more of something than they want.
■ **satiation** noun.

satiety /suh-**ty**-i-ti/ noun the state of being fully satisfied or of having had too much of something.

satin noun a smooth, glossy fabric.
■ **satiny** adjective.

satire /sa-ty-er/ noun 1 the use of humour, irony, exaggeration, or ridicule to reveal and criticize people's bad points. 2 a play or other piece of writing that uses satire.
■ **satirist** noun.

satirical or **satiric** adjective using satire.
■ **satirically** adverb.

satirize or **satirise** /sat-i-ryz/ verb (**satirizes**, **satirizing**, **satirized**) mock or criticize using satire.

satisfaction noun the feeling of pleasure that arises when you have the things you need or want or when the things you want to happen have happened.

satisfactory adjective acceptable.
■ **satisfactorily** adverb.

satisfy verb (**satisfies**, **satisfying**, **satisfied**)

THESAURUS

satanic adjective diabolical, fiendish, devilish, demonic, ungodly, hellish, infernal, wicked, evil, sinful.
OPPOSITES godly.

satire noun parody, burlesque, caricature, irony, lampoon, skit; informal spoof, take-off, send-up.

satirical adjective mocking, ironic, sardonic, critical, irreverent, disparaging, disrespectful.

satisfaction noun contentment, content, pleasure, gratification, fulfilment,

enjoyment, happiness, pride.

satisfactory adjective adequate, all right, acceptable, good enough, sufficient, reasonable, competent, fair, decent, average, passable, fine, in order, up to scratch, up to the mark.
OPPOSITES unsatisfactory.

satisfy verb 1 *a chance to satisfy his lust:* fulfil, gratify, meet, fill, indulge, appease, assuage, quench, slake, satiate. 2 *she satisfied herself that it was an accident:* convince, assure, reassure. 3 *products*

S

1 give someone the things they need or want or bring about the things they want to happen. **2** meet a particular demand, desire, or need.

satsuma /sat-soo-muh/ noun a kind of tangerine with a loose skin.

saturate verb (saturates, saturating, saturated) **1** soak thoroughly with a liquid. **2** make a substance combine with, dissolve, or hold the greatest possible quantity of another substance. **3** put more than is needed of a particular product into the market.
■ **saturation** noun.

saturated adjective Chemistry (of fats) having only single bonds between carbon atoms in their molecules and therefore being less easily processed by the body.

Saturday noun the day of the week before Sunday and following Friday.

Saturn noun the sixth planet from the sun in the solar system, circled by broad flat rings.

saturnine /sat-er-nyn/ adjective **1** (of a person or their manner) gloomy. **2** (of looks) dark and brooding.

satyr /sat-er/ noun (in Greek mythology) a lecherous woodland god, with a man's face and body and a horse's or goat's ears, tail, and legs.

sauce noun **1** a thick liquid served with food to add moistness and flavour. **2** informal cheeky talk or behaviour.
□ **sauce boat** a boat-shaped jug for serving sauce.

saucepan noun a deep cooking pan, with one long handle and a lid.

saucer noun a small shallow dish on which a cup stands.

saucy adjective (saucier, sauciest) informal **1** sexually suggestive in a light-hearted

way. **2** cheeky.
■ **saucily** adverb.

Saudi /sow-di/ noun (plural **Saudis**) a person from Saudi Arabia. • adjective relating to Saudi Arabia.

sauerkraut /sow-er-krowt/ noun a German dish of pickled cabbage.

sauna /saw-nuh/ noun **1** a small room used as a hot-air or steam bath for cleaning and refreshing the body. **2** a session in a sauna.

saunter verb (saunters, sauntering, sauntered) walk in a slow, relaxed way.
• noun a leisurely stroll.

sausage noun **1** a short tube of raw minced meat encased in a skin and grilled or fried before eating. **2** a tube of seasoned minced meat that is cooked or preserved and eaten cold in slices.
□ **sausage dog** Brit. informal a dachshund. **sausage meat** minced meat used in sausages or as a stuffing. **sausage roll** a portion of sausage meat baked in a roll of pastry.

sauté /soh-tay/ adjective fried quickly in shallow fat or oil. • verb (sautés, sautéing, sautéed or sautéd) cook in such a way.

Sauvignon /soh-vin-yon/ noun a type of white wine.

savage adjective **1** fierce and violent. **2** cruel and vicious. **3** primitive and uncivilized.
• noun **1** a member of a people seen as primitive and uncivilized. **2** a brutal person. • verb (savages, savaging, savaged) **1** attack ferociously; maul. **2** criticize severely.
■ **savagely** adverb **savagery** noun.

savannah or **savanna** noun a grassy plain in hot regions.

savant or **savante** /sav-uhnt/ noun a wise and knowledgeable person.

save[1] verb (saves, saving, saved) **1** rescue or

which satisfy EC law: comply with, meet, fulfil, answer, conform to, measure up to, come up to.
OPPOSITES frustrate.

saturate verb **1** rain had saturated the ground: soak, drench, waterlog. **2** the company has saturated the market: flood, glut, oversupply, overfill, overload.

saturated adjective **1** his trousers were saturated: soaked, soaking (wet), wet through, sopping (wet), sodden, dripping, wringing wet, drenched, soaked to the skin. **2** the saturated pitch: waterlogged, flooded, boggy, awash.
OPPOSITES dry.

sauce noun relish, condiment, ketchup, dip, dressing, jus, coulis, gravy.

savage adjective **1** savage dogs: ferocious, fierce, vicious, wild, feral. **2** a savage

assault: vicious, brutal, cruel, sadistic, ferocious, fierce, violent. **3** a savage attack on free trade: fierce, blistering, scathing, searing, stinging, devastating, withering, virulent, vitriolic.
OPPOSITES tame, mild.
• noun she described her assailants as savages: brute, beast, monster, barbarian, sadist, animal.
• verb **1** savaged by a dog: maul, attack, lacerate, claw, bite. **2** critics savaged the film: criticize, attack, lambaste, condemn, denounce, pillory, revile; informal pan; Brit. informal slate; N. Amer. informal trash.

save verb **1** the captain was saved by his crew: rescue, set free, free, liberate, deliver. **2** the house was saved from demolition: preserve, keep, protect, safeguard, salvage, retrieve, reclaim,

protect someone or something from harm or danger. **2** prevent someone from dying. **3** store or keep for future use. **4** (in computing) store data. **5** avoid, lessen, or guard against. **6** prevent an opponent from scoring a goal. **7** (in Christian use) prevent a soul from being damned. •**noun** an act of preventing an opponent's goal.
■ **saver** noun.

save² preposition & conjunction formal except.

saveloy /sav-uh-loy/ **noun** Brit. a smoked pork sausage.

saving noun **1** a reduction in money, time, or some other resource. **2** (**savings**) money saved. •**preposition** except.
□ **saving grace** a good quality that makes up for someone or something's faults.

saviour (US spelling **savior**) **noun 1** a person who saves someone or something from danger or harm. **2** (**Saviour**) (in Christianity) God or Jesus.

savoir faire /sav-war fair/ **noun** the ability to act appropriately in social situations.

savory noun a plant used as a herb in cookery.

savour (US spelling **savor**) **verb 1** eat or drink something slowly while enjoying its full flavour. **2** enjoy a feeling or experience thoroughly. •**noun** a characteristic flavour or smell.

savoury (US spelling **savory**) **adjective 1** (of food) salty or spicy rather than sweet. **2** morally acceptable or respectable. •**noun** (plural **savouries**) Brit. a savoury snack.

savoy noun a type of cabbage.

savvy informal **noun** intelligence and good judgement. •**adjective** having intelligence and good judgement.

saw¹ noun a tool with a long, thin jagged blade, used with a backwards and forwards movement to cut wood and other hard materials. •**verb** (**saws, sawing, sawed**; past participle Brit. **sawn** or N. Amer. **sawed**) cut through or cut off with a saw.

saw² past of SEE¹.

saw³ noun a proverb or wise saying.

sawdust noun powdery particles of wood produced by sawing.

sawmill noun a place where logs are sawn by machine.

sawtooth or **sawtoothed** adjective shaped like the jagged teeth of a saw.

sawyer noun a person who saws timber.

sax noun informal a saxophone.

saxifrage /saks-i-frayj/ noun a plant which grows on rocky or stony ground, with small red, white, or yellow flowers.

Saxon noun a member of a people from Germany that settled in southern England in the 5th and 6th centuries.

saxophone noun a metal wind instrument with a reed in the mouthpiece.
■ **saxophonist** noun.

say verb (**says, saying, said**) **1** speak words to communicate something. **2** (of a piece of writing or a symbol) convey information or instructions. **3** (of a clock or watch) indicate a time. **4** (**be said**) be reported. **5** assume something in order to work out what its consequences would be. •**noun** an opportunity to state your opinion.

saying noun a well-known statement expressing a general truth.

scab noun **1** a crust that forms over a wound as it heals. **2** informal, disapproving a person who refuses to take part in a strike.
■ **scabby** adjective.

scabbard noun a cover for the blade of a sword or dagger.

scabies noun a skin disease that causes itching and small red spots.

scabrous adjective **1** rough and covered with scabs. **2** indecent or sordid.

scaffold noun **1** (in the past) a raised wooden platform on which people stood when they were to be executed. **2** a structure made using scaffolding.

scaffolding noun **1** a structure made of wooden planks and metal poles, for people to stand on when building or repairing a

THESAURUS

rescue. **3** *start saving old newspapers:* put/set aside, put by/to one side, keep, retain, store, hoard; informal squirrel away. **4** *asking her saved a lot of trouble:* prevent, avoid, forestall, spare, stop, obviate, avert.

saving noun **1** *a considerable saving in cost:* reduction, cut, decrease, economy. **2** (**savings**) nest egg, capital, assets, funds, resources, reserves.

saviour noun rescuer, liberator, deliverer, champion, protector, redeemer.

savour verb *she savoured every moment:* relish, enjoy, appreciate, delight in, revel in, luxuriate in.

•**noun** *the subtle savour of wood smoke:* smell, aroma, fragrance, scent, perfume, bouquet, taste, flavour, tang, smack.

say verb **1** *he said her name:* speak, utter, voice, pronounce. **2** *'I must go,' she said:* declare, state, announce, observe, mention, comment, note, add. **3** *they said a prayer:* recite, repeat, utter, deliver, perform. **4** *her watch said one twenty:* indicate, show, read.
•**noun** *don't I have any say in the matter?* influence, sway, weight, voice, input.

saying noun proverb, maxim, aphorism, axiom, expression, phrase, formula, slogan, building. 2 the planks and poles used in such a structure.

scald verb 1 burn with very hot liquid or steam. 2 heat a liquid to near boiling point. 3 dip something briefly in boiling water. • noun an injury caused by hot liquid or steam.

scale¹ noun 1 each of the small overlapping plates protecting the skin of fish and reptiles. 2 a dry flake of skin. 3 a white deposit which is left in a kettle, water pipe, etc. when water containing lime is heated. 4 a hard deposit that forms on teeth. • verb (scales, scaling, scaled) 1 remove the scales from. 2 form or flake off in scales.

scale² noun 1 (usu. scales) an instrument for weighing. 2 either of the dishes on a simple set of scales.

scale³ noun 1 a range of values forming a system for measuring or grading something. 2 a measuring instrument based on such a system. 3 relative size or extent. 4 a ratio of size in a map, model, drawing, or plan. 5 Music an arrangement of notes in order of pitch. • verb (scales, scaling, scaled) 1 climb up or over something high and steep. 2 (scale something down or up) reduce (or increase) something in size, number, or extent. 3 represent something in a size that is larger or smaller than the original but exactly in proportion to it. □ to scale reduced or enlarged in proportion to something.

scallion noun N. Amer. a spring onion.

scallop /skol-luhp, skal-luhp/ noun 1 an edible shellfish with two hinged fan-shaped shells. 2 each of a series of small curves like the edge of a scallop shell, forming a decorative edging.

scalloped adjective (of the edge of something) decorated with a series of small curves.

scallywag noun informal a mischievous person.

scalp noun 1 the skin covering the top and back of the head. 2 (in the past, among American Indians) the scalp and hair cut away from an enemy's head as a battle trophy. • verb historical take the scalp of an enemy.

scalpel noun a knife with a small sharp blade, used by a surgeon.

scaly adjective (scalier, scaliest) 1 covered in scales. 2 (of skin) dry and flaking.

scam noun informal a dishonest scheme for making money.

scamp noun informal a mischievous person.

scamper verb (scampers, scampering, scampered) run with quick light steps.

scampi plural noun the tails of large prawns, covered in breadcrumbs or batter and fried.

scan verb (scans, scanning, scanned) 1 look at something quickly in order to find the parts that are most relevant or important. 2 move a detector or beam across. 3 convert a document or picture into digital form for storing or processing on a computer. 4 analyse the metre of a line of verse. 5 (of poetry) follow metrical rules. • noun 1 an act of scanning. 2 a medical examination using a scanner. 3 an image obtained by scanning.

scandal noun 1 an action or event that causes public outrage. 2 outrage or gossip arising from such an action or event. 3 an action or situation that you find shocking and unacceptable.

scandalize or **scandalise** verb (scandalizes, scandalizing, scandalized) shock other people by acting in way that is considered shameful or immoral.

scandalous adjective 1 causing public outrage. 2 shocking and unacceptable. ■ scandalously adverb.

Scandinavian adjective relating to the countries of Scandinavia, especially Norway, Sweden, and Denmark. • noun a person from Scandinavia.

scandium noun a soft silvery-white metallic element.

scanner noun 1 a machine that uses X-rays

catchphrase.

scale noun 1 *opposite ends of the social scale:* hierarchy, ladder, ranking, pecking order, order, spectrum. 2 *the scale of the map:* ratio, proportion. 3 *the scale of the disaster:* extent, size, scope, magnitude, dimensions, range, breadth, degree. • verb *thieves scaled the fence:* climb, ascend, clamber up, scramble up, shin (up), mount; N. Amer. shinny (up).

scan verb 1 *Adam scanned the horizon:* study, examine, scrutinize, inspect, survey, search, scour, sweep, watch. 2 *I scanned the* papers: glance through, look through, have a look at, run your eye over, cast your eye over, flick through, browse through. • noun 1 *a quick scan through the report:* glance, look, flick, browse. 2 *a brain scan:* examination, screening.

scandal noun 1 *a scandal that led him to resign:* affair, issue, incident, outrage, skeleton in the cupboard; informal ...-gate. 2 *it's a scandal:* disgrace, outrage, (crying) shame, sin. 3 *a name tarnished by scandal:* gossip, rumour(s), slander, libel, aspersions, muckraking; informal dirt.

S

or ultrasound to record images, used by doctors to examine the inside of someone's body. **2** a device that scans documents or pictures and converts them into digital data.

scansion noun **1** the action of scanning a line of verse to find out its rhythm. **2** the rhythm of a line of verse.

scant adjective barely reaching the amount specified or needed.

scanty adjective (**scantier, scantiest**) too little in size or amount for what is needed.
■ **scantily** adverb.

scapegoat noun a person who is blamed for the things other people do wrong. • verb make a scapegoat of.

scapula noun the shoulder blade.

scar¹ noun **1** a mark left on the skin or in body tissue after the healing of a wound. **2** a lasting effect left after an unpleasant experience. **3** a mark left at the point where a leaf or other part separates from a plant. • verb (**scars, scarring, scarred**) mark or be marked with a scar.

scar² noun a steep high cliff or outcrop of rock.

scarab /ska-ruhb/ noun **1** a kind of large beetle, seen as sacred in ancient Egypt. **2** an ancient Egyptian gem in the form of a scarab beetle.

scarce adjective **1** (of a resource) only available in small quantities that do not meet a demand. **2** rarely found.
■ **scarcity** noun.

scarcely adverb **1** only just. **2** just moments before. **3** definitely or very probably not.

scare verb (**scares, scaring, scared**)

1 frighten or become frightened. **2** (**scare someone away** or **off**) drive or keep someone away by frightening them. • noun **1** a sudden attack of fright. **2** a period of general alarm.

scarecrow noun an object made to look like a person, set up to scare birds away from crops.

scarf noun (plural **scarves** or **scarfs**) a length or square of fabric worn around the neck or head.

scarify verb (**scarifies, scarifying, scarified**) **1** rake out unwanted material from a lawn. **2** break up the surface of soil. **3** make shallow cuts in the skin.

scarlatina or **scarletina** noun scarlet fever.

scarlet noun a bright red colour.
□ **scarlet fever** an infectious disease that affects children, causing fever and a scarlet rash.

scarp noun a very steep slope.

scarper verb (**scarpers, scarpering, scarpered**) Brit. informal run away.

scarves plural of **SCARF**.

scary adjective (**scarier, scariest**) informal frightening.
■ **scarily** adverb.

scathing adjective severely critical.
■ **scathingly** adverb.

scatological adjective obsessed with excrement and excretion.
■ **scatology** noun.

scatter verb (**scatters, scattering, scattered**) **1** throw in various random directions. **2** separate and move off in different

---

THESAURUS

scant adjective little, little or no, minimal, limited, negligible, meagre, insufficient, inadequate.
OPPOSITES abundant, ample.

scapegoat noun whipping boy, Aunt Sally; informal fall guy; N. Amer. informal patsy.

scar noun **1** *the scar on his arm:* mark, blemish, disfigurement, discoloration, pockmark, pit, lesion, stitches.
2 *psychological scars:* trauma, damage, injury.
• verb *scarred for life:* disfigure, mark, blemish.

scarce adjective **1** *food was scarce:* in short supply, scant, meagre, sparse, hard to come by. **2** *wading birds are now scarce:* rare, few and far between, thin on the ground.
OPPOSITES plentiful.

scarcely adverb **1** *she could scarcely hear him:* hardly, barely, only just. **2** *I scarcely see her:* rarely, seldom, infrequently, not often, hardly ever; informal once in a blue moon. **3** *this could scarcely be an accident:* surely not, not, hardly.

scare verb *stop it, you're scaring me:* frighten, startle, alarm, terrify, unnerve, worry, intimidate, terrorize, cow; informal freak out; Brit. informal put the wind up; N. Amer. informal spook.
• noun *you gave me a scare:* fright, shock, start, turn, jump.

scared adjective frightened, afraid, fearful, nervous, panicky, terrified; informal in a cold sweat; N. Amer. informal spooked.

scary adjective (informal) frightening, terrifying, hair-raising, spine-chilling, blood-curdling, eerie, sinister; informal creepy, spine-tingling, spooky.

scatter verb **1** *scatter the seeds evenly:* spread, sprinkle, distribute, strew, disseminate, sow. **2** *the crowd scattered:* disperse, break up, disband, separate, dissolve. **3** *the floor was scattered with books:* cover, dot, sprinkle, spot, pepper, litter.
OPPOSITES gather, assemble.

directions. **3** (**be scattered**) be found at various places.

scatty or **scatterbrained** adjective informal disorganized and rather silly.

scavenge verb (**scavenges**, **scavenging**, **scavenged**) **1** search through waste for anything that can be used again. **2** (of an animal) search for and eat dead animals.
■ **scavenger** noun.

scenario noun (plural **scenarios**) **1** a possible sequence of events in the future. **2** a written outline of a film, play, or novel.

scene noun **1** the place where an incident happens. **2** a view or landscape as seen by a spectator. **3** an incident: *scenes of violence.* **4** a sequence of continuous action in a play, film, etc. **5** an area of activity or interest: *the literary scene.* **6** a public display of emotion or anger.
□ **behind the scenes** out of public view.

scenery noun **1** a landscape considered in terms of its appearance. **2** the background used to represent a place on a stage or film set.

scenic adjective having beautiful natural scenery.
■ **scenically** adverb.

scent noun **1** a distinctive smell, especially a pleasant one. **2** pleasant-smelling liquid worn on the skin; perfume. **3** a trail left by an animal, indicated by its smell. • verb

1 give a pleasant scent to. **2** find or recognize something by using the sense of smell. **3** sense that something is about to happen.
■ **scented** adjective.

sceptic /skep-tik/ (US spelling **skeptic**) noun a person who questions accepted opinions.
■ **scepticism** noun.

sceptical (US spelling **skeptical**) adjective not easily convinced; having doubts.
■ **sceptically** adverb.

sceptre /sep-ter/ (US spelling **scepter**) noun a decorated rod carried by a king or queen on ceremonial occasions.

schedule /shed-yool, sked-yool/ noun **1** a plan for doing something, with a list of intended events and times. **2** a timetable.
• verb (**schedules**, **scheduling**, **scheduled**) **1** plan for something to happen at a particular time. **2** (**scheduled**) (of a flight) forming part of a regular service rather than specially chartered.

schema /skee-muh/ noun (plural **schemata** /skee-muh-tuh/ or **schemas**) technical an outline of a plan or theory.

schematic adjective **1** (of a diagram) simplified and using symbols. **2** presented according to a plan.
■ **schematically** adverb.

scheme noun **1** a careful plan for achieving

scenario noun **1** *Walt wrote scenarios for various studios:* plot, outline, storyline, framework, screenplay, script. **2** *consider every possible scenario:* situation, chain of events, course of events.

scene noun **1** *the scene of the accident:* location, site, place, position. **2** *the scene is London in the 1890s:* background, setting, context, milieu, backdrop. **3** *scenes of violence:* incident, event, episode, happening. **4** *an impressive mountain scene:* view, vista, outlook, panorama, landscape, scenery. **5** *she made a scene:* fuss, exhibition of yourself, performance, tantrum, commotion, disturbance, row; informal to-do; Brit. informal carry-on. **6** *the political scene:* arena, stage, sphere, world, milieu, realm. **7** *a scene from a movie:* clip, section, segment, part, sequence, extract.

scenery noun **1** *beautiful scenery:* landscape, countryside, country, terrain, setting, surroundings, environment. **2** *scenery and costumes:* set, setting, backdrop.

scenic adjective picturesque, pretty, attractive, beautiful, charming, impressive, striking, spectacular, breathtaking, panoramic.

scent noun **1** *the scent of freshly cut hay:* smell, fragrance, aroma, perfume, savour,

odour. **2** *a bottle of scent:* perfume, fragrance, eau de toilette, eau de cologne. **3** *the hounds picked up the scent:* spoor, trail, track.
• verb *sharks soon scent the blood:* smell, nose out, detect, pick up, sense.

scented adjective perfumed, fragranced, fragrant, sweet-smelling, aromatic.

sceptic noun cynic, doubter, unbeliever, doubting Thomas.

sceptical adjective dubious, doubtful, doubting, cynical, distrustful, suspicious, disbelieving, unconvinced.
OPPOSITES certain, convinced.

scepticism noun doubt, a pinch of salt, disbelief, cynicism, distrust, suspicion, incredulity.

schedule noun **1** *our production schedule:* plan, programme, timetable, scheme. **2** *I have a busy schedule:* timetable, agenda, diary, calendar, itinerary.
• verb *a meeting has been scheduled:* arrange, organize, plan, programme, timetable, set up, line up; N. Amer. slate.

scheme noun **1** *fund-raising schemes:* plan, project, programme, strategy, stratagem, tactic; Brit. informal wheeze. **2** *his schemes and plots:* plot, intrigue, conspiracy, ruse, ploy, stratagem, manoeuvre, subterfuge, machinations; informal racket, scam.

S

something. **2** a secret or devious plan; a plot. **3** a system or pattern. •verb (**schemes, scheming, schemed**) make secret plans; plot.

scherzo /skair-tsoh/ noun (plural **scherzos** or **scherzi** /skair-tsi/) a short, lively piece of music.

schism /si-z'm, ski-z'm/ noun a disagreement or division between two groups or within an organization.
■ **schismatic** adjective.

schist /shist/ noun a metamorphic rock which consists of layers of different minerals.

schizoid /skit-soyd/ adjective having a mental condition similar to schizophrenia.

schizophrenia noun a mental disorder whose symptoms include a withdrawal from reality into fantasy.

schizophrenic adjective **1** suffering from schizophrenia. **2** having contradictory elements. •noun a schizophrenic person.

schmaltz noun informal the quality of being too sentimental.
■ **schmaltzy** adjective.

schnapps noun a strong alcoholic drink.

scholar noun **1** a person who is studying at an advanced level. **2** a student who has a scholarship.

scholarly adjective **1** relating to serious academic study. **2** very knowledgeable and keen on studying.

scholarship noun **1** academic work. **2** an amount of money given to a student to help pay for their education.

scholastic adjective having to do with schools and education.

school noun **1** a place where children are educated. **2** a place where instruction is given in a particular subject. **3** a group of artists, philosophers, etc. sharing similar ideas. **4** a large group of fish or sea mammals. •verb **1** formal or N. Amer. educate. **2** train in a particular skill or activity. □ **school of thought** a particular way of thinking.

schooling noun education received at school.

schooner /skoo-ner/ noun **1** a sailing ship with two or more masts. **2** Brit. a large glass for sherry.

sciatic /sy-at-ik/ adjective having to do with the hip or with the nerve which goes down the back of the thigh (the **sciatic nerve**).

sciatica noun pain affecting the back, hip, and leg, caused by pressure on the sciatic nerve.

science noun **1** study or knowledge of the physical and natural world, based on observation and experiment. **2** a particular branch of science. **3** a body of knowledge on any subject. □ **science fiction** fiction set in the future and dealing with imagined scientific advances. **science park** an area where a number of science-based companies are located.

scientific adjective **1** relating to or based on science. **2** systematic; methodical.
■ **scientifically** adverb.

scientist noun a person who studies or is an expert in science.

sci-fi noun science fiction.

scimitar /sim-i-ter/ noun a short sword with a curved blade.

scintillating adjective very skilful and exciting.

scion /sy-uhn/ noun **1** a young shoot or twig of a plant. **2** literary a descendant of a notable family.

scissors plural noun a device for cutting cloth and paper, consisting of two crossing blades pivoted in the middle.

THESAURUS

s

•verb *he schemed endlessly:* plot, conspire, intrigue, connive, manoeuvre, plan.

scheming adjective cunning, crafty, calculating, devious, conniving, wily, sly, tricky, artful.
OPPOSITES ingenuous, honest.

scholar noun academic, intellectual, learned person, man/woman of letters, authority, expert; informal egghead; N. Amer. informal pointy-head.

scholarly adjective learned, educated, erudite, academic, well read, intellectual, literary, highbrow.
OPPOSITES uneducated, illiterate.

scholarship noun **1** *a centre of scholarship:* learning, knowledge, erudition, education, academic study. **2** *a scholarship of £2,000:* grant, award, endowment; Brit. bursary.

school noun **1** *the village school:* college, academy, alma mater. **2** *the university's School of English:* department, faculty, division. **3** *the Columbia school of history:* tradition, approach, style, way of thinking, persuasion, creed, credo, doctrine, belief, opinion, point of view.
•verb *he schooled her in horsemanship:* train, teach, tutor, coach, instruct, drill.

science noun *the science of criminology:* subject, discipline, field, branch of knowledge, body of knowledge, area of study.

scientific adjective **1** *scientific research:* technological, technical, evidence-based, empirical. **2** *a more scientific approach:* systematic, methodical, organized, ordered, rigorous, exact, precise, accurate, mathematical.

sclerosis noun **1** abnormal hardening of body tissue. **2** (also **multiple sclerosis**) a serious disease of the nervous system that can cause partial paralysis.

scoff[1] verb speak about something in a scornful way.

scoff[2] verb informal eat something quickly and greedily.

scold verb angrily criticize or tell off.

sconce noun a candle holder attached to a wall.

scone /skon, skohn/ noun a small plain cake, usually eaten with butter.

scoop noun **1** an implement like a spoon, with a short handle and a deep bowl. **2** the bowl-shaped part of a digging machine. **3** informal a piece of news printed by one newspaper before its rivals. • verb **1** pick something up with a scoop. **2** create a hollow or hole in something. **3** pick someone or something up in a quick, smooth movement. **4** informal be quicker than other newspapers to print a piece of news.

scoot verb informal move or go quickly.

scooter noun **1** (also **motor scooter**) a light motorcycle. **2** a child's vehicle with two wheels and a long steering handle, which you move by pushing one foot against the ground.

scope noun **1** the opportunity or possibility for doing something. **2** the extent of the area or subject matter that something deals with.

scorch verb **1** burn something on the surface or edges. **2** (**scorched**) dried out and withered as a result of extreme heat.

scorcher noun informal a very hot day.

score noun **1** the number of points, goals, etc. achieved by a person or team in a game. **2** (plural **score**) a group or set of twenty. **3** (**scores of**) a lot of. **4** the written music for a composition. • verb (**scores, scoring, scored**) **1** win a point, goal, etc. in a game. **2** record the score during a game. **3** cut or scratch a mark on a surface. **4** (**score something out**) cross out a word or words. **5** arrange a piece of music.

scoreline noun Brit. the final score in a game.

scorn noun a strong feeling that someone or something is worthless; contempt. • verb **1** express scorn for. **2** reject in a contemptuous way.

scornful adjective showing or feeling scorn. ■ **scornfully** adverb.

Scorpio noun a sign of the zodiac (the Scorpion), 23 October–21 November.

scorpion noun a small creature with six legs, pincers, and a poisonous sting at the end of its tail.

Scot noun a person from Scotland.

Scotch noun (also **Scotch whisky**) whisky distilled in Scotland. • adjective dated Scottish.
□ **Scotch egg** Brit. a hard-boiled egg enclosed in sausage meat.

> **!** use **Scots** or **Scottish** rather than **Scotch** to refer to people or things from Scotland.

scotch verb decisively put an end to.

scot-free adverb without suffering any punishment or injury.

THESAURUS

scoff verb sneer, jeer, laugh; (**scoff at**) mock, deride, ridicule, dismiss, belittle; informal pooh-pooh.

scoop noun spoon, ladle, dipper.
□ **scoop out 1 hollow out**, gouge out, dig, excavate. **2 remove**, take out, spoon out, scrape out. **scoop up pick up**, gather up, lift, take up, snatch up, grab.

scope noun **1** the scope of the investigation: extent, range, breadth, reach, sweep, span, area, sphere, realm, compass, orbit, ambit, terms of reference, remit. **2** the scope for change is limited: opportunity, freedom, latitude, leeway, capacity, room (to manoeuvre).

scorch verb **1** trees were scorched by the fire: burn, sear, singe, char, blacken, discolour. **2** grass scorched by the sun: dry up, parch, wither, shrivel.

scorching adjective hot, red-hot, blazing, flaming, fiery, burning, blistering, searing; informal boiling, baking, sizzling.
OPPOSITES freezing, mild.

score noun **1** the final score was 4–3: result, outcome, total, tally, count. **2** an IQ score of 161: rating, grade, mark, percentage.
• verb **1** he's scored 13 goals this season: get, gain, chalk up, achieve, make, record, rack up, notch up; informal bag, knock up. **2** the piece was scored for horn and strings: arrange, set, adapt, orchestrate, write, compose. **3** score the wood in criss-cross patterns: scratch, cut, notch, incise, scrape, nick, gouge.
□ **score something out/through** cross out, strike out, delete, put a line through, obliterate.

scorn noun the scorn in his voice: contempt, derision, disdain, mockery, sneering.
OPPOSITES admiration, respect.
• verb **1** critics scorned the talks: deride, treat with contempt, mock, scoff at, sneer at, jeer at, laugh at. **2** they scorned my offers of help: spurn, rebuff, reject, ignore, shun, snub.
OPPOSITES admire, respect.

S

Scots adjective Scottish. •noun the form of English used in Scotland.

Scottie or **Scottie dog** noun informal a Scottish terrier.

Scottish adjective relating to Scotland or its people.
□ **Scottish terrier** a small breed of terrier with a rough coat.

scoundrel noun old use a dishonest or immoral person.

scour verb 1 clean by rubbing with rough material. 2 search a place thoroughly.

scourge /skerj/ noun 1 a cause of great suffering. 2 old use a whip. •verb (**scourges, scourging, scourged**) 1 cause great suffering to. 2 old use whip someone.

Scouse Brit. informal noun 1 the dialect or accent of people from Liverpool. 2 (also **Scouser**) a person from Liverpool.

scout noun 1 a person who is sent ahead to gather information about the enemy. 2 a member of the Scout Association, an organization for young people. 3 (also **talent scout**) a person whose job is searching for talented performers. •verb 1 search a place to find something or gather information. 2 act as a scout.

scowl noun a bad-tempered expression. •verb frown in an angry or bad-tempered way.

scrabble verb (**scrabbles, scrabbling,** scrabbled) 1 grope around with your fingers to find or hold on to something. 2 move quickly and awkwardly; scramble.

scraggy adjective thin and bony.

scram verb (**scrams, scramming, scrammed**) informal leave quickly.

scramble verb (**scrambles, scrambling, scrambled**) 1 move quickly and awkwardly, using hands as well as feet. 2 muddle. 3 put a transmission into a form that can only be understood by using a decoding device. 4 cook beaten eggs in a pan. 5 (of fighter aircraft) take off immediately in an emergency. •noun 1 an act of scrambling. 2 Brit. a motorcycle race over rough and hilly ground.

scrap[1] noun 1 a small piece or amount of something. 2 (**scraps**) bits of uneaten food left after a meal. 3 unwanted metal that can be used again. •verb (**scraps, scrapping, scrapped**) 1 abolish or cancel a plan, policy, etc. 2 remove from use.

scrap[2] noun a short fight or quarrel. •verb (**scraps, scrapping, scrapped**) be involved in a scrap.

scrapbook noun a book for sticking cuttings or pictures in.

scrape verb (**scrapes, scraping, scraped**) 1 drag something hard or sharp across a surface to remove dirt or waste matter.

THESAURUS

scour[1] verb the saucepan needs scouring: scrub, rub, clean, polish, buff, shine, burnish, grind, abrade.

scour[2] verb Christine scoured the shops: search, comb, hunt through, rummage through, look high and low in, ransack, turn upside-down.

scout noun 1 scouts reported that the Romans were advancing: lookout, outrider, spy. 2 a lengthy scout round the area: reconnaissance, reconnoitre, survey, exploration, search; informal recce; Brit. informal shufti.
•verb 1 I scouted around for some logs: search, look, hunt, ferret around, root around. 2 a patrol was sent to scout out the area: reconnoitre, explore, inspect, investigate, explore, survey, scan, study; informal check out, case.

scramble verb 1 we scrambled over the boulders: clamber, climb, crawl, claw your way, scrabble, struggle; N. Amer. shinny. 2 the speaker can scramble the words: muddle, confuse, mix up, jumble (up), disarrange, disorganize, disorder, disturb, mess up.
•noun 1 a short scramble over the rocks: clamber, climb. 2 the scramble for a seat: struggle, jostle, scrimmage, scuffle, tussle, free-for-all, jockeying, competition, race.

scrap noun 1 a scrap of paper: fragment,

piece, bit, snippet, shred, oddment, remnant. 2 there wasn't a scrap of evidence: bit, shred, speck, iota, particle, ounce, jot. 3 the foxes ate all our scraps: leftovers, crumbs, remains, remnants, residue. 4 a sculpture made from scrap: waste, rubbish, refuse, debris; N. Amer. garbage, trash; informal junk.
•verb 1 old computers are scrapped: throw away, throw out, dispose of, get rid of, discard, dispense with, bin, decommission, break up, demolish; informal chuck (away/out), ditch, dump, junk; Brit. informal get shot of; N. Amer. informal trash. 2 the scheme is to be scrapped: abandon, drop, abolish, withdraw, do away with, put an end to, cancel, axe; informal ditch, dump, junk.
OPPOSITES keep, preserve.

scrape verb 1 we scraped all the paint off the windows: rub, scratch, scour, grind, sand, sandpaper, abrade, file. 2 their boots scraped along the floor: grate, creak, rasp, scratch. 3 Ellen scraped her shins on the wall: graze, scratch, scuff, rasp, skin, cut, lacerate, bark, chafe.
•noun 1 the scrape of her key in the lock: grating, creaking, rasp, scratch. 2 a long scrape on his shin: graze, scratch, abrasion, cut, laceration, wound.

2 rub against a rough or hard surface.
3 just manage to achieve, succeed, or pass. • noun **1** an act or sound of scraping. **2** an injury or mark caused by scraping. **3** informal an awkward or difficult situation.

scrappy adjective disorganized, untidy, or incomplete.

scrapyard noun a place where scrap metal is collected.

scratch verb **1** make a long mark or wound on a surface with something sharp or pointed. **2** rub part of the body with your fingernails to relieve itching. **3** (**scratch something out**) cross out a word or words. **4** withdraw from a competition. **5** cancel or abandon a plan, project, etc. • noun **1** a mark or wound made by scratching. **2** informal a slight injury. • adjective put together from whatever is available: *a scratch squad.*
▫ **from scratch** from the very beginning. **up to scratch** to the required standard. **scratch card** a card with a section which you scrape to reveal whether a prize has been won.
■ **scratchy** adjective.

scrawl verb write in a hurried, careless way. • noun scrawled handwriting.

scrawny adjective (**scrawnier**, **scrawniest**) thin and bony.

scream verb make a loud, piercing cry or sound. • noun **1** a loud, piercing cry or sound. **2** (**a scream**) informal a very funny person or thing.

scree noun a mass of small loose stones on a mountain slope.

screech noun a loud, harsh cry or sound.

• verb make a screech.

screed noun **1** a long speech or piece of writing. **2** a layer of material applied to make a floor level.

screen noun **1** an upright partition used to divide a room or conceal something. **2** the front part of a television or computer monitor, on which images and data are displayed. **3** a blank surface on which films are projected. **4** (**the screen**) films or television. • verb **1** conceal or protect with a screen. **2** test a group of people for the presence of a disease. **3** show or broadcast a film or television programme.
▫ **screen printing** a process in which ink is forced through a screen of fine material to create a picture or pattern. **screen saver** a moving image displayed by a computer screen when the computer is switched on but has not been used for a particular length of time. **screen test** a filmed audition for a film part.

screenplay noun the script of a film, including acting instructions.

screenwriter noun a person who writes a screenplay.

screw noun **1** a metal pin with a spiral thread running around it, which is turned and pressed into a surface to join things together. **2** a ship's or aircraft's propeller. **3** informal a prison warder. • verb **1** fasten or tighten with a screw or screws. **2** rotate something to attach or remove it. **3** informal cheat or swindle.
▫ **screw someone/thing up 1** crush something into a tight mass. **2** informal make something fail or go wrong. **3** informal make

scratch verb **1** *the paintwork was scratched:* score, abrade, scrape, scuff. **2** *thorns scratched her skin:* graze, scrape, skin, cut, lacerate, bark, chafe.
• noun **1** *a scratch on the paintwork:* score, mark, line, scrape. **2** *he had scratches on his cheek:* graze, scrape, abrasion, cut, laceration.
▫ **up to scratch good enough,** up to the mark, up to standard, up to par, acceptable, satisfactory, adequate, passable, sufficient, all right; informal OK.

scream verb & noun shriek, screech, yell, howl, bawl, yelp, squeal, wail, squawk.

screen noun **1** *he dressed behind the screen:* partition, divider, windbreak. **2** *a computer with a 15-inch screen:* display, monitor, visual display unit. **3** *a screen to keep out mosquitoes:* mesh, net, netting. **4** *the hedge acts as a screen against the wind:* buffer, protection, shield, shelter, guard.
• verb **1** *the end of the hall had been screened off:* partition, divide, separate, curtain. **2** *the cottage was screened by the*

trees: conceal, hide, veil, shield, shelter, shade, protect. **3** *all blood is screened for the virus:* check, test, examine, investigate, vet; informal check out. **4** *the programme is screened on Thursday:* show, broadcast, transmit, televise, put out, air.

screw noun **1** *four steel screws:* bolt, fastener. **2** *the ship's twin screws:* propeller, rotor.
• verb **1** *he screwed the lid back on the jar:* tighten, turn, twist, wind. **2** *the bracket was screwed in place:* fasten, secure, fix, attach. **3** (informal) *she intended to screw more money out of them:* extort, force, extract, wrest, wring, squeeze; informal bleed.
▫ **screw something up 1** *Christina screwed up her face:* wrinkle, pucker, crumple, crease, furrow, contort, distort, twist.
2 (informal) *they'll screw up the whole thing:* wreck, ruin, destroy, damage, spoil, mess up; informal louse up, foul up; Brit. informal cock up.

S

someone emotionally disturbed.

screwdriver noun a tool with a tip that fits into the head of a screw to turn it.

screwy adjective informal rather odd or eccentric.

scribble verb (scribbles, scribbling, scribbled) write or draw carelessly or hurriedly. •noun a scribbled picture or piece of writing.

scribe noun (in the past) a person who copied out documents.

scrimmage noun a confused struggle or fight.

scrimp verb be very careful with money; economize.

script noun 1 the written text of a play, film, or broadcast. 2 handwriting as distinct from print. •verb write a script for.

scripture or **scriptures** noun 1 the sacred writings of Christianity contained in the Bible. 2 the sacred writings of another religion.
■ scriptural adjective.

scrofula noun the name in the past for a form of tuberculosis.
■ scrofulous adjective.

scroll noun a roll of parchment or paper for writing or painting on. •verb move data on a computer screen in order to view different parts of it.

Scrooge noun a person who is mean with money.

scrotum noun (plural scrota or scrotums) the pouch of skin containing the testicles.

scrounge verb (scrounges, scrounging, scrounged) informal try to get something from someone without having to pay or work for it.
■ scrounger noun.

scrub¹ verb (scrubs, scrubbing, scrubbed) rub something hard to clean it. •noun an act of scrubbing.

scrub² noun 1 vegetation consisting mainly of bushes and small trees. 2 land covered with such vegetation.
■ scrubby adjective.

scruff¹ noun the back of a person's or animal's neck.

scruff² noun Brit. informal a scruffy person.

scruffy adjective (scruffier, scruffiest) shabby

and untidy or dirty.
■ scruffiness noun.

scrum noun 1 (also scrummage) Rugby a formation in which players push against each other with heads down and try to gain possession of the ball when it is thrown in between them. 2 Brit. informal a disorderly crowd.

scrummy adjective informal delicious.

scrump verb Brit. informal steal fruit from an orchard or garden.

scrumptious adjective informal delicious.

scrumpy noun strong cider made in the west of England.

scrunch verb crush or squeeze into a tight mass.

scruple noun a feeling of doubt as to whether an action is morally right. •verb (not scruple to do) formal not hesitate to do something, even if it may be wrong.

scrupulous adjective 1 very careful and thorough. 2 very concerned to avoid doing wrong.
■ scrupulously adverb.

scrutinize or **scrutinise** verb (scrutinizes, scrutinizing, scrutinized) examine thoroughly.

scrutiny noun (plural scrutinies) close and critical examination.

scuba diving noun swimming underwater using an aqualung.

scud verb (scuds, scudding, scudded) move quickly, driven by the wind.

scuff verb 1 make a mark on the surface of something by scraping it against something rough. 2 drag your feet when walking. •noun a mark made by scuffing.

scuffle noun a short, confused fight or struggle. •verb (scuffles, scuffling, scuffled) take part in a scuffle.

scull noun 1 each of a pair of small oars used by a single rower. 2 a light, narrow boat propelled by a single rower. •verb propel a boat with sculls.

scullery noun (plural sculleries) a small room in an old house, used for washing dishes and laundry.

sculpt verb carve or shape.

sculptor noun (feminine sculptress) an artist who makes sculptures.

sculpture noun 1 the art of making

THESAURUS

scribble verb he scribbled a note: scrawl, scratch, dash off, jot (down), doodle, sketch.
•noun I can't read this scribble: scrawl, squiggle(s), jottings, doodle, doodlings.

script noun 1 her neat, tidy script: handwriting, writing, hand. 2 the script of the play: text, screenplay, libretto, score, lines, dialogue, words.

scrub verb 1 he scrubbed the kitchen floor: brush, scour, rub, clean, cleanse, wash. 2 (informal) the plans were scrubbed: abandon, scrap, drop, cancel, call off, axe; informal ditch, dump, junk.

scrutinize verb examine, inspect, survey, study, look at, peruse, investigate, explore, probe, enquire into, go into, check.

sculpture noun carving, statue, statuette,

S

three-dimensional figures and shapes by carving or shaping wood, stone, metal, etc. **2** a work of such a kind. •verb (**sculptures, sculpturing, sculptured**) **1** make or represent by sculpture. **2** (**sculptured**) pleasingly shaped, with strong, smooth lines.
■ **sculptural** adjective.

scum noun **1** a layer of dirt or froth on the surface of a liquid. **2** informal a worthless person or group of people.
■ **scummy** adjective.

scupper verb (**scuppers, scuppering, scuppered**) Brit. **1** informal stop something working or succeeding. **2** sink your own ship deliberately.

scurf noun flakes of skin.

scurrilous adjective rude and insulting; slanderous.

scurry verb (**scurries, scurrying, scurried**) move hurriedly with short, quick steps.

scurvy noun a disease caused by a lack of vitamin C.

scut noun the short tail of a hare, rabbit, or deer.

scuttle¹ noun a metal container used to store coal for a domestic fire.

scuttle² verb (**scuttles, scuttling, scuttled**) run hurriedly or secretively with short, quick steps.

scuttle³ verb (**scuttles, scuttling, scuttled**) **1** cause a scheme to fail. **2** sink your own ship deliberately.

scythe noun a tool with a long curved blade for cutting grass or corn. •verb (**scythes, scything, scythed**) cut with a scythe.

SE abbreviation south-east or south-eastern.

sea noun **1** the salt water that surrounds the land masses of the earth. **2** a particular area of sea. **3** a vast expanse or quantity. □ **at sea** very confused and uncertain. **sea anemone** a sea creature with stinging tentacles that make it resemble a flower. **sea change** a great or remarkable change in a situation. **sea cow** a manatee or other large plant-eating sea animal. **sea horse** a small sea fish that swims upright and has a

head rather like a horse's. **sea level** the average level of the sea's surface, used in calculating the height of land. **sea lion** a large seal with a mane on the neck and shoulders. **sea urchin** a small sea creature with a shell covered in spines.

seabird noun a bird that lives near the sea.

seaboard noun a region bordering the sea; the coastline.

seafaring adjective & noun travelling by sea.
■ **seafarer** noun.

seafood noun shellfish and sea fish as food.

seafront noun the part of a coastal town facing the sea.

seagoing adjective travelling on the sea.

seagull noun a gull.

seal¹ noun **1** a device or substance used to join two things together or to stop fluid getting in. **2** a piece of wax with a design stamped into it, attached to letters and documents to guarantee they are genuine. **3** a confirmation or guarantee: *a seal of approval.* •verb **1** fasten or close securely. **2** (**seal something off**) stop people entering and leaving an area. **3** coat a surface to stop fluid passing through it. **4** conclude; make definite.
■ **sealer** noun.

seal² noun a sea mammal with flippers and a streamlined body.

sealant noun material used to make something airtight or watertight.

seam noun **1** a line where two pieces of fabric are sewn together. **2** an underground layer of a mineral.
■ **seamed** adjective.

seaman noun (plural **seamen**) a sailor, especially one below the rank of officer.

seamless adjective smooth and without seams or obvious joins.
■ **seamlessly** adverb.

seamstress noun a woman who sews, especially as a job.

seamy adjective (**seamier, seamiest**) immoral and unpleasant.

seance /**say**-onss/ noun a meeting at which

S

THESAURUS

figure, figurine, effigy, bust, head, model.

sea noun **1** ocean, waves; informal the drink; Brit. informal the briny; literary the deep. **2** *a sea of roofs:* expanse, stretch, area, tract, sweep, carpet, mass.
OPPOSITES land.
•adjective *a sea story:* marine, ocean, oceanic, maritime, naval, nautical.
□ **at sea confused,** perplexed, puzzled, baffled, mystified, bemused, bewildered, nonplussed, dumbfounded, at a loss, lost; informal flummoxed, fazed.

seal noun *the seal round the bath:* sealant,

adhesive, mastic, joint.
•verb **1** *seal each bottle while hot:* stop up, seal up, cork, stopper, plug. **2** *they sealed the bargain:* clinch, secure, settle, conclude, complete, finalize, confirm.
□ **seal something off close off,** shut off, cordon off, fence off, isolate.

seam noun **1** *the seam was coming undone:* join, stitching, joint. **2** *a seam of coal:* layer, stratum, vein, lode.

seaman noun sailor, seafarer, mariner, boatman, hand, merchant seaman.
OPPOSITES landlubber.

people attempt to make contact with the dead.

seaplane noun an aircraft designed to land on and take off from water.

sear verb 1 scorch with a sudden intense heat. 2 (of pain) be experienced as a burning sensation.

search verb 1 try to find something by looking carefully and thoroughly. 2 examine something thoroughly in order to find something or someone. 2 look for information on the Internet by using a search engine. 3 (**searching**) investigating very deeply. •noun an act of searching. □ search engine a computer program that searches the Internet for web pages containing a specified word or words. search warrant a document authorizing a police officer to enter and search a place. ■ searcher noun searchingly adverb.

searchlight noun a powerful electric light with a concentrated beam that can be turned in any direction.

seascape noun a view or picture of the sea.

seashell noun the shell of a marine shellfish.

seashore noun an area of sandy, stony, or rocky land next to the sea.

seasick adjective suffering from nausea caused by the motion of a ship at sea. ■ seasickness noun.

seaside noun a place by the sea, especially a beach area or holiday resort.

season noun 1 each of the four divisions of the year (spring, summer, autumn, and winter). 2 a part of the year with particular weather, or when a particular sport is played. •verb 1 add salt, herbs, or spices to food. 2 dry wood for use as timber. 3 (**seasoned**) experienced. □ in season 1 (of food) available and ready

to eat. 2 (of a female mammal) ready to mate. season ticket a ticket that lets you travel within a particular period or gain admission to a series of events.

seasonable adjective usual or appropriate for a particular season of the year.

seasonal adjective 1 relating to or characteristic of a particular season of the year. 2 changing according to the season. ■ seasonally adverb.

seasoning noun salt or spices added to food to improve the flavour.

seat noun 1 a thing made or used for sitting on. 2 the part of a chair designed for sitting on. 3 a place for a person to sit in a vehicle, theatre, etc. 4 a person's bottom. 5 a place in an elected parliament or council. 6 Brit. a parliamentary constituency. 7 a site or location. 8 Brit. a large country house belonging to an aristocratic family. •verb 1 arrange for someone to sit somewhere. 2 (**seat yourself** or **be seated**) formal sit down. 3 (of a place) have enough seats for. □ seat belt a belt used to secure someone in the seat of a motor vehicle or aircraft.

seaweed noun plants growing in the sea or on rocks by the sea.

seaworthy adjective (of a boat) in a good enough condition to sail on the sea.

sebaceous /si-**bay**-shuhss/ adjective technical producing oil or fat.

secateurs /sek-uh-**terz**/ plural noun Brit. a cutting tool like a pair of strong scissors, used for pruning plants, bushes, etc.

secede verb (**secedes**, **seceding**, **seceded**) withdraw formally from an alliance or federation of states.

secession noun the action of seceding.

secluded adjective (of a place) sheltered and private.

THESAURUS

S

sear verb 1 *the heat of the blast seared his face:* scorch, burn, singe, char. 2 *sear the meat:* flash-fry, seal, brown.

search verb 1 *I searched for the key:* hunt, look, seek, forage, fish, look high and low, ferret, root, rummage. 2 *he searched the house:* look through, scour, go through, sift through, comb, turn upside down; Austral./NZ informal fossick through. 3 *the guards searched him:* examine, inspect, check, frisk. •noun *we continued our search:* hunt, look, quest, examination, exploration.

searching adjective penetrating, piercing, probing, keen, shrewd, sharp, intent.

seaside noun coast, shore, seashore, beach, sand, sands.

season noun *the seasons of the year:* period, time, time of year, spell, term.

•verb *a well seasoned dish:* flavour, add salt/pepper to, spice.

seasoned adjective experienced, practised, well versed, knowledgeable, established, veteran, hardened.
OPPOSITES inexperienced.

seasoning noun flavouring, salt and pepper, herbs, spices, condiments.

seat noun 1 *a wooden seat:* chair, bench, stool; (**seats**) seating. 2 *the seat of government:* headquarters, base, centre, nerve centre, hub, heart, location, site. 3 *the family's country seat:* residence, ancestral home, mansion. •verb 1 *they seated themselves round the table:* position, put, place, ensconce, install, settle. 2 *the hall seats 500:* have room for, contain, take, sit, hold, accommodate.

seclusion noun the state of being private and away from other people.

second[1] ordinal number **1** that is number two in a sequence; 2nd. **2** lower in position, rank, or importance. **3** (**seconds**) goods that are not of perfect quality. **4** a person who helps someone fighting in a duel or boxing match. **5** Brit. a place in the second highest grade in an exam for a degree.
•verb **1** formally support a nomination or resolution before voting or discussion. **2** express agreement with.
□ **second best** not quite as good as the best. **second class 1** the second-best accommodation in a train, ship, etc. **2** of a lower standard or quality than the best. **second-degree** (of burns) causing blistering but not permanent scars. **second-guess** predict someone's actions or thoughts by guesswork. **second-hand 1** having had a previous owner. **2** heard from another person. **second nature** a habit that has become instinctive. **second-rate** of bad quality. **second sight** the supposed ability to know what will happen in the future. **second thoughts** a change of opinion after reconsidering something. **second wind** fresh energy gained during exercise after having been out of breath.
■ **secondly** adverb.

second[2] noun **1** a unit of time equal to one sixtieth of a minute. **2** (**a second**) informal a very short time. **3** a measurement of an angle equal to one sixtieth of a minute.

second[3] /si-**kond**/ verb Brit. temporarily move a worker to another position or role.
■ **secondment** noun.

secondary adjective **1** coming after, or less important than, something else. **2** (of education) for children from the age of eleven to sixteen or eighteen.
■ **secondarily** adverb.

secret adjective **1** hidden from, or not known by, other people. **2** secretive. •noun **1** something that other people do not know about. **2** a method of achieving something that is not generally known.
□ **secret agent** a spy acting for a country. **secret police** a police force working in secret against a government's political opponents. **secret service** a government department concerned with spying.
■ **secrecy** noun **secretly** adverb.

secretariat /sek-ri-**tair**-i-uht/ noun a government office or department.

secretary noun (plural **secretaries**) **1** a person employed to type letters, keep records, etc. **2** an official of a society or other organization.
□ **Secretary of State 1** (in the UK) the head of a major government department. **2** (in the US) the government official

---

second[1] adjective **1** *the second day of the trial:* next, following, subsequent. **2** *a second pair of glasses:* additional, extra, alternative, another, spare, backup; N. Amer. alternate. **3** *second prize:* secondary, subordinate, subsidiary, lesser, inferior.
OPPOSITES first.
•noun *Eva had been working as his second:* assistant, attendant, helper, aide, supporter, auxiliary, second in command, number two, deputy, understudy; informal sidekick.
•verb *George seconded the motion:* support, vote for, back, approve, endorse.

second[2] noun *I'll be gone for a second:* moment, bit, little while, instant, flash; informal sec, jiffy; Brit. informal mo, tick.

secondary adjective **1** *a secondary issue:* less important, subordinate, lesser, minor, peripheral, incidental, subsidiary. **2** *secondary infections:* accompanying, attendant, concomitant, consequential, resulting, resultant.
OPPOSITES primary, main.

second-hand adjective **1** *second-hand clothes:* used, old, worn, pre-owned, nearly new, handed-down, hand-me-down, cast-off. **2** *second-hand information:* indirect.
OPPOSITES new, direct.
•adverb *I heard this second-hand:* indirectly; informal on the grapevine.
OPPOSITES directly.

secondly adverb furthermore, also, moreover, second, in the second place, next.

secrecy noun confidentiality, privacy, mystery, concealment, stealth.

secret adjective **1** *a secret plan:* confidential, top secret, classified, undisclosed, unknown, private, under wraps; informal hush-hush. **2** *a secret drawer in the table:* hidden, concealed, disguised. **3** *a secret campaign:* clandestine, covert, undercover, underground, surreptitious, cloak-and-dagger; informal hush-hush. **4** *a secret code:* cryptic, mysterious, abstruse, recondite, arcane, esoteric.
OPPOSITES public, open.
•noun **1** *it's a secret:* confidential matter, confidence, skeleton in the cupboard. **2** *the secrets of the universe:* mystery, enigma. **3** *the secret of their success:* recipe, magic formula, blueprint, key, answer, solution.
□ **in secret** secretly, in private, behind closed doors, under cover, furtively, stealthily, on the quiet, covertly.

secretive adjective uncommunicative, secret, unforthcoming, playing your cards close to your chest, reticent, tight-lipped.
OPPOSITES open, communicative.

S

responsible for foreign affairs.
■ **secretarial** adjective.

☑ *-ary*, not *-ery*: secretary.

secrete verb (**secretes**, **secreting**, **secreted**)
1 (of a cell, gland, or organ) produce a
liquid substance. **2** hide an object.
■ **secretion** noun.

secretive adjective inclined to hide your
feelings or not to give out information.
■ **secretively** adverb.

sect noun a small religious or political group
with different beliefs from those of the
larger group that they belong to.

sectarian adjective having to do with a sect
or group.
■ **sectarianism** noun.

section noun **1** any of the parts into which
something is divided. **2** a distinct group
within a larger body of people or things.
3 the shape that results from cutting
through something. • **verb** divide into
sections.

sector noun **1** a distinct area or part. **2** a
part of a circle between two lines drawn
from its centre to its circumference.

secular adjective not religious or spiritual.
■ **secularism** noun.

secure adjective **1** certain to remain safe.
2 fixed or fastened so as not to give way or
become loose. **3** free from fear or anxiety.
• **verb** (**secures**, **securing**, **secured**) **1** protect
against danger or threat. **2** firmly fix or
fasten. **3** succeed in obtaining.

■ **securely** adverb.

security noun (plural **securities**) **1** the state of
being or feeling secure. **2** the safety of a
state or organization. **3** a valuable item
offered as a guarantee that you will repay
a loan.

sedan noun **1** an enclosed chair carried
between two horizontal poles. **2** N. Amer. a
car for four or more people.

sedate adjective **1** calm and unhurried.
2 respectable and rather dull. • **verb**
(**sedates**, **sedating**, **sedated**) give someone
a sedative drug.
■ **sedately** adverb.

sedation noun the action of sedating
someone.

sedative adjective having the effect of
making someone calm or sleepy. • **noun** a
sedative drug.

sedentary /sed-uhn-tri/ adjective
1 involving a lot of sitting and not much
exercise. **2** sitting down a lot; taking little
exercise.

sedge noun a grass-like plant that grows in
wet ground.

sediment noun **1** matter that settles to the
bottom of a liquid. **2** material carried by
water or wind and deposited on land.
■ **sedimentary** adjective.

sedition noun things done or said to stir up
rebellion against a ruler or government.
■ **seditious** adjective.

seduce verb (**seduces**, **seducing**, **seduced**)
1 persuade someone to do something

THESAURUS

secretly adverb in secret, in private,
privately, behind closed doors, under cover,
furtively, stealthily, on the quiet, covertly.

sect noun group, cult, denomination, order,
splinter group, faction, camp.

section noun **1** *the separate sections of the
box*: part, bit, portion, segment, element,
unit, compartment, module. **2** *the last
section of the questionnaire*: passage,
subsection, chapter, subdivision, clause.
3 *the reference section of the library*:
department, area, division.

sector noun **1** *every sector of the industry*:
part, branch, arm, division, area,
department, field, sphere. **2** *the north-
eastern sector of the town*: district, quarter,
section, zone, region, area, belt.

secular adjective non-religious, lay,
temporal, civil, worldly, earthly, profane.
OPPOSITES sacred, religious.

secure adjective **1** *check that all bolts are
secure*: fastened, fixed, secured, done up,
closed, shut, locked. **2** *a place where
children feel secure*: safe, protected, safe
and sound, out of harm's way, in safe
hands, invulnerable, at ease, unworried,

relaxed, happy, confident. **3** *a secure
future*: certain, assured, reliable,
dependable, settled, fixed.
OPPOSITES loose, vulnerable, uncertain.
• **verb 1** *secure the handle to the main body*:
fix, attach, fasten, affix, connect, couple.
2 *the doors had been secured*: fasten, close,
shut, lock, bolt, chain, seal. **3** *the division
secured a major contract*: obtain, acquire,
gain, get; informal land.

security noun **1** *the security of our citizens*:
safety, protection. **2** *he could give her
security*: peace of mind, stability, certainty.
3 *security at the court was tight*: safety
measures, safeguards, surveillance,
defence, protection, policing. **4** *additional
security for your loan may be required*:
guarantee, collateral, surety, pledge, bond.
OPPOSITES insecurity.

sediment noun dregs, grounds, lees,
residue, deposit, silt.

seduce verb **1** *customers are seduced by the
advertising*: attract, allure, lure, tempt,
entice, beguile, inveigle, manipulate. **2** *he
tried to seduce her*: have your (wicked)
way with, take advantage of.

S

unwise. **2** persuade someone to have sex with you.
- **seduction** noun.

seductive adjective tempting and attractive.
- **seductively** adverb.

sedulous adjective showing great care or effort; diligent.

sedum /see-duhm/ noun a plant with fleshy leaves.

see[1] verb (**sees, seeing, saw**; past participle **seen**) **1** become aware of with the eyes. **2** experience or witness. **3** realize something after thinking or getting information. **4** think of in a particular way. **5** meet someone socially or by chance. **6** meet someone regularly as a boyfriend or girlfriend. **7** consult a specialist or professional. **8** guide or lead someone somewhere.
□ **see someone off** go with a person who is leaving to their point of departure. **see something through** carry on with a project until it is completed. **see-through** transparent or semi-transparent. **see to** deal with.

see[2] noun the district or position of a bishop or archbishop.

seed noun **1** a small, hard object produced by a plant, from which a new plant may grow. **2** the beginning of a feeling, process, etc. **3** any of the stronger competitors in a sports tournament who are kept from playing each other in the early rounds. **4** old use a man's semen. •verb **1** sow land with seeds. **2** remove the seeds from. **3** (be

seeded) be made a seed in a sports tournament.

seedling noun a young plant raised from seed.

seedy adjective (**seedier, seediest**) unpleasant because dirty or immoral.
- **seediness** noun.

seeing conjunction because; since.

seek verb (**seeks, seeking, sought**) **1** try to find or get. **2** ask for. **3** (**seek to do**) try or want to do. **4** (**seek someone/thing out**) search for and find someone or something.
- **seeker** noun.

seem verb **1** give the impression of being. **2** (**cannot seem to do**) be unable to do, despite having tried.

seeming adjective appearing to be real or true.
- **seemingly** adverb.

seemly adjective respectable or in good taste.

seen past participle of SEE[1].

seep verb (of a liquid) flow or leak slowly through a substance.
- **seepage** noun.

seer noun a person supposedly able to see visions of the future.

seersucker noun a fabric with a crinkled surface.

see-saw noun a long plank supported in the middle, on each end of which children sit and move up and down by pushing the ground with their feet. •verb repeatedly change between two states or positions.

seethe verb (**seethes, seething, seethed**)

THESAURUS

seductive adjective **tempting**, inviting, enticing, alluring, beguiling, attractive.

see verb **1** *he saw her in the street:* **discern**, spot, notice, catch sight of, glimpse, make out, pick out, spy; informal clap eyes on, clock; literary behold. **2** *I saw a programme about it:* **watch**, look at, view, catch. **3** *would you like to see the house?* **inspect**, view, look round, tour, survey, examine, scrutinize. **4** *I finally saw what she meant:* **understand**, grasp, comprehend, follow, realize, appreciate, recognize, work out, fathom; informal get, latch on to, tumble to, figure out; Brit. informal twig, suss (out). **5** *I must see what Victor is up to:* **find out**, discover, learn, ascertain, determine, establish. **6** *see that no harm comes to him:* **ensure**, make sure/certain, see to it, take care, mind. **7** *I see trouble ahead:* **foresee**, predict, forecast, prophesy, anticipate. **8** *later, I saw him in town:* **encounter**, meet, run into, come across, stumble across, happen on, chance on; informal bump into. **9** *you'd better see a doctor:* **consult**, confer with, talk to, have recourse to, call in, turn to. **10** *he's seeing someone else now:*

go out with, date, take out, be involved with; informal go steady with; dated court.
□ **see to attend to,** deal with, see about, take care of, look after, sort out, organize, arrange.

seed noun **pip,** stone, kernel.

seek verb **1** *he is seeking work:* **search for,** try to find, look for, be after, hunt for. **2** *he sought help from a motorist:* **ask for,** request, solicit, call for, appeal for, apply for. **3** *we constantly seek to improve the service:* **try,** attempt, endeavour, strive, work, do your best.

seem verb **appear (to be),** have the appearance/air of being, give the impression of being, look, sound, come across as, strike someone as.

seep verb **ooze,** trickle, exude, drip, dribble, flow, leak, drain, bleed, filter, percolate, soak.

seethe verb **1** *the water seethed with fish:* **teem,** swarm, boil, swirl, churn, surge, bubble, heave. **2** *I seethed at the injustice of it all:* **be angry,** be furious, be enraged, be incensed, be beside yourself, boil, rage,

S

1 be very angry but try not to show it. **2** be filled with a crowd that is moving about. **3** (of a liquid) boil or churn.

segment noun /seg-muhnt/ each of the parts into which something is divided.
• verb /seg-**ment**/ divide into segments.

segregate verb (**segregates, segregating, segregated**) **1** keep separate from the rest or from each other. **2** keep people of different races, sexes, or religions separate.
■ **segregation** noun.

segue /seg-way/ verb (**segues, segueing** or **seguing, segued**) move without interruption from one song or film scene to another.

seine /rhymes with rain/ noun a fishing net which hangs vertically in the water, with floats at the top.

seismic /syz-mik/ adjective **1** having to do with earthquakes. **2** enormous in size or effect.

seismology noun the study of earthquakes.
■ **seismologist** noun.

seize verb (**seized, seizing, seized**) **1** take hold of suddenly and forcibly. **2** (of the police) officially take possession of. **3** take an opportunity eagerly and decisively. **4** (**seize on**) take advantage of eagerly. **5** (often **seize up**) (of a machine) become jammed.

☑ **seize** is an exception to the usual rule of *i* before e except after c.

seizure noun **1** the action of seizing. **2** a sudden attack of illness, especially a stroke or an epileptic fit.

seldom adverb not often.

select verb carefully choose from a group.
• adjective **1** carefully chosen as being among the best. **2** used by, or made up of, wealthy people.
□ **select committee** a small parliamentary committee appointed for a special purpose.
■ **selector** noun.

selection noun **1** the action of selecting. **2** a number of selected things. **3** a range of things from which you can choose.

selective adjective **1** involving selection. **2** choosing carefully. **3** affecting some things and not others.
■ **selectively** adverb **selectivity** noun.

selenium /si-lee-ni-uhm/ noun a grey crystalline chemical element.

self noun (plural **selves**) **1** a person's essential being that distinguishes them from other people. **2** a person's particular nature or personality.

self-absorbed adjective obsessed with your own emotions or interests.

self-addressed adjective (of an envelope) addressed to yourself.

self-adhesive adjective sticking without needing to be moistened.

self-appointed adjective having taken up a position or role without the approval of other people.

self-assessment noun **1** assessment of your own performance. **2** a system in which you calculate yourself how much tax you owe.

self-assurance noun confidence in your

THESAURUS

rant, fume; informal be livid, foam at the mouth.

segment noun piece, bit, section, part, portion, division, slice, wedge.

segregate verb separate, set apart, keep apart, isolate, quarantine, partition, divide, discriminate against.
OPPOSITES integrate.

seize verb **1** *she seized the microphone:* grab, grasp, snatch, take hold of. **2** *rebels seized the air base:* capture, take, overrun, occupy, conquer, take over. **3** *the drugs were seized by customs:* confiscate, impound, commandeer, requisition, appropriate, expropriate. **4** *terrorists seized his wife:* kidnap, abduct, take captive, take prisoner, take hostage; informal snatch.
OPPOSITES liberate, relinquish, release.

seizure noun **1** *Napoleon's seizure of Spain:* capture, takeover, annexation, invasion, occupation. **2** *the seizure of banned goods:* confiscation, appropriation, expropriation. **3** *the seizure of UN staff:* kidnap, abduction. **4** *the baby suffered a seizure:*

convulsion, fit, spasm, paroxysm.
OPPOSITES liberation, release.

seldom adverb rarely, infrequently, hardly (ever), scarcely (ever); informal once in a blue moon.
OPPOSITES often.

select verb *select the correct tool for the job:* choose, pick (out), single out, sort out, take, adopt.
• adjective **1** *a small, select group:* choice, hand-picked, elite; informal top-flight. **2** *a very select area:* exclusive, privileged, wealthy; informal posh.
OPPOSITES inferior.

selection noun **1** *Jim made his selection:* choice, pick, option, preference. **2** *a wide selection of dishes:* range, array, diversity, variety, assortment, mixture. **3** *a selection of his poems:* anthology, assortment, collection, assemblage, miscellany, medley.

selective adjective discerning, discriminating, exacting, demanding, particular; informal choosy, picky.
OPPOSITES indiscriminate.

S

own abilities or character.
■ **self-assured** adjective.

self-aware adjective knowledgeable about your own character, feelings, motives, etc.
■ **self-awareness** noun.

self-catering adjective Brit. (of a holiday or accommodation) offering facilities for you to cook your own meals.

self-centred adjective obsessed with yourself and your affairs.

self-confessed adjective admitting to having certain characteristics.

self-confidence noun a feeling of trust in your abilities and judgement.
■ **self-confident** adjective.

self-conscious adjective nervous or awkward through being worried about what other people think of you.

self-contained adjective **1** complete in itself. **2** not depending on or influenced by other people.

self-control noun the ability to control your emotions or behaviour.
■ **self-controlled** adjective.

self-defeating adjective making things worse rather than achieving the desired aim.

self-defence noun defence of yourself.

self-denial noun not allowing yourself to have things that you want.

self-deprecating adjective modest about yourself.
■ **self-deprecation** noun.

self-destruct verb explode or disintegrate automatically.

self-destructive adjective causing harm to yourself.

self-determination noun the right or ability of a country or person to manage their own affairs.

self-discipline noun the ability to control your feelings and actions.
■ **self-disciplined** adjective.

self-doubt noun lack of confidence in yourself and your abilities.

self-effacing adjective not wanting to attract attention.

self-employed adjective working for yourself rather than for an employer.
■ **self-employment** noun.

self-esteem noun confidence in your own worth or abilities.

self-evident adjective obvious.

self-explanatory adjective not needing explanation; clearly understood.

self-expression noun the expression of

your feelings or thoughts.

self-fulfilling adjective (of a prediction) bound to come true because people behave in a way that makes it happen.

self-help noun reliance on your own efforts and resources to achieve things.

self-importance noun an exaggerated sense of your own value or importance.
■ **self-important** adjective.

self-indulgent adjective allowing yourself to have or do things that you like, especially to an excessive extent.
■ **self-indulgence** noun.

self-interest noun your personal interest or advantage.

selfish adjective concerned mainly with your own needs and wishes.
■ **selfishly** adverb **selfishness** noun.

selfless adjective concerned more with the needs and wishes of other people than with your own.

self-made adjective having become successful by your own efforts.

self-pity noun too much sorrow and concern for yourself and your own problems.
■ **self-pitying** adjective.

self-portrait noun a portrait by an artist of himself or herself.

self-possessed adjective calm, confident, and in control of your feelings.
■ **self-possession** noun.

self-raising flour noun Brit. flour that has baking powder already added.

self-reliance noun reliance on your own powers and resources.
■ **self-reliant** adjective.

self-respect noun pride and confidence in yourself.

self-righteous adjective certain that you are right or morally superior.

self-sacrifice noun the giving up of your own needs or wishes to help other people.
■ **self-sacrificing** adjective.

selfsame adjective (**the selfsame**) the very same.

self-satisfied adjective smugly pleased with yourself.
■ **self-satisfaction** noun.

self-seeking or **self-serving** adjective concerned only with your own welfare and interests.

self-service adjective (of a shop or restaurant) where customers choose goods for themselves and pay at a checkout.

self-styled adjective using a description or

S

THESAURUS

selfish adjective egocentric, egotistic, self-centred, self-absorbed, self-obsessed, wrapped up in yourself, solipsistic, self-

seeking, self-serving, mean, greedy, inconsiderate, thoughtless; informal looking after number one.

title that you have given yourself: *self-styled experts.*

self-sufficient adjective able to satisfy your basic needs without outside help.
■ **self-sufficiency** noun.

self-worth noun self-esteem.

sell verb (**sells, selling, sold**) **1** hand over something in exchange for money. **2** (of goods) be bought. **3** (**sell up**) sell all your property or assets. **4** persuade someone that something is good.
□ **sell out 1** sell all your stock of something. **2** (of tickets for an event) be all sold. **3** abandon your principles for reasons of convenience.
■ **seller** noun.

Sellotape noun Brit. trademark transparent adhesive tape.

selvedge /sel-vij/ noun an edge on woven fabric that prevents it from fraying or unravelling.

selves plural of **SELF**.

semantic adjective having to do with meaning.
■ **semantically** adverb.

semantics plural noun **1** the study of the meaning of words and phrases. **2** the meaning of words, phrases, etc.

semaphore noun a system of sending messages by holding the arms or two flags in positions that represent letters of the alphabet.

semblance noun the way that something looks or seems.

semen /see-muhn/ noun a fluid containing sperm that is produced by men and male animals.

semester noun a half-year term in a school or university.

semi noun (plural **semis**) informal **1** Brit. a semi-detached house. **2** a semi-final.

semi-automatic adjective (of a gun) able to load bullets automatically but not fire continuously.

semibreve noun Brit. a musical note that lasts as long as two minims or four crotchets.

semicircle noun a half of a circle.
■ **semicircular** adjective.

semicolon noun a punctuation mark (;)

indicating a bigger pause than that indicated by a comma.

semiconductor noun a solid which conducts electricity, but to a smaller extent than a metal.

semi-detached adjective Brit. (of a house) joined to another house on one side by a common wall.

semi-final noun (in sport) a match or round coming immediately before the final.
■ **semi-finalist** noun.

seminal adjective **1** strongly influencing later developments. **2** referring to semen.

seminar noun **1** a meeting for discussion or training. **2** a university class for discussion of topics with a teacher.

seminary noun (plural **seminaries**) a training college for priests or rabbis.

semiotics plural noun the study of signs and symbols.
■ **semiotic** adjective.

semi-precious adjective (of minerals) used as gems but less valuable than precious stones.

semiquaver noun Brit. a musical note lasting half as long as a quaver.

semi-skimmed adjective Brit. (of milk) having had some of the cream removed.

Semite /see-myt/ noun a member of a people speaking a Semitic language, especially the Jews and Arabs.

Semitic /si-mit-ik/ noun a group of languages that includes Hebrew and Arabic. • adjective relating to Semitic or Semites, especially the Jews and Arabs.

semitone noun Brit. a musical interval equal to half a tone.

semolina noun the hard grains left after flour has been milled, used to make puddings and pasta.

Semtex noun a powerful explosive.

senate noun **1** the smaller but higher law-making assembly in the US, France, etc. **2** the governing body of a university or college. **3** the state council of ancient Rome.

senator noun a member of a senate.

send verb (**sends, sending, sent**) **1** cause to

THESAURUS

sell verb **1** *they are selling their house:* put up for sale, put on the market, auction (off), trade in. **2** *he sells cakes:* trade in, deal in, traffic in, peddle, retail, market.
OPPOSITES buy.

seller noun vendor, dealer, retailer, trader, merchant, agent, hawker, pedlar, purveyor, supplier, stockist.
OPPOSITES buyer.

send verb **1** *they sent a message to HQ:*

dispatch, post, mail, email, consign, forward, transmit, convey, communicate, broadcast, radio. **2** *the pump sent out a jet of petrol:* propel, project, eject, deliver, discharge, spout, fire, shoot, release, fling, cast. **3** *it's enough to send you mad:* make, drive, turn.
OPPOSITES receive.

□ **send someone down** (informal) **send to prison**, imprison, jail, incarcerate, lock up,

go or be taken to a destination. **2** cause to move sharply or quickly. **3** put someone into a particular state.
□ **send someone down** Brit. **1** expel a student from a university. **2** informal sentence someone to imprisonment. **send-off** a gathering to say goodbye to someone who is leaving. **send someone up** informal make fun of someone by imitating them.

Senegalese /sen-i-guh-**leez**/ **noun** (plural **Senegalese**) a person from Senegal, a country in West Africa. •**adjective** relating to Senegal.

senescence /si-**ness**-uhnss/ **noun** the process of growing old and gradually deteriorating.
■ **senescent** adjective.

senile adjective suffering a loss of mental faculties because of old age.
■ **senility** noun.

senior adjective **1** having to do with older people. **2** Brit. having to do with schoolchildren above the age of about eleven. **3** US of the final year at a university or high school. **4** (after a name) referring to the elder of two with the same name in a family. **5** high or higher in status. •**noun 1** a person who is a stated number of years older than someone else: *she was two years his senior*. **2** a student at a senior school. **3** (in sport) a competitor of above a certain age or of the highest status.
□ **senior citizen** an old-age pensioner.

■ **seniority** noun.

senna noun a laxative prepared from the dried pods of a tree.

sensation noun **1** a feeling resulting from something that happens to or comes into contact with the body. **2** the ability to have such feelings. **3** a vague awareness or impression. **4** a widespread reaction of interest and excitement, or a person or thing that causes it.

sensational adjective **1** causing or trying to cause great public interest and excitement. **2** informal very impressive or attractive.
■ **sensationalism** noun **sensationalist** noun & adjective **sensationally** adverb.

sensationalize or **sensationalise** verb (**sensationalizes**, **sensationalizing**, **sensationalized**) present information in an exaggerated way to make it seem more interesting.

sense noun **1** any of the powers of sight, smell, hearing, taste, and touch, which allow the body to perceive things. **2** a feeling that something is the case. **3** (**sense of**) awareness of or sensitivity to. **4** a sensible and practical attitude or way of behaving. **5** a meaning of a word or expression. •**verb** (**senses, sensing, sensed**) **1** perceive by a sense or senses. **2** be vaguely aware of.
□ **make sense** be understandable or sensible.

confine, detain, intern; informal put away; Brit. informal bang up. **send for call**, summon, ask for, request, order. **send someone off** (Sport) **order off**, dismiss, show the red card; informal red-card, send for an early bath. **send someone/something up** (informal) **satirize**, ridicule, make fun of, parody, lampoon, mock, caricature, imitate, ape; informal take off, spoof, take the mickey out of.

send-off noun farewell, goodbye, adieu, leave-taking, funeral.
OPPOSITES welcome.

senior adjective **1** *senior school pupils:* older, elder. **2** *a senior officer:* superior, higher-ranking, more important; N. Amer. ranking.
OPPOSITES junior, subordinate.

sensation noun **1** *a sensation of heaviness:* feeling, sense, perception, impression. **2** *she caused a sensation:* commotion, stir, uproar, furore, scandal, impact; informal splash, to-do.

sensational adjective **1** *a sensational murder trial:* shocking, scandalous, appalling, fascinating, thrilling, exciting, interesting, dramatic, momentous, historic, newsworthy. **2** *sensational press reports:* overdramatized, melodramatic,

exaggerated, sensationalist, graphic, explicit, lurid; informal shock-horror, juicy. **3** (informal) *she looked sensational:* gorgeous, stunning, wonderful, superb, excellent, first-class; informal great, terrific, fantastic, tremendous, fabulous, out of this world; Brit. informal smashing.
OPPOSITES dull, understated, unremarkable.

sense noun **1** *the sense of touch:* feeling, faculty, awareness, sensation, recognition, perception. **2** *a sense of humour:* appreciation, awareness, understanding, comprehension. **3** *she had the sense to leave:* wisdom, common sense, wit, intelligence, judgement, reason, brain(s); informal gumption, nous, horse sense, savvy; Brit. informal loaf, common; N. Amer. informal smarts. **4** *I can't see the sense in this:* purpose, point, use, value, advantage, benefit. **5** *different senses of the word:* meaning, definition, nuance, drift, gist, thrust, tenor, message.
OPPOSITES stupidity.

•**verb** *she sensed their hostility:* detect, feel, observe, notice, recognize, pick up, be aware of, distinguish, make out; informal catch on to.

S

senseless adjective 1 lacking meaning, purpose, or common sense. 2 unconscious.

sensibility noun (plural **sensibilities**) 1 the ability to experience and understand emotion or art; sensitivity. 2 (**sensibilities**) the degree to which a person can be offended or shocked.

sensible adjective 1 having or showing common sense. 2 practical rather than decorative.
■ **sensibly** adverb.

sensitive adjective 1 quick to detect or be affected by slight changes. 2 appreciating the feelings of other people. 3 easily offended or upset. 4 secret or controversial.
■ **sensitively** adverb.

sensitivity noun (plural **sensitivities**) 1 the quality of being sensitive. 2 (**sensitivities**) a person's feelings which might be offended or hurt.

sensitize or **sensitise** verb (**sensitizes**, **sensitizing**, **sensitized**) make sensitive or aware.

sensor noun a device which detects or measures a light, heat, pressure, etc.

sensory adjective relating to sensation or the senses.

sensual adjective relating to the physical senses as a source of pleasure.
■ **sensuality** noun **sensually** adverb.

sensuous adjective 1 relating to or affecting the senses rather than the intellect. 2 attractive or pleasing physically.
■ **sensuously** adverb.

sent past and past participle of **SEND**.

sentence noun 1 a set of words that is complete in itself, conveying a statement, question, exclamation, or command. 2 the punishment given to someone found guilty by a court. • verb (**sentences**, **sentencing**, **sentenced**) say officially in a law court that an offender is to receive a particular punishment.

sententious /sen-ten-shuhss/ adjective given to making pompous comments on moral issues.

sentient adjective able to perceive or feel things.

sentiment noun 1 an opinion or feeling. 2 exaggerated feelings of tenderness, sadness, or nostalgia.

sentimental adjective having or causing exaggerated feelings of tenderness, sadness, or nostalgia.
■ **sentimentality** noun **sentimentally** adverb.

THESAURUS

senseless adjective pointless, futile, useless, needless, meaningless, absurd, foolish, insane, stupid, idiotic, mindless, illogical.
OPPOSITES wise.

sensible adjective practical, realistic, responsible, reasonable, commonsensical, rational, logical, sound, no-nonsense, level-headed, down-to-earth, wise.
OPPOSITES foolish.

sensitive adjective 1 *she's sensitive to changes in temperature:* responsive to, reactive to, sensitized to, aware of, conscious of, susceptible to, affected by, vulnerable to. 2 *sensitive skin:* delicate, fragile, tender, sore. 3 *the matter needs sensitive handling:* tactful, careful, thoughtful, diplomatic, delicate, subtle, kid-glove. 4 *he's sensitive about his bald patch:* touchy, oversensitive, hyper-sensitive, easily offended, thin-skinned, defensive, paranoid, neurotic. 5 *a sensitive issue:* difficult, delicate, tricky, awkward, problematic, ticklish, controversial, emotive.
OPPOSITES impervious, resilient, clumsy, thick-skinned, uncontroversial.

sensitivity noun 1 *the sensitivity of the skin:* responsiveness, sensitiveness, reactivity, susceptibility. 2 *the job calls for sensitivity:* tact, diplomacy, delicacy, subtlety, understanding. 3 *her sensitivity on the subject:* touchiness, oversensitivity,

hypersensitivity, defensiveness. 4 *the sensitivity of the issue:* delicacy, trickiness, awkwardness, ticklishness.

sensual adjective 1 *sensual pleasure:* physical, carnal, bodily, fleshly, animal. 2 *a very sensual woman:* passionate, sexual, physical, tactile, hedonistic.
OPPOSITES spiritual, passionless.

sensuous adjective 1 *big sensuous canvases:* rich, sumptuous, luxurious. 2 *sensuous lips:* voluptuous, sexy, seductive, luscious, lush, ripe.

sentence noun 1 *the judge delivered his sentence:* judgement, ruling, decision, verdict. 2 *a long sentence:* punishment, prison term; informal time, stretch.
• verb *they were sentenced to death:* condemn, doom, punish, convict.

sentiment noun 1 *the comments echo my own sentiments:* view, feeling, attitude, thought, opinion, belief. 2 *there's no room for sentiment:* sentimentality, emotion, softness; informal schmaltz, slush; Brit. informal soppiness; N. Amer. informal sappiness.

sentimental adjective 1 *she kept the vase for sentimental reasons:* nostalgic, emotional. 2 *the film is too sentimental:* mawkish, overemotional, cloying, sickly, romantic; Brit. twee; informal slushy, corny, schmaltzy; Brit. informal soppy; N. Amer. informal sappy.
OPPOSITES practical, gritty.

S

sentinel noun a guard whose job is to stand and keep watch.

sentry noun (plural **sentries**) a soldier whose job is to guard or control access to a place.

sepal /sep-uhl/ noun each of the leaf-like parts of a flower that surround the petals.

separable adjective able to be separated or treated separately.

separate adjective /sep-uh-ruht/ **1** forming a unit by itself. **2** different; distinct. •**verb** /sep-uh-rayt/ (**separates, separating, separated**) **1** move or come apart. **2** stop living together as a couple. **3** divide into distinct parts. **4** form a distinction or boundary between.
 ■ **separately** adverb.

☑ the middle is *-par-*, not *-per-*: separate.

separation noun **1** the action of separating. **2** the state in which a husband and wife remain married but live apart.

separatism noun separation of a group of people from a larger group.
 ■ **separatist** noun & adjective.

sepia /see-pi-uh/ noun a reddish-brown colour.

sepoy /see-poy/ noun historical an Indian soldier who served the British.

sepsis noun the infection of body tissues with harmful bacteria.

September noun the ninth month of the year.

septet noun a group of seven people playing music or singing together.

septic adjective (of a wound or a part of the body) infected with bacteria.
 □ **septic tank** an underground tank in which sewage is allowed to decompose before draining slowly into the soil.

septicaemia /sep-ti-**see**-mi-uh/ (US spelling

septicemia) noun blood poisoning caused by bacteria.

septuagenarian noun a person who is between 70 and 79 years old.

septum noun (plural **septa**) a partition separating two hollow areas in the body, such as that between the nostrils.

sepulchral adjective **1** having to do with a tomb or burial. **2** gloomy.

sepulchre /sep-uhl-ker/ (US spelling **sepulcher**) noun a stone tomb.

sequel noun **1** a book, film, or programme that continues the story of an earlier one. **2** something that takes place after or as a result of an earlier event.

sequence noun **1** a particular order in which things follow each other. **2** a set of things that follow each other in a particular order. •**verb** (**sequences, sequencing, sequenced**) arrange in a sequence.

sequential adjective following in a logical order or sequence.
 ■ **sequentially** adverb.

sequester verb (**sequesters, sequestering, sequestered**) **1** isolate or hide away. **2** sequestrate.

sequestrate verb (**sequestrates, sequestrating, sequestrated**) take legal possession of assets until a debt has been paid.
 ■ **sequestration** noun.

sequin noun a small, shiny disc sewn on to clothing for decoration.
 ■ **sequinned** (or **sequined**) adjective.

sequoia noun a redwood tree.

seraglio /si-**rah**-li-oh/ noun (plural **seraglios**) **1** the women's apartments in a Muslim palace. **2** a harem.

THESAURUS

separate adjective **1** *his personal life was separate from his job*: unconnected, unrelated, different, distinct, discrete, detached, divorced, disconnected, independent. **2** *the infirmary was separate from the school*: set apart, detached, cut off, segregated, isolated, free-standing, self-contained.
OPPOSITES linked, attached.
 •verb **1** *they separated the two youths*: split (up), break up, part, pull apart. **2** *the connectors can be separated*: disconnect, detach, disengage, uncouple, split. **3** *the wall that separated the two estates*: partition, divide, keep apart. **4** *the south aisle was separated off*: isolate, partition off, section off, close off, shut off, cordon off. **5** *they separated at the airport*: part (company), go their separate ways, split up, disperse, scatter. **6** *the road separated*:

fork, divide, branch, diverge. **7** *her parents separated*: split up, break up, part, divorce.
OPPOSITES unite, join, link, meet, merge, marry.

separately adverb individually, one by one, one at a time, singly, severally, apart, independently, alone, by yourself, on your own.

separation noun **1** *the separation of the two companies*: disconnection, splitting, division, breaking up. **2** *her parents' separation*: break-up, split, estrangement, divorce; Brit. informal bust-up.

sequel noun continuation, further episode, follow-up.

sequence noun **1** *the sequence of events*: succession, order, course, series, chain, train, progression, chronology, pattern, flow. **2** *a sequence from his film*: excerpt, clip, extract, section.

S

seraph noun (plural **seraphim** or **seraphs**) an angelic being associated with light and purity.
■ **seraphic** adjective.

Serbian noun **1** the language of the Serbs. **2** (also **Serb**) a person from Serbia.
• **adjective** relating to Serbia.

serenade noun a piece of music sung or played by a man for a woman he loves, outdoors and at night. • verb (**serenades, serenading, serenaded**) perform a serenade for.

serendipity noun the occurrence of something by chance in a fortunate way.
■ **serendipitous** adjective.

serene adjective calm and peaceful.
■ **serenely** adverb **serenity** noun.

serf noun (in the feudal system) an agricultural labourer who had to work on a particular estate and was not allowed to leave.
■ **serfdom** noun.

serge noun a hard-wearing woollen fabric.

sergeant noun **1** the rank of officer in the army or air force above corporal. **2** Brit. a police officer just below the rank of inspector.
□ **sergeant major** an officer in the British army who helps with administrative duties.

serial adjective **1** arranged in a series. **2** repeatedly committing the same offence or doing the same thing: *a serial killer.*
• **noun** a story published or broadcast in regular instalments.
□ **serial number** an identification number given to a manufactured item.

serialize or **serialise** verb (**serializes, serializing, serialized**) **1** publish or broadcast a story in regular instalments. **2** arrange in a series.
■ **serialization** noun.

series noun (plural **series**) **1** a number of related things coming one after another. **2** a sequence of related television or radio programmes.

serious adjective **1** dangerous or very bad: *a serious injury.* **2** needing careful consideration or action. **3** solemn or thoughtful. **4** sincere and in earnest.
■ **seriously** adverb **seriousness** noun.

sermon noun a talk on a religious or moral subject, especially one given during a church service.

serpent noun literary a large snake.

serpentine adjective winding or twisting like a snake.

serrated adjective having a jagged edge like the teeth of a saw.

serration noun a tooth or point of a serrated edge.

serried adjective (of rows of people or things) standing close together.

serum noun (plural **sera** or **serums**) a thin liquid which separates out when blood solidifies.

servant noun a person employed to perform domestic duties in a household or for a person.

serve verb (**serves, serving, served**) **1** perform duties or services for. **2** be employed as a member of the armed forces. **3** spend a period in a job or in prison. **4** present food or drink to. **5** (of

---

THESAURUS

series noun succession, sequence, string, chain, run, round, spate, wave, rash, course, cycle, row.

serious adjective **1** *a serious expression:* solemn, earnest, grave, sombre, unsmiling, stern, grim, humourless, stony. **2** *serious decisions:* important, significant, momentous, weighty, far-reaching. **3** *serious consideration:* careful, detailed, in-depth. **4** *a serious play:* intellectual, highbrow, heavyweight, deep, profound, literary, learned, scholarly; informal heavy. **5** *serious injuries:* severe, grave, bad, critical, acute, terrible, dire, dangerous. **6** *we're serious about equality:* sincere, earnest, genuine, wholehearted, resolute, committed, determined.
OPPOSITES light-hearted, trivial, superficial, lowbrow, minor, half-hearted.

seriously adverb **1** *Faye nodded seriously:* solemnly, earnestly, gravely, sombrely, sternly, grimly, humourlessly. **2** *seriously injured:* severely, gravely, badly, critically,

dangerously. **3** *seriously, I'm very pleased:* really, honestly, truthfully, truly, actually; Brit. informal straight up.

sermon noun address, homily, talk, speech, lecture.

servant noun attendant, domestic, maid, housemaid, retainer, lackey, flunkey, minion, slave, drudge; informal skivvy.

serve verb **1** *they served their masters faithfully:* work for, obey, do the bidding of. **2** *this job serves the community:* benefit, help, assist, aid, make a contribution to, do your bit for. **3** *he served his apprenticeship in Scotland:* carry out, perform, do, fulfil, complete, discharge, spend. **4** *serve the soup hot:* present, offer, give out, distribute, dish up, provide, supply. **5** *she served another customer:* attend to, deal with, see to, assist, help, look after. **6** *a saucer serving as an ashtray:* act, function, work, perform. **7** *official forms will serve in most cases:* suffice, do, be good enough, be adequate, fit/fill the bill, suit.

S

food or drink) be enough for. **6** attend to a customer in a shop. **7** fulfil a purpose. **8** treat in a particular way. **9** (in tennis, badminton, etc.) hit the ball or shuttlecock to begin play for each point of a game. •**noun** an act of serving in tennis, badminton, etc.
□ **serve someone right** be someone's deserved punishment.

server noun **1** a person or thing that serves. **2** a computer or program that controls or supplies information to a network of computers.

service noun **1** the action of serving. **2** a period of employment with an organization. **3** an act of assistance. **4** a ceremony of religious worship. **5** a system supplying a public need such as water or electricity. **6** a department or organization run by the state. **7** (**the services**) the armed forces. **8** a set of matching crockery. **9** (in tennis, badminton, etc.) a serve. **10** a routine inspection and maintenance of a vehicle or machine. **11** (**services** or **service area**) a roadside area with a petrol station, cafe, toilets, etc. for motorists. •**verb** (**services, servicing, serviced**) **1** perform routine maintenance or repair work on. **2** provide a service or services for someone. **3** pay interest on a debt.
□ **in service** dated employed as a servant.

service industry a business that provides a service rather than manufacturing things.
service station a garage selling petrol, oil, etc.

serviceable adjective **1** in working order. **2** useful and hard-wearing.

serviceman or **servicewoman** noun (plural **servicemen** or **servicewomen**) a member of the armed forces.

serviette noun Brit. a table napkin.

servile adjective **1** too willing to serve or please other people. **2** of a slave or slaves.
■ **servility** noun.

serving noun a quantity of food for one person.

servitude noun the state of being a slave, or of being under the complete control of someone more powerful.

servo noun a device in a vehicle which converts a force into a larger force.

sesame /sess-uh-mi/ noun a tropical plant grown for its oil-rich seeds.

session noun **1** a period devoted to a particular activity. **2** a meeting of a council, court, etc., or the period when such meetings are held.

set verb (**sets, setting, set**) **1** put in a particular place or position. **2** bring into a particular state. **3** give someone a task.

THESAURUS

service noun **1** *conditions of service:* **work,** employment, labour. **2** *he has done us a service:* **favour,** kindness, good turn, helping hand. **3** *the service was excellent:* **waiting,** serving, attendance, attention. **4** *products which give reliable service:* **use,** usage, functioning, operation. **5** *he took his car in for a service:* **overhaul,** check, maintenance. **6** *a marriage service:* **ceremony,** ritual, rite, liturgy. **7** *a range of local services:* **amenity,** facility, resource, utility. **8** *soldiers leaving the services:* **(armed) forces,** military, army, navy, air force.
•**verb** *the appliances are serviced regularly:* **overhaul,** check, go over, maintain.

session noun **1** *a session of the committee:* **meeting,** sitting, assembly, conclave; N. Amer. & NZ caucus. **2** *this parliamentary session:* **period,** time, term, year.

set[1] verb **1** *Beth set the bag on the table:* **put (down),** place, lay, deposit, position, settle, leave, stand, plant; informal stick, dump, park, plonk, pop. **2** *the fence is set in concrete:* **fix,** embed, insert, mount. **3** *a ring set with precious stones:* **adorn,** ornament, decorate, embellish. **4** *I'll set the table:* **lay,** prepare, arrange, fix. **5** *we set them some work:* **assign,** allocate, give, allot. **6** *they set a date for the election:* **arrange,** schedule, fix (on), settle on,

determine, designate, name, specify. **7** *he set his watch:* **adjust,** regulate, synchronize, calibrate, put right, correct. **8** *the adhesive will set in an hour:* **solidify,** harden, stiffen, thicken, gel, cake, congeal, coagulate, clot.
□ **set off/out set out,** start out, sally forth, leave, depart, embark, set sail; informal hit the road. **set something up 1** *a monument was set up:* **erect,** put up, construct, build. **2** *she set up her own business:* **establish,** start, begin, institute, found, create. **3** *set up a meeting:* **arrange,** organize, fix (up), schedule, timetable, line up.

set[2] noun **1** *a set of postcards:* **series,** collection, group, batch, arrangement, array, assortment, selection. **2** *the literary set:* **group,** circle, crowd, crew, band, fraternity, company, ring, camp, school, clique, faction; informal gang, bunch.

set[3] adjective **1** *a set routine:* **fixed,** established, predetermined, hard and fast, unvarying, unchanging, invariable, rigid, inflexible, strict, settled. **2** *she had very set ideas:* **inflexible,** rigid, fixed, entrenched. **3** *I was all set for the evening:* **ready,** prepared, organized, equipped, primed; informal geared up, psyched up.
OPPOSITES variable, flexible, unprepared.

S

4 decide on or fix a time or limit.
5 establish as an example or record.
6 adjust a device as required. **7** prepare a table for a meal. **8** harden into a solid, semi-solid, or fixed state. **9** arrange damp hair into the required style. **10** put a broken or dislocated bone into the right position for healing. **11** (of the sun, moon, etc.) appear to move towards and below the earth's horizon. • **noun 1** a number of things or people grouped together. **2** the way in which something is set. **3** a radio or television receiver. **4** (in tennis and similar games) a group of games counting as a unit towards a match. **5** a collection of scenery, furniture, etc., used for a scene in a play or film. • **adjective 1** fixed or arranged in advance. **2** firmly fixed and unchanging. **3** having a conventional or fixed wording. **4** ready, prepared, or likely to do something.
▫ **set about** start doing. **set something aside 1** temporarily stop using land for growing crops. **2** declare that a legal decision is no longer valid. **set off** begin a journey. **set something off** make a bomb or alarm go off. **set on** attack violently. **set out 1** begin a journey. **2** aim or intend to do something. **set piece 1** a formal or elaborate arrangement in a novel, film, etc. **2** Brit. a carefully organized move in a team game. **set square** a flat triangular piece of plastic or metal with a right angle, for drawing lines and angles. **set-top box** a device which converts a digital television signal into a form which can be viewed on an ordinary television. **set something up** establish a business or other organization.

setback noun a difficulty or problem that holds back progress.

sett noun a badger's burrow.

settee noun Brit. a long padded seat for more than one person.

setter noun a breed of dog trained to stand rigid when it scents game.

setting noun **1** the way or place in which something is set. **2** the metal in which a precious stone or gem is fixed to form a piece of jewellery. **3** a piece of music composed for particular words. **4** (also **place setting**) a complete set of crockery and cutlery for one person at a meal.

settle[1] verb (**settles, settling, settled**) **1** resolve a dispute or difficulty. **2** decide or arrange something finally. **3** make your home in a new place. **4** (often **settle down**) start to live in a more steady or secure way. **5** make or become calmer. **6** sit or rest comfortably or securely. **7** (often **settle in**) begin to feel comfortable in a new situation. **8** pay a debt. **9** (**settle for**) accept after negotiation.
■ **settler** noun.

settle[2] noun a wooden bench with a high back and arms.

settlement noun **1** the process of settling. **2** an agreement that is intended to settle a dispute. **3** a place where people establish a community.

seven cardinal number one more than six; 7. (Roman numeral: **vii** or **VII**.)

seventeen cardinal number one more than sixteen; 17. (Roman numeral: **xvii** or **XVII**.)
■ **seventeenth** ordinal number.

seventh ordinal number **1** at number seven in a sequence; 7th. **2** (**a seventh** or **one seventh**) each of seven equal parts of something.

seventy cardinal number (plural **seventies**) ten less than eighty; 70. (Roman numeral: **lxx** or **LXX**.)
■ **seventieth** ordinal number.

THESAURUS

setback noun **problem**, difficulty, hitch, complication, upset, blow; informal glitch, hiccup.
OPPOSITES breakthrough.

setting noun **surroundings**, position, situation, environment, background, backdrop, spot, place, location, locale, site, scene.

settle verb **1** *they settled the dispute:* **resolve**, sort out, clear up, end, fix, work out, iron out, set right, reconcile; informal patch up. **2** *she settled her affairs:* **put in order**, sort out, tidy up, arrange, organize, order, clear up. **3** *they settled on a date for the wedding:* **decide on**, set, fix, agree on, name, establish, arrange, choose, pick. **4** *she went to settle her bill:* **pay**, square, clear. **5** *he settled in London:* **make your home**, set up home, take up residence, put

down roots, establish yourself, live, move to. **6** *immigrants settled much of Australia:* **colonize**, occupy, populate. **7** *a brandy will settle your nerves:* **calm**, quieten, quiet, soothe, pacify, quell. **8** *a butterfly settled on the flower:* **land**, come to rest, alight, perch.
OPPOSITES stir up, take off.

settlement noun **1** *a pay settlement:* **agreement**, deal, arrangement, resolution, understanding, pact. **2** *the settlement of the dispute:* **resolution**, settling, solution, reconciliation. **3** *a frontier settlement:* **community**, colony, outpost, encampment, post, village.

settler noun **colonist**, frontiersman, pioneer, immigrant, newcomer, incomer.
OPPOSITES native.

sever verb (**severs**, **severing**, **severed**) **1** cut off, or cut into two pieces. **2** put an end to a connection or relationship.

several determiner & pronoun more than two but not many. •adjective separate or respective.
■ **severally** adverb.

severance noun **1** the ending of a connection, relationship, or period of employment. **2** the state of being separated or cut off.

severe adjective **1** (of something bad or difficult) very great. **2** strict or harsh. **3** very plain in style or appearance.
■ **severely** adverb **severity** noun.

sew verb (**sews**, **sewing**, **sewed**; past participle **sewn** or **sewed**) join or repair by making stitches with a needle and thread or a machine.

sewage /soo-ij/ noun human waste and water carried away from drains in sewers.

sewer /soo-er/ noun an underground channel for carrying away human waste and water from drains.
■ **sewerage** noun.

sex noun **1** either of the two main categories (male and female) into which humans and most other living things are divided. **2** the fact of being male or female. **3** the group of all members of either sex. **4** sexual intercourse.
□ **sex symbol** a celebrity famous for being sexually attractive. **sex something up** informal present something in a more interesting way.

sexagenarian noun a person between 60 and 69 years old.

sexism noun prejudice or discrimination on the basis of a person's sex.
■ **sexist** adjective & noun.

sexless adjective **1** not sexually attractive or active. **2** neither male nor female.

sextant noun an instrument for measuring angles and distances, used in navigation and surveying.

sextet noun **1** a group of six musicians. **2** a piece of music for a sextet.

sexton noun a person who looks after a church and churchyard.

sextuple adjective **1** made up of six parts or elements. **2** six times as much or as many.

sextuplet noun each of six children born at one birth.

sexual adjective **1** relating to sex, or to physical attraction or contact between individuals. **2** connected with the state of being male or female. **3** (of reproduction) involving the fusion of male and female cells.
□ **sexual harassment** the making of unwanted sexual advances or remarks to someone, especially at work. **sexual intercourse** sexual contact in which the man inserts his erect penis into the woman's vagina.
■ **sexually** adverb.

sexuality noun (plural **sexualities**) **1** capacity for sexual feelings. **2** a person's sexual preference.

sexy adjective (**sexier**, **sexiest**) **1** sexually

THESAURUS

sever verb **1** the head was severed from the body: cut off, chop off, detach, separate, amputate. **2** a knife had severed the artery: cut (through), rupture, split, pierce. **3** they severed diplomatic relations: break off, discontinue, suspend, end, cease, dissolve.
OPPOSITES join, maintain.

several adjective some, a number of, a few, various, assorted.

severe adjective **1** severe injuries: acute, very bad, serious, grave, critical, dangerous, life-threatening. **2** severe storms: fierce, violent, strong, powerful. **3** a severe winter: harsh, bitter, cold, freezing, icy, arctic. **4** severe criticism: harsh, scathing, sharp, strong, fierce, savage, devastating, withering. **5** his severe expression: stern, dour, grim, forbidding, disapproving, unsmiling, unfriendly, sombre, stony, cold, frosty. **6** a severe style of architecture: plain, simple, austere, unadorned, stark, clinical, uncluttered.
OPPOSITES minor, gentle, mild, friendly, ornate.

severely adverb **1** he was severely injured: badly, seriously, critically. **2** murderers

should be treated more severely: harshly, strictly, sternly, rigorously. **3** she looked severely at Harriet: sternly, grimly, dourly, disapprovingly.

sew verb stitch, tack, seam, hem, embroider.

sex noun **1** they talked about sex: sexual intercourse, lovemaking, making love, sexual relations, mating, copulation; formal fornication, coitus. **2** adults of both sexes: gender.

sexual adjective **1** the sexual organs: reproductive, genital, sex. **2** sexual activity: carnal, erotic.

sexuality noun **1** she had a powerful sexuality: sensuality, sexiness, seductiveness, eroticism, physicality, sexual appetite, passion, desire, lust. **2** I'm open about my sexuality: sexual orientation, sexual preference, leaning, persuasion.

sexy adjective **1** she's so sexy: sexually attractive, seductive, desirable, alluring; informal fanciable; Brit. informal fit; N. Amer. informal foxy. **2** sexy videos: erotic, sexually explicit, titillating, naughty, X-rated, rude, pornographic, crude; informal raunchy, steamy; euphemistic adult. **3** they weren't

S

attractive or exciting. **2** sexually aroused.
3 informal exciting and interesting.
■ **sexily** adverb **sexiness** noun.

shabby adjective (**shabbier, shabbiest**)
1 worn out or scruffy. **2** mean and unfair.
■ **shabbily** adverb **shabbiness** noun.

shack noun a roughly built hut or cabin.
• verb (**shack up with**) informal live with
someone as a lover.

shackle noun (**shackles**) **1** rings connected
by a chain, used to fasten a prisoner's
wrists or ankles together. **2** restraints or
restrictions. • verb (**shackles, shackling,
shackled**) **1** chain with shackles. **2** restrain;
limit.

shade noun **1** relative darkness and coolness
caused by shelter from direct sunlight. **2** a
colour, especially in terms of how light or
dark it is. **3** a variety. **4** a slight amount.
5 (**shades**) informal sunglasses. **6** literary a
ghost. • verb (**shades, shading, shaded**)
1 screen from direct light. **2** cover or
lessen the light of. **3** represent a darker
area with pencil or a block of colour.
4 change gradually into something else.

shadow noun **1** a dark area or shape
produced by an object coming between
light rays and a surface. **2** partial or
complete darkness. **3** sadness or gloom.
4 the slightest trace. **5** a weak or less good
version. **6** a person who constantly
accompanies or secretly follows another.
• verb **1** cast a shadow over. **2** follow and
observe secretly.
□ **shadow-boxing** boxing against an
imaginary opponent as a form of training.
Shadow Cabinet Brit. those members of the
main opposition party who would become
government ministers if their party won
the next election.
■ **shadowy** adjective.

shady adjective (**shadier, shadiest**) **1** giving,
or situated in, shade. **2** informal seeming to
be dishonest or illegal.

shaft noun **1** the long, narrow handle of a
tool or club, body of a spear or arrow, etc.
2 a ray of light or bolt of lightning. **3** a
narrow vertical passage giving access to a
mine, accommodating a lift, etc. **4** each of
the pair of poles between which a horse is
harnessed to a vehicle. **5** a rotating rod for
transmitting mechanical power in a
machine.

shag¹ noun coarse tobacco. • adjective (of pile
on a carpet) long and rough.

shag² noun a cormorant (seabird) with
greenish-black feathers.

shaggy adjective (**shaggier, shaggiest**) **1** (of
hair or fur) long, thick, and untidy.
2 having shaggy hair or fur.

shah noun (in the past) the title of the king
of Iran.

shake verb (**shakes, shaking, shook**; past

THESAURUS

feeling sexy: sexually aroused, sexually
excited, amorous, lustful, passionate;
informal turned on; Brit. informal randy.

shabby adjective **1** *a shabby little bar:* run
down, scruffy, dilapidated, squalid, sordid;
informal crummy; Brit. informal grotty; N. Amer.
informal shacky. **2** *a shabby grey coat:* scruffy,
old, worn out, threadbare, ragged, frayed,
tattered, battered, faded, moth-eaten;
informal tatty; N. Amer. informal raggedy. **3** *her
shabby treatment of Ben:* mean, unkind,
unfair, shameful, shoddy, unworthy,
contemptible, despicable, discreditable;
informal rotten.
OPPOSITES smart, decent.

shack noun hut, cabin, shanty, lean-to, shed,
hovel; Scottish bothy.

shade noun **1** *they sat in the shade:* shadow,
shelter, cover, cool. **2** *shades of blue:*
colour, hue, tone, tint, tinge. **3** *shades of
meaning:* nuance, gradation, degree,
difference, variation, variety, nicety,
subtlety, undertone, overtone. **4** *her skirt
was a shade too short:* little, bit, trace,
touch, modicum, tinge; informal tad,
smidgen. **5** *the window shade:* blind,
curtain, screen, cover, covering, awning,
canopy.
OPPOSITES light.

• verb *vines shaded the garden:* cast a
shadow over, shadow, shelter, cover,
screen.

shadow noun **1** *he saw her shadow in the
doorway:* silhouette, outline, shape,
contour, profile. **2** *he emerged from the
shadows:* shade, darkness, twilight, gloom.
• verb *he is shadowing a suspect:* follow,
trail, track, stalk, pursue; informal tail, keep
tabs on.

shady adjective **1** *a shady garden:* shaded,
shadowy, dim, dark, sheltered, leafy.
2 (informal) *shady deals:* suspicious, suspect,
questionable, dubious, irregular,
underhand; N. Amer. snide; informal fishy,
murky; Brit. informal dodgy; Austral./NZ informal
shonky.
OPPOSITES bright, honest.

shaft noun **1** *the shaft of a golf club:* pole,
shank, stick, rod, staff, handle, stem.
2 *shafts of sunlight:* ray, beam, gleam,
streak. **3** *a ventilation shaft:* tunnel,
passage, hole, bore, duct, well, flue, vent.

shake verb **1** *the building shook:* vibrate,
tremble, quiver, quake, shiver, shudder,
judder, wobble, rock, sway, convulse. **2** *she
shook the bottle:* jiggle, agitate; informal
wiggle, waggle. **3** *he shook his stick:*
brandish, wave, flourish, swing, wield.

S

participle **shaken**) **1** move quickly and jerkily up and down or to and fro. **2** tremble. **3** shock or upset. **4** get rid of or put an end to. •**noun 1** an act of shaking. **2** informal a milkshake.

□ **shake hands (with someone)** clasp someone's right hand in your own when meeting or leaving them, to congratulate them, or as a sign of agreement. **shake someone/thing up 1** stir someone into action. **2** make major changes to an institution or system.
■ **shaker** noun.

Shakespearean or **Shakespearian** adjective having to do with the English dramatist William Shakespeare or his works.

shaky adjective (**shakier**, **shakiest**) **1** shaking; unsteady. **2** not safe or certain.
■ **shakily** adverb.

shale noun soft rock formed from compressed mud or clay.

shall modal verb (3rd singular present **shall**)
1 used with *I* and *we* to express the future tense. **2** expressing a strong statement, intention, or order. **3** Brit. used in questions to make offers or suggestions: *shall we go?*

> ❗ the traditional rule is that you should use **shall** when forming the future tense with **I** and **we** (*I shall be late*) and **will** with **you**, **he**, **she**, **it**, and **they** (*he will not be there*).

shallot /shuh-lot/ noun a vegetable like a small onion.

shallow adjective **1** having a short distance between the top and the bottom; not deep. **2** not thinking or thought out seriously. •**noun** (**shallows**) a shallow area of water.
■ **shallowly** adverb.

shalwar = SALWAR.

sham noun **1** a thing that is not what it appears to be or is not as good as it seems. **2** a person who pretends to be something they are not. •**adjective** not genuine; false. •**verb** (**shams, shamming, shammed**) pretend.

shaman /shay-muhn/ noun (plural **shamans**) (in some societies) a person believed to be able to contact good and evil spirits.
■ **shamanic** adjective **shamanism** noun.

shamble verb (**shambles, shambling, shambled**) walk in a slow, shuffling, awkward way.

shambles noun informal a state of complete disorder.

shambolic adjective Brit. informal very disorganized.

shame noun **1** the feeling you have of embarrassment or distress when you know you have done something wrong or foolish. **2** loss of respect; dishonour. **3** a cause of shame. **4** a cause for regret or disappointment. •**verb** (**shames, shaming, shamed**) make someone feel shame.
□ **put someone/thing to shame** be much better than someone or something.

4 *what she saw shook her:* upset, distress, disturb, unsettle, disconcert, discompose, unnerve, throw off balance, agitate, fluster, shock, alarm, scare, worry; informal rattle.
OPPOSITES soothe.
•**noun 1** *camera shake:* judder, trembling, quivering, quake, tremor, shiver, shudder, wobble. **2** *he gave his coat a shake:* jiggle, joggle; informal waggle. **3** *a shake of his fist:* flourish, wave.

shaky adjective **1** *shaky legs:* unsteady, unstable, rickety, wobbly; Brit. informal wonky. **2** *I feel a bit shaky:* faint, dizzy, light-headed, giddy, weak, wobbly, in shock. **3** *the evidence is shaky:* unreliable, untrustworthy, questionable, dubious, doubtful, tenuous, suspect, flimsy, weak; informal iffy; Brit. informal dodgy.
OPPOSITES steady, stable, sound.

shallow adjective superficial, trivial, facile, insubstantial, lightweight, empty, trifling, surface, skin-deep, frivolous, foolish, silly.
OPPOSITES profound.

sham noun *it's all a sham:* pretence, fake, act, simulation, fraud, lie, counterfeit, humbug.
•**adjective** *a sham marriage:* fake, pretended, feigned, simulated, false,

artificial, bogus, insincere, affected, make-believe; informal pretend, put-on, phoney.
OPPOSITES genuine.
•**verb** *he's shamming:* pretend, fake, malinger; informal put it on; Brit. informal swing the lead.

shambles plural noun **1** *we have to sort out this shambles:* chaos, muddle, jumble, confusion, disorder, havoc. **2** *the room was a shambles:* mess, pigsty; informal disaster area; Brit. informal tip.

shame noun **1** *a sense of shame:* guilt, remorse, contrition. **2** *he brought shame on the family:* humiliation, embarrassment, indignity, mortification, disgrace, dishonour, discredit, ignominy, disrepute, infamy, scandal. **3** *it's a shame she never married:* pity, sad thing, bad luck; informal crime, sin.
OPPOSITES pride, honour.
•**verb 1** *you shamed your family:* disgrace, dishonour, discredit, blacken, drag through the mud. **2** *he was shamed in public:* humiliate, embarrass, humble, take down a peg or two, cut down to size; informal show up; N. Amer. informal make someone eat crow.
OPPOSITES honour.

S

shamefaced adjective showing shame.

shameful adjective causing a feeling of shame.
■ shamefully adverb.

shameless adjective showing no shame.
■ shamelessly adverb.

shammy noun (plural **shammies**) informal chamois leather.

shampoo noun 1 a liquid soap for washing the hair. 2 a similar substance for cleaning a carpet, car, etc. 3 an act of washing with shampoo. • verb (**shampoos, shampooing, shampooed**) wash or clean with shampoo.

shamrock noun a clover-like plant with three leaves on each stem, the national emblem of Ireland.

shandy noun (plural **shandies**) beer mixed with lemonade or ginger beer.

shanghai /shang-**hy**/ verb (**shanghais, shanghaiing, shanghaied**) informal force or trick into doing something.

shank noun 1 the lower part of the leg. 2 the shaft of a tool.
□ Shanks's pony your own legs as a means of transport.

shan't short form shall not.

shantung noun a type of silk fabric with a rough surface.

shanty¹ noun (plural **shanties**) a small roughly built hut.
□ shanty town a settlement in or near a town where poor people live in shanties.

shanty² noun (plural **shanties**) a song with alternating solo and chorus, sung by sailors when working.

shape noun 1 the form of something produced by its outline. 2 a piece of material, paper, etc. cut in a particular form. 3 a particular condition or state. 4 well-defined structure or arrangement. • verb (**shapes, shaping, shaped**) 1 give a shape to. 2 have a big influence on. □ shape up 1 develop in a particular way. 2 improve your fitness, behaviour, etc.

shapeless adjective lacking a definite or attractive shape.

shapely adjective having an attractive shape.

shard noun a sharp piece of broken pottery, glass, etc.

share noun 1 a part of a larger amount which is divided among or contributed to by a number of people. 2 any of the equal parts into which a company's wealth is divided, which can be bought by people in return for a proportion of the profits. 3 an amount thought to be normal or acceptable. • verb (**shares, sharing, shared**) 1 have or give a share of. 2 have, use, or experience jointly with others.
■ sharer noun.

shareholder noun an owner of shares in a company.

shark¹ noun a large and sometimes aggressive sea fish with a triangular fin on its back.

shark² noun informal a person who dishonestly obtains money from other people.

sharp adjective 1 having a cutting or

THESAURUS

shameful adjective 1 *shameful behaviour:* disgraceful, deplorable, despicable, contemptible, discreditable, reprehensible, unworthy, shabby, shocking, scandalous, outrageous, abominable, atrocious, appalling, inexcusable, unforgivable. 2 *a shameful secret:* embarrassing, mortifying, humiliating, ignominious.
OPPOSITES admirable.

shape noun 1 *the shape of the dining table:* form, appearance, configuration, structure, contours, lines, outline, silhouette, profile. 2 *a spirit in the shape of a fox:* guise, likeness, semblance, form, appearance, image. 3 *in good shape:* condition, health, trim, fettle, order; Brit. informal nick.
• verb 1 *the metal is shaped into tools:* form, fashion, make, mould, model. 2 *attitudes shaped by his report:* determine, form, fashion, mould, develop, influence, affect.

share noun *her share of the profits:* portion, part, division, quota, allowance, ration, allocation; informal cut, slice; Brit. informal whack.
• verb 1 *we share the bills:* split, divide, go halves on; informal go fifty-fifty on. 2 *they*

shared out the peanuts: apportion, divide up, allocate, portion out, measure out, carve up; Brit. informal divvy up. 3 *we all share in the learning process:* participate, take part, play a part, be involved, have a hand.

sharp adjective 1 *a sharp knife:* keen, razor-edged, sharpened, well honed. 2 *a sharp pain:* intense, acute, severe, agonizing, excruciating, stabbing, shooting, searing. 3 *a sharp taste:* tangy, piquant, acidic, acid, sour, tart, pungent. 4 *a sharp wind:* cold, chilly, icy, bitter, biting, brisk, keen, penetrating. 5 *sharp words:* harsh, bitter, cutting, spiteful, hurtful, cruel. 6 *a sharp photo:* clear, distinct, crisp, focused. 7 *a sharp increase:* sudden, abrupt, rapid, steep. 8 *she was sharp and witty:* astute, intelligent, bright, incisive, keen, quick-witted, shrewd, canny, perceptive, smart, quick; informal on the ball, quick on the uptake; N. Amer. informal heads-up.
OPPOSITES blunt, mild, sweet, soft, kind, indistinct, gradual, slow, stupid.
• adverb precisely, exactly, promptly, prompt, punctually; informal on the dot;

S

piercing edge or point. **2** tapering to a point or edge. **3** sudden and noticeable. **4** clear and definite. **5** producing a sudden, piercing feeling. **6** quick to understand, notice, or respond. **7** (of a taste or smell) strong and slightly bitter. **8** (of a note or key) higher by a semitone than a stated note or key. **9** (of musical sound) above true or normal pitch. •adverb **1** precisely. **2** suddenly or abruptly. •noun a musical note raised a semitone above natural pitch, shown by the sign ♯.
□ **sharp practice** dishonest business dealings.
■ **sharply** adverb **sharpness** noun.

sharpen verb make or become sharp.
■ **sharpener** noun.

sharpshooter noun a person skilled in shooting.

shatter verb (**shatters, shattering, shattered**) **1** break suddenly and violently into pieces. **2** damage or destroy. **3** upset someone greatly. **4** (**shattered**) Brit. informal completely exhausted.

shave verb (**shaves, shaving, shaved**) **1** remove hair by cutting it off close to the skin with a razor. **2** cut a thin slice or slices from something. **3** reduce something by a small amount. •noun an act of shaving.

shaven adjective shaved.

shaver noun an electric razor.

shaving noun a thin strip cut off a surface.

shawl noun a large piece of fabric worn by women over the shoulders or head or wrapped round a baby.

she pronoun **1** used to refer to a female person or animal previously mentioned or easily identified. **2** used to refer to a ship, country, or other thing thought of as female.

sheaf noun (plural **sheaves**) **1** a bundle of papers. **2** a bundle of grain stalks tied

together after reaping.

shear verb (**shears, shearing, sheared**; past participle **shorn** or **sheared**) **1** cut the wool off a sheep. **2** cut off something such as wool or grass with shears. **3** (**be shorn of**) have something taken away from you. **4** (**shear off**) tear or break off under pressure.
■ **shearer** noun.

> ❗ don't confuse **shear** with **sheer**, which is a verb meaning 'change course quickly' and also an adjective meaning 'nothing but; absolute'.

shears plural noun a cutting tool like very large scissors.

sheath noun (plural **sheaths**) **1** a cover for the blade of a knife or sword. **2** a condom. **3** a close-fitting covering.

sheathe verb (**sheathes, sheathing, sheathed**) **1** put a knife or sword into a sheath. **2** encase something in a close-fitting or protective covering.

shebang /shi-**bang**/ noun (**the whole shebang**) informal the whole thing.

shed[1] noun a simple building used for storage.

shed[2] verb (**sheds, shedding, shed**) **1** allow leaves, hair, skin, etc. to fall off naturally. **2** get rid of. **3** take off clothes. **4** give off light. **5** (of a vehicle) accidentally drop what it is carrying.
□ **shed tears** cry.

she'd short form she had or she would.

sheen noun a soft shine on a surface.

sheep noun (plural **sheep**) an animal with a thick woolly coat, kept in flocks for its wool or meat.
□ **sheep dip** a liquid in which sheep are dipped to clean and disinfect their wool.

sheepdog noun a breed of dog trained to guard and herd sheep.

N. Amer. informal on the button.
OPPOSITES roughly.

sharpen verb hone, whet, strop, grind, file.

shatter verb **1** the glasses shattered: smash, break, splinter, crack, fracture, fragment, disintegrate. **2** the announcement shattered their hopes: destroy, wreck, ruin, dash, crush, devastate, demolish, torpedo, scotch; informal do for, put paid to; Brit. informal scupper.

shattered adjective **1** he was shattered by the reviews: devastated, shocked, stunned, dazed, traumatized. **2** (informal) I feel too shattered to move: exhausted, tired, worn out, weary, fatigued, ready to drop; informal done in, all in, dead beat; Brit. informal knackered, whacked, zonked; N. Amer. informal pooped, tuckered out.

shave verb **1** he shaved his beard: cut off, crop, trim, barber. **2** shave off excess wood: plane, pare, whittle, scrape.

sheath noun covering, cover, case, casing, sleeve, scabbard.

shed[1] noun a shed in the garden: hut, lean-to, outhouse, outbuilding, cabin, shack.

shed[2] verb **1** the trees shed their leaves: drop, scatter, spill. **2** the caterpillar shed its skin: throw off, cast off, discard, slough off, moult. **3** we shed our clothes: take off, remove, discard, climb out of, slip out of; Brit. informal peel off. **4** the moon shed a watery light: cast, radiate, emit, give out.
OPPOSITES keep, put on.

sheen noun shine, lustre, gloss, patina, burnish, polish, shimmer.

S

sheepish adjective feeling embarrassed from shame or shyness.
■ **sheepishly** adverb.

sheepskin noun a sheep's skin with the wool on.

sheer[1] adjective **1** nothing but; absolute. **2** (of a cliff or wall) vertical or almost vertical. **3** (of fabric) very thin.

> ! don't confuse **sheer** with **shear**: see the note at SHEAR.

sheer[2] verb (**sheers, sheering, sheered**) **1** (especially of a boat) change course quickly. **2** move away from an unpleasant topic.

sheet[1] noun **1** a large rectangular piece of cotton or other fabric, used on a bed to lie on or under. **2** a broad flat piece of metal or glass. **3** a rectangular piece of paper. **4** a wide expanse or moving mass of water, flames, etc.
□ **sheet music** music printed on loose sheets of paper.

sheet[2] noun a rope attached to the lower corner of a sail.

sheikh or **sheik** /shayk/ noun a Muslim or Arab leader.

sheila noun Austral./NZ informal a girl or woman.

shekel noun the basic unit of money of modern Israel.

shelf noun (plural **shelves**) **1** a flat length of wood or other rigid material, fixed horizontally and used to display or store things. **2** a ledge of rock.
□ **off the shelf** taken from existing supplies, not made to order. **on the shelf** (of a woman) past an age when she might expect to be married. **shelf life** the length

of time for which an item to be sold can be stored.

shell noun **1** the hard protective outer case of an animal such as a shellfish or turtle. **2** the outer covering of an egg, nut kernel, or seed. **3** a metal case filled with explosive, to be fired from a large gun. **4** a hollow case. **5** an outer structure or framework. • verb **1** fire explosive shells at. **2** remove the shell or pod from. **3** (**shell something out**) informal pay an amount of money.
□ **shell shock** a mental condition which resembles a state of shock and can affect soldiers who have been in battle for a long time. **shell suit** Brit. an outfit consisting of a top and trousers with a soft lining and shiny outer layer.

she'll short form she shall or she will.

shellfish noun a water animal that has a shell and that can be eaten, such as a crab or oyster.

shelter noun **1** a place giving protection from bad weather or danger. **2** a place providing food and accommodation for the homeless. **3** protection from danger or bad weather. • verb (**shelters, sheltering, sheltered**) **1** provide with shelter. **2** find protection or take cover. **3** (**sheltered**) protected from the more unpleasant aspects of life. **4** (**sheltered**) Brit. (of accommodation) designed for elderly or disabled people, and staffed by a warden.

shelve verb (**shelves, shelving, shelved**) **1** decide not to continue with a plan for the time being. **2** place something on a shelf. **3** (of ground) slope downwards.

shelves plural of SHELF.

shenanigans plural noun informal

THESAURUS

sheer adjective **1** *the sheer audacity of the plan:* utter, complete, absolute, total, pure, downright, out-and-out. **2** *a sheer drop:* steep, abrupt, sharp, precipitous, vertical. **3** *a sheer dress:* thin, fine, gauzy, diaphanous, transparent, see-through, flimsy.
OPPOSITES gradual, thick.

sheet noun **1** *a sheet of ice:* layer, covering, blanket, coat, film, veneer, crust, skin, surface, stratum. **2** *a sheet of glass:* pane, panel, slab, plate, piece. **3** *a fresh sheet of paper:* page, leaf, piece. **4** *a sheet of water:* expanse, area, stretch, sweep.

shell noun **1** *peanut shells:* pod, hull, husk; N. Amer. shuck. **2** *the metal shell of the car:* body, case, casing, framework, hull, fuselage, hulk. • verb **1** *they were shelling peas:* pod, hull, husk; N. Amer. shuck. **2** *rebel artillery shelled the city:* bombard, fire on, attack, bomb, blitz.

shelter noun **1** *the trees provide shelter for animals:* protection, cover, shade, safety, security, refuge. **2** *a shelter for abandoned cats:* sanctuary, refuge, home, haven, safe house.
OPPOSITES exposure, danger.
• verb **1** *the hut sheltered him from the sun:* protect, shield, screen, cover, shade, defend, cushion, guard, insulate. **2** *the convoy sheltered in a bay:* take shelter, take refuge, take cover; informal hole up.
OPPOSITES expose.

sheltered adjective **1** *a sheltered stretch of water:* protected, tranquil, still, shady. **2** *a sheltered life:* protected, cloistered, insulated, privileged, secure, safe, quiet.

shelve verb postpone, put off, delay, defer, put back, reschedule, hold over/off, put to one side, suspend, stay, mothball; N. Amer. put over, table; informal put on ice, put on the back burner.
OPPOSITES execute, bring forward, revive.

S

mischievous behaviour.

shepherd noun a person who looks after sheep. •verb guide or direct someone. ◻ **shepherd's pie** Brit. a dish of minced meat under a layer of mashed potato. ■ **shepherdess** noun.

sherbet noun 1 Brit. a sweet fizzing powder eaten alone or made into a drink. 2 (in Arab countries) a drink of sweet diluted fruit juices.

sheriff noun 1 (also **high sheriff**) (in England and Wales) the chief executive officer in a county, working on behalf of a king or queen. 2 (in Scotland) a judge. 3 (in the US) an elected officer in a county, responsible for keeping the peace.

Sherpa noun (plural **Sherpa** or **Sherpas**) a member of a Himalayan people living on the borders of Nepal and Tibet.

sherry noun (plural **sherries**) a strong wine from southern Spain.

she's short form she is or she has.

Shetland pony noun a small breed of pony with a rough coat.

Shia /shi-uh/ noun (plural **Shia** or **Shias**) 1 one of the two main branches of Islam. The other is **Sunni**. 2 a Muslim who follows the Shia branch of Islam.

shiatsu /shi-at-soo/ noun a medical treatment from Japan in which pressure is applied with the hands to points on the body.

shibboleth /shib-buh-leth/ noun a long-standing belief or principle held by a group of people.

shied past and past participle of **shy²**.

shield noun 1 a broad piece of armour held for protection against blows or missiles. 2 a person or thing that acts as a protective barrier or screen. 3 a sports trophy consisting of an engraved metal plate mounted on a piece of wood. 4 a drawing or model of a shield used for displaying a coat of arms. •verb protect or hide.

shift verb 1 move or change from one position to another. 2 transfer blame or responsibility to someone else. 3 Brit. informal move quickly. •noun 1 a slight change in position or direction. 2 a period of time worked by someone who starts work as another finishes. 3 a straight dress without a fitted waist. 4 a key used to switch between two sets of characters or functions on a keyboard.

shiftless adjective lazy and lacking ambition.

shifty adjective informal seeming dishonest or untrustworthy.

Shiite /shee-It/ noun a follower of the Shia branch of Islam.

shilling noun 1 a former British coin worth one twentieth of a pound or twelve old pence (five p). 2 the basic unit of money of Kenya, Tanzania, and Uganda.

shilly-shally verb (**shilly-shallies, shilly-shallying, shilly-shallied**) be unable to make up your mind.

shimmer verb (**shimmers, shimmering, shimmered**) shine with a soft wavering light. •noun a soft wavering light or shine. ■ **shimmery** adjective.

shimmy verb (**shimmies, shimmying, shimmied**) move quickly and smoothly.

shin noun the front of the leg below the knee. •verb (**shins, shinning, shinned**) (**shin up** or **down**) climb quickly up or down by gripping with your arms and legs.

shindig noun informal a lively party.

shine verb (**shines, shining**, past and past participle **shone** or **shined**) 1 give out or reflect light. 2 direct a torch or other light somewhere. 3 (of a person's eyes) be bright with an emotion. 4 be very good at something. 5 (past and past participle **shined**)

THESAURUS S

shepherd verb usher, steer, herd, lead, take, escort, guide, conduct, marshal, walk.

shield noun a shield against radiation: protection, guard, defence, cover, screen, shelter.
•verb he shielded his eyes: protect, guard, defend, cover, screen, shade, shelter.
OPPOSITES expose.

shift verb 1 he shifted some chairs: move, transfer, transport, switch, relocate, reposition, rearrange. 2 the cargo has shifted: move, slide, slip, be displaced. 3 the wind shifted: veer, alter, change, turn. 4 (Brit.) this brush really shifts the dirt: get rid of, remove, get off, budge, lift. OPPOSITES leave.
•noun 1 a shift in public opinion: change, alteration, adjustment, variation, modification, revision, reversal, U-turn. 2 they worked three shifts: stint, stretch, spell.

shimmer verb the sea shimmered in the sunset: glint, glisten, twinkle, sparkle, flash, gleam, glow, glimmer, wink.
•noun a shimmer of moonlight: glint, twinkle, sparkle, flash, gleam, glow, glimmer, lustre, glitter.

shine verb 1 the sun shone: beam, gleam, radiate, glow, glint, glimmer, sparkle, twinkle, glitter, glisten, shimmer, flash. 2 she shone her shoes: polish, burnish, buff, rub up, brush, clean. 3 they shone at university: excel, stand out.
•noun linseed oil restores the shine: polish, gleam, gloss, lustre, sheen, patina.

polish. • **noun** a quality of brightness.
□ **take a shine to** informal develop a liking for.

shiner **noun** informal a black eye.

shingle¹ **noun** a mass of small rounded pebbles on a seashore.

shingle² **noun** a wooden tile used on walls or roofs.
■ **shingled** adjective.

shingles **noun** a disease in which painful blisters form along the path of a nerve.

Shinto **noun** a Japanese religion involving the worship of ancestors and nature spirits.

shiny adjective (**shinier, shiniest**) reflecting light.

ship **noun** a large boat for transporting people or goods by sea. • **verb** (**ships, shipping, shipped**) **1** transport goods on a ship or by other means. **2** (of a boat) take in water over the side.

shipbuilder **noun** a person or company that designs and builds ships.
■ **shipbuilding** noun.

shipment **noun** **1** the action of transporting goods. **2** an amount of goods shipped.

shipping **noun** **1** ships as a whole. **2** the transport of goods.

shipshape adjective orderly and neat.

shipwreck **noun** **1** the sinking or breaking up of a ship at sea. **2** a ship that has been lost or destroyed at sea. • **verb** (**be shipwrecked**) suffer a shipwreck.

shipyard **noun** a place where ships are built and repaired.

shire **noun** **1** Brit. a county in England. **2** (**the Shires**) country areas of England regarded as strongholds of traditional country life.
□ **shire horse** a heavy, powerful breed of horse.

shirk **verb** avoid work or a duty.
■ **shirker** noun.

shirred adjective (of fabric) gathered by

means of threads in parallel rows.

shirt **noun** a garment for the upper body, with a collar and sleeves and buttons down the front.

shirtsleeves plural noun (**in your shirtsleeves**) wearing a shirt without a jacket.

shirty adjective Brit. informal irritated or annoyed.

shish kebab **noun** a dish of pieces of meat and vegetables cooked and served on skewers.

shiver **verb** (**shivers, shivering, shivered**) shake slightly from fear, cold, or excitement. • **noun** a trembling movement.
■ **shivery** adjective.

shoal¹ **noun** a large number of fish swimming together.

shoal² **noun** **1** an area of shallow water. **2** a submerged sandbank that can be seen at low tide.

shock¹ **noun** **1** a sudden upsetting or surprising event or experience. **2** an unpleasant feeling of sudden surprise and distress. **3** a serious medical condition associated with a fall in blood pressure, caused by loss of blood, severe burns, etc. **4** a violent shaking movement caused by an impact, explosion, or earthquake. **5** an electric shock. • **verb** **1** greatly surprise and upset someone. **2** make someone feel outraged or disgusted.
□ **shock absorber** a device for absorbing jolts and vibrations on a vehicle. **shocking pink** a very bright shade of pink. **shock troops** troops trained to carry out sudden attacks. **shock wave** a moving wave of very high pressure caused by an explosion or by something travelling faster than sound.

shock² **noun** an untidy or thick mass of hair.

shocking adjective **1** causing shock or disgust. **2** Brit. informal very bad.
■ **shocker** noun **shockingly** adverb.

S

THESAURUS

shiny adjective glossy, bright, glassy, polished, gleaming, satiny, lustrous.
OPPOSITES matt.

ship noun boat, vessel, craft; literary barque.
• verb *goods are shipped within 24 hours:* deliver, send, dispatch, transport, carry, distribute.

shiver verb *she was shivering with fear:* tremble, quiver, shake, shudder, quake.
• noun *she gave a shiver:* shudder, twitch, start.

shock¹ noun **1** *the news came as a shock:* blow, upset, surprise, revelation, bolt from the blue, rude awakening, eye-opener.
2 *you gave me a shock:* fright, scare, start; informal turn. **3** *suffering from shock:*

trauma, collapse, breakdown, post-traumatic stress disorder. **4** *the first shock of the earthquake:* vibration, reverberation, shake, jolt, impact, blow.
• verb *the murder shocked the nation:* appal, horrify, outrage, scandalize, disgust, traumatize, distress, upset, disturb, stun, rock, shake.
OPPOSITES delight.

shock² noun *a shock of red hair:* mass, mane, mop, thatch, head, bush, tangle, cascade, halo.

shocking adjective appalling, horrifying, horrific, dreadful, awful, terrible, scandalous, outrageous, disgraceful, abominable, atrocious, disgusting, distressing, upsetting, disturbing, startling.

shoddy adjective (**shoddier, shoddiest**) **1** badly made or done. **2** dishonest or unfair.
■ **shoddily** adverb.

shoe noun **1** a covering for the foot with a stiff sole. **2** a horseshoe. •verb (**shoes, shoeing, shod**) **1** fit a horse with a shoe or shoes. **2** (**be shod**) be wearing shoes of a particular kind.
□ **shoe tree** a shaped block put into a shoe when it is not being worn, to keep it in shape.

shoehorn noun a curved piece of metal or plastic, used for easing your heel into a shoe. •verb force into a tight space.

shoelace noun a cord passed through holes or hooks on opposite sides of the opening in a shoe to fasten it.

shoestring noun (**on a shoestring**) informal with only a very small amount of money.

shogun noun (in the past, in Japan) a hereditary leader of the army.

shone past and past participle of **shine**.

shook past of **shake**.

shoot verb (**shoots, shooting, shot**) **1** kill or wound someone with a bullet, arrow, etc. **2** fire a gun. **3** move suddenly and rapidly. **4** direct a glance, question, or remark at someone. **5** (in sport) kick, hit, or throw the ball in an attempt to score a goal. **6** photograph or film a scene or film. **7** (**shooting**) (of a pain) sudden and piercing. **8** (of a boat) travel quickly down rapids. **9** move a bolt to fasten a door. **10** send out buds or shoots. **11** (**shoot up**) informal inject yourself with an illegal drug. •noun **1** a new part growing from a plant. **2** an occasion of taking photographs or making a film. **3** an occasion when a group of people hunt and shoot animals or birds as a sport.
□ **shooting star** a small rapidly moving

meteor that burns up on entering the earth's atmosphere. **shooting stick** a walking stick with a handle that unfolds to form a seat.

shooter noun **1** a person who uses a gun. **2** informal a gun.

shop noun **1** a building or part of a building where goods are sold. **2** a place where things are manufactured or repaired; a workshop. •verb (**shops, shopping, shopped**) **1** go to a shop or shops to buy goods. **2** (**shop around**) look for the best available price or rate for something. **3** Brit. informal inform on.
□ **shop floor** Brit. the area in a factory where things are made or put together by the workers. **shop-soiled** Brit. (of an article) dirty or damaged from being displayed or handled in a shop. **shop steward** Brit. a person elected by workers in a factory to represent them in dealings with the management. **talk shop** discuss work matters with a colleague when you are not at work.
■ **shopper** noun **shopping** noun.

shopkeeper noun the owner and manager of a shop.

shoplifting noun the stealing of goods from a shop.
■ **shoplifter** noun.

shore[1] noun **1** the land along the edge of a sea or other stretch of water. **2** (**shores**) literary a foreign country or region.
□ **on shore** on land.

shore[2] verb (**shores, shoring, shored**) (**shore something up**) **1** support or strengthen something. **2** hold something up with a prop or beam.

shoreline noun the line along which a sea or other stretch of water meets the land.

shorn past participle of **shear**.

short adjective **1** of a small length in space

THESAURUS

shoot verb **1** *they shot him in the street*: gun down, mow down, hit, wound, injure, shoot someone dead, kill. **2** *they shot at the police*: fire, open fire, snipe, let fly, bombard, shell. **3** *it can shoot bullets or grenades*: discharge, fire, launch, propel, release. **4** *a car shot past*: race, speed, flash, dash, rush, hurtle, streak, whizz, zoom, career, fly; informal belt, tear, zip, whip; Brit. informal bomb; N. Amer. informal hightail it, barrel. **5** *the film was shot in Tunisia*: film, photograph, take, make, record.
•noun *new shoots*: sprout, bud, runner, tendril.

shop noun store, retail outlet, boutique, emporium, department store, supermarket, hypermarket, superstore, chain store; N. Amer. mart, minimart.

shore noun seashore, beach, sand(s), shoreline, coast.

short adjective **1** *short people*: small, little, petite, tiny, diminutive, elfin; Scottish wee. **2** *a short report*: concise, brief, succinct, compact, pithy, abridged, abbreviated, condensed. **3** *a short visit*: brief, fleeting, lightning, quick, cursory. **4** *money is a bit short*: scarce, scant, meagre, sparse, insufficient, deficient, inadequate, lacking. **5** *he was rather short with her*: curt, sharp, abrupt, blunt, brusque, terse, offhand.
OPPOSITES tall, long, plentiful, courteous.
•adverb *she stopped short*: abruptly, suddenly, sharply, all of a sudden, unexpectedly, without warning.
□ **short of deficient in**, lacking, in need of, low on, short on, missing; informal strapped

or time. **2** small in height. **3** smaller than is usual or expected. **4** (**short of** or **on**) not having enough of. **5** not available in large enough quantities; scarce. **6** rude and abrupt. **7** (of odds in betting) reflecting a high level of probability. **8** (of pastry) containing a high proportion of fat to flour and therefore crumbly. • adverb not as far as expected or required. • noun Brit. a small drink of spirits. • verb have a short circuit. □ short-change cheat someone by giving them less than the correct change. short circuit a faulty connection in an electrical circuit in which the current flows along a shorter route than it should do. short-circuit cause a short circuit in. short cut a way of going somewhere or doing something that is quicker than usual. short-handed (or short-staffed) having fewer staff than you need or than is usual. short-lived lasting only a short time. short shrift abrupt and unsympathetic treatment. short-sighted Brit. **1** unable to see things clearly unless they are close to your eyes. **2** not thinking carefully about the consequences of something. short-tempered losing your temper quickly. stop short suddenly stop.
■ shortness noun.

shortage noun a lack of something needed.

shortbread or **shortcake** noun a rich, crumbly type of biscuit made with butter, flour, and sugar.

shortcoming noun a fault in someone's character or in a system.

shortcrust pastry noun Brit. crumbly pastry made with flour, fat, and a little water.

shorten verb make or become shorter.

shortening noun fat used for making pastry.

shortfall noun a situation in which something amounts to less than is required.

shorthand noun a way of writing very quickly when recording what someone is saying, by using abbreviations and symbols.

shortlist noun a list of selected candidates from which a final choice is made. • verb put on a shortlist.

shortly adverb **1** in a short time; soon. **2** abruptly or sharply.

shorts plural noun short trousers that reach to the thighs or knees.

shot[1] noun **1** the firing of a gun, arrow, etc. **2** (in sport) a hit, stroke, or kick of the ball as an attempt to score. **3** informal an attempt. **4** a photograph. **5** a film sequence photographed continuously by one camera. **6** a person with a particular level of ability in shooting. **7** (also **lead shot**) tiny lead pellets used in a shotgun. **8** a heavy ball thrown in the sport of shot put. **9** the launch of a rocket. **10** informal a small drink of spirits. **11** informal an injection of a drug or vaccine. □ like a shot informal without hesitation. shot put an athletic contest in which a very heavy round ball is thrown as far as possible.

shot[2] past and past participle of **SHOOT**. adjective woven with a warp and weft of different colours, giving a contrasting effect. □ shot through with filled with a quality.

shotgun noun a gun for firing small bullets at short range. □ shotgun wedding informal a wedding arranged quickly because the bride is pregnant.

should modal verb (3rd singular **should**) **1** used to indicate what is right or ought to be done. **2** used to indicate what is probable. **3** formal used to state what would happen if something else was the case: *if you should change your mind, I'll be at the hotel.* **4** used with *I* and *we* to express a polite request, opinion, or hope.

shoulder noun the joint between the upper arm and the main part of the body. • verb

---

THESAURUS

for, pushed for, minus.

shortage noun scarcity, dearth, poverty, insufficiency, deficiency, inadequacy, famine, lack, deficit, shortfall.
OPPOSITES abundance.

shortcoming noun fault, defect, flaw, imperfection, deficiency, limitation, failing, drawback, weakness, weak point, Achilles heel.
OPPOSITES strength.

shorten verb abbreviate, abridge, condense, contract, compress, reduce, shrink, diminish, cut (down), trim, pare (down), prune, curtail, truncate.
OPPOSITES lengthen.

shortly adverb soon, presently, in a little while, at any moment, in a minute, in next to no time, before long, by and by; N. Amer. momentarily; informal anon, any time now, in a jiffy; Brit. informal in a mo.

shot noun **1** *a shot rang out:* report, crack, bang, blast; (**shots**) gunfire, firing. **2** *a winning shot:* stroke, hit, strike, kick, throw. **3** *Mike was an excellent shot:* marksman, markswoman, shooter. **4** *a shot of us on holiday:* photograph, photo, snap, snapshot, picture, print, slide, still.

shoulder verb **1** *I shouldered the responsibility:* take on (yourself), undertake, accept, assume, bear, carry.

(**shoulders, shouldering, shouldered**) **1** take on a responsibility. **2** push aside with your shoulder. **3** carry on your shoulder.
□ **shoulder blade** either of the triangular bones at the top of the back.

shouldn't short form should not.

shout verb **1** speak or call out very loudly. **2** (**shout someone down**) prevent someone from being heard by shouting. •noun **1** a loud cry or call. **2** (**your shout**) Brit. informal your turn to buy a round of drinks.

shove verb (**shoves, shoving, shoved**) **1** push roughly. **2** place carelessly or roughly. **3** (**shove off**) informal go away. •noun a strong push.

shovel noun a tool resembling a spade with a broad blade and upturned sides, used for moving earth, snow, etc. •verb (**shovels, shovelling, shovelled**; US spelling **shovels, shoveling, shoveled**) move earth, snow, etc. with a shovel.

show verb (**shows, showing, showed**; past participle **shown** or **showed**) **1** be or make visible. **2** offer for inspection or viewing. **3** present an image of. **4** lead or guide. **5** behave in a particular way towards someone. **6** be evidence of; prove. **7** make someone understand something by explaining it or doing it yourself. **8** (also **show up**) informal arrive for an appointment. •noun **1** a stage performance involving singing and dancing. **2** an entertainment programme on television or radio. **3** an event or competition in which animals, plants, or products are displayed. **4** an impressive or pleasing sight. **5** a display of a quality or feeling. **6** a display intended to give a false impression.
□ **show business** the world of theatre, films, television, and pop music as a profession or industry. **show off** try to impress other people by talking about your abilities or possessions. **show something off** display something that you are proud of. **show-off** a person who tries to impress other people by showing off. **show trial** a public trial held to influence or please people, rather than to ensure that justice is done. **show someone/thing up 1** reveal someone or something to be bad or at fault. **2** informal humiliate someone.

showbiz noun informal show business.

showcase noun **1** an occasion for presenting someone or something to their best advantage. **2** a glass case used for displaying articles.

showdown noun a final argument, fight, or

THESAURUS

2 *another lad shouldered him aside:* push, shove, thrust, jostle, force, bulldoze, bundle.

shout verb *I heard a shout:* yell, cry (out), call (out), roar, howl, bellow, bawl, raise your voice; informal holler.
OPPOSITES whisper.
•noun *he shouted a warning:* yell, cry, call, roar, howl, bellow, bawl; informal holler.

shove verb **1** *she shoved him back:* push, thrust, propel, drive, force, ram, knock, elbow, shoulder. **2** *she shoved past him:* push (your way), force your way, barge (your way), elbow (your way), shoulder your way.
•noun *a hefty shove:* push, thrust, bump, jolt, barge.

show verb **1** *the stitches do not show:* be visible, be seen, be in view, be obvious. **2** *he wouldn't show the picture:* display, exhibit, put on show, put on display, put on view. **3** *Frank showed his frustration:* manifest, exhibit, reveal, convey, make known, communicate, express, make plain, make obvious, disclose, betray. **4** *I'll show you how to cook:* demonstrate, explain, describe, illustrate, teach, instruct. **5** *events show this to be true:* prove, demonstrate, confirm, substantiate, corroborate, verify, bear out. **6** *she showed them to their seats:* escort, accompany, take, conduct, lead, usher, guide, direct.
OPPOSITES conceal.

•noun **1** *a spectacular show of bluebells:* display, array, sight, spectacle. **2** *the motor show:* exhibition, display, fair, festival, parade; N. Amer. exhibit. **3** *a TV show:* programme, broadcast, presentation, production, episode. **4** *she's only doing it for show:* appearance, display, image. **5** *Drew made a show of looking busy:* pretence, outward appearance, (false) front, guise, pose.
□ **show off** (informal) put on airs, put on an act, swank, strut, grandstand, posture, draw attention to yourself. **show something off** display, show to advantage, exhibit, demonstrate, parade, draw attention to, flaunt. **show up 1** *cancers show up on X-rays:* be visible, be obvious, be seen, be revealed, appear. **2** (informal) *only two waitresses showed up:* turn up, appear, arrive, come, get here/there, put in an appearance, materialize. **show someone up** (informal) humiliate, embarrass, shame, put someone to shame, mortify. **show something up** expose, reveal, make obvious, highlight, emphasize, draw attention to.

showdown noun confrontation, clash, face-off.

shower noun **1** *a shower of rain:* fall, drizzle, sprinkling. **2** *a shower of missiles:* volley, hail, salvo, barrage.
•verb **1** *confetti showered down on us:* rain, fall, hail. **2** *she showered them with gifts:*

S

test, to settle a dispute.

shower noun 1 a short period of rain or snow. 2 a large number of things that fall or arrive together. 3 a device that creates a spray of water under which you stand to wash yourself. 4 an act of washing yourself in a shower. • verb (**showers, showering, showered**) 1 fall or make things fall in a shower. 2 (**shower someone with**) give large quantities of something to someone. 3 wash yourself in a shower.
■ **showery** adjective.

showgirl noun an actress who sings and dances in a musical or variety show.

showjumping noun the competitive sport of riding horses over a course of obstacles in an arena.

showman noun (plural **showmen**) 1 a person who is very good at entertaining people or getting their attention. 2 the manager or presenter of a circus, fair, etc.
■ **showmanship** noun.

shown past participle of SHOW.

showpiece noun an outstanding example of something.

showroom noun a room used to display cars, furniture, or other goods for sale.

showy adjective very bright or colourful and attracting a lot of attention.

shrank past of SHRINK.

shrapnel noun small metal fragments from an exploding shell or bomb.

shred noun 1 a strip of material that has been torn, cut, or scraped from something. 2 a very small amount. • verb (**shreds, shredding, shredded**) tear or cut into shreds.
■ **shredder** noun.

shrew noun 1 a small mouse-like animal with a long pointed snout. 2 a bad-tempered woman.

shrewd adjective having or showing good judgement.
■ **shrewdly** adverb **shrewdness** noun.

shrewish adjective (of a woman) bad-tempered or nagging.

shriek verb make a piercing cry. • noun a piercing cry.

shrike noun a songbird with a strong hooked bill.

shrill adjective high-pitched and piercing. • verb make a shrill noise.
■ **shrilly** adverb.

shrimp noun (plural **shrimp** or **shrimps**) a small edible shellfish.

shrine noun 1 a place connected with a holy person or event, where people go to pray. 2 a place containing a religious statue or object.

shrink verb (**shrinks, shrinking, shrank**; past participle **shrunk** or (especially as adjective) **shrunken**) 1 become or make smaller. 2 move back or away in fear or disgust. 3 (**shrink from**) be unwilling to do. • noun informal a psychiatrist.
□ **shrinking violet** informal a very shy person. **shrink-wrap** wrap in clinging plastic film.
■ **shrinkage** noun.

shrivel verb (**shrivels, shrivelling, shrivelled**; US spelling **shrivels, shriveling, shriveled**) wrinkle and shrink through loss of moisture.

shroud noun 1 a length of cloth in which a dead person is wrapped for burial. 2 a thing that closely surrounds or hides something. 3 (**shrouds**) a set of ropes supporting the mast of a sailing boat. • verb 1 wrap in a shroud. 2 cover or hide.

shrub noun a woody plant which is smaller than a tree and divided into separate stems

THESAURUS

S

deluge, flood, inundate, swamp, overwhelm, snow under.

show-off noun (informal) exhibitionist, extrovert, poser, poseur, swaggerer, self-publicist.

showy adjective ostentatious, flamboyant, gaudy, garish, brash, vulgar, loud, fancy, ornate; informal flash, flashy, bling-bling.
OPPOSITES restrained.

shred noun 1 her dress was torn to shreds: tatter, ribbon, rag, fragment, sliver. 2 not a shred of evidence: scrap, bit, speck, particle, ounce, jot, crumb, fragment, grain, drop, trace.
• verb grate, mince, grind.

shrewd adjective astute, sharp, smart, intelligent, clever, canny, perceptive; informal on the ball.
OPPOSITES stupid.

shriek verb & noun scream, screech, squeal, squawk, roar, howl, shout, yelp; informal holler.

shrink verb 1 the number of competitors shrank: get smaller, contract, diminish, lessen, reduce, decrease, dwindle, decline, fall off. 2 he doesn't shrink from naming names: recoil, shy away, flinch, be averse, be afraid, hesitate.
OPPOSITES expand, increase.

shrivel verb wither, shrink, wilt, dry up, dehydrate, parch, frazzle.

shroud noun a shroud of mist: covering, cover, cloak, mantle, blanket, layer, cloud, veil, winding sheet.
• verb shrouded by cloud: cover, envelop, veil, cloak, blanket, screen, conceal, hide, mask, obscure.

from near the ground.
■ **shrubby** adjective.

shrubbery noun (plural **shrubberies**) an area planted with shrubs.

shrug verb (**shrugs, shrugging, shrugged**)
1 raise your shoulders slightly and briefly as a sign that you do not know or care about something. **2** (**shrug something off**) treat something as unimportant. • noun an act of shrugging your shoulders.

shudder verb (**shudders, shuddering, shuddered**) tremble or shake violently.
• noun an act of shuddering.

shuffle verb (**shuffles, shuffling, shuffled**)
1 walk without lifting your feet completely from the ground. **2** move about restlessly while sitting or standing. **3** rearrange a pack of cards by sliding them over and under each other quickly. **4** rearrange people or things. • noun an act of shuffling.

shun verb (**shuns, shunning, shunned**) avoid or reject.

shunt verb **1** push or pull a railway vehicle from one set of tracks to another. **2** move something around or along. **3** move someone to a less important position.
■ **shunter** noun.

shut verb (**shuts, shutting, shut**) **1** move something into position to block an opening. **2** (**shut someone/thing in** or **out**) keep a person or animal in or out by closing a door, gate, etc. **3** prevent access to a place or along a route. **4** (with reference to a shop or other business) stop operating for business. **5** close a book, curtains, etc.
☐ **shut down** stop opening for business, or stop operating. **shut up** informal stop talking.

shutter noun **1** each of a pair of hinged panels inside or outside a window that can be closed for security or to keep out the light. **2** a device that opens and closes to expose the film in a camera. • verb

(**shutters, shuttering, shuttered**) close the shutters of a window or building.

shuttle noun **1** a form of transport that travels regularly between two places. **2** (in weaving) a bobbin for carrying the weft thread across the warp. • verb (**shuttles, shuttling, shuttled**) **1** travel regularly between places. **2** transport in a shuttle.

shuttlecock noun a light cone-shaped object that is struck with rackets in the game of badminton.

shy[1] adjective (**shyer, shyest**) nervous about meeting or talking to other people. • verb (**shies, shying, shied**) **1** (of a horse) turn aside in fright. **2** (**shy away from**) avoid doing something through lack of confidence.
■ **shyly** adverb.

shy[2] verb (**shies, shying, shied**) throw something at a target.

shyster noun informal a dishonest person, especially a lawyer.

SI abbreviation Système International, the international system of units of measurement.

Siamese adjective relating to Siam (the old name for Thailand).
☐ **Siamese cat** a breed of cat that has short pale fur with darker face, ears, feet, and tail. **Siamese twins** twins whose bodies are joined at birth.

sibilant adjective making a hissing sound.
■ **sibilance** noun.

sibling noun a brother or sister.

sibyl noun (in ancient Greece and Rome) a woman supposedly able to pass on messages from a god.
■ **sibylline** adjective.

sic adverb (after a copied word that seems odd or wrong) written exactly as it stands in the original.

THESAURUS   S

shudder verb *the ground shuddered:* shake, shiver, tremble, quiver, judder.
• noun *the truck's shudders and jolts:* shake, shiver, tremor, trembling, quivering, vibration, judder.

shuffle verb **1** *they shuffled along the passage:* shamble, dodder, drag your feet. **2** *she shuffled her feet:* scrape, drag, scuffle. **3** *he shuffled the cards:* mix (up), rearrange, jumble (up).

shun verb avoid, steer clear of, give a wide berth to, have nothing to do with; informal freeze out; Brit. informal send to Coventry.
OPPOSITES welcome.

shut verb *please shut the door:* close, pull to, push to, slam, fasten, put the lid on, lock, secure.
OPPOSITES open, unlock.

☐ **shut down cease activity,** close (down), cease trading; informal fold. **shut up** (informal) **be quiet,** keep quiet, stop talking, quieten down; informal shut it, shut your face/mouth/trap, belt up, give it a rest; Brit. informal shut your gob; N. Amer. informal save it. **shut someone/something up** (informal) **silence,** quieten down, hush, gag, muzzle.

shuttle verb commute, run, ply, go/travel back and forth, ferry.

shy adjective bashful, diffident, timid, reserved, introverted, retiring, self-effacing, withdrawn.
OPPOSITES confident.
☐ **shy away from flinch,** recoil, hang back, be loath, be reluctant, be unwilling, be disinclined, hesitate, baulk at.

sick adjective **1** physically or mentally ill. **2** wanting to vomit. **3** (**sick of**) bored by or annoyed about. **4** informal behaving in an abnormal or cruel way. **5** informal (of humour) dealing with unpleasant subjects in a way that is offensive. •noun Brit. informal vomit.

□ **be sick 1** be ill. **2** Brit. vomit.

sickbay noun a room set aside for sick people.

sickbed noun the bed of a person who is ill.

sicken verb **1** disgust or shock. **2** (**be sickening for**) start to develop an illness.

sickle noun a tool for cutting corn, with a semicircular blade and a short handle.

sickly adjective (**sicklier**, **sickliest**) **1** often ill. **2** looking or seeming unhealthy. **3** (of flavour, colour, etc.) so bright or sweet as to cause sickness.

sickness noun **1** the state of being ill. **2** a particular type of illness or disease. **3** nausea or vomiting.

side noun **1** a position to the left or right of an object, place, or central point. **2** either of the two halves into which something can be divided. **3** an upright or sloping surface of something that is not the top, bottom, front, or back. **4** each of the flat surfaces of a solid object, or either of the two surfaces of something flat and thin, e.g. paper. **5** either of the two surfaces of a record or the corresponding parts of a cassette tape. **6** a part near the edge of something. **7** a person or group opposing another in a dispute or contest. **8** a sports team. **9** a particular aspect. **10** Geometry each of the lines forming the boundary of a plane figure. •adjective additional or less important. •verb (**sides**, **siding**, **sided**) (**side with** or **against**) support or oppose in a conflict or dispute.

□ **side effect** a secondary effect of a drug. **side road** (or **street**) a minor road. **side-saddle** (of a rider) sitting with both feet on the same side of the horse. **take sides** support one person or cause against another.

sideboard noun **1** a piece of furniture with cupboards and drawers, used for storing crockery, glasses, etc. **2** (**sideboards**) Brit. sideburns.

sideburns plural noun a strip of hair growing down each side of a man's face in front of his ears.

sidecar noun a small, low vehicle attached to the side of a motorcycle for carrying passengers.

sidekick noun informal a person's assistant.

sidelight noun Brit. a small additional light on either side of a motor vehicle's headlights.

sideline noun **1** something you do in addition to your main job. **2** either of the two lines along the longer sides of a sports field or court. **3** (**the sidelines**) a position of watching a situation rather than being directly involved in it. •verb (**sidelines**,

THESAURUS

sick adjective **1** *the children are sick:* ill, unwell, poorly, ailing, indisposed; informal laid up, under the weather; Austral./NZ informal crook. **2** *he was feeling sick:* nauseous, queasy, bilious, green about the gills. **3** *I'm sick of this music:* fed up, bored, tired, weary. **4** (informal) *a sick joke:* macabre, tasteless, ghoulish, morbid, black, gruesome, gallows, cruel.
OPPOSITES well.

□ **be sick** (Brit.) **vomit**, heave; informal puke, throw up; N. Amer. informal barf, upchuck.

sicken verb **1** *the stench sickened him:* nauseate, make sick, turn someone's stomach, disgust; N. Amer. informal gross out. **2** *she sickened and died:* fall ill, catch something.
OPPOSITES please, recover.

sickening adjective nauseating, stomach-turning, repulsive, revolting, disgusting, offensive, off-putting, distasteful, obscene, gruesome, grisly; N. Amer. vomitous; informal gross.

sickness noun **1** *she was absent through sickness:* illness, disease, ailment, infection, malady, infirmity; informal bug, virus; Brit. informal lurgy. **2** *a wave of sickness:* nausea, biliousness, queasiness. **3** *sickness and diarrhoea:* nausea, vomiting, retching; informal throwing up, puking.

side noun **1** *the side of the road:* edge, border, verge, boundary, margin, fringe(s), flank, bank, perimeter, extremity, periphery, limit(s). **2** *the wrong side of the road:* half, part, carriageway, lane. **3** *the east side of the city:* district, quarter, area, region, part, neighbourhood, sector, zone. **4** *one side of the paper:* surface, face. **5** *his side of the argument:* point of view, viewpoint, perspective, opinion, standpoint, position, outlook, slant, angle. **6** *the losing side:* faction, camp, bloc, party. **7** *the players in their side:* team, squad, line-up.
OPPOSITES centre, end.

•adjective **1** *elaborate side pieces:* lateral, wing, flanking. **2** *a side issue:* subordinate, secondary, minor, peripheral, incidental, subsidiary.
OPPOSITES front, central.

□ **side with support**, take someone's part, stand by, back, be loyal to, defend, champion, ally yourself with.

sidelining, sidelined) remove from a team, game, or influential position.

sidelong adjective & adverb to or from one side; sideways.

sidereal /sy-deer-i-uhl/ adjective relating to the distant stars or their apparent positions in the sky.

sideshow noun a small show or stall at an exhibition, fair, or circus.

sidestep verb (sidesteps, sidestepping, sidestepped) 1 avoid dealing with a difficult issue. 2 avoid someone or something by stepping sideways.

sideswipe noun a critical or harsh remark made while discussing another matter.

sidetrack verb distract someone from the main issues of what they are discussing or doing.

sidewalk noun N. Amer. a pavement.

sideways adverb & adjective to, towards, or from the side.

siding noun a short track beside a main railway line, where trains are left.

sidle verb (sidles, sidling, sidled) walk in a secretive or timid way.

siege noun 1 a military operation in which forces surround a town and cut off its supplies. 2 a similar operation by a police team to force an armed person to surrender.

> ☑ remember, *i* before *e* in **siege** and **sieve**.

sienna noun a kind of earth used as a brown colouring in painting.

sierra /si-air-uh/ noun (in Spain and the US) a long chain of mountains with jagged peaks.

siesta noun an afternoon rest or nap.

sieve /siv/ noun a piece of mesh held in a frame, used for straining solids from liquids or separating coarser from finer particles. • verb (sieves, sieving, sieved) put a substance through a sieve.

sift verb 1 put a substance through a sieve. 2 examine something thoroughly to sort out what is important or useful.

sigh verb let out a long, deep breath expressing sadness, relief, etc. • noun such a breath.

sight noun 1 the ability to see. 2 the act of seeing something. 3 the area or distance within which you can see something. 4 a thing that you see. 5 (**sights**) places of interest to tourists. 6 (**a sight**) informal a person or thing that looks ridiculous or unattractive. 7 (also **sights**) a device that you look through to aim a gun or see with a telescope. • verb see or glimpse.
□ **raise** (or **lower**) **your sights** increase (or lower) your expectations. **set your sights on** have something as an ambition. **sight-read** read a musical score and play it without preparation.

> ! don't confuse **sight** with **site**, which means 'a place where something is located or happens'.

sighted adjective 1 having the ability to see; not blind. 2 having a particular kind of sight.

sightless adjective blind.

sightseeing noun the activity of visiting places of interest.
■ **sightseer** noun.

sign noun 1 an indication that something exists, is happening, or may happen. 2 a signal, gesture, or notice giving information or an instruction. 3 a symbol used to represent something in algebra, music, or other subjects. 4 each of the twelve divisions of the zodiac. • verb 1 write your name on something to show

sideways adverb 1 *I slid sideways:* to the side, laterally. 2 *the expansion slots are mounted sideways:* edgewise, edgeways, side first, end on.
• adjective 1 *sideways force:* lateral, sideward, on the side, side to side. 2 *a sideways look:* indirect, oblique, sidelong, surreptitious, furtive, covert, sly.

sift verb 1 *sift the flour into a large bowl:* sieve, strain, screen, filter. 2 *we sift out unsuitable applications:* separate out, filter out, sort out, weed out, get rid of, remove. 3 *sifting through the wreckage:* search, look, examine, inspect, scrutinize, pore over.

sight noun 1 *she has excellent sight:* eyesight, vision, eyes. 2 *her first sight of it:* view, glimpse, glance, look. 3 *historic sights:* landmark, place of interest, monument, spectacle, marvel, wonder.
• verb *one of the helicopters sighted wreckage:* glimpse, catch sight of, see, spot, spy, make out, pick out, notice, observe.

sign noun 1 *a sign of affection:* indication, signal, symptom, pointer, suggestion, intimation, mark, manifestation, demonstration, token. 2 *a sign of things to come:* warning, omen, portent, threat, promise. 3 *signs saying 'danger':* notice, board, placard, signpost. 4 *the dancers were daubed with signs:* symbol, figure, emblem, device, logo, character.
• verb 1 *he signed the letter:* write your name on, autograph, initial, countersign. 2 *the government signed the treaty:* endorse, validate, agree to, approve, ratify, adopt. 3 *he signed his name:* write, inscribe, pen.

S

that you have written it, or to authorize it. **2** recruit a sports player, musician, etc. by signing a contract. **3** use gestures to give information or instructions.
□ **sign language** a system of hand movements and facial expressions used to communicate with people who are deaf. **sign off** end a letter, broadcast, or other message. **sign on 1** commit yourself to a job. **2** Brit. register as unemployed. **sign someone on** employ someone. **sign up** commit yourself to a course, job, etc.
■ **signer** noun.

signal noun **1** a gesture, action, or sound giving information or an instruction. **2** a sign indicating a particular situation. **3** a device that uses lights or a movable arm to tell drivers to stop or beware on a road or railway. **4** an electrical impulse or radio wave that is sent or received. •**verb** (**signals, signalling, signalled**; US spelling **signals, signaling, signaled**) give a signal. •**adjective** noteworthy.
□ **signal box** Brit. a building beside a railway track from which signals and points are controlled.

signatory noun (plural **signatories**) a person who has signed an agreement.

signature noun **1** a person's name written in a distinctive way, used in signing something. **2** a distinctive product or quality by which someone or something can be recognized.
□ **signature tune** a tune announcing a particular television or radio programme.

signet noun (in the past) a small seal used to authorize an official document.

□ **signet ring** a ring with letters or a design set into it.

significance noun **1** importance. **2** the meaning of something.

significant adjective **1** important or large enough to have an effect or be noticed. **2** having a particular or secret meaning.
■ **significantly** adverb.

signify verb (**signifies, signifying, signified**) **1** be a sign of; mean. **2** make a feeling or intention known.
■ **signification** noun.

signing noun **1** Brit. a person who has recently been recruited to a sports team, record company, etc. **2** an event at which an author signs copies of their book. **3** the use of sign language.

signpost noun a sign on a post, giving information such as the direction and distance to a nearby place.

Sikh /seek/ noun a follower of a religion that developed from Hinduism.
■ **Sikhism** noun.

silage /sy-lij/ noun grass or other green crops that are stored in a silo without being dried, used as animal feed in the winter.

silence noun **1** complete lack of sound. **2** a situation in which someone is unwilling to speak or discuss something. •**verb** (**silences, silencing, silenced**) **1** stop someone from speaking. **2** make something silent.

silencer noun a device for reducing the noise made by a gun or exhaust system.

silent adjective **1** without any sound. **2** not speaking or not spoken aloud.
■ **silently** adverb.

silhouette noun a dark shape and outline

THESAURUS

signal noun **1** *a signal to stop:* gesture, sign, wave, cue, indication, warning, prompt, reminder. **2** *a clear signal that we're in trouble:* indication, sign, symptom, hint, pointer, clue, demonstration, evidence, proof.
•**verb 1** *the driver signalled to her:* gesture, sign, indicate, motion, wave, beckon, nod. **2** *they signalled their displeasure:* indicate, show, express, communicate. **3** *his death signals the end of an era:* mark, signify, mean, be a sign of, be evidence of.

significance noun importance, import, consequence, seriousness, gravity, weight, magnitude.
OPPOSITES insignificance.

significant adjective **1** *a significant fact:* notable, noteworthy, remarkable, important, of consequence. **2** *a significant increase:* large, considerable, sizeable, appreciable, conspicuous, obvious, sudden. **3** *a significant look:* meaningful,

expressive, eloquent, suggestive, knowing, telling.
OPPOSITES insignificant.

signify verb mean, denote, designate, represent, symbolize, stand for.

silence noun **1** *the silence of the night:* quietness, quiet, still, stillness, hush, tranquillity, peace. **2** *her silence was answer enough:* failure to speak, dumbness, reticence, taciturnity.
OPPOSITES sound, loquacity.
•**verb 1** *he silenced her with a kiss:* quieten, quiet, hush. **2** *dissidents have been silenced:* gag, muzzle, censor.

silent adjective **1** *the forest was silent:* quiet, still, hushed, noiseless, soundless, inaudible. **2** *the right to remain silent:* speechless, quiet, unspeaking, dumb, mute, taciturn, uncommunicative, tight-lipped. **3** *silent thanks:* unspoken, wordless.
OPPOSITES audible, noisy, spoken.

silhouette noun *silhouettes of aircraft:*

S

seen against a lighter background. • **verb**
(**silhouettes, silhouetting, silhouetted**)
show as a silhouette.

silica noun a hard substance formed from
silicon and oxygen that occurs as quartz
and is found in sandstone and other rocks.

silicon noun a chemical element that is a
semiconductor and is used to make
electronic circuits.
▢ **silicon chip** a microchip.

silicone noun a synthetic substance made
from silicon.

silk noun a fine, soft shiny fibre produced by
silkworms, made into thread or fabric.

silken adjective **1** smooth and shiny like silk.
2 made of silk.

silkworm noun a caterpillar that spins a
silk cocoon from which silk fibre is
obtained.

silky adjective (**silkier, silkiest**) smooth and
shiny like silk.

sill noun a shelf or slab at the foot of a
window or doorway.

silly adjective (**sillier, silliest**) showing a lack
of good judgement or common sense.
■ **silliness** noun.

silo noun (plural **silos**) **1** a tower used to store
grain. **2** a pit or airtight structure for
storing silage. **3** an underground chamber
in which a guided missile is kept ready for
firing.

silt noun fine sand or clay carried by running
water and deposited as a sediment. • **verb**
(**silt up**) fill or block with silt.
■ **silty** adjective.

silver noun **1** a shiny greyish-white precious
metal. **2** a shiny grey-white colour. **3** coins
made from silver or from a metal that
looks like silver. **4** silver dishes, containers,
or cutlery. • **verb** (**silvers, silvering, silvered**)
cover or plate with silver.

▢ **silver birch** a birch tree with silver-grey
bark. **silver jubilee** the twenty-fifth
anniversary of an important event. **silver
medal** a medal awarded for second place in
a race or competition. **silver plate 1** a thin
layer of silver applied as a coating to
another metal. **2** plates, dishes, etc. made
of or plated with silver. **silver wedding** Brit.
the twenty-fifth anniversary of a wedding.
■ **silvery** adjective.

silverfish noun (plural **silverfish**) a small
silvery wingless insect that lives in
buildings.

silverside noun the upper side of a cut of
beef from the outside of the leg.

silversmith noun a person who makes
silver articles.

SIM card noun a small card inside a mobile
phone that stores information such as
details of calls made and received.

simian adjective relating to or like apes or
monkeys. • **noun** an ape or monkey.

similar adjective like something but not
exactly the same.
■ **similarity** noun (plural **similarities**) **similarly**
adverb.

simile /sim-i-li/ noun a word or phrase that
compares one thing to another of a
different kind (e.g. *the family was as solid
as a rock*).

simmer verb (**simmers, simmering,
simmered**) **1** stay or cause to stay just
below boiling point. **2** be in a state of
anger or excitement which you only just
keep under control. **3** (**simmer down**)
become calmer and quieter.

simper verb (**simpers, simpering, simpered**)
smile in a coy and silly way. • **noun** a coy
and silly smile.

simple adjective (**simpler, simplest**) **1** easily

S

outline, contour(s), profile, form, shape.
• **verb** *silhouetted against the window:*
outline, define.

silly adjective **1** *don't be so silly:* foolish,
stupid, scatterbrained, frivolous, inane,
immature, childish, empty-headed; informal
dotty, scatty. **2** *that was a silly thing to do:*
unwise, imprudent, thoughtless, foolish,
stupid, unintelligent, idiotic, rash, reckless,
foolhardy, irresponsible; informal crazy, mad;
Brit. informal daft. **3** *he would worry about
silly things:* trivial, trifling, frivolous,
petty, small, insignificant, unimportant;
informal piffling.
OPPOSITES sensible, serious.

similar adjective **1** *you two are very similar:*
alike, the same; informal much of a
muchness. **2** *northern India and similar
areas:* comparable, like, corresponding,
equivalent.

OPPOSITES different, unlike.
▢ **similar to** like, much the same as,
comparable to.

similarity noun resemblance, likeness,
comparability, correspondence, parallel,
equivalence, uniformity.

simmer verb **1** *the soup was simmering on
the stove:* boil gently, cook gently, bubble.
2 *she was simmering with resentment:*
seethe, fume, smoulder.
▢ **simmer down** calm down, cool off/down.

simple adjective **1** *it's really pretty simple:*
straightforward, easy, uncomplicated,
uninvolved, undemanding, elementary,
child's play. **2** *simple language:* clear, plain,
straightforward, unambiguous,
understandable, comprehensible,
accessible; informal user-friendly. **3** *a simple
white blouse:* plain, unadorned, basic,

understood or done. **2** plain and basic.
3 composed of a single element; not
compound. **4** of very low intelligence.
□ **simple fracture** a fracture of a bone
without any breaking of the skin.

simpleton noun a foolish or unintelligent
person.

simplicity noun the quality of being simple.

simplify verb (**simplifies, simplifying,
simplified**) make something easier to do or
understand.
■ **simplification** noun.

simplistic adjective treating complex issues
as more simple than they really are.
■ **simplistically** adverb.

simply adverb **1** in a simple way. **2** just;
merely. **3** absolutely.

simulacrum /sim-yuu-**lay**-kruhm/ noun
(plural **simulacra** or **simulacrums**) something
that is similar to something else.

simulate verb (**simulates, simulating,
simulated**) **1** imitate the appearance or
nature of. **2** use a computer to create a
model of something or conditions that are
like those in real life. **3** pretend to have or
feel a particular emotion.
■ **simulation** noun **simulator** noun.

simultaneous adjective happening or done
at the same time.
■ **simultaneity** noun **simultaneously** adverb.

> ☑ the ending is -*eous*, not -*ious*:
> simultan*eous*.

sin noun **1** an act that breaks a religious or
moral law. **2** an act that causes strong
disapproval. ●verb (**sins, sinning, sinned**)
commit a sin.

since preposition in the period between a
time in the past and the present.
●**conjunction 1** during or in the time after.
2 because. ●**adverb 1** from the time
mentioned until the present. **2** ago.

sincere adjective (**sincerer, sincerest**) not
pretending anything or deceiving anyone;
genuine and honest.
■ **sincerely** adverb **sincerity** noun.

sine /*rhymes with* line/ noun Maths (in a
right-angled triangle) the ratio of the side
opposite a particular acute angle to the
hypotenuse.

sinecure /**sin**-i-kyoor/ noun a job for which
you are paid but which requires little or no
work.

sine qua non /see-nay kwah **nohn**/ noun a

THESAURUS

unsophisticated, no-frills, classic,
understated, uncluttered, restrained.
4 *simple country people*: unpretentious,
unsophisticated, ordinary, unaffected,
unassuming, natural, straightforward;
N. Amer. cracker-barrel.
OPPOSITES difficult, complex, fancy,
sophisticated.

simplicity noun **1** *the simplicity of the
recipes*: straightforwardness, ease. **2** *the
simplicity of the language*: clarity,
plainness, intelligibility, comprehensibility,
accessibility. **3** *the building's simplicity*:
austerity, plainness, spareness, clean lines.
4 *the simplicity of their lifestyle*: plainness,
modesty, naturalness.
OPPOSITES difficulty, complexity,
adornment, sophistication.

simplify verb make simpler, clarify, put
into words of one syllable, streamline;
informal dumb down.
OPPOSITES complicate.

simply adverb **1** *he always spoke simply and
forcefully*: straightforwardly, directly,
clearly, plainly, lucidly, unambiguously.
2 *she was dressed simply*: plainly, soberly,
unfussily, classically. **3** *they lived simply*:
modestly, plainly, quietly. **4** *they are
welcomed simply because they are rich*:
merely, just, purely, solely, only. **5** *she was
simply delighted*: utterly, absolutely,
completely, positively, just; informal plain.
OPPOSITES confusingly, elaborately.

simulate verb **1** *they simulated pleasure*:
feign, pretend, fake, affect, put on.
2 *simulating conditions in space*: imitate,
reproduce, replicate, duplicate, mimic.

simultaneous adjective concurrent,
happening at the same time,
contemporaneous, coinciding, coincident,
synchronized.
OPPOSITES separate.

simultaneously adverb at the same time,
at one and the same time, at once,
concurrently, (all) together, in unison, in
concert, in chorus.

sin noun **1** *a sin in the eyes of God*: wrong,
act of wickedness, transgression, crime,
offence, misdeed. **2** *the human capacity for
sin*: wickedness, wrongdoing, evil,
immorality, iniquity, vice, crime.
OPPOSITES virtue.
●verb *I have sinned*: transgress, do wrong,
misbehave, err, go astray.

sincere adjective **1** *our sincere gratitude*:
heartfelt, wholehearted, profound, deep,
true, honest. **2** *a sincere person*: honest,
genuine, truthful, direct, frank, candid;
informal straight, on the level; N. Amer. informal
on the up and up.

sincerely adverb genuinely, honestly, really,
truly, truthfully, wholeheartedly, earnestly.

sincerity noun genuineness, honesty,
truthfulness, integrity, directness,
openness, candour.

S

thing that is absolutely necessary.

sinew /**sin**-yoo/ noun a band of strong tissue that joins a muscle to a bone.
■ **sinewy** adjective.

sinful adjective **1** wicked. **2** disgraceful.
■ **sinfully** adverb **sinfulness** noun.

sing verb (**sings**, **singing**, **sang**; past participle **sung**) **1** make musical sounds with your voice; perform a song. **2** make a whistling sound.
□ **sing-song 1** a rising and falling sound in someone's voice. **2** informal an informal gathering for singing.
■ **singer** noun.

singalong noun an informal occasion when people sing together.

Singaporean noun a person from Singapore. • adjective relating to Singapore.

singe verb (**singes**, **singeing**, **singed**) burn the surface of something slightly. • noun a slight burn.

single adjective **1** one only. **2** designed for one person. **3** consisting of one part. **4** taken separately from others. **5** not involved in a romantic or sexual relationship. **6** Brit. (of a ticket) for an outward journey only. • noun **1** a single person or thing. **2** a short record or CD. **3** (**singles**) a game or competition for individual players. • verb (**singles**, **singling**, **singled**) (**single someone/thing out**) choose someone or something from a group for special treatment.
□ **single-breasted** (of a jacket or coat) fastened by one row of buttons at the centre of the front. **single file** a line of people moving one behind another. **single-handed** done without help from other people. **single-minded** determined to concentrate on one particular aim. **single parent** a person bringing up a child or children without a partner.

■ **singly** adverb.

singlet noun Brit. a vest or similar sleeveless garment.

singleton noun a single person or thing.

singular adjective **1** Grammar (of a word or form) referring to just one person or thing. **2** very good or interesting; remarkable. • noun Grammar the singular form of a word.
■ **singularity** noun **singularly** adverb.

Sinhalese /sin-huh-**leez**, sin-uh-**leez**/ noun (plural **Sinhalese**) **1** a member of an Indian people living in Sri Lanka. **2** the language of the Sinhalese. • adjective relating to the Sinhalese.

sinister adjective seeming evil or dangerous.

sink verb (**sinks**, **sinking**, **sank**; past participle **sunk**) **1** go down below the surface of liquid. **2** go or cause to go to the bottom of the sea. **3** move slowly downwards. **4** gradually decrease in amount or strength. **5** (**sink something into**) force something sharp through a surface. **6** (**sink in**) become fully understood. **7** pass into a particular state. **8** (**sink something into**) put money or resources into. • noun a fixed basin with a water supply and a drainage pipe.

sinker noun a weight used to keep a fishing line beneath the water.

sinner noun a person who sins.

Sino- /**sy**-noh/ combining form Chinese; Chinese and ...: *Sino-American*.

sinuous adjective **1** having many curves and turns. **2** moving in a graceful, swaying way.
■ **sinuously** adverb.

sinus /**sy**-nuhss/ noun a hollow space within the bones of the face that connects with the nostrils.

sinusitis noun inflammation of a sinus.

Sioux /soo/ noun (plural **Sioux**) a member of an American Indian people, many of whom

THESAURUS

S

sing verb **1** *he began to sing:* chant, trill, intone, croon, chorus. **2** *the birds were singing:* trill, warble, chirp, chirrup, cheep.

singe verb scorch, burn, sear, char.

singer noun vocalist, songster, songstress, soloist, chorister, cantor.

single adjective **1** *a single red rose:* sole, one, lone, solitary, unaccompanied, alone. **2** *every single word:* individual, separate, distinct. **3** *is she single?* unmarried, unwed, unattached, free, a bachelor, a spinster.
OPPOSITES double, multiple, married.
□ single someone/something out select, pick out, choose, decide on, target, earmark, mark out, separate out, set apart.

singly adverb one by one, one at a time, one after the other, individually, separately.
OPPOSITES together.

sinister adjective **1** *there was a sinister undertone in his words:* menacing, threatening, ominous, forbidding, baleful, frightening, alarming, disturbing, dark. **2** *a sinister motive:* evil, wicked, criminal, nefarious, villainous, base, malicious; informal shady.
OPPOSITES unthreatening, innocent.

sink verb **1** *the coffin sank below the waves:* submerge, founder, go down, be engulfed, drop, fall, descend. **2** *they sank their ships:* scuttle; Brit. scupper. **3** *the sun was sinking:* set, go down. **4** *Loretta sank into an armchair:* lower yourself, flop, collapse, drop, slump; informal plonk yourself. **5** *sink the pots into the ground:* embed, insert, drive, plant.
OPPOSITES float, rise.

live in South Dakota.

sip verb (**sips**, **sipping**, **sipped**) drink something in small mouthfuls. •**noun** a small mouthful of liquid.

siphon or **syphon** noun a tube used to move liquid from one container to another, using air pressure to maintain the flow. •**verb 1** draw off or move liquid by means of a siphon. **2** (**siphon something off**) take small amounts of money over a period of time.

sir noun **1** a polite form of address to a man. **2** used as a title for a knight or baronet.

sire noun **1** the male parent of an animal. **2** literary a father. **3** old use a respectful form of address to a king. •**verb** (**sires**, **siring**, **sired**) be the male parent of.

siren noun **1** a device that makes a loud prolonged warning sound. **2** Greek Mythology each of a group of creatures who were part woman, part bird, whose singing lured sailors on to rocks. **3** a woman whose attractiveness is regarded as dangerous to men.

sirloin noun the best part of a loin of beef.

sirocco /si-**rok**-koh/ noun (plural **siroccos**) a hot wind that blows from Africa to southern Europe.

sirup US spelling of **syrup**.

sisal /**sy**-z'l/ noun fibre made from the leaves of a tropical Mexican plant, used for ropes or matting.

sissy noun (plural **sissies**) informal a weak or cowardly person.

sister noun **1** a woman or girl in relation to other children of her parents. **2** a female friend or colleague. **3** a member of a religious order of women. **4** Brit. a senior female nurse.
□ **sister-in-law** (plural **sisters-in-law**) **1** the sister of a person's wife or husband. **2** the wife of a person's brother or brother-in-law.
■ **sisterly** adjective.

sisterhood noun **1** the relationship between sisters. **2** a bond of friendship and understanding between women. **3** a group

of women linked by a shared interest.

sit verb (**sits**, **sitting**, **sat**) **1** rest your weight on your bottom with your back upright. **2** be in a particular position or state. **3** serve as a member of a council, jury, or other official body. **4** (of a parliament, committee, or court of law) be carrying on its business. **5** Brit. take an exam. **6** (**sit for**) pose for an artist or photographer.
□ **sit-in** the occupation of a college or workplace as a form of protest.

> ❗ use **sitting** rather than **sat** with the verb 'to be': say *we were sitting there for hours* rather than *we were sat there for hours*.

sitar noun an Indian lute with a long neck.

sitcom noun a situation comedy.

site noun **1** a place where something is located or happens. **2** a website. •**verb** (**sites**, **siting**, **sited**) build or establish something in a particular place.

> ❗ don't confuse **site** with **sight**, which means 'the ability to see'.

sitter noun **1** a person who sits for a portrait. **2** a person who looks after children, pets, or a house while the parents or owners are away.

sitting noun **1** a period of time during which a court of law, committee, or parliament is carrying on its business. **2** a period of time when a group of people are served a meal. **3** a period of posing for a portrait.
□ **sitting duck** informal a person or thing that is easy to attack. **sitting room** a room for sitting and relaxing in. **sitting tenant** Brit. a tenant who has the legal right to remain living in a property.

situate verb (**situates**, **situating**, **situated**) **1** put in a particular place. **2** (**be situated**) be in a particular set of circumstances.

situation noun **1** a set of circumstances. **2** the location and surroundings of a place. **3** a job.
□ **situation comedy** a comedy series in

THESAURUS

sip verb *she sipped her martini:* drink, taste, sample, nip.
•**noun** *have a sip:* mouthful, swallow, drink, drop, dram, nip; informal swig.

sit verb **1** *you'd better sit down:* take a seat, be seated, perch, ensconce yourself, flop; informal take the load off your feet; Brit. informal take a pew. **2** *she sat the package on the table:* put, place, set, lay, deposit, rest, stand; informal stick, park. **3** *the committee sits on Saturday:* be in session, meet, be convened. **4** *she sits on the tribunal:* serve on, have a seat on, be a member of.

OPPOSITES stand.

site noun *the site of the battle:* location, place, position, situation, locality, whereabouts.
•**verb** *sited in an industrial area:* place, put, position, situate, locate.

situation noun **1** *their financial situation:* circumstances, state of affairs, state, condition. **2** *I'll fill you in on the situation:* the facts, how things stand, the lie of the land, what's going on; Brit. the state of play; N. Amer. the lay of the land; informal the score. **3** *the hotel's pleasant situation:* location,

S

which the same characters are involved in various amusing situations.

■ **situational** adjective.

six cardinal number **1** one more than five; 6. (Roman numeral: **vi** or **VI**.) **2** Cricket a hit that reaches the boundary without first hitting the ground, scoring six runs.
□ **at sixes and sevens** in a state of confusion. **knock someone for six** Brit. informal take someone completely by surprise.

sixpence noun Brit. (in the past) a coin worth six old pence (2½ p).

sixteen cardinal number one more than fifteen; 16. (Roman numeral: **xvi** or **XVI**.)
■ **sixteenth** ordinal number.

sixth ordinal number **1** being number six in a sequence; 6th. **2** (**a sixth** or **one sixth**) each of six equal parts of something.
□ **sixth-form college** Brit. a college for students aged 16 to 18. **sixth sense** a supposed ability to know things by intuition rather than using your sight, hearing, etc.

sixty cardinal number (plural **sixties**) ten more than fifty; 60. (Roman numeral: **lx** or **LX**.)
■ **sixtieth** ordinal number.

size¹ noun **1** the overall measurements or extent of something. **2** each of the series of standard measurements in which clothes, shoes, and other goods are made.
• verb (**sizes, sizing, sized**) **1** group things according to size. **2** (**size someone/thing up**) informal form a judgement of a person or thing.

size² noun a sticky solution used to glaze paper, stiffen textiles, and prepare plastered walls for decoration. • verb (**sizes, sizing, sized**) treat with size.

sizeable or **sizable** adjective fairly large.

sizzle verb (**sizzles, sizzling, sizzled**) **1** (of food) make a hissing sound when being fried. **2** (**sizzling**) informal very hot or exciting.

skate¹ noun an ice skate or roller skate.
• verb (**skates, skating, skated**) **1** move on skates. **2** (**skate over** or **round**) pass over or refer only briefly to.
■ **skater** noun.

skate² noun (plural **skate** or **skates**) an edible sea fish with a diamond-shaped body.

skateboard noun a short narrow board fitted with two small wheels at either end, on which a person can ride.
■ **skateboarder** noun **skateboarding** noun.

skedaddle verb (**skedaddles, skedaddling, skedaddled**) informal leave quickly.

skein noun a length of yarn held in a loose coil or knot.

skeletal adjective **1** having to do with a skeleton. **2** very thin.

skeleton noun **1** a framework of bone or cartilage supporting or containing the body of an animal. **2** a supporting framework or structure. • adjective referring to an essential or minimum number of people: *a skeleton staff.*
□ **skeleton in the cupboard** a shocking or embarrassing fact that someone wishes to keep secret. **skeleton key** a key designed to fit a number of locks.

skeptic US spelling of **SCEPTIC**.

skeptical US spelling of **SCEPTICAL**.

sketch noun **1** a rough drawing or painting. **2** a short humorous scene in a comedy show. **3** a brief written or spoken account. • verb **1** make a sketch of. **2** give a brief account of.

sketchbook noun a pad of drawing paper for sketching on.

sketchy adjective (**sketchier, sketchiest**) not thorough or detailed; rough.
■ **sketchily** adverb.

skew verb **1** suddenly change direction or move at an angle. **2** make something biased or distorted. • noun a bias towards one particular group or subject.
□ **skew-whiff** Brit. informal not straight; askew.

skewbald adjective (of a horse) having patches of white and brown.

skewer noun a long piece of metal or wood used for holding pieces of food together during cooking. • verb (**skewers, skewering, skewered**) hold or pierce with a pin or skewer.

ski noun (plural **skis**) each of a pair of long, narrow pieces of wood, metal, or plastic, attached to boots for travelling over snow. • verb (**skis, skiing, skied**) travel on skis.
□ **ski jump** a steep slope levelling off

S

THESAURUS

position, spot, site, setting, environment.

size noun dimensions, measurements, proportions, magnitude, largeness, area, expanse, breadth, width, length, height, depth.
□ **size someone/something up** (informal) assess, appraise, get the measure of, judge, take stock of, evaluate; Brit. informal suss out.

sizeable adjective large, substantial,

considerable, respectable, significant, goodly.
OPPOSITES small.

sizzle verb crackle, frizzle, sputter, hiss, spit.

sketch noun *a sketch of the proposed design:* drawing, outline, draft, diagram, design, plan; informal rough.
• verb *he sketched the garden:* draw, make a

before a sharp drop to allow a skier to leap through the air. **ski lift** a system of moving seats attached to an overhead cable, used for taking skiers to the top of a run.
■ **skier** noun.

> ☑ the plural of the noun is **skis**, without an e.

skid verb (**skids, skidding, skidded**) 1 (of a vehicle) slide sideways in an uncontrolled way. 2 slip; slide. •noun 1 an act of skidding. 2 a runner attached to the underside of a helicopter and some other aircraft.
□ **skid row** N. Amer. informal a run-down part of a town or city where homeless people and alcoholics live.

skiff noun a light rowing boat.

skilful (US spelling **skillful**) **adjective** having or showing skill.
■ **skilfully** adverb.

> ☑ there is only one *l* in the middle: ski/ful. The spelling with two *l*s is American.

skill noun 1 the ability to do something well. 2 a particular ability.

skilled adjective 1 having or showing skill. 2 (of work) needing special abilities or training.

skillet noun N. Amer. a frying pan.

skim verb (**skims, skimming, skimmed**) 1 remove a substance from the surface of a liquid. 2 move quickly and lightly over a surface or through the air. 3 read through quickly. 4 (**skim over**) deal with briefly.
□ **skimmed milk** milk from which the cream has been removed.

skimp verb spend less money or use less of something than is really needed in an attempt to economize.

skimpy adjective (**skimpier, skimpiest**) 1 not large enough in amount or size. 2 (of clothes) short and revealing.

skin noun 1 the thin layer of tissue forming the outer covering of the body. 2 the skin of a dead animal used for clothing or other items. 3 the peel or outer layer of a fruit or vegetable. •verb (**skins, skinning, skinned**) 1 remove the skin from. 2 graze a part of your body.
□ **by the skin of your teeth** only just. **have a thick skin** be unaffected by criticism or insults. **skin-deep** not deep or lasting; superficial. **skin-diving** swimming underwater without a diving suit, using an aqualung and flippers.

skinflint noun informal a very mean person.

skinhead noun a young person of a group with very short shaved hair.

skinny adjective (**skinnier, skinniest**) 1 (of a person) very thin. 2 (of a garment) tight-fitting.

skint adjective Brit. informal having little or no money.

skintight adjective (of a garment) very tight-fitting.

skip¹ verb (**skips, skipping, skipped**) 1 move along lightly, stepping from one foot to the other with a little jump. 2 Brit. jump repeatedly over a rope turned over the head and under the feet. 3 leave out or move quickly over. 4 fail to attend or deal with. •noun a skipping movement.

skip² noun Brit. a large open-topped container for holding and carrying away large unwanted items, builders' rubbish, etc.

skipper informal noun 1 the captain of a ship, boat, or aircraft. 2 the captain of a sports team. •verb (**skippers, skippering, skippered**) be captain of.

skirl noun a shrill sound made by bagpipes. •verb make such a sound.

skirmish noun a short period of fighting. •verb take part in a skirmish.

skirt noun a woman's garment that hangs

THESAURUS

drawing of, pencil, rough out, outline.

skilful adjective expert, accomplished, skilled, masterly, talented, deft, dexterous, handy; informal mean, crack, ace; N. Amer. informal crackerjack.
OPPOSITES incompetent.

skill noun expertise, accomplishment, skilfulness, mastery, talent, deftness, dexterity, prowess, competence, artistry.
OPPOSITES incompetence.

skim verb 1 *skim off the fat:* remove, scoop off, separate. 2 *the boat skimmed over the water:* glide, move lightly, slide, sail, skate. 3 *she skimmed through the newspaper:* glance, flick, flip, leaf, thumb, scan, run your eye over.

skin noun 1 *leopard skins:* hide, pelt, fleece.

2 *a banana skin:* peel, rind. 3 *milk with a skin on it:* film, layer, membrane, crust, covering, coating.
•verb 1 *skin the tomatoes:* peel, pare. 2 *he skinned his knee:* graze, scrape, abrade, bark, rub raw, chafe.

skinny adjective thin, underweight, scrawny, bony, gaunt, emaciated, skeletal, wasted, pinched, spindly, gangly; informal anorexic.

skip verb 1 *skipping down the path:* caper, prance, trip, dance, bound, bounce, gambol. 2 *we skipped the boring stuff:* omit, leave out, miss out, dispense with, pass over, skim over, disregard; informal give something a miss.

skirt verb 1 *he skirted the city:* go round, walk round, circle. 2 *the fields that skirt* from the waist and surrounds the lower body and legs. • verb 1 go round or past the edge of. 2 (also **skirt round**) avoid dealing with.

skirting or **skirting board** noun Brit. a wooden board running along the base of the walls of a room.

skit noun a short comedy sketch that makes fun of something by imitating it.

skitter verb (**skitters, skittering, skittered**) move lightly and quickly.

skittish adjective 1 (of a horse) nervous and tending to shy. 2 lively or changeable.
■ **skittishly** adverb.

skittle noun 1 (**skittles**) a game played with wooden pins set up to be bowled down with a ball. 2 a pin used in the game of skittles.

skive verb (**skives, skiving, skived**) Brit. informal avoid work or a duty by staying away or leaving early.
■ **skiver** noun.

skivvy noun (plural **skivvies**) Brit. informal a female domestic servant.

skua noun a large seabird like a gull.

skulduggery or **skullduggery** noun underhand behaviour.

skulk verb hide or move around in a secretive way.

skull noun the bony framework that surrounds and protects the brain.
□ **skull and crossbones** a picture of a skull with two thigh bones crossed below it, used in the past by pirates and now as a sign of danger.

skullcap noun a small close-fitting cap without a peak.

skunk noun an animal with black and white stripes that can spray foul-smelling liquid at attackers.

sky noun (plural **skies**) the region of the upper atmosphere seen from the earth.

skydiving noun the sport of jumping from an aircraft and performing movements in the air before landing by parachute.
■ **skydiver** noun.

skylark noun a lark that sings while flying.
• verb behave in a playful and mischievous way.

skylight noun a window set in a roof.

skyline noun an outline of land and buildings seen against the sky.

skyrocket verb (**skyrockets, skyrocketing, skyrocketed**) informal (of a price or amount) increase rapidly.

skyscraper noun a very tall building.

slab noun 1 a large, thick, flat piece of stone or concrete. 2 a thick slice of cake, bread, etc.

slack adjective 1 not taut or held tightly. 2 (of business or trade) quiet. 3 careless or lazy. 4 (of a tide) between the ebb and the flow. • noun 1 the part of a rope or line which is not held taut. 2 (**slacks**) casual trousers. • verb 1 (**slack off** or **up**) become slower or less intense. 2 Brit. informal work slowly or lazily.
■ **slacker** noun **slackly** adverb **slackness** noun.

slacken verb 1 make or become less active or intense. 2 make or become less tight.

slag noun 1 stony waste matter left when metal has been separated from ore by smelting or refining. 2 Brit. informal, disapproving a woman who has many sexual partners.
• verb (**slags, slagging, slagged**) (**slag someone/thing off**) Brit. informal criticize someone or something rudely.
□ **slag heap** a mound of waste material from a mine.

slain past participle of SLAY.

slake verb (**slakes, slaking, slaked**) satisfy a desire, thirst, etc.

slalom /slah-luhm/ noun a skiing or canoeing race following a winding course marked out by poles.

slam verb (**slams, slamming, slammed**) 1 shut forcefully and loudly. 2 put down with great force. 3 hit a ball with great force. 4 informal criticize severely. • noun a loud bang caused when a door is slammed.

slander noun the crime of saying something untrue that harms a person's reputation.
• verb (**slanders, slandering, slandered**) say something untrue and damaging about.
■ **slanderous** adjective.

slang noun very informal words and phrases that are more common in speech than in

S

THESAURUS

the park: border, edge, flank, line. 3 *he carefully skirted round the subject:* avoid, evade, sidestep, dodge, pass over, gloss over; informal duck; Austral./NZ informal duck-shove.

slab noun piece, block, hunk, chunk, lump, cake, tablet, brick, panel, plate, sheet.

slack adjective 1 *the rope went slack:* limp, loose. 2 *slack skin:* sagging, flabby, flaccid, loose, saggy. 3 *business is slack:* sluggish,

slow, quiet, slow-moving, flat, depressed, stagnant. 4 *slack procedure:* lax, negligent, careless, slapdash, slipshod; informal sloppy.
OPPOSITES taut, firm, busy, strict.
• verb (Brit. informal) *no slacking!* idle, shirk, be lazy, be indolent, waste time, lounge about; Brit. informal skive; N. Amer. informal goof off.

slam verb 1 *he slammed the door:* bang, shut with a bang. 2 *the car slammed into a lamp post:* crash, smash, plough, run, bump, writing and are used by a particular group of people.

□ **slanging match** Brit. an angry argument in which people insult each other.

■ **slangy** adjective.

slant verb **1** slope or lean. **2** present information from a particular point of view. •noun **1** a sloping position. **2** a point of view.

slap verb (**slaps, slapping, slapped**) **1** hit with the palm of your hand or a flat object. **2** hit against a surface with a slapping sound. **3** (**slap something on**) put something on a surface quickly or carelessly. •noun an act or sound of slapping. •adverb (also **slap bang**) informal suddenly and with great force.

□ **slap-up** Brit. informal (of a meal) large and extravagant.

slapdash adjective done too hurriedly and carelessly.

slapstick noun comedy consisting of deliberately clumsy actions and embarrassing situations.

slash verb **1** cut with a violent sweeping movement. **2** informal greatly reduce a price or quantity. •noun **1** a cut made with a wide sweeping stroke. **2** a slanting stroke (/) used between alternatives and in fractions and ratios.

slat noun each of a series of thin, narrow pieces of wood or other material, arranged so as to overlap or fit into each other.

■ **slatted** adjective.

slate noun a dark grey rock that is easily split into smooth, flat plates, used in building and in the past for writing on. •verb (**slates, slating, slated**) Brit. informal severely criticize.

slather verb (**slathers, slathering, slathered**) informal spread or smear thickly over.

slattern noun old use a dirty, untidy woman.

■ **slatternly** adjective.

slaughter noun **1** the killing of farm animals for food. **2** the killing of a large number of people in a cruel or violent way. •verb (**slaughters, slaughtering, slaughtered**) **1** kill animals for food. **2** kill a number of people in a cruel or violent way.

slaughterhouse noun a place where animals are killed for food.

Slav /slahv/ noun a member of a group of peoples in central and eastern Europe.

■ **Slavic** adjective.

slave noun **1** (in the past) a person who was the legal property of another and was forced to obey them. **2** a person who is strongly influenced or controlled by something. •verb (**slaves, slaving, slaved**) work very hard.

□ **slave-driver** informal a person who makes other people work very hard. **slave labour** very demanding work that is very badly paid.

slaver /sla-ver, slay-ver/ verb (**slavers, slavering, slavered**) let saliva run from the mouth. •noun saliva running from the mouth.

slavery noun **1** the state of being a slave. **2** the practice or system of owning slaves.

slavish adjective showing no attempt to be original.

■ **slavishly** adverb.

slay verb (**slays, slaying, slew**; past participle **slain**) old use or N. Amer. violently kill.

sleaze noun informal immoral or dishonest behaviour.

THESAURUS

collide with, hit, strike, ram; N. Amer. impact.

slant verb **1** *the floor slanted:* slope, tilt, incline, be at an angle, tip, lean, dip, pitch, shelve, list, bank. **2** *their findings were slanted in our favour:* bias, distort, twist, skew, weight.
•noun **1** *the slant of the roof:* slope, incline, tilt, gradient, pitch, angle, camber. **2** *a feminist slant:* point of view, viewpoint, standpoint, stance, angle, perspective, approach, view, attitude, position, bias.

slap *he slapped her hard:* smack, strike, hit, cuff, clip, spank; informal whack.
•noun *a slap across the face:* smack, blow, cuff, clip, spank; informal whack.

slash verb **1** *her tyres had been slashed:* cut, gash, slit, lacerate, knife. **2** (informal) *the company slashed prices:* reduce, cut, lower, bring down, mark down.
•noun *a slash across his temple:* cut, gash, slit, laceration, incision, wound.

slaughter verb **1** *the cattle were slaughtered:* kill, butcher, cull, put down. **2** *civilians are being slaughtered:* massacre, murder, butcher, kill, exterminate, wipe out, put to death, execute; literary slay.
•noun *a scene of slaughter:* massacre, (mass) murder, (mass) killing, (mass) execution, extermination, carnage, bloodshed, bloodletting, bloodbath; literary slaying.

slave noun *the work was done by slaves:* servant, lackey, drudge; Brit. informal skivvy, dogsbody; historical serf, vassal.
OPPOSITES freeman, master.
•verb *we slaved away:* toil, labour, sweat, work like a Trojan/dog, work your fingers to the bone; informal kill yourself, sweat blood, slog away; Brit. informal graft.

slavery noun enslavement, servitude, serfdom, bondage, captivity.
OPPOSITES freedom.

S

sleazy adjective (**sleazier**, **sleaziest**)
1 immoral or dishonest. **2** (of a place) dirty and seedy.

sled noun & verb (**sleds**, **sledding**, **sledded**)
N. Amer. = **SLEDGE**.

sledge noun **1** a vehicle on runners for travelling over snow or ice, sometimes pulled by dogs. **2** Brit. a toboggan. • verb (**sledges**, **sledging**, **sledged**) ride or carry on a sledge.

sledgehammer noun a large, heavy hammer.

sleek adjective **1** smooth and glossy. **2** having a wealthy and smart appearance. **3** elegant and streamlined.
■ **sleekly** adverb.

sleep noun a condition of rest in which the eyes are closed, the muscles are relaxed, and the mind is unconscious. • verb (**sleeps**, **sleeping**, **slept**) **1** be asleep. **2** (**sleep in**) remain asleep or in bed later than usual in the morning. **3** provide a particular number of people with beds. **4** (**sleep with**) have sex or be involved in a sexual relationship with. **5** (**sleep around**) have many sexual partners.
□ **put something to sleep** kill an animal painlessly. **sleeping bag** a warm padded bag for sleeping in when camping or travelling. **sleeping car** a railway carriage fitted with beds or berths. **sleeping partner** Brit. a partner who puts money into a business but is not involved in running it. **sleeping policeman** Brit. a hump in the road for slowing down traffic.
■ **sleepless** adjective.

sleeper noun **1** Brit. each of the wooden supports on which a railway track rests. **2** Brit. a ring or bar worn in a pierced ear to keep the hole from closing. **3** a train carrying sleeping cars.

sleepover noun a night spent by children at another person's house.

sleepwalk verb walk around while asleep.
■ **sleepwalker** noun.

sleepy adjective (**sleepier**, **sleepiest**) **1** ready for, or needing, sleep. **2** (of a place) without much activity.
■ **sleepily** adverb **sleepiness** noun.

sleet noun rain containing some ice, or snow melting as it falls. • verb (**it sleets**, **it is sleeting**, **it sleeted**) sleet falls.

sleeve noun **1** the part of a garment covering a person's arm. **2** a protective cover for a record. **3** a tube fitting over a rod or smaller tube.
□ **up your sleeve** kept secret and ready for use when needed.
■ **sleeveless** adjective.

sleigh noun a sledge pulled by horses or reindeer.

sleight /rhymes with slight/ noun (**sleight of hand**) **1** skilful use of the hands when performing magic tricks. **2** skilful deception.

slender adjective (**slenderer**, **slenderest**) **1** gracefully thin. **2** barely enough.

slept past and past participle of **SLEEP**.

sleuth /rhymes with truth/ noun informal a detective.
■ **sleuthing** noun.

slew¹ verb turn or slide violently or uncontrollably.

slew² past of **SLAY**.

slice noun **1** a thin, broad piece of food cut from a larger portion. **2** a portion or share. **3** a kitchen implement with a broad, flat blade for lifting cake, fish, etc. **4** (in sports) a sliced stroke or shot. • verb (**slices**,

THESAURUS

sleazy adjective **1** *sleazy politicians*: corrupt, immoral. **2** *a sleazy bar*: squalid, seedy, seamy, sordid, insalubrious.
OPPOSITES honest, reputable, upmarket.

sleek adjective **1** *his sleek dark hair*: smooth, glossy, shiny, shining, lustrous, silken, silky. **2** *the car's sleek lines*: streamlined, elegant, graceful.
OPPOSITES scruffy, crude.

sleep noun nap, doze, siesta, catnap; informal snooze, forty winks, shut-eye; Brit. informal kip; literary slumber.
OPPOSITES wakefulness.
• verb be asleep, doze, take a siesta, take a nap, catnap; informal snooze, get some shut-eye; Brit. informal kip; N. Amer. informal catch some Zs; literary slumber.
OPPOSITES wake up.
□ **go to sleep fall asleep**, get to sleep; informal drop off, nod off, drift off, crash out, flake out; N. Amer. informal sack out.

sleepy adjective **1** *she felt very sleepy*: drowsy, tired, somnolent, heavy-eyed; informal dopey. **2** *a sleepy little village*: quiet, peaceful, tranquil, placid, slow-moving, dull, boring.
OPPOSITES awake, alert.

slender adjective **1** *her tall, slender figure*: slim, lean, willowy, svelte, lissom, graceful, slight, thin, skinny. **2** *slender evidence*: meagre, limited, slight, scanty, scant, sparse, flimsy, insubstantial. **3** *the chances seemed slender*: faint, remote, tenuous, fragile, slim.
OPPOSITES plump, strong.

slice noun **1** *a slice of cake*: piece, portion, slab, wedge, rasher, sliver, wafer. **2** *a huge slice of public spending*: share, part, portion, tranche, percentage, proportion, allocation.
• verb *slice the cheese thinly*: cut, carve, divide.

S

slicing, sliced) **1** cut into slices. **2** cut with something sharp. **3** (in sport) hit the ball so that it spins or curves away to the side.

slick adjective **1** impressively smooth and efficient. **2** self-confident but insincere. **3** (of a surface) smooth, glossy, or slippery. •noun a smooth patch of oil. •verb make hair smooth and glossy with water, oil, or cream.
■ **slickly** adverb.

slide verb (**slides, sliding, slid**) **1** move along a smooth surface while remaining in contact with it. **2** move smoothly, quickly, or without being noticed. **3** become gradually lower or worse. •noun **1** a structure with a smooth sloping surface for children to slide down. **2** an act of sliding. **3** a rectangular piece of glass which you place an object on to look at it through a microscope. **4** a small piece of photographic film which you view using a projector.
□ **slide rule** a ruler with a sliding central strip, used for making calculations quickly. **sliding scale** a scale of fees, wages, etc. that varies according to some other factor.

slight adjective **1** small in degree. **2** not sturdy or strongly built. **3** lacking depth; trivial. •verb insult someone by treating them without proper respect or attention. •noun an insult.
■ **slightly** adverb.

slim adjective (**slimmer, slimmest**) **1** gracefully thin. **2** small in width and long and narrow in shape. **3** very small: *a slim chance.* •verb (**slims, slimming, slimmed**) Brit. make or become thinner.
■ **slimmer** noun.

slime noun an unpleasantly moist, soft, and slippery substance.

slimy adjective (**slimier, slimiest**) **1** like or covered by slime. **2** informal polite and flattering in a way that is not sincere.

sling noun **1** a loop of fabric used to support or raise a hanging weight. **2** a strap or loop used to hurl small missiles. •verb (**slings, slinging, slung**) **1** hang or carry with a sling or strap. **2** informal throw.

slingback noun a shoe held in place by a strap around the ankle.

slingshot noun a hand-held catapult.

slink verb (**slinks, slinking, slunk**) move quietly in a secretive way.

slinky adjective (**slinkier, slinkiest**) informal (of a woman's garment) close-fitting and sexy.

slip[1] verb (**slips, slipping, slipped**) **1** lose your balance and slide for a short distance. **2** accidentally slide out of position or from

THESAURUS

slick adjective **1** *a slick advertising campaign:* efficient, smooth, smooth-running, polished, well organized, well run, streamlined. **2** *a slick salesman:* glib, polished, assured, self-assured, smooth-talking, plausible; informal smarmy.
•verb *his hair was slicked down:* smooth, plaster, sleek, grease, oil, gel.

slide verb glide, slip, slither, skim, skate, skid, slew.

slight adjective **1** *the chance of success is slight:* small, tiny, minute, negligible, insignificant, minimal, remote, slim, faint. **2** *Elizabeth's slight figure:* slim, slender, delicate, dainty, fragile.
OPPOSITES good, plump.
•verb *he had been slighted:* insult, snub, rebuff, spurn, give someone the cold shoulder, cut (dead), scorn.
OPPOSITES respect.
•noun *an unintended slight:* insult, affront, snub, rebuff; informal put-down.
OPPOSITES compliment.

slightly adverb a little, a bit, somewhat, faintly, vaguely, a shade.
OPPOSITES very.

slim adjective **1** *tall and slim:* slender, lean, thin, willowy, sylphlike, svelte, lissom, trim. **2** *a slim silver bracelet:* narrow, slender. **3** *a slim chance:* slight, small, slender, faint, poor, remote.
OPPOSITES plump, wide, good.

•verb *I'm trying to slim:* lose weight, get into shape; N. Amer. slenderize.
OPPOSITES put on weight.

slimy adjective slippery, slithery, greasy; informal slippy, gloopy.

slink verb creep, sneak, steal, slip, slide, sidle, tiptoe.

sling verb **1** *a hammock was slung between two trees:* hang, suspend, string, swing. **2** (informal) *she slung her jacket on the sofa:* throw, toss, fling, hurl, cast, pitch, lob, flip; informal chuck, heave, bung.

slip verb **1** *she slipped on the ice:* slide, skid, slither, fall (over), lose your balance, tumble. **2** *the envelope slipped through Luke's fingers:* fall, drop, slide. **3** *we slipped out by a back door:* creep, steal, sneak, slide, sidle, slope, slink, tiptoe. **4** *she slipped the map into her pocket:* put, tuck, shove; informal pop, stick, stuff.
•noun **1** *a single slip could send them plummeting down:* false step, slide, skid, fall, tumble. **2** *a careless slip:* mistake, error, blunder, gaffe, oversight, omission, lapse; informal slip-up, boo-boo, howler; Brit. informal boob, clanger, bloomer; N. Amer. informal goof, blooper.
□ **slip up** (informal) make a mistake, blunder, get something wrong, make an error, err; informal make a boo-boo; Brit. informal boob, drop a clanger; N. Amer. informal goof up.

S

someone's grasp. **3** fail to grip a surface. **4** get gradually worse. **5** (usu. **slip up**) make a careless mistake. **6** move or place quietly, quickly, or secretly. **7** get free from. • noun **1** an act of slipping. **2** a minor or careless mistake. **3** a loose-fitting short petticoat. **4** Cricket a fielding position close behind the batsman to one side. □ slip knot a knot that can be undone by a pull, or that can slide along the rope on which it is tied. slip-on (of shoes or clothes) having no fastenings. slipped disc a displaced disc in the spine that presses on nearby nerves and causes pain. slip road Brit. a road entering or leaving a motorway or dual carriageway. ■ slippage noun.

slip² noun **1** a small piece of paper. **2** a cutting from a plant.

slipper noun a comfortable slip-on shoe worn indoors.

slippery adjective **1** difficult to hold firmly or stand on through being smooth, wet, or slimy. **2** (of a person) difficult to pin down. ■ slipperiness noun.

slippy adjective (**slippier**, **slippiest**) informal slippery.

slipshod adjective careless, thoughtless, or disorganized.

slipstream noun **1** a current of air or water driven back by a propeller or jet engine. **2** the partial vacuum created in the wake of a moving vehicle.

slipway noun a slope leading into water, used for launching and landing boats and ships.

slit noun a long, narrow cut or opening. • verb (**slits**, **slitting**, **slit**) make a slit in.

slither verb (**slithers**, **slithering**, **slithered**) **1** move smoothly over a surface with a twisting motion. **2** slide unsteadily on a loose or slippery surface. • noun a slithering movement. ■ slithery adjective.

sliver noun a small, narrow, sharp piece cut or split off a larger piece.

slob Brit. informal noun a lazy, untidy person. • verb (**slobs**, **slobbing**, **slobbed**) behave in a lazy, untidy way.

slobber verb (**slobbers**, **slobbering**, **slobbered**) have saliva dripping from the mouth. • noun saliva dripping from the mouth. ■ slobbery adjective.

sloe noun the small bluish-black fruit of the blackthorn.

slog verb (**slogs**, **slogging**, **slogged**) **1** work hard over a period of time. **2** move with difficulty or effort. **3** hit forcefully. **4** (**slog it out**) fight or compete fiercely. • noun a period of difficult, tiring work or travelling.

slogan noun a short, memorable phrase used in advertising or associated with a political group.

sloop noun a type of sailing boat with one mast.

slop verb (**slops**, **slopping**, **slopped**) **1** (of a liquid) spill over the edge of a container. **2** (**slop about** or **around**) Brit. informal spend time relaxing in casual or scruffy clothes. • noun (**slops**) **1** waste liquid that has to be emptied by hand. **2** unappetizing semi-liquid food.

slope noun **1** a surface with one end at a higher level than another. **2** a part of the side of a hill or mountain. • verb (**slopes**, **sloping**, **sloped**) **1** slant up or down. **2** (**slope off**) informal leave without attracting attention.

sloppy adjective (**sloppier**, **sloppiest**) **1** careless and disorganized. **2** containing too much liquid. **3** too sentimental. ■ sloppily adverb sloppiness noun.

slosh verb **1** (of liquid in a container) move around with a splashing sound. **2** move through liquid with a splashing sound.

---

slippery adjective **1** *the roads are slippery:* slithery, greasy, oily, icy, glassy, smooth, slimy, wet; informal slippy. **2** *a slippery customer:* sneaky, sly, devious, crafty, cunning, tricky, evasive, scheming, unreliable, untrustworthy; N. Amer. snide; informal shady, shifty; Brit. informal dodgy; Austral./NZ informal shonky.

slit noun **1** *three diagonal slits:* cut, incision, split, slash, gash. **2** *a slit in the curtains:* opening, gap, chink, crack, aperture, slot. • verb *he threatened to slit her throat:* cut, slash, split open, slice open.

slogan noun catchphrase, catchline, motto, jingle; N. Amer. informal tag line.

slope noun *the slope of the roof:* tilt, pitch, slant, angle, gradient, incline, inclination, fall, camber; N. Amer. grade. • verb *the garden sloped down to a stream:* tilt, slant, incline, lean, drop/fall away, descend, shelve, camber, rise, ascend, climb.

sloping adjective slanting, leaning, inclined, angled, cambered, tilted. OPPOSITES level.

sloppy adjective **1** *sloppy chicken curry:* runny, watery, liquid, mushy; informal gloopy. **2** *their defending was sloppy:* careless, slapdash, slipshod, untidy, slack, slovenly; informal slap-happy. **3** *sloppy letters:* sentimental, mawkish, romantic; informal slushy, schmaltzy; Brit. informal soppy; N. Amer. informal cornball, sappy, hokey.

3 pour liquid clumsily.

sloshed adjective informal drunk.

slot noun **1** a long, narrow opening into which something may be inserted. **2** a place in an arrangement or scheme. •**verb** (**slots, slotting, slotted**) **1** place into a slot. **2** (**slot in** or **into**) fit easily into a new role or situation.
□ **slot machine** a fruit machine or (Brit.) vending machine.

sloth /slohth/ noun **1** laziness. **2** a slow-moving animal that hangs upside down.
■ **slothful** adjective.

slouch verb stand, move, or sit in a lazy, drooping way. •**noun** a lazy, drooping posture.
□ **be no slouch** informal be fast or good at something.

slough[1] /rhymes with plough/ noun **1** a swamp. **2** a situation without progress or activity.

slough[2] /rhymes with rough/ verb (of an animal) cast off an old skin.

Slovakian (also **Slovak**) noun a person from Slovakia. •**adjective** relating to Slovakia.

Slovene /sloh-veen/ noun **1** a person from Slovenia. **2** the language of Slovenia.
■ **Slovenian** noun & adjective.

slovenly adjective **1** untidy and dirty. **2** careless.
■ **slovenliness** noun.

slow adjective **1** moving or capable of moving only at a low speed. **2** taking a long time. **3** (of a clock or watch) showing a time earlier than the correct time. **4** not quick to understand, think, or learn. •**verb** (often **slow down** or **up**) **1** reduce speed. **2** be less busy or active.

□ **slow motion** the showing of film or video more slowly than it was made or recorded.
slow-worm a small snake-like lizard.
■ **slowly** adverb **slowness** noun.

slowcoach noun Brit. informal a person who acts or moves slowly.

sludge noun thick, soft, wet mud or a similar mixture.
■ **sludgy** adjective.

slug[1] noun **1** a small creature like a snail without a shell. **2** informal a small amount of an alcoholic drink. **3** informal a bullet. •**verb** (**slugs, slugging, slugged**) informal gulp a drink.

slug[2] informal verb (**slugs, slugging, slugged**) **1** hit with a hard blow. **2** (**slug it out**) settle a dispute by fighting or competing fiercely.

sluggard noun a lazy, inactive person.

sluggish adjective **1** slow-moving or inactive. **2** not energetic or alert.
■ **sluggishly** adverb.

sluice /slooss/ noun **1** (also **sluice gate**) a sliding device for controlling the flow of water. **2** a channel for carrying off surplus water. •**verb** (**sluices, sluicing, sluiced**) wash or rinse with water.

slum noun **1** a rundown area of a city or town inhabited by very poor people. **2** a house or building which is unfit to be lived in. •**verb** (**slums, slumming, slummed**) (**slum it**) informal choose to spend time in uncomfortable conditions or at a low social level.

slumber verb (**slumbers, slumbering, slumbered**) sleep. •**noun** a sleep.

slump verb **1** sit, lean, or fall heavily and

THESAURUS

s

slot noun **1** *he slid a coin into the slot:* aperture, slit, crack, hole, opening. **2** *a mid-morning slot:* time, spot, period, niche, space; informal window.
•**verb** *he slotted a cassette into the machine:* insert, slide, fit, put, place.

slow adjective **1** *their slow walk home:* unhurried, leisurely, steady, sedate, sluggish, plodding. **2** *a slow process:* lengthy, time-consuming, long-drawn-out, protracted, prolonged, gradual. **3** *he's a bit slow:* stupid, unintelligent, obtuse; informal dense, dim, thick, slow on the uptake, dumb, dopey; Brit. informal dozy.
OPPOSITES fast, quick.
•**verb 1** *the traffic forced him to slow down:* reduce speed, go slower, decelerate, brake. **2** *this would slow down economic growth:* hold back/up, delay, retard, set back, check, curb.
OPPOSITES accelerate.

slowly adverb **1** *Rose walked off slowly:*

unhurriedly, without hurrying, steadily, at a leisurely pace, at a snail's pace. **2** *her health is improving slowly:* gradually, bit by bit, little by little, slowly but surely, step by step.
OPPOSITES quickly.

sluggish adjective lethargic, listless, lacking in energy, lifeless, inactive, slow, torpid, enervated.
OPPOSITES vigorous.

slum noun hovel; (**slums**) ghetto, shanty town.

slump verb **1** *he slumped into a chair:* sit heavily, flop, collapse, sink; informal plonk yourself. **2** *houses prices slumped:* fall, plummet, tumble, collapse, drop; informal crash, nosedive.
OPPOSITES rise, boom.
•**noun 1** *a slump in profits:* fall, drop, tumble, downturn, downswing, slide, decline, decrease; informal nosedive. **2** *an economic slump:* recession, decline,

limply. 2 fall in price, value, number, etc. suddenly and by a large amount. • noun an instance of slumping.

slung past and past participle of **SLING**.

slunk past and past participle of **SLINK**.

slur verb (**slurs, slurring, slurred**) 1 speak in a way that is difficult to understand. 2 perform a group of musical notes in a smooth, flowing way. • noun 1 an insult or accusation intended to damage someone's reputation. 2 a curved line indicating that notes are to be slurred.

slurp verb eat or drink with a loud sucking sound. • noun a slurping sound.

slurry noun (plural **slurries**) a semi-liquid mixture of water and manure, cement, or coal.

slush noun 1 partially melted snow or ice. 2 informal very sentimental talk or writing. □ slush fund a reserve of money used for something illegal. ■ slushy adjective.

slut noun disapproving a woman who has many sexual partners, or who is untidy and lazy. ■ sluttish adjective.

sly adjective (**slyer, slyest**) 1 cunning and deceitful. 2 (of a remark, glance, or expression) suggesting secret knowledge. ■ slyly adverb.

smack[1] noun 1 a sharp blow with the palm of the hand. 2 a loud, sharp sound. 3 a loud kiss. • verb 1 give someone a smack. 2 smash or drive into. 3 part your lips noisily. • adverb informal exactly or directly.

smack[2] verb (**smack of**) 1 seem to contain or involve something wrong or unpleasant. 2 smell or taste of.

smack[3] noun Brit. a sailing boat with one mast.

smack[4] noun informal heroin.

smacker noun informal 1 a loud kiss. 2 Brit. one pound sterling.

small adjective 1 of less than normal size. 2 not great in amount, number, strength, or power. 3 young. □ small arms guns that can be carried in the hands. small beer Brit. something unimportant. small fry young or unimportant people or things. the small hours the early hours of the morning after midnight. the small of the back the lower part of a person's back where the spine curves in. small print details printed so small that they are not easily noticed in an agreement or contract. small talk polite conversation about unimportant things. ■ smallness noun.

smallholding noun Brit. a piece of agricultural land that is smaller than a farm. ■ smallholder noun.

smallpox noun a serious disease which causes blisters that usually leave permanent scars.

smarmy adjective Brit. informal friendly or flattering in an unpleasant and insincere way.

smart adjective 1 clean, tidy, and stylish. 2 bright and fresh in appearance. 3 (of a place) fashionable and upmarket. 4 informal quick-witted. 5 chiefly N. Amer. cheekily clever.

depression, slowdown.
OPPOSITES rise, boom.

sly adjective 1 *she's very sly:* cunning, crafty, clever, wily, artful, tricky, scheming, devious, underhand, sneaky. 2 *a sly grin:* roguish, mischievous, impish, playful, wicked, arch, knowing. 3 *she took a sly sip of water:* surreptitious, furtive, stealthy, covert.
OPPOSITES open, straightforward.

smack noun *she gave him a smack:* slap, blow, cuff, clip, spank; informal whack.
• verb *he tried to smack her:* slap, strike, hit, cuff, clip, spank; informal whack.
• adverb (informal) *smack in the middle:* exactly, precisely, straight, right, directly, squarely, dead, plumb; informal slap, bang; N. Amer. informal smack dab.

small adjective 1 *a small flat:* little, compact, tiny, miniature, mini, minute, toy, baby, poky, cramped; Scottish wee; informal tiddly; Brit. informal titchy; N. Amer. informal little-bitty. 2 *a very small man:* short, little, petite, diminutive, elfin, tiny; Scottish wee; informal teeny, pint-sized. 3 *a few small changes:*

slight, minor, unimportant, trifling, trivial, insignificant, inconsequential, negligible; informal minuscule, piffling.
OPPOSITES big, tall, major.

smart adjective 1 *you look very smart:* well dressed, stylish, chic, fashionable, modish, elegant, dapper; N. Amer. trig; informal natty, snappy; N. Amer. informal fly. 2 *a smart restaurant:* fashionable, stylish, high-class, exclusive, chic, fancy; Brit. upmarket; N. Amer. high-toned; informal trendy, classy, swanky; Brit. informal swish; N. Amer. informal swank. 3 (informal) *he's very smart:* clever, bright, intelligent, quick-witted, shrewd, astute, perceptive; informal brainy, quick on the uptake. 4 *a smart pace:* brisk, quick, fast, rapid, lively, energetic, vigorous; informal cracking.
OPPOSITES untidy, downmarket, stupid, slow, gentle.
• verb 1 *her eyes were smarting:* sting, burn, tingle, prickle, hurt. 2 *she smarted at the accusations:* feel hurt, feel upset, take offence, feel aggrieved, feel indignant, be put out.

S

6 quick. •**verb 1** give a sharp, stinging pain.
2 feel upset and annoyed.
□ **smart card** a plastic card on which
information is stored in electronic form.
■ **smartish** adjective **smartly** adverb **smartness**
noun.

smarten verb (**smarten up**) make or become
smarter.

smash verb **1** break violently into pieces.
2 hit or collide forcefully. **3** (in sport) hit
the ball hard. **4** completely defeat or
destroy. •**noun 1** an act or sound of
smashing. **2** (also **smash hit**) informal a very
successful song, film, or show.

smashing adjective Brit. informal excellent.
■ **smasher** noun.

smattering noun **1** a small amount. **2** a
slight knowledge of a language.

smear verb **1** coat or mark with a greasy or
sticky substance. **2** blur or smudge. **3** make
false accusations about someone so as to
damage their reputation. •**noun 1** a greasy
or sticky mark. **2** a false accusation.
□ **smear test** Brit. a test to detect signs of
cervical cancer.

smell noun **1** the ability to sense different
things by means of the organs in the nose.
2 something sensed by the organs in the
nose; an odour. **3** an act of smelling. •**verb**
(**smells, smelling, smelt** or **smelled**) **1** sense
by means of the organs in the nose. **2** sniff
at something to find out its smell. **3** send
out a smell. **4** have a strong or unpleasant
smell. **5** sense or detect.
□ **smell a rat** informal suspect a trick.
smelling salts a strong-smelling liquid
formerly sniffed by people who felt faint.

smelly adjective (**smellier, smelliest**) having a
strong or unpleasant smell.

smelt[1] verb extract metal from its ore by
heating and melting it.

smelt[2] past and past participle of **SMELL**.

smidgen or **smidgeon** noun informal a tiny
amount.

smile verb (**smiles, smiling, smiled**) form
your features into a pleased, friendly, or
amused expression, with the corners of the
mouth turned up. •**noun** an act of smiling.

smirk verb smile in a smug or silly way.
•**noun** a smug or silly smile.

smite verb (**smites, smiting, smote;** past
participle **smitten**) **1** old use hit with a hard
blow. **2** (**be smitten**) be strongly attracted
to someone. **3** (**be smitten**) be severely
affected by a disease.

smith noun **1** a person who works in metal.
2 a blacksmith.

smithereens plural noun informal small
pieces.

smithy noun (plural **smithies**) a blacksmith's
workshop.

smock noun **1** a loose dress or blouse with
the upper part gathered into decorative
stitched pleats. **2** a loose overall worn to
protect your clothes.

smog noun fog or haze made worse by
pollution in the atmosphere.

smoke noun **1** a visible vapour in the air
produced by a burning substance. **2** an act
of smoking tobacco. **3** informal a cigarette or
cigar. **4** (**the Smoke** or **the Big Smoke**) Brit. a
big city. •**verb** (**smokes, smoking, smoked**)
1 give out smoke. **2** breathe smoke from a
cigarette, pipe, etc. in and out again.
3 preserve meat or fish by exposing it to
smoke. **4** (**smoke someone/thing out**) drive
someone or something out of a place by
using smoke. **5** (**smoked**) (of glass)
darkened.
■ **smokeless** adjective **smoker** noun.

smokescreen noun **1** something designed
to disguise your real intentions or

---

smash verb **1** *he smashed a window:* break,
shatter, splinter, crack; informal bust. **2** *she's
smashed the car:* crash, wreck; Brit. write
off; N. Amer. informal total. **3** *they smashed into
a wall:* crash, smack, slam, plough, run,
bump, hit, strike, ram, collide with; N. Amer.
impact.
•**noun** *a motorway smash:* crash, collision,
accident; N. Amer. wreck; informal pile-up; Brit.
informal shunt.

smear verb **1** *the table was smeared with
grease:* streak, smudge, mark. **2** *smear the
meat with olive oil:* cover, coat, grease.
3 *she smeared sunblock on her skin:* spread,
rub, daub, slap, smother, plaster. **4** *they are
trying to smear our reputation:* sully,
tarnish, blacken, drag through the mud,
damage, defame, malign, slander, libel;
N. Amer. slur.
•**noun 1** *smears of blood:* streak, smudge,

daub, dab, spot, patch, blotch, mark; informal
splodge. **2** *press smears about his closest
aides:* accusation, lie, untruth, slur,
slander, libel, defamation.

smell noun *the smell of the kitchen:* odour,
aroma, fragrance, scent, perfume, bouquet,
nose, stench, stink; Brit. informal pong, whiff.
•**verb 1** *he smelled her perfume:* scent, get a
sniff of, detect. **2** *the dogs smelled each
other:* sniff, nose. **3** *the cellar smells:* stink,
reek; Brit. informal pong.

smelly adjective foul-smelling, stinking,
reeking, rank, fetid, malodorous, pungent;
informal stinky; Brit. informal pongy.

smile verb *he smiled at her:* beam, grin
(from ear to ear), smirk, simper, leer.
OPPOSITES frown.
•**noun** *the smile on her face:* beam, grin,
smirk, simper, leer.

activities. **2** a cloud of smoke created to conceal military operations.

smokestack noun a chimney or funnel which takes away smoke produced by a locomotive, ship, factory, etc.

smoky adjective (**smokier, smokiest**) producing, filled with, or like smoke.

smolder US spelling of SMOULDER.

smooch verb informal kiss and cuddle.

smooth adjective **1** having an even and regular surface. **2** (of a liquid) without lumps. **3** (of movement) without jerks. **4** without difficulties. **5** charming in a very confident or flattering way. **6** (of a flavour) not harsh or bitter. • verb (also **smoothe**) (**smooths** or **smoothes, smoothing, smoothed**) **1** make something smooth. **2** (**smooth something over**) deal successfully with a problem.
☐ **smooth-talking** informal using very persuasive or flattering language.
■ **smoothly** adverb **smoothness** noun.

smoothie noun **1** a thick, smooth drink of fresh fruit with milk, yogurt, or ice cream. **2** informal a man with a charming, confident manner.

smorgasbord noun a meal at which you choose from a range of open sandwiches and savoury items.

smote past of SMITE.

smother verb (**smothers, smothering, smothered**) **1** suffocate someone by covering their nose and mouth. **2** (**smother someone/thing in** or **with**) cover someone or something thickly with. **3** be oppressively protective or loving towards someone.

smoulder (US spelling **smolder**) verb (**smoulders, smouldering, smouldered**) **1** burn slowly with smoke but no flame. **2** feel strong and barely hidden anger, hatred, lust, etc.

SMS abbreviation Short Message (or Messaging) Service, a system for sending and receiving text messages. • noun a message sent by SMS.

smudge verb (**smudges, smudging, smudged**) make or become blurred or smeared. • noun a smudged mark or image.
■ **smudgy** adjective.

smug adjective (**smugger, smuggest**) irritatingly pleased with yourself.
■ **smugly** adverb **smugness** noun.

smuggle verb (**smuggles, smuggling, smuggled**) **1** move goods illegally into or out of a country. **2** secretly convey.
■ **smuggler** noun.

smut noun **1** a small flake of soot or dirt. **2** indecent talk, writing, or pictures.
■ **smutty** adjective.

snack noun a small quantity of food eaten between meals or in place of a meal. • verb eat a snack.

snaffle noun a bit on a horse's bridle. • verb (**snaffles, snaffling, snaffled**) Brit. informal quickly take for yourself.

snag noun **1** an unexpected difficulty. **2** a sharp or jagged projection. **3** a small tear. • verb (**snags, snagging, snagged**) catch or tear on a snag.

snail noun a small, slow-moving creature with a spiral shell into which it can withdraw its whole body.

snake noun a reptile with no legs and a long slender body. • verb (**snakes, snaking, snaked**) move with the twisting motion of a snake.
☐ **snake in the grass** a person who pretends to be someone's friend but is secretly working against them.
■ **snaky** adjective.

THESAURUS

smooth adjective **1** *the smooth flat rocks:* even, level, flat, glassy, glossy, silky, polished. **2** *a smooth sauce:* creamy, fine, velvety. **3** *a smooth sea:* calm, still, tranquil, undisturbed, unruffled, even, flat, like a millpond. **4** *smooth operation:* steady, regular, uninterrupted, unbroken, straightforward, easy, effortless, trouble-free. **5** *a smooth, confident man:* suave, urbane, sophisticated, polished, debonair, courteous, gracious, glib, slick; informal smarmy.
OPPOSITES uneven, rough, lumpy, irregular, gauche.
• verb **1** *she smoothed the soil:* flatten, level (out/off), even out/off, press, roll, iron, plane. **2** *brokers smooth the passage of goods:* ease, facilitate, expedite, assist, aid.
OPPOSITES roughen, hinder.

smother verb **1** *she tried to smother her baby:* suffocate, asphyxiate, stifle, choke. **2** *we smothered the flames:* extinguish, put out, snuff out, douse, stamp out. **3** *we smothered ourselves with suncream:* smear, daub, spread, cover. **4** *she smothered a sigh:* stifle, muffle, strangle, suppress, hold back, fight back, swallow, conceal.

smug adjective self-satisfied, conceited, complacent, superior, pleased with yourself.

snack noun light meal, sandwich, refreshments, nibbles, titbit(s); informal bite (to eat).

snag noun *we've met a snag:* complication, difficulty, catch, hitch, obstacle, pitfall, problem, setback, disadvantage, drawback. • verb *thorns snagged his sweater:* catch, hook, tear.

S

snap verb (snaps, snapping, snapped)
1 break with a sharp cracking sound.
2 open or close with a brisk movement or
sharp sound. **3** (of an animal) make a
sudden bite. **4** say something quickly and
irritably. **5** suddenly lose self-control.
6 take a snapshot of. •noun **1** an act or
sound of snapping. **2** a snapshot. **3** Brit. a
card game in which players compete to call
'snap' as soon as two cards of the same
type are exposed. •adjective done on the
spur of the moment: *a snap decision.*
□ **snap something up** quickly buy
something that is in short supply. **snap out
of** informal get out of a bad mood by a
sudden effort.

snapdragon noun a plant with brightly
coloured flowers which have a mouth-like
opening.

snapper noun a sea fish noted for snapping
its jaws.

snappy adjective (snappier, snappiest) informal
1 short and clever or amusing: *snappy
slogans.* **2** neat and stylish. **3** irritable;
speaking sharply.
□ **make it snappy** do it quickly.

snapshot noun an informal photograph,
taken quickly.

snare noun **1** a trap for catching animals,
consisting of a loop of wire that pulls
tight. **2** a thing likely to lure someone into
trouble. **3** (also **snare drum**) a drum with a
length of wire stretched across the head to
produce a rattling sound. •verb (snares,
snaring, snared) catch in a snare or trap.

snarl verb **1** growl with bared teeth. **2** say
something aggressively. **3** (snarl something

up) make something tangled. •noun an act
of snarling.
□ **snarl-up** Brit. informal a traffic jam.

snatch verb **1** seize quickly in a rude and
eager way. **2** informal steal or kidnap.
3 quickly take the chance to have. •noun
1 an act of snatching. **2** a fragment of
music or talk.

snazzy adjective (snazzier, snazziest) informal
smart and stylish.

sneak verb (sneaks, sneaking, sneaked or
N. Amer. informal **snuck**) **1** move or take in a
secretive way. **2** Brit. informal tell someone in
authority of a person's wrongdoings.
3 (sneaking) (of a feeling) remaining
persistently in the mind. •noun Brit. informal
a telltale. •adjective secret or unofficial:
a sneak preview.

sneaker noun chiefly N. Amer. a soft shoe worn
for sports or casual occasions.

sneaky adjective (sneakier, sneakiest)
secretive in a sly or dishonest way.
■ **sneakily** adverb.

sneer noun a scornful or mocking smile or
remark. •verb (sneers, sneering, sneered)
smile or speak in a scornful or mocking
way.

sneeze verb (sneezes, sneezing, sneezed)
suddenly expel air from the nose and
mouth due to irritation of the nostrils.
•noun an act of sneezing.
□ **not to be sneezed at** informal worth having
or considering.

snick verb cut a small notch in. •noun a
small notch or cut.

snicker verb (snickers, snickering, snickered)
1 snigger. **2** (of a horse) make a gentle

THESAURUS

snap verb **1** *the ruler snapped:* break,
fracture, splinter, split, crack; informal bust.
2 *'Shut up!' Anna snapped:* bark, snarl,
growl, retort. **3** *photographers snapped the
royals:* photograph, picture, take, shoot,
film, capture.
•noun **1** *she closed her purse with a snap:*
click, crack, pop. **2** *holiday snaps:*
photograph, picture, photo, shot, snapshot,
print, slide.
□ **snap something up buy eagerly,** accept
eagerly, jump at, take advantage of, grab,
seize (on), pounce on.

snare noun *a fox caught in a snare:* trap, gin,
wire, net, noose.
•verb *game birds were snared:* trap, catch,
net, bag, ensnare, hook.

snatch verb **1** *she snatched the microphone:*
grab, seize, take hold of, take, pluck, grasp
at, clutch at. **2** (informal) *someone snatched
my bag:* steal, take, thieve; informal swipe,
nab, lift; Brit. informal nick, pinch, whip.
•noun **1** *brief snatches of sleep:* period,
spell, time, fit, bout, interval, stretch. **2** *a

snatch of conversation:* fragment, snippet,
bit, scrap, extract, excerpt, portion.

sneak verb **1** *I sneaked out:* creep, slink,
steal, slip, slide, sidle, tiptoe, pad. **2** *she
sneaked a camera in:* smuggle, spirit, slip.
•adjective *a sneak preview:* furtive, secret,
stealthy, sly, surreptitious, clandestine,
covert, private, quick, exclusive.

sneaking adjective **1** *a sneaking admiration
for him:* secret, private, hidden, concealed,
unvoiced. **2** *a sneaking feeling:* niggling,
nagging, lurking, insidious, lingering,
persistent.

sneaky adjective sly, crafty, cunning, wily,
scheming, devious, deceitful, underhand.
OPPOSITES honest.

sneer noun **1** *a sneer on her face:* smirk,
curled lip. **2** *the sneers of others:* jibe, jeer,
taunt, insult; informal dig.
•verb **1** *he looked at me and sneered:* smirk,
curl your lip. **2** *it is easy to sneer at them:*
scoff, laugh, scorn, disdain, mock, ridicule,
deride; N. Amer. slur.

S

high-pitched neigh. • **noun** a sound of snickering.

snide adjective disrespectful or mocking in an indirect way.

sniff verb **1** draw in air audibly through the nose. **2** (**sniff around** or **round**) informal investigate secretly. **3** (**sniff something out**) informal discover something by investigation. • **noun** an act of sniffing. □ **not to be sniffed at** informal worth having or considering. **sniffer dog** a dog trained to find drugs or explosives by smell.
■ **sniffer** noun **sniffy** adjective.

sniffle verb (**sniffles, sniffling, sniffled**) sniff slightly or repeatedly. • **noun 1** an act of sniffling. **2** a slight cold.
■ **sniffly** adjective.

snifter noun Brit. informal a small quantity of an alcoholic drink.

snigger verb (**sniggers, sniggering, sniggered**) give a half-suppressed laugh. • **noun** a half-suppressed laugh.

snip verb (**snips, snipping, snipped**) cut with small, quick strokes. • **noun 1** an act of snipping. **2** Brit. informal a bargain.

snipe verb (**snipes, sniping, sniped**) **1** shoot at someone from a hiding place at long range. **2** criticize someone in an unpleasant or petty way. • **noun** (plural **snipe** or **snipes**) a wading bird with brown feathers and a long straight bill.
■ **sniper** noun.

snippet noun a small piece or brief extract.

snitch informal verb **1** steal. **2** inform on someone. • **noun** an informer.

snivel verb (**snivels, snivelling, snivelled**; US spelling **snivels, sniveling, sniveled**) cry or complain in a whining way.

snob noun **1** a person who has great respect for people with social status or wealth and looks down on lower-class people. **2** a person who believes that they have superior taste in a particular area: *a wine snob.*
■ **snobbery** noun **snobbish** adjective **snobby** adjective.

snog Brit. informal verb (**snogs, snogging, snogged**) kiss. • **noun** an act or period of kissing.

snood noun a hairnet worn at the back of a woman's head.

snook noun (**cock a snook at**) Brit. informal

openly show contempt or disrespect for.

snooker noun **1** a game played with cues on a billiard table. **2** a position in a game of snooker or pool in which a player cannot make a direct shot at any permitted ball. • **verb** (**snookers, snookering, snookered**) **1** (in snooker or pool) put your opponent in a snooker. **2** (**be snookered**) Brit. informal be placed in an impossible position.

snoop informal verb look around or investigate secretly in order to find out something. • **noun** an act of snooping.
■ **snooper** noun.

snooty adjective (**snootier, snootiest**) informal behaving as if you are better or more important than other people.
■ **snootily** adverb.

snooze informal noun a short, light sleep. • **verb** (**snoozes, snoozing, snoozed**) have a snooze.

snore noun a snorting sound in a person's breathing while they are asleep. • **verb** (**snores, snoring, snored**) make a snorting sound while asleep.

snorkel noun a tube for a swimmer to breathe through while underwater.
■ **snorkelling** (US spelling **snorkeling**) noun.

snort verb **1** make a loud explosive sound by forcing breath out through the nose. **2** informal inhale cocaine. • **noun** a snorting sound.

snot noun informal mucus in the nose.

snotty adjective informal **1** full of, or covered with, mucus from the nose. **2** superior or arrogant.

snout noun **1** the projecting nose and mouth of an animal. **2** the projecting front or end of something such as a pistol.

snow noun **1** frozen water vapour in the atmosphere that falls in light white flakes. **2** (**snows**) falls of snow. • **verb 1** (**it snows, it is snowing, it snowed**) snow falls. **2** (**be snowed in** or **up**) be unable to leave a place because of heavy snow. **3** (**be snowed under**) be overwhelmed with a large quantity of something, especially work.

snowball noun a ball of packed snow. • **verb** increase rapidly in size, strength, or importance.

snowboard noun a board that resembles a

S

THESAURUS

sniff verb **1** *she sniffed and blew her nose:* inhale, snuffle. **2** *Tom sniffed the fruit:* smell, scent, get a whiff of.
• **noun 1** *she gave a loud sniff:* snuffle, snort. **2** *a sniff of fresh air:* smell, scent, whiff, lungful.
□ **sniff something out** (informal) detect, find, discover, bring to light, track down, dig up,

root out, uncover, unearth.

snigger verb & noun giggle, titter, snicker, chortle, laugh, sneer, smirk.

snobbish, snobby adjective elitist, superior, supercilious, arrogant, condescending, pretentious, affected; informal snooty, high and mighty, la-di-da, stuck-up; Brit. informal toffee-nosed.

short, broad ski, used for sliding downhill on snow.

■ **snowboarder** noun **snowboarding** noun.

snowbound adjective **1** unable to travel or go out because of snow. **2** (of a place) cut off by snow.

snowdrift noun a bank of deep snow heaped up by the wind.

snowdrop noun a plant with drooping white flowers that appear during late winter.

snowfall noun **1** a fall of snow. **2** the quantity of snow falling within a certain area in a given time.

snowflake noun each of the many ice crystals that fall as snow.

snowline noun the altitude above which some snow remains on the ground throughout the year.

snowman noun (plural **snowmen**) a model of a human figure made with compressed snow.

snowplough (US spelling **snowplow**) noun a device or vehicle for clearing roads of snow.

snowshoe noun a flat device attached to the sole of a boot and used for walking on snow.

snowy adjective (**snowier, snowiest**) **1** having a lot of snow. **2** pure white.

snub verb (**snubs, snubbing, snubbed**) **1** insult someone by ignoring them when you meet. **2** refuse to attend or accept something. •**noun** an act of snubbing. □ **snub nose** a nose that is short and turned up at the end.

snuck N. Amer. informal past and past participle of SNEAK.

snuff[1] verb **1** put out a candle. **2** (**snuff something out**) abruptly put an end to something. **3** (**snuff it**) Brit. informal die.

snuff[2] noun powdered tobacco that is sniffed up the nostril. •**verb** sniff at.

snuffle verb (**snuffles, snuffling, snuffled**)

1 breathe noisily through a partially blocked nose. **2** (of an animal) make repeated sniffing sounds. •**noun** a snuffling sound.

snug adjective (**snugger, snuggest**) **1** warm and cosy. **2** close-fitting. •**noun** Brit. a small, cosy bar in a pub or hotel.

■ **snugly** adverb.

snuggle verb (**snuggles, snuggling, snuggled**) settle into a warm, comfortable position.

so adverb **1** to such a great extent. **2** extremely; very much. **3** to the same extent; as. **4** that is the case. **5** similarly. **6** thus. •**conjunction 1** therefore. **2** (**so that**) with the result or aim that. **3** and then. **4** in the same way.

□ **or so** approximately. **so-and-so** (plural **so-and-sos**) informal **1** a person whose name you do not know. **2** a person that you do not like: *a nosy so-and-so.* **so-called** wrongly or inappropriately called a particular thing. **so long!** informal goodbye. **so-so** neither very good nor very bad.

soak verb **1** make something thoroughly wet by leaving it in liquid. **2** (of a liquid) spread completely throughout. **3** (**soak something up**) absorb a liquid. **4** (**soak something up**) expose yourself to something enjoyable. •**noun 1** a period of soaking. **2** informal a heavy drinker.

■ **soaking** adjective.

soap noun **1** a substance used with water for washing and cleaning. **2** informal a soap opera. •**verb** wash with soap. □ **soap opera** a television or radio serial that deals with the daily lives of a group of characters.

■ **soapy** adjective.

soapbox noun a box that someone stands on to speak in public.

soapstone noun a soft rock used for making ornaments.

S

THESAURUS

snub verb *sponsors find themselves snubbed by politicians:* rebuff, spurn, cold-shoulder, cut (dead), ignore, insult, slight; informal freeze out; N. Amer. informal stiff.
•**noun** *a very public snub:* rebuff, slap in the face; informal brush-off, put-down.

snug adjective **1** *our tents were snug:* cosy, comfortable, warm, sheltered, secure; informal comfy. **2** *a snug dress:* tight, skintight, close-fitting, figure-hugging. OPPOSITES bleak, loose.

soak verb **1** *soak the beans in water:* dip, immerse, steep, submerge, douse, marinate, souse. **2** *we got soaked outside:* drench, wet through, saturate, waterlog. **3** *the sweat soaked through his clothes:*

permeate, penetrate, impregnate, percolate, seep, spread. **4** *use towels to soak up the water:* absorb, suck up, blot, mop up.

soaking adjective drenched, wet (through), soaked (through), sodden, soggy, waterlogged, saturated, sopping, dripping, wringing. OPPOSITES parched.

soar verb **1** *the bird soared into the air:* rise, ascend, climb. **2** *the gulls soared on the winds:* glide, plane, float, hover. **3** *the cost of living soared:* increase, escalate, shoot up, spiral; informal go through the roof, skyrocket. OPPOSITES plummet.

soar verb **1** fly or rise high into the air.
2 increase rapidly.

sob verb (**sobs, sobbing, sobbed**) **1** cry with
loud gasps. **2** say while sobbing. • noun a
sound of sobbing.

sober adjective (**soberer, soberest**) **1** not
drunk. **2** serious. **3** (of a colour) not bright
or likely to attract attention. • verb (**sobers,
sobering, sobered**) **1** (**sober up**) make or
become sober after being drunk. **2** make or
become serious.
■ **soberly** adverb.

sobriety /suh-**bry**-uh-ti/ noun the state of
being sober.

sobriquet /**soh**-bri-kay/ or **soubriquet**
/**soo**-bri-kay/ noun a person's nickname.

soccer noun a form of football played with a
round ball which may not be handled
during play except by the goalkeepers.

sociable adjective **1** liking to talk to and do
things with other people. **2** friendly and
welcoming.
■ **sociability** noun **sociably** adverb.

social adjective **1** having to do with society
and its organization. **2** needing the
company of other people. **3** (of an activity)
in which people meet each other for
pleasure. **4** (of animals) breeding or living
in organized communities. • noun an
informal social gathering.
□ **social science 1** the study of human
society and social relationships. **2** a subject
within this field, such as economics. **social
security** (in the UK) money provided by
the state for poor or unemployed people.
social services services provided by the
state such as education and medical care.
social worker a person whose job is to help
improve the conditions of the poor, the
old, etc.

■ **socially** adverb.

socialism noun the theory that a country's
land, transport, industries, etc. should be
owned or controlled by the community as
a whole.
■ **socialist** noun & adjective.

socialite noun a person who mixes in
fashionable society.

socialize or **socialise** verb (**socializes,
socializing, socialized**) **1** mix socially with
other people. **2** make someone behave in a
socially acceptable way.

society noun (plural **societies**) **1** people living
together in an ordered community. **2** a
community of people. **3** (also **high society**)
people who are fashionable, wealthy, and
influential. **4** an organization formed for a
particular purpose. **5** the situation of being
in the company of other people.
■ **societal** adjective.

sociology noun the study of human society.
■ **sociological** adjective **sociologist** noun.

sock noun **1** a knitted garment for the foot
and lower part of the leg. **2** informal a hard
blow. • verb informal hit forcefully.
□ **pull your socks up** informal make an effort
to improve.

socket noun **1** a hollow in which something
fits or revolves. **2** an electrical device
which a plug or light bulb fits into.

sod noun **1** grass-covered ground. **2** a piece
of turf.

soda noun **1** (also **soda water**) carbonated
water. **2** N. Amer. a sweet fizzy drink. **3** a
compound of sodium.

sodden adjective **1** soaked through. **2** having
drunk too much alcohol: _whisky-sodden._

sodium noun a soft silver-white metallic
element.
□ **sodium bicarbonate** a white powder used

THESAURUS

sob verb weep, cry, snivel, whimper; Scottish
greet; informal blubber; Brit. informal grizzle.

sober adjective **1** _the driver was clearly
sober:_ clear-headed, teetotal, abstinent,
dry; informal on the wagon. **2** _a sober view of
life:_ serious, solemn, sensible, grave,
sombre, level-headed, businesslike, down-
to-earth. **3** _a sober suit:_ sombre, subdued,
severe, quiet, drab, plain.
OPPOSITES drunk, frivolous, sensational,
flamboyant.

so-called adjective supposed, alleged,
presumed, inappropriately named,
ostensible, reputed, self-styled.

sociable adjective friendly, amicable,
affable, companionable, gregarious, cordial,
warm, genial.
OPPOSITES unfriendly.

social adjective **1** _a social problem:_
communal, community, collective, group,

general, popular, civil, public. **2** _a social
club:_ recreational, leisure, entertainment.
OPPOSITES individual, professional.
• noun _the club has a social once a month:_
party, gathering, function, get-together,
celebration; informal do.

society noun **1** _a danger to society:_ the
community, the (general) public, the
people, the population, civilization,
humankind, mankind. **2** _an industrial
society:_ culture, community, civilization,
nation, population. **3** _Lady Angela will help
you enter society:_ high society, polite
society, the upper classes, the gentry, the
elite, the smart set; informal the upper crust.
4 _a local history society:_ club, association,
group, circle, institute, guild, lodge, league,
union, alliance. **5** _the society of others:_
company, companionship, fellowship,
friendship.

S

in fizzy drinks and as a raising agent in baking. **sodium chloride** the chemical name for salt. **sodium hydroxide** a strongly alkaline white compound; caustic soda.

sodomite noun a person who engages in sodomy.

sodomy noun anal intercourse.

sofa noun a long padded seat with a back and arms.

soft adjective **1** easy to mould, cut, compress, or fold. **2** not rough in texture. **3** quiet and gentle. **4** (of light or colour) not harsh. **5** not strict enough. **6** informal not needing much effort. **7** informal foolish. **8** (**soft on**) informal having romantic feelings for. **9** (of a drink) not alcoholic. **10** (of a drug) not likely to cause addiction. **11** (of water) free from mineral salts.
□ **have a soft spot for** be fond of. **soft focus** deliberate slight blurring in a photograph or film. **soft-hearted** kind and sympathetic. **softly-softly** Brit. cautious and patient. **soft-pedal** play down the unpleasant aspects of. **soft sell** the selling of something in a gently persuasive way. **soft-soap** informal use flattery to persuade someone. **soft top** a car with a roof that can be folded back. **soft touch** informal a person who is easily persuaded.
■ **softly** adverb **softness** noun.

softball noun a form of baseball played with a larger, softer ball.

soften verb **1** make or become soft or softer. **2** (**soften someone up**) make someone more likely to do or agree to something.

software noun programs and other operating information used by a computer.

softwood noun the wood from a conifer as opposed to that from a broadleaved tree.

soggy adjective (**soggier**, **soggiest**) very wet and soft.

soil noun **1** the upper layer of earth, in which plants grow. **2** the territory of a particular nation. •verb **1** make dirty. **2** bring discredit to.

soirée /swah-ray/ noun an evening social gathering.

sojourn /so-juhn/ literary noun a temporary stay. •verb stay temporarily.

solace /sol-iss/ noun comfort in a difficult time. •verb (**solaces**, **solacing**, **solaced**) give comfort to.

solar adjective having to do with the sun or its rays.
□ **solar eclipse** an eclipse in which the sun is hidden by the moon. **solar plexus** a network of nerves at the pit of the stomach. **solar system** the sun together with the planets, asteroids, comets, etc. in orbit around it.

solarium noun a room equipped with sunlamps or sunbeds.

sold past and past participle of SELL.

solder noun a soft alloy used for joining metals. •verb (**solders**, **soldering**, **soldered**) join with solder.
□ **soldering iron** an electrical tool for melting and applying solder.

soldier noun **1** a person who serves in an army. **2** a private in an army. **3** Brit. informal a strip of bread or toast for dipping into a boiled egg. •verb (**soldiers**, **soldiering**, **soldiered**) **1** serve as a soldier. **2** (**soldier on**) informal keep trying or working.
□ **soldier of fortune** a mercenary.
■ **soldierly** adjective.

soldiery noun soldiers as a group.

sole[1] noun **1** the underside of the foot. **2** the underside of a piece of footwear. •verb

THESAURUS

sofa noun settee, couch, divan, chaise longue, chesterfield.

soft adjective **1** *soft fruit*: mushy, squashy, pulpy, slushy, squelchy, squishy, doughy; informal gooey; Brit. informal squidgy. **2** *soft ground*: swampy, marshy, boggy, muddy, squelchy. **3** *a soft cushion*: squashy, spongy, supple, springy, elastic, resilient. **4** *soft fabric*: smooth, velvety, fleecy, downy, furry, silky. **5** *soft light*: dim, low, faint, subdued, muted. **6** *soft colours*: pale, pastel, muted, restrained, subdued, subtle. **7** *soft voices*: quiet, low, gentle, faint, muted, subdued, muffled, hushed, whispered. **8** *soft outlines*: blurred, vague, hazy, misty, foggy, nebulous, fuzzy, indistinct. **9** *soft words*: kind, gentle, sympathetic, soothing, tender, sensitive, affectionate, loving, warm, sweet, sentimental. **10** *she's too soft with her*

pupils: lenient, easy-going, tolerant, forgiving, forbearing, indulgent, liberal, lax.
OPPOSITES hard, firm, rough, harsh, lurid, strident, sharp, strict.

soften verb *the compensation should soften the blow*: ease, alleviate, relieve, soothe, take the edge off, cushion, lessen, diminish, blunt, deaden.

soil[1] noun **1** *acid soil*: earth, dirt, clay, ground, loam. **2** *British soil*: territory, land, region, country, domain, dominion.

soil[2] verb *he soiled his tie*: dirty, stain, smear, smudge, spoil, foul.

soldier noun fighter, trooper, serviceman, servicewoman, warrior; US GI; Brit. informal squaddie.

sole adjective only, one, single, solitary, lone, unique, exclusive.

(**soles, soling, soled**) put a new sole on a shoe.

sole[2] noun (plural **sole**) a kind of edible flatfish.

sole[3] adjective **1** one and only. **2** belonging or restricted to one person or group.
■ **solely** adverb.

solecism /sol-i-si-z'm/ noun **1** a grammatical mistake. **2** an example of bad manners or incorrect behaviour.

solemn adjective **1** formal and dignified. **2** serious. **3** deeply sincere.
■ **solemnly** adverb.

solemnity noun (plural **solemnities**) **1** the quality of being solemn. **2** (**solemnities**) solemn rites or ceremonies.

solemnize or **solemnise** verb (**solemnizes, solemnizing, solemnized**) **1** perform a ceremony. **2** mark an occasion with a ceremony.

solenoid noun a coil of wire which becomes magnetic when an electric current is passed through it.

solicit verb (**solicits, soliciting, solicited**) **1** try to obtain something from someone. **2** (of a prostitute) approach someone and offer sex for money.
■ **solicitation** noun.

solicitor noun Brit. a lawyer qualified to advise on property, wills, etc., instruct barristers, and represent clients in lower courts.

solicitous adjective showing interest or concern about a person's well-being.
■ **solicitously** adverb.

solicitude noun care or concern.

solid adjective (**solider, solidest**) **1** firm and stable in shape. **2** strongly built or made. **3** not hollow or having spaces or gaps. **4** consisting of the same substance throughout. **5** (of time) uninterrupted.

6 three-dimensional. •noun **1** a solid substance or object. **2** (**solids**) food that is not liquid.
□ **solid-state** (of an electronic device) using solid semiconductors, e.g. transistors, as opposed to valves.
■ **solidity** noun **solidly** adverb.

solidarity noun agreement and support resulting from shared interests, feelings, or opinions.

solidify verb (**solidifies, solidifying, solidified**) make or become hard or solid.
■ **solidification** noun.

soliloquy /suh-lil-uh-kwi/ noun (plural **soliloquies**) a speech in which a character speaks their thoughts aloud when alone on stage.

solipsism noun the view that the self is all that can be known to exist.
■ **solipsist** noun **solipsistic** adjective.

solitaire noun **1** Brit. a game for one player played by removing pegs from a board by jumping others over them. **2** N. Amer. the card game patience. **3** a single gem in a piece of jewellery.

solitary adjective **1** done or existing alone. **2** (of a place) secluded or isolated. **3** single.
□ **solitary confinement** the isolating of a prisoner in a separate cell as a punishment.

solitude noun the state of being alone.

solo noun (plural **solos**) **1** a piece of music or dance for one performer. **2** a flight undertaken by a single pilot. •adjective & adverb for or done by one person. •verb (**soloes, soloing, soloed**) perform a solo.
■ **soloist** noun.

solstice noun each of the two times in the year when the sun reaches its highest or lowest point in the sky at noon, marked by the longest and shortest days.

soluble adjective **1** (of a substance) able to

THESAURUS

solely adverb only, simply, purely, just, merely, uniquely, exclusively, entirely, wholly, alone.

solemn adjective **1** *a solemn occasion:* dignified, ceremonial, stately, formal, majestic, imposing, splendid, magnificent, grand. **2** *he looked very solemn:* serious, grave, sober, sombre, unsmiling, stern, grim, dour, humourless. **3** *a solemn promise:* sincere, earnest, honest, genuine, firm, heartfelt, wholehearted, sworn.
OPPOSITES frivolous, light-hearted, insincere.

solid adjective **1** *the plaster was solid:* hard, rock-hard, rigid, firm, solidified, set, frozen. **2** *solid gold:* pure, unadulterated, genuine. **3** *solid houses:* well built, sound, substantial, strong, sturdy, durable. **4** *a solid argument:* well founded, valid, sound,

logical, authoritative, convincing. **5** *solid support from their colleagues:* unanimous, united, consistent, undivided.
OPPOSITES liquid, alloyed, flimsy, untenable, half-hearted.

solidarity noun unanimity, unity, agreement, team spirit, accord, harmony, consensus; formal concord.

solitary adjective **1** *a solitary man:* lonely, unaccompanied, by yourself, on your own, alone, friendless, unsociable, withdrawn, reclusive; N. Amer. lonesome. **2** *solitary farmsteads:* isolated, remote, lonely, out of the way, in the back of beyond, outlying, off the beaten track, secluded; N. Amer. in the backwoods. **3** *a solitary piece of evidence:* single, lone, sole, only, one, individual.
OPPOSITES sociable.

be dissolved. **2** (of a problem) able to be solved.
■ **solubility** noun.

solution noun **1** a way of solving a problem. **2** the correct answer to a puzzle. **3** a mixture formed when a substance is dissolved in a liquid. **4** the process of dissolving.

solve verb (**solves**, **solving**, **solved**) find an answer to, or way of dealing with, a problem or mystery.

solvency noun the state of having more money than you owe.

solvent adjective **1** having more money than you owe. **2** able to dissolve other substances. •**noun** the liquid in which another substance is dissolved to form a solution.

Somali /suh-**mah**-li/ noun (plural **Somali** or **Somalis**) **1** a person from Somalia. **2** the language of the Somali. •**adjective** relating to Somalia.

somatic adjective having to do with the body rather than the mind.

sombre (US spelling **somber**) adjective **1** dark or dull. **2** very solemn or serious.
■ **sombrely** adverb.

sombrero noun (plural **sombreros**) a broad-brimmed felt or straw hat.

some determiner **1** an unspecified amount or number of. **2** unknown or unspecified. **3** approximately. **4** a considerable amount or number of. **5** used to express admiration. •**pronoun** a certain amount or number of people or things.

somebody pronoun someone.

some day or **someday** adverb at some time in the future.

somehow adverb **1** by one means or another. **2** for an unknown or unspecified reason.

someone pronoun **1** an unknown or unspecified person. **2** an important or famous person.

someplace adverb & pronoun N. Amer. informal somewhere.

somersault noun a movement in which a person turns head over heels and finishes on their feet. •**verb** perform a somersault.

something pronoun an unspecified or unknown thing or amount.

sometime adverb at some unspecified or unknown time. •**adjective** former.

sometimes adverb occasionally.

somewhat adverb to some extent.

somewhere adverb in or to an unspecified or unknown place. •**pronoun** some unspecified place.

somnambulism noun formal sleepwalking.
■ **somnambulist** noun.

somnolent adjective sleepy or drowsy.
■ **somnolence** noun.

son noun **1** a boy or man in relation to his parents. **2** a male descendant. **3** (**the Son**) Jesus.
□ **son-in-law** (plural **sons-in-law**) the husband of a person's daughter.

sonar noun a system for detecting objects underwater by giving out sound pulses.

sonata /suh-**nah**-tuh/ noun a piece of music for a solo instrument, sometimes with piano accompaniment.

song noun **1** a set of words set to music. **2** singing. **3** the musical phrases uttered by some birds, whales, and insects. **4** literary a poem.
□ **for a song** informal very cheaply. **on song** Brit. informal performing well.

songbird noun a bird with a musical song.

songster noun (feminine **songstress**) a person who sings.

sonic adjective relating to or using sound waves.
□ **sonic boom** an explosive noise caused by the shock wave from an object travelling faster than the speed of sound.
■ **sonically** adverb.

sonnet noun a poem of fourteen lines using a fixed rhyme scheme.

sonorous adjective **1** (of a sound) deep and full. **2** (of speech) using powerful language.
■ **sonority** noun **sonorously** adverb.

THESAURUS

solution noun **1** *a solution to the problem:* answer, result, resolution, key, explanation. **2** *a solution of salt and water:* mixture, blend, compound.

solve verb answer, resolve, work out, puzzle out, fathom, decipher, decode, clear up, straighten out, get to the bottom of, unravel, explain; informal figure out, crack; Brit. informal suss out.

sombre adjective **1** *sombre clothes:* dark, drab, dull, dingy, restrained, subdued, sober, funereal. **2** *a sombre expression:* solemn, earnest, serious, grave, sober,

unsmiling, stern, grim, dour, gloomy, sad, mournful, lugubrious.
OPPOSITES bright, cheerful.

somehow adverb one way or another, no matter how, by fair means or foul, by hook or by crook, come what may.

sometimes adverb occasionally, from time to time, now and then, every so often, once in a while, on occasion, at times, off and on.

song noun air, strain, ditty, chant, number, track, melody, tune.

soon adverb **1** in or after a short time. **2** early. **3** (**would sooner**) would rather.

soot noun a black powdery substance produced when wood, coal, etc. is burned.
■ **sooty** adjective.

soothe verb (**soothes, soothing, soothed**) **1** gently calm. **2** relieve pain or discomfort.

soothsayer noun a person supposed to be able to foresee the future.

sop noun a thing given or done to calm or please someone who is angry or disappointed. •verb (**sops, sopping, sopped**) (**sop something up**) soak up liquid.

sophism noun a false argument.

sophist noun a person who uses clever but false arguments.
■ **sophistry** noun.

sophisticate noun a sophisticated person.

sophisticated adjective **1** having experience and taste in matters of culture or fashion. **2** highly developed and complex.
■ **sophistication** noun.

sophomore noun N. Amer. a second-year university or high-school student.

soporific adjective causing drowsiness or sleep.

sopping adjective wet through.

soppy adjective (**soppier, soppiest**) Brit. informal **1** too sentimental. **2** feeble.
■ **soppily** adverb.

soprano noun (plural **sopranos**) the highest singing voice.

sorbet /sor-bay/ noun a water ice.

sorcerer noun (feminine **sorceress**) a person who practises magic.
■ **sorcery** noun.

sordid adjective **1** dishonest or immoral. **2** very dirty and unpleasant.
■ **sordidly** adverb.

sore adjective **1** painful or aching. **2** urgent: *in sore need.* **3** N. Amer. informal upset and angry. •noun a raw or painful place on the body. •adverb old use very: *sore afraid.* □ **sore point** an issue about which someone feels distressed or annoyed.
■ **soreness** noun.

sorely adverb extremely; badly.

sorghum /sor-guhm/ noun a cereal plant found in warm regions, grown for grain and animal feed.

sorority noun (plural **sororities**) N. Amer. a society for female students in a university or college.

sorrel noun **1** an edible plant with a bitter flavour. **2** a light reddish-brown colour.

sorrow noun **1** deep distress caused by loss or disappointment. **2** a cause of sorrow.

sorrowful adjective feeling or showing sorrow.
■ **sorrowfully** adverb.

sorry adjective (**sorrier, sorriest**) **1** feeling sympathy for someone else's misfortune. **2** feeling or expressing regret. **3** in a bad or pitiful state. **4** unpleasant and regrettable.

THESAURUS

soon adverb **shortly**, presently, in the near future, before long, in a little while, in a minute, in a moment; Brit. informal in a tick.

sooner adverb **1** *he should have done it sooner:* **earlier**, before now. **2** *I would sooner stay:* **rather**, preferably, given the choice.

soothe verb **1** *Rachel tried to soothe him:* **calm** (down), pacify, comfort, hush, quiet, settle (down), appease, mollify; Brit. quieten (down). **2** *an anaesthetic to soothe the pain:* **ease**, alleviate, relieve, take the edge off, allay, lessen, reduce.
OPPOSITES agitate, aggravate.

soothing adjective **relaxing**, restful, calm, calming, tranquil, peaceful.

sophisticated adjective **1** *sophisticated technology:* **advanced**, state-of-the-art, the latest, up-to-the-minute, cutting-edge, trailblazing, complex. **2** *a sophisticated woman:* **worldly**, worldly-wise, experienced, cosmopolitan, urbane, cultured, cultivated, polished, refined.
OPPOSITES crude, naive.

sophistication noun **worldliness**, experience, urbanity, culture, polish, refinement, elegance, style, poise, finesse, savoir faire.

sore adjective **1** *a sore leg:* **painful**, hurting, hurt, aching, throbbing, smarting, stinging, inflamed, sensitive, tender, raw. **2** (N. Amer. informal) *they were sore at us:* **upset**, angry, annoyed, cross, disgruntled, dissatisfied, irritated; informal aggravated, miffed, peeved; Brit. informal narked; N. Amer. informal ticked off.

sorrow noun **1** *he felt sorrow at her death:* **sadness**, unhappiness, misery, despondency, regret, despair, desolation, heartache, grief. **2** *the sorrows of life:* **trouble**, difficulty, problem, woe, affliction, trial, tribulation, misfortune.
OPPOSITES joy.

sorry adjective **1** *I was sorry to hear about his accident:* **sad**, moved, sorrowful, distressed. **2** *he felt sorry for her:* **full of pity**, sympathetic, compassionate, moved, concerned. **3** *I'm sorry I was rude:* **regretful**, apologetic, remorseful, contrite, repentant, rueful, penitent, guilty, shamefaced, ashamed.
OPPOSITES glad, unsympathetic, unrepentant.

S

sort noun **1** a category of people or things with a common feature or features. **2** informal a person: *a friendly sort.* • verb **1** arrange systematically in groups. **2** (often **sort someone/thing out**) separate someone or something from a mixed group. **3** (**sort something out**) deal with a problem or difficulty. ◻ **out of sorts** slightly unwell or unhappy.

> ❗ use **this sort of** to refer to a singular noun (e.g. *this sort of job*), and **these sorts of** to refer to a plural noun (e.g. *these sorts of questions*).

sorted adjective Brit. informal **1** organized; arranged. **2** emotionally stable.

sortie noun **1** an attack made by troops from a position of defence. **2** a flight by an aircraft on a military operation. **3** a short trip.

SOS noun **1** an international signal sent when in great trouble. **2** an urgent appeal for help.

sot noun old use a person who is regularly drunk.
■ **sottish** adjective.

sotto voce /sot-toh **voh**-chay/ adverb & adjective in a quiet voice.

soubriquet ⇒ SOBRIQUET.

soufflé /**soo**-flay/ noun a light, spongy dish made by mixing egg yolks with beaten egg whites.

sough /rhymes with cow or cuff/ verb literary (of the wind or sea) make a moaning, whistling, or rushing sound.

sought past and past participle of SEEK. ◻ **sought after** in great demand.

souk /sook/ noun an Arab market.

soul noun **1** the spiritual element of a person, believed by some to be immortal. **2** a person's inner nature. **3** emotional energy or power. **4** (**the soul of**) a perfect example of a particular quality. **5** an individual: *poor soul!* **6** a kind of music that expresses strong emotions, made popular by black Americans. ◻ **soul-destroying** unbearably dull and repetitive. **soul-searching** close examination of your emotions and motives.

soulful adjective expressing deep feeling.
■ **soulfully** adverb.

soulless adjective **1** lacking character or interest. **2** lacking human feelings.

soulmate noun a person ideally suited to another.

sound¹ noun **1** vibrations which travel through the air and are sensed by the ear. **2** a thing that can be heard. **3** an impression given by words. • verb **1** make sound. **2** make a sound to show or warn of something. **3** give a particular impression. **4** (**sound off**) express your opinions loudly or forcefully. ◻ **sound barrier** the point at which an aircraft approaches the speed of sound. **sound bite** a short, memorable extract from a speech or interview. **sound effect** a sound other than speech or music that is used in a play, film, etc. **sound wave** a wave by which sound travels through water, air, etc.
■ **soundless** adjective.

sound² adjective **1** in good condition. **2** based on solid judgement. **3** financially secure. **4** competent or reliable. **5** (of sleep) deep and unbroken. **6** severe or thorough.
■ **soundly** adverb.

sound³ verb **1** find out the depth of water

THESAURUS

sort noun *what sort of book is it?* type, kind, variety, class, category, style, form, genre, species, make, model.
• verb **1** *they sorted the books alphabetically:* classify, class, group, organize, arrange, order. **2** *the problem was soon sorted out:* resolve, settle, solve, fix, work out, straighten out, deal with, put right, set right, rectify, iron out.

soul noun **1** *his soul cried out:* spirit, psyche, (inner) self. **2** *their music lacked soul:* feeling, emotion, passion, animation, intensity, warmth, energy, vitality, spirit.

sound¹ noun **1** *the sound of a car:* noise, din, racket, row, resonance, reverberation. **2** *she did not make a sound:* utterance, cry, word, noise, peep. **3** *the sound of the flute:* tone, timbre, call, song, voice.
OPPOSITES silence.
• verb **1** *the buzzer sounded:* make a noise, resonate, resound, reverberate, go off, ring, chime, ping. **2** *drivers must sound their horns:* blow, blast, toot, ring, use, operate, activate, set off. **3** *it sounds a crazy idea:* appear, look (like), seem, give every indication of being.

sound² adjective **1** *your heart is sound:* healthy, in good condition/shape, fit, hale and hearty, in fine fettle, undamaged, unimpaired. **2** *a sound building:* well built, solid, substantial, strong, sturdy, durable, stable, intact. **3** *sound advice:* well founded, valid, reasonable, logical, weighty, authoritative, reliable. **4** *a sound judge of character:* reliable, dependable, trustworthy, fair, good. **5** *financially sound:* solvent, debt-free, in the black, in credit, creditworthy, secure. **6** *a sound sleep:* deep, undisturbed, uninterrupted, untroubled, peaceful.
OPPOSITES unhealthy, unsound, unsafe, unreliable, insolvent.

S

using a line, pole, or sound echoes.
2 (sound someone out) question someone about their opinions or feelings.

sound⁴ noun a narrow stretch of water connecting two larger areas of water.

sounding noun **1** a measurement of the depth of water. **2 (soundings)** information found out before taking action.
□ **sounding board** a person or group that you talk to in order to test out new ideas.

soundproof adjective preventing sound getting in or out. •verb make soundproof.

soundtrack noun the sound accompaniment to a film.

soup noun a savoury liquid dish made by boiling meat, fish, or vegetables. •verb **(soup something up)** informal make a car more powerful.
□ **soup kitchen** a place where free food is served to homeless or very poor people.

soupçon /soop-son/ noun a very small quantity of something.

sour adjective **1** having a sharp taste like lemon or vinegar. **2** (especially of milk) stale and unpleasant. **3** resentful or angry. •verb make or become sour.
□ **sour cream** cream that has been made sour by adding bacteria. **sour grapes** an attitude of pretending that something is worthless or undesirable because you cannot have it yourself.
■ **sourly** adverb **sourness** noun.

source noun **1** a place, person, or thing from which something originates. **2** a place where a river or stream starts. **3** a person, book, or document that provides information. •verb **(sources, sourcing, sourced)** obtain from a particular source.

sourpuss noun informal a bad-tempered or sulky person.

souse /sowss/ verb **(souses, sousing, soused) 1** soak in liquid. **2 (soused)** pickled or marinaded.

south noun **1** the direction which is on your right-hand side when you are facing east. **2** the southern part of a place. •adjective **1** lying towards or facing the south. **2** (of a wind) blowing from the south. •adverb to or towards the south.
■ **southward** adjective & adverb **southwards** adverb.

south-east noun the direction or region halfway between south and east. •adjective & adverb **1** towards or facing the south-east. **2** (of a wind) blowing from the south-east.
■ **south-eastern** adjective.

south-easterly adjective & adverb **1** in or towards the south-east. **2** (of a wind) blowing from the south-east.

southerly adjective & adverb **1** facing or moving towards the south. **2** (of a wind) blowing from the south.

southern adjective **1** situated in or facing the south. **2** coming from or characteristic of the south.

southerner noun a person from the south of a region.

south-west noun the direction or region halfway between south and west. •adjective & adverb **1** towards or facing the south-west. **2** (of a wind) blowing from the south-west.
■ **south-western** adjective.

south-westerly adjective & adverb **1** in or towards the south-west. **2** (of a wind) blowing from the south-west.

souvenir noun a thing that is kept as a reminder of a person, place, or event.

sou'wester /sow-wess-ter/ noun a waterproof hat with a brim that covers the back of the neck.

sovereign noun **1** a king or queen who is the supreme ruler of a country. **2** a former British gold coin worth one pound sterling. •adjective **1** possessing supreme power. **2** (of a country) independent.

sovereignty noun (plural **sovereignties**) **1** supreme power or authority. **2** a

S

THESAURUS

sour adjective **1** *sour wine:* acid, acidic, tart, bitter, sharp, vinegary, pungent. **2** *sour milk:* bad, off, turned, curdled, rancid, high, fetid. **3** *a sour old man:* embittered, resentful, jaundiced, bitter, cross, crabby, crotchety, cantankerous; informal grouchy.
OPPOSITES sweet, fresh, amiable.
•verb *the dispute soured relations:* spoil, mar, damage, harm, impair, wreck, upset, poison, blight.
OPPOSITES improve.

source noun **1** *the source of the river:* spring, origin. **2** *the source of the rumour:* origin, starting point, root, author, originator. **3** *historical sources:* reference, authority, informant, document.

souvenir noun memento, keepsake, reminder, memorial, trophy.

sovereign noun *the sovereign's prerogative:* ruler, monarch, potentate, overlord, king, queen, emperor, empress, prince, princess.
•adjective *a sovereign state:* autonomous, independent, self-governing, self-determining, non-aligned, free.

sovereignty noun **1** *their sovereignty over the islands:* power, rule, supremacy, dominion, jurisdiction, ascendancy, domination, authority, control. **2** *full sovereignty was achieved in 1955:* autonomy, independence, self-government, self-rule, home rule, self-determination, freedom.

self-governing state.

Soviet noun 1 a citizen of the former Soviet Union. 2 (**soviet**) an elected council in the former Soviet Union. • adjective having to do with the former Soviet Union.

sow[1] /soh/ verb (past **sowed**; past participle **sown** or **sowed**) 1 plant seed by scattering it on or in the earth. 2 spread or introduce something unwelcome.

sow[2] /sow/ noun an adult female pig.

soya bean noun an edible bean that is high in protein.

soy sauce noun a sauce made with fermented soya beans, used in Chinese and Japanese cooking.

sozzled adjective informal very drunk.

spa noun 1 a mineral spring considered to have health-giving properties. 2 a place with a mineral spring.

space noun 1 unoccupied ground or area. 2 a blank between typed or written words or characters. 3 the dimensions of height, depth, and width within which all things exist and move. 4 (also **outer space**) the universe beyond the earth's atmosphere. 5 an interval of time. 6 freedom to live and develop as you wish. • verb (**spaces, spacing, spaced**) 1 position items at a distance from one another. 2 (**be spaced out**) informal be confused or not completely conscious. □ **space shuttle** a spacecraft used for journeys between earth and craft which are orbiting the earth. **space station** a large spacecraft used as a base for manned operations in space.

spacecraft noun (plural **spacecraft** or **spacecrafts**) a vehicle used for travelling in space.

spaceman noun (plural **spacemen**) a male astronaut.

spaceship noun a manned spacecraft.

spacesuit noun a pressurized suit covering the whole body that allows an astronaut to survive in space.

spacious adjective (of a room or building) having plenty of space.

spade noun a tool with a rectangular metal blade and a long handle, used for digging. □ **call a spade a spade** speak plainly and frankly.

spades noun one of the four suits in a pack of playing cards, represented by a black heart-shaped figure with a small stalk. □ **in spades** informal in large amounts or to a high degree.

spadework noun hard or routine work done to prepare for something.

spaghetti /spuh-get-ti/ plural noun pasta made in long, thin strands.

spake old-fashioned past of SPEAK.

spam noun 1 (**Spam**) trademark a canned meat product made mainly from ham. 2 unwanted email sent to many Internet users.

span noun 1 the length of time for which something lasts. 2 width or extent from side to side. 3 a part of a bridge between the uprights supporting it. 4 the maximum distance between the tips of the thumb and little finger. • verb (**spans, spanning, spanned**) extend across or over.

spangle noun 1 a small piece of decorative glittering material. 2 a spot of bright colour or light.
■ **spangled** adjective **spangly** adjective.

Spaniard noun a person from Spain.

spaniel noun a breed of dog with a long silky coat and drooping ears.

Spanish noun the main language of Spain and of much of Central and South America. • adjective relating to Spain or Spanish.

spank verb slap someone on the buttocks with your hand or a flat object. • noun a slap on the buttocks.

spanking adjective 1 brisk. 2 informal impressive or pleasing. • noun a series of spanks.

spanner noun Brit. a tool for gripping and

THESAURUS

sow verb plant, scatter, disperse, strew, broadcast, seed.

space noun 1 *there was not enough space:* room, capacity, latitude, margin, leeway, play, elbow room, clearance. 2 *green spaces in London:* area, expanse, stretch, sweep, tract. 3 *a space between the timbers:* gap, interval, opening, aperture, cavity, niche. 4 *write your name in the appropriate space:* blank, gap, box, field. 5 *a space of seven years:* period, span, time, duration, stretch, course, interval, gap. 6 *the first woman in space:* outer space, deep space, the universe.
• verb *the chairs were spaced widely:*

position, arrange, range, array, spread, lay out, set.

spacious adjective roomy, capacious, commodious, voluminous, sizeable, generous.
OPPOSITES cramped.

span noun 1 *a six-foot wing span:* extent, length, width, reach, stretch, spread, distance, range. 2 *the span of one week:* period, space, time, duration, course, interval.
• verb 1 *an arch spanned the stream:* bridge, cross, traverse, pass over. 2 *his career spanned twenty years:* last, cover, extend, spread over.

S

turning a nut or bolt.

□ **spanner in the works** something that prevents a plan being carried out successfully.

spar¹ noun **1** a thick, strong pole used to support the sails on a ship. **2** the main supporting structure of an aircraft's wing.

spar² verb (**spars, sparring, sparred**) **1** make the motions of boxing without landing heavy blows, as a form of training. **2** argue in a friendly way.

spare adjective **1** additional to what is required for ordinary use. **2** not being used or occupied. **3** thin. •noun an item kept in case another is lost, broken, or worn out. •verb (**spares, sparing, spared**) **1** let someone have something that you have enough of. **2** refrain from killing or harming. **3** protect from something unpleasant.

□ **go spare** Brit. informal become very angry. **spare no expense** be prepared to pay any amount. **spare ribs** trimmed ribs of pork. **spare tyre** informal a roll of fat around a person's waist.

sparing adjective not wasteful; economical.
■ **sparingly** adverb.

spark noun **1** a small fiery particle produced by burning or caused by friction. **2** a flash of light produced by an electrical discharge. **3** a small amount of a quality or feeling. **4** a sense of liveliness and excitement. •verb **1** give out or produce sparks. **2** ignite a fire. **3** (usu. **spark something off**) cause something.

□ **spark plug** a device that produces a spark to ignite the fuel in a vehicle engine.
■ **sparky** adjective.

sparkle verb (**sparkles, sparkling, sparkled**) **1** shine brightly with flashes of light. **2** be attractively lively and witty. **3** (**sparkling**) (of a drink) fizzy. •noun **1** a glittering flash

of light. **2** attractive liveliness and wit.
■ **sparkly** adjective.

sparkler noun a hand-held firework that gives out sparks.

sparrow noun a small bird with brown and grey feathers.

sparrowhawk noun a small hawk that preys on small birds.

sparse adjective thinly scattered.
■ **sparsely** adverb **sparsity** noun.

spartan adjective not comfortable or luxurious.

spasm noun **1** a sudden involuntary contraction of a muscle. **2** a sudden period of an activity or sensation.

spasmodic adjective happening or done in brief, irregular bursts.
■ **spasmodically** adverb.

spastic adjective **1** relating to or affected by muscle spasm. **2** offensive having to do with cerebral palsy. •noun offensive a person with cerebral palsy.
■ **spasticity** noun.

> **!** say *person with cerebral palsy* rather than **spastic**, which many people find offensive.

spat¹ past and past participle of SPIT¹.

spat² noun informal a quarrel about something unimportant.

spat³ noun a cloth covering formerly worn by men over their ankles and shoes.

spate noun **1** a large number of similar things coming quickly one after another. **2** a sudden flood in a river.

spathe /spayth/ noun a large sheath enclosing the flower cluster of certain plants.

spatial adjective having to do with space.
■ **spatially** adverb.

spatter verb (**spatters, spattering,**

S

spare adjective **1** *a spare set of keys:* extra, supplementary, additional, second, other, alternative, emergency, reserve, backup, relief, substitute; N. Amer. alternate. **2** *they sold off the spare land:* surplus, superfluous, excess, leftover, redundant, unnecessary, unwanted; informal going begging. **3** *your spare time:* free, leisure, own. **4** *her spare, elegant form:* slender, lean, willowy, svelte, lissom, thin, skinny, gaunt, lanky, spindly.
•verb **1** *he couldn't spare any money:* afford, manage, part with, give, provide. **2** *they were spared by their captors:* pardon, let off, forgive, have mercy on, reprieve, release, free.

sparing adjective thrifty, economical, frugal, careful, prudent, cautious.
OPPOSITES lavish, extravagant.

spark noun *a spark of light:* flash, glint, twinkle, flicker, flare.
•verb *the arrest sparked off riots:* cause, give rise to, occasion, bring about, start, precipitate, prompt, trigger (off), provoke, stimulate, stir up.

sparkle verb & noun glitter, glint, glisten, twinkle, flicker, flash, shimmer.

sparkling adjective **1** *sparkling wine:* effervescent, fizzy, carbonated, aerated. **2** *a sparkling performance:* brilliant, dazzling, scintillating, exciting, exhilarating, stimulating, invigorating, vivacious, lively, vibrant.
OPPOSITES still, dull.

spate noun series, succession, run, cluster, string, rash, epidemic, outbreak, wave, flurry.

spattered) cover something with drops or spots of a liquid. • noun a spray or splash.

spatula noun an object with a broad, flat, blunt blade, used for mixing or spreading.

spawn verb 1 (of a fish, frog, etc.) release or deposit eggs. 2 give rise to. • noun the eggs of fish, frogs, etc.

spay verb sterilize a female animal by removing the ovaries.

speak verb (**speaks**, **speaking**, **spoke**; past participle **spoken**) 1 say something. 2 communicate, or be able to communicate, in a particular language. 3 (**speak up**) speak more loudly. 4 (**speak out** or **up**) express your opinions frankly and publicly.
□ speak in tongues speak in an unknown language during religious worship. speak volumes convey a great deal without using words.

speakeasy noun (plural **speakeasies**) (in the US during Prohibition) a secret illegal drinking club.

speaker noun 1 a person who speaks. 2 (**Speaker**) the person who is in charge of proceedings in a parliament. 3 a loudspeaker.

spear noun 1 a weapon with a pointed metal tip and a long shaft. 2 a pointed stem of asparagus or broccoli. • verb pierce with a spear or other pointed object.

spearhead verb lead a campaign or attack. • noun a person or group that leads a campaign or attack.

spearmint noun a type of garden mint, used in cooking.

spec noun informal 1 (**on spec**) without any specific preparation or plan. 2 a detailed working description.

special adjective 1 better or different from what is usual. 2 designed for or belonging to a particular person, place, or event. • noun 1 something designed or organized for a particular occasion or purpose. 2 a dish not on the regular menu but served on a particular day.
□ special constable a person trained to act as a police officer on particular occasions. special effects illusions created for films and television by camerawork, computer graphics, etc.

specialist noun an expert in a particular subject, area of activity, etc. • adjective involving detailed knowledge within a subject, area of activity, etc.
■ specialism noun.

speciality (US spelling **specialty**) noun (plural **specialities**) 1 a skill or area of study in which someone is an expert. 2 a product for which a person or region is famous. 3 (usu. **specialty**) a branch of medicine or surgery.

specialize or **specialise** verb (**specializes**, **specializing**, **specialized**) 1 concentrate on and become expert in a particular skill or area. 2 (**specialized**) adapted or designed for a particular purpose or area of activity.
■ specialization noun.

specially adverb 1 for a special purpose. 2 particularly.

specie /spee-shee/ noun money in the form of coins rather than notes.

species noun (plural **species**) 1 a group of animals or plants that are capable of breeding with each other. 2 a kind.

specific adjective 1 clearly defined or identified. 2 precise and clear. 3 (**specific to**) belonging or relating only to. • noun

THESAURUS

speak verb 1 *she refused to speak about it:* talk, converse, communicate, chat, have a word, gossip, commune, say anything/ something. 2 *she spoke her words carefully:* say, utter, state, declare, voice, express, pronounce, articulate, enunciate, verbalize. 3 *the Minister spoke for two hours:* give a speech, talk, lecture, hold forth; informal spout, sound off.

speaker noun speech-maker, lecturer, talker, orator, spokesperson, spokesman/ woman, reader, commentator, broadcaster, narrator.

special adjective 1 *a very special person:* exceptional, unusual, remarkable, outstanding, unique. 2 *our town's special character:* distinctive, distinct, individual, particular, specific, peculiar. 3 *a special occasion:* momentous, significant, memorable, important, historic. 4 *a special tool for cutting tiles:* specific, particular,

purpose-built, tailor-made, custom-built.
OPPOSITES ordinary, general.

specialist noun expert, authority, pundit, professional, connoisseur, master, maestro; informal buff.
OPPOSITES amateur.

speciality noun 1 *his speciality was watercolours:* strength, strong point, forte, métier, strong suit, party piece, pièce de résistance; informal bag, thing. 2 *a speciality of the region:* delicacy.

species noun type, kind, sort, breed, strain, variety, class, classification, category.

specific adjective 1 *a specific purpose:* particular, specified, fixed, set, determined, distinct, definite. 2 *I gave specific instructions:* detailed, explicit, express, clear-cut, unequivocal, precise, exact.
OPPOSITES general, vague.

(**specifics**) precise details.
- **specifically** adverb.

specification noun **1** the action of specifying. **2** (usu. **specifications**) a detailed description of the design and materials used to make something. **3** the standard of workmanship and materials in a piece of work.

specify verb (**specifies, specifying, specified**) state, identify, or require clearly and definitely.

specimen noun **1** an example of an animal, plant, object, etc. used for study or display. **2** a sample for medical testing. **3** a typical example of something. **4** informal a person of a specific type: *a sorry specimen.*

specious /spee-shuhss/ adjective seeming right or reasonable, but actually wrong.

speck noun a tiny spot or particle. • verb mark with small spots.

speckle noun a small spot or patch of colour. • verb (**speckles, speckling, speckled**) mark with speckles.

specs plural noun informal spectacles.

spectacle noun a visually striking performance or display.

spectacles plural noun Brit. a pair of glasses.

spectacular adjective very impressive, striking, or dramatic. • noun a spectacular performance or event.
- **spectacularly** adverb.

spectate verb (**spectates, spectating,**

spectated) be a spectator.

spectator noun a person who is watching a show, game, etc.

spectral adjective **1** like a spectre. **2** having to do with the spectrum.

spectre (US spelling **specter**) noun **1** a ghost. **2** a possible unpleasant or dangerous occurrence.

spectrum noun (plural **spectra**) **1** a band of colours produced by separating light into elements with different wavelengths, e.g. in a rainbow. **2** the entire range of wavelengths of light. **3** a range of sound waves or different types of wave. **4** an entire range of beliefs, ideas, etc.: *the political spectrum.*

speculate verb (**speculates, speculating, speculated**) **1** form a theory without firm evidence. **2** invest in stocks, property, etc. in the hope of gain but with the risk of loss.
- **speculation** noun **speculator** noun.

speculative adjective **1** based on theory or guesswork rather than knowledge. **2** (of an investment) risky.
- **speculatively** adverb.

speculum noun (plural **specula**) a metal instrument that is used to make an opening or canal in the body wider so that it can be examined.

speech noun **1** the expression of thoughts and feelings using spoken language. **2** a

---

specification noun **1** *clear specification of objectives:* statement, identification, definition, description, setting out. **2** *a shelter built to their specifications:* instruction, guideline, parameter, stipulation, requirement, condition, order, detail.

specify verb state, name, identify, define, set out, itemize, detail, list, spell out, stipulate, lay down.

specimen noun sample, example, model, instance, illustration, demonstration.

spectacle noun **1** *his love of spectacle:* display, show, pageantry, performance, exhibition, pomp and circumstance, extravaganza, spectacular. **2** *they were rather an odd spectacle:* sight, vision, scene, prospect, picture.

spectacular adjective **1** *a spectacular view:* striking, picturesque, eye-catching, breathtaking, arresting, glorious; informal out of this world. **2** *a spectacular victory:* impressive, magnificent, splendid, dazzling, sensational, dramatic, outstanding, memorable, unforgettable.
OPPOSITES dull, unimpressive.

spectator noun watcher, viewer, observer, onlooker, bystander, witness.

OPPOSITES participant.

spectre noun ghost, phantom, apparition, spirit, wraith, presence; informal spook.

speculate verb **1** *they speculated about my private life:* conjecture, theorize, hypothesize, guess, surmise, wonder, muse. **2** *investors speculate on the stock market:* gamble, venture, wager, invest, play the market; Brit. informal punt.

speculative adjective **1** *any discussion is largely speculative:* conjectural, suppositional, theoretical, hypothetical, tentative, unproven, unfounded, groundless, unsubstantiated. **2** *a speculative investment:* risky, hazardous, unsafe, uncertain, unpredictable; informal chancy.

speech noun **1** *the power of speech:* speaking, talking, verbal expression, verbal communication. **2** *her speech was slurred:* diction, elocution, articulation, enunciation, pronunciation, delivery, words. **3** *an after-dinner speech:* talk, address, lecture, discourse, oration, presentation, sermon. **4** *in popular speech:* language, parlance, tongue, idiom, dialect, vernacular; informal lingo.

S

formal talk given to an audience. **3** a sequence of lines written for one character in a play.
□ **speech therapy** treatment to help people with speech problems. **speech marks** inverted commas.

speechify verb (**speechifies, speechifying, speechified**) deliver a speech in a boring or pompous way.

speechless adjective unable to speak due to shock or strong emotion.

speed noun **1** the rate at which someone or something moves or operates. **2** a fast rate of movement or action. **3** each of the possible gear ratios of a vehicle or bicycle. **4** the sensitivity of photographic film to light. **5** informal an amphetamine drug. •verb (**speeds, speeding, speeded** or **sped**) **1** move quickly. **2** (**speed up**) move or work more quickly. **3** (of a motorist) travel at a speed greater than the legal limit. **4** old use make prosperous or successful.

speedboat noun a motorboat designed for high speed.

speedometer noun an instrument that indicates a vehicle's speed.

speedway noun Brit. a form of motorcycle racing in which the riders race around an oval dirt track.

speedwell noun a small plant with blue or pink flowers.

speedy adjective (**speedier, speediest**) done, happening, or moving quickly.
■ **speedily** adverb.

speleology /spee-li-**ol**-uh-ji/ noun the study or exploration of caves.
■ **speleologist** noun.

spell[1] verb (**spells, spelling, spelled** or chiefly Brit. **spelt**) **1** write or name the letters that form a word in correct sequence. **2** (of letters) form a word. **3** be a sign of. **4** (**spell something out**) explain something clearly and in detail.

spell[2] noun **1** a form of words with magical power. **2** a state of enchantment caused by a spell. **3** an ability to control or influence other people.

spell[3] noun a short period of time.

spellbound adjective with your attention completely held by something.
■ **spellbinding** adjective.

spellchecker noun a computer program which checks the spelling of words in an electronic document.

spelling noun **1** the process of spelling a word. **2** the way in which a word is spelled.

spend verb (**spends, spending, spent**) **1** pay out money to buy or hire goods or services. **2** pass time in a particular way. **3** use up energy or resources.
■ **spender** noun.

spendthrift noun a person who spends too much money or wastes money.

sperm noun (plural **sperm** or **sperms**) **1** semen. **2** a spermatozoon.
□ **sperm whale** a toothed whale that feeds largely on squid.

spermatozoon /sper-muh-tuh-**zoh**-on/ noun (plural **spermatozoa** /sper-muh-tuh-**zoh**-uh/) the male sex cell of an animal, that fertilizes the egg.

spermicide noun a contraceptive substance that kills spermatozoa.

spew verb **1** pour out in large quantities. **2** informal vomit.

sphagnum /**sfag**-nuhm/ noun a kind of moss that grows in boggy areas.

THESAURUS

speed noun **1** *the speed of their progress:* rate, pace, tempo, momentum, velocity; informal lick. **2** *the speed with which they responded:* rapidity, swiftness, promptness, briskness, haste, hurry.
OPPOSITES slowness.
•verb **1** *I sped home:* hurry, rush, dash, race, sprint, career, shoot, hurtle, hare, fly, zoom, hasten; informal tear, belt, pelt; Brit. informal bomb. **2** *a holiday will speed his recovery:* hasten, speed up, accelerate, advance, further, promote, boost, stimulate, aid, assist, facilitate.
OPPOSITES dawdle, slow, hinder.
□ **speed up hurry up**, accelerate, go faster, get a move on, put a spurt on, pick up speed; informal step on it.

speedy adjective fast, swift, quick, rapid, prompt, immediate, brisk, hasty, hurried, precipitate, rushed.
OPPOSITES slow.

spell[1] verb *the drought spelled disaster:* signal, signify, mean, amount to, add up to, constitute.
□ **spell something out explain**, make clear, clarify, specify, detail.

spell[2] noun **1** *the witch muttered a spell:* charm, incantation, formula, curse; N. Amer. hex; (**spells**) magic, sorcery, witchcraft. **2** *she surrendered to his spell:* influence, charm, magnetism, charisma, magic.
□ **put a spell on bewitch**, enchant, entrance, curse, jinx, witch; N. Amer. hex.

spell[3] noun **1** *a spell of dry weather:* period, time, interval, season, stretch, run; Brit. informal patch. **2** *a spell of dizziness:* bout, fit, attack.

spend verb **1** *she spent £185 on shoes:* pay out, expend; informal blow, splurge. **2** *the morning was spent gardening:* pass, occupy, fill, take up, while away. **3** *I've spent hours on this essay:* put in, devote, waste, squander.

S

sphere noun **1** a round solid figure in which every point on the surface is at an equal distance from the centre. **2** an area of activity or interest.

spherical adjective shaped like a sphere. ■ **spherically** adverb.

sphincter noun a ring of muscle surrounding an opening such as the anus.

sphinx noun an ancient Egyptian stone figure having a lion's body and a human or animal head.

spice noun **1** a strong-tasting substance used to flavour food. **2** an element that provides interest and excitement. •verb (**spices, spicing, spiced**) **1** flavour with spice. **2** (**spice something up**) make something more exciting or interesting.

spick and span adjective neat, clean, and well looked after.

spicy adjective (**spicier, spiciest**) **1** strongly flavoured with spice. **2** mildly indecent. ■ **spiciness** noun.

spider noun a small insect-like creature (an arachnid) with eight legs. ■ **spidery** adjective.

spiel /shpeel, speel/ noun informal an elaborate and insincere speech made in an attempt to persuade someone.

spigot noun **1** a small peg or plug. **2** the end of a section of a pipe that fits into the socket of the next one.

spike noun **1** a thin, pointed piece of metal or wood. **2** each of several metal points set into the sole of a sports shoe to prevent slipping. **3** a cluster of flower heads attached directly to a long stem. •verb (**spikes, spiking, spiked**) **1** impale on or pierce with a spike. **2** cover with sharp points. **3** informal secretly add alcohol or a drug to drink or food. ■ **spiky** adjective.

spill¹ verb (**spills, spilling, spilt** or **spilled**) **1** flow, or allow to flow, over the edge of a container. **2** move or empty out from a place. •noun **1** a quantity of liquid spilt.

2 informal a fall from a horse or bicycle. □ **spill the beans** informal reveal confidential information. **spill blood** kill or wound people. ■ **spillage** noun.

spill² noun a thin strip of wood or paper used for lighting a fire.

spin verb (**spins, spinning, spun**) **1** turn round quickly. **2** (of a person's head) have a dizzy sensation. **3** (of a ball) move through the air with a revolving motion. **4** draw out and twist the fibres of wool, cotton, etc. to convert them into yarn. **5** (of a spider, silkworm, etc.) produce silk or a web by forcing out a fine thread from a special gland. **6** (**spin something out**) make something last as long as possible. •noun **1** a spinning motion. **2** informal a brief trip in a vehicle for pleasure. **3** a favourable slant given to a news story. □ **spin doctor** informal a person employed by a political party to give a favourable interpretation of events to the media. **spin dryer** a machine that removes water from washed clothes by spinning them in a drum. **spinning wheel** a piece of equipment for spinning yarn or thread with a spindle driven by a wheel operated by hand or foot. **spin-off** something unexpected but useful resulting from an activity. ■ **spinner** noun.

spina bifida /spy-nuh **bi**-fi-duh/ noun a condition in which part of the spinal cord is exposed, sometimes causing paralysis.

spinach noun a plant with large dark green leaves which are eaten as a vegetable.

spinal adjective relating to the spine. □ **spinal column** the spine. **spinal cord** the nerve fibres enclosed in the spine and connected to the brain.

spindle noun **1** a slender rod with tapered ends used for spinning wool, flax, etc. by hand. **2** a rod around which something revolves.

spindly adjective long or tall and thin.

S

sphere noun **1** *a glass sphere*: globe, ball, orb, bubble. **2** *sphere of influence*: area, field, compass, orbit, range, scope, extent. **3** *the sphere of foreign affairs*: domain, realm, province, field, area, territory, arena, department.

spice noun **1** *the spices in curry powder*: seasoning, flavouring, condiment. **2** *the risk added spice to their affair*: excitement, interest, colour, piquancy, zest, an edge.

spicy adjective hot, tangy, peppery, piquant, spiced, highly seasoned, pungent. OPPOSITES bland.

spike noun prong, pin, barb, point, skewer, stake, spit.

spill verb **1** *Kevin spilled his drink*: knock over, tip over, upset, overturn. **2** *the bath water spilled on to the floor*: overflow, slop, slosh, splash, leak. **3** *students spilled out of the building*: stream, pour, surge, swarm, flood, throng, crowd.

spin verb **1** *the wheels are spinning*: revolve, rotate, turn, go round, whirl. **2** *she spun round to face him*: whirl, wheel, twirl, turn, swing, twist, swivel, pivot. •noun **1** *a spin of the wheel*: rotation, revolution, turn, whirl, twirl. **2** *a positive spin*: slant, angle, twist, bias. **3** *a spin in the car*: trip, jaunt, outing, excursion, journey, drive, ride, run, turn; informal tootle.

spindrift noun spray blown from the sea by the wind.

spine noun 1 a series of bones extending from the skull to the small of the back, enclosing the spinal cord; the backbone. 2 the part of a book that encloses the inner edges of the pages. 3 a hard pointed projection found on certain plants and animals.
□ **spine-chiller** a story or film that causes terror and excitement.
■ **spiny** adjective.

spineless adjective 1 lacking courage and determination. 2 having no backbone; invertebrate. 3 having no spines.

spinet noun a kind of small harpsichord.

spinnaker noun a large three-cornered sail used on a racing yacht when the wind is coming from behind.

spinney noun (plural **spinneys**) Brit. a small area of trees and bushes.

spinster noun disapproving a single woman beyond the usual age for marriage.
■ **spinsterhood** noun.

spiral adjective winding in a continuous curve around a central point or axis. • noun 1 a spiral curve, shape, or pattern. 2 a continuous rise or fall of prices, wages, etc. • verb (**spirals**, **spiralling**, **spiralled**; US spelling **spirals**, **spiraling**, **spiraled**) 1 follow a spiral course. 2 show a continuous increase or decrease.
■ **spirally** adverb.

spire noun a pointed structure on the top of a church tower.

spirit noun 1 the part of a person that consists of their character and feelings rather than their body. 2 a supernatural being. 3 typical character, quality, or mood.

4 (**spirits**) a person's mood or state of mind. 5 courage, energy, and determination. 6 the real meaning of something as opposed to its strict interpretation. 7 (also **spirits**) chiefly Brit. strong alcoholic drink, e.g. rum. 8 purified distilled alcohol, e.g. methylated spirit.
• verb (**spirits**, **spiriting**, **spirited**) (**spirit someone/thing away**) take someone or something away quickly and secretly.
□ **spirit level** a glass tube partially filled with a liquid, containing an air bubble whose position reveals whether a surface is perfectly level.

spirited adjective energetic and determined.
■ **spiritedly** adverb.

spiritual adjective 1 having to do with the human spirit as opposed to material or physical things. 2 having to do with religion or religious belief. • noun a religious song of a kind associated with black Christians of the southern US.
■ **spirituality** noun **spiritually** adverb.

spiritualism noun the belief that the spirits of the dead can communicate with the living.
■ **spiritualist** noun.

spirogyra /spy-ruh-jy-ruh/ noun a type of algae consisting of long green threads.

spit[1] verb (**spits**, **spitting**, **spat** or **spit**) 1 forcibly eject saliva, or food, liquid, etc., from the mouth. 2 say in a hostile way. 3 give out small bursts of sparks or hot fat. 4 (**it spits, it is spitting**) Brit. light rain falls. • noun 1 saliva. 2 an act of spitting.
□ **be the spitting image of** informal look exactly like.

spit[2] noun 1 a metal rod pushed through meat in order to hold and turn it while it is roasted. 2 a narrow point of land

THESAURUS

spine noun 1 *he injured his spine:* backbone, spinal column, back. 2 *cactus spines:* needle, quill, bristle, barb, spike, prickle, thorn.

spiral adjective *a spiral column:* coiled, helical, curling, winding, twisting.
• noun *a spiral of smoke:* coil, curl, twist, whorl, scroll, helix, corkscrew.
• verb *smoke spiralled up:* coil, wind, swirl, twist, snake.

spirit noun 1 *body and spirit:* soul, psyche, inner self, inner man/woman, mind. 2 *a spirit haunts the island:* ghost, phantom, spectre, apparition, presence. 3 *in good spirits:* mood, frame/state of mind, humour, temper. 4 *team spirit:* morale, esprit de corps. 5 *the spirit of the age:* ethos, essence, atmosphere, mood, feeling, climate. 6 *they played with spirit:* enthusiasm, energy, verve, vigour, dynamism, dash, sparkle, exuberance,

gusto, fervour, zeal, fire, passion; informal get-up-and-go. 7 *the spirit of the law:* real meaning, true meaning, essence, substance, idea.
OPPOSITES body, flesh.

spirited adjective lively, energetic, enthusiastic, vigorous, dynamic, passionate; informal feisty, gutsy; N. Amer. informal peppy.
OPPOSITES apathetic, lifeless.

spiritual adjective 1 *your spiritual self:* inner, mental, psychological, incorporeal, non-material. 2 *spiritual writings:* religious, sacred, divine, holy, devotional.
OPPOSITES physical, secular.

spit verb 1 *Cranston coughed and spat:* expectorate, hawk; Brit. informal gob. 2 *the fat began to spit:* sizzle, hiss, crackle, sputter.
• noun *spit dribbled from his mouth:* spittle, saliva, sputum, slobber, dribble; Brit. informal gob.

sticking out into the sea.

spite noun a desire to hurt, annoy, or offend someone. •verb (**spites, spiting, spited**) deliberately hurt, annoy, or offend someone.
□ **in spite of** without being affected by.

spiteful adjective deliberately hurtful; malicious.
■ **spitefully** adverb.

spitfire noun a person with a fierce temper.

spittle noun saliva.

spittoon noun a container for spitting into.

spiv noun Brit. informal a flashily dressed man who makes a living by dishonest business dealings.

splash verb **1** (of a liquid) fall in scattered drops. **2** make wet with scattered drops. **3** move around in water, causing it to fly about. **4** (**splash down**) (of a spacecraft) land on water. **5** prominently display a story or photograph in a newspaper or magazine. **6** (**splash out**) Brit. informal spend money freely. •noun **1** an instance of splashing. **2** a small quantity of liquid splashed on to a surface. **3** a small quantity of liquid added to a drink. **4** a bright patch of colour. **5** informal a prominent news story.
□ **make a splash** informal attract a lot of attention.

splatter verb (**splatters, splattering,**

splattered) splash with a sticky or thick liquid. •noun a splash of a sticky or thick liquid.

splay verb spread out wide apart.

spleen noun **1** an organ involved in producing and removing blood cells. **2** bad temper.

splendid adjective **1** magnificent; very impressive. **2** informal excellent.
■ **splendidly** adverb.

splendour (US spelling **splendor**) noun magnificent and impressive appearance.

splenetic adjective bad-tempered or spiteful.

splice verb (**splices, splicing, spliced**) **1** join ropes by weaving together the strands at the ends. **2** join pieces of film, tape, etc. at the ends. •noun a spliced join.

spliff noun informal a cannabis cigarette.

splint noun a rigid support for a broken bone.

splinter noun a small, thin, sharp piece of wood, glass, etc. broken off from a larger piece. •verb (**splinters, splintering, splintered**) break into splinters.
□ **splinter group** a small breakaway group.

split verb (**splits, splitting, split**) **1** break into parts by force. **2** divide into parts or

THESAURUS

spite noun *he said it out of spite:* malice, malevolence, ill will, vindictiveness, meanness, nastiness; informal bitchiness, cattiness.
OPPOSITES kindness.
•verb *he did it to spite me:* upset, hurt, wound.
OPPOSITES please.
□ **in spite of** despite, notwithstanding, regardless of, in defiance of, in the face of.

splash verb **1** *splash your face with water:* sprinkle, spray, shower, wash, squirt, daub, wet. **2** *his boots were splashed with rain:* spatter, splatter, speck, smear, stain, mark. **3** *waves splashing on the beach:* wash, break, lap, pound. **4** *children splashed in the water:* paddle, wade, wallow.
•noun **1** *a splash of rain:* spot, blob, smear, speck. **2** *a splash of lemonade:* drop, dash, bit, spot, soupçon, dribble; Scottish informal scoosh. **3** *a splash of colour:* patch, burst, streak.

splendid adjective **1** *splendid costumes:* magnificent, sumptuous, grand, imposing, superb, spectacular, resplendent, rich, lavish, ornate, gorgeous, glorious, dazzling, handsome, beautiful; informal plush; Brit. informal swish. **2** (informal) *a splendid holiday:* excellent, wonderful, marvellous, superb, glorious, lovely, delightful, first-class; informal super, great, amazing, fantastic,

terrific, tremendous; Brit. informal smashing, brilliant.
OPPOSITES simple, modest, awful.

splendour noun magnificence, sumptuousness, grandeur, resplendence, richness, glory, majesty.
OPPOSITES simplicity, modesty.

splinter noun *a splinter of wood:* sliver, chip, shard, fragment, shred; Scottish skelf.
•verb *the glass splintered:* shatter, smash, break into smithereens, fracture, split, crack, disintegrate.

split verb **1** *the force split the wood:* break, cut, burst, snap, crack. **2** *the ice split under him:* break, fracture, rupture, burst, snap, crack, come apart, splinter. **3** *her dress was split:* tear, rip, slash, slit. **4** *they split the profit:* share, divide up, distribute, dole out, parcel out, carve up, slice up. **5** *the path split:* fork, divide, branch, diverge. **6** *the band split up last year:* break up, separate, part, part company, go their separate ways.
OPPOSITES mend, join, unite, pool, converge, get together.
•noun **1** *a split in the rock face:* crack, fissure, cleft, crevice, break, fracture, breach. **2** *a split in the curtain:* rip, tear, cut, rent, slash, slit. **3** *a split in the Party:* division, rift, breach, schism, rupture, partition. **4** *the acrimonious split with his*

S

groups. **3** (often **split up**) end a marriage or other relationship. **4** (**be splitting**) informal (of a person's head) be suffering from a bad headache. • noun **1** a tear or crack. **2** an instance of splitting. **3** (**the splits**) a leap or seated position with the legs straight and at right angles to the body.
□ **split infinitive** Grammar an infinitive construction in which an adverb or other word is placed between *to* and the verb (e.g. *she used to secretly admire him*), traditionally regarded as bad English. **split-level** (of a room or building) having the floor divided into two levels. **split second** a very brief moment of time.

splodge or **splotch** noun Brit. a spot, splash, or smear.

splosh informal verb make a soft splashing sound. • noun a splashing sound.

splurge informal verb (**splurges**, **splurging**, **splurged**) spend extravagantly. • noun a sudden burst of extravagance.

splutter verb (**splutters**, **spluttering**, **spluttered**) **1** make a series of short explosive spitting or choking sounds. **2** say in a rapid, unclear way. • noun a spluttering sound.

spoil verb (**spoils**, **spoiling**, past and past participle **spoilt** (chiefly Brit.) or **spoiled**) **1** make something less good or enjoyable. **2** (of food) become unfit for eating. **3** harm the character of a child by not being strict enough. **4** treat with great or excessive kindness. **5** (**be spoiling for**) be very eager for. • noun (**spoils**) stolen goods.

spoiler noun **1** a flap on an aircraft wing which can be raised to create drag and slow it down. **2** a similar device on a car intended to improve roadholding at high speeds.

spoilsport noun a person who spoils the pleasure of other people.

spoke^1 noun each of the rods connecting the centre of a wheel to its rim.

spoke^2 past of SPEAK.

spoken past participle of SPEAK. • adjective speaking in a particular way: *a soft-spoken man.*
□ **be spoken for** be already claimed.

spokesman or **spokeswoman** noun (plural **spokesmen** or **spokeswomen**) a person who makes statements on behalf of a group.

spokesperson noun (plural **spokespersons** or **spokespeople**) a spokesman or spokeswoman.

spoliation /spoh-li-**ay**-shuhn/ noun **1** the action of destroying or ruining something. **2** the action of plundering.

sponge noun **1** a simple sea creature with no backbone and a soft porous body. **2** a piece of a light, absorbent substance used for washing, as padding, etc. **3** Brit. a cake made with little or no fat. • verb (**sponges**, **sponging** or **spongeing**, **sponged**) **1** wipe or clean with a wet sponge or cloth. **2** informal obtain money or food from other people without giving anything in return.
□ **sponge bag** Brit. a toilet bag.
■ **sponger** noun **spongy** adjective.

sponsor noun **1** a person or organization that helps pays for an event in return for advertising. **2** a person who promises to give money to a charity if another person completes a task or activity. **3** a person who proposes a new law. • verb be a sponsor for.
■ **sponsorship** noun.

☑ *-or, not -er:* sponsor.

spontaneous adjective **1** done or happening as a result of an impulse. **2** open, natural, and relaxed. **3** happening

---

THESAURUS

wife: break-up, split-up, separation, parting, estrangement, rift.
OPPOSITES join, merger, marriage.

spoil verb **1** *smoking spoils your complexion:* damage, ruin, impair, blemish, disfigure, blight, deface, harm, destroy, wreck. **2** *rain spoiled my plans:* ruin, wreck, upset, undo, mess up, sabotage, scotch, torpedo; informal muck up, screw up, do for, put the kibosh on; Brit. informal cock up, scupper. **3** *his sisters spoil him:* overindulge, pamper, indulge, mollycoddle, cosset, wait on someone hand and foot. **4** *stockpiled food may spoil:* go bad, go off, go rancid, turn, go sour, rot, perish.
OPPOSITES improve, enhance, further, neglect.

spoken adjective verbal, oral, vocal, unwritten, word-of-mouth.

OPPOSITES written.

spokesperson, spokesman, spokeswoman noun representative, voice, mouthpiece, agent, official; informal spin doctor.

sponsor noun backer, patron, promoter, benefactor, supporter, contributor.
• verb finance, fund, subsidize, back, promote, support, contribute to; N. Amer. informal bankroll.

spontaneous adjective **1** *a spontaneous display of affection:* unplanned, unpremeditated, impulsive, impromptu, spur-of-the-moment, unprompted; informal off-the-cuff. **2** *a spontaneous kind of person:* natural, uninhibited, relaxed, unselfconscious, unaffected.
OPPOSITES planned, inhibited.

without apparent external cause.
■ **spontaneity** noun **spontaneously** adverb.

spoof noun informal a humorous imitation of something.

spook informal **noun 1** a ghost. **2** N. Amer. a spy. •**verb** frighten.

spooky adjective (**spookier, spookiest**) informal sinister or ghostly.
■ **spookily** adverb.

spool noun a cylindrical device on which thread, film, etc. can be wound. •**verb** wind on to a spool.

spoon noun an implement consisting of a small, shallow bowl on a long handle, used for eating and serving food. •**verb** transfer food with a spoon.
□ **spoon-feed 1** feed someone with a spoon. **2** provide someone with so much help that they do not need to think for themselves.
■ **spoonful** noun.

spoonbill noun a tall wading bird that has a long bill with a very broad flat tip.

spoonerism noun a mistake in speech in which the initial sounds or letters of two or more words are accidentally swapped around, as in *you have hissed the mystery lectures*.

spoor noun the track or scent of an animal.

sporadic adjective happening at irregular intervals or only in a few places.
■ **sporadically** adverb.

spore noun a tiny reproductive cell produced by fungi and plants such as mosses and algae.

sporran noun a small pouch worn around the waist as part of men's Scottish Highland dress.

sport noun **1** a competitive activity which involves physical effort and skill. **2** informal a person who behaves well when teased or defeated. •**verb 1** wear a distinctive item. **2** literary amuse yourself or play in a lively way.
□ **sports car** a small, fast car. **sports jacket** a

man's informal jacket resembling a suit jacket.

sporting adjective **1** connected with or interested in sport. **2** fair and generous.
□ **sporting chance** a reasonable chance of winning or succeeding.
■ **sportingly** adverb.

sportive adjective playful; light-hearted.

sportsman or **sportswoman** noun (plural **sportsmen** or **sportswomen**) **1** a person who takes part in a sport. **2** a person who behaves in a fair and generous way.
■ **sportsmanship** noun.

sporty adjective (**sportier, sportiest**) informal **1** fond of or good at sport. **2** (of clothing) suitable for sport or casual wear. **3** (of a car) compact and fast.

spot noun **1** a small round mark on a surface. **2** a pimple. **3** a particular place, point, or position. **4** a small amount of something. •**verb** (**spots, spotting, spotted**) **1** notice or recognize, especially with difficulty or effort. **2** mark with spots.
□ **on the spot 1** immediately. **2** at the scene of an action or event. **spot check** a test made without warning on a person or thing selected at random. **spot on** completely accurate.
■ **spotted** adjective **spotter** noun **spotty** adjective.

spotless adjective absolutely clean or pure.
■ **spotlessly** adverb.

spotlight noun **1** a lamp projecting a narrow, strong beam of light directly on to a place or person. **2** (**the spotlight**) intense public attention. •**verb** (**spotlights, spotlighting**, past and past participle **spotlighted** or **spotlit**) light up with a spotlight.

spouse noun formal a husband or wife.

spout noun **1** a projecting tube or lip through or over which liquid can be poured from a container. **2** a stream of liquid flowing out. •**verb 1** send out or flow in a stream. **2** express your views in a lengthy and forceful way.
□ **up the spout** Brit. informal useless or ruined.

S

THESAURUS

sport noun game, physical recreation.
•**verb** *he was sporting a new tie:* wear, have on, dress in, show off, parade, flaunt.

sporting adjective sportsmanlike, generous, considerate, fair; Brit. informal decent.
OPPOSITES dirty, unfair.

sporty adjective (informal) athletic, fit, active, energetic.
OPPOSITES unfit, lazy.

spot noun **1** *a grease spot:* mark, patch, dot, fleck, smudge, smear, stain, blotch, splash; informal splodge. **2** *a spot on his nose:* pimple, pustule, blackhead, boil; informal zit; Scottish informal plook; (**spots**) acne. **3** *a secluded spot:* place, site, position,

situation, setting, location, venue.
•**verb** *she spotted him at the bar:* see, notice, observe, detect, make out, recognize, identify, locate, catch sight of, discern; Brit. informal clock; literary espy.

spotlight noun attention, glare of publicity, limelight, public eye.

spotted adjective spotty, dotted, polka-dot, freckled, mottled.

spotty adjective **1** *a spotty dress:* polka-dot, spotted, dotted. **2** (Brit.) *his spotty face:* pimply, pimpled, acned; Scottish informal plooky.

spouse noun partner, husband, wife, mate,

sprain verb wrench a joint violently so as to cause pain and swelling. • noun an instance of wrenching a joint.

sprang past of SPRING.

sprat noun a small sea fish of the herring family.

sprawl verb 1 sit, lie, or fall with your arms and legs spread out awkwardly. 2 spread out irregularly over a large area. • noun 1 a sprawling position or movement. 2 the disorganized expansion of a town or city.

spray noun 1 liquid sent through the air in tiny drops. 2 a liquid which can be forced out of an aerosol or other container in a spray. 3 a stem or small branch with flowers and leaves. 4 a small bunch of cut flowers worn on clothing. • verb 1 apply a spray of liquid to something. 2 scatter something over an area with great force.

spread verb (spreads, spreading, spread) 1 open out fully. 2 stretch out hands, fingers, wings, etc. 3 extend over a wide area or a specified period of time. 4 apply a substance in an even layer. • noun 1 the process of spreading. 2 the extent, width, or area covered by something. 3 the range of something. 4 a soft paste that can be spread on bread. 5 an article covering several pages of a newspaper or magazine. 6 informal a large and elaborate meal.
■ **spreader** noun.

spreadeagle verb (be spreadeagled) be stretched out with the arms and legs extended.

spreadsheet noun a computer program in which figures are arranged in a grid and used in calculations.

spree noun a short period of time spent doing a lot of a particular thing: a shopping spree.

sprig noun a small stem with leaves or flowers, taken from a bush or plant.

sprightly adjective (sprightlier, sprightliest) (of an old person) lively; energetic.
■ **sprightliness** noun.

spring verb (springs, springing, sprang or sprung; past participle sprung) 1 move suddenly upwards or forwards. 2 (spring from) come or appear from. 3 (spring up) suddenly develop or appear. 4 (sprung) having springs. • noun 1 the season after winter and before summer. 2 a spiral metal coil that returns to its former shape after being pressed or pulled. 3 a sudden jump upwards or forwards. 4 a place where water wells up from an underground source. 5 the quality of being elastic.
□ spring-clean clean a house or building thoroughly. spring-loaded containing a spring that presses one part against another. spring onion Brit. an onion taken from the ground before the bulb has formed.
■ **springy** adjective.

springboard noun 1 a flexible board from which a diver or gymnast jumps in order to push off more powerfully. 2 something that starts off an activity or enterprise.

springbok noun a southern African gazelle which leaps when disturbed.

sprinkle verb (sprinkles, sprinkling, sprinkled) 1 scatter or pour small drops or particles over an object or surface. 2 distribute something randomly

THESAURUS

consort; informal better half; Brit. informal other half.

sprawl verb stretch out, lounge, loll, slump, flop, slouch.

spray noun 1 a spray of water: shower, sprinkle, jet, squirt, mist, spume, foam, froth. 2 a perfume spray: aerosol, vaporizer, atomizer, sprinkler.
• verb 1 we sprayed water on the soil: sprinkle, dribble, drizzle. 2 spray the plants with weedkiller: water, mist, soak, douse, drench. 3 water sprayed into the air: spout, jet, gush, spurt, shoot, squirt.

spread verb 1 he spread the map out: lay out, open out, unfurl, unroll, roll out, straighten out, fan out, stretch out, extend. 2 the landscape spread out below: extend, stretch, sprawl. 3 papers were spread all over his desk: scatter, disperse, distribute. 4 he's spreading rumours: circulate, broadcast, put about, publicize, propagate, repeat. 5 the disease spread rapidly: travel, move, be borne, sweep,

diffuse, reproduce, be passed on, be transmitted. 6 she spread sun cream on her arms: smear, daub, plaster, apply, rub.
OPPOSITES fold up, suppress.
• noun 1 the spread of learning: expansion, proliferation, dissemination, diffusion, transmission, propagation. 2 a spread of six feet: span, width, extent, stretch, reach.

spree noun bout, orgy; informal binge, splurge.

spring verb 1 the cat sprang off her lap: leap, jump, bound, vault. 2 the branch sprang back: fly, whip, flick, whisk, kick, bounce. 3 all art springs from feelings: originate, derive, arise, stem, emanate, evolve.
• noun the mattress has lost its spring: springiness, bounce, resilience, elasticity, flexibility, stretch, stretchiness, give.

sprinkle verb 1 he sprinkled water on the cloth: splash, trickle, drizzle, spray, shower, drip. 2 sprinkle sesame seeds over the top: scatter, strew. 3 sprinkle the cake with icing sugar: dredge, dust.

S

throughout. •noun a small amount that is sprinkled.

sprinkler noun 1 a device for watering lawns. 2 an automatic fire extinguisher installed in a ceiling.

sprint verb run at full speed over a short distance. •noun 1 a period of sprinting. 2 a short, fast race.
■ sprinter noun.

sprite noun an elf or fairy.

spritzer noun a mixture of wine and soda water.

sprocket noun each of several projections on the rim of a wheel that engage with the links of a chain or with holes in film, paper, etc.

sprout verb produce shoots; begin to grow. •noun 1 a shoot of a plant. 2 a Brussels sprout.

spruce¹ adjective neat and smart. •verb (spruces, sprucing, spruced) (spruce someone/thing up) make someone or something smarter.

spruce² noun an evergreen tree with hanging cones.

sprung past and past participle of SPRING.

spry adjective (of an old person) lively.

spud noun informal a potato.

spume noun literary froth or foam.

spun past and past participle of SPIN.

spunk noun informal courage and determination.
■ spunky adjective.

spur noun 1 a spiked device worn on a rider's heel for urging a horse forward. 2 an encouragement. 3 an area of high ground that sticks out from a mountain. 4 a short branch road or railway line. •verb (spurs, spurring, spurred) 1 encourage someone to do something, or make

something happen faster or sooner. 2 urge a horse forward with spurs.
□ on the spur of the moment on a sudden impulse; without planning in advance.

spurious /rhymes with curious/ adjective 1 false or fake. 2 (of reasoning) apparently but not actually correct.
■ spuriously adverb.

spurn verb reject in a contemptuous way.

spurt verb 1 gush out in a stream. 2 move with a sudden burst of speed. •noun 1 a gushing stream. 2 a sudden burst of activity or speed.

sputter verb (sputters, sputtering, sputtered) make a series of soft explosive sounds. •noun a sputtering sound.

sputum noun saliva and mucus that is coughed up.

spy noun (plural spies) a person who secretly collects information about an enemy or competitor. •verb (spies, spying, spied) 1 be a spy. 2 (spy on) watch secretly. 3 see or notice.

spyglass noun a small telescope.

spyhole noun Brit. a peephole.

sq. abbreviation square.

squab noun a young pigeon that has not yet left the nest.

squabble noun a noisy quarrel about something unimportant. •verb (squabbles, squabbling, squabbled) have a squabble.

squad noun 1 a division of a police force. 2 a group of sports players from which a team is chosen. 3 a small group of soldiers.

squaddie noun (plural squaddies) Brit. informal a private soldier.

squadron noun 1 a unit of an air force. 2 a group of warships.

squalid adjective 1 very dirty and

THESAURUS

sprint verb run, race, rush, dash, bolt, fly, charge, shoot, speed; informal hotfoot it, leg it.
OPPOSITES walk.

sprout verb 1 the seeds begin to sprout: germinate, put/send out shoots, bud. 2 parsley sprouted from the pot: spring, come up, grow, develop, appear.

spur noun the spur of competition: stimulus, incentive, encouragement, inducement, impetus, motivation.
OPPOSITES disincentive.
•verb the thought spurred him into action: stimulate, encourage, prompt, prod, impel, motivate, move, galvanize, inspire, drive.
OPPOSITES discourage.

spurn verb reject, rebuff, scorn, turn down, treat with contempt, disdain, look down your nose at; informal turn your nose up at.
OPPOSITES welcome, accept.

spy noun a foreign spy: agent, mole, plant; N. Amer. informal spook.
•verb she spied a coffee shop: notice, observe, see, spot, sight, catch sight of, glimpse, make out, discern, detect.
□ spy on observe, keep under surveillance, eavesdrop on, watch, bug.

spying noun espionage, intelligence gathering, surveillance, infiltration.

squabble noun there was a brief squabble: quarrel, disagreement, row, argument, dispute, wrangle, clash, altercation; informal tiff, set-to, run-in, scrap, dust-up; Brit. informal barney, ding-dong; N. Amer. informal rhubarb.
•verb they squabbled over money: quarrel, row, argue, bicker, disagree; informal scrap.

squad noun 1 a maintenance squad: team, crew, gang, force. 2 a squad of marines: detachment, detail, unit, platoon, battery, troop, patrol, squadron, commando.

S

unpleasant. **2** immoral or dishonest.

squall noun **1** a sudden violent gust of wind. **2** a loud cry. •verb (of a baby) cry noisily and continuously.

squalor noun the state of being squalid.

squander verb (**squanders, squandering, squandered**) waste time, money, etc. in a reckless or foolish way.

square noun **1** a flat shape with four equal straight sides and four right angles. **2** an open area surrounded by buildings. **3** the product of a number multiplied by itself. **4** an L-shaped or T-shaped instrument used for obtaining or testing right angles. **5** informal an old-fashioned or boring person. •adjective **1** having the shape of a square. **2** having or forming a right angle. **3** (of a unit of measurement) equal to the area of a square whose side is of the unit specified: *2,000 square feet.* **4** referring to the length of each side of a square shape or object: *ten metres square.* **5** level or parallel. **6** broad and solid in shape. **7** fair or honest. **8** informal old-fashioned or boringly conventional. •verb (**squares, squaring, squared**) **1** make something square or rectangular. **2** (**squared**) marked out in squares. **3** multiply a number by itself. **4** (**square with**) make or be consistent with. **5** settle a bill or debt. **6** make the score of a game even. **7** (**square up**) take up the position of a person about to fight.
□ **square dance** a country dance that starts with four couples facing one another in a square. **square meal** a large and balanced meal. **square root** the number which produces a given number when multiplied by itself.
■ **squarely** adverb.

squash¹ verb **1** crush or squeeze something so that it becomes flat or distorted. **2** force into a restricted space. **3** stop something from continuing or developing. •noun **1** a state of being squashed. **2** Brit. a concentrated liquid mixed with water to make a fruit-flavoured drink. **3** (also **squash rackets**) a game in which two players use rackets to hit a small rubber ball against the walls of a closed court.
■ **squashy** adjective.

squash² noun a type of vegetable like a marrow.

squat verb (**squats, squatting, squatted**) **1** crouch or sit with the knees bent and the heels close to the thighs. **2** unlawfully occupy an uninhabited building or area of land. •adjective short or low and wide. •noun **1** a squatting position. **2** a building occupied by squatters.
■ **squatter** noun.

squaw noun offensive an American Indian woman or wife.

squawk verb **1** (of a bird) make a loud, harsh noise. **2** say something in a loud, ugly tone. •noun a squawking sound.

squeak noun a short, high-pitched sound or cry. •verb **1** make a squeak. **2** say something in a high-pitched tone.
■ **squeaky** adjective.

squeal noun a long, high-pitched cry or noise. •verb **1** make a squeal. **2** say something in a high-pitched tone. **3** (**squeal on**) informal inform on.

squeamish adjective **1** easily disgusted or made to feel sick. **2** having very strong moral views.

squeegee noun a scraping tool with a rubber-edged blade, used for cleaning windows.

squeeze verb (**squeezes, squeezing, squeezed**) **1** firmly press from opposite sides. **2** extract liquid from something by squeezing. **3** manage to get into or through a restricted space. •noun **1** an act of squeezing. **2** a hug. **3** a small amount of liquid extracted by squeezing. **4** a strong

---

S

THESAURUS

squander verb waste, throw away, misuse, fritter away, spend like water; informal blow, go through, splurge, pour down the drain.
OPPOSITES manage, make good use of, save.

square adjective *the sides were square at half-time:* level, even, drawn, equal, tied, level pegging; informal even-steven(s).
•verb **1** *this does not square with the data:* agree, tally, be in agreement, be consistent, match up, correspond, fit. **2** *Tom squared things with his boss:* resolve, sort out, settle, clear up, work out, iron out, straighten out, set right, rectify, remedy; informal patch up.

squash verb **1** *the fruit got squashed:* crush, squeeze, mash, pulp, flatten, compress, distort, pound, trample. **2** *she squashed her clothes inside the bag:* force, ram, thrust, push, cram, jam, stuff, pack, squeeze, wedge.

squeeze verb **1** *I squeezed the bottle:* compress, press, crush, squash, pinch, nip, grasp, grip, clutch. **2** *squeeze the juice from both oranges:* extract, press, force, express. **3** *Sally squeezed her feet into the sandals:* force, thrust, cram, ram, jam, stuff, pack, wedge, press, squash. **4** *we all squeezed into Steve's van:* crowd, crush, cram, pack, jam, squash, shove, push, force your way. •noun **1** *he gave her hand a squeeze:* press, pinch, nip, grasp, grip, clutch, hug. **2** *it was quite a squeeze:* crush, jam, squash, congestion.

squeezy adjective.

squelch verb make a soft sucking sound, e.g. by treading in thick mud. •noun a squelching sound.
■ **squelchy** adjective.

squib noun a small firework.

squid noun (plural **squid** or **squids**) a sea creature with a long body, eight arms, and two long tentacles.

squiffy adjective Brit. informal slightly drunk.

squiggle noun a short line that curls and loops irregularly.
■ **squiggly** adjective.

squint verb 1 look at someone or something with your eyes partly closed. 2 have a squint affecting one eye. •noun 1 a condition in which one eye looks in a different direction from the other. 2 informal a quick or casual look.

squire noun 1 a country gentleman. 2 (in the past) a young nobleman who acted as an attendant to a knight.

squirm verb 1 wriggle or twist the body from side to side. 2 be embarrassed or ashamed. •noun a wriggling movement.

squirrel noun a bushy-tailed rodent which lives in trees. •verb (**squirrels, squirrelling, squirrelled**; US spelling **squirrels, squirreling, squirreled**) (**squirrel something away**) hide money or valuables in a safe place.

squirt verb 1 force liquid out in a thin jet from a small opening. 2 wet with a jet of liquid. •noun 1 a thin jet of liquid. 2 informal a weak or insignificant person.

squish verb 1 make a soft squelching sound. 2 informal squash. •noun a soft squelching sound.
■ **squishy** adjective.

Sri Lankan noun a person from Sri Lanka. •adjective relating to Sri Lanka.

SS abbreviation 1 Saints. 2 steamship. •noun the Nazi special police force.

St abbreviation 1 Saint. 2 Street. 3 (**st**) stone (in weight).

stab verb (**stabs, stabbing, stabbed**) 1 thrust a knife or other pointed weapon into. 2 thrust a pointed object at. 3 (of a pain) cause a sudden sharp feeling. •noun 1 an act of stabbing. 2 a sudden sharp feeling or pain. 3 (**a stab at**) informal an attempt to do.

stability noun the state of being stable.

stabilize or **stabilise** verb (**stabilizes, stabilizing, stabilized**) make or become stable.
■ **stabilization** noun **stabilizer** noun.

stable[1] adjective 1 not likely to give way or overturn; firmly fixed. 2 not worsening in health after an injury or operation. 3 emotionally well balanced. 4 not likely to change or fail.
■ **stably** adverb.

stable[2] noun 1 a building in which horses are kept. 2 an establishment where racehorses are kept and trained. •verb (**stables, stabling, stabled**) put or keep a horse in a stable.

stablemate noun a horse from the same stable as another.

staccato /stuh-**kah**-toh/ adjective Music with each sound or note sharply separated from the others.

stack noun 1 a neat pile of objects. 2 a rectangular or cylindrical pile of hay, straw, etc. 3 informal a large quantity. 4 a chimney. •verb 1 arrange in a stack. 2 fill or cover with stacks of things. 3 cause aircraft to fly at different altitudes while waiting to land. 4 arrange a pack of cards dishonestly.

stadium noun (plural **stadiums** or **stadia**) a sports ground with rows of seats for spectators.

staff noun 1 the employees of an

---

stab verb *he stabbed him in the stomach:* knife, run through, skewer, spear, gore, spike, impale.
•noun 1 *a stab of pain:* twinge, pang, throb, spasm, cramp, prick, flash, thrill. 2 (informal) *a stab at writing:* attempt, try; informal go, shot, crack, bash.

stability noun 1 *the stability of the equipment:* firmness, solidity, steadiness. 2 *his mental stability:* balance (of mind), (mental) health, sanity, reason. 3 *the stability of their relationship:* strength, durability, lasting nature, permanence.

stable adjective 1 *a stable vehicle:* firm, solid, steady, secure. 2 *a stable person:* well balanced, of sound mind, compos mentis, sane, normal, rational. 3 *a stable*

relationship: secure, solid, strong, steady, firm, sure, steadfast, established, enduring, lasting.
OPPOSITES wobbly, unbalanced, rocky, changeable.

stack noun *a stack of boxes:* heap, pile, mound, mountain, pyramid, tower.
•verb 1 *Leo was stacking plates:* heap (up), pile (up), assemble, put together, collect. 2 *they stacked the shelves:* load, fill (up), pack, charge, stuff, cram, stock.

staff noun 1 *we'll take on new staff:* employees, workers, workforce, personnel, human resources, manpower, labour. 2 *a wooden staff:* stick, stave, pole, rod.
•verb *the centre is staffed by teachers:* man,

organization. **2** a group of military officers assisting an officer in command. **3** a long stick used as a support or weapon. **4** a rod or sceptre held as a symbol of office or authority. **5** Music a stave. • **verb** provide an organization with staff.
□ **staff nurse** Brit. an experienced nurse less senior than a sister.

stag noun a fully adult male deer.
□ **stag night** an all-male celebration held for a man who is about to get married.

stage noun **1** a point or step in a process or development. **2** a raised platform on which actors, entertainers, or speakers perform. **3** (**the stage**) the acting profession. **4** a platform on to which passengers or cargo can be landed from a boat. • **verb** (**stages, staging, staged**) **1** present a performance of a play. **2** organize an event.
□ **stage fright** nervousness before or during a performance. **stage-manage** arrange something carefully to create a certain effect. **stage manager** the person responsible for lighting and other technical arrangements for a play. **stage-struck** having a strong desire to become an actor. **stage whisper** a loud whisper by an actor on stage, intended to be heard by the audience. **staging post** a regular stop on a journey.

stagecoach noun a horse-drawn vehicle formerly used to carry passengers along a regular route.

stagehand noun a person who deals with the scenery or props for a play.

stagger verb (**staggers, staggering, staggered**) **1** walk or move unsteadily. **2** astonish. **3** spread over a period of time. • **noun** an unsteady walk.

stagnant adjective **1** (of water or air) not moving and having an unpleasant smell. **2** showing little activity.

stagnate verb (**stagnates, stagnating, stagnated**) become stagnant.
■ **stagnation** noun.

stagy or **stagey** adjective very theatrical or exaggerated.

staid adjective respectable and unadventurous.

stain verb **1** mark or discolour with something that is not easily removed. **2** damage someone's reputation. **3** colour with a dye or chemical. • **noun 1** a discoloured patch or mark. **2** a thing that damages someone's reputation. **3** a dye or chemical used to colour materials.
□ **stained glass** coloured glass used to form pictures or designs. **stainless steel** a form of steel containing chromium, resistant to tarnishing and rust.
■ **stainless** adjective.

stair noun **1** each of a set of fixed steps. **2** (**stairs**) a set of steps leading from one floor of a building to another.

staircase or **stairway** noun a set of stairs and its surrounding structure.

stairwell noun a shaft in which a staircase is built.

stake[1] noun a strong post driven into the ground to support a tree, form part of a fence, etc. • **verb** (**stakes, staking, staked**) **1** support with a stake. **2** (**stake something out**) mark an area with stakes to claim ownership. **3** (**stake someone/thing out**) informal keep a place or person under observation.

stake[2] noun **1** a sum of money gambled. **2** a share or interest in a business or situation. **3** (**stakes**) prize money, especially in horse racing. **4** (**stakes**) a competitive situation. • **verb** (**stakes, staking, staked**) gamble money or valuables.
□ **at stake 1** at risk. **2** in question.

stakeholder noun a person who has an interest in a business, project, etc., especially because they have invested money in it

stalactite noun a tapering structure hanging from the roof of a cave, formed of calcium salts deposited by dripping water.

stalagmite noun a tapering column rising from the floor of a cave, formed of calcium salts deposited by dripping water.

THESAURUS

people, crew, work, operate.

stage noun **1** *this stage of the development:* phase, period, juncture, step, point, level. **2** *the last stage of the race:* part, section, portion, stretch, leg, lap, circuit. **3** *a raised stage:* platform, dais, stand, rostrum, podium.

stagger verb **1** *he staggered to the door:* lurch, reel, sway, teeter, totter, stumble. **2** *I was absolutely staggered:* amaze, astound, astonish, surprise, stun, confound, daze, take aback; informal flabbergast; Brit. informal knock for six.

stain verb **1** *her clothing was stained with blood:* discolour, soil, mark, spot, spatter, splatter, smear, splash, smudge. **2** *the wood was stained:* colour, tint, dye, pigment.
• **noun 1** *a mud stain:* mark, spot, blotch, smudge, smear. **2** *a stain on his character:* blemish, taint, blot, smear, dishonour.

stake[1] noun *a stake in the ground:* post, pole, stick, spike, upright, support, cane.

stake[2] noun **1** *high stakes:* bet, wager, ante. **2** *a 40% stake in the business:* share, interest, ownership, involvement.
• **verb** *he staked his week's pay:* bet, wager, lay, put on, gamble.

S

stale adjective **1** (of food) no longer fresh. **2** no longer new and interesting. **3** no longer interested or motivated.
■ staleness noun.

stalemate noun **1** a situation in which further progress by opposing sides seems impossible. **2** Chess a position in which a player is not in check but can only move into check.

stalk[1] noun **1** the stem of a plant or support of a leaf, flower, or fruit. **2** a slender support or stem.

stalk[2] verb **1** follow or approach stealthily. **2** obsessively follow, watch, or try to communicate with a particular person. **3** walk in a proud, stiff, or angry way.
■ stalker noun.

stall noun **1** a stand or booth where goods are sold in a market. **2** a compartment for an animal in a stable or cowshed. **3** a compartment in which a horse is held before the start of a race. **4** a compartment in a set of toilets. **5** (**stalls**) Brit. the ground-floor seats in a theatre. **6** a seat in the choir or chancel of a church. •verb **1** (of a vehicle's engine) suddenly stop running. **2** stop making progress. **3** be vague or indecisive so as to gain more time to deal with something. **4** (of an aircraft) be moving too slowly to be controlled effectively.

stallion noun an adult male horse that has not been castrated.

stalwart adjective loyal, reliable, and hard-working. •noun a stalwart supporter or member of an organization.

stamen /stay-muhn/ noun a male fertilizing organ of a flower.

stamina noun the ability to keep up effort over a long period.

stammer verb (**stammers, stammering, stammered**) speak or say with difficulty, making sudden pauses and repeating the first letters of words. •noun a tendency to stammer.

stamp verb **1** bring down your foot heavily. **2** walk with heavy, forceful steps. **3** (**stamp something out**) decisively put an end to something. **4** press with a device that leaves a mark or pattern. •noun **1** a small piece of paper stuck to a letter or parcel to record payment of postage. **2** an instrument for stamping a pattern or mark. **3** a mark or pattern made by a stamp. **4** a characteristic impression or quality. **5** an act of stamping the foot.
□ stamp duty a tax on some legal documents. stamping ground a place you regularly visit or spend time in.

stampede noun **1** a sudden panicked rush of a number of horses, cattle, etc. **2** a sudden mass movement or reaction due to interest or panic. •verb (**stampedes, stampeding, stampeded**) take part in a stampede.

stance noun **1** the way in which someone stands. **2** an attitude or standpoint.

stanch US spelling of STAUNCH[2].

stanchion noun an upright bar, post, or frame forming a support or barrier.

stand verb (**stands, standing, stood**) **1** be or

THESAURUS

stale adjective **1** stale food: old, past its best, off, dry, hard, musty, rancid. **2** stale air: stuffy, musty, fusty, stagnant. **3** stale beer: flat, spoiled, off, insipid, tasteless. **4** stale jokes: overused, hackneyed, tired, worn out, overworked, threadbare, banal, clichéd; N. Amer. played out.
OPPOSITES fresh, original.

stalk verb **1** he was stalking a deer: trail, follow, shadow, track, go after, hunt; informal tail. **2** she stalked out: strut, stride, march, flounce, storm, stomp, sweep.

stall noun **1** a market stall: stand, table, counter, booth, kiosk. **2** stalls for larger animals: pen, coop, sty, corral, enclosure, compartment.
•verb **1** quit stalling: delay, play for time, procrastinate, hedge, drag your feet, filibuster, stonewall. **2** stall him for a bit: delay, divert, distract, hold off.

stalwart adjective staunch, loyal, faithful, committed, devoted, dedicated, reliable, dependable.
OPPOSITES disloyal, unfaithful, unreliable.

stamina noun endurance, staying power,

energy, toughness, determination, tenacity, perseverance, grit.

stammer verb stutter, stumble over your words, hesitate, falter, pause, splutter.

stamp verb **1** he stamped on my toe: trample, step, tread, tramp, crush, squash, flatten. **2** John stamped off, muttering: stomp, stump, clump. **3** the name is stamped on the cover: imprint, print, impress, punch, inscribe, emboss.
•noun the stamp of authority: mark, hallmark, sign, seal, sure sign, smack, savour, air.
□ stamp something out put an end to, end, stop, crush, put down, curb, quell, suppress, extinguish, stifle, abolish, get rid of, eliminate, eradicate, destroy, wipe out.

stance noun **1** a natural golfer's stance: posture, body position, pose, attitude. **2** a liberal stance: attitude, opinion, standpoint, position, approach, policy, line.

stand verb **1** the men stood up: rise, get to your feet, get up, pick yourself up. **2** today a house stands on the site: be situated, be located, be positioned, be sited, have been

S

become upright, supported by the feet.
2 place or be situated in a particular
position. **3** remain stationary, undisturbed,
or unchanged. **4** be in a particular state or
condition. **5** tolerate or like. **6** Brit. be a
candidate in an election. • **noun 1** an
attitude towards an issue. **2** a determined
effort to hold your ground or resist
something. **3** a structure for holding or
displaying something. **4** a large structure
for spectators to sit or stand in. **5** a raised
platform for a band, orchestra, or speaker.
6 a stall from which goods are sold or
displayed. **7** (**the stand**) the witness box in
a law court. **8** a stopping of motion or
progress.
□ **stand by 1** look on without becoming
involved. **2** support or remain loyal to. **3** be
ready to take action if needed. **stand down**
(or **aside**) resign from a position or office.
stand for 1 be an abbreviation of or symbol
for. **2** put up with. **stand in** deputize for
someone. **stand-off** a deadlock between
two opponents. **stand-offish** informal distant
and cold in manner. **stand out 1** stick out
or be easily noticeable. **2** be clearly better.
stand someone up informal fail to keep a
date with someone. **stand up for** speak or
act in support of.

❗ use **standing** rather than **stood** with the
verb 'to be': say *we were standing in a line
for hours* rather than *we were stood in a
line for hours*.

standard noun **1** a level of quality or
achievement. **2** a measure or model used to
make comparisons. **3** (**standards**) principles
of good behaviour. **4** a military or
ceremonial flag. • **adjective** used or accepted
as normal or average.
□ **standard-bearer 1** a leading figure in a
cause or movement. **2** a soldier who carries
a military or ceremonial flag. **standard
English** the dialect of English used by most
educated English speakers. **standard lamp** a
tall lamp that is placed on the floor.
standard of living the degree of comfort
that a person or community has.

standardize or **standardise** verb
(**standardizes**, **standardizing**, **standardized**)
make something fit in with a standard.
■ **standardization** noun.

standby noun (plural **standbys**) **1** readiness
for duty or action. **2** a person or thing
ready to be used in an emergency.
• **adjective** (of tickets) sold only at the last
minute.

standing noun **1** position, status, or
reputation. **2** duration or length. • **adjective**

THESAURUS

built. **3** *he stood the vase on the shelf:* put,
set, erect, place, position, prop, install,
arrange; informal park. **4** *my decision stands:*
remain in force, remain in operation, hold,
hold good, apply, be the case, exist. **5** *his
heart could not stand the strain:* withstand,
endure, bear, put up with, take, cope with,
handle, sustain, resist, stand up to.
6 (informal) *I won't stand cheek:* put up with,
endure, tolerate, accept, take, abide, stand
for, support, countenance; formal brook.
OPPOSITES sit, lie down.
• **noun 1** *the party's stand on immigration:*
attitude, stance, opinion, standpoint,
position, approach, policy, line. **2** *a stand
against tyranny:* opposition, resistance. **3** *a
mirror on a stand:* base, support, platform,
rest, plinth, tripod, rack, trivet. **4** *a
newspaper stand:* stall, counter, booth,
kiosk.
□ **stand by** wait, be prepared, be in (a state
of) readiness, be ready for action, be on
full alert, wait in the wings. **stand by
someone/something 1** *she stood by her
husband:* **remain/be loyal to**, stick with/by,
remain/be true to, stand up for, support,
back up, defend, stick up for. **2** *the
government must stand by its pledges:*
abide by, keep (to), adhere to, hold to,
stick to, observe, comply with. **stand for
mean**, be short for, represent, signify,

denote, symbolize. **stand in** **deputize**, act,
substitute, fill in, take over, cover, hold the
fort, step into the breach, replace, relieve,
take over from; informal sub, step into
someone's shoes; N. Amer. pinch-hit. **stand
out** **be noticeable**, be visible, be obvious,
be conspicuous, stick out, attract attention,
catch the eye, leap out; informal stick/stand
out a mile, stick/stand out like a sore
thumb.

standard noun **1** *the standard of her work:*
quality, level, calibre, merit, excellence. **2** *a
safety standard:* guideline, norm, yardstick,
benchmark, measure, criterion, guide,
touchstone. **3** *a standard to live by:*
principle, ideal; (**standards**) code of
behaviour, morals, ethics. **4** *the regiment's
standard:* flag, banner, ensign, colour(s).
• **adjective 1** *the standard way of doing it:*
normal, usual, typical, stock, common,
ordinary, customary, conventional,
established. **2** *the standard work on the
subject:* definitive, classic, recognized,
accepted.
OPPOSITES unusual, special.

standing noun **1** *his standing in the
community:* status, ranking, position,
reputation, stature. **2** *a person of some
standing:* prestige, rank, eminence,
seniority, repute, stature, esteem,
importance, account.

S

remaining in force or use: *a standing invitation.*

□ **standing joke** something that regularly causes amusement. **standing order** Brit. an instruction to a bank to make regular fixed payments to someone. **standing ovation** a long period of applause during which the audience rise to their feet.

standpoint noun an attitude towards a particular issue.

standstill noun a situation or condition without movement or activity.

stank past of **STINK**.

stanza noun a group of lines forming the basic unit in a poem.

staple¹ noun **1** a small piece of wire used to fasten papers together. **2** a small U-shaped metal bar driven into wood to hold things in place. •verb (**staples**, **stapling**, **stapled**) secure with a staple or staples.
■ **stapler** noun.

staple² noun **1** a main item of trade or production. **2** a main or important element. •adjective main or important.

star noun **1** a large ball of burning gas which appears as a glowing point in the night sky. **2** a simplified representation of a star with five or six points. **3** a famous entertainer or sports player. •verb (**stars**, **starring**, **starred**) **1** have someone as a leading performer. **2** have a leading role in a film, play, etc.
□ **Stars and Stripes** the national flag of the US. **star sign** a sign of the zodiac.
■ **stardom** noun.

starboard noun the side of a ship or aircraft that is on the right when you are facing forward.

starch noun **1** a carbohydrate which is obtained from potatoes, flour, rice, etc. and is an important part of the human diet. **2** powder or spray used to stiffen fabric. •verb stiffen with starch.

starchy adjective (**starchier**, **starchiest**) **1** containing a lot of starch. **2** informal stiff and formal in manner.

stare verb (**stares**, **staring**, **stared**) look with concentration and the eyes wide open. •noun an act of staring.

starfish noun (plural **starfish** or **starfishes**) a sea creature having five or more arms extending from a central point.

stark adjective **1** severe or bare in appearance. **2** unpleasantly or sharply clear. **3** complete; sheer: *stark terror.*
□ **stark naked** completely naked.
■ **starkly** adverb.

starkers adjective Brit. informal completely naked.

starlet noun informal a promising young actress or performer.

starling noun a bird with shiny dark speckled feathers.

starry adjective (**starrier**, **starriest**) full of or lit by stars.
□ **starry-eyed** full of unrealistic hopes or dreams.

starship noun (in science fiction) a spaceship for travel between stars.

start verb **1** begin to do or happen. **2** begin

THESAURUS

staple adjective main, principal, chief, major, primary, leading, foremost, first, most important, predominant, dominant, basic, prime; informal number-one.

star noun **1** *the sky was full of stars:* celestial/heavenly body, sun. **2** *the stars of the film:* principal, leading lady/man, lead, hero, heroine. **3** *a star of the world of chess:* celebrity, superstar, famous name, household name, leading light, VIP, personality, luminary; informal celeb, big shot, megastar.
OPPOSITES nobody.
•adjective **1** *a star pupil:* outstanding, exceptional. **2** *the star attraction:* top, leading, greatest, foremost, major, pre-eminent.
OPPOSITES poor, minor.

stare verb gaze, gape, goggle, glare, ogle, peer; informal gawk; Brit. informal gawp.

stark adjective **1** *a stark silhouette:* sharp, crisp, distinct, clear, clear-cut. **2** *a stark landscape:* desolate, bare, barren, empty, bleak. **3** *a stark room:* austere, severe, plain, simple, bare, unadorned. **4** *stark*

terror: sheer, utter, absolute, total, pure, downright, out-and-out, outright. **5** *the stark facts:* blunt, bald, bare, simple, plain, unvarnished, harsh, grim.
OPPOSITES fuzzy, indistinct, lush, ornate, disguised.
•adverb *stark naked:* completely, totally, utterly, absolutely, entirely, wholly, fully, quite, altogether, thoroughly.

start verb **1** *the meeting starts at 7.45:* begin, commence, get under way, get going, go ahead; informal kick off. **2** *this was how her illness started:* come into being/existence, begin, commence, be born, arise, originate, develop. **3** *she started her own charity:* establish, set up, found, create, bring into being, institute, initiate, inaugurate, introduce, open, launch. **4** *you can start the machine:* activate, switch/turn on, start up, fire up, boot up. **5** *the machine started:* begin working, start up, get going, spring into life. **6** *'Oh my!' she said, starting:* flinch, jerk, jump, twitch, wince.
OPPOSITES finish, stop, wind up, close down.
•noun **1** *the start of the event:* beginning,

S

to operate or start working. **3** make
something happen or start working.
4 begin to move or travel. **5** (**start out** or
up) begin a project or undertaking. **6** jump
or jerk from surprise. • **noun 1** an act of
beginning. **2** the point at which something
begins. **3** an advantage given to a
competitor at the beginning of a race. **4** a
sudden movement of surprise.

starter noun **1** a person or thing that starts.
2 the first course of a meal.

startle verb (**startles**, **startling**, **startled**)
make someone feel sudden shock or alarm.
■ **startled** adjective.

startling adjective very surprising.
■ **startlingly** adverb.

starve verb (**starves**, **starving**, **starved**)
1 suffer or die from hunger. **2** make
someone starve. **3** (**be starving** or **starved**)
informal feel very hungry. **4** (**be starved of**)
be deprived of.
■ **starvation** noun.

stash informal verb store safely in a secret
place. • **noun** a secret store.

stasis /stay-sis/ noun formal a period or state
when there is no activity or change.

state noun **1** the condition of someone or
something at a particular time. **2** a country
considered as an organized political
community. **3** an area forming part of a
federal republic. **4** (**the States**) the United
States of America. **5** the government of a
country. **6** the ceremonial procedures
associated with monarchy or government.
7 (**a state**) informal an agitated, untidy, or
dirty condition. • **verb** (**states**, **stating**,
stated) express definitely in speech or
writing.

□ **state-of-the-art** very up to date.
■ **stateless** adjective.

stately adjective (**statelier**, **stateliest**)
dignified, imposing, or grand.
□ **stately home** Brit. a large and fine house
occupied or formerly occupied by an
aristocratic family.

statement noun **1** a clear expression of
something in speech or writing. **2** an
account of events given to the police or in
court. **3** a list of amounts paid into and out
of a bank account.

stateroom noun **1** a private room on a ship.
2 a large room in a palace or public
building, for use on formal occasions.

stateside adjective & adverb informal relating
to or towards the US.

statesman or **stateswoman** noun (plural
statesmen or **stateswomen**) an experienced
and respected political leader.

static adjective not moving, acting, or
changing. • **noun 1** (also **static electricity**) an
electric charge acquired by an object that
is not a conductor of electricity. **2** crackling
or hissing on a telephone, radio, etc.
■ **statically** adverb.

station noun **1** a place where passenger
trains stop on a railway line. **2** a place
where an activity or service is based. **3** a
broadcasting company. **4** the place where
someone or something stands or is placed.
5 dated a person's social rank or position.
• **verb** put someone in a particular place or
position.
□ **station wagon** N. Amer. & Austral./NZ an
estate car.

THESAURUS

commencement, inception. **2** *the start of
her illness:* onset, emergence. **3** *a quarter
of an hour's start:* lead, head start,
advantage. **4** *she awoke with a start:* jerk,
twitch, spasm, jump.
OPPOSITES end, finish.

startle verb surprise, frighten, scare, alarm,
shock, give someone a fright, make
someone jump.
OPPOSITES put at ease.

starving adjective hungry, undernourished,
malnourished, starved, ravenous, famished.
OPPOSITES full.

state¹ noun **1** *the state of the economy:*
condition, shape, position, predicament,
plight. **2** *an autonomous state:* country,
nation, land, kingdom, realm, power,
republic. **3** *the country is divided into
thirty-two states:* province, region,
territory, canton, department, county,
district; Brit. shire. **4** *the power of the state:*
government, parliament, administration,

regime, authorities.

state² verb express, voice, utter, put into
words, declare, announce, make known,
put across/over, communicate, air.

stately adjective dignified, majestic,
ceremonious, courtly, imposing, solemn,
regal, grand.
OPPOSITES undignified.

statement noun declaration, expression,
affirmation, assertion, announcement,
utterance, communication, bulletin,
communiqué.

station noun **1** *a research station:*
establishment, base, camp, post, depot,
mission, site, facility, installation. **2** *a
police station:* office, depot, base,
headquarters; N. Amer. precinct, station
house. **3** *a radio station:* channel,
wavelength.
• **verb** *the regiment was stationed at
Woolwich:* base, post, establish, deploy,
garrison.

S

stationary adjective not moving or changing.

> ! don't confuse **stationary** and **stationery**: **stationary** means 'not moving or changing', whereas **stationery** means 'paper and other writing materials'.

stationer noun a person who sells stationery.

stationery noun paper and other materials needed for writing.

stationmaster noun a person in charge of a railway station.

statistic noun 1 (**statistics**) the collection and analysis of large amounts of information shown in numbers. 2 a fact or piece of data obtained from a study of statistics.
■ **statistician** noun.

statistical adjective relating to statistics.
■ **statistically** adverb.

statuary noun statues.

statue noun a model of a person or animal made of stone, metal, etc.

statuesque adjective (of a woman) attractively tall and dignified.

statuette noun a small statue.

stature noun 1 a person's height when they are standing. 2 importance or reputation.

status noun 1 a person's social or professional position. 2 high rank or social standing. 3 the situation at a particular time.
□ **status symbol** a possession intended to show a person's wealth or high status.

status quo /stay-tuhss **kwoh**/ noun the existing situation.

statute noun 1 a written law. 2 a rule of an organization or institution.

statutory adjective 1 required or permitted by law. 2 done or happening regularly and therefore expected.

staunch[1] adjective very loyal and committed.
■ **staunchly** adverb.

staunch[2] (US spelling **stanch**) verb stop or slow down a flow of blood.

stave noun 1 any of the lengths of wood fixed side by side to make a barrel, bucket, etc. 2 a strong stick, post, or pole. 3 (also **staff**) Music a set of five parallel lines which notes are written on or between. • verb (**staves, staving**, past and past participle **staved** or **stove**) 1 (**stave something in**) break something by forcing it inwards. 2 (past and past participle **staved**) (**stave something off**) stop or delay something bad or dangerous.

stay verb 1 remain in the same place. 2 remain in a particular state or position. 3 live somewhere temporarily as a visitor or guest. 4 stop, delay, or prevent. • noun 1 a period of staying somewhere. 2 a brace or support. 3 (**stays**) historical a corset stiffened by strips of whalebone.
□ **staying power** informal endurance or stamina. **stay of execution** a delay in carrying out the orders of a law court.

stead noun (**in someone's** or **something's stead**) instead of someone or something.
□ **stand someone in good stead** be useful to someone over time.

steadfast adjective not changing in your attitudes or aims.
■ **steadfastly** adverb.

steady adjective (**steadier, steadiest**)

stationary adjective static, parked, motionless, immobile, still, stock-still, at a standstill, at rest.
OPPOSITES moving, shifting.

stature noun 1 *small in stature:* height, size, build. 2 *an architect of international stature:* reputation, repute, standing, status, position, prestige, distinction, eminence, prominence, importance.

status noun 1 *the status of women:* standing, rank, position, level, place. 2 *wealth and status:* prestige, kudos, cachet, standing, stature, esteem, image, importance, authority, fame.

staunch[1] adjective *a staunch supporter:* stalwart, loyal, faithful, committed, devoted, dedicated, reliable.
OPPOSITES disloyal, unfaithful, unreliable.

staunch[2] verb *try to staunch the flow:* stem, stop, halt, check, curb; N. Amer. stanch.

stay verb 1 *he stayed where he was:* remain (behind), wait, linger, stick, be left, hold on, hang on; informal hang around; Brit. informal hang about. 2 *they won't stay hidden:* continue (to be), remain, keep, carry on being, go on being. 3 *our aunt is staying with us:* visit, stop (off/over), holiday, lodge; N. Amer. vacation.
OPPOSITES leave, stop being.
• noun *a stay at a hotel:* visit, stop, stopover, break, holiday; N. Amer. vacation.

steady adjective 1 *the ladder must be steady:* stable, firm, fixed, secure. 2 *keep the camera steady:* still, motionless, static, stationary. 3 *a steady gaze:* fixed, intent, unwavering, unfaltering. 4 *a steady income:* constant, regular, consistent, reliable. 5 *steady rain:* continuous, continual, unceasing, ceaseless, perpetual, unremitting, endless. 6 *a steady boyfriend:* regular, settled, firm, committed, long-term.
OPPOSITES unstable, loose, shaky, fluctuating, sporadic, occasional.
• verb 1 *he steadied the rifle:* stabilize, hold steady, brace, support, balance, rest. 2 *she*

S

1 firmly fixed, supported, or balanced.
2 not faltering or wavering. **3** sensible and
reliable. **4** regular, even, and continuous.
•verb (**steadies, steadying, steadied**) make
steady.
■ **steadily** adverb **steadiness** noun.

steak noun **1** high-quality beef cut into
thick slices for grilling or frying. **2** a thick
slice of other meat or fish. **3** poorer-quality
beef for stewing.

steal verb (**steals, stealing, stole**; past participle
stolen) **1** take something without
permission and without intending to
return it. **2** move quietly or secretively.
•noun informal a bargain.
▢ **steal the show** attract the most attention
and praise.

stealth noun cautious and secretive action
or movement.

stealthy adjective (**stealthier, stealthiest**)
cautious and secretive.
■ **stealthily** adverb.

steam noun **1** the hot vapour into which
water is converted when heated. **2** power
produced by steam under pressure.
3 momentum. •verb **1** give off or produce
steam. **2** (**steam up**) mist over with steam.
3 cook food by heating it in steam from
boiling water. **4** (of a ship or train) travel
under steam power. **5** informal move quickly
or forcefully.
■ **steamer** noun.

steamroller noun a heavy, slow vehicle
with a roller, used to flatten the surfaces
of roads. •verb (**steamrollers,
steamrollering, steamrollered**) **1** force
someone into doing or accepting
something. **2** forcibly pass a law.

steamship noun a ship that is propelled by
a steam engine.

steamy adjective (**steamier, steamiest**)
1 producing or filled with steam. **2** informal
involving passionate sexual activity.

steed noun literary a horse.

steel noun **1** a hard, strong metal that is a
mixture of iron and carbon. **2** strength and
determination. •verb mentally prepare
yourself for something difficult.
▢ **steel band** a band that plays music on
drums made from empty oil containers.

steelworks plural noun a factory where
steel is produced.

steely adjective (**steelier, steeliest**) **1** like
steel. **2** coldly determined.

steep[1] adjective **1** rising or falling sharply.
2 (of a rise or fall in an amount) very large
or rapid. **3** informal (of a price or demand)
too great.
■ **steepen** verb **steeply** adverb.

steep[2] verb **1** soak in water or other liquid.
2 (**be steeped in**) have a lot of a particular
quality or atmosphere.

steeple noun a church tower and spire.

steeplechase noun **1** a horse race with
ditches and hedges as jumps. **2** a race in
which runners must clear hurdles and
water jumps.
■ **steeplechaser** noun.

steeplejack noun a person who climbs tall
structures such as chimneys and steeples
to repair them.

steer[1] verb **1** guide or control the movement
of a vehicle, ship, etc. **2** direct or guide.
▢ **steer clear of** take care to avoid. **steering
wheel** a wheel that a driver turns in order
to steer a vehicle.

steer[2] noun a bullock.

steerage noun (in the past) the cheapest
accommodation in a ship.

steersman noun (plural **steersmen**) a person
who steers a boat or ship.

stegosaurus noun a plant-eating dinosaur
with large bony plates along the back.

stein /styn/ noun a large earthenware beer
mug.

stellar adjective having to do with a star or
stars.

stem[1] noun **1** the long, thin main part of a
plant or shrub, or support of a fruit,

S

THESAURUS

needed to steady her nerves: calm, soothe,
quieten, compose, settle, subdue, quell.

steal verb **1** burglars stole the TV: take,
thieve, help yourself to, pilfer, embezzle;
informal swipe, lift, filch; Brit. informal nick,
pinch, knock off; N. Amer. informal heist. **2** his
work was stolen by his tutor: plagiarize,
copy, pirate; informal rip off, lift, pinch, crib;
Brit. informal nick. **3** he stole out of the room:
creep, sneak, slink, slip, glide, tiptoe, slope.

stealth noun furtiveness, secretiveness,
secrecy, surreptitiousness.
OPPOSITES openness.

stealthy adjective furtive, secretive, secret,
surreptitious, sneaky, sly.

OPPOSITES open.

steep adjective **1** steep cliffs: sheer,
precipitous, abrupt, sharp, perpendicular,
vertical. **2** a steep increase: sharp, sudden,
dramatic.
OPPOSITES gentle, gradual, reasonable.

steeped adjective a city steeped in history:
imbued with, filled with, permeated with,
suffused with, soaked in, pervaded by.

steer verb guide, direct, manoeuvre, drive,
pilot, navigate.

stem[1] noun a plant stem: stalk, shoot, trunk.
▢ **stem from** come from, arise from,
originate from, have its origins in, spring
from, derive from.

flower, or leaf. **2** a long, thin supporting part of a wine glass, tobacco pipe, etc. **3** a vertical stroke in a letter or musical note. **4** the root or main part of a word. • verb (**stems**, **stemming**, **stemmed**) (**stem from**) come from or be caused by.

stem² verb (**stems**, **stemming**, **stemmed**) stop or slow down the flow or progress of something.

stench noun a strong and very unpleasant smell.

stencil noun a thin sheet with a pattern or letters cut out of it, used to produce a design by applying ink or paint through the holes. • verb (**stencils**, **stencilling**, **stencilled**; US spelling **stencils**, **stenciling**, **stenciled**) decorate or form something with a stencil.

stenographer /sti-nog-ruh-fer/ noun N. Amer. a shorthand typist.

stentorian adjective (of a person's voice) loud and powerful.

step noun **1** an act of lifting and putting down the foot or feet in walking. **2** the distance covered by a step. **3** a flat surface on which to place the feet when moving from one level to another. **4** a position or grade in a scale or ranking. **5** a measure or action taken to deal with something. • verb (**steps**, **stepping**, **stepped**) lift and put down your foot or feet.
□ **step down** resign from a job or post. **step in** become involved in a difficult situation. **stepping stone** a raised stone which you can step on when crossing a stream. **2** something that helps you make progress towards a goal. **step something up** increase the amount, speed, or strength of.

stepbrother noun a son of a person's stepfather or stepmother.

stepchild noun (plural **stepchildren**) a child of a person's husband or wife from a previous marriage.

stepdaughter noun a daughter of a person's husband or wife from a previous marriage.

stepfather noun a man who is married to a person's mother but is not his or her father.

stepladder noun a short free-standing folding ladder.

stepmother noun a woman who is married to a person's father but is not his or her mother.

steppe noun a large area of flat unforested grassland in SE Europe and Siberia.

stepsister noun a daughter of a person's stepfather or stepmother.

stepson noun a son of a person's husband or wife from a previous marriage.

stereo noun (plural **stereos**) **1** music or sound that come from two or more speakers and seems to surround you. **2** a CD player, record player, etc. that has two or more speakers. • adjective (also **stereophonic**) relating to this kind of sound.

stereotype noun an oversimplified idea of the typical characteristics of a person or thing. • verb (**stereotypes**, **stereotyping**, **stereotyped**) represent as a stereotype.
■ **stereotypical** adjective.

sterile adjective **1** not able to produce children, young, crops, or fruit. **2** not imaginative, creative, or exciting. **3** free from bacteria.
■ **sterility** noun.

sterilize or **sterilise** verb (**sterilizes**, **sterilizing**, **sterilized**) make sterile.
■ **sterilization** noun.

sterling noun British money. • adjective **1** excellent. **2** (of silver) of at least 92¼ per cent purity.

stern¹ adjective **1** grimly serious or strict. **2** severe.
■ **sternly** adverb.

THESAURUS

stem² verb *they stemmed the flow of blood:* stop, staunch, halt, check, curb; N. Amer. stanch.

step noun **1** *Frank took a step forward:* pace, stride. **2** *she heard a step on the stairs:* footstep, footfall, tread. **3** *the top step:* stair, tread; (**steps**) stairs, staircase, flight of stairs. **4** *resigning is a very serious step:* action, act, course of action, measure, move, operation. **5** *a significant step towards a ceasefire:* advance, development, move, movement, breakthrough. **6** *the first step on the managerial ladder:* stage, level, grade, rank, degree, phase.
• verb *she stepped forward:* walk, move, tread, pace, stride.
□ **step down resign**, stand down, give up your post/job, bow out, abdicate; informal

quit. **step in intervene**, become involved, intercede. **step something up increase**, intensify, strengthen, escalate, speed up, accelerate; informal up, crank up.

stereotype noun *the stereotype of the woman as carer:* conventional idea, standard image, cliché, formula.
• verb *bodybuilders are stereotyped as 'muscleheads':* typecast, pigeonhole, conventionalize, categorize, label, tag.

sterile adjective **1** *sterile desert:* unproductive, infertile, unfruitful, barren. **2** *sterile conditions:* hygienic, clean, pure, uncontaminated, sterilized, disinfected, germ-free, antiseptic.
OPPOSITES fertile, productive, septic.

stern adjective **1** *a stern expression:* unsmiling, frowning, serious, severe,

stern² noun the rear end of a ship or boat.

sternum noun the breastbone.

steroid /ste-royd, steer-oyd/ noun 1 any of a class of substances that includes certain hormones and vitamins. 2 an anabolic steroid.

stertorous /ster-tuh-ruhss/ adjective (of breathing) noisy and laboured.

stethoscope noun a device used by doctors for listening to the sound of a person's heart or breathing.

Stetson noun (trademark in the US) a hat with a high crown and a very wide brim, worn by cowboys and ranchers in the US.

stevedore noun a person employed at a dock to load and unload ships.

stew noun 1 a dish of meat and vegetables cooked slowly in a closed dish. 2 informal a state of anxiety or agitation. •verb 1 cook slowly in a closed dish. 2 Brit. (of tea) become strong and bitter with prolonged brewing. 3 informal be anxious or agitated.

steward noun 1 a person who looks after the passengers on a ship or aircraft. 2 an official who supervises arrangements at a large public event. 3 a person employed to manage a large house or estate. 4 a person responsible for supplies of food to a college, club, etc.
■ **stewardship** noun.

stewardess noun a woman who looks after the passengers on a ship or aircraft.

stick¹ noun 1 a thin piece of wood that has fallen or been cut from a tree. 2 a piece of wood used for support in walking or as a weapon. 3 a long, thin implement used in hockey, polo, etc. to hit the ball or puck. 4 a long, thin object or piece. 5 Brit. informal severe criticism or treatment. 6 (the sticks) informal remote country areas.
□ **stick insect** a long, slender insect that resembles a twig.

stick² verb (sticks, sticking, stuck) 1 push something pointed into or through something. 2 be fixed with its point embedded in something. 3 protrude or extend. 4 informal put something somewhere quickly or carelessly. 5 cling firmly to a surface; adhere. 6 (be stuck) be fixed or unable to move. 7 (be stuck) be unable to complete a task. 8 (be stuck with) informal be unable to get rid of or escape from. 9 (stick around) informal remain in or near a place. 10 (stick to) continue doing or using. 11 (stick up for) informal support.

sticker noun a sticky label or notice.

stickleback noun a small fish with sharp spines along its back.

stickler noun a person who insists on people behaving in a particular way.

sticky adjective (stickier, stickiest) 1 tending or designed to stick. 2 like glue in texture. 3 (of the weather) hot and humid.

stiff adjective 1 not easily bent. 2 difficult to

THESAURUS

forbidding, grim, unfriendly, austere, dour. 2 *stern measures*: strict, severe, stringent, harsh, drastic, hard, tough, extreme, draconian.
OPPOSITES genial, friendly, lenient, lax.

stick¹ noun 1 *a fire made of sticks*: branch, twig. 2 *he walks with a stick*: walking stick, cane, staff, crutch. 3 *the plants need supporting on sticks*: post, pole, cane, stake. 4 *he beat me with a stick*: club, cudgel, truncheon, baton, cane, switch, rod; Brit. informal cosh.

stick² verb 1 *he stuck his fork into the sausage*: thrust, push, insert, jab, poke, dig, plunge. 2 *the bristles stuck into his skin*: pierce, penetrate, puncture, prick, stab. 3 *the mug stuck to the mat*: adhere, cling. 4 *stick the stamp there*: attach, fasten, affix, fix, paste, glue, gum, tape. 5 *the wheels stuck fast*: jam, get jammed, catch, get caught, get trapped. 6 *that sticks in his mind*: remain, stay, linger, persist, continue, endure. 7 (Brit. informal) *I can't stick it*: tolerate, put up with, take, stand, stomach, endure, bear, abide.
□ **stick out** 1 *his front teeth stuck out*: protrude, jut (out), project, stand out, extend, poke out, bulge. 2 *they stuck out in their new clothes*: be conspicuous, be

obvious, stand out, attract attention, leap out; informal stick out a mile. **stick to** **abide by**, keep, adhere to, hold to, comply with, fulfil, stand by. **stick up for** **support**, take someone's side, side with, stand by, stand up for, defend.

sticky adjective 1 *sticky tape*: adhesive, self-adhesive, gummed. 2 *sticky clay*: tacky, gluey, gummy, treacly, glutinous; informal gooey. 3 *sticky weather*: humid, muggy, close, sultry, steamy, sweaty. 4 *a sticky situation*: awkward, difficult, tricky, ticklish, delicate, embarrassing, sensitive; informal hairy.
OPPOSITES dry, fresh, cool, easy.

stiff adjective 1 *stiff cardboard*: rigid, hard, firm. 2 *a stiff paste*: thick, firm, viscous, semi-solid. 3 *I'm stiff all over*: aching, achy, painful, arthritic. 4 *a rather stiff manner*: formal, reserved, wooden, forced, strained, stilted; informal starchy, uptight. 5 *a stiff fine*: harsh, severe, heavy, stringent, drastic, draconian; Brit. swingeing. 6 *stiff resistance*: vigorous, determined, strong, spirited, resolute, tenacious, dogged, stubborn. 7 *a stiff climb*: difficult, hard, arduous, tough, strenuous, laborious, exacting, tiring, demanding. 8 *a stiff breeze*: strong, fresh, brisk. 9 *a stiff drink*:

turn or operate. **3** unable to move easily and without pain. **4** not relaxed or friendly. **5** severe or strong. • **noun** informal a dead body.
◻ **stiff upper lip** the tendency to hide your feelings and not complain.
■ **stiffly** adverb **stiffness** noun.

stiffen verb **1** make or become stiff. **2** make or become stronger.

stifle verb (**stifles, stifling, stifled**) **1** prevent from breathing freely; suffocate. **2** restrain or suppress.

stifling adjective unpleasantly hot and stuffy.

stigma noun (plural **stigmas** or **stigmata**) **1** a mark or sign of disgrace. **2** (**stigmata**) marks on a person's body believed by some Christians to correspond to those left on Jesus's body by the Crucifixion. **3** the part of a plant that receives the pollen during pollination.

stigmatize or **stigmatise** verb (**stigmatizes, stigmatizing, stigmatized**) regard or treat as shameful.

stile noun an arrangement of steps in a fence or wall that allows people to climb over.

stiletto noun (plural **stilettos**) **1** a thin, high heel on a woman's shoe. **2** a short dagger with a tapering blade.

still adjective **1** not moving. **2** Brit. (of a drink) not fizzy. • **noun 1** deep, quiet calm. **2** a photograph or a single shot from a cinema film. **3** a piece of equipment for distilling alcoholic drinks such as whisky. • **adverb 1** even now or at a particular time.

2 nevertheless. **3** even. • **verb** make or become still.
◻ **still life** (plural **still lifes**) a painting or drawing of an arrangement of objects such as flowers or fruit.
■ **stillness** noun.

stillborn adjective (of a baby) born dead.
■ **stillbirth** noun.

stilt noun **1** either of a pair of upright poles that are used to walk raised above the ground. **2** each of a set of posts supporting a building.

stilted adjective (of speech or writing) stiff and unnatural.

Stilton noun trademark a kind of strong, rich blue cheese.

stimulant noun something that stimulates.

stimulate verb (**stimulates, stimulating, stimulated**) **1** cause a reaction in the body. **2** make more active or interested.
■ **stimulation** noun.

stimulus noun (plural **stimuli**) something that stimulates.

sting noun **1** a sharp-pointed part of an insect, capable of inflicting a wound by injecting poison. **2** a wound from a sting. **3** a sharp tingling sensation. • **verb** (**stings, stinging, stung**) **1** wound with a sting. **2** produce a stinging sensation. **3** upset someone.

stingray noun a ray (fish) with a poisonous spine at the base of the tail.

stingy /stin-ji/ adjective (**stingier, stingiest**) informal mean.

stink verb (**stinks, stinking, stank** or **stunk**;

strong, potent, alcoholic.
OPPOSITES flexible, limp, runny, supple, relaxed, informal, lenient, mild, half-hearted, easy, gentle, weak.

stifle verb suppress, smother, restrain, check, curb, silence, hinder, hamper, impede, prevent, inhibit.
OPPOSITES encourage, let out.

still adjective **1** *Polly lay still:* motionless, unmoving, stock-still, immobile, rooted to the spot, transfixed, static, stationary. **2** *a still night:* quiet, silent, calm, peaceful, serene, windless. **3** *the lake was still:* calm, flat, smooth, like a millpond.
OPPOSITES moving, active, noisy, rough.
• **adverb 1** *he's still here:* even now, yet. **2** *He's crazy. Still, he's harmless:* nevertheless, nonetheless, all the same, even so, but, however, despite that, in spite of that, for all that.
• **verb** *he stilled the crowd:* quieten, quiet, silence, hush, calm, settle, pacify, subdue.
OPPOSITES stir up.

stimulate verb encourage, prompt, motivate, trigger, spark, spur on, galvanize,

fire, inspire, excite; N. Amer. light a fire under.
OPPOSITES discourage.

stimulating adjective thought-provoking, interesting, inspiring, inspirational, lively, exciting, provocative.
OPPOSITES uninspiring, boring.

stimulus noun motivation, encouragement, impetus, prompt, spur, incentive, inspiration.
OPPOSITES deterrent, discouragement.

sting noun **1** *a bee sting:* prick, wound, injury. **2** *this cream will take the sting away:* pain, pricking, smart, soreness, hurt, irritation.
• **verb 1** *she was stung by a scorpion:* prick, wound. **2** *the smoke made her eyes sting:* smart, burn, hurt, be irritated, be sore. **3** *the criticism stung her:* upset, wound, hurt, pain, mortify.

stink verb *his clothes stank of sweat:* reek, smell.
• **noun** *the stink of sweat:* stench, reek; Brit. informal pong; N. Amer. informal funk.

S

past participle **stunk**) **1** have a strong, unpleasant smell. **2** informal be very bad or unpleasant. •**noun 1** a strong, unpleasant smell. **2** informal a row or fuss.
■ **stinker** noun.

stinking adjective **1** foul-smelling. **2** informal very unpleasant or bad. •**adverb** informal very: *stinking rich.*

stint verb (**stint on**) be very economical or mean about spending or providing something. •**noun** a period of work.

stipend /sty-pend/ noun a fixed regular sum paid as a salary to a priest, teacher, or official.

stipendiary adjective receiving a stipend; working for pay.

stipple verb (**stipples, stippling, stippled**) mark a surface with many small dots or specks.

stipulate verb (**stipulates, stipulating, stipulated**) demand or specify as part of an agreement.
■ **stipulation** noun.

stir verb (**stirs, stirring, stirred**) **1** move an implement round and round in a liquid or soft substance to mix it. **2** move slightly. **3** wake or get up. **4** (often **stir something up**) arouse a strong feeling in someone. **5** Brit. informal deliberately cause trouble by spreading rumours or gossip. •**noun 1** an act of stirring. **2** a disturbance or commotion.
□ **stir-fry** fry quickly over a high heat while stirring.
■ **stirrer** noun.

stirring adjective causing great excitement or strong emotion.

stirrup noun each of a pair of loops attached to a horse's saddle to support the rider's foot.

stitch noun **1** a loop of thread made by a single pass of the needle in sewing or knitting. **2** a method of sewing or knitting that produces a particular pattern. **3** a

sudden sharp pain in the side of the body, caused by strenuous exercise. •**verb** make or mend with stitches.
□ **in stitches** informal laughing uncontrollably. **stitch someone up** Brit. informal make someone appear to be guilty of something that they did not do.

stoat noun a small meat-eating animal of the weasel family.

stock noun **1** a supply of goods or materials available for sale or use. **2** farm animals; livestock. **3** money raised by selling shares in a company. **4** (**stocks**) shares in a company. **5** water in which bones, meat, fish, or vegetables have been simmered. **6** a person's ancestry. **7** a breed, variety, or population of an animal or plant. **8** the trunk or stem of a tree or shrub. **9** a plant with sweet-smelling lilac, pink, or white flowers. **10** (**the stocks**) (in the past) a wooden structure in which criminals were locked as a public punishment. •**adjective** common or conventional: *stock characters.* •**verb 1** have or keep a stock of. **2** provide or fill with a stock of something. **3** (**stock up**) collect stocks of something.
□ **stock car** a car used in a type of racing in which cars collide with each other. **stock exchange** (or **stock market**) a place where stocks and shares are bought and sold. **stock-in-trade** the typical thing a person or company uses or deals in. **stock-still** completely still. **take stock** assess your situation.

stockade noun a barrier or enclosure formed from wooden posts.

stockbroker noun a person who buys and sells stocks and shares on behalf of clients.

stocking noun **1** either of a pair of women's close-fitting nylon garments covering the foot and leg. **2** US or old use a long sock.
■ **stockinged** adjective.

stockist noun Brit. a retailer that sells goods of a particular type.

stockpile noun a large stock of goods or

THESAURUS

stint noun spell, stretch, turn, session, term, time, shift, tour of duty.

stipulate verb specify, set out, lay down, demand, require, insist on.

stir verb **1** *stir the mixture well:* mix, blend, beat, whip, whisk, fold in; N. Amer. muddle. **2** *James stirred in his sleep:* move, change your position, shift. **3** *a breeze stirred the leaves:* disturb, rustle, shake, move, agitate. **4** *the war stirred him to action:* spur, drive, rouse, prompt, propel, motivate, encourage, urge, impel, provoke. •**noun** *the news caused a stir:* commotion, disturbance, fuss, excitement, sensation; informal to-do, hoo-ha.

stock noun **1** *the shop doesn't carry much*

stock: merchandise, goods, wares. **2** *a stock of fuel:* store, supply, stockpile, reserve, hoard, cache, bank. **3** *farm stock:* animals, livestock, beasts, flocks, herds. **4** *his mother was of French stock:* descent, ancestry, origin(s), lineage, birth, extraction, family, blood, pedigree.
•**adjective** *the stock response:* usual, routine, predictable, set, standard, customary, familiar, conventional, traditional, stereotyped, clichéd, hackneyed, unoriginal, formulaic.
OPPOSITES non-standard, original.
•**verb** *we do not stock GM food:* sell, carry, keep (in stock), offer, supply, provide, furnish.

materials. • verb (**stockpiles, stockpiling, stockpiled**) gather together a large stock of.

stocktaking noun the process of listing all the stock held by a business.

stocky adjective (**stockier, stockiest**) (of a person) short and sturdy.

stodge noun Brit. informal food that is heavy and filling.
■ **stodgy** adjective.

stoic /stoh-ik/ noun a stoical person.
• adjective stoical.

stoical adjective enduring pain and hardship without complaining.
■ **stoically** adverb **stoicism** noun.

stoke verb (**stokes, stoking, stoked**) 1 add coal to a fire, furnace, etc. 2 encourage a strong emotion.
■ **stoker** noun.

stole¹ noun a woman's long scarf or shawl.

stole² past of STEAL.

stolen past participle of STEAL.

stolid adjective calm, dependable, and unemotional.
■ **stolidly** adverb.

stomach noun 1 the internal organ in which the first part of digestion occurs. 2 the front part of the body below the chest; the belly. 3 inclination or desire.
• verb 1 consume food or drink without feeling ill. 2 accept or approve of something.

stomp verb 1 tread heavily and noisily. 2 dance with stamping steps.

stone noun 1 the hard material that rock is made of. 2 a small piece of stone found on the ground. 3 a piece of stone shaped as a memorial, a boundary marker, etc. 4 a gem. 5 the hard seed of certain fruits. 6 (plural

stone) Brit. a unit of weight equal to 14 lb (6.35 kg). • verb (**stones, stoning, stoned**) 1 throw stones at. 2 remove the stone from a fruit. • adverb extremely or totally: *stone cold*.
□ **Stone Age** the prehistoric period when tools were made of stone. **a stone's throw** a short distance.

stoned adjective informal strongly affected by drugs or alcohol.

stonewall verb 1 refuse to answer questions, or give evasive replies. 2 Cricket bat very defensively.

stony adjective (**stonier, stoniest**) 1 full of stones. 2 made of or like stone. 3 cold and unfeeling.
■ **stonily** adverb.

stood past and past participle of STAND.

stooge noun 1 disapproving a less important person used by someone to do routine or unpleasant work. 2 a performer whose act involves being the butt of a comedian's jokes.

stool noun 1 a seat without a back or arms. 2 Medicine a piece of faeces.
□ **stool pigeon** informal a police informer.

stoop verb 1 bend the head or body forwards and downwards. 2 lower your standards to do something wrong. • noun a stooping posture.

stop verb (**stops, stopping, stopped**) 1 come or bring to an end. 2 prevent from happening or from doing something. 3 no longer move or operate. 4 (of a bus or train) call at a place to pick up or let off passengers. 5 block up a hole or leak. • noun 1 an act of stopping. 2 a place for a bus or train to stop at. 3 an object or part of a mechanism which prevents movement. 4 a

THESAURUS

stomach noun 1 *a pain in my stomach:* abdomen, belly, gut, middle; informal tummy, insides. 2 *his fat stomach:* paunch, belly, beer belly, girth; informal pot, tummy, spare tyre, middle-aged spread; N. Amer. informal bay window. 3 *no stomach for a fight:* appetite, taste, inclination, desire, wish.
• verb *they couldn't stomach it:* tolerate, put up with, take, stand, endure, bear, abide; informal hack; Brit. informal stick.

stone noun 1 *someone threw a stone:* rock, pebble, boulder. 2 *a precious stone:* gem, gemstone, jewel; informal rock, sparkler. 3 *a peach stone:* kernel, seed, pip, pit.

stoop verb *she stooped to pick up the pen:* bend, lean, crouch, bow, duck.
• noun *a man with a stoop:* hunch, round shoulders.

stop verb 1 *we can't stop the decline:* end, halt, finish, terminate, wind up,

discontinue, cut short, interrupt, nip in the bud, shut down. 2 *he stopped running:* cease, discontinue, desist from, break off, give up, abandon, cut out; informal quit, pack in; Brit. informal jack in. 3 *the car stopped:* pull up, draw up, come to a stop/halt, come to rest, pull in/over. 4 *the music stopped:* cease, end, come to an and, halt, finish, draw to a close, be over, conclude. 5 *the police stopped her leaving:* prevent, obstruct, impede, block, bar, preclude, dissuade from.
OPPOSITES start, begin, continue, allow, encourage.
• noun 1 *all business came to a stop:* halt, end, finish, close, standstill. 2 *a brief stop in the town:* break, stopover, stop-off, stay, visit. 3 *the next stop is Oxford Street:* stopping place, station, halt.
OPPOSITES start, beginning, continuation.

S

set of organ pipes.
□ **pull out all the stops** make a very great effort to achieve something. **stop press** Brit. news added to a newspaper at the last minute.

stopcock noun a valve which controls the flow of a liquid or gas through a pipe.

stopgap noun a temporary solution or substitute.

stoppage noun **1** an instance of being stopped. **2** an instance of industrial action. **3** a blockage. **4** (**stoppages**) Brit. deductions from wages for tax, National Insurance, etc.

stopper noun a plug for sealing a hole. •verb (**stoppers, stoppering, stoppered**) seal with a stopper.

stopwatch noun a watch with buttons that start and stop the display, used to time races.

storage noun **1** the action of storing. **2** space available for storing.
□ **storage heater** Brit. an electric heater that stores up heat during the night and releases it during the day.

store noun **1** an amount or supply kept to be used when needed. **2** (**stores**) equipment and food kept for use by an army, navy, etc. **3** a place where things are kept for future use or sale. **4** Brit. a large shop selling different types of goods. **5** N. Amer. a shop. •verb (**stores, storing, stored**) **1** keep for future use. **2** enter information in the memory of a computer.
□ **in store** about to happen. **set store by**

consider to be important.

storey (US spelling **story**) noun (plural **storeys** or **stories**) a particular level of a building.

> **!** don't confuse **storey** with **story**, which means 'an account of events told for entertainment'. In American English, the spelling **story** is used for both senses.

stork noun a tall long-legged bird with a long, heavy bill.

storm noun **1** a violent disturbance of the atmosphere with strong winds and rain, thunder, etc. **2** an uproar or controversy. •verb **1** move angrily or forcefully. **2** (of troops) suddenly attack and capture a place. **3** shout angrily.
□ **a storm in a teacup** Brit. great anger or excitement about something that is not very important.

stormy adjective (**stormier, stormiest**) **1** affected by a storm. **2** full of angry or violent outbursts of feeling.

story[1] noun (plural **stories**) **1** an account of imaginary or real events told for entertainment. **2** an item of news. **3** (also **storyline**) the plot of a novel, film, etc. **4** informal a lie.

> **!** don't confuse **story** with **storey**: see the note at **STOREY**.

story[2] US spelling of **STOREY**.

stoup /stoop/ noun a basin for holy water in a church.

stout adjective **1** rather fat or heavily built. **2** sturdy and thick. **3** brave and

---

THESAURUS

store noun **1** *a store of food:* stock, supply, stockpile, hoard, cache, reserve, bank, pool. **2** *a grain store:* storeroom, storehouse, repository, stockroom, depot, warehouse. **3** *ship's stores:* supplies, provisions, stocks, food, rations, materials, equipment, hardware. **4** *a DIY store:* shop, (retail) outlet, boutique, department store, supermarket, hypermarket, superstore, megastore.
•verb *rabbits don't store food:* keep, stockpile, lay in, set aside, put aside, put away/by, save, collect, accumulate, hoard; informal squirrel away.
OPPOSITES use, discard.

storehouse noun warehouse, depository, repository, store, storeroom, depot.

storm noun **1** *battered by a storm:* tempest, squall, gale, hurricane, tornado, cyclone, typhoon, thunderstorm, rainstorm, monsoon, hailstorm, snowstorm, blizzard. **2** *there was a storm over his remarks:* uproar, outcry, fuss, furore, rumpus, trouble; informal to-do, hoo-ha, ructions, stink; Brit. informal row.

•verb **1** *she stormed out:* stride, march, stomp, stamp, stalk, flounce, fling. **2** *police stormed the building:* attack, charge, rush, swoop on.

stormy adjective **1** *stormy weather:* blustery, squally, windy, gusty, blowy, thundery, wild, violent, rough, foul. **2** *a stormy debate:* angry, heated, fierce, furious, passionate, acrimonious.
OPPOSITES calm, fine, peaceful.

story noun **1** *an adventure story:* tale, narrative, account, history, anecdote, saga; informal yarn. **2** *the novel has a good story:* plot, storyline, scenario. **3** *the story appeared in the papers:* news, report, item, article, feature, piece. **4** *there have been a lot of stories going round:* rumour, whisper, allegation, speculation, gossip; Austral./NZ informal furphy.

stout adjective **1** *a short stout man:* fat, plump, portly, rotund, dumpy, corpulent; informal tubby; Brit. informal podgy; N. Amer. informal zaftig, corn-fed. **2** *stout leather shoes:* strong, sturdy, solid, robust, tough, durable, hard-wearing. **3** *stout resistance:*

S

determined. • **noun** a kind of strong, dark beer.

■ **stoutly** adverb.

stove¹ **noun** a device for cooking or heating.

stove² past and past participle of **STAVE**.

stow **verb 1** pack or store an object tidily. **2** (**stow away**) hide on a ship, aircraft, etc. to travel secretly and without paying.

stowaway **noun** a person who stows away.

straddle **verb** (**straddles, straddling, straddled**) **1** sit or stand with one leg on either side of. **2** extend across both sides of.

strafe /strahf, strayf/ **verb** (**strafes, strafing, strafed**) attack with gunfire or bombs from a low-flying aircraft.

straggle **verb** (**straggles, straggling, straggled**) **1** trail slowly behind the person or people in front. **2** grow or spread out in an untidy way.

■ **straggler** noun **straggly** adjective.

straight adjective **1** extending in one direction only; without a curve or bend. **2** level, upright, or symmetrical. **3** in proper order or condition. **4** honest and direct. **5** in continuous succession. **6** (of an alcoholic drink) undiluted. **7** informal

conventional or respectable. **8** informal heterosexual. • **adverb 1** in a straight line or in a straight way. **2** without delay. **3** clearly and logically.

□ **straight away** immediately. **straight-faced** having a serious expression. **straight-laced** ⇒ **STRAIT-LACED**.

straighten **verb** make or become straight.

straightforward **adjective 1** easy to do or understand. **2** honest and open.

■ **straightforwardly** adverb.

straightjacket ⇒ **STRAITJACKET**.

strain¹ **verb 1** make an unusually great effort. **2** injure a muscle, limb, etc. by making it work too hard. **3** make great or excessive demands on. **4** pour a mainly liquid substance through a sieve to separate out solid matter. • **noun 1** a force tending to strain something to an extreme degree. **2** an injury caused by straining a muscle, limb, etc. **3** a severe demand on strength or resources. **4** a state of tension or exhaustion. **5** the sound of a piece of music.

■ **strainer** noun.

strain² **noun 1** a breed or variety of an animal or plant. **2** a tendency in a person's character.

THESAURUS

determined, vigorous, forceful, spirited, committed, brave; informal gutsy.
OPPOSITES thin, flimsy, feeble.

straight adjective **1** *a long, straight road:* direct, linear, unswerving, undeviating. **2** *that picture isn't straight:* level, even, in line, aligned, square, vertical, upright, perpendicular, horizontal. **3** *we must get the place straight:* in order, tidy, neat, shipshape, orderly, organized, arranged, sorted out, straightened out. **4** *give me a straight answer:* honest, direct, frank, candid, truthful, sincere, forthright, straightforward, plain-spoken, blunt, unambiguous; informal upfront. **5** *straight brandy:* neat, undiluted, pure; N. Amer. informal straight up.
OPPOSITES winding, crooked, untidy, evasive.

• adverb **1** *he looked me straight in the eyes:* right, directly, squarely, full; informal smack, (slap) bang; N. Amer. informal spang, smack dab. **2** *she drove straight home:* directly, right. **3** *I told her straight:* frankly, directly, candidly, honestly, forthrightly, plainly, point-blank, bluntly, flatly; Brit. informal straight up. **4** *he can't think straight:* logically, rationally, clearly, lucidly, coherently, cogently.
□ **straight away at once**, right away, (right) now, this/that (very) minute, this/that instant, immediately, instantly, directly, forthwith, then and there; N. Amer. in short order; informal straight off, pronto; N. Amer.

informal lickety-split.

straighten verb **1** *Rory straightened his tie:* put straight, adjust, arrange, rearrange, tidy. **2** *we must straighten things out with Viola:* put right, sort out, clear up, settle, resolve, rectify, remedy; informal patch up.

straightforward adjective **1** *the process was remarkably straightforward:* uncomplicated, simple, plain sailing. **2** *a straightforward man:* honest, frank, candid, open, truthful, sincere, on the level, forthright, plain-speaking, direct; informal upfront; N. Amer. informal on the up and up.
OPPOSITES complicated, devious.

strain¹ verb **1** *take care that you don't strain yourself:* overtax, overwork, overextend, overreach, overdo it, exhaust, wear out; informal knacker, knock yourself out. **2** *you have strained a muscle:* injure, damage, pull, wrench, twist, sprain. **3** *strain the mixture:* sieve, sift, filter, screen.
• noun **1** *the rope snapped under the strain:* tension, tightness, tautness. **2** *muscle strain:* injury, sprain, wrench, twist. **3** *the strain of her job:* pressure, demands, burdens, stress; informal hassle. **4** *Melissa was showing signs of strain:* stress, (nervous) tension, exhaustion, fatigue, pressure, overwork.

strain² noun *a different strain of flu:* variety, kind, type, sort, breed, genus.

S

strained adjective **1** not relaxed or comfortable; showing signs of strain. **2** produced by deliberate effort; not graceful or spontaneous.

strait noun **1** (also **straits**) a narrow passage of water connecting two other large areas of water. **2** (**straits**) trouble or difficulty: *in dire straits.*

straitened adjective without enough money; poor.

straitjacket or **straightjacket** noun a strong garment with long sleeves which can be tied together to confine the arms of a violent person.

strait-laced or **straight-laced** adjective very strictly moral and conventional.

strand¹ verb **1** drive or leave a ship, whale, etc. aground on a shore. **2** leave someone or something without the means to move from a place. •noun literary a beach or shore.

strand² noun **1** a single thin length of thread, wire, etc. **2** an element that forms part of a complex whole.

strange adjective **1** unusual or surprising. **2** not previously visited or encountered.
■ **strangely** adverb.

stranger noun **1** a person that you do not know. **2** a person who does not know a particular place.

strangle verb (**strangles, strangling, strangled**) **1** kill or injure someone by squeezing their neck. **2** prevent from growing or developing.
■ **strangler** noun.

stranglehold noun **1** a firm grip around a person's neck that deprives them of oxygen. **2** complete or overwhelming control.

strangulation noun the action of strangling.

strap noun a strip of flexible material used for fastening, carrying, or holding on to.
•verb (**straps, strapping, strapped**) fasten or secure with a strap.
■ **strapless** adjective **strappy** adjective.

strapping adjective (of a person) big and strong.

stratagem noun a plan or scheme intended to outwit an opponent.

strategic adjective **1** forming part of a long-term plan to achieve something. **2** relating to the gaining of long-term military advantage. **3** (of weapons) for use against enemy territory rather than in battle.
■ **strategically** adverb.

strategy noun (plural **strategies**) **1** a plan designed to achieve a long-term aim. **2** the planning and directing of military activity in a war or battle.
■ **strategist** noun.

stratify verb (**stratifies, stratifying, stratified**) form or arrange into strata.
■ **stratification** noun.

stratosphere noun **1** the layer of the earth's atmosphere above the lowest layer, at a height of about 10–50 km. **2** informal the very highest levels of something.
■ **stratospheric** adjective.

stratum noun (plural **strata**) **1** a layer or series of layers of rock. **2** a level or class of society.

straw noun **1** dried stalks of grain. **2** a single dried stalk of grain. **3** a thin hollow tube used for sucking drink from a container. **4** a pale yellow colour.
▫ **clutch at straws** turn to something in desperation. **draw the short straw** be chosen to do something unpleasant. **the last (or final) straw** the final difficulty that makes a situation unbearable. **straw poll** an unofficial test of opinion.

THESAURUS

strained adjective **1** *relations were strained:* awkward, tense, uneasy, uncomfortable, edgy, difficult, troubled. **2** *a strained smile:* forced, unnatural, artificial, insincere, false, affected, put-on.
OPPOSITES friendly, genuine.

strait noun **1** channel, sound, narrows, stretch of water. **2** (**straits**) difficulty, trouble, crisis, mess, predicament, plight; informal hot water, jam, hole, fix, scrape.

strand noun thread, filament, fibre, length.

stranded adjective **1** *stranded on a desert island:* shipwrecked, wrecked, marooned, high and dry, grounded, aground, beached. **2** *stranded in a strange city:* helpless, abandoned, lost, adrift.

strange adjective **1** *strange things have been happening:* unusual, odd, curious, peculiar, queer, funny, bizarre, weird, uncanny, anomalous; informal fishy. **2** *visiting a strange house:* unfamiliar, unknown, new, novel.
OPPOSITES ordinary, familiar.

stranger noun newcomer, new arrival, visitor, guest, outsider, foreigner.

strangle verb throttle, choke, garrotte, asphyxiate.

strap noun *thick leather straps:* belt, tie, band, thong.
•verb *a bag was strapped to the bicycle:* tie, lash, secure, fasten, bind, make fast, truss.

strapping adjective big, strong, well built, brawny, burly, muscular; informal beefy.
OPPOSITES weedy.

strategic adjective planned, calculated, deliberate, tactical, judicious, prudent, shrewd.

strategy noun plan, grand design, game plan, policy, programme, scheme.

strawberry noun (plural **strawberries**) a sweet red fruit with seeds on the surface. □ **strawberry blonde** (of hair) light reddish-blonde.

stray verb move away aimlessly from a group or from the right course or place. • adjective 1 not in the right place; separated from a group. 2 (of a domestic animal) having no home or having wandered away from home. • noun a stray person or thing.

streak noun 1 a long, thin mark. 2 an element in someone's character: *a ruthless streak.* 3 a period of success or luck of a certain kind: *a winning streak.* • verb 1 mark with streaks. 2 move very fast. 3 informal run naked in a public place to shock or amuse people.
■ **streaker** noun **streaky** adjective.

stream noun 1 a small, narrow river. 2 a continuous flow of liquid, air, people, etc. 3 Brit. a group in which schoolchildren of the same age and ability are taught. • verb 1 move in a continuous flow. 2 run with tears, sweat, etc. 3 float out in the wind. 4 Brit. put schoolchildren in streams. □ **on stream** in operation or existence.

streamer noun a long, narrow flag or strip of decorative material.

streamline verb (**streamlines**, **streamlining**, **streamlined**) 1 (**be streamlined**) have a shape that allows quick, easy movement through air or water. 2 make an organization or system more efficient.

street noun a public road in a city, town, or village. □ **street value** the price something, especially drugs, would fetch if sold illegally.

streetcar noun N. Amer. a tram.

streetwalker noun a prostitute who seeks clients in the street.

streetwise adjective informal able to deal with the difficulties and dangers of life in a big city.

strength noun 1 the quality or state of being strong. 2 a good or useful quality or attribute. 3 the number of people making up a group. □ **on the strength of** on the basis of.

☑ remember the *g* before the *-th*: stren*g*th.

strengthen verb make or become stronger.

strenuous adjective needing or using a lot

---

stray verb 1 *the gazelle had strayed from the herd:* wander off, get separated, get lost, drift away. 2 *we strayed from our original topic:* digress, deviate, wander, get sidetracked, go off at a tangent, get off the subject.
• adjective 1 *a stray dog:* homeless, lost, abandoned, feral. 2 *a stray bullet:* random, chance, freak, unexpected.

streak noun 1 *a streak of light:* band, line, strip, stripe, vein, slash, ray, smear. 2 *a streak of self-destructiveness:* element, vein, strain, touch. 3 *a winning streak:* period, spell, stretch, run; Brit. informal patch.
• verb 1 *the sky was streaked with red:* stripe, band, fleck, smear, mark. 2 *Miranda streaked across the road::* race, speed, flash, shoot, dash, rush, hurtle, whizz, zoom, career, fly; informal belt, tear, zip, whip; Brit. informal bomb; N. Amer. informal barrel.

stream noun 1 *a mountain stream:* brook, rivulet, tributary; Scottish & N. English burn; N. English beck; S. English bourn; N. Amer. & Austral./NZ creek. 2 *a stream of boiling water:* jet, flow, rush, gush, surge, torrent, flood, cascade. 3 *a steady stream of visitors:* succession, series, string.
• verb 1 *tears were streaming down her face:* flow, pour, course, run, gush, surge, flood, cascade, spill. 2 *children streamed out of the classrooms:* pour, surge, flood, swarm, pile, crowd.

streamlined adjective 1 *streamlined cars:* aerodynamic, smooth, sleek. 2 *a*

streamlined organization: efficient, smooth-running, well run, slick.

street noun *road:* thoroughfare, avenue, drive, boulevard, lane; N. Amer. highway.

strength noun 1 *enormous physical strength:* power, muscle, might, brawn, force. 2 *Oliver began to regain his strength:* health, fitness, vigour, stamina. 3 *her great inner strength:* fortitude, resilience, spirit, backbone, courage, bravery, pluck, grit; informal guts. 4 *the strength of the retaining wall:* robustness, sturdiness, firmness, toughness, soundness, solidity, durability. 5 *political strength:* power, influence; informal clout. 6 *strength of feeling:* intensity, vehemence, force, depth. 7 *the strength of their argument:* force, weight, power, persuasiveness, soundness, cogency, validity. 8 *what are your strengths?* strong point, advantage, asset, forte, aptitude, talent, skill, speciality. 9 *the strength of the army:* size, extent, magnitude.
OPPOSITES weakness.

strengthen verb 1 *calcium strengthens growing bones:* make strong/stronger, build up, harden, toughen, fortify, stiffen, reinforce. 2 *the wind had strengthened:* become strong/stronger, gain strength, intensify, pick up.
OPPOSITES weaken.

strenuous adjective 1 *a strenuous climb:* difficult, arduous, hard, tough, taxing, demanding, exacting, exhausting, tiring,

S

of effort or exertion.
■ **strenuously** adverb.

streptococcus /strep-tuh-**kok**-kuhss/ noun
(plural **streptococci** /strep-tuh-**kok**-ky/) a
type of bacterium which can cause various
serious infections.
■ **streptococcal** adjective.

stress noun **1** pressure or tension exerted on
an object. **2** mental or emotional strain or
tension. **3** particular emphasis. **4** emphasis
given to a syllable or word in speech. •**verb**
1 emphasize. **2** subject to pressure, tension,
or strain.

stressful adjective causing mental or
emotional stress.
■ **stressfully** adverb.

stretch verb **1** be able to be made longer or
wider without tearing or breaking.
2 extend something without tearing or
breaking it. **3** extend part of the body to its
full length. **4** extend over an area or period
of time. **5** make demands on. •**noun 1** an
act of stretching. **2** the capacity to stretch
or be stretched; elasticity. **3** a continuous
expanse or period.
■ **stretchy** adjective.

stretcher noun a long framework covered
with canvas, used for carrying sick,
injured, or dead people. •**verb** (**stretchers,
stretchering, stretchered**) carry on a
stretcher.

strew verb (**strews, strewing**, past participle
strewn or **strewed**) **1** scatter untidily over
a surface or area. **2** (**be strewn with**) be
covered with untidily scattered things.

striated adjective marked with ridges or
furrows.
■ **striation** noun.

stricken North American or old-fashioned
past participle of **STRIKE**. •**adjective**
1 seriously affected by something
unpleasant. **2** showing great distress.

strict adjective **1** demanding that rules are
obeyed. **2** following rules or beliefs exactly.
■ **strictly** adverb **strictness** noun.

stricture noun **1** a rule restricting
behaviour or action. **2** a sternly critical
remark.

stride verb (**strides, striding, strode**; past
participle **stridden**) walk with long, decisive
steps. •**noun 1** a long, decisive step. **2** a step
made towards an aim.
□ **take something in your stride** deal calmly
with something difficult.

strident adjective **1** loud and harsh.
2 presenting a point of view in a way that
is too forceful.
■ **stridency** noun **stridently** adverb.

strife noun angry or bitter disagreement.

strike verb (**strikes, striking, struck**) **1** hit

THESAURUS

gruelling, back-breaking; Brit. informal
knackering. **2** *strenuous efforts:* vigorous,
energetic, forceful, strong, spirited,
intense, determined, resolute, dogged.
OPPOSITES easy, half-hearted.

stress noun **1** *he's under a lot of stress:*
strain, pressure, (nervous) tension, worry,
anxiety, trouble, difficulty; informal hassle.
2 *laying greater stress on education:*
emphasis, importance, weight.
•**verb 1** *they stress the need for reform:*
emphasize, draw attention to, underline,
underscore, point up, highlight. **2** *all the
staff were stressed:* overstretch, overtax,
pressurize, pressure, worry, harass; informal
hassle.
OPPOSITES play down.

stretch verb **1** *this material stretches:*
expand, give, be elastic, be stretchy. **2** *he
stretched the elastic:* pull (out), draw out,
extend, lengthen, elongate, expand.
3 *stretching the truth:* bend, strain, distort,
exaggerate, embellish. **4** *she stretched out
her arm:* reach out, hold out, extend,
straighten (out). **5** *she stretched out on the
sofa:* lie down, recline, lean back, sprawl,
lounge, loll. **6** *the desert stretches for miles:*
extend, spread, continue, go on.
OPPOSITES shorten, contract, fold up.
•**noun 1** *magnificent stretches of forest:*
expanse, area, tract, belt, sweep, extent.

2 *a four-hour stretch:* period, time, spell,
run, stint, session, shift.

strict adjective **1** *a strict interpretation of the
law:* precise, exact, literal, faithful,
accurate, careful, meticulous, rigorous.
2 *strict controls on spending:* stringent,
rigorous, severe, harsh, hard, rigid, tough.
3 *strict parents:* stern, severe, harsh,
uncompromising, authoritarian, firm. **4** *in
strict confidence:* absolute, utter, complete,
total.
OPPOSITES loose, liberal.

stride verb & noun step, pace, march.

strife noun conflict, friction, discord,
disagreement, dissension, dispute,
argument, quarrelling.
OPPOSITES peace.

strike verb **1** *the teacher struck Mary:* hit,
slap, smack, thump, punch, beat, bang;
informal clout, wallop, belt, whack, thwack,
bash, clobber, bop, biff; Austral./NZ informal
quilt. **2** *the car struck a tree:* crash into,
collide with, hit, run into, bump into,
smash into; N. Amer. impact. **3** *a thought
struck her:* occur to, come to (mind), dawn
on you, hit, spring to mind, enter your
head. **4** *you strike me as intelligent:* seem
to, appear to, give someone the impression
of being. **5** *train drivers are to strike:* take
industrial action, go on strike, down tools,
walk out.

someone or something with force. **2** attack suddenly. **3** (of a disaster) happen suddenly and have harmful effects on. **4** refuse to work as a form of organized protest. **5** discover gold, oil, etc. by digging or drilling. **6** light a match by rubbing it against a rough surface. **7** (of a clock) show the time by sounding a chime or stroke. **8** reach an agreement. • noun **1** an act of striking by employees. **2** a sudden attack. **3** an act of hitting a ball. □ **strike someone off** officially expel someone from a professional group. **strike out** start out on a new course. **strike up** begin to play a piece of music. **strike something up** begin a friendship or conversation with someone.

striker noun **1** an employee who is on strike. **2** (in soccer) a forward.

striking adjective **1** very noticeable. **2** dramatically good-looking.
■ **strikingly** adverb.

string noun **1** material consisting of threads twisted together to form a thin length. **2** a length of catgut or wire on a musical instrument, producing a note when it is made to vibrate. **3** (**strings**) the stringed instruments in an orchestra. **4** a sequence of similar items or events. • verb (**strings, stringing, strung**) **1** thread things together on a string. **2** (**be strung** or **be strung out**) be arranged in a long line. **3** fit strings to a musical instrument, bow, etc.
□ **with no strings attached** informal with no special conditions or restrictions. **string someone along** informal deliberately mislead someone. **string bean** any of various beans eaten in their pods. **string quartet** a chamber music group consisting of two violinists and a viola and cello player.

■ **stringed** adjective.

stringent adjective (of regulations or requirements) strict and precise.
■ **stringency** noun **stringently** adverb.

stringy adjective **1** like string. **2** (of meat) containing tough fibres that are difficult to chew.

strip¹ verb (**strips, stripping, stripped**) **1** remove all coverings or clothes from. **2** take off your clothes. **3** remove all the contents or fittings of a room, vehicle, etc. **4** remove paint from a surface. **5** (**strip someone of**) deprive someone of rank, power, or property. • noun **1** an act of undressing. **2** Brit. the identifying outfit worn by a sports team.

strip² noun **1** a long, narrow piece of cloth, paper, etc. **2** a long, narrow area of land. □ **strip light** Brit. a fluorescent lamp in the shape of a tube.

stripe noun a long, narrow band or strip of a different colour or texture from the areas next to it. • verb (**stripes, striping, striped**) mark with stripes.
■ **stripy** (or **stripey**) adjective.

stripling noun old use a young man.

stripper noun **1** a striptease performer. **2** a device or substance for stripping paint, varnish, etc. off a surface.

striptease noun a form of entertainment in which a performer gradually undresses to music in an erotic way.

strive verb (**strives, striving, strove** or **strived**; past participle **striven** or **strived**) try very hard to do or achieve something.

strobe noun a bright light which shines at rapid intervals.

strode past of STRIDE.

S

• noun **1** *a 48-hour strike:* industrial action, walkout. **2** *a military strike:* attack, assault, bombing.

striking adjective **1** *a striking resemblance:* noticeable, obvious, conspicuous, marked, unmistakable, strong, remarkable. **2** *Kenya's striking landscape:* impressive, imposing, magnificent, spectacular, breathtaking, marvellous, wonderful, stunning, sensational, dramatic.
OPPOSITES unremarkable.

string noun **1** *a ball of string:* twine, cord, yarn, thread. **2** *a string of brewers:* chain, group, consortium. **3** *he had a string of convictions:* series, succession, chain, sequence, run, streak. **4** *a string of wagons:* queue, procession, line, file, column, convoy, train, cavalcade. **5** (**strings**) *a guaranteed loan with no strings:* conditions, qualifications, provisions, provisos, caveats, stipulations, riders,

limitations, restrictions; informal catches.
• verb *lights were strung across the promenade:* hang, suspend, sling, stretch, run, thread, loop, festoon.

stringent adjective strict, firm, rigid, rigorous, severe, harsh, tough, tight, exacting, demanding.
OPPOSITES lax.

strip¹ verb **1** *he stripped and got into bed:* undress, strip off, take your clothes off, disrobe. **2** *stripping the paint off the door:* peel, remove, scrape, clean. **3** *I stripped down the engine:* dismantle, disassemble, take to bits/pieces, take apart. **4** *the house had been stripped:* empty, clear, clean out, plunder, rob, burgle, loot, pillage, ransack, sack.
OPPOSITES dress, reassemble.

strip² noun *a strip of paper:* (narrow) piece, band, belt, ribbon, slip, shred, stretch.

stroke noun **1** an act of hitting. **2** a sound made by a striking clock. **3** an act of stroking with the hand. **4** a mark made by drawing a pen, pencil, etc. across paper or canvas. **5** a short diagonal line separating characters or figures. **6** each of a series of repeated movements, e.g. in rowing or swimming. **7** a style of moving the arms and legs in swimming. **8** a sudden disabling attack caused by an interruption in the flow of blood to the brain. •verb (**strokes, stroking, stroked**) gently move your hand over.

stroll verb walk in a leisurely way. •noun a short leisurely walk.

strong adjective (**stronger, strongest**) **1** physically powerful. **2** done with or supplying great force. **3** able to withstand great force or pressure. **4** secure or stable. **5** great in power, influence, or ability. **6** great in intensity or degree. **7** having a lot of flavour. **8** (of a solution or drink) containing a large proportion of a substance. **9** used after a number to indicate the size of a group.
□ **going strong** informal continuing to be healthy, active, or successful.
■ **strongly** adverb.

strongbox noun a small metal box in which valuables are kept.

stronghold noun **1** a place of strong support for a cause or political party. **2** a place that has been strengthened against attack.

strongroom noun a room designed to protect valuable items against fire and theft.

strontium noun a soft silver-white metallic element.

stroppy adjective Brit. informal bad-tempered or argumentative.

strove past of STRIVE.

struck past and past participle of STRIKE.

structural adjective relating to or forming part of a structure.
■ **structurally** adverb.

structure noun **1** the putting together of different parts to form a whole. **2** a building or other object constructed from several parts. **3** good organization. •verb (**structures, structuring, structured**) put parts together to form a whole.

strudel /stroo-duhl/ noun a dessert of thin pastry rolled up round a fruit filling and baked.

struggle verb (**struggles, struggling,**

THESAURUS

stroke noun **1** *five hammer strokes:* blow, hit. **2** *light upward strokes:* movement, action, motion. **3** *broad brush strokes:* mark, line. **4** *he suffered a stroke:* thrombosis, seizure, apoplexy.
•verb *she stroked the cat:* caress, fondle, pat, pet, touch, rub, massage, soothe.

stroll verb & noun walk, amble, wander, meander, ramble, promenade, saunter; informal mosey.

strong adjective **1** *a strong lad:* powerful, sturdy, robust, athletic, tough, rugged, lusty. **2** *she isn't very strong:* well, healthy, fit. **3** *a strong character:* forceful, determined, spirited, self-assertive, tough, formidable, strong-minded; informal gutsy, feisty. **4** *a strong fortress:* secure, well built, well fortified, well protected, solid. **5** *strong cotton bags:* durable, hard-wearing, heavy-duty, tough, sturdy, well made, long-lasting. **6** *a strong interest in literature:* keen, passionate, fervent. **7** *strong feelings:* intense, forceful, passionate, ardent, fervent, deep-seated. **8** *strong arguments:* forceful, compelling, powerful, convincing, persuasive, sound, valid, cogent, well founded. **9** *a strong voice:* loud, powerful, forceful, resonant, sonorous, rich, deep, booming. **10** *strong language:* bad, foul, obscene, profane. **11** *a strong blue colour:* intense, deep, rich, bright, brilliant, vivid, vibrant. **12** *strong lights:* bright, brilliant, dazzling, glaring.

13 *strong coffee:* concentrated, undiluted. **14** *strong cheese:* highly flavoured, mature, ripe, piquant, tangy, spicy. **15** *strong drink:* alcoholic, intoxicating, hard, stiff.
OPPOSITES weak, gentle, mild.

stronghold noun **1** *the enemy stronghold:* fortress, fort, castle, citadel, garrison. **2** *a Tory stronghold:* bastion, centre, hotbed.

structure noun **1** *a vast Gothic structure:* building, edifice, construction, erection. **2** *the structure of local government:* construction, organization, system, arrangement, framework, form, formation, shape, composition, anatomy, make-up.
•verb *the programme is structured around periods of study:* arrange, organize, design, shape, construct, build.

struggle verb **1** *they struggled to do better:* strive, try hard, endeavour, make every effort. **2** *James struggled with the raiders:* fight, battle, grapple, wrestle, scuffle. **3** *she struggled over the dunes:* scramble, flounder, stumble, fight/battle your way, labour.
•noun **1** *the struggle for justice:* striving, endeavour, campaign, battle, crusade, drive, push. **2** *no signs of a struggle:* fight, scuffle, brawl, tussle, fracas; informal bust-up, ding-dong. **3** *many perished in the struggle:* conflict, fight, battle, confrontation, clash, hostilities, fighting, war, warfare, campaign. **4** *a struggle within the leadership:* contest, competition, fight,

S

struggled) **1** make great efforts to get free. **2** try hard to do something. **3** make your way with difficulty. •noun **1** an act of struggling. **2** a very difficult task.
■ **struggler** noun.

strum verb (**strums, strumming, strummed**) play a guitar or similar instrument by sweeping the thumb or a plectrum up or down the strings. •noun an instance of strumming.

strumpet noun old use a woman who has a lot of sexual partners.

strung past and past participle of STRING.

strut noun **1** a bar used to support or strengthen a structure. **2** a proud, confident walk. •verb (**struts, strutting, strutted**) walk in a proud and confident way.

strychnine /strik-neen/ noun a bitter and highly poisonous substance obtained from an Asian tree.

Stuart or **Stewart** adjective relating to the royal family ruling Scotland 1371–1714 and Britain 1603–1714.

stub noun **1** the remaining part of a pencil, cigarette, etc. after use. **2** the counterfoil of a cheque, ticket, etc. •verb (**stubs, stubbing, stubbed**) **1** accidentally bump your toe against something. **2** (often **stub something out**) put out a cigarette by pressing the lighted end against something.
■ **stubby** adjective.

stubble noun **1** short, stiff hairs growing on a man's face when he has not shaved for a while. **2** the cut stalks of cereal plants left in the ground after harvesting.
■ **stubbly** adjective.

stubborn adjective **1** determined not to

change your attitude or position. **2** difficult to move or remove.
■ **stubbornly** adverb **stubbornness** noun.

stucco noun plaster used for coating wall surfaces or moulding into decoration.
■ **stuccoed** adjective.

stuck past participle of STICK².
□ **stuck-up** informal having snobbish views and thinking that you are better than other people.

stud¹ noun **1** a piece of metal with a large head that projects from a surface. **2** Brit. a small projection fixed to the base of a shoe or boot to provide better grip. **3** a small piece of jewellery which is pushed through a pierced ear or nostril. **4** a fastener consisting of two buttons joined with a bar. •verb (**studs, studding, studded**) decorate with studs or similar small objects.

stud² noun **1** an establishment where horses are kept for breeding. **2** a stallion. **3** informal a man who has many sexual partners.

student noun **1** a person studying at a university or college. **2** a school pupil.

studio noun (plural **studios**) **1** a room from which television or radio programmes are broadcast. **2** a place where film or sound recordings are made. **3** a room where an artist works or where dancers practise.
□ **studio flat** Brit. a flat containing one main room.

studious adjective **1** spending a lot of time studying or reading. **2** done with careful effort.
■ **studiously** adverb.

study noun (plural **studies**) **1** the reading of books or examination of other materials to gain knowledge. **2** a detailed investigation

clash, rivalry, friction, feuding, conflict.

strut verb swagger, prance, parade, stride, sweep; N. Amer. informal sashay.
OPPOSITES slink.

stubborn adjective **1** *you're too stubborn to admit it:* obstinate, headstrong, wilful, strong-willed, pig-headed, inflexible, uncompromising, unbending; informal stiff-necked. **2** *stubborn stains:* indelible, permanent, persistent, tenacious, resistant.
OPPOSITES compliant, removable.

stuck adjective **1** *a message was stuck to his screen:* fixed, fastened, attached, glued, pinned. **2** *the gate was stuck:* jammed, immovable. **3** *if you get stuck, leave a blank:* baffled, beaten, at a loss; informal stumped, bogged down, flummoxed, bamboozled.

student noun **1** *a university student:* undergraduate, postgraduate. **2** *a former student:* pupil, schoolchild, schoolboy,

schoolgirl, scholar. **3** *a nursing student:* trainee, apprentice, probationer, novice, learner.

studio noun workshop, workroom, atelier.

studious adjective scholarly, academic, bookish, intellectual, erudite, learned, donnish; informal brainy.

study noun **1** *two years of study:* learning, education, schooling, scholarship, tuition, research. **2** *a study of global warming:* investigation, enquiry, research, examination, analysis, review, survey. **3** *Bob was in the study:* office, workroom, studio.
•verb **1** *Anil studied hard:* work, revise; informal swot, cram. **2** *he studied maths:* learn, read, be taught. **3** *Thomas studied ants:* investigate, research, look at, examine, analyse. **4** *she studied him thoughtfully:* scrutinize, examine, inspect, consider, regard, look at, observe, watch, survey; informal check out.

S

into a subject or situation. **3** a room used for reading and writing. **4** a piece of work done for practice or as an experiment. •verb (**studies, studying, studied**) **1** learn about something. **2** investigate a subject or situation in detail. **3** look at something closely in order to observe or read it. **4** (**studied**) done with careful effort.

stuff noun **1** material, articles, or activities of a particular kind, or of a mixed or unspecified kind. **2** basic characteristics. **3** (**your stuff**) informal the things that you are good at or responsible for. •verb **1** fill a container or space tightly with something. **2** fill out the skin of a dead animal or bird with material to restore its original appearance.

stuffing noun **1** a mixture used to stuff poultry or meat before cooking. **2** padding used to stuff cushions, furniture, or soft toys.

stuffy adjective (**stuffier, stuffiest**) **1** lacking fresh air or ventilation. **2** conventional and narrow-minded. **3** (of a person's nose) blocked up.

stultify verb (**stultifies, stultifying, stultified**) make someone feel bored or drained of energy.

stumble verb (**stumbles, stumbling, stumbled**) **1** trip and momentarily lose your balance. **2** walk unsteadily. **3** make a mistake in speaking. **4** (**stumble across** or **on**) find by chance. •noun an act of stumbling.

◻ **stumbling block** an obstacle.

stump noun **1** the part of a tree trunk left sticking out of the ground after the rest has fallen or been cut down. **2** a remaining piece. **3** Cricket each of the three upright pieces of wood which form a wicket. •verb informal baffle.

stumpy adjective (**stumpier, stumpiest**) short and thick; squat.

stun verb (**stuns, stunning, stunned**) **1** knock someone into a dazed or unconscious state. **2** greatly astonish or shock someone.

stung past and past participle of **STING**.

stunk past and past participle of **STINK**.

stunner noun informal a strikingly attractive or impressive person or thing.

stunning adjective very impressive or attractive.
■ **stunningly** adverb.

stunt¹ verb slow down the growth or development of.

stunt² noun **1** an action displaying spectacular skill and daring. **2** something unusual done to attract attention.

stuntman noun (plural **stuntmen**) a person taking an actor's place in performing dangerous stunts.

stupefy verb (**stupefies, stupefying, stupefied**) make someone unable to think properly.
■ **stupefaction** noun.

stupendous adjective very impressive.
■ **stupendously** adverb.

stupid adjective **1** lacking intelligence or

THESAURUS

stuff noun **1** *suede is tough stuff:* material, substance, fabric, cloth. **2** *first-aid stuff:* items, articles, objects, goods; informal things, bits and pieces, odds and ends. **3** *all my stuff is in the suitcase:* belongings, possessions, effects, paraphernalia; informal gear, things, kit; Brit. informal clobber.
•verb **1** *stuffing pillows:* fill, pack, pad, upholster. **2** *Robyn stuffed her clothes into a bag:* shove, thrust, push, ram, cram, squeeze, force, jam, pack, pile.

stuffing noun padding, wadding, filling, packing.

stuffy adjective **1** *a stuffy atmosphere:* airless, close, musty, stale. **2** *a stuffy young man:* staid, sedate, sober, priggish, strait-laced, conformist, conservative, old-fashioned; informal straight, starchy, fuddy-duddy.
OPPOSITES airy, clear, informal, modern.

stumble verb **1** *he stumbled and fell:* trip, lose your balance, lose your footing, slip. **2** *he stumbled back home:* stagger, totter, blunder, hobble.
◻ **stumble across/on** find, chance on, happen on, light on, come across/upon, discover, unearth, uncover; informal dig up.

stump verb (informal) baffle, perplex, puzzle, confound, defeat, put at a loss; informal flummox, fox, throw, floor.

stun verb **1** *the force of the blow stunned him:* daze, stupefy, knock out, lay out. **2** *she was stunned by the news:* astound, amaze, astonish, dumbfound, stupefy, stagger, shock, take aback; informal flabbergast, knock sideways.

stunning adjective beautiful, lovely, glorious, wonderful, marvellous, magnificent, superb, sublime, spectacular, fine, delightful; informal fantastic, terrific, tremendous, sensational, heavenly, divine, gorgeous, fabulous, awesome.
OPPOSITES ordinary.

stunt noun feat, exploit, trick.

stunted adjective small, undersized, underdeveloped, diminutive.

stupid adjective **1** *he's really stupid:* unintelligent, dense, foolish, slow, idiotic, simple-minded; informal thick, dim, dumb, dopey, dozy; Brit. informal daft. **2** *a stupid idea:* foolish, silly, senseless, idiotic, ill-advised, ill-considered, unwise; informal crazy, half-baked, cockeyed, hare-brained;

S

common sense. **2** dazed and unable to think clearly.
■ **stupidity** noun **stupidly** adverb.

stupor noun a state of being very dazed or nearly unconscious.

sturdy adjective (**sturdier, sturdiest**) **1** strong and solidly built or made. **2** confident and determined.
■ **sturdily** adverb **sturdiness** noun.

sturgeon /ster-juhn/ noun a very large fish with bony plates on the body, from whose roe (eggs) caviar is made.

stutter verb (**stutters, stuttering, stuttered**) **1** have difficulty talking because you are sometimes unable to stop repeating the first sounds of a word. **2** (of a machine or gun) produce a series of short, sharp sounds. • noun a tendency to stutter while speaking.
■ **stutterer** noun.

sty[1] noun (plural **sties**) a pigsty.

sty[2] or **stye** noun (plural **sties** or **styes**) an inflamed swelling on the edge of an eyelid.

Stygian /sti-ji-uhn/ adjective literary very dark.

style noun **1** a way of doing something. **2** a particular appearance, design, or arrangement. **3** a way of painting, writing, etc. characteristic of a particular period or person. **4** elegance and sophistication. **5** Botany a narrow extension of the ovary, carrying the stigma. • verb (**styles, styling, styled**) **1** design, make, or arrange in a particular form. **2** give a particular name, description, or title to.

stylish adjective having a good sense of style; fashionably elegant.
■ **stylishly** adverb.

stylist noun a person who designs fashionable clothes or cuts hair.

stylistic adjective relating to style.
■ **stylistically** adverb.

stylized or **stylised** adjective represented in an artificial style.

stylus noun (plural **styli** /sty-ly/) **1** a hard point that follows a groove in a gramophone record and transmits the

recorded sound for reproduction. **2** a pointed implement used for scratching or tracing letters or engraving.

stymie verb (**stymies, stymying** or **stymieing, stymied**) informal prevent or slow down the progress of.

styptic /stip-tik/ adjective able to make bleeding stop.

suave /swahv/ adjective (of a man) charming, confident, and elegant.
■ **suavely** adverb **suavity** noun.

sub informal noun **1** a submarine. **2** a subscription. **3** a substitute in a sports team. • verb (**subs, subbing, subbed**) act as a substitute.

subaltern /sub-uhl-tern/ noun an officer in the British army below the rank of captain.

subatomic adjective smaller than or occurring within an atom.

subconscious adjective concerning the part of the mind which you are not aware of but which influences your actions and feelings. • noun this part of the mind.
■ **subconsciously** adverb.

subcontinent noun a large part of a continent considered as a particular area, such as North America or southern Africa.

subcontract verb employ a firm or person outside your company to do work.
■ **subcontractor** noun.

subculture noun a distinct group within a society or class, having beliefs or interests that are different from those of the larger group.

subcutaneous adjective situated or applied under the skin.

subdivide verb (**subdivides, subdividing, subdivided**) divide a part into smaller parts.
■ **subdivision** noun.

subdue verb (**subdues, subduing, subdued**) **1** overcome, quieten, or control. **2** bring a group or country under control by force.

S

Brit. informal **potty**.
OPPOSITES intelligent, sensible.

sturdy adjective **1** *a sturdy lad:* strapping, well built, muscular, strong, hefty, brawny, powerful, solid, burly; informal beefy.
2 *sturdy boots:* robust, strong, well built, solid, stout, tough, durable, long-lasting, hard-wearing.
OPPOSITES feeble, flimsy.

style noun **1** *differing styles of management:* manner, way, technique, method, approach, system, form. **2** *dressing with style:* flair, elegance, taste, grace, poise,

polish, sophistication, dash; informal class.
3 *Laura travelled in style:* comfort, luxury.
4 *modern styles:* fashion, trend, vogue.
• verb *sportswear styled by Karl:* design, fashion, tailor, cut.

stylish adjective fashionable, modern, up to date, modish, smart, sophisticated, elegant, chic, dapper, dashing; informal trendy, natty; N. Amer. informal kicky, tony.
OPPOSITES unfashionable.

subdue verb conquer, defeat, vanquish, overcome, overwhelm, crush, beat, subjugate, suppress.

subdued adjective **1** quiet and thoughtful or depressed. **2** (of colour or lighting) soft; muted.

subedit verb (**subedits, subediting, subedited**) check and correct newspaper or magazine text before printing.
■ subeditor noun.

subhuman adjective not behaving like a human being.

subject noun /sub-jekt/ **1** a person or thing that is being discussed, studied, or dealt with. **2** a branch of knowledge that is studied or taught. **3** Grammar the word or words in a sentence that come before the verb and which the verb says something about, e.g. *Joe* in *Joe ran home.* **4** each of the people in a population ruled by a king or queen. •adjective /sub-jekt/ (**subject to**) **1** able to be affected by. **2** dependent or conditional on. **3** under the control or authority of. •adverb /sub-jekt/ (**subject to**) if certain conditions are fulfilled. •verb /suhb-jekt/ (**subject someone/thing to**) make someone or something undergo an unpleasant experience.
■ subjection noun.

subjective adjective based on or influenced by personal opinions.
■ subjectively adverb subjectivity noun.

sub judice /sub joo-di-si/ adjective being considered by a court of law and therefore not to be publicly discussed elsewhere.

subjugate verb (**subjugates, subjugating, subjugated**) bring someone under your control by force.
■ subjugation noun.

subjunctive adjective Grammar (of a verb) expressing what is imagined or wished or possible.

sublet verb (**sublets, subletting, sublet**) let a property or part of a property that you are already renting to someone else.

sublimate verb **1** direct energy, especially sexual energy, into socially acceptable activities such as exercise, work, or art. **2** Chemistry = **SUBLIME**.
■ sublimation noun.

sublime adjective **1** of great beauty or excellence. **2** extreme: *sublime confidence.* •verb (**sublimes, subliming, sublimed**) Chemistry (of a solid substance) change directly into vapour when heated.
■ sublimely adverb.

subliminal adjective affecting your mind without your being aware of it.
■ subliminally adverb.

sub-machine gun noun a hand-held lightweight machine gun.

submarine noun a streamlined warship designed to operate completely submerged in the sea. •adjective existing, occurring, or used under the surface of the sea.
■ submariner noun.

submerge verb (**submerges, submerging, submerged**) **1** push or hold something underwater. **2** go down below the surface of water. **3** completely cover or hide.

submerse verb submerge.
■ submersion noun.

submersible adjective designed to operate while submerged.

submicroscopic adjective too small to be seen by a microscope.

submission noun **1** the action of submitting. **2** a proposal or application submitted for consideration.

submissive adjective very obedient or passive.
■ submissively adverb.

THESAURUS

subdued adjective **1** *Lewis's subdued air:* sombre, downcast, sad, dejected, depressed, gloomy, despondent. **2** *subdued voices:* hushed, muted, quiet, low, soft, faint, muffled, indistinct. **3** *subdued lighting:* dim, muted, soft, low, mood. OPPOSITES cheerful, loud, bright.

subject noun **1** *the subject of this chapter:* theme, subject matter, topic, issue, question, concern. **2** *popular university subjects:* branch of study, discipline, field. **3** *British subjects:* citizen, national, resident, taxpayer, voter.
•verb *the prisoners were subjected to violence:* expose to, treat with, put through.
□ subject to conditional on, contingent on, dependent on.

subjective adjective personal, individual, emotional, biased, intuitive.
OPPOSITES objective.

submerge verb **1** *the U-boat submerged:* go under (water), dive, sink, plunge, blow its tanks. **2** *submerge the bowl in water:* immerse, plunge, sink. **3** *the farmland was submerged:* flood, deluge, swamp, inundate, overwhelm.
OPPOSITES surface, drain.

submission noun **1** *submission to authority:* yielding, capitulation, surrender, resignation, acceptance, consent, compliance, acquiescence, obedience, subjection, subservience, servility. **2** *a report for submission to the Board:* presentation, proffering, tendering, proposing. **3** *his original submission:* proposal, suggestion, proposition, entry, recommendation. **4** *the judge rejected his submission:* argument, assertion, contention, statement, claim, allegation.
OPPOSITES defiance, resistance.

S

submit verb (**submits, submitting, submitted**) **1** give in to the authority, control, or greater strength of someone or something. **2** present a proposal or application for consideration. **3** subject to a particular process or treatment.

subordinate adjective /suh-**bor**-di-nuht/ **1** lower in rank or position. **2** of less importance. • noun /suh-**bor**-di-nuht/ a person who is under the authority of someone else. • verb /suh-**bor**-di-nayt/ (**subordinates, subordinating, subordinated**) treat someone or something as less important than another.
■ subordination noun.

suborn verb pay or persuade someone to commit an unlawful act, especially perjury.

subplot noun a secondary plot in a play, novel, etc.

subpoena /suhb-**pee**-nuh/ Law noun a written order instructing someone to attend a court. • verb (**subpoenas, subpoenaing, subpoenaed**) summon someone with a subpoena.

subscribe verb (**subscribes, subscribing, subscribed**) **1** (often **subscribe to**) arrange to receive something regularly by paying in advance. **2** (**subscribe to**) contribute a sum of money to a project or cause. **3** (**subscribe to**) say you agree with an idea or proposal.
■ subscriber noun.

subscript adjective (of a letter, figure, or symbol) printed below the line.

subscription noun **1** money paid to subscribe to something. **2** the action of subscribing.

subsection noun a division of a section.

subsequent adjective coming after something.
■ subsequently adverb.

subservient adjective too ready to obey other people.
■ subservience noun.

subside verb (**subsides, subsiding, subsided**) **1** become less strong, violent, or severe. **2** (of water) go down to a lower level. **3** (of a building) sink lower into the ground. **4** (of the ground) cave in; sink. **5** (**subside into**) give way to a strong feeling.

subsidence noun the gradual caving in or sinking of an area of land.

subsidiary adjective **1** related but less important. **2** (of a company) controlled by another company. • noun (plural **subsidiaries**) a subsidiary company.

subsidize or **subsidise** verb (**subsidizes, subsidizing, subsidized**) **1** support an organization or activity financially. **2** pay part of the cost of producing something to reduce its price.

subsidy noun (plural **subsidies**) a sum of money given to help keep the price of a product or service low.

THESAURUS

submit verb **1** *she was forced to submit:* yield, give in/way, back down, cave in, capitulate, surrender. **2** *he refused to submit to their authority:* be governed by, abide by, comply with, accept, be subject to, agree to, consent to, conform to. **3** *we submitted an application:* put forward, present, offer, tender, propose, suggest, enter, put in, send in. **4** *they submitted that the judgement was incorrect:* contend, assert, argue, state, claim.
OPPOSITES resist, withdraw.

subordinate adjective inferior, junior, lower-ranking, lower, supporting.
• noun junior, assistant, second (in command), number two, deputy, aide, underling, minion.
OPPOSITES superior, senior.

subscribe verb *we subscribe to charity:* contribute, donate, give, pay.
□ subscribe to **support**, endorse, agree with, accept, go along with.

subscription noun membership fee, dues, annual payment, charge.

subsequent adjective following, ensuing, succeeding, later, future, coming, to come, next.
OPPOSITES previous.

subsequently adverb later (on), at a later date, afterwards, in due course, following this/that, eventually; formal thereafter.

subside verb **1** *wait until the storm subsides:* abate, let up, quieten down, calm, slacken (off), ease (up), relent, die down, diminish, decline. **2** *the flood has subsided:* recede, ebb, fall, go down, get lower. **3** *the house is gradually subsiding:* sink, settle, cave in, collapse, give way.
OPPOSITES intensify, rise.

subsidiary adjective *a subsidiary company:* subordinate, secondary, subservient, supplementary, peripheral, auxiliary.
OPPOSITES principal.
• noun *the firm's Spanish subsidiary:* branch, division, subdivision, derivative, offshoot.
OPPOSITES headquarters, holding company.

subsidize verb finance, fund, support, contribute to, give money to, underwrite, sponsor; informal shell out for; N. Amer. informal bankroll.

subsidy noun finance, funding, backing, support, grant, sponsorship, allowance, contribution, handout.

S

subsist verb maintain or support yourself at a basic level.

subsistence noun the action or fact of subsisting. •adjective (of production) at a level which is enough only for your own use, without any surplus for trade.

subsoil noun soil lying under the surface soil.

subsonic adjective relating to or flying at a speed less than that of sound.

substance noun 1 a type of solid, liquid, or gas that has particular qualities. 2 the real physical matter of which a person or thing consists. 3 solid basis in reality or fact. 4 the quality of being important, valid, or significant. 5 the most important or essential part or meaning.

substandard adjective below the usual or required standard.

substantial adjective 1 of considerable importance, size, or value. 2 strongly built or made. 3 concerning the essential points of something.

substantially adverb 1 to a great extent. 2 for the most part; mainly.

substantiate verb (**substantiates, substantiating, substantiated**) provide evidence to support or prove the truth of something.

substantive adjective real and meaningful.
■ **substantively** adverb.

substitute noun a person or thing that does something or is used in place of someone or something else. •verb (**substitutes, substituting, substituted**) make someone or something act as a substitute for.
■ **substitution** noun.

subsume verb (**subsumes, subsuming, subsumed**) include or absorb something in something else.

subterfuge noun secretive or dishonest actions.

subterranean adjective existing or happening under the earth's surface.

subtext noun an underlying theme in a piece of writing or speech.

subtitle noun 1 (**subtitles**) words displayed at the bottom of a cinema or television screen that translate what is being said. 2 a secondary title of a published work. •verb (**subtitles, subtitling, subtitled**) provide something with a subtitle or subtitles.

subtle adjective (**subtler, subtlest**) 1 so delicate or precise as to be difficult to analyse or describe. 2 capable of making fine distinctions. 3 making use of clever and indirect methods to achieve something.
■ **subtlety** noun **subtly** adverb.

subtotal noun the total of one set within a larger set of figures.

subtract verb take away a number or amount from another to calculate the difference.
■ **subtraction** noun.

subtropical adjective having to do with regions near or next to the tropics.

suburb noun a residential district that is outside the central part of a city.
■ **suburban** adjective.

suburbia noun suburbs, and the way of life of the people who live in them.

subversive adjective trying to damage or weaken the power of an established

THESAURUS

substance noun 1 *organic substances:* material, compound, matter, stuff. 2 *none of the objections has any substance:* significance, importance, import, validity, foundation. 3 *the substance of the tale is very thin:* content, subject matter, theme, message, essence. 4 *men of substance:* wealth, fortune, riches, affluence, prosperity, money, means.

substantial adjective 1 *substantial progress had been made:* considerable, real, significant, important, major, valuable, useful. 2 *substantial damages:* sizeable, considerable, significant, large, ample, appreciable. 3 *substantial Victorian villas:* sturdy, solid, stout, strong, well built, durable, long-lasting, hard-wearing.
OPPOSITES little, meagre, flimsy.

substitute noun *substitutes for permanent employees:* replacement, deputy, relief, proxy, reserve, surrogate, cover, stand-in, understudy; informal sub.
•adjective *a substitute teacher:* acting,

replacement, deputy, relief, reserve, surrogate, stand-in.
OPPOSITES permanent.
•verb 1 *curd cheese can be substituted for yogurt:* exchange, swap, use instead of, use as an alternative to, use in place of, replace with. 2 *the Senate was empowered to substitute for the President:* deputize, stand in, cover.

subtle adjective 1 *subtle colours:* understated, muted, subdued, delicate, soft. 2 *subtle distinctions:* fine, nice. 3 *a subtle change:* gentle, slight, gradual.
OPPOSITES gaudy, crude, dramatic.

subtlety noun delicacy, understatedness, refinement, mutedness, softness.

subversive adjective *subversive literature:* disruptive, troublemaking, insurrectionary, seditious, dissident.
•noun *he was suspected of being a subversive:* troublemaker, dissident, agitator, renegade.

S

system or institution. • **noun** a subversive person.
  ■ **subversively** adverb.

subvert verb damage or weaken the power of an established system or institution.
  ■ **subversion** noun.

subway noun 1 Brit. a passage under a road for use by pedestrians. 2 N. Amer. an underground railway.

sub-zero adjective (of temperature) lower than zero; below freezing.

succeed verb 1 achieve an aim or purpose. 2 gain wealth or status. 3 take over a job, role, or title from someone else. 4 come after and take the place of.

success noun 1 the achievement of an aim or purpose. 2 the gaining of wealth or status. 3 a person or thing that achieves success.

> ☑ double c and double s in **success**, **successful**, **succession**, and **successive**.

successful adjective 1 having achieved an aim or purpose. 2 having gained wealth or status.
  ■ **successfully** adverb.

succession noun 1 a number of people or things following one after the other. 2 the action, process, or right of inheriting a position or title.

successive adjective following one another or following others.
  ■ **successively** adverb.

successor noun a person or thing that succeeds another.

succinct /suhk-**singkt**/ adjective briefly and clearly expressed.
  ■ **succinctly** adverb.

succour /**suk**-ker/ (US spelling **succor**) noun help and support in difficult times. • **verb** give help and support to.

succulent adjective 1 (of food) tender, juicy, and tasty. 2 (of a plant) having thick fleshy leaves or stems that store water. • **noun** a succulent plant.
  ■ **succulence** noun.

succumb verb 1 give in to pressure or temptation. 2 die from the effect of a disease or injury.

such determiner & pronoun 1 of the type previously mentioned or about to be mentioned. 2 to so high a degree; so great. □ **such as** 1 for example. 2 of a kind that; like.

suchlike pronoun things of the type mentioned.

suck verb 1 draw something into your mouth by tightening your lip muscles to make a partial vacuum. 2 hold something in your mouth and draw at it by tightening your lip and cheek muscles. 3 draw something in a particular direction by creating a vacuum. 4 (**suck someone in** or **into**) involve someone in a situation or activity without them being able to choose or resist it. 5 (**suck up to**) informal do things to please someone in authority in order to gain advantage for yourself. 6 N. Amer. informal be very bad or unpleasant. • **noun** an act of sucking.

sucker noun 1 a rubber cup that sticks to a surface by suction. 2 an organ that allows an animal to cling to a surface by suction. 3 informal a person who is easily fooled. 4 (a **sucker for**) informal a person who is very fond of a particular thing. 5 a shoot springing from the base of a tree or other plant.

suckle verb (**suckles**, **suckling**, **suckled**) feed at the breast or a teat.

suckling noun a young child or animal that is still feeding on its mother's milk.

sucrose /**soo**-krohz/ noun the main substance in cane or beet sugar.

THESAURUS

succeed verb 1 *Darwin finally succeeded:* triumph, achieve success, be successful, do well, flourish, thrive; informal make it, make the grade. 2 *the plan succeeded:* be successful, turn out well, work (out), be effective; informal come off, pay off. 3 *he succeeded Gladstone as Prime Minister:* replace, take over from, follow, supersede.
  OPPOSITES fail, precede.

success noun 1 *the success of the scheme:* favourable outcome, triumph. 2 *the trappings of success:* prosperity, affluence, wealth, riches, opulence. 3 *a box-office success:* triumph, best-seller, sell-out; informal hit, smash, winner.
  OPPOSITES failure.

successful adjective 1 *a successful designer:* prosperous, affluent, wealthy, rich, famous, eminent, top, respected. 2 *successful companies:* flourishing, thriving, booming, buoyant, doing well, profitable, moneymaking, lucrative.

succession noun sequence, series, progression, chain, string, train, line, run.

successive adjective consecutive, in a row, sequential, in succession, running; informal on the trot.

succumb verb 1 *she finally succumbed to temptation:* yield, give in/way, submit, surrender, capitulate, cave in. 2 *he succumbed to the disease:* die from/of.
  OPPOSITES resist.

suck verb 1 *they sucked orange juice through straws:* sip, sup, siphon, slurp, drink. 2 *Fran sucked in a deep breath:* draw, pull, breathe, gasp.

suction noun the force produced when a partial vacuum is created by the removal of air.

Sudanese noun a person from Sudan. •adjective relating to Sudan.

sudden adjective happening or done quickly and unexpectedly.
■ **suddenly** adverb **suddenness** noun.

sudoku /soo-**dok**-koo, soo-**doh**-koo/ noun a type of number puzzle.

suds plural noun froth made from soap and water.

sue verb (**sues, suing, sued**) **1** start legal proceedings against someone that you claim has harmed you. **2** (**sue for**) formal appeal formally to a person for.

suede noun leather with the flesh side rubbed to give it a velvety surface.

suet noun hard white fat obtained from cattle, sheep, and other animals, used in cooking.

suffer verb (**suffers, suffering, suffered**) **1** experience something bad. **2** (**suffer from**) be affected by an illness or condition. **3** become worse in quality. **4** old use tolerate.
■ **sufferer** noun.

sufferance noun toleration, rather than genuine approval.

suffice verb (**suffices, sufficing, sufficed**) be enough or adequate.

sufficiency noun (plural **sufficiencies**) **1** the quality of being enough or adequate. **2** an adequate amount.

sufficient adjective enough; adequate.
■ **sufficiently** adverb.

suffix noun a part added on to the end of a word (e.g. -ly, -ation).

suffocate verb (**suffocates, suffocating, suffocated**) die or cause to die from lack of air or being unable to breathe.
■ **suffocation** noun.

suffrage /**suf**-frij/ noun the right to vote in political elections.

suffragette /suf-fruh-**jet**/ noun (in the past, when only men could vote) a woman who campaigned for the right to vote in an election.

suffuse verb (**suffuses, suffusing, suffused**) gradually spread through or over.
■ **suffusion** noun.

sugar noun **1** a sweet substance obtained from sugar cane or sugar beet. **2** a type of sweet soluble carbohydrate found in plant and animal tissue. •verb sweeten, sprinkle, or coat with sugar.
□ **sugar beet** a type of beet from which sugar is extracted. **sugar cane** a tropical grass with tall thick stems from which sugar is extracted. **sugar daddy** informal a rich older man who gives presents and money to a much younger woman.
■ **sugary** adjective.

suggest verb **1** put forward an idea or plan for people to consider. **2** make you think that something exists or is the case. **3** say or indicate something indirectly. **4** (**suggest itself**) (of an idea) come into your mind.

suggestible adjective quick to accept other people's ideas or suggestions.

suggestion noun **1** an idea or plan put forward for people to consider. **2** a thing that suggests that something is the case. **3** a slight trace or indication.

suggestive adjective **1** making you think of

THESAURUS

sudden adjective unexpected, unforeseen, immediate, instantaneous, instant, precipitous, abrupt, rapid, swift, quick.

suddenly adverb all of a sudden, all at once, abruptly, swiftly, unexpectedly, without warning, out of the blue.
OPPOSITES gradually.

sue verb take legal action (against), go to court, take to court, litigate.

suffer verb **1** *I hate to see him suffer:* hurt, ache, be in pain, be in distress, be upset, be miserable. **2** *he suffers from asthma:* be afflicted by, be affected by, be troubled with, have. **3** *England suffered a humiliating defeat:* undergo, experience, be subjected to, receive, endure, face. **4** *our reputation has suffered:* be impaired, be damaged, decline.

suffering noun hardship, distress, misery, adversity, pain, agony, anguish, trauma, torment, torture, hurt, affliction.
OPPOSITES pleasure, joy.

sufficient adjective & determiner enough, adequate, plenty of, ample.
OPPOSITES inadequate.

suggest verb **1** *Ruth suggested a holiday:* propose, put forward, recommend, advocate, advise. **2** *evidence suggests that voters are unhappy:* indicate, lead to the belief, demonstrate, show. **3** *what exactly are you suggesting?* hint, insinuate, imply, intimate.

suggestion noun **1** *some suggestions for tackling this problem:* proposal, proposition, recommendation, advice, counsel, hint, tip, clue, idea. **2** *the suggestion of a smirk:* hint, trace, touch, suspicion, ghost, semblance, shadow, glimmer. **3** *a suggestion that he knew about the plot:* insinuation, hint, implication.

suggestive adjective **1** *an odour suggestive of a brewery:* redolent, evocative, reminiscent, characteristic, indicative, typical. **2** *suggestive remarks:* indecent,

S

a particular thing. **2** hinting at sexual matters.
  ■ **suggestively** adverb.

suicide noun **1** the action of killing yourself intentionally. **2** a person who commits suicide.
  ■ **suicidal** adjective **suicidally** adverb.

suit noun **1** a set of clothes made of the same fabric, consisting of a jacket and trousers or a skirt. **2** a set of clothes for a particular activity. **3** any of the sets into which a pack of playing cards is divided (spades, hearts, diamonds, and clubs). **4** a lawsuit. • **verb 1** be right or good for. **2** (of clothes, colours, etc.) be right for someone's features or figure. **3** (**suit yourself**) do as you wish.

suitable adjective right or good for a particular person or situation.
  ■ **suitability** noun **suitably** adverb.

suitcase noun a case with a handle and a hinged lid, used for carrying clothes and other possessions.

suite noun **1** a set of rooms. **2** a set of furniture. **3** (in music) a set of instrumental compositions to be played one after the other.

suitor noun dated a man who pays attention to a woman because he wants to marry her.

sulfur US spelling of SULPHUR.

sulk verb be quietly bad-tempered and resentful because you are annoyed. • **noun** a period of sulking.

sulky adjective quietly bad-tempered and resentful.
  ■ **sulkily** adverb.

sullen adjective silent and bad-tempered.

  ■ **sullenly** adverb.

sully verb (**sullies, sullying, sullied**) literary spoil the purity or cleanness of something.

sulphate (US spelling **sulfate**) noun a salt or ester of sulphuric acid.

sulphide (US spelling **sulfide**) noun a compound of sulphur with another substance.

sulphur (US spelling **sulfur**) noun a chemical element in the form of yellow crystals, which easily catches fire.
  □ **sulphur dioxide** a poisonous gas formed by burning sulphur.

sulphuric (US spelling **sulfuric**) adjective containing sulphur.
  □ **sulphuric acid** a strong corrosive acid.

sulphurous (US spelling **sulfurous**) adjective containing or obtained from sulphur.

sultan noun a Muslim king or ruler.

sultana noun **1** Brit. a light brown seedless raisin. **2** the wife of a sultan.

sultry adjective **1** (of the weather) hot and humid. **2** suggesting sexual passion.

sum noun **1** a particular amount of money. **2** (also **sum total**) the total amount resulting from the addition of two or more numbers or amounts. **3** a calculation in arithmetic. • **verb** (**sums, summing, summed**) (**sum someone/thing up**) **1** describe the nature or character of someone or something concisely. **2** summarize something briefly.

summarize or **summarise** verb (**summarizes, summarizing, summarized**) give a summary of.

summary noun (plural **summaries**) a brief

indelicate, improper, unseemly, sexual, sexy, smutty, dirty.

suit noun **1** *a pinstriped suit:* outfit, ensemble. **2** *a medical malpractice suit:* legal action, lawsuit, (court) case, action, (legal/judicial) proceedings, litigation.
  • **verb 1** *blue really suits you:* look attractive on, look good on, become, flatter. **2** *savings schemes to suit all pockets:* be convenient for, be acceptable to, be suitable for, meet the requirements of; informal fit. **3** *recipes suited to students:* be appropriate, tailor, fashion, adjust, adapt, modify, fit, gear, design.

suitable adjective **1** *suitable employment:* acceptable, satisfactory, fitting; informal right up someone's street. **2** *a drama suitable for all ages:* appropriate, fitting, fit, acceptable, right. **3** *music suitable for a dinner party:* appropriate, suited, befitting, in keeping with. **4** *they treated him with suitable respect:* proper, seemly, decent, appropriate, fitting, correct, due.

OPPOSITES inappropriate.

suite noun apartment, flat, rooms.

sum noun **1** *a large sum of money:* amount, quantity, price, charge, fee, cost. **2** *the sum of two numbers:* total, sum total, grand total, tally. **3** *the sum of his wisdom:* entirety, totality, total, whole, beginning and end. **4** *we did sums at school:* calculation, problem; (**sums**) arithmetic, mathematics; Brit. informal maths; N. Amer. informal math.
  □ **sum someone/something up 1** *that just about sums him up:* evaluate, describe, encapsulate, summarize, put in a nutshell. **2** *he summed up his reasons:* summarize, make/give a summary of, precis, outline, recapitulate, review; informal recap.

summarize verb sum up, abridge, condense, outline, put in a nutshell, precis.

summary noun *a summary of the findings:* synopsis, precis, résumé, abstract, outline, rundown, summing-up, overview.

S

statement of the main points of something. •adjective 1 not including many details; brief. 2 (of a legal process or judgement) done or made immediately and without following the normal procedures.
■ summarily adverb.

summation noun 1 the process of adding things together. 2 the action of summing up. 3 a summary.

summer noun the season after spring and before autumn.
□ summer house a small building in a garden, used for relaxing in during hot weather.
■ summery adjective.

summit noun 1 the highest point of a hill or mountain. 2 the highest possible level of achievement. 3 a meeting between heads of government.

summon verb 1 order someone to be present. 2 urgently ask for help. 3 call people to attend a meeting. 4 make an effort to produce a quality or reaction from within yourself.

summons noun (plural **summonses**) 1 an order to appear in a law court. 2 an act of summoning.

sumo /soo-moh/ noun a Japanese form of wrestling.

sump noun the base of an internal-combustion engine, in which a reserve of oil is stored.

sumptuous adjective splendid and expensive-looking.
■ sumptuously adverb.

sun noun 1 (also **Sun**) the star round which the earth orbits. 2 any similar star. 3 the light or warmth received from the sun.
•verb (**suns, sunning, sunned**) (**sun yourself**) sit or lie outside in the heat of the sun.

sunbathe verb (**sunbathes, sunbathing, sunbathed**) sit or lie outside in the sun to get a suntan.

sunbeam noun a ray of sunlight.

sunbed noun Brit. 1 a long chair that you lie on when sunbathing. 2 a bed between two banks of sunlamps, which you lie on to get an artificial suntan.

sunblock noun a cream or lotion used on the skin for complete protection from sunburn.

sunburn noun inflammation of the skin caused by too much exposure to the ultraviolet rays of the sun.
■ sunburned (or **sunburnt**) adjective.

sundae noun a dish of ice cream with added fruit and syrup.

☑ -ae, not -ay: sundae.

Sunday noun the day of the week before Monday and following Saturday, observed by Christians as a day of worship.
□ Sunday school a class held on Sundays to teach children about Christianity or Judaism.

sunder verb (**sunders, sundering, sundered**) literary split apart.

sundial noun an instrument showing the time by the shadow cast by a pointer.

sundry adjective of various kinds. •noun (**sundries**) various items not important enough to be mentioned individually.

sunflower noun a tall plant with very large yellow flowers.

sung past participle of SING.

sunglasses plural noun glasses tinted to protect the eyes from sunlight.

sunk past participle of SINK.

sunken adjective 1 having sunk. 2 at a lower level than the surrounding area.

sunlamp noun a lamp giving off ultraviolet rays, under which you lie to get an artificial suntan.

sunlight noun light from the sun.
■ sunlit adjective.

Sunni noun (plural **Sunni** or **Sunnis**) 1 one of the two main branches of Islam. The other is SHIA. 2 a Muslim who follows the Sunni branch of Islam.

sunny adjective (**sunnier, sunniest**) 1 bright with or receiving a lot of sunlight. 2 cheerful.

sunrise noun 1 the time when the sun rises.

THESAURUS

summit noun 1 the summit of Mont Blanc: (mountain) top, peak, crest, crown, apex, tip, cap, hilltop. 2 the next superpower summit: meeting, conference, talk(s).
OPPOSITES base.

summon verb 1 he was summoned to the Embassy: send for, call for, request the presence of, ask, invite. 2 they were summoned as witnesses: summons, subpoena. 3 he summoned the courage to move closer: muster, gather, collect, rally, screw up.

sumptuous adjective lavish, luxurious, opulent, magnificent, resplendent, gorgeous, splendid; informal plush; Brit. informal swish.
OPPOSITES plain.

sunny adjective 1 a sunny day: bright, sunlit, clear, fine, cloudless. 2 a sunny disposition: cheerful, cheery, happy, bright, merry, joyful, bubbly, jolly.
OPPOSITES dull, miserable.

sunrise noun dawn, crack of dawn, daybreak, break of day, first light, early

2 the colours and light visible in the sky at sunrise.

sunroof noun a panel in the roof of a car that can be opened to let air in.

sunscreen noun a cream or lotion rubbed on to the skin to protect it from the sun.

sunset noun **1** the time when the sun sets. **2** the colours and light visible in the sky at sunset.

sunshade noun a light umbrella or awning giving protection from the sun.

sunshine noun sunlight unbroken by cloud.

sunspot noun a temporary darker and cooler patch on the sun's surface.

sunstroke noun heatstroke brought about by staying in the sun for too long.

suntan noun a golden-brown colouring of the skin caused by spending time in the sun.
■ **suntanned** adjective.

sup¹ verb (**sups, supping, supped**) dated or N. English take drink or liquid food by sips or spoonfuls. •noun a sip.

sup² verb (**sups, supping, supped**) old use eat supper.

super adjective informal excellent.

superannuate verb (**superannuates, superannuating, superannuated**) **1** arrange for someone to retire with a pension. **2** (**superannuated**) humorous too old to be effective or useful.

superannuation noun regular payment made by an employee into a fund from which a future pension will be paid.

superb adjective **1** very good; excellent. **2** magnificent or splendid.
■ **superbly** adverb.

supercharger noun a device that makes an engine more efficient by forcing extra air or fuel into it.
■ **supercharged** adjective.

supercilious adjective having a manner that shows you think you are better than other people.

superficial adjective **1** existing or happening at or on the surface. **2** apparent rather than real. **3** not thorough. **4** lacking the ability to think deeply about things.
■ **superficiality** noun **superficially** adverb.

superfluous/soo-per-floo-uhss/ adjective more than what is needed.
■ **superfluity** noun.

superglue noun a very strong quick-setting glue.

supergrass noun Brit. informal a person who secretly gives the police information about the criminal activities of a large number of people.

superhuman adjective having exceptional ability or powers.

superimpose verb (**superimposes, superimposing, superimposed**) lay one thing over another.
■ **superimposition** noun.

superintend verb manage or oversee.

superintendent noun **1** a person who supervises and controls a group or activity. **2** a senior police officer.

superior adjective **1** higher in status, quality, or power. **2** of high quality. **3** arrogant and conceited. •noun a person of higher rank or status.

THESAURUS

morning; N. Amer. sunup.

sunset noun nightfall, twilight, dusk, evening; N. Amer. sundown.

superb adjective **1** *a superb goal:* excellent, first-class, outstanding, marvellous, wonderful, splendid, admirable, fine, exceptional, glorious; informal great, fantastic, fabulous, terrific, super, awesome, ace; Brit. informal brilliant, smashing. **2** *a superb house:* magnificent, splendid, grand, impressive, imposing, awe-inspiring, breathtaking, gorgeous, beautiful.
OPPOSITES poor, unimpressive.

superficial adjective **1** *superficial burns:* surface, exterior, external, outer, slight. **2** *a superficial investigation:* cursory, perfunctory, casual, sketchy, desultory, token, slapdash, offhand, rushed, hasty, hurried. **3** *a superficial resemblance:* apparent, seeming, outward, ostensible, cosmetic, slight. **4** *a superficial person:* facile, shallow, flippant, empty-headed,

trivial, frivolous, silly, inane.
OPPOSITES deep, thorough, strong, intelligent.

superfluous adjective surplus (to requirements), redundant, unneeded, unnecessary, excess, extra, (to) spare, remaining, unused, left over, waste.
OPPOSITES necessary.

superior adjective **1** *a superior officer:* senior, higher-level, higher-ranking, higher. **2** *the superior candidate:* better, worthier, finer, preferred. **3** *superior chocolate:* top-quality, choice, select, exclusive, prime, fine, excellent, best, choicest, finest. **4** *a superior smile:* condescending, supercilious, patronizing, haughty, disdainful; informal high and mighty.
OPPOSITES junior, inferior, modest.
•noun *my immediate superior:* manager, chief, supervisor, senior, controller, foreman; informal boss.
OPPOSITES subordinate.

superiority noun the state of being superior.

superlative adjective 1 of the highest quality or degree. 2 (of an adjective or adverb) expressing the highest degree of a quality (e.g. *bravest*). • noun an exaggerated expression of praise.

superman noun (plural **supermen**) informal a man who is unusually strong or intelligent.

supermarket noun a large self-service shop selling foods and household goods.

supermodel noun a very successful and famous fashion model.

supernatural adjective not able to be explained by the laws of nature. • noun (**the supernatural**) supernatural events.
∎ **supernaturally** adverb.

supernova noun (plural **supernovae** /soo-per-**noh**-vee/ or **supernovas**) a star that undergoes an explosion, becoming suddenly very much brighter.

supernumerary adjective 1 present in more than the required number. 2 not belonging to a regular staff but employed for extra work.

superpower noun a very powerful and influential country.

superscript adjective (of a letter, figure, or symbol) printed above the line.

supersede verb (**supersedes**, **superseding**, **superseded**) take the place of.

| ☑ -*sede*, not -*cede*: super*sede*.

supersonic adjective involving or flying at a speed greater than that of sound.

superstar noun a very famous and successful performer or sports player.

superstition noun a belief in the supernatural, especially that particular things bring good or bad luck.

superstitious adjective believing in the supernatural and in the power of particular things to bring good or bad luck.
∎ **superstitiously** adverb.

superstore noun a very large out-of-town supermarket.

superstructure noun 1 a structure built on top of something else. 2 the part of a structure that is built above a supporting base or foundation.

supertanker noun a very large oil tanker.

supervene verb happen so as to interrupt or change an existing situation.

supervise verb be in charge of the carrying out of a task or the work done by a person, ensuring that everything is done correctly.
∎ **supervision** noun **supervisor** noun **supervisory** adjective.

supine adjective 1 lying face upwards. 2 failing to act as a result of laziness or weakness.

supper noun a light or informal evening meal.

supplant verb take the place of.

supple adjective (**suppler**, **supplest**) able to bend and move parts of your body easily; flexible.

supplement noun 1 a thing added to something else to improve or complete it. 2 a separate section added to a newspaper or magazine. 3 an additional charge payable for an extra service or facility. • verb add an extra thing or amount to.
∎ **supplemental** adjective.

supplementary adjective completing or improving something.

suppliant /**sup**-pli-uhnt/ noun a person who makes a humble request. • adjective making a humble request.

supplicate verb (**supplicates**, **supplicating**, **supplicated**) humbly ask for something.
∎ **supplicant** noun **supplication** noun.

supply verb (**supplies**, **supplying**, **supplied**)

THESAURUS

superiority noun supremacy, advantage, lead, dominance, primacy, ascendancy, eminence.

supernatural adjective 1 *supernatural powers:* paranormal, psychic, magic, magical, occult, mystic, mystical. 2 *a supernatural being:* ghostly, phantom, spectral, other-worldly, unearthly.

supersede verb replace, take the place of, take over from, succeed, supplant.

supervise verb oversee, be in charge of, superintend, preside over, direct, manage, run, look after, be responsible for, govern, keep an eye on, observe, monitor, mind.

supervisor noun manager, director, overseer, controller, superintendent, governor, chief, head, foreman; informal boss; Brit. informal gaffer.

supple adjective 1 *her supple body:* lithe, lissom, willowy, flexible, agile, acrobatic, nimble. 2 *supple leather:* pliable, flexible, soft, bendy, workable, stretchy, springy. OPPOSITES stiff, rigid.

supplement noun 1 *a dietary supplement:* extra, add-on, accessory, adjunct. 2 *a single room supplement:* surcharge, addition, increase. 3 *a supplement to the essay:* appendix, addendum, postscript, addition, coda. 4 *a special supplement with today's paper:* pull-out, insert.
• verb *he supplemented his income by teaching:* add to, augment, increase, boost, swell, amplify, enlarge, top up.

supply verb 1 *they supplied money to the rebels:* give, contribute, provide, furnish, donate, confer, dispense. 2 *the lake*

S

provide someone with something that is needed or wanted. •**noun** (plural **supplies**) **1** a stock or amount of something supplied or available. **2** the action of supplying. **3** (**supplies**) provisions and equipment necessary for a large group of people or for an expedition.
■ **supplier** noun.

support verb **1** carry all or part of the weight of. **2** give help, encouragement, or approval to. **3** confirm or back up. **4** provide someone with a home and the things they need in order to live. **5** like a particular sports team and watch or go to their matches. •**noun 1** encouragement, help, or approval. **2** a person or thing that supports. **3** the action of supporting.
■ **supporter** noun.

supportive adjective providing encouragement or emotional help.

suppose verb (**supposes, supposing, supposed**) **1** think that something is true or likely, but lack proof. **2** consider something as a possibility. **3** (**be supposed to do**) be required or expected to do.

supposedly adverb according to what is generally believed.

supposition noun a belief that something is likely to be true.

suppository noun (plural **suppositories**) a solid medical preparation designed to dissolve after being inserted into the rectum or vagina.

suppress verb **1** forcibly put an end to. **2** prevent from acting or developing. **3** stop something from being stated or published.
■ **suppressant** noun **suppression** noun.

☑ two *ps*: sup*press*.

suppurate verb (**suppurates, suppurating, suppurated**) form pus.
■ **suppuration** noun.

supremacist noun a person who believes that a particular group is superior to all others.

supremacy noun the state of being superior to all others.

THESAURUS

supplies the city with water: provide, furnish, serve, endow, equip, arm. **3** windmills supply their power needs: satisfy, meet, fulfil, cater for.
•**noun 1** a limited supply of food: stock, store, reserve, reservoir, stockpile, hoard, cache, fund, bank. **2** the supply of alcoholic liquor: provision, distribution, serving. **3** (**supplies**) provisions, stores, rations, food, necessities.

support verb **1** a roof supported by pillars: hold up, bear, carry, prop up, keep up, brace, shore up, underpin, buttress, reinforce. **2** he struggled to support his family: provide for, maintain, sustain, keep, take care of, look after. **3** she supported him to the end: stand by, defend, back, stand/stick up for. **4** there is evidence to support the argument: back up, substantiate, bear out, corroborate, confirm. **5** the money supports charitable projects: help, aid, assist, contribute to, back, subsidize, fund, finance; N. Amer. informal bankroll. **6** a candidate supported by local people: back, champion, favour, be in favour of, advocate, encourage, promote, endorse, espouse.
OPPOSITES neglect, contradict, oppose.
•**noun 1** bridge supports: pillar, post, prop, upright, brace, buttress, foundation. **2** I was lucky to have their support: encouragement, friendship, backing, endorsement, help, assistance, comfort. **3** thank you for your support: contributions, backing, donations, money, subsidy, funding, funds, finance, capital.
OPPOSITES opposition.

supporter noun **1** supporters of gun control: advocate, backer, adherent, promoter, champion, defender, upholder, campaigner. **2** the charity relies on its supporters: contributor, donor, benefactor, sponsor, backer, patron, subscriber, well-wisher. **3** the team's supporters: fan, follower, enthusiast, devotee, admirer.

supportive adjective encouraging, caring, sympathetic, reassuring, understanding, concerned, helpful.

suppose verb **1** I suppose he's used to it: assume, presume, expect, dare say, take it, guess. **2** suppose you had a spacecraft: imagine, assume, (let's) say, hypothesize, theorize, speculate.

supposed adjective **1** the supposed phenomena: alleged, reputed, rumoured, claimed, purported. **2** I'm supposed to meet him at 8.30: meant, intended, expected, required, obliged.

suppress verb **1** they will suppress any criticism: subdue, repress, crush, quell, quash, squash, stamp out, put down, crack down on. **2** she suppressed her irritation: conceal, restrain, stifle, smother, check, curb, contain. **3** the report was suppressed: censor, keep secret, conceal, hide, hush up, gag, withhold, cover up, stifle.
OPPOSITES allow, encourage, reveal.

supremacy noun control, power, rule, sovereignty, dominance, superiority, predominance, primacy, dominion, authority, mastery, ascendancy.

S

supreme adjective **1** highest in authority or rank. **2** very great or greatest; most important.
□ **supreme court** the highest law court in a country or state.
■ **supremely** adverb.

supremo noun (plural **supremos**) Brit. informal a person in overall charge.

surcharge noun an extra charge or payment.

surd noun Maths a number which cannot be expressed as a ratio of two whole numbers.

sure adjective **1** completely confident that you are right. **2** (**sure of** or **to do**) certain to receive, get, or do. **3** undoubtedly true. **4** steady and confident. • adverb informal certainly.
■ **sureness** noun.

surely adverb **1** it must be true that. **2** certainly.

surety noun (plural **sureties**) **1** a person who guarantees that somebody else will do something or pay a debt. **2** money given as a guarantee that someone will do something.

surf noun the breaking of large waves on a seashore or reef. • verb **1** stand or lie on a surfboard and ride on the crest of a wave towards the shore. **2** move from site to site on the Internet.
■ **surfer** noun **surfing** noun.

surface noun **1** the outside or top layer of something. **2** outward appearance. • verb (**surfaces**, **surfacing**, **surfaced**) **1** rise to the surface. **2** become apparent. **3** provide a road, floor, etc. with a top layer.

surfboard noun a long, narrow board used in surfing.

surfeit noun an amount that is more than is needed or wanted.

surge noun **1** a sudden powerful movement forwards or upwards. **2** a sudden increase. **3** a powerful rush of an emotion or feeling. • verb (**surges**, **surging**, **surged**) **1** move in a surge. **2** increase suddenly and powerfully.

surgeon noun a doctor who is qualified to practise surgery.

surgery noun (plural **surgeries**) **1** medical treatment that involves cutting open the body and repairing or removing parts. **2** Brit. a place where a doctor or nurse sees patients.

surgical adjective relating to or used in surgery.
□ **surgical spirit** Brit. methylated spirit used for cleaning the skin before injections or surgery.
■ **surgically** adverb.

surly adjective (**surlier**, **surliest**) bad-tempered and unfriendly.

surmise verb (**surmises**, **surmising**, **surmised**) suppose something without having evidence. • noun a guess.

surmount verb **1** overcome a difficulty or obstacle. **2** stand or be placed on top of.

surname noun an inherited name used by all the members of a family.

surpass verb be greater or better than.

surplice noun a white robe worn over a cassock by Christian ministers and people singing in church choirs.

THESAURUS

supreme adjective **1** *the supreme commander:* highest, chief, head, top, foremost, principal, superior, premier, first, prime. **2** *a supreme achievement:* extraordinary, remarkable, phenomenal, exceptional, outstanding, incomparable, unparalleled. **3** *the supreme sacrifice:* ultimate, greatest, highest, extreme, final, last.
OPPOSITES subordinate, insignificant.

sure adjective **1** *I'm sure they knew:* certain, positive, convinced, confident, definite, satisfied, persuaded. **2** *someone was sure to find out:* bound, likely, destined, fated. **3** *a sure winner:* guaranteed, unfailing, infallible, unerring, certain, inevitable; informal sure-fire. **4** *a sure sign that he's worried:* reliable, dependable, trustworthy, certain, unambiguous.
OPPOSITES uncertain, unlikely.

surface noun **1** *the surface of the wall:* outside, exterior, top, side, finish. **2** *the surface of polite society:* outward appearance, facade, veneer.

OPPOSITES inside, interior.
• verb **1** *a submarine surfaced:* come to the surface, come up, rise. **2** *the idea first surfaced in the sixties:* emerge, arise, appear, come to light, crop up, materialize, spring up.
OPPOSITES dive.

surge noun **1** *a surge of water:* gush, rush, outpouring, stream, flow. **2** *a surge in demand:* increase, rise, growth, upswing, upsurge, escalation, leap. **3** *a sudden surge of anger:* rush, storm, torrent, blaze, outburst, eruption.
• verb **1** *the water surged into people's homes:* gush, rush, stream, flow, burst, pour, cascade, spill, sweep, roll. **2** *the Dow Jones index surged 47.63 points:* increase, rise, grow, leap.

surpass verb excel, exceed, transcend, outdo, outshine, outstrip, outclass, eclipse, improve on, top, trump, cap, beat, better, outperform.

surplus noun an amount left over. •adjective more than what is needed or used.

surprise noun **1** a feeling of mild astonishment or shock caused by something unexpected. **2** an unexpected or astonishing thing. •verb (**surprises, surprising, surprised**) **1** make someone feel surprise. **2** attack or discover suddenly and unexpectedly.

> ☑ don't forget the first *r*, and note also that **surprise** can't be spelled with an *-ize* ending: surprise.

surreal adjective strange and having the qualities of a dream.
■ **surreally** adverb.

surrealism noun an artistic movement which combined normally unrelated images in a bizarre way.
■ **surrealist** noun & adjective.

surrender verb (**surrenders, surrendering, surrendered**) **1** give in to an opponent. **2** give up a right or possession. **3** (**surrender yourself to**) abandon yourself to a powerful emotion or influence. •noun an act of surrendering.

surreptitious adjective done secretly.
■ **surreptitiously** adverb.

surrogate noun a person who stands in for someone else.
❑ **surrogate mother** a woman who gives birth to a child on behalf of another woman.
■ **surrogacy** noun.

surround verb **1** be all round someone or something. **2** be associated with. •noun **1** a border or edging. **2** (**surrounds** or **surroundings**) the conditions or area around a person or thing.

surtax noun an extra tax on something already taxed.

surtitle noun a caption projected on a screen above the stage in an opera, translating the words that are being sung.

surveillance /ser-**vay**-luhnss/ noun close observation, especially of a suspected spy or criminal.

survey verb (**surveys, surveying, surveyed**) **1** look carefully and thoroughly at. **2** examine and record the features of an area of land in order to produce a map or description. **3** Brit. examine and report on the condition of a building. **4** question a group of people to find out their opinions. •noun **1** an investigation into the opinions or experience of a group of people, based on a series of questions. **2** a general view,

THESAURUS

surplus noun *food surpluses:* excess, surfeit, superfluity, oversupply, glut, remainder, residue, remains, leftovers.
OPPOSITES dearth.
•adjective *surplus cash:* excess, leftover, unused, remaining, extra, additional, spare, superfluous, redundant, unwanted, unneeded, dispensable.
OPPOSITES insufficient.

surprise noun **1** *Kate looked at me in surprise:* astonishment, amazement, wonder, bewilderment, disbelief. **2** *the test came as a big surprise:* shock, bolt from the blue, bombshell, revelation, eye-opener, rude awakening.
•verb **1** *I was so surprised that I dropped it:* astonish, amaze, startle, astound, stun, stagger, shock; informal bowl over, floor, flabbergast; Brit. informal knock for six. **2** *she surprised a burglar:* take by surprise, catch unawares, catch off guard, catch red-handed.

surprising adjective unexpected, unforeseen, astonishing, amazing, startling, astounding, staggering, incredible, extraordinary.

surrender verb **1** *the gunmen surrendered:* give up, give yourself up, give in, cave in, capitulate, concede (defeat), submit, lay down your arms/weapons. **2** *they surrendered power to the government:* give up, relinquish, renounce, cede, abdicate,

forfeit, sacrifice, hand over, turn over, yield.
OPPOSITES resist, seize.
•noun **1** *the surrender of the hijackers:* capitulation, submission, yielding. **2** *a surrender of power:* relinquishment, renunciation, abdication, resignation.

surround verb encircle, enclose, encompass, ring, hem in, confine, cut off, besiege, trap.

surrounding adjective neighbouring, enclosing, nearby, near, local, adjoining, adjacent.

surroundings plural noun environment, setting, background, backdrop, vicinity, locality, habitat.

survey verb **1** *he surveyed his work:* look at, look over, view, contemplate, regard, gaze at, stare at, eye, scrutinize, examine, inspect, scan, study; informal size up. **2** *they surveyed 4,000 drug users:* interview, question, canvass, poll, investigate, research, study. **3** *he was asked to survey the house:* inspect, assess, appraise, prospect.
•noun **1** *a survey of the current literature:* study, review, overview, examination. **2** *a survey of sexual behaviour:* poll, investigation, enquiry, study, probe, questionnaire, census, research. **3** *a thorough survey of the property:* inspection, assessment, appraisal.

S

examination, or description. **3** an act of surveying. **4** a map or report obtained by surveying.
■ surveyor noun.

survival noun **1** the state or fact of surviving. **2** an object or practice that has survived from an earlier time.

survive verb (**survives, surviving, survived**) **1** continue to live or exist. **2** remain alive after an accident or ordeal. **3** remain alive after someone has died.
■ survivor noun.

susceptibility noun (plural **susceptibilities**) the quality of being easily influenced or hurt.

susceptible adjective **1** (**susceptible to**) likely to be influenced or harmed by. **2** easily influenced by feelings or emotions.

sushi /soo-shi/ noun a Japanese dish consisting of balls of cold rice with raw seafood, vegetables, etc.

suspect verb **1** believe something to be likely or possible. **2** believe that someone is guilty of a crime or offence, without having definite proof. **3** feel that something may not be genuine or true.
• noun a person suspected of a crime or offence. • adjective possibly dangerous or false.

suspend verb **1** temporarily bring a stop to something. **2** temporarily stop someone from doing their job or attending school, as a punishment or during an investigation. **3** postpone or delay an

action, event, or judgement. **4** (**suspended**) (of a sentence given by a court) not enforced as long as no further offence is committed. **5** hang something in the air.

suspender noun **1** Brit. an elastic strap attached to a belt and fastened to the top of a stocking to hold it up. **2** (**suspenders**) N. Amer. braces for holding up trousers.

suspense noun a state or feeling of excited or anxious uncertainty about what may happen.

suspension noun **1** the action of suspending something or the state of being suspended. **2** a system of springs and shock absorbers which supports a vehicle on its wheels and makes it more comfortable to ride in. **3** a mixture in which particles are spread throughout a fluid.
□ suspension bridge a bridge which is suspended from cables running between towers.

suspicion noun **1** an idea that something is possible or likely or that someone has done something wrong. **2** a feeling of distrust. **3** a very slight trace.

suspicious adjective **1** having a feeling that someone has done something wrong. **2** making you feel that something is wrong. **3** not able to trust other people.
■ suspiciously adverb.

suss verb (**susses, sussing, sussed**) (often **suss someone/thing out**) Brit. informal realize or understand the true character or nature of.

sustain verb **1** strengthen or support

THESAURUS

survive verb **1** *he survived by escaping through a hole:* remain alive, live, sustain yourself, pull through, hold out, make it. **2** *the theatre must survive:* continue, remain, persist, endure, live on, persevere, abide, go on, carry on. **3** *he was survived by his sons:* outlive, outlast.

suspect verb **1** *I suspected she'd made a mistake:* have a suspicion, have a feeling, feel, be inclined to think, fancy, reckon, guess, surmise, have a hunch, fear. **2** *he had no reason to suspect me:* doubt, distrust, mistrust, have misgivings about, have qualms about, be suspicious of.
• adjective *a suspect package:* suspicious, dubious, doubtful, untrustworthy; informal fishy, funny; Brit. informal dodgy.

suspend verb **1** *the court case was suspended:* adjourn, interrupt, break off, cut short, discontinue; N. Amer. table. **2** *he was suspended from college:* exclude, debar, remove, expel, eject, rusticate. **3** *lights were suspended from the ceiling:* hang, sling, string, swing, dangle.

suspense noun tension, uncertainty, doubt, anticipation, excitement, anxiety, strain.

suspicion noun **1** *she had a suspicion that he didn't like her:* intuition, feeling, impression, inkling, hunch, fancy, notion, idea, theory, premonition; informal gut feeling. **2** *I confronted him with my suspicions:* misgiving, doubt, qualm, reservation, hesitation, question.
OPPOSITES trust.

suspicious adjective **1** *she gave him a suspicious look:* doubtful, unsure, dubious, wary, sceptical, mistrustful. **2** *a suspicious character:* suspect, dubious, unsavoury, disreputable; informal shifty, shady; Brit. informal dodgy. **3** *in suspicious circumstances:* strange, odd, questionable, irregular, funny, doubtful, mysterious, murky; informal fishy; Brit. informal dodgy.
OPPOSITES trusting, honest, innocent.

sustain verb **1** *her memories sustained her:* comfort, help, assist, encourage, support, give strength to, buoy up. **2** *they were unable to sustain a coalition:* continue, carry on, keep up, keep alive, maintain, preserve. **3** *she had bread and cheese to sustain her:* nourish, feed, nurture, keep alive, keep going. **4** *she sustained slight* someone physically or mentally. **2** keep something going over time or continuously. **3** experience something unpleasant. **4** carry the weight of an object.

sustainable adjective **1** able to be sustained. **2** (of industry, development, or agriculture) avoiding using up natural resources.
■ **sustainability** noun **sustainably** adverb.

sustenance noun **1** the food needed to keep someone alive. **2** the process of keeping something going.

suture noun a stitch holding together the edges of a wound or surgical cut. •**verb** (**sutures, suturing, sutured**) stitch up a wound or cut.

suzerainty /soo-zuh-rayn-ti/ noun the right of one country to rule over another country which has its own ruler but is not fully independent.

svelte adjective slender and elegant.

SW abbreviation south-west or south-western.

swab noun **1** a pad used for cleaning a wound or taking liquid from the body for testing. **2** a sample of liquid taken with a swab. •**verb** (**swabs, swabbing, swabbed**) **1** clean or take liquid from a wound or part of the body with a swab. **2** wash down a surface with water and a cloth or mop.

swaddle verb (**swaddles, swaddling, swaddled**) wrap in clothes or a cloth.
□ **swaddling clothes** (in the past) strips of cloth wrapped round a baby to calm it.

swag noun **1** a curtain hanging in a drooping curve. **2** informal property stolen by a burglar.

swagger verb (**swaggers, swaggering, swaggered**) walk or behave in a very confident or arrogant way. •**noun** a swaggering walk or way of behaving.

swain noun old use **1** a young male lover. **2** a country youth.

swallow¹ verb **1** contract the muscles of the mouth and throat so that food, drink, or saliva pass down the throat. **2** (**swallow someone/thing up**) surround or cover someone or something so that they disappear. **3** believe an untrue statement

without question. •**noun** an act of swallowing.

swallow² noun a fast-flying bird with a forked tail.

swam past of **swim**.

swamp noun an area of boggy or marshy land. •**verb** **1** flood an area with water. **2** overwhelm with too much of something.
■ **swampy** adjective.

swan noun a large white waterbird with a long flexible neck. •**verb** (**swans, swanning, swanned**) Brit. informal go around enjoying yourself in a way that makes other people jealous or annoyed.

swank informal verb show off your achievements, knowledge, or wealth. •**noun** the act of showing off.

swanky adjective (**swankier, swankiest**) informal stylishly luxurious and expensive.

swansong noun the final performance or activity of a person's career.

swap or **swop** verb (**swaps, swapping, swapped**) exchange or substitute something for something else. •**noun** an act of swapping.

sward noun literary an area of grass.

swarm noun **1** a large group of insects flying closely together. **2** a large number of honeybees that leave a hive with a queen in order to form a new colony. **3** a large group of people or things. •**verb** **1** move in or form a swarm. **2** (**swarm with**) be crowded or overrun with. **3** (**swarm up**) climb something rapidly by gripping with your hands and feet.

swarthy adjective (**swarthier, swarthiest**) having a dark skin.

swashbuckling adjective having many daring and romantic adventures.
■ **swashbuckler** noun.

swastika /swoss-ti-kuh/ noun an ancient symbol in the form of a cross with its arms bent at a right angle, used in the 20th century as the emblem of the Nazi party.

swat verb (**swats, swatting, swatted**) hit or crush something with a sharp blow from a flat object.

S

THESAURUS

injuries: **suffer**, experience, undergo, receive. **5** the allegation was not sustained: **confirm**, corroborate, substantiate, bear out, prove, authenticate, back up, uphold.

sustained adjective **continuous**, ongoing, steady, continual, constant, prolonged, persistent, non-stop, perpetual, relentless. OPPOSITES sporadic.

swallow verb **eat**, drink, gulp down, consume, devour, put away, quaff, slug; informal swig, swill, down; Brit. informal scoff.

swamp noun he got stuck in the swamp:

marsh, bog, fen, quagmire.
•**verb** **1** the rain was swamping the boat: **flood**, inundate, deluge, fill. **2** he was swamped by media attention: **overwhelm**, inundate, flood, deluge, engulf, snow under.

swap verb **exchange**, trade, barter, switch, change, replace.

swarm noun **1** a swarm of bees: **hive**, flock. **2** a swarm of reporters: **crowd**, horde, mob, throng, mass, army, herd, pack.
•**verb** reporters were swarming all over the

swatch noun a piece of fabric used as a sample.

swathe¹ /swayth/ (US spelling **swath** /swawth/) noun (plural **swathes** or **swaths**) 1 a broad strip or area. 2 a row or line of grass, corn, etc. as it falls when cut down.

swathe² /swayth/ verb (**swathes, swathing, swathed**) wrap in several layers of fabric.

sway verb 1 move slowly and rhythmically backwards and forwards or from side to side. 2 make someone change their opinion. • noun 1 a swaying movement. 2 influence or control over people. □ **hold sway** have power or influence.

swear verb (**swears, swearing, swore**; past participle **sworn**) 1 promise something solemnly or on oath. 2 use offensive or obscene language. □ **swear by** informal have or express great confidence in. **swear someone in** admit someone to a new post by making them take a formal oath. **swear word** an offensive or obscene word.

sweat noun moisture that comes out through the pores of the skin when you are hot, making a physical effort, or anxious. • verb (**sweats, sweating,** past and past participle **sweated** or N. Amer. **sweat**) 1 give off sweat. 2 (**sweat over**) make a lot of effort in doing something. 3 be very anxious. ■ **sweaty** adjective.

sweatband noun a band of absorbent material worn round the head or wrists to soak up sweat.

sweater noun a pullover with long sleeves.

sweatshirt noun a loose, warm cotton sweater.

sweatshop noun a factory or workshop employing workers for long hours in bad conditions.

swede noun 1 (**Swede**) a person from Sweden. 2 Brit. a round yellow root vegetable.

Swedish noun the language of Sweden. • adjective relating to Sweden.

sweep verb (**sweeps, sweeping, swept**) 1 clean an area by brushing away dirt or litter. 2 move quickly or forcefully. 3 (**sweep something away** or **aside**) remove or abolish something quickly and suddenly. 4 search an area. • noun 1 an act of sweeping. 2 a long, swift, curving movement. 3 a long curved stretch of road, river, etc. 4 the range or scope of something. 5 (also **chimney sweep**) a person who cleans out the soot from chimneys. ■ **sweeper** noun.

sweeping adjective 1 extending or performed in a long, continuous curve. 2 wide in range or effect. 3 (of a statement) too general.

sweepstake or **sweepstakes** noun a form of gambling in which the winner receives all the money bet by the other players.

sweet adjective 1 having the pleasant taste

THESAURUS

S

place: flock, crowd, throng, surge, stream.

swathe verb wrap, envelop, bandage, cover, shroud, drape, wind, enfold.

sway verb 1 *the curtains swayed in the breeze:* swing, shake, undulate, move to and fro. 2 *she swayed on her feet:* stagger, wobble, rock, lurch, reel, roll. 3 *we are swayed by the media:* influence, affect, manipulate, bend, mould. • noun 1 *the sway of her hips:* swing, roll, shake, undulation. 2 *a province under the sway of the Franks:* power, rule, government, sovereignty, dominion, control, jurisdiction, authority.

swear verb 1 *they swore to protect each other:* promise, vow, pledge, give your word, undertake, guarantee. 2 *she swore she would never go back:* insist, declare, proclaim, assert, maintain, emphasize, stress. 3 *Kate spilled her wine and swore:* curse, blaspheme, use bad language; informal cuss, eff and blind.

swearing noun bad language, strong language, cursing, blaspheming, obscenities, expletives, swear words; informal effing and blinding, four-letter words.

sweat noun *he was drenched with sweat:* perspiration. • verb 1 *she was sweating heavily:* perspire. 2 *I've sweated over this book:* work, labour, toil, slog, slave, work your fingers to the bone.

sweep verb 1 *she swept the floor:* brush, clean, scrub, mop, scour. 2 *he was swept out to sea:* carry, pull, drag, tow. 3 *riots swept the country:* engulf, overwhelm, flood, spread across. 4 *she swept down the stairs:* glide, sail, breeze, drift, race, speed, stride. • noun 1 *a sweep of his hand:* gesture, stroke, wave, movement. 2 *a long sweep of golden sand:* expanse, tract, stretch, extent. 3 *the broad sweep of our interests:* range, scope, compass, reach, spread, extent.

sweeping adjective 1 *sweeping changes:* extensive, wide-ranging, broad, comprehensive, wholesale, far-reaching, thorough, radical. 2 *sweeping statements:* general, blanket, unqualified, over-simplified, indiscriminate. OPPOSITES limited, focused.

sweet adjective 1 *sweet biscuits:* sugary, sweetened, sugared, honeyed, sickly, characteristic of sugar. **2** having a pleasant smell. **3** pleasing or satisfying. **4** charming and endearing. **5** kind and thoughtful. •noun Brit. **1** a small item of sweet food made with sugar, chocolate, etc. **2** a sweet dish forming a course of a meal. □ sweet-and-sour cooked with both sugar and vinegar. sweet pea a climbing plant of the pea family with colourful, sweet-smelling flowers. sweet pepper a large pepper with a mild or sweet flavour. sweet potato the pinkish-orange tuber of a tropical climbing plant, eaten as a vegetable. sweet-talk informal use charming or flattering words to persuade someone to do something. sweet tooth a great liking for sweet-tasting foods. ■ sweetly adverb sweetness noun.

sweetbread noun an animal's pancreas, eaten as food.

sweetcorn noun a kind of maize with sweet-tasting yellow kernels which are eaten as a vegetable.

sweeten verb **1** make or become sweet or sweeter. **2** make more pleasant or acceptable.

sweetener noun **1** a substance used to sweeten food or drink. **2** informal a bribe.

sweetheart noun a person you are in love with.

sweetmeat noun old use a sweet or other item of sweet food.

swell verb (**swells, swelling, swelled**; past participle **swollen** or **swelled**) **1** become larger or more rounded. **2** increase in strength, amount, or loudness. •noun **1** a slow, regular, rolling movement of the sea. **2** a full or gently rounded form. **3** a gradual increase in strength, amount, or loudness. •adjective N. Amer. informal, dated excellent.

swelling noun a place on the body that has swollen as a result of illness or an injury.

swelter verb (**swelters, sweltering, sweltered**) be uncomfortably hot.

swept past and past participle of **SWEEP**.

swerve verb (**swerves, swerving, swerved**) abruptly go off from a straight course. •noun an abrupt change of course.

swift adjective **1** happening quickly or promptly. **2** moving or able to move very fast. •noun a fast-flying bird with long, slender wings. ■ swiftly adverb swiftness noun.

swig verb (**swigs, swigging, swigged**) drink deeply and quickly. •noun a quick, deep drink.

swill verb Brit. **1** rinse something out with large amounts of water. **2** (of liquid) swirl round in a container or cavity. •noun waste food mixed with water for feeding to pigs.

swim verb (**swims, swimming, swam**; past participle **swum**) **1** move through water using your arms and legs. **2** be covered with liquid. **3** experience a dizzy, confusing feeling. •noun a period of swimming. ■ swimmer noun.

swimmingly adverb informal smoothly and satisfactorily.

swimsuit noun a woman's one-piece garment for swimming.

swindle verb (**swindles, swindling, swindled**) cheat someone in order to get money from them. •noun a dishonest scheme to get money from someone. ■ swindler noun.

swine noun **1** (plural **swine**) a pig. **2** (plural **swine** or **swines**) informal an unpleasant person. ■ swinish adjective.

THESAURUS

cloying. **2** *the sweet scent of roses:* fragrant, aromatic, perfumed. **3** *her sweet voice:* musical, melodious, dulcet, tuneful, soft, harmonious, silvery. **4** *life was still sweet:* pleasant, agreeable, delightful, nice, satisfying, gratifying, good. **5** *she has a sweet nature:* likeable, appealing, engaging, amiable, pleasant, agreeable, kind, thoughtful, considerate, delightful, lovely. **6** *she looks sweet:* cute, lovable, adorable, endearing, charming. OPPOSITES sour, savoury, harsh, disagreeable. •noun (Brit.) **1** *sweets for the children:* confectionery, bonbon; N. Amer. candy; informal sweetie; old use sweetmeat. **2** *a delicious sweet for the guests:* dessert, pudding; Brit. informal afters, pud.

sweetheart noun **1** *you look lovely, sweetheart:* darling, dear, dearest, love, beloved, sweet; informal honey, sweetie, sugar, baby, poppet. **2** *my high-school sweetheart:* lover, love, girlfriend, boyfriend, beloved; informal steady, flame.

swell verb **1** *her lip swelled up:* expand, bulge, distend, inflate, dilate, bloat, puff up, balloon, fatten, fill out. **2** *the population swelled:* grow, enlarge, increase, expand, rise, escalate, multiply, proliferate, snowball, mushroom. OPPOSITES shrink, decrease. •noun *a heavy swell on the sea:* surge, wave, roll.

swelling noun bump, lump, bulge, protuberance, protrusion, distension.

swift adjective **1** *a swift decision:* prompt, rapid, quick, sudden, immediate, instant, abrupt, hasty, hurried. **2** *swift runners:* fast, rapid, quick, speedy, brisk, lively. OPPOSITES slow, leisurely.

S

swing verb (**swings**, **swinging**, **swung**) **1** move backwards and forwards or from side to side while suspended. **2** move by grasping a support and leaping. **3** move in a smooth, curving line. **4** (**swing at**) attempt to hit. **5** change from one opinion, mood, or situation to another. **6** have a decisive influence on a vote or opinion. **7** informal succeed in bringing something about. • noun **1** a seat suspended by ropes or chains, on which you can sit and swing backwards and forwards. **2** an act of swinging. **3** a clear change in public opinion. **4** a style of jazz or dance music with an easy flowing rhythm.

swingeing /swin-jing/ adjective Brit. extreme or severe.

swinging adjective informal lively, exciting, and fashionable.

swipe informal verb (**swipes**, **swiping**, **swiped**) **1** hit or try to hit something with a swinging blow. **2** steal. **3** pass a swipe card through an electronic reader. • noun a swinging blow.
□ **swipe card** a plastic card carrying coded information which is read when the card is slid through an electronic device.

swirl verb move in a twisting or spiralling pattern. • noun a swirling movement or pattern.
■ **swirly** adjective.

swish verb move with a soft rushing sound. • noun a soft rushing sound or movement. • adjective Brit. informal impressively smart.

Swiss adjective relating to Switzerland. • noun (plural **Swiss**) a person from Switzerland.
□ **Swiss roll** Brit. a thin sponge cake spread with jam or cream and rolled up.

switch noun **1** a device for making and breaking an electrical connection. **2** a change or exchange. **3** a flexible shoot cut from a tree. • verb **1** change in position, direction, or focus. **2** exchange one thing for another. **3** (**switch something off** or **on**) turn an electrical device off or on. **4** (**switch off**) informal stop paying attention.

switchback noun Brit. a road that alternately slopes up and down very steeply.

switchblade noun N. Amer. a flick knife.

switchboard noun a device for putting phone calls made to an organization through to the right person.

swivel verb (**swivels**, **swivelling**, **swivelled**; US spelling **swivels**, **swiveling**, **swiveled**) turn around a central point. • noun a connecting device between two parts enabling one to revolve without turning the other.

swizz noun Brit. informal an instance of being mildly cheated or disappointed.

swollen past participle of SWELL.

swoon literary verb faint, especially from strong emotion. • noun an act of fainting.

swoop verb **1** move rapidly downwards through the air. **2** carry out a sudden raid. • noun an act of swooping.

swop ⇒ SWAP.

sword noun a weapon with a long, sharp metal blade.

swordfish noun (plural **swordfish** or **swordfishes**) a large sea fish with a sword-like snout.

swore past of SWEAR.

sworn past participle of SWEAR. • adjective **1** made after having sworn to tell the truth. **2** determined to remain so: *sworn enemies.*

swot Brit. informal verb (**swots**, **swotting**, **swotted**) study hard. • noun a person who spends a lot of time studying.

swum past participle of SWIM.

swung past and past participle of SWING.

sybarite /si-buh-ryt/ noun a person who is very fond of luxury.
■ **sybaritic** adjective.

sycamore noun **1** a tree with five-pointed leaves and seeds shaped like wings.

S

THESAURUS

swing verb **1** *the sign swung in the wind:* sway, move back and forth, oscillate, wave, rock, swivel, pivot, turn, rotate. **2** *Helen swung the bottle:* brandish, wave, flourish, wield. **3** *the road swings round:* curve, bend, veer, turn, bear, wind, twist, deviate, slew. **4** *the needle swings to the right:* rotate, swivel, pivot, turn.
• noun **1** *a swing of the pendulum:* oscillation, sway, wave. **2** *the swing to the Conservatives:* change, move, turnaround, turnabout, reversal. **3** *mood swings:* fluctuation, change, shift, variation, oscillation.

swirl verb whirl, eddy, billow, spiral, twist, twirl, circulate, revolve, spin.

switch noun **1** *the switch on top of the telephone:* button, lever, control. **2** *a switch from direct to indirect taxation:* change, move, shift, transition, transformation, reversal, turnaround, U-turn, changeover, transfer, conversion.
• verb **1** *he switched sides:* change, shift; informal chop and change. **2** *he managed to switch the envelopes:* exchange, swap, interchange, change round, rotate.

swoop verb **1** *pigeons swooped down after the grain:* dive, descend, pounce, plunge, pitch, nosedive. **2** *police swooped on the flat:* raid, descend on, pounce on, attack; N. Amer. informal bust.

2 N. Amer. a plane tree.

sycophant /**si**-kuh-fant/ noun a person who tries to gain favour with someone important by saying flattering things to them.
■ **sycophancy** noun **sycophantic** adjective.

syllable noun a unit of pronunciation having one vowel sound and forming all or part of a word.
■ **syllabic** adjective.

syllabub noun a dessert made of whipped cream flavoured with white wine or sherry.

syllabus noun (plural **syllabuses** or **syllabi** /**sil**-luh-by/) all the things covered in a course of study or teaching.

syllogism /**sil**-luh-ji-z'm/ noun a form of reasoning in which a conclusion is drawn from two propositions.

sylph noun **1** a slender woman or girl. **2** an imaginary spirit of the air.
■ **sylphlike** adjective.

sylvan adjective literary having to do with woods and trees.

symbiosis /sim-by-**oh**-siss/ noun (plural **symbioses** /sim-by-**oh**-seez/) Biology a situation in which two living things are connected with and dependent on each other to the advantage of both.
■ **symbiotic** adjective.

symbol noun **1** an object, person, or event that represents something else. **2** a letter, mark, or character used as a representation of something.

symbolic adjective **1** acting as a symbol. **2** involving the use of symbols or symbolism.
■ **symbolically** adverb.

symbolism noun the use of symbols to represent ideas or qualities.
■ **symbolist** noun & adjective.

symbolize or **symbolise** verb (**symbolizes**, **symbolizing**, **symbolized**) **1** be a symbol of. **2** represent something by means of symbols.

symmetrical adjective exactly the same on each side.

■ **symmetrically** adverb.

symmetry noun (plural **symmetries**) **1** the exact match in size or shape between two halves, parts, or sides of something. **2** the quality of being exactly the same or very similar.

sympathetic adjective **1** feeling or showing sympathy. **2** showing approval of an idea or action. **3** pleasing or likeable.
■ **sympathetically** adverb.

sympathize or **sympathise** verb (**sympathizes**, **sympathizing**, **sympathized**) **1** feel or express sympathy. **2** agree with an opinion.

sympathy noun (plural **sympathies**) **1** the feeling of being sorry for someone. **2** support for or approval of something. **3** understanding between people.
▢ **in sympathy** fitting in; in keeping.

symphonic adjective having the form of a symphony.

symphony noun (plural **symphonies**) a long, elaborate piece of music for a full orchestra.

symposium /sim-**poh**-zi-uhm/ noun (plural **symposia** /sim-**poh**-zi-uh/ or **symposiums**) a conference to discuss a particular academic subject.

symptom noun **1** a change in the body or mind which is the sign of a disease. **2** a sign of an undesirable situation.
■ **symptomatic** adjective.

synagogue /**sin**-uh-gog/ noun a building where Jews meet for worship and teaching.

synapse /**sy**-naps, si-**naps**/ noun a connection between two nerve cells.
■ **synaptic** adjective.

sync or **synch** noun informal synchronization.
▢ **in** (or **out of**) **sync** working well (or badly) together.

synchromesh noun a system of gear changing in which the gearwheels are made to revolve at the same speed during engagement.

synchronize or **synchronise** verb (**synchronizes**, **synchronizing**, **synchronized**)

S

THESAURUS

symbol noun **1** *the lotus is the symbol of purity:* representation, token, sign, emblem, figure, image, metaphor, allegory. **2** *the chemical symbol for helium:* sign, character, mark, letter. **3** *the Red Cross symbol:* logo, emblem, badge, stamp, trademark, crest, insignia, coat of arms, seal, device, monogram, hallmark, motif.

symmetrical adjective regular, uniform, consistent, even, equal, balanced, proportional.

sympathetic adjective **1** *a sympathetic listener:* compassionate, caring, concerned, understanding, sensitive, supportive. **2** *the*

most sympathetic character in the book: likeable, pleasant, agreeable, congenial.
OPPOSITES unsympathetic, unfeeling, unlikeable.

sympathize verb commiserate, show concern, offer condolences; (**sympathize with**) pity, feel sorry for, feel for, identify with, understand, relate to.

sympathy noun compassion, care, concern, commiseration, pity.
OPPOSITES indifference.

symptom noun indication, indicator, manifestation, sign, mark, feature, trait, clue, hint, warning, evidence, proof.

make things happen or operate at the same time or rate.

■ synchronization noun.

synchronous /sing-kruh-nuhss/ adjective existing or happening at the same time.

syncopate verb (syncopates, syncopating, syncopated) alter the beats or accents of music so that strong beats become weak and vice versa.

■ syncopation noun.

syndicate noun /sin-di-kuht/ a group of people or organizations who get together to promote a common interest. • verb /sin-di-kayt/ (syndicates, syndicating, syndicated) 1 control or manage an operation through a syndicate. 2 publish or broadcast something in a number of different ways at the same time.

■ syndication noun.

syndrome noun a set of medical symptoms which tend to occur together.

synergy noun the working together of two or more people or things to produce a combined effect that is greater than the sum of their separate effects.

synod noun an official meeting of Church ministers and members.

synonym /sin-uh-nim/ noun a word or phrase that means the same as another word or phrase in the same language.

synonymous /si-non-i-muhss/ adjective 1 (of a word or phrase) having the same meaning as another word or phrase in the same language. 2 closely associated.

synopsis noun (plural synopses) a brief summary or survey.

syntax noun the way in which words and phrases are put together to form sentences.

■ syntactic adjective syntactical adjective.

synthesis /sin-thuh-siss/ noun (plural syntheses /sin-thuh-seez/) 1 the combination of parts to form a connected whole. 2 the production of chemical compounds from simpler materials.

synthesize or **synthesise** verb (synthesizes, synthesizing, synthesized)

1 combine parts into a connected whole. 2 make something by chemical synthesis. 3 produce sound with a synthesizer.

synthesizer or **synthesiser** noun an electronic musical instrument that produces sounds by generating and combining signals of different frequencies.

synthetic adjective 1 made by chemical synthesis, especially to imitate a natural product. 2 not genuine.

■ synthetically adverb.

syphilis noun a disease caused by bacteria that are passed on during sex.

■ syphilitic adjective.

syphon ⇒ SIPHON.

Syrian noun a person from Syria. • adjective relating to Syria.

syringe noun a tube with a nozzle and a piston that is fitted with a hollow needle for injecting drugs or withdrawing blood.

syrup (US spelling **sirup**) noun 1 a thick sweet liquid made by dissolving sugar in boiling water. 2 a thick sweet liquid containing medicine or diluted to make a drink.

syrupy (US spelling **sirupy**) adjective 1 like syrup. 2 too sentimental.

system noun 1 a set of things that are connected or that work together. 2 an organized scheme or method. 3 (**the system**) the laws and rules that govern society.

systematic adjective done according to a system.

■ systematically adverb.

systematize or **systematise** verb (systematizes, systematizing, systematized) arrange things according to an organized system.

systemic /si-steem-ik/ adjective affecting the whole of a system.

systole /siss-tuh-li/ noun the stage of the heartbeat when the heart muscle contracts and pumps blood into the arteries.

■ systolic /si-stol-lik/ adjective.

THESAURUS

synthetic adjective artificial, fake, faux, imitation, mock, simulated, man-made, manufactured; informal pretend.
OPPOSITES natural.

system noun 1 a system of canals: structure, organization, arrangement, complex, network; informal set-up. 2 a system for regulating sales: method, technique, procedure, means, way, scheme, plan,

policy, programme, formula, routine. 3 (**the system**) the establishment, the administration, the authorities, the powers that be, bureaucracy, officialdom.

systematic adjective structured, methodical, organized, orderly, planned, regular, routine, standardized, standard, logical, coherent, consistent.
OPPOSITES unstructured, disorganized.

S

Tt

T or **t** noun (plural **Ts** or **T's**) the twentieth letter of the alphabet.
□ **to a T** informal to perfection. **T-bone** a large piece of steak containing a T-shaped bone. **T-shirt** a short-sleeved casual top. **T-square** a T-shaped instrument for drawing or testing right angles.

TA abbreviation Territorial Army.

ta exclamation Brit. informal thank you.

tab¹ noun **1** a small flap or strip of material attached to something. **2** informal, chiefly N. Amer. a restaurant bill.
□ **keep tabs on** informal keep a watch on.

tab² = TABULATOR.

tab³ noun informal a tablet containing an illegal drug.

tabard noun a sleeveless jacket consisting only of front and back pieces with a hole for the head.

tabby noun (plural **tabbies**) a grey or brownish cat with dark stripes.

tabernacle noun **1** a place of worship for some religions. **2** (in the Bible) a tent in which the Israelites kept the Ark of the Covenant during the Exodus.

table noun **1** a piece of furniture with a flat top and legs, for eating, writing, or working at. **2** a set of facts or figures arranged in rows and columns. **3** (**tables**) multiplication sums arranged in sets. • verb (**tables, tabling, tabled**) Brit. present something for discussion at a meeting.
□ **table tennis** a game played with small round bats and a small hollow ball which is hit across a table over a net. **turn the tables** reverse a situation.

tableau /**tab**-loh/ noun (plural **tableaux** /**tab**-lohz/) a group of models or motionless figures representing a scene.

tablecloth noun a cloth spread over a table.

table d'hôte /tah-bluh **doht**/ noun a restaurant menu or meal offered at a fixed price and with limited choices.

tableland noun a wide area of high, level ground; a plateau.

tablespoon noun a large spoon for serving food.

tablet noun **1** a pill. **2** a slab of stone or other hard material on which an inscription is written.

tabloid noun a newspaper that has small pages and is written in a popular style.

taboo noun (plural **taboos**) a social custom that prevents people from doing or talking about something. • adjective banned or restricted by social custom.

tabular adjective (of facts or figures) arranged in columns or tables.

tabulate verb (**tabulates, tabulating, tabulated**) arrange facts or figures in columns or tables.
■ **tabulation** noun.

tabulator noun a facility in a word-processing program, or a device on a typewriter, used for moving to fixed positions in a document when creating tables or columns.

tachograph noun an instrument used in commercial road vehicles to provide a record of their speed and the distance travelled.

tachometer /ta-**kom**-i-ter/ noun an instrument which measures the working speed of an engine.

tachycardia /ta-ki-**kar**-di-uh/ noun an abnormally fast heart rate.

tacit /**ta**-sit/ adjective understood or meant without being stated.
■ **tacitly** adverb.

taciturn /**ta**-si-tern/ adjective not saying very much.
■ **taciturnity** noun.

t

THESAURUS

table noun chart, diagram, figure, graphic, graph, plan, list.

taboo noun *the taboo against lying:* prohibition, proscription, veto, ban, interdict.
• adjective *taboo language:* forbidden, prohibited, banned, proscribed, outlawed, off limits, unmentionable, unspeakable, unutterable; informal no go.
OPPOSITES acceptable.

tack[1] noun **1** a small broad-headed nail. **2** N. Amer. a drawing pin. **3** a long stitch used to fasten fabrics together temporarily. **4** a course of action. **5** Sailing a sailing boat's course relative to the direction of the wind. • verb **1** fasten or fix with tacks. **2** (**tack something on**) casually add something to something else. **3** change course by turning a boat's head into and through the wind. **4** make a series of such changes of course while sailing.

tack[2] noun equipment used in horse riding.

tackle verb (**tackles, tackling, tackled**) **1** start to deal with a problem or task. **2** confront someone about a difficult issue. **3** (in soccer, hockey, rugby, etc.) try to take the ball from or prevent the movement of an opponent. • noun **1** the equipment needed for a task or sport. **2** a mechanism consisting of ropes, pulley blocks, and hooks for lifting heavy objects. **3** (in sport) an act of tackling an opponent. ■ tackler noun.

tacky adjective (**tackier, tackiest**) **1** (of glue, paint, etc.) not fully dry. **2** informal showing bad taste and quality.

taco noun (plural **tacos**) (in Mexican cookery) a folded tortilla filled with spicy meat or beans.

tact noun sensitivity and skill in dealing with other people.

tactful adjective having or showing tact. ■ tactfully adverb.

tactic noun **1** the method you use to achieve something. **2** (**tactics**) the art of organizing and directing the movement of soldiers and equipment during a war. ■ tactician noun.

tactical adjective **1** planned in order to achieve a particular end. **2** (of weapons) for use in direct support of military or naval operations. **3** (of voting) done to prevent the strongest candidate from winning, rather than indicating your true political choice. ■ tactically adverb.

tactile adjective **1** having to do with the sense of touch. **2** liking to touch other people in a friendly way.

tactless adjective thoughtless and insensitive. ■ tactlessly adverb.

tad adverb (**a tad**) informal to a small extent.

tadpole noun the larva of a frog or toad, which lives in water and has gills, a large head, and a tail.

taffeta noun a crisp shiny fabric.

tag noun **1** a label giving information about something. **2** an electronic device attached to someone to monitor their movements. **3** a nickname or commonly used description. **4** a nickname or identifying mark written as the signature of a graffiti artist. **5** a frequently repeated phrase. **6** a metal or plastic point at the end of a shoelace. **7** a chasing game played by children. • verb (**tags, tagging, tagged**) **1** attach a tag to. **2** (**tag something on**) add something to the end of something else as an afterthought. **3** (**tag along**) accompany someone without being invited.

tagliatelle /tal-yuh-**tel**-li/ plural noun pasta in narrow ribbons.

Tahitian /tah-**hee**-shuhn/ noun a person from Tahiti. • adjective relating to Tahiti.

tail noun **1** the part at the rear of an animal that sticks out and can be moved. **2** the rear part of an aircraft, with the tailplane and rudder. **3** the final, more distant, or

THESAURUS

tack noun *tacks held the carpet down:* pin, nail, staple, rivet.
• verb *a photo tacked to the wall:* pin, nail, staple, fix, fasten, attach, secure.
□ tack something on **add**, append, attach, join on, tag on.

tackle noun **1** *fishing tackle:* equipment, gear, apparatus, kit, hardware; informal things, clobber. **2** *a tackle by the scrum half:* interception, challenge, block, attack.
• verb **1** *we must tackle the problems:* deal with, take care of, attend to, see to, handle, manage, get to grips with, address, take on. **2** *he tackled an intruder:* confront, face up to, take on, challenge, attack, grab, struggle with, intercept, block, stop, bring down, floor, fell; informal have a go at.

tactful adjective diplomatic, discreet, considerate, sensitive, understanding, thoughtful, delicate, judicious, subtle.

tactic noun **1** *a tax-saving tactic:* scheme, plan, manoeuvre, method, trick, ploy. **2** (**tactics**) strategy, policy, campaign, game plan, planning, generalship, manoeuvres, logistics.

tactical adjective calculated, planned, strategic, prudent, politic, diplomatic, judicious, shrewd.

tactless adjective insensitive, inconsiderate, thoughtless, indelicate, undiplomatic, indiscreet, unsubtle, inept, gauche, blunt.

tag noun *a price tag:* label, ticket, badge, mark, tab, sticker, docket.
• verb *bottles tagged with stickers:* label, mark, ticket, identify, flag, indicate.

tail noun *the tail of the queue:* rear, end, back, extremity, bottom.
OPPOSITES head, front, start.
• verb (informal) *the detectives tailed him to his hide-out:* follow, shadow, stalk, trail, track, keep under surveillance.

weaker part. **4** (**tails**) the side of a coin without the image of a head on it. **5** (**tails**) informal a tailcoat. •**verb 1** informal secretly follow someone. **2** (**tail off** or **away**) gradually become smaller or weaker.

tailback noun Brit. a long queue of stationary traffic.

tailcoat noun Brit. a man's formal jacket with a long skirt divided at the back into tails and cut away in front.

tailgate noun **1** a hinged flap at the back of a truck. **2** the door at the back of an estate or hatchback car.

tailor noun a person who makes men's clothing for individual customers. •**verb 1** make clothes to fit individual customers. **2** make or adapt for a particular purpose or person.
□ **tailor-made** made for a particular purpose.

tailored adjective (of clothes) smart, fitted, and well cut.

tailplane noun Brit. a small wing at the tail of an aircraft.

tailspin noun a fast spinning motion made by a rapidly descending aircraft.

tailwind noun a wind blowing from behind.

taint verb **1** contaminate or pollute. **2** affect with a bad or unpleasant quality. •**noun** a trace of something bad or unpleasant.

Taiwanese noun (plural **Taiwanese**) a person from Taiwan. •**adjective** relating to Taiwan.

take verb (**takes**, **taking**, **took**; past participle **taken**) **1** reach for and hold. **2** occupy a place or position. **3** gain possession of by force. **4** carry or bring with you. **5** remove from a place. **6** subtract. **7** consume. **8** bring into a particular state. **9** experience or be affected by. **10** use as a route or a means of transport. **11** accept or receive. **12** require or use up. **13** act on an opportunity. **14** see or deal with in a particular way. **15** tolerate or endure. **16** study a subject. **17** do an exam or test. •**noun 1** a sequence of sound or vision photographed or recorded continuously. **2** a particular approach to something. **3** an amount gained.
□ **take after** look or behave like a parent or ancestor. **take someone/thing for granted 1** be too familiar with someone or something to appreciate them properly. **2** assume that something is true. **take**

---

tailor noun outfitter, couturier, costumier, dressmaker, fashion designer.
•**verb** *services can be tailored to requirements:* customize, adapt, adjust, modify, change, convert, alter, mould, gear, fit, shape, tune.

taint verb **1** *the wilderness is tainted by pollution:* contaminate, pollute, adulterate, infect, blight, spoil, soil, ruin. **2** *fraudulent firms taint our reputation:* tarnish, sully, blacken, stain, blot, damage.
OPPOSITES clean, improve.

take verb **1** *she took his hand:* grasp, get hold of, grip, clasp, clutch, grab. **2** *he took an envelope from his pocket:* remove, pull, draw, withdraw, extract, fish. **3** *a passage taken from my book:* extract, quote, cite, excerpt, derive, abstract, copy, cull. **4** *many prisoners were taken:* capture, seize, catch, arrest, apprehend, take into custody, carry off, abduct. **5** *someone's taken my car:* steal, remove, appropriate, make off with, pilfer, purloin; informal filch, swipe, snaffle; Brit. informal pinch, nick. **6** *take four from the total:* subtract, deduct, remove, discount; informal knock off, minus. **7** *all the seats had been taken:* occupy, use, utilize, fill, hold, reserve, engage; informal bag. **8** *he took notes:* write, note (down), jot (down), scribble, scrawl, record, register, document, minute. **9** *I took it back to London:* bring, carry, bear, transport, convey, move, transfer, shift, ferry; informal cart, tote. **10** *the priest took her home:* escort, accompany, help, assist, show, lead, guide, see, usher, convey.

11 *he took the train:* travel on/by, journey on, go via, use. **12** *I can't take much more:* endure, bear, tolerate, stand, put up with, abide, stomach, accept, allow, countenance, support, shoulder; formal brook.
OPPOSITES give, free, add.
□ **take after** resemble, look like, remind you of. **take something apart** dismantle, take to pieces, take apart, disassemble, break up. **take someone in** deceive, delude, hoodwink, mislead, trick, dupe, fool, cheat, defraud, swindle; informal con. **take something in** comprehend, understand, grasp, follow, absorb; informal get. **take off 1** *the plane took off:* become airborne, take to the air, leave the ground, lift off, blast off. **2** *the idea really took off:* succeed, do well, become popular, catch on, prosper, flourish. **take someone on 1** *there was no challenger to take him on:* compete against, oppose, challenge, confront, face. **2** *we took on extra staff:* engage, hire, employ, sign up. **take something on** undertake, accept, assume, shoulder, acquire. **take something over** assume control of, take charge of, take command of, seize, hijack, commandeer. **take something up 1** *he took up abstract painting:* begin, start, commence, engage in, practise. **2** *the meetings took up all her time:* consume, fill, absorb, use, occupy. **3** *her cousin took up the story:* resume, recommence, restart, carry on, continue, pick up, return to. **4** *he took up their offer of a job:* accept, say yes to, agree to, adopt.

t

someone/thing in **1** cheat or deceive someone. **2** make a garment tighter by altering its seams. **3** understand something. take off **1** become airborne. **2** leave hastily. take someone/thing off **1** remove clothing. **2** informal mimic someone. take-off an act of taking off. take someone/thing on **1** employ someone. **2** undertake a task. **3** begin to have a meaning or quality. take over begin to have control of or responsibility for something, in place of someone else. take to **1** get into the habit of. **2** start liking. **3** go to a place to escape danger. take something up **1** start to do something. **2** occupy time, space, or attention. **3** pursue a matter further.

takeaway noun Brit. **1** a restaurant or shop selling cooked food to be eaten elsewhere. **2** a meal of such food.

takeout noun N. Amer. a takeaway.

takeover noun an act of taking control of something from someone else.

takings plural noun money received by a shop for goods sold.

talc noun **1** talcum powder. **2** a soft mineral.

talcum powder noun a powder used to make the skin feel smooth and dry.

tale noun **1** a story. **2** a lie.

talent noun **1** natural ability or skill. **2** people possessing natural ability or skill. **3** an ancient weight and unit of currency. ■ talented adjective.

talisman noun (plural **talismans**) an object

thought to have magic powers and to bring good luck. ■ talismanic adjective.

talk verb **1** speak in order to give information or express ideas or feelings. **2** be able to speak. **3** (**talk something over** or **through**) discuss something thoroughly. **4** (**talk back**) reply in a defiant or cheeky way. **5** (**talk down to**) speak to someone in a superior way. **6** (**talk someone round**) persuade someone to accept or agree to something. **7** (**talk someone into** or **out of**) persuade someone to do or not to do something. ● noun **1** conversation. **2** a speech or lecture. **3** (**talks**) formal discussions. □ talking-to informal a telling-off.

talkative adjective fond of talking.

tall adjective **1** of great or more than average height. **2** measuring a stated distance from top to bottom. □ a tall order a difficult challenge. tall ship a sailing ship with high masts. a tall story an account of something that seems unlikely to be true.

tallow noun a hard substance made from animal fat, used in making candles and soap.

tally noun (plural **tallies**) **1** a current score or amount. **2** a record of a score or amount. ● verb (**tallies, tallying, tallied**) **1** agree or correspond. **2** calculate the total number of.

tally-ho exclamation a huntsman's cry to the hounds on sighting a fox.

Talmud /tal-muud/ noun a collection of

THESAURUS

takeover noun buyout, purchase, acquisition, merger, amalgamation.

tale noun story, narrative, anecdote, account, history, legend, fable, myth, saga; informal yarn.

talent noun flair, aptitude, facility, gift, knack, technique, bent, ability, forte, genius, brilliance.

talented adjective gifted, skilful, expert, accomplished, brilliant, consummate, able; informal ace.
OPPOSITES untalented, inept.

talk verb **1** I was talking to a friend: speak, chat, chatter, gossip, jabber; informal yak; Brit. informal natter. **2** they were able to talk in peace: converse, communicate, speak, confer, consult, negotiate, parley; informal have a confab.
● noun **1** he was bored with all this talk: chatter, gossip, prattle, jabbering; informal yak; Brit. informal nattering. **2** she needed a talk with Vi: conversation, chat, discussion, tête-à-tête, heart-to-heart, dialogue; informal confab, gossip. **3** (**talks**) negotiations, discussions, conference, summit, meeting, consultation, dialogue.

4 she gave a talk on her travels: lecture, speech, address, discourse, oration, presentation, report, sermon.

talkative adjective chatty, garrulous, loquacious, voluble, communicative; informal mouthy.
OPPOSITES taciturn.

tall adjective **1** a tall man: big, large, huge, towering, gigantic, giant, leggy, gangling. **2** tall buildings: high, big, lofty, towering, sky-high. **3** a tall tale: unlikely, improbable, exaggerated, far-fetched, implausible, dubious, unbelievable, incredible, untrue; informal cock and bull. **4** a tall order: demanding, exacting, difficult, unreasonable, impossible.
OPPOSITES short, low, wide, credible, easy.

tally noun a tally of the score: running total, count, record, reckoning, register, account, roll.
● verb these statistics tally with government figures: correspond, agree, accord, concur, coincide, match, fit, be consistent, conform, equate, parallel; informal square.
OPPOSITES disagree.

ancient writings on Jewish law and legend.

talon noun a curved claw.

tamarind noun a fruit with sticky brown pulp used in Asian cookery.

tamarisk noun a small tree with tiny leaves on slender branches.

tambourine noun a shallow drum with metal discs around the edge, which you play by shaking or hitting with your hand.

tame adjective 1 (of an animal) not dangerous or frightened of people. 2 not exciting, adventurous, or controversial. •verb (**tames, taming, tamed**) 1 make an animal tame. 2 make less powerful and easier to control.
■ **tamely** adverb.

Tamil noun 1 a member of a people living in parts of South India and Sri Lanka. 2 the language of the Tamils.

tamp verb firmly ram or pack a substance into something.

tamper verb (**tampers, tampering, tampered**) (**tamper with**) interfere with something without permission.

tampon noun a plug of soft material that a woman puts into her vagina to absorb blood during a period.

tan noun 1 a golden-brown shade of skin developed by pale-skinned people after being in the sun. 2 a yellowish-brown colour. •verb (**tans, tanning, tanned**) 1 become golden-brown from being in the sun. 2 convert animal skin into leather.

tandem noun a bicycle for two riders, one sitting behind the other. •adverb one behind another.
□ **in tandem** together or at the same time.

tandoori /tan-**door**-i/ adjective (of Indian food) cooked in a clay oven called a **tandoor.**

tang noun 1 a strong flavour or smell. 2 the projection on the blade of a tool that holds it firmly in the handle.
■ **tangy** adjective.

tangent noun 1 a straight line that touches a curve but does not cross it at that point. 2 Maths (in a right-angled triangle) the ratio

of the sides opposite and adjacent to a particular angle. 3 a completely different line of thought or action.

tangential /tan-jen-sh'l/ adjective 1 only slightly relevant. 2 relating to or along a tangent.

tangerine noun a small citrus fruit with a loose skin.

tangible adjective 1 able to be perceived by touch. 2 real.
■ **tangibility** noun **tangibly** adverb.

tangle verb (**tangles, tangling, tangled**) 1 twist together into a knotted mass. 2 (**tangle with**) informal come into conflict with. •noun 1 a twisted, knotted mass. 2 a muddle.

tango noun (plural **tangos**) a South American ballroom dance with abrupt pauses. •verb (**tangoes, tangoing, tangoed**) dance the tango.

tank noun 1 a large container for liquid or gas. 2 the container holding the fuel supply in a vehicle. 3 a clear container for keeping pet fish. 4 a heavy armoured fighting vehicle that moves on a continuous metal track.
□ **tank engine** a steam locomotive carrying fuel and water holders in its own frame, not in a separate wagon. **tank top** a sleeveless top worn over a shirt or blouse.

tankard noun a large beer mug, sometimes with a hinged lid.

tanker noun a ship, road vehicle, or aircraft for carrying liquids in bulk.

tannin noun a bitter-tasting substance present in tea, grapes, etc.

tannoy noun Brit. trademark a type of public address system.

tantalize or **tantalise** verb (**tantalizes, tantalizing, tantalized**) tease someone by showing or promising them something that they cannot have.

tantalum noun a hard silver-grey metallic element.

tantamount adjective (**tantamount to**) equivalent in seriousness to.

t

---

tame adjective 1 *a tame elephant:* domesticated, docile, broken, trained, gentle, mild, pet. 2 *a tame affair:* unexciting, uninteresting, uninspiring, dull, bland, flat, pedestrian, humdrum, boring.
OPPOSITES wild, exciting.
•verb 1 *wild rabbits can be tamed:* domesticate, break, train, master, subdue. 2 *she learned to tame her emotions:* subdue, curb, control, calm, master, moderate, discipline, suppress, temper, bridle.

tangible adjective real, actual, physical, solid, palpable, material, substantial, concrete, visible, definite, perceptible, discernible.
OPPOSITES abstract, theoretical.

tangle verb *the wool got tangled up:* entangle, snarl, catch, entwine, twist, knot, mat, jumble.
•noun 1 *a tangle of branches:* snarl, mass, knot, mesh, mishmash. 2 *the defence got into an awful tangle:* muddle, jumble, mix-up, confusion, shambles.

tantrum noun an uncontrolled outburst of anger and frustration.

Tanzanian /tan-zuh-**nee**-uhn/ noun a person from Tanzania. • adjective relating to Tanzania.

Taoiseach /tee-shuhkh/ noun the Prime Minister of the Irish Republic.

tap[1] noun a device for controlling the flow of liquid or gas from a pipe or container. • verb (**taps, tapping, tapped**) 1 make use of a supply or resource. 2 connect a device to a telephone so as to listen to conversations secretly. 3 draw liquid from a cask, barrel, etc. 4 draw sap from a tree by cutting into it.
☐ **on tap** 1 ready to be poured from a tap. 2 informal freely available whenever needed.

tap[2] verb (**taps, tapping, tapped**) hit with a quick, light blow. • noun a quick, light blow.
☐ **tap dancing** a style of dancing performed in shoes with metal pieces on the toes and heels.

tapas /**tap**-uhss/ plural noun small Spanish savoury dishes served with drinks at a bar.

tape noun 1 light, flexible material in a narrow strip, used to hold, fasten, or mark off something. 2 tape with magnetic properties, used for recording sound, pictures, or computer data. 3 a cassette or reel containing magnetic tape. • verb (**tapes, taping, taped**) 1 record sound or pictures on magnetic tape. 2 fasten, attach, or mark off with tape.
☐ **tape measure** a strip of tape marked for measuring the length of things. **tape recorder** a device for recording and then reproducing sounds on magnetic tape.

taper verb (**tapers, tapering, tapered**) 1 reduce in thickness towards one end. 2 (**taper off**) gradually lessen. • noun a thin candle.

tapestry noun (plural **tapestries**) a piece of thick fabric with a design woven or embroidered on it.

tapeworm noun a long ribbon-like worm which lives as a parasite in the intestines of a person or animal.

tapioca noun hard white grains of cassava, used for making puddings.

tapir /**tay**-peer/ noun a piglike animal with a short flexible snout.

tappet noun a moving part in a machine which transmits motion between a cam and another part.

taproot noun a tapering root that grows straight downwards, from which other roots grow.

tar noun 1 a dark, thick liquid distilled from wood or coal. 2 a similar substance formed by burning tobacco. • verb (**tars, tarring, tarred**) cover with tar.

taramasalata noun a dip made from the roe (eggs) of certain fish.

tarantula noun 1 a very large hairy spider found in warm parts of America. 2 a large black spider of southern Europe.

tardy adjective (**tardier, tardiest**) formal 1 late. 2 slow to act or respond.
■ **tardily** adverb **tardiness** noun.

tare noun the weight of a vehicle without its fuel or load.

target noun 1 a person, object, or place that is aimed at in an attack. 2 a board marked with a series of circles that you aim at in archery or shooting. 3 something that you aim to achieve. • verb (**targets, targeting, targeted**) 1 select as an object of attention or attack. 2 aim or direct.

☑ note that **targeted** and **targeting** have a single *t* in the middle.

tariff noun 1 a tax to be paid on a particular class of imports or exports. 2 a list of the charges made by a hotel, restaurant, etc.

☑ one *r*, double *f*: tariff.

THESAURUS

tantrum noun fit of temper, fit of rage, outburst, pet, paroxysm, frenzy; informal paddy, wobbly; N. Amer. informal hissy fit.

tap[1] noun *she turned the tap on:* valve, stopcock; N. Amer. faucet, spigot.
• verb 1 *their telephones were tapped:* bug, wiretap, monitor, overhear, eavesdrop on. 2 *the resources were to be tapped for our benefit:* draw on, exploit, milk, mine, use, utilize, turn to account.

tap[2] verb *she tapped on the door:* knock, rap, strike, beat, pat, drum.

tape noun 1 *a package tied with tape:* binding, ribbon, string, braid, band. 2 *they made a tape of the concert:* (audio) cassette, (tape) recording, video.
• verb 1 *a card was taped to the box:* bind,

stick, fix, fasten, secure, attach. 2 *police taped his confession:* record, tape-record, video.

target noun 1 *their profit target:* objective, goal, aim, mark, end, plan, intention, aspiration, ambition. 2 *she was the target for abuse:* victim, butt, recipient, focus, object, subject.
• verb 1 *he was targeted by a gunman:* pick out, single out, earmark, fix on, attack, aim at, fire at. 2 *the product is targeted at a specific market:* aim, direct, level, intend, focus.

tariff noun 1 *import tariffs:* tax, duty, toll, excise, levy, charge, rate, fee. 2 *the bar tariff:* price list, menu.

tarmac noun **1** (trademark in the UK) a mixture of broken stone and tar used for making road surfaces. **2** (**the tarmac**) a runway or other area with a tarmac surface. •verb (**tarmacs, tarmacking, tarmacked**) give a road or runway a tarmac surface.

tarn noun a small mountain lake.

tarnish verb **1** make metal lose its shine by exposure to air or damp. **2** make something less respected. •noun a film or stain formed on the exposed surface of metal.

tarot /ta-roh/ noun a set of cards used for fortune telling.

tarpaulin noun a sheet of heavy waterproof cloth.

tarragon noun a herb with narrow strong-tasting leaves.

tarry verb (**tarries, tarrying, tarried**) literary stay longer than intended.

tarsus noun (plural **tarsi** /tar-sy/) the group of small bones in the ankle and upper foot.

tart[1] noun an open pastry case containing a sweet or savoury filling. ■ **tartlet** noun.

tart[2] informal noun disapproving a woman who has many sexual partners. •verb Brit. **1** (**tart yourself up**) make yourself look attractive with clothes or make-up. **2** (**tart something up**) improve the appearance of something. ■ **tarty** adjective.

tart[3] adjective **1** sharp or acid in taste. **2** (of a remark or tone of voice) sharp or hurtful. ■ **tartly** adverb.

tartan noun **1** a pattern of coloured checks and intersecting lines. **2** cloth with a tartan pattern.

tartar[1] noun a person who is fierce or difficult to deal with.

tartar[2] noun **1** a hard deposit that forms on the teeth. **2** a deposit formed during the fermentation of wine.

tartare sauce noun a sauce consisting of mayonnaise mixed with chopped onions, gherkins, and capers.

task noun a piece of work to be done. □ **task force 1** an armed force organized for a special operation. **2** a group of people specially organized to deal with a particular problem. **take someone to task** criticize or reprimand someone.

taskmaster noun a person who gives someone a lot of difficult tasks.

tassel noun a tuft of threads that are knotted together at one end. ■ **tasselled** (US spelling **tasseled**) adjective.

taste noun **1** the sensation of flavour perceived in the mouth when it comes into contact with a particular substance. **2** the sense by which taste is perceived. **3** a small sample of food or drink. **4** a brief experience of something. **5** a liking for something. **6** the ability to pick out things that are of good quality or appropriate. •verb (**tastes, tasting, tasted**) **1** have a particular flavour. **2** perceive or recognize the flavour of. **3** test the flavour of. **4** have a brief experience of. □ **taste bud** any of the clusters of nerve endings on the tongue and in the mouth which provide the sense of taste. ■ **taster** noun.

THESAURUS

tarnish verb **1** *gold does not tarnish easily:* discolour, rust, oxidize, corrode, stain, dull, blacken. **2** *it tarnished his reputation:* sully, blacken, stain, blemish, ruin, disgrace, mar, damage, harm.
OPPOSITES polish, enhance.
•noun **1** *the tarnish on the candlesticks:* discoloration, oxidation, rust, verdigris. **2** *the tarnish on his reputation:* smear, stain, blemish, blot, taint, stigma.

tart[1] noun *a jam tart:* pastry, flan, quiche, tartlet, vol-au-vent, pie.

tart[2] (informal) verb **1** *she tarted herself up:* dress up, make up, smarten up; informal doll yourself up, titivate yourself. **2** *we must tart this place up a bit:* decorate, renovate, refurbish, redecorate, smarten up; informal do up, fix up.

tart[3] adjective **1** *a tart apple:* sour, sharp, acidic, zesty, tangy, piquant. **2** *a tart reply:* scathing, sharp, biting, cutting, sarcastic, acrimonious, nasty, rude, vicious, spiteful.
OPPOSITES sweet, kind.

task noun job, duty, chore, charge, assignment, detail, mission, engagement, occupation, undertaking, exercise.

taste noun **1** *a distinctive sharp taste:* flavour, savour, relish, tang, smack. **2** *a taste of brandy:* mouthful, drop, bit, sip, nip, touch, soupçon, dash. **3** *it's too sweet for my taste:* palate, appetite, stomach. **4** *a taste for adventure:* liking, love, fondness, fancy, desire, penchant, inclination. **5** *my first taste of prison:* experience, impression, exposure to, contact with, involvement with. **6** *the house was furnished with taste:* judgement, discrimination, discernment, refinement, elegance, grace, style. **7** *the photo was rejected on grounds of taste:* sensitivity, decorum, propriety, etiquette, nicety, discretion.
OPPOSITES dislike.
•verb **1** *Adam tasted the wine:* sample, test, try, savour. **2** *he could taste blood:* perceive, discern, make out, distinguish. **3** *a beer that tasted of cashews:* have the flavour, savour, smack, be reminiscent.

t

tasteful adjective showing good judgement of quality, appearance, or appropriate behaviour.
■ **tastefully** adverb.

tasteless adjective **1** having little or no flavour. **2** not showing good judgement of quality, appearance, or appropriate behaviour.
■ **tastelessly** adverb.

tasty adjective (**tastier, tastiest**) **1** (of food) having a pleasant flavour. **2** Brit. informal attractive; appealing.

tat noun Brit. informal tasteless or badly made articles.

tattered adjective old and torn.

tatters plural noun torn pieces of cloth, paper, etc.
□ **in tatters 1** torn in many places. **2** destroyed; ruined.

tattle noun gossip. • verb (**tattles, tattling, tattled**) engage in gossip.

tattoo¹ noun (plural **tattoos**) a permanent design made on the skin with a needle and ink. • verb (**tattoos, tattooing, tattooed**) give someone a tattoo.
■ **tattooist** noun.

tattoo² noun (plural **tattoos**) **1** Brit. a military display with music and marching. **2** a rhythmic tapping or drumming.

tatty adjective (**tattier, tattiest**) informal worn and shabby.

taught past and past participle of TEACH.

taunt noun a remark made in order to anger or upset someone. • verb anger or upset with taunts.

taupe /rhymes with rope/ noun a brownish-grey colour.

Taurus noun a sign of the zodiac (the Bull), 21 April–20 May.

taut adjective **1** stretched or pulled tight. **2** (of muscles or nerves) tense.
■ **tauten** verb **tautly** adverb.

tautology noun (plural **tautologies**) the saying of the same thing twice in different words.
■ **tautological** adjective **tautologous** adjective.

tavern noun old use an inn or pub.

tawdry adjective **1** showy but cheap and of bad quality. **2** sleazy or unpleasant.
■ **tawdriness** noun.

tawny adjective of an orange-brown or yellowish-brown colour.

tax noun money that must be paid to the state, charged as a proportion of income and profits or added to the cost of some goods and services. • verb **1** impose a tax on. **2** pay tax on a vehicle. **3** make heavy demands on. **4** accuse someone of doing something wrong.
□ **tax-deductible** allowed to be deducted from income before the amount of tax to be paid is calculated. **tax exile** a rich person who chooses to live somewhere with low rates of taxation. **tax haven** a country or independent area where low rates of taxes are charged. **tax return** a form on which a person states their income, used to assess how much tax they should pay.
■ **taxable** adjective.

taxation noun **1** the imposing of tax. **2** money paid as tax.

taxi noun (plural **taxis**) a vehicle which takes fare-paying passengers to the place of their choice. • verb (**taxies, taxiing** or **taxying, taxied**) (of an aircraft) move slowly along the ground before take-off or after landing.
□ **taxi rank** Brit. a place where taxis wait to be hired.

taxicab noun a taxi.

taxidermy noun the art of preparing and stuffing the skins of dead animals so that they look like living ones.
■ **taxidermist** noun.

taxing adjective physically or mentally demanding.

taxonomy noun **1** the branch of science concerned with classification. **2** a system of classifying things.
■ **taxonomic** adjective.

TB abbreviation tuberculosis.

tbsp or **tbs** abbreviation tablespoonful.

tea noun **1** a hot drink made by soaking the dried leaves of an evergreen Asian shrub in boiling water. **2** the dried leaves used to

THESAURUS

tasteful adjective stylish, refined, cultured, elegant, smart, chic, exquisite.
OPPOSITES tasteless.

tasty adjective delicious, palatable, luscious, mouth-watering, delectable, appetizing, tempting; informal yummy, scrumptious, moreish.
OPPOSITES bland.

taunt noun the taunts of his classmates: jeer, gibe, sneer, insult, barb; informal dig, put-down; (**taunts**) teasing, provocation, goading, derision, mockery.

• verb she taunted him about his job: jeer at, sneer at, scoff at, poke fun at, make fun of, get at, insult, tease, torment, ridicule, deride, mock; N. Amer. ride; informal rib, needle.

tax noun they have to pay tax: duty, excise, customs, dues, levy, tariff, toll, tithe, charge.

• verb his whining taxed her patience: strain, stretch, overburden, overload, overwhelm, try, wear out, exhaust, sap, drain, weary, weaken.

t

make tea. **3** Brit. a light afternoon meal of sandwiches, cakes, etc., with tea to drink. **4** Brit. a cooked evening meal.
□ **tea bag** a sachet of tea leaves on to which boiling water is poured to make tea. **tea room** a cafe serving tea, cakes, etc. **tea towel** (or **tea cloth**) Brit. a cloth for drying washed crockery, cutlery, etc. **tea tree** a shrub of Australia and New Zealand that produces an oil with antiseptic qualities.

teacake noun Brit. a kind of bun containing currants.

teach verb (**teaches, teaching, taught**) **1** give lessons in a particular subject to a class or pupil. **2** show someone how to do something. **3** make someone realize or understand something.
■ **teacher** noun.

teacup noun a cup from which you drink tea.

teak noun hard wood obtained from a tree native to India and SE Asia.

teal noun (plural **teal** or **teals**) a small freshwater duck.

team noun **1** a group of players forming one side in a game or sport. **2** two or more people working together. **3** two or more horses harnessed together to pull something. •verb **1** (**team up**) work together to achieve a shared goal. **2** (**team something with**) wear an item of clothing with another.
□ **team spirit** trust and cooperation among the members of a team.

teammate noun a fellow member of a team.

teamwork noun organized effort as a group.

teapot noun a pot with a handle, spout, and lid, in which tea is made.

tear¹ verb (**tears, tearing, tore**; past participle **torn**) **1** rip a hole or split in. **2** (usu. **tear something up**) pull something apart or to

pieces. **3** damage a muscle or ligament by overstretching it. **4** (**tear something down**) demolish or destroy something. **5** (**be torn**) be unsure about which of two options to choose. **6** informal move very quickly. **7** (**tear into**) attack verbally. •noun a hole or split caused by tearing.

tear² noun a drop of clear salty liquid produced in a person's eye when they are crying or when the eye is irritated.
□ **tear gas** gas that causes severe irritation to the eyes, used in warfare and riot control. **tear-jerker** informal a very sad book, film, or song.

tearaway noun Brit. a person who behaves in a wild or reckless way.

teardrop noun a single tear.

tearful adjective **1** crying or about to cry. **2** causing tears.
■ **tearfully** adverb.

tease verb (**teases, teasing, teased**) **1** playfully make fun of or attempt to provoke. **2** tempt sexually. **3** (**tease something out**) find out something by searching through a mass of information. **4** gently pull tangled wool, hair, etc. into separate strands. •noun a person who teases.
■ **teaser** noun.

teasel or **teazle** noun a tall prickly plant with spiny flower heads.

teaspoon noun a small spoon for adding sugar to hot drinks.

teat noun **1** a nipple on an animal's udder or similar organ. **2** Brit. a plastic nipple-shaped device for sucking milk from a bottle.

technetium /tek-**nee**-shi-uhm/ noun a radioactive metallic element that is produced artificially.

technical adjective **1** having to do with the techniques of a particular subject, art, or craft. **2** needing specialized knowledge. **3** having to do with the practical use of

teach verb educate, instruct, school, tutor, inform, coach, train, drill.

teacher noun educator, tutor, instructor, schoolteacher, master, mistress, schoolmarm, governess, coach, trainer, lecturer, professor, don, guide, mentor, guru.

team noun *the sales team:* group, squad, company, party, crew, troupe, band, side, line-up; informal bunch, gang.
•verb *ankle boots teamed with jeans:* match, coordinate, complement, pair up.
□ **team up join (forces)**, collaborate, work together, unite, combine, cooperate, link, ally, associate, club together.

tear verb **1** *your shirt's torn:* rip, split, slit, pull apart, pull to pieces, shred, rupture,

sever. **2** *his flesh was torn:* lacerate, cut (open), gash, slash, scratch, hack, pierce, stab. **3** *Gina tore the book from his hands:* snatch, grab, seize, rip, wrench, wrest, pull, pluck; informal yank.
•noun *a tear in her dress:* rip, hole, split, slash, slit, ladder, snag.

tease verb make fun of, laugh at, deride, mock, ridicule, guy, make a monkey (out) of, taunt, bait, goad, pick on; informal take the mickey out of, rag, have on, pull someone's leg; Brit. informal wind up.

technical adjective **1** *an important technical achievement:* practical, scientific, technological, high-tech. **2** *this might seem very technical:* specialist, specialized, scientific, complex, complicated, esoteric.

t

machinery and methods in science and industry. **4** according to the law or rules when applied strictly.
□ **technical college** a college specializing in applied sciences and other practical subjects.
■ **technically** adverb.

technicality noun (plural **technicalities**) **1** a small formal detail in a set of rules. **2** (**technicalities**) small details of how something works or is done. **3** the use of technical terms or methods.

technician noun **1** a person who looks after equipment or does practical work in a laboratory. **2** a person skilled in the technique of an art, science, craft, or sport.

Technicolor noun trademark a process of producing cinema films in colour.

technique noun **1** a particular way of carrying out a task. **2** a person's level of skill in doing something.

techno noun a style of fast, loud electronic dance music.

technology noun (plural **technologies**) **1** the application of scientific knowledge for practical purposes. **2** machinery or equipment developed from this knowledge. **3** the branch of knowledge concerned with applied sciences.
■ **technological** adjective **technologically** adverb **technologist** noun.

tectonic adjective Geology having to do with the earth's crust.

teddy or **teddy bear** noun (plural **teddies**) a soft toy bear.

Teddy boy noun (in Britain during the 1950s) a young man of a group who had their hair slicked up in a quiff and liked rock-and-roll music.

tedious adjective too long, slow, or dull.
■ **tediously** adverb.

tedium noun the state of being tedious.

tee noun **1** a place on a golf course from which the ball is struck at the beginning of each hole. **2** a small peg placed in the ground to support a golf ball before it is struck from a tee. **3** a mark aimed at in bowls. • verb (**tees**, **teeing**, **teed**) Golf **1** (**tee up**) place the ball on a tee ready to begin a

round or hole. **2** (**tee off**) begin a round or hole.

teem verb **1** (**teem with**) be swarming with. **2** (of rain) fall heavily.

teen informal adjective having to do with teenagers. • noun a teenager.

teenage adjective having to do with teenagers.
■ **teenaged** adjective.

teenager noun a person aged between 13 and 19 years.

teens plural noun the years of a person's age from 13 to 19.

teeny or **teensy** adjective (**teenier**, **teeniest**) informal tiny.

teepee ⇨ TEPEE.

tee shirt noun a T-shirt.

teeter verb (**teeters**, **teetering**, **teetered**) move or sway unsteadily.

teeth plural of TOOTH.

teethe verb (**teethes**, **teething**, **teethed**) (of a baby) develop its first teeth.
□ **teething troubles** problems that occur in the early stages of a new project.

teetotal adjective choosing not to drink alcohol.
■ **teetotaller** noun.

telecommunications noun the technology concerned with long-distance communication by means of cable, telephone, broadcasting, satellite, etc.

telegram noun a message sent by telegraph and delivered in written or printed form.

telegraph noun a system or device for transmitting messages from a distance along a wire. • verb send a message to someone by telegraph.
□ **telegraph pole** a tall pole used to carry telegraph or telephone wires.
■ **telegraphic** adjective.

telekinesis /te-li-ky-nee-siss/ noun the movement of objects supposedly as a result of using mental power.
■ **telekinetic** adjective.

telepathy noun the supposed communication of thoughts or ideas by means other than the known senses.
■ **telepathic** adjective.

telephone noun **1** a system for

THESAURUS

technique noun **1** *different techniques for solving the problem:* method, approach, procedure, system, way, means, strategy. **2** *I was impressed with his technique:* skill, ability, proficiency, expertise, artistry, craftsmanship, adroitness, deftness, dexterity.

tedious adjective boring, dull, monotonous, repetitive, unrelieved, unvaried, uneventful, lifeless, uninteresting, unexciting, uninspiring, lacklustre, dreary,

soul-destroying; informal deadly; N. Amer. informal dullsville.
OPPOSITES exciting.

teenager noun adolescent, youth, young person, minor, juvenile; informal teen.

telephone noun *Sophie picked up the telephone:* phone, handset, receiver; informal blower; N. Amer. informal horn.
• verb *he telephoned me:* phone, call, dial; Brit. ring (up); informal call up, give someone a buzz, get on the blower to; Brit. informal

transmitting voices over a distance using wire or radio. **2** an instrument used in a telephone system for speaking into. •**verb** (**telephones, telephoning, telephoned**) contact someone by telephone.

telephonist noun Brit. an operator of a telephone switchboard.

telephony /ti-**lef**-fuh-ni/ noun the working or use of telephones.

telephoto lens noun a lens that produces a magnified image of a distant object.

teleprinter noun Brit. a device for transmitting telegraph messages as they are keyed.

telesales plural noun the selling of goods or services over the telephone.

telescope noun an instrument designed to make distant objects appear nearer. •**verb** (**telescopes, telescoping, telescoped**) **1** (of an object made up of several tubes) slide into itself so as to become smaller. **2** condense or combine to occupy less space or time.
■ **telescopic** adjective.

teletext noun an information service transmitted to televisions.

telethon noun a long television programme broadcast to raise money for a charity.

televise verb (**televises, televising, televised**) show on television.

television noun **1** a system for transmitting visual images with sound and displaying them electronically on a screen. **2** (also **television set**) a device with a screen for receiving television signals. **3** the activity or medium of broadcasting on television.
■ **televisual** adjective.

telex noun **1** an international system in

which printed messages are transmitted and received by teleprinters. **2** a message sent by telex. •**verb** send a message to someone by telex.

tell verb (**tells, telling, told**) **1** communicate information to. **2** say that someone must do something. **3** relate a story. **4** (**tell on**) informal inform someone about a person's wrongdoings. **5** (**tell someone off**) reprimand someone. **6** establish that something is the case. **7** have a noticeable effect on someone.
□ **telling-off** (plural **tellings-off**) informal a reprimand.

teller noun **1** chiefly N. Amer. a person who deals with customers' transactions in a bank. **2** a person who counts votes. **3** a person who tells something.

telling adjective having a striking or revealing effect.
■ **tellingly** adverb.

telltale adjective revealing or betraying something: *telltale signs of stress.* •**noun** informal a person who reports things that other people have done wrong.

telly noun informal television.

temerity noun very confident behaviour that other people are likely to consider rude or disrespectful.

temp informal noun a person who is employed on a temporary basis. •**verb** work as a temp.

temper noun **1** a person's state of mind. **2** a tendency to become angry easily. **3** an angry state of mind. **4** the degree of hardness of a metal. •**verb** (**tempers, tempering, tempered**) **1** make something less extreme. **2** harden metal by heating and then cooling it.

THESAURUS

give someone a bell, give someone a tinkle; N. Amer. informal get someone on the horn.

television noun TV; informal the small screen; Brit. informal telly, the box; N. Amer. informal the tube.

tell verb **1** *why didn't you tell me?* inform, notify, let know, make aware, acquaint with, advise, put in the picture, brief, fill in, alert, warn; informal clue in/up. **2** *she told the story slowly:* relate, recount, narrate, report, recite, describe, sketch. **3** *she told him to leave:* instruct, order, command, direct, charge, enjoin, call on, require. **4** *it was hard to tell what he said:* ascertain, determine, work out, make out, deduce, discern, perceive, see, identify, recognize, understand, comprehend; informal figure out; Brit. informal suss out. **5** *he couldn't tell one from the other:* distinguish, differentiate, discriminate. **6** *the strain began to tell on him:* take its toll, leave its mark, affect.

telling adjective revealing, significant,

weighty, important, meaningful, influential, striking, potent, powerful, compelling.
OPPOSITES insignificant.

temper noun **1** *he walked out in a temper:* rage, fury, fit of pique, tantrum, bad mood, pet, sulk, huff; Brit. informal strop, paddy; N. Amer. informal hissy fit. **2** *a display of temper:* anger, fury, rage, annoyance, irritation, pique, petulance; Brit. informal stroppiness. **3** *she struggled to keep her temper:* composure, self-control, self-possession, calm, good humour; informal cool.
•**verb** *their idealism is tempered with realism:* moderate, modify, modulate, mitigate, alleviate, reduce, weaken, lighten, soften.
□ **lose your temper get angry,** fly into a rage, erupt; informal go mad, go bananas, have a fit, see red, fly off the handle, blow your top, hit the roof, lose your rag; Brit. informal go spare, throw a wobbly.

t

tempera noun a method of painting with powdered colours mixed with egg yolk.

temperament noun a person's nature in terms of the way it affects their behaviour.

temperamental adjective **1** tending to have sudden or unreasonable changes of mood. **2** relating to or caused by temperament.
■ **temperamentally** adverb.

temperance noun the practice of never drinking alcohol.

temperate adjective **1** (of a region or climate) having mild temperatures. **2** showing self-control.

temperature noun **1** the degree of heat in a place, substance, or object. **2** a body temperature above the normal.

> ☑ -era- in the middle: temperature.

tempest noun a violent windy storm.

tempestuous adjective **1** very stormy. **2** full of strong and changeable emotions.

template noun **1** a shaped piece of rigid material used as a pattern for cutting out, shaping, or drilling. **2** a model for others to copy.

temple¹ noun a building for the worship of a god or gods.

temple² noun the flat part either side of the head between the forehead and the ear.

tempo noun (plural **tempos** or **tempi** /tem-pi/) **1** the speed at which a passage of music is played. **2** the pace of an activity or process.

temporal adjective **1** relating to time. **2** having to do with the physical world rather than spiritual matters.
■ **temporally** adverb.

temporary adjective lasting for only a limited period.
■ **temporarily** adverb.

temporize or **temporise** verb (**temporizes**, **temporizing**, **temporized**) delay making a decision.

tempt verb **1** try to persuade someone to do something appealing but wrong. **2** (**be tempted to do**) have an urge or inclination to do.
□ **tempt fate** do something risky or dangerous.
■ **tempting** adjective **temptingly** adverb.

temptation noun **1** the action of tempting. **2** a tempting thing.

temptress noun a woman who sets out to make a man desire her.

ten cardinal number one more than nine; 10. (Roman numeral: **x** or **X**.)
□ **Ten Commandments** (in the Bible) the ten rules of conduct given by God to Moses.
■ **tenfold** adjective & adverb.

tenable adjective **1** able to be defended against attack or objection. **2** (of an academic post, grant, etc.) able to be held or used for a stated period.

tenacious adjective **1** firmly holding on to something. **2** continuing to exist or do something for longer than might be expected.
■ **tenaciously** adverb **tenacity** noun.

tenancy noun (plural **tenancies**) possession of land or property as a tenant.

tenant noun a person who rents land or property from a landlord. • verb occupy property as a tenant.

tench noun (plural **tench**) a freshwater fish of the carp family.

THESAURUS

temperamental adjective volatile, excitable, emotional, unpredictable, hot-headed, quick-tempered, impatient, touchy, moody, sensitive, highly strung.
OPPOSITES placid.

temple noun house of God, shrine, sanctuary, church, cathedral, mosque, synagogue.

temporarily adverb **1** *they are temporarily abroad:* for the time being, for the moment, for now, for the present, in the interim, provisionally, pro tem. **2** *he was temporarily blinded by the light:* briefly, for a short time, momentarily, fleetingly.
OPPOSITES permanently.

temporary adjective **1** *temporary accommodation:* provisional, short-term, interim, makeshift, stopgap, acting, fill-in, stand-in, caretaker. **2** *a temporary loss of self-control:* brief, short-lived, momentary, fleeting, passing, ephemeral.

OPPOSITES permanent, lasting.

tempt verb **1** *the manager tried to tempt me to stay:* entice, persuade, convince, inveigle, induce, cajole, coax, lure; informal sweet-talk. **2** *more customers are being tempted by credit:* attract, allure, appeal to, whet the appetite of, seduce.
OPPOSITES discourage, deter.

temptation noun **1** *Mary resisted the temptation to answer back:* desire, urge, itch, impulse, inclination. **2** *the temptations of London:* lure, enticement, attraction, draw, pull. **3** *the temptation of exotic travel:* allure, appeal, attraction, fascination.

tempting adjective enticing, alluring, attractive, appealing, inviting, seductive, beguiling, fascinating.
OPPOSITES off-putting, uninviting.

tenant noun occupant, resident, inhabitant, leaseholder, lessee, lodger; Brit. occupier.
OPPOSITES owner, freeholder.

tend[1] verb **1** frequently behave in a particular way or have certain characteristics. **2** go or move in a particular direction.

tend[2] verb care for or look after.

tendency noun (plural **tendencies**) an inclination to act in a particular way.

tendentious adjective formal expressing a strong, often controversial, opinion.

tender[1] adjective (**tenderer**, **tenderest**) **1** gentle and sympathetic. **2** (of food) easy to cut or chew. **3** (of a part of the body) sensitive. **4** young and vulnerable. **5** (of a plant) easily damaged by severe weather.
■ **tenderly** adverb **tenderness** noun.

tender[2] verb (**tenders**, **tendering**, **tendered**) **1** offer or present formally. **2** make a formal written offer to do work, supply goods, etc. for a stated fixed price. **3** offer money as payment. • noun a tendered offer.

tender[3] noun **1** a vehicle used by a fire service or the armed forces for carrying supplies. **2** a wagon attached to a steam locomotive to carry fuel and water. **3** a boat used to ferry people and supplies to and from a ship.

tenderize or **tenderise** verb (**tenderizes**, **tenderizing**, **tenderized**) make meat more tender by beating it or cooking it slowly.

tenderloin noun the tenderest part of a loin of pork or beef.

tendon noun a strong band or cord of tissue attaching a muscle to a bone.

tendril noun **1** a thin curling stem of a climbing plant, which twines round a support. **2** a slender ringlet of hair.

tenebrous adjective literary dark; shadowy.

tenement noun a building divided into flats.

tenet noun a central principle or belief.

tenner noun Brit. informal a ten-pound note.

tennis noun a game in which players use rackets to hit a ball over a net stretched across a grass or clay court.
□ **tennis elbow** inflammation of the tendons of the elbow caused by overuse of the forearm muscles.

tenon noun a projecting piece of wood that fits into a slot in another piece of wood.

tenor[1] noun the male singing voice below alto or countertenor.

tenor[2] noun the general meaning or character of something.

tenpin bowling noun a game in which ten skittles are bowled down with hard balls.

tense[1] adjective **1** feeling, causing, or showing anxiety and nervousness. **2** stretched tight or rigid. • verb (**tenses**, **tensing**, **tensed**) make or become tense.
■ **tensely** adverb.

tense[2] noun Grammar a set of forms of a verb that indicate the time or completeness of the action referred to.

tensile adjective **1** relating to tension. **2** capable of being drawn out or stretched.

tension noun **1** a situation that is strained

---

tend[1] verb **1** *I tend to get very involved in my work:* be inclined, be apt, be disposed, be prone, be liable. **2** *younger voters tended towards the tabloid press:* incline, lean, gravitate, prefer, favour; N. Amer. trend.

tend[2] verb *she tended her cattle:* look after, take care of, minister to, attend to, see to, watch over, keep an eye on, mind, protect, guard.
OPPOSITES neglect.

tendency noun inclination, propensity, proclivity, proneness, aptness, likelihood, bent, leaning, liability.

tender[1] adjective **1** *a gentle, tender man:* caring, kind, kind-hearted, soft-hearted, compassionate, sympathetic, warm, gentle, mild, benevolent. **2** *a tender kiss:* affectionate, fond, loving, romantic, emotional; informal lovey-dovey. **3** *simmer until the meat is tender:* soft, succulent, juicy, melt-in-the-mouth. **4** *her ankle was swollen and tender:* sore, sensitive, inflamed, raw, painful, hurting, aching, throbbing. **5** *the tender age of fifteen:* young, youthful, impressionable, inexperienced; informal wet behind the ears.

OPPOSITES hard-hearted, callous, tough.

tender[2] verb *she tendered her resignation:* offer, proffer, present, put forward, propose, suggest, advance, submit, hand in.
• noun *contractors were invited to submit tenders:* bid, offer, quotation, quote, estimate, price.

tense adjective **1** *tense muscles:* taut, tight, rigid, stretched, strained, stiff. **2** *Loretta was feeling tense:* anxious, nervous, on edge, edgy, strained, stressed, under pressure, ill at ease, uneasy, restless, worked up, keyed up, overwrought, jumpy, nervy; informal a bundle of nerves, jittery, twitchy, uptight. **3** *a tense moment:* nerve-racking, stressful, anxious, worrying, fraught, charged, strained, nail-biting.
OPPOSITES slack, relaxed, calm.
• verb *Hebden tensed his muscles:* tighten, tauten, flex, contract, brace, stiffen.
OPPOSITES relax.

tension noun **1** *the tension of the rope:* tightness, tautness, rigidity, pull. **2** *the tension was unbearable:* strain, stress, anxiety, pressure, worry, nervousness,

t

because of differing views or aims.
2 mental or emotional strain. **3** the state of being stretched tight. **4** voltage of a particular magnitude: *high tension.*

tent noun a portable shelter made of cloth and supported by poles and cords.
■ **tented** adjective.

tentacle noun a long, thin, flexible part extending from the body of certain animals, used for feeling or holding things or moving about.

tentative adjective **1** done without confidence. **2** not certain or fixed.
■ **tentatively** adverb.

tenterhook noun (**on tenterhooks**) in a state of nervous suspense.

tenth ordinal number **1** that is number ten in a sequence; 10th. **2** (**a tenth** or **one tenth**) each of ten equal parts into which something is divided.

tenuous adjective very slight or weak.
■ **tenuously** adverb.

tenure noun **1** the conditions under which land or buildings are held or occupied. **2** the period of time when someone holds a job or position. **3** the right to stay permanently in a particular job.

tenured adjective having permanent employment in a particular job.

tepee or **teepee** noun a cone-shaped tent used by American Indians.

tepid adjective **1** lukewarm. **2** unenthusiastic.

tequila /ti-**kee**-luh/ noun a clear Mexican alcoholic spirit.

tercentenary noun (plural **tercentenaries**) a three-hundredth anniversary.

term noun **1** a word or phrase used to describe a thing or to express an idea.

2 (**terms**) requirements or conditions. **3** (**terms**) relations between people: *we're on good terms.* **4** a period for which something lasts. **5** each of the periods in the year during which teaching is given in a school or college. **6** (also **full term**) the completion of a normal length of pregnancy. **7** Maths each of the quantities in a ratio, equation, etc. •verb call by a particular term.
□ **come to terms with** become able to accept or deal with.
■ **termly** adjective & adverb.

termagant noun a bossy woman.

terminal adjective **1** having to do with or situated at the end. **2** (of a disease) predicted to lead to death. •noun **1** the station at the end of a railway or bus route. **2** a departure and arrival building for passengers at an airport. **3** a point at which connection can be made in an electric circuit. **4** a keyboard and screen joined to a central computer system.
■ **terminally** adverb.

terminate verb (**terminates, terminating, terminated**) **1** bring or come to an end. **2** (of a train or bus service) end its journey.

termination noun **1** the ending of something. **2** a medical procedure to end a pregnancy at an early stage.

terminology noun (plural **terminologies**) a set of terms relating to a subject.
■ **terminological** adjective.

terminus noun (plural **termini** /**ter**-mi-**ny**/ or **terminuses**) **1** Brit. a railway or bus terminal. **2** a final point or end.

termite noun a small insect which eats wood and lives in colonies in large nests of earth.

THESAURUS

jumpiness, edginess, restlessness, suspense, uncertainty. **3** *months of tension between the military and the government:* strained relations, strain, ill feeling, friction, antagonism, antipathy, hostility.

tentative adjective **1** *tentative arrangements:* provisional, unconfirmed, preliminary, exploratory, experimental. **2** *he took a few tentative steps:* hesitant, uncertain, cautious, timid, hesitating, faltering, shaky, unsteady, halting.
OPPOSITES definite, confident.

term noun **1** *scientific terms:* word, expression, phrase, name, title, designation, label, description. **2** *the terms of the contract:* condition, stipulation, specification, provision, proviso, restriction, qualification. **3** *the President is elected for a four-year term:* period, length of time, spell, stint, duration, stretch, run, session.

•verb *he has been termed the father of modern theology:* call, name, entitle, title, style, designate, describe as, dub, label, tag.

terminal adjective **1** *a terminal illness:* incurable, untreatable, inoperable, fatal, lethal, mortal, deadly. **2** *a terminal bonus may be payable:* final, last, concluding, closing, end.
OPPOSITES curable, initial.
•noun **1** *a railway terminal:* station, last stop, end of the line, depot; Brit. terminus. **2** *a computer terminal:* workstation, VDU, visual display unit.

terminate verb **1** *treatment was terminated:* bring to an end, bring to a close, close, conclude, finish, stop, wind up, discontinue, cease, cut short, abort, axe; informal pull the plug on. **2** *the pregnancy was terminated:* abort, end.
OPPOSITES begin, start, continue.

t

tern noun a white seabird with long pointed wings and a forked tail.

ternary adjective composed of three parts.

terpsichorean /terp-si-kuh-**ree**-uhn/ adjective relating to dancing.

terrace noun 1 a paved area next to a house; a patio. 2 Brit. a row of houses built in one block. 3 each of a series of flat areas on a slope, used for growing plants and crops. 4 Brit. a flight of wide, shallow steps for standing spectators in a stadium. • verb (**terraces**, **terracing**, **terraced**) make sloping land into terraces.
■ **terraced** adjective **terracing** noun.

terracotta noun brownish-red earthenware that has not been glazed.

terra firma noun dry land; the ground.

terrain noun a stretch of land seen in terms of its physical features.

terrapin noun a small freshwater turtle.

terrarium /ter-**rair**-i-uhm/ noun a glass container in which plants are grown, or in which small reptiles or amphibians are kept.

terrestrial adjective 1 having to do with the earth or dry land. 2 (of an animal or plant) living on or in the ground. 3 (of television broadcasting) not using a satellite.

terrible adjective 1 very bad, serious, or unpleasant. 2 troubled or guilty. 3 causing terror.

terribly adverb 1 extremely. 2 very badly.

terrier noun a small, lively breed of dog.

terrific adjective 1 of great size, amount, or strength. 2 informal excellent.
■ **terrifically** adverb.

terrify verb (**terrifies**, **terrifying**, **terrified**) make someone feel very frightened.

terrine /tuh-**reen**/ noun a mixture of chopped savoury food that is pressed into a container and served cold.

territorial adjective 1 relating to a territory or area. 2 (of an animal) having a territory which it defends.
□ **Territorial Army** (in the UK) a military reserve force of volunteers.
■ **territorially** adverb.

territory noun (plural **territories**) 1 an area controlled by a ruler or state. 2 a division of a country. 3 an area defended by an animal against others. 4 an area in which a person has special rights, responsibilities, or knowledge.

terror noun 1 extreme fear. 2 a cause of terror. 3 the use of terror to intimidate people. 4 informal a person causing trouble or annoyance.

terrorism noun the unofficial or unauthorized use of violence and intimidation in the attempt to achieve political aims.
■ **terrorist** noun & adjective.

terrorize or **terrorise** verb (**terrorizes**, **terrorizing**, **terrorized**) threaten and frighten over a period of time.

terry noun a towelling fabric.

terse adjective (**terser**, **tersest**) using few words.
■ **tersely** adverb.

tertiary /**ter**-shuh-ri/ adjective 1 third in order or level. 2 Brit. relating to university education.

tessellated adjective decorated with mosaics.
■ **tessellation** noun.

THESAURUS

terrain noun land, ground, territory, topography, landscape, countryside, country.

terrestrial adjective earthly, worldly, mundane, earthbound.

terrible adjective 1 *a terrible crime:* dreadful, awful, appalling, horrific, horrible, horrendous, atrocious, monstrous, sickening, heinous, vile. 2 *he was in terrible pain:* severe, extreme, intense, excruciating, agonizing, unbearable. 3 *the film was terrible:* very bad, dreadful, awful, frightful, atrocious, poor; informal pathetic, pitiful, useless, lousy, appalling; Brit. informal chronic, rubbish, pants.
OPPOSITES minor, slight, excellent.

terribly adverb 1 *he played terribly:* very badly, atrociously, awfully, dreadfully, appallingly, execrably; informal abysmally, pitifully. 2 (informal) *I shall miss you terribly:* very much, greatly, a great deal, a lot; informal loads.

terrific adjective 1 *a terrific bang:* tremendous, huge, massive, gigantic, colossal, mighty, considerable; informal mega, whopping; Brit. informal ginormous. 2 (informal) *a terrific game of top-quality football:* marvellous, wonderful, sensational, outstanding, superb, excellent, first-rate, dazzling, out of this world, breathtaking; informal great, fantastic, fabulous, super, ace, wicked, awesome; Brit. informal brilliant.

terrify verb frighten, horrify, petrify, scare, strike terror into, paralyse, transfix.

territory noun 1 *British overseas territories:* region, area, enclave, country, state, land, dependency, colony, dominion. 2 *mountainous territory:* terrain, land, ground, countryside. 3 *the territory of biblical scholarship:* domain, province, department, field, preserve, sphere, arena, realm, world.

terror noun fear, dread, horror, fright, alarm, panic, shock.

t

test noun **1** a procedure intended to establish how reliable or good something is, or whether something is present. **2** a short examination of skill or knowledge. **3** a medical examination of part of the body. **4** a difficult situation. **5** (**Test** or **Test match**) an international cricket or rugby match. •**verb 1** subject someone or something to a test. **2** make great demands on someone's endurance or patience.
□ **test case** Law a case that sets an example for future cases. **test tube** a thin glass tube used to hold material in laboratory tests. **test-tube baby** informal a baby conceived by in vitro fertilization.
■ **tester** noun.

testament noun **1** a person's will. **2** evidence or proof. **3** (**Testament**) each of the two divisions of the Bible.
■ **testamentary** adjective.

testate adjective having made a valid will before dying.

testicle noun either of the two oval organs that produce sperm in male mammals, enclosed in the scrotum.
■ **testicular** adjective.

testify verb (**testifies**, **testifying**, **testified**) **1** give evidence as a witness in a law court. **2** (**testify to**) be evidence or proof of.

testimonial noun **1** a formal statement of a person's good character and qualifications. **2** a public tribute to someone.

testimony noun (plural **testimonies**) **1** a formal statement, especially one given in a court of law. **2** (**testimony to**) evidence or proof of.

testis /tess-tiss/ noun (plural **testes** /tess-teez/) a testicle.

testosterone noun a hormone that stimulates the development of male physical characteristics.

testy adjective (**testier**, **testiest**) easily irritated.
■ **testily** adverb.

tetanus noun a disease that causes the muscles to stiffen and go into spasms.

tetchy adjective (**tetchier**, **tetchiest**) bad-tempered and irritable.
■ **tetchily** adverb.

tête-à-tête /tet-ah-**tet**/ noun a private conversation between two people.
•**adjective & adverb** happening privately between two people.

tether verb (**tethers**, **tethering**, **tethered**) tie an animal to a post with a rope or chain.
•**noun** a rope or chain used to tether an animal.

tetrahedron /tet-ruh-**hee**-druhn/ noun (plural **tetrahedra** or **tetrahedrons**) a solid figure with four triangular faces.

Teutonic /tyoo-**ton**-ik/ adjective often disapproving German.

text noun **1** a book or other written or printed work. **2** the main part of a work as distinct from illustrations, notes, etc. **3** written or printed words or computer data. **4** a text message. •**verb** send someone a text message.
□ **text message** an electronic message sent and received via mobile phone.
■ **textual** adjective.

textbook noun a book used for the study of a subject. •**adjective** done in exactly the recommended way.

textile noun any type of cloth or fabric.

texture noun the feel, appearance, or consistency of a surface, substance, or fabric. •**verb** (**textures**, **texturing**, **textured**) give a rough or raised texture to.
■ **textural** adjective.

Thai /ty/ noun (plural **Thai** or **Thais**) **1** a person from Thailand. **2** the official language of Thailand.

thalidomide /thuh-**lid**-uh-myd/ noun a sedative drug which was found to cause abnormalities in the fetus when taken by pregnant women.

thallium noun a soft silvery-white metallic element whose compounds are very poisonous.

than conjunction & preposition **1** used to introduce the second part of a comparison. **2** used to introduce an exception or

THESAURUS

test noun **1** *a series of scientific tests:* trial, experiment, check, examination, assessment, evaluation, appraisal, investigation. **2** *candidates must take a test:* exam, examination; N. Amer. quiz.
•**verb** *a small-scale prototype was tested:* try out, trial, put through its paces, experiment with, check, examine, assess, evaluate, appraise, investigate, sample.

testify verb swear, attest, give evidence, state on oath, declare, assert, affirm.

testimonial noun reference, letter of recommendation, commendation.

testimony noun evidence, sworn statement, attestation, affidavit, statement, declaration, assertion.

testing adjective difficult, challenging, tough, hard, demanding, taxing, stressful. OPPOSITES easy.

text noun **1** *a text which explores pain and grief:* book, work, textbook. **2** *the pictures relate well to the text:* words, content, body, wording, script, copy.

textiles plural noun fabrics, cloths, materials.

texture noun feel, touch, appearance, finish,

contrast. **3** used in expressions indicating one thing happening immediately after another.

thane noun an Anglo-Saxon or medieval Scottish landowner or nobleman.

thank verb **1** express gratitude to. **2** ironic blame or hold responsible.
□ **thank you** a polite expression of gratitude.

> ☑ **thank you** is a two-word phrase: don't spell it as one word.

thankful adjective pleased and relieved.
■ **thankfulness** noun.

thankfully adverb **1** in a thankful way. **2** fortunately.

thankless adjective **1** (of a job or task) unpleasant and unlikely to be appreciated by other people. **2** not showing or feeling gratitude.

thanks plural noun **1** an expression of gratitude. **2** = thank you.
□ **thanks to** due to.

thanksgiving noun **1** the expression of gratitude to God. **2** (**Thanksgiving**) (in North America) a national holiday held in November in the US and October in Canada.

that pronoun & determiner **1** (plural **those**) used to refer to a person or thing seen or heard or already mentioned or known. **2** (plural **those**) referring to the more distant of two things. • pronoun used instead of which, who, when, etc. to introduce a clause that defines or identifies something. • adverb to such a degree; so. • conjunction introducing a statement or suggestion.

thatch noun a roof covering of straw, reeds, etc. • verb cover with thatch.
■ **thatcher** noun.

thaw verb **1** make or become liquid or soft after being frozen. **2** make or become friendlier. • noun **1** a period of warmer weather that thaws ice and snow. **2** an increase in friendliness.

the determiner **1** used to refer to one or more

people or things already mentioned or easily understood; the definite article. **2** used to refer to someone or something that is the only one of its kind. **3** used to refer to something in a general rather than specific way.

theatre (US spelling **theater**) noun **1** a building in which plays are performed. **2** the writing and production of plays. **3** the dramatic quality of a play or event. **4** a room where specific things are done: *an operating theatre.* **5** the area in which something happens: *a theatre of war.*

theatrical adjective **1** having to do with acting or the theatre. **2** exaggerated and too dramatic. • noun (**theatricals**) theatrical performances or behaviour.
■ **theatricality** noun **theatrically** adverb.

theatrics noun theatricals.

thee old-fashioned or dialect form of **you**, as the singular object of a verb or preposition.

theft noun the action or crime of stealing.

their possessive determiner **1** belonging to or associated with the people or things previously mentioned or easily identified. **2** belonging to or associated with a person whose sex is not specified.

> ❗ don't confuse **their** with **there**, which means 'in or to that place' or **they're**, which is short for 'they are'.

theirs possessive pronoun used to refer to something belonging to or associated with two or more people or things previously mentioned.

> ☑ no apostrophe: **theirs**.

them pronoun **1** used as the object of a verb or preposition to refer to two or more people or things previously mentioned or easily identified. **2** referring to a person whose sex is not specified.

thematic adjective arranged according to subject, or connected with a subject.
■ **thematically** adverb.

theme noun **1** a subject which a person

THESAURUS t

surface, grain, consistency.

thank verb express your gratitude to, say thank you to, show your appreciation to.

thankful adjective grateful, relieved, pleased, glad.

thanks plural noun *they expressed their thanks and wished her well:* gratitude, appreciation, acknowledgement, recognition, credit.
□ **thanks to as a result of,** owing to, due to, because of, through, on account of, by virtue of.

thaw verb melt, unfreeze, defrost, soften,

liquefy.
OPPOSITES freeze.

theatrical adjective **1** *a theatrical career:* stage, dramatic, thespian, show-business; informal showbiz. **2** *Henry looked over his shoulder with theatrical caution:* exaggerated, ostentatious, stagy, showy, melodramatic, affected.

theft noun robbery, stealing, larceny, shoplifting, burglary, embezzlement, raid, hold-up; informal smash-and-grab; N. Amer. informal heist.

theme noun **1** *the theme of her speech:*

speaks, writes, or thinks about. **2** a prominent or recurring melody in a piece of music. **3** an idea that is often repeated in a work of art or literature. **4** (also **theme tune** or **music**) a piece of music played at the beginning and end of a film or programme.
□ **theme park** a large amusement park based around a particular idea.
■ **themed** adjective.

themselves pronoun **1** used as the object of a verb or preposition to refer to a group of people or things previously mentioned as the subject of the clause. **2** they or them personally. **3** used instead of 'himself' or 'herself' to refer to a person whose sex is not specified.

❗ note that you should use **themselves** rather than **themself** to refer to a person whose sex is not specified, e.g. *helping someone to help themselves*, not *helping someone to help themself*.

then adverb **1** at that time. **2** after that. **3** also. **4** therefore.

thence or **from thence** adverb formal **1** from a place or source previously mentioned. **2** as a consequence.

thenceforth or **thenceforward** adverb formal from that time, place, or point onward.

theocracy noun (plural **theocracies**) a system of government by priests.
■ **theocratic** adjective.

theodolite /thi-od-uh-lyt/ noun an instrument used in surveying for measuring horizontal and vertical angles.

theologian /thi-uh-loh-juhn/ noun a person who is an expert in or is studying theology.

theology noun (plural **theologies**) **1** the study of God and religious belief. **2** a system of religious beliefs and theory.
■ **theological** adjective **theologist** noun.

theorem noun a scientific or mathematical rule or proposition that can be proved by reasoning.

theoretical adjective **1** concerned with the theory of a subject rather than its practical application. **2** based on theory rather than experience or practice.
■ **theoretically** adverb.

theoretician noun a person who develops or studies the theoretical framework of a subject.

theorist noun a theoretician.

theorize or **theorise** verb (**theorizes**, **theorizing**, **theorized**) form a theory or theories about something.

theory noun (plural **theories**) **1** an idea or system of ideas intended to explain something. **2** a set of principles on which an activity is based.

therapeutic /the-ruh-**pyoo**-tik/ adjective **1** relating to the healing of disease. **2** having a good effect on the body or mind.
■ **therapeutically** adverb.

therapy noun (plural **therapies**) **1** treatment of a physical problem or illness. **2** treatment of mental or emotional problems using psychological methods.
■ **therapist** noun.

there adverb **1** in, at, or to that place or position. **2** on that issue.
□ **there is** (or **there are**) used to indicate that something exists or is true.

❗ don't confuse **there** with **their** or **they're**: see the note at **THEIR**.

thereabouts adverb near that place, time, or amount.

thereafter adverb after that time.

thereby adverb by that means; as a result of that.

therefore adverb for that reason.

THESAURUS

subject, topic, argument, idea, thrust, thread, motif, keynote. **2** *the first violin takes up the theme:* melody, tune, air, motif, leitmotif.

then adverb **1** *I was living in Cairo then:* at that time, in those days, at that point (in time), at that moment, on that occasion. **2** *she won the first and then the second game:* next, after that, afterwards, subsequently; formal thereafter.

theoretical adjective hypothetical, speculative, academic, conjectural, suppositional, notional, unproven.
OPPOSITES actual, real, practical.

theory noun **1** *that confirms my theory:* hypothesis, thesis, conjecture, supposition, speculation, postulation, proposition, premise, opinion, view, belief, contention.

2 *modern economic theory:* principles, ideas, concepts, philosophy, ideology, thinking.

therapeutic adjective healing, curative, remedial, medicinal, restorative, health-giving.
OPPOSITES harmful.

therapist noun psychologist, psychiatrist, psychotherapist, analyst, psychoanalyst, counsellor; informal shrink.

therapy noun **1** *complementary therapies:* treatment, remedy, cure. **2** *he's currently in therapy:* psychotherapy, psychoanalysis, counselling.

therefore adverb consequently, because of that, for that reason, that being the case, so, as a result, hence, accordingly.

therein adverb formal in that place, document, or respect.

thereof adverb formal of the thing just mentioned.

there's short form 1 there is. 2 there has.

thereupon adverb formal immediately or shortly after that.

therewith adverb old use or formal 1 with or in the thing mentioned. 2 soon or immediately after that.

thermal adjective 1 relating to heat. 2 (of a garment) designed to keep the body warm by stopping heat from escaping. • noun an upward current of warm air.
■ **thermally** adverb.

thermodynamics noun the study of the relationship between heat and other forms of energy.
■ **thermodynamic** adjective.

thermometer noun an instrument for measuring temperature, usually containing mercury or alcohol which expands when heated.

thermonuclear adjective relating to or using nuclear fusion reactions that occur at very high temperatures.

Thermos noun trademark a vacuum flask.

thermostat noun a device that automatically controls temperature or activates a device at a set temperature.
■ **thermostatic** adjective **thermostatically** adverb.

thesaurus /thi-**saw**-ruhss/ noun a book containing lists of words which have the same or a similar meaning.

these plural of **THIS.**

thesis noun (plural **theses**) 1 a statement or theory that is put forward to be supported or proved. 2 a long piece of work involving research, written as part of a university degree.

thespian noun an actor or actress. • adjective relating to drama and the theatre.

they pronoun 1 used to refer to two or more people or things previously mentioned or easily identified. 2 people in general. 3 used to refer to a person whose sex is not specified (in place of either 'he' or 'he or she').

they'd short form 1 they had. 2 they would.

they'll short form 1 they shall. 2 they will.

they're short form they are.

> ! don't confuse **they're** with **their** or **there**: see the note at **THEIR.**

they've short form they have.

thiamine or **thiamin** noun vitamin B_1, found in grains, nuts, beans, and liver.

thick adjective 1 with opposite sides or surfaces relatively far apart. 2 (of a garment or fabric) made of heavy material. 3 made up of a large number of things or people close together. 4 (**thick with**) filled or covered with. 5 (of the air or atmosphere) difficult to see through or breathe. 6 (of something liquid or semi-liquid) relatively firm in consistency. 7 informal stupid. 8 (of a voice) hoarse or husky. 9 (of an accent) strong and difficult to understand. 10 informal having a very close, friendly relationship. • noun (**the thick**) the middle or the busiest part.
□ **through thick and thin** under all circumstances.
■ **thickly** adverb.

thicken verb make or become thick or thicker.

thicket noun a dense group of bushes or trees.

thickness noun 1 the distance through an object, as distinct from width or height. 2 the state or quality of being thick. 3 a layer of material.

thickset adjective heavily built.

thief noun (plural **thieves**) a person who steals another person's property.

> ☑ *i* before *e* except after *c*: th*ief*.

thieve verb (**thieves, thieving, thieved**) steal things.
■ **thievery** noun.

THESAURUS t

thesis noun 1 *the central thesis of his lecture:* theory, contention, argument, proposal, proposition, premise, assumption, hypothesis, supposition. 2 *a doctoral thesis:* dissertation, essay, paper, treatise, composition, study; N. Amer. theme.

thick adjective 1 *thick stone walls:* broad, wide, deep, stout, bulky, hefty, chunky, solid, plump. 2 *the station was thick with people:* crowded, full, packed, teeming, seething, swarming, crawling, crammed, thronged, bursting at the seams, solid, overflowing; informal jam-packed, chock-a-block, stuffed; Austral./NZ informal chocker. 3 *the thick vegetation:* plentiful, abundant, profuse, luxuriant, bushy, rich, riotous, exuberant, rank, rampant, dense; informal jungly. 4 *a thick paste:* semi-solid, firm, stiff, heavy, viscous, gelatinous. 5 *thick fog:* dense, heavy, opaque, impenetrable, soupy, murky.
OPPOSITES thin, slender, sparse.

thicken verb stiffen, condense, solidify, set, gel, congeal, clot, coagulate.

thief noun robber, burglar, housebreaker, shoplifter, pickpocket, mugger, kleptomaniac; informal crook.

thieve verb steal, take, purloin, help

thigh noun the part of the leg between the hip and the knee.

thimble noun a small covering that you wear to protect the end of the finger and push the needle in sewing.

thin adjective (**thinner, thinnest**) **1** having opposite surfaces or sides close together. **2** (of a garment or fabric) made of light material. **3** having little flesh or fat on the body. **4** having few parts or members in relation to the area covered or filled. **5** not dense or heavy. **6** containing a lot of liquid and not much solid substance. **7** (of a sound) faint and high-pitched. **8** weak and inadequate. •verb (**thins, thinning, thinned**) (often **thin out**) make or become less thick or dense.
■ **thinly** adverb **thinness** noun.

thine pronoun & possessive determiner old use your or yours.

thing noun **1** an inanimate object. **2** an unspecified object, action, activity, etc. **3** (**your things**) personal belongings. **4** (**the thing**) informal what is needed or required. **5** (**your thing**) informal your special interest.

think verb (**thinks, thinking, thought**) **1** have a particular opinion, belief, or idea. **2** use or direct your mind. **3** (**think of** or **about**) take into account or consideration. **4** intend. **5** (**think something over**) consider something carefully. **6** (**think something up**) informal invent something. •noun an act of thinking. □ **think better of** reconsider and decide not to do. **think tank** a group of experts providing advice and ideas.
■ **thinker** noun.

thinner noun a solvent used to thin paint or other solutions.

third ordinal number **1** that is number three in a sequence; 3rd. **2** (**a third** or **one third**) each of three equal parts into which something is divided. **3** Brit. a place in the third grade in an exam for a degree. □ **third-degree** (of burns) of the most severe kind, affecting tissue below the skin. **the third degree** lengthy and harsh questioning. **third party 1** a person besides the two main ones involved in a situation. **2** Brit. (of insurance) covering damage or injury suffered by someone other than the person who is insured. **Third World** the developing countries of Asia, Africa, and Latin America.
■ **thirdly** adverb.

thirst noun **1** a feeling of needing or

THESAURUS

yourself to, snatch, pilfer, embezzle, misappropriate; informal rob, swipe, nab, lift; Brit. informal nick, pinch, knock off; N. Amer. informal heist.

thin adjective **1** *a thin white line:* narrow, fine, attenuated. **2** *a thin cotton nightdress:* lightweight, light, fine, delicate, flimsy, diaphanous, gossamer, sheer, filmy, transparent, gauzy, see-through. **3** *a tall, thin woman:* slim, lean, slender, willowy, svelte, sylphlike, spare, slight, skinny, underweight, scrawny, scraggy, bony, gaunt, emaciated, skeletal, lanky, spindly, gangly; informal anorexic. **4** *thin soup:* watery, weak, runny, sloppy.
OPPOSITES thick, broad, fat.
•verb **1** *some paint must be thinned down:* dilute, water down, weaken. **2** *the crowds were beginning to thin out:* disperse, dissipate, scatter.
OPPOSITES thicken, gather.

thing noun **1** *the room was full of strange things:* object, article, item, artefact, commodity; informal doodah, whatsit, whatchamacallit, thingummy, thingy; Brit. informal gubbins. **2** (**things**) *I'll collect my things:* belongings, possessions, stuff, property, worldly goods, effects, paraphernalia, bits and pieces, luggage, baggage; informal gear, junk; Brit. informal clobber. **3** (**things**) *his gardening things:* equipment, apparatus, gear, kit, tackle, stuff, implements, tools, utensils, accoutrements.

think verb **1** *I think he's gone home:* believe, be of the opinion, be of the view, be under the impression, expect, imagine, anticipate, suppose, fancy; informal reckon, figure. **2** *his family was thought to be rich:* consider, judge, hold, reckon, deem, presume, estimate, regard as, view as. **3** *Jack thought for a moment:* ponder, reflect, deliberate, consider, meditate, contemplate, muse, brood. **4** *she thought of all the visits she had made:* recall, remember, recollect, call to mind. **5** *I can't think how bad it must be:* imagine, picture, visualize, envisage.
□ **think something up devise**, dream up, come up with, invent, create, concoct, make up, hit on.

thinker noun intellectual, philosopher, scholar, sage, ideologist, theorist, intellect, mind; informal brain.

thinking adjective *a thinking man:* intelligent, sensible, reasonable, rational, logical, analytical, thoughtful.
OPPOSITES stupid, irrational.
•noun *the thinking behind the campaign:* reasoning, idea(s), theory, thoughts, philosophy, beliefs, opinion(s), view(s).

thirst noun *his thirst for knowledge:* craving, desire, longing, yearning, hunger, hankering, eagerness, lust, appetite; informal yen, itch.
□ **thirst for crave**, want, covet, desire, hunger for, lust after, hanker after, wish

wanting to drink. **2** the state of not having enough water to drink. **3** (**thirst for**) a strong desire for. • verb **1** (**thirst for** or **after**) have a strong desire for. **2** old use feel a need to drink.

thirsty adjective (**thirstier, thirstiest**) **1** feeling or causing thirst. **2** (**thirsty for**) having a strong desire for.
■ thirstily adverb.

thirteen cardinal number one more than twelve; 13. (Roman numeral: **xiii** or **XIII**.)
■ thirteenth ordinal number.

thirty cardinal number (plural **thirties**) ten less than forty; 30. (Roman numeral: **xxx** or **XXX**.)
■ thirtieth ordinal number.

this pronoun & determiner (plural **these**) **1** used to identify a specific person or thing close at hand, just mentioned, or being indicated or experienced. **2** referring to the nearer of two things close to the speaker. • adverb to the degree or extent indicated.

thistle noun a plant with a prickly stem and leaves and purple flowers.

thistledown noun the light fluffy down of thistle seeds.

thither adverb old use to or towards that place.

tho' or **tho** informal spelling of **THOUGH**.

thong noun **1** a narrow strip used as a fastening or as the lash of a whip. **2** a pair of knickers like a G-string.

thorax noun (plural **thoraces** /thor-uh-seez/ or **thoraxes**) **1** the part of the body between the neck and the abdomen. **2** the middle section of an insect's body, to which the legs and wings are attached.
■ thoracic adjective.

thorium noun a white radioactive metallic element.

thorn noun **1** a stiff sharp-pointed projection on a plant. **2** a thorny bush, shrub, or tree.
□ a thorn in someone's side (or flesh) a source of continual annoyance or trouble.

thorny adjective (**thornier, thorniest**) **1** having many thorns. **2** causing difficulty.

thorough adjective **1** complete with regard to every detail. **2** very careful and complete. **3** absolute; utter.
■ thoroughly adverb.

thoroughbred adjective descended from animals that were all of the same breed. • noun a thoroughbred animal.

thoroughfare noun a road or path between two places.

thoroughgoing adjective **1** thorough. **2** complete; absolute.

those plural of **THAT**.

thou pronoun old use you (as the singular subject of a verb).

though conjunction **1** despite the fact that; although. **2** however; but. • adverb however.

thought[1] noun **1** an idea or opinion produced by thinking, or occurring suddenly in the mind. **2** the process of thinking. **3** (**thought of**) intention, hope, or idea of. **4** the forming of opinions, or the opinions so formed.

thought[2] past and past participle of **THINK**.

thoughtful adjective **1** absorbed in thought.

THESAURUS

for, long for.

thirsty adjective longing for a drink, dry, dehydrated; informal parched, gasping.

thorn noun prickle, spike, barb, spine.

thorough adjective **1** *a thorough investigation:* rigorous, in-depth, exhaustive, minute, detailed, close, meticulous, methodical, careful, complete, comprehensive. **2** *he is slow but thorough:* meticulous, scrupulous, assiduous, conscientious, painstaking, punctilious, methodical, careful. **3** *the child is being a thorough nuisance:* utter, downright, absolute, complete, total, out-and-out, real, perfect, proper; Brit. informal right; Austral./NZ informal fair.
OPPOSITES superficial, cursory, careless.

though conjunction *though she smiled bravely, she looked tired:* although, even though, even if, despite the fact that, notwithstanding (the fact) that, for all that.
• adverb *You can't always do that. You can try, though:* nevertheless, nonetheless, even so, however, be that as it may, for all

that, despite that, having said that; informal still and all.

thought noun **1** *what are your thoughts on the matter?* idea, notion, opinion, view, impression, feeling, theory. **2** *he gave up any thought of taking a degree:* hope, aspiration, ambition, dream, intention, idea, plan, design, aim. **3** *it only took a moment's thought:* thinking, contemplation, musing, pondering, consideration, reflection, deliberation, meditation. **4** *have you no thought for others?* consideration, understanding, regard, sensitivity, compassion, sympathy, care, concern.

thoughtful adjective **1** *a thoughtful expression:* pensive, reflective, contemplative, musing, meditative, philosophical, preoccupied. **2** *how very thoughtful of you!* considerate, caring, attentive, understanding, sympathetic, solicitous, concerned, helpful, obliging, accommodating, kind, compassionate.
OPPOSITES vacant, inconsiderate.

t

2 showing careful consideration. **3** showing consideration for other people.
■ **thoughtfully** adverb.

thoughtless adjective **1** not showing consideration for other people. **2** without considering the consequences.
■ **thoughtlessly** adverb.

thousand cardinal number **1** the product of a hundred and ten; 1,000. (Roman numeral: **m** or **M**.) **2** (**thousands**) informal an unspecified large number.
■ **thousandth** ordinal number.

thrall noun the state of being in another person's power.

thrash verb **1** beat repeatedly and violently with a stick or whip. **2** move in a violent or uncontrolled way. **3** informal defeat heavily. **4** (**thrash something out**) discuss an issue frankly and thoroughly.

thread noun **1** a thin strand of cotton or other fibres used in sewing or weaving. **2** a spiral ridge on the outside of a screw or bolt or on the inside of a hole, to allow two parts to be screwed together. **3** a theme running through a situation or piece of writing. •verb **1** pass a thread through. **2** weave in and out of obstacles.

threadbare adjective thin and tattered with age.

threat noun **1** a stated intention to inflict harm on someone. **2** a person or thing likely to cause harm. **3** the possibility of trouble or danger.

threaten verb **1** make a threat to. **2** put at risk. **3** seem likely to produce an unwelcome result.
■ **threatening** adjective **threateningly** adverb.

three cardinal number one more than two; 3. (Roman numeral: **iii** or **III**.)
□ **three-dimensional** having or appearing to have length, breadth, and depth.
■ **threefold** adjective & adverb.

threepence /thrup-uhnss/ noun Brit. the sum of three old pence before decimalization (1971).
■ **threepenny** adjective.

threesome noun a group of three people.

threnody /thren-uh-di/ noun (plural **threnodies**) a song, piece of music, or poem expressing grief or regret.

thresh verb **1** separate grains of corn from the rest of the plant. **2** move in an uncontrolled way.
■ **thresher** noun.

threshold noun **1** a strip of wood or stone forming the bottom of a doorway. **2** a level or point marking the start of something.

> ☑ there is only one *h* in the middle: threshold.

threw past of **THROW**.

> ! don't confuse **threw** with **through**, which means 'in one side of an opening or place and out of the other'.

thrice adverb old use three times.

thrift noun the quality of spending money very carefully, so that none is wasted.
■ **thrifty** adjective.

thrill noun **1** a sudden feeling of excitement

THESAURUS

thrash verb **1** *she thrashed him with a whip:* hit, beat, strike, batter, thump, hammer, pound; informal belt. **2** *he was thrashing around in pain:* flail, writhe, thresh, jerk, toss, twist, twitch.

thread noun **1** *a needle and thread:* cotton, yarn, filament, fibre. **2** *she lost the thread of the conversation:* train of thought, drift, direction, theme, tenor.
•verb **1** *he threaded the rope through a pulley:* pass, string, work, ease, push, poke. **2** *she threaded her way through the tables:* weave, inch, squeeze, navigate, negotiate.

threat noun **1** *Maggie ignored his threats:* threatening remark, warning, ultimatum. **2** *a possible threat to aircraft:* danger, peril, hazard, menace, risk. **3** *the company faces the threat of liquidation:* possibility, chance, probability, likelihood, risk.

threaten verb **1** *how dare you threaten me?* menace, intimidate, browbeat, bully, terrorize. **2** *these events could threaten the stability of Europe:* endanger, jeopardize, imperil, put at risk. **3** *the grey skies threatened snow:* herald, bode, warn of,

presage, foreshadow, indicate, point to, be a sign of, signal.

threshold noun **1** *the threshold of the church:* doorstep, entrance, entry, gate. **2** *on the threshold of a new era:* start, beginning, commencement, brink, verge, dawn, inception, day one, opening, debut. **3** *the human threshold of pain:* limit, minimum.

thrifty adjective frugal, economical, sparing, careful with money, provident, prudent, abstemious, parsimonious, penny-pinching.
OPPOSITES extravagant.

thrill noun *the thrill of jumping out of an aeroplane:* excitement, stimulation, pleasure, tingle; informal buzz, kick; N. Amer. informal charge.
OPPOSITES boredom.
•verb **1** *his words thrilled her:* excite, stimulate, arouse, rouse, inspire, delight, exhilarate, intoxicate, stir, electrify, move; informal give someone a buzz, give someone a kick; N. Amer. informal give someone a charge. **2** *he thrilled at the sound of her voice:* feel excited, tingle; informal get a buzz

t

and pleasure. **2** an exciting or enjoyable experience. **3** a wave of emotion or sensation. • verb **1** give someone a thrill. **2** (**thrill to**) experience something exciting. ■ thrilling adjective.

thriller noun a novel, play, or film with an exciting plot, typically involving crime or spying.

thrive verb (**thrives, thriving, thrived** or **throve**; past participle **thrived** or **thriven**) **1** grow or develop well. **2** be successful; flourish.

throat noun **1** the passage which leads from the back of the mouth to the lungs and stomach. **2** the front part of the neck.

throaty adjective (**throatier, throatiest**) sounding deep and husky. ■ throatily adverb.

throb verb (**throbs, throbbing, throbbed**) **1** beat or sound with a strong, regular rhythm. **2** feel pain in a series of pulsations. • noun a strong, regular beat or sound.

throes plural noun severe or violent pain and struggle. □ **in the throes of** in the middle of doing or dealing with something difficult.

thrombosis noun (plural **thromboses**) the formation of a blood clot in a blood vessel or the heart.

throne noun **1** a chair for a king or queen, used during ceremonies. **2** (**the throne**) the power or rank of a king or queen.

throng noun a large, densely packed crowd. • verb gather somewhere in large numbers.

throttle noun a device controlling the flow of fuel or power to an engine. • verb (**throttles, throttling, throttled**) **1** attack or kill by choking or strangling. **2** control an engine or vehicle with a throttle.

through preposition & adverb **1** in one side and out of the other side of an opening or place. **2** continuing in time towards. **3** from beginning to end. **4** by means of. • adjective **1** (of public transport) continuing to the final destination. **2** (of traffic, roads, etc.) passing straight through a place. **3** having successfully reached the next stage of a competition. **4** informal having finished an activity, relationship, etc.

❗ don't confuse **through** with **threw**, which is the past of **throw**.

throughout preposition & adverb all the way through.

throughput noun the amount of material or number of items passing through a process.

throve past of THRIVE.

throw verb (**throws, throwing, threw**; past

out of, get a kick out of; N. Amer. informal get a charge out of.
OPPOSITES bore.

thrilling adjective exciting, stimulating, stirring, action-packed, rip-roaring, gripping, electrifying, riveting, fascinating, dramatic, hair-raising.
OPPOSITES boring.

thrive verb flourish, prosper, burgeon, bloom, blossom, do well, advance, succeed, boom.
OPPOSITES decline, wither.

thriving adjective flourishing, prospering, growing, developing, blooming, healthy, successful, booming, profitable; informal going strong.
OPPOSITES declining.

throb verb her arms and legs throbbed with tiredness: pulsate, beat, pulse, palpitate, pound, thud, thump, drum, judder, vibrate, quiver.
• noun the throb of the ship's engines: pulsation, beat, pulse, palpitation, pounding, thudding, thumping, drumming, juddering, vibration, quivering.

throng noun throngs of people blocked her way: crowd, horde, mass, army, herd, flock, drove, swarm, sea, troupe, pack; informal gaggle, bunch, gang.
• verb **1** the pavements were thronged with

tourists: fill, crowd, pack, cram, jam. **2** people thronged to see the play: flock, stream, swarm, troop. **3** visitors thronged round him: crowd, cluster, mill, swarm, congregate, gather.

throttle verb choke, strangle, garrotte.

through preposition **1** he got the job through an advertisement: by means of, by way of, by dint of, via, using, thanks to, by virtue of, as a result of, as a consequence of, on account of, owing to. **2** he worked through the night: throughout, for the duration of, until/to the end of, all.

throughout preposition **1** the event had repercussions throughout Europe: all over, in every part of, everywhere in. **2** Rose had been very fit throughout her life: all through, for the duration of, for the whole of, until the end of, all.

throw verb **1** hurl, toss, fling, pitch, cast, lob, launch, bowl; informal chuck, heave, sling, bung. **2** he threw the door open: push, thrust, fling, bang. **3** a chandelier threw its light over the walls: cast, send, give off, emit, radiate, project. **4** his intervention threw me: disconcert, unnerve, fluster, ruffle, put off, throw off balance, unsettle, confuse; informal rattle, faze.

participle **thrown**) **1** send through the air with a rapid movement of the arm and hand. **2** move or place hurriedly or roughly. **3** project, direct, or cast light, an expression, etc. in a particular direction. **4** send suddenly into a particular position or condition. **5** upset or confuse. •noun **1** an act of throwing. **2** a small rug or light cover for furniture.

□ **throw something away** (or **out**) get rid of something. **throw up** informal vomit.

throwaway adjective **1** intended to be thrown away after use. **2** (of a remark) said without careful thought.

throwback noun a person or thing that resembles someone or something that existed in the past.

thrum verb (**thrums**, **thrumming**, **thrummed**) make a continuous rhythmic humming sound. •noun a thrumming sound.

thrush[1] noun a bird with a brown back and spotted breast.

thrush[2] noun an infection of the mouth and throat or the genitals.

thrust verb (**thrusts**, **thrusting**, **thrust**) **1** push suddenly or violently. **2** make your way forcibly. •noun **1** a sudden or violent lunge or attack. **2** the main point of an argument. **3** the force produced by an engine to push forward a jet, rocket, etc.

thrusting adjective aggressively ambitious.

thud noun a dull, heavy sound. •verb (**thuds**, **thudding**, **thudded**) move, fall, or strike with a thud.

thug noun a violent man.
■ **thuggery** noun **thuggish** adjective.

thulium noun a soft silvery-white metallic element.

thumb noun the short, thick first digit of the hand. •verb **1** turn over pages with your thumb. **2** ask for a free ride in a passing vehicle by signalling with your thumb.

□ **thumb index** lettered notches cut into the side of a book to help you find the section you want. **thumbs up** (or **down**) informal an indication of approval (or disapproval). **under someone's thumb** under someone's control.

thumbnail noun the nail of the thumb.
□ **thumbnail sketch** a brief, concise description.

thumbscrew noun an instrument of torture that crushes the thumbs.

thump verb **1** hit heavily with your fist or a blunt object. **2** put down forcefully. **3** (of a person's heart) beat strongly. •noun a dull, heavy blow or noise.

thumping adjective informal very big.

thunder noun **1** a loud rumbling or crashing noise heard after a lightning flash due to the expansion of rapidly heated air. **2** a loud, deep noise. •verb **1** (**it thunders**, **it is thundering**, **it thundered**) thunder is sounding. **2** make a loud, deep noise. **3** speak loudly and angrily.

thunderbolt noun a flash of lightning with a crash of thunder at the same time.

thunderclap noun a sudden crash of thunder.

thundercloud noun a cloud charged with electricity and producing thunder and lightning.

thunderous adjective **1** very loud. **2** (of a person's expression) very angry or threatening.

THESAURUS

•noun **lob**, toss, pitch, bowl.
□ **throw something away/out discard**, dispose of, get rid of, scrap, dump, jettison; informal chuck (away/out), ditch, bin, junk; Brit. informal get shot of. **throw someone out expel**, eject, evict, drive out, force out, oust, remove, get rid of, depose, topple, unseat, overthrow; informal boot out, kick out; Brit. informal turf out.

thrust verb **1** *a spear was thrust into the sack:* shove, push, force, plunge, stick, drive, ram. **2** *fame had been thrust on him:* force, foist, impose, inflict. **3** *he thrust his way past her:* push, shove, force, elbow, shoulder, barge.
•noun **1** *a hard thrust:* shove, push, lunge, poke. **2** *a thrust by the Third Army:* advance, push, drive, attack, assault, onslaught, offensive. **3** *only one engine is producing thrust:* force, propulsion, power, impetus. **4** *the thrust of the speech:* gist, substance, drift, message, import, tenor.

thug noun ruffian, hooligan, bully boy, hoodlum, gangster, villain; informal tough, bruiser, heavy; Brit. informal rough, bovver boy; N. Amer. informal hood, goon.

thump verb **1** *he thumped the policeman:* hit, punch, strike, smack; informal whack, wallop, bash, biff, bop, clobber; Brit. informal slosh; N. Amer. informal slug. **2** *her heart thumped with fright:* throb, pound, thud, hammer.
•noun **1** *a thump in the eye:* blow, punch, box, cuff, smack; informal whack, wallop, bash, biff; Brit. informal slosh; N. Amer. informal boff, slug. **2** *she put the box down with a thump:* thud, clunk, clonk, crash, smack, bang.

thunder noun rumble, boom, roar, pounding, thud, crash, reverberation.
•verb **1** *below me the surf thundered:* rumble, boom, roar, pound, thud, thump, bang. **2** *'Answer me!' he thundered:* shout, roar, bellow, bark, bawl.

thunderstorm noun a storm with thunder and lightning.

thunderstruck adjective very surprised or shocked.

Thursday noun the day of the week before Friday and following Wednesday.

thus adverb formal 1 as a result or consequence of this; therefore. 2 in this way. 3 to this point; so.

thwack verb hit with a sharp blow. • noun a sharp blow.

thwart verb prevent someone from accomplishing something.

thy or (before a vowel) **thine** possessive determiner old use your.

thyme /rhymes with time/ noun a low-growing, sweet-smelling plant used in cooking.

thymus /**thy**-muhss/ noun (plural **thymi** /**thy**-my/) a gland in the neck which produces white blood cells for the immune system.

thyroid noun a large gland in the neck which produces hormones regulating growth and development.

tiara noun a jewelled ornamental band worn above the forehead.

Tibetan noun a person from Tibet. • adjective relating to Tibet.

tibia noun (plural **tibiae** /**ti**-bi-ee/ or **tibias**) the inner of the two bones between the knee and the ankle.

tic noun a recurring spasm in the muscles of the face.

tick¹ noun 1 Brit. a mark (✓) used to show that something is correct or has been chosen or checked. 2 a regular short, sharp sound. 3 Brit. informal a moment. • verb 1 Brit. mark with a tick. 2 make regular ticking sounds. 3 (**tick away** or **by** or **past**) (of time) keep passing. 4 (**tick over**) (of an engine) run slowly while the vehicle is not moving. 5 (**tick someone off**) Brit. informal tell someone off.

tick² noun a tiny insect-like creature which attaches itself to the skin and sucks blood.

ticker noun 1 informal a person's heart. 2 N. Amer. a machine that prints out data on a strip of paper.
□ **ticker tape** strips of paper on which data is printed by a machine.

ticket noun 1 a piece of paper or card giving you the right to travel on public transport or letting you in to a place or an event. 2 an official notice that you have committed a parking or driving offence. 3 a label attached to a product, giving its price, size, etc.

ticking noun a hard-wearing material used to cover mattresses.

tickle verb (**tickles, tickling, tickled**) 1 lightly touch in a way that causes itching or twitching and often laughter. 2 be appealing or amusing to. • noun an act of tickling, or the sensation of being tickled.
■ **tickly** adjective.

ticklish adjective 1 sensitive to being tickled. 2 needing care and tact.

tidal adjective relating to or affected by tides.
□ **tidal wave** a huge sea wave caused by an earthquake, storm, etc.
■ **tidally** adverb.

tidbit US spelling of TITBIT.

tiddler noun Brit. informal a small fish.

tiddly adjective informal 1 slightly drunk. 2 Brit. little; tiny.

tiddlywinks plural noun a game in which small plastic counters are flicked into a cup.

tide noun 1 the alternate rising and falling of the sea due to the attraction of the moon and sun. 2 a powerful surge of feeling or trend of events. • verb (**tides, tiding, tided**) (**tide someone over**) help someone through a difficult period.

tidings plural noun literary news; information.

tidy adjective (**tidier, tidiest**) 1 arranged

THESAURUS

t

thus adverb 1 *the studio handled production, thus cutting its costs:* consequently, so, therefore, accordingly, hence, as a result. 2 *legislation forbids such data being held thus:* like this/that, in this/that way, so, like so, as follows.

thwart verb foil, frustrate, forestall, stop, check, block, prevent, defeat, impede, obstruct, derail, snooker; informal put paid to, do for, stymie; Brit. informal scupper.
OPPOSITES help.

ticket noun 1 *a bus ticket:* pass, permit, authorization, token, coupon, voucher. 2 *a price ticket:* label, tag, sticker, tab, slip, docket.

tickle verb 1 stroke, pet, chuck. 2 *something*

tickled his imagination: stimulate, interest, appeal to, arouse, excite. 3 *the idea tickled Lewis:* amuse, entertain, divert, please, delight.

tide noun 1 current, flow, stream, ebb. 2 *the tide of history:* course, movement, direction, trend, current, drift, run.

tidy adjective 1 *a tidy room:* neat, orderly, well ordered, well kept, in apple-pie order, uncluttered, straight. 2 *a very tidy person:* organized, neat, methodical, meticulous.
OPPOSITES messy, disorganized.
• verb *I'd better tidy up the living room:* put in order, clear up, sort out, straighten (up), clean up, spruce up.
OPPOSITES mess up.

neatly and in order. **2** liking to keep yourself and your possessions neat and in order. **3** informal (of a sum of money) large. •**verb** (**tidies, tidying, tidied**) (often **tidy up**) make a place tidy. •**noun** (plural **tidies**) **1** an act of tidying. **2** a container for holding small objects.
■ **tidily** adverb **tidiness** noun.

tie verb (**ties, tying, tied**) **1** attach or fasten with string, cord, ribbon, etc. **2** form into a knot or bow. **3** restrict to a particular situation or place. **4** connect or link. **5** achieve the same score or ranking as another competitor. •**noun** (plural **ties**) **1** a strip of material worn beneath a collar and tied in a knot at the front. **2** a thing that ties. **3** a result in a game or match in which two or more competitors are equal. **4** Brit. a sports match in which the winners go on to the next round.
◻ **tie-dye** produce patterns on fabric by tying knots in it before it is dyed. **tie in** fit or be in harmony. **tie someone/thing up** **1** restrict someone's movement by tying their arms or legs. **2** bring something to a conclusion. **3** informal occupy someone so that they have no time for other activities.

tiebreaker (also **tiebreak**) noun a means of deciding a winner from competitors who are equal at the end of a game or match.

tied adjective Brit. **1** (of accommodation) rented by someone on condition that they work for the owner. **2** (of a pub) owned and controlled by a brewery.

tiepin noun an ornamental pin for holding a tie in place.

tier noun one of a series of rows or levels placed one above and behind the other.
■ **tiered** adjective.

tiff noun informal a quarrel about something unimportant.

tiffin noun dated or Indian a snack or light meal.

tiger noun a large cat with a yellow coat striped with black, native to the forests of Asia.

tight adjective **1** firmly fixed, closed, or fastened. **2** (of clothes) fitting very closely. **3** well sealed against water or air. **4** (of a rope, fabric, or surface) stretched so as to leave no slack. **5** (of an area or space) allowing little room for movement. **6** closely packed together. **7** (of a form of control) very strict. **8** (of money or time) limited. •**adverb** very closely or firmly.
◻ **tight-fisted** informal not willing to spend your money. **tight-knit** (or **tightly knit**) (of a group of people) closely connected so as to each other through family or social relationships. **tight-lipped** unwilling to express emotion or give away information.
■ **tightly** adverb **tightness** noun.

tighten verb make or become tight or tighter.

tightrope noun a rope or wire stretched high above the ground, on which acrobats balance.

tights plural noun a close-fitting garment made of stretchy material, covering the hips, legs, and feet.

tigress noun a female tiger.

tikka /tik-uh, tee-kuh/ noun an Indian dish of meat or vegetables marinated in spices.

tilde /til-duh/ noun an accent (˜) placed over the Spanish *n* or Portuguese *a* or *o* to change the way they are pronounced.

tile noun a thin square or rectangular piece of fired clay, concrete, cork, etc., used for covering roofs, floors, or walls. •**verb** (**tiles, tiling, tiled**) cover with tiles.
■ **tiler** noun.

till¹ less formal way of saying **UNTIL**.

THESAURUS

tie verb **1** *he tied the boat to the jetty*: bind, tie up, tether, hitch, strap, truss, fetter, rope, make fast, moor, lash. **2** *he bent to tie his shoelaces*: do up, lace, knot. **3** *women can feel tied by childcare responsibilities*: restrict, restrain, limit, tie down, constrain, cramp, hamper, handicap, hamstring, encumber, shackle. **4** *a pay deal tied to productivity*: link, connect, couple, relate, join, marry. **5** *they tied for second place*: draw, be equal, be even.
•**noun** **1** *he tightened the ties of his robe*: lace, string, cord, fastening. **2** *family ties*: bond, connection, link, relationship, attachment, affiliation. **3** *pets can be a tremendous tie*: restriction, constraint, curb, limitation, restraint, hindrance, encumbrance, handicap, obligation, commitment. **4** *a tie for first place*: draw, dead heat.

tier noun **1** *six tiers of seats*: row, rank, bank, line, layer, level. **2** *a tier of management*: grade, gradation, echelon, rung on the ladder.

tight adjective **1** *a tight grip*: firm, secure. **2** *the rope was pulled tight*: taut, rigid, stiff, tense, stretched, strained. **3** *tight jeans*: close-fitting, narrow, figure-hugging, skintight; informal sprayed on. **4** *a tight mass of fibres*: compact, compressed, dense, solid. **5** *a tight space*: small, tiny, narrow, limited, restricted, confined, cramped, constricted. **6** *a tight joint*: sealed, sound, impenetrable, impervious.
OPPOSITES slack, loose, roomy, leaky.

tighten verb **1** *he tightened his grip*: strengthen, harden. **2** *she tightened the rope*: stretch, tauten, strain, stiffen, tense.
OPPOSITES loosen, slacken, relax.

till² noun a cash register or drawer for money.

till³ verb prepare and cultivate land for crops.

tiller noun a horizontal bar fitted to a boat's rudder and used for steering.

tilt verb 1 slip or move into a sloping position. 2 (**tilt at**) (in the past, in jousting) thrust at someone with a lance. • noun 1 a tilting position or movement. 2 a leaning or bias. 3 (in the past) a joust. 4 (**tilt at**) an attempt at winning something.
□ (at) full tilt with maximum speed or force.

tilth noun soil that has been prepared for crops.

timber noun 1 wood prepared for use in building and carpentry. 2 a wooden beam used in building.

timbre /**tam**-ber/ noun the quality of the sound in a voice or piece of music.

time noun 1 the continuing and unlimited progress of existence and events in the past, present, and future. 2 a point or period within this. 3 a point of time as measured in hours and minutes past midnight or noon. 4 the right or agreed moment to do something. 5 time as a resource to be used. 6 an instance of something happening or being done. 7 (**times**) (following a number) expressing multiplication. 8 the rhythmic pattern or tempo of a piece of music. • verb (**times, timing, timed**) 1 arrange a time for. 2 do at a particular time. 3 measure the time taken by.
□ behind the times not using the latest

ideas or techniques. for the time being until some other arrangement is made. in time 1 not late. 2 eventually. on time punctual, or punctually. time-honoured (of a custom or tradition) respected or valued because it has existed for a long time. time off time spent away from your usual work or studies. time-server a person who makes little effort at work because they are waiting to leave or retire. time signature a sign at the start of a piece of music showing the number of beats in a bar.

timekeeper noun 1 a person who records the amount of time taken by a process or activity. 2 a person regarded in terms of their punctuality.
■ timekeeping noun.

timeless adjective not affected by the passing of time.

timely adjective done or happening at a good or appropriate time.
■ timeliness noun.

timepiece noun a clock or watch.

timer noun 1 a device that records how long something is taking. 2 a device that stops or starts a machine at a preset time.

timescale noun the time allowed for or taken by a process or events.

timeshare noun an arrangement in which joint owners use a property as a holiday home at different times.

timetable noun a list or plan of times at which events are scheduled to take place. • verb (**timetables, timetabling, timetabled**) schedule events to take place at particular times.

timid adjective not brave or confident.
■ timidity noun timidly adverb.

THESAURUS

tilt verb the ground seemed to tilt: slope, tip, lean, list, bank, slant, incline, pitch, cant, angle.
• noun a tilt of some 45°: slope, list, camber, gradient, bank, slant, incline, pitch, cant, bevel, angle.

timber noun 1 houses built of timber: wood; N. Amer. lumber. 2 the timbers of wrecked ships: beam, spar, plank, batten, lath, board, joist, rafter.

time noun 1 the best time to leave: moment, point (in time), occasion, instant, juncture, stage. 2 he worked there for a time: while, spell, stretch, stint, interval, period, length of time, duration, phase. 3 the time of the dinosaurs: era, age, epoch, period, years, days.
• verb the meeting is timed for 4 o'clock: schedule, arrange, set, organize, fix, book, line up, timetable, plan; N. Amer. slate.
□ all the time **constantly**, the entire time, around the clock, day and night, {morning, noon, and night}, {day in, day out}, always,

without a break, ceaselessly, endlessly, incessantly, perpetually, permanently, continuously, continually, eternally; informal 24-7. at times **occasionally**, sometimes, from time to time, now and then, every so often, once in a while, on occasion, off and on, at intervals, periodically.

timeless adjective lasting, enduring, classic, ageless, permanent, perennial, abiding, unchanging, unvarying, never-changing, eternal, everlasting.
OPPOSITES ephemeral.

timely adjective opportune, well timed, convenient, appropriate, expedient, seasonable, propitious.
OPPOSITES ill-timed.

timetable noun schedule, programme, agenda, calendar, diary.
• verb schedule, arrange, programme, organize, fix, time, line up; Brit. diarize; N. Amer. slate.

timid adjective fearful, afraid, faint-hearted,

timorous adjective easily frightened.

timpani or **tympani** /tim-puh-ni/ plural noun kettledrums.

tin noun **1** a silvery-white metal. **2** an airtight container with a lid, made of tinplate or aluminium. **3** Brit. a sealed tinplate or aluminium container for preserving food. **4** Brit. an open metal container for baking food. •verb (**tins**, **tinning**, **tinned**) **1** cover another metal with a thin layer of tin. **2** (**tinned**) Brit. (of food) preserved in a tin.
□ **tin whistle** a metal musical instrument like a small flute.

tincture noun **1** a medicine made by dissolving a drug in alcohol. **2** a slight trace.

tinder noun dry material used in lighting a fire.

tinderbox noun (in the past) a box containing tinder, flint, and other items for lighting fires.

tine noun a prong or sharp point.

tinfoil noun metal foil used for covering or wrapping food.

tinge noun a slight trace of a colour, feeling, or quality. •verb (**tinges**, **tinging** or **tingeing**, **tinged**) give a tinge to.

tingle verb (**tingles**, **tingling**, **tingled**) have a slight prickling or stinging feeling. •noun a slight prickling or stinging sensation.
■ **tingly** adjective.

tinker noun (in the past) a person who travelled from place to place mending pots, kettles, etc. •verb (**tinkers**, **tinkering**, **tinkered**) (**tinker with**) casually try to repair or improve.

tinkle verb (**tinkles**, **tinkling**, **tinkled**) make or cause to make a light, clear ringing sound. •noun a tinkling sound.

tinnitus /tin-ni-tuhss/ noun a ringing or buzzing in the ears.

tinny adjective **1** having a thin, metallic sound. **2** made of thin or poor-quality metal.

tinplate noun thin sheets of steel or iron coated with a layer of tin.

tinpot adjective informal not important or effective.

tinsel noun thin strips of shiny metal foil attached to a length of thread, used to decorate a Christmas tree.

tint noun **1** a shade of a colour. **2** a dye for colouring the hair. •verb **1** colour something slightly. **2** dye hair with a tint.

tintinnabulation noun a ringing or tinkling sound.

tiny adjective (**tinier**, **tiniest**) very small.

tip¹ noun **1** the pointed or rounded end of something slender or tapering. **2** a small part fitted to the end of an object.
□ **tip-top** of the very best quality.
■ **tipped** adjective.

tip² verb (**tips**, **tipping**, **tipped**) **1** overbalance so as to fall or turn over. **2** be or put in a sloping position. **3** empty out the contents of a container by holding it at an angle.
•noun **1** Brit. a place where rubbish is left. **2** informal a dirty or untidy place.

tip³ noun **1** a small extra amount of money that you give to someone for their good service in a restaurant, taxi, etc. **2** a piece of practical advice. **3** a prediction about the likely winner of a race or contest. •verb

THESAURUS

timorous, nervous, scared, frightened, shy, diffident.
OPPOSITES bold.

tinge verb **1** *white blossom tinged with pink*: tint, colour, stain, shade, wash. **2** *his optimism is tinged with realism*: influence, affect, touch, flavour, colour.
•noun **1** *a blue tinge*: tint, colour, shade, tone, hue. **2** *a tinge of cynicism*: trace, note, touch, suggestion, hint, flavour, element, streak, suspicion, soupçon.

tinker verb fiddle, play about, mess about, adjust, try to mend; Brit. informal muck about.

tint noun **1** *an apricot tint*: shade, colour, tone, hue, tinge, cast, flush, blush. **2** *a hair tint*: dye, colourant, colouring, wash.
•verb dye, colour, tinge.

tiny adjective minute, minuscule, microscopic, very small, mini, diminutive, miniature, baby, toy, dwarf; Scottish wee; informal teeny, tiddly; Brit. informal titchy; N. Amer. informal little-bitty.
OPPOSITES huge.

tip¹ noun **1** *the tip of the spear*: point, end, extremity, head, spike, prong, nib. **2** *the tips of the mountains*: peak, top, summit, apex, crown, crest, pinnacle.
•verb *mountains tipped with snow*: cap, top, crown, surmount.

tip² verb **1** *the boat tipped over*: overturn, turn over, topple (over), fall (over), keel over, capsize, roll over. **2** *a whale could tip over a small boat*: upset, overturn, topple over, turn over, push over, upend, capsize; informal roll. **3** *the car tipped to one side*: lean, tilt, list, slope, bank, slant, incline, pitch, cant. **4** *she tipped the water into the trough*: pour, empty, drain, dump, discharge, decant.
•noun (Brit.) *rubbish must be taken to the tip*: dump, rubbish dump, landfill site.

tip³ noun **1** *a generous tip*: gratuity, baksheesh, present, gift, reward. **2** *useful tips*: piece of advice, suggestion, word of advice, pointer, hint; informal wrinkle.

t

(**tips, tipping, tipped**) **1** give a tip to. **2** Brit. predict that a particular horse, competitor, etc. is likely to win something. **3** (**tip someone off**) informal give someone secret information.

tipple informal **noun** an alcoholic drink. • **verb** (**tipples, tippling, tippled**) drink alcohol regularly.
■ **tippler** noun.

tipster noun a person who gives tips as to the likely winner of a race or contest.

tipsy adjective slightly drunk.
■ **tipsily** adverb.

tiptoe verb (**tiptoes, tiptoeing, tiptoed**) walk quietly and carefully with your heels raised.
□ **on tiptoe** (or **tiptoes**) with your heels raised.

tirade noun a long angry speech.

tire¹ verb (**tires, tiring, tired**) **1** make or become in need of rest or sleep. **2** (**tire of**) become impatient or bored with.

tire² US spelling of **TYRE**.

tired adjective **1** in need of sleep or rest. **2** (**tired of**) bored with. **3** (of a statement or idea) boring because it has been said or used too often.
■ **tiredness** noun.

tireless adjective having or showing great effort or energy.
■ **tirelessly** adverb.

tiresome adjective making you feel impatient or bored.
■ **tiresomely** adverb.

'tis short form literary it is.

tissue /**ti**-shoo/ noun **1** any of the distinct types of material of which animals or plants are made. **2** a disposable paper handkerchief.
□ **a tissue of lies** a story that is full of lies. **tissue paper** a very thin, soft paper.

tit¹ noun a small bird that searches for food among leaves and branches.

tit² noun (**tit for tat**) a situation in which

you insult or hurt someone because they have done the same to you.

Titan noun **1** any of a family of giant gods in Greek mythology. **2** (**titan**) a person of very great strength, intelligence, or importance.

titanic adjective of exceptional strength, size, or power.

titanium noun a silver-grey metal used in making strong alloys.

titbit (US spelling **tidbit**) noun **1** a small piece of tasty food. **2** a small item of very interesting information.

titch noun Brit. informal a small person.
■ **titchy** adjective.

tithe noun (in the past) one tenth of what people produced or earned in a year, taken as a tax to support the Church.

titillate verb (**titillates, titillating, titillated**) make someone feel interested or mildly excited, especially sexually.
■ **titillation** noun.

☑ one *t*, two *l*s: titi**ll**ate. Also, don't confuse **titillate** with **titivate**, which means 'make smarter or more attractive'.

titivate verb (**titivates, titivating, titivated**) informal make smarter or more attractive.
■ **titivation** noun.

title noun **1** the name of a book, piece of music, or other work. **2** a name that describes someone's position or job. **3** a word, such as *Dr*, *Mrs*, or *Lord*, used before or instead of someone's name to indicate their rank or profession. **4** a descriptive name that someone has earned or chosen. **5** the position of being the champion of a major sports competition. **6** a caption or credit in a film or broadcast. • **verb** (**titles, titling, titled**) give a title to.
□ **title deed** a legal document giving evidence of someone's right to own a property. **title role** the part in a play or film from which the title is taken.

titled adjective having a title indicating nobility, e.g. *Lord* or *Lady*.

THESAURUS

t

tire verb **1** *he began to tire:* get tired, weaken, flag, droop. **2** *the journey had tired him:* fatigue, tire out, exhaust, wear out, drain, weary; informal knock out, take it out of; Brit. informal knacker. **3** *they tired of his difficult behaviour:* weary, get tired, get fed up, get sick, get bored.

tired adjective **1** *tired from travelling:* exhausted, worn out, weary, fatigued, ready to drop, drained; informal all in, dead beat, shattered; Brit. informal knackered, whacked; N. Amer. informal pooped, tuckered out; Austral./NZ informal stonkered. **2** *are you tired of having him here?* fed up with, weary of, bored with/by, sick (and tired)

of; informal up to here with. **3** *tired jokes:* hackneyed, overused, stale, clichéd, predictable, unimaginative, unoriginal, dull, boring; informal corny.
OPPOSITES energetic, lively, fresh.

tiring adjective exhausting, wearying, taxing, draining, hard, arduous, strenuous, onerous, gruelling; informal killing; Brit. informal knackering.

title noun **1** *the title of the article:* heading, label, inscription, caption, subheading, legend. **2** *the title of Duke of Marlborough:* name, designation, form of address, rank, office, position; informal moniker, handle. **3** *an Olympic title:* championship,

titration noun the calculation of the amount of a substance in a solution by measuring the volume of a reagent required to react with it.

titter verb (**titters, tittering, tittered**) laugh quietly. •noun a short, quiet laugh.

tittle-tattle noun gossip.

titular /tit-yuu-ler/ adjective **1** holding a formal position or title without any real authority. **2** relating to a title.

tizzy noun (plural **tizzies**) informal a state of nervous excitement or worry.

TNT abbreviation trinitrotoluene, a high explosive.

to preposition **1** expressing direction or position in relation to a particular location, point, or condition. **2** Brit. (in telling the time) before the hour mentioned. **3** identifying the person or thing affected by an action. **4** identifying a particular relationship between one person or thing and another. **5** indicating a rate of return on something: *ten miles to the gallon.* **6** indicating that two things are attached. •infinitive marker used with the base form of a verb to indicate that the verb is in the infinitive. •adverb so as to be closed or nearly closed. □ **to and fro** backwards and forwards or from side to side. **to-do** informal a fuss or commotion.

> ! don't confuse **to** with **too** or **two**. **To** mainly means 'in the direction of' (as in *the next train to London*), while **too** means 'excessively' (as in *she was driving too fast*) or 'in addition', and **two** is the number meaning 'one less than three'.

toad noun an amphibian with a short body, short legs, and no tail.

toadstool noun a fungus with a rounded cap on a stalk.

toady noun (plural **toadies**) a person who is too polite and respectful to someone in order to gain their favour. •verb (**toadies, toadying, toadied**) act in a way that is too polite and respectful.

toast noun **1** sliced bread that has been held against a source of heat until it is brown and crisp. **2** an act of raising glasses at a gathering and drinking together in honour of a person or thing. **3** a person who is greatly respected or admired. •verb **1** make bread brown and crisp by holding it against a source of heat. **2** drink a toast to.

toaster noun an electrical device for making

toast.

tobacco noun (plural **tobaccos**) a preparation of the dried nicotine-rich leaves of an American plant, used for smoking or chewing.

tobacconist noun Brit. a shopkeeper who sells cigarettes and tobacco.

toboggan noun a light, narrow vehicle on runners, used for sliding downhill over snow or ice. ■ **tobogganist** noun.

toccata /tuh-kah-tuh/ noun a piece of music for a keyboard instrument designed to show the performer's skill and technique.

tod noun (**on your tod**) Brit. informal on your own.

today adverb **1** on or in the course of this present day. **2** at the present period of time. •noun **1** this present day. **2** the present period of time.

toddle verb (**toddles, toddling, toddled**) **1** (of a young child) move with short unsteady steps while learning to walk. **2** informal walk or go about in a leisurely way.

toddler noun a young child who is just beginning to walk.

toddy noun (plural **toddies**) a drink of spirits mixed with hot water.

toe noun **1** any of the five digits at the end of the foot. **2** the lower end, tip, or point of something. □ **on your toes** ready and alert. **toe the line** be obedient.

toecap noun a piece of steel or leather fitted over the front part of a boot or shoe.

toehold noun a small foothold.

toenail noun a nail on the upper surface of the tip of each toe.

toff noun Brit. informal, disapproving a rich, upper-class person.

toffee noun a kind of firm sweet which softens when sucked or chewed, made by boiling together sugar and butter. □ **toffee-nosed** Brit. informal snobbish.

tofu /toh-foo/ noun a soft white substance made from mashed soya beans.

tog[1] informal noun (**togs**) clothes. •verb (**be togged up**) be fully dressed for a particular occasion or activity.

tog[2] noun Brit. a unit for measuring the warmth of duvets or quilts.

toga noun a loose outer garment made of a

THESAURUS

crown, first place.

toast noun **1** *he raised his glass in a toast:* tribute, salutation; old use pledge. **2** *he was the toast of the West End:* darling, favourite, pet, heroine, hero, talk; Brit.

informal blue-eyed boy/girl.
•verb *we toasted the couple with champagne:* drink (to) the health of, salute, honour, pay tribute to; old use pledge.

single piece of cloth, worn in ancient
Rome.

together adverb **1** with or near to another
person or people. **2** so as to touch,
combine, or be united. **3** regarded as a
whole. **4** (of two people) married or in a
sexual relationship. **5** at the same time.
6 without interruption. • adjective informal
level-headed and well organized.
■ **togetherness** noun.

toggle noun a narrow piece of wood or
plastic attached to a garment, pushed
through a loop to act as a fastener.

Togolese /toh-guh-**leez**/ noun (plural
Togolese) a person from Togo, a country in
West Africa. • adjective relating to Togo.

toil verb **1** work very hard. **2** move
somewhere slowly and with difficulty.
• noun exhausting work.

toilet noun **1** a large bowl for urinating or
defecating into. **2** old use the process of
washing yourself, dressing, brushing your
hair, etc.
□ **toilet bag** Brit. a waterproof bag for
toothpaste, soap, etc., used when
travelling. **toilet-train** teach a young child
to use the toilet. **toilet water** a diluted
form of perfume.

toiletries plural noun articles used in

washing and taking care of your body, such
as soap and shampoo.

token noun **1** a thing that represents a
feeling, fact, or quality. **2** a voucher that
can be exchanged for goods or services. **3** a
disc used to operate a machine. • adjective
involving little effort or commitment and
done only for show.

tokenism noun the practice of doing
something in a superficial way, so as to be
seen to be obeying the law or satisfying a
particular group of people.
■ **tokenistic** adjective.

told past and past participle of TELL.

tolerable adjective **1** able to be tolerated.
2 fairly good.
■ **tolerably** adverb.

tolerance noun **1** the ability to accept
things you do not like or agree with. **2** an
allowable amount of variation in the
dimensions of a machine or part.

tolerant adjective **1** able to accept things
you do not like or agree with. **2** able to
cope with particular conditions.

tolerate verb (**tolerates, tolerating,
tolerated**) **1** allow someone to do
something you do not like or agree with.
2 patiently accept something unpleasant.
3 be able to be exposed to a drug, toxin,

together adverb **1** *friends who work
together:* with each other, in conjunction,
jointly, in cooperation, in collaboration, in
partnership, in combination, in league, side
by side; informal in cahoots. **2** *they both spoke
together:* simultaneously, at the same time,
at once, concurrently, as a group, in
unison, in chorus.
OPPOSITES separately, successively.
• adjective (informal) *she looks a very together
young woman:* level-headed, well adjusted,
sensible, practical, realistic, mature, stable,
full of common sense, well organized,
efficient, methodical, self-confident, self-
assured; informal unflappable.
OPPOSITES disorganized.

toil verb **1** *she toiled all night:* work, labour,
slave, strive; informal slog, beaver; Brit. informal
graft. **2** *she began to toil up the path:*
struggle, drag yourself, trudge, slog, plod;
N. Amer. informal schlep.
OPPOSITES rest, relax.
• noun *a life of toil:* hard work, labour,
exertion, slaving, drudgery, effort, {blood,
sweat, and tears}; informal slog, elbow
grease; Brit. informal graft.

toilet noun lavatory, WC, (public)
convenience, cloakroom, powder room,
latrine, privy, urinal; N. Amer. bathroom,
washroom, rest room, men's/ladies' room,
comfort station; Brit. informal loo, the Ladies,
the Gents; N. Amer. informal can, john; Austral./NZ

informal dunny.

token noun **1** *a token of our appreciation:*
symbol, sign, emblem, badge, mark,
representation, indication, expression,
demonstration. **2** *a book token:* voucher,
coupon, note.
• adjective *token resistance:* symbolic,
nominal, perfunctory, slight, minimal,
superficial, emblematic, indicative.

tolerance noun **1** *an attitude of tolerance
towards people:* acceptance, open-
mindedness, broad-mindedness,
forbearance, patience, charity,
understanding. **2** *the plant's tolerance of
pollution:* endurance, resilience, resistance,
immunity. **3** *a 1% maximum tolerance in
measurement:* deviation, variation, play,
inaccuracy, imprecision.

tolerant adjective open-minded, forbearing,
broad-minded, liberal, unprejudiced,
unbiased, patient, long-suffering,
understanding, charitable, lenient, easy-
going.
OPPOSITES intolerant, strict.

tolerate verb **1** *a regime unwilling to
tolerate dissent:* allow, permit, condone,
accept, swallow, countenance. **2** *he couldn't
tolerate her moods any longer:* endure, put
up with, bear, take, stand, support,
stomach, abide; Brit. informal stick.

t

etc. without a bad reaction.
■ **toleration** noun.

toll[1] noun **1** a charge you have to pay for the use of certain roads or bridges. **2** the number of deaths or casualties arising from an accident, war, etc. **3** the cost or damage resulting from something.

toll[2] verb (of a bell) sound with slow, even strokes, especially as a sign that someone has died. •noun a single ring of a bell.

tom or **tomcat** noun a male domestic cat.

tomahawk noun a light axe used in the past by American Indians.

tomato noun (plural **tomatoes**) a red fruit eaten as a vegetable or in salads.

☑ no e on the end: tomato.

tomb noun **1** a burial place consisting of a stone structure built above ground, or an underground vault. **2** a monument to a dead person, built over their burial place.

tombola noun Brit. a game in which tickets are drawn from a revolving drum to win prizes.

tomboy noun a girl who enjoys rough, noisy activities traditionally associated with boys.
■ **tomboyish** adjective.

tombstone noun a flat stone with an inscription, standing or laid over a grave.

tome noun a large, serious book.

tomfoolery noun silly behaviour.

tomography /tuh-**mog**-ruh-fi/ noun a technique for seeing a cross section through a human body or other solid object using X-rays or ultrasound.
■ **tomographic** adjective.

tomorrow adverb on the day after today. •noun **1** the day after today. **2** the future.

☑ one m, two rs: tomorrow.

tom-tom noun a drum beaten with the hands.

ton /tun/ noun **1** (also **long ton**) a unit of weight equal to 2,240 lb avoirdupois (1016.05 kg). **2** (also **short ton**) N. Amer. a unit of weight equal to 2,000 lb avoirdupois (907.19 kg). **3** a metric ton. **4** a unit of measurement of a ship's weight equal to 2,240 lb or 35 cubic feet (0.99 cubic metres). **5** (also **tons**) informal a large number or amount. **6** Brit. informal a speed of one hundred miles per hour.

tonal adjective **1** relating to tone. **2** (of music) written using traditional keys and harmony.
■ **tonality** noun **tonally** adverb.

tone noun **1** the quality of a musical sound. **2** the feeling or mood expressed in a person's voice. **3** general character. **4** a particular brightness, deepness, or shade in a colour. **5** firmness in a resting muscle. **6** a basic interval in classical Western music, equal to two semitones. •verb (**tones, toning, toned**) **1** (often **tone something up**) give greater strength or firmness to a part of your body. **2** (**tone something down**) make a statement or piece of writing less harsh, extreme, or strong.
□ **tone deaf** unable to hear differences in musical pitch.

toner noun **1** a liquid applied to the skin to reduce oiliness. **2** a type of powder or ink used in photocopiers.

tongs plural noun a tool with two arms that are joined at one end, used for picking up and holding things.

tongue noun **1** the fleshy organ in the mouth, used for tasting, licking, swallowing, and speaking. **2** a person's way of speaking: *a sharp tongue*. **3** a language. **4** a strip of leather or fabric under the laces in a shoe.
□ **tongue and groove** wooden boards which are joined by means of interlocking ridges and grooves down their sides. **tongue-tied** too shy or embarrassed to speak. **tongue-twister** a sequence of words that are difficult to pronounce. **with tongue in cheek** not seriously meaning what you are saying.

tonic noun **1** a drink taken as a kind of

THESAURUS

t

toll[1] noun **1** *a motorway toll:* charge, fee, payment, levy, tariff, tax. **2** *the toll of dead and injured:* number, count, tally, total, sum. **3** *the toll on the environment has been high:* harm, damage, hurt, injury, detriment, adverse effect, cost, price, loss.

toll[2] verb *I heard the bell toll:* ring, sound, clang, chime, strike, peal.

tomb noun burial chamber, vault, crypt, catacomb, sepulchre, mausoleum, grave.

tone noun **1** *the tone of the tuba:* sound, timbre, voice, colour, tonality. **2** *the impatient tone of his letter:* mood, air, feel, flavour, note, attitude, character. **3** *a*

dialling tone: note, signal, bleep. **4** *tones of lavender and rose:* shade, colour, hue, tint, tinge.
•verb *the shirt toned well with her cream skirt:* harmonize, go, blend, coordinate, team, match, suit, complement.
□ **tone something down 1** *the colour needs to be toned down:* soften, lighten, mute, subdue. **2** *the papers refused to tone down their criticism:* moderate, modify, temper, soften, modulate.

tonic noun stimulant, boost, restorative, refresher, fillip; informal shot in the arm, pick-me-up, bracer.

medicine, to make you feel energetic and healthy. **2** something that makes you feel happier or healthier. **3** (also **tonic water**) a fizzy drink with a slightly bitter flavour, often mixed with gin.

tonight adverb on the evening or night of the present day. • noun the evening or night of the present day.

tonnage noun **1** weight in tons. **2** the size or carrying capacity of a ship measured in tons.

tonne /tun/ noun a metric ton.

tonsil noun each of two small masses of tissue in the throat.

tonsillectomy noun (plural **tonsillectomies**) an operation to remove the tonsils.

tonsillitis noun inflammation of the tonsils.

tonsure noun a circular area on a monk's or priest's head where the hair is shaved off.

too adverb **1** to a higher degree than is desirable, allowed, or possible; excessively. **2** in addition.

> **!** don't confuse **too** with **to** or **two**: see the note at **TO**.

took past of **TAKE**.

tool noun **1** an object or device used to carry out a particular function. **2** a thing that helps you to do your job or achieve something. • verb **1** impress a design on leather with a heated tool. **2** equip an organization with tools for industrial production.

toot noun a short sound made by a horn, trumpet, or similar instrument. • verb make a toot.

tooth noun (plural **teeth**) **1** each of the hard white projections in the mouth, used for biting and chewing. **2** a projecting part such as a cog on a gearwheel or a point on a saw or comb.
■ **toothed** adjective **toothless** adjective.

toothache noun pain in a tooth.

toothbrush noun a small long-handled brush for cleaning your teeth.

toothpaste noun a paste for cleaning the teeth.

toothpick noun a thin, pointed piece of wood or plastic for removing bits of food from between your teeth.

toothsome adjective **1** (of food) appetizing or tasty. **2** informal attractive.

toothy adjective having large or prominent teeth.

tootle verb (**tootles, tootling, tootled**) **1** make a series of sounds on a horn, trumpet, etc. **2** walk or drive somewhere without hurrying.

top[1] noun **1** the highest or uppermost point, part, or surface. **2** a thing placed on, fitted to, or covering the upper part of something. **3** (**the top**) the highest or most important level or position. **4** the utmost degree. **5** a garment covering the upper part of the body. • adjective highest in position, status, or degree. • verb (**tops, topping, topped**) **1** be more, better, or taller than. **2** be at the highest place or rank in. **3** reach the top of a hill or rise. **4** provide with a top or topping.
□ **on top of 1** so as to cover. **2** in command or control of. **3** in addition to. **over the top** Brit. informal excessive or exaggerated. **top hat** a man's tall formal black hat. **top-heavy** too heavy at the top and therefore likely to fall. **top something up 1** add to a number or amount to bring it up to a certain level. **2** fill up a partly full container.

top[2] noun a toy shaped like a cone with a point at the base, that can be made to spin.

topaz noun a colourless yellow or pale blue precious stone.

topcoat noun **1** an overcoat. **2** an outer coat of paint.

THESAURUS

too adverb **1** *invasion would be too risky:* excessively, overly, unduly, immoderately, inordinately, unreasonably, extremely, very. **2** *he was unhappy, too, you know:* also, as well, in addition, into the bargain, besides, furthermore, moreover.

tool noun implement, utensil, instrument, device, apparatus, gadget, appliance, machine, contrivance, contraption; informal gizmo.

top noun **1** *the top of the cliff:* summit, peak, pinnacle, crest, crown, brow, head, tip, apex. **2** *the top of the coffee jar:* lid, cap, cover. **3** *he was at the top of his profession:* height, peak, pinnacle, zenith, culmination, climax, prime.
OPPOSITES bottom, base.
• adjective **1** *the top floor:* highest, topmost,

uppermost. **2** *top scientists:* foremost, leading, principal, pre-eminent, greatest, best, finest, elite. **3** *the organization's top management:* chief, principal, main, leading, highest, ruling, commanding, most powerful, most important. **4** *a top hotel:* prime, premier, excellent, superior, choice, select, five-star, grade A, best, finest. **5** *at top speed:* maximum, greatest, utmost.
OPPOSITES bottom, lowest, minimum.
• verb **1** *sales topped £1 billion:* exceed, surpass, go beyond, better, beat, outstrip, outdo, outshine, eclipse. **2** *their CD is currently topping the charts:* lead, head, be at the top of. **3** *mousse topped with cream:* cover, cap, coat, finish, garnish.
□ **top something up** fill, refill, refresh, freshen, replenish, recharge, resupply.

t

topiary noun (plural **topiaries**) **1** the art of clipping evergreen shrubs into interesting shapes. **2** shrubs clipped in this way.

topic noun a subject that you talk, write, or learn about.

topical adjective **1** relating to or dealing with current affairs. **2** relating to a particular subject.
■ **topicality** noun **topically** adverb.

topknot noun a knot of hair arranged on the top of the head.

topless adjective having the breasts uncovered.

topography noun **1** the arrangement of the physical features of an area of land. **2** the representation of these features on a map.
■ **topographical** (or **topographic**) adjective.

topping noun a layer of food poured or spread over another food.

topple verb (**topples**, **toppling**, **toppled**) **1** overbalance and fall down. **2** remove a government or leader from power.

topsoil noun the top layer of soil.

topspin noun a fast forward spin given to a moving ball.

topsy-turvy adjective & adverb **1** upside down. **2** in a state of confusion.

tor noun a small steep hill or rocky peak.

Torah /**tor**-uh, tor-**ah**/ noun (in Judaism) the law of God as revealed to Moses and recorded in the Pentateuch.

torch noun **1** Brit. a portable lamp powered by a battery. **2** (in the past) a piece of wood or cloth soaked in fat and set on fire.
• verb informal set fire to.

tore past of TEAR¹.

toreador noun a bullfighter.

torment noun /**tor**-ment/ **1** great suffering. **2** a cause of suffering. • verb /tor-**ment**/ **1** make someone suffer very much. **2** annoy or tease in a cruel or unkind way.
■ **tormentor** noun.

torn past participle of TEAR¹.

tornado noun (plural **tornadoes** or **tornados**) a violent rotating wind storm.

torpedo noun (plural **torpedoes**) a long narrow underwater missile. • verb (**torpedoes**, **torpedoing**, **torpedoed**) attack using torpedoes.

torpid adjective inactive and having no energy.
■ **torpidity** noun.

torpor noun the state of being inactive and having no energy.

torque /tork/ noun a force causing rotation.

torrent noun **1** a strong, fast-moving stream of water or other liquid. **2** a large outpouring.

torrential adjective (of rain) falling rapidly and heavily.

torrid adjective **1** very hot and dry. **2** full of sexual passion. **3** full of difficulty.

torsion noun the state of being twisted.

torso noun (plural **torsos**) the trunk of the human body.

tort noun Law a wrongful act or a violation of a right.

tortellini /tor-tuhl-**lee**-ni/ plural noun stuffed pasta parcels rolled into small rings.

tortilla /tor-**tee**-yuh/ noun **1** (in Mexican cookery) a thin, flat maize pancake. **2** (in Spanish cookery) an omelette.

tortoise /**tor**-tuhss/ noun a slow-moving reptile with a hard, round shell into which it can draw its head and legs.

tortoiseshell noun **1** the semi-transparent mottled yellow and brown shell of certain turtles, used to make jewellery or ornaments. **2** a domestic cat with markings resembling tortoiseshell. **3** a butterfly with mottled orange, yellow, and black markings.

tortuous adjective **1** full of twists and turns.

THESAURUS

topic noun subject, theme, issue, matter, point, question, concern, argument, thesis.

topical adjective current, up to date, up to the minute, contemporary, recent, relevant, in the news.
OPPOSITES out of date.

topple verb **1** she toppled off the chair: fall, tumble, tip, overbalance, overturn, keel over, lose your balance. **2** protesters toppled a statue: knock over, upset, push over, tip over, upend. **3** a plot to topple the government: overthrow, oust, unseat, overturn, bring down, defeat, get rid of, dislodge, eject.

torment noun emotional torment: agony, suffering, torture, pain, anguish, misery, distress, trauma.
• verb **1** she was tormented by shame: torture, afflict, rack, harrow, plague, haunt, distress, agonize. **2** she began to torment the boys: tease, taunt, bait, provoke, harass, bother, persecute; informal needle.

torn adjective **1** a torn shirt: ripped, rent, cut, slit, ragged, tattered. **2** she was torn between the two options: wavering, vacillating, irresolute, dithering, uncertain, unsure, undecided, in two minds.

tornado noun whirlwind, cyclone, typhoon, storm, hurricane; N. Amer. informal twister.

torrent noun **1** a torrent of water: flood, deluge, spate, cascade, rush. **2** a torrent of abuse: outburst, outpouring, stream, flood, volley, barrage, tide.
OPPOSITES trickle.

2 very long and complicated.
■ **tortuously** adverb.

torture noun 1 severe pain inflicted on someone, especially to make them say something. 2 great suffering or anxiety. • verb (**tortures, torturing, tortured**) subject someone to torture.
■ **torturer** noun **torturous** adjective.

Tory noun (plural **Tories**) a member or supporter of the British Conservative Party.

toss verb 1 throw lightly or casually. 2 move something from side to side or backwards and forwards. 3 jerk your head or hair backwards. 4 throw a coin into the air and see which side is facing upwards when it lands, using this to help decide something. 5 shake or turn food in a liquid to coat it lightly. • noun an act of tossing.
□ **toss-up** 2 a situation in which any of two or more outcomes is equally possible. 1 the tossing of a coin to make a decision.

tot¹ noun 1 a very young child. 2 Brit. a small drink of spirits.

tot² verb (**tots, totting, totted**) (**tot something up**) Brit. add up numbers or amounts.

total adjective 1 consisting of the whole number or amount. 2 complete. • noun a total number or amount. • verb (**totals, totalling, totalled**; US spelling **totals, totaling, totaled**) 1 amount to a total

number. 2 find the total of.
■ **totality** noun **totally** adverb.

totalitarian adjective (of a system of government) consisting of only one leader or party and having complete power and control over the people.
■ **totalitarianism** noun.

totalizator or **totalisator** noun 1 a device showing the number of bets and amount of money staked on a race. 2 the system of betting based on this; the tote.

tote¹ noun (**the tote**) informal a system of betting based on the use of the totalizator, in which winnings are calculated according to the amount staked rather than odds offered.

tote² verb (**totes, toting, toted**) informal carry.

totem noun a natural object or animal believed to have spiritual meaning and adopted as an emblem by a particular society.
□ **totem pole** a pole on which totems are hung or on which images of totems are carved.
■ **totemic** adjective.

totter verb (**totters, tottering, tottered**) 1 move in an unsteady way. 2 shake or rock as if about to collapse.

toucan /too-kuhn/ noun a tropical bird with a massive bill and brightly coloured feathers.

touch verb 1 bring your fingers or another

THESAURUS

torture noun 1 *the torture of political prisoners:* abuse, ill-treatment, mistreatment, maltreatment, persecution, cruelty, atrocity. 2 *the torture of losing a loved one:* torment, agony, suffering, pain, anguish, misery, distress, heartbreak, trauma.
• verb 1 *the forces routinely tortured suspects:* abuse, ill-treat, mistreat, maltreat, persecute. 2 *he was tortured by grief:* torment, rack, afflict, harrow, plague, distress, trouble.

toss verb 1 *he tossed his tools into the boot:* throw, hurl, fling, sling, pitch, lob, launch; informal heave, chuck, bung. 2 *he tossed a coin:* flip, flick, spin. 3 *the ship tossed about on the waves:* pitch, lurch, rock, roll, plunge, reel, sway. 4 *toss the ingredients together:* mix, combine, stir, turn, shake.

total adjective 1 *the total cost:* entire, complete, whole, full, combined, aggregate, gross, overall. 2 *a total disaster:* utter, complete, absolute, thorough, perfect, downright, out-and-out, outright, sheer, unmitigated.
OPPOSITES partial, net.
• noun *a total of £16:* sum, aggregate, whole, entirety, totality.
• verb 1 *the prize money totalled £33,050:*

add up to, amount to, come to, run to, make. 2 *he totalled up his score:* add, count, reckon, tot up, compute, work out.

totally adverb completely, entirely, wholly, thoroughly, fully, utterly, absolutely, perfectly, unreservedly, unconditionally, downright, one hundred per cent.
OPPOSITES partly.

touch verb 1 *his feet touched the floor:* contact, meet, brush, graze, come up against, be in contact with, border, abut. 2 *he touched her cheek:* feel, pat, tap, stroke, fondle, caress, pet, handle. 3 *sales touched twenty grand:* reach, attain, come to, make, rise to, soar to, sink to, plummet to; informal hit. 4 *nobody can touch him when he's on form:* compare with, be on a par with, equal, match, rival, measure up to, better, beat; informal hold a candle to. 5 *you're not supposed to touch the computer:* handle, hold, pick up, move, use, meddle with, play about with, fiddle with, interfere with, tamper with, disturb. 6 *Lisa felt touched by her kindness:* affect, move, stir.
• noun 1 *her touch on his shoulder:* tap, pat, contact, stroke, caress. 2 *his political touch:* skill, expertise, dexterity, deftness, adroitness, adeptness, ability, talent, flair,

t

part of your body into contact with.
2 come into or be in physical contact with.
3 have an effect on. **4** (**be touched**) feel
moved with gratitude or sympathy because
of someone's actions or situation. **5** harm
or interfere with. **6** use or consume.
7 (**touched**) informal mad. •noun **1** an act or
way of touching. **2** the ability to become
aware of something and learn what it is
like through physical contact, especially
with the fingers. **3** a small amount. **4** a
distinctive detail or feature. **5** a distinctive
or skilful way of dealing with something.
□ **in touch 1** in or into communication.
2 having up-to-date knowledge. **out of
touch** lacking up-to-date knowledge or
awareness. **touch-and-go** (of a particular
outcome) possible but very uncertain.
touch down (of an aircraft or spacecraft)
land. **touch on** deal briefly with. **touch-type**
type using all of your fingers and without
needing to look at the keys. **touch
something up** make small improvements to
something.

touchdown noun **1** the moment at which
an aircraft touches down. **2** (in rugby) an
act of scoring by touching the ball down
behind the opponents' goal line.

touché /too-**shay**/ exclamation used to
acknowledge a good point made at your
own expense.

touching adjective making you feel
gratitude or sympathy; moving.

touchline noun (in football) the boundary
line on each side of the field.

touchstone noun a standard by which
something is judged.

touchy adjective **1** quick to take offence.
2 (of a situation or issue) needing careful
treatment.

tough adjective **1** strong enough to
withstand wear and tear. **2** able to deal
with pain or difficulty. **3** strict. **4** involving
problems or difficulties. **5** (of a person)
rough or violent. •noun informal a rough or
violent man.
■ **toughness** noun.

toughen verb make or become tough.

toupee /**too**-pay/ noun a small wig or
hairpiece worn to cover a bald spot.

tour noun **1** a journey for pleasure in which
several different places are visited. **2** a
short trip to view or inspect something. **3** a
series of plays, matches, etc. performed in
several different places. •verb make a tour
of.

tour de force /toor duh **forss**/ noun (plural
tours de force /toor duh **forss**/) a
performance or achievement accomplished
with great skill.

tourism noun the business of organizing
and operating holidays and visits to places
of interest.

tourist noun **1** a person who travels for
pleasure. **2** Brit. a member of a touring
sports team.

touristy adjective informal visited by a lot of
tourists.

tournament noun **1** a series of contests
between a number of competitors. **2** a
medieval sporting event in which knights
jousted with blunted weapons.

tourney /**toor**-ni, **ter**-ni/ noun (plural

THESAURUS

facility, proficiency, knack. **3** *there was a
touch of bitterness in her voice:* trace, bit,
suggestion, suspicion, hint, scintilla, tinge,
dash, taste, spot, drop, dab, soupçon. **4** *the
gas lights are a nice touch:* detail, feature,
point, element, addition. **5** *have you been
in touch with him?* contact,
communication, correspondence.
□ **touch on/upon refer to**, mention,
comment on, remark on, bring up, raise,
broach, allude to, cover, deal with.

touching adjective moving, affecting, heart-
warming, emotional, emotive, poignant,
sad, tear-jerking.

tough adjective **1** *tough leather:* durable,
strong, resilient, sturdy, rugged, solid,
stout, robust, hard-wearing, long-lasting,
heavy-duty, well built, made to last. **2** *he'll
survive—he's pretty tough:* robust,
resilient, strong, hardy, rugged, fit; informal
hard. **3** *tough sentencing for offenders:*
strict, stern, severe, stringent, rigorous,
hard, firm, hard-hitting, uncompromising.
4 *the training was pretty tough:* difficult,

hard, strenuous, onerous, gruelling,
exacting, arduous, demanding, taxing,
tiring, exhausting, punishing. **5** *tough
questions:* difficult, hard, knotty, thorny,
tricky.
OPPOSITES weak, lenient, light, easy.
•noun *a gang of toughs:* ruffian, thug,
hoodlum, hooligan, bully boy; Brit. rough;
informal heavy, bruiser; Brit. informal yob.

tour noun **1** *a three-day walking tour:* trip,
excursion, journey, expedition, jaunt,
outing, trek, safari. **2** *a tour of the factory:*
visit, inspection, walkabout.
•verb **1** *this hotel is well placed for touring
Devon:* travel round, explore, holiday in;
informal do. **2** *the Prince toured a local
factory:* visit, inspect, go round, walk
round.

tourist noun holidaymaker, traveller,
sightseer, visitor, backpacker, globetrotter,
tripper; N. Amer. vacationer.
OPPOSITES local.

tournament noun competition, contest,
championship, meeting, event.

tourneys) a joust or tournament.

tourniquet /**toor**-ni-kay, **tor**-ni-kay/ noun a cord or tight bandage tied round a limb to stop the flow of blood through an artery.

tousle verb (**tousles, tousling, tousled**) make someone's hair untidy.

tout /towt/ verb **1** try to sell. **2** try to persuade people of something's value. **3** Brit. resell a ticket for a popular event at a higher price than you paid for it. •noun a person who buys up tickets for an event to resell them at a profit.

tow verb use a vehicle or boat to pull another vehicle or boat along. •noun an act of towing.
□ in tow **1** (also **on tow**) being towed. **2** accompanying or following someone.

towards or **toward** preposition **1** in the direction of. **2** getting nearer to. **3** in relation to. **4** contributing to the cost of.

towel noun a piece of absorbent cloth used for drying. •verb (**towels, towelling, towelled**; US spelling **towels, toweling, toweled**) dry someone or something with a towel.

towelling (US spelling **toweling**) noun absorbent cloth used for towels.

tower noun **1** a tall, narrow building or part of a building, especially of a church or castle. **2** a tall structure containing special equipment. •verb (**towers, towering, towered**) **1** rise to or reach a great height. **2** (**towering**) very important or influential. **3** (**towering**) very great: *a towering rage.*
□ **tower block** Brit. a tall modern building containing many floors of offices or flats.

town noun **1** a settlement larger than a village and generally smaller than a city. **2** the central part of a town or city containing its shopping area.
□ **go to town** informal do something thoroughly or enthusiastically. **town crier** (in the past) a person employed to shout out public announcements in the streets.

town hall the building where local government offices are located.

township noun (in South Africa) a suburb or city occupied chiefly by black people.

towpath noun a path beside a river or canal, originally used as a pathway for horses towing barges.

toxaemia /tok-**see**-mi-uh/ (US spelling **toxemia**) noun a form of blood poisoning.

toxic adjective **1** poisonous. **2** relating to or caused by poison.
■ **toxicity** noun.

toxicology noun the branch of science concerned with how poisons work.
■ **toxicologist** noun.

toxin noun a poison caused by a germ, to which the body reacts by producing antibodies.

toy noun an object for a child to play with. •verb (**toy with**) **1** casually consider an idea. **2** fiddle with something. •adjective (of a breed of dog) very small.
□ **toy boy** Brit. informal a male lover who is much younger than his partner.

trace verb (**traces, tracing, traced**) **1** find by careful investigation. **2** find or describe the origin or development of. **3** follow the course or position of something with your eye or finger. **4** copy something by drawing over its lines on a piece of transparent paper placed on top of it. **5** draw a pattern or outline. •noun **1** a mark or other sign of the existence or passing of something. **2** a very small amount. **3** a barely noticeable indication. **4** a line or pattern on paper or a screen showing information recorded by a machine.
□ **trace element** a chemical element that is present in tiny amounts.

THESAURUS

tow verb pull, haul, drag, draw, tug, lug.

towards preposition **1** *they were driving towards her flat:* in the direction of, to, on the way to, on the road to. **2** *towards evening dark clouds gathered:* just before, shortly before, near, around, approaching, getting on for. **3** *her attitude towards politics:* with regard to, regarding, in/with regard to, in relation to, concerning, about, apropos.

tower verb *snow-capped peaks towered over the valley:* soar, rise, rear, overshadow, overhang, hang over, dominate.

toxic adjective poisonous, dangerous, harmful, injurious, noxious, pernicious, deadly, lethal.
OPPOSITES harmless.

toy noun *playing with their toys:* plaything, game.
•adjective *a toy gun:* model, imitation, replica, miniature.
□ **toy with 1** *I was toying with the idea:* think about, consider, flirt with, entertain the possibility of; informal kick around. **2** *Adam toyed with his glasses:* fiddle with, play with, fidget with, twiddle, finger.

trace verb **1** *police hope to trace the owner:* track down, find, discover, detect, unearth, turn up, hunt down, ferret out, run to ground. **2** *she traced a pattern in the sand:* draw, outline, mark.
•noun **1** *no trace had been found of the missing plane:* sign, mark, indication, evidence, clue, vestige, remains, remnant. **2** *a trace of bitterness crept into her voice:* bit, touch, hint, suggestion, suspicion, shadow, dash, tinge; informal smidgen, tad.

t

tracer noun a bullet or shell whose course is made visible by a trail of flames or smoke.

tracery noun (plural **traceries**) **1** a decorative design of holes and outlines in stone. **2** a delicate branching pattern.

trachea /truh-kee-uh/ noun (plural **tracheae** /truh-kee-ee/ or **tracheas**) the tube carrying air between the larynx and the lungs; the windpipe.

tracheotomy /tra-ki-ot-uh-mi/ or **tracheostomy** /tra-ki-oss-tuh-mi/ noun (plural **tracheotomies**) a surgical cut in the windpipe, made to enable someone to breathe when their windpipe is blocked.

track noun **1** a rough path or small road. **2** a course or circuit for racing. **3** a line of marks left on the ground by a person, animal, or vehicle as they move along. **4** a continuous line of rails on a railway. **5** a section of a CD, record, or cassette tape containing one song or piece of music. **6** a strip or rail along which something may be moved. • verb **1** follow the trail or movements of. **2** (**track someone/thing down**) find someone or something after a thorough search. **3** follow a particular course. **4** (of a camera) move along with the subject being filmed. □ **keep** (or **lose**) **track of** keep (or fail to keep) fully aware of or informed about. **on the right** (or **wrong**) **track** following a course that is likely to result in success (or failure). **track events** athletic events that take place on a running track. **track record** someone's past achievements. ■ **tracker** noun.

tracksuit noun an outfit consisting of a sweatshirt and loose trousers.

tract¹ noun **1** a large area of land. **2** a system of connected organs or tissues in the body along which something passes.

tract² noun a short piece of religious writing in the form of a pamphlet.

tractable adjective **1** (of a person) easy to

control or influence. **2** (of a difficulty) easy to resolve.

traction noun **1** the action of pulling a thing along a surface. **2** the power used in pulling. **3** a way of treating a broken bone by gradually pulling it back into position. **4** the grip of a tyre on a road or a wheel on a rail. □ **traction engine** a steam or diesel-powered road vehicle used for pulling heavy loads.

tractor noun a powerful motor vehicle with large rear wheels, used for pulling farm machinery.

trade noun **1** the buying and selling of goods and services. **2** a particular area of commercial activity. **3** a job requiring special skills and training. • verb (**trades, trading, traded**) **1** buy and sell goods and services. **2** exchange. **3** (**trade something in**) exchange a used article as part of the payment for another. **4** (**trade on**) take advantage of. **5** (**trade something off**) exchange something of value as part of a compromise. □ **trade union** (or Brit. **trades union**) an association formed within an industry or particular workplace to protect the rights of the workers. **trade wind** a wind blowing steadily towards the equator. ■ **trader** noun.

trademark noun **1** a symbol, word, or words chosen to represent a company or product. **2** a distinctive characteristic.

tradesman noun (plural **tradesmen**) **1** a person who has a small shop. **2** a person working at a skilled trade.

tradition noun **1** the passing on of customs or beliefs from generation to generation. **2** a long-established custom or belief passed on in this way. **3** a method or style established by an artist, writer, or movement, and followed by others.

traditional adjective having to do with or

THESAURUS

track noun **1** *a gravel track:* path, footpath, lane, trail, route. **2** *the final lap of the track:* course, racecourse, racetrack, velodrome; Brit. circuit. **3** *he found the tracks of a fox:* traces, marks, prints, footprints, trail, spoor. **4** *the railway tracks:* rail, line. **5** *the album's title track:* song, recording, number, piece.
• verb *he tracked a bear for 40 km:* follow, trail, pursue, shadow, stalk; informal tail. □ **track someone/something down discover**, find, detect, hunt down, unearth, uncover, turn up, dig up, ferret out, run to ground.

trade noun **1** *the trade in stolen cattle:* dealing, buying and selling, commerce, traffic, business. **2** *the glazier's trade:*

occupation, work, craft, job, career, profession, business, line (of work), métier.
• verb **1** *he made his fortune trading in diamonds:* deal, do business, bargain, negotiate, traffic, buy and sell. **2** *the business is trading at a loss:* operate, run, do business, deal. **3** *I traded the old machine for a newer model:* swap, exchange, barter, part-exchange.

trader noun dealer, merchant, buyer, seller, vendor, purveyor, supplier, trafficker.

tradition noun custom, practice, convention, ritual, observance, way, usage, habit, institution, unwritten law; formal praxis.

traditional adjective customary, long-

following tradition.
■ **traditionally** adverb.

traditionalism noun the upholding of tradition, especially so as to resist change.
■ **traditionalist** noun & adjective.

traduce verb (**traduces**, **traducing**, **traduced**) formal say things about someone that are unpleasant or untrue.

traffic noun 1 vehicles moving on public roads. 2 the movement of ships or aircraft. 3 the commercial transportation of goods or passengers. 4 the messages or signals sent through a communications system. 5 the action of trading in something illegal. •verb (**trafficks**, **trafficking**, **trafficked**) buy or sell something illegal. □ **traffic jam** a congestion in the flow of traffic so that it is at or almost at a standstill. **traffic lights** a set of automatically operated lights for controlling the flow of traffic. **traffic warden** Brit. an official who locates and reports on cars breaking parking regulations.
■ **trafficker** noun.

tragedian /truh-jee-di-uhn/ noun 1 a person who writes tragedies for the theatre. 2 a person who acts in tragedies.

tragedy noun (plural **tragedies**) 1 a very sad event or situation. 2 a serious play with an unhappy ending.

tragic adjective 1 very sad. 2 relating to tragedy in a literary work.
■ **tragically** adverb.

tragicomedy noun (plural **tragicomedies**) a play or novel containing elements of both comedy and tragedy.
■ **tragicomic** adjective.

trail noun 1 a line of marks or signs left behind by someone or something as it moves along. 2 a track or scent used in following someone or hunting an animal. 3 a path through rough country. 4 a route planned or followed for a particular purpose. 5 a long thin part stretching behind or hanging down from something. •verb 1 draw or be drawn along behind. 2 follow the trail of. 3 walk or move slowly or wearily. 4 (**trail away** or **off**) become gradually quieter and then stop. 5 be losing to an opponent in a contest. 6 (of a plant) grow along the ground or so as to hang down.

trailblazer noun 1 a person who is the first to do something new. 2 a person who finds a new way through wild country.
■ **trailblazing** adjective.

trailer noun 1 an unpowered vehicle pulled by another. 2 the rear section of an articulated truck. 3 N. Amer. a caravan. 4 an extract from a film or programme used to advertise it.

train verb 1 teach a person or animal a particular skill or type of behaviour. 2 be taught a particular skill. 3 make or become physically fit through a course of exercise. 4 (**train something on**) point something at. 5 make a plant grow in a particular direction or into a required shape. •noun 1 a series of railway carriages or wagons

---

established, time-honoured, classic, wonted, accustomed, standard, regular, normal, conventional, habitual, ritual, age-old, folk.

traffic noun 1 *the increased use of railways for goods traffic:* transport, freight, shipping. 2 *the traffic in stolen art:* trade, dealing, commerce, business, buying and selling.
•verb *he confessed to trafficking in ivory:* trade, deal, do business, buy and sell.

tragedy noun disaster, calamity, catastrophe, cataclysm, misfortune, adversity.

tragic adjective 1 *a tragic accident:* disastrous, calamitous, catastrophic, cataclysmic, devastating, terrible, dreadful, awful, appalling, horrendous, fatal. 2 *a tragic tale:* sad, unhappy, pathetic, moving, distressing, painful, harrowing, heart-rending, sorry.
OPPOSITES fortunate, happy.

trail noun 1 *a trail of clues:* series, string, chain, succession, sequence. 2 *wolves on the trail of their prey:* track, spoor, path,

scent, traces, marks, signs, prints, footprints. 3 *the plane's vapour trail:* wake, tail, stream. 4 *nature trails:* path, way, footpath, track, route.
•verb 1 *her robe trailed along the ground:* drag, sweep, be drawn, dangle. 2 *the roses trailed over the banks:* hang, droop, fall, spill, cascade. 3 *Sharpe suspected they were trailing him:* follow, pursue, track, shadow, stalk, hunt; informal tail. 4 *the defending champions were trailing 10–5:* lose, be down, be behind, lag behind.
OPPOSITES lead.

train verb 1 *an engineer trained in remote-sensing techniques:* instruct, teach, coach, tutor, school, educate, prime, drill, ground. 2 *she's training to be a hairdresser:* study, learn, prepare, take instruction. 3 *with the Olympics in mind, athletes are training hard:* exercise, work out, get into shape, practise. 4 *she trained the gun on him:* aim, point, direct, level, focus.
•noun *a bizarre train of events:* chain, string, series, sequence, succession, set, course.

t

moved by a locomotive. **2** a number of vehicles or animals moving in a line. **3** a series of connected events, thoughts, etc. **4** a long piece of trailing material attached to the back of a formal dress or robe. □ **in train** in progress.

trainee noun a person undergoing training for a job or profession.

trainer noun **1** a person who trains people or animals. **2** Brit. a soft shoe for sports or casual wear.

trainspotter noun Brit. a person who collects locomotive numbers as a hobby.
■ **trainspotting** noun.

traipse verb (**traipses, traipsing, traipsed**) walk or move wearily or reluctantly. • noun a boring walk.

trait /trayt, tray/ noun a distinguishing quality or characteristic.

traitor noun a person who betrays their country, an organization, or a cause.
■ **traitorous** adjective.

trajectory noun (plural **trajectories**) the path followed by a moving object.

tram or **tramcar** noun Brit. a passenger vehicle powered by electricity and running on rails laid in a road.

tramlines plural noun rails for a tram.

trammel noun (**trammels**) literary restrictions on someone's freedom. • verb (**trammels, trammelling, trammelled**; US spelling **trammels, trammeling, trammeled**) restrict or limit.

tramp noun **1** a homeless person who travels around and lives by begging or doing casual work. **2** the sound of heavy steps. **3** a long walk. **4** N. Amer. informal a woman who has a lot of sexual partners. • verb **1** walk heavily or noisily. **2** walk over a long distance.

trample verb (**tramples, trampling, trampled**) **1** tread on and crush. **2** (**trample**

on or **over**) treat with contempt.

trampoline noun a strong fabric sheet connected by springs to a frame, used as a springboard and landing area in doing acrobatic or gymnastic exercises.
■ **trampolining** noun.

trance noun a half-conscious state in which someone does not respond to things happening around them.

tranche /rhymes with branch/ noun one of the parts into which something is divided, especially an amount of money.

tranquil adjective free from disturbance; calm.
■ **tranquillity** (or **tranquility**) noun **tranquilly** adverb.

tranquillize or **tranquillise** (US spelling **tranquilize**) verb (**tranquillizes, tranquillizing, tranquillized**) give a calming or sedative drug to.

tranquillizer or **tranquilliser** (US spelling **tranquilizer**) noun a drug taken to reduce tension or anxiety.

transact verb conduct or carry out business.

transaction noun **1** an act of buying or selling. **2** the process of carrying out business.

transatlantic adjective **1** crossing the Atlantic. **2** concerning countries on either side of the Atlantic.

transceiver noun a combined radio transmitter and receiver.

transcend verb **1** be or go beyond the range or limits of. **2** be superior to.

transcendent adjective **1** going beyond normal or physical human experience. **2** (of God) existing apart from the material world.
■ **transcendence** noun.

transcendental adjective going beyond the limits of human knowledge in a religious

THESAURUS

trainer noun coach, instructor, teacher, tutor, handler.

trait noun characteristic, attribute, feature, quality, habit, mannerism, idiosyncrasy, peculiarity.

traitor noun betrayer, back-stabber, double-crosser, renegade, Judas, quisling, fifth columnist, turncoat, defector; informal snake in the grass.

tramp verb **1** men were tramping through the shrubbery: trudge, plod, stamp, trample, lumber; informal traipse. **2** he spent ten days tramping through the jungle: trek, walk, hike, slog, march, roam, ramble, rove; informal traipse; N. Amer. informal schlep.
• noun **1** a dirty old tramp: vagrant, vagabond, homeless person, down-and-out, traveller, drifter; N. Amer. hobo; N. Amer. informal

bum. **2** the tramp of boots: tread, step, footstep, footfall. **3** a tramp round York: trek, walk, hike, slog, march, roam, ramble; N. Amer. informal schlep.

trample verb tread, stamp, walk, squash, crush, flatten.

trance noun daze, stupor, hypnotic state, dream, reverie.

tranquil adjective **1** a tranquil village: peaceful, calm, restful, quiet, still, relaxing, undisturbed. **2** Martha smiled, perfectly tranquil: calm, serene, relaxed, unruffled, unperturbed, unflustered, untroubled, composed; informal unflappable.
OPPOSITES busy, excitable.

transaction noun deal, bargain, agreement, undertaking, arrangement, negotiation, settlement.

t

or spiritual context.

■ **transcendentally** adverb.

transcontinental adjective crossing or extending across a continent or continents.

transcribe verb (**transcribes, transcribing, transcribed**) **1** put thoughts, speech, or data into written form, or into a different written form. **2** arrange a piece of music for a different instrument or voice.

transcript noun a written or printed version of material that was originally spoken or presented in another form.

transcription noun **1** a transcript. **2** the process of transcribing. **3** a transcribed piece of music.

transducer noun a device that produces an electrical signal from another form of energy such as pressure or brightness.

transept noun (in a cross-shaped church) either of the two parts extending at right angles from the nave.

transfer verb (**transfers, transferring, transferred**) **1** move someone or something from one place to another. **2** move to another department, job, etc. **3** change to another place, route, or means of transport during a journey. **4** pass a property, right, or responsibility to another person. •noun **1** an act of transferring. **2** Brit. a small coloured picture or design on paper, which can be transferred to another surface by being pressed or heated.

■ **transference** noun.

transfigure verb (**be transfigured**) be transformed into something more beautiful or spiritual.

■ **transfiguration** noun.

transfix verb **1** make motionless with horror, wonder, or astonishment. **2** pierce with a sharp object.

transform verb **1** change or be changed in nature, form, or appearance. **2** change the voltage of an electric current.

■ **transformation** noun.

transformer noun a device for changing the voltage of an electric current.

transfusion noun a medical process in which someone is given a supply of

someone else's blood.

transgress verb go beyond the limits of what is morally, socially, or legally acceptable.

■ **transgression** noun **transgressor** noun.

transient adjective **1** lasting only for a short time. **2** staying or working in a place for a short time only. •noun a transient person.

■ **transience** noun **transiently** adverb.

transistor noun **1** a silicon-based device which is able to amplify or rectify electric currents. **2** (also **transistor radio**) a portable radio using circuits containing transistors.

transit noun **1** the carrying of people or things from one place to another. **2** an act of passing through or across a place.

transition noun **1** the process of changing from one state or condition to another. **2** a period of such change.

■ **transitional** adjective.

transitive adjective (of a verb) able to take a direct object, e.g. *saw* in *he saw the donkey*.

■ **transitivity** noun.

transitory adjective lasting for only a short time.

translate verb (**translates, translating, translated**) **1** express the sense of words or a piece of writing in another language. **2** (**translate into**) change or be changed into another form.

translation noun **1** the action of translating. **2** a piece of writing or word that is translated.

translator noun a person who translates writing or speech from one language into another.

transliterate verb (**transliterates, transliterating, transliterated**) write a letter or word using the corresponding letters of a different alphabet or language.

■ **transliteration** noun.

translucent adjective allowing light to pass through partially; semi-transparent.

■ **translucence** (or **translucency**) noun.

transmission noun **1** the passing of

t

THESAURUS

transfer verb move, take, bring, shift, convey, remove, carry, transport, relocate.

transform verb change, alter, convert, revolutionize, overhaul, reconstruct, rebuild, reorganize, rearrange, rework.

transition noun change, passage, move, transformation, conversion, shift, metamorphosis, alteration, changeover, switch.

transitional adjective **1** *a transitional period:* intermediate, interim, changeover, changing, fluid, unsettled. **2** *the*

transitional government: interim, temporary, provisional, pro tem, acting, caretaker.

translate verb interpret, convert, render, put, change, express, decipher, reword, decode, gloss, explain.

translation noun interpretation, rendition, conversion, change, alteration, adaptation.

transmission noun **1** *the transmission of knowledge:* transfer, communication, passing on, conveyance, dissemination, spread, circulation, relaying. **2** *the* something from one place or person to another. **2** a transmitted programme or signal. **3** the mechanism by which power is passed from an engine to the axle in a motor vehicle.

transmit verb (**transmits, transmitting, transmitted**) **1** cause to pass from one place or person to another. **2** broadcast or send out an electrical signal or a radio or television programme. **3** allow heat, light, etc. to pass through a material.

transmitter noun a device used to produce and transmit electromagnetic waves carrying messages or signals, especially those of radio or television.

transmogrify verb (**transmogrifies, transmogrifying, transmogrified**) humorous change into something completely different.

transmute verb (**transmutes, transmuting, transmuted**) change in form, nature, or substance.
■ **transmutation** noun.

transom noun **1** the flat surface forming the stern of a boat. **2** a strengthening crossbar.

transparency noun (plural **transparencies**) **1** the condition of being transparent. **2** a positive transparent photograph printed on plastic or glass, and viewed using a slide projector.

transparent adjective **1** allowing light to pass through so that objects behind can be distinctly seen. **2** obvious or evident.
■ **transparently** adverb.

transpire verb (**transpires, transpiring, transpired**) **1** come to be known. **2** take place; happen. **3** (of a plant or leaf) give off water vapour through pores in the surface layer.
■ **transpiration** noun.

transplant verb **1** take living tissue or an organ and implant it in another part of the body or in another body. **2** transfer to another place or situation. • noun **1** an operation in which an organ or tissue is transplanted. **2** a person or thing that has been transplanted.
■ **transplantation** noun.

transport verb **1** carry people or goods from one place to another by means of a vehicle, aircraft, or ship. **2** (**be transported**) be overwhelmed with a strong emotion. **3** (in the past) send someone to a distant place as a punishment. • noun **1** a system or method of carrying people or goods from one place to another. **2** the action of transporting. **3** a large vehicle, ship, or aircraft for carrying troops or stores. **4** (**transports**) very strong emotions.
■ **transportation** noun **transporter** noun.

transpose verb (**transposes, transposing, transposed**) **1** cause two or more things to change places with each other. **2** move something to a different place or context. **3** write or play music in a different key from the original.
■ **transposition** noun.

transsexual or **transexual** noun a person who emotionally and psychologically feels that they belong to the opposite sex.

transubstantiation noun (in Christian thinking) the doctrine that the bread and wine served in the service of Holy Communion become the actual body and blood of Jesus after they have been blessed.

transverse adjective placed or extending across something.
■ **transversely** adverb.

transvestite noun a person, especially a man, who likes to dress in clothes worn by the opposite sex.
■ **transvestism** noun.

trap noun **1** a device, pit, or enclosure

THESAURUS

transmission of the film: broadcasting, airing, televising. **3** a live transmission: broadcast, programme, show.

transmit verb **1** the use of computers to transmit information: transfer, communicate, pass on, hand on, convey, impart, channel, carry, relay, dispatch, disseminate, spread, circulate. **2** the programme will be transmitted on Sunday: broadcast, send out, air, televise.

transparent adjective **1** transparent blue water: clear, translucent, limpid. **2** fine transparent fabrics: see-through, sheer, filmy, gauzy, diaphanous. **3** a transparent attempt to buy votes: obvious, blatant, unambiguous, unequivocal, clear, plain, apparent, unmistakable, manifest, conspicuous, patent.

OPPOSITES opaque, obscure.

transplant verb **1** these ideas were transplanted to America: transfer, move, remove, shift, relocate, take, replant. **2** kidneys are frequently transplanted: transfer, implant, graft.

transport verb the blocks were transported by lorry: convey, carry, take, transfer, move, shift, send, deliver, bear, ship, ferry; informal cart.
• noun the transport of crude oil: conveyance, carriage, delivery, shipping, freight, shipment, haulage.

trap noun **1** an animal caught in a trap: snare, net, mesh, gin; N. Amer. deadfall. **2** the question was set as a trap: trick, ploy, ruse, deception, subterfuge; informal set-up.
• verb **1** police trapped the men: snare,

designed to catch and hold animals. **2** an unpleasant situation from which you cannot escape. **3** a trick causing someone to say or do something which they do not intend. **4** a container or device used to collect a particular thing. **5** a light, two-wheeled carriage pulled by a horse or pony. •verb (**traps, trapping, trapped**) **1** catch and hold in a trap. **2** trick into doing something.

trapdoor noun a hinged or removable panel in a floor, ceiling, or roof.

trapeze noun a horizontal bar hanging on two ropes high above the ground, used by acrobats in a circus.

trapezium noun (plural **trapezia** or **trapeziums**) (in geometry) a quadrilateral with one pair of sides parallel.

trapper noun a person who traps wild animals.

trappings plural noun **1** the signs or objects associated with a particular situation or role. **2** a horse's ornamental harness.

Trappist noun a monk belonging to an order that speaks only at certain times.

trash noun **1** N. Amer. waste material. **2** poor-quality writing, art, etc. **3** N. Amer. a person or people of very low social status. •verb informal wreck or destroy.
□ **trash can** N. Amer. a dustbin.
■ **trashy** adjective.

trauma /traw-muh/ noun (plural **traumas**) **1** a deeply disturbing experience. **2** emotional shock following a stressful event. **3** (in medicine) physical injury.
■ **traumatic** adjective.

traumatize or **traumatise** verb (**be traumatized**) suffer lasting shock as a result of a disturbing experience or injury.

travail or **travails** noun old use a situation involving a lot of hard work or difficulty.

travel verb (**travels, travelling, travelled**; US spelling **travels, traveling, traveled**) **1** go from one place to another, especially over a long distance. **2** journey along a particular road or through a particular region. •noun **1** the action of travelling. **2** (**travels**) journeys over a long distance.
□ **travel agent** a person or agency that makes the necessary arrangements for travellers.

traveller (US spelling **traveler**) noun **1** a person who is travelling or who often travels. **2** Brit. a Gypsy or other travelling person.
□ **traveller's cheque** a cheque for a fixed amount that can be exchanged for cash in foreign countries.

travelogue noun a film, book, or talk about a person's travels.

traverse verb (**traverses, traversing, traversed**) travel or extend across or through.

travesty noun (plural **travesties**) a ridiculous or shocking version of something.

trawl verb **1** catch fish with a trawl net. **2** search through something thoroughly. •noun **1** an act of trawling. **2** a large wide-mouthed fishing net dragged by a boat along the bottom of the sea.

trawler noun a fishing boat used for trawling.

tray noun a flat container with a raised rim, used for carrying plates, cups, etc.

treacherous adjective **1** guilty of or involving betrayal. **2** having hidden or unpredictable dangers.
■ **treacherously** adverb **treachery** noun.

treacle noun Brit. **1** molasses. **2** golden syrup.
■ **treacly** adjective.

tread verb (**treads, treading, trod**; past participle **trodden** or **trod**) **1** walk in a particular way. **2** press down or crush with your feet. **3** walk on or along. •noun **1** a way or the

---

entrap, capture, catch, ambush. **2** *a rat trapped in a barn:* confine, cut off, corner, shut in, pen in, hem in, imprison. **3** *I hoped to trap him into an admission:* trick, dupe, deceive, fool, hoodwink.

trash noun **1** (N. Amer.) *the entrance was blocked with trash:* rubbish, refuse, waste, litter, junk; N. Amer. garbage. **2** (informal) *they read trash:* rubbish, nonsense, trivia, pulp fiction, pap; N. Amer. garbage; informal drivel.

trauma noun **1** *the trauma of divorce:* shock, upheaval, distress, stress, strain, pain, anguish, suffering, upset, ordeal. **2** *trauma to the liver:* injury, damage, wound.

traumatic adjective disturbing, shocking, distressing, upsetting, painful, agonizing, hurtful, stressful, devastating, harrowing.

travel verb journey, tour, take a trip, voyage, go sightseeing, globetrot, backpack, trek.
•noun (**travels**) travelling, journeys, expeditions, trips, tours, excursions, voyages, treks, wanderings, jaunts.

traveller noun tourist, tripper, holidaymaker, sightseer, globetrotter, backpacker, passenger, commuter; N. Amer. vacationer.

tread verb **1** *he trod purposefully down the hall:* walk, step, stride, pace, march, tramp, plod, stomp, trudge. **2** *the snow had been trodden down by the horses:* crush, flatten, press down, squash, trample on, stamp on.
•noun *we heard his heavy tread on the stairs:* step, footstep, footfall, tramp.

t

sound of walking. **2** the top surface of a step or stair. **3** the part of a vehicle tyre that grips the road. **4** the part of the sole of a shoe that touches the ground.
□ **tread water** stay in an upright position in deep water by moving the feet with a walking movement.

treadle noun a lever which you work with your foot to operate a machine.

treadmill noun **1** a job or situation that is tiring or boring and difficult to escape from. **2** a large wheel turned by the weight of people or animals treading on steps fitted into it, used in the past to drive machinery. **3** a device used for exercise consisting of a continuous moving belt on which you walk or run.

treason or **high treason** noun the crime of betraying your country.
■ **treasonable** adjective.

treasure noun **1** a quantity of precious coins, gems, or other valuable objects. **2** a very valuable object. **3** informal a much loved or highly valued person. • verb (**treasures, treasuring, treasured**) **1** look after carefully. **2** value highly.
□ **treasure hunt** a game in which players search for hidden objects by following a trail of clues. **treasure trove** a store of valuable or pleasant things.

treasurer noun a person appointed to manage the finances of a society, company, etc.

treasury noun (plural **treasuries**) **1** the funds or revenue of a state, institution, or society. **2** (**Treasury**) (in some countries)

the government department responsible for the overall management of the economy.

treat verb **1** behave towards or deal with in a certain way. **2** give medical care or attention to. **3** use a substance or process to protect or preserve something, or give it particular properties. **4** present or discuss a subject. **5** (**treat someone to**) provide a person with food, drink, or entertainment that you have paid for. **6** (**treat yourself**) do or have something very enjoyable.
• noun a gift or event that gives someone great pleasure.

treatise /tree-tiss/ noun a formal piece of writing on a subject.

treatment noun **1** a way of behaving towards someone or dealing with something. **2** medical care for an illness or injury. **3** the use of a substance or process to preserve or give particular properties to something. **4** the presentation or discussion of a subject.

treaty noun (plural **treaties**) a formal agreement between states.

treble¹ adjective **1** consisting of three parts. **2** multiplied or occurring three times.
• pronoun an amount which is three times as large as usual. • verb (**trebles, trebling, trebled**) make or become treble.

treble² noun **1** a high-pitched voice, especially a boy's singing voice. **2** the high-frequency output of a radio or audio system.
□ **treble clef** (in music) a clef placing G above middle C on the second-lowest line of the stave.

THESAURUS

treason noun treachery, disloyalty, betrayal, sedition, subversion, mutiny, rebellion. OPPOSITES allegiance, loyalty.

treasure noun **1** *a casket of treasure:* riches, valuables, jewels, gems, gold, silver, precious metals, money, cash, wealth, fortune. **2** *art treasures:* masterpiece, gem, pearl, jewel.
• verb *I treasure the photographs:* cherish, hold dear, prize, set great store by, value greatly.

treasury noun storehouse, repository, treasure house, exchequer, fund, mine, bank, coffers, purse.

treat verb **1** *Charlotte treated him badly:* behave towards, act towards, use, deal with, handle. **2** *police are treating the fires as arson:* regard, consider, view, look on, put down as. **3** *the book treats its subject with insight:* deal with, tackle, handle, discuss, explore, investigate. **4** *she was treated in hospital:* tend, nurse, attend to, give medical attention to. **5** *a cream used to treat sunburn:* cure, heal, remedy. **6** *he*

treated her to lunch: buy, take out for, stand, give, pay for, entertain, wine and dine; informal foot the bill for. **7** *delegates were treated to dance performances:* entertain with/to, regale with, fete with, amuse with.
• noun **1** *a birthday treat:* celebration, entertainment, amusement, surprise. **2** *I bought you some chocolate as a treat:* present, gift, titbit, delicacy, luxury, indulgence, extravagance; informal goody. **3** *it was a real treat to see them:* pleasure, delight, thrill, joy.

treatment noun **1** *the company's treatment of its workers:* behaviour towards, conduct towards, handling of, dealings with. **2** *she's responding well to treatment:* medical care, therapy, nursing, medication, drugs. **3** *her treatment of the topic:* discussion, handling, investigation, exploration, consideration, study, analysis.

treaty noun agreement, settlement, pact, deal, entente, concordat, accord, protocol, compact, convention; formal concord.

tree noun a plant consisting of a thick wooden stem and a number of branches, that can grow to a great height and live for many years.
▫ **tree diagram** a diagram with a structure of branching lines. **tree house** a structure built in the branches of a tree for children to play in.

treeline noun a height up a mountain above which trees do not grow.

trefoil noun **1** a small plant with yellow flowers and clover-like leaves. **2** a shape or design in the form of three rounded lobes like a clover leaf.

trek noun a long, difficult journey, especially one made on foot. •**verb** (**treks, trekking, trekked**) go on a trek.
■ **trekker** noun.

trellis noun a framework of bars used as a support for climbing plants.

tremble verb (**trembles, trembling, trembled**) **1** shake in a way that you cannot control, usually as a result of fear, excitement, or weakness. **2** be in a state of great worry or fear. •**noun** a trembling feeling, movement, or sound.

tremendous adjective **1** very great in amount, scale, or force. **2** informal very good or impressive.
■ **tremendously** adverb.

tremolo noun (plural **tremolos**) a wavering effect in singing or created in certain musical instruments.

tremor noun **1** a quivering movement that cannot be controlled. **2** (also **earth tremor**) a slight earthquake. **3** a sudden feeling of fear or excitement.

tremulous adjective **1** shaking or quivering slightly. **2** nervous.

trench noun **1** a long, narrow ditch. **2** a ditch dug by troops to provide shelter from enemy fire. **3** (also **ocean trench**) a long, deep depression in the ocean bed.
▫ **trench coat** a belted, double-breasted raincoat.

trenchant adjective (of something said or written) expressed strongly and clearly.
■ **trenchantly** adverb.

trencher noun (in the past) a flat piece of wood from which food was served or eaten.

trend noun **1** a general direction in which something is developing or changing. **2** a fashion.

trendsetter noun a person who leads the way in fashion or ideas.

trendy adjective (**trendier, trendiest**) informal very fashionable.

trepidation noun a feeling of fear or nervousness.

trespass verb **1** enter someone's land or property without their permission. **2** (**trespass on**) take advantage of someone's time, good nature, etc. **3** (**trespass against**) old use do wrong or harm to. •**noun 1** Law the entering of someone's land or property without their permission. **2** old use a bad or wrongful act.
■ **trespasser** noun.

tress noun literary a long lock of hair.

trestle noun a structure consisting of a horizontal bar on sloping legs, used in pairs to support a surface such as a table top.

triad noun **1** a group of three people or things. **2** a Chinese secret society involved in criminal activity.

trial noun **1** a formal examination in a court of law to decide if someone is guilty of a crime. **2** a test of performance, qualities, or suitability. **3** (**trials**) an event in which horses or dogs compete or perform. **4** something that tests a person's endurance or patience. •**verb** (**trials,**

THESAURUS

trek noun journey, trip, expedition, safari, hike, march, tramp, walk.

tremble verb **1** *Joe's hands were trembling:* shake, quiver, twitch. **2** *the entire building trembled:* shudder, shake, judder, vibrate, wobble, rock, move, sway.

tremendous adjective **1** *tremendous sums of money:* huge, enormous, immense, colossal, massive, prodigious, stupendous; informal whopping, astronomical; Brit. informal ginormous. **2** (informal) *a tremendous result:* excellent, first-class, outstanding, marvellous, wonderful, splendid, superb, admirable; informal great, fantastic, fabulous, terrific, super, awesome, ace; Brit. informal brilliant, smashing.
OPPOSITES tiny, poor.

trench noun ditch, channel, trough,

excavation, furrow, rut, conduit.

trend noun **1** *an upward trend in unemployment:* tendency, movement, drift, swing, shift, course, current, direction, inclination, leaning. **2** *the latest trend in music:* fashion, vogue, style, mode, craze, mania, rage; informal fad, thing.

trespass verb intrude, encroach, invade, enter without permission.

trial noun **1** *a county court trial:* case, lawsuit, hearing, tribunal, litigation, proceedings. **2** *the drug is undergoing clinical trials:* test, experiment, pilot study, examination, check, assessment, audition, evaluation, appraisal; informal dry run. **3** *trials and tribulations:* trouble, affliction, ordeal, tribulation, difficulty, problem, misfortune, mishap, misadventure.

trialling, trialled; US spelling trials, trialing, trialed) test something to assess its suitability or performance.
□ on trial 1 being tried in a court of law. 2 undergoing tests. trial and error the process of trying out various methods until you find one that works well.

triangle noun 1 a figure with three straight sides and three angles. 2 a musical instrument consisting of a steel rod bent into a triangle, sounded with a rod. 3 an emotional relationship involving a couple and a third person.
■ **triangular** adjective.

triangulation noun the division of an area into a series of triangles in order to determine distances and relative positions.

triathlon noun an athletic contest involving three different events, typically swimming, cycling, and long-distance running.
■ **triathlete** noun.

tribalism noun behaviour and attitudes that result from a system in which people belong to tribes.

tribe noun 1 a group of people within a traditional society sharing customs and beliefs and led by a chief. 2 informal a large number of people.
■ **tribal** adjective.

tribesman noun (plural **tribesmen**) a member of a tribe in a traditional society.

tribulation noun trouble, suffering, or difficulty.

tribunal noun 1 Brit. a group of people established to settle disputes. 2 a court of justice.

tribune noun (in ancient Rome) an official chosen by the ordinary people to protect their interests.

tributary noun (plural **tributaries**) a river or stream that flows into a larger river or lake.

tribute noun 1 an act, statement, or gift intended to show respect or admiration for someone. 2 historical payment made by a state to a more powerful one.

trice noun (in a trice) in a moment.

tricentenary noun (plural **tricentenaries**) a three-hundredth anniversary.

triceps /try-seps/ noun (plural **triceps**) the large muscle at the back of the upper arm.

triceratops /try-se-ruh-tops/ noun a large plant-eating dinosaur with two large horns.

trichology /tri-kol-uh-ji/ noun the branch of medicine concerned with the hair and scalp.
■ **trichologist** noun.

trick noun 1 something intended to deceive or outwit someone. 2 a skilful act performed to entertain people. 3 an illusion. 4 a habit or mannerism. 5 (in card games) a single round of play. •verb cunningly deceive or outwit someone.
■ **trickery** noun.

trickle verb (**trickles, trickling, trickled**) 1 (of a liquid) flow in a small stream. 2 come or go slowly or gradually. •noun 1 a small flow of liquid. 2 a small number of people or things moving slowly.

trickster noun a person who cheats or deceives people.

tricksy adjective clever or mischievous.

tricky adjective (**trickier, trickiest**) 1 difficult or awkward. 2 likely to deceive you; crafty.

tricolour /tri-kuh-ler/ (US spelling **tricolor**) noun a flag with three bands of different colours, especially the French national flag.

tricycle noun a vehicle similar to a bicycle but having three wheels.

trident noun a three-pronged spear.

tried past and past participle of TRY.

triennial adjective lasting for or happening every three years.

trier noun a person who always tries hard.

THESAURUS

tribe noun ethnic group, people, family, clan, race, dynasty, house, nation.

tribunal noun court, board, panel, committee.

tribute noun accolade, praise, commendation, salute, testimonial, homage, congratulations, compliments, plaudits.
OPPOSITES criticism, condemnation.

trick noun 1 *a mean trick:* stratagem, ploy, ruse, scheme, device, manoeuvre, dodge, subterfuge, swindle, fraud; informal con, set-up, scam, sting. 2 *he's playing a trick on us:* practical joke, prank; informal leg-pull, spoof, put-on. 3 *it was probably a trick of the light:* illusion, figment of the imagination, mirage. 4 *the tricks of the trade:* knack, skill, technique, secret, art.
•verb *tricked by villains:* deceive, delude, hoodwink, mislead, take in, dupe, fool, cheat, defraud, swindle; informal con, diddle, take for a ride, shaft, do; N. Amer. informal sucker.

trickle verb *blood was trickling from two cuts:* dribble, drip, ooze, leak, seep, spill.
OPPOSITES pour, gush.
•noun *trickles of water:* dribble, drip, thin stream, rivulet.

tricky adjective 1 *a tricky situation:* difficult, awkward, problematic, delicate, ticklish, sensitive; informal sticky. 2 *a tricky politician:* cunning, crafty, wily, devious, sly, scheming, calculating, deceitful.
OPPOSITES straightforward, honest.

t

trifle noun **1** something of little value or importance. **2** a small amount. **3** Brit. a cold dessert of sponge cake and fruit with layers of custard, jelly, and cream. •verb (**trifles, trifling, trifled**) (**trifle with**) treat without seriousness or respect.

trifling adjective unimportant; trivial.

trigger noun **1** a small lever that sets off a gun or other mechanism when pulled. **2** an event that causes something to happen. •verb (**triggers, triggering, triggered**) **1** cause a device to function. **2** make something happen.
□ **trigger-happy** tending to fire a gun on the slightest provocation.

trigonometry noun the branch of mathematics concerned with the relationships between the sides and angles of triangles.

trilby noun (plural **trilbies**) Brit. a man's soft felt hat with a narrow brim.

trill noun a high warbling sound. •verb make a high warbling sound.

trillion cardinal number **1** a million million (1,000,000,000,000 or 10^{12}). **2** Brit. dated a million million million (1,000,000,000,000,000,000 or 10^{18}).
■ **trillionth** ordinal number.

trilobite /try-luh-byt/ noun a fossil sea creature with a rear part divided into segments.

trilogy noun (plural **trilogies**) a group of three related novels, plays, or films.

trim verb (**trims, trimming, trimmed**) **1** cut away unwanted parts from something.
2 reduce the size, amount, or number of. **3** decorate something along its edges. **4** adjust a sail. •noun **1** decoration along the edges of something. **2** the upholstery or interior lining of a car. **3** an act of trimming. **4** good condition. •adjective (**trimmer, trimmest**) neat and smart.
□ **in trim** slim and fit.

trimaran /try-muh-ran/ noun a yacht with three hulls side by side.

trimming noun **1** (**trimmings**) small pieces trimmed off. **2** decoration, or the traditional accompaniments to something.

trinity noun (plural **trinities**) **1** (**the Trinity** or **the Holy Trinity**) (in Christian belief) the three persons (Father, Son, and Holy Spirit) that make up God. **2** a group of three people or things.

trinket noun a small inexpensive ornament or item of jewellery.

trio noun (plural **trios**) **1** a set or group of three. **2** a group of three musicians.

trip verb (**trips, tripping, tripped**) **1** catch your foot on something and stumble or fall. **2** (**trip up**) make a mistake. **3** walk, run, or dance with quick, light steps. **4** make a mechanism start working. **5** informal experience hallucinations as a result of taking a drug such as LSD. •noun **1** a journey to a place and back again, especially for pleasure. **2** an instance of tripping or falling. **3** informal a period of hallucinations caused by taking a drug such as LSD. **4** a device that trips a mechanism.

THESAURUS

trifle noun **triviality,** thing of no consequence, bagatelle, inessential, nothing, technicality; (**trifles**) trivia, minutiae.

trifling adjective **trivial,** unimportant, insignificant, inconsequential, petty, minor, of little/no account, footling, incidental; informal piffling.
OPPOSITES important.

trigger verb **start,** set off, initiate, spark (off), activate, touch off, provoke, precipitate, prompt, stir up, cause, give rise to, lead to, set in motion, bring about.

trim verb **1** his hair had been trimmed: **cut,** crop, bob, shorten, clip, snip, shear, dock, lop off, prune, shave, pare. **2** gloves trimmed with fake fur: **decorate,** adorn, ornament, embellish, edge, border, fringe. •noun **1** white curtains with a blue trim: **decoration,** ornamentation, adornment, embellishment, border, edging, piping, fringe, frill. **2** hair in need of a trim: **haircut,** cut, clip, snip.
•adjective **1** a very trim garden: **neat,** tidy, orderly, uncluttered, well kept, well
maintained, immaculate, spick and span, spruce, dapper. **2** her trim figure: **slim,** slender, lean, sleek, willowy.
OPPOSITES untidy, messy.
□ **in trim fit,** in good health, in fine fettle, slim, in shape.

trimming noun **1** a black dress with lace trimming: **decoration,** ornamentation, adornment, borders, edging, piping, fringes, frills. **2** (**trimmings**) **accompaniments,** extras, frills, accessories, accoutrements, trappings, paraphernalia, garnish.

trio noun **threesome,** three, triumvirate, triad, troika, trinity, trilogy.

trip verb **1** he tripped on the stones: **stumble,** lose your footing, catch your foot, slip, fall (down), tumble. **2** they tripped up the steps: **skip,** dance, prance, bound, spring, scamper.
•noun **1** a trip to Paris: **excursion,** outing, jaunt, holiday, break, visit, tour, journey, expedition, voyage, drive, run; informal spin. **2** trips cause many accidents: **stumble,** slip, fall, misstep.

t

tripartite adjective **1** consisting of three parts. **2** shared by or involving three parties.

tripe noun **1** the stomach of a cow or sheep used as food. **2** informal nonsense.

triplane noun an early type of aircraft with three pairs of wings, one above the other.

triple adjective **1** consisting of three parts, things, or people. **2** having three times the usual size, quality, or strength. • noun a thing that is three times as large as usual or is made up of three parts. • verb (**triples**, **tripling**, **tripled**) make or become triple. ◻ **triple jump** an athletic event in which competitors perform a hop, a step, and a jump from a running start.
■ **triply** adverb.

triplet noun **1** each of three children born at the same birth. **2** a group of three musical notes to be performed in the time of two or four.

triplicate adjective /trip-li-kuht/ existing in three copies or examples. • verb /trip-li-kayt/ (**triplicates, triplicating, triplicated**) **1** make three copies of. **2** multiply by three.

tripod noun a three-legged stand for a camera or other device.

tripper noun Brit. informal a person who goes on a pleasure trip.

triptych /trip-tik/ noun a picture or carving on three panels.

tripwire noun a wire that is stretched close to the ground and sets off a trap or alarm when disturbed.

trite adjective (of a remark or idea) unoriginal and dull.

triumph noun **1** a great victory or achievement. **2** joy or satisfaction resulting from a success or victory. **3** a very successful example of something. • verb be successful or victorious.
■ **triumphal** adjective.

triumphant adjective **1** having won a battle or contest. **2** joyful after a victory or achievement.
■ **triumphantly** adverb.

triumvirate /try-um-vi-ruht/ noun a group of three powerful or important people or things.

trivet noun a metal stand on which hot dishes are placed.

trivia plural noun unimportant details or pieces of information.

trivial adjective of little value or importance.
■ **triviality** noun (plural **trivialities**) **trivially** adverb.

trivialize or **trivialise** verb (**trivializes, trivializing, trivialized**) make something seem less important or complex than it really is.
■ **trivialization** noun.

trod past and past participle of TREAD.

trodden past participle of TREAD.

troglodyte noun a person who lives in a cave.

troika noun **1** a Russian vehicle pulled by a team of three horses side by side. **2** a group of three people working together.

Trojan noun an inhabitant of ancient Troy in Asia Minor (present-day Turkey). • adjective relating to Troy.
◻ **Trojan Horse** something intended to weaken or defeat an enemy secretly.

troll¹ noun (in stories) an ugly giant or dwarf.

troll² verb fish by trailing a baited line along behind a boat.

trolley noun (plural **trolleys**) **1** Brit. a large metal basket with wheels, for transporting heavy or bulky items. **2** a small table on wheels.

trolleybus noun Brit. a bus powered by electricity obtained from overhead wires.

trollop noun dated or humorous a woman who has a lot of sexual partners.

trombone noun a large brass wind instrument with a sliding tube which you move to produce different notes.
■ **trombonist** noun.

THESAURUS

triple adjective **1** *a triple alliance:* threefold, tripartite, three-way. **2** *triple the going rate:* three times, treble.

triumph noun **1** *Napoleon's triumphs:* victory, win, conquest, success, achievement. **2** *his eyes shone with triumph:* jubilation, exultation, elation, delight, joy, happiness, glee, pride, satisfaction.
OPPOSITES defeat, disappointment.
• verb *he triumphed in the Grand Prix:* win, succeed, come first, be victorious, carry the day, prevail.
OPPOSITES lose.
◻ **triumph over defeat,** beat, conquer, trounce, vanquish, overcome, overpower, overwhelm, get the better of; informal lick.

triumphant adjective **1** *the triumphant team:* victorious, successful, winning, conquering. **2** *a triumphant expression:* jubilant, exultant, celebratory, elated, joyful, delighted, gleeful, proud, cock-a-hoop.
OPPOSITES unsuccessful, defeated, despondent.

trivial adjective unimportant, insignificant, inconsequential, minor, of no account, of no importance, petty, trifling, footling, negligible; informal piffling.
OPPOSITES important, significant.

troop noun 1 (**troops**) soldiers or armed forces. 2 a unit of troops. 3 a group of people or animals. •verb come or go as a group.

trooper noun 1 a soldier in a cavalry or armoured unit. 2 US a state police officer.

trophy noun (plural **trophies**) 1 a cup or other object awarded as a prize. 2 a souvenir of an achievement.

tropic noun 1 the line of latitude 23°26′ north (**tropic of Cancer**) or south (**tropic of Capricorn**) of the equator. 2 (**the tropics**) the region between the tropics of Cancer and Capricorn.

tropical adjective 1 having to do with the tropics. 2 very hot and humid.
■ **tropically** adverb.

trot verb (**trots, trotting, trotted**) 1 (of a horse) move at a pace faster than a walk. 2 run at a moderate pace with short steps. 3 (**trot something out**) informal repeat something that has been said many times before. •noun 1 a trotting pace. 2 a period of trotting.
◻ **on the trot** Brit. informal one after another.

troth noun (**plight your troth**) old use promise to marry.

trotter noun a pig's foot.

troubadour /troo-buh-dor/ noun a travelling singer and poet in medieval France.

trouble noun 1 difficulty or problems. 2 effort that you make to do something. 3 a cause of worry or inconvenience. 4 a situation in which you can be punished or blamed. 5 a situation in which people are angry or violent. •verb (**troubles, troubling, troubled**) 1 cause distress or inconvenience to. 2 (**troubled**) feeling anxious or experiencing problems. 3 (**trouble to do**) make the effort required to do.

troublemaker noun a person who regularly causes trouble.

troubleshooter noun a person who investigates and solves problems or faults.
■ **troubleshooting** noun.

troublesome adjective causing difficulty or problems.

trough noun 1 a long, narrow open container for animals to eat or drink out of. 2 (in weather forecasting) a long region of low atmospheric pressure. 3 a point of low activity or achievement.

trounce verb (**trounces, trouncing, trounced**) defeat heavily.

troupe noun a touring group of entertainers.

trouper noun 1 an entertainer with many years of experience. 2 a reliable and uncomplaining person.

THESAURUS

troop noun 1 *a troop of musicians:* group, party, band, gang, body, company, troupe, crowd, squad, unit. 2 (**troops**) soldiers, armed forces, soldiery, servicemen, servicewomen.
•verb *we trooped out of the hall:* walk, march, file, flock, crowd, throng, stream, swarm.

trophy noun 1 *a swimming trophy:* cup, medal, prize, award. 2 *trophies from his travels:* souvenir, memento, keepsake, spoils, booty.

tropical adjective hot, sweltering, humid, sultry, steamy, sticky, oppressive, stifling.
OPPOSITES cold.

trot verb run, jog, scuttle, scurry, bustle, scamper.

trouble noun 1 *you've caused enough trouble:* difficulty, problems, bother, inconvenience, worry, anxiety, distress, stress, agitation, unpleasantness, harassment; informal hassle. 2 *she poured out all her troubles:* problem, misfortune, difficulty, trial, tribulation, woe, grief, heartache, misery, affliction, suffering. 3 *he's gone to a lot of trouble:* bother, inconvenience, fuss, effort, exertion, work, labour. 4 *I wouldn't want to be a trouble to her:* nuisance, bother, inconvenience, irritation, problem, trial, pest; informal headache, pain, drag. 5 *you're too gullible,*

that's your trouble: shortcoming, weakness, failing, fault. 6 *he had heart trouble:* disease, illness, sickness, ailment, complaint, problem, disorder, disability. 7 *the crash was due to engine trouble:* malfunction, failure, breakdown. 8 *a match marred by crowd trouble:* disturbance, disorder, unrest, fighting, scuffles, breach of the peace.
•verb 1 *this matter had been troubling her for some time:* worry, bother, concern, disturb, upset, agitate, distress, perturb, annoy, nag, prey on someone's mind; informal bug. 2 *he was troubled by ill health:* afflict, burden, suffer from, be cursed with. 3 *there is nothing you need trouble about:* worry, upset yourself, fret, be anxious, be concerned. 4 *I'm sorry to trouble you:* inconvenience, bother, impose on, disturb, put out, disoblige; informal hassle.

troublesome adjective 1 *a troublesome problem:* annoying, irritating, exasperating, maddening, infuriating, bothersome, tiresome, nagging, difficult, awkward; N. Amer. informal pesky. 2 *a troublesome child:* difficult, awkward, uncooperative, rebellious, unmanageable, unruly, obstreperous, disruptive, disobedient, naughty, recalcitrant.
OPPOSITES simple, cooperative.

t

trousers plural noun an outer garment that covers the body from the waist down and has a separate part for each leg.

trousseau /troo-soh/ noun (plural **trousseaux** or **trousseaus** /troo-sohz/) clothes and other belongings collected by a bride for her marriage.

trout noun (plural **trout** or **trouts**) an edible fish of the salmon family.

trove noun a store of valuable things.

trowel noun 1 a small tool with a curved scoop for lifting plants or earth. 2 a small tool with a flat blade for applying mortar or plaster.

troy noun a system of weights used mainly for precious metals and gems, with a pound of 12 ounces.

truant noun a pupil who stays away from school without permission or explanation. • verb (also **play truant**) stay away from school without permission or explanation. ■ **truancy** noun.

truce noun an agreement between enemies to stop fighting for a certain time.

truck¹ noun 1 a large road vehicle for carrying goods. 2 Brit. an open railway vehicle for carrying goods. ■ **trucker** noun.

truck² noun (**have no truck with**) refuse to have any dealings or association with.

truculent /truk-yuu-luhnt/ adjective quick to argue or fight. ■ **truculence** noun **truculently** adverb.

trudge verb (**trudges, trudging, trudged**) walk slowly and with heavy steps. • noun a difficult or long and tiring walk.

true adjective (**truer, truest**) 1 in accordance with fact or reality. 2 rightly so called: *true love*. 3 real or actual. 4 accurate and exact. 5 (**true to**) in keeping with what is usual or expected. 6 loyal or faithful. 7 upright or level. ■ **truly** adverb.

☑ note that there's no e in **truly**.

truffle noun 1 an underground fungus that is eaten as a delicacy. 2 a soft chocolate sweet.

trug noun Brit. a wooden basket for carrying flowers, fruit, and vegetables.

truism noun a statement that is obviously true and says nothing new or interesting.

trump noun (in card games) a card of the suit chosen to rank above the others. • verb 1 play a trump on a card of another suit. 2 beat by saying or doing something better. 3 (**trump something up**) invent a false accusation or excuse. □ **come** (or **turn**) **up trumps** Brit. informal 1 unexpectedly do very well. 2 be especially generous or helpful.

trumpery adjective old use showy but worthless.

trumpet noun 1 a brass musical instrument with a flared end. 2 the loud cry of an elephant. • verb (**trumpets, trumpeting, trumpeted**) 1 announce widely or enthusiastically. 2 (of an elephant) make its characteristic loud cry. 3 play a trumpet. □ **blow your own trumpet** talk boastfully about your achievements. ■ **trumpeter** noun.

truncate verb (**truncates, truncating, truncated**) shorten by cutting off the top or end. ■ **truncation** noun.

truncheon noun Brit. a short, thick stick carried as a weapon by a police officer.

trundle verb (**trundles, trundling, trundled**) move or roll slowly and heavily.

trunk noun 1 the main woody stem of a tree. 2 a person's or animal's body apart from the limbs and head. 3 the long nose of an elephant. 4 a large box for storing or transporting articles. 5 N. Amer. the boot of a car. □ **trunk call** Brit. dated a long-distance telephone call. **trunk road** an important main road.

THESAURUS

truce noun ceasefire, armistice, cessation, peace.

true adjective 1 *what I say is true:* correct, accurate, right, verifiable, the case, so. 2 *true craftsmanship:* genuine, authentic, real, actual, bona fide, proper. 3 *true repentance:* sincere, genuine, real, unfeigned, heartfelt. 4 *a true friend:* loyal, faithful, constant, devoted, trustworthy, reliable, dependable. 5 *a true reflection of life:* accurate, faithful, telling it like it is, realistic, factual, lifelike.
OPPOSITES untrue, false, disloyal, inaccurate.

truly adverb 1 *tell me truly what you want:* truthfully, honestly, frankly, candidly, openly. 2 *I'm truly grateful:* sincerely, genuinely, really, indeed, heartily, profoundly. 3 *a truly dreadful song:* really, absolutely, simply, utterly, totally, perfectly, thoroughly, completely. 4 *this is truly a miracle:* without (a) doubt, unquestionably, certainly, surely, definitely, undeniably, really, actually, in fact.

trumpet verb proclaim, announce, declare, noise abroad, shout from the rooftops.
OPPOSITES keep quiet about.

trunk noun 1 *the trunk of a tree:* stem, bole, stock, stalk. 2 *his powerful trunk:* torso, body. 3 *an elephant's trunk:* proboscis,

trunks plural noun men's shorts worn for swimming or boxing.

truss noun **1** a framework which supports a roof, bridge, or other structure. **2** a padded belt worn to support a hernia. •**verb 1** tie someone up tightly. **2** tie up the wings and legs of a bird before cooking.

trust noun **1** firm belief in the truth, reliability, or ability of someone or something. **2** responsibility for someone or something. **3** an arrangement by which someone manages property for the benefit of another person or people. **4** an organization or company managed by trustees. •**verb 1** have trust in. **2** (**trust someone with**) allow someone to have, use, or look after. **3** (**trust someone/thing to**) give someone or something to another person for safekeeping. **4** (**trust to**) rely on luck, fate, etc. **5** expect or hope.
□ **trust fund** a fund of money or property that is held for someone by a trust.

trustee noun a person who is given legal powers to manage property for the benefit of others.

trustful adjective having total trust in someone.
■ **trustfully** adverb.

trusting adjective tending to trust other people; not suspicious.
■ **trustingly** adverb.

trustworthy adjective honest and reliable.
■ **trustworthiness** noun.

trusty adjective (**trustier, trustiest**) old use or humorous reliable or faithful.

truth noun (plural **truths**) **1** the quality or state of being true. **2** true facts. **3** a fact or belief that is accepted as true.

truthful adjective **1** telling or expressing the truth. **2** accurate; true to life.
■ **truthfully** adverb **truthfulness** noun.

try verb (**tries, trying, tried**) **1** make an attempt to do something. **2** (also **try something out**) test something new or different. **3** attempt to open a door. **4** (**try something on**) put on an item of clothing to see if it fits or looks good. **5** put someone on trial. •**noun** (plural **tries**) **1** an attempt. **2** an act of testing something new or different. **3** Rugby an act of touching the ball down behind the opposing goal line to score points.
□ **try someone's patience** make someone feel irritated or annoyed.

> **!** when writing, it is better to use **try to** rather than **try and** (*we should try to help them* rather than *we should try and help them*).

trying adjective difficult or annoying.

tryst /trist/ noun literary a private, romantic meeting between lovers.

tsar, **czar**, or **tzar** /zar/ noun an emperor of Russia before 1917.
■ **tsarist** adjective.

tsetse fly /tset-si/ noun an African

nose, snout. **4** *an enormous tin trunk*: chest, box, crate, coffer, case, portmanteau.

trust noun *good relationships are built on trust*: confidence, belief, faith, certainty, assurance, conviction, credence, reliance.
OPPOSITES distrust, mistrust, doubt.
•**verb 1** *I should never have trusted her*: have faith in, have (every) confidence in, believe in, pin your hopes/faith on. **2** *he can be trusted to carry out an impartial investigation*: rely on, depend on, bank on, count on, be sure of. **3** *I trust we shall meet again*: hope, expect, take it, assume, presume. **4** *they won't trust their money to strangers*: entrust, consign, commit, give, hand over, turn over, assign.
OPPOSITES distrust, mistrust, doubt.

trusting adjective trustful, unsuspecting, unquestioning, naive, innocent, childlike, ingenuous, wide-eyed, credulous, gullible, easily taken in.
OPPOSITES distrustful, suspicious.

trustworthy adjective reliable, dependable, honest, as good as your word, above suspicion; informal on the level.
OPPOSITES unreliable.

truth noun **1** *he doubted the truth of her*

statement: accuracy, correctness, authenticity, veracity, verity. **2** *truth is stranger than fiction*: fact(s), reality, real life, actuality.
OPPOSITES lies, fiction, falsehood.

truthful adjective true, accurate, correct, factual, faithful, reliable.
OPPOSITES deceitful, untrue.

try verb **1** *try to help him*: attempt, endeavour, make an effort, strive, do your best, do your utmost, aim; informal have a go, go all out. **2** *try it and see what you think*: test, sample, taste, inspect, investigate, examine, appraise, evaluate, assess; informal check out. **3** *Mary tried everyone's patience*: tax, strain, test, stretch, sap, drain, exhaust, wear out.
•**noun** *I'll have one last try*: attempt, effort, endeavour; informal go, shot, crack, stab, bash.

trying adjective **1** *a trying day*: stressful, taxing, demanding, difficult, challenging, pressured, frustrating, fraught; informal hellish. **2** *Steve was very trying*: annoying, irritating, exasperating, maddening, infuriating, tiresome, troublesome.
OPPOSITES easy.

t

bloodsucking fly which transmits diseases.

tsp abbreviation teaspoonful.

tsunami /tsoo-**nah**-mi/ noun a tidal wave caused by an underwater earthquake or other disturbance.

tub noun 1 a low, wide, open container with a flat bottom. 2 a small plastic or cardboard container for food.
□ tub-thumping informal loud, aggressive expression of opinions.

tuba noun a large low-pitched brass wind instrument.

tubby adjective (**tubbier**, **tubbiest**) informal (of a person) short and rather fat.

tube noun 1 a long, hollow cylinder for conveying or holding something. 2 a flexible container sealed at one end and having a cap at the other. 3 (**the Tube**) Brit. trademark the underground railway system in London.

tuber noun a thick underground part of the stem or root of some plants, from which new plants grow.

tubercular adjective relating to, or suffering from, tuberculosis.

tuberculosis /tyoo-ber-kyuu-**loh**-siss/ noun a serious infectious disease in which small swellings (**tubercles**) appear, especially in the lungs.

tubular adjective 1 long, round, and hollow like a tube. 2 made from a tube or tubes.

TUC abbreviation Trades Union Congress.

tuck verb 1 push, fold, or turn between two surfaces. 2 put neatly into a small space. 3 (**tuck someone in** or **up**) settle someone in bed by pulling the edges of the bedclothes under the mattress. 4 (**tuck in** or **into**) informal eat food heartily. • noun 1 a flattened, stitched fold in a garment or material. 2 Brit. informal food eaten by children at school as a snack.

tucker noun Austral./NZ informal food.

Tudor adjective relating to the royal family which ruled England 1485–1603.

Tuesday noun the day of the week before Wednesday and following Monday.

tufa noun 1 rock formed as a deposit from mineral springs. 2 rock formed from volcanic ash.

tuffet noun 1 a tuft or clump. 2 a footstool

or low seat.

tuft noun a bunch of threads, grass, or hair held or growing together at the base.
■ tufted adjective tufty adjective.

tug verb (**tugs**, **tugging**, **tugged**) pull hard or suddenly. • noun 1 a hard or sudden pull. 2 (also **tugboat**) a small, powerful boat for towing larger boats and ships.
□ tug of war a contest in which two teams pull at opposite ends of a rope.

tuition noun teaching or instruction.

tulip noun a plant with brightly coloured cup-shaped flowers.

tulle /tyool/ noun a soft, fine net material, used for making veils and dresses.

tumble verb (**tumbles**, **tumbling**, **tumbled**) 1 fall suddenly or clumsily. 2 move in a headlong way. 3 decrease rapidly in amount or value. • noun 1 a sudden or clumsy fall. 2 an untidy or confused arrangement.
□ tumble dryer a machine that dries washed clothes by turning them in hot air inside a revolving drum.

tumbledown adjective (of a building) ruined or falling into ruin.

tumbler noun 1 a drinking glass with straight sides and no handle or stem. 2 an acrobat. 3 a part of a lock that holds the bolt until lifted by a key.

tumbril noun an open cart of a kind used to take prisoners to the guillotine during the French Revolution.

tumescent /tyuu-**mess**-uhnt/ adjective swollen or becoming swollen.

tumid adjective (of a part of the body) swollen.

tummy noun (plural **tummies**) informal a person's stomach or abdomen.
□ tummy button the navel.

tumour (US spelling **tumor**) noun an abnormal growth of tissue in the body.

tumult noun 1 a loud, confused noise. 2 confusion or disorder.

tumultuous /tyuu-**mul**-tyuu-uhss/ adjective 1 very loud and showing strong feelings: *tumultuous applause*. 2 excited, confused,

THESAURUS

tuck verb push, insert, slip, thrust, stuff, stick, cram; informal pop.

tug verb 1 *Ben tugged at her sleeve:* pull, pluck, tweak, twitch, jerk, catch hold of; informal yank. 2 *she tugged him towards the door:* drag, pull, lug, draw, haul, heave, tow, trail.

tuition noun instruction, teaching, coaching, tutoring, tutelage, lessons,

education, schooling, training.

tumble verb 1 *he tumbled over:* fall (over/down), topple over, lose your balance, take a spill, trip (up), stumble. 2 *oil prices tumbled:* plummet, plunge, dive, nosedive, drop, slump, slide; informal crash.
OPPOSITES rise.

tumour noun cancer, growth, lump,

or disorderly.

tumulus /tyoo-myuu-luhss/ noun (plural **tumuli** /tyoo-myuu-ly/) an ancient burial mound.

tun noun a large beer or wine cask.

tuna noun (plural **tuna** or **tunas**) a large edible fish of warm seas.

tundra noun the vast, flat, treeless regions of Europe, Asia, and North America in which the soil under the surface is permanently frozen.

tune noun **1** a sequence of notes that form a piece of music; a melody. **2** correct musical pitch. •verb (**tunes, tuning, tuned**) **1** adjust a musical instrument to the correct pitch. **2** adjust a radio or television to a particular frequency. **3** adjust an engine so that it runs smoothly and efficiently. **4** adjust or adapt to a purpose or situation. □ **tuning fork** a two-pronged steel device which produces a specific note when hit against a surface.

tuneful adjective having a pleasing tune. ▪ **tunefully** adverb.

tuneless adjective not having a pleasing tune. ▪ **tunelessly** adverb.

tuner noun **1** a person or device that tunes musical instruments. **2** a part of a stereo system that receives radio broadcasts.

tungsten noun a hard grey metal used to make electric light filaments.

tunic noun **1** a loose sleeveless garment reaching to the thighs or knees. **2** a close-fitting short coat worn as part of a uniform.

Tunisian noun a person from Tunisia. •adjective relating to Tunisia.

tunnel noun a passage built underground for a road or railway or by a burrowing animal. •verb (**tunnels, tunnelling, tunnelled**; US spelling **tunnels, tunneling, tunneled**) dig a tunnel. □ **tunnel vision 1** a condition in which things cannot be seen properly if they are not straight ahead. **2** informal the tendency to focus only on a single aspect of a situation.

tunny noun (plural **tunny** or **tunnies**) a tuna.

tuppence ⇒ TWOPENCE.

turban noun a long length of material worn wound round the head by Muslim and Sikh men.

▪ **turbaned** (or **turbanned**) adjective.

turbid adjective (of a liquid) cloudy or muddy; not clear.

turbine noun a machine in which a wheel or rotor is made to revolve by a fast-moving flow of water, air, etc.

turbocharger or **turbo** noun a supercharger driven by a turbine powered by the engine's exhaust gases. ▪ **turbocharged** adjective.

turbofan noun a jet engine in which a turbine-driven fan provides additional thrust.

turbojet noun a jet engine in which the exhaust gases also operate a device for compressing the air drawn into the engine.

turboprop noun a jet engine in which a turbine is used to drive a propeller.

turbot noun (plural **turbot** or **turbots**) an edible flatfish.

turbulence noun **1** violent or unsteady movement of air or water. **2** conflict or confusion.

turbulent adjective **1** involving a lot of conflict, disorder, or confusion. **2** (of air or water) moving unsteadily or violently. ▪ **turbulently** adverb.

tureen noun a deep covered dish from which soup is served.

turf noun (plural **turfs** or **turves**) **1** grass and earth held together by its roots. **2** a piece of turf cut from the ground. **3** (**the turf**) horse racing. **4** (**your turf**) informal your territory. •verb **1** (**turf someone out**) Brit. informal force someone to leave. **2** cover with turf. □ **turf accountant** Brit. a bookmaker.

turgid adjective **1** (of language) pompous and boring. **2** swollen or full.

Turk noun a person from Turkey.

turkey noun (plural **turkeys**) a large game bird bred for food.

Turkish noun the language of Turkey. •adjective relating to Turkey or its language. □ **Turkish bath** a period of sitting in a room filled with very hot air or steam, followed by washing and massage. **Turkish delight** a sweet consisting of flavoured gelatin coated in icing sugar.

turmeric /ter-muh-rik/ noun a bright yellow powder obtained from a plant, used in Asian cookery.

THESAURUS

malignancy; Medicine carcinoma, sarcoma.

tune noun she hummed a tune: melody, air, strain, theme, song, jingle, ditty. •verb a body clock tuned to the tides: attune, adapt, adjust, regulate.

tunnel noun underground passage, underpass, subway, shaft, burrow, hole, warren, labyrinth. •verb dig, burrow, mine, bore, drill.

turbulent adjective tempestuous, stormy, unstable, unsettled, tumultuous, chaotic, anarchic, lawless. OPPOSITES peaceful.

turf noun grass, lawn, sod; literary sward.

turmoil noun a state of great disturbance, confusion, or uncertainty.

turn verb 1 move around a central point. 2 move so as to face or go in a different direction. 3 make or become: *she turned pale.* 4 shape on a lathe. 5 twist or sprain an ankle. •noun 1 an act of turning. 2 a bend in a road, river, etc. 3 a place where a road meets or branches off another. 4 the time when a member of a group must or is allowed to do something. 5 a time when one period of time ends and another begins. 6 a short walk or ride. 7 a brief feeling of illness. 8 a short performance. □ be turned out be dressed in a particular way. do someone a good turn do something that is helpful for someone. to a turn to exactly the right degree. turn someone/thing down 1 reject an offer made by someone. 2 reduce the volume or strength of sound, heat, etc. produced by a device. turn in informal go to bed. turn someone in hand someone over to the authorities. turn something off switch something off. turn on suddenly attack. turn someone/thing on 1 switch something on. 2 informal excite someone sexually. turn out 1 prove to be the case. 2 be present at an event. turn something out switch off an electric light. turn over (of an engine) start to run. turn up 1 be found. 2 arrive. turn something up increase the volume or strength of sound, heat, etc. produced by a device. turn-up Brit. 1 the end of a trouser leg folded upwards on the outside. 2 informal an unusual or unexpected event.

turncoat noun a person who deserts one party or cause in order to join an opposing one.

turning noun a place where a road branches off another.
□ turning point a time when a decisive change happens, especially one with good results.

turnip noun a round root which is eaten as a vegetable.

turnkey noun (plural **turnkeys**) old use a jailer.

turnout noun the number of people attending or taking part in an event.

turnover noun 1 the amount of money taken by a business in a particular period. 2 the rate at which employees leave a workforce and are replaced. 3 the rate at which goods are sold and replaced in a

---

THESAURUS

turmoil noun confusion, upheaval, turbulence, tumult, disorder, disturbance, ferment, chaos, mayhem.
OPPOSITES peace, order.

turn verb 1 *the wheels were still turning:* go round, revolve, rotate, spin, roll, circle, wheel, whirl, gyrate, swivel, pivot. 2 *I turned and headed back:* change direction, change course, make a U-turn, turn about/round, wheel round. 3 *the path turned to right and left:* bend, curve, wind, twist, meander, snake, zigzag. 4 *Emma turned red:* become, go, grow, get. 5 *the milk had turned:* (go) sour, go off, curdle, become rancid, go bad, spoil.
•noun 1 *a turn of the wheel:* rotation, revolution, spin, whirl, gyration, swivel. 2 *a turn to the left:* change of direction, veer, divergence. 3 *we're approaching the turn:* bend, corner, junction, twist, dog-leg; Brit. hairpin bend. 4 *you'll get your turn:* opportunity, chance, say, stint, time, try; informal go, shot, stab, crack. 5 *she did me some good turns:* service, deed, act, favour, kindness, disservice, wrong.
□ turn someone/something down 1 *his novel was turned down:* reject, spurn, rebuff, refuse, decline. 2 *Pete turned the sound down:* reduce, lower, decrease, lessen, mute. turn into become, develop into, turn out to be, be transformed into, change into. turn something into convert, change, transform, make, adapt, modify. turn something off/out switch off, shut off, put off, extinguish, deactivate; informal kill, cut. turn something on switch on, put on, start up, activate, trip. turn out 1 *a huge crowd turned out:* come, be present, attend, appear, turn up, arrive, assemble, gather; informal show up. 2 *it turned out that she had been abroad:* transpire, emerge, come to light, become apparent. 3 *things didn't turn out well:* happen, occur, come about, develop, work out, come out, end up; informal pan out. turn up 1 *the documents turned up:* be found, be discovered, be located, reappear. 2 *the police turned up:* arrive, appear, present yourself; informal show (up). 3 *something better will turn up:* present itself, occur, happen, crop up. turn something up 1 *she turned up the volume:* increase, raise, amplify, intensify. 2 *they turned up lots of information:* discover, uncover, unearth, find, dig up, expose.

turning noun junction, turn-off, side road, exit; N. Amer. turnout.

turning point noun watershed, critical moment, decisive moment, moment of truth, crossroads, crisis.

turnout noun 1 *the lecture attracted a good turnout:* attendance, audience, house, congregation, crowd, gate, gathering. 2 *his turnout was very elegant:* outfit, clothing, dress, garb, attire, ensemble; informal get-up.

turnover noun 1 *a turnover of £2 million:* gross revenue, income, yield, sales. 2 *staff turnover:* replacement, change, movement.

t

shop. **4** a small pie made by folding a piece of pastry over on itself to enclose a filling.

turnpike noun US & historical a road on which a toll is charged.

turnstile noun a gate with revolving arms allowing only one person at a time to pass through.

turntable noun a circular revolving platform or support, e.g. for the record in a record player.

turpentine noun a liquid obtained from certain trees, used to thin paint and clean brushes.

turpitude noun formal wickedness.

turps noun informal turpentine.

turquoise noun **1** a greenish-blue or sky-blue semi-precious stone. **2** a greenish-blue colour.

turret noun **1** a small tower at the corner of a building or wall. **2** an armoured tower for a gun in a ship, aircraft, or tank. ■ **turreted** adjective.

turtle noun a reptile with a bony or leathery shell, that lives in the sea. ◻ **turn turtle** (of a boat) turn upside down. **turtle dove** a small dove with a soft call.

turtleneck noun **1** Brit. a high, round, close-fitting neck on a garment. **2** N. Amer. a polo neck.

turves plural of TURF.

tusk noun a long, pointed tooth which protrudes from the closed mouth of an elephant, walrus, or wild boar.

tussle noun a short struggle or scuffle. ● verb (**tussles, tussling, tussled**) be involved in a tussle.

tussock noun a dense clump or tuft of grass.

tutelage /tyoo-ti-lij/ noun formal **1** protection or authority. **2** instruction.

tutelary /tyoo-ti-luh-ri/ adjective formal acting as a protector, guardian, or patron.

tutor noun **1** a person who teaches a single pupil or a very small group. **2** Brit. a university or college teacher with extra responsibility for students. ● verb act as a tutor to.

tutorial noun a period of teaching by a university or college tutor. ● adjective relating to a tutor.

tutu noun a female ballet dancer's very short, stiff skirt that sticks out from the waist.

tuxedo /tuk-see-doh/ noun (plural **tuxedos** or **tuxedoes**) chiefly N. Amer. a man's dinner jacket.

TV abbreviation television.

twaddle noun informal silly talk or writing.

twain old-fashioned form of TWO.

twang noun **1** a strong ringing sound made by the plucked string of a musical instrument. **2** a distinctive nasal way of speaking. ● verb make a twang. ■ **twangy** adjective.

tweak verb **1** twist or pull with a small but sharp movement. **2** informal improve by making small adjustments. ● noun an act of tweaking.

twee adjective Brit. too sentimental or sweet.

tweed noun a rough woollen cloth flecked with mixed colours. ■ **tweedy** adjective.

tweet noun the chirp of a small or young bird. ● verb make a chirping noise.

tweeter noun a loudspeaker that reproduces high frequencies.

tweezers plural noun a small pair of pincers for plucking out hairs and picking up small objects.

twelfth ordinal number being number twelve in a sequence; 12th.

twelve cardinal number two more than ten; 12. (Roman numeral: **xii** or **XII**.)

twenty cardinal number (plural **twenties**) ten less than thirty; 20. (Roman numeral: **xx** or **XX**.) ◻ **twenty-twenty vision** normal vision. ■ **twentieth** ordinal number.

twerp noun informal a silly person.

twice adverb **1** two times. **2** double in degree or quantity.

twiddle verb (**twiddles, twiddling, twiddled**) fiddle with something in an aimless or nervous way. ◻ **twiddle your thumbs** have nothing to do. ■ **twiddly** adjective.

twig¹ noun a slender woody shoot growing from a branch or stem of a tree or shrub.

twig² verb (**twigs, twigging, twigged**) Brit. informal understand or realize something.

twilight noun **1** the soft glowing light from the sky when the sun is below the horizon. **2** a period or state of gradual decline. ■ **twilit** adjective.

twill noun a fabric with a slightly ridged surface.

THESAURUS

tutor noun *a history tutor*: teacher, instructor, coach, educator, lecturer, trainer, mentor.
● verb *he was tutored at home*: teach, instruct, educate, school, coach, train, drill.

twilight noun **1** *we arrived at twilight*: dusk, sunset, sundown, nightfall, evening, close of day. **2** *it was scarcely visible in the twilight*: half-light, semi-darkness, gloom. OPPOSITES dawn.

twin noun **1** each of two children born at the same birth. **2** a thing that is exactly like another. • **adjective** forming or being one of a pair of twins. • **verb** (**twins, twinning, twinned**) link or combine as a pair.

twine noun strong string consisting of strands twisted together. • **verb** (**twines, twining, twined**) wind round something.

twinge noun **1** a sudden, sharp pain. **2** a brief, sharp pang of emotion.

twinkle verb (**twinkles, twinkling, twinkled**) **1** shine with a gleam that changes constantly from bright to faint. **2** (of a person's eyes) sparkle with amusement or liveliness. • **noun** a twinkling sparkle or gleam.
■ **twinkly** adjective.

twinset noun a woman's matching cardigan and jumper.

twirl verb spin quickly and lightly round. • **noun** an act of twirling.
■ **twirly** adjective.

twist verb **1** bend, curl, or distort. **2** force out of the natural position. **3** have a winding course. **4** deliberately change the meaning of. **5** (**twisted**) unpleasantly abnormal; perverted. • **noun 1** an act of twisting. **2** a thing with a spiral shape. **3** a new or unexpected development or treatment. **4** (**the twist**) a dance with a twisting movement of the body, popular in the 1960s.
□ **twist someone's arm** informal forcefully persuade someone to do something.
■ **twister** noun.

twit[1] noun Brit. informal a silly person.

twit[2] verb (**twits, twitting, twitted**) informal tease good-humouredly.

twitch verb make a short jerking movement. • **noun** a twitching movement.

twitcher noun Brit. informal a keen birdwatcher.

twitchy adjective informal nervous.

twitter verb (**twitters, twittering, twittered**) **1** (of a bird) make a series of short, high sounds. **2** talk rapidly in a nervous or silly way. • **noun** a twittering sound.

two cardinal number one less than three; 2. (Roman numeral: **ii** or **II**.)
□ **put two and two together** draw a conclusion from what is known or evident. **two-dimensional** having or appearing to have length and breadth but no depth. **two-faced** insincere and deceitful. **two-time** be unfaithful to a husband, wife, or lover.
■ **twofold** adjective & adverb.

> **!** don't confuse **two** with **to** or **too**: see the note at **to**.

twopence or **tuppence** /tup-puhnss/ noun Brit. the sum of two pence before decimalization (1971).
■ **twopenny** (or **tuppenny**) adjective.

twosome noun a set of two people or things.

tycoon noun a wealthy, powerful person in business or industry.

tying present participle of **TIE**.

tyke or **tike** noun informal a mischievous child.

tympani ⇒ **TIMPANI**.

tympanum noun (plural **tympanums** or **tympana**) the eardrum.

THESAURUS

twin noun *a sitting room that was the twin of her own:* **duplicate**, double, carbon copy, likeness, mirror image, replica, lookalike, clone, match, pair; informal spitting image, dead ringer.
• **adjective 1** *the twin towers of the stadium:* **matching**, identical, paired. **2** *the twin aims of conservation and recreation:* **twofold**, double, dual, related, linked, connected, parallel, complementary.
• **verb** *the company twinned its brewing with distilling:* **combine**, join, link, couple, pair.

twinkle verb & noun **glitter**, sparkle, shine, glimmer, shimmer, glint, gleam, glisten, flicker, flash, wink.

twist verb **1** *the impact twisted the chassis:* **crumple**, crush, buckle, mangle, warp, deform, distort, contort. **2** *he twisted round in his seat:* **turn**, swivel, spin, pivot, rotate, revolve, twiddle. **3** *I twisted my ankle:* **sprain**, wrench, turn, rick, crick. **4** *she twisted her hair round her finger:* **wind**, twirl, coil, curl, wrap. **5** *the wires were twisted together:* **intertwine**, interlace, weave, plait, braid, coil, wind. **6** *the road twisted and turned:* **wind**, bend, curve, turn, meander, weave, zigzag, snake.
• **noun 1** *the twist of a dial:* **turn**, twirl, spin. **2** *the twists of the road:* **bend**, curve, turn, zigzag, dog-leg. **3** *the twists of the plot:* **convolution**, complication, complexity, intricacy, surprise, revelation.

twitch verb **1** *he twitched and then lay still:* **jerk**, convulse, have a spasm, quiver, tremble, shiver, shudder. **2** *he twitched the note out of my hand:* **snatch**, tweak, pluck, pull, tug; informal yank.
• **noun 1** *a twitch of her lips:* **spasm**, convulsion, quiver, tremor, shiver, shudder, tic. **2** *he gave a twitch at his moustache:* **pull**, tug, tweak; informal yank.

tycoon noun **magnate**, mogul, businessman, captain of industry, industrialist, financier, entrepreneur; informal, derogatory fat cat.

t

type noun **1** a category of people or things that share particular qualities or features. **3** informal a person of a particular nature: *a sporty type.* **4** printed characters or letters.
•verb **(types, typing, typed)** write using a typewriter or computer.
■ **typist** noun.

typecast verb **(be typecast)** (of an actor) always be cast in the same type of role.

typeface noun a particular design of printed letters or numbers.

typescript noun a typed copy of a written work.

typeset verb **(typeset, typesetting, typeset)** arrange or generate the data or type for text to be printed.
■ **typesetter** noun.

typewriter noun a machine with keys that are pressed to produce characters similar to printed ones.
■ **typewriting** noun **typewritten** adjective.

typhoid noun an infectious fever that causes red spots on the chest and severe pain in the intestines.

typhoon noun a tropical storm with very high winds.

typhus noun an infectious disease that causes a purple rash, headaches, fever, and usually delirium.

typical adjective **1** having the distinctive qualities of a particular type of person or thing. **2** characteristic of a particular person or thing.

■ **typically** adverb.

typify verb **(typifies, typifying, typified)** be typical of.

typo noun (plural **typos**) informal a small error in typed or printed writing.

typography noun **1** the setting and arrangement of printed characters. **2** the style and appearance of printed material.
■ **typographer** noun **typographical** (or **typographic**) adjective.

tyrannical adjective using power in a cruel or unfair way.
■ **tyrannically** adverb.

tyrannize or **tyrannise** verb **(tyrannizes, tyrannizing, tyrannized)** rule or dominate in a cruel or unfair way.

tyrannosaurus rex noun a large meat-eating dinosaur that walked on its strong hind legs.

tyranny noun (plural **tyrannies**) cruel and oppressive government or rule.

> ☑ one *r*, two *ns* : tyranny.

tyrant noun a cruel and oppressive ruler.

tyre (US spelling **tire**) noun a rubber covering, usually inflated, that fits round a wheel.

tyro noun (plural **tyros**) a beginner or novice.

tzar ⇨ TSAR.

tzatziki /tsat-see-ki/ noun a Greek side dish of yogurt with cucumber and garlic.

THESAURUS

type noun **1** *six types of coffee:* kind, sort, variety, class, category, set, genre, species, order, breed. **2** *italic type:* print, typeface, characters, lettering, font; Brit. fount.

typical adjective **1** *a typical example of art deco:* representative, characteristic, classic, quintessential, archetypal. **2** *a fairly typical day:* normal, average, ordinary, standard,

regular, routine, run-of-the-mill, conventional, unremarkable; informal bog-standard.
OPPOSITES unusual, exceptional.

tyranny noun despotism, absolute power, autocracy, dictatorship, totalitarianism, fascism, oppression, repression, subjugation, enslavement.

t

Uu

U or **u** noun (plural **Us** or **U's**) the twenty-first letter of the alphabet. • abbreviation Brit. (in film classification) universal.
□ **U-boat** a German submarine of the First or Second World War. **U-turn 1** the turning of a vehicle in a U-shaped course so as to face the opposite way. **2** a complete change in policy.

ubiquitous /yoo-**bi**-kwi-tuhss/ adjective appearing or found everywhere.
■ **ubiquitously** adverb **ubiquity** noun.

udder noun the bag-like milk-producing organ of female cattle, sheep, horses, etc.

UFO noun (plural **UFOs**) a mysterious object seen in the sky that some people believe is carrying beings from outer space (short for *unidentified flying object*).

Ugandan noun a person from Uganda.
• adjective relating to Uganda.

ugly adjective (**uglier**, **ugliest**) **1** unpleasant or unattractive in appearance. **2** hostile or threatening.
□ **ugly duckling** a person who unexpectedly turns out to be beautiful or talented.
■ **ugliness** noun.

UK abbreviation United Kingdom.

Ukrainian /yoo-**kray**-ni-uhn/ noun a person from Ukraine. • adjective relating to Ukraine.

ukulele or **ukelele** /yoo-kuh-**lay**-li/ noun a small four-stringed guitar.

ulcer noun an open sore on the body or on an internal organ.

■ **ulcerated** adjective **ulceration** noun.

ulna noun (plural **ulnae** /**ul**-nee/ or **ulnas**) the thinner and longer of the two bones in the human forearm.

ulterior adjective other than what is obvious or admitted: *she had an ulterior motive.*

ultimate adjective **1** happening at the end of a process. **2** being the best or most extreme example of its kind. **3** basic or fundamental. • noun (**the ultimate**) the best of its kind that is imaginable.
■ **ultimately** adverb.

ultimatum noun a final warning that action will be taken against you if you do not agree to another party's demands.

ultramarine noun a brilliant deep blue colour or pigment.

ultrasonic adjective involving sound waves with a frequency above the upper limit of human hearing.

ultrasound noun sound or other vibrations with an ultrasonic frequency, used in medical scans.

ultraviolet adjective (of electromagnetic radiation) having a wavelength just shorter than that of violet light.

ululate verb (**ululates**, **ululating**, **ululated**) howl or wail.
■ **ululation** noun.

umber noun a dark brown or yellowish-brown colour.

umbilical adjective relating to the navel or

THESAURUS

ubiquitous adjective everywhere, omnipresent, all over the place, all-pervasive, universal, worldwide, global. OPPOSITES rare.

ugly adjective **1** unattractive, unsightly, ill-favoured, hideous, plain, unprepossessing, horrible, ghastly, repellent; N. Amer. homely; Brit. informal no oil painting. **2** *things got pretty ugly:* unpleasant, nasty, disagreeable, alarming, dangerous, perilous, threatening, menacing, hostile, ominous, sinister. OPPOSITES beautiful, pleasant.

ultimate adjective **1** *the ultimate collapse of the Empire:* eventual, final, concluding, terminal, end. **2** *ultimate truths:* fundamental, basic, primary, elementary, absolute, central, crucial, essential, pivotal. **3** *the ultimate gift for cat lovers:* best, ideal, greatest, supreme, quintessential.

ultimately adverb **1** *the cost will ultimately fall on us:* eventually, in the end, in the long run, at length, finally, in time, one day. **2** *two ultimately contradictory reasons:* fundamentally, basically, primarily, essentially, at heart, deep down.

u

umbilical cord.

□ **umbilical cord** a flexible tube which connects a developing fetus with the placenta while it is in the womb.

umbilicus noun the navel.

umbra noun (plural **umbras** or **umbrae** /um-bree/) the shadow cast by the earth or the moon in an eclipse.

umbrage noun (**take umbrage**) take offence; become annoyed.

umbrella noun a folding device used as protection against rain. •adjective including or containing many different parts.

umlaut /uum-lowt/ noun a mark (¨) placed over a vowel in some languages to indicate how it should sound.

umpire noun (in certain sports) an official who supervises a game to make sure that players keep to the rules. •verb (**umpires, umpiring, umpired**) be the umpire of.

umpteen cardinal number informal very many.
■ **umpteenth** ordinal number.

UN abbreviation United Nations.

unabashed adjective not embarrassed or ashamed.

unabated adjective not reduced in intensity or strength.

unable adjective not able to do something.

unacceptable adjective not satisfactory or allowable.
■ **unacceptably** adverb.

unaccountable adjective 1 unable to be explained. 2 not having to explain your actions or decisions.
■ **unaccountably** adverb.

unaccustomed adjective 1 not usual. 2 (**unaccustomed to**) not familiar with or used to.

unadulterated adjective not mixed with any different or extra elements.

unaided adjective without any help.

unalloyed adjective complete; total: *unalloyed delight.*

unambiguous adjective not open to more than one interpretation.
■ **unambiguously** adverb.

unanimous adjective 1 fully in agreement.

2 (of an opinion, decision, or vote) held or carried by everyone involved.
■ **unanimity** noun **unanimously** adverb.

unannounced adjective without warning or notice.

unappetizing or **unappetising** adjective not inviting or attractive.

unapproachable adjective not welcoming or friendly.

unarguable adjective not able to be disagreed with.
■ **unarguably** adverb.

unarmed adjective not equipped with or carrying weapons.

unassailable adjective unable to be attacked, questioned, or defeated.

unassuming adjective not drawing attention to yourself or your abilities.

unattached adjective without a husband or wife or established lover.

unattended adjective not being supervised or looked after.

unauthorized or **unauthorised** adjective not having official permission or approval.

unavailing adjective achieving little or nothing.

unavoidable adjective not able to be avoided or prevented.
■ **unavoidably** adverb.

unaware adjective having no knowledge of a situation or fact.

unawares adverb so as to surprise someone; unexpectedly.

unbalanced adjective emotionally or mentally disturbed.

unbearable adjective not able to be endured.
■ **unbearably** adverb.

unbeknown or **unbeknownst** adjective (**unbeknown to**) without the knowledge of.

unbelievable adjective 1 unlikely to be true. 2 extraordinary.
■ **unbelievably** adverb.

unbeliever noun a person without religious belief.

---

umpire noun referee, judge, line judge, linesman, touch judge, adjudicator, arbitrator, moderator; informal ref.

unable adjective incapable, powerless, impotent, inadequate, incompetent, unqualified, unfit.

unanimous adjective 1 *doctors were unanimous about the effects:* in agreement, of one mind, in accord, united, undivided. 2 *a unanimous vote:* uniform, consistent, united.
OPPOSITES split.

unarmed adjective defenceless,

unprotected, unguarded.
OPPOSITES armed.

unaware adjective ignorant, oblivious, unconscious, unwitting, unsuspecting, uninformed, unenlightened, innocent; informal in the dark.
OPPOSITES aware.

unbelievable adjective incredible, inconceivable, unthinkable, unimaginable, unconvincing, far-fetched, implausible, improbable; informal hard to swallow.
OPPOSITES believable.

unbending adjective unwilling to compromise or change your mind.

unbiased or **unbiassed** adjective showing no prejudice.

unbidden adjective without having been invited.

unborn adjective not yet born.

unbounded adjective having no limits.

unbowed adjective not having given in or been defeated.

unbridgeable adjective (of a gap or difference between people) not able to be made smaller or less significant.

unbridled adjective uncontrolled: *unbridled lust.*

unburden verb (**unburden yourself**) confide in someone about your worries or problems.

uncalled adjective (**uncalled for**) not fair or appropriate; unnecessary.

uncanny adjective (**uncannier, uncanniest**) strange or mysterious.
■ **uncannily** adverb.

unceasing adjective not ceasing; continuous.
■ **unceasingly** adverb.

unceremonious adjective rude or abrupt.
■ **unceremoniously** adverb.

uncertain adjective 1 not known, reliable, or definite. 2 not completely confident or sure.
□ in no uncertain terms clearly and forcefully.
■ **uncertainly** adverb **uncertainty** noun.

uncharitable adjective unkind or unsympathetic to other people.
■ **uncharitably** adverb.

uncharted adjective (of an area of land or sea) not mapped or surveyed.

unchristian adjective 1 not in line with the teachings of Christianity. 2 not generous or fair.

uncle noun the brother of your father or mother or the husband of your aunt.
□ Uncle Sam the United States.

unclean adjective 1 dirty. 2 immoral. 3 (of food) forbidden by a religion.

uncomfortable adjective 1 not physically comfortable. 2 uneasy or awkward.
■ **uncomfortably** adverb.

uncommon adjective 1 out of the ordinary; unusual. 2 remarkably great.
■ **uncommonly** adverb.

uncomprehending adjective unable to understand something.
■ **uncomprehendingly** adverb.

uncompromising adjective unwilling to compromise.
■ **uncompromisingly** adverb.

unconcern noun a lack of worry or interest.
■ **unconcerned** adjective.

unconditional adjective not subject to any conditions.
■ **unconditionally** adverb.

unconfined adjective 1 not confined to a limited space. 2 (of joy or excitement) very great.

unconscionable /un-**kon**-shuh-nuh-b'l/ adjective formal not right or reasonable.
■ **unconscionably** adverb.

THESAURUS

unbiased adjective impartial, unprejudiced, neutral, non-partisan, disinterested, objective, even-handed, fair.

unbroken adjective 1 *the last unbroken window:* undamaged, unharmed, unscathed, untouched, sound, intact, whole. 2 *an unbroken chain of victories:* uninterrupted, continuous, endless, constant, unremitting, ongoing. 3 *his record is still unbroken:* unbeaten, undefeated, unsurpassed, unrivalled, unmatched, supreme.

uncanny adjective 1 *the silence was uncanny:* eerie, unnatural, unearthly, other-worldly, ghostly, strange, abnormal, weird; informal creepy, spooky. 2 *an uncanny resemblance:* striking, remarkable, extraordinary, exceptional, incredible.

uncertain adjective 1 *the effects are uncertain:* unknown, debatable, open to question, in doubt, unsure, in the balance, up in the air, unpredictable, unforeseeable; informal iffy. 2 *Ed was uncertain about the decision:* unsure, doubtful, dubious, undecided, irresolute, hesitant, vacillating, vague, unclear, ambivalent, in two minds.
OPPOSITES certain, predictable, sure.

unclear adjective uncertain, unsure, unsettled, up in the air, in doubt, ambiguous, equivocal, indefinite, vague, mysterious, obscure, hazy, nebulous.
OPPOSITES clear, evident.

uncomfortable adjective 1 *an uncomfortable chair:* painful, awkward, lumpy, confining, cramped. 2 *I felt uncomfortable in her presence:* uneasy, awkward, nervous, tense, edgy, restless, embarrassed, anxious; informal rattled, twitchy.
OPPOSITES comfortable, relaxed.

uncommon adjective unusual, abnormal, rare, atypical, exceptional, unconventional, unfamiliar, strange, extraordinary, peculiar, scarce, few and far between, isolated, infrequent.
OPPOSITES common.

unconditional adjective unquestioning, unqualified, unreserved, unlimited, unrestricted, wholehearted, complete, total, entire, full, absolute, unequivocal.

u

unconscious adjective 1 not awake and aware of your surroundings. 2 done or existing without you realizing. 3 (**unconscious of**) unaware of. • noun the part of the mind which you are not aware of but which affects behaviour and emotions.
■ **unconsciously** adverb **unconsciousness** noun.

unconstitutional adjective not allowed by the constitution of a country or the rules of an organization.
■ **unconstitutionally** adverb.

unconstrained adjective not restricted or limited.

uncontrollable adjective not able to be controlled.
■ **uncontrollably** adverb.

unconventional adjective not fitting in with what is generally done or believed.
■ **unconventionally** adverb.

unconvincing adjective failing to convince or impress.
■ **unconvincingly** adverb.

uncooperative adjective unwilling to help other people or do what they ask.

uncoordinated adjective 1 clumsy. 2 badly organized.

uncouth adjective lacking good manners.

uncover verb (**uncovers, uncovering, uncovered**) 1 remove a cover or covering from. 2 discover something previously secret or unknown.

unction noun 1 formal the smearing of someone with oil or ointment as part of a religious ceremony. 2 excessive politeness or flattery.

unctuous adjective excessively polite or flattering.
■ **unctuously** adverb.

undaunted adjective not discouraged by difficulty or danger.

undeceive verb tell someone that an idea or belief is mistaken.

undecided adjective 1 not having made a decision. 2 not yet settled or resolved.

undemonstrative adjective not tending to express feelings openly.

undeniable adjective unable to be denied or disputed.
■ **undeniably** adverb.

under preposition 1 extending or directly below. 2 at a lower level or grade than. 3 expressing control by another person. 4 in accordance with rules. 5 used to express grouping or classification. 6 undergoing a process. • adverb extending or directly below something.
□ **under way** 1 having started and making progress. 2 (of a boat) moving through the water.

underachieve verb (**underachieves, underachieving, underachieved**) do less well than is expected.

underarm adjective & adverb done with the arm or hand below shoulder level.

undercarriage noun the wheeled structure which supports an aircraft when it is on the ground.

underclass noun the lowest social class, consisting of very poor and unemployed people.

underclothes plural noun underwear.

undercoat noun a layer of paint applied before the top layer.

undercover adjective & adverb involving secret work for investigation or spying.

undercurrent noun an underlying feeling or influence.

undercut verb (**undercuts, undercutting, undercut**) 1 offer products or services at a lower price than a competitor. 2 weaken or undermine.

underdog noun a competitor thought to have little chance of winning a fight or contest.

underdone adjective not cooked enough.

THESAURUS

unconscious adjective 1 *she made sure he was unconscious:* knocked out, senseless, comatose, inert; informal out cold, out for the count. 2 *an unconscious desire:* subconscious, instinctive, involuntary, uncontrolled, subliminal; informal gut. 3 *blissfully unconscious of these problems:* unaware of, oblivious to, insensible to, impervious to, unaffected by.
OPPOSITES conscious, voluntary, aware.

uncouth adjective uncivilized, uncultured, rough, coarse, crude, loutish, boorish, rude, discourteous, disrespectful, bad-mannered, ill-bred.
OPPOSITES civilized.

uncover verb 1 *she uncovered the sandwiches:* expose, reveal, lay bare, unwrap, unveil, strip. 2 *they uncovered a plot:* discover, detect, come across, stumble on, chance on, find, turn up, unearth, dig up.

under preposition 1 *they hid under a bush:* below, beneath, underneath. 2 *the rent is under £250:* less than, lower than, below. 3 *branch managers are under the retail director:* subordinate to, answerable to, responsible to, subject to, junior to, inferior to.
OPPOSITES above, over.

undercover adjective secret, covert, clandestine, underground, surreptitious, furtive, cloak-and-dagger, stealthy; informal hush-hush.
OPPOSITES overt.

u

underdressed adjective wearing clothes that are too plain or casual.

underestimate verb (**underestimates, underestimating, underestimated**) **1** estimate something to be smaller or less important than it really is. **2** think of someone as less capable than they really are. •noun an estimate that is too low. ■ underestimation noun.

underfoot adverb **1** on the ground. **2** constantly present and in the way.

undergarment noun a piece of underwear.

undergo verb (**undergoes, undergoing, underwent**; past participle **undergone**) experience something unpleasant or difficult.

undergraduate noun a student at a university who has not yet taken a first degree.

underground adjective & adverb **1** beneath the surface of the ground. **2** in secrecy or hiding. •noun **1** Brit. an underground railway. **2** a secret group working against the government or an enemy.

undergrowth noun a mass of shrubs and other plants growing closely together.

underhand adjective done in a secret or dishonest way.

underlay noun material laid under a carpet.

underlie verb (**underlies, underlying, underlay**; past participle **underlain**) lie or be situated under.

underline verb (**underlines, underlining, underlined**) **1** draw a line under. **2** emphasize.

underling noun disapproving a person of lower status.

undermine verb (**undermines, undermining, undermined**) **1** damage or weaken. **2** wear away the base or foundation of.

underneath preposition & adverb **1** situated directly below. **2** so as to be concealed by. •noun the part or side facing towards the ground.

underpants plural noun a piece of underwear covering the lower part of the body and having two holes for the legs.

underpart noun a lower part.

underpass noun a road or tunnel passing under another road or a railway.

underpin verb (**underpins, underpinning, underpinned**) **1** support or form the basis for an argument, claim, etc. **2** support a structure from below.

underplay verb represent something as being less important than it really is.

underprivileged adjective not having the same rights or standard of living as the majority of the population.

underrated verb rated less highly than is deserved.

underscore verb underline.

undersea adjective found or situated below the surface of the sea.

undersecretary noun (plural **undersecretaries**) (in the UK) a junior minister or senior civil servant.

undersell verb (**undersells, underselling, undersold**) sell something at a lower price than a competitor.

underside noun the bottom or lower side or surface of something.

undersigned noun formal the person or people who have signed the document in question.

undersized or **undersize** adjective of less than the usual size.

understaffed adjective having too few members of staff.

understand verb (**understands,**

THESAURUS

underestimate verb underrate, undervalue, miscalculate, misjudge, do an injustice to.
OPPOSITES overestimate.

undergo verb experience, go through, submit to, face, be subjected to, receive, endure, brave, bear, withstand, weather.

underground adjective **1** an underground car park: subterranean, buried, sunken, basement. **2** underground organizations: secret, clandestine, surreptitious, covert, undercover, closet, cloak-and-dagger, resistance, subversive.
•noun **1** he took the underground: metro; N. Amer. subway; Brit. informal tube.
2 information from the French underground: resistance, partisans, guerrillas, freedom fighters.

underline verb **1** she underlined a phrase:

underscore, mark, pick out, emphasize, highlight. **2** the programme underlines the benefits of exercise: emphasize, stress, highlight, accentuate, accent, focus on, spotlight.

underlying adjective fundamental, basic, primary, central, essential, principal, elementary, initial.

undermine verb weaken, diminish, reduce, impair, mar, spoil, ruin, damage, sap, shake, threaten, subvert, compromise, sabotage.
OPPOSITES strengthen, support.

understand verb **1** he couldn't understand anything we said: comprehend, grasp, take in, see, apprehend, follow, make sense of, fathom; informal work out, figure out, make head or tail of, get; Brit. informal twig, suss.
2 she understood how hard he'd worked:

u

understanding, **understood**) 1 know or realize the real or intended meaning or cause of. 2 know how someone feels or why they behave in a particular way. 3 interpret or view in a particular way. 4 believe that something is the case because of information that you have received.

understandable adjective 1 able to be understood. 2 natural, reasonable, or forgivable.
■ **understandably** adverb.

understanding noun 1 the ability to understand something. 2 a person's intellect. 3 the way in which a person looks at a situation. 4 sympathetic awareness or tolerance. 5 an informal or unspoken agreement or arrangement. • adjective sympathetically aware of other people's feelings.
■ **understandingly** adverb.

understate verb (**understates**, **understating**, **understated**) represent something as being smaller or less significant than it really is.
■ **understatement** noun.

understated adjective pleasingly subtle.

understudy noun (plural **understudies**) an actor who learns another's role in order to take their place if necessary. • verb (**understudies**, **understudying**, **understudied**) be an understudy for.

undertake verb (**undertake**, **undertaking**, **undertook**; past participle **undertaken**) 1 begin an activity. 2 formally guarantee or promise.

undertaker noun a person whose job is preparing dead bodies for burial or cremation and making arrangements for funerals.

undertaking noun 1 a formal promise to do something. 2 a task.

undertone noun 1 a subdued or muted tone. 2 an underlying quality or feeling.

undertow noun a current under the surface of water.

underused adjective not used as much as it could or should be.
■ **underuse** noun.

underwater adjective & adverb situated, happening, or used beneath the surface of the water.

underwear noun clothing worn under other clothes next to the skin.

underweight adjective below a normal or

know, realize, recognize, acknowledge, appreciate, be aware of, be conscious of. 3 *I understand that you wish to go:* believe, gather, take it, hear (tell), notice, see, learn.

understandable adjective 1 *make the issues understandable to the layman:* comprehensible, intelligible, clear, plain, unambiguous, transparent, user-friendly, straightforward, explicit, coherent. 2 *an understandable desire:* unsurprising, expected, predictable, inevitable, reasonable, acceptable, logical, rational, normal, natural, justifiable, excusable, pardonable, forgivable.
OPPOSITES incomprehensible, surprising, illogical, abnormal, unforgivable.

understanding noun 1 *test your understanding of the language:* comprehension, grasp, mastery, appreciation, knowledge, awareness, skill, expertise, proficiency; informal know-how. 2 *a young man of brilliant understanding:* intellect, intelligence, brainpower, judgement, insight, intuition, acumen, sagacity, wisdom; informal nous. 3 *it was my understanding that this was free:* belief, perception, view, conviction, feeling, opinion, intuition, impression. 4 *he treated me with understanding:* sympathy, compassion, pity, feeling, concern, consideration, kindness, sensitivity, decency, goodwill. 5 *we had a tacit understanding:* agreement, arrangement, deal, bargain, settlement, pledge, pact.
OPPOSITES ignorance, indifference.
• adjective *an understanding friend:* sympathetic, compassionate, sensitive, considerate, kind, thoughtful, tolerant, patient, forbearing, lenient, forgiving.

understate verb play down, underrate, underplay, trivialize, minimize, diminish, downgrade, brush aside, gloss over.
OPPOSITES exaggerate.

undertake verb 1 *we undertook a survey of the site:* set about, embark on, go about, engage in, take on, be responsible for, get down to, get to grips with, tackle, attempt; informal have a go at. 2 *the Minister undertook to attend:* promise, pledge, vow, give your word, swear, guarantee, contract, give an assurance, commit yourself.

undertaker noun funeral director; N. Amer. mortician.

undertaking noun 1 *a risky undertaking:* enterprise, venture, project, campaign, scheme, plan, operation, endeavour, effort, task. 2 *sign this undertaking to comply with the rules:* promise, pledge, agreement, oath, covenant, vow, commitment, guarantee, assurance.

underwater adjective submerged, sunken, undersea, submarine.

underwear noun underclothes, undergarments, underthings, lingerie; informal undies; Brit. informal smalls.

u

desirable weight.

underwent past of **UNDERGO**.

underwhelmed verb humorous not very impressed.

underworld noun **1** the world of criminals or of organized crime. **2** (in myths and legends) the home of the dead, imagined as being under the earth.

underwrite verb (**underwrites, underwriting, underwrote;** past participle **underwritten**) **1** accept legal responsibility for an insurance policy. **2** accept financial responsibility for an undertaking.
■ **underwriter** noun.

undesirable adjective harmful, offensive, or unpleasant. •noun an unpleasant or offensive person.

undeterred adjective persevering despite setbacks.

undeviating adjective constant and steady.

undies plural noun informal pieces of underwear.

undisputed adjective not disputed or called into question.

undistinguished adjective not particularly good or successful.

undivided adjective **1** not divided or broken into parts. **2** complete; total: *my undivided attention.*

undo verb (**undoes, undoing, undid;** past participle **undone**) **1** unfasten or loosen. **2** reverse the effects of something previously done. **3** formal cause the downfall or ruin of.

undoing noun formal a person's ruin or downfall.

undoubted adjective not questioned or doubted.
■ **undoubtedly** adverb.

undreamed or Brit. **undreamt** adjective

(**undreamed of**) not previously thought to be possible.

undress verb **1** (also **get undressed**) take off your clothes. **2** take the clothes off someone else. •noun formal the state of being naked or only partially clothed.

undue adjective more than is reasonable or necessary.
■ **unduly** adverb.

undulate verb (**undulates, undulating, undulated**) **1** move with a smooth wave-like motion. **2** have a wavy form or outline.
■ **undulation** noun.

undying adjective lasting forever.

unearth verb **1** find in the ground by digging. **2** discover by investigation or searching.

unearthly adjective **1** unnatural or mysterious. **2** informal very early and therefore inconvenient or annoying.

unease noun anxiety or discontent.

uneasy adjective (**uneasier, uneasiest**) anxious or uncomfortable.
■ **uneasily** adverb **uneasiness** noun.

unedifying adjective distasteful or unpleasant.

unemployable adjective not having enough skills or qualifications to get paid employment.

unemployed adjective without a paid job but available to work.

unemployment noun **1** the state of being unemployed. **2** the number or proportion of unemployed people.

unencumbered adjective not burdened or held back.

unending adjective seeming to last forever.

unenviable adjective difficult, undesirable,

THESAURUS

underwrite verb sponsor, support, back, insure, indemnify, subsidize, pay for, finance, fund; N. Amer. informal bankroll.

undesirable adjective unpleasant, disagreeable, nasty, unwelcome, unwanted, unfortunate.
OPPOSITES pleasant.

undo verb **1** *he undid his shirt:* unfasten, unbutton, unhook, untie, unlace, unlock, unbolt, loosen, detach, free, open. **2** *they will undo a decision by the lords:* cancel, reverse, overrule, overturn, repeal, rescind, countermand, revoke, annul, invalidate, negate. **3** *she undid much of the good work:* ruin, undermine, overturn, scotch, sabotage, spoil, impair, mar, destroy, wreck; informal blow; Brit. informal scupper.
OPPOSITES fasten, ratify, enhance.

undoubtedly adverb doubtless, indubitably, unquestionably, indisputably,

undeniably, incontrovertibly, without (a) doubt, clearly.

unearth verb **1** *workmen unearthed an artillery shell:* dig up, excavate, exhume, disinter, root out. **2** *I unearthed an interesting fact:* discover, uncover, find, come across, hit on, bring to light, expose, turn up.

uneasy adjective **1** *the doctor made him feel uneasy:* worried, anxious, troubled, disturbed, nervous, nervy, tense, edgy, apprehensive, fearful, uncomfortable, unsettled; informal jittery. **2** *an uneasy peace:* tense, awkward, strained, fraught, precarious, unstable, insecure.
OPPOSITES calm, stable.

unemployed adjective jobless, out of work, unwaged, redundant, laid off, on benefit; Brit. signing on; N. Amer. on welfare; Brit. informal on the dole, resting.

u

or unpleasant.

unequal adjective **1** not equal. **2** not fair or even. **3** (**unequal to**) not having the ability to meet a challenge.
■ **unequally** adverb.

unequalled (US spelling **unequaled**) adjective better or greater than all others.

unequivocal adjective leaving no doubt; unambiguous.
■ **unequivocally** adverb.

unerring adjective always right or accurate.
■ **unerringly** adverb.

uneven adjective **1** not level or smooth. **2** not regular or equal.
■ **unevenly** adverb **unevenness** noun.

uneventful adjective not marked by interesting or exciting events.
■ **uneventfully** adverb.

unexceptionable adjective not able to be objected to, but not particularly new or exciting.

unexceptional adjective not out of the ordinary; usual.
■ **unexceptionally** adverb.

unexpected adjective not expected or thought likely to happen.
■ **unexpectedly** adverb.

unexpurgated adjective (of a written work) complete and containing all the original material.

unfailing adjective reliable or never changing.
■ **unfailingly** adverb.

unfair adjective not fair or just.
■ **unfairly** adverb **unfairness** noun.

unfaithful adjective **1** having sex with someone who is not your husband, wife, or usual partner. **2** disloyal.

unfathomable adjective incapable of being fully understood.

unfavourable (US spelling **unfavorable**) adjective **1** not approving. **2** not good or likely to lead to success.
■ **unfavourably** adverb.

unfazed adjective informal not worried or confused by something unexpected.

unfeasible adjective not able to be done or achieved.
■ **unfeasibly** adverb.

unfit adjective **1** unsuitable. **2** not in good physical condition.

unflagging adjective not becoming weak or tired.

unflappable adjective informal calm in a crisis.

unflinching adjective not afraid or hesitant.
■ **unflinchingly** adverb.

unfold verb **1** open or spread out from a folded position. **2** reveal or be revealed.

unforeseen adjective not anticipated or predicted; unexpected.
■ **unforeseeable** adjective.

> ☑ remember the e before the r: unforeseen.

unforgettable adjective very memorable.
■ **unforgettably** adverb.

unforgivable adjective so bad as to be unable to be forgiven.
■ **unforgivably** adverb.

unforgiving adjective **1** not willing to forgive. **2** (of conditions) harsh.

unforthcoming adjective **1** not willing to give out information. **2** not available when needed.

unfortunate adjective **1** unlucky. **2** regrettable or inappropriate. • noun a

THESAURUS

uneven adjective **1** *uneven ground:* bumpy, rough, lumpy, stony, rocky, rutted. **2** *uneven teeth:* irregular, crooked, lopsided, askew, asymmetrical. **3** *uneven quality:* inconsistent, variable, fluctuating, irregular, erratic, patchy.
OPPOSITES flat, regular.

unfair adjective **1** *the trial was unfair:* unjust, prejudiced, biased, discriminatory, one-sided, unequal, uneven, unbalanced, partisan. **2** *his comments were unfair:* undeserved, unmerited, unreasonable, unjustified; Brit. informal out of order. **3** *unfair play:* unsporting, dirty, underhand, dishonourable, dishonest.
OPPOSITES fair, just, justified.

unfasten verb undo, open, disconnect, remove, untie, unbutton, unzip, loosen, free, unlock, unbolt.

unfit adjective **1** *the film is unfit for children:* unsuitable, inappropriate, not designed.

2 *unfit for duty:* incapable of, not up to, not equal to, unequipped, inadequate; informal not cut out for. **3** *I am unfit:* unhealthy, out of condition/shape.
OPPOSITES fit, suitable, capable, healthy.

unfold verb **1** *May unfolded the map:* open out, spread out, flatten, straighten out, unroll. **2** *I watched the events unfold:* develop, evolve, happen, take place, occur.
OPPOSITES fold up.

unfortunate adjective **1** *unfortunate people:* unlucky, hapless, wretched, forlorn, poor, pitiful; informal down on your luck. **2** *an unfortunate start to our holiday:* unwelcome, disadvantageous, unfavourable, unlucky, adverse, unpromising, inauspicious. **3** *an unfortunate remark:* regrettable, inappropriate, unsuitable, tactless, injudicious.
OPPOSITES fortunate, lucky, auspicious,

u

person who suffers bad luck.
■ **unfortunately** adverb.

unfounded adjective having no basis in fact.

unfurl verb open something that is rolled or folded.

ungainly adjective clumsy; awkward.
■ **ungainliness** noun.

ungodly adjective 1 immoral or disrespectful to God. 2 informal very early or late, and therefore annoying.

ungovernable adjective impossible to control or govern.

ungrateful adjective not grateful.
■ **ungratefully** adverb.

unguarded adjective 1 without protection. 2 not well considered; careless: *an unguarded remark*.

unguent /ung-yuu-uhnt/ noun a soft greasy or thick substance used as ointment or for lubrication.

ungulate noun the name in zoology for a hoofed mammal.

unhappy adjective (**unhappier, unhappiest**) 1 not happy. 2 unfortunate.
■ **unhappily** adverb **unhappiness** noun.

unharmed adjective not harmed.

unhealthy adjective (**unhealthier, unhealthiest**) 1 not having good health. 2 not good for your health.
■ **unhealthily** adverb.

unheard adjective 1 not heard or listened to. 2 (**unheard of**) previously unknown.

unhelpful adjective not helpful.
■ **unhelpfully** adverb.

unheralded adjective not previously announced, expected, or recognized.

unhesitating adjective without doubt or hesitation.
■ **unhesitatingly** adverb.

unhinged adjective mentally ill or unbalanced.

unholy adjective 1 sinful; wicked. 2 unnatural and likely to be harmful. 3 informal dreadful.

unhurried adjective moving or doing things in a leisurely way.
■ **unhurriedly** adverb.

unhurt adjective not hurt or harmed.

unicameral adjective (of a parliament) consisting of only one main part.

unicorn noun (in stories) a creature like a horse with a single long horn on its forehead.

unicycle noun a cycle with a single wheel.
■ **unicyclist** noun.

unidentified adjective not recognized or identified.

unification noun the process of uniting or of being united.

uniform noun the distinctive clothing worn by members of the same organization or school. •adjective not varying; the same in all cases and at all times.
■ **uniformed** adjective **uniformity** noun **uniformly** adverb.

unify verb (**unifies, unifying, unified**) make or become united.

unilateral adjective done by or affecting only one person or group.
■ **unilaterally** adverb.

unimaginable adjective impossible to imagine or understand.
■ **unimaginably** adverb.

THESAURUS

well chosen.

ungainly adjective awkward, clumsy, graceless, inelegant, gawky, gauche, uncoordinated.
OPPOSITES graceful.

unhappy adjective 1 *why are you looking so unhappy?* sad, miserable, sorrowful, dejected, despondent, disconsolate, morose, heartbroken, down, dispirited, downhearted, depressed, melancholy, mournful, gloomy, glum; informal down in the mouth, fed up, blue. 2 *I was unhappy with the service:* dissatisfied, displeased, discontented, disappointed, disgruntled. 3 *an unhappy coincidence:* unfortunate, unlucky, ill-starred, ill-fated, doomed; informal jinxed.
OPPOSITES happy, pleased, cheerful, lucky.

unhealthy adjective 1 *an unhealthy lifestyle:* harmful, detrimental, destructive, injurious, damaging, noxious, poisonous. 2 *he's pretty unhealthy:* sick, poorly, ill, unwell, unfit, ailing, weak, frail, infirm,

washed out, run down. 3 *an unhealthy obsession:* abnormal, morbid, macabre, twisted, unwholesome, warped, depraved, unnatural; informal sick.

uniform adjective 1 *a uniform temperature:* constant, consistent, steady, invariable, unchanging, stable, static, regular, fixed, even. 2 *pieces of uniform size:* identical, matching, similar, equal, same, like, consistent.
OPPOSITES variable.
•noun *a soldier in uniform:* costume, outfit, suit, ensemble, livery, regalia; informal get-up, rig, gear.

unify verb unite, combine, bring together, join, merge, fuse, amalgamate, coalesce, consolidate.
OPPOSITES separate.

uninteresting adjective boring, dull, unexciting, tiresome, tedious, dreary, lifeless, humdrum, colourless, bland, insipid, banal, dry.
OPPOSITES interesting, exciting.

u

unimaginative adjective not using or showing imagination or new ideas; dull. ■ **unimaginatively** adverb.

unimpeachable adjective not able to be doubted or criticized.

unimportant adjective not important. ■ **unimportance** noun.

uninhabited adjective having no people living there. ■ **uninhabitable** adjective.

uninhibited adjective saying or doing things without concern about what other people think.

uninitiated adjective without knowledge or experience of something.

uninspired adjective 1 not original or exciting; dull. 2 feeling no excitement. ■ **uninspiring** adjective.

unintelligible adjective impossible to understand. ■ **unintelligibility** noun **unintelligibly** adverb.

unintentional adjective not done on purpose. ■ **unintentionally** adverb.

uninterested adjective not interested or concerned.

> ! don't confuse **uninterested** and **disinterested**. Disinterested means 'impartial' , while **uninterested** means 'not interested'.

uninterrupted adjective not interrupted; continuous.

union noun 1 the act of uniting two or more things. 2 a trade union. 3 a club, society, or association. 4 (also **Union**) a political unit consisting of a number of states or provinces with the same central government. 5 a state of harmony or agreement. 6 a marriage. □ Union Jack (or **Union Flag**) the national

flag of the United Kingdom.

unionist noun 1 a member of a trade union. 2 (**Unionist**) a person in favour of the union of Northern Ireland with Great Britain.

unionize or **unionise** verb (**unionizes, unionizing, unionized**) make or become members of a trade union. ■ **unionization** noun.

unique adjective 1 being the only one of its kind. 2 (**unique to**) belonging or connected to one particular person, group, or place. 3 very special or unusual. ■ **uniquely** adverb.

unisex adjective designed to be suitable for both sexes.

unison noun (**in unison**) at the same time; together.

unit noun 1 a single thing or group that is complete in itself but can also form part of something larger. 2 a device, part, or item of furniture with a particular function: *a sink unit.* 3 a self-contained section of a building or group of buildings. 4 a subdivision of a larger military grouping. 5 a quantity used as a standard measure. □ unit trust Brit. a company that invests money in various different businesses on behalf of individuals, who can buy small units.

Unitarian noun a member of a Christian Church that believes that God is one being and rejects the idea of the Trinity.

unitary adjective 1 forming a single unit or entity. 2 relating to a unit or units.

unite verb (**unites, uniting, united**) 1 join together with others in order to do something as a group. 2 bring people or things together to form a unit or whole. ■ **united** adjective.

unity noun (plural **unities**) 1 the state of

THESAURUS

union noun 1 *the union of art and nature:* unification, joining, merger, fusion, amalgamation, coalition, combination, synthesis, blend. 2 *a trade union:* association, league, guild, confederation, federation.
OPPOSITES separation, parting.

unique adjective 1 *each town has its unique quality:* distinctive, individual, special, particular, specific, idiosyncratic, single, sole, lone, unrepeated, solitary, exclusive; informal one-off. 2 *a unique insight into history:* remarkable, special, notable, unequalled, unparalleled, unmatched, unsurpassed, incomparable.
OPPOSITES common.

unit noun 1 *the family is the fundamental unit of society:* component, element, constituent, subdivision. 2 *a unit of*

currency: quantity, measure, denomination. 3 *a guerrilla unit:* group, detachment, contingent, division, cell, faction, department, office, branch.

unite verb 1 *uniting the nation:* unify, join, link, connect, combine, amalgamate, fuse, weld, bond, bring together. 2 *environmentalists and activists united:* join together, join forces, combine, band together, ally, cooperate, collaborate, work together, team up. 3 *he sought to unite comfort with elegance:* merge, mix, blend, mingle, combine.
OPPOSITES divide.

unity noun 1 *European unity:* union, unification, integration, amalgamation, coalition, federation, confederation. 2 *unity between opposing factions:* harmony, accord, cooperation,

u

being united or forming a whole. **2** a thing forming a complex whole. **3** Maths the number one.

universal adjective **1** affecting or done by all people or things in the world or in a particular group. **2** true or right in all cases.
■ universality noun universally adverb.

universe noun the whole of space and everything in it.

university noun (plural **universities**) an institution where students study for a degree, and where academic research is done.

unjust adjective not just; unfair.
■ unjustly adverb.

unjustifiable adjective impossible to justify.
■ unjustifiably adverb.

unjustified adjective not justified; unfair.

unkempt adjective having an untidy appearance.

unkind adjective not caring or kind.
■ unkindly adverb unkindness noun.

unknowing adjective not knowing or aware.
■ unknowingly adverb.

unknown adjective not known or familiar.
• noun an unknown person or thing.
□ unknown quantity a person or thing that is not known about and whose actions or effects are unpredictable. Unknown Soldier an unidentified member of a country's armed forces killed in war, buried in a national memorial to represent all those killed but unidentified.

unladylike adjective not typical of a well-mannered woman or girl.

unlawful adjective not obeying or allowed by law or rules.
■ unlawfully adverb.

unleaded adjective (of petrol) without added lead.

unleash verb release something from a leash or restraint; set free.

unleavened adjective (of bread) flat because made without yeast.

unless conjunction except when; if not.

unlike preposition **1** different from; not like. **2** in contrast to. **3** not characteristic of.
• adjective different from each other.

unlikely adjective (unlikelier, unlikeliest) **1** not likely to happen. **2** not what you would expect.
■ unlikelihood noun.

unlimited adjective not limited or restricted.

unload verb remove goods from a vehicle, ship, aircraft, or container.

unlock verb undo the lock of a door, container, etc. using a key.

unlooked adjective (unlooked for) not planned or expected.

unloose or **unloosen** verb (unlooses, unloosing, unloosed) release something.

unlucky adjective (unluckier, unluckiest)

THESAURUS

collaboration, agreement, consensus, solidarity. **3** *the organic unity of the universe:* oneness, singleness, wholeness, uniformity, homogeneity.
OPPOSITES division, discord.

universal adjective general, common, widespread, ubiquitous, comprehensive, global, worldwide, international.

universally adverb always, without exception, by everyone, in all cases, everywhere, worldwide, globally, internationally, commonly, generally.

universe noun cosmos, macrocosm, space, infinity, nature, all existence.

unkind adjective **1** *everyone was being unkind to him:* unpleasant, disagreeable, nasty, mean, cruel, vicious, spiteful, catty, malicious, callous, unsympathetic; informal bitchy. **2** *unkind weather:* inclement, intemperate, rough, severe, filthy.

unknown adjective **1** *the outcome was unknown:* undisclosed, unrevealed, secret, undetermined, undecided. **2** *unknown country:* unexplored, uncharted, unmapped, undiscovered. **3** *persons unknown:* unidentified, unnamed, anonymous. **4** *firearms were unknown to the Indians:* unfamiliar, unheard of, new, novel, strange. **5** *unknown artists:* obscure, unheard of, unsung, minor, undistinguished.
OPPOSITES known, familiar.

unlike preposition **1** *England is totally unlike Jamaica:* different from, dissimilar to. **2** *unlike Lyn, Chris was a bit of a radical:* in contrast to, as opposed to.
OPPOSITES similar to.

unlikely adjective improbable, doubtful, dubious, questionable, unconvincing, implausible, far-fetched, unrealistic, incredible, unbelievable, inconceivable.
OPPOSITES probable, believable.

unload verb **1** *we unloaded the van:* unpack, empty. **2** *they unloaded the cases from the lorry:* remove, offload, discharge, dump.
OPPOSITES load.

unlucky adjective **1** *the unlucky victim:* unfortunate, hapless, ill-fated. **2** *an unlucky number:* unfavourable, inauspicious, unpropitious, ominous, jinxed.
OPPOSITES fortunate, favourable.

u

having, bringing, or resulting from bad luck.
■ **unluckily** adverb.

unmade adjective Brit. (of a road) without a hard, smooth surface.

unmanageable adjective difficult or impossible to manage or control.

unmanned adjective not having or needing a crew or staff.

unmarked adjective 1 not marked. 2 not noticed.

unmarried adjective not married.

unmask verb reveal the true character of.

unmatched adjective not matched or equalled.

unmentionable adjective too embarrassing or shocking to be spoken about.

unmerciful adjective showing no mercy.
■ **unmercifully** adverb.

unmetalled adjective Brit. (of a road) not having a hard surface.

unmindful adjective (**unmindful of**) not conscious or aware of.

unmissable adjective that should not or cannot be missed.

unmistakable or **unmistakeable** adjective not able to be mistaken for anything else.
■ **unmistakably** adverb.

unmitigated adjective complete: *an unmitigated disaster.*

unmoved adjective not affected by emotion or excitement.

unnameable adjective too bad or frightening to mention.

unnatural adjective 1 different from what is found in nature or what is normal in society. 2 not spontaneous.
■ **unnaturally** adverb.

unnecessary adjective not necessary, or more than is necessary.
■ **unnecessarily** adverb.

unnerve verb (**unnerves, unnerving, unnerved**) make someone feel fearful or

lacking in confidence.

unnoticeable adjective not easily seen or noticed.

unnoticed adjective not being or having been seen or noticed.

unobtainable adjective not able to be obtained.

unobtrusive adjective not conspicuous or attracting attention.
■ **unobtrusively** adverb.

unofficial adjective not officially authorized or confirmed.
■ **unofficially** adverb.

unopposed adjective not opposed or challenged.

unorthodox adjective different from what is usual, traditional, or accepted.

unpack verb take things out of a suitcase, bag, or package.

unpaid adjective 1 (of a debt) not yet paid. 2 done without payment. 3 not receiving payment for work done.

unpalatable adjective 1 not pleasant to taste. 2 difficult to accept.

unparalleled adjective having no equal; exceptional.

unpardonable adjective (of a fault or offence) unforgivable.
■ **unpardonably** adverb.

unperturbed adjective not concerned or worried about something.

unpick verb 1 undo the sewing of stitches or a garment. 2 carefully analyse the different elements of something.

unpleasant adjective 1 not pleasant or comfortable. 2 not friendly or kind.
■ **unpleasantly** adverb **unpleasantness** noun.

unplug verb (**unplugs, unplugging, unplugged**) disconnect an electrical device from a socket.

unpopular adjective not liked or popular.
■ **unpopularity** noun.

unprecedented adjective never done or

---

u

unnatural adjective 1 *the life of a battery hen is completely unnatural:* abnormal, unusual, uncommon, extraordinary, strange, unorthodox, exceptional, irregular, untypical. 2 *an unnatural colour:* artificial, man-made, synthetic, manufactured. 3 *her voice sounded unnatural:* affected, artificial, stilted, forced, false, fake, insincere; informal put on, phoney.
OPPOSITES normal, genuine.

unnecessary adjective unneeded, inessential, not required, uncalled for, unwarranted, dispensable, optional, extraneous, expendable, redundant.
OPPOSITES necessary.

unpleasant adjective 1 *a very unpleasant situation:* disagreeable, irksome, distressing, nasty, horrible, terrible, awful, dreadful, invidious, objectionable. 2 *an unpleasant man:* unlikeable, unlovable, disagreeable, unfriendly, rude, impolite, obnoxious, nasty, spiteful, mean, insufferable, objectionable, unbearable, annoying, irritating. 3 *an unpleasant taste:* unappetizing, unpalatable, unsavoury, unappealing, disgusting, revolting, nauseating, sickening.
OPPOSITES agreeable, likeable.

unpopular adjective disliked, friendless, unloved, unwelcome, avoided, ignored, known before.

unpredictable adjective not able to be predicted; changeable.
■ **unpredictability** noun **unpredictably** adverb.

unprejudiced adjective without prejudice; unbiased.

unpremeditated adjective not planned beforehand.

unprepared adjective not ready or able to deal with something.

unprepossessing adjective not attractive or interesting.

unprincipled adjective without moral principles.

unprintable adjective (of words or comments) too rude or offensive to be published.

unproductive adjective 1 not able to produce the required quantity of goods or crops. 2 not achieving much; not very useful.

unprofessional adjective not in accordance with professional standards or behaviour.
■ **unprofessionally** adverb.

unprofitable adjective 1 not making a profit. 2 not helpful or useful.

unprompted adjective without being prompted; spontaneous.

unpronounceable adjective too difficult to pronounce.

unproven or **unproved** adjective not proved or tested.

unprovoked adjective (of an attack or crime) not directly provoked.

unqualified adjective 1 not having the necessary qualifications or requirements. 2 complete.

unquantifiable adjective impossible to express or measure in terms of quantity.

unquestionable adjective not able to be denied or doubted.
■ **unquestionably** adverb.

unquestioned adjective not denied or doubted.

unravel verb (**unravels**, **unravelling**, **unravelled**; US spelling **unravels**, **unraveling**, **unraveled**) 1 undo twisted, knitted, or woven threads. 2 (of threads) become undone. 3 solve a mystery or puzzle.

unreadable adjective 1 not clear enough to

read. 2 too dull or difficult to be worth reading.

unreal adjective 1 strange and not seeming real. 2 not related to reality; unrealistic.
■ **unreality** noun.

unrealistic adjective 1 not showing things in a way that is accurate and true to life. 2 not having a sensible understanding of what can be achieved.
■ **unrealistically** adverb.

unreasonable adjective 1 not based on good sense. 2 beyond what is achievable or acceptable.
■ **unreasonably** adverb.

unrecognizable or **unrecognisable** adjective not able to be recognized.

unrelenting adjective 1 not stopping or becoming less severe. 2 not giving in to requests.
■ **unrelentingly** adverb.

unreliable adjective not able to be relied on.
■ **unreliability** noun **unreliably** adverb.

unrelieved adjective lacking variation or change.

unremarkable adjective not particularly interesting or surprising.

unremitting adjective never stopping or easing.

unrepeatable adjective 1 not able to be repeated. 2 too offensive or shocking to be said again.

unrepentant adjective showing no shame or regret for your actions.

unrequited adjective (of love) not given in return.

unreserved adjective 1 without any doubts or reservations. 2 not set apart or booked in advance.
■ **unreservedly** adverb.

unrest noun 1 a situation in which people are feeling discontented and rebellious. 2 a state of uneasiness.

unrivalled (US spelling **unrivaled**) adjective greater or better than all others.

unroll verb open out something that is rolled up.

unruffled adjective calm and undisturbed.

unruly adjective (**unrulier**, **unruliest**) difficult to control; disorderly.
■ **unruliness** noun.

u

THESAURUS

rejected, shunned, out of favour.

unravel verb 1 *he unravelled the strands:* untangle, disentangle, separate out, unwind, untwist. 2 *detectives are trying to unravel the mystery:* solve, resolve, clear up, puzzle out, get to the bottom of, explain, clarify; informal figure out.
OPPOSITES entangle.

unreal adjective imaginary, fictitious,

pretend, make-believe, made-up, dreamed-up, mock, false, illusory, mythical, fanciful, hypothetical, theoretical; informal phoney.
OPPOSITES real.

unrest noun disturbance, trouble, turmoil, disruption, disorder, chaos, anarchy, dissatisfaction, dissent, strife, agitation, protest, rebellion, uprising, rioting.
OPPOSITES peace, contentment.

unsafe adjective **1** not safe; dangerous. **2** (of a decision in a court of law) not based on good evidence.

unsatisfactory adjective not good enough.
■ **unsatisfactorily** adverb.

unsaturated adjective Chemistry (of fats) having double or triple bonds between carbon atoms in their molecules and therefore being more easily processed by the body.

unsavoury (US spelling **unsavory**) adjective **1** unpleasant to taste, smell, or look at. **2** not respectable.

unscathed adjective without suffering any injury, damage, or harm.

unschooled adjective lacking schooling or training.

unscientific adjective not using proper scientific methods.
■ **unscientifically** adverb.

unscrew verb unfasten something by twisting it or undoing screws.

unscrupulous adjective without moral principles; dishonest or unfair.
■ **unscrupulously** adverb.

unseasonable adjective (of weather) unusual for the time of year.
■ **unseasonably** adverb.

unseasonal adjective unusual or inappropriate for the time of year.

unseat verb **1** make someone fall from a saddle or seat. **2** remove someone from a position of power.

unseeing adjective having your eyes open but not noticing anything.

unseemly adjective (of behaviour or actions) not proper or appropriate.

unseen adjective **1** not seen or noticed. **2** (of a passage for translation in an exam) not previously read or prepared.

unselfconscious adjective not self-

conscious; not shy or embarrassed.
■ **unselfconsciously** adverb.

unselfish adjective putting other people's needs before your own.
■ **unselfishly** adverb.

unserviceable adjective not in working order; unfit for use.

unsettle verb (**unsettles, unsettling, unsettled**) make someone anxious or uneasy.

unsettled adjective **1** frequently changing, or likely to change. **2** anxious or uneasy. **3** not yet resolved.

unshakeable or **unshakable** adjective (of a belief or feeling) firm and unable to be changed.

unshaven adjective not having shaved.

unsightly adjective unpleasant to look at; ugly.

unskilled adjective not having or needing special skill or training.

unsociable adjective not enjoying the company of other people.

unsocial adjective (of hours of work) not falling within the normal working day.

unsolicited adjective not asked for.

unsophisticated adjective **1** not having much experience in matters of culture or fashion. **2** not complicated or highly developed; basic.

unsound adjective **1** not safe or strong; in bad condition. **2** not based on reliable evidence or reasoning.

unsparing adjective **1** very severe or harsh. **2** giving generously.

unspeakable adjective too bad or horrific to express in words.
■ **unspeakably** adverb.

unspoilt or **unspoiled** adjective (of a place) beautiful because it has not been changed or built on.

unstable adjective **1** likely to fall or

THESAURUS

unsafe adjective **1** *the building was unsafe:* dangerous, risky, hazardous, high-risk, treacherous, insecure, unsound, harmful, injurious, toxic. **2** *the verdict was unsafe:* unreliable, insecure, unsound, open to doubt, questionable, doubtful, dubious, suspect; informal iffy; Brit. informal dodgy.
OPPOSITES safe, harmless, secure.

unsatisfactory adjective disappointing, displeasing, inadequate, unacceptable, poor, bad, substandard, weak, mediocre, not up to par, defective, deficient; informal leaving a lot to be desired.

unscrupulous adjective dishonest, deceitful, devious, underhand, unethical, immoral, shameless, exploitative, corrupt, unprincipled, dishonourable, disreputable; informal crooked, shady.

unsettle verb disturb, disconcert, unnerve, upset, disquiet, perturb, alarm, dismay, trouble, bother, agitate, fluster, ruffle, shake (up), throw; informal rattle, faze.

unsightly adjective unattractive, ugly, unprepossessing, hideous, horrible, repulsive, revolting, offensive, grotesque.
OPPOSITES attractive.

unsociable adjective unfriendly, uncongenial, unneighbourly, unapproachable, introverted, reserved, withdrawn, retiring, aloof, distant, remote, detached; informal stand-offish.
OPPOSITES sociable, friendly.

unstable adjective **1** *icebergs are notoriously unstable:* unsteady, rocky, wobbly, rickety, shaky, unsafe, insecure, precarious. **2** *unstable coffee prices:* changeable,

u

collapse. **2** likely to change; unsettled.
3 tending to experience mental health
problems or sudden changes of mood.

unsteady adjective **1** liable to fall or shake;
not firm. **2** not uniform or even.
■ **unsteadily** adverb.

unstick verb (**unsticks, unsticking, unstuck**)
separate things that have been stuck
together.
□ **come unstuck** informal fail.

unstinting adjective given or giving freely
or generously.

unsuccessful adjective not successful.
■ **unsuccessfully** adverb.

unsuitable adjective not right or
appropriate for a particular purpose or
occasion.
■ **unsuitability** noun **unsuitably** adverb.

unsung adjective not celebrated or praised.

unsure adjective having doubts about
something; not certain.

unsurpassed adjective better or greater
than any other.

unsurprising adjective expected and so not
causing surprise.
■ **unsurprisingly** adverb.

unsuspecting adjective not aware of the
presence of danger.

unsustainable adjective **1** not able to be
maintained at the current level.
2 upsetting the ecological balance by using
up natural resources.

unswerving adjective not changing or
becoming weaker.

unsympathetic adjective **1** not
sympathetic. **2** not showing approval of an
idea or action. **3** not likeable.
■ **unsympathetically** adverb.

unsystematic adjective not done or acting
according to a fixed plan.
■ **unsystematically** adverb.

untapped adjective (of a resource) available
but not yet used.

untenable adjective (of a theory or view)
not able to be defended against criticism
or attack.

unthinkable adjective too unlikely or
unpleasant to be considered a possibility.

unthinking adjective not thinking about
the effects of what you do or say.
■ **unthinkingly** adverb.

untidy adjective (**untidier, untidiest**) **1** not
arranged tidily. **2** not inclined to be neat.
■ **untidily** adverb **untidiness** noun.

untie verb (**unties, untying, untied**) undo or
unfasten something that is tied.

until preposition & conjunction up to the time
or event mentioned.

> ☑ just one **l** at the end: unti**l**.

untimely adjective **1** happening or done at
an unsuitable time. **2** (of a death or end)
happening too soon or sooner than normal.

unto preposition old use **1** to. **2** until.

untold adjective **1** too much or too many to
be counted. **2** (of a story) not told to
anyone.

untouchable adjective **1** not able to be
touched. **2** not able to be criticized or
rivalled. ●noun offensive a member of the
lowest Hindu caste (social class).

THESAURUS

volatile, variable, fluctuating, irregular,
unpredictable, erratic. **3** *he was mentally
unstable:* unbalanced, of unsound mind,
mentally ill, deranged, demented,
disturbed, unhinged.
OPPOSITES stable, steady, firm.

unsuccessful adjective **1** *an unsuccessful
attempt:* failed, abortive, ineffective,
fruitless, profitless, unproductive, vain,
futile. **2** *an unsuccessful business:*
unprofitable, loss-making. **3** *an
unsuccessful candidate:* failed, losing,
beaten, unlucky.

unsuitable adjective **1** *an unsuitable
product:* inappropriate, ill-suited,
inapposite, unacceptable, unfitting,
incompatible, out of place, out of keeping.
2 *an unsuitable moment:* inopportune,
badly timed, unfortunate, difficult,
infelicitous.
OPPOSITES appropriate, opportune.

unsure adjective **1** *she felt very unsure:*
unconfident, unassertive, insecure,
hesitant, diffident, anxious, apprehensive.

2 *Sally was unsure what to do:* undecided,
uncertain, irresolute, dithering, in two
minds, in a quandary, vacillating. **3** *some
teachers are unsure about the proposed
strike:* dubious, doubtful, sceptical,
uncertain, unconvinced.
OPPOSITES confident.

untangle verb disentangle, unravel,
unsnarl, straighten out, untwist, unknot,
sort out.
OPPOSITES tangle.

unthinkable adjective unimaginable,
inconceivable, unbelievable, incredible,
implausible, out of the question,
impossible, unconscionable, unreasonable.

untidy adjective **1** *untidy hair:* scruffy,
tousled, dishevelled, unkempt, messy,
rumpled, bedraggled, uncombed, tangled,
matted. **2** *the room was untidy:* disordered,
messy, disorganized, cluttered, in chaos,
haywire, in disarray; informal higgledy-
piggledy.
OPPOSITES tidy, neat, orderly.

u

❗ the official term today for the lowest Hindu social class is **scheduled caste**.

untouched adjective **1** not handled, used, or consumed. **2** not affected, changed, or damaged.

untoward adjective unexpected and unwanted.

untrammelled (US spelling **untrammeled**) adjective not restricted or hampered.

untrue adjective **1** false. **2** not faithful or loyal.

untrustworthy adjective unable to be trusted.

unused adjective **1** not used. **2** (**unused to**) not accustomed to.

unusual adjective **1** not often done or happening. **2** exceptional.
■ **unusually** adverb.

unutterable adjective too great or bad to describe.
■ **unutterably** adverb.

unvarnished adjective **1** not varnished. **2** plain and straightforward.

unveil verb **1** show or announce something publicly for the first time. **2** remove a veil or covering from.

unwaged adjective Brit. unemployed or doing unpaid work.

unwanted adjective not wanted.

unwarrantable adjective not reasonable or justifiable.

unwarranted adjective not justified.

unwavering adjective not changing or becoming weaker.

unwelcome adjective not wanted.

unwell adjective ill.

unwholesome adjective **1** harmful to health. **2** unpleasant or unnatural.

unwieldy adjective hard to move or manage because of its size, shape, or weight.

unwilling adjective not willing.
■ **unwillingly** adverb **unwillingness** noun.

unwind verb (**unwinds, unwinding, unwound**) **1** undo something that has been wound or twisted. **2** relax after a period of work or tension.

unwise adjective foolish.
■ **unwisely** adverb.

unwitting adjective **1** not aware of the full facts. **2** unintentional.
■ **unwittingly** adverb.

unwonted /un-**wohn**-tid/ adjective not usual or expected.

unworldly adjective **1** having little awareness of the realities of life. **2** not seeming to belong to this world.

unworthy adjective not deserving effort, attention, or respect.
■ **unworthiness** noun.

unwrap verb (**unwraps, unwrapping, unwrapped**) remove the wrapping from.

unwritten adjective (of a rule or law) generally known about and accepted, although not made official.

unyielding adjective **1** not bending or breaking; firm. **2** (of a person) not changing their mind.

unzip verb (**unzips, unzipping, unzipped**) **1** unfasten the zip of. **2** Computing decompress a file.

up adverb **1** towards a higher place or position. **2** to the place where someone is.

THESAURUS

untoward adjective unexpected, unforeseen, surprising, unusual, inappropriate, inconvenient, unwelcome, unfavourable, adverse, unfortunate, infelicitous.

untrue adjective false, invented, made up, fabricated, concocted, trumped up, erroneous, wrong, incorrect, inaccurate.
OPPOSITES true, correct.

unusual adjective **1** *an unusual sight:* uncommon, abnormal, atypical, unexpected, surprising, unfamiliar, different, strange, odd, curious, queer, extraordinary, unorthodox, unconventional, peculiar; informal weird, offbeat. **2** *a man of unusual talent:* remarkable, extraordinary, exceptional, particular, outstanding, notable, noteworthy, distinctive, striking, significant, special, unique, unparalleled, prodigious.
OPPOSITES common.

unwarranted adjective **1** *the criticism is unwarranted:* unjustified, indefensible, inexcusable, unforgivable, unpardonable, uncalled for, unnecessary, unjust, groundless. **2** *an unwarranted invasion of privacy:* unauthorized, unsanctioned, unapproved, uncertified, unlicensed, illegal, unlawful, illicit, illegitimate, criminal, actionable.
OPPOSITES justified.

unwieldy adjective awkward, unmanageable, unmanoeuvrable, cumbersome, clumsy, massive, heavy, hefty, bulky.

unwilling adjective **1** *unwilling conscripts:* reluctant, unenthusiastic, hesitant, resistant, grudging, involuntary, forced. **2** *he was unwilling to take on responsibility:* disinclined, reluctant, averse, loath; (**be unwilling to do something**) baulk at, demur at, shy away from, flinch from, shrink from, not have the heart to, have qualms about, have misgivings about, have reservations about.
OPPOSITES willing, keen.

u

3 at or to a higher level or value. **4** into the desired condition or position. **5** out of bed. **6** (of the sun) visible in the sky.
●**preposition 1** from a lower to a higher point of. **2** from one end of a street to another. ●**adjective 1** directed or moving towards a higher place or position. **2** at an end. ●**verb** (**ups, upping, upped**) increase a level or an amount.
□ **up-and-coming** likely to be successful. **up to date** using or aware of the latest developments and trends.

upbeat adjective positive and cheerful or enthusiastic.

upbraid verb scold or criticize.

upbringing noun the way in which a person is taught and looked after as a child.

upcoming adjective forthcoming.

update verb (**updates, updating, updated**) **1** make something more modern. **2** give someone the latest information on something. ●**noun** an act of updating, or an updated version of something.

upend verb set something on its end or upside down.

upfront informal adjective **1** not trying to hide your thoughts or intentions; frank. **2** (of a payment) made in advance. ●**adverb** (usu. **up front**) (of a payment) in advance.

upgrade verb (**upgrades, upgrading, upgraded**) raise something to a higher standard or rank. ●**noun** an act of

upgrading, or an upgraded version of something.

upheaval noun a big change that causes a lot of upset or disruption.

uphill adverb towards the top of a slope.
●**adjective 1** sloping upwards. **2** difficult: *an uphill struggle.*

uphold verb (**upholds, upholding, upheld**) **1** confirm or support something which has been questioned. **2** maintain a custom or practice.

upholster verb (**upholsters, upholstering, upholstered**) provide an armchair, sofa, etc. with a soft, padded covering.
■ **upholsterer** noun.

upholstery noun **1** the soft, padded covering on an armchair, sofa, etc. **2** the art of upholstering furniture.

upkeep noun the process or cost of keeping something in good condition or of supporting a person.

upland or **uplands** noun an area of high or hilly land.

uplift verb make someone feel hope or happiness. ●**noun 1** an act of lifting or raising something. **2** a feeling of hope or happiness.
■ **uplifting** adjective.

upload verb transfer data to a larger computer system.

upmarket adjective chiefly Brit. expensive or of high quality.

upon more formal term for **on**.

upper adjective **1** situated above another

THESAURUS

upbeat adjective cheerful, optimistic, cheery, positive, confident, hopeful, bullish, buoyant.
OPPOSITES pessimistic, negative.

upbringing noun childhood, early life, formative years, teaching, instruction, rearing.

update verb **1** *security measures are continually updated:* modernize, upgrade, improve, overhaul. **2** *I'll update him on developments:* brief, bring up to date, inform, fill in, tell, notify, keep posted; informal clue in, put in the picture, bring/keep up to speed.

upgrade verb improve, modernize, update, reform.
OPPOSITES downgrade.

upheaval noun disturbance, disruption, trouble, turbulence, disorder, confusion, turmoil.

uphill adjective **1** *an uphill path:* upward, rising, ascending, climbing. **2** *an uphill job:* difficult, hard, tough, demanding, arduous, taxing, exacting, stiff, gruelling, onerous.
OPPOSITES downhill.

uphold verb **1** *the court upheld his claim:* confirm, endorse, sustain, approve,

support, back (up). **2** *they've a tradition to uphold:* maintain, sustain, continue, preserve, protect, keep, hold to, keep alive, keep going.
OPPOSITES overturn, oppose.

upkeep noun **1** *the upkeep of the road:* maintenance, repair(s), servicing, care, preservation, conservation, running. **2** *the child's upkeep:* (financial) support, maintenance, keep, subsistence, care.

uplifting adjective inspiring, stirring, inspirational, rousing, moving, touching, affecting, cheering, heartening, encouraging.

upper adjective **1** *the upper floor:* higher, superior, top. **2** *the upper echelons of the party:* senior, superior, higher-level, higher-ranking, top.
OPPOSITES lower.

upper-class adjective aristocratic, noble, patrician, titled, blue-blooded, high-born, elite; Brit. county; informal upper-crust, top-drawer; Brit. informal posh.

upright adjective **1** *an upright position:* vertical, perpendicular, plumb, straight (up), erect, on end, on your feet. **2** *an upright member of the community:* honest,

u

part. **2** higher in position or status.
3 situated on higher ground. •**noun** the part of a boot or shoe above the sole.
□ **have the upper hand** have an advantage or control over someone. **upper case** capital letters. **upper class** the social group with the highest status. **the Upper House** (in the UK) the House of Lords.

uppercut noun a punch delivered with an upward motion and the arm bent.

uppermost adjective & adverb highest in place, rank, or importance.

uppity adjective informal behaving as if you are more important than you really are.

upright adjective 1 in a vertical position. **2** greater in height than breadth. **3** strictly honest and respectable. **4** (of a piano) having vertical strings. •**adverb** in or into an upright position. •**noun** a vertical post, structure, or line.

uprising noun a rebellion.

upriver ⇨ **UPSTREAM**.

uproar noun 1 a loud noise or disturbance made by people who are angry or upset about something. **2** a public expression of outrage.

uproarious adjective 1 very noisy and lively. **2** very funny.
■ **uproariously adverb.**

uproot verb 1 pull a tree or other plant out

of the ground. **2** move someone from their home or usual surroundings.

upscale adjective N. Amer. upmarket.

upset verb (**upsets, upsetting, upset**) **1** make someone unhappy, disappointed, or worried. **2** knock something over. **3** disrupt or disturb a situation or arrangement.
•**noun 1** a difficult or unexpected result or situation. **2** a state of being upset.
•**adjective 1** unhappy, disappointed, or worried. **2** (of a person's stomach) not digesting food normally.

upshot noun the eventual outcome or conclusion of something.

upside noun the positive aspect of something.
□ **upside down** with the upper part where the lower part should be.

upstage verb (**upstages, upstaging, upstaged**) draw attention away from someone so that people notice you instead.
•**adverb & adjective** at or towards the back of a stage.

upstairs adverb & adjective on or to an upper floor. •**noun** an upper floor.

upstanding adjective very respectable and responsible.

upstart noun disapproving a person who thinks they are more important than they really are.

THESAURUS

honourable, upstanding, respectable, high-minded, law-abiding, worthy, righteous, decent, good, virtuous, principled.
OPPOSITES flat, horizontal, dishonourable.

uprising noun rebellion, revolt, insurrection, mutiny, revolution, insurgence, rioting, coup.

uproar noun 1 *the uproar in the kitchen continued:* commotion, disturbance, rumpus, disorder, confusion, chaos, tumult, mayhem, pandemonium, bedlam, noise, din, clamour, hubbub, racket; informal hullabaloo; Brit. informal row. **2** *there was an uproar when he was dismissed:* outcry, furore, fuss, commotion, hue and cry, rumpus; informal hullabaloo, stink, ructions; Brit. informal row.
OPPOSITES calm.

upset verb 1 *the accusation upset her:* distress, trouble, perturb, dismay, sadden, grieve, disturb, unsettle, disconcert, disquiet, worry, bother, agitate, fluster, throw, ruffle, unnerve, shake. **2** *he upset the soup:* knock over, overturn, upend, tip over, topple, spill. **3** *the dam will upset the ecological balance:* disrupt, interfere with, disturb, throw into confusion, mess up.
OPPOSITES calm, reassure.
•**noun 1** *a legal dispute will cause upset:* distress, trouble, dismay, disquiet, worry,

bother, agitation, hurt, grief. **2** *a stomach upset:* disorder, complaint, ailment, illness, sickness; informal bug; Brit. informal lurgy.
OPPOSITES reassurance.
•**adjective 1** *I was upset by the news:* distressed, troubled, perturbed, dismayed, disturbed, unsettled, disconcerted, worried, bothered, anxious, agitated, flustered, ruffled, unnerved, shaken, saddened, grieved; informal cut up, choked; Brit. informal gutted. **2** *an upset stomach:* disturbed, unsettled, queasy, bad, poorly; informal gippy.
OPPOSITES unperturbed, calm.

upside down adjective 1 *an upside-down canoe:* upturned, upended, wrong side up, overturned, inverted, capsized. **2** *they left the flat upside down:* in disarray, in disorder, jumbled up, in a muddle, untidy, disorganized, in chaos, in confusion; informal higgledy-piggledy.

up to date adjective 1 *up-to-date equipment:* modern, contemporary, the latest, state-of-the-art, new, up-to-the-minute, advanced. **2** *the newsletter will keep you up to date:* informed, up to speed, in the picture, in touch, au fait, conversant, familiar, knowledgeable, acquainted; informal clued up.
OPPOSITES out of date, old-fashioned.

u

upstate adjective & adverb US in or to a part of a state remote from its large cities.

upstream or **upriver** adverb & adjective at or to a point nearer the source of a stream or river.

upsurge noun an increase.

uptake noun the action of taking up or making use of something.
□ **be quick (or slow) on the uptake** informal be quick (or slow) to understand something.

uptight adjective informal nervously tense or angry, and unable to express your feelings.

upturn noun an improvement or upward trend. •verb (**be upturned**) be turned upwards or upside down.

upward adjective & adverb towards a higher level.
■ **upwards** adverb.

upwind adverb & adjective into the wind.

uranium /yuu-**ray**-ni-uhm/ noun a radio-active metallic element used as a fuel in nuclear reactors.

Uranus /yoo-**ray**-nuhss, **yoo**-ruh-nuhss/ noun the seventh planet from the sun in the solar system.

urban adjective having to do with a town or city.

urbane /er-**bayn**/ adjective (of a man) confident, polite, and sophisticated.
■ **urbanity** noun.

urchin noun a poor child dressed in ragged clothes.

Urdu /**oor**-doo, er-doo/ noun a language of Pakistan and India.

ureter /yuu-**ree**-ter/ noun the duct by which urine passes from the kidney to the bladder.

urethra /yuu-**ree**-thruh/ noun the duct by which urine passes out of the body, and which in males also carries semen.
■ **urethral** adjective.

urge verb (**urges, urging, urged**)
1 encourage or earnestly ask someone to do something. **2** strongly recommend.
•noun a strong desire or impulse.

urgent adjective needing immediate action or attention.
■ **urgency** noun **urgently** adverb.

urinal noun a container into which men urinate, attached to the wall in a public toilet.

urinate verb (**urinates, urinating, urinated**) pass urine out of the body.
■ **urination** noun.

urine /**yoo**-rin, yoo-ryn/ noun a yellowish liquid that is stored in the bladder and which contains waste substances that are passed with it out of the body.
■ **urinary** adjective.

URL abbreviation uniform (or universal) resource locator, the address of a World Wide Web page.

urn noun **1** a container for storing a cremated person's ashes. **2** a metal container with a tap, in which tea or coffee is made and kept hot.

ursine adjective having to do with bears.

Uruguayan /yoor-uh-**gwy**-uhn/ noun a person from Uruguay. •adjective relating to Uruguay.

US abbreviation United States.

us pronoun used by a speaker to refer to himself or herself and one or more other people as the object of a verb or preposition.

USA abbreviation United States of America.

usable or **useable** adjective able to be used.
■ **usability** noun.

usage noun the using of something.

use verb (**uses, using, used**) **1** do something

THESAURUS

urban adjective town, city, municipal, metropolitan, built-up, inner-city, suburban.
OPPOSITES rural.

urge verb **1** *she urged him to try:* encourage, exhort, press, entreat, implore, call on, appeal to, beg, plead with. **2** *I urge caution in interpreting these results:* advise, counsel, advocate, recommend.
•noun *his urge to travel:* desire, wish, need, compulsion, longing, yearning, hankering, craving, hunger, thirst; informal yen, itch.

urgent adjective pressing, acute, dire, desperate, critical, serious, grave, intense, crying, burning, compelling, extreme, high-priority, life-and-death.

usage noun **1** *energy usage:* consumption, use. **2** *the usage of equipment:* use,

utilization, operation, manipulation, running, handling. **3** *English usage:* language, expression, phraseology, parlance, idiom.

use verb **1** *she used her key to open the door:* utilize, employ, avail yourself of, work, operate, wield, ply, apply, put into service. **2** *the court will use its discretion:* exercise, employ, bring into play, practise, apply. **3** *she was using me:* take advantage of, exploit, manipulate, take liberties with, impose on, abuse, capitalize on, profit from, trade on, milk; informal cash in on, walk all over. **4** *we have used up our funds:* consume, get/go through, exhaust, deplete, expend, spend.
•noun **1** *the use of such weapons:* utilization, application, employment,

u

with an object or adopt a method in order to achieve a purpose. **2** (**use something up**) consume all of something. **3** take unfair advantage of a person or situation. **4** (**used to**) did something repeatedly in the past, or existed or happened in the past. **5** (**be** or **get used to**) be or become familiar with something through experience. **6** (**used**) second-hand. • **noun 1** the using of something. **2** the ability to use a part of the body. **3** a purpose for something, or a way in which something can be used. **4** value.

useful adjective able to be used for a practical purpose or in several ways.
■ **usefully** adverb **usefulness** noun.

useless adjective **1** serving no purpose. **2** informal having no ability or skill.
■ **uselessly** adverb.

user noun a person who uses or operates something.
□ **user-friendly** easy for people to use or understand.

usher noun **1** a person who shows people to their seats in a theatre or cinema or in church. **2** an official in a law court who swears in jurors and generally keeps order. • verb (**ushers, ushering, ushered**) guide someone somewhere.

usherette noun a woman who shows people to their seats in a cinema or theatre.

USSR abbreviation historical Union of Soviet Socialist Republics.

usual adjective happening or done typically, regularly, or frequently.
■ **usually** adverb.

> ☑ remember that **usually** is spelled with a double *l*.

usurp /yuu-zerp/ verb take over someone's position or power without having the right to do so.
■ **usurper** noun.

usury /yoo-zhuh-ri/ noun formal the practice of lending money at unreasonably high rates of interest.
■ **usurer** noun.

utensil noun a tool or container, especially for household use.

uterus /yoo-tuh-ruhss/ noun the womb.
■ **uterine** adjective.

utilitarian adjective useful or practical rather than attractive.

utilitarianism noun the doctrine that the right course of action is the one that will lead to the greatest happiness of the greatest number of people.

utility noun (plural **utilities**) **1** the state of being useful or profitable. **2** an organization supplying electricity, gas, water, or sewerage to the public.
□ **utility room** a room where a washing machine and other domestic equipment are kept.

utilize or **utilise** verb (**utilizes, utilizing,**

THESAURUS

operation, manipulation. **2** *his use of other people for his own ends:* exploitation, manipulation, abuse. **3** *what is the use of that?* advantage, benefit, good, point, object, purpose, sense, reason, service, utility, help, gain, avail, profit, value, worth.

used adjective *a used car:* second-hand, pre-owned, nearly new, old, worn, hand-me-down, cast-off.
OPPOSITES new.
□ **used to accustomed to**, no stranger to, familiar with, at home with, in the habit of, experienced in, versed in, conversant with, acquainted with.

useful adjective **1** *a useful tool:* functional, practical, handy, convenient, utilitarian, serviceable, of service; informal nifty. **2** *a useful experience:* beneficial, advantageous, helpful, worthwhile, profitable, rewarding, productive, constructive, valuable, fruitful.
OPPOSITES useless, disadvantageous.

useless adjective **1** *it was useless to try:* futile, pointless, to no avail, vain, to no purpose, unavailing, hopeless, ineffectual, fruitless, unprofitable, unproductive.
2 (informal) *he was useless at his job:* incompetent, inept, ineffective, incapable,

inadequate, hopeless, bad; informal a dead loss.
OPPOSITES useful, beneficial, competent.

usher verb *she ushered him to a seat:* escort, accompany, take, show, see, lead, conduct, guide.
• noun *ushers showed them to their seats:* guide, attendant, escort.

usual adjective normal, customary, accustomed, wonted, habitual, routine, regular, standard, typical, established, set, stock, conventional, traditional, expected, familiar.
OPPOSITES unusual, exceptional.

usually adverb normally, generally, habitually, customarily, routinely, typically, ordinarily, commonly, as a rule, in general, more often than not, mainly, mostly.

utensil noun implement, tool, instrument, device, apparatus, gadget, appliance, contrivance, contraption; informal gizmo.

utility noun usefulness, use, benefit, value, advantage, help, practicality, effectiveness, service.

utilize verb use, employ, avail yourself of, press into service, bring into play, deploy, draw on, exploit.

u

utilized) make practical and effective use of.

■ **utilization** noun.

utmost adjective most extreme; greatest. •noun (**the utmost**) the greatest or most extreme extent or amount.

Utopia /yoo-toh-pi-uh/ noun an imagined world or society where everything is perfect.

utopian adjective idealistic.

utter¹ adjective complete; absolute.

■ **utterly** adverb.

utter² verb (**utters, uttering, uttered**) make a sound, or say something.

utterance noun 1 a word, statement, or sound uttered. 2 the action of saying or uttering something.

uttermost = UTMOST.

uvula /yoo-vyuu-luh/ noun (plural **uvulae** /yoo-vyuu-lee/) a small piece of flesh that hangs down at the top of the throat.

uxorious /uk-sor-i-uhss/ adjective (of a man) very fond of his wife.

THESAURUS

utmost adjective greatest, highest, maximum, most, extreme, supreme, paramount.

Utopia noun paradise, heaven, Eden, Shangri-La, idyll, nirvana.

utter¹ adjective *that's utter nonsense:* complete, total, absolute, thorough, perfect, downright, out-and-out, outright, sheer, arrant, positive, prize, pure, unmitigated, unadulterated, unqualified.

utter² verb say, speak, voice, mouth, express, articulate, pronounce, enunciate, emit, let out, give, produce.

utterance noun remark, comment, word, statement, observation, declaration, pronouncement.

u

V or **v** noun (plural **Vs** or **V's**) **1** the twenty-second letter of the alphabet. **2** the Roman numeral for five. • abbreviation **1** volts. **2** (**v**) versus.
□ **V-neck** a V-shaped neckline. **V-sign 1** an insulting gesture made with the first two fingers pointing up and the back of the hand facing outwards. **2** a similar sign made with the palm facing outwards, used as a symbol of victory.

vacancy noun (plural **vacancies**) **1** a job or position that is available. **2** an available room in a hotel, guest house, etc. **3** empty space.

vacant adjective **1** empty. **2** (of a job or position) available. **3** showing no intelligence or interest.
■ **vacantly** adverb.

vacate verb (**vacates**, **vacating**, **vacated**) **1** go out of a place, leaving it empty. **2** give up a position.

vacation noun **1** a period when universities, law courts, etc. are closed. **2** N. Amer. a holiday. **3** the action of vacating a place. • verb N. Amer. take a holiday.

vaccinate verb (**vaccinates**, **vaccinating**, **vaccinated**) give a person or animal an injection of a vaccine to protect them against a disease.
■ **vaccination** noun.

vaccine /**vak**-seen/ noun a substance injected into the body that causes the production of antibodies and so provides

immunity against a disease.

vacillate /**va**-si-layt/ verb (**vacillates**, **vacillating**, **vacillated**) keep changing your mind about something.
■ **vacillation** noun.

vacuous adjective showing a lack of thought or intelligence.
■ **vacuity** noun.

vacuum /**vak**-yuum/ noun (plural **vacuums** or **vacua** /**vak**-yuu-uh/) **1** a completely empty space in which there is no air or other matter. **2** a gap left by the loss of someone or something important. • verb clean a surface using a vacuum cleaner.
□ **vacuum cleaner** an electrical machine that collects dust by means of suction. **vacuum flask** a container with a double wall enclosing a vacuum, used for keeping drinks hot or cold.

vagabond noun a person who has no settled home or job.

vagary /**vay**-guh-ri/ noun (plural **vagaries**) a change that is difficult to predict or control.

vagina /vuh-**jy**-nuh/ noun (in a woman or girl) a tube leading from the external genitals to the womb.
■ **vaginal** adjective.

vagrant /**vay**-gruhnt/ noun a person who has no settled home or job. • adjective having no settled home or job.
■ **vagrancy** noun.

vague adjective **1** not certain or definite.

THESAURUS

vacancy noun opening, position, post, job, opportunity.

vacant adjective **1** *a vacant house*: empty, unoccupied, not in use, free, unfilled, uninhabited, untenanted. **2** *a vacant look*: blank, expressionless, unresponsive, emotionless, impassive, vacuous, empty, glazed.
OPPOSITES full, occupied, expressive.

vacate verb **1** *he was forced to vacate the premises*: leave, move out of, evacuate, quit, depart from. **2** *he will be vacating his post next year*: resign from, leave, stand

down from, give up, bow out of, relinquish, retire from; informal quit.
OPPOSITES occupy, take up.

vacation noun holiday, trip, tour, break, leave, time off, recess.

vagrant noun tramp, drifter, down-and-out, beggar, itinerant, wanderer, nomad, traveller; N. Amer. hobo; N. Amer. informal bum.

vague adjective **1** *a vague shape*: indistinct, indefinite, indeterminate, unclear, ill-defined, hazy, fuzzy, misty, blurry, out of focus, shadowy, obscure. **2** *a vague description*: imprecise, rough, approximate,

V

2 saying things or thinking in a way that is not clear.
■ **vaguely** adverb **vagueness** noun.

vain adjective **1** having too high an opinion of yourself. **2** useless or meaningless.
□ **in vain** without success.
■ **vainly** adverb.

vainglorious adjective literary boastful or vain.
■ **vainglory** noun.

valance /**va**-luhnss/ noun a length of fabric fitted over the base of the bed under the mattress.

vale noun literary a valley.

valediction /va-li-**dik**-sh'n/ noun **1** the action of saying farewell. **2** a farewell statement.

valedictory /va-li-**dik**-tuh-ri/ adjective (especially of a speech) saying farewell.

valency /**vay**-luhn-si/ or **valence** noun (plural **valencies**) Chemistry the combining power of an element, especially as measured by the number of hydrogen atoms it can displace or combine with.

valentine noun **1** a card that you send to a person you love on St Valentine's Day (14 February). **2** a person to whom you send such a card.

valerian /vuh-**leer**-i-uhn/ noun **1** a plant with small pink, red, or white flowers. **2** a sedative drug obtained from valerian roots.

valet /**va**-lay, va-**lit**/ noun **1** a person who looks after a man's clothes and other personal needs. **2** N. Amer. a person employed to clean or park cars. •**verb** (**valets, valeting, valeted**) **1** clean a car as a professional service. **2** act as a valet to.

valetudinarian /va-li-tyoo-di-**nair**-i-uhn/ noun a person who is in bad health, or worries too much about their health.

valiant adjective showing courage or determination.
■ **valiantly** adverb.

valid adjective **1** (of a reason, argument, etc.) sound or logical. **2** legally binding or acceptable.
■ **validity** noun.

validate verb (**validates, validating, validated**) make valid, or show to be valid.
■ **validation** noun.

valise /vuh-**leez**/ noun a small travelling bag or suitcase.

Valium noun trademark a tranquillizing drug used to relieve anxiety.

valley noun (plural **valleys**) a low area between hills or mountains.

valour (US spelling **valor**) noun great courage in the face of danger.
■ **valorous** adjective.

valuable adjective **1** worth a lot of money. **2** very useful or important. •**noun** (**valuables**) valuable items.

valuation noun an estimation of how much something is worth.

value noun **1** the importance or usefulness of something. **2** the amount of money that something is worth. **3** (**values**) standards of behaviour. **4** Maths the amount represented by a letter or symbol. **5** the relative length of the sound represented by a musical note. •**verb** (**values, valuing, valued**) **1** estimate how much something is worth. **2** consider something to be important or useful.
□ **value added tax** a tax on the amount by which goods rise in value at each stage of production.

THESAURUS

inexact, non-specific, ambiguous, hazy, uncertain. **3** *she was so vague in life:* absent-minded, forgetful, dreamy, abstracted; informal scatty, not with it.
OPPOSITES clear, precise, certain, sharp.

vain adjective **1** *their flattery made him vain:* conceited, proud, arrogant, boastful, cocky, narcissistic, immodest; informal big-headed. **2** *a vain attempt:* futile, useless, pointless, ineffective, fruitless, unproductive, unsuccessful, failed, abortive.
OPPOSITES modest, successful.
□ **in vain** unsuccessfully, to no avail, to no purpose, fruitlessly.

valid adjective **1** *a valid criticism:* well founded, sound, reasonable, rational, logical, justifiable, defensible, cogent, credible, forceful. **2** *a valid contract:* legally binding, lawful, official, in force, in effect.
OPPOSITES invalid.

valley noun dale, vale, hollow, gully, gorge, ravine, canyon, rift; Brit. combe; Scottish glen.

valuable adjective **1** *a valuable watch:* precious, costly, high-priced, expensive, dear, priceless. **2** *a valuable contribution:* useful, helpful, beneficial, invaluable, productive, worthwhile, worthy, important.
OPPOSITES cheap, worthless, useless.

valuables plural noun precious items, costly items, prized possessions, treasures.

value noun **1** *houses exceeding £250,000 in value:* price, cost, worth, market price. **2** *the value of adequate preparation:* worth, usefulness, advantage, benefit, gain, profit, good, help. **3** (**values**) principles, ethics, morals, standards, code of behaviour.
•**verb 1** *his estate was valued at £45,000:* evaluate, assess, estimate, appraise, price. **2** *she valued his opinion:* think highly of, have a high opinion of, rate highly, esteem, set great store by, respect.
OPPOSITES despise.

v

valve noun 1 a device for controlling the flow of a liquid or gas through a pipe or duct. 2 a mechanism that varies the length of the tube in a brass musical instrument. 3 a structure in the heart or a vein which allows blood to flow in one direction only.

vamp[1] verb (**vamp something up**) informal improve something by adding something more interesting to it.

vamp[2] noun informal a woman who uses her sexual attractiveness to control men.
■ **vampish** adjective.

vampire noun 1 (in stories) a dead person that leaves their grave at night to drink the blood of living people. 2 (also **vampire bat**) a bloodsucking bat found mainly in tropical America.
■ **vampirism** noun.

van[1] noun 1 a motor vehicle used for moving goods or a group of people. 2 Brit. a railway carriage used for large luggage, mail, etc.

van[2] noun (**the van**) the leading part of an advancing group of people.

vanadium noun a hard grey metallic chemical element, used to make some types of steel.

vandal noun a person who deliberately destroys or damages property.
■ **vandalism** noun.

vandalize or **vandalise** verb (**vandalizes, vandalizing, vandalized**) deliberately destroy or damage property.

vane noun a broad blade that is moved by wind or water, forming part of a windmill, propeller, or turbine.

vanguard noun 1 the leading part of an advancing army. 2 a group of people leading the way in new developments or ideas.

vanilla noun a substance obtained from the pods of a tropical plant, used as a flavouring or scent.

vanish verb 1 disappear suddenly and completely. 2 gradually cease to exist.

vanity noun (plural **vanities**) 1 too much pride in your own appearance or achievements. 2 the quality of being pointless or futile.

vanquish verb literary defeat completely.

vantage or **vantage point** noun a place or position giving the best view.

vapid adjective offering no stimulation or challenge.
■ **vapidity** noun.

vaporize or **vaporise** verb (**vaporizes, vaporizing, vaporized**) convert something into vapour.
■ **vaporization** noun **vaporizer** noun.

vapour (US spelling **vapor**) noun 1 moisture suspended in the air. 2 Physics a gaseous substance that can be made into liquid by pressure alone.

variable adjective 1 not consistent or having a fixed pattern. 2 able to be changed or adapted. • noun a variable element, feature, or quantity.
■ **variability** noun **variably** adverb.

variance noun 1 the fact or quality of being different or inconsistent. 2 the state of disagreeing or quarrelling.

variant noun a version that varies from other forms of the same thing.

variation noun 1 a change or slight difference in condition, amount, or level. 2 a different or distinct form or version. 3 a new but still recognizable version of a musical theme.

varicose adjective (of a vein) swollen, twisted, and lengthened, as a result of bad circulation.

varied adjective involving a number of different types or elements.

variegated /vair-i-gay-tid/ adjective having irregular patches or streaks of a different

---

THESAURUS

vanish verb 1 *he vanished into the darkness:* disappear, be lost to sight, become invisible, recede from view. 2 *all hope vanished:* fade (away), evaporate, melt away, end, cease to exist, pass away, die out.
OPPOSITES appear, materialize.

vanity noun conceit, self-love, self-admiration, egotism, narcissism, pride, arrogance, boastfulness, cockiness, swagger; informal big-headedness.
OPPOSITES modesty.

variable adjective changeable, shifting, fluctuating, irregular, inconstant, inconsistent, fluid, unstable; informal up and down.
OPPOSITES constant.

variant noun *variants of the same idea:* variation, form, alternative, version, adaptation, alteration, modification.
• adjective *a variant spelling:* alternative, other, different, divergent.

variation noun 1 *regional variations in farming:* difference, dissimilarity, disparity, contrast, discrepancy, imbalance. 2 *opening times are subject to variation:* change, alteration, modification. 3 *there was very little variation from the pattern:* deviation, variance, divergence, departure, fluctuation.

varied adjective diverse, assorted, mixed, miscellaneous, sundry, wide-ranging, disparate, motley.
OPPOSITES similar, unchanging.

V

colour or colours.
■ **variegation** noun.

☑ remember the *e* in the middle: variegated.

variety noun (plural **varieties**) **1** the quality of being varied. **2** (**a variety of**) a number of things of the same type that are distinct in character. **3** a thing which differs in some way from others of the same general class. **4** a form of entertainment involving singing, dancing, and comedy.

various adjective of different kinds or sorts. •determiner & pronoun more than one; individual and separate.
■ **variously** adverb.

varnish noun a liquid applied to wood to give a hard, clear, shiny surface when dry. •verb put varnish on.

vary verb (**varies, varying, varied**) **1** differ in size, degree, or nature from something else of the same general class. **2** change from one form or state to another. **3** alter something to make it less uniform.

vascular adjective referring to the system of vessels for carrying blood or (in plants) the tissues carrying sap, water, and nutrients.

vas deferens /vass def-uh-renz/ noun (plural **vasa deferentia** /vay-suh def-uh-**ren**-shuh/) the duct carrying sperm from a testicle to the urethra.

vase noun a container for displaying cut flowers.

vasectomy /vuh-**sek**-tuh-mi/ noun (plural **vasectomies**) the surgical cutting and sealing of part of each vas deferens as a means of sterilization.

Vaseline noun trademark a type of petroleum jelly used as an ointment and lubricant.

vassal noun (in the feudal system) a man who promised to support and fight for a

king or lord in return for holding a piece of land.

vast adjective of very great extent or quantity; immense.
■ **vastly** adverb **vastness** noun.

VAT abbreviation value added tax.

vat noun a large tank or tub used to hold liquid.

Vatican noun the official residence of the Pope in Rome.

vaudeville /**vaw**-duh-vil/ noun a type of entertainment featuring a mixture of musical and comedy acts.

vault[1] noun **1** a large room used for storage, especially in a bank. **2** a chamber beneath a church or in a graveyard, used for burials. **3** a roof in the form of an arch or a series of arches.
■ **vaulted** adjective.

vault[2] verb leap or spring using your hands or a pole to push yourself. •noun an act of vaulting.

vaunted adjective praised or boasted about.

VC abbreviation Victoria Cross.

VCR abbreviation video cassette recorder.

VDU abbreviation Brit. visual display unit.

veal noun meat from a young calf.

vector noun **1** Maths a quantity having direction as well as magnitude. **2** the carrier of a disease or infection.

Veda /**vay**-duh, **vee**-duh/ noun the most ancient Hindu scriptures.

veer verb (**veers, veering, veered**) **1** change direction suddenly. **2** (of the wind) change direction clockwise around the points of the compass.

vegan noun a person who does not eat or use any animal products.

vegetable noun **1** a plant used as food. **2** offensive a person who is incapable of normal mental or physical activity as a

THESAURUS

variety noun **1** *the lack of variety in the curriculum:* diversity, variation, diversification, change, difference. **2** *a wide variety of flowers:* assortment, miscellany, range, array, collection, selection, mixture, medley. **3** *fifty varieties of pasta:* sort, kind, type, class, category, style, form, make, model, brand, strain, breed. OPPOSITES uniformity.

various adjective diverse, different, differing, varied, assorted, mixed, sundry, miscellaneous, disparate, motley. OPPOSITES similar.

vary verb **1** *estimates of the cost vary:* differ, be dissimilar, disagree. **2** *rates of interest vary over time:* fluctuate, rise and fall, go up and down, change, alter, shift, swing. **3** *the diaphragm is used for varying the*

aperture: modify, change, alter, adjust, regulate, control, set.

vast adjective huge, extensive, broad, wide, boundless, enormous, immense, great, massive, colossal, gigantic, mammoth, giant, mountainous; informal mega, whopping; Brit. informal ginormous. OPPOSITES tiny.

vault[1] noun **1** *the vault under the church:* cellar, basement, crypt, undercroft, catacomb, burial chamber. **2** *valuables stored in the vault:* strongroom, safe deposit.

vault[2] verb *he vaulted over the gate:* jump, leap, spring, bound, clear.

veer verb turn, swerve, swing, weave, wheel, change direction, change course, deviate.

v

result of brain damage.

☑ *vege-*, not *vega-*: vegetable.

vegetal adjective relating to plants.

vegetarian noun a person who does not eat meat or fish. •adjective eating or including no meat or fish.
■ vegetarianism noun.

vegetate verb (**vegetates, vegetating, vegetated**) spend your time in a dull way that involves little mental stimulation.

vegetation noun plants.

vegetative adjective 1 relating to vegetation. 2 Medicine alive but showing no sign of brain activity or responsiveness.

vehement /**vee**-uh-muhnt/ adjective showing strong feeling.
■ vehemence noun vehemently adverb.

vehicle noun a car, lorry, truck, etc. used for transporting people or goods on land.
■ vehicular /vi-**hik**-yuu-ler/ adjective.

veil noun 1 a piece of thin material worn to protect or hide the face. 2 the part of a nun's headdress that covers the head and shoulders. 3 a thing that hides or disguises. •verb 1 cover with a veil. 2 (**veiled**) partially hidden or disguised.

vein noun 1 any of the tubes that carry blood from all parts of the body towards the heart. 2 a blood vessel. 3 (in plants) a thin rib running through a leaf. 4 (in insects) a hollow rib forming part of the supporting framework of a wing. 5 a streak of a different colour in wood, marble, cheese, etc. 6 a fracture in rock containing a deposit of minerals or ore. 7 a source of a particular quality: *a vein of humour.*
■ veined adjective.

Velcro noun trademark a fastener consisting of two strips of fabric covered with tiny hooks.

veld or **veldt** /velt/ noun open uncultivated country or grassland in southern Africa.

vellum noun fine parchment made from animal skin.

velociraptor /vi-**los**-si-rap-ter/ noun a small meat-eating dinosaur.

velocity noun (plural **velocities**) speed in a particular direction.

velodrome noun a track used for cycle racing.

velour /vuh-**loor**/ noun a thick, soft fabric resembling velvet.

velvet noun a fabric with a soft, short pile on one side.
■ velvety adjective.

velveteen noun a cotton fabric resembling thin velvet.

venal /**vee**-n'l/ adjective open to bribery.
■ venality noun.

vend verb sell small items.
□ vending machine a machine from which you can buy drinks, snacks, etc. by inserting coins.

vendetta noun 1 a feud in which the family of a murdered person seeks vengeance on the murderer or the murderer's family. 2 a long and bitter quarrel.

vendor (US spelling **vender**) noun 1 a person selling small items. 2 Law a person who is selling a property.

veneer noun 1 a thin covering of fine wood applied to a cheaper wood or other material. 2 an outward appearance that hides the true nature of a person or thing.
■ veneered adjective.

venerable adjective given great respect because of age, wisdom, or character.

venerate verb (**venerates, venerating, venerated**) respect someone highly.
■ veneration noun.

venereal disease noun a disease caught by having sex with an infected person.

Venetian adjective relating to Venice.
□ venetian blind a window blind consisting of horizontal slats which can be turned to control the amount of light that passes through.

Venezuelan /ve-ni-**zway**-luhn/ noun a person from Venezuela. •adjective relating to Venezuela.

vengeance noun an act of harming or punishing someone in return for what they have done to you or someone close to you.
□ with a vengeance with great intensity.

THESAURUS

vehicle noun 1 *a stolen vehicle:* means of transport, conveyance. 2 *a vehicle for the communication of ideas:* channel, medium, means, agent, instrument, mechanism, organ, apparatus.

veil noun *a thin veil of cloud:* covering, screen, curtain, mantle, cloak, mask, blanket, shroud, canopy, cloud, pall.
•verb *the peak was veiled in mist:* cover, surround, swathe, enfold, envelop, conceal, hide, obscure, screen, shield, cloak, blanket, shroud.

vein noun 1 *veins of quartz:* layer, seam, lode, stratum, deposit. 2 *he closes his article in a humorous vein:* mood, humour, attitude, tone, spirit, character, feel, flavour, quality, atmosphere, manner, way, style.

velocity noun speed, pace, rate, tempo, rapidity.

vengeance noun revenge, retribution, retaliation, requital, reprisal, an eye for an eye.
OPPOSITES forgiveness.

V

vengeful adjective wanting to punish or harm someone in return for something they have done.

venial /vee-ni-uhl/ adjective (of a fault or offence) slight and able to be forgiven.

venison noun meat from a deer.

Venn diagram noun a diagram representing mathematical sets as circles, with overlapping sections representing elements shared between sets.

venom noun 1 the poisonous liquid produced by some animals that bite or sting, such as snakes and scorpions. 2 a strong feeling of hatred or bitterness.

venomous adjective 1 producing venom. 2 full of hatred or bitterness.
■ **venomously** adverb.

venous /vee-nuhss/ adjective relating to a vein or the veins.

vent[1] noun an opening that allows air, gas, or liquid to pass out of or into a confined space. •verb 1 allow yourself to express a strong emotion. 2 let air, gas, or liquid pass through a vent.

vent[2] noun a slit in a garment.

ventilate verb (**ventilates, ventilating, ventilated**) cause air to enter and circulate freely in a room or building.
■ **ventilation** noun.

ventilator noun 1 an opening or a machine for ventilating a room or building. 2 a machine that pumps air in and out of a person's lungs to help them to breathe.

ventral adjective having to do with the underside or abdomen.

ventricle noun each of the two larger and lower cavities of the heart.

ventriloquist /ven-**tril**-uh-kwist/ noun an entertainer who can make their voice seem to come from elsewhere.
■ **ventriloquism** noun.

venture noun 1 a business enterprise involving considerable risk. 2 a risky or daring journey or undertaking. •verb (**ventures, venturing, ventured**) 1 dare to do something dangerous or risky. 2 dare to say something.

venturesome adjective literary willing to take on something risky or difficult.

venue noun the place where an event or meeting is held.

Venus noun the second planet from the sun in the solar system.
□ **Venus flytrap** a plant with hinged leaves that spring shut on and digest insects which land on them.

veracious adjective formal truthful.

veracity noun the quality of being truthful and accurate.

veranda or **verandah** noun a roofed structure with an open front along the outside of a house.

verb noun a word expressing an action or occurrence.

verbal adjective 1 relating to or in the form of words. 2 spoken rather than written. 3 relating to a verb.
■ **verbally** adverb.

verbalize or **verbalise** verb (**verbalizes, verbalizing, verbalized**) express something in words.

verbatim /ver-**bay**-tim/ adverb & adjective in exactly the same words as were used originally.

verbena noun a garden plant with brightly coloured flowers.

verbiage noun speech or writing that is too long or detailed.

verbose adjective using more words than are needed.
■ **verbosity** noun.

verdant adjective green with grass or other lush vegetation.

verdict noun 1 a decision made by a jury in a court of law about whether someone is innocent or guilty. 2 an opinion or judgement formed after trying or testing something.

verdigris /ver-di-gree/ noun a bright bluish-green substance formed on copper or brass by oxidation.

verdure noun literary lush green vegetation.

THESAURUS

venomous adjective poisonous, toxic, dangerous, deadly, lethal, fatal.
OPPOSITES harmless.

vent noun an air vent: outlet, inlet, opening, aperture, hole, gap, orifice, space, duct, flue, shaft, well, passage, airway.
•verb the crowd vented their fury: let out, release, pour out, utter, express, air, voice.

venture noun a business venture: enterprise, undertaking, project, scheme, operation, endeavour, speculation.

•verb 1 we ventured across the moor: set out, go, travel, journey. 2 may I venture an opinion? put forward, advance, proffer, offer, air, suggest, volunteer, submit, propose. 3 I ventured to invite her: dare, be so bold as, presume, have the audacity, have the nerve, take the liberty of.

verbal adjective oral, spoken, word-of-mouth, stated, said, unwritten.

verdict noun judgement, adjudication, decision, finding, ruling, sentence.

verge noun **1** Brit. a grass edging by the side of a road or path. **2** a limit beyond which a particular thing will happen: *I was on the verge of tears.* •verb (**verges**, **verging**, **verged**) (**verge on**) be very close or similar to.

verger noun an official in a church who acts as a caretaker and attendant.

verify verb (**verifies**, **verifying**, **verified**) make sure or show that something is true and accurate.
■ **verifiable** adjective **verification** noun.

verily adverb old use truly; certainly.

verisimilitude noun the appearance of being true or real.

veritable adjective genuine.
■ **veritably** adverb.

verity noun (plural **verities**) formal truthfulness, or a truth.

vermicelli /ver-mi-**chel**-li/ plural noun **1** pasta made in long thin threads. **2** Brit. shreds of chocolate used to decorate cakes.

vermilion noun a bright red colour.

vermin noun wild animals or birds which carry disease or harm crops.
■ **verminous** adjective.

vermouth /ver-**muhth**/ noun a red or white wine flavoured with herbs.

vernacular noun the language or dialect spoken by the ordinary people of a country or region.

vernal adjective relating to the season of spring.

verruca /vuh-**roo**-kuh/ noun a contagious wart on the sole of the foot.

versatile adjective able to adapt or be adapted to many different functions or activities.
■ **versatility** noun.

verse noun **1** writing arranged with a metrical rhythm. **2** a group of lines that form a unit in a poem or song. **3** each of the short numbered divisions of a chapter in the Bible.

versed adjective (**versed in**) experienced or skilled in.

versify verb (**versifies**, **versifying**, **versified**) write verse, or turn a piece of writing into verse.
■ **versification** noun.

version noun **1** a particular form of something which differs from other forms of the same type of thing. **2** an account of something told from a particular person's point of view.

verso /**ver**-soh/ noun (plural **versos**) a left-hand page of an open book, or the back of a loose document.

versus preposition **1** against. **2** as opposed to.

vertebra /**ver**-ti-bruh/ noun (plural **vertebrae** /**ver**-ti-bray, **ver**-ti-bree/) each of the series of small bones forming the backbone.

vertebrate noun an animal having a backbone, e.g. a mammal, bird, reptile, amphibian, or fish.

vertex noun (plural **vertices** /**ver**-ti-seez/ or **vertexes**) **1** the highest point. **2** a meeting point of two lines that form an angle.

vertical adjective going straight up or down, at a right angle to a horizontal line or surface. •noun a vertical line or surface.
■ **vertically** adverb.

vertiginous /ver-**tij**-i-nuhss/ adjective very high or steep.

vertigo /**ver**-ti-goh/ noun a feeling of giddiness caused by looking down from a great height.

vervain noun a plant with small blue, white, or purple flowers, used in herbal medicine.

verve noun energy, spirit, and style.

very adverb in a high degree. •adjective

THESAURUS

verge noun **1** *the verge of the lake:* edge, border, margin, side, brink, rim, lip, fringe, boundary, perimeter. **2** *I was on the verge of tears:* brink, threshold, edge, point. □ **verge on** approach, border on, be close/near to, resemble, be tantamount to, tend towards, approximate to.

verify verb confirm, prove, substantiate, corroborate, back up, bear out, justify, support, uphold, testify to, validate, authenticate.
OPPOSITES refute.

versatile adjective **1** *a versatile player:* adaptable, flexible, all-round, multi-talented, resourceful. **2** *a versatile device:* adjustable, adaptable, multi-purpose, all-purpose.

verse noun **1** *Elizabethan verse:* poetry, lyrics. **2** *a verse he'd composed:* poem, lyric,
rhyme, ditty, lay. **3** *a poem with sixty verses:* stanza.
OPPOSITES prose.

version noun **1** *his version of events:* account, report, statement, description, record, story, rendering, interpretation, explanation, understanding, reading, impression, side. **2** *the English version will be published next year:* edition, translation, impression. **3** *they have replaced coal-burning fires with gas versions:* type, sort, kind, form, equivalent, variety, variant, design, model, style.

vertical adjective upright, erect, perpendicular, plumb, on end, standing.
OPPOSITES flat, horizontal.

very adverb *that's very kind of you:* extremely, exceedingly, exceptionally, extraordinarily, tremendously, immensely,

V

1 actual; precise. **2** extreme. **3** mere.

vespers noun a Christian service of evening prayer.

vessel noun **1** a ship or large boat. **2** a tube or duct carrying a liquid within the body, or within a plant. **3** old use a bowl, cup, or other container for liquids.

vest noun **1** Brit. a sleeveless garment or undergarment worn on the upper part of the body. **2** N. Amer. & Austral. a waistcoat or sleeveless jacket. •verb (**vest something in**) give someone power or property, or the legal right to hold power or own property. □ **vested interest** a personal reason for wanting something to happen.

vestibule noun a room or hall just inside the outer door of a building.

vestige noun **1** a last remaining trace of something. **2** the smallest amount. ■ **vestigial** adjective.

vestment noun a robe worn by ministers or members of the choir during church services.

vestry noun (plural **vestries**) a small room in a church, used as an office and for changing into ceremonial robes.

vet noun a person qualified to treat sick or injured animals. •verb (**vets, vetting, vetted**) find out about someone's background and past before employing them.

vetch noun a plant of the pea family grown as food for farm animals.

veteran noun **1** a person who has had many years of experience in a particular field. **2** a person who used to serve in the armed forces.

veterinarian noun N. Amer. a vet.

veterinary /vet-uhn-ri, vet-uh-ri-nuh-ri/ adjective relating to the treatment of diseases and injuries in animals. □ **veterinary surgeon** a vet.

> ☑ note the -er- before the -in-: veterinary.

veto /vee-toh/ noun (plural **vetoes**) **1** the right or power to reject a ruling or decision made by others. **2** a refusal to allow something. •verb (**vetoes, vetoing, vetoed**) use a veto against, or refuse to allow.

vex verb make someone annoyed or worried. ■ **vexation** noun **vexatious** adjective.

vexed adjective **1** (of an issue) difficult to deal with and causing a lot of debate. **2** annoyed or worried.

VHF abbreviation very high frequency.

VHS abbreviation trademark video home system.

via preposition **1** travelling through a particular place on the way to a destination. **2** by way of; through. **3** by means of.

viable adjective **1** capable of working successfully. **2** (of a plant, animal, or cell) able to live. ■ **viability** noun.

viaduct noun a long bridge-like structure carrying a road or railway across a valley or other low ground.

vial noun a small cylindrical glass bottle for medicine etc.

viands plural noun old use food.

vibe or **vibes** noun informal the atmosphere of a place, or a feeling passing between people.

vibrant adjective **1** full of energy and enthusiasm. **2** (of sound) strong or

---

THESAURUS

acutely, abundantly, singularly, decidedly, highly, remarkably, really; informal awfully, terribly, majorly, seriously, mega, ultra; Brit. informal ever so, well, dead, jolly; N. Amer. informal real, mighty.
OPPOSITES slightly.
•adjective **1** those were his very words: **exact,** actual, precise. **2** the very thought of food made her feel ill: mere, simple, pure, sheer.

vessel noun **1** a fishing vessel: **boat,** ship, craft. **2** a cooking vessel: **container,** receptacle, basin, bowl, pan, pot, jug.

vestige noun remnant, fragment, relic, echo, trace, mark, legacy, reminder.

vet verb check up on, screen, investigate, examine, scrutinize, inspect, look over, assess, evaluate, appraise; informal check out.

veteran noun a veteran of many political campaigns: old hand, past master, doyen, doyenne; informal old-timer; N. Amer. informal vet.
OPPOSITES novice.

•adjective a veteran diplomat: long-serving, seasoned, old, hardened, practised, experienced; informal battle-scarred.

veto noun parliament's right of veto: rejection, dismissal, prohibition, embargo, proscription, ban.
OPPOSITES approval.
•verb the president vetoed the bill: reject, turn down, throw out, dismiss, prohibit, forbid, proscribe, disallow, embargo, ban; informal kill.
OPPOSITES approve.

viable adjective feasible, workable, practicable, practical, realistic, achievable, attainable; informal doable.
OPPOSITES impracticable.

vibrant adjective **1** a vibrant performance: spirited, lively, energetic, vigorous, storming, dynamic, passionate, fiery; informal feisty. **2** vibrant colours: vivid, bright, striking, brilliant, glowing, strong, rich.
OPPOSITES lifeless, pale.

V

resonant. **3** (of colour) bright.
■ **vibrancy** noun **vibrantly** adverb.

vibraphone noun an electrical percussion instrument giving a vibrato effect.

vibrate verb (**vibrates, vibrating, vibrated**) **1** move with rapid small movements to and fro. **2** (of a sound) resonate.
■ **vibration** noun.

vibrato /vi-**brah**-toh/ noun a rapid, slight variation in pitch in singing or playing some musical instruments.

vicar noun (in the Church of England) a minister in charge of a parish.

vicarage noun a vicar's house.

vicarious /vi-**kair**-i-uhss/ adjective experienced in the imagination rather than directly: *a vicarious thrill.*
■ **vicariously** adverb.

vice[1] noun **1** immoral or wicked behaviour. **2** criminal activities that involve sex or drugs. **3** a bad personal characteristic. **4** a bad habit.

vice[2] (US spelling **vise**) noun a metal tool with movable jaws which are used to hold an object firmly in place while work is done on it.

vice- combining form next in rank to; deputy: *vice-president.*

viceroy noun a person sent by a king or queen to govern a colony.

vice versa adverb reversing the order of the items just mentioned.

vicinity noun (plural **vicinities**) the area near or surrounding a place.

vicious adjective **1** cruel or violent. **2** (of an animal) wild and dangerous.
□ **vicious circle** a situation in which one problem leads to another, which then makes the first one worse.
■ **viciously** adverb **viciousness** noun.

☑ no *s* in the middle: vicious.

vicissitudes /vi-**sis**-si-tyoodz/ plural noun the ups and downs and changes in your life.

victim noun a person who is harmed or killed as a result of a crime, injustice, or accident.

victimize or **victimise** verb (**victimizes, victimizing, victimized**) single someone out for cruel or unfair treatment.
■ **victimization** noun.

victor noun a person who defeats an opponent in a battle, game, or competition.

Victorian adjective relating to the reign of Queen Victoria (1837–1901).

victorious adjective having won a victory.

victory noun (plural **victories**) an act of defeating an opponent.

victuals /vi-t'lz/ plural noun old use food and provisions.

video noun (plural **videos**) **1** a system of recording and reproducing moving images using magnetic tape. **2** a film or other recording on magnetic tape. **3** Brit. a video recorder. ●verb (**videoes, videoing, videoed**) film or make a video recording of.
□ **video game** a computer game played on a television screen. **video recorder** a machine linked to a television, used for recording programmes and playing videotapes.

videotape noun **1** magnetic tape for recording and reproducing visual images and sound. **2** a cassette on which this magnetic tape is held. ●verb (**videotapes, videotaping, videotaped**) record on videotape.

vie verb (**vies, vying, vied**) compete eagerly with others in order to do or achieve something.

Vietnamese noun (plural **Vietnamese**) **1** a person from Vietnam. **2** the language of Vietnam. ●adjective relating to Vietnam.

view noun **1** the ability to see something or

---

vibrate verb shake, tremble, shiver, quiver, shudder, throb, pulsate.

vice noun **1** *youngsters may be driven to vice:* immorality, wrongdoing, wickedness, evil, iniquity, villainy, corruption, misconduct, sin, depravity. **2** *smoking is my only vice:* fault, failing, flaw, defect, shortcoming, weakness, deficiency, foible, frailty.
OPPOSITES virtue.

vicious adjective **1** *a vicious killer:* brutal, ferocious, savage, violent, ruthless, merciless, heartless, callous, cruel, cold-blooded, inhuman, barbaric, bloodthirsty. **2** *a vicious hate campaign:* malicious, spiteful, vindictive, cruel, bitter, acrimonious, hostile, nasty, catty.
OPPOSITES gentle, kindly.

victim noun sufferer, injured party,

casualty, fatality, loss, survivor.

victorious adjective triumphant, conquering, vanquishing, winning, champion, successful.
OPPOSITES unsuccessful, losing.

victory noun success, triumph, conquest, win, coup; informal walkover.
OPPOSITES defeat, loss.

vie verb compete, contend, struggle, fight, battle, jockey.

view noun **1** *the view from her flat:* outlook, prospect, panorama, vista, scene, scenery, landscape. **2** *we agree with this view:* opinion, viewpoint, belief, judgement, thinking, notion, idea, conviction, persuasion, attitude, feeling, sentiment. **3** *the church came into view:* sight, perspective, vision, visibility.

V

to be seen from a particular position.
2 something seen from a particular position, especially natural scenery. **3** an attitude or opinion. • **verb 1** look at or inspect. **2** have a particular attitude towards.
□ **in view of** because or as a result of. **with a view to** with the intention of.
■ **viewer** noun.

viewfinder noun a device on a camera that you look through to see what will appear in the picture.

viewpoint noun an opinion.

viewscreen noun the screen on a television or computer on which images and information are displayed.

vigil /**vi**-jil/ noun a period of staying awake through the night to keep watch or pray.

vigilant adjective keeping careful watch for possible danger or difficulties.
■ **vigilance** noun **vigilantly** adverb.

vigilante /vi-ji-**lan**-ti/ noun a member of a group of people who take it on themselves to prevent crime or punish criminals without legal authority.
■ **vigilantism** noun.

vignette /vee-**nyet**/ noun **1** a brief, vivid description or episode. **2** a small illustration or photograph which fades into its background without a definite border.

vigorous adjective **1** strong, healthy, and full of energy. **2** involving physical strength, effort, or energy.
■ **vigorously** adverb.

vigour (US spelling **vigor**) noun **1** physical strength and good health. **2** effort, energy, and enthusiasm.

Viking noun a member of the Scandinavian

people who settled in parts of Britain and elsewhere in NW Europe between the 8th and 11th centuries.

vile adjective **1** very unpleasant. **2** wicked.
■ **vilely** adverb.

vilify verb (**vilifies, vilifying, vilified**) speak or write about someone in a very unpleasant way.
■ **vilification** noun.

villa noun **1** Brit. a rented holiday home abroad. **2** (especially in southern Europe) a large country house in its own grounds. **3** a large house in ancient Rome.

village noun a small community of streets and houses in a country area.
■ **villager** noun.

villain noun **1** a bad person. **2** a bad character in a novel or play whose actions are important to the plot.
■ **villainous** adjective **villainy** noun.

villein /**vil**-luhn, vil-**layn**/ noun (in medieval England) a poor man who had to work for a lord in return for a small piece of land on which to grow food.

vim noun informal energy; enthusiasm.

vinaigrette /vi-ni-**gret**, vi-nay-**gret**/ noun a salad dressing consisting of oil mixed with vinegar.

vindicate verb (**vindicates, vindicating, vindicated**) **1** clear someone of blame or suspicion. **2** show something to be right or justified.
■ **vindication** noun.

vindictive adjective having or showing a strong or inappropriate desire for revenge.
■ **vindictiveness** noun.

vine noun a climbing plant, especially one

THESAURUS

• **verb 1** *they viewed the landscape:* **look at,** observe, eye, gaze at, contemplate, regard, scan, survey, inspect, scrutinize; informal check out; N. Amer. informal eyeball. **2** *the law was viewed as a last resort:* **consider,** regard, look on, see, perceive, judge, deem, reckon.

viewer noun **watcher,** spectator, onlooker, observer; (**viewers**) audience, crowd.

vigilant adjective **watchful,** observant, attentive, alert, eagle-eyed, on the lookout, on your guard; informal beady-eyed.
OPPOSITES inattentive.

vigorous adjective **1** *the child was vigorous:* **robust,** healthy, hale and hearty, strong, sturdy, fit, hardy, tough, energetic, lively, active. **2** *a vigorous defence:* **strenuous,** powerful, forceful, spirited, determined, aggressive, passionate; informal punchy, feisty.
OPPOSITES weak, feeble.

vigorously adverb **strenuously,** strongly,

powerfully, forcefully, energetically, heartily, all out, fiercely, hard; informal like mad; Brit. informal like billy-o.

vigour noun **health,** strength, robustness, energy, life, vitality, spirit, passion, determination, dynamism, drive; informal oomph, get-up-and-go.
OPPOSITES lethargy.

vile adjective **foul,** nasty, unpleasant, bad, horrid, repulsive, disgusting, hateful, nauseating; informal gross.
OPPOSITES pleasant.

villain noun **criminal,** lawbreaker, offender, felon, miscreant, wrongdoer, rogue, scoundrel, reprobate; informal crook, baddy.

vindicate verb **1** *he was vindicated by the jury:* **acquit,** clear, absolve, exonerate; informal let off. **2** *our concerns were vindicated:* **justify,** warrant, substantiate, confirm, corroborate, prove, defend, support, back, endorse.
OPPOSITES incriminate.

that produces grapes.

vinegar noun a sour liquid made from wine, cider, or beer, used as a seasoning or for pickling.
■ **vinegary** adjective.

vineyard /vin-yard/ noun a plantation of grapevines producing grapes used in winemaking.

vintage noun 1 the year or place in which wine was produced. 2 a wine of high quality made from the crop of a single identified district in a good year. 3 the harvesting of grapes for winemaking. 4 the grapes or wine of a particular season. 5 the time that something was produced.
•adjective 1 referring to vintage wine. 2 referring to something from the past of high quality.

vintner noun a wine merchant.

vinyl noun a type of strong flexible plastic, used in making floor coverings, paints, and gramophone records.

viol /vy-uhl/ noun an early instrument like a violin, but with six strings.

viola[1] /vi-oh-luh/ noun an instrument of the violin family, larger than the violin and tuned to a lower pitch.

viola[2] /vy-uh-luh/ noun a plant of a group that includes pansies and violets.

violate verb (**violates, violating, violated**) 1 break a rule or formal agreement. 2 treat something with disrespect. 3 rape or sexually assault someone.
■ **violation** noun.

violence noun 1 actions using physical force and intended to hurt or kill someone or to cause damage. 2 an unpleasant or destructive natural force. 3 strength of emotion.

violent adjective 1 using or involving violence. 2 very forceful or powerful.
■ **violently** adverb.

violet noun 1 a small plant with purple or blue flowers. 2 a bluish-purple colour.

violin noun a musical instrument with four strings, that you play with a bow.
■ **violinist** noun.

violoncello /vy-uh-luhn-**chel**-loh/ formal term for **CELLO**.

VIP noun a very important person.

viper noun a poisonous snake with large fangs and a patterned body.

virago /vi-**rah**-goh/ noun (plural **viragos** or **viragoes**) a domineering, violent, or bad-tempered woman.

viral adjective having to do with a virus or viruses.

virgin noun 1 a person who has never had sex. 2 (**the Virgin**) the Virgin Mary, mother of Jesus. •adjective 1 having had no sexual experience. 2 not yet used, touched, or spoiled: *virgin forest*. 3 (of olive oil) made from the first pressing of olives.
■ **virginal** adjective **virginity** noun.

Virgo noun a sign of the zodiac (the Virgin), 23 August–22 September.

virile adjective (of a man) having strength, energy, and a strong sex drive.
■ **virility** noun.

virology noun the scientific study of viruses.
■ **virologist** noun.

virtual adjective 1 almost or nearly the thing described, but not completely. 2 not existing in reality but made by computer

THESAURUS

vintage adjective 1 *vintage French wine:* high-quality, quality, choice, select, superior. 2 *vintage motor vehicles:* classic, ageless, timeless, old, antique, heritage, historic.

violate verb 1 *this violates human rights:* contravene, breach, infringe, break, transgress, disobey, defy, flout, disregard, ignore. 2 *the tomb was violated:* desecrate, profane, defile, degrade, debase, damage, vandalize, deface, destroy.
OPPOSITES respect.

violation noun 1 *a traffic violation:* contravention, breach, infringement, transgression, defiance, flouting, disregard. 2 *the violation of the relics:* desecration, defilement, damage, vandalism, destruction.

violence noun 1 *police violence:* brutality, savagery, cruelty, barbarity. 2 *the violence of the blow:* force, power, strength, might. 3 *the violence of his passion:* intensity, severity, strength, force, vehemence, power, ferocity, fury.

violent adjective 1 *a violent alcoholic:* brutal, vicious, savage, rough, aggressive, threatening, fierce, ferocious. 2 *a violent blow:* powerful, forceful, hard, sharp, smart, strong, vigorous, mighty, hefty. 3 *violent jealousy:* intense, extreme, strong, powerful, unbridled, uncontrollable, ungovernable, consuming, passionate.
OPPOSITES gentle, weak, mild.

virgin adjective 1 *virgin forest:* untouched, unspoilt, untainted, pristine, spotless, unpolluted, undefiled, perfect, intact, unexplored, uncharted. 2 *virgin girls:* chaste, celibate, abstinent, pure, uncorrupted, undefiled, innocent, immaculate.

virtual adjective effective, near (enough), essential, practical, to all intents and purposes, in all but name, implied, unacknowledged.

V

software to appear to do so.

□ **virtual reality** a system in which images that look like real objects are created by computer.

■ **virtually** adverb.

virtue noun **1** behaviour showing high moral standards. **2** a good or useful quality. **3** old use virginity or chastity.

□ **by virtue of** because or as a result of.

virtuoso /ver-tyoo-**oh**-soh/ noun (plural **virtuosi** /ver-tyoo-**oh**-si/ or **virtuosos**) a person highly skilled in music or another art.

■ **virtuosity** noun.

virtuous adjective **1** having high moral standards. **2** old use chaste.

■ **virtuously** adverb.

virulent adjective **1** (of a disease or poison) very harmful in its effects. **2** bitterly hostile or critical.

■ **virulence** noun **virulently** adverb.

virus noun **1** a submicroscopic organism which can cause disease. **2** an infection or disease caused by a virus. **3** a piece of code introduced secretly into a computer system in order to damage or destroy data.

visa noun a note on your passport indicating that you are allowed to enter, leave, or stay in a country.

visage /**vi**-zij/ noun literary a person's facial features or expression.

vis-à-vis /veez-ah-**vee**/ preposition in relation to.

viscera /**vis**-suh-ruh/ plural noun the internal organs of the body.

visceral adjective **1** relating to deep inward feelings rather than to the intellect. **2** relating to the viscera.

■ **viscerally** adverb.

viscid /**viss**-id/ adjective technical sticky.

viscose noun a smooth synthetic fabric made from cellulose.

viscosity noun the state of being viscous.

viscount /**vy**-kownt/ noun a British nobleman ranking above a baron and below an earl.

■ **viscountess** noun.

viscous /**viss**-kuhss/ adjective having a thick, sticky consistency between solid and liquid.

vise US spelling of VICE².

visibility noun **1** the state of being able to see or be seen. **2** the distance you can see, as determined by light and weather conditions.

visible adjective able to be seen or noticed.

■ **visibly** adverb.

vision noun **1** the ability to see. **2** the ability to think about the future with imagination or wisdom. **3** an experience of seeing something in a dream, trance, etc. **4** the images seen on a television screen. **5** a person or sight of unusual beauty.

visionary adjective **1** thinking about the future with imagination or wisdom. **2** relating to supernatural or dreamlike visions. ● noun (plural **visionaries**) a person with imaginative and original ideas about the future.

visit verb (**visits**, **visiting**, **visited**) **1** go to spend time with a person or in a place. **2** view a website or web page. **3** (**visit with**) N. Amer. chat with someone. **4** (**visit something on**) literary cause something harmful or unpleasant to affect someone. ● noun an act of visiting.

■ **visitor** noun.

THESAURUS

virtually adverb effectively, all but, more or less, practically, almost, nearly, close to, verging on, just about, as good as, essentially, to all intents and purposes.

virtue noun **1** *the simple virtue of peasant life:* goodness, righteousness, morality, integrity, dignity, rectitude, honour. **2** *promptness was not one of his virtues:* good point, good quality, strong point, asset, forte, attribute, strength, talent. **3** *I can see no virtue in this:* merit, advantage, benefit, usefulness, strength.
OPPOSITES vice, failing, disadvantage.

visible adjective observable, perceptible, noticeable, detectable, discernible, in sight, in view, on display, evident, apparent, manifest, plain.
OPPOSITES invisible.

vision noun **1** *her vision was blurred:* eyesight, sight, observation, eyes, view, perspective. **2** *visions of the ancestral pilgrims:* apparition, spectre, phantom,

ghost, wraith, manifestation, hallucination, illusion, mirage; informal spook. **3** *visions of a better future:* dream, reverie, plan, hope, fantasy, delusion, pipe dream. **4** *his speech lacked vision:* imagination, creativity, inventiveness, innovation, inspiration, intuition, perception, insight.

visit verb **1** *I visited my uncle:* call on, go to see, look in on, stay with, holiday with, stop by, drop by; informal pop in on, drop in on, look up. **2** *Alex was visiting America:* stay in, stop over in, spend time in, holiday in, vacation in, tour, explore, see; informal do.
● noun **1** *she paid a visit to her mum:* (social) call. **2** *a visit to the museum:* trip, tour of, look round, stopover, stay, holiday, break, vacation.

visitor noun **1** *I am expecting a visitor:* guest, caller, company. **2** *the monument attracts many visitors:* tourist, traveller, holidaymaker, tripper, vacationer,

visitation noun **1** an official or formal visit. **2** the appearance of a god, goddess, etc. **3** a disaster or difficulty seen as a punishment from God.

visor or **vizor** noun **1** a movable part of a helmet that can be pulled down to cover the face. **2** a screen for protecting the eyes from light.

vista noun a pleasing view.

visual adjective relating to seeing or sight. •noun a picture, piece of film, or display used to illustrate or accompany something. □ **visual display unit** Brit. a device that displays information from a computer on a screen.
■ **visually** adverb.

visualize or **visualise** verb (**visualizes**, **visualizing**, **visualized**) form an image of something in the mind.
■ **visualization** noun.

vital adjective **1** absolutely necessary. **2** essential for life. **3** full of energy. •noun (**vitals**) the body's important internal organs.
□ **vital statistics** informal the measurements of a woman's bust, waist, and hips.
■ **vitally** adverb.

vitality noun the state of being strong and active.

vitalize or **vitalise** verb (**vitalizes**, **vitalizing**, **vitalized**) give strength and energy to.

vitamin noun any of a group of natural substances which are present in many foods and are essential for normal nutrition.

vitiate /vi-shee-ayt/ verb (**vitiates**, **vitiating**, **vitiated**) formal make something less good or effective.

viticulture noun the cultivation of grapevines.

vitreous adjective containing or like glass. □ **vitreous humour** the transparent jelly-like tissue that fills the eyeball.

vitrify verb (**vitrifies**, **vitrifying**, **vitrified**) convert into glass or a glass-like substance by exposure to heat.

vitriol noun **1** very cruel or bitter remarks. **2** old use sulphuric acid.
■ **vitriolic** adjective.

vituperation noun bitter and abusive language.
■ **vituperative** adjective.

viva[1] /vee-vuh/ exclamation long live!

viva[2] /vy-vuh/ or **viva voce** /vy-vuh voh-chi/ noun Brit. an oral exam for an academic qualification.

vivacious adjective attractively lively.
■ **vivaciously** adverb **vivacity** noun.

vivarium noun (plural **vivaria**) a place for keeping animals in natural conditions for study or as pets.

vivid adjective **1** producing powerful feelings or strong, clear images in the mind. **2** (of a colour) very deep or bright.
■ **vividly** adverb **vividness** noun.

vivify verb (**vivifies**, **vivifying**, **vivified**) formal make more lively or interesting; enliven.

viviparous /vi-vi-puh-ruhss/ adjective (of an animal) giving birth to live young.

vivisection noun the performance of operations on live animals for scientific research.

vixen noun **1** a female fox. **2** a spirited or hot-tempered woman.

viz. adverb namely; in other words.

vizier /vi-zeer/ noun (in the past) an important official in some Muslim countries.

vizor ⇒ **visor**.

vocabulary noun (plural **vocabularies**) **1** all the words used in a particular language or activity. **2** all the words known to a person. **3** a list of words and their meanings, provided with a piece of technical or foreign writing.

THESAURUS

sightseer, pilgrim, foreigner, stranger.

vista noun view, scene, prospect, panorama, sight, scenery, landscape.

visual adjective **1** *visual defects*: optical, ocular, eye, vision, sight. **2** *a visual indication that the alarm works*: visible, observable, perceptible, discernible.
OPPOSITES acoustic.

visualize verb envisage, conjure up, picture, call to mind, see, imagine, dream up.

vital adjective **1** *it is vital that action is taken*: essential, critical, crucial, indispensable, all-important, imperative, mandatory, high-priority. **2** *he is young and*

vital: lively, energetic, active, sprightly, spirited, vivacious, exuberant, dynamic, vigorous; informal full of beans.
OPPOSITES unimportant, listless.

vitality noun life, energy, spirit, vivacity, exuberance, dynamism, vigour, passion, drive; informal get-up-and-go.

vivid adjective **1** *a vivid blue*: bright, colourful, brilliant, radiant, vibrant, strong, bold, deep, intense, rich, warm. **2** *a vivid account*: graphic, realistic, lifelike, faithful, authentic, striking, evocative, arresting, colourful, dramatic, memorable, powerful, stirring, moving, haunting.
OPPOSITES dull, vague.

V

vocal adjective 1 relating to the human voice. 2 expressing opinions or feelings freely or loudly. 3 (of music) consisting of or including singing. • noun (also **vocals**) a part of a piece of music that is sung. □ **vocal cords** strips of muscle in the throat that vibrate to produce the voice. ■ **vocally** adverb.

vocalist noun a singer.

vocalize or **vocalise** verb (**vocalizes, vocalizing, vocalized**) 1 make a sound or say a word. 2 express something with words. ■ **vocalization** noun.

vocation noun 1 a strong feeling that you ought to pursue a particular career or occupation. 2 a person's career or occupation. ■ **vocational** adjective.

vocative /vok-uh-tiv/ noun Grammar the case of nouns, pronouns, and adjectives used in addressing a person or thing.

vociferous /vuh-sif-uh-ruhss/ adjective expressing opinions in a loud and forceful way. ■ **vociferously** adverb.

vodka noun a clear alcoholic spirit, originally from Russia.

vogue noun the fashion or style current at a particular time. ■ **voguish** adjective.

voice noun 1 the sound produced in a person's larynx and uttered through the mouth, as speech or song. 2 the ability to speak or sing. 3 a vocal part in a piece of music. 4 Grammar a form of a verb showing the relation of the subject to the action. • verb (**voices, voicing, voiced**) express something in words.

□ **voice box** the larynx. **voice-over** a piece of speech in a film or broadcast that is spoken by a person who is not seen on the screen. ■ **voiceless** adjective.

voicemail noun an electronic system which can store messages from telephone callers.

void adjective 1 not valid or legally binding. 2 completely empty. 3 (**void of**) free from; lacking. • noun a completely empty space. • verb 1 empty waste matter from the bladder or bowels. 2 declare to be not valid or legally binding.

voile /voyl, vwahl/ noun a thin, semi-transparent fabric.

volatile adjective 1 liable to change rapidly and unpredictably. 2 (of a substance) easily evaporated at normal temperatures. ■ **volatility** noun.

vol-au-vent /vol-oh-von/ noun a small round case of puff pastry filled with a savoury mixture.

volcanic adjective relating to or produced by a volcano or volcanoes.

volcano noun (plural **volcanoes** or **volcanos**) a mountain with an opening through which lava, rock, and gas are forced from the earth's crust.

vole noun a small mouse-like rodent.

volition noun a person's will or power of independent action.

volley noun (plural **volleys**) 1 a number of bullets, arrows, etc. fired at one time. 2 a series of questions, insults, etc. directed rapidly at someone. 3 (in sport) an act of hitting the ball before it touches the ground. • verb (**volleys, volleying, volleyed**) hit the ball before it touches the ground.

THESAURUS

vocal adjective 1 *vocal sounds:* spoken, said, voiced, uttered, articulated, oral. 2 *a vocal critic:* vociferous, outspoken, forthright, plain-spoken, blunt, frank, candid, passionate, vehement, vigorous.

vocation noun calling, life's work, mission, purpose, profession, occupation, career, job, employment, trade, craft, line (of work).

vogue noun fashion, trend, fad, fancy, craze, rage, enthusiasm, passion.

voice noun 1 *the voice of the people:* opinion, view, feeling, wish, desire, vote. 2 *a powerful voice for conservation:* mouthpiece, representative, spokesperson, agent, vehicle. • verb *they voiced their opposition:* express, communicate, declare, state, vent, utter, say, speak, articulate; informal come out with.

void noun *the void of space:* vacuum, emptiness, nothingness, blankness, (empty) space, gap, cavity, chasm, gulf.

• verb *the contract was voided:* invalidate, annul, nullify, negate, quash, cancel, countermand, repeal, revoke, rescind, retract, withdraw, reverse. OPPOSITES validate, fill. • adjective 1 *vast void spaces:* empty, vacant, blank, bare, clear, free. 2 *the election was void:* invalid, null, ineffective, worthless. OPPOSITES full, valid.

volatile adjective 1 *a volatile personality:* unpredictable, temperamental, capricious, fickle, impulsive, emotional, excitable, turbulent, erratic, unstable. 2 *the atmosphere is too volatile for an election:* tense, strained, fraught, uneasy, charged, uncomfortable, explosive, inflammatory, turbulent. OPPOSITES stable, calm.

volley noun barrage, cannonade, battery, bombardment, salvo, burst, storm, hail, shower, deluge, torrent.

V

volleyball noun a team game in which a ball is hit by hand over a net and must be kept from touching the ground.

volt noun the basic unit of electric potential.

voltage noun an electrical force expressed in volts.

volte-face /volt-**fass**/ noun an abrupt and complete change of attitude or policy.

voluble adjective talking easily and at length.
■ volubility noun volubly adverb.

volume noun 1 the amount of space occupied by something or enclosed within a container. 2 the amount or quantity of something. 3 degree of loudness. 4 a book, especially one forming part of a larger work or series.

voluminous adjective 1 (of clothing) loose and full. 2 (of writing) very lengthy.

voluntary adjective 1 done or acting of your own free will. 2 working or done without payment. • noun (plural **voluntaries**) an organ solo played before, during, or after a church service.
■ voluntarily adverb.

volunteer noun 1 a person who freely offers to do something. 2 a person who does work without being paid. 3 a person who freely joins the armed forces. • verb (**volunteers, volunteering, volunteered**) 1 freely offer to do something. 2 say or suggest something without being asked.

voluptuary noun (plural **voluptuaries**) a person who loves luxury and pleasure.

voluptuous /vuh-**lup**-tyuu-uhss/ adjective 1 (of a woman) curvaceous and sexually attractive. 2 giving sensual pleasure.
■ voluptuously adverb.

vomit verb (**vomits, vomiting, vomited**) 1 bring up food from the stomach through the mouth. 2 send out in an uncontrolled stream. • noun food vomited from the stomach.

voodoo noun a religious cult practised mainly in the Caribbean and involving sorcery and possession by spirits.

voracious adjective 1 wanting or eating great quantities of food. 2 doing something eagerly and enthusiastically.
■ voraciously adverb voracity noun.

vortex noun (plural **vortexes** or **vortices** /**vor**-ti-seez/) a whirling mass of water or air.

votary noun (plural **votaries**) 1 a person who has dedicated themselves to God or religious service. 2 a devoted follower or supporter.

vote noun 1 a formal choice made between two or more candidates or courses of action. 2 (**the vote**) the right to take part in an election. • verb (**votes, voting, voted**) give or register a vote.
■ voter noun.

votive adjective offered to a god as a sign of thanks.

vouch verb (**vouch for**) 1 state that something is true or accurate. 2 state that someone is who they claim to be, or that they are of good character.

voucher noun a piece of paper that entitles you to a discount, or that may be exchanged for goods or services.

vouchsafe verb (**vouchsafes, vouchsafing, vouchsafed**) formal give or say in a gracious or superior way.

vow noun a solemn promise. • verb solemnly

THESAURUS

volume noun 1 *a volume from the library:* book, publication, tome, work, title. 2 *a syringe of known volume:* capacity, mass, bulk, extent, size, dimensions. 3 *a huge volume of water:* quantity, amount, mass, bulk, measure. 4 *she turned the volume down:* loudness, sound, amplification.

voluntarily adverb of your own free will, of your own volition, by choice, by preference, spontaneously, willingly, readily, freely.
OPPOSITES compulsorily.

voluntary adjective 1 *attendance is voluntary:* optional, discretionary, elective, non-compulsory. 2 *voluntary work:* unpaid, unsalaried, for free, without charge, for nothing, honorary.
OPPOSITES compulsory, paid.

volunteer verb 1 *I volunteered my services:* offer, tender, proffer, put forward, put up, venture. 2 *he volunteered as a driver:* offer your services, present yourself, make

yourself available, come forward.
OPPOSITES withdraw, refuse.

vomit verb 1 *he needed to vomit:* be sick, spew, fetch up, heave, retch, gag; informal throw up, puke; N. Amer. informal barf. 2 *I vomited my breakfast:* bring up, regurgitate, spew up; informal throw up, puke up; Brit. informal sick up.
• noun *a coat stained with vomit:* sick; informal puke, spew; N. Amer. informal barf.

vote noun 1 *a rigged vote:* ballot, poll, election, referendum, plebiscite, show of hands. 2 *in 1918 women got the vote:* suffrage, franchise, voting rights, voice, say.
• verb *I vote we have one more game:* suggest, propose, recommend, advocate, move, submit.

voucher noun coupon, token, ticket, pass, chit, slip, stub, docket; Brit. informal chitty.

vow noun *a vow of silence:* promise, pledge, oath, bond, covenant, commitment, word

V

promise to do something.

vowel noun a letter of the alphabet representing a sound in which the mouth is open and the tongue is not touching the top of the mouth, the teeth, or the lips (in English *a*, *e*, *i*, *o*, and *u*).

voyage noun a long journey by sea or in space. •verb (**voyages, voyaging, voyaged**) go on a voyage.
■ **voyager** noun.

voyeur /vwa-yer, voy-er/ noun **1** a person who gains sexual pleasure from watching other people when they are naked or having sex. **2** a person who enjoys seeing the pain or distress of other people.
■ **voyeurism** noun **voyeuristic** adjective.

vs abbreviation versus.

vulcanized or **vulcanised** adjective (of rubber) hardened by being treated with sulphur at a high temperature.

vulgar adjective **1** lacking sophistication or good taste. **2** referring to sex or bodily functions in a rude or inappropriate way.
□ **vulgar fraction** Brit. a fraction shown by numbers above and below a line, not decimally.
■ **vulgarity** noun **vulgarly** adverb.

vulgarize or **vulgarise** verb (**vulgarizes, vulgarizing, vulgarized**) spoil something by making it less refined or exclusive.

Vulgate noun the main Latin version of the Bible, prepared in the 4th century.

vulnerable adjective able to be attacked or harmed.
■ **vulnerability** noun **vulnerably** adverb.

vulpine adjective having to do with foxes, or like a fox.

vulture noun a large bird of prey that feeds mainly on dead animals.

vulva noun the female external genitals.

vying present participle of **vie**.

THESAURUS

(of honour).
•verb *I vowed to do better:* promise, pledge, swear, undertake, make a commitment, give your word, guarantee.

voyage noun journey, trip, cruise, passage, sail, crossing, expedition, odyssey.

vulgar adjective **1** *a vulgar joke:* rude, crude, dirty, filthy, smutty, naughty, indecent, obscene, coarse, risqué; informal blue. **2** *the decor was lavish but vulgar:* tasteless, crass, tawdry, ostentatious, flamboyant, showy, gaudy, garish; informal flash, tacky.

3 *it was vulgar for a woman to whistle:* impolite, ill-mannered, boorish, uncouth, unsophisticated, unrefined.
OPPOSITES clean, tasteful, decent.

vulnerable adjective **1** *a vulnerable city:* in danger, in peril, in jeopardy, at risk, unprotected, undefended, unguarded, open to attack, exposed, defenceless. **2** *he is vulnerable to criticism:* exposed, open, liable, prone, prey, susceptible, subject, an easy target.
OPPOSITES invulnerable, safe.

Ww

W or **w** noun (plural **Ws** or **W's**) the twenty-third letter of the alphabet. •**abbreviation 1** watts. **2** West or Western.

wacky or **whacky** adjective (**wackier, wackiest**) informal funny or amusing in a slightly odd way.

wad noun **1** a lump or bundle of a soft material. **2** a bundle of paper or banknotes. •verb (**wads, wadding, wadded**) **1** press a soft material into a wad. **2** line or fill with soft material.

waddle verb (**waddles, waddling, waddled**) walk with short steps and a clumsy swaying motion. •noun a waddling way of walking.

wade verb (**wades, wading, waded**) **1** walk through water or mud. **2** (**wade through**) read or deal with something that is boring or takes a long time. **3** (**wade in** or **into**) informal attack or intervene in a forceful way.

wader noun **1** a long-legged bird that feeds in shallow water. **2** (**waders**) high waterproof boots.

wafer noun **1** a very thin, light, sweet biscuit. **2** a thin disc of unleavened bread used in the Christian service of Holy Communion.

waffle[1] Brit. informal verb (**waffles, waffling, waffled**) speak or write at length without saying anything interesting or important. •noun lengthy talk or writing that does not say anything interesting or important.

waffle[2] noun a small, crisp batter cake, eaten hot with butter or syrup.

waft verb pass easily or gently through the air. •noun a gentle movement of air.

wag verb (**wags, wagging, wagged**) move rapidly to and fro. •noun **1** a wagging movement. **2** informal a person who likes making jokes.
■ **waggish** adjective.

wage noun (also **wages**) a fixed regular payment for work. •verb (**wages, waging, waged**) carry on a war or campaign.

wager more formal term for **BET**.

waggle verb (**waggles, waggling, waggled**) move with short, quick movements from side to side or up and down.

wagon or Brit. **waggon** noun **1** a vehicle, especially a horse-drawn one, for transporting goods. **2** Brit. a railway vehicle for carrying goods in bulk.
□ **on the wagon** informal not drinking alcohol.

wagtail noun a slender bird with a long tail that it frequently wags up and down.

waif noun **1** a poor, helpless person, especially a child. **2** a person who is thin and pale.

wail noun **1** a long high-pitched cry of pain, grief, or anger. **2** a sound resembling this. •verb make a wail.

wain noun old use a wagon or cart.

wainscot /wayn-skuht/ noun an area of wooden panelling on the lower part of the walls of a room.

waist noun **1** the part of the human body below the ribs and above the hips. **2** a narrow part in the middle of something.

waistband noun a strip of cloth forming the waist of a skirt or pair of trousers.

waistcoat noun Brit. a waist-length garment with buttons down the front and no sleeves or collar.

THESAURUS

waddle verb toddle, totter, wobble, shuffle.

wade verb **1** they waded in the water: paddle, wallow, splosh; informal splosh. **2** I had to wade through some hefty documents: plough, plod, trawl, labour, toil.

wag verb **1** the dog's tail wagged: swing, swish, switch, sway, shake; informal waggle. **2** he wagged his stick at them: shake, wave,

wiggle, flourish, brandish.

wage noun the workers' wages: pay, salary, stipend, fee, remuneration, income, earnings.
•verb they waged war on the guerrillas: engage in, carry on, conduct, execute, pursue, prosecute, proceed with.

wail noun & verb howl, cry, bawl, moan,

waistline noun the measurement around a person's body at the waist.

wait verb **1** stay in a particular place or delay doing anything until a particular time or event. **2** be delayed or postponed. **3** (**wait on**) act as an attendant to. **4** serve people at a meal or in a restaurant. • noun a period of waiting.

waiter or **waitress** noun a person whose job is to serve customers at their tables in a restaurant.

waive verb (**waives**, **waiving**, **waived**) choose not to insist on a claim or right.

waiver noun an instance of waiving a right or claim, or a document recording this.

wake[1] verb (**wakes**, **waking**, **woke**; past participle **woken**) **1** (often **wake up**) stop sleeping. **2** bring to life, or make more alert. **3** (**wake up to**) become aware of. • noun **1** a party held after a funeral. **2** a gathering held beside the body of someone who has died.

wake[2] noun a trail of disturbed water or air left by a ship or aircraft. □ **in the wake of** following as a result of.

wakeful adjective **1** not sleeping. **2** alert and aware of possible dangers. ■ **wakefulness** noun.

waken verb wake from sleep.

walk verb **1** move fairly slowly using the legs. **2** travel over a route or area on foot. **3** accompany someone on foot. **4** take a dog out for exercise. • noun **1** a journey on foot. **2** a fairly slow rate of movement on foot. **3** a person's way of walking. **4** a path for walking. □ **walking stick** a stick used for support when walking. **walk of life** the position in society that someone holds. ■ **walker** noun.

walkabout noun **1** chiefly Brit. an informal stroll among a crowd by an important visitor. **2** Austral. a journey (originally on foot) made by an Australian Aboriginal in order to live in the traditional way.

walkie-talkie noun a portable two-way radio.

Walkman noun (plural **Walkmans** or **Walkmen**) trademark a personal stereo.

walkout noun a sudden angry departure as a protest or strike.

walkover noun an easy victory.

walkway noun a raised passageway or a wide path.

wall noun **1** a continuous upright structure forming a side of a building or room, or enclosing or dividing an area of land. **2** a barrier. **3** the outer layer or lining of an organ or cavity in the body. • verb enclose or block with walls. □ **go to the wall** informal (of a business) fail. **wall-eyed** informal having an eye that squints outwards.

wallaby noun (plural **wallabies**) an Australian animal like a small kangaroo.

wallet noun a small flat, folding holder for money and plastic cards.

THESAURUS

groan, yowl, whine, lament.

wait verb **1** *we'll wait in the airport:* **stay (put)**, remain, rest, stop, halt, pause, linger, loiter; informal stick around. **2** *she had to wait until her bags arrived:* **stand by**, hold back, bide your time, mark time, kill time, waste time, kick your heels, twiddle your thumbs; informal hold on, hang around, sit tight. **3** *that job will have to wait:* **be postponed**, be delayed, be put off, be deferred; informal be put on the back burner, be put on ice.
• noun *a long wait:* **delay**, hold-up, interval, interlude, pause, break, suspension, stoppage, halt, interruption, lull, gap.

waiter, waitress noun **server**, steward, stewardess, attendant, butler, servant; N. Amer. waitperson.

waive verb **1** *he waived his right to a hearing:* **give up**, abandon, renounce, relinquish, surrender, sacrifice, turn down. **2** *the manager waived the rules:* **disregard**, ignore, overlook, set aside, forgo.

wake[1] verb **1** *at 4.30 a.m. Mark woke up:* **awake**, waken, stir, come to, come round. **2** *she woke her husband:* **rouse**, waken. OPPOSITES go to sleep, send to sleep.

• noun **vigil**, watch, funeral. □ **wake up to realize**, become aware of, become conscious of.

wake[2] noun *the cruiser's wake:* **backwash**, slipstream, trail, path, track. □ **in the wake of in the aftermath of**, after, subsequent to, following, as a result of, as a consequence of, on account of, because of.

walk verb **1** *they walked along the road:* **stroll**, saunter, amble, trudge, plod, hike, tramp, trek, march, stride, troop, wander, ramble, promenade, traipse; informal mosey, hoof it. **2** *he walked her home:* **accompany**, escort, guide, show, see, take.
• noun **1** *country walks:* **ramble**, hike, tramp, march, stroll, promenade, constitutional, turn. **2** *her elegant walk:* **gait**, step, stride, tread. **3** *the riverside walk:* **path**, pathway, footpath, track, walkway, promenade, footway, pavement, trail, towpath.

walker noun **rambler**, hiker, trekker, stroller, pedestrian.

wallet noun **purse**, case, pouch, holder; N. Amer. billfold, pocketbook.

w

wallflower noun **1** a plant with sweet-smelling flowers that bloom in early spring. **2** informal a girl who has no one to dance with at a party.

wallop informal verb (**wallops, walloping, walloped**) hit very hard. •noun a heavy blow.

wallow verb **1** roll about or lie in mud or water. **2** (of a boat or aircraft) roll from side to side. **3** (**wallow in**) indulge in. •noun **1** an act of wallowing. **2** an area of mud or shallow water where animals go to wallow.

wallpaper noun **1** paper pasted in strips over the walls of a room as decoration. **2** a background pattern or picture on a computer screen.

wally noun (plural **wallies**) Brit. informal a stupid person.

walnut noun an edible nut with a wrinkled shell.

walrus noun a large sea mammal with downward-pointing tusks.

waltz noun a ballroom dance in triple time performed by a couple. •verb **1** dance a waltz. **2** move in a casual or inconsiderate way.

waltzer noun a fairground ride in which cars are carried round a track that moves up and down.

wan /rhymes with gone/ adjective **1** (of a person) pale and appearing ill or exhausted. **2** (of light) pale or weak. **3** (of a smile) lacking enthusiasm; strained. ■ **wanly** adverb.

wand noun a long, thin rod, especially one

used in casting magic spells or performing tricks.

wander verb (**wanders, wandering, wandered**) **1** move in a leisurely, casual, or aimless way. **2** move slowly away from the correct place. •noun a period of wandering. ■ **wanderer** noun.

wanderlust noun a strong desire to travel.

wane verb (**wanes, waning, waned**) **1** (of the moon) appear to decrease in size day by day. **2** become weaker. □ **on the wane** becoming weaker.

wangle verb (**wangles, wangling, wangled**) informal get something by using persuasion or a clever plan.

want verb **1** have a desire to possess or do. **2** (**be wanted**) (of a suspected criminal) be searched for by the police. **3** (also **want for**) lack or be short of. **4** feel sexual desire for. •noun **1** lack or shortage. **2** poverty. **3** a desire for something.

wanting adjective **1** not having something required or desired. **2** not good enough.

wanton adjective **1** (of a cruel or violent action) deliberate and unprovoked. **2** having many sexual partners. ■ **wantonly** adverb.

WAP abbreviation Wireless Application Protocol, a means of enabling a mobile phone to browse the Internet.

wapiti /wop-i-ti/ noun (plural **wapitis**) a large North American red deer.

war noun **1** a state of armed conflict between different nations, states, or groups. **2** a long contest between rivals or campaign against something. •verb (**wars,**

THESAURUS

wander verb **1** *I wandered around the estate:* stroll, amble, saunter, walk, potter, ramble, meander, roam, range, drift; Scottish & Irish stravaig; informal traipse, mosey. **2** *we are wandering from the point:* stray, depart, diverge, deviate, digress, drift, get sidetracked.

wane verb decline, diminish, decrease, dwindle, shrink, tail off, ebb, fade, lessen, peter out, fall off, recede, slump, weaken, wither, evaporate, die out.
OPPOSITES wax, grow.

want verb desire, wish for, hope for, fancy, care for, like, long for, yearn for, crave, hanker after, hunger for, thirst for, cry out for, covet; informal have a yen for, be dying for.
•noun **1** *his want of vigilance:* lack, absence, non-existence, dearth, deficiency, inadequacy, insufficiency, paucity, shortage, scarcity. **2** *a time of want:* need, austerity, privation, deprivation, poverty, destitution. **3** *her wants would be taken care of:* wish, desire, demand, longing,

fancy, craving, need, requirement; informal yen.

wanting adjective deficient, inadequate, lacking, insufficient, imperfect, flawed, unsound, substandard, inferior, second-rate.
OPPOSITES sufficient.

wanton adjective deliberate, wilful, malicious, gratuitous, unprovoked, motiveless, arbitrary, unjustifiable, senseless.
OPPOSITES justifiable.

war noun **1** *the Napoleonic wars:* conflict, warfare, combat, fighting, action, bloodshed, struggle, fight, campaign, hostilities, jihad, crusade. **2** *the war against drugs:* campaign, crusade, battle, fight, struggle.
OPPOSITES peace.
•verb *rival Emperors warred against each other:* fight, battle, combat, wage war, take up arms, feud, quarrel, struggle, contend, wrangle, cross swords.

W

warring, warred) be involved in a war.
□ **be on the warpath** be very angry with someone. **war crime** an action that breaks accepted international rules of war.

warble verb (**warbles, warbling, warbled**) sing in a trilling or quavering voice.

warbler noun a small songbird with a warbling song.

ward noun 1 a room in a hospital for one or more patients. 2 a division of a city or borough that is represented by a councillor or councillors. 3 a young person looked after by a guardian appointed by their parents or a court. 4 a ridge or bar in a lock that engages with grooves on a key.
• verb (**ward someone/thing off**) prevent someone or something from harming you.

warden noun 1 a person supervising a place or procedure. 2 Brit. the head of certain schools, colleges, etc. 3 N. Amer. a prison governor.

warder noun (feminine **wardress**) Brit. a prison guard.

wardrobe noun 1 a large, tall cupboard for hanging clothes in. 2 a person's entire collection of clothes. 3 the costume department of a theatre or film company.

wardroom noun the room on a warship where the officers eat.

ware noun 1 pottery of a particular type. 2 manufactured articles. 3 (**wares**) articles offered for sale.

warehouse noun 1 a large building for storing raw materials or manufactured goods. 2 a large wholesale or retail store.

warfare noun the activity of fighting a war.

warhead noun the explosive head of a missile, torpedo, etc.

warhorse noun informal a very experienced soldier, politician, etc.

warlike adjective 1 hostile. 2 intended for war.

warlock noun a man who practises witchcraft.

warlord noun a military commander, especially one controlling a region.

warm adjective 1 at a fairly high temperature. 2 helping the body to stay warm. 3 enthusiastic, affectionate, or kind. 4 (of a colour) containing red, yellow, or orange tones. 5 (of a scent or trail) fresh and easy to follow. • verb 1 make or become warm. 2 (**warm to** or **towards**) become more interested in or enthusiastic about.
• noun (**the warm**) a warm place or area.
□ **warm-blooded** (of animals) keeping a constant body temperature by their body's chemical processes. **warm up** prepare for physical exertion by doing gentle stretches and exercises. **warm something up** entertain an audience before the arrival of the main act.
■ **warmly** adverb.

warmonger noun a person who tries to bring about war.

warmth noun 1 the quality of being warm. 2 enthusiasm, affection, or kindness. 3 strength of emotion.

warn verb 1 tell someone of a possible danger or problem. 2 advise someone not to do something. 3 (**warn someone off**) order someone to keep away.

THESAURUS

ward noun 1 *the surgical ward:* room, unit, department, area. 2 *a marginal ward in Westminster:* district, constituency, division, quarter, zone, parish. 3 *the boy is my ward:* dependant, charge, protégé.

warden noun 1 *the flats have a resident warden:* superintendent, caretaker, porter, steward, custodian, watchman, concierge, doorman, commissionaire. 2 *a game warden:* ranger, keeper, guardian, protector. 3 *he was handcuffed to a warden:* prison officer, guard, jailer, warder, keeper; informal screw. 4 (Brit.) *the college warden:* principal, head, governor, master, mistress, rector, provost, dean, president, director, chancellor.

warehouse noun storeroom, depot, depository, stockroom, magazine, granary; informal lock-up.

wares plural noun goods, merchandise, products, produce, stock, commodities.

warfare noun fighting, war, combat, conflict, action, hostilities.

warm adjective 1 *a warm kitchen:* hot, cosy, snug. 2 *a warm day:* balmy, summery, sultry, hot, mild, temperate. 3 *warm water:* tepid, lukewarm. 4 *a warm sweater:* thick, chunky, thermal, winter, woolly. 5 *a warm welcome:* friendly, cordial, amiable, genial, kind, pleasant, fond, welcoming, hospitable, hearty.
OPPOSITES cold, chilly, light, hostile.
• verb *warm the soup in that pan:* heat (up), reheat.
OPPOSITES chill.

warmth noun 1 *the warmth of the fire:* heat, cosiness, snugness. 2 *the warmth of their welcome:* friendliness, amiability, geniality, cordiality, kindness, tenderness, fondness.

warn verb 1 *David warned her that it was too late:* inform, notify, tell, alert, apprise, make someone aware, remind; informal tip off. 2 *police are warning galleries to be alert:* advise, exhort, urge, counsel, caution.

w

warning noun **1** a statement or event that indicates a possible danger or problem. **2** advice against wrong or foolish behaviour. **3** advance notice.

warp verb **1** make or become bent or twisted. **2** make abnormal or strange. •noun **1** a distortion or twist in shape. **2** the lengthwise threads on a loom over and under which the weft threads are passed to make cloth.

warrant noun **1** an official authorization allowing police, soldiers, etc. to make an arrest, search premises, etc. **2** a document that entitles you to receive goods, money, or services. **3** justification or authority. •verb **1** justify or make necessary. **2** officially state or guarantee. □ **warrant officer** a rank of military officer below the commissioned officers.

warranty noun (plural **warranties**) a written guarantee promising to repair or replace an article if necessary within a stated period.

warren noun **1** a network of interconnecting rabbit burrows. **2** a complex network of paths or passages.

warrior noun a brave or experienced soldier or fighter.

warship noun an armed ship designed to take part in warfare at sea.

wart noun a small, hard growth on the skin. ■ **warty** adjective.

warthog noun an African wild pig with warty lumps on the face.

wary adjective (**warier**, **wariest**) cautious about possible dangers or problems. ■ **warily** adverb **wariness** noun.

was 1st and 3rd person singular past of **BE**.

wash verb **1** clean with water and usually soap or detergent. **2** (of water) flow freely in a particular direction. **3** (**wash over**) happen all around someone without affecting them very much. **4** informal seem convincing or genuine. •noun **1** an act of washing. **2** a quantity of clothes needing to be washed. **3** the water or air disturbed by a moving boat or aircraft. **4** a medicinal or cleansing solution. **5** a thin coating of paint. □ **be washed out 1** be postponed or cancelled because of rain. **2** (**washed out**) pale and tired. **wash your hands of** take no further responsibility for. **wash up 1** Brit. wash crockery and cutlery after use. **2** (**washed up**) informal no longer effective or successful.

washbasin noun a basin for washing your

---

warning noun **1** *the earthquake came without warning:* (**advance**) **notice**, alert, hint, signal, sign, alarm bells; informal a tip-off. **2** *a health warning:* **caution**, notification, information, exhortation, advice. **3** *a warning of things to come:* **omen**, premonition, foreboding, prophecy, prediction, forecast, token, portent, signal, sign. **4** *his sentence is a warning to other drunk drivers:* **example**, deterrent, lesson, caution, message, moral. **5** *she received a written warning:* **reprimand**, caution, remonstrance, admonition, censure; informal dressing-down, talking-to, telling-off.

warp verb **1** *timber which is too dry will warp:* **buckle**, twist, bend, distort, deform, curve, bow, contort. **2** *he warped the mind of her child:* **corrupt**, twist, pervert, deprave.
OPPOSITES straighten.

warrant noun **1** *a warrant for his arrest:* **authorization**, order, writ, mandate, licence, permit, summons. **2** *a travel warrant:* **voucher**, chit, slip, ticket, coupon, pass.
•verb **1** *the charges warranted a severe sentence:* **justify**, deserve, vindicate, call for, sanction, permit, authorize, excuse, account for, legitimize, support, license, merit, qualify for, rate. **2** *we warrant that the texts do not infringe copyright:* **guarantee**, promise, affirm, swear, vouch, vow, pledge, undertake, declare, testify.

warranty noun **guarantee**, assurance, promise, commitment, undertaking, pledge, agreement, covenant.

warrior noun **fighter**, soldier, serviceman, combatant.

wary adjective **1** *he was trained to be wary:* **cautious**, careful, circumspect, on your guard, chary, alert, on the lookout, attentive, heedful, watchful, vigilant, observant. **2** *we are wary of strangers:* **suspicious**, chary, leery, careful, distrustful.
OPPOSITES inattentive, trustful.

wash verb **1** *he washed in the bath:* **clean yourself**, bathe, shower. **2** *she washed her hands:* **clean**, cleanse, scrub, wipe, shampoo, lather, sluice, swill, douse, swab, disinfect. **3** *she washed off the blood:* **remove**, expunge, eradicate, sponge off, scrub off, wipe off, rinse off. **4** *the women were washing clothes:* **launder**, clean, rinse. **5** *waves washed against the hull:* **splash**, lap, dash, break, beat, surge, ripple, roll. **6** *the wreckage was washed downriver:* **sweep**, carry, convey, transport, deposit.
OPPOSITES dirty.
•noun **1** *that shirt should go in the wash:* **laundry**, washing. **2** *the wash of a motor boat:* **backwash**, wake, trail, path.
□ **wash something away erode**, abrade, wear away, eat away, undermine.

W

hands and face.

washboard noun a ridged or corrugated board formerly used for scrubbing clothes when washing them.

washer noun 1 a person or device that washes. 2 a small flat ring fixed between a nut and bolt.

washing noun clothes, sheets, towels, etc. that need washing or have just been washed.

□ washing-up Brit. crockery, cutlery, etc. that need washing.

washout noun informal a disappointing failure.

washroom noun N. Amer. a room with washing and toilet facilities.

washstand noun a piece of furniture formerly used to hold a bowl or basin for washing the hands and face.

wasn't short form was not.

wasp noun a stinging winged insect with a black and yellow striped body.

□ wasp waist a very narrow waist.

waspish adjective sharply irritable.

■ waspishly adverb.

wassail /wos-sayl/ old use noun lively festivities involving the drinking of a lot of alcohol. • verb 1 celebrate with a lot of alcohol. 2 go carol-singing at Christmas.

wastage noun 1 the process of wasting. 2 an amount wasted. 3 (also **natural wastage**) Brit. the reduction in the size of a workforce through people resigning or retiring.

waste verb (**wastes, wasting, wasted**) 1 use more of something than is necessary. 2 fail to make good use of. 3 (**be wasted on**) not be appreciated by. 4 (often **waste away**)

gradually become weaker and thinner. 5 (**wasted**) informal under the influence of alcohol or illegal drugs. • adjective 1 discarded because no longer useful or required. 2 (of land) not used, cultivated, or built on. • noun 1 an instance of wasting. 2 material that is not wanted or useful. 3 a large area of barren, uninhabited land.

□ lay waste to completely destroy.

■ waster noun.

wasteful adjective using more of something than is necessary.

■ wastefully adverb.

wasteland noun a barren or empty area of land.

wastrel noun literary a lazy person who spends their time or money wastefully.

watch verb 1 look at attentively. 2 keep under careful observation. 3 be cautious about. 4 (**watch for**) look out for. 5 (**watch out**) be careful. • noun 1 a small clock worn on a strap on your wrist. 2 an instance of watching. 3 a period of keeping watch during the night. 4 a shift worked by firefighters or police officers.

□ keep watch be alert for danger or trouble.

■ watchable adjective watcher noun.

watchdog noun 1 a dog kept to guard property. 2 a person or group that monitors the practices of companies providing a particular service.

watchful adjective alert to possible difficulty or danger.

■ watchfully adverb watchfulness noun.

watchman noun (plural **watchmen**) a man employed to look after an empty building.

watchtower noun a tower built as a high

THESAURUS

waste verb 1 *he doesn't like to waste money:* squander, misspend, misuse, fritter away, throw away, lavish, dissipate; informal blow, splurge. 2 *kids are wasting away in the streets:* grow weak, grow thin, shrink, wilt, fade, flag, deteriorate. 3 *the disease wasted his legs:* emaciate, atrophy, wither, shrivel, shrink, weaken.

OPPOSITES conserve, thrive.

• adjective 1 *waste material:* unwanted, excess, superfluous, left over, scrap, unusable, unprofitable. 2 *waste ground:* uncultivated, barren, desert, arid, bare, desolate.

• noun 1 *a waste of money:* misuse, misapplication, abuse, extravagance, lavishness. 2 *household waste:* rubbish, refuse, litter, debris, junk, sewage, effluent; N. Amer. garbage, trash. 3 (**wastes**) desert, wasteland, wilderness, emptiness, wilds.

wasteful adjective prodigal, profligate,

uneconomical, extravagant, lavish, excessive, imprudent, improvident, spendthrift.

OPPOSITES frugal.

watch verb 1 *she watched him as he spoke:* observe, view, look at, eye, gaze at, peer at, contemplate, inspect, scrutinize, scan; informal check out, get a load of, recce, eyeball. 2 *he was being watched by the police:* spy on, keep in sight, keep under surveillance, track, monitor, tail; informal keep tabs on, stake out. 3 *we stayed to watch the boat:* guard, mind, protect, look after, keep an eye on, take care of, shield, defend.

OPPOSITES ignore, neglect.

• noun 1 *Bill looked at his watch:* wristwatch, timepiece, chronometer. 2 *we kept watch on the yacht:* guard, vigil, lookout, an eye, observation, surveillance.

watchdog noun ombudsman, monitor, scrutineer, inspector, supervisor.

w

observation point.

watchword noun a word or phrase expressing a central aim or belief.

water noun **1** the liquid which forms the seas, lakes, rivers, and rain. **2** (**waters**) an area of sea under the authority of a particular country. **3** (**waters**) fluid that passes from a woman's body shortly before she gives birth. •verb (**waters, watering, watered**) **1** pour water over a plant. **2** give a drink of water to an animal. **3** (of the eyes or mouth) produce tears or saliva. **4** dilute a drink with water. **5** (**water something down**) make something less forceful or controversial.

□ **hold water** (of a theory) seem valid or reasonable. **water buffalo** a kind of Asian buffalo used for carrying heavy loads. **water cannon** a device that sends out a powerful jet of water, used to make a crowd disperse. **water closet** dated a flush toilet. **water ice** a frozen dessert consisting of fruit juice or purée in a sugar syrup. **watering can** a portable container with a long spout, used for watering plants. **watering hole** informal a pub or bar. **water lily** a plant that grows in water, with large round floating leaves. **water meadow** a meadow that is periodically flooded by a stream or river. **water polo** a game played by swimmers in a pool, who try to throw the ball into their opponents' net. **water table** the level below which the ground is saturated with water. **water tower** a tower that raises up a water tank to create enough pressure to distribute the water through pipes.

■ **waterless** adjective **watery** adjective.

waterbed noun a bed with a water-filled mattress.

watercolour (US spelling **watercolor**) noun **1** artists' paint that is thinned with water. **2** a picture painted with watercolours.

watercourse noun a stream or artificial water channel.

watercress noun a kind of cress which grows in running water.

waterfall noun a place where a stream of water falls from a height.

waterfowl plural noun ducks, geese, or other large birds living in water.

waterfront noun a part of a town or city alongside an area of water.

waterhole noun a water-filled hollow

where animals drink.

waterline noun the level normally reached by the water on the side of a ship.

waterlogged adjective saturated with water.

watermark noun a faint design made in some paper that can be seen when held against the light.

watermelon noun a very large fruit with smooth green skin, red pulp, and watery juice.

watermill noun a mill worked by a waterwheel.

waterproof adjective unable to be penetrated by water. •noun Brit. a waterproof garment. •verb make waterproof.

watershed noun **1** an area of land that separates waters flowing to different rivers, seas, etc. **2** a turning point in a situation.

waterski noun (plural **waterskis**) each of a pair of skis that let you skim the surface of the water when towed by a motorboat. •verb (**waterskis, waterskiing, waterskied**) travel on waterskis.

■ **waterskier** noun.

waterspout noun a column of water formed by a whirlwind over the sea.

watertight adjective **1** not allowing any water to pass through. **2** unable to be called into question.

waterway noun a river, canal, or other route for travel by water.

waterwheel noun a large wheel driven by flowing water, used to work machinery or to raise water to a higher level.

waterworks noun a place with equipment for managing a water supply.

watt noun the basic unit of power.

wattage noun an amount of electrical power expressed in watts.

wattle[1] noun rods interlaced with twigs or branches, used for making fences, walls, etc.
□ **wattle and daub** wattle covered with mud or clay, formerly used in building walls.

wattle[2] noun a fleshy part hanging from the head or neck of the turkey and some other birds.

THESAURUS

water verb **1** *water the plants:* sprinkle, moisten, dampen, wet, spray, splash. **2** *my mouth watered:* moisten, salivate.
□ **water something down 1** *staff had watered down the drinks:* dilute, thin (out), weaken, adulterate. **2** *the proposals were watered down:* **tone down**, temper, mitigate, moderate, soften, tame.

waterfall noun falls, cascade, cataract, rapids.

watery adjective runny, thin, diluted, weak, tasteless, bland.

wave verb (**waves, waving, waved**) **1** move your hand, or something held in it, to and fro, especially when greeting someone. **2** move to and fro with a swaying motion. • noun **1** a ridge of water moving along the surface of the sea or breaking on the shore. **2** a sudden occurrence of or increase in a phenomenon or emotion. **3** a gesture made by waving your hand. **4** a slightly curling lock of hair. **5** a regular to-and-fro motion of particles of matter involved in transmitting sound, light, heat, etc.

waveband noun a range of wavelengths used in radio transmission.

wavelength noun **1** the distance between successive crests of a wave of sound, light, radio, etc. **2** a person's way of thinking.

wavelet noun a small wave.

waver verb (**wavers, wavering, wavered**) **1** move in a quivering way; flicker. **2** begin to weaken; falter. **3** be indecisive.

wavy adjective (**wavier, waviest**) having a series of wave-like curves.

wax¹ noun **1** a soft solid substance used for making candles or polishes. **2** a substance produced by bees to make honeycombs; beeswax. • verb polish or treat with wax. ■ **waxen** adjective **waxy** adjective.

wax² verb **1** (of the moon) gradually appear to increase in size. **2** literary become larger or stronger. **3** literary speak or write in a particular way: *they waxed lyrical.*

waxwork noun **1** a lifelike dummy made of

wax. **2** (**waxworks**) an exhibition of waxworks.

way noun **1** a method, style, or manner of doing something. **2** a road, track, or path. **3** a route or means taken in order to reach, enter, or leave a place. **4** a direction. **5** the distance in space or time between two points. **6** condition or state. **7** (**ways**) parts into which something divides. • adverb informal at or to a considerable distance or extent.
□ **by the way** used to introduce a comment that is not connected to the current subject of conversation. **give way 1** yield. **2** collapse or break under pressure. **3** (**give way to**) be replaced by. **in the way** obstructing someone's progress. **make way** allow room for someone or something else. **way-out** informal very unconventional.

wayfarer noun literary a person who travels on foot.

waylay verb (**waylays, waylaying, waylaid**) **1** intercept someone in order to attack them. **2** stop someone and talk to them.

wayside noun the edge of a road.

wayward adjective unpredictable and hard to control.

WC abbreviation Brit. water closet.

we pronoun **1** used by a speaker to refer to himself or herself and one or more other people considered together. **2** people in general.

weak adjective **1** lacking strength and

THESAURUS

wave verb **1** *he waved his flag:* flap, wag, shake, swish, swing, brandish, flourish, wield. **2** *the grass waved in the breeze:* ripple, flutter, undulate, stir, flap, sway, shake, quiver. **3** *the waiter waved them closer:* gesture, signal, beckon, motion. • noun **1** *she gave him a friendly wave:* signal, sign, motion, gesture. **2** *he surfs the big waves:* breaker, roller, comber, boomer, ripple; (**waves**) swell, surf. **3** *a wave of emigration:* rush, flow, surge, flood, stream, tide, deluge, spate. **4** *a wave of self-pity:* surge, rush, stab, upsurge, sudden feeling.

waver verb **1** *the candlelight wavered in the draught:* flicker, quiver. **2** *his voice wavered:* falter, wobble, tremble, quaver. **3** *he wavered between the choices:* hesitate, dither, be irresolute, be undecided, vacillate, blow hot and cold; Brit. haver, hum and haw; informal shilly-shally, sit on the fence.

way noun **1** *a way of reducing the damage:* method, process, procedure, technique, system, plan, strategy, scheme, means, mechanism, approach. **2** *she kissed him in her brisk way:* manner, style, fashion, mode. **3** *I've changed my ways:* practice,

wont, habit, custom, convention, routine, trait, attribute, peculiarity, idiosyncrasy, conduct, behaviour, manner, style. **4** *which way leads home?* route, course, direction, track, path, access, gate, exit, entrance, door. **5** *a short way downstream:* distance, length, stretch, journey. **6** *April is a long way away:* time, stretch, term, span, duration. **7** *a car coming the other way:* direction, bearing, course, orientation, line, tack. **8** *in some ways, he may be better off:* respect, regard, aspect, facet, sense, detail, point, particular. **9** *the country is in a bad way:* state, condition, situation, circumstances, position, predicament, plight; informal shape.
□ **give way 1** *the government gave way and passed the bill:* yield, back down, give in, surrender, concede defeat, submit; informal throw in the towel/sponge, cave in. **2** *the door gave way:* collapse, give, cave in, fall in, come apart, crumple.

weak adjective **1** *they are too weak to move:* feeble, frail, delicate, fragile, infirm, debilitated, decrepit, exhausted; informal weedy. **2** *bats have weak eyes:* inadequate, poor, feeble, defective, faulty, deficient, imperfect, substandard. **3** *a weak excuse:*

W

energy. **2** likely to break or give way under pressure. **3** not secure or stable. **4** lacking power, influence, or ability. **5** (of a liquid or solution) heavily diluted.
∎ **weakly** adverb.

weaken verb make or become weak.

weakling noun a weak person or animal.

weakness noun **1** the state of being weak. **2** a fault. **3** (**weakness for**) a liking for something that you find difficult to resist.

weal noun a red swollen mark left on flesh by a blow or pressure.

wealth noun **1** a large amount of money, property, or possessions. **2** the state of being rich. **3** a large amount of something desirable.

wealthy adjective (**wealthier**, **wealthiest**) rich.

wean verb **1** make a young mammal used to food other than its mother's milk. **2** (**wean someone off**) make someone give up a habit or addiction. **3** (**be weaned on**) be strongly influenced by something from an early age.

weapon noun **1** a thing used to cause physical harm or damage. **2** a means of gaining an advantage or defending yourself.
∎ **weaponry** noun.

wear verb (**wears**, **wearing**, **wore**; past participle **worn**) **1** have something on your body as clothing, decoration, or protection. **2** have a particular facial expression. **3** damage something by continuous use or rubbing. **4** (**wear off**) stop being effective or strong. **5** (**wear someone out**) exhaust someone. **6** (**wearing**) mentally or physically tiring. **7** (**wear on**) (of time) pass in a slow or boring way. •noun

---

THESAURUS

unconvincing, tenuous, implausible, unsatisfactory, poor, inadequate, feeble, flimsy, lame, hollow; informal pathetic. **4** *a weak bridge:* fragile, frail, rickety, insubstantial, wobbly, unstable, ramshackle, jerry-built, shoddy. **5** *I was too weak to be a rebel:* spineless, craven, cowardly, timid, irresolute, indecisive, ineffectual, meek, tame, soft, faint-hearted; informal yellow, gutless. **6** *a weak light:* dim, pale, wan, faint, feeble, muted. **7** *a weak voice:* indistinct, muffled, muted, hushed, faint, low. **8** *weak coffee:* watery, dilute, watered down, thin.
OPPOSITES strong, powerful, convincing, solid, resolute, bright, loud.

weaken verb **1** *the virus weakened him:* enfeeble, debilitate, incapacitate, sap, tire, exhaust. **2** *our morale weakened:* decrease, dwindle, diminish, wane, ebb, subside, peter out, fizzle out, tail off, decline, falter. **3** *the move weakened her authority:* impair, undermine, compromise, lessen.
OPPOSITES strengthen, bolster.

weakness noun **1** *with old age came weakness:* frailty, feebleness, fragility, delicacy, debility, incapacity, decrepitude; informal weediness. **2** *he has worked on his weaknesses:* fault, flaw, defect, deficiency, failing, shortcoming, imperfection, Achilles heel. **3** *a weakness for champagne:* fondness, liking, partiality, love, penchant, predilection, inclination, taste. **4** *he was accused of weakness:* timidity, cravenness, cowardliness, indecision, irresolution, ineffectuality, ineffectiveness, impotence. **5** *the weakness of this argument:* inadequacy, implausibility, poverty, untenability, transparency, flimsiness, hollowness.

wealth noun **1** *a gentleman of wealth:* affluence, prosperity, riches, means, fortune, money, cash, capital, treasure, finance; informal wherewithal, dough, bread. **2** *a wealth of information:* abundance, profusion, plethora, mine, store; informal lot, load, mountain, stack, ton; Brit. informal shedload.
OPPOSITES poverty, dearth.

wealthy adjective rich, affluent, moneyed, well off, well-to-do, prosperous; informal well heeled, rolling in it, made of money, loaded, flush.
OPPOSITES poor.

wear verb **1** *he wore a suit:* dress in, be clothed in, have on, sport. **2** *Barbara wore a smile:* bear, have (on your face), show, display, exhibit, give, put on, assume. **3** *the bricks have been worn down:* erode, abrade, rub away, grind away, wash away, crumble (away), eat away (at). **4** *the tyres are wearing well:* last, endure, hold up, bear up.
•noun **1** *you won't get much wear out of that:* use, service, value; informal mileage. **2** *evening wear:* clothes, garments, dress, attire, garb, wardrobe; informal get-up, gear, togs; Brit. informal kit, clobber. **3** *the varnish will withstand wear:* damage, friction, abrasion, erosion.
□ **wear off** *the novelty soon wore off:* fade, diminish, lessen, dwindle, decrease, wane, peter out, fizzle out, pall, disappear, vanish. **wear out** deteriorate, become worn, fray, become threadbare, go into holes. **wear someone out** tire out, fatigue, weary, exhaust, drain, sap, enervate; informal whack, poop, shatter, do in; Brit. informal knacker.

wearing adjective tiring, exhausting, wearying, fatiguing, enervating, draining, sapping, demanding, exacting, taxing, gruelling, punishing.

W

1 clothing of a particular type. **2** damage caused by continuous use.
■ **wearer** noun.

wearisome adjective making you feel tired or bored.

weary adjective (**wearier, weariest**) **1** tired. **2** causing tiredness. **3** (**weary of**) bored with. • verb (**wearies, wearying, wearied**) **1** make someone weary. **2** (**weary of**) grow bored with.
■ **wearily** adverb **weariness** noun.

weasel noun a small, slender meat-eating animal with reddish-brown fur.

weather noun the state of the atmosphere in terms of temperature, wind, rain, etc. • verb (**weathers, weathering, weathered**) **1** wear something away by long exposure to the weather. **2** come safely through a difficult or dangerous situation.
□ **make heavy weather of** informal have unnecessary difficulty in dealing with. **under the weather** informal slightly unwell.

weathercock noun a weathervane in the form of a cockerel.

weatherman noun (plural **weathermen**) a man who gives a description and forecast of weather conditions on television or radio.

weathervane noun a revolving pointer that shows the direction of the wind.

weave¹ verb (**weaves, weaving, wove**; past participle **woven** or **wove**) **1** make fabric by interlacing long threads with others. **2** make facts, events, etc. into a story. • noun a particular way in which fabric is woven.
■ **weaver** noun.

weave² verb (**weaves, weaving, weaved**) move from side to side to get around obstructions.

web noun **1** a network of fine threads made by a spider to catch its prey. **2** a complex system of interconnected elements. **3** (**the Web**) the World Wide Web. **4** the skin between the toes of a bird or animal living in water.
□ **web page** a document that can be accessed via the Internet.

webbed adjective (of an animal's feet) having the toes connected by a web.

webbing noun strong fabric used for making straps, belts, etc.

webcam noun (trademark in the US) a video camera connected to a computer, so that the film produced may be viewed on the Internet.

webcast noun a live video broadcast of an event transmitted on the Internet.

weblog noun a personal website on which someone regularly writes about their interests, experiences, etc.

website noun a location on the Internet that maintains one or more web pages.

wed verb (**weds, wedding, wedded** or **wed**) **1** formal or literary marry. **2** (**wedded**) having to do with marriage. **3** combine two desirable factors or qualities. **4** (**be wedded to**) be entirely devoted to a particular activity or belief.

we'd short form **1** we had. **2** we should or we would.

wedding noun a marriage ceremony.

wedge noun **1** a piece of wood, metal, etc. with a thick end that tapers to a thin edge. **2** a golf club for hitting the ball as high as possible into the air. **3** a shoe with a fairly high heel forming a solid block with the sole. • verb (**wedges, wedging, wedged**) **1** fix in position using a wedge. **2** force

---

THESAURUS

weary adjective **1** *he was weary after cycling:* **tired**, worn out, exhausted, fatigued, sapped, spent, drained; informal done in, ready to drop, bushed, shattered; Brit. informal knackered, whacked; N. Amer. informal pooped. **2** *a weary journey:* **tiring**, exhausting, fatiguing, enervating, draining, sapping, demanding, taxing, arduous, gruelling. OPPOSITES fresh, keen, refreshing.

weather noun *what's the weather like?* **conditions**, climate, elements, forecast, outlook.
• verb *we weathered the recession:* **survive**, come through, ride out, pull through, withstand, endure, rise above; informal stick out.

weave¹ verb **1** *flowers were woven into their hair:* **entwine**, lace, twist, knit, braid, plait. **2** *he weaves colourful plots:* **invent**, make up, fabricate, construct, create, spin.

weave² verb *he had to weave his way through the crowds:* **thread**, wind, wend, dodge, zigzag.

web noun **1** *a spider's web:* **mesh**, net, lattice, lacework, gauze, gossamer. **2** *a web of friendships:* **network**, nexus, complex, tangle, chain.

wedded adjective **1** *wedded bliss:* **married**, matrimonial, marital, conjugal, nuptial. **2** *he is wedded to his work:* **dedicated**, devoted, attached, fixated.

wedding noun **marriage** (**service**), nuptials, union.

wedge noun **1** *the door was secured by a wedge:* **chock**, stop. **2** *a wedge of cheese:* **triangle**, segment, slice, section, chunk, lump, slab, hunk, block, piece.
• verb *she wedged her case between two bags:* **squeeze**, cram, jam, ram, force, push, shove; informal stuff, bung.

w

into a narrow space.
▫ **the thin end of the wedge** informal something unimportant in itself which is likely to lead to a more serious or unpleasant situation.

wedlock noun formal the state of being married.

Wednesday noun the day of the week before Thursday and following Tuesday.

> ☑ Remember the *d* before the *n*: We*d*nesday.

wee adjective Scottish little.

weed noun **1** a wild plant growing where it is not wanted. **2** informal cannabis. **3** (**the weed**) informal tobacco. **4** Brit. informal a weak or skinny person. **5** (**weeds**) old use black clothes worn by a widow in mourning for her husband. •verb **1** remove weeds from. **2** (**weed someone/thing out**) remove unwanted members or items.

weedkiller noun a substance used to destroy weeds.

weedy adjective (**weedier**, **weediest**) **1** Brit. informal thin and weak. **2** containing or covered with many weeds.

week noun **1** a period of seven days. **2** the five days from Monday to Friday, when many people work. **3** Brit. a week after a stated day.

weekday noun a day of the week other than Saturday or Sunday.

weekend noun Saturday and Sunday.

weekly adjective & adverb happening or produced once a week.

weeny adjective (**weenier**, **weeniest**) informal tiny.

weep verb (**weeps**, **weeping**, **wept**) **1** shed tears; cry. **2** (of a wound) produce liquid. •noun a period of shedding tears.

weepy adjective (**weepier**, **weepiest**) informal **1** tearful. **2** sentimental.

weevil noun a small beetle which eats crops

or stored food.

weft noun (in weaving) the threads that are passed over and under the warp threads to make cloth.

weigh verb **1** find out how heavy someone or something is. **2** have a particular weight. **3** (**weigh something out**) measure and take out a portion of a particular weight. **4** (**weigh someone down**) be a burden to someone. **5** (**weigh on**) be depressing or worrying to. **6** (**weigh in**) (of a boxer or jockey) be officially weighed before or after a contest. **7** (often **weigh something up**) consider something carefully. **8** (often **weigh against**) influence a decision or action. **9** (**weigh in**) informal join in something enthusiastically or forcefully.

weighbridge noun a machine on to which vehicles are driven to be weighed.

weight noun **1** the heaviness of a person or thing. **2** the quality of being heavy. **3** a unit used for expressing how much something weighs. **4** a piece of metal known to weigh a definite amount and used on scales to find out how heavy something is. **5** a heavy object. **6** ability to influence decisions. **7** the importance attached to something. •verb **1** make heavier or keep in place with a weight. **2** (**be weighted**) be arranged so as to give one party an advantage.
■ **weightless** adjective.

weighting noun **1** adjustment made to take account of special circumstances. **2** Brit. additional wages paid to allow for a higher cost of living in a particular area.

weightlifting noun the sport or activity of lifting heavy weights.
■ **weightlifter** noun.

weighty adjective (**weightier**, **weightiest**) **1** heavy. **2** very serious and important. **3** very influential.

weir /rhymes with here/ noun a low dam built across a river to control its flow.

weird adjective **1** informal very strange.

---

weep verb cry, shed tears, sob, snivel, whimper, wail, bawl, keen; Scottish greet; informal boohoo, blub.
OPPOSITES rejoice.

weigh verb **1** *she weighed the vegetables:* put on the scales. **2** *he weighed 118 kg:* tip the scales at. **3** *he has to weigh up the possibilities:* consider, contemplate, think about, mull over, chew over, reflect on, ruminate about, muse on, assess, examine, review, explore, take stock of. **4** *they need to weigh benefit against risk:* balance, evaluate, compare, juxtapose, contrast.

weight noun **1** *the weight of the book:* mass, heaviness, load, burden. **2** *his personal recommendation will carry great weight:* influence, force, leverage, sway, pull,

power, authority; informal clout. **3** *a weight off her mind:* burden, load, millstone, trouble, worry. **4** *the weight of the evidence is against him:* most, bulk, majority, preponderance, body, lion's share.

weird adjective **1** *weird apparitions:* uncanny, eerie, unnatural, supernatural, unearthly, other-worldly, ghostly, mysterious, strange, abnormal, unusual; informal creepy, spooky, freaky. **2** *a weird sense of humour:* bizarre, odd, curious, strange, quirky, outlandish, eccentric, unconventional, unorthodox, idiosyncratic, surreal, crazy, absurd, grotesque, peculiar; informal wacky, freaky; N. Amer. informal wacko.
OPPOSITES normal, conventional.

W

2 mysterious or strange in a frightening way; eerie.
■ **weirdly** adverb **weirdness** noun.

> ☑ *weird* is an exception to the usual rule of *i* before *e* except after *c*.

weirdo noun (plural **weirdos**) informal a strange or eccentric person.

welch ⇨ WELSH.

welcome noun **1** an instance or way of greeting someone. **2** a pleased or approving reaction. • verb (**welcomes**, **welcoming**, **welcomed**) **1** greet someone in a polite or friendly way when they arrive somewhere. **2** be glad to receive or hear of. • adjective **1** gladly received. **2** very pleasing because much needed or wanted. **3** allowed or invited to do a particular thing.

weld verb **1** join together metal parts by heating the surfaces and pressing or hammering them together. **2** make two things combine into a whole. • noun a welded joint.
■ **welder** noun.

welfare noun **1** the general health, happiness, and safety of a person or group.

2 organized help given to people in need.
◻ **welfare state** a system under which the state provides pensions, health care, etc.

well[1] adverb **1** in a good way. **2** thoroughly. **3** to a great extent or degree. **4** very probably. **5** without difficulty. **6** with good reason. • adjective **1** in good health. **2** in a satisfactory state or position. **3** sensible; advisable. • exclamation used to express surprise, anger, resignation, etc.
◻ **as well 1** in addition. **2** with equal reason or an equally good result. **well advised** sensible; wise. **well appointed** having a high standard of equipment or furnishing. **well-being** the state of being comfortable, healthy, or happy. **well disposed** having a sympathetic or friendly attitude. **well heeled** informal wealthy. **well nigh** almost. **well off 1** wealthy. **2** in a good situation. **well read** having read widely. **well spoken** having an educated and refined voice. **well-to-do** wealthy. **well-wisher** a person who wants someone else to be happy or successful.

> **!** **well** is often used with a past participle such as *known* or *dressed* to form adjectives such as **well known, well**

THESAURUS

welcome noun *a welcome from the vicar:* greeting, salutation, reception, hospitality, the red carpet.
• verb **1** *welcome your guests in their own language:* greet, salute, receive, meet, usher in. **2** *we welcomed their decision:* be pleased by, be glad about, approve of, applaud, appreciate, embrace.
OPPOSITES resent, object to.
• adjective *welcome news:* pleasing, good, agreeable, encouraging, gratifying, heartening, promising, favourable, pleasant.
OPPOSITES unwelcome.

weld verb fuse, bond, stick, join, attach, seal, splice, melt, solder.

welfare noun **1** *the welfare of children:* well-being, health, comfort, security, safety, protection, success, interest, good. **2** *we cannot claim welfare:* social security, benefit, public assistance, pension, credit, support, sick pay, unemployment benefit; Brit. informal the dole.

well[1] adverb **1** *please behave well:* satisfactorily, nicely, correctly, properly, fittingly, suitably, appropriately. **2** *they get on well together:* amicably, agreeably, pleasantly, nicely, happily, harmoniously, amiably, peaceably; informal famously. **3** *he plays the piano well:* skilfully, ably, competently, proficiently, adeptly, deftly, expertly, excellently. **4** *treat your employees well:* decently, fairly, kindly, generously. **5** *mix the ingredients well:* thoroughly,

completely, effectively, rigorously, carefully. **6** *I know her quite well:* intimately, thoroughly, deeply, profoundly, personally. **7** *they studied the car market well:* carefully, closely, attentively, rigorously, in depth, exhaustively, in detail, meticulously, scrupulously, methodically, comprehensively, fully, extensively. **8** *they speak well of him:* admiringly, highly, approvingly, favourably, appreciatively, warmly, enthusiastically, glowingly. **9** *she lives well:* comfortably, in luxury, prosperously. **10** *you may well be right:* quite possibly, conceivably, probably. **11** *he is well over forty:* considerably, very much, a great deal, substantially, easily, comfortably, significantly. **12** *she could well afford it:* easily, comfortably, readily, effortlessly.
OPPOSITES badly, negligently, disparagingly, barely.
• adjective **1** *she was completely well again:* healthy, fine, fit, robust, strong, vigorous, blooming, thriving, in fine fettle; informal in the pink. **2** *all is not well:* satisfactory, all right, fine, in order, as it should be, acceptable; informal OK, hunky-dory.
OPPOSITES poorly, unsatisfactory.
◻ **as well too**, also, in addition, into the bargain, besides, furthermore, moreover, to boot. **as well as together with**, along with, besides, plus, and, with, on top of, not to mention.

dressed, etc. Write these adjectives without a hyphen when they come after a noun or pronoun (*she is well known*) but with a hyphen when they come directly in front of a noun (*a well-known writer*).

well² noun **1** a shaft sunk into the ground to obtain water, oil, or gas. **2** a hollow made to hold liquid. **3** a space in the middle of a building for stairs, a lift, etc. •verb (often **well up**) **1** (of a liquid) rise up to the surface. **2** (of an emotion) develop and become stronger.

we'll short form we shall or we will.

well built adjective (of a person) strong and sturdy.

wellington noun Brit. a knee-length waterproof rubber or plastic boot.

welly or **wellie** noun Brit. informal a wellington boot.

Welsh noun the language of Wales. •adjective relating to Wales.
□ **Welsh rarebit** (or **Welsh rabbit**) a dish of melted cheese on toast.

welsh or **welch** verb (**welsh on**) fail to repay a debt or fulfil an obligation.

welt noun **1** a leather rim to which the sole of a shoe is attached. **2** a red swollen mark left on the skin by a blow or pressure.

welter noun a large and confused or disorganized number of items.

welterweight noun a weight in boxing between lightweight and middleweight.

wench noun old use or humorous a girl or young woman.

wend verb (**wend your way**) go slowly or by an indirect route.

Wendy house noun Brit. a toy house large enough for children to play in.

went past of GO.

wept past and past participle of WEEP.

were 2nd person singular past, plural past, and past subjunctive of BE.

we're short form we are.

weren't short form were not.

werewolf /wair-wuulf/ noun (plural **werewolves**) (in stories) a person who periodically changes into a wolf, especially when there is a full moon.

west noun **1** the direction in which the sun sets. **2** the western part of a place. **3** (**the West**) Europe and North America.

•adjective & adverb **1** towards or facing the west. **2** (of a wind) blowing from the west.
■ **westward** adjective & adverb **westwards** adverb.

westerly adjective & adverb **1** facing or moving towards the west. **2** (of a wind) blowing from the west.

western adjective **1** situated in or facing the west. **2** (**Western**) having to do with the west, in particular Europe and North America. •noun a film or novel about cowboys in western North America.

westerner noun a person from the west of a region.

westernize or **westernise** verb (**westernizes, westernizing, westernized**) bring under the influence of Europe and North America.

wet adjective (**wetter, wettest**) **1** covered or soaked with liquid. **2** (of the weather) rainy. **3** not yet having dried or hardened. **4** Brit. informal feeble. •verb (**wets, wetting, wet** or **wetted**) **1** cover or touch with liquid. **2** urinate in or on. •noun **1** (**the wet**) rainy weather. **2** liquid that makes something damp. **3** Brit. informal a feeble person.
□ **wet blanket** informal a person who spoils other people's enjoyment by being disapproving or unenthusiastic. **wet nurse** a woman employed to breastfeed another woman's child.
■ **wetly** adverb **wetness** noun.

wether noun a castrated ram.

wetland noun (also **wetlands**) swampy or marshy land.

wetsuit noun a close-fitting rubber garment covering the entire body, worn in water sports or diving.

we've short form we have.

whack informal verb **1** hit forcefully. **2** (**whacked**) Brit. completely exhausted. **3** (**whacking**) Brit. very large. •noun **1** a sharp blow. **2** Brit. a share or contribution.

whacky ⇨ WACKY.

whale noun (plural **whales**) a very large sea mammal with a blowhole on top of the head for breathing.
□ **have a whale of a time** informal enjoy yourself very much.

whalebone noun a hard substance growing

THESAURUS   W

well² noun *she drew water from the well:* borehole, spring, waterhole, shaft.
•verb *tears welled from her eyes:* flow, spill, stream, gush, roll, cascade, flood, spout, burst, issue.

wet adjective **1** *wet clothes:* damp, moist, soaked, drenched, saturated, sopping, dripping, soggy, waterlogged, squelchy. **2** *it*

was cold and wet: rainy, pouring, teeming, showery, drizzly. **3** *the paint is still wet:* sticky, tacky.
OPPOSITES dry, fine.
•verb *wet the clothes before ironing them:* dampen, moisten, sprinkle, spray, splash, soak, saturate, flood, douse, drench.
OPPOSITES dry.

in plates in the upper jaw of some whales, used by them to strain plankton from the seawater.

whaler noun **1** a ship used for hunting whales. **2** a sailor who hunts and kills whales.

whaling noun the practice of hunting and killing whales.

whammy noun (plural **whammies**) informal an event with a powerful and unpleasant effect.

wharf /worf/ noun (plural **wharves** or **wharfs**) a level area where ships are moored to load and unload.

what pronoun & determiner **1** asking for information about something. **2** whatever. **3** used to emphasize something surprising or remarkable. • pronoun **1** asking someone to repeat something. **2** the thing or things that. • adverb to what extent?

whatever or **whatsoever** pronoun & determiner everything or anything that; no matter what. • pronoun used for emphasis instead of 'what' in questions. • adverb at all; of any kind.

whatnot noun informal an unspecified item or items.

wheat noun a cereal crop whose grain is ground to make flour.

wheatear noun a small songbird.

wheatgerm noun a nutritious food consisting of the centre parts of grains of wheat.

wheatmeal noun flour made from wheat from which some of the bran and germ has been removed.

wheedle verb (**wheedles**, **wheedling**, **wheedled**) try to persuade someone to do something by flattering them or saying nice things that you do not mean.

wheel noun **1** a revolving circular object that is fixed below a vehicle to enable it to move along, or that forms part of a machine. **2** (**the wheel**) a steering wheel. **3** a turn or rotation. • verb **1** push or pull a vehicle with wheels. **2** carry on a vehicle with wheels. **3** fly or turn in a wide curve. **4** turn round quickly. **5** (**wheel something out**) informal resort to something that has been frequently seen or heard before. □ **wheel and deal** take part in commercial or political scheming.

wheelbarrow noun a small cart with a wheel at the front and two handles at the rear.

wheelbase noun the distance between the front and rear axles of a vehicle.

wheelchair noun a chair on wheels for a person who is ill or disabled.

wheeler-dealer noun a person who wheels and deals.

wheelwright noun a person who makes or repairs wooden wheels.

wheeze verb (**wheezes**, **wheezing**, **wheezed**) **1** breathe with a whistling or rattling sound in the chest. **2** make a rattling or spluttering sound. • noun **1** a sound of wheezing. **2** Brit. informal a clever or amusing scheme or trick.
■ **wheezy** adjective.

whelk noun a shellfish with a pointed spiral shell.

whelp noun old use **1** a puppy. **2** disapproving a boy or young man. • verb give birth to a puppy.

when adverb **1** at what time? **2** in what circumstances? **3** at which time or in which situation. • conjunction **1** at or during the time that. **2** at any time that; whenever. **3** in view of the fact that. **4** although; whereas.

whence or **from whence** adverb formal **1** from what place or source? **2** from which or from where. **3** to the place from which. **4** as a consequence of which.

whenever or formal **whensoever** conjunction **1** at whatever time or on whatever occasion. **2** every time that. • adverb used for emphasis instead of 'when' in questions.

where adverb **1** in or to what place or position? **2** in what direction or respect? **3** at, in, or to which. **4** in or to a place or situation in which.

whereabouts adverb where or approximately where? • noun the place where someone or something is.

whereas conjunction **1** in contrast or comparison with the fact that. **2** taking into consideration the fact that.

whereby adverb by which.

wherefore old use adverb for what reason? • adverb & conjunction as a result of which.

wherein adverb formal **1** in which. **2** in what place or respect?

whereof adverb formal of what or which.

whereupon conjunction immediately after which.

wherever or formal **wheresoever** adverb

THESAURUS

wharf noun quay, pier, dock, berth, landing, jetty, harbour, dockyard.

wheedle verb coax, cajole, persuade, inveigle, charm, flatter; informal sweet-talk.

wheel verb **1** *she wheeled the trolley away:*

push, trundle, roll. **2** *birds wheeled overhead:* turn, go round, circle, orbit.

whereabouts noun location, position, site, situation, spot, point, home, address, neighbourhood.

1 in or to whatever place. **2** used for emphasis instead of 'where' in questions. • **conjunction** in every case when.

wherewithal noun the money or other resources needed for something.

wherry /rhymes with sherry/ noun (plural **wherries**) a light rowing boat or barge.

whet /wet/ verb (**whets, whetting, whetted**) **1** sharpen a blade. **2** stimulate someone's interest or appetite.

whether conjunction **1** expressing a doubt or choice between alternatives. **2** indicating that a statement applies whichever of the alternatives mentioned is the case.

whetstone noun a stone used for sharpening cutting tools.

whey /way/ noun the watery part of milk that remains after curds have formed.

which pronoun & determiner **1** asking for information specifying one or more people or things from a set. **2** used to refer to something previously mentioned when introducing a clause giving further information.

whichever determiner & pronoun **1** any which; that or those which. **2** regardless of which.

whiff noun **1** a smell that is smelt only briefly or faintly. **2** Brit. informal an unpleasant smell. **3** a trace or hint of something bad or exciting. **4** a puff or breath of air or smoke.

Whig noun historical a member of a British political party that became the Liberal Party.

while noun **1** (**a while**) a period of time. **2** (**a while**) for some time. **3** (**the while**) meanwhile. • **conjunction 1** at the same time as. **2** whereas. **3** although. • **adverb** during which. • **verb** (**whiles, whiling, whiled**) (**while something away**) pass time in a leisurely way.
□ **worth while** (or **worth your while**) worth the time or effort spent.

whilst conjunction & adverb chiefly Brit. while.

whim noun a sudden desire or change of mind.

whimper verb (**whimpers, whimpering, whimpered**) make low, feeble sounds

expressing fear, pain, or discontent. • **noun** a whimpering sound.

whimsical adjective **1** playfully unusual. **2** showing sudden changes of mood or behaviour.
■ **whimsically** adverb.

whimsy noun (plural **whimsies**) **1** playfully unusual behaviour or humour. **2** an odd or unusual thing. **3** a whim.

whin noun chiefly N. English gorse.

whine noun **1** a long, high-pitched complaining cry. **2** a long, high-pitched sound. • **verb** (**whines, whining, whined**) give or make a whine.
■ **whiny** adjective.

whinge Brit. informal verb (**whinges, whingeing, whinged**) complain persistently and irritably. • **noun** an act of whingeing.

whinny noun (plural **whinnies**) a gentle, high-pitched neigh. • **verb** (**whinnies, whinnying, whinnied**) (of a horse) make a whinny.

whip noun **1** a length of leather or cord fastened to a handle, used for beating a person or urging on an animal. **2** an official of a political party who is appointed to keep parliamentary discipline among its members. **3** a written notice from a party whip telling members how to vote in a debate. **4** a dessert made from cream or eggs beaten into a light fluffy mass. • **verb** (**whips, whipping, whipped**) **1** hit a person or animal with a whip. **2** beat or move violently. **3** move or take out fast or suddenly. **4** beat cream, eggs, etc. into a froth.
□ **the whip hand** a position of power or control over someone. **whipping boy** a person who is blamed or punished for other people's faults. **whip-round** Brit. informal a collection of money. **whip someone/thing up 1** make or prepare something very quickly. **2** deliberately excite or provoke someone.

whiplash noun **1** injury caused by a severe jerk to the head. **2** the flexible part of a whip.

whippersnapper noun informal a young and inexperienced but overconfident person.

while noun we chatted for a while: time, spell, stretch, stint, span, interval, period; Brit. informal patch.
• **verb** tennis helped to while away the time: pass, spend, occupy, use up, kill.

whim noun impulse, urge, notion, fancy, caprice, vagary, inclination.

whine verb **1** a child was whining: wail, whimper, cry, mewl, moan, howl, yowl. **2** the lift began to whine: hum, drone, beep. **3** he's always whining about

something: complain, grouse, grouch, grumble, moan, carp; informal gripe, bellyache, whinge.

whip noun he used a whip on his dogs: lash, scourge, strap, belt.
• **verb 1** he whipped the boy: flog, lash, scourge, strap, belt, thrash, beat. **2** then whip the cream: whisk, beat. **3** he whipped his listeners into a frenzy: rouse, stir up, excite, galvanize, electrify, stimulate, inspire, fire up, inflame, provoke.

W

whippet noun a small, slender breed of dog.

whippoorwill /wip-per-wil/ noun an American bird with a distinctive call.

whirl verb **1** move rapidly round and round. **2** (of the head or mind) seem to spin round. •noun **1** a rapid movement round and round. **2** busy or hurried activity.

whirligig noun **1** a toy that spins round. **2** a roundabout at a fair.

whirlpool noun a current of water that whirls in a circle.

whirlwind noun **1** a column of air moving rapidly round and round. **2** a situation in which many things happen very quickly. •adjective very quick and unexpected: *a whirlwind romance.*

whirr or **whir** verb (**whirs** or **whirrs**, **whirring**, **whirred**) (of something rapidly rotating or moving) make a low, continuous, regular sound. •noun a whirring sound.

whisk verb **1** beat eggs, cream, etc. with a light, rapid movement. **2** move or take suddenly and quickly. •noun **1** a device for whisking eggs, cream, etc. **2** a bunch of grass, twigs, etc. for flicking away dust or flies.

whisker noun **1** each of the long hairs or bristles growing from the face of an animal. **2** (**whiskers**) the hair growing on a man's face. **3** (**a whisker**) informal a very small amount.

whisky (Irish & US spelling **whiskey**) noun (plural **whiskies**) a strong alcoholic drink distilled from malted grain.

> ☑ Scotch whis*k*y, but Irish whis*k*ey.

whisper verb (**whispers**, **whispering**, **whispered**) **1** speak very softly. **2** literary rustle or murmur softly. •noun **1** something whispered. **2** a very soft voice. **3** literary a soft rustling or murmuring. **4** a rumour or piece of gossip. **5** a slight trace.

whist noun a card game in which points are scored according to the number of tricks won.

whistle noun **1** a clear, high-pitched sound made by forcing breath between the lips or teeth. **2** any similar high-pitched sound. **3** a device used to produce a whistling sound. •verb (**whistles**, **whistling**, **whistled**) **1** give out a whistle. **2** move rapidly with a whistling sound. **3** blow a whistle. □ whistle-stop very fast and with only brief pauses.

Whit noun Whitsun. □ Whit Sunday a Christian festival held on the seventh Sunday after Easter.

whit noun a very small part or amount.

white adjective **1** having the colour of milk or fresh snow. **2** very pale. **3** relating to people with light-coloured skin. **4** Brit. (of coffee or tea) with milk. **5** (of wine) yellowish in colour. **6** innocent and pure. •noun **1** white colour. **2** the visible pale part of the eyeball around the iris. **3** the outer part which surrounds the yolk of an egg; the albumen. **4** a white person. □ white blood cell a cell in the blood or lymph which acts against foreign substances and disease. white-collar relating to work in an office or other professional environment. white elephant a useless or troublesome possession. white flag a white flag waved as a symbol of surrender or truce. white-hot so hot that it glows white. white lie a harmless lie told to avoid hurting someone's feelings. white magic magic used only for good purposes. White Paper (in the UK) a government report giving information or proposals on an issue. white sauce a sauce made with flour, butter, and milk or stock. white spirit Brit. a colourless liquid distilled from petroleum, used as a paint thinner and solvent. ■ whiteness noun.

whitebait noun the young of various sea fish used as food.

THESAURUS

whirl verb **1** *leaves whirled in the wind:* rotate, circle, wheel, turn, revolve, orbit, spin, twirl. **2** *they whirled past:* hurry, race, dash, rush, run, sprint, bolt, career, charge, shoot, hurtle, hare, fly, speed; informal tear, belt; Brit. informal bomb. **3** *his mind was whirling:* spin, reel, swim. •noun **1** *a whirl of dust:* swirl, flurry, eddy. **2** *the mad social whirl:* hurly-burly, activity, round, bustle, rush, flurry. **3** *Laura's mind was in a whirl:* spin, daze, muddle, jumble, confusion; informal dither.

whisk verb **1** *the cable car will whisk you to the top:* speed, hurry, rush, sweep, hurtle, shoot. **2** *she whisked the cloth away:* pull, snatch, pluck, tug, jerk; informal whip, yank.

3 *whisk the egg yolks:* whip, beat, mix. •noun *an egg whisk:* beater, mixer, blender.

whisper verb *Alison whispered in his ear:* murmur, mutter, mumble, speak softly, breathe. OPPOSITES shout. •noun **1** *she spoke in a whisper:* murmur, mutter, mumble, low voice, undertone. **2** *I heard a whisper that he's left town:* rumour, story, report, gossip, speculation, suggestion, hint; informal buzz. OPPOSITES shout.

white adjective *her face went white:* pale, pallid, wan, ashen, chalky, pasty, peaky, washed out, ghostly, deathly.

W

whiten verb make or become white.
■ **whitener** noun.

whitewash noun **1** a solution of lime or chalk and water, used for painting walls white. **2** a deliberate concealment of mistakes or faults. • **verb 1** paint with whitewash. **2** conceal mistakes or faults.

whither adverb formal or old use **1** to what place or state. **2** what is the likely future of?

whiting noun (plural **whiting**) a sea fish with white flesh eaten as food.

Whitsun or **Whitsuntide** noun the weekend or week including Whit Sunday.

whittle verb (**whittles, whittling, whittled**) **1** carve wood by cutting small slices from it. **2** (**whittle something away** or **down**) gradually reduce something.

whizz verb (**whizzes, whizzing, whizzed**) **1** move quickly through the air. **2** move or go fast. • **noun** informal a person who is very clever at something.
□ **whizz-kid** informal a young person who is very successful or skilful.

who pronoun **1** what or which person or people? **2** introducing a clause giving further information about a person or people previously mentioned.

> **!** the rule is that you should use **who** as the subject of a verb (*who decided this?*) and **whom** as the object of a verb or preposition (*whom do you think we should support?*). When speaking, however, it's acceptable to use **who** instead of **whom**, as in *who do you think we should support?*

whoa /woh/ exclamation used as a command to a horse to stop or slow down.

who'd short form **1** who had. **2** who would.

whodunnit (US spelling **whodunit**) noun informal a crime story in which the identity of the murderer is not revealed until the end.

whoever or formal **whosoever** pronoun **1** the person or people who; any person

who. **2** regardless of who. **3** used for emphasis instead of 'who' in questions.

whole adjective **1** complete; entire. **2** in one piece. • noun **1** a thing that is complete in itself. **2** (**the whole**) all of something. □ **on the whole** taking everything into account; in general.
■ **wholeness** noun.

wholefood noun Brit. food that has been processed as little as possible and is free from additives.

wholehearted adjective completely sincere and committed.
■ **wholeheartedly** adverb.

wholemeal adjective Brit. (of flour or bread) made from whole grains of wheat including the husk.

wholesale noun the selling of goods in large quantities to be sold to the public by others. • **adjective & adverb 1** being sold in such a way. **2** done to a very large number of people or things. • **verb** (**wholesales, wholesaling, wholesaled**) sell goods wholesale.
■ **wholesaler** noun.

wholesome adjective **1** good for health or well-being. **2** morally good.

wholly adverb entirely; fully.

> ☑ two *l*s, no e: who**ll**y, not *-ely*.

whom pronoun used instead of 'who' as the object of a verb or preposition.

whoop noun a loud cry of joy or excitement. • **verb** give or make a whoop. □ **whooping cough** an illness which mainly affects children, marked by coughs followed by a noisy drawing in of breath.

whoopee exclamation informal expressing excitement or joy.

whoosh verb move quickly with a rushing sound. • **noun** a whooshing movement.

whopper noun informal **1** something that is very large. **2** a blatant lie.

whopping adjective informal very large.

whore /rhymes with door/ noun **1** a

THESAURUS

whole adjective **1** *the whole report:* entire, complete, full, unabridged, uncut. **2** *the eggs emerge whole:* intact, in one piece, unbroken, undamaged, flawless, unmarked, perfect.
OPPOSITES incomplete.
• noun **1** *a single whole:* entity, unit, body, ensemble. **2** *the whole of the year:* all, every part, the lot, the sum.
□ **on the whole overall**, all in all, all things considered, for the most part, in the main, in general, by and large, normally, usually, almost always, typically, ordinarily.

wholehearted adjective unqualified, unreserved, unconditional, complete, full,

total, absolute.
OPPOSITES half-hearted.

wholesale adverb *the images were removed wholesale:* extensively, on a large scale, comprehensively, indiscriminately, without exception.
OPPOSITES selectively.
• adjective *wholesale destruction:* extensive, widespread, large-scale, wide-ranging, comprehensive, total, mass, indiscriminate.
OPPOSITES partial.

wholly adverb completely, totally, absolutely, entirely, fully, thoroughly, utterly, downright, in every respect; informal one hundred per cent.

W

prostitute. **2** disapproving a woman who has many sexual partners.

whorl /worl, werl/ **noun 1** each of the turns in a spiral or coil. **2** a spiral or coil. **3** a coil of leaves, flowers, or branches encircling a stem.

who's short form **1** who is. **2** who has.

> **!** don't confuse **who's** with **whose**. **Who's** is short for either **who is** or **who has**, as in *he has a son who's a doctor* or *who's done the reading?*, whereas **whose** means 'belonging to which person' or 'of whom or which', as in *whose is this?* or *he's a man whose opinion I respect.*

whose possessive determiner & pronoun **1** belonging to or associated with which person. **2** of whom or which.

why adverb **1** for what reason or purpose? **2** on account of which; the reason that. •exclamation expressing surprise, annoyance, etc.

wick noun a length of cord in a candle, lamp, or lighter which carries liquid fuel to the flame.

wicked adjective **1** very bad; evil. **2** playfully mischievous. **3** informal excellent; wonderful. ■ **wickedly** adverb **wickedness** noun.

wicker noun twigs plaited or woven to make items such as furniture and baskets. ■ **wickerwork** noun.

wicket noun **1** Cricket each of the two sets of three stumps with two bails across the top that are defended by a batsman. **2** a small door or gate.

wicketkeeper noun Cricket a fielder positioned close behind a batsman's wicket.

wide adjective (**wider**, **widest**) **1** of great or more than average width. **2** having a particular width. **3** open to the full extent. **4** including a great variety of people or things. **5** spread among a large number or over a large area. **6** at a distance from a point or mark. **7** (in football) at or near the side of the field. •adverb **1** to the full extent. **2** far from the target. □ **wide awake** fully awake. **wide boy** Brit. informal a man involved in petty criminal activities. ■ **widely** adverb.

widen verb make or become wider.

widespread adjective spread among a large number or over a large area.

widgeon ⇨ WIGEON.

widget noun informal a small gadget or mechanical device.

widow noun a woman whose husband has died and who has not married again. •verb (**be widowed**) become a widow or widower.

widower noun a man whose wife has died and who has not married again.

width noun **1** the measurement or extent of something from side to side. **2** wide range or extent.

widthways or **widthwise** adverb in a direction parallel with a thing's width.

wield verb **1** hold and use a weapon or tool. **2** have power or influence.

> ☑ remember, the usual rule is *i* before *e* except after *c*: w*ie*ld.

wife noun (plural **wives**) the woman a man is married to. ■ **wifely** adjective.

wig noun a covering for the head made of real or artificial hair.

wigeon or **widgeon** noun a duck with mainly reddish-brown and grey feathers.

wiggle verb (**wiggles**, **wiggling**, **wiggled**) move with short movements up and down or from side to side. •noun a wiggling movement. ■ **wiggly** adjective.

THESAURUS

wicked adjective **1** *wicked deeds:* evil, sinful, immoral, wrong, bad, iniquitous, corrupt, base, vile, villainous, criminal, nefarious; informal crooked. **2** *a wicked sense of humour:* mischievous, playful, naughty, impish, roguish, puckish, cheeky. OPPOSITES virtuous.

wide adjective **1** *a wide river:* broad, extensive, spacious, vast, spread out. **2** *a wide range of opinion:* comprehensive, ample, broad, extensive, large, exhaustive, all-inclusive. **3** *his shot was wide:* off target, off the mark, inaccurate. OPPOSITES narrow.
•adverb **1** *he opened his eyes wide:* fully, to the fullest/furthest extent, as far/much as possible. **2** *he shot wide:* off target, wide of the mark/target, inaccurately.

widen verb broaden, open up/out, expand, extend, enlarge.

widespread adjective general, extensive, universal, common, global, worldwide, omnipresent, ubiquitous, across the board, predominant, prevalent, rife, broad. OPPOSITES limited.

width noun breadth, thickness, span, diameter, girth.

wield verb **1** *he was wielding a sword:* brandish, flourish, wave, swing, use, employ, handle. **2** *he has wielded power since 1972:* exercise, exert, hold, maintain, command, control.

wife noun spouse, partner, mate, consort, bride; informal better half, missus; Brit. informal other half.

w

wigwam noun a tent consisting of animal skins fixed over a framework of poles, formerly lived in by some North American Indian peoples.

wild adjective **1** (of animals or plants) living or growing in their natural environment. **2** (of scenery or a region) not lived in or changed by people. **3** lacking discipline or control. **4** not based on reason or evidence. **5** informal very enthusiastic or excited. • noun **1** (**the wild**) a natural state. **2** (**the wilds**) a remote area.
□ **wild card 1** a playing card which can take on any value, suit, or colour that the player holding it needs. **2** Computing a character that will match any character or sequence of characters in a search. **3** an opportunity to enter a sports competition without having qualified in the usual way. **wild goose chase** a hopeless search for something that you will never find.
■ **wildly** adverb **wildness** noun.

wildcat adjective (of a strike) sudden and unofficial.

wildebeest /wil-duh-beest/ noun a gnu (a kind of antelope).

wilderness noun a wild, uninhabited, and unwelcoming region.

wildfire noun (**spread like wildfire**) spread very fast.

wildfowl plural noun birds that are hunted for sport or food.

wildlife noun all the animals, birds, and insects that naturally inhabit a particular region.

wiles plural noun cunning methods used by someone to get what they want.

wilful (US spelling **willful**) adjective **1** (of a bad act) deliberate. **2** stubborn and determined.
■ **wilfully** adverb **wilfulness** noun.

will¹ modal verb (3rd singular present **will**; past **would**) **1** expressing the future tense. **2** expressing a request. **3** expressing desire, consent, or willingness. **4** expressing facts about ability or capacity.

> **!** the traditional rule is that you should use **shall** when forming the future tense with **I** and **we** (*I shall be late*) and **will** with **you**, **he, she, it,** and **they** (*he will not be there*). Nowadays, people do not follow this rule so strictly and are more likely to use the shortened forms **I'll, she'll,** etc.

will² noun **1** the power you have to decide on something and take action. **2** (also **willpower**) the ability to control your thoughts and actions in order to achieve something. **3** a desire or intention. **4** a legal document in which someone gives instructions about what should be done with their money and property after their death. • verb **1** intend or desire that something should happen. **2** bring something about by using your mental powers. **3** leave money or property to someone in a will.
□ **at will** whenever or in whatever way you like.

willing adjective **1** ready, eager, or prepared to do something. **2** given or done readily.
■ **willingly** adverb **willingness** noun.

THESAURUS

wild adjective **1** *wild animals:* untamed, undomesticated, feral, fierce, ferocious, savage. **2** *wild flowers:* uncultivated, native, indigenous. **3** *wild hill country:* uninhabited, unpopulated, uncultivated, rugged, rough, inhospitable, desolate, barren. **4** *a wild night:* stormy, squally, tempestuous, turbulent, boisterous. **5** *wild behaviour:* uncontrolled, unrestrained, undisciplined, unruly, rowdy, disorderly, riotous. **6** *Bill's wild schemes:* foolish, ridiculous, ludicrous, stupid, foolhardy, idiotic, madcap, absurd, silly, impractical, impracticable, unworkable; informal crazy, crackpot. **7** *a wild guess:* random, arbitrary, haphazard, uninformed.
OPPOSITES tame, cultivated, calm, disciplined.

wilderness noun **1** *the Siberian wilderness:* wilds, wastes, desert. **2** *a litter-strewn wilderness:* wasteland.

wilful adjective **1** *wilful destruction:* deliberate, intentional, premeditated, planned, conscious. **2** *a wilful child:* headstrong, strong-willed, obstinate, stubborn, pig-headed, recalcitrant, uncooperative; Brit. informal bloody-minded, bolshie.
OPPOSITES accidental, amenable.

will noun **1** *the will to succeed:* determination, strength of character, resolve, single-mindedness, drive, commitment, dedication, doggedness, tenacity, staying power. **2** *they stayed against their will:* desire, wish, preference, inclination, intention. **3** *God's will:* wish, desire, decision, choice, decree, command. • verb **1** *do what you will:* want, wish, please, see fit, think fit/best, like, choose, prefer. **2** *God willed it:* decree, order, ordain, command.

willing adjective **1** *I'm willing to give it a try:* ready, prepared, disposed, inclined, minded, happy, glad, pleased, agreeable, amenable; informal game. **2** *willing help:* readily given, ungrudging.
OPPOSITES reluctant.

willingly adverb voluntarily, of your own free will, of your own accord, readily, without reluctance, ungrudgingly,

W

will-o'-the-wisp noun **1** a thing that is impossible to obtain. **2** a faint flickering light seen at night over marshy ground, thought to result from natural gases burning.

willow noun a tree which has narrow leaves and produces catkins.

willowy adjective tall and slim.

willy-nilly adverb **1** whether you like it or not. **2** without any direction or plan.

wilt verb **1** (of a plant) become limp through heat or lack of water. **2** feel tired and weak.

wily /rhymes with highly/ adjective clever in a cunning or crafty way.

wimp noun informal a person who is not strong, brave, or confident.
■ **wimpish** adjective **wimpy** adjective.

wimple noun a cloth headdress covering the head, neck, and sides of the face, worn in the past by women and still today by some nuns.

win verb (**wins, winning, won**) **1** be the most successful in a contest or conflict. **2** gain something as a result of success in a contest or conflict. **3** gain someone's attention, support, or love. **4** (**win someone over**) gain someone's agreement or support by persuading them that you are right. •noun a victory in a game or contest.

wince verb (**winces, wincing, winced**) flinch slightly on feeling pain or distress. •noun an act of wincing.

winceyette noun Brit. a soft brushed cotton fabric.

winch noun a hauling or lifting device consisting of a rope or chain winding around a rotating drum. •verb hoist or haul something with a winch.

wind[1] noun **1** a natural movement of the air. **2** breath needed to play an instrument or do exercise. **3** wind or woodwind instruments forming a band or section of an orchestra. **4** Brit. air or gas in the stomach or intestines. •verb **1** make someone unable to breathe easily for a short time. **2** Brit. pat a baby on its back to help it bring up air swallowed while feeding.
□ **get wind of** informal hear a rumour of. **put the wind up** Brit. informal alarm or frighten. **wind instrument 1** a musical instrument which you play by blowing into it. **2** a woodwind instrument as distinct from a brass instrument. **wind tunnel** a tunnel-like structure in which a strong current of air is created, to test the effect of wind and air flow on vehicles.
■ **windy** adjective.

wind[2] verb (**winds, winding, wound**) **1** move in or take a twisting or spiral course. **2** pass something around a thing or person so as to encircle or enfold them. **3** (with reference to something long) twist or be twisted around itself or a central thing. **4** make a clockwork device work by turning a key or handle. **5** turn a key or handle repeatedly. **6** move an audio tape, videotape, or film backwards or forwards.
□ **wind down 1** (of a clockwork mechanism) gradually lose power. **2** (also **wind something down**) draw or bring something gradually to an end. **3** informal relax. **wind up** informal end up in a particular situation or place. **wind someone/thing up 1** gradually bring something to an end. **2** Brit. informal tease or irritate someone.

windbag noun informal a person who talks a

THESAURUS

cheerfully, happily, gladly, with pleasure.
OPPOSITES reluctantly.

willingness noun readiness, inclination, will, wish, desire.
OPPOSITES reluctance.

wilt verb **1** the roses had begun to wilt: droop, sag, become limp, flop. **2** we were wilting in the heat: languish, flag, droop, become listless.
OPPOSITES flourish.

win verb **1** Steve won the race: come first in, take first prize in, triumph in, be successful in. **2** she was determined to win: come first, be victorious, carry/win the day, come out on top, succeed, triumph, prevail. **3** he won a cash prize: earn, gain, secure, collect, pick up, walk away/off with, carry off; informal land, net, bag, scoop.
OPPOSITES lose.
•noun victory, triumph, conquest.
OPPOSITES defeat.

wince verb grimace, pull a face, flinch, blench, start.

wind[1] noun **1** the trees were swaying in the wind: breeze, current of air, gale, hurricane, gust, draught; informal blow; literary zephyr. **2** Jez got his wind back: breath; informal puff.

wind[2] verb **1** the road winds up the mountain: twist (and turn), bend, curve, loop, zigzag, weave, snake. **2** he wound a towel around his waist: wrap, furl, entwine, lace. **3** Anne wound the wool into a ball: coil, roll, twist, twine.
□ **wind something up 1** Richard wound up the meeting: conclude, bring to an end/close, terminate; informal wrap up. **2** the company has been wound up: close (down), dissolve, put into liquidation.

windfall noun bonanza, jackpot, pennies from heaven, godsend.

lot but without saying anything interesting or important.

windbreak noun a screen providing shelter from the wind.

windcheater noun Brit. a wind-resistant jacket with a close-fitting neck and cuffs.

windfall noun **1** a piece of unexpected good fortune. **2** an apple or other fruit blown from a tree by the wind.

windlass noun a winch used on a ship or in a harbour.

windmill noun a building with sails or vanes that turn in the wind and generate power to grind corn, generate electricity, or draw water.

window noun **1** an opening in a wall, fitted with glass to let in light and allow people to see out. **2** a framed area on a computer screen for viewing information. □ **window dressing 1** the arrangement of an attractive display in a shop window. **2** the presentation of something in a superficially attractive way to give a good impression. **window-shop** spend time looking at the goods displayed in shop windows.

windowpane noun a pane of glass in a window.

windowsill noun a ledge or sill at the bottom of a window.

windpipe noun the tube carrying air down the throat and into the lungs; the trachea.

windscreen noun Brit. a glass screen at the front of a motor vehicle.

windshield noun N. Amer. a windscreen.

windsock noun a light, flexible cone mounted on a mast to show the direction and strength of the wind.

windsurfing noun the sport of riding on a sailboard on water. ■ **windsurf** verb **windsurfer** noun.

windswept adjective exposed to strong winds.

windward adjective & adverb facing the wind, or on the side facing the wind.

wine noun an alcoholic drink made from fermented grape juice.

winery noun (plural **wineries**) an establishment where wine is made.

wing noun **1** a kind of limb used by a bird, bat, or insect for flying. **2** a rigid structure projecting from both sides of an aircraft and supporting it in the air. **3** a part of a large building. **4** a group or faction within an organization. **5** (**the wings**) the sides of a theatre stage out of view of the audience. **6** the part of a soccer or rugby field close to the sidelines. **7** Brit. the part of a car above and extending slightly over a wheel. **8** an air force unit of several squadrons. ●verb **1** fly, or move quickly as if flying. **2** shoot a bird so as to wound it in the wing. **3** (**wing it**) informal speak or act without preparation. □ **wing nut** a nut with a pair of projections for the fingers to turn it on a screw. ■ **winged** adjective.

winger noun an attacking player on the wing in soccer, hockey, etc.

wingspan noun the full extent from tip to tip of the wings of an aircraft, bird, etc.

wink verb **1** close and open one eye quickly as a private signal. **2** shine with an unsteady light; flash on and off. ●noun an act of winking.

winkle noun a small edible shellfish with a spiral shell. ●verb (**winkles, winkling, winkled**) (**winkle something out**) Brit. **1** extract something with difficulty. **2** get information from someone who is reluctant to give it.

winning adjective attractive. ●noun (**winnings**) money won by gambling. ■ **winningly** adverb.

winnow verb **1** remove people or things from a group until only the best ones are left. **2** blow air through grain in order to remove the chaff.

wino noun (plural **winos**) informal a person who sits all day in the streets drinking alcohol.

winsome adjective appealing.

winter noun the coldest season of the year,

windy adjective breezy, blowy, fresh, blustery, gusty, wild, stormy, squally. OPPOSITES still.

wing noun **1** *the east wing of the house:* part, section, side, annexe, extension. **2** *the radical wing of the party:* faction, camp, caucus, arm, branch, group, section, set. ●verb **1** *a seagull winged its way over the sea:* fly, glide, soar. **2** *she was shot at and winged:* wound, graze, hit.

wink verb **1** *he winked an eye at her:* blink, flutter, bat. **2** *the diamond winked in the moonlight:* sparkle, twinkle, flash, glitter, gleam, shine, scintillate.

winner noun victor, champion, conqueror, vanquisher, medallist; informal champ, top dog. OPPOSITES loser.

winning adjective **1** *the winning team:* victorious, successful, triumphant, undefeated, conquering, first, top. **2** *a winning smile:* engaging, charming, appealing, endearing, sweet, cute, winsome, attractive, prepossessing, fetching, disarming, captivating.

winnings plural noun prize money, gains, booty, spoils, proceeds, profits, takings, purse.

W

after autumn and before spring. •verb
(**winters, wintering, wintered**) spend the
winter in a particular place.

wintry adjective cold or bleak.

wipe verb (**wipes, wiping, wiped**) 1 clean or
dry something by rubbing it with a cloth
or your hand. 2 remove something from a
surface in this way. 3 erase data from a
computer, tape, etc. •noun 1 an act of
wiping. 2 an absorbent cleaning cloth.
◻ wipe someone/thing out 1 remove or
eliminate something. 2 kill a large number
of people.
▪ wiper noun.

wire noun 1 metal in the form of a thin
flexible strand. 2 a length of wire used for
fencing, to carry an electric current, etc.
3 a concealed listening device. 4 informal a
telegram. •verb (**wires, wiring, wired**)
1 install electric circuits or wires in a room
or building. 2 fasten or reinforce with
wire. 3 informal send a telegram to.

wireless adjective using radio, microwaves,
etc. (as opposed to wires) to transmit
signals. •noun dated 1 a radio.
2 broadcasting using radio signals.

wiretapping noun the secret tapping of
telephone lines in order to listen to other
people's conversations.

wiring noun a system of wires providing
electric circuits for a device or building.

wiry adjective 1 resembling wire. 2 lean,
tough, and sinewy.

wisdom noun 1 the quality of being wise.
2 the knowledge that a particular society
or culture has gained over a period of
time.
◻ wisdom tooth each of the four molars at
the back of the mouth which usually

appear at about the age of twenty.

wise[1] adjective 1 having or showing
experience, knowledge, and good
judgement. 2 (**wise to**) informal aware of.
•verb (**wises, wising, wised**) (**wise up**)
informal become aware of something.
▪ wisely adverb.

wise[2] noun old use the manner or extent of
something.

wisecrack informal noun a witty remark or
joke. •verb make a wisecrack.

wish verb 1 feel a strong desire for
something. 2 silently express a hope that
something will happen. 3 say that you
hope that someone will be happy,
successful, etc. •noun 1 a desire or hope.
2 (**wishes**) an expression of hope that
someone will be happy, successful, etc. 3 a
thing wished for.

wishbone noun a forked bone between the
neck and breast of a bird.

wishful adjective wishing for something to
happen.
◻ wishful thinking expectations that are
based on optimistic wishes rather than
facts.

wishy-washy adjective not firm or forceful;
feeble.

wisp noun a small, thin bunch or strand of
something.
▪ wispy adjective.

wisteria /wi-**steer**-i-uh/ noun a climbing
plant with hanging clusters of bluish-lilac
flowers.

wistful adjective having a feeling of vague
or regretful longing.
▪ wistfully adverb wistfulness noun.

wit noun 1 (also **wits**) the ability to think

THESAURUS

wipe verb 1 *Beth wiped the table:* rub, mop,
sponge, swab, clean, dry, polish. 2 *he wiped
the marks off the window:* rub off, clean
off, remove, erase, efface.

wisdom noun 1 *we questioned the wisdom
of the decision:* understanding,
intelligence, sagacity, sense, common
sense, shrewdness, astuteness, judgement,
prudence, circumspection, logic, rationale,
soundness, advisability. 2 *the wisdom of
the East:* knowledge, learning, erudition,
scholarship, philosophy, lore.
OPPOSITES folly.

wise adjective *a wise old man:* sage,
sagacious, intelligent, clever, learned,
knowledgeable, enlightened, astute, smart,
shrewd, sharp-witted, canny, knowing,
sensible, prudent, discerning, perceptive.
OPPOSITES foolish.

wish verb 1 *they can do as they wish:* want,
desire, feel inclined, feel like, care, choose,
please, think fit. 2 *I wish you to send them*

a message: want, desire, require.
•noun 1 *his wish to own a Mercedes:* desire,
longing, yearning, whim, craving, hunger,
hope, aspiration, aim, ambition, dream;
informal hankering, yen. 2 *her parents'
wishes:* request, requirement, bidding,
instruction, direction, demand, order,
command, want, desire, will.
◻ wish for **desire**, want, hope for, covet,
dream of, long for, yearn for, crave, hunger
for, aspire to, set your heart on, seek,
fancy, hanker after; informal have a yen for.

wit noun 1 *he needed all his wits to escape:*
intelligence, shrewdness, astuteness,
cleverness, canniness, sense, judgement,
acumen, insight, brains, mind; informal nous.
2 *my sparkling wit:* wittiness, humour,
drollery, repartee, badinage, banter,
wordplay, jokes, witticisms, quips, puns.
3 *she's such a wit:* comedian, humorist,
comic, joker; informal wag.

w

quickly and make good decisions. **2** a natural talent for using words and ideas in a quick and funny way. **3** a witty person. □ **at your wits' end** not knowing what to do.

witch noun a woman believed to have evil magic powers. □ **witch doctor** a person believed to have magic powers that cure illness. **witch hazel** a lotion made from the bark and leaves of a shrub, used for treating injuries on the skin. **witch-hunt** a campaign against a person who holds unpopular views.

witchcraft noun the use of evil magic powers.

with preposition **1** accompanied by. **2** in the same direction as. **3** possessing; having. **4** indicating the instrument used to perform an action or the material used for a purpose. **5** in opposition to or competition with. **6** indicating the way or attitude in which a person does something. **7** in relation to. □ **with it** informal **1** up to date or fashionable. **2** alert and able to understand.

withdraw verb (**withdraws, withdrawing, withdrew**; past participle **withdrawn**) **1** remove or take away. **2** leave or cause to leave a place. **3** stop taking part in an

activity. **4** take back something you have said. **5** take money out of an account. **6** go away to another place in search of quiet or privacy. **7** stop taking an addictive drug. **8** (**withdrawn**) very shy or reserved. ■ **withdrawal** noun.

wither verb (**withers, withering, withered**) **1** (of a plant) become dry and shrivelled. **2** become shrunken or wrinkled from age or disease. **3** become weaker; decline. **4** (**withering**) scornful.

withers plural noun the highest part of a horse's back, at the base of the neck.

withhold verb (**withholds, withholding, withheld**) **1** refuse to give. **2** hold back an emotion or reaction.

☑ remember to double the *h*: with**h**old.

within preposition **1** before a particular period of time has passed. **2** inside the range or bounds of something. **3** inside something. ● adverb inside.

without preposition not accompanied by, using, or having. ● adverb old use outside.

withstand verb (**withstands, withstanding, withstood**) remain undamaged by; resist.

witless adjective foolish; stupid.

witness noun **1** a person who sees an event take place. **2** a person who gives evidence in a court of law. **3** a person who is present

THESAURUS

witch noun **1** *the witch cast a spell:* sorceress, enchantress, hex, Wiccan. **2** (informal) *she's a right old witch:* hag, crone, harpy, harridan, she-devil; informal battleaxe.

witchcraft noun sorcery, (black) magic, wizardry, spells, incantations, necromancy, Wicca.

withdraw verb **1** *she withdrew her hand from his:* remove, extract, pull out, take out, take back. **2** *the ban on advertising was withdrawn:* abolish, cancel, lift, set aside, end, stop, remove, reverse, revoke, rescind, repeal, annul. **3** *she withdrew the allegation:* retract, take back, go back on, recant, repudiate, renounce, back down, climb down, backtrack, back-pedal, do a U-turn, eat your words. **4** *the troops withdrew from the city:* retreat, pull out of, evacuate, quit, leave. **5** *his partner withdrew from the project:* pull out of, back out of, bow out of. **6** *they withdrew to their rooms:* retire, retreat, adjourn, decamp, leave, depart, absent yourself; formal repair.
OPPOSITES insert, introduce, deposit, enter.

withdrawal noun **1** *the withdrawal of subsidies:* removal, abolition, cancellation, discontinuation, termination, elimination. **2** *the withdrawal of the troops:* departure, pull-out, exit, exodus, evacuation, retreat.

wither verb **1** *the flowers withered in the sun:* shrivel (up), dry up, wilt, droop, go

limp, fade, perish. **2** *the muscles in his leg withered:* waste (away), shrivel (up), shrink, atrophy. **3** *her confidence withered:* diminish, dwindle, shrink, lessen, fade, wane, evaporate, disappear.
OPPOSITES thrive, grow.

withering adjective scornful, contemptuous, scathing, stinging, devastating, humiliating, mortifying.
OPPOSITES admiring.

withhold verb **1** *he withheld the information:* hold back, keep back, refuse to give, retain, hold on to, hide, conceal, keep secret; informal sit on. **2** *she could not withhold her tears:* suppress, repress, hold back, fight back, choke back, control, check, restrain, contain.
OPPOSITES release.

withstand verb resist, weather, survive, endure, cope with, stand, tolerate, bear, defy, brave, hold out against.

witness noun *witnesses claimed that he started the fight:* observer, onlooker, eyewitness, spectator, viewer, watcher, bystander, passer-by.
● verb **1** *who witnessed the incident?* see, observe, watch, view, notice, spot, be present at, attend. **2** *the will is correctly witnessed:* countersign, sign, endorse, validate.

W

at the signing of a document and signs it themselves to confirm this. •**verb 1** be a witness to. **2** be the place, period, etc. in which an event takes place.

witter verb (**witters, wittering, wittered**) Brit. informal talk for a long time about unimportant things.

witticism noun a witty remark.

witty adjective (**wittier, wittiest**) able to say clever and amusing things.
∎ **wittily** adverb.

wives plural of **WIFE**.

wizard noun **1** a man who has magical powers. **2** a person who is very skilled in something.
∎ **wizardry** noun.

wizened adjective shrivelled or wrinkled with age.

WMD abbreviation weapon (or weapons) of mass destruction.

woad noun a plant whose leaves were used in the past to make blue dye.

wobble verb (**wobbles, wobbling, wobbled**) **1** move unsteadily from side to side. **2** (of the voice) tremble. •noun a wobbling movement or sound.
∎ **wobbly** adjective.

woe noun literary **1** great sadness or distress. **2** (**woes**) troubles.
□ **woe betide someone** a person will be in trouble if they do a particular thing.

woebegone /woh-bi-gon/ adjective looking sad or miserable.

woeful adjective **1** very sad. **2** very bad.
∎ **woefully** adverb.

wok noun a bowl-shaped frying pan used in Chinese cookery.

woke past of **WAKE**[1].

woken past participle of **WAKE**[1].

wold noun an area of high, open land.

wolf noun (plural **wolves**) a wild animal of the dog family, that lives and hunts in packs. •**verb** (**wolfs, wolfing, wolfed**) eat food quickly and greedily.
□ **cry wolf** keep raising false alarms, so that when you really need help you are ignored. **wolf whistle** a whistle with a rising and falling note, used by a man to show that he finds a woman sexually attractive.
∎ **wolfish** adjective.

wolfhound noun a large breed of dog originally used to hunt wolves.

wolfram noun tungsten or its ore.

wolverine noun a heavily built meat-eating animal found in cold northern areas.

woman noun (plural **women**) an adult human female.
∎ **womanhood** noun **womanly** adjective.

womanize or **womanise** verb (**womanizes, womanizing, womanized**) (of a man) have a lot of casual affairs with women.
∎ **womanizer** noun.

womankind noun women as a whole.

womb noun the organ in a woman's body in which a baby develops before it is born.

wombat noun an Australian animal resembling a small bear with short legs.

won past and past participle of **WIN**.

wonder verb (**wonders, wondering,**

THESAURUS

witty adjective humorous, amusing, droll, funny, comic, jocular, sparkling, scintillating, entertaining, clever, quick-witted.

wizard noun **1** *the wizard cast a spell:* sorcerer, warlock, magus, (black) magician, enchanter. **2** *a financial wizard:* genius, expert, master, virtuoso, maestro, marvel; informal hotshot, whizz-kid; Brit. informal dab hand; N. Amer. informal maven.

wobble verb **1** *the table wobbled:* rock, teeter, jiggle, sway, see-saw, shake. **2** *he wobbled across to the door:* teeter, totter, stagger, lurch. **3** *her voice wobbled:* tremble, shake, quaver, quiver, waver.

wobbly adjective **1** *a wobbly table:* unsteady, unstable, shaky, rocky, rickety, unsafe, precarious; informal wonky. **2** *her legs were a bit wobbly:* shaky, quivery, weak, unsteady; informal like jelly.
OPPOSITES stable.

woe noun **1** *a tale of woe:* misery, sorrow, distress, sadness, unhappiness, heartache, heartbreak, despair, adversity, misfortune,

disaster, suffering, hardship. **2** *financial woes:* trouble, difficulty, problem, trial, tribulation, misfortune, setback, reverse.
OPPOSITES joy.

woman noun lady, female; Scottish & N. English lass; Irish colleen; informal chick; N. Amer. informal sister, dame, broad; Austral./NZ informal sheila; literary damsel.

womanly adjective **1** *womanly virtues:* feminine, female. **2** *her womanly figure:* voluptuous, curvaceous, shapely, ample, buxom, full-figured; informal curvy, busty.
OPPOSITES manly, boyish.

wonder noun **1** *she was speechless with wonder:* awe, admiration, fascination, surprise, astonishment, amazement. **2** *the wonders of nature:* marvel, miracle, phenomenon, sensation, spectacle, beauty, curiosity.
•verb **1** *I wondered what was on her mind:* ponder, think about, meditate on, reflect on, muse on, speculate about, conjecture, be curious about. **2** *people wondered at such bravery:* marvel, be amazed, be astonished, stand in awe, be dumbfounded;

w

wondered) **1** be interested to know about something. **2** feel doubt. **3** feel amazement and admiration. • noun **1** a feeling of amazement and admiration. **2** a person or thing that causes such a feeling.
□ no wonder it is not surprising.

wonderful adjective very good, pleasant, or remarkable.
■ wonderfully adverb.

wonderland noun a place full of wonderful things.

wondrous adjective literary inspiring wonder.

wonky adjective informal **1** not straight; crooked. **2** unsteady or faulty.

wont /wohnt/ noun (your wont) formal your normal behaviour. • adjective (wont to) literary in the habit of doing something.

won't short form will not.

wonted /wohn-tid/ adjective literary usual.

woo verb (woos, wooing, wooed) **1** (of a man) try to make a woman love him. **2** try to get someone's support or custom.

wood noun **1** the hard material forming the trunk and branches of a tree. **2** (also woods) a small forest.
■ woody adjective.

woodbine noun Brit. honeysuckle.

woodcock noun (plural woodcock) a woodland bird with a long beak and brown feathers.

woodcut noun a print made with a block of wood in which a design has been cut.

woodcutter noun a person who cuts down trees for wood.

wooded adjective (of land) covered with woods.

wooden adjective **1** made of wood. **2** acting or speaking in a stiff and awkward way.

■ woodenly adverb.

woodland or **woodlands** noun land covered with trees.

woodlouse noun (plural woodlice) a small insect-like creature with a grey segmented body.

woodpecker noun a bird with a strong bill that pecks at tree trunks to find insects.

woodturning noun the activity of shaping wood with a lathe.

woodwind noun wind instruments other than brass instruments forming a section of an orchestra.

woodwork noun **1** the wooden parts of a room, building, or other structure. **2** the activity of making things from wood.
■ woodworker noun.

woodworm noun the larva of a kind of beetle, that bores into wood.

woof[1] noun the barking sound made by a dog. • verb bark.

woof[2] = WEFT.

woofer noun a loudspeaker that reproduces low frequencies.

wool noun the fine, soft hair forming the coat of a sheep.

woollen (US spelling woolen) adjective **1** made of wool. **2** relating to the production of wool. • noun (woollens) woollen clothes.

woolly adjective **1** made of wool. **2** covered with wool or hair resembling wool. **3** resembling wool. **4** confused or unclear. • noun (plural woollies) informal a woollen jumper or cardigan.

woozy adjective informal unsteady, dizzy, or dazed.
■ woozily adverb.

word noun **1** a unit of language which has

---

informal be flabbergasted.

wonderful adjective marvellous, magnificent, superb, glorious, sublime, lovely, delightful; informal super, great, fantastic, terrific, tremendous, sensational, fabulous, awesome, magic, wicked; Brit. informal smashing, brilliant; N. Amer. informal peachy, dandy, neat; Austral./NZ informal beaut, bonzer.

woo verb **1** *Richard wooed Joan:* pay court to, pursue, chase (after); dated court, romance, seek the hand of. **2** *the party wooed voters with promises:* seek, pursue, curry favour with, try to win, try to attract, try to cultivate. **3** *an attempt to woo him out of retirement:* entice, tempt, coax, persuade, wheedle, seduce; informal sweet-talk.

wood noun **1** *polished wood:* timber, planks, logs; N. Amer. lumber. **2** *a walk through the woods:* forest, woodland, trees, copse,

coppice, grove; Brit. spinney.

wooded adjective forested, afforested, tree-covered; literary sylvan.

wooden adjective **1** *a wooden door:* wood, timber. **2** *wooden acting:* stilted, stiff, unnatural, awkward, flat, stodgy, lifeless, soulless. **3** *her face was wooden:* expressionless, impassive, poker-faced, emotionless, blank, vacant, unresponsive.

wool noun fleece, hair, coat.

word noun **1** *the Italian word for 'ham':* term, name, expression, designation. **2** *his words were meant kindly:* remark, comment, observation, statement, utterance. **3** *I've got three weeks to learn my words:* script, lines, lyrics, libretto. **4** *I give you my word:* promise, assurance, guarantee, undertaking, pledge, vow, oath, bond. **5** *I want a word with you:* talk, conversation, chat, tête-à-tête, heart-to-heart, one-to-one, discussion; informal

w

meaning and is used with others to form sentences. **2** a remark or statement. **3** (**words**) angry talk. **4** (**the word**) a command, slogan, or signal. **5** (**your word**) your account of the truth of something that happened. **6** (**your word**) a thing that you promise. **7** news. •**verb** express something in particular words.
▢ **in a word** briefly. **word of mouth** talking as a way of passing on information. **word processor** a computer or program for creating and printing a document or piece of text. **word class** a category in which a word is placed according to its function in grammar; a part of speech.

wording noun the way in which something is worded.

wordy adjective using too many words.

wore past of **WEAR**.

work noun **1** activity involving mental or physical effort done in order to achieve a result. **2** the activity or job that a person does in order to earn money. **3** a task or tasks to be done. **4** a thing or things done or made. **5** (**works**) a place where industrial or manufacturing processes are carried out. **6** (**works**) activities involving the building or repair of something. **7** (**works**) the mechanism of a clock or other machine. •**verb 1** do work as your job. **2** make someone do work. **3** (of a machine or system) function properly. **4** (of a machine) be in operation. **5** have the desired result. **6** bring a material or mixture to a desired shape or consistency. **7** cultivate land, or extract materials from a mine or quarry. **8** move something gradually or with difficulty into another position.
▢ **get worked up** become stressed or angry. **work out 1** develop in the desired way. **2** do energetic physical exercise. **work something out 1** solve something. **2** plan something in detail. **work permit** an official document giving a foreigner permission to take a job in a country. **work-to-rule** a situation in which people refuse to do overtime or extra work, as a form of protest. **work up to** proceed gradually towards something more demanding or advanced.

workaday adjective ordinary.

THESAURUS

confab. **6** *there's no word from the hospital:* news, information, communication, intelligence, message, report, communiqué, dispatch, bulletin; literary tidings.
•**verb** *the question was carefully worded:* phrase, express, put, couch, frame, formulate, style.

wording noun phrasing, phraseology, language, words, expression, terminology.

wordy adjective long-winded, verbose, lengthy, rambling, garrulous, voluble; informal windy; Brit. informal waffly.
OPPOSITES succinct.

work noun **1** *a day's work in the fields:* labour, toil, slog, drudgery, exertion, effort; informal grind, sweat; Brit. informal graft. **2** *I'm looking for work:* employment, job, post, position, situation, occupation, profession, career, vocation, calling. **3** *haven't you got any work?* tasks, jobs, duties, assignments, projects, chores. **4** *works of literature:* composition, piece, creation, opus. **5** *this is the work of a radical faction:* handiwork, doing, act, deed. **6** *a lifetime spent doing good works:* deeds, acts, actions, turns. **7** *the complete works of Shakespeare:* writings, oeuvre, canon, output. **8** *a car works:* factory, plant, mill, workshop, facility. **9** *the works of a clock:* mechanism, machinery, workings, parts, movement, action; informal insides.
OPPOSITES leisure, pleasure.
•**verb 1** *staff worked late into the night:* labour, toil, exert yourself, slave (away); informal slog (away), beaver away; Brit. informal graft. **2** *he worked in education for years:* be employed, have a job, earn your living, do business. **3** *farmers worked the land:* cultivate, farm, till, plough. **4** *his car was working perfectly:* function, go, run, operate; informal behave. **5** *how do I work this machine?* operate, use, handle, control, manipulate, run. **6** *their ploy worked:* succeed, turn out well, go as planned, get results, be effective; informal come off, pay off, do the trick. **7** *blusher can work miracles:* achieve, accomplish, bring about, produce, perform. **8** *he worked the crowd into a frenzy:* stir (up), excite, drive, move, rouse, fire, galvanize; whip up, agitate. **9** *work the mixture into a paste:* knead, squeeze, form; mix, stir, blend. **10** *he worked the blade into the padlock:* manipulate, manoeuvre, guide, squeeze, edge. **11** *he worked his way through the crowd:* manoeuvre, make, thread, wind, weave, wend, elbow.
OPPOSITES rest, fail.
▢ **work something out 1** *work out what you can afford:* calculate, compute, reckon up, determine. **2** *I'm trying to work out what she meant:* understand, comprehend, puzzle out, sort out, make sense of, get to the bottom of, make head or tail of, unravel, decipher, decode; informal figure out; Brit. informal suss out. **3** *they worked out a plan:* devise, formulate, draw up, put together, develop, construct, arrange, organize, contrive, concoct; hammer out, negotiate.

W

workbench noun a bench at which carpentry and other work is done.

worker noun 1 a person who works. 2 a neuter or undeveloped female bee, wasp, ant, etc., large numbers of which perform the basic work of a colony.

workforce noun the people working or available for work in a particular area, firm, or industry.

workhouse noun (in the past in the UK) a place where poor people were given accommodation and food in return for work.

working adjective 1 having paid employment. 2 doing manual work. 3 functioning or able to function. 4 used as a basis for work or discussion and likely to be changed later. • noun 1 a mine from which minerals are being extracted. 2 (workings) the way in which a machine, organization, or system operates. □ working class the social group consisting mainly of people who do manual or industrial work. working party a group set up to study and report on a particular question and make recommendations.

workload noun the amount of work to be done by someone or something.

workman noun (plural workmen) a man employed to do manual work.

workmanlike adjective showing efficient skill.

workout noun a session of energetic physical exercise.

workshop noun 1 a room or building in which things are made or repaired. 2 a meeting for discussion and activity on a particular subject or project.

workstation noun a desktop computer that is part of a network.

worktop noun Brit. a flat surface for working on in a kitchen.

world noun 1 (the world) the earth with all its countries and peoples. 2 all that belongs to a particular region, period, or area of activity. □ world-weary bored with or cynical about life. World Wide Web an information system on the Internet which allows documents to be connected to each other using hypertext links.

worldly adjective 1 relating to material things rather than spiritual ones. 2 experienced and sophisticated. □ worldly-wise having a lot of experience of life.

worldwide adjective & adverb throughout the world.

worm noun 1 an earthworm or other creeping or burrowing creature with a long, thin body and no limbs. 2 (worms) long, thin creatures that live as parasites in a person's or animal's intestines. • verb 1 move by crawling or wriggling. 2 (worm your way into) gradually move into. 3 (worm something out of) cleverly obtain information from someone who is reluctant to give it. □ worm cast a small spiral of earth or sand thrown up at the surface by a burrowing worm.

wormwood noun a plant with a bitter flavour, used in drinks such as vermouth.

worn past participle of WEAR. • adjective thin or damaged as a result of wear. □ worn out 1 exhausted. 2 damaged by wear, and no longer usable.

worried adjective feeling anxiety or concern. ■ worriedly adverb.

THESAURUS

worker noun employee, member of staff, workman, labourer, hand, operator, operative, agent, wage-earner, bread-winner, proletarian.

workshop noun 1 *an ideal set of tools for a workshop:* workroom, studio, factory, works, plant, industrial unit. 2 *a workshop on combating stress:* study group, discussion group, seminar, forum, class.

world noun 1 *he travelled the world:* earth, globe, planet, sphere. 2 *the academic world:* sphere, society, circle, arena, milieu, province, domain, preserve, realm, field. 3 (the world) *the world would hear of her achievements:* everyone, people, mankind, humankind, humanity, the public, all and sundry.

worldly adjective 1 *worldly pursuits:* earthly, terrestrial, temporal, mundane, mortal, human, material, physical. 2 *a*

worldly man: sophisticated, experienced, worldly-wise, knowledgeable, knowing, enlightened, mature, seasoned, cosmopolitan, urbane, cultured. OPPOSITES spiritual, naive.

worldwide adjective global, international, intercontinental, universal, ubiquitous. OPPOSITES local.

worn adjective shabby, worn out, threadbare, in tatters, falling to pieces, ragged, frayed, moth-eaten, scruffy, having seen better days. OPPOSITES new, smart.

worried adjective anxious, troubled, bothered, concerned, uneasy, fretful, agitated, nervous, edgy, tense, apprehensive, fearful, afraid, frightened; Brit. informal in a stew, in a flap. OPPOSITES carefree.

W

worrisome adjective causing anxiety or concern.

worry verb (worries, worrying, worried) 1 feel or cause to feel troubled over unwelcome things that have happened or may happen. 2 annoy or disturb. 3 (of a dog) repeatedly push at and bite something. 4 (of a dog) chase and attack livestock. •noun (plural worries) 1 the state of being worried. 2 a source of anxiety. ■ worrier noun.

worse adjective 1 less good, satisfactory, or pleasing. 2 more serious or severe. 3 more ill or unhappy. •adverb 1 less well. 2 more seriously or severely. •noun a worse event or circumstance.

worsen verb make or become worse.

worship noun 1 the practice of praising and praying to God or a god or goddess. 2 religious rites and ceremonies. 3 a strong feeling of admiration and respect for someone. •verb (worships, worshipping, worshipped; US spelling worships, worshiping, worshiped) 1 offer praise and prayers to God or a god or goddess. 2 feel great admiration and respect for. ■ worshipper noun.

worshipful adjective 1 feeling or showing great respect and admiration. 2 (Worshipful) Brit. a title given to Justices of the Peace.

worst adjective most bad, severe, or serious. •adverb 1 most severely or seriously. 2 least well. •noun the worst part, event, or circumstance.

worsted /wuus-tid/ noun a smooth woollen fabric of good quality.

worth adjective 1 equivalent in value to a particular sum or item. 2 deserving to be treated in a particular way. •noun 1 the value of someone or something. 2 an amount of something that is equivalent to a particular sum of money.

worthless adjective 1 having no practical or financial value. 2 having no good qualities.

worthwhile adjective worth the time, money, or effort spent.

worthy adjective (worthier, worthiest) 1 deserving effort, attention, or respect. 2 (worthy of) deserving or good enough for. 3 well intended but too serious and dull. •noun (plural worthies) humorous an important person. ■ worthily adverb worthiness noun.

THESAURUS

worry verb 1 *she worries about his health:* tbe anxious, be concerned, fret, agonize, brood, panic, lose sleep, get worked up; informal get in a flap, get in a state. 2 *is something worrying you?* trouble, bother, make anxious, disturb, distress, upset, concern, unsettle, perturb, scare, prey on someone's mind; informal bug, get to. •noun 1 *I'm beside myself with worry:* anxiety, distress, concern, unease, disquiet, nerves, agitation, edginess, tension, apprehension, fear, misgiving; informal butterflies. 2 *the rats are a worry:* problem, cause for concern, nuisance, pest, trial, trouble, bane, bugbear; informal pain, headache, hassle.
OPPOSITES peace of mind.

worsen verb 1 *insomnia can worsen a patient's distress:* aggravate, add to, intensify, increase, compound, magnify, heighten, inflame, exacerbate. 2 *the recession worsened:* deteriorate, degenerate, decline; informal go downhill.
OPPOSITES improve.

worship noun 1 *the worship of saints:* reverence, veneration, adoration, glorification, exaltation, devotion, praise, thanksgiving, homage, honour. 2 *morning worship:* service, rite, prayer, praise, devotion, observance. •verb 1 *they worship pagan gods:* revere, pray to, pay homage to, honour, adore, venerate, praise, glorify, exalt. 2 *he absolutely worshipped her:* love, cherish,

treasure, hold dear, esteem, adulate, idolize, deify, hero-worship, lionize; informal put on a pedestal.
OPPOSITES mock, despise, shun.

worth noun 1 *evidence of the rug's worth:* value, price, cost, valuation, estimate. 2 *the intrinsic worth of education:* benefit, good, advantage, use, value, virtue, desirability, sense.

worthless adjective 1 *the item was worthless:* valueless. 2 *a mountain of worthless information:* useless, pointless, meaningless, senseless, inconsequential, ineffective, ineffectual, fruitless, unproductive, unavailing, valueless. 3 *his worthless son:* good-for-nothing, ne'er-do-well, useless, despicable, contemptible, degenerate; informal no-good, lousy.
OPPOSITES valuable, useful, worthy.

worthwhile adjective valuable, useful, of service, beneficial, rewarding, advantageous, positive, helpful, profitable, gainful, fruitful, productive, constructive, effective.

worthy adjective *a worthy citizen:* good, righteous, virtuous, moral, ethical, upright, respectable, upstanding, high-minded, principled, reputable, decent.
OPPOSITES disreputable.
•noun *local worthies:* dignitary, personage, grandee, VIP, notable, pillar of society, luminary, leading light; informal bigwig.
OPPOSITES nobody.

w

would modal verb (3rd singular present **would**)
1 past of **WILL**[1]. 2 indicating the result of an imagined event. 3 expressing a desire or inclination. 4 expressing a polite request. 5 expressing an opinion or assumption. 6 literary expressing a wish or regret.
□ **would-be** wishing to be a particular type of person: *a would-be actress.*

wouldn't short form would not.

wound[1] noun 1 an injury to the body caused by a cut, blow, or bullet. 2 an injury to a person's feelings. •verb 1 inflict a wound on. 2 injure someone's feelings.

wound[2] past and past participle of **WIND**[2].

wove past of **WEAVE**[1].

woven past participle of **WEAVE**[1].

wow informal **exclamation** expressing great surprise or admiration. •verb impress someone very much.

WPC abbreviation woman police constable.

wrack[1] ⇒ **RACK**.

wrack[2] noun a brown seaweed.

wraith /rayth/ noun a ghost.

wrangle noun a long dispute or argument. •verb (**wrangles, wrangling, wrangled**) be involved in a wrangle.

wrap verb (**wraps, wrapping, wrapped**) 1 enclose something in paper or soft material. 2 encircle or wind round. •noun 1 a loose outer garment or piece of material. 2 paper or material used for wrapping.
□ **under wraps** kept secret. **wrap**

someone/thing up 1 (also **wrap up**) dress someone in or put on warm clothes. 2 bring a meeting or deal to a close.
■ **wrapper** noun.

wrasse /rass/ noun (plural **wrasse** or **wrasses**) a brightly coloured sea fish with thick lips and strong teeth.

wrath /roth/ noun extreme anger.
■ **wrathful** adjective.

wreak verb 1 cause a lot of damage or harm. 2 take revenge on someone.

wreath noun (plural **wreaths**) 1 an arrangement of flowers or leaves fastened in a ring. 2 a curl or ring of smoke or cloud.

wreathe verb (**wreathes, wreathing, wreathed**) 1 (**be wreathed**) be surrounded or encircled. 2 move with a curling motion.

wreck noun 1 the destruction of a ship at sea. 2 a ship destroyed at sea. 3 a building, vehicle, etc. that has been destroyed or badly damaged. 4 N. Amer. a road or rail crash. 5 a person in a very bad state. •verb 1 destroy or badly damage. 2 spoil a plan. 2 cause a ship to sink or break up.

wreckage noun the remains of something that has been badly damaged.

wren noun 1 a very small bird with a cocked tail. 2 (in the UK) a member of the former Women's Royal Naval Service.

wrench verb 1 pull or twist something suddenly and violently. 2 twist and injure a part of the body. •noun 1 a sudden

---

THESAURUS

would-be adjective aspiring, budding, promising, prospective, potential, hopeful, keen, eager, ambitious; informal wannabe.

wound noun 1 *a chest wound:* injury, cut, gash, laceration, graze, scratch, abrasion, puncture, lesion; Medicine trauma. 2 *the wounds inflicted by the media:* insult, blow, slight, offence, affront, hurt, damage, injury.
•verb 1 *he was critically wounded:* injure, hurt, harm, lacerate, cut, graze, gash, stab, slash, wing. 2 *her words had wounded him:* hurt, insult, slight, offend, affront, distress, grieve, pain, sting.

wrap verb 1 *she wrapped herself in a towel:* enclose, enfold, envelop, encase, cover, fold, wind, swathe, bundle, swaddle. 2 *I wrapped the vase carefully:* pack, package, parcel up, bundle (up), gift-wrap.
•noun *he put a wrap round her:* shawl, stole, cloak, cape, mantle, scarf.

wrath noun anger, rage, temper, fury, outrage, spleen, resentment, (high) dudgeon, indignation; literary ire.
OPPOSITES happiness.

wreath noun garland, circlet, chaplet, crown, festoon, lei, ring, loop, circle.

wreathe verb 1 *a pulpit wreathed in holly:* festoon, garland, drape, cover, deck, decorate, ornament, adorn. 2 *blue smoke wreathed upwards:* spiral, coil, loop, wind, curl, twist, snake.

wreck noun 1 *salvage teams landed on the wreck:* shipwreck, sunken ship, hull. 2 *the wreck of a stolen car:* wreckage, debris, ruins, remains, burnt-out shell.
•verb 1 *he had wrecked her car:* destroy, break, demolish, crash, smash up, write off; N. Amer. informal trash, total. 2 *the crisis wrecked his plans:* ruin, spoil, disrupt, undo, put a stop to, frustrate, blight, crush, dash, destroy, scotch, shatter, devastate, sabotage; informal mess up, screw up, put paid to, stymie; Brit. informal scupper.

wrench noun 1 *she felt a wrench on her shoulders:* tug, pull, jerk, jolt, heave; informal yank. 2 *hold the piston with a wrench:* spanner. 3 *leaving was an immense wrench:* blow, ache, trauma, pang.
•verb 1 *he wrenched the gun from her:* tug, pull, jerk, wrest, heave, twist, force, prise; N. Amer. pry; informal yank. 2 *she wrenched her ankle:* sprain, twist, turn, strain, rick, crick.

W

violent twist or pull. **2** a feeling of sadness on leaving a place or person. **3** an adjustable tool used for gripping and turning nuts or bolts.

wrest verb **1** forcibly pull something from someone's grasp. **2** succeed in taking power or control from someone after a struggle.

wrestle verb (**wrestles, wrestling, wrestled**) **1** take part in a fight or contest that involves close grappling with your opponent. **2** struggle with a difficulty or problem. **3** struggle to move an object. •noun **1** a wrestling bout or contest. **2** a hard struggle.
■ **wrestler** noun **wrestling** noun.

wretch noun **1** an unfortunate person. **2** informal an unpleasant person.

wretched adjective **1** in a very unhappy or unfortunate state. **2** of bad quality.
■ **wretchedly** adverb.

wriggle verb (**wriggles, wriggling, wriggled**) **1** twist and turn with quick short movements. **2** (**wriggle out of**) use excuses to avoid doing something. •noun a wriggling movement.
■ **wriggly** adjective.

wring verb (**wrings, wringing, wrung**) **1** squeeze and twist something to force water out of it. **2** twist and break an animal's neck. **3** squeeze someone's hand tightly. **4** (**wring something from** or **out of**) obtain something from someone with difficulty.
■ **wringer** noun.

wringing adjective very wet.

wrinkle noun a slight line or fold, especially in fabric or a person's skin. •verb (**wrinkles, wrinkling, wrinkled**) make or become covered with wrinkles.
■ **wrinkly** adjective.

wrist noun the joint connecting the hand with the lower part of the arm.

wristwatch noun a watch worn on a strap round the wrist.

writ¹ noun an official document from a court or other legal authority, ordering someone to do or not to do something.

writ² old-fashioned past participle of **WRITE**.
□ **writ large** in an obvious or exaggerated form.

write verb (**writes, writing, wrote**; past participle **written**) **1** mark letters, words, or other symbols on a surface with a pen, pencil, etc. **2** write and send a letter to someone. **3** compose a written or musical work. **4** fill out a cheque or similar document.
□ **write something off 1** decide that something is useless or a failure. **2** decide not to pursue a debt. **write-off** Brit. a vehicle that is too badly damaged to be repaired. **write-up** a newspaper review of a recent event, performance, etc.
■ **writer** noun.

writhe /ryth/ verb (**writhes, writhing, writhed**) twist or squirm in pain or embarrassment.

writing noun **1** the activity or skill of writing. **2** a sequence of letters or symbols forming words. **3** (**writings**) books or other written works.

wrong adjective **1** not correct or true;

THESAURUS

wrestle verb grapple, fight, struggle, scuffle, tussle, brawl; informal scrap.

wretched adjective **1** *I felt so wretched without you:* miserable, unhappy, sad, heartbroken, grief-stricken, distressed, desolate, devastated, disconsolate, downcast, dejected, depressed, melancholy, forlorn. **2** *wretched living conditions:* harsh, hard, grim, difficult, poor, pitiful, piteous, pathetic, tragic, miserable, bleak, cheerless, hopeless, sorry, sordid; informal crummy.
OPPOSITES cheerful, comfortable.

wriggle verb *she tried to hug him but he wriggled:* squirm, writhe, wiggle, thresh, flounder, flail, twitch, twist and turn, snake, worm.
□ **wriggle out of** avoid, shirk, dodge, evade, sidestep; escape; informal duck.

wrinkle noun *fine wrinkles around her mouth:* crease, fold, pucker, line, crinkle, furrow, ridge, groove; informal crow's feet.
•verb *his coat tails wrinkled up:* crease, pucker, gather, crinkle, crumple, rumple,

ruck up, scrunch up.

write verb **1** *he wrote her name in the book:* put in writing, put down, jot down, note (down), take down, record, inscribe, sign, scribble, scrawl, pen, pencil. **2** *I wrote a poem:* compose, draft, think up, formulate, compile, pen, dash off, produce. **3** *he promised to write:* correspond, communicate, get in touch, keep in contact; informal drop someone a line.

writer noun author, wordsmith; informal scribbler, scribe, pen-pusher, hack.

writing noun **1** *I can't read his writing:* handwriting, hand, script, calligraphy, lettering, print, printing; informal scribble, scrawl. **2** *this fear did not show in her writing:* written work, compositions, books, publications, papers, articles, essays, oeuvre.

wrong adjective **1** *the wrong answer:* incorrect, mistaken, erroneous, inaccurate, inexact, imprecise; informal off beam, out. **2** *he knew he had said the wrong thing:* inappropriate, unsuitable, ill-advised, ill-

W

mistaken or in error. **2** unjust, dishonest, or immoral. **3** in a bad or abnormal condition. • **adverb 1** in a mistaken or unwelcome way or direction. **2** with an incorrect result. • **noun** an unjust, dishonest, or immoral action. • **verb** treat someone unfairly.
□ **wrong-foot 1** (in a game) catch an opponent off balance. **2** place someone in a difficult situation by saying or doing something unexpected. **wrong-headed** having bad judgement.
■ **wrongly** adverb **wrongness** noun.

wrongdoing noun illegal or dishonest behaviour.
■ **wrongdoer** noun.

wrongful adjective not fair, just, or legal.
■ **wrongfully** adverb.

wrote past tense of **WRITE**.

wrought /rawt/ old-fashioned past and past participle of **WORK**. • **adjective 1** (of

metals) beaten out or shaped by hammering. **2** made in a particular way: *well wrought.*
□ **wrought iron** tough iron suitable for forging or rolling.

wrung past and past participle of **WRING**.

wry adjective (**wryer, wryest** or **wrier, wriest**) **1** using dry, mocking humour. **2** (of a person's face) twisted into an expression of disgust, disappointment, or annoyance. **3** bending or twisted to one side.
■ **wryly** adverb.

wunderkind /vuun-der-kind/ noun a person who is very successful at a young age.

Wurlitzer /wer-lit-ser/ noun trademark a large pipe organ or electric organ.

WWI abbreviation World War I.

WWII abbreviation World War II.

WWW abbreviation World Wide Web.

THESAURUS

considered, ill-judged, unwise, infelicitous; informal out of order. **3** *I've done nothing wrong:* bad, dishonest, illegal, unlawful, illicit, criminal, corrupt, unethical, immoral, wicked, sinful, iniquitous, nefarious, reprehensible; informal crooked.
4 *there's something wrong with the engine:* amiss, awry, out of order, not right, faulty, defective.
OPPOSITES right, correct, appropriate, legal.
• **adverb** *she guessed wrong:* incorrectly, wrongly, inaccurately, erroneously, mistakenly.
• **noun 1** *the difference between right and wrong:* immorality, sin, wickedness, evil, illegality, unlawfulness, crime, corruption,

villainy, dishonesty, injustice, misconduct, transgression. **2** *an attempt to make up for past wrongs:* misdeed, offence, injury, crime, transgression, sin, injustice, outrage, atrocity.
OPPOSITES right.
• **verb** *she was determined to forget the man who had wronged her:* mistreat, ill-use, ill-treat, do an injustice to, abuse, harm, hurt, injure.

wrongdoer noun offender, lawbreaker, criminal, felon, delinquent, villain, culprit, evil-doer, sinner, transgressor, malefactor, miscreant, rogue, scoundrel; informal crook, wrong 'un.

W

XxYyZz

X or **x** noun (plural **Xs** or **X's**) **1** the twenty-fourth letter of the alphabet. **2** an X-shaped written symbol, used to show that an answer is wrong, or to symbolize a kiss. **3** the Roman numeral for ten.
□ **X chromosome** a sex chromosome, two of which are normally present in female cells and one in male cells. **X certificate** (in the past) a classification of a film as suitable for adults only. **x-rated** pornographic or indecent. **X-ray 1** an electromagnetic wave of very short wavelength, which is able to pass through many solids and so make it possible to see into or through them. **2** an image of the internal structure of an object produced by passing X-rays through it.

xenon /zen-on/ noun an inert gaseous element, present in small amounts in the air.

xenophobia /zen-uh-foh-bi-uh/ noun dislike or fear of people from other countries.
■ **xenophobic** adjective.

Xerox /zeer-oks/ noun trademark **1** a process for copying documents using an electric charge and dry powder. **2** a copy made using such a process. •verb (**xerox**) copy a document by such a process.

Xmas noun informal Christmas.

xylophone /zy-luh-fohn/ noun a musical instrument consisting of a row of bars which you hit with small hammers.

Y or **y** noun (plural **Ys** or **Y's**) the twenty-fifth letter of the alphabet.
□ **Y chromosome** a sex chromosome which is normally present only in male cells. **Y-fronts** Brit. trademark men's or boys' underpants with a seam at the front in the shape of an upside-down Y.

yacht /yot/ noun **1** a medium-sized sailing boat. **2** a boat with an engine, equipped for cruising.
■ **yachting** noun **yachtsman** noun (plural **yachtsmen**) **yachtswoman** noun (plural **yachtswomen**).

yahoo /yah-hoo/ noun informal a rude or bad-mannered person.

yak[1] noun a large ox with shaggy hair and large horns, found in Tibet and central Asia.

yak[2] or **yack** verb (**yaks, yakking, yakked**) informal talk continuously about something unimportant.

yam noun the tuber of a tropical plant, eaten as a vegetable.

yang noun (in Chinese philosophy) the active male force in the universe.

Yank noun informal an American.

yank informal verb pull quickly and hard. •noun a sudden hard pull.

Yankee noun informal **1** an American. **2** US a person from New England or one of the northern states. **3** historical a Federal soldier in the Civil War.

yap verb (**yaps, yapping, yapped**) give a sharp, high-pitched bark. •noun a sharp, high-pitched bark.

yard[1] noun **1** a unit of length equal to 3 feet (0.9144 metre). **2** a square or cubic yard. **3** a long piece of wood slung across a ship's mast for a sail to hang from.

yard[2] noun **1** Brit. a piece of enclosed ground next to a building. **2** an area of land used for a particular purpose. **3** N. Amer. the garden of a house.

yardarm noun either end of a ship's yard supporting a sail.

Yardie noun informal a member of a Jamaican gang of criminals.

yardstick noun a standard used for judging how good or successful something is.

yarmulke or **yarmulka** /yar-muul-kuh/

THESAURUS

xenophobic adjective jingoistic, chauvinistic, flag-waving, nationalistic, isolationist, prejudiced, bigoted, intolerant.
yank verb & noun (informal) jerk, pull, tug, wrench.
yardstick noun standard, measure, gauge, indicator, test, touchstone, barometer, benchmark.

noun a skullcap worn by Jewish men.

yarn noun **1** thread used for knitting, weaving, or sewing. **2** informal a long story.

yashmak noun a veil concealing all of the face except the eyes, worn by some Muslim women.

yaw verb (of a moving ship or aircraft) turn unsteadily from side to side. • noun a yawing movement.

yawn verb **1** open your mouth wide and take a deep breath, usually when tired or bored. **2** (**yawning**) wide open. • noun an act of yawning.

yd abbreviation yard.

ye¹ plural of THOU.

ye² old use = THE.

yea adverb old use yes.

year noun **1** the period of 365 days (or 366 days in leap years) starting from January 1. **2** a period of this length starting at a different point. **3** the time taken by the earth to go around the sun. **4** (**your years**) your age or time of life. **5** (**years**) informal a very long time. **6** a set of students who enter and leave a school or college at the same time.

yearbook noun a book published annually, giving details of the previous year's events.

yearling noun an animal between one and two years old.

yearly adjective & adverb happening or produced once a year or every year.

yearn verb have a strong feeling of longing for something.
■ **yearning** noun & adjective.

yeast noun **1** a fungus which can convert sugar into alcohol and carbon dioxide. **2** a substance formed from this, used to make bread dough rise and to ferment beer and wine.
■ **yeasty** adjective.

yell noun a loud, sharp call or cry. • verb

shout loudly.

yellow adjective **1** of the colour of egg yolks or ripe lemons. **2** informal cowardly. • noun a yellow colour. • verb (of paper, fabric, etc.) become slightly yellow with age.
□ **yellow card** (in soccer) a yellow card shown by the referee to a player being cautioned. **yellow fever** a tropical disease that causes fever and jaundice and often death.
■ **yellowish** adjective.

yellowhammer noun a bird with a yellow head, neck, and breast.

yelp noun a short, sharp cry. • verb give a yelp or yelps.

Yemeni /yem-uh-ni/ noun a person from Yemen. • adjective relating to Yemen.

yen¹ noun (plural **yen**) the basic unit of money of Japan.

yen² noun informal a strong desire to have or do something.

yeoman /yoh-muhn/ noun (plural **yeomen**) (in the past) a man having his own house and small area of farming land.
□ **Yeoman of the Guard** a member of the British king or queen's ceremonial bodyguard.

yes exclamation **1** used to give a response in favour of something. **2** used to respond to someone who is talking to you. • noun (plural **yeses** or **yesses**) a decision or vote in favour of something.
□ **yes-man** a person who always agrees with people in authority.

yesterday adverb on the day before today. • noun **1** the day before today. **2** the recent past.

yesteryear noun literary last year or the recent past.

yet adverb **1** up until now or then. **2** as soon as this. **3** from now into the future. **4** referring to something that will or may

THESAURUS

yarn noun **1** thread, cotton, wool, fibre, filament. **2** (informal) **story**, tale, saga; informal spiel, shaggy-dog story.

yawning adjective gaping, wide, cavernous, deep, huge, vast.

yearly adjective annual.
• adverb annually, once a year, per annum, each/every year.

yearn verb long, pine, crave, desire, want, wish, hanker, covet, hunger, thirst, ache; informal itch.

yell verb he yelled in agony: **shout**, cry out, howl, wail, scream, shriek, screech, yelp, squeal, roar, bawl.
• noun a yell of rage: **shout**, cry, howl, scream, shriek, screech, yelp, squeal, roar.

yellow adjective golden, gold, blonde,

fair, flaxen.

yes adverb certainly, very well, of course, by all means, sure, all right, absolutely, indeed, affirmative, agreed, roger; Scottish & N. English, aye; Nautical aye aye; informal yeah, yep, uh-huh, okay, OK; Brit. informal righto, righty-ho; N. Amer. informal surely.
OPPOSITES no.

yet adverb **1** he hasn't made up his mind yet: **so far**, as yet, up to now, up till now. **2** don't celebrate just yet: (**right**) **now**, at this time, already, so soon. **3** he did nothing, yet he seemed happy: **nevertheless**, nonetheless, even so, but, however, still, notwithstanding, despite that, in spite of that, for all that, all the same, just the same, at the same time. **4** yet more advice: **even**, still.

y

happen. **5** still; even. **6** in spite of that.
•**conjunction** but at the same time.

yeti noun a large hairy creature like a bear or a man, said to live in the highest part of the Himalayas.

yew noun an evergreen tree with poisonous red fruit.

Yiddish noun a language used by Jews from central and eastern Europe. •**adjective** relating to Yiddish.

yield verb **1** produce or provide a natural or industrial product. **2** produce a result or financial gain. **3** give way to demands or pressure. **4** give up possession of. **5** give way under force or pressure. •**noun** an amount or result yielded.

> ☑ remember, *i* before *e* except after *c*: *yield*.

yin noun (in Chinese philosophy) the passive female presence in the universe.

yob or **yobbo** noun (plural **yobs** or **yobbos**) Brit. informal a rude and aggressive young man.
■ **yobbish** adjective.

yodel verb (**yodels, yodelling, yodelled**; US spelling **yodels, yodeling, yodeled**) sing or call in a style that alternates rapidly between a normal voice and a very high voice. •**noun** a song or call of this type.
■ **yodeller** noun.

yoga noun a system involving breathing exercises and the holding of particular body positions, followed for fitness and relaxation and based on Hindu philosophy.
■ **yogic** adjective.

yogi noun (plural **yogis**) a person who is skilled in yoga.

yogurt, yoghurt, or **yoghourt** noun a thick liquid food made from milk with bacteria added.

yoke noun **1** a piece of wood fastened over

the necks of two animals and attached to a plough or cart in order for them to pull it. **2** a frame fitting over a person's neck and shoulders, used for carrying buckets or baskets. **3** something that limits freedom or is difficult to bear. **4** a part of a garment that fits over the shoulders and to which the main part of the garment is attached. •**verb** (**yokes, yoking, yoked**) join together or attach to a yoke.

yokel noun an unsophisticated country person.

yolk noun the yellow part in the middle of an egg.

Yom Kippur /yom kip-**poor**/ noun an important day in the Jewish religion in which people pray and fast.

yon old use or dialect **determiner & adverb** that. •**pronoun** that person or thing.

yonder old use or dialect **adverb** over there. •**determiner** that or those.

yonks plural noun Brit. informal a very long time.

yore noun (**of yore**) literary in the past; long ago.

Yorkshire pudding noun an item of food made from baked batter, eaten with roast beef.

Yorkshire terrier noun a small breed of terrier with a long grey and brown coat.

you pronoun **1** used to refer to the person or people that the speaker is talking to. **2** used to refer to any person in general.

you'd short form **1** you had. **2** you would.

you'll short form you will or you shall.

young adjective (**younger, youngest**) **1** having lived or existed for only a short time. **2** relating to or characteristic of young people. •**plural noun** young children or animals; offspring.

youngster noun a young person.

your possessive determiner **1** belonging to or

THESAURUS

yield verb **1** *such projects yield poor returns:* produce, bear, give, provide, afford, return, bring in, earn, realize, generate, deliver, pay out. **2** *the duke was forced to yield:* surrender, capitulate, submit, admit defeat, back down, give in.
OPPOSITES withhold, resist.
•**noun** *we expected a higher yield:* profit, gain, return, dividend, earnings.
□ **yield to give in to**, give way to, submit to, comply with, agree to, consent to, go along with, grant, permit, allow; informal cave in to; formal accede to.

yob, yobbo noun (Brit. informal) lout, thug, hooligan, tearaway, vandal, ruffian, troublemaker; Austral. larrikin; informal tough, bruiser, yahoo; Brit. informal lager lout; Scottish informal ned.

young adjective **1** *young people:* youthful, juvenile, junior, adolescent, teenage, in your salad days. **2** *she's very young for her age:* immature, childish, inexperienced, naive, green, wet behind the ears. **3** *a young industry:* fledgling, developing, budding, in its infancy, emerging.
OPPOSITES old, mature.
•**noun 1** *a robin feeding its young:* offspring, progeny, family, babies, litter, brood. **2** *the young don't care nowadays:* young people, children, boys and girls, youngsters, youth, the younger generation, juveniles, minors; informal kids.

youngster noun child, teenager, adolescent, youth, juvenile, minor, junior, boy, girl; Scottish & N. English lass, lassie; informal lad, kid, whippersnapper, teen.

y

associated with the person or people that the speaker is talking to. **2** belonging to or associated with any person in general.

> ❗ don't confuse **your** meaning 'belonging to you' (as in *let me talk to your daughter*) with the form **you're**, which is short for **you are** (as in *you're a good cook*).

you're short form you are.

yours possessive pronoun used to refer to something belonging to or associated with the person or people that the speaker is talking to.

> ☑ no apostrophe: **yours**.

yourself pronoun (plural **yourselves**) **1** used as the object of a verb or preposition when this is the same as the subject of the clause and the subject is the person or people being spoken to. **2** you personally.

youth noun (plural **youths**) **1** the period between childhood and adult age. **2** the qualities of energy, freshness, etc. associated with being young. **3** a young man. **4** young people.
▢ **youth club** a club where young people can meet and take part in various activities. **youth hostel** a place providing cheap overnight accommodation, especially for young people.

youthful adjective **1** young or seeming young. **2** characteristic of young people.
■ **youthfully** adverb **youthfulness** noun.

you've short form you have.

yowl /rhymes with fowl/ noun a loud wailing cry of pain or distress. • **verb** make such a cry.

yo-yo noun (plural **yo-yos**) (trademark in the UK) a toy consisting of a pair of joined discs with a groove between them in which string is attached and wound, which can be spun down and up as the string unwinds and rewinds. • **verb** (**yo-yoes, yo-yoing, yo-yoed**) move up and down repeatedly.

ytterbium /it-ter-bi-uhm/ noun a silvery-white metallic element.

yttrium /it-tri-uhm/ noun a greyish-white

metallic element.

yucca noun a plant with long, stiff pointed leaves, native to the southern US and Mexico.

Yugoslav /yoo-guh-slahv/ noun a person from any of the states of the former Yugoslavia.
■ **Yugoslavian** noun & adjective.

Yule or **Yuletide** noun old use Christmas.

yummy adjective (**yummier, yummiest**) informal delicious.

yuppie or **yuppy** noun (plural **yuppies**) informal a young middle-class professional person who earns a lot of money.

Z or **z** noun (plural **Zs** or **Z's**) the twenty-sixth letter of the alphabet.

Zambian noun a person from Zambia.
• **adjective** relating to Zambia.

zany adjective (**zanier, zaniest**) amusingly unconventional or unusual.

zap informal verb (**zaps, zapping, zapped**) **1** destroy completely. **2** move very fast. **3** use a remote control to change television channels.

zeal noun great energy and enthusiasm for a cause or aim.

zealot /zel-uht/ noun a person who follows a religion, cause, or policy very strictly and enthusiastically.
■ **zealotry** noun.

zealous /zel-uhss/ adjective showing great energy and enthusiasm for a cause or aim.
■ **zealously** adverb.

zebra noun an African wild horse with black and white stripes.
▢ **zebra crossing** Brit. an area of road marked with broad white stripes, where pedestrians can cross.

zeitgeist /zyt-gysst/ noun the general spirit or mood of a particular period of history.

Zen noun a type of Buddhism that emphasizes the value of meditation and intuition.

zenith noun **1** the time at which someone or something is most powerful or successful.

THESAURUS

youth noun **1** *he was a fine athlete in his youth:* early years, teens, teenage years, adolescence, boyhood, girlhood, childhood, minority. **2** *local youths:* young man, boy, juvenile, teenager, adolescent, junior, minor; informal lad, kid. **3** *the youth of the nation:* young people, young, younger generation, next generation; informal kids.
OPPOSITES adulthood, old age.

youthful adjective young, boyish, girlish, fresh-faced, young-looking, spry, sprightly, vigorous, active.
OPPOSITES elderly.

yowl verb wail, howl, yelp, shriek, scream, cry.

zany adjective eccentric, unconventional, odd, bizarre, weird, mad, crazy, comic, madcap, quirky, idiosyncratic; informal wacky, oddball, off the wall; Brit. informal daft; N. Amer. informal kooky, wacko.

zeal noun enthusiasm, passion, ardour, fervour, fire, devotion, gusto, vigour, energy.
OPPOSITES apathy.

zealous adjective fervent, ardent, fanatical, passionate, committed, dedicated, enthusiastic, keen, avid, fierce.

2 the point in the sky directly overhead. **3** the highest point in the sky reached by the sun or moon.

zephyr noun literary a soft, gentle breeze.

Zeppelin noun a large German airship of the early 20th century.

zero cardinal number (plural **zeros**) **1** the figure 0; nought. **2** a temperature of 0°C (32°F), marking the freezing point of water. **3** a point on a scale of measurement from which a positive or negative quantity is reckoned. •verb (**zeroes, zeroing, zeroed**) (**zero in on**) take aim at or focus attention on.
□ **zero hour** the time at which a military operation or important event is set to begin. **zero tolerance** the policy of applying laws against antisocial behaviour very strictly.

zest noun **1** great enthusiasm and energy. **2** excitement or stimulation. **3** the outer coloured part of the peel of an orange or lemon.

zigzag noun a line or course having sharp alternate right and left turns. •adjective & adverb veering to right and left alternately. •verb (**zigzags, zigzagging, zigzagged**) move in a zigzag.

zilch pronoun informal nothing.

zillion cardinal number informal a very large number of people or things.
■ **zillionth** ordinal number.

Zimbabwean noun a person from Zimbabwe. •adjective relating to Zimbabwe.

Zimmer frame noun trademark a metal frame that people use to help them walk.

zinc noun a silvery-white metallic element used in making brass and to coat iron and steel.

zing noun informal energy, enthusiasm, or liveliness.
■ **zingy** adjective.

Zionism noun a movement for the development of a Jewish nation in Israel.
■ **Zionist** noun & adjective.

zip noun **1** Brit. a fastener consisting of two flexible interlocking strips of metal or plastic, closed or opened by pulling a slide along them. **2** informal energy; liveliness. •verb (**zips, zipping, zipped**) **1** fasten with a zip. **2** informal move quickly. **3** Computing compress a file so that it takes up less space.
□ **zip code** US a postcode.

zipper noun chiefly N. Amer. a zip fastener.

zippy adjective informal **1** speedy, fresh, or lively. **2** bright, fresh, or lively.

zircon noun a brown or semi-transparent mineral.

zirconium noun a hard silver-grey metallic element.

zit noun informal a spot on the skin.

zither /zi-*ther*/ noun a musical instrument with numerous strings stretched across a flat box, which you hold horizontally and play with your fingers and a plectrum.

zodiac noun an area in the sky in which the sun, moon, and planets appear to lie, divided by astrologers into twelve equal divisions or signs.
■ **zodiacal** /zuh-**dy**-uh-k'l/ adjective.

zombie noun **1** informal a person who seems to be only partly alive. **2** (in stories) a dead body that has been brought back to life by magic.

zone noun **1** an area that has particular characteristics or a particular use. **2** (also **time zone**) an area where a common standard time is used. •verb (**zones, zoning, zoned**) divide something into zones.
■ **zonal** adjective.

zoo noun a place where wild animals are kept for study, conservation, or display to the public.

zookeeper noun a person employed to look after the animals in a zoo.

zoology noun **1** the scientific study of animals. **2** the animal life of a particular area or time.
■ **zoological** adjective **zoologist** noun.

zoom verb **1** move or travel very quickly. **2** (of a camera) change smoothly from a long shot to a close-up or vice versa.
□ **zoom lens** a lens allowing a camera to zoom.

zucchini /zuu-**kee**-ni/ noun (plural **zucchini** or **zucchinis**) N. Amer. a courgette.

Zulu noun **1** a member of a South African people. **2** the language of the Zulus.

zygote noun Biology a cell resulting from the joining of two gametes.

THESAURUS

zero noun **1** *the answer is zero:* nought, nothing, nil, o. **2** *there was absolutely zero I could do about it:* nothing (at all), nil, none; N. English nowt; informal zilch, not a dicky bird; Brit. informal damn all, not a sausage; N. Amer. informal zip, nada.

zigzag verb twist, meander, snake, wind, weave, swerve.

zone noun area, sector, section, belt, stretch, region, territory, district, quarter, neighbourhood.

zoom verb (informal) hurry, rush, dash, race, speed, sprint, career, shoot, hurtle, hare, fly; informal tear, belt; Brit. informal bomb.